In the name of God,
the Most Gracious, the Most Merciful.
All praise is due to God, the Lord of the Universe,
and peace and prayers be upon
His Final Prophet and Messenger.

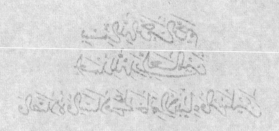

In the name of God,
the Most Gracious, the Most Merciful.
All praise is due to God, the Lord of the Universe,
and peace and prayers be upon
His Final Prophet and Messenger

The Quran

English Translation, Commentary and Parallel Arabic Text

Translation and Commentary by
Maulana Wahiduddin Khan

Edited by
Farida Khanam

Goodword Books

First published by Goodword Books 2011
Reprinted 2011

Arabic version:
al-Tadhkir al-Qawim fi Tafsir al-Quran al-Hakim (2009)

Urdu version:
Tazkirul Quran (1986)

Hindi version:
Tazkirul Quran (2008)

Goodword Books
1, Nizamuddin West Market
New Delhi - 110 013
Tel. +9111-41827083
email: info@goodwordbooks.com

Center for Peace and Spirituality USA
2665 Byberry Road, Bensalem, PA 19020, USA
Tel. 215-240-4298
email: cps@alrisala.org, www.alrisala.org

IPCI: Islamic Vision
434 Coventry Road, Small Heath, Birmingham B10 0UG, U.K.
Tel. 0121-773-0137
email: info@ipci-iv.co.uk

see our complete catalogue at

www.goodwordbooks.com
www.goodword.net

Printed and bound in India by Replika Press

CONTENTS

THE QURAN

vi Contents

INTRODUCTION

The Quran is the Book of God. It has been preserved in its entirety for all time to come. Although written originally in Arabic, it has been made accessible, thanks to translations, to those who have no knowledge of Arabic. While no substitute for the original, translations serve the signal purpose of spreading the word of God far beyond the Arabic-speaking peoples to a far broader spectrum of humanity.

The Quran is apparently in the Arabic language, but in reality, it is in the language of nature, that is, the language in which God directly addressed all human beings at the time of Creation. This divine invocation of humanity is ever-present in the consciousness of all human beings, that is why the Quran is universally understandable—to some on a conscious plane, and to others at the subconscious level. This reality has been described in the Quran as 'clear revelations in the hearts of those who have been given knowledge.' This verse goes on to say that 'none deny Our revelations save the wrongdoers' (29:49).

This means that the Divine Reality, explained by the Quran on a conscious plane, pre-exists in man at the level of the subconscious. The message of the Quran is not, therefore, something which is alien to man. It is in fact a verbal expression of that same Divine Reality which is in consonance with man's own nature and with which he is already familiar. The Quran explains this by saying that those born in later times were all initially born at the time of the creation of Adam and, at that time, God had directly addressed all these human souls.

This event is thus alluded to in the Quran:

'[Prophet], when your Lord brought forth the offspring from the loins of the Children of Adam and made them bear witness about themselves, He said, 'Am I not your Lord?' and they replied, 'Yes, we bear witness that You are.' So you cannot say on the Day of Resurrection, 'We were not aware of this' (7:172).

In the following verse, the Quran makes further mention of the dialogue between God and man:

'Surely We offered Our trust to the heavens and the earth, and the hills, but they shrank from bearing it and were afraid of it. And man undertook it. But he has proved a tyrant and a fool' (33:72).

The Quran, for man, is in essence already known to him, rather than an entirely unknown entity. In reality, the Quran is the unfolding of the human mind.

When one whose nature is alive—having saved himself from later conditioning—reads the Quran, those brain cells will be activated wherein God's first address lies preserved. If we keep this in mind, it will not be difficult to appreciate that the translation of the Quran is a valid means of understanding it.

If God's address was the First Covenant, the Quran is the Second Covenant. Each testifies to the veracity of the other. If one has little, or even no grasp of the Arabic language, and can read the scriptures only in translation, he should not anticipate that he will be frustrated in his understanding of the Quran, for the Quranic concept of man as the natural recipient of God's word has become a reality in modern times. The science of the genetic code and the findings of anthropology both fully support this viewpoint.

The Creation Plan of God

Every book has its objective and the objective of the Quran is to make man aware of the Creation plan of God. That is, to tell man why God created this world; what the purpose is of settling man on earth; what is required from man in his pre-death life span, and what he is going to confront after death. Man is born as an eternal creature. When God created man as such, He divided his life span into two periods, the pre-death period, which is a time of trial, and the post-death period, which is the time for receiving the rewards or punishment merited by one's actions during one's lifetime. These take the form of eternal paradise or eternal hell. The purpose of the Quran is to make man aware of this reality. This is the theme of this divine Book, which serves to guide man through his entire journey through life into the after-life.

It would be correct to say that man is a seeker by birth. These questions lurk in everyone's mind: Who am I? What is the purpose of my life? What is the reality of life and death? What is the secret of man's success and failure? etc. According to the Quran, the answer to these questions is that the present world is the testing ground and whatever man has been endowed with in his pre-death period is all a part of the test. The Hereafter is the place where the result of the test will be taken into account by the Almighty and whatever man receives in the life after death, by way of reward or punishment, will be commensurate with his deeds in this world. The secret of man's success in this life is to understand God's creation plan and map out his life accordingly.

A Book of Divine Warning

The Quran is a book of divine warning. A combination of lessons and admonitions, it would be even more appropriately called a book of wisdom. The Quran does not follow the pattern of the traditional didactic book. In fact, when the average reader picks up the Quran, it appears to him to be a collection of fragmentary statements. Apparently this feeling is not unreal. But this arrangement of the Quran is not due to any shortcoming, but is rather in conformance with the Quranic plan of retaining its original form in order to fulfill its purpose of conveying the message of truth to the reader who may, in his forays into the scriptures, read only one page, one verse or one line at a time.

One vital aspect of the Quran is that it is a reminder of the blessings granted by the Supreme Benefactor. The most important of these are the exceptional qualities with which God endowed man when He created him. Another great blessing is that He settled him on the earth, a planet where all kinds of support systems existed for his benefit. The purpose of the Quran is to ensure that, while enjoying these blessings of nature, man will keep his Benefactor in mind: he must acknowledge the munificence of his Creator. It is in so doing that man will gain entry into eternal paradise; ignoring his Benefactor, on the other hand, will lead man straight to hell. The Quran is indeed a reminder of this inescapable reality.

There are some who think that the presence of a realized person is essential for an understanding of the Quran. That is, it is solely with the assistance of a spiritual person that the meaning of the Quran may be revealed. This is to underestimate both man and the Quran. The Quran addresses man's mind and the mind is man's greatest faculty. Discovering the Quran, therefore, on a purely intellectual level is sufficient to arrive at its meaning. Indeed, at the intellectual level, the Quran becomes an open book But those who discover the Quran at any lower level cannot be said to have discovered it at all. Falling back instead on their community traditions for instruction and enlightenment cannot compare with the ideal approach to religion that the Quran so consistently offers.

The Inner Spirit and God Realization

One important quality of the Quran is that it gives us only basic, but essential principles, often resorting to reiteration to emphasize them. On the contrary, non-basics, or matters relating only to form, constitute only a negligible part of the scriptures. This is in consonance with the Quranic scheme, the importance of form being entirely secondary. To the Quran, only those precepts are important which figure as fundamental guidelines. This aspect of the Quran is so clear that its reader cannot but appreciate it.

The truth is that the inner spirit is of the utmost importance in the building of the Islamic personality. Once the inner spirit is developed, correct form will naturally ensue. But form on its own can never produce the inner spirit. That is why the aim of the Quran is to initiate and bring to fruition an intellectual revolution within man. The expression used by the Quran for this intellectual revolution is *ma'rifah* (realization of truth) (5:83).

The Quran stresses the importance of man's discovery of truth at the level of realization. True faith in God is what one achieves at such a level. Where there is no realization, there is no faith.

The Word of God

When you read the Quran, you will repeatedly find it stated that it is the word of God. Apparently this is a plain fact. But when seen in context, it is an extraordinary statement. There are many books in the world which are believed to be sacred. But, except for the Quran, we do not find any religious book which thus projects itself as the word of God. This kind of statement, appearing uniquely in the Quran, gives a point of departure to the reader. He then studies it as an exceptional book, rather than as a common book written by human beings. We find recurring in the Quran statements worded more or less as follows, 'O man, it is your Lord, who is addressing you. Listen to His words and follow Him.' Even this style of address is quite exceptional. This kind of direct divine invocation is not present in any other book. It leaves a lasting impression on man. He feels his Lord is directly addressing him. This feeling compels man to take the assertions of the Quran with extreme seriousness, rather than treat them like everyday statements in an ordinary book. The style of compilation of the Quran is also unique. Books written by human beings usually have their material arranged in order from A to Z, according to the topic. But the Quran does not follow a pattern of this kind, so that to the common man it appears to be lacking in order. When looked at in reality, however, it will emerge as an extremely coherent and orderly book, and quite majestic in its style of writing. While reading the Quran, we feel that its writer is on a very high pedestal from where He is looking down and addressing the whole of humanity, which is His special concern. This address focuses on different groups of human beings, while encompassing all of them.

One special aspect of the Quran is that at any moment its reader can consult its Writer, put his questions and receive answers, for the Writer of the Quran is God Himself. He is a living God. As man's Creator, He directly hears and answers man's call.

Jihad *is a Peaceful Ideological Struggle*

Those who are introduced to the Quran only through the media, generally have the impression that the Quran is a book of *jihad*, and *jihad* to them is an attempt to achieve one's goal by means of violence. But this idea is based on a misunderstanding. Anyone who reads the Quran for himself will easily appreciate that its message has nothing to do with violence. The Quran is, from beginning to end, a book which promulgates peace and in no way countenances violence. It is true that *jihad* is one of the teachings of the Quran. But *jihad*, taken in its correct sense, is the name of peaceful struggle rather than of any kind of violent action. The Quranic concept of jihad is expressed in the following verse, 'Do greater *jihad* (i.e strive more strenuously) with the help of this [Quran]' (25:52).

Obviously, the Quran is not a weapon, but a book which gives us an introduction to the divine ideology of peaceful struggle. The method of such a struggle, according to the Quran, is 'to speak to them a word to reach their very soul' (4:63).

So, the desired approach, acccording to the Quran, is one which moves man's heart and mind. That is, in addressing people's minds, it satisfies them, convinces them of the veracity of the Quran and, in short, brings about an intellectual revolution within them. This is the mission of the Quran. And this mission can be performed only by means of rational arguments. This target can never be achieved by means of violence or armed action.

It is true that there are certain verses in the Quran, which convey injunctions similar to the following, 'Slay them wherever you find them' (2:191).

Referring to such verses, there are some who attempt to give the impression that Islam is a religion of war and violence. This is totally untrue. Such verses relate, in a restricted sense, to those who have unilaterally attacked the Muslims. The above verse does not convey the general command of Islam.

The truth of the matter is that the Quran was not revealed in the complete form in which it exists today. It was revealed from time to time, according to the circumstances, over a time span of 23 years. If this is divided into years of war and peace, the period of peace amounts to 20 years, while that of state of war amounts only to 3 years. The revelations during these 20 peaceful years were the peaceful teachings of Islam as are conveyed in the verses regarding the realization of God, worship, morality, justice, etc.

This division of commands into different categories is a natural one and is found in all religious books. For instance, the Gita, the holy book of the Hindus, pertains to wisdom and moral values. Yet along with this is the exhortation of Krishna to Arjuna, encouraging him to fight (Bhagavad Gita, 3:30). This does not mean that believers in the Gita should wage wars all the time. Mahatma Gandhi, after all, derived his philosophy of non-violence from the same Gita. The exhortation to wage war in the Gita applies only to exceptional cases where circumstances leave no choice. But for general day-to-day existence it gives the same peaceful commands as derived from it by Mahatma Gandhi.

Similarly, Jesus Christ said, 'Do not think that I came to bring peace on Earth. I did not come to bring peace, but a sword.' (Matthew, 10:34).

It would not be right to conclude that the religion preached by Christ was one of war and violence, for such utterances relate purely to particular occasions. So far as general life is concerned, Christ taught peaceful values, such as the building up of a good character, loving each other, helping the poor and needy, etc.

The same is true of the Quran. When the Prophet Muhammad emigrated from Makkah to Madinah, the idolatrous tribes were aggressive towards him. But the Prophet always averted their attacks by the exercise of patience and the strategy of avoidance. However on certain occasions no other options existed, save that of defence. Therefore, he had to do battle on certain occasions. It was these circumstances, which occasioned those revelations relating to war. These commands, being specific to certain circumstances, had no general application. They were not meant to be valid for all time to come. That is why; the permanent status of the Prophet has been termed a 'mercy for all mankind.' (21:107)

Islam is a religion of peace in the fullest sense of the word. The Quran calls its way 'the paths of peace' (5:16). It describes reconciliation as the best policy (4:128), and states that God abhors any disturbance of the peace (2:205). We can say that it is no exaggeration to say that Islam and violence are contradictory to each other. The concept of Islamic violence is so obviously unfounded that prima facie it stands rejected. The fact that violence is not sustainable, in the present world, is sufficient indication that violence, as a principle, is quite alien to the scheme of things in Islam. Islam claims to be an eternal religion and, as such, could never afford to uphold any principle, which could not stand up to the test of time. Any attempt to bracket violence with Islam amounts, therefore, to casting doubt upon the very eternity of the Islamic religion. Islamic terrorism is a contradiction in terms, much like 'pacifist' terrorism. And the truth of the matter is that, all the teachings of Islam are based, directly or indirectly, on the principle of peace.

A Revealed Book

The Quran is a book of God revealed to the Prophet Muhammad. It did not come to him in the form of a complete book, but in parts over a period of 23 years. The first part was revealed in 610 AD, when the Prophet Muhammad was in Makkah. Subsequently, different parts continued to be revealed regularly, the final part being revealed in 632, when the Prophet was in Madinah.

There are 114 chapters in the Quran, both long and short. The verses number about 6600. To meet the needs of recitation, the Quran was divided into 30 parts. These parts were finally set in order under the guidance of the Angel Gabriel, through whom God had revealed the Quran.

When the Quran was revealed in the first quarter of the 7th century, paper had already been invented. This paper, known as papyrus, was made by hand from the fibres of certain trees. Whenever any part of the Quran was revealed, it was written down on papyrus, or in Arabic, *qirtas* (6:7). During this process, people committed the verses to memory, the Quran being the only Islamic literature which was recited in prayer, as well as being read out for the purposes of *da'wah*. In this way, the Quran continued to be simultaneously memorized as well as written down. This method of preservation continued during the lifetime of the Prophet Muhammad. In this way, the Quran was preserved during the lifetime of the Prophet.

The third caliph, 'Uthman ibn 'Affan, had several copies prepared. He sent these to different cities, where they were kept in the great mosques. People not only recited from these copies, but also prepared more copies from them.

The writing of the Quran by hand continued till the printing press was invented and paper began to be manufactured on a large scale, thanks to the industrial revolution. Then, the Quran began to be printed. Printing methods went on improving and so the printing of the Quran also improved. Now printed copies of the Quran have become so common that they can be found in every home, mosque, library and bookstore. Today anyone can find a beautiful copy of the Quran, wherever he might be, in any part of the globe.

Maulana Wahiduddin Khan

sk@skhan.org

CHRONOLOGICAL TABLE
OF THE QURAN

570   Birth of the Prophet Muhammad (the Prophet's father died a few months before his birth)

576   Death of the Prophet's mother Aminah, when the Prophet is six year old

578   Death of the Prophet's grandfather, 'Abdul Muttalib

595   The Prophet's marriage to Khadijah

610   The Prophet receives the first revelation of the Quran at Mount al-Nur near Makkah

613   First public preaching.

615   Migration of some of the [...] het to Abyssinia (Ethiopia) to avoid pers[...] he Makkans

616-619   The Banu Hashim boy[...] s family

619   Death of the Prophet'[...] e Abu Talib

619   The Prophet visits T[...] ople there give him humiliating treatmen[...]

620   The Prophet's Nigh[...] nd then to the Seven Heavens

622   The Prophet's migration (*hijrah*) from Makkah to Madinah, which marks the beginning of the Islamic calendar

624   Battle of Badr: the pagan Makkans were defeated by the Muslims

625   Battle of Uhud: the Muslims were defeated by the pagan Makkans

628   The Peace Treaty of Hudaybiyyah. Ten year no-war pact with pagan Makkans, allowing peaceful preaching of Islam. As a result many came into the fold of Islam

630   No-war pact broken by the pagan Makkans. Makkah's surrender— the Prophet forgives the Makkans and entire population enters the fold of Islam

631   'The Year of Embassies'—Islam accepted by Arabian tribes. The

Map of Arabian Peninsula showing places at the time of the
revelation of the Quran, 610-632.

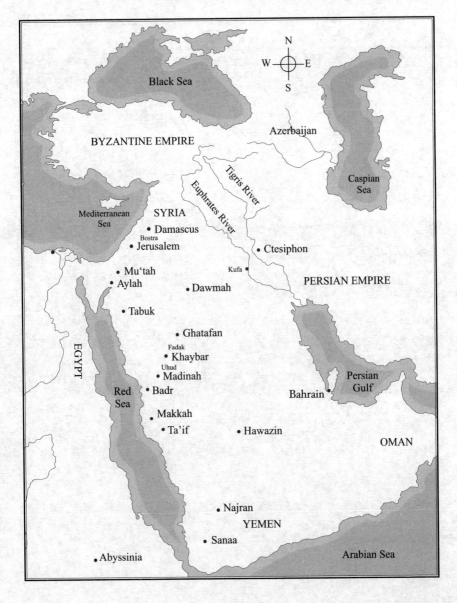

The Quran

The Quran

1. THE OPENING

سُورَةُ ٱلْفَاتِحَة

¹ In the name of God,
the Most Gracious, the Most Merciful

بِسْمِ ٱللَّهِ ٱلرَّحْمَٰنِ ٱلرَّحِيمِ

² All praise is due to God, the Lord of the Universe; ³ the Beneficent, the Merciful; ⁴ Lord of the Day of Judgement. ⁵ You alone we worship, and to You alone we turn for help. ⁶ Guide us to the straight path: ⁷ the path of those You have blessed; not of those who have incurred <u>Your wrath</u>, nor of those who have gone astray.[a]

ٱلْحَمْدُ لِلَّهِ رَبِّ ٱلْعَٰلَمِينَ ﴿١﴾ ٱلرَّحْمَٰنِ ٱلرَّحِيمِ ﴿٢﴾ مَٰلِكِ يَوْمِ ٱلدِّينِ ﴿٣﴾ إِيَّاكَ نَعْبُدُ وَإِيَّاكَ نَسْتَعِينُ ﴿٤﴾ ٱهْدِنَا ٱلصِّرَٰطَ ٱلْمُسْتَقِيمَ ﴿٥﴾ صِرَٰطَ ٱلَّذِينَ أَنْعَمْتَ عَلَيْهِمْ غَيْرِ ٱلْمَغْضُوبِ عَلَيْهِمْ وَلَا ٱلضَّآلِّينَ ﴿٧﴾

---

[a] The best way to begin any task is in the name of God, the Lord, the Being who is the source of all blessings, and whose blessings and mercy are continually pouring upon His creation. To commence any undertaking in His name is to pray that God, in His infinite mercy, should come to one's assistance and bring one's work to a successful conclusion. This is man's acknowledgement of the fact that he is God's servant, and also brings divine assurance of success.

The Quran has a special and characteristic way of expressing a believer's inner sentiments in the most appropriate words. The invocation of God, in the opening chapter of the Quran, constitutes a supplication of this nature. The feelings which are naturally aroused in one after discovering the truth are expressed in these lines. Man's existence is a very great gift of God. We can estimate its greatness by the fact that man would never exchange it, or even any apart of it—his eyes or hands, or any organ of his body—for the greatest treasures of the world.

Even these basic gifts of God (organs of the body) are more precious than the kingdoms of the kings. When man looks at the world around him, he cannot fail to notice God's power and mercy abundantly in evidence everywhere. Wherever he casts his glance, he finds extraordinary order and supervision. Everything has been extraordinarily and astonishingly adapted to man's needs. This observation shows that the great cosmic machine cannot be in vain. Therefore, one realizes that there must come a day when the grateful and the ungrateful are rewarded for the way they have lived their lives in this world. One spontaneously entreats God in words to this effect, 'Lord, You are the Master of the Day of Judgement. I have submitted to You and humbly seek Your help; have mercy on me. Lord, show us the path that is, to You, the true path. Enable us to tread the path of Your chosen servants. Help us to avoid the path of those who have gone astray, and the path of those who have incurred Your wrath due to their obstinacy.'

God requires His servant to live his life with such feelings and emotions. The opening chapter of the Quran is a miniature portrayal of Islamic belief; the rest of the Quran is an enlargement of this picture.

2. THE HEIFER

In the name of God,
the Most Gracious, the Most Merciful

¹ *Alif Lam Mim*

² This is the Book; there is no doubt in it. It is a guide for those who are mindful of God, ³ who believe in the unseen, and are steadfast in prayer, and spend out of what We have provided them with; ⁴ those who believe in the revelation sent down to you and in what was sent before you, and firmly believe in the life to come—⁵ they are the people who are rightly following their Lord and it is they who shall be successful.*

ᵃ There is no doubt that the Quran is a book of guidance. But it guides only those who are sincere in their search for truth, and who are anxious to be guided. The search for truth is inherent in man's nature; one has simply to uncover one's own true nature in order to find it. True searching and true finding are but the initial and the advanced stages of the same journey. One who searches for truth unravels the closed faculties of his own inner self. Thus with God's help, the vague yearnings of his nature begin to receive a definite response.

The awakening within one of these sincere yearnings is an attempt to discern the world of meanings (the hidden world) behind the world of forms (the present world). When this leads to a discovery, it is transformed into faith in the unseen. That which is initially an urge to submit to some superior power, later takes on the form of bowing to the Almighty. That which is initially a wish to sacrifice oneself for some greater good, later takes the form of spending one's wealth for the cause of God. That which is initially a quest to comprehend the final outcome of life beyond this world, finds an answer in the form of faith in the life to come.

To discover truth is to raise one's consciousness to the level of the supreme reality. Those who find truth in this way become complex-free souls. They come to see truth as it really is. Wherever truth is, and whoever proclaims it, they immediately recognize and accept it. No rigidity, convention or prejudice, can come between them and the truth. God gives His protection to people having this nature. His universal order embraces them, so that they may be guided on a sure course in this world. Heaven will be their final destination in the life to come. Only those who seek truth can find it. Those who seek it shall surely find it. On this path, there is no divide between seeking and finding.

⁶ As for those who are bent on denying the truth, it makes no difference to them whether you warn them or not, they will not believe. ⁷ God has sealed their hearts and their ears, and over their eyes there is a covering. They will have a terrible punishment.*

إِنَّ ٱلَّذِينَ كَفَرُوا۟ سَوَآءٌ عَلَيْهِمْ ءَأَنذَرْتَهُمْ أَمْ لَمْ تُنذِرْهُمْ لَا يُؤْمِنُونَ ۝ خَتَمَ ٱللَّهُ عَلَىٰ قُلُوبِهِمْ وَعَلَىٰ سَمْعِهِمْ وَعَلَىٰٓ أَبْصَٰرِهِمْ غِشَٰوَةٌ وَلَهُمْ عَذَابٌ عَظِيمٌ ۝

→ God determines?
God solidifies the reality of those who deny?

ᵃ If one closes one's eyes, one will not be able to see. If one blocks one's ears, one will not be able to hear. However clear the call of truth may be, it can be understood and accepted only if one opens one's mind to it. God's inaudible call present in the universe, and the audible expression of that call by the preacher of God's word, cannot touch those who have closed minds. *determined punishment*

The call of truth in its pure, unadulterated form is founded on reality; it is in accord with nature. When it is made, none can fail to recognize it. If one hears it with an open mind, one will know in one's heart that it is nothing else but truth. However, where society is rigidly bound by age-old conventions, people are less concerned with opening their minds to divine realities than they are with supporting the vested interests of the existing system.

As God's emissary, the preacher is neither a representative nor a supporter of the conventional structures of society. His call, being new and unfamiliar, poses itself as a threat to material security. Much as people are urged by him to submit to the will of God, they baulk at doing so, because it would mean demolishing the world they have made for themselves. It is difficult also for him to convey his message to highly placed individuals who are afraid that, if they follow an 'insignificant' person, they will thereby suffer some diminution of their own personal glory. The two greatest obstacles then to the success of the preacher are people's worldliness and arrogance.

It is these mental states, which prevent people from accepting the truth; the Quran has called them 'seals' over people's hearts. The minds of those who do not consider the call of truth seriously, who are proud and worldly in their attitude, are covered with an invisible veil which makes them impervious to the truth. When one is prejudiced against something, one cannot see its rationality, even if there are clear signs in support of it.

INVISIBLE VEIL TO TRUTH

8 There are some who say, 'We believe in God and the Last Day,' yet they are not believers. 9 They seek to deceive God and the believers, but they only deceive themselves, though they do not realize it. 10 In their hearts is a disease, which God has increased. They will have a painful punishment, because they have been lying. 11 When they are told, 'Do not cause corruption in the land,' they say, 'We are only promoters of peace,' 12 but it is they who are really causing corruption, though they do not realize it. 13 And when they are told, 'Believe as other people have believed,' they say, 'Are we to believe just as fools believe?' Surely they are the fools, even though they do not realize it.[a]

وَمِنَ ٱلنَّاسِ مَن يَقُولُ ءَامَنَّا بِٱللَّهِ وَبِٱلْيَوْمِ ٱلْأَخِرِ وَمَا هُم بِمُؤْمِنِينَ ۝ يُخَٰدِعُونَ ٱللَّهَ وَٱلَّذِينَ ءَامَنُوا۟ وَمَا يَخْدَعُونَ إِلَّآ أَنفُسَهُمْ وَمَا يَشْعُرُونَ ۝ فِى قُلُوبِهِم مَّرَضٌ فَزَادَهُمُ ٱللَّهُ مَرَضًا ۖ وَلَهُمْ عَذَابٌ أَلِيمٌۢ بِمَا كَانُوا۟ يَكْذِبُونَ ۝ وَإِذَا قِيلَ لَهُمْ لَا تُفْسِدُوا۟ فِى ٱلْأَرْضِ قَالُوٓا۟ إِنَّمَا نَحْنُ مُصْلِحُونَ ۝ أَلَآ إِنَّهُمْ هُمُ ٱلْمُفْسِدُونَ وَلَٰكِن لَّا يَشْعُرُونَ ۝ وَإِذَا قِيلَ لَهُمْ ءَامِنُوا۟ كَمَآ ءَامَنَ ٱلنَّاسُ قَالُوٓا۟ أَنُؤْمِنُ كَمَآ ءَامَنَ ٱلسُّفَهَآءُ ۗ أَلَآ إِنَّهُمْ هُمُ ٱلسُّفَهَآءُ وَلَٰكِن لَّا يَعْلَمُونَ ۝

a For those who put worldly interests and expediency first, total and unconditional devotion to truth appears unwise, for their true allegiance is to their worldly interests; only on a superficial level can they attach themselves to the truth. They consider themselves clever. They think they are safeguarding themselves in this world, and also qualifying to be considered among the pious. But this is no more than wishful thinking; it is a figment of their imagination rather than a real fact of life. Every test in life removes them further from the path of true religion and brings them closer to their own world-oriented 'religion'. Their hypocrisy is like a cancer which keeps on growing. They consider true believers, who act in the interests of truth, to be ruining themselves for no good reason. They call their own policy, on the other hand, one of reform; they prize it because it enables them to pursue a safe course without clashing with anyone; but this just shows how distorted their reasoning is. If they were to think deeply, they would realize that on earth reform can only come from man giving himself up to God alone, while obstructing any movement aimed at consolidating man's relationship with the will of his Lord amounts to creating disorder on earth. Their seemingly profitable business is in fact running at a loss. For, they are forsaking pure truth for an adulterated version of it, which can benefit none.

¹⁴ When they meet those who believe, they say, 'We believe.' But when they are alone with their evil leaders, they say, 'We are really with you; we were only mocking.' ¹⁵ God will requite them for their mockery, and draw them on, for a while, to wander blindly in their insolence. ¹⁶ Such are those who have taken misguidance in exchange for guidance; but their bargain does not profit them, nor have they found true guidance.

¹⁷ They are like those who kindled a fire, and when it lighted up all around them, God took away their sight and left them in utter darkness, unable to see—¹⁸ deaf, dumb, and blind: they will never return [to the right path].^a

وَإِذَا لَقُواْ ٱلَّذِينَ ءَامَنُواْ قَالُوٓاْ ءَامَنَّا وَإِذَا خَلَوْاْ إِلَىٰ شَيَـٰطِينِهِمْ قَالُوٓاْ إِنَّا مَعَكُمْ إِنَّمَا نَحْنُ مُسْتَهْزِءُونَ ۝ ٱللَّهُ يَسْتَهْزِئُ بِهِمْ وَيَمُدُّهُمْ فِى طُغْيَـٰنِهِمْ يَعْمَهُونَ ۝ أُوْلَـٰٓئِكَ ٱلَّذِينَ ٱشْتَرَوُاْ ٱلضَّلَـٰلَةَ بِٱلْهُدَىٰ فَمَا رَبِحَت تِّجَـٰرَتُهُمْ وَمَا كَانُواْ مُهْتَدِينَ ۝ مَثَلُهُمْ كَمَثَلِ ٱلَّذِى ٱسْتَوْقَدَ نَارًا فَلَمَّآ أَضَآءَتْ مَا حَوْلَهُ ذَهَبَ ٱللَّهُ بِنُورِهِمْ وَتَرَكَهُمْ فِى ظُلُمَـٰتٍ لَّا يُبْصِرُونَ ۝ صُمٌّ بُكْمٌ عُمْىٌ فَهُمْ لَا يَرْجِعُونَ ۝

^a In a dark room black and white look the same, but as soon as the lights are turned on, black appears as black, and white as white. The same is true of the message of God, which was revealed to the prophets. The divine scriptures are God's beacons to the world. When this light is shed upon mankind, guidance and error clearly appear for what they are. It becomes evident what good and evil deeds consist of, and what their consequences are. But some people, instead of bowing to the truth, want the truth to be subservient to them. The light of God only serves to confuse them. Their hidden jealousy and pride take hold of them. As soon as they see themselves in the divine mirror, their negative sentiments are aroused. Deep-rooted prejudices overcome their senses. They have eyes, but cannot see; they have ears, but cannot hear; they have tongues, but cannot speak. They can neither hear the call of truth, nor respond to it in any way, nor can they find their way by any sign from God. Instead of reflecting upon the call of truth, as they should do, they evade it either by attaching no importance to it, or by not listening to it at all.

¹⁹ Or their case is like that of heavy rain pouring down from the clouds, accompanied by darkness, thunder and lightning; they thrust their fingers in their ears at the sound of thunderclaps for fear of death. God thus encompasses those who deny the truth. ²⁰ The lightning almost takes away their sight: whenever it flashes upon them, they walk on, but as soon as darkness falls around them, they stand still. Indeed, if God pleased, He could take away their hearing and their sight: God has power over all things.ᵃ

أَوْ كَصَيِّبٍ مِّنَ ٱلسَّمَآءِ فِيهِ ظُلُمَٰتٌ وَرَعْدٌ وَبَرْقٌ يَجْعَلُونَ أَصَٰبِعَهُمْ فِىٓ ءَاذَانِهِم مِّنَ ٱلصَّوَٰعِقِ حَذَرَ ٱلْمَوْتِ وَٱللَّهُ مُحِيطٌۢ بِٱلْكَٰفِرِينَ ۝ يَكَادُ ٱلْبَرْقُ يَخْطَفُ أَبْصَٰرَهُمْ كُلَّمَآ أَضَآءَ لَهُم مَّشَوْا۟ فِيهِ وَإِذَآ أَظْلَمَ عَلَيْهِمْ قَامُوا۟ وَلَوْ شَآءَ ٱللَّهُ لَذَهَبَ بِسَمْعِهِمْ وَأَبْصَٰرِهِمْ إِنَّ ٱللَّهَ عَلَىٰ كُلِّ شَىْءٍ قَدِيرٌ ۝

ᵃ Fear is another factor which prevents them from acknowledging the truth. Rain is a wonderful blessing of God. But with rain, come thunder and lightning, which terrify faint-hearted people. God's word as revealed to His prophets affects them similarly. On the one hand, it holds out to man the promise of great success, but on the other hand, its acceptance places man temporarily at risk: there is the fear of losing one's worldly position; of clashing with the conventional set-up. Fear of these things sometimes makes one halt, and sometimes makes one move hesitantly on. But such caution cannot help one. Those who do not respond to God's call open-heartedly shall be deprived of God's blessings in this world as well as in the Hereafter.

²¹ People, worship your Lord, who created you and those before you, so that you may become righteous, ²² who made the earth a bed, and the sky a canopy; and it is He who sends down rain from above for the growth of every kind of food for your sustenance. And do not knowingly set up rivals to God. ²³ If you are in doubt about the revelation We have sent down to Our servant, then produce a single chapter like it, and call upon your helpers besides God, if you are truthful. ²⁴ But if you cannot do it, and you can never do it, then guard yourselves against the Fire whose fuel is men and stones, prepared for those who deny the truth.ᵃ

يَـٰٓأَيُّهَا ٱلنَّاسُ ٱعْبُدُواْ رَبَّكُمُ ٱلَّذِى خَلَقَكُمْ وَٱلَّذِينَ مِن قَبْلِكُمْ لَعَلَّكُمْ تَتَّقُونَ ۝ ٱلَّذِى جَعَلَ لَكُمُ ٱلْأَرْضَ فِرَٰشًا وَٱلسَّمَآءَ بِنَآءً وَأَنزَلَ مِنَ ٱلسَّمَآءِ مَآءً فَأَخْرَجَ بِهِۦ مِنَ ٱلثَّمَرَٰتِ رِزْقًا لَّكُمْ فَلَا تَجْعَلُواْ لِلَّهِ أَندَادًا وَأَنتُمْ تَعْلَمُونَ ۝ وَإِن كُنتُمْ فِى رَيْبٍ مِّمَّا نَزَّلْنَا عَلَىٰ عَبْدِنَا فَأْتُواْ بِسُورَةٍ مِّن مِّثْلِهِۦ وَٱدْعُواْ شُهَدَآءَكُم مِّن دُونِ ٱللَّهِ إِن كُنتُمْ صَـٰدِقِينَ ۝ فَإِن لَّمْ تَفْعَلُواْ وَلَن تَفْعَلُواْ فَٱتَّقُواْ ٱلنَّارَ ٱلَّتِى وَقُودُهَا ٱلنَّاسُ وَٱلْحِجَارَةُ أُعِدَّتْ لِلْكَـٰفِرِينَ ۝

ᵃ God alone has created man and all that is in the heavens and on earth. He has invested the world with profound significance and He constantly looks after its needs. The proper course for a man is to take God as his Creator, Master and Sustainer, and not attempt to set up anyone as a partner with Him; that is, a man should give himself up entirely to God. But since He is invisible, it often happens that man gives importance to some visible object and worships that instead of God. He equates the created with the Creator—sometimes just a part of it and sometimes creation in its entirety, at times calling it by the name of God and at times doing so without taking God's name.

Therein lies man's basic error. The prophets taught man to glorify God alone, and forsake the other things that he had elevated to a position of glory. People whose hearts are attached to objects other than God consider the call of true religion repugnant. They have become so greatly attached to their supposed 'deities' that they cannot believe that they are unreal. They cannot believe that the truth is what is proclaimed by a mortal just like themselves.

²⁵ Give the good news to those who believe and do good works, that they will have Gardens through which rivers flow: whenever they are given fruit to eat they will say, 'This is what we were provided with before,' because they were given similar things. And there will be pure spouses for them, and they will abide there forever.ᵃ

وَبَشِّرِ ٱلَّذِينَ ءَامَنُوا۟ وَعَمِلُوا۟ ٱلصَّٰلِحَٰتِ أَنَّ لَهُمْ جَنَّٰتٍ تَجْرِى مِن تَحْتِهَا ٱلْأَنْهَٰرُ ۖ كُلَّمَا رُزِقُوا۟ مِنْهَا مِن ثَمَرَةٍ رِّزْقًا ۙ قَالُوا۟ هَٰذَا ٱلَّذِى رُزِقْنَا مِن قَبْلُ ۖ وَأُتُوا۟ بِهِۦ مُتَشَٰبِهًا ۖ وَلَهُمْ فِيهَآ أَزْوَٰجٌ مُّطَهَّرَةٌ ۖ وَهُمْ فِيهَا خَٰلِدُونَ ۝

ᵃ The call of truth is indisputably marked with a divine radiance. Its inimitable style and its irrefutable reasoning go to show that it is a message from God. Those who deny it, irrespective of this, shall find no refuge in God's universe. Those who find God in the word of God are already given a glimpse of the next world. They are the ones who shall be admitted into the gardens of Paradise.

²⁶ God does not disdain to give a parable about a gnat or a smaller creature. The faithful know that it is the truth from their Lord, but those who deny the truth ask, 'What could God mean by this parable?' He lets many go astray through it, and guides many by it. But He makes only the disobedient go astray: ²⁷ those who break God's covenant after they have pledged to keep it, and sever whatever God has ordered to be joined, and spread corruption in the land—it is they who are the losers. ²⁸ How can you disbelieve in God when you were dead [lifeless] and He gave you life? He will let you die once more, then bring you back to life again, whereupon you will be returned to Him.ᵃ

﴿ إِنَّ ٱللَّهَ لَا يَسْتَحْىِۦٓ أَن يَضْرِبَ مَثَلًا مَّا بَعُوضَةً فَمَا فَوْقَهَا فَأَمَّا ٱلَّذِينَ ءَامَنُواْ فَيَعْلَمُونَ أَنَّهُ ٱلْحَقُّ مِن رَّبِّهِمْ وَأَمَّا ٱلَّذِينَ كَفَرُواْ فَيَقُولُونَ مَاذَآ أَرَادَ ٱللَّهُ بِهَٰذَا مَثَلًا يُضِلُّ بِهِۦ كَثِيرًا وَيَهْدِى بِهِۦ كَثِيرًا وَمَا يُضِلُّ بِهِۦٓ إِلَّا ٱلْفَٰسِقِينَ ۝ ٱلَّذِينَ يَنقُضُونَ عَهْدَ ٱللَّهِ مِنۢ بَعْدِ مِيثَٰقِهِۦ وَيَقْطَعُونَ مَآ أَمَرَ ٱللَّهُ بِهِۦٓ أَن يُوصَلَ وَيُفْسِدُونَ فِى ٱلْأَرْضِ أُوْلَٰٓئِكَ هُمُ ٱلْخَٰسِرُونَ ۝ كَيْفَ تَكْفُرُونَ بِٱللَّهِ وَكُنتُمْ أَمْوَٰتًا فَأَحْيَٰكُمْ ثُمَّ يُمِيتُكُمْ ثُمَّ يُحْيِيكُمْ ثُمَّ إِلَيْهِ تُرْجَعُونَ ۝

ᵃ Man's first duty to God is to be true to the covenant made between the Creator and His creatures at the beginning of the world, namely, that man should remain God's servant. Then, his conduct towards his fellow men should be such that all the ties that God has enjoined man to keep may be consolidated. Thirdly, man should not turn people away from following the divine call raised by one of God's servants by inventing groundless arguments against it. The message of truth seeks to harmonize man with his own nature: those who prevent others from receiving it are guilty of spreading corruption in the land.

God has created man from nothing. This is a favour great enough to make man completely surrender himself to God. But God has not just created man and left it at that: He has given him an earth made to suit his needs perfectly. But there is more to the matter than merely this. Immediately after his demise, he will be brought before the Lord of the Universe to be judged. This state of affairs demands that he devote himself entirely to God; that he remember and obey God throughout his life, forever remaining His humble servant.

When the divine message is so clear and reasonable, why do people not accept it? The chief cause is unwillingness to learn. This manifests itself in various ways: deliberate denigration of God's message, attempts to belittle it by finding flaws ▶

²⁹ It is He who created everything on the earth for you: then He turned towards heaven and fashioned it into the seven heavens. He has knowledge of all things.

³⁰ When your Lord said to the angels, 'I am putting a successor on earth,' they said, 'Will You place someone there who will cause corruption on it and shed blood, while we glorify You with Your praise and extol Your holiness?' [God] answered, 'Surely, I know that which you do not know.'ᵃ

هُوَ ٱلَّذِى خَلَقَ لَكُم مَّا فِى ٱلْأَرْضِ جَمِيعًا ثُمَّ ٱسْتَوَىٰٓ إِلَى ٱلسَّمَآءِ فَسَوَّىٰهُنَّ سَبْعَ سَمَٰوَٰتٍ وَهُوَ بِكُلِّ شَىْءٍ عَلِيمٌ ۝ وَإِذْ قَالَ رَبُّكَ لِلْمَلَٰٓئِكَةِ إِنِّى جَاعِلٌ فِى ٱلْأَرْضِ خَلِيفَةً قَالُوٓاْ أَتَجْعَلُ فِيهَا مَن يُفْسِدُ فِيهَا وَيَسْفِكُ ٱلدِّمَآءَ وَنَحْنُ نُسَبِّحُ بِحَمْدِكَ وَنُقَدِّسُ لَكَ قَالَ إِنِّىٓ أَعْلَمُ مَا لَا تَعْلَمُونَ ۝

in it, or misrepresenting it as irrational or concerned with mere trivialities. One who is not willing to learn from sound advice does not think seriously about it. When some argument is presented to him, he looks at it superficially and sets about finding some shortcomings in it. But those who are willing to learn take the trouble to give those arguments serious thought and they do not take long to realize that they are faced with the truth. It does not make any difference to them that the truth has been explained in parables of mere gnats, and other equally insignificant creatures.

ᵃ The literal meaning of '*khalifah*' or 'caliph' is 'one who takes another's place'— a successor. In the age of hereditary rule, it was generally used for a monarch who took the place of his predecessor. According to this usage, the word came to refer to one invested with power. When God created man to dwell on earth, He decreed that he might enjoy freedom of will. The angels became apprehensive of man being corrupted by this grant of power and free will and, as a consequence, spreading evil and causing bloodshed in the world. History showed that their fears were well founded. God was also fully aware of this possibility. But He had a particular reason for investing man with power and freedom on earth. If many human beings were to be corrupted by their power, there would also be a substantial number who, in spite of their power and freedom on earth, would acknowledge God's greatness and power and their own helplessness. Such people would, of their own free will, adopt the path of submission and obedience to God. Although comparatively few in number, they would be specially prized above all others. They would be just like the food grains at harvest time, which, although greatly outweighed in bulk by chaff and straw, are the truly valued part of the crop. (Indeed if the chaff and straw are permitted to grow, it is solely so that people may have access to grain.)

³¹ He taught Adam all the names,^a then He set them before the angels and said, 'Tell Me the names of these, if what you say be true.' ³² They said, 'Glory be to You; we have no knowledge except whatever You have taught us. You are the All Knowing, the All Wise.' ³³ Then He said, 'O Adam, tell them their names.' When Adam had told them the names, God said to the angels, 'Did I not say to you: I know the secrets of the heavens and of the earth, and I know what you reveal and what you conceal?'^b

وَعَلَّمَ ءَادَمَ ٱلْأَسْمَآءَ كُلَّهَا ثُمَّ عَرَضَهُمْ عَلَى ٱلْمَلَـٰئِكَةِ فَقَالَ أَنۢبِـُٔونِى بِأَسْمَآءِ هَـٰٓؤُلَآءِ إِن كُنتُمْ صَـٰدِقِينَ ۝ قَالُوا۟ سُبْحَـٰنَكَ لَا عِلْمَ لَنَآ إِلَّا مَا عَلَّمْتَنَآ إِنَّكَ أَنتَ ٱلْعَلِيمُ ٱلْحَكِيمُ ۝ قَالَ يَـٰٓـَٔادَمُ أَنۢبِئْهُم بِأَسْمَآئِهِمْ فَلَمَّآ أَنۢبَأَهُم بِأَسْمَآئِهِمْ قَالَ أَلَمْ أَقُل لَّكُمْ إِنِّىٓ أَعْلَمُ غَيْبَ ٱلسَّمَـٰوَٰتِ وَٱلْأَرْضِ وَأَعْلَمُ مَا تُبْدُونَ وَمَا كُنتُمْ تَكْتُمُونَ ۝

^a The mixture of good and evil in mankind became evident when God, in His omnipotence, brought all the progeny of Adam before their first father. He said to the angels, 'Look, these are the progeny of Adam. Can you give me the name of each one of them, and say what sort of people they will be?' The angels, having no knowledge of them, were unable to answer. Then God told Adam their names and characteristics, and then commanded him to pass the knowledge on to the angels. When Adam had explained to them the nature of the human race, they realized that, besides the wicked and the corrupt, there would also be among their number great, righteous and pious souls.

^b Man's greatest crimes, after the denial of his Lord, are spreading corruption and causing bloodshed in the world. Neither an individual nor a group has God's permission to indulge in such actions as may disrupt the order of nature established by God. For example, no man should take the life of another: all actions of this nature disqualify mankind from receiving God's mercy. In short, preserving the system of nature is 'to reform' it, while upsetting this system is equal 'to spreading corruption'.

³⁴ When We said to the angels, 'Bow down before Adam,' they all bowed except for Iblis [Satan]. He refused and acted proudly and became an unbeliever. ³⁵ We said, 'O Adam! live with your wife in Paradise and eat freely from it anywhere you may wish. Yet do not approach this tree lest you become wrongdoers.' ³⁶ But Satan caused them both to slip through this and thus brought about the loss of their former state. We said, 'Go down from here as enemies to each other; and on earth you shall have your abode and your livelihood for a while!' ᵃ

وَإِذْ قُلْنَا لِلْمَلَٰٓئِكَةِ ٱسْجُدُوا۟ لِءَادَمَ فَسَجَدُوٓا۟ إِلَّآ إِبْلِيسَ أَبَىٰ وَٱسْتَكْبَرَ وَكَانَ مِنَ ٱلْكَٰفِرِينَ ۝ وَقُلْنَا يَٰٓـَٔادَمُ ٱسْكُنْ أَنتَ وَزَوْجُكَ ٱلْجَنَّةَ وَكُلَا مِنْهَا رَغَدًا حَيْثُ شِئْتُمَا وَلَا تَقْرَبَا هَٰذِهِ ٱلشَّجَرَةَ فَتَكُونَا مِنَ ٱلظَّٰلِمِينَ ۝ فَأَزَلَّهُمَا ٱلشَّيْطَٰنُ عَنْهَا فَأَخْرَجَهُمَا مِمَّا كَانَا فِيهِ وَقُلْنَا ٱهْبِطُوا۟ بَعْضُكُمْ لِبَعْضٍ عَدُوٌّ وَلَكُمْ فِى ٱلْأَرْضِ مُسْتَقَرٌّ وَمَتَٰعٌ إِلَىٰ حِينٍ ۝

ᵃ When God made Adam stand up in front of the angels including Iblis (Satan), and tested them by commanding them to bow down before Adam, He was giving the first man on earth a practical demonstration of the two paths that would be open to his progeny. Either they would follow the example of the angels and bow to God's commandments, even if it meant bowing before someone they held inferior to themselves; or else they would be proud like Satan, and refuse to bow to others. This is the test that man faces throughout his entire life. Here on earth man is constantly faced with two alternative courses of action. He can either follow the course set by the angels and carry out God's commandments by bowing before truth and justice in all that he does; or he can act as Satan did and, letting himself be controlled by arrogance and contempt, refuse to concede the right of others.

³⁷ Then Adam received some words [of prayer] from his Lord and He accepted his repentance. He is the Forgiving One, the Merciful. ³⁸ We said, 'Go down, all of you, from here: then when guidance comes to you from Me, anyone who follows My guidance will have no fear, nor will they grieve— ³⁹ those who deny and reject Our signs shall be the inhabitants of the Fire; therein shall they abide forever.' ª

فَتَلَقَّىٰٓ ءَادَمُ مِن رَّبِّهِۦ كَلِمَٰتٍ فَتَابَ عَلَيْهِ إِنَّهُۥ هُوَ ٱلتَّوَّابُ ٱلرَّحِيمُ ۝ قُلْنَا ٱهْبِطُوا۟ مِنْهَا جَمِيعًا فَإِمَّا يَأْتِيَنَّكُم مِّنِّى هُدًى فَمَن تَبِعَ هُدَاىَ فَلَا خَوْفٌ عَلَيْهِمْ وَلَا هُمْ يَحْزَنُونَ ۝ وَٱلَّذِينَ كَفَرُوا۟ وَكَذَّبُوا۟ بِـَٔايَٰتِنَآ أُو۟لَٰٓئِكَ أَصْحَٰبُ ٱلنَّارِ هُمْ فِيهَا خَٰلِدُونَ ۝

ª The practical lesson of the forbidden tree demonstrates how man goes astray by letting himself be deceived by Satan, and exceeding the bounds that God has laid down for him. As soon as he eats of the 'forbidden fruit', he is deprived of God's grace or, in other words, Paradise. But this loss is not an irretrievable one. Man still has an opportunity to turn in repentance to his Lord, rectify his actions and seek forgiveness for his sins. When he turns to the Lord in repentance, God relents towards him, and cleanses him of his sins, as if he had never committed them.

The preacher of truth is an 'Adam'; it is for people to bow before him. If, carried away by pride and prejudice, they refuse to acknowledge his position, they are following in Satan's footsteps. Such a denial amounts to having failed the test devised for man by God.

God does not become plainly visible in this world; He reveals Himself through His signs, thereby testing his creatures. It is only those who can interpret His signs who will discover God Himself.

⁴⁰ Children of Israel, remember the favours I have bestowed upon you, and fulfil the covenant that you made with Me. I shall fulfil the covenant I made with you. Fear Me alone. ⁴¹ And believe in the message I have sent down which fulfils that [predictions about the last prophet in their Scripture] which you already possess and do not be foremost among those who deny its truth. Do not sell My revelations for a paltry price; fear Me alone.[a]

يَٰبَنِىٓ إِسۡرَٰٓءِيلَ ٱذۡكُرُواْ نِعۡمَتِىَ ٱلَّتِىٓ أَنۡعَمۡتُ عَلَيۡكُمۡ وَأَوۡفُواْ بِعَهۡدِىٓ أُوفِ بِعَهۡدِكُمۡ وَإِيَّٰىَ فَٱرۡهَبُونِ ۝ وَءَامِنُواْ بِمَآ أَنزَلۡتُ مُصَدِّقٗا لِّمَا مَعَكُمۡ وَلَا تَكُونُوٓاْ أَوَّلَ كَافِرِۭ بِهِۦ وَلَا تَشۡتَرُواْ بِـَٔايَٰتِى ثَمَنٗا قَلِيلٗا وَإِيَّٰىَ فَٱتَّقُونِ ۝

---

[a] The greatest favour that God bestows upon a people is to send His prophet to them, thus opening for them the road to eternal salvation. Prior to the times of the Prophet Muhammad—the last of the prophets—this favour was the privilege of the Children of Israel. However, soon their religion ceased to be something that they accepted as a matter of conscious decision, and they let it deteriorate into a set of lifeless rituals passed on from one generation to the next. With the coming of the Prophet Muhammad the reality came to light. Those whose sensitivity to truth was still alive recognized the veracity of his prophethood and followed him. But those for whom religion had become a hereditary tradition found his message unfamiliar and failed to recognize the truth when they heard it; they rejected it and turned against the Prophet.

In view of the clear prophecies in the Torah of the coming of an Arab Prophet, it would not have been difficult for the Israelites to recognize the truth of his prophethood and believe in him; but to believe in him was not in their worldly interests. Over hundreds of years an ecclesiastical structure had developed, in which the Israelites had held pride of place. Being the successors of saints and prophets, they were looked up to for spiritual leadership. People also paid tribute and presented offerings to them all the year round. It appeared to them that if they accepted the Arab Prophet, their privileged religious position would come to an end and their whole profit structure would be demolished.

⁴² Do not mix truth with falsehood, or hide the truth when you know it. ⁴³ Attend to your prayers, give the *zakat* [prescribed alms] and bow down with those who bow down. ⁴⁴ Do you admonish others to do good and forget this yourselves? Yet you read the Book. Will you not then understand? ⁴⁵ Seek help with patience and prayer; this is indeed an exacting discipline, but not to the humble, ⁴⁶ who know for certain that they will meet their Lord, and that they will return to Him.ᵃ

وَلَا تَلْبِسُوا۟ ٱلْحَقَّ بِٱلْبَٰطِلِ وَتَكْتُمُوا۟ ٱلْحَقَّ وَأَنتُمْ تَعْلَمُونَ ۞ وَأَقِيمُوا۟ ٱلصَّلَوٰةَ وَءَاتُوا۟ ٱلزَّكَوٰةَ وَٱرْكَعُوا۟ مَعَ ٱلرَّٰكِعِينَ ۞ ۞ أَتَأْمُرُونَ ٱلنَّاسَ بِٱلْبِرِّ وَتَنسَوْنَ أَنفُسَكُمْ وَأَنتُمْ تَتْلُونَ ٱلْكِتَٰبَ أَفَلَا تَعْقِلُونَ ۞ وَٱسْتَعِينُوا۟ بِٱلصَّبْرِ وَٱلصَّلَوٰةِ وَإِنَّهَا لَكَبِيرَةٌ إِلَّا عَلَى ٱلْخَٰشِعِينَ ۞ ٱلَّذِينَ يَظُنُّونَ أَنَّهُم مُّلَٰقُوا۟ رَبِّهِمْ وَأَنَّهُمْ إِلَيْهِ رَٰجِعُونَ ۞

ᵃ As the Israelites were considered representatives of revealed religion in the Arab world, people used to ask them about the Arab Prophet. Pretending innocence, they would put forward such points as would turn people away from the Prophet and his mission. They used to preach to people, exhorting them to follow the truth and live their lives according to it; in practice, however, they failed to accept the truth when their turn came to do so.

When a positive response to the call of God means relinquishing positions of high honour and prestige, then those who have gained religious rank through worldly elevation find it extremely difficult to follow this course. For the truly devout, however, these considerations are not a hindrance. The fulfillment that others find in worldly pleasures, true believers find in remembering God, in spending for His cause, in obeying His commandments and being steadfast in treading His path. They know full well that it is God's punishment that is to be feared, not worldly loss.

47 Children of Israel, remember My blessing which I have bestowed on you, and how I favoured you above all other people. 48 Guard yourselves against the Day on which no soul shall in the least avail another, when neither intercession nor ransom shall be accepted from it nor shall help be given to it. 49 Remember when We delivered you from Pharaoh's people, who subjected you to grievous torment, slaying your sons and sparing only your daughters—surely in that there was a great trial for you from your Lord—50 and when We divided the sea for you and saved you and drowned Pharaoh's people, while you looked on. 51 We appointed for Moses forty nights [on Mount Sinai], and in his absence you took to worshipping the calf, and thus became transgressors. 52 Yet after that We pardoned you, so that you might be grateful.[a]

يَـٰبَنِىٓ إِسْرَٰٓءِيلَ ٱذْكُرُوا۟ نِعْمَتِىَ ٱلَّتِىٓ أَنْعَمْتُ عَلَيْكُمْ وَأَنِّى فَضَّلْتُكُمْ عَلَى ٱلْعَـٰلَمِينَ ۝ وَٱتَّقُوا۟ يَوْمًا لَّا تَجْزِى نَفْسٌ عَن نَّفْسٍ شَيْـًٔا وَلَا يُقْبَلُ مِنْهَا شَفَـٰعَةٌ وَلَا يُؤْخَذُ مِنْهَا عَدْلٌ وَلَا هُمْ يُنصَرُونَ ۝ وَإِذْ نَجَّيْنَـٰكُم مِّنْ ءَالِ فِرْعَوْنَ يَسُومُونَكُمْ سُوٓءَ ٱلْعَذَابِ يُذَبِّحُونَ أَبْنَآءَكُمْ وَيَسْتَحْيُونَ نِسَآءَكُمْ وَفِى ذَٰلِكُم بَلَآءٌ مِّن رَّبِّكُمْ عَظِيمٌ ۝ وَإِذْ فَرَقْنَا بِكُمُ ٱلْبَحْرَ فَأَنجَيْنَـٰكُمْ وَأَغْرَقْنَآ ءَالَ فِرْعَوْنَ وَأَنتُمْ تَنظُرُونَ ۝ وَإِذْ وَٰعَدْنَا مُوسَىٰٓ أَرْبَعِينَ لَيْلَةً ثُمَّ ٱتَّخَذْتُمُ ٱلْعِجْلَ مِنۢ بَعْدِهِۦ وَأَنتُمْ ظَـٰلِمُونَ ۝ ثُمَّ عَفَوْنَا عَنكُم مِّنۢ بَعْدِ ذَٰلِكَ لَعَلَّكُمْ تَشْكُرُونَ ۝

---

[a] The Israelites were chosen by God. He selected them for a special task: they were to receive God's scriptures and pass His commandments on to the rest of mankind. In relation to this office, they were granted many other blessings and facilities: victory over their enemies, forgiveness of their sins, special help in times of peril, divine provision for their physical needs, and so on. This misled later generations of Jews into thinking that they were God's chosen people, and were assured of salvation in the next world. But such matters as salvation are not a hereditary right of any group. Successive generations are to be judged on their own merits. On the Day of Judgement people will be judged individually, according to their actions. To think that anything other than good deeds will avail one, is to underestimate the rigours of that Day.

⁵³ Remember when We gave Moses the Scripture, and the criterion [to distinguish between right and wrong], so that you might be guided. ⁵⁴ When Moses said to his people, 'O my people, you have indeed wronged yourselves by worshipping the calf; turn in repentance to your Creator and slay [the culprits] among you. That course is best for you in the sight of your Maker.' He relented towards you. He is the Forgiving One, the Merciful. ⁵⁵ Remember when you said, 'Moses, we will not believe in you until we see God with our own eyes,' a thunderbolt struck you while you were looking on. ⁵⁶ Then We brought you back to life after your death, so that you might be grateful. ⁵⁷ Then We caused the clouds to provide shade for you and sent down for you manna and quails, saying, 'Eat the good things We have provided for you.' Indeed, they did not wrong Us, but they wronged themselves.ᵃ

وَإِذْ ءَاتَيْنَا مُوسَى ٱلْكِتَٰبَ وَٱلْفُرْقَانَ لَعَلَّكُمْ تَهْتَدُونَ ۝ وَإِذْ قَالَ مُوسَىٰ لِقَوْمِهِۦ يَٰقَوْمِ إِنَّكُمْ ظَلَمْتُمْ أَنفُسَكُم بِٱتِّخَاذِكُمُ ٱلْعِجْلَ فَتُوبُوٓاْ إِلَىٰ بَارِئِكُمْ فَٱقْتُلُوٓاْ أَنفُسَكُمْ ذَٰلِكُمْ خَيْرٌ لَّكُمْ عِندَ بَارِئِكُمْ فَتَابَ عَلَيْكُمْ إِنَّهُۥ هُوَ ٱلتَّوَّابُ ٱلرَّحِيمُ ۝ وَإِذْ قُلْتُمْ يَٰمُوسَىٰ لَن نُّؤْمِنَ لَكَ حَتَّىٰ نَرَى ٱللَّهَ جَهْرَةً فَأَخَذَتْكُمُ ٱلصَّٰعِقَةُ وَأَنتُمْ تَنظُرُونَ ۝ ثُمَّ بَعَثْنَٰكُم مِّنۢ بَعْدِ مَوْتِكُمْ لَعَلَّكُمْ تَشْكُرُونَ ۝ وَظَلَّلْنَا عَلَيْكُمُ ٱلْغَمَامَ وَأَنزَلْنَا عَلَيْكُمُ ٱلْمَنَّ وَٱلسَّلْوَىٰ كُلُواْ مِن طَيِّبَٰتِ مَا رَزَقْنَٰكُمْ وَمَا ظَلَمُونَا وَلَٰكِن كَانُوٓاْ أَنفُسَهُمْ يَظْلِمُونَ ۝

ᵃ True piety is to worship God alone, to believe in Him though one has not seen Him, to live in fear of Judgement Day, to subsist on the pure things of the earth, to prevent whomsoever one can from falling into sin. It is those who adopt this way of life who will be successful in the next world.

⁵⁸ Remember when We said, 'Enter this land and eat freely wherever you will. Make your way through the gates, bowing down and saying, "God! Forgive us our sins." We shall forgive you your sins and We shall give abundance to those who do good.' ⁵⁹ But the wrongdoers changed the words to something other than what they had been told. So We sent down upon the transgressors a punishment from heaven, because they were disobedient. ⁶⁰ When Moses prayed for water for his people, We said to him, 'Strike the rock with your staff!' And there gushed out from it twelve springs. Each tribe knew its drinking-place. [We said], 'Eat and drink what God has provided and do not act wrongfully in the land, spreading corruption.'ᵃ

وَإِذْ قُلْنَا ٱدْخُلُوا۟ هَٰذِهِ ٱلْقَرْيَةَ فَكُلُوا۟ مِنْهَا حَيْثُ شِئْتُمْ رَغَدًا وَٱدْخُلُوا۟ ٱلْبَابَ سُجَّدًا وَقُولُوا۟ حِطَّةٌ نَّغْفِرْ لَكُمْ خَطَٰيَٰكُمْ ۚ وَسَنَزِيدُ ٱلْمُحْسِنِينَ ۝ فَبَدَّلَ ٱلَّذِينَ ظَلَمُوا۟ قَوْلًا غَيْرَ ٱلَّذِى قِيلَ لَهُمْ فَأَنزَلْنَا عَلَى ٱلَّذِينَ ظَلَمُوا۟ رِجْزًا مِّنَ ٱلسَّمَآءِ بِمَا كَانُوا۟ يَفْسُقُونَ ۝ ۞ وَإِذِ ٱسْتَسْقَىٰ مُوسَىٰ لِقَوْمِهِۦ فَقُلْنَا ٱضْرِب بِّعَصَاكَ ٱلْحَجَرَ ۖ فَٱنفَجَرَتْ مِنْهُ ٱثْنَتَا عَشْرَةَ عَيْنًا ۖ قَدْ عَلِمَ كُلُّ أُنَاسٍ مَّشْرَبَهُمْ ۖ كُلُوا۟ وَٱشْرَبُوا۟ مِن رِّزْقِ ٱللَّهِ وَلَا تَعْثَوْا۟ فِى ٱلْأَرْضِ مُفْسِدِينَ ۝

ᵃ God bestowed special blessings upon the Israelites. They should have shown their gratitude by remaining obedient to Him, but they did quite the opposite. They were given possession of a great city and told to enter it—not in a vainglorious manner—but in humility and repentance; but instead they started rejoicing in their victory.

⁶¹ When you said, 'Moses, we cannot bear to eat only one kind of food, so pray to your Lord to bring forth for us some of the earth's produce, its herbs and cucumbers, its garlic, lentils, and onions.'ᵃ Moses said, 'Would you take a lesser thing in exchange for what is better? Go to some town and there you will find all that you demand.' Abasement and destitution were stamped upon them, and they incurred the wrath of God, for having rejected His signs, and they killed His prophets unjustly, because they were rebels and transgressors.ᵇ

وَإِذْ قُلْتُمْ يَٰمُوسَىٰ لَن نَّصْبِرَ عَلَىٰ طَعَامٍ وَٰحِدٍ فَٱدْعُ لَنَا رَبَّكَ يُخْرِجْ لَنَا مِمَّا تُنۢبِتُ ٱلْأَرْضُ مِنۢ بَقْلِهَا وَقِثَّآئِهَا وَفُومِهَا وَعَدَسِهَا وَبَصَلِهَا ۖ قَالَ أَتَسْتَبْدِلُونَ ٱلَّذِى هُوَ أَدْنَىٰ بِٱلَّذِى هُوَ خَيْرٌ ۚ ٱهْبِطُوا۟ مِصْرًا فَإِنَّ لَكُم مَّا سَأَلْتُمْ ۗ وَضُرِبَتْ عَلَيْهِمُ ٱلذِّلَّةُ وَٱلْمَسْكَنَةُ وَبَآءُو بِغَضَبٍ مِّنَ ٱللَّهِ ۗ ذَٰلِكَ بِأَنَّهُمْ كَانُوا۟ يَكْفُرُونَ بِـَٔايَٰتِ ٱللَّهِ وَيَقْتُلُونَ ٱلنَّبِيِّـۧنَ بِغَيْرِ ٱلْحَقِّ ۗ ذَٰلِكَ بِمَا عَصَوا۟ وَّكَانُوا۟ يَعْتَدُونَ ۝

ᵃ Divine provision was given to them in the form of manna and quails so that, free from the struggle for a livelihood, they would be able to devote themselves entirely to carrying out God's commandments; but they took to demanding spicy, cooked foods instead. Discontented with the basic necessities of life, they sought to indulge in worldly luxury. So hardened did they become that even clear signs of God could not move their hearts. They opposed and even killed those servants of God who sought to admonish them.

ᵇ The reason for the Israelite's heedlessness was that they thought salvation was their birthright, whereas God will not judge anyone on an ethnic or hereditary basis. Jews will be judged according to the same divine law as non-Jews. Heaven is for those who prove themselves worthy of it by their actions; it is not the monopoly of any clan or community. Man's harmony with nature comes from his leading a life of thanksgiving, humility and contentment; by his remaining steadfast in the face of adversity. Ingratitude, hot-headedness, pride and greed only spread evil in the world, and lead to deviation from the natural order established by God.

⁶² The believers, the Jews, the Christians, and the Sabaeans—all those who believe in God and the Last Day and do good deeds—will be rewarded by their Lord; they shall have no fear, nor shall they grieve. *a*

إِنَّ ٱلَّذِينَ ءَامَنُواْ وَٱلَّذِينَ هَادُواْ وَٱلنَّصَـٰرَىٰ وَٱلصَّـٰبِـِٔينَ مَنْ ءَامَنَ بِٱللَّهِ وَٱلْيَوْمِ ٱلْأَخِرِ وَعَمِلَ صَـٰلِحًا فَلَهُمْ أَجْرُهُمْ عِندَ رَبِّهِمْ وَلَا خَوْفٌ عَلَيْهِمْ وَلَا هُمْ يَحْزَنُونَ ۝

---

a Four communities are mentioned in this verse: Muslims, who are the followers of the Prophet Muhammad; Jews who follow the Prophet Moses; Christians, who follow the Prophet Jesus; and Sabeans, who adhered to the teachings of John the Baptist, the Prophet Yahya. The last-mentioned sect resided in Iraq in ancient times, but is now extinct. They were people of the Book, and offered their prayers facing the Ka'bah in Makkah.

Here the Muslims have not been mentioned separately, but have been grouped with other communities associated with prophets. This means that all ethnic groups are equal in the sight of God; no community is inherently superior to any other. Only true belief and righteous actions are rewarded with salvation. This is a rule that applies consistently to every community. No one, whether he calls himself Muslim, Jew, Christian or Sabaean, is exempt from this rule. Belonging to a particular community gives no special status in the eyes of God. God elevates to a high rank only those who have sought to mould their own lives according to His divine scheme.

The lives of those who associate with a prophet during his lifetime are always based on true belief and righteous actions. At that time certain people hear the Prophet's call. Their spirits are moved by his message: an intellectual revolution takes place within them, filling them with new resolve. Their whole pattern of life changes. Where, previously, they had been guided by personal desires, they now base their lives on the teachings of God, and may truly call themselves followers of the prophets; these are the ones to whom the prophets gave good tidings of eternal blessings in the next world.

The situation changes, however, as time passes. For the generations that follow, religion becomes a kind of national heritage. Tidings, which had been given on the basis of faith and righteous actions come to be considered to be the result of ethnic affiliations. People reckon that they have a special relationship with God that others do not enjoy: one who belongs to a particular community is sure to be saved, notwithstanding the standard of his faith and deeds; paradise is for us, hell for them. But God does not have a special relationship with any particular community. He has regard solely for man's thoughts and deeds. In the Hereafter, people will be judged according to their deeds and character, and not on the basis of the group to which they belong.

63 [Children of Israel], We made a covenant with you and raised the mountain high above you, saying, 'Hold fast to what We have given you and bear its contents in mind, so that you may guard yourselves [against evil].' 64 Yet after that you turned away, and but for God's grace and mercy, you would have surely been among the losers. 65 You are aware of those who transgressed in the matter of the Sabbath, whereupon We said to them, 'Be as apes, despised!' 66 We made their fate an example to their own generation and to those who followed them and a lesson to those who fear God.[a]

وَإِذْ أَخَذْنَا مِيثَٰقَكُمْ وَرَفَعْنَا فَوْقَكُمُ ٱلطُّورَ خُذُوا۟ مَآ ءَاتَيْنَٰكُم بِقُوَّةٍ وَٱذْكُرُوا۟ مَا فِيهِ لَعَلَّكُمْ تَتَّقُونَ ۝ ثُمَّ تَوَلَّيْتُم مِّنۢ بَعْدِ ذَٰلِكَ فَلَوْلَا فَضْلُ ٱللَّهِ عَلَيْكُمْ وَرَحْمَتُهُۥ لَكُنتُم مِّنَ ٱلْخَٰسِرِينَ ۝ وَلَقَدْ عَلِمْتُمُ ٱلَّذِينَ ٱعْتَدَوْا۟ مِنكُمْ فِى ٱلسَّبْتِ فَقُلْنَا لَهُمْ كُونُوا۟ قِرَدَةً خَٰسِئِينَ ۝ فَجَعَلْنَٰهَا نَكَٰلًا لِّمَا بَيْنَ يَدَيْهَا وَمَا خَلْفَهَا وَمَوْعِظَةً لِّلْمُتَّقِينَ ۝

[a] A covenant was made with Moses' people that they would faithfully carry out the divine teachings given to them in the form of the Ten Commandments. The Talmud tells how, at this time, God turned a mountain upside down, holding it above them and told them either to accept the teachings of the Torah, or be destroyed there and then. The same is the case with everyone who embraces true faith. To have faith is to make a contract with God that one will live and die in accordance with His will. What a grave pledge this is. On the one hand there is man—a tiny, helpless speck in God's world—and on the other, God, whose might upholds the universe. If man keeps his word, he will be granted God's eternal blessings. But if he turns away from his commitment, he is in grave danger of being cast into hell-fire, never to emerge again.

Everyone who believes in God should go through the same experience as Moses' people. Everyone who binds himself to the contract of faith should live in the fear of breaking his religious vows, thereby bringing catastrophe down upon himself.

Sometimes those entrusted with the law of God go astray by contradicting it in practice, while finding words to make it appear that they are following it to the letter. The Israelites, for instance, were commanded to keep holy the Sabbath day, and refrain from worldly pursuits on that day. But they violated it and went about their work on the Sabbath as on any other day. Furthermore, they sought to justify their actions and made out that what they were doing conformed to the will of God. This audacity incurred God's displeasure and they were turned into apes. Whenever one turns against the law of God, one puts oneself on a par with animals who follow no code of ethics. Those who play games with divine law, should fear being deprived of their human dignity, and being brought down to the level of animals.

⁶⁷ When Moses said to his people, 'God commands you to sacrifice a heifer,' they said, 'Are you making a mockery of us?' He answered, 'God forbid that I should be so ignorant!' ⁶⁸ They said, 'Ask your Lord to make it clear to us what sort of heifer she should be.' He answered, 'God says she should be neither too old nor too young, but in between, so do as you are commanded.' ⁶⁹ They said, 'Call on your Lord for us, to show us what colour she should be.' He answered, 'God says she should be a bright yellow heifer, pleasing to the eye.' ⁷⁰ They said, 'Ask your Lord to make it clear to us the exact type of heifer she should be, for to us all heifers look alike. If God wills, we shall be rightly guided.' ⁷¹ Moses answered, 'Your Lord says, she should be a heifer which has not been yoked to plough the land or water the fields, a heifer free from any blemish.' 'Now you have told us the truth,' they answered, and they sacrificed it, though they would rather not have done it.ᵃ

وَإِذْ قَالَ مُوسَىٰ لِقَوْمِهِۦٓ إِنَّ ٱللَّهَ يَأْمُرُكُمْ أَن تَذْبَحُوا۟ بَقَرَةً ۖ قَالُوٓا۟ أَتَتَّخِذُنَا هُزُوًا ۖ قَالَ أَعُوذُ بِٱللَّهِ أَنْ أَكُونَ مِنَ ٱلْجَٰهِلِينَ ۝ قَالُوا۟ ٱدْعُ لَنَا رَبَّكَ يُبَيِّن لَّنَا مَا هِىَ ۚ قَالَ إِنَّهُۥ يَقُولُ إِنَّهَا بَقَرَةٌ لَّا فَارِضٌ وَلَا بِكْرٌ عَوَانٌۢ بَيْنَ ذَٰلِكَ ۖ فَٱفْعَلُوا۟ مَا تُؤْمَرُونَ ۝ قَالُوا۟ ٱدْعُ لَنَا رَبَّكَ يُبَيِّن لَّنَا مَا لَوْنُهَا ۚ قَالَ إِنَّهُۥ يَقُولُ إِنَّهَا بَقَرَةٌ صَفْرَآءُ فَاقِعٌ لَّوْنُهَا تَسُرُّ ٱلنَّٰظِرِينَ ۝ قَالُوا۟ ٱدْعُ لَنَا رَبَّكَ يُبَيِّن لَّنَا مَا هِىَ إِنَّ ٱلْبَقَرَ تَشَٰبَهَ عَلَيْنَا وَإِنَّآ إِن شَآءَ ٱللَّهُ لَمُهْتَدُونَ ۝ قَالَ إِنَّهُۥ يَقُولُ إِنَّهَا بَقَرَةٌ لَّا ذَلُولٌ تُثِيرُ ٱلْأَرْضَ وَلَا تَسْقِى ٱلْحَرْثَ مُسَلَّمَةٌ لَّا شِيَةَ فِيهَا ۚ قَالُوا۟ ٱلْـَٰٔنَ جِئْتَ بِٱلْحَقِّ ۚ فَذَبَحُوهَا وَمَا كَادُوا۟ يَفْعَلُونَ ۝

ᵃ Another mistake that the Israelites had made was to destroy the simplicity of divine religion by involving themselves in complicated theological wrangling. They had to learn to interpret God's will in a straightforward manner and obey it immediately. This was another lesson that was taught under the pretext of this murder case: hair-splitting to define the exact scope of divine edicts will only make things difficult for everyone; additional conditions will only complicate the carrying out of what had originally been a simple commandment.

⁷² Then, when you [Israelites] killed someone and started to blame one another—God brought to light what you concealed—⁷³ We said, 'Strike [the corpse] with a part of it.' Thus God restores the dead to life and shows you His signs, so that you may understand.^a

وَإِذْ قَتَلْتُمْ نَفْسًا فَٱدَّٰرَٰٓءْتُمْ فِيهَا ۖ وَٱللَّهُ مُخْرِجٌ مَّا كُنتُمْ تَكْتُمُونَ ۝ فَقُلْنَا ٱضْرِبُوهُ بِبَعْضِهَا ۚ كَذَٰلِكَ يُحْىِ ٱللَّهُ ٱلْمَوْتَىٰ وَيُرِيكُمْ ءَايَٰتِهِۦ لَعَلَّكُمْ تَعْقِلُونَ ۝

---

^a A murder was committed among the Israelites in Moses' time. The method that God revealed to His prophet to identify the killer was that an animal should be sacrificed, and the dead man's corpse be struck with a piece of it. The dead man would then name the murderer.

The third lesson in this instance was that life after death is no less a reality than life before death. Just as the dead corpse was revived, so every soul will be raised up in the Hereafter and given new life.

74 Then your hearts became as hard as rock or even harder: for, there are rocks from which streams gush forth; and, there are some that cleave asunder and water flows out from them, while others fall down for fear of God. God is not unaware of what you do.[a]

ثُمَّ قَسَتْ قُلُوبُكُم مِّنۢ بَعْدِ ذَٰلِكَ فَهِىَ كَٱلْحِجَارَةِ أَوْ أَشَدُّ قَسْوَةً ۚ وَإِنَّ مِنَ ٱلْحِجَارَةِ لَمَا يَتَفَجَّرُ مِنْهُ ٱلْأَنْهَٰرُ ۚ وَإِنَّ مِنْهَا لَمَا يَشَّقَّقُ فَيَخْرُجُ مِنْهُ ٱلْمَآءُ ۚ وَإِنَّ مِنْهَا لَمَا يَهْبِطُ مِنْ خَشْيَةِ ٱللَّهِ ۗ وَمَا ٱللَّهُ بِغَٰفِلٍ عَمَّا تَعْمَلُونَ ۝

---

[a] Those who seek to find loopholes in God's commandments become more and more insensitive. God is another name for the most supreme of beings. If man's faith is a living faith, belief in God shakes his soul so deeply that his verbosity is replaced by stunned silence. But when the heart is hardened, people begin to manipulate the divine scriptures, for they are used to doing the same with human writings. Such brazenness on their part increases their insensitivity, leading to hardening of their hearts. Their hearts are not moved before the might of their Lord. Their souls become resistant to any excitement at the thought of God. They remain rigid as the most impervious of rocks.

Three aspects of the symbolic meaning of rocks have been mentioned in this verse:

1. One sees in the mountains how streams flow over the rocks, finally to join together to form a river. This is symbolic of a certain type of human being: one in whose heart fear of God is lodged, like water in the bosom of a mountain. This fear of the Lord flows from his eyes in the form of tears, as streams flow down the crags of the hillside.

2. Some rocks seem to be nothing more than dry boulders; but when cracked, reveal huge pools of water beneath them—wells from which people quench their thirst. This is on a parallel with one who, at first sight, appears to be far from the Lord. But then he is struck by some calamity, which shakes his soul. With floods of tears in his eyes he hastens to turn towards God.

3. Sometimes one sees landslides on mountain sides, with great slabs of rocks crashing down the slopes. This is comparable to a human being who has adopted an unjust attitude towards another. But, the moment he is reminded of the command of God, he immediately submits to it. He is not willing to give in to another human being. But when man's issues become God's affairs, he surrenders to Him in all humility.

In nature, there is a message in every single thing, for God has created the world as a source of admonition and remembrance for man, to demonstrate to him how to make his life conform to the divine will. While throughout the universe, this message is conveyed in the language of silent examples, in the Quran it has been expressly set forth.

⁷⁵ Do you then hope that they will believe in you when some of them have already heard the word of God and then, after having understood it, they knowingly perverted it? ⁷⁶ When they meet the faithful, they say, 'We are believers.' But when alone, they say to each other, 'Must you tell them what God has revealed to us? They will only use it to argue against you before your Lord! Have you no sense?' ⁷⁷ Do they not know that God knows all that they conceal and all that they disclose?^a

۞ أَفَتَطْمَعُونَ أَن يُؤْمِنُواْ لَكُمْ وَقَدْ كَانَ فَرِيقٌ مِّنْهُمْ يَسْمَعُونَ كَلَـٰمَ ٱللَّهِ ثُمَّ يُحَرِّفُونَهُۥ مِنۢ بَعْدِ مَا عَقَلُوهُ وَهُمْ يَعْلَمُونَ ۝ وَإِذَا لَقُواْ ٱلَّذِينَ ءَامَنُواْ قَالُوٓاْ ءَامَنَّا وَإِذَا خَلَا بَعْضُهُمْ إِلَىٰ بَعْضٍ قَالُوٓاْ أَتُحَدِّثُونَهُم بِمَا فَتَحَ ٱللَّهُ عَلَيْكُمْ لِيُحَآجُّوكُم بِهِۦ عِندَ رَبِّكُمْ أَفَلَا تَعْقِلُونَ ۝ أَوَلَا يَعْلَمُونَ أَنَّ ٱللَّهَ يَعْلَمُ مَا يُسِرُّونَ وَمَا يُعْلِنُونَ ۝

---

^a One of the reasons for the promptness with which the people of Madinah recognized the Prophet Muhammad, and believed in him, was that they had often heard from their Jewish neighbours of the coming of a final prophet. They had, therefore, been expecting his arrival. The Jews then were responsible for the Muslims' initial fervour for Islam. It was only natural that the Muslims, in their turn, should hope that the Jews would unhesitatingly accept the prophethood of Muhammad. With every hope of a positive response, it was with sublime feelings that they called on the Jews to join them in their belief in the Prophet.

How shocked the Muslims were, then, when they found that, contrary to their expectations, the Jews were not ready to accept their invitation to accept Islam. Rather, their efforts had the opposite effect, for the Prophet's opponents took the opportunity to ask the Muslims, 'How are you so sure about the prophethood of Muhammad? If he were truly a prophet, the Jews would have been the first to believe in him, for their knowledge of what is written in the scriptures is greater than yours.'

But acceptance of a truth is not dependent upon knowledge alone; one has also to be sincere. As for the Jews, they had already altered their own scriptures, though they knew them to be the word of God. Seeking out loopholes in any part of the Holy scriptures that did not conform to their wishes, they altered the word of God at will; religion was subordinated to their worldly interests.

However true something may be, if one is bent on denial and intentional distortion, one is sure to find some justification or the other for it. Such a perverse attitude finally leads to deliberate misrepresentation of the true word of God. One who has such irreverent attitude towards the divine scriptures can never appreciate the gravity of matters concerning God: he hears the word of God, but he can always find words to show that the commandment does not apply to him; he believes in God, but his insensitivity makes him commit acts of flagrant rebellion against Him which no one who really believes that God is watching over him, and hearing what he says, would ever dare to perpetrate.

⁷⁸ There are among them unlettered people who have no real knowledge of the Scriptures, knowing only their own wishful thinking and following only conjecture. ⁷⁹ Woe to those who write the scripture with their own hands, and then declare, 'This is from God,' in order to sell it for a paltry price. Woe to them because of what their own hands have written, and woe to them for what they have earned. ⁸⁰ They say, 'The Fire is not going to touch us, and [even if it does], it will only be for a few days!' Say [to them], 'Have you received a promise from God—for God never breaks His promise—or do you attribute something to God which you do not know?' ⁸¹ Truly, those who do evil and are encompassed by their misdeeds, shall be the inmates of the Fire. Therein they shall abide forever, ⁸² but those who believe and do good works are the heirs of Paradise; there they shall abide forever.ᵃ

وَمِنْهُمْ أُمِّيُّونَ لَا يَعْلَمُونَ ٱلْكِتَٰبَ إِلَّآ أَمَانِيَّ وَإِنْ هُمْ إِلَّا يَظُنُّونَ ۝ فَوَيْلٌ لِّلَّذِينَ يَكْتُبُونَ ٱلْكِتَٰبَ بِأَيْدِيهِمْ ثُمَّ يَقُولُونَ هَٰذَا مِنْ عِندِ ٱللَّهِ لِيَشْتَرُوا۟ بِهِۦ ثَمَنًا قَلِيلًا ۖ فَوَيْلٌ لَّهُم مِّمَّا كَتَبَتْ أَيْدِيهِمْ وَوَيْلٌ لَّهُم مِّمَّا يَكْسِبُونَ ۝ وَقَالُوا۟ لَن تَمَسَّنَا ٱلنَّارُ إِلَّآ أَيَّامًا مَّعْدُودَةً ۚ قُلْ أَتَّخَذْتُمْ عِندَ ٱللَّهِ عَهْدًا فَلَن يُخْلِفَ ٱللَّهُ عَهْدَهُۥٓ ۖ أَمْ تَقُولُونَ عَلَى ٱللَّهِ مَا لَا تَعْلَمُونَ ۝ بَلَىٰ مَن كَسَبَ سَيِّئَةً وَأَحَٰطَتْ بِهِۦ خَطِيٓـَٔتُهُۥ فَأُو۟لَٰٓئِكَ أَصْحَٰبُ ٱلنَّارِ ۖ هُمْ فِيهَا خَٰلِدُونَ ۝ وَٱلَّذِينَ ءَامَنُوا۟ وَعَمِلُوا۟ ٱلصَّٰلِحَٰتِ أُو۟لَٰٓئِكَ أَصْحَٰبُ ٱلْجَنَّةِ ۖ هُمْ فِيهَا خَٰلِدُونَ ۝

ᵃ The Arabic word for 'false notions' is *amani*. According to Ibn 'Abbas, Fara' and Mujahid—some of the most reliable of the Quranic commentators—the word refers to the mythical tales invented by Jewish scholars. The overall aim of these stories was to prove that Paradise was reserved for the Jews. Added to this, statements in support of the theory that the Jews were God's 'chosen people' were attributed to venerated Jewish saints. It was made out that certain magical properties were inherent in their religion, ensuring salvation by virtue of mere adherence to the run-of-the-mill rites of Judaism.

Such sacred recipes for cheap salvation are very attractive to the masses, for they give credence to the popular notion based on wishful thinking that there is no need to discipline oneself—no need to lead a responsible life; superstitious charms and magical remedies are enough to cure one's spiritual ills and have one admitted to heaven. The scholars who taught these tales, attributing them to past saints, became highly regarded for the theories they expounded were designed to win popular support. ▶

83 Remember when We made a covenant with the Children of Israel, 'Worship none but God and be good to your parents and to relatives and orphans and the needy. And speak kindly to people. Attend to your prayers and pay the zakat [prescribed alms].' But with the exception of a few, you turned away [in aversion] and paid no heed.ᵃ

وَإِذْ أَخَذْنَا مِيثَاقَ بَنِىٓ إِسْرَٰٓءِيلَ لَا تَعْبُدُونَ إِلَّا ٱللَّهَ وَبِٱلْوَٰلِدَيْنِ إِحْسَانًا وَذِى ٱلْقُرْبَىٰ وَٱلْيَتَٰمَىٰ وَٱلْمَسَٰكِينِ وَقُولُوا۟ لِلنَّاسِ حُسْنًا وَأَقِيمُوا۟ ٱلصَّلَوٰةَ وَءَاتُوا۟ ٱلزَّكَوٰةَ ثُمَّ تَوَلَّيْتُمْ إِلَّا قَلِيلًا مِّنكُمْ وَأَنتُم مُّعْرِضُونَ ﴿٨٣﴾

Facilitation of eternal salvation became for them a lucrative source of worldly income. People flocked to support them. They were showered with offerings, for they ushered others along the path to a paradise that did not have to be earned; in return they received worldly wealth that they did not have to labour for.

This has been a failing in the people of the Book in every age. They wanted to live in a dream world, thinking that they had no obligations save the perfunctory performance of certain empty rituals, and deluding themselves into believing that they had certain inalienable rights given by God. Such people cannot accept the call of true religion, for truth demolishes all their wishful thinking, and makes them face the stark realities of life.

ᵃ Man's first duty to God is to become His worshipper without ascribing any partners to Him. Secondly, he should show kindness to others. Kindness starts at home, with one's parents and family, extends to one's neighbours and relatives, and finally reaches out to everyone with whom one comes into contact. There is only one proper way to deal with others, and that is with justice and well-wishing.

Where one is really tested is in one's dealings with 'orphans and the needy', that is, with the weaker members of society. As for the strong, their strength itself guarantees that they will be given deferential treatment. But so far as the weak are concerned there is no such incentive to deal with them justly. Therefore, one should be especially careful to behave well towards them. People who are good to those who wield no worldly power and possess scant resources, do so for God's sake alone, for they have no other incentive.

There are various reasons for having little inclination to show kindness when dealing with the weak. Benefactors frequently regard themselves as 'superior' persons and, when they are not shown what they consider to be due deference, they tend to treat people less fortunate than themselves with disdain. Then the thought of a permanent liability is often so irksome to them that they resort to ill-mannered behaviour to rid themselves of a burdensome obligation.

This attitude leaves no room for the notion that the weak also have their self-respect. When the benefactor is not shown what he considers to be due deference, he regards the beneficiary as unworthy and incompetent. This thinking finds expression in various ways.

84 When We made a covenant with you, We said, 'You shall not shed each other's blood, nor turn your people out of their homes.' You consented to this and bore witness. 85 Yet, here you are, slaying one another and driving some of your own people from their homelands, aiding one another against them, committing sin and aggression; but if they came to you as captives, you would ransom them. Surely their very expulsion was unlawful for you. Do you believe in one part of the Book and deny another part of it? Those of you who act thus shall be rewarded with disgrace in this world and with a severe punishment on the Day of Resurrection. God is never unaware of what you do. 86 Such are they who buy the life of this world at the price of the Hereafter. Their punishment shall not be lightened for them, nor shall they be helped.ᵃ

وَإِذْ أَخَذْنَا مِيثَاقَكُمْ لَا تَسْفِكُونَ دِمَاءَكُمْ وَلَا تُخْرِجُونَ أَنفُسَكُم مِّن دِيَارِكُمْ ثُمَّ أَقْرَرْتُمْ وَأَنتُمْ تَشْهَدُونَ ۝ ثُمَّ أَنتُمْ هَٰؤُلَاءِ تَقْتُلُونَ أَنفُسَكُمْ وَتُخْرِجُونَ فَرِيقًا مِّنكُم مِّن دِيَارِهِمْ تَظَاهَرُونَ عَلَيْهِم بِٱلْإِثْمِ وَٱلْعُدْوَانِ وَإِن يَأْتُوكُمْ أُسَارَىٰ تُفَادُوهُمْ وَهُوَ مُحَرَّمٌ عَلَيْكُمْ إِخْرَاجُهُمْ أَفَتُؤْمِنُونَ بِبَعْضِ ٱلْكِتَابِ وَتَكْفُرُونَ بِبَعْضٍ فَمَا جَزَاءُ مَن يَفْعَلُ ذَٰلِكَ مِنكُمْ إِلَّا خِزْيٌ فِى ٱلْحَيَوٰةِ ٱلدُّنْيَا وَيَوْمَ ٱلْقِيَامَةِ يُرَدُّونَ إِلَىٰ أَشَدِّ ٱلْعَذَابِ وَمَا ٱللَّهُ بِغَافِلٍ عَمَّا تَعْمَلُونَ ۝ أُوْلَٰئِكَ ٱلَّذِينَ ٱشْتَرَوُاْ ٱلْحَيَوٰةَ ٱلدُّنْيَا بِٱلْآخِرَةِ فَلَا يُخَفَّفُ عَنْهُمُ ٱلْعَذَابُ وَلَا هُمْ يُنصَرُونَ ۝

ᵃ Before the advent of Islam, three Jewish tribes inhabited the area around Madinah: the Banu Nadir, the Banu Qurayzah, and the Banu Qaynuqa'. Despite the fact that all of them adhered to Mosaic law, ignorant prejudices had divided them into two groups. They had become enmeshed, along with the polytheist tribes of Madinah—al-Aws and the Khazraj—in political manoeuvering. The Banu Nadir and the Banu Qurayzah had aligned themselves with the Aws tribe, and the Banu Qaynuqa' with the Khazraj. Divided into two camps in this manner, the three Jewish tribes were constantly at war with one another. ▶

⁸⁷To Moses We gave the Book and sent a succession of messengers after him. We gave Jesus, son of Mary, clear signs and strengthened him with the Holy Spirit. But, whenever a messenger came to you with something which you did not desire, you grew arrogant, calling some liars and slaying others. ⁸⁸They say, 'Our hearts are impenetrably wrapped [against whatever you say],' but God has rejected them for their denial; they have but little faith.ᵃ

وَلَقَدْ ءَاتَيْنَا مُوسَى ٱلْكِتَبَ وَقَفَّيْنَا مِنۢ بَعْدِهِۦ بِٱلرُّسُلِ ۖ وَءَاتَيْنَا عِيسَى ٱبْنَ مَرْيَمَ ٱلْبَيِّنَتِ وَأَيَّدْنَهُ بِرُوحِ ٱلْقُدُسِ ۗ أَفَكُلَّمَا جَآءَكُمْ رَسُولٌۢ بِمَا لَا تَهْوَىٰٓ أَنفُسُكُمُ ٱسْتَكْبَرْتُمْ فَفَرِيقًا كَذَّبْتُمْ وَفَرِيقًا تَقْتُلُونَ ۝ وَقَالُواْ قُلُوبُنَا غُلْفُۢ ۚ بَل لَّعَنَهُمُ ٱللَّهُ بِكُفْرِهِمْ فَقَلِيلًا مَّا يُؤْمِنُونَ ۝

The basic teachings of Islamic law demand the total renunciation of pagan ways, the suppressing of one's selfish desires and the controlling of one's worldly needs—that is why the commands of Islamic law are ignored in politics. Obedience to them would bring about true piety, but people do not like to involve themselves in such arduous practices. They prefer to put on a pretence of piety by conducting certain superficial rituals. This is tantamount to issuing a self-made edition of divine religion; it is to disregard the Hereafter and attach importance to the worldly aspect of religion in the hope that zeal in performing actions which promise worldly fame and honour will qualify them for the reward reserved for true piety. But such brazen distortion of religion can only earn one God's wrath; it does not merit any reward from God.

ᵃ The Torah was the Book of God revealed to the Jews. Gradually, however, they ceased to treat it as a source of divine guidance and came to regard it as a sacred relic of their national heritage, a symbol of ethnic superiority; it became more a guarantee of salvation than a guide as to how salvation could be earned. After Moses, several prophets arose among the Jewish people—Joshua, David, Zachariah, John the Baptist and finally Jesus, to name but a few—all of whom pointed out to the Jews that it was not enough just to revere the Torah as a holy book. Its teachings had to be actually practised. It is futile to believe in the sacredness of the holy scriptures if one does not implement their message in one's everyday life. But the Jews, the very people who held the Torah in such high esteem, were extremely intolerant of the Prophet's exhortations. The reason for such a reaction on their part was that they had allowed self-interest and worldly ambitions to rule their lives, while passing themselves off as bearers and upholders of the true faith. As long as religion served to consolidate their worldly status, they welcomed it, but were loath to accept the message of truth—presented to them in all its purity—which they saw as a threat to the hegemony they had secured for themselves on the basis of religion. It was their egoism which came in the way of true religiosity. ▶

89 And now that a Book has come to them from God, fulfilling that [predictions about the final prophet in their scriptures] which is with them, they deny it—whereas previously they used to pray for victory against the disbelievers—yet when there came to them that which they recognized as the truth, they rejected it. God's rejection is the due of all who deny the truth. 90 What they have sold their souls for is evil: to the denial of God's own revelation, grudging that He should reveal His bounty to whom He chooses from among His servants! They have incurred wrath upon wrath. Humiliating punishment awaits those who deny the truth.*a*

وَلَمَّا جَآءَهُمْ كِتَبٌ مِّنْ عِندِ ٱللَّهِ مُصَدِّقٌ لِّمَا مَعَهُمْ وَكَانُواْ مِن قَبْلُ يَسْتَفْتِحُونَ عَلَى ٱلَّذِينَ كَفَرُواْ فَلَمَّا جَآءَهُم مَّا عَرَفُواْ كَفَرُواْ بِهِۦ فَلَعْنَةُ ٱللَّهِ عَلَى ٱلْكَفِرِينَ ۝ بِئْسَمَا ٱشْتَرَوْاْ بِهِۦٓ أَنفُسَهُمْ أَن يَكْفُرُواْ بِمَآ أَنزَلَ ٱللَّهُ بَغْيًا أَن يُنَزِّلَ ٱللَّهُ مِن فَضْلِهِۦ عَلَىٰ مَن يَشَآءُ مِنْ عِبَادِهِۦ فَبَآءُو بِغَضَبٍ عَلَىٰ غَضَبٍ وَلِلْكَفِرِينَ عَذَابٌ مُّهِينٌ ۝

Instead of being the first to believe in it, they rejected the message as well as the messenger, subjecting God's prophets to scorn and victimisation. They called them impostors and even went to the extent of killing them.

a The Jews of Arabia behaved similarly with the Prophet Muhammad. They had seen prophecies of the coming of a final prophet in their scriptures, and had eagerly anticipated his arrival. When he comes, they used to say, we will join with him in a grand alliance against the pagans and idolators. But these proved to be empty words on their part, a pretence aimed at consolidating their status as undisputed guardians of divine faith. When the Prophet came, the truth of their position was exposed. They were shown to be steeped in bigotry, reluctant to believe in a prophet who did not come from the Jewish race. They could not dispute the authentic indications presented by the Quran in support of his prophethood; all they could say was, 'It all sounds very impressive, but our ancestral religion is good enough for us. Our hearts are sealed and we will not accept anything besides the faith we have inherited from our forefathers.'

⁹¹ When they are told, 'Believe in what God has revealed,' they say, 'We believe in what was revealed to us,' while they deny the truth in what has been sent down after that, even though it is the Truth, confirming that which they already have. Say, 'Why did you kill God's prophets in the past, if you were true believers? ⁹² Moses came to you with clear signs, but in his absence you worshipped the calf and became wrongdoers.' ⁹³ When We made a covenant with you and raised the mountain above you saying, 'Hold firmly to what We have given you and listen,' you said, 'We hear, but we disobey,' and their hearts were filled with the love of the calf, because of their refusal to acknowledge the truth. Say, 'Evil is that to which your faith enjoins you if you are indeed believers.'ᵃ

وَإِذَا قِيلَ لَهُمْ ءَامِنُوا بِمَا أَنزَلَ ٱللَّهُ قَالُوا نُؤْمِنُ بِمَا أُنزِلَ عَلَيْنَا وَيَكْفُرُونَ بِمَا وَرَآءَهُ وَهُوَ ٱلْحَقُّ مُصَدِّقًا لِّمَا مَعَهُمْ قُلْ فَلِمَ تَقْتُلُونَ أَنۢبِيَآءَ ٱللَّهِ مِن قَبْلُ إِن كُنتُم مُّؤْمِنِينَ ۝ وَلَقَدْ جَآءَكُم مُّوسَىٰ بِٱلْبَيِّنَٰتِ ثُمَّ ٱتَّخَذْتُمُ ٱلْعِجْلَ مِنۢ بَعْدِهِ وَأَنتُمْ ظَٰلِمُونَ ۝ وَإِذْ أَخَذْنَا مِيثَٰقَكُمْ وَرَفَعْنَا فَوْقَكُمُ ٱلطُّورَ خُذُوا مَآ ءَاتَيْنَٰكُم بِقُوَّةٍ وَٱسْمَعُوا قَالُوا سَمِعْنَا وَعَصَيْنَا وَأُشْرِبُوا فِى قُلُوبِهِمُ ٱلْعِجْلَ بِكُفْرِهِمْ قُلْ بِئْسَمَا يَأْمُرُكُم بِهِۦ إِيمَٰنُكُمْ إِن كُنتُم مُّؤْمِنِينَ ۝

ᵃ The Jews were not ready to accept the Quran, because they thought they were already rightly guided. They were sure that the very fact that they belonged to the largest group of the followers of truth, that is, the Israelites, that would be enough to earn them salvation. But, in fact, this was a feeling of ethnic superiority which they mistook for love of truth.

The communal values of their group came to occupy the position of pure truth. That was why, when the truth appeared in its original form, they failed to accept it. Had their aim been to find pure truth, they would not have found it difficult, since predictions about it had appeared in their own sacred book, (the Torah) to the effect that now it was the Quran that was the Book of Truth to be followed and not the religion of their own group.

94 Say, 'If God's abode of the Hereafter is for you alone, to the exclusion of all others, then wish for death, if you are truthful.' 95 But they will never wish for death, because of what their own hands have sent on before them; God is fully aware of the wrongdoers. 96 You will find them clinging to life more eagerly than any other people, even the polytheists. Any of them would wish to be given a life of a thousand years, though even such a long life would not save them from [Our] punishment; and God sees all that they do.[a]

قُل إِن كَانَتْ لَكُمُ ٱلدَّارُ ٱلْآخِرَةُ عِندَ ٱللَّهِ خَالِصَةً مِّن دُونِ ٱلنَّاسِ فَتَمَنَّوُاْ ٱلْمَوْتَ إِن كُنتُمْ صَـٰدِقِينَ ۝ وَلَن يَتَمَنَّوْهُ أَبَدًا بِمَا قَدَّمَتْ أَيْدِيهِمْ وَٱللَّهُ عَلِيمٌ بِٱلظَّـٰلِمِينَ ۝ وَلَتَجِدَنَّهُمْ أَحْرَصَ ٱلنَّاسِ عَلَىٰ حَيَوٰةٍ وَمِنَ ٱلَّذِينَ أَشْرَكُواْ يَوَدُّ أَحَدُهُمْ لَوْ يُعَمَّرُ أَلْفَ سَنَةٍ وَمَا هُوَ بِمُزَحْزِحِهِ مِنَ ٱلْعَذَابِ أَن يُعَمَّرَ وَٱللَّهُ بَصِيرٌۢ بِمَا يَعْمَلُونَ ۝

[a] The fact that the Israelites were not really concerned with truth is proved by their own history. It was they who had slain their own prophets, such as Zachariah and John the Baptist, the only reason for these actions being that these prophets had criticized the Israelites' mode of living, and sought to bring them back to the divine way (Nehemiah, 9:26). They had seen Moses perform undeniable miracles, but when he was not with them in person, having left them to spend forty days on Mount Sinai, they started worshipping the golden calf; it had only been his personal authority which had kept them under control. When the Mount was raised threateningly above their heads, they temporarily agreed to do 'all that the Lord hath spoken' (Exodus, 19:5, 8, 16, 18), but, after that, most of them returned to their disobedient ways. If they had really been seeking God, their attention would have been entirely focused on the life after death; but, in fact, they, more than all the others, were obsessed with the love of the present world.

⁹⁷ Say, 'Anyone who is an enemy of Gabriel—who by God's leave has brought down to your heart [the Quran] fulfilling that [predictions about the last prophet in the earlier revelations] which precedes it, and is a guidance and good news for the faithful—⁹⁸ whoever is an enemy of God, His angels, or His messengers, or of Gabriel or Michael, will surely find that God too is the enemy of those who deny the truth.'ᵃ

قُلْ مَن كَانَ عَدُوًّا لِّجِبْرِيلَ فَإِنَّهُۥ نَزَّلَهُۥ عَلَىٰ قَلْبِكَ بِإِذْنِ ٱللَّهِ مُصَدِّقًا لِّمَا بَيْنَ يَدَيْهِ وَهُدًى وَبُشْرَىٰ لِلْمُؤْمِنِينَ ۝ مَن كَانَ عَدُوًّا لِّلَّهِ وَمَلَٰٓئِكَتِهِۦ وَرُسُلِهِۦ وَجِبْرِيلَ وَمِيكَىٰلَ فَإِنَّ ٱللَّهَ عَدُوٌّ لِّلْكَٰفِرِينَ ۝

ᵃ Owing to their own rebelliousness, the Israelites had severe punishments meted out to them in ancient times. It was God's way to warn them of these impending punishments beforehand, and such warnings came to them through the prophets, who were acting on the words of the Archangel Gabriel. The moral was that people had to follow God's commandments; if they persisted in a sinful life, they would be exposing themselves to His wrath. But, instead of heeding these admonitions, the Israelites came to regard Gabriel as their enemy, because it had always been he who gave prior warning through the prophets about impending doom. Consequently, when the Prophet Muhammad proclaimed that he was receiving his revelation through Gabriel, they said, 'So, it is our old enemy Gabriel, who always brings commands from heaven against us! That explains why the scriptures, the birthright of the Israelites, are being conveyed to one who belongs to another tribe.'

Now angels, being the rarefied creatures that they are, do not hold grudges against ordinary mortals; they descend to earth only by divine command in order to carry out the tasks assigned to them by their Creator—in this case, the revelation of the Scriptures to the prophet whom God Himself had chosen. Given the clear proofs that the Arab Prophet had had the same revelation communicated to him as had been received by Abraham, Moses and Jesus, and that it tallied with the previous divine scriptures, there were no grounds for the Israelites to reject the divine message. Their negative reaction was the result of their having lead insincere, unrestricted lives, which had become dominated by self-interest, empty convention and racial prejudice. Religion had been adhered to only on a superficial level, just to keep up the pretence that the Israelites were, in fact, faithfully treading the path of God.

⁹⁹ We have sent down clear signs to you and no one will reject them except the wicked. ¹⁰⁰ Why is it that, whenever they make a covenant, some of them cast it aside? Most of them do not believe. ¹⁰¹ Whenever a messenger from God has come to them, fulfilling that [predictions] which they already had, some of those to whom the Book was given have cast off the Book of God behind their backs as if they had no knowledge.*

وَلَقَدۡ أَنزَلۡنَآ إِلَيۡكَ ءَايَٰتِۭ بَيِّنَٰتٖ وَمَا يَكۡفُرُ بِهَآ إِلَّا ٱلۡفَٰسِقُونَ ۝ أَوَكُلَّمَا عَٰهَدُواْ عَهۡدٗا نَّبَذَهُۥ فَرِيقٞ مِّنۡهُمۚ بَلۡ أَكۡثَرُهُمۡ لَا يُؤۡمِنُونَ ۝ وَلَمَّا جَآءَهُمۡ رَسُولٞ مِّنۡ عِندِ ٱللَّهِ مُصَدِّقٞ لِّمَا مَعَهُمۡ نَبَذَ فَرِيقٞ مِّنَ ٱلَّذِينَ أُوتُواْ ٱلۡكِتَٰبَ كِتَٰبَ ٱللَّهِ وَرَآءَ ظُهُورِهِمۡ كَأَنَّهُمۡ لَا يَعۡلَمُونَ ۝

---

* Perversion sets in the People of the Book for just one reason. They come to believe that by uttering mere words, or by performing lifeless rituals, they will be able to earn salvation, but salvation can be earned only by performing righteous actions.

During this stage of decline, superstition comes to be more highly regarded than actual good deeds. People begin to expect mysterious kinds of results or benefits by performing senseless rituals. This thinking, initially centreing on salvation, later comes to dominate the entire national policy of the group. A realistic approach is thus replaced by a superstitious approach.

Now those who merely make an outward show of following their religion are inevitably averse to responding in earnest to the proclamation of true, unadulterated religion. For such people, the call is seen as a threat to the worldly honour and status that they enjoy owing to their worldly interpretation of religion. Due to their negativism, they begin to make such representations as are outwardly correct but which, in terms of the inner reality, are totally meaningless. There is no doubt about it that the coming of the angels and messengers was entirely a part of the divine plan. All arguments point to the fact that the Arab Prophet received the same message as was sent down to Abraham, Moses and Jesus, and that the revelation received by the Arab Prophet tallied exactly with the predictions made in previous divine scriptures. This proves beyond all doubt that it was sent by God Himself. People make many protestation of their faith, but all these mouthings being hollow and meaningless, they bear no relation to true faith and piety.

102 They pursued what the devils falsely attributed to the kingdom of Solomon. Solomon was not an unbeliever: it is the devils who are unbelievers. They taught people witchcraft, and that which was sent down to Harut and Marut, the two angels in Babylon. But these two taught no one until they had said, 'We are but a trial, therefore, do not disbelieve [in God's guidance].' So men learnt from them that by which they caused discord between man and wife; but they harmed no one thereby, except by the command of God; [on the contrary], these people learned that which would harm them and do them no good, knowing full well that whoever acquired [this knowledge] would have no share in the Hereafter. Evil indeed was the [price] for which they sold their souls, if only they had known it. 103 And had they but believed and been mindful of God, His reward would have been far better for them, if they had but known it.ᵃ

وَٱتَّبَعُواْ مَا تَتْلُواْ ٱلشَّيَـٰطِينُ عَلَىٰ مُلْكِ سُلَيْمَـٰنَ وَمَا كَفَرَ سُلَيْمَـٰنُ وَلَـٰكِنَّ ٱلشَّيَـٰطِينَ كَفَرُواْ يُعَلِّمُونَ ٱلنَّاسَ ٱلسِّحْرَ وَمَا أُنزِلَ عَلَى ٱلْمَلَكَيْنِ بِبَابِلَ هَـٰرُوتَ وَمَـٰرُوتَ وَمَا يُعَلِّمَانِ مِنْ أَحَدٍ حَتَّىٰ يَقُولَا إِنَّمَا نَحْنُ فِتْنَةٌ فَلَا تَكْفُرْ فَيَتَعَلَّمُونَ مِنْهُمَا مَا يُفَرِّقُونَ بِهِۦ بَيْنَ ٱلْمَرْءِ وَزَوْجِهِۦ وَمَا هُم بِضَآرِّينَ بِهِۦ مِنْ أَحَدٍ إِلَّا بِإِذْنِ ٱللَّهِ وَيَتَعَلَّمُونَ مَا يَضُرُّهُمْ وَلَا يَنفَعُهُمْ وَلَقَدْ عَلِمُواْ لَمَنِ ٱشْتَرَىٰهُ مَا لَهُۥ فِى ٱلْأَخِرَةِ مِنْ خَلَـٰقٍ وَلَبِئْسَ مَا شَرَوْاْ بِهِۦٓ أَنفُسَهُمْ لَوْ كَانُواْ يَعْلَمُونَ ۝ وَلَوْ أَنَّهُمْ ءَامَنُواْ وَٱتَّقَوْاْ لَمَثُوبَةٌ مِّنْ عِندِ ٱللَّهِ خَيْرٌ لَّوْ كَانُواْ يَعْلَمُونَ ۝

ᵃ When superstition and apathy set in in the declining Jewish race, certain individuals exploited this tendency in order to make commercial gains, by providing success-seekers with magical prescriptions. To make their business flourish, these unscrupulous profiteers attributed their art to Solomon, saying that the extraordinary powers he exercised over the spirits and winds were, in fact, based on his knowledge of magic, and claimed that this knowledge had been passed on to them by the spirits. This claim to authority accounted in great measure for the rapid spread of sorcery, which soon developed into a highly popular art among the Jews.

When angels came to Lot's people, who were practising homosexuals, they came in the garb of handsome boys in order to test them. Similarly, angels were sent to the Jews in Babylon in the garb of holymen to teach them magic, at the same time making it quite clear that they were only putting the Jews to the test, this being a form of knowledge that should not be practised. But the Jews took no heed of this warning: they practised magic with great fervour and even used it for illicit ends.

¹⁰⁴ Believers, do not say to the Prophet, 'Ra'ina' but say, 'Unzurna,' and listen to him with attention. For those who deny the truth, there is a painful punishment.ᵃ ¹⁰⁵ They who deny the truth from among the People of the Book, or from among those who associate partners with God, do not desire that any good should be sent down to you from your Lord. But God singles out for His grace whom He wills—for God is limitless in His great bounty.ᵇ ¹⁰⁶ If We abrogate a verse or cause it to be forgotten, We will replace it by a better one or one similar to it. Do you not know that God has power over all things?

يَـٰٓأَيُّهَا ٱلَّذِينَ ءَامَنُواْ لَا تَقُولُواْ رَٰعِنَا وَقُولُواْ ٱنظُرْنَا وَٱسْمَعُواْ وَلِلْكَـٰفِرِينَ عَذَابٌ أَلِيمٌ ۝ مَا يَوَدُّ ٱلَّذِينَ كَفَرُواْ مِنْ أَهْلِ ٱلْكِتَـٰبِ وَلَا ٱلْمُشْرِكِينَ أَن يُنَزَّلَ عَلَيْكُم مِّنْ خَيْرٍ مِّن رَّبِّكُمْ وَٱللَّهُ يَخْتَصُّ بِرَحْمَتِهِۦ مَن يَشَآءُ وَٱللَّهُ ذُو ٱلْفَضْلِ ٱلْعَظِيمِ ۝ مَا نَنسَخْ مِنْ ءَايَةٍ أَوْ نُنسِهَا نَأْتِ بِخَيْرٍ مِّنْهَآ أَوْ مِثْلِهَآ أَلَمْ تَعْلَمْ أَنَّ ٱللَّهَ عَلَىٰ كُلِّ شَىْءٍ قَدِيرٌ ۝

ᵃ Another gambit of those who deny the truth was to sit in the Prophet's company and, by playing on words, make a mockery of his teachings. For instance, instead of using the unambiguous Arabic word for 'May we have your attention'—'unzurna'—they would say 'ra'ina'. 'Ra'ina', when pronounced properly, has much the same meaning as 'unzurna', but with the protraction of the second vowel, it becomes 'raeena', meaning 'our shepherd,' and with the protraction of the first it becomes 'raaina', which means idiot.

ᵇ The Muslims were told therefore to avoid ambiguous words, and to be quite clear in their speech; words with a derisive shade of meaning should be especially avoided. Furthermore, they were enjoined to pay close attention to what the Prophet said and to try to understand it on their own, without resorting to excessive questioning; receptiveness rather than obstinacy was to mark their attitude to his instructions. This was the way to gain faith, and it was the consolidation and strengthening of faith that was to be sought. The believers were also told not to be jealous of another person's valuable possessions, for it was God Himself who had bestowed that particular blessing on His servant. God Himself decreed that the Prophet be the recipient of divine revelation. If one were earnest in seeking to learn from him, one could share in the blessing he received.

107 Do you not know that the kingdom of the heavens and the earth belongs to God alone? And that there is no protector or helper for you besides God? 108 Do you [all] want to question your messenger just as Moses was questioned previously? Anyone who exchanges faith for unbelief has strayed from the right path.

109 Many among the People of the Book wish, through envy, to lead you back to unbelief, now that you have embraced the faith and the truth has been made plain to them. But you should pardon them and bear with them until God gives His command. Truly, God has power over all things.ᵃ

أَلَمْ تَعْلَمْ أَنَّ ٱللَّهَ لَهُۥ مُلْكُ ٱلسَّمَـٰوَٰتِ وَٱلْأَرْضِ ۗ وَمَا لَكُم مِّن دُونِ ٱللَّهِ مِن وَلِيٍّ وَلَا نَصِيرٍ ۝ أَمْ تُرِيدُونَ أَن تَسْـَٔلُوا۟ رَسُولَكُمْ كَمَا سُئِلَ مُوسَىٰ مِن قَبْلُ ۗ وَمَن يَتَبَدَّلِ ٱلْكُفْرَ بِٱلْإِيمَـٰنِ فَقَدْ ضَلَّ سَوَآءَ ٱلسَّبِيلِ ۝ وَدَّ كَثِيرٌ مِّنْ أَهْلِ ٱلْكِتَـٰبِ لَوْ يَرُدُّونَكُم مِّنۢ بَعْدِ إِيمَـٰنِكُمْ كُفَّارًا حَسَدًا مِّنْ عِندِ أَنفُسِهِم مِّنۢ بَعْدِ مَا تَبَيَّنَ لَهُمُ ٱلْحَقُّ ۖ فَٱعْفُوا۟ وَٱصْفَحُوا۟ حَتَّىٰ يَأْتِيَ ٱللَّهُ بِأَمْرِهِۦٓ ۗ إِنَّ ٱللَّهَ عَلَىٰ كُلِّ شَىْءٍ قَدِيرٌ ۝

ᵃ One who has discovered the truth by the help of God has to face stiff opposition when he starts to communicate it to others. One reason is that acceptance of truth entails negation of the self. People of high social status always find this hard, and none more so than the People of the Book, who considered prophethood to be their exclusive right. Unable to conceive of a prophet coming amongst people other than them, they tried various ploys to turn people away from the Arab prophet. One of the theological objections that they raised to his teachings was on the subject of abrogation. Some of the Quranic injunctions differ from Mosaic law, so they would say, 'Does God make mistakes in His revelations, that He sends down one commandment, and then replaces it with another? This shows that what your Prophet Muhammad is teaching is not from God, but is his own creation.' So intensive had this propaganda campaign become that even some simple-minded Muslims were affected, and started raising the issue with the Prophet.

¹¹⁰ Attend to your prayers and pay the prescribed alms; any good you store up for yourselves, you will find it with God. Certainly, God sees what you do. ¹¹¹ They declare, 'None shall ever enter Heaven unless he be a Jew or a Christian.' This is their own wishful thinking. [Prophet], say, 'Produce your evidence if you are telling the truth.' ¹¹² Indeed, those who submit themselves to God and act righteously shall be rewarded by their Lord: they shall have no fear, nor shall they grieve.ᵃ

وَأَقِيمُواْ ٱلصَّلَوٰةَ وَءَاتُواْ ٱلزَّكَوٰةَ وَمَا تُقَدِّمُواْ لِأَنفُسِكُم مِّنْ خَيْرٍ تَجِدُوهُ عِندَ ٱللَّهِ إِنَّ ٱللَّهَ بِمَا تَعْمَلُونَ بَصِيرٌ ۝ وَقَالُواْ لَن يَدْخُلَ ٱلْجَنَّةَ إِلَّا مَن كَانَ هُودًا أَوْ نَصَٰرَىٰ تِلْكَ أَمَانِيُّهُمْ قُلْ هَاتُواْ بُرْهَٰنَكُمْ إِن كُنتُمْ صَٰدِقِينَ ۝ بَلَىٰ مَنْ أَسْلَمَ وَجْهَهُ لِلَّهِ وَهُوَ مُحْسِنٌ فَلَهُۥ أَجْرُهُۥ عِندَ رَبِّهِۦ وَلَا خَوْفٌ عَلَيْهِمْ وَلَا هُمْ يَحْزَنُونَ ۝

ᵃ Once the Jews had set their minds against the message of Islam as being worthless, they became alarmed by the heartfelt acclaim with which many were receiving it. They considered themselves the only ones qualified to pass decrees on truth and falsehood: how could others be allowed to believe in what they themselves had chosen to disbelieve? The first step that they took was to incite the polytheists to rise up against the Muslims. Secondly, they tried to mislead Muslim converts about their new religion, putting doubts into their minds in the hope that they would revert to the religion of their forefathers. It was only natural that this should provoke the Muslims, but God told them that this was not the time for violent reaction. Muslims should always be patient, since patience prevents one from taking negative retaliatory measures in the heat of the moment. They should be steadfast in prayers, for prayer brings one closer to God. They should never fail in the payment of the prescribed alms (zakat), for a society in which the rich are willing to share with the poor will be based on compassion; there will be a real sense of togetherness among its members.

The Jews used to tell new Muslim converts that if they had to forsake their ancestral religion, they should become Jews or Christians. Being the descendants of saints and prophets throughout history, they were the ones who would go to heaven. But the Quran tells us that one does not merit entry into heaven by dint of belonging to a certain community. Everyone will be judged according to his own actions. National status is of no significance in the sight of God. To be sincere in one's faith is to become so devoted to God that everything else assumes secondary importance. Prejudices, personal loyalties, material or worldly interests should not come in the way of responding to the call of truth.

113 The Jews say, 'The Christians have no ground to stand on,' and the Christians say, 'The Jews have no ground to stand on.' Yet they both recite the Book, and those who have no knowledge say the same; God will judge between them on the Day of Resurrection concerning their disputes. 114 Who could be more wicked than someone who prevents God's name from being mentioned in His places of worship, and seeks to bring about their ruin, while it behoves these men to enter them with fear in their hearts? There is disgrace in store for them in this world and a great punishment in the next.ᵃ

وَقَالَتِ ٱلْيَهُودُ لَيْسَتِ ٱلنَّصَرَىٰ عَلَىٰ شَىْءٍ وَقَالَتِ ٱلنَّصَرَىٰ لَيْسَتِ ٱلْيَهُودُ عَلَىٰ شَىْءٍ وَهُمْ يَتْلُونَ ٱلْكِتَٰبَ كَذَٰلِكَ قَالَ ٱلَّذِينَ لَا يَعْلَمُونَ مِثْلَ قَوْلِهِمْ فَٱللَّهُ يَحْكُمُ بَيْنَهُمْ يَوْمَ ٱلْقِيَٰمَةِ فِيمَا كَانُوا۟ فِيهِ يَخْتَلِفُونَ ۝ وَمَنْ أَظْلَمُ مِمَّن مَّنَعَ مَسَٰجِدَ ٱللَّهِ أَن يُذْكَرَ فِيهَا ٱسْمُهُۥ وَسَعَىٰ فِى خَرَابِهَآ أُو۟لَٰٓئِكَ مَا كَانَ لَهُمْ أَن يَدْخُلُوهَآ إِلَّا خَآئِفِينَ لَهُمْ فِى ٱلدُّنْيَا خِزْىٌ وَلَهُمْ فِى ٱلْءَاخِرَةِ عَذَابٌ عَظِيمٌ ۝

ᵃ To the Israelites the criterion of truth was their association with the prophets and saints. That was why they believed that their community was in the right while other communities were in the wrong. As for the Christians, they considered themselves unique in that God's 'beloved son' had been sent to them. Even the polytheists of Makkah thought of themselves as superior to others, basing their claim on the fact that they were the guardians of God's Sacred House. Thus every nation had set its own self-styled religious standards, according to which they themselves inevitably appeared to be in the right, and everyone else in the wrong. Their actions, however, did not substantiate their claims. For one thing, they had become divided into sects, though all of them swore allegiance to the divine scriptures. They took every opportunity to deny others the right to enter places of worship, though they would say that they were doing this to protect the sanctity of these places. In fact they were ruining them, for places of worship become derelict when people are denied the right of worship there. If a worshipper has the correct attitude, he will never deny the right to worship to those who come to do so; he will never persecute those who come to serve the Lord. When one is truly conscious of God's greatness and one's own helplessness before Him, one's humility will show in one's dealings with others: one will not seek to harm one's fellow men in any way, let alone deny them their fundamental right to worship God.

115 The East and the West belong to God. Whichever way you turn, there is the Face of God. God is all pervading and all knowing. 116 They say, 'God has taken a son.' Glory be to Him! Everything in the heavens and the earth belongs to Him; all things are obedient to Him. 117 He is the Originator of the heavens and the earth, and when He decrees something, He says only, 'Be!' and it is.

118 Those who are devoid of knowledge say, 'Why does God not speak to us or show us a sign?' The same demand was made by those before them; their hearts are all alike. We have made the signs clear to those whose faith is firm. 119 We have sent you with the truth, bearing good news and giving warning. You will not be held accountable for the people of the Fire.[a]

وَلِلَّهِ ٱلْمَشْرِقُ وَٱلْمَغْرِبُ ۚ فَأَيْنَمَا تُوَلُّواْ فَثَمَّ وَجْهُ ٱللَّهِ ۚ إِنَّ ٱللَّهَ وَٰسِعٌ عَلِيمٌ ۝ وَقَالُواْ ٱتَّخَذَ ٱللَّهُ وَلَدًا ۗ سُبْحَٰنَهُۥ ۖ بَل لَّهُۥ مَا فِى ٱلسَّمَٰوَٰتِ وَٱلْأَرْضِ ۖ كُلٌّ لَّهُۥ قَٰنِتُونَ ۝ بَدِيعُ ٱلسَّمَٰوَٰتِ وَٱلْأَرْضِ ۖ وَإِذَا قَضَىٰٓ أَمْرًا فَإِنَّمَا يَقُولُ لَهُۥ كُن فَيَكُونُ ۝ وَقَالَ ٱلَّذِينَ لَا يَعْلَمُونَ لَوْلَا يُكَلِّمُنَا ٱللَّهُ أَوْ تَأْتِينَآ ءَايَةٌ ۗ كَذَٰلِكَ قَالَ ٱلَّذِينَ مِن قَبْلِهِم مِّثْلَ قَوْلِهِمْ ۘ تَشَٰبَهَتْ قُلُوبُهُمْ ۗ قَدْ بَيَّنَّا ٱلْأَيَٰتِ لِقَوْمٍ يُوقِنُونَ ۝ إِنَّآ أَرْسَلْنَٰكَ بِٱلْحَقِّ بَشِيرًا وَنَذِيرًا ۖ وَلَا تُسْـَٔلُ عَنْ أَصْحَٰبِ ٱلْجَحِيمِ ۝

---

[a] Another error into which they fell was to liken God to man. A human being, for instance, cannot be in two places at the same time, and, in consequence, people think that God is also to be found only in some particular place. But God is everywhere. True, He has prescribed a direction for us to face when we worship, but this is a purely organizational requirement for prayer; it does not mean that God is to be found in only one direction and not in any other. Another outcome of this basic misconception of God's nature is people's attributing a son to Him. But only those who have needs beget sons, and God is above all such imperfections and limitations. He is complete in Himself. Such beliefs do not stem from God; man has invented them himself.

120 Neither the Christians nor the Jews will be pleased with you until you follow their ways. Say, 'God's guidance is the only true guidance.' If you followed their desires after the knowledge which has come to you, you would not have any patron or supporter against God. 121 Those whom We have given this Book follow it as it ought to be followed; it is they who [truly] believe in it; those who deny it will be the losers.*

وَلَن تَرْضَىٰ عَنكَ ٱلْيَهُودُ وَلَا ٱلنَّصَـٰرَىٰ حَتَّىٰ تَتَّبِعَ مِلَّتَهُمْ قُلْ إِنَّ هُدَى ٱللَّهِ هُوَ ٱلْهُدَىٰ وَلَئِنِ ٱتَّبَعْتَ أَهْوَآءَهُم بَعْدَ ٱلَّذِى جَآءَكَ مِنَ ٱلْعِلْمِ مَا لَكَ مِنَ ٱللَّهِ مِن وَلِىٍّ وَلَا نَصِيرٍ ۝ ٱلَّذِينَ ءَاتَيْنَـٰهُمُ ٱلْكِتَـٰبَ يَتْلُونَهُۥ حَقَّ تِلَاوَتِهِۦٓ أُوْلَـٰٓئِكَ يُؤْمِنُونَ بِهِۦ وَمَن يَكْفُرْ بِهِۦ فَأُوْلَـٰٓئِكَ هُمُ ٱلْخَـٰسِرُونَ ۝

---

a All those whom God has sent to preach truth on earth have been confronted with the same kind of reaction. 'If you are God's envoy,' people say to them, 'Why are you not blessed with great worldly treasures?' Such people themselves can think only in worldly terms, so they expect God's messenger to come up to their materialistic standards. They cannot conceive of someone being God's messenger who is not endowed with worldly grandeur. This is the reason the prophets of God have had to face opposition throughout the ages. How, people think, could a great God, whose kingdom encompasses everything, starting with the earth and going to the furthest expanse of the heavens, have chosen such an ordinary person as His messenger? The signs of God were reflected in the lives and teachings of His prophets; indeed, the prophets' words and deeds, based as they were on truth, were manifestations of God's signs. But people could not see such signs because they were too materialistic in their thinking. Their minds were moulded in such a manner that they acknowledged only tangible, visible signs of greatness; the invisible, but intensely meaningful signs that God gave His prophets meant nothing to them. When the preacher comes armed with forceful arguments based on truth, his hearers fail to comprehend them because of their negative mindset.

In ancient times the Jews and Christians had been the bearers of divinely revealed religion on earth. When they went into decline, however, their religion was reduced to a set of ethnic customs: piety lay in belonging to their community and impiety in being apart from it. Their sole criterion for judging between truth and falsehood was the individual's relation to his own community. This sectarian attitude prevented them from accepting genuine unadulterated religion when it was presented to them. True religion can be accepted only by those who are alive to their own true, human natures unlike those who, having suppressed their own true natures, have forsaken natural religion for artificial dogmas.

¹²² Children of Israel, remember My favour which I have bestowed upon you, and how I preferred you above all other people; ¹²³ and fear a Day when no human being shall avail another. Nor shall ransom be accepted from any of them, nor shall intercession be of any use to them, and none shall be succoured. ¹²⁴ When his Lord tested Abraham with certain commands and he fulfilled them, He said, 'I will make you a leader of men.' Abraham asked, 'And what of my descendants?' He answered, 'My covenant does not extend to the transgressors.'ᵃ

يَـٰبَنِىٓ إِسْرَٰٓءِيلَ ٱذْكُرُوا۟ نِعْمَتِىَ ٱلَّتِىٓ أَنْعَمْتُ عَلَيْكُمْ وَأَنِّى فَضَّلْتُكُمْ عَلَى ٱلْعَٰلَمِينَ ۝ وَٱتَّقُوا۟ يَوْمًا لَّا يَجْزِى نَفْسٌ عَن نَّفْسٍ شَيْـًٔا وَلَا يُقْبَلُ مِنْهَا عَدْلٌ وَلَا تَنفَعُهَا شَفَٰعَةٌ وَلَا هُمْ يُنصَرُونَ ۝ ۞ وَإِذِ ٱبْتَلَىٰٓ إِبْرَٰهِـۧمَ رَبُّهُۥ بِكَلِمَٰتٍ فَأَتَمَّهُنَّ قَالَ إِنِّى جَاعِلُكَ لِلنَّاسِ إِمَامًا قَالَ وَمِن ذُرِّيَّتِى قَالَ لَا يَنَالُ عَهْدِى ٱلظَّٰلِمِينَ ۝

ᵃ The Children of Israel were selected by God to perform a very special task: they were to call other nations to turn to God, impressing on them the fact that they were answerable to their Lord for their actions. God sent innumerable prophets from amongst them to help and guide them in the performance of this task—Abraham, Jacob, Joseph, Moses, David, Solomon, Zachariah, John the Baptist and Jesus, to name just a few. Over the centuries, however, the community of the Children of Israel began to degenerate. They took their privileged position, which was in fact due solely to the lofty task that had been entrusted to them, to be an indication of ethnic superiority. They thus lost their right to be representatives of divine religion on earth. The coming of the Arab prophet signified the replacement of the Children of Israel by the Children of Ishmael as God's chosen people: it was they who were chosen to carry on the task of communicating God's word to other nations of the world. Those among the Children of Israel who were truly pious and God-fearing soon realized that the teachings of the Prophet Muhammad came to him from God. They recognized that the word he preached emanated from the same source that had inspired the prophets before him. Those who denied him were acting solely out of prejudice: they refused to accept that any other nation besides their own could have been selected to benefit by God's favour.

These people were warned, through the Arab prophet, that in the next world value would be attached solely to true faith borne out by earnest actions. In this world one person is able to bear the burden of another; sometimes intercession is accepted; sometimes one can free oneself by giving compensation; sometimes a helper is at hand to see one through a difficult situation. In the next world, however, none of these mitigating factors will be allowed to come into play. ▶

¹²⁵ And We made the House [the Ka‘bah] a place of assembly and a sanctuary for mankind, [saying], 'Make the place where Abraham stood a place of worship.' We commanded Abraham and Ishmael, 'Purify My House for those who walk round it, those who stay there for devotion, and those who bow down and prostrate themselves.'^a

وَإِذْ جَعَلْنَا ٱلْبَيْتَ مَثَابَةً لِّلنَّاسِ وَأَمْنًا وَٱتَّخِذُوا۟ مِن مَّقَامِ إِبْرَٰهِـۧمَ مُصَلًّى وَعَهِدْنَآ إِلَىٰٓ إِبْرَٰهِـۧمَ وَإِسْمَـٰعِيلَ أَن طَهِّرَا بَيْتِىَ لِلطَّآئِفِينَ وَٱلْعَـٰكِفِينَ وَٱلرُّكَّعِ ٱلسُّجُودِ ﴿١٢٥﴾

There, God's justice will apply to one and all equally, for no ethnic group holds a monopoly over the next world. Take the example of Abraham, patriarch of both the Arabs and the Jews. He was granted leadership of mankind only after he had undergone very severe tests, and had shown himself to be faithful and true to God under all circumstances. What God had demanded of Abraham was the most difficult sacrifice—his son's life—and when God finally intervened before Abraham could actually sacrifice his own son, it was because Abraham had demonstrated his perfect willingness to make any sacrifice demanded of him by God, no matter how great or how terrible it might have been. The rule that applied to Abraham applies to every generation: only those who prove themselves worthy will be granted a share in God's covenant; those who do not will meet the same fate as any other offenders in God's sight, regardless of the nation to which they belong. One who is willing to make soul-searing sacrifices for God's cause shows his utmost dedication to it: it is only just and natural, then, that he should become the leader of his people.

^a Every year, the faithful come from all over the world to visit the Ka‘bah in Makkah, where no one is allowed to harm even the lowliest living creature; for Makkah has been made into a sacred place of worship for all time. Since people come to this place to remember God in an atmosphere of peace and solitude, it has to be cleansed of all impurities, and all activities that are contrary to this basic purpose are banned. Here the faithful bow and prostrate themselves, their greatest mark of respect for their Creator being the circumambulation of the Ka‘bah.

[126] And when Abraham prayed, 'My Lord, make this city a city of peace, and provide its inhabitants with fruits, such of them as believe in God and the Last Day.' God said, 'As for those who deny the truth, I will grant them benefits for a short while and then subject them to the punishment of the Fire—an evil destination.'[a]

وَإِذْ قَالَ إِبْرَاهِـٰمُ رَبِّ ٱجْعَلْ هَـٰذَا بَلَدًا ءَامِنًا وَٱرْزُقْ أَهْلَهُۥ مِنَ ٱلثَّمَرَٰتِ مَنْ ءَامَنَ مِنْهُم بِٱللَّهِ وَٱلْيَوْمِ ٱلْأَخِرِ قَالَ وَمَن كَفَرَ فَأُمَتِّعُهُۥ قَلِيلًا ثُمَّ أَضْطَرُّهُۥٓ إِلَىٰ عَذَابِ ٱلنَّارِ وَبِئْسَ ٱلْمَصِيرُ ۝

---

[a] In ancient times Arabia was the most arid land on earth: its sandy surfaces and barren rocks were totally unsuitable for any kind of cultivation. Worse, it was totally exposed to attacks from the outside world. Four thousand years ago Abraham was commanded to take his family into an 'uncultivable valley', in that part of Arabia known as Hijaz, and settle them there.

Abraham bowed to the will of God without slightest hesitation. When he had taken his family to that 'uncultivable and inhospitable valley' he prayed to God, 'O my God, I have done as was commanded. Now listen to the call of your servant and make this town a place of peace, and make special provision for the material needs of its citizens; for the land that they inhabit is uncultivable.' Abraham's prayer was answered: the land of Hijaz has remained an abode of peace and plenty up to the present day.

The believer's whole life should be an act of worship. In whatever far-off corner of the world he lives, he should at all times remember that, one day, he shall have to return to the Lord. He should cause no harm to his fellow men, and as for the earth he lives on, it should be thought of as a place of worship, and kept free of all pollution. Although physically in this world, his heart and mind should always be focused on God—his life should revolve around Him alone; his whole life should be that of submission to Him. True religion makes certain demands on everyone, sometimes even requires that his children be taken to a place as arid and uncultivable as Abraham's valley. Whatever is entailed, he should faithfully carry out God's commandments and only then pray to God that He should make his efforts successful. It may well be that God will make fountains gush forth from a dry desert, and lush crops spring forth from a barren land.

Whatever splendour and glory one is accorded in this life, these things in themselves do not signify that one is considered fit by God for the leadership of mankind. Everything given to man is a means of testing him and there is no one who is exempt from God's trial. Leadership indicates that one has been selected by God to represent Him in the nations of the world, and it is only for those who have been found fit by God to represent His divine religion on earth.

127 And when Abraham and Ishmael were laying the foundations of the House, [they prayed], 'Our Lord, accept this from us; for You are All Hearing, All Knowing. 128 Lord, make us submissive to You; make of our descendants a nation that will submit to You. Teach us our rites of worship and turn to us with mercy; You are the Forgiving One and the Merciful.*

وَإِذْ يَرْفَعُ إِبْرَاهِـمُ ٱلْقَوَاعِدَ مِنَ ٱلْبَيْتِ وَإِسْمَـعِيلُ رَبَّنَا تَقَبَّلْ مِنَّا إِنَّكَ أَنتَ ٱلسَّمِيعُ ٱلْعَلِيمُ ﴿١٢٧﴾ رَبَّنَا وَٱجْعَلْنَا مُسْلِمَيْنِ لَكَ وَمِن ذُرِّيَّتِنَا أُمَّةً مُّسْلِمَةً لَّكَ وَأَرِنَا مَنَاسِكَنَا وَتُبْ عَلَيْنَا إِنَّكَ أَنتَ ٱلتَّوَّابُ ٱلرَّحِيمُ ﴿١٢٨﴾

* God ordained that a universal centre of Islamic *dawah* be established in Hijaz. Almighty God chose Abraham and his family to establish this centre and make provision for its functioning. The words which Abraham and Ishmael uttered when they were building the house of God in Makkah were, in addition to being supplications to God, an indication of their unwavering fidelity to God's scheme of things. It is prayer of this kind that is most pleasing to God, so He accepted their prayer and a permanent fountain of spiritual life for the whole world gushed forth from the barren desert of Arabia. The name of this fountain was Islam. As for the people who inhabited this desert, the offspring of Ishmael, God made them enthusiastic proponents of the Islamic cause: He enabled them to propagate His word far and wide. Through them, he informed mankind how they should please their Lord, so that He might turn to them in mercy. It was to the Children of Ishmael that the final prophet was sent, and for the first time in history, the entire prophetic pattern was recorded for posterity, so that future generations could follow it.

¹²⁹ Our Lord, send forth to them a messenger of their own to recite Your revelations to them,^a to teach them the Scripture^b and wisdom,^c and purify^d them. You are the Mighty, the Wise One.'

¹³⁰ Who but a foolish man would turn away from the religion of Abraham? We chose him in this world, and in the Hereafter he shall be among the righteous.

رَبَّنَا وَٱبْعَثْ فِيهِمْ رَسُولاً مِّنْهُمْ يَتْلُواْ عَلَيْهِمْ ءَايَٰتِكَ وَيُعَلِّمُهُمُ ٱلْكِتَٰبَ وَٱلْحِكْمَةَ وَيُزَكِّيهِمْ ۚ إِنَّكَ أَنتَ ٱلْعَزِيزُ ٱلْحَكِيمُ ۝ وَمَن يَرْغَبُ عَن مِّلَّةِ إِبْرَٰهِـۧمَ إِلَّا مَن سَفِهَ نَفْسَهُۥ ۚ وَلَقَدِ ٱصْطَفَيْنَٰهُ فِى ٱلدُّنْيَا ۖ وَإِنَّهُۥ فِى ٱلْءَاخِرَةِ لَمِنَ ٱلصَّٰلِحِينَ ۝

^a The first and foremost task of God's messenger is to interpret His signs, which are proofs of His greatness and power. God has introduced innumerable signs into human nature as well as into the outside world to enable human beings to know their Creator. But these signs have to be unveiled by God's messenger: he shares his divine insight with them so that they may have a glimpse of God's glory.

^b 'The Scripture' refers here to the Quran. The second task of the prophet is to become a recipient of revelation from God. He has to communicate this divine message to man.

^c 'Wisdom' here refers to insight. When this insight is produced within man, he is able to see more deeply into the signs of God. When he moulds himself according to the teachings of the Quran, the light of insight burns within him, producing a sublime level of consciousness. This enables him to arrive at right conclusions in all matters as desired by God.

^d 'Purification', or *tazkiah*, means 'to free something from unfavourable elements'. In this context it means enabling human beings to purify themselves of all negative influences resulting from their conditioning. The final aim of a prophet is to fashion such souls as are totally absorbed in love for and devotion to God; that are free from all kinds of complexes; that derive their spiritual nourishment from the world around them, something which God Himself has made available to His believing servants.

¹³¹ When his Lord said to him, 'Surrender!' he responded, 'I have surrendered to the Lord of the Universe,' ¹³² and Abraham enjoined his sons to do the same, as did Jacob, 'My sons, God has chosen this religion for you; so do not let death overtake you, except when you are in a state of submission.' ᵃ

إِذْ قَالَ لَهُۥ رَبُّهُۥٓ أَسْلِمْ قَالَ أَسْلَمْتُ لِرَبِّ ٱلْعَٰلَمِينَ ۝ وَوَصَّىٰ بِهَآ إِبْرَٰهِـۧمُ بَنِيهِ وَيَعْقُوبُ يَٰبَنِىَّ إِنَّ ٱللَّهَ ٱصْطَفَىٰ لَكُمُ ٱلدِّينَ فَلَا تَمُوتُنَّ إِلَّا وَأَنتُم مُّسْلِمُونَ ۝

ᵃ The message taught by the Prophet Muhammad was exactly the same as had been taught by Abraham. But those People of the Book, who prided themselves on being followers of Abraham, led the opposition against the Prophet. Why did they act in this manner? The reason was that the religion that the Prophet taught, and which Abraham had taught before him, was the religion of Islam. Now, Islam means total submission to God, and it was this religion that Abraham handed down to his offspring. But the religion that the People of the Book practised had nothing to do with total submission to God. Having lapsed into permissiveness and, unwilling to change this lifestyle, they had allowed their religion to degenerate into a series of hollow rituals, which they fondly believed would make it easy for them to enter paradise. In the religion that the Prophet Muhammad taught, however, one could gain salvation only by virtue of one's actions. The People of the Book, for their part, thought that their affiliation to a nation of saints and prophets would be sufficient to earn them redemption. There was a world of difference then between Islam, the true religion of Abraham, and the religion that the People of the Book practised and attributed to him. True religion means acceptance of divine guidance, as revealed to man through the prophets, whereas the religion practised by the People of the Book was based on their own national legacy, a collection of national traditions, which had accumulated over generations.

¹³³ Were you present when Jacob faced the hour of death and he asked his sons, 'Who will you worship after me?' They answered, 'We will worship your God and the God of your fathers, Abraham and Ishmael and Isaac: the one God; we have submitted ourselves to Him.' ¹³⁴ Those were a people that have passed away; what they did is theirs and what you have done is yours. You will not be answerable for their deeds.[a]

أَمْ كُنتُمْ شُهَدَآءَ إِذْ حَضَرَ يَعْقُوبَ ٱلْمَوْتُ إِذْ قَالَ لِبَنِيهِ مَا تَعْبُدُونَ مِنْ بَعْدِى قَالُوا۟ نَعْبُدُ إِلَٰهَكَ وَإِلَٰهَ ءَابَآئِكَ إِبْرَٰهِۦمَ وَإِسْمَٰعِيلَ وَإِسْحَٰقَ إِلَٰهًا وَٰحِدًا وَنَحْنُ لَهُۥ مُسْلِمُونَ ۝ تِلْكَ أُمَّةٌ قَدْ خَلَتْ لَهَا مَا كَسَبَتْ وَلَكُم مَّا كَسَبْتُمْ وَلَا تُسْـَٔلُونَ عَمَّا كَانُوا۟ يَعْمَلُونَ ۝

---

[a] Attaching oneself to saints and prophets, living or dead, lulls one into a false sense of security. It leads one to imagine that just as one has been attached to them in this life, one will remain attached to them in the next. It makes one feel that their surplus of good deeds will make up for one's own shortcomings. The People of the Book were immersed in this form of wishful thinking to the extent that they had invented a dogma of ancestral salvation, pinning all their hopes on the holiness of their elders. But it is sheer self-deception to think that one person will receive the reward of another's actions. In reality, everyone will reap the rewards, and bear the burden of punishment for his own actions. No one will be made to share in the reward, or punishment, which is awarded to another by virtue of his actions on earth.

One who submits to God finds that he has to face all kinds of difficulties in this life. His worldly hopes and ambitions will not necessarily be fulfilled. Yet one who is firm in the faith will not be put off by adversity; he will persevere, making sure that he leaves this world as a believer, so that he can look forward to God's blessings in the next world.

135 They say, 'Be Jews or Christians, and you shall be rightly guided.' Say, 'By no means! We believe in the faith of Abraham, who was ever inclined [to God]; he was not one of those who set up partners with God.' 136 Say, 'We believe in God and what was revealed to us; and what was revealed to Abraham, Ishmael, Isaac, Jacob, and their descendants, and what was given to Moses and Jesus and what was given to the [other] prophets by their Lord. We make no distinction between any of them. It is to Him that we surrender ourselves.'[a]

وَقَالُوا۟ كُونُوا۟ هُودًا أَوْ نَصَـٰرَىٰ تَهْتَدُوا۟ قُلْ بَلْ مِلَّةَ إِبْرَٰهِـۧمَ حَنِيفًا وَمَا كَانَ مِنَ ٱلْمُشْرِكِينَ ۝ قُولُوٓا۟ ءَامَنَّا بِٱللَّهِ وَمَآ أُنزِلَ إِلَيْنَا وَمَآ أُنزِلَ إِلَىٰٓ إِبْرَٰهِـۧمَ وَإِسْمَـٰعِيلَ وَإِسْحَـٰقَ وَيَعْقُوبَ وَٱلْأَسْبَاطِ وَمَآ أُوتِىَ مُوسَىٰ وَعِيسَىٰ وَمَآ أُوتِىَ ٱلنَّبِيُّونَ مِن رَّبِّهِمْ لَا نُفَرِّقُ بَيْنَ أَحَدٍ مِّنْهُمْ وَنَحْنُ لَهُۥ مُسْلِمُونَ ۝

---

[a] The religion that the Prophet Muhammad taught was the religion of the Prophet Abraham, the very religion to which the Jews and the Christians claimed allegiance. Why was it, then, that they turned away from the Prophet Muhammad? The reason for this was that the religion brought by the Prophet, taught people to take on the hue of God; to devote themselves to Him entirely. With the People of the Book, religion had a different meaning. For them religion was reduced to a symbol of national pride. The message brought by the Prophet hurt their pride, so they turned against him. Those who consider their own race superior to others cannot accept the truth when it manifests itself in some nation other than their own. They would believe in prophets who came from amongst their own people, but not in those who appeared among other people outside their own community. The only personalities that they acknowledged were those who belonged to their own race. Those who look at religion as worship of God, on the other hand, recognize the truth of every piece of wisdom that God sends down, no matter who teaches it. For the theologians to realize that the Prophet was God's final messenger was not a matter of insuperable difficulty. There was nothing to prevent them from seeing the truth of his religion. They should have proclaimed what, deep down in their hearts, they knew to be true. But they did not accept him as the final prophet, as was enjoined by God, for the simple reason that they were more concerned about their own position and prestige. Just as the people of old received their just deserts as individuals, so will latter-day generations receive what they merit on their own account, for truth is an individual, not an ancestral matter. The mistake of the People of the Book was to think that contemporary and succeeding generations would be rewarded for the good deeds of their ancestors. The idea of original sin held by Christians implied that sins were handed down from one generation to the next. Such beliefs have no basis in truth. Everyone will be rewarded by God according to his or her own personal actions; no one can be held responsible for the deeds of others.

137 If they believe as you have believed, then are they rightly guided; but if they turn back, then know that they are entrenched in hostility. God will surely suffice to defend you against them, for He is All Hearing, All Knowing. 138 We take on God's own dye. Who has a better dye than God's? We worship Him alone. 139 Say, 'Do you dispute with us about God, while He is our Lord and your Lord? We have our actions and you have your actions. We are devoted to Him alone. 140 Do you claim that Abraham and Ishmael and Isaac and Jacob and their descendants were all Jews or Christians?' Say, 'Do you know better or does God? And who could be more unjust than one who conceals a testimony given to him by God? God is not unaware of what you do.' 141 Those were a people that have passed away; theirs is what they did and yours what you have done. You shall not be answerable for their deeds.a

فَإِنْ ءَامَنُواْ بِمِثْلِ مَآ ءَامَنتُم بِهِۦ فَقَدِ ٱهْتَدَواْ ۖ وَّإِن تَوَلَّوْاْ فَإِنَّمَا هُمْ فِى شِقَاقٍ ۖ فَسَيَكْفِيكَهُمُ ٱللَّهُ ۚ وَهُوَ ٱلسَّمِيعُ ٱلْعَلِيمُ ۝ صِبْغَةَ ٱللَّهِ ۖ وَمَنْ أَحْسَنُ مِنَ ٱللَّهِ صِبْغَةً ۖ وَنَحْنُ لَهُۥ عَـٰبِدُونَ ۝ قُلْ أَتُحَآجُّونَنَا فِى ٱللَّهِ وَهُوَ رَبُّنَا وَرَبُّكُمْ وَلَنَآ أَعْمَـٰلُنَا وَلَكُمْ أَعْمَـٰلُكُمْ وَنَحْنُ لَهُۥ مُخْلِصُونَ ۝ أَمْ تَقُولُونَ إِنَّ إِبْرَٰهِـۧمَ وَإِسْمَـٰعِيلَ وَإِسْحَـٰقَ وَيَعْقُوبَ وَٱلْأَسْبَاطَ كَانُواْ هُودًا أَوْ نَصَـٰرَىٰ ۗ قُلْ ءَأَنتُمْ أَعْلَمُ أَمِ ٱللَّهُ ۗ وَمَنْ أَظْلَمُ مِمَّن كَتَمَ شَهَـٰدَةً عِندَهُۥ مِنَ ٱللَّهِ ۗ وَمَا ٱللَّهُ بِغَـٰفِلٍ عَمَّا تَعْمَلُونَ ۝ تِلْكَ أُمَّةٌ قَدْ خَلَتْ ۖ لَهَا مَا كَسَبَتْ وَلَكُم مَّا كَسَبْتُمْ ۖ وَلَا تُسْـَٔلُونَ عَمَّا كَانُواْ يَعْمَلُونَ ۝

---

a If faith is to be of the kind which pleases God, it must be identical with that of the Companions of the Prophet. What was so special about that faith was that it amounted to acceptance of the truth on an abstract level; it was belief in truth for the sake of truth. This had become a rarity in a society which, revering the words of the ancient prophets, regarded as truth whatever had been sanctified by centuries-old tradition. Continued belief in such 'truth', embellished as it was by myth and legend, became a matter of national pride; to regard it in any other light would have been to deny a great legacy from the past. Unlike the ancient prophets, who were great figures, eulogised in their nations' history, the Prophet Muhammad came afresh to the world with no accumulation of tradition behind him to lend weight to his words. When truth stands on its own, unsupported by history or tradition, as it was in the time of the Prophet, those who accept it do so for the pure and simple reason that it is the truth. This is the kind of belief that God recognizes and accepts. This is true faith; only faith of such strength and purity is acceptable to God.

142 The foolish will ask, 'What has made them turn away from their direction of prayer which they used to face?' Say, 'The East and the West belong to God. He guides whom He pleases to the right path.'*a*

سَيَقُولُ ٱلسُّفَهَآءُ مِنَ ٱلنَّاسِ مَا وَلَّىٰهُمْ عَن قِبْلَتِهِمُ ٱلَّتِى كَانُوا۟ عَلَيْهَا قُل لِّلَّهِ ٱلْمَشْرِقُ وَٱلْمَغْرِبُ يَهْدِى مَن يَشَآءُ إِلَىٰ صِرَٰطٍ مُّسْتَقِيمٍ ۝

---

a The *qiblah* is the direction which Muslims face when praying. This direction has to do with the form, rather than the reality, of worship. A *qiblah* is appointed so that prayer may assume an organized pattern. God can change it as He pleases, for in whichever direction one turns, one faces Him. The direction that He lays down is the one that we should face in our prayer, irrespective of what direction it may be. Before the coming of Islam people had prayed towards Jerusalem. This old *qiblah* had come to be thought of as sacred and inviolable. In the second year after the Prophet's emigration to Madinah, he was commanded to alter the direction of prayer, and face Makkah instead of Jerusalem. Some people found this change difficult to accept. How, they thought, could another place be the *qiblah* when Jerusalem had held this position for time immemorial? The opponents of Islam used the change of the *qiblah* as an excuse to spread all sorts of rumours about the Prophet. 'Previous prophets have always faced Jerusalem in their prayer,' they said. 'How is it that this prophet has gone against them? This goes to show that the only purpose of his mission is to spite the Jews.' Some poured scorn on Muhammad's claim to prophethood. 'He seems to be in two minds about his own mission,' they said. 'Sometimes he faces Jerusalem, sometimes Makkah.' Others said, 'Well, if the Ka'bah in Makkah is the real *qiblah*, then all the prayers which Muslims have made facing towards Jerusalem have been wasted.'

These were the sort of objections that the Prophet's opponents made. True believers, those who were not caught up in the externals of religion, did not let such things disturb them. They realized that it was not the direction of prayer that really mattered, but God's commandment. God could lay down any *qiblah*, whenever He liked. Whatever He prescribed should be followed. The commandment regarding the change of *qiblah* was revealed seventeen months after the Prophet's emigration to Madinah. The Prophet was praying with a group of his companions at the time. As soon as God's commandment was revealed, all of them turned, still praying, from Jerusalem to Makkah—a 160 degree turn from north-west to south.

¹⁴³Thus We have made you a middle nation,^a so that you may act as witnesses for mankind, and the Messenger may be a witness for you. We decreed your former prayer direction towards which you used to face only in order that We might make a clear distinction between the Messenger's true followers and those who were to turn their backs on him. This was indeed a hard test for all but those whom God has guided. God will never let your faith go to waste. God is compassionate and merciful to mankind.

وَكَذَٰلِكَ جَعَلْنَٰكُمْ أُمَّةً وَسَطًا لِّتَكُونُوا۟ شُهَدَآءَ عَلَى ٱلنَّاسِ وَيَكُونَ ٱلرَّسُولُ عَلَيْكُمْ شَهِيدًا ۗ وَمَا جَعَلْنَا ٱلْقِبْلَةَ ٱلَّتِى كُنتَ عَلَيْهَآ إِلَّا لِنَعْلَمَ مَن يَتَّبِعُ ٱلرَّسُولَ مِمَّن يَنقَلِبُ عَلَىٰ عَقِبَيْهِ ۚ وَإِن كَانَتْ لَكَبِيرَةً إِلَّا عَلَى ٱلَّذِينَ هَدَى ٱللَّهُ ۗ وَمَا كَانَ ٱللَّهُ لِيُضِيعَ إِيمَٰنَكُمْ ۚ إِنَّ ٱللَّهَ بِٱلنَّاسِ لَرَءُوفٌ رَّحِيمٌ ۝

---

^a Acting as intermediaries, the prophets used to receive guidance from God and convey it to the people. This process continued for thousands of years until the arrival of the Prophet Muhammad, with whom the chain of prophethood ended. But, even after the end of the prophethood, the conveying of God's message to the people had, and still has to be continued. Generation after generation, innumerable people are born and, before they die, they must be told about the reality of life and the divine commandments. After the death of the Prophet, this responsibility had to be discharged by the Muslims. Now, with the end of the prophethood, the entire Muslim community stands between God and the people, a position formerly occupied by the prophets.

This is not a reward for superiority but a massive responsibility, so that all of the Muslims' social and community-based planning must of necessity be *dawah*-oriented. Muslims should be most eager to carry out this mission, should make it their principal goal and be ready to sacrifice their all for it.

The change of *qiblah* was a sign that God had removed the Children of Israel from their position of spiritual leadership and appointed in their place the followers of Muhammad. Now the Ka'bah shall remain, until the end of time, the rallying point for the call of divine religion, a centre for all true believers in God, with Muslims acting as a 'middle nation' (*ummat wasat*), or intermediaries, between God and man. It is for them to communicate the word of God to their fellow human beings, just as the Prophet had done in his time. This is a responsibility which is eternally incumbent upon the Muslim community. Their success, in this world and in the Hereafter, depends upon how effectively they discharge it.

144 We have frequently seen you turn your face towards heaven. So We will make you turn in a direction for prayer that will please you. So turn your face now towards the Sacred Mosque: and wherever you may be, turn your faces towards it. Those who were given the Book know this to be the truth from their Lord. God is not unaware of what they do. 145 But even if you should produce every kind of sign for those who have been given the Book, they would never accept your prayer direction, nor would you accept their prayer direction: nor would any of them accept one another's direction. If, after all the knowledge you have been given, you yield to their desires, then, you shall surely become a transgressor.[a]

قَدْ نَرَىٰ تَقَلُّبَ وَجْهِكَ فِى ٱلسَّمَآءِ
فَلَنُوَلِّيَنَّكَ قِبْلَةً تَرْضَىٰهَا ۚ فَوَلِّ وَجْهَكَ
شَطْرَ ٱلْمَسْجِدِ ٱلْحَرَامِ ۚ وَحَيْثُ مَا
كُنتُمْ فَوَلُّوا۟ وُجُوهَكُمْ شَطْرَهُۥ ۗ وَإِنَّ
ٱلَّذِينَ أُوتُوا۟ ٱلْكِتَٰبَ لَيَعْلَمُونَ أَنَّهُ
ٱلْحَقُّ مِن رَّبِّهِمْ ۗ وَمَا ٱللَّهُ بِغَٰفِلٍ عَمَّا
يَعْمَلُونَ ۝ وَلَئِنْ أَتَيْتَ ٱلَّذِينَ أُوتُوا۟
ٱلْكِتَٰبَ بِكُلِّ ءَايَةٍ مَّا تَبِعُوا۟ قِبْلَتَكَ ۚ
وَمَآ أَنتَ بِتَابِعٍ قِبْلَتَهُمْ ۚ وَمَا بَعْضُهُم
بِتَابِعٍ قِبْلَةَ بَعْضٍ ۚ وَلَئِنِ ٱتَّبَعْتَ
أَهْوَآءَهُم مِّنۢ بَعْدِ مَا جَآءَكَ مِنَ
ٱلْعِلْمِ ۙ إِنَّكَ إِذًا لَّمِنَ ٱلظَّٰلِمِينَ ۝

[a] Not until the Prophet Muhammad received divine revelation on a particular matter, did he change the pattern of previous prophets. Faithful to this principle, he initially made Jerusalem his prayer direction, or the *qiblah,* for prophets since the time of Solomon had prayed in that direction. The coming of Islam signalled the removal of the Jews from their position as torch-bearers of the true faith. The true faith had also to be separated and made distinct from Jewish tradition, so that it could appear in a new and unmistakably pure form. For this reason the Prophet eagerly awaited instructions to change the *qiblah.* In the second year after his emigration to Madinah, he received the commandment. The prophets who hailed from among the Jewish people had been informed that one day God would alter the *qiblah,* and they had passed the knowledge on to the Jews. It was something, therefore, that Jewish theologians should have expected. Yet only a few of them, such as 'Abdullah ibn Salam and Mukhairiq, confirmed the authenticity of this commandment and acknowledged that God had revealed the truth through the Prophet Muhammad. The reason for the majority's refusal to follow the Prophet was the fact that they were used to behave as they wished. They had certain romantic notions about the special position occupied by their own people, and they had made these the bedrock of their life and creed. Those who give free rein to their own desires will never follow the path of reason. In their perversity, they want the kind of satisfaction from the denial of God's signs, which God would have wished them to derive from their acceptance.

¹⁴⁶ Those to whom We have given the Book recognize it just as they recognize their own sons. But, some of them knowingly conceal the truth. ¹⁴⁷ Truth is what comes from your Lord; therefore, do not be of those who doubt.ᵃ

ٱلَّذِينَ ءَاتَيْنَـٰهُمُ ٱلْكِتَـٰبَ يَعْرِفُونَهُۥ كَمَا يَعْرِفُونَ أَبْنَآءَهُمْ وَإِنَّ فَرِيقًا مِّنْهُمْ لَيَكْتُمُونَ ٱلْحَقَّ وَهُمْ يَعْلَمُونَ ۝ ٱلْحَقُّ مِن رَّبِّكَ فَلَا تَكُونَنَّ مِنَ ٱلْمُمْتَرِينَ ۝

ᵃ Whenever God reveals some truth to the world, it is supported by clear arguments. No one can then fail to recognize it to be the truth. Those who do not make the truth their own, show that they had never realised God, for, if they had, they would have recognized His word when they heard it.

Those who find words to reject the truth think that they have discovered strong arguments to justify their stand. They think that they are standing on firm logical ground. But very soon they realize that those words were nothing but imaginary props, which they themselves had devised to give false satisfaction to their egos.

148 Each community has its own direction in which it turns: vie, then, with one another in doing good works. Wherever you may be, God will bring you all before Him. God has power over all things. 149 Wherever you set out from, turn your face in the direction of the Sacred Mosque—this is the truth from your Lord: He is not unaware of what you do—150 wherever you come from, turn your face to the Sacred Mosque; wherever you may be, turn your faces towards it, so that people will not have any argument against you except for the wrongdoers among them. Do not fear them; fear Me, so that I may perfect My favour to you and you may be rightly guided.[a]

وَلِكُلٍّ وِجْهَةٌ هُوَ مُوَلِّيهَا ۖ فَٱسْتَبِقُوا۟ ٱلْخَيْرَٰتِ ۚ أَيْنَ مَا تَكُونُوا۟ يَأْتِ بِكُمُ ٱللَّهُ جَمِيعًا ۚ إِنَّ ٱللَّهَ عَلَىٰ كُلِّ شَىْءٍ قَدِيرٌ ۝ وَمِنْ حَيْثُ خَرَجْتَ فَوَلِّ وَجْهَكَ شَطْرَ ٱلْمَسْجِدِ ٱلْحَرَامِ ۖ وَإِنَّهُ لَلْحَقُّ مِن رَّبِّكَ ۗ وَمَا ٱللَّهُ بِغَٰفِلٍ عَمَّا تَعْمَلُونَ ۝ وَمِنْ حَيْثُ خَرَجْتَ فَوَلِّ وَجْهَكَ شَطْرَ ٱلْمَسْجِدِ ٱلْحَرَامِ ۚ وَحَيْثُ مَا كُنتُمْ فَوَلُّوا۟ وُجُوهَكُمْ شَطْرَهُ لِئَلَّا يَكُونَ لِلنَّاسِ عَلَيْكُمْ حُجَّةٌ إِلَّا ٱلَّذِينَ ظَلَمُوا۟ مِنْهُمْ فَلَا تَخْشَوْهُمْ وَٱخْشَوْنِى وَلِأُتِمَّ نِعْمَتِى عَلَيْكُمْ وَلَعَلَّكُمْ تَهْتَدُونَ ۝

---

[a] When the Ka'bah in Makkah was appointed as the prayer direction, or *qiblah*, the People of the Book started discussing whether the East was God's direction or the West. They saw the matter as one of direction alone, but this was nothing other than sheer ignorance on their part. The selection of the House of God as the *qiblah* was not merely the specification of a certain direction for prayer; it was a sign that the time had come for God to reveal His greatest favour to man. It had been decided a long time ago, that, in answer to the prayer of Abraham and Ishmael (see 2:129), God would send a final Prophet to the world. The path to life everlasting was now being thrown open to all: God was showing His ultimate favour to mankind. The bringing of religion to its final stage of perfection in Islam does not mean that previous religions were incomplete. They too were complete in themselves, but none of them was preserved in its original and authentic form. God had revealed true religion time and time again, but on each occasion mankind had rebelled against it and either distorted it or allowed it to fall into oblivion. Now it was revealed in its ultimate and indelible form. Divine religion that had deteriorated into a set of mythological tales was now incorporated into history in the form of solid facts. Up till then, no pattern of true religion had been preserved for posterity; now, it was placed before mankind in a permanent, living and practical form. The change of *qiblah*, rather than denoting a change from one direction of worship to another, more sacred one, showed the completion of God's guidance to mankind.

¹⁵¹ Thus We have sent among you a Messenger of your own to recite Our revelations to you, purify you and teach you the Book and wisdom, and to teach you what you did not know. ¹⁵² So remember Me; I will remember you. Be thankful to Me and do not be ungrateful.^a

كَمَآ أَرْسَلْنَا فِيكُمْ رَسُولاً مِّنكُمْ يَتْلُواْ عَلَيْكُمْ ءَايَٰتِنَا وَيُزَكِّيكُمْ وَيُعَلِّمُكُمُ ٱلْكِتَٰبَ وَٱلْحِكْمَةَ وَيُعَلِّمُكُم مَّا لَمْ تَكُونُواْ تَعْلَمُونَ ۞ فَٱذْكُرُونِىٓ أَذْكُرْكُمْ وَٱشْكُرُواْ لِى وَلَا تَكْفُرُونِ ۞

---

^a It was at the time of the construction of the Ka'bah that Abraham and Ishmael prayed for a prophet to be born among the people of Makkah. The prayer was answered, and the coming of the final prophet, whose focus would be Makkah, was decreed. God's messengers who came to the world used to prophesy his coming.

Now that he had come, the Ka'bah in Makkah was made the prayer direction for all nations. This was God's sign, indicating that the prophet, whose coming had been anticipated, had finally arrived. As for the sincere—they needed no further proof, but even the conclusiveness of this sign was not enough to silence those who gave no thought to God. It is those who fear God who are guided on the path to Him. God remembers those who remember Him. Only those who are filled with fear of Him are free of fear of all else besides Him.

¹⁵³ You who believe, seek help through patience and prayer; surely, God is with the steadfast. ¹⁵⁴ Do not say that those who are killed in God's cause are dead; they are alive, but you are not aware of it. ¹⁵⁵ We shall certainly test you with fear and hunger, and loss of property, lives and crops. Give good news to those who endure with fortitude.ᵃ

يَـٰٓأَيُّهَا ٱلَّذِينَ ءَامَنُوا۟ ٱسْتَعِينُوا۟ بِٱلصَّبْرِ وَٱلصَّلَوٰةِ إِنَّ ٱللَّهَ مَعَ ٱلصَّـٰبِرِينَ ۝ وَلَا تَقُولُوا۟ لِمَن يُقْتَلُ فِى سَبِيلِ ٱللَّهِ أَمْوَٰتٌۢ بَلْ أَحْيَآءٌ وَلَـٰكِن لَّا تَشْعُرُونَ ۝ وَلَنَبْلُوَنَّكُم بِشَىْءٍ مِّنَ ٱلْخَوْفِ وَٱلْجُوعِ وَنَقْصٍ مِّنَ ٱلْأَمْوَٰلِ وَٱلْأَنفُسِ وَٱلثَّمَرَٰتِ وَبَشِّرِ ٱلصَّـٰبِرِينَ ۝

ᵃ One who has adopted religion in the real sense of the word has truly discovered God. He lives in a permanent state of thanksgiving and remembrance of his Lord. Such a life alone is a source of peace and happiness. But peace and happiness will materialize in their complete form only in the next eternal world. This world has not been created for reward: it has been created for the trial of man. This world being a testing ground, God's servants face obstacles in their path so that the earnest among them may be distinguished from those who are not serious and sincere. These obstacles present themselves in normal, everyday situations of life— human temptations, family demands, worldly interests, social pressure—these are the things that provide the real test of life. First one has to realize in what manner one is being tested; then one has to avoid the pitfalls by remembering God and thanking Him for the blessings of life.

There is only one way to succeed in the trials of life, and that is through patience and prayer. This entails attaching oneself to God and conscientiously adhering to the path of truth, enduring all the setbacks that afflict one on the way. Those who do not waver from the path despite all the difficulties it presents—who stay with God even when no worldly benefit seems to accrue therefrom—are the ones who will finally emerge successful from the trials of life. God has reserved the eternal blessings of the next life for those who show themselves willing to sacrifice this life for the next.

A preacher of truth has to make the greatest sacrifices in the path of God. Suffering and affliction are his lot because of his hearers' negative response to the criticism and admonition, which are inseparable parts of such preaching. There are few in this world who are willing to be reproved and warned. The sincere preacher also incurs the animosity of mercenary individuals, who are doing brisk business in the name of religion. The sincerity of the true preacher becomes a threat to the status of hypocrites, therefore, they turn hostile to the preacher. Becoming a preacher of God's word, then, is tantamount to putting one's hand into a fire. One who takes this task upon himself is exposing himself to prejudice, economic ruin and even expulsion from his own land. He is placing both his life and his property in the utmost peril. It is inevitable that one who follows God's path is persecuted in this world. But it is those who lose all for God's sake who are the true finders; it is those who give their lives for Him who inherit life everlasting. For those who do not seek to make their paradise in this ephemeral world, God has prepared an eternal paradise in the next.

¹⁵⁶ Those who say, when afflicted with a calamity, 'We belong to God and to Him we shall return,' ¹⁵⁷ are the ones who will have blessings and mercy from their Lord: it is they who are on the right path!ᵃ

الَّذِينَ إِذَآ أَصَٰبَتْهُم مُّصِيبَةٌ قَالُوٓاْ إِنَّا لِلَّهِ وَإِنَّآ إِلَيْهِ رَٰجِعُونَ ۝ أُوْلَٰٓئِكَ عَلَيْهِمْ صَلَوَٰتٌ مِّن رَّبِّهِمْ وَرَحْمَةٌ وَأُوْلَٰٓئِكَ هُمُ ٱلْمُهْتَدُونَ ۝

ᵃ On the death of a loved one, one goes in a state of prayerfulness, deep thinking and contemplation. The experience reminds him that there is very little time at his disposal and that at any moment death can come calling.

However, we are so involved in worldly things that we never stop to think about the day which is fast approaching us. The Prophet Muhammad said, 'People are asleep, they will wake up only when they die.' All of a sudden, death will bring you standing face to face with God, at which time you will be held accountable for all your deeds.

That will be the moment you realise that what you were doing was one thing and that what you should have been doing was quite another. The Prophet Muhammad once said that on the Day of Judgement, a man's foot would not move unless he had answered four questions: Where he earned his money from, and where he spent it; how he spent his youth and how he used his knowledge.

The Creator has divided human life into two parts: the pre-death and post-death periods. The pre-death period is very short (like the tip of an iceberg) in comparison to the post-death period, which is eternal. The pre-death period is the preparatory phase in which you prepare yourself to become eligible to enter Paradise in the post-death period.

This worldly life is a 'test' for everyone, whether poor or rich, powerful or powerless, strong or weak. Man is required to pass in all these tests and trials by leading a need-based life rather than a desire and greed-based life, so that in the life hereafter, God will allow him to enter Paradise, to live there forever in close proximity to his Creator.

On the death of a loved one, one should not go into a state of mourning. The Quran gives us great hope in moments of grief and loss: It says that God will reunite all the righteous members of the family in Paradise.

Moreover, if a member of the family has reached a higher level of Paradise, all the righteous members of that family will be 'upgraded', so that they may all enjoy eternal bliss and nearness to God. This idea gives great solace and it acts as an incentive and encouragement to do good work, and lead a pious and righteous life.

The Prophet Muhammad said that when a man dies, everything connected with him is cut off except three things: Continuous charity, knowledge from which benefit is derived and virtuous children who pray for him.

¹⁵⁸Safa and Marwah are among the symbols set up by God; there is nothing wrong if anyone goes on a pilgrimage to the House, or performs a minor pilgrimage, in walking to and fro between them. Of anyone who does good of his own accord, God is appreciative, and aware.^a

﴿ إِنَّ ٱلصَّفَا وَٱلْمَرْوَةَ مِن شَعَآئِرِ ٱللَّهِ ۖ فَمَنْ حَجَّ ٱلْبَيْتَ أَوِ ٱعْتَمَرَ فَلَا جُنَاحَ عَلَيْهِ أَن يَطَّوَّفَ بِهِمَا ۚ وَمَن تَطَوَّعَ خَيْرًا فَإِنَّ ٱللَّهَ شَاكِرٌ عَلِيمٌ ﴿١٥٨﴾

---

^a Prophet Abraham was a native of Iraq. Acting at God's behest, he took his wife Hajar and his infant son Ishmael, and left them in the place now known as Makkah. There was no habitation there at that time and there was no water. Thirst forced Hajar to go far afield in search of water. Distressed, she ran back and forth between the hills of Safa and Marwah. After seven unsuccessful attempts, she returned to her dwelling. There she found a spring, now known as the spring of Zamzam, flowing from the ground. This was a symbolic event, showing us how Almighty God looks after His servants. If one persists in the service of God, finally reaching a stage where there is nothing but burning sand beneath one's feet, then God in His mercy will cause a refreshing spring to gush forth from the dryness of the desert sands. When Muslims perform the pilgrimage to Makkah, they repeat Hajar's historic quest between these hills, thus commemorating the profound relevance of the event to everyone who struggles in the path of God.

God's signs were displayed so clearly in the Prophet Muhammad's life and teachings, that it was not difficult to see that he had been sent by God. Yet the Jewish intelligentsia denied him. They were prevented from believing in him by the fear that if they accepted an Arab prophet, their religious hegemony would come to an end. People would stop looking up to the Jews as their leaders. Old established religious traditions, and the interests, which had come to be associated with them, (the Jews being the main beneficiaries) would be destroyed. They deemed it wise to conceal the truth, for they thought that they would lose their worldly status were they to accept it; but it would have been much wiser for them to have proclaimed it. They forgot that God's servants are required to put truth before their worldly interests. One who becomes destitute for the sake of the Lord gains succour from the inexhaustible treasures of divine grace.

The doors of God's mercy are always open to His servants. He will always forgive one who comes to his senses and mends his erring ways, proclaiming the truth as God wishes it to be proclaimed. Only those who persevere in their disbelief till the day they die will be deprived of His mercy.

159 Those who conceal the evidence of the truth and the guidance We have revealed, after We have made them clear to people in the Scripture, will be rejected by God and so do others. 160 But from those who repent and mend their ways and make known the truth, I will certainly accept their repentance: I am the Ever Relenting, the Most Merciful. 161 Those who deny the truth, and die as deniers, on them shall be the curse of God and of angels and of men altogether. 162 Under it they shall remain forever; their punishment shall not be lightened, nor shall they be granted respite.

163 Your God is one God. There is no deity save Him. He is the Compassionate, the Merciful.[a]

إِنَّ ٱلَّذِينَ يَكْتُمُونَ مَآ أَنزَلْنَا مِنَ ٱلْبَيِّنَٰتِ وَٱلْهُدَىٰ مِنۢ بَعْدِ مَا بَيَّنَّٰهُ لِلنَّاسِ فِى ٱلْكِتَٰبِ أُو۟لَٰٓئِكَ يَلْعَنُهُمُ ٱللَّهُ وَيَلْعَنُهُمُ ٱللَّٰعِنُونَ ۝ إِلَّا ٱلَّذِينَ تَابُوا۟ وَأَصْلَحُوا۟ وَبَيَّنُوا۟ فَأُو۟لَٰٓئِكَ أَتُوبُ عَلَيْهِمْ وَأَنَا ٱلتَّوَّابُ ٱلرَّحِيمُ ۝ إِنَّ ٱلَّذِينَ كَفَرُوا۟ وَمَاتُوا۟ وَهُمْ كُفَّارٌ أُو۟لَٰٓئِكَ عَلَيْهِمْ لَعْنَةُ ٱللَّهِ وَٱلْمَلَٰٓئِكَةِ وَٱلنَّاسِ أَجْمَعِينَ ۝ خَٰلِدِينَ فِيهَا لَا يُخَفَّفُ عَنْهُمُ ٱلْعَذَابُ وَلَا هُمْ يُنظَرُونَ ۝ وَإِلَٰهُكُمْ إِلَٰهٌ وَٰحِدٌ لَّآ إِلَٰهَ إِلَّا هُوَ ٱلرَّحْمَٰنُ ٱلرَّحِيمُ ۝

---

[a] Mankind has only one God: He is the only worthy focus of man's attention. Our very existence on earth, and all the benefits we derive from the world around us, are manifestations of His unbounded grace and mercy. In return, we should become God's devoted servants, living for Him, dying for Him, and setting all our hopes on winning His eternal favour. Man owes everything to his Creator. If he becomes conscious of this, his Lord will mean everything to him, as a mother means everything to her infant.

164 In the creation of the heavens and the earth; in the alternation of night and day; in the ships that sail the ocean bearing cargoes beneficial to man; in the water which God sends down from the sky and with which He revives the earth after its death, scattering over it all kinds of animals; in the courses of the winds, and in the clouds pressed into service between earth and sky, there are indeed signs for people who use their reason.^a

إِنَّ فِى خَلْقِ ٱلسَّمَـٰوَٰتِ وَٱلْأَرْضِ وَٱخْتِلَـٰفِ ٱلَّيْلِ وَٱلنَّهَارِ وَٱلْفُلْكِ ٱلَّتِى تَجْرِى فِى ٱلْبَحْرِ بِمَا يَنفَعُ ٱلنَّاسَ وَمَآ أَنزَلَ ٱللَّهُ مِنَ ٱلسَّمَآءِ مِن مَّآءٍ فَأَحْيَا بِهِ ٱلْأَرْضَ بَعْدَ مَوْتِهَا وَبَثَّ فِيهَا مِن كُلِّ دَآبَّةٍ وَتَصْرِيفِ ٱلرِّيَـٰحِ وَٱلسَّحَابِ ٱلْمُسَخَّرِ بَيْنَ ٱلسَّمَآءِ وَٱلْأَرْضِ لَـَٔايَـٰتٍ لِّقَوْمٍ يَعْقِلُونَ ۝

---

^a The vast universe spread out before us serves as a magnificent introduction to God. The existence of a limitless world in the form of the earth and the heavens is a proof that there must be a Creator behind it. Despite apparently different and contrasting elements, all things work together in absolute harmony, showing that their Creator and Sustainer is the one and only God. Then the fact that every single thing benefits the rest of the universe, in some manner or the other, shows that all things have been designed according to a definite and absolutely conscious plan. Apparently lifeless objects are invested with life through a natural process: this shows that death is only a temporary phase in this universe. Here death is always followed by new life. Every variety of animate creature flourishes in this world in huge numbers. All are being sustained by varied forms of the same food and drink, indicating the unfathomable power of God. The atmosphere totally encompassing the earth shows that man's life is entirely in his Creator's hands. Everything in this universe has been tamed to cater to man's needs. This is indicative of the fact that man's Creator is a highly compassionate being. Even before an individual has been born into the world, all his requirements have already been taken care of.

The presence of all these signs in the universe are reflections of the Creator in His creation. The universe displays God's very existence and His oneness on a vast scale; it is an amalgam of every aspect of perfection, so that no one with any vision or even a grain of intelligence can fail to discover Him in it. But these signs, spread all over the universe, serve as proofs of God's existence and His role as sustainer of the entire universe, only to one who sincerely reflects on these signs. For, to be able to arrive at the truth, one has to be sincere in one's search for it, and one has to rise above worldly considerations before drawing one's conclusions. This can be achieved only by total absorption, not in externals, but in the search for the inner reality that lies beneath the outward surface of things.

165 Yet there are some who set up equals with God and adore them with the adoration due to God, but those who believe love God most. If only the wrongdoers could see— as they will see when they face the punishment—that all power belongs to God, and that God is severe in punishment.[a]

وَمِنَ ٱلنَّاسِ مَن يَتَّخِذُ مِن دُونِ ٱللَّهِ أَندَادًا يُحِبُّونَهُمْ كَحُبِّ ٱللَّهِ ۖ وَٱلَّذِينَ ءَامَنُوٓا۟ أَشَدُّ حُبًّا لِّلَّهِ ۗ وَلَوْ يَرَى ٱلَّذِينَ ظَلَمُوٓا۟ إِذْ يَرَوْنَ ٱلْعَذَابَ أَنَّ ٱلْقُوَّةَ لِلَّهِ جَمِيعًا وَأَنَّ ٱللَّهَ شَدِيدُ ٱلْعَذَابِ ﴿١٦٥﴾

[a] By their nature and circumstances, human beings always look for an external support—a being, who may compensate for their feelings of helplessness, and may serve as a source of confidence and conviction. To make someone a part of one's life in this capacity is akin to accepting that being as a deity. When a being (or an object) is taken as a deity, it is assumed to be someone or something worthy of being worshipped. It necessarily entails that all one's feelings of love and devotion become exclusively reserved for that being or object. Their own nature compels human beings to have some focus for all their feelings of love, devotion and reverence. And whatever becomes the focus of these emotions is held to be God. (That is, that object has been accorded the status of divinity). Since God remains invisible in this present world, one who judges things by appearances tends to accord some visible being the status due only to the Almighty. Such beings are generally leaders who, because of certain marks of distinction, become the centre of public attention. This vacuum in human nature was in actual fact to be filled by God Almighty, but many people chose something or someone other than God for this purpose.

This happens when ordinary human beings, seeing someone surrounded by visible pomp and splendour, are impressed by certain special talents or qualities; when they find certain individuals occupying 'seats' sanctified by centuries-old traditions; when at times they are impressed by the large following which certain people enjoy and when they see public figures surrounded with the halo of mysterious legends. Being ordinary mortals themselves, they come thus to regard certain persons as possessing extraordinary power and therefore superior to the common man.

But the truth is that in this universe of God, no one save God possesses any power or greatness. Man may continue to receive the status of divinity only for so long as God remains invisible. But when God appears on Doomsday, the state of affairs will change so drastically that people will flee from one another. Today people take great pride in their association with and devotion to great men. They think that they are clinging to a firm rock which will surely help them in the Hereafter. Such association will prove meaningless on Doomsday—as if they had never existed at all.

Man will look at his past life in despair, but he will be utterly helpless to rectify the situation. He will be able to do nothing but regret his past deeds.

166 When they face their punishment, those who have been followed will disown their followers, and all their ties shall be cut asunder, 167 those who followed will say, 'If we could only return to the world, we would disown them as they have disowned us.' God will thus show them their actions as a cause of bitter regret and remorse. They shall never emerge from the Fire.

168 O mankind, eat whatever is lawful and wholesome on the earth; and do not follow in the footsteps of Satan; for he is indeed your avowed enemy. 169 He bids you only to do evil and to commit deeds of abomination and to attribute to God something of which you have no knowledge. 170 But when they are told, 'Follow what God has sent down,' they answer, 'We will follow the ways of our fathers,' even though their fathers did not use their reason, and were devoid of all guidance.[a]

إِذْ تَبَرَّأَ ٱلَّذِينَ ٱتُّبِعُوا۟ مِنَ ٱلَّذِينَ ٱتَّبَعُوا۟ وَرَأَوُا۟ ٱلْعَذَابَ وَتَقَطَّعَتْ بِهِمُ ٱلْأَسْبَابُ ۝ وَقَالَ ٱلَّذِينَ ٱتَّبَعُوا۟ لَوْ أَنَّ لَنَا كَرَّةً فَنَتَبَرَّأَ مِنْهُمْ كَمَا تَبَرَّءُوا۟ مِنَّا ۗ كَذَٰلِكَ يُرِيهِمُ ٱللَّهُ أَعْمَٰلَهُمْ حَسَرَٰتٍ عَلَيْهِمْ ۖ وَمَا هُم بِخَٰرِجِينَ مِنَ ٱلنَّارِ ۝ يَٰٓأَيُّهَا ٱلنَّاسُ كُلُوا۟ مِمَّا فِى ٱلْأَرْضِ حَلَٰلًا طَيِّبًا وَلَا تَتَّبِعُوا۟ خُطُوَٰتِ ٱلشَّيْطَٰنِ ۚ إِنَّهُۥ لَكُمْ عَدُوٌّ مُّبِينٌ ۝ إِنَّمَا يَأْمُرُكُم بِٱلسُّوٓءِ وَٱلْفَحْشَآءِ وَأَن تَقُولُوا۟ عَلَى ٱللَّهِ مَا لَا تَعْلَمُونَ ۝ وَإِذَا قِيلَ لَهُمُ ٱتَّبِعُوا۟ مَآ أَنزَلَ ٱللَّهُ قَالُوا۟ بَلْ نَتَّبِعُ مَآ أَلْفَيْنَا عَلَيْهِ ءَابَآءَنَآ ۗ أَوَلَوْ كَانَ ءَابَآؤُهُمْ لَا يَعْقِلُونَ شَيْـًٔا وَلَا يَهْتَدُونَ ۝

---

[a] What is polytheism? It is the worship of something other than God in order to satisfy one's feelings of devotion and veneration. God is the greatest and most essential need of man. The urge to worship God is so integral to human nature that no one can live without Him. Man's going astray does not mean that he abandons God altogether. What actually happens is that the real God is replaced by a false god. That is why the Islamic law holds unlawful all those things which, in any degree, lead to deviation, i.e. diverting man's natural desire for God in some other direction.

The polytheists set certain animals free in the name of their deities. These animals are not used for food or service. This is akin to according divinity to an object; a divinity which is a prerogative of none save God. It is akin to diluting man's natural feelings of reverence and devotions meant only for God, and which should be exclusively reserved for God alone. Satan encourages human beings to channelise their feelings of awe and reverence on to different paths in order that their attachment to God may be weakened.

¹⁷¹ Those who deny the truth are like animals which hear nothing in your call but the sound of a voice, without understanding its meaning. They are deaf, dumb and blind. They understand nothing.ᵃ

وَمَثَلُ ٱلَّذِينَ كَفَرُواْ كَمَثَلِ ٱلَّذِى يَنْعِقُ بِمَا لَا يَسْمَعُ إِلَّا دُعَاءً وَنِدَآءً صُمٌّ بُكْمٌ عُمْىٌ فَهُمْ لَا يَعْقِلُونَ ۝

ᵃ Once an object, which is not God, is accepted as God as a result of man's superstitious attitude, many other accompanying evils ensue. An animal may come to be regarded as possessing supernatural powers—something possessed only by God. That animal is then held to be a means of achieving proximity to God and is expected to be a source of blessings.

In the next generation all these superstitious beliefs become firmly rooted in the human psyche and are upheld with great zeal and fervour as the sacred way of the forefathers. At this stage, people become resistant to any rational analysis of these superstitious beliefs. The situation deteriorates further with succeeding generations. People reach a level where they are totally unable to hear or understand any argument put forward to them. They act as if they have neither eyes nor ears to see and hear, nor brains to give thought to any argument presented to them.

¹⁷²Believers, eat the wholesome things which We have provided for you and give thanks to God, if it is Him you worship. ¹⁷³He has forbidden you only carrion, blood, and the flesh of swine; also any flesh that is consecrated other than in the name of God. But for one who is driven by necessity, neither craving nor transgressing, it is no sin. For God is forgiving and merciful.ᵃ

يَـٰٓأَيُّهَا ٱلَّذِينَ ءَامَنُوا۟ كُلُوا۟ مِن طَيِّبَـٰتِ مَا رَزَقْنَـٰكُمْ وَٱشْكُرُوا۟ لِلَّهِ إِن كُنتُمْ إِيَّاهُ تَعْبُدُونَ ۝ إِنَّمَا حَرَّمَ عَلَيْكُمُ ٱلْمَيْتَةَ وَٱلدَّمَ وَلَحْمَ ٱلْخِنزِيرِ وَمَآ أُهِلَّ بِهِۦ لِغَيْرِ ٱللَّهِ فَمَنِ ٱضْطُرَّ غَيْرَ بَاغٍ وَلَا عَادٍ فَلَآ إِثْمَ عَلَيْهِ إِنَّ ٱللَّهَ غَفُورٌ رَّحِيمٌ ۝

ᵃ Human beings should feel thankful and obedient to God while eating food and drinking water. They should express themselves thus, 'In accordance with God's commandment, we are eating and drinking what God has provided us with.' These emotions evoke in a man the feeling of true devotion to his Maker. But this psychological make-up changes in the case of self-styled beliefs. In that case man's attention is diverted to the supposed properties of the things he consumes. Therefore, the same divine blessing which is meant to produce feelings of thanksgiving, evoke instead feelings of veneration for material objects. Under the influence of such false beliefs, man comes to accord the position of Creator to the created. If something is held unlawful by God, it is not owing to the sacredness of that thing but rather because it is something impure or the divine law has testified to its uncleanness, e.g. carrion, blood, swine or an animal sacrificed in the name of some idol instead of in the name of God. In cases of extreme necessity where a man's life may be at stake, he may eat food otherwise forbidden, for instance when suffering extreme hunger and when no other food is available, or in illness, or other such circumstances as may compel him to do so. However, it is essential that such forbidden food should not be taken simply for the pleasure of the palate. That is, one must remain within the bare limits of necessity.

174 Those who conceal any part of the Scriptures which God has revealed in order to gain some paltry end, simply fill their bellies with Fire. On the Day of Resurrection, God will neither speak to them nor purify them. They will have a painful punishment. 175 Those are the ones who have taken error in exchange for guidance and punishment for forgiveness. How little do they seem to fear the Fire! 176 That is because God has sent down the Book with the truth. And those who pursue differences in the Scriptures go much too far in dissension.[a]

إِنَّ ٱلَّذِينَ يَكْتُمُونَ مَا أَنزَلَ ٱللَّهُ مِنَ ٱلْكِتَٰبِ وَيَشْتَرُونَ بِهِۦ ثَمَنًا قَلِيلًا أُوْلَٰٓئِكَ مَا يَأْكُلُونَ فِى بُطُونِهِمْ إِلَّا ٱلنَّارَ وَلَا يُكَلِّمُهُمُ ٱللَّهُ يَوْمَ ٱلْقِيَٰمَةِ وَلَا يُزَكِّيهِمْ وَلَهُمْ عَذَابٌ أَلِيمٌ ۝ أُوْلَٰٓئِكَ ٱلَّذِينَ ٱشْتَرَوُاْ ٱلضَّلَٰلَةَ بِٱلْهُدَىٰ وَٱلْعَذَابَ بِٱلْمَغْفِرَةِ فَمَآ أَصْبَرَهُمْ عَلَى ٱلنَّارِ ۝ ذَٰلِكَ بِأَنَّ ٱللَّهَ نَزَّلَ ٱلْكِتَٰبَ بِٱلْحَقِّ وَإِنَّ ٱلَّذِينَ ٱخْتَلَفُواْ فِى ٱلْكِتَٰبِ لَفِى شِقَاقٍ بَعِيدٍ ۝

---

[a] When superstitious beliefs about prohibitions have been accepted by the masses as religious beliefs and held sacred, the religious scholars of the community fail to muster enough courage to declare openly that those beliefs have nothing to do with true religion, for they are afraid that if they did so, they would be severing themselves from the general public to whom they owe their popularity. They may revel in such compromises as bring them wealth and honour, but in the eyes of God, they are the worst offenders. Hiding the truth for worldly considerations is not one of those offences that God will ignore in the Hereafter. These are in fact crimes that deprive man of God's mercy. Worse still are those, who, instead of accepting the truth when it is presented to them start engaging in meaningless discussions. They develop a propensity to divisiveness and ultimately they stray so far from the truth that there remains no chance of their returning.

177 Virtue does not consist in whether you face towards the East or the West; virtue means believing in God, the Last Day, the angels, the Book and the prophets; the virtuous are those who, despite their love for it, give away their wealth to their relatives and to orphans and the very poor, and to travellers and those who ask [for charity], and to set slaves free, and who attend to their prayers and pay the alms, and who keep their pledges when they make them, and show patience in hardship and adversity, and in times of distress. Such are the true believers; and such are the God-fearing.ᵃ

﴿ لَيْسَ ٱلْبِرَّ أَن تُوَلُّوا۟ وُجُوهَكُمْ قِبَلَ ٱلْمَشْرِقِ وَٱلْمَغْرِبِ وَلَٰكِنَّ ٱلْبِرَّ مَنْ ءَامَنَ بِٱللَّهِ وَٱلْيَوْمِ ٱلْءَاخِرِ وَٱلْمَلَٰئِكَةِ وَٱلْكِتَٰبِ وَٱلنَّبِيِّۦنَ وَءَاتَى ٱلْمَالَ عَلَىٰ حُبِّهِۦ ذَوِى ٱلْقُرْبَىٰ وَٱلْيَتَٰمَىٰ وَٱلْمَسَٰكِينَ وَٱبْنَ ٱلسَّبِيلِ وَٱلسَّآئِلِينَ وَفِى ٱلرِّقَابِ وَأَقَامَ ٱلصَّلَوٰةَ وَءَاتَى ٱلزَّكَوٰةَ وَٱلْمُوفُونَ بِعَهْدِهِمْ إِذَا عَٰهَدُوا۟ وَٱلصَّٰبِرِينَ فِى ٱلْبَأْسَآءِ وَٱلضَّرَّآءِ وَحِينَ ٱلْبَأْسِ أُو۟لَٰئِكَ ٱلَّذِينَ صَدَقُوا۟ وَأُو۟لَٰئِكَ هُمُ ٱلْمُتَّقُونَ ﴾ ١٧٧

ᵃ There is no doubt that there are certain accepted forms of religious conduct but, in essence, a religious act is aimed at discovering God as the light of the earth and the heavens, One who is closer to man than his jugular vein. What brings man closer to God is not the mere adherence to outward religious forms but such actions as he performs, in total sincerity, for the sake of God alone. Man must discover God in a way that He becomes a part and parcel of his being. All his actions must aim at earning God's pleasure. His attachment to God should be so great that, even in the most trying circumstances, he must not waver from the straight path. In short, the Almighty's pleasure can be earned only by displaying true faithfulness and not just by turning our faces in one or the other direction.

Believing in God is to trust in God in the full sense of the word. Believing in the Hereafter means giving the utmost importance to the life of the Hereafter instead of to the life of this world. Believing in the angels means believing in God's emissaries who are running this world at the divine command. Believing in the Book means believing that God has sent His guidance for man, which man must follow. Believing in the prophets is to accept these mortals as God's chosen messengers.

The faith in all these matters must so deeply pervade the believer's psyche that he helps the needy and others in distress by spending his wealth, says his prayers by surrendering himself totally to God, and pays the poor due—his only motivation being to earn God's pleasure. One of the characteristics of a true believer is that when he enters into a contract, he fulfills it, treating it as if he has entered into a covenant with God. ▶

178 Believers, retribution is prescribed for you in cases of murder: the free man for the free man, the slave for the slave, the female for the female. If the offender is granted some remission by the heir of the slain person, the agreed penalty should be equitably exacted and should be discharged in a handsome manner. This is an alleviation from your Lord and an act of grace. He who transgresses after this shall have a painful punishment. 179 In [this law of] retribution there is life for you, O people of understanding, so that perhaps you will be mindful of God.ᵃ

يَـٰٓأَيُّهَا ٱلَّذِينَ ءَامَنُوا۟ كُتِبَ عَلَيْكُمُ ٱلْقِصَاصُ فِى ٱلْقَتْلَى ٱلْحُرُّ بِٱلْحُرِّ وَٱلْعَبْدُ بِٱلْعَبْدِ وَٱلْأُنثَىٰ بِٱلْأُنثَىٰ فَمَنْ عُفِىَ لَهُۥ مِنْ أَخِيهِ شَىْءٌ فَٱتِّبَاعٌۢ بِٱلْمَعْرُوفِ وَأَدَآءٌ إِلَيْهِ بِإِحْسَـٰنٍ ذَٰلِكَ تَخْفِيفٌ مِّن رَّبِّكُمْ وَرَحْمَةٌ فَمَنِ ٱعْتَدَىٰ بَعْدَ ذَٰلِكَ فَلَهُۥ عَذَابٌ أَلِيمٌ ۝ وَلَكُمْ فِى ٱلْقِصَاصِ حَيَوٰةٌ يَـٰٓأُو۟لِى ٱلْأَلْبَـٰبِ لَعَلَّكُمْ تَتَّقُونَ ۝

His trust in God is so great, even in the most dire of circumstances, that he always adheres to the godly path. These are the characteristics of a true believer. One who possesses these qualities will earn God's blessing in this world as well as in the Hereafter.

ᵃ Islam has laid down the principle of retaliation in like measure (*qisas*). For example, 'an eye for an eye and a tooth for a tooth'. Retribution for a killer means the forfeiture of his own life. In this way, on the one hand, a capital crime like the taking of life is effectively discouraged, for the fear of losing one's own life deters one from taking another's life and, as a result, the life of all the members of a society become protected. The killing of the killer guarantees the saving of lives in a society. Thus the objective of *qisas* is the protection of the members of society, and not revenge. Moreover, the vengeful feelings of the family of the murdered person are cooled, thus obviating the possibility of any further injurious activity. However, *qisas* in Islam permits a settlement to be arrived at between the killer and the killed. The heirs of the deceased person may, of course, opt for the execution of the killer, but they may also, if they so wish, accept blood-money instead, or even forgive him. The main aim of these alternatives is to guarantee the prevalence of brotherly feeling in Islamic society, and to prevent an atmosphere of rivalry taking root. Then the principle of blood-money has the special advantage of giving the bereaved family monetary compensation for the death of one of its members.

180 It is prescribed that when death approaches any of you and he is leaving behind wealth, he shall make a will in favour of his parents and relatives equitably. This is a duty for all who fear God. 181 Anyone who alters it once he has heard it shall be accountable for his crime. Surely, God is all hearing and all knowing. 182 But if anyone apprehends partiality or an injustice on the part of a testator, it shall be no sin for him to bring about a settlement between the parties. God is forgiving and merciful.[a]

كُتِبَ عَلَيْكُمْ إِذَا حَضَرَ أَحَدَكُمُ الْمَوْتُ إِن تَرَكَ خَيْرًا الْوَصِيَّةُ لِلْوَالِدَيْنِ وَالْأَقْرَبِينَ بِالْمَعْرُوفِ حَقًّا عَلَى الْمُتَّقِينَ ۝ فَمَنۢ بَدَّلَهُ بَعْدَمَا سَمِعَهُ فَإِنَّمَا إِثْمُهُ عَلَى الَّذِينَ يُبَدِّلُونَهُ إِنَّ اللَّهَ سَمِيعٌ عَلِيمٌ ۝ فَمَنْ خَافَ مِن مُّوصٍ جَنَفًا أَوْ إِثْمًا فَأَصْلَحَ بَيْنَهُمْ فَلَا إِثْمَ عَلَيْهِ إِنَّ اللَّهَ غَفُورٌ رَّحِيمٌ ۝

---

[a] After someone's death the problem arises as to how to deal with his or her wealth. The Islamic injunction in this regard is to distribute it in a just and equitable manner to the heirs. One who fears God should follow this injunction regarding the disposal of intestate property in the spirit of justice. This will create a brotherly atmosphere in society, preventing litigation and quarrels over property.

Where there is a member of a family, like an orphaned grandson, or any other needy member of the family who does not inherit under the Islamic inheritance scheme, the testator may provide for him, as he has been given the power to dispose of up to one third of his property by making a will in his favour. Islam approves of every lawful device for keeping society free from litigation and quarrels. But unless this is the objective, the changing of the provisions of a will is unlawful.

¹⁸³ Believers, fasting has been prescribed for you, just as it was prescribed for those before you, so that you may guard yourselves against evil. ¹⁸⁴ Fast for a specified number of days, but if any one among you is ill or on a journey, let him fast the same number of days later. For those who can fast only with extreme difficulty, there is a way to compensate—the feeding of a needy person. But he who does good of his own accord shall be well rewarded; but to fast is better for you, if you only knew.^a

يَـٰٓأَيُّهَا ٱلَّذِينَ ءَامَنُوا۟ كُتِبَ عَلَيْكُمُ ٱلصِّيَامُ كَمَا كُتِبَ عَلَى ٱلَّذِينَ مِن قَبْلِكُمْ لَعَلَّكُمْ تَتَّقُونَ ۝ أَيَّامًا مَّعْدُودَٰتٍ ۚ فَمَن كَانَ مِنكُم مَّرِيضًا أَوْ عَلَىٰ سَفَرٍ فَعِدَّةٌ مِّنْ أَيَّامٍ أُخَرَ ۚ وَعَلَى ٱلَّذِينَ يُطِيقُونَهُۥ فِدْيَةٌ طَعَامُ مِسْكِينٍ ۖ فَمَن تَطَوَّعَ خَيْرًا فَهُوَ خَيْرٌ لَّهُۥ ۚ وَأَن تَصُومُوا۟ خَيْرٌ لَّكُمْ ۖ إِن كُنتُمْ تَعْلَمُونَ ۝

---

^a The main aim of fasting is to reduce man's dependence on material things and strengthen his spiritual resolve, so that he may enter the higher realms of faith and piety. In this way, fasting during Ramadan is a unique opportunity to concentrate on doing good and abstaining from evil. The heart of the believer is thus gladdened and his mind is set at rest.

Although the fast is prescribed for just one month every year, the spirit of fasting is far more enduring. It brings man closer to God by showing him how to withdraw from the world while still being a part of it. It shows man the way to fulfil his spiritual obligations in the turmoil of the materialistic world. In that sense, fasting during Ramadan is a way of attaining peace of mind.

Ramadan is the month of heightened God-consciousness, of attaining piety and training ourselves to be the best possible human beings. Instead of indulging in gossiping, lying, slandering and generally exhibiting all other traits of bad character, one is focused on improving one's character by cultivating good habits. In doing so the believer's inner self inches closer day by day towards a state of righteousness, worshipfulness, devotion and piety, which elevates the soul to a condition of superior spiritual bliss.

It is a path which the Prophet Muhammad himself had laid down. During Ramadan he would engage himself in prayer and praise the Almighty throughout the day, especially while breaking the fast at sunset. Just before sunset, when the fast reaches its climax, the believer experiences closeness to his Creator. Perhaps for this reason, the Prophet Muhammad included the fasting person at the time of breaking his fast in the five kinds of people whose supplications were never turned down by God. (The others were a just ruler, an oppressed person, a parent who prays for his children and one who travels for the sake of God.) ▶

185 The month of Ramadan is the month when the Quran was sent down as guidance for mankind with clear proofs of guidance and the criterion by which to distinguish right from wrong. Therefore, whoever of you is present in that month, let him fast; but he who is ill or on a journey shall fast a similar number of days later on. God desires ease for you, not hardship. He desires you to fast the whole month, so that you may glorify Him for His having guided you and so that you may be grateful to Him.[a]

شَهْرُ رَمَضَانَ ٱلَّذِىٓ أُنزِلَ فِيهِ ٱلْقُرْءَانُ هُدًى لِّلنَّاسِ وَبَيِّنَتٍ مِّنَ ٱلْهُدَى وَٱلْفُرْقَانِ ۚ فَمَن شَهِدَ مِنكُمُ ٱلشَّهْرَ فَلْيَصُمْهُ ۖ وَمَن كَانَ مَرِيضًا أَوْ عَلَى سَفَرٍ فَعِدَّةٌ مِّنْ أَيَّامٍ أُخَرَ ۗ يُرِيدُ ٱللَّهُ بِكُمُ ٱلْيُسْرَ وَلَا يُرِيدُ بِكُمُ ٱلْعُسْرَ وَلِتُكْمِلُوا۟ ٱلْعِدَّةَ وَلِتُكَبِّرُوا۟ ٱللَّهَ عَلَىٰ مَا هَدَىٰكُمْ وَلَعَلَّكُمْ تَشْكُرُونَ ۝

The Prophet Muhammad divided the month of fasting into three parts. He called the first ten days 'blessings', the next ten days 'forgiveness' and the last ten days 'freedom from Hellfire.' The Prophet also said, 'The best days of this world are the last ten days of Ramadan.' Therefore, during the last ten days the Prophet's family would join him in what they called, 'the tightening of his belt'—in its figurative sense—indicating total seriousness of devotion.

[a] Fasting serves as training for two things at the same time—inculcating the spirit of thanksgiving and instilling the fear of God in the heart of the believer. Food and water are great blessings of God, yet man is incapable of attaching due importance to them. While fasting, he goes hungry and thirsty the whole day, then at sunset, in a state of extreme hunger and thirst, he eats and drinks to his fill. He then realizes through his own experience how great are the blessings of God which are present in the form of food and water. This experience produces boundless feelings of gratitude towards his Lord. On the other hand, fasting also serves as a form of training for a God-fearing life, which entails abstaining from all kinds of sins and evil deeds, which God has forbidden. A total abstention from food and drink from dawn until sunset is an exercise in making God one's guardian. The entire life of the believer is a life of fasting. During the month of Ramadan he receives his training by temporarily, abstaining from certain things, so that for the rest of his life he may permanently renounce all those things of which God disapproves. The Quran is a great blessing of God to man. It is through fasting that man enables himself to be truly thankful to God, and to lead a godly life in accordance with the teachings enshrined in the Quran.

¹⁸⁶ When My servants ask you about Me, say that I am near. I respond to the call of one who calls, whenever he calls to Me: let them, then, respond to Me, and believe in Me, so that they may be rightly guided. ¹⁸⁷ It has been made lawful for you to go to your wives on the night of the fast: they are like a garment for you, and you are like a garment for them. God is aware that you were deceiving yourselves and He has turned in mercy towards you and pardoned you. So you may now consort with them and seek what God has ordained for you. Eat and drink until the white thread of dawn becomes distinct from the black. Then resume the fast until nightfall, and do not approach them during the nights of your devotional retreat in the mosques. These are the limits set by God, so do not approach them. Thus He makes clear His commandments to mankind, so that they may guard themselves [against evil].^a

وَإِذَا سَأَلَكَ عِبَادِى عَنِّى فَإِنِّى قَرِيبٌ أُجِيبُ دَعْوَةَ ٱلدَّاعِ إِذَا دَعَانِ فَلْيَسْتَجِيبُواْ لِى وَلْيُؤْمِنُواْ بِى لَعَلَّهُمْ يَرْشُدُونَ ۝ أُحِلَّ لَكُمْ لَيْلَةَ ٱلصِّيَامِ ٱلرَّفَثُ إِلَىٰ نِسَآئِكُمْ هُنَّ لِبَاسٌ لَّكُمْ وَأَنتُمْ لِبَاسٌ لَّهُنَّ عَلِمَ ٱللَّهُ أَنَّكُمْ كُنتُمْ تَخْتَانُونَ أَنفُسَكُمْ فَتَابَ عَلَيْكُمْ وَعَفَا عَنكُمْ فَٱلْـَٰنَ بَٰشِرُوهُنَّ وَٱبْتَغُواْ مَا كَتَبَ ٱللَّهُ لَكُمْ وَكُلُواْ وَٱشْرَبُواْ حَتَّىٰ يَتَبَيَّنَ لَكُمُ ٱلْخَيْطُ ٱلْأَبْيَضُ مِنَ ٱلْخَيْطِ ٱلْأَسْوَدِ مِنَ ٱلْفَجْرِ ثُمَّ أَتِمُّواْ ٱلصِّيَامَ إِلَى ٱلَّيْلِ وَلَا تُبَٰشِرُوهُنَّ وَأَنتُمْ عَٰكِفُونَ فِى ٱلْمَسَٰجِدِ تِلْكَ حُدُودُ ٱللَّهِ فَلَا تَقْرَبُوهَا كَذَٰلِكَ يُبَيِّنُ ٱللَّهُ ءَايَٰتِهِ لِلنَّاسِ لَعَلَّهُمْ يَتَّقُونَ ۝

^a Fasting by its very nature is an act of patience, and patience involves putting up with all kinds of difficulties in order to carry out God's commandments. This helps man to attain that state of mind which brings him closer to God. Only those find God who surrender themselves totally to Him, only the words of those reach God whose 'wavelength' matches that of God.

The command to fast is followed by the command, 'Do not consume one another's property by unjust means' (see 2.188). This shows the essence of fasting. The real aim of fasting is to create such a feeling of subservience that when God commands us to abstain from anything, we must do so forthwith. The lesson fasting gives us is that even if God wants us to stay away from lawful things, we must show no hesitation in obeying His command. Thus one who abstains from lawful things if God wants him to do so, will have no difficulty in abstaining from unlawful things if God so commands.

¹⁸⁸ Do not consume one another's property by unjust means, nor offer it as a bribe to the authorities, so that you may deliberately and wrongfully devour a part of other people's wealth.[a]

¹⁸⁹ They ask you about the phases of the moon.[b] Say, 'They are a means of determining time for the regulation of people's affairs and for the pilgrimage.' Piety does not consist in entering your houses from the rear.[c] Indeed, one who guards himself against evil out of fear of God is the truly righteous one. Enter your houses by their doors and be mindful of God, so that you may prosper.

وَلَا تَأْكُلُوٓا۟ أَمْوَٰلَكُم بَيْنَكُم بِٱلْبَٰطِلِ وَتُدْلُوا۟ بِهَآ إِلَى ٱلْحُكَّامِ لِتَأْكُلُوا۟ فَرِيقًا مِّنْ أَمْوَٰلِ ٱلنَّاسِ بِٱلْإِثْمِ وَأَنتُمْ تَعْلَمُونَ ۞ يَسْـَٔلُونَكَ عَنِ ٱلْأَهِلَّةِ ۖ قُلْ هِىَ مَوَٰقِيتُ لِلنَّاسِ وَٱلْحَجِّ ۗ وَلَيْسَ ٱلْبِرُّ بِأَن تَأْتُوا۟ ٱلْبُيُوتَ مِن ظُهُورِهَا وَلَٰكِنَّ ٱلْبِرَّ مَنِ ٱتَّقَىٰ ۗ وَأْتُوا۟ ٱلْبُيُوتَ مِنْ أَبْوَٰبِهَا ۚ وَٱتَّقُوا۟ ٱللَّهَ لَعَلَّكُمْ تُفْلِحُونَ ۝

[a] Thus the life of a believer is one of renunciation. For his entire life he has to keep himself away from certain things. The month of Ramadan serves as training for this. A life of restraint during the month of fasting gives us the lesson that the true servant of God is one who worships God at the level of *taqwa*, and lives a life of piety and fear of God. God will answer the call only of those who bring themselves closer to Him by living a life of sacrifice.

[b] The waxing and waning of the moon are meant to serve only as measures of time. The superstitious believe that the days when the moon is waxing are auspicious while the days of the moon's waning are inauspicious. The moon, in fact, is an almanac of nature appearing in the sky so that people may plan the timings of their worldly affairs as well as their worship. But there are many people who have come to regard mere outward observance as religiosity.

[c] The ancient Arabs believed (a mere supposition) that, after the donning of *ihram* to perform Hajj, nothing should come between them and the sky, for they thought it was against the etiquette of *ihram*. Due to this superstitious custom, when the Arabs left their homes after donning *ihram*, they did not enter their houses by the doors, but climbed over the walls to reach the courtyard during or after the pilgrimage. This is disapproved of, for there is no virtue in observing any such outward rituals in the name of religion. True religiosity is to fear God and remain within the bounds laid down by Him.

¹⁹⁰ And fight*a* in God's cause against those who wage war against you, but do not commit aggression—for surely, God does not love aggressors. ¹⁹¹ Slay them wherever you find them [those who fight against you];*a* drive them out of the places from which they drove you, for [religious] persecution is worse than killing. Do not fight them at the Sacred Mosque unless they fight you there. If they do fight you, slay them—such is the reward for those who deny the truth—¹⁹² but if they desist, then surely God is most forgiving and merciful. ¹⁹³ Fight them until there is no more *fitna*b [religious persecution] and religion belongs to God alone. If they desist, then let there be no hostility, except towards aggressors.

وَقَٰتِلُواْ فِى سَبِيلِ ٱللَّهِ ٱلَّذِينَ يُقَٰتِلُونَكُمْ وَلَا تَعْتَدُوٓاْ إِنَّ ٱللَّهَ لَا يُحِبُّ ٱلْمُعْتَدِينَ ۝ وَٱقْتُلُوهُمْ حَيْثُ ثَقِفْتُمُوهُمْ وَأَخْرِجُوهُم مِّنْ حَيْثُ أَخْرَجُوكُمْ وَٱلْفِتْنَةُ أَشَدُّ مِنَ ٱلْقَتْلِ وَلَا تُقَٰتِلُوهُمْ عِندَ ٱلْمَسْجِدِ ٱلْحَرَامِ حَتَّىٰ يُقَٰتِلُوكُمْ فِيهِ فَإِن قَٰتَلُوكُمْ فَٱقْتُلُوهُمْ كَذَٰلِكَ جَزَآءُ ٱلْكَٰفِرِينَ ۝ فَإِنِ ٱنتَهَوْاْ فَإِنَّ ٱللَّهَ غَفُورٌ رَّحِيمٌ ۝ وَقَٰتِلُوهُمْ حَتَّىٰ لَا تَكُونَ فِتْنَةٌ وَيَكُونَ ٱلدِّينُ لِلَّهِ فَإِنِ ٱنتَهَوْاْ فَلَا عُدْوَٰنَ إِلَّا عَلَى ٱلظَّٰلِمِينَ ۝

---

a The fighting (*qital*) mentioned here refers to that which took place during the life of the Prophet Muhammad. The Prophet's Makkan opponents, not content with just expelling the Prophet and his companions from Makkah, their home-town, also prevented them from living and working peacefully in the neighbouring town of Yathrib (Madinah) where they had gone to settle. Without any provocation, they repeatedly attacked the Muslims who then had to fight in self-defence. When aggression has already been committed by opponents, believers are obliged to defend themselves. Initiating hostilities is not permitted for Muslims. Only defensive war is permitted in Islam. Even defensive war has to be openly declared by an established state.

b The Quranic exhortation to do battle against religious persecution (*fitnah*) has been explained by 'Abdullah ibn 'Umar, a senior companion of the Prophet. He said that this verse referred to the coercive religious system that prevailed in the ancient world. (*Fathul Bari*, vol. 8, p. 60).

Temporary in nature, the war against *fitnah* was thus one of limited duration, meant to be engaged in only until its specific purpose had been served. In the wake of the Islamic revolution, religious persecution was replaced by intellectual freedom. As 'Abdullah ibn 'Umar said, they had already put an end to *fitnah*, therefore, except in cases where self-defence had become inevitable, the Quran did not give permission for violence.

¹⁹⁴ A sacred month for a sacred month: violation of sanctity calls for fair retribution. Thus you may exact retribution from whoever transgresses against you, in proportion to his transgression.[a] Fear God and know that God is with those who are mindful of Him. ¹⁹⁵ Spend for God's cause: do not cast yourselves into destruction by your own hands. Do good, God loves the doers of good.[b]

ٱلشَّهْرُ ٱلْحَرَامُ بِٱلشَّهْرِ ٱلْحَرَامِ وَٱلْحُرُمَٰتُ قِصَاصٌ ۚ فَمَنِ ٱعْتَدَىٰ عَلَيْكُمْ فَٱعْتَدُوا۟ عَلَيْهِ بِمِثْلِ مَا ٱعْتَدَىٰ عَلَيْكُمْ ۚ وَٱتَّقُوا۟ ٱللَّهَ وَٱعْلَمُوٓا۟ أَنَّ ٱللَّهَ مَعَ ٱلْمُتَّقِينَ ۝ وَأَنفِقُوا۟ فِى سَبِيلِ ٱللَّهِ وَلَا تُلْقُوا۟ بِأَيْدِيكُمْ إِلَى ٱلتَّهْلُكَةِ ۛ وَأَحْسِنُوٓا۟ ۚ إِنَّ ٱللَّهَ يُحِبُّ ٱلْمُحْسِنِينَ ۝

[a] Fighting during the sacred months (Muharram, Rajab, Dhu'l-Qada, Dhu'l-Hijjah) or fighting within the precincts of Makkah is forbidden. But if opponents commit aggression in these months, believers may fight back in self-defence. But while fighting, believers must abstain from all atrocities, they should not transgress any bounds set by God—if they truly fear God—even at times of great provocation as in a state of war.

[b] More than anything else, the struggle for the cause of God demands the expenditure of money. It is the sacrifice of wealth, which man finds most difficult. That is why the Quran enjoins us to regard the cause of God as our own cause and to spend generously for the cause of religion. If we fail to do so, we are inviting our own destruction in this world as well as in the next. If man does not surrender all that he has to God, why should God give what He has to him?

Man thinks that the best use of his wealth is to spend it on himself or his family. But the Quran calls this the way to destruction. The proper use of wealth is to spend generously for the cause of religion. This will make man deserving of God's blessings. He will receive divine succour in this world and will be rewarded with paradise in the hereafter.

196 Perform the Hajj and the minor pilgrimage [*umrah*] for the sake of God. If you are prevented from doing so, then make whatever offering you can afford and do not shave your heads until the offering has reached the place of sacrifice. But if any of you is ill, or has an ailment of the head, he should compensate by fasting or almsgiving or sacrifice. In times of peace, if any of you combines the minor pilgrimage with the Hajj, he should make whatever offering he can afford, but if he lacks the means, then let him fast three days during the pilgrimage and for seven days after his return; that is, ten days in all. That is incumbent upon anyone whose family does not live near the Sacred Mosque. Fear God and know that God is severe in punishment.*a*

وَأَتِمُّوا۟ ٱلْحَجَّ وَٱلْعُمْرَةَ لِلَّهِ ۚ فَإِنْ أُحْصِرْتُمْ فَمَا ٱسْتَيْسَرَ مِنَ ٱلْهَدْىِ ۖ وَلَا تَحْلِقُوا۟ رُءُوسَكُمْ حَتَّىٰ يَبْلُغَ ٱلْهَدْىُ مَحِلَّهُۥ ۚ فَمَن كَانَ مِنكُم مَّرِيضًا أَوْ بِهِۦٓ أَذًى مِّن رَّأْسِهِۦ فَفِدْيَةٌ مِّن صِيَامٍ أَوْ صَدَقَةٍ أَوْ نُسُكٍ ۚ فَإِذَآ أَمِنتُمْ فَمَن تَمَتَّعَ بِٱلْعُمْرَةِ إِلَى ٱلْحَجِّ فَمَا ٱسْتَيْسَرَ مِنَ ٱلْهَدْىِ ۚ فَمَن لَّمْ يَجِدْ فَصِيَامُ ثَلَٰثَةِ أَيَّامٍ فِى ٱلْحَجِّ وَسَبْعَةٍ إِذَا رَجَعْتُمْ ۗ تِلْكَ عَشَرَةٌ كَامِلَةٌ ۗ ذَٰلِكَ لِمَن لَّمْ يَكُنْ أَهْلُهُۥ حَاضِرِى ٱلْمَسْجِدِ ٱلْحَرَامِ ۚ وَٱتَّقُوا۟ ٱللَّهَ وَٱعْلَمُوٓا۟ أَنَّ ٱللَّهَ شَدِيدُ ٱلْعِقَابِ ﴿١٩٦﴾

---

a The Hajj pilgrimage takes place once a year, in the month of Dhu'l-Hijjah, whereas 'umrah (the minor pilgrimage) may be performed at any time. Be it Hajj or 'umrah, any worship, when performed purely for God, is valuable in the eyes of God. When the true worshipper of God undertakes a religious duty like Hajj, he spiritually experiences in its rites worship a surrender to a Being whom he loves and fears more than anything else. The greatest concern of such a worshipper is to escape God's punishment in the Hereafter. Thus a believer is one who lives not for the satisfaction of his desires, but for a worthy goal. His goal is to completely abstain from all that God has forbidden. He must refrain from all kinds of misdeeds and quarrels with his fellow men. The Hajj pilgrimage successfully serves the purpose of this moral training. That is why the believers are especially enjoined to undertake it.

The pilgrims take provisions with them to meet their requirements during the journey. However, we are reminded that the best provision for a believer is to live in fear of God. Going in fear of God (*taqwa*) relates to the intellect. It has nothing to do with the observance of certain outward forms. It is, in fact, a state of heightened consciousness. When man finds his Lord at the level of the keenest awareness, his mind is filled with God's greatness and beauty. Then at the spiritual level, that state which may be described as God-fearing (*taqwa*, or God conscious-ness) is produced.

197 The pilgrimage is in the appointed months. Whoever intends to perform it during them must abstain from indecent speech, from all wicked conduct, and from quarrelling while on the pilgrimage. Whatever good you may do, God is aware of it. Make provision for yourselves—but surely, the best of all provision is God-consciousness. Always be mindful of Me, you that are endowed with understanding.

198 You will be committing no sin if [during the pilgrimage] you seek to obtain any bounty from your Lord. When you return from Arafat, remember God at the sacred place, and remember Him as He has guided you. Before this you were surely astray. 199 Then press on from where the pilgrims stream forth and ask God's forgiveness. God is ever forgiving and most merciful. 200 When you have performed the acts of worship prescribed for you, celebrate the praises of God as you celebrated the praises of your fathers, or even more fervently than that. There are some who say, 'Our Lord, give us abundance in this world.' These shall have no share in the world to come.[a]

ٱلْحَجُّ أَشْهُرٌ مَّعْلُومَـٰتٌ فَمَن فَرَضَ فِيهِنَّ ٱلْحَجَّ فَلَا رَفَثَ وَلَا فُسُوقَ وَلَا جِدَالَ فِى ٱلْحَجِّ وَمَا تَفْعَلُوا۟ مِنْ خَيْرٍ يَعْلَمْهُ ٱللَّهُ وَتَزَوَّدُوا۟ فَإِنَّ خَيْرَ ٱلزَّادِ ٱلتَّقْوَىٰ وَٱتَّقُونِ يَـٰٓأُو۟لِى ٱلْأَلْبَـٰبِ ۝ لَيْسَ عَلَيْكُمْ جُنَاحٌ أَن تَبْتَغُوا۟ فَضْلًا مِّن رَّبِّكُمْ فَإِذَآ أَفَضْتُم مِّنْ عَرَفَـٰتٍ فَٱذْكُرُوا۟ ٱللَّهَ عِندَ ٱلْمَشْعَرِ ٱلْحَرَامِ وَٱذْكُرُوهُ كَمَا هَدَىٰكُمْ وَإِن كُنتُم مِّن قَبْلِهِ لَمِنَ ٱلضَّآلِّينَ ۝ ثُمَّ أَفِيضُوا۟ مِنْ حَيْثُ أَفَاضَ ٱلنَّاسُ وَٱسْتَغْفِرُوا۟ ٱللَّهَ إِنَّ ٱللَّهَ غَفُورٌ رَّحِيمٌ ۝ فَإِذَا قَضَيْتُم مَّنَـٰسِكَكُمْ فَٱذْكُرُوا۟ ٱللَّهَ كَذِكْرِكُمْ ءَابَآءَكُمْ أَوْ أَشَدَّ ذِكْرًا فَمِنَ ٱلنَّاسِ مَن يَقُولُ رَبَّنَآ ءَاتِنَا فِى ٱلدُّنْيَا وَمَا لَهُۥ فِى ٱلْأَخِرَةِ مِنْ خَلَـٰقٍ ۝

a Fear of God is the basic element of worship. As long as one remains in this frame of mind, it does not matter if the order of a rite is changed by mistake in performing the rites of pilgrimage, or if one attends to some private business while in the holy land. What is important is that one should enter into the spirit of pilgrimage—fear of God, remembrance of Him, prayerfulness, thanksgiving and wholehearted submission to God. While on a pilgrimage, one should make sure not to do anything which runs counter to this spirit. There should be no feeling of superiority over fellow pilgrims, that is, one should 'press on from where the pilgrims stream forth.' ▶

²⁰¹ But there are others who pray, 'Our Lord, grant us good in this world as well as good in the world to come,^a and protect us from the torment of the Fire.' ²⁰² They shall have a good share from what they have earned. God is swift in His reckoning. ²⁰³ Remember God during the appointed days; for one who hastens to leave in two days, it shall be no sin; and for one who stays on, it shall be no sin for him either. This is for one who fears God. Have fear of God, and know that you shall all be gathered before Him.^b

وَمِنْهُم مَّن يَقُولُ رَبَّنَآ ءَاتِنَا فِى ٱلدُّنْيَا حَسَنَةً وَفِى ٱلْأَخِرَةِ حَسَنَةً وَقِنَا عَذَابَ ٱلنَّارِ ۩ أُوْلَٰٓئِكَ لَهُمْ نَصِيبٌ مِّمَّا كَسَبُوا۟ ۚ وَٱللَّهُ سَرِيعُ ٱلْحِسَابِ ۩ ۞ وَٱذْكُرُوا۟ ٱللَّهَ فِىٓ أَيَّامٍ مَّعْدُودَٰتٍ ۚ فَمَن تَعَجَّلَ فِى يَوْمَيْنِ فَلَآ إِثْمَ عَلَيْهِ وَمَن تَأَخَّرَ فَلَآ إِثْمَ عَلَيْهِ ۚ لِمَنِ ٱتَّقَىٰ ۗ وَٱتَّقُوا۟ ٱللَّهَ وَٱعْلَمُوٓا۟ أَنَّكُمْ إِلَيْهِ تُحْشَرُونَ ۩

Making too much of one's forefathers, praising their great deeds, is also against the spirit of pilgrimage: pilgrimage is for the glory of God, not for praise of the self. What place can such attitudes and activities have in Hajj, the very lesson of which is the equality of man before one, supreme God. If one does not assimilate this lesson during the pilgrimage, what chance is there of one applying it throughout the rest of one's life?

^a Prayers, especially those offered during the pilgrimage, are an outward manifestation of an inward state. Whatever one cherishes in one's heart, one expresses in prayer. One who has set his mind on worldly riches and grandeur will concentrate on little else when he prays to God, whereas one who seeks the next world, with its infinite happiness and blessings, will make this the central theme of his devotions.

This prayer on the part of the believer is not a request for worldly riches. Material gain and worldly wealth are only parts of a 'test paper'. And no one would like to pray to increase the difficulty of his 'test paper'. This prayer is more like asking God to give him what is best for man in the eyes of God in this world and what is best for man in the eyes of God in the Hereafter.

Therefore, the best prayer for man is to say to his Lord, 'O my God, give me in this world whatever You see is good for this world, and give me in the next life whatever You see is good for that world and save me from eternal doom.'

^b 'You shall be gathered before Him' is the greatest lesson of pilgrimage, given in the plains of Arafat where millions of pilgrims gather annually. This gathering symbolizes the final gathering of all human beings on Doomsday. Practical results are always produced by actions, not by words.

²⁰⁴ There are some men whose views on the affairs of this life may please you. They even call on God to witness whatever is in their heart, yet they are the most contentious of quarrellers. ²⁰⁵ When he turns away, he sets out to spread corruption in the land, destroying crops and cattle. God does not love corruption.^a

وَمِنَ ٱلنَّاسِ مَن يُعْجِبُكَ قَوْلُهُ فِى ٱلْحَيَوٰةِ ٱلدُّنْيَا وَيُشْهِدُ ٱللَّهَ عَلَىٰ مَا فِى قَلْبِهِۦ وَهُوَ أَلَدُّ ٱلْخِصَامِ ۞ وَإِذَا تَوَلَّىٰ سَعَىٰ فِى ٱلْأَرْضِ لِيُفْسِدَ فِيهَا وَيُهْلِكَ ٱلْحَرْثَ وَٱلنَّسْلَ ۗ وَٱللَّهُ لَا يُحِبُّ ٱلْفَسَادَ ۞

---

^a Those who have adopted opportunism as their religion are always able to impress people with words. Why? Because it is in their own selfish interest to do so. For them it is not right or wrong that matters; there is no set standard guiding them. They just go by what is calculated to make a favourable impression on the listener. They have no problem in painting a glowing picture on the outside, despite the fact that in their heart of hearts they are bereft of the warmth of true sincerity; they owe no loyalty to truth; they are loyal only to their own interests.

Why is it that judged by his words a person appears to be a great reformer, while his actions result only in corruption in the land. It can all be traced to the contradiction in himself. He may have an array of words to demonstrate his love for truth, but in practice he belies his words, and acts out of self-interest. So there is bound to be a dichotomy between his words and his actions. He can convey a sense of idealism in speech, but when he gets down to actually doing things, he is drawn by the force of his self-interest to feather his own nest at the expense of others. The one who spoke of peace and reconciliation acts in a manner that leads to strife and conflict. He plays on people's emotions, saying things which will make him popular, with no regard for the real situation. Such are they who have sold themselves for the world. Even when the truth is made plain to them, they do not follow it. They see no benefit for themselves, no furtherance of their own interests, in following truth. Only when there is sufficient gain to be had do they uphold the truth; otherwise they deny it. Behind an obsequious exterior they hide a proud ego. That is why they can never acknowledge truth if it comes from a preacher whom they consider inferior to them.

There are others who sell their lives, not for themselves, but for God; it is to find favour with Him that they strive. They do no accept the demands of their own selves, but the commands of God. At any cost to themselves, they give what they have in the divine cause. It is God's true faith that they seek, so they leave conventional, ancestral religion by the wayside; even though such a move will make them lose in popularity. Their guideline is truth, and they stick to it, despite the fury of the people which pours on them from all sides.

206 When he is told, 'Have fear of God,' he is seized by pride which drives him to wrongdoing. Hell shall be enough for him. A dreadful resting place. 207 But there are others who would dedicate themselves to seeking the pleasure of God. God is compassionate to His servants.

208 Believers, surrender yourselves totally to God, and do not follow in the footsteps of Satan; surely, he is your sworn enemy. 209 But if you lapse after the clear signs that have come to you, then know that God is mighty and wise. 210 Are they only waiting for God as well as the angels to come down to them under canopies of clouds, so that the matter will be settled? All things return to God. 211 Ask the Children of Israel how many clear signs We have given them. Anyone who changes God's blessing once it has come to him will find God is stern in punishment. 212 The life of this world is made to appear attractive for those who deny the truth and they scoff at those who believe. But those who fear God shall be above them on the Day of Resurrection: God bestows His bounties on whoever He pleases without stinting.[a]

وَإِذَا قِيلَ لَهُ ٱتَّقِ ٱللَّهَ أَخَذَتْهُ ٱلْعِزَّةُ بِٱلْإِثْمِ ۚ فَحَسْبُهُۥ جَهَنَّمُ ۚ وَلَبِئْسَ ٱلْمِهَادُ ۝ وَمِنَ ٱلنَّاسِ مَن يَشْرِى نَفْسَهُ ٱبْتِغَآءَ مَرْضَاتِ ٱللَّهِ ۚ وَٱللَّهُ رَءُوفٌۢ بِٱلْعِبَادِ ۝ يَٰٓأَيُّهَا ٱلَّذِينَ ءَامَنُوا۟ ٱدْخُلُوا۟ فِى ٱلسِّلْمِ كَآفَّةً وَلَا تَتَّبِعُوا۟ خُطُوَٰتِ ٱلشَّيْطَٰنِ ۚ إِنَّهُۥ لَكُمْ عَدُوٌّ مُّبِينٌ ۝ فَإِن زَلَلْتُم مِّنۢ بَعْدِ مَا جَآءَتْكُمُ ٱلْبَيِّنَٰتُ فَٱعْلَمُوٓا۟ أَنَّ ٱللَّهَ عَزِيزٌ حَكِيمٌ ۝ هَلْ يَنظُرُونَ إِلَّآ أَن يَأْتِيَهُمُ ٱللَّهُ فِى ظُلَلٍ مِّنَ ٱلْغَمَامِ وَٱلْمَلَٰٓئِكَةُ وَقُضِىَ ٱلْأَمْرُ ۚ وَإِلَى ٱللَّهِ تُرْجَعُ ٱلْأُمُورُ ۝ سَلْ بَنِىٓ إِسْرَٰٓءِيلَ كَمْ ءَاتَيْنَٰهُم مِّنْ ءَايَةٍۭ بَيِّنَةٍ ۗ وَمَن يُبَدِّلْ نِعْمَةَ ٱللَّهِ مِنۢ بَعْدِ مَا جَآءَتْهُ فَإِنَّ ٱللَّهَ شَدِيدُ ٱلْعِقَابِ ۝ زُيِّنَ لِلَّذِينَ كَفَرُوا۟ ٱلْحَيَوٰةُ ٱلدُّنْيَا وَيَسْخَرُونَ مِنَ ٱلَّذِينَ ءَامَنُوا۟ ۘ وَٱلَّذِينَ ٱتَّقَوْا۟ فَوْقَهُمْ يَوْمَ ٱلْقِيَٰمَةِ ۗ وَٱللَّهُ يَرْزُقُ مَن يَشَآءُ بِغَيْرِ حِسَابٍ ۝

---

a There are two ways of adopting Islam as one's religion. One is to do so without any consideration for one's own interests and reservations; to do what Islam enjoins on one and refrain from what it forbids. This is to enter Islam wholeheartedly. The other way is to take up Islam, only to the extent that it does not clash with one's everyday life; and only so long as it serves, or at least does not harm one's own interests. One who adopts the latter course does not let Islam undermine the habits he is accustomed to, the creeds he cherishes, the profits he craves, the honour he thrives on or the leadership he seeks to preserve and consolidate. ▶

²¹³ Mankind was once a single community, [but then people developed differences], so God sent prophets to them as bearers of good tidings and warning, and sent down with them the Book containing the truth, so that He might judge between their disputes. It was only those to whom it [the scripture] was given who disagreed about it after clear signs had come to them, because of rivalry between them. God by His will guided the believers to the truth about which the others had disputed. God guides whom He will to a straight path.^a

كَانَ ٱلنَّاسُ أُمَّةً وَٰحِدَةً فَبَعَثَ ٱللَّهُ ٱلنَّبِيِّنَ مُبَشِّرِينَ وَمُنذِرِينَ وَأَنزَلَ مَعَهُمُ ٱلْكِتَٰبَ بِٱلْحَقِّ لِيَحْكُمَ بَيْنَ ٱلنَّاسِ فِيمَا ٱخْتَلَفُوا۟ فِيهِ وَمَا ٱخْتَلَفَ فِيهِ إِلَّا ٱلَّذِينَ أُوتُوهُ مِنۢ بَعْدِ مَا جَآءَتْهُمُ ٱلْبَيِّنَٰتُ بَغْيًۢا بَيْنَهُمْ فَهَدَى ٱللَّهُ ٱلَّذِينَ ءَامَنُوا۟ لِمَا ٱخْتَلَفُوا۟ فِيهِ مِنَ ٱلْحَقِّ بِإِذْنِهِۦ وَٱللَّهُ يَهْدِى مَن يَشَآءُ إِلَىٰ صِرَٰطٍ مُّسْتَقِيمٍ ﴿٢١٣﴾

His initial enthusiasm for Islam cools when it requires him to make radical changes in his pattern of thought, or forgo personal preferences and desires. He slides back, adhering to Islam in name alone, without letting it harm his interests, or interfere with his life in any way. If it is arguments that he seeks to make him truly believe in the message of Islam, then arguments have been provided in full measure. If it is miracles he is looking for, he has God's entire universe before him. But those who cannot bring themselves to accept clear arguments will not be won over by miracles of this nature. What else is the doubter waiting for, but that God Himself should appear, along with all the angels? When that happens, a sudden surge of belief will not benefit anyone, for that will be a time when fates are sealed, not forged. The whole point of man's being tested in this world is that he should believe in God, without having seen Him and solely by virtue of His arguments. It is believing without seeing that will profit man, not seeing and believing.

Those who put their own interests first and Islam second, and those who unconditionally enter into Islam are people of very different mettle. It is usually the former who accumulate all the worldly splendours in this life, while the latter remain bereft of things of worldly importance. The mere possession of material resources makes the former group feel justified in assuming an air of superiority. They may look down upon the true believers, but this state of affairs is quite short-lived. The world will end, to give way to a new and finer system in which they will be brought low, and the great will be cut down to size, and those who had been considered lowly will occupy high places in the heavenly world.

^a Religion, as revealed by God, is one religion. Yet men differ on this point, putting a variety of interpretations upon divine religion, so that it may fit in with their mental make-up. In this way different viewpoints, all claiming allegiance to one divine scripture, come into existence. ▶

214 Do you think that you will enter Paradise without having suffered like those who passed away before you? Affliction and hardship befell them and so shaken were they that the Messenger and the believers with him would exclaim, 'When will God's help come?' Surely the help of God is near.[a]

أَمْ حَسِبْتُمْ أَن تَدْخُلُوا۟ ٱلْجَنَّةَ وَلَمَّا يَأْتِكُم مَّثَلُ ٱلَّذِينَ خَلَوْا۟ مِن قَبْلِكُم مَّسَّتْهُمُ ٱلْبَأْسَاءُ وَٱلضَّرَّاءُ وَزُلْزِلُوا۟ حَتَّىٰ يَقُولَ ٱلرَّسُولُ وَٱلَّذِينَ ءَامَنُوا۟ مَعَهُۥ مَتَىٰ نَصْرُ ٱللَّهِ أَلَآ إِنَّ نَصْرَ ٱللَّهِ قَرِيبٌ

When this happens, God chooses one of His servants to proclaim the truth on earth. He talks in human language, and appears no different from everyone else, but those who are bent on finding truth appreciate the divine quality in his words. Forgetting their differences, they flock to his standard. Others, however, stick stubbornly to their self-contrived interpretations of religion. Why, they contend should we accept what is taught to us by another? Their claim to have a monopoly over truth makes them proud and prejudiced. It causes them to deny truth itself—the very thing that they in their complacency claimed to monopolize.

[a] Truth, supported by clear proofs, is revealed to men, yet still they refuse to accept it. Why is this? It is because they see truth as destructive to the dream world they have built up; they view it as damaging to their own interests and honour, as threatening to the comfortable, secure lives to which they have become accustomed. But in order to be faithful to God, we are required to make sacrifices of this nature. It is the road that men are reluctant to tread, because of its dangers and difficulties. But that is the only road which leads to Paradise. The price of Paradise is one's own self. There is only one way to earn Paradise, and that is by total self-abnegation. This involves changing the very foundation of one's life, thinking and acting in accordance with the pattern God has laid down, and giving up former habits. This task cannot be performed without exhorting others to do good deeds, and criticising their misdeeds. People in every age have been especially averse to criticism and admonition of this nature. Teachers of truth, then, have to be prepared for adverse reactions from their congregations.

²¹⁵ They will ask you what they should spend on others. Say, 'Whatever you give should be for parents, close relatives, orphans, the needy, and travellers. God is well aware of whatever good you do.'[a] ²¹⁶ Fighting [in defence] is ordained for you, abhorrent as it may be to you. You may dislike something although it is good for you,[b] or like something although it is bad for you: God knows but you do not.[c]

يَسْـَٔلُونَكَ مَاذَا يُنفِقُونَ قُلْ مَآ أَنفَقْتُم مِّنْ خَيْرٍ فَلِلْوَٰلِدَيْنِ وَٱلْأَقْرَبِينَ وَٱلْيَتَٰمَىٰ وَٱلْمَسَٰكِينِ وَٱبْنِ ٱلسَّبِيلِ وَمَا تَفْعَلُوا۟ مِنْ خَيْرٍ فَإِنَّ ٱللَّهَ بِهِۦ عَلِيمٌ ۝ كُتِبَ عَلَيْكُمُ ٱلْقِتَالُ وَهُوَ كُرْهٌ لَّكُمْ وَعَسَىٰٓ أَن تَكْرَهُوا۟ شَيْـًٔا وَهُوَ خَيْرٌ لَّكُمْ وَعَسَىٰٓ أَن تُحِبُّوا۟ شَيْـًٔا وَهُوَ شَرٌّ لَّكُمْ وَٱللَّهُ يَعْلَمُ وَأَنتُمْ لَا تَعْلَمُونَ ۝

[a] Man thinks that the best utilization of his life and wealth is for the benefit of his family. He is happy to expend his wealth for his own desires and ambitions. But Islam urges him to spend for the cause of God, which is quite a different form of expenditure, involving spending on others rather than just on oneself. Another tendency is to expend all one's energy on attaining a high worldly position—something which meets the eye—while everlasting reward, which we as yet cannot see, should be one's most important goal. What man may dislike might be pleasing to God. For that alone will benefit us in the next, infinitely vaster world. In God's sight, evil lies in man giving preference to his own pleasure rather than the pleasure of his Creator. Evil may benefit a person in this temporal world; in the hereafter it will do him only harm.

[b] The same is true of all aspects of life. People like to lead free and unrestricted lives, but it is better for them to adhere to God's laws. They make friends with those who praise them. But they would be better advised to become endeared to their critics—those who are kind enough to point out their faults. In order to save face in the eyes of men, they defy truth, though they would do better to seek honour with God; and God honours only those who uphold the truth. Sacrifice and struggle are things that they shy away from; they prefer a religion which promises paradise without such total involvement. But it would be better for them to engage themselves in the sacrifice and struggle which it entails, for that will benefit them in the long run. The trouble is, they are deeply enmeshed in the present life and its issues, whereas they would be wiser paying attention to matters lying beyond death.

[c] 'God knows but you do not' means that God is above superficial feelings and impulses, whereas the thinking of human beings is a conditioned thinking. Consequently, they fail to think objectively. Under the influence of prejudiced opinions they are diverted from the right path. God's decision is totally objective. Human beings, spurred on by base emotions, tend to arrive at biased, unrealistic conclusions. Therefore, we must surrender our opinions in the face of divine commands.

²¹⁷ They ask you about fighting in the sacred month. Say, 'To fight [in a sacred month] is a grave matter; but barring people from the path of God, to deny Him, and expelling people from the Sacred Mosque are far graver in His sight; and persecution is worse than killing.' They will not stop fighting you until they make you renounce your faith, if they can. Whoever of you turns back from his faith and dies as a denier of the truth will have his deeds come to nothing in this world and the Hereafter, and he will be an inhabitant of the Fire, to abide therein forever.ᵃ

يَسْـَٔلُونَكَ عَنِ ٱلشَّهْرِ ٱلْحَرَامِ قِتَالٍ فِيهِ قُلْ قِتَالٌ فِيهِ كَبِيرٌ وَصَدٌّ عَن سَبِيلِ ٱللَّهِ وَكُفْرٌ بِهِ وَٱلْمَسْجِدِ ٱلْحَرَامِ وَإِخْرَاجُ أَهْلِهِ مِنْهُ أَكْبَرُ عِندَ ٱللَّهِ وَٱلْفِتْنَةُ أَكْبَرُ مِنَ ٱلْقَتْلِ وَلَا يَزَالُونَ يُقَٰتِلُونَكُمْ حَتَّىٰ يَرُدُّوكُمْ عَن دِينِكُمْ إِنِ ٱسْتَطَٰعُوا وَمَن يَرْتَدِدْ مِنكُمْ عَن دِينِهِ فَيَمُتْ وَهُوَ كَافِرٌ فَأُوْلَٰئِكَ حَبِطَتْ أَعْمَٰلُهُمْ فِي ٱلدُّنْيَا وَٱلْءَاخِرَةِ وَأُوْلَٰئِكَ أَصْحَٰبُ ٱلنَّارِ هُمْ فِيهَا خَٰلِدُونَ ۝

ᵃ In Rajab, 2 A.H., a group of the Prophet's companions clashed with a group of the Quraysh (the pagan Makkans), at Nakhlah, which lies between Makkah and Taif. One of the Quraysh was slain. The believers had been under the impression that it was the thirtieth of Jumada al-Thani, the month before Rajab, but Jumada al-Thani had only twenty-nine days that year. The new moon had risen the evening before; it was the first day of Rajab. Now, Rajab is counted among the sacred months, and Arab feeling ran high with regard to the age-old tradition of respect for these months. With this unintentional violation, opponents were able to hurl accusations at the Prophet and his followers. 'Look, they don't even respect the sacred months, so far gone are they in their contumacy.' True, the Quran says in reply, fighting in the sacred months is a sin. But this was just by chance and by mistake. The faithful were not aware that Rajab had begun. Besides, the people who were making this accusation were the very ones who deliberately and persistently engaged in far more criminal activities than fighting in the sacred month.

There is nothing more abhorrent in the sight of God than one who is involved in far greater crimes attempting to discredit another by exaggerating the latter's minor mistakes. When the call to truth was raised among the Quraysh, not only did they deny it themselves, but they sought to prevent others from following it. Their prejudice and antipathy knew no bounds: they even closed the doors of God's House to the servants of the Lord. In their efforts to force the Prophet's followers to forsake their faith, the Quraysh also turned them out of their houses, and tormented them with extreme forms of cruelty. And remember, persecution of a person on account of his faith is a crime worse than any other crime in the eyes of God.

²¹⁸ But those who have believed, migrated, and striven for God's cause, can look forward to God's mercy: God is forgiving and merciful.[a]

إِنَّ ٱلَّذِينَ ءَامَنُوا۟ وَٱلَّذِينَ هَاجَرُوا۟ وَجَٰهَدُوا۟ فِى سَبِيلِ ٱللَّهِ أُو۟لَٰٓئِكَ يَرْجُونَ رَحْمَتَ ٱللَّهِ ۚ وَٱللَّهُ غَفُورٌ رَّحِيمٌ ﴿٢١٨﴾

---

[a] When the faithful are persecuted in this way, and forced to leave their homes, they sometimes even have to take to arms in self-defence. So when the believers were debarred from worship by the polytheists, they were repeatedly subjected to aggression, such circumstances compelled them at times to take up arms in self-defence. This was a two-sided process which separated the people of God from the enemies of God. On the one hand, some were exposed as servants only of themselves; for who else but who has no fear of God—pursuing only his own selfish ends—would persecute God's servants? On the other hand, out of this persecution came emigration and peaceful missionary struggle—acts of true faith on the part of those who remained devoted to God through all torment and oppression; there were others, of course, who, unable to withstand the pressure, forsook their faith. (That is, such persecution gave the believers the opportunity to show the strength of their faith, and in spite of the adverse atmosphere, their continuing trust in God. This made them stand out from those who, weak in faith, proved unable to withstand the pressure, and lost their trust in God.)

219 They ask you [Prophet] about intoxicants and gambling.[a] Say, 'There is great sin in both, although they have some benefit for people: but their harm is greater than their benefit.' They ask you what they should spend [in God's cause]. Say, 'Whatever is surplus to your needs.' Thus God makes His commandments clear to you so that you may reflect

۞ يَسْـَٔلُونَكَ عَنِ ٱلْخَمْرِ وَٱلْمَيْسِرِ ۖ قُلْ فِيهِمَآ إِثْمٌ كَبِيرٌ وَمَنَٰفِعُ لِلنَّاسِ وَإِثْمُهُمَآ أَكْبَرُ مِن نَّفْعِهِمَا ۗ وَيَسْـَٔلُونَكَ مَاذَا يُنفِقُونَ قُلِ ٱلْعَفْوَ ۗ كَذَٰلِكَ يُبَيِّنُ ٱللَّهُ لَكُمُ ٱلْأَيَٰتِ لَعَلَّكُمْ تَتَفَكَّرُونَ ٢١٩

---

[a] The answers to the above questions reveal certain fundamental principles: firstly, if something does more harm than good, it should be eschewed: secondly, any wealth in excess of one's actual needs should be spent for the cause of God: thirdly, in one's dealings with others, one should avoid any action which could lead to evil, and engage only in such activity as will bring some positive benefit to society.

Let us concede that after drinking wine a person becomes elated. And gambling could be looked upon as an easy way of making money without having to work hard for it. But, viewed from a purely moral angle, drinking and gambling lead to such spiritual danger as far outweighs any benefits they may confer. The same rule applies to other human activities. If they are calculated to be more harmful than beneficial, they are to be avoided. Social celebrations, political initiatives, personal enterprises, all the activities of one's life, in fact, should be evaluated in terms of this standard, before one ever considers engaging in them.

²²⁰ upon this world and the Hereafter. They ask you about orphans. Say, 'Promotion of their welfare is an act of great goodness. There is no harm in your living together with them, for they are your brothers. God knows the mischief-maker from the reformer. If God had so willed, He would have afflicted you with hardship. Surely, God is mighty and wise.'[a]

فِى ٱلدُّنْيَا وَٱلْأَخِرَةِ وَيَسْـَٔلُونَكَ عَنِ ٱلْيَتَـٰمَىٰ قُلْ إِصْلَاحٌ لَّهُمْ خَيْرٌ وَإِن تُخَالِطُوهُمْ فَإِخْوَٰنُكُمْ وَٱللَّهُ يَعْلَمُ ٱلْمُفْسِدَ مِنَ ٱلْمُصْلِحِ وَلَوْ شَآءَ ٱللَّهُ لَأَعْنَتَكُمْ إِنَّ ٱللَّهَ عَزِيزٌ حَكِيمٌ ۝

---

[a] Who can truly call himself a true believer? He who makes the next world his goal and who is constantly striving to find favour with his Lord. Such a man does not make worldly possessions his aim in life. This does not mean, however, that he renounces the world, for a certain number of material things are an obvious necessity. It simply means that when he makes a living and engages in worldly activities, he does so only in so far as such action is related to acquiring the bare necessities of life. His purpose in life is never to amass wealth. His purpose, on the contrary, is to gain the blessing of his Lord. So, out of whatever he has, he keeps only what he really needs for himself and spends the rest for the cause of God.

If we were to attempt to state, in explicit, legal terms, how men should deal with their fellowmen and how they should conduct their business, this would be too complicated in the context of daily living. It is, therefore, more useful to lay down some, fundamental guidelines: to wish others well and to keep in mind not just our own interests, but also the interests of those with whom we have to deal, thinking of them as brothers. God will never take us to task if we act in a manner which is conducive to harmony and justice.

²²¹ Do not marry women who associate partners with God until they believe. A believing bondwoman is better than a woman who associates partners with God, however pleasing she may appear to you. Nor give believing women in marriage to men who associate partners with God, till they have believed; a believing bondman is certainly better than a man who associates partners with God, even though he may please you. Such people call you to Hell-fire; but God calls you to Paradise and to forgiveness. He makes His messages clear to people, so that they might bear them in mind.ᵃ

وَلَا تَنكِحُوا۟ ٱلْمُشْرِكَٰتِ حَتَّىٰ يُؤْمِنَّ وَلَأَمَةٌ مُّؤْمِنَةٌ خَيْرٌ مِّن مُّشْرِكَةٍ وَلَوْ أَعْجَبَتْكُمْ ۗ وَلَا تُنكِحُوا۟ ٱلْمُشْرِكِينَ حَتَّىٰ يُؤْمِنُوا۟ ۚ وَلَعَبْدٌ مُّؤْمِنٌ خَيْرٌ مِّن مُّشْرِكٍ وَلَوْ أَعْجَبَكُمْ ۗ أُو۟لَٰٓئِكَ يَدْعُونَ إِلَى ٱلنَّارِ ۖ وَٱللَّهُ يَدْعُوٓا۟ إِلَى ٱلْجَنَّةِ وَٱلْمَغْفِرَةِ بِإِذْنِهِۦ ۖ وَيُبَيِّنُ ءَايَٰتِهِۦ لِلنَّاسِ لَعَلَّهُمْ يَتَذَكَّرُونَ ۞

ᵃ To illustrate the purpose of the matrimonial bond, the relationship between man and woman may be likened to that of a farmer and his field. This means that it is not just for selfish enjoyment that a couple takes the marriage vow. Just as a farmer's task of planting his fields is a serious matter, so also is the husband/wife relationship a serious one. Various factors have to be taken into account, certain guidelines followed.

The first thing to be taken into consideration when choosing a spouse is belief. The relationship between a husband and wife is an extremely delicate one, balanced precariously within a network of social, domestic and psychological factors. For such a close, intricate relationship to flourish there has to be harmony of belief. A Muslim who marries someone of another faith may have to compromise on his beliefs, in which case it will be his faith that suffers; and if he refuses to do so, it will be his marriage which will flounder. Secondly, a husband and his wife should consort and cohabit according to the pattern of creation. Just as revelation is an expression of God's will, so is nature, for it follows divine commands to the letter. Natural laws are for us to follow, just as revealed laws are to be obeyed. And one should fear God at all times, always remembering that He knows a person's inner and outer states, and that eventually one is going to be brought before Him.

²²² They ask you about menstruation. Say, 'It is an impurity, so keep away from women during it and do not approach them until they are cleansed; when they are cleansed you may approach them as God has ordained. God loves those who turn to Him in penitence and He loves those who keep themselves clean. ²²³ Your wives are your fields. Go, then, into your fields as you will. Do good deeds, and fear God, and know that you shall meet Him.' Give good tidings to the believers.ᵃ

وَيَسْـَٔلُونَكَ عَنِ ٱلْمَحِيضِ قُلْ هُوَ أَذًى فَٱعْتَزِلُوا۟ ٱلنِّسَآءَ فِى ٱلْمَحِيضِ وَلَا تَقْرَبُوهُنَّ حَتَّىٰ يَطْهُرْنَ فَإِذَا تَطَهَّرْنَ فَأْتُوهُنَّ مِنْ حَيْثُ أَمَرَكُمُ ٱللَّهُ إِنَّ ٱللَّهَ يُحِبُّ ٱلتَّوَّٰبِينَ وَيُحِبُّ ٱلْمُتَطَهِّرِينَ ﴿٢٢٢﴾ نِسَآؤُكُمْ حَرْثٌ لَّكُمْ فَأْتُوا۟ حَرْثَكُمْ أَنَّىٰ شِئْتُمْ وَقَدِّمُوا۟ لِأَنفُسِكُمْ وَٱتَّقُوا۟ ٱللَّهَ وَٱعْلَمُوٓا۟ أَنَّكُم مُّلَٰقُوهُ وَبَشِّرِ ٱلْمُؤْمِنِينَ ﴿٢٢٣﴾

ᵃ Doing good works means acting with the Hereafter in mind. In the knowledge that there is an eternal side to life, which is more important than the temporal side, it is for eternity that we should strive. Should our actions on earth profit us in this life, but be harmful to our everlasting life, we shall have lived our lives in vain. What we do on earth will be judged after death. We should take care to ensure that our deeds measure up well on God's scale of justice, for if they fail to do so, there is no way we can avoid His punishment.

²²⁴ Do not make God a pretext, when you swear by Him, to avoid doing good, being righteous and making peace between people. God is all hearing and all knowing. ²²⁵ God will not call you to account for any oaths you uttered unintentionally, but He will take you to task for what is intended in your hearts. God is most forgiving and forbearing.[a]

وَلَا تَجْعَلُوا۟ ٱللَّهَ عُرْضَةً لِّأَيْمَـٰنِكُمْ أَن تَبَرُّوا۟ وَتَتَّقُوا۟ وَتُصْلِحُوا۟ بَيْنَ ٱلنَّاسِ ۗ وَٱللَّهُ سَمِيعٌ عَلِيمٌ ۝ لَّا يُؤَاخِذُكُمُ ٱللَّهُ بِٱللَّغْوِ فِىٓ أَيْمَـٰنِكُمْ وَلَـٰكِن يُؤَاخِذُكُم بِمَا كَسَبَتْ قُلُوبُكُمْ ۗ وَٱللَّهُ غَفُورٌ حَلِيمٌ ۝

---

[a] Swayed by anger and obstinacy, sometimes an individual swears an oath that he will not do anything which would benefit a certain person. In ancient times, a variety of such oaths was very common among the Arabs. They swore oaths that they would refrain from such and such a good deed, so that when they were called upon to join in some good act, they would decline, saying that they had already taken an oath to the contrary. To refrain from good acts is in itself bad enough, but swearing to this in the name of God is much worse. For God is a being who is all merciful and all good. Then attaching the name of God to the non-performance of good works is sinful. Perversion at all events is bad. But if perverse acts are done in the name of God, there is a manifold increase in the evil perpetuated.

226 For those who swear that they will not approach their wives, there shall be a waiting period of four months: if they revert to conciliation, surely, God is most forgiving and ever merciful; 227 but if they decide upon divorce, God is all hearing and all knowing. 228 Divorced women should wait for three menstrual cycles; it is unlawful for them, if they believe in God and the Last Day, to hide what God has created in their wombs. Their husbands have the right to take them back within that time, if they desire to be reconciled. The wives have rights corresponding to those which the husbands have, according to what is recognized to be fair, but men have a rank above them. God is almighty and all wise.[a]

لِّلَّذِينَ يُؤْلُونَ مِن نِّسَآئِهِمْ تَرَبُّصُ أَرْبَعَةِ أَشْهُرٍ فَإِن فَآءُو فَإِنَّ ٱللَّهَ غَفُورٌ رَّحِيمٌ ۝ وَإِنْ عَزَمُواْ ٱلطَّلَٰقَ فَإِنَّ ٱللَّهَ سَمِيعٌ عَلِيمٌ ۝ وَٱلْمُطَلَّقَٰتُ يَتَرَبَّصْنَ بِأَنفُسِهِنَّ ثَلَٰثَةَ قُرُوٓءٍ وَلَا يَحِلُّ لَهُنَّ أَن يَكْتُمْنَ مَا خَلَقَ ٱللَّهُ فِىٓ أَرْحَامِهِنَّ إِن كُنَّ يُؤْمِنَّ بِٱللَّهِ وَٱلْيَوْمِ ٱلْءَاخِرِ وَبُعُولَتُهُنَّ أَحَقُّ بِرَدِّهِنَّ فِى ذَٰلِكَ إِنْ أَرَادُوٓاْ إِصْلَٰحًا وَهُنَّ مِثْلُ ٱلَّذِى عَلَيْهِنَّ بِٱلْمَعْرُوفِ وَلِلرِّجَالِ عَلَيْهِنَّ دَرَجَةٌ وَٱللَّهُ عَزِيزٌ حَكِيمٌ ۝

---

[a] There are certain people who keep swearing oaths inadvertently, out of sheer habit. This is quite wrong. A believer must refrain from doing so. However, between husband and wife, such thoughtless oaths have been held legally invalid, due to the delicacy of the marital relationship. But the case of solemn, intentional oaths is different. If a man intentionally swears by God that he will not go to his wife, this is taken seriously and then Islamic law will take its course. In the family system, both the man and the woman have duties as well as rights. Each of them must, as well as demanding his or her rights, honour the rights of others. That is, if we want others to fulfill their obligations to us, we must also fulfill obligations to them. If one misuses his power and advantageous position to act unjustly towards others, then he cannot save himself from God's chastisement.

229 Divorce may be pronounced twice, and then a woman must be retained honourably or released with kindness.[a] It is not lawful for you to take away anything of what you have given your wives, unless both fear that they would not be able to observe the bounds set by God. In such a case it shall be no sin for either of them if the woman opts to give something for her release. These are the bounds set by God; do not transgress them. Those who transgress the bounds of God are wrongdoers. 230 And if man finally divorces his wife, he cannot remarry her until she has married another man. Then if the next husband divorces her, there will be no blame on either of them if the former husband and wife return to one another, provided they think that they can keep within the bounds set by God. These are the bounds prescribed by God, which He makes clear to men of understanding.[b]

ٱلطَّلَٰقُ مَرَّتَانِ ۖ فَإِمْسَاكٌ بِمَعْرُوفٍ أَوْ تَسْرِيحٌ بِإِحْسَٰنٍ ۗ وَلَا يَحِلُّ لَكُمْ أَن تَأْخُذُوا۟ مِمَّآ ءَاتَيْتُمُوهُنَّ شَيْـًٔا إِلَّآ أَن يَخَافَآ أَلَّا يُقِيمَا حُدُودَ ٱللَّهِ ۖ فَإِنْ خِفْتُمْ أَلَّا يُقِيمَا حُدُودَ ٱللَّهِ فَلَا جُنَاحَ عَلَيْهِمَا فِيمَا ٱفْتَدَتْ بِهِۦ ۗ تِلْكَ حُدُودُ ٱللَّهِ فَلَا تَعْتَدُوهَا ۚ وَمَن يَتَعَدَّ حُدُودَ ٱللَّهِ فَأُو۟لَٰٓئِكَ هُمُ ٱلظَّٰلِمُونَ ۝ فَإِن طَلَّقَهَا فَلَا تَحِلُّ لَهُۥ مِنۢ بَعْدُ حَتَّىٰ تَنكِحَ زَوْجًا غَيْرَهُۥ ۗ فَإِن طَلَّقَهَا فَلَا جُنَاحَ عَلَيْهِمَآ أَن يَتَرَاجَعَآ إِن ظَنَّآ أَن يُقِيمَا حُدُودَ ٱللَّهِ ۗ وَتِلْكَ حُدُودُ ٱللَّهِ يُبَيِّنُهَا لِقَوْمٍ يَعْلَمُونَ ۝

---

[a] Divorce is an abnormal event which takes place in an abnormal situation. But, in this most emotional matter too, the Quran commands us to adhere to going in fear of God (taqwa), and to being both just and kind. From this we may gauge what kind of behaviour God desires from a believer in this life.

We are commanded to break the marriage bond, if this has become unavoidable, in three stages and not all at once.

[b] This course takes three months to finalize. The prescribing of a very seriously thought-out procedure in such an extremely emotional matter shows what the behaviour of a believer should be in cases of difference and discord. His behaviour with his opponent should be dispassionate, well-considered, and the result of patient decision-making rather than impulsive action resulting from some hasty or rash decision. Thus the procedure for divorce has an important lesson for life in general.

²³¹ Once you divorce women, and they have reached the end of their waiting period, then either retain them in all decency or part from them decently. Do not retain them in order to harm them or to wrong them. Whoever does this, wrongs his own soul. Do not make a mockery of God's revelations. Remember the favours God has bestowed upon you, and the Book and the wisdom He has revealed to exhort you. Fear God and know that God is aware of everything.ᵃ

²³² When you divorce women and they reach the end of their waiting period, do not prevent them from marrying other men, if they have come to an honourable agreement. This is enjoined on every one of you who believes in God and the Last Day; it is more wholesome and purer for you. God knows, but you do not know.

وَإِذَا طَلَّقْتُمُ ٱلنِّسَآءَ فَبَلَغْنَ أَجَلَهُنَّ فَأَمْسِكُوهُنَّ بِمَعْرُوفٍ أَوْ سَرِّحُوهُنَّ بِمَعْرُوفٍ وَلَا تُمْسِكُوهُنَّ ضِرَارًا لِّتَعْتَدُواْ وَمَن يَفْعَلْ ذَٰلِكَ فَقَدْ ظَلَمَ نَفْسَهُۥ وَلَا تَتَّخِذُوٓاْ ءَايَٰتِ ٱللَّهِ هُزُوًا وَٱذْكُرُواْ نِعْمَتَ ٱللَّهِ عَلَيْكُمْ وَمَآ أَنزَلَ عَلَيْكُم مِّنَ ٱلْكِتَٰبِ وَٱلْحِكْمَةِ يَعِظُكُم بِهِۦ وَٱتَّقُواْ ٱللَّهَ وَٱعْلَمُوٓاْ أَنَّ ٱللَّهَ بِكُلِّ شَىْءٍ عَلِيمٌ ۝ وَإِذَا طَلَّقْتُمُ ٱلنِّسَآءَ فَبَلَغْنَ أَجَلَهُنَّ فَلَا تَعْضُلُوهُنَّ أَن يَنكِحْنَ أَزْوَٰجَهُنَّ إِذَا تَرَٰضَوْاْ بَيْنَهُم بِٱلْمَعْرُوفِ ذَٰلِكَ يُوعَظُ بِهِۦ مَن كَانَ مِنكُمْ يُؤْمِنُ بِٱللَّهِ وَٱلْيَوْمِ ٱلْءَاخِرِ ذَٰلِكُمْ أَزْكَىٰ لَكُمْ وَأَطْهَرُ وَٱللَّهُ يَعْلَمُ وَأَنتُمْ لَا تَعْلَمُونَ ۝

ᵃ Even after taking a decision as regards separation, one must continue to consider the possibility of reconciliation. Even when relationships have to be finally severed, one must not take this as an end to all human relations. Even at such trying turns we have to fully adhere to God's law. In carrying out the commands of the Islamic law, no legal loopholes or excuses should be sought to evade their execution. In the observance of the law, the spirit behind the words must be given great importance. For instance what the husband had given to his wife during their marriage should not be taken back after separation. If before their separation they showed goodwill towards each other, they should also be on their best behaviour during their separation.

A man once divorced his wife and did not return to her during the time of waiting. After this period had come to an end, he had second thoughts and, along with some other prospective husbands, he too made her a proposal of marriage. The woman was willing to remarry her former husband, but her brother objected to it. He sought to thwart their reunion, but the Quran decreed that when both agreed between themselves in a lawful manner, they should not be prevented from being reunited.

ᵇ Literally 'when you have divorced wives and they reach the end of their waiting period'.

²³³ And the [divorced] mothers should nurse their children for two whole years, if they wish to complete the period of nursing; and during that period the father of the child shall be responsible for the maintenance of the mother in a reasonable manner. No soul is charged with more than it can bear. No mother should be made to suffer on account of her child, and no father should be made to suffer on account of his child. The same duties devolve upon the father's heir [in case of the death of the father]. But if, after consultation, they choose by mutual agreement to wean the child, there shall be no blame on them. Nor shall it be any offence for you if you desire to engage a wet-nurse for your children, provided you hand over what you have agreed to pay, in a reasonable manner. Have fear of God and know that God is observant of all your actions.ᵃ

* وَٱلۡوَٰلِدَٰتُ يُرۡضِعۡنَ أَوۡلَٰدَهُنَّ حَوۡلَيۡنِ كَامِلَيۡنِ لِمَنۡ أَرَادَ أَن يُتِمَّ ٱلرَّضَاعَةَ وَعَلَى ٱلۡمَوۡلُودِ لَهُۥ رِزۡقُهُنَّ وَكِسۡوَتُهُنَّ بِٱلۡمَعۡرُوفِ لَا تُكَلَّفُ نَفۡسٌ إِلَّا وُسۡعَهَا لَا تُضَآرَّ وَٰلِدَةٌۢ بِوَلَدِهَا وَلَا مَوۡلُودٌ لَّهُۥ بِوَلَدِهِۦ وَعَلَى ٱلۡوَارِثِ مِثۡلُ ذَٰلِكَ فَإِنۡ أَرَادَا فِصَالًا عَن تَرَاضٍ مِّنۡهُمَا وَتَشَاوُرٍ فَلَا جُنَاحَ عَلَيۡهِمَا وَإِنۡ أَرَدتُّمۡ أَن تَسۡتَرۡضِعُوٓاْ أَوۡلَٰدَكُمۡ فَلَا جُنَاحَ عَلَيۡكُمۡ إِذَا سَلَّمۡتُم مَّآ ءَاتَيۡتُم بِٱلۡمَعۡرُوفِ وَٱتَّقُواْ ٱللَّهَ وَٱعۡلَمُوٓاْ أَنَّ ٱللَّهَ بِمَا تَعۡمَلُونَ بَصِيرٌ ۝

ᵃ After divorce, many matters remain to be cleared up. Sometimes the husband and wife wish to remarry; or maybe the woman wishes to have a new husband. On no account should obstacles be placed in their path. A woman may well have children from her former husband. Maybe they are infants, who have to be suckled. This being the case, the man and the woman should not cause trouble for one another. Rather than make the matter an emotional issue between them, they should settle it by mutual counsel and consent. This is how a believer should settle matters involving conflict and separation. The interests of both parties should be respected, with neither party seeking to inconvenience the other. Attempts should be made to settle the dispute in a manner acceptable to both sides. This is the cleaner, purer way of settling disputes, a method befitting those whose souls have been purified by true belief.

Unless a person believes in God and fears His judgement, he will not be inclined to heed admonishment, no matter how correct and relevant it may be. He will set out to find a loophole in the advice he has been given and make up some excuse ▶

²³⁴ If any of you die and leave widows, the widows should wait for four months and ten days. When they have reached the end of their waiting period you will not be blamed for what they may reasonably choose to do with themselves: God is aware of what you do. ²³⁵ It shall be no offence for you to hint at a proposal of marriage [to divorced or widowed women] or to cherish them in your hearts. God knows that you will bear them in mind. But do not enter into any secret arrangement with them, beyond conveying some indication to them of your inclination. Do not proceed with tying the marriage-knot before the end of their waiting period. Know that God has knowledge of all your thoughts. Therefore, take heed and bear in mind that God is forgiving and forbearing.ᵃ

وَٱلَّذِينَ يُتَوَفَّوْنَ مِنكُمْ وَيَذَرُونَ أَزْوَٰجًا يَتَرَبَّصْنَ بِأَنفُسِهِنَّ أَرْبَعَةَ أَشْهُرٍ وَعَشْرًا فَإِذَا بَلَغْنَ أَجَلَهُنَّ فَلَا جُنَاحَ عَلَيْكُمْ فِيمَا فَعَلْنَ فِىٓ أَنفُسِهِنَّ بِٱلْمَعْرُوفِ وَٱللَّهُ بِمَا تَعْمَلُونَ خَبِيرٌ ۝ وَلَا جُنَاحَ عَلَيْكُمْ فِيمَا عَرَّضْتُم بِهِۦ مِنْ خِطْبَةِ ٱلنِّسَآءِ أَوْ أَكْنَنتُمْ فِىٓ أَنفُسِكُمْ عَلِمَ ٱللَّهُ أَنَّكُمْ سَتَذْكُرُونَهُنَّ وَلَٰكِن لَّا تُوَاعِدُوهُنَّ سِرًّا إِلَّآ أَن تَقُولُوا۟ قَوْلًا مَّعْرُوفًا وَلَا تَعْزِمُوا۟ عُقْدَةَ ٱلنِّكَاحِ حَتَّىٰ يَبْلُغَ ٱلْكِتَٰبُ أَجَلَهُۥ وَٱعْلَمُوٓا۟ أَنَّ ٱللَّهَ يَعْلَمُ مَا فِىٓ أَنفُسِكُمْ فَٱحْذَرُوهُ وَٱعْلَمُوٓا۟ أَنَّ ٱللَّهَ غَفُورٌ حَلِيمٌ ۝

or the other for not applying it to himself. One who believes in God and the Last Day, knows, however, that the matter does not end there. Finally it will come before God, at which point the erring individual will not be able to make any excuses for having shirked his responsibilities.

ᵃ While explaining the laws of marriage and divorce the Quran repeatedly enjoins going in fear of God and being kind to others. This shows that to carry out any command in its true spirit, individuals are required to go beyond the wording of that command, in its purely legal sense. Rather they must have feelings of goodwill, well-wishing, kindness and justice for one another. At the same time they must always go in fear of God: if they do not behave properly with their fellow men, they will incur God's displeasure. On Judgement Day neither will excuses come to their rescue, nor will they be able to hide anything from God.

236 You will not be blamed [for not paying the dower money] if you divorce women when you have not yet consummated the marriage or fixed a dower money upon them, but make fair provision for them, the affluent according to his means and the straitened according to his means; this is binding on righteous men. 237 If you divorce them before the marriage is consummated, but after their dower money has been settled, give them the half of their dower money, unless they [the women] agree to forego it, or the man [the husband] in whose hand lies the marriage knot foregoes it. To forego is nearer to righteousness. Do not neglect any chance of behaving benevolently towards each other. God is observant of whatever you do.[a]

لَّا جُنَاحَ عَلَيْكُمْ إِن طَلَّقْتُمُ ٱلنِّسَآءَ مَا لَمْ تَمَسُّوهُنَّ أَوْ تَفْرِضُواْ لَهُنَّ فَرِيضَةً وَمَتِّعُوهُنَّ عَلَى ٱلْمُوسِعِ قَدَرُهُ وَعَلَى ٱلْمُقْتِرِ قَدَرُهُ مَتَٰعَۢا بِٱلْمَعْرُوفِ حَقًّا عَلَى ٱلْمُحْسِنِينَ ۝ وَإِن طَلَّقْتُمُوهُنَّ مِن قَبْلِ أَن تَمَسُّوهُنَّ وَقَدْ فَرَضْتُمْ لَهُنَّ فَرِيضَةً فَنِصْفُ مَا فَرَضْتُمْ إِلَّآ أَن يَعْفُونَ أَوْ يَعْفُوَاْ ٱلَّذِي بِيَدِهِۦ عُقْدَةُ ٱلنِّكَاحِ وَأَن تَعْفُوٓاْ أَقْرَبُ لِلتَّقْوَىٰ وَلَا تَنسَوُاْ ٱلْفَضْلَ بَيْنَكُمْ إِنَّ ٱللَّهَ بِمَا تَعْمَلُونَ بَصِيرٌ ۝

---

[a] If the bride-gift is fixed at the time of marriage, but separation takes place before the consummation of the marriage, according to the Islamic law, half the dower fixed shall be paid by the man to the woman. But the spirit of goodwill calls for both husband and wife to adopt a liberal rather than a legal attitude. The woman should feel that, when the marriage has not been consummated she should, as the law requires, remit half the amount of the bride-gift due to her. While the man should feel, that although he is legally entitled to deduct half of the amount, he should rather hand over all of it as a gesture of goodwill. This attitude of liberality and goodwill is required in all matters of life. A truly Muslim society is that in which its members are more interested in giving to one another, rather than in taking from one another. Furthermore, this attitude of liberality should be evinced in times of enmity as well as in friendship.

238 Be ever mindful of prayers, especially the middle prayer; and stand up before God in submissive devotion. 239 When you are exposed to danger, pray on foot or while riding; when you are safe again, remember God, for He has taught you what you did not know. 240 If any of you die and leave widows, make a bequest for them of a year's maintenance without causing them to leave their homes; but if they leave of their own accord, you will not be blamed for what they may reasonably choose to do with themselves. God is almighty and wise.[a]

حَٰفِظُوا۟ عَلَى ٱلصَّلَوَٰتِ وَٱلصَّلَوٰةِ ٱلْوُسْطَىٰ وَقُومُوا۟ لِلَّهِ قَٰنِتِينَ ۞ فَإِنْ خِفْتُمْ فَرِجَالًا أَوْ رُكْبَانًا فَإِذَآ أَمِنتُمْ فَٱذْكُرُوا۟ ٱللَّهَ كَمَا عَلَّمَكُم مَّا لَمْ تَكُونُوا۟ تَعْلَمُونَ ۞ وَٱلَّذِينَ يُتَوَفَّوْنَ مِنكُمْ وَيَذَرُونَ أَزْوَٰجًا وَصِيَّةً لِّأَزْوَٰجِهِم مَّتَٰعًا إِلَى ٱلْحَوْلِ غَيْرَ إِخْرَاجٍ فَإِنْ خَرَجْنَ فَلَا جُنَاحَ عَلَيْكُمْ فِى مَا فَعَلْنَ فِى أَنفُسِهِنَّ مِن مَّعْرُوفٍ وَٱللَّهُ عَزِيزٌ حَكِيمٌ ۞

[a] The word hafizu (literally 'guard') is used to denote yet another aspect of prayer. It is as if prayer were an object to be guarded just the way wealth is. Great care in observing the proper timings of prayer, even in times of the greatest danger, and refraining from all such actions as may mar the spirit of prayer—all this is implied by the 'guarding' of prayer. The third aspect of prayer is humility. It is the essence of prayer. Prayer is the standing of His servants before their Lord. Therefore, it is essential that at times of prayer that state of mind should be induced in the suppliant, which prevails when the most humble stands before the Most High.

[b] This shows that there is a middle prayer, and then prayers before and after. In this verse the prayers before and after have to be taken to refer to at least four in number, for the word used in the Arabic language, salawat (plural of salat) denotes three or more in number. The first possible number where one prayer may become a middle prayer between the prayers is four. In this way, with one prayer becoming the middle prayer, there are two sets of two prayers on either side. The middle prayer, according to the majority of the exegetes, is the afternoon ('asr) prayer.

Prayer is the essence of religion. It is the microcosm of a believing life which, when extended, becomes a complete Islamic life. Here the three most important aspects of prayer have been briefly described: 1. Prayer is obligatory five times a day. 2. Praying is of great importance. 3. Humility is the real essence of prayer.

241 For divorced women a provision according to what is fair shall also be made. This is an obligation binding on the righteous. 242 Thus God makes His commandments clear to you, so that you may understand.[a]

وَلِلْمُطَلَّقَٰتِ مَتَٰعٌۢ بِٱلْمَعْرُوفِ ۖ حَقًّا عَلَى ٱلْمُتَّقِينَ ﴿٢٤١﴾ كَذَٰلِكَ يُبَيِّنُ ٱللَّهُ لَكُمْ ءَايَٰتِهِۦ لَعَلَّكُمْ تَعْقِلُونَ ﴿٢٤٢﴾

---

[a] Setting forth injunctions regarding social matters, the Quran states, 'This is an obligation binding on the righteous.' This shows us an important aspect of Islamic law. In mutual matters there are certain rights on which the law has been laid down. But there are further mutual rights which go beyond fixed boundaries. These rights can be seen as such only by those who are God-fearing. The more one is God-fearing, the more sensitive one is in discharging one's duties with regard to giving others their dues.

²⁴³ Have you not seen those who fled their homes in their thousands for fear of death, whereupon God said to them, 'Die!' and later brought them back to life? Surely God is bountiful to mankind, but most of them are ungrateful. ²⁴⁴ Fight [in defence] in God's cause and remember that He is all hearing and all knowing.ᵃ

۞ أَلَمْ تَرَ إِلَى ٱلَّذِينَ خَرَجُواْ مِن دِيَٰرِهِمْ وَهُمْ أُلُوفٌ حَذَرَ ٱلْمَوْتِ فَقَالَ لَهُمُ ٱللَّهُ مُوتُواْ ثُمَّ أَحْيَٰهُمْ إِنَّ ٱللَّهَ لَذُو فَضْلٍ عَلَى ٱلنَّاسِ وَلَٰكِنَّ أَكْثَرَ ٱلنَّاسِ لَا يَشْكُرُونَ ۝ وَقَٰتِلُواْ فِي سَبِيلِ ٱللَّهِ وَٱعْلَمُوٓاْ أَنَّ ٱللَّهَ سَمِيعٌ عَلِيمٌ ۝

ᵃ The Muslims left Makkah for Madinah as a result of severe persecution at the hands of the Makkans. In Madinah they were free to live in accordance with their religion. But the opponents of Islam did not leave matters at that. They began launching armed onslaughts on the Muslims in order to uproot them from Madinah. The Muslims at that time were far less in number and had fewer resources as compared to their opponents. This discouraged them from going ahead and facing the enemy. On this occasion God reminded them of an event in the history of the Israelites, where in the trials of life, fear of defeat was defeat itself.

The Philistines, a neighbouring people, once attacked the Israelites and defeated them, slaying more than four thousand Hebrews. The Israelites were so greatly stricken with fear that they abandoned their homes and ran away. 'Thus the glory departed from Israel,' and in the words of the Bible, 'All the houses of Israel trembled with fear and beseeched the Lord.' Twenty years passed in this state. Then they all gave serious thought as to why they had been defeated by the Philistines. Their prophet Samuel said to them, 'If you return to the Lord with all your hearts, then put away the foreign gods... from among you, and prepare your hearts for the Lord, and serve Him only; and He will deliver you out of the hand of the Philistines' (1 Samuel 7:3).

So they put away the foreign gods and served only their Lord. Now the Philistines drew near to battle against Israel, 'But the Lord thundered on that day, with a great thunder upon the Philistines and discomfited them; and they were smitten before Israel' (Samuel 7:10).

Abandoning the path of trust in God leads to the moral death of nations and communities, while opting for the path of trust in God leads to their regeneration.

245 Who will give God a generous loan? He will multiply it many times over. It is God who withholds, and God who gives abundantly, and it is to Him that you shall all be returned.

246 Have you not heard of what the chiefs of the Children of Israel demanded of one of their prophets after Moses? They said, 'Appoint for us a king, and we will fight for the cause of God.' He replied, 'What if you refuse to fight, when ordered to do so?' 'Why should we not fight for the cause of God,' they replied, 'when we have been driven forth from our homes and our children?' But when at last they were commanded to fight, they all refused, except a few of them. God knows the wrongdoers.ᵃ

مَّن ذَا ٱلَّذِى يُقْرِضُ ٱللَّهَ قَرْضًا حَسَنًا فَيُضَٰعِفَهُۥ لَهُۥٓ أَضْعَافًا كَثِيرَةً ۚ وَٱللَّهُ يَقْبِضُ وَيَبْصُۜطُ وَإِلَيْهِ تُرْجَعُونَ ﴿٢٤٥﴾ أَلَمْ تَرَ إِلَى ٱلْمَلَإِ مِنۢ بَنِىٓ إِسْرَٰٓءِيلَ مِنۢ بَعْدِ مُوسَىٰٓ إِذْ قَالُوا۟ لِنَبِىٍّ لَّهُمُ ٱبْعَثْ لَنَا مَلِكًا نُّقَٰتِلْ فِى سَبِيلِ ٱللَّهِ ۖ قَالَ هَلْ عَسَيْتُمْ إِن كُتِبَ عَلَيْكُمُ ٱلْقِتَالُ أَلَّا تُقَٰتِلُوا۟ ۖ قَالُوا۟ وَمَا لَنَآ أَلَّا نُقَٰتِلَ فِى سَبِيلِ ٱللَّهِ وَقَدْ أُخْرِجْنَا مِن دِيَٰرِنَا وَأَبْنَآئِنَا ۖ فَلَمَّا كُتِبَ عَلَيْهِمُ ٱلْقِتَالُ تَوَلَّوْا۟ إِلَّا قَلِيلًا مِّنْهُمْ ۗ وَٱللَّهُ عَلِيمٌۢ بِٱلظَّٰلِمِينَ ﴿٢٤٦﴾

ᵃ Spending for the cause of God's religion is called giving a 'generous loan.' This spending is purely for God: no other interest is involved. God called for a loan to be given to Him and he called it a 'generous loan' because He would return it many times over.

The facing of difficulties and setbacks by a believer is in no way a deprivation. It is indeed akin to opening a new door to God's blessings. At a later stage, by spending his life and wealth for the cause of God, he becomes deserving of those blessings of God, that no one would ordinarily receive.

About three hundred years after the death of Moses, the Israelites were again subjugated by the polytheistic neighbouring nations. After having remained in that state of subjugation for about a quarter of a century, they felt the urge to bring back their period of glory. For this purpose they needed a leader around whom they could rally in order to fight their enemies. So their Prophet Samuel appointed a man called Talut in the Quran and Saul in the Bible. Tall, wise and strong, Saul was distinguished in physique, and commanding in appearance. Although he was superior both in mind and body, the Hebrews were loath to accept his leadership and raised all kinds of petty objections, one of which was that he belonged to the tribe of Benjamin, the smallest tribe in Israel. Moreover, he was not rich. Out of sheer selfishness, each one of them, instead of desiring the good of the people as a whole—as a leader should—wanted to be leader and king himself.

247 Their prophet said to them, 'God has now appointed Talut to be your king.' But they replied, 'How can he be king over us when we are worthier of kingship than he and he has not even been granted an abundance of wealth?' He said, 'God has chosen him over you, and has given him great knowledge and physique.*a* God grants kingship to whoever He pleases: God is magnanimous and all knowing.' 248 Their prophet also said to them, 'The sign of his kingship is that the Ark [of the Covenant] shall come to you. Therein shall be tranquillity from your Lord, and the relics which the House of Moses and the House of Aaron left behind. It will be borne by the angels. There is a sign in this for you, if you believe.'

وَقَالَ لَهُمْ نَبِيُّهُمْ إِنَّ ٱللَّهَ قَدْ بَعَثَ لَكُمْ طَالُوتَ مَلِكًا قَالُوٓا۟ أَنَّىٰ يَكُونُ لَهُ ٱلْمُلْكُ عَلَيْنَا وَنَحْنُ أَحَقُّ بِٱلْمُلْكِ مِنْهُ وَلَمْ يُؤْتَ سَعَةً مِّنَ ٱلْمَالِ قَالَ إِنَّ ٱللَّهَ ٱصْطَفَىٰهُ عَلَيْكُمْ وَزَادَهُۥ بَسْطَةً فِى ٱلْعِلْمِ وَٱلْجِسْمِ وَٱللَّهُ يُؤْتِى مُلْكَهُۥ مَن يَشَآءُ وَٱللَّهُ وَٰسِعٌ عَلِيمٌ ﴿٢٤٧﴾ وَقَالَ لَهُمْ نَبِيُّهُمْ إِنَّ ءَايَةَ مُلْكِهِۦٓ أَن يَأْتِيَكُمُ ٱلتَّابُوتُ فِيهِ سَكِينَةٌ مِّن رَّبِّكُمْ وَبَقِيَّةٌ مِّمَّا تَرَكَ ءَالُ مُوسَىٰ وَءَالُ هَٰرُونَ تَحْمِلُهُ ٱلْمَلَٰٓئِكَةُ إِنَّ فِى ذَٰلِكَ لَءَايَةً لَّكُمْ إِن كُنتُم مُّؤْمِنِينَ ﴿٢٤٨﴾

---

a Stirring up controversies on all issues was indicative of their degeneration. God's decrees are based on knowledge and broadmindedness. Therefore, only that person will be held to be a true believer who is broadminded in his thinking and who takes decisions on the basis of realities rather than prejudices and other petty considerations. The restoration of the Ark of the Covenant was an extraordinary testimony to the appointment of Talut (Saul) by God's own will.

b The Israelites had a sacred chest, or box, known as the Ark of the Covenant (*at-tabut*), which they had had in their possession from the time they left Egypt. It contained the Ten Commandments engraved on stone, as well as relics of Moses and Aaron. This was a possession sacred to Israel. It served as a visible symbol of God's gracious presence. It guided them on their journey, and led them on from victory to victory. It was lost to the enemy in the early part of Samuel's ministry. But in the town where this Ark was placed, plague and pestilence broke out and the Philistines were terrified. Subsequently, they placed it on a driverless cart drawn by two cows. The beasts took it of their own accord to Bayt ash-Shamsh, a city of Judah. The Israelites were immensely overjoyed at its miraculous restoration.

249 When Talut set out with his forces, he said to them, 'God will test you with a river: whoever drinks from it is not with me and whoever does not drink is with me. There will, however, be no blame upon one who sips only a handful from it.' But, except for a few of them, they all drank from it. When he and those who believed along with him had crossed the river, they said, 'We have no strength today against Goliath and his warriors.' But those of them who believed that they would meet God replied, 'Many a small group, by God's command has prevailed against a large group. God is indeed with the steadfast.' [a]

فَلَمَّا فَصَلَ طَالُوتُ بِالْجُنُودِ قَالَ إِنَّ اللَّهَ مُبْتَلِيكُم بِنَهَرٍ فَمَن شَرِبَ مِنْهُ فَلَيْسَ مِنِّي وَمَن لَّمْ يَطْعَمْهُ فَإِنَّهُ مِنِّي إِلَّا مَنِ اغْتَرَفَ غُرْفَةً بِيَدِهِ فَشَرِبُوا مِنْهُ إِلَّا قَلِيلًا مِّنْهُمْ فَلَمَّا جَاوَزَهُ هُوَ وَالَّذِينَ آمَنُوا مَعَهُ قَالُوا لَا طَاقَةَ لَنَا الْيَوْمَ بِجَالُوتَ وَجُنُودِهِ قَالَ الَّذِينَ يَظُنُّونَ أَنَّهُم مُّلَاقُوا اللَّهِ كَم مِّن فِئَةٍ قَلِيلَةٍ غَلَبَتْ فِئَةً كَثِيرَةً بِإِذْنِ اللَّهِ وَاللَّهُ مَعَ الصَّابِرِينَ ﴿٢٤٩﴾

---

[a] About three hundred years after Moses and about one thousand years before Christ the Philistines attacked the Israelites and annexed most of the region of Palestine. After a period of time the Israelites wished to take some action against the Philistines, so that they might recover their lands from them. At that time there was a prophet called Samuel among them. Living in an ancient city in Syria, known as Rama, Samuel was in charge of the community matters of the Israelites. Therefore, a delegation met him and said to him, 'Now that you have aged, you should appoint a king from amongst us, in order that we may wage war against our enemies under the command of our leader.'

Although Samuel did not have a good opinion of the character of the Israelites, he agreed to their request and promised to appoint a King for them. Therefore, he appointed a brave youth, Saul, who belonged to the tribe of Benjamin.

Saul (Talut) set forth with the army to meet the enemy. On the way they had to cross the river Jordan. Since Saul was aware of the weaknesses of the Israelites, he employed a simple method to test them. He gave the order that, while crossing the river, no one was to drink more than a handful of water from it. The majority of the Israelites failed the test. However, God was with them and they emerged victorious under the leadership of Saul. A decisive role was played in this battle by David, a young Israelite soldier who was one of those who had full confidence in God. The feat he performed was to kill the enemy's supreme commander, Goliath (Jalut). Upon the fall of Goliath, the Philistine army broke ranks and fled.

²⁵⁰ When they met Goliath and his warriors, they said, 'Our Lord, bestow patience upon us, make us stand firm, and help us against those who deny the truth.' ²⁵¹ And so by the command of God they defeated them.ᵃ David killed Goliath, and God gave him kingship and wisdom, and imparted to him the knowledge of whatever He willed. Had it not been for God's repelling some people by means of others, the earth would have been filled with corruption.ᵇ But God is bountiful to His creatures.

وَلَمَّا بَرَزُوا۟ لِجَالُوتَ وَجُنُودِهِۦ قَالُوا۟ رَبَّنَآ أَفْرِغْ عَلَيْنَا صَبْرًا وَثَبِّتْ أَقْدَامَنَا وَٱنصُرْنَا عَلَى ٱلْقَوْمِ ٱلْكَـٰفِرِينَ ۝ فَهَزَمُوهُم بِإِذْنِ ٱللَّهِ وَقَتَلَ دَاوُۥدُ جَالُوتَ وَءَاتَىٰهُ ٱللَّهُ ٱلْمُلْكَ وَٱلْحِكْمَةَ وَعَلَّمَهُۥ مِمَّا يَشَآءُ ۗ وَلَوْلَا دَفْعُ ٱللَّهِ ٱلنَّاسَ بَعْضَهُم بِبَعْضٍ لَّفَسَدَتِ ٱلْأَرْضُ وَلَـٰكِنَّ ٱللَّهَ ذُو فَضْلٍ عَلَى ٱلْعَـٰلَمِينَ ۝

ᵃ What is essential to gain a victory in any such encounter is that the participants must have the capacity to persevere, whatever the odds, and must obey their leader. Saul forbade his soldiers to drink water from the river in order to test their obedience and perseverence. According to the Bible, only 600 out of the whole army were able to refrain from drinking water. Those who could not resist drinking it were confirmed in their moral weakness. That was why they were all the more terrified at the sight of the apparently strong army of their enemies. But those who had not drunk the river water had by their obedience confirmed their patience and endurance. Then they realized that God alone brought defeat or granted victory. In the words of the Bible, 'Then all this assembly shall know that the Lord does not save with sword and spear, for the battle is the Lord's and He will give you into our hands' (1 Samuel, 17:47).

ᵇ Power makes people arrogant and consequently they start committing injustice. If power continued to remain with one individual or one group for a long time, the earth would be filled with corruption and injustice. That is why God compensates for this by changing the people invested with power and giving it by turns to different groups or individuals. He removes the group in power, investing power in a new group, raised from amongst the powerless. Thus whenever the group in power transgresses all limits in oppression, the oppressed group knows that the time of God's succour is at hand. Then, provided they fulfill the conditions of patience and obedience and join in the divine plan, they will prevail against a larger group by God's succour, despite their being smaller in number and with less resources. The fear of God is not something negative. It is in fact a kind of knowledge which illumines people's minds and enables them to see things in their real form.

²⁵² These are the revelations of God which We recite to you in all truth, for you are truly one of the messengers. ²⁵³ Of these messengers, We have given something additional among them.ᵃ There are some to whom God spoke directly and others He exalted in rank. We gave Jesus, son of Mary clear signs, and strengthened him with the holy spirit. Had God pleased, those who succeeded them would not have fought against one another after the clear signs had come to them. But they disagreed among themselves; some believed, while others did not. Yet had God willed, they would not have fought against one another; but God does whatever He wills.ᵇ

تِلْكَ ءَايَٰتُ ٱللَّهِ نَتْلُوهَا عَلَيْكَ بِٱلْحَقِّ وَإِنَّكَ لَمِنَ ٱلْمُرْسَلِينَ ۞ تِلْكَ ٱلرُّسُلُ فَضَّلْنَا بَعْضَهُمْ عَلَىٰ بَعْضٍ مِّنْهُم مَّن كَلَّمَ ٱللَّهُ وَرَفَعَ بَعْضَهُمْ دَرَجَٰتٍ وَءَاتَيْنَا عِيسَى ٱبْنَ مَرْيَمَ ٱلْبَيِّنَٰتِ وَأَيَّدْنَٰهُ بِرُوحِ ٱلْقُدُسِ وَلَوْ شَآءَ ٱللَّهُ مَا ٱقْتَتَلَ ٱلَّذِينَ مِنۢ بَعْدِهِم مِّنۢ بَعْدِ مَا جَآءَتْهُمُ ٱلْبَيِّنَٰتُ وَلَٰكِنِ ٱخْتَلَفُوا۟ فَمِنْهُم مَّنْ ءَامَنَ وَمِنْهُم مَّن كَفَرَ وَلَوْ شَآءَ ٱللَّهُ مَا ٱقْتَتَلُوا۟ وَلَٰكِنَّ ٱللَّهَ يَفْعَلُ مَا يُرِيدُ ۞

ᵃ Literally 'We favoured some above others'.

ᵇ When God sends one of his messenger to bring the truth to mankind, his call is marked by signs so unmistakable that his congregation has no difficulty in recognizing his message to be from God. Yet, in spite of this, people give no credence to his words. The first to deny God's messenger are those who are followers of past prophets. Each prophet received certain special favours from God in order to facilitate the communication of his message according to the varying exigencies of the different historical periods in which he lived. But the followers, attaching too much importance to the miracle bestowed by God on a particular prophet, came to believe that their particular prophet was superior to all others. They felt that none could surpass the prophet they believed in. They consequently saw no reason to listen to the contemporary prophet whose name had yet to be hallowed by tradition.

For instance, believers in Moses rejected Jesus. Followers of the latter disbelieved in the Prophet Muhammad. In the case of Moses, his followers held him to be greater than all other prophets, because he had had the distinction of being addressed directly by God. Believers in Jesus considered him peerless, because he had been born to a virgin mother.

Those who have come to reform and revitalize the Muslim community since the passing of the Final Prophet have fared no better. They have been treated with total irreverence, as creatures of no account whatsoever, for the simple reason ▶

²⁵⁴ Believers, spend out of what We have given you, before the Day comes when there will be neither trading, friendship nor intercession. Truly, it is those who deny the truth who are the wrongdoers.ᵃ

يَـٰٓأَيُّهَا ٱلَّذِينَ ءَامَنُوٓا۟ أَنفِقُوا۟ مِمَّا رَزَقْنَـٰكُم مِّن قَبْلِ أَن يَأْتِىَ يَوْمٌ لَّا بَيْعٌ فِيهِ وَلَا خُلَّةٌ وَلَا شَفَـٰعَةٌ وَٱلْكَـٰفِرُونَ هُمُ ٱلظَّـٰلِمُونَ ۝

that their contemporaries believed themselves to be successors of earlier saints and thus were in no need of further religious counselling, particularly by someone who appeared to be inferior to their own predecessors.

When communities begin to go into a decline, they become preoccupied with wordly interests, yet they do not wish to forfeit their 'right' to salvation, and as a form of psychological defence, attach themselves mentally to hallowed religious personalities. They fondly imagine that the lofty status of their saintly patrons will ensure their redemption in the next world, no matter how unethical their conduct might have been in this world.

It is this false sense of security which gives such people the audacity to oppose those who call them to God. It is imaginable that God might have arranged human destiny in such a way that man, having no freedom to demur, was obliged invariably to bow to His will. But this was not part of God's scheme for mankind. God gave man freedom of action in order to put him to the divine test: He wished to see if man could find his way to his Maker, while He Himself remained invisible. For this reason, man is required to be able to recognize the word of God, albeit uttered by the human tongue, and to penetrate the veil of outward forms in order to reach the hidden, inner truth.

ᵃ Only one who spends for the cause of God finds God. When he finds Him, he comes into possession of a light which leads him on to the straight and undeviating path to paradise—the final destination of a true believer. On the other hand, one who wants God without paying this price, remains in darkness forever.

'Spending for God's cause' relates here to any kind of sacrifice made for the sake of God, and not merely to spending one's wealth: for instance, devoting one's life to the cause of God; sacrificing one's material interests and considerations to go ahead along God's path. When one accepts an ideology at the cost of sacrifice, then it shows that one is sincere about it. Sincerity is a matter of great importance, for, regardless of the issue, it is only when one is sincere that one can delve deeply into the subject; then all its secrets are laid bare before one. It is this element of sincerity that enables a real relationship to be created between the man and his goal. In consequence, all the aspects of that goal are revealed to him.

²⁵⁵ God: there is no deity save Him, the Living, the Eternal One. Neither slumber nor sleep overtakes Him. To Him belong whatsoever is in the heavens and whatsoever is on the earth. Who can intercede with Him except by His permission? He knows all that is before them and all that is behind them. They can grasp only that part of His knowledge which He wills. His throne extends over the heavens and the earth; and their upholding does not weary Him. He is the Sublime, the Almighty One! ²⁵⁶ There shall be no compulsion in religion: true guidance has become distinct from error. But whoever refuses to be led by Satan and believes in God has grasped the strong handhold that will never break. God is all hearing and all knowing. ²⁵⁷ God is the patron of the faithful. He leads them from darkness to the light. As for those who deny the truth, their supporter is Satan, who brings them out of light into darkness. They are the heirs of the Fire, and there they will remain forever.ᵃ

ٱللَّهُ لَآ إِلَـٰهَ إِلَّا هُوَ ٱلْحَىُّ ٱلْقَيُّومُ لَا تَأْخُذُهُ سِنَةٌ وَلَا نَوْمٌ لَّهُ مَا فِى ٱلسَّمَـٰوَٰتِ وَمَا فِى ٱلْأَرْضِ مَن ذَا ٱلَّذِى يَشْفَعُ عِندَهُ إِلَّا بِإِذْنِهِ يَعْلَمُ مَا بَيْنَ أَيْدِيهِمْ وَمَا خَلْفَهُمْ وَلَا يُحِيطُونَ بِشَىْءٍ مِّنْ عِلْمِهِ إِلَّا بِمَا شَآءَ وَسِعَ كُرْسِيُّهُ ٱلسَّمَـٰوَٰتِ وَٱلْأَرْضَ وَلَا يَـُٔودُهُ حِفْظُهُمَا وَهُوَ ٱلْعَلِىُّ ٱلْعَظِيمُ ۝ لَآ إِكْرَاهَ فِى ٱلدِّينِ قَد تَّبَيَّنَ ٱلرُّشْدُ مِنَ ٱلْغَىِّ فَمَن يَكْفُرْ بِٱلطَّـٰغُوتِ وَيُؤْمِن بِٱللَّهِ فَقَدِ ٱسْتَمْسَكَ بِٱلْعُرْوَةِ ٱلْوُثْقَىٰ لَا ٱنفِصَامَ لَهَا وَٱللَّهُ سَمِيعٌ عَلِيمٌ ۝ ٱللَّهُ وَلِىُّ ٱلَّذِينَ ءَامَنُوا يُخْرِجُهُم مِّنَ ٱلظُّلُمَـٰتِ إِلَى ٱلنُّورِ وَٱلَّذِينَ كَفَرُوٓا أَوْلِيَآؤُهُمُ ٱلطَّـٰغُوتُ يُخْرِجُونَهُم مِّنَ ٱلنُّورِ إِلَى ٱلظُّلُمَـٰتِ أُو۟لَـٰٓئِكَ أَصْحَـٰبُ ٱلنَّارِ هُمْ فِيهَا خَـٰلِدُونَ ۝

ᵃ Unlike sincere devotees, there are some who never accept religion at the cost of the surrender of their being. They are never serious in matters of religion, and as a result believe that intercession by certain religious seers or the performance of certain rituals, or the observance of certain forms is enough to earn salvation in the Hereafter. Due to their insincerity about the Hereafter, they fail to understand that Doomsday is the Day of the manifestation of God's power and majesty. Hoping that the performance of certain superficial rituals might earn them God Almighty's pleasure is indeed an underestimation of God's divinity. This only increases their sinfulness in the eyes of God. The truth comes to one in the form of arguments, and one who is not sincere summarily rejects them. This is one of Satan's temptations. Guidance comes only to those who scrupulously resist Satan's temptations and, recognizing the divine arguments, wholeheartedly concur in them.

²⁵⁸ Have you not heard of him who argued with Abraham about his Lord because God had bestowed the kingdom upon him? Abraham said, 'My Lord is the one who gives life and brings death.' He answered, 'I [too] give life and bring death!' Abraham said, 'God brings up the sun from the east, so bring it up yourself from the west.' Then the disbeliever was confounded. God does not guide the wrongdoers.ᵃ

أَلَمْ تَرَ إِلَى ٱلَّذِى حَآجَّ إِبْرَٰهِـۧمَ فِى رَبِّهِۦٓ أَنْ ءَاتَىٰهُ ٱللَّهُ ٱلْمُلْكَ إِذْ قَالَ إِبْرَٰهِـۧمُ رَبِّىَ ٱلَّذِى يُحْىِۦ وَيُمِيتُ قَالَ أَنَا۠ أُحْىِۦ وَأُمِيتُ قَالَ إِبْرَٰهِـۧمُ فَإِنَّ ٱللَّهَ يَأْتِى بِٱلشَّمْسِ مِنَ ٱلْمَشْرِقِ فَأْتِ بِهَا مِنَ ٱلْمَغْرِبِ فَبُهِتَ ٱلَّذِى كَفَرَ وَٱللَّهُ لَا يَهْدِى ٱلْقَوْمَ ٱلظَّٰلِمِينَ ۝

ᵃ In the modern age, the right to govern a people is secured by popular support. However, that was not the case in pre-democratic times, when kings sanctioned their rule over their subjects by laying claim to being some kind of divine incarnation. Nimrod, a king of ancient Iraq, was a case in point. A contemporary of Abraham, he was one of those monarchs who used this method to back up his right of sovereignty over the people. The sun was believed by his people to be the Chief of the gods and was thus revered by them as an object of worship. Nimrod claimed that he was an incarnation of the sun-god, a position which gave him a divine right to worldly sovereignty. When Abraham preached the message of the One God in the land of Iraq, his teachings had no direct connection with politics or government in the country. All he did was to impress upon the people that there was but One God; He was their sole Lord and Master. There were no partners with Him in the godhead, so mankind should worship Him alone, fearing Him and placing their hopes in Him. Though Abraham's message was apolitical, it nevertheless appeared to Nimrod as a threat to his political claims, for according to the message taught by Abraham, even the sun was part of God's creation. It had no power of its own, but was controlled by God Almighty. Had his subjects accepted Abraham's message of the One God, it would have amounted to demolishing the theological base on which the edifice of his political power rested. It was for this reason that Nimrod turned vehemently against Abraham and his teachings.

The dialogue conducted between Abraham and Nimrod shows us the method adopted by the prophets in the communication of their message. First of all, Abraham pointed out that his Lord had control over life and death. Immediately, Nimrod disputed this, claiming himself to have power over life and death. Abraham, of course, could have answered this claim made by Nimrod, but he did not want the conversation to deteriorate into a heated polemical discussion. So, instead of persisting with this point, he changed the subject and chose another example, one with which Nimrod would not be able to argue. Abraham did not consider Nimrod his enemy or rival. ▶

²⁵⁹ Or of him who, when passing by a town the roofs of which had caved in, exclaimed, 'How will God restore it to life after its destruction?' Thereupon God caused him to die, and after a hundred years, brought him back to life. God asked, 'How long have you remained in this state?' He answered, 'I have remained a day or part of a day.' God said, 'No, you have remained in this state for a hundred years. Now look at your food and your drink; they have not rotted. Look at your ass. We will make you a sign to mankind. Look at the bones—how We set them together, then clothe them with flesh!' When it had all become clear to him, he said, 'Now I know that God has power over all things.'

أَوْ كَٱلَّذِى مَرَّ عَلَىٰ قَرْيَةٍ وَهِىَ خَاوِيَةٌ عَلَىٰ عُرُوشِهَا قَالَ أَنَّىٰ يُحْىِۦ هَـٰذِهِ ٱللَّهُ بَعْدَ مَوْتِهَا ۖ فَأَمَاتَهُ ٱللَّهُ مِائَةَ عَامٍ ثُمَّ بَعَثَهُ ۖ قَالَ كَمْ لَبِثْتَ ۖ قَالَ لَبِثْتُ يَوْمًا أَوْ بَعْضَ يَوْمٍ ۖ قَالَ بَل لَّبِثْتَ مِائَةَ عَامٍ فَٱنظُرْ إِلَىٰ طَعَامِكَ وَشَرَابِكَ لَمْ يَتَسَنَّهْ ۖ وَٱنظُرْ إِلَىٰ حِمَارِكَ وَلِنَجْعَلَكَ ءَايَةً لِّلنَّاسِ ۖ وَٱنظُرْ إِلَى ٱلْعِظَامِ كَيْفَ نُنشِزُهَا ثُمَّ نَكْسُوهَا لَحْمًا ۚ فَلَمَّا تَبَيَّنَ لَهُۥ قَالَ أَعْلَمُ أَنَّ ٱللَّهَ عَلَىٰ كُلِّ شَىْءٍ قَدِيرٌ ۝

Rather, he had compassion for him as a *madu'* (addressee) and earnestly wished to communicate to him the message of Truth. It was this compassion which showed Abraham the correct method to be adopted in addressing the Iraqi king.

Since the present world is a place where man is being tested, there are always different options open to everyone. This causes people to construe situations in different ways. For instance, should one be endowed with worldly wealth and power, one may consider these to be a personal success, the outcome of one's own talent. One may, on the other hand, look at them purely as blessings from God. The former way of seeing things amounts to grave injustice, while the latter shows a grateful disposition. For one who is thankless in his outlook, everything in this world will only serve to lead him further astray. Everything he experiences will only add to his pride and conceit. But for those who are grateful for what they have been given, everything they experience in this world leads them closer to God. The world, and all that it contains, serves to stimulate their faith in God.

²⁶⁰ When Abraham said, 'Show me, my Lord, how You revive the dead!' God said, 'Do you not believe?' Abraham answered, 'Yes, indeed I do believe, but just to reassure my heart.' Then God said, 'Take four birds, and train them to come back to you. Then place them separately on each hilltop, and call them: they will come flying to you. Know that God is almighty and wise.'[a]

وَإِذْ قَالَ إِبْرَٰهِـۧمُ رَبِّ أَرِنِي كَيْفَ تُحْىِ ٱلْمَوْتَىٰ قَالَ أَوَلَمْ تُؤْمِن قَالَ بَلَىٰ وَلَٰكِن لِّيَطْمَئِنَّ قَلْبِى قَالَ فَخُذْ أَرْبَعَةً مِّنَ ٱلطَّيْرِ فَصُرْهُنَّ إِلَيْكَ ثُمَّ ٱجْعَلْ عَلَىٰ كُلِّ جَبَلٍ مِّنْهُنَّ جُزْءًا ثُمَّ ٱدْعُهُنَّ يَأْتِينَكَ سَعْيًا ۚ وَٱعْلَمْ أَنَّ ٱللَّهَ عَزِيزٌ حَكِيمٌ ۝

---

[a] The two experiences of resurrection after death mentioned here relate to the prophets. It is generally thought that in the first incident, the prophet in question was Ezra (Uzayr) (5th century BC), while in the second, as the Quran itself makes clear, it was Abraham, who lived between the years 2160 and 1985 BC. Prophets are sent by God in order to inform mankind of realities which, for ordinary people, lie beyond the realm of human vision, being screened by a veil of cause and effect. This veil is removed, however, in the case of the prophets, since it is their task to inform others of these realities. This can be done with far greater conviction if they have actually witnessed with their own eyes the facts which they attempt to convey to the rest of mankind. Their hearers, also, are more likely to believe in their message, rather than treating it purely as hearsay.

Prophets have generally been endowed with prophethood around the age of forty. Prior to this, they have shown impeccable honesty in their dealings with their fellows. Having provided practical proof of their truthfulness, the time then came for them to inform mankind of those realities of life which God, in order to test men, has kept hidden from them. These truthful human beings, known as prophets, communicated to mankind the message revealed to them by God, while providing evidence based on nature and reason to back up their teachings. The prophets have always been fully sincere in what they taught. It is shown by the fact that they themselves have never wavered from the truth, despite the severe hardships which they had to endure as a result of following this course. If they had simply concocted their message, they would not have proved so persistent in their adherence to it, for the mendacious usually crack under pressure and abandon the subject. Neither does something, which has been formulated by the human mind, as opposed to being inspired by God, conform so perfectly to the phenomena of the outside world.

²⁶¹ Those who spend their wealth for God's cause may be compared to a grain of corn which sprouts into seven ears, with a hundred grains in each ear: for God grants manifold increase to whom He wills;ᵃ God is infinite and all knowing. ²⁶² Those who spend their wealth for God's cause and do not follow their almsgiving with taunts and insults shall be rewarded by their Lord;ᵇ they shall have no fear, nor shall they grieve.

مَّثَلُ ٱلَّذِينَ يُنفِقُونَ أَمْوَٰلَهُمْ فِى سَبِيلِ ٱللَّهِ كَمَثَلِ حَبَّةٍ أَنۢبَتَتْ سَبْعَ سَنَابِلَ فِى كُلِّ سُنۢبُلَةٍ مِّائَةُ حَبَّةٍ وَٱللَّهُ يُضَٰعِفُ لِمَن يَشَآءُ وَٱللَّهُ وَٰسِعٌ عَلِيمٌ ۝ ٱلَّذِينَ يُنفِقُونَ أَمْوَٰلَهُمْ فِى سَبِيلِ ٱللَّهِ ثُمَّ لَا يُتْبِعُونَ مَآ أَنفَقُواْ مَنًّا وَلَآ أَذًى لَّهُمْ أَجْرُهُمْ عِندَ رَبِّهِمْ وَلَا خَوْفٌ عَلَيْهِمْ وَلَا هُمْ يَحْزَنُونَ ۝

ᵃ Every act committed by man is like a seed planted in the ground. If one does something in order to be admired by others, it is as though one is planting a seed in the earth of this world. If, on the other hand, one acts in order to please God, then one has sown a seed in the everlasting fields of the Hereafter, where it will blossom and bear fruit. In this world, one seed produces a thousand grains of corn. Likewise in the harvest of the Hereafter, man will reap rewards far in excess of what he has sown.

ᵇ One who spends his wealth in order to gain worldly fame and prestige, and who seeks to be recompensed in this ephemeral world, will have no share in the rewards of the life everlasting. Those who spend for the cause of God, on the other hand, adopt a different approach. They do not, for one, taunt their beneficiaries with reminders of the favours they have bestowed. Indeed, having spent from their wealth for the cause of God, they do not consider themselves to have bestowed any favour at all upon anyone. And they do not show any displeasure if a gracious response is not forthcoming from those to whom they have been generous. ▶

²⁶³ A kind word and forgiveness is better than a charitable deed followed by hurtful words: God is self-sufficient and forbearing. ²⁶⁴ Believers, do not cancel out your charitable deeds with reminders and hurtful words, like one who spends his wealth only to be seen by people, and not believing in God and the Last Day. Such men are like a rock covered with earth: a shower falls upon it and leaves it hard and bare.ᵃ They will gain nothing from their works. God does not guide those who deny the truth.

۞ قَوْلٌ مَّعْرُوفٌ وَمَغْفِرَةٌ خَيْرٌ مِّن صَدَقَةٍ يَتْبَعُهَآ أَذًى ۗ وَٱللَّهُ غَنِيٌّ حَلِيمٌ ﴿٢٦٣﴾ يَٰٓأَيُّهَا ٱلَّذِينَ ءَامَنُوا۟ لَا تُبْطِلُوا۟ صَدَقَٰتِكُم بِٱلْمَنِّ وَٱلْأَذَىٰ كَٱلَّذِى يُنفِقُ مَالَهُۥ رِئَآءَ ٱلنَّاسِ وَلَا يُؤْمِنُ بِٱللَّهِ وَٱلْيَوْمِ ٱلْءَاخِرِ ۖ فَمَثَلُهُۥ كَمَثَلِ صَفْوَانٍ عَلَيْهِ تُرَابٌ فَأَصَابَهُۥ وَابِلٌ فَتَرَكَهُۥ صَلْدًا ۖ لَّا يَقْدِرُونَ عَلَىٰ شَىْءٍ مِّمَّا كَسَبُوا۟ ۗ وَٱللَّهُ لَا يَهْدِى ٱلْقَوْمَ ٱلْكَٰفِرِينَ ﴿٢٦٤﴾

This is because their hopes are pinned on being rewarded in full by God, so what do they care if human beings show appreciation or not? Moreover, if they are unable to accede to a request for monetary assistance, at least they do not rebuff the suppliant. Instead, they find kind words with which to excuse themselves, for they know that God hears everything they say. Their fear of God makes them circumspect in the choice of words they utter to their fellow human beings.

ᵃ Some soil (earth) may collect on the surface of a boulder. Outwardly, it appears as though this is good, fertile soil, but when a gust of wind brings a rain-shower down upon it, then the earth is washed away, leaving the rock exposed to the elements. The same is true of one who has donned a superficial robe of piety, without that piety having permeated his entire being. Should he be addressed rudely by someone asking for financial help, or should his ego receive a wounding blow, he becomes so irritated that he exceeds all bounds of decency in his response. Incidents of this nature are like the showers of rain which wash away his outward garb of piety, leaving his true nature exposed to the outside world.

To do things for God's sake, is to give priority to the invisible over the visible world. It is to set one's sights on an unseen world, over and above the world which meets the eye. This requires a loftiness of vision. Those who show such sublimity of vision have the door of God's realization opened to them.

²⁶⁵ But those who spend their wealth in order to gain God's approval, and to strengthen their souls are like a garden on elevated ground. When heavy rain falls on it, it doubles its produce; and if heavy rain does not fall, then light rain suffices. God sees what you do.ᵃ

وَمَثَلُ ٱلَّذِينَ يُنفِقُونَ أَمْوَٰلَهُمُ ٱبْتِغَآءَ مَرْضَاتِ ٱللَّهِ وَتَثْبِيتًا مِّنْ أَنفُسِهِمْ كَمَثَلِ جَنَّةٍ بِرَبْوَةٍ أَصَابَهَا وَابِلٌ فَآتَتْ أُكُلَهَا ضِعْفَيْنِ فَإِن لَّمْ يُصِبْهَا وَابِلٌ فَطَلٌّ وَٱللَّهُ بِمَا تَعْمَلُونَ بَصِيرٌ ﴿٢٦٥﴾

ᵃ If an individual has some goal in mind, his own striving towards the attainment of that goal further strengthens his will-power and increases the mental resolve which enables him to reach his objective. Should it be the objects of his own desires towards which his efforts are directed, then the more he exerts himself, the more he will set his heart on them. However, should it be the will of God that holds pride of place in determining his actions, then it will be God on whom his heart is set. One acts at all events under conditions which are sometimes difficult and sometimes comparatively easy. But the more difficult the conditions one encounters, the greater will be the increase in one's will-power and the stronger one's connection to that on which one's heart is set. One who spends for the cause of God under normal conditions will certainly have his reward from God. However, when spending for God's cause is done in adverse circumstances, which call for a special exercise of will-power, the reward which God grants on such occasions will be commensurately greater. For instance, if the outlay of one's wealth is done on something from which no worldly benefit will be forthcoming, then in that case it is done solely for the sake of God. Then one may have to give to a person to whom one would rather not give anything. Again it is done just to please God. One may have a grudge against someone, yet one still extends to him the hand of friendship. All these acts strengthen one's bond with the Lord, opening the way to His special grace and succour.

²⁶⁶ Would any of you, being a man well advanced in age with helpless children to support, like to have a garden of dates and grapes, watered by rivers and containing all kinds of fruits, stricken by a fiery whirlwind and utterly scorched? Thus God makes His signs clear to you, so that you may reflect.ᵃ

أَيَوَدُّ أَحَدُكُمْ أَن تَكُونَ لَهُ جَنَّةٌ مِّن نَّخِيلٍ وَأَعْنَابٍ تَجْرِى مِن تَحْتِهَا ٱلْأَنْهَارُ لَهُ فِيهَا مِن كُلِّ ٱلثَّمَرَٰتِ وَأَصَابَهُ ٱلْكِبَرُ وَلَهُ ذُرِّيَّةٌ ضُعَفَآءُ فَأَصَابَهَآ إِعْصَارٌ فِيهِ نَارٌ فَٱحْتَرَقَتْ كَذَٰلِكَ يُبَيِّنُ ٱللَّهُ لَكُمُ ٱلْءَايَٰتِ لَعَلَّكُمْ تَتَفَكَّرُونَ ﴿٢٦٦﴾

ᵃ When an individual plants an orchard in his youth, he does so in the hope that he will enjoy its fruits when he grows old. How unfortunate, then, is one who sees his beautiful orchard reduced to rubble towards the end of his days, just when he stands in greatest need of it. Now time has run out on him and he has no chance of nurturing new saplings. This is exactly what will happen to those who engage themselves in a religious cause, purely out of lust for worldly prestige and profit. Outwardly, they appear to be engaged in pious works, but it is only in their form that their actions differ from those of the run-of-the-mill materialists of this world. In reality, there is no difference between the two types of people. Normally, people seeking worldly fame and prestige, choose worldly means of attaining their goals, whereas hypocritical people choose religious means of advancement towards the same worldly ends. All are aiming at the same mundane goals; only the ways in which they go about achieving them are different. People guided by worldly motives in all their actions will find no reward awaiting them in the Hereafter. God's signs take an abtruse form. Only those who cultivate in themselves a capacity for reflection are able to decipher these signs and, through them, come to know God.

267 Believers, give charitably from the good things which you have earned and what We produce for you from the earth; not worthless things which you yourselves would only reluctantly accept. Know that God is self-sufficient and praiseworthy. 268 Satan threatens you with the prospect of poverty and commands you to do foul deeds. But God promises His forgiveness and His bounty. God is bountiful and all knowing.[a]

يَٰٓأَيُّهَا ٱلَّذِينَ ءَامَنُوٓا۟ أَنفِقُوا۟ مِن طَيِّبَٰتِ مَا كَسَبْتُمْ وَمِمَّآ أَخْرَجْنَا لَكُم مِّنَ ٱلْأَرْضِ ۖ وَلَا تَيَمَّمُوا۟ ٱلْخَبِيثَ مِنْهُ تُنفِقُونَ وَلَسْتُم بِـَٔاخِذِيهِ إِلَّآ أَن تُغْمِضُوا۟ فِيهِ ۚ وَٱعْلَمُوٓا۟ أَنَّ ٱللَّهَ غَنِىٌّ حَمِيدٌ ۝ ٱلشَّيْطَٰنُ يَعِدُكُمُ ٱلْفَقْرَ وَيَأْمُرُكُم بِٱلْفَحْشَآءِ ۖ وَٱللَّهُ يَعِدُكُم مَّغْفِرَةً مِّنْهُ وَفَضْلًا ۗ وَٱللَّهُ وَٰسِعٌ عَلِيمٌ ۝

[a] There are two ways of spending one's earnings in this world. One is to spend in ways shown by Satan. Another is to spend in ways shown by God. What Satan does is to impress on the minds of human beings the importance of personal requirements, and bring about conviction that all their earnings are best spent on personal comforts and luxuries. When Satan sees that any individual has more wealth than is necessary for his personal needs, he kindles in him another desire, that of indulging in showy activities. At the instigation of Satan, man spends all his money on ostentatious living and feels happy that he has spent his money in the best possible way.

What is desired of man is that he should not regard his wealth as his personal possession but rather as something that belongs only to God. He should spend as much of his wealth as is necessary for his actual needs and the rest he should spend on achieving higher goals. He should give this surplus wealth to the weaker of God's servants and also spend for the cause of God's religion. When he spends for the weaker section of society, he hopes that in the Hereafter, when he appears empty-handed before God, he will not be deprived of God's blessings. Similarly, when he spends his wealth for the cause of God's religion, he allies himself with God's mission.

²⁶⁹ He grants wisdom to whom He will; and whoever is granted wisdom has indeed been granted abundant wealth. Yet none bear this in mind except those endowed with understanding.

²⁷⁰ Whatever you spend and whatever vows you make are known to God, but the wrongdoers shall have no helpers. ²⁷¹ If you give charity openly, it is good, but if you keep it secret and give to the needy in private, that is better for you, and it will atone for some of your bad deeds. God is aware of all that you do. ²⁷² It is not your responsibility to make them follow the right path; God guides whomever He pleases. Whatever wealth you spend is to your own benefit, provided that you spend only to seek the favour of God. Whatever wealth you spend [for God's cause] shall be repaid to you in full and you shall not be wronged.ᵃ

يُؤۡتِى ٱلۡحِكۡمَةَ مَن يَشَآءُ ۚ وَمَن يُؤۡتَ ٱلۡحِكۡمَةَ فَقَدۡ أُوتِىَ خَيۡرٗا كَثِيرٗا ۗ وَمَا يَذَّكَّرُ إِلَّآ أُوْلُواْ ٱلۡأَلۡبَٰبِ ﴿٢٦٩﴾ وَمَآ أَنفَقۡتُم مِّن نَّفَقَةٍ أَوۡ نَذَرۡتُم مِّن نَّذۡرٖ فَإِنَّ ٱللَّهَ يَعۡلَمُهُۥ ۗ وَمَا لِلظَّٰلِمِينَ مِنۡ أَنصَارٍ ﴿٢٧٠﴾ إِن تُبۡدُواْ ٱلصَّدَقَٰتِ فَنِعِمَّا هِىَ ۖ وَإِن تُخۡفُوهَا وَتُؤۡتُوهَا ٱلۡفُقَرَآءَ فَهُوَ خَيۡرٞ لَّكُمۡ ۚ وَيُكَفِّرُ عَنكُم مِّن سَيِّـَٔاتِكُمۡ ۗ وَٱللَّهُ بِمَا تَعۡمَلُونَ خَبِيرٞ ﴿٢٧١﴾ ۞ لَّيۡسَ عَلَيۡكَ هُدَىٰهُمۡ وَلَٰكِنَّ ٱللَّهَ يَهۡدِى مَن يَشَآءُ ۗ وَمَا تُنفِقُواْ مِنۡ خَيۡرٖ فَلِأَنفُسِكُمۡ ۚ وَمَا تُنفِقُونَ إِلَّا ٱبۡتِغَآءَ وَجۡهِ ٱللَّهِ ۚ وَمَا تُنفِقُواْ مِنۡ خَيۡرٖ يُوَفَّ إِلَيۡكُمۡ وَأَنتُمۡ لَا تُظۡلَمُونَ ﴿٢٧٢﴾

ᵃ One who spends his money for the sake of God in the way that He has commanded him to do, proves that he has been blessed with wisdom. Wisdom here means knowledge and understanding of the Quran. The biggest folly is to be so enamoured of one's wealth that one fails to spend for the cause of God, and the greatest wisdom lies in recognizing that monetary interests do not present any obstacle to one's engaging oneself in God's work. One should consider God's cause as one's own. One who lives within the cocoon of personal interests and considerations cannot possess the insight which would enable him to see higher realities and experience higher states of consciousness. On the contrary, one who goes ahead towards God by ignoring all personal considerations raises himself above all limitations. His consciousness reaches the divine level of God, who is independent (free from all wants), praiseworthy, all-sufficient, and wise.

Man is thus enabled to see things as they are. For he goes beyond the limitations which serve as obstacles to seeing things in their true form. However true any argument may be, its truth dawns upon one only when one can see it with an open mind.

²⁷³ The needy, who are too engrossed in God's cause to be able to travel about the land in search of a livelihood, are considered by those who are unaware of their condition to be free from want, because they refrain from begging. But they can be known from their appearance. They do not make insistent demands upon people. Whatever wealth you spend, God knows it. ²⁷⁴ Those who spend their wealth night and day, both privately and publicly, will receive their reward from their Lord. They shall have no fear, nor shall they grieve.ᵃ

لِلْفُقَرَآءِ ٱلَّذِينَ أُحْصِرُوا۟ فِى سَبِيلِ ٱللَّهِ لَا يَسْتَطِيعُونَ ضَرْبًا فِى ٱلْأَرْضِ يَحْسَبُهُمُ ٱلْجَاهِلُ أَغْنِيَآءَ مِنَ ٱلتَّعَفُّفِ تَعْرِفُهُم بِسِيمَٰهُمْ لَا يَسْـَٔلُونَ ٱلنَّاسَ إِلْحَافًا وَمَا تُنفِقُوا۟ مِنْ خَيْرٍ فَإِنَّ ٱللَّهَ بِهِۦ عَلِيمٌ ٢٧٣ ٱلَّذِينَ يُنفِقُونَ أَمْوَٰلَهُم بِٱلَّيْلِ وَٱلنَّهَارِ سِرًّا وَعَلَانِيَةً فَلَهُمْ أَجْرُهُمْ عِندَ رَبِّهِمْ وَلَا خَوْفٌ عَلَيْهِمْ وَلَا هُمْ يَحْزَنُونَ ٢٧٤

ᵃ The greatest way to spend money for the cause of God is to extend monetary help to those of God's servants who have devoted themselves wholly to the cause of His religion, thus leaving themselves no time to earn for their personal needs. Just as a successful businessman has little free time for anything except his business, similarly one who serves the cause of religion full time has no time to work to make money for himself. Furthermore, each job shapes in a particular way the thinking of the person involved. One who involves himself in business develops the relevant skills, so that he is able to easily understand the complexities of commerce. But that same person will not be able to understand the nuances of religion's cause. Similarly, a religious worker will not be able to successfully run a business, for he cannot concentrate on business matters due to his attention being diverted elsewhere. However, a society needs both kinds of activities. The solution to this problem is for those who possess monetary resources to arrange a share for those who, because of their religious commitments, are unable to provide for their own economic needs. This is like a tacit division of labour, which takes place between the two groups purely in order to earn God's pleasure. The missionary, having devoted himself to God, does not ask anything from others, nor does he expect anything from them. On the other hand, those who are monetarily strong, knowing that they have amassed wealth through not devoting themselves to the cause of religion (which they should have done), think that they should, by way of compensation, give a share of their wealth to their brothers in faith.

Spending for a peaceful religious struggle which brings no fame or laurels makes one all the more deserving of God's blessings. For such spending is only to seek God's pleasure.

275 Those who live on usury shall rise up before God like men whom Satan has demented by his touch; for they say, 'Buying and selling is only a kind of usury.'[a] But God has made trade lawful and made usury unlawful. Therefore, he who desists because of the admonition that has come to him from his Lord may retain what he has received in the past; and it will be for God to judge him. Those who revert to it shall be the inmates of the Fire; they shall abide therein forever.[b]

ٱلَّذِينَ يَأْكُلُونَ ٱلرِّبَوٰا۟ لَا يَقُومُونَ إِلَّا كَمَا يَقُومُ ٱلَّذِى يَتَخَبَّطُهُ ٱلشَّيْطَٰنُ مِنَ ٱلْمَسِّ ذَٰلِكَ بِأَنَّهُمْ قَالُوٓا۟ إِنَّمَا ٱلْبَيْعُ مِثْلُ ٱلرِّبَوٰا۟ وَأَحَلَّ ٱللَّهُ ٱلْبَيْعَ وَحَرَّمَ ٱلرِّبَوٰا۟ فَمَن جَآءَهُۥ مَوْعِظَةٌ مِّن رَّبِّهِۦ فَٱنتَهَىٰ فَلَهُۥ مَا سَلَفَ وَأَمْرُهُۥٓ إِلَى ٱللَّهِ وَمَنْ عَادَ فَأُو۟لَٰٓئِكَ أَصْحَٰبُ ٱلنَّارِ هُمْ فِيهَا خَٰلِدُونَ ﴿٢٧٥﴾

[a] The word 'riba' in the original is translated here as 'usury', which means the practice of lending money to people at unfairly high rates of interest.

[b] The injunction to give alms (zakat) symbolizes the economic relationship between God's servants. Alms-giving means recognizing one another's rights, and going to the extent of giving a share in one's own income to one's fellow men.

A religion which aims at creating a worthwhile social set-up can never accept a money-loving society based on usury. In a well-ordered society, mutual exchanges take place according to the rules of business and not on the principle of usury. Business may be based on the principle of profit-making, but profit comes as a result of hard work and at the cost of taking risks. But profit coming from usury betokens selfishness and hoarding.

One who deals in usury does so to increase his wealth without there being any risk of loss involved. The personality developed in this process is selfish and materially-minded. A believer, on the contrary, does not make a profit out of others' needs. Rather he shares his wealth with them. The personality developed in such a person is totally different from that of the usurer, for the believer is a well-wisher of his fellow men and he rises above the sphere of his own interests.

276 God blights usury and blesses charitable deeds. God does not love the ungrateful wrongdoer. 277 Those who believe, do good deeds, attend to their prayers and engage in almsgiving, shall be rewarded by their Lord and shall have no fear, nor shall they grieve.[a]

يَمۡحَقُ ٱللَّهُ ٱلرِّبَوٰاْ وَيُرۡبِي ٱلصَّدَقَٰتِۗ وَٱللَّهُ لَا يُحِبُّ كُلَّ كَفَّارٍ أَثِيمٍ ۞ إِنَّ ٱلَّذِينَ ءَامَنُواْ وَعَمِلُواْ ٱلصَّٰلِحَٰتِ وَأَقَامُواْ ٱلصَّلَوٰةَ وَءَاتَوُاْ ٱلزَّكَوٰةَ لَهُمۡ أَجۡرُهُمۡ عِندَ رَبِّهِمۡ وَلَا خَوۡفٌ عَلَيۡهِمۡ وَلَا هُمۡ يَحۡزَنُونَ ۝

---

[a] Man has not been sent into this world to hoard wealth. All the good things of this life are meant for the next world. Man has been sent into this world so that it may be judged whether or not he has developed those qualities that would qualify him to inherit the world of Paradise in the Hereafter. Those adjudged fit to dwell in Paradise will be separated from the unfit, and the latter will be consigned to hell.

Practicing charity (*sadaqah*) means giving one's wealth to the needy for the sake of God, while engaging in usury means giving one's wealth in order to exploit others. *Sadaqah* is an indication of the fact that man wants to see the massive array of God's blessings in the next world, whereas usury is indicative of the fact that he wants to amass fortunes in this world itself. The alms-giver and the usurer are two different types of individuals. It is not possible that they will both have the same fate in the Hereafter. Only those find the world who have worked hard for it; similarly, only those will find the Hereafter who have sacrificed their wealth in order to receive God's blessings in the Hereafter.

278 Believers, have fear of God, and give up what is still due to you from usury, if you are true believers. 279 For, if you do not do so, then know that you are at war with God and His Messenger. But if you repent, you may retain your capital. Do not wrong [others] and you will not be wronged. 280 If the debtor is in straitened circumstances, then grant him respite till a time of ease. If you were to write it off as an act of charity, that would be better for you, if only you knew.*

يَـٰٓأَيُّهَا ٱلَّذِينَ ءَامَنُوا۟ ٱتَّقُوا۟ ٱللَّهَ وَذَرُوا۟ مَا بَقِىَ مِنَ ٱلرِّبَوٰٓا۟ إِن كُنتُم مُّؤْمِنِينَ ۝ فَإِن لَّمْ تَفْعَلُوا۟ فَأْذَنُوا۟ بِحَرْبٍ مِّنَ ٱللَّهِ وَرَسُولِهِۦ ۖ وَإِن تُبْتُمْ فَلَكُمْ رُءُوسُ أَمْوَٰلِكُمْ لَا تَظْلِمُونَ وَلَا تُظْلَمُونَ ۝ وَإِن كَانَ ذُو عُسْرَةٍ فَنَظِرَةٌ إِلَىٰ مَيْسَرَةٍ ۚ وَأَن تَصَدَّقُوا۟ خَيْرٌ لَّكُمْ ۖ إِن كُنتُمْ تَعْلَمُونَ ۝

---

a The basic principle of the reformation of a society is for its members to treat each other with justice. There should be neither oppressor nor oppressed. Usury is a form of open economic oppression, that is why Islam has held it unlawful. Business based on the principle of usury, if engaged in under Islamic rule, is deemed to be a criminal offence. However, just as a usurer is not allowed to make anyone the target of his economic oppression, others should also refrain from subjecting him to their oppression.

An offender in one field is not deprived of his rights in other fields. Any action taken against any usurer may consist only of withholding the interest due to him. His capital should be returned to him. While giving general commands, Islam makes full concessions to human weaknesses. That is why we have been commanded that if a debtor has fallen upon hard times, he must be granted respite till he is able to repay his debt. We have also been enjoined that if the debtor is insolvent, we should have the courage to write off his debt as charity.

One who is forbearing shall deserve a reward from God. This is beneficial in this world too. An atmosphere of mutual compassion, sympathy and well-wishing is produced which is good for all members of society.

²⁸¹ Fear the Day when you shall be made to return to God; then every soul shall be paid in full what it has earned; and they shall not be wronged.ᵃ

وَٱتَّقُواْ يَوْمًا تُرْجَعُونَ فِيهِ إِلَى ٱللَّهِ ثُمَّ تُوَفَّىٰ كُلُّ نَفْسٍ مَّا كَسَبَتْ وَهُمْ لَا يُظْلَمُونَ ۝

ᵃ However, the imposition of law alone is not a guarantee of social reforms. For a real reform it is essential that the spirit of God-fearing (*taqwa*) prevails in society. That is why, while giving legal commands, the Quran places faith, *taqwa* and the Hereafter in the foreground.

Even a secular system will run successfully only when its citizens possess the necessary national character. Similarly, the Islamic system is truly brought into being when a considerable number of its members possess the spirit of *taqwa*. National character, or *taqwa* is, in fact, another name for the willingness of the individuals to uphold the desired system. If we do not find public acceptance of a system to a certain degree, it cannot be imposed by the power of law alone. Furthermore, according to Islam, what is actually most desirable is the reform of the individual. Society is not the target of reform according to Islam. The reform of society is only a by-product. The Quran calls to faith, to *taqwa*, to genuine concern for the Hereafter. This call is realized in the individual and not in a social system. That is why the actual addressee of the Quranic call is the individual. The reform of society is in actual fact a social manifestation of the reform of a number of individuals.

²⁸²Believers, when you contract a debt for a stated term, put it down in writing; have a scribe write it down with fairness between you.ᵃ No scribe should refuse to write: let him write as God has taught him, let the debtor dictate, and let him fear God, his Lord, and not diminish [the debt] at all. If the debtor is weak in mind or body, or unable to dictate, then in fairness let his guardian dictate for him. Call in two of your men as witnesses. But if two men cannot be found, then call one man and two women out of those you approve of as witnesses, so that if one of the two women should forget the other can remind her. Let the witnesses not refuse when they are summoned. Do not be disinclined to write down your debts, be they small or large, together with the date of payment. This is more just in the sight of God; it is more reliable as testimony, and more likely to prevent doubts arising between you, unless it be ready merchandise which you give or take from hand to hand, then it will not be held against you for not writing it down. Have witnesses present whenever you trade with one another, and let no harm be done to either scribe or witness, for if you did cause them harm, it would be a crime on your part. Be mindful of God; He teaches you: He has full knowledge of everything.

يَـٰٓأَيُّهَا ٱلَّذِينَ ءَامَنُوٓا۟ إِذَا تَدَايَنتُم بِدَيْنٍ إِلَىٰٓ أَجَلٍ مُّسَمًّى فَٱكْتُبُوهُ وَلْيَكْتُب بَّيْنَكُمْ كَاتِبٌۢ بِٱلْعَدْلِ وَلَا يَأْبَ كَاتِبٌ أَن يَكْتُبَ كَمَا عَلَّمَهُ ٱللَّهُ فَلْيَكْتُبْ وَلْيُمْلِلِ ٱلَّذِى عَلَيْهِ ٱلْحَقُّ وَلْيَتَّقِ ٱللَّهَ رَبَّهُ وَلَا يَبْخَسْ مِنْهُ شَيْـًٔا فَإِن كَانَ ٱلَّذِى عَلَيْهِ ٱلْحَقُّ سَفِيهًا أَوْ ضَعِيفًا أَوْ لَا يَسْتَطِيعُ أَن يُمِلَّ هُوَ فَلْيُمْلِلْ وَلِيُّهُۥ بِٱلْعَدْلِ وَٱسْتَشْهِدُوا۟ شَهِيدَيْنِ مِن رِّجَالِكُمْ فَإِن لَّمْ يَكُونَا رَجُلَيْنِ فَرَجُلٌ وَٱمْرَأَتَانِ مِمَّن تَرْضَوْنَ مِنَ ٱلشُّهَدَآءِ أَن تَضِلَّ إِحْدَىٰهُمَا فَتُذَكِّرَ إِحْدَىٰهُمَا ٱلْأُخْرَىٰ وَلَا يَأْبَ ٱلشُّهَدَآءُ إِذَا مَا دُعُوا۟ وَلَا تَسْـَٔمُوٓا۟ أَن تَكْتُبُوهُ صَغِيرًا أَوْ كَبِيرًا إِلَىٰٓ أَجَلِهِۦ ذَٰلِكُمْ أَقْسَطُ عِندَ ٱللَّهِ وَأَقْوَمُ لِلشَّهَـٰدَةِ وَأَدْنَىٰٓ أَلَّا تَرْتَابُوٓا۟ إِلَّآ أَن تَكُونَ تِجَـٰرَةً حَاضِرَةً تُدِيرُونَهَا بَيْنَكُمْ فَلَيْسَ عَلَيْكُمْ جُنَاحٌ أَلَّا تَكْتُبُوهَا وَأَشْهِدُوٓا۟ إِذَا تَبَايَعْتُمْ وَلَا يُضَآرَّ كَاتِبٌ وَلَا شَهِيدٌ وَإِن تَفْعَلُوا۟ فَإِنَّهُۥ فُسُوقٌۢ بِكُمْ وَٱتَّقُوا۟ ٱللَّهَ وَيُعَلِّمُكُمُ ٱللَّهُ وَٱللَّهُ بِكُلِّ شَىْءٍ عَلِيمٌ ﴿٢٨٢﴾

ᵃ Where there is a cash transaction between two parties, the matter ends there itself. But contracting a debt is a different matter. In such a case, if the transaction is purely verbal, there is a possibility of differences arising due to the absence of written proof. ▶

[283] If you are on a journey and do not find any literate person, something should be handed over as security. If one of you entrusts another with something, let the trustee restore the pledge to its owner; and let him fear God, his Lord. Do not conceal testimony. If someone does conceal it, in his heart he commits a crime. God knows what you do.

۞ وَإِن كُنتُمۡ عَلَىٰ سَفَرٍ وَلَمۡ تَجِدُواْ كَاتِبًا فَرِهَٰنٌ مَّقۡبُوضَةٌۖ فَإِنۡ أَمِنَ بَعۡضُكُم بَعۡضًا فَلۡيُؤَدِّ ٱلَّذِي ٱؤۡتُمِنَ أَمَٰنَتَهُۥ وَلۡيَتَّقِ ٱللَّهَ رَبَّهُۥۗ وَلَا تَكۡتُمُواْ ٱلشَّهَٰدَةَۚ وَمَن يَكۡتُمۡهَا فَإِنَّهُۥٓ ءَاثِمٌ قَلۡبُهُۥۗ وَٱللَّهُ بِمَا تَعۡمَلُونَ عَلِيمٌ ۝

Either party will present the matter according to his own perceptions, for there is no clear or absolute basis on which a proper decision may be arrived at. As a result, differences and complaints arise between the two parties at the time of payment. The only solution is to write down the particulars of the loan and then have witnesses testify to it. If any differences arise, this document would become the basis for a final decision. For a believer this would be a strategic safeguard based on *taqwa* and justice. In abiding by the written conditions and making a proper payment of dues, he acquits himself before the people and before God.

Believers are witnesses of God's religion. Just as they are not allowed to knowingly hide anything from God, they should similarly never conceal any evidence they may possess. Concealing evidence is to nurture a criminal mentality and to shirk the role they can play in making just decisions. Man's conscience demands that the truth should be acknowledged and untruth should be proclaimed to be such. In matters of justice, one who withholds evidence for the sake of prestige or some other worldly considerations, is like a criminal who becomes a witness to his own crime.

²⁸⁴ All that the heavens and the earth contain belongs to God, whether you disclose what is in your minds or keep it hidden. God will bring you to account for it. He will forgive whom He will and punish whom He pleases: He has power over all things. ²⁸⁵ The Messenger believes in what has been sent down to him from his Lord, and [so do] believers. They all believe in God and His angels, His scriptures, and His messengers. They say, 'We do not differentiate between any of His messengers. We hear and obey. Grant us Your forgiveness, Lord, to You we shall all return!' ᵃ

لِّلَّهِ مَا فِي ٱلسَّمَٰوَٰتِ وَمَا فِي ٱلْأَرْضِ وَإِن تُبْدُواْ مَا فِىٓ أَنفُسِكُمْ أَوْ تُخْفُوهُ يُحَاسِبْكُم بِهِ ٱللَّهُ فَيَغْفِرُ لِمَن يَشَآءُ وَيُعَذِّبُ مَن يَشَآءُ وَٱللَّهُ عَلَىٰ كُلِّ شَيْءٍ قَدِيرٌ ۝ ءَامَنَ ٱلرَّسُولُ بِمَآ أُنزِلَ إِلَيْهِ مِن رَّبِّهِ وَٱلْمُؤْمِنُونَ كُلٌّ ءَامَنَ بِٱللَّهِ وَمَلَٰٓئِكَتِهِ وَكُتُبِهِ وَرُسُلِهِ لَا نُفَرِّقُ بَيْنَ أَحَدٍ مِّن رُّسُلِهِ وَقَالُواْ سَمِعْنَا وَأَطَعْنَا غُفْرَانَكَ رَبَّنَا وَإِلَيْكَ ٱلْمَصِيرُ ۝

ᵃ Everything in the universe is under God's command. Right from dust particles to the stars, all are bound by God's decreed plan. They must follow the path set for them by God. Man alone is the creature who finds that he may choose different paths of his own free will. But man does not possess freedom in an absolute sense: if he has freedom, it is so that he may be put to the test. Man has also to submit to the will of God like the rest of the universe. The life of restraint that the rest of the universe is obliged to follow must be followed voluntarily by man. He should not be deceived by the appearance of there being no one before or behind him. The truth of the matter is that at all times man is watched over by the Lord of the universe. He watches each and every thing, whether great or small, whether within him or without.

286 God does not charge a soul with more than it can bear. It shall be requited for whatever good and whatever evil it has done. [They pray], 'Our Lord, do not take us to task if we forget or make a mistake! Our Lord, do not place on us a burden like the one You placed on those before us! Our Lord, do not place on us a burden we have not the strength to bear! Pardon us; and forgive us; and have mercy on us. You are our Lord and Sustainer, so help us against those who deny the truth.'[a]

لَا يُكَلِّفُ ٱللَّهُ نَفْسًا إِلَّا وُسْعَهَا لَهَا مَا كَسَبَتْ وَعَلَيْهَا مَا ٱكْتَسَبَتْ رَبَّنَا لَا تُؤَاخِذْنَا إِن نَّسِينَا أَوْ أَخْطَأْنَا رَبَّنَا وَلَا تَحْمِلْ عَلَيْنَا إِصْرًا كَمَا حَمَلْتَهُ عَلَى ٱلَّذِينَ مِن قَبْلِنَا رَبَّنَا وَلَا تُحَمِّلْنَا مَا لَا طَاقَةَ لَنَا بِهِ وَٱعْفُ عَنَّا وَٱغْفِرْ لَنَا وَٱرْحَمْنَا أَنتَ مَوْلَىٰنَا فَٱنصُرْنَا عَلَى ٱلْقَوْمِ ٱلْكَـٰفِرِينَ

---

[a] Who is that man who measures up to the standards of the Almighty? He is one who is a man of faith, who submits and obeys. Faith means a conscious surrender to God, while obedience means practical surrender. For this to become a reality, man must enshrine God within himself as his Creator and Sustainer. He must be one to discover the reality that the system of the universe is not soulless or mechanical. Rather it is a live system, which is run by God's devoted workers. He must be one to recognize those servants of God chosen by Him to communicate this message to mankind. The Book revealed by God for the guidance of mankind must be accepted by him and become a part of his thoughts in the real sense. When faith in God, His angels, His Books and His messengers is firmly rooted in his heart and mind, he wholeheartedly surrenders himself to treading the path shown by God.

This faith and obedience should not be a matter of rituals or just an outward show. Rather, faith and obedience should be so inseparable from his soul that he starts to remember God at all times, and his whole life becomes entirely dependent on God.

3. THE FAMILY OF 'IMRAN

سورة العمران

In the name of God,
the Most Gracious, the Most Merciful

بِسْمِ اللَّهِ الرَّحْمَٰنِ الرَّحِيمِ

[1] *Alif Lam Mim*

[2] God! There is no deity save Him, the Living, the Sustainer. [3] He has sent down the Book to you with truth, which fulfils [the predictions] in the Scriptures that preceded it: He sent down the Torah and the Gospel [4] in the past as guidance for mankind; He has [also] sent down the Standard by which to discern the true from the false. Surely those who deny God's signs will suffer severe punishment. God is mighty and capable of retribution.[a]

الٓمٓ ۝ اللَّهُ لَآ إِلَٰهَ إِلَّا هُوَ ٱلْحَىُّ ٱلْقَيُّومُ ۝ نَزَّلَ عَلَيْكَ ٱلْكِتَٰبَ بِٱلْحَقِّ مُصَدِّقًا لِّمَا بَيْنَ يَدَيْهِ وَأَنزَلَ ٱلتَّوْرَىٰةَ وَٱلْإِنجِيلَ ۝ مِن قَبْلُ هُدًى لِّلنَّاسِ وَأَنزَلَ ٱلْفُرْقَانَ ۗ إِنَّ ٱلَّذِينَ كَفَرُواْ بِـَٔايَٰتِ ٱللَّهِ لَهُمْ عَذَابٌ شَدِيدٌ ۗ وَٱللَّهُ عَزِيزٌ ذُو ٱنتِقَامٍ ۝

---

[a] The Creator and Sustainer of the universe is not a mechanical God. He is, in fact, a live and conscious Being. He has sent guidance for man throughout the ages, including the Torah and the Bible, which were revealed to the former prophets. But man has always put different constructions upon divine teachings. Thus, through his self-styled interpretations, he has divided one religion into many. Ultimately, in accordance with God's plan, the final book in the form of the Quran was sent down to man. The Quran is not only a genuine book of guidance but also serves as the criterion or standard of right and wrong. It tells us which is the true religion and which is the religion devised by human beings through misinterpretation. Now those who, denying the book of the Almighty, refuse to abandon the religion devised by human beings, are deserving of His punishment. These are the people to whom God granted eyes, but who failed to see the light (sent by God in the form of this book). These are the people to whom their Creator granted minds, but who failed to understand the truth when it came to them in the form of arguments. Bowing to the truth required them to bow to the Prophet and to God, and they thought that by surrendering to the Supreme Being and His Prophet they would diminish in stature. To save their petty 'greatness', they refused to bow to the Truth.

⁵ Nothing on earth or in the heavens is hidden from God: ⁶ it is He who shapes you in the womb as He will. There is no deity save Him, the Mighty, the Wise One.ᵃ

إِنَّ ٱللَّهَ لَا يَخْفَىٰ عَلَيْهِ شَىْءٌ فِى ٱلْأَرْضِ وَلَا فِى ٱلسَّمَآءِ ۗ ﴿٥﴾ هُوَ ٱلَّذِى يُصَوِّرُكُمْ فِى ٱلْأَرْحَامِ كَيْفَ يَشَآءُ ۚ لَآ إِلَـٰهَ إِلَّا هُوَ ٱلْعَزِيزُ ٱلْحَكِيمُ ﴿٦﴾

ᵃ Only God can truly tell us what He is in His Being and in His attributes. And He has made this so clear in His Book, that any reader who is eager for knowledge of Him will certainly gain enlightenment from it. Again, it is only God who can truly give guidance to man. The right course of action for man can be determined only by a Being who has not only known man from his birth to his death, but also knows what has gone before his birth and what will happen after his death. It is, therefore, only God who, after placing the nature of man in the perspective of the entire universe, may decree what kind of conduct will guarantee man's success in this world and the next, for a sound human mentality can only be one which is in harmony with the rest of the world and in complete accord with the vaster system of the cosmos. It is only God who has the power and the knowledge to ordain what it befits human beings to strive for in the present world. This being so, the only realistic approach for man is to trust in His Maker and accept and follow His guidance wholeheartedly and with full confidence.

⁷ It is He who has sent down the Book to you. Some of its verses are clear and precise in meaning—they are the basis of the Book—while others are allegorical. Those with deviation in their hearts pursue the allegorical, so as to create dissension by seeking to explain it: but no one knows its meaning except God. Those who are firmly grounded in knowledge say, 'We believe in it: it is all from our Lord.' But only the wise take heed.ᵃ

هُوَ ٱلَّذِىٓ أَنزَلَ عَلَيْكَ ٱلْكِتَٰبَ مِنْهُ ءَايَٰتٌ مُّحْكَمَٰتٌ هُنَّ أُمُّ ٱلْكِتَٰبِ وَأُخَرُ مُتَشَٰبِهَٰتٌ فَأَمَّا ٱلَّذِينَ فِى قُلُوبِهِمْ زَيْغٌ فَيَتَّبِعُونَ مَا تَشَٰبَهَ مِنْهُ ٱبْتِغَآءَ ٱلْفِتْنَةِ وَٱبْتِغَآءَ تَأْوِيلِهِۦ وَمَا يَعْلَمُ تَأْوِيلَهُۥٓ إِلَّا ٱللَّهُ وَٱلرَّٰسِخُونَ فِى ٱلْعِلْمِ يَقُولُونَ ءَامَنَّا بِهِۦ كُلٌّ مِّنْ عِندِ رَبِّنَا وَمَا يَذَّكَّرُ إِلَّآ أُوْلُواْ ٱلْأَلْبَٰبِ ٧

ᵃ There are two kinds of subjects dealt with in the Quran, one pertaining to the known human world, like historical events, signs from the universe and commandments for worldly life; the other pertaining to unseen matters which are not comprehensible by man in this life, for instance, God's attributes, and the states of Heaven and Hell, etc. The first are clear revelations, quite precise in their meaning, since they have been couched in a direct style. The second relate to the unknown world (for man) and cannot, therefore, be expressed in everyday language. That is why they are framed in an allegorical style. For instance, if we say, 'man's hand', this is an example of the expression of a fact, but if we say, 'God's hand', this is an example of an allegory. Those who do not understand this difference fall into the error of interpreting allegorical verses quite literally. This will only lead man astray; he will never arrive at the truth. Whereas a 'human hand' may be precisely understood, a 'divine hand' cannot, because of our present limited thinking capacity.

8 'Our Lord, do not let our hearts deviate after You have guided us. Bestow upon us Your mercy. Surely You are a Munificent Giver. 9 Our Lord, You will surely gather all mankind on the Day of whose coming there is no doubt. God never fails to fulfill His promise.' a

رَبَّنَا لَا تُزِغْ قُلُوبَنَا بَعْدَ إِذْ هَدَيْتَنَا وَهَبْ لَنَا مِن لَّدُنكَ رَحْمَةً إِنَّكَ أَنتَ ٱلْوَهَّابُ ۞ رَبَّنَآ إِنَّكَ جَامِعُ ٱلنَّاسِ لِيَوْمٍ لَّا رَيْبَ فِيهِ إِنَّ ٱللَّهَ لَا يُخْلِفُ ٱلْمِيعَادَ ۞

a The correct academic and intellectual stand regarding the allegorical part of the Quran is for man to acknowledge his limitations. One should be content to have an abstract understanding of the things which cannot be grasped precisely by the senses. When, due to his imperfect sensory perception, man cannot have a total understanding of those realities, the practical approach should be not to make any attempt to determine the precise meaning in these matters. Instead, man should pray to God to save him from entanglement in fruitless discussions. He should pray to God to grant him such wisdom as will enable him to recognize his place and be content to repose his faith in those realities, without knowing all of their details. A Day is soon to come when these realities will come into full view, but it is not possible for man to comprehend them as long as he is still being put to the test in this life, by his Lord.

The path of the intellect may be a slippery one, where the intellectual may slip and fall in failing to see things in their right perspective. He understands reality, but only when he looks at it from the proper angle. When he does so from another angle, it is quite possible that he will fail to assess it properly and will be a prey to misunderstandings. The greater wisdom for man is to learn the secret of seeing things from the correct standpoint.

¹⁰ As for those who deny the truth, their wealth and children will not help them against God. They will be fuel for the Fire. ¹¹ Their end will be like Pharaoh's people and those before them; they denied Our signs, so God seized them in their sinfulness: God is stern in punishment. ¹² Say to those who deny the truth, 'You shall be overcome and driven into Hell—an evil resting place!' *ᵃ*

إِنَّ ٱلَّذِينَ كَفَرُواْ لَن تُغۡنِيَ عَنۡهُمۡ أَمۡوَٰلُهُمۡ وَلَآ أَوۡلَٰدُهُم مِّنَ ٱللَّهِ شَيۡـًٔا وَأُوْلَٰٓئِكَ هُمۡ وَقُودُ ٱلنَّارِ ۝ كَدَأۡبِ ءَالِ فِرۡعَوۡنَ وَٱلَّذِينَ مِن قَبۡلِهِمۡ كَذَّبُواْ بِـَٔايَٰتِنَا فَأَخَذَهُمُ ٱللَّهُ بِذُنُوبِهِمۡ وَٱللَّهُ شَدِيدُ ٱلۡعِقَابِ ۝ قُل لِّلَّذِينَ كَفَرُواْ سَتُغۡلَبُونَ وَتُحۡشَرُونَ إِلَىٰ جَهَنَّمَ وَبِئۡسَ ٱلۡمِهَادُ ۝

ᵃ When the call of Truth goes out, it appears to people to be of no value. On the one hand, there are all the assets of worldly comfort and grandeur, while, on the other hand, there is the caravan of truth, having no foothold in society, and no worldly interests attached to it. In such a situation, joining the caravan of truth amounts to detachment from the social circle and depriving oneself of all material benefits. That is why, in order to safeguard his interests, man turns away from the truth. If it means abandoning his friends and relatives, he is not ready to join a lone preacher (da'i). But all the material considerations that appear important today will cease to matter on the Day of Judgement. Their importance will last only so long as dealings are between man and man. The Day the veil of Doomsday is rent asunder, and all issues are to be settled between man and God, all worldly things will become insignificant—as if they had never existed. The missionary in this world appears to be powerless, but in reality, he is powerful, because God is backing him. The denier appears to be influential in this world, but is, in fact, totally powerless, because his strength is nothing but a temporary delusion.

13 There was a sign for you in the two groups which met face to face [at Badr], one party fighting for the cause of God and the other made up of those who deny the truth. The faithful saw with their own eyes that the others were twice their number: but God strengthens with His succour whom He wills. In this, there is indeed a lesson for all who have eyes to see.[a]

قَدْ كَانَ لَكُمْ ءَايَةٌ فِى فِئَتَيْنِ ٱلْتَقَتَا فِئَةٌ تُقَٰتِلُ فِى سَبِيلِ ٱللَّهِ وَأُخْرَىٰ كَافِرَةٌ يَرَوْنَهُم مِّثْلَيْهِمْ رَأْىَ ٱلْعَيْنِ وَٱللَّهُ يُؤَيِّدُ بِنَصْرِهِۦ مَن يَشَآءُ إِنَّ فِى ذَٰلِكَ لَعِبْرَةً لِّأُوْلِى ٱلْأَبْصَٰرِ ﴿١٣﴾

---

[a] The battle of Badr in the fourteenth year of the prophethood was a worldly example of what will happen in the next world. Those who deny the truth greatly exceeded the believers in numbers and in strength. In fact, the believers were so few in number that they were powerless. In spite of this, those who denied the truth suffered a crushing defeat and the believers achieved a decisive victory. This is a clear proof that God is always on the side of the believers. In the face of such a great difference in resources, an extraordinary victory cannot be achieved without God's succour. This serves as a demonstration from God that truth does not go unsupported. It is also a clear indication to those who deny the truth of how they are placed in this world. There are obvious signs in the words and deeds of the preacher that the Truth he preaches comes from God. But the arrogant find refuge in fine words to refute this. They live by false explanations, until finally they leave for the next world, only to learn that the words in which they had taken refuge were utterly meaningless from the standpoint of reality.

¹⁴ The satisfaction of worldly desires through women, and children, and heaped-up treasures of gold and silver, and pedigreed horses, and cattle and lands is attractive to people. All this is the provision of the worldly life; but the most excellent abode is with God. ¹⁵ Say, 'Shall I tell you of something better than all of these? For the God-fearing, there are Gardens in nearness to their God with rivers flowing through them where they shall live forever with pure spouses and the goodwill of God. God is watching His servants —ᵃ

زُيِّنَ لِلنَّاسِ حُبُّ ٱلشَّهَوَٰتِ مِنَ ٱلنِّسَاءِ وَٱلْبَنِينَ وَٱلْقَنَٰطِيرِ ٱلْمُقَنطَرَةِ مِنَ ٱلذَّهَبِ وَٱلْفِضَّةِ وَٱلْخَيْلِ ٱلْمُسَوَّمَةِ وَٱلْأَنْعَٰمِ وَٱلْحَرْثِ ۗ ذَٰلِكَ مَتَٰعُ ٱلْحَيَوٰةِ ٱلدُّنْيَا ۖ وَٱللَّهُ عِندَهُۥ حُسْنُ ٱلْمَـَٔابِ ۝ قُلْ أَؤُنَبِّئُكُم بِخَيْرٍ مِّن ذَٰلِكُمْ ۚ لِلَّذِينَ ٱتَّقَوْا عِندَ رَبِّهِمْ جَنَّٰتٌ تَجْرِى مِن تَحْتِهَا ٱلْأَنْهَٰرُ خَٰلِدِينَ فِيهَا وَأَزْوَٰجٌ مُّطَهَّرَةٌ وَرِضْوَٰنٌ مِّنَ ٱللَّهِ ۗ وَٱللَّهُ بَصِيرٌۢ بِٱلْعِبَادِ ۝

ᵃ This world is a place of trial. God, wishing to ascertain which of His creatures are capable of rising above worldly attractions, has so willed it that man should be attracted to and find gratification in the things of this world, but at the same time be faced with the choice of clinging to them or renouncing them in favour of the unseen things of the next world. This is not an easy choice, for he sees that worldly acquisitions lead him to an honourable place in society. By possessing material resources, he can have all that he wants in life. This gives him the impression that it is these things that are of consequence. All his interests and activities centre around his family, his wealth and his property. This presents the greatest obstacle to advancing towards the demands of the Hereafter. The aura of importance surrounding worldly things makes him oblivious of all that pertains to the next life. He is so engrossed in building the future of his children in this world, that he no longer remembers the fact that there is any 'future' beyond this present life, to which he should give thought. Providing all comforts for his home in this world becomes so dear to him that it never occurs to him that there is any other home save this, to which he should pay heed. Making money, accumulating riches and possessing property in this world seem so estimable to him, that he fails to realize that there is any 'wealth' other than this, to which he should devote his life. However, all these things with the external glitter of this present life will be of no use to him in the next, eternal life. It is only one who makes the permanent life of the Hereafter the focus of his attention who will realize the insignificance of these worldly things.

¹⁶ those who say, "Lord, we believe in You, forgive us our sins and keep us from the punishment of the Fire," ¹⁷ those who are steadfast, truthful, obedient, and those who spend [for God's cause] and who pray before dawn for forgiveness.'ᵃ

ٱلَّذِينَ يَقُولُونَ رَبَّنَآ إِنَّنَآ ءَامَنَّا فَٱغْفِرْ لَنَا ذُنُوبَنَا وَقِنَا عَذَابَ ٱلنَّارِ ﴿١٦﴾ ٱلصَّٰبِرِينَ وَٱلصَّٰدِقِينَ وَٱلْقَٰنِتِينَ وَٱلْمُنفِقِينَ وَٱلْمُسْتَغْفِرِينَ بِٱلْأَسْحَارِ ﴿١٧﴾

ᵃ He will be filled with the conviction that the matters of the next world are entirely in the hands of his Lord and all the glitter of this world will appear meaningless. As a result, God will be the entity he fears most and he will be desirous of the next life more than anything else. He will not follow his mundane desires, but will rather determine his course of action, keeping in view the court of the Almighty. There will be no discrepancy between his words and his actions. His wealth will no longer remain his, but will be devoted to the cause of God. Whatever difficulties he faces in the path of his Creator, he will adhere to that path with total steadfastness, because he will have the conviction that no one can give him succour if he turns away from God. His heart will be filled with His remembrance, and he will start calling upon Him spontaneously. God will be his companion in his solitude. In the presence of His greatness and perfection, his own being will appear completely insignificant. He will have no words to utter but—'O my God, forgive me.'

¹⁸ God bears witness that there is no deity save Him, as do the angels and those who possess knowledge. He is the upholder of justice. There is no diety save Him, the Mighty, the Wise One. ¹⁹ The only true religion in God's sight is complete submission to God. And those who were given the Book disagreed only out of rivalry, after knowledge had been given to them—he who denies God's signs should know that God is swift in His reckoning.ᵃ

شَهِدَ ٱللَّهُ أَنَّهُ لَا إِلَٰهَ إِلَّا هُوَ وَٱلْمَلَٰئِكَةُ وَأُوْلُواْ ٱلْعِلْمِ قَآئِمَاً بِٱلْقِسْطِ لَا إِلَٰهَ إِلَّا هُوَ ٱلْعَزِيزُ ٱلْحَكِيمُ ۝ إِنَّ ٱلدِّينَ عِندَ ٱللَّهِ ٱلْإِسْلَٰمُ وَمَا ٱخْتَلَفَ ٱلَّذِينَ أُوتُواْ ٱلْكِتَٰبَ إِلَّا مِنۢ بَعْدِ مَا جَآءَهُمُ ٱلْعِلْمُ بَغْيَاۢ بَيْنَهُمْ وَمَن يَكْفُرْ بِـَٔايَٰتِ ٱللَّهِ فَإِنَّ ٱللَّهَ سَرِيعُ ٱلْحِسَابِ ۝

ᵃ The God of the universe is the One and only God and He likes justice. This assertion is made in all the revealed scriptures which are still in their original form. The vast universe run by its Master through His unseen agents, the angels, is exactly what it ought to be and as perfect as it can be. According to established knowledge, the universe seems to be a completely unitary system. This would indicate that it has a single Planner. Moreover, everything in the universe being in its right place is a proof that its Lord loves justice and righteousness rather than injustice and wrongdoing. Then how can God, who has maintained justice in the vaster universe, allow injustice in human matters?

Each and every part of the universe is in a complete state of 'surrender', that is, all its functions are performed in accordance with the appointed plan of God. Exactly the same performance is required of man. Man must recognize his Lord and mould his life in accordance with God's plan. Making anyone else, save God, the centre of his attention or nurturing the thought that God's judgement can be based on anything other than justice is inconceivable in the present universe.

²⁰ If they dispute with you, say, 'I have submitted my whole being to God and so have those who follow me.' And ask those who have been given the Book, as well as the unlettered, 'Do you submit yourselves to God in the same way?' If they submit themselves to Him, they are on the right path; but if they turn away, your duty is only to convey the message. God is observant of all His servants. ²¹ Those who deny God's signs and kill the prophets unjustly and kill those who enjoin justice—give them warning of a woeful punishment— ²² their deeds will come to nothing in this world as well as in the hereafter; they will have no supporters.ᵃ

فَإِنْ حَآجُّوكَ فَقُلْ أَسْلَمْتُ وَجْهِيَ لِلَّهِ وَمَنِ ٱتَّبَعَنِ ۗ وَقُل لِّلَّذِينَ أُوتُواْ ٱلْكِتَٰبَ وَٱلْأُمِّيِّـۧنَ ءَأَسْلَمْتُمْ ۚ فَإِنْ أَسْلَمُواْ فَقَدِ ٱهْتَدَواْ ۖ وَّإِن تَوَلَّوْاْ فَإِنَّمَا عَلَيْكَ ٱلْبَلَٰغُ ۗ وَٱللَّهُ بَصِيرٌۢ بِٱلْعِبَادِ ۝ إِنَّ ٱلَّذِينَ يَكْفُرُونَ بِـَٔايَٰتِ ٱللَّهِ وَيَقْتُلُونَ ٱلنَّبِيِّـۧنَ بِغَيْرِ حَقٍّ وَيَقْتُلُونَ ٱلَّذِينَ يَأْمُرُونَ بِٱلْقِسْطِ مِنَ ٱلنَّاسِ فَبَشِّرْهُم بِعَذَابٍ أَلِيمٍ ۝ أُوْلَٰٓئِكَ ٱلَّذِينَ حَبِطَتْ أَعْمَٰلُهُمْ فِى ٱلدُّنْيَا وَٱلْأَخِرَةِ وَمَا لَهُم مِّن نَّٰصِرِينَ ۝

ᵃ The call of the Quran is the call of the same true version of Islam, the religion of submission to God, as was revealed to all the other prophets. Those who deny this do so, not because its truth is not clear to them, but because of their own sense of superiority. Acknowledging its veracity amounts, as they see it, to accepting the intellectual superiority of the proponent of the Quran. And their jealousy and arrogance do not allow of such an acknowledgement. Instead of accepting the truth, they want to exterminate the dayee himself. However, this is not possible in this world of God. All their plans to censor the dayees' words will fail, and when God's scales of justice are put in place, they will see that those actions, which had given them the conviction of securing success and salvation, are quite without value. True argument is one of God's signs. One who does not bow to a true argument, fails to bow to God. Such dissenters will enter the next world divested of all support.

²³ Have you not seen those who received a portion of the Book? When they are invited to accept the judgement of God's Book, a group of them turns away in aversion. ²⁴ That is because they say, 'The Fire will touch us only for a limited number of days.' Thus the false beliefs which they have invented have deluded them in the matter of their religion.ᵃ

أَلَمْ تَرَ إِلَى ٱلَّذِينَ أُوتُوا نَصِيبًا مِنَ ٱلْكِتَٰبِ يُدْعَوْنَ إِلَىٰ كِتَٰبِ ٱللَّهِ لِيَحْكُمَ بَيْنَهُمْ ثُمَّ يَتَوَلَّىٰ فَرِيقٌ مِّنْهُمْ وَهُم مُّعْرِضُونَ ﴿٢٣﴾ ذَٰلِكَ بِأَنَّهُمْ قَالُوا لَن تَمَسَّنَا ٱلنَّارُ إِلَّا أَيَّامًا مَّعْدُودَٰتٍ وَغَرَّهُمْ فِي دِينِهِم مَّا كَانُوا يَفْتَرُونَ ﴿٢٤﴾

ᵃ God's guidance is one and the same as that revealed to various prophets from time to time in various languages. The same guidance was revealed to the Final Prophet in the form of the Quran. Due to this uniformity in content, recognizing the call of the Quran is not difficult for the People of the Book, i.e. believers in other revealed scriptures. The only difference between the Quranic call and former divine scriptures lies in the fact that the Quran has purified the religion of God of all human interpolations. Then why is it that many people deny the call of the Quran? It is because the Quranic call does not appear to them to be a serious matter, vis à vis their self-styled concepts by which they feel that they have safeguarded themselves from the fire of hell. It is as a result of this mindset that they think that, even if they do not recognize the truth, their salvation is still not at risk. But when the divine scales are put in place, they will realize how deluded they were in their wishful thinking.

²⁵ How will it be when We gather them all together upon a Day which is sure to come, when every human being shall be repaid in full for what he has done? They will not be wronged. ²⁶ Say, 'Lord, sovereign of all sovereignty. You bestow sovereignty on whom you will and take it away from whom You please; You exalt whoever You will and abase whoever You will. All that is good lies in Your hands. You have the power to will anything. ²⁷ You cause the night to pass into the day, and the day into the night; You bring forth the living from the lifeless and the lifeless from the living. You give without measure to whom You will.'[a]

فَكَيْفَ إِذَا جَمَعْنَاهُمْ لِيَوْمٍ لَّا رَيْبَ فِيهِ وَوُفِّيَتْ كُلُّ نَفْسٍ مَّا كَسَبَتْ وَهُمْ لَا يُظْلَمُونَ ۞ قُلِ ٱللَّهُمَّ مَالِكَ ٱلْمُلْكِ تُؤْتِى ٱلْمُلْكَ مَن تَشَآءُ وَتَنزِعُ ٱلْمُلْكَ مِمَّن تَشَآءُ وَتُعِزُّ مَن تَشَآءُ وَتُذِلُّ مَن تَشَآءُ بِيَدِكَ ٱلْخَيْرُ إِنَّكَ عَلَىٰ كُلِّ شَىْءٍ قَدِيرٌ ۞ تُولِجُ ٱلَّيْلَ فِى ٱلنَّهَارِ وَتُولِجُ ٱلنَّهَارَ فِى ٱلَّيْلِ وَتُخْرِجُ ٱلْحَىَّ مِنَ ٱلْمَيِّتِ وَتُخْرِجُ ٱلْمَيِّتَ مِنَ ٱلْحَىِّ وَتَرْزُقُ مَن تَشَآءُ بِغَيْرِ حِسَابٍ ۞

---

[a] All kinds of honour and power lie in the hand of God. Those who are considered insignificant by the leaders of the time can be entitled to the highest honour and eminence by the grace of God. In the eyes of God, it is those who regard such attainments as being purely and simply the gifts of God who are deserving of honour and power. The most undeserving of honour and power are those who consider them to be their own acquisitions. In the vaster universe, God daily performs the miracle, on a colossal scale, of bringing darkness after light and light after darkness (i.e. the alternation of day and night). He brings into existence life from dead elements and causes living things to die. There is nothing surprising about it if this same power of God manifests itself among human beings. But those who exchange falsehoods in the name of truth always turn against the call of truth.

The preacher of truth may ultimately be rendered homeless and his economic resources may be cut off. But such an individual is always under the direct guardianship of God, who provides for him His special succour. While others are provided for according to their efforts, a messenger of truth is provided for by God 'without measure'.

²⁸ Let not the believers take those who deny the truth for their allies in preference to the believers— anyone who does that will isolate himself completely from God— unless it be to protect yourselves against them in this way. God admonishes you to fear Him: for, to God shall all return. ²⁹ Say, 'God knows everything that is in your heart, whether you conceal it or reveal it; He knows everything that the heavens and earth contain; God has power over all things.' ᵃ

لَا يَتَّخِذِ ٱلْمُؤْمِنُونَ ٱلْكَٰفِرِينَ أَوْلِيَآءَ مِن دُونِ ٱلْمُؤْمِنِينَ ۖ وَمَن يَفْعَلْ ذَٰلِكَ فَلَيْسَ مِنَ ٱللَّهِ فِى شَىْءٍ إِلَّآ أَن تَتَّقُوا۟ مِنْهُمْ تُقَىٰةً ۗ وَيُحَذِّرُكُمُ ٱللَّهُ نَفْسَهُۥ ۗ وَإِلَى ٱللَّهِ ٱلْمَصِيرُ ۝ قُلْ إِن تُخْفُوا۟ مَا فِى صُدُورِكُمْ أَوْ تُبْدُوهُ يَعْلَمْهُ ٱللَّهُ ۗ وَيَعْلَمُ مَا فِى ٱلسَّمَٰوَٰتِ وَمَا فِى ٱلْأَرْضِ ۗ وَٱللَّهُ عَلَىٰ كُلِّ شَىْءٍ قَدِيرٌ ۝

ᵃ A believer treats all human beings with justice and fairness, without differentiating between Muslims and non-Muslims. But friendship with non-Muslims who are at war with Islam is not lawful. In the eyes of God, it is our intention that matters: when our intention is sincere, God does not take us to task for our actions. The key factor, worthy of consideration in all matters, is the fear of God. One should always give proper thought to one's behaviour, whatever the issue, because one is accountable to God for everything. Whoever is proved wrong on the divine scale cannot escape punishment. Nothing pertaining to human beings escapes the eyes of God, whether in public or in private. When the veil of the divine test is cast aside, the world of the Hereafter will appear before mankind and the fruits of all man's actions will be before him. This sight will be so dreadful that all the things of this world which had appeared so pleasing to him, will now be the very things from which he will want to distance himself. What is most important in the eyes of God is whether Islam is implanted in one's heart or not. A believer is one whose love for God springs from his heart, who loves God truly in his heart of hearts. It is people such as those who deserve God's love and attention. One who forms such a bond with God is forgiven by Him for his failings. God is hard on the arrogant. But He is gentle with those who adopt modesty as their way of life.

30 On the Day when every human being will find himself faced with all the good that he has done, and with all the evil that he has done, many will wish that there were a long space of time between himself and that [Day]. God admonishes you to fear Him, but God is compassionate towards His servants. ³¹ Say, 'If you love God, follow me and God will love you and forgive you your sins. God is most forgiving, and most merciful.' ³² Say, 'Obey God and the Messenger,' and if they turn away, God does not love those who deny the truth.ᵃ

يَوْمَ تَجِدُ كُلُّ نَفْسٍ مَّا عَمِلَتْ مِنْ خَيْرٍ مُّحْضَرًا وَمَا عَمِلَتْ مِن سُوءٍ تَوَدُّ لَوْ أَنَّ بَيْنَهَا وَبَيْنَهُۥ أَمَدًۢا بَعِيدًا وَيُحَذِّرُكُمُ ٱللَّهُ نَفْسَهُۥ وَٱللَّهُ رَءُوفٌۢ بِٱلْعِبَادِ ۝ قُلْ إِن كُنتُمْ تُحِبُّونَ ٱللَّهَ فَٱتَّبِعُونِى يُحْبِبْكُمُ ٱللَّهُ وَيَغْفِرْ لَكُمْ ذُنُوبَكُمْ وَٱللَّهُ غَفُورٌ رَّحِيمٌ ۝ قُلْ أَطِيعُواْ ٱللَّهَ وَٱلرَّسُولَ فَإِن تَوَلَّوْاْ فَإِنَّ ٱللَّهَ لَا يُحِبُّ ٱلْكَٰفِرِينَ ۝

ᵃ It is a psychological reality that one who loves someone cannot at the same time love the enemy of the beloved. It is also a fact that when the beloved is a Being who has the status of one's Creator and Sustainer, then this love will necessarily bring about in the lover the desire to obey that Being in all matters. If the love of God does not produce in him feelings of obeisance to Him, then such a love is false. A believer who is one in name only will be included among the deniers. God Himself has testified to the Prophet's total obedience to Him in all matters. So the authentic example of a life of God-worship in this world is only such as was handed down to us by His messenger.

33 God chose Adam and Noah and the family of Abraham and the family of 'Imran above all His creatures. 34 They are the offspring of one another. God hears all and knows all. 35 Remember when the wife of 'Imran said, 'My Lord, I have dedicated what is in my womb entirely to Your service. So accept this from me. You are the One who hears and knows all.' 36 When she gave birth, she said, 'My Lord, I have given birth to a girl'—God knew very well what she had given birth to: a male is not like a female—'I have named her Mary and placed her and her children in Your protection from the rejected Satan.' 37 Her Lord graciously accepted her and made her grow in goodness and entrusted her to the care of Zachariah. Every time Zachariah visited her in her chamber he found some provision with her. He asked, 'Mary, where did this provision come from?' She replied, 'This is from God. God provides for whoever He wills without measure.' 38 Thereupon Zachariah prayed to his Lord, saying, 'Lord, grant me by Your own grace virtuous offspring. You are the hearer of all prayers.' 39 As he stood praying in the chamber, the angels called out to him, saying, 'God gives you the good news of John, who shall confirm the Word from God, and [shall be] outstanding among men, and utterly chaste, and a prophet from among the righteous.'

۞ إِنَّ ٱللَّهَ ٱصْطَفَىٰٓ ءَادَمَ وَنُوحًا وَءَالَ إِبْرَٰهِيمَ وَءَالَ عِمْرَٰنَ عَلَى ٱلْعَٰلَمِينَ ۝ ذُرِّيَّةًۢ بَعْضُهَا مِنۢ بَعْضٍ وَٱللَّهُ سَمِيعٌ عَلِيمٌ ۝ إِذْ قَالَتِ ٱمْرَأَتُ عِمْرَٰنَ رَبِّ إِنِّى نَذَرْتُ لَكَ مَا فِى بَطْنِى مُحَرَّرًا فَتَقَبَّلْ مِنِّىٓ إِنَّكَ أَنتَ ٱلسَّمِيعُ ٱلْعَلِيمُ ۝ فَلَمَّا وَضَعَتْهَا قَالَتْ رَبِّ إِنِّى وَضَعْتُهَآ أُنثَىٰ وَٱللَّهُ أَعْلَمُ بِمَا وَضَعَتْ وَلَيْسَ ٱلذَّكَرُ كَٱلْأُنثَىٰ وَإِنِّى سَمَّيْتُهَا مَرْيَمَ وَإِنِّىٓ أُعِيذُهَا بِكَ وَذُرِّيَّتَهَا مِنَ ٱلشَّيْطَٰنِ ٱلرَّجِيمِ ۝ فَتَقَبَّلَهَا رَبُّهَا بِقَبُولٍ حَسَنٍ وَأَنۢبَتَهَا نَبَاتًا حَسَنًا وَكَفَّلَهَا زَكَرِيَّا كُلَّمَا دَخَلَ عَلَيْهَا زَكَرِيَّا ٱلْمِحْرَابَ وَجَدَ عِندَهَا رِزْقًا قَالَ يَٰمَرْيَمُ أَنَّىٰ لَكِ هَٰذَا قَالَتْ هُوَ مِنْ عِندِ ٱللَّهِ إِنَّ ٱللَّهَ يَرْزُقُ مَن يَشَآءُ بِغَيْرِ حِسَابٍ ۝ هُنَالِكَ دَعَا زَكَرِيَّا رَبَّهُۥ قَالَ رَبِّ هَبْ لِى مِن لَّدُنكَ ذُرِّيَّةً طَيِّبَةً إِنَّكَ سَمِيعُ ٱلدُّعَآءِ ۝ فَنَادَتْهُ ٱلْمَلَٰٓئِكَةُ وَهُوَ قَآئِمٌ يُصَلِّى فِى ٱلْمِحْرَابِ أَنَّ ٱللَّهَ يُبَشِّرُكَ بِيَحْيَىٰ مُصَدِّقًۢا بِكَلِمَةٍ مِّنَ ٱللَّهِ وَسَيِّدًا وَحَصُورًا وَنَبِيًّا مِّنَ ٱلصَّٰلِحِينَ ۝

40 'Lord,' said Zachariah, 'how shall I have a son when I am now overtaken by old age and my wife is barren?' 'Such is the will of God,' replied [the angel], 'He does what He pleases.' 41 He said, 'My Lord, grant me a sign.' [The angel] said, 'Your sign is that you will not be able to speak to people for three days except by signs. Remember your Lord much and glorify Him morning and evening.' 42 The angels said, 'Mary, God has selected you and purified you. He has selected you over [all] the women of your time. 43 O Mary! Remain truly devout to your Sustainer, and prostrate yourself in worship, and bow down with those who bow down [before Him].' 44 This is an account of the unseen, which We reveal to you. You were not with them when they drew lots as to which of them should be Mary's guardian and you were not with them when they disputed with one another.[a]

قَالَ رَبِّ أَنَّىٰ يَكُونُ لِى غُلَٰمٌ وَقَدْ بَلَغَنِىَ ٱلْكِبَرُ وَٱمْرَأَتِى عَاقِرٌ قَالَ كَذَٰلِكَ ٱللَّهُ يَفْعَلُ مَا يَشَآءُ ۝ قَالَ رَبِّ ٱجْعَل لِّىٓ ءَايَةً قَالَ ءَايَتُكَ أَلَّا تُكَلِّمَ ٱلنَّاسَ ثَلَٰثَةَ أَيَّامٍ إِلَّا رَمْزًا وَٱذْكُر رَّبَّكَ كَثِيرًا وَسَبِّحْ بِٱلْعَشِىِّ وَٱلْإِبْكَٰرِ ۝ وَإِذْ قَالَتِ ٱلْمَلَٰٓئِكَةُ يَٰمَرْيَمُ إِنَّ ٱللَّهَ ٱصْطَفَىٰكِ وَطَهَّرَكِ وَٱصْطَفَىٰكِ عَلَىٰ نِسَآءِ ٱلْعَٰلَمِينَ ۝ يَٰمَرْيَمُ ٱقْنُتِى لِرَبِّكِ وَٱسْجُدِى وَٱرْكَعِى مَعَ ٱلرَّٰكِعِينَ ۝ ذَٰلِكَ مِنْ أَنۢبَآءِ ٱلْغَيْبِ نُوحِيهِ إِلَيْكَ وَمَا كُنتَ لَدَيْهِمْ إِذْ يُلْقُونَ أَقْلَٰمَهُمْ أَيُّهُمْ يَكْفُلُ مَرْيَمَ وَمَا كُنتَ لَدَيْهِمْ إِذْ يَخْتَصِمُونَ ۝

---

[a] God blessed Zachariah (Zakariyya) with an offspring in his old age; provided sustenance to Mary in her shrine; created Jesus without a father, and brought into being chaste and upright people who were descendants of Abraham, so that they could be chosen to communicate the message of God to human beings. God did not grant these blessings to His people for no good reason: He found them so deserving that he showered them with His blessings. These were the people who had no material expectations from their children; their happiness rested upon their children's dedication and devotion to the cause of God. These were the people who wanted their children to be safe from Satan and join the band of believers. They were not given to jealousy and ill-will on seeing goodness in others. It was through their good influence that their children too were in control of their selves and became one with those who truly remembered God: who chose the right way, abandoning the path that leads one astray. Such are the people whom God provides for out of His special mercy, and who have His special blessings showered upon them.

⁴⁵ When the angels said, 'O Mary, your Lord gives you good news of a Word from Him. His name is the Messiah, Jesus, son of Mary, honoured in this world and in the next and one of those who are granted nearness to God. ⁴⁶ And he shall speak to men in his cradle, and as a grown man, and shall be one of the righteous.' ⁴⁷ 'Lord,' she said, 'how can I have a child when no man has touched me?' [The angel] replied, 'Thus it is: God creates what He wills: when He wills a thing He need only say, "Be," and it is. ⁴⁸ God will instruct him in the Book and in wisdom and in the Torah and in the Gospel.ᵃ

إِذْ قَالَتِ ٱلْمَلَٰٓئِكَةُ يَٰمَرْيَمُ إِنَّ ٱللَّهَ يُبَشِّرُكِ بِكَلِمَةٍ مِّنْهُ ٱسْمُهُ ٱلْمَسِيحُ عِيسَى ٱبْنُ مَرْيَمَ وَجِيهًا فِى ٱلدُّنْيَا وَٱلْأَخِرَةِ وَمِنَ ٱلْمُقَرَّبِينَ ۝ وَيُكَلِّمُ ٱلنَّاسَ فِى ٱلْمَهْدِ وَكَهْلًا وَمِنَ ٱلصَّٰلِحِينَ ۝ قَالَتْ رَبِّ أَنَّىٰ يَكُونُ لِى وَلَدٌ وَلَمْ يَمْسَسْنِى بَشَرٌ قَالَ كَذَٰلِكِ ٱللَّهُ يَخْلُقُ مَا يَشَآءُ إِذَا قَضَىٰٓ أَمْرًا فَإِنَّمَا يَقُولُ لَهُۥ كُن فَيَكُونُ ۝ وَيُعَلِّمُهُ ٱلْكِتَٰبَ وَٱلْحِكْمَةَ وَٱلتَّوْرَىٰةَ وَٱلْإِنجِيلَ ۝

ᵃ The Jews were chosen by God for the special mission of being the bearers of divine guidance so that, along with following the path of God, they should also communicate this guidance to others. But the rot set in in the Jews in later times. Then a time came when they were no longer worthy of being the bearers of divine guidance. God then took away this trust from them and gave it to the other branch of Abraham's dynasty, the Banu Isma'il. Before the enforcement of this decree, it was necessary to prove to them that they were no longer to be trusted. Jesus Christ was sent by God for this purpose. His extraordinary birth and his performance of extraordinary miracles were meant to convince the Jews of his messengership (i.e. that he had been sent by God) and that he was speaking on behalf of God.

⁴⁹ He will make him a messenger to the Children of Israel. He will say: "I have come to you with a sign from your Lord. I will make the shape of a bird out of clay for you and then breathe into it and, by God's leave, it will become a living bird. And by God's leave I will heal the blind and the leper and bring the dead to life. I will tell you what you eat and what you store up in your homes. Surely in this there is a sign for you, if you are believers. ⁵⁰ I come to fulfill [the prediction] of the Torah which preceded me and to make lawful for you some of what was forbidden to you and I come to you with a sign from your Lord. So fear God and obey me. ⁵¹ God is my Lord and your Lord, so worship Him. That is the straight path.'" *a*

وَرَسُولاً إِلَىٰ بَنِىٓ إِسْرَٰٓءِيلَ أَنِّى قَدْ جِئْتُكُم بِـَٔايَةٍ مِّن رَّبِّكُمْ أَنِّىٓ أَخْلُقُ لَكُم مِّنَ ٱلطِّينِ كَهَيْـَٔةِ ٱلطَّيْرِ فَأَنفُخُ فِيهِ فَيَكُونُ طَيْرًا بِإِذْنِ ٱللَّهِ وَأُبْرِئُ ٱلْأَكْمَهَ وَٱلْأَبْرَصَ وَأُحْىِ ٱلْمَوْتَىٰ بِإِذْنِ ٱللَّهِ وَأُنَبِّئُكُم بِمَا تَأْكُلُونَ وَمَا تَدَّخِرُونَ فِى بُيُوتِكُمْ إِنَّ فِى ذَٰلِكَ لَءَايَةً لَّكُمْ إِن كُنتُم مُّؤْمِنِينَ ۝ وَمُصَدِّقًا لِّمَا بَيْنَ يَدَىَّ مِنَ ٱلتَّوْرَىٰةِ وَلِأُحِلَّ لَكُم بَعْضَ ٱلَّذِى حُرِّمَ عَلَيْكُمْ وَجِئْتُكُم بِـَٔايَةٍ مِّن رَّبِّكُمْ فَٱتَّقُوا۟ ٱللَّهَ وَأَطِيعُونِ ۝ إِنَّ ٱللَّهَ رَبِّى وَرَبُّكُمْ فَٱعْبُدُوهُ هَٰذَا صِرَٰطٌ مُّسْتَقِيمٌ ۝

---

a Jesus Christ was not only given extraordinary signs from God, but he spoke in so effective, persuasive and logical a manner that no one in his time could equal him. When he spoke for the first time in the temple, 'all that heard him were astonished at his understanding and answers.' (Luke 2:47). It was on account of his miraculous personality and his astonishing powers of speech that, although he was born without a father, no one dared to abuse him on this score. However, the Jews had become so insensitive and insolent that, in spite of very clear proofs, they refused to believe in him. 'Surely in this there is a sign for you, if you are believers' means that the proof, as presented, although complete in itself, would make sense only to one who wanted to believe; who had the ability to come out of his self and ponder over its veracity; whose nature was so receptive that the question of personal prestige did not become an obstacle to the acceptance of truth.

⁵²When Jesus perceived their denial, he said, 'Who will be my helpers in God's cause?' The disciples said, 'We are God's helpers, we believe in God. Bear witness that we have surrendered ourselves. ⁵³Our Lord, we believe in what You have sent down and we follow the messenger, so count us among those who bear witness.' ⁵⁴And they schemed but God also schemed and God is the Best of Schemers.ᵃ

* فَلَمَّآ أَحَسَّ عِيسَىٰ مِنْهُمُ ٱلْكُفْرَ قَالَ مَنْ أَنصَارِىٓ إِلَى ٱللَّهِ قَالَ ٱلْحَوَارِيُّونَ نَحْنُ أَنصَارُ ٱللَّهِ ءَامَنَّا بِٱللَّهِ وَٱشْهَدْ بِأَنَّا مُسْلِمُونَ ۝ رَبَّنَآ ءَامَنَّا بِمَآ أَنزَلْتَ وَٱتَّبَعْنَا ٱلرَّسُولَ فَٱكْتُبْنَا مَعَ ٱلشَّـٰهِدِينَ ۝ وَمَكَرُوا۟ وَمَكَرَ ٱللَّهُ وَٱللَّهُ خَيْرُ ٱلْمَـٰكِرِينَ ۝

ᵃ The religious leaders of the Israelites refused to believe in Jesus Christ. In any society, it is the leading lights who have access to all resources, and, in addition to being in possession of religious seats, they become the representatives of religion in the eyes of the people. This being so, if someone is rejected by these influential people, not only is he deprived of life's resources, but even after losing all for the sake of truth, he remains a heretic in people's eyes. In such circumstances, the most difficult of tasks is to support a preacher of truth. It means testifying to his veracity in a general atmosphere of suspicion and opposition. It amounts to siding with the truth when it stands alone and unsupported.

When the truth is presented in all its purity, all those who are leading a life of untruth feel on the defensive—especially those who, by having pasted the label of truth on their lives, have secured a position of honour in society. It is such as they who rise to suppress the call of truth, setting the people against the caller by putting wrong constructions on his words.

When this does not work, they finally plan to resort to the use of power in order to annihilate both the call and the caller. But God's succour is always with the preacher. That is why no opposition to him succeeds in suppressing the truth, and he is able to complete his mission. Those who oppose the call of truth are mischief-makers in the eyes of God. This is because they stop potential believers from reaching the path of Paradise. No evil can be greater than obstructing the path of those intent upon entering God's Paradise.

⁵⁵ God said, 'O Jesus, I shall take you to Me and will raise you up to Me and shall clear you [of the calumnies] of the disbelievers, and shall place those who follow you above those who deny the truth, until the Day of Judgement; then to Me shall all return and I will judge between you regarding your disputes. ⁵⁶ Those who deny the truth shall be sternly punished in this world and in the world to come: there shall be none to help them.' ⁵⁷ As for those who have believed and do good works, they shall be given their reward in full. God does not love evil-doers. ⁵⁸ This which We recite to you is a revelation and a wise reminder.[a]

إِذْ قَالَ ٱللَّهُ يَـٰعِيسَىٰٓ إِنِّي مُتَوَفِّيكَ وَرَافِعُكَ إِلَيَّ وَمُطَهِّرُكَ مِنَ ٱلَّذِينَ كَفَرُواْ وَجَاعِلُ ٱلَّذِينَ ٱتَّبَعُوكَ فَوْقَ ٱلَّذِينَ كَفَرُوٓاْ إِلَىٰ يَوْمِ ٱلْقِيَـٰمَةِ ثُمَّ إِلَيَّ مَرْجِعُكُمْ فَأَحْكُمُ بَيْنَكُمْ فِيمَا كُنتُمْ فِيهِ تَخْتَلِفُونَ ۝ فَأَمَّا ٱلَّذِينَ كَفَرُواْ فَأُعَذِّبُهُمْ عَذَابًا شَدِيدًا فِي ٱلدُّنْيَا وَٱلْأَخِرَةِ وَمَا لَهُم مِّن نَّـٰصِرِينَ ۝ وَأَمَّا ٱلَّذِينَ ءَامَنُواْ وَعَمِلُواْ ٱلصَّـٰلِحَـٰتِ فَيُوَفِّيهِمْ أُجُورَهُمْ وَٱللَّهُ لَا يُحِبُّ ٱلظَّـٰلِمِينَ ۝ ذَٰلِكَ نَتْلُوهُ عَلَيْكَ مِنَ ٱلْأَيَـٰتِ وَٱلذِّكْرِ ٱلْحَكِيمِ ۝

---

[a] Jesus Christ was born into the Jewish community, but the Jews did not affirm his prophethood. Instead, they made out a false case against him and took him to the Roman court in Palestine. The court decreed to have him crucified, but God saved him and the Roman soldiers crucified another person who resembled Christ, taking him to be Christ. To punish this crime of the Jews, God decreed that the believers in Jesus Christ, would forever, till Doomsday, have dominion over the Jewish people. This is what was decreed by God for this world. The Hereafter however, is a different matter.

⁵⁹ Jesus in the sight of God is like Adam. He created him from dust; then said to him, 'Be!' and he was. ⁶⁰ This is the truth from your Lord, so do not be among the doubters.ᵃ

إِنَّ مَثَلَ عِيسَىٰ عِندَ ٱللَّهِ كَمَثَلِ ءَادَمَ خَلَقَهُۥ مِن تُرَابٍ ثُمَّ قَالَ لَهُۥ كُن فَيَكُونُ ۝ ٱلْحَقُّ مِن رَّبِّكَ فَلَا تَكُن مِّنَ ٱلْمُمْتَرِينَ ۝

ᵃ The Christians believe that Christ is the son of God, and that he is different from all other human beings. Since his very birth was quite exceptional in that he had no father, how could he be a human being like any other? They hold that his uncommon birth itself shows that he was not the son of man but of God. But this contention can be shown to be invalid by comparing the birth of Christ with the birth of the first man. (All of us, the Christians too, believe that Adam was the first man.) He was not born in the normal way, i.e. having a father and mother, but came into existence directly by God's command. Then when Adam, born without a father, is not God's son, how could Jesus Christ, who was also born without a father, be the son of God?

⁶¹ And if anyone should argue with you about this [truth] after the knowledge you have received, say to them, 'Come! Let us gather our sons and your sons, our women and your women, and ourselves and yourselves; and then let us pray earnestly and invoke the curse of God upon the liars. ⁶² This is the true account. There is no deity save Him. God is Mighty and Wise.' ⁶³ And if they turn away, God knows well the evil-doers.ᵃ

فَمَنْ حَاجَّكَ فِيهِ مِنْ بَعْدِ مَا جَاءَكَ مِنَ ٱلْعِلْمِ فَقُلْ تَعَالَوْاْ نَدْعُ أَبْنَاءَنَا وَأَبْنَاءَكُمْ وَنِسَاءَنَا وَنِسَاءَكُمْ وَأَنفُسَنَا وَأَنفُسَكُمْ ثُمَّ نَبْتَهِلْ فَنَجْعَل لَّعْنَتَ ٱللَّهِ عَلَى ٱلْكَٰذِبِينَ ۝ إِنَّ هَٰذَا لَهُوَ ٱلْقَصَصُ ٱلْحَقُّ وَمَا مِنْ إِلَٰهٍ إِلَّا ٱللَّهُ وَإِنَّ ٱللَّهَ لَهُوَ ٱلْعَزِيزُ ٱلْحَكِيمُ ۝ فَإِن تَوَلَّوْاْ فَإِنَّ ٱللَّهَ عَلِيمٌۢ بِٱلْمُفْسِدِينَ ۝

ᵃ Najran (about 150 miles north of Sanaʿ towards Yemen) was a great centre of Christianity at the time of the revelation of the Quran. In the 10th year of the Hijra, a Christian deputation came from Najran, to discuss Christian beliefs with the Prophet Muhammad. The Prophet presented many arguments to them. He asked how Christ could be God's son, when God is a living being who would never die, whereas Jesus would eventually be overcome by death. They could not counter his arguments but, nevertheless, stood their ground.

When the Prophet saw that they were not going to accept his arguments, however sound they might be, he gave them a final challenge. He said that if they really believed that they were right (in believing Christ to be the son of God) they should be ready for a *mubahalah,* i.e., a solemn meeting, in which both sides should summon not only their men, but their women and children, to pray earnestly to God, and invoke the curse of God on those who lied. Those who were pure and sincere in their faith would not hesitate.

The next day the Prophet came out of his home accompanied by his grandsons, Hasan and Husayn, and his daughter Fatimah, and son-in-law ʿAli. On seeing this the Christians were so impressed that they sought some time to reconsider. In their consultations one of their religious scholars said: 'You know God has promised to send a Prophet among the Ishmaelites. Suppose he be the same prophet. In that case, the only result of engaging in a *mubahalah* with him would be the destruction of all our people and its effect would even extend to our next generations. By God, I am seeing such faces as could move mountains with their prayers. So it is better to enter into certain peace treaties with him and go back to our homes.'

64 Say, 'People of the Book, let us come to a word common to us that we shall worship none but God and that we shall associate no partner with Him and that none of us shall take others, besides God, for lords.' And if they turn away, say, 'Bear witness that we have submitted to God.' 65 People of the Book, why do you dispute about Abraham when the Torah and Gospel were only sent down after him. Do you not use your reason? 66 You are those who disputed about things of which you had some knowledge. Must you now argue about things of which you have no knowledge? God knows, but you do not know.ᵃ

قُلْ يَـٰٓأَهْلَ ٱلْكِتَـٰبِ تَعَالَوْا۟ إِلَىٰ كَلِمَةٍ سَوَآءٍۭ بَيْنَنَا وَبَيْنَكُمْ أَلَّا نَعْبُدَ إِلَّا ٱللَّهَ وَلَا نُشْرِكَ بِهِۦ شَيْـًٔا وَلَا يَتَّخِذَ بَعْضُنَا بَعْضًا أَرْبَابًا مِّن دُونِ ٱللَّهِ ۚ فَإِن تَوَلَّوْا۟ فَقُولُوا۟ ٱشْهَدُوا۟ بِأَنَّا مُسْلِمُونَ ۝ يَـٰٓأَهْلَ ٱلْكِتَـٰبِ لِمَ تُحَآجُّونَ فِىٓ إِبْرَٰهِيمَ وَمَآ أُنزِلَتِ ٱلتَّوْرَىٰةُ وَٱلْإِنجِيلُ إِلَّا مِنۢ بَعْدِهِۦٓ ۚ أَفَلَا تَعْقِلُونَ ۝ هَـٰٓأَنتُمْ هَـٰٓؤُلَآءِ حَـٰجَجْتُمْ فِيمَا لَكُم بِهِۦ عِلْمٌ فَلِمَ تُحَآجُّونَ فِيمَا لَيْسَ لَكُم بِهِۦ عِلْمٌ ۚ وَٱللَّهُ يَعْلَمُ وَأَنتُمْ لَا تَعْلَمُونَ ۝

ᵃ The concept of monotheism is not only a basic teaching of the Prophet Muhammad but is also enshrined as an established reality, even in the interpolated versions of the Torah and the Bible. Judged on this established criterion, Islam, unlike Judaism and Christianity, is proved to be a perfectly true religion. Monotheism implies belief in only one God. He alone should be worshipped. No one should be associated with Him. No man should be accorded that special place which is the sole prerogative of the Lord of the Universe. This concept of monotheism is preserved in its pure form only in Islam in the Quran. Other religions, while accepting monotheism ideologically, also adopted almost everything that ran counter to it. While believing in God as the Sustainer, in practice they accorded that status to their saints.

⁶⁷ Abraham was neither a Jew nor a Christian. He was an upright man, one who had surrendered himself to God. He was not one of those who associate partners with God. ⁶⁸ Surely, the people who are closest to Abraham are those who followed him and this Prophet [Muhammad], and those who believe in him. God is the guardian of the believers. ⁶⁹ Some of the People of the Book wish to lead you astray but they only lead themselves astray, though they do not realise it. ⁷⁰ People of the Book! Why do you deny God's signs, having been witnesses thereof? ⁷¹ People of the Book! Why do you mix truth with falsehood and knowingly conceal the truth? ᵃ

مَا كَانَ إِبْرَٰهِيمُ يَهُودِيًّا وَلَا نَصْرَانِيًّا وَلَٰكِن كَانَ حَنِيفًا مُّسْلِمًا وَمَا كَانَ مِنَ ٱلْمُشْرِكِينَ ۞ إِنَّ أَوْلَى ٱلنَّاسِ بِإِبْرَٰهِيمَ لَلَّذِينَ ٱتَّبَعُوهُ وَهَٰذَا ٱلنَّبِىُّ وَٱلَّذِينَ ءَامَنُوا۟ وَٱللَّهُ وَلِىُّ ٱلْمُؤْمِنِينَ ۞ وَدَّت طَّآئِفَةٌ مِّنْ أَهْلِ ٱلْكِتَٰبِ لَوْ يُضِلُّونَكُمْ وَمَا يُضِلُّونَ إِلَّآ أَنفُسَهُمْ وَمَا يَشْعُرُونَ ۞ يَٰٓأَهْلَ ٱلْكِتَٰبِ لِمَ تَكْفُرُونَ بِـَٔايَٰتِ ٱللَّهِ وَأَنتُمْ تَشْهَدُونَ ۞ يَٰٓأَهْلَ ٱلْكِتَٰبِ لِمَ تَلْبِسُونَ ٱلْحَقَّ بِٱلْبَٰطِلِ وَتَكْتُمُونَ ٱلْحَقَّ وَأَنتُمْ تَعْلَمُونَ ۞

ᵃ The Makkan polytheists called their religion the faith of Abraham. Jews and Christians too bracketed their religious history with that of Abraham. In every age people have used the names of their prophets and saints to justify their own additions to and inventions in religion. After the passage of time, people fail to differentiate between the original religion and its later version. The later version is ultimately taken to be the real religion. The atmosphere surrounding it is such that, when the call to return to true and pure religion is given, its opponents find the easiest way to discredit it is by making public allegations that the caller is against the religion handed down to them by their saints. One who is the true representative of the religion of 'saints' is now rejected in the name of former saints. This is because what his opponents hold up as their yardstick is not actually the original version of religion as given by the saints of the past. Instead it is the body of alterations and additions made by later followers and subsequently accepted as the 'religion of the saints'. This is like drawing a veil of falsehood over the truth. That is, making pronouncements which are invalid from the religious and logical point of view. But since the public does not have the ability to analyze them, it deems them to be right and is thus distanced from the truth. The *hanif* (monotheist) is one who treads the straight path of monotheism and the *non-hanif* is one who deviates from the straight path, going instead into by-lanes. Sometimes the secondary aspects of religion are so emphasized by the interpretation put upon them that they appear to be the main foci, the actual core of religion. In this way its fundamentals lose their significance and people stray from the straight thoroughfare of monotheism into the byways of unimportant issues.

72 Some of the People of the Book say to one another, 'Believe in what is revealed to the faithful in the morning and deny it in the evening, so that they [the Muslims] may themselves abandon their faith [in confusion]. 73 Believe only in those who follow your own religion.' Say to them, 'Surely, the true guidance is the guidance from God.' [But you think it is impossible that] someone else may be granted [revelation] such as you were granted—or else that they should contend against you before your Lord. Say, 'All grace is in the hands of God; He grants it to whom He wills: for God is boundless, and all knowing, 74 He singles out for His mercy whoever He pleases. God is the Lord of exceeding bounty.' a

وَقَالَت طَّآئِفَةٌ مِّنْ أَهْلِ ٱلْكِتَٰبِ ءَامِنُوا بِٱلَّذِىٓ أُنزِلَ عَلَى ٱلَّذِينَ ءَامَنُوا وَجْهَ ٱلنَّهَارِ وَٱكْفُرُوٓا ءَاخِرَهُۥ لَعَلَّهُمْ يَرْجِعُونَ ۝ وَلَا تُؤْمِنُوٓا إِلَّا لِمَن تَبِعَ دِينَكُمْ قُلْ إِنَّ ٱلْهُدَىٰ هُدَى ٱللَّهِ أَن يُؤْتَىٰٓ أَحَدٌ مِّثْلَ مَآ أُوتِيتُمْ أَوْ يُحَآجُّوكُمْ عِندَ رَبِّكُمْ قُلْ إِنَّ ٱلْفَضْلَ بِيَدِ ٱللَّهِ يُؤْتِيهِ مَن يَشَآءُ وَٱللَّهُ وَٰسِعٌ عَلِيمٌ ۝ يَخْتَصُّ بِرَحْمَتِهِۦ مَن يَشَآءُ وَٱللَّهُ ذُو ٱلْفَضْلِ ٱلْعَظِيمِ ۝

a A community into which prophets and reformers have been born and in which religion has held sway for a considerable period of time, is often mistaken in thinking that their ethos and the truth are synonymous (that is, whatever they believe and practise is nothing but the truth). It comes to believe that guidance has something to do with a particular community rather than being a matter of principle, and is unwilling to accept such truth as has been revealed elsewhere. This was the case with the Jews. Under the influence of historical traditions, they began to believe that whoever was one of them was on the right path, and that whoever was not, was misguided. Even today, they tend to forget that truth is something that comes from God and not from an individual or a community. Although they are ostensibly adherents of a divine religion, in reality for them their community is supreme, while God is relegated to a secondary place. This mentality casts such a veil over their eyes that they become unable to see any merit outside their own fraternity. Even in the face of clear signs and arguments, they doubt the veracity of any outsider, and strongly oppose any call of truth which comes from without. In obedience to their false standards, they try to stifle such a call.

They would not hesitate to adopt unjust methods to curb the activities of the preacher. They would even resort to spreading false propaganda to cast doubt upon his veracity. Going against God's commandments, they adopt two separate criteria of behaviour, one for the members of their own community and another for outsiders.

⁷⁵ Among the people of the Book there are some who, if you entrust them with a heap of gold, will return it to you. But there are others of them who, if you entrust them with a single *dinar*, will not return it to you, unless you keep demanding it from them. That is because they say, 'We are under no obligation towards the gentiles.' They deliberately tell lies about God. ⁷⁶ Indeed God loves those who honour their covenants and fear Him. God loves the righteous.ᵃ

۞ وَمِنْ أَهْلِ ٱلْكِتَٰبِ مَنْ إِن تَأْمَنْهُ بِقِنطَارٍ يُؤَدِّهِۦ إِلَيْكَ وَمِنْهُم مَّنْ إِن تَأْمَنْهُ بِدِينَارٍ لَّا يُؤَدِّهِۦٓ إِلَيْكَ إِلَّا مَا دُمْتَ عَلَيْهِ قَآئِمًا ۗ ذَٰلِكَ بِأَنَّهُمْ قَالُوا۟ لَيْسَ عَلَيْنَا فِى ٱلْأُمِّيِّۧنَ سَبِيلٌ وَيَقُولُونَ عَلَى ٱللَّهِ ٱلْكَذِبَ وَهُمْ يَعْلَمُونَ ۝ بَلَىٰ مَنْ أَوْفَىٰ بِعَهْدِهِۦ وَٱتَّقَىٰ فَإِنَّ ٱللَّهَ يُحِبُّ ٱلْمُتَّقِينَ ۝

ᵃ Being particularly chosen to represent His religion is one of the special blessings of God. Such a choice is not based on one's belonging to a certain community. The recipient of this blessing is one whom God selects for his spiritual virtues. And God likes one who is so attached to Him and who so fears Him that He becomes his Keeper, and his Lord in the true sense of these words. Indeed, when the believer enters into a covenant with his Creator, he is not able to go back.

God's chosen servants are those who fulfill their trusts and do not break their promises. It is people such as these who are showered with God's blessings. On the contrary, those who are careless in the fulfillment of trusts and are negligent about keeping their promises are of no value in the eyes of God. They will be denied God's mercies and blessings.

⁷⁷ Those who sell out God's covenant and their oaths for a paltry price will have no share in the life to come on the Day of Resurrection. God will neither speak to them nor cast a look upon them on the Day of Judgement, nor will He purify them. For them there shall be a grievous punishment.ᵃ

إِنَّ ٱلَّذِينَ يَشْتَرُونَ بِعَهْدِ ٱللَّهِ وَأَيْمَـٰنِهِمْ ثَمَنًا قَلِيلاً أُوْلَـٰئِكَ لَا خَلَـٰقَ لَهُمْ فِى ٱلْأَخِرَةِ وَلَا يُكَلِّمُهُمُ ٱللَّهُ وَلَا يَنظُرُ إِلَيْهِمْ يَوْمَ ٱلْقِيَـٰمَةِ وَلَا يُزَكِّيهِمْ وَلَهُمْ عَذَابٌ أَلِيمٌ ۝

ᵃ On embracing the faith, the individual enters into a covenant with God that he will obey Him and that, living among human beings, and pledging himself to a life of constraint, he will fulfill all the responsibilities that God's law imposes upon him. Such a life can be adhered to only by one who has risen above worldly interests. One who is ready to overlook the divine pact whenever his self suffers or his worldly interests are endangered barters the world for the Hereafter at a very paltry price: whenever the question arises of choosing either the world or the Hereafter, he always prefers the world. How can one who attaches so little value to the Hereafter be deserving of God's mercies in the next world?

78 There are some among them who distort the Book by the way they speak to make you think that what they say is from the Book, whereas it is not. They say it is from God whereas it is not. Thus they tell a lie about God and they know it. 79 No one to whom God has given the Scriptures and on whom He has bestowed wisdom and prophethood would say to men, 'Worship me instead of God.' [He would say rather], 'Be devoted servants of God, for you have taught and studied the Scriptures.' 80 Nor would he enjoin you to take the angels and the prophets as your lords; how could he command you to be disbelievers after you have submitted to God.ᵃ

وَإِنَّ مِنْهُمْ لَفَرِيقًا يَلْوُونَ أَلْسِنَتَهُم بِٱلْكِتَٰبِ لِتَحْسَبُوهُ مِنَ ٱلْكِتَٰبِ وَمَا هُوَ مِنَ ٱلْكِتَٰبِ وَيَقُولُونَ هُوَ مِنْ عِندِ ٱللَّهِ وَمَا هُوَ مِنْ عِندِ ٱللَّهِ وَيَقُولُونَ عَلَى ٱللَّهِ ٱلْكَذِبَ وَهُمْ يَعْلَمُونَ ۝ مَا كَانَ لِبَشَرٍ أَن يُؤْتِيَهُ ٱللَّهُ ٱلْكِتَٰبَ وَٱلْحُكْمَ وَٱلنُّبُوَّةَ ثُمَّ يَقُولَ لِلنَّاسِ كُونُوا۟ عِبَادًا لِّى مِن دُونِ ٱللَّهِ وَلَٰكِن كُونُوا۟ رَبَّٰنِيِّۦنَ بِمَا كُنتُمْ تُعَلِّمُونَ ٱلْكِتَٰبَ وَبِمَا كُنتُمْ تَدْرُسُونَ ۝ وَلَا يَأْمُرَكُمْ أَن تَتَّخِذُوا۟ ٱلْمَلَٰٓئِكَةَ وَٱلنَّبِيِّۦنَ أَرْبَابًا أَيَأْمُرُكُم بِٱلْكُفْرِ بَعْدَ إِذْ أَنتُم مُّسْلِمُونَ ۝

ᵃ Those who buy the world in exchange for the Hereafter do not deny religion or the Hereafter outright. Rather, they fully associate themselves with their religion. Then how do they reconcile these two conflicting spheres? This is done in a devious way, that is, by putting a self-styled construction upon revealed teachings. Aspirants to material honour and glory pervert the teachings of their religion in order to justify their worldly ways, sometimes by altering the wordings of revelations and sometimes by a wilful misinterpretation supportive of their selfish interests. Instead of changing themselves, they change the book of God, so that whatever it takes to give a religious aura to their irreligious lives may be shown to be contained therein. The most heinous crime in the eyes of God is to attribute to God something which He has not said.

The simplest and most certain testimony of the truth of any teaching is that it brings God's servants closer to their Lord, that it directs people's feelings of love and fear towards God. On the contrary, any teaching which produces a personal cult or any other cult for that matter, or which diverts peoples' finer feelings and emotions towards anything other than God, should be considered based on falsehood, even if it be couched in religious terms.

81 When God made a covenant with the prophets, He said, 'Here is the Book and the wisdom which I have given you. When there comes to you a messenger fulfilling that [predictions about him in their Scripture] which is with you, you must believe in him and help him. Do you then affirm this and accept the responsibility I have laid upon you in these terms?' They said, 'We will affirm it.' God said, 'Then bear witness, and I will bear witness with you.' 82 Now whoever turns away after this, are surely transgressors. 83 Do they seek a religion other than the religion of God, when everything in the heavens and the earth has submitted to Him, willingly or unwillingly? To Him they shall all return.[a]

وَإِذْ أَخَذَ ٱللَّهُ مِيثَٰقَ ٱلنَّبِيِّـۧنَ لَمَآ ءَاتَيْتُكُم مِّن كِتَٰبٍ وَحِكْمَةٍ ثُمَّ جَآءَكُمْ رَسُولٌ مُّصَدِّقٌ لِّمَا مَعَكُمْ لَتُؤْمِنُنَّ بِهِۦ وَلَتَنصُرُنَّهُۥ قَالَ ءَأَقْرَرْتُمْ وَأَخَذْتُمْ عَلَىٰ ذَٰلِكُمْ إِصْرِى قَالُوٓاْ أَقْرَرْنَا قَالَ فَٱشْهَدُواْ وَأَنَا۠ مَعَكُم مِّنَ ٱلشَّٰهِدِينَ ۝ فَمَن تَوَلَّىٰ بَعْدَ ذَٰلِكَ فَأُوْلَٰٓئِكَ هُمُ ٱلْفَٰسِقُونَ ۝ أَفَغَيْرَ دِينِ ٱللَّهِ يَبْغُونَ وَلَهُۥٓ أَسْلَمَ مَن فِى ٱلسَّمَٰوَٰتِ وَٱلْأَرْضِ طَوْعًا وَكَرْهًا وَإِلَيْهِ يُرْجَعُونَ ۝

---

[a] Discovering God is to find an eternal reality. It is to become a co-traveller or a travelling companion of the whole universe. Those who find God in this way, can rise above all kinds of prejudices. They recognize truth in all situations, whether the call of truth comes through an 'Israelite prophet' or an 'Ishmaelite prophet'. But those who lead their lives on the level of community-oriented thinking can recognize the truth only when it comes to them from a member of their own community. If God selects as His messenger someone from outside their community, then the message he brings does not lodge in their minds, not even when their own hearts bear witness to the veracity of that message. Even if such 'believers' regard themselves as true believers, they will find their names deleted from the list of believers in the Hereafter. This is because they recognized the truth only in relation to their community rather than in relation to God. Not acknowledging a message of truth, which has been testified to by their own hearts, is the worst crime in the eyes of God. Such people will be condemned in the Hereafter and all creatures will join in this condemnation.

84 Say, 'We believe in God and in what has been sent down to us and to Abraham, Ishmael, Isaac, Jacob and the Tribes. We believe in what has been given to Moses, Jesus and the prophets from their Lord. We make no distinction between any of them. It is to Him that we have surrendered ourselves.' 85 If anyone seeks a religion other than Islam [submission to God], it will not be accepted from him; he will be among the losers in the Hereafter. 86 How would God bestow His guidance upon people who have opted for unbelief after having embraced the faith and having borne witness that this Messenger is true and [after] all evidence of the truth has come to them? For, God does not guide such wrongdoers: 87 such people will be rewarded with rejection by God, by the angels, by all mankind. 88 In this state they shall abide forever; their punishment shall not be lightened nor shall they be granted respite. 89 Except for those who afterwards repent and reform. God is forgiving and merciful; 90 but as for those who are bent on denying the truth after accepting the true faith and grow in their refusal to acknowledge the truth, their repentance will not be accepted. They are the ones who have gone far astray. 91 Those who reject faith and die in the state of rejection will not be saved, even if they offer as ransom enough gold to fill the entire earth. Painful punishment is in store for them and they will have no supporters.[a]

قُلْ ءَامَنَّا بِٱللَّهِ وَمَآ أُنزِلَ عَلَيْنَا وَمَآ أُنزِلَ عَلَىٰٓ إِبْرَٰهِيمَ وَإِسْمَٰعِيلَ وَإِسْحَٰقَ وَيَعْقُوبَ وَٱلْأَسْبَاطِ وَمَآ أُوتِيَ مُوسَىٰ وَعِيسَىٰ وَٱلنَّبِيُّونَ مِن رَّبِّهِمْ لَا نُفَرِّقُ بَيْنَ أَحَدٍ مِّنْهُمْ وَنَحْنُ لَهُ مُسْلِمُونَ ۝ وَمَن يَبْتَغِ غَيْرَ ٱلْإِسْلَٰمِ دِينًا فَلَن يُقْبَلَ مِنْهُ وَهُوَ فِى ٱلْأَخِرَةِ مِنَ ٱلْخَٰسِرِينَ ۝ كَيْفَ يَهْدِى ٱللَّهُ قَوْمًا كَفَرُوا۟ بَعْدَ إِيمَٰنِهِمْ وَشَهِدُوٓا۟ أَنَّ ٱلرَّسُولَ حَقٌّ وَجَآءَهُمُ ٱلْبَيِّنَٰتُ وَٱللَّهُ لَا يَهْدِى ٱلْقَوْمَ ٱلظَّٰلِمِينَ ۝ أُو۟لَٰٓئِكَ جَزَآؤُهُمْ أَنَّ عَلَيْهِمْ لَعْنَةَ ٱللَّهِ وَٱلْمَلَٰٓئِكَةِ وَٱلنَّاسِ أَجْمَعِينَ ۝ خَٰلِدِينَ فِيهَا لَا يُخَفَّفُ عَنْهُمُ ٱلْعَذَابُ وَلَا هُمْ يُنظَرُونَ ۝ إِلَّا ٱلَّذِينَ تَابُوا۟ مِنۢ بَعْدِ ذَٰلِكَ وَأَصْلَحُوا۟ فَإِنَّ ٱللَّهَ غَفُورٌ رَّحِيمٌ ۝ إِنَّ ٱلَّذِينَ كَفَرُوا۟ بَعْدَ إِيمَٰنِهِمْ ثُمَّ ٱزْدَادُوا۟ كُفْرًا لَّن تُقْبَلَ تَوْبَتُهُمْ وَأُو۟لَٰٓئِكَ هُمُ ٱلضَّآلُّونَ ۝ إِنَّ ٱلَّذِينَ كَفَرُوا۟ وَمَاتُوا۟ وَهُمْ كُفَّارٌ فَلَن يُقْبَلَ مِنْ أَحَدِهِم مِّلْءُ ٱلْأَرْضِ ذَهَبًا وَلَوِ ٱفْتَدَىٰ بِهِۦٓ أُو۟لَٰٓئِكَ لَهُمْ عَذَابٌ أَلِيمٌ وَمَا لَهُم مِّن نَّٰصِرِينَ ۝

---

[a] Not acknowledging any truth external to their community appears to be a bid to save their faith. But in actuality it destroys their faith. ▶

⁹²Never will you attain to righteousness unless you spend for the cause of God out of what you cherish; and whatever you spend is known to God. ⁹³All food was lawful for the Children of Israel, except whatever Israel had made unlawful for himself before the Torah was sent down. Say to them, 'Bring the Torah then and read it, if you are truthful. ⁹⁴Those who, after this, persist in making up lies and attributing them to God are transgressors.' ⁹⁵Say, 'God speaks the Truth, so follow the faith of Abraham. He was an upright man and he was not one of the polytheists.' ⁹⁶The first House to be built for mankind was the one at Bakkah [Makkah]. It is a blessed place; a source of guidance for the whole world. ⁹⁷There are clear signs in it; it is the place where Abraham stood. Anyone who enters it will be secure. Pilgrimage to the House is a duty to God for anyone who is able to undertake it. Anyone who disbelieves should remember that God is independent of all creatures.ᵃ

لَن تَنَالُوا۟ ٱلۡبِرَّ حَتَّىٰ تُنفِقُوا۟ مِمَّا تُحِبُّونَ ۚ وَمَا تُنفِقُوا۟ مِن شَىۡءٍ فَإِنَّ ٱللَّهَ بِهِۦ عَلِيمٌ ۝ ٩٢ كُلُّ ٱلطَّعَامِ كَانَ حِلًّا لِّبَنِىٓ إِسۡرَٰٓءِيلَ إِلَّا مَا حَرَّمَ إِسۡرَٰٓءِيلُ عَلَىٰ نَفۡسِهِۦ مِن قَبۡلِ أَن تُنَزَّلَ ٱلتَّوۡرَىٰةُ ۗ قُلۡ فَأۡتُوا۟ بِٱلتَّوۡرَىٰةِ فَٱتۡلُوهَآ إِن كُنتُمۡ صَٰدِقِينَ ۝ ٩٣ فَمَنِ ٱفۡتَرَىٰ عَلَى ٱللَّهِ ٱلۡكَذِبَ مِنۢ بَعۡدِ ذَٰلِكَ فَأُو۟لَٰٓئِكَ هُمُ ٱلظَّٰلِمُونَ ۝ ٩٤ قُلۡ صَدَقَ ٱللَّهُ ۗ فَٱتَّبِعُوا۟ مِلَّةَ إِبۡرَٰهِيمَ حَنِيفًا وَمَا كَانَ مِنَ ٱلۡمُشۡرِكِينَ ۝ ٩٥ إِنَّ أَوَّلَ بَيۡتٍ وُضِعَ لِلنَّاسِ لَلَّذِى بِبَكَّةَ مُبَارَكًا وَهُدًى لِّلۡعَٰلَمِينَ ۝ ٩٦ فِيهِ ءَايَٰتُۢ بَيِّنَٰتٌ مَّقَامُ إِبۡرَٰهِيمَ ۖ وَمَن دَخَلَهُۥ كَانَ ءَامِنًا ۗ وَلِلَّهِ عَلَى ٱلنَّاسِ حِجُّ ٱلۡبَيۡتِ مَنِ ٱسۡتَطَاعَ إِلَيۡهِ سَبِيلًا ۚ وَمَن كَفَرَ فَإِنَّ ٱللَّهَ غَنِىٌّ عَنِ ٱلۡعَٰلَمِينَ ۝ ٩٧

God's true believer lives on God's continuous inspiration, so that one who confines himself to self-worship and community-worship will be blocking all paths to God's blessing entering into him. After being deprived of God's inspiration, what will there be left with which to nurture his faith?

ᵃAccording to the Jews' self-made set of religious laws, eating the meat of the camel and the rabbit was illegal, while it was quite licit in Islam. So the Jews would ask, if Islam was a revealed religion, why it was that the lawful and the unlawful were different in Islam from what had been laid down in the former revealed religions. Similarly, they would ask how it was that a religion revealed by God could command the direction of prayer to be the Ka'bah instead of al-Bayt al-Maqdis (Jerusalem), which had remained the direction for prayer in the teachings of all the prophets up till then. They in fact refused to believe that God could reveal a religion in which the Ka'bah was held to be the direction for prayer.

⁹⁸ Say, 'People of the Book, why do you reject God's revelations when God is witness to all that you do?' ⁹⁹ Say, 'People of the Book, why do you turn the believers away from the path of God, seeking to make it crooked, while you are witnesses thereof? God is not unaware of what you do.' *a*

قُلْ يَٰٓأَهْلَ ٱلْكِتَٰبِ لِمَ تَكْفُرُونَ بِـَٔايَٰتِ ٱللَّهِ وَٱللَّهُ شَهِيدٌ عَلَىٰ مَا تَعْمَلُونَ ۝ قُلْ يَٰٓأَهْلَ ٱلْكِتَٰبِ لِمَ تَصُدُّونَ عَن سَبِيلِ ٱللَّهِ مَنْ ءَامَنَ تَبْغُونَهَا عِوَجًا وَأَنتُمْ شُهَدَآءُ وَمَا ٱللَّهُ بِغَٰفِلٍ عَمَّا تَعْمَلُونَ ۝

---

a When the call of truth comes in all its purity, the interests of those who contrived to convince others that their self-styled religion had indeed been revealed by God are put at risk. People serving their own interests oppose the new messenger by raising different kinds of objections based on fallacies in order to turn others away from the true message. In their self-styled religion the basics of faith are not stressed. Instead, by giving importance to hair-splitting arguments on the relative aspects of religion, the acme of virtue is equated with full adherence to a man-made religious form. For example, they would shun rabbit's meat, saying that it was not consumed by their saints, although along with this, many illegal things would have been legalized by them. They would consider it of the utmost importance to face exactly in the direction of al-Bayt al-Maqdis, like a compass needle pointing to the pole. But they would show no interest in making their daily activities God-oriented. Virtue, however, hinges upon the making of sacrifices and not on the mere fact of opting for a religious form. God's true servant is one who offers his Lord the gift of love, and for whom no material thing is dearer than God. He is ever ready to pay the price of losing his prestige by recognizing the truth; he is ever ready to spend his wealth for the cause of God. Whoever is ready to pay the price of sacrificing his most cherished ambitions will be counted among the virtuous and considered a God-worshipper in the eyes of God.

¹⁰⁰ O believers, if you yield to some of those who were given the Scripture, they will cause you to renounce the truth after you have believed. ¹⁰¹ But how can you deny the truth when God's revelations are being conveyed to you and His own Messenger is in your midst? He who holds fast to God is indeed guided to the straight path. ¹⁰² Believers, fear God as is His due, and when death comes, be in a state of complete submission to Him.^a

يَٰٓأَيُّهَا ٱلَّذِينَ ءَامَنُوٓاْ إِن تُطِيعُواْ فَرِيقًا مِّنَ ٱلَّذِينَ أُوتُواْ ٱلْكِتَٰبَ يَرُدُّوكُم بَعْدَ إِيمَٰنِكُمْ كَٰفِرِينَ ۝ وَكَيْفَ تَكْفُرُونَ وَأَنتُمْ تُتْلَىٰ عَلَيْكُمْ ءَايَٰتُ ٱللَّهِ وَفِيكُمْ رَسُولُهُۥ ۗ وَمَن يَعْتَصِم بِٱللَّهِ فَقَدْ هُدِىَ إِلَىٰ صِرَٰطٍ مُّسْتَقِيمٍ ۝ يَٰٓأَيُّهَا ٱلَّذِينَ ءَامَنُواْ ٱتَّقُواْ ٱللَّهَ حَقَّ تُقَاتِهِۦ وَلَا تَمُوتُنَّ إِلَّا وَأَنتُم مُّسْلِمُونَ ۝

---

^a This world is a place of trial. Here, man is forever exposed to Satan's evil temptations. So there is always the possibility of Satan's succeeding in turning one from belief to unbelief. Then, while in this state—devoid of the true spirit of faith—one's time of departure from this world might come, making it almost impossible for one to make amends. That is why it is always necessary for man to be cautious: he must become his own keeper.

The actual mainspring of religion is fear of God (*taqwa*), that is, adopting till one's dying day an unshakeable sense of accountability to God for all of one's actions. This is the true and straight path. Any turning away from this path occurs when certain parts of the religion are modified in order to change the order of priorities, e.g. what is important is relegated to a secondary place, and vice versa. Such deviation mostly occurs when some secondary aspect is taken to be a fundamental part of religion and is stressed in a manner which should be reserved for the fear of God and concern for the Hereafter. Whenever such alterations are made in a religion, it necessarily results in differences which lead to serious schisms, with one group stressing one particular secondary aspect and another group stressing another particular secondary aspect—all of which culminates in the community splitting up into a number of sects. While an attitude inspired by the fear of God (*taqwa*) focuses all attention on the one and only God, in the absence of such fear, it is purely trivial matters which are thrust to the forefront. When peripheral issues are thus given importance, the upshot is disunity—and this is what brings on all the evils that push man to the brink of Hell. Disunity in a group must, therefore, be eschewed at all costs, for it will lead to calamity both in this world and in the Hereafter. It must be conceded that it is only when all of the emphasis is on *taqwa* that unity is a natural consequence.

¹⁰³ Hold fast to the cord of God and let nothing divide you. Remember the blessings He has bestowed upon you; you were enemies and then He united your hearts and by His grace you became brothers; you were on the brink of an abyss of Fire and He rescued you from it. Thus God makes His signs clear to you, so that you may find guidance.[a]

¹⁰⁴ Let there be a group among you who call others to good, and enjoin what is right, and forbid what is wrong: those who do this shall be successful.[b]

وَٱعْتَصِمُوا۟ بِحَبْلِ ٱللَّهِ جَمِيعًا وَلَا تَفَرَّقُوا۟ ۚ وَٱذْكُرُوا۟ نِعْمَتَ ٱللَّهِ عَلَيْكُمْ إِذْ كُنتُمْ أَعْدَآءً فَأَلَّفَ بَيْنَ قُلُوبِكُمْ فَأَصْبَحْتُم بِنِعْمَتِهِۦٓ إِخْوَٰنًا وَكُنتُمْ عَلَىٰ شَفَا حُفْرَةٍ مِّنَ ٱلنَّارِ فَأَنقَذَكُم مِّنْهَا ۗ كَذَٰلِكَ يُبَيِّنُ ٱللَّهُ لَكُمْ ءَايَٰتِهِۦ لَعَلَّكُمْ تَهْتَدُونَ ۝ وَلْتَكُن مِّنكُمْ أُمَّةٌ يَدْعُونَ إِلَى ٱلْخَيْرِ وَيَأْمُرُونَ بِٱلْمَعْرُوفِ وَيَنْهَوْنَ عَنِ ٱلْمُنكَرِ ۚ وَأُو۟لَٰٓئِكَ هُمُ ٱلْمُفْلِحُونَ ۝

---

[a] Before the advent of Islam there were two tribes, the Aws and Khazraj, inhabiting Madinah. Both were Arabs, but they continuously waged war against each other. Attacks and counter-attacks had considerably weakened them. When they accepted Islam, all hostilities ended: they became like brothers. The reason for this is that one who denies the truth is faithful only to his own self, while a believer gives his allegiance solely to God. In a society where individuals are faithful only to their own selves or to their groups, many allegiances naturally come into existence. The result is strife and dissension. On the contrary, in a society where all its members bow only to one God, everyone is directed towards a single focal point. All being bound by one and the same cord, mutual clashes and strife cease altogether.

[b] This command pertains, on the one hand, to the common man and on the other to the intellectuals and the educated class. The educated should be strenuous in their efforts to enjoin goodness and forbid wrong in the community. Their keen awareness of the need for reform should ensure their continuing concern with the state of the people: they must encourage everyone to follow the path of goodness and shun the path of evil.

However, for such an effort to succeed, the public must be submissive; they must be willing to listen to their elders. They must show respect for them, follow them as they are bid and stop where they are told to stop, thus surrendering themselves to their religious reformers. A Muslim community's success thus depends respectively upon the attitudes of the religious elders and of the public. It is in an atmosphere of listening and obeying that society can be reformed, ensuring success both in this world as well as in the next. In short, elders motivated by the true religious spirit, should never shirk their responsibility towards their community of enjoining goodness upon them and forbidding evil.

¹⁰⁵ Do not be like those who, after they had been given clear evidence, split into factions and differed among themselves: a terrible punishment awaits such people. ¹⁰⁶ On the Day when some faces are bright and some faces are dark, it will be said to those with darkened faces, 'Did you reject faith after accepting it? Taste, then, this punishment for having denied the truth!' ¹⁰⁷ But as for those with shining faces, they shall abide forever in God's grace. ¹⁰⁸ These are God's revelations; We recite them to you in all truth. God desires no injustice to mankind. ¹⁰⁹ His is all that the heavens and the earth contain. To God shall all things return.

¹¹⁰ You are indeed the best community that has ever been brought forth for [the good of] mankind. You enjoin what is good, and forbid what is evil, and you believe in God. If the People of the Book had also believed, it would have surely been better for them. Some of them are true believers, but most of them are disobedient.ᵃ

وَلَا تَكُونُوا كَٱلَّذِينَ تَفَرَّقُوا وَٱخْتَلَفُوا مِنۢ بَعْدِ مَا جَآءَهُمُ ٱلْبَيِّنَٰتُ ۚ وَأُو۟لَٰٓئِكَ لَهُمْ عَذَابٌ عَظِيمٌ ۝ يَوْمَ تَبْيَضُّ وُجُوهٌ وَتَسْوَدُّ وُجُوهٌ ۚ فَأَمَّا ٱلَّذِينَ ٱسْوَدَّتْ وُجُوهُهُمْ أَكَفَرْتُم بَعْدَ إِيمَٰنِكُمْ فَذُوقُوا ٱلْعَذَابَ بِمَا كُنتُمْ تَكْفُرُونَ ۝ وَأَمَّا ٱلَّذِينَ ٱبْيَضَّتْ وُجُوهُهُمْ فَفِى رَحْمَةِ ٱللَّهِ هُمْ فِيهَا خَٰلِدُونَ ۝ تِلْكَ ءَايَٰتُ ٱللَّهِ نَتْلُوهَا عَلَيْكَ بِٱلْحَقِّ ۗ وَمَا ٱللَّهُ يُرِيدُ ظُلْمًا لِّلْعَٰلَمِينَ ۝ وَلِلَّهِ مَا فِى ٱلسَّمَٰوَٰتِ وَمَا فِى ٱلْأَرْضِ ۚ وَإِلَى ٱللَّهِ تُرْجَعُ ٱلْأُمُورُ ۝ كُنتُمْ خَيْرَ أُمَّةٍ أُخْرِجَتْ لِلنَّاسِ تَأْمُرُونَ بِٱلْمَعْرُوفِ وَتَنْهَوْنَ عَنِ ٱلْمُنكَرِ وَتُؤْمِنُونَ بِٱللَّهِ ۗ وَلَوْ ءَامَنَ أَهْلُ ٱلْكِتَٰبِ لَكَانَ خَيْرًا لَّهُم ۚ مِّنْهُمُ ٱلْمُؤْمِنُونَ وَأَكْثَرُهُمُ ٱلْفَٰسِقُونَ ۝

ᵃ The benefit the intellectuals have of being imbued with this spirit is that all their attention remains focussed on goodness, that is, on the basics of religion. They have thus no time for hair-splitting arguments about secondary aspects of religion. Those who become the heralds of God's greatness and arise both as warners and as harbingers of glad tidings have not the time to waste their expertise on matters of no significance. In this way, the task of exhorting people to lead a life of righteousness and forbidding evil engages them in finding solutions to real problems. Verbal jousting over supposed problems seems to them meaningless and futile, just as a farmer finds the game of chess a futile exercise, a waste of time. In showing willingness to be obedient to well-intentioned religious elders, the people are saved from schism and strife. Submitting to an authority unites all of them. Unity becomes a common attribute of believers, and unity, without doubt is the greatest of all powers in this world.

111 They can do you very little harm; if they come out to fight you, they will show you their backs; then they shall not be helped—112 abasement shall attend them wherever they are found, unless they make a covenant with God or with man. They have incurred God's wrath and have been utterly humbled, because they have persistently disbelieved in God's signs and killed prophets unjustly. This resulted from their disobedience and their habit of transgression.[a]

لَن يَضُرُّوكُمْ إِلَّا أَذًى وَإِن يُقَٰتِلُوكُمْ يُوَلُّوكُمُ ٱلْأَدْبَارَ ثُمَّ لَا يُنصَرُونَ ۞ ضُرِبَتْ عَلَيْهِمُ ٱلذِّلَّةُ أَيْنَ مَا ثُقِفُوٓاْ إِلَّا بِحَبْلٍ مِّنَ ٱللَّهِ وَحَبْلٍ مِّنَ ٱلنَّاسِ وَبَآءُو بِغَضَبٍ مِّنَ ٱللَّهِ وَضُرِبَتْ عَلَيْهِمُ ٱلْمَسْكَنَةُ ذَٰلِكَ بِأَنَّهُمْ كَانُواْ يَكْفُرُونَ بِـَٔايَٰتِ ٱللَّهِ وَيَقْتُلُونَ ٱلْأَنۢبِيَآءَ بِغَيْرِ حَقٍّ ذَٰلِكَ بِمَا عَصَواْ وَّكَانُواْ يَعْتَدُونَ ۞

---

[a] Subsequently, God sent His religion in its original form through the Prophet Muhammad. Now the Muslims have undertaken the obligation of guiding people to the true religion of submission to God. The assignment of this role demands that they be true believers in God. It devolves upon them to enjoin goodness upon the world and to inform mankind of whatever is evil in the eyes of God. Since this is a mission assigned by Almighty God, He Himself has guaranteed to help His emissaries surmount all obstacles to their performing this task. Those who come forward for this divine mission have God's pledge that their opponents will not be able to inflict any real harm upon them.

113 Yet they are not all alike. Of the People of the Book there are some who stand by their covenant; they recite the word of God during the night and prostrate themselves before Him, 114 who believe in God and the Last Day, who enjoin justice and forbid evil and vie with each other in good works. These are righteous men 115 and they will not be denied [the reward] for whatever good deeds they do: God knows the righteous.*

۞ لَيْسُوا۟ سَوَآءً مِّنْ أَهْلِ ٱلْكِتَٰبِ أُمَّةٌ قَآئِمَةٌ يَتْلُونَ ءَايَٰتِ ٱللَّهِ ءَانَآءَ ٱلَّيْلِ وَهُمْ يَسْجُدُونَ ۝ يُؤْمِنُونَ بِٱللَّهِ وَٱلْيَوْمِ ٱلْءَاخِرِ وَيَأْمُرُونَ بِٱلْمَعْرُوفِ وَيَنْهَوْنَ عَنِ ٱلْمُنكَرِ وَيُسَٰرِعُونَ فِى ٱلْخَيْرَٰتِ وَأُو۟لَٰٓئِكَ مِنَ ٱلصَّٰلِحِينَ ۝ وَمَا يَفْعَلُوا۟ مِنْ خَيْرٍ فَلَن يُكْفَرُوهُ وَٱللَّهُ عَلِيمٌۢ بِٱلْمُتَّقِينَ ۝

---

a This refers here to the conduct of the People of the Book (believers in former revealed scriptures), and their immediate recognition and acceptance, in all humility, of the divine truth as proclaimed from the lips of the Last Prophet. At that time there was, on the one hand, the religion of Moses, invested with all the strength of historical grandeur and sanctity of tradition. On the other hand stood the religion of the Prophet Muhammad, which had yet to acquire the force of argument, historical grandeur and traditional sanctity to support it. This difference between Moses' religion and the religion of the Prophet of the time posed the greatest obstacle to the acknowledgment of the latter's religion. Yet this obstacle was successfully overcome and the religion of the contemporary Prophet was welcomed.

116 As for those who deny the truth, neither their possessions nor their children shall avail them in the least against God. They will be inmates of the Fire. They will remain there for ever; 117 that which they spend in pursuit of the life of this world is like a biting frosty blast which smites the harvest of a people who have wronged themselves, and destroys it. God is not unjust to them; they are unjust to their own souls.ᵃ

إِنَّ ٱلَّذِينَ كَفَرُواْ لَن تُغْنِىَ عَنْهُمْ أَمْوَٰلُهُمْ وَلَآ أَوْلَٰدُهُم مِّنَ ٱللَّهِ شَيْـًٔا وَأُوْلَٰٓئِكَ أَصْحَٰبُ ٱلنَّارِ هُمْ فِيهَا خَٰلِدُونَ ۝ مَثَلُ مَا يُنفِقُونَ فِى هَٰذِهِ ٱلْحَيَوٰةِ ٱلدُّنْيَا كَمَثَلِ رِيحٍ فِيهَا صِرٌّ أَصَابَتْ حَرْثَ قَوْمٍ ظَلَمُوٓاْ أَنفُسَهُمْ فَأَهْلَكَتْهُ ۚ وَمَا ظَلَمَهُمُ ٱللَّهُ وَلَٰكِنْ أَنفُسَهُمْ يَظْلِمُونَ ۝

ᵃ The love of wealth and children becomes an obstacle to accepting a religion, which entails all kinds of sacrifices. And adherence to God's religion is not a matter of engaging in hollow pretences of piety carried out in the public eye. Just as a gust of chill air ravages the whole harvest, so will the tempest of the Last Day (qiyamah) render valueless all such ostentatious acts.

There were some among the Jews who believed in the Prophet Muhammad. And a few God-fearing people are more precious in the eyes of God than a host of ungodly people.

But merely being a member of a community formed of one race in the name of a prophet, is not enough to earn one salvation. What is actually required of an individual is that he binds himself by a covenant with God. By 'covenant' is meant faith—the sacred bond between God and man. That is to say, personal actions and not community relationship make one deserving of God's mercy and blessings.

All the responsibilities that faith implies are included in this pledge. Remembering God in one's solitude, worshipping Him, leading one's life keeping in view the Hereafter, enjoining goodness upon the people around one, discouraging people from committing evil, working unstintingly for the cause of God—all such actions fulfil the divine covenant. Those who follow such a course are upright people in the eyes of God. God has full knowledge of their actions, for which He will reward them, and He will greatly honour them on the Day of Judgement.

[118] Believers, do not take outsiders as your intimate friends, they will spare no effort to harm you.[a] They love to see you suffer; their hatred is evident from the words which fall from their mouths. But what their hearts conceal is far worse. We have made Our signs clear to you; will you not understand?[b]

يَـٰٓأَيُّهَا ٱلَّذِينَ ءَامَنُواْ لَا تَتَّخِذُواْ بِطَانَةً مِّن دُونِكُمْ لَا يَأْلُونَكُمْ خَبَالاً وَدُّواْ مَا عَنِتُّمْ قَدْ بَدَتِ ٱلْبَغْضَآءُ مِنْ أَفْوَٰهِهِمْ وَمَا تُخْفِى صُدُورُهُمْ أَكْبَرُ قَدْ بَيَّنَّا لَكُمُ ٱلْءَايَـٰتِ إِن كُنتُمْ تَعْقِلُونَ ۝

[a] This refers only to people whose enmity has become apparent from their behaviour and their utterances (Tabari).

[b] The Muslims believed in the same divine faith as was given to the former People of the Book by their prophets. The religion of both was one in terms of actual reality, but the People of the Book opposed the believers. The reason being that they had formed a self-styled religion, which they attributed to their prophets. It was due to this self-styled religion that they had been enjoying a position of leadership with the people. In a true religion of God, all attention remains centred on God, whereas in a self-styled religion, people's attention is diverted to the founders of the religion and the commentators. Upholders of the latter form of faith never tolerate the call of true religion, because this would amount to displacing themselves from their position of eminence. In such a situation, true believers should refrain from negative reaction and adhere steadily to the path of patience and piety (taqwa). Patience (sabr) entails holding fast to the truth under all circumstances, and taqwa entails regarding God, and no other, as the only decisive power. If believers give proof of maintaining this kind of positive attitude, no enmity, however great, can harm them.

¹¹⁹ It is you who love them, but they do not love you;[a] you believe in all the revealed Books. When they meet you, they say, 'We believe,' but when they are alone, they bite their fingertips with rage. Say, 'Die of rage!' God is aware of what your hearts contain. ¹²⁰ Whenever something good happens to you, it grieves them; but when evil befalls you, they rejoice. If you persevere and fear God, their designs will never harm you in the least: God encompasses all that they do.[b]

هَـٰٓأَنتُمْ أُوْلَآءِ تُحِبُّونَهُمْ وَلَا يُحِبُّونَكُمْ وَتُؤْمِنُونَ بِٱلْكِتَـٰبِ كُلِّهِۦ وَإِذَا لَقُوكُمْ قَالُوٓاْ ءَامَنَّا وَإِذَا خَلَوْاْ عَضُّواْ عَلَيْكُمُ ٱلْأَنَامِلَ مِنَ ٱلْغَيْظِ قُلْ مُوتُواْ بِغَيْظِكُمْ إِنَّ ٱللَّهَ عَلِيمٌۢ بِذَاتِ ٱلصُّدُورِ ۝ إِن تَمْسَسْكُمْ حَسَنَةٌ تَسُؤْهُمْ وَإِن تُصِبْكُمْ سَيِّئَةٌ يَفْرَحُواْ بِهَا وَإِن تَصْبِرُواْ وَتَتَّقُواْ لَا يَضُرُّكُمْ كَيْدُهُمْ شَيْئًا إِنَّ ٱللَّهَ بِمَا يَعْمَلُونَ مُحِيطٌ ۝

---

[a] This refers to the contemporary Jews or Christians.

[b] The existence of love in the hearts of true believers for the People of the Book and the lack of love in the hearts of the latter for the believers shows who really subscribes to the truth and who does not. God is all mercy and justice. God is the Creator and Sustainer of all human beings, so whoever finds God in the real sense of the word, will open his heart to all God's creatures. For him all human beings equally become the family of God. Then he begins to like for everyone what he likes for himself. But those who have not found God in the real sense of the word, those who have not subordinated their will to the will of God and who live only on the plane of the self, regard life's possessions as paramount, both at the personal and the communal level. This mentality makes them inimical to anyone who appears to be against their interests—who is not, in short, a member of their own community. In spite of believing in God, they tend to forget that this world was made by God, and that no strategy can be effective here without God's approval.

¹²¹ When you set out at dawn from your home to assign battle positions to the believers—God hears all and knows all. ¹²² When two groups from among you were about to lose heart, God was their protector. In God let the faithful put their trust. ¹²³ God had already helped you at Badr, when you were weak. Fear God, so that you may be grateful. ¹²⁴ [And remember] when you said to the believers, 'Does it not suffice that your Lord helps you by sending down three thousand angels?ᵃ

وَإِذْ غَدَوْتَ مِنْ أَهْلِكَ تُبَوِّئُ الْمُؤْمِنِينَ مَقَاعِدَ لِلْقِتَالِ ۗ وَاللَّهُ سَمِيعٌ عَلِيمٌ ﴿١٢١﴾ إِذْ هَمَّت طَّآئِفَتَانِ مِنكُمْ أَن تَفْشَلَا وَاللَّهُ وَلِيُّهُمَا ۗ وَعَلَى اللَّهِ فَلْيَتَوَكَّلِ الْمُؤْمِنُونَ ﴿١٢٢﴾ وَلَقَدْ نَصَرَكُمُ اللَّهُ بِبَدْرٍ وَأَنتُمْ أَذِلَّةٌ ۖ فَاتَّقُوا اللَّهَ لَعَلَّكُمْ تَشْكُرُونَ ﴿١٢٣﴾ إِذْ تَقُولُ لِلْمُؤْمِنِينَ أَلَن يَكْفِيَكُمْ أَن يُمِدَّكُمْ رَبُّكُم بِثَلَاثَةِ ءَالَافٍ مِّنَ الْمَلَٰئِكَةِ مُنزَلِينَ ﴿١٢٤﴾

ᵃ These verses were revealed after the Battle of Uhud which took place in the third year after *hijrah*. The enemy forces numbered three thousand, while the Muslims who rose in defence were initially only one thousand in number. When three hundred hypocritical Muslims, led by 'Abdullah ibn Ubayy, deserted, some of the Madinan Muslims were disheartened at this, so the Prophet reminded them that they had come forth to defend themselves, relying on God rather than only on themselves.

If, due to the severity of circumstances, believers show some temporary weakness, God does not leave them to fend for themselves. He sends His special succour to restore their faith. This special succour of God was sent to the whole group of believers at a time when, by exploiting the weakness of the Muslims, the enemies had overcome them, and had every opportunity to crush the Muslim forces completely. But the enemy army, in spite of being victorious, retreated from the battlefield. This astonishing event in military history took place because of the special divine succour, which diverted the enemy towards 'Makkah' rather than 'Madinah' (the Muslim area). It was the defeated who pursued the victorious.

125 If you remain patient and God-fearing, and the enemy should fall upon you all of a sudden, Your Lord will reinforce you with five thousand angels clearly marked!' 126 and God ordained this only as good news for you so that your hearts might be comforted—help comes only from God, the Powerful, the Wise One— 127 and so that He might cut off a portion of those who are bent on denying the truth or abase them so that they might be turned back frustrated. 128 You have no say in this affair to decide whether He will relent towards them or He will punish them: they are wrongdoers. 129 Whatever is in the heavens and whatever is on the earth belong to God. He forgives whoever He pleases and punishes whoever He pleases. God is most forgiving and ever merciful.ᵃ

بَلَىٰٓ إِن تَصْبِرُواْ وَتَتَّقُواْ وَيَأْتُوكُم مِّن فَوْرِهِمْ هَٰذَا يُمْدِدْكُمْ رَبُّكُم بِخَمْسَةِ ءَالَٰفٍ مِّنَ ٱلْمَلَٰٓئِكَةِ مُسَوِّمِينَ ۝ وَمَا جَعَلَهُ ٱللَّهُ إِلَّا بُشْرَىٰ لَكُمْ وَلِتَطْمَئِنَّ قُلُوبُكُم بِهِۦ وَمَا ٱلنَّصْرُ إِلَّا مِنْ عِندِ ٱللَّهِ ٱلْعَزِيزِ ٱلْحَكِيمِ ۝ لِيَقْطَعَ طَرَفًا مِّنَ ٱلَّذِينَ كَفَرُوٓاْ أَوْ يَكْبِتَهُمْ فَيَنقَلِبُواْ خَآئِبِينَ ۝ لَيْسَ لَكَ مِنَ ٱلْأَمْرِ شَىْءٌ أَوْ يَتُوبَ عَلَيْهِمْ أَوْ يُعَذِّبَهُمْ فَإِنَّهُمْ ظَٰلِمُونَ ۝ وَلِلَّهِ مَا فِى ٱلسَّمَٰوَٰتِ وَمَا فِى ٱلْأَرْضِ يَغْفِرُ لِمَن يَشَآءُ وَيُعَذِّبُ مَن يَشَآءُ وَٱللَّهُ غَفُورٌ رَّحِيمٌ ۝

ᵃ Believers should never be upset at any lack of manpower or resources. When small in number, they should have the conviction that God will amply compensate for this by sending angels down to help them. When confronted with inadequate resources, they should trust God to create such situations as will compensate for this deficiency. Success depends more on patience and being God-fearing (taqwa) than on material resources. Those who fear and trust God can receive His divine succour in two ways: first, by His causing a section of the enemy to be brought to repentance and submission, thus reducing their number; and second, by His bringing about their outright defeat. The first kind of God's succour comes by way of dawah work. God opens to the truth the hearts of those opponents, who have some receptivity in them, and thus they join the believers. In this way they weaken the enemy forces and strengthen the believers' ranks. By the second method, God gives strength and courage to the believers and enables them to emerge victorious.

¹³⁰ Believers, do not devour usury multiplied many times over. Fear God, so that you may prosper—¹³¹ guard yourself against the Fire prepared for those who deny the truth—¹³² and obey God and the Messenger, so that you may be given mercy. ¹³³ And vie with one another for your Lord's forgiveness and for a Paradise as vast as the heavens and the earth, which has been prepared for the God-fearing, ¹³⁴ for those who spend, both in prosperity and adversity, who restrain their anger and are forgiving towards their fellow men—God loves those who do good works.ᵃ

يَـٰٓأَيُّهَا ٱلَّذِينَ ءَامَنُوا۟ لَا تَأْكُلُوا۟ ٱلرِّبَوٰٓا۟ أَضْعَـٰفًا مُّضَـٰعَفَةً ۖ وَٱتَّقُوا۟ ٱللَّهَ لَعَلَّكُمْ تُفْلِحُونَ ۝ وَٱتَّقُوا۟ ٱلنَّارَ ٱلَّتِىٓ أُعِدَّتْ لِلْكَـٰفِرِينَ ۝ وَأَطِيعُوا۟ ٱللَّهَ وَٱلرَّسُولَ لَعَلَّكُمْ تُرْحَمُونَ ۝ ۞ وَسَارِعُوٓا۟ إِلَىٰ مَغْفِرَةٍ مِّن رَّبِّكُمْ وَجَنَّةٍ عَرْضُهَا ٱلسَّمَـٰوَٰتُ وَٱلْأَرْضُ أُعِدَّتْ لِلْمُتَّقِينَ ۝ ٱلَّذِينَ يُنفِقُونَ فِى ٱلسَّرَّآءِ وَٱلضَّرَّآءِ وَٱلْكَـٰظِمِينَ ٱلْغَيْظَ وَٱلْعَافِينَ عَنِ ٱلنَّاسِ ۗ وَٱللَّهُ يُحِبُّ ٱلْمُحْسِنِينَ ۝

ᵃ Engaging in usury is the ultimate in money worship. A usurer thinks day in and day out as to how to double and quadruple his money. But what he ought to pursue relentlessly is not the acquisition of material things but his entry into Paradise in the Hereafter. He ought to be ever eager to attain God's mercy and blessing, but not by increasing his worldly wealth in order to guarantee himself a life of grandeur in this world. Honour and success are of no importance when compared to Paradise, the pleasure and enjoyment of which are immeasurable. Wise is the one who pursues God's Paradise. Hastening towards it means giving away more and more of one's wealth for the cause of God. The way to worldly success is to *increase* one's riches, while the way to success in the Hereafter is to *decrease* one's riches. If the inspiration to tread the former path is the love of money, the inspiration towards the latter is the love of God and His Messenger. If the 'wealth' of the former is worldly profit, the 'wealth' of the latter is the profit of the Hereafter. Where those desirous of riches have the fear of worldly loss, those of a spiritual bent of mind fear loss in the Hereafter.

135 And who, when they have committed an indecency or have wronged their souls, remember God and pray that their sins be forgiven— for who but God can forgive sins?— and do not knowingly persist in their misdeeds, 136 their recompense is forgiveness from their Lord, and Gardens with rivers flowing through them, where they will abide forever. How excellent will be the reward of those who do good works. 137 There are many examples [of the communities] that have passed away before you: travel through the land, and see what was the end of those who rejected the Truth. 138 This Quran is an exposition for the people and a guidance and admonition for those who fear God.[a]

وَٱلَّذِينَ إِذَا فَعَلُوا۟ فَٰحِشَةً أَوْ ظَلَمُوٓا۟ أَنفُسَهُمْ ذَكَرُوا۟ ٱللَّهَ فَٱسْتَغْفَرُوا۟ لِذُنُوبِهِمْ وَمَن يَغْفِرُ ٱلذُّنُوبَ إِلَّا ٱللَّهُ وَلَمْ يُصِرُّوا۟ عَلَىٰ مَا فَعَلُوا۟ وَهُمْ يَعْلَمُونَ ۝ أُو۟لَٰٓئِكَ جَزَآؤُهُم مَّغْفِرَةٌ مِّن رَّبِّهِمْ وَجَنَّٰتٌ تَجْرِى مِن تَحْتِهَا ٱلْأَنْهَٰرُ خَٰلِدِينَ فِيهَا وَنِعْمَ أَجْرُ ٱلْعَٰمِلِينَ ۝ قَدْ خَلَتْ مِن قَبْلِكُمْ سُنَنٌ فَسِيرُوا۟ فِى ٱلْأَرْضِ فَٱنظُرُوا۟ كَيْفَ كَانَ عَٰقِبَةُ ٱلْمُكَذِّبِينَ ۝ هَٰذَا بَيَانٌ لِّلنَّاسِ وَهُدًى وَمَوْعِظَةٌ لِّلْمُتَّقِينَ ۝

_____

[a] Those who fear God lead their lives as if God is watching over them, that is, as if all their actions are performed so as to be more and more pleasing in the eyes of God. Instead of leading a life of licentiousness, they lead a life of constraint. The requirements of the religion of God become their own requirements and for that they spend in charity under all circumstances, irrespective of whether they have much or little. When enraged, they control themselves. When there is a cause for complaint, they forgive instead of reacting negatively. They too fall into error, but that is only temporary. They immediately realize their mistake and return to God, spontaneously invoking His forgiveness and seeking His mercy. Whatever has been stated verbally in the Quran is borne out by the events of Islamic history. But advice is heeded only by those who are keen to have it.

¹³⁹ And do not become faint of heart,
nor grieve—you will have the upper
hand, if you are believers—¹⁴⁰ if you
have suffered a wound, they too have
suffered a similar wound. We bring
these days to men by turns, so that
God may know those who believe,
and choose witnesses from among
you; and God does not love the
unjust, ¹⁴¹ so that God may purge
those who believe and wipe out
those who deny the truth.^a

وَلَا تَهِنُوا وَلَا تَحْزَنُوا وَأَنتُمُ ٱلْأَعْلَوْنَ
إِن كُنتُم مُّؤْمِنِينَ ۝ إِن يَمْسَسْكُمْ
قَرْحٌ فَقَدْ مَسَّ ٱلْقَوْمَ قَرْحٌ مِّثْلُهُۥ
وَتِلْكَ ٱلْأَيَّامُ نُدَاوِلُهَا بَيْنَ ٱلنَّاسِ
وَلِيَعْلَمَ ٱللَّهُ ٱلَّذِينَ ءَامَنُوا وَيَتَّخِذَ
مِنكُمْ شُهَدَآءَ وَٱللَّهُ لَا يُحِبُّ ٱلظَّٰلِمِينَ
۝ وَلِيُمَحِّصَ ٱللَّهُ ٱلَّذِينَ ءَامَنُوا
وَيَمْحَقَ ٱلْكَٰفِرِينَ ۝

---

^a Accepting faith amounts to making a pledge to lead one's life according to God's
commandments. God has promised the believers success in this world and Paradise
in the next. Besides this, He will confer upon those who have suffered rejection
in this world, the foremost honour of being chosen as witnesses in His court. And
it will be on the basis of their evidence that the eternal fate of all human beings
will be decided. But one will not receive this status merely on the strength of verbal
claims to have embraced the faith; each individual will have necessarily to prove
his genuineness in terms of the patience he has exercised on earth and his struggle
for the cause of God. Difficulties and obstacles will be placed by others in the path
of the believer in both cases, that is, whether he wants to base his personal life on
faith and belief or stand before others as a witness of the religion of God.
Persevering in God's cause while facing all odds and difficulties along the way is
a form of struggle, or *jihad*, while standing by one's pledges and never taking an
emotional step are a form of patience, or *sabr*. Whichever group struggles while
remaining patient and peaceful will be successful in this world of God as well as
in the Hereafter. It is people such as these who are deserving candidates for
Paradise.

¹⁴² Do you suppose that you would enter the Garden, without God knowing those among you who would strive hard for His cause and endure with fortitude? ¹⁴³ You were longing for death, before you met it. Now you have seen it with your own eyes.^a

أَمْ حَسِبْتُمْ أَن تَدْخُلُواْ ٱلْجَنَّةَ وَلَمَّا يَعْلَمِ ٱللَّهُ ٱلَّذِينَ جَهَدُواْ مِنكُمْ وَيَعْلَمَ ٱلصَّبِرِينَ ۝ وَلَقَدْ كُنتُمْ تَمَنَّوْنَ ٱلْمَوْتَ مِن قَبْلِ أَن تَلْقَوْهُ فَقَدْ رَأَيْتُمُوهُ وَأَنتُمْ تَنظُرُونَ ۝

^a When an individual resolves to follow the path of God, he is confronted with many kinds of problems and difficulties created by others. Sometimes these problems produce in him a state of uncertainty; sometimes they make him think of opting for a policy of expediency; sometimes they arouse negative feelings within him; sometimes he is tempted to embrace such a version of God's religion as has great public appeal. Herein lies the test of man in the present world. Whatever reaction man shows on such occasions serves as an indicator of whether he is false or true in his acceptance of faith. If his actions correspond to his verbal claim of faith, he is true, and if not, he is false. Becoming God's witness is the final destination of this journey.

Let us imagine a servant of God who comes forward as a preacher of truth before the people. He himself fully practises what he preaches. People may regard him as insignificant, but he does not mind. He faces difficulties, but he is not discouraged; he perseveres in sending out the call of truth. He is neither disheartened nor given to negative thinking. Even when he has to pay the price with his life and property, his stand is not shaken. This test is a momentous one; but it is as a result of his passing this test that God selects him to be a witness in His divine court. When, despite all sorts of adverse situations, man continues to perform the task of conveying the divine message, he proves that he is convinced of the truth of the message he preaches. Furthermore, this also shows that the message he conveys to others is not just a trivial matter, but an extremely serious one.

144 Muhammad is only a messenger. Messengers have passed away before him. If he should die, or be killed, will you turn back on your heels? Those who turn on their heels do not harm the Lord in the least. God will reward the grateful. 145 No soul shall die except with God's permission and at an appointed time. And if one desires the rewards of this world, We shall grant it to him; and if one desires the rewards of the life to come, We shall grant it to him. We will reward the grateful.ª

وَمَا مُحَمَّدٌ إِلَّا رَسُولٌ قَدْ خَلَتْ مِن قَبْلِهِ ٱلرُّسُلُ أَفَإِيْن مَّاتَ أَوْ قُتِلَ ٱنقَلَبْتُمْ عَلَىٰ أَعْقَابِكُمْ وَمَن يَنقَلِبْ عَلَىٰ عَقِبَيْهِ فَلَن يَضُرَّ ٱللَّهَ شَيْئًا وَسَيَجْزِى ٱللَّهُ ٱلشَّٰكِرِينَ ۞ وَمَا كَانَ لِنَفْسٍ أَن تَمُوتَ إِلَّا بِإِذْنِ ٱللَّهِ كِتَٰبًا مُّؤَجَّلًا وَمَن يُرِدْ ثَوَابَ ٱلدُّنْيَا نُؤْتِهِ مِنْهَا وَمَن يُرِدْ ثَوَابَ ٱلْءَاخِرَةِ نُؤْتِهِ مِنْهَا وَسَنَجْزِى ٱلشَّٰكِرِينَ ۞

ª During the battle of Uhud, a cry was raised that the Messenger had been slain. This news seriously depressed certain Muslims. But the real servants of God are those whose religiosity is not based on a human personality. God requires a religiosity that attaches His servants with all their hearts and souls to the one God. A believer is one who follows Islam for the truth of its principles rather than for the support of some human individual. One who enters the fold of Islam in this way, finds it such a blessing that his spirit overflows with feelings of gratitude to God. He begins to regard the Hereafter, and not this world, as his all in all. Life becomes to him a transient thing, for he knows that he is going to be faced with death at any point of time. He is able to discern the universe as a divine workshop, where each happening takes place at God's will and where God is both the Giver and the Taker.

146 How many a prophet has fought with many devout men alongside him! They did not lose heart, despite all that they had to suffer in God's path. They neither weakened nor yielded. God loves the patient! 147 All they said was, 'Our Lord, forgive us our sins and our excesses. Make our feet firm, and help us against those who deny the truth,' 148 and so God gave them both the rewards of this life and the excellent recompense of the life to come: God loves those who do good.ᵃ

وَكَأَيِّن مِّن نَّبِيٍّ قَٰتَلَ مَعَهُۥ رِبِّيُّونَ كَثِيرٌ فَمَا وَهَنُوا۟ لِمَآ أَصَابَهُمْ فِى سَبِيلِ ٱللَّهِ وَمَا ضَعُفُوا۟ وَمَا ٱسْتَكَانُوا۟ ۗ وَٱللَّهُ يُحِبُّ ٱلصَّٰبِرِينَ ۝ وَمَا كَانَ قَوْلَهُمْ إِلَّآ أَن قَالُوا۟ رَبَّنَا ٱغْفِرْ لَنَا ذُنُوبَنَا وَإِسْرَافَنَا فِىٓ أَمْرِنَا وَثَبِّتْ أَقْدَامَنَا وَٱنصُرْنَا عَلَى ٱلْقَوْمِ ٱلْكَٰفِرِينَ ۝ فَـَٔاتَىٰهُمُ ٱللَّهُ ثَوَابَ ٱلدُّنْيَا وَحُسْنَ ثَوَابِ ٱلْءَاخِرَةِ ۗ وَٱللَّهُ يُحِبُّ ٱلْمُحْسِنِينَ ۝

ᵃ People who realize these truths are the true followers of the path of God. If God wills, they are invested with honour and power in this world as well, and so far as the eternal and superior rewards of the Hereafter are concerned, these too are reserved for them. However, this status is earned only when the believer has passed all the tests, when his eyes are set on God, even when all the apparent supports have crumbled away. His life being at risk fails to depress him. He does not retreat even when he sees the destruction of his worldly position before his very eyes. He regards any loss he incurs as the result of his own shortcomings. He holds himself responsible for it, and seeks forgiveness from God. When he is blessed with some good thing, he knows that it comes from God and he is thankful to Him. Such people become deserving candidates for all kinds of blessings showered upon them by their Creator. They who have thus discovered God are the most precious of souls and have themselves wholeheartedly enrolled in God's plan. Remaining united at crucial moments and adhering strictly and with patience to the truth are the qualities that make believers deserving of divine succour.

¹⁴⁹ Believers, if you yield to those who deny the truth, they will cause you to turn back on your heels and you will turn into losers. ¹⁵⁰ No, indeed! it is God who is your protector: He is the best supporter. ¹⁵¹ We will strike awe into the hearts of those who deny the truth, because they have associated partners with God, for which He has sent down no authority. Their abode shall be the Fire, and evil indeed is the abode of the wrongdoers.ᵃ

يَـٰٓأَيُّهَا ٱلَّذِينَ ءَامَنُوٓا۟ إِن تُطِيعُوا۟ ٱلَّذِينَ كَفَرُوا۟ يَرُدُّوكُمْ عَلَىٰٓ أَعْقَـٰبِكُمْ فَتَنقَلِبُوا۟ خَـٰسِرِينَ ۝ بَلِ ٱللَّهُ مَوْلَىٰكُمْ ۖ وَهُوَ خَيْرُ ٱلنَّـٰصِرِينَ ۝ سَنُلْقِى فِى قُلُوبِ ٱلَّذِينَ كَفَرُوا۟ ٱلرُّعْبَ بِمَآ أَشْرَكُوا۟ بِٱللَّهِ مَا لَمْ يُنَزِّلْ بِهِۦ سُلْطَـٰنًا ۖ وَمَأْوَىٰهُمُ ٱلنَّارُ ۚ وَبِئْسَ مَثْوَى ٱلظَّـٰلِمِينَ ۝

ᵃ The temporary defeat of the Muslims at the battle of Uhud gave an opportunity to the opponents of Islam to prove their stand that the credo of the Prophet and his companions was not a divine matter. It was just the boyish enthusiasm of certain people and now they were suffering for it. Their enemies would point out that had it pertained to God, they would never have been defeated at the hands of their opponents. However, such happenings, even if the results of the Muslims' own errors, are, at all events, 'test papers' from God. A happening like that of Uhud must take place in this world in order to find out who are the ones who truly trust in God and who are the ones who are to fall by the wayside. Such happenings serve as a two-sided trial for the believer. He passes the test only if he perseveres at all times, is not influenced by the adverse remarks of others and is not discouraged by temporary setbacks.

¹⁵² And God made good His promise to you when by His leave you were about to destroy your foes, but then your courage failed you and you disagreed among yourselves [concerning the Prophet's direction] and disobeyed it, after He had brought you within sight of what you wished for—some of you desired the goods of this world and some of you desired the Hereafter—then in order that He might put you to the test, He prevented you from defeating your foes. But now He has pardoned you: God is most gracious to the believers. ¹⁵³ When you were running away and did not look back at anyone, while the Messenger was calling to you from behind, He paid you back with one sorrow after another, so that you might not grieve for what you lost, nor for what befell you. God is aware of what you do.ᵃ

وَلَقَدْ صَدَقَكُمُ ٱللَّهُ وَعْدَهُۥ إِذْ تَحُسُّونَهُم بِإِذْنِهِۦ حَتَّىٰ إِذَا فَشِلْتُمْ وَتَنَٰزَعْتُمْ فِى ٱلْأَمْرِ وَعَصَيْتُم مِّنۢ بَعْدِ مَآ أَرَىٰكُم مَّا تُحِبُّونَ مِنكُم مَّن يُرِيدُ ٱلدُّنْيَا وَمِنكُم مَّن يُرِيدُ ٱلْءَاخِرَةَ ثُمَّ صَرَفَكُمْ عَنْهُمْ لِيَبْتَلِيَكُمْ وَلَقَدْ عَفَا عَنكُمْ وَٱللَّهُ ذُو فَضْلٍ عَلَى ٱلْمُؤْمِنِينَ ۝ إِذْ تُصْعِدُونَ وَلَا تَلْوُۥنَ عَلَىٰ أَحَدٍ وَٱلرَّسُولُ يَدْعُوكُمْ فِىٓ أُخْرَىٰكُمْ فَأَثَٰبَكُمْ غَمًّۢا بِغَمٍّ لِّكَيْلَا تَحْزَنُوا۟ عَلَىٰ مَا فَاتَكُمْ وَلَا مَآ أَصَٰبَكُمْ وَٱللَّهُ خَبِيرٌۢ بِمَا تَعْمَلُونَ ۝

ᵃ When believers show steadfastness at crucial moments, God sends His special succour, that is, He strikes terror into the hearts of those who deny the truth. Any person or group who adheres to anything other than the true divine religion is standing in fact on quicksand. For, there is no other real base to build on in this world except the truth revealed by God. As such, whenever one has proved to be standing firmly on the ground of God's religion, the ranks of those who deny the truth begin to show signs of disarray. Lacking sound arguments, those who deny the truth, unlike the believers, suffer from feelings of uncertainty and inferiority. This lack of conviction finally leads to their downfall. They are ultimately defeated at the hands of true believers. But in the case of the Muslims, their weakness and defeat are traceable solely to their disunity arising from dissension. Yet unity cannot come about in a society solely on the basis of uniformity of opinion. It takes united action also, even in the face of divisive opinions, to ensure total cohesiveness within a community. Only when a community thinks on this level can it remain united and powerful. When people start breaking up into factions, just because of disagreements, the resulting weakness will most certainly lead to defeat.

¹⁵⁴ Then, after sorrow He sent down peace [of mind] upon you in the shape of drowsiness that overcame some of you, but there were others who were anxious only about themselves. They entertained false notions about God, like the notions of the days of ignorance. 'Have we any say in the matter?' they asked. Say to them, 'All is in the hands of God.' They conceal in their hearts what they would not reveal to you. They say, 'Had we had any say in the matter, none of us would have been killed here.' Say to them, 'Had you stayed in your homes, those whose death had been decreed would nevertheless have gone forth to the places where they were destined to die.' And all this befell you so that God might test what is in your minds. And in order to purify what was in your hearts. For God is aware of your innermost thoughts.^a

ثُمَّ أَنزَلَ عَلَيْكُم مِّنۢ بَعْدِ ٱلْغَمِّ أَمَنَةً نُّعَاسًا يَغْشَىٰ طَآئِفَةً مِّنكُمْ ۖ وَطَآئِفَةٌ قَدْ أَهَمَّتْهُمْ أَنفُسُهُمْ يَظُنُّونَ بِٱللَّهِ غَيْرَ ٱلْحَقِّ ظَنَّ ٱلْجَٰهِلِيَّةِ ۖ يَقُولُونَ هَل لَّنَا مِنَ ٱلْأَمْرِ مِن شَىْءٍ ۗ قُلْ إِنَّ ٱلْأَمْرَ كُلَّهُۥ لِلَّهِ ۗ يُخْفُونَ فِىٓ أَنفُسِهِم مَّا لَا يُبْدُونَ لَكَ ۖ يَقُولُونَ لَوْ كَانَ لَنَا مِنَ ٱلْأَمْرِ شَىْءٌ مَّا قُتِلْنَا هَٰهُنَا ۗ قُل لَّوْ كُنتُمْ فِى بُيُوتِكُمْ لَبَرَزَ ٱلَّذِينَ كُتِبَ عَلَيْهِمُ ٱلْقَتْلُ إِلَىٰ مَضَاجِعِهِمْ ۖ وَلِيَبْتَلِىَ ٱللَّهُ مَا فِى صُدُورِكُمْ وَلِيُمَحِّصَ مَا فِى قُلُوبِكُمْ ۚ وَٱللَّهُ عَلِيمٌۢ بِذَاتِ ٱلصُّدُورِ

^a The most important thing for the believer, in life's trials and tribulations, is to remain calm and composed, so that he may draw up his plans with full concentration. Such composure and concentration derive from complete trust placed in God. Even on the most earth-shaking of occasions, when people find it impossible to sleep, the believers are able to revitalize themselves with the soothing effect of sleep. This was demonstrated on the occasion of Uhud when, despite the severest of conditions, they were able to have a good night's sleep. Rested and refreshed, they then pursued the enemy forces as far as Hamraul-Asad, some eight miles from Madinah. Severely wounded and defeated, they would not have been able to take any further action, had calm not descended upon them. This hot pursuit awed the enemy, who turned about and retreated to Makkah. This is the state in which the believers live, whereas those who have not made God their guardian and protector in the full sense of these words, inevitably fear for their own lives. Bereft of any concern for religion, they are engrossed in their own selves. Such people are never blessed with composure through divine succour.

155 Those of you who turned away on the day the two hosts met [in battle] were made to slip by Satan on account of some of their deeds. But God has pardoned them: God is forgiving and forbearing.[a]

إِنَّ ٱلَّذِينَ تَوَلَّوْا مِنكُمْ يَوْمَ ٱلْتَقَى ٱلْجَمْعَانِ إِنَّمَا ٱسْتَزَلَّهُمُ ٱلشَّيْطَانُ بِبَعْضِ مَا كَسَبُوا وَلَقَدْ عَفَا ٱللَّهُ عَنْهُمْ إِنَّ ٱللَّهَ غَفُورٌ حَلِيمٌ ۝

[a] On the occasion of Uhud, 'Abdullah ibn Ubayy counselled that the defence of Madinah should be undertaken within the walls, instead of the Muslims boldly coming out to meet the enemy. The Prophet, however, at the instance of some other sincere Muslims, went out of the city to meet the enemy, posting his men strategically on Mount Uhud. The battle began well for the Muslims, but turned to near defeat because of the disobedience of a band of fifty archers who had been given the task of guarding a certain pass. Seeing the imminent Muslim victory, they abandoned their posts, attracted by the prospects of booty. When this victory turned into defeat, the hypocrites who had deserted the Muslims even before the battle started, on the pretext that their counsel had not been accepted by the Prophet, began to say that, had their words been heeded, this calamity could have been averted. But death is decreed by God and comes regardless of circumstances. No precautionary measure can save one from death. Such happenings, whatever their apparent reason, are wrought by God, in order that His true believers may turn to Him in repentance and become worthy of further blessings from Him. Such happenings also serve to reveal the truth about those who are not the true servants of God.

When the fifty archers posted at the Mount Uhud pass saw that the Muslims had won the battle, a large number of them insisted on going in pursuit of booty. Although 'Abdullah ibn Jubayr and a few other companions pointed out that it was against the orders of the Prophet, they deserted their posts, leaving behind eleven men. Satan thus made inroads by using the dissension already evident among them. However, when they admitted their error, they were forgiven by God, and after the initial setback, God's succour came to them too. The Almighty struck terror into the hearts of their enemies, which resulted in their retreat, although they were just a few miles from Madinah. Had God's succour not come, there was nothing to stop them from forcing their entry into Madinah and uprooting the nascent tree of Islam.

156 Believers, do not be like those who are bent on denying the truth and who say of their brothers, when they travel about the land or go forth to war, 'Had they but remained with us, they would not have died, or been slain'—for God will cause such thoughts to become a source of bitter regret in their hearts, since it is God who gives life and causes death. And God sees all that you do. 157 If you are killed or die in God's cause, then surely forgiveness from God and His grace are better than all that one could amass. 158 For, indeed, if you die or are killed, it is to God that you shall be gathered.ᵃ

يَـٰٓأَيُّهَا ٱلَّذِينَ ءَامَنُوا۟ لَا تَكُونُوا۟ كَٱلَّذِينَ كَفَرُوا۟ وَقَالُوا۟ لِإِخْوَٰنِهِمْ إِذَا ضَرَبُوا۟ فِى ٱلْأَرْضِ أَوْ كَانُوا۟ غُزًّى لَّوْ كَانُوا۟ عِندَنَا مَا مَاتُوا۟ وَمَا قُتِلُوا۟ لِيَجْعَلَ ٱللَّهُ ذَٰلِكَ حَسْرَةً فِى قُلُوبِهِمْ ۗ وَٱللَّهُ يُحْىِۦ وَيُمِيتُ ۗ وَٱللَّهُ بِمَا تَعْمَلُونَ بَصِيرٌ ۝ وَلَئِن قُتِلْتُمْ فِى سَبِيلِ ٱللَّهِ أَوْ مُتُّمْ لَمَغْفِرَةٌ مِّنَ ٱللَّهِ وَرَحْمَةٌ خَيْرٌ مِّمَّا يَجْمَعُونَ ۝ وَلَئِن مُّتُّمْ أَوْ قُتِلْتُمْ لَإِلَى ٱللَّهِ تُحْشَرُونَ ۝

ᵃ All that happens in this world is by the will of God. However, everything takes place under the veil of cause and effect. Incidents appear to have a cause behind them but, actually, they occur at the will of God. Man's faith is put to the test through apparent causes, which make it difficult to see the hidden hand of God in all things. The non-believer is the one who is lost in trying to understand the causes and effects, while the believer is one who penetrates their veil to discover the actual reality. One who claims to be a believer, yet regards life and death, success and failure as the results of human strategies, is not true to his claim. When a non-believer suffers a setback, he grieves over it, thinking that had he adopted this or that course, he could have been saved. But when a believer confronts the same situation, he resigns himself to it by accepting it as the will of God. When a man has the conviction that everything happens by God's will, then all other human causes appear insignificant and not worthy of further consideration.

Those, on the other hand, who hold worldly resources important devote their whole lives to providing for the things of this world. But the only things of true value are those which will be theirs in the Hereafter—that is, God's forgiveness and Paradise. Paradise is something which can be attained only at the cost of one's life. Man's existence on earth is the exact price he has to pay to enter Paradise. If he fails to make this sacrifice, he cannot be certain of his fate in the Hereafter.

159 It is by God's grace that you were gentle with them—for if you had been harsh and hard-hearted, they would surely have deserted you—so bear with them and pray for forgiveness for them. Take counsel with them in the conduct of affairs; then, when you have decided upon a course of action, place your trust in God: for God loves those who place their trust in Him. 160 If God helps you, none can overcome you, but if He withdraws His help from you, who is there who can help you besides Him? In God, then, let the believers place their trust! [a]

فَبِمَا رَحْمَةٍ مِّنَ ٱللَّهِ لِنتَ لَهُمْ وَلَوْ كُنتَ فَظًّا غَلِيظَ ٱلْقَلْبِ لَٱنفَضُّوا۟ مِنْ حَوْلِكَ فَٱعْفُ عَنْهُمْ وَٱسْتَغْفِرْ لَهُمْ وَشَاوِرْهُمْ فِى ٱلْأَمْرِ فَإِذَا عَزَمْتَ فَتَوَكَّلْ عَلَى ٱللَّهِ إِنَّ ٱللَّهَ يُحِبُّ ٱلْمُتَوَكِّلِينَ ۝ إِن يَنصُرْكُمُ ٱللَّهُ فَلَا غَالِبَ لَكُمْ وَإِن يَخْذُلْكُمْ فَمَن ذَا ٱلَّذِى يَنصُرُكُم مِّنۢ بَعْدِهِۦ وَعَلَى ٱللَّهِ فَلْيَتَوَكَّلِ ٱلْمُؤْمِنُونَ ۝

---

[a] The gentle way the Prophet is asked to deal with the believers (in this context those who had disobeyed him in quitting their posts, incurring defeat in the battle) is equally essential in any Muslim leader. Moderation is indispensable for him. This lenient attitude is required not only in normal, daily life but also in dealings between Muslims and non-Muslims, even where, due to the disobedience of certain people, a victory turns into a defeat. Unless the leader shows broad-mindedness and high thinking, a powerful polity cannot be established. Mistakes, however grave their outcome, if committed without any evil intention, are pardonable. The leader, therefore, should overlook this type of error while dealing with people. He should be such a great well-wisher of his people that he should pray to God for their guidance. Indeed, the good leader so values his people that he takes decisions on matters of importance only after consulting them.

¹⁶¹ It is not for any Prophet to hold back anything; he who hides anything away shall bring it forth on the Day of Resurrection, when every human being shall be repaid in full for whatever he has done, and none shall be wronged. ¹⁶² Can one who seeks the pleasure of God, be like one who incurs the wrath of God and whose abode shall be Hell—an evil destination? ¹⁶³ All have a different standing in the eyes of God, and God is observant of all their actions.ᵃ

وَمَا كَانَ لِنَبِيٍّ أَن يَغُلَّ وَمَن يَغْلُلْ يَأْتِ بِمَا غَلَّ يَوْمَ ٱلْقِيَٰمَةِ ثُمَّ تُوَفَّىٰ كُلُّ نَفْسٍ مَّا كَسَبَتْ وَهُمْ لَا يُظْلَمُونَ ۝ أَفَمَنِ ٱتَّبَعَ رِضْوَٰنَ ٱللَّهِ كَمَن بَآءَ بِسَخَطٍ مِّنَ ٱللَّهِ وَمَأْوَىٰهُ جَهَنَّمُ وَبِئْسَ ٱلْمَصِيرُ ۝ هُمْ دَرَجَٰتٌ عِندَ ٱللَّهِ وَٱللَّهُ بَصِيرٌ بِمَا يَعْمَلُونَ ۝

ᵃ The Prophet forgave the forty Muslims who had disobeyed his orders on the occasion of the battle of Uhud. However, people doubted that the Prophet had really forgiven them. They thought that he had done so only outwardly, for show, and that later he would show his anger. These verses tell us that the Prophet's inner feelings did not differ from his outward behaviour. His actions never belied his words. This also indicates what a Muslim leader should be like. His heart should be free of malice, jealousy, hatred, etc., even at a time when such a grave mistake is being made by his people as was made by the Prophet's companions on the occasion of the battle of Uhud. He should not even keep any malice hidden in his heart. He should live with his people, after his act of forgiveness, as if nothing had ever been amiss. Moreover, when Muslims trustingly handed over all their affairs to him, he should not exploit their lives and their wealth to serve his own personal ends. This would be crossing the limits, showing no fear of God's wrath. How could one, dedicated to leading people along the path of God's will, ever think of meeting God, if he himself had gone against His will?

164 Indeed, God has conferred a great favour on the believers in sending a Messenger from among themselves, to recite His revelations to them, and purify them, and teaches them the Book and wisdom, for, before that they were surely in manifest error.[a]

لَقَدْ مَنَّ ٱللَّهُ عَلَى ٱلْمُؤْمِنِينَ إِذْ بَعَثَ فِيهِمْ رَسُولاً مِّنْ أَنفُسِهِمْ يَتْلُواْ عَلَيْهِمْ ءَايَـٰتِهِۦ وَيُزَكِّيهِمْ وَيُعَلِّمُهُمُ ٱلْكِتَـٰبَ وَٱلْحِكْمَةَ وَإِن كَانُواْ مِن قَبْلُ لَفِى ضَلَـٰلٍ مُّبِينٍ ﴿١٦٤﴾

---

[a] The example set by the Prophet throughout his life must be followed by all reformers till Doomsday. For the task of reformation to be successful, it is essential that the targeted people should feel as if the reformer is one of themselves in every respect. His language, his style of speaking, his style of living— all should be familiar to them. No such feelings should be created between him and his addressee that may lead, in one way or another, to the latter becoming distanced from him, or to the addressee and the reformer becoming rivals.

The first task to be performed among the people is to foster in them the ability to read the signs of God spread everywhere within and without their own selves. God's signs should become part of their very mental make-up.

The second task is to purify people. This end is achieved by the reformer speaking to them in person and giving them the opportunity to spend time in his company. The message can, of course, be put across through general discourses and writing, but this would only be in principle; whereas by resorting to individual communication the message can be conveyed in a more precise and detailed way. Then there is the question of the personality of the dayee, which should always lend weight to the message. Individual meetings thus serve the purpose of the purification of the addressees, or madu'.

The third task is to introduce to the madu' the shariah—the book of guidance on how life should be led in this world.

The fourth task is to impart wisdom, that is, to unveil the secrets of religion and to highlight the truths hidden between the lines.

165 What! When a misfortune befalls you, after you had yourself inflicted twice as heavy losses, you say, 'How has this come about?' Say, 'It was your own fault.' Truly, God has the power to will anything: 166 the misfortune which befell you on the day when the two armies met happened by God's leave, so that He might mark out the [true] believers 167 and know those who acted hypocritically.' When they were told, 'Come, fight in God's cause and defend yourselves,' they replied, 'If we knew that fighting would take place, we would surely follow you.' They were that day nearer to unbelief than to belief. The words they utter bear no relation to what is in their hearts. God knows well what they conceal.*a*

أَوَلَمَّآ أَصَـٰبَتْكُم مُّصِيبَةٌ قَدْ أَصَبْتُم مِّثْلَيْهَا قُلْتُمْ أَنَّىٰ هَـٰذَا قُلْ هُوَ مِنْ عِندِ أَنفُسِكُمْ إِنَّ ٱللَّهَ عَلَىٰ كُلِّ شَىْءٍ قَدِيرٌ ﴿١٦٥﴾ وَمَآ أَصَـٰبَكُمْ يَوْمَ ٱلْتَقَى ٱلْجَمْعَانِ فَبِإِذْنِ ٱللَّهِ وَلِيَعْلَمَ ٱلْمُؤْمِنِينَ ﴿١٦٦﴾ وَلِيَعْلَمَ ٱلَّذِينَ نَافَقُوا۟ وَقِيلَ لَهُمْ تَعَالَوْا۟ قَـٰتِلُوا۟ فِى سَبِيلِ ٱللَّهِ أَوِ ٱدْفَعُوا۟ قَالُوا۟ لَوْ نَعْلَمُ قِتَالًا لَّٱتَّبَعْنَـٰكُمْ هُمْ لِلْكُفْرِ يَوْمَئِذٍ أَقْرَبُ مِنْهُمْ لِلْإِيمَـٰنِ يَقُولُونَ بِأَفْوَٰهِهِم مَّا لَيْسَ فِى قُلُوبِهِمْ وَٱللَّهُ أَعْلَمُ بِمَا يَكْتُمُونَ ﴿١٦٧﴾

---

a In the confrontation between truth and untruth, truth is always destined to have the final victory, because truth always has God on its side. However, this world being a world of trial, mischief-mongers too have full freedom of action. That is why at times, by exploiting some weakness of the believers—for instance, mutual dissension—they are able to inflict temporary harm on them. Yet such happenings, though tragic in appearance, have a good side to them as well, for in this way Muslims are put to the test. In the face of unfavourable situations, the insincere fall away, while the true believers persevere because of their total trust in God.

In this way, it becomes clear who are the trustworthy and who are not. Furthermore, God's mercy is all the more focussed upon them, when, after incurring loss due to their inadvertent mistakes, the believers turn to God once again in all patience and humility.

¹⁶⁸ Those who stayed behind, said of their brothers, 'Had they listened to us, they would not have been killed.' Say to them, 'Ward off death from yourselves, then, if what you say be true!'ᵃ

ٱلَّذِينَ قَالُوا۟ لِإِخْوَٰنِهِمْ وَقَعَدُوا۟ لَوْ أَطَاعُونَا مَا قُتِلُوا۟ قُلْ فَٱدْرَءُوا۟ عَنْ أَنفُسِكُمُ ٱلْمَوْتَ إِن كُنتُمْ صَٰدِقِينَ ١٦٨

ᵃ Those who participate in the encounter of truth and untruth in such a way as to make real sacrifices for the sake of truth, are scorned by worldly people as having destroyed themselves for no good reason. But this is a foolish assessment. Incurring a seeming loss in God's path is a positive happening, because those who have sacrificed everything for God are the ones most deserving of God's rewards.

The foolish speak of those who sacrifice their lives in the path of God as if it is only they who die, as if those who are striving towards worldly ends do not taste death. This is entirely meaningless and those who speak of such things are never serious. Their hearts tell them that they have made a great mistake in not making sacrifices for the cause of truth, but by speaking ill of those who have done so, they want to keep up a pretence that they are in the right. But death is decreed for all human beings by God. It will certainly visit everyone at the appointed time. Whichever path one follows, none can escape from the clutches of death. People realize their mistake in their hearts, but they do not want to acknowledge it. In order to justify their course of action, they utter such words as even their own hearts attest to as being false.

¹⁶⁹ Do not think of those who have been killed in God's cause as dead. They are alive, and well provided for by their Lord; ¹⁷⁰ they are joyful because of what God has bestowed on them of His grace and they rejoice that those they left behind, who have not yet joined them, that they shall have no fear, nor shall they grieve; ¹⁷¹ rejoicing in God's grace and bounty. [They know that] God will not fail to requite the believers. ¹⁷² Those who responded to the call of God and the Messenger, despite their having received an injury, and such of them as did good deeds and feared God, shall have a great reward.^a

وَلَا تَحْسَبَنَّ ٱلَّذِينَ قُتِلُوا۟ فِى سَبِيلِ ٱللَّهِ أَمْوَٰتًۢا بَلْ أَحْيَآءٌ عِندَ رَبِّهِمْ يُرْزَقُونَ ﴿١٦٩﴾ فَرِحِينَ بِمَآ ءَاتَىٰهُمُ ٱللَّهُ مِن فَضْلِهِۦ وَيَسْتَبْشِرُونَ بِٱلَّذِينَ لَمْ يَلْحَقُوا۟ بِهِم مِّنْ خَلْفِهِمْ أَلَّا خَوْفٌ عَلَيْهِمْ وَلَا هُمْ يَحْزَنُونَ ﴿١٧٠﴾ ۞ يَسْتَبْشِرُونَ بِنِعْمَةٍ مِّنَ ٱللَّهِ وَفَضْلٍ وَأَنَّ ٱللَّهَ لَا يُضِيعُ أَجْرَ ٱلْمُؤْمِنِينَ ﴿١٧١﴾ ٱلَّذِينَ ٱسْتَجَابُوا۟ لِلَّهِ وَٱلرَّسُولِ مِنۢ بَعْدِ مَآ أَصَابَهُمُ ٱلْقَرْحُ ۚ لِلَّذِينَ أَحْسَنُوا۟ مِنْهُمْ وَٱتَّقَوْا۟ أَجْرٌ عَظِيمٌ ﴿١٧٢﴾

---

^a The martyrdom of the believers was derided by the hypocrites. They said that Muslims were being slain meaninglessly at the instance of their leader—the Prophet. God says that, on the contrary, what they call death is in fact the true, real life, which they have entered through the gateway of death. The non-believers know only the profit and loss of this world. That is why sacrificing their lives for the cause of the Hereafter appears to them as self-destruction. But they ought to know that the believers' 'dead' have a far better 'life' than those among the non-believers who are alive: in the Hereafter, they rejoice in the bliss they have attained through sacrifice for the cause of God.

Satan's way is to take in hand those people whom he finds closer to him, and prevent them from advancing towards religion, by showing them the 'dreadful' consequences of such a step. People who give in to Satan's influences thus become his agents. They exaggerate the power and the resources of the opponents of Islam in order to awe the believers. But such kinds of propaganda only serve to benefit the believers. Their conviction is strengthened all the more that their God will not abandon them in a difficult situation.

173 Those who, on being told that, 'the enemy has gathered against you a great force, so fear them,' only grew stronger in their faith and replied, 'God is sufficient for us. He is the best guardian.' 174 They returned home with God's favour and blessings, without having been touched by evil; for they pursued God's pleasure. And God's bounty is infinite. 175 It is Satan who instills fear [into you] of his followers; do not fear them. But fear Me, if you are true believers.[a]

ٱلَّذِينَ قَالَ لَهُمُ ٱلنَّاسُ إِنَّ ٱلنَّاسَ قَدْ جَمَعُواْ لَكُمْ فَٱخْشَوْهُمْ فَزَادَهُمْ إِيمَٰنًا وَقَالُواْ حَسْبُنَا ٱللَّهُ وَنِعْمَ ٱلْوَكِيلُ ۝ فَٱنقَلَبُواْ بِنِعْمَةٍ مِّنَ ٱللَّهِ وَفَضْلٍ لَّمْ يَمْسَسْهُمْ سُوٓءٌ وَٱتَّبَعُواْ رِضْوَٰنَ ٱللَّهِ وَٱللَّهُ ذُو فَضْلٍ عَظِيمٍ ۝ إِنَّمَا ذَٰلِكُمُ ٱلشَّيْطَٰنُ يُخَوِّفُ أَوْلِيَآءَهُۥ فَلَا تَخَافُوهُمْ وَخَافُونِ إِن كُنتُم مُّؤْمِنِينَ ۝

---

[a] The battle of Uhud took place at a distance of two miles from Madinah. After the battle, the enemy, led by Abu Sufyan, marched back and camped at a place called Hamra-ul-Asad, at a distance of eight miles from Madinah. After having camped there, it occurred to those who denied the truth that they had made a great mistake in leaving Uhud, as it was there that they had the best opportunity to pursue the Muslims as far as Madinah and crush their power forever. In the meantime, they met a trader's caravan belonging to the tribe of Abdul Qays, going on to Madinah. They gave the people of the caravan some money and induced them to spread rumours in Madinah that would strike terror into the hearts of the Muslims. When they reached Madinah, they started saying that they had seen themselves that the Makkans were gathering a large force and intended to attack Madinah once again. However, the Muslims' total trust in God was a guarantee that the planning of the enemies would prove counter-productive. The rumour about the Makkans actually benefited the Muslims, as they were now forewarned of their enemies' intentions. Consequently, the Prophet along with his companions immediately marched towards Hamra-ul-Asad, prior to the Makkan army advancing on Madinah. When the Makkans learnt that the Muslim force was advancing towards them, they thought that the Muslims had mustered fresh forces. They immediately fled to Makkah, giving up all thoughts of attacking Madinah again.

176 And let not those grieve you who vie with one another in denying the truth: they cannot harm God in the least; it is God's will that they will have no share in the life to come—a severe punishment awaits them. 177 Those who have bought a denial of truth at the price of faith can in no way harm God; painful punishment awaits them. 178 Let not those who deny the truth think that Our granting them respite is good for them: Our granting them respite will only cause them to increase in disobedience—shameful punishment awaits them.[a]

وَلَا يَحْزُنكَ ٱلَّذِينَ يُسَٰرِعُونَ فِى ٱلْكُفْرِ إِنَّهُمْ لَن يَضُرُّوا۟ ٱللَّهَ شَيْـًٔا يُرِيدُ ٱللَّهُ أَلَّا يَجْعَلَ لَهُمْ حَظًّا فِى ٱلْءَاخِرَةِ وَلَهُمْ عَذَابٌ عَظِيمٌ ۝ إِنَّ ٱلَّذِينَ ٱشْتَرَوُا۟ ٱلْكُفْرَ بِٱلْإِيمَٰنِ لَن يَضُرُّوا۟ ٱللَّهَ شَيْـًٔا وَلَهُمْ عَذَابٌ أَلِيمٌ ۝ وَلَا يَحْسَبَنَّ ٱلَّذِينَ كَفَرُوٓا۟ أَنَّمَا نُمْلِى لَهُمْ خَيْرٌ لِّأَنفُسِهِمْ إِنَّمَا نُمْلِى لَهُمْ لِيَزْدَادُوٓا۟ إِثْمًا وَلَهُمْ عَذَابٌ مُّهِينٌ ۝

---

[a] The real problem is that, being veiled from our eyes, life is not what it appears to be. People are concerned with saving themselves from 'hell' (the difficulties and problems of this world) and devote all their attention to attaining the 'paradise' of this world. But it would be wiser to aim for the Paradise of the next world and in so doing save oneself from the Hell of the next world. Wealth, property and the trappings of honour are things that everyone can see with his own eyes. That is why man relentlessly pursues these goals, exerting himself to the utmost, so as not to be deprived of them. But the actual human dilemma is the question of the Hereafter. This real problem has been screened from our eyes, because human beings have to be put to the test by God. However, God has His way of informing people of it. This is done by selecting His messengers from amongst men, so that they may make people aware of the realities beyond death. The real test of man is to discover the truth in the message of the preacher (da'i) appointed by God. He may see the actual reality in a verbal message. He may hear the divine voice in the voice of a human being. God speaks through His messengers—human beings. Now man has to acknowledge a man like himself as one receiving the divine message.

179 On no account will God leave the believers in the condition in which they are now, until He separates the evil from the good. Nor will God reveal to you the unseen. But God chooses those of his messengers whom He will. Therefore, believe in God and His messengers, for if you have faith and guard yourselves against evil, you shall have a great reward.[a]

مَّا كَانَ ٱللَّهُ لِيَذَرَ ٱلْمُؤْمِنِينَ عَلَىٰ مَآ أَنتُمْ عَلَيْهِ حَتَّىٰ يَمِيزَ ٱلْخَبِيثَ مِنَ ٱلطَّيِّبِ ۗ وَمَا كَانَ ٱللَّهُ لِيُطْلِعَكُمْ عَلَى ٱلْغَيْبِ وَلَٰكِنَّ ٱللَّهَ يَجْتَبِي مِن رُّسُلِهِۦ مَن يَشَآءُ ۖ فَـَٔامِنُوا۟ بِٱللَّهِ وَرُسُلِهِۦ ۚ وَإِن تُؤْمِنُوا۟ وَتَتَّقُوا۟ فَلَكُمْ أَجْرٌ عَظِيمٌ ۝

[a] Having faith implies not being obsessed with one's own self. Such an obsession amounts to assigning the position of greatness to one's own self rather than to God. A believer should not be engrossed in the world, as this would mean that he did not attach real importance to the Hereafter. A believer should eschew arrogance, miserliness, injustice, and even love for and deep attachment to anything other than God. He should instead adopt the ways of God-worship, humility, generosity and justice. This would show that he is sincere in his faith and that he has actually dedicated himself to God and the Hereafter. Failure to do so means that he is not sincere in his faith. In spite of a formal acceptance of faith, he would in fact be living in this world very much like the non-believers. The division into good and bad souls in the Hereafter will be based on reality rather than on ostentatious behaviour.

We find that wicked people too have been given full freedom. But it is only so that they can reveal their entirely perverse nature (what lies within them). Yet, however hard they may try, they can never succeed in vanquishing the believers. They have the power to use their freedom only where they themselves are concerned, not against others.

¹⁸⁰ Let not those who are niggardly with what God has granted them out of His bounty think that it is good for them. Indeed, it is evil for them. What they are niggardly about shall be hung about their necks like a collar on the Day of Resurrection. It is God who will inherit the heavens and the earth: God is aware of all that you do. ¹⁸¹ God has indeed heard the words of those who said, 'Behold, God is poor while we are rich!' We shall record what they have said—and their slaying of the prophets unjustly—and We shall say, 'Taste the torment of burning. ¹⁸² In return for what your own hands have wrought—for never does God do the least wrong to His creatures!ᵃ

وَلَا تَحْسَبَنَّ ٱلَّذِينَ يَبْخَلُونَ بِمَآ ءَاتَىٰهُمُ ٱللَّهُ مِن فَضْلِهِۦ هُوَ خَيْرًا لَّهُم ۖ بَلْ هُوَ شَرٌّ لَّهُمْ ۖ سَيُطَوَّقُونَ مَا بَخِلُوا۟ بِهِۦ يَوْمَ ٱلْقِيَٰمَةِ ۗ وَلِلَّهِ مِيرَٰثُ ٱلسَّمَٰوَٰتِ وَٱلْأَرْضِ ۗ وَٱللَّهُ بِمَا تَعْمَلُونَ خَبِيرٌ ۝ لَّقَدْ سَمِعَ ٱللَّهُ قَوْلَ ٱلَّذِينَ قَالُوٓا۟ إِنَّ ٱللَّهَ فَقِيرٌ وَنَحْنُ أَغْنِيَآءُ ۘ سَنَكْتُبُ مَا قَالُوا۟ وَقَتْلَهُمُ ٱلْأَنۢبِيَآءَ بِغَيْرِ حَقٍّ وَنَقُولُ ذُوقُوا۟ عَذَابَ ٱلْحَرِيقِ ۝ ذَٰلِكَ بِمَا قَدَّمَتْ أَيْدِيكُمْ وَأَنَّ ٱللَّهَ لَيْسَ بِظَلَّامٍ لِّلْعَبِيدِ ۝

ᵃ One comes to be called a believer by just repeating some words (*kalimah*), but so far as God is concerned, the would-be Muslim becomes a believer only when he sacrifices his life and his wealth for His cause. Without such a sacrifice, nobody's faith is credible in the eyes of God. One thinks that by safeguarding one's money one is safeguarding one's worldly future. But man's real future is that which pertains to the Hereafter. And money amassed for worldly purposes will only prove to be a curse for the hoarder.

[183] To those who say, 'God has commanded us not to believe in any messenger unless he brings down to us an offering to be consumed by fire,' say, 'Messengers before me have come to you with clear signs, including the one you demand. Why did you kill them, if you are telling the truth?' [184] If they deny you, so have other messengers been denied before you, who came with clear signs, scriptures and enlightening book. [185] Every human being is bound to taste death: and you shall receive your rewards in full on the Day of Resurrection. He who is kept away from the Fire and is admitted to Paradise, will surely triumph; for the life of this world is nothing but an illusory enjoyment.[a]

ٱلَّذِينَ قَالُوٓاْ إِنَّ ٱللَّهَ عَهِدَ إِلَيْنَآ أَلَّا نُؤْمِنَ لِرَسُولٍ حَتَّىٰ يَأْتِيَنَا بِقُرْبَانٍ تَأْكُلُهُ ٱلنَّارُ قُلْ قَدْ جَآءَكُمْ رُسُلٌ مِّن قَبْلِي بِٱلْبَيِّنَٰتِ وَبِٱلَّذِي قُلْتُمْ فَلِمَ قَتَلْتُمُوهُمْ إِن كُنتُمْ صَٰدِقِينَ ۝ فَإِن كَذَّبُوكَ فَقَدْ كُذِّبَ رُسُلٌ مِّن قَبْلِكَ جَآءُو بِٱلْبَيِّنَٰتِ وَٱلزُّبُرِ وَٱلْكِتَٰبِ ٱلْمُنِيرِ ۝ كُلُّ نَفْسٍ ذَآئِقَةُ ٱلْمَوْتِ وَإِنَّمَا تُوَفَّوْنَ أُجُورَكُمْ يَوْمَ ٱلْقِيَٰمَةِ فَمَن زُحْزِحَ عَنِ ٱلنَّارِ وَأُدْخِلَ ٱلْجَنَّةَ فَقَدْ فَازَ وَمَا ٱلْحَيَوٰةُ ٱلدُّنْيَآ إِلَّا مَتَٰعُ ٱلْغُرُورِ ۝

---

[a] Those who do not adopt the religion of sacrifice justify their stand in various ways. For instance, they say, 'This wealth has been granted to us by God. Then why should we not spend it for our personal needs and worldly comforts?' Sometimes their insensitivity leads them to such extremes that they attempt to discredit the preacher himself on one pretext or the other, or by trying to find loopholes in his message. The need for them to sacrifice their lives and wealth does not arise, if they can prove that the preacher is not a genuine one. These justifications appear to be in the form of valid arguments but, in fact, they are only excuses to avoid fulfilling the requirements of faith. Therefore, whatever truth is presented, they will always find words to counter the preacher's arguments, and to justify their own actions. These people are oblivious of the fact that their final end is death. And death will completely overturn the whole state of affairs. It will nullify all the false props. Then man will find himself standing at exactly that point where he actually is and not where he has shown himself to be. In other words, he will be cut down to size. Success and failure in this world are one and the same thing in terms of reality. Neither are the blessings of this world a proof of one's being in the right, nor are the difficulties, problems and setbacks of this world a proof of one's being in the wrong. Both are forms of divine trial and not signs of one's spiritual advancement or decline.

¹⁸⁶ You will surely be tried and tested in your possessions and your persons, and you shall surely hear many hurtful things from those who were given the Book before you and from those who set up partners with God, but if you endure with fortitude and restrain yourselves, that indeed is a matter of strong determination.^a

۞ لَتُبْلَوُنَّ فِى أَمْوَٰلِكُمْ وَأَنفُسِكُمْ وَلَتَسْمَعُنَّ مِنَ ٱلَّذِينَ أُوتُوا۟ ٱلْكِتَٰبَ مِن قَبْلِكُمْ وَمِنَ ٱلَّذِينَ أَشْرَكُوٓا۟ أَذًى كَثِيرًا وَإِن تَصْبِرُوا۟ وَتَتَّقُوا۟ فَإِنَّ ذَٰلِكَ مِنْ عَزْمِ ٱلْأُمُورِ ۝

---

^a A man has to make the journey of faith in a world where he might be hurt in many ways, both by his own people as well as strangers. But under no circumstances should he fall prey to negative thoughts. He should rather confront every difficult situation as it comes and keep going on. He might be even provoked, but nonetheless he should restrain himself. He should bear every setback without resorting to vengeance. There might be many an occasion when his heart, unable to take any more suffering might tell him to break the bonds of God and act as his heart bids him. Still, the fear of God should stop him from taking such a step even then.

The demands of religion inevitably require the ultimate sacrifice—which would mean sacrificing one's life and wealth. In such a situation, one has to uphold religion by making sacrifices for its cause, though that might mean adopting the most difficult of the courses open to one. On the journey of faith, this is a tremendous test of courage and high-mindedness. Indeed, becoming a true believer is a trial which requires patience and piety. One who successfully qualifies in this test is the believer for whom the gates of Paradise will be thrown open in the Hereafter.

187 God made a covenant with those who were given the Book to make it known to people and not conceal it. But they cast it behind their backs and bartered it for a paltry price: what an evil bargain they made! 188 Those who exult in their misdeeds and love to be praised for what they have not done should not suppose that they are secure from punishment; they shall suffer a grievous punishment. 189 The kingdom of the heavens and the earth belongs to God; God has power over all things.a

وَإِذْ أَخَذَ ٱللَّهُ مِيثَٰقَ ٱلَّذِينَ أُوتُواْ ٱلْكِتَٰبَ لَتُبَيِّنُنَّهُۥ لِلنَّاسِ وَلَا تَكْتُمُونَهُۥ فَنَبَذُوهُ وَرَآءَ ظُهُورِهِمْ وَٱشْتَرَوْاْ بِهِۦ ثَمَنًا قَلِيلًا ۖ فَبِئْسَ مَا يَشْتَرُونَ ۝ لَا تَحْسَبَنَّ ٱلَّذِينَ يَفْرَحُونَ بِمَآ أَتَواْ وَّيُحِبُّونَ أَن يُحْمَدُواْ بِمَا لَمْ يَفْعَلُواْ فَلَا تَحْسَبَنَّهُم بِمَفَازَةٍ مِّنَ ٱلْعَذَابِ ۖ وَلَهُمْ عَذَابٌ أَلِيمٌ ۝ وَلِلَّهِ مُلْكُ ٱلسَّمَٰوَٰتِ وَٱلْأَرْضِ ۗ وَٱللَّهُ عَلَىٰ كُلِّ شَىْءٍ قَدِيرٌ ۝

---

a When a decline sets in in the bearers of a revealed Book, it in no way means that they have entirely severed their bond with God or His messenger. This is not possible, because religion becomes a part of the traditions of a community. It becomes a great national asset and a matter of tremendous pride. And once such a communal and national link is established with something, disassociation from it is just not possible for any group. However, this association with traditions in the name of religion is purely formal and lacks in genuine religiosity, for all worldly activities continue to be engaged in in the name of religion. Even when members of certain societies have nothing to do with religion, they want to be called religious. They want to take credit for things they have not done. Having no real concern for eternal salvation, they develop such concepts as appear to show that their salvation is certain. They follow a self-made religion, but call themselves upholders of divine religion. They are busy in activities serving worldly ends, but call these activities Hereafter-oriented. They call their self-styled politics divinely guided politics, declaring that they have been moved to action for the betterment of the *ummah* (community), whereas, in reality they do little more than serve their own national interests.

One cannot save oneself from the chastisement of God by giving one's irreligiousness the name of religion. When man remains engrossed in worldly pursuits, oblivious of matters which are important in view of the Hereafter, he is going astray, but when he engages himself in worldly pursuits in the name of God, or the Prophet, he is adding insult to injury, because he wants to be given credit for a faith which is hollow and actions which are false.

¹⁹⁰ There are signs in the creation of the heavens and the earth, and in the alternation of night and day for people of understanding; ¹⁹¹who remember God while standing, sitting and [lying] on their sides, and who ponder over the creation of the heavens and the earth, saying, 'Lord, You have not created all this without purpose. Glory be to You! Save us from the torment of the Fire. ¹⁹² Lord, those whom You condemn to enter the Fire You have surely brought to disgrace. Wrongdoers will have no supporters.ᵃ

إِنَّ فِى خَلْقِ ٱلسَّمَٰوَٰتِ وَٱلْأَرْضِ وَٱخْتِلَٰفِ ٱلَّيْلِ وَٱلنَّهَارِ لَأَيَٰتٍ لِّأُوْلِى ٱلْأَلْبَٰبِ ۝ ٱلَّذِينَ يَذْكُرُونَ ٱللَّهَ قِيَٰمًا وَقُعُودًا وَعَلَىٰ جُنُوبِهِمْ وَيَتَفَكَّرُونَ فِى خَلْقِ ٱلسَّمَٰوَٰتِ وَٱلْأَرْضِ رَبَّنَا مَا خَلَقْتَ هَٰذَا بَٰطِلًا سُبْحَٰنَكَ فَقِنَا عَذَابَ ٱلنَّارِ ۝ رَبَّنَآ إِنَّكَ مَن تُدْخِلِ ٱلنَّارَ فَقَدْ أَخْزَيْتَهُۥ ۖ وَمَا لِلظَّٰلِمِينَ مِنْ أَنصَارٍ ۝

ᵃ The universe with its whole existence is a silent declaration of God's presence. When man removes the man-made veils from his eyes and unstops his ears, he starts seeing and hearing this silent announcement all around him. It then appears improbable to him that, in a universe where the stars and the planets have continued to exist for millions of years, man may cease to exist within fifty or a hundred years, taking with him to his grave all his desires and aspirations. In a world which abounds in the beauties of nature, with the fragrance of flowers, where countless meaningful blessings, like air, water and the sun have been provided, should man's end be nothing but only sorrow and suffering? Then he also finds it unthinkable that, in a world of limitless possibilities where, just by sowing seeds in the ground, a whole forest of trees comes into existence, one should fail to receive the fruits of virtuous actions; that in a world where the sun shines daily after the dark night, centuries go by without being illuminated by the lustre of fairness and justice; that in a world where earthquakes and tempests lie dormant, man should continue to perpetrate tyranny and oppression without ever being checked.

¹⁹³ Lord, we have heard a caller calling to the true faith saying, "Believe in your Lord," and we believed. Lord, forgive us our sins and remove from us our bad deeds and make us die with the virtuous. ¹⁹⁴ Our Lord! Grant us what You have promised to us through Your messengers, and do not humiliate us on the Day of Resurrection. Surely, You never fail to fulfill Your promise.'^a

رَبَّنَآ إِنَّنَا سَمِعْنَا مُنَادِيًا يُنَادِى لِلْإِيمَـٰنِ أَنْ ءَامِنُوا۟ بِرَبِّكُمْ فَـَٔامَنَّا رَبَّنَا فَٱغْفِرْ لَنَا ذُنُوبَنَا وَكَفِّرْ عَنَّا سَيِّـَٔاتِنَا وَتَوَفَّنَا مَعَ ٱلْأَبْرَارِ ۝ رَبَّنَا وَءَاتِنَا مَا وَعَدتَّنَا عَلَىٰ رُسُلِكَ وَلَا تُخْزِنَا يَوْمَ ٱلْقِيَـٰمَةِ ۗ إِنَّكَ لَا تُخْلِفُ ٱلْمِيعَادَ ۝

---

^a Those who think deeply, seeking a more profound reality, find it unthinkable that a meaningful universe should have a meaningless end. They discover, that the message conveyed by the preacher is the announcement, in human language, of the same reality, which is being silently proclaimed by the whole universe. The greatest issue is that when the truth is unveiled, and the 'sun' of justice makes its appearance, they should not be left deprived and destitute. So when the truth appears, they rush towards it, remembering God. By breaking all personal bonds and ridding their thoughts of worldly considerations, they become one with the preacher of truth; so that in the next world, when the 'darkness' and the 'light' of the universe are separated, the Lord of the universe will make them inhabit the light, and will not abandon them to fumble eternally in the dark.

The true measure of wisdom and unwisdom is wholly different from the one devised by human beings on their own. Here a wise man is one who lives in the remembrance of God, who can discover the divine meaningfulness at work in the creation plan of the universe. On the contrary, the unwise man is one who keeps his mind engaged in other more material things, who lives in this world as if he is totally unaware of the creation plan of the Lord of the Universe.

¹⁹⁵ Their Lord accepted their prayer, saying, 'I will deny no man or woman among you the reward of their labours. You are members one of another. I will certainly forgive the sins of those who emigrated and were expelled from their homes, who suffered persecution in My cause, who fought and were killed. I will certainly admit them to Gardens through which rivers flow, as a reward from God: with God is the best reward.' ¹⁹⁶ Do not be deceived by the actions of those who deny the truth in the land: ¹⁹⁷ this is only a brief enjoyment, after which Hell shall be their abode—what an evil resting place! [a]

فَٱسْتَجَابَ لَهُمْ رَبُّهُمْ أَنِّى لَا أُضِيعُ عَمَلَ عَٰمِلٍ مِّنكُم مِّن ذَكَرٍ أَوْ أُنثَىٰ بَعْضُكُم مِّنۢ بَعْضٍ فَٱلَّذِينَ هَاجَرُوا۟ وَأُخْرِجُوا۟ مِن دِيَٰرِهِمْ وَأُوذُوا۟ فِى سَبِيلِى وَقَٰتَلُوا۟ وَقُتِلُوا۟ لَأُكَفِّرَنَّ عَنْهُمْ سَيِّـَٔاتِهِمْ وَلَأُدْخِلَنَّهُمْ جَنَّٰتٍ تَجْرِى مِن تَحْتِهَا ٱلْأَنْهَٰرُ ثَوَابًا مِّنْ عِندِ ٱللَّهِ وَٱللَّهُ عِندَهُۥ حُسْنُ ٱلثَّوَابِ ۝ لَا يَغُرَّنَّكَ تَقَلُّبُ ٱلَّذِينَ كَفَرُوا۟ فِى ٱلْبِلَٰدِ ۝ مَتَٰعٌ قَلِيلٌ ثُمَّ مَأْوَىٰهُمْ جَهَنَّمُ وَبِئْسَ ٱلْمِهَادُ ۝

---

^a The responsible life of the believers deprives them of any liberties that might be taken with the self. In their mission of communicating the Truth, many of their hearers turn hostile when they find that the success of such a mission entails a negation of their own existence. This state of affairs sometimes becomes so calamitous that believers are rendered homeless in their own homeland, having to suffer the oppression of their opponents. If they adopt the divine religion, it must be at the cost of their lives and property. In order to succeed in these tests, the believers should never place the considerations of this world above those of the Hereafter. Difficulties and unpleasantness should be suffered patiently. Negative feelings should be suppressed and any reaction should be refrained from. Believers must remain steadfast in their encounters with their opponents. It is this steadfastness, which draws God's succour towards them. Besides this, it is necessary that all believers be united, joining together to face enemy onslaughts with all the strength of perfect union. Faith is in fact a test of patience, and only those who fear God can pass this test.

¹⁹⁸ Those who fear their Lord shall have gardens through which rivers flow, wherein they will abide forever: and a goodly welcome from their Lord. God's recompense is best for the virtuous. ¹⁹⁹ Some of the People of the Book believe in God, and in what has been revealed to you and what was revealed to them. They humble themselves before God and do not sell God's revelations for a trifling price. These shall be rewarded by their Lord: God is swift in reckoning! ²⁰⁰ Believers, endure, vie with each other in endurance, stand firm in your faith and fear God, so that you may succeed.ᵃ

لَـٰكِنِ ٱلَّذِينَ ٱتَّقَوْا۟ رَبَّهُمْ هُمْ جَنَّـٰتٌ تَجْرِى مِن تَحْتِهَا ٱلْأَنْهَـٰرُ خَـٰلِدِينَ فِيهَا نُزُلًا مِّنْ عِندِ ٱللَّهِ ۗ وَمَا عِندَ ٱللَّهِ خَيْرٌ لِّلْأَبْرَارِ ۝ وَإِنَّ مِنْ أَهْلِ ٱلْكِتَـٰبِ لَمَن يُؤْمِنُ بِٱللَّهِ وَمَا أُنزِلَ إِلَيْكُمْ وَمَا أُنزِلَ إِلَيْهِمْ خَـٰشِعِينَ لِلَّهِ لَا يَشْتَرُونَ بِـَٔايَـٰتِ ٱللَّهِ ثَمَنًا قَلِيلًا ۗ أُو۟لَـٰئِكَ لَهُمْ أَجْرُهُمْ عِندَ رَبِّهِمْ ۗ إِنَّ ٱللَّهَ سَرِيعُ ٱلْحِسَابِ ۝ يَـٰٓأَيُّهَا ٱلَّذِينَ ءَامَنُوا۟ ٱصْبِرُوا۟ وَصَابِرُوا۟ وَرَابِطُوا۟ وَٱتَّقُوا۟ ٱللَّهَ لَعَلَّكُمْ تُفْلِحُونَ ۝

ᵃ It often happens in this world that those who have no fear of God and have no concern for the Hereafter come into positions of dominance. All kinds of honour and glory surround them. On the other hand, the believers are often powerless. No share of worldly glory comes their way. But this state of affairs is temporary in nature. The situation will reverse itself with the advent of Doomsday. Those who lived in this world without any fear of God and gathered around them the honour and glory of the world will find themselves cast into the pit of humiliation. And those who had been denied worldly honour and successes, because of their attachment to God, will be the possessors of all kinds of eternal honour and success in the next world. They will be God's guests and there is nothing greater on this earth and in the heavens than being God's guests.

4. WOMEN

In the name of God,
the Most Gracious, the Most Merciful

¹ O mankind! Fear your Lord, who created you from a single soul. He created its mate from it and from the two of them spread countless men and women [throughout the earth]. Fear God, in whose name you appeal to one another, and be mindful of your obligations in respect of ties of kinship. God is always watching over you.ᵃ

ᵃ All human beings are one and the same by birth. Ultimately, everyone can trace his origin to the same man and woman as father and mother. It is, therefore, necessary that all human beings should have a feeling of affinity with each other and live with fairness and goodwill like the members of one extended family. This racial unity becomes more compact in family relationships and the importance of decent behaviour among kinsfolk becomes further heightened. Good behaviour between fellow human beings is important, not merely from the moral point of view, but rather as a matter of personal concern to man himself. This is so, because everyone is governed by the Great, Almighty God, who as the Reckoner for one and all, will decide the eternal future of all human beings in the Hereafter, requiting them according to their actions in this world. Man should, therefore, not consider his dealings with others as a matter between man and man, but as a matter between man and God. He should fear the grip of God and should adhere to the bounds set by God so as to save himself from His wrath.

According to a *hadith*, God proclaimed, 'I shall associate Myself with one who strengthens the ties of kinship and detach Myself from one who severs them.' This shows that man's attachment to God is being tested by the criterion of his relations with other human beings. One who goes in fear of God while dealing with the rights of others, is one who truly venerates Him; one who loves other human beings, is one who really loves his Creator. The virtues of fair dealing and compassion are general requirements of human society, but so vital are they to maintaining good family relations that in importance they stand second only to God.

² Give the orphans the possessions that belong to them, do not exchange good things with bad and do not consume their property, adding it to your own. Surely, this is a great crime. ³ If you fear that you cannot deal fairly with orphan girls, you may marry women of your choice, two or three or four; but if you fear that you might not be able to treat them with equal fairness, then only one—or [from among] those whom you rightfully possess. That is more likely to keep you from committing an injustice. ⁴ And give the women their dowers willingly, but if they, of their own accord, remit any part of it to you, you may make use of it with pleasure and goodwill.ᵃ

وَءَاتُواْ ٱلۡيَتَٰمَىٰٓ أَمۡوَٰلَهُمۡ وَلَا تَتَبَدَّلُواْ ٱلۡخَبِيثَ بِٱلطَّيِّبِ وَلَا تَأۡكُلُوٓاْ أَمۡوَٰلَهُمۡ إِلَىٰٓ أَمۡوَٰلِكُمۡ إِنَّهُۥ كَانَ حُوبًا كَبِيرًا ۝ وَإِنۡ خِفۡتُمۡ أَلَّا تُقۡسِطُواْ فِي ٱلۡيَتَٰمَىٰ فَٱنكِحُواْ مَا طَابَ لَكُم مِّنَ ٱلنِّسَآءِ مَثۡنَىٰ وَثُلَٰثَ وَرُبَٰعَ فَإِنۡ خِفۡتُمۡ أَلَّا تَعۡدِلُواْ فَوَٰحِدَةً أَوۡ مَا مَلَكَتۡ أَيۡمَٰنُكُمۡ ذَٰلِكَ أَدۡنَىٰٓ أَلَّا تَعُولُواْ ۝ وَءَاتُواْ ٱلنِّسَآءَ صَدُقَٰتِهِنَّ نِحۡلَةً فَإِن طِبۡنَ لَكُمۡ عَن شَيۡءٍ مِّنۡهُ نَفۡسًا فَكُلُوهُ هَنِيٓـًٔا مَّرِيٓـًٔا ۝

ᵃ Orphan boys and girls are the weakest members of a family or society and, therefore, dealing with them appropriately is the toughest test of one's being imbued with the fear of God.

Orphans deserve to be treated in a manner which is just and compassionate and whereby their rights are ensured the maximum protection. It is a major sin for a joint property to be divided in such a way that some are given valuable shares, while others are given worthless shares, only for the purpose of tallying the listed items.

⁵ Do not give those who are of immature mind your property which God has granted you as a means of support: make provision for them out of it, and clothe them, and give them good advice. ⁶ Keep a close check on orphans till they attain the age of marriage; then, if you find them to be mature of mind, hand over their property to them. Do not consume it by wasteful spending, before they come of age. If the guardian is affluent, let him abstain altogether, and if he is poor, let him have for himself what is just and reasonable. When you hand over their property to them, call witnesses in their presence; God is sufficient as a Reckoner.ᵃ

وَلَا تُؤْتُوا۟ ٱلسُّفَهَآءَ أَمْوَٰلَكُمُ ٱلَّتِى جَعَلَ ٱللَّهُ لَكُمْ قِيَٰمًا وَٱرْزُقُوهُمْ فِيهَا وَٱكْسُوهُمْ وَقُولُوا۟ لَهُمْ قَوْلًا مَّعْرُوفًا ۝ وَٱبْتَلُوا۟ ٱلْيَتَٰمَىٰ حَتَّىٰٓ إِذَا بَلَغُوا۟ ٱلنِّكَاحَ فَإِنْ ءَانَسْتُم مِّنْهُمْ رُشْدًا فَٱدْفَعُوٓا۟ إِلَيْهِمْ أَمْوَٰلَهُمْ وَلَا تَأْكُلُوهَآ إِسْرَافًا وَبِدَارًا أَن يَكْبَرُوا۟ وَمَن كَانَ غَنِيًّا فَلْيَسْتَعْفِفْ وَمَن كَانَ فَقِيرًا فَلْيَأْكُلْ بِٱلْمَعْرُوفِ فَإِذَا دَفَعْتُمْ إِلَيْهِمْ أَمْوَٰلَهُمْ فَأَشْهِدُوا۟ عَلَيْهِمْ وَكَفَىٰ بِٱللَّهِ حَسِيبًا ۝

ᵃ Property is meant neither for luxury nor for the manifestation of pride. It is a means of livelihood for man, supporting his existence in the world. As such, it is not proper on the one hand to consider its acquisition one's goal in life, while on the other, it is extremely important that any wasteful use of property should be checked and earnest efforts be made, when it falls into the wrong hands, to restore it to its rightful owner. Any misappropriation of anyone's belongings is akin to creating a breach in God's arrangement of bestowing a livelihood upon His servants. In the case of an orphan, who happens to be the weakest member of society, it becomes even more imperative that his property be well-protected and he be dealt with in fairness and justice. It is also necessary that a justified settlement with orphans should be recorded in writing and witnessed so that the executor's responsibility may be honourably discharged with no question of future disputes or complaints. Whenever one takes someone's affairs in hand, he must proceed with the realization that any injustice he may commit is in the knowledge of God. It is possible that the person whose affairs are being settled is weak and cannot deal effectively with unjust treatment, but surely God will catch hold of the arbiter on the Day of Reckoning and punish him severely for any unjustified settlement. This is inevitable and none can escape it.

7 Men shall have a share in what parents and relatives leave behind, and women shall have a share in what parents and relatives leave behind, whether it be little or much. This is ordained [by God]. 8 If other relatives, orphans or needy people are present at the time of the division, then provide for them out of it, and speak kindly to them. 9 Those who are concerned about the fate of their own helpless children if they should die and leave them behind should show the same concern for orphans. Let them fear God and uphold justice. 10 Those who consume the property of orphans unjustly are actually swallowing fire into their own bellies; soon they will burn in the blazing Flame.[a]

لِّلرِّجَالِ نَصِيبٌ مِّمَّا تَرَكَ ٱلۡوَٰلِدَانِ وَٱلۡأَقۡرَبُونَ وَلِلنِّسَآءِ نَصِيبٌ مِّمَّا تَرَكَ ٱلۡوَٰلِدَانِ وَٱلۡأَقۡرَبُونَ مِمَّا قَلَّ مِنۡهُ أَوۡ كَثُرَ نَصِيبًا مَّفۡرُوضًا ٧ وَإِذَا حَضَرَ ٱلۡقِسۡمَةَ أُوْلُواْ ٱلۡقُرۡبَىٰ وَٱلۡيَتَٰمَىٰ وَٱلۡمَسَٰكِينُ فَٱرۡزُقُوهُم مِّنۡهُ وَقُولُواْ لَهُمۡ قَوۡلًا مَّعۡرُوفًا ٨ وَلۡيَخۡشَ ٱلَّذِينَ لَوۡ تَرَكُواْ مِنۡ خَلۡفِهِمۡ ذُرِّيَّةً ضِعَٰفًا خَافُواْ عَلَيۡهِمۡ فَلۡيَتَّقُواْ ٱللَّهَ وَلۡيَقُولُواْ قَوۡلًا سَدِيدًا ٩ إِنَّ ٱلَّذِينَ يَأۡكُلُونَ أَمۡوَٰلَ ٱلۡيَتَٰمَىٰ ظُلۡمًا إِنَّمَا يَأۡكُلُونَ فِي بُطُونِهِمۡ نَارًا وَسَيَصۡلَوۡنَ سَعِيرًا ١٠

---

a In this world a man may usurp a weak person's right. But every unlawful acquisition that he makes is like filling up his belly with fire. The fact that whatever is usurped is like fire may not be apparent here, but it will become evident in the Hereafter. Man has been given freedom of action in this world, but he cannot manipulate the result of his actions. One who wishes to be saved from evil consequences should not do wrong to others. He should adopt the culture of beneficence and, according to his capacity, be a giver to others. If one is not in a position to benefit others in any way, one should, according to Islamic standards, at least not hurt anyone's feelings. One should speak plainly and truthfully, or else remain silent.

11 Concerning your children, God enjoins you that a male shall receive a share equivalent to that of two females. But if there are more than two females, then their share is two thirds of the inheritance. If there is only one, she will receive the half. Each of your parents receives a sixth of what you leave if you have children. If you are childless and your heirs are your parents, your mother receives a third. If you have brothers [or sisters] your mother receives a sixth, after [the deduction of] any bequest you make or the repayment of any debts with regard to your father and your sons. You do not know which of them is going to benefit you more: but this fixing of portions is by God and He is all knowing and all wise.[a]

يُوصِيكُمُ ٱللَّهُ فِىٓ أَوْلَٰدِكُمْ ۖ لِلذَّكَرِ مِثْلُ حَظِّ ٱلْأُنثَيَيْنِ ۚ فَإِن كُنَّ نِسَآءً فَوْقَ ٱثْنَتَيْنِ فَلَهُنَّ ثُلُثَا مَا تَرَكَ ۖ وَإِن كَانَتْ وَٰحِدَةً فَلَهَا ٱلنِّصْفُ ۚ وَلِأَبَوَيْهِ لِكُلِّ وَٰحِدٍ مِّنْهُمَا ٱلسُّدُسُ مِمَّا تَرَكَ إِن كَانَ لَهُۥ وَلَدٌ ۚ فَإِن لَّمْ يَكُن لَّهُۥ وَلَدٌ وَوَرِثَهُۥٓ أَبَوَاهُ فَلِأُمِّهِ ٱلثُّلُثُ ۚ فَإِن كَانَ لَهُۥٓ إِخْوَةٌ فَلِأُمِّهِ ٱلسُّدُسُ ۚ مِنۢ بَعْدِ وَصِيَّةٍ يُوصِى بِهَآ أَوْ دَيْنٍ ۗ ءَابَآؤُكُمْ وَأَبْنَآؤُكُمْ لَا تَدْرُونَ أَيُّهُمْ أَقْرَبُ لَكُمْ نَفْعًا ۚ فَرِيضَةً مِّنَ ٱللَّهِ ۗ إِنَّ ٱللَّهَ كَانَ عَلِيمًا حَكِيمًا ۝

---

[a] Man-made laws have some bias or the other. During the ancient tribal age, a boy was of considerable importance in the social order. Since he was a source of strength to the tribe, he was awarded the sole right of inheritance, depriving the girl completely. This has come to be resented in modern times and consequently the boy and the girl are now both considered equal. But, if the ancient principle was unjustified, the present principle is unrealistic. A law free from all types of inequity can be expected only from God, to whom is attributed infinite knowledge and wisdom. The divine laws enjoined by God on this subject are not only a real source of social justice, but relate in the most profound way to the life Hereafter as well.

[12] You will inherit half of what your wives leave, provided they have left no children. But if they leave children then you inherit a quarter of what they leave, after payment of any bequests they may have made or any debts they may have incurred. Your wives shall inherit one quarter of what you leave if you are childless. But if you leave children, your wives shall inherit one eighth, after payment of any bequest or debts. If a man or woman has no direct heirs [neither children or parents] but has left a brother or a sister, they shall each inherit one sixth, but if they are more than two, they share one third between them, after payment of any bequests or debts, so that no harm is done to anyone. That is a commandment from God: God is all knowing and forbearing. [13] These are the limits set by God. Anyone who obeys God and His Messenger will be admitted to Gardens through which rivers flow, to live there forever. That will be the supreme achievement. [14] But anyone who disobeys God and His Messenger and transgresses His limits shall be cast into a Fire, wherein he will abide forever. And he shall have a humiliating punishment.[a]

وَلَكُمْ نِصْفُ مَا تَرَكَ أَزْوَٰجُكُمْ إِن لَّمْ يَكُن لَّهُنَّ وَلَدٌ ۚ فَإِن كَانَ لَهُنَّ وَلَدٌ فَلَكُمُ ٱلرُّبُعُ مِمَّا تَرَكْنَ ۚ مِنۢ بَعْدِ وَصِيَّةٍ يُوصِينَ بِهَآ أَوْ دَيْنٍ ۚ وَلَهُنَّ ٱلرُّبُعُ مِمَّا تَرَكْتُمْ إِن لَّمْ يَكُن لَّكُمْ وَلَدٌ ۚ فَإِن كَانَ لَكُمْ وَلَدٌ فَلَهُنَّ ٱلثُّمُنُ مِمَّا تَرَكْتُم ۚ مِّنۢ بَعْدِ وَصِيَّةٍ تُوصُونَ بِهَآ أَوْ دَيْنٍ ۗ وَإِن كَانَ رَجُلٌ يُورَثُ كَلَٰلَةً أَوِ ٱمْرَأَةٌ وَلَهُ أَخٌ أَوْ أُخْتٌ فَلِكُلِّ وَٰحِدٍ مِّنْهُمَا ٱلسُّدُسُ ۚ فَإِن كَانُوٓا۟ أَكْثَرَ مِن ذَٰلِكَ فَهُمْ شُرَكَآءُ فِى ٱلثُّلُثِ ۚ مِنۢ بَعْدِ وَصِيَّةٍ يُوصَىٰ بِهَآ أَوْ دَيْنٍ غَيْرَ مُضَآرٍّ ۚ وَصِيَّةً مِّنَ ٱللَّهِ ۗ وَٱللَّهُ عَلِيمٌ حَلِيمٌ ﴿١٢﴾ تِلْكَ حُدُودُ ٱللَّهِ ۚ وَمَن يُطِعِ ٱللَّهَ وَرَسُولَهُ يُدْخِلْهُ جَنَّٰتٍ تَجْرِى مِن تَحْتِهَا ٱلْأَنْهَٰرُ خَٰلِدِينَ فِيهَا ۚ وَذَٰلِكَ ٱلْفَوْزُ ٱلْعَظِيمُ ﴿١٣﴾ وَمَن يَعْصِ ٱللَّهَ وَرَسُولَهُ وَيَتَعَدَّ حُدُودَهُ يُدْخِلْهُ نَارًا خَٰلِدًا فِيهَا وَلَهُ عَذَابٌ مُّهِينٌ ﴿١٤﴾

---

[a] Payment of the dues of orphans, abiding by wills, release of the inheritance to the inheritors, etc., are among those matters on which a man's being sent to hell or heaven depends. To make out a will disposing of one-third part of one's property is permissible by Islamic law. But anyone making out a will with the intention of depriving a person of his rightful inheritance, would be committing a sin that could condemn him to Hell. Man has to follow the law of God in this regard and not his own personal desires or family expediencies.

¹⁵ If any of your women commit fornication, call in four male witnesses from among yourselves against them; if they testify to their guilt, confine them to the house until death releases them or until God gives them another way out. ¹⁶ If two men commit a like abomination, punish them both. If they repent and mend their ways, leave them alone. God is forgiving and merciful.ᵃ

وَٱلَّـٰتِى يَأْتِينَ ٱلْفَـٰحِشَةَ مِن نِّسَآئِكُمْ فَٱسْتَشْهِدُوا۟ عَلَيْهِنَّ أَرْبَعَةً مِّنكُمْ فَإِن شَهِدُوا۟ فَأَمْسِكُوهُنَّ فِى ٱلْبُيُوتِ حَتَّىٰ يَتَوَفَّىٰهُنَّ ٱلْمَوْتُ أَوْ يَجْعَلَ ٱللَّهُ لَهُنَّ سَبِيلًا ۝ وَٱلَّذَانِ يَأْتِيَـٰنِهَا مِنكُمْ فَـَٔاذُوهُمَا ۖ فَإِن تَابَا وَأَصْلَحَا فَأَعْرِضُوا۟ عَنْهُمَآ ۗ إِنَّ ٱللَّهَ كَانَ تَوَّابًا رَّحِيمًا ۝

ᵃ If a man or a woman commits an act considered a sin according to Islamic tenets, he or she will be dealt with in accordance with the rule of law, and not arbitrarily. It is unjust to declare anyone a criminal without fulfilling the legal conditions, nor is there permission to proceed summarily against even a proven criminal. The purpose of punishment is to uphold justice, and justice cannot be upheld through tyranny and injustice. Moreover, if a sinner pleads guilty and reforms himself, it becomes essential to adopt a sympathetic and forgiving attitude towards him. It is not proper to assess anyone on the basis of his past. When God Himself pardons those who sincerely repent, and turns in His benevolence to those who reform and improve, mere mortals have no right to taunt and ridicule former delinquents. One who taunts and ridicules them may yet prove to be a transgressor himself.

¹⁷ But God undertakes to accept repentance only from those who do evil out of ignorance and those who repent soon after. God turns towards such people with mercy; He is all knowing and all wise. ¹⁸ Forgiveness is not for those who continue to do evil deeds until, when death comes upon one of them, he says: 'Now I repent!' nor from those who die as deniers of the truth. We have prepared a painful punishment for them.ᵃ

إِنَّمَا ٱلتَّوْبَةُ عَلَى ٱللَّهِ لِلَّذِينَ يَعْمَلُونَ ٱلسُّوٓءَ بِجَهَٰلَةٍ ثُمَّ يَتُوبُونَ مِن قَرِيبٍ فَأُو۟لَٰٓئِكَ يَتُوبُ ٱللَّهُ عَلَيْهِمْ ۗ وَكَانَ ٱللَّهُ عَلِيمًا حَكِيمًا ۝ وَلَيْسَتِ ٱلتَّوْبَةُ لِلَّذِينَ يَعْمَلُونَ ٱلسَّيِّـَٔاتِ حَتَّىٰٓ إِذَا حَضَرَ أَحَدَهُمُ ٱلْمَوْتُ قَالَ إِنِّى تُبْتُ ٱلْـَٰٔنَ وَلَا ٱلَّذِينَ يَمُوتُونَ وَهُمْ كُفَّارٌ أُو۟لَٰٓئِكَ أَعْتَدْنَا لَهُمْ عَذَابًا أَلِيمًا ۝

ᵃ Repentance does not mean simply uttering certain words like, 'I repent' or 'tawbah'. It should not be mere lip service. It means the intense realization of one's wrongdoing. If a sinner sincerely repents the error of his ways, he experiences an agonizing condition at par with self-punishment. God will surely pardon one who thus repents due to His intense fear. However, He does not accept the repentance of those who daringly and insensitively and knowingly continue to disobey and transgress, paying no heed to any warning and saying 'I repent' only when death is staring them in the face. Nor does the repentance of those who admit their sins only after witnessing the horrors of the Hereafter have any meaning for the Almighty.

The essence of contrition is that the wrongdoer should turn to his Lord, so that the Lord also turns to him. Repentance (tawbah) is for one who commits a wrongful act under the influence of a momentary emotion or passion, but who is soon made by his conscience to realize his fault; who renounces evil ways and returns to righteousness, reforming his life according to the divine law. This shows genuine penitence. One who thus repents is like the man who, after straying away, returns to his home.

¹⁹ Believers, it is not lawful for you to inherit women against their will, nor should you detain them wrongfully, so that you may take away a part of what you have given them, unless they are guilty of something clearly outrageous. Live with them in accordance with what is fair and kind; if you dislike them, it may be that you dislike something which God might make a source of abundant good. ²⁰ If you desire to replace one wife with another, do not take any part of her dower back: even if you have given her a treasure. Would you take it by slandering her and with manifest sinfulness?^a

يَٰٓأَيُّهَا ٱلَّذِينَ ءَامَنُواْ لَا يَحِلُّ لَكُمۡ أَن تَرِثُواْ ٱلنِّسَآءَ كَرۡهٗا ۖ وَلَا تَعۡضُلُوهُنَّ لِتَذۡهَبُواْ بِبَعۡضِ مَآ ءَاتَيۡتُمُوهُنَّ إِلَّآ أَن يَأۡتِينَ بِفَٰحِشَةٖ مُّبَيِّنَةٖ ۚ وَعَاشِرُوهُنَّ بِٱلۡمَعۡرُوفِ ۚ فَإِن كَرِهۡتُمُوهُنَّ فَعَسَىٰٓ أَن تَكۡرَهُواْ شَيۡـٔٗا وَيَجۡعَلَ ٱللَّهُ فِيهِ خَيۡرٗا كَثِيرٗا ۝ وَإِنۡ أَرَدتُّمُ ٱسۡتِبۡدَالَ زَوۡجٖ مَّكَانَ زَوۡجٖ وَءَاتَيۡتُمۡ إِحۡدَىٰهُنَّ قِنطَارٗا فَلَا تَأۡخُذُواْ مِنۡهُ شَيۡـًٔا ۚ أَتَأۡخُذُونَهُۥ بُهۡتَٰنٗا وَإِثۡمٗا مُّبِينٗا ۝

---

^a Undoubtedly, the successors of a deceased person have the right to inherit his property. But his widow is not to be treated as a part of the inheritance and exploited as the successors decide. Property is inanimate and therefore without feeling, and, as such is a proper object of inheritance, but human beings have sensate, independent existences, and therefore possess the right to decide their future according to their own choice.

If there is any physical or temperamental shortcoming in a woman, it should be tolerated so that she may have the opportunity to use her other natural talents to play her part in the building up of the household. One should overlook the unpleasant aspects of her personality and try to adjust amicably. The secret of the progress and solidarity of any family or society is that its members should ignore the shortcomings and deficiencies of each other and give everyone the chance to exercise his or her abilities. Those who adopt the way of patience and tolerance in this world for the sake of God, are the people who will be granted admission to Paradise in the Hereafter.

When one does not like one's life companion and, rather than be tolerant, decides to separate, it often happens that one exaggerates the shortcomings of the other to justify one's decision. Allegations are fabricated so that the weaker person should become nervous and leave. Similarly, while severing the marriage bond, trumped up reasons are presented to the other party. But these activities are against the covenant. A covenant is considered sacred by God and whether written or unwritten, it is essentially binding. It applies equally to both parties, leaving them no choice of their own.

²¹ How can you take it when you have been intimate with one another, and she has taken a solemn pledge from you? ²² Do not marry women whom your fathers married, except for what has already taken place in the past. This is indeed a shameful deed, a loathsome thing and an evil practice.ᵃ

وَكَيْفَ تَأْخُذُونَهُۥ وَقَدْ أَفْضَىٰ بَعْضُكُمْ إِلَىٰ بَعْضٍ وَأَخَذْنَ مِنكُم مِّيثَٰقًا غَلِيظًا ۞ وَلَا تَنكِحُوا۟ مَا نَكَحَ ءَابَآؤُكُم مِّنَ ٱلنِّسَآءِ إِلَّا مَا قَدْ سَلَفَ إِنَّهُۥ كَانَ فَٰحِشَةً وَمَقْتًا وَسَآءَ سَبِيلًا ۞

ᵃ The maxim 'the past is past' relates not just to marriage, but stands out as a general principle of wisdom. Whenever any change takes place in life, whether at the family or the national level, many affairs of the past, looked at by modern standards, appear to be wrong on all such occasions. Orders based on things which have now become irrelevant give rise to innumerable problems. The right approach is, therefore, to forget the past and direct one's efforts to reforming the present and future.

The advice in verse 19, 'if you dislike them, it may be that you dislike something which God might make a source of abundant good' may appear here with regard to the relationship between husband and wife, but it is a form of general guidance as well. It is commonly found that the Quran, while giving guidance on a specific matter, also sets forth profound advice of a general nature which may concern a human being's entire life.

Living collectively is an essential condition for human life in this world. No one can survive alone. However, due to the variations of temperament among individuals, some irritants inevitably crop up. In such a situation the only practicable approach is to ignore complaints, avoid friction and endeavour to maintain peaceable relationships.

It often happens that one detects some shortcoming in his companion and becomes annoyed with it. Instead, if he ponders over the matter, it will be evident that there are few situations which do not have their unfavourable aspects. Adversities sometimes become a test of patience; sometimes act as a stimulus to turn to God in repentance and sometimes their very vexing nature teaches an important lesson.

²³ You are forbidden to take as wives your mothers, daughters, sisters, paternal and maternal aunts, your brothers' daughters and your sisters' daughters, your foster mothers and foster sisters, your wives' mothers and stepdaughters in your protection and the daughters of your wives with whom you have consummated your marriage; but if you have not consummated your marriage then you will not be blamed [if you marry their daughters.] You are also forbidden to marry the spouses of your sons or two sisters together, except what has already passed. Surely, God is ever-forgiving and merciful. ²⁴ Also forbidden are married women, except those who have passed into your hands as prisoners of war. This is a commandment of God to you. All women other than these are lawful to you, provided you seek them with your wealth in honest wedlock, not in fornication. When you consummate your marriage with them, give the dowers due to them. And there is no sin for you in what you do by mutual agreement after the fixing of the dower. God is all knowing and wise.ᵃ

حُرِّمَتْ عَلَيْكُمْ أُمَّهَٰتُكُمْ وَبَنَاتُكُمْ وَأَخَوَٰتُكُمْ وَعَمَّٰتُكُمْ وَخَٰلَٰتُكُمْ وَبَنَاتُ ٱلْأَخِ وَبَنَاتُ ٱلْأُخْتِ وَأُمَّهَٰتُكُمُ ٱلَّٰتِي أَرْضَعْنَكُمْ وَأَخَوَٰتُكُم مِّنَ ٱلرَّضَٰعَةِ وَأُمَّهَٰتُ نِسَآئِكُمْ وَرَبَٰٓئِبُكُمُ ٱلَّٰتِي فِي حُجُورِكُم مِّن نِّسَآئِكُمُ ٱلَّٰتِي دَخَلْتُم بِهِنَّ فَإِن لَّمْ تَكُونُوا۟ دَخَلْتُم بِهِنَّ فَلَا جُنَاحَ عَلَيْكُمْ وَحَلَٰٓئِلُ أَبْنَآئِكُمُ ٱلَّذِينَ مِنْ أَصْلَٰبِكُمْ وَأَن تَجْمَعُوا۟ بَيْنَ ٱلْأُخْتَيْنِ إِلَّا مَا قَدْ سَلَفَ إِنَّ ٱللَّهَ كَانَ غَفُورًا رَّحِيمًا ۞ ٢٣ وَٱلْمُحْصَنَٰتُ مِنَ ٱلنِّسَآءِ إِلَّا مَا مَلَكَتْ أَيْمَٰنُكُمْ كِتَٰبَ ٱللَّهِ عَلَيْكُمْ وَأُحِلَّ لَكُم مَّا وَرَآءَ ذَٰلِكُمْ أَن تَبْتَغُوا۟ بِأَمْوَٰلِكُم مُّحْصِنِينَ غَيْرَ مُسَٰفِحِينَ فَمَا ٱسْتَمْتَعْتُم بِهِۦ مِنْهُنَّ فَـَٔاتُوهُنَّ أُجُورَهُنَّ فَرِيضَةً وَلَا جُنَاحَ عَلَيْكُمْ فِيمَا تَرَٰضَيْتُم بِهِۦ مِنۢ بَعْدِ ٱلْفَرِيضَةِ إِنَّ ٱللَّهَ كَانَ عَلِيمًا حَكِيمًا ٢٤

ᵃ Many natural desires make themselves felt in human beings—sexuality between man and woman being one of these. Islamic law, which fixes a limitation for all human emotions, has determined the limits for sexual relationships also. According to this divine dictate, only that sexual alliance between man and woman is valid which is established through a standard solemn social agreement in the form of marriage. It requires, moreover, that along with the satisfaction of natural desire, an environment of chastity must also prevail in the family life. For this purpose certain close relations have been declared prohibited to keep them beyond and above sexual desires.

²⁵ If any of you cannot afford to marry a free believing woman let him marry one of his believing maids whom he possesses. God best knows your faith. You are one of another. So marry them with their owner's permission, and give them their dower according to what is fair, neither committing fornication nor taking secret paramours. And if, after they are married, they commit adultery they shall have half the punishment prescribed for a free woman. This is for those of you who fear lest he should fall into sin. But that it is better for you to practise self restraint. God is most forgiving and merciful.[a]

وَمَن لَّمْ يَسْتَطِعْ مِنكُمْ طَوْلًا أَن يَنكِحَ ٱلْمُحْصَنَٰتِ ٱلْمُؤْمِنَٰتِ فَمِن مَّا مَلَكَتْ أَيْمَٰنُكُم مِّن فَتَيَٰتِكُمُ ٱلْمُؤْمِنَٰتِ ۚ وَٱللَّهُ أَعْلَمُ بِإِيمَٰنِكُم ۚ بَعْضُكُم مِّنۢ بَعْضٍ ۚ فَٱنكِحُوهُنَّ بِإِذْنِ أَهْلِهِنَّ وَءَاتُوهُنَّ أُجُورَهُنَّ بِٱلْمَعْرُوفِ مُحْصَنَٰتٍ غَيْرَ مُسَٰفِحَٰتٍ وَلَا مُتَّخِذَٰتِ أَخْدَانٍ ۚ فَإِذَآ أُحْصِنَّ فَإِنْ أَتَيْنَ بِفَٰحِشَةٍ فَعَلَيْهِنَّ نِصْفُ مَا عَلَى ٱلْمُحْصَنَٰتِ مِنَ ٱلْعَذَابِ ۚ ذَٰلِكَ لِمَنْ خَشِىَ ٱلْعَنَتَ مِنكُمْ ۚ وَأَن تَصْبِرُوا۟ خَيْرٌ لَّكُمْ ۗ وَٱللَّهُ غَفُورٌ رَّحِيمٌ

---

[a] Matters of external glamour are not the scale by which to judge the honour and importance of an individual. The real standard of greatness is the unseen faith in man's heart which is in the knowledge of God alone. Thus, whether someone is great or otherwise is beyond the comprehension of man. This unknown aspect will be judged and made known in the court of God. Realization of this fact takes away one's superiority complex, which is usually the root cause of most social evils.

²⁶ God wishes to explain things to you and guide you to the ways of those who have gone before you and to turn to you in mercy. God is all knowing and all wise. ²⁷ He wishes to turn towards you in mercy, but those who follow their own passions want you to drift far away from the right path. ²⁸ God wishes to lighten your burdens, for, man has been created weak.ᵃ

يُرِيدُ ٱللَّهُ لِيُبَيِّنَ لَكُمْ وَيَهْدِيَكُمْ سُنَنَ ٱلَّذِينَ مِن قَبْلِكُمْ وَيَتُوبَ عَلَيْكُمْ ۗ وَٱللَّهُ عَلِيمٌ حَكِيمٌ ۝ وَٱللَّهُ يُرِيدُ أَن يَتُوبَ عَلَيْكُمْ وَيُرِيدُ ٱلَّذِينَ يَتَّبِعُونَ ٱلشَّهَوَٰتِ أَن تَمِيلُوا۟ مَيْلًا عَظِيمًا ۝ يُرِيدُ ٱللَّهُ أَن يُخَفِّفَ عَنكُمْ ۚ وَخُلِقَ ٱلْإِنسَٰنُ ضَعِيفًا ۝

ᵃ There is nothing new about the moral standards laid down in the Quran. In every age God has been proclaiming them through His messengers and believing people in every age have followed them. But since the ancient heavenly books could not remain untampered with, the divine modes of living were consequently lost or obscured. God, however, revealed them again in the Arabic language through His final Messenger. Today, when any group of people follows them, it joins that eternal caravan of righteous humanity which, favoured with the grace of God, adhered steadfastly to the divine path.

In every group of people certain traditions become rooted as a matter of centuries-old practice and people become too accustomed to them to think of them critically. When an original thinker tries to bring in social reform, he is bitterly opposed by traditionalists. They find it difficult to leave their familiar ways and adopt unfamiliar ones. They become hostile to any effort at reformation which would distance them from the ways of their forefathers. In such cases the reaction of the religious class is by far the strongest.

When the core of a religion becomes weak, it is vitiated by hair-splitting arguments, and a structure of elaborate rules based on form is built up. Devoid of the real spirit, people keep following the old rituals, thinking that they are adhering to the religion of God. This religion of human creation is gradually identified with their forefathers and becomes sacred. Ultimately, the simple and natural religion of God is so heavily veiled that it becomes difficult to recognize it as the original religion. The situation being such, any movement for the revival of the simple and natural religion faces bitter opposition; people find their ritualistic dogma threatened and negated by it.

Those whose dogma is based on self-styled faith viciously oppose any effort to revive God's simple and straightforward religion, because they anticipate that such an effort may lead to the end of their dominance and leadership.

²⁹ Believers, do not wrongfully consume each other's wealth, but trade with it by mutual consent. Do not kill one another, for God is most merciful to you. ³⁰ If anyone does these things through transgression and injustice, We shall cast him into the Fire; and that is easy for God. ³¹ If you shun the great sins you have been forbidden, We shall cancel out your minor misdeeds and admit you to a place of honour.ᵃ

يَـٰٓأَيُّهَا ٱلَّذِينَ ءَامَنُوا۟ لَا تَأْكُلُوٓا۟ أَمْوَٰلَكُم بَيْنَكُم بِٱلْبَـٰطِلِ إِلَّآ أَن تَكُونَ تِجَـٰرَةً عَن تَرَاضٍ مِّنكُمْ ۚ وَلَا تَقْتُلُوٓا۟ أَنفُسَكُمْ ۚ إِنَّ ٱللَّهَ كَانَ بِكُمْ رَحِيمًا ۝ وَمَن يَفْعَلْ ذَٰلِكَ عُدْوَٰنًا وَظُلْمًا فَسَوْفَ نُصْلِيهِ نَارًا ۚ وَكَانَ ذَٰلِكَ عَلَى ٱللَّهِ يَسِيرًا ۝ إِن تَجْتَنِبُوا۟ كَبَآئِرَ مَا تُنْهَوْنَ عَنْهُ نُكَفِّرْ عَنكُمْ سَيِّـَٔاتِكُمْ وَنُدْخِلْكُم مُّدْخَلًا كَرِيمًا ۝

ᵃ One of the profitable ways in which the possessions of one person are shared by another is through the system of demand and supply; another way is through payment for services rendered. Trading and the provision of services are, according to Islamic law, the right way of earning a livelihood. Any income gained by other means, such as theft, deceit, lies, bribery, usury, gambling, etc., is unlawful in the sight of God. These are nothing but different ways of plundering and those who do so at the expense of honest means of earning may be successful in this world, but all that will be in store for them in the Hereafter will be fire and brimstone.

Similarly, reverence must be shown for human life. Human beings deserve justice. The right to execute a person lies in the hands of only an established government, which may punish the accused after he has been proved guilty according to the law of God. Apart from this, anyone who tries to deprive a man of his life, commits an unlawful act, for which God will prescribe severe punishment. Going beyond all limits and torturing unjustifiably are the most heinous crimes in the eyes of God. Those who desist from such unlawful acts will receive special favour from Him and will enter the eternal world of the Hereafter, after being pardoned for minor negligence and weaknesses in this world.

³² Do not covet the bounties which God has bestowed more abundantly on some of you than on others. Men shall be rewarded according to their deeds, and women shall be rewarded according to their deeds. You should rather ask God for His bounty. God has knowledge of all things. ³³ We have appointed heirs for everything that parents and close relatives leave behind. As for those with whom you have entered into agreements, let them, too, have their due. God is witness to all things.ᵃ

وَلَا تَتَمَنَّوْاْ مَا فَضَّلَ ٱللَّهُ بِهِۦ بَعْضَكُمْ عَلَىٰ بَعْضٍۚ لِّلرِّجَالِ نَصِيبٌ مِّمَّا ٱكْتَسَبُواْۖ وَلِلنِّسَآءِ نَصِيبٌ مِّمَّا ٱكْتَسَبْنَۚ وَسْـَٔلُواْ ٱللَّهَ مِن فَضْلِهِۦٓۚ إِنَّ ٱللَّهَ كَانَ بِكُلِّ شَيْءٍ عَلِيمًا ﴿٣٢﴾ وَلِكُلٍّ جَعَلْنَا مَوَٰلِيَ مِمَّا تَرَكَ ٱلْوَٰلِدَانِ وَٱلْأَقْرَبُونَۚ وَٱلَّذِينَ عَقَدَتْ أَيْمَٰنُكُمْ فَـَٔاتُوهُمْ نَصِيبَهُمْۚ إِنَّ ٱللَّهَ كَانَ عَلَىٰ كُلِّ شَيْءٍ شَهِيدًا ﴿٣٣﴾

ᵃ Disparity, i.e. the difference between individuals in this world, is in accordance with God's creation plan. Some are physically and mentally less endowed than others; some are born in favourable and some in unfavourable conditions; some have powerful resources and some barely exist with just minimal resources. The latter become jealous of the former, finding them in a superior position. This situation leads to envy, enmity and conflict in social life. But it is totally wrong to make an assessment of oneself or of others judging solely by externals, as these are of importance only in this world. One receives them only to leave them behind. The issues of real importance, i.e. success and achievement in the Hereafter, have nothing to do with worldly possessions. Success in the Hereafter depends rather on those actions which have been performed in this world with the sole intention of seeking God's pleasure. It is, therefore, most wise to insulate oneself from envy, and to pray to God for strength, and to continue to direct one's efforts towards success in the Hereafter.

Wherever a group of people live together, whether as a family or as a country, it is necessary to have a leader to take charge. Authority will undisputedly rest in one single person. According to God's plan for this world, man has been chosen to become the head of the family and has been endowed with the inborn abilities needed to discharge this responsibility. The biological and physiological differences between man and woman are in conformity with God's creation plan. If there are some who wish to go against God's plan, they will only cause perversion and discord. For, nature will continue to go ahead creating men and women according to the divine scheme of things, whereby men will be endowed with the qualities needed as protectors and guardians and women will have the quality of submission to be able to assist them without prejudice to the faculties that nature has endowed them with. But, if men and women are given opposite and conflicting roles to perform in social activities, the result will be nothing but perversion in social life.

34 Men are protectors of women, because God has made some of them excel others and because they spend their wealth on them. So virtuous women are obedient and guard in the husband's absence what God would have them guard. As for those from whom you apprehend infidelity, admonish them, then refuse to share their beds, and finally hit them [lightly]. Then if they obey you, take no further action against them. For God is High, Great. 35 If you fear any breach between a man and his wife, appoint one arbiter from his family and one arbiter from her family. If they both want to set things right, God will bring about a reconciliation between them: He is all knowing and all aware.[a]

الرِّجَالُ قَوَّٰمُونَ عَلَى ٱلنِّسَاءِ بِمَا فَضَّلَ ٱللَّهُ بَعْضَهُمْ عَلَىٰ بَعْضٍ وَبِمَآ أَنفَقُواْ مِنْ أَمْوَٰلِهِمْ ۚ فَٱلصَّٰلِحَٰتُ قَٰنِتَٰتٌ حَٰفِظَٰتٌ لِّلْغَيْبِ بِمَا حَفِظَ ٱللَّهُ ۚ وَٱلَّٰتِى تَخَافُونَ نُشُوزَهُنَّ فَعِظُوهُنَّ وَٱهْجُرُوهُنَّ فِى ٱلْمَضَاجِعِ وَٱضْرِبُوهُنَّ ۖ فَإِنْ أَطَعْنَكُمْ فَلَا تَبْغُواْ عَلَيْهِنَّ سَبِيلًا ۗ إِنَّ ٱللَّهَ كَانَ عَلِيًّا كَبِيرًا ۝ وَإِنْ خِفْتُمْ شِقَاقَ بَيْنِهِمَا فَٱبْعَثُواْ حَكَمًا مِّنْ أَهْلِهِ وَحَكَمًا مِّنْ أَهْلِهَآ إِن يُرِيدَآ إِصْلَٰحًا يُوَفِّقِ ٱللَّهُ بَيْنَهُمَآ ۗ إِنَّ ٱللَّهَ كَانَ عَلِيمًا خَبِيرًا ۝

***

[a] A good woman is one who, conducting herself according to God's plan, accepts the role of man as leader. Similarly, a good man is one who, discharging his role, does not forget that God is always watching him. The divine court of judgement does not differentiate between man and woman. The gender-based difference is meant only to ensure the effective management of worldly life and bears no relation to the requital and rewards of the Hereafter. Man should try to discharge all his responsibilities towards woman, and if there is such a woman who does not recognize the administrative capacity of the man, it must not lead to a revengeful attitude in the man, nor should he start maligning her with allegations. However, under specific circumstances, if the man finds her guilty of immoral conduct, he should try to reform her. The process of this reform has to start with counselling, then if need be, he may cease to talk to and relate with her and lastly, he may reprove her with light punishment.

When two persons have differences between them, their minds become prejudiced. They do not think about each other objectively. In such a situation, the best way of resolving the matter is to bring in an arbiter who is not involved with the issue personally, and who will be able to think without bias and reach a decision based on the facts of the case.

³⁶ Worship God: and do not associate partners with Him. Be good to your parents, to relatives, to orphans, to the needy, and the neighbour who is a kinsman, and the neighbour who is not related to you and your companions and the wayfarers and those whom you rightfully possess.ᵃ God does not like arrogant, boastful people, ³⁷ who are miserly and enjoin others to be the same and conceal the riches which God has given them of His bounty. We have prepared a humiliating punishment for those who deny the truth.ᵇ

۞ وَٱعْبُدُواْ ٱللَّهَ وَلَا تُشْرِكُواْ بِهِ شَيْـًٔا وَبِٱلْوَٰلِدَيْنِ إِحْسَٰنًا وَبِذِى ٱلْقُرْبَىٰ وَٱلْيَتَٰمَىٰ وَٱلْمَسَٰكِينِ وَٱلْجَارِ ذِى ٱلْقُرْبَىٰ وَٱلْجَارِ ٱلْجُنُبِ وَٱلصَّاحِبِ بِٱلْجَنۢبِ وَٱبْنِ ٱلسَّبِيلِ وَمَا مَلَكَتْ أَيْمَٰنُكُمْ ۗ إِنَّ ٱللَّهَ لَا يُحِبُّ مَن كَانَ مُخْتَالًا فَخُورًا ٣٦ ٱلَّذِينَ يَبْخَلُونَ وَيَأْمُرُونَ ٱلنَّاسَ بِٱلْبُخْلِ وَيَكْتُمُونَ مَآ ءَاتَىٰهُمُ ٱللَّهُ مِن فَضْلِهِ ۗ وَأَعْتَدْنَا لِلْكَٰفِرِينَ عَذَابًا مُّهِينًا ٣٧

ᵃ Literally 'what your right hands possess'.

ᵇ Whatever man possesses is provided by God. This reality demands that man should surrender himself to God and become His worshipper. Such a person naturally becomes humble and his humility is expressed in his relations with the other human beings interacting in his life. He behaves decently with his mother and father and feels the watchful presence of God while dealing with all those who come into contact with him. He pays everybody's due in accordance with his relationship and need. To overlook a person, in whatever capacity he has to deal with him, appears to him as if he himself is taking the risk of being overlooked by God.

One who does not surrender to God, develops an overweening sense of pride. He thinks that whatever he possesses is the outcome of his labour and intelligence. Consequently, he considers that his earnings belong to him alone. To become associated with poor relatives and destitutes becomes a matter of degradation for him. He spends lavishly to satisfy his desires and serves his own interests, but becomes mean about such expenditure as does not satisfy his ego. He is very generous in matters which give him publicity, but quite a miser in the case of unpublicized religious causes.

³⁸ And [God does not like] those who spend their wealth for the sake of ostentation, who do not believe in God or the Last Day. Whoever has Satan as his companion has an evil companion. ³⁹ What harm could befall them if they believed in God and the Last Day, and spent out of what God bestowed on them? God knows them well. ⁴⁰ God does not wrong anyone by as much as a grain's weight. If there be a good deed, He will repay twofold, and will bestow out of His own bounty an immense reward.ᵃ

وَٱلَّذِينَ يُنفِقُونَ أَمۡوَٰلَهُمۡ رِئَآءَ ٱلنَّاسِ وَلَا يُؤۡمِنُونَ بِٱللَّهِ وَلَا بِٱلۡيَوۡمِ ٱلۡأَخِرِ وَمَن يَكُنِ ٱلشَّيۡطَٰنُ لَهُۥ قَرِينٗا فَسَآءَ قَرِينٗا ۝ وَمَاذَا عَلَيۡهِمۡ لَوۡ ءَامَنُواْ بِٱللَّهِ وَٱلۡيَوۡمِ ٱلۡأَخِرِ وَأَنفَقُواْ مِمَّا رَزَقَهُمُ ٱللَّهُ وَكَانَ ٱللَّهُ بِهِمۡ عَلِيمًا ۝ إِنَّ ٱللَّهَ لَا يَظۡلِمُ مِثۡقَالَ ذَرَّةٖ وَإِن تَكُ حَسَنَةٗ يُضَٰعِفۡهَا وَيُؤۡتِ مِن لَّدُنۡهُ أَجۡرًا عَظِيمٗا ۝

ᵃ Those who become proud instead of humble after receiving the bounties of God and those who spend their God-given wealth on making selfish investments instead of on good causes as approved by God, are fellow travellers of Satan. Having been lured by the fleeting gains of this life, they lose interest in the eternal gain promised by God. For such persons, there shall be nothing but severe punishment in the Hereafter.

Man declares unimportant that which he does not practice. This is self-centred theorizing and an effort at self-justification. All such endeavours are futile and worthless in the eyes of God.

⁴¹ What will they do when We bring a witness from each community and bring you as a witness against these people? ⁴² On that Day, those who were bent on denying the truth and disobeyed the Messenger will wish that the earth were made level above them. They will not be able to hide anything from God.ᵃ

فَكَيْفَ إِذَا جِئْنَا مِن كُلِّ أُمَّةٍ بِشَهِيدٍ وَجِئْنَا بِكَ عَلَىٰ هَٰؤُلَاءِ شَهِيدًا ۝ يَوْمَئِذٍ يَوَدُّ ٱلَّذِينَ كَفَرُوا۟ وَعَصَوُا۟ ٱلرَّسُولَ لَوْ تُسَوَّىٰ بِهِمُ ٱلْأَرْضُ وَلَا يَكْتُمُونَ ٱللَّهَ حَدِيثًا ۝

ᵃ A dayee or a messenger of Truth happens to be just an ordinary person at the start of his mission. He is not surrounded by any pomp and show. That is why he is rejected by the prominent leaders and intellectuals of society: they fail to apprehend that a man devoid of any outward splendour could be so important that God might choose him to communicate His message to mankind.

But when Doomsday approaches and the divine court is ready to deliver its verdict, they will be bewildered to see that that very ordinary man, whom they had rejected as being of no value, has been given the honour of becoming God's witness and has been set above the nations. In that court the rejecters will stand in the enclosure of the accused, while that ordinary man rejected by them will occupy the seat of God's spokesman. It will be such a terrible and hard moment for the defaulters that they will wish that the earth would rend itself asunder and swallow them up. But their repentance and sense of humiliation will not at that point serve any purpose. The whole record of their speech, actions and thoughts will be with God and they will be told that their rejection of truth was not due to ignorance but pride, that they considered themselves superior to the preacher of truth, and that the acceptance of reality, despite its having been laid before them, appeared to them like setting their own greatness at naught.

43 Believers, do not approach your prayers when you are drunk, until you understand what you say,[a] nor when you are in a state of impurity, —except when you are on a journey—till you have bathed. And if you are ill, or on a journey or have relieved yourselves or when you have consorted with women and you cannot find any water, then find some clean sand and wipe your face and your hands with it.[b] God is gracious and forgiving.

يَـٰٓأَيُّهَا ٱلَّذِينَ ءَامَنُوا۟ لَا تَقْرَبُوا۟ ٱلصَّلَوٰةَ وَأَنتُمْ سُكَـٰرَىٰ حَتَّىٰ تَعْلَمُوا۟ مَا تَقُولُونَ وَلَا جُنُبًا إِلَّا عَابِرِى سَبِيلٍ حَتَّىٰ تَغْتَسِلُوا۟ وَإِن كُنتُم مَّرْضَىٰٓ أَوْ عَلَىٰ سَفَرٍ أَوْ جَآءَ أَحَدٌ مِّنكُم مِّنَ ٱلْغَآئِطِ أَوْ لَـٰمَسْتُمُ ٱلنِّسَآءَ فَلَمْ تَجِدُوا۟ مَآءً فَتَيَمَّمُوا۟ صَعِيدًا طَيِّبًا فَٱمْسَحُوا۟ بِوُجُوهِكُمْ وَأَيْدِيكُمْ ۗ إِنَّ ٱللَّهَ كَانَ عَفُوًّا غَفُورًا ۞

---

[a] This verse appears here to underline the initial prohibition of intoxicants or wine, but it also reveals an important reality about prayer. Prayer does not mean the mere repetition of certain words and motions with accuracy; it must also reflect the concentration of the mind. The individual must say his prayers sincerely. When he is submitting himself to God with his utterances and his body, his mind and intention should also be in submission to Him. Along with his physical obeisance, his consciousness should inhere in his prayer.

[b] Islamic law has granted exceptional relaxations under exceptional conditions. Sickness, travelling and non-availability of water—these are three exceptional conditions for man. It has, therefore, been permitted that, if there is any risk to health, one may perform dry ablution (tayammum). The purpose of ablution is to create the spirit of purity: Tayammum is a way of maintaining that spirit when the usual ablution is not possible.

⁴⁴ Do you not know of those who were in possession of a portion of the Book? They buy up error and want you to lose your way.ᵃ ⁴⁵ God is quite aware as to who your enemies are; God suffices as a patron, and God suffices as a supporter. ⁴⁶ Some Jews take words out of their context and say, 'We have heard, but we disobey,' or 'Hear without listening.' And they say 'Look at us,' twisting the phrase with their tongues so as to disparage religion. But if they had said, 'We hear and we obey,' and 'Listen to us and look at us with favour,' that would have been better and more proper for them. God has rejected them for their defiance so that they shall not believe, except a few of them.ᵇ

أَلَمْ تَرَ إِلَى ٱلَّذِينَ أُوتُواْ نَصِيبًا مِّنَ ٱلْكِتَٰبِ يَشْتَرُونَ ٱلضَّلَٰلَةَ وَيُرِيدُونَ أَن تَضِلُّواْ ٱلسَّبِيلَ ۝ وَٱللَّهُ أَعْلَمُ بِأَعْدَآئِكُمْ وَكَفَىٰ بِٱللَّهِ وَلِيًّا وَكَفَىٰ بِٱللَّهِ نَصِيرًا ۝ مِّنَ ٱلَّذِينَ هَادُواْ يُحَرِّفُونَ ٱلْكَلِمَ عَن مَّوَاضِعِهِۦ وَيَقُولُونَ سَمِعْنَا وَعَصَيْنَا وَٱسْمَعْ غَيْرَ مُسْمَعٍ وَرَٰعِنَا لَيًّا بِأَلْسِنَتِهِمْ وَطَعْنًا فِى ٱلدِّينِ وَلَوْ أَنَّهُمْ قَالُواْ سَمِعْنَا وَأَطَعْنَا وَٱسْمَعْ وَٱنظُرْنَا لَكَانَ خَيْرًا لَّهُمْ وَأَقْوَمَ وَلَٰكِن لَّعَنَهُمُ ٱللَّهُ بِكُفْرِهِمْ فَلَا يُؤْمِنُونَ إِلَّا قَلِيلًا ۝

ᵃ They took the words of their divine Book and recited them to solicit blessings without trying to understand their meaning or applying them to their lives.

ᵇ The book of God is given to a community so that it may rectify the thinking and conduct of its people. But when the bearers of the Divine Book, like the Jews, suffer from decline, they begin to take misguidance in place of guidance from it. The commands of God become the subject of futile hair-splitting discussions; concocted philosophies are produced in the name of theology, and wrongdoers alter the divine book to justify the religious validity of their actions. They detach the words of God from their context and interpret them on the basis of their own assumptions.

The Jews having received a portion of the Book means that they were able to read the words of the Book, but could not mould their actions according to those words, thereby defeating the real purpose of the Scriptures. They remained the bearers of the Book so far as its words were concerned, but in the matter of practice they adopted the ways of other worldly communities. Moreover, while the others practised worldliness in the name of worldliness, the Jews adopted the same worldly ways but had the audacity to try to justify their practices by misquoting the Divine Book.

47 O People of the Book, believe in what We have sent down, fulfilling [the predictions] that is with you, before We destroy [your sense of] direction, so as to confound or reject you, as We rejected those who broke the Sabbath: God's command is always carried out. 48 God will not forgive anyone for associating something with Him, while He will forgive whoever He wishes for anything besides that. Whoever ascribes partners to God is guilty of a monstrous sin. 49 Have you not seen those who consider themselves pure? It is indeed God who purifies whoever He pleases and none shall be wronged by as much as a hair's breadth. 50 See how they attribute their own lying inventions to God. This is in itself a flagrant sin! [a]

يَٰٓأَيُّهَا ٱلَّذِينَ أُوتُوا۟ ٱلْكِتَٰبَ ءَامِنُوا۟ بِمَا نَزَّلْنَا مُصَدِّقًا لِّمَا مَعَكُم مِّن قَبْلِ أَن نَّطْمِسَ وُجُوهًا فَنَرُدَّهَا عَلَىٰٓ أَدْبَارِهَآ أَوْ نَلْعَنَهُمْ كَمَا لَعَنَّآ أَصْحَٰبَ ٱلسَّبْتِ ۚ وَكَانَ أَمْرُ ٱللَّهِ مَفْعُولًا ۝ إِنَّ ٱللَّهَ لَا يَغْفِرُ أَن يُشْرَكَ بِهِۦ وَيَغْفِرُ مَا دُونَ ذَٰلِكَ لِمَن يَشَآءُ ۚ وَمَن يُشْرِكْ بِٱللَّهِ فَقَدِ ٱفْتَرَىٰٓ إِثْمًا عَظِيمًا ۝ أَلَمْ تَرَ إِلَى ٱلَّذِينَ يُزَكُّونَ أَنفُسَهُم ۚ بَلِ ٱللَّهُ يُزَكِّى مَن يَشَآءُ وَلَا يُظْلَمُونَ فَتِيلًا ۝ ٱنظُرْ كَيْفَ يَفْتَرُونَ عَلَى ٱللَّهِ ٱلْكَذِبَ ۖ وَكَفَىٰ بِهِۦٓ إِثْمًا مُّبِينًا ۝

---

[a] The Jews were thought to be the representatives of the religion of God. Hence, when non-Jewish Arabs started supporting the Prophet, the Jews became his opponents to save the facade of their religiousness. In this way their being misguided did not remain confined to themselves and they began to raise controversies about the life and teachings of the Prophet. This was to confuse people and to prove that he was not the Messenger of God but a self-proclaimed proponent of religion working towards fulfilling his ambition of becoming a leader. God is, however, not indifferent in this matter: He will surely side with the faithful and make them successful against misguided opponents.

Accursedness is, in fact, the extreme form of man's insensibility. When he becomes too insensitive to distinguish between right and wrong, this has been called the state of being accursed.

An individual often hears something without its registering upon him. This happens at a time when he is not serious about heeding the divine message. As this attitude becomes more established, the person becomes irresponsive, as if the features of his face had been obliterated and he is seeing and listening with the back of his head where there are neither eyes nor ears. Such blindness and deafness to the truth and reality indicate that God has deprived that person of His blessings due to his constant negligence of truth and reality. God had provided him with ears, but he could not listen; God had given him eyes, but he failed to observe. God, therefore, made him exactly the same as what the individual had actually turned himself into. This extreme stage of insensitivity takes the form of 'maskh', that is, a metamorphosis from a superior state to an extremely inferior state; man, the most superior form of creature, is degraded to the level of the beasts.

⁵¹ Have you not seen those who were in possession of a portion of the Book? They believe in idols and devils. They say of those who deny the truth, 'They are more rightly guided than the believers.' ⁵² Those are the ones God has rejected: you will not find anyone to help those God has rejected. ⁵³ Have they a share in God's kingdom? If they did, they would not give others so much as the groove of a date stone.ᵃ

أَلَمْ تَرَ إِلَى ٱلَّذِينَ أُوتُواْ نَصِيبًا مِّنَ ٱلْكِتَٰبِ يُؤْمِنُونَ بِٱلْجِبْتِ وَٱلطَّٰغُوتِ وَيَقُولُونَ لِلَّذِينَ كَفَرُواْ هَٰٓؤُلَآءِ أَهْدَىٰ مِنَ ٱلَّذِينَ ءَامَنُواْ سَبِيلًا ۝ أُوْلَٰٓئِكَ ٱلَّذِينَ لَعَنَهُمُ ٱللَّهُ وَمَن يَلْعَنِ ٱللَّهُ فَلَن تَجِدَ لَهُۥ نَصِيرًا ۝ أَمْ لَهُمْ نَصِيبٌ مِّنَ ٱلْمُلْكِ فَإِذًا لَّا يُؤْتُونَ ٱلنَّاسَ نَقِيرًا ۝

ᵃ The Jews, thinking that they belonged to the race of prophets, projected their community as a sacred one. In consequence, they laid claim to honour and privilege which they justified by the invention of numerous stories and parables. By their own lights, everyone who was Jewish by faith was destined for deliverance and would not be consigned to the fire of Hell. Clearly, their lives were dominated by wishful thinking.

The Quranic statement that 'it is indeed God who purifies whoever He pleases' rejects such notion that 'those who consider themselves pure' are actually and necessarily so. It clarifies that no one may have honour and privilege on the basis of his links with a race or community; these things depend on the divine law of justice. One who, adhering to the divine law, proves himself deserving of honour, will have honour conferred upon him, but one who, by his actions, fails to do so, will never be honoured—no matter which race or community he belongs to.

The belief in community-based salvation, whether created by the Jews or any other group, is totally without foundation. To invent such a belief and associate it with God is an attempt to associate falsehood with Him. He has never imparted such teaching. God does not discriminate between people on the basis of group, community or race. Such discrimination is a great injustice, whereas God dispenses absolute justice: He does not deal unjustly with anyone.

When decadence sets in among the People of the Book, its adherents begin to live a life of wishful thinking instead of following the commands of God. This leads to superstition gaining ground. What can be achieved only through the performance of good deeds, they attempt to gain through sorcery, false beliefs and communion with evil spirits. Such deviators consider religion as a matter of 'sacred words' and 'special relations with saintly personages,' which may bring miraculous results merely by pronouncing those words or practising the relevant rituals. They continue to pay lip service to religion, but in practice, they follow the path of Satan.

54 Do they envy others because of what God has given them out of His bounty? We granted the House of Abraham the Book and wisdom and We granted them a great kingdom. 55 Some of them believed in it and some held back from it. Hell will suffice as a blazing Fire. 56 We shall send those who reject Our revelations to the Fire. When their skins are burnt up, We shall replace them with new ones so that they may continue to taste the punishment. God is mighty and wise. 57 As for those who believe and do good works, We shall make them enter Gardens through which rivers flow, to dwell therein forever; therein they shall have pure spouses, and We shall admit them into a dense shade.[a]

أَمْ يَحْسُدُونَ ٱلنَّاسَ عَلَىٰ مَآ ءَاتَىٰهُمُ ٱللَّهُ مِن فَضْلِهِۦ فَقَدْ ءَاتَيْنَآ ءَالَ إِبْرَٰهِيمَ ٱلْكِتَٰبَ وَٱلْحِكْمَةَ وَءَاتَيْنَٰهُم مُّلْكًا عَظِيمًا ۝ فَمِنْهُم مَّنْ ءَامَنَ بِهِۦ وَمِنْهُم مَّن صَدَّ عَنْهُ وَكَفَىٰ بِجَهَنَّمَ سَعِيرًا ۝ إِنَّ ٱلَّذِينَ كَفَرُوا۟ بِـَٔايَٰتِنَا سَوْفَ نُصْلِيهِمْ نَارًا كُلَّمَا نَضِجَتْ جُلُودُهُم بَدَّلْنَٰهُمْ جُلُودًا غَيْرَهَا لِيَذُوقُوا۟ ٱلْعَذَابَ إِنَّ ٱللَّهَ كَانَ عَزِيزًا حَكِيمًا ۝ وَٱلَّذِينَ ءَامَنُوا۟ وَعَمِلُوا۟ ٱلصَّٰلِحَٰتِ سَنُدْخِلُهُمْ جَنَّٰتٍ تَجْرِى مِن تَحْتِهَا ٱلْأَنْهَٰرُ خَٰلِدِينَ فِيهَآ أَبَدًا لَّهُمْ فِيهَآ أَزْوَٰجٌ مُّطَهَّرَةٌ وَنُدْخِلُهُمْ ظِلًّا ظَلِيلًا ۝

---

[a] In real life, the hypocrites tread the path of selfish desires and give in to satanic inducements, but outwardly, bearing the label of religion, they think that their actions are truly guided by God's religion. In such an atmosphere, whenever the pure Truth is presented to them, they become its bitterest opponents. They feel that their religious status is being negated by that call. On the other hand, the existence of non-believers around them poses no such challenge and, therefore, their attitude towards them remains lax. But the preacher of truth cannot expect any leniency from them, for they become infuriated with jealousy over someone else having been granted religious representation, when they alone had formerly had a monopoly of religion. They quite forget that God chooses the representatives of His religion on the basis of purity of soul, inner piety and a sound heart, and not because of any outward show of piety.

Being accursed is to be deprived of the grace and succour of God. Just as starvation and thirst wreck one's physical existence, similarly deprivation of God's grace and succour wrecks one's spiritual existence. A cursed person becomes so insensitive that he loses the ability to distinguish between truth and untruth. He fails to recognize and accept explicit signs and cannot differentiate between absurd argumentation and logical argument.

58 God commands you to hand back your trusts to their rightful owners, and when you judge between people, to judge with fairness. God's instructions to you are excellent. God hears and sees all things. 59 Believers, obey God and obey the Messenger and those who have been entrusted with authority among you. If you are in dispute over any matter, refer it to God and the Messenger, if you truly believe in God and the Last Day: this is best, and best in the end. 60 Have you not seen those who profess to believe in what has been revealed to you and [to other prophets] before you? They seek the judgement of evil people, although they were commanded not to obey them. And Satan wants to lead them far astray.[a]

۞ إِنَّ ٱللَّهَ يَأْمُرُكُمْ أَن تُؤَدُّواْ ٱلْأَمَٰنَٰتِ إِلَىٰٓ أَهْلِهَا وَإِذَا حَكَمْتُم بَيْنَ ٱلنَّاسِ أَن تَحْكُمُواْ بِٱلْعَدْلِ ۚ إِنَّ ٱللَّهَ نِعِمَّا يَعِظُكُم بِهِۦٓ ۗ إِنَّ ٱللَّهَ كَانَ سَمِيعًۢا بَصِيرًا ٥٨ يَٰٓأَيُّهَا ٱلَّذِينَ ءَامَنُوٓاْ أَطِيعُواْ ٱللَّهَ وَأَطِيعُواْ ٱلرَّسُولَ وَأُوْلِى ٱلْأَمْرِ مِنكُمْ ۖ فَإِن تَنَٰزَعْتُمْ فِى شَىْءٍ فَرُدُّوهُ إِلَى ٱللَّهِ وَٱلرَّسُولِ إِن كُنتُمْ تُؤْمِنُونَ بِٱللَّهِ وَٱلْيَوْمِ ٱلْءَاخِرِ ۚ ذَٰلِكَ خَيْرٌ وَأَحْسَنُ تَأْوِيلاً ٥٩ أَلَمْ تَرَ إِلَى ٱلَّذِينَ يَزْعُمُونَ أَنَّهُمْ ءَامَنُواْ بِمَآ أُنزِلَ إِلَيْكَ وَمَآ أُنزِلَ مِن قَبْلِكَ يُرِيدُونَ أَن يَتَحَاكَمُوٓاْ إِلَى ٱلطَّٰغُوتِ وَقَدْ أُمِرُوٓاْ أَن يَكْفُرُواْ بِهِۦ وَيُرِيدُ ٱلشَّيْطَٰنُ أَن يُضِلَّهُمْ ضَلَٰلَۢا بَعِيدًا ٦٠

---

[a] Every responsibility is a trust which must be properly discharged. Our dealings with everyone should be just and fair, no matter whether they be friend or foe. Even if the way of trustworthiness and justice appears to run counter to one's interests and worldly considerations, one has to adhere to the path of justice and truth. Our gain lies in following not the dictates of the self, but the directives of God. If there are opportunities of forming the government, the Muslims must establish a proper Islamic government, but if such opportunities do not exist, they should concentrate on leading a religious life under the guidance of reliable persons selected from among themselves. Any differences between them should be resolved in the light of instructions given by God and the Prophet. Everyone does have the right to differ, but no one is permitted to defy a collective decision. Societal order and system are the primary needs of Muslim society.

⁶¹ When they are told, 'Come to what God has sent down and to the Messenger,' you see the hypocrites turn away from you. ⁶² How will it be when an affliction befalls them because of what they themselves have done? They will come to you, swearing by God, saying that they were seeking nothing but goodwill and conciliation. ⁶³ But God knows all that is in their hearts; so ignore what they say, admonish them and speak to them in such terms as will address their minds.ᵃ

وَإِذَا قِيلَ لَهُمْ تَعَالَوْاْ إِلَىٰ مَآ أَنزَلَ ٱللَّهُ وَإِلَى ٱلرَّسُولِ رَأَيْتَ ٱلْمُنَـٰفِقِينَ يَصُدُّونَ عَنكَ صُدُودًا ۝ فَكَيْفَ إِذَآ أَصَـٰبَتْهُم مُّصِيبَةٌۢ بِمَا قَدَّمَتْ أَيْدِيهِمْ ثُمَّ جَآءُوكَ يَحْلِفُونَ بِٱللَّهِ إِنْ أَرَدْنَآ إِلَّآ إِحْسَـٰنًا وَتَوْفِيقًا ۝ أُوْلَـٰٓئِكَ ٱلَّذِينَ يَعْلَمُ ٱللَّهُ مَا فِى قُلُوبِهِمْ فَأَعْرِضْ عَنْهُمْ وَعِظْهُمْ وَقُل لَّهُمْ فِىٓ أَنفُسِهِمْ قَوْلًۢا بَلِيغًا ۝

ᵃ During the early period of Madinah there used to be two courts where judgement on controversial issues might be sought: one pre-dating Islam and controlled by the leaders of the Jews, and the other set up by the Prophet, established after the Migration. Those Muslims who were not ready to sacrifice their interests for the sake of religion and were aware that their cases were too flimsy to be awarded favourable decisions by the court of the Prophet, used to approach the court of Ka'b ibn Ashraf, a leader of the Jews. Such an attitude is totally against the spirit of the faith. If an individual is unwilling to accept God's judgement, and aspires to be favoured with a decision to his own liking, his claim to faith is false, whatever repertoire of beautiful words he may draw on to justify his stand. However, while avoiding confrontation with such people, efforts to reform them must be effectively continued.

64 All the messengers We sent were meant to be obeyed by God's leave. If they had come to you and sought forgiveness from God whenever they wronged themselves, and the Messenger had prayed for forgiveness for them, they would have found that God is ever-forgiving and merciful. 65 By your Lord, they will not be true believers until they seek your arbitration in their disputes and find within themselves no doubt about what you decide and accept it wholeheartedly.*

وَمَآ أَرْسَلْنَا مِن رَّسُولٍ إِلَّا لِيُطَاعَ بِإِذْنِ ٱللَّهِ ۚ وَلَوْ أَنَّهُمْ إِذ ظَّلَمُوٓاْ أَنفُسَهُمْ جَآءُوكَ فَٱسْتَغْفَرُواْ ٱللَّهَ وَٱسْتَغْفَرَ لَهُمُ ٱلرَّسُولُ لَوَجَدُواْ ٱللَّهَ تَوَّابًا رَّحِيمًا ۝ فَلَا وَرَبِّكَ لَا يُؤْمِنُونَ حَتَّىٰ يُحَكِّمُوكَ فِيمَا شَجَرَ بَيْنَهُمْ ثُمَّ لَا يَجِدُواْ فِىٓ أَنفُسِهِمْ حَرَجًا مِّمَّا قَضَيْتَ وَيُسَلِّمُواْ تَسْلِيمًا ۝

---

a A prophet is not sent to the world to raise a group of followers who will wax eloquent in his praise and cover him in glory. A prophet comes so that people should learn the code of conduct for their lives and adopt it in practice. One should be so thoroughly committed to doing so, that even in controversial situations, when conflicting interests have caused strained relations, one will not fail to obey the Prophet's teachings. The true believer will simply suppress his ego and conscientiously follow the guidance of the Prophet. He will willingly accept his ways, even if they are detrimental to his interests and run counter to his way of thinking. He will remain mentally alert to any inadvertent mistake on his part, soon realizing that he had strayed from the Prophet's path to the path of Satan. He will immediately repent, mend his ways and seek forgiveness. On the contrary, one who is not able to adhere to the straight path of the faith, when the dictates of faith clash with his feelings and desires, cannot be expected to remain steadfast in times of harder trial. At such trying times one has to give proof of one's faith by making sacrifices for it.

66 If We had commanded them, 'Lay down your lives or leave your dwellings,' they would have not done it, save a few of them. If they had done what they were instructed to do, it would have been better for them, as well as more strengthening [for their faith], 67 and We would have given them a great reward of Our own, 68 and guided them to a straight path. 69 Whoever obeys God and the Messenger will be among those He has blessed: the messengers, the truthful, the witnesses, and the righteous. What excellent companions these are! 70 That is God's favour. Sufficient is God's infinite knowledge.[a]

وَلَوْ أَنَّا كَتَبْنَا عَلَيْهِمْ أَنِ ٱقْتُلُوٓاْ أَنفُسَكُمْ أَوِ ٱخْرُجُواْ مِن دِيَٰرِكُم مَّا فَعَلُوهُ إِلَّا قَلِيلٌ مِّنْهُمْ وَلَوْ أَنَّهُمْ فَعَلُواْ مَا يُوعَظُونَ بِهِۦ لَكَانَ خَيْرًا لَّهُمْ وَأَشَدَّ تَثْبِيتًا ۝ وَإِذًا لَّأَتَيْنَٰهُم مِّن لَّدُنَّآ أَجْرًا عَظِيمًا ۝ وَلَهَدَيْنَٰهُمْ صِرَٰطًا مُّسْتَقِيمًا ۝ وَمَن يُطِعِ ٱللَّهَ وَٱلرَّسُولَ فَأُوْلَٰٓئِكَ مَعَ ٱلَّذِينَ أَنْعَمَ ٱللَّهُ عَلَيْهِم مِّنَ ٱلنَّبِيِّـۧنَ وَٱلصِّدِّيقِينَ وَٱلشُّهَدَآءِ وَٱلصَّٰلِحِينَ وَحَسُنَ أُوْلَٰٓئِكَ رَفِيقًا ۝ ذَٰلِكَ ٱلْفَضْلُ مِنَ ٱللَّهِ وَكَفَىٰ بِٱللَّهِ عَلِيمًا ۝

---

[a] By pursuing a course of selfishness and opportunism in life, the individual incurs the greatest loss, i.e. he fails to find the straight path (as explicitly laid down in the Book of God and sayings of the Prophet) which could have led him to his Lord. One who does not think objectively, who is opportunistic in his thinking, will fail to find that straight path, no matter how clearly it may have been shown to him. This results from his viewing religion, not from a correct perspective, but from the standpoint of his own desires and convenience, so that an image of religion moulded by his own perceptions is formed in his mind. Though a claimant of faith, he remains deprived of it. How could such a person be eligible for Paradise, which is to be inhabited only by those who have embraced the Faith, rising above all considerations of self-interest and expediency, who have stood by the covenant of God, being witnesses for the truth to the ultimate extent, and having lead totally pious lives?

⁷¹ You who believe, take your precautions and then go forth in small groups or go forth all together. ⁷² Among you are some who lag behind and if you encounter a setback, they say, 'God has been gracious to me; I was not present with them.' ⁷³ But if, by God's grace, good fortune should be your lot, they will say, 'If only I had been with them I should have achieved a great success,' as if no affection had existed between you and them.ᵃ

يَـٰٓأَيُّهَا ٱلَّذِينَ ءَامَنُوا۟ خُذُوا۟ حِذْرَكُمْ فَٱنفِرُوا۟ ثُبَاتٍ أَوِ ٱنفِرُوا۟ جَمِيعًا ۞ وَإِنَّ مِنكُمْ لَمَن لَّيُبَطِّئَنَّ فَإِنْ أَصَـٰبَتْكُم مُّصِيبَةٌ قَالَ قَدْ أَنْعَمَ ٱللَّهُ عَلَىَّ إِذْ لَمْ أَكُن مَّعَهُمْ شَهِيدًا ۞ وَلَئِنْ أَصَـٰبَكُمْ فَضْلٌ مِّنَ ٱللَّهِ لَيَقُولَنَّ كَأَن لَّمْ تَكُن بَيْنَكُمْ وَبَيْنَهُۥ مَوَدَّةٌ يَـٰلَيْتَنِى كُنتُ مَعَهُمْ فَأَفُوزَ فَوْزًا عَظِيمًا ۞

ᵃ This world is a place of trial; hence everyone has freedom of action here. Even miscreants have the opportunity to oppress believers without any justification. Believers, however, pass the test of sincere faith by remaining steadfastly on the straight path, patiently bearing all persecution. They have to be ever vigilant against the enemies of God, organizing their defence both through peaceful policies as well as by strategic preparations, and guarding themselves from enemies both individually and collectively. Moreover, among the rank and file of Muslims, there may be persons, as was apparent during the battle of Uhud, who desire success in the Hereafter, without incurring any risk of loss in this world. They participate enthusiastically in activities which show the possibility of some worldly gain, but find some excuse or the other to justify their refusal to join a religious struggle which entails worldly loss. These Muslims have this mentality because they live on the same materialistic plane as before, despite having accepted Islam. They lack the conviction that it is the Hereafter that is of real importance and not the success or failure of this world. The true believer for the cause of God is one who aspires only to the Hereafter and sacrifices the benefits and conveniences of this world to make progress along the path of God. The real believer is not one who wants to be ranked among those who wish to be hailed as believers without enduring the slightest of injury or who have achieved fame and honour by eloquent lip service to religion. The real struggle is one which is purely for the cause of God.

74 Let those who would exchange the life of this world for the Hereafter, fight for the cause of God; whoever fights for the cause of God, whether he is slain or is victorious, to him We shall give a great reward. 75 And how should you not fight for the cause of God, and for the helpless old men, women, and children who say, 'Deliver us, Lord, from this city of wrongdoers, grant us a protector out of Your grace and grant us a supporter out of Your grace?' 76 The believers fight for the cause of God, while those who reject faith fight for Satan. Then fight the allies of Satan: Satan's scheming is truly weak.[a]

فَلْيُقَاتِلْ فِى سَبِيلِ ٱللَّهِ ٱلَّذِينَ يَشْرُونَ ٱلْحَيَوٰةَ ٱلدُّنْيَا بِٱلْءَاخِرَةِ وَمَن يُقَاتِلْ فِى سَبِيلِ ٱللَّهِ فَيُقْتَلْ أَوْ يَغْلِبْ فَسَوْفَ نُؤْتِيهِ أَجْرًا عَظِيمًا ۝ وَمَا لَكُمْ لَا تُقَاتِلُونَ فِى سَبِيلِ ٱللَّهِ وَٱلْمُسْتَضْعَفِينَ مِنَ ٱلرِّجَالِ وَٱلنِّسَآءِ وَٱلْوِلْدَٰنِ ٱلَّذِينَ يَقُولُونَ رَبَّنَآ أَخْرِجْنَا مِنْ هَٰذِهِ ٱلْقَرْيَةِ ٱلظَّالِمِ أَهْلُهَا وَٱجْعَل لَّنَا مِن لَّدُنكَ وَلِيًّا وَٱجْعَل لَّنَا مِن لَّدُنكَ نَصِيرًا ۝ ٱلَّذِينَ ءَامَنُوا۟ يُقَٰتِلُونَ فِى سَبِيلِ ٱللَّهِ وَٱلَّذِينَ كَفَرُوا۟ يُقَٰتِلُونَ فِى سَبِيلِ ٱلطَّٰغُوتِ فَقَٰتِلُوٓا۟ أَوْلِيَآءَ ٱلشَّيْطَٰنِ إِنَّ كَيْدَ ٱلشَّيْطَٰنِ كَانَ ضَعِيفًا ۝

---

[a] One who struggles, facing all difficulties and setbacks to warn people of the perils of Hell and guides them towards Paradise, refrains from picking quarrels with anyone on materialistic or political issues, but even then he is opposed and challenged by evil-doers. The followers of the path of Satan would fight with a servant of God for the simple reason that his utterances assail their egos, and with the spread of his message, they anticipate economic and political danger for themselves. They cannot find any valid argument to counter his arguments, so they resort to violence and aggression.

⁷⁷ Have you not seen those to whom it was said, 'Restrain your hands, say your prayers and pay the prescribed alms?' And when they have been ordered to fight, some of them have felt afraid of human beings just as they should be afraid of God, or they are even more afraid. They say, 'Our Lord, why have You ordered us to fight? If You would only postpone it for a little while longer!' Say, 'The benefits of this world are negligible and the Hereafter will be better for one who fears God; and you shall not be wronged in the slightest.ᵃ

أَلَمْ تَرَ إِلَى ٱلَّذِينَ قِيلَ لَهُمْ كُفُّوٓاْ أَيْدِيَكُمْ وَأَقِيمُواْ ٱلصَّلَوٰةَ وَءَاتُواْ ٱلزَّكَوٰةَ فَلَمَّا كُتِبَ عَلَيْهِمُ ٱلْقِتَالُ إِذَا فَرِيقٌ مِّنْهُمْ يَخْشَوْنَ ٱلنَّاسَ كَخَشْيَةِ ٱللَّهِ أَوْ أَشَدَّ خَشْيَةً وَقَالُواْ رَبَّنَا لِمَ كَتَبْتَ عَلَيْنَا ٱلْقِتَالَ لَوْلَآ أَخَّرْتَنَآ إِلَىٰ أَجَلٍ قَرِيبٍ قُلْ مَتَـٰعُ ٱلدُّنْيَا قَلِيلٌ وَٱلْأَخِرَةُ خَيْرٌ لِّمَنِ ٱتَّقَىٰ وَلَا تُظْلَمُونَ فَتِيلاً

٧٧

ᵃ The opponents of Islam in Makkah used to persecute Muslims before the Migration. They resorted to all kinds of aggression and injustice against the Muslims, such as assault, destruction of their means of livelihood, stopping them from praying in the Kabah, not permitting them to spread the word of God, compelling them to leave their homes, etc. Whoever accepted Islam was subjected to all types of pressures to abandon his new faith and return to his ancestral religion. This unjust and aggressive stance of the opponents of Islam had, in principle, made it basically legitimate for the Muslims to take up arms against them; and therefore, the oppressed Muslims approached the Prophet repeatedly to seek his permission to fight. But the Prophet always restrained them, saying that he had not been given permission for armed confrontation. Instead, he advised the Muslims to be patient, say their prayers (salat) and pay the obligatory alms (zakat). The reason for this restraint was that premature and untimely action is not the way of Islam. The Muslims were not powerful enough in Makkah to take decisive action against their enemies. An armed confrontation at that time would have intensified their affliction. It would have amounted to giving the Makkans justification to declare open war against the Muslims, instead of there being just stray incidents of tyranny at the individual level. A practical step may be taken only when the necessary preparations have been made for it. Before reaching this stage, the faithful are required only to fulfil their personal obligations, which must be attended to under all circumstances. These obligations are to seek closeness with God, pay others their rightful dues and endure the difficulties encountered in the path of religion.

⁷⁸ Wherever you may be, death will overtake you, even if you be in strongly built towers.' If some good befalls them, they say, 'This is from God,' and if ill befalls them, they say, 'This is from you.' Tell them, 'All is from God.' But what is wrong with these people that they fail to understand anything? ⁷⁹ Whatever good befalls you, it is from God: and whatever ill befalls you is from yourself. We have sent you forth as a messenger to mankind; and God suffices as a witness.[a]

أَيْنَمَا تَكُونُوا۟ يُدْرِككُّمُ ٱلْمَوْتُ وَلَوْ كُنتُمْ فِى بُرُوجٍ مُّشَيَّدَةٍ وَإِن تُصِبْهُمْ حَسَنَةٌ يَقُولُوا۟ هَـٰذِهِۦ مِنْ عِندِ ٱللَّهِ وَإِن تُصِبْهُمْ سَيِّئَةٌ يَقُولُوا۟ هَـٰذِهِۦ مِنْ عِندِكَ قُلْ كُلٌّ مِّنْ عِندِ ٱللَّهِ فَمَالِ هَـٰٓؤُلَآءِ ٱلْقَوْمِ لَا يَكَادُونَ يَفْقَهُونَ حَدِيثًا ۝ مَّآ أَصَابَكَ مِنْ حَسَنَةٍ فَمِنَ ٱللَّهِ وَمَآ أَصَابَكَ مِن سَيِّئَةٍ فَمِن نَّفْسِكَ وَأَرْسَلْنَـٰكَ لِلنَّاسِ رَسُولًا وَكَفَىٰ بِٱللَّهِ شَهِيدًا ۝

---

[a] When the Quranic instructions pertaining to sacrifice were revealed, the opportunists found them to be disturbing to the pattern of their lives. They started pretentious talk to hide their own weakness. The debacle at Uhud, they said, was due to the poor strategy of the Prophet, and thus they tried to misguide people about his ability to lead. Whenever something favourable happened, they associated it with the grace of God, simply to exhibit their faith in Islam; but to escape from the practical demands of Islam, they tried to prove the Prophet wrong. It is possible for man to show faith in God and continue to follow the dictates of his desires; but once he accepts allegiance with the messenger of God, it becomes necessary to stand by the side of the dayee, which is indeed a most difficult proposition.

⁸⁰ He who obeys the Messenger obeys God. As for those who turn away, know that We have not sent you to be their keeper. ⁸¹ They say: 'We obey you,' but as soon as they leave you, a group of them plan together by night against what you say. God records whatever they scheme. So ignore them, and put your trust in God. God is sufficient as a trustee.ᵃ

مَّن يُطِعِ ٱلرَّسُولَ فَقَدْ أَطَاعَ ٱللَّهَ ۖ وَمَن تَوَلَّىٰ فَمَآ أَرْسَلْنَٰكَ عَلَيْهِمْ حَفِيظًا ۝ وَيَقُولُونَ طَاعَةٌ فَإِذَا بَرَزُوا۟ مِنْ عِندِكَ بَيَّتَ طَآئِفَةٌ مِّنْهُمْ غَيْرَ ٱلَّذِى تَقُولُ ۖ وَٱللَّهُ يَكْتُبُ مَا يُبَيِّتُونَ ۖ فَأَعْرِضْ عَنْهُمْ وَتَوَكَّلْ عَلَى ٱللَّهِ ۚ وَكَفَىٰ بِٱللَّهِ وَكِيلًا ۝

ᵃ The acknowledgment of the dayee is to accept 'a human being like oneself'. This is why people may accept God, but do not extend their acceptance to God's dayee. The real test, however, is to acknowledge and accept the dayee and stand by his side. Unless one takes him to be truly a messenger of God, one cannot be serious towards him. Then is no point in agreeing to lend support to the dayee to his face, and then continue to go one's own way afterwards, or going to the extent of spreading irresponsible rumours about him. Those who behave so carelessly towards him cannot expect to be exonerated in the Hereafter by pleading ignorance. The veracity of the dayee, if one ponders upon it, is self-evident in his utterances, which are God-inspired.

⁸² Do they not ponder on the Quran? If it had been from anyone other than God, they would have found much inconsistency in it.ᵃ ⁸³ When they hear any news, whether of peace or of something fearful, they spread it about; whereas if they referred it to the Messenger and to the men in charge, those of them who would have investigated it and could have arrived at the truth of the matter. But for God's grace and mercy, all but a few of you would have followed Satan.ᵇ

أَفَلَا يَتَدَبَّرُونَ ٱلْقُرْءَانَ ۚ وَلَوْ كَانَ مِنْ عِندِ غَيْرِ ٱللَّهِ لَوَجَدُواْ فِيهِ ٱخْتِلَٰفًا كَثِيرًا ۝ وَإِذَا جَآءَهُمْ أَمْرٌ مِّنَ ٱلْأَمْنِ أَوِ ٱلْخَوْفِ أَذَاعُواْ بِهِۦ ۖ وَلَوْ رَدُّوهُ إِلَى ٱلرَّسُولِ وَإِلَىٰٓ أُوْلِى ٱلْأَمْرِ مِنْهُمْ لَعَلِمَهُ ٱلَّذِينَ يَسْتَنۢبِطُونَهُۥ مِنْهُمْ ۗ وَلَوْلَا فَضْلُ ٱللَّهِ عَلَيْكُمْ وَرَحْمَتُهُۥ لَٱتَّبَعْتُمُ ٱلشَّيْطَٰنَ إِلَّا قَلِيلًا ۝

ᵃ A clear proof of the Quran being the Divine Book is that none of its statements contradict any established truth. It does not contain anything which is against human nature. It does not conflict with any fact known through the earlier divine books. There is no sign of any part of its content contradicting any fact verified by the body of knowledge established by observation and experimentation. The Quran's total conformity with factual realities is the definite proof that it is the message revealed by God. The Quran being free from contradictions will appear as such to one who ponders over the matter. For truth, to appear as truth, depends on the sincerity with which one tries to understand it, but one who does not ponder over it will ceaselessly raise baseless objections against this Book—and he may do so till the period of human trial is brought to an end by the onset of Doomsday.

ᵇ The truly Islamic society is one whose members have done sufficient self-analysis to acknowledge their shortcomings. They are ready to place their affairs in the charge of members who are more competent than themselves and accept their leadership. The quality of self-assessment is the factor that deters the members of a society from following the path of Satan. A person devoid of this virtue jumps into the fray without having the capacity to handle complicated issues. He brings destruction upon himself as well as upon his own people. In matters of collective application and significance, it is more important to be silent than to be vocal. Spreading rumours on the basis of hearsay amounts to extending help to Satan.

84 So fight for the cause of God. You are responsible only for yourself. Urge on the believers. God may fend off the power [violence] of those who deny the truth, for He is stronger in might and stronger in inflicting punishment. 85 Whoever rallies to a good cause shall have a share in its blessing; and whoever rallies to an evil cause shall be answerable for his part in it: for, indeed, God watches over everything.ᵃ

فَقَٰتِلْ فِى سَبِيلِ ٱللَّهِ لَا تُكَلَّفُ إِلَّا نَفْسَكَ وَحَرِّضِ ٱلْمُؤْمِنِينَ عَسَى ٱللَّهُ أَن يَكُفَّ بَأْسَ ٱلَّذِينَ كَفَرُواْ وَٱللَّهُ أَشَدُّ بَأْسًا وَأَشَدُّ تَنكِيلًا ۝ مَّن يَشْفَعْ شَفَٰعَةً حَسَنَةً يَكُن لَّهُۥ نَصِيبٌ مِّنْهَا وَمَن يَشْفَعْ شَفَٰعَةً سَيِّئَةً يَكُن لَّهُۥ كِفْلٌ مِّنْهَا وَكَانَ ٱللَّهُ عَلَىٰ كُلِّ شَىْءٍ مُّقِيتًا ۝

ᵃ One form that religiosity takes is the public observance of certain outward rites and, without making any changes in one's life, regarding oneself as a religious person. Such a 'religion' is resented by no one; no one feels any need to oppose it. Another form of religion is that which calls for sacrifice; one that entails one's lifestyle being disturbed. Whenever this latter kind of religiousness is invoked, people become divided. One group which opposes this is made up of those who have established their leadership in the religious field by observing certain rites which do not call for any sacrifice of their worldly interests. They follow the maxim that speaking in defence of truth amounts to damaging one's worldly interests, whereas either remaining silent or opposing the truth brings great worldly benefits. They therefore oppose the religion of sacrifice, as it would bring them down from their established positions. There is quite another group, however, which consists of those who have a live conscience and who judge matters by rising above considerations of gain and expediency. They do not hesitate to accept a reality proved by argument. True Muslims are directed not to let their social relationships be affected and constrained due to such differences and not to adopt a discourteous attitude towards others. A Muslim's attitude is expected to be free from reactionary impulses. He knows that it is for God to judge and requite as He wishes.

⁸⁶ When you are greeted by anyone, respond with a better greeting or at least return it; God takes account of all things. ⁸⁷ He is God: there is no deity other than Him. He will gather you all together on the Day of Resurrection, there is no doubt about it. Whose word can be truer than God's?

⁸⁸ How is it that you are divided into two groups regarding the hypocrites, when God Himself cast them back [to disbelief] because of their misdeeds? Do you seek to guide those whom God allows to go astray? You cannot guide those whom God allows to go astray. ⁸⁹ They want you to deny the Truth, so that you may become all alike. Do not take them as your allies until they emigrate in the way of God. If they turn back (to enmity), seize them and kill them wherever you may find them; and take no friend or helper from among them.ᵃ

وَإِذَا حُيِّيتُم بِتَحِيَّةٍ فَحَيُّوا بِأَحْسَنَ مِنْهَآ أَوْ رُدُّوهَآ ۗ إِنَّ ٱللَّهَ كَانَ عَلَىٰ كُلِّ شَىْءٍ حَسِيبًا ۝ ٱللَّهُ لَآ إِلَٰهَ إِلَّا هُوَ لَيَجْمَعَنَّكُمْ إِلَىٰ يَوْمِ ٱلْقِيَٰمَةِ لَا رَيْبَ فِيهِ ۗ وَمَنْ أَصْدَقُ مِنَ ٱللَّهِ حَدِيثًا ۝ ۞ فَمَا لَكُمْ فِى ٱلْمُنَٰفِقِينَ فِئَتَيْنِ وَٱللَّهُ أَرْكَسَهُم بِمَا كَسَبُوٓا ۚ أَتُرِيدُونَ أَن تَهْدُوا مَنْ أَضَلَّ ٱللَّهُ ۖ وَمَن يُضْلِلِ ٱللَّهُ فَلَن تَجِدَ لَهُۥ سَبِيلًا ۝ وَدُّوا لَوْ تَكْفُرُونَ كَمَا كَفَرُوا فَتَكُونُونَ سَوَآءً ۖ فَلَا تَتَّخِذُوا مِنْهُمْ أَوْلِيَآءَ حَتَّىٰ يُهَاجِرُوا فِى سَبِيلِ ٱللَّهِ ۚ فَإِن تَوَلَّوْا فَخُذُوهُمْ وَٱقْتُلُوهُمْ حَيْثُ وَجَدتُّمُوهُمْ ۖ وَلَا تَتَّخِذُوا مِنْهُمْ وَلِيًّا وَلَا نَصِيرًا ۝

ᵃ During difficult times the only guarantee of keeping alive the message of the Truth is for the dayee, despite trying conditions, to remain firm in his commitment and carry on his mission, even if there happens to be no one to support him. In such circumstances, the determination of the dayee makes him eligible for God's special reward. During the second expedition of Badr, which took place only one month after the battle of Uhud, the state of affairs in Madinah was so gloomy that only seventy men came forward to fight along with the Prophet. This small troop, however, received special succour from God, filling the Makkans with awe, making them retreat without fighting, thus averting what could have been a disastrous encounter. God's resolve is to weaken the non-believers, but this resolve is expressed only when the standard bearers of His own religion, though deprived of means and support, step forward to counter the enemy onslaught.

⁹⁰ But make an exception of those who seek refuge with people with whom you have a treaty, or who come over to you because their hearts forbid them to fight against you or against their own people. Had God pleased, He would have given them power over you, so that they would have taken up arms against you. Therefore, if they keep away from you and cease their hostility and propose peace to you, God does not allow you to harm them. ⁹¹ You will find others who wish to be safe from you, and from their own people, yet whenever they find an opportunity of inflicting harm, they plunge into it. So if they neither withdraw, nor offer you peace, nor restrain themselves from fighting you, seize and kill them wherever you encounter them. Over such people We have given you clear authority.[a]

إِلَّا ٱلَّذِينَ يَصِلُونَ إِلَىٰ قَوْمٍ بَيْنَكُمْ وَبَيْنَهُم مِّيثَٰقٌ أَوْ جَآءُوكُمْ حَصِرَتْ صُدُورُهُمْ أَن يُقَٰتِلُوكُمْ أَوْ يُقَٰتِلُوٓاْ قَوْمَهُمْ ۚ وَلَوْ شَآءَ ٱللَّهُ لَسَلَّطَهُمْ عَلَيْكُمْ فَلَقَٰتَلُوكُمْ ۚ فَإِنِ ٱعْتَزَلُوكُمْ فَلَمْ يُقَٰتِلُوكُمْ وَأَلْقَوْاْ إِلَيْكُمُ ٱلسَّلَمَ فَمَا جَعَلَ ٱللَّهُ لَكُمْ عَلَيْهِمْ سَبِيلًا ۝ سَتَجِدُونَ ءَاخَرِينَ يُرِيدُونَ أَن يَأْمَنُوكُمْ وَيَأْمَنُوٓاْ قَوْمَهُمْ كُلَّ مَا رُدُّوٓاْ إِلَى ٱلْفِتْنَةِ أُرْكِسُواْ فِيهَا ۚ فَإِن لَّمْ يَعْتَزِلُوكُمْ وَيُلْقُوٓاْ إِلَيْكُمُ ٱلسَّلَمَ وَيَكُفُّوٓاْ أَيْدِيَهُمْ فَخُذُوهُمْ وَٱقْتُلُوهُمْ حَيْثُ ثَقِفْتُمُوهُمْ ۚ وَأُوْلَٰئِكُمْ جَعَلْنَا لَكُمْ عَلَيْهِمْ سُلْطَٰنًا مُّبِينًا ۝

[a] After a person accepts God's religion, he repeatedly encounters such situations in his life whereby the sincerity of his decision is tested. 'Migration' is one such test. It implies that when worldly gains and convenience appear to be obstacles in the path of religion, one should thrust them aside and move ahead towards God. If the situation demands, the individual should abandon his relatives and home as well. If he is able to move ahead in the path of truth in the moment of trial, by ignoring personal gains and expediency, he consolidates his attachment to truth. One who adopts this course, enhances his sensitivity to truth and continues to move closer to it. But one who does not, diminishes his receptiveness to truth. The hard demands of religion divide people into several groups: simple people, opponents and hypocrites. Muslims must deal with them accordingly. They should be firm in eradicating evil through peaceful means but lenient in the discharge of moral responsibilities. They should be considerate to the weak and try to influence others instead of becoming swayed themselves. They should not challenge a group who wants to make peace with them.

92 No believer should kill another believer, unless it be by mistake. Anyone who kills a believer by mistake should free a believing slave and pay blood money to the victim's relatives unless they forego it as an act of charity. If the victim belongs to a people at war with you, but is a believer, then the compensation is to free a believing slave. If he belongs to a people with whom you have a treaty, then blood-money should be handed over to his relatives and a believing slave set free. Anyone who lacks the means must fast for two consecutive months. Such is the penance imposed by God. God is all knowing and wise. 93 If anyone kills a believer deliberately, his reward shall be eternal Hell. God will condemn him and reject him, and prepare for him a terrible punishment.[a]

وَمَا كَانَ لِمُؤْمِنٍ أَن يَقْتُلَ مُؤْمِنًا إِلَّا خَطَـًٔا ۚ وَمَن قَتَلَ مُؤْمِنًا خَطَـًٔا فَتَحْرِيرُ رَقَبَةٍ مُّؤْمِنَةٍ وَدِيَةٌ مُّسَلَّمَةٌ إِلَىٰٓ أَهْلِهِۦٓ إِلَّآ أَن يَصَّدَّقُوا۟ ۚ فَإِن كَانَ مِن قَوْمٍ عَدُوٍّ لَّكُمْ وَهُوَ مُؤْمِنٌ فَتَحْرِيرُ رَقَبَةٍ مُّؤْمِنَةٍ ۖ وَإِن كَانَ مِن قَوْمٍ بَيْنَكُمْ وَبَيْنَهُم مِّيثَٰقٌ فَدِيَةٌ مُّسَلَّمَةٌ إِلَىٰٓ أَهْلِهِۦ وَتَحْرِيرُ رَقَبَةٍ مُّؤْمِنَةٍ ۖ فَمَن لَّمْ يَجِدْ فَصِيَامُ شَهْرَيْنِ مُتَتَابِعَيْنِ تَوْبَةً مِّنَ ٱللَّهِ ۗ وَكَانَ ٱللَّهُ عَلِيمًا حَكِيمًا ۝ وَمَن يَقْتُلْ مُؤْمِنًا مُّتَعَمِّدًا فَجَزَآؤُهُۥ جَهَنَّمُ خَٰلِدًا فِيهَا وَغَضِبَ ٱللَّهُ عَلَيْهِ وَلَعَنَهُۥ وَأَعَدَّ لَهُۥ عَذَابًا عَظِيمًا ۝

---

[a] Killing is a heinous and irreversible crime. One who deliberately kills another therefore brings down upon himself the wrath of God, who, leaving him no scope for atonement will curse him into Hell fire. Accidental killing, however, is more leniently punished. If one unintentionally kills someone, but then, fully realizing the gravity of the crime, sincerely seeks God's forgiveness and makes due monetary compensation, one may hope for divine clemency. One positive development arising from having faced up to the enormity of the crime is the desire for self-reform. To this end God has given man His directives. Self-punishment is a starting point and may be achieved by the observance of a continuous fast.

⁹⁴ Believers, when you go forth in the cause of God, make due investigation and do not say to those who offer you the greeting of peace, 'You are no believer!' because you seek the good things of this life. With God there are good things in plenty. You yourself were in the same position before, but God conferred His special favour on you. Therefore, take care to investigate. Surely God is well-aware of what you do.ᵃ

يَـٰٓأَيُّهَا ٱلَّذِينَ ءَامَنُوٓا۟ إِذَا ضَرَبْتُمْ فِى سَبِيلِ ٱللَّهِ فَتَبَيَّنُوا۟ وَلَا تَقُولُوا۟ لِمَنْ أَلْقَىٰٓ إِلَيْكُمُ ٱلسَّلَـٰمَ لَسْتَ مُؤْمِنًا تَبْتَغُونَ عَرَضَ ٱلْحَيَوٰةِ ٱلدُّنْيَا فَعِندَ ٱللَّهِ مَغَانِمُ كَثِيرَةٌ كَذَٰلِكَ كُنتُم مِّن قَبْلُ فَمَنَّ ٱللَّهُ عَلَيْكُمْ فَتَبَيَّنُوٓا۟ إِنَّ ٱللَّهَ كَانَ بِمَا تَعْمَلُونَ خَبِيرًا ۝

ᵃ In essence, these verses primarily lay down the law on premeditated and unpremeditated modes of crime, but they also suggest ways, under the divine law, of dealing with and checking other serious crimes in the public realm.

Just as it is our duty not to deprive our fellow men of their lives, we are also commanded that we should not disgrace others, or rob or deprive them of their livelihood or victimize them in any manner such as would seriously disturb their peace of mind.

If one commits any such damaging acts against others by mistake, one should be quick to accept the blame. Proof of the realisation of guilt would be sincere repentance before God and providing compensation for the loss of the affected person. But if one indulges in acts such as are deliberately intended to harm and harass others, this would be regarded as the equivalent of an act of deliberate homicide, the only difference being in its degree of gravity.

⁹⁵ Those believers who stay behind—apart from those forced by necessity—are not equal to those who strive hard in God's cause with their possessions and their persons. God has given those who strive with their goods and their persons a higher rank than those who stayed behind. God has promised all a good reward; but far greater is the recompense of those who strive for Him *a*—

لَّا يَسْتَوِى ٱلْقَاعِدُونَ مِنَ ٱلْمُؤْمِنِينَ غَيْرُ أُوْلِى ٱلضَّرَرِ وَٱلْمُجَاهِدُونَ فِى سَبِيلِ ٱللَّهِ بِأَمْوَالِهِمْ وَأَنفُسِهِمْ فَضَّلَ ٱللَّهُ ٱلْمُجَاهِدِينَ بِأَمْوَالِهِمْ وَأَنفُسِهِمْ عَلَى ٱلْقَاعِدِينَ دَرَجَةً وَكُلًّا وَعَدَ ٱللَّهُ ٱلْحُسْنَىٰ وَفَضَّلَ ٱللَّهُ ٱلْمُجَاهِدِينَ عَلَى ٱلْقَاعِدِينَ أَجْرًا عَظِيمًا ۝

---

a Muslims broadly fall into two categories as far the level of their actions is concerned. One category is comprised of those who adopt the Islamic way of life, remaining within the confines of obligatory injunctions. They worship God and live discreetly, heeding what is lawful and what is unlawful. The second category includes those who live at the level of sacrifice. They follow Islam and exert themselves to convey its message to other people, willingly enduring the difficulties of their endeavour. They place their lives and prossessions in jeopardy for the cause of Islam. They do not confine themselves to obeying obligatory injunctions, but move far beyond—offering their very existence for the sake of Islam. Muslims in both the categories are sincere and will be recipients of their respective shares of God's grace; however, the status of the second category of Muslims is different from the first. Their offerings in the path of God were not in measurable terms, so neither will God's requital of their efforts be measurable. These Muslims joined the mission of God without any consideration for expediency; accordingly, God's grace and mercy will, in return, be immeasurable.

⁹⁶ high ranks conferred by Him as well as forgiveness and mercy. God is forgiving and merciful.

⁹⁷ When the angels take the souls of those who have wronged themselves, they will ask, 'What was wrong with you?' They will answer, 'We were too weak on earth.' The angels will say, 'Was God's earth not spacious enough for you to have migrated to some other place?' These are the ones whose abode shall be Hell, an evil destination—⁹⁸ except such weak ones among men, women and children, as are incapable of adopting any plan or of finding any way out.ᵃ

دَرَجَٰتٍ مِّنْهُ وَمَغْفِرَةً وَرَحْمَةً ۚ وَكَانَ ٱللَّهُ غَفُورًا رَّحِيمًا ۝ إِنَّ ٱلَّذِينَ تَوَفَّىٰهُمُ ٱلْمَلَٰئِكَةُ ظَالِمِىٓ أَنفُسِهِمْ قَالُوا۟ فِيمَ كُنتُمْ ۖ قَالُوا۟ كُنَّا مُسْتَضْعَفِينَ فِى ٱلْأَرْضِ ۚ قَالُوٓا۟ أَلَمْ تَكُنْ أَرْضُ ٱللَّهِ وَٰسِعَةً فَتُهَاجِرُوا۟ فِيهَا ۚ فَأُو۟لَٰٓئِكَ مَأْوَىٰهُمْ جَهَنَّمُ ۖ وَسَآءَتْ مَصِيرًا ۝ إِلَّا ٱلْمُسْتَضْعَفِينَ مِنَ ٱلرِّجَالِ وَٱلنِّسَآءِ وَٱلْوِلْدَٰنِ لَا يَسْتَطِيعُونَ حِيلَةً وَلَا يَهْتَدُونَ سَبِيلًا ۝

ᵃ A believer naturally wants a free environment where his believing personality may find full opportunities to express itself. If he finds the environment unfavourable, he had better change his surroundings. This change of place is called *hijrah* (emigration). Thus, in the real spirit of *hijrah*, one should remove oneself from an unfavourable to a favourable situation. Let us take the example of a person who is associated with an organisation which is dominated by certain personalities. He realises that he may exist there only as a glorifier of those personalities and not as a glorifier of God. Now, if for the sake of self-interest he compromises with that atmosphere and fails to proclaim the truth as he sees it, and then, still in the same state, he breathes his last, it might be said that in that case, he had perpetrated an injustice against his soul.

⁹⁹ God may well pardon them. God is ever-pardoning and ever forgiving. ¹⁰⁰ Whoever emigrates for the cause of God will find many places of refuge in the land and plentiful provision. Those who leave home for the cause of God and His Messenger; but is then overtaken by death, shall be recompensed by God. God is most forgiving and ever-merciful.[a]

فَأُوْلَٰٓئِكَ عَسَى ٱللَّهُ أَن يَعْفُوَ عَنْهُمْ ۚ وَكَانَ ٱللَّهُ عَفُوًّا غَفُورًا ۝ وَمَن يُهَاجِرْ فِى سَبِيلِ ٱللَّهِ يَجِدْ فِى ٱلْأَرْضِ مُرَٰغَمًا كَثِيرًا وَسَعَةً ۚ وَمَن يَخْرُجْ مِنۢ بَيْتِهِۦ مُهَاجِرًا إِلَى ٱللَّهِ وَرَسُولِهِۦ ثُمَّ يُدْرِكْهُ ٱلْمَوْتُ فَقَدْ وَقَعَ أَجْرُهُۥ عَلَى ٱللَّهِ ۗ وَكَانَ ٱللَّهُ غَفُورًا رَّحِيمًا ۝

---

[a] When a call of truth is raised, which demands that the believers respond to the call and expend their energies and their wealth on spreading this message, they refuse to come out of their cocoons of self-interest and expediency. Thus they fail to join the caller for truth and become his supporters. If they continue to remain in this state till the moment of their death, they will appear before God as having done an injustice to their own lives. However, those who are really helpless and incapable of extending any support are exempted from this condition.

¹⁰¹ When you [believers] are travelling in the land, you will not be blamed for shortening your prayers, if you fear the disbelievers may harm you. They are your avowed enemies. ¹⁰² When you are among the believers and lead them in prayer, let only part of them stand up along with you, armed with their weapons. After they have prostrated themselves, let them withdraw to the rear to stand guard and then let another party, who have not yet prayed, come forward and pray with you. And let them also be on their guard, armed with their weapons. Those who deny the truth want you to be negligent of your arms and your baggage, so that they may fall upon you suddenly. It is no offence for you to lay aside your arms when overtaken by heavy rain or illness, and always take every precaution for defence. God has prepared a humiliating punishment for those who deny the truth.ᵃ

وَإِذَا ضَرَبْتُمْ فِى ٱلْأَرْضِ فَلَيْسَ عَلَيْكُمْ جُنَاحٌ أَن تَقْصُرُواْ مِنَ ٱلصَّلَوٰةِ إِنْ خِفْتُمْ أَن يَفْتِنَكُمُ ٱلَّذِينَ كَفَرُوٓاْ إِنَّ ٱلْكَٰفِرِينَ كَانُواْ لَكُمْ عَدُوًّا مُّبِينًا ۝ وَإِذَا كُنتَ فِيهِمْ فَأَقَمْتَ لَهُمُ ٱلصَّلَوٰةَ فَلْتَقُمْ طَآئِفَةٌ مِّنْهُم مَّعَكَ وَلْيَأْخُذُوٓاْ أَسْلِحَتَهُمْ فَإِذَا سَجَدُواْ فَلْيَكُونُواْ مِن وَرَآئِكُمْ وَلْتَأْتِ طَآئِفَةٌ أُخْرَىٰ لَمْ يُصَلُّواْ فَلْيُصَلُّواْ مَعَكَ وَلْيَأْخُذُواْ حِذْرَهُمْ وَأَسْلِحَتَهُمْ وَدَّ ٱلَّذِينَ كَفَرُواْ لَوْ تَغْفُلُونَ عَنْ أَسْلِحَتِكُمْ وَأَمْتِعَتِكُمْ فَيَمِيلُونَ عَلَيْكُم مَّيْلَةً وَٰحِدَةً وَلَا جُنَاحَ عَلَيْكُمْ إِن كَانَ بِكُمْ أَذًى مِّن مَّطَرٍ أَوْ كُنتُم مَّرْضَىٰٓ أَن تَضَعُوٓاْ أَسْلِحَتَكُمْ وَخُذُواْ حِذْرَكُمْ إِنَّ ٱللَّهَ أَعَدَّ لِلْكَٰفِرِينَ عَذَابًا مُّهِينًا

ᵃ All acts of religion, whether in the nature of prayer (salat) and alms-giving (zakat) or the propagation of God's word or the struggle for God's cause, have the ultimate purpose of remembering God. Their aim is to create a man who lives with the thought of God at every moment and under all situations; who fears God in moments of apprehension and longs for Him in moments of hope; who relies solely on God; whose attention is diverted towards God. If he achieves something, he believes it to be from God and if he suffers deprivation, he takes it as being God's command. The whole of his inner existence should be lost in the majesty and grace of God. This orientation is such an important matter that, even in such critical times as war, one is directed to say one's prayer in some form or the other so that, even though face to face with death, one may be reminded of what is of real value, to be carried along with one to the Hereafter.

¹⁰³ When you have finished the prayer, remember God while standing, and sitting, and lying on your sides. When you feel secure, say your prayers in the prescribed form. Believers are under the obligation to say their prayers at the appointed hours. ¹⁰⁴ Do not relent in the pursuit of the enemy. If you are suffering hardships, they too are suffering similar hardships, but what you can hope for from God, they cannot. God is all knowing and wise.^a

فَإِذَا قَضَيْتُمُ ٱلصَّلَوٰةَ فَٱذْكُرُوا۟ ٱللَّهَ قِيَـٰمًا وَقُعُودًا وَعَلَىٰ جُنُوبِكُمْ ۚ فَإِذَا ٱطْمَأْنَنتُمْ فَأَقِيمُوا۟ ٱلصَّلَوٰةَ ۚ إِنَّ ٱلصَّلَوٰةَ كَانَتْ عَلَى ٱلْمُؤْمِنِينَ كِتَـٰبًا مَّوْقُوتًا ۝ وَلَا تَهِنُوا۟ فِى ٱبْتِغَآءِ ٱلْقَوْمِ ۖ إِن تَكُونُوا۟ تَأْلَمُونَ فَإِنَّهُمْ يَأْلَمُونَ كَمَا تَأْلَمُونَ ۖ وَتَرْجُونَ مِنَ ٱللَّهِ مَا لَا يَرْجُونَ ۗ وَكَانَ ٱللَّهُ عَلِيمًا حَكِيمًا ۝

---

^a Though Muslims rely entirely on God, they have been instructed to be ready with the necessary means of defence against their enemies. This is so because help from God reaches the recipient through tangible means. If the Muslims did not prepare for their defence, it would be like not taking hold of the receptacle through which God's help could reach them. The difficulties faced by the Muslims in this world are a part of God's scheme to create such conditions of trial as will enable Him to judge who remains steadfast and who is a reckless victimiser of his fellow men. During the struggle between truth and untruth, sometimes the believers are defeated and harmed. This causes pessimism among some of them. But in such adversities, God's providence lies hidden; they occur so that man's repentance will be the greater and, in turning to God, he will make himself more deserving of His benevolence.

105 We have sent the Book down to you with the truth so that you may judge among mankind by means of what God has shown you. And do not be an advocate for the treacherous. 106 Ask God for forgiveness: He is most forgiving and merciful.[a]

إِنَّآ أَنزَلْنَآ إِلَيْكَ ٱلْكِتَٰبَ بِٱلْحَقِّ لِتَحْكُمَ بَيْنَ ٱلنَّاسِ بِمَآ أَرَىٰكَ ٱللَّهُ وَلَا تَكُن لِّلْخَآئِنِينَ خَصِيمًا ۝ وَٱسْتَغْفِرِ ٱللَّهَ إِنَّ ٱللَّهَ كَانَ غَفُورًا رَّحِيمًا ۝

---

[a] Living along with others is a need felt by every human being. It is this need that creates the nation or the community. A man has his strength enhanced a thousand times by association with his own community. However, something which initially came into existence as a human need for social cohesion, gradually takes on the status of a social religion. The community or the nation becomes a goal in itself. This leads to the mentality, 'My community right or wrong. It is my community, whether based on truth or falsehood.' Thus people consider their own circle as important and that of others as unimportant. It is considered that a man belonging to their own circle, even if he is in the wrong, must be supported, while another associated with a different group or community, though right and justified, receives no support.

A group with this mentality can be said to have taken communal expediencies and group bias as the criteria by which to judge right and wrong. On the contrary one should regard God's command as the standard by which to make judgements. If someone errs, he must be checked without prejudice or favouritism. If someone stands for truth, he must be supported—even though associated with another group. Even in a situation where two persons are involved, one from one's own group and the other from some other group, matters must be looked into on the basis of truth and untruth, ignoring all other considerations. One should always associate oneself with the truth.

241

107 And do not plead on behalf of those who are dishonest to themselves. Surely God does not love one who is treacherous and sinful. 108 They feel ashamed before men but do not feel ashamed before God, despite His being present with them when they plot at night, uttering things of which He does not approve; and indeed God is fully aware of what they do.[a]

وَلَا تُجَٰدِلْ عَنِ ٱلَّذِينَ يَخْتَانُونَ أَنفُسَهُمْ إِنَّ ٱللَّهَ لَا يُحِبُّ مَن كَانَ خَوَّانًا أَثِيمًا ۝ يَسْتَخْفُونَ مِنَ ٱلنَّاسِ وَلَا يَسْتَخْفُونَ مِنَ ٱللَّهِ وَهُوَ مَعَهُمْ إِذْ يُبَيِّتُونَ مَا لَا يَرْضَىٰ مِنَ ٱلْقَوْلِ وَكَانَ ٱللَّهُ بِمَا يَعْمَلُونَ مُحِيطًا ۝

---

[a] Abandoning the truth is like abandoning oneself. A man is dishonest to himself before he is dishonest to someone else. This is so because, in the hearts and minds of every human being, God has implanted a conscience as His representative. Whenever any individual intends to go against the truth, he is stopped by this invisible representative of God. He has first to suppress and ignore this inner voice, and only then is it possible for him to leave the path of justice for that of injustice. All too often he lends support to some erring person due to importance having been attached to him. Social relations and expediencies lead him to turn a blind eye to the other's misdeeds and, therefore, knowing full well that the other is not on the right path, he becomes his supporter. Refusal to distance himself from a person known to be following the path of untruth happens at the cost of distancing himself from God. When one supports untruth to seek the esteem of another human being in this world, one loses God's company in the Hereafter.

¹⁰⁹ You might argue on their behalf in the life of this world: but who will argue on their behalf with God on the Day of Resurrection and who will be their defender? ¹¹⁰ Yet anyone who does evil or wrongs his own soul and then asks God for forgiveness will find God forgiving and merciful. ¹¹¹ He who commits sin does so against his own soul. God is all knowing and wise.[a]

هَـٰٓأَنتُمْ هَـٰٓؤُلَآءِ جَـٰدَلْتُمْ عَنْهُمْ فِى ٱلْحَيَوٰةِ ٱلدُّنْيَا فَمَن يُجَـٰدِلُ ٱللَّهَ عَنْهُمْ يَوْمَ ٱلْقِيَـٰمَةِ أَمْ مَّن يَكُونُ عَلَيْهِمْ وَكِيلًا ۝ وَمَن يَعْمَلْ سُوٓءًا أَوْ يَظْلِمْ نَفْسَهُۥ ثُمَّ يَسْتَغْفِرِ ٱللَّهَ يَجِدِ ٱللَّهَ غَفُورًا رَّحِيمًا ۝ وَمَن يَكْسِبْ إِثْمًا فَإِنَّمَا يَكْسِبُهُۥ عَلَىٰ نَفْسِهِۦ وَكَانَ ٱللَّهُ عَلِيمًا حَكِيمًا ۝

---

[a] This world is a place of trial. Everyone may commit mistakes here, both with regard to God as well as to His servants. When someone errs, the right course is that he should sincerely repent and seek the guidance of God, beg for His forgiveness and pray to be assisted to perform only virtuous deeds in future. One who seeks God's shelter so sincerely, will certainly receive it from Him. By the grace of God, his religious sensibility will be sharpened and he will be enabled to live more prudently in this world.

On the other hand, a person may do some wrong, but does not care to admit it; he rather attempts to justify himself. He then gathers his supporters and fights with those who simply intended to inform him of his mistake. Such arrogant, unrepentant individuals and their supporters are the worst criminals in the eyes of God. Their eloquence, used to hide their wrongs, will become meaningless, and the host of supporters, who propped up their arrogance, will be of no avail in the Hereafter.

¹¹² And anyone who commits an offence or a sin, then charges an innocent person with it, shall certainly bear the guilt of a calumny and a manifest sin. ¹¹³ If it were not for the grace of God and His mercy to you, some of them had resolved to lead you astray but they lead astray no one but themselves. Nor can they do you any harm. God has sent down to you the Book and Wisdom and has taught you what you did not know. God's favour to you has been great indeed.ᵃ

وَمَن يَكْسِبْ خَطِيئَةً أَوْ إِثْمًا ثُمَّ يَرْمِ بِهِۦ بَرِيٓـًٔا فَقَدِ ٱحْتَمَلَ بُهْتَـٰنًا وَإِثْمًا مُّبِينًا ۝ وَلَوْلَا فَضْلُ ٱللَّهِ عَلَيْكَ وَرَحْمَتُهُۥ لَهَمَّت طَّآئِفَةٌ مِّنْهُمْ أَن يُضِلُّوكَ وَمَا يُضِلُّونَ إِلَّآ أَنفُسَهُمْ وَمَا يَضُرُّونَكَ مِن شَىْءٍ وَأَنزَلَ ٱللَّهُ عَلَيْكَ ٱلْكِتَـٰبَ وَٱلْحِكْمَةَ وَعَلَّمَكَ مَا لَمْ تَكُن تَعْلَمُ وَكَانَ فَضْلُ ٱللَّهِ عَلَيْكَ عَظِيمًا ۝

ᵃ A man steals something, but when faced with the possibility of getting caught, he hides it in someone else's house. He then raises the alarm that so and so has committed a theft. Similarly, a man may intend to outrage the modesty of a woman, but when that pious woman does not relent, he defames her with all sorts of fabricated stories. Again, two persons start a business in partnership. After some time, one of them feels that his personal interests are being harmed in the venture and, therefore, manages to get it closed down, putting the blame on his partner. All such activities are deliberate efforts to implicate others in order to lay the blame at their door. But these misdemeanours only increase the guilt of the person concerned; they do not absolve him of his responsibility. To such wrongdoers God gives the opportunity to reform; through His immense bounty they are advised to accept their faults without argument, not to be arrogant in their dealings because of the strength of their supporters, but to remain humble out of fear for God, and if there happens to be any chance of retaliation, not to exult, but to pray that God may save them from becoming tyrants.

¹¹⁴ There is no good in most of their secret talk, except in the case of those who enjoin charity and kindness, or reconciliation between people. If anyone does that, seeking the pleasure of God, We will give him an immense reward. ¹¹⁵ But if anyone opposes the Messenger after his guidance has become clear to him, and follows a path other than that of the faithful, We shall let him pursue his chosen path and shall cast him into Hell: an evil destination.ᵃ

۞ لَّا خَيْرَ فِى كَثِيرٍ مِّن نَّجْوَىٰهُمْ إِلَّا مَنْ أَمَرَ بِصَدَقَةٍ أَوْ مَعْرُوفٍ أَوْ إِصْلَٰحٍ بَيْنَ ٱلنَّاسِ ۚ وَمَن يَفْعَلْ ذَٰلِكَ ٱبْتِغَآءَ مَرْضَاتِ ٱللَّهِ فَسَوْفَ نُؤْتِيهِ أَجْرًا عَظِيمًا ۝ وَمَن يُشَاقِقِ ٱلرَّسُولَ مِنۢ بَعْدِ مَا تَبَيَّنَ لَهُ ٱلْهُدَىٰ وَيَتَّبِعْ غَيْرَ سَبِيلِ ٱلْمُؤْمِنِينَ نُوَلِّهِۦ مَا تَوَلَّىٰ وَنُصْلِهِۦ جَهَنَّمَ ۖ وَسَآءَتْ مَصِيرًا ۝

ᵃ The issuing of a genuine call to the truth amounts to the establishment of God's balance of justice on the earth. Everyone feels that he is being weighed in its scale. Such a call removes the veneer from man and leaves him as he actually is. This state of affairs is so hard upon those who are thus exposed that they become infuriated to an extreme degree. The preacher of God's word has to bear the brunt of this.

People who find themselves valueless in the scales of truth are overcome with feelings of haughtiness and pride. They lose no time in opposing and obstructing any move that casts doubt on their being lovers of the truth. They spread all kinds of rumours against the call and the caller. They dissuade others from extending any financial help to the dayees . They relentlessly try to discourage God's servants from rallying around the conveyor of the divine message by creating doubts about his message.

On the other hand, to those who have kept their consciences alive, God gives the ability to surrender before the preacher of God's word, to extend their full support to him and mould their lives in accordance with his guidance. For them their God-given faculty of speech is used to openly acknowledge the truth; they urge people to expend their time and wealth on that mission, they encourage people to use their energies in charity and welfare activities and strive to persuade them to extinguish personal enmities and grievances. The acknowledgement of truth awakens a positive psychology within them as a natural result of which they feel disposed to engage in positive activities.

116 Surely, God will not forgive the ascribing of partners to Him. He forgives whoever He will for anything other than that. Whoever ascribes partners to God has strayed far indeed.[a] 117 They [the polytheists] call upon female deities, and they invoke none but Satan, the rebellious one,[b]

إِنَّ ٱللَّهَ لَا يَغْفِرُ أَن يُشْرَكَ بِهِۦ وَيَغْفِرُ مَا دُونَ ذَٰلِكَ لِمَن يَشَآءُ ۚ وَمَن يُشْرِكْ بِٱللَّهِ فَقَدْ ضَلَّ ضَلَٰلًۢا بَعِيدًا ۝ إِن يَدْعُونَ مِن دُونِهِۦٓ إِلَّآ إِنَٰثًا وَإِن يَدْعُونَ إِلَّا شَيْطَٰنًا مَّرِيدًا ۝

---

[a] Opposition to the call of truth and victimization of the followers of the giver of that call are unforgivable offences in the eyes of God. While all other sinful acts may have been committed out of human weakness, the act of opposing the call of Truth is entirely due to insolence and haughtiness: insolence and rebellion are crimes that God will not forgive unless man confesses his mistakes and gives up his rebellious stance. Whenever the call of truth is brought to people in its pure and original form (without making concessions to people's whims and wishes) it always is a divine mission supported by the special succour of God. To oppose such a mission is to stand in opposition to God Almighty. And can any individual succeed if he takes a stand against God?

One who firmly believes in God has his actions rooted in Him. He may err occasionally but, when he turns to God, he rejoins his real roots. On the other hand, one who has associated himself with anyone besides God, is as if deprived of the true base in this universe. An individual who has not established his roots in the one God may perform some good actions, but such actions do not emanate from the divine source; they have only a surface value and are easily nullified by the slightest jolt. That is why a good action based in monotheism unfolds its results in the Hereafter, whereas that based in polytheism is swept away in this world itself.

[b] Man's real challenge in this world is from Satan. Though Satan has no real power, he can lure human beings with fanciful promises to fulfil wishful, imaginary desires and thus manage to make them deviate from the straight path of truth. Satan's way of misguiding is of two main types: one is superstition and the other is interference in God's creation. Faith in superstition means expectation of such results from something as have no relation with that thing. For instance, on the basis of self-styled suppositions, one may believe that someone other than God is the controller of the affairs of the world, while it is a well-established fact that no one enjoys any power save God. Superstition can also take the form of being fully involved in worldly activities and then, by wishful thinking, hoping to achieve success in the Hereafter without having worked hard for it.

[118] whom God has rejected. He said [to God], 'I will assuredly take a number of Your servants, [119] and shall lead them astray, and fill them with vain desires and order them to slit the ears of cattle. I shall order them to tamper with God's creation. Whoever chooses Satan as a patron instead of God is utterly ruined: [120] he holds out promises to them, and fills them with vain desires: but Satan's promises are nothing but delusion. [121] Hell shall be their home: they shall find no refuge from it. [122] As for those who believe and do good works. We shall admit them to Gardens through which rivers flow; wherein they will abide forever. This is a promise from God; and whose word could be truer than God's?[a]

لَّعَنَهُ ٱللَّهُ ۘ وَقَالَ لَأَتَّخِذَنَّ مِنْ عِبَادِكَ نَصِيبًا مَّفْرُوضًا ۝ وَلَأُضِلَّنَّهُمْ وَلَأُمَنِّيَنَّهُمْ وَلَآمُرَنَّهُمْ فَلَيُبَتِّكُنَّ ءَاذَانَ ٱلْأَنْعَٰمِ وَلَآمُرَنَّهُمْ فَلَيُغَيِّرُنَّ خَلْقَ ٱللَّهِ ۚ وَمَن يَتَّخِذِ ٱلشَّيْطَٰنَ وَلِيًّا مِّن دُونِ ٱللَّهِ فَقَدْ خَسِرَ خُسْرَانًا مُّبِينًا ۝ يَعِدُهُمْ وَيُمَنِّيهِمْ ۖ وَمَا يَعِدُهُمُ ٱلشَّيْطَٰنُ إِلَّا غُرُورًا ۝ أُوْلَٰٓئِكَ مَأْوَىٰهُمْ جَهَنَّمُ وَلَا يَجِدُونَ عَنْهَا مَحِيصًا ۝ وَٱلَّذِينَ ءَامَنُوا۟ وَعَمِلُوا۟ ٱلصَّٰلِحَٰتِ سَنُدْخِلُهُمْ جَنَّٰتٍ تَجْرِى مِن تَحْتِهَا ٱلْأَنْهَٰرُ خَٰلِدِينَ فِيهَآ أَبَدًا ۖ وَعْدَ ٱللَّهِ حَقًّا ۚ وَمَنْ أَصْدَقُ مِنَ ٱللَّهِ قِيلًا ۝

---

[a] Another way of Satan's misleading man is by interfering in the divine scheme of things. God has created man with the innate desire to direct all his attention to God. Interfering with this involves diverting man's attention towards things other than God or else encouraging him to acquire things by other self-devised ways and not through the natural course set by God (for instance, homosexuality). In this manner Satan interferes with man's observance of God's divine plan for the entire universe.

¹²³ It is not your desires, nor the desires of the People of the Book, that shall prevail. Anyone who commits evil will be rewarded accordingly. He will not find any protector or patron for himself besides God. ¹²⁴ Anyone who performs good deeds, whether it be a man or woman, provided that he is a believer, shall enter Paradise. No one shall suffer the least injustice.ᵃ

لَّيْسَ بِأَمَانِيِّكُمْ وَلَآ أَمَانِيِّ أَهْلِ ٱلْكِتَٰبِ مَن يَعْمَلْ سُوٓءًا يُجْزَ بِهِۦ وَلَا يَجِدْ لَهُۥ مِن دُونِ ٱللَّهِ وَلِيًّا وَلَا نَصِيرًا ۝ وَمَن يَعْمَلْ مِنَ ٱلصَّٰلِحَٰتِ مِن ذَكَرٍ أَوْ أُنثَىٰ وَهُوَ مُؤْمِنٌ فَأُوْلَٰٓئِكَ يَدْخُلُونَ ٱلْجَنَّةَ وَلَا يُظْلَمُونَ نَقِيرًا ۝

ᵃ When the People of the Book, that is, believers in God and the Hereafter, become engrossed in the world, they do not do so by refusing to believe in God and the existence of the Hereafter. What they do is believe in these realities in the formal sense while, in practice, devoting all their efforts to worldly acquisition. They are very serious about the attainment of worldly honour and glory. They know that to achieve success in this world one must struggle. But for the attainment of Paradise, wishful thinking alone is believed to suffice. For instance, through the blessing of some saint, association with a certain group, recitation of some words and phrases, in short, by such cheap formulae or superficial actions, it is hoped that they will be saved from the raging fire of Hell and be ushered into Heaven. Such wishful thinking, in whatever beautiful words it may have been couched, is not going to come to their rescue. God's system is established on such firm grounds that all divine verdicts are based on realities and not on wishful thinking. In God's court everyone will be judged exactly in accordance with his actions. There will be nothing other than the law of justice promulgated by God Himself to influence His decisions.

¹²⁵ Who is better in faith than one who submits himself wholly to God, acts righteously, and follows the religion of Abraham, the upright in faith, whom God chose for a friend? ¹²⁶ To God belongs all that the heavens and earth contain. God has knowledge of all things.ᵃ

وَمَنْ أَحْسَنُ دِينًا مِّمَّنْ أَسْلَمَ وَجْهَهُۥ لِلَّهِ وَهُوَ مُحْسِنٌ وَٱتَّبَعَ مِلَّةَ إِبْرَٰهِيمَ حَنِيفًا ۗ وَٱتَّخَذَ ٱللَّهُ إِبْرَٰهِيمَ خَلِيلًا ﴿١٢٥﴾ وَلِلَّهِ مَا فِى ٱلسَّمَٰوَٰتِ وَمَا فِى ٱلْأَرْضِ وَكَانَ ٱللَّهُ بِكُلِّ شَىْءٍ مُّحِيطًا ﴿١٢٦﴾

ᵃ Who is that servant of God upon whom God will shower His blessings? One historical example is that of Abraham. It is believers like Abraham who submit themselves fully to their Lord; who reserve their loyalties exclusively for God; who carry out their affairs in the world with justice and modesty, scrupulously avoiding injustice and arrogance. Man's face represents his whole personality. Turning one's face towards God means turning towards Him with one's whole existence.

God is the Lord of the universe. He is the possessor of all kinds of powers. However, He has chosen to remain invisible in this world. Man commits all kinds of evil deeds, because he does not see God. He assumes that he is free to do as he pleases. If one were to realize that human beings are utterly powerless, one would experience the same state of utter helplessness as one will undergo on the Day of Judgement, when all the realities are laid bare before one.

127 They consult you concerning women. Say, 'God has given you directions concerning them. The commandment given to you in the Book concerns the orphan girls to whom you do not give what is prescribed for them, and whom you nevertheless desire to marry, and about helpless children. He has instructed you to deal justly with orphans. God has knowledge of all the good you do. 128 If a woman fears ill-treatment or indifference on the part of her husband, it shall be no offence for her to seek a reconciliation, for reconciliation is best. But people are prone to selfish greed. If you do good and fear Him, surely God is aware of what you do.*

وَيَسْتَفْتُونَكَ فِى ٱلنِّسَآءِ ۖ قُلِ ٱللَّهُ يُفْتِيكُمْ فِيهِنَّ وَمَا يُتْلَىٰ عَلَيْكُمْ فِى ٱلْكِتَٰبِ فِى يَتَٰمَى ٱلنِّسَآءِ ٱلَّٰتِى لَا تُؤْتُونَهُنَّ مَا كُتِبَ لَهُنَّ وَتَرْغَبُونَ أَن تَنكِحُوهُنَّ وَٱلْمُسْتَضْعَفِينَ مِنَ ٱلْوِلْدَٰنِ وَأَن تَقُومُوا۟ لِلْيَتَٰمَىٰ بِٱلْقِسْطِ ۚ وَمَا تَفْعَلُوا۟ مِنْ خَيْرٍ فَإِنَّ ٱللَّهَ كَانَ بِهِۦ عَلِيمًا ۝ وَإِنِ ٱمْرَأَةٌ خَافَتْ مِنۢ بَعْلِهَا نُشُوزًا أَوْ إِعْرَاضًا فَلَا جُنَاحَ عَلَيْهِمَآ أَن يُصْلِحَا بَيْنَهُمَا صُلْحًا ۚ وَٱلصُّلْحُ خَيْرٌ ۗ وَأُحْضِرَتِ ٱلْأَنفُسُ ٱلشُّحَّ ۚ وَإِن تُحْسِنُوا۟ وَتَتَّقُوا۟ فَإِنَّ ٱللَّهَ كَانَ بِمَا تَعْمَلُونَ خَبِيرًا ۝

---

a When people asked the Prophet about the injunctions of the *shariah* on various social matters, he was instructed by God that great emphasis must be laid on goodness, justice, fraternity and piety. This is because any law serves its purpose only when the person who has to enforce it is God-fearing and truly desirous of justice. In the absence of such an attitude, despite the actual enforcement of law, no real reform can be brought about. Moreover, social reform can take place only when the evil-doer realizes that he is ultimately accountable to God and that, even if he manages to fool the people and save himself from the consequences of his crime in this world, he cannot escape from God's grip. As for the doer of good works, he should carry on his efforts irrespective of whether or not he is appreciated by the people, in the belief that God is certainly watching him and will definitely reward him for his endeavours. The dread of Hell will deter him from injustice and the hope of Paradise will give him the courage to endure the loss which is invariably faced in the process of living a truthful life.

129 You will never be able to treat your wives with equal fairness, however much you may desire to do so, but do not ignore one wife altogether, leaving her suspended [between marriage and divorce]. And if you make amends and act righteously, surely God is most forgiving and merciful. 130 If they decide to separate, God will compensate both out of His own abundance: God is bountiful and wise.[a]

وَلَن تَسۡتَطِيعُوٓاْ أَن تَعۡدِلُواْ بَيۡنَ ٱلنِّسَآءِ وَلَوۡ حَرَصۡتُمۡ فَلَا تَمِيلُواْ كُلَّ ٱلۡمَيۡلِ فَتَذَرُوهَا كَٱلۡمُعَلَّقَةِ وَإِن تُصۡلِحُواْ وَتَتَّقُواْ فَإِنَّ ٱللَّهَ كَانَ غَفُورًا رَّحِيمًا ۝ وَإِن يَتَفَرَّقَا يُغۡنِ ٱللَّهُ كُلًّا مِّن سَعَتِهِۦ وَكَانَ ٱللَّهُ وَٰسِعًا حَكِيمًا ۝

---

[a] The differences emerging between husband and wife or between any other two persons largely result from greed. One party, without any consideration for the other, wants his demands to be fulfilled. This mentality leads to distrust between the two. The proper course is for each party to give thought to the other's problems and making due allowances, try to reach some consensus. Just as God desires people to be considerate to one another, similarly He shows the maximum consideration to His servants. God does not seize man for his natural weaknesses but rather takes man to task for his deliberate excesses and acts of injustice out of haughtiness and insolence. If man fears God and has the urge of reform in his heart, all his acts done with the right intentions would be considered pardonable in the Hereafter. Besides, one should never nurture such thoughts in his mind that it is he who is behind the success of such and such a person and that if he had not helped that person, success could never have been achieved. One must remember the fact that God alone is the provider. He alone is behind every success and achievement, and His help may come under diverse sets of circumstances.

131 All that the heavens and the earth contain belongs to God. We have commanded those who were given the Scripture before you, and We command you to fear God. If you deny Him, know that all that the heavens and the earth contain belongs to God. God is self-sufficient and praiseworthy.[a]

وَلِلَّهِ مَا فِى ٱلسَّمَـٰوَٰتِ وَمَا فِى ٱلْأَرْضِ وَلَقَدْ وَصَّيْنَا ٱلَّذِينَ أُوتُواْ ٱلْكِتَـٰبَ مِن قَبْلِكُمْ وَإِيَّاكُمْ أَنِ ٱتَّقُواْ ٱللَّهَ وَإِن تَكْفُرُواْ فَإِنَّ لِلَّهِ مَا فِى ٱلسَّمَـٰوَٰتِ وَمَا فِى ٱلْأَرْضِ وَكَانَ ٱللَّهُ غَنِيًّا حَمِيدًا ۝

---

[a] The virtuous life that a believer is expected to live is possible only when he has become a God-worshipper in his very heart and soul. Discovering God as the Lord of the universe; fearing and trusting God alone; diverting one's full attention to the Hereafter—these are the things which enable man to lead a godly life, as desired by God, in this world. This is the life which will make him successful in the life to come. That is why these were the things most focussed on in the teachings of the prophets.

¹³² All that the heavens and the earth contain belongs to God; and none is as worthy of trust as God. ¹³³ If He wanted, He could remove you altogether and replace you with other people: He has the full power to do so. ¹³⁴ If one desires the rewards of this world [let him remember that] with God are the rewards of [both] this world and the life to come: and God is indeed all hearing, all seeing.ᵃ

وَلِلَّهِ مَا فِي ٱلسَّمَٰوَٰتِ وَمَا فِي ٱلْأَرْضِ وَكَفَىٰ بِٱللَّهِ وَكِيلًا ۝ إِن يَشَأْ يُذْهِبْكُمْ أَيُّهَا ٱلنَّاسُ وَيَأْتِ بِـَٔاخَرِينَ ۚ وَكَانَ ٱللَّهُ عَلَىٰ ذَٰلِكَ قَدِيرًا ۝ مَّن كَانَ يُرِيدُ ثَوَابَ ٱلدُّنْيَا فَعِندَ ٱللَّهِ ثَوَابُ ٱلدُّنْيَا وَٱلْءَاخِرَةِ ۚ وَكَانَ ٱللَّهُ سَمِيعًا بَصِيرًا ۝

ᵃ The present world is a world of trial. Here everyone is being tested to find out who is good and who is bad. To serve this purpose the present world has been built to provide for every kind of freedom. In this world one even has the liberty to label one's misdeeds as good deeds. Here people have every opportunity to be involved in all kinds of sinful acts, yet pass themselves off as pious people. Here people find beautiful words to justify themselves. Here it is possible to refute an open truth and find a beautiful explanation to justify its denial. Here it is possible for one to build his life on honour-seeking, popularity, hoarding, self-interest, expediency, self-glorification, and yet succeed in convincing others that he is engaged in the genuine cause of truth. Here it is possible for a person to exploit God's religion for the achievement of his worldly and material purposes, and yet continue to flourish in this world. Here it is possible to abandon what is lawful in favour of what is unlawful; to take the path of tyranny instead of justice, and yet go scot free. In all these instances, if man wanted, he could bind himself either to truth and justice or to injustice and haughtiness. The truth is that, of all the aspects of man's relationship with God, what is of most importance is whether man fears God or not. Because it is fear of God which enables the individual to lead a responsible life. Without the fear of God, there is nothing to check one from following the path of evil. This is particularly true in a world where evil can be couched in beautiful words to mislead the people; in a world where great personal advancement can be achieved on the basis of injustice; where every tyrant finds fine words to hide his tyranny.

135 Believers, be strict in upholding justice and bear witness for the sake of God, even though it be against yourselves, your parents, or your kindred. Be they rich or poor, God knows better about them both. Do not, then, follow your own desires, lest you swerve from justice. If you conceal the truth or evade it, then remember that God is well aware of all that you do.[a]

بِسْمِ ٱللَّهِ ٱلرَّحْمَٰنِ ٱلرَّحِيمِ ۞ يَـٰٓأَيُّهَا ٱلَّذِينَ ءَامَنُوا۟ كُونُوا۟ قَوَّٰمِينَ بِٱلْقِسْطِ شُهَدَآءَ لِلَّهِ وَلَوْ عَلَىٰٓ أَنفُسِكُمْ أَوِ ٱلْوَٰلِدَيْنِ وَٱلْأَقْرَبِينَ ۚ إِن يَكُنْ غَنِيًّا أَوْ فَقِيرًا فَٱللَّهُ أَوْلَىٰ بِهِمَا ۖ فَلَا تَتَّبِعُوا۟ ٱلْهَوَىٰٓ أَن تَعْدِلُوا۟ ۚ وَإِن تَلْوُۥٓا۟ أَوْ تُعْرِضُوا۟ فَإِنَّ ٱللَّهَ كَانَ بِمَا تَعْمَلُونَ خَبِيرًا ۝١٣٥

---

[a] In life it often happens that man is confronted with a situation where, on the one hand, lies the path of desire and self-interest, and on the other hand, lies the path of justice. Now those who are unmindful of God, those who have no conviction that God is watching them on all such occasions follow the path of their desire. They consider it an achievement to ignore the call of truth and take to the path of self-interest and worldly considerations. But those who fear God, who regard God as their guardian, have their eyes always set on truth and justice and act according to their demands. They sincerely desire that they may leave this world having done no injustice to anyone, having fully adhered to the path of truth and justice.

This desire for truth and justice is so heightened in them that it becomes impossible for them to tolerate any behaviour which does not measure up to the standard of absolute justice. When confronted with wrongdoing, they dare to proclaim the demands of truth and justice, even if such a stand amounts to adversely affecting the interests of their family or goes against their own worldly considerations. They say only what justice would demand. It is also very wrong from the standpoint of justice to give influential persons their due while denying the rights of those who are weak and without influence. A true believer is one who deals justly with everyone, whether weak or powerful.

136 Believers, believe in God and His
Messenger and in the Scripture He
sent down to His Messenger, as well
as what He sent down before. He
who denies God, His angels, His
Scriptures, His messengers and the
Last Day has surely gone far astray.ᵃ

يَـٰٓأَيُّهَا ٱلَّذِينَ ءَامَنُوٓاْ ءَامِنُواْ بِٱللَّهِ
وَرَسُولِهِۦ وَٱلۡكِتَـٰبِ ٱلَّذِى نَزَّلَ عَلَىٰ
رَسُولِهِۦ وَٱلۡكِتَـٰبِ ٱلَّذِىٓ أَنزَلَ مِن
قَبۡلُ وَمَن يَكۡفُرۡ بِٱللَّهِ وَمَلَـٰٓئِكَتِهِۦ
وَكُتُبِهِۦ وَرُسُلِهِۦ وَٱلۡيَوۡمِ ٱلۡأٓخِرِ فَقَدۡ
ضَلَّ ضَلَـٰلَۢا بَعِيدًا ﴿١٣٦﴾

ᵃ 'Believers, believe' is like saying, 'Muslims become Muslims!' Calling oneself a
Muslim or regarding oneself as such does not suffice for one to be held a Muslim
in the eyes of God. A true Muslim is only that person who has made God the
centre of his life and the source of his trust and confidence. A Muslim is one who
believes in the Prophet and his guidance to the exclusion of all else. A Muslim
is one who adheres to the revealed Scripture in such a manner that his thinking
and his feelings become totally subordinated to it. A Muslim is one to whom belief
in the angels means that he is surrounded by God's guardians who are constantly
watching him. A Muslim is one whose belief in the Hereafter is so profound that
he begins to examine all his words and deeds in the balance of the Hereafter. One
who becomes a believer in this sense is, in the eyes of God, on the right path, on
the straight path to success in the Hereafter. One who does not become a believer
in this sense has gone astray, however much he may consider himself a Muslim,
a believer.

¹³⁷ As for those who come to believe, and then deny the truth, and again come to believe, and again deny the truth, and thereafter grow stubborn in their denial of the truth—God will never forgive them, nor will He guide them. ¹³⁸ Warn the hypocrites that for them there is a painful punishment. ¹³⁹ As for those who take the deniers of the truth for their allies rather than the believers—do they seek honour in their company? Surely all honour belongs to God.^a

إِنَّ ٱلَّذِينَ ءَامَنُوا۟ ثُمَّ كَفَرُوا۟ ثُمَّ ءَامَنُوا۟ ثُمَّ كَفَرُوا۟ ثُمَّ ٱزْدَادُوا۟ كُفْرًا لَّمْ يَكُنِ ٱللَّهُ لِيَغْفِرَ لَهُمْ وَلَا لِيَهْدِيَهُمْ سَبِيلًا ۝ بَشِّرِ ٱلْمُنَٰفِقِينَ بِأَنَّ لَهُمْ عَذَابًا أَلِيمًا ۝ ٱلَّذِينَ يَتَّخِذُونَ ٱلْكَٰفِرِينَ أَوْلِيَآءَ مِن دُونِ ٱلْمُؤْمِنِينَ ۚ أَيَبْتَغُونَ عِندَهُمُ ٱلْعِزَّةَ فَإِنَّ ٱلْعِزَّةَ لِلَّهِ جَمِيعًا ۝

^a This tussle between belief and unbelief continues through life. In dealing with any matter the human mind starts thinking along two lines: it tilts either to the demands of desires or of truth and justice. If on such occasions the thinking and feeling of a person take to the path of desires, this will amount to a denial of the faith he professes to believe in. On the other hand, if he makes his thinking and feelings subservient to the demands of truth and justice, this would amount to his becoming a true Muslim.

Whenever any matter of truth is brought before people, it is met with two kinds of responses: one from a person, who adopts the attitude of modesty and acknowledges the truth, and the other from a person who is so proud and haughty that he denies the truth. The first response stems from *iman* and faith, while the other stems from faithlessness. One who is not a true believer loves worldly honour and prestige. He, therefore, feels attracted to like-minded people who—even if they be the deniers of the truth—will add to his honour and glory. One so enamoured of worldly affairs is not interested in those whose association does not add to his honour and prestige, even if they be true God-worshippers.

140 He has instructed you in the Book that, when you hear people deny or ridicule God's revelations, you must not sit with them unless they engage in other talk, or else you yourselves shall become like them. God will gather all the hypocrites and those who deny the truth together in Hell.[a]

وَقَدْ نَزَّلَ عَلَيْكُمْ فِي ٱلْكِتَٰبِ أَنْ إِذَا سَمِعْتُمْ ءَايَٰتِ ٱللَّهِ يُكْفَرُ بِهَا وَيُسْتَهْزَأُ بِهَا فَلَا تَقْعُدُواْ مَعَهُمْ حَتَّىٰ يَخُوضُواْ فِي حَدِيثٍ غَيْرِهِ إِنَّكُمْ إِذَا مِّثْلُهُمْ إِنَّ ٱللَّهَ جَامِعُ ٱلْمُنَٰفِقِينَ وَٱلْكَٰفِرِينَ فِي جَهَنَّمَ جَمِيعًا ١٤٠

---

[a] Whenever the call of God is addressed to any human group, its basis is so strong that it is not possible to refute it by arguments. Therefore, those who do not want to accept it, attempt to show its worthlessness by ridiculing it. By heaping contempt upon it, they want to convey to others that this message is not worthy of being accepted. Those who act like this, demonstrate by their behaviour that they do not regard truth to be a serious matter. And when people are not serious about something, arguing with them is of no use. On such occasions it is better to remain silent and wait for the time when the addressees are in the right state of mind to give their attention to the missionary call.

We should withdraw from any company where the divine call is held in low esteem. Being a part of such company, where truth is taken to be a subject of ridicule, will be a clear indication that we are not serious about truth.

141 The hypocrites wait to see what happens to you and, if God grants you a victory, they say, 'Were we not on your side?' And if those who deny the truth have a share of it [victory] they say to them, 'Did we not help you win, and protect you from the believers?' God will judge between you [all] on Resurrection Day. And never will God allow those who deny the truth to harm the believers.[a]

ٱلَّذِينَ يَتَرَبَّصُونَ بِكُمْ فَإِن كَانَ لَكُمْ فَتْحٌ مِّنَ ٱللَّهِ قَالُوٓاْ أَلَمْ نَكُن مَّعَكُمْ وَإِن كَانَ لِلْكَٰفِرِينَ نَصِيبٌ قَالُوٓاْ أَلَمْ نَسْتَحْوِذْ عَلَيْكُمْ وَنَمْنَعْكُم مِّنَ ٱلْمُؤْمِنِينَ فَٱللَّهُ يَحْكُمُ بَيْنَكُمْ يَوْمَ ٱلْقِيَٰمَةِ وَلَن يَجْعَلَ ٱللَّهُ لِلْكَٰفِرِينَ عَلَى ٱلْمُؤْمِنِينَ سَبِيلاً ۝

---

[a] The hypocrite is one who is outwardly religious but inwardly irreligious. Having no principles, he watches out for opportunities to turn events to his own advantage. He associates himself with any group which may help him realise his worldly ambitions, be it composed of believers or of those who deny the truth. Into whichever gathering he goes, he speaks to please everybody. For reasons of worldly convenience or expediency he has to associate himself at times with believers, but he is not their well-wisher. Since the very existence of true believers becomes a criterion of Truth in a society, those who stand on the ground of false religiosity want such criteria as expose their false religiosity to be demolished. However, the evil wishers of the believers can make mischief only in this world. Believers will be safe from their mischief in the Hereafter.

A hypocrite is bracketed with those who deny the truth, because in God's judgement, there is no difference between outward religiosity and blatant irreligiosity. This is because although both the states may appear to be different, in reality they are identical. To God, what is of importance is the inward state (the reality) and not the outward appearance.

142 The hypocrites seek to outwit God—but it is He who outwits them. And when they stand up for prayer, they do so reluctantly and to be seen by others, and they hardly remember God at all. 143 They vacillate between the two, belonging neither to one side nor the other. But for him whom God allows to go astray you can never find the way for him. 144 Do not take deniers of the truth [who are at war with you] for your allies in preference to believers. Would you give God a clear proof against yourselves? 145 The hypocrites shall surely be in the lowest depth of the Fire; and you will find no helper for them. 146 But those who repent and mend their ways, who hold fast to God and are sincere in their worship of God will be joined with the believers; and God will bestow a great reward upon the believers. 147 Why should God punish you, if you render thanks to Him and believe in Him? God is appreciative and aware.*

إِنَّ ٱلْمُنَٰفِقِينَ يُخَٰدِعُونَ ٱللَّهَ وَهُوَ خَٰدِعُهُمْ وَإِذَا قَامُوٓاْ إِلَى ٱلصَّلَوٰةِ قَامُواْ كُسَالَىٰ يُرَآءُونَ ٱلنَّاسَ وَلَا يَذْكُرُونَ ٱللَّهَ إِلَّا قَلِيلًا ۝ مُّذَبْذَبِينَ بَيْنَ ذَٰلِكَ لَآ إِلَىٰ هَٰٓؤُلَآءِ وَلَآ إِلَىٰ هَٰٓؤُلَآءِ وَمَن يُضْلِلِ ٱللَّهُ فَلَن تَجِدَ لَهُۥ سَبِيلًا ۝ يَٰٓأَيُّهَا ٱلَّذِينَ ءَامَنُواْ لَا تَتَّخِذُواْ ٱلْكَٰفِرِينَ أَوْلِيَآءَ مِن دُونِ ٱلْمُؤْمِنِينَ أَتُرِيدُونَ أَن تَجْعَلُواْ لِلَّهِ عَلَيْكُمْ سُلْطَٰنًا مُّبِينًا ۝ إِنَّ ٱلْمُنَٰفِقِينَ فِي ٱلدَّرْكِ ٱلْأَسْفَلِ مِنَ ٱلنَّارِ وَلَن تَجِدَ لَهُمْ نَصِيرًا ۝ إِلَّا ٱلَّذِينَ تَابُواْ وَأَصْلَحُواْ وَٱعْتَصَمُواْ بِٱللَّهِ وَأَخْلَصُواْ دِينَهُمْ لِلَّهِ فَأُوْلَٰٓئِكَ مَعَ ٱلْمُؤْمِنِينَ وَسَوْفَ يُؤْتِ ٱللَّهُ ٱلْمُؤْمِنِينَ أَجْرًا عَظِيمًا ۝ مَّا يَفْعَلُ ٱللَّهُ بِعَذَابِكُمْ إِن شَكَرْتُمْ وَءَامَنتُمْ وَكَانَ ٱللَّهُ شَاكِرًا عَلِيمًا ۝

---

* Those who have not surrendered themselves to God succumb to worldly interests. They will associate themselves with anyone, be he religious or irreligious, by whom their worldly interests are served. Such people's words and deeds, however religious they may appear to be, are not to please God, but to show others that they too are believers. Opportunism is their real religion, but they are at pains to show people that they are God-worshippers. These people want to prove themselves to be godly although they are not.

148 God does not love the utterance of evil words except in the case of someone who has been wronged. God hears all and knows all. 149 Whether you reveal any good or hide it, or pardon any evil, God is forgiving and all powerful.[a]

* لَّا يُحِبُّ ٱللَّهُ ٱلْجَهْرَ بِٱلسُّوٓءِ مِنَ ٱلْقَوْلِ إِلَّا مَن ظُلِمَ ۚ وَكَانَ ٱللَّهُ سَمِيعًا عَلِيمًا ۝ إِن تُبْدُواْ خَيْرًا أَوْ تُخْفُوهُ أَوْ تَعْفُواْ عَن سُوٓءٍ فَإِنَّ ٱللَّهَ كَانَ عَفُوًّا قَدِيرًا ۝

---

[a] In spite of knowing Islam to be the true religion, the hypocrites do not want to abandon their worldly interests. Due to this mentality they are distracted, being fully devoted neither to the demands of their religion nor to their worldly interests. They fall between two stools, vacillating between faith and infidelity—between the interests of this world and the Hereafter. Such people remain deprived of God's succour, which can be earned only by perseverance in God's cause.

Such hypocritical people cannot save themselves from the wrath of God, regardless of how many showy actions they may have performed. In spite of the observance of Islam for appearance's sake, they are far from it in respect of reality. That is why their reward will be meted out to them in accordance with what they were in reality, and not what they were in terms of appearance. However, even if one errs, God does not become one's enemy. If wrongdoers are ashamed of their misdeeds, change their life style, divert their full attention to God and take to His path wholeheartedly, then He will surely forgive them.

In life one often comes to know about some shortcoming or fault, or vice of oneself, be it of a religious or worldly nature, through the people around oneself. But God disapproves of public criticism that defames the person concerned. Everyone has the right to give his counsel with the motive of reforming that individual. But the counselling should be done in private, not in public. If something needs to be said in public to check that vice from spreading in society, the wrongdoer should not be named. The reference to the vice should be in general terms.

Day in and day out God overlooks people's crimes. His servants too should follow this divine principle. However, one who has been oppressed or who has suffered a wrong is permitted to tell people about the wrong or oppression he has suffered. Nevertheless, it is better for him to exercise patience and forgive the one who wronged him. In this way the victim shows that he cares for the loss of the Hereafter more than any loss incurred in this world. For the thought of a greater loss renders a small loss insignificant. This is what happens with a true believer who really dreads the onset of Doomsday.

150 Those who deny God and His messengers and seek to make a distinction between God and His messengers and say, 'We believe in some messengers and disbelieve in others', and desire to adopt a position in between. 151 Those indeed are they who are denying the truth beyond doubt, and We have prepared a humiliating punishment for the deniers. 152 To those who believe in God and His messengers, and make no distinction between any of them, to those—We shall surely give them their rewards. God is most forgiving and merciful.ᵃ

إِنَّ ٱلَّذِينَ يَكْفُرُونَ بِٱللَّهِ وَرُسُلِهِۦ وَيُرِيدُونَ أَن يُفَرِّقُواْ بَيْنَ ٱللَّهِ وَرُسُلِهِۦ وَيَقُولُونَ نُؤْمِنُ بِبَعْضٍ وَنَكْفُرُ بِبَعْضٍ وَيُرِيدُونَ أَن يَتَّخِذُواْ بَيْنَ ذَٰلِكَ سَبِيلًا ۞ أُوْلَٰٓئِكَ هُمُ ٱلْكَٰفِرُونَ حَقًّا ۚ وَأَعْتَدْنَا لِلْكَٰفِرِينَ عَذَابًا مُّهِينًا ۞ وَٱلَّذِينَ ءَامَنُواْ بِٱللَّهِ وَرُسُلِهِۦ وَلَمْ يُفَرِّقُواْ بَيْنَ أَحَدٍ مِّنْهُمْ أُوْلَٰٓئِكَ سَوْفَ يُؤْتِيهِمْ أُجُورَهُمْ ۗ وَكَانَ ٱللَّهُ غَفُورًا رَّحِيمًا ۞

ᵃ The Makkans believed in the prophethood of Abraham. Similarly, the Jews and the Christians believed respectively in the prophethood of Moses and Jesus. But none of them would acknowledge the prophethood of Muhammad. All of them were willing to accept the prophets of the past, but none of them were ready to accept the Prophet of their own times—mindful as they were of the fact that the prophets they believed in had also been faced with the same hostile reactions in their times as were now being faced by the Arab prophet. All such attempts to reject the contemporary prophet amounted to finding a middle course between truth-worship and self-worship, so that entry to Paradise should be secured without any sacrifice of self-interest.

The truth of the matter is that the prophethood of the past is an established fact. Whereas, to acknowledge the contemporary prophet one needs to undertake a new intellectual journey. The prophethood of the past after the passage of time becomes so accepted that it becomes a part of one's thinking process right from the time of one's birth. But the prophet of the day is a controversial personality. He appears to be an 'ordinary human being.' So, to believe in a prophet in the garb of an ordinary human being, it is essential for man to have a complete change of mindset. He has to find God again at the level of awareness. Belief in the prophet of the past entails only a belief in one's own heritage, following in the footsteps of one's forefathers. Their faith was not by choice, but by birth. They had not made a conscious discovery of God. So, belief in the prophet of the past is only a continuation of one's forefather's ways, while belief in the prophet of one's own times means a conscious acceptance of faith. What is of importance in the eyes of God is the faith adopted by choice and not by birth.

¹⁵³ The People of the Book ask you to bring down for them a book from heaven. Of Moses they demanded a greater thing than that. They said to him: 'Show us God face to face.' A thunderbolt struck them for their wickedness. After that, they took to worshipping the [golden] calf, after all evidence of the truth had come to them! Yet We pardoned even that and bestowed on Moses clear authority. ¹⁵⁴ And We raised above them the Mount, while making a covenant with them, and We said to them. 'Enter the gate humbly,' and We also commanded them, 'Transgress not in the matter of the Sabbath.' We took from them a firm covenant.^a

يَسۡـَٔلُكَ أَهۡلُ ٱلۡكِتَٰبِ أَن تُنَزِّلَ عَلَيۡهِمۡ كِتَٰبٗا مِّنَ ٱلسَّمَآءِ فَقَدۡ سَأَلُواْ مُوسَىٰٓ أَكۡبَرَ مِن ذَٰلِكَ فَقَالُوٓاْ أَرِنَا ٱللَّهَ جَهۡرَةٗ فَأَخَذَتۡهُمُ ٱلصَّٰعِقَةُ بِظُلۡمِهِمۡ ثُمَّ ٱتَّخَذُواْ ٱلۡعِجۡلَ مِنۢ بَعۡدِ مَا جَآءَتۡهُمُ ٱلۡبَيِّنَٰتُ فَعَفَوۡنَا عَن ذَٰلِكَ وَءَاتَيۡنَا مُوسَىٰ سُلۡطَٰنٗا مُّبِينٗا ۝ وَرَفَعۡنَا فَوۡقَهُمُ ٱلطُّورَ بِمِيثَٰقِهِمۡ وَقُلۡنَا لَهُمُ ٱدۡخُلُواْ ٱلۡبَابَ سُجَّدٗا وَقُلۡنَا لَهُمۡ لَا تَعۡدُواْ فِي ٱلسَّبۡتِ وَأَخَذۡنَا مِنۡهُم مِّيثَٰقًا غَلِيظٗا ۝

^a God's prophet is a man amongst human beings. He appears before the people as a common man. That is why people fail to understand how they can take a common man to be a representative of God Almighty; how they can believe that this man—one from amongst themselves—is a person appointed by God Himself to speak on His behalf. So they demand that he show them his message being revealed by God, or heaven itself testifying to the truth of his message, otherwise they will not believe in it. But demands such as these show their utter insincerity. Because man's trial demands that he believe in these things without seeing them; that he discover the inner realities. In such a situation, it makes no sense to believe after seeing.

Even if God were to alter the system of nature to fulfil their demand by showing them the realities, that would be of no use because these realities would be shown to them only for a time and not permanently. So the human freedom which had led them to rebelliousness would continue, with the result that, at the time of the miracles, they would be awed into belief but afterwards they would continue to misuse their freedom as before. The history of the Israelites furnishes ample proof of this.

The extraordinary situation thus referred to in the Quran, 'We raised above them the Mount' was created by God on Mount Tur to take a solemn covenant from the Jews. They were enjoined to enter their synagogue with humility and pray to God in all humbleness and submissiveness, and to ensure that their struggle for livelihood conformed strictly to the bounds set by God. But the Jews broke this entire covenant they had made with God. ▶

155 But they broke their covenant; and they rejected the signs of God; and put the prophets to death without justification, and said, 'Our hearts are sealed.' It is God who has sealed their hearts, on account of their denial of the truth. Except for a few of them, they have no faith. 156 They denied the truth and uttered a monstrous slander against Mary.[a]

فَبِمَا نَقْضِهِم مِّيثَـٰقَهُمْ وَكُفْرِهِم بِـَٔايَـٰتِ ٱللَّهِ وَقَتْلِهِمُ ٱلْأَنۢبِيَآءَ بِغَيْرِ حَقٍّ وَقَوْلِهِمْ قُلُوبُنَا غُلْفٌ ۚ بَلْ طَبَعَ ٱللَّهُ عَلَيْهَا بِكُفْرِهِمْ فَلَا يُؤْمِنُونَ إِلَّا قَلِيلًا ۝ وَبِكُفْرِهِمْ وَقَوْلِهِمْ عَلَىٰ مَرْيَمَ بُهْتَـٰنًا عَظِيمًا ۝

'Yet We pardoned even that and bestowed on Moses clear authority.' This is the case with all the prophets. The prophet is like an ordinary human being but for his utterances; it is in his utterances that he gives clear arguments which adequately prove his status as God's messenger. But the unjust man always manages to find an explanation of God's signs by which he may refute them and then continue to lead a life of transgression far from God's ways.

[a] The Jews had Scriptures revealed to them in which they were asked to surrender to the will of God in this world, in return for which God would grant them Paradise in the next. They forgot the first part and came to regard the second part as their birthright. All kinds of rot set in among the Jewish community. Moreover, they were so greatly convinced of the notion that salvation was their birthright that they considered it unnecessary to acknowledge the new Prophet. They would say ironically, 'Our hearts are sealed.' This not only showed their inability to acknowledge the new Prophet, but also their conviction that, whatever their misconduct with the Prophet, their salvation was not going to be endangered.

157 They declared, 'We have put to death the Messiah, Jesus, son of Mary, the Messenger of God.' They did not kill him, nor did they crucify him, but it only seemed to them [as if it had been so]. And those who differ in this matter are in doubt concerning it. They have no definite knowledge about it, but only follow mere conjecture. But they certainly did not kill him. 158 God raised him towards Himself. God is almighty and wise.a

وَقَوْلِهِمْ إِنَّا قَتَلْنَا ٱلْمَسِيحَ عِيسَى ٱبْنَ مَرْيَمَ رَسُولَ ٱللَّهِ وَمَا قَتَلُوهُ وَمَا صَلَبُوهُ وَلَٰكِن شُبِّهَ لَهُمْ وَإِنَّ ٱلَّذِينَ ٱخْتَلَفُوا۟ فِيهِ لَفِى شَكٍّ مِّنْهُ مَا لَهُم بِهِۦ مِنْ عِلْمٍ إِلَّا ٱتِّبَاعَ ٱلظَّنِّ وَمَا قَتَلُوهُ يَقِينًۢا ۝ بَل رَّفَعَهُ ٱللَّهُ إِلَيْهِ وَكَانَ ٱللَّهُ عَزِيزًا حَكِيمًا ۝

---

a Those who suffer from false convictions are emboldened to commit all kinds of crimes. They have no qualms about breaking the divine covenant to which they are bound by their belief in God. Despite clear arguments from God they are not willing to mend their ways. One who calls upon them to accept the truth exposes their ungodly ways, so they do not hesitate to perpetrate any kind of aggression against him. They will go even to the extent of false calumny against the dayee in order to dishonour him. The Jews went so far as to try to kill the Prophet Jesus and then boasted, 'We have put to death the Messiah, Jesus, son of Mary.' However, whatever plots these people may hatch against the dayee, they can never succeed. God's power and his immutable system of nature is always there to support His envoys. Despite all plots and all opposition, they receive every kind of divine succour until they have completed the divine mission.

Those who opt for an antagonistic attitude to the call of the truth have their very capacity to accept the truth taken away by God, until one day they are brought as criminals before the divine court by the angels.

¹⁵⁹ There is none among the People of the Book but will believe in it before his death; and on the Day of Resurrection he shall be a witness against them. ¹⁶⁰ Because of the wrongdoings of the Jews, We forbade them certain good things that had been allowed to them before; for having frequently debarred others from God's path; ¹⁶¹ for taking usury, when they had been forbidden to do so. And because of their devouring people's wealth wrongfully. We have prepared a painful punishment for those of them who [continue to] deny the truth. ¹⁶² But to those of them, who are firmly grounded in knowledge, and the believers, who truly believe in what is revealed to you, and what was revealed before you. To those who pray regularly and pay the *zakat* [prescribed alms] and believe in God and the Last Day, We will surely give a great reward.^a

وَإِن مِّنْ أَهْلِ ٱلْكِتَٰبِ إِلَّا لَيُؤْمِنَنَّ بِهِۦ قَبْلَ مَوْتِهِۦ وَيَوْمَ ٱلْقِيَٰمَةِ يَكُونُ عَلَيْهِمْ شَهِيدًا ۝ فَبِظُلْمٍ مِّنَ ٱلَّذِينَ هَادُوا۟ حَرَّمْنَا عَلَيْهِمْ طَيِّبَٰتٍ أُحِلَّتْ لَهُمْ وَبِصَدِّهِمْ عَن سَبِيلِ ٱللَّهِ كَثِيرًا ۝ وَأَخْذِهِمُ ٱلرِّبَوٰا۟ وَقَدْ نُهُوا۟ عَنْهُ وَأَكْلِهِمْ أَمْوَٰلَ ٱلنَّاسِ بِٱلْبَٰطِلِ وَأَعْتَدْنَا لِلْكَٰفِرِينَ مِنْهُمْ عَذَابًا أَلِيمًا ۝ لَّٰكِنِ ٱلرَّٰسِخُونَ فِى ٱلْعِلْمِ مِنْهُمْ وَٱلْمُؤْمِنُونَ يُؤْمِنُونَ بِمَآ أُنزِلَ إِلَيْكَ وَمَآ أُنزِلَ مِن قَبْلِكَ وَٱلْمُقِيمِينَ ٱلصَّلَوٰةَ وَٱلْمُؤْتُونَ ٱلزَّكَوٰةَ وَٱلْمُؤْمِنُونَ بِٱللَّهِ وَٱلْيَوْمِ ٱلْءَاخِرِ أُو۟لَٰٓئِكَ سَنُؤْتِيهِمْ أَجْرًا عَظِيمًا ۝

---

^a When a group opts for a self-styled religion instead of the divine religion, it decides upon certain self-styled signs to show its religious status. According to the temperament and circumstances of its members, it formulates new rules about what is lawful and what is unlawful, and by sedulously observing them, it shows that it adheres to religion more than others do. The religion of such people is based on excessive care for certain outward forms, as opposed to paying proper attention to the spirit of the religion's rules. By fully observing the form they are completely satisfied that they have been following their religion to the letter. Such so-called adherents of religion are not afraid of deriving worldly benefits from the ways forbidden by God and they are not afraid of putting obstacles in the path of the divine caller. Such people will be bracketed with the patently irreligious, far from being grouped along with truly religious people.

There were certain people among the Jews, like 'Abdullah ibn Salam, who believed in the Prophet Muhammad and fully supported him. Those who are not caught up in human interpolations in their religion; who have discovered the original divine religion; who have risen above the mentality of prejudice, blind imitation of their community's ways and opportunism, find no obstacle to their recognizing the truth and surrendering themselves to it. They can see the truth despite all kinds of mental blocks. These are the people who will be ushered into the Paradise God has prepared for them.

163 We have sent revelation to you [Prophet] as We did to Noah and the prophets who came after him, to Abraham, Ishmael, Isaac, Jacob, and the Tribes, to Jesus, Job, Jonah, Aaron, and Solomon and David, to whom We gave the Psalms. 164 We have told you about some messengers sent previously, while We have not yet told you about others. God spoke to Moses directly. 165 They were messengers, bearing good news and giving warning, so that mankind would have no excuse before God, after the coming of the messengers. God is mighty, wise. [a]

۞ إِنَّآ أَوْحَيْنَآ إِلَيْكَ كَمَآ أَوْحَيْنَآ إِلَىٰ نُوحٍ وَٱلنَّبِيِّـۧنَ مِنۢ بَعْدِهِۦ ۚ وَأَوْحَيْنَآ إِلَىٰٓ إِبْرَٰهِيمَ وَإِسْمَٰعِيلَ وَإِسْحَٰقَ وَيَعْقُوبَ وَٱلْأَسْبَاطِ وَعِيسَىٰ وَأَيُّوبَ وَيُونُسَ وَهَٰرُونَ وَسُلَيْمَٰنَ ۚ وَءَاتَيْنَا دَاوُۥدَ زَبُورًا ۝ وَرُسُلًا قَدْ قَصَصْنَٰهُمْ عَلَيْكَ مِن قَبْلُ وَرُسُلًا لَّمْ نَقْصُصْهُمْ عَلَيْكَ ۚ وَكَلَّمَ ٱللَّهُ مُوسَىٰ تَكْلِيمًا ۝ رُّسُلًا مُّبَشِّرِينَ وَمُنذِرِينَ لِئَلَّا يَكُونَ لِلنَّاسِ عَلَى ٱللَّهِ حُجَّةٌۢ بَعْدَ ٱلرُّسُلِ ۚ وَكَانَ ٱللَّهُ عَزِيزًا حَكِيمًا ۝

a God created man, and then He created Paradise and Hell. Man was later settled on the earth. Here man has freedom to do as he wishes. But this freedom is not forever. It is temporary and meant for his trial. It is so that good and bad may be distinguished from one another. God is watching those who, despite being granted freedom, can adopt realistic attitudes, and surrender themselves to the will of God, and who are the people who misuse their freedom and prove themselves to be rebels. Both kinds of people have been mixed in this world. Both have equal opportunity to gain fully from the blessings of God. But, after the completion of the appointed time of trial, those groups will be separated from one another. The first group will be lodged in the Gardens of Paradise forever, while the second group will be consigned to Hell for all eternity.

This plan devised by God for human existence put man in an extremely delicate situation, for the outcome of his brief stay in this world was going to appear in one of two extreme forms—either eternal comfort or eternal chastisement. That is why, besides other natural arrangements for divine guidance, God also arranged to send to mankind His messengers and His Scriptures, so that no one should remain unaware of the reality of life. No one may then attempt to excuse his misconduct on the plea that he was not informed of the divine plan of how human beings were expected to lead their lives.

From start to finish, this divine plan necessitated all of the prophets bringing the same message and the same mission to mankind. For, when all human beings without exception are to be weighed in the divine scale, how could their 'test papers' be different from one another? The truth is that the message brought by all the prophets was one and the same and they communicated that same message to all human beings: that everyone is standing at a perilous watershed. On one side of it is Paradise and on the other is Hell. If one steps to one side, one will reach Paradise; if one steps to the other, one will fall into the gorge of Hell. All the prophets had this identical message.

¹⁶⁶ But God bears witness to what He has sent down to you. He has sent it down with His knowledge. The angels too bear witness. And God suffices as a witness. ¹⁶⁷ Those who are bent on denying the truth and on turning others away from the path of God have strayed far from the right path.ᵃ

لَّـٰكِنِ ٱللَّهُ يَشْهَدُ بِمَآ أَنزَلَ إِلَيْكَ أَنزَلَهُۥ بِعِلْمِهِۦ وَٱلْمَلَـٰٓئِكَةُ يَشْهَدُونَ وَكَفَىٰ بِٱللَّهِ شَهِيدًا ۞ إِنَّ ٱلَّذِينَ كَفَرُوا۟ وَصَدُّوا۟ عَن سَبِيلِ ٱللَّهِ قَدْ ضَلُّوا۟ ضَلَـٰلًۢا بَعِيدًا ۞

ᵃ However, according to the requirements of the age, different prophets received different kinds of succour from God. This is still how God functions, so that those of his servants who came forward to spread His message will likewise, according to their circumstances, receive special divine succour, in order that they may effectively continue to carry out their *dawah* responsibilities.

At the time when the Prophet Muhammad was chosen as a Messenger by God, the Jews enjoyed the status of representatives of the divine religion. For their part, they had supposed themselves to be the chosen people, the sole custodians of divine religion. As such, they occupied all the religious positions of honour. Not wishing to acknowledge any other's greatness save their own, they refused to believe that the Arab prophet had been sent by God to communicate His message to mankind. They thought that they had a monopoly over religion; that, if they did not testify to a person's being a representative of God, he would lack all credibility. They had forgotten that this was God's universe, its system tended by God's obedient angels. Thus the real validation comes from God, and is supported by the entire system of the universe. Indeed, it is God, with His entire universe, who supports His messenger, rather than someone's self-styled suppositions.

168 God will not forgive those who deny the truth and act wrongfully, nor will He guide them, 169 to any path other than the path of Hell, wherein they shall abide forever. That is easy enough for God. 170 Mankind! The Messenger has brought you the truth from your Lord, so believe for your own good. And if you deny the truth, know that to God belongs all that the heavens and the earth contain. God is all knowing and wise.[a]

إِنَّ ٱلَّذِينَ كَفَرُواْ وَظَلَمُواْ لَمْ يَكُنِ ٱللَّهُ لِيَغْفِرَ لَهُمْ وَلَا لِيَهْدِيَهُمْ طَرِيقًا ۝ إِلَّا طَرِيقَ جَهَنَّمَ خَالِدِينَ فِيهَآ أَبَدًا ۚ وَكَانَ ذَلِكَ عَلَى ٱللَّهِ يَسِيرًا ۝ يَأَيُّهَا ٱلنَّاسُ قَدْ جَآءَكُمُ ٱلرَّسُولُ بِٱلْحَقِّ مِن رَّبِّكُمْ فَـَٔامِنُواْ خَيْرًا لَّكُمْ ۚ وَإِن تَكْفُرُواْ فَإِنَّ لِلَّهِ مَا فِى ٱلسَّمَٰوَٰتِ وَٱلْأَرْضِ ۚ وَكَانَ ٱللَّهُ عَلِيمًا حَكِيمًا ۝

---

[a] Those who respond negatively to the call of God by ignoring and rejecting it show quite clearly that they have strayed far from true submission to God. They say such things as are refuted by the entire universe, and take up a position against a plan which is supported by the Lord of the universe. Obviously, there is no greater foolishness than this. Such perverse behaviour leads them into denying and rejecting God rather than acknowledging Him and submitting to Him. Day by day they are removed further away from the truth, until they ultimately fall into the pit of eternal damnation.

The denial of the call of God is the denial of oneself. The call of God is made in such clear terms that no one should find any difficulty in understanding it. Moreover, those who deny the call of God are, as it were, showing their audacity in the face of God Himself. Impudence and presumptuousness are the greatest crimes in the eyes of God.

If man were to keep the windows of his heart open, the divine call would appear to him an exact answer to his own quest. He would feel that the truth which had been veiled in human interpretations had been brought to him in its pure and original form by the arrangement of God Himself, and that it was an expression of God's own wisdom and knowledge rather than its being a matter of the personal ambition of a human being.

¹⁷¹ People of the Book! Do not go to extremes in your religion. Say nothing but the truth about God. The Christ Jesus, son of Mary, was only a messenger of God and His word, conveyed to Mary, a spirit from Him. So believe in God and His messengers and do not say: 'There are three [gods].' Desist, it will be better for you. Indeed, God is the one and only God. His Holiness is far above having a son. To Him belongs whatever is in the heavens and whatever is on the earth. And God is sufficient as a guardian.^a

يَـٰٓأَهْلَ ٱلْكِتَـٰبِ لَا تَغْلُوا۟ فِى دِينِكُمْ وَلَا تَقُولُوا۟ عَلَى ٱللَّهِ إِلَّا ٱلْحَقَّ إِنَّمَا ٱلْمَسِيحُ عِيسَى ٱبْنُ مَرْيَمَ رَسُولُ ٱللَّهِ وَكَلِمَتُهُۥٓ أَلْقَىٰهَآ إِلَىٰ مَرْيَمَ وَرُوحٌ مِّنْهُ فَـَٔامِنُوا۟ بِٱللَّهِ وَرُسُلِهِۦ وَلَا تَقُولُوا۟ ثَلَـٰثَةٌ ٱنتَهُوا۟ خَيْرًا لَّكُمْ إِنَّمَا ٱللَّهُ إِلَـٰهٌ وَٰحِدٌ سُبْحَـٰنَهُۥٓ أَن يَكُونَ لَهُۥ وَلَدٌ لَّهُۥ مَا فِى ٱلسَّمَـٰوَٰتِ وَمَا فِى ٱلْأَرْضِ وَكَفَىٰ بِٱللَّهِ وَكِيلًا

^a It is a human weakness to see any outstanding aspect in anything and then hold exaggerated views about it. This is exceeding the limits in determining its actual position. This is called excess. All forms of polytheism and personality cults are the result of committing this excess.

Exaggeration in religion means according an inflated status to things and personalities associated with the religion in question. The Quran enjoins us to keep everything in its proper place and to refrain from according a higher status to things and people than they actually deserve. Everything should be seen as it is, without the viewer indulging in excesses of any sort: for instance, calling a servant of God—created without a father—the son of God; or regarding someone to whom God has granted special honour and status as an extraordinary, infallible being. Similarly, if God enjoins one to abstain from the luxuries and glitter of the world, then taking this injunction on simple living to the extreme of renouncing the world is yet another form of excess.

Another form of excess is taking an injunction regarding some aspect of life and exaggerating it so greatly as to develop a full-fledged religious philosophy on its basis. All such forms in which a religious injunction or precept is elevated from its real position and accorded an excessively high status will bring about an exaggeration in religion.

¹⁷² Surely, the Messiah would never disdain to be accounted a servant of God. Nor would the angels who are nearest to Him. If any do disdain to worship Him, and grow arrogant, He will in any case gather them all before Him. ¹⁷³ Those who believe and do good works will be fully recompensed by Him. And He will give them yet more out of His bounty; and as for those who were disdainful and proud, He will punish them with a painful punishment. And they will not find anyone to help or protect them against God.^a ¹⁷⁴ Men, you have received clear evidence from your Lord. We have sent down a clear light to you.^b

لَن يَسْتَنكِفَ ٱلْمَسِيحُ أَن يَكُونَ عَبْدًا لِّلَّهِ وَلَا ٱلْمَلَـٰٓئِكَةُ ٱلْمُقَرَّبُونَ وَمَن يَسْتَنكِفْ عَنْ عِبَادَتِهِ وَيَسْتَكْبِرْ فَسَيَحْشُرُهُمْ إِلَيْهِ جَمِيعًا ۞ فَأَمَّا ٱلَّذِينَ ءَامَنُوا۟ وَعَمِلُوا۟ ٱلصَّـٰلِحَـٰتِ فَيُوَفِّيهِمْ أُجُورَهُمْ وَيَزِيدُهُم مِّن فَضْلِهِ ۖ وَأَمَّا ٱلَّذِينَ ٱسْتَنكَفُوا۟ وَٱسْتَكْبَرُوا۟ فَيُعَذِّبُهُمْ عَذَابًا أَلِيمًا وَلَا يَجِدُونَ لَهُم مِّن دُونِ ٱللَّهِ وَلِيًّا وَلَا نَصِيرًا ۞ يَـٰٓأَيُّهَا ٱلنَّاسُ قَدْ جَآءَكُم بُرْهَـٰنٌ مِّن رَّبِّكُمْ وَأَنزَلْنَآ إِلَيْكُمْ نُورًا مُّبِينًا ۞

---

^a God alone possesses all power. All human beings are His helpless servants. By scaling the heights of awareness, man discovers that God is all powerful and man is quite powerless. Prophets and angels have reached the highest stage of such awareness. That is why their realization of God's greatness and powerfulness and of their own helplessness surpasses that of all others. The real test of man lies in his ability to acknowledge this. One who has realized his own helplessness has, in essence, found out how he relates to God.

The aware person is one who has eyes: he will reach his destination successfully. The unaware person is one who is blind. He will wander around going astray until he falls into the pit of abomination.

^b When a divine call is made to human beings, it is so loud and clear that it amounts to wiping out darkness and illuminating life's realities to the ultimate extent. It comes so well fortified with arguments that it is not possible to deny it. The deniers may ridicule it, but they cannot counter it with logic. When God makes the sun rise, light and darkness are separated from one another. This divine power is expressed in the call of truth also. After this divine call, truth and untruth are so clearly separated from one another that no one in his senses finds it difficult to understand. However, in order to see the sun, man has to open his eyes. Similarly, to receive guidance from the divine call, it is necessary to pay full attention to it. One who does not pay heed will remain deprived of it, even as the divine call is being made.

175 As for those who believe in God and hold fast to Him, He will admit them to His mercy and His grace; He will guide them towards Him on a straight path.[a] 176 They ask you for instruction. Say, 'God instructs you concerning the indirect heirs. If a person dies childless but has a sister, she receives half of what he leaves, and he is her heir if she dies childless. If there are two sisters, they receive two-thirds of what he leaves. If there are brothers and sisters, the share of each male shall be that of two females. God makes things clear to you, so that you will not go astray. God has knowledge of all things.'[b]

فَأَمَّا ٱلَّذِينَ ءَامَنُوا۟ بِٱللَّهِ وَٱعْتَصَمُوا۟ بِهِۦ فَسَيُدْخِلُهُمْ فِى رَحْمَةٍ مِّنْهُ وَفَضْلٍ وَيَهْدِيهِمْ إِلَيْهِ صِرَٰطًا مُّسْتَقِيمًا ۝ يَسْتَفْتُونَكَ قُلِ ٱللَّهُ يُفْتِيكُمْ فِى ٱلْكَلَٰلَةِ إِنِ ٱمْرُؤٌا۟ هَلَكَ لَيْسَ لَهُۥ وَلَدٌ وَلَهُۥٓ أُخْتٌ فَلَهَا نِصْفُ مَا تَرَكَ وَهُوَ يَرِثُهَآ إِن لَّمْ يَكُن لَّهَا وَلَدٌ فَإِن كَانَتَا ٱثْنَتَيْنِ فَلَهُمَا ٱلثُّلُثَانِ مِمَّا تَرَكَ وَإِن كَانُوٓا۟ إِخْوَةً رِّجَالًا وَنِسَآءً فَلِلذَّكَرِ مِثْلُ حَظِّ ٱلْأُنثَيَيْنِ يُبَيِّنُ ٱللَّهُ لَكُمْ أَن تَضِلُّوا۟ وَٱللَّهُ بِكُلِّ شَىْءٍ عَلِيمٌۢ ۝

---

[a] It is also necessary to hold on firmly to the truth. Because in this world of trial Satan is pursuing man and, by deceiving him in many ways, keeps turning him away from the Truth. If man does not resolve to support the truth by fighting Satan's deceptions, then certainly Satan will be able to induce him to enter his fold. However, in this world of trial man is not left all alone. Those who wish to tread the divine path will receive divine guidance at every turn. By the help of God they will succeed in reaching their destination. When man gives all importance to the Truth alone, by the blessing of God this ability to persevere on the straight path of pure truth is engendered within him. He is thus saved from deviating to other paths that will lead him astray.

[b] Giving the injunction regarding inheritance the Quran states, 'God makes things clear to you so that you will not go astray.' This shows that inheritance is not a simple matter. This is one of those areas in which disobeying the divine injunction will lead you astray from the straight and narrow path of guidance.

5. THE TABLE

In the name of God,
the Most Gracious, the Most Merciful

¹ Believers, fulfill your obligations. All livestock is lawful for you, other than that which is hereby announced to you. You are forbidden to kill game while you are on a pilgrimage— God commands what He will.ᵃ

يَـٰٓأَيُّهَا ٱلَّذِينَ ءَامَنُوٓاْ أَوْفُواْ بِٱلْعُقُودِ أُحِلَّتْ لَكُم بَهِيمَةُ ٱلْأَنْعَـٰمِ إِلَّا مَا يُتْلَىٰ عَلَيْكُمْ غَيْرَ مُحِلِّى ٱلصَّيْدِ وَأَنتُمْ حُرُمٌ إِنَّ ٱللَّهَ يَحْكُمُ مَا يُرِيدُ ١

ᵃ A believer's life is a regulated life. Although he is free in the world to do whatever he likes, in spite of this, he admits the supremacy and Lordship of God and makes himself subject to regulation. Of his own he ties himself in the bondage of a vow. In the matter of God or His subjects he has taken it upon himself not to act independently but according to God's commandments. He should have as food only those things that God has permitted and give up eating those things which God has forbidden. If on some occasions even permitted things are forbidden, as is evident from orders applicable while in the state of *ihram* or during sacred months, he should willingly accept this. If something becomes the symbol of some religious reality, then it should be respected, because respecting such a thing is equivalent to respecting religion itself. And all this should be done out of fear of God and for no other reason.

² Believers, violate neither the sanctity of God's signs, the Sacred Month, the sacrificial animals, the animals wearing garlands [indicating they are to be sacrificed] nor those on their way to the Sacred House seeking the bounty and pleasure of their Lord. When, on completion of your pilgrimage, you take off the garb of the pilgrim, you may hunt. Do not let the enmity of those who barred you from the Sacred Mosque lead you into sin. Help one another in goodness and in piety. Do not help one another in sin and transgression. Fear God! God is severe in punishment.[a]

يَـٰٓأَيُّهَا ٱلَّذِينَ ءَامَنُوا۟ لَا تُحِلُّوا۟ شَعَـٰٓئِرَ ٱللَّهِ وَلَا ٱلشَّهْرَ ٱلْحَرَامَ وَلَا ٱلْهَدْىَ وَلَا ٱلْقَلَـٰٓئِدَ وَلَآ ءَآمِّينَ ٱلْبَيْتَ ٱلْحَرَامَ يَبْتَغُونَ فَضْلًا مِّن رَّبِّهِمْ وَرِضْوَٰنًا ۚ وَإِذَا حَلَلْتُمْ فَٱصْطَادُوا۟ ۚ وَلَا يَجْرِمَنَّكُمْ شَنَـَٔانُ قَوْمٍ أَن صَدُّوكُمْ عَنِ ٱلْمَسْجِدِ ٱلْحَرَامِ أَن تَعْتَدُوا۟ ۘ وَتَعَاوَنُوا۟ عَلَى ٱلْبِرِّ وَٱلتَّقْوَىٰ ۖ وَلَا تَعَاوَنُوا۟ عَلَى ٱلْإِثْمِ وَٱلْعُدْوَٰنِ ۚ وَٱتَّقُوا۟ ٱللَّهَ ۖ إِنَّ ٱللَّهَ شَدِيدُ ٱلْعِقَابِ ۝

[a] In normal circumstances, man carries out God's commands. But under extraordinary circumstances, he becomes a different man. For example, the occasion arises when somebody's opposition irritates him. Then one who seemed to fear God in normal circumstances, suddenly changed into one who is fearless of God. Then man forgets the limits of justice and wants to degrade and defeat his opponent in whatever way possible. But this type of revengeful, inimical action is not legitimate in the eyes of God, even if it were in retaliation for being prevented from performing the pilgrimage to the Sacred Mosque in Makkah. If others co-opearate with one who indulges in such oppressive activity this will amount to helping in the commission of a sin. Those who fear God will support others only in righteous deeds. It is the most difficult task in the present world to support those who are on the right path and ignore those who are not on the right path as they have all the wordly glories by their side. But it is by virtue of man's success in this very task that his fate will be decided.

3 You are forbidden carrion, blood and pork; and any flesh over which the name of any other than God is invoked; and any creature which has been strangled, or killed by a blow or in a fall, or has been gored to death or half-eaten by a wild animal, saving that which you make lawful [by slaughtering properly while it was still alive] and what has been slaughtered at an altar. You are forbidden to make the division of [meat] by means of divining arrows: that is sinful conduct. Those who deny the truth have this day despaired of ever harming your religion. So do not fear them. Fear Me. Today I have completed your religion for you and completed My blessing upon you. I have chosen for you Islam as your religion. But if anyone is forced by hunger to eat something which is forbidden, not intending to commit a sin, he will find God forgiving and merciful.[a]

حُرِّمَتْ عَلَيْكُمُ ٱلْمَيْتَةُ وَٱلدَّمُ وَلَحْمُ ٱلْخِنزِيرِ وَمَآ أُهِلَّ لِغَيْرِ ٱللَّهِ بِهِۦ وَٱلْمُنْخَنِقَةُ وَٱلْمَوْقُوذَةُ وَٱلْمُتَرَدِّيَةُ وَٱلنَّطِيحَةُ وَمَآ أَكَلَ ٱلسَّبُعُ إِلَّا مَا ذَكَّيْتُمْ وَمَا ذُبِحَ عَلَى ٱلنُّصُبِ وَأَن تَسْتَقْسِمُوا۟ بِٱلْأَزْلَٰمِ ذَٰلِكُمْ فِسْقٌ ٱلْيَوْمَ يَئِسَ ٱلَّذِينَ كَفَرُوا۟ مِن دِينِكُمْ فَلَا تَخْشَوْهُمْ وَٱخْشَوْنِ ٱلْيَوْمَ أَكْمَلْتُ لَكُمْ دِينَكُمْ وَأَتْمَمْتُ عَلَيْكُمْ نِعْمَتِى وَرَضِيتُ لَكُمُ ٱلْإِسْلَٰمَ دِينًا فَمَنِ ٱضْطُرَّ فِى مَخْمَصَةٍ غَيْرَ مُتَجَانِفٍ لِّإِثْمٍ فَإِنَّ ٱللَّهَ غَفُورٌ رَّحِيمٌ ۝

[a] Some animals, due to their being harmful from the point of view of health and morality, are not fit to be consumed by human beings as food. That is the sole reason for Almighty God having forbidden pork. Similarly, there are many things in the body of an animal besides its flesh that are not fit to be eaten. Blood is one of these. Accordingly, in Islam a certain method of slaughtering an animal (dhabh) is prescribed in order to ensure that after slaughtering all of the animal's blood oozes out. In other methods of killing an animal, except dhabh, the blood of the animal remains absorbed in its flesh and does not get fully separated. For the same reason, in the Islamic law, the consumption of all types of dead animals is also forbidden, because the blood of a dead animal immediately gets absorbed in its flesh. Similarly, meat that is somehow polluted by polytheistic belief is forbidden; for example, the meat of an animal slaughtered by invoking any name other than that of God or the meat of animals in order to attain nearness to (or to appease) anybody other than God. However, God by His special grace has made the allowance that any starving person who has to choose between death and taking forbidden food may opt for the latter. ►

4 If they ask you what has been made lawful for them, say, 'All good things have been made lawful for you;' and what you have taught your birds and beasts of prey to catch, training them as God has taught you. So eat what they catch for you, but first pronounce God's name over it. Fear God, for God is swift in taking account.[a]

يَسۡـَٔلُونَكَ مَاذَآ أُحِلَّ لَهُمۡ قُلۡ أُحِلَّ لَكُمُ ٱلطَّيِّبَـٰتُ وَمَا عَلَّمۡتُم مِّنَ ٱلۡجَوَارِحِ مُكَلِّبِينَ تُعَلِّمُونَهُنَّ مِمَّا عَلَّمَكُمُ ٱللَّهُ فَكُلُوا۟ مِمَّآ أَمۡسَكۡنَ عَلَيۡكُمۡ وَٱذۡكُرُوا۟ ٱسۡمَ ٱللَّهِ عَلَيۡهِ وَٱتَّقُوا۟ ٱللَّهَ إِنَّ ٱللَّهَ سَرِيعُ ٱلۡحِسَابِ ۝

'Today I have perfected your religion for you' i.e. the commandments that were to be given to you have all been given. Whatever was destined to be sent to you has all been sent. Here there is no mention about the perfection of religion in the absolute sense; it is only a declaration of the completion of the process of revelation of the Quran which was started earlier. This mentions the completion of revelation and that of the religion. Therefore, the wording is not 'Today I have perfected the religion,' but rather 'Today I have completed your religion for you.' The fact is that the religion of God was given to man in every period in perfect form. God has never sent imperfect religion to man.

God has put the people following the Quran on such a firm footing that by virtue of their latent potential they have gone beyond the reach of any external danger. Now if that community comes to any harm, it will be due to its internal weaknesses and not due to any external attacks. And the greatest guarantee of being free from internal weaknesses is that its members should have fear of God at heart.

[a] All those things which are considered clean and perfectly formed in the eyes of nature, and all those animals whose nature is compatible with human nature, are all legitimate and permissible for human consumption. This is subject to the condition that for any external reason they have not developed any defect from the viewpoint of health or in the light of the Islamic law. However, the human mind is not capable of properly applying this principle. Therefore, the principle has been set forth along with its correct application. Hunting by a trained hunting animal is permissible because he catches the hunted animals on behalf of his master. In other words, he has learnt man's nature. Such an animal, so to say, has become a substitute for man.

⁵Today, all good things have been made lawful to you. The food of the People of the Book is lawful to you, and your food is lawful to them. The chaste believing women and the chaste women of the people who were given the Book before you, are lawful to you, provided that you give them their dowers, and marry them, neither committing fornication nor taking them as mistresses. The deeds of anyone who rejects the faith will come to nothing, and in the Hereafter he will be among the losers.[a]

اَلْيَوْمَ أُحِلَّ لَكُمُ الطَّيِّبَٰتُ وَطَعَامُ الَّذِينَ أُوتُوا الْكِتَٰبَ حِلٌّ لَّكُمْ وَطَعَامُكُمْ حِلٌّ لَّهُمْ وَالْمُحْصَنَٰتُ مِنَ الْمُؤْمِنَٰتِ وَالْمُحْصَنَٰتُ مِنَ الَّذِينَ أُوتُوا الْكِتَٰبَ مِن قَبْلِكُمْ إِذَآ ءَاتَيْتُمُوهُنَّ أُجُورَهُنَّ مُحْصِنِينَ غَيْرَ مُسَٰفِحِينَ وَلَا مُتَّخِذِىٓ أَخْدَانٍ وَمَن يَكْفُرْ بِالْإِيمَٰنِ فَقَدْ حَبِطَ عَمَلُهُ وَهُوَ فِى الْءَاخِرَةِ مِنَ الْخَٰسِرِينَ ۞

[a] However elaborate the Law relating to forbidden and permissible things is made, it is finally man's intention which debars him from certain things and leads him towards certain others. It is not the provisions of Law that act as a watchdog but man himself. If a man himself is not so inclined, then in spite of accepting the Law, he will try to find ways to escape its provisions. It is only the fear of God which compels a man to give proper regard to the Law in its true spirit. That is why it has been said while explaining the Law relating to prohibitions and permissions: 'Fear God, for God is swift in taking account.'

It is not ever permissible for a Muslim woman to marry a non-Muslim man. But Muslim males have been permitted, subject to certain special conditions to marry women belonging to communities, who are in possession of the Holy scriptures. The wisdom underlying this provision is that a woman is by nature easily influenced. It may be expected of her that once she enters marital life, she may be influenced by her Muslim husband and Muslim society, and thus her marriage may become a starting point for her entry into Islam. (See also note on 2:221).

'The deeds of anyone who rejects the faith will come to nothing' i.e. without Faith, good deeds have no reality or value. A good deed is that which is performed for the sake of God. A deed which is not for the sake of God is actually for one's own self. Why would God give any value to a deed done for one's own self?

6 Believers, when you rise to pray, wash your faces and your hands up to the elbows and wipe your heads and [wash] your feet up to the ankles. If you are in a state of impurity, take a full bath. But if you are sick or on a journey or when you have just relieved yourselves, or you have consorted with your spouses, you can find no water, take some clean sand and rub your faces and hands with it. God does not wish to place any burden on you; He only wishes to purify you and perfect His favour to you, in order that you may be grateful.[a]

يَـٰٓأَيُّهَا ٱلَّذِينَ ءَامَنُوٓاْ إِذَا قُمْتُمْ إِلَى ٱلصَّلَوٰةِ فَٱغْسِلُواْ وُجُوهَكُمْ وَأَيْدِيَكُمْ إِلَى ٱلْمَرَافِقِ وَٱمْسَحُواْ بِرُءُوسِكُمْ وَأَرْجُلَكُمْ إِلَى ٱلْكَعْبَيْنِ ۚ وَإِن كُنتُمْ جُنُبًا فَٱطَّهَّرُواْ ۚ وَإِن كُنتُم مَّرْضَىٰٓ أَوْ عَلَىٰ سَفَرٍ أَوْ جَآءَ أَحَدٌ مِّنكُم مِّنَ ٱلْغَآئِطِ أَوْ لَـٰمَسْتُمُ ٱلنِّسَآءَ فَلَمْ تَجِدُواْ مَآءً فَتَيَمَّمُواْ صَعِيدًا طَيِّبًا فَٱمْسَحُواْ بِوُجُوهِكُمْ وَأَيْدِيكُم مِّنْهُ ۚ مَا يُرِيدُ ٱللَّهُ لِيَجْعَلَ عَلَيْكُم مِّنْ حَرَجٍ وَلَـٰكِن يُرِيدُ لِيُطَهِّرَكُمْ وَلِيُتِمَّ نِعْمَتَهُۥ عَلَيْكُمْ لَعَلَّكُمْ تَشْكُرُونَ ۝

[a] The purpose of *salat* (prayers) is to purify a man of all evils. Ablution, or *wudu*, is the preparation of the body for this religious rite. When a man intends to offer prayers, he first goes in search of water. Water is a great gift of God which is the best thing for washing all the impurities out of man. Similarly, *salat* is a 'divine spring' in which a man bathes and purifies himself of evil emotions and vicious thoughts.

Initiating the process of ablution (*wudu*) when a man puts water on his hands, he is, in effect, praying, 'O, God! Save these hands of mine from indulging in evil, and let whatever evil deeds I have indulged in through them be washed off.' Then he rinses his mouth and washes his face. At that time his soul prays silently, 'O, God! Kindly remove the bad effects of any improper food I have put in my mouth; the evil words I have uttered, and the evil things I have seen.' Thereafter, when he takes water in his hands and massages his head with his hands, his whole existence is moulded by the prayers, 'O, God! Wash away the bad effects of the evil ideas conceived by my mind and wrong plans devised by me, and cleanse and purify my mind.' When he washes his feet, this action of his becomes the entreaty before his Lord, that He may cleanse his feet of the dust of evil and make them (his feet) never tread any path except the path of righteousness and justice. In this way, the whole process of ablution assumes, so to say, the practical shape of the prayer, 'O, God! Make me a person who turns away from wrongs and one who keeps himself clear of evils.' ▶

7 Remember God's favour to you, and the covenant, which He made with you when you said, 'We hear and we obey.' Fear God. God has full knowledge of the innermost thoughts of men. 8 Believers, be steadfast in the cause of God and bear witness with justice. Do not let your enmity for others turn you away from justice. Deal justly; that is nearer to being God-fearing. Fear God. God is aware of all that you do.[a]

وَٱذْكُرُوا۟ نِعْمَةَ ٱللَّهِ عَلَيْكُمْ وَمِيثَٰقَهُ ٱلَّذِى وَاثَقَكُم بِهِۦٓ إِذْ قُلْتُمْ سَمِعْنَا وَأَطَعْنَا ۖ وَٱتَّقُوا۟ ٱللَّهَ ۚ إِنَّ ٱللَّهَ عَلِيمٌۢ بِذَاتِ ٱلصُّدُورِ ﴿٧﴾ يَٰٓأَيُّهَا ٱلَّذِينَ ءَامَنُوا۟ كُونُوا۟ قَوَّٰمِينَ لِلَّهِ شُهَدَآءَ بِٱلْقِسْطِ ۖ وَلَا يَجْرِمَنَّكُمْ شَنَـَٔانُ قَوْمٍ عَلَىٰٓ أَلَّا تَعْدِلُوا۟ ۚ ٱعْدِلُوا۟ هُوَ أَقْرَبُ لِلتَّقْوَىٰ ۖ وَٱتَّقُوا۟ ٱللَّهَ ۚ إِنَّ ٱللَّهَ خَبِيرٌۢ بِمَا تَعْمَلُونَ ﴿٨﴾

In normal circumstances, ablution is enough to create feelings of cleanliness in man, but the state of impurity (resulting from sex) is an extraordinary condition. So, in this state, washing of the whole body (ghusl) has been prescribed. However, God does not like to cause his subjects any unnecessary hardship. Therefore, in case of any practical difficulties in taking a full bath, dry ablution (tayammum) has been declared as sufficient to revive the feeling of cleanliness. The simplicity of the methods prescribed for ablution and bathing is a great blessing of God. In this way physical cleanliness is linked with purity under the Islamic law. In case of any difficulties, permission for dry ablution is an additional blessing, because this saves one from the excesses of which many other religions suffered.

[a] Faith is the vow which binds God and His subject. The subject vows that he will remain God-fearing in his life in this world, and God guarantees that He will be His subject's guardian in this world and in the Hereafter. God's subject has to prove his fulfillment of his vow in two ways. First, he should become steadfast on the path of God. On every occasion his lifestyle should give the response which is expected of a subject to his Lord. When he observes the universe, his mind should be filled with the realisation of God's glories and powers. When he looks at himself, he should realise that his existence is entirely due to God's grace and His mercy. If his emotions erupt, they should erupt for the sake of God. If his attention is focused on anybody, it should be on God. His love should be for God. His fears should be linked with God. The remembrance of God should be uppermost in his mind. He should be given to prayer and obedience to God, and should spend his assets for the cause of God. In devoting his life to God, he should feel pleasure. ▶

⁹ God has promised those who believe and do good deeds forgiveness and a great reward; ¹⁰ but those who deny the truth and deny Our signs are destined for Hell. ¹¹ Believers, remember the blessings which God bestowed upon you when a certain people were about to lay hands on you and He held back their hands from you. Have fear of God and in God let the believers place their trust.

¹² God made a covenant with the Children of Israel; and raised among them twelve leaders. God said, 'Surely, I am with you. If you attend to your prayers and pay the alms and believe in My messengers and support them, and give a generous loan to God, I will certainly forgive you your sins and admit you into Gardens through which rivers flow. Whoever among you denies the truth after this shall go astray from the straight path.'ᵃ

وَعَدَ ٱللَّهُ ٱلَّذِينَ ءَامَنُوا۟ وَعَمِلُوا۟ ٱلصَّٰلِحَٰتِ هُم مَّغْفِرَةٌ وَأَجْرٌ عَظِيمٌ ۝ وَٱلَّذِينَ كَفَرُوا۟ وَكَذَّبُوا۟ بِـَٔايَٰتِنَا أُو۟لَٰٓئِكَ أَصْحَٰبُ ٱلْجَحِيمِ ۝ يَٰٓأَيُّهَا ٱلَّذِينَ ءَامَنُوا۟ ٱذْكُرُوا۟ نِعْمَتَ ٱللَّهِ عَلَيْكُمْ إِذْ هَمَّ قَوْمٌ أَن يَبْسُطُوٓا۟ إِلَيْكُمْ أَيْدِيَهُمْ فَكَفَّ أَيْدِيَهُمْ عَنكُمْ وَٱتَّقُوا۟ ٱللَّهَ وَعَلَى ٱللَّهِ فَلْيَتَوَكَّلِ ٱلْمُؤْمِنُونَ ۝ ۞ وَلَقَدْ أَخَذَ ٱللَّهُ مِيثَٰقَ بَنِىٓ إِسْرَٰٓءِيلَ وَبَعَثْنَا مِنْهُمُ ٱثْنَىْ عَشَرَ نَقِيبًا وَقَالَ ٱللَّهُ إِنِّى مَعَكُمْ لَئِنْ أَقَمْتُمُ ٱلصَّلَوٰةَ وَءَاتَيْتُمُ ٱلزَّكَوٰةَ وَءَامَنتُم بِرُسُلِى وَعَزَّرْتُمُوهُمْ وَأَقْرَضْتُمُ ٱللَّهَ قَرْضًا حَسَنًا لَّأُكَفِّرَنَّ عَنكُمْ سَيِّـَٔاتِكُمْ وَلَأُدْخِلَنَّكُمْ جَنَّٰتٍ تَجْرِى مِن تَحْتِهَا ٱلْأَنْهَٰرُ فَمَن كَفَرَ بَعْدَ ذَٰلِكَ مِنكُمْ فَقَدْ ضَلَّ سَوَآءَ ٱلسَّبِيلِ ۝

The second condition for the fulfillment of the vow of God's subject is that his dealings with his fellow-beings should be based on justice and fair play. Justice means meting out to a person that treatment which he actually deserves—no more and no less. In his dealings he should follow the dictates of justice and not his desires. He should be bound by this principle to the extent that he should adhere to justice even when dealing with his enemies; even when grievances and bitter memories are apt to divert him from the path of justice.

ᵃ In the world, God makes His appearance felt through symbols, i.e. in the shape of such arguments as cannot be contradicted by man. When an argument of God is presented to a man and he indulges in verbal jugglery instead of accepting it, this amounts to denying the signs of God. Such people will receive severe punishment at God's behest. And those who accept the argument will deserve a reward from God.

13 Since they broke their solemn pledge, We laid on them Our curse and hardened their hearts. They distorted the meaning of the revealed words, taking them out of their context, and forgot much of what they were enjoined. You will constantly discover treachery on their part, except for a few of them. But pardon them, and bear with them; truly, God loves the doers of good.[a]

فِيمَا نَقْضِهِم مِّيثَـٰقَهُمْ لَعَنَّـٰهُمْ وَجَعَلْنَا قُلُوبَهُمْ قَـٰسِيَةً يُحَرِّفُونَ ٱلْكَلِمَ عَن مَّوَاضِعِهِ وَنَسُواْ حَظًّا مِّمَّا ذُكِّرُواْ بِهِۦ وَلَا تَزَالُ تَطَّلِعُ عَلَىٰ خَآئِنَةٍ مِّنْهُمْ إِلَّا قَلِيلًا مِّنْهُمْ فَٱعْفُ عَنْهُمْ وَٱصْفَحْ إِنَّ ٱللَّهَ يُحِبُّ ٱلْمُحْسِنِينَ

---

[a] A pledge was taken from the Children of Israel by their prophet that they would lead a godly life, and twelve chiefs from their twelve tribes were appointed to keep a watch over them. The pledge taken from the Children of Israel was that they would make themselves godly by offering *salat* (prayers); that they would discharge the rights of others in the shape of *zakat* (obligatory alms-giving); align themselves on the side of God by supporting His prophets; and spend their assets in support of the struggle for the religion of God. It was only after undertaking all this and after establishing a collective system among themselves for ensuring the continued fulfillment of these duties that they were entitled to God's company and support, and entitled to enter the aesthetic atmosphere of paradise, after being purified. One attains paradise by the performance of good deeds and not due to any racial relationship.

The requirements mentioned in this pledge are the very same basic requirements of religion. This is the highway which leads all human beings towards God and His paradise. But when the communities blessed with Divine Scriptures go astray, they turn to the right or left of this highway. Now, it happens that with the help of self-made interpretations the concepts of religion are changed. In the name of ceremonial prayers irrelevant discussions are started. Ways of salvation which are supposed to lead a man to his destination without discharging the claims or rights of his fellowmen, are sought. In the name of the call for truth, meaningless worldly activities find favour with such communities. They devise various means of justifying worldly expenditure. In other words, they concoct a religion of their own, keeping purely worldly considerations in view, and start calling it the religion of God. Once a group reaches this stage in its wrong-doing, God withdraws His attention from it. Deprived of Divine guidance, such people reach the stage where they understand only the language of their base desires and remain preoccupied with satisfying their desires, until the angel of death approaches in order to catch hold of them and take them to the court of God.

14 We also made a covenant with those who say, 'We are Christians.' But they too have forgotten much of what they were enjoined. So, We have put enmity and hatred between them till the Day of Judgement; and soon God will declare to them what they have been doing.[a]

وَمِنَ ٱلَّذِينَ قَالُوٓاْ إِنَّا نَصَٰرَىٰٓ أَخَذْنَا مِيثَٰقَهُمْ فَنَسُواْ حَظًّا مِّمَّا ذُكِّرُواْ بِهِۦ فَأَغْرَيْنَا بَيْنَهُمُ ٱلْعَدَاوَةَ وَٱلْبَغْضَآءَ إِلَىٰ يَوْمِ ٱلْقِيَٰمَةِ وَسَوْفَ يُنَبِّئُهُمُ ٱللَّهُ بِمَا كَانُواْ يَصْنَعُونَ ١٤

---

[a] When The People of the Book (i.e. those communities blessed with Divine Scriptures) go astray, they disregard the clear-cut, eternal parts of the Scriptures and hasten to embrace those parts which are of purely local or topical interest. This leads to conflict and results in degradation in the Hereafter.

Whenever such groups leave the right path, infirmities become apparent. They start adopting a religion of their own imagining, casting aside their time-honoured authentic religion. Dissatisfied with the clear commandments given by God and His prophets on religious laws, spirituality and politics, they delve into them to find new points of contention. This opens up the door to differences and sectarianism. Sometimes, to justify worldly desires, sometimes to perfect the 'imperfect' religion of God, sometimes just to move with the times, dissatisfied elements introduce new elements into religion which are not really part of it. In this way, different new editions of religion take shape—some spiritual, some political, and so on. Around each one of them, like-minded persons start gathering and finally they form a sect. Succeeding generations start protecting this new version, treating it as if it were the heritage of their forefathers. A stage comes when it will clearly be perpetuated until Doomsday, because man tends to treat the past as sacred, and once something is sanctified by time and tradition, it takes on an aura of being eternal.

Sectarianism in the name of religion on the one hand becomes sacred and eternal and on the other comes to be regarded as God's command and gives licence for harbouring hatred and indulging in violence against others.

¹⁵ People of the Book! Our Messenger has come to make clear to you much of what you have hidden of the Scriptures and to forgive you much. A light has now come to you from God and a clear Book, ¹⁶ whereby God guides to the ways of peace all who seek His good pleasure, bringing them from darkness to the light, by His will, and guiding them to a straight path.ᵃ

يَـٰٓأَهْلَ ٱلْكِتَـٰبِ قَدْ جَآءَكُمْ رَسُولُنَا يُبَيِّنُ لَكُمْ كَثِيرًا مِّمَّا كُنتُمْ تُخْفُونَ مِنَ ٱلْكِتَـٰبِ وَيَعْفُواْ عَن كَثِيرٍ قَدْ جَآءَكُم مِّنَ ٱللَّهِ نُورٌ وَكِتَـٰبٌ مُّبِينٌ ۝ يَهْدِى بِهِ ٱللَّهُ مَنِ ٱتَّبَعَ رِضْوَٰنَهُۥ سُبُلَ ٱلسَّلَـٰمِ وَيُخْرِجُهُم مِّنَ ٱلظُّلُمَـٰتِ إِلَى ٱلنُّورِ بِإِذْنِهِۦ وَيَهْدِيهِمْ إِلَىٰ صِرَٰطٍ مُّسْتَقِيمٍ ۝

ᵃ The People of the Book made two mistakes in their religion. One is that they omitted some teachings from it by means either of deliberate misinterpretation or distortion. For instance, they made certain changes in their Book obviating the necessity to accept any further prophet for their salvation; their attachment to the religion of their forfathers was considered enough for their salvation. The other mistake which they made in the name of religion, was that they imposed upon themselves restrictions which had not been ordained by God: for example, the petty rites of sacrifice, which were not commanded by their prophets, but which were concocted by their scholars by means of their hair-splitting interpretations. The Quran came to them as a blessing. It revived or renewed their Divine religion, when they had been groping in the darkness on a path which they deludedly thought was leading them towards paradise, when it was actually taking them towards the wrath of God. The Quran pulled them out of this darkness. On the one hand, the Quran presented their lost teachings in their original form, and on the other hand, liberated them from the unnecessary religious restrictions by which they had shackled themselves. Now those who obey and follow their desires will remain groping in the dark, and those who seek the pleasure of God, will find the right path. With the help of God's guidance, they will be successful in pulling themselves out of darkness and enter the brightness of light. The fact of Truth being Truth and falsehood being falsehood is clarified perfectly, but it is always in terms of reasoning, and reasoning appeals to the minds of only those people who keep their minds open.

The false deities (other than the one and only God) set up by human beings are such that they are not capable of creating or destroying anything by themselves. This fact is in itself enough to establish that there is no deity except the one and only God. How can beings that have no powers over creation and death be God?

¹⁷ In blasphemy indeed are those who say, 'God is Christ, the son of Mary.' Say, 'Who then could prevent God if He so willed from destroying Christ, son of Mary, and his mother and everyone on earth? The kingdom of the heavens and the earth and everything between them belong to God. He creates what He will and God has power over all things.' ¹⁸ The Jews and the Christians say, 'We are the children of God and His beloved ones.' Say, 'Then why does He punish you for your sins? Indeed, you are but human beings among those He has created. He forgives whom He pleases and punishes whom He pleases. The kingdom of the heavens and the earth and all that is between them, belong to God and all shall return to Him.'ᵃ

لَّقَدْ كَفَرَ ٱلَّذِينَ قَالُوٓاْ إِنَّ ٱللَّهَ هُوَ ٱلْمَسِيحُ ٱبْنُ مَرْيَمَ قُلْ فَمَن يَمْلِكُ مِنَ ٱللَّهِ شَيْئًا إِنْ أَرَادَ أَن يُهْلِكَ ٱلْمَسِيحَ ٱبْنَ مَرْيَمَ وَأُمَّهُۥ وَمَن فِى ٱلْأَرْضِ جَمِيعًا وَلِلَّهِ مُلْكُ ٱلسَّمَٰوَٰتِ وَٱلْأَرْضِ وَمَا بَيْنَهُمَا يَخْلُقُ مَا يَشَآءُ وَٱللَّهُ عَلَىٰ كُلِّ شَىْءٍ قَدِيرٌ ۝ وَقَالَتِ ٱلْيَهُودُ وَٱلنَّصَٰرَىٰ نَحْنُ أَبْنَٰٓؤُاْ ٱللَّهِ وَأَحِبَّٰٓؤُهُۥ قُلْ فَلِمَ يُعَذِّبُكُم بِذُنُوبِكُم بَلْ أَنتُم بَشَرٌ مِّمَّنْ خَلَقَ يَغْفِرُ لِمَن يَشَآءُ وَيُعَذِّبُ مَن يَشَآءُ وَلِلَّهِ مُلْكُ ٱلسَّمَٰوَٰتِ وَٱلْأَرْضِ وَمَا بَيْنَهُمَا وَإِلَيْهِ ٱلْمَصِيرُ ۝

ᵃ A community which is blessed with the Book and a prophet, and proves that it accepts them, receives many blessings from God—special help and victory over opponents; domination on the earth; God's pardon and the promise of paradise, etc. In the case of the earlier generations of a community, this is a reward for their actions; they surrendered their existence to God, therefore, God blessed them with His bounties. However, in the case of later generations, the position changes. Now the whole matter assumes a national or communal character. Whereas the earlier people enjoyed the blessings of God by virtue of their performance, the later generations assume that they are entitled to the same blessings—whatever their actions—simply because they belong to a certain community or race. Then they start believing that they are the specially favoured people of God, and whatever they do, they will definitely receive the bounties of God. With a view to removing this misunderstanding on the part of the people of the Book, God has specifically ordained that the rewards meant for them will start right here in this world. Such people can see in the present world itself how their God is going to deal with them in the future world. If, in this world, they are enjoying supremacy over their enemies, then it means that they are the favourite group of God, and if their enemies prevail over them, then it means that the reverse is true. If a group which is in possession of the Book is repeatedly vanquished and remains downtrodden in this world, in spite of being large in number, it should never entertain the hope of enjoying a high position and honours in the Hereafter.

¹⁹ People of the Book, Our Messenger has come to you to make things clear to you after an interval between the messengers, lest you say, 'No bearer of glad tidings and no warner has come to us.' So a bearer of glad tidings and a warner has indeed come to you. God has the power to do all things.ᵃ

يَـٰٓأَهْلَ ٱلْكِتَـٰبِ قَدْ جَآءَكُمْ رَسُولُنَا يُبَيِّنُ لَكُمْ عَلَىٰ فَتْرَةٍ مِّنَ ٱلرُّسُلِ أَن تَقُولُوا۟ مَا جَآءَنَا مِنۢ بَشِيرٍ وَلَا نَذِيرٍ فَقَدْ جَآءَكُم بَشِيرٌ وَنَذِيرٌ وَٱللَّهُ عَلَىٰ كُلِّ شَىْءٍ قَدِيرٌ ۝

ᵃ Considering any community as a favourite community of God is an absolutely meaningless thought. Before God the reckoning is individual to individual and not community to community. Everybody will get his reward before God according to his deeds. In the eyes of God, every man is a human being irrespective of his belonging to this community or that. Every man's future will be decided on the basis of his performance in this world of test and trial. Paradise is not the native place of any community; nor is hell the prison for any particular community. It is the way of God that He, on His behalf, raises certain individuals who acquaint the people with the realities of life; warn them of hell and give them the good news of paradise. It is only by supporting these 'warners' and 'bringers of good news' and cooperating with them that man finds God, and not in any other way.

²⁰ Remember when Moses said to his people, 'O my people! Remember God's favour to you, He has raised up prophets among you, made you kings, and granted you [favours] such as He has not granted to anyone else in the world. ²¹ O my people! Enter the holy land which God has assigned for you. Do not turn back, or you will be the losers.' ²² They said, 'Moses, in that land there is a powerful people. Never shall we enter it until they leave it: if they leave, then we shall certainly enter it.' ²³ Thereupon two God-fearing men whom God had blessed said, 'Go into them through the gate—for as soon as you enter, you shall surely be victorious! Put your trust in God if you are true believers.' ²⁴ They said, 'We will never enter it, Moses, as long as they are there. Go, you and your Lord, and fight, and we will stay here.'ᵃ

وَإِذْ قَالَ مُوسَىٰ لِقَوْمِهِۦ يَٰقَوْمِ ٱذْكُرُوا۟ نِعْمَةَ ٱللَّهِ عَلَيْكُمْ إِذْ جَعَلَ فِيكُمْ أَنۢبِيَآءَ وَجَعَلَكُم مُّلُوكًا وَءَاتَىٰكُم مَّا لَمْ يُؤْتِ أَحَدًا مِّنَ ٱلْعَٰلَمِينَ ۝ يَٰقَوْمِ ٱدْخُلُوا۟ ٱلْأَرْضَ ٱلْمُقَدَّسَةَ ٱلَّتِى كَتَبَ ٱللَّهُ لَكُمْ وَلَا تَرْتَدُّوا۟ عَلَىٰٓ أَدْبَارِكُمْ فَتَنقَلِبُوا۟ خَٰسِرِينَ ۝ قَالُوا۟ يَٰمُوسَىٰٓ إِنَّ فِيهَا قَوْمًا جَبَّارِينَ وَإِنَّا لَن نَّدْخُلَهَا حَتَّىٰ يَخْرُجُوا۟ مِنْهَا فَإِن يَخْرُجُوا۟ مِنْهَا فَإِنَّا دَٰخِلُونَ ۝ قَالَ رَجُلَانِ مِنَ ٱلَّذِينَ يَخَافُونَ أَنْعَمَ ٱللَّهُ عَلَيْهِمَا ٱدْخُلُوا۟ عَلَيْهِمُ ٱلْبَابَ فَإِذَا دَخَلْتُمُوهُ فَإِنَّكُمْ غَٰلِبُونَ وَعَلَى ٱللَّهِ فَتَوَكَّلُوٓا۟ إِن كُنتُم مُّؤْمِنِينَ ۝ قَالُوا۟ يَٰمُوسَىٰٓ إِنَّا لَن نَّدْخُلَهَآ أَبَدًا مَّا دَامُوا۟ فِيهَا فَٱذْهَبْ أَنتَ وَرَبُّكَ فَقَٰتِلَآ إِنَّا هَٰهُنَا قَٰعِدُونَ ۝

ᵃ It is the way of God that He chooses a group in order to convey His message to the people. He sends His prophet and His Book to this group and assigns them the task of conveying this message to others. Just as a particular person is the recipient of revelation, similarly a particular group is made the bearer of the revelation. In ancient times this special position was enjoyed by the Children of Israel and after the advent of the last of the prophets, his followers (ummah) were appointed to this position.

Just as God requires of a community that it should represent His religion, similarly He also wants the community representing His religion to enjoy honours and high position in this world, so that it should be demonstrated to the people that in the new world coming into existence after Doomsday, prominence and distinction will be conferred only upon the 'People of the Truth'. All others will be subdued and distanced from God's blessings. However, this worldly benefit is not conferred on this group unconditionally: the group has first to face the test of entitlement. It has to prove that it has full faith in God under all circumstances and bows to His will and pleasure even if that tries their patience to the very limits.

²⁵ Moses supplicated, 'Lord, I have power over none but myself and my brother; so separate us from the disobedient people.' ²⁶ God said, 'The land is forbidden to them for forty years, while they wander around the earth, bewildered; do not grieve over these wicked people.'ᵃ

قَالَ رَبِّ إِنِّى لَآ أَمْلِكُ إِلَّا نَفْسِى وَأَخِى ۖ فَٱفْرُقْ بَيْنَنَا وَبَيْنَ ٱلْقَوْمِ ٱلْفَـٰسِقِينَ ۝ قَالَ فَإِنَّهَا مُحَرَّمَةٌ عَلَيْهِمْ ۛ أَرْبَعِينَ سَنَةً ۛ يَتِيهُونَ فِى ٱلْأَرْضِ ۚ فَلَا تَأْسَ عَلَى ٱلْقَوْمِ ٱلْفَـٰسِقِينَ ۝

ᵃ At the time the Children of Israel left Egypt under the leadership of Moses and reached the Sinai desert, a tyrant community, the Amaliqa, was ruling Syria and Palestine areas. God informed the Children of Israel that the tyrant people had come to the end of their epoch, that they should enter that country and that with the help of God they would overcome the tyrant people after some negligible resistence. But, the Israelites were so terror-striken by the tyrant community that they were not prepared to enter its country. This meant that they were more afraid of human beings than of God. Thereafter, they became worthless in the eyes of God. God then decided that for forty years (1440 B.C. to 1400 B.C.) they would wander in the desert, by which time all those who were of the age of twenty years or more would have died and during this period a new generation living under new conditions would have grown up. And it actually happened like that. In the forty years spent in the desert, all the people of advanced age died. Thereafter, their new generations under the leadership of Yusha' bin Nun (Joshua) conquered Syria and Palestine. This Yusha' was one of the the two righteous Israelites who had previously advised their community to trust in God and enter the Amaliqa's country.

The Children of Israel had told Moses that if they invaded that country (of the Amalekites) they themselves would be defeated and their children would be treated as so much loot. But, these very children, after growing up, entered that country and captured it. The children acquired this strength because, for a long period, they had faced the hardships of desert life. Those very conditions which had been considered by the fathers of the children to be so dangerous as to spell death for their children actually held for them the secret of life.

To live in favourable conditions is evidently very pleasant. But, the fact is that the best latent talents of a man emerge when he has to struggle with circumstances for his life. In Egypt, the Children of Israel had been living in peace for centuries. The result of this was that they had become a dead community. But after their exile, the desert life which they had to live was a total challenge for them. Those who spent their lives from childhood to youth in such circumstances were naturally a different kind of people. The desert conditions had fostered in them simplicity courage, diligence and realism; and these are the qualities which infuse life into a community. If a community becomes 'dead' as a result of the prevailing circumstances, then it is placed in extraordinary circumstances in order to revive it.

²⁷ Relate to them, the true story of the two sons of Adam. When they both presented an offering, it was accepted from one of them and not from the other. The latter said, 'I shall kill you!' The former said, 'God accepts [things] only from the righteous. ²⁸ If you raise your hand to kill me, I will not raise mine to kill you. I fear God, the Lord of the Universe, ²⁹ and I want you to bear your sins against me as well as your own sins and become an inhabitant of the Fire. Such is the reward of the wrongdoers.' ^a

﷽ وَٱتْلُ عَلَيْهِمْ نَبَأَ ٱبْنَىْ ءَادَمَ بِٱلْحَقِّ إِذْ قَرَّبَا قُرْبَانًا فَتُقُبِّلَ مِنْ أَحَدِهِمَا وَلَمْ يُتَقَبَّلْ مِنَ ٱلْآخَرِ قَالَ لَأَقْتُلَنَّكَ ۖ قَالَ إِنَّمَا يَتَقَبَّلُ ٱللَّهُ مِنَ ٱلْمُتَّقِينَ ۝ لَئِنۢ بَسَطتَ إِلَىَّ يَدَكَ لِتَقْتُلَنِى مَآ أَنَا۠ بِبَاسِطٍ يَدِىَ إِلَيْكَ لِأَقْتُلَكَ ۖ إِنِّىٓ أَخَافُ ٱللَّهَ رَبَّ ٱلْعَلَمِينَ ۝ إِنِّىٓ أُرِيدُ أَن تَبُوٓأَ بِإِثْمِى وَإِثْمِكَ فَتَكُونَ مِنْ أَصْحَبِ ٱلنَّارِ ۚ وَذَلِكَ جَزَٰٓؤُا۟ ٱلظَّلِمِينَ ۝

^a The real reward for the deeds performed for the sake of God will be given in the Hereafter. However, sometimes even in this world certain occurrences show whether human actions have gained God's approval. This happened in the case of Adam's sons, Abel and Cain (Habil and Qabil). Abel's offerings from his flocks of sheep and goats were accepted by God and he was duly blessed, but Cain's offerings of his agricultural produce were not, and he remained unblessed. Cain then became so jealous of his younger brother that he threatened to kill him. Abel said that Cain's offering had been rejected because Cain had no heartfelt fear of God and should, therefore, reform himself instead of threatening him. But, jealousy and enmity blur the truth and one can think only of how to eliminate one's supposed enemy.

Abel told Cain that he might raise his hand to murder him, but that he would not retaliate, because God had prohibited any fighting between one Muslim and another. Even if a Muslim wanted to assassinate his brother, the brother should not consider it legitimate to kill his attacker. This obviated the mutual clash which was otherwise inevitable, as well as the resulting endless chain of action and reaction in Muslim society. If two Muslims are bent on each other's destruction, the guilt is divided between the two. But if one Muslim carries out his intention, while the other remains immersed in prayer, the attacker will not only shoulder the burden of his own sin, but also that of any sin which his victim might have commmitted had he not remained patient and prayerful.

³⁰ His lower self persuaded him to kill his brother, and he killed him and he became one of the lost. ³¹ Then God sent a raven, which scratched the earth, so that He might show him how to hide the corpse of his brother. 'Alas!' he cried, 'Am I not able even to be like this raven, so that I may hide the corpse of my brother?' And he repented.ª

فَطَوَّعَتۡ لَهُۥ نَفۡسُهُۥ قَتۡلَ أَخِيهِ فَقَتَلَهُۥ فَأَصۡبَحَ مِنَ ٱلۡخَٰسِرِينَ ۝ فَبَعَثَ ٱللَّهُ غُرَابٗا يَبۡحَثُ فِي ٱلۡأَرۡضِ لِيُرِيَهُۥ كَيۡفَ يُوَٰرِي سَوۡءَةَ أَخِيهِ ۚ قَالَ يَٰوَيۡلَتَىٰٓ أَعَجَزۡتُ أَنۡ أَكُونَ مِثۡلَ هَٰذَا ٱلۡغُرَابِ فَأُوَٰرِيَ سَوۡءَةَ أَخِي ۖ فَأَصۡبَحَ مِنَ ٱلنَّٰدِمِينَ ۝

ª Whatever a man receives in this world is bestowed by God. Therefore, one who, out of being jealous inflicts harm upon another who is better situated in life attempts, in effect, to nullify God's plan. Such a person is to some extent given the scope to do whatever he likes in this world of trial, but in the eyes of God, he is the worst sinner. Abel drew the attention of his elder brother Cain to this fact. This created some hesitation in Cain's mind. He realised that if he was bent on killing his younger brother, it was without any justification. But the feeling of jealousy in him did not cool down. He invented excuses to justify his action. Ultimately, his inner struggle resolved itself by returning to his self-devised justification and he proceeded to kill his brother. The voice of conscience is the voice of God. A question arising in a man's conscience about any action of his amounts in fact to his facing a test. A man is successful if he gives a positive response to the voice of his conscience, but if, in taking the shelter of false excuses, he suppresses the voice of his conscience, then he has failed.

It has been recorded in a tradition of the Prophet that transgression and the killing of kindred are sins for which punishment starts right here in this world. The punishment for the unjustified atrocity committed by Cain against his brother was given to him not only in the Hereafter but in this very world where he was immediately plunged into misery. It has come to us through Mujahid that Cain, after committing the murder, was afflicted by his lower leg becoming stuck to his thigh. He remained lying on the ground, unattended and uncared for, until he died in ignominy and distress. (*Tafsir ibn Kathir*).

Cain was instructed by means of a crow how to bury the dead body under the ground. This points to the fact that man was less knowledgeable than the animals about the ways of nature. And, if he follows his emotions, there is no worse transgressor than he. Furthermore, it is implied that if, rather than committing a crime, a man buries the intention in his heart, he will not have to face the shame of it afterwards. A man should curb and bury his bad intentions in his heart and not allow them to emerge and become a reality. A man, before bringing his evil designs to fruition, has simply to bury the intention. If, not, he will be confronted with the problem of burying the dead body, which, even after burial, will be treated by God as not having been buried.

³² That was why We laid it down for the Children of Israel that whoever killed a human being—except as a punishment for murder or for spreading corruption in the land—shall be regarded as having killed all mankind, and that whoever saved a human life shall be regarded as having saved all mankind. Our messengers came to them with clear signs, but many of them continued to commit excesses in the land.ᵃ

مِنْ أَجْلِ ذَٰلِكَ كَتَبْنَا عَلَىٰ بَنِىٓ إِسْرَٰٓءِيلَ أَنَّهُۥ مَن قَتَلَ نَفْسًۢا بِغَيْرِ نَفْسٍ أَوْ فَسَادٍ فِى ٱلْأَرْضِ فَكَأَنَّمَا قَتَلَ ٱلنَّاسَ جَمِيعًا وَمَنْ أَحْيَاهَا فَكَأَنَّمَآ أَحْيَا ٱلنَّاسَ جَمِيعًا ۚ وَلَقَدْ جَآءَتْهُمْ رُسُلُنَا بِٱلْبَيِّنَٰتِ ثُمَّ إِنَّ كَثِيرًا مِّنْهُم بَعْدَ ذَٰلِكَ فِى ٱلْأَرْضِ لَمُسْرِفُونَ ۝

ᵃ When one person kills another, he is the killer of not only one person but of all human beings, because he contravenes the law of respect for human life upon which the lives of all human beings depend. Similarly, when someone saves another from oppression, he is not the saviour of just one person but of all human beings, because he is protecting the principle of respect for life of all hman beings, which holds that nobody has the right to raise his hand to another. If one person attacks the honour, property or life of another, it means that abnormal conditions have developed in the society. It is necessary for Muslims to look at even one incident of this nature as if the life, property and honour of all people are in danger. In a society, the tradition of respect for each other's life is formed as a result of a long history, and once this tradition is violated, it will be a very long time before it can be revived. Those who establish the tradition of violence in a society are the worst enemies of that society.

33 Those that make war against God and His Messenger and spread disorder in the land shall be put to death or crucified or have their hands and feet cut off on alternate sides, or be banished from the country. They shall be disgraced in this world, and then severely punished in the Hereafter, 34 except for those who repent before you gain power over them: for you must know that God is forgiving and merciful.

35 Believers, fear God and seek ways to come closer to Him and strive for His cause, so that you may prosper. 36 As for those who reject Faith, if they had everything on earth, and twice as much again and offered it to ransom themselves from the torment of the Day of Resurrection, it shall not be accepted from them— they will have a painful punishment. 37 They will want to get out of the Fire but they will be unable to do so: theirs shall be a lasting punishment.[a]

إِنَّمَا جَزَٰٓؤُاْ ٱلَّذِينَ يُحَارِبُونَ ٱللَّهَ وَرَسُولَهُۥ وَيَسْعَوْنَ فِى ٱلْأَرْضِ فَسَادًا أَن يُقَتَّلُوٓاْ أَوْ يُصَلَّبُوٓاْ أَوْ تُقَطَّعَ أَيْدِيهِمْ وَأَرْجُلُهُم مِّنْ خِلَٰفٍ أَوْ يُنفَوْاْ مِنَ ٱلْأَرْضِ ذَٰلِكَ لَهُمْ خِزْىٌ فِى ٱلدُّنْيَا وَلَهُمْ فِى ٱلْأَخِرَةِ عَذَابٌ عَظِيمٌ ۝ إِلَّا ٱلَّذِينَ تَابُواْ مِن قَبْلِ أَن تَقْدِرُواْ عَلَيْهِمْ فَٱعْلَمُوٓاْ أَنَّ ٱللَّهَ غَفُورٌ رَّحِيمٌ ۝ يَٰٓأَيُّهَا ٱلَّذِينَ ءَامَنُواْ ٱتَّقُواْ ٱللَّهَ وَٱبْتَغُوٓاْ إِلَيْهِ ٱلْوَسِيلَةَ وَجَٰهِدُواْ فِى سَبِيلِهِۦ لَعَلَّكُمْ تُفْلِحُونَ ۝ إِنَّ ٱلَّذِينَ كَفَرُواْ لَوْ أَنَّ لَهُم مَّا فِى ٱلْأَرْضِ جَمِيعًا وَمِثْلَهُۥ مَعَهُۥ لِيَفْتَدُواْ بِهِۦ مِنْ عَذَابِ يَوْمِ ٱلْقِيَٰمَةِ مَا تُقُبِّلَ مِنْهُمْ وَلَهُمْ عَذَابٌ أَلِيمٌ ۝ يُرِيدُونَ أَن يَخْرُجُواْ مِنَ ٱلنَّارِ وَمَا هُم بِخَٰرِجِينَ مِنْهَا وَلَهُمْ عَذَابٌ مُّقِيمٌ ۝

---

[a] The principle on which God has created the system of this world is that everybody should discharge his duty, and nobody should unnecessarily interfere in the sphere of others. All inanimate objects and animals follow this natural law. Human beings also have been given clear instructions to this effect through the prophets. But human beings who, unlike other creatures, have been given freedom for the time being, rebel, and in that way create a disturbance in the system of Nature. Such people are the worst criminals in the eyes of God. And those who declare war against God and His prophet are still worse criminals. Such people frequently indulge in acts of terrorism. This runs counter to God's call to His subjects to refrain from creating disturbances. It also negates His invitation to them to lead their lives according to divine Nature. For such people there is a terrible punishment in this world and an all-consuming fire in the Hereafter.

³⁸ Cut off the hands of thieves, whether they are male or female, as a [deterrent] punishment from God for what they have done. God is almighty and wise. ³⁹ But God will surely turn in mercy to him who repents after his transgression and reforms. Surely, God is most forgiving and ever merciful. ⁴⁰ Do you not know that the kingdom of the heavens and earth belongs to God? He punishes whom He will and forgives whom He pleases. God has power over all things.ᵃ

وَٱلسَّارِقُ وَٱلسَّارِقَةُ فَٱقْطَعُوٓاْ أَيْدِيَهُمَا جَزَآءًۢ بِمَا كَسَبَا نَكَـٰلًا مِّنَ ٱللَّهِ ۗ وَٱللَّهُ عَزِيزٌ حَكِيمٌ ﴿٣٨﴾ فَمَن تَابَ مِنۢ بَعْدِ ظُلْمِهِۦ وَأَصْلَحَ فَإِنَّ ٱللَّهَ يَتُوبُ عَلَيْهِ ۗ إِنَّ ٱللَّهَ غَفُورٌ رَّحِيمٌ ﴿٣٩﴾ أَلَمْ تَعْلَمْ أَنَّ ٱللَّهَ لَهُۥ مُلْكُ ٱلسَّمَـٰوَٰتِ وَٱلْأَرْضِ يُعَذِّبُ مَن يَشَآءُ وَيَغْفِرُ لِمَن يَشَآءُ ۗ وَٱللَّهُ عَلَىٰ كُلِّ شَىْءٍ قَدِيرٌ ﴿٤٠﴾

ᵃ The greatest achievement for a man is his nearness to God. This nearness in its real and perfect shape will be his in the Hereafter. However, when a man's righteous action brings him nearness to God, he experiences this in this world purely in the form of heavenly feeling. The way to attain this nearness is through *taqwa* (fear of God) and *jihad* (struggle) i.e. becoming a worshipper or devotee of God through fear of God and struggling to make efforts for His cause. There are some moments in the life of a man when he finds himself in between Truth and untruth. In taking the direction of Truth, he has to surrender his ego and the structure of his worldly considerations seems to become insecure, while in adopting the way of untruth, his ego remains intact and his worldly considerations seem to be perfectly safe. In the former case, a man fears God and, overlooking all other considerations sticks to God; tolerating every difficulty and unpleasantness, he moves ahead towards God—these are the things which bless him with nearness to God. First hand experience of this nearness at that time takes the shape of aesthetic heavenly realization. On the contrary, the person who is not ready to adopt the path of fearing God and struggling to make efforts for the cause of God, drifts away from Him, and brings upon himself afflictions from which he can never get relief.

The punitive system in Islam for social crimes has been formulated keeping in view two special aspects—one is punishment for a man's crime and the other is the deterrent effect of that punishment. However, if a criminal is truly repentant after committing a crime, seeks God's pardon and completely refrains from such misdemeanours in future, then it may be hoped that God will forgive him in the Hereafter.

The matter of reward is entirely in the hands of God. There is no cause to fear, however, that despite an individual having reformed only later in his life, his earlier transgressions will not be pardoned. Nor is it true that there is some force, other than God's will which, by recommendation or intervention, can change one's destiny. Everything rests with God and He alone in His perfect wisdom and power decides the fate of everyone.

⁴¹ Messenger, do not be grieved by those who vie with one another in denying the truth; those who say with their tongues, 'We believe,' but have no faith in their hearts; from among the Jews also, there are those who listen eagerly to any lies. They listen to you to convey to others [religious leaders] who do not come to you [out of pride and conceit]. They [these leaders] take words out of their context and say, 'If this be given to you, receive it, but if not, then beware!' If anyone's trial is intended by God, you cannot in the least prevail against God on his behalf. Those whose hearts God does not intend to purify shall be subjected to disgrace in this world and a severe punishment in the Hereafter.ᵃ

ﱡ يَٰٓأَيُّهَا ٱلرَّسُولُ لَا يَحْزُنكَ ٱلَّذِينَ يُسَٰرِعُونَ فِى ٱلْكُفْرِ مِنَ ٱلَّذِينَ قَالُوٓاْ ءَامَنَّا بِأَفْوَٰهِهِمْ وَلَمْ تُؤْمِن قُلُوبُهُمْ ۚ وَمِنَ ٱلَّذِينَ هَادُواْ ۖ سَمَّٰعُونَ لِلْكَذِبِ سَمَّٰعُونَ لِقَوْمٍ ءَاخَرِينَ لَمْ يَأْتُوكَ ۖ يُحَرِّفُونَ ٱلْكَلِمَ مِنۢ بَعْدِ مَوَاضِعِهِۦ ۖ يَقُولُونَ إِنْ أُوتِيتُمْ هَٰذَا فَخُذُوهُ وَإِن لَّمْ تُؤْتَوْهُ فَٱحْذَرُواْ ۚ وَمَن يُرِدِ ٱللَّهُ فِتْنَتَهُۥ فَلَن تَمْلِكَ لَهُۥ مِنَ ٱللَّهِ شَيْـًٔا ۚ أُوْلَٰٓئِكَ ٱلَّذِينَ لَمْ يُرِدِ ٱللَّهُ أَن يُطَهِّرَ قُلُوبَهُمْ ۚ لَهُمْ فِى ٱلدُّنْيَا خِزْىٌ ۖ وَلَهُمْ فِى ٱلْءَاخِرَةِ عَذَابٌ عَظِيمٌ ﴿٤١﴾

ᵃ Within Madinah there were two kinds of people who opposed the Islamic mission—one the hypocrites and the other the Jews. The hypocrites, feeling that the real Islamic mission was harmful to their interests and purposes, merely put on a show of having adopted Islam. The Jews for their part, occupying as they did the thrones of the representatives of religion, felt that the Islamic mission was pulling them down from their elevated positions. Both these types of people considered the true Islamic mission to be their common enemy. Therefore, they joined hands in running a campaign against Islam. The more prominent of them, considering it beneath their dignity to attend meetings held by the Prophet Muhammad, stayed away from them, but their inferiors were set the task of hearing him and conveying the happenings to their leaders. These people used then to invest them with wrong meanings in order to defame him and his mission. Their arrogance had made them so brazen that they did not hesitate to take God's message out of its proper context and draw from it inferences which suited their interests. ▶

⁴² They listen eagerly to falsehood, and devour forbidden things voraciously. If they come to you, then judge between them or avoid them. If you avoid them, they can in no way harm you, but if you do judge, judge them with fairness: God loves those that deal justly.*

سَمَّعُونَ لِلْكَذِبِ أَكَّلُونَ لِلسُّحْتِ فَإِن جَآءُوكَ فَٱحْكُم بَيْنَهُمْ أَوْ أَعْرِضْ عَنْهُمْ وَإِن تُعْرِضْ عَنْهُمْ فَلَن يَضُرُّوكَ شَيْئًا وَإِنْ حَكَمْتَ فَٱحْكُم بَيْنَهُم بِٱلْقِسْطِ إِنَّ ٱللَّهَ يُحِبُّ ٱلْمُقْسِطِينَ ۝

Such are those who do not bow to God and His Prophet, their attitude being to accept only whatever suits their interests. This is the most disturbing trend for a man. Those who give preference to their vested interests and personal considerations over the Truth, who want to see themselves in high positions at any cost, who devise destructive plots to suppress the Truth — to the point of distorting God's message to justify their action — develop a mentality which blocks their capacity to accept the Truth. They desert God, so God deserts them. Such people, being deprived of God's guidance, remain enmeshed in falsehood, until they reach the world of the Fire.

The servant of God, who has arisen with the message of God's true religion, should not become discouraged by opposition. The activities of opponents are not actually against the missionary but against God, and can therefore never be successful. What God requires from missionary activity is that people should be made fully aware of the real facts. And this task is certainly fulfilled with God's assistance.

ª The common form of bribe (*suht*) is that which is taken directly as such. For example, there were ancient religious scholars who used to give false decrees and opinions after taking bribes. However, there is another form of corruption in which there is no direct give-and-take transaction but it is the biggest and worst out of all the various forms of corruption. This is the distorting of the provisions of religion by opportunists to suit popular tastes so that they may have honour and glory conferred upon them by an admiring public, and receive contributions and offerings from all and sundry.

Presenting religion in its pure form is always at the cost of unpopularity with the public. On the contrary, a version of religion which without materially disrupting people's lives, confers the advantages of religion, is very popular and attracts large crowds. The purveyors of a 'religion' which does not oblige potential followers to give up or modify their world-oriented lives, and guarantees admission to paradise with the help of some trivial formalities, very soon become the favourites of the public. ▶

43 But why do they come to you for judgement when they have the Torah, which enshrines God's own judgement? Yet, in spite of that, they turn their backs; and certainly they will not believe.[a]

وَكَيْفَ يُحَكِّمُونَكَ وَعِندَهُمُ ٱلتَّوْرَىٰةُ فِيهَا حُكْمُ ٱللَّهِ ثُمَّ يَتَوَلَّوْنَ مِنۢ بَعْدِ ذَٰلِكَ وَمَآ أُوْلَـٰٓئِكَ بِٱلْمُؤْمِنِينَ ٤٣

The same is true of those who present a 'religion' which gives sanctity to national and communal interests and all the accompanying frenzy of material activities; which gives a man the opportunity, under the banner of religion, to engage himself in glory-seeking activities.

[a] The ancient Jewish leaders had become a centre of attraction for the people by dispensing this type of religion. They presented to the people the religion of their choice and the people responded with everything from monetary co-operation to the conferment of honours and glory. Given these circumstances, the raising of the voice of true religion by the Prophet Muhammad seemed intolerable to them, as this amounted to the demolition of the structure of their vested interests. They were so displeased with the Prophet that they were in no way interested in hearing anything good about him. On the contrary, if they heard any bad news about him, they took immense interest in it and spread it with their own additions. The condition of those who fall victim to such evil is that even if they are inclined to take a religious decision on any matter, they do so in the hopes that the outcome will be in line with their own desires. If not, they disassociate themselves from it, in spite of knowing full well that the real decision makers are God and His Prophet. They forget that their rejection of the matter in hand amounts to a denial of Faith and Islam itself.

⁴⁴ We have revealed the Torah, in which there is guidance and light. By it the prophets who were obedient to Us judged the Jews, and so did the rabbis and the priests, according to God's Book which had been entrusted to their care; and to which they were witnesses. Have no fear of man; fear Me, and do not sell My revelations for a paltry sum. Those who do not judge by what God has sent down are deniers of truth.ᵃ

إِنَّآ أَنزَلْنَا ٱلتَّوْرَىٰةَ فِيهَا هُدًى وَنُورٌ
يَحْكُمُ بِهَا ٱلنَّبِيُّونَ ٱلَّذِينَ أَسْلَمُواْ
لِلَّذِينَ هَادُواْ وَٱلرَّبَّٰنِيُّونَ وَٱلْأَحْبَارُ بِمَا
ٱسْتُحْفِظُواْ مِن كِتَٰبِ ٱللَّهِ وَكَانُواْ
عَلَيْهِ شُهَدَآءَ فَلَا تَخْشَوُاْ ٱلنَّاسَ
وَٱخْشَوْنِ وَلَا تَشْتَرُواْ بِـَٔايَٰتِى ثَمَنًا
قَلِيلًا وَمَن لَّمْ يَحْكُم بِمَآ أَنزَلَ ٱللَّهُ
فَأُوْلَٰٓئِكَ هُمُ ٱلْكَٰفِرُونَ ۝

ᵃ The purpose of God's Book coming to the world was to guide the people to the way of eternal welfare, and to bring them out of the darkness of desire-worship and into the light of Truth-worship. Those who are God-fearing consider the Book of God as a holy covenant between God and His subjects, and as such, they know that there cannot, on their behalf, be any increase in the benefits it confers or any lessening of the strictness of its ordinances. As it is in the nature of a trust with them, they carry out its instructions.

God's Book conveys His will with regard to His subjects. Its guidance must be followed in all matters and disputes must be settled in accordance with its instructions. Allowing worldly desires and self interest to reign supreme and only playing lip service to God's book amounts to a rejection of God's word. Self-styled Muslims who act in this way are sinners in God's eyes. As rejecters of God's supremacy and defaulters on their pledge to obey God, they are destroyers of Truth. Intentional violators of Islamic law, can lay no claim to God's approval.

⁴⁵ We prescribed for them in [the Torah]: a life for a life, an eye for an eye, a nose for a nose, an ear for an ear, a tooth for a tooth, and a wound for a wound. But, if anyone forgoes it, this shall be for him an expiation. Those who do not judge by what God has sent down are wrongdoers! ⁴⁶ We caused Jesus, son of Mary to follow in their footsteps, fulfilling what had been revealed before him in the Torah. We gave him the Gospel, which contained guidance and light, fulfilling what was revealed before it in the Torah: a guide and an admonition to the God-fearing. ⁴⁷ Therefore, let those who follow the Gospel judge according to what God has revealed in it. Those who do not judge by what God has sent down are rebellious.ᵃ

وَكَتَبْنَا عَلَيْهِمْ فِيهَآ أَنَّ ٱلنَّفْسَ بِٱلنَّفْسِ وَٱلْعَيْنَ بِٱلْعَيْنِ وَٱلْأَنفَ بِٱلْأَنفِ وَٱلْأُذُنَ بِٱلْأُذُنِ وَٱلسِّنَّ بِٱلسِّنِّ وَٱلْجُرُوحَ قِصَاصٌ فَمَن تَصَدَّقَ بِهِۦ فَهُوَ كَفَّارَةٌ لَّهُۥ وَمَن لَّمْ يَحْكُم بِمَآ أَنزَلَ ٱللَّهُ فَأُو۟لَٰٓئِكَ هُمُ ٱلظَّٰلِمُونَ ۝ وَقَفَّيْنَا عَلَىٰٓ ءَاثَٰرِهِم بِعِيسَى ٱبْنِ مَرْيَمَ مُصَدِّقًا لِّمَا بَيْنَ يَدَيْهِ مِنَ ٱلتَّوْرَىٰةِ وَءَاتَيْنَٰهُ ٱلْإِنجِيلَ فِيهِ هُدًى وَنُورٌ وَمُصَدِّقًا لِّمَا بَيْنَ يَدَيْهِ مِنَ ٱلتَّوْرَىٰةِ وَهُدًى وَمَوْعِظَةً لِّلْمُتَّقِينَ ۝ وَلْيَحْكُمْ أَهْلُ ٱلْإِنجِيلِ بِمَآ أَنزَلَ ٱللَّهُ فِيهِ وَمَن لَّمْ يَحْكُم بِمَآ أَنزَلَ ٱللَّهُ فَأُو۟لَٰٓئِكَ هُمُ ٱلْفَٰسِقُونَ ۝

ᵃ In connection with justice (and the relevant penal action) it is the requirement of the Islamic law that its rules should be enforced without any individual's status being taken into account. However, sometimes a man's violence is not the result of his mischievous intent, but occurs accidentally under the influence of emotional stress. Under such circumstances, if the victim of violence pardons the perpetrator of violence, that will be deemed an act of magnanimity towards the latter and will contribute to creating an atmosphere of broad-mindedness in society.

⁴⁸ We have sent down the Book to you with the truth, fulfilling [the predictions] revealed in the previous scriptures and determining what is true therein, and as a guardian over it. Judge, therefore, between them by what God has revealed, and do not follow their vain desires turning away from the truth that has come to you. To every one of you We have ordained a law and a way, and had God so willed, He would have made you all a single community, but He did not so will, in order that He might try you by what He has given you. Vie, then, with one another in doing good works; to God you shall all return; then He will make clear to you about what you have been disputing.ᵃ

وَأَنزَلْنَا إِلَيْكَ ٱلْكِتَبَ بِٱلْحَقِّ مُصَدِّقًا لِّمَا بَيْنَ يَدَيْهِ مِنَ ٱلْكِتَبِ وَمُهَيْمِنًا عَلَيْهِ فَٱحْكُم بَيْنَهُم بِمَا أَنزَلَ ٱللَّهُ وَلَا تَتَّبِعْ أَهْوَآءَهُمْ عَمَّا جَآءَكَ مِنَ ٱلْحَقِّ لِكُلٍّ جَعَلْنَا مِنكُمْ شِرْعَةً وَمِنْهَاجًا وَلَوْ شَآءَ ٱللَّهُ لَجَعَلَكُمْ أُمَّةً وَحِدَةً وَلَكِن لِّيَبْلُوَكُمْ فِى مَآ ءَاتَىٰكُمْ فَٱسْتَبِقُوا۟ ٱلْخَيْرَتِ إِلَى ٱللَّهِ مَرْجِعُكُمْ جَمِيعًا فَيُنَبِّئُكُم بِمَا كُنتُمْ فِيهِ تَخْتَلِفُونَ ۞

ᵃ Here 'the Book' means the original and basic teachings of religion. This Book of God is a single entity and has been revealed to all the prophets with some changes in respect of language and the order of commandments. However, as regards the outward structure in which the realities of religion are presented, there are differences in the teachings of the various prophets. The reason is not that there are stages in the revelation of the religion which indicate the actual evolution of the religion itself, i.e. it is not that prior to this a less developed or imperfect religion was revealed and thereafter a more developed and entirely perfect religion was revealed. The truth is that with any considerable passage of time, the internal reality of religion is lost and public rituals and formal ceremonies assume the strength of the internal reality, eventually becoming 'holy'. People begin to consider the repetition of such rituals, accompanied by external trappings, as real worship. That is why the external framework was changed from time to time, so that the mentality of considering this framework as the real substance of religion should be eradicated and so that nothing other than God should become the centre of one's attention. According to the Quran, this came about simply for the purpose of putting people to the test. The reason for this strategy is the Divine Wisdom of putting mankind on trial and not the Divine Wisdom of the evolution of religion.

An example of this is the change of *qiblah*. The Children of Israel were commanded to turn towards the 'Holy House' (Jerusalem) while saying their prayers. This command was only for the sake of being consistent about the direction. But thereafter they gradually developed the idea that prayer meant simply facing towards Jerusalem. ▶

⁴⁹Judge between them by what God has sent down and do not be led by their desires. Beware of them lest they turn you away from a part of that what God has revealed to you. If they reject your judgement, know that God intends to punish them for the sins they have committed. Indeed a large number of the people are disobedient.[a]

وَأَنِ ٱحْكُم بَيْنَهُم بِمَآ أَنزَلَ ٱللَّهُ وَلَا تَتَّبِعْ أَهْوَآءَهُمْ وَٱحْذَرْهُمْ أَن يَفْتِنُوكَ عَنۢ بَعْضِ مَآ أَنزَلَ ٱللَّهُ إِلَيْكَ ۖ فَإِن تَوَلَّوْاْ فَٱعْلَمْ أَنَّمَا يُرِيدُ ٱللَّهُ أَن يُصِيبَهُم بِبَعْضِ ذُنُوبِهِمْ ۗ وَإِنَّ كَثِيرًا مِّنَ ٱلنَّاسِ لَفَٰسِقُونَ ۝

Then the earlier commandment was changed and the Ka'bah was made the *qiblah*. Now, some people adhered to the earlier tradition, while others followed God's guidance. In this way, the change of *qiblah* made it clear as to who worshipped walls and doors and who were the genuine worshippers of God (see 2:143).

Now there is no possibility of the occurrence of such a change, because the structure would have to be changed by a prophet and now no other prophet is going to be raised. However, as far as the real purpose is concerned, it is to remain as it is. Even now, before God, His true worshipper will be the one who, though following the structural formalities, will not give them the status of real purpose; who, freeing his mind from outward ceremonial, will say his prayers directly to God. This has to be achieved through rigorous mental discipline.

The disputes existing in religion in the name of outward formalities have arisen because people's negligence has made them ignorant of the true facts. If they were to become aware of the truth — as it will present itself in the Hereafter—all the disputes would come to an end right now.

[a] The Quran and other Divine Scriptures are not separate books. They are the different editions of a single Book of God which has been named *al-kitab* here. All editions of the Book revealed by God were one and the same as regards content. However, the bearers of the previous scriptures could not in the later periods preserve them in their original form. Therefore, God revealed His Book (*muhaymin*) i.e. the Quran, the authentic expression of His will, — a touchstone which reveals which sections of the other scriptures have retained their original form and which have been changed.

50 Is it pagan laws that they wish to be judged by? Who is a better judge than God for men whose faith is firm? [a]

أَفَحُكْمَ ٱلْجَٰهِلِيَّةِ يَبْغُونَ ۚ وَمَنْ أَحْسَنُ مِنَ ٱللَّهِ حُكْمًا لِّقَوْمٍ يُوقِنُونَ ۞

---

[a] The Jews had formulated a new self-made religion by mingling their own innovations with the true religion of God. Their self interests were linked with this self-devised religion. Therefore, they were not at all ready to give it up and adopt the pure religion introduced by the Prophet. Instead of bowing down before the Truth, they took to harassing the flag-bearer of Truth, so that he should kneel down before them, give up the true religion of God and accept the religion devised by them. Had it been the will of God, He could have tied the hands of these transgressors at the very first instance and they would not have succeeded in harassing him. But God allowed them some respite to put their evil plans into action. This was done so as to make it abundantly clear that these claimants of so-called righteousness were the worst type of irreligious people; being devotees not of God but of their own self-interests. This act of God, though it constituted a hard test for the missionary of Truth, was the only way a decision might be reached as to who deserved paradise and who deserved hell.

It is the weakness of the human being that he wants to fulfill his desires. Being governed by God's commandments is, therefore, not tolerable to him. He then goes so far as to use self-devised interpretations of the Divine religion to make it conform to his desires. Pure religion is acceptable only to those who do not view things in the light of their desires, preferring to make the moral choice of rising above them. The word of God is undoubtedly the truest word. But in this present world of trial, every Truth is hidden behind the curtain of doubt. It is the test of a man that he should be able to tear asunder this curtain, that he should be able to make the unseen observable to himself, so that he may be in possession of the Truth. One who is caught up in outward doubts is a failure and one who brushes aside the veil of apparent doubts and finds the Truth has achieved success.

⁵¹ Believers, do not take the Jews and Christians as allies. They are allies with one another. Whoever of you takes them as an ally shall become one of them. God does not guide the wrongdoers.^a

♦ يَـٰٓأَيُّهَا ٱلَّذِينَ ءَامَنُوا۟ لَا تَتَّخِذُوا۟ ٱلْيَهُودَ وَٱلنَّصَـٰرَىٰٓ أَوْلِيَآءَ ۘ بَعْضُهُمْ أَوْلِيَآءُ بَعْضٍ ۚ وَمَن يَتَوَلَّهُم مِّنكُمْ فَإِنَّهُۥ مِنْهُمْ ۗ إِنَّ ٱللَّهَ لَا يَهْدِى ٱلْقَوْمَ ٱلظَّـٰلِمِينَ ۝

---

^a In Arabia, in the early days of Islam, the Jews and Christians held a monopoly of the major economic resources of the country, and made efforts day and night to uproot the Muslims, who were as yet a newly emerging force. The people, deeply impressed by the centuries of history which reinforced the greatness of the Jews and the Christians, saw them as having such power that they could never be overthrown. The weaker members of the Muslim community did not, therefore, want to take part in Islamic efforts in such a way as to displease them, for if this struggle ended in defeat for the Muslims, they would have to face the vengeful retaliation of these powerful enemies. In order to protect themselves from future danger, they lived in a state of dual loyalty, which itself was not without its hazards. They lost sight of the fact that worshipping the Truth solely in unimportant matters would not stand them in good stead if, once faced with danger, they lent their support to upholders of falsehood: their fate would inevitably be no different from the fate of those they had co-operated with whenever they felt imperiled.

⁵² You will see those whose minds are diseased hastening towards them, saying, 'We fear lest a misfortune befall us.' But God may well bring about victory or make a decision which is favourable to you. Then they will repent of the thoughts, which they secretly harboured in their hearts. ⁵³ Then the believers will say, 'Are these the men who swore their strongest oaths by God, that they were with you?' Their works will come to nothing and they will lose all. ⁵⁴ Believers, if any among you renounce the faith, God will replace them by others who love Him and are loved by Him, who will be kind and considerate towards believers and firm and unyielding towards those who deny the truth. They will strive hard for the cause of God and will in no way take to heart the reproaches of the fault finder. Such is God's bounty, which He gives to anyone He wishes. God is bountiful and all-knowing.ᵃ

فَتَرَى ٱلَّذِينَ فِى قُلُوبِهِم مَّرَضٌ يُسَٰرِعُونَ فِيهِمْ يَقُولُونَ نَخْشَىٰٓ أَن تُصِيبَنَا دَآئِرَةٌ فَعَسَى ٱللَّهُ أَن يَأْتِىَ بِٱلْفَتْحِ أَوْ أَمْرٍ مِّنْ عِندِهِۦ فَيُصْبِحُواْ عَلَىٰ مَآ أَسَرُّواْ فِىٓ أَنفُسِهِمْ نَٰدِمِينَ ۝ وَيَقُولُ ٱلَّذِينَ ءَامَنُوٓاْ أَهَٰٓؤُلَآءِ ٱلَّذِينَ أَقْسَمُواْ بِٱللَّهِ جَهْدَ أَيْمَٰنِهِمْ إِنَّهُمْ لَمَعَكُمْ حَبِطَتْ أَعْمَٰلُهُمْ فَأَصْبَحُواْ خَٰسِرِينَ ۝ يَٰٓأَيُّهَا ٱلَّذِينَ ءَامَنُواْ مَن يَرْتَدَّ مِنكُمْ عَن دِينِهِۦ فَسَوْفَ يَأْتِى ٱللَّهُ بِقَوْمٍ يُحِبُّهُمْ وَيُحِبُّونَهُۥٓ أَذِلَّةٍ عَلَى ٱلْمُؤْمِنِينَ أَعِزَّةٍ عَلَى ٱلْكَٰفِرِينَ يُجَٰهِدُونَ فِى سَبِيلِ ٱللَّهِ وَلَا يَخَافُونَ لَوْمَةَ لَآئِمٍ ذَٰلِكَ فَضْلُ ٱللَّهِ يُؤْتِيهِ مَن يَشَآءُ وَٱللَّهُ وَٰسِعٌ عَلِيمٌ ۝

ᵃ In a person's life, the most critical moment is when he has to make some sacrifice in order to stay resolutely on the path of Islam. If such occasions arise in human life, it is so that individuals may have the opportunity to make a clear avowal of their confirmation or rejection of Islam. God wants a man to prove his Islamism not only in danger-free conditions, but also when he is required to suppress his emotions or face danger to his life and property. Only on his success in this test does a man become entitled to be included by God among His faithful and loyal subjects. It is by providing proof of his Islamism on such occasions that a man's previous deeds are validated. If he is unable to do so, he renders all his previous deeds valueless.

Every test in this world is a test of intention. What man has to do to prove his intention is simply to ignore dangers; in that way he takes the first step on the path towards God. Then God's help comes to him immediately thereafter. But one who does not provide proof of his intention and does not take the first step in the direction of God, is a transgressor in His eyes. Such individuals cannot then expect to be sent God's unilateral help.

⁵⁵ Your helpers are only God and His Messenger and the believers who say their prayers and pay the alms and bow down in worship. ⁵⁶ Those who ally themsleves with God, His Messenger, and the believers must know that God's party is sure to triumph.^a

إِنَّمَا وَلِيُّكُمُ ٱللَّهُ وَرَسُولُهُۥ وَٱلَّذِينَ ءَامَنُوا۟ ٱلَّذِينَ يُقِيمُونَ ٱلصَّلَوٰةَ وَيُؤْتُونَ ٱلزَّكَوٰةَ وَهُمْ رَٰكِعُونَ ۝ وَمَن يَتَوَلَّ ٱللَّهَ وَرَسُولَهُۥ وَٱلَّذِينَ ءَامَنُوٓا۟ فَإِنَّ حِزْبَ ٱللَّهِ هُمُ ٱلْغَٰلِبُونَ ۝

^a If after embracing the Faith, one does not fulfill the requirements of Faith, one has, in the eyes of God, turned away from religion. The truly faithful people are those whose entire beings are so pervaded by Faith that they develop a relation with God at the level of love. Fulfillment of Islamic objectives should be so dear to them that there should be nothing but sympathy and kindness in their hearts for their brothers in Islam. They should become so kind-hearted towards Muslims that their powers and talents should never be used against them.

Islamic life is a purposeful life and is therefore a life of struggle. It is the mission of a Muslim to convey the religion of God to all God's subjects, guiding the world to keep away from the path leading to hell and to tread the path leading to paradise. In the course of carrying out this task, one has naturally to face different types of difficulties and suffer ignomiy. Ultimately, two groups are formed—one consisting of those whose hearts are set in this world and the other whose focus is the Hereafter. A regular tug-of-war starts between these two groups. The test of man is that in all moments of difficulty and strife, he proves to be one who places complete reliance on God and, without caring for anybody except God, continues his spiritual journey, until that Day arrives when he shall stand accountable before God.

The attention of such people centres almost entirely on God. They are steadfast in observing *salat* (prayer); they offer *zakat* (prescribed alms), and their relations with others are based on mutual well-wishing. Their bowing down before God shows that in their worldly affairs there is no egoism or arrogance. They invariably adopt an attitude of humility and on all occasions do as God desires. When people of this type come together at any one place in considerable numbers, they are destined to become dominant in that region.

⁵⁷ Believers! Do not seek the friendship of those who were given the Book before you or the disbelievers who ridicule your religion and make a jest of it.ᵃ Have fear of God, if you are true believers. ⁵⁸ When you call them to prayer, they treat it as a jest and a diversion. This is because they are devoid of understanding. ⁵⁹ Say, 'People of the Book! Do you resent us only because we believe in God and in what has been revealed to us and to others before, and because most of you are disobedient?' ⁶⁰ Say, 'Shall I tell you who will receive a worse reward from God? Those whom God has rejected and with whom He has been angry. They were condemned as apes and swine and those who worship the evil. These are in the worst plight and farthest astray from the right path.'ᵃ

يَـٰٓأَيُّهَا ٱلَّذِينَ ءَامَنُوا۟ لَا تَتَّخِذُوا۟ ٱلَّذِينَ ٱتَّخَذُوا۟ دِينَكُمْ هُزُوًا وَلَعِبًا مِّنَ ٱلَّذِينَ أُوتُوا۟ ٱلْكِتَـٰبَ مِن قَبْلِكُمْ وَٱلْكُفَّارَ أَوْلِيَآءَ ۚ وَٱتَّقُوا۟ ٱللَّهَ إِن كُنتُم مُّؤْمِنِينَ ۝ وَإِذَا نَادَيْتُمْ إِلَى ٱلصَّلَوٰةِ ٱتَّخَذُوهَا هُزُوًا وَلَعِبًا ۚ ذَٰلِكَ بِأَنَّهُمْ قَوْمٌ لَّا يَعْقِلُونَ ۝ قُلْ يَـٰٓأَهْلَ ٱلْكِتَـٰبِ هَلْ تَنقِمُونَ مِنَّآ إِلَّآ أَنْ ءَامَنَّا بِٱللَّهِ وَمَآ أُنزِلَ إِلَيْنَا وَمَآ أُنزِلَ مِن قَبْلُ وَأَنَّ أَكْثَرَكُمْ فَـٰسِقُونَ ۝ قُلْ هَلْ أُنَبِّئُكُم بِشَرٍّ مِّن ذَٰلِكَ مَثُوبَةً عِندَ ٱللَّهِ ۚ مَن لَّعَنَهُ ٱللَّهُ وَغَضِبَ عَلَيْهِ وَجَعَلَ مِنْهُمُ ٱلْقِرَدَةَ وَٱلْخَنَازِيرَ وَعَبَدَ ٱلطَّـٰغُوتَ ۚ أُو۟لَـٰٓئِكَ شَرٌّ مَّكَانًا وَأَضَلُّ عَن سَوَآءِ ٱلسَّبِيلِ ۝

ᵃ When the call for true and pure religion goes out those who claim, on the basis of a self-made religion, to have a monopoly of devotion to God, develop such an extreme aversion to it that they lose all sense of rationality. They even ridicule things that are unanimously treated as sacred. This was how some people of Madinah behaved. They did not hesitate even to ridicule the *adhan* (the call to prayer). Any relation between Muslims and such insensate and frivolous people can be in connection only with missionary activity and can never be that of friendship.

The result of such people's lack of fear of God is that they consider pure Muslims to be criminals and, notwithstanding all of their own crimes, they blatantly hold, before God, that their dealings are absolutely fair. Such insensitivity blunts their conscience when it comes to distinguishing between Truth and falsehood and prevents their amending this state of affairs. In outward form, they may appear to be human beings but, with regard to their inner qualities, they are the worst animals. ▶

⁶¹ When they come to you they say, 'We believe,' but they come [with the resolve] to deny the truth and leave in the same state. God knows best what they are concealing.ᵃ

وَإِذَا جَآءُوكُمْ قَالُوٓاْ ءَامَنَّا وَقَد دَّخَلُواْ بِٱلْكُفْرِ وَهُمْ قَدْ خَرَجُواْ بِهِۦ ۚ وَٱللَّهُ أَعْلَمُ بِمَا كَانُواْ يَكْتُمُونَ ﴿٦١﴾

A man's delicate, subtle feelings, such as modesty, broadmindedness, the desire for cleanliness, etc., which function as the watch-guards of God within him and prevent him from evil action, get smothered. The last stage of his downfall comes when his whole life is corroded by satanic ways. When a group reaches this stage, and is distanced from God's grace to the furthest possible extent, its own nature becomes distorted and it becomes a curse to itself and to the rest of humanity. Having drifted so far away from the right path of nature, it starts living like the animals.

What prevents a man from following the dictates of his desires is his moral fibre. But when obstinacy and enmity dominate him, his ability to think becomes suppressed and then there is nothing to combat the pressure of his desires. He may be a human being in appearance but, inside he is an animal; a man with deep insight, just by looking at him, can tell what animal is hidden inside the human exterior.

ᵃ There were certain of the Jews of Madinah who were impressed by Islam. Moreover, considering the increasing domination of Islam, they did not want to incur its open enmity. Although in their hearts these people were steadfast in the religion of their forefathers, they used to make a show of being believers by their utterances. Such people forget that their dealings are not actually with any human being but with God, and God is the Being who knows what is inside one's heart. When He deals with anyone, it will be based on reality and not on any words which that person chose to utter to protect his own interests.

There were two types of prominent Jews—one the rabbis and the other the holy men. The latter were *ahbar*, i.e. scholars and interpreters. Both types remained busy day and night in the work of religion, for their leadership was propped up solely by religious work and they received substantial amounts in the name of religion. But, the real secret of their leadership and public acclaim was their presentation of a popular version of religion rather than the true religion favoured by God. They spoke and acted ostensibly for the sake of religion, but in reality their words and deeds were worldly-wise. Worse, they gave to the people, in the name of religion, whatever they wanted for themselves, knowing full well that in actuality those things were unconnected with religion.

⁶²You see many among them vie with one another in sin and transgression and practice what is unlawful. It is vile indeed what they have been doing! ⁶³Why do their rabbis and scholars not forbid them to utter sinful words or to consume what is unlawful? Their actions are indeed vile.ᵃ

وَتَرَىٰ كَثِيرًا مِّنْهُمْ يُسَٰرِعُونَ فِى ٱلْإِثْمِ وَٱلْعُدْوَٰنِ وَأَكْلِهِمُ ٱلسُّحْتَ لَبِئْسَ مَا كَانُوا۟ يَعْمَلُونَ ۝ لَوْلَا يَنْهَىٰهُمُ ٱلرَّبَّٰنِيُّونَ وَٱلْأَحْبَارُ عَن قَوْلِهِمُ ٱلْإِثْمَ وَأَكْلِهِمُ ٱلسُّحْتَ لَبِئْسَ مَا كَانُوا۟ يَصْنَعُونَ ۝

ᵃ The favoured religion of God is that of *taqwa* (fear of God). In other words, a man should live in society in such a way that he utters no words of sin; in his activities he should avoid forbidden ways and he should behave with entire fairness towards those with whom he has dealings. But a man's selfishness puts him on the path of world-worship; he wants to lead a life in which he is not troubled by having to distinguish between right and wrong, and in which he needs to worry only about his own worldly interests. The general run of the Jewish people mindlessly trod this path of self-centredness. This being so, it was the duty of the foremost among them to alert them to their wrongdoing and to wean them away from this course. Instead of this, they reached a tacit understanding with the common people. They started disseminating among them a particular type of religion which guaranteed their salvation and promised them a high status, without their having to change their actual way of living in any way. These prominent people did not disturb the current lives of the common people, but used to recite to them false stories of the supremacy of the Jewish community; giving a religious colour to their communal events and conveying to them the glad news that they only had to repeat a number of ritual actions and palaces would be built for them in paradise. Before God, it is the most evil deed to disseminate this type of religion among the people, in which change in their actual lives is not required, and to delude them into thinking that, by publicly performing certain showy rites, their entry into paradise will be guaranteed.

⁶⁴ The Jews say, 'The hand of God is tied up.' May their own hands be tied up and may they be cursed for what they say. No indeed! His hands are both outstretched: He bestows as He will. What is revealed to you from your Lord will surely increase in most of them their obstinate rebellion and denial of truth; and We have sown among them enmity and hatred till the Day of Resurrection. Whenever they kindle the fire of war, God puts it out. They spread evil in the land, but God does not love the evil-doers.ᵃ

وَقَالَتِ ٱلْيَهُودُ يَدُ ٱللَّهِ مَغْلُولَةٌ غُلَّتْ أَيْدِيهِمْ وَلُعِنُواْ بِمَا قَالُواْ بَلْ يَدَاهُ مَبْسُوطَتَانِ يُنفِقُ كَيْفَ يَشَآءُ وَلَيَزِيدَنَّ كَثِيرًا مِّنْهُم مَّآ أُنزِلَ إِلَيْكَ مِن رَّبِّكَ طُغْيَـٰنًا وَكُفْرًا وَأَلْقَيْنَا بَيْنَهُمُ ٱلْعَدَٰوَةَ وَٱلْبَغْضَآءَ إِلَىٰ يَوْمِ ٱلْقِيَٰمَةِ كُلَّمَآ أَوْقَدُواْ نَارًا لِّلْحَرْبِ أَطْفَأَهَا ٱللَّهُ وَيَسْعَوْنَ فِى ٱلْأَرْضِ فَسَادًا وَٱللَّهُ لَا يُحِبُّ ٱلْمُفْسِدِينَ ۞

ᵃ In the Quran, when stress was laid on spending in charity for God's sake and when people were urged to give gratuitous loans to God, the Jews made this the subject of ridicule. They used to say that God is a pauper and his subjects are rich; God's hands are empty these days. They knew full well that God was above suffering a shortage of anything; so such statements were not directed against God, but against the Prophet and the Quran, and were meant actually to show that the Prophet was not the true Prophet and that Quran was not the Book of God. According to them, had the Quran truly been sent down on behalf of God, its content would have been quite different. But those who hold forth in this way only prove that they are devoid of the spirit of real religion; they are living in a state of insensitivity.

When the Jews refused to accept the guidance offered by the Quran, it was not a simple refusal. It was actually a claim that they already enjoyed salvation and did not need any further guidance. An extreme type of egotism develops in people who have such a conceited mentality. In their dealings with others, even in their everyday lives, they are not prepared to give up their ego. As a result, the whole of society falls a prey to mutual differences and enmity.

The call of a prophet is that man should also adopt that religion of obedience to God which has already been adopted by all things of the universe. This means keeping a peaceful balance in the world (*islah*). Now, those who place impediments in the way of the prophetic call seek to create a disturbance in this world of God. However, man has the freedom only to deal with his own inner turmoil. Nobody has that right over another's fate.

65 If only the People of the Book would believe and be mindful of God, We would surely pardon their sins and We would surely admit them into the Gardens of Bliss. 66 If they had observed the Torah and the Gospel and what was revealed to them from their Lord, they would surely have been nourished from above and from below. There are some among them who are on the right course; but there are many among them who do nothing but evil.*

وَلَوْ أَنَّ أَهْلَ ٱلْكِتَٰبِ ءَامَنُوا۟ وَٱتَّقَوْا۟ لَكَفَّرْنَا عَنْهُمْ سَيِّئَاتِهِمْ وَلَأَدْخَلْنَٰهُمْ جَنَّٰتِ ٱلنَّعِيمِ ۝ وَلَوْ أَنَّهُمْ أَقَامُوا۟ ٱلتَّوْرَىٰةَ وَٱلْإِنجِيلَ وَمَا أُنزِلَ إِلَيْهِم مِّن رَّبِّهِمْ لَأَكَلُوا۟ مِن فَوْقِهِمْ وَمِن تَحْتِ أَرْجُلِهِم مِّنْهُمْ أُمَّةٌ مُّقْتَصِدَةٌ وَكَثِيرٌ مِّنْهُمْ سَآءَ مَا يَعْمَلُونَ ۝

---

a The root cause of all waywardness is man's reckless bravado. But once a man fears God, he immediately understands the power emanating from Him and his bravado vanishes. His fear of God immediately makes him grasp what is God's will, and he there and then accepts it. All impure impulses are thus driven out. When a man makes himself wholly attentive to God, he thereby becomes entitled to God's attention. That is, God washes away all his human weaknesses and, after his death, He lodges him in the flourishing gardens of paradise. It is man's psychological weaknesses which are the evils preventing him from advancing on the way towards paradise, but with the help of God, one can overcome such weaknesses and ultimately reach the goal of eternal bliss.

Whenever the call for Truth goes out, those who enjoy positions of prominence in the prevailing system feel perturbed. They fear that by complying with it, their economic interests and high positions will be jeopardized. But, such an attitude is only the result of their narrow-mindedness. Such people forget that what they are faced with, and which they fear, has appeared only to test their entitlement to God's blessings: the decision about their worthiness to receive His blessings will depend not on their self-centred devices, but on their receptiveness to the call for Truth. In other words, their rejection of it, in the interests of retaining their high status, is the very act which, in God's eyes, rules out their ever meriting His favour.

It invariably happens in the case of those communities that are the bearers of Divine Scriptures that, by making additions to or deletions in the original, they form a self-made religion; and after a long passage of time, its members become so familiar with it that they consider it to be the true religion of God. Given this history, when the straightforward and true religion of God is presented to them, they find it unfamiliar and become perturbed by it. This was the condition of Jews and Christians. So, a large majority of them failed to be impressed by the truth of Islam. Only a few people, such as Najashi (Negus) the King of Abyssinia and 'Abdullah ibn Salam, etc,. who were already on the path of moderation, immediately understood the truth of Islam. They came forward to embrace Islam, as if they had already been moving in this direction and, simply in order to maintain the continuity of their journey, they had joined the caravan of Muslims.

⁶⁷O Messenger, deliver whatever has been sent down to you by your Lord. If you do not do so, you will not have conveyed His message. God will defend you from mankind. For God does not guide those who deny the truth.ᵃ

۞ يَـٰٓأَيُّهَا ٱلرَّسُولُ بَلِّغْ مَآ أُنزِلَ إِلَيْكَ مِن رَّبِّكَ ۖ وَإِن لَّمْ تَفْعَلْ فَمَا بَلَّغْتَ رِسَالَتَهُۥ ۚ وَٱللَّهُ يَعْصِمُكَ مِنَ ٱلنَّاسِ ۗ إِنَّ ٱللَّهَ لَا يَهْدِى ٱلْقَوْمَ ٱلْكَـٰفِرِينَ ۝

ᵃ When the Prophet Muhammad appeared in Arabia, it was not the case that there was nobody professing religion there at that time. The whole of Arabian society was founded on religion. It was in the name of religion that many people had assumed positions of prominence and leadership. Being holders of high religious positions was the symbol of a high status in society and something to be proud of. In spite of this, the Prophet had to endure the worst type of opposition from the people of Arabia. The reason for this was the prevalence among them of a new self-made religion which had usurped the real religion of God. In this region, centuries of tradition had resulted in the formation of various seats of power and centres of vested interests. This being the situation, when the Prophet gave a call for pure religion, the people felt that it was damaging to their religious status. They were afraid that once this pure religion took root, the old religious order which had given them prominent status would be destroyed.

Such a state of affairs is very hard on the preacher of the word of God. Openly pursuing his religious activities becomes equivalent to struggling against the established religious authorities of the time. He feels that if he makes no compromises in propagating true religion, he shall have to face the most severe reaction; he will be ridiculed; he will be degraded; he will become impoverished, violent action will be taken against him; and he will be deprived of all assistance and support.

Now he has two ways open to him. He can either take worldly considerations into account, in which case successful communication of the word of God appears impossible. Or he can ignore the constraints of worldly considerations, in which case in fulfilling his responsibilities, God's promise of help will assist him to concentrate. God promises that if he focuses fully on preaching, His help will be enough in case of any difficulties created by the addressee community. The purveyor of God's will should simply trust in God.

The reaction of the addressee community is natural and the preacher has to face it at all events. But its sphere is limited to the scope of God's Law relating to the trial of man. It can never happen that opponents gain control of the situation to the extent of stopping the preacher's work or preventing its completion. Achieving the target of such work is the plan of God. So, it will inevitably be completed. Thereafter, acceptance by the addressee group is its own responsibility, and can be effective only to the extent the addressees desire.

68 Say, 'People of the Book, you have no ground to stand on until you observe the Torah and the Gospel and what is revealed to you from your Lord.' What is revealed to you from your Lord will surely increase many of them in rebellion and in their denial of the truth. But do not grieve for those who deny the truth. 69 Believers, Jews, Sabaeans and Christians—whoever believes in God and the Last Day and does what is right—shall have nothing to fear nor shall they grieve.[a]

قُلْ يَٰٓأَهْلَ ٱلْكِتَٰبِ لَسْتُمْ عَلَىٰ شَىْءٍ حَتَّىٰ تُقِيمُواْ ٱلتَّوْرَىٰةَ وَٱلْإِنجِيلَ وَمَا أُنزِلَ إِلَيْكُم مِّن رَّبِّكُمْ وَلَيَزِيدَنَّ كَثِيرًا مِّنْهُم مَّا أُنزِلَ إِلَيْكَ مِن رَّبِّكَ طُغْيَٰنًا وَكُفْرًا فَلَا تَأْسَ عَلَى ٱلْقَوْمِ ٱلْكَٰفِرِينَ ۝ إِنَّ ٱلَّذِينَ ءَامَنُواْ وَٱلَّذِينَ هَادُواْ وَٱلصَّٰبِـُٔونَ وَٱلنَّصَٰرَىٰ مَنْ ءَامَنَ بِٱللَّهِ وَٱلْيَوْمِ ٱلْءَاخِرِ وَعَمِلَ صَٰلِحًا فَلَا خَوْفٌ عَلَيْهِمْ وَلَا هُمْ يَحْزَنُونَ ۝

---

[a] The members of the Jewish community, thriving on stories of the excellence of their community and the supposed holiness of their elders, had not subjected themselves and their personal affairs to the will of God. Moreover, as a result of wishful thinking, they were convinced of their salvation before God. But their wishful thinking had no value in His eyes, for they were not ruled by His religion. What actually carries weight with God is being punctilious about carrying out His commandments and founding one's life on His religion.

When people who indulge in wishful thinking and false hopes are confronted by the message that, before God, it is intentions and deeds that carry weight and not wishes and false hopes, they react strongly against it. In this call they see the demolition of their castles in the air and this imagined state of affairs becomes a trial for them. It follows that they become strong opponents of such a call. Their self-centredness, hidden in the garb of showy devotion to God, comes out into the open. While they should have taken Divine nourishment from this call for Truth, they are instead spurred on by it to disbelief and arrogance.

The generations succeeding the early followers of the prophets of ancient times gradually assumed the shape of a regular group or community. They no longer followed the examples set by the prophets; instead they perpetuated legends eulogizing their past glories and supremacy. Every group began to regard itself as the best of all, believing that their salvation was certain and that their status before God was the highest of all. But the fact is that such groupist religions have no value in the eyes of God. Every individual's case will be separately presented before God and the decision about his future will be wholly based on his own deeds and not on any other basis.

Upholding the Book of God means having full faith in God; being overwhelmed by the fear of the Hereafter; and leading a life of a righteous character among one's fellow human beings. ▶

70 We made a covenant with the Children of Israel and sent forth messengers among them. But whenever a messenger came to them with a message that was not to their liking, some they accused of lying, while others they put to death, 71 and they imagined that no harm would come to them; and so they became blind and deaf [of heart]. God turned to them in mercy; yet again many of them became blind and deaf. God is fully aware of their actions.[a]

لَقَدْ أَخَذْنَا مِيثَقَ بَنِى إِسْرَءِيلَ وَأَرْسَلْنَا إِلَيْهِمْ رُسُلًا كُلَّمَا جَاءَهُمْ رَسُولٌ بِمَا لَا تَهْوَىٰ أَنفُسُهُمْ فَرِيقًا كَذَّبُوا۟ وَفَرِيقًا يَقْتُلُونَ ۝ وَحَسِبُوٓا۟ أَلَّا تَكُونَ فِتْنَةٌ فَعَمُوا۟ وَصَمُّوا۟ ثُمَّ تَابَ ٱللَّهُ عَلَيْهِمْ ثُمَّ عَمُوا۟ وَصَمُّوا۟ كَثِيرٌ مِّنْهُمْ وَٱللَّهُ بَصِيرٌۢ بِمَا يَعْمَلُونَ ۝

This is the true religion and everybody is required to adopt it in his way of living. The community blessed with the Book of God has great merit in the world so long as its members adopt God's true religion. On deviating from this they become completely undeserving before God—even less meritorious than open deniers and polytheists.

[a] God had taken the pledge of faith and obedience from the Jews through Moses. They fulfilled this pledge for just a few days. Thereafter, their behaviour started deteriorating. Then, God raised reformers among them to remind them of their pledge. But their waywardness and arrogance went on increasing. They went to the extent of silencing the admonishers themselves, and killed many people. When their arrogance went beyond all limits, God caused them to be subjected to the rule of Nebuchadnezzar, the ruler of Babylon and Nineveh (Iraq). He attacked and destroyed their holy city of Jerusalem in 586 B.C., and enslaving the Jews, he took them to his country as bonded labour. After this event, the hearts of the Jews were softened and they sought God's pardon. Now, God helped them through Cyrus (the King of Iran) who captured their area in 539 B.C. by attacking the Chaldeans and defeating them. Thereafter, he freed the Jews from their exile and allowed them to go back to their country and settle there.

Now, the Jews got a new lease of life and progressed considerably, but after a very short time they once again fell into the ways of recklessness and arrogance. Again, God warned them through prophets and reformers, but they did not come to their senses. They went to the extent of killing John (Yahya) and also a man whom they understood to be Jesus. Now, the wrath of God broke loose on them and, in the year 70 A.D., they were defeated by the Roman Emperor, Titus, who attacked their country and destroyed them. After this, the Jews could never stand on their own.

72 Indeed, they are deniers of the truth who say, 'God is the Christ, the son of Mary.' For the Christ himself said, 'Children of Israel, serve God, my Lord and your Lord.' If anyone associates anything with God, God will forbid him the Garden and the Fire will be his home. The wrongdoers shall have no helpers.ᵃ

لَقَدْ كَفَرَ ٱلَّذِينَ قَالُوٓا۟ إِنَّ ٱللَّهَ هُوَ ٱلْمَسِيحُ ٱبْنُ مَرْيَمَ وَقَالَ ٱلْمَسِيحُ يَٰبَنِىٓ إِسْرَٰٓءِيلَ ٱعْبُدُوا۟ ٱللَّهَ رَبِّى وَرَبَّكُمْ إِنَّهُۥ مَن يُشْرِكْ بِٱللَّهِ فَقَدْ حَرَّمَ ٱللَّهُ عَلَيْهِ ٱلْجَنَّةَ وَمَأْوَىٰهُ ٱلنَّارُ وَمَا لِلظَّٰلِمِينَ مِنْ أَنصَارٍ ۝

ᵃ The bearers of divine scriptures in later periods developed the belief that they were the special people of God and that whatever they did, they would not have to face any reckoning. In the teachings of God, there are clear statements against such beliefs, but they became blind and deaf to them. They built around themselves such barriers of self-made beliefs and fictitious stories that God's warnings went unnoticed. The history of the Jews shows that whenever a community bearing the scriptures was made to suffer subjugation by its 'enemies', this was designed as a testing period for it. Light punishment administered to the community was meant to awaken its moral sense. If feelings of devotion to God were then aroused in its members, there was a cessation of the punishment, but if this did not happen, God rejected them, cast them away and did not turn His attention towards them ever again.

Almighty God granted Jesus the power to perform extraordinary miracles. This was done so that people should recognize him as a prophet and have faith in him. But it turned out otherwise. Jesus had been sent by God purely for the guidance of the people, but looking to his miracles, the Christians developed the belief that he was God and that God was incarnate in him. The Jews for their part ignored him, relegating him to the position of a magician and conjurer. While the latter group rejected him, the former group was inspired by him to establish polytheistic beliefs.

73 They are deniers of the truth who say, 'God is one of three.' There is only One God. If they do not desist from so saying, a painful punishment is bound to befall such of them as are bent on denying the truth. 74 Why do they not turn to God and ask for His forgiveness? God is forgiving and merciful. 75 Christ, son of Mary, was no more than a messenger. Many messengers passed away before him. His mother was a virtuous woman; and they both ate food [like other mortals]. See how We make the signs clear to them! See how they turn away! 76 Say, 'Do you worship something other than God, that has no power to do you harm or good? God alone is the All Hearing and All Knowing.'ᵃ

لَّقَدْ كَفَرَ ٱلَّذِينَ قَالُوٓا۟ إِنَّ ٱللَّهَ ثَالِثُ ثَلَٰثَةٍ وَمَا مِنْ إِلَٰهٍ إِلَّآ إِلَٰهٌ وَٰحِدٌ وَإِن لَّمْ يَنتَهُوا۟ عَمَّا يَقُولُونَ لَيَمَسَّنَّ ٱلَّذِينَ كَفَرُوا۟ مِنْهُمْ عَذَابٌ أَلِيمٌ ٧٣ أَفَلَا يَتُوبُونَ إِلَى ٱللَّهِ وَيَسْتَغْفِرُونَهُ وَٱللَّهُ غَفُورٌ رَّحِيمٌ ٧٤ مَّا ٱلْمَسِيحُ ٱبْنُ مَرْيَمَ إِلَّا رَسُولٌ قَدْ خَلَتْ مِن قَبْلِهِ ٱلرُّسُلُ وَأُمُّهُ صِدِّيقَةٌ كَانَا يَأْكُلَانِ ٱلطَّعَامَ ٱنظُرْ كَيْفَ نُبَيِّنُ لَهُمُ ٱلْآيَٰتِ ثُمَّ ٱنظُرْ أَنَّىٰ يُؤْفَكُونَ ٧٥ قُلْ أَتَعْبُدُونَ مِن دُونِ ٱللَّهِ مَا لَا يَمْلِكُ لَكُمْ ضَرًّا وَلَا نَفْعًا وَٱللَّهُ هُوَ ٱلسَّمِيعُ ٱلْعَلِيمُ ٧٦

ᵃ Only that Being can be worth worshipping who is Himself not dependent on anybody and who has the power to benefit or harm others. Food is the most significant symbol of man's dependence. One who is dependent for his food is dependent about everything. One who takes food is a completely dependent being. How can such a being be God? The same is true of conferring benefits or inflicting harm. Somebody's receiving benefits or suffering harm are events which require the co-ordination of universal factors for them to come into effect. No ordinary human being is capable of organizing such universal factors. Therefore, no human being can elevate himself to a position where he may be treated as worthy of worship.

When a man makes somebody the centre of his veneration and love, the underlying feeling is that that 'somebody' enjoys a high status in this world of God and that he will be helpful to him before God. But all such hopes are false. In this world of test and trial, the fact that all except God are helpless is not absolutely clear. That is why man suffers from such a misapprehension. But in the Hereafter, when the truth is revealed, man will see that, except for God, all the supports on which he had relied were absolutely valueless.

⁷⁷ Say, 'People of the Book! Do not go to extremes in your religion and do not follow the whims of those who went astray before you—they caused many to go astray and themselves strayed away from the right path.' [a]

قُل يَـٰٓأَهۡلَ ٱلۡكِتَـٰبِ لَا تَغۡلُوا۟ فِى دِينِكُمۡ غَيۡرَ ٱلۡحَقِّ وَلَا تَتَّبِعُوٓا۟ أَهۡوَآءَ قَوۡمٍ قَدۡ ضَلُّوا۟ مِن قَبۡلُ وَأَضَلُّوا۟ كَثِيرًا وَضَلُّوا۟ عَن سَوَآءِ ٱلسَّبِيلِ ۝

---

[a] In the eyes of Jesus's early disciples 'Jesus was a man who was from God.' They considered him a human being and a prophet. When his religion spread out from Syria, it had to encounter the philosophy of Egypt and Greece. Such persons accepted Christianity and entered the Christian fold as were under the influence of the philosophic thought of the time. As a result of internal causes and external factors, a new era began in Christianity when efforts were made to describe Christianity in the prevalent philosophic style of the times.

In the civilized world of those days, the philosophers of Egypt and Greece were dominant. Their thinking greatly influenced the intelligentsia of those days. The Greek philosophers had formed an imaginary concept of the universe. They used to interpret reality on three levels—existence, life and knowledge. Christian theologians were themselves impressed by these ideas and wanted to attract the intellectuals of the times towards Christianity. They tried, therefore, to mould their religion on the lines of current thinking. They offered an interpretation of Christianity which directly related it in essence to the aforesaid three levels. They hoped that in so doing the people could equate Christianity with their own way of thinking and accordingly accept it. They said that religious reality also manifested itself in the 'Trinity'. 'Existence' was the 'Father', 'Life' was the 'son' and 'knowledge' was the 'Holy Spirit'. In order to complete the religion thus interpreted, many ideas were imported into it, for example, the belief that Jesus was the embodied manifestation of *kalam* (word). After the descent of Adam every human being had become a sinner and God's son had to atone for this by acquiescing in his own crucifixion, etc. In this way, in the fourth century A.D., having been moulded to fit Egyptian, Greek and Roman concepts, what is now known as Christianity came into being.

78 Those of the Children of Israel who were bent on denying the truth were cursed by David and Jesus, the son of Mary. That was because they disobeyed and were given to transgression; 79 they would not prevent one another from doing the wrong things they did. Evil indeed were their deeds.[a]

لُعِنَ ٱلَّذِينَ كَفَرُواْ مِن بَنِىٓ إِسۡرَٰٓءِيلَ عَلَىٰ لِسَانِ دَاوُۥدَ وَعِيسَى ٱبۡنِ مَرۡيَمَ ذَٰلِكَ بِمَا عَصَواْ وَّكَانُواْ يَعۡتَدُونَ ۝ كَانُواْ لَا يَتَنَاهَوۡنَ عَن مُّنكَرٍ فَعَلُوهُ لَبِئۡسَ مَا كَانُواْ يَفۡعَلُونَ ۝

---

[a] Frequently the reason for a people's deviation from the right path of God is that they have been impressed by the thoughts of communities which have gone astray and seek to emulate them; while accepting the religion of God, they interpret it in such a way that it appears to be in consonance with current thinking. Thus, in the name of God's religion, they adopt an ungodly religion. The Christians adapted their religion to the ideas of polytheistic communities and described it as God's favoured religion. Sometimes this happens, when religion is cast in the mould of national aspirations. An example of this second type of deviation is presented by the Jews. They interpreted God's religion in such a way that it should legitimize their worldliness. For Muslims there is no scope for inserting such interpretations in the text of God's Book. But outside the text, they are free to follow the example of previous communities.

Faith makes a man sensitive about transgression and evil. When he sees anyone committing transgression or indulging in evil, he becomes perturbed and immediately wants to prevent him from behaving in this way. He relates to evil people in terms of separation and not of friendship. But when his faith weakens, he remains sensitive only about his own self. Now, only that which adversely affects his own self-interest appears to him to be evil. He remains neutral about the evils which are directed towards others.

80 You see many among them allying themselves with those who deny the truth. Evil is that which their souls have sent on ahead for them. They have incurred the wrath of God and shall suffer eternal punishment. 81 Had they believed in God and the Prophet and what was revealed to him, they would not have taken those who deny the truth as their allies, but many of them are disobedient. 82 You will find that the bitterest in their enmity to the faithful are the Jews and the polytheists; the nearest in affection to them are those who say, 'We are Christians.' That is because there are priests and monks among them; and because they are free from pride.*a*

تَرَىٰ كَثِيرًا مِّنْهُمْ يَتَوَلَّوْنَ ٱلَّذِينَ كَفَرُوا۟ لَبِئْسَ مَا قَدَّمَتْ هُمْ أَنفُسُهُمْ أَن سَخِطَ ٱللَّهُ عَلَيْهِمْ وَفِى ٱلْعَذَابِ هُمْ خَٰلِدُونَ ﴿٨٠﴾ وَلَوْ كَانُوا۟ يُؤْمِنُونَ بِٱللَّهِ وَٱلنَّبِىِّ وَمَآ أُنزِلَ إِلَيْهِ مَا ٱتَّخَذُوهُمْ أَوْلِيَآءَ وَلَٰكِنَّ كَثِيرًا مِّنْهُمْ فَٰسِقُونَ ﴿٨١﴾ ۞ لَتَجِدَنَّ أَشَدَّ ٱلنَّاسِ عَدَٰوَةً لِّلَّذِينَ ءَامَنُوا۟ ٱلْيَهُودَ وَٱلَّذِينَ أَشْرَكُوا۟ وَلَتَجِدَنَّ أَقْرَبَهُم مَّوَدَّةً لِّلَّذِينَ ءَامَنُوا۟ ٱلَّذِينَ قَالُوٓا۟ إِنَّا نَصَٰرَىٰ ذَٰلِكَ بِأَنَّ مِنْهُمْ قِسِّيسِينَ وَرُهْبَانًا وَأَنَّهُمْ لَا يَسْتَكْبِرُونَ ﴿٨٢﴾

---

a The Children of Israel faced this downfall, but that did not stop them from making self-righteous utterances and the elect among them went on making fine speeches. But they were not serious about rushing to intervene when they saw somebody indulging in tyranny and evil, or about trying to prevent such actions. David (Dawud) said of the Children of Israel of his period that not one of them was righteous, and from his discourses it is clear that the Jews used to talk peace with their neighbours, describing the law of God and reaffirming their pledge to God, when their hearts were actually full of ill intent. Jesus likewise castigated the Jews of his time, calling them hypocritical scholars who had usurped the dwellings of widows, while at the same time prolonging their prayers. He lamented the fact that they paid the tithes of mint leaves, anise and cummin seeds, while ignoring the weighty provisions of the shariat, i.e. justice, mercy and faith. He called them 'blind guides' who 'strain at a gnat and swallow a camel'. He scorned them for being apparently righteous, while from within they were entirely hypocritical and faithless. (Matthew 23).

The Jews did as Jesus said—they used to describe the law of God, offer prolonged prayers and paid their tithes from their crops. But all that was purely lip service. They used to carry out harmless commands with a show of piety, but when the question arose of treating others with justice, or when they were required to have mercy on a down-trodden person, or when there was the need to crush self-interest in order to carry out God's command, then they used to be guilty of backsliding. And if anyone pointed out their mistakes, they became his enemies. It was such behaviour which caused them to incur God's wrath and curses.

83 When they listen to what has been sent down to the Messenger, you see their eyes overflowing with tears, because of the Truth they recognize. They say, 'Our Lord, we believe, so count us among those who bear witness. 84 Why should we not believe in God and in the truth that has come down to us? We yearn for our Lord to admit us among the righteous.' 85 And for their words God will reward them with Gardens through which rivers flow, wherein they shall abide forever. That is the reward of those who do good. 86 But those who deny the truth and deny Our signs will become the inmates of Hell.ᵃ

وَإِذَا سَمِعُوا۟ مَآ أُنزِلَ إِلَى ٱلرَّسُولِ تَرَىٰٓ أَعْيُنَهُمْ تَفِيضُ مِنَ ٱلدَّمْعِ مِمَّا عَرَفُوا۟ مِنَ ٱلْحَقِّ يَقُولُونَ رَبَّنَآ ءَامَنَّا فَٱكْتُبْنَا مَعَ ٱلشَّٰهِدِينَ ۝ وَمَا لَنَا لَا نُؤْمِنُ بِٱللَّهِ وَمَا جَآءَنَا مِنَ ٱلْحَقِّ وَنَطْمَعُ أَن يُدْخِلَنَا رَبُّنَا مَعَ ٱلْقَوْمِ ٱلصَّٰلِحِينَ ۝ فَأَثَٰبَهُمُ ٱللَّهُ بِمَا قَالُوا۟ جَنَّٰتٍ تَجْرِى مِن تَحْتِهَا ٱلْأَنْهَٰرُ خَٰلِدِينَ فِيهَا ۚ وَذَٰلِكَ جَزَآءُ ٱلْمُحْسِنِينَ ۝ وَٱلَّذِينَ كَفَرُوا۟ وَكَذَّبُوا۟ بِـَٔايَٰتِنَآ أُو۟لَٰٓئِكَ أَصْحَٰبُ ٱلْجَحِيمِ ۝

ᵃ In this verse paradise is declared the reward for certain 'words' uttered by people (fa athabahumu'llah bima qalu). But what were these 'words' which made the speakers of them entitled to eternal paradise? What they said represented and gave expression to their entire being. It was the sound of the outflow of their personality. They heard God's message in such a way that they found the whole truth enshrined in it. It penetrated their hearts and minds. It caused in them a revolution which changed the entire focus of their wishes and aspirations—to the extent that all barriers of prejudice and interests broke down. They identified themselves with Truth in such a way that they lost their separate identity. They became its witness and to become a witness meant truth embedding itself within them. The Quran was not a mere book for them but a living sign of the Lord of the Universe. This Divine experience, although expressed in words, was not just a matter of words: it was a turmoil, an earthquake which affected their entire existence. So much so that tears flowed from their eyes. ▶

⁸⁷Believers, do not forbid the wholesome good things, which God made lawful to you. Do not transgress; God does not love the transgressors. ⁸⁸Eat the lawful and wholesome things, which God has given you. Fear God, in whom you believe.^a

يَـٰٓأَيُّهَا ٱلَّذِينَ ءَامَنُوا۟ لَا تُحَرِّمُوا۟ طَيِّبَـٰتِ مَآ أَحَلَّ ٱللَّهُ لَكُمْ وَلَا تَعْتَدُوٓا۟ۚ إِنَّ ٱللَّهَ لَا يُحِبُّ ٱلْمُعْتَدِينَ ۝ وَكُلُوا۟ مِمَّا رَزَقَكُمُ ٱللَّهُ حَلَـٰلًا طَيِّبًاۚ وَٱتَّقُوا۟ ٱللَّهَ ٱلَّذِىٓ أَنتُم بِهِۦ مُؤْمِنُونَ ۝

Words spoken about reality do not merely make a statement: they are the highest form in which to give meaningful shape to a man's actions and feelings, and, in the entire known universe, only man has the capacity to comprehend the refinement and significance of words and to use them to the best effect. 'Words' are the best of man's being. 'Word' is eloquent action. Therefore, when a man proves and expresses his servitude to God at the level of 'words', he establishes a certain entitlement to paradise.

The strongest reasons for non-acceptance of Truth by a man are his ego and pride. Those who have pride hidden in their hearts show the strongest reaction against the call for Truth, refusing to accept it at any cost and going so far as to become its most dangerous antagonists. On the other hand, those who are not filled with pride, while they may be flawed by any other evil, they cannot oppose the Truth to this extent.

^a The connection between man and God is a live relationship which is established on a psychological level. It is internal in nature. But when religion is on the decline, and this internal relationship becomes weakened, then the mentality develops that one must try to build up such a relationship from external sources. One of these is giving up worldly pleasures—in effect, renunciation or monasticism. It is assumed that staying away from material things will cause a man to come nearer to God. Some of the Prophet Muhammad's companions were influenced by such monastic thoughts. They intended to give up eating meats and sleeping at nights, to castrate themselves and leave their homes to lead the life of hermits. Some of them went to the extent of taking a vow or oath to this effect. But people were prohibited from doing this and were told that one could not attain nearness to God just by treating permitted things (halal) as forbidden things (haram). Whatever a man achieves, is done by his remaining within natural limits, and not by his inventing stricter limits.

⁸⁹ God will not call you to account for your meaningless oaths, but He will call you to account for the oaths, which you swear in earnest. The expiation for a broken oath is the feeding of ten needy men with such food as you normally offer to your own people; or the clothing of ten needy men; or the freeing of one slave. Anyone who lacks the means shall fast for three days. That is the expiation of your breaking the oaths that you have sworn. Do keep your oaths. Thus God explains to you His commandments, so that you may be grateful.ᵃ

لَا يُؤَاخِذُكُمُ ٱللَّهُ بِٱللَّغْوِ فِىٓ أَيْمَٰنِكُمْ وَلَٰكِن يُؤَاخِذُكُم بِمَا عَقَّدتُّمُ ٱلْأَيْمَٰنَ فَكَفَّٰرَتُهُۥٓ إِطْعَامُ عَشَرَةِ مَسَٰكِينَ مِنْ أَوْسَطِ مَا تُطْعِمُونَ أَهْلِيكُمْ أَوْ كِسْوَتُهُمْ أَوْ تَحْرِيرُ رَقَبَةٍ فَمَن لَّمْ يَجِدْ فَصِيَامُ ثَلَٰثَةِ أَيَّامٍ ذَٰلِكَ كَفَّٰرَةُ أَيْمَٰنِكُمْ إِذَا حَلَفْتُمْ وَٱحْفَظُوٓا۟ أَيْمَٰنَكُمْ كَذَٰلِكَ يُبَيِّنُ ٱللَّهُ لَكُمْ ءَايَٰتِهِۦ لَعَلَّكُمْ تَشْكُرُونَ ۝

ᵃ According to Islam, real monasticism consists of fear of and gratitude to God. Fear of God causes one to abstain from things prohibited by Him. If the desire awakens in man to enjoy the pleasure of some forbidden (haram) thing, the fear of God will restrain him from satisfying that desire. Again, if he becomes so angry with someone that he feels like killing him, it is the fear of God which stays his hand. His heart may tell him that he should lead an unrestricted life, but the fear of God's wrath compels him to remain within God's prescribed limits. The same is true of gratitude. When the grateful man receives some worldly good things, when he is blessed with health, wealth, position, worldly goods and his share of popularity, these things do not lead him into self-aggrandizement or boasting; he takes everything to be God's gift and concedes that all the benefits he enjoys are by the grace of God. He is overwhelmed by feelings of gratitude and humility. These are the emotions which join him with God. By fearing God and being grateful to Him, man comes close to Him. Keeping away from material things is definitely a virtue, but the act of distancing oneself from them has to be a mental and not just a physical process.

⁹⁰ Believers, intoxicants and gambling and [occult dedication of] stones and divining arrows are abominations devised by Satan. Avoid them, so that you may prosper. ⁹¹ Satan seeks to sow enmity and hatred among you by means of wine and gambling, and to keep you from the remembrance of God and from your prayers. Will you not then abstain?ᵃ

يَـٰٓأَيُّهَا ٱلَّذِينَ ءَامَنُوٓا۟ إِنَّمَا ٱلْخَمْرُ وَٱلْمَيْسِرُ وَٱلْأَنصَابُ وَٱلْأَزْلَـٰمُ رِجْسٌ مِّنْ عَمَلِ ٱلشَّيْطَـٰنِ فَٱجْتَنِبُوهُ لَعَلَّكُمْ تُفْلِحُونَ ۝ إِنَّمَا يُرِيدُ ٱلشَّيْطَـٰنُ أَن يُوقِعَ بَيْنَكُمُ ٱلْعَدَـٰوَةَ وَٱلْبَغْضَآءَ فِى ٱلْخَمْرِ وَٱلْمَيْسِرِ وَيَصُدَّكُمْ عَن ذِكْرِ ٱللَّهِ وَعَنِ ٱلصَّلَوٰةِ فَهَلْ أَنتُم مُّنتَهُونَ ۝

ᵃ The imbibing of intoxicants, gambling and frequenting abodes where beings other than God are worshipped or offered sacrifices and the drawing of lots, in which seeking help from someone other than God is involved—all these are base, satanic actions. These things lead a man to his mental and physical downfall. Intoxicants destroy the refined human feelings existing in a man. Similarly, the throwing of arrows, the drawing of lots, etc., are actions which are based either on superficial thoughts or on superstitious beliefs.

Islam wants man to become a rememberer and worshipper of God; making himself completely obedient to God and His Prophet. For this purpose, a man's being serious is absolutely necessary. But the above-mentioned misdeeds are the greatest destroyers of seriousness. Islam wants to create a man who recognizes and understands realities, who in living his life, rises above materialism, whereas intoxicants make a man forgetful of realities, arrows and the drawing of lots plunge a man into the dark abysses of superstition, and gambling leads man into materialism to an extent which is criminal. Islam wants to create a man who elevates himself on the basis of facts and realities, but intoxicants promote an excessive lack of awareness of what is proper and gambling promotes excessive selfishness. These are the two root causes of disturbances and riots. Those who lose their moral awareness also lose their respect for others' dignity and property. Such people become brazen to the ultimate extent, indulging in tyranny and injustice and unduly harassing others. Similarly, gambling is the worst form of exploitation and selfishness in that it enables a man to rob many people, thus enriching himself and achieving great material success. A drunkard is devoid of any awareness of others' trouble or grief, while for a gambler, others are only subjects of exploitation. A society where such people exist will be vitiated by clashes and enmity, and its members will live in an atmosphere of mutual mistrust and recrimination.

⁹² Obey God and obey the Messenger, and be ever on your guard [against evil]. But if you turn away, then know that Our Messenger's duty is only to deliver the message clearly. ⁹³ Those who believe and do good deeds will not be blamed for what they may have consumed [in the past], so long as they fear God and believe in Him and do good works; so long as they fear God and believe in Him, so long as they fear God and do good deeds. For God loves those who do good.

⁹⁴ Believers, God will test you with game which come within the reach of your hands and spears, so that He may know those who fear Him, even if they cannot see Him. Anyone who oversteps the limits after this will have a painful punishment.ᵃ

وَأَطِيعُوا۟ ٱللَّهَ وَأَطِيعُوا۟ ٱلرَّسُولَ وَٱحْذَرُوا۟ ۚ فَإِن تَوَلَّيْتُمْ فَٱعْلَمُوٓا۟ أَنَّمَا عَلَىٰ رَسُولِنَا ٱلْبَلَـٰغُ ٱلْمُبِينُ ۝ لَيْسَ عَلَى ٱلَّذِينَ ءَامَنُوا۟ وَعَمِلُوا۟ ٱلصَّـٰلِحَـٰتِ جُنَاحٌ فِيمَا طَعِمُوٓا۟ إِذَا مَا ٱتَّقَوا۟ وَّءَامَنُوا۟ وَعَمِلُوا۟ ٱلصَّـٰلِحَـٰتِ ثُمَّ ٱتَّقَوا۟ وَّءَامَنُوا۟ ثُمَّ ٱتَّقَوا۟ وَّأَحْسَنُوا۟ ۗ وَٱللَّهُ يُحِبُّ ٱلْمُحْسِنِينَ ۝ يَـٰٓأَيُّهَا ٱلَّذِينَ ءَامَنُوا۟ لَيَبْلُوَنَّكُمُ ٱللَّهُ بِشَىْءٍ مِّنَ ٱلصَّيْدِ تَنَالُهُۥٓ أَيْدِيكُمْ وَرِمَاحُكُمْ لِيَعْلَمَ ٱللَّهُ مَن يَخَافُهُۥ بِٱلْغَيْبِ ۚ فَمَنِ ٱعْتَدَىٰ بَعْدَ ذَٰلِكَ فَلَهُۥ عَذَابٌ أَلِيمٌ ۝

ᵃ During Hajj or 'umrah (the pilgrimage to the Ka'bah) it is the rule that before reaching the Ka'bah, people are required to put on *ahram* (specified dress) at and from some specified places (*miqat*). Thereafter, on the journey towards the Ka'bah, pilgrims come across many birds and animals which they could easily hunt, but this has been declared *haram* (forbidden). Hunting personally, or through others, is prohibited in these conditions. According to tradition, this verse was revealed during the Hudaybiyyah journey, when the Muslims were clad in *ihram* with the intention of performing 'umrah. At that time, many birds and animals were roaming about so close that they could have been easily hunted down with arrows or spears. The Muslims wanted to hunt, as they normally did, to meet their requirements. But they immediately stopped on receiving this order. This order, which is applicable under *ihram,* has to be followed by the common man in day-to-day life.

95 Believers, do not kill any game while you are on a pilgrimage. Anyone of you who kills game deliberately shall make compensation with an animal which is the equivalent of what he has killed, to be determined by two just men from among you, as an offering brought to the Ka'bah; or he shall, in expiation, either feed the poor or do the equivalent of that in fasting, so that he may taste the consequence of his deeds. God forgives what is past, but if anyone relapses into wrongdoing, God will exact His retribution. God is mighty, the Lord of retribution.[a]

يَـٰٓأَيُّهَا ٱلَّذِينَ ءَامَنُوا۟ لَا تَقْتُلُوا۟ ٱلصَّيْدَ وَأَنتُمْ حُرُمٌ ۚ وَمَن قَتَلَهُۥ مِنكُم مُّتَعَمِّدًا فَجَزَآءٌ مِّثْلُ مَا قَتَلَ مِنَ ٱلنَّعَمِ يَحْكُمُ بِهِۦ ذَوَا عَدْلٍ مِّنكُمْ هَدْيًۢا بَـٰلِغَ ٱلْكَعْبَةِ أَوْ كَفَّـٰرَةٌ طَعَامُ مَسَـٰكِينَ أَوْ عَدْلُ ذَٰلِكَ صِيَامًا لِّيَذُوقَ وَبَالَ أَمْرِهِۦ ۗ عَفَا ٱللَّهُ عَمَّا سَلَفَ ۚ وَمَنْ عَادَ فَيَنتَقِمُ ٱللَّهُ مِنْهُ ۗ وَٱللَّهُ عَزِيزٌ ذُو ٱنتِقَامٍ ۝

---

[a] The real purpose of this order is that God may know those who fear Him, even if they cannot see Him. God has placed human beings in this world, but has concealed Himself from their eyes. Now, He wants to see who, without seeing Him, is so reality-conscious as to behave righteously, as if he were actually seeing Him with all His powers, unlike those who, not finding God before them, become fearless and behave as they please. This is experienced not only during the short period of the pilgrimage, but also on a daily basis in human relations. A man may gain such control over another that it is quite possible for him to threaten his life, ruin him financially or falsely defame and degrade him. Now, under these conditions, there may conversely be a man who, in spite of having such control and similar opportunity, holds his peace and stays his hands out of fear of God. Of these two, the latter has proved that he fears God without seeing Him, while the former has proved otherwise. The latter has countless divine blessings in store for him, while there shall be a terrible punishment for the former.

⁹⁶ To hunt and to eat the fish of the sea is made lawful for you, a provision made for you and for seafarers. But you are forbidden the game of the land while you are on a pilgrimage. Have fear of God, before whom you shall all be gathered.ᵃ

أُحِلَّ لَكُمْ صَيْدُ ٱلْبَحْرِ وَطَعَامُهُۥ مَتَٰعًا لَّكُمْ وَلِلسَّيَّارَةِ وَحُرِّمَ عَلَيْكُمْ صَيْدُ ٱلْبَرِّ مَا دُمْتُمْ حُرُمًا وَٱتَّقُوا۟ ٱللَّهَ ٱلَّذِىٓ إِلَيْهِ تُحْشَرُونَ ۝

ᵃ Hunting is prohibited (*haram*) while in the state of *ihram*. This prohibition was ordained, not because of any feature inherent in the thing prohibited, but as a matter of human trial. In order to test man, God chose to ban certain items symbolically. However, wherever the Law-Giver felt that the trial might cause unnecessary hardship to His subjects, the Law was relaxed. For example, for pilgrims who travel by sea or river to the House of God, it is legitimate to fish in the waters and eat the catch if, during the voyage, there is nothing else available to them. Indeed, they have no alternative if they are to save their lives.

⁹⁷ God has made the Ka'bah, the Sacred House, a means of support as well as the sacred month and the sacrificial animals with their garlands. That is so that you may know that God has knowledge of whatever is in the heavens and on the earth and that He is fully aware of all things. ⁹⁸ Know that God is severe in punishment, yet most forgiving and merciful. ⁹⁹ The Messenger's sole duty is to convey the message. God knows what you reveal and what you hide. ¹⁰⁰ Say, 'The bad and the good are not alike, even though the abundance of the bad may appear pleasing to you. So fear God, O men of understanding, so that you may prosper.'[a]

۞ جَعَلَ ٱللَّهُ ٱلْكَعْبَةَ ٱلْبَيْتَ ٱلْحَرَامَ قِيَـٰمًا لِّلنَّاسِ وَٱلشَّهْرَ ٱلْحَرَامَ وَٱلْهَدْىَ وَٱلْقَلَـٰٓئِدَ ۚ ذَٰلِكَ لِتَعْلَمُوٓا۟ أَنَّ ٱللَّهَ يَعْلَمُ مَا فِى ٱلسَّمَـٰوَٰتِ وَمَا فِى ٱلْأَرْضِ وَأَنَّ ٱللَّهَ بِكُلِّ شَىْءٍ عَلِيمٌ ۝ ٱعْلَمُوٓا۟ أَنَّ ٱللَّهَ شَدِيدُ ٱلْعِقَابِ وَأَنَّ ٱللَّهَ غَفُورٌ رَّحِيمٌ ۝ مَّا عَلَى ٱلرَّسُولِ إِلَّا ٱلْبَلَـٰغُ ۗ وَٱللَّهُ يَعْلَمُ مَا تُبْدُونَ وَمَا تَكْتُمُونَ ۝ قُل لَّا يَسْتَوِى ٱلْخَبِيثُ وَٱلطَّيِّبُ وَلَوْ أَعْجَبَكَ كَثْرَةُ ٱلْخَبِيثِ ۚ فَٱتَّقُوا۟ ٱللَّهَ يَـٰٓأُو۟لِى ٱلْأَلْبَـٰبِ لَعَلَّكُمْ تُفْلِحُونَ ۝

---

[a] The Ka'bah is the eternal centre for Islam and the Islamic community. By declaring it essential to turn towards the Ka'bah to say one's prayers (salat,), God has linked each and every Muslim with the centrality of the Ka'bah. Then by means of Hajj (pilgrimage) it has been made the international meeting place of Islam. The symbolic rites to be performed in connection with the pilgrimage to the Ka'bah are of great importance, not because of any inherent holiness in them, but because they are the signs of the trial of man. When a subject of God carries out His commandments on these symbolic rites, he reminds himself that though God is not apparently visible, He is actively present—He gives commands; He keeps a watch on His subjects; He is aware of all our actions. These thoughts develop fear of God in man and make him able to remain a true subject of God throughout the vicissitudes of his life.

It is a human weakness to give the utmost importance to the drawing of crowds, and to accumulating an abundance of showy worldly goods, etc. In the eyes of God, however, importance attaches only to quality. Quantity has no value for Him. Those who rush towards 'abundance' and attach no value to truth think they are very clever, but in reality they are unwise. One who orders his life in fear of God and not on account of material considerations or worldly cares, is the one who is truly successful.

101 Believers, do not ask questions about things which, if they were made known to you, would only become burdensome for you; but if you ask them when the Quran is being revealed, they shall be made plain to you—God has kept silent about them: God is most forgiving and forbearing. 102 Other people before you enquired about such things, but when they were disclosed to them, they refused to carry them out.*a*

يَـٰٓأَيُّهَا ٱلَّذِينَ ءَامَنُوا۟ لَا تَسْـَٔلُوا۟ عَنْ أَشْيَآءَ إِن تُبْدَ لَكُمْ تَسُؤْكُمْ وَإِن تَسْـَٔلُوا۟ عَنْهَا حِينَ يُنَزَّلُ ٱلْقُرْءَانُ تُبْدَ لَكُمْ عَفَا ٱللَّهُ عَنْهَا ۗ وَٱللَّهُ غَفُورٌ حَلِيمٌ ۝ قَدْ سَأَلَهَا قَوْمٌ مِّن قَبْلِكُمْ ثُمَّ أَصْبَحُوا۟ بِهَا كَـٰفِرِينَ ۝

---

a It has been recorded in the traditions that when the order regarding Hajj was received, the Prophet Muhammad said in a sermon 'O, people! Hajj has been made compulsory for you.' On hearing this, a person from the Banu Asad tribe got up and asked: 'O, Prophet of God! Is it for every year?' The Prophet Muhammad was very angry and said, 'By the Lord in whose hands my life is! Had I said "'Yes", it would have become compulsory for every year, and having become compulsory for every year, you would not have been able to perform it every year and thus committed denial of truth. So, leave out whatever I leave out. When I order anything to be done, do it, and when I prohibit you from doing anything, don't do it.' (*Tafsir ibn Kathir*).

103 God has ordained no sanctity about animals described as *bahirah*, or *sa'ibah*, or *wasilah* or *ham*.[a] Those who deny the truth invent falsehoods about God. Most of them do not use their reason: 104 when it is said to them, 'Come to what God has sent down and to the Messenger.' They reply, 'The faith we have inherited from our fathers is sufficient for us.' Even though their forefathers knew nothing and were not guided! 105 Believers, take care of your own souls. The misguided cannot harm you as long as you are guided. All of you will return to God. Then He will make you realize that which you used to do.[b]

مَا جَعَلَ ٱللَّهُ مِنْ بَحِيرَةٍ وَلَا سَآئِبَةٍ وَلَا وَصِيلَةٍ وَلَا حَامٍ وَلَٰكِنَّ ٱلَّذِينَ كَفَرُواْ يَفْتَرُونَ عَلَى ٱللَّهِ ٱلْكَذِبَ وَأَكْثَرُهُمْ لَا يَعْقِلُونَ ۞ وَإِذَا قِيلَ لَهُمْ تَعَالَوْاْ إِلَىٰ مَآ أَنزَلَ ٱللَّهُ وَإِلَى ٱلرَّسُولِ قَالُواْ حَسْبُنَا مَا وَجَدْنَا عَلَيْهِ ءَابَآءَنَآ أَوَلَوْ كَانَ ءَابَآؤُهُمْ لَا يَعْلَمُونَ شَيْئًا وَلَا يَهْتَدُونَ ۞ يَٰٓأَيُّهَا ٱلَّذِينَ ءَامَنُواْ عَلَيْكُمْ أَنفُسَكُمْ لَا يَضُرُّكُم مَّن ضَلَّ إِذَا ٱهْتَدَيْتُمْ إِلَى ٱللَّهِ مَرْجِعُكُمْ جَمِيعًا فَيُنَبِّئُكُم بِمَا كُنتُمْ تَعْمَلُونَ ۞

---

[a] These are different categories of domestic animals which the pre-Islamic Arabs used to dedicate to their deities.

[b] The ban on raising unnecessary questions in force at the time of the revelation of the Quran is applicable even today. The best and correct thing to do is to keep any order that is given in its original form. There should be no attempt, by raising unnecessary questions, to extend or reduce the limits of its restriction. Making a brief command more detailed, making an absolute command a limited one and making efforts to make an indefinite order definite, are additions in religion which God and the Prophet have prohibited.

The former elders of a community attain holy status after a certain passage of time. Many kinds of wrong practices occur in the name of these long deceased people. So much so that if they had established the custom of venerating sheeps and camels, their successors would go on doing so without giving any thought to it. Such misguided behaviour, which is based on a tradition of holiness, is so firmly and deeply rooted that it is very difficult to dissuade people from it. It is possible to rise above such psychological complications only when a man acquires a firm belief, in the real sense, that finally he has to appear before God. One holding such a belief man accepts today itself what he will be compelled to accept after death; but acceptance at that time will be of no use to anyone.

106 Believers, when death approaches you, let two just men from among you act as witnesses when you make your testaments; or two men from another tribe, if the calamity of death overtakes you while you are travelling in the land. Detain them after prayers, and if you doubt their honesty, let them swear by God, 'We will not sell our testimony for any price, even to a kinsman. And we will not conceal the testimony of God. If we did, we would indeed be guilty of sin.'[a]

يَـٰٓأَيُّهَا ٱلَّذِينَ ءَامَنُوا۟ شَهَـٰدَةُ بَيْنِكُمْ إِذَا حَضَرَ أَحَدَكُمُ ٱلْمَوْتُ حِينَ ٱلْوَصِيَّةِ ٱثْنَانِ ذَوَا عَدْلٍ مِّنكُمْ أَوْ ءَاخَرَانِ مِنْ غَيْرِكُمْ إِنْ أَنتُمْ ضَرَبْتُمْ فِى ٱلْأَرْضِ فَأَصَـٰبَتْكُم مُّصِيبَةُ ٱلْمَوْتِ تَحْبِسُونَهُمَا مِنۢ بَعْدِ ٱلصَّلَوٰةِ فَيُقْسِمَانِ بِٱللَّهِ إِنِ ٱرْتَبْتُمْ لَا نَشْتَرِى بِهِۦ ثَمَنًا وَلَوْ كَانَ ذَا قُرْبَىٰ وَلَا نَكْتُمُ شَهَـٰدَةَ ٱللَّهِ إِنَّآ إِذًا لَّمِنَ ٱلْءَاثِمِينَ ﴿١٠٦﴾

---

[a] If a man is on a journey and he senses that the time of his death is approaching, he should seek out two Muslims and hand over his personal possessions to them with proper instructions about bequeathing them to his inheritors. If he cannot find two Muslims in time, he should do likewise with two non-Muslims. These two persons should bring his possessions and hand them over to his heirs. At that time, if the inheritors have any doubts about the statement of the witnesses, they (the latter) should be detained in a mosque and should be made to take an oath before the general body of Muslims, which will testify that whatever they have said on behalf of the deceased was correct. If the inheritors are not satisfied with the statement on oath of the witnesses, then two of the inheritors should take an oath to that effect. Thereafter, a decision should be taken in accordance with their declaration. The giving of this right to the inheritors amounts to the establishment of a check, due to which no one will dare to commit a breach of trust.

¹⁰⁷ If it turns out that both prove dishonest, two others should take their place from amongst those whose rights have been usurped and let them swear by God, saying, 'Our testimony is indeed truer than the testimony of these two. And we have not been guilty of any misstatement for then indeed we would be transgressors.' ¹⁰⁸ That makes it more likely that people will bear true witness, or else they will fear that their oaths will be contradicted by the oaths of others. Heed God and listen; God does not guide a rebellious, disobedient people.ᵃ

فَإِنْ عُثِرَ عَلَىٰ أَنَّهُمَا ٱسْتَحَقَّآ إِثْمًا فَـَٔاخَرَانِ يَقُومَانِ مَقَامَهُمَا مِنَ ٱلَّذِينَ ٱسْتَحَقَّ عَلَيْهِمُ ٱلْأَوْلَيَٰنِ فَيُقْسِمَانِ بِٱللَّهِ لَشَهَٰدَتُنَآ أَحَقُّ مِن شَهَٰدَتِهِمَا وَمَا ٱعْتَدَيْنَآ إِنَّآ إِذًا لَّمِنَ ٱلظَّٰلِمِينَ ﴿١٠٧﴾ ذَٰلِكَ أَدْنَىٰٓ أَن يَأْتُوا۟ بِٱلشَّهَٰدَةِ عَلَىٰ وَجْهِهَآ أَوْ يَخَافُوٓا۟ أَن تُرَدَّ أَيْمَٰنٌۢ بَعْدَ أَيْمَٰنِهِمْ ۗ وَٱتَّقُوا۟ ٱللَّهَ وَٱسْمَعُوا۟ ۗ وَٱللَّهُ لَا يَهْدِى ٱلْقَوْمَ ٱلْفَٰسِقِينَ ﴿١٠٨﴾

ᵃ In the Islamic law, such instructions are given concerning day-to-day life as provide lessons in a wider sphere of existence.. After a person's death the division of his property is a family and economic matter. But this has been made a source of training in two important respects. One is that people should adopt the attitude of not giving consideration in their dealings to connections and relations: they should take into account only rights and truth. They should see what the truth is and not question who is favoured by it and who is not. The other is that every procedure should be treated as giving evidence before God. Anything which is in the custody of man is in God's trust, because man saw it given by God with his own eyes, preserved it in his memory as given by God and now has to declare it with the help of the tongue given by God. Under these circumstances it will be a breach of trust if a man does not state the facts as he has seen them or committed them to memory.

¹⁰⁹ The Day when God assembles the messengers and asks them, 'What was the response you received [from the people]?' they will reply, 'We have no knowledge of it. You alone know what is hidden.'ᵃ

۞ يَوْمَ يَجْمَعُ ٱللَّهُ ٱلرُّسُلَ فَيَقُولُ مَاذَآ أُجِبْتُمْ قَالُواْ لَا عِلْمَ لَنَآ إِنَّكَ أَنتَ عَلَّامُ ٱلْغُيُوبِ ۝

ᵃ Those who embraced the faith on the strength of their prophets' teachings later fell away from the true religion and concocted their own religion in the name of the prophet. In spite of this, every group treated itself as the *ummah* (community) of its prophet, though after deviating from the real teachings of that prophet, they ceased to have any link with him. The Jews claim to have a connection with Moses and the Christians with Jesus, though their present religions are unconnected with those prophets. This fact has become obscure in the present world of trial. But, on the Day of Judgement, all will be made clear. On that Day, God will assemble all the prophets and, in the presence of their communities, He will ask them what teachings they gave their community and how the community adopted them. In this way, it will be made clear to every community before its prophet as to how far its members contravened their prophet's teachings on the religion of God, and it will be shown how they had falsely linked their self-made religion with the prophet.

110 Then God will say, 'Jesus, son of Mary, remember My favour to you and to your mother: how I strengthened you with the holy spirit, so that you could speak to people in childhood and in maturity; and how I taught you the Book, and wisdom, the Torah and the Gospel; how by My leave you fashioned from clay the shape of a bird and blew upon it, so that, by My leave, it became a bird, and healed the blind and the leper by My permission, and when you brought forth the dead by My permission; and how I prevented the Children of Israel from harming you when you came to them with clear signs, when those of them who denied the truth said, "This is sheer magic." [a]

إِذْ قَالَ ٱللَّهُ يَـٰعِيسَى ٱبْنَ مَرْيَمَ ٱذْكُرْ نِعْمَتِى عَلَيْكَ وَعَلَىٰ وَٰلِدَتِكَ إِذْ أَيَّدتُّكَ بِرُوحِ ٱلْقُدُسِ تُكَلِّمُ ٱلنَّاسَ فِى ٱلْمَهْدِ وَكَهْلًا ۖ وَإِذْ عَلَّمْتُكَ ٱلْكِتَـٰبَ وَٱلْحِكْمَةَ وَٱلتَّوْرَىٰةَ وَٱلْإِنجِيلَ ۖ وَإِذْ تَخْلُقُ مِنَ ٱلطِّينِ كَهَيْـَٔةِ ٱلطَّيْرِ بِإِذْنِى فَتَنفُخُ فِيهَا فَتَكُونُ طَيْرًۢا بِإِذْنِى ۖ وَتُبْرِئُ ٱلْأَكْمَهَ وَٱلْأَبْرَصَ بِإِذْنِى ۖ وَإِذْ تُخْرِجُ ٱلْمَوْتَىٰ بِإِذْنِى ۖ وَإِذْ كَفَفْتُ بَنِى إِسْرَٰٓءِيلَ عَنكَ إِذْ جِئْتَهُم بِٱلْبَيِّنَـٰتِ فَقَالَ ٱلَّذِينَ كَفَرُوا۟ مِنْهُمْ إِنْ هَـٰذَآ إِلَّا سِحْرٌ مُّبِينٌ ۝

[a] Among those prophets, there is the example of Jesus, who is an intermediate link between the earlier prophets and the last of the prophets. Jesus was given very special miracles to perform. Those who had embraced the faith through him were very few in number and his opponents, the Jews, enjoyed worldly power. In spite of this, they could not inflict any harm on him and were not successful in destroying his companions. The result of these miracles should have been that people should have accepted the religion brought by him. But what actually happened was that his opponents ignored him, saying that the miracles performed by him were merely feats of magic. On the contrary, those who embraced his faith later on gave him the status of a god. On Judgement Day, it will be made clear to those who claim to be his followers that whatever feats Jesus had performed were all done at God's behest. It was God who saved him from the dangers presented by his opponents. When this was the true state of affairs and Jesus himself will testify to this, standing before them, then his people will have to explain who had given them the religion which they had wrongly attributed to Jesus.

111 [Remember the time], when I inspired the disciples to believe in Me and in My messenger, they replied, "We believe, bear witness that we have submitted."'*a* 112 When the disciples said, 'O Jesus, son of Mary! Can your Lord send down to us from heaven a table spread with food?'*b* He replied, 'Have fear of God, if you are true believers.' 113 They said, 'We want to eat from it, so that we may satisfy our hearts and know that you have told us the truth, and that we should be witnesses of it.'

وَإِذْ أَوْحَيْتُ إِلَى ٱلْحَوَارِيِّنَ أَنْ ءَامِنُوا۟ بِى وَبِرَسُولِى قَالُوٓا۟ ءَامَنَّا وَٱشْهَدْ بِأَنَّنَا مُسْلِمُونَ ۝ إِذْ قَالَ ٱلْحَوَارِيُّونَ يَـٰعِيسَى ٱبْنَ مَرْيَمَ هَلْ يَسْتَطِيعُ رَبُّكَ أَن يُنَزِّلَ عَلَيْنَا مَآئِدَةً مِّنَ ٱلسَّمَآءِ قَالَ ٱتَّقُوا۟ ٱللَّهَ إِن كُنتُم مُّؤْمِنِينَ ۝ قَالُوا۟ نُرِيدُ أَن نَّأْكُلَ مِنْهَا وَتَطْمَئِنَّ قُلُوبُنَا وَنَعْلَمَ أَن قَدْ صَدَقْتَنَا وَنَكُونَ عَلَيْهَا مِنَ ٱلشَّـٰهِدِينَ ۝

a It is the dayee who performs the duty of calling upon people to Truth. But a positive response to this call cannot be given unless it is God-inspired. Even after being convinced of the veracity of the call, a man still does not necessarily proceed to accept it, as many impediments still remain—the appearance of the missionary as a common man; the fear that on acceptance of the call the structure of the life already built up will crumble, the question that if this is the Truth, whether certain great men were strangers to the Truth, etc. This is a critical juncture where a man is unable to take a decision, even having reached the stage of decision-making. This is the point at which God helps him. He holds the hands of a person in whom He sees some goodness and leads him across the borders of doubt and ushers him into the area of certainty.

b Man is constantly being provided with the provisions for his life by God. In fact, the whole earth has become a table laid with provisions for man. But the demand made by the believers in Jesus for food to be sent down from the sky caused a severe warning to be given to them. The reason for this is that the provisions we receive under normal conditions are routed through a veil of cause and effect, while the demand of the believers involved the removal of that veil. This is again the way of God, because if this veil is removed, how can the conditions for human trial be perpetuated?

114 Jesus, son of Mary, said, 'O God, our Lord! Send down for us a table spread with food from heaven, so that it may be a feast for us, for the first of us and for the last of us: a sign from You. Give us our sustenance, for You are the best of sustainers.' 115 God replied, 'I will certainly send it down to you, but whosoever of you deny the truth thereafter will be punished with a punishment such as I have never meted out to anyone else in the world.' a

قَالَ عِيسَى ٱبْنُ مَرْيَمَ ٱللَّهُمَّ رَبَّنَا أَنزِلْ عَلَيْنَا مَآئِدَةً مِّنَ ٱلسَّمَآءِ تَكُونُ لَنَا عِيدًا لِّأَوَّلِنَا وَءَاخِرِنَا وَءَايَةً مِّنكَ وَٱرْزُقْنَا وَأَنتَ خَيْرُ ٱلرَّٰزِقِينَ ۝ قَالَ ٱللَّهُ إِنِّى مُنَزِّلُهَا عَلَيْكُمْ فَمَن يَكْفُرْ بَعْدُ مِنكُمْ فَإِنِّىٓ أُعَذِّبُهُۥ عَذَابًا لَّآ أُعَذِّبُهُۥٓ أَحَدًا مِّنَ ٱلْعَٰلَمِينَ ۝

---

a The fact is that crops flourishing in the fields, or the emergence of a tree, stout and green, from beneath the earth are all as miraculous events as the descent to us of a platter containing food from the midst of the clouds. But the miraculous nature of these events is not apparent to us because they appear from behind a veil. It is the test of man that he should be able to see the reality by tearing down that veil. He should be able to look upon the basic elements of foodstuffs emerging from the earth as if they were descending from heaven. If a person insists that he will accept the Divine Truth only on 'seeing' it, then he is saying, as it were, that he will receive God's grace without undergoing His trial, and that is not possible according to the way of God.

¹¹⁶ When God says, 'Jesus, son of Mary, did you say to people, "Take me and my mother as two deities besides God"?' He will answer, 'Glory be to You! How could I ever say that to which I have no right? If I had ever said so, You would surely have known it. You know what is in my mind, while I do not know anything that is within Yours. You alone are the knower of unseen things— ¹¹⁷ I told them only what You commanded me to, "Worship God, my Lord and your Lord." I was a witness to what they did as long as I remained among them, and when You took my soul, You were the watcher over them. You are the witness of all things, ¹¹⁸ and if You punish them, they are surely Your servants; and if You forgive them, You are surely the Mighty and Wise.' [a]

وَإِذْ قَالَ ٱللَّهُ يَٰعِيسَى ٱبْنَ مَرْيَمَ ءَأَنتَ قُلْتَ لِلنَّاسِ ٱتَّخِذُونِى وَأُمِّىَ إِلَٰهَيْنِ مِن دُونِ ٱللَّهِ قَالَ سُبْحَٰنَكَ مَا يَكُونُ لِىٓ أَنْ أَقُولَ مَا لَيْسَ لِى بِحَقٍّ إِن كُنتُ قُلْتُهُ فَقَدْ عَلِمْتَهُۥ تَعْلَمُ مَا فِى نَفْسِى وَلَآ أَعْلَمُ مَا فِى نَفْسِكَ إِنَّكَ أَنتَ عَلَّٰمُ ٱلْغُيُوبِ ۝ مَا قُلْتُ لَهُمْ إِلَّا مَآ أَمَرْتَنِى بِهِۦٓ أَنِ ٱعْبُدُوا۟ ٱللَّهَ رَبِّى وَرَبَّكُمْ وَكُنتُ عَلَيْهِمْ شَهِيدًا مَّا دُمْتُ فِيهِمْ فَلَمَّا تَوَفَّيْتَنِى كُنتَ أَنتَ ٱلرَّقِيبَ عَلَيْهِمْ وَأَنتَ عَلَىٰ كُلِّ شَىْءٍ شَهِيدٌ ۝ إِن تُعَذِّبْهُمْ فَإِنَّهُمْ عِبَادُكَ وَإِن تَغْفِرْ لَهُمْ فَإِنَّكَ أَنتَ ٱلْعَزِيزُ ٱلْحَكِيمُ ۝

---

[a] When the Day of Judgement arrives, man will come to know without being told what is right and what is wrong. People will witness with their own eyes that all powers are with the one and only God. He has no partner in being our Creator and Lord. No one but Him has any powers and there is no one except Him who deserves to be worshipped and obeyed. Under these circumstances, when God asks His prophets with what message they were sent to the world, then it will amount to asking about something which would have already become known to the people. The answer to this question will be so clear at that time that, without anybody's saying anything, the whole atmosphere of the Judgement Day will have been shouting it out. This question and answer will serve only to increase the abasement of the people being judged by God. It will be for the purpose of clarifying in the presence of the prophets that the religion concocted by them in the name of prophets was not at all connected with their teachings.

119 God will say, 'This is the Day when the truthful will benefit from their truthfulness. They shall forever dwell in Gardens through which rivers flow. God is pleased with them and they with Him: that is the supreme triumph.' 120 The kingdom of the heavens and the earth and everything in them belongs to God: He has power over all things.a

قَالَ ٱللَّهُ هَٰذَا يَوْمُ يَنفَعُ ٱلصَّٰدِقِينَ صِدْقُهُمْ لَهُمْ جَنَّٰتٌ تَجْرِى مِن تَحْتِهَا ٱلْأَنْهَٰرُ خَٰلِدِينَ فِيهَآ أَبَدًا رَّضِىَ ٱللَّهُ عَنْهُمْ وَرَضُوا۟ عَنْهُ ذَٰلِكَ ٱلْفَوْزُ ٱلْعَظِيمُ ۝ لِلَّهِ مُلْكُ ٱلسَّمَٰوَٰتِ وَٱلْأَرْضِ وَمَا فِيهِنَّ وَهُوَ عَلَىٰ كُلِّ شَىْءٍ قَدِيرٌ ۝

---

a This world has been created for the sake of putting man to the test. Therefore, everybody has freedom here. Here man may prosper even after linking with God and his prophet a religion which is not connected with God and His prophet. Here, even on the strength of imaginary hopes and false wishes, the right to paradise can be claimed. Here, it is possible for a man to create a great fanfare about his leadership and to 'prove' that whatever he does is exactly according to the religion of God. But, no such thing will be useful on the Day of Judgement. What will be useful on the Day of Judgment will be that man should prove truthful in the eyes of God. The test of the community bearing the Divine Scripture is not whether they are the claimants of faith or not. Their real test is a demonstration of their ability to prove their claim to Faith.

6. THE CATTLE

In the name of God,
the Most Gracious, the Most Merciful

¹ Praise be to God, who has created
the heavens and the earth and
brought into being darkness and
light. Yet those who deny the truth
set up equals to their Lord!ᵃ

ᵃ The system inherent in the governance of heaven and earth is so perfect in its
coordination and its unitary nature—despite the magnitude of the task—that it
proclaims aloud the fact that its Creator and Organiser can be none other than the
one and only God. Witness how unimaginably great is this universe in its vastness,
wisdom and meaningfulness. The flawlessly regulated revolution of the earth in
space around the bright sphere of the Sun and, hence the coming into existence
of light and darkness and day and night are events beyond human comprehension.
Now, why should there be any question of God—who has organised the universe
to perfection—having any shortcoming which would necessitate His having a
partner to give Him assistance? The fact is that the wonderful system by which
everything in the world is regulated is in itself proof that its Lord (God) is one and
one alone, and this same system also demonstrates that God is so great that He
does not need any assistant either in His creation or in His control of what He has
created.

334

2 It is He who has created you out of clay, and then has decreed a term [for you]—a term known [only] to Him. Yet you are still in doubt— 3 He is God both in the heavens and on earth. He has knowledge of all that you hide and all that you reveal. He knows what you do; 4 yet every time a sign comes to them from their Lord, they turn away from it.[a]

هُوَ ٱلَّذِى خَلَقَكُم مِّن طِينٍ ثُمَّ قَضَىٰٓ أَجَلًا ۖ وَأَجَلٌ مُّسَمًّى عِندَهُۥ ۖ ثُمَّ أَنتُمْ تَمْتَرُونَ ۝ وَهُوَ ٱللَّهُ فِى ٱلسَّمَٰوَٰتِ وَفِى ٱلْأَرْضِ ۖ يَعْلَمُ سِرَّكُمْ وَجَهْرَكُمْ وَيَعْلَمُ مَا تَكْسِبُونَ ۝ وَمَا تَأْتِيهِم مِّنْ ءَايَةٍ مِّنْ ءَايَٰتِ رَبِّهِمْ إِلَّا كَانُوا۟ عَنْهَا مُعْرِضِينَ ۝

---

[a] The age of the present world is limited. Here life cannot be devoid of grief. Here unpleasantness goes along with pleasantness. Evil cannot be separated from goodness nor goodness from evil. In such circumstances, man is unable to understand how the eternal world of the Hereafter, which will be free from grief (35:34) can come into existence. If the world of the Hereafter is to be created with some matter other than that of this world, that is something beyond man's ken; but if the other world of the Hereafter is to be created from the matter of this world, it has to be conceded that this world in itself lacks the capacity to bring into existence a world of total perfection.

The very existence of the raiser of this issue is in itself an answer to this question. The body of a human being is wholly made of earth elements but it has unique properties, none of which is found in the earth. Man hears; he speaks; and he thinks; he performs wonderful acts, though the earth with which he is made is not capable of performing these acts. From earthen elements a non-earthly creature has wondrously emerged. This is a matter confirmed by everyday experience. In view of this, how strange it is that man should harbour doubts about the advent of the Hereafter. If a living and active man comes into existence from earth; if fragrant flowers and luscious fruits emerge from earth, then why cannot a more perfect world emerge from our present world?

The message of God and the Hereafter, issued directly by God Himself, is accompanied by clear signs which establish it as a true call from the Almighty. Its being on the lines of nature on which the system of God's eternal world is established; its being supported by arguments that cannot be countered by anybody; its being backed by a preacher of God's word whose seriousness and sincerity are above doubt; its repeated survival of the destructive plans of its opponents, despite their superior power—all these are clear indications of its being based on truth. Inspite of all this, man does not believe in it and is not willing to support it. The reason for this is that all these proofs, in spite of all their clarity, always appear through a veil of cause and effect. When these signs come to a man's attention, he attributes them to certain causes and pays no heed to them. He does not become inclined to accept their validity. ▶

⁵ They have rejected truth whenever it came to them, yet [more] news will reach them concerning what they have been making a mockery of. ⁶ Have they not seen how many generations We destroyed before them? We established them on the earth more firmly than you, and We sent the clouds over them, pouring down abundant rain; and made the rivers flow at their feet. Yet We destroyed them for their sins, and raised up other generations after them.ᵃ

فَقَدْ كَذَّبُوا بِالْحَقِّ لَمَّا جَاءَهُمْ فَسَوْفَ يَأْتِيهِمْ أَنبَٰٓؤُا۟ مَا كَانُوا۟ بِهِ يَسْتَهْزِءُونَ ۝ أَلَمْ يَرَوْا۟ كَمْ أَهْلَكْنَا مِن قَبْلِهِم مِّن قَرْنٍ مَّكَّنَّٰهُمْ فِى ٱلْأَرْضِ مَا لَمْ نُمَكِّن لَّكُمْ وَأَرْسَلْنَا ٱلسَّمَآءَ عَلَيْهِم مِّدْرَارًا وَجَعَلْنَا ٱلْأَنْهَٰرَ تَجْرِى مِن تَحْتِهِمْ فَأَهْلَكْنَٰهُم بِذُنُوبِهِمْ وَأَنشَأْنَا مِنۢ بَعْدِهِمْ قَرْنًا ءَاخَرِينَ ۝

Instead of accepting the call he would say that had this call been on behalf of God, then God and His angels would have been visible to the naked eye. But this idea is absolutely meaningless, because when God and His angels appear in all their glory, it will be the time for the final rendering of accounts and not for giving a call of Truth or for preaching about the greatness of God.

ᵃ Those who have firmly established themselves in this world, having accumulated many material goods for themselves, and who see the manifestations of their own greatness and popularity around them, are always liable to be a prey to misunderstanding. They look down upon the things God has gathered around the caller of Truth as compared to the things around them. This overweening confidence on their part increases to such an extent that they even become unafraid of God. They make fun of the warning given by the missionary of Truth that, if their arrogance continued, their material achievements would not be able to save them from God's scourge. Their treatment of the *dayee* as a non-entity makes his warnings also insignificant. Even historic instances of God's having destroyed materially well set up people, as if their lives were of no value whatsoever, fail to teach them a lesson. The recurrence of events in which one set of people face decline while another set rises shows that the rule of 'crime and punishment' is prevalent here, but man does not learn a lesson from this. The succeeding generations repeat those very same actions as were indulged in by their predecessors, due to which they were destroyed.

⁷ But even if We had sent down to you a Book written on parchment, and they had touched it with their own hands—those who deny the truth would still have said, 'This is mere magic.' ⁸ They ask, 'Why has an angel not been sent down to him?' If We did send down an angel, the matter would be settled and they would not have been granted any respite. ⁹ Indeed, if We had sent an angel as messenger, We would have made him in the form of a man as well, and would have thus added to their confusion.ᵃ

وَلَوْ نَزَّلْنَا عَلَيْكَ كِتَبًا فِى قِرْطَاسٍ فَلَمَسُوهُ بِأَيْدِيهِمْ لَقَالَ ٱلَّذِينَ كَفَرُوٓاْ إِنْ هَٰذَآ إِلَّا سِحْرٌ مُّبِينٌ ۝ وَقَالُواْ لَوْلَآ أُنزِلَ عَلَيْهِ مَلَكٌ وَلَوْ أَنزَلْنَا مَلَكًا لَّقُضِىَ ٱلْأَمْرُ ثُمَّ لَا يُنظَرُونَ ۝ وَلَوْ جَعَلْنَٰهُ مَلَكًا لَّجَعَلْنَٰهُ رَجُلًا وَلَلَبَسْنَا عَلَيْهِم مَّا يَلْبِسُونَ ۝

ᵃ The reason for a man going astray in this world is that here he has complete freedom to reject the Truth. He even has the opportunity to give fine justifications for erroneous thoughts, words and deeds. Man enjoys full freedom in this world of trial to accept or reject the Truth as he pleases. If the preacher of God's word appears in the shape of an ordinary man, the 'reason' given for ignoring him could be that his effectiveness hinges on a talent for leadership and has nothing to do with Truth or righteousness. Similarly, if a book complete in every detail, comes down from the sky, he will say, 'This is mere magic,' to justify his rejection of it.

The people of Makkah used to ask, if the Prophet was appointed to convey God's message, why God's angels were not with him to testify. A man talks like this because he is not serious about the call of God's message. If he is serious, he will immediately come to know that this world is a place of trial. The test can be carried out only when realities are hidden behind a curtain. If the hidden realities were revealed and God and His angels made their appearance, there would be no question of prophethood or of giving the call of Truth, because thereafter nobody would dare to deny the realities. In the present world, because of their devotion to externals, people are unable to recognise the Messenger of God from the importance of his message. God's Messenger appears to them like an ordinary man suddenly emerging and claiming very high status. They assess him on the basis of his outward appearance and, finding him insignificant in that respect, they deny him.

¹⁰ Messengers have been mocked before you, but those who scoffed were overtaken by the very thing they scoffed at. ¹¹ Say, 'Travel about the land and see what was the end of the deniers.'

¹² Say, 'To whom belongs all that is in the heavens and earth?' Say, 'To God. He has taken it upon Himself to be merciful. That He will gather you on the Day of Resurrection is beyond all doubt. Those who have forfeited their souls will never have faith.' ¹³ To Him belongs all that dwells in the night and the day. He is the All Hearing and the All Knowing.ᵃ

وَلَقَدِ ٱسْتُهْزِئَ بِرُسُلٍ مِّن قَبْلِكَ فَحَاقَ بِٱلَّذِينَ سَخِرُوا۟ مِنْهُم مَّا كَانُوا۟ بِهِۦ يَسْتَهْزِءُونَ ۝ قُلْ سِيرُوا۟ فِى ٱلْأَرْضِ ثُمَّ ٱنظُرُوا۟ كَيْفَ كَانَ عَٰقِبَةُ ٱلْمُكَذِّبِينَ ۝ قُل لِّمَن مَّا فِى ٱلسَّمَٰوَٰتِ وَٱلْأَرْضِ قُل لِّلَّهِ كَتَبَ عَلَىٰ نَفْسِهِ ٱلرَّحْمَةَ لَيَجْمَعَنَّكُمْ إِلَىٰ يَوْمِ ٱلْقِيَٰمَةِ لَا رَيْبَ فِيهِ ٱلَّذِينَ خَسِرُوٓا۟ أَنفُسَهُمْ فَهُمْ لَا يُؤْمِنُونَ ۝ وَلَهُۥ مَا سَكَنَ فِى ٱلَّيْلِ وَٱلنَّهَارِ وَهُوَ ٱلسَّمِيعُ ٱلْعَلِيمُ ۝

ᵃ In this world communicating the Word of God is a task of some complexity. This is because God has ordained that the Truth be veiled in doubt, so that man may find reasons for rejecting it alongside arguments in support of its acceptance. The real test of man is that he should be able to tear down the veil of doubt and raise himself to the position of certainty. He should eschew doubt in all its guises and take a firm hold of the divine Truth. Believing without seeing is the real test of man. When reality is made visible, its acceptance has no value.

Man denies the obvious truth. On obtaining power, he degrades others. One man makes another the victim of his tyranny. Why is this so? Does man wield absolute power in this world? Is there nobody here to stay his hand? Is there a combination of opposites in God's regime, given that He seems to have filled man's world with oppression and injustice and the rest of the world with mercy and meaningfulness? No, it is not so. God, who is the Lord of Heaven and earth, is also the Lord of that creature who toils during the day and rests at night. Just as God's grace is given unstintingly to the universe, so also is it given to human beings. The difference is that for the rest of the world, His grace is fully in evidence right from the first day, whereas for the world of human beings, His grace will be fully shown on the Day of Judgement.

¹⁴ Say, 'Shall I take as my protector someone other than God, Creator of the heavens and the earth, who feeds all and is fed by none?' Say, 'I have been commanded to be the first of those who submit. Do not be one of the polytheists.' ¹⁵ Say, 'I will never disobey my Lord, for I fear the punishment of a dreadful Day.' ¹⁶ Anyone from whom punishment is averted on that Day has been shown great mercy by God. That is a supreme achievement.ᵃ

قُلْ أَغَيْرَ ٱللَّهِ أَتَّخِذُ وَلِيًّا فَاطِرِ ٱلسَّمَـٰوَٰتِ وَٱلْأَرْضِ وَهُوَ يُطْعِمُ وَلَا يُطْعَمُ ۗ قُلْ إِنِّي أُمِرْتُ أَنْ أَكُونَ أَوَّلَ مَنْ أَسْلَمَ ۖ وَلَا تَكُونَنَّ مِنَ ٱلْمُشْرِكِينَ ۝ قُلْ إِنِّي أَخَافُ إِنْ عَصَيْتُ رَبِّي عَذَابَ يَوْمٍ عَظِيمٍ ۝ مَّن يُصْرَفْ عَنْهُ يَوْمَئِذٍ فَقَدْ رَحِمَهُۥ ۚ وَذَٰلِكَ ٱلْفَوْزُ ٱلْمُبِينُ ۝

ᵃ Man is a creature with a will of his own and that is why voluntary worship is required of him. Those who do not choose to exercise their will rightly, do not deserve a share in God's bounties, not having fulfilled the purpose of their creation. After the period of trial is over, all human beings will be gathered in a new world. On that Day God will take into His hands the direct control of the rest of the world. On that Day God's scale of justice will be operative. On that Day those who admitted the reality and surrendered themselves to God will come to the fore and those who did not, having led a life of arrogance and obstinacy in the world, will be the losers.

Whenever a man adopts an arrogant stance, it is on the basis of some backing. But the things on which his arrogance depends for support have no value in this universe. Nothing has any power here, for the sole possessor of power is God. All are dependent on Him and He is not dependent on anyone. So, on the Day of Judgement, only those who had sought out the real support, who had made the true faith the religion of their lives, will be successful.

17 If God should let any harm touch you, no one could remove it except He; while if He should let some good touch you, know that He has the power to do all that He wills. 18 He reigns Supreme over His servants; and He is the All Wise, the All Aware.[a]

وَإِن يَمْسَسْكَ ٱللَّهُ بِضُرٍّ فَلَا كَاشِفَ لَهُۥ إِلَّا هُوَ ۖ وَإِن يَمْسَسْكَ بِخَيْرٍ فَهُوَ عَلَىٰ كُلِّ شَىْءٍ قَدِيرٌ ۝ وَهُوَ ٱلْقَاهِرُ فَوْقَ عِبَادِهِۦ ۚ وَهُوَ ٱلْحَكِيمُ ٱلْخَبِيرُ ۝

---

[a] The different parts of the vast universe spread out before us are so interconnected that for an event to occur, the coordination of the whole universe is necessary. This being so, no human being is capable of causing any event to occur, because no human being is in control of the universe. Here, even a small event takes place only when countless universal factors combine to set it in motion, and God alone is the controller of these factors. Amidst these universal factors, man is only the possessor of a will. The fact is that in this world whether one receives blessings or afflictions, both conditions come about by the direct orders of God. In view of this, it is utter foolishness for a man to think that he can save one or destroy another. It is also quite meaningless for a man to fear or build his hopes on anybody except God.

¹⁹ Ask them, 'What carries the most weight as a witness?' Tell them it is God. He is a witness between you and me. Say, 'This Quran has been revealed to me so that through it I may warn you and whoever it reaches. Do you really bear witness that there are other deities beside God?' Say, 'I do not bear witness to this.' Say, 'He is only one God, and I disown whatever you associate with Him.' [a]

قُلْ أَيُّ شَيْءٍ أَكْبَرُ شَهَادَةً قُلِ اللَّهُ شَهِيدٌ بَيْنِي وَبَيْنَكُمْ وَأُوحِيَ إِلَيَّ هَذَا الْقُرْآنُ لِأُنذِرَكُم بِهِ وَمَن بَلَغَ أَئِنَّكُمْ لَتَشْهَدُونَ أَنَّ مَعَ اللَّهِ آلِهَةً أُخْرَى قُل لَّا أَشْهَدُ قُلْ إِنَّمَا هُوَ إِلَهٌ وَاحِدٌ وَإِنَّنِي بَرِيءٌ مِّمَّا تُشْرِكُونَ ۩

---

[a] In the on-going struggle between the proponents, on the one hand of Truth and on the other of falsehood, the only decisive factor is the Book of God. There is nobody who knows the full facts or has any real authority except God. So God, the only Being who is capable of settling this dispute, has given an arbiter to the people in the form of the Quran. Now, man has only one course open to him. If he is not aware of the veracity of the Quran, he should investigate and satisfy himself that it is the Book of God. When he comes to know that it is really the Book of God, he should necessarily be satisfied with whatever is advocated therein. One who is not in agreement with the decision of the Quran runs the risk of being forced to accept its verdict in the Hereafter after much degradation and punishment.

The Quran has been revealed so that, before the arrival of the time of Judgement, people may be made aware of what awaits them. The Prophet Muhammad performed this task during his prophethood and the same work has to be continued by his followers (ummah) till Doomsday. The Quran tells us in advance how God is going to treat people in the eternal world of the Hereafter. Those who are assigned the task of delivering this message to the people will be free of the responsibility once they have fully conveyed the message; but those to whom it is delivered will be free in the eyes of God only when they have accepted it and reformed themselves accordingly. The missionary's responsibility ends with his 'preaching', while that of the addressee ends only on his 'fulfilling his religious obligations'.

²⁰ Those to whom We have given the Scriptures know this as they know their own sons. But those who have ruined their souls will not believe. ²¹ Who does greater wrong than he who invents a lie against God and denies His signs? Assuredly, the wrongdoers will not succeed. ²² On the Day when We gather them all together, We will say to those who associated [others with Us], 'Where are those partners that you claimed?' ²³ Then they will have no excuse but to say, 'By God our Lord, we have never been polytheists.' ²⁴ See how they lie to themselves, and how those [the deities] they invented have deserted them.ᵃ

ٱلَّذِينَ ءَاتَيْنَـٰهُمُ ٱلْكِتَـٰبَ يَعْرِفُونَهُۥ كَمَا يَعْرِفُونَ أَبْنَآءَهُمُ ٱلَّذِينَ خَسِرُوٓا۟ أَنفُسَهُمْ فَهُمْ لَا يُؤْمِنُونَ ۝ وَمَنْ أَظْلَمُ مِمَّنِ ٱفْتَرَىٰ عَلَى ٱللَّهِ كَذِبًا أَوْ كَذَّبَ بِـَٔايَـٰتِهِۦٓ إِنَّهُۥ لَا يُفْلِحُ ٱلظَّـٰلِمُونَ ۝ وَيَوْمَ نَحْشُرُهُمْ جَمِيعًا ثُمَّ نَقُولُ لِلَّذِينَ أَشْرَكُوٓا۟ أَيْنَ شُرَكَآؤُكُمُ ٱلَّذِينَ كُنتُمْ تَزْعُمُونَ ۝ ثُمَّ لَمْ تَكُن فِتْنَتُهُمْ إِلَّآ أَن قَالُوا۟ وَٱللَّهِ رَبِّنَا مَا كُنَّا مُشْرِكِينَ ۝ ٱنظُرْ كَيْفَ كَذَبُوا۟ عَلَىٰٓ أَنفُسِهِمْ وَضَلَّ عَنْهُم مَّا كَانُوا۟ يَفْتَرُونَ ۝

ᵃ Reality is a familiar thing for man, because it is part of man's own nature and it speaks the same silent language throughout the universe. This was truer of the Jews and the Christians, because their Prophets and their scriptures had clearly heralded the advent of the last of the Prophets and the Quran. So, for them to know about this was as good as knowing their own sons.

In spite of things being so clear, why do people not accept the Truth? It is because of the fear of some immediate loss. The cost of acceptance of the Truth is that man has to pull himself down from a high status; he has to come out of the sphere of conformism and give up ready-made advantages. When a man is not ready to make these sacrifices, he does not accept the Truth, and for the sake of instant gain, he pushes himself into a position of eternal loss.

If he has a false sense of satisfaction with the stand he has taken, it is because in this world of trial he is always successful in finding explanations and justifications in his support; he readily finds the words to reject arguments in favour of the Truth—so much so that he feels free to wilfully misinterpret truth and claim that the 'real Truth' is that which he has adopted. ▶

²⁵ Among them are some who listen to you, but We have placed veils over their hearts and deafness in their ears which prevent them from understanding what you say. Even if they saw all the signs, they would still not believe in them. When those who deny the truth come to dispute with you, they will say, 'This is nothing but ancient fables,' ²⁶ and they bar others from believing and themselves keep away. But they ruin no one but themselves, though they fail to realize this.ᵃ

وَمِنْهُم مَّن يَسْتَمِعُ إِلَيْكَ وَجَعَلْنَا عَلَىٰ قُلُوبِهِمْ أَكِنَّةً أَن يَفْقَهُوهُ وَفِي ءَاذَانِهِمْ وَقْرًا وَإِن يَرَوْا۟ كُلَّ ءَايَةٍ لَّا يُؤْمِنُوا۟ بِهَا حَتَّىٰ إِذَا جَآءُوكَ يُجَٰدِلُونَكَ يَقُولُ ٱلَّذِينَ كَفَرُوٓا۟ إِنْ هَٰذَآ إِلَّآ أَسَٰطِيرُ ٱلْأَوَّلِينَ ۝ وَهُمْ يَنْهَوْنَ عَنْهُ وَيَنْـَٔوْنَ عَنْهُ وَإِن يُهْلِكُونَ إِلَّآ أَنفُسَهُمْ وَمَا يَشْعُرُونَ ۝

Whenever a man makes entities other than God the centre of his attention, a magical halo gradually forms around them. He indulges in such wishful thinking as gives him the illusion that he has a firm hold of a very strong support. But, on the Day of Judgement, when all the veils are torn asunder, and when he sees that all the supports except that of God were absolutely false, he will have no alternative but to contradict his own statements. In other words, such people at that time will become witnesses against their own falsity. In the Hereafter they will become the rejecters of those very things of which they had been proud of being attached to. The edifice of false beliefs and explanations they had constructed will be so totally destroyed that it will seem never to have existed.

ᵃ In the present world of trial, man has every opportunity to find pretexts or justifications for anything that suits his interests. There are some who appear to listen to God's message, but if from the outset they are prejudiced, the truth falls on deaf ears and so fails to touch their hearts. They set up mental barriers and, because of this, have no idea of their religious duties, even after they have been carefully explained to them. Arguments, no matter how clearly stated, fail to convince them because, whenever they allow anything of religious significance to cross these barriers, it is with the intention of disputing it, rather than receiving guidance from it. They have no intention of hearing or understanding anything of moral import. As a result, the relevant aspects of any such issue do not come within their mental grasp. Moreover, they are ever ready to present religious matters in a contorted manner. Correct arguments have no influence upon them. Due to their perverseness, they seek out in all ethical questions certain facts which they can misrepresent in order to delude themselves and others that they are on the right path.

²⁷ If you could only see when they are set before the Fire. They will say, 'If only we could be sent back. Then we would not deny the signs of our Lord and we would be of the believers.' ²⁸ The truth they used to hide will become all too clear to them. But if they were sent back, they would return to what they had been forbidden. For they are indeed liars.^a

وَلَوْ تَرَىٰ إِذْ وُقِفُواْ عَلَى ٱلنَّارِ فَقَالُواْ يَٰلَيْتَنَا نُرَدُّ وَلَا نُكَذِّبَ بِـَٔايَٰتِ رَبِّنَا وَنَكُونَ مِنَ ٱلْمُؤْمِنِينَ ۝ بَلْ بَدَا لَهُم مَّا كَانُواْ يُخْفُونَ مِن قَبْلُ ۖ وَلَوْ رُدُّواْ لَعَادُواْ لِمَا نُهُواْ عَنْهُ وَإِنَّهُمْ لَكَٰذِبُونَ ۝

^a For people who have this temperament, all moralizing is in vain, because in this world of trial there is no such rule as prevents them from fabricating counter arguments. Even if they do not manage to concoct such arguments, they will contemptuously ignore the truth, saying, 'What is new in this? This is the same old story which we have been hearing for such a long time.' In this way, even after being convinced of the veracity of moral precepts, they will find some excuse to reject them. Before God such people are doubly guilty, because not only do they themselves refrain from admitting the Truth, but they also make the Divine argument seem dubious to people in general by distorting its true meaning; they have so little understanding themselves that they are unable to make any profound analysis of the subject.

In the life of this world, such people make very tall claims, and because they lose nothing by denying the Truth, they mislead themselves and others.

But on the Day of Judgement, when they are called to account and threatened with Hellfire, the Truth will overwhelm them. Suddenly they will start accepting those very principles which they had denied in this life.

²⁹ They say, 'There is nothing beyond our life in this world: we shall not be raised up again from the dead.' ³⁰ If you could only see when they are made to stand before their Lord! He will ask them, 'Is this [second life] not the truth?' They will say, 'Yes, by our Lord!' He will say, 'Then, taste the punishment that comes from your having refused to acknowledge the truth!'[a]

وَقَالُوٓاْ إِنْ هِيَ إِلَّا حَيَاتُنَا ٱلدُّنْيَا وَمَا نَحْنُ بِمَبْعُوثِينَ ۝ وَلَوْ تَرَىٰٓ إِذْ وُقِفُواْ عَلَىٰ رَبِّهِمْ قَالَ أَلَيْسَ هَٰذَا بِٱلْحَقِّ قَالُواْ بَلَىٰ وَرَبِّنَا قَالَ فَذُوقُواْ ٱلْعَذَابَ بِمَا كُنتُمْ تَكْفُرُونَ ۝

[a] Whenever a man denies the Truth or follows the desires of his self, it is because he does not live his life in this world on the understanding that he will be resurrected after death and made to stand before the Lord of the universe to give an account of himself in everyday life. Man has been given a certain power which he uses unhesitatingly. He has the material prop of wealth, and friends and companions on whom he relies. He has been given a brain, which he uses to think out arrogant strategies and find clever pretexts for his transgressions. The success of his initiatives deceives him; he starts placing false reliance on things other than God, and imagines that the position he enjoys today is of a perennial nature. He forgets that whatever he has been given in this world is only by way of trial and is not a matter of entitlement.

This type of life is thoroughly sinful, whether led in open denial of the Hereafter or without actually uttering the words of denial. On what basis does man rush towards worldly things—thinking them his own? Man has not paid any fee for the sunlight in which he walks or for the air he breathes. No part or ingredient of the earth from which he derives the wherewithal to live has been made by him. None of the favourite things towards which he rushes can he call his own. When these things have not been created by man, should not the Lord of all these things have any right over man? The fact is that man's very utilisation of the present world makes it only logical that he should be made to stand before his Lord on the day of reckoning.

³¹ Those indeed are the losers who deny the meeting with God. When the Hour comes on them suddenly, they cry, 'Alas for us, that we neglected it!' They shall bear their burdens on their backs. Evil are the burdens they shall bear. ³² The life of this world is but a sport and a pastime. Surely the Home of the Hereafter is best for those who fear God. Will you not understand?ᵃ

³³ We know that what they say grieves you. It is not you that the wrongdoers are rejecting, rather it is the signs of God that they reject. ³⁴ Other messengers have been denied before you, and they bore their rejection and persecution steadfastly, until Our help came to them. There is no one who can change the words of God. You have already received some account of those messengers.

قَدْ خَسِرَ ٱلَّذِينَ كَذَّبُواْ بِلِقَآءِ ٱللَّهِ حَتَّىٰٓ إِذَا جَآءَتْهُمُ ٱلسَّاعَةُ بَغْتَةً قَالُواْ يَـٰحَسْرَتَنَا عَلَىٰ مَا فَرَّطْنَا فِيهَا وَهُمْ يَحْمِلُونَ أَوْزَارَهُمْ عَلَىٰ ظُهُورِهِمْ أَلَا سَآءَ مَا يَزِرُونَ ۝ وَمَا ٱلْحَيَوٰةُ ٱلدُّنْيَآ إِلَّا لَعِبٌ وَلَهْوٌ وَلَلدَّارُ ٱلْآخِرَةُ خَيْرٌ لِّلَّذِينَ يَتَّقُونَ أَفَلَا تَعْقِلُونَ ۝ قَدْ نَعْلَمُ إِنَّهُ لَيَحْزُنُكَ ٱلَّذِى يَقُولُونَ فَإِنَّهُمْ لَا يُكَذِّبُونَكَ وَلَـٰكِنَّ ٱلظَّـٰلِمِينَ بِـَٔايَـٰتِ ٱللَّهِ يَجْحَدُونَ ۝ وَلَقَدْ كُذِّبَتْ رُسُلٌ مِّن قَبْلِكَ فَصَبَرُواْ عَلَىٰ مَا كُذِّبُواْ وَأُوذُواْ حَتَّىٰٓ أَتَىٰهُمْ نَصْرُنَا وَلَا مُبَدِّلَ لِكَلِمَـٰتِ ٱللَّهِ وَلَقَدْ جَآءَكَ مِن نَّبَإِيْ ٱلْمُرْسَلِينَ ۝

ᵃ A life lived on the assumption that the world belongs to God is a truly God-fearing life, i.e. a life of *taqwa*, whereas a life in which no such assumption is made is one of sinfulness, being entirely given over to worldly pleasures and trivialities. The latter pleasure-seeking life will last—in terms of eternity—for only a matter of days and, with death, will come to an end, whereas the God-fearing life, regulated by God's eternal principles, will continue to stand man in good stead both in this world and the next. In the present world man denies these realities but, as soon as the freedom given to him under test conditions ends, he will be compelled to accept them, though acceptance at that time will be of no avail.

35 If you find their rejection hard to bear, then seek a tunnel into the ground or a ladder into the sky, if you can, and bring them a sign. Had God so willed, He would indeed have given them all [His] guidance. So do not be among the ignorant. 36 Only they who listen can respond to a call; and as for the dead, God will raise them up, and then they will all return to Him.[a]

وَإِن كَانَ كَبُرَ عَلَيْكَ إِعْرَاضُهُمْ فَإِنِ اسْتَطَعْتَ أَن تَبْتَغِيَ نَفَقًا فِى ٱلْأَرْضِ أَوْ سُلَّمًا فِى ٱلسَّمَآءِ فَتَأْتِيَهُم بِـَٔايَةٍ وَلَوْ شَآءَ ٱللَّهُ لَجَمَعَهُمْ عَلَى ٱلْهُدَىٰ فَلَا تَكُونَنَّ مِنَ ٱلْجَٰهِلِينَ ۝ إِنَّمَا يَسْتَجِيبُ ٱلَّذِينَ يَسْمَعُونَ وَٱلْمَوْتَىٰ يَبْعَثُهُمُ ٱللَّهُ ثُمَّ إِلَيْهِ يُرْجَعُونَ ۝

---

[a] Abu Jahl said to the Prophet, 'O, Muhammad! By God, we do not reject you. Only we deny that which you have brought.' That is, the people of Makkah who had not embraced the faith nevertheless admitted that he was a righteous person. But, to say of a person that his utterances were marked by Truth and reality amounted to glorifying him, and they were not prepared to give him such high honour. When they called him, 'truthful and honest' they had the mental satisfaction that he was a man of their own level, but admitting that God's own discourse emanated from his lips amounted to according him a status higher than their own, and such an admission is the most difficult one for any man to make.

In the present world, God does not appear directly in His original shape. He appears before man in the shape of arguments, signs and symbols. Therefore, not accepting arguments in support of the Truth, or turning a blind eye to the signs in its favour amounts to a refusal to accept God, or to turning one's eyes away from the face of God. However, it is not part of God's plan to appear along with compelling miracles, for if His call were to be presented in this context, freedom of action would come to an end; for the purpose of maintaining test conditions, an atmosphere of freedom of action must be perpetuated. The da'i should not be put out by the fact that he has only the weight of arguments to offer or that he possesses no extraordinary powers of control. Instead of being worried on this account, he should exercise patience. The making of efforts in connection with the mission of truth, is on the one hand, a test of the da'i's patience and, on the other, a test of the addressees as to whether they are able to see a glimpse of God's representative in a man like themselves. Are they able to recognise the majesty of God's message in the words coming out of a man's mouth; do they bow down before arguments that are devoid of material strength, as they will bow down before a strong and powerful God? For those who have life in them, the whole universe is full of God's signs, but those who have extinguished the fire of their sensitivities will not be able to learn a lesson from anything except the terrors of Doomsday.

³⁷ They ask, 'Why has no sign been sent down to him from his Lord?' Say, 'God alone has the power to send down a sign.' But most of them do not understand: ³⁸ there is not an animal that moves about on the earth, nor a bird that flies on its two wings, but are creatures like you. We have left out nothing in the Book—they shall all be gathered before their Lord. ³⁹ Those who reject Our signs are deaf and dumb, [groping along] in darkness. God lets anyone He wishes go astray and sets whoever He will on a straight path.ᵃ

وَقَالُوا۟ لَوْلَا نُزِّلَ عَلَيْهِ ءَايَةٌ مِّن رَّبِّهِۦ قُلْ إِنَّ ٱللَّهَ قَادِرٌ عَلَىٰٓ أَن يُنَزِّلَ ءَايَةً وَلَـٰكِنَّ أَكْثَرَهُمْ لَا يَعْلَمُونَ ۝ وَمَا مِن دَآبَّةٍ فِى ٱلْأَرْضِ وَلَا طَـٰٓئِرٍ يَطِيرُ بِجَنَاحَيْهِ إِلَّآ أُمَمٌ أَمْثَالُكُم مَّا فَرَّطْنَا فِى ٱلْكِتَـٰبِ مِن شَىْءٍ ثُمَّ إِلَىٰ رَبِّهِمْ يُحْشَرُونَ ۝ وَٱلَّذِينَ كَذَّبُوا۟ بِـَٔايَـٰتِنَا صُمٌّ وَبُكْمٌ فِى ٱلظُّلُمَـٰتِ مَن يَشَإِ ٱللَّهُ يُضْلِلْهُ وَمَن يَشَأْ يَجْعَلْهُ عَلَىٰ صِرَٰطٍ مُّسْتَقِيمٍ ۝

ᵃ If the brief import of these verses is expanded, it will be as follows: They ask us why extraordinary signs do not accompany the Prophet in order to establish that his message is truthful. God has the full power to present all types of signs. But the real question is not that of signs but of people's ignorance. God's countless signs are spread out here everywhere. When people are not able to learn anything from these existing signs, what advantage can they derive from the presentation of a new sign? The various types of animals moving about on the earth and the birds flying in the air are signs for you. What God requires of these living creatures is the same as He requires of you, and God has written down His requirements for all living creatures—for human beings in terms of Islamic law and for other creatures by way of their instincts. Creatures like birds and animals carry out God's writ to the letter, but man is not prepared to accept God's writ. Therefore, the question is not of signs but of blindness. What is the justification for man to adopt any religion other than the one adopted by all of God's creatures? The fact is that those who are inclined to act properly do so without demanding any new signs and those who are not so inclined demand signs in spite of already being surrounded by innumerable signs. Such people are inevitably destined to be assembled on Doomsday and shown how all types of animals, having adopted the realistic approach, trod the path of God; it was human beings who deviated from it.

The animal kingdom is synonymous with the world of nature. Animals are on the constant look-out for food but, in obtaining it, there is no persecution by one animal on another. Needs are satisfied but without selfishness. ▶

40 Say, 'Tell me if the punishment of God came upon you or the Hour overtook you, would you call upon any other than God, if you are truthful?' 41 Indeed, it is on Him that you would call, and He could remove that [affliction] which made you call on Him, if He will, and then you would forget [the false deities] which you associate with Him!' a

قُلْ أَرَءَيْتَكُمْ إِنْ أَتَىٰكُمْ عَذَابُ ٱللَّهِ أَوْ أَتَتْكُمُ ٱلسَّاعَةُ أَغَيْرَ ٱللَّهِ تَدْعُونَ إِن كُنتُمْ صَٰدِقِينَ ۝ بَلْ إِيَّاهُ تَدْعُونَ فَيَكْشِفُ مَا تَدْعُونَ إِلَيْهِ إِن شَآءَ وَتَنسَوْنَ مَا تُشْرِكُونَ ۝

Even if one animal is troubled by another, there is no hostility or enmity. Among them tasks are performed, but there is no ambition to get the credit for them. Unlike animals, man is arrogant. He is not prepared to be regulated by God's plan. God's requirement of man is the same as that which is fulfilled by the animals. Then why is it necessary for man to demand a miracle? Are not there living signs in the shape of animals which provide an example of God's methods and also corroborate for mankind the truth of the Prophet's teachings?

a History bears witness to the fact that a man starts invoking the name of God in crucial moments; even one who relied on beings other than God or did not believe in God's existence at all. This is nature's testament to God's existence and His being the absolute authority. Under extraordinary circumstances, when the outward veils are removed and when man dismisses all superficial thoughts, he does not remember anything except God. In other words, on reaching the point of helplessness, every man admits the existence of God. But the Quran demands that man should follow a course of acceptance and obedience *at a time when there is no apparent compulsion to do so*.

All animals other than man instinctively lead realistic lives. But what pushes man towards realism and the admission of the truth is the psychology of fear. In the world of animals all things are accomplished by instinct. The same role is played by fear of God (*taqwa*) in the world of human beings.

42 We sent messengers before you [Prophet] to many communities and afflicted their people with suffering and hardship, so that they might humble themselves. 43 When the affliction decreed by Us befell them, they did not humble themselves, but rather their hearts hardened, for Satan had made all their doings seem fair to them. 44 When they had forgotten Our admonition, We granted them all that they desired; but just as they were rejoicing in what they were given, We seized them suddenly and they were plunged into despair. 45 The wrongdoers were thus annihilated. All praise be to God, the Lord of the Worlds.[a]

وَلَقَدْ أَرْسَلْنَآ إِلَىٰ أُمَمٍ مِّن قَبْلِكَ فَأَخَذْنَٰهُم بِٱلْبَأْسَآءِ وَٱلضَّرَّآءِ لَعَلَّهُمْ يَتَضَرَّعُونَ ۝ فَلَوْلَآ إِذْ جَآءَهُم بَأْسُنَا تَضَرَّعُوا۟ وَلَٰكِن قَسَتْ قُلُوبُهُمْ وَزَيَّنَ لَهُمُ ٱلشَّيْطَٰنُ مَا كَانُوا۟ يَعْمَلُونَ ۝ فَلَمَّا نَسُوا۟ مَا ذُكِّرُوا۟ بِهِۦ فَتَحْنَا عَلَيْهِمْ أَبْوَٰبَ كُلِّ شَىْءٍ حَتَّىٰٓ إِذَا فَرِحُوا۟ بِمَآ أُوتُوٓا۟ أَخَذْنَٰهُم بَغْتَةً فَإِذَا هُم مُّبْلِسُونَ ۝ فَقُطِعَ دَابِرُ ٱلْقَوْمِ ٱلَّذِينَ ظَلَمُوا۟ وَٱلْحَمْدُ لِلَّهِ رَبِّ ٱلْعَٰلَمِينَ ۝

---

[a] When a man is faced with the truth and he does not accept it, God does not seize him immediately, but gives him some jolts by way of monetary loss or physical trouble, so that he should review his way of life, and his thinking should be revolutionised. Life's events are not mere happenings but vibrant messages from God sent to wake a man up from his sleep of forgetfulness. But man learns nothing from these things. He consoles himself by saying that these are normal ups and downs and that such ups and downs do occur in life. In this way, Satan all too often diverts the mind of the individual from possible divine disfavour and pushes him into negligence of his religious duties by providing him with plausible justifications. When a man indulges in this type of behaviour again and again, his heart loses all sensitivity to what is true or false, right or wrong. His conscience eventually becomes totally blunted.

When a man ignores the warnings received from God, His approach towards him changes. Now, God's decision for him is that the doors to comfort and success should be opened for him; he should be granted prosperity in full measure; his honour and popularity should increase. This is in reality, a punishment, so that the evil hidden in him should come out clearly. The purpose of this is that man should feel satisfied with himself and become more and more insensitive and much bolder in ignoring the Truth. And, as a result, his meriting punishment is fully established. When this purpose is achieved, God's retribution suddenly overwhelms him. He is deprived of worldly life and presented before the court of the Hereafter, so that he may be awarded the punishment of Hell. ▶

⁴⁶ Say, 'If God should take away your hearing and your sight and seal your hearts, who is the deity who could restore it to you save God?' See how We explain the signs to them in diverse ways, yet they turn away. ⁴⁷ Ask them, 'Tell me, if the punishment of God came upon you suddenly or predictably, would any but the wrongdoers be destroyed?'ᵃ

قُلْ أَرَءَيْتُمْ إِنْ أَخَذَ ٱللَّهُ سَمْعَكُمْ وَأَبْصَرَكُمْ وَخَتَمَ عَلَىٰ قُلُوبِكُم مَّنْ إِلَٰهٌ غَيْرُ ٱللَّهِ يَأْتِيكُم بِهِ ۗ ٱنظُرْ كَيْفَ نُصَرِّفُ ٱلْآيَٰتِ ثُمَّ هُمْ يَصْدِفُونَ ۝ قُلْ أَرَءَيْتَكُمْ إِنْ أَتَىٰكُمْ عَذَابُ ٱللَّهِ بَغْتَةً أَوْ جَهْرَةً هَلْ يُهْلَكُ إِلَّا ٱلْقَوْمُ ٱلظَّٰلِمُونَ ۝

This world is God's world. Here the right to have one's greatness extolled belongs to only one Being. So, if a man ignores the divine truth, he is in fact disrespecting God. In a world overarched by the majesty of the Almighty, he wants to establish his own greatness. In this way he is indulging in unparalleled transgression. He is being insolent to God before whom no behaviour other than that of the utmost humility is proper.

ᵃ The granting of ears, eyes and heart to man indicates what his Creator wants from him. The Creator wants man to hear and see His signs and accept them using rational arguments. If a man does not utilise these God-given capabilities for the purpose they are meant, then he is running the risk that he may be declared incapable and his capabilities may be snatched from him. How helpless is one who is rendered blind, deaf and mentally disabled because such a person will remain of no social value. But there is a kind of helplessness greater than this: it is to have ears but be deaf to the Truth; it is to have eyes but be blind to the Truth; it is to have a heart in one's breast but be incapable of understanding the Truth. This deprivation is much more serious than the first kind, because it makes a man debased and worthless in respect of the Hereafter; there is no shortcoming more heinous than this.

If a man is warned of the result of the denial of truth, and has the bravado to respond insolently, it is because, being well placed in the world, he thinks that he need not fear the scourge of God. Indeed, he imagines he is exempt from divine retribution. And the more daring ones, such as he, challenge God's messenger and say, 'If you are truthful, bring down upon us God's wrath, and let us see.' They do not understand that if God vents His anger, it will be on them and not on anyone else.

48 We send the messengers only to give good news and to warn, so those who believe and reform themselves need have no fear, nor will they grieve. 49 Chastisement will befall those who reject Our signs because of their disobedience. 50 Say, 'I do not say to you that I possess the treasures of God, nor do I know the unseen, nor do I say to you that I am an angel. I follow only that which is revealed to me.' Say, 'Are the blind and the seeing alike? Can you not then think?' [a]

وَمَا نُرْسِلُ ٱلْمُرْسَلِينَ إِلَّا مُبَشِّرِينَ وَمُنذِرِينَ فَمَنْ ءَامَنَ وَأَصْلَحَ فَلَا خَوْفٌ عَلَيْهِمْ وَلَا هُمْ يَحْزَنُونَ ۝ وَٱلَّذِينَ كَذَّبُواْ بِـَٔايَٰتِنَا يَمَسُّهُمُ ٱلْعَذَابُ بِمَا كَانُواْ يَفْسُقُونَ ۝ قُل لَّا أَقُولُ لَكُمْ عِندِى خَزَآئِنُ ٱللَّهِ وَلَا أَعْلَمُ ٱلْغَيْبَ وَلَا أَقُولُ لَكُمْ إِنِّى مَلَكٌ إِنْ أَتَّبِعُ إِلَّا مَا يُوحَىٰ إِلَىَّ قُلْ هَلْ يَسْتَوِى ٱلْأَعْمَىٰ وَٱلْبَصِيرُ أَفَلَا تَتَفَكَّرُونَ ۝

---

[a] The preacher of God's word appears in the world not only as one who gives good news, but also as a warner. In other words, the basis on which a man is tested before God is that he should recognise the Truth conveyed in the language of admonition and reform himself accordingly. If he fails to recognise the Truth and demands magic feats and charms as a condition for acceptance, he merely proves his moral blindness; and for such blind people, there is no fate but havoc and destruction in this world of God.

⁵¹ Warn by it those who fear to be gathered before their Lord, when they have no guardian or intercessor besides God, so that they may become God-fearing. ⁵² Do not send away those who call upon their Lord in the morning and in the evening, seeking only His grace. You are not by any means accountable for them, nor are they accountable for you. If you turn them away, you yourself will become one of the unjust.ᵃ

وَأَنذِرْ بِهِ ٱلَّذِينَ يَخَافُونَ أَن يُحْشَرُوٓا۟ إِلَىٰ رَبِّهِمْ لَيْسَ لَهُم مِّن دُونِهِۦ وَلِىٌّ وَلَا شَفِيعٌ لَّعَلَّهُمْ يَتَّقُونَ ۝ وَلَا تَطْرُدِ ٱلَّذِينَ يَدْعُونَ رَبَّهُم بِٱلْغَدَوٰةِ وَٱلْعَشِىِّ يُرِيدُونَ وَجْهَهُۥ مَا عَلَيْكَ مِنْ حِسَابِهِم مِّن شَىْءٍ وَمَا مِنْ حِسَابِكَ عَلَيْهِم مِّن شَىْءٍ فَتَطْرُدَهُمْ فَتَكُونَ مِنَ ٱلظَّٰلِمِينَ ۝

ᵃ Admonition is effective only for those who live in fear of God. Only one who is concerned about possible danger can be warned about imminent calamity. On the contrary, those who live reckless lives are never serious about admonition, and that is why they are never prepared to heed advice.

Recklessness or fearlessness arises from two factors—one is worship of the world and the other is worship of ancestors. Those who are lost in worldly things or are satisfied with worldly success do not even remember that one day, when they die, they shall have to appear before their Creator and Lord, and so do not consider the Hereafter as anything significant. Remembrance of the Hereafter does not, therefore, find a place in their thinking. Their temperament is such that they ignore such things, considering them unimportant.

Another category of individuals includes those who consider recommendation the key to Paradise. They presume that the 'great ones' for whom they have developed an attachment will be their supporters and commenders in the Hereafter and that no matter how unfavourable the conditions, that will be sufficient for their salvation. Such people live in the fond hope that since they have grasped the hands of some 'holy' personalities and since they are with the group which is ostensibly loved and favoured by God, no affair of theirs can go awry. It is this mentality which makes them unafraid of the Hereafter. They are not ready to give serious consideration to anything which may throw doubt on their position in the life to come.

53 In this way We try some of them by means of others, so that they may ask, 'Are these [lowly ones] whom God has singled out for His favours from among us? Does God not know best who are the grateful ones?'^a

وَكَذَٰلِكَ فَتَنَّا بَعْضَهُم بِبَعْضٍ لِّيَقُولُوٓاْ أَهَٰٓؤُلَآءِ مَنَّ ٱللَّهُ عَلَيْهِم مِّنۢ بَيْنِنَآ ۗ أَلَيْسَ ٱللَّهُ بِأَعْلَمَ بِٱلشَّٰكِرِينَ ۝

---

^a Those who have achieved wealth and popularity prefer to give weightage to the considerations of their worldly interests, rather than support the pure and unadulterated call of Truth, because, according to them, supporting the Truth would amount to demolition of the entire structure of their vested interests. Moreover, when they see that Truth is upheld by people of ordinary status, their way of thinking is further strengthened. They feel that by associating with the Truth they will be lowering their own status. Instead of testing the Truth on the touchstone of Truth, they judge it by their own criteria, i.e. by their own private and personal touchstone, and when the Truth does not measure up to this, they ignore it.

⁵⁴ When those who believe in Our revelations come to you, say, 'Peace be upon you. Your Lord has taken it upon Himself to be merciful. So that if any one among you does evil in ignorance and repents thereafter and makes amends, then He is most forgiving and ever merciful.' ⁵⁵ Thus We make plain Our signs, so that the path of the evil-doers might be laid bare.ᵃ

وَإِذَا جَاءَكَ ٱلَّذِينَ يُؤۡمِنُونَ بِـَٔايَـٰتِنَا فَقُلۡ سَلَـٰمٌ عَلَيۡكُمۡ ۖ كَتَبَ رَبُّكُمۡ عَلَىٰ نَفۡسِهِ ٱلرَّحۡمَةَ ۖ أَنَّهُۥ مَنۡ عَمِلَ مِنكُمۡ سُوٓءَۢا بِجَهَـٰلَةٍ ثُمَّ تَابَ مِنۢ بَعۡدِهِۦ وَأَصۡلَحَ فَأَنَّهُۥ غَفُورٌ رَّحِيمٌ ۝ وَكَذَٰلِكَ نُفَصِّلُ ٱلۡـَٔايَـٰتِ وَلِتَسۡتَبِينَ سَبِيلُ ٱلۡمُجۡرِمِينَ ۝

ᵃ During the period of the Prophet Muhammad, there were those who demanded miracles before accepting his bona fides. Unlike them, there were others who embraced the faith on hearing him recite the verses of the Quran. This sort of test of man goes on in every era. In the present world God does not appear in physical form. He advances His arguments through the medium of the bearer of truth, casting them in verbal form, so that they may be presented to mankind. Now, one in whom nature is alive is able to see the glow of God in these arguments and he accepts it and bows down before it. But, those who have shrouded their nature in artificial veils fail to find God through His 'words'. They are unable to see God through reasoning and therefore they want God to appear before them physically, in an observable shape. But this is not possible in the present world of trial. Here, only that person will find God who is able to recognise Him while He is still invisible. One who insists on witnessing God in physical form in this world faces spiritual destitution of the most extreme kind.

Those who sedulously avoid the truth by adopting a wrong approach, accuse those who accept the Truth of various kinds of wrongdoing, so that they may prove themselves to be much better than them. They are unable to see their own transgressions but, if a truthful person happens to commit any slight mistake, they try to exaggerate it with a view to establishing that those who have rallied to the quest for truth are unreliable. The truth is quite the reverse. Believers who have abjured untruth and accepted truth tread the path of faith and righteousness. In this way, in accordance with the will of God, they become entitled to receive inspiration for the betterment of their present position and share the bounties of God. Unlike them, those who steer clear of the truth only prove by their actions that they are not interested in adopting the way of faith and righteousness. Even when such people are deprived of God's guidance, their bravado does not come to an end, and it is their effrontery which constitutes the greatest crime in this world of God.

God expresses Himself in the language of 'symbols'. Symbols are useful only to one who has the desire to read or interpret them. Similarly, guidance will be available only to one who is eager to have it. One who shows no interest in guidance has no other option but to go astray.

⁵⁶ Say, 'I am forbidden to worship those you call upon besides God.' Say, 'I do not follow your whims and desires. If I did, I would go astray and cease to be rightly guided.' ⁵⁷ Say, 'I stand by the clear evidence from my Lord, yet you deny it. What you seek to hasten is not within my power. Judgement is for God alone. He declares the truth. He is the best of judges.' [a]

قُل إِنِّي نُهِيتُ أَنْ أَعْبُدَ ٱلَّذِينَ تَدْعُونَ مِن دُونِ ٱللَّهِ قُل لَّآ أَتَّبِعُ أَهْوَآءَكُمْ قَدْ ضَلَلْتُ إِذًا وَمَآ أَنَا۠ مِنَ ٱلْمُهْتَدِينَ ۝ قُلْ إِنِّي عَلَىٰ بَيِّنَةٍ مِّن رَّبِّي وَكَذَّبْتُم بِهِۦ مَا عِندِي مَا تَسْتَعْجِلُونَ بِهِۦٓ إِنِ ٱلْحُكْمُ إِلَّا لِلَّهِ يَقُصُّ ٱلْحَقَّ وَهُوَ خَيْرُ ٱلْفَٰصِلِينَ

[a] Man's own wishful thinking—which he presumes to be a reality, is all too often raised to the status of something worth worshipping. Sometimes, just to save himself from the consequences of his negligence of religious duties, he accepts someone as God's favourite and treats him as one who is supposed to support him before God and recommend his case to Him. Sometimes he imagines such a person to have charismatic, supernatural greatness in him, and that he could make up for his own shortcomings by attaching himself to him. Sometimes, due to his easy-going nature, he invents a god who is easy of access and who can easily be pleased with small things.

But all such things are mere suppositions and suppositions can never lead anyone to reality. However, there are some who become so blinkered by cheap demands that they even challenge those who have rallied to the side of the real Lord of the Universe. They challenge them thus: 'If all greatness and majesty belong to the one and only God whom you represent, then arrange to let His retribution come down upon us. Let us see.' They dare to behave in this way, because they observe that they are much more surrounded by worldly glories than the *da'is* who work for the acceptance of God's unity. They forget that the material amenities available to them are due to their devotion to worldly considerations and worldly interests, whereas the missionaries of God, who are bereft of all these things, are in such a condition because their yearning for the Hereafter has prevented them from stooping to the level of devotion to worldly goals.

⁵⁸ Say, 'If what you seek to hasten were within my power, the matter would be settled between you and me. God best knows the evil-doers.' ⁵⁹ He holds the keys to the unseen; none knows them but He. He has knowledge of all that land and sea contain. No leaf falls without His knowledge, nor is there a single grain in the darkness of the earth, or anything, wet or dry, but is recorded in a clear Record.ᵃ

قُل لَّوۡ أَنَّ عِندِى مَا تَسۡتَعۡجِلُونَ بِهِۦ لَقُضِىَ ٱلۡأَمۡرُ بَيۡنِى وَبَيۡنَكُمۡ وَٱللَّهُ أَعۡلَمُ بِٱلظَّٰلِمِينَ ۝ وَعِندَهُۥ مَفَاتِحُ ٱلۡغَيۡبِ لَا يَعۡلَمُهَآ إِلَّا هُوَ وَيَعۡلَمُ مَا فِى ٱلۡبَرِّ وَٱلۡبَحۡرِ وَمَا تَسۡقُطُ مِن وَرَقَةٍ إِلَّا يَعۡلَمُهَا وَلَا حَبَّةٍ فِى ظُلُمَٰتِ ٱلۡأَرۡضِ وَلَا رَطۡبٍ وَلَا يَابِسٍ إِلَّا فِى كِتَٰبٍ مُّبِينٍ ۝

ᵃ The present world is one of test and trial. Therefore, what is truly significant here is not the material conditions in which a man lives, but whether he is taking a stand on the rationale of truth or on suppositions and false hopes. In the final analysis, only that person will be successful who takes a stand on the real rationale of Truth. The people who rely on suppositions in this world of God will be ultimately reduced to a state of utter helplessness. How could the final fate of the world, which is functioning under the strict control of the Almighty, become relegated to an abyss of false hopes?

⁶⁰ It is He who gathers you in at night and knows all that you do by day; then He raises you up during the day so that an appointed term may be completed. Then to Him you shall return and He will declare to you all that you used to do.ᵃ

وَهُوَ ٱلَّذِى يَتَوَفَّىٰكُم بِٱلَّيْلِ وَيَعْلَمُ مَا جَرَحْتُم بِٱلنَّهَارِ ثُمَّ يَبْعَثُكُمْ فِيهِ لِيُقْضَىٰٓ أَجَلٌ مُّسَمًّى ثُمَّ إِلَيْهِ مَرْجِعُكُمْ ثُمَّ يُنَبِّئُكُم بِمَا كُنتُمْ تَعْمَلُونَ ۝

ᵃ God has created this world in such a way that it provides practical examples of those facts to which the attention of human beings is called. If a man does not close his eyes and does not screen off his mind with false veils, he will find in the whole universe practical demonstrations of the Quran's challenge to man's thinking processes.

Branches emerge from a tree trunk and leaves sprout from the branches, but there is a difference in their respective joints. In other words, the Creator knows that the branches have to remain attached to the trunk, while the leaves have to detach themselves and fall down. If this were not so, the leaves would fail to separate from the branches and the entire system of bringing new life to the tree every year would be upset. Similarly, when a seed is sown, the earth in which it is placed already possesses all the ingredients from which it derives nourishment and finally grows into a full-fledged tree. Then, how is it possible that God who is aware of the conditions of such things as a leaf and a seed could be unaware of the human condition?

⁶¹ He is the Absolute Master over His servants. He sends forth guardians [angels] who watch over you until, when death approaches one of you, Our angels take his soul, and they never fail in their duty. ⁶² Then they will all be returned to God, their true Lord. The Judgement is His alone. He is the swiftest reckoner.ᵃ

وَهُوَ ٱلْقَاهِرُ فَوْقَ عِبَادِهِۦ ۚ وَيُرْسِلُ عَلَيْكُمْ حَفَظَةً حَتَّىٰٓ إِذَا جَآءَ أَحَدَكُمُ ٱلْمَوْتُ تَوَفَّتْهُ رُسُلُنَا وَهُمْ لَا يُفَرِّطُونَ ۝ ثُمَّ رُدُّوٓا۟ إِلَى ٱللَّهِ مَوْلَىٰهُمُ ٱلْحَقِّ ۚ أَلَا لَهُ ٱلْحُكْمُ وَهُوَ أَسْرَعُ ٱلْحَـٰسِبِينَ ۝

ᵃ Our earth is a unique phenomenon in the whole universe. The system prevailing here has been made congenial to the conditions of God's creatures—human beings. A major part of the interior of the earth consists of fire but it does not burst open. The sun is at exactly the right distance mathematically, and does not move closer or farther away. A man always needs air and water; so air has been spread over the earth in gaseous form and water has been stored under the surface of the earth in liquid form. There are countless similar arrangements that are constantly maintained in the right proportions on the earth. If there were even a slight variation in these, it would be impossible for a human being to live here.

Sleep is a wonderful thing. Man roams about here and there; he sees and speaks; but when he sleeps all his senses become suspended, just as if life had oozed out of them. When he has had his full sleep and wakes up, he becomes as active as before. This is, so to say, an example of life and death. This event demonstrates how a man will die and how he will be resurrected, i.e. be brought back to life. These events prove that all men are in the power of God and soon that Day will come when God will take fateful decisions about them in the exercise of His powers.

63 Say, 'Who is it who delivers you from the dark depths of land and sea when you call out to Him humbly and in secret, saying, "If He rescues us from this, we shall most certainly be among the grateful."?'[a] 64 Say, 'It is God who delivers you from it and from every other distress, yet you associate partners with Him.' 65 Say, 'He has the power to send punishment on you from above your heads or from beneath your feet, or to divide you in sects and make you taste one another's violence.' See how We explain Our revelations in various ways, so that they may understand.

قُلْ مَن يُنَجِّيكُم مِّن ظُلُمَٰتِ ٱلْبَرِّ وَٱلْبَحْرِ تَدْعُونَهُۥ تَضَرُّعًا وَخُفْيَةً لَّئِنْ أَنجَىٰنَا مِنْ هَٰذِهِۦ لَنَكُونَنَّ مِنَ ٱلشَّٰكِرِينَ ۝ قُلِ ٱللَّهُ يُنَجِّيكُم مِّنْهَا وَمِن كُلِّ كَرْبٍ ثُمَّ أَنتُمْ تُشْرِكُونَ ۝ قُلْ هُوَ ٱلْقَادِرُ عَلَىٰٓ أَن يَبْعَثَ عَلَيْكُمْ عَذَابًا مِّن فَوْقِكُمْ أَوْ مِن تَحْتِ أَرْجُلِكُمْ أَوْ يَلْبِسَكُمْ شِيَعًا وَيُذِيقَ بَعْضَكُم بَأْسَ بَعْضٍ ٱنظُرْ كَيْفَ نُصَرِّفُ ٱلْأَيَٰتِ لَعَلَّهُمْ يَفْقَهُونَ ۝

[a] No other living creature in this world faces so many troubles as human beings do. This is so, because man is intended to be subjected to adverse conditions so that all artificial, unreal thoughts are driven out of his mind, and he is able to see his own true nature. The fact is that whenever a man confronts any major trouble, he starts single-mindedly calling upon God. At that time, all the man-made veils are swept away from his mind. He comes to realise that in this world man is completely humble and helpless, and it is God alone who has all the power. But as soon as his troubles are eased, he reverts to his usual neglect and recklessness and becomes the same man as he was earlier.

[b] Basically, polytheism (shirk) is the reposing of one's faith in some entity other than God, while monotheism is directing of man's entire faith solely towards God. One form of polytheism is that which involves worship of deities and of other phenomena. But exhibiting ingratitude instead of gratitude is also 'shirk'. The more common form of shirk is that whereby a man makes a deity of himself; he starts having faith only in himself. When a man proves to be vain, it is as if he has faith in his efforts alone. When a man considers his earnings as actually having been generated by him, he in fact has faith only in his own talents. When a man overlooks another's right, he thinks that nobody can inflict any punishment on him for doing so. When a man dares to oppress another, he thinks that he has full powers over the wronged person and there is nobody to prevent him from doing whatever he likes to him. All these are forms of vanity and pride. And pride is—before God— the worst type of shirk, because indulging in this amounts to placing oneself in the position of God.

⁶⁶ Your people have rejected the message We have sent through you, though it is the truth. Say 'I am not your keeper. ⁶⁷ Every prophecy has its fixed time to be fulfilled: and soon you will come to know.'

⁶⁸ When you see people engaged in finding fault with Our revelations, withdraw from them until they turn to some other topic. Should Satan cause you to forget this, take leave of the wrongdoers as soon as you remember. ⁶⁹ The God-fearing are not in any way held accountable for the wrongdoers; their only duty is to remind them, so that they may fear God.ᵃ

وَكَذَّبَ بِهِ قَوْمُكَ وَهُوَ ٱلْحَقُّ قُل لَّسْتُ عَلَيْكُم بِوَكِيلٍ ۞ لِّكُلِّ نَبَإٍ مُّسْتَقَرٌّ وَسَوْفَ تَعْلَمُونَ ۞ وَإِذَا رَأَيْتَ ٱلَّذِينَ يَخُوضُونَ فِىٓ ءَايَٰتِنَا فَأَعْرِضْ عَنْهُمْ حَتَّىٰ يَخُوضُوا۟ فِى حَدِيثٍ غَيْرِهِۦ وَإِمَّا يُنسِيَنَّكَ ٱلشَّيْطَٰنُ فَلَا تَقْعُدْ بَعْدَ ٱلذِّكْرَىٰ مَعَ ٱلْقَوْمِ ٱلظَّٰلِمِينَ ۞ وَمَا عَلَى ٱلَّذِينَ يَتَّقُونَ مِنْ حِسَابِهِم مِّن شَىْءٍ وَلَٰكِن ذِكْرَىٰ لَعَلَّهُمْ يَتَّقُونَ ۞

ᵃ If due consideration were to be given to the human condition, no one would ever be proud. Man is buffeted by winds which can turn into a cyclone at any time and completely wreck his life; he stands on land which can at any time be rent apart by earthquakes; he lives in a society which is so fraught with internal enmities that even a spark is enough to push the whole of society into a bloodbath.

⁷⁰ Leave alone those for whom religion is only a sport and pastime and are deceived by the life of this world, but continue to remind them with the Quran, lest a soul be held in pledge because of what it has wrought, having no helper or intercessor besides God. Whatever ransom they may offer, it will not be accepted. Such are those that are damned by their own actions: they will have boiling water to drink and a painful punishment for their denial of truth.ᵃ

وَذَرِ ٱلَّذِينَ ٱتَّخَذُوا۟ دِينَهُمْ لَعِبًا وَلَهْوًا وَغَرَّتْهُمُ ٱلْحَيَوٰةُ ٱلدُّنْيَا وَذَكِّرْ بِهِۦٓ أَن تُبْسَلَ نَفْسٌۢ بِمَا كَسَبَتْ لَيْسَ لَهَا مِن دُونِ ٱللَّهِ وَلِىٌّ وَلَا شَفِيعٌ وَإِن تَعْدِلْ كُلَّ عَدْلٍ لَّا يُؤْخَذْ مِنْهَآ أُو۟لَٰٓئِكَ ٱلَّذِينَ أُبْسِلُوا۟ بِمَا كَسَبُوا۟ لَهُمْ شَرَابٌ مِّنْ حَمِيمٍ وَعَذَابٌ أَلِيمٌۢ بِمَا كَانُوا۟ يَكْفُرُونَ ۝

ᵃ 'Abdullah ibn 'Abbas says that God fixed a religious festival day ('Id) for every community, the purpose being that on that day they should glorify God, offer prayers to Him and fill the whole day with His remembrance. Those who came later made their religious festival ('Id) a day of fun and frolic. (Tafsir Kabir).

There is a purpose behind every religious activity and then there is its outward aspect too. The purpose of 'Id is the collective demonstration of the glorification of God and His remembrance. But too much attention is paid to the externals of 'Id—for example, the wearing of good clothes, arrangements for group activities, etc. Now, making 'Id a mere event of fun and frolic amounts to neglecting its real purpose, which becomes forgotten in the fuss which is made about its outward and material aspects, such as a show of good clothes and possessions, the hustle and bustle of shopping, arrangements for entertainment, and the pomp which goes with a show of one's position, etc.

71 Say, 'Instead of God, shall we call upon that which can neither benefit us nor harm us? Are we to turn upon our heels after God has guided us, like one who, beguiled by devils in the land, wanders bewildered, his companions calling him to the right path, saying, "Come to us"?' Say, 'God's guidance is the only guidance. We are commanded to surrender ourselves to the Lord of the Universe, 72 say our prayers regularly and to fear God.' He it is to whom you will be gathered.' a

قُلْ أَنَدْعُواْ مِن دُونِ ٱللَّهِ مَا لَا
يَنفَعُنَا وَلَا يَضُرُّنَا وَنُرَدُّ عَلَىٰ أَعْقَابِنَا
بَعْدَ إِذْ هَدَىٰنَا ٱللَّهُ كَٱلَّذِى ٱسْتَهْوَتْهُ
ٱلشَّيَٰطِينُ فِى ٱلْأَرْضِ حَيْرَانَ لَهُۥ
أَصْحَٰبٌ يَدْعُونَهُۥٓ إِلَى ٱلْهُدَى ٱئْتِنَا
قُلْ إِنَّ هُدَى ٱللَّهِ هُوَ ٱلْهُدَى
وَأُمِرْنَا لِنُسْلِمَ لِرَبِّ ٱلْعَٰلَمِينَ ٧١
وَأَنْ أَقِيمُواْ ٱلصَّلَوٰةَ وَٱتَّقُوهُ وَهُوَ
ٱلَّذِىٓ إِلَيْهِ تُحْشَرُونَ ٧٢

---

a When communities go astray, all religious acts undergo this change. People ignore the true objective of the religious act and lay stress on externals. Now, those who reach the stage of making religion a source of worldly fun and frolic and are completely oblivious to its intended purpose, prove by their deeds that they are neither serious nor sincere about religion. And those who are not serious about such matters cannot have anything explained to them in this connection, as this goes against their temperament. Moreover, possession of material things gives them the illusion that they are the possessors of truth also. Here, they observe that all their needs are adequately fulfilled. Everywhere they are the life and soul of the gathering. There is no void in their lives. So, they presume that in the Hereafter also they will be successful. Such people, because of their misapprehensions, are not serious about the Hereafter.

But, they should know that whatever they perpetrate will not be without consequences. They will be undone by their own actions. Their very arrogance will very soon rebound on them and there will be no mitigation of their suffering.

73 It was He who created the heavens and the earth for a true purpose. On the Day when He says, 'Be,' it shall be: His word is the truth. All sovereignty shall be His on the Day when the trumpet is sounded. The Knower of the unseen and the visible, He is the Wise, the Aware One.[a] 74 Remember when Abraham said to his father, Azar, 'Do you take idols as your gods? I see that you and your people have clearly gone astray.'[b]

وَهُوَ ٱلَّذِى خَلَقَ ٱلسَّمَٰوَٰتِ وَٱلْأَرْضَ بِٱلْحَقِّ وَيَوْمَ يَقُولُ كُن فَيَكُونُ قَوْلُهُ ٱلْحَقُّ وَلَهُ ٱلْمُلْكُ يَوْمَ يُنفَخُ فِى ٱلصُّورِ عَٰلِمُ ٱلْغَيْبِ وَٱلشَّهَٰدَةِ وَهُوَ ٱلْحَكِيمُ ٱلْخَبِيرُ ۝ وَإِذْ قَالَ إِبْرَٰهِيمُ لِأَبِيهِ ءَازَرَ أَتَتَّخِذُ أَصْنَامًا ءَالِهَةً إِنِّى أَرَىٰكَ وَقَوْمَكَ فِى ضَلَٰلٍ مُّبِينٍ ۝

---

[a] There are two kinds of travellers in the desert. One puts his entire trust in God. When he goes astray, he begs God's assistance and soon has his feet set on the right path once again. The other has faith in entities other than God. When he loses his way in the desert, he is hardly aware that he is wandering aimlessly and ignores the calls of the faithful who would gladly re-direct him. The reason for this difference in outlook is that the former traveller keeps an open mind. He has no difficulty in seeing which is the right path, and if he chances to stray from it, he is willing to accept God's guidance in order to return to it. The latter traveller, however, is lost right from the beginning, because he has fallen under the influence of Satan. His mind, therefore, works in a perverse way. The result is that he may listen, but he does not hear, and he may look, but he does not see.

[b] The seeking of things other than God is a futile pursuit of entities that have no power to benefit or harm anybody. Heaven and earth, along with the systems prevailing in them, deny the existence of any being having any powers except the one and only Supreme Being. Similarly, man makes worldly glories his purpose in life and, in his efforts to achieve this purpose, tramples upon the requirements of truth and justice. All this is absolutely wrong. This would mean that this world is but a showplace for selfish and egoistic persons. But, the fact is that the perfect system prevalent in this universe reveals resplendent glimpses of the Perfect God and it is quite unimaginable that such a Perfect Being as He would create a showplace without meaning.

The present situation existing in this world is purely temporary. God may at any moment promulgate a new command and break down the existing system. Then man's present freedom will come to an end and God's authority will prevail over human beings as it does today over all the other creatures in the universe. At that point only those who have surrendered themselves to God during the test period will be successful, i.e. those who feared God without any pressure being brought to bear on them before they bowed down to Him in body and soul.

75 In this way We showed Abraham Our kingdom of the heavens and the earth, so that he might have certainty of faith. 76 When night descended on him, he saw a star. He said, 'This is my Lord!' Then when it set he said, 'I do not love things that set.' 77 When he saw the moon rise and spread its light, he said, 'This is my Lord.' But when it set, he said, 'If my Lord does not guide me, I will be one of the misguided people.' 78 Then, when he saw the sun shining, he said, 'This is my Lord! This is the greatest of all!' Then when it set, he said, 'My people, I disown all that you worship besides God. 79 I have set my face with single-minded devotion, towards Him who has created the heavens and the earth, and I am not one of the polytheists.'[a]

وَكَذَٰلِكَ نُرِىٓ إِبْرَٰهِيمَ مَلَكُوتَ ٱلسَّمَٰوَٰتِ وَٱلْأَرْضِ وَلِيَكُونَ مِنَ ٱلْمُوقِنِينَ ۝ فَلَمَّا جَنَّ عَلَيْهِ ٱلَّيْلُ رَءَا كَوْكَبًا قَالَ هَٰذَا رَبِّى فَلَمَّآ أَفَلَ قَالَ لَآ أُحِبُّ ٱلْءَافِلِينَ ۝ فَلَمَّا رَءَا ٱلْقَمَرَ بَازِغًا قَالَ هَٰذَا رَبِّى فَلَمَّآ أَفَلَ قَالَ لَئِن لَّمْ يَهْدِنِى رَبِّى لَأَكُونَنَّ مِنَ ٱلْقَوْمِ ٱلضَّآلِّينَ ۝ فَلَمَّا رَءَا ٱلشَّمْسَ بَازِغَةً قَالَ هَٰذَا رَبِّى هَٰذَآ أَكْبَرُ فَلَمَّآ أَفَلَتْ قَالَ يَٰقَوْمِ إِنِّى بَرِىٓءٌ مِّمَّا تُشْرِكُونَ ۝ إِنِّى وَجَّهْتُ وَجْهِىَ لِلَّذِى فَطَرَ ٱلسَّمَٰوَٰتِ وَٱلْأَرْضَ حَنِيفًا وَمَآ أَنَا۠ مِنَ ٱلْمُشْرِكِينَ ۝

[a] One night Abraham was looking up at the sky in search of signs of the one and only God. Soon, the planet Venus, whom his community was worshipping as God, appeared shining before him in all its brightness. A thought arose in his mind—not as a question, but as an expression of astonishment— 'Is this the thing which could be my Lord? Is this the one we should worship?' But then, he saw it setting, i.e. disappearing from his sight. He exclaimed over this and asked how a thing which shone momentarily and then disappeared could be treated as worthy of worship. This was an argument based on observation which testified to the truth of his own belief. He had the same experience with the sun and the moon. Everything shines for some time, leaves people wonderstruck and then vanishes. He presented these astronomical observations (which were for him a clear verification of the principle of the unity of God) before his community in his preaching as an argument, adopting the method which is known in philosophical terminology as 'accusative logic', that is, repeating the words of the addressee and then convincing him. This method has been used in the Quran at other places also, for example, in verse 97, chapter 20, entitled, Ta Ha.

The signs of creation spread throughout the universe are not only a source of enhancement of Faith, but also provide strong arguments for the call for Truth.

⁸⁰ His people argued with him. He said, 'Are you arguing with me about God, while He has guided me? I have no fear of any partner you ascribe to Him, unless my Lord should wish otherwise. My Lord encompasses all things in His knowledge, so will you not pay heed? ⁸¹ Why should I fear what you associate with Him, while you do not fear to associate with God that for which He has sent down to you no authority? Tell me, if you know the truth, which side has more right to feel secure.ᵃ

وَحَآجَّهُ قَوْمُهُ ۚ قَالَ أَتُحَٰجُّوٓنِّي فِي ٱللَّهِ وَقَدْ هَدَىٰنِ ۚ وَلَآ أَخَافُ مَا تُشْرِكُونَ بِهِۦٓ إِلَّآ أَن يَشَآءَ رَبِّي شَيْـًٔا ۗ وَسِعَ رَبِّي كُلَّ شَيْءٍ عِلْمًا ۗ أَفَلَا تَتَذَكَّرُونَ ⁨٨٠⁩ وَكَيْفَ أَخَافُ مَآ أَشْرَكْتُمْ وَلَا تَخَافُونَ أَنَّكُمْ أَشْرَكْتُم بِٱللَّهِ مَا لَمْ يُنَزِّلْ بِهِۦ عَلَيْكُمْ سُلْطَٰنًا ۚ فَأَيُّ ٱلْفَرِيقَيْنِ أَحَقُّ بِٱلْأَمْنِ ۖ إِن كُنتُمْ تَعْلَمُونَ ⁨٨١⁩

ᵃ The story of Abraham narrated here is not the story of his search for Truth but that of his observation of Truth. Abraham was born in Iraq four thousand years ago in an environment in which the sun, moon and stars were worshipped. However, Nature's guidance and God's special help kept Abraham away from polytheism. His keen vigilant eyes observed signs in the phenomena spread throughout the universe which supported the idea of the oneness of God (tawhid). Everywhere in the mirror of the universe, the face of the one God would appear before him. Feeling sorry for his community, he used to ask them why they were blind to reality, in spite of the facts revealed before them.

Whenever a thing or person is given the status of the worshipped one (ma'bud), it naturally follows that the concepts of mysterious pre-eminence and greatness become attached to that thing or person. People start thinking that, in the scheme of the universe, this being has a high status such as is not enjoyed by anybody else. Pleasing him brings good fortune, while displeasing him does the reverse. Accordingly, when Abraham said that his community's deities were valueless and that in this world of God they had absolutely no powers, people were afraid that, as a result of this 'insolence', they might be subjected to some suffering and they started arguing with Abraham. They warned him against such talk and said that the vengeance of these deities would be wreaked upon him—he would become blind, go mad, would face destruction, etc.

⁸² It is those who have faith, and do not mix their faith with wrongdoing, who will be secure, and it is they who are rightly guided.' ⁸³ This is the reasoning We gave to Abraham against his people—We raise in rank anyone We please—your Lord is wise and aware. ⁸⁴ We gave him Isaac and Jacob, each of whom We guided as We had guided Noah before. Among his descendants were David and Solomon, and Job, Joseph, Moses and Aaron. Thus do We reward the righteous.^a

ٱلَّذِينَ ءَامَنُوا۟ وَلَمْ يَلْبِسُوٓا۟ إِيمَـٰنَهُم بِظُلْمٍ أُو۟لَـٰٓئِكَ لَهُمُ ٱلْأَمْنُ وَهُم مُّهْتَدُونَ ۝ وَتِلْكَ حُجَّتُنَآ ءَاتَيْنَـٰهَآ إِبْرَٰهِيمَ عَلَىٰ قَوْمِهِۦ نَرْفَعُ دَرَجَـٰتٍ مَّن نَّشَآءُ إِنَّ رَبَّكَ حَكِيمٌ عَلِيمٌ ۝ وَوَهَبْنَا لَهُۥٓ إِسْحَـٰقَ وَيَعْقُوبَ كُلًّا هَدَيْنَا وَنُوحًا هَدَيْنَا مِن قَبْلُ وَمِن ذُرِّيَّتِهِۦ دَاوُۥدَ وَسُلَيْمَـٰنَ وَأَيُّوبَ وَيُوسُفَ وَمُوسَىٰ وَهَـٰرُونَ وَكَذَٰلِكَ نَجْزِى ٱلْمُحْسِنِينَ ۝

---

^a In this world there is only one Supreme Being—God, whose majesty and greatness are based on sound arguments. All other kinds of so-called greatness and the reverence for them are based on superstitious beliefs. God's supremacy stands by virtue of its own strength, while all other godheads owe their existence to the acceptance of their followers. If their followers refused to accept them, they would become non-existent.

Looking to externals, the worshippers of these deities are misled into believing that they are more securely situated than the worshippers of the one and only God. But this is the worst type of misunderstanding. It is one who goes by sound arguments who is in the really safe position. But if it is by compromising with worldly considerations and customs that he attempts to better his situation, this has no value from the point of view of his final fate.

Sometimes the domination of false deities becomes so universal that even the worshippers of the real God are overwhelmed by it and make compromises. Worldly considerations and material interests are so closely linked with these false deities that, to all appearances, it seems that there is no other way to have a respectable life than to effect a compromise with the structure formed under them. But this procedure amounts to such an adulteration of one's own faith that it makes one's sincerity doubtful in the eyes of God.

⁸⁵ Zachariah, John, Jesus, and Elijah—every one of them was righteous—⁸⁶ Ishmael, Elisha, Jonah, and Lot—We favoured each one of them above other people,*^{a 87} and also some of their forefathers, their offspring, and their brothers: We chose them and guided them to a straight path. ⁸⁸ This is the guidance of God: He gives that guidance to whichever of His servants He pleases. If they had associated other deities with Him, surely all they did would have been of no avail.*^b

وَزَكَرِيَّا وَيَحْيَىٰ وَعِيسَىٰ وَإِلْيَاسَ ۖ كُلٌّ مِّنَ ٱلصَّـٰلِحِينَ ۝ وَإِسْمَـٰعِيلَ وَٱلْيَسَعَ وَيُونُسَ وَلُوطًا ۚ وَكُلًّا فَضَّلْنَا عَلَى ٱلْعَـٰلَمِينَ ۝ وَمِنْ ءَابَآئِهِمْ وَذُرِّيَّـٰتِهِمْ وَإِخْوَٰنِهِمْ ۖ وَٱجْتَبَيْنَـٰهُمْ وَهَدَيْنَـٰهُمْ إِلَىٰ صِرَٰطٍ مُّسْتَقِيمٍ ۝ ذَٰلِكَ هُدَى ٱللَّهِ يَهْدِى بِهِۦ مَن يَشَآءُ مِنْ عِبَادِهِۦ ۚ وَلَوْ أَشْرَكُوا۟ لَحَبِطَ عَنْهُم مَّا كَانُوا۟ يَعْمَلُونَ ۝

---

*^a Excellence, or superiority, is not anyone's racial or national prerogative. It is a gift of God to only those individuals who keep themselves righteous according to God's guidance, who avoid all sorts of polytheism (*shirk*) and who throw themselves, body and soul, into the task of 'preaching (admonition) without remuneration.' These are the people who make the Book of God their real guide. They identify themselves with the Book to such an extent that the divine mysteries reveal themselves to them; the result of which process is known as wisdom (*hikmah*). These are the people whom God picks out, then commissions some of them, whom He likes, with the task of conveying His message, as prophets during the age of prophethood, and thereafter as *da'is*. God's reward either to prophets or *da'i* will be entirely on the basis of righteous action (*ihsan*).

*^b The task of giving the call of Truth is undertaken only by those people who have become so selfless and so immersed in this work that they have no material expectations whatsoever of their addressees. Then the preacher cannot stage protests or run a campaign of demands pitted against the very person or group of persons to whom he is conveying the message of the Hereafter. Such an action on the part of the messenger of Truth would risk his exhortations being treated as ridiculous in the eyes of his addressees, and in society at large his call could never thus attain the status of a serious effort to convey the Word of God.

⁸⁹ Those are the ones to whom We gave the Scripture, wisdom, and prophethood. If these people [the Makkans] reject it, We shall entrust it to a people who will never refuse to acknowledge it.^a ⁹⁰ Those [the previous prophets] were the people whom God guided. Follow their guidance then and say, 'I ask no reward for this from you: it is only a reminder for all mankind.'

أُوْلَٰٓئِكَ ٱلَّذِينَ ءَاتَيْنَٰهُمُ ٱلْكِتَٰبَ وَٱلْحُكْمَ وَٱلنُّبُوَّةَ فَإِن يَكْفُرْ بِهَا هَٰٓؤُلَآءِ فَقَدْ وَكَّلْنَا بِهَا قَوْمًا لَّيْسُوا۟ بِهَا بِكَٰفِرِينَ ۝ أُوْلَٰٓئِكَ ٱلَّذِينَ هَدَى ٱللَّهُ فَبِهُدَىٰهُمُ ٱقْتَدِهْ قُل لَّآ أَسْـَٔلُكُمْ عَلَيْهِ أَجْرًا إِنْ هُوَ إِلَّا ذِكْرَىٰ لِلْعَٰلَمِينَ ۝

^a In Makkah, a few individuals had embraced the faith on the strength of the Prophet Muhammad's preaching. But, as a community, the people had rejected him. Thereafter, God the Almighty softened the hearts of the people of Madinah towards his call; and they embraced the faith as a community; so much so that it became possible for him to go to Madinah and establish a centre of Islam there. This aid from Almighty God was granted to the Prophet Muhammad in its complete form. However, God can give this aid even to the successors of the Prophet who rise to follow his call. This is something which God has always done according to the requirement of His da'is.

⁹¹ They do not make a just estimate of God, when they say, 'God has not revealed anything to any human being.' Say, 'Who revealed the Book which Moses brought, a light and guidance for the people, which you made into separate sheets, showing some but hiding many? You have been taught things that neither you nor your forefathers had known before.' Say, 'God has sent it;' then leave them toying away with their speculation.ᵃ

وَمَا قَدَرُواْ ٱللَّهَ حَقَّ قَدْرِهِۦ إِذْ قَالُواْ مَآ أَنزَلَ ٱللَّهُ عَلَىٰ بَشَرٍ مِّن شَيْءٍ ۗ قُلْ مَنْ أَنزَلَ ٱلْكِتَٰبَ ٱلَّذِى جَآءَ بِهِۦ مُوسَىٰ نُورًا وَهُدًى لِّلنَّاسِ ۖ تَجْعَلُونَهُۥ قَرَاطِيسَ تُبْدُونَهَا وَتُخْفُونَ كَثِيرًا ۖ وَعُلِّمْتُم مَّا لَمْ تَعْلَمُوٓاْ أَنتُمْ وَلَآ ءَابَآؤُكُمْ ۖ قُلِ ٱللَّهُ ۖ ثُمَّ ذَرْهُمْ فِى خَوْضِهِمْ يَلْعَبُونَ ۝

ᵃ When the call of the Prophet Muhammad reached the people of Makkah, some of them asked certain Jews what they thought about it and whether God's Word had really been revealed to the Prophet Mohammad. The Jews replied that God had not made revelations to any human being. This is obviously very strange, because the Jews themselves accepted a series of prophets, thus tacitly admitting that God's word had indeed been revealed from time to time to human beings. But when a man blindly opposes anything, he will go to the extent of contradicting his own accepted ideas in the heat of attempting to defeat his opponent.

⁹² This is a blessed Book which We have revealed, confirming what came before it, so that you may warn the Mother of Cities [Makkah] and the people around it. Those who believe in the Hereafter do believe in it, and they are ever-mindful of their prayers.ᵃ

وَهَـٰذَا كِتَـٰبٌ أَنزَلْنَـٰهُ مُبَارَكٌ مُّصَدِّقُ ٱلَّذِى بَيْنَ يَدَيْهِ وَلِتُنذِرَ أُمَّ ٱلْقُرَىٰ وَمَنْ حَوْلَهَا ۚ وَٱلَّذِينَ يُؤْمِنُونَ بِٱلْأَخِرَةِ يُؤْمِنُونَ بِهِۦ ۖ وَهُمْ عَلَىٰ صَلَاتِهِمْ يُحَافِظُونَ ۝

ᵃ This brazen disregard for the truth developed in the Jews because they had disintegrated God's Book page by page. They used to call attention to certain teachings of God, while there were others which they deliberately omitted to mention. For example, they used repeatedly to listen to and recite all verses relating to rewards, while omitting those verses which mentioned the deeds which merited rewards. They used to make special mention of those verses from which they could draw support for the petty details of their politics, while ignoring the verses in which instructions were given about quiet reformation. They used to elaborate upon those verses which gave them the opportunity to display their verbal hair-splitting talents, while cursorily passing over verses in which the eternal realities of religion were set forth. Frequent public airings were given to such verses as gave an indication of their superiority, while verses in which their responsibilities were mentioned used to be neglected. In those who disintegrate God's Book 'page by page' in this way, a tendency to insolent bravado naturally develops. They indulge in frivolous and trivial discussions, then bicker, and make contradictory statements. One cannot expect real co-operation from them. If people do not do justice to God's Book, how can they be just while dealing with human beings?

The call of religion is actually a call to awaken people. The caller, however perfect he may be, can be effective and make an impact on the listener's heart only when the listener has a fearing heart in his breast and considers the Hereafter a matter of the utmost gravity. If these elementary qualities are not found in the listener, then the giver of the call cannot offer him any benefit.

⁹³ Who could do greater wrong than someone who invents a lie against God or who says, 'It has been revealed to me,' while nothing has been revealed to him, or someone who says, 'I will send down the like of what God has sent down'? If you could only see the wrongdoers in the throes of death when the angels are stretching out their hands, saying, 'Give up your souls. Today you will be repaid with a humiliating punishment for saying false things about God and being arrogant about His signs.'^a

وَمَنْ أَظْلَمُ مِمَّنِ ٱفْتَرَىٰ عَلَى ٱللَّهِ كَذِبًا أَوْ قَالَ أُوحِيَ إِلَيَّ وَلَمْ يُوحَ إِلَيْهِ شَيْءٌ وَمَن قَالَ سَأُنزِلُ مِثْلَ مَا أَنزَلَ ٱللَّهُ وَلَوْ تَرَىٰ إِذِ ٱلظَّٰلِمُونَ فِي غَمَرَٰتِ ٱلْمَوْتِ وَٱلْمَلَٰئِكَةُ بَاسِطُوٓا۟ أَيْدِيهِمْ أَخْرِجُوٓا۟ أَنفُسَكُمُ ٱلْيَوْمَ تُجْزَوْنَ عَذَابَ ٱلْهُونِ بِمَا كُنتُمْ تَقُولُونَ عَلَى ٱللَّهِ غَيْرَ ٱلْحَقِّ وَكُنتُمْ عَنْ ءَايَٰتِهِۦ تَسْتَكْبِرُونَ ۝

---

^a When God chooses one of His subjects for the purpose of conveying His will to mankind, He blesses him with capability to do dawah work. A glimpse of the fear of the Hereafter is seen in his character. The power of divine reasoning emerging in his talk, he is successful in discharging his task of conveying God's message in the best manner possible, even in the face of tremendous opposition. His whole existence is a sign of God in this world of God. But those who are lost in worldly glories are unable to understand the greatness of one who urges them to accept the realities of the Hereafter. By their own worldly material standards, their own personality appears to them to be greater than that of God's messenger. This inclines them towards haughtiness or conceit, and from those of such a mentality, irrational behaviour is to be expected.

⁹⁴ And now you have returned to Us, alone as We created you at first, leaving behind all that We gave you. Nor do We see with you your intercessors, those you claimed were your partners with God. The link between you is cut and that which you presumed has failed you.[a]

وَلَقَدْ جِئْتُمُونَا فُرَادَىٰ كَمَا خَلَقْنَاكُمْ أَوَّلَ مَرَّةٍ وَتَرَكْتُم مَّا خَوَّلْنَاكُمْ وَرَاءَ ظُهُورِكُمْ وَمَا نَرَىٰ مَعَكُمْ شُفَعَاءَكُمُ ٱلَّذِينَ زَعَمْتُمْ أَنَّهُمْ فِيكُمْ شُرَكَٰٓؤُا۟ لَقَد تَّقَطَّعَ بَيْنَكُمْ وَضَلَّ عَنكُم مَّا كُنتُمْ تَزْعُمُونَ ۝

---

[a] This haughtiness which develops in a man is due to his worldly position and the material goods that are available to him in the world. He forgets that whatever blessings come his way, are only for the purpose of testing him and that too during a finite period. As soon as the time of death arrives, all these things will suddenly be snatched from him. Thereafter, his will be a lone existence, just as it was at the time of his birth. Immediately after death man will reach that stage where he will have neither wealth nor position; where he will have neither his companions nor his intermediaries; there will be only God and himself. None of the things he was proud of in the world will be there to save him from God's scourge.

Many people try to charm their way through life with the magic of words. Every man seeks and finds words to show his existence to be justified and righteous. He portrays the path he treads as straightaway leading towards correct goals. But when the revolution of the Hereafter unveils the realities, how utterly meaningless will his words appear.

⁹⁵ It is God who splits the seed and the fruit-stone. He brings forth the living from the dead, and the dead from the living. That is God. How then can you, deluded, turn away from the truth?ᵃ

﴿ إِنَّ ٱللَّهَ فَالِقُ ٱلْحَبِّ وَٱلنَّوَىٰ يُخْرِجُ ٱلْحَيَّ مِنَ ٱلْمَيِّتِ وَمُخْرِجُ ٱلْمَيِّتِ مِنَ ٱلْحَيِّ ذَٰلِكُمُ ٱللَّهُ فَأَنَّىٰ تُؤْفَكُونَ ﴾

ᵃ When anyone has to manufacture a motor car or any other such complex mechanism, he manufactures every part of it separately. Then he assembles these parts and gives them the requisite finish. But when God causes a tree to grow or creates a human being, the methodology is different. He produces the entity in its totality all at one time. In God's workshop the whole tree or the whole man issues forth from the one seed or the one drop and then proceeds to grow. This is a unique process which no human being can set in motion. This proves that there exists a Being superior to the human being, a Being whose plan is superior to all other plans.

⁹⁶ He causes the break of day, and has made the night for rest and He made the sun and the moon to a precise measure. That is the measure determined by the Almighty and the All Knowing. ⁹⁷ It is He who has set up for you the stars so that you might be guided by them in the midst of the darkness of land and sea. We have made the signs clear for people who want to understand.[a]

فَالِقُ ٱلْإِصْبَاحِ وَجَعَلَ ٱلَّيْلَ سَكَنًا وَٱلشَّمْسَ وَٱلْقَمَرَ حُسْبَانًا ۚ ذَٰلِكَ تَقْدِيرُ ٱلْعَزِيزِ ٱلْعَلِيمِ ۝ وَهُوَ ٱلَّذِى جَعَلَ لَكُمُ ٱلنُّجُومَ لِتَهْتَدُوا۟ بِهَا فِى ظُلُمَٰتِ ٱلْبَرِّ وَٱلْبَحْرِ ۗ قَدْ فَصَّلْنَا ٱلْءَايَٰتِ لِقَوْمٍ يَعْلَمُونَ ۝

---

[a] The volume of the sun is 1.2 million times that of the earth, and the earth itself is four times larger than the moon. The moon is about two hundred and fifty thousand miles away from the earth and revolves around it. The earth is at a distance of about 95 million miles from the sun and is moving round the latter in two ways—one in rotation on its axis and the other in orbit around the sun. Similarly, there is the revolution of other stars which are at vast distances from us and each other but all moving with extreme regularity. Due to this system of the universe, day and night come into existence; systems based on the measurement of time take shape; in turn, it becomes possible for man to regulate his life on land and sea. This gigantic system runs with such exactitude that no discrepancy has crept into it even after millions of years. This proves the immanence of a Being whose powers are of unlimited greatness.

These large-scale signs of God show that the Maker of this workshop is extremely knowledgeable. No ignorant being could erect such a complex structure. He is all-powerful; otherwise the running of this enormous workshop in this manner would not have been possible. Its planning is absolutely perfect; without such planning, it would not have been possible to have such meaningfulness and harmony in such a colossal universe.

God's world is full of His signs and arguments. But reasoning or argument is the name of theoretical reasoning and not that of a hammer. So, acceptance of an argument by a man is possible only when he is really serious, i.e. when he is consciously ready to accept the argument, irrespective of whether it goes in his favour or against him.

⁹⁸ It is He who first produced you from a single soul, then gave you a place to stay [in life] and a resting place [after death]. We have made Our revelations clear to those who are men of understanding.ᵃ

وَهُوَ ٱلَّذِىٓ أَنشَأَكُم مِّن نَّفْسٍ وَٰحِدَةٍ فَمُسْتَقَرٌّ وَمُسْتَوْدَعٌ ۗ قَدْ فَصَّلْنَا ٱلْءَايَٰتِ لِقَوْمٍ يَفْقَهُونَ ۝

ᵃ Man-made workshops, or factories, are not capable of making a machine which can start giving birth to similar countless machines. Our factories have to manufacture such machines one after another. But in the workshop of God, such an event takes place every day. The seed of a tree is sown and then generations of trees go on multiplying out of that simple, original seed. This is the case with human beings also. Starting with a man and a woman, billions and billions of human beings have started coming into existence—and there is no end to this process. This observation shows that the power of God, who created the universe, is limitless. He is capable of this rare feat of creation by which, primarily, one entity is brought into existence and thereafter it continuously replicates itself in countless numbers. Similarly, God can create a great and perfect world out of this present world. The concept of the Hereafter is not a far-fetched theory; belief in it amounts to acceptance of the possible occurrence of certain future events on the strength of the present observation of similar events taking place every day.

⁹⁹ It is He who sends down water from the sky. With it We produce vegetation of all kinds; out of green foliage, We produce clustered grain; and from the date-palm, out of its sheath, We produce bunches of dates hanging low. We produce vineyards and olive groves and pomegranates, alike yet different. Look at their fruit as He causes it to grow and ripen. In this are signs for people who believe.ᵃ

وَهُوَ ٱلَّذِىٓ أَنزَلَ مِنَ ٱلسَّمَآءِ مَآءً فَأَخْرَجْنَا بِهِۦ نَبَاتَ كُلِّ شَىْءٍ فَأَخْرَجْنَا مِنْهُ خَضِرًا نُّخْرِجُ مِنْهُ حَبًّا مُّتَرَاكِبًا وَمِنَ ٱلنَّخْلِ مِن طَلْعِهَا قِنْوَانٌ دَانِيَةٌ وَجَنَّٰتٍ مِّنْ أَعْنَابٍ وَٱلزَّيْتُونَ وَٱلرُّمَّانَ مُشْتَبِهًا وَغَيْرَ مُتَشَٰبِهٍ ٱنظُرُوٓا۟ إِلَىٰ ثَمَرِهِۦٓ إِذَآ أَثْمَرَ وَيَنْعِهِۦٓ إِنَّ فِى ذَٰلِكُمْ لَءَايَٰتٍ لِّقَوْمٍ يُؤْمِنُونَ ۝

ᵃ Earth, or mud, is apparently a dead and inert thing. Then rain falls on it. Soon after the absorption of water, a new lush green world springs out of the earth. Sundry varieties of crops and different kinds of fruit-bearing trees come forth from it. This event also is an example of the coming world after this world. As soon as water permeates the earth, the emergence of a fresh, beautiful and fragrant carpet of colours from the earth indicates the potential which the Creator of the World has implanted here. The righteous deeds which a man performs in this world of today are on a parallel with this. When God's grace rains down, this potential will become a reality—flourishing and producing the burgeoning crops of the Hereafter.

Man, in the beginning, is nurtured in the womb of his mother and thereafter makes his entry into the present world. The grave is also, so to say, a sort of 'womb', to which man is ultimately consigned. Thereafter, he opens his eyes in another, future world, so that he may be sent to Heaven or Hell according to his deeds. Glimpses of and arguments in favour of the unseen hidden world, which man must necessarily accept, are already there in the present tangible and visible world. But only that person will accept it who is already mentally prepared to do so. It is only when a man has travelled half the distance along the path towards Faith (iman) that it is possible for the call to the faith to enter freely into his mind and to be acceptable to him. Exhortations to believe in God will not in any way benefit a man who has been travelling in a direction opposite to that of Faith.

100 They have set up jinns as associates with God, even though He created them! They have even dared, in their ignorance, to attribute sons and daughters to Him. Hallowed be He and exalted far above what they ascribe to Him, 101 the Originator of the heavens and the earth. How could He have a son when He has no consort? He created everything and is aware of everything! 102 This is God, your Lord, there is no God but Him, the Creator of all things, so worship Him; He is the guardian of all things.[a]

وَجَعَلُواْ لِلَّهِ شُرَكَآءَ ٱلْجِنَّ وَخَلَقَهُمْ وَخَرَقُواْ لَهُۥ بَنِينَ وَبَنَٰتٍ بِغَيْرِ عِلْمٍ سُبْحَٰنَهُۥ وَتَعَٰلَىٰ عَمَّا يَصِفُونَ ۝ بَدِيعُ ٱلسَّمَٰوَٰتِ وَٱلْأَرْضِ أَنَّىٰ يَكُونُ لَهُۥ وَلَدٌ وَلَمْ تَكُن لَّهُۥ صَٰحِبَةٌ وَخَلَقَ كُلَّ شَىْءٍ وَهُوَ بِكُلِّ شَىْءٍ عَلِيمٌ ۝ ذَٰلِكُمُ ٱللَّهُ رَبُّكُمْ لَآ إِلَٰهَ إِلَّا هُوَ خَٰلِقُ كُلِّ شَىْءٍ فَٱعْبُدُوهُ وَهُوَ عَلَىٰ كُلِّ شَىْءٍ وَكِيلٌ ۝

---

[a] Since ancient times it has been a weakness on the part of man to find some distinction or mysticism in a thing and then to consider that thing to be a partner of God and start worshipping it in order to seek its help or save himself from any harm it may do him. It was because of this mentality that many people started worshipping angels, stars and jinns, though the clear proof of their not being gods is that they do not possess the capacity to create. They have neither created themselves, nor are they capable of creating any other thing. They were themselves created by some other Being. So, the question is, whether the Creator will be accepted as God, or His creatures will usurp the position of His godhead.

A tree receives the things it requires for its sustenance in perfect proportions. This is the condition of all things in the universe. When it is a fact that they receive things, (whatever be their nature) because a Giver gives them to them, then it naturally follows that the Giver will be the One who is aware of all things at all times. If He were not aware of them, how could He fulfil the needs of every single thing exactly according to its requirements? Now, for what purpose should God—the Possessor of such superlative attributes—take anybody as a partner in his godhead?

¹⁰³ No vision can grasp Him, but He takes in over all vision; He is the Subtle and Aware One. ¹⁰⁴ Clear insights have come to you from your Lord. Whoever, therefore, chooses to see, does so for his own good; and whoever chooses to remain blind, does so to his own loss. Say, 'I am not here as your keeper.' *ᵃ*

لَا تُدْرِكُهُ ٱلْأَبْصَـٰرُ وَهُوَ يُدْرِكُ ٱلْأَبْصَـٰرَ ۖ وَهُوَ ٱللَّطِيفُ ٱلْخَبِيرُ ۝ قَدْ جَآءَكُم بَصَآئِرُ مِن رَّبِّكُمْ ۖ فَمَنْ أَبْصَرَ فَلِنَفْسِهِۦ ۖ وَمَنْ عَمِىَ فَعَلَيْهَا ۚ وَمَآ أَنَا۠ عَلَيْكُم بِحَفِيظٍ ۝

ᵃ Man wants to see God in a tangible shape and when God does not manifest Himself in this way, he presumes other tangible things to be gods and thus satisfies his appearance-loving instinct. But this shows a very poor appreciation of God's Being. After all, how can God, who is so great as to have created this gigantic universe with its highly regulated systems, be so ordinary as to present Himself to a weak human creature in a form that will be visible to his eyes and touchable with his hands? Man must rather discover God through his heart and see Him with the eye of his faith. Only one who is satisfied with observation through insight will discover God. One who insists on His being visible to the naked eye will never truly find God, just like the person who fails to recognise a flower by its fragrance and insists on referring to chemical standards.

105 This is how We explain Our revelations in various ways—so that they might come to the point of saying, 'You have read this out to us,' and that We might make it clear [that this is the truth] to those who are eager to know.

106 Follow what has been revealed to you from your Lord: there is no deity but Him; and ignore the polytheists.[a]

وَكَذَٰلِكَ نُصَرِّفُ ٱلْءَايَٰتِ وَلِيَقُولُواْ دَرَسْتَ وَلِنُبَيِّنَهُۥ لِقَوْمٍ يَعْلَمُونَ ۝ ٱتَّبِعْ مَآ أُوحِىَ إِلَيْكَ مِن رَّبِّكَ لَآ إِلَٰهَ إِلَّا هُوَ وَأَعْرِضْ عَنِ ٱلْمُشْرِكِينَ ۝

---

[a] There are some who have the urge to acquire knowledge and learn; who are in search of Truth. There are others who have acquired wealth and power and consider themselves successful to the point of feeling that there is nothing lacking in them which needs to be compensated for. When the call of Truth is given, it is mostly the former kind of people who accept it, unlike the latter who do not attach any significance to it. They never give it any serious thought, and therefore its importance does not become clear to them. The call of Truth provides answers for those who earnestly go in quest of the truth, and gives those who are not so inclined, a logical conclusion to their arguments. With regard to the former, the aim is to enable them to accept the truth; as for the others, it is meant to make them concede that at least the divine message had been conveyed to them in full.

107 If God had willed, they would not have associated anything with Him. We did not appoint you over them as their keeper, nor are you their guardian. 108 Do not revile those [beings] whom they invoke instead of God, lest they, in their hostility, revile God out of ignorance. Thus to every people We have caused their actions to seem fair. To their Lord they shall all return, and He will declare to them all that they have done.[a]

وَلَوْ شَاءَ ٱللَّهُ مَآ أَشْرَكُوا۟ وَمَا جَعَلْنَٰكَ عَلَيْهِمْ حَفِيظًا وَمَآ أَنتَ عَلَيْهِم بِوَكِيلٍ ۝ وَلَا تَسُبُّوا۟ ٱلَّذِينَ يَدْعُونَ مِن دُونِ ٱللَّهِ فَيَسُبُّوا۟ ٱللَّهَ عَدْوًۢا بِغَيْرِ عِلْمٍ كَذَٰلِكَ زَيَّنَّا لِكُلِّ أُمَّةٍ عَمَلَهُمْ ثُمَّ إِلَىٰ رَبِّهِم مَّرْجِعُهُمْ فَيُنَبِّئُهُم بِمَا كَانُوا۟ يَعْمَلُونَ ۝

---

[a] Those who reject the divine message invent different excuses to justify their doing so. In these circumstances, it may occur to the preacher that he should change the way he conveys his message, so that it becomes acceptable to the addressees. But this would not be proper. He should adhere to the style which has been directly taught to him by God, because the real purpose of his activity is to link man with God and not to win people over and draw them into his sphere by hook or by crook. On the other hand, neither is it proper to respond to the addressee's obduracy with abusive outbursts.

The individual develops a bias in favour of the particular traditions to which he is born, or the kind of thinking with which he has become familiar. According to this, he develops a particular frame of mind which affects all his thinking process. This frame of mind presents the greatest impediment to the acceptance of Truth. Unless it can be altered, that door of his mind, through which the voice of Truth might enter, will never open.

[109] They swear a solemn oath by God that if there should come to them a sign, they will believe in it. Say, 'Signs are granted only by God.' How can you tell that if a sign be given to them, they will indeed believe in it?

[110] We will turn away their hearts and eyes from the Truth, since they refused to believe in it in the first instance. We will let them wander blindly in their insolence.[a]

وَأَقْسَمُواْ بِٱللَّهِ جَهْدَ أَيْمَٰنِهِمْ لَئِن جَآءَتْهُمْ ءَايَةٌ لَّيُؤْمِنُنَّ بِهَا ۚ قُلْ إِنَّمَا ٱلْءَايَٰتُ عِندَ ٱللَّهِ ۖ وَمَا يُشْعِرُكُمْ أَنَّهَآ إِذَا جَآءَتْ لَا يُؤْمِنُونَ ۝ وَنُقَلِّبُ أَفْـِٔدَتَهُمْ وَأَبْصَٰرَهُمْ كَمَا لَمْ يُؤْمِنُواْ بِهِۦٓ أَوَّلَ مَرَّةٍ وَنَذَرُهُمْ فِى طُغْيَٰنِهِمْ يَعْمَهُونَ ۝

---

[a] The truth may be laid before a man with all its supporting arguments and he will still reject it. There is just one reason for this, i.e. his looking at things perversely instead of looking at them in a straightforward manner. An argument may be most rational and based on sound reasoning, but if one is not inclined to accept it, he will find some words or the other to reject it. For example, instead of viewing the arguments of a preacher as definitive, he will start discussing whether all the previous great men were all wrong and strangers to the Truth, and will go on to raise other similar points.

It is extremely difficult for one who has developed such a temperament to arrive at the right path. He can give the wrong colour to any subject and seek an excuse to reject it. In order to contradict theoretical arguments, he will find the excuse that they were against the creed of his ancestors. Similarly, in order to allege the falsity of physical observations, he will voice the opinion that they are optical illusions or mere conjuring tricks. This attitude, which impedes the acceptance of theoretical arguments, will likewise obstruct the acceptance of physical facts in support of the truth. One who is determined to remain unreceptive to the truth will, as always, have to go without guidance.

Such deniers are arrogant in nature. They want to see themselves set above others at any cost. When a preacher appears before them with a message of Truth, it frequently happens that he is a stranger in those surroundings and has none of the elegant trappings of the times. So, forming any connection with him amounts to degrading one's position. Those with a superiority complex are therefore unable to accept him. Offering a variety of excuses, they reject him.

111 Even if We sent down angels to them, and caused the dead to speak to them, and We gathered together everything in front of them, they would still not believe, unless God had so willed. But most of them behave ignorantly.[a] 112 In like manner We have assigned for every prophet an opponent, Satans from among men and jinn, who make evil suggestions to each other by means of specious words in order to deceive—had it been your Lord's will, they would not have done so; so leave them alone to their fabrication,[b]

وَلَوْ أَنَّنَا نَزَّلْنَآ إِلَيْهِمُ ٱلْمَلَٰٓئِكَةَ وَكَلَّمَهُمُ ٱلْمَوْتَىٰ وَحَشَرْنَا عَلَيْهِمْ كُلَّ شَىْءٍ قُبُلًا مَّا كَانُوا۟ لِيُؤْمِنُوٓا۟ إِلَّآ أَن يَشَآءَ ٱللَّهُ وَلَٰكِنَّ أَكْثَرَهُمْ يَجْهَلُونَ ۝ وَكَذَٰلِكَ جَعَلْنَا لِكُلِّ نَبِىٍّ عَدُوًّا شَيَٰطِينَ ٱلْإِنسِ وَٱلْجِنِّ يُوحِى بَعْضُهُمْ إِلَىٰ بَعْضٍ زُخْرُفَ ٱلْقَوْلِ غُرُورًا وَلَوْ شَآءَ رَبُّكَ مَا فَعَلُوهُ فَذَرْهُمْ وَمَا يَفْتَرُونَ ۝

---

[a] Wisdom lies in man's acceptance of God's plan and in preparing himself to regulate his mind according to that plan. Conversely, it would be foolish for a man to have a self-made standard instead of God's plan and to maintain that he will accept anything which conforms to that standard and will reject anything which does not. For such a man there is nothing but perdition in this world. In this world of God man can reach his goal only by adopting the ways laid down by God—not by departing from them.

[b] Ibn Jarir has quoted Abu Dharr al-Ghifari as saying, 'I attended a meeting of the Prophet Muhammad. It was a long meeting. He asked me, "O, Abu Dharr, have you said your prayers?" I replied, "No, O Prophet of God." He said, "Get up and offer salah of two rakat." Thereupon, I offered salah and joined the meeting again. Then he (the Prophet) asked, "O Abu Dharr, did you seek the protection of God against the Satans among human beings and jinns?" I replied, "No, O Prophet of God. Are there Satans among human beings also?" The Prophet said, "Yes, those Satans are worse than those among the jinns."' (Ibn Kathir, Tafsir).

Here, 'Satans among human beings' refers to those people who have attained respectability and popularity on the basis of self-made religion, and who will stop at nothing to disprove the call of Truth. When the call of the Truth is given in its purest form, they feel that they are being stripped of all protection. The straight path for them would have been to accept the Truth on its being clarified. But, compared to acceptance of the Truth, their position is dearer to them. To save their position, they set about proving the dubiousness of the preacher and his call. They make allegations that are themselves baseless, but because they express themselves so beautifully, many people are influenced and are filled with doubt.

¹¹³ in order that the hearts of those who do not believe in the life to come might incline towards those suggestions and, being pleased, persist in their sinful ways.^a

وَلِتَصْغَىٰ إِلَيْهِ أَفْئِدَةُ ٱلَّذِينَ لَا يُؤْمِنُونَ بِٱلْآخِرَةِ وَلِيَرْضَوْهُ وَلِيَقْتَرِفُوا۟ مَا هُم مُّقْتَرِفُونَ ۝

---

^a If a preacher of Truth can present the Truth in the language of rational arguments, the proponents of falsehood may also utter such beautiful words against the Truth as could appear to be valid arguments in its disfavour. Both liars and tellers of the truth having at their command the same range of plausible expressions with which to support their arguments creates a situation in which man is put to the test. He must at all events pass the test of being able to distinguish between true and false arguments, and then accept true arguments, having rejected whatever is baseless. This state of affairs will necessarily continue till Doomsday.

The 'Satans' among human beings misuse their intelligence to deceive others, but only those who have no fears about the Hereafter are influenced by them. Anxiety about the Hereafter makes a man serious and the reality of things can never remain hidden from one who sincerely serves God. But those who are devoid of any cares about the Hereafter are not serious about Truth and, as such, they are unable to understand the difference between solid argument and triviality.

114 Should I seek a judge other than God, when it is He who has revealed the Book, clearly explained. Those to whom We gave the Book earlier know that it is the truth revealed by your Lord. Therefore, have no doubts.

115 The Word of your Lord is perfected in truth and justice. None can change His words. He is the All Hearing, the All Knowing. 116 If you obey the majority of those on earth, they will lead you astray from God's way. They follow nothing but conjecture. They are only guessing. 117 Your Lord knows best who has strayed from His Way and He knows best those who are guided.*a*

أَفَغَيْرَ ٱللَّهِ أَبْتَغِى حَكَمًا وَهُوَ ٱلَّذِى أَنزَلَ إِلَيْكُمُ ٱلْكِتَـٰبَ مُفَصَّلاً وَٱلَّذِينَ ءَاتَيْنَـٰهُمُ ٱلْكِتَـٰبَ يَعْلَمُونَ أَنَّهُۥ مُنَزَّلٌ مِّن رَّبِّكَ بِٱلْحَقِّ فَلَا تَكُونَنَّ مِنَ ٱلْمُمْتَرِينَ ۝ وَتَمَّتْ كَلِمَتُ رَبِّكَ صِدْقًا وَعَدْلاً لَّا مُبَدِّلَ لِكَلِمَـٰتِهِۦ وَهُوَ ٱلسَّمِيعُ ٱلْعَلِيمُ ۝ وَإِن تُطِعْ أَكْثَرَ مَن فِى ٱلْأَرْضِ يُضِلُّوكَ عَن سَبِيلِ ٱللَّهِ إِن يَتَّبِعُونَ إِلَّا ٱلظَّنَّ وَإِنْ هُمْ إِلَّا يَخْرُصُونَ ۝ إِنَّ رَبَّكَ هُوَ أَعْلَمُ مَن يَضِلُّ عَن سَبِيلِهِۦ وَهُوَ أَعْلَمُ بِٱلْمُهْتَدِينَ ۝

---

a Rules about the sacrifice of animals were given in the Quran, it being specified where sacrificed animals might be eaten. There was also a ban on eating animals which had died of natural or other causes. On this some people commented, 'The religion of Muslims is strange; they consider animals sacrificed by their hands as permitted and consider dead animals, i.e. those killed by God, as prohibited.' In this statement there is no argument—only verbal gymnastics. But many people were deceived by it and started looking at Islam with suspicion. This always happens. In every age there are only a few people who can place matters in their true perspective. Many people become lost in a verbal labyrinth. They take illusory things to be real, only because these are described in beautiful words.

But this is a world in which God has made Himself clear about all basic realities. So, going astray on the pretext of ignorance is not pardonable. God's discourse is a clear touchstone by which every man can test all statements and ascertain whether they are mere verbal tricks or are based on facts. God has made true statements about all the essential matters of the past, present and future. He has shown the way of perfect justice in regard to all aspects of human relations. If a man is really serious, it is not at all difficult for him to know what is right and what is wrong. Only those whose thinking processes work under the influence of something other than God's revelation will have doubts. For one who brings his thinking in line with Divine realities, there is no possibility of deviance of thought. ▶

118 Eat then, only that over which God's name has been pronounced, if you truly believe in His revelations.

119 Why should you not eat what has been consecrated in God's name, when He has already explained to you what He has forbidden you, unless you are compelled by necessity? Surely, many mislead others by their desires through lack of knowledge. But your Lord best knows the transgressors.[a]

فَكُلُوا۟ مِمَّا ذُكِرَ ٱسْمُ ٱللَّهِ عَلَيْهِ إِن كُنتُم بِـَٔايَٰتِهِۦ مُؤْمِنِينَ ۝ وَمَا لَكُمْ أَلَّا تَأْكُلُوا۟ مِمَّا ذُكِرَ ٱسْمُ ٱللَّهِ عَلَيْهِ وَقَدْ فَصَّلَ لَكُم مَّا حَرَّمَ عَلَيْكُمْ إِلَّا مَا ٱضْطُرِرْتُمْ إِلَيْهِ ۗ وَإِنَّ كَثِيرًا لَّيُضِلُّونَ بِأَهْوَآئِهِم بِغَيْرِ عِلْمٍ ۗ إِنَّ رَبَّكَ هُوَ أَعْلَمُ بِٱلْمُعْتَدِينَ ۝

Even after this Divine explanation, if a man goes astray, God knows his condition very well. He knows that person who, in order to maintain his status, attaches no significance to any reality beyond himself; that person whose bias has deprived him of any capacity to understand godly matters; that person who, due to his inclination for cheap display, pays no attention to the voice of Truth; that person who, being a prey to feelings of jealousy, remains a stranger to the Truth.

[a] Whatever there is in the world is all 'others' property' for us, because all of it belongs to God. We have no right to possess or use anything unless it is obtained and utilized in the manner shown by God. This holds good for animals also.

Animals provide valuable food for us, but the question arises as to how we acquired the right to use them as food. God creates animals and He alone rears them and brings them to maturity. Then, how does it become permissible for us to use them as our food? Taking God's name at the time of sacrificing an animal is the answer to this very question. But the taking of God's name is not a verbal formality. It is, in fact, the recognition of God's ownership rights over the animal and a demonstration of our gratitude to Him for his gift. Taking God's name at the time of sacrifice is the symbol of this admission and of our gratitude—the 'price' on payment of which an animal in the eyes of our Lord becomes sacrificeable for us. However, one who faces accidental compulsion has been exempted by God from this restriction.

When man neglects God's commands on the subject of what is permitted or prohibited, legal or illegal, superstitions begin to take the place of divine injunctions. On the basis of superstitious ideas, people form divergent opinions. There are some self-devised philosophies behind these superstitions, and on their basis some formalities become established. It is necessary for those who want to become God's obedient servants to completely give up these superstitions, in practice as well as in theory.

120 Eschew all sin, open or secret: Those who commit sin will receive due punishment for their sins, 121 and do not eat anything over which God's name has not been pronounced, for that surely is disobedience. The devils inspire their followers to argue with you. If you obey them, you will become of those who associate partners with God.*

وَذَرُواْ ظَاهِرَ ٱلْإِثْمِ وَبَاطِنَهُۥٓ إِنَّ ٱلَّذِينَ يَكْسِبُونَ ٱلْإِثْمَ سَيُجْزَوْنَ بِمَا كَانُواْ يَقْتَرِفُونَ ۝ وَلَا تَأْكُلُواْ مِمَّا لَمْ يُذْكَرِ ٱسْمُ ٱللَّهِ عَلَيْهِ وَإِنَّهُۥ لَفِسْقٌ وَإِنَّ ٱلشَّيَٰطِينَ لَيُوحُونَ إِلَىٰٓ أَوْلِيَآئِهِمْ لِيُجَٰدِلُوكُمْ وَإِنْ أَطَعْتُمُوهُمْ إِنَّكُمْ لَمُشْرِكُونَ ۝

---

a In the matter of eating and drinking and other everyday routines, every community develops a customary religion. People have strong feelings about this customary or traditional religion because of the testimonies of ancestors and of great men of the past, which exist in its support. Deviation from this becomes synonymous with turning away from the religion of the revered forefathers. So, when the call of Truth clashes with this customary religion, all sorts of objections are raised against it. The great men of the day seek out such aspects of established practices as will convince the general public that their customary religion is correct and the 'new religion' is wrong. But God is aware of everything. On Doomsday, when He lays bare the realities, every individual will see whether he has been standing on the firm ground of reality or on the thin ice of superstition.

122 Can he who was dead, to whom We gave life, and a light whereby he could walk among people be like him who is in utter darkness from which he can never emerge? Thus the deeds of those who deny the truth have been made fair-seeming to them.

123 Thus We have placed leaders of the wicked in every town to plot therein. Yet it is only against themselves that they scheme, though they may not perceive it.*a*

أَوَمَن كَانَ مَيْتًا فَأَحْيَيْنَاهُ وَجَعَلْنَا لَهُ نُورًا يَمْشِي بِهِ فِي ٱلنَّاسِ كَمَن مَّثَلُهُ فِي ٱلظُّلُمَاتِ لَيْسَ بِخَارِجٍ مِّنْهَا كَذَٰلِكَ زُيِّنَ لِلْكَافِرِينَ مَا كَانُوا۟ يَعْمَلُونَ ۝ وَكَذَٰلِكَ جَعَلْنَا فِي كُلِّ قَرْيَةٍ أَكَابِرَ مُجْرِمِيهَا لِيَمْكُرُوا۟ فِيهَا وَمَا يَمْكُرُونَ إِلَّا بِأَنفُسِهِمْ وَمَا يَشْعُرُونَ ۝

---

a In the eyes of God that person has life who accepts the light of guidance which appears before him and makes it the illumination of his path. Conversely, that person is lifeless who remains deprived of the light of guidance and roams about groping in the darkness of falsehood.

The lifeless person is one who is so caught up in the net of superstitions and prejudice that true, straight facts do not fall within the scope of his understanding. He is so unaware of the true nature of things that he is unable to distinguish between meaningless argument and real discourse. He is so engrossed in self-aggrandisement that it is not possible for him to accept the Truth coming from any source other than that of tradition. Customary and traditional ideas so dominate his mind that he is unable to assess things by any other standard. Due to these weaknesses, he is left groping in the dark. Though apparently alive, he becomes virtually a dead person.

In direct contrast to this, one who opens his heart to guidance becomes free of all psychological knots; it takes him no time at all to recognise the Truth. The veils of words fail to hide the face of reality from his eyes. The problems of taste and habit do not attain such a position in his life as to come between the Truth and himself. Truth becomes a bright reality for him; his gaze does not falter looking at it and he does not remain indolent once he has discovered it. He himself treads the path of light and endeavours to make others walk in that light.

124 When a sign comes to them, they say, 'We will not believe in it until we are given what God's messengers have been given.' But God knows best whom to appoint as His Messenger. Humiliation before God and severe torment will befall the evil-doers for their scheming.[a]

وَإِذَا جَآءَتْهُمْ ءَايَةٌ قَالُوا۟ لَن نُّؤْمِنَ حَتَّىٰ نُؤْتَىٰ مِثْلَ مَآ أُوتِىَ رُسُلُ ٱللَّهِ ٱللَّهُ أَعْلَمُ حَيْثُ يَجْعَلُ رِسَالَتَهُۥ سَيُصِيبُ ٱلَّذِينَ أَجْرَمُوا۟ صَغَارٌ عِندَ ٱللَّهِ وَعَذَابٌ شَدِيدٌۢ بِمَا كَانُوا۟ يَمْكُرُونَ

---

[a] Those who have captured public attention by claiming self-made things to be God's religion, become inimical toward every voice which calls upon people to adhere to true religion. Every such voice appears to them to be a no-confidence motion directed against themselves. The luminaries of the time then ferret out trivial points by which to defame the call of Truth, so as to prevent the general public from being influenced by it. They give wrong direction to the reasoning of Truth and cause the public to become doubtful. They even try to denigrate the personality of the preacher by casting baseless aspersions on him. But such efforts only increase their guilt; they are unable to harm the preacher and his call in any way. The righteous person is one who sees the Truth, even when worldly glories have not graced it. Accepting the Truth when it is surrounded by worldly glories, amounts to accepting the worldly glories and not the Truth.

¹²⁵ When God desires to guide someone, He opens his breast to Islam; and whoever He wills to let go astray, He causes his breast to be constricted as if he had to climb up to the skies. That is how God heaps ignominy upon those who refuse to believe.

¹²⁶ This is the straight path leading to your Lord. We have made the signs clear for thinking men. ¹²⁷ They shall dwell in the Home of Peace with their Lord; He will be their Protector as a recompense for what they have been doing.ᵃ

فَمَن يُرِدِ ٱللَّهُ أَن يَهْدِيَهُ يَشْرَحْ صَدْرَهُ لِلْإِسْلَٰمِ وَمَن يُرِدْ أَن يُضِلَّهُ يَجْعَلْ صَدْرَهُ ضَيِّقًا حَرَجًا كَأَنَّمَا يَصَّعَّدُ فِى ٱلسَّمَآءِ كَذَٰلِكَ يَجْعَلُ ٱللَّهُ ٱلرِّجْسَ عَلَى ٱلَّذِينَ لَا يُؤْمِنُونَ ۝ وَهَٰذَا صِرَٰطُ رَبِّكَ مُسْتَقِيمًا قَدْ فَصَّلْنَا ٱلْءَايَٰتِ لِقَوْمٍ يَذَّكَّرُونَ ۝ لَهُمْ دَارُ ٱلسَّلَٰمِ عِندَ رَبِّهِمْ وَهُوَ وَلِيُّهُم بِمَا كَانُوا۟ يَعْمَلُونَ ۝

ᵃ Truth by its very nature is so clear that it is not difficult for anyone to understand it. Still, in every age, in spite of the Truth being made clear, countless people do not accept it. This is due to a flawed mentality. One person attaches himself to 'holy' beings to the extent that he fears that leaving them will completely destroy him. In the case of another, the fear of the breakdown of the system of his worldly interests is so strong within him that it becomes impossible for him to proceed towards the Truth. Yet another feels that if he accepts anything against the established custom of the time, he might become a stranger to the whole atmosphere of his own society. Man is overcome by such thoughts to the extent that acceptance of Truth appears synonymous with climbing a steep and difficult slope and, simply by looking at it, he loses heart.

The case of individuals who do not suffer from any psychological complications is entirely different; they place Truth higher than everything else. They are seekers of the Truth right from the very beginning. So, when the Truth appears before them, they recognise it without delay and, ignoring all excuses and suspicions, they accept it.

God reveals His Truth before the people in the shape of signs and symbols. Now, those who have weaknesses in their hearts, make self-made interpretations of these signs to justify their rejection of them, whereas those who have open hearts, discover in these signs their real depth, and make them the nourishment of their minds. Their lives are immediately launched on that straight path which is traversed under the direct guidance of God and which leads a man to enduring success. ▶

128 On the day when He gathers them all together, He will say, 'Company of jinn, you took away many followers among mankind.' And their adherents among mankind will say, 'Our Lord, we benefited from one another, but now we have reached the end of the term which You determined for us.' He will say, 'The Fire shall be your home, and there you shall remain forever, except as God wills. Surely your Lord is wise and all knowing.

129 And in like manner We shall keep the wrongdoers close to others as a punishment for their misdeeds.[a]

وَيَوْمَ يَحْشُرُهُمْ جَمِيعًا يَـٰمَعْشَرَ ٱلْجِنِّ قَدِ ٱسْتَكْثَرْتُم مِّنَ ٱلْإِنسِ ۖ وَقَالَ أَوْلِيَآؤُهُم مِّنَ ٱلْإِنسِ رَبَّنَا ٱسْتَمْتَعَ بَعْضُنَا بِبَعْضٍ وَبَلَغْنَآ أَجَلَنَا ٱلَّذِىٓ أَجَّلْتَ لَنَا ۚ قَالَ ٱلنَّارُ مَثْوَىٰكُمْ خَٰلِدِينَ فِيهَآ إِلَّا مَا شَآءَ ٱللَّهُ ۗ إِنَّ رَبَّكَ حَكِيمٌ عَلِيمٌ ۝ وَكَذَٰلِكَ نُوَلِّى بَعْضَ ٱلظَّٰلِمِينَ بَعْضًۢا بِمَا كَانُوا۟ يَكْسِبُونَ ۝

What God values above all else is a man's good deeds. One who obeys God will deserve God's help and will be led to His Abode of Peace. This Abode of Peace is God's Paradise, where man will lead a life of eternal peace, secure from every kind of grief or trouble. God's help will be given to individuals in the life after death according to their deeds. Moreover, if a considerable number of people become obedient to God in the world, this group will be given a share of God's grace in this world also.

[a] If someone is misled by another, it is not a one-sided affair. Both the individuals for their part think that they are fulfilling some purpose. When Satan deceives a man and wins him over to his side, he tries to fulfil his challenge to God at the beginning of creation that he would make a large part of God's creation fall a prey to his temptations (17:61). Those who surrender themselves to Satan have definite self-interests in mind. There are some who promote their business dealings through magic in the name of jinn, or connect their poetry or charms with some jinn master and thus establish superiority over the general public. Similarly, the supporters of all such movements as rise under satanic inducements, extend their support to them because they expect that in this way they can easily establish their leadership in society. Satanic slogans, as compared to the Divine call, have always proved to be more attractive to the general masses.

¹³⁰ Company of jinn and mankind! Did messengers not come from among you to recite My revelations to you, and warn you of the meeting of this Day?' They will say, 'We bear witness against ourselves.' It was the life of this world that deceived them and so they will bear witness against themselves, that they rejected the truth. ¹³¹ Your Lord would not destroy a community for its wrongdoing, so long as its people were still unaware.ᵃ

يَٰمَعۡشَرَ ٱلۡجِنِّ وَٱلۡإِنسِ أَلَمۡ يَأۡتِكُمۡ رُسُلٌ مِّنكُمۡ يَقُصُّونَ عَلَيۡكُمۡ ءَايَٰتِى وَيُنذِرُونَكُمۡ لِقَآءَ يَوۡمِكُمۡ هَٰذَا قَالُواْ شَهِدۡنَا عَلَىٰٓ أَنفُسِنَا وَغَرَّتۡهُمُ ٱلۡحَيَوٰةُ ٱلدُّنۡيَا وَشَهِدُواْ عَلَىٰٓ أَنفُسِهِمۡ أَنَّهُمۡ كَانُواْ كَٰفِرِينَ ۝ ذَٰلِكَ أَن لَّمۡ يَكُن رَّبُّكَ مُهۡلِكَ ٱلۡقُرَىٰ بِظُلۡمٍ وَأَهۡلُهَا غَٰفِلُونَ ۝

ᵃ On Doomsday, when the veil is torn from reality, it will be clear that those who had gone astray, or had misguided others, did not do so because of any misunderstanding. The reason for this was not their being unaware of the truth but their deliberately ignoring it. They could not rise above worldly pomp and show; they could not forego timely benefits. The guidance provided by God through His special subjects was so clear that nobody could have remained unaware of realities, but their worship of the world drew a veil over their eyes; in spite of knowing, they became unaware; in spite of listening, they did not hear.

In the Hereafter, they will be shorn of the artificial supports on the strength of which they had remained careless of the Truth. Then it will be pointed out how the Truth had appeared before them and how they had rejected it with the help of false words; how, though their mistake had been explained to them, they still thought that they had been successful in justifying their stand by clever misrepresentations.

¹³² For all are degrees of rank according to their deeds; your Lord is not unaware of anything they do.

¹³³ Your Lord is the self-sufficient One, the merciful. If He wills, He can take you away and replace you by anyone He pleases, just as He raised you from the offspring of other people. ¹³⁴ That which you are promised shall surely come to pass and you cannot prevent it. ¹³⁵ Say, 'O my people! Go on acting in your way; indeed I am going to act in my way; soon you will know whose end will be best in the Hereafter.' Surely, the wrongdoers shall not prosper.ᵃ

وَلِكُلٍّ دَرَجَٰتٌ مِّمَّا عَمِلُوا۟ وَمَا رَبُّكَ بِغَٰفِلٍ عَمَّا يَعْمَلُونَ ۝ وَرَبُّكَ ٱلْغَنِىُّ ذُو ٱلرَّحْمَةِ إِن يَشَأْ يُذْهِبْكُمْ وَيَسْتَخْلِفْ مِنۢ بَعْدِكُم مَّا يَشَآءُ كَمَآ أَنشَأَكُم مِّن ذُرِّيَّةِ قَوْمٍ ءَاخَرِينَ ۝ إِنَّ مَا تُوعَدُونَ لَءَاتٍ وَمَآ أَنتُم بِمُعْجِزِينَ ۝ قُلْ يَٰقَوْمِ ٱعْمَلُوا۟ عَلَىٰ مَكَانَتِكُمْ إِنِّى عَامِلٌ فَسَوْفَ تَعْلَمُونَ مَن تَكُونُ لَهُۥ عَٰقِبَةُ ٱلدَّارِ إِنَّهُۥ لَا يُفْلِحُ ٱلظَّٰلِمُونَ ۝

ᵃ In the life of this world we see that there is a difference between the status of one man and another. This difference is exactly in proportion to the efforts made and the struggle engaged in by each of them. A man's wisdom, his diligence and accommodation of interests will determine the degree of his success in this life.

The same state of affairs exists in the case of the Hereafter. In the Hereafter also, the award of status will relate exactly to the deeds performed by human beings in the world. A man has to spend time and money on the Hereafter also, just as he spends time and money on the world. In the matter of the Hereafter, too, he has to behave wisely, as he has been behaving in the world; he has to look after his interests and take care of delicate situations, just as he had been doing in the world. God, in whose hands lies the power of taking decisions in the Hereafter, is fully aware of the condition of each and every individual. It will not be difficult for Him to give everyone whatever he is entitled to.

Through this world of trial which God has created, He has opened the door to immense and valuable possibilities for man, who by performing good deeds in the short temporary life of this world, can earn superlative rewards in the eternal life of the Hereafter. There is no benefit to God in this system. If the present generation does not accept God's creation plan, He can raise in their place others who will accept His creation plan and enlist themselves in its support. Even the sands of the desert and the leaves of the trees can be raised by Him as His faithful subjects.

In a world based entirely on Truth and Justice, the fact that freedom is enjoyed by tyrants and arrogant people as well as virtuous people, in itself proves that this freedom is not by way of reward but by way of trial. ▶

136 They set aside for God a share in what He has produced, such as crops and livestock, and they say, 'This is for God'—so they claim!—and 'this is for our associate-gods? Their associate-gods' share does not reach God, whereas God's share reaches their associate-gods. How ill they judge! [a]

137 And in like manner, their associate gods have made killing their children seem fair to many pagans, so that they may ruin them and cause confusion in their religion. Had God pleased, they would not have done so; so leave them to their false inventions.

وَجَعَلُوا۟ لِلَّهِ مِمَّا ذَرَأَ مِنَ ٱلْحَرْثِ وَٱلْأَنْعَٰمِ نَصِيبًا فَقَالُوا۟ هَٰذَا لِلَّهِ بِزَعْمِهِمْ وَهَٰذَا لِشُرَكَآئِنَا ۖ فَمَا كَانَ لِشُرَكَآئِهِمْ فَلَا يَصِلُ إِلَى ٱللَّهِ ۖ وَمَا كَانَ لِلَّهِ فَهُوَ يَصِلُ إِلَىٰ شُرَكَآئِهِمْ ۗ سَآءَ مَا يَحْكُمُونَ ۝ وَكَذَٰلِكَ زَيَّنَ لِكَثِيرٍ مِّنَ ٱلْمُشْرِكِينَ قَتْلَ أَوْلَٰدِهِمْ شُرَكَآؤُهُمْ لِيُرْدُوهُمْ وَلِيَلْبِسُوا۟ عَلَيْهِمْ دِينَهُمْ ۖ وَلَوْ شَآءَ ٱللَّهُ مَا فَعَلُوهُ ۖ فَذَرْهُمْ وَمَا يَفْتَرُونَ ۝

One who refuses to accept the Truth and still does not apparently lose anything, should not brag about his apparent good fortune, for this condition is purely temporary.

Very soon the time will come when everything on the strength of which he behaved with arrogance, will be taken away from him. And he will be pushed towards eternal destruction, from which he will never be able to emerge, and where he will have the opportunity neither to perform good deeds nor to save himself from the final result of his misdeeds.

[a] Man invents tangible deities because he does not have full faith in the intangible Supreme Being—God. In ancient times polytheists did, however, pay lip service to God, while reserving their real faith for their deities. This was evident from the inequitable way in which they apportioned their sacrificial offerings of grain and livestock to their deities on the one hand, and to God on the other. It was always the deities who were given preference in terms of the quantity and quality of the offerings, and never God. Moreover, when those who in reality are idolaters are 'worshipping' God, they devote a part of their prayers to that person, living or dead, whom they idolize. But when they worship the latter, they do not even mention the name of God. They will readily lavish upon a partner that ecstatic devotion which they should reserve for God. In any meeting held to extol God's greatness, the majesty and glory of the partner will somehow find a place; but in any meeting held to describe the greatness of the partner, there will be absolutely no mention of the majesty and glory of God. ▶

¹³⁸ They also say, 'These animals and these crops are forbidden. None may eat them except those we permit.' So they claim! There are some animals they exempt from labour and some over which they do not pronounce God's name, thus committing a sin against Him. He will requite them for the falsehoods they invent.

¹³⁹ They say, 'What is in the wombs of such and such cattle is exclusively for our males and is forbidden to our females. But if it is stillborn, they may have a share of it.' God will soon punish them for their [false] attribution. He is wise, and all-knowing.ᵃ

وَقَالُوا هَـٰذِهِۦٓ أَنۡعَـٰمٌ وَحَرۡثٌ حِجۡرٌ لَّا يَطۡعَمُهَآ إِلَّا مَن نَّشَآءُ بِزَعۡمِهِمۡ وَأَنۡعَـٰمٌ حُرِّمَتۡ ظُهُورُهَا وَأَنۡعَـٰمٌ لَّا يَذۡكُرُونَ ٱسۡمَ ٱللَّهِ عَلَيۡهَا ٱفۡتِرَآءً عَلَيۡهِۚ سَيَجۡزِيهِم بِمَا كَانُوا۟ يَفۡتَرُونَ ۝ وَقَالُوا۟ مَا فِى بُطُونِ هَـٰذِهِ ٱلۡأَنۡعَـٰمِ خَالِصَةٌ لِّذُكُورِنَا وَمُحَرَّمٌ عَلَىٰٓ أَزۡوَٰجِنَاۖ وَإِن يَكُن مَّيۡتَةً فَهُمۡ فِيهِ شُرَكَآءُۚ سَيَجۡزِيهِمۡ وَصۡفَهُمۡۚ إِنَّهُۥ حَكِيمٌ عَلِيمٌ ۝

The importance of the 'partner' sometimes dominates minds to such an extent that a man will with pleasure sacrifice even his children for it—something which he will not do for the sake of God. All such acts are carried out in the name of God's religion, but falsely so, because this amounts to attributing to God such precepts as had never been laid down by Him.

ᵃ In ancient times, the people of Arabia used to attribute their religion to Abraham and Ishmael. But, in practice, the religion prevalent there was a self-made one, which their leaders had invented and introduced among them. The offering of their produce and cattle made in the name of God and His alleged partners were subject to strict restrictions of their own conception. For instance, if a freed animal was sacrificed and if a live offspring came out of its womb, then it was held that its meat could be eaten only by males and should not be eaten by females, whereas if the offspring was a dead one, it could be eaten by both males and females. Similarly, it was forbidden to ride on the back of certain animals or to place loads on them. In respect of some animals, it was their belief that God's name should not be taken while riding, slaughtering or milking them.

Such people are far removed from the real requirements of religion, i.e. the human being's devotion to God and his concern about the Hereafter. Every day, they go beyond the limits fixed by God, but take care to strictly observe rules about irrelevant matters of minor importance. This is one of Satan's complex strategies. ▶

¹⁴⁰ Losers indeed are they who kill their children foolishly and without knowledge and declare as forbidden what God has provided for them as sustenance—a fabrication against God: they have gone astray and have not chosen to be rightly guided.ᵃ

قَدْ خَسِرَ ٱلَّذِينَ قَتَلُوٓاْ أَوْلَٰدَهُمْ سَفَهًا بِغَيْرِ عِلْمٍ وَحَرَّمُوٓاْ مَا رَزَقَهُمُ ٱللَّهُ ٱفْتِرَآءً عَلَى ٱللَّهِ قَدْ ضَلُّواْ وَمَا كَانُواْ مُهْتَدِينَ ۝

He alienates people from the real religion by introducing unrelated matters among them in the name of religion. By creating a tendency to extremism in them, he instils the misunderstanding in man that he (the latter) is steadfast in God's religion. Extremism in the outer formalities of prayers is the special product of this psychology. A man devoid of sincerity and humility pays meticulous attention to externals, imagining that he has performed the act of prayer to the utmost perfection.

ᵃ How misguided such people are, is clear from the fact that many of them thought the savage act of killing one's own progeny was quite proper. Such misapprehensions deprive people of the clear provisions made by God, so that while fighting over ordinary problems, they overlook matters which are of greater importance, but which might still be understood by the use of common sense.

¹⁴¹ It is He who has produced gardens, both trellised and untrellised, and date palms and field crops, all varying in taste, and the olive and the pomegranate, both similar and dissimilar. Eat their fruits when they bear fruit and give away what is due of them on the day of their harvest. Do not waste anything. He does not love the wasteful!

¹⁴² Of the cattle there are some for carrying burdens and some for food. Eat what God has provided for you and do not follow in Satan's footsteps, for he is a declared enemy of yours.ᵃ

وَهُوَ ٱلَّذِىٓ أَنشَأَ جَنَّـٰتٍ مَّعْرُوشَـٰتٍ وَغَيْرَ مَعْرُوشَـٰتٍ وَٱلنَّخْلَ وَٱلزَّرْعَ مُخْتَلِفًا أُكُلُهُۥ وَٱلزَّيْتُونَ وَٱلرُّمَّانَ مُتَشَـٰبِهًا وَغَيْرَ مُتَشَـٰبِهٍ ۚ كُلُوا۟ مِن ثَمَرِهِۦٓ إِذَآ أَثْمَرَ وَءَاتُوا۟ حَقَّهُۥ يَوْمَ حَصَادِهِۦ ۖ وَلَا تُسْرِفُوٓا۟ ۚ إِنَّهُۥ لَا يُحِبُّ ٱلْمُسْرِفِينَ ۝

وَمِنَ ٱلْأَنْعَـٰمِ حَمُولَةً وَفَرْشًا ۚ كُلُوا۟ مِمَّا رَزَقَكُمُ ٱللَّهُ وَلَا تَتَّبِعُوا۟ خُطُوَٰتِ ٱلشَّيْطَـٰنِ ۚ إِنَّهُۥ لَكُمْ عَدُوٌّ مُّبِينٌ ۝

ᵃ God has created different types of food for man, some spreading out over the ground, like melons, and leafy vegetables; some growing on climbing plants like the grapes on the vine; and some growing high up in the trees, like dates and mangoes. Similarly, different kinds of animals, both big and small, have been created to fulfil the needs of man, for example, camels, horses, sheep and goats.

Man, the birds and animals and all the green, growing things have come into existence quite independently of each other, but man sees that there is a strong harmony between himself and all the rest of God's creations. If a man's body needs nourishment, then outside, on the green trees, wonderful food packets are hanging. If his palate yearns for something delicious to eat, he has only to pluck fruits and then eat them. If his eyes have an aesthetic longing for scenic beauty, then the entire background of nature presents a panorama of scenic beauty and charm. If he needs to eat, ride or despatch goods, then such animals are available here as can serve his transport needs as well as provide him with valuable food. In this way, the entire existence of the universe has become a proclamation of the unity of God, because this uniformity observed in the various phenomena of the universe would not be possible unless its Creator and Lord were one.

When a man sees that this great universal provision for him has been arranged without his necessarily deserving it, his heart is filled with gratitude for this freely given blessing. In consequence, this whole matter becomes nourishment for man's God-fearing instinct, or piety (taqwa). It is the rule of nature that every privilege be accompanied by responsibility. This reminds man of reward and punishment, and induces him to live in this world with the active realisation that one day he has to appear before God to give an account of himself. If these feelings really take hold of a man, then, of necessity, two tendencies will develop in him. ▶

¹⁴³ God has created four kinds of livestock of either sex: two of sheep and two of goats. Ask them, 'Is it the two males He has forbidden or the two females or what the wombs of the two females contain? Tell me on the basis of knowledge, if you are truthful.'

¹⁴⁴ Again, of the camels there are two, and of the oxen two. Ask them, 'Is it the two males He has forbidden, or the two females or what the wombs of the two females contain? Were you present when God enjoined this on you?' Who is more unjust than one who, without knowledge, fabricates a lie against God, so that he may lead people astray without knowledge? Surely, God does not guide the wrongdoers.ᵃ

ثَمَٰنِيَةَ أَزْوَٰجٍ مِّنَ ٱلضَّأْنِ ٱثْنَيْنِ
وَمِنَ ٱلْمَعْزِ ٱثْنَيْنِ قُلْ ءَآلذَّكَرَيْنِ
حَرَّمَ أَمِ ٱلْأُنثَيَيْنِ أَمَّا ٱشْتَمَلَتْ عَلَيْهِ
أَرْحَامُ ٱلْأُنثَيَيْنِ نَبِّـُٔونِي بِعِلْمٍ إِن
كُنتُمْ صَٰدِقِينَ ۞ وَمِنَ ٱلْإِبِلِ
ٱثْنَيْنِ وَمِنَ ٱلْبَقَرِ ٱثْنَيْنِ قُلْ
ءَآلذَّكَرَيْنِ حَرَّمَ أَمِ ٱلْأُنثَيَيْنِ أَمَّا
ٱشْتَمَلَتْ عَلَيْهِ أَرْحَامُ ٱلْأُنثَيَيْنِ أَمْ
كُنتُمْ شُهَدَآءَ إِذْ وَصَّىٰكُمُ ٱللَّهُ
بِهَٰذَا فَمَنْ أَظْلَمُ مِمَّنِ ٱفْتَرَىٰ عَلَى
ٱللَّهِ كَذِبًا لِّيُضِلَّ ٱلنَّاسَ بِغَيْرِ عِلْمٍ
إِنَّ ٱللَّهَ لَا يَهْدِي ٱلْقَوْمَ ٱلظَّٰلِمِينَ

One is—whatever he receives—to appreciate that his Lord has a hand in it, and the other is to spend strictly according to his needs and not in excess of this or without occasion. But what Satan does is to divert a man's mind from the right direction and enmesh it in diverse irrelevant matters.

ᵃ By nature, there is in man the consciousness of God and the realisation of what is permitted and what is forbidden. Man, in pursuance of his internal urge, wants to make a Supreme Being his God and wants to distinguish between permitted and forbidden things. Satan knows this fact very well. He knows that if a man is allowed to go his own way under normal conditions, he will adopt the straight path of nature. So, in order to blunt man's natural instinct, he introduces different types of false customs. In the name of God, he invents some imaginary gods. In the name of what is permitted and forbidden, he devises some baseless prohibition. In this way, Satan tries to entangle man in these imaginary matters, so that he should not arrive at the real truth, but stray from the right path; then, seeing himself apparently progressing, he should think that he is on the right path, even though it might be a crooked line and not the straight right path. Those who fall a victim to Satan's misleading, are transgressors in the eyes of God. God had given them the understanding by which they could have differentiated between Truth and falsehood. But their prejudices warp their minds and, in spite of having the capacity to understand, they remain far removed from the truth.

145 Say [O Prophet], 'In all that has been revealed to me, I do not find a ban on anything to eat, except for carrion, flowing blood and pork, all these being unclean or profane, on which the name of someone other than God has been invoked.' But if anyone is forced by necessity, being neither disobedient nor exceeding the limit, then surely your Lord is most forgiving and merciful.*

قُل لَّآ أَجِدُ فِى مَآ أُوحِىَ إِلَىَّ مُحَرَّمًا عَلَىٰ طَاعِمٍ يَطْعَمُهُۥٓ إِلَّآ أَن يَكُونَ مَيْتَةً أَوْ دَمًا مَّسْفُوحًا أَوْ لَحْمَ خِنزِيرٍ فَإِنَّهُۥ رِجْسٌ أَوْ فِسْقًا أُهِلَّ لِغَيْرِ ٱللَّهِ بِهِۦ ۚ فَمَنِ ٱضْطُرَّ غَيْرَ بَاغٍ وَلَا عَادٍ فَإِنَّ رَبَّكَ غَفُورٌ رَّحِيمٌ ﴿١٤٥﴾

---

a Among the animals reared by the Arabs for the sake of their meat and milk, etc., four kinds were very well known—sheep, goats, camels and cows. With reference to them, they had framed different types of prohibitory regulations. But they had no authority to back these up save their polytheistic customs. The banning of the meat of the sheep, goat, camel or cow, whether male or female, has no rationality in it. All the meat on them is the best food for man. They do not even have any dirty habits which could make them undesirable for human consumption. Even in the teachings coming down from heaven there is no mention of their being forbidden. Then, why does it happen that different types of restrictive regulations gain currency? The reason for this is satanic inducements.

¹⁴⁶ We forbade the Jews all animals with claws and the fat of sheep [and goats] and oxen, except what is on their backs and in their intestines and what adheres to their bones. That is the penalty We imposed on them for their disobedience. And We assuredly are true to Our word.

¹⁴⁷ So, if they accuse you of lying, say, 'The mercy of your Lord is all-encompassing. His punishment cannot be averted from sinful men.'^a

وَعَلَى ٱلَّذِينَ هَادُواْ حَرَّمْنَا كُلَّ ذِى ظُفُرٍ وَمِنَ ٱلْبَقَرِ وَٱلْغَنَمِ حَرَّمْنَا عَلَيْهِمْ شُحُومَهُمَآ إِلَّا مَا حَمَلَتْ ظُهُورُهُمَآ أَوِ ٱلْحَوَايَآ أَوْ مَا ٱخْتَلَطَ بِعَظْمٍ ذَٰلِكَ جَزَيْنَٰهُم بِبَغْيِهِمْ وَإِنَّا لَصَٰدِقُونَ ۝ فَإِن كَذَّبُوكَ فَقُل رَّبُّكُمْ ذُو رَحْمَةٍ وَٰسِعَةٍ وَلَا يُرَدُّ بَأْسُهُ عَنِ ٱلْقَوْمِ ٱلْمُجْرِمِينَ ۝

---

^a According to the divine *Shariah* (Islamic regulations), the truly forbidden things have always been the same as mentioned in the foregoing verse, viz. carrion, out-pouring blood, the meat of pigs and animals slaughtered in the name of any thing or being other than God. Anything else which is forbidden falls into a sub-group of the above-mentioned as a matter of detail.

But along with this, among God's prohibitory laws, another principle is at work, namely, that when a community blessed with His Book adopts the way of arrogance instead of obedience, it is subjected to new difficulties by way of punishment, i.e. such things as were not originally forbidden them in the Divine Shariah are now banned.

One way in which this change comes about is that in such a community, leaders arise who are completely ignorant of the reality of the religion. They are conversant only with its outward formalities. The meticulousness which they should apply to the meaningful realities of religion is reserved by them for outward formalities and rites. The result is that unnecessary hair-splitting over externals becomes a set pattern in religion. Such leaders devise self-made outward standards of religion. By a process of extreme exaggeration, they make a simple commandment complicated and a legitimate thing unlawful.

For instance, when arrogance set in among the Jews, certain scholars arose among them who, by their hair-splitting arguments, made the rule that for an animal to be deemed fit to eat, it should possess two qualities—one, that its hooves should be cloven or divided, and second, that it should be a cud-chewing animal. Even if one of these conditions was not fulfilled, that animal, according to them, was forbidden. Due to this self-imposed condition, even animals like the camel and the rabbit, etc., were unnecessarily banned. Similarly, by taking up an extreme position about the importance attached to claws, they unnecessarily placed ostriches, swans and ducks in the forbidden category. These unnatural restrictions narrowed their lives, whereas God had intended to give them wider latitude. ▶

¹⁴⁸ Those who associate partners with God will surely say, 'Had God pleased, neither we nor our fathers would have served other gods besides Him; nor would we have made anything unlawful.' Likewise those who lived before them argued falsely until they came to taste Our punishment! Say, 'Have you any knowledge? If so, produce it before us. You follow nothing but conjecture. You are merely guessing.'

¹⁴⁹ Say, 'God alone has the conclusive proof. If He had willed, He could have guided every one of you.' ^a

سَيَقُولُ ٱلَّذِينَ أَشْرَكُواْ لَوْ شَاءَ ٱللَّهُ مَآ أَشْرَكْنَا وَلَآ ءَابَآؤُنَا وَلَا حَرَّمْنَا مِن شَىْءٍ ۚ كَذَٰلِكَ كَذَّبَ ٱلَّذِينَ مِن قَبْلِهِمْ حَتَّىٰ ذَاقُواْ بَأْسَنَا ۗ قُلْ هَلْ عِندَكُم مِّنْ عِلْمٍ فَتُخْرِجُوهُ لَنَآ ۖ إِن تَتَّبِعُونَ إِلَّا ٱلظَّنَّ وَإِنْ أَنتُمْ إِلَّا تَخْرُصُونَ ۝ قُلْ فَلِلَّهِ ٱلْحُجَّةُ ٱلْبَٰلِغَةُ ۖ فَلَوْ شَاءَ لَهَدَىٰكُمْ أَجْمَعِينَ ۝

After rejecting the Truth, man is not immediately seized upon by God. He finds himself free and his life as full as before. For this reason, he erroneously imagines that he is not going to lose anything by not accepting the Truth. He forgets that if he remains safe, it is simply because of the merciful forbearance of God. In spite of man's arrogance, God gives him the opportunity to redeem himself till the very last moment. Finally, when he has not changed his behaviour, all of a sudden God swoops down on him—sometimes in this world and sometimes both in this world and the Hereafter.

^a The unadulterated missionary call for Truth always stands out as something rather strange. On the one hand, there is the customary religion which enjoys prominence in all social institutions. Centuries of traditions are behind it to lend it weight. On the other hand, there is the call for Truth, which has no time-honoured conventions in its favour. It is difficult, therefore, for people to understand that customary religion, which has such an elevated status and great popularity, will not be to God's liking. The common presumption is that it has been possible for the customary religion to flourish to this extent because it suited God's will and pleasure: had it not been so, it would not have spread and endured to this extent. They raise the question of whether God's favoured religion will be one already enjoying a high status everywhere in this world of God or one which has no standing whatsoever.

¹⁵⁰ Say, 'Come, bring your witnesses, who can testify that God forbade [all] this.' If they bear witness [falsely], do not bear witness with them; nor yield to the wishes of those who deny Our signs, nor of those who do not believe in the life to come and set up others as equals with their Lord.ᵃ

قُلْ هَلُمَّ شُهَدَآءَكُمُ ٱلَّذِينَ يَشْهَدُونَ أَنَّ ٱللَّهَ حَرَّمَ هَٰذَا ۖ فَإِن شَهِدُوا۟ فَلَا تَشْهَدْ مَعَهُمْ ۚ وَلَا تَتَّبِعْ أَهْوَآءَ ٱلَّذِينَ كَذَّبُوا۟ بِـَٔايَٰتِنَا وَٱلَّذِينَ لَا يُؤْمِنُونَ بِٱلْأَخِرَةِ وَهُم بِرَبِّهِمْ يَعْدِلُونَ ۝

ᵃ God has made this world like one great examination hall in which He has left it up to man to do well or badly in the questions of right and wrong. Of course, differentiating between Truth and falsehood should always be based on real reasoning and not on conjecture or on references to popular custom. But man is not bound to opt for the path of logic. For, instead of forcibly imposing His will on man, God adopted the method of teaching man about what is right or what is wrong and left it to him to tread the right or the wrong path. This means that in the life of the world, argument (reasoning) is God's representative. When a man bows before a correct or sound argument, it is as if he is bowing down before God, and when he refuses to do so, it is as if he is rejecting God.

The reason why a man does not accede to reasoning is that he is unable to rise above his desires. In order to justify his actions, he is prepared to declare falsehood to be truth. His recklessness goes to the extent of ignoring God's signs. He becomes careless of the fact that finally God is going to have him in His grasp, and gives to other things the importance which he should give to God alone.

151 Say, 'Come! I will tell you what your Lord has really forbidden you! Do not associate anything with Him; be good to your parents; and do not kill your children for fear of poverty—We shall provide sustenance for you as well as for them—refrain from committing indecent deeds, whether openly or in secret; and do not kill the life which God has made sacred, save by right. That is what He has enjoined upon you, so that you may understand.ᵃ

۞ قُل تَعَالَوۡاۡ أَتۡلُ مَا حَرَّمَ رَبُّكُمۡ عَلَيۡكُمۡ أَلَّا تُشۡرِكُواۡ بِهِۦ شَيۡـًٔا وَبِٱلۡوَٰلِدَيۡنِ إِحۡسَٰنًا وَلَا تَقۡتُلُوۡاۡ أَوۡلَٰدَكُم مِّنۡ إِمۡلَٰقٍ نَّحۡنُ نَرۡزُقُكُمۡ وَإِيَّاهُمۡ وَلَا تَقۡرَبُواۡ ٱلۡفَوَٰحِشَ مَا ظَهَرَ مِنۡهَا وَمَا بَطَنَ وَلَا تَقۡتُلُواۡ ٱلنَّفۡسَ ٱلَّتِي حَرَّمَ ٱللَّهُ إِلَّا بِٱلۡحَقِّ ذَٰلِكُمۡ وَصَّىٰكُم بِهِۦ لَعَلَّكُمۡ تَعۡقِلُونَ ۝

ᵃ In the name of Divine restrictions, people introduce different types of formal and outward restrictions, and by paying particular attention to these formalities, they feel satisfied that they have completely fulfilled their duty to God. But the regulations that God requires man to obey are real and substantial, and are not just formal rites.

The first requirement is that man should accept as his God the one and only God. The greatness of anybody except Him should not dominate his mind. He should not have faith in anybody except Him; he should not entertain hopes of anybody except Him; he should not be afraid of anybody except Him; and he should not feel intense love for anybody except Him.

If an individual's parents are weak and needy, while he is strong, and if he treats them well, this is not the outcome of self-interest but of righteousness. In this way, the question of discharging the rights of parents becomes the first test of a man's adoption of God's religion, not just at the level of mere talk but as a matter of practical action. If he places emphasis on the parents' rights rather than on their weakness, if his love for his friends and his wife and children does not take him away from his parents, he has, as it were given the first proof that his behaviour will be subject to principles and regard for rights and not to self-interest and self-consideration.

But there are many who, out of greed, act oppressively, in that they do not allow God-created provision to reach all of God's subjects in the proper manner. Then, when the artificially created problems of scarcity of essential commodities arise, they take the lives of unborn children. All such action amounts to negating God's system of provision.

Moreover, there are many wrongs that are so lewd in nature that no special knowledge is required to understand their evil, and man's nature and his conscience are enough to indicate that it is not proper for such acts to be perpetrated upon anyone. ▶

152 Stay well away from an orphan's property, except with the best intentions, before he comes of age.' Give full measure and weight, according to justice—We never charge a soul with more than it can bear—when you speak, observe justice, even though it concerns a close relative; and fulfil the covenants of God. That is what He has enjoined upon you so that you may take heed. 153 [He has enjoined], 'This is My straight path; so follow it, and do not follow other ways: that will lead you away from His path.' That is what He enjoins upon you, so that you may guard yourselves.ᵃ

وَلَا تَقْرَبُواْ مَالَ ٱلْيَتِيمِ إِلَّا بِٱلَّتِى هِىَ أَحْسَنُ حَتَّىٰ يَبْلُغَ أَشُدَّهُ ۖ وَأَوْفُواْ ٱلْكَيْلَ وَٱلْمِيزَانَ بِٱلْقِسْطِ ۖ لَا نُكَلِّفُ نَفْسًا إِلَّا وُسْعَهَا ۖ وَإِذَا قُلْتُمْ فَٱعْدِلُواْ وَلَوْ كَانَ ذَا قُرْبَىٰ ۖ وَبِعَهْدِ ٱللَّهِ أَوْفُواْ ۚ ذَٰلِكُمْ وَصَّىٰكُم بِهِۦ لَعَلَّكُمْ تَذَكَّرُونَ ۝ وَأَنَّ هَٰذَا صِرَٰطِى مُسْتَقِيمًا فَٱتَّبِعُوهُ ۖ وَلَا تَتَّبِعُواْ ٱلسُّبُلَ فَتَفَرَّقَ بِكُمْ عَن سَبِيلِهِۦ ۚ ذَٰلِكُمْ وَصَّىٰكُم بِهِۦ لَعَلَّكُمْ تَتَّقُونَ ۝

Under these circumstances, if someone indulges in acts of shamelessness, he proves, as it were, that he is devoid of even the most rudimentary humanity. Every human being's life is sacred. It is not legitimate to take the life of any man unless he commits a crime in terms of the Creator's law, in which case it would be legitimate to take his life on the fulfilment of certain conditions. All these things are so clear that no one who exercises his mind could fail to realize this.

ᵃ The orphan is the least likely to receive good treatment, because he is the weakest member of any society. In his case, any of the factors which would predispose an individual to behave well towards others are unlikely to come into play. Shouldering responsibility in the case of an 'orphan' can be done only by one who has become a man of character purely out of principle and not on the basis of self-interest. Such a person who is the well-wisher of an orphan will also give exceptionally good treatment to other people.

All things in the universe are so interrelated as to ensure that giving and taking are done on an equitable basis and are mutually beneficial. This very principle has to be adopted by man in his life. If an individual has to measure out something for others, he should measure it out properly and, if he has to weigh out something, he should weigh it out properly. It should never happen that he uses one scale for himself and a different scale for others.

It happens from time to time that a man is required to express an opinion against somebody. On such occasions, the way to win God's approval is to utter such views as meet the standards of justice. Whether the person in question is one of his own or a stranger; whether his relations with him are friendly or inimical, whether or not his interests are linked with him, he should remain uninfluenced by all these factors and should say only what is right and proper. ▶

154 Then We gave Moses the Book, completing [Our favour] to the righteous, explaining everything clearly, as guidance and mercy, so that they might believe in meeting their Lord.

155 This is a Book which We have revealed as a blessing—follow it and fear your Lord, so that you may receive mercy—156 and not say, 'The Book was only sent down to the two groups before us and we were indeed unaware of their teachings,' 157 or you may say, 'If the Book had been sent down to us, we would surely have followed its guidance better than they did.' There has now come to you clear evidence from your Lord, and guidance and mercy. Who, then, is more unjust than one who rejects the signs of God and turns away from them? We shall requite those who turn away from Our signs with a painful punishment, for their turning away.*

ثُمَّ ءَاتَيْنَا مُوسَى ٱلْكِتَبَ تَمَامًا عَلَى ٱلَّذِىٓ أَحْسَنَ وَتَفْصِيلًا لِّكُلِّ شَىْءٍ وَهُدًى وَرَحْمَةً لَّعَلَّهُم بِلِقَآءِ رَبِّهِمْ يُؤْمِنُونَ ۝ وَهَذَا كِتَبٌ أَنزَلْنَهُ مُبَارَكٌ فَٱتَّبِعُوهُ وَٱتَّقُوا۟ لَعَلَّكُمْ تُرْحَمُونَ ۝ أَن تَقُولُوٓا۟ إِنَّمَآ أُنزِلَ ٱلْكِتَبُ عَلَى طَآئِفَتَيْنِ مِن قَبْلِنَا وَإِن كُنَّا عَن دِرَاسَتِهِمْ لَغَفِلِينَ ۝ أَوْ تَقُولُوٓا۟ لَوْ أَنَّآ أُنزِلَ عَلَيْنَا ٱلْكِتَبُ لَكُنَّآ أَهْدَىٰ مِنْهُمْ فَقَدْ جَآءَكُم بَيِّنَةٌ مِّن رَّبِّكُمْ وَهُدًى وَرَحْمَةٌ فَمَنْ أَظْلَمُ مِمَّن كَذَّبَ بِـَٔايَتِ ٱللَّهِ وَصَدَفَ عَنْهَا سَنَجْزِى ٱلَّذِينَ يَصْدِفُونَ عَنْ ءَايَتِنَا سُوٓءَ ٱلْعَذَابِ بِمَا كَانُوا۟ يَصْدِفُونَ ۝

Every man is bound by certain vows. Some are in writing and others are purely verbal. But a man's Faith, his humanity and his nobility demand that right action should be taken in the fulfilment of pledges of any form. The Muslim is duty-bound to fulfil both the written and the verbal kind—all this is very clear. Heavenly revelation and man's mind both bear testimony to this being proper. But, only that person will learn a lesson from divine revelation who himself wants to learn.

These commandments (verses 151-53) are basic sections of the divine Shariah. To follow these within their strict and direct meaning is in fact to follow the straight highway of God. But if, by means of hair-splitting, different by-ways are introduced and if all emphasis is laid on them, this amounts to going astray on various paths (other than the straight highway) which will never lead a man towards God.

* The Book which is revealed on behalf of God contains many details, but its purpose is but one and that is that man should firmly believe that he has to face God. In other words, he should spend life in the world in such a way that he should always treat himself as being answerable to God for his each and every action. His life should be a responsible life and not a free and unrestricted life. This was the purpose of previous Books and this is likewise the aim of the Quran. ▶

158 Are they waiting for the angels or your Lord to come down to them, or for some of your Lord's signs to come? The day when some of the signs of your Lord shall come, it shall not profit any human being who did not believe before, or who did not do any good by his faith. Say to them, 'Wait then, we too are waiting.' [a]

هَلْ يَنظُرُونَ إِلَّا أَن تَأْتِيَهُمُ ٱلْمَلَـٰٓئِكَةُ أَوْ يَأْتِيَ رَبُّكَ أَوْ يَأْتِيَ بَعْضُ ءَايَـٰتِ رَبِّكَ يَوْمَ يَأْتِي بَعْضُ ءَايَـٰتِ رَبِّكَ لَا يَنفَعُ نَفْسًا إِيمَـٰنُهَا لَمْ تَكُنْ ءَامَنَتْ مِن قَبْلُ أَوْ كَسَبَتْ فِي إِيمَـٰنِهَا خَيْرًا قُلِ ٱنتَظِرُوٓا۟ إِنَّا مُنتَظِرُونَ ﴿١٥٨﴾

God has given full freedom to human beings, while keeping the rest of the world under His direct orders and subject to His regulation. The method devised by Him for human guidance is to make people aware of Truth and falsehood through the Prophets as well as His Books which are couched in the language of reason.

In the world, God's will appears before the people in the shape of reasoning. Here, acceptance of this reasoning means acceptance of God and rejection of this reasoning amounts to rejection of God.

[a] With the advent of the explosion of Doomsday, all hidden realities will reveal themselves to the people. At that time, man will be compelled to accept God and act only at His behest, but acceptance at that time will have no value. Only that acceptance is real acceptance which takes place at the stage of the Almighty still being unseen. True faith lies in accepting, without seeing, that which one is compelled to accept after seeing. One who accepts after seeing has, as it were, not accepted at all.

If those enjoying the power to choose today make themselves subject to God's will, they will be rewarded by God with Paradise. But, if they bow down before God only after the arrival of Doomsday, their bowing down will amount to proving their guilt with more force. This will mean that, by their own admission, they did not accept something which was really worth accepting; they did not perform such tasks as were really worth performing.

¹⁵⁹ Have nothing to do with those who have split up their religion into sects. Their case rests with God; He will tell them about what they used to do.

¹⁶⁰ Whoever does a good deed will be repaid tenfold, but those who do a bad deed will only be repaid with its equivalent and they shall not be wronged.ᵃ

إِنَّ ٱلَّذِينَ فَرَّقُواْ دِينَهُمْ وَكَانُواْ شِيَعًا لَّسْتَ مِنْهُمْ فِي شَىْءٍ إِنَّمَآ أَمْرُهُمْ إِلَى ٱللَّهِ ثُمَّ يُنَبِّئُهُم بِمَا كَانُواْ يَفْعَلُونَ ۞ مَن جَآءَ بِٱلْحَسَنَةِ فَلَهُۥ عَشْرُ أَمْثَالِهَا وَمَن جَآءَ بِٱلسَّيِّئَةِ فَلَا يُجْزَىٰٓ إِلَّا مِثْلَهَا وَهُمْ لَا يُظْلَمُونَ ۞

ᵃ Adherence to religion requires that the individual should not give a higher status to anyone in his life than God. He should build relations on the basis of recognition of the Truth and not on the basis of self-interest, and the first symbol of that is the proper treatment of parents. He should consider the provision made by God as a divine gift and should not meddle with His system. In this connection a man's misguidance leads him into the foolishness of the killing of children. He should be shown deeds of shamelessness so that his heart's sensitivity to evil remains alive. He should not exploit the weak: the acid test of this is how he treats an orphan. In the discharge of duties and in matters of give and take, he should strike a just balance. He should always speak with justice. He should spend his life with the feeling that he is bound by a divine pledge, and that he is never free of its responsibilities. This is the straightforward way for a man to spend his life—one which is liked by God. Man should keep himself on this straight path without deviating to the right or left.

The Ten Commandments mentioned above (verses 151-153) are simple and natural. Every man's mind testifies to their truth. If stress is laid on these things, there can never be differences or sectarianism. But when communities decline, such leaders are born among them as wilfully misinterpret these straightforward precepts and this is what fragments religious unity.

If unnecessary discussions are introduced into the Faith of monotheism—e.g. whether God has a body or is bodyless; if there is hair-splitting on the subject of orphans, i.e. what is the definition of orphanhood; if the point is raised that Divine commands cannot be carried out unless the government is overthrown and as such the first task is changing the 'un-Islamic' government—there will be no end to the difficulties created and it will be impossible to achieve a general consensus on these points. Then different schools of thought will form; separate sects will take shape; long-established unity will turn into internal discord. ▶

161 Say, 'My Lord has guided me to a straight path, and to an upright religion, the religion of Abraham the upright, who was not of those who associate partners with God.'

162 Say, 'My prayer and my sacrifice and my life and my death are all for God, the Lord of the worlds; 163 He has no partner. So am I commanded, and I am the first of those who submit.' [a]

قُلْ إِنَّنِي هَدَانِي رَبِّي إِلَىٰ صِرَٰطٍ مُّسْتَقِيمٍ دِينًا قِيَمًا مِّلَّةَ إِبْرَٰهِيمَ حَنِيفًا وَمَا كَانَ مِنَ ٱلْمُشْرِكِينَ ۝ قُلْ إِنَّ صَلَاتِي وَنُسُكِي وَمَحْيَايَ وَمَمَاتِي لِلَّهِ رَبِّ ٱلْعَٰلَمِينَ ۝ لَا شَرِيكَ لَهُ وَبِذَٰلِكَ أُمِرْتُ وَأَنَا۠ أَوَّلُ ٱلْمُسْلِمِينَ ۝

To devote one's full attention to this simple and natural religion is the best act of righteousness. But for this purpose, a man has to fight with his self; even if the atmosphere is unpropitious, one has to remain firm by exercising patience and making sacrifices. This is an arduous task, and that is why the reward for it is multiplied many times over by God. Those who practice evil, those who adopt paths other than that specified by God, indulge in the worst type of crime. However, God does not take excessive measures against them. He gives them a punishment commensurate with their crime.

[a] In the pages of the Quran, God has revealed His religion in the uncorrupted state in which He had given it to Abraham and other prophets. Now, one who wants to be blessed by the Grace of God and His support should adopt this religion. He should dedicate his prayers to God; he should have a relation with God at the level of sacrifice; if he lives, he should live for the sake of God, and when he is overtaken by death, he should by that time have unreservedly become a subject of God, in body and soul. The vast universe with its heavenly bodies follows this religion of obedience to God. Then, how can a man adopt a path other than this? In the world of obedience to God, how can arrogance directed against God lead to success? This is a matter which concerns every individual. Nobody can share another's reward or suffer another's punishment. The individual should be as serious about this as he is about all matters which concern him personally.

164 Say, 'Shall I seek a lord other than God, while He is the Lord of all things?' Everyone must bear the consequence of what he does, and no bearer of a burden can bear the burden of another. Then to your Lord you will return, and He will inform you of what you used to dispute about. 165 It is He who has made you successors [of others] on the earth and has exalted some of you over the others in degrees of rank, so that He may test you by that which He has given you. Your Lord is swift in punishment; yet surely He is forgiving, and merciful.*a*

قُلْ أَغَيْرَ ٱللَّهِ أَبْغِى رَبًّا وَهُوَ رَبُّ كُلِّ شَىْءٍ ۚ وَلَا تَكْسِبُ كُلُّ نَفْسٍ إِلَّا عَلَيْهَا ۚ وَلَا تَزِرُ وَازِرَةٌ وِزْرَ أُخْرَىٰ ۚ ثُمَّ إِلَىٰ رَبِّكُم مَّرْجِعُكُمْ فَيُنَبِّئُكُم بِمَا كُنتُمْ فِيهِ تَخْتَلِفُونَ ۝ وَهُوَ ٱلَّذِى جَعَلَكُمْ خَلَٰئِفَ ٱلْأَرْضِ وَرَفَعَ بَعْضَكُمْ فَوْقَ بَعْضٍ دَرَجَٰتٍ لِّيَبْلُوَكُمْ فِى مَا ءَاتَىٰكُمْ ۗ إِنَّ رَبَّكَ سَرِيعُ ٱلْعِقَابِ وَإِنَّهُ لَغَفُورٌ رَّحِيمٌ ۝

---

a The system of this world is that one person goes away and another takes his place. One community is thrust aside and another community takes its place and captures the resources of the land. These incidents remind us again and again that here nobody's dominance is permanent. But man's behaviour is strange. When he sees some opportunity to advance himself, he forgets the fate of his forebears. He fabricates different types of arguments to justify oppression and arrogance. But when God lays bare the realities, man will see that his actions—which he had considered strong enough to justify his position—were meaningless.

The reason for man's arrogance in this world is that he thinks of the good things of this life as God's reward. The fact is that whatever a man receives in this life is meant to be a test and not a reward. If a man considers the good things available to him in this life as his due, this will cause him to be proud, but if he considers them as a means of testing him, this will develop a sense of humility in him. While a proud mentality is marked by haughtiness, a humble attitude is marked by the willingness to obey God.

7. THE HEIGHTS

In the name of God,
the Most Gracious, the Most Merciful

¹ *Alif Lam Mim Sad*

² This Book has been sent down to you—let there be no heaviness in your heart about it—so that you may warn by means of it and it is a reminder to the believers.*

³ Follow what has been sent down to you by your Lord and do not follow any protector other than Him. How seldom you take heed.*

---

*The Book of God is, in essence, a book of guidance. But as such it is of value only to the few who have kept their consciences alive. For the others it amounts only to a warning of the impending grievous fate towards which they are moving because of their arrogance. The preacher of truth is concerned to see that what he sees as the absolute truth is being rejected by the majority of the people who consider it a falsehood. What is paramount in his eyes is treated by people with unconcern, as if it had no substance, as if it were completely unreal.

*This is a world of trial. Here everybody has the opportunity and the liberty to accept or reject the truth as he pleases, and even find clever words to justify his stand. But this position is a temporary one. As soon as the period of trial comes to an end, it will be revealed to all that the preacher's words were based on eternal truths; that it was sheer bias and egotism on his opponents' part which prevented them from seeing the Truth at the core of his arguments. It will become clear at that time that the arguments advanced by them to contradict the preacher's words were simply a falsification of the facts and not a form of reasoning in any real sense.

⁴ How many towns We have destroyed. Our scourge fell upon them by night or at midday when they were resting: ⁵ and when Our scourge fell upon them, their only cry was, 'We were indeed wrongdoers!' ⁶ Then shall We question those to whom Our message was sent and those through whom We sent it ⁷ with full knowledge, We shall tell them what they did, for We have never been away from them. ⁸ Truth alone will be of weight that Day. Those whose scales are heavy shall be successful, ⁹ and those whose good deeds are light [in the balance] will be the ones who have lost themselves because they wrongfully rejected Our signs.^a

وَكَم مِّن قَرْيَةٍ أَهْلَكْنَٰهَا فَجَآءَهَا بَأْسُنَا بَيَٰتًا أَوْ هُمْ قَآئِلُونَ ۝ فَمَا كَانَ دَعْوَىٰهُمْ إِذْ جَآءَهُم بَأْسُنَآ إِلَّآ أَن قَالُوٓاْ إِنَّا كُنَّا ظَٰلِمِينَ ۝ فَلَنَسْـَٔلَنَّ ٱلَّذِينَ أُرْسِلَ إِلَيْهِمْ وَلَنَسْـَٔلَنَّ ٱلْمُرْسَلِينَ ۝ فَلَنَقُصَّنَّ عَلَيْهِم بِعِلْمٍ وَمَا كُنَّا غَآئِبِينَ ۝ وَٱلْوَزْنُ يَوْمَئِذٍ ٱلْحَقُّ فَمَن ثَقُلَتْ مَوَٰزِينُهُ فَأُوْلَٰٓئِكَ هُمُ ٱلْمُفْلِحُونَ ۝ وَمَنْ خَفَّتْ مَوَٰزِينُهُ فَأُوْلَٰٓئِكَ ٱلَّذِينَ خَسِرُوٓاْ أَنفُسَهُم بِمَا كَانُواْ بِـَٔايَٰتِنَا يَظْلِمُونَ ۝

---

^a In this world the importance of an individual is gauged by the material splendour surrounding him, and his ability to influence people with his impressive words, and thus have a massive following. Since the preacher is not generally in such a happy position, his word is valueless in the eyes of worldly people, while the words of his opponents, who bask in material grandeur have a greater impact. But when Doomsday uncovers all the facts, the position will be just the opposite. Now, all the weight will be on the side of the Truth: Untruth will be divested of all its arguments and will be rendered valueless.

10 We established you in the land and provided you with a means of livelihood there: yet you are seldom thankful. 11 We created you, then We shaped you and then We said to the angels, 'Prostrate yourselves before Adam,' and they all prostrated themselves, except Satan. He was not among those who prostrated themselves.ᵃ

وَلَقَدْ مَكَّنَّٰكُمْ فِى ٱلْأَرْضِ وَجَعَلْنَا لَكُمْ فِيهَا مَعَٰيِشَ ۗ قَلِيلًا مَّا تَشْكُرُونَ ۝ وَلَقَدْ خَلَقْنَٰكُمْ ثُمَّ صَوَّرْنَٰكُمْ ثُمَّ قُلْنَا لِلْمَلَٰئِكَةِ ٱسْجُدُوا۟ لِءَادَمَ فَسَجَدُوٓا۟ إِلَّآ إِبْلِيسَ لَمْ يَكُن مِّنَ ٱلسَّٰجِدِينَ ۝

ᵃ Whatever God has bestowed upon man in this world has been given for the purpose of eliciting his gratitude. But this is the very thing which man does not offer to his Lord. The reason for this is that Satan contrives to distort his feelings and steers him away from any expression of gratitude.

It becomes evident from the story of Adam and Satan what the real criterion is for the judgement of one's case. Man is being judged at the point where feelings of jealousy and pride develop in the human heart. In this world of trial it happens again and again that one man rises above another; sometimes one man receives a greater share of wealth and honour as compared to his fellow men. Sometimes, in a deal between two persons, it happens that one of them considers his discharging of the other's legitimate rights as degrading to himself. On all such occasions man is being judged whether he responds positively or reacts negatively.

¹² God asked, 'What prevented you from prostrating yourself when I commanded you to?' He replied, 'I am better than he is; You created me from fire, while You created him from clay.' ¹³ God said, 'Get down from here! This is no place for your arrogance. Get out! You are contemptible!' ¹⁴ Satan said, 'Give me respite until the Day of Resurrection,' ¹⁵ and God replied, 'You are granted respite.' ¹⁶ Then Satan said, 'Because You have put me in the wrong, I will lie in ambush for them on Your straight path: ¹⁷ then I will surely come upon them from before them and from behind them and from their right and from their left, and then You will find most of them ungrateful.' ¹⁸ He said, 'Get out of here, despised, and rejected! I shall fill Hell with all of those who follow you.'ᵃ

قَالَ مَا مَنَعَكَ أَلَّا تَسْجُدَ إِذْ أَمَرْتُكَ ۖ قَالَ أَنَا۠ خَيْرٌ مِّنْهُ خَلَقْتَنِي مِن نَّارٍ وَخَلَقْتَهُۥ مِن طِينٍ ۝ قَالَ فَٱهْبِطْ مِنْهَا فَمَا يَكُونُ لَكَ أَن تَتَكَبَّرَ فِيهَا فَٱخْرُجْ إِنَّكَ مِنَ ٱلصَّٰغِرِينَ ۝ قَالَ أَنظِرْنِىٓ إِلَىٰ يَوْمِ يُبْعَثُونَ ۝ قَالَ إِنَّكَ مِنَ ٱلْمُنظَرِينَ ۝ قَالَ فَبِمَآ أَغْوَيْتَنِى لَأَقْعُدَنَّ لَهُمْ صِرَٰطَكَ ٱلْمُسْتَقِيمَ ۝ ثُمَّ لَءَاتِيَنَّهُم مِّنۢ بَيْنِ أَيْدِيهِمْ وَمِنْ خَلْفِهِمْ وَعَنْ أَيْمَٰنِهِمْ وَعَن شَمَآئِلِهِمْ ۖ وَلَا تَجِدُ أَكْثَرَهُمْ شَٰكِرِينَ ۝ قَالَ ٱخْرُجْ مِنْهَا مَذْءُومًا مَّدْحُورًا ۖ لَّمَن تَبِعَكَ مِنْهُمْ لَأَمْلَأَنَّ جَهَنَّمَ مِنكُمْ أَجْمَعِينَ ۝

ᵃ Sometimes God chooses a messenger to convey His word to the people, but his status as a guide is not readily acceptable to them. For this would imply that they were inferior to the messenger as they had failed to arrive at the truth. On such occasions Satan stirs up feelings of jealousy and pride. Puffed up with the feeling: 'I am better,' a man is not prepared to acknowledge the superiority of his brother. In the eyes of God, this amounts to treading the path of Satan. In such instances, one who treads the path of jealousy and pride makes himself deserving of the fate of hell, while one who remains humble proves that he deserves to find an abode in the gardens of Paradise. Whatever a man receives comes from God. So, the admission of someone else's superiority is in fact an admission of the propriety of God's endowments. Thus, denying the superiority of a well-endowed person is like the denial of God's own decree. Similarly, when one man yields to another on the basis of some truth, he is not bowing down before just some man but before God; he does so in response to God's command and not because of the other's personal superiority.

¹⁹ To Adam He said, 'You and your wife, dwell in the Garden and eat and drink there from wherever you wish, but do not approach this tree, lest you become wrongdoers.' ²⁰ But Satan tempted them so that he might reveal to them their nakedness which had been hidden from them. He said, 'Your Lord has forbidden you to approach this tree lest you should become angels or become of the immortals,' ²¹ and he swore to them, 'Surely, I am your well-wisher.'ᵃ

وَيَٰٓـَٔادَمُ ٱسْكُنْ أَنتَ وَزَوْجُكَ ٱلْجَنَّةَ فَكُلَا مِنْ حَيْثُ شِئْتُمَا وَلَا تَقْرَبَا هَٰذِهِ ٱلشَّجَرَةَ فَتَكُونَا مِنَ ٱلظَّٰلِمِينَ ۞ فَوَسْوَسَ لَهُمَا ٱلشَّيْطَٰنُ لِيُبْدِىَ لَهُمَا مَا وُۥرِىَ عَنْهُمَا مِن سَوْءَٰتِهِمَا وَقَالَ مَا نَهَىٰكُمَا رَبُّكُمَا عَنْ هَٰذِهِ ٱلشَّجَرَةِ إِلَّآ أَن تَكُونَا مَلَكَيْنِ أَوْ تَكُونَا مِنَ ٱلْخَٰلِدِينَ ۞ وَقَاسَمَهُمَآ إِنِّى لَكُمَا لَمِنَ ٱلنَّٰصِحِينَ ۞

ᵃ Paradise with all its vast expanses was open to Adam and his spouse. There were innumerable types of good things in it. And they had all the freedom to use them in whatever manner they liked. In the midst of countless permitted things, they were prohibited the use of only one thing. Satan used this prohibition as a vantage point from which to attack them. He incited them to wrongdoing by saying that the thing from which they were kept away was the most important thing in Paradise, the whole secret of holiness and eternity was hidden therein. Adam and his spouse were influenced by Satan's continuous urging and finally ate the fruit of the forbidden tree. But, when they did this, the result was entirely the opposite of what they had expected. This disobedience of theirs removed the cloak of safety from their bodies. They became absolutely helpless in a world where they had had every convenience and total safety.

This indicates the special weapon used by Satan to deceive man into distancing himself from God's grace and succour. His strategy was to belittle in the eyes of man the extensive world of legitimate gifts from God and to inflate the importance of the few prohibited things, by presenting them in an attractive light, all the while reassuring man of the immense advantages concealed within them. In performing this task, Satan treats everybody according to his tastes and circumstances. He will misguide some by making them hate health-giving food and teaching them that, if they want to have wonderful health, they should take to drinking wines; a man may feel that he should consolidate his own position in order to defeat his opponent, but Satan will poison his mind by suggesting that the most effective method of defeating his opponent is to start destructive activities against him; for another there will be ample opportunities to adopt the policy of self-improvement, but Satan will teach him that indulging in protests and demands is the shortest way to achieve success; yet another might have countless religious tasks before him which he may perform without there being any clash with the Government of the day, but Satan will create the misunderstanding that only if un-Islamic rulers are unseated can Islam's perfect system prevail there and then throughout the whole country; and so on.

²² Thus he cunningly seduced them. When they tasted the tree's fruit, their nakedness became exposed to them and they started covering themselves with the leaves of the garden. Their Lord called out to them, 'Did I not forbid you to approach that tree, and did I not say to you that Satan was surely your open enemy?' ²³ They replied, 'Our Lord, we have wronged our souls: if You do not forgive us and have mercy on us, we shall be among the lost.' ²⁴ He said, 'Go down from here as enemies to each other. For a while, there is an abode for you and a provision on earth. ²⁵ There you will live; there you will die; from there you will be raised up again.' *ᵃ*

فَدَلَّىٰهُمَا بِغُرُورٍ ۚ فَلَمَّا ذَاقَا ٱلشَّجَرَةَ بَدَتْ لَهُمَا سَوْءَٰتُهُمَا وَطَفِقَا يَخْصِفَانِ عَلَيْهِمَا مِن وَرَقِ ٱلْجَنَّةِ ۖ وَنَادَىٰهُمَا رَبُّهُمَآ أَلَمْ أَنْهَكُمَا عَن تِلْكُمَا ٱلشَّجَرَةِ وَأَقُل لَّكُمَآ إِنَّ ٱلشَّيْطَٰنَ لَكُمَا عَدُوٌّ مُّبِينٌ ﴿٢٢﴾ قَالَا رَبَّنَا ظَلَمْنَآ أَنفُسَنَا وَإِن لَّمْ تَغْفِرْ لَنَا وَتَرْحَمْنَا لَنَكُونَنَّ مِنَ ٱلْخَٰسِرِينَ ﴿٢٣﴾ قَالَ ٱهْبِطُوا۟ بَعْضُكُمْ لِبَعْضٍ عَدُوٌّ ۖ وَلَكُمْ فِي ٱلْأَرْضِ مُسْتَقَرٌّ وَمَتَٰعٌ إِلَىٰ حِينٍ ﴿٢٤﴾ قَالَ فِيهَا تَحْيَوْنَ وَفِيهَا تَمُوتُونَ وَمِنْهَا تُخْرَجُونَ ﴿٢٥﴾

ᵃ Both Adam and Satan have been sent to the earth as each other's enemies. Now the battle which goes on between them will continue till Doomsday. Satan constantly strives to bring human beings on to his path and to deprive man of God's grace, just as he himself had been deprived of it. But man should place himself in opposition to him; he should sabotage the plans of Satan. He should ignore his call and rush to obey the call of God.

The fight between Adam and Satan makes itself manifest in the formation of human beings into two groups. Some succumb to the inducements of Satan and fall in line with him, while others who respond to God's call incur the risk of all the companions of Satan contriving to vilify and defeat them. It has been seen in every age that true devotees of truth, who are always small in number, remain victims of the direst enmity of those who deny the truth. The reason for this is Satan's inimical actions. He turns people against the true believers, in different ways filling their hearts with a burning hatred for them. Thus certain people become Satan's tools and start harassing these devotees of truth. ▶

²⁶ O children of Adam! We have sent down to you clothes to cover your nakedness, and to be pleasing to the eye; but the raiment of righteousness is the best. That is one of the signs of God. So that people may take heed.^a

يَٰبَنِىٓ ءَادَمَ قَدْ أَنزَلْنَا عَلَيْكُمْ لِبَاسًا يُوَٰرِى سَوْءَٰتِكُمْ وَرِيشًا وَلِبَاسُ ٱلتَّقْوَىٰ ذَٰلِكَ خَيْرٌ ذَٰلِكَ مِنْ ءَايَٰتِ ٱللَّهِ لَعَلَّهُمْ يَذَّكَّرُونَ ٢٦

The real sin of Satan was his refusal to acknowledge the favour bestowed upon Adam by God. It is Satan's effort to create in every man a temperament similar to his own. He instigates the younger ones not to give due regard to their elders. In the course of social or business transactions, when one party is honour-bound to give the other his dues, Satan persuades the former not to honour his pledge. When a servant of God brings the message of truth, Satan introduces different types of doubts into the hearts of the people and induces them not to accept it. If there is a dispute between two parties and if one of them is ready to pay an amount commensurate with his circumstances, Satan insidiously persuades the other party not to accept this offer, but rather to make such huge demands as the other party cannot meet, so that the fight continues unabated.

In this way, due to the misguidance of Satan, enmity between people prevails everywhere. Two opposing groups form among human beings and Satan sees to it that the confrontation between them will be unending.

^a God has created the system of the world in such a way that its externals are the signs of an inner reality. By pondering over outward things, a man can arrive at hidden truths. One such outer emblem is human attire.

God has given clothes to man which protect him as well as being a means of improving his looks and prestige. This is indicative of the fact that a form of clothing is necessary for man's spiritual existence as well. This clothing is righteousness born of the fear of God (taqwa), which represents the inner personality of a man. This vestment of taqwa on the one hand protects man from the attacks of Satan and, on the other, enhances his inner self and makes him capable of inhabiting the fine and aesthetic world of Paradise. What is this righteousness, or taqwa? It is fear of God, acknowledging of the Truth, adhering to uniform criteria for oneself and others, considering oneself a subject of God, behaving with modesty and humility, leading a Hereafter-oriented life instead of going astray in the world. When a man develops these virtues he 'dresses' his inner self. While the outer body is covered by a garment made of cloth, the inner self, the soul, is clad in taqwa. But if his behaviour is the opposite, he is, as it were, laying his inner self bare.

²⁷ Children of Adam, do not let Satan seduce you, just as he turned your parents out of the Garden: he deprived them of their garment in order to make them aware of their nakedness. He and his forces watch you from where you do not see them! We have made the devils friends of those who do not believe.

²⁸ And when they commit an indecency, they say, 'This is what our fathers used to do and God has enjoined it on us.' Say, 'God does not enjoin what is indecent. Would you attribute to God something of which you have no knowledge?'^a

يَـٰبَنِىٓ ءَادَمَ لَا يَفْتِنَنَّكُمُ ٱلشَّيْطَـٰنُ كَمَآ أَخْرَجَ أَبَوَيْكُم مِّنَ ٱلْجَنَّةِ يَنزِعُ عَنْهُمَا لِبَاسَهُمَا لِيُرِيَهُمَا سَوْءَٰتِهِمَآ إِنَّهُۥ يَرَىٰكُمْ هُوَ وَقَبِيلُهُۥ مِنْ حَيْثُ لَا تَرَوْنَهُمْ إِنَّا جَعَلْنَا ٱلشَّيَـٰطِينَ أَوْلِيَآءَ لِلَّذِينَ لَا يُؤْمِنُونَ ۝ وَإِذَا فَعَلُوا۟ فَـٰحِشَةً قَالُوا۟ وَجَدْنَا عَلَيْهَآ ءَابَآءَنَا وَٱللَّهُ أَمَرَنَا بِهَا قُلْ إِنَّ ٱللَّهَ لَا يَأْمُرُ بِٱلْفَحْشَآءِ أَتَقُولُونَ عَلَى ٱللَّهِ مَا لَا تَعْلَمُونَ ۝

---

^a The way that Satan leads a man astray is by misinforming him. He shows the prohibited tree as the fountainhead of all advantages. He approaches man by such innocuous ways that he has no suspicion that he is about to be misled. Satan knows all the weak points, delicate places in the moral armour of human beings and he takes care to attack those very spots.

Which people is Satan successful in misguiding? He is successful with those who are unable to give proof of faith on occasions of trial; with those who do not carefully ponder over the signs of God; with those who reject valid arguments; and with those who cannot abide by the demands of truth in preference to their own personal inclinations. They do not recognize Truth as such if it does not promote their interests.

²⁹ Say, 'My Lord has commanded you to act justly. Turn your faces up toward Him at every time and place of worship, and call upon Him, making yourselves sincere towards Him in religion. As He brought you into being, so shall you return.' ³⁰ Some He has guided and some have earned misguidance: they have taken devils rather than God as their patrons, thinking that they are rightly guided.ᵃ

قُلْ أَمَرَ رَبِّى بِٱلْقِسْطِ وَأَقِيمُوا۟ وُجُوهَكُمْ عِندَ كُلِّ مَسْجِدٍ وَٱدْعُوهُ مُخْلِصِينَ لَهُ ٱلدِّينَ كَمَا بَدَأَكُمْ تَعُودُونَ ۝ فَرِيقًا هَدَىٰ وَفَرِيقًا حَقَّ عَلَيْهِمُ ٱلضَّلَٰلَةُ إِنَّهُمُ ٱتَّخَذُوا۟ ٱلشَّيَٰطِينَ أَوْلِيَآءَ مِن دُونِ ٱللَّهِ وَيَحْسَبُونَ أَنَّهُم مُّهْتَدُونَ ۝

ᵃ The word 'justice' (*qist*) signifies a form of behaviour which fulfills every moral criterion. It is what it should be. Worship in the form of prayer is a natural urge in every man; he wants to accept some Being as supreme and to prostrate himself before Him. In this matter justice will be done only if he worships the one true God who is his Creator, Lord and Sustainer. Man wants to have some Being at the core of his conviction. In this case, justice will consist in his making God, who is all-Powerful, the basis of his trust. Similarly, acceptance of further life after death will be justice in the absolute sense, because when a man is born, he comes into existence from non-existence. So believing in the life after death (resurrection) will amount to believing in the very reality which every man has already experienced at the time of his birth in this world.

Man looks to the luminaries of former times for support, so that he may reject the preacher of Truth. The greatness of these ancient forebears has been historically established and in the eyes of all and sundry their being in the right is taken for granted. As opposed to this, the preacher of Truth before them is a new preacher who has not yet been sanctified by historical testimony. When the individual looks at the ancients, who are revered as saints because of their illustrious history, and compares them to the new missionary of Truth with no tradition behind him, he rejects him outright, believing himself to be on the right path. But this sort of misunderstanding cannot provide an excuse in the eyes of God, for, in rejecting the missionary, one is not really following God: one is merely following Satan in the name of God.

³¹ O Children of Adam, dress yourself properly whenever you are at worship: and eat and drink but do not be wasteful: God does not like wasteful people. ³² Say, 'Who has forbidden the adornment of God, which He has brought forth for His servants and good things, clean and pure, which God has provided for His servants?' Say, 'They are [lawful] for the believers in the present life but they shall be exclusively for them on the Day of Resurrection.' Thus We explain Our signs for a people who understand. ³³ Say, 'My Lord has forbidden indecency, both open and hidden, sin and wrongful oppression and that, without His sanction, you associate things with Him, and that you say things about Him without knowledge.' ᵃ

ٱلْفَوَٰحِشَ مَا ظَهَرَ مِنْهَا وَمَا بَطَنَ وَٱلْإِثْمَ وَٱلْبَغْىَ بِغَيْرِ ٱلْحَقِّ وَأَن تُشْرِكُوا۟ بِٱللَّهِ مَا لَمْ يُنَزِّلْ بِهِۦ سُلْطَٰنًا وَأَن تَقُولُوا۟ عَلَى ٱللَّهِ مَا لَا تَعْلَمُونَ ۝

یَٰبَنِىٓ ءَادَمَ خُذُوا۟ زِينَتَكُمْ عِندَ كُلِّ مَسْجِدٍ وَكُلُوا۟ وَٱشْرَبُوا۟ وَلَا تُسْرِفُوٓا۟ إِنَّهُۥ لَا يُحِبُّ ٱلْمُسْرِفِينَ ۝ قُلْ مَنْ حَرَّمَ زِينَةَ ٱللَّهِ ٱلَّتِىٓ أَخْرَجَ لِعِبَادِهِۦ وَٱلطَّيِّبَٰتِ مِنَ ٱلرِّزْقِ قُلْ هِىَ لِلَّذِينَ ءَامَنُوا۟ فِى ٱلْحَيَوٰةِ ٱلدُّنْيَا خَالِصَةً يَوْمَ ٱلْقِيَٰمَةِ كَذَٰلِكَ نُفَصِّلُ ٱلْأَيَٰتِ لِقَوْمٍ يَعْلَمُونَ ۝ قُلْ إِنَّمَا حَرَّمَ رَبِّىَ

ᵃ Some Arab tribes used to perform their circumambulation of the Ka'bah completely bare-bodied, thinking that it brought them nearer to God. Similarly, during the pre-Islamic period (the days of ignorance) they used to abstain from certain things such as goat's milk or meat, while starting out on Hajj, imagining that they were performing great and righteous deeds. This type of misguided action has been indulged in by people of every period. Such individuals do not include the requirements of religion in their everyday life; only on certain occasions, by paying special heed to certain irrelevant, pointless actions, they make a great show of conducting themselves according to the religion of God, and contend that by attending to trivialities, they are fulfilling God's will to the maximum extent.

God wants man to abstain from being a spendthrift; that is, he should not transgress the limits laid down by God. He should not hold permitted things as forbidden and vice versa. He should eschew shameful acts. He should abstain from whatever is evidently evil in the light of common sense. He should shun all excesses. Whenever Truth appears before him, he should accede to it, ignoring all else. He should fully cleanse himself of polytheism (ascribing partners to God). With no one should he have the sublime relationship, which is the actual right of the one and only God. It should not happen that he adopts the path of his choice and then attributes it to God without any reason; he should consistently remain a subject of God; as such he should not adopt any ways which are not proper for him as a servant of God. ▶

34 For all people a term has been set: and when [the end of] their term approaches, they can neither delay it by a single moment, nor can they advance it. 35 Children of Adam! If messengers come to you from among yourselves, reciting My revelations to you, then those that take warning and mend their ways, on such shall come no fear nor shall they grieve. 36 But those who deny and scorn Our revelations shall be the inmates of Hell, where they shall remain forever.ᵃ

وَلِكُلِّ أُمَّةٍ أَجَلٌ ۖ فَإِذَا جَاءَ أَجَلُهُمْ لَا يَسْتَأْخِرُونَ سَاعَةً ۖ وَلَا يَسْتَقْدِمُونَ ۝ يَـٰبَنِىٓ ءَادَمَ إِمَّا يَأْتِيَنَّكُمْ رُسُلٌ مِّنكُمْ يَقُصُّونَ عَلَيْكُمْ ءَايَـٰتِى ۙ فَمَنِ ٱتَّقَىٰ وَأَصْلَحَ فَلَا خَوْفٌ عَلَيْهِمْ وَلَا هُمْ يَحْزَنُونَ ۝ وَٱلَّذِينَ كَذَّبُوا۟ بِـَٔايَـٰتِنَا وَٱسْتَكْبَرُوا۟ عَنْهَآ أُو۟لَـٰٓئِكَ أَصْحَـٰبُ ٱلنَّارِ ۖ هُمْ فِيهَا خَـٰلِدُونَ ۝

In the Hereafter, God's bounties will be received as a reward; as such they will be given only to those subjects of God whom God decides to send to Paradise. Unlike these divine rewards, the bounties that are received in the world are available only for a limited period for the purposes of human trial. So one receives a share in them only in terms of his 'test paper.' The way to fulfill the requirements of this test is not to keep away from the worldly provisions that God has provided him for this purpose, but to use them within the limits specified for them. Man should respond to the blessing of God with gratitude and not by renunciation or a display of bravado.

ᵃ According to the creation plan one has the opportunity to perform well or badly in the present world till the period of one's trial is over.

But as far as a community or a nation is concerned, there is no such limit for the enforcement of God's decision. This decision is taken on the basis of that community's response after the truth has been introduced to it. The community whose period is over, is sometimes destroyed by the inflicting of an extraordinary retributive punishment and sometimes it is punished by being displaced from its position of honour and supremacy.

The decision about Heaven or Hell as the final destination for a man is taken on the basis of his response after the truth has appeared before him, supported by arguments whose rationality is testified to by his intellect. This means conveying the message in the full sense. Even after that, if a man refuses to accept the Truth, he does so out of egotism. His desire to maintain his superiority prevents him from lowering himself in comparison to the Truth. For such a man, before God, there is no fate except Hell.

37 Who does a greater wrong than he who invents lies against God or rejects His revelations? Such people will have what has been decreed for them. And when Our messengers come to them to take away their souls, they shall ask them, 'Where are those you used to call upon besides God?' They will answer, 'They have deserted us;' and they will bear witness against themselves that they were disbelievers?[a]

فَمَنْ أَظْلَمُ مِمَّنِ ٱفْتَرَىٰ عَلَى ٱللَّهِ كَذِبًا أَوْ كَذَّبَ بِـَٔايَٰتِهِ ۚ أُوْلَٰٓئِكَ يَنَالُهُمْ نَصِيبُهُم مِّنَ ٱلْكِتَٰبِ ۖ حَتَّىٰٓ إِذَا جَآءَتْهُمْ رُسُلُنَا يَتَوَفَّوْنَهُمْ قَالُوٓاْ أَيْنَ مَا كُنتُمْ تَدْعُونَ مِن دُونِ ٱللَّهِ ۖ قَالُواْ ضَلُّواْ عَنَّا وَشَهِدُواْ عَلَىٰٓ أَنفُسِهِمْ أَنَّهُمْ كَانُواْ كَٰفِرِينَ ۝

[a] Whenever a man rejects the truth, he does so imagining that he has something to back him up. He may rely on wealth and power, or on respect and popularity. He may feel confident that all his personal matters are in such good order that rejection of the Truth will not harm him in any way. He may take pride in having the intelligence to find eloquent expressions with which to present his own ideas, as if they came directly from God. But these are all great misapprehensions. He has erroneously regarded as supports—on which he could depend for salvation—the things actually meant for his trial.

But on Doomsday, when all these false props desert him, it will not be difficult for him to understand that he was actually rejecting the Truth merely due to ignorance, though he kept quoting 'principles' to justify his rejection.

³⁸ God will say, 'Enter the Fire and join the bands of jinn and men that have gone before you.' Every time a host enters [the fire], it will curse its fellow-host, then, when they are all gathered there, the last of them will say of the first, 'Our Lord, it was they who led us astray: give them double punishment in the Fire,'—God will say, 'Every one of you will have double punishment, though you do not know it'—³⁹ then the preceding one will say to the succeeding one, You are no better than us: so taste the punishment you have earned.' ^a

قَالَ ٱدْخُلُواْ فِىٓ أُمَمٍ قَدْ خَلَتْ مِن قَبْلِكُم مِّنَ ٱلْجِنِّ وَٱلْإِنسِ فِى ٱلنَّارِ كُلَّمَا دَخَلَتْ أُمَّةٌ لَّعَنَتْ أُخْتَهَا حَتَّىٰٓ إِذَا ٱدَّارَكُواْ فِيهَا جَمِيعًا قَالَتْ أُخْرَىٰهُمْ لِأُولَىٰهُمْ رَبَّنَا هَـٰٓؤُلَآءِ أَضَلُّونَا فَـَٔاتِهِمْ عَذَابًا ضِعْفًا مِّنَ ٱلنَّارِ قَالَ لِكُلٍّ ضِعْفٌ وَلَـٰكِن لَّا تَعْلَمُونَ ۝ وَقَالَتْ أُولَىٰهُمْ لِأُخْرَىٰهُمْ فَمَا كَانَ لَكُمْ عَلَيْنَا مِن فَضْلٍ فَذُوقُواْ ٱلْعَذَابَ بِمَا كُنتُمْ تَكْسِبُونَ ۝

^a In this verse 'community'(*ummah*) means those leaders who misguide and 'fellow community' *(ukht)* means the misguided general public. In the Hereafter when the wrong-thinking leaders and their misguided followers from the general public are cast into Hell, this will present a great lesson-giving scene. In the world they posed as each other's well-wishers and as being ready to make sacrifices for each other. Such leaders used to respect each and every wish of the general public and the general public made heroes of their leaders. But, when they are trapped in the fire of Hell, all the artificial veils will drop from their eyes. Then everybody will be seen in his true colours. The followers will say to their leaders, 'May you be accursed! How terrible was your leadership which showed us false spectacles and thereafter thrust us into such horrible affliction!' In reply to this, the leaders will say, 'You wanted a religion to your liking and finding such a religion with us, you rushed towards us. Otherwise, during that very period there were such servants of God as were calling you towards the path of real success. You heard their call, but did not pay attention to them.'

The leaders will tell their followers, 'You are in no way better than us. We established leadership in pursuance of our desires, and you followed us for the sake of your desires. So, in point of fact, both of us are in the same position. So, here you will be liable to receive the same punishment as has been laid down for us in accordance with our deeds.' ▶

⁴⁰ The gates of Heaven shall not be opened for those who rejected Our signs and arrogantly spurned them; nor shall they enter Paradise until a camel shall pass through the eye of a needle. That is how We repay the evil-doers—⁴¹ Hell shall be their bed, and over them will be coverings of fire—thus shall We reward the wrongdoers.ᵃ

إِنَّ ٱلَّذِينَ كَذَّبُوا بِآيَٰتِنَا وَٱسْتَكْبَرُوا عَنْهَا لَا تُفَتَّحُ لَهُمْ أَبْوَٰبُ ٱلسَّمَآءِ وَلَا يَدْخُلُونَ ٱلْجَنَّةَ حَتَّىٰ يَلِجَ ٱلْجَمَلُ فِي سَمِّ ٱلْخِيَاطِ ۚ وَكَذَٰلِكَ نَجْزِي ٱلْمُجْرِمِينَ ۝ لَهُم مِّن جَهَنَّمَ مِهَادٌ وَمِن فَوْقِهِمْ غَوَاشٍ ۚ وَكَذَٰلِكَ نَجْزِي ٱلظَّٰلِمِينَ ۝

The followers will tell God that the leaders had misled them and as such the latter should be given double the punishment that they received. The reply will be that the leaders were already being given double punishment but that they did not know it. The fact is that in Hell whatever punishment is given to anybody will be felt to be so severe that he will think that nobody else is in such terrible agony. Everyone will feel himself the worst afflicted.

In the world self-interested leaders and self-interested followers are inter-linked in strong bonds of friendship. Each group expresses fine opinions about the other, and each finds words for the good of the other. But, in the Hereafter the one group will hate the other. Each will try to push the other towards the direst of fates.

ᵃ Why is it that when God's missionaries give the call to Truth, the egotism of their addressees prevents them from accepting their call? The reason for this is that the call-givers' sole strength is argument, while the addressee has the support of material glories. The call-giver stands on the basis of argument, while the addressees stand on a tangible material basis. The force of argument is both intangible and invisible. This difference fosters egotism, causing people to consider the call-giver lower in status than themselves and giving them a 'reason' to ignore him.

The admission of such people to the mercy of God is as impossible as the passing of a camel through the eye of a needle. They ignore God, so God ignores them. God gave them glimpses of Himself through the call-giver; He appeared before them in the form of arguments; but they attached no importance to these signs and refused to bow down before them. How can such people have a share in God's bounty?

⁴²But those who believed and did good deeds—and We do not burden any soul with more than it can bear—such are the heirs of the Garden and there they will remain forever. ⁴³And We shall remove whatever rancour may be in their hearts. At their feet shall flow rivers. And they shall say, 'All praise belongs to God who has guided us to this. Had God not guided us, we would never have found the way. The messengers of our Lord brought the Truth.' A voice will call out to them, 'This is the Garden which you have inherited by your labours.'ᵃ

وَٱلَّذِينَ ءَامَنُواْ وَعَمِلُواْ ٱلصَّٰلِحَٰتِ لَا نُكَلِّفُ نَفْسًا إِلَّا وُسْعَهَآ أُوْلَٰٓئِكَ أَصْحَٰبُ ٱلْجَنَّةِ هُمْ فِيهَا خَٰلِدُونَ ۝ وَنَزَعْنَا مَا فِى صُدُورِهِم مِّنْ غِلٍّ تَجْرِى مِن تَحْتِهِمُ ٱلْأَنْهَٰرُ وَقَالُواْ ٱلْحَمْدُ لِلَّهِ ٱلَّذِى هَدَىٰنَا لِهَٰذَا وَمَا كُنَّا لِنَهْتَدِىَ لَوْلَآ أَنْ هَدَىٰنَا ٱللَّهُ لَقَدْ جَآءَتْ رُسُلُ رَبِّنَا بِٱلْحَقِّ وَنُودُوٓاْ أَن تِلْكُمُ ٱلْجَنَّةُ أُورِثْتُمُوهَا بِمَا كُنتُمْ تَعْمَلُونَ ۝

ᵃ The position in Hell will be that people who were friends in this world will hate and curse each other. But, the atmosphere in Heaven will be entirely different. Here, all people's hearts will be open to each other. Fountains of love and well-wishing for others will emerge from every heart. For the man in Hell, his past will be a bitter memory, while for the man in Heaven his past will be a pleasant memory.

The future life of evil people will start with their hearts being a graveyard of regret and frustration. Their past will be solely composed of bitter memories. In contrast to this, the condition of good people will be that their minds will be full of the remembrance of God on whom they had rightly relied. They will be happy to find the intimation given by the flag-bearers of Truth to be absolutely correct. They will thankfully recognize God's grace in His having blessed them and inspired them to support those who summoned them to accept the Truth.

44 The people of the Garden will call out to the people of the Fire, 'We have found that what our Lord promised us is true. Have you, too, found that what your Lord promised you is true?' They will say, 'Yes, we have!' Then a crier shall call out among them saying, 'The curse of God is upon the wrongdoers— 45 who turned people away from the path of God and sought to make it appear crooked, and who denied the Hereafter.'[a]

وَنَادَىٰٓ أَصْحَٰبُ ٱلْجَنَّةِ أَصْحَٰبَ ٱلنَّارِ أَن قَدْ وَجَدْنَا مَا وَعَدَنَا رَبُّنَا حَقًّا فَهَلْ وَجَدتُّم مَّا وَعَدَ رَبُّكُمْ حَقًّا ۖ قَالُوا۟ نَعَمْ ۚ فَأَذَّنَ مُؤَذِّنٌۢ بَيْنَهُمْ أَن لَّعْنَةُ ٱللَّهِ عَلَى ٱلظَّٰلِمِينَ ۝ ٱلَّذِينَ يَصُدُّونَ عَن سَبِيلِ ٱللَّهِ وَيَبْغُونَهَا عِوَجًا وَهُم بِٱلْءَاخِرَةِ كَٰفِرُونَ ۝

---

[a] The question was asked in early times how with Heaven and Hell being far away from each other—heaven above the skies and Hell at the lowest possible level—it would be possible for the voices of the people in heaven to reach the people in hell. But, in this age of mass communication, this question has become a relative matter. Now, man has come to know that it is possible to see far-away things and to hear voices from far away. What was not clear in ancient times has now become fully understandable in the light of modern experience and observation. This indicates that if any statement of the Quran defies analysis in the light of today's knowledge, no conclusion should be drawn about it. It is quite possible that, with the increase in knowledge, it may become an accepted fact tomorrow, though today it seems to be strange and unknowable.

However, this does not mean that, in the Hereafter, a connection will be established between the respective inmates of heaven and hell by means of modern radio or television. It only means that modern discoveries have shown that, in this universe of God, certain arrangements make it possible for two men situated far away from each other to see and talk to each other without any difficulty.

A man can feel the weight of an argument only if he is serious and sincere about it. Those who do not attach significance to the Hereafter, are unable to see the point of arguments about the after-life. The reality of the Hereafter is supported by extremely strong arguments, but with their non-serious minds they can only ferret out defects in it. They produce different types of objections to it and, as a result, not only do they themselves entertain different suspicions and doubts about it, but they incline others towards incredulity. Such people are, in the eyes of God, guilty in the extreme. In the Hereafter, they will suffer the scourge of God, though in this world they may consider themselves entitled to His grace. ▶

46 A barrier will divide the two groups, and on the heights there will be men who recognize each group by their marks. They will call out to the people of the Garden, 'Peace be with you.' They will not have yet entered, but they will be hoping [to do so], 47 and when they turn their eyes towards the inmates of the Fire, they will say, 'Our Lord, do not include us among the wrongdoers!'[a] 48 And the people of the heights[b] will call out to men they recognize by their marks, 'What use have your great numbers and your false pride been?

وَبَيْنَهُمَا حِجَابٌ وَعَلَى ٱلْأَعْرَافِ رِجَالٌ يَعْرِفُونَ كُلًّا بِسِيمَٰهُمْ وَنَادَوْاْ أَصْحَٰبَ ٱلْجَنَّةِ أَن سَلَٰمٌ عَلَيْكُمْ لَمْ يَدْخُلُوهَا وَهُمْ يَطْمَعُونَ ۞ وَإِذَا صُرِفَتْ أَبْصَٰرُهُمْ تِلْقَآءَ أَصْحَٰبِ ٱلنَّارِ قَالُواْ رَبَّنَا لَا تَجْعَلْنَا مَعَ ٱلْقَوْمِ ٱلظَّٰلِمِينَ ۞ وَنَادَىٰٓ أَصْحَٰبُ ٱلْأَعْرَافِ رِجَالًا يَعْرِفُونَهُم بِسِيمَٰهُمْ قَالُواْ مَآ أَغْنَىٰ عَنكُمْ جَمْعُكُمْ وَمَا كُنتُمْ تَسْتَكْبِرُونَ ۞

Howsoever strong and convincing an argument may be, doubt can always be cast upon its veracity by clever utterances. People in general are unable to differentiate between a real argument and sophistry. So, they move away from Truth on hearing such talk. But those who, in spite of being capable of understanding the Truth, alienate people from it by indulging in such clever utterances, will be far removed from God's grace on the Day of Reckoning.

[a] It happens in the world that believers and those who deny the truth alike are recipients of both the bounties and the afflictions sent down by God. But, it will not be so in the Hereafter. There, a barrier will be set up between the two. There, the joys of the bounties savoured by the people of Paradise will not reach the people of Hell, and similarly the woes afflicting the people of Hell will not reach the people of Heaven.

[b] According to al-Qurtubi, 'the people of the heights' in this verse refers to shuhada'. That is, those special servants of God who, in the service of the religion of God, were witness to the deeds of the nations of the world. Some accepted their call, while others rejected it. These preachers of the divine message have been mentioned in the Quran in many different terms such as 'warner', 'bearer of glad tidings', 'the caller', etc. This group, originally formed of the prophets, was later made up of those special servants of God who followed the example of the prophets and performed dawah for the people of their times.

The Final Judgement on human beings, which is going to take place in the hereafter, will be based on the task performed by the witnesses (shahadah) for the people of the world. This task of witness divides the people of the world into two groups: one which accepts the divine message and the other which rejects it. On the Day of Judgement these two opposing groups will be separated from each other. ▶

49 See! are these not the people you sworn would never earn God's mercy? "Enter the Garden! No fear shall come upon you nor shall you grieve."' 50 The people of the Fire shall call out to the people of heaven, 'Pour out some water on us, or give us something out of that which God has bestowed upon you.' But the blessed will reply, 'God has forbidden all that to those who denied the truth.

أَهَٰٓؤُلَآءِ ٱلَّذِينَ أَقْسَمْتُمْ لَا يَنَالُهُمُ ٱللَّهُ بِرَحْمَةٍ ٱدْخُلُوا۟ ٱلْجَنَّةَ لَا خَوْفٌ عَلَيْكُمْ وَلَآ أَنتُمْ تَحْزَنُونَ ۞ وَنَادَىٰٓ أَصْحَٰبُ ٱلنَّارِ أَصْحَٰبَ ٱلْجَنَّةِ أَنْ أَفِيضُوا۟ عَلَيْنَا مِنَ ٱلْمَآءِ أَوْ مِمَّا رَزَقَكُمُ ٱللَّهُ قَالُوٓا۟ إِنَّ ٱللَّهَ حَرَّمَهُمَا عَلَى ٱلْكَٰفِرِينَ ۞

Then according to their deeds, they will be judged and will be destined to two different sets of consequences.

Though this judgement will be entirely God's judgement, the announcement of it will be made by those special servants of God who had undertaken the task of calling people to God. This will be a matter of a great honour to them. On the Day of Judgement, high platforms will be raised for 'the people of the heights' to stand on. From there they will be able to see everyone, and will pronounce God's judgement to the people.

Those who bore witness to people (shuhada') and those who called people to truth (du'at), strove very hard in the world to convey the message of God to people. They dedicated their entire lives to this mission, as if it were their own personal work. For this reason, they will be honoured on the Day of Judgement by being asked to announce the final result of their call to the people to truth. They ranked high in the world according to their mission, and they will be referred to as high-ranked on the Day of Judgement, according to the result of their actions.

The conveying of the message of Truth to everyone, the responsibility for which has been placed on the Muslims, is not like an optional subject, which you may either take up or make some excuse to leave off. This is a responsibility of such a nature that it has to be discharged at all costs.

No excuse made by the followers of the Prophet will be heard and found acceptable by God. Even other religious acts and deeds will not be enough for the salvation of the believers, if they have ignored the responsibility of conveying the message of Truth to all the people.

Thousands of men and women are dying every day without having had the message of God conveyed to them; without having had the opportunity to accept it, they have missed their chance of improving their lives in the Hereafter. In such a situation it is the grave responsibility of the believers to desist from making excuses and seriously take up the mission of proclaiming the divine truth.

51 Who treated religion as a pastime and an idle sport and whom the life of the world had beguiled.' On that Day We shall forget them, as they forgot their meeting of that Day with Us, for they denied Our revelations.[a]

اَلَّذِينَ اتَّخَذُوا دِينَهُمْ لَهْوًا وَلَعِبًا وَغَرَّتْهُمُ الْحَيَوٰةُ الدُّنْيَا ۚ فَالْيَوْمَ نَنسَىٰهُمْ كَمَا نَسُوا لِقَآءَ يَوْمِهِمْ هَٰذَا وَمَا كَانُوا بِـَٔايَٰتِنَا يَجْحَدُونَ ۝

[a] The world offers a spread of two types of food—one worldly and the other other-worldly. There is one kind of man whose soul derives nourishment from seeing his 'self' receive prominence. He feels very happy when he is surrounded by worldly glories. He considers himself successful on procuring and becoming the owner of worldly material goods. This man is completely forgetful of God and the life of the Hereafter. If anything relating to God is brought to his attention, he will consider it insignificant and ignore it. He will deal with it superficially, as if it were not a serious matter but a trivial charade.

For such a person there will be no share in the bounties of Hereafter. He has fostered such a soul in himself as could derive nourishment only from worldly materials. Then, how can his soul be nourished by the things of the Hereafter? For one who has not lived for the Hereafter in his life today cannot be held deserving for God's blessings in the Hereafter.

The other kind of person is one who has been lost in unseen realities; whose soul could relish the remembrance of the Hereafter; whose bread and butter will be living in God and breathing in the atmosphere of God. This will be the man for whom the Hereafter will be a place where he will find all the good things he desires. But just as he had found God in the world of the unseen, so will he find God in the seen world of the Hereafter.

Why does it happen that, in this world of God, man forgets God? The reason is that God makes His appearance felt in the world through signs which come within human grasp only on reflection. Man leans towards outward things and ignores the signs pointing to God. But any such action amounts to forsaking the Hereafter for the sake of the world. And one who takes no account of the Hereafter in the life before death will be deprived of the Hereafter even in the life after death.

When people show blatant disregard for something which has been presented to them by God as the Truth, they in effect are treating God Himself as being so unimportant as to be undeserving of any serious consideration. They may possibly be deceived by the divine forces underlying Truth remaining invisible, but they nevertheless risk being ignored by God on the Day of Reckoning, just as they — imagining that no harm could come to them thereby—ignored God in this life.

⁵² And surely We have brought them a Book which We have expounded with knowledge, a guide and a mercy for those who believe. ⁵³ Do they wait for the fulfillment of that of which it warns? On the Day when that fulfillment comes, those who had neglected it before will say, 'The messengers of our Lord did indeed bring the truth. Have we then any intercessors who would intercede for us? Or, could we be sent back so that we might act differently from the way we used to?' They have indeed ruined their souls and what they invented has forsaken them.ᵃ

وَلَقَدْ جِئْنَـٰهُم بِكِتَـٰبٍ فَصَّلْنَـٰهُ عَلَىٰ عِلْمٍ هُدًى وَرَحْمَةً لِّقَوْمٍ يُؤْمِنُونَ ۝ هَلْ يَنظُرُونَ إِلَّا تَأْوِيلَهُۥ ۚ يَوْمَ يَأْتِى تَأْوِيلُهُۥ يَقُولُ ٱلَّذِينَ نَسُوهُ مِن قَبْلُ قَدْ جَآءَتْ رُسُلُ رَبِّنَا بِٱلْحَقِّ فَهَل لَّنَا مِن شُفَعَآءَ فَيَشْفَعُواْ لَنَآ أَوْ نُرَدُّ فَنَعْمَلَ غَيْرَ ٱلَّذِى كُنَّا نَعْمَلُ ۚ قَدْ خَسِرُوٓاْ أَنفُسَهُمْ وَضَلَّ عَنْهُم مَّا كَانُواْ يَفْتَرُونَ ۝

ᵃ The Quran warns mankind of the life after death. It tells of the reckoning of the Hereafter. But, man is not awakened. These intimations of the Quran are not merely 'news,' but the inevitable realities of the universe. However, they have not yet appeared as factual events. They are still hidden in the veil of the future. Unmindfully, man thinks that this is nothing but meaningless talk and ignores it, considering it unimportant.

But these messages are on behalf of God who is all-knowing. Those who have not vitiated their nature and whose eyes are not covered by artificial veils will find the tenor of the Quran to be in consonance with the voice of their hearts. They will find that this is the very thing which their nature was already in search of. For them the Quran will become a treasure of life and Faith.

The position of those who do not take the warnings of the Quran seriously will be entirely different. They will linger in this slumber until that event breaks upon them of which they are being warned. At that time, man will suddenly come to know that he has become completely helpless. The problems to which he gave importance and in which he was therefore embroiled will now appear to be baseless. The things on which he was relying will have ceased to be with him. The rosy hopes on which he was living will all prove to be false. ▶

The Heights

⁵⁴ Your Lord is God, who created the heavens and the earth in six Days [periods] and then settled Himself firmly on the throne. He throws the veil of night over the day, each seeking the other in rapid succession. It was He who created the sun, the moon and the stars, and made them subservient to His will. His is the creation, His the command. Blessed be God, Lord of the universe!ᵃ

إِنَّ رَبَّكُمُ ٱللَّهُ ٱلَّذِى خَلَقَ ٱلسَّمَٰوَٰتِ وَٱلْأَرْضَ فِى سِتَّةِ أَيَّامٍ ثُمَّ ٱسْتَوَىٰ عَلَى ٱلْعَرْشِ يُغْشِى ٱلَّيْلَ ٱلنَّهَارَ يَطْلُبُهُۥ حَثِيثًا وَٱلشَّمْسَ وَٱلْقَمَرَ وَٱلنُّجُومَ مُسَخَّرَٰتٍۭ بِأَمْرِهِۦٓ أَلَا لَهُ ٱلْخَلْقُ وَٱلْأَمْرُ تَبَارَكَ ٱللَّهُ رَبُّ ٱلْعَٰلَمِينَ

The belief in the Hereafter appears to be an abstract idea. So, man does not become serious about it. But, in the life after death, when the Hereafter with all its terror will be thrust upon man, everyone will be compelled at that time to accept what he had not earlier been ready to accept. Man will then come to know that what he was being told earlier in the language of arguments was absolute fact and that, not being serious about it, he could not grasp its significance.

When all those things on which he was relying in the world, leave man in the lurch, he will want to be sent back to earth, so that he may lead his life in a proper manner. But such an opportunity does not come to anyone twice.

ᵃ God is the Creator of the earth, the sky and all things. This creation could have been haphazard, i.e. all things could have been created, then left in confusion. But He did not do so. He linked all things in an absolutely perfect, well-organised and wisely regulated system, and activated them in such a way that everything kept working exactly in the manner in which it ought to, if it had to serve the collective interest.

Man is also a small part of this world. Then, what should be his role in this well-formed environment? His role should be the same as that of all other things. He should devote himself to the Creator's plan, in the way that the whole Universe has surrendered itself to this plan in all obedience.

All things of the universe take part in the plan of God with the utmost degree of efficiency (*ihsan*). So, man should also devote himself to this to the same degree. Here nothing exceeds the prescribed limits. So, it is necessary also for man not to exceed the limits of justice and Truth prescribed by God. Furthermore, man has the additional attributes of the power of speech and consciousness. So, even at the level of speech and consciousness, the expression of his surrender to his Lord is also necessary. The recognition and realisation of God should be so deeply embedded in man that they come to be expressed again and again. He should call out to God as a subject calls out to his Creator and Lord. He should be so conscious of God's godhead that nothing except God should remain at the centre of his hopes or fears. He should fear only God and link his hopes to Him alone. To associate one's fears and hopes with God is the ultimate stage of obedience to God.

⁵⁵ Call on your Lord with humility and in secret—He does not love the transgressors: ⁵⁶ do not spread corruption on the earth after it has been set in order—pray to Him with fear and hope, God's mercy is close to those who do good.ᵃ

ادْعُوا رَبَّكُمْ تَضَرُّعًا وَخُفْيَةً ۚ إِنَّهُ لَا يُحِبُّ الْمُعْتَدِينَ ۝ وَلَا تُفْسِدُوا فِي الْأَرْضِ بَعْدَ إِصْلَاحِهَا وَادْعُوهُ خَوْفًا وَطَمَعًا ۚ إِنَّ رَحْمَتَ اللَّهِ قَرِيبٌ مِّنَ الْمُحْسِنِينَ ۝

ᵃ The greatest achievement of man is that he should be able to attain God's mercy. But the grace of God falls to the lot of those who associate themselves with God to such an extent that all their emotions without exception are directed towards Him. They should call out only to Him and behave with humility towards Him alone. They should entertain hopes of receiving things from Him, and fear Him alone lest things be taken away. People who do so seek closeness to God and God awards them a place close to Him.

57 It is God who sends forth the winds as harbingers of His mercy, and when they have gathered up the heavy clouds, We drive them on to a dead land where We cause rain to fall, bringing out all kinds of fruit, just as We will raise the dead to life. Perhaps you will take heed. 58 Vegetation comes out of good land in abundance by the will of its Lord, but out of bad land only scantily. Thus We explain Our signs in diverse ways for those who give thanks.[a]

وَهُوَ ٱلَّذِى يُرْسِلُ ٱلرِّيَاحَ بُشْرًۢا بَيْنَ يَدَىْ رَحْمَتِهِۦ حَتَّىٰٓ إِذَآ أَقَلَّتْ سَحَابًا ثِقَالًا سُقْنَٰهُ لِبَلَدٍ مَّيِّتٍ فَأَنزَلْنَا بِهِ ٱلْمَآءَ فَأَخْرَجْنَا بِهِۦ مِن كُلِّ ٱلثَّمَرَٰتِ ۚ كَذَٰلِكَ نُخْرِجُ ٱلْمَوْتَىٰ لَعَلَّكُمْ تَذَكَّرُونَ ۝ وَٱلْبَلَدُ ٱلطَّيِّبُ يَخْرُجُ نَبَاتُهُۥ بِإِذْنِ رَبِّهِۦ ۖ وَٱلَّذِى خَبُثَ لَا يَخْرُجُ إِلَّا نَكِدًا ۚ كَذَٰلِكَ نُصَرِّفُ ٱلْءَايَٰتِ لِقَوْمٍ يَشْكُرُونَ ۝

[a] God has made the world in such a way that its material occurrences symbolize its spiritual aspects.

When rain falls anywhere, the water reaches every part of that place. But in respect of its use, conditions in different lands vary. When one region gets water, lush green fields emerge from it. There may be another region which, even after getting rain, remains unaffected, and nothing but wild bushes will grow there.

The same is the position of that spiritual rainfall which comes down on behalf of God in the shape of His guidance. The message of this guidance reaches the ears of every man but its benefits accrue to everybody according to his receptivity. One who is receptive to accepting the Truth, derives full advantage from it; he gets a new lease of life from it; his nature is suddenly activated. His contact with his Almighty Lord is established. His parched soul blooms with divine inspiration.

Just the opposite is the condition of the person who has lost his natural receptivity. The rainfall of guidance, in spite of its immense possibilities, does not benefit him at all; he remains as dry as he was earlier. If at all there is any crop, it is only a scanty growth of wild bushes. The rainfall of guidance breeds in him jealousy, haughtiness, a tendency to employ meaningless sophistry, and opposition to the truth. Thus he fails to accept the truth and support it. In order to absorb the rainwater, the land must necessarily be dry. If the land is not dry, the rain water will simply pass over it, and will not be absorbed in it. In the same way, the guidance of God becomes rooted only in that man who is desirous of it; one who has emptied his soul of the dross of this world. Unlike him, one who is careless of God's guidance and whose heart is engrossed in other interests and other glories may encounter God's guidance, but it will not permeate him. It will not become the nutrition of his soul; it will not water the land of his soul and help to grow the garden of God in it.

⁵⁹ We sent Noah to his people. He said, 'O my people, worship God; you have no other god but He. I fear for you the punishment of a dreadful Day,' ⁶⁰ but the leading men of his people said, 'Truly, we see that you are obviously lost in error!' ⁶¹ Said [Noah], 'O my people! I am not in error. Indeed, I am a messenger from the Lord of the Worlds, ⁶² I am conveying my Lord's messages to you and giving you sincere advice. I know things from God that you do not. ⁶³ Do you find it so strange that a message should come from your Lord through a man from among yourselves, so that he may warn you and so that you may fear God and be shown mercy?' ⁶⁴ But they denied him, so We saved him and those with him in the Ark, and We drowned those who rejected Our signs. They were indeed a blind people.ᵃ

لَقَدْ أَرْسَلْنَا نُوحًا إِلَىٰ قَوْمِهِۦ فَقَالَ يَٰقَوْمِ ٱعْبُدُوا۟ ٱللَّهَ مَا لَكُم مِّنْ إِلَٰهٍ غَيْرُهُۥٓ إِنِّىٓ أَخَافُ عَلَيْكُمْ عَذَابَ يَوْمٍ عَظِيمٍ ۝ قَالَ ٱلْمَلَأُ مِن قَوْمِهِۦٓ إِنَّا لَنَرَىٰكَ فِى ضَلَٰلٍ مُّبِينٍ ۝ قَالَ يَٰقَوْمِ لَيْسَ بِى ضَلَٰلَةٌ وَلَٰكِنِّى رَسُولٌ مِّن رَّبِّ ٱلْعَٰلَمِينَ ۝ أُبَلِّغُكُمْ رِسَٰلَٰتِ رَبِّى وَأَنصَحُ لَكُمْ وَأَعْلَمُ مِنَ ٱللَّهِ مَا لَا تَعْلَمُونَ ۝ أَوَعَجِبْتُمْ أَن جَآءَكُمْ ذِكْرٌ مِّن رَّبِّكُمْ عَلَىٰ رَجُلٍ مِّنكُمْ لِيُنذِرَكُمْ وَلِتَتَّقُوا۟ وَلَعَلَّكُمْ تُرْحَمُونَ ۝ فَكَذَّبُوهُ فَأَنجَيْنَٰهُ وَٱلَّذِينَ مَعَهُۥ فِى ٱلْفُلْكِ وَأَغْرَقْنَا ٱلَّذِينَ كَذَّبُوا۟ بِـَٔايَٰتِنَآ إِنَّهُمْ كَانُوا۟ قَوْمًا عَمِينَ ۝

ᵃ After Adam, for about one thousand years his descendants adhered to the monotheistic faith (faith in the oneness of God). Thereafter, according to a tradition as told by 'Abdullah ibn 'Abbas, people started making the likenesses of their ancient great ones, so that the memory of their feats and their prayers would remain fresh in their minds. The names of these revered figures were Wudd, Suwa', Yaguth, Ya'uq and Nasr. Gradually, these great men acquired the status of gods among these people who inhabited ancient Iraq. When this evil increased to this extent in them, God sent Noah to reform them, appointing him as His Prophet. But they refused to accept Noah. They were not ready to adopt the way of righteousness and fear of God (taqwa).

According to the Quran, the reason for this refusal was that it was very difficult for them to understand that a man who was apparently like them had been selected to deliver God's message on His behalf. Compared to the great men whose religion they were ostensibly following and whose greatness had become recognised in the annals of history, Noah, their contemporary, with no glory attached to his name, appeared to them to be just an ordinary man. So, his community refused to accept him. They did not hesitate to call the prophet of the time foolish and misguided, because according to them, he had deviated from the religion of their great ones. The well-wishing on the part of Noah, the strength of his arguments, his reasoning, his being staunchly on the path of Truth—none of these things could influence them. ▶

⁶⁵ To the people of 'Ad We sent their brother, Hud.[a] He said, 'O my people, worship God, you have no other god but He. Then will you not be God-fearing?' ⁶⁶ The leading men of his people who refused to acknowledge the truth, said, 'We can see you are a foolish man, and we think you are lying.' ⁶⁷ He said, 'My people, I am by no means a fool, but rather am a messenger from the Lord of the Universe, ⁶⁸ I am conveying my Lord's messages to you and I am your sincere and honest adviser.[b]

۞ وَإِلَىٰ عَادٍ أَخَاهُمْ هُودًا ۗ قَالَ يَٰقَوْمِ ٱعْبُدُوا۟ ٱللَّهَ مَا لَكُم مِّنْ إِلَٰهٍ غَيْرُهُۥ ۚ أَفَلَا تَتَّقُونَ ۝ قَالَ ٱلْمَلَأُ ٱلَّذِينَ كَفَرُوا۟ مِن قَوْمِهِۦٓ إِنَّا لَنَرَىٰكَ فِى سَفَاهَةٍ وَإِنَّا لَنَظُنُّكَ مِنَ ٱلْكَٰذِبِينَ ۝ قَالَ يَٰقَوْمِ لَيْسَ بِى سَفَاهَةٌ وَلَٰكِنِّى رَسُولٌ مِّن رَّبِّ ٱلْعَٰلَمِينَ ۝ أُبَلِّغُكُمْ رِسَٰلَٰتِ رَبِّى وَأَنَا۠ لَكُمْ نَاصِحٌ أَمِينٌ ۝

When Noah had fully conveyed the divine message, and was rejected by the people, the community was drowned in the great flood. The reason for this punishment was that they had falsified and denied God's signs. They wanted God's message to be conveyed to them through an established personality instead of an 'ordinary person.' But, in the eyes of God, this was blindness. God has given man insight so that he should recognise the Truth in the shape of 'signs' and not through any tangible object. Those who do not recognise Truth in the shape of signs, are in the eyes of God blind in spite of having eyes. Such people have no share in the grace of God.

[a] Iram, Noah's grandson was one of the believers who were saved in Noah's Ark. He was the forefather of a tribe known as 'Ad. These people, settled in Yemen, were initially adherents of the religion of Noah. But later on when they strayed from the right path, God appointed Hud to be their prophet. But in the eyes of the leaders of the community, he did not appear to possess that greatness which they thought should inhere in prophets. So they felt that either he was a fool or that he was making a false claim.

[b] Literally 'I am your well-wisher.' This utterance of the prophet shows that the relationship between the call-giver and his addressees is not that of a rival or a competitor. It is a relationship of well-wishing and trust. The call-giver should be such that he should have nothing in his heart except good wishes for his addressees. Howsoever rude and unpleasant the behaviour that he comes across in his addressees may be, the call-giver should remain their well-wisher till the last moment. Then, while delivering his message, he should not have the feeling that he is bestowing upon another something which belongs to him. He should feel rather that it belongs to others and that he is holding it in trust for them, and that, by delivering it, he is relieving himself of a great responsibility.

⁶⁹ Do you find it strange that a Message should come from your Lord, through one of your own men, to warn you? Remember how He made you successors of Noah's people, and increased you greatly in stature. Remember the favours of God, so that you may prosper.'

⁷⁰ They said, 'Have you come to tell us to serve God alone and to forsake the gods our forefathers served? Bring us then what you threaten us with, if you are truthful.'ᵃ

أَوَعَجِبْتُمْ أَن جَآءَكُمْ ذِكْرٌ مِّن رَّبِّكُمْ عَلَىٰ رَجُلٍ مِّنكُمْ لِيُنذِرَكُمْ وَٱذْكُرُوٓاْ إِذْ جَعَلَكُمْ خُلَفَآءَ مِنۢ بَعْدِ قَوْمِ نُوحٍ وَزَادَكُمْ فِى ٱلْخَلْقِ بَصْۜطَةً فَٱذْكُرُوٓاْ ءَالَآءَ ٱللَّهِ لَعَلَّكُمْ تُفْلِحُونَ ۝ قَالُوٓاْ أَجِئْتَنَا لِنَعْبُدَ ٱللَّهَ وَحْدَهُۥ وَنَذَرَ مَا كَانَ يَعْبُدُ ءَابَآؤُنَا فَأْتِنَا بِمَا تَعِدُنَآ إِن كُنتَ مِنَ ٱلصَّٰدِقِينَ ۝

ᵃ The basis of the missionary call of the prophets has always been to remind man of the bounties conferred on him, and to warn him that if he did not remain grateful to God, he would have to suffer the scourge of God. Communal and material issues are never made the topics of their missionary discourses by prophets. They try their best to ensure that in the discussions between them and their addressees nothing but truths of real concern are taken up; their community should see them as preachers of the cause of the one God and the Hereafter and in no other form.

'Remember the favours of God, so that you may prosper.' This shows that the bounties of the Hereafter are merited only by one who has admitted God's grace in the world. Paradise is the greatest expression of God's grace and bountifulness. So, the Paradise of the Hereafter will be attained by one who has found and recognised God's attribute of grace and magnanimity. This realisation is the real price of Paradise.

[71] He said, 'Your Lord's wrath and indignation have already fallen upon you. Would you dispute with me about mere names, which you and your fathers have invented, and for which God has revealed no authority? Wait then if you will: I am waiting alongside you.' [72] Then We saved him and those who were with him, by Our mercy; We annihilated those who denied Our signs and would not believe.[a]

قَالَ قَدْ وَقَعَ عَلَيْكُم مِّن رَّبِّكُمْ رِجْسٌ وَغَضَبٌ أَتُجَٰدِلُونَنِي فِي أَسْمَآءٍ سَمَّيْتُمُوهَآ أَنتُمْ وَءَابَآؤُكُم مَّا نَزَّلَ ٱللَّهُ بِهَا مِن سُلْطَٰنٍ فَٱنتَظِرُوٓاْ إِنِّي مَعَكُم مِّنَ ٱلْمُنتَظِرِينَ ۝ فَأَنجَيْنَٰهُ وَٱلَّذِينَ مَعَهُۥ بِرَحْمَةٍ مِّنَّا وَقَطَعْنَا دَابِرَ ٱلَّذِينَ كَذَّبُواْ بِـَٔايَٰتِنَا وَمَا كَانُواْ مُؤْمِنِينَ ۝

---

[a] Man is able to imagine virtues or qualities through names. If a good word is attached to a person, he appears to be good and if a bad word is attached to him he appears to be bad. Things or beings other than God who become the centre of the attention of men come to be such because of these names. Certain individuals come to be called by such names as *ghaus-e-pak* (holy hearer of plaints), *ganj bakhsh* (granter of treasure), *gharib nawaz* (benefactor of the poor), or *mushkil kusha* (solver of difficulties). Gradually these names become so attached to their personalities that people start believing that the person called *ghaus* really has the power to hear plaints and pleas; and that the person known as *mushkil kusha* can really solve difficulties. But the truth is that names of this kind are all devised by human beings. There is nobody existing who carries these names. There is no religious or rational argument in their favour.

The above kind of tradition in names is that which is prevalent among the ignorant masses. However, there is a civilized form of this tradition which is popular among educated people. In this, too, extraordinary words are attached to certain personalities, for example, *qudsi sifat* (having the attributes of angels), *mahbub-e-khuda* (beloved of God), *sutun-e-Islam* (pillar of Islam), *najat dehenda-e-millat* (saviour of the community), etc. Gradually, these words become integral parts of the names of the respective persons. People start considering them as being as extraordinary as their conferred names and titles indicate.

Whatever, as a result of long-standing conventions, has acquired the holiness attaching to the past, assumes great importance and loftiness in the eyes of the people. Compared to it, the call of today's preacher appears to be trivial. So, they ignore the present missionary considering him unimportant. They are confident that nothing will harm them, as they consider themselves the inheritors of the glory of their forefathers.

Recklessness in respect of God gradually makes a man insensitive. He does not remain capable of reforming himself through the language of admonition or remembrance. It will be only when he hears the voice of God pronouncing the verdict of divine retribution that he will become aware of his own shortcomings.

73 To the Thamud We sent their brother Salih. He said, 'O my people, worship God; you have no other god but Him. A veritable proof has come to you from your Lord: this is God's she-camel, a sign for you, so let her feed in God's land and do not harm her in any way, or you will be overwhelmed by a painful punishment.[a]

وَإِلَىٰ ثَمُودَ أَخَاهُمْ صَٰلِحًا ۗ قَالَ يَٰقَوْمِ
ٱعْبُدُوا۟ ٱللَّهَ مَا لَكُم مِّنْ إِلَٰهٍ غَيْرُهُۥ ۖ
قَدْ جَآءَتْكُم بَيِّنَةٌ مِّن رَّبِّكُمْ ۖ هَٰذِهِۦ
نَاقَةُ ٱللَّهِ لَكُمْ ءَايَةً ۖ فَذَرُوهَا
تَأْكُلْ فِىٓ أَرْضِ ٱللَّهِ ۖ وَلَا تَمَسُّوهَا
بِسُوٓءٍ فَيَأْخُذَكُمْ عَذَابٌ أَلِيمٌ ٧٣

[a] After the destruction of the 'Ad community, certain righteous people redeemed by God settled in the Hajr, the area in the north west of Arabia. Their race increased and they made immense progress in the fields of agriculture and construction. They constructed palaces in the plains and by chiselling the hills, made stone houses. But later on they fell victim to the evils that generally follow a community's material development and worldly well-being, i.e. debauchery, obliviousness of the Hereafter, heedlessness about the limits laid down by God, self-conceit and disregard for the greatness of God. At this juncture God raised Salih so that he might warn them of the chastisement of God. But they did not accept the admonition. They were not willing to mend their ways. In the universe, where all things are living in complete obedience to God, they opted to live in arrogance and disobey God: where everything strictly observed the limits set by God, man wanted to lead his life by transgressing His limits. Their transgression created disturbances in the reformed world. Therefore, they were held unfit to inhabit the world.

For the purpose of testing the community of Thamud, God assigned a she-camel to them and commanded them not to harm her, or else they would be destroyed. It would have been quite possible for God to appoint a terrifying lion for this purpose. But God appointed a she-camel instead of a lion. The reason for this is that the test of a man's fear of God is always taken at the level of a 'she camel' and not at the level of a 'lion'. In society there are always some people who are like the camel of God. These are the weak individuals who do not have the material strength which could act as a deterrent to oppression. Through these people, God tests the true faith of His people. And the certificates of Heaven and Hell are given on the basis of the results of these tests.

74 Remember when He made you successors to the 'Ad and settled you in the land. You built palaces on its plains and carved houses out of the mountains. Remember God's blessings and do not spread corruption in the land,' 75 but the arrogant leaders of his people said to the believers who were deemed weak, 'Do you know for certain that Salih is one sent from his Lord?' They replied, 'We believe in the message which has been sent through him.' 76 The arrogant leaders said, 'We reject what you believe in.'*a*

وَٱذۡكُرُوٓاْ إِذۡ جَعَلَكُمۡ خُلَفَآءَ مِنۢ بَعۡدِ عَادٖ وَبَوَّأَكُمۡ فِي ٱلۡأَرۡضِ تَتَّخِذُونَ مِن سُهُولِهَا قُصُورٗا وَتَنۡحِتُونَ ٱلۡجِبَالَ بُيُوتٗاۖ فَٱذۡكُرُوٓاْ ءَالَآءَ ٱللَّهِ وَلَا تَعۡثَوۡاْ فِي ٱلۡأَرۡضِ مُفۡسِدِينَ ٧٤ قَالَ ٱلۡمَلَأُ ٱلَّذِينَ ٱسۡتَكۡبَرُواْ مِن قَوۡمِهِۦ لِلَّذِينَ ٱسۡتُضۡعِفُواْ لِمَنۡ ءَامَنَ مِنۡهُمۡ أَتَعۡلَمُونَ أَنَّ صَٰلِحٗا مُّرۡسَلٞ مِّن رَّبِّهِۦۚ قَالُوٓاْ إِنَّا بِمَآ أُرۡسِلَ بِهِۦ مُؤۡمِنُونَ ٧٥ قَالَ ٱلَّذِينَ ٱسۡتَكۡبَرُوٓاْ إِنَّا بِٱلَّذِيٓ ءَامَنتُم بِهِۦ كَٰفِرُونَ ٧٦

a The people of Thamud perfected the art of construction. They were definitely well versed in related branches of knowledge, for example, mathematics, geometry and engineering, otherwise such development could not have been possible. But they were held guilty not of material developments but of spreading disturbance on the earth. This means that God does not prohibit progress within legitimate limits. But, in the matter of how he conducts his life, man should follow the balanced system which God has enforced in the whole universe.

When a prophet comes to the world, he is a controversial figure in his time rather than an established personality. Moreover, he is not surrounded by worldly glories. He is not the occupier of any of the important seats of the time. That is why his contemporaries, unable to understand his prophethood, reject him. They find it difficult to believe that one whom they know as an ordinary person is the very individual whom God has chosen to deliver His message.

'We are believers in that with which he has been sent.' This reply of Salih's companions tells us the difference between them and others. Those who deny the truth looked at the personality of Salih while the believers looked at the real message. Since, for those who denied the truth, no outward glory surrounded the personality of Salih, they ignored him. The believers, on the contrary, saw glimpses of Truth in Salih's message, so they immediately accepted his words and became his companions.

⁷⁷ So they hamstrung the she-camel, and insolently defied the commandment of their Lord, saying, 'O Salih! Bring upon us what you threaten us with if you are indeed a messenger.' ⁷⁸ So the earthquake overwhelmed them, and morning found them prostrate in their dwelling places. ⁷⁹ He left them, saying, 'My people, I delivered my Lord's messages to you and counselled you sincerely, but you do not like sincere advisors.'ᵃ

فَعَقَرُواْ ٱلنَّاقَةَ وَعَتَوْاْ عَنْ أَمْرِ رَبِّهِمْ وَقَالُواْ يَٰصَٰلِحُ ٱئْتِنَا بِمَا تَعِدُنَآ إِن كُنتَ مِنَ ٱلْمُرْسَلِينَ ۝ فَأَخَذَتْهُمُ ٱلرَّجْفَةُ فَأَصْبَحُواْ فِى دَارِهِمْ جَٰثِمِينَ ۝ فَتَوَلَّىٰ عَنْهُمْ وَقَالَ يَٰقَوْمِ لَقَدْ أَبْلَغْتُكُمْ رِسَالَةَ رَبِّى وَنَصَحْتُ لَكُمْ وَلَٰكِن لَّا تُحِبُّونَ ٱلنَّٰصِحِينَ ۝

ᵃ Truth always reveals itself on the strength of arguments and not on the strength of worldly glories. Those who are capable of seeing the Truth in the shape of arguments immediately find it, while those perpetually awed by outward glories remain doubtful. They never receive God's guidance to become supporters of truth.

The killer of Salih's she-camel was an arrogant member of that community. But this action was attributed to the entire community and it was said, 'They hamstrung the she-camel.' This shows that if one member among a group performs a bad deed and other people do not condemn such deeds, all of them are treated as a party to this criminal action.

The community which succumbs to desire is not at all impressed by realistic talk. It is not prepared to support anyone who invites its members to engage in serious and sincere action. On the contrary, huge crowds gather around people who utter pleasant words and trade in false promises. They are not attracted towards true well-wishers, but rush towards the exploiters.

80 We sent Lot, who said to his people, 'How can you commit an abomination such as no one in the world has ever done before you? 81 You lust after men rather than women! You transgress all bounds!' 82 The only answer given by his people was, 'Turn them out of your town. They are people who regard themselves to be pure.' 83 So We saved him and his family—except for his wife. She was one of those who stayed behind. [a]

وَلُوطًا إِذْ قَالَ لِقَوْمِهِ أَتَأْتُونَ ٱلْفَٰحِشَةَ مَا سَبَقَكُم بِهَا مِنْ أَحَدٍ مِّنَ ٱلْعَٰلَمِينَ ۝ إِنَّكُمْ لَتَأْتُونَ ٱلرِّجَالَ شَهْوَةً مِّن دُونِ ٱلنِّسَآءِ ۚ بَلْ أَنتُمْ قَوْمٌ مُّسْرِفُونَ ۝ وَمَا كَانَ جَوَابَ قَوْمِهِ إِلَّا أَن قَالُوٓا۟ أَخْرِجُوهُم مِّن قَرْيَتِكُمْ ۖ إِنَّهُمْ أُنَاسٌ يَتَطَهَّرُونَ ۝ فَأَنجَيْنَٰهُ وَأَهْلَهُۥٓ إِلَّا ٱمْرَأَتَهُۥ كَانَتْ مِنَ ٱلْغَٰبِرِينَ ۝

[a] Lot was Abraham's nephew. The community to which he was sent as a prophet was settled on the banks of the river Jordan in southern Syria. The prosperity of the community led its members into an excessive love of luxury, and evil behaviour which went to extremes in sexual promiscuity and even homosexuality. The prophet warned them against this open shamelessness.

The universe has a scheme of nature. This scheme is called the reformed state (islah) in Quranic terminology. Going against this means a disturbance in the balance of things (fasad) in this universe. It is only man who takes undue advantage of his freedom and goes against the way of nature. The community of Lot also committed such a disruption of the divine order. The natural form of sexual relationship is that of a husband and wife. This means following the way of islah. As opposed to this, if a sexual relation develops between man and man, and a woman and a woman, this amounts to transgressing the limits fixed by God. This is what is called fasad in the Quran.

Only a few people close to Lot had any faith in him. The rest of the people were sunk in debauchery. They even said: 'When these people consider us dirty and want to keep themselves pure, why should the clean live with the unclean? They had better leave our town.' This statement of theirs smacked of their haughtiness. They had the courage to say this because they were in the majority and enjoyed material superiority; they thus considered themselves safe.

When God's retribution visited Lot's community, the Prophet Lot's wife was one of the victims. This shows the unbiased justice of God in the matter of reward and punishment. In the judicial balance of God there is no regard for relationships or friendships. God's decision was so unbiased that it did not spare even Noah's son, Abraham's father, Lot's wife and the Prophet Muhammad's uncle. On the other hand, when Pharaoh's wife performed righteous deeds, she was admitted to Paradise.

⁸⁴ We rained down on them a shower [of brimstone]. Then see what was the end of the evil-doers.

⁸⁵ To Midian We sent their brother Shu'ayb. He said, 'O my people, worship God; you have no other god but Him. A clear Sign has indeed come to you from your Lord. So give full measure and full weight, and do not deliver short. Do not corrupt the land after it has been set in order. This is for your own good, if you are true believers.ᵃ

وَأَمْطَرْنَا عَلَيْهِم مَّطَرًا ۖ فَٱنظُرْ كَيْفَ كَانَ عَـٰقِبَةُ ٱلْمُجْرِمِينَ ۝ وَإِلَىٰ مَدْيَنَ أَخَاهُمْ شُعَيْبًا ۗ قَالَ يَـٰقَوْمِ ٱعْبُدُوا۟ ٱللَّهَ مَا لَكُم مِّنْ إِلَـٰهٍ غَيْرُهُۥ ۖ قَدْ جَآءَتْكُم بَيِّنَةٌ مِّن رَّبِّكُمْ ۖ فَأَوْفُوا۟ ٱلْكَيْلَ وَٱلْمِيزَانَ وَلَا تَبْخَسُوا۟ ٱلنَّاسَ أَشْيَآءَهُمْ وَلَا تُفْسِدُوا۟ فِى ٱلْأَرْضِ بَعْدَ إِصْلَـٰحِهَا ۚ ذَٰلِكُمْ خَيْرٌ لَّكُمْ إِن كُنتُم مُّؤْمِنِينَ ۝

ᵃ One of the sons of Abraham was Madyan who was born of his third wife, Quatura. The people of Midian (or Madyan), his decendants, settled on the Arabian coast of the Red Sea. These people believed in God and professed to be of Abraham's religion. But, five hundred years after the time of Abraham, they fell into wrong ways. They were a trading community; so their evil found expression in their dealings. They did not maintain the principles of honesty in weights, measures and transactions.

Injustice in dealing with others is against the balanced system (islah) enforced by God. God has caused the system of this world to work on the basis of perfect justice. Here, there is nothing like taking more from others and giving less in return. Here everything functions on the principles of justice to the point of mathematical exactness. If this does not happen, then it would amount to creating a disturbance in the well-balanced world of God.

86 Do not lie in ambush on every pathway, threatening people, barring those who believe from the Way of God, seeking to make it appear crooked. Remember when you were few in number and He multiplied you. Consider the fate of those who used to spread corruption. 87 And if there is a group of you which believes in My message and others who disbelieve it, be patient until God shall judge between us. He is the best of judges.'

88 The arrogant leaders of his people said, 'Shu'ayb, we will expel you and your fellow believers from our town unless you return to our faith.' He said, 'Even though we detest it? 89 We would be inventing lies against God if we returned to your faith after God has delivered us from it. It is not for us to return to it unless God our Lord so willed. Our Lord encompasses all things in His knowledge. We have put our trust in God. Our Lord, expose the truth [and judge] between us and our people, You are the best judge.'[a]

وَلَا تَقْعُدُواْ بِكُلِّ صِرَٰطٍ تُوعِدُونَ وَتَصُدُّونَ عَن سَبِيلِ ٱللَّهِ مَنْ ءَامَنَ بِهِۦ وَتَبْغُونَهَا عِوَجًا ۚ وَٱذْكُرُوٓاْ إِذْ كُنتُمْ قَلِيلًا فَكَثَّرَكُمْ ۖ وَٱنظُرُواْ كَيْفَ كَانَ عَٰقِبَةُ ٱلْمُفْسِدِينَ ﴿٨٦﴾ وَإِن كَانَ طَآئِفَةٌ مِّنكُمْ ءَامَنُواْ بِٱلَّذِىٓ أُرْسِلْتُ بِهِۦ وَطَآئِفَةٌ لَّمْ يُؤْمِنُواْ فَٱصْبِرُواْ حَتَّىٰ يَحْكُمَ ٱللَّهُ بَيْنَنَا ۚ وَهُوَ خَيْرُ ٱلْحَٰكِمِينَ ﴿٨٧﴾ ۞ قَالَ ٱلْمَلَأُ ٱلَّذِينَ ٱسْتَكْبَرُواْ مِن قَوْمِهِۦ لَنُخْرِجَنَّكَ يَٰشُعَيْبُ وَٱلَّذِينَ ءَامَنُواْ مَعَكَ مِن قَرْيَتِنَآ أَوْ لَتَعُودُنَّ فِى مِلَّتِنَا ۚ قَالَ أَوَلَوْ كُنَّا كَٰرِهِينَ ﴿٨٧﴾ قَدِ ٱفْتَرَيْنَا عَلَى ٱللَّهِ كَذِبًا إِنْ عُدْنَا فِى مِلَّتِكُم بَعْدَ إِذْ نَجَّىٰنَا ٱللَّهُ مِنْهَا ۚ وَمَا يَكُونُ لَنَآ أَن نَّعُودَ فِيهَآ إِلَّآ أَن يَشَآءَ ٱللَّهُ رَبُّنَا ۚ وَسِعَ رَبُّنَا كُلَّ شَىْءٍ عِلْمًا ۚ عَلَى ٱللَّهِ تَوَكَّلْنَا ۚ رَبَّنَا ٱفْتَحْ بَيْنَنَا وَبَيْنَ قَوْمِنَا بِٱلْحَقِّ وَأَنتَ خَيْرُ ٱلْفَٰتِحِينَ ﴿٨٨﴾

[a] When the people of Midian went to extremes in their wrongful ways, God sent Shu'ayb to them with His message. He exhorted them to adopt the way of righteousness and honesty in their dealings. With the help of clear arguments, He made them fully aware of the necessity for honesty. But they were not willing to accept the admonition. Not only that, they were not ready to accept the mission of Shu'ayb. They distorted his preachings and created misunderstanding among the people about him. They even resorted to violent means to dissuade the people from supporting him. In the end the retribution of God descended upon them and they were destroyed. In the eyes of God, matters relating to the consideration of the rights of fellow human beings and honesty in mutual dealings are so important that a community, in spite of claiming to be believers, was destroyed. God is the best Judge and His judgement cannot be biased.

90 The leading men of his people who were bent on denying the truth, said, 'If you follow Shu'ayb, you will certainly be the losers.' 91 Thereupon an earthquake overtook them and morning found them lying flattened in their homes; 92 those who had denied Shu'ayb became as though they had never lived there. Those who denied Shu'ayb, were themselves the losers.ᵃ

وَقَالَ ٱلۡمَلَأُ ٱلَّذِينَ كَفَرُوا۟ مِن قَوۡمِهِۦ لَئِنِ ٱتَّبَعۡتُمۡ شُعَيۡبًا إِنَّكُمۡ إِذًا لَّخَٰسِرُونَ ۝ فَأَخَذَتۡهُمُ ٱلرَّجۡفَةُ فَأَصۡبَحُوا۟ فِى دَارِهِمۡ جَٰثِمِينَ ۝ ٱلَّذِينَ كَذَّبُوا۟ شُعَيۡبًا كَأَن لَّمۡ يَغۡنَوۡا۟ فِيهَا ٱلَّذِينَ كَذَّبُوا۟ شُعَيۡبًا كَانُوا۟ هُمُ ٱلۡخَٰسِرِينَ ۝

ᵃ Shu'ayb's community was not guilty of denying God, but of misrepresenting Him, i.e. it had attributed to God a religion which was not sent by Him. This has been the position of the communities of all the prophets. The communities of the prophets were no different from those to whom God had earlier revealed His religion. But, by means of self-made changes and additions, they made it into something else. They changed the religion of God into the religion of their desires and started calling it the religion of God.

The religious leaders of today, who have the support of the people and are in power, do realize that they cannot argue with the prophets, as they would not succeed. But since they do not want someone to usurp them of their importance, they look for a way to silence them.

Allowances can be made for a person so long as the Truth is not clear to him. But after the Truth has been made clear, and if a man still chooses to be arrogant, he loses any right to sympathy. In this world, punishment is given on this basis; and on this same basis, punishment will be decided according to the guilt of the people in the Hereafter.

⁹³ So he turned away from them, saying, 'My people, I delivered my Lord's messages to you and gave you sincere advice, so why should I grieve for people who refused to believe?'

⁹⁴ Whenever We sent a prophet to a town, We afflicted its people with suffering and adversity, so that they might humble themselves [before God], ⁹⁵ and then We changed their hardship into ease until they grew affluent and said, 'Our fathers had also experienced adversity and prosperity,' then We seized them suddenly, unawares.ᵃ

فَتَوَلَّىٰ عَنْهُمْ وَقَالَ يَٰقَوْمِ لَقَدْ أَبْلَغْتُكُمْ رِسَٰلَٰتِ رَبِّي وَنَصَحْتُ لَكُمْ ۖ فَكَيْفَ ءَاسَىٰ عَلَىٰ قَوْمٍ كَٰفِرِينَ ۝ وَمَآ أَرْسَلْنَا فِى قَرْيَةٍ مِّن نَّبِىٍّ إِلَّآ أَخَذْنَآ أَهْلَهَا بِٱلْبَأْسَآءِ وَٱلضَّرَّآءِ لَعَلَّهُمْ يَضَّرَّعُونَ ۝ ثُمَّ بَدَّلْنَا مَكَانَ ٱلسَّيِّئَةِ ٱلْحَسَنَةَ حَتَّىٰ عَفَوا۟ وَّقَالُوا۟ قَدْ مَسَّ ءَابَآءَنَا ٱلضَّرَّآءُ وَٱلسَّرَّآءُ فَأَخَذْنَٰهُم بَغْتَةً وَهُمْ لَا يَشْعُرُونَ ۝

ᵃ According to the tradition (of the Prophet), a believer goes on getting into difficulties until he becomes clear of sins, and a hypocrite is like a donkey who does not know why his owner has tied him and why he has let him loose. (*Tafsir ibn Kathir*).

God imposes various types of difficulties on man so that his heart may soften, he may give up his reliance on anything other than God, and his haughtiness—which prevents him from accepting the Truth from outside may diminish. In this way, by God's arrangements, the psychology of shortcomings and helplessness is instilled in man, so that he may give his full attention to the voice of Truth. The general public as well as the prophet's addressees undergo this treatment. However, according to the usual procedure of God, all this happens garbed in doubt. For example, if some trouble affects somebody, it does so as part of the cause-and-effect process. This sort of occurrence poses a test for many people. They ignore it, saying that this was bound to happen and it happened. When they do not learn a lesson from these difficulties, God changes their conditions for the better. Now such people are pushed towards more severe misunderstandings. They firmly believe this to be a part of the occurrences of the time; a matter of the usual ups and downs which people are subjected to, under normal conditions; otherwise they would not have experienced good days after bad days. So they are thus prevented from learning a lesson from the first set of circumstances as well as from the second set.

To be blessed with progress even after being guilty of arrogance is very dangerous. It is a sign of the fact that God has decided to catch hold of the culprit at the point where he has become most fearless of God's punishment. ▶

96 Had the people of those towns believed in and feared God, We would have showered upon them blessings from heaven and earth, but they rejected the truth. So We seized them on account of their misdeeds. 97 Do the people of these towns now feel secure against the coming of Our punishment upon them by night while they are asleep? 98 Or, do they feel secure against the coming of Our punishment upon them in the forenoon while they are at play? 99 Do they feel secure against God's devising? No one feels secure against God's devising except for those doomed to ruin. 100 Does it not guide the people who inherit the land from former people that We can punish them for their sins if We will? And seal up their hearts so that they would not be able to lend an ear to words of guidance? *a*

وَلَوْ أَنَّ أَهْلَ ٱلْقُرَىٰٓ ءَامَنُوا۟ وَٱتَّقَوْا۟ لَفَتَحْنَا عَلَيْهِم بَرَكَٰتٍ مِّنَ ٱلسَّمَآءِ وَٱلْأَرْضِ وَلَٰكِن كَذَّبُوا۟ فَأَخَذْنَٰهُم بِمَا كَانُوا۟ يَكْسِبُونَ ۝ أَفَأَمِنَ أَهْلُ ٱلْقُرَىٰٓ أَن يَأْتِيَهُم بَأْسُنَا بَيَٰتًا وَهُمْ نَآئِمُونَ ۝ أَوَأَمِنَ أَهْلُ ٱلْقُرَىٰٓ أَن يَأْتِيَهُم بَأْسُنَا ضُحًى وَهُمْ يَلْعَبُونَ ۝ أَفَأَمِنُوا۟ مَكْرَ ٱللَّهِ فَلَا يَأْمَنُ مَكْرَ ٱللَّهِ إِلَّا ٱلْقَوْمُ ٱلْخَٰسِرُونَ ۝ أَوَلَمْ يَهْدِ لِلَّذِينَ يَرِثُونَ ٱلْأَرْضَ مِنۢ بَعْدِ أَهْلِهَآ أَن لَّوْ نَشَآءُ أَصَبْنَٰهُم بِذُنُوبِهِمْ وَنَطْبَعُ عَلَىٰ قُلُوبِهِمْ فَهُمْ لَا يَسْمَعُونَ ۝

The real reward of a God-fearing life will come in the Hereafter. However, if God wishes, He gives the initial reward in this world also in the shape of well-being and respect.

a It happens again and again that a community reaches a high level of honour and prosperity and thereafter faces decline. It is removed from the scene and in its place another community occupies the same position of honour and prosperity that the former community enjoyed.

This event is a sign of God, which should remind man of His supremacy. It shows that all the strings controlling gains and losses are in the hands of a supreme being. He may award good fortune to one or take it away from another. Making use of the powers of observation and thinking bestowed on him by God, man can easily understand these facts. He will realise that had the real source of power not been in other hands, the group which once managed to attain ascendancy would never have allowed others to replace it. If man can learn such lessons, he will find divine nourishment in the rise and fall of nations. But whenever a community falls from grace and another community rises in its place, the members of the rising community entertain the misunderstanding that whatever happened to the previous community was the fate particular to that community, and that it was never going to happen to them.

¹⁰¹ We have told you the stories of those towns: their messengers came to them with clear signs, but they were never going to believe in something they had already rejected. Thus God seals up the hearts of those who deny the truth. ¹⁰² We found most of them untrue to their covenants, indeed We found most of them to be defiant.ᵃ

¹⁰³ After them We sent Moses with Our signs to Pharaoh and his chiefs. But they willfully rejected them. Consider the end of the evil-doers. ¹⁰⁴ Moses said, 'Pharaoh, I am a messenger from the Lord of the Universe, ¹⁰⁵ duty-bound to say nothing about God but the truth, and I have brought you a clear sign from your Lord. Let the Children of Israel go with me.' ¹⁰⁶ [Pharaoh] said, 'If you come with a sign, then produce it, if you are telling the truth.'

تِلْكَ ٱلْقُرَىٰ نَقُصُّ عَلَيْكَ مِنْ أَنۢبَآئِهَا ۚ وَلَقَدْ جَآءَتْهُمْ رُسُلُهُم بِٱلْبَيِّنَٰتِ فَمَا كَانُوا۟ لِيُؤْمِنُوا۟ بِمَا كَذَّبُوا۟ مِن قَبْلُ ۚ كَذَٰلِكَ يَطْبَعُ ٱللَّهُ عَلَىٰ قُلُوبِ ٱلْكَٰفِرِينَ ﴿١٠١﴾ وَمَا وَجَدْنَا لِأَكْثَرِهِم مِّنْ عَهْدٍ ۖ وَإِن وَجَدْنَآ أَكْثَرَهُمْ لَفَٰسِقِينَ ﴿١٠٢﴾ ثُمَّ بَعَثْنَا مِنۢ بَعْدِهِم مُّوسَىٰ بِـَٔايَٰتِنَآ إِلَىٰ فِرْعَوْنَ وَمَلَإِيْهِ فَظَلَمُوا۟ بِهَا ۖ فَٱنظُرْ كَيْفَ كَانَ عَٰقِبَةُ ٱلْمُفْسِدِينَ ﴿١٠٣﴾ وَقَالَ مُوسَىٰ يَٰفِرْعَوْنُ إِنِّى رَسُولٌ مِّن رَّبِّ ٱلْعَٰلَمِينَ ﴿١٠٤﴾ حَقِيقٌ عَلَىٰٓ أَن لَّآ أَقُولَ عَلَى ٱللَّهِ إِلَّا ٱلْحَقَّ ۚ قَدْ جِئْتُكُم بِبَيِّنَةٍ مِّن رَّبِّكُمْ فَأَرْسِلْ مَعِىَ بَنِىٓ إِسْرَٰٓءِيلَ ﴿١٠٥﴾ قَالَ إِن كُنتَ جِئْتَ بِـَٔايَةٍ فَأْتِ بِهَآ إِن كُنتَ مِنَ ٱلصَّٰدِقِينَ ﴿١٠٦﴾

ᵃ God has blessed man with the powers of observation, hearing and thinking, so that he may learn lessons and, with their help, may understand the signs of God. But when a man does not utilize these powers for the purpose for which they were intended, then it inevitably happens that the sensitivity of his heart starts waning until his feelings become blunted; the seal of insensitivity is thus fixed on his heart and mind. Now, his position becomes that of one who does not see in spite of having eyes, does not hear in spite of having ears and does not understand in spite of having a mind; and in spite of being a human being, he loses his humanity.

The human race began with the followers of Adam. Thereafter, when they fell into wrong ways, the prophets of God came to admonish them. Now those who reformed themselves on the advent of the prophets were saved and those who refused to be reformed were destroyed. Again the following generations forgot the vows of submission to God made to their prophets, and they suffered the same consequences as those of the later generations of Adam's followers. Such a state of affairs has occurred again and again, so much so that the history of the greater part of the human race has become that of disobedience and the breaking of pledges.

107 Then Moses threw down his staff and suddenly, unmistakably, it appeared as a serpent, 108 and he drew forth his hand, and it appeared [shining] white to the beholders. 109 The chiefs of Pharaoh's people said, 'This is most surely a skillful magician, 110 who seeks to drive you from your land!' Pharaoh said, 'What then do you advise?' 111 They said, 'Let him and his brother wait awhile, and send into the cities summoners, 112 who should bring to you every skillful magician.' *a*

فَأَلْقَىٰ عَصَاهُ فَإِذَا هِىَ ثُعْبَانٌ مُّبِينٌ ۝ وَنَزَعَ يَدَهُ فَإِذَا هِىَ بَيْضَآءُ لِلنَّٰظِرِينَ ۝ قَالَ ٱلْمَلَأُ مِن قَوْمِ فِرْعَوْنَ إِنَّ هَٰذَا لَسَٰحِرٌ عَلِيمٌ ۝ يُرِيدُ أَن يُخْرِجَكُم مِّنْ أَرْضِكُمْ فَمَاذَا تَأْمُرُونَ ۝ قَالُوٓا أَرْجِهْ وَأَخَاهُ وَأَرْسِلْ فِى ٱلْمَدَآئِنِ حَٰشِرِينَ ۝ يَأْتُوكَ بِكُلِّ سَٰحِرٍ عَلِيمٍ ۝

---

a A prophet's discourse is initially addressed to the leaders of the day; to those who enjoy leadership of thought in their environment. Such people, thanks to their superior intellect, are in a better position to understand the message of Truth in all its profundity. But, history shows that they have invariably always been antagonistic to the prophet's call, i.e. they utilize their mental talents to assign a wrong meaning to the message of Truth. For example, they declare a sign which had appeared on the strength of God's intervention to have appeared by the force of magic, or, in order to disparage the prophetic movement, give it a political colour and say that such preachers are simply seeking power. As the general public are unable to analyse matters, such talk leads them into becoming suspicious of the Truth. But to raise such frivolous points against the messenger of Truth is a great crime. In this way, the leading lights of the day may be able to preserve their leadership, but it will be at the cost of the Hereafter.

God is the Truth. So it is not proper for one who comes forward in the name of God to speak of anything other than truth and justice. If he does otherwise, he will lose the right to represent God and will be liable to be punished rather than rewarded by God.

Moses was sent (by God) to both the Children of Israel and to the Pharaoh and his Copt community. At that time the Children of Israel suffered from many weaknesses. However, they basically supported Moses. Unlike them, Pharaoh and his community, (with the exception of a few) rejected him. Finally, after 40 years of attempting to propagate God's command, Moses was commanded to migrate from Egypt along with the Children of Israel. He asked Pharaoh to allow the Children of Israel to leave the country, so that they might be able to pray to the one and only God in the open atmosphere of the desert (Exodus-16). Moses was the representative of Truth, but Pharaoh considered him to be merely practising magic and decided to overcome him through his own magicians.

¹¹³ And the magicians came to Pharaoh and asked, 'Shall we have a reward, if we should prevail?' ¹¹⁴ Pharaoh replied, 'Certainly, and you shall also become my courtiers.' ¹¹⁵ They said, 'Moses, will you first throw, or shall we?' ¹¹⁶ He said, 'You throw [first]!' When they made their cast, they bewitched the eyes of the people and struck them with awe, for they showed a great [feat of] magic.ᵃ

وَجَآءَ ٱلسَّحَرَةُ فِرْعَوْنَ قَالُوٓاْ إِنَّ لَنَا لَأَجْرًا إِن كُنَّا نَحْنُ ٱلْغَٰلِبِينَ ۝ قَالَ نَعَمْ وَإِنَّكُمْ لَمِنَ ٱلْمُقَرَّبِينَ ۝ قَالُوا۟ يَٰمُوسَىٰٓ إِمَّآ أَن تُلْقِىَ وَإِمَّآ أَن نَّكُونَ نَحْنُ ٱلْمُلْقِينَ ۝ قَالَ أَلْقُواْ فَلَمَّآ أَلْقَوْا۟ سَحَرُوٓا۟ أَعْيُنَ ٱلنَّاسِ وَٱسْتَرْهَبُوهُمْ وَجَآءُو بِسِحْرٍ عَظِيمٍ ۝

ᵃ Prophet's are given miracles according to the mindset of their contemporaries. In ancient Egypt magic captivated the minds of the people, so Moses was given the miracle of magic.

As planned by Pharaoh, on the occasion of the national festival, all their great magicians assembled.

The magicians asked Moses whether they should perform their feat first, or whether he would like to start the proceedings. Moses asked them to demonstrate their magic first, and they accepted. This shows that a prophet never takes the initiative in taking action against his enemy. Till the last moment he gives his opponents the opportunity to open hostilities. When his opponents, in this way, have already taken upon themselves the responsibility of initiating action, at that time the prophet uses all the powers at his command to subdue them. Presenting the ideology of Islam theoretically, a prophet takes the first step, but he never takes the initiative when it could lead to an offensive action.

¹¹⁷ Then We inspired Moses, saying, 'Throw down your staff.' And it immediately swallowed up their false devices. ¹¹⁸ Thus the truth prevailed and what they had produced came to nothing: ¹¹⁹ Pharaoh and his men were defeated and utterly humiliated. ¹²⁰ And the sorcerers prostrated themselves ¹²¹ and said, 'We believe in the Lord of the Universe, ¹²² the Lord of Moses and Aaron!' *a*

۞ وَأَوْحَيْنَا إِلَىٰ مُوسَىٰ أَنْ أَلْقِ عَصَاكَ ۖ فَإِذَا هِيَ تَلْقَفُ مَا يَأْفِكُونَ ۝ فَوَقَعَ ٱلْحَقُّ وَبَطَلَ مَا كَانُوا۟ يَعْمَلُونَ ۝ فَغُلِبُوا۟ هُنَالِكَ وَٱنقَلَبُوا۟ صَٰغِرِينَ ۝ وَأُلْقِيَ ٱلسَّحَرَةُ سَٰجِدِينَ ۝ قَالُوٓا۟ ءَامَنَّا بِرَبِّ ٱلْعَٰلَمِينَ ۝ رَبِّ مُوسَىٰ وَهَٰرُونَ ۝

---

a In Egypt, the mission of Moses continued for about forty years. This competition with the magicians took place in the last stage of this period. We can imagine from this that the magicians must have been aware of Moses' message. However, the veil covering their eyes had not fallen away. When they saw Moses' superiority in the field in which they specialised, then all the veils were torn apart. They could see that this was not a case of magic but of Divine prophethood. They voluntarily and spontaneously prostrated themselves before God.

When the sticks and ropes were thrown down by the magicians, they appeared to the people to be moving snakes, due to an optical illusion. But when Moses' staff turned into a snake and started moving along the ground, the magician's sticks and ropes turned back into sticks and ropes. The magicians knew the limits of magic. In this event, the magicians realised actually how insignificant were man's devices, even in their most perfect forms, and how Great and all-Powerful was God. Thereafter, Pharaoh—with all his authority—appeared valueless to them. The same magicians who, before witnessing God's greatness, were desirous of rewards from Pharaoh, ignored Pharaoh's threat of the worst punishment as if it were of no account.

¹²³ Pharaoh said, 'You dare believe in Him before I have given you permission? Behold, this is indeed a plot which you have devised in this city in order to drive its people out. But you shall soon know the consequences, ¹²⁴ I will cut off your hands and feet on alternate sides and then crucify you all!' ¹²⁵ They replied, 'We shall surely return to our Lord. ¹²⁶ You would punish us only because we believed in the signs of our Lord when they were shown to us. Our Lord, pour patience upon us, and cause us to die in a state of submission to You.'ᵃ

قَالَ فِرْعَوْنُ ءَامَنتُم بِهِۦ قَبْلَ أَنْ ءَاذَنَ لَكُمْ إِنَّ هَٰذَا لَمَكْرٌ مَّكَرْتُمُوهُ فِي ٱلْمَدِينَةِ لِتُخْرِجُواْ مِنْهَآ أَهْلَهَا فَسَوْفَ تَعْلَمُونَ ۝ لَأُقَطِّعَنَّ أَيْدِيَكُمْ وَأَرْجُلَكُم مِّنْ خِلَٰفٍ ثُمَّ لَأُصَلِّبَنَّكُمْ أَجْمَعِينَ ۝ قَالُوٓاْ إِنَّآ إِلَىٰ رَبِّنَا مُنقَلِبُونَ ۝ وَمَا تَنقِمُ مِنَّآ إِلَّآ أَنْ ءَامَنَّا بِـَٔايَٰتِ رَبِّنَا لَمَّا جَآءَتْنَا رَبَّنَآ أَفْرِغْ عَلَيْنَا صَبْرًا وَتَوَفَّنَا مُسْلِمِينَ ۝

ᵃ To sacrifice one's life for the sake of Truth amounts to bearing the final testimony to the Truth as the Truth. With the help of God, the magicians were enabled to make this sacrifice. The magicians, by offering themselves for the worst punishment, proved that their faith in Moses was not a matter of excuse or conspiracy, but a genuine acknowledgement of the truth. But, this supreme action of the magicians stung Pharaoh's pride. Supporting Moses against him amounted to insulting Pharaoh before the whole community. So, Pharaoh was enraged at them. He, therefore, decided to take stern action against the magicians, as any haughty person in a position of power would do. Both the magicians as well as Pharaoh were defeated in the field of arguments. But the magicians, by admitting their defeat, became entitled to God's eternal rewards, while Pharaoh made it a prestige issue. In order to satisfy his false egotism, he could do little but oppress truth-loving individuals and in the Hereafter be himself consigned to God's eternal punishment.

Pharaoh considered the question of acceptance or non-acceptance of Moses' call as one involving his 'permission', while the magicians treated it as a 'sign' (from God). It is always the attitude of a haughty person that his opinion overrides arguments and proofs. Such people never receive inspiration to accept the Truth.

At this critical juncture, the strength shown by the magicians was entirely due to God's help, and the prayer which fell from their lips was entirely inspired. When a subject of God surrenders himself body and soul to God, he becomes so close to Him that he starts receiving special blessings from God. He utters such words as are God-inspired in the full sense. ▶

¹²⁷ The chiefs of Pharaoh's people said, 'Will you allow Moses and his people to spread corruption in the land, and to forsake you and your gods?' He replied, 'We shall kill their male children and spare only the females. We have complete power over them.' [a]

وَقَالَ ٱلۡمَلَأُ مِن قَوۡمِ فِرۡعَوۡنَ أَتَذَرُ مُوسَىٰ وَقَوۡمَهُۥ لِيُفۡسِدُواْ فِى ٱلۡأَرۡضِ وَيَذَرَكَ وَءَالِهَتَكَ قَالَ سَنُقَتِّلُ أَبۡنَآءَهُمۡ وَنَسۡتَحۡىِۦ نِسَآءَهُمۡ وَإِنَّا فَوۡقَهُمۡ قَٰهِرُونَ ۝

The magicians' prayer, 'Our Lord, pour patience upon us, and cause us to die in a state of submission to You,' meant 'We have entirely surrendered to You, O God. Now, we have done whatever it is in our power to do, and we leave the rest to You.' When a subject of God prays like this from the bottom of his heart, certainly God is sufficient for him to solve all his difficulties.

[a] For the Children of Israel Pharaoh's rule created a problem, and they asked their prophet to solve it for them. But the solution suggested by the Prophet was that they should turn towards God. This indicates the difference in the way of thinking of worldly leaders and that of the Prophet regarding communal problems. Worldly leaders seek the solution to such problems at the government level, either by way of compromise with the government or by a clash with the government. But the solution offered by the Prophet was that whatever was happening should be tolerated and God's help should be solicited; without expecting anything from the powers that be, one should turn to God.

128 Moses said to his people, 'Turn to God for help and be patient. The earth belongs to God. He gives it to those of His servants whom He chooses, and the future belongs to the God-fearing.' 129 They replied, 'We were being persecuted before you came to us, and we are still being persecuted.' He said, 'Your Lord may well destroy your enemy and make you successors to the land. Then He will see how you conduct yourselves.' *a*

قَالَ مُوسَىٰ لِقَوْمِهِ ٱسْتَعِينُوا بِٱللَّهِ وَٱصْبِرُوٓا إِنَّ ٱلْأَرْضَ لِلَّهِ يُورِثُهَا مَن يَشَاءُ مِنْ عِبَادِهِ ۖ وَٱلْعَـٰقِبَةُ لِلْمُتَّقِينَ ۝ قَالُوٓا أُوذِينَا مِن قَبْلِ أَن تَأْتِيَنَا وَمِنۢ بَعْدِ مَا جِئْتَنَا ۚ قَالَ عَسَىٰ رَبُّكُمْ أَن يُهْلِكَ عَدُوَّكُمْ وَيَسْتَخْلِفَكُمْ فِى ٱلْأَرْضِ فَيَنظُرَ كَيْفَ تَعْمَلُونَ ۝

a Then the prophet also explained why he was presenting a solution which was against the general way of thinking of the community; though these problems apparently stemmed from the ruling authority and were resolvable only by that ruling authority, the more important point for consideration was how power and authority came to be wielded. Nobody wields power simply as a result of strategies; power is bestowed or taken away directly by God. This being so, it follows that the solution to the problem also lies in God.

Then, this power, regardless of whoever it is bestowed upon, is in fact a test for the recipient. In this world, being powerful is as much of a test as being powerless. Today, if one has received power, it is because he is being tested on whether he will become haughty and tyrannical, or will behave with justice and modesty. If empowerment is conferred upon others, even then the purpose will be to test others. If, due to its incompetence, one group has power taken away from it and handed over to another group, and if this other group also proves incompetent, power will likewise be taken away from it and given to yet another group.

The prosperity and power for which a man pines in this world are in fact, assets that are attainable in the real sense only in the Hereafter: thus in the world these things are conferred on human beings solely to put them to the test, while in the Hereafter they will be given to the righteous people as rewards.

130 We afflicted Pharaoh's people with shortages of food and famine so that they might take heed, 131 then when something good came to them, they said, 'It is our due!'—but when something bad came, they ascribed it as an ill-omen to Moses and those with him. Surely their [evil] fortune had been decreed by God, but most of them did not know this. 132 They said, 'Whatever miracles you work to bewitch us, we will not believe in you.' a

وَلَقَدْ أَخَذْنَآ ءَالَ فِرْعَوْنَ بِٱلسِّنِينَ وَنَقْصٍ مِّنَ ٱلثَّمَرَٰتِ لَعَلَّهُمْ يَذَّكَّرُونَ ۝ فَإِذَا جَآءَتْهُمُ ٱلْحَسَنَةُ قَالُوا۟ لَنَا هَٰذِهِۦ ۖ وَإِن تُصِبْهُمْ سَيِّئَةٌ يَطَّيَّرُوا۟ بِمُوسَىٰ وَمَن مَّعَهُۥٓ ۗ أَلَآ إِنَّمَا طَٰٓئِرُهُمْ عِندَ ٱللَّهِ وَلَٰكِنَّ أَكْثَرَهُمْ لَا يَعْلَمُونَ ۝ وَقَالُوا۟ مَهْمَا تَأْتِنَا بِهِۦ مِنْ ءَايَةٍ لِّتَسْحَرَنَا بِهَا فَمَا نَحْنُ لَكَ بِمُؤْمِنِينَ ۝

---

a Words have necessarily to be used to pronounce a thing right or wrong or to label a man innocent or guilty. But, the user of the words is man and in this present world of trial, he has been given the power to use these words in any way he pleases.

The most critical part of the freedom given to him is his having the ability to justify his calling the Truth falsehood or falsehood the Truth. He can classify as magic what is clearly a miracle wrought by a prophet, and then ignore it. If God gives him some blessing, he can express this in a way which suggests that whatever he received was due solely to his own capabilities and efforts. If God sends some warning as a punishment to him for his ignoring the Truth, he is free to say that it was due to the inauspicious presence of those very God-worshipping servants whom he had ill-treated and on whose account he had been sent that warning. Everything flows from God so that man should learn a lesson from it. But by using certain words, man gives the opposite meaning to every admonition and thus remains deprived of its inherent lesson.

'Whatever sign you might bring, we will not embrace the Faith.' This statement made by Pharaoh shows that in spite of the Truth being apparent in an abundantly clear and perfect shape, only that person becomes a recipient of it who is open to it. In other words, the reality of Truth reveals itself only to that person who is serious about the Truth; who has the inclination and willingness to receive and accept the Truth, wherever and in whatever form it is offered. Unlike him, one who is not serious about this matter; whose mental condition is such that he is satisfied with the statusquo will not be capable of seeing the Truth as such; so he will not be able to accept it. Being happy with the condition in which a man finds himself makes him unaware of the things outside himself; he is ignorant in spite of having knowledge; he does not hear in spite of having ears.

Man will certainly find the Truth if his mind is free from negatively conditioned thinking. But, mostly people have been subjected to such mental conditioning and that is why the Truth eludes them.

¹³³ Then We afflicted them with storms, and locusts, and lice, and frogs, and blood: so many clear signs. But they were steeped in arrogance, for they were a people given to sin. ¹³⁴ Whenever a plague struck them, they would say, 'Moses, pray to your Lord for us by virtue of the promise He has made to you: if you remove this plague from us, we will surely believe in you and let the Children of Israel go with you,' ¹³⁵ but whenever We removed the plague from them, giving them time to make good their promise, they would break their word.ᵃ

فَأَرْسَلْنَا عَلَيْهِمُ ٱلطُّوفَانَ وَٱلْجَرَادَ وَٱلْقُمَّلَ وَٱلضَّفَادِعَ وَٱلدَّمَ ءَايَٰتٍ مُّفَصَّلَٰتٍ فَٱسْتَكْبَرُواْ وَكَانُواْ قَوْمًا مُّجْرِمِينَ ۝ وَلَمَّا وَقَعَ عَلَيْهِمُ ٱلرِّجْزُ قَالُواْ يَٰمُوسَى ٱدْعُ لَنَا رَبَّكَ بِمَا عَهِدَ عِندَكَ لَئِن كَشَفْتَ عَنَّا ٱلرِّجْزَ لَنُؤْمِنَنَّ لَكَ وَلَنُرْسِلَنَّ مَعَكَ بَنِىٓ إِسْرَٰٓءِيلَ ۝ فَلَمَّا كَشَفْنَا عَنْهُمُ ٱلرِّجْزَ إِلَىٰٓ أَجَلٍ هُم بَٰلِغُوهُ إِذَا هُمْ يَنكُثُونَ ۝

ᵃ Moses performed his prophetic mission in Egypt for about forty years. There were two parts of his mission—one, to give the message of the oneness of God to Pharaoh and secondly, to lead the Children of Israel out of Egypt, settle them in the Sinai Desert and give them religious training in that untainted atmosphere. The Children of Israel (the progeny of Joseph) at that time were in the the grip of the Copt ruler (Pharaoh). The Copts used to utilise them as labourers in their agricultural and construction works. So, the Copt rulers did not want the Israelites to leave Egypt.

Initially, when Moses demanded that Pharaoh should allow the Children of Israel to leave Egypt along with him, Pharaoh and his courtiers gave his request a political colour and accused Moses of intending to remove the Copt from Egypt (7:110). This was absolutely meaningless, because Moses's plan was to remove himself from Egypt. At that time Pharaoh and his companions had an inflated opinion of their power and that is why they saw even a straight proposition in a crooked way.

But, in later stages, God subjected Pharaoh and his community to all types of calamities. For many years they had continuously to face famines; they had severe hail-storms with lightning and thunder; swarms of locusts invaded their country and ate up their crops and gardens and completely destroyed all greenery; lice so proliferated that clothes and beds became infested with them; and in the houses and on the pathways, frogs were hopping about everywhere; the water in the rivers and lakes became bloody. When Pharaoh and his community began to suffer these strange afflictions, they asked Moses to pray to his Lord to relieve them of these troubles, then they would allow the Children of Israel to leave with Moses. Moses's demand, which had earlier appeared to the Copts as a political conspiracy to evict them, now appeared to them simply as a migration of the Children of Israel themselves.

¹³⁶ So We exacted retribution from them and drowned them in the sea, because they rejected Our signs and paid no heed to them; ¹³⁷ We made the people who were considered weak inheritors of the eastern parts and western parts of the land which We had blessed. Thus your Lord's good promise to the Children of Israel was fulfilled, because of their patience, and We destroyed all that Pharaoh and his people had built and all that they had raised high.ᵃ

فَٱنتَقَمۡنَا مِنۡهُمۡ فَأَغۡرَقۡنَٰهُمۡ فِى ٱلۡيَمِّ بِأَنَّهُمۡ كَذَّبُواْ بِـَٔايَٰتِنَا وَكَانُواْ عَنۡهَا غَٰفِلِينَ ۞ وَأَوۡرَثۡنَا ٱلۡقَوۡمَ ٱلَّذِينَ كَانُواْ يُسۡتَضۡعَفُونَ مَشَٰرِقَ ٱلۡأَرۡضِ وَمَغَٰرِبَهَا ٱلَّتِى بَٰرَكۡنَا فِيهَاۖ وَتَمَّتۡ كَلِمَتُ رَبِّكَ ٱلۡحُسۡنَىٰ عَلَىٰ بَنِىٓ إِسۡرَٰٓءِيلَ بِمَا صَبَرُواْۖ وَدَمَّرۡنَا مَا كَانَ يَصۡنَعُ فِرۡعَوۡنُ وَقَوۡمُهُۥ وَمَا كَانُواْ يَعۡرِشُونَ ۞

ᵃ Punishment was inflicted on the communities addressed by the Prophet because of their denial of the signs (*ayat*) of God. The believers in the Prophet on the other hand, were entitled to special succour from God, thanks to their patience in the face of all kinds of provocations from their contemporaries (the addressees of the Prophet) and their remaining steadfast on the path of God.

By 'signs' is meant those arguments which establish Truth as Truth. But man, due to his egotism or pride is unable to accept them. Instead of paying full attention to the arguments presented to him, he diverts his attention to the preacher, the presenter of arguments. He fails to counter the arguments, but the person who is presenting them is not a historically established figure, neither is he covered in worldly glory, so the addressee finds it easier to ridicule the presenter instead of his arguments. He (the addressee) thinks that if he listens to the arguments, it will amount to making his status inferior to that of the preacher. Therefore, in order to maintain his pride and superiority vis à vis the *dai*, he refuses to acknowledge the superiority of the Truth. This is the real point on which man is being tested. In the present world, God reveals Himself indirectly in the form of signs and reason. In the Hereafter, He will reveal His Being directly, then no one will dare to deny Him. But only that faith is of value when it stems from man's discovery of the truth when God is as yet unseen.

ᵇ Man concocts a great deal of hocus-pocus when he feels himself in a safe position. But when his defences are down and he is put in a position of real helplessness, he suddenly becomes realistic. Now he himself understands those things which he had earlier failed to grasp, even after having had them explained to him. But acknowledgement, while still having the power of denial, is real acknowledgement. Acknowledgement after being deprived of words, is no acknowledgement at all. ▶

138 We brought the Children of Israel across the sea and they came upon a people who were devoted to their idols. They said, 'Moses, give us a god just like the gods these people have.' He said, 'You are indeed an ignorant people: 139 what they are engaged in is doomed to destruction and all their works are in vain.'*

وَجَوَزْنَا بِبَنِى إِسْرَٰٓءِيلَ ٱلْبَحْرَ فَأَتَوْاْ
عَلَىٰ قَوْمٍ يَعْكُفُونَ عَلَىٰٓ أَصْنَامٍ هُّمْ
قَالُوٓاْ يَٰمُوسَى ٱجْعَل لَّنَآ إِلَٰهًا كَمَا
لَهُمْ ءَالِهَةٌ ۚ قَالَ إِنَّكُمْ قَوْمٌ تَجْهَلُونَ
(١٣٨) إِنَّ هَٰٓؤُلَآءِ مُتَبَّرٌ مَّا هُمْ فِيهِ
وَبَٰطِلٌ مَّا كَانُوْا يَعْمَلُونَ (١٣٩)

Believing in God only when He reveals Himself proves man's sinfulness instead of making him eligible for reward. Such belief proves that if man did not accept the truth, it was entirely due to his heedlessness. Had he been serious about it, he would have found no difficulty in doing so.

Moreover, the most prominent quality of God's faithful servant is patience. In fact, the life of faith is entirely one of patience. Accepting truth on receiving it from someone like himself; establishing one's life on truth and principles instead of on personal desires and ambitions; ignoring suffering for the sake of God; not losing courage on being provoked by the opponents of the truth—all these are stages of faith and one can never successfully pass through these stages without exercising patience.

Pharaoh was proud of his power, his wealth, his orchards and his palatial buildings. But after the emigration of Moses, Pharaoh and his army were drowned in the sea. Locusts devastated the lush green orchards and earthquakes ravaged the palatial buildings. By contrast, a few generations after their emigration, the Israelites came to possess Syria and Palestine during the times of David and Solomon. Those who deny God's signs invariably invite the wrath of God and those who exercise patience are bound to receive God's succour.

¹⁴⁰ He said, 'Shall I seek a deity for you other than God, while it is He who has exalted you above all peoples? ¹⁴¹ We delivered you from Pharaoh's people, who afflicted you with dreadful torment, slaying your male children and sparing only your daughters. That was surely a great trial for you by your Lord.'^a

قَالَ أَغَيْرَ ٱللَّهِ أَبْغِيكُمْ إِلَٰهًا وَهُوَ فَضَّلَكُمْ عَلَى ٱلْعَٰلَمِينَ ۞ وَإِذْ أَنجَيْنَٰكُم مِّنْ ءَالِ فِرْعَوْنَ يَسُومُونَكُمْ سُوٓءَ ٱلْعَذَابِ يُقَتِّلُونَ أَبْنَآءَكُمْ وَيَسْتَحْيُونَ نِسَآءَكُمْ وَفِى ذَٰلِكُم بَلَآءٌ مِّن رَّبِّكُمْ عَظِيمٌ ۞

---

^a The Israelites crossed the northern end of the Red Sea and reached the Sinai Peninsula. Then they travelled Southwards along the banks of the sea. During this journey, they witnessed a community engaged in polytheism. On seeing this, some of the Israelites demanded that Moses make an idol for them.

The greatest weakness of man is to attach importance to appearances, thus becoming unable to devote his attention to the Invisible God. That is why he cannot detach himself from things which can be seen with the naked eye. The unenlightened bow down before deities of stone and metals, while the civilized devote their attention to a particular personality or a community or a cultural structure, etc. When a group of Israelites asked Moses to make tangible idols, Moses replied, 'All their devotion is going to be wasted.' What he meant was that when his mission was to make people worship the one God, how could he possibly carve idols for his community?

The Israelites were given superiority over all mankind. This 'superiority' is not used here in the racial sense, but refers rather to their mission. It conveys the same sense as the Quranic phrase "you are the best community" applied to the *ummah* of the Prophet Muhammad. It is the way of God that He selects a community to become the bearer of the Book of God and, through this community, He conveys His message to other nations. In ancient times this office was held by the Israelites, but after the coming of the Final Prophet, this office was given to the Muslim community.

The opportunity Pharaoh had of oppressing the Israelites was a test for the Israelites and not a punishment. Believers are subjected to such trials in order to shake them and awaken them by shock treatment. It thus becomes clear who are the people who turn away from the true religion of God because of having to face difficult circumstances and who are the people who can adhere strictly to God's religion by exercising patience in times of adversity.

¹⁴² We appointed thirty nights for Moses, then added ten more: the term set by his Lord was fulfilled in forty nights. Moses said to his brother Aaron, 'Take my place among my people: act rightly and do not follow the way of those who spread corruption.'[a]

وَوَاعَدْنَا مُوسَىٰ ثَلَٰثِينَ لَيْلَةً وَأَتْمَمْنَٰهَا بِعَشْرٍ فَتَمَّ مِيقَٰتُ رَبِّهِۦٓ أَرْبَعِينَ لَيْلَةً ۚ وَقَالَ مُوسَىٰ لِأَخِيهِ هَٰرُونَ ٱخْلُفْنِى فِى قَوْمِى وَأَصْلِحْ وَلَا تَتَّبِعْ سَبِيلَ ٱلْمُفْسِدِينَ ۝

---

[a] Moses was given *dawah* commands in Egypt, while laws were communicated to him after he reached the Sinai desert. This shows the order of divine injunctions. In general situations, what is required of the believers is to rectify their personal life and live as true devotees of God, and along with this, they must invite others to accept monotheism and the Hereafter-oriented life. But when the believers acquire the position of an independent community and have the freedom to organize themselves as the Israelites did in the Sinai desert, then it becomes incumbent on them to establish their social life on the basis of the Islamic law.

When Moses appointed Aaron as guardian of the Israelites in his absence, he said to him, 'Take my place among my people: act rightly and do not follow the way of those who spread corruption.' This shows the basic principle of shouldering one's responsibilities as the head of the community.

143 And when Moses came at Our appointed time and his Lord spoke to him, he said, 'My Lord, show Yourself to me so that I may look at You.' He replied, 'You cannot see Me, but look at the mountain; if it remains firmly in its place, then only will you see Me.' And when his Lord manifested Himself on the mountain, He broke it into pieces and Moses fell down unconscious. And when he recovered, he said, 'Glory be to You, I turn towards You, and I am the first to believe.'

144 He replied, 'Moses, I have chosen you of all mankind for My messages and My Words. Hold fast to what I have given you, and be among the grateful!' [a]

وَلَمَّا جَاءَ مُوسَىٰ لِمِيقَٰتِنَا وَكَلَّمَهُۥ رَبُّهُۥ قَالَ رَبِّ أَرِنِىٓ أَنظُرْ إِلَيْكَ قَالَ لَن تَرَىٰنِى وَلَٰكِنِ ٱنظُرْ إِلَى ٱلْجَبَلِ فَإِنِ ٱسْتَقَرَّ مَكَانَهُۥ فَسَوْفَ تَرَىٰنِى فَلَمَّا تَجَلَّىٰ رَبُّهُۥ لِلْجَبَلِ جَعَلَهُۥ دَكًّا وَخَرَّ مُوسَىٰ صَعِقًا فَلَمَّآ أَفَاقَ قَالَ سُبْحَٰنَكَ تُبْتُ إِلَيْكَ وَأَنَا۠ أَوَّلُ ٱلْمُؤْمِنِينَ ﴿١٤٣﴾ قَالَ يَٰمُوسَىٰٓ إِنِّى ٱصْطَفَيْتُكَ عَلَى ٱلنَّاسِ بِرِسَٰلَٰتِى وَبِكَلَٰمِى فَخُذْ مَآ ءَاتَيْتُكَ وَكُن مِّنَ ٱلشَّٰكِرِينَ ﴿١٤٤﴾

---

[a] Moses wanted to see God, but when he learnt that it was not possible to do so, he turned to God in repentance and reposed his faith in God, the unseen. Thus man is put to the test of believing in God without seeing Him. Seeing God is a reward reserved for the Hereafter, so how is it possible to see God in this present world?

Moses received his first prophetic call on the mountainside. The next time he was again called to the mountain to receive the commands of the Torah. This is an indication that the best place to receive divine inspiration is the environment of nature rather than that of human society. Where man emerges from the hubbub of this noisy world of human beings and reaches the quiet world of the trees, mountains and rivers, he begins to feel himself closer to God.

His mind is free from mundane problems; it is not preoccupied with worldly thoughts, so this is the best moment for him to think without any bias or complexes which might affect his thinking. Then he can be in true communion with God.

¹⁴⁵ And We wrote for him upon the Tablets an admonition and details of all things, then [bade him], 'Hold fast to them; and command your people to follow them in their best sense. Soon I shall show you the home of the wicked.ᵃ

وَكَتَبْنَا لَهُ فِي ٱلْأَلْوَاحِ مِن كُلِّ شَيْءٍ مَّوْعِظَةً وَتَفْصِيلًا لِّكُلِّ شَيْءٍ فَخُذْهَا بِقُوَّةٍ وَأْمُرْ قَوْمَكَ يَأْخُذُوا۟ بِأَحْسَنِهَا ۚ سَأُو۟رِيكُمْ دَارَ ٱلْفَٰسِقِينَ

ᵃ A prophet is also a man like other men. He is not a supernatural creature. His only special characteristic is that he is successful in preserving his inborn abilities intact. Therefore he is chosen by God to become the bearer of His message and may be trusted to represent Him among the people. In this sense, Moses was the best person of his community. Therefore, God chose him as His prophet, and revealed His message to him.

God's revelation provides the necessary guidance for one's life. But these divine messages come down in the form of words, and in the present world of trial, there is always the possibility of putting a wrong or distorted construction upon these words to suit one's own desires. But one who is serious and sincere in this matter of guidance and fears God for His chastisement or censure, will be able to draw from those words the same meaning which God wanted to convey. Thus it is only one who is desirous of finding the True Path who will receive divine inspiration from God's words. 'Soon I shall show you the homes of the wicked.' That is, during your journey you will pass through the ruins of those communities that had been destroyed. They had been given God's guidance, but they transgressed in their ways. They could not stay strong and firm in their belief, for they failed to ignore the pressures of circumstances and succumbed to their own personal desires and ambitions. So they earned God's displeasure and were destroyed. Likewise, if the Children of Israel also disobeyed God, they would meet the same fate. God is not partial to any community in the balance of Divine justice; there is no difference between one community and another.

In this world one has the opportunity to interpret God's words according to one's own whims and fancies and even put distorted interpretations upon them. But this is the kind of insolence which places even those who profess to be obedient on the list of disobedient persons in the eyes of God.

146 I will turn away from My signs all those who are arrogant in the land without any right, so that even if they see all the signs they will not believe in them. If they see the right path, they shall not walk upon it: but if they see the path of error, they shall choose it for their path, because they have given the lie to Our signs and paid no heed to them.*a*

سَأَصْرِفُ عَنْ ءَايَٰتِيَ ٱلَّذِينَ يَتَكَبَّرُونَ فِى ٱلْأَرْضِ بِغَيْرِ ٱلْحَقِّ وَإِن يَرَوْاْ كُلَّ ءَايَةٍ لَّا يُؤْمِنُواْ بِهَا وَإِن يَرَوْاْ سَبِيلَ ٱلرُّشْدِ لَا يَتَّخِذُوهُ سَبِيلًا وَإِن يَرَوْاْ سَبِيلَ ٱلْغَىِّ يَتَّخِذُوهُ سَبِيلًا ذَٰلِكَ بِأَنَّهُمْ كَذَّبُواْ بِـَٔايَٰتِنَا وَكَانُواْ عَنْهَا غَٰفِلِينَ ۝

a There are two ways of leading one's life in this world. One way is to keep one's eyes and ears open. Then one can see things as they really are. When truth appears, one will recognise it, for lessons are sure to be found in the signs of God which are in evidence everywhere in the universe. The other way to lead one's life is to have a superiority complex. One who has such a complex lives as if he is the owner of this world. He does not care for anything except for his personal interests. He thinks that all the good things he is receiving in this world are thanks to his own ability and his own efforts. Therefore, he does not consider others' needs. This attitude on his part comes in the way of his recognising and accepting the truth.

The former type of man is mentally receptive to his environment. With his openness of mind he can understand the relevance of God's signs and loses no time in moulding himself accordingly. Unlike him, the latter type of man is not receptive to his environment because of his pride and self-righteousness. He is confronted with the truth but, attaching no importance to it, he ignores it. Nature sings its melodies in silent language, but he pays no attention to it. He is not inclined towards any form of truth, which is outside his own beliefs. The world of the Hereafter is not for people of this category. Just as he ignored the message of God in this world of trials, so will he be ignored by God in the eternal world of the Hereafter, while those of the former type will be bountifully rewarded by God.

Treading the path of misguidance is the result of man's following the desires of his own self. The path of guidance can be arrived at when one rises above the influence of the self and one's surroundings: it is a path opted for purely for the sake of God.

The self-centred person who appreciates nothing but the fulfillment of his own desires rushes headlong towards the path of transgression. The right path appears strange and alien to his temperament, so he will fail to follow it.

One who feels himself to be superior finds it easy to accept any proposition which does not diminish his sense of superiority. But where he thinks he will not receive due importance, he becomes disinterested.

147 The actions of those who denied Our signs and the Meeting of the Hereafter will come to nothing— they shall be requited only, according to their deeds.'

148 In his absence, the people of Moses made a calf from their ornaments, an image which made a lowing sound. Could they not see that it did not speak to them or guide them in any way? Yet they took to worshipping it: they were evil-doers. 149 When they were afflicted with remorse, and realized that they had indeed gone astray, they said, 'If our Lord does not have mercy on us and forgive us, we shall be among the lost.'[a]

وَٱلَّذِينَ كَذَّبُواْ بِـَٔايَٰتِنَا وَلِقَآءِ ٱلْأَخِرَةِ حَبِطَتْ أَعْمَٰلُهُمْ هَلْ يُجْزَوْنَ إِلَّا مَا كَانُواْ يَعْمَلُونَ ۝ وَٱتَّخَذَ قَوْمُ مُوسَىٰ مِنۢ بَعْدِهِۦ مِنْ حُلِيِّهِمْ عِجْلًا جَسَدًا لَّهُۥ خُوَارٌ أَلَمْ يَرَوْاْ أَنَّهُۥ لَا يُكَلِّمُهُمْ وَلَا يَهْدِيهِمْ سَبِيلًا ٱتَّخَذُوهُ وَكَانُواْ ظَٰلِمِينَ ۝ وَلَمَّا سُقِطَ فِىٓ أَيْدِيهِمْ وَرَأَوْاْ أَنَّهُمْ قَدْ ضَلُّواْ قَالُواْ لَئِن لَّمْ يَرْحَمْنَا رَبُّنَا وَيَغْفِرْ لَنَا لَنَكُونَنَّ مِنَ ٱلْخَٰسِرِينَ ۝

---

[a] There was a clever man named Samiri among the Israelites. When Moses left for the mountain, leaving his people in the care of Aaron, Samiri started misleading them. He collected pieces of jewellery from the people and moulded them into the shape of a calf. The sculpting art of the ancient Egyptians was such that when air passed through it, a bellowing sound came out of the calf's mouth. People are generally awed by strange things. So this 'miracle' of the calf led them to believe that there was something sacred about it and they began worshipping it. Thanks to Samiri's engaging way of speaking, people started gathering around him. His influence increased to such an extent that he soon acquired a large number of followers, except for Aaron and a few of his companions. Nobody dared to openly protest against him. In the face of this mass following, even the protests of Aaron were not strong enough to sway the people and no other member of the community had the courage to speak up.

This has always been the reaction of the public from ancient times to the present day. A clever person by his sheer eloquence may draw a huge crowd, even on some non-issue. The public who are attracted to trivialities which are unrelated to the facts do not have the ability to think deeply enough to analyse what is true and what is not. That is why they rally to the side of such a person, thus adding to his popularity and importance. And if anyone attempts to reveal the truth, he is simply ignored in the same way as Aaron was.

150 When Moses returned to his people in anger and great sorrow, he said, 'What an awful sin you have committed in my absence. Did you want to hasten your Lord's command?' He threw down the Tablets and seized his brother by the head, pulling him towards himself. Aaron said, 'Son of my mother, the people oppressed me and almost killed me. Do not give my enemies cause to gloat over me. Do not number me among the wrongdoers.' 151 He said, 'My Lord, forgive me and my brother and admit us to Your mercy. You are the Most Merciful of the merciful.' a

وَلَمَّا رَجَعَ مُوسَىٰ إِلَىٰ قَوْمِهِ غَضْبَٰنَ أَسِفًا قَالَ بِئْسَمَا خَلَفْتُمُونِي مِنۢ بَعْدِىٓ أَعَجِلْتُمْ أَمْرَ رَبِّكُمْ وَأَلْقَى ٱلْأَلْوَاحَ وَأَخَذَ بِرَأْسِ أَخِيهِ يَجُرُّهُۥٓ إِلَيْهِ قَالَ ٱبْنَ أُمَّ إِنَّ ٱلْقَوْمَ ٱسْتَضْعَفُونِي وَكَادُوا۟ يَقْتُلُونَنِي فَلَا تُشْمِتْ بِىَ ٱلْأَعْدَآءَ وَلَا تَجْعَلْنِي مَعَ ٱلْقَوْمِ ٱلظَّٰلِمِينَ ۞ قَالَ رَبِّ ٱغْفِرْ لِى وَلِأَخِى وَأَدْخِلْنَا فِى رَحْمَتِكَ وَأَنتَ أَرْحَمُ ٱلرَّٰحِمِينَ ۞

---

a When Moses came down from the Mountain and saw the Israelites worshipping the golden calf, he held Aaron responsible for this, under the impression that he had neglected his duty as a reformer. Moses caught hold of him in anger but Aaron clarified his position and told him that he had done all he could to show them the right path. But they had not listened to him. So Moses checked himself, and started praying to God for Aaron. Many misunderstandings take place between believers, but after clarification they return to normalcy, just as if no misunderstanding had ever taken place.

¹⁵² Those who took to worshipping the calf will be afflicted by their Lord's wrath, and be disgraced in the life of this world. This is the way We requite those who invent falsehoods. ¹⁵³ As for those who committed evils, and thereafter repented and believed, they shall find your Lord forgiving and merciful.ᵃ

إِنَّ ٱلَّذِينَ ٱتَّخَذُواْ ٱلْعِجْلَ سَيَنَالُهُمْ غَضَبٌ مِّن رَّبِّهِمْ وَذِلَّةٌ فِى ٱلْحَيَوٰةِ ٱلدُّنْيَا وَكَذَٰلِكَ نَجْزِى ٱلْمُفْتَرِينَ ۝ وَٱلَّذِينَ عَمِلُواْ ٱلسَّيِّئَاتِ ثُمَّ تَابُواْ مِنۢ بَعْدِهَا وَءَامَنُواْ إِنَّ رَبَّكَ مِنۢ بَعْدِهَا لَغَفُورٌ رَّحِيمٌ ۝

ᵃ This action of the Israelites has been called false representation (*iftira*). Why was it so called? The reason is that they had committed this wrongful act in the name of Truth. Their case was not of the rejection of truth but of the exploition of Truth in order to gain material benefits. They used to justify such acts in religious terms. Like the polytheists, they said that God had become incarnate in the form of the idol they had made themselves, so they believed that worshipping it was as good as worshipping God. Moreover, Samiri also fabricated a dream, saying that in it he had seen Gabriel and collected a handful of earth from the footprint of his horse and put it in the statue of the calf, which caused a sound to come from its mouth. Samiri and his companions fabricated falsehoods and attributed them to God. Such action amounted to the making of false allegations (*iftira*) about God.

When the People of the Book indulge in such irreligious acts in the name of religion, they incur the wrath of God. Such people are punished not only in the Hereafter but also in this life. As for the Israelites, Moses instructed the leaders of each tribe to find out those who were initially responsible for this wrongdoing. The guilty were thus caught and put to death by their own tribesmen. Only those who, greatly ashamed of their actions, admitted their guilt and sincerely repented, were not punished.

The Israelites were punished for their wrongdoing by their own people. However, such punishment is sometimes meted out by other people or communities, especially when they can also inflict humiliation or ignominy.

Being truly ashamed of sin is the real essence of repentance (*tawbah*). This strong feeling of shame is a guarantee that the individual resolves in the innermost recesses of his heart that he will never indulge in such an act in future. When a sinner displays this feeling of shame and proves his determination never to repeat the act in question, it is as if he has embraced the faith afresh. After a period of backsliding, he re-enters the fold of God's religion.

154 When his anger had subsided, Moses took up the Tablets upon which was inscribed a pledge of guidance and mercy for those who fear their Lord.[a]

وَلَمَّا سَكَتَ عَن مُّوسَى ٱلْغَضَبُ أَخَذَ ٱلْأَلْوَاحَ ۖ وَفِى نُسْخَتِهَا هُدًى وَرَحْمَةٌ لِّلَّذِينَ هُمْ لِرَبِّهِمْ يَرْهَبُونَ ١٥٤

---

[a] The Book of God is one of guidance and grace. It is the best guide for man in the life of this world and a certain source of God's grace in the Hereafter. But the Book of God can benefit only those who fear God, who constantly think of how their fate will be decided by God. These are the people who are the real seekers after Truth. So when the Truth comes before them, they accept it without suffering from any psychological complexes. God becomes the centre of their hopes and fears. Their lives and their possessions are all then devoted to God.

Their fear of God awakens their consciousness. All barriers are removed from their eyes. They do not fail to recognize God's signs when these appear before them. In short, they live in fear and not in contentment and complacency.

155 And Moses chose from his people seventy men for Our appointment. When they were seized with violent quaking, he prayed, 'O my Lord! If it had been Your will, You could have destroyed both them and me long ago. But would You destroy us for the deeds of the foolish ones among us? This is no more than Your trial: by it You cause whom You will to stray, and You lead whom You will to the right path. You are our Protector. Forgive us, therefore, and have mercy on us, for You are the best of those who forgive. 156 Grant us good things, both in this life and in the hereafter. To You alone we turn.' He replied, 'As for My punishment, I smite with it anyone I will. But My mercy encompasses all things. I shall prescribe it for those who do their duty, pay the *zakat* and who believe in Our signs. *a*

وَٱخْتَارَ مُوسَىٰ قَوْمَهُۥ سَبْعِينَ رَجُلًا لِّمِيقَـٰتِنَا ۖ فَلَمَّآ أَخَذَتْهُمُ ٱلرَّجْفَةُ قَالَ رَبِّ لَوْ شِئْتَ أَهْلَكْتَهُم مِّن قَبْلُ وَإِيَّـٰىَ ۖ أَتُهْلِكُنَا بِمَا فَعَلَ ٱلسُّفَهَآءُ مِنَّآ ۖ إِنْ هِىَ إِلَّا فِتْنَتُكَ تُضِلُّ بِهَا مَن تَشَآءُ وَتَهْدِى مَن تَشَآءُ ۚ أَنتَ وَلِيُّنَا فَٱغْفِرْ لَنَا وَٱرْحَمْنَا ۖ وَأَنتَ خَيْرُ ٱلْغَـٰفِرِينَ ۞ ۞ وَٱكْتُبْ لَنَا فِى هَـٰذِهِ ٱلدُّنْيَا حَسَنَةً وَفِى ٱلْءَاخِرَةِ إِنَّا هُدْنَآ إِلَيْكَ ۚ قَالَ عَذَابِىٓ أُصِيبُ بِهِۦ مَنْ أَشَآءُ ۖ وَرَحْمَتِى وَسِعَتْ كُلَّ شَىْءٍ ۚ فَسَأَكْتُبُهَا لِلَّذِينَ يَتَّقُونَ وَيُؤْتُونَ ٱلزَّكَوٰةَ وَٱلَّذِينَ هُم بِـَٔايَـٰتِنَا يُؤْمِنُونَ ۞

---

a The making of a calf by the Israelites for the purposes of worship revealed that they did not have that conviction and faith in God that they should have had. So they were called by God to Mount Sinai to which Moses, along with seventy representatives of the Children of Israel, once again went at the appointed time. There God created conditions by means of thunder, lightning and earthquakes such as made them turn to God in total submission. The Children of Israel cried and wailed before God and repented collectively. They vowed that they would truly carry out the commandments of the Torah. On this occasion, Moses prayed, 'O, my Lord, ordain for us good in this world and in the Hereafter.' God said, 'I inflict My punishment on whomsoever I will and My mercy embraces all things.' Moses' prayer was for his entire community, in general, but in His reply God made it clear that salvation and success did not depend on belonging to any particular community. This would be decided in respect of every individual on the basis of his deeds. God is the most merciful, yet one who does not perform righteous deeds cannot escape God's chastisement, irrespective of his belonging to any special group.

157 Also for those who follow the Messenger—the unlettered prophet they find described in the Torah that is with them, and in the Gospel—who commands them to do right and forbids them to do wrong, who makes good things lawful to them and bad things unlawful, who will relieve them of their burdens and of the shackles that weigh upon them. Those that believe in him and honour him, those that aid him and follow the light sent down with him, shall surely triumph.'ᵃ

ٱلَّذِينَ يَتَّبِعُونَ ٱلرَّسُولَ ٱلنَّبِيَّ ٱلْأُمِّيَّ ٱلَّذِي يَجِدُونَهُ مَكْتُوبًا عِندَهُمْ فِى ٱلتَّوْرَىٰةِ وَٱلْإِنجِيلِ يَأْمُرُهُم بِٱلْمَعْرُوفِ وَيَنْهَىٰهُمْ عَنِ ٱلْمُنكَرِ وَيُحِلُّ لَهُمُ ٱلطَّيِّبَٰتِ وَيُحَرِّمُ عَلَيْهِمُ ٱلْخَبَٰٓئِثَ وَيَضَعُ عَنْهُمْ إِصْرَهُمْ وَٱلْأَغْلَٰلَ ٱلَّتِى كَانَتْ عَلَيْهِمْ فَٱلَّذِينَ ءَامَنُوا۟ بِهِۦ وَعَزَّرُوهُ وَنَصَرُوهُ وَٱتَّبَعُوا۟ ٱلنُّورَ ٱلَّذِىٓ أُنزِلَ مَعَهُۥٓ أُو۟لَٰٓئِكَ هُمُ ٱلْمُفْلِحُونَ ۝

ᵃ To the knowledge of the Israelites, whatever prophets had come, had all without exception been from their own community. Now, according to God's plan the last prophet was to be appointed from the Children of Isma'il, a fact which God had already conveyed to the Israelites through their prophets. They were given these tidings, so that when the last prophet appeared, they should not have to undergo any great trial, but be able to recognize him readily and rally to his cause. Many predictions on this subject are still extant in their Books.

The Prophet Muhammad was unlettered, so that no one might doubt his credibility. If he had been educated, people would have had their doubts that he had invented everything himself, while attributing it to God. Furthermore, according to Jewish tradition, it was predicted in the scriptures that the Final Prophet would be unlettered, so that people would have no difficulty in recognizing him as a prophet of God.

The real spirit of religion is the fear of God and concern for the Hereafter. But in the later generations (of a prophet or a reformer) when the inner spirit became less ardent, and the utmost importance was attached to the form, the Prophet Muhammad brought the pure religion, free of all human additions and interpolations.

When a prophet appears, the greatest virtue lies in believing in him. But this Faith does not simply mean reciting a few words as if performing a ritual. It, in fact, amounts to abandoning the soulless structure of rituals in favour of a living religion, having direct appeal to human nature. Man's links with the former religious structure rest simply on the strength of historical traditions and racial customs. But when he accepts a new religion (of a new prophet) it involves a conscious decision on his part. He leaves behind him soulless rituals and opts for the reality. This appears to be a simple matter, but this has proved to be the most difficult step to take in every age. (That is, people find it most difficult to see beyond appearances).

¹⁵⁸ Say, 'People, I am God's Messenger to you all, He has sovereignty over the heavens and the earth. There is no god but Him. He ordains life and death, so believe in God and His Messenger, the unlettered prophet who believes in God and His words. Follow him so that you may be rightly guided.' ¹⁵⁹ Yet there is a group among the people of Moses who guide with truth and act justly in accordance with it.^a

قُلْ يَا أَيُّهَا ٱلنَّاسُ إِنِّي رَسُولُ ٱللَّهِ إِلَيْكُمْ جَمِيعًا ٱلَّذِي لَهُ مُلْكُ ٱلسَّمَوَٰتِ وَٱلْأَرْضِ لَا إِلَهَ إِلَّا هُوَ يُحْىِۦ وَيُمِيتُ فَآمِنُوا بِٱللَّهِ وَرَسُولِهِ ٱلنَّبِيِّ ٱلْأُمِّيِّ ٱلَّذِي يُؤْمِنُ بِٱللَّهِ وَكَلِمَٰتِهِۦ وَٱتَّبِعُوهُ لَعَلَّكُمْ تَهْتَدُونَ ۝ وَمِن قَوْمِ مُوسَىٰ أُمَّةٌ يَهْدُونَ بِٱلْحَقِّ وَبِهِۦ يَعْدِلُونَ ۝

---

^a 'Say, "People, I am God's Messenger to you all,"' does not mean that all other prophets were sent to their own community while the Prophet Muhammad was sent to all the nations. This statement is not meant to compare one prophet with any other, but is simply a statement of fact. In fact, the prophethood of the Prophet Muhammad has two distinct aspects. One is direct and the other through his community, the '*ummah*'. He was sent to convey the divine message directly to people living in Arabia (6:92) and he was to convey the message indirectly to the whole world (22:78).

In principle, this was the nature of the task assigned to all the prophets of God. But the religion brought by other prophets did not remain in its original, pristine condition, hence it was not possible for them to become the givers of good tidings or to warn the people of the consequences of their actions in the life to come, that being the main duty of a prophet.

About the Arab Prophet there is a prediction in the Bible that all the tribes of the earth will be blessed through him (Genesis, Ch. 12) It has been possible for his blessings to reach all nations because the religion brought by him has been preserved in its original state. The religion brought by Moses and Jesus Christ has been distorted. Therefore, its voice may reach everybody, but its blessings will not. ▶

160 We divided them up into twelve tribes, each a whole community, and We revealed Our will to Moses, when his people asked for water, saying, 'Strike the rock with your staff.' Twelve springs gushed from it and each tribe knew its drinking place. We caused the clouds to draw their shadow over them and sent down for them manna and quails, saying, 'Eat the good things We have given you.' They did not wrong Us; rather it was themselves they wronged.*

وَقَطَّعْنَٰهُمُ ٱثْنَتَىْ عَشْرَةَ أَسْبَاطًا أُمَمًا وَأَوْحَيْنَآ إِلَىٰ مُوسَىٰٓ إِذِ ٱسْتَسْقَىٰهُ قَوْمُهُۥٓ أَنِ ٱضْرِب بِّعَصَاكَ ٱلْحَجَرَ فَٱنۢبَجَسَتْ مِنْهُ ٱثْنَتَا عَشْرَةَ عَيْنًا قَدْ عَلِمَ كُلُّ أُنَاسٍ مَّشْرَبَهُمْ وَظَلَّلْنَا عَلَيْهِمُ ٱلْغَمَٰمَ وَأَنزَلْنَا عَلَيْهِمُ ٱلْمَنَّ وَٱلسَّلْوَىٰ كُلُوا۟ مِن طَيِّبَٰتِ مَا رَزَقْنَٰكُمْ وَمَا ظَلَمُونَا وَلَٰكِن كَانُوٓا۟ أَنفُسَهُمْ يَظْلِمُونَ ﴿١٦٠﴾

A number of Jewish tribes were settled in Arabia, who were proud of having God's holy Book.

Such people resist accepting any external truth. Their feeling that they are in possession of the greatest Truth hinders them from accepting any Truth brought to them by any other. The large majority of the Jews were blinded by obstinacy and prejudice, except for a few people like 'Abdullah ibn Salam, who could look upon Islam with an open mind. They vouched for its veracity without caring for their worldly honour and surrendered themselves wholeheartedly to it.

'The unlettered prophet who believes in God and His words.' This statement indicates the difference between the philosopher's concept of God and the prophet's concept of God. The philosopher's God is an abstract spirit. Accepting Him is like accepting the force of gravity in the universe. But the force of gravity neither speaks nor gives commands, whereas the God of the prophet is a living and conscious God. He speaks to human beings; He commands His subjects and decides on reward or punishment on the basis of obedience or disobedience to His commands.

a God took the Israelites from the polytheistic atmosphere of Egypt and settled them in the desert of Sinai. Here they were organised and divided into twelve groups. Each group had a leader and all were under the charge of Moses.

Then, the Children of Israel were specially provided with all the necessities of life. Water was provided for them from mountain springs. For their food, 'manna and quails' were sent down and these were readily available to them right in front of their tents. For their regular settlement one entire city, Ariho, (in the Jordan valley) was given to them.

God then advised them that He had arranged for all their necessities and that they should therefore desist from being greedy for the pleasures of the world and the flesh and should not rush towards unholy things; instead, they should adopt the way of contentment and gratefulness towards God.

¹⁶¹ When they were told, 'Settle down in the town and eat wherever you wish in it, and pray for forgiveness and enter the gate in humility: We shall forgive you your sins and shall bestow further favours upon those who do good,' ¹⁶² the transgressors among them substituted something else for the word they had been given. So We sent them a punishment from heaven for their wrongdoing.ᵃ

وَإِذْ قِيلَ لَهُمُ ٱسْكُنُوا۟ هَٰذِهِ ٱلْقَرْيَةَ وَكُلُوا۟ مِنْهَا حَيْثُ شِئْتُمْ وَقُولُوا۟ حِطَّةٌ وَٱدْخُلُوا۟ ٱلْبَابَ سُجَّدًا نَّغْفِرْ لَكُمْ خَطِيٓـَٰٔتِكُمْ ۚ سَنَزِيدُ ٱلْمُحْسِنِينَ ۝ فَبَدَّلَ ٱلَّذِينَ ظَلَمُوا۟ مِنْهُمْ قَوْلًا غَيْرَ ٱلَّذِى قِيلَ لَهُمْ فَأَرْسَلْنَا عَلَيْهِمْ رِجْزًا مِّنَ ٱلسَّمَآءِ بِمَا كَانُوا۟ يَظْلِمُونَ ۝

ᵃ Literally, 'Enter the gate bowing down or kneeling down.' The Jews were asked to enter their place of worship with humility and modesty and to worship their Lord; they were enjoined to remember the majesty and supremacy of God and admit their shortcomings before Him. But the Jews forgot the admonition of God. Instead of adopting the way shown by God, they followed a path devised by themselves in the name of God. They adopted the way of arrogance instead of treading the path of humility. Their utterances were not of gratitude but of insolence.

When the Jews went to this extent in their wrongdoing, God withdrew His grace from them. They were surrounded by different kinds of punishments instead of God's blessings.

163 Ask them about the town which was by the sea and what befell its people when they broke the Sabbath. On their Sabbath the fish came to them near the surface, but on week-days they never came near them—thus We tried them because of their disobedience. 164 When some of them asked, 'Why do you admonish a people whom God is going to destroy or to afflict with a severe punishment?' They answered, 'In order to be free from blame before your Lord, and that they may perhaps fear Him.'ᵃ

وَسْـَٔلْهُمْ عَنِ ٱلْقَرْيَةِ ٱلَّتِى كَانَتْ حَاضِرَةَ ٱلْبَحْرِ إِذْ يَعْدُونَ فِى ٱلسَّبْتِ إِذْ تَأْتِيهِمْ حِيتَانُهُمْ يَوْمَ سَبْتِهِمْ شُرَّعًا وَيَوْمَ لَا يَسْبِتُونَ لَا تَأْتِيهِمْ كَذَٰلِكَ نَبْلُوهُم بِمَا كَانُوا۟ يَفْسُقُونَ ۝ وَإِذْ قَالَتْ أُمَّةٌ مِّنْهُمْ لِمَ تَعِظُونَ قَوْمًا ٱللَّهُ مُهْلِكُهُمْ أَوْ مُعَذِّبُهُمْ عَذَابًا شَدِيدًا قَالُوا۟ مَعْذِرَةً إِلَىٰ رَبِّكُمْ وَلَعَلَّهُمْ يَتَّقُونَ ۝

ᵃ It is a sin to do anything which God has prohibited. But to perform a prohibited act by attempting to legalize it through some trick amounts to adding insult to injury. By violating the rule of the Sabbath, the Jews had committed a double sin. Such people must suffer divine retribution; that is, they are deprived of the bounties which God has set apart for human beings alone. In this world such people fall from the level of humanity to the level of the animals.

¹⁶⁵ Therefore when they forgot what they had been reminded of, We saved those who had tried to prevent the doing of evil. And We meted out a severe punishment to the transgressors because they were rebellious. ¹⁶⁶ And then, when they disdainfully persisted in doing what they had been forbidden to do, We said to them, 'Be as apes, despised!' *ᵃ*

فَلَمَّا نَسُوا۟ مَا ذُكِّرُوا۟ بِهِۦٓ أَنجَيۡنَا ٱلَّذِينَ يَنۡهَوۡنَ عَنِ ٱلسُّوٓءِ وَأَخَذۡنَا ٱلَّذِينَ ظَلَمُوا۟ بِعَذَابٍۭ بَـِٔيسٍۭ بِمَا كَانُوا۟ يَفۡسُقُونَ ۝ فَلَمَّا عَتَوۡا۟ عَن مَّا نُهُوا۟ عَنۡهُ قُلۡنَا لَهُمۡ كُونُوا۟ قِرَدَةً خَـٰسِـِٔينَ ۝

ᵃ This was the fate of those who contravened the rule of the Sabbath. But 'God made them apes,' does not mean that their faces became the faces of apes; it means that their character became ape-like; their hearts and thinking were like those of apes instead of human beings. *(Tafsir al-Qurtubi).*

Now, man's becoming an ape means that he becomes so insensitive after taking action again and again against the dictates of his wisdom and conscience, that any fine feelings are completely driven out of him. Whatever desire takes shape in his heart, he puts it into action. Whenever anyone comes into his ambit, he will attack his honour and property. If he has a complaint against anybody, he will immediately set about degrading that person. If he has any differences with anybody, he will start denigrating him. If he finds somebody to be an impediment in his way, he will immediately start fighting with him. A true man is one who applies the bridle of God to himself, and an ape is one who unrestrictedly starts doing whatever his base self asks him to do.

Preventing others from doing evil is, in fact, a way of proclaiming that one has discharged one's responsibility. So, when God's scourge falls upon a group, those people who are extremely disgusted with evil, to the extent of becoming its preventers, are saved from this punishment.

A human being is a creature into whom the Creator has infused intelligence and conscience. In a human being when some desire takes shape, his wisdom and conscience immediately becomes activated and the question arises as to whether the fulfillment of that desire is proper or not. In the case of an ape, however, there is no impediment between his wish and its fulfillment. Whatever comes into his mind he immediately does it. It is not necessary for him to think about his wish, nor need he be ashamed after pursuing it.

167 Then your Lord declared that, until the Day of Resurrection, He would send others against them to inflict terrible suffering on them. Your Lord is swift in retribution; yet surely He is most forgiving and merciful. 168 We split them up into sections on the earth. Some of them are righteous while some of them are otherwise, and We tested them with blessings and misfortunes, so that they might return to the right path.[a]

وَإِذْ تَأَذَّنَ رَبُّكَ لَيَبْعَثَنَّ عَلَيْهِمْ إِلَىٰ يَوْمِ ٱلْقِيَـٰمَةِ مَن يَسُومُهُمْ سُوٓءَ ٱلْعَذَابِ إِنَّ رَبَّكَ لَسَرِيعُ ٱلْعِقَابِ وَإِنَّهُۥ لَغَفُورٌ رَّحِيمٌ ۝ وَقَطَّعْنَـٰهُمْ فِى ٱلْأَرْضِ أُمَمًا مِّنْهُمُ ٱلصَّـٰلِحُونَ وَمِنْهُمْ دُونَ ذَٰلِكَ وَبَلَوْنَـٰهُم بِٱلْحَسَنَـٰتِ وَٱلسَّيِّـَٔاتِ لَعَلَّهُمْ يَرْجِعُونَ ۝

[a] When a great reward is given for the performance of a task, it follows that the punishment for non-performance of that task will be equally great. This is the case in respect of a community which has been made the bearer of the Holy Book. God had elevated the Jews to this status. So, besides being made promises of bounties in the Hereafter, they were granted extraordinary benefits in the world as well. But the Jews continuously indulged in disobedience, committing irreligious acts in the name of practicing religion. The result was that God deposed them from their elevated status. It was decided that so long as the world existed, they would continue to experience God's punishment, and whatever was going to happen in the Hereafter would be further to that.

This does not mean that till Doomsday, they would never have good fortune. As is clarified in these verses themselves, they would have intervals of good days, but such periods would themselves be a sort of divine curse on them, in as much as it would be an opportunity for them to indulge in more insolence and thus become liable for more punishment.

This universal law of God was not solely for the Jews. It was applicable to even that later group which was raised, after the deposition of the Jews, to the elevated position of God's witnesses. If Muslims find that they are being dominated by those who deny the truth and polytheists, and that their various groups have become scattered, then they must revert to God, because this shows that they have incurred God's displeasure.

¹⁶⁹ They were succeeded by generations who inherited the Scripture and took to the fleeting gains of this world, saying, 'We shall certainly be forgiven.' If there came to them similar fleeting gains again, they would take them. Was a pledge not taken from them, written in the Scripture, that they would not say anything but the truth about God? And they have studied whatever is in it. Surely the Home of the Hereafter is better for those who fear Him. Will you not understand?^a

فَخَلَفَ مِنۢ بَعۡدِهِمۡ خَلۡفٌ وَرِثُواْ
ٱلۡكِتَٰبَ يَأۡخُذُونَ عَرَضَ هَٰذَا ٱلۡأَدۡنَىٰ
وَيَقُولُونَ سَيُغۡفَرُ لَنَا وَإِن يَأۡتِهِمۡ عَرَضٌ
مِّثۡلُهُۥ يَأۡخُذُوهُ أَلَمۡ يُؤۡخَذۡ عَلَيۡهِم
مِّيثَٰقُ ٱلۡكِتَٰبِ أَن لَّا يَقُولُواْ عَلَى ٱللَّهِ
إِلَّا ٱلۡحَقَّ وَدَرَسُواْ مَا فِيهِ وَٱلدَّارُ
ٱلۡأٓخِرَةُ خَيۡرٌ لِّلَّذِينَ يَتَّقُونَ أَفَلَا
تَعۡقِلُونَ ﴿١٦٩﴾

---

^a During the time of Moses, Jews were given the commandments of God, the event having taken place at the foot of a hill. At that time such conditions were created that the Jews felt as if the hill was about to fall on them. This was to impress upon them that giving a pledge to God was a very serious matter, and that if they did not fulfil the conditions of the pledge, they had to remember that the other party to this pledge was that majestic Being who, if He so desired, could cause the hill to fall on them.

At that time, there were many people among the Jews who were God-fearing and righteous in their deeds. But, later on, they gradually adopted the world as the goal of their life. They started accumulating wealth without having any scruples about its being legitimate or otherwise. Even then, they used to read the Holy Book, but by means of self-devised interpretations, they gave it such a colour that God Himself appeared to be supporting their rebellious way of life. Their insensitiveness increased to the extent that they took satisfaction in declaring, 'We are a pious community; we are the progeny of prophets; God will forgive us in the name of His favourite subjects.'

170 As for those who hold fast to the Book and are steadfast in prayer, We shall not deny the righteous their reward. 171 When We suspended the mountain over them as if it were a canopy, and they thought it was going to fall down on them, We said, 'Hold on firmly to what We have given you and remember what is in it, so that you may remain conscious of God.'

172 When your Lord brought forth offspring from the loins of the Children of Adam and made them bear witness about themselves, He said, 'Am I not your Lord?' They replied, 'We bear witness that You are.' This He did, lest you should say on the Day of Resurrection, 'We had no knowledge of that.'ᵃ

وَٱلَّذِينَ يُمَسِّكُونَ بِٱلْكِتَٰبِ وَأَقَامُوا۟ ٱلصَّلَوٰةَ إِنَّا لَا نُضِيعُ أَجْرَ ٱلْمُصْلِحِينَ ۝ وَإِذْ نَتَقْنَا ٱلْجَبَلَ فَوْقَهُمْ كَأَنَّهُ ظُلَّةٌ وَظَنُّوٓا۟ أَنَّهُ وَاقِعٌۢ بِهِمْ خُذُوا۟ مَآ ءَاتَيْنَٰكُم بِقُوَّةٍ وَٱذْكُرُوا۟ مَا فِيهِ لَعَلَّكُمْ تَتَّقُونَ ۝ وَإِذْ أَخَذَ رَبُّكَ مِنۢ بَنِىٓ ءَادَمَ مِن ظُهُورِهِمْ ذُرِّيَّتَهُمْ وَأَشْهَدَهُمْ عَلَىٰٓ أَنفُسِهِمْ أَلَسْتُ بِرَبِّكُمْ قَالُوا۟ بَلَىٰ شَهِدْنَآ أَن تَقُولُوا۟ يَوْمَ ٱلْقِيَٰمَةِ إِنَّا كُنَّا عَنْ هَٰذَا غَٰفِلِينَ ۝

ᵃ This happens in the case of every prophet's community. In the beginning, its individuals are God-fearing and pious. But in later generations, this spirit vanishes. They become just like other worldly people. Religion is still amongst them. The Holy Book is still read and taught. But all this is done in the context of a national heritage and not as a real fulfilment of a pledge to God. They proceed in the way of the world and in practice forget the Hereafter. Being completely unmindful of right or wrong, they make their desire their religion. At the same time they are proud of being the best of all communities. They are the members of the community of one who is God's favourite; they are the inheritors of the Holy Book; by the grace of the belief in monotheism they shall certainly be granted salvation.

But the truth is that man should hold fast to God's Word; he should regularly say his prayers. And the sign of holding fast God's Book and of having said his prayers sincerely is that he should have become a maintainer of peace and harmony (muslihun).

Communion with God's Book and God's worship are what makes a man opposed to one who disturbs the peace.

¹⁷³ Or lest you say, 'Our forefathers associated others with God before our time, and we are only the descendants who came after them. So are You going to destroy us for what those inventors of falsehood did?' ¹⁷⁴ We explain Our signs in detail thus, so that perhaps they may return to Us.ᵃ

أَوْ تَقُولُوٓاْ إِنَّمَآ أَشْرَكَ ءَابَآؤُنَا مِن قَبْلُ وَكُنَّا ذُرِّيَّةً مِّنۢ بَعْدِهِمْ أَفَتُهْلِكُنَا بِمَا فَعَلَ ٱلْمُبْطِلُونَ ۝ وَكَذَٰلِكَ نُفَصِّلُ ٱلْأَيَـٰتِ وَلَعَلَّهُمْ يَرْجِعُونَ ۝

ᵃ If an animal is separated from its father and mother and it is brought up in a strange atmosphere, even after growing up it retains the characteristics of its species. The way it behaves in all its dealings is rooted in its instinct. The same is true of the human being as regards his 'God-consciousness'. In the soul of a human being the consciousness of a Creator and Lord has been instilled so deeply that he never loses it.

However, there is one difference between animals and human beings. Animals are not capable of going against their nature. They are compelled to do whatever their inner nature urges them to do. But the case of a human being is different. This awareness is embedded in his nature, but he is completely free in the matter of action, even although his mind and his conscience start pointing out to him what is right and what is wrong. A human being has, therefore, the power and the option either to follow his inner voice, or to ignore it and start doing whatever he likes.

It is on such occasions of moral choice that man is on trial and on the basis of its result, decisions regarding heaven or hell are taken. The one who lends his ears to the voice of God and does whatever He tells him to do through the silent language of 'Nature', passes the test. The doors of heaven (Paradise) will be thrown open for him after death, whereas one who ignores the voice of God speaking at Nature's level, will be held guilty in the eyes of God and he will be ignored by God, just as he ignored God's voice. This voice of inner nature is, in itself, evidence of the existence of God. Now, nobody has the excuse of ignorance and nobody can say that he is just doing whatever has been done since ancient times. Man brings the consciousness of God along with him from his birth. This consciousness remains preserved even with changes in his circumstances. In view of this, what excuse has anyone to follow the path of misguidance?

¹⁷⁵ Recite to them the tale of the man to whom We gave Our signs, but who then cast them to one side and Satan overtook him. And he became one of those who went astray—¹⁷⁶ if it had been Our will, We could have used these signs to exalt him, but instead he clung to the earth and followed his own desires—he was like a dog that pants whether you chase it away or leave it alone. Such are those who reject Our signs. Tell them this story so that they may reflect. ¹⁷⁷ How evil is the case of those who deny Our signs. They only wrong themselves: ¹⁷⁸ anyone whom God guides has been rightly guided; while those He lets go astray will surely be the losers.^a

وَٱتْلُ عَلَيْهِمْ نَبَأَ ٱلَّذِىٓ ءَاتَيْنَٰهُ ءَايَٰتِنَا فَٱنسَلَخَ مِنْهَا فَأَتْبَعَهُ ٱلشَّيْطَٰنُ فَكَانَ مِنَ ٱلْغَاوِينَ ۞ وَلَوْ شِئْنَا لَرَفَعْنَٰهُ بِهَا وَلَٰكِنَّهُۥٓ أَخْلَدَ إِلَى ٱلْأَرْضِ وَٱتَّبَعَ هَوَىٰهُ ۚ فَمَثَلُهُۥ كَمَثَلِ ٱلْكَلْبِ إِن تَحْمِلْ عَلَيْهِ يَلْهَثْ أَوْ تَتْرُكْهُ يَلْهَث ۚ ذَّٰلِكَ مَثَلُ ٱلْقَوْمِ ٱلَّذِينَ كَذَّبُوا۟ بِـَٔايَٰتِنَا ۚ فَٱقْصُصِ ٱلْقَصَصَ لَعَلَّهُمْ يَتَفَكَّرُونَ ۞ سَآءَ مَثَلًا ٱلْقَوْمُ ٱلَّذِينَ كَذَّبُوا۟ بِـَٔايَٰتِنَا وَأَنفُسَهُمْ كَانُوا۟ يَظْلِمُونَ ۞ مَن يَهْدِ ٱللَّهُ فَهُوَ ٱلْمُهْتَدِى ۖ وَمَن يُضْلِلْ فَأُو۟لَٰٓئِكَ هُمُ ٱلْخَٰسِرُونَ ۞

---

^a During the period of the Prophet Muhammad there was a man of great moral and intellectual distinction called Umayyah ibn Abi as-Salt. When he came to know that there were predictions in the Holy Books of the Christians and Jews about the coming of a prophet, he felt that he himself was that prophet. Later, when he was informed about the claim to prophethood made by the Prophet Muhammad and he heard the fine discourse revealed to him, he was greatly disappointed, and became an opponent of the Prophet. The proper use of the superior qualities given by God to Umayyah ibn Abi as-Salt would have been to recognise the Prophet of God and then become his companion. But because of the blessings of God already showered on him, he formed the idea that God should have showered the blessing of prophethood on him rather than on anyone else. He saw worldly benefit in the rejection of the Prophet of God while, on the contrary, acceptance of the Prophet would have led to benefit in the Hereafter. Had he gone in the direction of acceptance, he could have made the angels his fellow travellers. But when he walked the path of jealousy and pride, there was nobody except Satan to give him company. This example is applicable to all those people who ignore the Truth or refuse to accept it on the basis of jealousy and haughtiness. ▶

179 We created many of the jinn and mankind for hell. They have hearts they do not understand with; they have eyes they do not see with; and they have ears they do not hear with. Such people are like cattle—no, they are even more misguided. Such are the heedless.[a]

وَلَقَدْ ذَرَأْنَا لِجَهَنَّمَ كَثِيرًا مِّنَ ٱلْجِنِّ وَٱلْإِنسِ لَهُمْ قُلُوبٌ لَّا يَفْقَهُونَ بِهَا وَلَهُمْ أَعْيُنٌ لَّا يُبْصِرُونَ بِهَا وَلَهُمْ ءَاذَانٌ لَّا يَسْمَعُونَ بِهَآ أُوْلَٰٓئِكَ كَٱلْأَنْعَٰمِ بَلْ هُمْ أَضَلُّ أُوْلَٰٓئِكَ هُمُ ٱلْغَٰفِلُونَ

A man's becoming like this amounts to falling down from the status of humanity to the status of a dog. A dog pants on good treatment as well as on bad. This is the condition of such a man. When God blessed him, he became arrogant and when He did not bless him, he still remained arrogant. Actually, he should have been grateful and obliged to God for His blessing, and when he did not receive some blessing, he should have reconciled himself to God's dispensation and turned back to Him.

God does not openly appear to guide people, He shows His way to the people by means of signs. Those who have the ability to recognize Truth as it appears in the shape of signs and arguments, and are ready to surrender to it, are the ones who avail of guidance in this world. And for those who do not attach importance to signs and arguments, there is nothing but eternal destruction.

[a] The Truth is a thing which a man has to discover by himself. God has given everyone a heart (mind), eyes and ears. Man arrives at the Truth by utilizing these faculties. The man who does not do so will be unable to discover the Truth, howsoever close it may be to him.

Discovery of the Truth is the conscious and deliberate act of every man. Only one who has kept the doors of his heart (mind) open for the purpose, will be able to understand the Truth. Only one who has not covered his eyes with artificial veils will be able to see it. Only one who has not plugged his ears will hear its voice. Such people will recognise the voice of Truth and will surrender themselves before it. And one whose case is opposite to this will remain mindless like the animals. It will not be possible for him to be moved by even the weightiest of arguments. Flashes of God's brilliant light will appear before him, but he will not be able to see them. The melody of Divine song will come to his ears, but he will be prevented from hearing it. Truth is available to those who are awake; for neglectful people, no truth is Truth.

478

¹⁸⁰ God has the Most Excellent Names. Call on Him by His Names and keep away from those who distort them. They shall be requited for what they do. ¹⁸¹ Of those We have created there are some who give true guidance and act justly. ¹⁸² We shall gradually seize those who reject Our signs from a place they do not recognize. ¹⁸³ For though I give them rein for a while, My strategy is sure.ᵃ

¹⁸⁴ Have they not reflected that their companion is not mad?ᵇ He is only a plain warner. ¹⁸⁵ Have they not looked into the realms of the heavens and the earth and all that God created, and seen that the end of their time might be near? What will they believe in if they do not believe in this? ¹⁸⁶ No one can guide those whom God lets go astray: He leaves them blundering about in their arrogance.

وَلِلَّهِ ٱلْأَسْمَاءُ ٱلْحُسْنَىٰ فَٱدْعُوهُ بِهَا وَذَرُوا۟ ٱلَّذِينَ يُلْحِدُونَ فِىٓ أَسْمَـٰٓئِهِۦ سَيُجْزَوْنَ مَا كَانُوا۟ يَعْمَلُونَ ۝ وَمِمَّنْ خَلَقْنَآ أُمَّةٌ يَهْدُونَ بِٱلْحَقِّ وَبِهِۦ يَعْدِلُونَ ۝ وَٱلَّذِينَ كَذَّبُوا۟ بِـَٔايَـٰتِنَا سَنَسْتَدْرِجُهُم مِّنْ حَيْثُ لَا يَعْلَمُونَ ۝ وَأُمْلِى لَهُمْ إِنَّ كَيْدِى مَتِينٌ ۝ أَوَلَمْ يَتَفَكَّرُوا۟ مَا بِصَاحِبِهِم مِّن جِنَّةٍ إِنْ هُوَ إِلَّا نَذِيرٌ مُّبِينٌ ۝ أَوَلَمْ يَنظُرُوا۟ فِى مَلَكُوتِ ٱلسَّمَـٰوَٰتِ وَٱلْأَرْضِ وَمَا خَلَقَ ٱللَّهُ مِن شَىْءٍ وَأَنْ عَسَىٰٓ أَن يَكُونَ قَدِ ٱقْتَرَبَ أَجَلُهُمْ فَبِأَىِّ حَدِيثٍ بَعْدَهُۥ يُؤْمِنُونَ ۝ مَن يُضْلِلِ ٱللَّهُ فَلَا هَادِىَ لَهُۥ وَيَذَرُهُمْ فِى طُغْيَـٰنِهِمْ يَعْمَهُونَ ۝

ᵃ The reason for man's being misguided in respect of God is that, although he accepts His existence, he often frames a wrong image of God in his mind. He attributes some things to God which do not befit His glory. For example, imagining things as in the case of a human being, he formulates the idea of God's close ones. Looking at Kings, he assumes the existence of deputies and assistants of God, just as there are regents and advisers of Kings. In the matter of God's decisions, he assumes such things as fulfil his desires, but which are not in accordance with God's justice. Attributing to God such matters as are not consistent with His Majesty and Glory amounts to distortion of the names of God.

God does not seize a person immediately for his wrongdoing. In this way, he is given the opportunity either to take a lesson from God's warnings and reform himself, or to become still more fearless so that his guilt becomes well-established.

ᵇ A man with a mission is a man of principle. His thinking is unconditioned thinking. He has risen above all kinds of worldly interests. Truth becomes his sole concern. ▶

187 They ask you [Prophet] about the Last Hour, 'When will it come?' Say, 'Knowledge about it rests only with my Lord; He alone will reveal when its time will come, it lies heavy on the heavens and the earth: it will suddenly overtake you.' They will put questions to you as though you had full knowledge of it. Say, 'Knowledge about it rests only with God, though most people do not realize it.' 188 Say, 'I myself have no power to benefit or do harm, save as God pleases. If I had knowledge of the unseen, I would have availed myself of an abundance of good, and no harm would have touched me. I am but a warner and a bearer of good tidings for those who will believe.' *a*

يَسْـَٔلُونَكَ عَنِ ٱلسَّاعَةِ أَيَّانَ مُرْسَىٰهَا ۖ قُلْ إِنَّمَا عِلْمُهَا عِندَ رَبِّى ۖ لَا يُجَلِّيهَا لِوَقْتِهَآ إِلَّا هُوَ ۚ ثَقُلَتْ فِى ٱلسَّمَٰوَٰتِ وَٱلْأَرْضِ ۚ لَا تَأْتِيكُمْ إِلَّا بَغْتَةً ۗ يَسْـَٔلُونَكَ كَأَنَّكَ حَفِىٌّ عَنْهَا ۖ قُلْ إِنَّمَا عِلْمُهَا عِندَ ٱللَّهِ وَلَٰكِنَّ أَكْثَرَ ٱلنَّاسِ لَا يَعْلَمُونَ ۝ قُل لَّآ أَمْلِكُ لِنَفْسِى نَفْعًا وَلَا ضَرًّا إِلَّا مَا شَآءَ ٱللَّهُ ۚ وَلَوْ كُنتُ أَعْلَمُ ٱلْغَيْبَ لَٱسْتَكْثَرْتُ مِنَ ٱلْخَيْرِ وَمَا مَسَّنِىَ ٱلسُّوٓءُ ۚ إِنْ أَنَا۠ إِلَّا نَذِيرٌ وَبَشِيرٌ لِّقَوْمٍ يُؤْمِنُونَ ۝

He sacrifices his life and property for a goal, which does not appear to yield any result in this world. That is why a man with a mission is called crazy, out of his mind. A prophet of God was the greatest man with a mission of his time. So, people in every age have called the prophets of God fanatics.

To call a missionary of God's religion a madman is the greatest of all transgressions, because the message with which he comes is one which is corroborated by the entire heaven and earth. He calls mankind towards God who is supremely manifest in His Creations in the Universe. He informs people of the Hereafter which, in heaven and on the earth, is equal in gravity to a full pregnancy in a woman's womb. But people are not serious about the truth. So, a man who sacrifices his life for the sake of the truth appears mad to them. Had they known the real value of truth, they would never have used the word 'mad'.

a 'On which day will Doomsday occur?' Questions of this sort are produced by non-serious minds. Only the sincere will believe in the Day of Judgement, without wanting to know the exact date of its occurrence. As this world is a place of testing, Doomsday will be indicated here in terms of caution and warning alone.

¹⁸⁹ It was He who created you from a single soul, and from it made its mate so that he may find comfort in her. Once he has covered her, she conceives and goes about with a light burden. When it grows heavy, they both call to God, their Lord, 'If You bestow on us a healthy child, we will surely be grateful,' ¹⁹⁰ yet when He grants them a healthy child, they begin to ascribe to others a share in the gift they have received. But God is far above what they associate with Him! ¹⁹¹ Do they associate with Him those who create nothing and are themselves created? ¹⁹² They can give them no help, nor can they help themselves. ¹⁹³ It makes no difference whether you call on them or remain silent. If you call them to the right path, they will not follow you. ¹⁹⁴ Those whom you call on besides God are but creatures like yourselves. Call upon them, then, and let them respond to you, if what you say is true.^a

هُوَ ٱلَّذِى خَلَقَكُم مِّن نَّفْسٍ وَٰحِدَةٍ وَجَعَلَ مِنْهَا زَوْجَهَا لِيَسْكُنَ إِلَيْهَا فَلَمَّا تَغَشَّىٰهَا حَمَلَتْ حَمْلًا خَفِيفًا فَمَرَّتْ بِهِۦ فَلَمَّآ أَثْقَلَت دَّعَوَا ٱللَّهَ رَبَّهُمَا لَئِنْ ءَاتَيْتَنَا صَٰلِحًا لَّنَكُونَنَّ مِنَ ٱلشَّٰكِرِينَ ۝ فَلَمَّآ ءَاتَىٰهُمَا صَٰلِحًا جَعَلَا لَهُۥ شُرَكَآءَ فِيمَآ ءَاتَىٰهُمَا فَتَعَٰلَى ٱللَّهُ عَمَّا يُشْرِكُونَ ۝ أَيُشْرِكُونَ مَا لَا يَخْلُقُ شَيْـًٔا وَهُمْ يُخْلَقُونَ ۝ وَلَا يَسْتَطِيعُونَ لَهُمْ نَصْرًا وَلَآ أَنفُسَهُمْ يَنصُرُونَ ۝ وَإِن تَدْعُوهُمْ إِلَى ٱلْهُدَىٰ لَا يَتَّبِعُوكُمْ سَوَآءٌ عَلَيْكُمْ أَدَعَوْتُمُوهُمْ أَمْ أَنتُمْ صَٰمِتُونَ ۝ إِنَّ ٱلَّذِينَ تَدْعُونَ مِن دُونِ ٱللَّهِ عِبَادٌ أَمْثَالُكُمْ فَٱدْعُوهُمْ فَلْيَسْتَجِيبُوا۟ لَكُمْ إِن كُنتُمْ صَٰدِقِينَ ۝

^a This vast universe itself introduces its Creator. This introduction in no case admits of the concept of polytheism. In the universe countless items or parts are found separately; but all these parts combine and become a harmonious whole. There is no contradiction or clash among them. This perfect harmony could not be possible unless the Creator and Lord of this universe were one and in control of its functioning.

Look at the case of man and woman. Man and woman both are born as independent beings. But at the same time both are complementary to each other in the full sense of the word. This harmony is so perfect that each of them feels that he or she was created for the other. This is a most wonderful example of harmony in this world. This harmony is a clear proof that both the male and the female were created by one and the same God. Had there been more than one Being in action in the universe, this perfect harmony between two different and opposite entities would not have been possible.

195 Have they feet to walk with? Have they hands to hold with? Have they eyes to see with? Have they ears to hear with? Say, 'Call upon those you associate with God as partners, then all of you contrive against me and give me no respite. 196 My protector is God who sent down the Book, for it is He who protects the righteous.[a]

أَلَهُمْ أَرْجُلٌ يَمْشُونَ بِهَا ۖ أَمْ لَهُمْ أَيْدٍ يَبْطِشُونَ بِهَا ۖ أَمْ لَهُمْ أَعْيُنٌ يُبْصِرُونَ بِهَا ۖ أَمْ لَهُمْ ءَاذَانٌ يَسْمَعُونَ بِهَا ۗ قُلِ ٱدْعُوا۟ شُرَكَآءَكُمْ ثُمَّ كِيدُونِ فَلَا تُنظِرُونِ ۝ إِنَّ وَلِۦَّۧ ٱللَّهُ ٱلَّذِى نَزَّلَ ٱلْكِتَٰبَ ۖ وَهُوَ يَتَوَلَّى ٱلصَّٰلِحِينَ ۝

[a] But how surprising it is that in this world, where there are so many arguments in favour of one God, man makes polytheism his religion. By this miraculous harmony between two human beings, a child is born. Now some hold the belief that this has happened due to the blessing of some living or dead saint, some attribute it to certain supposed deities; some say that it was the result of some action and reaction between certain blind forces of matter, while others thought that it was the result of their own striving that had come to them in the shape of a beautiful baby.

Behind the idols of stone or metal set up by polytheists is the 'philosophy' that these are external manifestations and in them their alleged god has become incarnate. By this token, the worship of these manifestations amounts to the worship of the god whom they are supposed to represent. However, at the level of the common people, polytheism takes the shape of people considering these idols themselves as holy. These idols are not capable of walking or talking or seeing or hearing, but superstitious man presumes they will be of use to him and will fulfil his needs.

197 'Those whom you call on besides Him have no power to help you, nor can they help themselves.' 198 If you call them to the right path, they will not hear you. You find them looking towards you, but they do not see you.ᵃ

وَٱلَّذِينَ تَدْعُونَ مِن دُونِهِۦ لَا يَسْتَطِيعُونَ نَصْرَكُمْ وَلَآ أَنفُسَهُمْ يَنصُرُونَ ۝ وَإِن تَدْعُوهُمْ إِلَى ٱلْهُدَىٰ لَا يَسْمَعُواْ وَتَرَىٰهُمْ يَنظُرُونَ إِلَيْكَ وَهُمْ لَا يُبْصِرُونَ ۝

ᵃ However, this is not restricted only to known types of idols. This is the condition of all things—things which are given the status of objects of worship—from one's native country and community to personalities, whether dead or alive, to whom those feelings are attached, whereas in reality, these feelings should be attached to the one and only God. All come into the same category (that is, it amounts to according them the status of God.) What is the reality of all these things? None has its own power; none of them has legs, hands or eyes of its own making. Every 'leg-owner' has been given a leg; if this limb is snatched away, he cannot make another leg again. Every 'hand owner' has been given a hand; if this hand does not remain with him, he cannot make another hand. Every 'eye-owner' has had an eye gifted to him; if this eye is lost, it is not possible for him to make another eye for himself.

God alone is man's Sustainer and Saviour. In this world He remains invisible but in the world of the Hereafter, He will reveal Himself, then man will see with his own eyes that it was God who alone was the provider and the sustainer of human beings. It was only because of his foolishness that he had attributed this to other supposed deities. These associates have no power of their own to take care even of themselves, so what can they do for others? It is God alone who helps His servants in this world and it is He who will also help His faithful servants in the world to come.

¹⁹⁹ Be tolerant; enjoin what is right; and avoid the ignorant. ²⁰⁰ If an evil impulse from Satan provokes you, seek refuge with God; He is all hearing, and all knowing. ²⁰¹ When any evil suggestion from Satan touches those who fear God, they are instantly alerted and become watchful; ²⁰² but the followers of devils are led relentlessly into error by them. They never desist.

²⁰³ When you do not bring them a sign, they say, 'Why do you not invent one?' Say, 'I follow only what is revealed to me by my Lord. This Book is an enlightenment from your Lord and a guide and mercy to true believers.'ᵃ

خُذِ ٱلْعَفْوَ وَأْمُرْ بِٱلْعُرْفِ وَأَعْرِضْ عَنِ ٱلْجَٰهِلِينَ ۝ وَإِمَّا يَنزَغَنَّكَ مِنَ ٱلشَّيْطَٰنِ نَزْغٌ فَٱسْتَعِذْ بِٱللَّهِ إِنَّهُۥ سَمِيعٌ عَلِيمٌ ۝ إِنَّ ٱلَّذِينَ ٱتَّقَوْا۟ إِذَا مَسَّهُمْ طَٰٓئِفٌ مِّنَ ٱلشَّيْطَٰنِ تَذَكَّرُوا۟ فَإِذَا هُم مُّبْصِرُونَ ۝ وَإِخْوَٰنُهُمْ يَمُدُّونَهُمْ فِى ٱلْغَىِّ ثُمَّ لَا يُقْصِرُونَ ۝ وَإِذَا لَمْ تَأْتِهِم بِـَٔايَةٍ قَالُوا۟ لَوْلَا ٱجْتَبَيْتَهَا قُلْ إِنَّمَآ أَتَّبِعُ مَا يُوحَىٰٓ إِلَىَّ مِن رَّبِّى هَٰذَا بَصَآئِرُ مِن رَّبِّكُمْ وَهُدًى وَرَحْمَةٌ لِّقَوْمٍ يُؤْمِنُونَ ۝

ᵃ Calling people to monotheism, the Hereafter, a virtuous life and justice is to call people to good ('urf). That is, it is calling people to those good deeds, the goodness of which can be verified by reason. But people have found leading an upright life most difficult. The desire for immediate gain makes them opt for worldly gain. Very often they exploit religion to achieve their worldly interests. In such a state of affairs when the call for pure Truth is given to them, they are afraid that their interests will be affected so they oppose it with all their might.

What should a preacher (da'i) do in such a situation? The only right response from him on such occasions, is avoidance. That is, he should continue spreading the message without stirring up any clash or confrontation. If he fails to do so, 'dawah' will be turned into debate. His time and energies will be wasted in debating with his addressees. That is why, in order to preserve the purity of the call, it is essential that the da'i exercise patience in all unpleasant situations and continue his work along positive lines.

However, in this present world, no one is exempt from the attacks of self and Satan. What saves him on all such occasions is the fear of God. Fear of God makes one extremely sensitive. It is this sensitivity which is man's greatest shield in this world of trial. Whenever any evil thought comes to his mind, or he is afflicted by a negative psychology, it is his sensitivity which immediately alerts him against it. Instantly his eyes are opened and he seeks God's forgiveness and resolves never to commit such perverse acts again. ▶

²⁰⁴ When the Quran is read, listen to it with attention, and hold your peace, so that you may receive mercy.' ²⁰⁵ Remember your Lord deep in your very soul, in all humility and awe, without raising your voice, morning and evening—do not be one of the heedless— ²⁰⁶ [even] the ones [angels] who live in the presence of your Lord are not too proud to worship Him: they glorify Him and prostrate themselves before Him.ᵃ

وَإِذَا قُرِئَ ٱلْقُرْءَانُ فَٱسْتَمِعُوا۟ لَهُۥ وَأَنصِتُوا۟ لَعَلَّكُمْ تُرْحَمُونَ ۝ وَٱذْكُر رَّبَّكَ فِى نَفْسِكَ تَضَرُّعًا وَخِيفَةً وَدُونَ ٱلْجَهْرِ مِنَ ٱلْقَوْلِ بِٱلْغُدُوِّ وَٱلْءَاصَالِ وَلَا تَكُن مِّنَ ٱلْغَـٰفِلِينَ ۝ إِنَّ ٱلَّذِينَ عِندَ رَبِّكَ لَا يَسْتَكْبِرُونَ عَنْ عِبَادَتِهِۦ وَيُسَبِّحُونَهُۥ وَلَهُۥ يَسْجُدُونَ ۩ ۝

On the contrary, those whose hearts are free from the fear of God are never on guard against Satan's attacks. Satan leads them on and on to the pit of destruction without their ever being conscious of it. Sensitivity is man's greatest shield. While insensitivity renders one defenceless against Satan's attacks.

ᵃ The Makkans used to ask the Prophet that if he was a Prophet of God why he did not bring miracles from God. It would indeed have been very easy for God to send His messenger with miracles. But if the Prophet had come with miracles, the real purpose of his coming would have been defeated. For instance, let's suppose he was given a modern car with loudspeakers fixed to it in order to facilitate the communication of his message. One thousand five hundred years ago such a car would surely be a breathtaking miracle. Had this been so, people's attention would have been diverted from the message. The real purpose of the coming of the prophet was that God's word should serve to produce deep thinking in the people so that they might use their mental faculties to give deep thought to the words of God in order to purify their souls and establish contact with God. But given miracles, their attention would have been diverted, and they would have been lost in miracles instead of in God.

True religion consists of paying attention to the word of God, in order to establish a profound relation with God. The devotee's heart is softened. He becomes one who always remembers God. His heart and mind are overwhelmed with God's majesty, making him truly modest and fearful of God.

We are told to develop an angelic character in order that we may find the company of angels in the next life. When man frees himself from arrogance, he is so engrossed with God's marvels expressed in creation that he cannot but remember God always from the innermost recesses of his heart. He attains the level of angels. The highest point for human achievement in his world is that, being a human being, one comes to develop an angelic character.

8. THE SPOILS OF WAR

In the name of God,
the Most Gracious, the Most Merciful

بِسْمِ اللهِ الرَّحْمَٰنِ الرَّحِيمِ

¹ They ask you about the spoils of war. Say, 'They belong to God and His Messenger. So fear God, and set things right among yourselves, and obey God and His Messenger, if you are true believers: ² true believers are those whose hearts tremble with awe at the mention of God, and whose faith grows stronger as they listen to His revelations. They are those who put their trust in their Lord, ³ who pray regularly and give in alms out of what We have provided for them.⁴ Such are the true believers. They have a high standing with their Lord, His forgiveness and an honourable provision made for them.'ᵃ

يَسْـَٔلُونَكَ عَنِ ٱلْأَنفَالِ قُلِ ٱلْأَنفَالُ لِلَّهِ وَٱلرَّسُولِ فَٱتَّقُوا۟ ٱللَّهَ وَأَصْلِحُوا۟ ذَاتَ بَيْنِكُمْ وَأَطِيعُوا۟ ٱللَّهَ وَرَسُولَهُۥٓ إِن كُنتُم مُّؤْمِنِينَ ۝ إِنَّمَا ٱلْمُؤْمِنُونَ ٱلَّذِينَ إِذَا ذُكِرَ ٱللَّهُ وَجِلَتْ قُلُوبُهُمْ وَإِذَا تُلِيَتْ عَلَيْهِمْ ءَايَٰتُهُۥ زَادَتْهُمْ إِيمَٰنًا وَعَلَىٰ رَبِّهِمْ يَتَوَكَّلُونَ ۝ ٱلَّذِينَ يُقِيمُونَ ٱلصَّلَوٰةَ وَمِمَّا رَزَقْنَٰهُمْ يُنفِقُونَ ۝ أُو۟لَٰٓئِكَ هُمُ ٱلْمُؤْمِنُونَ حَقًّا لَّهُمْ دَرَجَٰتٌ عِندَ رَبِّهِمْ وَمَغْفِرَةٌ وَرِزْقٌ كَرِيمٌ ۝

ᵃ This chapter was revealed after the battle of Badr (2 A.H.). In this battle the Muslims were victorious and thereafter considerable spoils of war fell to their lot. After the battle a dispute arose over the distribution of the booty.

All such quarrels go against the God-fearing spirit. The fear of God develops the psychology of responsibility in man. The attention of a believer is focussed on his duties and not on his rights. Instead of looking at himself, he should look towards God. His heart softens in obedience to God and His prophet. He becomes a praying and worshipping subject of God. He derives satisfaction from giving to people and not from snatching things away from them. These qualities create in man the attitude of realism and readiness to admit the truth. The inevitable result of realism and admission of truth is that all mutual quarrels vanish and if at all quarrels emerge incidentally, a warning given once is enough to set matters right.

⁵ As it was your Lord who rightfully brought you forth from your house, even though some of the believers disliked it, ⁶ and they disputed with you concerning the truth after it had become manifest, as though they were being driven to their death with open eyes. ⁷ God promised you that one of the two parties would fall to you, and you wished that the one without sting should be yours, but God wanted to establish the truth by His words and cut off the root of those who denied the truth—⁸ so that He might prove the truth to be true and the false to be false, however much the wrongdoers might dislike it.ᵃ

كَمَآ أَخْرَجَكَ رَبُّكَ مِن بَيْتِكَ بِٱلْحَقِّ وَإِنَّ فَرِيقًا مِّنَ ٱلْمُؤْمِنِينَ لَكَٰرِهُونَ ۝ تُجَٰدِلُونَكَ فِى ٱلْحَقِّ بَعْدَ مَا تَبَيَّنَ كَأَنَّمَا يُسَاقُونَ إِلَى ٱلْمَوْتِ وَهُمْ يَنظُرُونَ ۝ وَإِذْ يَعِدُكُمُ ٱللَّهُ إِحْدَى ٱلطَّآئِفَتَيْنِ أَنَّهَا لَكُمْ وَتَوَدُّونَ أَنَّ غَيْرَ ذَاتِ ٱلشَّوْكَةِ تَكُونُ لَكُمْ وَيُرِيدُ ٱللَّهُ أَن يُحِقَّ ٱلْحَقَّ بِكَلِمَٰتِهِۦ وَيَقْطَعَ دَابِرَ ٱلْكَٰفِرِينَ ۝ لِيُحِقَّ ٱلْحَقَّ وَيُبْطِلَ ٱلْبَٰطِلَ وَلَوْ كَرِهَ ٱلْمُجْرِمُونَ ۝

ᵃ In Sha'ban, (2 A.H.) the eighth month of the Islamic calendar, it came to be known that a commercial caravan of the Quraysh, carrying goods worth about fifty thousand guineas, was returning from Syria to Makkah. It was on a route which passed close by Madinah. It was feared that the Muslims might attack this caravan of their enemies. So, the chief of the caravan, Abu Sufyan ibn Harb, sent word to the people of Makkah that they should rush to him with aid, otherwise the Muslims would capture the caravan. This news created a lot of fervour in Makkah. So, a troop of 950 horsemen (600 of them fully armoured) set out from Makkah for Madinah.

The Prophet was also receiving all the news. Now the Muslims of Madinah were in between two groups—one was the caravan returning from Syria, and the other was the army advancing from Makkah to Madinah. One section of the Muslims had the idea that they should advance towards the caravan. Since this caravan had only 40 guards, it could be overcome and its goods captured. But God's plan was different. In fact, God wanted to crush the strength of those who deny the truth rather than permit the Muslims to make some material gain. God, therefore, created special conditions and caused all the chiefs of the opponents to set out from Makkah and reach Badr, a place 20 miles from Madinah, so that they should finally perish forever after clashing with the Muslims. When the Prophet informed the Muslims of God's plan, they all agreed and proceeded towards Badr. Their strength was only 313 and they were ill-equipped. But God gave them special aid, and they routed the army of the Quraysh. Seventy of their chiefs were killed and seventy were taken prisoner. ▶

⁹ When you prayed to your Lord for help, He answered, 'I am sending to your aid a thousand angels in succession.' ¹⁰ God only did this to give you good news, and so that your hearts might be set at rest, for help comes from God alone. Surely, God is Mighty and Wise. ¹¹ He brought drowsiness upon you to give you His reassurance and sent down water from the sky upon you, so that He might thereby purify you and remove Satan's pollution from you, and make your hearts strong and your feet firm.ᵃ

إِذْ تَسْتَغِيثُونَ رَبَّكُمْ فَٱسْتَجَابَ لَكُمْ أَنِّى مُمِدُّكُم بِأَلْفٍ مِّنَ ٱلْمَلَـٰٓئِكَةِ مُرْدِفِينَ ۝ وَمَا جَعَلَهُ ٱللَّهُ إِلَّا بُشْرَىٰ وَلِتَطْمَئِنَّ بِهِۦ قُلُوبُكُمْ ۚ وَمَا ٱلنَّصْرُ إِلَّا مِنْ عِندِ ٱللَّهِ ۚ إِنَّ ٱللَّهَ عَزِيزٌ حَكِيمٌ ۝ إِذْ يُغَشِّيكُمُ ٱلنُّعَاسَ أَمَنَةً مِّنْهُ وَيُنَزِّلُ عَلَيْكُم مِّنَ ٱلسَّمَآءِ مَآءً لِّيُطَهِّرَكُم بِهِۦ وَيُذْهِبَ عَنكُمْ رِجْزَ ٱلشَّيْطَـٰنِ وَلِيَرْبِطَ عَلَىٰ قُلُوبِكُمْ وَيُثَبِّتَ بِهِ ٱلْأَقْدَامَ ۝

The battlefield of Badr became the scene of Islam's victory over the deniers of the Truth. Whenever it happens that there is material benefit on the one hand and religious benefit on the other, this division itself proves that God's will and pleasure centre upon religious benefit and not upon material benefit. The target of Islamic effort is never the attainment of economic advantages. The purpose of Islamic struggle is always to break the strength of falsehood, either by ideological superiority or, through material power as dictated by the circumstances.

ᵃ The battle of Badr took place under very critical conditions. Only 313 Muslims were pitted against about one thousand well-armed enemies. The Muslims were scantily armed. The enemies had already reached the venue of battle (Badr) and had captured a vantage point and the spring of water. Seeing this, the Muslims were beset by doubts that perhaps they would not be supported by God in the mission for which they had been sacrificing their lives. Had truth been on their side, God would not have helped the enemies on this critical occasion and all the favourable opportunities would have slipped from their grasp and passed on to their enemies. But at that time, Almighty God caused heavy rains to fall in the area of Badr. Muslims made ponds and stored the water. The enemy had deprived Muslims of the water of the land; God then arranged for them to have water from the sky. God furthermore blessed them with an extraordinary favour—that of sleep. Sleep is very necessary for a man to be refreshed, but the conditions in the battlefield are so terrible that it is impossible to have sound sleep. In spite of this, Almighty God blessed them with His special succour; on the eve of the battle, He made it possible for them to have sound sleep. In the night they slept free of all mental pressure and got up in the morning fully refreshed. Out of conditions which were causing Muslims to have misgivings, God created such possibilities that they developed new faith and a sense of self-reliance.

¹² When your Lord commanded the angels, saying, 'I am with you, so make those who believe stand firm. I will instill fear in the hearts of those who deny the truth: so strike their necks and strike all their finger joints!' ¹³ That was because they defied God and His Messenger. He who defies God and His Messenger shall be severely punished by God. ¹⁴ That is your punishment, taste it then; and know that for those who deny the truth there is the punishment of the Fire.ᵃ

إِذْ يُوحِى رَبُّكَ إِلَى ٱلْمَلَـٰٓئِكَةِ أَنِّى مَعَكُمْ فَثَبِّتُوا۟ ٱلَّذِينَ ءَامَنُوا۟ سَأُلْقِى فِى قُلُوبِ ٱلَّذِينَ كَفَرُوا۟ ٱلرُّعْبَ فَٱضْرِبُوا۟ فَوْقَ ٱلْأَعْنَاقِ وَٱضْرِبُوا۟ مِنْهُمْ كُلَّ بَنَانٍ ۝ ذَٰلِكَ بِأَنَّهُمْ شَآقُّوا۟ ٱللَّهَ وَرَسُولَهُ ۚ وَمَن يُشَاقِقِ ٱللَّهَ وَرَسُولَهُ فَإِنَّ ٱللَّهَ شَدِيدُ ٱلْعِقَابِ ۝ ذَٰلِكُمْ فَذُوقُوهُ وَأَنَّ لِلْكَـٰفِرِينَ عَذَابَ ٱلنَّارِ ۝

ᵃ At the time of confrontation what is required of the people of Truth is steadfastness. They should not be disheartened under any circumstances. The gift readily given by God in return for this steadfastness is the striking of terror into the hearts of the enemies of Truth, and nothing can save from defeat any such group as is terror-stricken by its opponents.

15 Believers, when you meet in battle those who deny the truth, never turn your backs on them: 16 whoever turns his back on such an occasion, unless it be as a stratagem of war, or in an endeavour to join another group [of the believers] will indeed draw down upon himself the wrath of God, and Hell shall be his abode and the worst indeed is that destination.[a]

يَٰٓأَيُّهَا ٱلَّذِينَ ءَامَنُوٓاْ إِذَا لَقِيتُمُ ٱلَّذِينَ كَفَرُواْ زَحْفًا فَلَا تُوَلُّوهُمُ ٱلْأَدْبَارَ ۝ وَمَن يُوَلِّهِمْ يَوْمَئِذٍ دُبُرَهُۥٓ إِلَّا مُتَحَرِّفًا لِّقِتَالٍ أَوْ مُتَحَيِّزًا إِلَىٰ فِئَةٍ فَقَدْ بَآءَ بِغَضَبٍ مِّنَ ٱللَّهِ وَمَأْوَىٰهُ جَهَنَّمُ وَبِئْسَ ٱلْمَصِيرُ ۝

---

[a] When the clash between believers and those who deny the truth reaches the battlefield, it is a moment of reckoning for both the parties. If at that critical moment a believing individual or group, turns tail and flees from the battlefield, it amounts to committing the worst kind of crime. Such people consider it more important to save themselves rather than to defend the Truth. They do this when what is at stake is the life of that Truth which they have admitted as the greatest Truth and which they have embraced in all good faith.

On such critical occasions, even a minor defection can cause a major debacle. One person's or one group's flight from the battlefield lowers the morale of the whole army. One person's running away can finally turn into a mass stampede. However, the exception to this is when a soldier or an army unit retreats for some strategic purpose, perhaps to leave one front and join another. Retreat is undoubtedly an unpardonable crime, but when carried out on strategic grounds, it is legitimate.

The aforesaid commandment originally relates to battle. However, other similar cases may also come within its purview. For example, a missionary may call people to engage in the peaceful and constructive propagation of Islam, but after some time, when he sees that his call is not very popular, he may lose patience and, abandoning the constructive approach, may rush towards that type of Islam through which fame and status among the general public can very soon become a reality.

Running away from the battlefield occurs consciously and with intention. But 'running away' from the struggle going on outside the battlefield often takes place at the unconscious level. Man happens to be result-loving by nature. He likes to be admired for his work. He wants his work to be accepted and recognised. Such a temperament gradually removes him from the tasks from which an immediate result does not seem to follow. Barely conscious of the factors working within him, he is attracted towards such things as apparently give him the hope of immediate honour and success. Every deviation of this type is an example of what has been described in the above-mentioned verse as 'running away from the battlefield.'

¹⁷ You did not kill them; it was God who killed them; and when you [Prophet] threw [sand] at them it was not you, but God who threw it so that He might confer on the believers a great favour from Himself. Surely, God is all hearing, all-knowing—¹⁸ that is what happened—and God will surely undermine the design of those who deny the truth. ¹⁹ If you were seeking a judgement, a judgement has now come to you. If you desist, it will be the better for you. But if you return [to hostility] We too will return. And your host will avail you naught, however numerous it may be, and [know] that surely God is with the believers.[a]

فَلَمْ تَقْتُلُوهُمْ وَلَٰكِنَّ ٱللَّهَ قَتَلَهُمْ ۚ وَمَا رَمَيْتَ إِذْ رَمَيْتَ وَلَٰكِنَّ ٱللَّهَ رَمَىٰ ۚ وَلِيُبْلِيَ ٱلْمُؤْمِنِينَ مِنْهُ بَلَآءً حَسَنًا ۚ إِنَّ ٱللَّهَ سَمِيعٌ عَلِيمٌ ۝ ذَٰلِكُمْ وَأَنَّ ٱللَّهَ مُوهِنُ كَيْدِ ٱلْكَٰفِرِينَ ۝ إِن تَسْتَفْتِحُوا۟ فَقَدْ جَآءَكُمُ ٱلْفَتْحُ ۖ وَإِن تَنتَهُوا۟ فَهُوَ خَيْرٌ لَّكُمْ ۖ وَإِن تَعُودُوا۟ نَعُدْ وَلَن تُغْنِىَ عَنكُمْ فِئَتُكُمْ شَيْـًٔا وَلَوْ كَثُرَتْ وَأَنَّ ٱللَّهَ مَعَ ٱلْمُؤْمِنِينَ ۝

---

[a] It has been handed down in traditions that, when the battle of Badr was in full swing the words uttered by the Prophet, in prayer, were: 'O, my Lord! If this class of people is killed, You will never be worshipped on earth.'

Helping believers is a responsibility borne by Almighty God. By His devices He renders ineffective whatever conspiracies their enemies hatch. He causes them to be overwhelmed so that the faithful may dominate. But when does this happen? This happens when the believers merge their will with that of God, in such a way that God's will and their will become one and the same. When a subject of God aligns himself with God in such a way, whatever belongs to God becomes his, because he would have already given to God whatever was his.

Before leaving for Badr, the chiefs of Makkah went to the House of God and, catching hold of the curtain of the Ka'bah, prayed like this: 'O, God help the better of the two armies; the more respectable of the two groups; and the better of the two tribes.' At the battle of Badr, the chiefs of Makkah were totally defeated and the Faithful were completely victorious. So, by the very standard set by the chiefs themselves, it was proved that, before God it was not they who were superior and more honourable but the followers of Islam. In spite of this, they did not accept Islam. For those who conduct themselves in this way, there shall be grave punishment both in the Hereafter and in this world.

'Bless with victory the side which is superior and the more honourable of the two.' This was ostensibly a prayer, but in fact was an expression of boastful self-confidence. The rationale behind this was that they were the Trustees of the Ka'bah; they were the progeny of Abraham and Ishmael. When they had such superior factors on their side, victory was bound to be theirs. But, before God, real value is attached to personal deeds and not to external connections. However great an external connection may be, it will be of no avail to anybody on Judgement Day.

20 Believers, obey God and His Messenger, and do not turn away from him now that you have heard all. 21 Do not be like those who say, 'We hear,' but pay no heed to what they hear— 22 the worst creatures in God's eyes are those who are deaf and dumb, and who possess no understanding. 23 If God had found any good in them, He would certainly have made them hear; but being as they are, even if He makes them hear, they will turn away in aversion.*a*

يَٰٓأَيُّهَا ٱلَّذِينَ ءَامَنُوٓاْ أَطِيعُواْ ٱللَّهَ وَرَسُولَهُۥ وَلَا تَوَلَّوْاْ عَنْهُ وَأَنتُمْ تَسْمَعُونَ ۞ وَلَا تَكُونُواْ كَٱلَّذِينَ قَالُواْ سَمِعْنَا وَهُمْ لَا يَسْمَعُونَ ۞ إِنَّ شَرَّ ٱلدَّوَآبِّ عِندَ ٱللَّهِ ٱلصُّمُّ ٱلْبُكْمُ ٱلَّذِينَ لَا يَعْقِلُونَ ۞ وَلَوْ عَلِمَ ٱللَّهُ فِيهِمْ خَيْرًا لَّأَسْمَعَهُمْ وَلَوْ أَسْمَعَهُمْ لَتَوَلَّواْ وَّهُم مُّعْرِضُونَ ۞

---

a When a Truth is presented before a man, ideally he apprehends it with all the human faculties granted to him by God. He gives his full attention to it, he feels the weight of its veracity and then he utters that correct response which a man's nature should present in the face of Truth. One who behaves in this way has been receptive to the presented matter in the manner of a true human being. However, there is the type of individual who listens as if he has no ears to hear with. His mind fails to grasp the veracity of what he hears. And so he is unable to give the requisite response in view of the facts. One who behaves in this way has heard the presented matter as if he were an animal.

The truth becomes clear only to one who hears it with a receptive mind. By contrast, one whose temperament is flawed by jealousy, haughtiness, self-interest and love of outward show will not regard the issue of Truth as worth considering and will not pay serious attention to it. So, he will certainly fail to discover its veracity.

Faith on the face of it, is a statement of trust in God. But in reality it is a human decision. Faith is not merely repetition of words of testimony, but the verbal expression of one's inner feeling. If a man's condition is really the same as that declared by his words, he is a real believer in the eyes of God. A believer is the most serious human being and as such can never, by his words, show himself to be something other than what his inner condition actually is.

A man whose faith reflects his inner reality, will, as soon as he admits his faith, make God his object of worship and will be a follower of His commands in all aspects of his life. For him oral acceptance of faith will be not just a verbal profession, but an indicator of the direction of his journey. Just the opposite is the condition of one who heard the voice of Truth, but did not let it enter his soul and did not let it become part of his heart-beats, even though he had no answer for its arguments. Outwardly he may have uttered the words, 'Yes, it is true,' but, his real life, even after that, remained the same as it had been earlier. This second attitude is hypocritical, and before God such a hypocritical 'faith' has no value.

24 Believers, obey God and the Messenger when he calls you to that which gives you life. Know that God stands between man and his heart, and you shall all be gathered in His presence. 25 And beware of an affliction that will not smite exclusively those among you who have done wrong. Know that God is severe in exacting retribution.a

يَٰٓأَيُّهَا ٱلَّذِينَ ءَامَنُواْ ٱسۡتَجِيبُواْ لِلَّهِ وَلِلرَّسُولِ إِذَا دَعَاكُمۡ لِمَا يُحۡيِيكُمۡۖ وَٱعۡلَمُوٓاْ أَنَّ ٱللَّهَ يَحُولُ بَيۡنَ ٱلۡمَرۡءِ وَقَلۡبِهِۦ وَأَنَّهُۥٓ إِلَيۡهِ تُحۡشَرُونَ ۝ وَٱتَّقُواْ فِتۡنَةً لَّا تُصِيبَنَّ ٱلَّذِينَ ظَلَمُواْ مِنكُمۡ خَآصَّةٗۖ وَٱعۡلَمُوٓاْ أَنَّ ٱللَّهَ شَدِيدُ ٱلۡعِقَابِ ۝

---

a Here the 'call of life' means the call for the struggle to convey the Truth to others. Initially this struggle starts by preaching by word of mouth or by means of the pen. But the belligerent attitude of those to whom the call is given takes this struggle to various other stages, even to the extent of migration or war. Man formulates his religious life in accordance with his ideas, at the individual level. He makes his life so consistent with his circumstances that it appears to be an island of safety for him. He has the feeling that if he exerts himself to reform others, this well-established abode will be destroyed; his well organised life will be disturbed and the regulation of his time and the system devised by him to govern his property—keeping his personal requirements in view—will be upset.

Such fears prevent him from making efforts to call upon others to the Truth and to sacrifice his life and property for that cause. But this is utter stupidity. The fact is that the abode of peace which he considers his 'life' is his graveyard, and hidden in the sacrifice in which he sees his death, lies the secret of his life. Giving the call to the people and their reformation are extremely important tasks, provided that they are aimed at the Hereafter and are not for worldly purposes. It makes a dead religion a living religion. It links man with God at the highest level. It introduces man to such religious experiences as he could never have if he remained in his individual shell. If, in spite of hearing such an important call on behalf of God, people are still unmindful of it, they incur the risk of creating a psychological barrier between themselves and the Truth; they risk losing their natural capacity to hear the voice of Truth, to rush towards it and discover their Lord.

Man's life is social in nature. Nobody can go on living on his own on an isolated island. If a man is content with his personal righteousness, he always incurs the risk that, as a result of perversion in society, he himself will also be affected, for he is also a part of the same society. His struggle to reform the people would serve as a practical demonstration that he was not involved directly or indirectly with evil people. Every evil starts in a small way and then gradually becomes greatly enlarged. If it happens that when an evil is in the initial stages, it is opposed by a number of people at that time, it will be easily crushed. But once the evil has spread, it becomes so deep-rooted that it becomes impossible to eliminate it.

26 Remember when you were few in number and were accounted weak in the land, ever fearing the onslaught of your enemies, but He provided you with shelter, and supported you with His help and provided you with good things, so that you might be grateful. 27 Do not betray God and His Messenger, and do not knowingly violate your trusts. 28 Know that your wealth and children are a trial and that there is an immense reward with God.[a]

وَاذْكُرُوٓا۟ إِذْ أَنتُمْ قَلِيلٌ مُّسْتَضْعَفُونَ فِى ٱلْأَرْضِ تَخَافُونَ أَن يَتَخَطَّفَكُمُ ٱلنَّاسُ فَـَٔاوَىٰكُمْ وَأَيَّدَكُم بِنَصْرِهِۦ وَرَزَقَكُم مِّنَ ٱلطَّيِّبَـٰتِ لَعَلَّكُمْ تَشْكُرُونَ ۝ يَـٰٓأَيُّهَا ٱلَّذِينَ ءَامَنُوا۟ لَا تَخُونُوا۟ ٱللَّهَ وَٱلرَّسُولَ وَتَخُونُوٓا۟ أَمَـٰنَـٰتِكُمْ وَأَنتُمْ تَعْلَمُونَ ۝ وَٱعْلَمُوٓا۟ أَنَّمَآ أَمْوَٰلُكُمْ وَأَوْلَـٰدُكُمْ فِتْنَةٌ وَأَنَّ ٱللَّهَ عِندَهُۥٓ أَجْرٌ عَظِيمٌ ۝

---

[a] In Makkah, Muslims were in a state of helplessness. They were always in fear of being uprooted at any time. They were like a weakling who is oppressed in every way and denied even his legitimate rights. At last the way to Madinah opened for them. They were given the opportunity to go to Madinah, form a centre of their own there and live in freedom and with respect in that atmosphere.

This providing of easy circumstances after difficulties is meant to infuse feelings of gratefulness in man. When a man's living conditions reach the point where he feels himself helpless, at that time suddenly God's help appears and everything changes for the better. It happens in this way so that man should firmly believe that whatever happened was at the behest of God, and on the basis of this realisation, he should be overflowing with gratitude for the Grace of God.

Man embraces faith in God and His Prophet. In this way, he vows that he will tread the path of God and His Prophet. But, while adopting the way of Faith, the compulsions of his property and children come in the way. Then, he shuns the requirements of Faith and gives all his attention to property and children. This is an open betrayal of his pledge of Faith. The gravity of this betrayal becomes painfully obvious when it is realised that the things for which man betrays God are in themselves gifts from God.

What are a man's property and his children? Are they not gifts from God? They are a trust given by God to his subject. The best use of this trust is that when its Donor wants it, it should be willingly surrendered to Him. But when God exhorts the people to rise and strive with all their might in the cause of His religion, they make an excuse of that very trust of God which they should have sacrificed for God's religion and thus fulfilled their pledge of Faith to Him. In this way, after being on the verge of success, they add their names to the list of failures.

An action becomes a crime in the eyes of God only when it is perpetrated in the full knowledge that it is wrong. ▶

²⁹ Believers, if you fear God, He will grant you the ability to discriminate between right and wrong, and will forgive you your sins: for God is limitless in His great bounty. ³⁰ Remember how those who bent on denying the truth plotted against you to imprison you or kill you or expel you: they schemed—but God also schemed. God is the best of schemers.ᵃ

يَٰٓأَيُّهَا ٱلَّذِينَ ءَامَنُوٓاْ إِن تَتَّقُواْ ٱللَّهَ يَجْعَل لَّكُمْ فُرْقَانًا وَيُكَفِّرْ عَنكُمْ سَيِّـَٔاتِكُمْ وَيَغْفِرْ لَكُمْ ۗ وَٱللَّهُ ذُو ٱلْفَضْلِ ٱلْعَظِيمِ ۝ وَإِذْ يَمْكُرُ بِكَ ٱلَّذِينَ كَفَرُواْ لِيُثْبِتُوكَ أَوْ يَقْتُلُوكَ أَوْ يُخْرِجُوكَ ۚ وَيَمْكُرُونَ وَيَمْكُرُ ٱللَّهُ ۖ وَٱللَّهُ خَيْرُ ٱلْمَٰكِرِينَ ۝

If a deed is clearly wrong, yet the doer of that deed refuses to desist, he shall have to face serious consequences. This is because willfully repeating a wrong action amounts to flouting God's will. God can never forgive such extreme behaviour.

ᵃ If a man fears God, he does whatever God has commanded him to do and refrains from doing whatever God has prohibited; he is inspired to be able to distinguish truth from falsehood. (The word used in the original for the ability to make this distinction is *furqan*). (*Tafsir ibn Kathir*).

The greatest stimulus to the proper use of human capabilities is fear. Man, in a state of fear, becomes extremely realistic in all matters. Fear removes all veils from his mind so thoroughly that he is able to rise above all omissions, mistakes and misunderstandings and can then form the most correct opinions. This is exactly what happens to that subject of God who goes in fear (*taqwa*) of the Lord of all the universe.

This ability to tell right from wrong (*furqan*) is almost the same as inner realisation (*ma'rifah*) or insight (*basirah*). Insight creates an inner light in a man which enables him to see everything in its reality without his being deceived by its outward aspects. Whenever a man involves himself in anything to the point of always being careful about it, a particular sort of sensitivity develops in him which makes him recognise the favourable and unfavourable aspects of that matter. This applies to everyone, whether he be a religious man, a trader, a doctor or an engineer. If a man becomes totally devoted to his work, his inner realisation becomes so intense that, he cuts through all confusion, and straightaway understands the reality of the matter.

Development of this Divine insight (*furqan*) in a man is the greatest guarantee that he will be safe from evils; it will enable him to place his relations with God, on a sound footing and he will finally become entitled to the grace of God. ▶

³¹ Whenever Our revelations are recited to them, they say, 'We have heard them. If we wished, we could produce the like. They are nothing but the fables of the ancients.' ³² They also said, 'God, if this really is the truth from You, then rain down upon us stones from heaven, or send us some other painful punishment.'ᵃ

وَإِذَا تُتْلَىٰ عَلَيْهِمْ ءَايَٰتُنَا قَالُوا۟ قَدْ سَمِعْنَا لَوْ نَشَآءُ لَقُلْنَا مِثْلَ هَٰذَآ إِنْ هَٰذَآ إِلَّآ أَسَٰطِيرُ ٱلْأَوَّلِينَ ۝ وَإِذْ قَالُوا۟ ٱللَّهُمَّ إِن كَانَ هَٰذَا هُوَ ٱلْحَقَّ مِنْ عِندِكَ فَأَمْطِرْ عَلَيْنَا حِجَارَةً مِّنَ ٱلسَّمَآءِ أَوِ ٱئْتِنَا بِعَذَابٍ أَلِيمٍ ۝

The development of this capacity to distinguish between truth and falsehood indicates that a man has attached himself to the truth to the extent that no difference remains between him and the Truth: the Truth and he have become complementary to each other. Thereafter his being saved becomes as necessary as the saving of Truth. Such people come directly under God's protection. Now, plotting against them amounts to undermining the Truth itself. One who schemes against God is invariably unsuccessful, no matter how great the devices he employs.

ᵃ Literally, 'We can also produce such a discourse. If we speak untruths why do stones not rain down upon us?' All such talk arises from haughtiness. When a man finds himself in a safe position in this world; when he observes that he has lost nothing by denying the Truth or by ignoring it, a certain false self-confidence is created in him. He thinks that whatever he has been doing is perfectly right. This feeling makes him utter such words as are not uttered by anyone in normal circumstances.

This daring on the part of such people can manifest itself only because of God's law of respite. God certainly punishes the guilty, but He follows the principle of seizing a man only when the work of clarifying to him Truth and falsehood has been fully performed. Before the completion of this task, nobody is struck down. Furthermore, if during the process of the missionary call, even one or two people at a time are influenced and start reforming themselves, God withholds His retribution so that all those who wish to respond positively to the call of truth may have the time and opportunity to do so.

33 But God would not punish them while you [Prophet] were in their midst, nor would He punish them so long as they sought forgiveness. 34 Yet why should God not punish them when they debar people from the Sacred Mosque, although they are not its guardians? Its rightful guardians are those who fear God, though most of them do not realize it. 35 Their prayers at the Sacred House are nothing but whistling and clapping of hands. 'So taste the punishment because of your denial.'[a]

وَمَا كَانَ ٱللَّهُ لِيُعَذِّبَهُمْ وَأَنتَ فِيهِمْ وَمَا كَانَ ٱللَّهُ مُعَذِّبَهُمْ وَهُمْ يَسْتَغْفِرُونَ ۝ وَمَا لَهُمْ أَلَّا يُعَذِّبَهُمُ ٱللَّهُ وَهُمْ يَصُدُّونَ عَنِ ٱلْمَسْجِدِ ٱلْحَرَامِ وَمَا كَانُوٓاْ أَوْلِيَآءَهُۥٓ إِنْ أَوْلِيَآؤُهُۥٓ إِلَّا ٱلْمُتَّقُونَ وَلَٰكِنَّ أَكْثَرَهُمْ لَا يَعْلَمُونَ ۝ وَمَا كَانَ صَلَاتُهُمْ عِندَ ٱلْبَيْتِ إِلَّا مُكَآءً وَتَصْدِيَةً فَذُوقُواْ ٱلْعَذَابَ بِمَا كُنتُمْ تَكْفُرُونَ ۝

---

[a] It does not happen that when communities are diverted from the true path, all forms of religion disappear from among them. It always happens during such a period that when religion based on the fear of God is submerged, its place is taken by a false, ostentatious religion. Now, the community relates not to the religion per se but to the hallowed personalities of the past. By attaching themselves to these personalities and by occupying their revered seats, they think that they have attained the greatness which those personalities enjoyed on historical grounds. Such people are hollow inside, but by performing showy deeds on the strength of big names, they think that they are undertaking tremendous religious feats.

The people of Makkah were suffering from this psychological affliction. They were proud that they were the inheritors of the House of God; that they were the descendants of the great Prophets, Abraham and Ishmael; they had the honour of being the servants of the Kabah. So, they thought that when they had such religious honours and performed such 'religious' deeds, it was not possible that God would cast them into hell.

³⁶ Those who are bent on denying the truth are spending their wealth in debarring others from the path of God. They will continue to spend it in this way till, in the end, this spending will become a source of intense regret for them, and then they will be overcome. And those who denied the truth will be gathered together in Hell. ³⁷ So that God may separate the bad from the good, He will heap the wicked one upon another and then cast them into Hell. These will surely be the losers.^a

إِنَّ ٱلَّذِينَ كَفَرُواْ يُنفِقُونَ أَمْوَٰلَهُمْ لِيَصُدُّواْ عَن سَبِيلِ ٱللَّهِ ۚ فَسَيُنفِقُونَهَا ثُمَّ تَكُونُ عَلَيْهِمْ حَسْرَةً ثُمَّ يُغْلَبُونَ ۗ وَٱلَّذِينَ كَفَرُوٓاْ إِلَىٰ جَهَنَّمَ يُحْشَرُونَ ۝ لِيَمِيزَ ٱللَّهُ ٱلْخَبِيثَ مِنَ ٱلطَّيِّبِ وَيَجْعَلَ ٱلْخَبِيثَ بَعْضَهُۥ عَلَىٰ بَعْضٍ فَيَرْكُمَهُۥ جَمِيعًا فَيَجْعَلَهُۥ فِي جَهَنَّمَ ۚ أُوْلَٰٓئِكَ هُمُ ٱلْخَٰسِرُونَ ۝

---

^a Among human beings some are clean and pure, while some are unclean. Some souls draw nourishment from the things that are liked by God, while others have a taste for things that are the favourites of their base selves or of Satan. Under normal conditions, both types of people live together. On the face of it, there appears to be no difference between them. So, Almighty God causes a struggle between True and false, so that the people of both types separate from each other and it becomes clear as to who is who.

During this struggle it becomes clear as to who immediately accepts the Truth when it comes before him and who rejects it; who, in dealing with others remains within the limit of justice, and who resorts to injustice; who remains modest and humble in the world and who becomes arrogant, who spends money for the cause of Truth and who spends as a matter of prejudice and show. The actions of those who expend their efforts in ways other than the way of Truth are glorified and made handsome in their eyes by Satan in such a way that they start thinking that they are performing superior acts; that they are proceeding towards a glorious future. But this misunderstanding is short-lived. Very soon man reaches the stage when he comes to know that whatever he had done was merely a wastage of his energy and money. The future towards which he was proceeding was only one of unfulfilled longing and frustration, though on the basis of false hopes he had considered it a journey towards a bright future.

When the call for pure religion is given, all those people who had gained a position of leadership on the basis of adulterated religion feel adversely affected by that call. So, they spend all their energy in protecting the custom-based, traditional structure which had conferred the position of superiority on them. But such people necessarily fail when opposed by the unadulterated Truth, sometimes in the field of argument and sometimes in the field of action as well. The activities of this world have been designed just to separate pure and impure souls from each other. When this process of sorting out is over, God will send the pure souls to paradise and assemble the impure souls and thrust them into hell.

38 Tell those who are bent on denying the truth that if they desist, their past shall be forgiven, but if they persist in sin, they have an example in the fate of those who went before. **39** Fight them until there is no more [religious] persecution, and religion belongs wholly to God: if they desist, then surely God is watchful of what they do,[a] **40** but if they turn away, know that God is your Protector; the Best of Protectors and the Best of Helpers![b]

قُل لِّلَّذِينَ كَفَرُوٓاْ إِن يَنتَهُواْ يُغْفَرْ لَهُم مَّا قَدْ سَلَفَ وَإِن يَعُودُواْ فَقَدْ مَضَتْ سُنَّتُ ٱلْأَوَّلِينَ ۝ وَقَٰتِلُوهُمْ حَتَّىٰ لَا تَكُونَ فِتْنَةٌ وَيَكُونَ ٱلدِّينُ كُلُّهُۥ لِلَّهِ فَإِنِ ٱنتَهَوْاْ فَإِنَّ ٱللَّهَ بِمَا يَعْمَلُونَ بَصِيرٌ ۝ وَإِن تَوَلَّوْاْ فَٱعْلَمُوٓاْ أَنَّ ٱللَّهَ مَوْلَىٰكُمْ نِعْمَ ٱلْمَوْلَىٰ وَنِعْمَ ٱلنَّصِيرُ ۝

[a] "And religion is wholly for God" in this connection those traditions are worth noting which are enshrined in *Sahih al-Bukhari*. When, after the fourth Caliph Ali ibn Abi Talib, political conflict ensued between Abdullah ibn Zubayr and the Umayyads, Abdullah ibn Umar, one of the senior-most companions of the Prophet, held himself aloof from the battle. People approached him and, quoting the verse of *qital-al-fitna*, asked him why he was not joining in the battle. Abdullah ibn Umar replied that *'fitna'* as mentioned in the Quran did not refer to political infighting, but rather to the religious coercive system, that had already been put an end to by them. (*Fathul Bari*, 8/60) From this we learn that the war against *fitna* was a war of limited duration, temporary in nature, meant to be engaged in only until its specific purpose had been served.

[b] It is a principle of Islam that the individual is rewarded according to his deeds. However, by His grace Almighty God has made special exemptions to this general principle: when a man is truly repentant, he will not be punished thereafter for his earlier deeds. Suppose a man spent his life in ungodliness, then he received the light of guidance, became a true believer and adopted the righteous life. In this case, he will be forgiven for the evil deeds done by him earlier; he will not be seized on the basis of his earlier crimes.

This very principle is also operative in collective and political matters. Sometimes the struggle between Truth and falsehood develops into a clash. During this clash the opponents commit atrocities on the believers. Finally, the supporters of the truth are dominant and the opponents are overcome and subdued. In this matter also, the principle of Islam is the same as stated above, that is, people will not be punished for committing atrocities in the past. Rather, if, after the victory anybody indulges in criminal acts will, after due procedure, receive the punishment prescribed in the Islamic law for such a criminal.

In ancient times the establishment of chieftains and rulers was based on polytheism. Today, rulers hold sway as representatives of the people, but in the past they ruled as representatives of God or God's so called partners. ▶

⁴¹ Know that one-fifth of your battle gains belongs to God and the Messenger, to his close relatives and orphans, to the needy and travellers, if you believe in God and the revelation We sent down to Our servant on the Decisive Day, the day when the two forces met. God has power over all things.ᵃ

وَٱعْلَمُوٓاْ أَنَّمَا غَنِمْتُم مِّن شَىْءٍ فَأَنَّ لِلَّهِ خُمُسَهُۥ وَلِلرَّسُولِ وَلِذِى ٱلْقُرْبَىٰ وَٱلْيَتَـٰمَىٰ وَٱلْمَسَـٰكِينِ وَٱبْنِ ٱلسَّبِيلِ إِن كُنتُمْ ءَامَنتُم بِٱللَّهِ وَمَآ أَنزَلْنَا عَلَىٰ عَبْدِنَا يَوْمَ ٱلْفُرْقَانِ يَوْمَ ٱلْتَقَى ٱلْجَمْعَانِ ۗ وَٱللَّهُ عَلَىٰ كُلِّ شَىْءٍ قَدِيرٌ ۝

Consequently, in ancient society, polytheism enjoyed a position of power. Polytheists used to harass the believers in the one God. Persecution (*fitnah*) was common. So God commanded His Prophet and His companions to disrupt the link between polytheism and power so that the polytheists should be deprived of the power to persecute the monotheists. Accordingly, the universal revolution brought about by the Prophet snapped forever the link between polytheism and the political system. Now, polytheism is simply a religious practice in some parts of the world and is not a political theory on the basis of which governments are formed.

In Arabia an end had to be put to both polytheists and polytheism, so that the precincts of Makkah and Madinah could be made the eternal centre of pure monotheism.

ᵃ In ancient times it was the custom that after a battle whatever enemy property (*ghanimah*) the victors could lay their hands on was treated as their property. However, Islam laid down the rule that whatever one got from the battlefield should be brought back and deposited with the chief.

After gathering all the spoils of war in this way, one-fifth part of it was kept aside in the name of God. This was received by the Prophet, who acted on God's behalf, and was spent in this way: one part was spent on himself, then on his relatives who supported him in his religious mission in difficult times, then on the destitute, orphans, the needy and travellers. The remaining four-fifths were distributed among the soldiers.

Islam wants man to develop the outlook of considering whatever he gets as God-given. In the battle of Badr a weak group overcoming an extremely powerful group was extraordinary proof of the fact that whatever happened was at the behest of God.

Keeping a share of booty for other deserving brethren teaches the lesson that the bases for entitlement to a share in property are not merely effort and inheritance; there are other bases which do not fall within these spheres. The acknowledgement of others' entitlement amounts to one's admitting that everything belongs to God and not to oneself. ▶

42 You were on the nearer side of the valley, and they were on the farther side, and the caravan was below you. Had you wished to set a time by mutual agreement, you would certainly have disagreed on the timing. However, the encounter took place, so that God might settle a matter which had already been ordained, so that he who was to perish might perish after clear evidence of the truth, and he who was to live might live in clear evidence of the truth. Surely, God is all hearing and all-knowing.[a]

إِذْ أَنتُم بِٱلْعُدْوَةِ ٱلدُّنْيَا وَهُم بِٱلْعُدْوَةِ ٱلْقُصْوَىٰ وَٱلرَّكْبُ أَسْفَلَ مِنكُمْ وَلَوْ تَوَاعَدتُّمْ لَٱخْتَلَفْتُمْ فِى ٱلْمِيعَٰدِ وَلَٰكِن لِّيَقْضِيَ ٱللَّهُ أَمْرًا كَانَ مَفْعُولًا لِّيَهْلِكَ مَنْ هَلَكَ عَنۢ بَيِّنَةٍ وَيَحْيَىٰ مَنْ حَىَّ عَنۢ بَيِّنَةٍ وَإِنَّ ٱللَّهَ لَسَمِيعٌ عَلِيمٌ ۝

The third important lesson taught by this law of *ghanimah* is that the basis of ownership is not possession but principle. Nobody will become the owner of a thing merely on the basis of it having accidentally come into his possession. In spite of being in possession of something, the individual must hand over the item to the responsible persons and should be content with receiving whatever is due to him as a matter of principle and as per the law.

[a] It is the intention of Almighty God that the Truth being true and falsehood being false should be absolutely clear to the people. Initially, this work is done through the call given in the language of argument. The missionary, by using powerful but easily understood arguments, proves the Truth being true and falsehood being false. The completion of this work is finally effected by extraordinary happenings. Such events take either the shape of a heavenly miracle or domination on earth. The latter event took place at the battle of Badr.

The Quraysh set out from Makkah to lend their assistance to their trading caravan coming in from Syria. The Muslims set out from Madinah to attack this caravan, but it deviated from the usual path, going along the seacoast, and thus escaped being attacked. The two parties then reached Badr and confronted each other. This happened at the behest of God. Both the parties were made to clash with each other and the victory was awarded to the people of the Faith. In this way, the veracity of the Prophet and that of his mission became abundantly clear to the people. It was finally clear to those who were true seekers of the truth that this was the real Truth while those who remained disaffected because of psychological complications persisted in their stand and thus proved that they deserved to be eliminated.

43 God showed them to you in your dream as small in number. If He had shown them to you as many, you would have lost heart and disputed about the matter; but God saved you. He has full knowledge of what is in the human heart. 44 When at the time of your encounter He made them appear few in your eyes, and made you appear few in their eyes, it was so that God might bring about that which had been decreed. Everything returns to God.[a]

إِذْ يُرِيكَهُمُ ٱللَّهُ فِى مَنَامِكَ قَلِيلًا وَلَوْ أَرَىٰكَهُمْ كَثِيرًا لَّفَشِلْتُمْ وَلَتَنَٰزَعْتُمْ فِى ٱلْأَمْرِ وَلَٰكِنَّ ٱللَّهَ سَلَّمَ إِنَّهُۥ عَلِيمٌۢ بِذَاتِ ٱلصُّدُورِ ۝ وَإِذْ يُرِيكُمُوهُمْ إِذِ ٱلْتَقَيْتُمْ فِىٓ أَعْيُنِكُمْ قَلِيلًا وَيُقَلِّلُكُمْ فِىٓ أَعْيُنِهِمْ لِيَقْضِىَ ٱللَّهُ أَمْرًا كَانَ مَفْعُولًا وَإِلَى ٱللَّهِ تُرْجَعُ ٱلْأُمُورُ ۝

---

[a] At Badr the Quraysh had a large army. Had the Muslims seen their real numbers, some of them would have said that they should fight, while others would have asked not to fight. In this way differences would have cropped up and the real task would have remained unfinished. So, God showed their numbers to Muslims as fewer while he showed the number of Muslims to the Quraysh as more. In this way it was possible for the Muslims to fight fearlessly. When God wants a task to be performed, He sends help and arranges for its completion.

The events that occur during the course of action occur at God's behest, so that He may judge the reaction of the person concerned to the conditions set by Him.

⁴⁵ Believers! When you encounter a party, remain firm and remember God much, so that you may succeed. ⁴⁶ Obey God and His Messenger, and avoid dissension, lest you falter and are no longer held in awe. Have patience: God is with those who are patient. ⁴⁷ Do not be like those who left their homes full of conceit and showing off to others. They debar others from the path of God: but God has knowledge of all their actions.ᵃ

يَـٰٓأَيُّهَا ٱلَّذِينَ ءَامَنُوٓاْ إِذَا لَقِيتُمْ فِئَةً فَٱثْبُتُواْ وَٱذْكُرُواْ ٱللَّهَ كَثِيرًا لَّعَلَّكُمْ تُفْلِحُونَ ۝ وَأَطِيعُواْ ٱللَّهَ وَرَسُولَهُۥ وَلَا تَنَـٰزَعُواْ فَتَفْشَلُواْ وَتَذْهَبَ رِيحُكُمْ وَٱصْبِرُوٓاْ إِنَّ ٱللَّهَ مَعَ ٱلصَّـٰبِرِينَ ۝ وَلَا تَكُونُواْ كَٱلَّذِينَ خَرَجُواْ مِن دِيَـٰرِهِم بَطَرًا وَرِئَآءَ ٱلنَّاسِ وَيَصُدُّونَ عَن سَبِيلِ ٱللَّهِ وَٱللَّهُ بِمَا يَعْمَلُونَ مُحِيطٌ ۝

ᵃ Success ensues with the help of God. But God's help always arrives in this world in the garb of the cause and effect process, and not otherwise. If Muslims prepare themselves as far as possible, fulfilling all the conditions laid down by God for success, then God grants them success after compensating for any shortcomings that they might have. But if they do not exert themselves to the full as commanded by God, He never sends His help in such circumstances.

What are these factors which will lead to success? Firstly Muslims should not initiate aggression. Then they should set about strengthening their roots until the enemy comes to attack them. When things reach the stage of a clash, they should prove to be staunch and unflinching, keeping in mind the remembrance of God—in other words, the real goal,—so that their morale may remain intact; they should keep themselves fully organised under the command of their chief, ignoring mutual differences instead of enlarging upon them and becoming divided; they should impress the enemy with their unity; they should exercise patience, i.e., they should adopt a sensible approach instead of being emotional; they should not take any immature step in the hope of quick success; their eyes should be on the final goal and not on immediate gain.

Receiving God's succour is thus a matter of cause and effect. If we are willing to surrender our will wholeheartedly to the will of God, then alone are we held deserving to receive divine succour. The present world is one of trial. Here, God achieves His will from behind the veil of the 'unseen.' That is why when He helps the believers, it is done from behind the screen of 'cause and effect.' If the Muslims go on taking steps without making preliminary preparations and suffer from differences and dissension, they should never hope that God will appear all of a sudden and solve all their problems on the spot. Even if the Muslims find themselves in better conditions than those of their opponents, it should not happen that, like those who deny the truth they become boastful of their power; fall a prey to haughtiness and ostentation and, in claiming superiority, go to the extent of opposing the call of Truth because it does not suit their whims and fancies.

⁴⁸ Satan made their deeds seem fair to them and said, 'None of the people shall prevail against you this day; I shall be your protector!' But when the two forces came in sight of each other, he turned on his heels, saying, 'This is where I leave you: I see what you do not, and I fear God—God is severe in His punishment.' ⁴⁹ The hypocrites and those whose hearts were perverted said, 'These people [the believers] must be deluded by their religion.' But he who places his trust in God [knows that], God is Almighty and Wise.ᵃ

وَإِذْ زَيَّنَ لَهُمُ ٱلشَّيْطَٰنُ أَعْمَٰلَهُمْ وَقَالَ لَا غَالِبَ لَكُمُ ٱلْيَوْمَ مِنَ ٱلنَّاسِ وَإِنِّي جَارٌ لَّكُمْ ۖ فَلَمَّا تَرَآءَتِ ٱلْفِئَتَانِ نَكَصَ عَلَىٰ عَقِبَيْهِ وَقَالَ إِنِّي بَرِيٓءٌ مِّنكُمْ إِنِّيٓ أَرَىٰ مَا لَا تَرَوْنَ إِنِّيٓ أَخَافُ ٱللَّهَ ۚ وَٱللَّهُ شَدِيدُ ٱلْعِقَابِ ۝ إِذْ يَقُولُ ٱلْمُنَٰفِقُونَ وَٱلَّذِينَ فِي قُلُوبِهِم مَّرَضٌ غَرَّ هَٰٓؤُلَآءِ دِينُهُمْ ۚ وَمَن يَتَوَكَّلْ عَلَى ٱللَّهِ فَإِنَّ ٱللَّهَ عَزِيزٌ حَكِيمٌ ۝

ᵃ The Quraysh of Makkah considered themselves adherents of the Truth and the companions of the Prophet adherents of falsehood. They were so certain about this, that they prayed standing before the Kabah, 'O God! Give success to the one of these two parties which is in the right and destroy the party which is in the wrong.' However this faith of theirs was false. This type of faith always develops due to glorification (taz'in) of wrong action. Satan taught the people of Makkah that they were the followers of the recognised, well-known prophets, Abraham and Ishmael, while the Muslims were the followers of a person whose very claim to being a prophet was controversial; they were the inheritors of the Ka'bah, while the Muslims had been banished from the land of the Ka'bah. Satan having created such ideas in the hearts of the Makkans, infused false faith in them. They thought that whatever they were doing was done rightly and that, at all events, God would come to their assistance.

On the one hand, the Makkan opponents considered their false conviction to be true on the basis of the above-mentioned factors. On the other hand, when they saw that the Prophet's companions had engaged themselves on the Islamic front with stronger conviction and the will to self-sacrifice, they set about trying to show that their true faith was unreliable by saying that it was merely religious fanaticism; that they were going mad under the influence of the eloquent utterances of the Prophet.

But, when there was a clash between the two groups and God's succour came down in favour of the Muslims, Satan fled, abandoning the opponents of Islam. By the Grace of God, the Muslims' hearts became strengthened.

God certainly helps those who rely on Him. But, God's help appears only when believers prove their faith in God to such a great extent that those who deny the truth feel justified in saying that they (the Faithful) have gone mad.

50 If you could see, when the angels take the souls of those who are bent on denying the truth [at death], how they strike their faces and backs: saying 'Taste the punishment of the Burning! 51 This is the punishment for what your hands committed—for, God never does the least wrong to His servants.' 52 Like Pharaoh's people and those that have gone before them, they rejected God's signs and God seized them for their sins. God is strong, and severe in punishment! 53 God would never withdraw a favour that He had conferred upon a people unless they change what is in their hearts. God is all hearing and all-knowing.*a*

وَلَوْ تَرَىٰٓ إِذْ يَتَوَفَّى ٱلَّذِينَ كَفَرُوٓاْ ٱلْمَلَـٰٓئِكَةُ يَضْرِبُونَ وُجُوهَهُمْ وَأَدْبَـٰرَهُمْ وَذُوقُواْ عَذَابَ ٱلْحَرِيقِ ۝ ذَٰلِكَ بِمَا قَدَّمَتْ أَيْدِيكُمْ وَأَنَّ ٱللَّهَ لَيْسَ بِظَلَّـٰمٍ لِّلْعَبِيدِ ۝ كَدَأْبِ ءَالِ فِرْعَوْنَ ۚ وَٱلَّذِينَ مِن قَبْلِهِمْ ۚ كَفَرُواْ بِـَٔايَـٰتِ ٱللَّهِ فَأَخَذَهُمُ ٱللَّهُ بِذُنُوبِهِمْ ۗ إِنَّ ٱللَّهَ قَوِىٌّ شَدِيدُ ٱلْعِقَابِ ۝ ذَٰلِكَ بِأَنَّ ٱللَّهَ لَمْ يَكُ مُغَيِّرًا نِّعْمَةً أَنْعَمَهَا عَلَىٰ قَوْمٍ حَتَّىٰ يُغَيِّرُواْ مَا بِأَنفُسِهِمْ ۙ وَأَنَّ ٱللَّهَ سَمِيعٌ عَلِيمٌ ۝

---

a The granting of God's bounty depends upon eligibility for entitlement to such bounty. At the national or community level, bounty is commensurate with the worth of the individuals making up the larger entity. Collective bounty or blessings are given according to the status of a community assessed at the level of its individuals. This means that if a group wants to have God's collective grace, it should bend its entire energies to the improvement of the inner selves of its individuals. Similarly, if a community finds that collective bounties are taken away from it, instead of running after the bounties themselves, it should pursue its individuals, because of the fact that it is due to deterioration in individuals that it is deprived of bounties, and only on the reformation of individuals can it have God's grace restored.

When a community adopts the way of tyranny instead of justice and the way of arrogance instead of modesty, then a pronouncement of Truth is made before it so that it is given a warning. This declaration, in view of its perfect clarity, is a sign from God. Accepting it amounts to accepting God, just as its rejection amounts to rejection of God. When the call of God reveals itself to the extent of a sign (*ayah*), and appears before people, and still they reject it, they necessarily become liable for punishment. Though the beginning of this punishment starts in this world, the punishment of the world is far more lenient than the punishment that man is going to face after death. The beatings of the angels, humiliation before all the creatures, burning in the fire of hell—all these stages are so terrible that one cannot even imagine them in the present conditions.

When a man adopts the ways of tyranny and arrogance, he receives at first a warning. When he does not learn a lesson from it, he is finally struck down by the severe punishment of God.

54 Like Pharaoh's people and those who went before them, they denied their Lord's signs: We destroyed them for their sins, and We drowned Pharaoh's people—they were all evil-doers.

55 The worst creatures in the sight of God are those who reject Him and will not believe; 56 those with whom you have made a covenant, and who break their covenant on every occasion and have no fear [of God]. 57 Should you encounter them in war, then deal with them in such a manner that those that follow them should abandon their designs and may take warning. 58 And if you learn of treachery on the part of any people, throw their treaty back at them, so as to be on equal terms, for God does not love the treacherous.[a]

كَدَأْبِ ءَالِ فِرْعَوْنَ ۙ وَالَّذِينَ مِن قَبْلِهِمْ ۚ كَذَّبُوا بِـَٔايَٰتِ رَبِّهِمْ فَأَهْلَكْنَٰهُم بِذُنُوبِهِمْ وَأَغْرَقْنَآ ءَالَ فِرْعَوْنَ ۚ وَكُلٌّ كَانُوا ظَٰلِمِينَ ۝ إِنَّ شَرَّ ٱلدَّوَآبِّ عِندَ ٱللَّهِ ٱلَّذِينَ كَفَرُوا فَهُمْ لَا يُؤْمِنُونَ ۝ ٱلَّذِينَ عَٰهَدتَّ مِنْهُمْ ثُمَّ يَنقُضُونَ عَهْدَهُمْ فِى كُلِّ مَرَّةٍ وَهُمْ لَا يَتَّقُونَ ۝ فَإِمَّا تَثْقَفَنَّهُمْ فِى ٱلْحَرْبِ فَشَرِّدْ بِهِم مَّنْ خَلْفَهُمْ لَعَلَّهُمْ يَذَّكَّرُونَ ۝ وَإِمَّا تَخَافَنَّ مِن قَوْمٍ خِيَانَةً فَٱنۢبِذْ إِلَيْهِمْ عَلَىٰ سَوَآءٍ ۚ إِنَّ ٱللَّهَ لَا يُحِبُّ ٱلْخَآئِنِينَ ۝

---

[a] The Jews of Madinah had already become guilty by rejecting the prophethood of the Prophet Muhammad. The gravity of their guilt was further increased by their breaking of the pledge. After the emigration to Madinah, there had been a written agreement between the Prophet and the Jews of Madinah that both the sides would be neutral in matters relating to each other. But the Jews started conspiring against him, secretly joining hands and collaborating with his enemies. This was breach of trust in addition to the rejection of truth. Punishment awaits such people in the Hereafter. And in this world they will be discouraged from creating further mischief.

If the Muslims have a treaty with a community, but they want to cancel it for fear of its being breached by that community, it is necessary that they should first inform those co-signatories, so that it is known in advance that the treaty no longer exists between them.

The position is different when there is not merely the fear of a beach of trust but there has been a clear contravention of the treaty. In such a case it is permissable to start retaliatory action without informing the other party. The campaign of Makkah is an example of this type. The Quraysh had unilaterally contravened the Hudaibiyah treaty by joining the Banu Bakr's aggression against an ally of the Prophet Muhammad, namely, the Banu Khuza'a. So the Prophet quietly proceeded against the Quraysh without giving them advance information.

⁵⁹ Let not the deniers think that they will ever get away. They cannot frustrate [God's purpose]. They have not the power to do so. ⁶⁰ Prepare any strength you can muster against them, and any cavalry with which you can overawe God's enemy and your own enemy as well, and others besides them whom you do not know, but who are known to God. Anything you spend in the way of God will be repaid to you in full. You will not be wronged. ⁶¹ Then if they should be inclined to make peace, make peace with them, and put your trust in God. Surely, it is He who is All Hearing and All Knowing. ⁶² Should they seek to deceive you, God is enough for you: it was He who strengthened you with His help, and rallied the faithful around you, and bound their hearts together.ᵃ

وَلَا تَحْسَبَنَّ ٱلَّذِينَ كَفَرُوا۟ سَبَقُوٓا۟ إِنَّهُمْ لَا يُعْجِزُونَ ۝ وَأَعِدُّوا۟ لَهُم مَّا ٱسْتَطَعْتُم مِّن قُوَّةٍ وَمِن رِّبَاطِ ٱلْخَيْلِ تُرْهِبُونَ بِهِۦ عَدُوَّ ٱللَّهِ وَعَدُوَّكُمْ وَءَاخَرِينَ مِن دُونِهِمْ لَا تَعْلَمُونَهُمُ ٱللَّهُ يَعْلَمُهُمْ وَمَا تُنفِقُوا۟ مِن شَىْءٍ فِى سَبِيلِ ٱللَّهِ يُوَفَّ إِلَيْكُمْ وَأَنتُمْ لَا تُظْلَمُونَ ۝ وَإِن جَنَحُوا۟ لِلسَّلْمِ فَٱجْنَحْ لَهَا وَتَوَكَّلْ عَلَى ٱللَّهِ إِنَّهُۥ هُوَ ٱلسَّمِيعُ ٱلْعَلِيمُ ۝ وَإِن يُرِيدُوٓا۟ أَن يَخْدَعُوكَ فَإِنَّ حَسْبَكَ ٱللَّهُ هُوَ ٱلَّذِىٓ أَيَّدَكَ بِنَصْرِهِۦ وَبِٱلْمُؤْمِنِينَ ۝

ᵃ Islam relies not on the use of force but on the demonstration of force to inspire awe in the enemy. That is why the believers were commanded to equip themselves with power so that the enemy might be demoralized and refrain from aggression. Those who spend their resources in strengthening Islam intellectually and materially will be rewarded many times over by their Lord. The secret of success in Islam does not lie in military confrontation but in the preaching of its principles—hence the command that whenever there is an offer of peace by the other party, it should be accepted, setting aside every doubt or suspicion, because doubt or suspicion is in any case an uncertain thing, but the benefit of a cease-fire is certain: it permits the dawah work of Islam to start in a peaceful atmosphere. The stoppage of war thus facilitates the ideological expansion of Islam.

Islam in itself is the greatest power. If the belief in God and the Hereafter is engendered in a group, then all those psychological drawbacks which cause differences and clashes are driven out of them. Thereafter, it necessarily happens that all of them join together and become one, and it is a fact that the greatest strength lies in unity. A united group, though small, will overcome a group larger than itself. Mutual integration is the most difficult task. The sign of a divinely—aided group is that its members are united; nothing succeeds in disuniting them.

⁶³ Even if you had spent all that is on the earth, you could not have bound their hearts together, but God has bound them together. Surely, He is Mighty and Wise.

⁶⁴ O Prophet! God is sufficient for you and the believers who follow you. ⁶⁵ Prophet, urge the believers to fight; if there are twenty of you who are steadfast, they will overcome two hundred, and if there are a hundred of you, they will overcome a thousand of those who deny the truth, for they are devoid of understanding. ⁶⁶ God has now lightened your burden, for He knows that there is weakness in you. If there are a hundred of you who are steadfast, they will overcome two hundred; and if there are a thousand of you, they will overcome two thousand by God's will. God is with the steadfast.[a]

وَأَلَّفَ بَيْنَ قُلُوبِهِمْ لَوْ أَنفَقْتَ مَا فِى ٱلْأَرْضِ جَمِيعًا مَّآ أَلَّفْتَ بَيْنَ قُلُوبِهِمْ وَلَٰكِنَّ ٱللَّهَ أَلَّفَ بَيْنَهُمْ إِنَّهُۥ عَزِيزٌ حَكِيمٌ ۝ يَٰٓأَيُّهَا ٱلنَّبِىُّ حَسْبُكَ ٱللَّهُ وَمَنِ ٱتَّبَعَكَ مِنَ ٱلْمُؤْمِنِينَ ۝ يَٰٓأَيُّهَا ٱلنَّبِىُّ حَرِّضِ ٱلْمُؤْمِنِينَ عَلَى ٱلْقِتَالِ إِن يَكُن مِّنكُمْ عِشْرُونَ صَٰبِرُونَ يَغْلِبُوا۟ مِا۟ئَتَيْنِ وَإِن يَكُن مِّنكُم مِّا۟ئَةٌ يَغْلِبُوٓا۟ أَلْفًا مِّنَ ٱلَّذِينَ كَفَرُوا۟ بِأَنَّهُمْ قَوْمٌ لَّا يَفْقَهُونَ ۝ ٱلْـَٰٔنَ خَفَّفَ ٱللَّهُ عَنكُمْ وَعَلِمَ أَنَّ فِيكُمْ ضَعْفًا فَإِن يَكُن مِّنكُم مِّا۟ئَةٌ صَابِرَةٌ يَغْلِبُوا۟ مِا۟ئَتَيْنِ وَإِن يَكُن مِّنكُمْ أَلْفٌ يَغْلِبُوٓا۟ أَلْفَيْنِ بِإِذْنِ ٱللَّهِ وَٱللَّهُ مَعَ ٱلصَّٰبِرِينَ ۝

---

[a] The reason for a lesser number of believers overcoming a large number of those who deny the truth has been explained by saying that the believers possessed *fiqh*, while those who deny the truth were devoid of it. The literal meaning of *fiqh* is understanding. This means the insight and wisdom which a man acquires as a result of faith. Faith in God is like the lighting of a lamp in a dark room. The lamp lights up the room in a such way that everything in it is seen clearly. Similarly, faith blesses man with a divine consciousness, after which he starts seeing all realities in their original shape.

As a result of faith, man understands the reality of life and death. He comes to know that the most important thing is not the life of this world but the life of the Hereafter. This makes him fearless. He looks at death as if it is a door through which he may enter Paradise.

A believer is God-fearing and he is anxious about the Hereafter. Such a temperament purifies him of all types of negative feelings. He rises above obstinacy, hatred, prejudice, revenge and haughtiness. The case of those who deny the truth is just the opposite. One who denies the truth acts emotionally, while the believer acts realistically. One who denies the truth carries out his dealings with narrow-mindedness, while the believer displays broad-mindedness.

⁶⁷ It is not right for a Prophet to keep captives unless he has battled strenuously in the land. You desire the gain of this world, while God desires for you the Hereafter—God is mighty and wise. ⁶⁸ Had it not been for a writ from God that had already gone forth, you would have been severely punished on account of what you took. ⁶⁹ So eat of that which you have gained in war as lawful and good, and fear God. Surely, God is most forgiving and merciful.^a

مَا كَانَ لِنَبِيٍّ أَن يَكُونَ لَهُ أَسْرَىٰ حَتَّىٰ يُثْخِنَ فِى ٱلْأَرْضِ تُرِيدُونَ عَرَضَ ٱلدُّنْيَا وَٱللَّهُ يُرِيدُ ٱلْأَخِرَةَ وَٱللَّهُ عَزِيزٌ حَكِيمٌ ۝ لَّوْلَا كِتَٰبٌ مِّنَ ٱللَّهِ سَبَقَ لَمَسَّكُمْ فِيمَآ أَخَذْتُمْ عَذَابٌ عَظِيمٌ ۝ فَكُلُواْ مِمَّا غَنِمْتُمْ حَلَٰلًا طَيِّبًا وَٱتَّقُواْ ٱللَّهَ إِنَّ ٱللَّهَ غَفُورٌ رَّحِيمٌ ۝

---

^a At the battle of Badr, the Muslims killed seventy of the Quraysh's greatest men and captured another seventy. Many of these captives were chiefs. After the battle, a consultation was held to decide the fate of these prisoners. The majority of the companions were for ransoming them. These enemies were continuously hostile. But the Muslims lacked the resources to defend themselves. So, it was thought that the ransom could be utilised to purchase armaments. 'Umar ibn al-Khattab and Sa'd ibn Ma'az were against this opinion. 'Umar said: 'O, Prophet of God, these prisoners are the leaders of those who deny the truth. The real strength of our enemies has fallen into our hands. They should be killed so that the problem is solved once and for all.' However, the Prophet Muhammad acted on the first opinion.

Later on, those verses were revealed in which there were comments on the battle. While the ransom was declared legitimate by God, displeasure was expressed on that transaction. Releasing the war prisoners on a ransom was apparently a matter of mercy and grace, but it was not in accordance with the long term plan of God. God planned to root out paganism and polytheism and had caused all the leaders of the Quraysh (except Abu Lahab and Abu Sufyan) to gather on the field of Badr, arranging matters in such a way that they came entirely under the control of the Muslims. Had these leaders been killed at that time, the resistance of paganism and polytheism to montheism would have been completely buried in Badr itself. The result of releasing these leaders was that they were able to re-organise themselves and continue the resistance movement.

This decision was against the Muslims' war strategy, and could have become the cause of the most serious difficulties for them. These leaders, along with their followers, could have completely finished the entire mission of Islam. But God had ordained that the Last Prophet and his companions should necessarily overcome everything. That is the reason why, in spite of this shortcoming in strategy, the Quraysh were not able to overcome the Faithful.

⁷⁰ Prophet, tell those you have taken captive: 'If God knows of any good in your hearts, He will give you something better than what has been taken from you, and He will forgive you: God is Forgiving and Merciful.' ⁷¹ And if they would betray you, they betrayed God before, and He gave [you] power over them. God is aware and wise.ᵃ

يَـٰٓأَيُّهَا ٱلنَّبِىُّ قُل لِّمَن فِىٓ أَيْدِيكُم مِّنَ ٱلْأَسْرَىٰٓ إِن يَعْلَمِ ٱللَّهُ فِى قُلُوبِكُمْ خَيْرًا يُؤْتِكُمْ خَيْرًا مِّمَّآ أُخِذَ مِنكُمْ وَيَغْفِرْ لَكُمْ ۗ وَٱللَّهُ غَفُورٌ رَّحِيمٌ ۝ وَإِن يُرِيدُوا۟ خِيَانَتَكَ فَقَدْ خَانُوا۟ ٱللَّهَ مِن قَبْلُ فَأَمْكَنَ مِنْهُمْ ۗ وَٱللَّهُ عَلِيمٌ حَكِيمٌ ۝

ᵃ Releasing the prisoners at the battle of Badr was a strategic error. But, for the prisoners themselves, this amounted to giving them a new lease of life. This meant that the people who had become liable to be killed due to their opposition of the Truth, were given a further opportunity to re-think the Islamic call and their improper behaviour towards it. This respite opened up for them the door of self-rectification. Now one consequence of this event could have been that the flames of revenge flared up in the hearts of the prisoners due to the defeat they had suffered; they could have become eager to avenge the ignominy and loss they had suffered on the payment of ransom. In this case, they would have repeated the same wrong action as a result of which they had become liable to be seized upon by God. They would have expended their energy in opposing Islam, the result of which action would have been destruction in the world and punishment in the Hereafter.

The second possibility was that they could have thought over the extraordinary happenings on the battlefield of Badr, i.e. why did it happen that, in spite of having inferior and fewer armaments, the Muslims were clearly victorious? This clearly indicated that God was in favour of the religion of the Muslims and disfavoured that of the Quraysh. If this second line of thinking developed, it would make them change their previous behaviour and adopt the religion which they had not earlier been able to adopt and in this way become eligible for God's reward in this world and also in the Hereafter. History shows that there were a number of individuals among the Quraysh in whose hearts this question had arisen and sooner or later they joined Islam. 'Abbas ibn 'Abdul Muttalib had embraced Islam when he was a prisoner. Some others also joined the Islamic circle later. These people lowered themselves in the eyes of their own prejudiced group, but they honoured themselves in the eyes of God. They suffered worldly harm, but became possessors of the benefit of the Hereafter.

On the release of the prisoners, the Muslims had the suspicion that the latter, instead of being grateful for the Muslims' magnanimity, would engage in conspiracies, adopt destructive ways and create impediments in the way of Islam. But the Quran did not give importance to these suspicions, because a movement launched for the cause of pure Truth is not an ordinary movement. It is a Divine affair. God Himself is behind it; and nobody has the power to fight God.

⁷²Those who have believed and migrated and struggled for God's cause with their possessions and persons, and those who have given refuge and help, are the friends and protectors of one another. But as for those who have come to believe without having migrated —you are in no way responsible for their protection until they migrate. If they seek your help in the matter of religion, it is incumbent on you to help them, except against a people with whom you have a pact. God sees what you do. ⁷³Those who deny the truth support one another. If you fail to do likewise, there will be great disorder and corruption in the land.ᵃ

إِنَّ ٱلَّذِينَ ءَامَنُوا۟ وَهَاجَرُوا۟ وَجَٰهَدُوا۟ بِأَمْوَٰلِهِمْ وَأَنفُسِهِمْ فِى سَبِيلِ ٱللَّهِ وَٱلَّذِينَ ءَاوَوا۟ وَّنَصَرُوٓا۟ أُو۟لَٰٓئِكَ بَعْضُهُمْ أَوْلِيَآءُ بَعْضٍ وَٱلَّذِينَ ءَامَنُوا۟ وَلَمْ يُهَاجِرُوا۟ مَا لَكُم مِّن وَلَٰيَتِهِم مِّن شَىْءٍ حَتَّىٰ يُهَاجِرُوا۟ وَإِنِ ٱسْتَنصَرُوكُمْ فِى ٱلدِّينِ فَعَلَيْكُمُ ٱلنَّصْرُ إِلَّا عَلَىٰ قَوْمٍ بَيْنَكُمْ وَبَيْنَهُم مِّيثَٰقٌ وَٱللَّهُ بِمَا تَعْمَلُونَ بَصِيرٌ ۝ وَٱلَّذِينَ كَفَرُوا۟ بَعْضُهُمْ أَوْلِيَآءُ بَعْضٍ إِلَّا تَفْعَلُوهُ تَكُن فِتْنَةٌ فِى ٱلْأَرْضِ وَفَسَادٌ كَبِيرٌ ۝

ᵃ Generally when a man helps another, it is because that other person belongs to his family or group or class. But after the *hijrah* (migration to Madinah) the Islamic society formed in Madinah was such that those who were householders gave their houses to people with whom their relation was based only on religion. The people who left their hearths and homes and migrated to Madinah had done all this for the sake of God and the Hereafter, and those who allowed these strangers to share their money and property also did so, in order that God should be pleased with them and send them to paradise in the Hereafter.

This was a society in which relations of family or race were not important as compared to faith. People used to help each other, not for worldly benefit, but for the sake of the Hereafter. They used to give to each other without expecting any return from the receiver, but only expecting a reward from God. That society is truly Islamic where relations are established not on the basis of family relations or the prejudices of groupism, but on the basis of Truth; where the people are the supporters and helpers of each other for the sole reason that they are brothers in religion and not because some worldly consideration is linked with them.

74 Those who have believed and migrated and striven for the cause of God, as well as those who have given them refuge and support, are the true believers; they shall have forgiveness and an honourable provision. 75 And those who have believed later on, and emigrated and struggled for God's sake alongside you are also a part of you. But as to blood relations, they are nearer one to another in the Book of God. God has full knowledge of all things.ᵃ

وَٱلَّذِينَ ءَامَنُواْ وَهَاجَرُواْ وَجَهَدُواْ فِى سَبِيلِ ٱللَّهِ وَٱلَّذِينَ ءَاوَواْ وَّنَصَرُوٓاْ أُوْلَٰٓئِكَ هُمُ ٱلْمُؤْمِنُونَ حَقًّا ۚ لَّهُم مَّغْفِرَةٌ وَرِزْقٌ كَرِيمٌ ۝ وَٱلَّذِينَ ءَامَنُواْ مِنۢ بَعْدُ وَهَاجَرُواْ وَجَهَدُواْ مَعَكُمْ فَأُوْلَٰٓئِكَ مِنكُمْ ۚ وَأُوْلُواْ ٱلْأَرْحَامِ بَعْضُهُمْ أَوْلَىٰ بِبَعْضٍ فِى كِتَٰبِ ٱللَّهِ ۗ إِنَّ ٱللَّهَ بِكُلِّ شَىْءٍ عَلِيمٌۢ ۝

ᵃ Having faith in God means deciding to lead one's life purely for His sake. People who do so, frequently become strangers among those who live for things other than God. This alienation sometimes leads to the decision to migrate due to a wholly inimical atmosphere; one's whole life thus becomes one of struggle and sacrifice. These migrants are the true believers in the eyes of God—their faith being of the highest order. Next come those who support these migrants in God's cause.

In order to become a real Muslim, at least one of the following courses of action should be entered upon. Either the potential devotee should attach himself to Islam to such an extent that, if required, he will forsake his well-established life. Or he should loosen his purse strings in order to come to the aid of those who choose to migrate. If necessary he should even invite them to share in his earnings and property. True faith will thus become a reality for people on their becoming either *muhajirs* (migrants in God's cause) or *ansars* (helpers or supporters).

These are the two kinds of people for whom, before God, there is pardon or forgiveness (*maghfirah*) and respectable sustenance (*rizq karim*). The Paradise of the Hereafter is an extremely refined world; it is a perfect world; and the people eligible to be settled in a perfect world should also be perfect. No human being can attain such perfection in view of human weaknesses. However, God has promised that one who fulfils one test out of the two tests mentioned above shall have allowances made for his shortcomings and, by His grace, will be sent to Paradise. Helping and supporting those who become brothers through religion is very important. However, this will not affect the rights of blood relations and the distribution of inheritance among them. Under the influence of personal desire, a man may treat some things as essential for his family members, but this has no importance in the eyes of God. However, God himself has laid down in His Book laws regarding the rights of family members and rules of inheritance applicable to them. These will in any case hold good, and nothing can become an excuse for violating them.

9. REPENTANCE

¹ This is a declaration of immunity from God and His Messenger to the polytheists, with whom you had made agreements. ² So go about in the land for four months, but know that you cannot frustrate the plan of God and that God will disgrace those who deny the truth.ᵃ

بَرَآءَةٌ مِّنَ ٱللَّهِ وَرَسُولِهِۦٓ إِلَى ٱلَّذِينَ عَـٰهَدتُّم مِّنَ ٱلْمُشْرِكِينَ ۞ فَسِيحُوا۟ فِى ٱلْأَرْضِ أَرْبَعَةَ أَشْهُرٍ وَٱعْلَمُوٓا۟ أَنَّكُمْ غَيْرُ مُعْجِزِى ٱللَّهِ وَأَنَّ ٱللَّهَ مُخْزِى ٱلْكَـٰفِرِينَ ۞

ᵃ The opportunity that people have been given to live and settle in the present world, is not on the basis of any right but is only for the purpose of trial. As long as God wishes, He keeps a man on the earth and when, in His wisdom, He judges, the period of his test to be over, He causes death to overtake him and he is carried away from here.

³ This is a proclamation from God and His Messenger to the people on the day of the Pilgrimage, that God is free of all obligation to the polytheists, and so is His Messenger. If you repent, it will be better for you, but if you turn away, then know that you cannot frustrate the plan of God. Proclaim a grievous punishment to those who are bent on denying the truth. ⁴ As for those who have honoured the treaty you made with them and who have not supported anyone against you: fulfill your agreement with them to the end of their term. God loves those who are righteous.ᵃ

وَأَذَٰنٌ مِّنَ ٱللَّهِ وَرَسُولِهِۦٓ إِلَى ٱلنَّاسِ يَوْمَ ٱلْحَجِّ ٱلْأَكْبَرِ أَنَّ ٱللَّهَ بَرِىٓءٌ مِّنَ ٱلْمُشْرِكِينَ ۙ وَرَسُولُهُۥ ۚ فَإِن تُبْتُمْ فَهُوَ خَيْرٌ لَّكُمْ ۖ وَإِن تَوَلَّيْتُمْ فَٱعْلَمُوٓاْ أَنَّكُمْ غَيْرُ مُعْجِزِى ٱللَّهِ ۗ وَبَشِّرِ ٱلَّذِينَ كَفَرُواْ بِعَذَابٍ أَلِيمٍ ۝ إِلَّا ٱلَّذِينَ عَٰهَدتُّم مِّنَ ٱلْمُشْرِكِينَ ثُمَّ لَمْ يَنقُصُوكُمْ شَيْـًٔا وَلَمْ يُظَٰهِرُواْ عَلَيْكُمْ أَحَدًا فَأَتِمُّوٓاْ إِلَيْهِمْ عَهْدَهُمْ إِلَىٰ مُدَّتِهِمْ ۚ إِنَّ ٱللَّهَ يُحِبُّ ٱلْمُتَّقِينَ ۝

ᵃ The Prophet testified to the Truth to the fullest extent to his hearers. After the completion of his divine task, those who still did not embrace the Faith, lost their right to live on God's earth. They had been kept here for the purpose of trial; on completion of the process of preaching and argumentation, the trial was over. Thereafter, why should they have had any lenience shown to them? This is why, after the completion of the work of the prophets, some sort of destructive calamity befell the unbelievers and they were annihilated.

This is exactly what happened to the addressees of the Prophet Muhammad. But, it was not any calamity from the sky which descended upon them. The above-mentioned principle of God was implemented, in this case within the framework of a cause and effect system. First of all, by means of the superior Quranic style of expression and the superior character of the Prophet, the call to the Truth was conveyed to them. Then by giving domination to the monotheists over the Makkan polytheists, the process of argument was completed in their case. When all this was done and still they persisted in rejecting the Truth, they were accused of continuous breach of trust and violation of their pledge and an ultimatum was issued to them that they should reform themselves in four months time; otherwise they would be annihilated.

All this was settled on the principles of God-fearing (taqwa) and not on the principle of national politics. The polytheists were silenced at the level of arguments; then they would be warned in advance that they would be given a number of months' respite to reconsider the matter; the door was kept open for them till the last moment, so that those who repented might join those blessed by God; the case of some tribes who had not violated their agreement was kept separate from the case of those who had.

⁵ When the forbidden months have passed, kill the polytheists [who are at war with you] wherever you find them.ᵃ Take them captive, and besiege them, and lie in wait for them at every place of ambush. But if they repent, and take to prayer regularly and pay the alms, then let them go their way. God is forgiving and merciful. ⁶ If any one of the polytheists seeks asylum with you, grant him asylum so that he may hear the word of God; then convey him to a place of safety. That is because they are a people who have no knowledge.ᵇ

فَإِذَا ٱنسَلَخَ ٱلْأَشْهُرُ ٱلْحُرُمُ فَٱقْتُلُوا۟ ٱلْمُشْرِكِينَ حَيْثُ وَجَدتُّمُوهُمْ وَخُذُوهُمْ وَٱحْصُرُوهُمْ وَٱقْعُدُوا۟ لَهُمْ كُلَّ مَرْصَدٍ فَإِن تَابُوا۟ وَأَقَامُوا۟ ٱلصَّلَوٰةَ وَءَاتَوُا۟ ٱلزَّكَوٰةَ فَخَلُّوا۟ سَبِيلَهُمْ إِنَّ ٱللَّهَ غَفُورٌ رَّحِيمٌ ۝ وَإِنْ أَحَدٌ مِّنَ ٱلْمُشْرِكِينَ ٱسْتَجَارَكَ فَأَجِرْهُ حَتَّىٰ يَسْمَعَ كَلَٰمَ ٱللَّهِ ثُمَّ أَبْلِغْهُ مَأْمَنَهُ ذَٰلِكَ بِأَنَّهُمْ قَوْمٌ لَّا يَعْلَمُونَ ۝

ᵃ The command to do battle given here after the lapse of four months of respite was not about an ordinary fight. This was God's retribution imposed on those who denied the truth due to their rejection of the Prophet. By rejecting God's prophet even after the completion of the process of arguments, they had made themselves liable to be left with no option but to accept the faith or fight. This was a special principle of God which related to the addressees of the Prophet and not to the general people. However, even after the completion of the process of preaching, this order was not made applicable immediately; even at the last stage they were given four months' respite.

Revenge does not know pardon. One with a revengeful mentality is satisfied only when he sees his opponent disgraced and destroyed. But the action taken against the polytheists of Arabia was not in any way connected with any type of revenge; it was based on an absolutely realistic principle. That is the reason why, in spite of the order being so severe, it was always open to them to embrace the Islamic religion and save themselves from punishment and acquire a respectable position in the Islamic brotherhood. For anybody's repentance to be acceptable, only two practical conditions were enough—prayer (salat) and religious alms-giving (zakat). In times of conflict, if any individual from amongst the enemies says that he wants to understand Islam, Muslims have been ordered to give him protection, to give him an opportunity to be in their atmosphere and to try to see that the message of Islam is implanted in his heart. Even then, if he does not accept Islam, he should be led back to his place of residence under their protection. ▶

7 How can there be a treaty with the polytheists on the part of God and His Messenger, except for those with whom you entered into a treaty at the Sacred Mosque? As long as they act straight with you, act straight with them. God loves those who are righteous. 8 How [can there be a treaty] for, if they get the upper hand over you, they will respect neither kinship nor covenant. They [try to] please you with their tongues but their hearts reject you; most of them are perfidious.ᵃ

كَيْفَ يَكُونُ لِلْمُشْرِكِينَ عَهْدٌ عِندَ ٱللَّهِ وَعِندَ رَسُولِهِۦٓ إِلَّا ٱلَّذِينَ عَٰهَدتُّمْ عِندَ ٱلْمَسْجِدِ ٱلْحَرَامِ ۖ فَمَا ٱسْتَقَٰمُواْ لَكُمْ فَٱسْتَقِيمُواْ لَهُمْ ۚ إِنَّ ٱللَّهَ يُحِبُّ ٱلْمُتَّقِينَ ۝ كَيْفَ وَإِن يَظْهَرُواْ عَلَيْكُمْ لَا يَرْقُبُواْ فِيكُمْ إِلًّا وَلَا ذِمَّةً ۚ يُرْضُونَكُم بِأَفْوَٰهِهِمْ وَتَأْبَىٰ قُلُوبُهُمْ وَأَكْثَرُهُمْ فَٰسِقُونَ ۝

In wartime, it is usually unwise to give such a concession to the enemy, because it is quite possible that an enemy spy, taking advantage of this concession, may enter the Muslim camp and try to find out its strategic secrets. But, Islam holds that, the question of preaching in order to invite people towards the right path is so important that, in spite of this risk, its door should never be closed.

If a man indulges in transgression unknowingly or out of ignorance, he will be treated with all possible lenience until his unawareness or ignorance is rectified.

ᵃ When the Muslims attained a strong position, the Quraysh entered into treaties with them. However, the Quraysh were not happy with these agreements. They thought that their execution of these treaties with their 'enemy' was very much to their detriment. That is why they were always on the look-out for opportunities to violate their agreements and cause harm to Muslims or at least defame them. Obviously, when there is a clear breach of a treaty by one party, the carrying out of the agreement by the other party is no longer obligatory.

This was the thinking of the Quraysh who felt that, with the rise of the Muslims, their leadership was at stake. However, there were other tribes (Banu Kinana, Banu Khuza'a, Banu Dhamra) who, unhampered by this psychological complication, had executed agreements with the Muslims and fulfilled them. When a period of respite of four months was announced, about nine months remained until the expiry of the periods of these agreements. The order was that these agreements be honoured till the last date, because that was the requirement of God-fearing. But after the expiry of this period, no such agreement was entered into with anybody and there were only two alternatives before the polytheists—either to embrace Islam or be ready for war.

⁹ They have sold God's revelations for a paltry price, and barred others from His path. How evil is what they have been doing! ¹⁰ Where believers are concerned, they respect no tie of kinship or treaty. They are people who overstep the limits. ¹¹ If they repent and keep up their prayers and pay the alms, then they are your brethren in faith. We make Our messages clear for people who are willing to learn.ᵃ

ٱشْتَرَوْاْ بِـَٔايَٰتِ ٱللَّهِ ثَمَنًا قَلِيلًا فَصَدُّواْ عَن سَبِيلِهِۦٓ إِنَّهُمْ سَآءَ مَا كَانُواْ يَعْمَلُونَ ۝ لَا يَرْقُبُونَ فِى مُؤْمِنٍ إِلًّا وَلَا ذِمَّةً وَأُوْلَٰٓئِكَ هُمُ ٱلْمُعْتَدُونَ ۝ فَإِن تَابُواْ وَأَقَامُواْ ٱلصَّلَوٰةَ وَءَاتَوُاْ ٱلزَّكَوٰةَ فَإِخْوَٰنُكُمْ فِى ٱلدِّينِ وَنُفَصِّلُ ٱلْـَٔايَٰتِ لِقَوْمٍ يَعْلَمُونَ ۝

ᵃ The basis of social life rests on two things: kinship or mutual commitments or agreements. Man honours such rights as are based on blood relationships and the rights of those with whom he has agreements, in terms of his commitments to them. But when a man is overcome by the temptation of worldly interest, and its considerations, he forgets both these duties. For the sake of his petty interests, he forgets the rights of blood relations as well as rights flowing from agreements. Such people are transgressors; they are guilty in the eyes of God. Even if they escape the consequences in the world, they will not be able to save themselves from seizure by God in the Hereafter, unless they repent and desist from arrogance. However wicked an individual may have been in the past, he becomes a respectable member of the Islamic brotherhood if he makes amends and reforms himself. Thereafter, there remains no difference between him and other Muslims.

[12] But if they break faith after pledging it and revile your religion, then fight these leaders of unbelief,[a] so that they may desist, for they have no regard for their pledged word.[b] [13] Will you not fight against those who have broken their oaths and conspired to banish the Messenger? They were the first to attack you. Do you fear them? Surely God is more deserving of your fear, if you are true believers. [14] Fight them: God will punish them at your hands, and will disgrace them. He will help you to overcome them and heal the hearts of the faithful; [15] He will remove the rage from their hearts. God will turn in His mercy to whom He wills. God is all knowing and wise.[c]

وَإِن نَّكَثُوٓاْ أَيْمَـٰنَهُم مِّنۢ بَعْدِ عَهْدِهِمْ وَطَعَنُواْ فِى دِينِكُمْ فَقَـٰتِلُوٓاْ أَئِمَّةَ ٱلْكُفْرِ إِنَّهُمْ لَآ أَيْمَـٰنَ لَهُمْ لَعَلَّهُمْ يَنتَهُونَ ۝ أَلَا تُقَـٰتِلُونَ قَوْمًا نَّكَثُوٓاْ أَيْمَـٰنَهُمْ وَهَمُّواْ بِإِخْرَاجِ ٱلرَّسُولِ وَهُم بَدَءُوكُمْ أَوَّلَ مَرَّةٍ ۚ أَتَخْشَوْنَهُمْ ۚ فَٱللَّهُ أَحَقُّ أَن تَخْشَوْهُ إِن كُنتُم مُّؤْمِنِينَ ۝ قَـٰتِلُوهُمْ يُعَذِّبْهُمُ ٱللَّهُ بِأَيْدِيكُمْ وَيُخْزِهِمْ وَيَنصُرْكُمْ عَلَيْهِمْ وَيَشْفِ صُدُورَ قَوْمٍ مُّؤْمِنِينَ ۝ وَيُذْهِبْ غَيْظَ قُلُوبِهِمْ ۗ وَيَتُوبُ ٱللَّهُ عَلَىٰ مَن يَشَآءُ ۗ وَٱللَّهُ عَلِيمٌ حَكِيمٌ ۝

---

[a] The phrase 'leaders of disbelief' referred to the Quraysh who, because of their position of leadership in Arabia, led the movement of opposition against Islam. This was the first prominent group to oppose the movement of Islam, wherever it arose. Its members, feeling that its superior position was being adversely affected by the pure call of Truth, were clever enough to pick out trivial points in the divine call in order to discredit it and they had the resources to thrust the Muslims into different types of difficulties in order to discourage them.

[b] 'They have no regard for their pledged word' is a very meaningful sentence. The pledges and treaties of those who oppose Islam out of enmity and obstinacy are uncertain and unreliable. The attitude is that of constant irritation with their opponent. There is no consistency in them. Even if they execute an agreement they are unable to uphold and maintain it for long due to the vagaries of their temperament. It does not take long for them to be overcome by their negative feelings and break their pledges.

[c] The root of all wisdom is fear of God. The fear of God develops in man the readiness to accept the Truth; it awakens in man a certain consciousness that enables him to see realities in their original form. That is why it does not take the God-fearing man long to understand the Divine plan. He comes to know the will of God and dedicates himself to it with full confidence. He starts moving on that right path which ultimately leads to success. The fear of God makes a man's eye tearful, and before God, it is only the tearful eye which is destined to be cooled in this world as well as in the Hereafter.

¹⁶ Do you [O believers] think that you will be spared without God identifying which of you have struggled and did not take anyone for friends and protectors except God, His Messenger, and the believers? God is fully aware of all your actions.^a

أَمْ حَسِبْتُمْ أَن تُتْرَكُواْ وَلَمَّا يَعْلَمِ ٱللَّهُ ٱلَّذِينَ جَهَدُواْ مِنكُمْ وَلَمْ يَتَّخِذُواْ مِن دُونِ ٱللَّهِ وَلَا رَسُولِهِۦ وَلَا ٱلْمُؤْمِنِينَ وَلِيجَةً وَٱللَّهُ خَبِيرٌۢ بِمَا تَعْمَلُونَ ۝

---

^a In the present world, when a man makes something the purpose of his life, he encounters many problems and demands in his efforts to achieve it. If the man is bent upon his purpose, he utilizes all his strength in overcoming these problems and fulfilling these demands. This is called *jihad*. In this world everyone has to face this *jihad*. Everyone has to prove how ardent he is about his purpose at the level of *jihad*; only then is it possible for him to succeed in achieving it.

It is this struggle in the path of God which indicates to what extent the individual is serious about his purpose. To one who claims to have faith, events which test his faith occur again and again. Sometimes his heart becomes influenced by feelings of ill-will and jealousy towards somebody but his faith urges him to rid himself of all such feelings. Sometimes unpleasant words are on the tip of his tongue but his faith requires that he should hold his tongue at that time. Sometimes, in the course of his dealings, a right has to be honoured which is unpleasant to him, but faith exhorts him to fulfil all entitlements as a matter of justice, whether pleasant or unpleasant. Moreover, the call for truth sometimes reaches the stage when faith commands him to sacrifice his life and property to ensure its success. Going on fulfilling the requirements of faith at any cost, is known as *jihad*.

In the present world, when a man adopts a broad-based purpose, he has necessarily to focus on the centralism of his purpose; he has to be loyal to his leader; and he should completely identify himself with the fellow-travellers on the same path. These things are fraught with a sense of purposefulness. Without these, the claim to lead a purposeful life would be false. Similarly, when a man seriously introduces religion into his life, it will necessarily happen that God, His Prophet and the faithful will become his friends and supporters (*walijah*); he will be at one with them in every respect.

This matter becomes more critical when it is kept in view that its Assessor has full knowledge of its open and the hidden aspects. He will, therefore, deal with every individual in accordance with inner reality and not in accordance with his apparent outward aspect.

¹⁷ It is not right that the polytheists should frequent God's places of worship while they are self-confessed unbelievers. It is they whose works shall come to nothing and they shall abide in Hell. ¹⁸ Only he should tend God's houses of worship who believes in God and the Last Day, and is constant in prayer, and spends in charity, and stands in awe of none but God: such people may hope to be among the rightly guided.^a

مَا كَانَ لِلْمُشْرِكِينَ أَن يَعْمُرُوا۟ مَسَٰجِدَ ٱللَّهِ شَٰهِدِينَ عَلَىٰٓ أَنفُسِهِم بِٱلْكُفْرِ أُو۟لَٰٓئِكَ حَبِطَتْ أَعْمَٰلُهُمْ وَفِى ٱلنَّارِ هُمْ خَٰلِدُونَ ۝ إِنَّمَا يَعْمُرُ مَسَٰجِدَ ٱللَّهِ مَنْ ءَامَنَ بِٱللَّهِ وَٱلْيَوْمِ ٱلْءَاخِرِ وَأَقَامَ ٱلصَّلَوٰةَ وَءَاتَى ٱلزَّكَوٰةَ وَلَمْ يَخْشَ إِلَّا ٱللَّهَ فَعَسَىٰٓ أُو۟لَٰٓئِكَ أَن يَكُونُوا۟ مِنَ ٱلْمُهْتَدِينَ ۝

---

^a At the time when the Quran was revealed, the position in Arabia was that the Muslims had gathered round the Prophet Muhammad and the polytheists around the Ka'bah. Till that time the histories of glories which we are now acquainted with had not yet become attached to the name of the Prophet Muhammad. He appeared to the people like an ordinary man. On the other hand, the Sacred Mosque of Makkah, because of the thousands of years of history attached to it, appeared to them a symbol of greatness and holiness. The polytheists saw themselves as being servants and retainers of the holiest shrine. On the contrary, when they saw the Muslims, they thought of them, under the circumstances prevailing at that time, as a group of people gathered around a madman.

¹⁹ Do you regard giving water to pilgrims and tending the Sacred Mosque as being equal to the deeds of those who believe in God and the Last Day and who strive in God's path? They are not equal in the sight of God. God does not guide such unjust people. ²⁰ Those who have believed and have migrated, and have striven for God's sake with their possessions and persons, stand much higher in God's esteem. It is they who will triumph; ²¹ their Lord gives them the good news of His mercy and His pleasure and gardens of eternal bliss. ²² There they will dwell for ever. Truly there is an immense reward with God.

²³ Believers, do not take your fathers and your brothers for allies if they choose denial of truth in preference to faith. Those among you who ally themselves with them are wrongdoers.ᵃ

۞ أَجَعَلْتُمْ سِقَايَةَ ٱلْحَاجِّ وَعِمَارَةَ ٱلْمَسْجِدِ ٱلْحَرَامِ كَمَنْ ءَامَنَ بِٱللَّهِ وَٱلْيَوْمِ ٱلْأَخِرِ وَجَٰهَدَ فِى سَبِيلِ ٱللَّهِ لَا يَسْتَوُۥنَ عِندَ ٱللَّهِ وَٱللَّهُ لَا يَهْدِى ٱلْقَوْمَ ٱلظَّٰلِمِينَ ۝ ٱلَّذِينَ ءَامَنُوا۟ وَهَاجَرُوا۟ وَجَٰهَدُوا۟ فِى سَبِيلِ ٱللَّهِ بِأَمْوَٰلِهِمْ وَأَنفُسِهِمْ أَعْظَمُ دَرَجَةً عِندَ ٱللَّهِ وَأُو۟لَٰٓئِكَ هُمُ ٱلْفَآئِزُونَ ۝ يُبَشِّرُهُمْ رَبُّهُم بِرَحْمَةٍ مِّنْهُ وَرِضْوَٰنٍ وَجَنَّٰتٍ لَّهُمْ فِيهَا نَعِيمٌ مُّقِيمٌ ۝ خَٰلِدِينَ فِيهَآ أَبَدًا إِنَّ ٱللَّهَ عِندَهُۥٓ أَجْرٌ عَظِيمٌ ۝ يَٰٓأَيُّهَا ٱلَّذِينَ ءَامَنُوا۟ لَا تَتَّخِذُوٓا۟ ءَابَآءَكُمْ وَإِخْوَٰنَكُمْ أَوْلِيَآءَ إِنِ ٱسْتَحَبُّوا۟ ٱلْكُفْرَ عَلَى ٱلْإِيمَٰنِ وَمَن يَتَوَلَّهُم مِّنكُمْ فَأُو۟لَٰٓئِكَ هُمُ ٱلظَّٰلِمُونَ ۝

ᵃ But this idea of the polytheists was absolutely wrong. They were making the mistake of comparing the outward appearances of things with the realities. Supplying drinking water to the visitors of the Sacred Mosque; cleaning the Mosque and lighting it; covering the Ka'bah, attending to its floor and walls—all these are outward, showy deeds. How can they be equal to the deeds of a man who discovers God and spends the rest of his life caring about the Hereafter; who dedicates his life and property to God; who denies all other greatness and makes God his great one? The real discoverers of Truth are not those who discover it at the meaningless level of outward show, but those who are attached to Truth at the level of self-sacrifice and not simply at the level of superficial exhibitionism.

There are two types of attachment: one is to ritual, in which a man performs deeds of a showy nature, but does not offer himself or his wealth for the cause of God. The other is one in which a man is so serious about his faith that if he is required to renounce anything for its sake, he does so willingly, and whatever he is required to give, he gives willingly. One who evinces the second kind of attachment will, after death, be blessed by God with great munificence.

²⁴ Say, 'If your fathers and your sons and your brothers and your spouses and your tribe, and the worldly goods which you have acquired, and the commerce which you fear will decline, and the homes you love are dearer to you than God and His Messenger and the struggle for His cause, then wait until God fulfills His decree. God does not guide the disobedient people.'ᵃ

قُلْ إِن كَانَ ءَابَآؤُكُمْ وَأَبْنَآؤُكُمْ وَإِخْوَٰنُكُمْ وَأَزْوَٰجُكُمْ وَعَشِيرَتُكُمْ وَأَمْوَٰلٌ ٱقْتَرَفْتُمُوهَا وَتِجَٰرَةٌ تَخْشَوْنَ كَسَادَهَا وَمَسَٰكِنُ تَرْضَوْنَهَآ أَحَبَّ إِلَيْكُم مِّنَ ٱللَّهِ وَرَسُولِهِ وَجِهَادٍ فِى سَبِيلِهِۦ فَتَرَبَّصُوا۟ حَتَّىٰ يَأْتِىَ ٱللَّهُ بِأَمْرِهِۦ ۗ وَٱللَّهُ لَا يَهْدِى ٱلْقَوْمَ ٱلْفَٰسِقِينَ ۝

ᵃ For human beings, their families, their wealth and their economic interests have the greatest value. They consider these things the most important. They prefer these things to all other things and sacrifice their all for them. This sort of life is of the worldly type, and whatever the worldly person receives, he receives only in this world. There is nothing for him in the eternal life after death. As opposed to this, the other type of life is that in which a man gives the greatest importance to God, His Prophet and to efforts for the cause of God and, for the sake of these things, he is ready to leave everything else. It is the latter which is the God-worshipping life and for God's worshippers, the doors of paradise will remain eternally open in the Hereafter.

The first sort of life is based on worldly connections and worldly interests. The second is based on Faith. Whatever a man chooses to adopt as the basis of his life, it is always at the cost of having to leave all other things for its sake; he has to develop relations with some people and break off relations with others. Certain losses are absolutely unbearable to him and at the risk of his life and at the cost of the greater part of his wealth, he tries to avert them, but as regards certain other losses, he is not perturbed by their occurrence. Those who invest their all in worldly affairs, achieve worldly success. Similarly, the Hereafter will be the achievement of those who sacrifice everything else for its sake.

Giving up a materially advantageous thing in favour of something apparently less advantageous is a serious matter. So much so that a man's belief or disbelief comes to be determined on that basis. Just as in this world of God, open infidels are not destined to succeed, similarly there is no possibility of success for those who make tall claims of faith, but when faced with a critical situation, give preference to the world-oriented way. If such claimants of faith have any misconceptions about themselves, they will come to know of their fate at the time God pronounces His verdict.

²⁵ Indeed, God has helped you on many occasions. On the day of Hunayn, when you took pride in your great numbers, they proved of no avail to you—for the earth, despite all its vastness, became [too] narrow for you and you turned back, in retreat. ²⁶ God caused His tranquillity to descend upon His Messenger and the faithful: and sent down forces which you did not see: He punished those who denied the truth—for such is the recompense of all who deny the truth—²⁷ then after that, God will turn in His mercy to whom He wills: God is forgiving and merciful.ᵃ

لَقَدْ نَصَرَكُمُ ٱللَّهُ فِى مَوَاطِنَ كَثِيرَةٍ وَيَوْمَ حُنَيْنٍ إِذْ أَعْجَبَتْكُمْ كَثْرَتُكُمْ فَلَمْ تُغْنِ عَنكُمْ شَيْئًا وَضَاقَتْ عَلَيْكُمُ ٱلْأَرْضُ بِمَا رَحُبَتْ ثُمَّ وَلَّيْتُم مُّدْبِرِينَ ۝ ثُمَّ أَنزَلَ ٱللَّهُ سَكِينَتَهُ عَلَى رَسُولِهِ وَعَلَى ٱلْمُؤْمِنِينَ وَأَنزَلَ جُنُودًا لَّمْ تَرَوْهَا وَعَذَّبَ ٱلَّذِينَ كَفَرُوا وَذَٰلِكَ جَزَآءُ ٱلْكَٰفِرِينَ ۝ ثُمَّ يَتُوبُ ٱللَّهُ مِنۢ بَعْدِ ذَٰلِكَ عَلَىٰ مَن يَشَآءُ وَٱللَّهُ غَفُورٌ رَّحِيمٌ ۝

ᵃ In Ramadan of the year 8 Hijrah, the Muslims successfully subdued the Quraysh and conquered Makkah. This was a virtually bloodless entry into Makkah. But in the very next month of Shawwal of the year 8 Hijrah, they were defeated by the polytheistic tribes of Hawazin and Thaqif, though at the conquest of Makkah, the number of Muslims was only ten thousand, while in the battle against the Hawazin and the Thaqif their number was twelve thousand. The reason for this was that when the Muslims had marched against the Quraysh, they had set out simply relying on God. But while proceeding to fight against the Hawazin and the Thaqif, they were proud of the fact that they were the conquerors of Makkah; that they had an army of twelve thousand men; that now nobody could defeat them. They were successful when they had reposed confidence in God; when they reposed confidence in themselves, they had to face defeat.

Reliance on oneself develops a sort of a haughtiness in a man which results in carelessness of external facts. He falls short in carrying out disciplinary regulations. Due to overweening self-confidence, he starts acting in an unrealistic manner, the result of which is necessarily defeat in this world of cause and effect. As opposed to this, having confidence in God is reliance on the greatest power. This develops humility in a man; he becomes extremely realistic; and realism is the key to all success.

²⁸ Believers, know that the polytheists are impure, so they should not approach the Sacred Mosque after this year onwards. If you should fear destitution, God will enrich you out of His bounty, if He so wishes. God is aware and wise.^a

يَـٰٓأَيُّهَا ٱلَّذِينَ ءَامَنُوٓاْ إِنَّمَا ٱلۡمُشۡرِكُونَ نَجَسٞ فَلَا يَقۡرَبُواْ ٱلۡمَسۡجِدَ ٱلۡحَرَامَ بَعۡدَ عَامِهِمۡ هَـٰذَاۚ وَإِنۡ خِفۡتُمۡ عَيۡلَةٗ فَسَوۡفَ يُغۡنِيكُمُ ٱللَّهُ مِن فَضۡلِهِۦٓ إِن شَآءَۚ إِنَّ ٱللَّهَ عَلِيمٌ حَكِيمٞ ﴿٢٨﴾

---

^a Initially, when the entry of polytheists into the Sacred Mosque of Makkah was banned, Muslims were worried because, Arabia being a non-agricultural country, its economy was based on trade and commerce, and trade is based on mutually harmonious relations. Muslims thought that when the entry of polytheists into the Sacred Mosque ended, trade relations with them would also come to an end. But they did not keep in view the possibility that these very polytheists might soon embrace Islam. And that is exactly what happened. Due to the general acceptance of Islam by Arabs, trade activities were restored in a new form. Moreover, the result of this initial sacrifice was that finally Islam became an international religion. The doors of their economy, which seemed to be closed at a local level, were opened at a universal level.

²⁹ Fight those from among the People of the Book who believe neither in God, nor in the Last Day, nor hold as unlawful what God and His Messenger have declared to be unlawful, nor follow the true religion, until they pay the tax willingly and agree to submit. ³⁰ The Jews say, 'Ezra is the son of God,' and the Christians say, 'The Messiah is the son of God.' These are but their baseless utterances. They imitate the assertions made in earlier times by those who deny the truth. May God destroy them! How far astray they have been led! ᵃ

قَٰتِلُوا۟ ٱلَّذِينَ لَا يُؤْمِنُونَ بِٱللَّهِ وَلَا بِٱلْيَوْمِ ٱلْءَاخِرِ وَلَا يُحَرِّمُونَ مَا حَرَّمَ ٱللَّهُ وَرَسُولُهُۥ وَلَا يَدِينُونَ دِينَ ٱلْحَقِّ مِنَ ٱلَّذِينَ أُوتُوا۟ ٱلْكِتَٰبَ حَتَّىٰ يُعْطُوا۟ ٱلْجِزْيَةَ عَن يَدٍ وَهُمْ صَٰغِرُونَ ۝ وَقَالَتِ ٱلْيَهُودُ عُزَيْرٌ ٱبْنُ ٱللَّهِ وَقَالَتِ ٱلنَّصَٰرَى ٱلْمَسِيحُ ٱبْنُ ٱللَّهِ ذَٰلِكَ قَوْلُهُم بِأَفْوَٰهِهِمْ يُضَٰهِـُٔونَ قَوْلَ ٱلَّذِينَ كَفَرُوا۟ مِن قَبْلُ قَٰتَلَهُمُ ٱللَّهُ أَنَّىٰ يُؤْفَكُونَ ۝

ᵃ If faith is active and alive, man attributes every event to God. He is able to understand a thing only when he forms an opinion about it with reference to God. He appreciates and understands the sweet smell of a flower when he finds the fragrance of God in it. He discovers the sum only when he comes to know of its donor. Every greatness seems to him the blessing of God. Every good reminds him of God's Grace. Contrary to this, if man's relation with God is reduced to the stage of a feeble belief, then God will become an unknown entity in the sphere of his active consciousness; he will start imagining God on the pattern of the visible things of the world.

Those of feeble belief start seeing their Creator in the same way as they see the things of the world known to them. They bring the Creator down to the level of the created ones. This was the condition of the ancient Jews and the Christians during the period of their deviation from the true faith. At that time the concept of God they had was relegated to the position of a flimsy belief. Accordingly they started giving to their great ones and saints the status which they should have given to the All Knowing God, Who is Aware of the Unseen. They saw that the Greek and Roman nations had made the sun their god and had presumed the existence of a son of that god. So, they too felt that this was the highest ranking title for their great ones. They made their own interpretation of the words *ab* (father) and *ibn* (son) appearing in their Holy Books and started calling God 'the father' and each of their prophets His 'son,' though the fact is that God is One and only One; He is incomparable; He alone deserves to be accepted as the Greatest and most worthy of being worshipped.

³¹ They have taken their learned men and their monks for their lords besides God. So have they taken the Messiah, son of Mary, although they were commanded to worship only the One God. There is no deity but He. He is far above whatever they set up as His partners! ^a

ٱتَّخَذُوٓاْ أَحْبَارَهُمْ وَرُهْبَٰنَهُمْ أَرْبَابًا مِّن دُونِ ٱللَّهِ وَٱلْمَسِيحَ ٱبْنَ مَرْيَمَ وَمَآ أُمِرُوٓاْ إِلَّا لِيَعْبُدُوٓاْ إِلَٰهًا وَٰحِدًا لَّآ إِلَٰهَ إِلَّا هُوَ سُبْحَٰنَهُۥ عَمَّا يُشْرِكُونَ ۝

---

^a God has invariably ruled that when a community has had his divine call directly conveyed to it by a prophet, its right to exist is taken away from it if, after all the necessary preaching and argumentation has been done, it persists in its wrongful approach, just as in a state, an individual forfeits his right to live if his being a rebel is established. But as far as other groups are concerned, they are to be dealt with as is deemed proper and in accordance with normal international principles.

³² They want to extinguish God's light with their mouths, but God seeks only to perfect His light, no matter how those who deny the truth may abhor it. ³³ It is He who has sent His Messenger with guidance and the religion of Truth, so that He may make it prevail [ideologically] over every other religion, however much the polytheists may hate this.ᵃ

يُرِيدُونَ أَن يُطْفِئُوا نُورَ ٱللَّهِ بِأَفْوَٰهِهِمْ وَيَأْبَى ٱللَّهُ إِلَّآ أَن يُتِمَّ نُورَهُ وَلَوْ كَرِهَ ٱلْكَٰفِرُونَ ۝ هُوَ ٱلَّذِىٓ أَرْسَلَ رَسُولَهُ بِٱلْهُدَىٰ وَدِينِ ٱلْحَقِّ لِيُظْهِرَهُ عَلَى ٱلدِّينِ كُلِّهِ وَلَوْ كَرِهَ ٱلْمُشْرِكُونَ ۝

ᵃ In these verses, God has announced His firm resolve to keep His religion completely safe till Doomsday.

When Almighty God settled human beings on the earth, He furnished them with His Guide Book. Later, when people fell into the ways of neglect and worldliness, they changed the words of God to suit their desires. For example, presuming their great revered men to be mediators with and recommenders to God, they adopted the belief that whatever they did, their holy men would, on the strength of their recommendation, be their saviours before God. They also believed that heaven or hell existed right there in the present world and that there was nothing beyond this world. Whatever the people themselves wanted, they attributed it to God and wrote it in God's Book. Thereafter, God sent another prophet who rid the divine religion of all man-made impurities and presented it again in its true form. Subsequent generations made changes in that as well. This happened again and again. Finally, Almighty God decided to send a final Prophet, and through him create such conditions that the religion of God should remain safe in its original form forever.

This task—the greatest in the history of prophethood—was achieved through the Prophet Muhammad.

At the time when the Prophet Muhammad appeared, many self-made religions had been devised. The polytheists of Arabia had a religion which they called the religion of Moses. The Christians had a religion which they called the religion of Jesus. These were all concocted editions of God's religion, and had been wrongly claimed to be the religion sent by God. God rejected all these religions and established the religion revealed to Prophet Muhammad as the sole authentic edition of His religion which would remain valid until Doomsday.

Today Islam is the only religion in the text of which no changes could be made. Islam is the only religion which is historically authentic. Islam is the only religion whose teachings are found in a living language. The candle lit by God in the shape of Islam has never been dimmed or extinguished. It is there in its entirety before the world, maintaining its ideological superiority over all other religions.

34 Believers, many religious scholars and monks wrongfully appropriate people's possessions and turn people away from God's path! Tell those who hoard gold and silver instead of giving in God's cause that they will have a painful punishment: 35 on the Day their treasure is heated up in the fire of hell, their foreheads and their sides and their backs shall be branded with it, and they will be told, 'This is what you hoarded up for yourselves. Taste then what you were hoarding.'*a*

﴿ يَٰٓأَيُّهَا ٱلَّذِينَ ءَامَنُوٓاْ إِنَّ كَثِيرًا مِّنَ ٱلْأَحْبَارِ وَٱلرُّهْبَانِ لَيَأْكُلُونَ أَمْوَٰلَ ٱلنَّاسِ بِٱلْبَٰطِلِ وَيَصُدُّونَ عَن سَبِيلِ ٱللَّهِ ۗ وَٱلَّذِينَ يَكْنِزُونَ ٱلذَّهَبَ وَٱلْفِضَّةَ وَلَا يُنفِقُونَهَا فِى سَبِيلِ ٱللَّهِ فَبَشِّرْهُم بِعَذَابٍ أَلِيمٍ ﴿٣٤﴾ يَوْمَ يُحْمَىٰ عَلَيْهَا فِى نَارِ جَهَنَّمَ فَتُكْوَىٰ بِهَا جِبَاهُهُمْ وَجُنُوبُهُمْ وَظُهُورُهُمْ ۖ هَٰذَا مَا كَنَزْتُمْ لِأَنفُسِكُمْ فَذُوقُواْ مَا كُنتُمْ تَكْنِزُونَ ﴿٣٥﴾

---

a One way of taking wealth from others is by doing so rightfully, i.e. one may offer real service to another or give him some real benefit and then take money from him in return. This is perfectly legitimate. The wrongful way of taking the wealth of others is to obtain it by deceiving them. This latter way is illegitimate and invites God's wrath.

Taking others' wealth wrongfully is that action which is known as exploitation in modern times. The ancient religious leaders indulged in the large-scale exploitation of the general public. They spread false stories among the people to ensure that they entertained extraordinary hopes of holy persons and, treating them as holy persons, would seek their blessings, and present them with offerings and gifts. In the name of service to religion they used to extract money from people, though the faith they presented to the people was their own brand of religion and not at all that which was sent down by God. They used to collect huge donations in the name of the revival of the community. Whatever they did on this pretext aroused false hopes, so that they could maintain their leadership. They even used to attribute mysterious qualities to the charms and talismans which they prepared and then sold to the people, though they themselves did not rely on these charms in their own crucial affairs.

There are only certain legitimate uses of the wealth received by man—spending on his actual needs and giving away for the cause of God whatever is surplus, i.e. exceeding his actual needs. Any ways of spending other than these two will lead to retributive punishment for man—whether he spends his money lavishly or hoards it. ▶

³⁶ On the Day God created heaven and earth, He decreed that the number of months should be twelve in number. Out of these, four are sacred. That is the true religion. Do not wrong your souls in these months. Fight the polytheists all together, as they fight you all together, and know that God is with the righteous.[a]

إِنَّ عِدَّةَ ٱلشُّهُورِ عِندَ ٱللَّهِ ٱثْنَا عَشَرَ شَهْرًا فِى كِتَٰبِ ٱللَّهِ يَوْمَ خَلَقَ ٱلسَّمَٰوَٰتِ وَٱلْأَرْضَ مِنْهَآ أَرْبَعَةٌ حُرُمٌ ذَٰلِكَ ٱلدِّينُ ٱلْقَيِّمُ فَلَا تَظْلِمُوا۟ فِيهِنَّ أَنفُسَكُمْ وَقَٰتِلُوا۟ ٱلْمُشْرِكِينَ كَآفَّةً كَمَا يُقَٰتِلُونَكُمْ كَآفَّةً وَٱعْلَمُوٓا۟ أَنَّ ٱللَّهَ مَعَ ٱلْمُتَّقِينَ ۝

Those who have established their leadership in a group on the basis of a self-made religion and exploit people in the name of God's religion abhor the call for truth which attempts to revive the true and unadulterated religion of God. Within the framework of such a religion, it seems to them that their religious position would lose credibility.

They feel that if this religion prevails among the people, their religious trading might come out into the open and be publicly unmasked. As soon as such a movement is set in motion, they come to know of it and set about opposing it.

[a] Religious commandments can be carried out by everyone individually. But it is required by Almighty God that all the people of Faith should perform them together, so that a collective spirit is created in them. For the purpose of promoting this collectivism, definite timings and dates have been fixed for the performance of the religious rites of prayers, etc. Had these dates been appointed according to the solar calendar, there could have been uniformity in the time of their occurrence. For example, the days of fasting would always have come in one particular season and likewise Hajj. But, whereas uniformity creates inertia in man, change introduces new inspiration for action. Therefore, the natural lunar calendar has been adopted to provide the basis for the collective pattern of religious matters.

On account of this principle, the dates of Hajj (pilgrimage) fall in different seasons —sometimes in summer and sometimes in winter. In ancient times when the congregation for Hajj was most important from the commercial point of view, the occurrence of Hajj in different seasons appeared to be harmful.

Worldly considerations appeared to the Arab people more important than religious imperatives. They wanted to adopt a system by which Hajj would fall in one suitable season. At that time they came to know of the adjustments possible in the calculation (kabisa) of the Jews and Christians. They approved of this, as it was exactly according to their wishes, and they therefore adopted it. This meant displacing months and replacing one month by another, for example, replacing the month of Safar by the month of Muharram and vice versa. ▶

37 The postponing of [sacred months] is but one more instance of [their] refusal to acknowledge the truth—by which those who are bent on denying the truth are led astray. They declare this to be permissible in one year and forbidden in another year, so that they may adjust the months which God has sanctified, thus making lawful what God has forbidden. Their evil deed seems fair to them: God does not guide those who deny the truth.[a]

إِنَّمَا ٱلنَّسِيٓءُ زِيَادَةٌ فِى ٱلْكُفْرِ يُضَلُّ بِهِ ٱلَّذِينَ كَفَرُوا۟ يُحِلُّونَهُۥ عَامًا وَيُحَرِّمُونَهُۥ عَامًا لِّيُوَاطِـُٔوا۟ عِدَّةَ مَا حَرَّمَ ٱللَّهُ فَيُحِلُّوا۟ مَا حَرَّمَ ٱللَّهُ زُيِّنَ لَهُمْ سُوٓءُ أَعْمَـٰلِهِمْ وَٱللَّهُ لَا يَهْدِى ٱلْقَوْمَ ٱلْكَـٰفِرِينَ ۝

'Fight the polytheists all together, as they fight you all together.' This means that just as the infidels unite on their refusal to fear God, the Muslims should unite on their fear of God *(taqwa)*: If they join together for negative purposes, the Muslims should join together for positive ends. If they become one for the sake of the world, the Muslims should become one for the sake of the Hereafter.

a The Arabs derived two advantages from this method of transposition *(nasi')*—one was the diverting of the Hajj season to suit commercial requirements and the other was that if fighting against an enemy had to be started in forbidden months (i.e. Muharram, Rajab, Dhu'l-Qa'dah and Dhu'l-Hijjah), replacing a haram month by a non-haram month legitimised the opening of hostilities. Abraham's method had formerly been the backbone of Arab tradition, but since the Arabs' thinking was dominated by commercial considerations and tribal requirements, the *nasi'* method found favour with them and they adopted it in their affairs.

³⁸ Believers, what is the matter with you that when you are asked to go forth in the cause of God, you cling slothfully to the land? Do you prefer the life of this world to the Hereafter? But little is the comfort of this life, compared to that of the Hereafter. ³⁹ If you do not go forth, He will punish you sternly and replace you by other people. You will not harm Him in the least. God has power over all things.[a]

يَـٰٓأَيُّهَا ٱلَّذِينَ ءَامَنُوا۟ مَا لَكُمْ إِذَا قِيلَ لَكُمُ ٱنفِرُوا۟ فِى سَبِيلِ ٱللَّهِ ٱثَّاقَلْتُمْ إِلَى ٱلْأَرْضِ أَرَضِيتُم بِٱلْحَيَوٰةِ ٱلدُّنْيَا مِنَ ٱلْءَاخِرَةِ فَمَا مَتَـٰعُ ٱلْحَيَوٰةِ ٱلدُّنْيَا فِى ٱلْءَاخِرَةِ إِلَّا قَلِيلٌ ۞ إِلَّا تَنفِرُوا۟ يُعَذِّبْكُمْ عَذَابًا أَلِيمًا وَيَسْتَبْدِلْ قَوْمًا غَيْرَكُمْ وَلَا تَضُرُّوهُ شَيْـًٔا ۗ وَٱللَّهُ عَلَىٰ كُلِّ شَىْءٍ قَدِيرٌ ۞

---

[a] These verses were revealed while the Prophet was at Tabuk (9 Hijra). At this juncture the behaviour displayed by the hypocrites *(munafiqun)* of Madinah gives us an idea of the role played by people of fickle faith when they join the Islamic society.

In reality there are two stages of connection with Islam. In one, all of man's loyalties become attached to Islam; it becomes a question of life and death for him. In the other, man's real interests are elsewhere and he only superficially accepts Islam. In the first category are the real believers—the people of faith. In the second are those known, in the terminology of the Shariah, as *munafiq* (hypocrites). The condition of the believer is that he steadfastly holds to Islam in normal circumstances as well as at times when sacrifice is required. By contrast, the hypocrite seems to be very much to the fore in making a show of his religiousness, when Islam makes no special demands on him, but as soon as he has to fulfil demands of Islam at the level of sacrifice, he backs away.

40 If you do not support him [Muhammad], know that God did support him when those who denied the truth expelled him when the two[a] of them were in the cave, he [Muhammad] told his companion, 'Do not worry; for God is with us.' So God sent His tranquillity down on him and aided him with forces invisible to you and placed the word of those who disbelieved lowest, while God's word remained supreme. God is powerful and wise.[b]

إِلَّا تَنصُرُوهُ فَقَدْ نَصَرَهُ ٱللَّهُ إِذْ أَخْرَجَهُ ٱلَّذِينَ كَفَرُوا۟ ثَانِيَ ٱثْنَيْنِ إِذْ هُمَا فِى ٱلْغَارِ إِذْ يَقُولُ لِصَـٰحِبِهِۦ لَا تَحْزَنْ إِنَّ ٱللَّهَ مَعَنَا فَأَنزَلَ ٱللَّهُ سَكِينَتَهُۥ عَلَيْهِ وَأَيَّدَهُۥ بِجُنُودٍ لَّمْ تَرَوْهَا وَجَعَلَ كَلِمَةَ ٱلَّذِينَ كَفَرُوا۟ ٱلسُّفْلَىٰ وَكَلِمَةُ ٱللَّهِ هِىَ ٱلْعُلْيَا وَٱللَّهُ عَزِيزٌ حَكِيمٌ ۝

[a] The 'second of two' is an allusion to the prophet's immigration, in the company of Abu Bakr, from Makkah to Madinah in the year 622 A.D.

[b] The reason for this difference is that the true believer keeps the goal of the Hereafter before him, and does not set a higher value upon the things of this world, than upon the eternal bounties of the Hereafter. So if anything of a worldly nature impedes him, he ignores it and proceeds towards the goals of religion. Unlike him, the hypocrite likes that type of Islam in which, without damaging one's worldly interests, one gets the credit for Islamism. Therefore, whenever an occasion arises when he has to lose the world for Islam, he tilts towards the world, even if in this process, he loses his grip on the rope of Islam.

The struggles between Islam and non-Islam that arise from time to time in the present world are between two groups, but in reality it is an affair of God. On every such occasion, God Himself supports Islam. This is expressed in the shape of a cause-and-effect event, so that the credit of doing service to religion may be given to those people who have completely surrendered themselves to God.

⁴¹ Go forth, whether lightly or heavily equipped, and strive and struggle, with your goods and your persons, for the cause of God. That is better for you, if you only knew.ᵃ

آنفِرُوا۟ خِفَافًا وَثِقَالًا وَجَٰهِدُوا۟ بِأَمْوَٰلِكُمْ وَأَنفُسِكُمْ فِى سَبِيلِ ٱللَّهِ ذَٰلِكُمْ خَيْرٌ لَّكُمْ إِن كُنتُمْ تَعْلَمُونَ

ᵃ Among the hypocrites of Madinah there was a group who were Muslims of weak belief. Finding Islam to be the truth, they had accepted it. But they used to act only on those teachings of Islam which were not against their worldly interests. When the demands of Islam clashed with their worldly pursuits, they ignored Islamic imperatives and upheld worldly requirements. In Madinan society one who adhered to Islam, even when it meant making sacrifices, was known as a believer, while one who did not want to go to the extent of sacrifice for the sake of Islam was called a hypocrite.

The Tabuk affair was a symbolic event which showed who was a believer and who was a hypocrite in the eyes of God. On this occasion it was necessary to set out against a great and organised power, the Romans. The midsummer heat was at its fiercest and the crops were almost ready to be reaped; despite all the unfavourable circumstances, it was necessary to reach the faraway border of Syria. Then, among the Muslims some had property and some were without property; some were free and some were tied down by their domestic circumstances. But the order was that they should at all events set out without making any kind of excuse. The reason for this was that, before God, quantity did not matter; but whatever a man had should be offered. This is, in fact, the cost of paradise, howsoever small or great it may apparently be in the eyes of the people.

The particular sign of a hypocrite is that when he sees that after undertaking a journey without hardships he will receive great credit for Islamic service, he will immediately be willing to set forth. However, if the journey is likely to be beset with hardships, and if there is no likelihood of achieving honour or success, even after facing those hardships, he is not inclined to take part in such a religious campaign.

If a genuine religious campaign is the option, but an individual, preferring to dissociate himself from it, makes all kinds of excuses, this clearly proves that he has not given top priority in his life to God's religion. Making excuses in itself implies that there is something which has more importance in the individual's view than the purpose before him. Obviously, making excuses is going to make a man appear unreliable in the eyes of God, and will take away his opportunity of being on God's list of most cherished creatures. Hypocrisy is in fact being neglectful of God, while caring more for His subjects. If a man comes to realise the power of God, he will never behave like this.

⁴² Had the gain been immediate and the journey shorter, they would have followed you: but the distance seemed too great for them. Yet they will swear by God, 'Had we been able, we would have gone out with you.' They bring ruin upon themselves. God knows that they are surely lying.

⁴³ May God pardon you! Why did you permit them to do so before it had become clear to you which ones were truthful, so that you might recognize the liars? ᵃ

لَوۡ كَانَ عَرَضًا قَرِيبًا وَسَفَرًا قَاصِدًا لَّٱتَّبَعُوكَ وَلَٰكِنۢ بَعُدَتۡ عَلَيۡهِمُ ٱلشُّقَّةُ ۚ وَسَيَحۡلِفُونَ بِٱللَّهِ لَوِ ٱسۡتَطَعۡنَا لَخَرَجۡنَا مَعَكُمۡ يُهۡلِكُونَ أَنفُسَهُمۡ وَٱللَّهُ يَعۡلَمُ إِنَّهُمۡ لَكَٰذِبُونَ ۝ عَفَا ٱللَّهُ عَنكَ لِمَ أَذِنتَ لَهُمۡ حَتَّىٰ يَتَبَيَّنَ لَكَ ٱلَّذِينَ صَدَقُواْ وَتَعۡلَمَ ٱلۡكَٰذِبِينَ ۝

ᵃ A hypocrite is one who remains to the fore in the profitable and undemanding aspects of Islam, but who recoils when he feels that his interests are being affected. On such occasions, what such weaklings rely on is excuses. They try to hide their inaction by attractive explanations. In view of collective considerations, if the chief of believers accepts their excuses, they are very happy, thinking that they have successfully hidden their reluctance behind a veil of words. But they forget that their real dealings are not with a human being but with God, and He very well knows the truth about every man. God sometimes reveals the hidden aspects of such persons in this world, but in the Hereafter the truth about everyone is going to be laid bare.

44 Those who believe in God and the Last Day will never ask you to exempt them from striving with their wealth and their lives—God best knows the righteous—45 only those seek exemption who do not truly believe in God and the Last Day, and whose hearts have become a prey to doubt. Because they doubt, they waver. 46 If they had wished to go forth, they would surely have made some preparation for it, but God disliked their setting out [and being raised high in God's eyes] and held them back. They were told to stay behind with those who stay behind. 47 Had they gone forth with you, they would only have proved a source of evil for you, and would have run back and forth among you, seeking to sow discord among you: and among you there were some who would have willingly listened to them. God knows the evil-doers.[a]

لَا يَسْتَأْذِنُكَ ٱلَّذِينَ يُؤْمِنُونَ بِٱللَّهِ وَٱلْيَوْمِ ٱلْآخِرِ أَن يُجَٰهِدُوا۟ بِأَمْوَٰلِهِمْ وَأَنفُسِهِمْ ۗ وَٱللَّهُ عَلِيمٌ بِٱلْمُتَّقِينَ ۝ إِنَّمَا يَسْتَأْذِنُكَ ٱلَّذِينَ لَا يُؤْمِنُونَ بِٱللَّهِ وَٱلْيَوْمِ ٱلْآخِرِ وَٱرْتَابَتْ قُلُوبُهُمْ فَهُمْ فِى رَيْبِهِمْ يَتَرَدَّدُونَ ۝ ۞ وَلَوْ أَرَادُوا۟ ٱلْخُرُوجَ لَأَعَدُّوا۟ لَهُۥ عُدَّةً وَلَٰكِن كَرِهَ ٱللَّهُ ٱنۢبِعَاثَهُمْ فَثَبَّطَهُمْ وَقِيلَ ٱقْعُدُوا۟ مَعَ ٱلْقَٰعِدِينَ ۝ لَوْ خَرَجُوا۟ فِيكُم مَّا زَادُوكُمْ إِلَّا خَبَالًا وَلَأَوْضَعُوا۟ خِلَٰلَكُمْ يَبْغُونَكُمُ ٱلْفِتْنَةَ وَفِيكُمْ سَمَّٰعُونَ لَهُمْ ۗ وَٱللَّهُ عَلِيمٌۢ بِٱلظَّٰلِمِينَ ۝

[a] At a time when a son is ill or there is a daughter's marriage, nobody spares himself or his money; he will sacrifice his life and his wealth for the sole purpose of being of use to his kinsfolk. This is not the time for sheltering behind excuses. Similarly, the truly religious individual will never put forward excuses, when some occasion arises which demands sacrifice for religion. The restless emotions of faith in his heart await such a crucial moment when he will have the chance to sacrifice himself and prove his loyalty before God. Then, such an occasion having arisen, how would such a person try to hide behind an excuse?

The believer is God-fearing in nature, fear being the strongest feeling in man. The feeling of fear overcomes all other feelings. A man becomes extremely realistic and serious about anything to which he relates to. For this reason, one who has become a believer in God at the level of fear wastes no time in understanding what his reaction should be on particular occasions.

The benefits of the Hereafter not being present before a human being, he entertains doubts about making any sacrifices for it. But to tear off this veil of doubt is the real test of man in this world.

⁴⁸ They have already tried to sow dissension, and hatched plots against you, until the truth became manifest and God's will prevailed, much to their disgust.^a

لَقَدِ ٱبْتَغَوُاْ ٱلْفِتْنَةَ مِن قَبْلُ وَقَلَّبُواْ لَكَ ٱلْأُمُورَ حَتَّىٰ جَآءَ ٱلْحَقُّ وَظَهَرَ أَمْرُ ٱللَّهِ وَهُمْ كَٰرِهُونَ ۝

---

^a Adopting a religion may be done either with sincerity or with hypocrisy. Adopting religion sincerely means that a man makes religion the focus of his life, with a prime right over his life and property. Without sincerity, the adherent has a purely formal, external relation with religion, feeling no need to face all kinds of adversity for its sake.

Admission of one's mistakes amounts to acceptance of one's being inferior to another: to do so is the most difficult thing for a man. That is why man always tries to somehow prove the correctness of his stand. Accordingly, those who accept Islam hypocritically are always in search of an opportunity to taunt sincere believers and to prove themselves as being in the right as compared to them.

The hypocrites of Madinah were continuously engaged in such efforts. For example, when the Muslims were defeated in the battle of Uhud, the hypocrites who had remained behind in Madinah started circulating propaganda against the Prophet Muhammad to the effect that he had no experience of warfare or strategic affairs; that, spurred on by his own enthusiasm, he had taken the youngsters of the community to a dangerous place and had senselessly caused them to be killed.

Among human beings there are very few people who are capable of deeply analysing problems and realising that the mere fact of a statement being cast in grammatically correct language does not in itself furnish proof of its being meaningfully correct. Many people are simple minded, and if something is presented to them in beautiful words, they are very soon affected by it. It is the presence of the hypocritical type of people in a Muslim group that is the cause of the weakening of that group. In their attempt to prove themselves right, such people frequently distort what they have to say so as give it a colour suited to their purpose. Influenced by such artifice, simple-minded people begin to be beset by doubts and uncertainty.

In spite of the hypocrites' efforts to oppose Islam, when the Muslims were victorious in the battle of Badr, 'Abdullah ibn Ubayy and his companions are reported to have said, 'This thing has got going now.' The domination of Islam being obvious, they should have placed credence on the veracity of Islam, but even that fed their jealousy.

⁴⁹ Some of them say, 'Give us leave to stay behind and do not put us to trial.' Surely, they have already fallen into trial. Surely, Hell shall engulf those who deny the truth. ⁵⁰ If good befalls you, it grieves them, but if a misfortune befalls you, they say, 'We took our precautions beforehand!' They turn away rejoicing.ᵃ

وَمِنْهُم مَّن يَقُولُ ٱئْذَن لِّي وَلَا تَفْتِنِّي ۚ أَلَا فِي ٱلْفِتْنَةِ سَقَطُوا ۗ وَإِنَّ جَهَنَّمَ لَمُحِيطَةٌ بِٱلْكَٰفِرِينَ ۞ إِن تُصِبْكَ حَسَنَةٌ تَسُؤْهُمْ ۖ وَإِن تُصِبْكَ مُصِيبَةٌ يَقُولُوا قَدْ أَخَذْنَا أَمْرَنَا مِن قَبْلُ وَيَتَوَلَّوا وَّهُمْ فَرِحُونَ ۞

ᵃ When there was a general call to set out for the campaign of Tabuk, one Jud ibn Qais of Madinah came to the Prophet Muhammad and said: 'Please excuse me from taking part in this campaign. This is a Roman area. There after seeing the Roman women, I will be caught in trying circumstances (*fitna*).' But, making excuses on such occasions in itself amounts to being affected in *fitna*, because in moments of adversity, far from seeking excuses to lag behind, the urge to sacrifice himself for the sake of religion should well up inside a man. To give such an excuse a religious and moral colour is a greater evil, since it amounts to adding fraud to inaction.

This type of attitude develops in an individual because he is more attached to his worldly interests than to the Hereafter. In times of danger, such people hold themselves back from treading the path of religion. Then, when the real proponents of Truth suffer any loss due to their uncompromising, principled behaviour, these people are happy, feeling that it is good that they adopted the policy of keeping themselves safe. On the contrary, if it happens that the real supporters of truth face dangers and yet are successful, then they are unhappy, because this occurrence proves that the policy they had adopted was not correct.

⁵¹ Say, 'Nothing can befall us, except what God has ordained for us. He is our Supreme Lord. In God let the faithful put their trust.' ⁵² Say, 'Are you waiting for anything to befall us except one of the two best things [Victory in this world or Paradise in the next]? But we expect that God will send His punishment to you either directly from Himself, or by our hands. So wait, if you will; we too, are waiting with you.'ᵃ

قُل لَّن يُصِيبَنَا إِلَّا مَا كَتَبَ ٱللَّهُ لَنَا هُوَ مَوْلَىٰنَا ۚ وَعَلَى ٱللَّهِ فَلْيَتَوَكَّلِ ٱلْمُؤْمِنُونَ ۝ قُلْ هَلْ تَرَبَّصُونَ بِنَا إِلَّا إِحْدَى ٱلْحُسْنَيَيْنِ ۖ وَنَحْنُ نَتَرَبَّصُ بِكُمْ أَن يُصِيبَكُمُ ٱللَّهُ بِعَذَابٍ مِّنْ عِندِهِۦ أَوْ بِأَيْدِينَا ۖ فَتَرَبَّصُوٓا۟ إِنَّا مَعَكُم مُّتَرَبِّصُونَ ۝

ᵃ For true men of faith, there is no question of failure in this world. Their success lies in God being pleased with them and this is a certainty, in both good times and bad. If any trouble befalls a believer, this increases his inclination towards God. If he receives some benefit, this creates the feeling of obligation and gratitude in him and, by being grateful to God, he becomes entitled to further blessings from Him.

'So wait, if you will; we too, are waiting with you.' On the face of it, this is a statement of believers, but in fact these are God's words addressed to unbelievers. God is telling them in a warning tone that although they have been waiting for the destruction of the believers, the fact is that in God's scheme they are destined to achieve eternal success, and what is going to happen to them (the opponents) is that after their being given a long rope to fully and finally establish their guilt, they will be consigned to eternal degradation and punishment.

⁵³ Say, 'Whether you give willingly or unwillingly, your offerings shall not be accepted by God, for you are indeed a disobedient people.' ⁵⁴ The only reason their contributions are not accepted is that they have denied God and His Messenger, they come to the prayer half heartedly, and they offer contributions unwillingly.ᵃ

قُلْ أَنفِقُواْ طَوْعًا أَوْ كَرْهًا لَّن يُتَقَبَّلَ مِنكُمْ إِنَّكُمْ كُنتُمْ قَوْمًا فَٰسِقِينَ ۝ وَمَا مَنَعَهُمْ أَن تُقْبَلَ مِنْهُمْ نَفَقَٰتُهُمْ إِلَّا أَنَّهُمْ كَفَرُواْ بِٱللَّهِ وَبِرَسُولِهِۦ وَلَا يَأْتُونَ ٱلصَّلَوٰةَ إِلَّا وَهُمْ كُسَالَىٰ وَلَا يُنفِقُونَ إِلَّا وَهُمْ كَٰرِهُونَ ۝

ᵃ In Madinah the majority of all the people who had embraced Islam, were sincere believers. However, there were a number of people who had embraced Islam to go with the tide of the times, but who lacked that spirit of surrender which is the characteristic of true faith in and true attachment to God. These are the people who are known as hypocrites.

These hypocrites consisted mostly of the wealthy class. It was this wealth which was behind their hypocrisy. Those who do not have anything to lose are ready and willing to accept that Islam in which one has to lose one's all. But those who have something to lose generally become anxious about their worldly considerations. They somehow carry out those commandments of Islam which do not involve any sacrifice, but they find themselves unable to go ahead and accept any requirements of Islam which might involve loss of life and property, or when the question of becoming a believer at the level of sacrifice arises.

But lagging behind in accepting the Islam of sacrifice renders even their prayers and fasting valueless. The rite of prayer (*ibadah*)—the worship performed in mosques—is intimately related with worship outside the mosque. If the individual's life outside the mosque is devoid of the real spirit of religion, his life inside the mosque will also be empty of the true religious spirit and, obviously, action without such spirit has no value before God. God accepts nothing but righteous action. All else is devoid of merit in His eyes.

55 Do not let their wealth and children impress you. For God seeks to punish them through these things in the life of this world, so that their souls shall depart while they are still denying the truth. 56 They swear by God that they are believers like you; but they are not. They are afraid [to appear in their true colours]: 57 if they could find a place of refuge, or a cave or any hiding-place, they would run there with frantic haste.

58 Among them there are some who find fault with you concerning the distribution of alms. If a share is given to them, they are pleased, but if they receive nothing, they grow resentful. 59 If only they had been content with what God and His Messenger had given them and had said, 'God is sufficient for us. God will give us out of His bounty, and so will His Messenger. To God alone do we turn with hope!' a

فَلَا تُعْجِبْكَ أَمْوَٰلُهُمْ وَلَآ أَوْلَٰدُهُمْ إِنَّمَا يُرِيدُ ٱللَّهُ لِيُعَذِّبَهُم بِهَا فِى ٱلْحَيَوٰةِ ٱلدُّنْيَا وَتَزْهَقَ أَنفُسُهُمْ وَهُمْ كَٰفِرُونَ ۞ وَيَحْلِفُونَ بِٱللَّهِ إِنَّهُمْ لَمِنكُمْ وَمَا هُم مِّنكُمْ وَلَٰكِنَّهُمْ قَوْمٌ يَفْرَقُونَ ۞ لَوْ يَجِدُونَ مَلْجَـًٔا أَوْ مَغَٰرَٰتٍ أَوْ مُدَّخَلًا لَّوَلَّوْا۟ إِلَيْهِ وَهُمْ يَجْمَحُونَ ۞ وَمِنْهُم مَّن يَلْمِزُكَ فِى ٱلصَّدَقَٰتِ فَإِنْ أُعْطُوا۟ مِنْهَا رَضُوا۟ وَإِن لَّمْ يُعْطَوْا۟ مِنْهَآ إِذَا هُمْ يَسْخَطُونَ ۞ وَلَوْ أَنَّهُمْ رَضُوا۟ مَآ ءَاتَٰهُمُ ٱللَّهُ وَرَسُولُهُۥ وَقَالُوا۟ حَسْبُنَا ٱللَّهُ سَيُؤْتِينَا ٱللَّهُ مِن فَضْلِهِۦ وَرَسُولُهُۥٓ إِنَّآ إِلَى ٱللَّهِ رَٰغِبُونَ ۞

---

a If a man basks in the glories of wealth and has many minions constantly in attendance, the general public will envy him. But the fact is that such people are the most unlucky. Their condition is such that their wealth and status become fetters, rendering them unable to proceed fully towards God's religion; they forget God and busy themselves with worldly affairs until they meet with death, which mercilessly divests them of their wealth and high position.

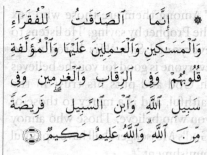

60 Alms are only for: the poor and the destitute, for those who collect *zakat,* for conciliating people's hearts, for freeing slaves, for those in debt, for spending for God's cause, and for travellers in need. It is a legal obligation enjoined by God. God is all-knowing and wise.[a]

---

[a] Here the items of expenditure of prescribed alms or religious charity (*zakat*) have been enumerated. According to the Quran these are eight in number:

1. Poor (*fuqara'*): For those who have nothing.

2. Destitute (*masakin*): For those who have less than their needs.

3. Officials (*'amilun*): For those who have been appointed by the Islamic government to collect money given in charity and to maintain its accounts.

4. The winning of hearts (*mu'allafati'l qulub*): For those who need encouragement to accept Islam or for those who are weak in their faith.

5. Freeing slaves (*riqab*): For the freeing of slaves or for the release of prisoners or the payment of ransom.

6. For those in debt (*gharamin*): For those who are in debt or those bearing the burden of surety.

7. Spending for God's cause (*fi sabilil'lah*): For missionary work and endeavour for the cause of God. Peaceful *dawah* work falls into this category.

8. Travellers (*ibn as-sabil*): For those who become needy during a journey, even though they may be well off when at home.

In any collective system, when the funds are distributed in charity, it always happens that certain people have complaints about violation of their rights or unjustified distribution. But such complaints expose the weakness of the complainant himself. Howsoever righteous the person responsible for distribution might be, people who are greedy and narrow in their way of thinking will somehow fabricate false grounds for such complaints.

Yet this type of complaint works most of all against the complainant himself. It impedes the process of the arousal of the intellectual potential of the individual. If a man reconciles himself to whatever he possesses and concentrates his thinking on God, then fresh courage will develop in him; positive talents which are latent in him will awaken. He will put the amounts received by him to better use; instead of depending on donations, he will develop self-confidence; he will start seeking out new economic opportunities, relying on God; instead of being bored or dissatisfied with others, he will develop the attitude of making companions of them and will work together with them, etc.

⁶¹ Among them are those who vex the Prophet by saying, 'He listens to everyone.' Say, 'His listening to everyone is good for you; he believes in God and puts his trust in the faithful, and is a mercy to those of you who believe. Those who annoy God's Messenger shall have a painful punishment.'[a]

وَمِنْهُمُ ٱلَّذِينَ يُؤْذُونَ ٱلنَّبِيَّ وَيَقُولُونَ هُوَ أُذُنٌ قُلْ أُذُنُ خَيْرٍ لَّكُمْ يُؤْمِنُ بِٱللَّهِ وَيُؤْمِنُ لِلْمُؤْمِنِينَ وَرَحْمَةٌ لِّلَّذِينَ ءَامَنُوا مِنكُمْ وَٱلَّذِينَ يُؤْذُونَ رَسُولَ ٱللَّهِ هُمْ عَذَابٌ أَلِيمٌ ۝

---

[a] The hypocrites of Madinah used to deride Islamic personalities in private, but when they appeared before Muslims they assured them, on oath, that they were loyal to Islam. The reason for this was that the Muslims were powerful in Madinah. They were in a position to harm the interests of hypocrites. So the hypocrites wanted to give the impression that they were with the Muslims.

This reveals the reality of a hypocritical character. The religiosity of a hypocrite derives from the fear of human beings and not from the fear of God. He becomes a man of character and justice where there is pressure from other human beings or there is the fear of a reaction from the public. But where there is no such risk and there is only the fear of God to prevent him from the misuse of his words and deeds, he becomes a completely changed man. He becomes a man who is not interested in being a man of character and does not feel the necessity to adopt the way of justice.

⁶² They swear by God in order to please you [believers]: but it would be more fitting for them to please God and His Messenger, if they are believers. ⁶³ Do they not know that whoever opposes God and His Messenger shall abide forever in the fire of Hell? That is the supreme humiliation.

⁶⁴ The hypocrites are afraid lest a chapter [of the Quran] be sent down about them, telling them what is in their hearts—say, 'Go on mocking. God will surely bring to light what you are dreading.' ᵃ

يَحْلِفُونَ بِٱللَّهِ لَكُمْ لِيُرْضُوكُمْ وَٱللَّهُ وَرَسُولُهُۥٓ أَحَقُّ أَن يُرْضُوهُ إِن كَانُواْ مُؤْمِنِينَ ۞ أَلَمْ يَعْلَمُوٓاْ أَنَّهُۥ مَن يُحَادِدِ ٱللَّهَ وَرَسُولَهُۥ فَأَنَّ لَهُۥ نَارَ جَهَنَّمَ خَٰلِدًا فِيهَا ذَٰلِكَ ٱلْخِزْىُ ٱلْعَظِيمُ ۞ يَحْذَرُ ٱلْمُنَٰفِقُونَ أَن تُنَزَّلَ عَلَيْهِمْ سُورَةٌ تُنَبِّئُهُم بِمَا فِى قُلُوبِهِمْ قُلِ ٱسْتَهْزِءُوٓاْ إِنَّ ٱللَّهَ مُخْرِجٌ مَّا تَحْذَرُونَ ۞

ᵃ Those who are engrossed in worldly considerations and therefore are not able to support God's religion—rising above their reservations—are generally people of status in society. In order to keep their position intact, they try to spoil the image of those who have risen in true Islam. They run campaigns of false propaganda against them, devising different ways to distort their image, such as ferreting out various points in their statements which they claim to be objectionable.

Such people forget that this is a very serious matter. For their part they are simply opposing the people of Faith, but it amounts to opposing God Himself; it is like setting themselves up as adversaries of God. Had these people admitted their wrongdoing, instead of trying to establish their innocence, and had they been the well-wishers of the believers at least in their hearts, they would perhaps have been treated as pardonable. But having adopted an obstinate and inimical attitude, they have written their names on the list of God's enemies. Now, for them, there is nothing but dishonour and divine retribution.

Fear of God softens a person's heart. He patiently listens even to people's baseless utterances—to such an extent that the hypocrites start saying that that person seems to be a simpleton, that he is unable to fully understand the points being made.

⁶⁵If you ask them, they will say, 'We were only joking and playing with words.' Say, 'Would you make a mockery of God and of His Revelations and of His Messenger? ⁶⁶ Make no excuses; you rejected the faith after you accepted it.' If We pardon some of you, We will punish others amongst you, for they are guilty.'^a

وَلَئِن سَأَلْتَهُمْ لَيَقُولُنَّ إِنَّمَا كُنَّا نَخُوضُ وَنَلْعَبُ قُلْ أَبِاللَّهِ وَءَايَـٰتِهِ وَرَسُولِهِ كُنتُمْ تَسْتَهْزِءُونَ ۝ لَا تَعْتَذِرُواْ قَدْ كَفَرْتُم بَعْدَ إِيمَـٰنِكُمْ إِن نَّعْفُ عَن طَآئِفَةٍ مِّنكُمْ نُعَذِّبْ طَآئِفَةَ بِأَنَّهُمْ كَانُواْ مُجْرِمِينَ ۝

^a At the time of the battle of Tabuk, those who had set out with the Prophet Muhammad were treated as staunch and courageous people, while those who remained behind at home were considered hypocrites and cowards.

The hypocrites who stayed at home started ridiculing the Prophet and his companions in order to belittle the action taken by them. Some said, 'In these reciters of the Quran, we see nothing except that they are the hungriest among us, the most extreme liars among us and the worst cowards among us.' Some asked, 'Do you think that fighting the Romans is like internal fighting among the Arabs? By God! Tomorrow all these people will be seen tied and bound.' Others said, 'This gentleman thinks that he will conquer and capture the palaces and castles of Rome. It's a pity.' *(Tafsir ibn Kathir).*

When the Prophet Muhammad came to know about this, he called them and asked them about it. They said, 'We were simply talking jocularly. In reply to this, the Quran has this to say: 'Would you make a mockery of God and of His Revelations and His Messenger?'

The message of God is always conveyed through some human being. If this man is apparently ordinary in the eyes of the observers, they start to mock him. But this mockery is not against that man; it is against God Himself. Those who do this only prove that they are not serious about God's religion. Such people are most guilty in the eyes of God. Their false justifications will never be successful in hiding the reality.

Hypocrisy and apostasy *(irtidad)* after accepting Islam are two aspects of the same fact. If a man, after adopting Islam, openly becomes an infidel (disbeliever) then this is *irtidad*; and if in his mind and heart, he is far away from Islam but before other people shows himself as a Muslim, this is hypocrisy. The fate of such hypocrites before God is the same as of those who have committed *irtidad*. However, if they sincerely admit their wrongs and reform themselves before death, God may relent towards them.

⁶⁷ The hypocrites, both men and women, are all alike. They enjoin what is evil, forbid what is right and they are niggardly when it comes to spending for the cause of God. They have forgotten God, so He has forgotten them. The hypocrites are the disobedient ones. ⁶⁸ God has promised the hypocrites, both men and women, and those who deny the truth, the Fire of Hell. They shall abide in it forever. That is a sufficient recompense for them. God has rejected them. They shall have everlasting punishment.ᵃ

ٱلْمُنَـٰفِقُونَ وَٱلْمُنَـٰفِقَـٰتُ بَعْضُهُم مِّنۢ بَعْضٍ ۚ يَأْمُرُونَ بِٱلْمُنكَرِ وَيَنْهَوْنَ عَنِ ٱلْمَعْرُوفِ وَيَقْبِضُونَ أَيْدِيَهُمْ ۚ نَسُوا۟ ٱللَّهَ فَنَسِيَهُمْ ۗ إِنَّ ٱلْمُنَـٰفِقِينَ هُمُ ٱلْفَـٰسِقُونَ ٦٧ وَعَدَ ٱللَّهُ ٱلْمُنَـٰفِقِينَ وَٱلْمُنَـٰفِقَـٰتِ وَٱلْكُفَّارَ نَارَ جَهَنَّمَ خَـٰلِدِينَ فِيهَا ۚ هِىَ حَسْبُهُمْ ۚ وَلَعَنَهُمُ ٱللَّهُ ۖ وَلَهُمْ عَذَابٌ مُّقِيمٌ ٦٨

ᵃ God has blessed previous communities with status and wealth. These things nourished their pride, haughtiness and insensitivity. Their successors did not take a lesson from the plight that befell them. They too chose for themselves a share in worldly effects as their predecessors had done before them. This has been the condition of the common man in every period. He does not give importance to the requirements of Truth. The requirements of his children and his property are everything for him.

The condition of the hypocrite in point of fact is also the same. Outwardly, he appears to be like the true believers, but the level of his existence is the same as that of an ordinary worldly person. The result is that, leaving aside a certain amount of exhibitionism, in real life he is just like any other average human being.

The hypocrite is emotionally more attached to worldly individuals than to religious people. His heart constricts if he has to spend anything for the Hereafter. But he does not hesitate to go ahead and spend on worldly affairs. He does not like the progress of truth, but if it is a question of the progress of untruth, he eagerly tolerates it. In spite of outward religiousness, he is forgetful of God and the Hereafter, as if God and the Hereafter have no value for him.

Such people are never safe from God's wrath simply on the basis of their outward show of Islam. They will be cursed in the world and punished in the Hereafter. They will be deprived of God's grace in the world as well as in the Hereafter.

Complete attachment to God is the only thing which gives value to a man's deeds. A deed performed without this will be as valueless in the Hereafter as a body without a soul, which in spite of its resemblance to a human body is in reality without meaning.

⁶⁹ Like those before you who were stronger than you, possessed more wealth and children; they enjoyed their share in this life as you have enjoyed yours; like them, you have indulged in idle talk. It is they whose works shall come to nothing in this world and in the life to come—and it is they who shall be the losers. ⁷⁰ Have they never heard the stories about their predecessors, the peoples of Noah, ʿAd, Thamud, Abraham, Midian, and of the ruined cities? Their messengers brought them clear evidence of the truth. It was not God who wronged them; they wronged themselves.ᵃ

كَٱلَّذِينَ مِن قَبْلِكُمْ كَانُوٓاْ أَشَدَّ مِنكُمْ قُوَّةً وَأَكْثَرَ أَمْوَٰلاً وَأَوْلَٰداً فَٱسْتَمْتَعُواْ بِخَلَٰقِهِمْ فَٱسْتَمْتَعْتُم بِخَلَٰقِكُمْ كَمَا ٱسْتَمْتَعَ ٱلَّذِينَ مِن قَبْلِكُم بِخَلَٰقِهِمْ وَخُضْتُمْ كَٱلَّذِى خَاضُوٓاْ أُوْلَٰٓئِكَ حَبِطَتْ أَعْمَٰلُهُمْ فِى ٱلدُّنْيَا وَٱلْءَاخِرَةِ وَأُوْلَٰٓئِكَ هُمُ ٱلْخَٰسِرُونَ ۝ أَلَمْ يَأْتِهِمْ نَبَأُ ٱلَّذِينَ مِن قَبْلِهِمْ قَوْمِ نُوحٍ وَعَادٍ وَثَمُودَ وَقَوْمِ إِبْرَٰهِيمَ وَأَصْحَٰبِ مَدْيَنَ وَٱلْمُؤْتَفِكَٰتِ أَتَتْهُمْ رُسُلُهُم بِٱلْبَيِّنَٰتِ فَمَا كَانَ ٱللَّهُ لِيَظْلِمَهُمْ وَلَٰكِن كَانُوٓاْ أَنفُسَهُمْ يَظْلِمُونَ ۝

ᵃ The characteristics of people hypocritically connected with Islam are carelessness about the Hereafter, interest in worldly affairs, avoidance of cooperation with goodness, and an inclination towards exhibitionism. Because of these common characteristics, they remain very well united. These things give them subjects of common interest for discussion, and provide them with a field for mutual cooperation. This becomes a basis for close relations between them.

The reverse is true of genuine believers, because the love of God is embedded in their hearts. Their greatest care is for the Hereafter. They have connections with worldly things only to the extent necessary and not as a goal. If any work which is pleasing to God is under way, their hearts are immediately attracted towards it. On the contrary, any work of an evil nature arouses disgust and loathing in them. Their life and their assets are first and foremost for the sake of God and not for themselves. They commemorate God and spend for His cause.

71 The believers, both men and women, are friends to each other; they enjoin what is good and forbid evil, they attend to their prayers and pay the alms and obey God and His Messenger. On these God will have mercy, for God is almighty and wise. 72 God has promised the believers, both men and women, Gardens through which rivers flow, wherein they will abide, and fine dwelling places in Gardens of eternity. But the good pleasure of God is greater still. That is the supreme achievement.*a*

وَٱلْمُؤْمِنُونَ وَٱلْمُؤْمِنَٰتُ بَعْضُهُمْ أَوْلِيَآءُ بَعْضٍ يَأْمُرُونَ بِٱلْمَعْرُوفِ وَيَنْهَوْنَ عَنِ ٱلْمُنكَرِ وَيُقِيمُونَ ٱلصَّلَوٰةَ وَيُؤْتُونَ ٱلزَّكَوٰةَ وَيُطِيعُونَ ٱللَّهَ وَرَسُولَهُۥٓ أُو۟لَٰٓئِكَ سَيَرْحَمُهُمُ ٱللَّهُ إِنَّ ٱللَّهَ عَزِيزٌ حَكِيمٌ ۝ وَعَدَ ٱللَّهُ ٱلْمُؤْمِنِينَ وَٱلْمُؤْمِنَٰتِ جَنَّٰتٍ تَجْرِى مِن تَحْتِهَا ٱلْأَنْهَٰرُ خَٰلِدِينَ فِيهَا وَمَسَٰكِنَ طَيِّبَةً فِى جَنَّٰتِ عَدْنٍ وَرِضْوَٰنٌ مِّنَ ٱللَّهِ أَكْبَرُ ذَٰلِكَ هُوَ ٱلْفَوْزُ ٱلْعَظِيمُ ۝

---

a The common qualities of the people of faith as mentioned in the above verse bring them together. They all run towards God. Everyone's focus of obedience is the Prophet of God. When they meet each other, these are the things of common interest on which they talk; and solely on these bases are their mutual relations built up. These are the things which provide them with the goal towards which they have to strive unitedly; this furnishes them with the target towards which they have to move all together.

The life of the people of Faith in this world is symbolic of their life in the Hereafter. In this world, the people of faith live like so many flourishing trees standing in a lush green garden; everyone adds to the beauty of the other. Every believer is the well-wisher and companion of other believers, so much so, that the whole atmosphere becomes that of an abode of peace and tranquillity. This godly life will turn into the heavenly life in the Hereafter. There, the believer will not only reap the harvest sown by him, but will also receive such bounty by the special grace of God as he had never hitherto imagined.

⁷³ O Prophet, strive against those who deny the truth and the hypocrites, and be firm against them. Their abode shall be Hell: an evil destination. ⁷⁴ They swear by God that they did not, yet they uttered the words of denial of truth after they had accepted Islam. They meditated a plot which they were unable to carry out, and being spiteful was their only response to God, who had enriched them out of His bounty, and to His Messenger. If they repent, it will indeed be better for them. If they turn away, God will punish them with grievous suffering in this world and the Hereafter, and there will be no one on earth to protect or help them.^a

يَـٰٓأَيُّهَا ٱلنَّبِىُّ جَـٰهِدِ ٱلْكُفَّارَ وَٱلْمُنَـٰفِقِينَ وَٱغْلُظْ عَلَيْهِمْ ۚ وَمَأْوَىٰهُمْ جَهَنَّمُ ۖ وَبِئْسَ ٱلْمَصِيرُ ۝ يَحْلِفُونَ بِٱللَّهِ مَا قَالُوا۟ وَلَقَدْ قَالُوا۟ كَلِمَةَ ٱلْكُفْرِ وَكَفَرُوا۟ بَعْدَ إِسْلَـٰمِهِمْ وَهَمُّوا۟ بِمَا لَمْ يَنَالُوا۟ ۚ وَمَا نَقَمُوٓا۟ إِلَّآ أَنْ أَغْنَىٰهُمُ ٱللَّهُ وَرَسُولُهُۥ مِن فَضْلِهِ ۚ فَإِن يَتُوبُوا۟ يَكُ خَيْرًا لَّهُمْ ۖ وَإِن يَتَوَلَّوْا۟ يُعَذِّبْهُمُ ٱللَّهُ عَذَابًا أَلِيمًا فِى ٱلدُّنْيَا وَٱلْـَٔاخِرَةِ ۚ وَمَا لَهُمْ فِى ٱلْأَرْضِ مِن وَلِىٍّ وَلَا نَصِيرٍ ۝

---

^a According to a tradition, during the period of the Prophet Muhammad, there were about eighty hypocrites in Madinah. This indicates that the *jihad* ordered here against hypocrites did not mean waging (*qital*) war on them. Had it been so, the Prophet would have had them eliminated. According to a *hadith* narrated by Ibn 'Abbas, here *jihad* meant striving by word of mouth. Hence, according to the majority of Muslims, *jihad* with the sword against hypocrites is not in accordance with the Shariah.

Hypocrisy is the adoption of Islam in such a way that it is subservient to personal interests and worldly considerations. When hypocrites see that true believers have adopted Islam in a manner devoid of self-interest and worldly consideration and invite others also to accept the true Islam, they feel that this Islam amounts to degrading their form of Islam. Therefore, they begin to hate such preachers (*da'is*). They become the enemies of the inviters to that very Islam in the name of which they have flourishing business.

This enmity of hypocrites expresses itself by way of conspiracy and ridicule. If they observe that somebody has ill feelings towards the believers, the hypocrites encourage and incite these feelings with a view to making sure that fighting breaks out against the believers. They make fun of sincere people of faith. They utter words which belittle their sacrifices. They trivialize and distort their doings in order to spoil their image among the people. During the Tabuk journey, it once happened that the Prophet Muhammad's camel strayed from a camp site and a search was started by some of the Muslims. ▶

75 There are some among them who pledged themselves to God, saying, 'If God gives us something out of His bounty, we shall certainly give alms and be righteous,' 76 but when He bestowed His favours on them they grew niggardly, and turned away in aversion. 77 So He caused hypocrisy to settle in their hearts until the Day of their meeting with Him, because they broke their word to God, and because they lied.*

﷽ وَمِنْهُم مَّنْ عَٰهَدَ ٱللَّهَ لَئِنْ ءَاتَىٰنَا مِن فَضْلِهِۦ لَنَصَّدَّقَنَّ وَلَنَكُونَنَّ مِنَ ٱلصَّٰلِحِينَ ۝ فَلَمَّآ ءَاتَىٰهُم مِّن فَضْلِهِۦ بَخِلُوا۟ بِهِۦ وَتَوَلَّوا۟ وَّهُم مُّعْرِضُونَ ۝ فَأَعْقَبَهُمْ نِفَاقًا فِى قُلُوبِهِمْ إِلَىٰ يَوْمِ يَلْقَوْنَهُۥ بِمَآ أَخْلَفُوا۟ ٱللَّهَ مَا وَعَدُوهُ وَبِمَا كَانُوا۟ يَكْذِبُونَ ۝

When the hypocrites came to know of this, they mockingly said, 'This gentleman tells about happenings in the skies, but he is not aware of the whereabouts of his camel.'

The hypocritical Muslims become the accomplices and instruments of Satan in order to defeat the believers. But, God is ever the supporter of true believers, and He saves them in spite of all the conspiracies of hypocrites. The fate of the hypocrites is that, their transgressions having been established beyond doubt, they become liable for punishment in this world as well as in the Hereafter.

a Tha'laba ibn Hathib Ansari requested the Prophet Muhammad to pray to God to bless him with wealth. The Prophet said that to be grateful to God for less wealth is better than acquiring a lot of wealth and then being unable to be grateful to Him. But Tha'laba repeated his request several times. So, the Prophet prayed, 'O God, bless Tha'laba with wealth.' Thereafter, Tha'laba reared a goat. The breed of goats increased to such an extent that the land of Madinah could not provide enough fodder for his goats. Tha'laba then shifted to a valley outside Madinah. Now Tha'laba started becoming remiss in his Islamic observances.

First of all he missed the congregational prayers. Then he missed the Friday prayers. A stage came when an official on behalf of the Prophet Muhammad approached Tha'laba to collect alms (*zakat*) and he refused, saying, 'This is nothing but a capital tax (*jizyah*); this is in no way different from the tax levied on those who deny the truth.'

⁷⁸ Do they not know that God knows what they conceal and what they talk about in secret? That God knows all that is hidden?

⁷⁹ As for those who ridicule such believers as give alms freely for the sake of God and taunt those who find nothing to give save that which they earn through their toil, God will cause their ridicule to rebound on them: they shall have a painful punishment. ⁸⁰ It is the same whether or not you ask forgiveness for them. Even if you ask forgiveness for them seventy times, God will not forgive them, for they have denied God and His Messenger. God does not guide the evil-doers.ᵃ

أَلَمۡ يَعۡلَمُوٓاْ أَنَّ ٱللَّهَ يَعۡلَمُ سِرَّهُمۡ وَنَجۡوَىٰهُمۡ وَأَنَّ ٱللَّهَ عَلَّٰمُ ٱلۡغُيُوبِ ۝ ٱلَّذِينَ يَلۡمِزُونَ ٱلۡمُطَّوِّعِينَ مِنَ ٱلۡمُؤۡمِنِينَ فِى ٱلصَّدَقَٰتِ وَٱلَّذِينَ لَا يَجِدُونَ إِلَّا جُهۡدَهُمۡ فَيَسۡخَرُونَ مِنۡهُمۡ سَخِرَ ٱللَّهُ مِنۡهُمۡ وَلَهُمۡ عَذَابٌ أَلِيمٌ ۝ ٱسۡتَغۡفِرۡ لَهُمۡ أَوۡ لَا تَسۡتَغۡفِرۡ لَهُمۡ إِن تَسۡتَغۡفِرۡ لَهُمۡ سَبۡعِينَ مَرَّةً فَلَن يَغۡفِرَ ٱللَّهُ لَهُمۡ ذَٰلِكَ بِأَنَّهُمۡ كَفَرُواْ بِٱللَّهِ وَرَسُولِهِۦ وَٱللَّهُ لَا يَهۡدِى ٱلۡقَوۡمَ ٱلۡفَٰسِقِينَ ۝

ᵃ That person is a hypocrite in the eyes of God who prays to God for the blessing of wealth and when God makes him wealthy, forgets to keep aside God's share. When a man has no wealth, he finds fault with wealthy persons, saying that they are wasting wealth in improper ways; and that if he were to be blessed with wealth by God, he would spend it on good and charitable causes. But when he receives wealth, his mentality changes. He forgets what he had said earlier and what feelings he had expressed. Now, he thinks that his wealth is the result of his own diligence and talents, which gives him the right to sole possession of it. He forgets to set aside God's share in his wealth.

Such people, in order to cover up their weaknesses, indulge in further arrogance by ridiculing those who spend their wealth for the cause of God. If a person spends more, they belittle him by calling him ostentatious, and of one who can spend only a little, in view of his circumstances, they ask derisively whether God was in need of this man's charity. Those people who are in this way obsessed with their own greatness, are never able to see the higher realities outside themselves.

⁸¹ Those who stayed at home were glad that they were left behind by God's Messenger. They hated the thought of striving for God's cause with their possessions and their persons. They said, 'Do not go forth in this heat.' Say, 'The Fire of Hell is far hotter.' If only they could understand. ⁸² Let them laugh a little and weep much in return for their misdeeds.ᵃ

فَرِحَ ٱلْمُخَلَّفُونَ بِمَقْعَدِهِمْ خِلَٰفَ رَسُولِ ٱللَّهِ وَكَرِهُوٓا۟ أَن يُجَٰهِدُوا۟ بِأَمْوَٰلِهِمْ وَأَنفُسِهِمْ فِى سَبِيلِ ٱللَّهِ وَقَالُوا۟ لَا تَنفِرُوا۟ فِى ٱلْحَرِّ قُلْ نَارُ جَهَنَّمَ أَشَدُّ حَرًّا لَّوْ كَانُوا۟ يَفْقَهُونَ ۝ فَلْيَضْحَكُوا۟ قَلِيلًا وَلْيَبْكُوا۟ كَثِيرًا جَزَآءًۢ بِمَا كَانُوا۟ يَكْسِبُونَ ۝

ᵃ The battle of Tabuk occurred in an extremely hot season. From Madinah to the Syrian border three hundred miles had to be travelled. The hypocritical Muslims asked others not to undertake such a long journey in such extremely hot weather. In saying this they forgot that, after hearing the call of God, refusal to set out for fear of some danger amounted to putting oneself in greater danger. It was like running away from the sun and taking refuge in the flames of a fire.

Those who are fonder of themselves and their wealth than God are very pleased with themselves if, by their attractive devices, they manage to remain 'Muslims' and at the same time there is no danger to their lives and property. They consider themselves wise and treat those people as foolish who struggle so hard for the cause of God that they have no time for themselves.

But this is absolute nonsense. They may laugh now, but they will end up crying, because in the life to come after death, their 'cleverness' is going to prove to be the worst type of foolishness. At that time they will feel extremely sorry that, though they wanted paradise, they refused to part with the very asset which whould have gained them entry into it.

83 So [Prophet], if God brings you back to a group of them, and should they ask your leave to go forth with you, say, 'You shall never go forth with me and shall never fight an enemy with me. You chose to sit at home the first time, so sit now with those who remain behind.' 84 And never [O Muhammad] pray for one of them who dies, nor stand by his grave. For they denied God and His Messenger, and died rebellious.

85 Do not let their wealth and their children dazzle you. God only wants to punish them through these things in this world, and let their souls depart while they deny the truth. 86 When a chapter is revealed enjoining, 'Believe in God and strive for the cause of God along with His Messenger,' the wealthy among them ask you to exempt them saying, 'Let us stay with those who are to stay behind.'[a]

فَإِن رَّجَعَكَ ٱللَّهُ إِلَىٰ طَآئِفَةٍ مِّنْهُمْ فَٱسْتَـْٔذَنُوكَ لِلْخُرُوجِ فَقُل لَّن تَخْرُجُواْ مَعِىَ أَبَدًا وَلَن تُقَٰتِلُواْ مَعِىَ عَدُوًّا إِنَّكُمْ رَضِيتُم بِٱلْقُعُودِ أَوَّلَ مَرَّةٍ فَٱقْعُدُواْ مَعَ ٱلْخَٰلِفِينَ ۝ وَلَا تُصَلِّ عَلَىٰ أَحَدٍ مِّنْهُم مَّاتَ أَبَدًا وَلَا تَقُمْ عَلَىٰ قَبْرِهِۦٓ إِنَّهُمْ كَفَرُواْ بِٱللَّهِ وَرَسُولِهِۦ وَمَاتُواْ وَهُمْ فَٰسِقُونَ ۝ وَلَا تُعْجِبْكَ أَمْوَٰلُهُمْ وَأَوْلَٰدُهُمْ إِنَّمَا يُرِيدُ ٱللَّهُ أَن يُعَذِّبَهُم بِهَا فِى ٱلدُّنْيَا وَتَزْهَقَ أَنفُسُهُمْ وَهُمْ كَٰفِرُونَ ۝ وَإِذَآ أُنزِلَتْ سُورَةٌ أَنْ ءَامِنُواْ بِٱللَّهِ وَجَٰهِدُواْ مَعَ رَسُولِهِ ٱسْتَـْٔذَنَكَ أُوْلُواْ ٱلطَّوْلِ مِنْهُمْ وَقَالُواْ ذَرْنَا نَكُن مَّعَ ٱلْقَٰعِدِينَ ۝

---

[a] Hypocrites of this kind are always those who, because of their policy of expediency, gather around themselves the resources of position and wealth. Due to this, the general run of Muslims are impressed by their worldly position. Their glamorous lives and their glib talk make them seem great in the eyes of the common man. This can create moments of grave trial for an Islamic society, because, in a truly Islamic society, such people ought to be ignored rather than being given places of honour.

The real Islamic society will not be willing to accord a position of honour to those about whom it is abundantly clear that they are Muslims in name only, being in fact loyal only to their own vested interests and worldly considerations. The fate of such people is that in Islamic functions they find a place only on the back benches; they have no share in the congregational affairs of Muslims, being held unfit to grace religious offices. Any society in which such people have been able to attain a position of honour can never be looked upon with favour by God.

⁸⁷ They preferred to be with [the women], who remained behind [at home]: their hearts are sealed and so they do not understand. ⁸⁸ But the Messenger and those who shared his faith strove hard with their possessions and their lives. It is they who shall have all kinds of good, and it is they who shall surely prosper. ⁸⁹ God has prepared for them Gardens through which rivers flow, in which they shall abide forever. That is the supreme triumph.ᵃ

رَضُوا بِأَن يَكُونُوا مَعَ ٱلْخَوَالِفِ وَطُبِعَ عَلَىٰ قُلُوبِهِمْ فَهُمْ لَا يَفْقَهُونَ ۝ لَـٰكِنِ ٱلرَّسُولُ وَٱلَّذِينَ ءَامَنُوا مَعَهُۥ جَـٰهَدُوا بِأَمْوَٰلِهِمْ وَأَنفُسِهِمْ ۚ وَأُوْلَـٰٓئِكَ لَهُمُ ٱلْخَيْرَٰتُ ۖ وَأُوْلَـٰٓئِكَ هُمُ ٱلْمُفْلِحُونَ ۝ أَعَدَّ ٱللَّهُ لَهُمْ جَنَّـٰتٍ تَجْرِى مِن تَحْتِهَا ٱلْأَنْهَـٰرُ خَـٰلِدِينَ فِيهَا ۚ ذَٰلِكَ ٱلْفَوْزُ ٱلْعَظِيمُ ۝

ᵃ A hypocrite, due to his being materially minded, gathers around him many worldly effects; a crowd of supporters is also seen around him. These things greatly impress the superficial kind of person. But, for those who look into things more deeply, such showy glamour is not enviable but serves rather to teach a lesson. Such an accumulation of goods hinders the hypocrite from coming closer to God. God's favourite servant is one who proceeds towards Him without any reservation or worldly consideration. But those who are immersed in worldly glories are unable to rise above these things. Whenever they are inclined to proceed towards God, they feel as if that would be at the cost of material gains. Since they cannot muster enough courage to undertake this sacrifice, they cannot be loyal to God. Their worldly benefits are gained at the horrible price of entering the Hereafter deprived of everything.

The condition of such people is that when God's religion asks them to forget themselves and attach themselves to God, they are unable to bury their inflated egos. When God's religion tells them to tread a path devoid of personal glory, they lag behind, prefering to take care of their fame and popularity. When the struggle for God's religion demands the sacrifice of life and property, their lives and property appear so valuable to them that they are unable to sacrifice them for any non-worldly goal.

This attitude goes on hardening to the point where their hearts lose all sensitivity. Falling victim to insensitivity, they lose the urge which pulls them towards God and which does not allow them to reconcile with anything other than God.

In contrast to this, the true believers allot the highest position to God and as such everything other than God appears worthless to them. They are always ready to move ahead towards God by undertaking every kind of sacrifice. These are the people for whom God's graces and bounties exist. Nothing stands between them and the eternal paradise of God, save death.

⁹⁰ Some of the desert Arabs, too, came to make excuses, asking to be granted exemption. Those who lied to God and His Messenger stayed behind at home. Those who denied the truth among them will be afflicted with a painful chastisement, ⁹¹ but no blame shall attach to the weak, the sick, and those who have no means to spend, provided they are sincere to God and His Messenger. There is no reason to reproach those who do good deeds; God is most forgiving and merciful.ᵃ

وَجَآءَ ٱلْمُعَذِّرُونَ مِنَ ٱلْأَعْرَابِ لِيُؤْذَنَ لَهُمْ وَقَعَدَ ٱلَّذِينَ كَذَبُوا۟ ٱللَّهَ وَرَسُولَهُۥ سَيُصِيبُ ٱلَّذِينَ كَفَرُوا۟ مِنْهُمْ عَذَابٌ أَلِيمٌ ۝ لَّيْسَ عَلَى ٱلضُّعَفَآءِ وَلَا عَلَى ٱلْمَرْضَىٰ وَلَا عَلَى ٱلَّذِينَ لَا يَجِدُونَ مَا يُنفِقُونَ حَرَجٌ إِذَا نَصَحُوا۟ لِلَّهِ وَرَسُولِهِۦ مَا عَلَى ٱلْمُحْسِنِينَ مِن سَبِيلٍ وَٱللَّهُ غَفُورٌ رَّحِيمٌ ۝

ᵃ When the struggle to obey the call of religion demands that people forfeit their lives and property, and if at that time they lag behind in spite of having the ability to make such a sacrifice, this is the worst type of crime. This proves people's insensitivity to the call of religion. Such behaviour on the part of a Muslim amounts to his being a traitor to God and His Prophet. Such people do not deserve any share in God's graces. If they were unwilling to spare anything from whatever they had for the sake of God, then how do they expect that God will give them whatever He has? Nobody can receive anything unless he or she pays the price for it.

However, God forgives handicapped persons and invalids. One who is ill, who has nothing to contribute to the mission or who does not possess the resources required for the journey will be forgiven by God. Moreover, it is quite possible that in spite of not doing anything, they may be given credit for everything, as has been recorded in a tradition (*hadith*) of the Prophet Muhammad: while returning from the battle of Tabuk, he said to his companions, 'There are certain people in Madinah, about whom you may say that they have not trodden any path or that they have not traversed any valley but who were nevertheless shoulder to shoulder alongwith you.'

⁹²Nor [does any blame] attach to those who came to you to be provided with mounts, and when you said, 'I can find no mounts for you,' they went back, and tears welled up in their eyes with sadness, since they could not find any way to contribute. ⁹³The blameworthy are those who are men of wealth and yet ask for exemption. They are content to be with those [women] who stay behind. God has sealed their hearts: they do not understand.

⁹⁴They will make excuses to you when you return to them. Say, 'Do not make excuses, we will not believe you. God has already informed us about you. God will see your actions, as will His Messenger. Then you will be returned to the One who knows the seen and the unseen and He will tell you all that you used to do.' ᵃ

وَلَا عَلَى ٱلَّذِينَ إِذَا مَآ أَتَوْكَ لِتَحْمِلَهُمْ قُلْتَ لَآ أَجِدُ مَآ أَحْمِلُكُمْ عَلَيْهِ تَوَلَّوْا وَّأَعْيُنُهُمْ تَفِيضُ مِنَ ٱلدَّمْعِ حَزَنًا أَلَّا يَجِدُوا مَا يُنفِقُونَ ۞ إِنَّمَا ٱلسَّبِيلُ عَلَى ٱلَّذِينَ يَسْتَـْٔذِنُونَكَ وَهُمْ أَغْنِيَآءُ رَضُوا بِأَن يَكُونُوا مَعَ ٱلْخَوَالِفِ وَطَبَعَ ٱللَّهُ عَلَىٰ قُلُوبِهِمْ فَهُمْ لَا يَعْلَمُونَ ۞ يَعْتَذِرُونَ إِلَيْكُمْ إِذَا رَجَعْتُمْ إِلَيْهِمْ قُل لَّا تَعْتَذِرُوا لَن نُّؤْمِنَ لَكُمْ قَدْ نَبَّأَنَا ٱللَّهُ مِنْ أَخْبَارِكُمْ وَسَيَرَى ٱللَّهُ عَمَلَكُمْ وَرَسُولُهُ ثُمَّ تُرَدُّونَ إِلَىٰ عَٰلِمِ ٱلْغَيْبِ وَٱلشَّهَٰدَةِ فَيُنَبِّئُكُم بِمَا كُنتُمْ تَعْمَلُونَ ۞

ᵃ Now, who are those fortunate people whose inaction is regarded as action and who are therefore rewarded for it? They are those who, while not physically participating because of some incapacity, give proof of three things—heartfelt solidarity with the participants (nush); doing at least by word of mouth whatever is possible for them to do (ihsan); and, sorrowfulness about their shortcomings that is so intense that it gushes out in the form of tears (huzn).

If an individual relegates something to an unimportant category in his life and does so again and again, it can happen that the very consciousness of its importance vanishes from his heart. The demands of that task keep coming before him, but there being no urge left in his heart to accomplish it, he fails to come to grips with it. This growing insensitivity is termed in the Quran 'the sealing of hearts'.

'God has already informed us about you.' This statement makes it clear that the hypocrites referred to here are those present at the time of revelation of the Quran, that is, the Prophet's contemporaries. According to *Tabaqat ibn Sa'd*, there were eighty individuals about whose hypocritical character God had informed the Prophet through His revelation. ▶

⁹⁵ When you return, they will swear to you by God so that you may leave them alone, so leave them alone. They are unclean, and Hell will be their home as a reward for their actions—⁹⁶ they will swear to you, so that you may be pleased with them. But [even] if you are pleased with them, God is not pleased with rebellious people.ᵃ

سَيَحْلِفُونَ بِٱللَّهِ لَكُمْ إِذَا ٱنقَلَبْتُمْ إِلَيْهِمْ لِتُعْرِضُوا۟ عَنْهُمْ فَأَعْرِضُوا۟ عَنْهُمْ إِنَّهُمْ رِجْسٌ وَمَأْوَىٰهُمْ جَهَنَّمُ جَزَآءً بِمَا كَانُوا۟ يَكْسِبُونَ ۝ يَحْلِفُونَ لَكُمْ لِتَرْضَوْا۟ عَنْهُمْ فَإِن تَرْضَوْا۟ عَنْهُمْ فَإِنَّ ٱللَّهَ لَا يَرْضَىٰ عَنِ ٱلْقَوْمِ ٱلْفَٰسِقِينَ ۝

However, in spite of this knowledge, the behaviour which the companions of the Prophet were allowed to adopt towards them was to overlook and ignore them. The issue of meting out punishment to them was kept by God in His own Hands. However, the only severity shown to the hypocrites of Madinah was that the excuses they offered were not accepted. So much so that when Tha'laba ibn Hatib Ansari, a hypocrite, offered *zakat*, it was not accepted from him. 'Abdullah ibn Ubayy's son wanted to take drastic action against his father for his hypocritical actions, but the Prophet restrained him, saying, 'Leave him. By God, as long as he is amongst us, we will treat him properly.' *(Tabaqat ibn Sa'd)*

ᵃ The orders regarding the hypocrites of later periods were the same. However, there was one difference. The treatment given to the hypocrites of the early period was based on the state of their hearts. But the treatment given to the later hypocrites will be based on external proof. The approach of overlooking and ignoring them will be proper only if external proof of their hypocrisy is available. No action will be taken against them on the basis of their intention or the condition of their hearts. If the later hypocrites present any excuses, their excuses and their charities, etc., will also be accepted. Leaving their fate to be decided by God, such action will be taken against them as is warranted in the normal course of law.

Paradise is attainable on the basis of personal deeds and not on the basis of having joined any class or group of Muslims. All the hypocrites were a part of the Mulsim *ummah*; they used to offer prayers and observe the ritual of fasting along with the Muslims, but in spite of that, God decalred them to be bound for Hell.

⁹⁷ The desert Arabs are more stubborn in their denial of truth and hypocrisy, and are the least likely to be aware of the limits which God has revealed to His Messenger. God is all knowing and wise. ⁹⁸ Some desert Arabs regard what they give for the cause of God as a fine and wait for some misfortune to befall you. May ill-fortune befall them! God hears all and knows all.ᵃ

ٱلْأَعْرَابُ أَشَدُّ كُفْرًا وَنِفَاقًا وَأَجْدَرُ أَلَّا يَعْلَمُوا۟ حُدُودَ مَآ أَنزَلَ ٱللَّهُ عَلَىٰ رَسُولِهِۦ ۗ وَٱللَّهُ عَلِيمٌ حَكِيمٌ ۝ وَمِنَ ٱلْأَعْرَابِ مَن يَتَّخِذُ مَا يُنفِقُ مَغْرَمًا وَيَتَرَبَّصُ بِكُمُ ٱلدَّوَآئِرَ ۚ عَلَيْهِمْ دَآئِرَةُ ٱلسَّوْءِ ۗ وَٱللَّهُ سَمِيعٌ عَلِيمٌ ۝

ᵃ A tradition of the Prophet says, 'One who settles in a village will become hard in nature.' There is an intellectual atmosphere in a city; educational institutes are established there, discussion of learning and the arts is a regular feature of city life, whereas the people in villages do not have these opportunities for self-improvement. Moreover, their manner of living and the means of their livelihood are also inferior in comparison. Consequently, a deep and mature consciousness does not develop in these people of the countryside. There is harshness in their temperament and superficiality in their thinking. They find it difficult to understand the dialectics of religion and cannot absorb its truth.

God is aware of everything; at the same time He is Wise and Merciful also. He is fully aware of this weakness on the part of country people (villagers), or in other words, the general public, and in His wisdom and Mercy allows them full latitude on this account. Therefore, God does not demand from them deep realisation (ma'rifah) or a high level of religiosity. If they are well-intentioned, God will accept their simple faith.

⁹⁹ There are also those among them who believe in God and the Last Day and regard what they spend for the cause of God as a means of bringing them nearer to God and of deserving the prayers of the Messenger. This shall certainly be for them a means of drawing near to God. God will admit them into His mercy; God is indeed most forgiving and merciful.

¹⁰⁰ As for those who led the way, the first of the emigrants and the supporters, as well as those who nobly followed them, God is well pleased with them, and they are well pleased with Him; He has prepared for them Gardens through which rivers flow, where they shall dwell forever. That is the supreme achievement.ᵃ

وَمِنَ ٱلْأَعْرَابِ مَن يُؤْمِنُ بِٱللَّهِ وَٱلْيَوْمِ ٱلْآخِرِ وَيَتَّخِذُ مَا يُنفِقُ قُرُبَٰتٍ عِندَ ٱللَّهِ وَصَلَوَٰتِ ٱلرَّسُولِ ۚ أَلَآ إِنَّهَا قُرْبَةٌ لَّهُمْ ۚ سَيُدْخِلُهُمُ ٱللَّهُ فِى رَحْمَتِهِ ۚ إِنَّ ٱللَّهَ غَفُورٌ رَّحِيمٌ ۝ وَٱلسَّٰبِقُونَ ٱلْأَوَّلُونَ مِنَ ٱلْمُهَٰجِرِينَ وَٱلْأَنصَارِ وَٱلَّذِينَ ٱتَّبَعُوهُم بِإِحْسَٰنٍ رَّضِىَ ٱللَّهُ عَنْهُمْ وَرَضُوا۟ عَنْهُ وَأَعَدَّ لَهُمْ جَنَّٰتٍ تَجْرِى تَحْتَهَا ٱلْأَنْهَٰرُ خَٰلِدِينَ فِيهَآ أَبَدًا ۚ ذَٰلِكَ ٱلْفَوْزُ ٱلْعَظِيمُ ۝

ᵃ Religion for the general public is acceptance of God from the bottom of their hearts; keeping the realisation fresh in their minds that they have to face the Hereafter one day; spending a part of their earnings for the sake of God. They think that in this way they will be able to attain closeness to God and His blessings, and may seek the blessings of the Prophet who is a representative of God. This is the ordinary, superficial level of their religiousness, but if a man's heart is pure and he is well-intentioned, God will accept this simple kind of devotion from him.

But, if the common people, becoming completely neglectful of God and His commands, lose all connection with religion, so much so that spending for the cause of religion appears to them a sort of fine and they are terrified of the progress of Islam, then they are undoubtedly unpardonable. Because of the low level of understanding of the common people, they may be excused if they are not capable of deep and noble religiousness. But if their lack of understanding assumes the shape of arrogance or disloyalty towards Islam, then under no circumstances, can they be pardoned.

¹⁰¹ Some of the desert Arabs around you are hypocrites as are some of the people of Madinah—they are obdurate in their hypocrisy. You do not know them, but We know them. We shall cause them to suffer doubly and then they will be subjected to a great punishment.ᵃ

وَمِمَّنْ حَوْلَكُم مِّنَ ٱلْأَعْرَابِ مُنَٰفِقُونَ وَمِنْ أَهْلِ ٱلْمَدِينَةِ مَرَدُواْ عَلَى ٱلنِّفَاقِ لَا تَعْلَمُهُمْ نَحْنُ نَعْلَمُهُمْ سَنُعَذِّبُهُم مَّرَّتَيْنِ ثُمَّ يُرَدُّونَ إِلَىٰ عَذَابٍ عَظِيمٍ ۝

ᵃ When the call goes out for God's religion, the atmosphere can be either inimical or propitious. If inimical, those who issue the call become aliens, or *muhajirs*, in their own hometown; if propitious, they risk neither life nor property and can lend their support to the *muhajirs*. These helpers are called *ansar*. The conditions in the early period at Makkah were such that those of the townspeople who were Muslims were forced into the position of *muhajirs* while the conditions in Madinah were such that those of the townspeople who were Muslims were able to become *ansars*.

God's approval is attainable by anyone willing to pay the price of being a *muhajir* or an *ansar*; either he should concentrate so much on treading God's path that he loses hold of all worldly strings; or if he is a person of some means, he should utilize his wealth to alleviate the deprivation of the first category of people. The Muslims of Makkah (companions of the Prophet) were the perfect examples of individuals willing to suffer this deprivation, going to the extent of emigration, while the Muslims of Madinah were the perfect examples of extending full support to the deprived people for the sake of receiving God's blessings. Those among the later Muslims who follow their predecessors in this matter will join this divine group. God causes some people to be deprived in order to see that they turn to Him. Similarly, God saves others from deprivation in order that they may help the deprived ones and thus join those who spend for the sake of God. This is the plan of God. Those who do not come up to this standard are, in actual fact, not 'pleased' with God's plan. So God will not be 'pleased' with them in the Hereafter.

'They are well pleased with Him.' That is, it was by God's will that they were placed in such circumstances that they had to adopt religion at the cost of sacrificing everything they had. And still they remained steadfastly on the path of religion. Similarly, others were placed in circumstances which required them to share their belongings with their brothers in religion—with whom they had only the relationship of a common cause and not of blood-relationship—and still they willingly did this. Such are those who attain the pleasure of God and it is they who will be settled in the eternal gardens of paradise. ▶

102 There are others who have confessed their wrongdoing, who have done some good deeds and some bad ones. It is likely that God will turn to them in mercy. Surely, God is most forgiving, merciful. 103 Take alms out of their wealth to cleanse them and purify them, and pray for them; your prayer will be a comfort to them. God is all hearing, all knowing.[a]

وَءَاخَرُونَ ٱعْتَرَفُوا بِذُنُوبِهِمْ خَلَطُوا عَمَلًا صَٰلِحًا وَءَاخَرَ سَيِّئًا عَسَى ٱللَّهُ أَن يَتُوبَ عَلَيْهِمْ إِنَّ ٱللَّهَ غَفُورٌ رَّحِيمٌ ۝ خُذْ مِنْ أَمْوَٰلِهِمْ صَدَقَةً تُطَهِّرُهُمْ وَتُزَكِّيهِم بِهَا وَصَلِّ عَلَيْهِمْ إِنَّ صَلَوٰتَكَ سَكَنٌ لَّهُمْ وَٱللَّهُ سَمِيعٌ عَلِيمٌ ۝

A hypocrite is one who claims to be a Muslim, but when the question arises of paying the price of *hijrah* (supporting the callers to the faith) for the sake of religion, he does not find it in his heart to do so.

[a] The proof of sincere repentance is a greater urge to serve the cause of religion. To absolve themselves of sin, they offered a part of their cherished property for the cause of God. On seeing such a positive response from them, the Prophet was asked not to reproach them but rather to give them psychological support, pray for them so that the burden (of guilt) in their hearts was lightened and their confidence in their faith restored.

Doing wrong is not the real evil in the eyes of God; persistence in that wrong is the real evil. One who begins to justify his wrongs ruins himself, while one who admits his mistakes and tries his best to atone for them with good deeds is worthy of being pardoned by God.

104 Do they not know that God accepts the repentance of His servants and receives their alms, and that God is the Forgiving, the Merciful One? 105 Say, 'Do as you will. God will watch your conduct and so will His Messenger and the believers. Soon you will be brought back to Him who knows what is hidden and what is manifest: then He will show you the truth of all that you have done.' 106 [There are yet] others whose cases are deferred until it is God's will to judge them. He will either punish them, or turn in mercy to them; God is all knowing and wise.[a]

أَلَمْ يَعْلَمُوٓاْ أَنَّ ٱللَّهَ هُوَ يَقْبَلُ ٱلتَّوْبَةَ عَنْ عِبَادِهِۦ وَيَأْخُذُ ٱلصَّدَقَٰتِ وَأَنَّ ٱللَّهَ هُوَ ٱلتَّوَّابُ ٱلرَّحِيمُ ﴿١٠٤﴾ وَقُلِ ٱعْمَلُواْ فَسَيَرَى ٱللَّهُ عَمَلَكُمْ وَرَسُولُهُۥ وَٱلْمُؤْمِنُونَ وَسَتُرَدُّونَ إِلَىٰ عَٰلِمِ ٱلْغَيْبِ وَٱلشَّهَٰدَةِ فَيُنَبِّئُكُم بِمَا كُنتُمْ تَعْمَلُونَ ﴿١٠٥﴾ وَءَاخَرُونَ مُرْجَوْنَ لِأَمْرِ ٱللَّهِ إِمَّا يُعَذِّبُهُمْ وَإِمَّا يَتُوبُ عَلَيْهِمْ وَٱللَّهُ عَلِيمٌ حَكِيمٌ ﴿١٠٦﴾

---

[a] After committing a wrong, the individual has two options: either to admit his mistake or shamelessly persist. One who admits his mistakes becomes increasingly modest and once again he becomes entitled to God's grace and blessings. On the contrary, one who is emboldened by his persistence in his sinful ways invites the wrath of God. In order to prove that the path he has opted for is the right path, he invents false arguments in self-defence. In this way his attempt to falsely justify one mistake will lead him on to making more and more mistakes. This is why God's grace awaits the former type of individual, while His wrath awaits the latter.

¹⁰⁷ Then there are those who built a mosque to cause harm, to spread apostasy and disunity among the believers—as an outpost for those who from the outset warred on God and His Messenger. They swear, 'Our intentions were nothing but good,' but God bears witness that they are lying. ¹⁰⁸ Do not set foot in it. Only a house of worship, founded from the very first day upon piety, is worthy of your setting foot therein. In it are men who love to be purified and God loves those who purify themselves.ᵃ

وَٱلَّذِينَ ٱتَّخَذُوا۟ مَسْجِدًا ضِرَارًا وَكُفْرًا وَتَفْرِيقًا بَيْنَ ٱلْمُؤْمِنِينَ وَإِرْصَادًا لِّمَنْ حَارَبَ ٱللَّهَ وَرَسُولَهُ مِن قَبْلُ وَلَيَحْلِفُنَّ إِنْ أَرَدْنَا إِلَّا ٱلْحُسْنَى وَٱللَّهُ يَشْهَدُ إِنَّهُمْ لَكَٰذِبُونَ ۝ لَا تَقُمْ فِيهِ أَبَدًا لَّمَسْجِدٌ أُسِّسَ عَلَى ٱلتَّقْوَىٰ مِنْ أَوَّلِ يَوْمٍ أَحَقُّ أَن تَقُومَ فِيهِ فِيهِ رِجَالٌ يُحِبُّونَ أَن يَتَطَهَّرُوا۟ وَٱللَّهُ يُحِبُّ ٱلْمُطَّهِّرِينَ ۝

ᵃ There are two foundations for the building of life. One is piety (taqwa) and the other is self-centredness. In the first case the whole structure of life is built on a firm foundation of being God-fearing.

In this case all the activities of the individual are influenced by one central thought. That is, he has to be accountable for all his words and deeds to a Being Who is aware of all things, whether open or hidden, and Who is to award punishments or rewards accordingly. One who considers himself accountable to God has erected his building on a solid foundation that will never be shaken.

In contrast to him is the man who builds on the crumbling edge of an abyss. Free from all fears and apprehensions, he leads a self-oriented life in the world. He does not accept any restrictions, and speaks and acts at will.

The example of the life of such a person can be compared to a building which has been constructed on the brink of a gorge which is about to cave in; all of a sudden it will collapse, carrying all the building's residents down into its depths.

[109] Who is better, he who founds his building on the fear of God and His good pleasure, or he who builds on the brink of a crumbling precipice, so that his house is ready to fall with him into the Fire of Hell? God does not guide the wrongdoers: [110] the building which they have built will never cease to be a source of deep disquiet in their hearts, until their hearts are cut to pieces. God is all knowing and wise.

[111] God has bought from the believers their lives and their wealth in return for the Garden. They fight for the cause of God and they kill and are killed. It is a promise binding on Him in the Torah, the Gospel and the Quran, and who is truer to his promise than God? Rejoice then in the bargain you have made. That is the supreme achievement.[a]

أَفَمَنْ أَسَّسَ بُنْيَٰنَهُۥ عَلَىٰ تَقْوَىٰ مِنَ ٱللَّهِ وَرِضْوَٰنٍ خَيْرٌ أَم مَّنْ أَسَّسَ بُنْيَٰنَهُۥ عَلَىٰ شَفَا جُرُفٍ هَارٍ فَٱنْهَارَ بِهِۦ فِى نَارِ جَهَنَّمَ وَٱللَّهُ لَا يَهْدِى ٱلْقَوْمَ ٱلظَّٰلِمِينَ ۝ لَا يَزَالُ بُنْيَٰنُهُمُ ٱلَّذِى بَنَوْا۟ رِيبَةً فِى قُلُوبِهِمْ إِلَّآ أَن تَقَطَّعَ قُلُوبُهُمْ وَٱللَّهُ عَلِيمٌ حَكِيمٌ ۝ إِنَّ ٱللَّهَ ٱشْتَرَىٰ مِنَ ٱلْمُؤْمِنِينَ أَنفُسَهُمْ وَأَمْوَٰلَهُم بِأَنَّ لَهُمُ ٱلْجَنَّةَ يُقَٰتِلُونَ فِى سَبِيلِ ٱللَّهِ فَيَقْتُلُونَ وَيُقْتَلُونَ وَعْدًا عَلَيْهِ حَقًّا فِى ٱلتَّوْرَىٰةِ وَٱلْإِنجِيلِ وَٱلْقُرْءَانِ وَمَنْ أَوْفَىٰ بِعَهْدِهِۦ مِنَ ٱللَّهِ فَٱسْتَبْشِرُوا۟ بِبَيْعِكُمُ ٱلَّذِى بَايَعْتُم بِهِۦ وَذَٰلِكَ هُوَ ٱلْفَوْزُ ٱلْعَظِيمُ ۝

---

[a] The most heinous crime of the people who build their lives on the basis of self-oriented behaviour came to light in the form of the Dhirar Mosque in Madinah. At that time there were already two mosques in Madinah, the Mosque of the Prophet or al-Masjid an-Nabawi, which was inside the town, and the Quba' Mosque, which was in the suburbs.

The hypocrites constructed a third mosque to divert people's attention. Although acts of this kind are apparently performed in the name of religion, in reality, their aim is to maintain the hypocrites' leadership by supporting their opposition to the call of Truth. Those who are unable to accede to the call of truth on account of their self-centredness, try to create a front against it, so that they may indulge in destructive activities. This divides Muslims in two groups. These negative acts, carried out in the name of religion, go to the extent of bringing recognized personalities on to their stage in order to gain credibility among the people.

In their blind enmity, these people forget that opposition to the Truth amounts, in fact, to opposition to God. This can never succeed in God's world. The only fate ordained for them is their meeting with death in despair and frustration and being deprived of God's Grace forever. ▶

¹¹² [The believers are] those who turn to God in repentance; who worship and praise Him; who go about in the land serving His cause, who bow down, who prostrate themselves, who enjoin good and forbid evil, and who observe the limits set by God. Give good news to the believers! ^a

ٱلتَّـٰٓئِبُونَ ٱلۡعَـٰبِدُونَ ٱلۡحَـٰمِدُونَ السَّـٰٓئِحُونَ ٱلرَّٰكِعُونَ ٱلسَّـٰجِدُونَ ٱلۡءَامِرُونَ بِٱلۡمَعۡرُوفِ وَٱلنَّاهُونَ عَنِ ٱلۡمُنكَرِ وَٱلۡحَـٰفِظُونَ لِحُدُودِ ٱللَّهِ وَبَشِّرِ ٱلۡمُؤۡمِنِينَ ۝

Becoming a true believer in God entails the 'selling' of oneself to God. One gives one's life and property to God so that He may grant one eternal paradise in return. This is what is meant by surrendering oneself totally to God. A real attachment to anything is always at the level of complete surrender. It is this degree of commitment that is required with regard to God. None can receive the eternal bounties of paradise without complete surrender.

When an individual adopts God's religion in this spirit, it does not remain separate from his life. Rather it becomes a matter of his personal concern. It forms the centre of his interests, concern and apprehensions. If the cause of religion demands his property, he is willing to offer it. If he is required to devote his time and his talents to it, he is willing to do so.

^a Those who unconditionally surrender to God develop the qualities mentioned in the above verse. Their sensitivity is awakened to such an extent that they are able to pinpoint their mistakes in no time and admit them immediately. They are obeisance personified in the eyes of God. They are so engrossed in thoughts of God's Majesty that this begins to find expression spontaneously, springing from the innermost recesses of their hearts. They become spiritual travellers, that is, they go from the human world to the divine world of nature which is a source of peace and tranquillity

What true believers love most is bowing down to God. They try to lead anyone they come in contact with towards the path of righteousness. When they find anyone taking to evil ways, they do their utmost to stop him from doing so. They become extremely vigilant in observing the limits set by God. They are like the gardener who is extra careful about his garden or his orchard. These are the people to whom God sends His glad tidings of eternal divine reward in the form of paradise.

God's paradise is far more precious than any other precious thing. But God's paradise is like a pledge: it is not like an immediate cash reward. It is due to the delayed fulfillment of this pledge, (that is, it comes after death and not in this world) that people set paradise aside and rush towards petty, ephemeral benefits.

¹¹³It is not proper for the Prophet and those who believe to seek forgiveness for polytheists, even though they are close relatives, after it has become clear to them that they have earned the punishment of Hell. ¹¹⁴Abraham's asking forgiveness for his father was only because of a promise he had made to him, but when it became clear to him, that he was God's enemy, he disassociated himself from him. Surely, Abraham was most tender-hearted and forbearing. ¹¹⁵God would never lead a people astray after He has guided them and until He has made clear to them what they should guard against. God has knowledge of all things; ¹¹⁶surely to God belongs the kingdom of the heavens and of the earth. He gives life and death. You have none besides God to protect or help you.^a

مَا كَانَ لِلنَّبِيِّ وَالَّذِينَ ءَامَنُوٓاْ أَن يَسْتَغْفِرُواْ لِلْمُشْرِكِينَ وَلَوْ كَانُوٓاْ أُوْلِى قُرْبَىٰ مِنۢ بَعْدِ مَا تَبَيَّنَ لَهُمْ أَنَّهُمْ أَصْحَـٰبُ ٱلْجَحِيمِ ۝ وَمَا كَانَ ٱسْتِغْفَارُ إِبْرَٰهِيمَ لِأَبِيهِ إِلَّا عَن مَّوْعِدَةٍ وَعَدَهَآ إِيَّاهُ فَلَمَّا تَبَيَّنَ لَهُۥٓ أَنَّهُۥ عَدُوٌّ لِّلَّهِ تَبَرَّأَ مِنْهُ إِنَّ إِبْرَٰهِيمَ لَأَوَّٰهٌ حَلِيمٌ ۝ وَمَا كَانَ ٱللَّهُ لِيُضِلَّ قَوْمًۢا بَعْدَ إِذْ هَدَىٰهُمْ حَتَّىٰ يُبَيِّنَ لَهُم مَّا يَتَّقُونَ إِنَّ ٱللَّهَ بِكُلِّ شَيْءٍ عَلِيمٌ ۝ إِنَّ ٱللَّهَ لَهُۥ مُلْكُ ٱلسَّمَـٰوَٰتِ وَٱلْأَرْضِ يُحْىِۦ وَيُمِيتُ وَمَا لَكُم مِّن دُونِ ٱللَّهِ مِن وَلِىٍّ وَلَا نَصِيرٍ ۝

^a Abraham, being a very compassionate person, was greatly concerned about the salvation of humanity. Swayed by these sentiments, he had made a pledge to pray to God for his pagan father. But, when he was made aware of God's will, he desisted. God has instilled in every human being a natural instinct for discerning evil. When an individual receives a message which is intended to stop him from committing an evil deed, his whole inner being testifies to its truth. A silent check is produced in his heart. For 'God would never lead a people astray after He has guided them.' But if the man ignores this impulse arising from within, and does not save himself, in spite of the hint given him by nature, his natural sensitivity gradually goes on weakening, till a time comes when it dies altogether. This danger threatens Muslims as well as non-Muslims.

¹¹⁷ God turned in mercy to the Prophet, and the emigrants and the helpers who followed him in the hour of hardship. After the hearts of a group of them had almost faltered, He turned towards them, for He was compassionate and merciful towards them.^a

لَّقَد تَّابَ ٱللَّهُ عَلَى ٱلنَّبِيِّ وَٱلْمُهَٰجِرِينَ وَٱلْأَنصَارِ ٱلَّذِينَ ٱتَّبَعُوهُ فِى سَاعَةِ ٱلْعُسْرَةِ مِنۢ بَعْدِ مَا كَادَ يَزِيغُ قُلُوبُ فَرِيقٍ مِّنْهُمْ ثُمَّ تَابَ عَلَيْهِمْ إِنَّهُۥ بِهِمْ رَءُوفٌ رَّحِيمٌ

---

^a On the occasion of the battle of Tabuk, there was a group which surrendered its best asset to Islam: their crops. It was harvest time, but they left everything behind and set out on a journey which involved a march of three hundred miles in intense heat in order to face the most powerful empire of the time. The shortage of mounts, equipment and goods was so acute that several men had to take turns on each camel, and for food they had often to rest content with one date per person. However, they were only being tested for their resolve and dedication to the cause of God. After God had seen their mettle, He caused the enemy to fall a prey to terror. They retreated from the battlefield without any confrontation and the Muslims returned victorious without having shed any blood. There was another group which consisted of the confessors (9:102). These people could not set out on this journey due to their engagement in worldly activities. However, they very soon realised that they had made a serious mistake, to which they unreservedly confessed. They were truly ashamed of their misdeed and sincerely repented of it. The flood of tears flowing from their eyes compensated for their shortcomings. God enveloped them in His mercy, because they had admitted their mistake in all sincerity.

¹¹⁸ He has turned with mercy to the three whose case was deferred, when the earth, for all its spaciousness, closed in upon them, and their own souls seemed straitened to them and they realised that there was no refuge from God except in Him. He turned to them so that they might turn to Him. God is the Ever Forgiving, the Most Merciful.^a

وَعَلَى ٱلثَّلَٰثَةِ ٱلَّذِينَ خُلِّفُوا۟ حَتَّىٰٓ إِذَا ضَاقَتْ عَلَيْهِمُ ٱلْأَرْضُ بِمَا رَحُبَتْ وَضَاقَتْ عَلَيْهِمْ أَنفُسُهُمْ وَظَنُّوٓا۟ أَن لَّا مَلْجَأَ مِنَ ٱللَّهِ إِلَّآ إِلَيْهِ ثُمَّ تَابَ عَلَيْهِمْ لِيَتُوبُوٓا۟ إِنَّ ٱللَّهَ هُوَ ٱلتَّوَّابُ ٱلرَّحِيمُ

^a A third group consisted of those who were left behind. These were three youths, Ka'b ibn Malik, Mararah ibn Rubay and Hilal ibn Umayyah. Though they regarded their inability to proceed on this journey as a shortcoming, their feelings of repentance and turning towards God had not been as intense as was required in this first stage. That is why they were punished by a social boycott. Now even with this boycott these three had a number of options. They could have remained happy and contented; they could have remained engrossed in their homes and gardens; they could have become rebellious; they could have formed their own separate group in collaboration with disgruntled elements, thus forming an island, a happy world cut off from the general body of Muslims. But they refrained from doing so. The thought of having earned the displeasure of God and His Prophet disturbed their minds so greatly that they failed to find a moment's peace. For them this was an option, not a compulsion. For they could have escaped by rebelling against this boycott and joining any other group. But their response being positive, they naturally turned to God for forgiveness. They repented and prayed to God. Their hearts were truly softened. After a period of 50 days of prayer God showed them His mercy and they were pardoned.

[119] Believers, fear God and stand with the truthful. [120] It was not proper for the people of Madinah and those desert Arabs around them to hold back from following God's Messenger, and to prefer their own lives to his life. This is because whenever they suffer from thirst or weariness or hunger for God's cause, and whenever they take any step which provokes those who deny the truth, or inflicts any loss upon the enemy, it shall be counted as a good deed in the sight of God—God will not deny the righteous their reward— [121] and whenever they spend anything [for the sake of God], be it little or much, and whenever they traverse the land [in God's cause]— it is recorded to their credit, and God will grant them the best reward for all that they have been doing.[a]

يَـٰٓأَيُّهَا ٱلَّذِينَ ءَامَنُوا۟ ٱتَّقُوا۟ ٱللَّهَ وَكُونُوا۟ مَعَ ٱلصَّـٰدِقِينَ ۝ مَا كَانَ لِأَهْلِ ٱلْمَدِينَةِ وَمَنْ حَوْلَهُم مِّنَ ٱلْأَعْرَابِ أَن يَتَخَلَّفُوا۟ عَن رَّسُولِ ٱللَّهِ وَلَا يَرْغَبُوا۟ بِأَنفُسِهِمْ عَن نَّفْسِهِۦ ذَٰلِكَ بِأَنَّهُمْ لَا يُصِيبُهُمْ ظَمَأٌ وَلَا نَصَبٌ وَلَا مَخْمَصَةٌ فِى سَبِيلِ ٱللَّهِ وَلَا يَطَـُٔونَ مَوْطِئًا يَغِيظُ ٱلْكُفَّارَ وَلَا يَنَالُونَ مِنْ عَدُوٍّ نَّيْلًا إِلَّا كُتِبَ لَهُم بِهِۦ عَمَلٌ صَـٰلِحٌ إِنَّ ٱللَّهَ لَا يُضِيعُ أَجْرَ ٱلْمُحْسِنِينَ ۝ وَلَا يُنفِقُونَ نَفَقَةً صَغِيرَةً وَلَا كَبِيرَةً وَلَا يَقْطَعُونَ وَادِيًا إِلَّا كُتِبَ لَهُمْ لِيَجْزِيَهُمُ ٱللَّهُ أَحْسَنَ مَا كَانُوا۟ يَعْمَلُونَ ۝

---

[a] Our life is social in nature. That is why everyone, according to his tastes and aptitudes, forms a circle of his own in which to spend his days and nights. It is necessary for those who fear God and want to tread the path of faith to befriend those who are sincere, truthful, and God-fearing, and who are consistent in their words and deeds. By keeping company with such people, one is transformed into a truthful person too. On the contrary, if one seeks the company of insincere, hypocritical persons, one will necessarily come under their influence. There are times when Islam has to be served by risking one's life; there are times when Islam has to be served at the cost of suffering the pangs of hunger and thirst; there are times when one is exhausted struggling for the cause of God; there are times when one has to serve God and His prophet by sacrificing one's peace of mind. On such occasions one feels like opting for the safer course and hesitates to go ahead and answer the call of one's faith. One is oblivious of the fact that those were the very opportunities to give practical proof of one's attachment to God, when by doing so, one could have expected to be found worthy of paradise.

¹²² It is not right that all the believers should go out [in time of war] all together. Why, then, does not a party from every group come to [the Prophet] in order to acquire a deeper knowledge of religion and to warn their people, so that they can guard themselves against evil? ^a

وَمَا كَانَ ٱلْمُؤْمِنُونَ لِيَنفِرُواْ كَآفَّةً فَلَوْلَا نَفَرَ مِن كُلِّ فِرْقَةٍ مِّنْهُمْ طَآئِفَةٌ لِّيَتَفَقَّهُواْ فِى ٱلدِّينِ وَلِيُنذِرُواْ قَوْمَهُمْ إِذَا رَجَعُوٓاْ إِلَيْهِمْ لَعَلَّهُمْ يَحْذَرُونَ ۞

^a In this verse, a deeper knowledge of Islam *(li yatafaqqahu fi'ddin),* does imply education in the traditional sense, which would mean acquiring a detailed knowledge of the form of religion, that is the ritual part, because then the study of religion becomes synonymous with the study of problems relating to the formal aspects of religion.

Understanding *(tafaqquh)* in religion implies deep knowledge of the fundamentals of religion, a knowledge which makes one enlightened, which makes one fully aware of the eternal teachings of religion and helps one to build one's life on the concept of the Hereafter.

This verse tells us that the aim of developing an understanding in religion is to acquire the ability to deliver the divine message to the people. The word 'warn' *(inzar)* used here means to make people aware of the consequences in the Hereafter of their actions.

This shows that Islamic education should prepare individuals for the role of preachers *(da'is),* so that their addressees may fear God and make Him their sole concern in their present lives. Islamic learning is basically to prepare messengers to convey the word of God to others and is not merely the study of the problems of jurisprudence or of Islamic laws as is commonly understood.

From this point of view, Islamic education should come under two headings:

1. The Quran and the traditions of the Prophet.

2. Such studies as are necessary from the point of view of the addressee—who is the target of the Divine Call, for instance, the language of the addressee, and his mindset.

¹²³ Believers! Fight against those deniers of the truth who are near you. Deal firmly with them. Know that God is with those who fear Him. ¹²⁴ Whenever a chapter is sent down, there are some of them who say, 'Which of you has had his faith increased by it?' But, as for those who believe, it increases their faith and they rejoice, ¹²⁵ but as for those with sickness in their hearts, it adds defilement to their defilement and they die in a state of denial of truth. ¹²⁶ Do they not see that they are tried every year once or twice? Yet they do not repent, nor would they be admonished. ¹²⁷ Whenever a chapter is revealed, they glance at each other, asking, 'Is anyone watching?' Then they turn away. God has turned their hearts away, because they are people who do not understand.^a

يَٰٓأَيُّهَا ٱلَّذِينَ ءَامَنُواْ قَٰتِلُواْ ٱلَّذِينَ يَلُونَكُم مِّنَ ٱلْكُفَّارِ وَلْيَجِدُواْ فِيكُمْ غِلْظَةً ۚ وَٱعْلَمُوٓاْ أَنَّ ٱللَّهَ مَعَ ٱلْمُتَّقِينَ ۝ وَإِذَا مَآ أُنزِلَتْ سُورَةٌ فَمِنْهُم مَّن يَقُولُ أَيُّكُمْ زَادَتْهُ هَٰذِهِۦٓ إِيمَٰنًا ۚ فَأَمَّا ٱلَّذِينَ ءَامَنُواْ فَزَادَتْهُمْ إِيمَٰنًا وَهُمْ يَسْتَبْشِرُونَ ۝ وَأَمَّا ٱلَّذِينَ فِى قُلُوبِهِم مَّرَضٌ فَزَادَتْهُمْ رِجْسًا إِلَىٰ رِجْسِهِمْ وَمَاتُواْ وَهُمْ كَٰفِرُونَ ۝ أَوَلَا يَرَوْنَ أَنَّهُمْ يُفْتَنُونَ فِى كُلِّ عَامٍ مَّرَّةً أَوْ مَرَّتَيْنِ ثُمَّ لَا يَتُوبُونَ وَلَا هُمْ يَذَّكَّرُونَ ۝ وَإِذَا مَآ أُنزِلَتْ سُورَةٌ نَّظَرَ بَعْضُهُمْ إِلَىٰ بَعْضٍ هَلْ يَرَىٰكُم مِّنْ أَحَدٍ ثُمَّ ٱنصَرَفُواْ ۚ صَرَفَ ٱللَّهُ قُلُوبَهُم بِأَنَّهُمْ قَوْمٌ لَّا يَفْقَهُونَ ۝

---

^a 'Fight against those deniers of the truth who are near you.' These words indicate that the Islamic struggle is not an unplanned effort, but that order has to be kept in view in it. First, efforts would be made to overcome nearby obstacles and thereafter distant impediments would be tackled. From this, it is deduced that the very first struggle should be undertaken with a man's own 'self', because the thing nearest to a man is his 'self'; anything outside this focus would come later. Then, again, the foremost thing required in relation to the aggressors is firmness of a kind to instill a deterrent fear in the them: 'If this happens it will create fear in their hearts.' (*Tafsir Jasas*).

Moreover, it is necessary that all action against aggressors should be carried out in fear of God (*taqwa*). It is only such action which guarantees God's help to believers. The moment they lose their fear of God, they will be deprived of God's help; they will be far away from God and God will be far away from them.

Fear of God is a meeting point between God and His subject. When a man fears God, he brings himself to the point where God wants to see him; to which God had called him. Under these circumstances, it is only such fear which can take a man closer to God.

¹²⁸ There has come to you a Messenger of your own. Your suffering distresses him: he is deeply concerned for your welfare and full of kindness and mercy towards the believers. ¹²⁹ But if they turn away, say, 'God suffices me: there is no deity but He: in Him I have put my trust. He is the Lord of the Glorious Throne.'^a

لَقَدْ جَآءَكُمْ رَسُولٌ مِّنْ أَنفُسِكُمْ عَزِيزٌ عَلَيْهِ مَا عَنِتُّمْ حَرِيصٌ عَلَيْكُم بِٱلْمُؤْمِنِينَ رَءُوفٌ رَّحِيمٌ ۝ فَإِن تَوَلَّوْا۟ فَقُلْ حَسْبِيَ ٱللَّهُ لَآ إِلَٰهَ إِلَّا هُوَ عَلَيْهِ تَوَكَّلْتُ وَهُوَ رَبُّ ٱلْعَرْشِ ٱلْعَظِيمِ ۝

---

^a The Quran tells us that God's messenger is extremely kind and affectionate towards people. He is so perturbed by others' suffering that it is as if he himself were affected by it. He is extremely anxious to give guidance to others. What moves him to convey the message of truth to the people is nothing but his great desire for their welfare—far from his having any personal ambition or there being any national problem.

According to a tradition narrated by 'Abdullah ibn Mas'ud, the Prophet Muhammad said, 'People are falling into the fire like flies and I am trying to keep them away from it by holding on to their waists.' (Musnad Ahmad).

In this depiction of the Prophet, we can see the mental and moral makeup of the eternal preacher of truth. He should have two prominent features. Firstly, his reliance should be solely on the one and only God. Secondly, he should have in his heart feelings only of love and well-wishing for the addressee. There might be many grievances against the addressee, there might be national or communal or material quarrels between the preacher (da'i) and the addressee (mad'u), yet, in spite of this, the preacher must ignore all points of conflict and must not allow any feelings to be aroused in him other than those of affection and kindness.

The preacher should rise above the psychology of reaction. He should unilaterally become the well-wisher of his congregation, regardless of any objectionable behaviour on their part and call them to the Truth.

10. JONAH

In the name of God,
the Most Gracious, the Most Merciful

[1] *Alif Lam Ra*

These are the verses of the Book of Wisdom. [2] Does it seem strange to people that We have sent revelation to a man from among themselves, saying, 'Warn mankind and give glad tidings to the believers that they have a true rank [of honour] with their Lord?' Those who deny the truth say, 'This man is clearly a sorcerer.'[a]

الر تِلْكَ ءَايَتُ ٱلْكِتَبِ ٱلْحَكِيمِ ۝ أَكَانَ لِلنَّاسِ عَجَبًا أَنْ أَوْحَيْنَا إِلَىٰ رَجُلٍ مِّنْهُمْ أَنْ أَنذِرِ ٱلنَّاسَ وَبَشِّرِ ٱلَّذِينَ ءَامَنُوٓا أَنَّ لَهُمْ قَدَمَ صِدْقٍ عِندَ رَبِّهِمْ قَالَ ٱلْكَفِرُونَ إِنَّ هَذَا لَسَحِرٌ مُّبِينٌ ۝

---

[a] A prophet's call is always based on sound and strong reasoning. Thanks to his extraordinary manner of expression, he is himself proof of his speaking on behalf of God. In spite of this, people of every period have rejected the prophets. The reason for this is man's passion for external appearances. In the eyes of his contemporaries, a prophet is an ordinary man like other ordinary men. The glories of history, which later on become attached to his name, have not yet gathered around him. So, his contemporaries overlook him, considering him to be an ordinary man. They are unable either to look at the prophet as one deputed by God or to appreciate him in view of the history that is going to take shape in future. Yet the fact remains that everyone will be compelled to realise his prophetic greatness in due course.

A prophet's call is entirely miraculous and leaves its hearers bereft of any argument. It is quite spell-binding. Finding themselves helpless in the field of arguments, the prophet's hearers start maligning his message. In this way they cast doubts upon the veracity of his words. Thinking like simpletons, they scorn the call as nothing but makebelieve. They call it verbal witchcraft and as such of no consequence.

The real mission of a prophet is warning others (*inzar*) and giving good news (*tabshir*). That is, warning people of God's retribution and giving good news of Paradise to those who are ready to live in the world in fear of God. The prophet appears in the world in order to make people aware of the fact that man is not free and all-powerful in this world and that the story of his life is not going to end with his death. Indeed, there is eternal life after death and man should take the utmost care to prepare for this. One who is unmindful of this or adopts an attitude of insolence, will reach the world after death in such a condition that nothing will await him there except agony and misery. ▶

³ Truly, your Lord is God who created the heavens and the earth in six days [periods], then He ascended the Throne, disposing the whole affair. No one may intercede with Him save with His permission. Such is God, your Lord, so worship Him alone. Will you not take heed? ⁴ To Him you shall all return. God's promise is true; He originates Creation, then He restores it, so that He may reward with justice those who believe and do good works. Those who have denied the truth shall have boiling water to drink, and a painful punishment, because of their denial.ᵃ

إِنَّ رَبَّكُمُ ٱللَّهُ ٱلَّذِى خَلَقَ ٱلسَّمَٰوَٰتِ وَٱلْأَرْضَ فِى سِتَّةِ أَيَّامٍ ثُمَّ ٱسْتَوَىٰ عَلَى ٱلْعَرْشِ يُدَبِّرُ ٱلْأَمْرَ مَا مِن شَفِيعٍ إِلَّا مِنۢ بَعْدِ إِذْنِهِۦ ذَٰلِكُمُ ٱللَّهُ رَبُّكُمْ فَٱعْبُدُوهُ أَفَلَا تَذَكَّرُونَ ۝ إِلَيْهِ مَرْجِعُكُمْ جَمِيعًا وَعْدَ ٱللَّهِ حَقًّا إِنَّهُۥ يَبْدَؤُا۟ ٱلْخَلْقَ ثُمَّ يُعِيدُهُۥ لِيَجْزِىَ ٱلَّذِينَ ءَامَنُوا۟ وَعَمِلُوا۟ ٱلصَّٰلِحَٰتِ بِٱلْقِسْطِ وَٱلَّذِينَ كَفَرُوا۟ لَهُمْ شَرَابٌ مِّنْ حَمِيمٍ وَعَذَابٌ أَلِيمٌۢ بِمَا كَانُوا۟ يَكْفُرُونَ ۝

One for whom outward appearance is all-important thinks that honour and glory attach to those who are in possession of worldly power, who are the possessors of worldly wealth. The Prophet says that this is deceptive; that such honour and glory exist only amongst fellow-human beings in this ephemeral worldly life. Real honour and glory are to be achieved in the eternal life in the presence of God; only such honour and glory are both real and eternal.

ᵃ Studies indicate that the appearance of the many different kinds of natural phenomena in the universe did not occur at one time, but gradually over a period. The Quran divides this phase—the divine creation into six periods. This proves that the creation of the universe was done according to a conscious plan. Then, the study of the universe shows that it is running according to hard and fast laws. Everything behaves in exactly the manner in which it is required to behave, in consideration of overall requirements. This is clear proof of the fact that this universe is made to function by an Active and Alive Planner who directly controls it at all times. This wonderfully regulated system of the universe itself makes the powerful statement that its Lord is so Perfect and so Great that there is no question of any recommendation being useful to Him. The universe reflects the image of its Creator in the mirror of its amazing characteristics.

The system of justice (qist) prevails throughout the universe. Here, whatever one does, one is confronted with commensurate results; everyone is rewarded according to whatever he has done. This is true of material results; but in the matter of moral outcome, the picture of the world seems to be entirely different. A man performs righteous deeds, but he does not receive the fruits of his righteousness. ▶

⁵ It is He who made the sun radiate a brilliant light and the moon shed its lustre, and ordained for it stages so that you may learn to count out the years and [to make other such] reckoning of time. God has not created all these without a purpose. He makes plain His revelations to men of understanding.ᵃ

هُوَ ٱلَّذِى جَعَلَ ٱلشَّمْسَ ضِيَآءً وَٱلْقَمَرَ نُورًا وَقَدَّرَهُۥ مَنَازِلَ لِتَعْلَمُوا۟ عَدَدَ ٱلسِّنِينَ وَٱلْحِسَابَ مَا خَلَقَ ٱللَّهُ ذَٰلِكَ إِلَّا بِٱلْحَقِّ يُفَصِّلُ ٱلْءَايَٰتِ لِقَوْمٍ يَعْلَمُونَ ۝

A man indulges in arrogance, and his arrogance goes on unpunished. Why is it that God's will, which is operative in the case of His other creatures, does not seem to be operative in the case of human beings?

The reason for this is that the manifestation of godly justice in the life of human beings has been deferred by God till the life Hereafter. The first life has been given to man for the performance of deeds. The second life will be given to him so that he may be requited for his deeds; and the possibility of the occurrence of the second life (the life of the hereafter) is as certain as that of the first life.

ᵃ The sun is at the most appropriate distance from our earth. That is why it has been a treasure-like source of light and heat for us. If a difference were to occur in this alignment, the sun would not be the sun for us: it would become the fire of hell. Instead of being the messenger of life, it would be the messenger of death. The moon rotates in its orbit in a precise, mathematical way. In spite of its being devoid of its own light, it not only gives us cool light, reflected from the sun, but also provides us with a natural calender of months and days. These astronomical signs prove that there is strong purposefulness in the universe, and the fate of the purposeful universe cannot be purposeless.

Then, the appearance of day after night indicates, in the language of symbolism, the moral fact that, according to the law prevailing in this world of ours, light should prevail after the reign of darkness; the brightness of light should follow upon darkness. Where, before, human rights had been trampled upon, there will now ensue a sytem whereby rights will be honoured. Divine justice will dominate in place of human arrogance. Such a time is destined to come, when the prevalence of evil will come to an end and the recognition of truth will prevail everywhere.

⁶ In the alternation of night and day, and in all that God has created in the heavens and the earth, there are signs for a God-fearing people.^a ⁷ Those who entertain no hope of meeting Us, being pleased and contented with the life of this world, and those who give no heed to Our signs, ⁸ shall have their abode in the Fire in requital for their deeds.^b

إِنَّ فِى ٱخْتِلَٰفِ ٱلَّيْلِ وَٱلنَّهَارِ وَمَا خَلَقَ ٱللَّهُ فِى ٱلسَّمَٰوَٰتِ وَٱلْأَرْضِ لَءَايَٰتٍ لِّقَوْمٍ يَتَّقُونَ ۝ إِنَّ ٱلَّذِينَ لَا يَرْجُونَ لِقَآءَنَا وَرَضُوا۟ بِٱلْحَيَوٰةِ ٱلدُّنْيَا وَٱطْمَأَنُّوا۟ بِهَا وَٱلَّذِينَ هُمْ عَنْ ءَايَٰتِنَا غَٰفِلُونَ ۝ أُو۟لَٰٓئِكَ مَأْوَىٰهُمُ ٱلنَّارُ بِمَا كَانُوا۟ يَكْسِبُونَ ۝

---

^a God has revealed the realities of the Hereafter by means of symbols. Similarly, in the present world, God reveals Himself in the form of arguments, and not as a tangible manifestation. So, we can find God only in the manner and shape in which He reveals Himself and not in any other form.

In this world, God has offered mankind His guidance. But only those who are ready to follow it according to the godly plan, are destined to receive this guidance. Only those who are ready to understand the truth presented in the language of reason and accept it will be inspired to tread the right path. Those who do not bow down before true argument fail to bow down, as it were, before God; it is like not accepting God. Such people may expect nothing but Hell as their reward.

In the heavens and on the earth, there are countless signs which become the elements of a lesson for those who are God-fearing. Fear, or apprehension, is a thing which makes a man serious. Unless a man is serious, he will not pay full attention to matters of importance and will not understand their various aspects.

The whole universe is held together in a creative balance. This is a clear indication of the fact that the Lord of the universe is One who has absolute power over man. Similarly, the initial life which we are now experiencing provides clear proof of the fact that a second life is also possible. The appearance of material results in the present world and the non-appearance of moral results warrants the taking shape of another world where the moral results will be clearly in evidence. This is an unassailable truth, but this can be grasped only by one who looks at life in fear and apprehension.

^b For whom is hell meant? It is for those who have forgotten that they will have to face God; those who have contented themselves with the temporary amenities of this world as opposed to the eternal bounties of the Hereafter; those who are satisfied with the things that purely as a matter of trial they have received in this world; those who attach themselves to ungodly things to such an extent that they become completely unmindful of the realities revealed by God. All this amounts to treading the path of hell in the eyes of God, and those who adopt the way of hell will not arrive anywhere except in hell.

⁹ Those who believe and do good deeds will be guided by their Lord because of their faith. Rivers shall flow at their feet in the Gardens of Bliss. ¹⁰ In that [state of happiness] they will call out; 'Glory be to You, O God!', while their greeting in it will be: 'Peace!' And the close of their call will be, 'All praise is due to God, the Lord of the Universe!'ᵃ

إِنَّ ٱلَّذِينَ ءَامَنُواْ وَعَمِلُواْ ٱلصَّٰلِحَٰتِ يَهْدِيهِمْ رَبُّهُم بِإِيمَٰنِهِمْ تَجْرِى مِن تَحْتِهِمُ ٱلْأَنْهَٰرُ فِى جَنَّٰتِ ٱلنَّعِيمِ ۝ دَعْوَىٰهُمْ فِيهَا سُبْحَٰنَكَ ٱللَّهُمَّ وَتَحِيَّتُهُمْ فِيهَا سَلَٰمٌ وَءَاخِرُ دَعْوَىٰهُمْ أَنِ ٱلْحَمْدُ لِلَّهِ رَبِّ ٱلْعَٰلَمِينَ ۝

ᵃ Literally, 'On account of their faith, God will lead them towards the goal of Paradise.' This shows that Faith is guidance for man; it prevents him from taking wrong paths and makes him tread the right way until it leads him to the real goal.

Faith is discovery of God. The thread of knowledge comes within the grasp of one who is blessed with faith. He becomes capable of starting his thinking from the right place on all matters. Never allowing his thoughts to err, he attains correctness in his thinking. Furthermore, belief in God is not simply acceptance of a bookish philosophy; it is belief in God Who is alive and Who is going to finally assemble all human beings before Him to take a final reckoning. In this way, Faith inculcates in man a sense of anxiety or apprehension about his future fate and this makes him extremely serious. He is forced to look at all his actions in the light of their being right or wrong, so that he may adopt only the right direction. In this way, Faith provides man with the right way of thinking as well as the power to distinguish between right and wrong, which acts as his permanent practical guide.

The Paradise of the Hereafter is for those who have, in this world, proved themselves to be deserving of it. The Hereafter is a place where one will directly experience and become directly immersed in the glories of God. So, the opportunity to live in Paradise will be given only to those who, in this world, had immersed themselves in the indirect manifestations of the glories of God. In the Hereafter, human hearts will be full of well-wishing and peace-desiring for each other. So, only those who, in this world had proved that in their hearts they had only such feelings for others, will find their abode in Paradise.

¹¹ Had God hastened the punishment of men as He hastens the good, the end of their term of life would already have been reached. We leave those who do not hope to meet Us groping along in their arrogance.ᵃ

وَلَوْ يُعَجِّلُ ٱللَّهُ لِلنَّاسِ ٱلشَّرَّ ٱسْتِعْجَالَهُم بِٱلْخَيْرِ لَقُضِىَ إِلَيْهِمْ أَجَلُهُمْ ۖ فَنَذَرُ ٱلَّذِينَ لَا يَرْجُونَ لِقَآءَنَا فِى طُغْيَٰنِهِمْ يَعْمَهُونَ ۝

ᵃ It is the law of God that when an individual performs a praiseworthy deed, it is immediately included in the record of his deeds. But if he commits an act which warrants punishment, God gives him respite so that better counsel should prevail, and he may at some point reform himself. This law of God is a great mercy to human beings; otherwise man is a great transgressor and is always ready to perform evil deeds, and if people were immediately seized upon for their evil deeds, their lives would very soon come to an end and the face of the earth would become devoid of human existence.

Those who lead their lives as if they are not required to face God after death, live with arrogance in this world. They are those who lead their lives free of the fear of God's scourge, thinking that they are at liberty to practice as much deceit and spread as much chaos as they like. The fact is that man should realise that there is one Power over and above all powerful ones—every man is helpless before Him— He will one day seize upon all human beings and everybody will be compelled to accept His verdict.

¹² Whenever any trouble befalls a person, he prays to Us all the time, lying on his side, sitting or standing; but when We remove his trouble, he goes on his way as if he had never prayed to Us for the removal of his trouble. Thus it is that the doings of the transgressors are made to look fair to them.ᵃ

وَإِذَا مَسَّ ٱلْإِنسَٰنَ ٱلضُّرُّ دَعَانَا لِجَنۢبِهِۦ أَوْ قَاعِدًا أَوْ قَآئِمًا فَلَمَّا كَشَفْنَا عَنْهُ ضُرَّهُۥ مَرَّ كَأَن لَّمْ يَدْعُنَآ إِلَىٰ ضُرٍّ مَّسَّهُۥ كَذَٰلِكَ زُيِّنَ لِلْمُسْرِفِينَ مَا كَانُوا۟ يَعْمَلُونَ ۝

ᵃ The system of this world is so designed that from time to time man is hit by some calamity or accident. He begins to realise that he is absolutely helpless against external forces. At that time he spontaneously starts calling upon God; he admits his humbleness compared to God's Power. But, he is humble only so long as he is in trouble.

The moment he gets relief from trouble, he becomes as negligent and arrogant as he was earlier. God does not accept the obeisance of such people, because only that obeisance is acceptable which is offered in a free atmosphere. Obeisance offered under the pressure of compelling circumstances has no value in the eyes of God.

Man is a creature who likes justification. He seeks justification for every action of his. If a man chooses to be arrogant, his mentality will be inclined towards that. He will, in practice indulge in arrogance, and his mind will provide him with beautiful words in order to prove his arrogance justified. This is known as *taz'in*. Man expresses his misdeeds in beautiful words and is satisfied that he is in the right. But, this is like a man holding a burning lump of coal in his hand and thinking that it will not burn him simply because he calls it a red flower.

¹³ And indeed, before your time We destroyed [whole] generations when they [persistently] did evil; their messengers came to them with clear signs, but they would not believe. Thus We requite the guilty.ᵃ

وَلَقَدْ أَهْلَكْنَا ٱلْقُرُونَ مِن قَبْلِكُمْ لَمَّا ظَلَمُواْ وَجَاءَتْهُمْ رُسُلُهُم بِٱلْبَيِّنَتِ وَمَا كَانُواْ لِيُؤْمِنُواْ كَذَٰلِكَ نَجْزِى ٱلْقَوْمَ ٱلْمُجْرِمِينَ ۝

ᵃ The prophets addressed their communities with clear arguments, (baiyinat), but they did not accept them. This shows that the missionary call—given on behalf of God—rests on the basis of reasoning. People have to recognize the prophet at the level of arguments and reasoning. Those who want to find him basking in outward glories surrounded with huge numbers of supporters will never be able to find him, because he will not be there at all. The prophet does not perform miracles, but engages rather in the process of argument. At the stage of the missionary call, all work is done on this basis. Individuals and groups transgress in not recognizing the Divine call appearing in the form of arguments or reasoning. They reject it, not having found it in accordance with their self-devised standards. Due to this behaviour, such people are punished by the law of God.

The communities of the past which had incurred God's retribution for their rejection of the prophets, were not actually total rejectors of prophethood. All these communities had accepted some prophet or the other of earlier periods, but they rejected the prophet of their own times. In the case of the earlier prophets, the corroborative historical facts had accumulated to back them. They had become objects of national prestige, and public predilections favoured them, while the contemporary prophet was as yet devoid of all such additional attributes. They recognised that past prophet who had as a result of tradition over the generations, become their national prophet, and connecting with him was synonymous with linking themselves with a tower of greatness. They recognised their national prophet as such, and rejected that prophet who could be recognised only through his reasoning and arguments. In the eyes of God, this was such a serious crime that those who were declared to be rejecters of the prophet were destroyed.

¹⁴ Then We made you their successors in the land, so that We might observe how you would conduct yourselves.

¹⁵ When Our clear revelations are recited to them, those who do not expect to meet Us say, 'Bring us a different Quran, or make some changes in it.' Say, 'It is not for me to change it of my own accord. I follow only what is revealed to me. I fear, if I were to disobey my Lord, the punishment on a Dreadful Day.'ᵃ

ثُمَّ جَعَلْنَٰكُمْ خَلَٰئِفَ فِى ٱلْأَرْضِ مِنۢ بَعْدِهِمْ لِنَنظُرَ كَيْفَ تَعْمَلُونَ ۝ وَإِذَا تُتْلَىٰ عَلَيْهِمْ ءَايَاتُنَا بَيِّنَٰتٍ قَالَ ٱلَّذِينَ لَا يَرْجُونَ لِقَآءَنَا ٱئْتِ بِقُرْءَانٍ غَيْرِ هَٰذَآ أَوْ بَدِّلْهُ قُلْ مَا يَكُونُ لِىٓ أَنْ أُبَدِّلَهُۥ مِن تِلْقَآئِ نَفْسِىٓ إِنْ أَتَّبِعُ إِلَّا مَا يُوحَىٰٓ إِلَىَّ إِنِّىٓ أَخَافُ إِنْ عَصَيْتُ رَبِّى عَذَابَ يَوْمٍ عَظِيمٍ ۝

ᵃ 'Then We made you their successors (khala'if, sing. khalifah) in the land.' The real meaning of khalifah is 'one who comes afterwards'. This word 'successor' is specially used for coming into power after another. This succession is in relation to human beings and not in relation to God. In the Quran, wherever the word khilafah has been used, it is in connection with succession to some creature and not in connection with succession to God. Making somebody a successor is solely for the purpose of putting him to the test and is not meant to confer any honour. Making somebody a successor means giving one an opportunity to work after another; it is placing one community in the arena of testing in place of another community. For example, in India, the native Rajas were replaced by Mughals. Then they were removed and the Britishers were made their successors. Later, they (the British) were made to leave the country, making way for the majority community. In all these cases, the 'one coming afterwards' was the successor (khalifah) of the earlier one.

16 Say, 'If God had so wished, I would not have recited it to you, nor would He have brought it to your knowledge. Indeed, I have spent a whole lifetime among you before it came to me. How can you not use your reason?' 17 Who is more unjust than the man who invents a falsehood about God or denies His signs? Surely, the guilty shall never prosper.*a*

قُل لَّوۡ شَآءَ ٱللَّهُ مَا تَلَوۡتُهُۥ عَلَيۡكُمۡ وَلَآ أَدۡرَىٰكُم بِهِۦ ۖ فَقَدۡ لَبِثۡتُ فِيكُمۡ عُمُرًا مِّن قَبۡلِهِۦٓ ۚ أَفَلَا تَعۡقِلُونَ ١٦ فَمَنۡ أَظۡلَمُ مِمَّنِ ٱفۡتَرَىٰ عَلَى ٱللَّهِ كَذِبًا أَوۡ كَذَّبَ بِـَٔايَٰتِهِۦٓ ۚ إِنَّهُۥ لَا يُفۡلِحُ ٱلۡمُجۡرِمُونَ ١٧

---

a The Quraysh of Makkah believed in God and the Prophet. They claimed to be the followers of the cult of Abraham (Ibrahim). So much so that many of the religious terms of Islam, for example, *salat* (prayers), *sawm* (fasting), *zakat* (alms-giving), *hajj* (pilgrimage), etc. are the same as had already been prevalent among them. In spite of this, why did they insist that they would accept the Quran only if it were replaced or amended?

The reason for this was that the Quran enshrined God's pure religion, while the Quraysh had adopted an adulterated variant of it in the name of God's religion.

A blow was dealt to their polytheistic concept of God by the Quranic principle of the oneness of God. In the light of the Quranic concept of prayer and obeisance to God, their prayer appeared to be simply child's play. They had made the prophet the sign of national prestige, while the Quran wanted them to accept and follow a prophet who had to be given the status of a guide in all practical matters. They had taken it for granted that their service to the Ka'bah was the greatest proof of their righteousness, whereas the Quran said that righteousness prevails when a man has the fear of God in his heart and, keeping the Hereafter in view, acts accordingly.

A man mouths pious sounding words but ignores the Truth. The reason for this is that, at heart, he has no scruples. If a man is scrupulous enough to realise that he is answerable to God for all his utterances and deeds, he will immediately become serious, and a person who is serious will look at matters realistically. He cannot ignore moral questions or look at them in a superficial manner.

¹⁸ Instead of God they worship what neither harms nor benefits them, and they say: 'These are our intercessors with God.' Say, 'Do you inform God about something in heavens and on earth that He does not know? Glory be to Him; may He be Exalted over whatever they associate [with Him]!' ^a

وَيَعْبُدُونَ مِن دُونِ ٱللَّهِ مَا لَا يَضُرُّهُمْ وَلَا يَنفَعُهُمْ وَيَقُولُونَ هَٰٓؤُلَآءِ شُفَعَٰٓؤُنَا عِندَ ٱللَّهِ قُلْ أَتُنَبِّئُونَ ٱللَّهَ بِمَا لَا يَعْلَمُ فِى ٱلسَّمَٰوَٰتِ وَلَا فِى ٱلْأَرْضِ سُبْحَٰنَهُۥ وَتَعَٰلَىٰ عَمَّا يُشْرِكُونَ ﴿١٨﴾

---

^a The events that occur in this world of ours seem, outwardly, to be the result of certain material causes, but the reality is that God's control and management have been the underlying factors in all these events. In this world nobody has any personal or intrinsic power at all. A man is a monotheist (believing in the oneness of God) if he goes beyond the outwardly apparent phenomena and reaches the invisible God through them. As opposed to this, he is a polytheist (believing in partners to God) if he can go no further than outwardly apparent phenomena and if he confers on created things the status of their Creator.

In this world nobody except God has the power to grant benefits or to inflict harm. A person who realises this truth devotes all his attention to God. He worships only God; he fears only Him and reposes his hopes in Him alone; he makes the one and only God his all. Unlike him, those who are preoccupied by mere things, make somebody other than God their God, according to their inclinations, and attach to these false gods such hopes and fears as should have been directed towards the one and only God. One form of these wrongful ideas is the belief in 'recommendation.' People suppose that there are some superior beings among human beings and among creatures other than human beings, who are holy in the eyes of God; God hears their recommendation and on the basis of this, He takes a decision about granting worldly provision and salvation in the after-life. But this kind of belief is false; it amounts to an underestimation of God's godliness.

God is free of every kind of *shirk* (imputing partners to God). No such belief befits the image of the qualities of God as is introduced and projected by the immense universe created by Him. Any such belief would mean that God is not what He seems to be in the mirror of His creative attributes, or that there is a contradiction in His attributes. Obviously, neither of these alternatives is possible.

¹⁹ Mankind was only one community, but then they differed, and had it not been for a prior word from your Lord, their differences would have been settled for them.^a

وَمَا كَانَ ٱلنَّاسُ إِلَّا أُمَّةً وَاحِدَةً فَٱخْتَلَفُوا ۚ وَلَوْلَا كَلِمَةٌ سَبَقَتْ مِن رَّبِّكَ لَقُضِيَ بَيْنَهُمْ فِيمَا فِيهِ يَخْتَلِفُونَ ﴿١٩﴾

---

^a God initially grounded human existence in the religion of nature. At that time, the religion of all humanity was one and the same. But, people had their differences and devised different forms of religions. The reason for this is the misuse of the freedom given to the people for the purpose of testing them. If God were to reveal Himself, human arrogance would come to an end on observing His powers, and suddenly unity would replace differences, because extremity of fear demolishes a a multiplicity of opinions. But God will not intervene in this state of affairs before Judgement Day. God had created the present world for the sake of putting human beings to the test, and to maintain the atmosphere of testing, it is necessary to keep the reality concealed, so that people should have the opportunity to use their wisdom in both right and wrong directions.

²⁰ They ask, 'Why has no sign been sent down to him from his Lord?' Tell them, 'God alone has knowledge of the unseen. So wait; I too will wait with you.' ²¹ Whenever We let mankind taste mercy after some adversity has afflicted them, they forthwith turn to devising false arguments against Our signs. Say, 'God is swifter in His devising! Our angels are recording your intrigues.' ᵃ

وَيَقُولُونَ لَوْلَا أُنزِلَ عَلَيْهِ ءَايَةٌ مِّن رَّبِّهِۦ فَقُلْ إِنَّمَا ٱلْغَيْبُ لِلَّهِ فَٱنتَظِرُوٓاْ إِنِّى مَعَكُم مِّنَ ٱلْمُنتَظِرِينَ ۝ وَإِذَآ أَذَقْنَا ٱلنَّاسَ رَحْمَةً مِّنۢ بَعْدِ ضَرَّآءَ مَسَّتْهُمْ إِذَا لَهُم مَّكْرٌ فِىٓ ءَايَاتِنَا قُلِ ٱللَّهُ أَسْرَعُ مَكْرًا إِنَّ رُسُلَنَا يَكْتُبُونَ مَا تَمْكُرُونَ ۝

ᵃ When the people of Makkah persisted in their rejections of the Truth, God caused them to be plagued by a famine which went on for seven years. At last it ended, but only after the the Prophet Muhammad had prayed for this. This was a sign from God from which they should have learned the lesson that on rejecting the Prophet, they would come within the ambit of God's scourge. But their mindset was such that, as long as the famine continued, they kept lamenting and beseeching, but when the famine ended, they started saying, 'These are the vagaries of the times which occur now and then to everybody. This has nothing to do with the acceptance or rejection of the Prophet.'

People make demands for signs or miracles from the Prophet. But the real question is not that of the occurrence of miracles, but that of learning the lesson that a sign is there for observation and not for compulsion. Even after the appearance of a sign, a man has the option of either accepting it or rejecting it.

However, when God's last sign appears, man will have no power against it. This last sign will appear as God's retribution after the conclusive phase of the process of *dawah* and it will appear in different forms for different prophets. In the case of the last of the prophets, the Prophet Muhammad, on the basis of various considerations, this sign took the form of those who deny the truth being overcome and the believers being made to dominate them.

When a man indulges in arrogance and this does not seem to cause any harm to him, he becomes more insolent. He thinks that he is beyond God's grasp, though this is in accordance with God's plan. God gives an arrogant man a long rope so that he may indulge in extremes of arrogance without any fear; and during this period, God's agents, in concealment and silence, go on recording his utterances and deeds, until his time is up and the angel of death suddenly appears and catches hold of him in order to present him before God to be judged by Him.

²² It is God who enables you to travel on land and sea. And when you are sailing on ships and rejoicing in the favourable wind, a storm arrives, and the waves surge upon those on board from every side and they think they are encompassed, then they make a fervent appeal to God, saying in all sincerity, 'If You deliver us from this, we will surely be of the thankful.' *ᵃ*

هُوَ ٱلَّذِى يُسَيِّرُكُمْ فِى ٱلْبَرِّ وَٱلْبَحْرِ حَتَّىٰ إِذَا كُنتُمْ فِى ٱلْفُلْكِ وَجَرَيْنَ بِهِم بِرِيحٍ طَيِّبَةٍ وَفَرِحُوا بِهَا جَاءَتْهَا رِيحٌ عَاصِفٌ وَجَاءَهُمُ ٱلْمَوْجُ مِن كُلِّ مَكَانٍ وَظَنُّوا أَنَّهُمْ أُحِيطَ بِهِمْ دَعَوُا ٱللَّهَ مُخْلِصِينَ لَهُ ٱلدِّينَ لَئِنْ أَنجَيْتَنَا مِنْ هَٰذِهِ لَنَكُونَنَّ مِنَ ٱلشَّٰكِرِينَ ۝

ᵃ Man is an extremely sensitive being. He cannot bear trouble. This is why he immediately becomes serious as soon as he faces a moment of difficulty. At that time, all artificial veils are removed from his mind. In times of adversity a man readily admits truths which he was reluctant to admit at a time when he had no worries.

An example of this is a voyage by sea. When the sea is calm and the boat is sailing towards its destination, it is most pleasant at that moment for its passengers. This develops a false confidence in them. They think that everything is all right and nobody can cause any disturbance.

Thereafter, strong sea-winds arise. High, mountain-like waves surround the boat from every side. In such conditions, even the biggest ship is tossed about like an ordinary plank of wood. To all appearances it seems that there is no alternative but destruction. At this point, those who deny the truth in God admit His existence, worshippers of false gods start calling on the one and only God, while those who rely on their own strength and devices leave aside everything else and also start remembering the one and only God. This is empirical proof based on experience that belief in the unity of God is the only natural belief.

This experience shows that whatever philosophy a man might present for not accepting God, it is simply theorising born of a carefree atmosphere. If a man realises that opportunities have been given to him in the world only for the time being for the purpose of testing him, he will immediately become serious; all the artificial walls erected in his mind will fall down; and he will have no option left but to accept the one and only God.

That time is fast approaching when man will start trembling on witnessing the majesty of God, and he will be compelled to admit the veracity of all godly matters. But, the wise man is one who is able to see in the experiences of his present life the realities of the coming life, and who will, of his own free will, accept today what he will be forced to accept tomorrow: accepting tomorrow under compulsion will be of no avail to him.

[23] But when He has delivered them, they begin, wrongfully to commit excesses in the land. O you men, your excesses only affect your own selves. Have the enjoyment of the present life. Then to Us you shall return; and We will inform you of all that you have done.

فَلَمَّآ أَنجَىٰهُمْ إِذَا هُمْ يَبْغُونَ فِى ٱلْأَرْضِ بِغَيْرِ ٱلْحَقِّ ۗ يَٰٓأَيُّهَا ٱلنَّاسُ إِنَّمَا بَغْيُكُمْ عَلَىٰٓ أَنفُسِكُم ۖ مَّتَٰعَ ٱلْحَيَوٰةِ ٱلدُّنْيَا ۖ ثُمَّ إِلَيْنَا مَرْجِعُكُمْ فَنُنَبِّئُكُم بِمَا كُنتُمْ تَعْمَلُونَ ٢٣

[24] The life of the world is like the water which We send down from the sky, and which is absorbed by the plants of the earth, from which men and cattle eat. But when the earth has taken on its finest appearance, and looks beautiful, and its people think they have it under their control, then by day or by night, Our command comes to it and We convert it into a field of stubble, as if nothing had existed there the day before. Thus We make plain Our revelations for those who reflect.[a]

إِنَّمَا مَثَلُ ٱلْحَيَوٰةِ ٱلدُّنْيَا كَمَآءٍ أَنزَلْنَٰهُ مِنَ ٱلسَّمَآءِ فَٱخْتَلَطَ بِهِۦ نَبَاتُ ٱلْأَرْضِ مِمَّا يَأْكُلُ ٱلنَّاسُ وَٱلْأَنْعَٰمُ حَتَّىٰٓ إِذَآ أَخَذَتِ ٱلْأَرْضُ زُخْرُفَهَا وَٱزَّيَّنَتْ وَظَنَّ أَهْلُهَآ أَنَّهُمْ قَٰدِرُونَ عَلَيْهَآ أَتَىٰهَآ أَمْرُنَا لَيْلًا أَوْ نَهَارًا فَجَعَلْنَٰهَا حَصِيدًا كَأَن لَّمْ تَغْنَ بِٱلْأَمْسِ ۚ كَذَٰلِكَ نُفَصِّلُ ٱلْءَايَٰتِ لِقَوْمٍ يَتَفَكَّرُونَ ٢٤

---

[a] The life of this world is for the purpose of putting man to the test. Therefore, here man has been given complete freedom and all sorts of opportunities. Apparently, a man is free to do whatever he likes and to shape his own future in whatever way he likes. But in the midst of these preoccupations, certain events unfold which teach lessons to thoughtful persons and which indicate the fact that all this is temporary and will very soon be taken away from them. One such example is that of green vegetation on the earth. When there is rain, the earth becomes lush green with different kinds of vegetation. Man is pleased with this; he starts thinking that things are completely under his control and very soon he will be the owner of a rich crop. Exactly at the same time, some calamity suddenly befalls him, for example, a tornado strikes, there is snowfall or there is a plague of locusts and in this way the whole crop is destroyed in a moment.

The same is true of man's life. Man is born with a fine body. The worldly factors are in his favour and he shapes for himself a very successful and glorious life. Now he develops confidence in himself; he thinks that his affairs are under his control. But one day, or one night, he suddenly meets with death. A person who considers himself powerful, suddenly finds himself in a condition of total helplessness and powerlessness. If man keeps this reality in view, he will never be arrogant in this world; he will never be guilty of oppression or injustice.

²⁵ God calls man to the home of peace and He guides whom He wills to a straight path. ²⁶ Those who do good works shall have a good reward and more besides. No darkness and no ignominy shall cover their faces. They are destined for Paradise wherein they shall dwell forever.ᵃ

وَٱللَّهُ يَدْعُوٓا۟ إِلَىٰ دَارِ ٱلسَّلَـٰمِ وَيَهْدِى مَن يَشَآءُ إِلَىٰ صِرَٰطٍ مُّسْتَقِيمٍ ۝

لِّلَّذِينَ أَحْسَنُوا۟ ٱلْحُسْنَىٰ وَزِيَادَةٌ ۖ وَلَا يَرْهَقُ وُجُوهَهُمْ قَتَرٌ وَلَا ذِلَّةٌ ۚ أُو۟لَـٰٓئِكَ أَصْحَـٰبُ ٱلْجَنَّةِ ۖ هُمْ فِيهَا خَـٰلِدُونَ ۝

ᵃ Man is deceived by the apparent conditions of the world. He considers a transient thing as a permanent one. He begins to think that a life of happiness and the comforts which he likes to have are within his reach in this present world itself. In reality, the world of human wishes is going to take shape in the Hereafter, but it will be available only to those who try to attain it in accordance with the method shown by God.

Even supposing that a man manages to obtain everything he wants in the world, he still has no power to keep his life free of trouble and sorrow. Here some fear is attached to every happiness: every success here soon falls prey to some trouble; a life free of trouble and sorrow is that unique life which would be available to man only in the atmosphere of Paradise. Those who are able to discover this secret will be the ones who will follow the path to Paradise and ultimately reach the eternal heaven of God.

27 But as for those who have done evil deeds, the recompense shall be in proportion. They will have none to defend them against God. Ignominy shall cover them, as though their faces were veiled by the night's own darkness. It is they who are destined for the fire, where they will live forever.[a]

وَٱلَّذِينَ كَسَبُواْ ٱلسَّيِّئَاتِ جَزَآءُ سَيِّئَةٍ بِمِثْلِهَا وَتَرْهَقُهُمْ ذِلَّةٌ مَّا لَهُم مِّنَ ٱللَّهِ مِنْ عَاصِمٍ كَأَنَّمَآ أُغْشِيَتْ وُجُوهُهُمْ قِطَعًا مِّنَ ٱلَّيْلِ مُظْلِمًا أُوْلَٰٓئِكَ أَصْحَٰبُ ٱلنَّارِ هُمْ فِيهَا خَٰلِدُونَ ٢٧

---

[a] The life of comfort and happiness which is so favoured by man will be available to God's loyal subjects in a perfect form in Paradise. But there is a still higher grade of comfort and happiness which is much higher than that commonly acknowledged; and that is the glimpse of the Lord of the Universe which will specially be available to the people of Paradise. God, Who is the Creator of comforts and pleasure is certainly the greatest treasure of all comforts and pleasure. It has been handed down in a *hadith* that when the people of Paradise have entered Paradise and when the people of Hell have entered Hell, a call-giver will give the call: 'O, people of Paradise! There is one promise of God which remains to be fulfilled, and He wants to fulfil it now.' On hearing this, the people of Paradise will say, 'What is it? Haven't our scales of virtue been made heavier? Haven't our faces been brightened? Has not God admitted us to Paradise and saved us from the fire?' Thereafter, the veil will be lifted away from them, and they will be able to see their Lord. So, by God! No bounty that had been granted them will be more pleasant or more favourable to them than the sight of God, and nothing else will cool their eyes more than this. (*Tafsir ibn Kathir*).

There is no worse position that man can find himself in than being in a state of helplessness which is destined to be eternal; it is the equivalent of being plunged into a failure so absolute that it can never be turned back into success. Those who are condemned to be the inhabitants of hell in the Hereafter, shall have to face this condition. Man will be given punishment commensurate with his evil deeds, and his desperation at his eternal deprivation will be so severe that even his face will be blackened on account of it, as if immersed in layers of darkness.

28 On the Day when We gather them all together, We shall say to those who ascribed partners to God, 'Keep to your places, you and your partners!' Then We shall separate them from one another and their partner-gods will say, 'It was not us that you worshipped. 29 God suffices as a witness between us and you. We were entirely unaware that you worshipped us.' 30 Then every soul shall realize what it has done. They shall be returned to God, their true Master, and anything they had invented will forsake them.ᵃ

وَيَوْمَ نَحْشُرُهُمْ جَمِيعًا ثُمَّ نَقُولُ لِلَّذِينَ أَشْرَكُوا مَكَانَكُمْ أَنتُمْ وَشُرَكَآؤُكُمْ فَزَيَّلْنَا بَيْنَهُمْ وَقَالَ شُرَكَآؤُهُم مَّا كُنتُمْ إِيَّانَا تَعْبُدُونَ ﴿٢٨﴾ فَكَفَىٰ بِٱللَّهِ شَهِيدًا بَيْنَنَا وَبَيْنَكُمْ إِن كُنَّا عَنْ عِبَادَتِكُمْ لَغَٰفِلِينَ ﴿٢٩﴾ هُنَالِكَ تَبْلُوا كُلُّ نَفْسٍ مَّآ أَسْلَفَتْ وَرُدُّوٓا إِلَى ٱللَّهِ مَوْلَىٰهُمُ ٱلْحَقِّ وَضَلَّ عَنْهُم مَّا كَانُوا يَفْتَرُونَ ﴿٣٠﴾

ᵃ All of the observances of *shirk* (attributing partners to God) are based on false hopes. Events which occur by God's will are attributed by man to false gods, which in his self-delusion he makes the centre of his obeisance and worship. He depends so much on these false gods of his that he thinks that even in the Hereafter they will come to his help against God and save him from God's scourge.

These are but false hopes, but in the world their falsehood does not become clear, because due to the conditions of man's trial here, a veil of secrecy covers every reality. Here man has the opportunity to attribute the various events to his imaginary gods and thus be satisfied with their 'godliness.' But in the Hereafter all realities will be laid bare. There, it will become clear that in this universe nobody has power except the one and only God.

In the present world, man is living under the misunderstanding that, with the help of his leaders and false gods, he will be successful in the stages of the Hereafter, but in the Hereafter it will suddenly be clear to him that this confidence of his was absolutely false. Here, everybody will be requited according to what he himself has done and all imaginary supports will disappear as if they had never existed.

³¹ Say, 'Who provides [sustenance] for you from heaven and earth? Who is it who controls the ears and the eyes? Who brings forth the living from the dead, and the dead from the living? And who governs all affairs?' They will say, 'God'. Then say, 'Will you not then fear Him? ³² That is God, your true Lord. What is there, besides the truth, but error? How then can you turn away?' ³³ Thus the Word of your Lord is proved true against those who are disobedient. They will not believe.ᵃ

قُلْ مَن يَرْزُقُكُم مِّنَ ٱلسَّمَآءِ وَٱلْأَرْضِ أَمَّن يَمْلِكُ ٱلسَّمْعَ وَٱلْأَبْصَٰرَ وَمَن يُخْرِجُ ٱلْحَيَّ مِنَ ٱلْمَيِّتِ وَيُخْرِجُ ٱلْمَيِّتَ مِنَ ٱلْحَيِّ وَمَن يُدَبِّرُ ٱلْأَمْرَ فَسَيَقُولُونَ ٱللَّهُ فَقُلْ أَفَلَا تَتَّقُونَ ۝ فَذَٰلِكُمُ ٱللَّهُ رَبُّكُمُ ٱلْحَقُّ فَمَاذَا بَعْدَ ٱلْحَقِّ إِلَّا ٱلضَّلَٰلُ فَأَنَّىٰ تُصْرَفُونَ ۝ كَذَٰلِكَ حَقَّتْ كَلِمَتُ رَبِّكَ عَلَى ٱلَّذِينَ فَسَقُوٓا۟ أَنَّهُمْ لَا يُؤْمِنُونَ ۝

ᵃ Man needs sustenance. How does he receive it? It is through the coordinated action of the universe. The whole universe, with the utmost harmony, acts in a particular direction. Then only is it possible to make available to man that provision without which it would not be possible for him to survive on this earth. Studies show that every phenomenon in the universe is a product of a great and harmonious coordination among numerous elements of different and opposite nature. According to the polytheists' stand, this universal coordination of such a high degree becomes unexplainable. For these supposed partners in 'godhead' are responsible for only one part of the functioning of the universe. And a 'god' of one part can never cause an event which comes into existence through harmonious coordination of all parts.

Moreover, there is the example of the wonderful capabilities bestowed upon man that are represented by his ears and eyes. These could not be treated as the endowment of any false god. The false gods and goddesses themselves are either devoid of these capabilities, or even if these are found in any supposed god, he is not their creator. Even these can be taken away as they are taken away from ordinary human beings. Similarly, it is not possible for these false gods to give life to lifeless things or to make living things lifeless. There is no proof of this and no worshippers of theirs hold this belief about them. Then how will it be possible for man to get such things from them? How strange it is that man believes in a great God but, in spite of that, he attributes such things to God as nullify His superior qualities. The reason for this is that he has no fear of God. As a result of his false ideas, he has consoled himself that God is not going to make him give an account of himself, and if the stage of reckoning comes, there are such beings who, in his support, will recommend him to God and save him. Fear makes a man serious; if a man's heart is devoid of fear, nothing can stop him from adopting the way of injustice. Such a man becomes arrogant and an arrogant man never admits the Truth.

³⁴ Ask then, 'Can any of your partner-gods originate creation, and then reproduce it?' Say, 'It is God who originates creation and then restores it: how then are you so misled?' ³⁵ Say, 'Does any of your partner-gods guide one to the Truth?' Say, 'It is God who guides to the truth. Then, is He who guides to the truth more worthy to be followed or one who cannot find the way himself unless he be guided? What is the matter with you? How ill you judge!' ³⁶ Most of them follow nothing but mere conjecture. But conjecture is of no use against the Truth. God is well aware of what they do.ᵃ

قُلْ هَلْ مِن شُرَكَآئِكُم مَّن يَبْدَؤُاْ ٱلْخَلْقَ ثُمَّ يُعِيدُهُۥ قُلِ ٱللَّهُ يَبْدَؤُاْ ٱلْخَلْقَ ثُمَّ يُعِيدُهُۥ فَأَنَّىٰ تُؤْفَكُونَ ۞ قُلْ هَلْ مِن شُرَكَآئِكُم مَّن يَهْدِىٓ إِلَى ٱلْحَقِّ قُلِ ٱللَّهُ يَهْدِى لِلْحَقِّ أَفَمَن يَهْدِىٓ إِلَى ٱلْحَقِّ أَحَقُّ أَن يُتَّبَعَ أَمَّن لَّا يَهِدِّىٓ إِلَّآ أَن يُهْدَىٰ فَمَا لَكُمْ كَيْفَ تَحْكُمُونَ ۞ وَمَا يَتَّبِعُ أَكْثَرُهُمْ إِلَّا ظَنًّا إِنَّ ٱلظَّنَّ لَا يُغْنِى مِنَ ٱلْحَقِّ شَيْئًا إِنَّ ٱللَّهَ عَلِيمٌۢ بِمَا يَفْعَلُونَ ۞

ᵃ Except for God, no being who has been given the status of godhead, either from among human beings or non-human beings, has the power to bring anything into existence. It is only God whose creative power stands proved; and when God's creativity has once been proved, it also stands to reason that He can and will repeat His acts of creation in the Hereafter. Then it is futile to pay attention to the so-called other partners. From them, man cannot obtain anything either in his first life or in his second.

This is also the case with guidance. It is only God who sends guidance. The utterances of the prophets, presented by them as God's guidance, were definitely such. As opposed to this, the condition of partners is that either they are entirely incapable of giving knowledge about right or wrong to human beings, or due to their own shortcomings and limitations, they are themselves in need of guidance, leave alone giving guidance to others. Given this state of affairs, man should revert to the one and only God and dismiss from his mind any imaginary partners.

The tenets of polytheism are based not on any real knowledge but on suppositions or imagination. Without any basis, people have been wrongly persuaded that certain beings possess godly qualities, though such an important assessment of such beings can be formed only on the basis of real knowledge and not simply on conjecture or guesswork.

37 This Quran is not such as could have been produced by anyone but God. It fulfills that [the predictions] which came before it and gives a fuller explanation of the [earlier] Revelations. There is no doubt about it: it is from the Lord of the Universe. 38 Do they say, 'He has fabricated it?' Say, 'Bring me one chapter like it. Call on whom you may besides God to help you, if what you say be true!' 39 Indeed, they are denying something which they cannot comprehend; the reality not yet having dawned on them. Likewise those before them rejected the truth. But see what was the end of the wrongdoers.[a]

وَمَا كَانَ هَٰذَا ٱلْقُرْءَانُ أَن يُفْتَرَىٰ مِن دُونِ ٱللَّهِ وَلَٰكِن تَصْدِيقَ ٱلَّذِى بَيْنَ يَدَيْهِ وَتَفْصِيلَ ٱلْكِتَٰبِ لَا رَيْبَ فِيهِ مِن رَّبِّ ٱلْعَٰلَمِينَ ۝ أَمْ يَقُولُونَ ٱفْتَرَىٰهُ قُلْ فَأْتُوا۟ بِسُورَةٍ مِّثْلِهِ وَٱدْعُوا۟ مَنِ ٱسْتَطَعْتُم مِّن دُونِ ٱللَّهِ إِن كُنتُمْ صَٰدِقِينَ ۝ بَلْ كَذَّبُوا۟ بِمَا لَمْ يُحِيطُوا۟ بِعِلْمِهِ وَلَمَّا يَأْتِهِمْ تَأْوِيلُهُ كَذَٰلِكَ كَذَّبَ ٱلَّذِينَ مِن قَبْلِهِمْ فَٱنظُرْ كَيْفَ كَانَ عَٰقِبَةُ ٱلظَّٰلِمِينَ ۝

---

[a] The Quran is its own proof. With its superior literary style, it is quite inimitable; and this in itself is enough to prove that it presents superhuman discourse. Had it been the work of a human being, it would certainly have been possible for other human beings also to create a similar discourse by their own efforts.

The second proof of the Quran being a divine discourse is that it fulfills the prophesies made about it while waiting for a final book of guidance. The Quran has appeared in answer to this expectation. Then why should anyone have any doubt about it? Moreover, it is the details of the 'Book' which elucidate and present in correct and unadulterated form the divine teachings which are the essence of all divine scriptures. This is a clear indication which shows that the Quran has come from God, on whose behalf the previous divine scriptures had come.

Claims that the Quran is not the product of divine wisdom, its having been authored by a human being, can be instantly dismissed by asking the claimants to produce a book the equal of the Quran or even a chapter as excellent as those of the Quran. Neither they nor anyone else will be able to do so. Despite their claims having been proved incorrect, they still challenge the Quran. And if they do so, it is because they are devoid of any fear of the consequences of rejecting the Quran. They are not afraid that, by rejecting the Quran, they will have to suffer severe retribution. Their antagonistic behaviour is caused by the flippant attitude developed in them due to their fearlessness and not because of any kind of rational or cogent line of reasoning.

⁴⁰ Some of them will believe in it [the Quran], while others will not. And your Lord is fully aware of the evildoers. ⁴¹ If they should reject you, say, 'My deeds are mine and your deeds are yours. You are not accountable for my actions, nor am I accountable for what you do.'ᵃ

وَمِنْهُم مَّن يُؤْمِنُ بِهِ وَمِنْهُم مَّن لَّا يُؤْمِنُ بِهِ وَرَبُّكَ أَعْلَمُ بِالْمُفْسِدِينَ ۝ وَإِن كَذَّبُوكَ فَقُل لِّى عَمَلِى وَلَكُمْ عَمَلُكُمْ أَنتُم بَرِيُّونَ مِمَّا أَعْمَلُ وَأَنَا۠ بَرِىٓءٌ مِّمَّا تَعْمَلُونَ ۝

ᵃ One who does not embrace the Faith is, in the eyes of God, *mufsid* (a disturber of the peace) because it is only by disturbing his nature that it is possible for anyone to prevent himself from accepting the truth. Such a man curbs the voice of his conscience; he does not put to use his thinking capacity; he ignores clear reasoning by uttering false words; he is not receptive even after listening and does not try to understand even after having had everything explained to him. He gives preference to his prejudices, and his self-interests overwhelm the truth.

Those who argue falsely, and at length, go on arguing till the last, saying: 'You mind your own business and I'll mind mine.' To make such a statement seems to them like a way of avoiding defeat. But a missionary performs his work, rising above the psychology of victory or defeat. So, when he observes that the opponent has stooped to adopt an adamant and stubborn attitude and finds that there is no use in arguing further, he disassociates himself by saying that real decision is with God; and that his opponent's final fate will be in accordance with his position in God's assessment.

⁴²Some of them appear to be listening to you; but can you make the deaf hear, incapable as they are of understanding? ⁴³Some of them look fixedly at you; but can you make the blind see, bereft as they are of sight? ⁴⁴Surely, God does not wrong people at all, but people wrong themselves.

⁴⁵And on the Day when He shall gather them together, it will seem to them as if they had not tarried in the world longer than an hour of a day. They will recognize one another; lost indeed will be those who considered it a lie that they were destined to meet God, and did not follow the right path.*ᵃ*

وَمِنْهُم مَّن يَسْتَمِعُونَ إِلَيْكَ أَفَأَنتَ تُسْمِعُ ٱلصُّمَّ وَلَوْ كَانُوا لَا يَعْقِلُونَ ۝ وَمِنْهُم مَّن يَنظُرُ إِلَيْكَ أَفَأَنتَ تَهْدِى ٱلْعُمْىَ وَلَوْ كَانُوا لَا يُبْصِرُونَ ۝ إِنَّ ٱللَّهَ لَا يَظْلِمُ ٱلنَّاسَ شَيْئًا وَلَـٰكِنَّ ٱلنَّاسَ أَنفُسَهُمْ يَظْلِمُونَ ۝ وَيَوْمَ يَحْشُرُهُمْ كَأَن لَّمْ يَلْبَثُوا إِلَّا سَاعَةً مِّنَ ٱلنَّهَارِ يَتَعَارَفُونَ بَيْنَهُمْ قَدْ خَسِرَ ٱلَّذِينَ كَذَّبُوا بِلِقَآءِ ٱللَّهِ وَمَا كَانُوا مُهْتَدِينَ ۝

---

*ᵃ*Certain rejectors of Truth are clearly such right from the beginning. But the clever ones among them make a show of attentively listening, as if they really want to understand things, though in their hearts they maintain that they do not have to understand. They look at the signs of the veracity of the Prophet as if they want to observe them with an open heart, though they are already determined not to observe and not to accept. The preacher is thus misled into thinking that they are about to accept the Truth. But, in the eyes of God, they are people who are deaf in spite of having ears and blind in spite of having eyes. Such people do not receive inspiration from God to accept the Truth.

God has blessed man with superior capacities. If he utilises these capacities, he will never go astray. But man, finding himself free, misunderstands things. He falls to indulging in utter arrogance. This happens because he fails to understand God's plan. The things given to him purely for the purpose of putting him to the test are taken by him to be rightfully his.

46 Whether We show you something of what We have promised them or cause you to die [before that], to Us they shall return. God is Witness to all that they do.

47 Every nation has a messenger. Once their messenger has come, judgement will be passed upon them in all fairness and they will not be wronged.ᵃ

وَإِمَّا نُرِيَنَّكَ بَعْضَ ٱلَّذِى نَعِدُهُمْ أَوْ نَتَوَفَّيَنَّكَ فَإِلَيْنَا مَرْجِعُهُمْ ثُمَّ ٱللَّهُ شَهِيدٌ عَلَىٰ مَا يَفْعَلُونَ ۝ وَلِكُلِّ أُمَّةٍ رَّسُولٌ فَإِذَا جَآءَ رَسُولُهُمْ قُضِىَ بَيْنَهُم بِٱلْقِسْطِ وَهُمْ لَا يُظْلَمُونَ ۝

ᵃ Today, the Hereafter is not before man; today, a man desirous of seeing it has to see it with the eye of his imagination. Therefore, to a man who is not serious about the Hereafter, it will appear to be a far-away thing. But when the Hereafter sweeps over him as the greatest reality, and when he starts seeing it in all its rigour with his own eyes, he will forget his arrogance. At that time, all those worldly matters which had made him neglectful and careless about the Hereafter, will appear to him lowly, frivolous and contemptible.

The Hereafter will not occur in any strange world, but in this thoroughly-familiar world of ours. Then, man will find himself in the same atmosphere in which he had earlier rejected the Truth; he will find himself among the same persons on the strength of whose support he indulged in arrogance. But, at that time, none of them will be of any avail. Everything will be fresh in his mind, as if no time had elapsed at all.

The relation between a preacher and his hearers is the most delicate of all affairs. If the preacher has come forward in actuality to bring the Truth, he is God's representative in this world. Accepting him is like accepting God and rejecting him amounts to rejection of God. Such events cannot be without consequences. After the appearance of the preacher of Truth, it necessarily follows that the divine discourse which falls from his lips, will leave his hearers speechless. This is the first victory of Truth over falsehood. The second victory will take place in the Hereafter when his opponents, by God's grace, will be powerless before Him. The first event necessarily occurs right here in this world. The second event also occurs to a certain extent in this world, if God wishes to reveal it in the present world.

This sort of happening is bound to take place with every group when, prior to its being directly presented before God, it is indirectly presented before God's representative in this world. In this way, God sees who surrenders himself to Him.

⁴⁸ They say, 'When will this promise come to pass—if you speak the truth?' ⁴⁹ Say, 'I have no control over any harm or benefit to myself, except by the will of God. For every people, however, there is an appointed term. When the end of their term arrives, they cannot postpone it for an hour, nor can they advance it.' *ᵃ*

وَيَقُولُونَ مَتَىٰ هَٰذَا ٱلۡوَعۡدُ إِن كُنتُمۡ صَٰدِقِينَ ﴿٤٨﴾ قُل لَّآ أَمۡلِكُ لِنَفۡسِى ضَرًّا وَلَا نَفۡعًا إِلَّا مَا شَآءَ ٱللَّهُ لِكُلِّ أُمَّةٍ أَجَلٌ إِذَا جَآءَ أَجَلُهُمۡ فَلَا يَسۡتَـٔۡخِرُونَ سَاعَةً وَلَا يَسۡتَقۡدِمُونَ ﴿٤٩﴾

ᵃ Man finds himself free in this world. It seems to him that whatever he may do, there is nobody to catch hold of him and nobody to punish him. This state of affairs makes him unheeding, so much so that when the preacher warns him on behalf of God about the outcome of his deeds, he ridicules the missionary and asks, 'When will the warning of retribution for my arrogance which you have been giving me materialise?'

The reason behind all such talk is nothing but foolishness; because this punishment is executed not on behalf of the preacher but on behalf of God; and at all times God is revealing in this world of His that His way is not that of inordinate haste.

If a boat has a hole in it and if a sailor heedlessly sets sail in it, then in accordance with the law of God, it will sink. But such a boat does not sink immediately. It does so only at its appointed time and according to God's law. Such instances abound in the world and they acquaint man with the methods of God. But, in spite of observing all this, man says, 'If all such deeds entail God's punishment, why does not this punishment come soon?' The reason for asking such pointless questions is that man is not serious about God's scourge.

⁵⁰ Say, 'If His punishment comes upon you in the dead of night, or by the light of day, how will the guilty escape it? ⁵¹ Will you believe in it only after it has overtaken you, although it was your wish to hurry it on?' ⁵² Then the evil-doers will be told, 'Taste the everlasting punishment. Have you not been rewarded according to your deeds?'ᵃ

قُلْ أَرَءَيْتُمْ إِنْ أَتَىٰكُمْ عَذَابُهُۥ بَيَٰتًا أَوْ نَهَارًا مَّاذَا يَسْتَعْجِلُ مِنْهُ ٱلْمُجْرِمُونَ ۝ أَثُمَّ إِذَا مَا وَقَعَ ءَامَنتُم بِهِۦٓ ءَآلْـَٰٔنَ وَقَدْ كُنتُم بِهِۦ تَسْتَعْجِلُونَ ۝ ثُمَّ قِيلَ لِلَّذِينَ ظَلَمُوا۟ ذُوقُوا۟ عَذَابَ ٱلْخُلْدِ هَلْ تُجْزَوْنَ إِلَّا بِمَا كُنتُمْ تَكْسِبُونَ ۝

ᵃ Earthquakes and storms are God-managed events. These events show that whenever an issue arises between God and man, the power of deciding rests entirely with the former. But man does not take this factor into consideration. He sees only that the Law of God is not immediately coming into effect; and this being so, he remains neglectful. But when God's decision comes into force, man will find himself ready to accept everything, though accepting at that time will be of no avail, because that will be the time when one is faced with the consequences of deeds already performed, with no account taken of the performance of fresh deeds.

⁵³ They enquire of you if this will really happen. Tell them, 'Yes, by my Lord. Most certainly it will happen, and you cannot avert it.' *ᵃ*

وَيَسْتَنْبِئُونَكَ أَحَقٌّ هُوَ قُلْ إِى وَرَبِّى إِنَّهُ لَحَقٌّ وَمَآ أَنتُم بِمُعْجِزِينَ ۝

ᵃ The Prophet Muhammad told the Arab people that if they did not reform themselves, they would be set upon by the punishment of the Hereafter. In answer to that they started ridiculing his warning. This does not mean that they were not believers in the Hereafter. In fact, they were not disregarding the fact of the Hereafter itself, but rather dismissing the Prophet Muhammad's warning as valueless. At that time the greatness of the Prophet Muhammad had not yet come to be recognised. In the eyes of his addressees, he appeared to be in the shape of an 'ordinary' human being. They failed to understand how they would be liable for God's punishment on rejecting this 'ordinary' man's words. They were doubtful of his being the representative of God and the Hereafter. This comparison was not between acceptance of the Hereafter and denial of the Hereafter but between the religion of a celebrated personality and the religion of an insignificant personality. They allied themselves with the established great ones of the past.

They considered themselves to be following the religion of the recognised personalities. As against the recognised personalities of the past, when they saw their contemporary Prophet, he appeared to be an ordinary human being. They were not able to understand that their association with those great personalities would not be sufficient for their salvation and that it would be necessary for them to associate themselves with that person who was not apparently vested with greatness. This was the psychology which emboldened them to ridicule the Prophet Muhammad.

54 If every wrongdoer possessed all that was on the earth, he would seek to ransom himself with it: when they see the punishment, they will repent in secret. But judgement will be passed upon them in all fairness, and they will not be wronged. 55 Assuredly, everything that is in the heavens and on the earth belongs to God. Assuredly, God's promise is true. Yet most of them do not realize it. 56 He gives life and brings about death, and to Him you shall all return.[a]

وَلَوْ أَنَّ لِكُلِّ نَفْسٍ ظَلَمَتْ مَا فِى ٱلْأَرْضِ لَٱفْتَدَتْ بِهِۦ وَأَسَرُّوا۟ ٱلنَّدَامَةَ لَمَّا رَأَوُا۟ ٱلْعَذَابَ وَقُضِىَ بَيْنَهُم بِٱلْقِسْطِ وَهُمْ لَا يُظْلَمُونَ ۝ أَلَآ إِنَّ لِلَّهِ مَا فِى ٱلسَّمَـٰوَٰتِ وَٱلْأَرْضِ أَلَآ إِنَّ وَعْدَ ٱللَّهِ حَقٌّ وَلَـٰكِنَّ أَكْثَرَهُمْ لَا يَعْلَمُونَ ۝ هُوَ يُحْىِۦ وَيُمِيتُ وَإِلَيْهِ تُرْجَعُونَ ۝

---

[a] Man is a sensitive being. He cannot bear trouble. As long as he is not confronted with retribution, he ridicules the Truth; he spurns it with unconcern. But when the retribution of the Hereafter is before him, he will be stricken with such terror that everything will appear insignificant to him. Even if he possessed the wealth of the entire world and all the bounties of the world, all that will appear so valueless to him seeing the punishment before him that he will fervently desire that he should be relieved of that chastisement in exchange for all the bounties.

But the issue in the Hereafter is not that of bargaining. It is the question of facing the consequences for the deeds performed. It is an essential part of God's plan regarding life and death. It is the demand of Divine Justice that it should happen; and God's omnipotence is the sure guarantee that it will take place.

The seeming delay in the occurrence of this is only due to having to await that appointed hour, when the period of the present test will be over, and all human beings will be presented before God to face their final fate.

⁵⁷ O mankind! There has come to you an admonition from your Lord, a cure for what is in the hearts, and a guide and a blessing to true believers. ⁵⁸ Say, 'In the grace and mercy of God let them rejoice, for these are better than the worldly riches which they hoard.' *a*

يَـٰٓأَيُّهَا ٱلنَّاسُ قَدْ جَآءَتْكُم مَّوْعِظَةٌ مِّن رَّبِّكُمْ وَشِفَآءٌ لِّمَا فِى ٱلصُّدُورِ وَهُدًى وَرَحْمَةٌ لِّلْمُؤْمِنِينَ ۝ قُلْ بِفَضْلِ ٱللَّهِ وَبِرَحْمَتِهِۦ فَبِذَٰلِكَ فَلْيَفْرَحُواْ هُوَ خَيْرٌ مِّمَّا يَجْمَعُونَ ۝

---

a Man is a psychological being. If psychologically he is vitiated, his whole life is affected. The guidance revealed by God in the form of the divine Book is an absolute mercy to all humanity. It consists of the best advice and guidance, but it is necessary for a man to be its recipient that he should not have lost his power of right thinking. As for one who has perverted his faculty of right thinking, the principles enshrined in the divine Book will fail to guide him.

The things of the present world and its glories and grandeur are 'cash' benefits in the eyes of man. Man relishes their taste and savours them at every moment. In comparison to this, the bounties of the Hereafter count as mere 'promises'. Man only hears about them; he does not experience them. For this reason, many people rush towards and fall all-out on the 'ready' benefits of world. But those who think deeply will be happy with the thought that God, by revealing His guidance, has opened for them the doors to attaining eternal bounties.

⁵⁹ Say, 'Have you considered the provision God has sent down for you, and have you made some of it unlawful and some lawful?' Say, 'Has God given you permission [to do this], or are you inventing falsehoods about God?' ⁶⁰ What will they think, those who invent falsehoods about God, on the Day of Resurrection? God is bountiful to men: yet most of them are not grateful.

⁶¹ In whatever activity you may be engaged, and whichever part of the Quran you recite, and whatever deed you do, We are witness to it when you are engaged in it. Not the smallest particle on the earth or in heaven is hidden from your Lord; and there is nothing smaller or bigger but is recorded in a clear Book.^a

قُلْ أَرَءَيْتُم مَّآ أَنزَلَ ٱللَّهُ لَكُم مِّن رِّزْقٍ فَجَعَلْتُم مِّنْهُ حَرَامًا وَحَلَٰلًا قُلْ ءَآللَّهُ أَذِنَ لَكُمْ أَمْ عَلَى ٱللَّهِ تَفْتَرُونَ ﴿٥٩﴾ وَمَا ظَنُّ ٱلَّذِينَ يَفْتَرُونَ عَلَى ٱللَّهِ ٱلْكَذِبَ يَوْمَ ٱلْقِيَٰمَةِ إِنَّ ٱللَّهَ لَذُو فَضْلٍ عَلَى ٱلنَّاسِ وَلَٰكِنَّ أَكْثَرَهُمْ لَا يَشْكُرُونَ ﴿٦٠﴾ وَمَا تَكُونُ فِى شَأْنٍ وَمَا تَتْلُوا۟ مِنْهُ مِن قُرْءَانٍ وَلَا تَعْمَلُونَ مِنْ عَمَلٍ إِلَّا كُنَّا عَلَيْكُمْ شُهُودًا إِذْ تُفِيضُونَ فِيهِ وَمَا يَعْزُبُ عَن رَّبِّكَ مِن مِّثْقَالِ ذَرَّةٍ فِى ٱلْأَرْضِ وَلَا فِى ٱلسَّمَآءِ وَلَا أَصْغَرَ مِن ذَٰلِكَ وَلَآ أَكْبَرَ إِلَّا فِى كِتَٰبٍ مُّبِينٍ ﴿٦١﴾

^a All of God's gifts to man—whether agricultural produce or other things which are useful to man—are divine provision (*rizq*). As man utilizes them in the way shown by God, he develops a feeling of gratitude towards his Maker. But Satan wants man to fail to remember God while making use of divine provisions. In ancient times Satan induced people to associate with these provisions the rites due to false gods and goddesses so that in availing of them, they would forget the remembrance of their true Lord. In the present age Satan is achieving this purpose by advancing material explanations for things. God-gifted things are being shown to people as resulting from certain material factors, so that when they receive these things, they will not treat these bounties as the provision (*rizq*) of God but as the outcome of worldly toils.

⁶² Those who are close to God shall certainly have no fear, nor shall they grieve. ⁶³ For those who believe and are mindful of God, ⁶⁴ there is good news in this life and in the Hereafter: the Word of God shall never change. That is the supreme triumph. ⁶⁵ Do not let their words grieve you. Surely, all might and glory belongs to God alone; He is the all-hearing, the all-knowing.^a

أَلَا إِنَّ أَوْلِيَاءَ ٱللَّهِ لَا خَوْفٌ عَلَيْهِمْ وَلَا هُمْ يَحْزَنُونَ ۝ ٱلَّذِينَ ءَامَنُوا وَكَانُوا يَتَّقُونَ ۝ لَهُمُ ٱلْبُشْرَىٰ فِي ٱلْحَيَوٰةِ ٱلدُّنْيَا وَفِي ٱلْآخِرَةِ لَا تَبْدِيلَ لِكَلِمَٰتِ ٱللَّهِ ذَٰلِكَ هُوَ ٱلْفَوْزُ ٱلْعَظِيمُ ۝ وَلَا يَحْزُنكَ قَوْلُهُمْ إِنَّ ٱلْعِزَّةَ لِلَّهِ جَمِيعًا هُوَ ٱلسَّمِيعُ ٱلْعَلِيمُ ۝

---

^a Giving the call for Truth is a very difficult task. The preacher has to totally devote himself to Truth alone, and only then can he become a preacher (*da'i*), in the true sense. When the preacher presents God's religion in its original form and makes it very clear with the help of sound reasoning, then all those who follow their self-made religion become perturbed and infuriated. Showing themselves to be pious established leaders, they try to degrade the preacher. They treat everything, such as baseless propaganda, conspiracies, even violent actions as all being permissible in opposing him. The freedom granted to them in the present world gives them the opportunity to go on doing whatever they want to do against the preacher. A stage comes when all the power of materialism is ranged against the preacher's arguments. And because the preacher's opponents are vested with so much worldly power, they feel they can suppress his voice.

This state of affairs is undoubtedly very trying. For it happens that, on the one hand, the opponents of Truth appear to be successful and thus become emboldened. On the other hand an errant thought crosses the mind of the preacher: 'Is God neutral on this issue? Has He disassociated Himself after drawing me into this battle between truth and falsehood?'

But this is not so. It is not possible that God would cease to support the truth. The opponent's becoming bereft of sound reasoning and all the strength of reasoning being totally on the side of the preacher are sure proofs that God is with the preacher of Truth. It is so, because reason is God's representative in the present world. If anyone has the power of reasoning, then it is as if God is with him. The opponents have the opportunity of committing aggression and violence, simply due to the freedom given to them for the sake of testing them. As soon as the world of trial comes to an end, this position will change. At that time superiority and respect will be accorded to those who took a stand on the basis of reasoning, while others who failed to do so will be dishonoured. The group of true preachers of God are the friends of God. God gives them good news of a sublime life in the Hereafter in which they neither suffer any regrets about their past life nor have any fears about their future life.

⁶⁶ Surely, all who are in the heavens and on the earth belong to Him. What do those follow, who appeal to associates instead of to God? They merely follow conjecture and they are only guessing. ⁶⁷ It is He who has made the night dark for you so that you may rest in it, and the day a source of light. Surely, there are signs in this for a people who listen.ᵃ

أَلَا إِنَّ لِلَّهِ مَن فِي ٱلسَّمَٰوَٰتِ وَمَن فِي ٱلْأَرْضِ ۗ وَمَا يَتَّبِعُ ٱلَّذِينَ يَدْعُونَ مِن دُونِ ٱللَّهِ شُرَكَآءَ ۚ إِن يَتَّبِعُونَ إِلَّا ٱلظَّنَّ وَإِنْ هُمْ إِلَّا يَخْرُصُونَ ۝ هُوَ ٱلَّذِي جَعَلَ لَكُمُ ٱلَّيْلَ لِتَسْكُنُوا۟ فِيهِ وَٱلنَّهَارَ مُبْصِرًا ۚ إِنَّ فِي ذَٰلِكَ لَءَايَٰتٍ لِّقَوْمٍ يَسْمَعُونَ ۝

ᵃ Who has created heaven and earth; and who is sustaining them?—These questions have been the central point of the human quest in every age. But finding the correct answers to these questions will be possible only when a man is able to see beyond the physical world, and nobody possesses eyes which can see beyond the physical world. This is why every answer which man himself devises is based on mere guesswork and conjecture and not on any knowledge based on facts.

In this world, those who speak on the basis of real knowledge are known as prophets. These are the particular people who have direct contact with the world above. God Himself, on His own, informs them of the reality of things. Therefore, prophets' knowledge is the only knowledge on which one can rely with certainty.

We have no direct means of testing the veracity of the Prophet's claims. However, there certainly exists an indirect means; and that is the signs (*ayat*) of the universe. These signs, in effect, corroborate the inner realities explained by the Prophet.

For instance, we see that on earth, day follows night and night follows day. This phenomenon of rotation has come into existence due to an extremely stable system which is regulated with mathematical precision. Moreover, this phenomenon is wonderfully favourable to our life. There appears to be a clearly purposeful plan at work behind it. This state of affairs is definitely a proof of the existence of a Being who is vested with Absolute power, who is Benevolent and Merciful, and about whom the prophets have been giving us information throughout the ages.

Those who, according to their own ideas, follow 'partners' are not following any factual reality, but only their own conjecture and imagination. The reality revealed through the prophets is corroborated by the entire universe, but there is nobody here to corroborate or uphold the claim of the polytheists, or those who attribute partners to God (*mushriks*).

⁶⁸ They say, 'God has begotten a son.' Glory be to Him. He is the Self-Sufficient One; everything in the heavens and on the earth belongs to Him. Do you have any authority for this? Would you ascribe to God something which you do not know? *a*

قَالُوا۟ ٱتَّخَذَ ٱللَّهُ وَلَدًا ۗ سُبْحَٰنَهُۥ ۖ هُوَ ٱلْغَنِىُّ ۖ لَهُۥ مَا فِى ٱلسَّمَٰوَٰتِ وَمَا فِى ٱلْأَرْضِ ۚ إِنْ عِندَكُم مِّن سُلْطَٰنٍۭ بِهَٰذَآ ۚ أَتَقُولُونَ عَلَى ٱللَّهِ مَا لَا تَعْلَمُونَ ۝

---

a Imagining the sons and daughters of God is like imagining God on the lines of a human being. Man is the victim of shortcomings and limitations; he therefore needs children so that, through them he can compensate for these shortcomings and limitations. But imagining such a position in respect of God is absolutely baseless.

The pattern of God's creations itself confirms the existence of a Creator. The image of God which should be projected is that of one who is perfect to the final degree; one who is free of all kinds of flaws and deficiencies. Had God not been a perfect being, had He been full of shortcomings and defects, He would not have been able to create a universe like the present one and would not have been able to control it in the present, precisely regulated manner.

This means that all the signs of heaven and the earth establish the existence of the one God, the concept of which has been presented by the prophets. But the concept of God devised for themselves by the polytheists has absolutely no proof in the present universe. Now, obviously, the polytheists' acceptance of an unproved god shows that such people can never be successful, because how can a god who is actually non-existent come to help anybody or fulfil anybody's wishes? God, who is really in existence, is not accepted by the polytheists and the god they accept does not exist anywhere. Under these circumstances, how can the the polytheists be successful in the present universe? Their only possible fate will be to finally become helpless and without support and forever suffer disgrace and disappointment.

⁶⁹ Say, 'Those who invent falsehoods about God shall not prosper.' ⁷⁰ Their portion is short-lived enjoyment in this world; but to Us they shall return. Then We shall make them taste a severe punishment, because of their denial of truth.ᵃ

قُلْ إِنَّ ٱلَّذِينَ يَفْتَرُونَ عَلَى ٱللَّهِ ٱلْكَذِبَ لَا يُفْلِحُونَ ۝ مَتَٰعٌ فِى ٱلدُّنْيَا ثُمَّ إِلَيْنَا مَرْجِعُهُمْ ثُمَّ نُذِيقُهُمُ ٱلْعَذَابَ ٱلشَّدِيدَ بِمَا كَانُوا۟ يَكْفُرُونَ ۝

ᵃ In the present world nobody loses anything by rejection of the Truth or *shirk* (assigning partners to God). This leads to great misunderstanding. But, this state of affairs comes about simply because of the respite given to man during his period of trial. In the present world man has been given freedom of action, so that he may be put to the test. The moment the period of testing is over, the present condition will also come to an end. At that time man will see that he has been left with none of those things of which he considered himself the owner, and on account of which he had become arrogant.

It has been recorded in a tradition of the Prophet Muhammad that God apostrophied wisdom, saying, 'O, wisdom! In this universe I have not created anything superior to you, anything more beautiful or any creature better than you.' The necessary consequence of the grant of such a great boon to a human being is that his responsibility should also be great. That is why rejection of truth is the greatest crime before God. When Truth is proved by reasoning, it becomes necessary for man to accept it. If, even after the truth has been proved by arguments, a man rejects it, then he is committing an unpardonable crime. When God has given to man the wisdom by which he may recognise the Truth as Truth and falsehood as falsehood, in such a situation there can be no excuse for his wrongdoing before God.

⁷¹ Tell them the story of Noah. He said to his people, 'My people, if my presence among you and my preaching to you of God's revelations offends you, know that I put my trust in God, so agree on your course of action, along with your partner-gods, and let no hesitation deflect you from it, then put it into effect against me, and give me no respite. ⁷² If you turn away from me, remember I demand no recompense from you. Only God will reward me and I have been commanded to submit completely to Him.' ᵃ

وَاتْلُ عَلَيْهِمْ نَبَأَ نُوحٍ إِذْ قَالَ لِقَوْمِهِ يَقَوْمِ إِن كَانَ كَبُرَ عَلَيْكُم مَّقَامِي وَتَذْكِيرِي بِآيَاتِ ٱللَّهِ فَعَلَى ٱللَّهِ تَوَكَّلْتُ فَأَجْمِعُوا أَمْرَكُمْ وَشُرَكَاءَكُمْ ثُمَّ لَا يَكُنْ أَمْرُكُمْ عَلَيْكُمْ غُمَّةً ثُمَّ ٱقْضُوا إِلَيَّ وَلَا تُنظِرُونِ ﴿٧١﴾ فَإِن تَوَلَّيْتُمْ فَمَا سَأَلْتُكُم مِّنْ أَجْرٍ إِنْ أَجْرِيَ إِلَّا عَلَى ٱللَّهِ وَأُمِرْتُ أَنْ أَكُونَ مِنَ ٱلْمُسْلِمِينَ ﴿٧٢﴾

ᵃ Noah (Nuh) was a Prophet of the most ancient period. As long as he was silent, his community respected him, but when he came forward as a call-giver of the Truth and started telling the people what to do and what not to do, he became *persona non grata* in the eyes of his community, so much so that they gave him the ultimatum: 'Either you give up this call-giving and tendering of advice or else we will not allow you to stay in this land of ours.'

Noah said that they were saying all this because they were treating his message as the affair of a human being, while this was actually God's own concern. He said that, in order to fight with him, they would have to fight God. He further said, 'If you don't believe it, then what you can do is gather your companions and partners and formulate any unanimous plan against me, and then carry it out with all your might. Then you will see that your every plan against me is a failure.' In the present world, the standard confirming the veracity of a caller for truth is that he fulfills his mission at all costs and nobody succeeds in thwarting him.

73 Then they rejected him; then We delivered him and those with him in the Ark, and We made them successors; while We drowned the others who belied Our signs. Observe then the fate of those who had been forewarned.ᵃ

فَكَذَّبُوهُ فَنَجَّيْنَٰهُ وَمَن مَّعَهُۥ فِى ٱلْفُلْكِ وَجَعَلْنَٰهُمْ خَلَٰٓئِفَ وَأَغْرَقْنَا ٱلَّذِينَ كَذَّبُواْ بِـَٔايَٰتِنَا ۖ فَٱنظُرْ كَيْفَ كَانَ عَٰقِبَةُ ٱلْمُنذَرِينَ ٧٣

ᵃ One who comes forward on behalf of God with the call for the Truth, does so always on the strength of argument. Although reasoning (argument) pertains to the intellect, man fails to realise its greatness. In spite of having no answer to it, he refuses to bow down before it.

One of the considerations of the task which a messenger of Truth has to carry out is that he should not make any economic or material demands upon the community he addresses, even if this means great sacrifice on his part. This is so that the relation between them may remain that of the missionary and his addressee. It should not turn into group or material rivalry.

When Noah had finally delivered his message in its entirety to his community, and still his community was adamant and arrogant, they were drowned in turbulent flood waters so that the earth was rid of them, while the Faithful (adherents of Noah) were given the opportunity to live in the world as inheritors of the earth. This, in Quranic terminology, is described as 'khalifah.' Before the flood, the community of Noah was the khalifah of the earth; after the flood those faithful to Noah were made the successors of the earth.

74 After him We sent other messengers to their respective peoples, and they brought them clear proofs. But they would not believe in the truth, because they had rejected it before. Thus We seal up the hearts of the transgressors.ᵃ

75 Then We sent forth Moses and Aaron with Our signs to Pharaoh and his nobles, but they behaved arrogantly, for they were wicked people. 76 When the truth came to them from Us, they said, 'This is plain sorcery.'ᵇ

ثُمَّ بَعَثْنَا مِنْ بَعْدِهِ رُسُلاً إِلَىٰ قَوْمِهِمْ فَجَآءُوهُم بِٱلْبَيِّنَٰتِ فَمَا كَانُوا۟ لِيُؤْمِنُوا۟ بِمَا كَذَّبُوا۟ بِهِۦ مِن قَبْلُ كَذَٰلِكَ نَطْبَعُ عَلَىٰ قُلُوبِ ٱلْمُعْتَدِينَ ۝ ثُمَّ بَعَثْنَا مِنۢ بَعْدِهِم مُّوسَىٰ وَهَٰرُونَ إِلَىٰ فِرْعَوْنَ وَمَلَإِيْهِۦ بِـَٔايَٰتِنَا فَٱسْتَكْبَرُوا۟ وَكَانُوا۟ قَوْمًا مُّجْرِمِينَ ۝ فَلَمَّا جَآءَهُمُ ٱلْحَقُّ مِنْ عِندِنَا قَالُوٓا۟ إِنَّ هَٰذَا لَسِحْرٌ مُّبِينٌ ۝

ᵃ In this verse 'transgressors' refers to those who, once having rejected the Truth, stick to that position, make it a prestige issue and then go on continuously ignoring the Truth so that their religious knowledge and their being on the right path do not become doubtful in others' eyes.

Those who display this sort of behaviour are punished in this world by having their hearts sealed, that is, under the law of God, their psychology becomes gradually affected and finally they lose their sensitivity to the matter of Truth. The little sensitivity which they had earlier is ultimately benumbed. They do not remain capable of being anxious about Truth and untruth, or accepting the Truth rather than untruth. The history of Noah and the succeeding prophets bears testimony to this.

The condition of any preacher of Truth who comes forward on behalf of God is such that he is not surrounded by outward worldly glories. The only strength he possesses is the power of reasoning. Those who are capable of recognising Truth in the language of reason are the only ones who acknowledge the preacher of Truth. Those whom the language of argument cannot influence are incapable of accepting or supporting the preacher of Truth.

ᵇ Because of their arrogance, Pharaoh and the chiefs of his people did not accept the word of Moses and Aaron. They judged all matters by the standard of power and glory instead of seeing them in the light of reason. Due to this self-established standard, they considered themselves of a high status and Moses and Aaron of a lower status. This mentality prevented them from accepting the Truth as presented to them by Moses and Aaron whom they regarded as inferior persons.

⁷⁷ Moses replied, 'Do you speak thus of the truth after it has been brought to you? Can this be sorcery? Sorcerers never prosper.' ⁷⁸ They said, 'Have you come to turn us away from what we found our forefathers following, so that the two of you might become supreme in this land? We will never believe in you.' ^a

قَالَ مُوسَىٰٓ أَتَقُولُونَ لِلْحَقِّ لَمَّا جَآءَكُمْ أَسِحْرٌ هَٰذَا وَلَا يُفْلِحُ ٱلسَّٰحِرُونَ ۝ قَالُوٓاْ أَجِئْتَنَا لِتَلْفِتَنَا عَمَّا وَجَدْنَا عَلَيْهِ ءَابَآءَنَا وَتَكُونَ لَكُمَا ٱلْكِبْرِيَآءُ فِى ٱلْأَرْضِ وَمَا نَحْنُ لَكُمَا بِمُؤْمِنِينَ ۝

^a When the language of reasoning was not understood by Pharaoh, he (Moses) drew his hand out of his armpit and it shone brightly. Pharaoh had no answer for this. So, he tried to hide his defeat at the hands of Moses by giving the false impression that what Moses said and did was not the Truth but a form of magic. It is true that there is some outward similarity between magic and miracles. But very soon it becomes clear that magic is simply a feat, a trick. On the contrary, a miracle is real. Magic finally proves to be magic and a miracle finally establishes itself as a miracle.

On this occasion Pharaoh made two more statements calculated to divert his people from the call of Moses—one being that Moses wanted them to turn away from the religion of their ancestors. Pharaoh should have tried to understand the Message of Moses in terms of Truth and untruth. But he tested it by the ancestral and non-ancestral standard, so that he should not have to admit his wrong approach. By keeping to ancestral and non-ancestral matters, he had some justification for continuing to act as he did.

The second point that Pharaoh made was that Moses and Aaron wanted to establish their supremacy in their country. This was only a political stunt to deceive the public, because in the very first instance Moses had made it clear to Pharaoh that his sole purpose was to deliver the message of God to him and thereafter to leave Egypt for the Sinai desert along with the Israelites. This being so, the allegation that Moses was planning to usurp the rule of Egypt was obviously untrue.

⁷⁹ Then Pharaoh said, 'Bring me every skilled magician!' ⁸⁰ When the magicians came, Moses said to them, 'Cast down whatever you are going to cast down.' ⁸¹ And when they had done so, Moses said, 'What you have wrought is mere sorcery. Surely, God will bring it to nothing. Truly, God does not support the work of mischief-makers; ⁸² God establishes the truth by His words, however much the sinners may dislike it.' *ᵃ*

وَقَالَ فِرْعَوْنُ ٱئْتُونِي بِكُلِّ سَٰحِرٍ عَلِيمٍ ۝ فَلَمَّا جَآءَ ٱلسَّحَرَةُ قَالَ لَهُم مُّوسَىٰٓ أَلْقُوا۟ مَآ أَنتُم مُّلْقُونَ ۝ فَلَمَّآ أَلْقَوْا۟ قَالَ مُوسَىٰ مَا جِئْتُم بِهِ ٱلسِّحْرُ إِنَّ ٱللَّهَ سَيُبْطِلُهُۥٓ إِنَّ ٱللَّهَ لَا يُصْلِحُ عَمَلَ ٱلْمُفْسِدِينَ ۝ وَيُحِقُّ ٱللَّهُ ٱلْحَقَّ بِكَلِمَٰتِهِۦ وَلَوْ كَرِهَ ٱلْمُجْرِمُونَ ۝

ᵃ When Pharaoh called upon expert magicians to perform, it was not because he thought that he would actually subdue Moses with their help. His action, rather than being a rational course to follow, was more the result of his over-anxiety to reject Moses. The plan to prove God's Prophet wrong with the help of magicians was one whose failure could be foreseen. But when a man does not want to accept the truth and is bent upon rejecting it, this desire takes him to such extremes that he takes ill-advised steps to do so: he constructs a dam of tiny splinters to hold back a rising flood, though he knows full well that tiny splinters will be absolutely useless in this instance.

So things happened as they were bound to happen. The magicians threw down on the ground ropes and sticks, which crept towards the people like snakes. Then Moses threw down his stick. This turned into a huge snake which started running along the ground. This 'snake' was not merely a snake; it was, in fact, a force of God which had appeared to establish truth as Truth and falsehood as falsehood. So, as soon as it appeared, the magicians' ropes reverted to their original form.

Thus Pharaoh was defeated in an arena he himself had chosen. But even then, Pharaoh did not accept defeat. He found words to contradict Moses as he had earlier done.

83 But none save a few youths declared their faith in Moses, [while others held back] for fear that Pharaoh and his nobles would persecute them. Pharaoh was high and mighty in the land. And one who transgressed all bounds. 84 Moses said, 'O my people; if you believe in God, [and] if you have surrendered yourselves to Him, then in Him alone put your trust.' 85 They said, 'In God we put our trust. Our Lord, make us not a trial [the subject of persecution] for the oppressors. 86 And deliver us by Your mercy from the people who deny the truth.' a

فَمَآ ءَامَنَ لِمُوسَىٰٓ إِلَّا ذُرِّيَّةٌ مِّن قَوْمِهِۦ عَلَىٰ خَوْفٍ مِّن فِرْعَوْنَ وَمَلَإِيْهِمْ أَن يَفْتِنَهُمْ ۚ وَإِنَّ فِرْعَوْنَ لَعَالٍ فِى ٱلْأَرْضِ وَإِنَّهُۥ لَمِنَ ٱلْمُسْرِفِينَ ۝ وَقَالَ مُوسَىٰ يَٰقَوْمِ إِن كُنتُمْ ءَامَنتُم بِٱللَّهِ فَعَلَيْهِ تَوَكَّلُوٓا۟ إِن كُنتُم مُّسْلِمِينَ ۝ فَقَالُوا۟ عَلَى ٱللَّهِ تَوَكَّلْنَا رَبَّنَا لَا تَجْعَلْنَا فِتْنَةً لِّلْقَوْمِ ٱلظَّٰلِمِينَ ۝ وَنَجِّنَا بِرَحْمَتِكَ مِنَ ٱلْقَوْمِ ٱلْكَٰفِرِينَ ۝

---

a Acceptance of thinking which breaks fresh ground is always at the cost of the individual having to face numerous unforeseen problems in his society. That is why elderly people exercise caution in accepting any new idea. For a number of reasons elderly people are overwhelmed by a variety of considerations. In spite of admitting the correctness of a new idea, they are unable to proceed further and support it.

But the younger generation are generally free from such considerations. So it has always happened throughout history that only those who have not yet attained old age have gone ahead and accepted a new and revolutionary call. This happened likewise in the case of Moses.

The youth supporting Moses, on the one hand, risked the retribution of Pharaoh. On the other, they received no encouragement from the elders of their own community. Though these elders accepted the prophethood of Moses, they looked to their own interests, and did not want their sons and daughters to give enthusiastic support to Moses and thus incur the wrath of Pharaoh as a result.

However, the existence of such a state of affairs does not call for people to sit quietly, without taking any counter measures. They should keep in view God's support and favour, rather than human opposition. Relying on God, they should rise in defence of that Truth which they personally found impossible to support.

87 We revealed [Our will] to Moses and his brother, saying, 'Set aside for your people some houses in the city and turn them into places of worship, and be constant in prayer! And give [O Moses] the good news to the believers.' [a]

وَأَوْحَيْنَآ إِلَىٰ مُوسَىٰ وَأَخِيهِ أَن تَبَوَّءَا لِقَوْمِكُمَا بِمِصْرَ بُيُوتًا وَٱجْعَلُوا بُيُوتَكُمْ قِبْلَةً وَأَقِيمُوا ٱلصَّلَوٰةَ وَبَشِّرِ ٱلْمُؤْمِنِينَ ۝

---

[a] The word 'qiblah' in Arabic means a place to be turned towards or a centre of attention. Here, the statement 'build houses in the city' means that some houses or suitable portions of these houses in the settlements of Israelites should be set apart for use as centres for the missionary efforts of Moses; religious gatherings could be held there for consultation, and planning could be done there for God's word to be spread peacefully.

Pharaoh, the ruler of Egypt, was very displeased by Moses' sermons about the unity of God and the Hereafter. He imposed the most severe restrictions on him (Moses), so much so that it became very difficult for Moses to continue his dawah activities openly. At that time it was commanded that, instead of clashing with Pharaoh, the Israelites should continue their activities within a close circle; they should form small missionary and organisational centres in their settlements; and continue their work in a limited sphere without creating any disturbance.

The second command which was given to them under these circumstances was to say their prayers regularly, in order to develop a bond with God and to seek His help. They were to arrange to pray, both individually as well as collectively. Prayer is in fact a method of seeking the help of God by getting close to Him. By becoming engrossed in prayer, a servant of God brings himself to the position of humility and modesty, and it is in this position that he meets God; there is no other point from which he can meet God.

The secret of the welfare and salvation of the Israelites was hidden in this plan which was shown to them. This command was, in a way, a piece of good news for them, indicating that God was going to bring them out of the prevailing conditions into which their enemies had thrust them.

⁸⁸ Moses prayed, 'Our Lord, You have bestowed upon Pharaoh and his nobles pomp and wealth in the present life, whereby they lead people astray from Your path. Our Lord, destroy their riches and harden their hearts, so that they shall not believe until they are faced with grievous punishment.' [a]

وَقَالَ مُوسَىٰ رَبَّنَآ إِنَّكَ ءَاتَيْتَ فِرْعَوْنَ وَمَلَأَهُۥ زِينَةً وَأَمْوَٰلًا فِى ٱلْحَيَوٰةِ ٱلدُّنْيَا رَبَّنَا لِيُضِلُّوا۟ عَن سَبِيلِكَ رَبَّنَا ٱطْمِسْ عَلَىٰ أَمْوَٰلِهِمْ وَٱشْدُدْ عَلَىٰ قُلُوبِهِمْ فَلَا يُؤْمِنُوا۟ حَتَّىٰ يَرَوُا۟ ٱلْعَذَابَ ٱلْأَلِيمَ ۝

---

[a] Those who are anxious about the Hereafter are generally slow to accumulate worldly things as compared to those who, completely neglecting the Hereafter, rush towards worldly benefits. A lessening of worldly prosperity is the cost of being mindful of the Hereafter and material prosperity is attained at the cost of being neglectful of the Hereafter.

Moreover, one who has worldly glory and worldly things in abundance, develops a superiority complex. The result is that such people lose the innate capacity to recognise and appreciate the Truth when expounded by another and to bow down before it. Had they considered as a gift from God the resources they possessed, they would have spent them in supporting the cause of Truth. But, they consider these gifts of God stemming from their own talents. So, they utilise them to suppress the Truth and in this way maintain their supremacy.

'Whereby they lead people astray from Your path.' means that they used the wealth and resources granted by God solely for the purpose of alienating God's subjects from Him: instead of devoting them to the service of Truth, they utilized them in the service of falsehood. Here, for the sake of making statements more forcefully, the style of discourse has changed.

Moses called upon Pharaoh and his entourage to accept the true religion, and with the help of his great talents and God's asssistance, he made his message clear down to the last detail. In spite of this, Pharaoh and his nobles did not accept the message of Moses. At that time Moses prayed: 'O, God, give Pharaoh and others such punishment as arrogant people are destined to receive in accordance with Your law.' The curse of a prophet, although issuing from the mouth of God's representative, is actually a declaration made by God Himself.

⁸⁹ God said, 'Your prayer is granted, so continue, then, both of you, steadfastly on the right path, and do not follow the path of those who have no knowledge.'^a

قَالَ قَدْ أُجِيبَت دَّعْوَتُكُمَا فَٱسْتَقِيمَا وَلَا تَتَّبِعَآنِّ سَبِيلَ ٱلَّذِينَ لَا يَعْلَمُونَ ۞

---

^a The aforesaid prayer of Moses was accepted. However, as recorded in some traditions, there was a span of forty years between the prayer of Moses and the destruction of Pharaoh. (*at-Tafsir an-Nasafi*). This means that, even after that, for a long time the same conditions, in which Moses and his companions found themselves helpless, continued to prevail, while Pharaoh and his court continued as ever to enjoy a position of pomp and glory. Under these circumstances, if a man is unaware of God's way of allowing some respite to arrogant people, he will, in haste, give up his main task and fall a victim to disappointment and frustration.

⁹⁰ So We brought the Children of Israel across the sea. Pharaoh and his troops pursued them arrogantly and aggressively. When he was about to drown, [Pharaoh] exclaimed, 'I believe that there is no deity save Him in whom the Children of Israel believe, and I am of those who surrender themselves to Him!' ᵃ

وَجَـٰوَزْنَا بِبَنِىٓ إِسْرَٰٓءِيلَ ٱلْبَحْرَ فَأَتْبَعَهُمْ فِرْعَوْنُ وَجُنُودُهُۥ بَغْيًا وَعَدْوًا ۖ حَتَّىٰٓ إِذَآ أَدْرَكَهُ ٱلْغَرَقُ قَالَ ءَامَنتُ أَنَّهُۥ لَآ إِلَـٰهَ إِلَّا ٱلَّذِىٓ ءَامَنَتْ بِهِۦ بَنُوٓاْ إِسْرَٰٓءِيلَ وَأَنَا۠ مِنَ ٱلْمُسْلِمِينَ ۝

ᵃ The mission of Moses in Egypt was two-sided—firstly to call upon Pharaoh and his people to accept the oneness of God and the Hereafter and, secondly, to lead the Israelites out of Egypt into the open atmosphere of the desert and to train them there. When the call for the Truth, meant for Pharaoh, had been fully accomplished in accordance with God's command, Moses was commanded to set out from Egypt along with the Israelites. In order to reach the Sinai desert, they found it necessary to cross the Red Sea. When the Children of Israel reached the bank of the sea under the leadership of Moses, of God's command Moses struck the water with his staff. The waters parted and rose up to the right and left. They stayed like that and in between a dry path appeared. Moses and the Children of Israel easily crossed over by means of this path.

While in pursuit of the Children of Israel, Pharaoh forged ahead with his army. When he reached the bank of the sea, he saw that Moses and the Children of Israel were passing along a dry path. The wide stretch of the sea had been torn asunder and had given way to Moses and his companions. This event was, in fact, a sign from God. Pharaoh should have learned the lesson from this that Moses stood for the Truth and that God was with him. But he treated the separating of the waters as an ordinary mundane event instead of treating it as a Godly miracle. He saw only the sea between himself and Moses, though in fact God Himself was standing there. Thus an event in which there was a message of obedience (to God) and inclination (towards Him) for Pharaoh, merely caused an increase in his arrogance. He saw the 'sea' but did not see 'God.' He thought that he too could cross the sea as Moses and his companions had done.

⁹¹'Only now? When you had always been a rebel, and a wrongdoer. ⁹² So We shall save your body this day, so that you may serve as a sign for those who come after you: for many people are indeed heedless of Our signs.'ᵃ

ءَآلۡـَٔنَ وَقَدۡ عَصَيۡتَ قَبۡلُ وَكُنتَ مِنَ الۡمُفۡسِدِينَ ۝ فَالۡيَوۡمَ نُنَجِّيكَ بِبَدَنِكَ لِتَكُونَ لِمَنۡ خَلۡفَكَ ءَايَةً وَإِنَّ كَثِيرًا مِّنَ النَّاسِ عَنۡ ءَايَٰتِنَا لَغَٰفِلُونَ ۝

ᵃ With this thought, Pharaoh and his army entered the sea. The water of the sea had split in two only for the sake of Moses and his companions and not for Pharaoh and his followers. So, when Pharaoh and his army reached the middle of the sea, both sides of the water joined, in compliance with God's command, and Pharaoh along with his army was drowned. While drowning, he declared his acceptance of faith, but it was useless, because in the eyes of Almighty God, only a voluntary embracing of the Faith is reliable and acceptable and not a compulsory profession of Faith.

The result of disobedience to God arising from arrogance is destruction. Examples of such incidents used to occur from time to time during the period of the Prophet. However, some examples of this type have been given historical shape by God, so that they might continue to give lessons to man in later ages after the time of the prophets had ended. One of these historical examples from the period of Moses is that of Pharaoh (Rameses II) whose mummified body was found by archaeologists in the ancient Egyptian town of Thebes. It is now kept on display in the museum at Cairo.

93 We settled the Children of Israel in a blessed land, and We provided them with good things. And it was not until knowledge [of God's revelation] was granted to them that they began to hold divergent views. Your Lord will judge between them on the Day of Resurrection concerning that in which they differed. [a]

وَلَقَدۡ بَوَّأۡنَا بَنِىٓ إِسۡرَٰٓءِيلَ مُبَوَّأَ صِدۡقٍ وَرَزَقۡنَٰهُم مِّنَ ٱلطَّيِّبَٰتِ فَمَا ٱخۡتَلَفُوا۟ حَتَّىٰ جَآءَهُمُ ٱلۡعِلۡمُ إِنَّ رَبَّكَ يَقۡضِى بَيۡنَهُمۡ يَوۡمَ ٱلۡقِيَٰمَةِ فِيمَا كَانُوا۟ فِيهِ يَخۡتَلِفُونَ ٩٣

---

[a] The Israelites were the bearers of God's religion in ancient times. God granted them the favour of saving them from their enemy, Pharaoh. Then He caused them to be led to the open atmosphere of Sinai. There, by His instrumentality, water and provisions were made available to them. Through this training in the desert, a new powerful generation came into being. This generation, after Moses, constituted a great nation, and in the fertile areas of Syria, Jordan and Palestine, established the Israelite empire, which remained in existence for several centuries.

The result of this favour should have been that the Children of Israel should have remained obedient to God and grateful to Him and should have made the service of religion the purpose of their lives. But in spite of clear guidance, they had gone astray.

What was it that is called here 'going astray'? It was having differences among themselves. They possessed the knowledge revealed by God which was the only Truth. But they had differences in the correct construction to be put on this knowledge and became divided (at-Tafsir an-Nasafi). As long as a community is one, religion remains united. But, later on, differences develop among them in the explanation of the knowledge of God's revelation (al-'ilm). Some insist on one opinion and others on another. In order to establish the truth of its way of thinking, every faction resorts to unnecessary discussions, speeches and public debates, so much so that a stage is reached when the real knowledge of God's revelation (al-'ilm) remains bound in books and all its strength becomes dissipated in interpretations and explanations. In this way, in spite of being from the same mould, people become divisively opinionated by becoming involved in the subsidiary aspects of religious teachings.

'Your Lord will judge between them on the Day of Resurrection' is apparently in the transitive form, but actually it is in the intransitive form. The idea is that on Judgement Day, when God makes His appearance, all men and women will forget their differences and accept the one and only Truth. Had they been God-fearing, they would have converged on one opinion. Fearlessness leads to a multiplicity of opinions, while fear results in a convergence of opinion.

⁹⁴ If you are in any doubt concerning what We have sent down to you, then question those who have read the Book before you: the Truth has come to you from your Lord, so do not be one of the doubters—⁹⁵do not be one who rejects God's signs, for then you would become one of the losers.ᵃ

فَإِن كُنتَ فِى شَكٍّ مِّمَّآ أَنزَلْنَآ إِلَيْكَ فَسْـَٔلِ ٱلَّذِينَ يَقْرَءُونَ ٱلْكِتَٰبَ مِن قَبْلِكَ ۚ لَقَدْ جَآءَكَ ٱلْحَقُّ مِن رَّبِّكَ فَلَا تَكُونَنَّ مِنَ ٱلْمُمْتَرِينَ ﴿٩٤﴾ وَلَا تَكُونَنَّ مِنَ ٱلَّذِينَ كَذَّبُوا۟ بِـَٔايَٰتِ ٱللَّهِ فَتَكُونَ مِنَ ٱلْخَٰسِرِينَ ﴿٩٥﴾

ᵃ Prophets have always come to the world with the divine Truth without any kind of human addition, but obedience to such a call has always been the most difficult task for man. Bowing to the call for pure Truth has to be at the cost of negating one's own self; in order to accept the Truth, one has to lower one's own status in comparison with that of the preacher, and doing so is undoubtedly a most difficult proposition. That is why it never happens that as soon as the call to accept the Truth is issued, people start flocking towards it. Truth in this world has always been received with opposition and distaste.

Considering this disrespect for Truth, the preacher of Truth sometimes entertains doubts about whether he himself has erred in some way. In this verse, the preacher has been instructed to guard himself against such thinking.

A very clear proof of these doubts being unfounded is that previous prophets and dayees also had to face very similar situations in the past. Those who are aware of their history know full well that, in this world, it has never happened that when a prophet comes forward, he immediately gains public popularity. Then, if similar situations arise in the case of dayees of later ages, why should that cause anxiety or worry?

If a man's mind testifies to the truth of something, and if even then he gives it up, simply because of the opposition of others, then this amounts to a refusal to accept the signs of God. God appears before man through His signs, so that the acceptance of whatever is established by means of reasoning, is God's right over man. So, what will be the fate of one who denies God's right—if not loss and destruction?

⁹⁶ Those against whom your Lord's word has been confirmed will never believe; ⁹⁷ not even if every Sign were to come to them—until they see the painful punishment. ⁹⁸ Why was there no other people, save the people of Jonah, who should have believed so that their belief would have benefited them. Once they believed, We lifted the torment of shame from them during their worldly life and let them enjoy Our provision for a while.ᵃ

إِنَّ ٱلَّذِينَ حَقَّتْ عَلَيْهِمْ كَلِمَتُ رَبِّكَ لَا يُؤْمِنُونَ ۝ وَلَوْ جَآءَتْهُمْ كُلُّ ءَايَةٍ حَتَّىٰ يَرَوُاْ ٱلْعَذَابَ ٱلْأَلِيمَ ۝ فَلَوْلَا كَانَتْ قَرْيَةٌ ءَامَنَتْ فَنَفَعَهَآ إِيمَٰنُهَآ إِلَّا قَوْمَ يُونُسَ لَمَّآ ءَامَنُواْ كَشَفْنَا عَنْهُمْ عَذَابَ ٱلْخِزْيِ فِى ٱلْحَيَوٰةِ ٱلدُّنْيَا وَمَتَّعْنَٰهُمْ إِلَىٰ حِينٍ ۝

ᵃ When the Truth appears before a man, his mind testifies to its correctness. But, in order to achieve what is right, man has to give something, and on this score man is not ready to give. In order to do so, man has to belittle himself in comparison with the other person; he has to acknowledge the other's interests; he has to sacrifice his own prestige to be able to accept the Truth. Whatever proposition should have been readily accepted by him is the very thing which he denies and rejects. Man's psychology is so formed that once he takes a direction, his whole mind takes the same direction. That is why, after a man's deviation from the Truth, every passing day, he becomes more and more conditioned in his way of thinking, so much so that he does not remain capable of turning towards the Truth.

Such people, with a view to justifying their stand, make efforts to give the impression that theirs is the correct way of thinking but, in fact, it is the result of obstinacy and prejudice, arising from worldly considerations. However, at the moment of God's retribution, this bubble will burst. The intensity of fear man feels will force him to bow down before that very thing which previously he had not been ready to accept so long as he felt fearless.

In past ages, the prophets had been faced the same situation, i.e. their addressee communities did not embrace the Faith till the last moment. However, the moment they were seized by God's retribution, they cried out that they were embracing the Faith. As long as God was calling to them in the language of reasoning, they did not accept, but when God caused them to be struck down by His powers, they declared their acceptance there and then. But such acceptance is not effective in the eyes of God. God requires acceptance when a man bows down on the strength of reasoning and not when he feels coerced. ▶

⁹⁹ Had your Lord pleased, all the people on earth would have believed in Him, without exception. So will you compel people to become believers? ¹⁰⁰ No soul can believe except by the will of God. He will place the filth [of doubt] upon those who do not use their reason.ᵃ

وَلَوْ شَاءَ رَبُّكَ لَآمَنَ مَن فِى ٱلْأَرْضِ كُلُّهُمْ جَمِيعًا ۚ أَفَأَنتَ تُكْرِهُ ٱلنَّاسَ حَتَّىٰ يَكُونُوا۟ مُؤْمِنِينَ ۝ وَمَا كَانَ لِنَفْسٍ أَن تُؤْمِنَ إِلَّا بِإِذْنِ ٱللَّهِ ۚ وَيَجْعَلُ ٱلرِّجْسَ عَلَى ٱلَّذِينَ لَا يَعْقِلُونَ ۝

Jonah (Yunus) was sent to Nineveh, an old city in Iraq. He started preaching there, but its denizens did not embrace the Faith. Finally, according to the tradition of the prophets, he migrated. While leaving Nineveh, he told people that they would face God's retribution. After the departure of Jonah, the preliminary signs of retribution appeared. At that time they did not behave as the community of Hud had done. On seeing the clouds of retribution gather, the latter had said, 'This cloud is coming to bring rain for us.' Unlike this, the community of Jonah immediately experienced an awakening. All its members, along with their cattle, women and children, assembled on a stretch of open ground and started praying to God in all humility. Thereafter the punishment was averted. The acceptance of Faith just prior to the meting out of punishment is also acceptable provided it is as perfect as that of the community of Jonah.

ᵃ 'Had your Lord pleased, all the people on earth would have believed in Him,' means that it was possible for God to have made the system of the world of human beings one in which everything is completely regulated by the commands of God. But, with regard to human beings this is not at all the scheme of God, which is to keep man in a free atmosphere, give him the opportunity to obey God of his own free will and voluntarily perform the tasks which the rest of the world does under compulsion. The eternal bounties of Paradise are to be obtained at the cost of this voluntary obedience.

'No soul can believe except by the will of God,' means that, in the present world, man will be granted the blessing of Faith only on his adopting the method laid down by God for this purpose. In the present world, the way for man to be blessed with Faith is by his using his mind to understand the call to the Faith. The mind of an individual which is swamped by worldly considerations is as if immersed in mud. There is no question of such a person being blessed with the bounty of Faith.

101 Say, 'Look at whatever [exists] in heavens and on earth.' But signs and warnings do not benefit the unbelievers. 102 What can they be waiting for but the punishment that came to those before them? Say, 'So wait; I am one of those waiting with you.' 103 Then We shall save Our messengers and those who believe. Thus We have made it incumbent upon Ourself to save the believers.[a]

104 Say, 'O people, if you are in doubt concerning my religion, then [know that] I do not worship those whom you worship instead of God, but rather I worship God who will cause you to die, for I am commanded to be one of the believers.' 105 And set your face towards the [true] faith in all uprightness, and do not be one of those who ascribe partners to God;[b]

قُلِ ٱنظُرُواْ مَاذَا فِى ٱلسَّمَٰوَٰتِ وَٱلْأَرْضِ وَمَا تُغْنِى ٱلْءَايَٰتُ وَٱلنُّذُرُ عَن قَوْمٍ لَّا يُؤْمِنُونَ ۝ فَهَلْ يَنتَظِرُونَ إِلَّا مِثْلَ أَيَّامِ ٱلَّذِينَ خَلَوْاْ مِن قَبْلِهِمْ قُلْ فَٱنتَظِرُوٓاْ إِنِّى مَعَكُم مِّنَ ٱلْمُنتَظِرِينَ ۝ ثُمَّ نُنَجِّى رُسُلَنَا وَٱلَّذِينَ ءَامَنُواْ كَذَٰلِكَ حَقًّا عَلَيْنَا نُنجِ ٱلْمُؤْمِنِينَ ۝ قُلْ يَٰٓأَيُّهَا ٱلنَّاسُ إِن كُنتُمْ فِى شَكٍّ مِّن دِينِى فَلَآ أَعْبُدُ ٱلَّذِينَ تَعْبُدُونَ مِن دُونِ ٱللَّهِ وَلَٰكِنْ أَعْبُدُ ٱللَّهَ ٱلَّذِى يَتَوَفَّىٰكُمْ وَأُمِرْتُ أَنْ أَكُونَ مِنَ ٱلْمُؤْمِنِينَ ۝ وَأَنْ أَقِمْ وَجْهَكَ لِلدِّينِ حَنِيفًا وَلَا تَكُونَنَّ مِنَ ٱلْمُشْرِكِينَ ۝

[a] In the universe surrounding us, there are innumerable signs which prove God's existence. Moreover, in the world, events (such as cyclones and tornadoes) occur as warnings and this should make a man serious in his state of trial, that is, in a world where man has the discretion to accept or disown the Truth. So, what man does is this: he concocts some explanations of his own for these events so as to divert attention from their true significance and thus remains deprived of guidance.

When man does not understand the language of reasoning, it is as if he is waiting for the veil of testing to be removed and for God to appear to give His final verdict. But when that day comes, it will be entirely different from the present day. Today, those who accept and those who reject are apparently in the same condition. But when the Day of Judgement arrives, only those who had proved themselves to be Truth-worshippers will be at peace, while all of the others will be overwhelmed by their punishment and they will find no escape route which could give them some respite.

[b] The preacher first of all gives his sermon in the language of reason. But if his hearers, even after hearing his arguments remain in doubt, what he must do finally is to express the veracity of his message in sterner language. ▶

[106] and do not invoke besides God what can neither help nor harm you. If you do, you will be one of the wrongdoers. [107] If God inflicts harm on you, no one can remove it but He, and if He intends good for you, no one can withhold His bounty; He grants His bounty to any of His servants whom He will. He is the Most Forgiving, and the Most Merciful.[a]

وَلَا تَدْعُ مِن دُونِ ٱللَّهِ مَا لَا يَنفَعُكَ وَلَا يَضُرُّكَ فَإِن فَعَلْتَ فَإِنَّكَ إِذًا مِّنَ ٱلظَّٰلِمِينَ ۝ وَإِن يَمْسَسْكَ ٱللَّهُ بِضُرٍّ فَلَا كَاشِفَ لَهُۥ إِلَّا هُوَ وَإِن يُرِدْكَ بِخَيْرٍ فَلَا رَآدَّ لِفَضْلِهِۦ يُصِيبُ بِهِۦ مَن يَشَآءُ مِنْ عِبَادِهِۦ وَهُوَ ٱلْغَفُورُ ٱلرَّحِيمُ ۝

When a preacher of the Oneness of God tells the polytheists (those who ascribe partners to God): 'I do not worship that which you worship' this is not simply a declaration, but an argument in itself. It means: 'I am also a man like you. I have a mind as you have. Then, why is it that the veracity of something which is understandable to me is not understandable to you?'

If Truth is understandable at the level of one man, it proves that it should be understandable to others also. In spite of this, if others reject it, then it must surely be due to some shortcoming on their part and not to any deficiency in the call to the Truth. If a thing seen by one who has eyes, is not seen by another who likewise has eyes, it simply proves that the latter is not the true possessor of eyes, because it is not possible in this world that a thing which is seen by one person having eyes cannot be seen by another person in spite of his also having eyes.

[a] Death testifies to the fact that man is completely powerless in this world. Death proves all those things false, on the strength of which man opts for the way of arrogance and denial of God. Death introduces man, on the one hand, to his helplessness and on the other to God's majestic power. It shows that in this world there is nobody who has the power to grant benefits or inflict harm. If a man has a mind capable of learning lessons from events, then the event of death is enough to reform him. It makes a man a perfect worshipper of God.

A time comes for every man when, helpless, he surrenders himself to death. Similarly, it is not within the power of any man, whether it concerns benefit or harm, to cause things to happen as he wants. He receives the desired benefit in any case; and remains safe from undesirable harm in any case.

This state of affair shows that man is a powerless creature: he lives in a world where there is some Being who rules over him.

¹⁰⁸ Say, 'Mankind, Truth has come to you from your Lord! Anyone who accepts guidance is guided only for his own sake; and he who goes astray does so at his own peril. I am not appointed as your keeper.' ¹⁰⁹ Follow what is revealed to you, [O Prophet], and be steadfast until God gives His judgement. He is the Best of Judges.^a

قُلْ يَـٰٓأَيُّهَا ٱلنَّاسُ قَدْ جَآءَكُمُ ٱلْحَقُّ مِن رَّبِّكُمْ ۖ فَمَنِ ٱهْتَدَىٰ فَإِنَّمَا يَهْتَدِى لِنَفْسِهِۦ ۖ وَمَن ضَلَّ فَإِنَّمَا يَضِلُّ عَلَيْهَا ۖ وَمَآ أَنَا۠ عَلَيْكُم بِوَكِيلٍ ۞ وَٱتَّبِعْ مَا يُوحَىٰٓ إِلَيْكَ وَٱصْبِرْ حَتَّىٰ يَحْكُمَ ٱللَّهُ ۚ وَهُوَ خَيْرُ ٱلْحَـٰكِمِينَ ۞

^a The real task of the call of Truth—conveying the message of God to a specific group—is fulfilled when the preacher proves that he is quite serious about his goals and finally makes the Truth known, with the help of sound reasoning.

If the preacher rationalises the question of Truth according to the standard of the time, he bears full testimony to the Truth, and unmindful of gain or loss, he continues his preaching, tolerating all kinds of trouble and unpleasantness. Thereafter, the process of conclusive argument in relation to the addressee-community is completed; after which nobody will have the excuse of ignorance before God.

The real work of a preacher lies in his adherence to divine revelations, that is, in conducting himself personally at the behest of our Lord and also repeatedly calling upon others to strive to bow to the will of the Lord in order to earn His pleasure. The preacher must keep this up continuously with patience, wisdom and well-wishing. After this, all the stages that remain are directly under the purview of God. Any further step on the part of the preachers will be proper only when God Himself has taken some decision upon it and has made His will quite clear.

God's decision always appears in the shape of circumstances. When, according to God's assessment, a preacher's missionary work has reached the required stage, God causes such changes in the situation as enable the preacher to enter the next phase of his preaching.

11. HUD

In the name of God,
the Most Gracious, the Most Merciful

Alif Lam Ra

[This is] a Book, with verses which are fundamental [in nature], and then expounded in detail by One who is all wise and all aware. ²[It teaches] that you should worship none but God. I am sent to you from Him to warn you and to give you good tidings. ³ Seek forgiveness from your Lord; then turn towards Him [in repentance]. He will make generous provision for you for an appointed term and will bestow His grace on all who merit it! But if you turn away, then I fear for you the torment of a dreadful Day: ⁴ to God you shall all return; and He has power over all things.ᵃ

الٓر ۚ كِتَٰبٌ أُحْكِمَتْ ءَايَٰتُهُۥ ثُمَّ فُصِّلَتْ مِن لَّدُنْ حَكِيمٍ خَبِيرٍ ﴿١﴾ أَلَّا تَعْبُدُوٓا۟ إِلَّا ٱللَّهَ ۚ إِنَّنِى لَكُم مِّنْهُ نَذِيرٌ وَبَشِيرٌ ﴿٢﴾ وَأَنِ ٱسْتَغْفِرُوا۟ رَبَّكُمْ ثُمَّ تُوبُوٓا۟ إِلَيْهِ يُمَتِّعْكُم مَّتَٰعًا حَسَنًا إِلَىٰٓ أَجَلٍ مُّسَمًّى وَيُؤْتِ كُلَّ ذِى فَضْلٍ فَضْلَهُۥ ۖ وَإِن تَوَلَّوْا۟ فَإِنِّىٓ أَخَافُ عَلَيْكُمْ عَذَابَ يَوْمٍ كَبِيرٍ ﴿٣﴾ إِلَى ٱللَّهِ مَرْجِعُكُمْ ۖ وَهُوَ عَلَىٰ كُلِّ شَىْءٍ قَدِيرٌ ﴿٤﴾

ᵃ The message of the Quran is that man should not worship anyone except the one and only God. He should make the one and only God his everything; he should fear Him alone and repose his hopes in Him alone; his mind and heart should obey Him alone. In the affairs of his life, he should give prior consideration to His will and pleasure. He should be willing to place himself in the position of a worshipper and give God the status of the worshipped one.

The task of the prophet is, in fact, that of making man aware of this position. This has been powerfully and lucidly described in the Quran. Now, what is expected of man is that he should give the correct response to the divine message. He should not ignore it under the influence of such feelings as jealousy, hauteur, vested interest or self-centredness, but duly accept it and turn towards God. He should seek God's pardon for his past sins and, for the future, he should solicit God's help. ▶

624

⁵ See how they cover themselves up to hide [their thoughts] from Him. But when they cover themselves up with their garments, He knows what they hide and what they reveal. He knows their innermost thoughts. ⁶ There is not a living creature on the earth but it is for God to provide its sustenance. He knows its dwelling and its [final] resting place. All this is recorded in a clear book.ᵃ

أَلَا إِنَّهُمْ يَثْنُونَ صُدُورَهُمْ لِيَسْتَخْفُوا۟ مِنْهُ أَلَا حِينَ يَسْتَغْشُونَ ثِيَابَهُمْ يَعْلَمُ مَا يُسِرُّونَ وَمَا يُعْلِنُونَ إِنَّهُۥ عَلِيمٌۢ بِذَاتِ ٱلصُّدُورِ ۞ وَمَا مِن دَآبَّةٍ فِى ٱلْأَرْضِ إِلَّا عَلَى ٱللَّهِ رِزْقُهَا وَيَعْلَمُ مُسْتَقَرَّهَا وَمُسْتَوْدَعَهَا كُلٌّ فِى كِتَٰبٍ مُّبِينٍ ۝

If food is presented to a man and he accepts it, it means that he intends to stimulate his physical growth. On the contrary, if he does not accept the food, it is as if he means to stunt his physical growth. The same holds for the call to the Truth. When a man accepts the Truth, in reality he accepts that Divine provision which enters into him and causes the righteous growth of his soul and his body, and finally takes him to that stage of his spiritual progress which entitles him to enter the Gardens of Paradise.

One who does not accept the call to the Truth has, in effect, deprived his soul of the opportunities afforded by Divine uplift. While the acceptor of Truth lives in modesty, the rejecter of Truth will be flawed by hauteur. While the acceptor of Truth will spend each moment of his life in the remembrance of God, the denier of God will spend his time in the remembrance of beings other than God. While the acceptor of Truth adopts the way of obedience to God on all occasions in his life, the denier will instead adopt the way of arrogance. The result of this will be that the former will leave this world with a healthy and developed soul and will be treated as deserving of being settled in the rarefied atmosphere of Paradise. The soul of the latter will be unhealthy and under-developed and will deserve only to be thrown on to the garbage dump of hell.

ᵃ When the call to the unity of God (tawhid) was made to certain chiefs of the Quraysh, they rose and, nonchalantly donning their mantles, they left.

This is, in fact, a way of ignoring something. When a man considers a preacher lowly in comparison to himself, he behaves in this way. But he forgets that Almighty God knows very well the psychology of his doing so. This is not only ignoring a man (the preacher) but amounts also to ignoring God Himself, Who knows all open and hidden matters.

And then, what will be man's condition when he faces God? He will see that God, whom he had ignored, was the Being who gave him all that he possessed—even those things on the strength of which he had ignored the word of God. Man is living in God's world and ultimately he has to return to his Maker. But he lives as if he has no connection with God today and will have nothing to do with Him in future.

7 Enthroned above the waters, it was He who created the heavens and the earth in six Days [periods], in order to test which of you is best in conduct. If you say, 'You will [all] be raised up after death,' those who deny the truth will say, 'This is just sheer sorcery!' 8 If We defer their punishment till an appointed time, they ask, 'What is holding it back?' On the Day when it overtakes them, there will be nothing to avert it from them; and what they used to mock at shall encompass them.[a]

وَهُوَ ٱلَّذِى خَلَقَ ٱلسَّمَٰوَٰتِ وَٱلْأَرْضَ فِى سِتَّةِ أَيَّامٍ وَكَانَ عَرْشُهُۥ عَلَى ٱلْمَآءِ لِيَبْلُوَكُمْ أَيُّكُمْ أَحْسَنُ عَمَلًا وَلَئِن قُلْتَ إِنَّكُم مَّبْعُوثُونَ مِنۢ بَعْدِ ٱلْمَوْتِ لَيَقُولَنَّ ٱلَّذِينَ كَفَرُوٓا۟ إِنْ هَٰذَآ إِلَّا سِحْرٌ مُّبِينٌ ۝ وَلَئِنْ أَخَّرْنَا عَنْهُمُ ٱلْعَذَابَ إِلَىٰٓ أُمَّةٍ مَّعْدُودَةٍ لَّيَقُولُنَّ مَا يَحْبِسُهُۥٓ أَلَا يَوْمَ يَأْتِيهِمْ لَيْسَ مَصْرُوفًا عَنْهُمْ وَحَاقَ بِهِم مَّا كَانُوا۟ بِهِۦ يَسْتَهْزِءُونَ ۝

[a] The present world was created by God in six days, that is, in six stages or six periods. There was a period when its surface was covered with water. In this part of God's domain, only water was seen everywhere at that time. Then, at God's behest, patches of land emerged and water filled the great hollows which became the seas and the oceans. In this way it was possible for various species of life to come into existence on the earth.

God has the power to give an ideal shape to things and events, but He has chosen to fashion this world in a less than ideal way, so that it may serve as a testing ground for man. Indeed, God's purpose in creating the world and settling human beings upon it was to single out the doers of good deeds. 'Good deed' is actually another name for a realistic deed, i.e. one which a man is required to perform in accordance with reality, without there being any pressure upon him to do. The realistic person is one who appreciates the hidden hand of God by peering through the cause-and-effect veil which, by design, He has drawn over His creations; he is one who, in spite of apparently having power, renders himself powerless; one who, in spite of having the option of leading an arrogant life, becomes obedient to God.

In the present world, the selection of such realistic persons continues unremittingly. When the period of this selection is over, the present system will be replaced by another standard system in which all good things will be allotted only to those who perform good deeds, leaving all bad things for the wrongdoers.

Almighty God does not immediately catch hold of those who deny the truth and the arrogant in view of His rule of giving respite; i.e. He gives them respite to the fullest possible extent, so that they may be warned and reform themselves, or finally prove themselves guilty. This rule of respite becomes a cause of misunderstanding to certain arrogant people. They forget their real position of powerlessness and start indulging in tall talk. But, when they are smitten by God's scourge, they will there and then come to know how helpless they are in comparison to God.

⁹ When We bestow upon man a measure of Our grace and then take it away from him, he yields to despair and becomes ungrateful. ¹⁰ And if, after adversity, We let him taste good fortune he says, 'All my ills are gone.' He becomes exultant and boastful. ¹¹ Not so those who are patient and do good deeds. They shall have forgiveness and a great reward.ᵃ

وَلَئِنْ أَذَقْنَا ٱلْإِنسَـٰنَ مِنَّا رَحْمَةً ثُمَّ نَزَعْنَـٰهَا مِنْهُ إِنَّهُۥ لَيَـُٔوسٌ كَفُورٌ ۝ وَلَئِنْ أَذَقْنَـٰهُ نَعْمَآءَ بَعْدَ ضَرَّآءَ مَسَّتْهُ لَيَقُولَنَّ ذَهَبَ ٱلسَّيِّـَٔاتُ عَنِّىٓ إِنَّهُۥ لَفَرِحٌ فَخُورٌ ۝ إِلَّا ٱلَّذِينَ صَبَرُواْ وَعَمِلُواْ ٱلصَّـٰلِحَـٰتِ أُوْلَـٰٓئِكَ لَهُم مَّغْفِرَةٌ وَأَجْرٌ كَبِيرٌ ۝

ᵃ In the present world, man is given ease and hardship by turns. But here, neither is comfort given as a reward nor is hardship imposed as a punishment. The purpose of both is to put human beings to the test. This world is a great examination hall. The purpose of whatever happens to man here is to see what sort of responses he offers to different testing conditions.

That man is a failure whose behaviour is such that when he receives some worldly bounties from God, he becomes proud; he behaves with haughtiness towards those who appear to him of a lower status than himself. Similarly, that person is also a failure who displays ingratitude when some bounty is taken away from him or he becomes the victim of some affliction. Even after being deprived of something, a man still possesses many things granted to him by God. But man forgets them and becomes so desperate over that one loss, it is as if he had been robbed of everything.

On the contrary, those who fully measure up to the standards of Faith are individuals who are patient and righteous in their deeds. That is, in spite of every setback, they keep their emotional balance and continue to exercise moderation; they continue to do whatever they are required to do as subjects of God.

What is patience? It is a man's conduct being shaped by principles and not by the conditions and situations in which he finds himself. Whatever may be the condition, he should rise above them and formulate his views purely in the light of Truth. He should have the courage to live on the level of his Faith and moral awareness, unaffected by the prevailing conditions. This sort of life is one of piety. Those who establish their piety in this way will be the ones who will share God's bounties in the future life and have a place in God's eternal Gardens.

¹² You may [feel the inclination] to leave aside a part of what is revealed to you and you may be distressed because they say, 'Why has no treasure been sent down to him, why has no angel come with him?' But you are only to give warning. God is the guardian of all things. ¹³ If they say, 'He has invented it himself.' Say, 'If you are truthful, produce ten invented chapters like it, and call on whom you can besides God, to help you.' ¹⁴ But if they do not respond to you, then know that this [Quran] is sent down with God's knowledge and that there is no deity but Him. Will you then surrender yourselves to Him? ^a

فَلَعَلَّكَ تَارِكٌ بَعْضَ مَا يُوحَىٰ إِلَيْكَ وَضَآئِقٌ بِهِۦ صَدْرُكَ أَن يَقُولُوا۟ لَوْلَآ أُنزِلَ عَلَيْهِ كَنزٌ أَوْ جَآءَ مَعَهُۥ مَلَكٌ إِنَّمَآ أَنتَ نَذِيرٌ وَٱللَّهُ عَلَىٰ كُلِّ شَىْءٍ وَكِيلٌ ۝ أَمْ يَقُولُونَ ٱفْتَرَىٰهُ قُلْ فَأْتُوا۟ بِعَشْرِ سُوَرٍ مِّثْلِهِۦ مُفْتَرَيَٰتٍ وَٱدْعُوا۟ مَنِ ٱسْتَطَعْتُم مِّن دُونِ ٱللَّهِ إِن كُنتُمْ صَٰدِقِينَ ۝ فَإِلَّمْ يَسْتَجِيبُوا۟ لَكُمْ فَٱعْلَمُوٓا۟ أَنَّمَآ أُنزِلَ بِعِلْمِ ٱللَّهِ وَأَن لَّآ إِلَٰهَ إِلَّا هُوَ فَهَلْ أَنتُم مُّسْلِمُونَ ۝

---

^a When the Prophet Muhammad started opposing the ascribing of partners to God (*shirk*) and called upon the people to accept the oneness of God (*tawhid*), his addressees became perturbed. This was because the people most adversely affected by his statements were their great ones—the great ones whose religion they had adopted and were proud to venerate. The position was that these leading lights of ancient Arabia had attained pre-eminence in their eyes through a historical process, while as yet no historical greatness was attached to the Prophet Muhammad. He appeared to them at that time as a man of no consequence. So, the people of Arabia were greatly upset that an ordinary man was making statements which made their leaders lose in credibility.

Under these circumstances the thought crosses the preacher's mind that he should at least temporarily give up being critical in his approach and present his message in a more palatable way. 'You may (feel the inclination) to leave aside a part of what is revealed to you' means this very portion of the revelations, which contained criticism of polytheistic beliefs. But, Almighty God wants to clarify everything. And if, as a result of fully clarifying the Truth, the preacher is made the butt of ridicule and opposed, this inimical reaction on the part of the addressees is the cost a man has to pay in this world for becoming the preacher of unadulterated Truth.

The most certain proof of the veracity of God's messenger is his inimitable discourse. Those who scorned the Prophet and who rejected the idea that this apparently ordinary man possessed that Truth, which even their great ones did not have, were told that they should not test the Prophet's veracity on the basis of his material condition, but should appreciate that his missionary discourse was so great that neither they nor their leaders could produce the like of it. ▶

15 Those who desire the life of this world and all its finery shall be repaid in full in this life for their deeds—nothing shall be denied them. 16 These are the people who, in the world to come, shall have nothing but Hellfire and all that they used to do shall be in vain.^a

مَن كَانَ يُرِيدُ ٱلْحَيَوٰةَ ٱلدُّنْيَا وَزِينَتَهَا نُوَفِّ إِلَيْهِمْ أَعْمَٰلَهُمْ فِيهَا وَهُمْ فِيهَا لَا يُبْخَسُونَ ۝ أُوْلَٰٓئِكَ ٱلَّذِينَ لَيْسَ لَهُمْ فِى ٱلْءَاخِرَةِ إِلَّا ٱلنَّارُ وَحَبِطَ مَا صَنَعُواْ فِيهَا وَبَٰطِلٌ مَّا كَانُواْ يَعْمَلُونَ ۝

This inimitable distinction is a definite proof of the fact that the Prophet was speaking for and on behalf of God. In spite of this clear sign of the Prophet's veracity, why are people still hesitating to become the obedient servants of God?

^a There are two kinds of religion—one adulterated and the other unadulterated. The former, although a compromise between religion and worldliness, displays the label of religion. This is why in every period big institutions come into existence on its basis and through them, people with vested interests receive worldly benefits in the name of 'religion'.

The case of unadulterated religion is just the opposite. When its call goes out, it is to project a purely theoretical Truth; it is not surrounded by economic interests and leadership considerations. This being so, when the call of unadulterated religion reaches those who have attained a high status and great respect in the name of adulterated religion, they are horrified, because they feel that, on adopting it, they will lose all their worldly benefits.

People often engage themselves in worldly activities in the name of religion. The call of pure religion among such people amounts to exposing them for what they really are. The call of truth is, in fact, a subtle test paper for its addressees. Now the very people who were engaged in activities in the name of religion resist the call of truth. Their resistance to the divine message shows that their 'religious' observances were, in fact, interest-oriented worldly activities. Had they been sincere in their service to religion, they would have lost no time in recognizing the Truth in its unadulterated form.

The call of Truth thus serves as a discriminator between sincere and insincere people. The sincere are ready to make any sacrifice for the true cause of religion. But the insincere favour only that religion which ensures the safety of their worldly gains. They cannot even contemplate losing their material assets. They want to spend their time and energy only on those religious activities which bring them fame, honour and all other worldly benefits. Obviously such efforts cannot bear fruit in the Hereafter.

¹⁷ Can they be compared to those who possess a clear proof from their Lord, followed up by a witness from Him, preceded by the Book of Moses, as a guide and a mercy? These people believe in it; whereas those groups that deny its truth are promised the Fire. Therefore, have no doubt about it. It is the truth from your Lord, but most people do not believe it.^a

أَفَمَن كَانَ عَلَىٰ بَيِّنَةٍ مِّن رَّبِّهِۦ وَيَتْلُوهُ شَاهِدٌ مِّنْهُ وَمِن قَبْلِهِۦ كِتَٰبُ مُوسَىٰٓ إِمَامًا وَرَحْمَةً أُوْلَٰٓئِكَ يُؤْمِنُونَ بِهِۦ وَمَن يَكْفُرْ بِهِۦ مِنَ ٱلْأَحْزَابِ فَٱلنَّارُ مَوْعِدُهُۥ فَلَا تَكُ فِي مِرْيَةٍ مِّنْهُ إِنَّهُ ٱلْحَقُّ مِن رَّبِّكَ وَلَٰكِنَّ أَكْثَرَ ٱلنَّاسِ لَا يُؤْمِنُونَ ۝

^a When the Prophet Muhammad called upon the people of Arabia to accept the oneness of God, only a few individuals accepted it, while many rejected it. This is what happens in every period with the call to the Truth.

God created every man with an upright nature as befits his human status. In every corner of the world, there are signs which proclaim the existence of his Creator and give indications of His creation scheme. Moreover, a long line of God's prophets, one of whom was Moses, have been coming into the world, right from the beginning of the human era, to convey the divine message to man. The scripture brought by Moses is still extant in some form or the other.

Now, one who is serious and sincere will have the ability to learn lessons from things, and will be so familiar with the Truth that, whenever a preacher presents the Truth to him, he will immediately recognise it. His heart and mind will bear testimony to that call of Truth; he will go ahead and readily adopt it, as if it were the very voice of his heart. But the condition of most people is that they do not look upon things with any great seriousness. They mar their lives by indulging in superficial show and ephemeral interests. Their being busy in unnecessary engagements never gives them the chance to pause and give thought to the missionary and his message. So when they are called to the Truth, they are unable to recognise it. Due to their perverted, spoiled temperament, they reject or even oppose it. Such are those who have failed to appreciate God and God's scheme of creation. In the Hereafter, they shall have nothing but the Fire of Hell in store for them.

Human nature, the events occurring on earth or in the skies, as well as previous scriptures, all bear testimony to the Quran's veracity. In spite of this, if the majority of people reject it, then the reason for this shall have to be sought in those who reject it, rather than in the pages of the Quran.

¹⁸ Who does greater wrong than the one who fabricates a lie against God? Such people shall be brought before their Lord, and the witnesses will say, 'These are the ones who lied about their Lord.' Surely God's rejection is merited by such wrongdoers.ᵃ

وَمَنْ أَظْلَمُ مِمَّنِ ٱفْتَرَىٰ عَلَى ٱللَّهِ كَذِبًا أُوْلَٰئِكَ يُعْرَضُونَ عَلَىٰ رَبِّهِمْ وَيَقُولُ ٱلْأَشْهَٰدُ هَٰٓؤُلَآءِ ٱلَّذِينَ كَذَبُوا۟ عَلَىٰ رَبِّهِمْ أَلَا لَعْنَةُ ٱللَّهِ عَلَى ٱلظَّٰلِمِينَ ۝

ᵃ Here the invention of a falsehood does not refer to the Being of God, but to His word. God did not appear before us Himself, in order to give His message, but had it announced through the mouth of a human being. This human being at that time happened apparently to be an ordinary man, but there were clearly godly glimpses in his discourse. If, in their judgement of him, people had taken into account his discourse, they would have found God in its greatness. But thanks to people's superficiality and appearance-loving nature, their view was contorted by the ordinary position of the preacher. The prophet's being 'ordinary' (in terms of worldly glory) was visible to them, but they were unable to see the extraordinary nature of the message given by him. They considered it as emanating from an 'ordinary' man and heaped scorn upon it; they raised false objections to what he had to say and then ignored it as if it were of no importance whatsoever.

19 Such as those who turn others away from the path of God and seek to make it appear crooked: these are the ones who deny the Hereafter. 20 They can never frustrate God on earth, nor have they any protectors besides God. They will be subjected to double punishment, for they could neither hear nor see. 21 It is such as these who have ruined their souls, and that which they fabricated shall fail them. 22 In the Hereafter, it is they who shall be the greatest losers.[a]

ٱلَّذِينَ يَصُدُّونَ عَن سَبِيلِ ٱللَّهِ وَيَبْغُونَهَا عِوَجًا وَهُم بِٱلْآخِرَةِ هُمْ كَٰفِرُونَ ﴿١٩﴾ أُوْلَٰٓئِكَ لَمْ يَكُونُواْ مُعْجِزِينَ فِى ٱلْأَرْضِ وَمَا كَانَ لَهُم مِّن دُونِ ٱللَّهِ مِنْ أَوْلِيَآءَ يُضَٰعَفُ لَهُمُ ٱلْعَذَابُ مَا كَانُواْ يَسْتَطِيعُونَ ٱلسَّمْعَ وَمَا كَانُواْ يُبْصِرُونَ ﴿٢٠﴾ أُوْلَٰٓئِكَ ٱلَّذِينَ خَسِرُوٓاْ أَنفُسَهُمْ وَضَلَّ عَنْهُم مَّا كَانُواْ يَفْتَرُونَ ﴿٢١﴾ لَا جَرَمَ أَنَّهُمْ فِى ٱلْآخِرَةِ هُمُ ٱلْأَخْسَرُونَ ﴿٢٢﴾

---

[a] The real reasons for people's sinful behaviour and their failure to treat the divine message with due respect were their lack of any firm belief in the Hereafter and their having no fear in their hearts for Almighty God. It was this fearlessness which caused them to treat the divine message without the seriousness it deserved. And anything about which an individual is not serious will fail to elicit the correct response from him.

But such insincerity and lack of seriousness will vanish when people stand before the Lord of the Universe on the Day of Judgement. At that time they will have lost their present freedom. The worldly goods and resources on the strength of which they had become arrogant, will turn into God's tape-recorders, which will start giving evidence against them. At that time it will be abundantly clear that the reason for their rejection of God's preacher was not that they were unable to understand him, but rather that they were not serious about him. The horror of Doomsday will suddenly make them serious. At that time, in the face of their own helplessness, they will understand all that they had been unable to understand while living in the world in an atmosphere of freedom.

God has blessed man with fine capabilities and talents. If he utilises them, he can understand any subject in depth. In his worldly matters, he actually utilises these talents, but when it comes to the Hereafter, he becomes deaf, in spite of having ears. He becomes blind, in spite of having eyes.

Man's success depends entirely upon his sincerity. Those who are sincere in worldly matters are successful in them. Similarly, those who are sincere in matters of the Hereafter will be successful in the Hereafter.

²³ Those who have believed and done good deeds and humbled themselves before their Lord are destined for Paradise, and they will live in it forever. ²⁴ These two groups are like the blind and the deaf as compared with those who can see and hear. Can the two be equal? Will you not then understand? ª

إِنَّ ٱلَّذِينَ ءَامَنُواْ وَعَمِلُواْ ٱلصَّـٰلِحَـٰتِ وَأَخْبَتُوٓاْ إِلَىٰ رَبِّهِمْ أُوْلَـٰٓئِكَ أَصْحَـٰبُ ٱلْجَنَّةِ هُمْ فِيهَا خَـٰلِدُونَ ۞ مَثَلُ ٱلْفَرِيقَيْنِ كَٱلْأَعْمَىٰ وَٱلْأَصَمِّ وَٱلْبَصِيرِ وَٱلسَّمِيعِ هَلْ يَسْتَوِيَانِ مَثَلًا أَفَلَا تَذَكَّرُونَ ۞

ª Being humble is the essence of Faith. Faith is neither something hereditary nor does it consist of the mere recitation of certain phrases. Faith is a discovery. When a man finds God by living in a state of keen awareness and in comparison realizes his position of helplessness, the feeling which takes possession of him at that time is known as humility (ikhbat). Humility is the necessary result of one's realisation and recognition of one's own position of powerlessness in comparison with God.

Faith, humility and righteous deeds—all three are different aspects of the same reality. Faith is the conscious discovery of God and His perfect attributes. Humility is the state of the heart which necessarily develops in man as a result of the discovery of God. When man thinks in godly terms, when his heart is full of godly feelings, the natural result is that the external aspect of his life becomes moulded in the shape of godly, or righteous deeds. One who is the embodiment of Faith, humility and righteous deeds is the very person desired by God and as such will find his abode in the eternal gardens of paradise.

Testing conditions of the highest order have been created in this world in order to find out which group used their senses of hearing and observation to discover the truth and moulded themselves accordingly. These are the sincere people of this world: they applied their reason and found the truth. The others did not properly use their senses of hearing and observation, so that naturally they did not acquire any knowledge of the truth and, that being so, did not mould themselves according to it. They are the blind and the deaf. Obviously, these are two different types of people and their ultimate fate cannot be the same.

²⁵ We sent Noah to his people. He said, 'I have come to you with a clear warning: ²⁶ worship none but God. I fear lest punishment befall you on a woeful Day.' ²⁷ The leaders of his people, who refused to acknowledge the truth, said, 'We regard you only as a human being like ourselves. We do not see that anyone follows you but the lowliest of us, those of immature judgement. We see no superior merit in you; in fact we believe you are a liar.'ᵃ

وَلَقَدْ أَرْسَلْنَا نُوحًا إِلَىٰ قَوْمِهِ إِنِّى لَكُمْ نَذِيرٌ مُّبِينٌ ۝ أَن لَّا تَعْبُدُوٓا۟ إِلَّا ٱللَّهَ إِنِّىٓ أَخَافُ عَلَيْكُمْ عَذَابَ يَوْمٍ أَلِيمٍ ۝ فَقَالَ ٱلْمَلَأُ ٱلَّذِينَ كَفَرُوا۟ مِن قَوْمِهِ مَا نَرَىٰكَ إِلَّا بَشَرًا مِّثْلَنَا وَمَا نَرَىٰكَ ٱتَّبَعَكَ إِلَّا ٱلَّذِينَ هُمْ أَرَاذِلُنَا بَادِىَ ٱلرَّأْىِ وَمَا نَرَىٰ لَكُمْ عَلَيْنَا مِن فَضْلٍ بَلْ نَظُنُّكُمْ كَٰذِبِينَ ۝

ᵃ Numerous prophets of God have appeared in this world and it has been their mission to acquaint man with God's scheme of creation—the scheme by which man has been kept in the present world for the purpose of putting him to the test. Here, one has the opportunity to worship different things, but what is desired from man is that he should become the worshipper of God. Those who do not become God's worshippers have failed in the test and shall have to face severe punishment in the life after death. This is precisely what Noah told the people of his community. So, he became the 'clear warner' for them, but his community did not accept what he had to say.

The reason for this was the propensity of the people to be taken in by appearances. In theory, man is a prey to many kinds of misguidance. But, in fact, there has been only one way of human beings going astray throughout the ages and that is their clinging to appearances coupled with their worldly approach to all matters. World-oriented people, in accordance with their temperament, assume worldly things to be the standard by which to determine Truth and untruth. Either consciously or unconsciously, they presume that the possessor of worldly outward glories is in possession of the Truth and one who is deprived of worldly glories is also deprived of the Truth.

When God's missionary makes his appearance, he seems to his contemporaries to be only a human being among other human beings. From the worldly point of view he has no special signs of greatness around him. And since, till then, no material benefits had become attached to the religion he presents to people, it is mostly destitute people who have nothing to lose by adopting the 'new religion,' who enter the fold of that religion. This state of affairs becomes a trial for the great ones of the time. They presume that since the adherents of the new religion have no worldly glory, neither can they be in possession of the Truth, so much so that there are certain people in the community who do not hesitate to call them impostors and liars.

²⁸ He said, 'O my people, tell me: if I have clear evidence from my Lord and He has favoured me with grace from Himself, which you have been unable to recognize, can we force it on you against your will? ²⁹ O my people, I do not ask you for any money for this; my reward comes only from God. I will not drive away those who believe; they shall surely meet their Lord. Yet I see that you are a people who act out of ignorance.ᵃ

قَالَ يَٰقَوْمِ أَرَءَيْتُمْ إِن كُنتُ عَلَىٰ بَيِّنَةٍ مِّن رَّبِّى وَءَاتَىٰنِى رَحْمَةً مِّنْ عِندِهِۦ فَعُمِّيَتْ عَلَيْكُمْ أَنُلْزِمُكُمُوهَا وَأَنتُمْ لَهَا كَٰرِهُونَ ۝ وَيَٰقَوْمِ لَآ أَسْـَٔلُكُمْ عَلَيْهِ مَالًا إِنْ أَجْرِىَ إِلَّا عَلَى ٱللَّهِ وَمَآ أَنَا۠ بِطَارِدِ ٱلَّذِينَ ءَامَنُوٓا۟ إِنَّهُم مُّلَٰقُوا۟ رَبِّهِمْ وَلَٰكِنِّىٓ أَرَىٰكُمْ قَوْمًا تَجْهَلُونَ ۝

ᵃ Here 'baiyyinah' means argument, while 'rahmah' means prophethood. (Tafsir an-Nafasi). When a prophet preaches to a community, he takes a stand on these two things. After the Prophet, a preacher will be a true preacher only when he takes a stand on precisely these two things, with the difference that whatever inspiration he has will be what he indirectly received from the Prophet, while the Prophet received it directly from God.

When a community ignores the messenger of God, thinking that from the worldly point of view he has nothing of value for them, at that very time he is in a position to give them very great and valuable things, i.e. argument and guidance. The greatness of reasoning and guidance is totally at the command of the messenger. This is an important part of his inner and intangible greatness, but how can those whose eyes are fixed on outward glamour appreciate it?

³⁰ My people, who would support me against God if I were to drive them off? Will you not take heed? ³¹ I do not say to you that I possess God's treasures, or that I have knowledge of the unseen, or that I am an angel. Nor do I say concerning those upon whom you look with contempt, that God will not bestow any good upon them— God knows best what is in their hearts. If I did, I would certainly be one of the wrongdoers.'ᵃ

وَيَـٰقَوْمِ مَن يَنصُرُنِى مِنَ ٱللَّهِ إِن طَرَدتُّهُمْ ۚ أَفَلَا تَذَكَّرُونَ ۝ وَلَآ أَقُولُ لَكُمْ عِندِى خَزَآئِنُ ٱللَّهِ وَلَآ أَعْلَمُ ٱلْغَيْبَ وَلَآ أَقُولُ إِنِّى مَلَكٌ وَلَآ أَقُولُ لِلَّذِينَ تَزْدَرِىٓ أَعْيُنُكُمْ لَن يُؤْتِيَهُمُ ٱللَّهُ خَيْرًا ۖ ٱللَّهُ أَعْلَمُ بِمَا فِىٓ أَنفُسِهِمْ ۖ إِنِّىٓ إِذًا لَّمِنَ ٱلظَّـٰلِمِينَ ۝

ᵃ The task of calling upon people to bow to God relates purely to the Hereafter. In order to ensure its success, it is absolutely necessary that there should be no disputes relating to money, land or property between the call-giver and his addressees. The call-giver himself has to shoulder the responsibility of maintaining a normal atmosphere between himself and his addressees, and for that purpose, he should unilaterally put an end to all types of material and economic disputes. That preacher who, on the one hand, makes a plea for the acceptance of Truth and, on the other, agitates and makes demands about worldly things is not a preacher in the real sense but a charlatan. He can have no value in the eyes either of his addressees or of God.

The test of the addressee is that he should be able to see the greatness of Truth in an ordinary man. Conversely, the preacher should not welcome an irreligious person simply because he possesses property and status, nor should he disregard a religious person simply because he does not possess the trappings of worldly pomp and glory. If a preacher does so, it means that by word of mouth he delivers sermons about the importance of the Hereafter, while in practice he proves himself to be one who attaches greater importance to the world. Obviously, this amounts to contradicting oneself, and the word of such a person has no value in the eyes of others.

³² 'Noah,' they replied, 'you have argued with us, and argued to excess. Now bring down upon us what you threaten us with, if you speak the truth!?' ³³ He said, 'It is God who will bring it down upon you, if He wishes, and you will not be able to escape. ³⁴ My advice will not benefit you, no matter how sincerely I want to advise you, if God lets you go astray. He is your Lord and you will all return to Him.' *ᵃ*

قَالُوا۟ يَٰنُوحُ قَدْ جَٰدَلْتَنَا فَأَكْثَرْتَ جِدَٰلَنَا فَأْتِنَا بِمَا تَعِدُنَآ إِن كُنتَ مِنَ ٱلصَّٰدِقِينَ ۝ قَالَ إِنَّمَا يَأْتِيكُم بِهِ ٱللَّهُ إِن شَآءَ وَمَآ أَنتُم بِمُعْجِزِينَ ۝ وَلَا يَنفَعُكُمْ نُصْحِىٓ إِنْ أَرَدتُّ أَنْ أَنصَحَ لَكُمْ إِن كَانَ ٱللَّهُ يُرِيدُ أَن يُغْوِيَكُمْ هُوَ رَبُّكُمْ وَإِلَيْهِ تُرْجَعُونَ ۝

ᵃ Noah did not indulge in disputes or debating sessions (*jidal*) with his community. He used simply to present his righteous message to them in a serious manner. But his serious call appeared to his community to be quite the opposite. The reason for this is man's weakness: when he himself is affected, he loses all seriousness. He does not see things in the light of reason or proof. He straightaway rejects the Truth without giving it serious consideration. Even the solid reasoning of the preacher appears to him to be meaningless discussion and *jidal*.

The statement, 'Noah, you have argued with us, and argued to excess' is not intended to indicate what Noah said, but rather shows how little importance was attached to his word by his hearers.

Similarly, the demand for their own punishment made by Noah's opponents was not really seriously meant, but was intended rather to ridicule Noah. What is really meant was, 'See, this person is talking of something which is never going to happen.' They thought that their position was so strong that there was no scope for any punishment to be meted out to them. Adopting this attitude, they said, 'Bring on us that punishment of which you have been warning us, as a result of our rejection.' And since, according to them, such punishment was never going to occur, their statement implied: 'We are based on Truth and you on untruth.'

Noah replied that they were looking at the matter in the context of his personality and it was because he was a weak person, that they were unable to understand how any punishment could ever come upon them. He added that had they looked at the matter in relation to God, they would not have taken this stand, because then they would have realised that God's retribution against the transgressor in this world was as certain as the rising of the sun and as terrible as the eruption of an earthquake. ▶

35 If they say, 'He has invented it himself,' say to them, 'If I have indeed invented this myself, then may I be punished for my sin; I am innocent of the crimes that you commit.'

36 God's will was revealed to Noah, 'No more of your people will believe in you than those who already believe; do not grieve, therefore, over what they have been doing. 37 Build the Ark under Our eyes and in accordance with Our revelation. Do not plead with Me concerning the evil-doers. They shall certainly be drowned.' a

أَمْ يَقُولُونَ ٱفْتَرَىٰهُ قُلْ إِنِ ٱفْتَرَيْتُهُۥ فَعَلَىَّ إِجْرَامِى وَأَنَا۠ بَرِىٓءٌ مِّمَّا تُجْرِمُونَ ۞ وَأُوحِىَ إِلَىٰ نُوحٍ أَنَّهُۥ لَن يُؤْمِنَ مِن قَوْمِكَ إِلَّا مَن قَدْ ءَامَنَ فَلَا تَبْتَئِسْ بِمَا كَانُوا۟ يَفْعَلُونَ ۞ وَٱصْنَعِ ٱلْفُلْكَ بِأَعْيُنِنَا وَوَحْيِنَا وَلَا تُخَٰطِبْنِى فِى ٱلَّذِينَ ظَلَمُوٓا۟ إِنَّهُم مُّغْرَقُونَ ۞

Acceptance of the message of the missionary of Truth mostly depends on the hearer not looking at it in the context of the messenger's personality, but rather valuing it on the basis of its content. Since Noah's community took his word as that of an ordinary man, he said that with that mentality they would never be able to discover the real value of what he had to say. Therefore, the only option now left to them was to wait for the Day when God would appear right in front of them.

a Those who said that the Prophet was himself guilty of invention, and that his message had not been sent by God, did not actually disbelieve in revelation or inspiration; they even accepted the previous prophets. Then why did they speak in this way? This was, in fact, not a rejection of Revelation but a rejection of the receiver of Revelation. The individual who spoke on behalf of God appeared to them to be an ordinary man. With their tendency to worship appearances, they were unable to understand how such an ordinary man could be the person whom God had chosen as His messenger.

The Prophet Noah said, 'If I have invented this myself, then may I be punished for my sin! I am innocent of the crimes that you commit.' These are, in fact, the words of parting, when the addressee does not accept the preacher's word through argument.

If, in spite of clear explanation, the addressee is bent upon rejecting the word of the preacher, then the preacher feels that the final option should be to keep quiet, after stating that both preacher and addressee are bound to be presented before their real Lord and that everybody will be exposed for what he is and everybody will be treated according to what he deserves. When reasoning has run its full course, the preacher is left with no option but to speak in terms of firm faith and keep himself aloof.

³⁸ So he began to build the Ark, and whenever leaders of his people passed by, they scoffed at him. He said, 'If you are scoffing at us, we shall scoff at you [and your ignorance], just as you scoff at us: ³⁹ you will soon come to know who will receive a humiliating punishment, and find unleashed against him an everlasting punishment.'^a

وَيَصْنَعُ ٱلْفُلْكَ وَكُلَّمَا مَرَّ عَلَيْهِ مَلَأٌ مِّن قَوْمِهِ سَخِرُواْ مِنْهُ قَالَ إِن تَسْخَرُواْ مِنَّا فَإِنَّا نَسْخَرُ مِنكُمْ كَمَا تَسْخَرُونَ ۞ فَسَوْفَ تَعْلَمُونَ مَن يَأْتِيهِ عَذَابٌ يُخْزِيهِ وَيَحِلُّ عَلَيْهِ عَذَابٌ مُّقِيمٌ ۞

---

^a The faith required of man is one at which he has arrived as a conscious and voluntary decision. Those who do not accept the Faith, in spite of the Prophet's best missionary efforts, prove that they are not yet ready to become the Faithful of God of their own free will. The second stage for such people is having their freedom taken away and then being directly presented before God in all His Majesty, so that what they had not accepted as believers they should have to accept as criminals and be made to face the punishment befitting their arrogance.

After hundreds of years of Noah's missionary efforts, this stage had come for his community. Thereafter, Noah was told that, after having fully discharged the responsibility of preaching God's word he should build an Ark, so that when the flood sent by God came to drown the arrogant people, he and his companions in Faith could take refuge in it.

Noah then built a large boat with three decks. This took several years. While Noah was working on the boat along with his companions, the arrogant people of the community used to see it as they came and went. They thought that all talk of punishment was simply imaginary, and when they saw that a boat was even being built for protection from that imaginary punishment, they started ridiculing Noah much more.

When a man amasses wealth by means of arrogance and injustice, one who is enamoured of appearances will take him to be successful, judging by his worldly assets. But one who knows that the world is subject to moral laws, will see in the aforesaid person's temporary success a glimpse of his total destruction in the Hereafter.

Such superficial people of Noah's community made fun of him but, in reality, they were themselves about to become the subject of ridicule.

⁴⁰ When Our command came, and water gushed forth in torrents, We said to Noah, 'Take into the Ark a pair from every species, and your own family—except those on whom the sentence has already been passed, and all the true believers.' But only a few believed along with him. ⁴¹ Noah said, 'Embark on it. In the name of God, it shall set sail and cast anchor. Truly, my Lord is forgiving and merciful.'ᵃ

حَتَّىٰ إِذَا جَاءَ أَمْرُنَا وَفَارَ ٱلتَّنُّورُ قُلْنَا ٱحْمِلْ فِيهَا مِن كُلٍّ زَوْجَيْنِ ٱثْنَيْنِ وَأَهْلَكَ إِلَّا مَن سَبَقَ عَلَيْهِ ٱلْقَوْلُ وَمَنْ ءَامَنَ وَمَآ ءَامَنَ مَعَهُۥ إِلَّا قَلِيلٌ ۞ وَقَالَ ٱرْكَبُوا۟ فِيهَا بِسْمِ ٱللَّهِ مَجْرَىٰهَا وَمُرْسَىٰهَآ إِنَّ رَبِّى لَغَفُورٌ رَّحِيمٌ ۞

ᵃ When the Ark was ready, stormy winds started blowing at God's behest. Torrents of water started gushing out of the ground and there was continuous rainfall. So much so that there was water everywhere and all the people were drowned. The only survivors were a few human beings and some animals who had boarded Noah's Ark. Even Noah's son was drowned. In the eyes of God a man's worth is judged according to his deeds and not according to relationship, even if the relationship is with a prophet.

When all those destined to perish had drowned, God commanded the storm to stop and it stopped; the water drained into seas and rivers and the earth again became habitable.

⁴² The Ark sailed along with them through mountainous waves. Noah called out to his son who stood apart, 'O my son! Embark with us and do not be among the deniers!' ⁴³ He replied, 'I shall seek refuge on a mountain, which will save me from the water.' Noah cried, 'Today there is no refuge for anyone from God's command except for those to whom He shows mercy!' Thereupon, a wave swept in between them, and Noah's son was among those who were drowned. ⁴⁴ A voice cried out, 'Earth, swallow up your waters. O sky, cease your rain.' The waters receded. The command was fulfilled. The Ark came to rest on Mount Judi. It was said, 'Away with the wrong-doing people.'ᵃ

وَهِىَ تَجْرِى بِهِمْ فِى مَوْجٍ كَٱلْجِبَالِ وَنَادَىٰ نُوحٌ ٱبْنَهُۥ وَكَانَ فِى مَعْزِلٍ يَٰبُنَىَّ ٱرْكَب مَّعَنَا وَلَا تَكُن مَّعَ ٱلْكَٰفِرِينَ ۝ قَالَ سَـَٔاوِىٓ إِلَىٰ جَبَلٍ يَعْصِمُنِى مِنَ ٱلْمَآءِ قَالَ لَا عَاصِمَ ٱلْيَوْمَ مِنْ أَمْرِ ٱللَّهِ إِلَّا مَن رَّحِمَ وَحَالَ بَيْنَهُمَا ٱلْمَوْجُ فَكَانَ مِنَ ٱلْمُغْرَقِينَ ۝ وَقِيلَ يَٰٓأَرْضُ ٱبْلَعِى مَآءَكِ وَيَٰسَمَآءُ أَقْلِعِى وَغِيضَ ٱلْمَآءُ وَقُضِىَ ٱلْأَمْرُ وَٱسْتَوَتْ عَلَى ٱلْجُودِىِّ وَقِيلَ بُعْدًا لِّلْقَوْمِ ٱلظَّٰلِمِينَ ۝

ᵃ On the occasion of Noah's flood, a strange happening was to be seen: those who had taken refuge by climbing tall peaks were drowned, while those who boarded the Ark were safe, in spite of the fact that the boat had been tossed about on a terrible stormy sea. The reason for this was neither in the peaks themselves nor in the Ark itself. The reason was that this was a matter of God's will. Had God's command focussed on the peaks, they would have saved those who had taken refuge on them, while those who had boarded the Ark would have lost their lives. But on this occasion, God's command focussed on the Ark. So, those who were on it were safe and those who sought refuge in other things were drowned.

The system of 'cause and effect' in this world is only a veil; otherwise, whatever is happening happens by the direct orders of God. It is the test of a human being that he should be able to tear asunder the outward veil and see the reality; he should discover the divine powers working behind the screen of cause and effect.

45 Noah called out to his Lord, saying, 'My Lord, my son was a part of my family. Your promise was surely true. You are the most just of all judges.' 46 God said, 'Noah, he was not one of your family. For, indeed, he was unrighteous in his conduct. Do not question Me about something of which you have no knowledge; I admonish you lest you become like an ignorant man.' 47 He said, 'My Lord, I take refuge with You from asking You something of which I have no knowledge. If You do not forgive me and show me mercy, I shall be one of the losers.'[a]

وَنَادَىٰ نُوحٌ رَّبَّهُۥ فَقَالَ رَبِّ إِنَّ ٱبْنِى مِنْ أَهْلِى وَإِنَّ وَعْدَكَ ٱلْحَقُّ وَأَنتَ أَحْكَمُ ٱلْحَٰكِمِينَ ۝ قَالَ يَٰنُوحُ إِنَّهُۥ لَيْسَ مِنْ أَهْلِكَ إِنَّهُۥ عَمَلٌ غَيْرُ صَٰلِحٍ فَلَا تَسْـَٔلْنِ مَا لَيْسَ لَكَ بِهِۦ عِلْمٌ إِنِّىٓ أَعِظُكَ أَن تَكُونَ مِنَ ٱلْجَٰهِلِينَ ۝ قَالَ رَبِّ إِنِّىٓ أَعُوذُ بِكَ أَنْ أَسْـَٔلَكَ مَا لَيْسَ لِى بِهِۦ عِلْمٌ وَإِلَّا تَغْفِرْ لِى وَتَرْحَمْنِىٓ أَكُن مِّنَ ٱلْخَٰسِرِينَ ۝

---

[a] Among those who were drowned in the great flood of Noah, was Kan'an, Noah's son. Noah wanted him to board his Ark, but he refused to do so out of sheer stubbornness. Then Noah prayed to God for his protection and the answer was that such questions should be avoided as showing a lack of understanding, on the part of Noah, of God's plan.

The fact is that God does not treat as redeemed the children of holy men or those who attach themselves to certain 'holy men', nor does He settle them in the Gardens of Paradise. God's decisions regarding redemption are based purely on deeds and not on relationships, descent or group attachments.

In this world, family relationships are of great importance. This will not be so in the Hereafter, there moral relationships outweigh all else. Noah's flood had occurred in order that all divisions of human beings other than moral ones be abolished, and all doers of righteous deeds be saved by accommodating them in the Divine Ark, while the unrighteous were consigned to the merciless waves. There will be a repetition of such an event on Doomsday, only on a larger scale and to the uttermost degree.

48 God said, 'Noah, go ashore in peace; Our blessings upon you and upon the people who are with you and upon some of the descendants of those who are with you. [As for the unrighteous] We shall grant provision for a time, then a grievous punishment from Us shall afflict them.' 49 These are tidings of the unseen that We reveal to you, [O Prophet], which you did not know before, nor did your people, so be patient: the future belongs to the God-fearing.*

قِيلَ يَـٰنُوحُ ٱهْبِطْ بِسَلَـٰمٍ مِّنَّا وَبَرَكَـٰتٍ عَلَيْكَ وَعَلَىٰٓ أُمَمٍ مِّمَّن مَّعَكَ ۚ وَأُمَمٌ سَنُمَتِّعُهُمْ ثُمَّ يَمَسُّهُم مِّنَّا عَذَابٌ أَلِيمٌ ۝ تِلْكَ مِنْ أَنۢبَآءِ ٱلْغَيْبِ نُوحِيهَآ إِلَيْكَ ۖ مَا كُنتَ تَعْلَمُهَآ أَنتَ وَلَا قَوْمُكَ مِن قَبْلِ هَـٰذَا ۖ فَٱصْبِرْ ۖ إِنَّ ٱلْعَـٰقِبَةَ لِلْمُتَّقِينَ ۝

*When all the evil people were drowned, the flood abated. The water was gradually absorbed in the ground or drained away into the seas. Noah's Ark ran aground on Mount Judi. Noah and his companions then disembarked. At God's command the earth again became lush green and well-populated.

The people among whom Noah appeared were those who believed in Adam's prophethood. After Noah his people stayed on the right path, but only in the beginning. When later generations began to stray, prophets were again sent to them. These later prophets appeared in the communities who had accepted the prophethood of Noah. In spite of this, since they did not accept any prophet of their own times, and did not reform themselves, they were destroyed. This means that for the purpose of salvation, it is not enough to accept a prophet or to associate oneself with a prophet. Rather such Faith is required as is an active and live Faith, and has the power to turn a man's life into one of righteous action.

The history of Noah teaches the lesson that lovers of falsehood may appear to be all-powerful and they may be very long-lived, but they are nevertheless destined to face destruction. On the contrary, men of Faith may be very few in number and may appear to be quite powerless, but by God's will, these are the very people who will ultimately share His graces in the present world, in the beginning and, finally, in the Hereafter.

⁵⁰ To 'Ad We sent their brother Hud. He said, 'O my people, worship God alone; you have no god but Him. You do nothing but fabricate lies. ⁵¹ I ask of you nothing in return for this [Message]. My recompense is with Him who has created me. Why do you not use your reason? ⁵² My people, seek forgiveness of your Lord and turn to Him in repentance. He will send from the sky abundant rain upon you; He will add strength to your strength. Do not turn away from Him as evil-doers.'ᵃ

وَإِلَىٰ عَادٍ أَخَاهُمْ هُودًا ۗ قَالَ يَٰقَوْمِ ٱعْبُدُوا۟ ٱللَّهَ مَا لَكُم مِّنْ إِلَٰهٍ غَيْرُهُۥٓ ۖ إِنْ أَنتُمْ إِلَّا مُفْتَرُونَ ۝ يَٰقَوْمِ لَآ أَسْـَٔلُكُمْ عَلَيْهِ أَجْرًا ۖ إِنْ أَجْرِىَ إِلَّا عَلَى ٱلَّذِى فَطَرَنِىٓ ۚ أَفَلَا تَعْقِلُونَ ۝ وَيَٰقَوْمِ ٱسْتَغْفِرُوا۟ رَبَّكُمْ ثُمَّ تُوبُوٓا۟ إِلَيْهِ يُرْسِلِ ٱلسَّمَآءَ عَلَيْكُم مِّدْرَارًا وَيَزِدْكُمْ قُوَّةً إِلَىٰ قُوَّتِكُمْ وَلَا تَتَوَلَّوْا۟ مُجْرِمِينَ ۝

ᵃ The Prophet Hud, successor of Noah, was chosen to guide the 'Ad community, of which he himself was a member. This has always been God's way in the matter of prophets. The wisdom of this is that, being of their own brethen, these prophets are thoroughly conversant with the psychology, conditions and language of the community, and can, therefore, very effectively discharge their function as missionaries of Truth.

Hud gave to his community the message that they should worship the one and only God. Furthermore, he pointed out that their 'religion' was simply a lie of their own fabrication. This shows that a prophet's way of preaching was not simply to present his message in a 'positive manner,' but also at the same time to resort to open criticism because, unless untruth is exposed as such by means of criticism and analysis, the Truth being Truth cannot be properly understood.

In the case of the prophets in all ages, if they were to be accepted by their opponents, it was necessary for them to be highly placed officials with great wealth at their disposal and for them to reside in dwellings of great grandeur. But this standard of judging a preacher of Truth is not correct. The right standard by which to test the veracity of the preacher is to see whether he is serious and sincere in his mission; whether his message is rational in every detail; whether he is above every worldly interest; whether whatever he says is fully based on reality; and whether his message is perfectly consistent with the universal system; so that accepting it amounts to stepping on to the highway to success. ▶

⁵³ They replied, 'Hud, you have not brought us any clear evidence and we shall not forsake our deities merely at your behest, nor will we believe in you. ⁵⁴ We can only say that some of our gods have stricken you with evil.' He said, 'I call God to witness, and you also bear witness, that I disown those which you associate with God. ^a

قَالُوا يَٰهُودُ مَا جِئْتَنَا بِبَيِّنَةٍ وَمَا نَحْنُ بِتَارِكِىٓ ءَالِهَتِنَا عَن قَوْلِكَ وَمَا نَحْنُ لَكَ بِمُؤْمِنِينَ ۝ إِن نَّقُولُ إِلَّا ٱعْتَرَىٰكَ بَعْضُ ءَالِهَتِنَا بِسُوٓءٍۗ قَالَ إِنِّىٓ أُشْهِدُ ٱللَّهَ وَٱشْهَدُوٓا أَنِّى بَرِىٓءٌ مِّمَّا تُشْرِكُونَ ۝

'He will add strength to your strength.' This statement does not mean an increase in material power, because in those days the 'Ad community was already very powerful. The Quran states that when the Prophet warned them about God's punishment, they said, 'Who is stronger than us?' (41:15). So, from the point of view of the call to truth, the promise of an increase in material power could not have been very attractive to them.

In this verse, an increase in power means the addition of the power of Faith to material power. The Prophet meant to say that if they adopted the life of Faith, they would attain moral and spiritual power; with their present material strength, if they attained moral and spiritual power, their total power would not decrease but rather increase many times over.

^a The Prophet Hud's community raised the point that he had no proof or argument in favour of his being right. This does not really mean that Hud had no argument to prove the truth of his message. He certainly had such arguments, but it did not appear to be so to his opponents. The reason for this was that man is generally unable to test statements purely on the basis of reason or rationality, but sees them from a point of view opposite to that of the presenter of the statements. Since the presenter at that time did not appear to the people to be a man of considerable status, his word did not carry any weight with them.

When anyone sets out to invite others to pure unadulterated religion, leaving aside the well-established religion of the day, it invariably happens that in the prevailing atmosphere he becomes a stranger and is reduced to insignificance. People even look upon him as if he were suffering from some mental illness. This was what happened in the case of the Prophet Hud. That is why his people were emboldened to say, 'We think that some curse has been cast on you by our holy men.' But after the completion of theoretical arguments, the proof of the veracity of the preacher of Truth is always such that his opponents are unable to subdue him, in spite of every effort.

⁵⁵ So scheme against me, all of you together, and then grant me no respite. ⁵⁶ I have put my trust in God, my Lord and your Lord. For there is no living creature which He does not hold by its forelock. My Lord is on the straight path.ᵃ

مِن دُونِهِۦ فَكِيدُونِى جَمِيعًا ثُمَّ لَا تُنظِرُونِ ۝ إِنِّى تَوَكَّلْتُ عَلَى ٱللَّهِ رَبِّى وَرَبِّكُم مَّا مِن دَآبَّةٍ إِلَّا هُوَ ءَاخِذٌۢ بِنَاصِيَتِهَآ إِنَّ رَبِّى عَلَىٰ صِرَٰطٍ مُّسْتَقِيمٍ ۝

ᵃ The communities into which God's prophets had come were all believers in God. In other words, the missionary projected himself as a God-worshipper, while his addressees also made the same claim. So the question arises: in which group is God present? The simple answer to this question is that God is on a straight highway (*as-sirat al-mustaqim*). So, the religion which is going on the straight path will directly reach God and that which is going on crooked paths will be diverted on to by-paths and can never be successful in reaching God.

When Hud said, 'My Lord is on the straight path,' he was saying in other words that the path towards which he was calling them was 'the highway of religion.' But his people, in the name of religion, had adopted by-ways around the highway of religion and were running headlong along them. Such a headlong course does not take a man towards God; it takes him here and there and leaves him astray.

In the light of these verses, the straight path shown by Hud comprises the following: belief in the unity of God, worship of God, seeking God's pardon, repentance, turning towards God (*tawbah*), gratitude for God's grace, placing trust in God, treating God as our Sustainer, treating God as the only possessor of all power, accepting God's watchfulness over oneself, and remaining humble.

All these are the basic teachings of religion. Following these teachings and making them the centre of one's attention amounts to treading the highway of religion. One who treads this path straightaway reaches God. On the contrary, if a man gives importance to other things, it is as if he is taking the side paths to the right or the left of the highway and hastening along them. Such a course takes a man away from God, not closer to God.

⁵⁷ 'If you turn away, I have conveyed to you the message with which I was sent. My Lord will make another people your successors and you cannot harm Him in the least. For my Lord is guardian over all things.' ⁵⁸ When Our command came, We delivered Hud and those who believed with him by Our special mercy. We saved them from a severe punishment. ⁵⁹ Such were the 'Ad who denied the signs of their Lord and disobeyed His messengers and followed the bidding of every headstrong enemy of truth. ⁶⁰ They were pursued by a curse in this world as they will be on the Day of Resurrection. Indeed, the 'Ad denied their Lord. So away with the 'Ad, the people of Hud!ᵃ

فَإِن تَوَلَّوْا۟ فَقَدْ أَبْلَغْتُكُم مَّآ أُرْسِلْتُ بِهِۦٓ إِلَيْكُمْ ۚ وَيَسْتَخْلِفُ رَبِّى قَوْمًا غَيْرَكُمْ وَلَا تَضُرُّونَهُۥ شَيْـًٔا ۚ إِنَّ رَبِّى عَلَىٰ كُلِّ شَىْءٍ حَفِيظٌ ٥٧ وَلَمَّا جَآءَ أَمْرُنَا نَجَّيْنَا هُودًا وَٱلَّذِينَ ءَامَنُوا۟ مَعَهُۥ بِرَحْمَةٍ مِّنَّا وَنَجَّيْنَٰهُم مِّنْ عَذَابٍ غَلِيظٍ ٥٨ وَتِلْكَ عَادٌ ۖ جَحَدُوا۟ بِـَٔايَٰتِ رَبِّهِمْ وَعَصَوْا۟ رُسُلَهُۥ وَٱتَّبَعُوٓا۟ أَمْرَ كُلِّ جَبَّارٍ عَنِيدٍ ٥٩ وَأُتْبِعُوا۟ فِى هَٰذِهِ ٱلدُّنْيَا لَعْنَةً وَيَوْمَ ٱلْقِيَٰمَةِ ۗ أَلَآ إِنَّ عَادًا كَفَرُوا۟ رَبَّهُمْ ۗ أَلَا بُعْدًا لِّعَادٍ قَوْمِ هُودٍ ٦٠

ᵃ Those who ignore God's word, are ignored by God. This happens to a lesser degree in the present world but, on Doomsday, this will be a total reality. At that time all the arrogant and insolent people will be denied God's grace; the grace of God will be shared only by those who lived in the world as His loyal and obedient subjects.

God has introduced the principle of succession (istikhlaf) in this world, that is, the removal of a community from its position of prominence and the installing of another community in its place. This temporary prominence in the world is for the purpose of putting people to the test. In the Hereafter, in the perfect world of God, such prominence will be granted only to people of true Faith as an everlasting reward.

The system of this world of trial has been formulated in such a way that, here, a man is always placed between good and bad. He has the option to follow either of these two ways. Furthermore, evil is largely dominant in this world. Only the strength of theoretical arguments is on the side of goodness. On the contrary, material power weighs in on the side of evil, and that too in such great measure that its flag-bearers develop attitudes of arrogance and hauteur and create such an atmosphere of pressure in the environment that the common man loses the courage to proceed towards the Truth.

61 To the Thamud We sent their brother Salih. He said, 'My people, worship God! You have no god but Him. It was He who brought you into being from the earth and settled you upon it and so ask His forgiveness. Turn to Him in repentance. My Lord is near and responsive.' 62 They said, 'O Salih! We had great hopes in you. Do you forbid us to worship what our fathers worshipped? We are in grave doubt, amounting to suspicion, concerning that to which you call us.' 63 He said, 'O my people, tell me: if I have clear evidence from my Lord, and He has granted His mercy, who then will support me against God, if I disobey Him? You would only make my loss greater.'[a]

﴿ وَإِلَىٰ ثَمُودَ أَخَاهُمْ صَـٰلِحًا ۚ قَالَ
يَـٰقَوْمِ ٱعْبُدُواْ ٱللَّهَ مَا لَكُم مِّنْ إِلَـٰهٍ
غَيْرُهُۥ ۖ هُوَ أَنشَأَكُم مِّنَ ٱلْأَرْضِ
وَٱسْتَعْمَرَكُمْ فِيهَا فَٱسْتَغْفِرُوهُ ثُمَّ تُوبُوٓاْ
إِلَيْهِ ۚ إِنَّ رَبِّى قَرِيبٌ مُّجِيبٌ ۝ قَالُواْ
يَـٰصَـٰلِحُ قَدْ كُنتَ فِينَا مَرْجُوًّا قَبْلَ
هَـٰذَآ ۖ أَتَنْهَىٰنَآ أَن نَّعْبُدَ مَا يَعْبُدُ
ءَابَآؤُنَا وَإِنَّنَا لَفِى شَكٍّ مِّمَّا تَدْعُونَآ
إِلَيْهِ مُرِيبٍ ۝ قَالَ يَـٰقَوْمِ أَرَءَيْتُمْ إِن
كُنتُ عَلَىٰ بَيِّنَةٍ مِّن رَّبِّى وَءَاتَىٰنِى مِنْهُ
رَحْمَةً فَمَن يَنصُرُنِى مِنَ ٱللَّهِ إِنْ
عَصَيْتُهُۥ ۖ فَمَا تَزِيدُونَنِى غَيْرَ تَخْسِيرٍ ۝

---

[a] The Prophet Salih the successor of Ad called upon his community to worship the one and only God. Indeed, this had been the aim of all the prophets in every age. But, Salih's community did not accept his message. The reason for this was that he was talking of linking them directly to God, while they held that they were linked to their great and holy men in the name of God.

Now, since Salih's sole strength was the power of reasoning, his community was not impressed by the significance of what he had to say. The importance of the religion which Salih was urging them towards would have been clear if they had given due consideration to God's revelation and signs. But the members of his community were willing to give due recognition only to that religion which had come down to them through the records and traditions of the leading lights of their community. The result was that the community, in spite of being overwhelmed by his arguments, were in a dilemma of doubt.

Like all other prophets, as Salih grew up in his community he was recognised as one who was distinctive in personality and intelligence. It was hoped that, on growing up, he would prove to be a useful member of society. But, things took a different turn and he started criticising the religion prevalent at that time. Seeing this, his people were greatly disappointed in him. They said, 'We were under the impression that you would be a pillar of our established religious system. On the contrary, we see that you are bent upon proving our religious system baseless.' In every period God's true missionaries had to face this sort of reaction on the part of their communities.

⁶⁴ My people! This she-camel of God is a sign for you. So leave her alone to graze on God's earth. And do her no harm, lest you should be instantly afflicted with a torment.' ⁶⁵ But they hamstrung her. He [Salih] said, 'Enjoy yourselves in your homes for three more days. This warning will not prove false.' ⁶⁶ Then when Our command came by Our grace, We saved Salih and those who believed along with him from the disgrace of that day. Surely, your Lord is powerful and mighty. ⁶⁷ The wrongdoers were overtaken by a dreadful blast and they lay dead in their homes, ⁶⁸ as if they had never dwelt there. The Thamud denied their Lord; cursed are the tribe of Thamud.^a

وَيَٰقَوۡمِ هَٰذِهِۦ نَاقَةُ ٱللَّهِ لَكُمۡ ءَايَةٗ فَذَرُوهَا تَأۡكُلۡ فِىٓ أَرۡضِ ٱللَّهِ وَلَا تَمَسُّوهَا بِسُوٓءٖ فَيَأۡخُذَكُمۡ عَذَابٞ قَرِيبٞ ٦٤ فَعَقَرُوهَا فَقَالَ تَمَتَّعُوا۟ فِى دَارِكُمۡ ثَلَٰثَةَ أَيَّامٖۖ ذَٰلِكَ وَعۡدٌ غَيۡرُ مَكۡذُوبٖ ٦٥ فَلَمَّا جَآءَ أَمۡرُنَا نَجَّيۡنَا صَٰلِحٗا وَٱلَّذِينَ ءَامَنُوا۟ مَعَهُۥ بِرَحۡمَةٖ مِّنَّا وَمِنۡ خِزۡىِ يَوۡمِئِذٍۚ إِنَّ رَبَّكَ هُوَ ٱلۡقَوِىُّ ٱلۡعَزِيزُ ٦٦ وَأَخَذَ ٱلَّذِينَ ظَلَمُوا۟ ٱلصَّيۡحَةُ فَأَصۡبَحُوا۟ فِى دِيَٰرِهِمۡ جَٰثِمِينَ ٦٧ كَأَن لَّمۡ يَغۡنَوۡا۟ فِيهَآۗ أَلَآ إِنَّ ثَمُودَا۟ كَفَرُوا۟ رَبَّهُمۡۗ أَلَا بُعۡدٗا لِّثَمُودَ ٦٨

---

^a Salih repeatedly told his community that he was the Lord's messenger and that if they did not accept what he had to say, they would be seized upon by God. However, his community did not take his words seriously, even although they did not disbelieve in God and prophethood. The reason was that Salih had only theoretical reasoning to prove his prophethood, and it is a weakness of human beings that they are hardly ready to give up a familiar thing in favour of an unfamiliar thing merely on the basis of theoretical argument.

When Salih's community were not ready to bow to his word, at their demand a tangible miracle was performed as a final sign. This was a she-camel which came out of a solid rock before their very eyes. It is the law of God that the appearance of such a sign indicates that the period of testing is coming to an end. Salih thereupon, announced that they should repent and accept his word: otherwise all of them would be destroyed. But those who are not impressed by theoretical arguments, fail to learn a lesson even from tangible signs. So, even then, Salih's community did not refrain from arrogance and they even went to the extent of slaying the she-camel. Thereafter, there being no question of any further respite for them, Salih was commanded to leave his community which, at that time, was settled in Western Arabia. Accompanied by his sincere companions, he therefore left for Syria. Subsequently, a horrible earthquake swallowed up the entire community, killing everyone.

⁶⁹ Our messengers came to Abraham with good news and greeted him with, 'Peace.' He too said, 'Peace be on you,' and hastened to bring a roasted calf. ⁷⁰ But when he saw that they made no move to eat,^a he found this strange and became afraid of them. They said, 'Do not be afraid, for we have been sent to the people of Lot.' ⁷¹ His wife, who was standing nearby, laughed when We gave her the good news of Isaac, and after Isaac, Jacob. ⁷² She said, 'Alas! Shall I bear a child in this old age, while my husband here is also old? This is indeed a strange thing!' ⁷³ They said, 'Are you astonished at God's command? May the mercy of God and His blessings be upon you, O people of this house. Surely, He is praiseworthy and glorious.'^b

وَلَقَدْ جَآءَتْ رُسُلُنَآ إِبْرَٰهِيمَ بِٱلْبُشْرَىٰ قَالُوا۟ سَلَٰمًا قَالَ سَلَٰمٌ فَمَا لَبِثَ أَن جَآءَ بِعِجْلٍ حَنِيذٍ ﴿٦٩﴾ فَلَمَّا رَءَآ أَيْدِيَهُمْ لَا تَصِلُ إِلَيْهِ نَكِرَهُمْ وَأَوْجَسَ مِنْهُمْ خِيفَةً قَالُوا۟ لَا تَخَفْ إِنَّآ أُرْسِلْنَآ إِلَىٰ قَوْمِ لُوطٍ ﴿٧٠﴾ وَٱمْرَأَتُهُۥ قَآئِمَةٌ فَضَحِكَتْ فَبَشَّرْنَٰهَا بِإِسْحَٰقَ وَمِن وَرَآءِ إِسْحَٰقَ يَعْقُوبَ ﴿٧١﴾ قَالَتْ يَٰوَيْلَتَىٰٓ ءَأَلِدُ وَأَنَا۠ عَجُوزٌ وَهَٰذَا بَعْلِى شَيْخًا إِنَّ هَٰذَا لَشَىْءٌ عَجِيبٌ ﴿٧٢﴾ قَالُوٓا۟ أَتَعْجَبِينَ مِنْ أَمْرِ ٱللَّهِ رَحْمَتُ ٱللَّهِ وَبَرَكَٰتُهُۥ عَلَيْكُمْ أَهْلَ ٱلْبَيْتِ إِنَّهُۥ حَمِيدٌ مَّجِيدٌ ﴿٧٣﴾

---

^a Literally 'their hands did not reach towards the meal'.

^b Once when Abraham was about a hundred years old, several very handsome young men entered his house. Considering them as guests, he immediately arranged for their food. They were not human beings, but angels of God. They had come with the dual purpose of giving the good news of children to Abraham, and destroying Lot's community, who had gone to the furthest extremes in their arrogance and rejection of the Truth. Conveying to Abraham and his wife the good news of Isaac (Ishaq), a son, and Jacob (Ya'qub), a grandson, did not simply mean giving the good news of children in the usual sense. No, indeed, this amounted to the bringing into existence of a line of righteous and mission-oriented human beings. It is a matter of historical record that generally it is a 'family' that rises in the service of religion. The history of the prophets and the events in the lives of the true followers who came after them demonstrate this fact. This is because one to whom Truth is revealed is an ordinary person in the eyes of his contemporaries, and this makes it difficult for the common people to recognise his status and support him. But from within his own family, personal relationships become an additional force. What outsiders are unable to see—due to their love of externals—the family members clearly appreciate, thanks to the element of attachment. Not finding it difficult to understand his real position, they become supporters of his mission.

74 When the fear had left Abraham, and the glad tidings had been conveyed to him, he began to plead with Us for Lot's people, 75 for Abraham was forbearing, tender-hearted and oft-returning to God. 76 We said, 'Abraham, cease your pleading: the command of your Lord has gone forth. There shall fall upon them a punishment which none can avert!'[a]

77 When Our messengers came to Lot, he was uneasy on this account and felt powerless to protect them. He said, 'This is a dreadful day.'

فَلَمَّا ذَهَبَ عَنْ إِبْرَٰهِيمَ ٱلرَّوْعُ وَجَآءَتْهُ ٱلْبُشْرَىٰ يُجَٰدِلُنَا فِى قَوْمِ لُوطٍ ۝ إِنَّ إِبْرَٰهِيمَ لَحَلِيمٌ أَوَّٰهٌ مُّنِيبٌ ۝ يَٰٓإِبْرَٰهِيمُ أَعْرِضْ عَنْ هَٰذَآ ۖ إِنَّهُۥ قَدْ جَآءَ أَمْرُ رَبِّكَ ۖ وَإِنَّهُمْ ءَاتِيهِمْ عَذَابٌ غَيْرُ مَرْدُودٍ ۝ وَلَمَّا جَآءَتْ رُسُلُنَا لُوطًا سِىٓءَ بِهِمْ وَضَاقَ بِهِمْ ذَرْعًا وَقَالَ هَٰذَا يَوْمٌ عَصِيبٌ ۝

---

[a] Abraham's conversation took place with those angels who had come to destroy Lot's community. These angels had come to carry out God's orders, and God made it clear that they came at His behest. A part of this conversation between the Prophet Abraham and the angels is given in chapter 29 (verse 32) and a detailed account of this also appears in the Bible (Genesis, chapter 18).

Abraham's prayer in favour of Lot's community being spared was not accepted. Similarly, Noah's earlier prayer that his son be spared had not been accepted.

Prayer amounts to presenting oneself before God. If Noah's son or Lot's community had had the urge to pray, and had they prayed to God to be given respite, then God would certainly have pardoned them and would have sent them His blessing. Revoking of punishment is possible, as we find from the example of the community of Jonah (Yunus). But if the punishment is revoked, it will be done on the strength of the prayers of the persons who have to suffer punishment, and not in answer to the prayer of any other person, even if that other person be a prophet. The reason for this is that a prayer for pardon is not a recommendation, in the usual sense, which one person makes in favour of another person and which, due to the holiness of the former, is accepted in favour of the latter.

One person should certainly pray for another; in every period, prophets and righteous people have prayed for others. But this is, in fact, an expression of the forbearance, kind-heartedness and the inclination towards God of the person who prays. A servant of God has fear of God at heart, starts trembling when he sees God's punishment, and starts praying for himself and for others. However, prayer by others will be effective only when the affected person himself fears God and invokes His grace.

78 His people, who were used to committing foul deeds, came running to him. He said, 'My people, here are my daughters. They are purer for you, [if you marry] so have some fear of God and do not disgrace me before my guests. Is there not a single right-minded man among you?' 79 They replied, 'You know we have no need of your daughters. You know very well what we are seeking.'[a]

وَجَاءَهُۥ قَوْمُهُۥ يُهْرَعُونَ إِلَيْهِ وَمِن قَبْلُ كَانُوا۟ يَعْمَلُونَ ٱلسَّيِّئَاتِ قَالَ يَٰقَوْمِ هَٰٓؤُلَآءِ بَنَاتِى هُنَّ أَطْهَرُ لَكُمْ فَٱتَّقُوا۟ ٱللَّهَ وَلَا تُخْزُونِ فِى ضَيْفِىٓ أَلَيْسَ مِنكُمْ رَجُلٌ رَّشِيدٌ ۝ قَالُوا۟ لَقَدْ عَلِمْتَ مَا لَنَا فِى بَنَاتِكَ مِنْ حَقٍّ وَإِنَّكَ لَتَعْلَمُ مَا نُرِيدُ ۝

---

[a] The angels who had come to Lot were the angels of retribution. But they entered the town in the shape of very handsome youths. This was intended to establish the guilt of Lot's community quite finally. When a man continuously indulges in an evil, he becomes completely insensitive about it. This was the case with Lot's community. They were now openly indulging in evil deeds. So, when they saw that handsome young men had come to Lot's house, they rushed to his house full of lustful, lewd feelings. With utter shamelessness, they started demanding that the young men be handed over to them.

When Lot saw the miscreants coming in this manner, he was extremely ashamed. He said, 'Here are the daughters of the community. You may marry any of them you like and satisfy your natural instincts.' The elderly persons of a community speak of the daughters of the community as if they were their own offspring. In this sense, Lot referred to the daughters of the community as his own daughters.

But they rejected Lot's legitimate offer, and continued to press for what was illegitimate. This finally established that these were evil, guilty people and certainly deserved to be destroyed. So, thereafter, all of them were annihilated.

'Is there not a single right-minded man among you?' This is generally the last utterance of a servant of God who has no material power to restrain miscreants, when all rational persuasion has failed to hold them back. At that time, by uttering such words, he invokes the prestige of the community and awakens its conscience. In spite of this, if his hearers remain insensitive, it means that there is not an iota of humanity or honour left in them.

⁸⁰ He said, 'If only I had the strength to stop you or could take refuge in some powerful support!' ⁸¹ They said, 'Lot, we are your Lord's messengers. By no means shall they reach you! So depart with your family while it is yet night and let none of you look back. But your wife will suffer the fate that befalls the others. Their appointed time is the morning: is the morning not near?' ⁸² When Our command came, We turned that town upside down and We rained upon it stones of clay, layer upon layer, ⁸³ marked for them by the decree of your Lord. The punishment of the unjust was not far off.^a

قَالَ لَوْ أَنَّ لِى بِكُمْ قُوَّةً أَوْ ءَاوِىٓ إِلَىٰ رُكْنٍ شَدِيدٍ ۝ قَالُوا۟ يَٰلُوطُ إِنَّا رُسُلُ رَبِّكَ لَن يَصِلُوٓا۟ إِلَيْكَ ۖ فَأَسْرِ بِأَهْلِكَ بِقِطْعٍ مِّنَ ٱلَّيْلِ وَلَا يَلْتَفِتْ مِنكُمْ أَحَدٌ إِلَّا ٱمْرَأَتَكَ ۖ إِنَّهُۥ مُصِيبُهَا مَآ أَصَابَهُمْ ۚ إِنَّ مَوْعِدَهُمُ ٱلصُّبْحُ ۚ أَلَيْسَ ٱلصُّبْحُ بِقَرِيبٍ ۝ فَلَمَّا جَآءَ أَمْرُنَا جَعَلْنَا عَٰلِيَهَا سَافِلَهَا وَأَمْطَرْنَا عَلَيْهَا حِجَارَةً مِّن سِجِّيلٍ مَّنضُودٍ ۝ مُّسَوَّمَةً عِندَ رَبِّكَ ۖ وَمَا هِىَ مِنَ ٱلظَّٰلِمِينَ بِبَعِيدٍ ۝

^a At first, Lot considered the young men who came to him as human beings. When he became anxious, thinking he was in danger, one of them clarified that they were angels and had been sent by God. In other words, this was not an affair of human beings but a divine matter. As the angels put it, 'These people will not be able to harm you or us.' When the townspeople persisted in advancing, one of the angels moved his arm, whereupon all of them became blind and turned back saying, 'Run away! Lot's guests appear to be great magicians.'

When God decides to destroy a community because of their arrogance, His will prevails throughout the entire area where they live. On such an occasion, all the living things settled there are affected by God's retribution. However, by God's special grace, those who had uttered the truth to these arrogant people, are saved. Conveying the message of God to man provides the best guarantee of avoiding being seized upon by God in this world as well as in the Hereafter.

It is recorded in a tradition that, at heart, Lot's wife was not on his side. But at the last moment, when Lot was leaving the town, saying that by morning God's punishment would be meted out there, she joined Lot's caravan. However, while Lot's people were still on the way, the terrible noise of an earthquake and a storm could be heard from behind. Lot and his trustworthy companions did not pay any attention to what was happening in the rear. But Lot's wife turned to look behind her. When she saw a dust-storm and heard the noise, she uttered the words, 'Alas! my community!' At that moment a stone hit her as a punishment and she dropped dead there and then. ▶

84 To the people of Midian, We sent their brother Shu'ayb. He said, 'My people, worship God. You have no deity other than Him. Do not give short measure and short weight. I see you are prospering. I fear for you the punishment of a fateful Day. 85 O my people, [always] give full measure and weight, in all fairness and do not defraud people by making short delivery, and do not spread corruption in the land. 86 What God leaves with you is the best for you, if you are believers. I have not been appointed as your keeper.'[a]

٭ وَإِلَىٰ مَدْيَنَ أَخَاهُمْ شُعَيْبًا ۚ قَالَ يَٰقَوْمِ ٱعْبُدُوا۟ ٱللَّهَ مَا لَكُم مِّنْ إِلَٰهٍ غَيْرُهُۥ ۖ وَلَا تَنقُصُوا۟ ٱلْمِكْيَالَ وَٱلْمِيزَانَ ۚ إِنِّىٓ أَرَىٰكُم بِخَيْرٍ وَإِنِّىٓ أَخَافُ عَلَيْكُمْ عَذَابَ يَوْمٍ مُّحِيطٍ ۝ وَيَٰقَوْمِ أَوْفُوا۟ ٱلْمِكْيَالَ وَٱلْمِيزَانَ بِٱلْقِسْطِ ۖ وَلَا تَبْخَسُوا۟ ٱلنَّاسَ أَشْيَآءَهُمْ وَلَا تَعْثَوْا۟ فِى ٱلْأَرْضِ مُفْسِدِينَ ۝ بَقِيَّتُ ٱللَّهِ خَيْرٌ لَّكُمْ إِن كُنتُم مُّؤْمِنِينَ ۚ وَمَآ أَنَا۠ عَلَيْكُم بِحَفِيظٍ ۝

This incident has a lesson in it. One who is not really loyal to God and His Prophet will not be safeguarded by joining the caravan of righteous people under the influence of some factor other than the fear of God. His weakness will come to light somewhere or the other and he will be doomed.

[a] The Midian (Madyan) region, to which the Prophet Shu'ayb was sent, lay between Hijaz and Syria. His addressing his community as 'people of faith' shows that they claimed to be believers. In other words, it was a Muslim community of that time; they were the *ummah* of the prophet who preceded Shu'ayb; but now after a long passage of time, in their later generations there had been a decline in their piety.

Shu'ayb told them that, if they were to be taken as people of the Faith, their claim would be acceptable before God only if they fulfilled the requirements of their claim, failing which, their claim had no value.

He said that their faith demanded that they worship the one and only God, adhere to justice and fair play in their transactions and choose for others what they desired for themselves. Every one of them had to discharge his obligations fully to others and there should be no shortcoming in this. They should live on the earth as God wanted His subjects to live, remaining contented with their legitimately gained earnings and not try to gain more through disobedience. If they did all this, they would be treated as believers in the eyes of God. Otherwise, there was the likelihood of their being smitten by God's punishment.

Shu'ayb also advised them not to give short measure, or engage in any other kind of fraudulent practices. His reference to their prosperity shows that in his community, some were poor and some were rich; there were some who received more, while others received less. Had all his addressees received less, then who would have been the prosperous ones? ►

87 They said, 'Shu'ayb, does your prayer tell you that we should abandon what our forefathers worshipped and that we should stop disposing of our belongings as we please? You are indeed the only wise and rightly-guided man!' [a]

قَالُواْ يَـٰشُعَيْبُ أَصَلَوٰتُكَ تَأْمُرُكَ أَن نَّتْرُكَ مَا يَعْبُدُ ءَابَآؤُنَآ أَوْ أَن نَّفْعَلَ فِىٓ أَمْوَٰلِنَا مَا نَشَـٰٓؤُاْ ۖ إِنَّكَ لَأَنتَ ٱلْحَلِيمُ ٱلرَّشِيدُ ۝

This shows that the addressees mentioned here were people of status with influence. Prophets come for the guidance of everyone, but their words are especially directed towards the upper echelons of the community, as defined by their wealth and intellect, because the general public goes along with them. Mostly they follow in the footsteps of their 'great ones,' so that, the conveying of the divine message to the elite amounts to reaching the general public also.

[a] Sometimes it happens that people use the word 'salat' (prayer) when they actually mean 'religion.' Here they had used the word salat because salat is the most prominent and clear sign of religion. (Safwat at-Tafasir).

Shu'ayb's community claimed to be religious. They used to say their prayers also. But they had associated shirk (ascribing partners to God) with their religion and prayers, and in its name had allowed foul play in their transactions. Shu'ayb urged them to be true worshippers of God and to adhere to fair play in their dealings and said that if there is polytheism along with religion and there is foul play in transactions along with prayers, then such religion and such prayer have no value in the eyes of God.

Such talk was likely to expose the false pretensions of the community about their piety. Their stand—that they were religious in spite of their wrongdoing—was adversely affected by this. Being already acclaimed as 'worshippers', they became irritated and said, 'Are you the only worshipper of God? Were the holy great ones whose ways we have adopted ignorant? Doesn't anybody else except you know what prayer is and what its requirements are? Perhaps you think that you are the only wise and righteous person in the whole world!' In the eyes of Shu'ayb's community, only those who had become great by virtue of long-standing tradition, or who occupied seats of high status appeared to be truly great. That is why they had the courage to taunt Shu'ayb in this manner.

[88] [Shu'ayb] said, 'O my people! What do you think? If I have clear evidence from my Lord, and He has sustained me with fair sustenance from Himself [should I not guide you?]. I have no desire to do, out of opposition to you, what I am asking you not to do. I only want to reform you as far as I can. Nor can I succeed without God's help. In Him I have put my trust and to Him I turn. [89] O my people, do not let your opposition to me bring upon you a fate similar to the peoples of Noah or Hud or Salih; nor is it long since the people of Lot were punished! [90] Seek forgiveness of your Lord and turn to Him in repentance. For my Lord is indeed merciful and loving.' [a]

قَالَ يَٰقَوْمِ أَرَءَيْتُمْ إِن كُنتُ عَلَىٰ بَيِّنَةٍ مِّن رَّبِّى وَرَزَقَنِى مِنْهُ رِزْقًا حَسَنًا ۚ وَمَآ أُرِيدُ أَنْ أُخَالِفَكُمْ إِلَىٰ مَآ أَنْهَىٰكُمْ عَنْهُ ۚ إِنْ أُرِيدُ إِلَّا ٱلْإِصْلَٰحَ مَا ٱسْتَطَعْتُ ۚ وَمَا تَوْفِيقِى إِلَّا بِٱللَّهِ ۚ عَلَيْهِ تَوَكَّلْتُ وَإِلَيْهِ أُنِيبُ ۝ وَيَٰقَوْمِ لَا يَجْرِمَنَّكُمْ شِقَاقِى أَن يُصِيبَكُم مِّثْلُ مَآ أَصَابَ قَوْمَ نُوحٍ أَوْ قَوْمَ هُودٍ أَوْ قَوْمَ صَٰلِحٍ ۚ وَمَا قَوْمُ لُوطٍ مِّنكُم بِبَعِيدٍ ۝ وَٱسْتَغْفِرُوا۟ رَبَّكُمْ ثُمَّ تُوبُوٓا۟ إِلَيْهِ ۚ إِنَّ رَبِّى رَحِيمٌ وَدُودٌ ۝

---

[a] There are two types of acceptance of a precept—one is routine or unconscious acceptance by imitation and the other is acceptance after finding it to be right. In the first case, man accepts something because others accept it. In the second case, man accepts it because, on the basis of reasoning, he found that it was right. While the former is only a formal acceptance, the latter is conscious discovery.

Discovery of Truth at the level of reason is the real asset of a believer. This leads to that live, active belief which prompts him and enables him to stand in the midst of people and start representing the Truth to them, unmindful of everything else. Conscious discovery of truth is a substitute for everything else. One who receives this bounty is never in need of anything else.

An unbeliever is satisfied with material achievement. But the believer is satisfied only when his reason is addressed. On receiving sustenance of this kind (conscious discovery), it becomes impossible for anyone to take a stand against it. Contradiction between talk and action is the result of formal faith, while consistency in talk and action is the result of conscious faith.

In his interpretation of the word 'shiqaq,' meaning 'opposition,' Hasan al-Basri, the famous Sufi, says, 'Should your enmity against me make you leave the path of Faith, you will be liable to receive the punishment meted out to the unbelievers.' (Al-Qurtubi). ▶

⁹¹ They replied, 'Shu'ayb, we do not understand much of what you say. In fact, we see that you are powerless among us.^a Were it not for your clan, we would have stoned you,^b for you are not strong against us.'

قَالُوا۟ يَـٰشُعَيْبُ مَا نَفْقَهُ كَثِيرًا مِّمَّا تَقُولُ وَإِنَّا لَنَرَىٰكَ فِينَا ضَعِيفًا ۖ وَلَوْلَا رَهْطُكَ لَرَجَمْنَـٰكَ ۖ وَمَآ أَنتَ عَلَيْنَا بِعَزِيزٍ ۝

Since the missionary appears as an ordinary man to the people, his critical approach is extremely disturbing to those who have attained a high status in society. That an ordinary man should venture to criticise them and their great ones seems unconscionable to them. That is why they develop a hatred for the preacher and become obdurate towards him.

The development of such a mentality in a man amounts to his being put to a severe test, because he considers even a godly message insignificant if it is brought by an 'ordinary' preacher. In the process of ignoring a human being, he ignores God Himself.

^a In a tradition of the Prophet Muhammad, Shu'ayb has been called the orator among the prophets (*khatib al-ambiya*'). He used to explain facts to the people of his community in their own understandable language in the most effective manner. Then, why did they not understand what he said? The reason for this was that the mindset of the community had been so vitiated that their way of thinking was quite different from that of Shu'ayb. Therefore, what he had to say seemed incomprehensible. The community was engrossed in obeisance to human beings whereas Shu'ayb called upon them to do obeisance to the one and only God. They were under the impression that belief in saints or great ones was enough for their salvation. But Shu'ayb's dictum was that salvation can be attained only through the belief in the one God and the performance of good deeds. The community members thought that since they considered themselves believers, they really were believers. Shu'ayb said however, that a believer was one who was so by God's assessment. In the eyes of the community *salat* (prayer) was merely a sort of ineffective formal supplement. Shu'ayb declared, on the contrary, that *salat* was a reckoner of man's life, his income and expenditure. The community thought that Faith was merely a spiritless acceptance, whereas he said that faith was that which was acquired by a live consciousness. In this way, a barrier had developed between Shu'ayb and the community when it came to understanding his true and straightforward words.

^b 'Were it not for your clan, we would have stoned you.' This statement reveals the great extent to which Shu'ayb's community had grown insensitive and become immersed in the love of outward, showy concerns. The truth of the matter was that when Shu'ayb exposed the religious pretensions of the community, its members became his enemies. ▶

⁹² He said, 'My people, is my tribe mightier to you than God? You put Him behind you, turning your backs on Him! Surely, my Lord encompasses all that you do. ⁹³ My people, do what you will and so shall I. You will certainly come to know who will receive a punishment to disgrace him, and who is a liar. Wait on; I shall wait on with you.'

⁹⁴ When Our command came, We saved Shu'ayb and those who believed with him as a mercy from Ourself, while the blast overtook the wrongdoers, so that they lay dead in their homes, ⁹⁵ as though they had never dwelt therein. Oh, away with the people of Midian, just as happened with the Thamud! [a]

قَالَ يَٰقَوْمِ أَرَهْطِىٓ أَعَزُّ عَلَيْكُم مِّنَ اللَّهِ وَاتَّخَذْتُمُوهُ وَرَآءَكُمْ ظِهْرِيًّا إِنَّ رَبِّى بِمَا تَعْمَلُونَ مُحِيطٌ ۝ وَيَٰقَوْمِ ٱعْمَلُوا۟ عَلَىٰ مَكَانَتِكُمْ إِنِّى عَٰمِلٌ سَوْفَ تَعْلَمُونَ مَن يَأْتِيهِ عَذَابٌ يُخْزِيهِ وَمَنْ هُوَ كَٰذِبٌ وَٱرْتَقِبُوٓا۟ إِنِّى مَعَكُمْ رَقِيبٌ ۝ وَلَمَّا جَآءَ أَمْرُنَا نَجَّيْنَا شُعَيْبًا وَٱلَّذِينَ ءَامَنُوا۟ مَعَهُۥ بِرَحْمَةٍ مِّنَّا وَأَخَذَتِ ٱلَّذِينَ ظَلَمُوا۟ ٱلصَّيْحَةُ فَأَصْبَحُوا۟ فِى دِيَٰرِهِمْ جَٰثِمِينَ ۝ كَأَن لَّمْ يَغْنَوْا۟ فِيهَآ أَلَا بُعْدًا لِّمَدْيَنَ كَمَا بَعِدَتْ ثَمُودُ ۝

At that time he had no crowds surrounding him to deter them from attacking him. He did not possess wealth and status with which to impress his listeners. He had at his command only the strength of Truth and reasonableness, but with such people Truth and reasonableness did not carry any weight.

In these circumstances, they would have certainly made a fatal attack on him, had it not been for the fear of tribal revenge. In the tribal era, the killing of a member of a tribe meant that, according to tribal custom, the entire tribe would rise to avenge that killing. This fear restrained Shu'ayb's community from taking any extreme step, just as in the present age people remain safe from the mischief of miscreants, because the latter fear that if they commit a crime, they will have to face the police force and the courts.

[a] The people of Shu'ayb's community considered themselves Lords of Midian, taking things which had been given to them for the purpose of putting them to the test as their inalienable right. With all this in mind, they planned aggressive measures against Shu'ayb. They even threatened to banish him and his companions from their land (7:88). But in the land which they considered their very own and of which they had become landlords, a terrible earthquake with horrifying tremors erupted at God's behest; as a result of which, the whole region was destroyed. They were annihilated in their own domain, as if they had never existed.

However, those members of the community who had accepted Shu'ayb's word, and had become his companions, were saved by special divine intervention.

96 We sent forth Moses with Our signs and with manifest authority, 97 to Pharaoh and his nobles. But they followed the command of Pharaoh and the command of Pharaoh was not rightly directed. 98 He shall stand at the head of his people on the Day of Resurrection, and shall lead them into the Fire. Evil is the place to which they shall be led. 99 A curse followed them in this world, and shall follow them on the Day of Resurrection. What a foul gift to be given! [a]

وَلَقَدْ أَرْسَلْنَا مُوسَىٰ بِـَٔايَـٰتِنَا وَسُلْطَـٰنٍ مُّبِينٍ ۝ إِلَىٰ فِرْعَوْنَ وَمَلَإِيْهِۦ فَٱتَّبَعُوٓاْ أَمْرَ فِرْعَوْنَ وَمَآ أَمْرُ فِرْعَوْنَ بِرَشِيدٍ ۝ يَقْدُمُ قَوْمَهُۥ يَوْمَ ٱلْقِيَـٰمَةِ فَأَوْرَدَهُمُ ٱلنَّارَ وَبِئْسَ ٱلْوِرْدُ ٱلْمَوْرُودُ ۝ وَأُتْبِعُواْ فِى هَـٰذِهِۦ لَعْنَةً وَيَوْمَ ٱلْقِيَـٰمَةِ بِئْسَ ٱلرِّفْدُ ٱلْمَرْفُودُ ۝

---

[a] Moses presented his call to the Truth in the best possible manner and to the greatest possible extent. He not only struck Pharaoh and his companions dumb, but also showed them a clear outward proof of his veracity in the shape of the miracle of the staff. Even so, the community of Pharaoh still sided with him and were not ready to support Moses.

The reason for this was that, in their eyes, power and worldly goods were all-important; and they did not find Moses in possession of any of these things. They were no doubt amazed at what he had to say but, when they compared Moses with Pharaoh, they found in the former a lack of resources and material belongings, while in the latter they saw pomp and glory. This comparison became decisive for them; and in spite of Moses' arguments and miracles, they were not ready to leave Pharaoh and go along with Moses.

Those who, in this world, preferred to be with one who possessed things of material greatness, will be placed alongside that individual, even in the Hereafter, but unlike the position in this world, this will be bad company, because in the Hereafter he will have been shorn of all his assets. Now his existence will be a symbol of dishonour and destruction. He will take his adherents to the same fire to which he was destined by God as result of his leading others astray.

100 We relate to you such accounts of earlier towns: some of them are still standing; while others have ceased to exist; 101 We did not wrong them; they wronged themselves; the deities they called on besides God availed them nothing: when God's command came upon them, they only added to their ruin.[a]

ذَٰلِكَ مِنْ أَنۢبَآءِ ٱلْقُرَىٰ نَقُصُّهُۥ عَلَيْكَ مِنْهَا قَآئِمٌ وَحَصِيدٌ ۝ وَمَا ظَلَمْنَٰهُمْ وَلَٰكِن ظَلَمُوٓاْ أَنفُسَهُمْ ۖ فَمَآ أَغْنَتْ عَنْهُمْ ءَالِهَتُهُمُ ٱلَّتِى يَدْعُونَ مِن دُونِ ٱللَّهِ مِن شَىْءٍ لَّمَّا جَآءَ أَمْرُ رَبِّكَ ۖ وَمَا زَادُوهُمْ غَيْرَ تَتْبِيبٍ ۝

---

[a] In ancient chronicles events relating to Kings and military generals have been mentioned but events relating to prophets and their communities find no place therein. History as written by man has omitted those very things which, in the eyes of the Creator, were most worthy of mention. However, the Quran describes at great length the *dawah* work performed by the prophets and the reactions of their addressees to the call. Other matters have been ignored by the Quran as being of no importance.

Of the areas destroyed during the age of prophethood, some are still in existence, for example, Egypt, which was the domain of Pharaoh. However, there were communities like that of Hud and Lot whose settlements along with their inhabitants were completely obliterated. Only a few signs of these are still extant in the shape of ruins or artefacts uncovered by excavations.

The destruction of these settlements seems to be an act of tyranny. But viewed in the context of the reason for its happening, it will appear to be consistent with reality: it was the outcome of their evil deeds—the punishment meted out to them after their having sinned.

Whenever a man indulges in arrogance and transgression, he does so on the strength of some notion. He considers some things or beings as supports and thinks that they will continue to be so in difficult times. But these supports will be such for only so long as God gives them leave. When, according to the law of God, the period of respite ends and God announces His final verdict, then man will come to know that the assumptions which, in his foolishness, he had made about his 'supports' were all false.

¹⁰²Such is the punishment of your Lord when He seizes the towns in the midst of their sins: His punishing grip is terrible and severe. ¹⁰³ In that is a sign for him who fears the punishment of the Hereafter. That is a Day for which mankind shall be gathered together, a Day when all will be present. ¹⁰⁴ We will only postpone it until a predetermined time, ¹⁰⁵ and when that Day arrives, no soul shall speak but by His leave. Among those some shall be damned, and others shall be blessed.ᵃ

وَكَذَٰلِكَ أَخْذُ رَبِّكَ إِذَآ أَخَذَ ٱلْقُرَىٰ وَهِيَ ظَـٰلِمَةٌ ۚ إِنَّ أَخْذَهُۥٓ أَلِيمٌ شَدِيدٌ ﴿١٠٢﴾ إِنَّ فِى ذَٰلِكَ لَآيَةً لِّمَنْ خَافَ عَذَابَ ٱلْآخِرَةِ ۚ ذَٰلِكَ يَوْمٌ مَّجْمُوعٌ لَّهُ ٱلنَّاسُ وَذَٰلِكَ يَوْمٌ مَّشْهُودٌ ﴿١٠٣﴾ وَمَا نُؤَخِّرُهُۥٓ إِلَّا لِأَجَلٍ مَّعْدُودٍ ﴿١٠٤﴾ يَوْمَ يَأْتِ لَا تَكَلَّمُ نَفْسٌ إِلَّا بِإِذْنِهِۦ ۚ فَمِنْهُمْ شَقِىٌّ وَسَعِيدٌ ﴿١٠٥﴾

ᵃ In the present world, the opportunity to live and to settle is available to man for the sole reason that he has to be put to the test. Those who continue to deny the truth even after the conclusion of the preaching process by the prophets, lose their right to remain on God's earth any further. That is why God destroyed the rejecters of the Prophet (29:40). Mostly this destruction took place in the form of the severest natural calamities. For example, cyclones, floods or earthquakes which, under normal conditions, remain within a limit, were made to wreak havoc to an unlimited extent. Such destruction of communities as took place in the past were called 'climatic pulsation' by the scholars of geographic history, as if whatever happened was the result of a geographical upheaval. However, they are unable to explain why such 'climatic pulsations' (changes) occurred only in the past and why these do not occur now, after the end of the period of prophethood.

The fact is that these events were not merely geographical events in the simple sense. They were manifestations of God's will. This proves that the system of the present world is based on justice. Here, according to the law of nature itself, a transgressor will perforce receive punishment for his transgression, while the righteous one will receive a reward for his just behaviour. To call these events 'climatic pulsation' amounts to consigning them to the geographical realm. On the contrary, if these are treated as forms of divine retribution, they can teach great lessons about the fear of God and create anxiety about the Hereafter.

The events that occurred during the age of the prophets, were, so to say, small signs prior to the advent of the great Doomsday. In these cases it so happened that those who denied the truth were given respite for some period. Thereafter, God's verdict was made manifest and all were destroyed. Only those were saved who, being the supporters of the truth, were treated as favoured in the eyes of God. Others who were, in the assessment of God, arrogant and, therefore, disfavoured, were directly afflicted by God's retribution; so much so that the recommendations of the prophets could not save them, as proved by the examples of Noah and Abraham.

106 The wretched ones will be in the
Fire sighing and groaning,
107 remaining in it timelessly, for ever,
as long as the heavens and earth
endure, except as your Lord wills.
Your Lord carries out whatever He
wills. 108 Those who are blessed shall
abide in the Garden; they will dwell
therein as long as the heavens and
the earth endure, except as your
Lord wills. Such bounty shall be
unending. 109 Have no doubt as to
what they worship. They worship
nothing but what their fathers
worshipped before [them]. We shall
certainly give them their share in
full, without diminishing anything.[a]

فَأَمَّا ٱلَّذِينَ شَقُواْ فَفِى ٱلنَّارِ لَهُمْ فِيهَا
زَفِيرٌ وَشَهِيقٌ ۝ خَٰلِدِينَ فِيهَا مَا
دَامَتِ ٱلسَّمَٰوَٰتُ وَٱلْأَرْضُ إِلَّا مَا
شَآءَ رَبُّكَ إِنَّ رَبَّكَ فَعَّالٌ لِّمَا يُرِيدُ
۝ ۞ وَأَمَّا ٱلَّذِينَ سُعِدُواْ فَفِى ٱلْجَنَّةِ
خَٰلِدِينَ فِيهَا مَا دَامَتِ ٱلسَّمَٰوَٰتُ
وَٱلْأَرْضُ إِلَّا مَا شَآءَ رَبُّكَ عَطَآءً غَيْرَ
مَجْذُوذٍ ۝ فَلَا تَكُ فِى مِرْيَةٍ مِّمَّا
يَعْبُدُ هَٰٓؤُلَآءِ مَا يَعْبُدُونَ إِلَّا كَمَا
يَعْبُدُ ءَابَآؤُهُم مِّن قَبْلُ وَإِنَّا
لَمُوَفُّوهُمْ نَصِيبَهُمْ غَيْرَ مَنقُوصٍ ۝

[a] What has been mentioned in the Quran as being of the utmost importance, and
has been the most often repeated, is that human beings will not be spared the final
reckoning, but after death will be presented in God's court. There everybody will
be consigned either to Paradise or to Hell, according to his performance in this
world.

The reason for giving this point so much importance and repeating it so often is
the 'doubts' which people have. People see that there are countless individuals on
the earth who do not carry out God's instructions; there are countless individuals
who act independently of God's instructions; many persons live self-centred lives
instead of God-oriented lives, without any loss to themselves; all of them are still
successful. Here, apparently, it is nowhere to be seen that those loyal to God
receive special rewards and those disobedient to God have to face punishment.

For this reason, people start entertaining doubts. They are unable to believe that
people are destined to meet any fate other than what they have gone on witnessing
with their own eyes. Here the Quran states that people's upholding of untruth is
not because they had studied the problem from every aspect and had found untruth
reasonable. It was rather because of their adherence to customs and tradition
instead of being open to arguments and reasonableness. ▶

¹¹⁰ We certainly gave the Book to Moses, but differences arose about it:ᵃ had it not been that a word had gone forth before from your Lord, Judgement would indeed have been passed on them then and there: yet they are in grave doubt about it. ¹¹¹ Your Lord will reward each one of them in full for their deeds. He is well-aware of all their actions.

وَلَقَدْ ءَاتَيْنَا مُوسَى ٱلْكِتَٰبَ فَٱخْتُلِفَ فِيهِ ۚ وَلَوْلَا كَلِمَةٌ سَبَقَتْ مِن رَّبِّكَ لَقُضِىَ بَيْنَهُمْ ۚ وَإِنَّهُمْ لَفِى شَكٍّ مِّنْهُ مُرِيبٍ ۝ وَإِنَّ كُلًّا لَّمَّا لَيُوَفِّيَنَّهُمْ رَبُّكَ أَعْمَٰلَهُمْ ۚ إِنَّهُۥ بِمَا يَعْمَلُونَ خَبِيرٌ ۝

If, in spite of this, they are not faced with the result of their actions, it is because of the respite they are given for being tested; for the life on earth before death is a life of trial. So, to make the test valid, the opportunity is given to man here till the time of his death to say whatever he likes and to do whatever he likes.

Death marks the end of this period. Death means that man is transported from the place of testing to the place of judgement. There everyone will receive whatever he actually deserves and everyone will lose whatever he had assembled around himself without deserving it.

ᵃ This means that the addressees of the Book given by God to Moses had diverse opinions about its statements. Some of them rejected them and some of them accepted them. (at-Tabari).

Whenever a statement is made, a man has two alternatives—one is to make the correct interpretation of it and the other is to make the wrong interpretation of it. If the hearers are really serious, they will inevitably arrive at the one correct interpretation. Their seriousness will guarantee their unity of opinion. On the contrary, if they are not serious, they will not give the statement any importance and will interpret it differently according to their own individual thinking. One will say this and the other will say that. In this way their levity will lead them to differences of opinion.

This happened in the case of all the prophets. God has nevertheless tolerated this, because He has created the present world as a place for the performance of deeds and the coming world as a place for reward or retribution. That is the way of God. That is why people are given full respite here. The present state of affairs is entirely due to this respite being given so that human beings may be tested and not due to God being under any compulsion.

112 Therefore stand firm [in the straight path] as you are commanded, along with those who have turned to God with you, and do not exceed the bounds, for He sees everything you do. 113 Do not incline toward those who do wrong, lest the Fire touch you. For [then] you would have none to protect you from God, and you will not be helped. 114 Say your prayers morning and evening, and during parts of the night; surely good makes amends for evil. This is a reminder for people who pay heed. 115 Be steadfast; for surely, God does not let the wages of the righteous be wasted.[a]

فَٱسْتَقِمْ كَمَآ أُمِرْتَ وَمَن تَابَ مَعَكَ وَلَا تَطْغَوْاْ إِنَّهُۥ بِمَا تَعْمَلُونَ بَصِيرٌ ۝ وَلَا تَرْكَنُوٓاْ إِلَى ٱلَّذِينَ ظَلَمُواْ فَتَمَسَّكُمُ ٱلنَّارُ وَمَا لَكُم مِّن دُونِ ٱللَّهِ مِنْ أَوْلِيَآءَ ثُمَّ لَا تُنصَرُونَ ۝ وَأَقِمِ ٱلصَّلَوٰةَ طَرَفَيِ ٱلنَّهَارِ وَزُلَفًا مِّنَ ٱلَّيْلِ إِنَّ ٱلْحَسَنَٰتِ يُذْهِبْنَ ٱلسَّيِّئَاتِ ذَٰلِكَ ذِكْرَىٰ لِلذَّٰكِرِينَ ۝ وَٱصْبِرْ فَإِنَّ ٱللَّهَ لَا يُضِيعُ أَجْرَ ٱلْمُحْسِنِينَ ۝

[a] The initial response to a call for the Truth is that it is ignored. Thereafter opposition starts and then it soon goes beyond all limits. This is a very critical situation for the call-givers. At that time the believers begin to consider different ways of thinking. One way is to become irritated and to imagine that, with the help of force, they should clash with those on whom theoretical reasoning had proved ineffective. The other way is to amend their message suitably in order to make it acceptable to the addressees, by omitting those portions which displease them.

The first way amounts to going to extremes, while the second means compromising with falsehood, and both of these are equally wrong in the eyes of God; especially the second approach (i.e. amendment of the message in order to make it acceptable) which amounts to a sin, because that which is most desired by Almighty God is the unequivocal declaration of Truth, and in the case of compromises, there cannot be any such declaration.

Whenever obstacles arise in the path of giving the call to the Truth, the call-giver should turn towards God as much as possible, because He, being Omnipotent, is the sole and certain means of solving all problems.

116 Why, then, were there not among the generations before you upright men who would speak out against the [spread of] corruption on earth—except for the few whom We saved? But the wrongdoers pursued their worldly pleasures and thus became guilty. 117 Your Lord would never unjustly destroy communities while their people were trying to reform.*a*

فَلَوْلَا كَانَ مِنَ ٱلْقُرُونِ مِن قَبْلِكُمْ أُوْلُوا۟ بَقِيَّةٍ يَنْهَوْنَ عَنِ ٱلْفَسَادِ فِى ٱلْأَرْضِ إِلَّا قَلِيلًا مِّمَّنْ أَنجَيْنَا مِنْهُمْ ۗ وَٱتَّبَعَ ٱلَّذِينَ ظَلَمُوا۟ مَآ أُتْرِفُوا۟ فِيهِ وَكَانُوا۟ مُجْرِمِينَ ۝ وَمَا كَانَ رَبُّكَ لِيُهْلِكَ ٱلْقُرَىٰ بِظُلْمٍ وَأَهْلُهَا مُصْلِحُونَ ۝

---

a Here 'generation before you' means previous People of the Book, i.e. believing communities. A community faces ruination when the worldly good things given by God to its people with the purpose of developing feelings of gratitude in them, become instead a source of lust and create the urge to seek after material things. Under these circumstances, the tasks which need to be carried out for the reformation of the Muslim community are known in the terminology of the Islamic law as *al-Amr bi'l-Ma'ruf wa'n-Nahy 'an al-Munkar,* that is, exhorting righteousness and preventing individuals from indulging in sinful acts.

This admonition specifies the responsibility placed on a Muslim with regard to his immediate neighbours. This means that in a Muslim society, there should always be some individuals who should remind Muslims of God and the Hereafter, who should keep a watch on people's morals and who should try to keep them on the right path in all their dealings.

The non-existence of such righteous individuals in a community is generally for one of two reasons—either the whole community has morally deteriorated and there is not a single righteous person left in it. Or else, there may still be certain righteous people, but due to the all-pervasive evil, they may not be able to find the courage to open their mouths. They may be afraid that if they spoke the Truth, they would lose the respect of their community.

In both the above-mentioned cases, the community loses God's esteem and becomes liable to be afflicted by God's retribution in one form or the other.

¹¹⁸ If your Lord had wished, He would have made mankind into one community. As it is, they will not cease to dispute,—¹¹⁹ and to this end He has created them [all], except for those to whom your Lord has shown mercy. The word of your Lord shall be fulfilled, 'I will fill Hell with jinn and men all together.'ᵃ

وَلَوْ شَاءَ رَبُّكَ لَجَعَلَ ٱلنَّاسَ أُمَّةً وَاحِدَةً وَلَا يَزَالُونَ مُخْتَلِفِينَ ۝ إِلَّا مَن رَّحِمَ رَبُّكَ وَلِذَٰلِكَ خَلَقَهُمْ وَتَمَّتْ كَلِمَةُ رَبِّكَ لَأَمْلَأَنَّ جَهَنَّمَ مِنَ ٱلْجِنَّةِ وَٱلنَّاسِ أَجْمَعِينَ ۝

ᵃ In our world, there are innumerable creatures besides human beings. All these creatures follow the one fixed path of nature at all times. Similarly, God could have created human beings as compulsory followers of the straight path too. But this is in no way God's scheme with regard to human beings. God's plan was that they would be so created that they should, of their own accord, be able independently to make correct moral choices. The difference in the world of human beings (i.e. some of them adopting one way and others adopting an other way) is, in fact, due to this special plan of God.

This plan was certainly a risky one, because it meant that many people had the opportunity to misuse their freedom and thus make themselves liable to be cast into hell. But, with the help of this very plan, such noble souls could be chosen as could be treated as deserving the special grace of God. God has blessed the entire universe with His bounties. Now, God devised this plan so that He might give His creatures the benefit of His grace, saying, 'You are entitled to this.'

God's grace will be granted to that person whose consciousness is so alert that he recognizes in the power given to him by way of testing him his real powerlessness. Such a person will be able to see through the veil of human power and have a glimpse of God's power behind it. Such perceptiveness takes away the capacity for arrogance in a man. So much so that, when God grants him His Grace saying, 'This is your entitlement,' in his awareness of reality he cries out, 'O God! This is also a manifestation of Your grace, otherwise my deeds have no value.'

¹²⁰ We have told you the stories of the prophets to make your heart firm and in these accounts truth has come to you, with an exhortation and a reminder for the believers. ¹²¹ Say to those who do not believe, you do things in your way and we are doing things in our way, ¹²² and wait, we too are waiting.' ¹²³ The knowledge of the secret of the heavens and the earth belongs to God alone, and to Him shall all affairs be referred. So worship Him and put your trust in Him alone. Your Lord is not unaware of what you do.^a

وَكُلًّا نَّقُصُّ عَلَيْكَ مِنْ أَنۢبَآءِ ٱلرُّسُلِ مَا نُثَبِّتُ بِهِۦ فُؤَادَكَ ۚ وَجَآءَكَ فِى هَـٰذِهِ ٱلْحَقُّ وَمَوْعِظَةٌ وَذِكْرَىٰ لِلْمُؤْمِنِينَ ۝ وَقُل لِّلَّذِينَ لَا يُؤْمِنُونَ ٱعْمَلُوا۟ عَلَىٰ مَكَانَتِكُمْ إِنَّا عَـٰمِلُونَ ۝ وَٱنتَظِرُوٓا۟ إِنَّا مُنتَظِرُونَ ۝ وَلِلَّهِ غَيْبُ ٱلسَّمَـٰوَٰتِ وَٱلْأَرْضِ وَإِلَيْهِ يُرْجَعُ ٱلْأَمْرُ كُلُّهُۥ فَٱعْبُدْهُ وَتَوَكَّلْ عَلَيْهِ ۚ وَمَا رَبُّكَ بِغَـٰفِلٍ عَمَّا تَعْمَلُونَ ۝

---

^a The events in the lives of the prophets have been narrated in the Quran, so that the later dayees should learn a lesson from them. In these events the preacher sees that their addressee-communities quarrelled with them, abused them by giving a twist to their straightforward discourses, subjected them to all sorts of hardship and rejected them as if they had no value at all.

But, finally God helped them and their word carried the day. All the attacks of their opponents failed. The different fates of the believers and unbelievers became manifest in their initial form in this world itself, and will appear in their most perfect form in the Hereafter.

With the help of these examples, the call-giver acquires the confidence, based on history, that there is no question of his being disappointed by or being terrified of the difficulties faced by him while calling for the Truth. Such difficulties always arise in dawah work, but he knows that he too will finally be successful, just as success was achieved by all the previous prophets.

12. JOSEPH

In the name of God,
the Most Gracious, the Most Merciful

[1] *Alif Lam Ra*

These are verses from the clear
Book. [2] We have sent down the
Quran in Arabic, so that you may
understand. [3] We recount to you the
best of narratives in revealing this
Quran to you, even though you were
unaware of it before it came.[a]

---

[a] The Quran has been revealed for the guidance of the whole world. However, since
its first addressees were the Arabs, it was revealed in the Arabic language. Now it
is the duty of those who have Faith in it to translate its teachings into every
language and to convey them to all the nations of the world.

The Quran's teachings have been communicated in different modes and styles:
sometimes in the language of reasoning based on the phenomena of nature,
sometimes in the language of warning and good tidings, and sometimes in the
language of history. The message of chapter 12, is conveyed in the form of the story
of Joseph (Yusuf). In this chapter, people of Faith are told, by means of a prophet's
story, that God is all-powerful. He helps those who come forward to promote the
cause of Truth, finally making them successful in spite of the intrigues of
opponents, on the condition that the people should be God-fearing and should
have the quality of patience; they should have the fear of God in their hearts and
regardless of the circumstances, should persevere on the path of Truth.

⁴ When Joseph told his father, 'My father, I saw eleven stars, and the sun and moon: I saw them prostrate themselves before me,' ⁵ he replied, 'My son, do not relate your dream to your brothers, lest they plot evil against you—Satan is the sworn enemy of man.ᵃ

إِذْ قَالَ يُوسُفُ لِأَبِيهِ يَٰٓأَبَتِ إِنِّى رَأَيْتُ أَحَدَ عَشَرَ كَوْكَبًا وَٱلشَّمْسَ وَٱلْقَمَرَ رَأَيْتُهُمْ لِى سَٰجِدِينَ ۝ قَالَ يَٰبُنَىَّ لَا تَقْصُصْ رُءْيَاكَ عَلَىٰٓ إِخْوَتِكَ فَيَكِيدُوا۟ لَكَ كَيْدًا ۖ إِنَّ ٱلشَّيْطَٰنَ لِلْإِنسَٰنِ عَدُوٌّ مُّبِينٌ ۝

ᵃ According to a *hadith* of the Prophet Muhammad, there are three kinds of dreams—those of wish fulfillment, fear of Satan and good tidings from God. A common man's dream may be of any of these kinds, but a Prophet's dream is always from God. Sometimes it is direct in meaning and sometimes it is purely symbolic.

Joseph lived in the nineteenth century B.C. His father, Jacob, was a resident of Palestine. Joseph and his brother Benjamin (Bin Yamin) were born of the same mother, while their ten older brothers had different mothers. In Joseph's dream the sun and the moon stood for his parents and the eleven stars meant his eleven brothers. This dream predicted that prophethood would be conferred on Joseph and it also signified that the political power and worldly glory ordained for him would be decreed by God after his reaching Egypt; after which all his family members would be compelled to recognize his greatness.

Looking at Joseph's personality and his popularity, his ten step brothers were jealous of him, so his father Jacob (Ya'qub), on hearing his dream, immediately advised Joseph not to mention it to his stepbrothers, as they would otherwise become even more hostile towards him.

Feeling jealous of a person on account of his greatness shows an evil nature. One who has this trait in him ought to turn to God in repentance, because this is a proof that he is not reconciled to God's will; he is following the lead of Satan rather than God's guidance.

⁶ You shall be chosen by your Lord and He will impart to you some understanding of the inner meaning of events. He will bestow the full measure of His blessings upon you and upon the House of Jacob—even as He formerly bestowed it in full measure upon your forefathers, Abraham and Isaac. Truly, your Sustainer is all-knowing and wise!ᵃ

وَكَذَٰلِكَ يَجْتَبِيكَ رَبُّكَ وَيُعَلِّمُكَ مِن تَأْوِيلِ ٱلْأَحَادِيثِ وَيُتِمُّ نِعْمَتَهُۥ عَلَيْكَ وَعَلَىٰٓ ءَالِ يَعْقُوبَ كَمَآ أَتَمَّهَا عَلَىٰٓ أَبَوَيْكَ مِن قَبْلُ إِبْرَٰهِيمَ وَإِسْحَٰقَ إِنَّ رَبَّكَ عَلِيمٌ حَكِيمٌ ٦

ᵃ Here the expression 'He will bestow the full measure of His blessings upon you' applies to Joseph as it had previously applied to Abraham. The difference between the two was that Joseph was invested with political power, while Abraham was not. There was, however, an all-important factor common to both, namely, the prophethood conferred upon each of them by God. That was the sense in which God's 'blessings' had been bestowed in 'full measure'. It was the prophethood, that is, the conferring of special divine guidance, which would lead them to a high status in the Hereafter. God's guidance to man is, in effect, the perfection of His favour to him. This favour is available directly to His prophets and indirectly to their true followers.

⁷ Surely, in Joseph and his brothers there are signs for the inquirers. ⁸ They said [to each other], 'Surely Joseph and his brother [Benjamin] are dearer to our father than ourselves, although we are a band. Truly, our father is clearly mistaken. ⁹ Therefore, let us put Joseph to death or cast him away to some [far-off] land, so that our father's attention should turn only to us, and you can thereafter become a righteous people.' ¹⁰ One of them said, 'Do not kill Joseph, but if you must do something, cast him into the bottom of a well; some of the travellers will pick him up.' ᵃ

۞ لَّقَدۡ كَانَ فِى يُوسُفَ وَإِخۡوَتِهِۦٓ ءَايَٰتٌ لِّلسَّآئِلِينَ ۝ إِذۡ قَالُوا۟ لَيُوسُفُ وَأَخُوهُ أَحَبُّ إِلَىٰٓ أَبِينَا مِنَّا وَنَحۡنُ عُصۡبَةٌ إِنَّ أَبَانَا لَفِى ضَلَٰلٍ مُّبِينٍ ۝ ٱقۡتُلُوا۟ يُوسُفَ أَوِ ٱطۡرَحُوهُ أَرۡضًا يَخۡلُ لَكُمۡ وَجۡهُ أَبِيكُمۡ وَتَكُونُوا۟ مِنۢ بَعۡدِهِۦ قَوۡمًا صَٰلِحِينَ ۝ قَالَ قَآئِلٌ مِّنۡهُمۡ لَا تَقۡتُلُوا۟ يُوسُفَ وَأَلۡقُوهُ فِى غَيَٰبَتِ ٱلۡجُبِّ يَلۡتَقِطۡهُ بَعۡضُ ٱلسَّيَّارَةِ إِن كُنتُمۡ فَٰعِلِينَ ۝

ᵃ In the course of the last days of the Prophet Muhammad in Makkah, when Abu Talib and Khadijah had passed away, the people of Makkah intensified their opposition to him. In that period, some Makkans asked him about Joseph, whose name they had heard from some Jews during their travels. They asked him this question just to ridicule him, but God Almighty turned the thrust of this question against the interrogators themselves. By means of this story they were indirectly informed that they were treading in the footsteps of Joseph's stepbrothers, while by the Grace of God, the prophet's future would be like that of Joseph in Egypt.

Jacob could see that among his children Joseph was the ablest and most pious. In him he could see the personality of a future prophet. For this reason, he was very much attached to Joseph. But his other ten sons looked at the matter from the worldly point of view. They thought that the most important in the eyes of their father should have been their collective group, because only that was capable of helping and supporting the family. In ancient tribal times the number (particularly male) of family members was of the utmost importance in defending and supporting the family. This one-sided view of theirs assumed such proportions that they thought that if they removed Joseph from the scene, they would have their father's undivided attention.

When they sat together to devise plans against Joseph, one of his brothers proposed that instead of killing Joseph, he should be pushed into some dry well. This was a special plan of God Almighty. It is the way of God, when a group is bent upon oppressing someone unjustly, that He makes them adopt such a moderate course as may open up new possibilities for their victim.

¹¹ They said to their father, 'Why do you not trust us with Joseph? We are indeed his well-wishers. ¹² Send him with us tomorrow, so that he may play and enjoy himself. We will look after him.' ¹³ [Jacob] said, 'It would indeed grieve me if you took him away with you, and I fear lest the wolf should devour him while you are off your guard.' ¹⁴ They said, 'Surely, if the wolf devoured him while we were a strong party, we should indeed be great losers.' ᵃ

قَالُوا۟ يَٰٓأَبَانَا مَا لَكَ لَا تَأْمَنَّا عَلَىٰ يُوسُفَ وَإِنَّا لَهُۥ لَنَٰصِحُونَ ۝ أَرْسِلْهُ مَعَنَا غَدًا يَرْتَعْ وَيَلْعَبْ وَإِنَّا لَهُۥ لَحَٰفِظُونَ ۝ قَالَ إِنِّى لَيَحْزُنُنِىٓ أَن تَذْهَبُوا۟ بِهِۦ وَأَخَافُ أَن يَأْكُلَهُ ٱلذِّئْبُ وَأَنتُمْ عَنْهُ غَٰفِلُونَ ۝ قَالُوا۟ لَئِنْ أَكَلَهُ ٱلذِّئْبُ وَنَحْنُ عُصْبَةٌ إِنَّآ إِذًا لَّخَٰسِرُونَ ۝

ᵃ The reply given by Jacob to his sons shows that he had already guessed that it was not a question of Joseph playing and enjoying himself in some meadow, but that Joseph's brothers had hatched a conspiracy against him. But a man who fears God is one who trusts in God. He had sensed what was going to happen, but he considered the power of God to be above everything else. With full faith in his Lord's omnipotence, and in spite of sensing clear dangers, he consigned Joseph to the care of his brothers.

This was the picture of a God-fearing person. By contrast, Joseph's brothers presented a picture of people whose hearts are completely devoid of the fear of God. In making their plans to destroy a servant of God quite unjustifiably, they had forgotten that this was a world in which nobody had any power except God.

They tried to present themselves as well-wishers simply on the basis of beautiful words, but before God, a person is treated as a well-wisher solely on the basis of his deeds.

¹⁵ And so, when they went away with him, they decided to cast him into the dark depths of a well. Then We revealed to him Our will, 'You shall [one day] tell them of this deed of theirs, when they do not realize who you are.' ¹⁶ And at nightfall they came to their father, weeping. ¹⁷ They said, 'Father, we went off racing and left Joseph with our belongings, and the wolf devoured him. But you will not believe us, even though we are telling the truth.' ¹⁸ And they showed him their brother's shirt, stained with false blood. 'No!' he cried. 'Your souls have tempted you to do something evil! But it is best to be patient: God alone can help me bear the loss you speak of.' ᵃ

فَلَمَّا ذَهَبُوا بِهِ وَأَجْمَعُوا أَن يَجْعَلُوهُ فِي غَيَابَتِ ٱلْجُبِّ وَأَوْحَيْنَآ إِلَيْهِ لَتُنَبِّئَنَّهُم بِأَمْرِهِمْ هَٰذَا وَهُمْ لَا يَشْعُرُونَ ۝ وَجَآءُوٓ أَبَاهُمْ عِشَآءً يَبْكُونَ ۝ قَالُوا يَٰأَبَانَآ إِنَّا ذَهَبْنَا نَسْتَبِقُ وَتَرَكْنَا يُوسُفَ عِندَ مَتَٰعِنَا فَأَكَلَهُ ٱلذِّئْبُ وَمَآ أَنتَ بِمُؤْمِنٍ لَّنَا وَلَوْ كُنَّا صَٰدِقِينَ ۝ وَجَآءُو عَلَىٰ قَمِيصِهِ بِدَمٍ كَذِبٍ قَالَ بَلْ سَوَّلَتْ لَكُمْ أَنفُسُكُمْ أَمْرًا فَصَبْرٌ جَمِيلٌ وَٱللَّهُ ٱلْمُسْتَعَانُ عَلَىٰ مَا تَصِفُونَ ۝

ᵃ The story of Joseph is definitely more detailed than what has been described in the Quran. But the real purpose of the Quran is to convey moral advice and not to engage in story telling. So, it deals with only those aspects that are useful for the purpose of giving moral lessons and omits other parts, leaving them for the historians to compile.

According to traditions, Joseph was in the dry well for three days. During these three days, he was probably shown his future through dreams. In one of them, he saw himself coming out of the well and reaching a high position of honour and glory. Ultimately, such a wide gap develops between his position and the position of his brothers that they are unable to recognize him when they see him. All this was revealed by his dream.

What Joseph's brothers did was an act of extreme provocation. Unlike them, Joseph entrusted his fate to God and, sitting quietly in the dry well at a deserted place, waited for God's help to arrive. Joseph's father, Jacob, for his part, took the course of noble patience. According to some commentaries he is reported to have told his sons that had a wolf devoured Joseph, it would certainly have torn his shirt. He meant, what a noble wolf it was who took away Joseph and removed his blood-stained shirt to hand it over to them undamaged.

¹⁹ And there came a caravan of travellers and they sent their water-drawer to draw water from the well. He let down his bucket into the well and he exclaimed, 'Oh, what a lucky find, here is a boy!' They hid him like a piece of merchandise, but God knew well what they did. ²⁰ Later they sold him for a paltry sum, a few pieces of silver [*dirhams*]: So little did they value him.*

وَجَآءَتْ سَيَّارَةٌ فَأَرْسَلُواْ وَارِدَهُمْ فَأَدْلَىٰ دَلْوَهُۥ قَالَ يَٰبُشْرَىٰ هَٰذَا غُلَٰمٌ وَأَسَرُّوهُ بِضَٰعَةً وَٱللَّهُ عَلِيمٌۢ بِمَا يَعْمَلُونَ ۝ وَشَرَوْهُ بِثَمَنٍۭ بَخْسٍ دَرَٰهِمَ مَعْدُودَةٍ وَكَانُواْ فِيهِ مِنَ ٱلزَّٰهِدِينَ ۝

---

a After pushing Joseph into the dry well, the brothers returned home. Three days later, a caravan of traders, which was going from Midian to Egypt, happened to pass by that place. A member of the caravan set out in search of water and let his bucket down into the dry well. Joseph (who was about 16 years old at the time) caught hold of it and was pulled up.

This was the age of the slave trade. So the people of the caravan were very happy because they could carry this lad to Egypt and sell him very profitably. Accordingly, when they reached Egypt, they put Joseph on sale along with other saleable commodities. There, a man, finding Joseph attractive in appearance and demeanour, bought him for twenty dirhams.

Joseph's brothers exiled him and pushed him into a well. The people of the caravan sold him as a slave. Thereafter the wife of a highly-placed officer of Egypt (Zulaykha) had him imprisoned. But God Almighty made all these stages stepping stones of honour and glory for him. What a tremendous difference there is between human knowledge and the divine knowledge of God!

²¹ The Egyptian who bought him said to his wife, 'Lodge him honourably, he may prove of benefit to us, or we may even adopt him as our son.' Thus We established Joseph in the land, so that We might teach him the true meaning of events. God has power over all things. However, most people do not know this. ²² And when he reached maturity, We bestowed on him right judgement and knowledge. Thus We reward those who do good.*ᵃ*

وَقَالَ ٱلَّذِى ٱشۡتَرَىٰهُ مِن مِّصۡرَ لِٱمۡرَأَتِهِۦٓ أَكۡرِمِى مَثۡوَىٰهُ عَسَىٰٓ أَن يَنفَعَنَآ أَوۡ نَتَّخِذَهُۥ وَلَدٗاۚ وَكَذَٰلِكَ مَكَّنَّا لِيُوسُفَ فِى ٱلۡأَرۡضِ وَلِنُعَلِّمَهُۥ مِن تَأۡوِيلِ ٱلۡأَحَادِيثِۚ وَٱللَّهُ غَالِبٌ عَلَىٰٓ أَمۡرِهِۦ وَلَٰكِنَّ أَكۡثَرَ ٱلنَّاسِ لَا يَعۡلَمُونَ ۝ وَلَمَّا بَلَغَ أَشُدَّهُۥٓ ءَاتَيۡنَٰهُ حُكۡمٗا وَعِلۡمٗاۚ وَكَذَٰلِكَ نَجۡزِى ٱلۡمُحۡسِنِينَ ۝

ᵃ It is said that an officer of the Egyptian government, Potiphar, bought Joseph. He recognized Joseph's great personality hidden behind an ordinary exterior. He could make out that Joseph was not really a slave but a member of a noble family who, for whatever the reason, had fallen into the hands of the caravan and been sold into slavery. So he asked his wife not to keep Joseph as a slave, but as a family member. He further said that the youth appeared to be a promising young man, capable of managing the affairs of his household and property.

Moreover, Potiphar was childless and wanted to adopt somebody as his son. So he intended to adopt Joseph as his son if he lived up to his expectations.

When Joseph was about forty years old, God blessed him with prophethood on the one hand and with power and authority on the other. He received this reward owing to his righteous deeds. The door of God's blessings is always open for righteous people! The only difference is that during the age of prophethood, a deserving person could have been given prophethood as a result of his righteous deeds but, in later periods, (after the Prophet Muhammad, the last messenger of God) he may receive all bounties except that of prophethood.

²³ However, the woman in whose house he lived, wanted to seduce him. One day she bolted the doors and said, 'Come!' He replied, 'God forbid! Truly [your husband] is my master and has treated me honourably. Wrongdoers certainly never prosper.' ²⁴ She started towards him, and he would have succumbed to her, if he had not seen a sign from his Lord—We did this in order to keep evil and indecency away from him, for he was truly one of Our chosen servants.ᵃ

وَرَٰوَدَتۡهُ ٱلَّتِى هُوَ فِى بَيۡتِهَا عَن نَّفۡسِهِۦ وَغَلَّقَتِ ٱلۡأَبۡوَٰبَ وَقَالَتۡ هَيۡتَ لَكَ ۚ قَالَ مَعَاذَ ٱللَّهِ ۖ إِنَّهُۥ رَبِّى أَحۡسَنَ مَثۡوَاىَ ۖ إِنَّهُۥ لَا يُفۡلِحُ ٱلظَّٰلِمُونَ ۝ وَلَقَدۡ هَمَّتۡ بِهِۦ ۖ وَهَمَّ بِهَا لَوۡلَآ أَن رَّءَا بُرۡهَٰنَ رَبِّهِۦ ۚ كَذَٰلِكَ لِنَصۡرِفَ عَنۡهُ ٱلسُّوٓءَ وَٱلۡفَحۡشَآءَ ۚ إِنَّهُۥ مِنۡ عِبَادِنَا ٱلۡمُخۡلَصِينَ ۝

ᵃ Zulaykha, the wife of the nobleman, was charmed by the beauty of Joseph. She constantly tried to seduce him and one day, finding the opportunity, she closed the door of the room.

This was a very critical occasion for an unmarried youth, but Joseph had preserved his godly nature and this nature came to his rescue on this occasion. The capacity to distinguish between truth and untruth, right and wrong, is ingrained in every human being by birth and this serves as a warning on all such occasions. To ignore it amounts to ignoring the voice of God. One who does so is deprived of God's succour so that his moral strength gradually ebbs away. On the contrary, one who immediately bows down before the divine call, as soon as it is given, can count on God's help; this improves his moral fibre and on future occasions he becomes stronger in the face of evil.

What prevented Joseph from indulging in evil was in fact the fear of God but, at that time, invoking God before Zulaykha would have been ineffective. This was not an occasion for a declaration of Truth but an occasion when he had to save himself in a critical situation. In view of this situation he referred to Zulaykha's husband. He said that 'her husband was his master and he had maintained him in his house with due honour. Therefore, it was not possible for him to besmirch the honour of his benefactor.'

²⁵ They both ran to the door and, in the struggle, she tore his shirt at the back. They found her husband at the door. She cried, 'Shall not the man who wished to violate your wife be thrown into prison or sternly punished?' ²⁶ Joseph said, 'It was she who sought to seduce me.' One of her household testified, 'If his shirt is torn at the front then she is speaking the truth, and he is lying. ²⁷ But if it is torn from behind then she is lying, and he speaks the truth.' ²⁸ So when he saw his shirt torn from behind [her husband] said, 'This is the guile of you women. Your guile is great indeed. ²⁹ Joseph, overlook this: but you [wife], ask forgiveness for your sin, for you have done wrong.' ^a

وَٱسْتَبَقَا ٱلْبَابَ وَقَدَّتْ قَمِيصَهُ مِن دُبُرٍ وَأَلْفَيَا سَيِّدَهَا لَدَا ٱلْبَابِ قَالَتْ مَا جَزَآءُ مَنْ أَرَادَ بِأَهْلِكَ سُوٓءًا إِلَّآ أَن يُسْجَنَ أَوْ عَذَابٌ أَلِيمٌ ۞ قَالَ هِىَ رَٰوَدَتْنِى عَن نَّفْسِى وَشَهِدَ شَاهِدٌ مِّنْ أَهْلِهَآ إِن كَانَ قَمِيصُهُ قُدَّ مِن قُبُلٍ فَصَدَقَتْ وَهُوَ مِنَ ٱلْكَٰذِبِينَ ۞ وَإِن كَانَ قَمِيصُهُ قُدَّ مِن دُبُرٍ فَكَذَبَتْ وَهُوَ مِنَ ٱلصَّٰدِقِينَ ۞ فَلَمَّا رَءَا قَمِيصَهُ قُدَّ مِن دُبُرٍ قَالَ إِنَّهُ مِن كَيْدِكُنَّ إِنَّ كَيْدَكُنَّ عَظِيمٌ ۞ يُوسُفُ أَعْرِضْ عَنْ هَٰذَا وَٱسْتَغْفِرِى لِذَنۢبِكِ إِنَّكِ كُنتِ مِنَ ٱلْخَاطِـِٔينَ ۞

---

^a Joseph ran towards the door to save himself and Zulaykha also ran after him and caught hold of his shirt from behind. In this chaos the back of his shirt was torn. However, Joseph was able to open the door and came out. It so happened that Zulaykha's husband was there outside the door. On seeing him, Zulaykha put all the blame on Joseph. She did not hesitate to make a false accusation against a person for whom she had been professing love only a moment earlier.

Joseph said that the matter was entirely the opposite of what Zulaykha claimed. Now the question was to decide as to who was in the wrong. No third person was present on this occasion who could have been an eyewitness. At that time a wise person of the household offered good advice. (In all probability this person was already aware of the situation. Moreover, he might have already seen that Joseph's shirt was torn from behind and not from in front.) He told all those concerned that, in the absence of an eyewitness, circumstantial evidence should be relied upon and the circumstantial evidence was that Joseph's shirt was a clear proof of the fact that in this case it was not Joseph, but Zulaykha who had made improper advances.

³⁰ Women in the town began to gossip, 'The nobleman's wife is trying to seduce her slave! Love for him consumes her heart! Indeed! We see her in manifest error.' ³¹ When she heard of their intrigues, she sent for them and prepared a party for them. She gave a knife to each of them [to cut fruits, etc.] and then asked Joseph to appear before them. When the women saw him, they were greatly amazed [at his beauty], and they cut their hands, exclaiming, 'God preserve us! This is no human being but a noble angel!' ³² She said, 'This is he about whom you have been blaming me! And, indeed, I did try to make him yield to me, but he was unyielding. Now, however, if he does not do as I bid him, he shall certainly be put in prison and be humiliated.' ³³ Joseph said, 'O my Lord! I would prefer prison to what these women are inviting me to do. And if You do not avert their guile from me, I may yield to them and so become one of the ignorant.' ³⁴ So his Lord answered him and warded off their guile. He is All Hearing and All Knowing.ᵃ

۞ وَقَالَ نِسْوَةٌ فِى ٱلْمَدِينَةِ ٱمْرَأَتُ ٱلْعَزِيزِ تُرَٰوِدُ فَتَىٰهَا عَن نَّفْسِهِۦ قَدْ شَغَفَهَا حُبًّا إِنَّا لَنَرَىٰهَا فِى ضَلَٰلٍ مُّبِينٍ ۝ فَلَمَّا سَمِعَتْ بِمَكْرِهِنَّ أَرْسَلَتْ إِلَيْهِنَّ وَأَعْتَدَتْ لَهُنَّ مُتَّكَـًٔا وَءَاتَتْ كُلَّ وَٰحِدَةٍ مِّنْهُنَّ سِكِّينًا وَقَالَتِ ٱخْرُجْ عَلَيْهِنَّ فَلَمَّا رَأَيْنَهُۥٓ أَكْبَرْنَهُۥ وَقَطَّعْنَ أَيْدِيَهُنَّ وَقُلْنَ حَٰشَ لِلَّهِ مَا هَٰذَا بَشَرًا إِنْ هَٰذَآ إِلَّا مَلَكٌ كَرِيمٌ ۝ قَالَتْ فَذَٰلِكُنَّ ٱلَّذِى لُمْتُنَّنِى فِيهِ وَلَقَدْ رَٰوَدتُّهُۥ عَن نَّفْسِهِۦ فَٱسْتَعْصَمَ وَلَئِن لَّمْ يَفْعَلْ مَآ ءَامُرُهُۥ لَيُسْجَنَنَّ وَلَيَكُونًا مِّنَ ٱلصَّٰغِرِينَ ۝ قَالَ رَبِّ ٱلسِّجْنُ أَحَبُّ إِلَىَّ مِمَّا يَدْعُونَنِىٓ إِلَيْهِ وَإِلَّا تَصْرِفْ عَنِّى كَيْدَهُنَّ أَصْبُ إِلَيْهِنَّ وَأَكُن مِّنَ ٱلْجَٰهِلِينَ ۝ فَٱسْتَجَابَ لَهُۥ رَبُّهُۥ فَصَرَفَ عَنْهُ كَيْدَهُنَّ إِنَّهُۥ هُوَ ٱلسَّمِيعُ ٱلْعَلِيمُ ۝

ᵃ Certain ladies of noble families were invited by Zulaykha to meet Joseph and they saw in him a handsome young man. Joseph also could have seen these ladies as a means of satisfying the desires of his lower self. But even in the most exciting of circumstances, he did not see them as such.

The ladies were all so thrilled by his extremely charming personality, that, in their extreme state of absorption, they injured their hands with knives while cutting fruit. But Joseph's whole attention was directed towards God. God's greatness and Majesty so dominated his senses that nothing could divert his attention. What a difference there is between one human being and another.

35 Yet, even after all the evidence they had seen, they thought it right to jail him for a time. 36 Two young men entered the prison along with him. One of them said, 'I saw myself [in a dream] I was pressing wine.' The other said, 'I dreamed I was carrying bread on my head from which the birds were eating. Tell us their meaning; for we see that you are one who does good [to all].'ᵃ

ثُمَّ بَدَا لَهُم مِّنۢ بَعْدِ مَا رَأَوُا۟ ٱلْأَيَـٰتِ لَيَسْجُنُنَّهُۥ حَتَّىٰ حِينٍ ۝ وَدَخَلَ مَعَهُ ٱلسِّجْنَ فَتَيَانِ ۖ قَالَ أَحَدُهُمَآ إِنِّىٓ أَرَىٰنِىٓ أَعْصِرُ خَمْرًا ۖ وَقَالَ ٱلْأَخَرُ إِنِّىٓ أَرَىٰنِىٓ أَحْمِلُ فَوْقَ رَأْسِى خُبْزًا تَأْكُلُ ٱلطَّيْرُ مِنْهُ ۚ نَبِّئْنَا بِتَأْوِيلِهِۦٓ ۖ إِنَّا نَرَىٰكَ مِنَ ٱلْمُحْسِنِينَ ۝

ᵃ When the ladies of high status of Egypt failed to attract Joseph's attention towards themselves, they deemed it only right and proper that he should be sent to prison. At that time Joseph was a slave, and it was not necessary (according to the custom of the time) to follow court procedure before sending a slave to prison. The masters themselves had the power to have their slaves incarcerated in accordance with their own decisions.

But the prison proved to be a stepping-stone for him. So far he had been introduced to only a few high ranking households. Now it became possible that the news of his personality would reach the king of Egypt himself.

It so happened that two youths were also sent to the same prison where he was kept confined. Both of them were connected with the royal palace. Both of them had a dream in the prison and they asked Joseph to interpret these dreams. Joseph did so and his interpretation proved to be true. Thereafter one of them was released from the prison and returned to the royal palace. At the opportune moment, he told the king that there was a righteous person in the prison who gave the correct interpretation of dreams. Joseph's imprisonment thus became a preliminary stepping-stone for access to the royal palace.

³⁷ Joseph said to them, 'I shall inform you of the interpretation of your dreams before your meal is brought to you. This is a part of the knowledge that my Lord has taught me. I have renounced the religion of the people who do not believe in God and who deny the Hereafter. ³⁸ I follow the religion of my fathers, Abraham, Isaac and Jacob; and it is not for us to associate anyone with God as a partner. This is of God's grace upon us and upon mankind; even though most men are not grateful. ³⁹ O my two fellow-prisoners! Are many diverse lords better, or God, the One, the Almighty? ⁴⁰ All those you worship instead of Him are mere names you and your forefathers have invented, names for which God has sent down no authority: all power belongs to God alone, and He orders you to worship none but Him: this is the true faith, though most people do not realize it.^a

قَالَ لَا يَأْتِيكُمَا طَعَامٌ تُرْزَقَانِهِۦٓ إِلَّا نَبَّأْتُكُمَا بِتَأْوِيلِهِۦ قَبْلَ أَن يَأْتِيَكُمَا ذَٰلِكُمَا مِمَّا عَلَّمَنِى رَبِّىٓ إِنِّى تَرَكْتُ مِلَّةَ قَوْمٍ لَّا يُؤْمِنُونَ بِٱللَّهِ وَهُم بِٱلْأَخِرَةِ هُمْ كَٰفِرُونَ ۝ وَٱتَّبَعْتُ مِلَّةَ ءَابَآءِى إِبْرَٰهِيمَ وَإِسْحَٰقَ وَيَعْقُوبَ مَا كَانَ لَنَآ أَن نُّشْرِكَ بِٱللَّهِ مِن شَىْءٍ ذَٰلِكَ مِن فَضْلِ ٱللَّهِ عَلَيْنَا وَعَلَى ٱلنَّاسِ وَلَٰكِنَّ أَكْثَرَ ٱلنَّاسِ لَا يَشْكُرُونَ ۝ يَٰصَٰحِبَىِ ٱلسِّجْنِ ءَأَرْبَابٌ مُّتَفَرِّقُونَ خَيْرٌ أَمِ ٱللَّهُ ٱلْوَٰحِدُ ٱلْقَهَّارُ ۝ مَا تَعْبُدُونَ مِن دُونِهِۦٓ إِلَّآ أَسْمَآءً سَمَّيْتُمُوهَآ أَنتُمْ وَءَابَآؤُكُم مَّآ أَنزَلَ ٱللَّهُ بِهَا مِن سُلْطَٰنٍ إِنِ ٱلْحُكْمُ إِلَّا لِلَّهِ أَمَرَ أَلَّا تَعْبُدُوٓا۟ إِلَّآ إِيَّاهُ ذَٰلِكَ ٱلدِّينُ ٱلْقَيِّمُ وَلَٰكِنَّ أَكْثَرَ ٱلنَّاسِ لَا يَعْلَمُونَ ۝

---

^a The young prisoners approached Joseph in order to know the interpretation of their dreams. The manner in which they put their questions to Joseph was a clear indication that they were impressed by his personality and relied on his opinion. This approach was natural in the case of a righteous and principled person like Joseph.

Joseph, with his missionary spirit, immediately realised that this was the best opportunity to convey the message of truth to these youths. But, after hearing the interpretation of their dreams, their attention might have been diverted from Joseph. So he adopted a wise approach and delayed the interpretation for some time. Thereafter he talked to them briefly about the unity of God and, in view of the mentality of the addressees, he used superior reasoning to convey his message to them.

⁴¹ O my two fellow-prisoners, one of you will serve wine to his lord, the other of you will be crucified and birds will feed off his head. The matter about which you have been seeking my opinion has been so decreed.' ⁴² He said to the one he thought would be saved, 'Mention me to your master.' However Satan made him forget to mention him to his master, and so Joseph remained in prison for a number of years.^a

يَـٰصَحِبَيِ ٱلسِّجْنِ أَمَّا أَحَدُكُمَا فَيَسْقِى رَبَّهُۥ خَمْرًا ۖ وَأَمَّا ٱلْآخَرُ فَيُصْلَبُ فَتَأْكُلُ ٱلطَّيْرُ مِن رَّأْسِهِۦ ۚ قُضِىَ ٱلْأَمْرُ ٱلَّذِى فِيهِ تَسْتَفْتِيَانِ ۝ وَقَالَ لِلَّذِى ظَنَّ أَنَّهُۥ نَاجٍ مِّنْهُمَا ٱذْكُرْنِى عِندَ رَبِّكَ فَأَنسَـٰهُ ٱلشَّيْطَـٰنُ ذِكْرَ رَبِّهِۦ فَلَبِثَ فِى ٱلسِّجْنِ بِضْعَ سِنِينَ ۝

---

^a Of the two youths who were put in jail, one was a bread maker and the other was a wine-server to the king of Egypt. Both were accused of trying to poison the food of the king. On investigation, the wine-server proved to be innocent of the allegation. He was released from the jail and was again appointed as a wine-server to the king. His dream meant that he was serving wine to the king in dream and after few days he would really serve wine while awake. The bread maker was proved guilty. He was hanged and left for the birds to peck at his body and, in this way, be a lesson to the people.

Both the interpretations of Joseph proved to be correct but, after reaching the palace, the wine-server forgot to mention Joseph to the king as promised. He remembered his promise only when the king had a dream and asked his courtiers to interpret it.

43 The king said, 'I saw [in a dream] seven fat cows which seven lean ones were eating, also seven green ears of corn and seven others which were dry. Tell me the meaning of this vision, my nobles, if you can interpret visions.' 44 They said, 'These are confusing dreams and we do not know the interpretation of such dreams.' 45 Then one of the two men who had been released and who, after a long time, remembered, said, 'I shall tell you its interpretation; therefore, give me leave to go [to Joseph in prison].'ᵃ

وَقَالَ ٱلْمَلِكُ إِنِّي أَرَىٰ سَبْعَ بَقَرَٰتٍ سِمَانٍ يَأْكُلُهُنَّ سَبْعٌ عِجَافٌ وَسَبْعَ سُنۢبُلَٰتٍ خُضْرٍ وَأُخَرَ يَابِسَٰتٍ ۖ يَٰٓأَيُّهَا ٱلْمَلَأُ أَفْتُونِي فِي رُءْيَٰىَ إِن كُنتُمْ لِلرُّءْيَا تَعْبُرُونَ ۝ قَالُوٓاْ أَضْغَٰثُ أَحْلَٰمٍ ۖ وَمَا نَحْنُ بِتَأْوِيلِ ٱلْأَحْلَٰمِ بِعَٰلِمِينَ ۝ وَقَالَ ٱلَّذِى نَجَا مِنْهُمَا وَٱدَّكَرَ بَعْدَ أُمَّةٍ أَنَا۟ أُنَبِّئُكُم بِتَأْوِيلِهِۦ فَأَرْسِلُونِ ۝

ᵃ Though the king of Egypt was a polytheist and a wine drinker, God made him see a true dream of the future. This shows how God helps the preacher of truth. One way is to make the potential convert see a dream which impresses upon him the preacher's importance. As a result his heart is softened and fresh opportunities are opened up for the dayee.

Only when the king's wine-server heard about the king's dream was he reminded of the incident in prison. He related his personal experience to the king and the courtiers of how Joseph's interpretation of his own dream and that of another prisoner had proved to be absolutely true. Thereafter, with the permission of the king, he went to the prison to ask Joseph about the interpretation of the king's dream. The introduction of this aspect of Joseph's personality provided a way for him to be released from prison. God could have arranged for his immediate release as soon as the wine-server was out of prison. He could have made the drink-server fulfil his promise and mention Joseph to the king as soon as he was back in the palace. But every work of God is performed at the ordained time. It is not the way of God to perform any task before the time appointed for it.

⁴⁶ 'O truthful Joseph!' he said, 'Tell us the meaning of a dream in which seven fat cows are being eaten by seven lean ones, and there are seven green ears of corn and seven others which are dry, so that I may return to my people and inform them.' ⁴⁷ Joseph said, 'You shall sow for seven consecutive years as usual, but leave in the ear the harvest that you reap, except for a little which you may eat. ⁴⁸ Then there will follow seven years of great hardship which will consume all but a little of what you stored. ⁴⁹ Then a year will come after that when people will have abundant rain and when once more they will press [wine and oil].' ᵃ

يُوسُفُ أَيُّهَا ٱلصِّدِّيقُ أَفْتِنَا فِى سَبْعِ بَقَرَٰتٍ سِمَانٍ يَأْكُلُهُنَّ سَبْعٌ عِجَافٌ وَسَبْعِ سُنۢبُلَٰتٍ خُضْرٍ وَأُخَرَ يَابِسَٰتٍ لَّعَلِّىٓ أَرْجِعُ إِلَى ٱلنَّاسِ لَعَلَّهُمْ يَعْلَمُونَ ﴿٤٦﴾ قَالَ تَزْرَعُونَ سَبْعَ سِنِينَ دَأَبًا فَمَا حَصَدتُّمْ فَذَرُوهُ فِى سُنۢبُلِهِۦٓ إِلَّا قَلِيلًا مِّمَّا تَأْكُلُونَ ﴿٤٧﴾ ثُمَّ يَأْتِى مِنۢ بَعْدِ ذَٰلِكَ سَبْعٌ شِدَادٌ يَأْكُلْنَ مَا قَدَّمْتُمْ لَهُنَّ إِلَّا قَلِيلًا مِّمَّا تُحْصِنُونَ ﴿٤٨﴾ ثُمَّ يَأْتِى مِنۢ بَعْدِ ذَٰلِكَ عَامٌ فِيهِ يُغَاثُ ٱلنَّاسُ وَفِيهِ يَعْصِرُونَ ﴿٤٩﴾

ᵃ The interpretation Joseph gave to the king's dream was that the seven fat cows and the seven green ears of corn stood for seven years when there would be consistently good harvests. Animals would multiply and vegetation would flourish immensely. Thereafter, there would be scarcity and famine for seven years, during which period the previously reserved resources would be exhausted and only some portion for future sowing would be left. These succeeding seven years were represented by lean cows and withered ears of corn and these would consume the previous fat cows and green ears of corn.

Along with the interpretation Joseph also indicated the means to overcome this calamity. He advised that the produce during the first seven years should be preserved with the utmost care and should be used with the utmost economy. He said that the corn in excess of the food requirement should be left in the ear of corn to keep it safe from pests and in this way, the produce of seven years would be sufficient for fourteen years. Furthermore he gave the good news that the year following the seven years of famine would again be a year of good harvests. There would be copious rain in these years and people would have plenty of milk and fruit.

God Almighty caused the king to have a strange dream and through Joseph indicated its correct interpretation. In this way Joseph was provided with an opportunity to attain a very high status in the Government of Egypt.

⁵⁰ The king said, 'Bring him to me.' When the king's messenger came to Joseph, he said, 'Go back to your master and ask him about the women who cut their hands: my Lord knows well their guile.' ⁵¹ The king asked the women, 'What was the truth of the affair in which you tried to seduce Joseph?' The women said, 'God forbid! We know no evil of him.' The wife of the nobleman said, 'The truth has now come to light. It was I who tried to seduce him; he is surely an honest man.' [a]

وَقَالَ ٱلْمَلِكُ ٱئْتُونِى بِهِۦ ۖ فَلَمَّا جَآءَهُ ٱلرَّسُولُ قَالَ ٱرْجِعْ إِلَىٰ رَبِّكَ فَسْـَٔلْهُ مَا بَالُ ٱلنِّسْوَةِ ٱلَّـٰتِى قَطَّعْنَ أَيْدِيَهُنَّ ۚ إِنَّ رَبِّى بِكَيْدِهِنَّ عَلِيمٌ ۝ قَالَ مَا خَطْبُكُنَّ إِذْ رَٰوَدتُّنَّ يُوسُفَ عَن نَّفْسِهِۦ ۚ قُلْنَ حَـٰشَ لِلَّهِ مَا عَلِمْنَا عَلَيْهِ مِن سُوٓءٍ ۚ قَالَتِ ٱمْرَأَتُ ٱلْعَزِيزِ ٱلْـَٰٔنَ حَصْحَصَ ٱلْحَقُّ أَنَا۠ رَٰوَدتُّهُۥ عَن نَّفْسِهِۦ وَإِنَّهُۥ لَمِنَ ٱلصَّـٰدِقِينَ ۝

---

[a] After his release from prison, Joseph had to play a role at the national level. So it was necessary that his personality should become well-known country-wide. This was achieved through the incident of the king's dream. The king was so anxious to know the interpretation of his peculiar dream that he made a public announcement and gathered all the scholars; the priests and wise people of the country assembled in his court to give their interpretation of this dream. But they all failed to do so. In this way the incident of the dream became a matter of general fame.

As soon as Joseph gave the interpretation of the dream, and it was liked by the king, he suddenly came to be known by the whole populace.

After hearing the whole history of Joseph's imprisonment, the king made inquiries of the concerned women. All of them unanimously declared him to be innocent. The wife of the nobleman of Egypt (Zulaykha) did not spare herself in the admission of truth. She declared in clear terms that her friends were telling the truth. She said that she had been entirely to blame in this matter and that Joseph was totally innocent. This admission on the part of the wife of the nobleman was such a noble action that it would not have been surprising if she had been guided towards the true faith thereafter.

⁵² 'From this,' said Joseph, '[The nobleman] should know that I did not betray him in his absence, and that God does not guide the plotting of the treacherous. ⁵³ I am not trying to absolve myself: for man's very soul incites him to evil unless my Lord bestows His mercy. Indeed, my Lord is forgiving and merciful.' *ᵃ*

ذَٰلِكَ لِيَعْلَمَ أَنِّى لَمْ أَخُنْهُ بِٱلْغَيْبِ وَأَنَّ ٱللَّهَ لَا يَهْدِى كَيْدَ ٱلْخَآئِنِينَ ۞ وَمَآ أُبَرِّئُ نَفْسِىٓ إِنَّ ٱلنَّفْسَ لَأَمَّارَةٌۢ بِٱلسُّوٓءِ إِلَّا مَا رَحِمَ رَبِّىٓ إِنَّ رَبِّى غَفُورٌ رَّحِيمٌ ۞

ᵃ When the king called Joseph to his court, he did not leave the prison immediately but said that first of all that incident on the pretext of which he had been imprisoned should be investigated. Though he was completely innocent before God, as a consequence of the aforesaid incident, he was accused of being disloyal and dishonest towards his master. This was a critical issue, because he had to render the service of prophethood to the people, that is, he was required to convey the message of guidance entrusted to him to the subjects of God. Prior to his appearing before the general public, it was necessary that this allegation against him should be disproved; because one whom the people do not consider trustworthy in his dealings will not be considered trustworthy in the role of God's envoy.

A man of faith has two options before him at all times. He has to choose between man and God. Sometimes it happens that, when dealing with human beings, he has to utter some words of clarification which appear to be a tall claim on his part, although even at that time his heart is full of feelings of humility and modesty, and even if, when he looks at himself in relation to God, he is nothing but humble. The concept of God keeps a believer balanced at every moment. Joseph's above-mentioned utterance gives a picture of this unique character of a believer's personality.

⁵⁴ The king said, 'Bring him to me. I will take him for my special service.' And when he had spoken to him, he said, 'From now on you will dwell with us, honoured and trusted.' ⁵⁵ Joseph said, 'Place in my charge the storehouses of the land; for I am a good and knowledgeable custodian.' ⁵⁶ Thus We caused Joseph to be established in a position of authority in the land. He could dwell therein wherever he pleased. We bestow Our mercy on whomever We please, and We do not allow the reward of the righteous to go to waste. ⁵⁷ Yet the reward of the hereafter is best for those who believe and are mindful of God.^a

وَقَالَ ٱلْمَلِكُ ٱئْتُونِى بِهِۦ أَسْتَخْلِصْهُ لِنَفْسِى ۖ فَلَمَّا كَلَّمَهُۥ قَالَ إِنَّكَ ٱلْيَوْمَ لَدَيْنَا مَكِينٌ أَمِينٌ ۝ قَالَ ٱجْعَلْنِى عَلَىٰ خَزَآئِنِ ٱلْأَرْضِ ۖ إِنِّى حَفِيظٌ عَلِيمٌ ۝ وَكَذَٰلِكَ مَكَّنَّا لِيُوسُفَ فِى ٱلْأَرْضِ يَتَبَوَّأُ مِنْهَا حَيْثُ يَشَآءُ ۚ نُصِيبُ بِرَحْمَتِنَا مَن نَّشَآءُ ۖ وَلَا نُضِيعُ أَجْرَ ٱلْمُحْسِنِينَ ۝ وَلَأَجْرُ ٱلْأَخِرَةِ خَيْرٌ لِّلَّذِينَ ءَامَنُوا۟ وَكَانُوا۟ يَتَّقُونَ ۝

---

^a 'Place in my charge the storehouses of the land.' (The original Arabic word translated here as storehouses [or granaries] literally means 'treasure'). Seeing that he had the attention of the king, Joseph made this request to him, so that with the help of government resources he should be empowered to construct large granaries throughout the whole country, where surplus corn acquired from the farmers and could be stored for the first seven years. The king agreed to this and, exercising his constitutional royal authority, gave Joseph all kinds of power to facilitate this task.

The king of Egypt was a polytheist. Verse 76 shows that after the appointment of Joseph the religion of the same king prevailed in Egypt for about ten years. This tradition of the Prophet of God shows that acceptance of a subordinate post under a non-Muslim government is not against Islam. On the same basis our predecessors accepted the posts of 'Qazi' under tyrant kings. (*Tafsir an-Nasafi*).

What was Joseph's purpose in assuming authority in Egypt? The information given in the Quran indicates that his purpose seems to have been to save the subjects of God from famine and then, as a result of this, to create opportunities for the Children of Israel to settle in Egypt.

⁵⁸ Joseph's brothers arrived and presented themselves before him. He recognized them, but they did not know him. ⁵⁹ When he had made provision for them, he told them, 'Bring me your brother on your father's side. Do you not see that I give you full measure and that I am the best of hosts? ⁶⁰ But if you do not bring him to me, you shall have no grain from me, nor shall you ever approach me again.' ⁶¹ They replied, 'We shall try to persuade his father to send him with us. We shall do [our utmost]!' ᵃ

وَجَاءَ إِخْوَةُ يُوسُفَ فَدَخَلُواْ عَلَيْهِ فَعَرَفَهُمْ وَهُمْ لَهُ مُنكِرُونَ ۝ وَلَمَّا جَهَّزَهُم بِجَهَازِهِمْ قَالَ ٱئْتُونِى بِأَخٍ لَّكُم مِّنْ أَبِيكُمْ أَلَا تَرَوْنَ أَنِّى أُوفِى ٱلْكَيْلَ وَأَنَا۠ خَيْرُ ٱلْمُنزِلِينَ ۝ فَإِن لَّمْ تَأْتُونِى بِهِۦ فَلَا كَيْلَ لَكُمْ عِندِى وَلَا تَقْرَبُونِ ۝ قَالُواْ سَنُرَٰوِدُ عَنْهُ أَبَاهُ وَإِنَّا لَفَاعِلُونَ ۝

ᵃ There were bumper crops during the first seven years of Joseph's power. He had big granaries constructed throughout the whole country in which he stored surplus corn bought from the farmers every year. Thereafter when the years of famine commenced, he arranged to have this corn stored in the capital and started selling it at a fair price.

This famine prevailed not only in Egypt but also in the surrounding areas, that is, in Syria, Palestine. Transjordan, etc. When the news spread far and wide that corn was being sold at a fair price in Egypt, Joseph's brothers also came to Egypt to purchase corn. Although they were seeing Joseph after twenty years, they saw a resemblance to their brother in him. But immediately this thought vanished from their minds, because they could not understand how someone whom they had pushed into a dry well could assume the highest office of Egypt.

Joseph arranged one camel-load of corn per head for his brothers. Now they wanted to have one more camel-load of corn in Benjamin's name too. They said that one of their brothers had been detained by their old father to be with him, therefore they said that it would be very kind of him if Benjamin's share could also be given to them.

Joseph said that it was against his principles to hand over the share of an absentee. He also said that when they came again, they should bring their brother with them and then only could they have his share. Joseph added, 'You have experienced my generosity. Even after this, are you reluctant to bring your brother with you? If you are unable to bring this brother the next time, it will be presumed that you were telling a lie and only wanted to get one more camel-load of corn by deceit. The punishment for this will be that in future you will be deprived of even your own share of corn.'

[62] Joseph said to his servants, 'Put their money back into their saddlebags, so that they will recognize it when they return home to their family; thus they may come back.' [63] When they returned to their father, they said, 'Our father, any [further] measure of grain has been denied us, so send our brother [Benjamin] along with us, so that we may obtain our measure [of grain]; and, we shall guard him well.' [64] He replied, 'Am I to trust you with him as I once trusted you with his brother? But God is the best of guardians, the Most Merciful of all.' [a]

وَقَالَ لِفِتْيَٰنِهِ ٱجْعَلُوا۟ بِضَٰعَتَهُمْ فِى رِحَالِهِمْ لَعَلَّهُمْ يَعْرِفُونَهَآ إِذَا ٱنقَلَبُوٓا۟ إِلَىٰٓ أَهْلِهِمْ لَعَلَّهُمْ يَرْجِعُونَ ۝ فَلَمَّا رَجَعُوٓا۟ إِلَىٰٓ أَبِيهِمْ قَالُوا۟ يَٰٓأَبَانَا مُنِعَ مِنَّا ٱلْكَيْلُ فَأَرْسِلْ مَعَنَآ أَخَانَا نَكْتَلْ وَإِنَّا لَهُۥ لَحَٰفِظُونَ ۝ قَالَ هَلْ ءَامَنُكُمْ عَلَيْهِ إِلَّا كَمَآ أَمِنتُكُمْ عَلَىٰٓ أَخِيهِ مِن قَبْلُ فَٱللَّهُ خَيْرٌ حَٰفِظًا وَهُوَ أَرْحَمُ ٱلرَّٰحِمِينَ ۝

---

[a] Joseph probably felt that it was discourteous to take the price of the corn from his brothers, or he perhaps thought that a lack of money might prevent them from coming back again. Therefore, he instructed his men that whatever amount his brothers had paid towards the corn should be quietly put among their belongings, so that when they went home and opened their bundles, they would find it and come again with their brother, Benjamin.

Jacob, on the one hand, expressed his lack of trust in his sons where Benjamin was concerned. On the other hand, he also said that neither they nor anybody else had any power. Whatever God wished was bound to happen. But this happening is caused by human hands, so that an evil person, by performing evil deeds, may lay bare the truth about himself, while the good person, by performing righteous deeds, may have his name listed among the righteous.

⁶⁵ When they opened their packs, they discovered that their money had been returned to them. They said, 'Our father, what more do we desire than this? This money of ours has been returned to us, so we shall [again] buy food for our family and we shall guard our brother, and we shall obtain an additional camel-load of grain. This [that we bring now] is a small quantity.' ⁶⁶ He [Jacob] said, 'I will never send him with you until you give me a solemn pledge, before God, that you will indeed bring him back to me, unless you yourselves are trapped [in a compulsive situation].' And when they had given him their solemn pledge, [Jacob] said, 'God shall be witness to all that we say.'^a

وَلَمَّا فَتَحُوا۟ مَتَٰعَهُمْ وَجَدُوا۟ بِضَٰعَتَهُمْ رُدَّتْ إِلَيْهِمْ قَالُوا۟ يَٰٓأَبَانَا مَا نَبْغِى هَٰذِهِۦ بِضَٰعَتُنَا رُدَّتْ إِلَيْنَا وَنَمِيرُ أَهْلَنَا وَنَحْفَظُ أَخَانَا وَنَزْدَادُ كَيْلَ بَعِيرٍ ذَٰلِكَ كَيْلٌ يَسِيرٌ ۝ قَالَ لَنْ أُرْسِلَهُۥ مَعَكُمْ حَتَّىٰ تُؤْتُونِ مَوْثِقًا مِّنَ ٱللَّهِ لَتَأْتُنَّنِى بِهِۦٓ إِلَّآ أَن يُحَاطَ بِكُمْ فَلَمَّآ ءَاتَوْهُ مَوْثِقَهُمْ قَالَ ٱللَّهُ عَلَىٰ مَا نَقُولُ وَكِيلٌ ۝

---

^a On reaching home, when they found their money in their bags of corn, they were very happy. They told their father that he should send Benjamin with them. They promised to take care of him. They said that they would bring one more camel-load of corn as his share. They also said that the corn they had now brought was not sufficient for their needs.

Perhaps according to the distribution system introduced by Joseph, outsiders were each allowed one camel-load of corn.

⁶⁷ 'O my sons! Do not all of you enter [the city] by one gate; enter by separate gates. I cannot help you in any way against God; judgement is His alone. In Him I have put my trust. In Him let the faithful put their trust.' ⁶⁸ They entered [safely] as their father had told them. However, he had no power to guard them against God's decree. It was only a wish in Jacob's soul which he had thus fulfilled. He was possessed of knowledge which We had given him. But most people have no knowledge.^a

وَقَالَ يَٰبَنِىَّ لَا تَدْخُلُوا۟ مِنۢ بَابٍ وَٰحِدٍ وَٱدْخُلُوا۟ مِنْ أَبْوَٰبٍ مُّتَفَرِّقَةٍ ۖ وَمَآ أُغْنِى عَنكُم مِّنَ ٱللَّهِ مِن شَىْءٍ ۖ إِنِ ٱلْحُكْمُ إِلَّا لِلَّهِ ۖ عَلَيْهِ تَوَكَّلْتُ ۖ وَعَلَيْهِ فَلْيَتَوَكَّلِ ٱلْمُتَوَكِّلُونَ ۝ وَلَمَّا دَخَلُوا۟ مِنْ حَيْثُ أَمَرَهُمْ أَبُوهُم مَّا كَانَ يُغْنِى عَنْهُم مِّنَ ٱللَّهِ مِن شَىْءٍ إِلَّا حَاجَةً فِى نَفْسِ يَعْقُوبَ قَضَىٰهَا ۚ وَإِنَّهُۥ لَذُو عِلْمٍ لِّمَا عَلَّمْنَٰهُ وَلَٰكِنَّ أَكْثَرَ ٱلنَّاسِ لَا يَعْلَمُونَ ۝

---

^a The ancient capital of Egypt was a city around which there was a rampart with many gates in it. Jacob's advice to his sons that they should not enter the city through the same gate, but through different gates was based on the fear that some enemy of theirs might try to kill them (*Tafsir an-Nasafi*).

Verse 73 of this chapter clarifies the matter of this fear. In this Joseph's brothers profess that they are innocent by saying that they had not come there to fight or steal. Joseph's brothers had come to Egypt from foreign lands; their way of dressing was different from that of the local people; because of their appearance they would appear to be outsiders to the people of Egypt; the entry of eleven such persons together would have created suspicion in the eyes of the people. So in order to save them from any unnecessary clash with the local people, Jacob advised them not to band together in one group while entering the city.

A believer's eyes are ever on the supreme power of God; he observes that in this universe nobody has any power except God. At the same time he knows that this world is a testing ground. Owing to the exigencies of this test God has hidden all matters behind the veil of cause and effect. For this reason, Jacob advised his sons to take worldly precautions. But he also said that whatever happened, would happen at the instance of God, because nobody except God had any real power.

⁶⁹ When they presented themselves before Joseph, he took his brother [Benjamin] aside. He said, 'I am your brother, so do not feel distressed about whatever they have been doing.' ⁷⁰ And when he had given them their provisions, he placed a drinking-cup in his brother's pack. Then a crier called out after them, 'Men of the caravan! You have committed theft!' ⁷¹ They said, turning towards him, 'What is it that you have lost?' ⁷² 'We miss the royal measuring bowl,' he replied. 'He who brings it shall have a camel-load of corn. I pledge my word for it.' ⁷³ They said, 'By God, you [ought to] know we have not come here to cause any trouble in the land. We are not thieves!' ⁷⁴ The Egyptians asked them, 'And if we find that you are lying, what penalty shall we mete out to you?' ⁷⁵ They replied, 'The penalty should be that he in whose saddlebag it is found, should be held [as bondman] to atone for the crime. That is how we punish the wrongdoers.' ᵃ

وَلَمَّا دَخَلُوا۟ عَلَىٰ يُوسُفَ ءَاوَىٰٓ إِلَيْهِ أَخَاهُ قَالَ إِنِّىٓ أَنَا۠ أَخُوكَ فَلَا تَبْتَئِسْ بِمَا كَانُوا۟ يَعْمَلُونَ ۝ فَلَمَّا جَهَّزَهُم بِجَهَازِهِمْ جَعَلَ ٱلسِّقَايَةَ فِى رَحْلِ أَخِيهِ ثُمَّ أَذَّنَ مُؤَذِّنٌ أَيَّتُهَا ٱلْعِيرُ إِنَّكُمْ لَسَـٰرِقُونَ ۝ قَالُوا۟ وَأَقْبَلُوا۟ عَلَيْهِم مَّاذَا تَفْقِدُونَ ۝ قَالُوا۟ نَفْقِدُ صُوَاعَ ٱلْمَلِكِ وَلِمَن جَآءَ بِهِۦ حِمْلُ بَعِيرٍ وَأَنَا۠ بِهِۦ زَعِيمٌ ۝ قَالُوا۟ تَٱللَّهِ لَقَدْ عَلِمْتُم مَّا جِئْنَا لِنُفْسِدَ فِى ٱلْأَرْضِ وَمَا كُنَّا سَـٰرِقِينَ ۝ قَالُوا۟ فَمَا جَزَٰٓؤُهُۥٓ إِن كُنتُمْ كَـٰذِبِينَ ۝ قَالُوا۟ جَزَٰٓؤُهُۥ مَن وُجِدَ فِى رَحْلِهِۦ فَهُوَ جَزَٰٓؤُهُۥ كَذَٰلِكَ نَجْزِى ٱلظَّـٰلِمِينَ ۝

ᵃ At the time of departure of Joseph's brothers, Joseph out of kindness put his drinking cup (which was perhaps made of silver) in his brother Benjamin's possessions. This was not known to Benjamin or to the courtiers. Thereafter, by the will of God, it happened that the royal measure for measuring the corn (which was also perhaps very costly) was misplaced somewhere. When the royal servants did not find it after making a search, they suspected Joseph's brothers who had left just then. One of the officials called back the caravan. In the course of inquiries they themselves (Joseph's brothers) suggested as a punishment for theft (which was prevalent among them), according to the law of Abraham, that the thief himself should remain with the owner for a year as a slave.

⁷⁶ He [the herald] searched their bags before his brother's and then took out the cup from his brother's bag. In this way, We devised a plan on behalf of Joseph. He could not have detained his brother under the King's law, unless God so willed. We exalt whoever We please: but above those who have knowledge there is One all knowing.^a

فَبَدَأَ بِأَوْعِيَتِهِمْ قَبْلَ وِعَاءِ أَخِيهِ ثُمَّ اسْتَخْرَجَهَا مِن وِعَاءِ أَخِيهِ ۚ كَذَٰلِكَ كِدْنَا لِيُوسُفَ ۖ مَا كَانَ لِيَأْخُذَ أَخَاهُ فِي دِينِ الْمَلِكِ إِلَّا أَن يَشَاءَ اللَّهُ ۚ نَرْفَعُ دَرَجَاتٍ مِّن نَّشَاءُ ۗ وَفَوْقَ كُلِّ ذِي عِلْمٍ عَلِيمٌ ۝

---

^a Joseph did not want his younger brother to depart. When Benjamin's packs were being readied, Joseph put his drinking cup in his younger brother's packs. This was no malicious subterfuge on the part of Joseph, but was done out of great affection for his younger brother. Previously Joseph had done something similar when he put all the money which they had brought to buy grain in his brothers' packs. The brothers only realized it when they opened their packs once they were back home. This time too, as a gesture of affection and love to his brother, he put his drinking cup in his younger brother's pack. This was neither known to Benjamin nor to the courtiers. In the meantime, the weighing cup of the king had been misplaced and the courtiers suspected Joseph's brothers of stealing it. When they opened their packs, they found Joseph's drinking cup in Benjamin's bag. This was not the cup they were looking for, but it was a similar one. The difference in these two cups can be understood by the two different words used for them in the Quran. The drinking cup belonging to Joseph is called *siqayah*, while the royal measuring bowl is called *suwa'* (verse 72). The cup which was recovered from Benjamin's bag was a *siqayah* not a *suwa'*, as a feminine pronoun, 'ha' (*istakhrajaha*) used for the cup here refers to the drinking cup of Joseph, and not to the lost measuring bowl of the king. This was not, therefore, a trick on the part of Joseph to prevent his brother from leaving, but in the words of Quran, it was an inspiration from God: 'We devised a plan on behalf of Joseph'.

In this instance, if the law of the king of Egypt had been observed, Benjamin would not have been given into the custody of Joseph but would instead have been beaten and the cost of the stolen item recovered from him, for that was the punishment regularly meted out to thieves. This incident did not come about by Joseph's intention. It happened due to divine arrangement: God attributed it to Himself, 'We devised a plan on behalf of Joseph' (*kazalika kidna li yusufa*).

⁷⁷ They said, 'If he is a thief, a brother of his had [also] committed theft before him.' But Joseph kept his secret and revealed nothing to them. He said [to himself], 'Your deed was worse. God best knows the things you speak of.' ⁷⁸ They said, 'O exalted one, he has a very aged father, take one of us in his place. We can see that you are a very good man.' ⁷⁹ He replied, 'God forbid that we should take anyone other than the person on whom we found our property. In that case, we would clearly be wrongdoers.'ᵃ

﴾ قَالُوٓا۟ إِن يَسْرِقْ فَقَدْ سَرَقَ أَخٌ لَّهُۥ مِن قَبْلُ ۚ فَأَسَرَّهَا يُوسُفُ فِى نَفْسِهِۦ وَلَمْ يُبْدِهَا لَهُمْ ۚ قَالَ أَنتُمْ شَرٌّ مَّكَانًا ۖ وَٱللَّهُ أَعْلَمُ بِمَا تَصِفُونَ ٧٧ قَالُوا۟ يَٰٓأَيُّهَا ٱلْعَزِيزُ إِنَّ لَهُۥٓ أَبًا شَيْخًا كَبِيرًا فَخُذْ أَحَدَنَا مَكَانَهُۥٓ ۖ إِنَّا نَرَىٰكَ مِنَ ٱلْمُحْسِنِينَ ٧٨ قَالَ مَعَاذَ ٱللَّهِ أَن نَّأْخُذَ إِلَّا مَن وَجَدْنَا مَتَٰعَنَا عِندَهُۥٓ إِنَّآ إِذًا لَّظَٰلِمُونَ ٧٩

ᵃ According to commentators of the Quran, in his childhood Joseph quietly removed an idol from his grandmother's house and broke it. This showed his antipathy for polytheism. But because it was a parallel to Benjamin's act, his brothers gave it the colour of theft, and making this an excuse to blacken Benjamin's name, they said, 'A brother of his had [also] committed theft before him.'

Joseph's brothers showed great humility to Joseph, who occupied a very high position in Egypt, addressing him as 'O exalted one', etc. But the Joseph of Canaan, who was in their eyes only a village boy, was being wrongly alleged to be a thief.

Joseph knew very well that due to the drinking cup placed by him in Benjamin's pack, his brother was unnecessarily being accused of being a thief. But for timely reasons, he kept quiet and allowed matters (i.e. what was going on between his brothers and the royal officers) to take their own course.

When he was obliged to say something, he did not refer to Benjamin as 'one who has stolen something belonging to us,' but 'the person on whom we found our property.'

⁸⁰ When they had lost all hope of [persuading] him, they withdrew, conferring among themselves. The eldest said, 'Do you not know that your father took from you a pledge in God's name. You have already failed with regard to Joseph, so I shall never leave the land until my father permits me to, or God decides [things] for me. He is the best judge! ⁸¹ Return to your father and say, "Father, your son has committed a theft. We testify only to what we know. How could we guard against the unforeseen? ⁸² Inquire of [the people of] the city where we lodged, and of the caravan with which we travelled. We are telling you the truth."' ^a

فَلَمَّا ٱسْتَيْـَٔسُواْ مِنْهُ خَلَصُواْ نَجِيًّا ۖ قَالَ كَبِيرُهُمْ أَلَمْ تَعْلَمُوٓاْ أَنَّ أَبَاكُمْ قَدْ أَخَذَ عَلَيْكُم مَّوْثِقًا مِّنَ ٱللَّهِ وَمِن قَبْلُ مَا فَرَّطتُمْ فِى يُوسُفَ ۖ فَلَنْ أَبْرَحَ ٱلْأَرْضَ حَتَّىٰ يَأْذَنَ لِىٓ أَبِىٓ أَوْ يَحْكُمَ ٱللَّهُ لِى ۖ وَهُوَ خَيْرُ ٱلْحَٰكِمِينَ ۝ ٱرْجِعُوٓاْ إِلَىٰٓ أَبِيكُمْ فَقُولُواْ يَٰٓأَبَانَآ إِنَّ ٱبْنَكَ سَرَقَ وَمَا شَهِدْنَآ إِلَّا بِمَا عَلِمْنَا وَمَا كُنَّا لِلْغَيْبِ حَٰفِظِينَ ۝ وَسْـَٔلِ ٱلْقَرْيَةَ ٱلَّتِى كُنَّا فِيهَا وَٱلْعِيرَ ٱلَّتِىٓ أَقْبَلْنَا فِيهَا ۖ وَإِنَّا لَصَٰدِقُونَ ۝

---

^a Among Joseph's stepbrothers there was perhaps one brother who was different from the others. He was the same brother who had advised in the initial stage that Joseph should not be killed but pushed into a dry well, so that any caravan passing by could take him with it. That brother faced the same situation in Egypt and he separated himself from the others. His sense of honour prevented him from facing his father before whom he had already been proven guilty of losing a brother. He did not want him to think him guilty of losing yet another brother.

⁸³ Jacob said, 'No, but you have yourselves contrived a story. But it is best to be patient. God may well bring them all back to me [in the end]. For He is indeed full of knowledge and wisdom.'^a ⁸⁴ And he turned away from them, crying, 'Alas for Joseph!' His eyes went white with grief, and he was filled with sorrow. ⁸⁵ They said, 'By God, will you keep on remembering Joseph until your health is ruined, and you die?' ⁸⁶ He said 'I only complain of my anguish and my sorrow to God. God has made known to me things that you do not know. ⁸⁷ Go, my sons, and seek news of Joseph and his brother. Do not despair of God's mercy; none but those who deny the truth despair of God's mercy.'^b

قَالَ بَلْ سَوَّلَتْ لَكُمْ أَنفُسُكُمْ أَمْرًا فَصَبْرٌ جَمِيلٌ عَسَى ٱللَّهُ أَن يَأْتِيَنِي بِهِمْ جَمِيعًا إِنَّهُۥ هُوَ ٱلْعَلِيمُ ٱلْحَكِيمُ ۝ وَتَوَلَّىٰ عَنْهُمْ وَقَالَ يَـٰٓأَسَفَىٰ عَلَىٰ يُوسُفَ وَٱبْيَضَّتْ عَيْنَاهُ مِنَ ٱلْحُزْنِ فَهُوَ كَظِيمٌ ۝ قَالُوا۟ تَٱللَّهِ تَفْتَؤُا۟ تَذْكُرُ يُوسُفَ حَتَّىٰ تَكُونَ حَرَضًا أَوْ تَكُونَ مِنَ ٱلْهَـٰلِكِينَ ۝ قَالَ إِنَّمَآ أَشْكُوا۟ بَثِّى وَحُزْنِىٓ إِلَى ٱللَّهِ وَأَعْلَمُ مِنَ ٱللَّهِ مَا لَا تَعْلَمُونَ ۝ يَـٰبَنِىَّ ٱذْهَبُوا۟ فَتَحَسَّسُوا۟ مِن يُوسُفَ وَأَخِيهِ وَلَا تَا۟يْـَٔسُوا۟ مِن رَّوْحِ ٱللَّهِ إِنَّهُۥ لَا يَا۟يْـَٔسُ مِن رَّوْحِ ٱللَّهِ إِلَّا ٱلْقَوْمُ ٱلْكَـٰفِرُونَ ۝

---

^a By saying this Jacob exposed the evil in the hearts of Joseph's brothers. When they left their father, they had taken Benjamin with them, promising his complete safety; and when a cup was discovered among Benjamin's belongings, they could not even say in his defence that just the finding of the cup did not prove him to be a thief. Perhaps somebody had put it in his baggage; or it might have been packed up in his baggage by mistake. Instead, they confirmed the Egyptians' suspicion about Benjamin's alleged guilt by their referring to a theft formerly committed by his brother.

^b Jacob was heartbroken on losing his two very dear sons. But at the same time he pinned his hopes on the Grace of God. He was certain that Joseph's dream predicted the future and that it would definitely come true. That is why he asked his sons to go and search for Joseph and also to try to have Benjamin released.

88 When his brothers presented themselves before Joseph, they pleaded, 'Exalted one, distress has afflicted us and our family and we have brought only a paltry sum; but give us full measure. Be charitable to us. Truly, God rewards the charitable.' 89 He said, 'Are you aware of what you did to Joseph and his brother in ignorance?' 90 They exclaimed, 'Are you indeed Joseph?' He replied, 'I am Joseph and this is my brother. God has indeed been gracious to us. The truth is that God does not waste the reward of those who do good, who are righteous and steadfast.'[a]

فَلَمَّا دَخَلُوا عَلَيْهِ قَالُوا يَٰٓأَيُّهَا ٱلْعَزِيزُ مَسَّنَا وَأَهْلَنَا ٱلضُّرُّ وَجِئْنَا بِبِضَٰعَةٍ مُّزْجَىٰةٍ فَأَوْفِ لَنَا ٱلْكَيْلَ وَتَصَدَّقْ عَلَيْنَآ إِنَّ ٱللَّهَ يَجْزِى ٱلْمُتَصَدِّقِينَ ۝ قَالَ هَلْ عَلِمْتُم مَّا فَعَلْتُم بِيُوسُفَ وَأَخِيهِ إِذْ أَنتُمْ جَٰهِلُونَ ۝ قَالُوٓا أَءِنَّكَ لَأَنتَ يُوسُفُ قَالَ أَنَا۠ يُوسُفُ وَهَٰذَآ أَخِى قَدْ مَنَّ ٱللَّهُ عَلَيْنَآ إِنَّهُۥ مَن يَتَّقِ وَيَصْبِرْ فَإِنَّ ٱللَّهَ لَا يُضِيعُ أَجْرَ ٱلْمُحْسِنِينَ ۝

---

[a] 'God does not waste the reward of those who do good, who are righteous and steadfast.' This is the moral lesson and substance of the whole story of Joseph. Almighty God wanted to set a clear example showing that one who adopts the God-fearing way in his worldly dealings and who avoids the ways of impatience will ultimately achieve success with His help. Joseph's story was made a tangible example of this reality.

In Egypt, the first seven years of prosperity and the succeeding seven years of scarcity had both occurred at the instance of God. Had it been the will of God, He would have made all the years prosperous years. Similarly, the incidents of Joseph's being pushed into the well and his coming out of it and reaching Egypt both occurred under the watchful eye of God. Had God so desired, He would have arranged for Joseph to acquire a position of authority in Egypt without making him pass through the stage of being abandoned in a dry well. But, if these extraordinary incidents had not occurred, then in this world of 'cause and affect' how could he have established the example of the fact that He helps those who place their trust in Him and adhere to the path of righteousness and patience?

There are two types of incidents: one which has an element of fame attaching to it and the other, which has no such element. Both incidents may be similar in nature, but one becomes famous while the other one remains unknown. God's succour of this same nature may also be received by any number of righteous people. But the special feature of God's succour in the case of Joseph was that it had a legendary quality about it, and that is why it came to be so widely known and appreciated.

⁹¹ [The brothers] said, 'By God! Most certainly God has raised you high above us, and we have indeed been guilty!' ⁹² He said, 'No blame [shall fall] on you this day; may God forgive you! And He is the Most Merciful of those who show mercy. ⁹³ Go with this shirt of mine and cast it upon my father's face. He will recover his sight; thereupon come [back] to me with all your family.'ᵃ

قَالُواْ تَٱللَّهِ لَقَدْ ءَاثَرَكَ ٱللَّهُ عَلَيْنَا وَإِن كُنَّا لَخَٰطِـِٔينَ ۝ قَالَ لَا تَثْرِيبَ عَلَيْكُمُ ٱلْيَوْمَ يَغْفِرُ ٱللَّهُ لَكُمْ وَهُوَ أَرْحَمُ ٱلرَّٰحِمِينَ ۝ ٱذْهَبُواْ بِقَمِيصِى هَٰذَا فَأَلْقُوهُ عَلَىٰ وَجْهِ أَبِى يَأْتِ بَصِيرًا وَأْتُونِى بِأَهْلِكُمْ أَجْمَعِينَ ۝

ᵃ When the truth came out into the open, Joseph's brothers acknowledged Joseph's greatness and freely admitted their guilt. In the same way, Joseph also showed such broadmindedness as a true God-worshipper is expected to show on such occasions. He did not condemn his brothers. He completely forgot and forgave the bitter experiences of the past and once again entered into fraternal relations with his brothers.

In this incident there is an example of a combination of divine and human help. And through this incident, circumstances were created which favoured the Children of Israel leaving Palestine and reaching Egypt where they attained a position of honour and prosperity. It was during the time of Joseph that the family of Jacob shifted to Egypt and for the next five hundred years they lived there with dignity and honour. According to the Bible, the number of members of Jacob's family who went to Egypt was sixty seven.

⁹⁴ When the caravan set out from Egypt, their father [in Canaan] said, 'You may think I am senile, but I certainly perceive the breath of Joseph.' ⁹⁵ They said, 'By God, you still persist in your illusions!' ⁹⁶ But when the bearer of the good news arrived and cast the shirt on Jacob's face, his eyesight returned and he said, 'Did I not tell you that I know from God what you do not know?' ⁹⁷ They said, 'O our father! Ask forgiveness for our sins—we were truly in the wrong.' ⁹⁸ He said, 'I shall certainly ask my Lord to forgive you. Surely, He is the Most Forgiving and Merciful.'^a

وَلَمَّا فَصَلَتِ ٱلْعِيرُ قَالَ أَبُوهُمْ إِنِّى لَأَجِدُ رِيحَ يُوسُفَ لَوْلَآ أَن تُفَنِّدُونِ ۝ قَالُوا۟ تَٱللَّهِ إِنَّكَ لَفِى ضَلَٰلِكَ ٱلْقَدِيمِ ۝ فَلَمَّآ أَن جَآءَ ٱلْبَشِيرُ أَلْقَىٰهُ عَلَىٰ وَجْهِهِۦ فَٱرْتَدَّ بَصِيرًا قَالَ أَلَمْ أَقُل لَّكُمْ إِنِّىٓ أَعْلَمُ مِنَ ٱللَّهِ مَا لَا تَعْلَمُونَ ۝ قَالُوا۟ يَٰٓأَبَانَا ٱسْتَغْفِرْ لَنَا ذُنُوبَنَآ إِنَّا كُنَّا خَٰطِـِٔينَ ۝ قَالَ سَوْفَ أَسْتَغْفِرُ لَكُمْ رَبِّىٓ إِنَّهُۥ هُوَ ٱلْغَفُورُ ٱلرَّحِيمُ ۝

---

^a After the separation from his father, Joseph lived in the neighbouring country of Egypt for more than 20 years, but Jacob remained unaware of it. But during his last days, when Joseph's garment was being brought back from Egypt, Jacob started smelling the garment's fragrance before it reached him. This shows that a prophet's knowledge is not his own personal affair but a gift from God. Had it been a question of his personal knowledge, Jacob would have come to know much earlier that his son was in Egypt, but this did not happen. He came to know about Joseph's whereabouts only when God made him aware of them.

The conversation between Jacob's family members as recorded in this chapter at various places gives an indication that, in the eyes of his family members, Jacob did not inspire the awe befitting a prophet. Those who adore their ancestors, holding them holy, are not ready to admit the greatness of the living guide. The reason for this is that a halo of exaggerated stories and anecdotes of magical charms is woven round the venerated leaders of the past; an artificial image of the holy person is thus impressed on the minds of the people. As the living guide does not measure up to this artificial image, he does not appear to be a great man to his contemporaries.

⁹⁹ Then, when they presented themselves before Joseph, he drew his parents to him and said, 'Welcome to Egypt, in safety, if God wills!' ¹⁰⁰ He helped his parents to a couch and they all fell down on their knees before him. He said, 'My father, this is the interpretation of my dream. My Lord has made it come true!ᵃ He was kind to me when He let me out of prison and brought you from the desert after Satan had brought about discord between me and my brethren. My Lord is the best planner in achieving what He will; He is All Knowing, and Truly Wise.'ᵇ

فَلَمَّا دَخَلُوا۟ عَلَىٰ يُوسُفَ ءَاوَىٰٓ إِلَيْهِ أَبَوَيْهِ وَقَالَ ٱدْخُلُوا۟ مِصْرَ إِن شَآءَ ٱللَّهُ ءَامِنِينَ ۝ وَرَفَعَ أَبَوَيْهِ عَلَى ٱلْعَرْشِ وَخَرُّوا۟ لَهُۥ سُجَّدًا ۖ وَقَالَ يَـٰٓأَبَتِ هَـٰذَا تَأْوِيلُ رُءْيَـٰىَ مِن قَبْلُ قَدْ جَعَلَهَا رَبِّى حَقًّا ۖ وَقَدْ أَحْسَنَ بِىٓ إِذْ أَخْرَجَنِى مِنَ ٱلسِّجْنِ وَجَآءَ بِكُم مِّنَ ٱلْبَدْوِ مِنۢ بَعْدِ أَن نَّزَغَ ٱلشَّيْطَـٰنُ بَيْنِى وَبَيْنَ إِخْوَتِىٓ ۚ إِنَّ رَبِّى لَطِيفٌ لِّمَا يَشَآءُ ۚ إِنَّهُۥ هُوَ ٱلْعَلِيمُ ٱلْحَكِيمُ ۝

ᵃ Here the 'couch' does not mean a royal throne but the seat where Joseph used to sit and discharge the duties of his post; here prostration (*sajdah*) does not mean lying face down in the usual sense but bowing down and kneeling (*ruku'*). This form of obeisance to a great man was prevalent in ancient times.

ᵇ God, in order to fulfil His plan, makes such dispositions that a common man cannot even hazard a guess about them.

[101] Then Joseph prayed, 'My Lord, You have given me power and taught me the interpretation of dreams. Creator of the heavens and the earth, You are my patron in this world and the Hereafter! Make me die in submission to You and admit me among the righteous.'[a]

۞ رَبِّ قَدْ ءَاتَيْتَنِى مِنَ ٱلْمُلْكِ وَعَلَّمْتَنِى مِن تَأْوِيلِ ٱلْأَحَادِيثِ فَاطِرَ ٱلسَّمَٰوَٰتِ وَٱلْأَرْضِ أَنتَ وَلِيِّۦ فِى ٱلدُّنْيَا وَٱلْءَاخِرَةِ تَوَفَّنِى مُسْلِمًا وَأَلْحِقْنِى بِٱلصَّٰلِحِينَ ﴿١٠١﴾

---

[a] The one who rejects the truth looks at everything from the point of view of the human being, while a believer looks at everything in relation to God. Joseph received a high administrative post and he ascribed it to God's generosity. He had the ability to interpret dreams but said that God had taught him all he knew. His own near and dear ones caused him trouble; even then he looked at this from the point of view that these were subtle devices of God by means of which He planned his intellectual and spiritual development.

His sense of the majesty of God had obliterated all feelings of personal superiority. Even on reaching the zenith of worldly glory, he uttered these words, 'O, God! Your being is all-powerful. It is You who fulfill all my needs. Kindly help me in the world as well as in the Hereafter. Include me among those people who have had the inspiration to submit to Your will in the world and in the Hereafter and are worthy of Your eternal reward.'

¹⁰² These are tidings of the unseen that We reveal to you, [O Prophet], though you were not present with them when they plotted and agreed upon a plan. ¹⁰³ Yet most men will not become believers, no matter how eager you may be. ¹⁰⁴ You shall not ask them for any reward for this. It is but a reminder for all mankind.ᵃ

ذَٰلِكَ مِنْ أَنۢبَآءِ ٱلْغَيْبِ نُوحِيهِ إِلَيْكَ ۖ وَمَا كُنتَ لَدَيْهِمْ إِذْ أَجْمَعُوٓا۟ أَمْرَهُمْ وَهُمْ يَمْكُرُونَ ۝ وَمَآ أَكْثَرُ ٱلنَّاسِ وَلَوْ حَرَصْتَ بِمُؤْمِنِينَ ۝ وَمَا تَسْـَٔلُهُمْ عَلَيْهِ مِنْ أَجْرٍ ۚ إِنْ هُوَ إِلَّا ذِكْرٌ لِّلْعَٰلَمِينَ ۝

ᵃ The story of Joseph is in itself a proof of the Quran being the revelation of God and not the discourse of a human being. This incident occurred about two and half thousand years prior to the advent of the Prophet Muhammad. He had neither witnessed this train of events himself, nor was it recorded in history books so that he could have read about it, nor could he have heard it from others. It was found only on the pages of the Torah, and before the age of the printing press, the Torah was a book which was known only to a few Jewish scholars at Jewish centres and not to anybody else.

Moreover, the events pertaining to Joseph's life have been described in the Quran in such a way that, in spite of their tallying basically with the descriptions in the Torah, they differ in respect of details. This difference is in itself a proof of the Quran being the revelation of God, because throughout the Quran its description appears to be very rational and natural. The descriptions given in the Quran are clearly consistent with Jacob's and Joseph's prophetic character, while the descriptions given in the Torah are not. Similarly, many very important aspects, for instance, Joseph's speech in the prison (5: 37-40), which is mentioned in the Quran, find no place in the Bible or in the Talmud: even certain historical errors that are found in the Bible are not repeated in the Quran. For example, the Bible says that the king of Egypt in Joseph's period was Pharaoh. In actual fact, the dynasty which assumed the title of Pharaoh became the rulers of Egypt only five hundred years after Joseph. During the period of Joseph, Egypt was ruled by an Arab dynasty, the Hyksos, known as the shepherd kings. (See Bible, chapter 'Genesis').

The refusal to accept the Truth here is due to an apparent lack of reason. But as soon as a convincing argument is presented to an individual, he should immediately accept it. Most often the real reason for denial of the Truth is stubbornness. People do not accept the Truth because they do not want to do so. Acceptance of the Truth generally involves humbling oneself and this is a very difficult task for a human being. This is one reason why arrogant people never change their ways, in spite of valid arguments or reasoning being used to convince them. They will tolerate the downgrading of the truth, but they are not ready to humble themselves; they forget that those who keep a low profile in this world will be glorified in the Hereafter, whereas one who does not do so will be forever reduced to insignificance in the next world.

105 And there are many signs in the heavens and the earth that they pass by and give no heed to—106 and most of them, even when they profess belief in God, attribute partners to Him. 107 Do they feel secure that the all-encompassing punishment of God will not come upon them, or that the Last Hour will not come upon them suddenly when they least expect it? 108 Say, 'This is my way; on the basis of sure knowledge, I call on you to have faith in God, I and those who follow me. God is Holy; I am not one of those who associate partners with God.' *a*

وَكَأَيِّن مِّن ءَايَةٍ فِى ٱلسَّمَـٰوَٰتِ وَٱلْأَرْضِ يَمُرُّونَ عَلَيْهَا وَهُمْ عَنْهَا مُعْرِضُونَ ۝ وَمَا يُؤْمِنُ أَكْثَرُهُم بِٱللَّهِ إِلَّا وَهُم مُّشْرِكُونَ ۝ أَفَأَمِنُوٓا أَن تَأْتِيَهُمْ غَٰشِيَةٌ مِّنْ عَذَابِ ٱللَّهِ أَوْ تَأْتِيَهُمُ ٱلسَّاعَةُ بَغْتَةً وَهُمْ لَا يَشْعُرُونَ ۝ قُلْ هَٰذِهِۦ سَبِيلِىٓ أَدْعُوٓا إِلَى ٱللَّهِ عَلَىٰ بَصِيرَةٍ أَنَا۠ وَمَنِ ٱتَّبَعَنِى وَسُبْحَٰنَ ٱللَّهِ وَمَآ أَنَا۠ مِنَ ٱلْمُشْرِكِينَ ۝

a After the Truth, has been made plain, those who do not accept it, say that the requisite sound arguments in its favour were not forthcoming and had such reasoning been put forward, they would have accepted it. In other words, according to them, the reason for their denial lay outside them and not within them. That is to say, that they had failed to accept the truth, not because of any lack of receptivity on their part, but because of a lack of arguments in support of the truth.

But just the opposite is true. The Truth is so clear that when it appears, all the signs of the earth and the heavens corroborate it. It becomes the most established and proven fact in the universe. But, in order to find the Truth, an observant eye and a receptive mind are vital and these are the very virtues which are non-existent in those who deny the truth.

When a man shows arrogance with regard to the Truth, the reason for it is mostly polytheism (*shirk*). The position taken by most people is that while accepting God, they also love some living or dead beings in whom they have placed their trust and to whom they give a position of greatness. In this way, everyone has appointed for himself some 'great ones' other than God. They lead their lives relying on these 'great ones', though before God all of them are small. Ultimately, the only things which will save one, will be one's personal deeds and not the exaltedness of the 'great ones'.

A prophet's mission is to exhort his hearers to turn to the one and only God. He sets out on this mission because of his realization of the truth. In other words, the prophetic call is that which links a man with the one and only God. The veracity of this call is so abundantly evident to him that it bespeaks a deep realization of godhood and acts as an inspiration to him.

Man takes his temporary satisfaction to be permanent in nature, though nobody has any guarantee of how long he will live. ▶

¹⁰⁹ All the messengers We sent before you [Muhammad] were human beings to whom We made revelations; they were men chosen from the people of their towns. Did they not travel across the earth and see the end of those before them? Those who are mindful of God prefer the life to come. Will you not then understand? ¹¹⁰ When the messengers lost all hopes and thought that they had been told lies, Our help came to them: We saved whoever We pleased, but Our punishment will not be averted from the guilty.ᵃ

وَمَآ أَرْسَلْنَا مِن قَبْلِكَ إِلَّا رِجَالًا نُّوحِىٓ إِلَيْهِم مِّنْ أَهْلِ ٱلْقُرَىٰٓ أَفَلَمْ يَسِيرُوا۟ فِى ٱلْأَرْضِ فَيَنظُرُوا۟ كَيْفَ كَانَ عَٰقِبَةُ ٱلَّذِينَ مِن قَبْلِهِمْ وَلَدَارُ ٱلْءَاخِرَةِ خَيْرٌ لِّلَّذِينَ ٱتَّقَوْا۟ أَفَلَا تَعْقِلُونَ ۝ حَتَّىٰٓ إِذَا ٱسْتَيْـَٔسَ ٱلرُّسُلُ وَظَنُّوٓا۟ أَنَّهُمْ قَدْ كُذِبُوا۟ جَآءَهُمْ نَصْرُنَا فَنُجِّىَ مَن نَّشَآءُ وَلَا يُرَدُّ بَأْسُنَا عَنِ ٱلْقَوْمِ ٱلْمُجْرِمِينَ ۝

Nobody knows when death will come and prove all his claims false; and when the upheaval of Doomsday will upset his well-made world. Man thinks that a sure and certain fate is in store for him, though in fact at every moment of his life, he is standing on the shore of an uncertain future.

ᵃ History shows that even those who believed in prophethood also rejected it, when a person in their own community was made a prophet and stood right in front of them. The reason for this was that the prophet of the past had by then become a historically accepted prophet, while the contemporary prophet's merits were as yet unproven. The acceptance of a historical prophet has never proved difficult, while the reverse is true of any prophet who is still a figure of controversy.

The deserted settlements of the communities of the 'Ad, Thamud, Midian and Lot lay in ruins around the land of the Quraysh, who could not fail to see them in their travels. These ruins were a silent reminder of the punishment which God had meted out to these communities: they were destroyed only because they failed to recognize a prophet during the controversial stage of prophethood. But, in spite of this, the Quraysh did not learn a lesson from them. The reason for this was that it is man's weakness to do wrong and then, on the basis of some weak arguments, excise his name from the list of wrongdoers.

Verse 110 of this chapter is clarified by verse 214 of the second chapter, in which it is stated, 'Do you think that you will enter Paradise without having suffered like those who passed away before you? Affliction and hardship befell them and so shaken were they, that the Messenger and the believers with him would exclaim, "When will God's help come? Surely the help of God is near."' ▶

111 In their stories there is a lesson for men of understanding. This [Quran] is no invented tale, but a confirmation of the previous [scripture] and a detailed explanation of all things as well as guidance and mercy to true believers.[a]

لَقَدْ كَانَ فِى قَصَصِهِمْ عِبْرَةٌ لِّأُوْلِى ٱلْأَلْبَٰبِ مَا كَانَ حَدِيثًا يُفْتَرَىٰ وَلَٰكِن تَصْدِيقَ ٱلَّذِى بَيْنَ يَدَيْهِ وَتَفْصِيلَ كُلِّ شَىْءٍ وَهُدًى وَرَحْمَةً لِّقَوْمٍ يُؤْمِنُونَ ۝

God always helps one who spreads the word of God. But this help brings in its wake punishment for the rejectors of truth. That is why help comes only when the missionary struggle (dawah) has reached its final stage. There are times when this delay makes the preachers feel frustrated and they despair of God's succour.

'And surely, the abode of the Hereafter is better for those who fear God'. This shows that God's succour for His envoy is symbolic of His choicest blessings upon them in the Hereafter.

God always helps those who call upon others to accept the Truth: in this world God makes their call supreme. They are thus successful in fulfilling their mission, in spite of all kinds of conspiracies and the opposition of their enemies. This honour and glory will be theirs in the Hereafter, but in a far more perfect and absolute form.

[a] The stories of previous prophets and their communities are the stories of all mankind, as far as moral lessons are concerned. If a man exercises his wisdom he will be able to derive lessons for the present period from past incidents. He will amend his way of life on seeing the fate of others.

The Quran is not a book concocted by a man. It is a Book revealed by God. It is exactly in accordance with the predictions that were made in the previous scriptures. It contains all the necessary guidance required by man.

If man follows this guidance, he shall certainly be blessed by God both in this world and in the Hereafter.

13. THUNDER

In the name of God,
the Most Gracious, the Most Merciful

¹ *Alif Lam Mim Ra*

These are the verses of the Book. What is sent down to you from your Lord is the truth, yet most men do not believe in it.*a*

a The Quran enjoins the acceptance of the one and only God. Those who do not believe in God advance the argument that if God is in existence, He should be visible to everyone. But our known universe shows that a thing's invisibility does not prove that it has no existence at all. An example of this is the force of gravity. There are innumerable stars and many planets in space. Human knowledge claims that in between these astronomical bodies there is an ethereal and intangible force of gravity (or force of attraction) which is balancing them in the vastness of space. So man believes in the force of gravity in spite of its being intangible and unseen. Then how can he be justified in denying the existence of God, simply because of His being unseen?

This is the case with Revelation and prophethood. When an observer of the universe studies its phenomena, he finds that everything here functions according to a system. It appears as if all things are bound by a special order. This 'order' does not exist in the things themselves. Certainly, it comes from outside. In other words, the whole universe seeks instruction from 'outside' for its working. This external instruction in the case of our world (leaving out of account its human population) is generally referred to as the Law of Nature. In the case of human beings, this external instruction, or guidance, comes in the form of revelation and inspiration.

The Universe is, so to say, a machine and the Quran is its 'Guide Book'. The former is the example of God's regulation of affairs and the latter is the example of God's detailing of signs. There is perfect consistency between these two. Whatever exists in the universe in physical form, exists in the Quran in verbal form. This consistency simultaneously proves two things—first, that there is a Creator of this universe and second, that the Quran is the Book of that Creator and not the creation of the limited mind of a human being.

² It was God who raised the heavens with no visible supports, and then established Himself on the throne; He has regulated the sun and the moon, so that each will pursue its course for an appointed time; He ordains all things and makes plain His revelations, so that you may be certain of meeting your Lord; ³ it was He who spread out the earth and placed upon it mountains and rivers, and fruits of every kind in male and female pairs. He drew the veil of night over the day. In all this, truly, there are signs for people who reflect.ᵃ

ٱللَّهُ ٱلَّذِى رَفَعَ ٱلسَّمَٰوَٰتِ بِغَيْرِ عَمَدٍ تَرَوْنَهَا ثُمَّ ٱسْتَوَىٰ عَلَى ٱلْعَرْشِ وَسَخَّرَ ٱلشَّمْسَ وَٱلْقَمَرَ كُلٌّ يَجْرِى لِأَجَلٍ مُّسَمًّى يُدَبِّرُ ٱلْأَمْرَ يُفَصِّلُ ٱلْآيَٰتِ لَعَلَّكُم بِلِقَآءِ رَبِّكُمْ تُوقِنُونَ ۞ وَهُوَ ٱلَّذِى مَدَّ ٱلْأَرْضَ وَجَعَلَ فِيهَا رَوَٰسِىَ وَأَنْهَٰرًا وَمِن كُلِّ ٱلثَّمَرَٰتِ جَعَلَ فِيهَا زَوْجَيْنِ ٱثْنَيْنِ يُغْشِى ٱلَّيْلَ ٱلنَّهَارَ إِنَّ فِى ذَٰلِكَ لَآيَٰتٍ لِّقَوْمٍ يَتَفَكَّرُونَ ۞

ᵃ When we observe the earth, we will find that the conditions here appear to be most suitable for human settlement and growth. The earth is spread out beneath human beings like a natural floor. Deep oceans cater to human needs on the one hand and on the other there are the mountain ranges, so that both of them together help in maintaining a balance on the earth. The plants and trees could have grown independently, but they have been paired off, and pollination must play its part between them so that flowers, fruits and seeds will grow. The position of the earth is that, apart from its annual revolution around the sun, it rotates continuously on its axis. This rotation is completed in twenty-four hours, resulting in the creation of night and day. Anyone who seriously gives consideration to signs of this kind will be forced to accept that this earth is under an authoritative and powerful Lord. And He, by His own will, has made it subject to purposeful planning. Without conscious planning, this meaningfulness on earth would not have been at all possible.

⁴ On the earth are diverse tracts, adjoining one another: vineyards and cornfields and groves of palm, the single and the clustered. Their fruits are nourished by the same water; yet We make the taste of some excel that of others. In this also are signs for people who understand.^a

وَفِى ٱلْأَرْضِ قِطَعٌ مُّتَجَٰوِرَٰتٌ وَجَنَّٰتٌ مِّنْ أَعْنَٰبٍ وَزَرْعٌ وَنَخِيلٌ صِنْوَانٌ وَغَيْرُ صِنْوَانٍ يُسْقَىٰ بِمَآءٍ وَٰحِدٍ وَنُفَضِّلُ بَعْضَهَا عَلَىٰ بَعْضٍ فِى ٱلْأُكُلِ إِنَّ فِى ذَٰلِكَ لَءَايَٰتٍ لِّقَوْمٍ يَعْقِلُونَ ۝

---

^a 'Abdullah ibn 'Abbas says that one strip of land is fertile while another is barren. One strip of land produces crops while one nearby does not. Mujahid says that the same is the case with mankind. There are good people in this world and also bad, though the origin of all is one. There is a strange phenomenon on this earth: the soil in different places may be similar and may be watered by the same water, but in one place it will produce a tree whose fruit is sweet, while in another place it will produce a tree whose fruit is sour. One tree may have a high yield and another a low yield. This is a parallel in nature to the human condition. It is like all human beings, although cast in the same mould, showing a marked difference from one individual to another when it comes to deriving any benefit from the divine guidance which is consistently offered to all. One will receive the full benefit of such guidance, and thus have his entire life enriched by it, while another may avail of only a part of it or even reject it altogether. In other words, the same 'seeds' of guidance when 'sown' in different individuals will produce outcomes as different as the sweet and sour fruits of our analogy.

⁵ If anything can astonish you, you should surely be astonished at their asking, 'What? When we become dust, shall we be created anew?' These are the ones who deny their Lord: around their necks there shall be fetters. They are the inheritors of the Fire, and shall abide therein forever.ᵃ

۞ وَإِن تَعْجَبْ فَعَجَبٌ قَوْلُهُمْ أَءِذَا كُنَّا تُرَٰبًا أَءِنَّا لَفِى خَلْقٍ جَدِيدٍ ۗ أُوْلَٰٓئِكَ ٱلَّذِينَ كَفَرُواْ بِرَبِّهِمْ ۖ وَأُوْلَٰٓئِكَ ٱلْأَغْلَٰلُ فِىٓ أَعْنَاقِهِمْ ۖ وَأُوْلَٰٓئِكَ أَصْحَٰبُ ٱلنَّارِ ۖ هُمْ فِيهَا خَٰلِدُونَ ۝

ᵃ The case of those who deny the life after death is very strange. While accepting the occurrence of an event once, they deny the occurrence of the same event on future occasions. Those who do not accept the occurrence of life after death, or a second life, express their surprise at those who believe in a second life. They think that acceptance of a second life is irrational, whereas the position is just the opposite, because an unbeliever can only reject second life. As far as the first life is concerned, it is not possible for anybody to reject it, because it is evident to everybody as a real event. So, if the occurrence of the first life is possible, why should the occurrence of a second life be impossible?

There are few who would actually reject the existence of God. Mostly people believe in a Creator, but they do not accept the Hereafter. But after the denial of the Hereafter, the acceptance of a Creator has no value.

God is not only the Creator of this universe, but He Himself is the Truth. God's Being necessarily warrants that whatever He does, should be done with Rectitude and Justice. The Hereafter is, in fact, a manifestation of God's attribute of Justice. Acceptance of God is acceptance in the real sense only when it is followed by acceptance of the Hereafter. Belief in God remains incomplete without acceptance of the Hereafter.

People's rejection of the straightforward and true message of Truth is mostly due to their being victims of bias, prejudice and egoism. They are slaves of their own ideas. Thus mentally shackled, they are unable to give due consideration to any external reality. This condition has been described as being 'chained by the neck' – the chain being the symbol of slavery. Those who are bent on making prisoners of themselves in this world can expect nothing other than remaining prisoners in the Hereafter.

⁶ They demand that you hasten on the evil rather than the good, although there have been many examples of punishment before them—your Lord is full of forgiveness for mankind, despite their wrongdoings, but He is truly severe in punishment.ᵃ

وَيَسْتَعْجِلُونَكَ بِٱلسَّيِّئَةِ قَبْلَ ٱلْحَسَنَةِ وَقَدْ خَلَتْ مِن قَبْلِهِمُ ٱلْمَثُلَٰتُ وَإِنَّ رَبَّكَ لَذُو مَغْفِرَةٍ لِّلنَّاسِ عَلَىٰ ظُلْمِهِمْ وَإِنَّ رَبَّكَ لَشَدِيدُ ٱلْعِقَابِ ۝

ᵃ The Prophet Muhammad used to tell the people of Makkah to follow the guidance of God, otherwise they would be seized upon by Him. In reply to this they would say, 'O, God! If whatever Muhammad declares is true, then shower pieces of stone on us from the sky.' Apparently this prayer was addressed to God but, in fact, it was directed at the Prophet. At that time he appeared to be worthless to the people of Makkah. It was very difficult for them to believe that God would punish them on their rejecting such an ordinary man. Any imposition of punishment for their rejecting 'Muhammad' appeared to them such a distant possibility that they used to say, quite ridiculously, 'We want that the punishment with which you are threatening us to actually be meted out to us.'

God says that His punishment is definitely going to overtake them due to their rejection of Truth. It is due to their being misguided that they wanted it to happen earlier. In fact, they should have spent this period of respite in giving careful consideration to the call of the Quran, rather than invite the punishment of God before time.

People want to see the punishment of God with their own eyes and then accept it. But this is a demand made in sheer blindness. If they have observing eyes, then whatever happened with others should be enough to teach them a lesson. Many communities have passed before them who, like them, rejected the prophets of their age and finally they had to face punishment for this.

By the law of God man is allowed respite to perform certain deeds. Unfortunately, this law of respite has made people arrogant. But there is a limit to respite. After this limit nothing awaits them except a horrible punishment from which they will not be able to save themselves.

7 Those who deny the truth ask, 'Why has no sign been sent down to him by His Lord?' But you are only a warner; every people has its guide.*

وَيَقُولُ ٱلَّذِينَ كَفَرُواْ لَوْلَآ أُنزِلَ عَلَيْهِ ءَايَةٌ مِّن رَّبِّهِۦٓ إِنَّمَآ أَنتَ مُنذِرٌ وَلِكُلِّ قَوْمٍ هَادٍ ۝

---

* Today, throughout the world, there are more than a billion people who accept the Prophet Muhammad as a prophet of God. But in his lifetime the people of Makkah could not understand that God had made him His prophet. The reason for this was that in the preliminary stage, his prophethood was a controversial issue. But now, in this advanced stage of history, his prophethood is no longer controversial. It is now as easy to believe in the prophethood as it was difficult to believe in it at an earlier, controversial stage.

The standards by which the people of Makkah lived were those of wealth, power and popularity. By these standards the Prophet Muhammad did not appear to them to be in any way exceptional, so they wanted him to have some extraordinary sign which would be a definite proof of his prophethood. In response to this it was said that these people demanded something which was not in accordance with God's plan and as such it would remain beyond human reach.

The present world is a place of trial. Here guidance is not available in the form of such clear signs that there is no scope for human doubt, because if that were so, the purpose of the divine test would be defeated. Here the only possibility is for man to take guidance in the shape of 'information' and accept it after examining it. One who does not pass this test will never have his share of guidance.

God raises in every community a man from among them so that he may deliver the message in a language familiar to them. This arrangement was made for the convenience of the different communities. But it often happened that the communities were affected in the opposite manner: they rejected God's prophets. Their vision was clouded by the ordinary nature of the messenger. Their eyes could not see the extraordinary nature of the message itself.

⁸ God knows what every female bears. He knows of every change within the womb. For everything He has a proper measure; ⁹ He is the knower of the unseen and the visible, the Great, the Most-Exalted. ¹⁰ It makes no difference whether you converse in secret or aloud, whether you hide under the cloak of night or walk about freely in the light of day.ᵃ

اللَّهُ يَعْلَمُ مَا تَحْمِلُ كُلُّ أُنثَىٰ وَمَا تَغِيضُ ٱلْأَرْحَامُ وَمَا تَزْدَادُ وَكُلُّ شَىْءٍ عِندَهُۥ بِمِقْدَارٍ ۝ عَٰلِمُ ٱلْغَيْبِ وَٱلشَّهَٰدَةِ ٱلْكَبِيرُ ٱلْمُتَعَالِ ۝ سَوَآءٌ مِّنكُم مَّنْ أَسَرَّ ٱلْقَوْلَ وَمَن جَهَرَ بِهِۦ وَمَنْ هُوَ مُسْتَخْفٍ بِٱلَّيْلِ وَسَارِبٌۢ بِٱلنَّهَارِ ۝

ᵃ The womb of a mother is a wonderful factory. The wonderful aspect of the human produce is that it conforms to a 'fixed proportion'. There is a constant balance between 'demand and supply'.

For instance, this wonderful plant which has been working for thousands of years, produces men as well as women, but a constant proportion is maintained between these two sexes. It never happens that this plant produces males only or females only. An event like war sometimes temporarily disturbs this proportion. But it has been observed, strangely enough, that after a certain period this original proportion is soon restored.

The same is true of the balance of talent in the men and women coming out of this plant. Research has shown that those being born are not of a uniform capacity. There is a great diversity in their talents. This diversity is of importance in civilization, because persons of diverse capacities are required to manage the affairs of a civilization. The plant of mothers is quietly and successfully producing persons with different talents, as if it were receiving 'orders' from outside which led to how the persons in the womb were constituted. If there had not been this diversity in the production of human beings, the whole system of civilization would have descended into chaos and all development would have ceased.

The existence of this planning in the working of the mother's womb clearly shows that there is a Planner behind it. Without conscious planning, a system marked by such regularity could never exist.

This also proves that the Creator and Lord of this world is a Being Who is aware not only of whatever is plain for everyone to see, but also of what is unseen and hidden. Whatever happens in a woman's womb is apparently a secret matter. But the above-mentioned details show that God is completely aware of it. Then this Being Who is aware of the open and hidden aspects of everything is bound to know the hidden, and open aspects pertaining to human beings. Belief in angels is also proved by this, because it is an extension of the present system of keeping 'watch'.

¹¹ Each has guardian angels before him and behind him, who watch him at God's command. God does not change the condition of a people's lot, unless they change what is in their hearts. But when God decrees punishment for a people, none can ward it off. Besides Him, they have no protector.ᵃ

¹² It is He who shows you the lightning, inspiring fear and hope, and gathers up the heavy clouds; ¹³ and the thunder glorifies Him with His praise and the angels do so too in awe of Him, and He sends His thunderbolts to strike anyone He pleases, yet they dispute about God, who is inexorable in His power.ᵇ

لَهُۥ مُعَقِّبَٰتٌ مِّنۢ بَيْنِ يَدَيْهِ وَمِنْ خَلْفِهِۦ يَحْفَظُونَهُۥ مِنْ أَمْرِ ٱللَّهِ إِنَّ ٱللَّهَ لَا يُغَيِّرُ مَا بِقَوْمٍ حَتَّىٰ يُغَيِّرُوا۟ مَا بِأَنفُسِهِمْ وَإِذَآ أَرَادَ ٱللَّهُ بِقَوْمٍ سُوٓءًا فَلَا مَرَدَّ لَهُۥ وَمَا لَهُم مِّن دُونِهِۦ مِن وَالٍ ﴿١١﴾ هُوَ ٱلَّذِى يُرِيكُمُ ٱلْبَرْقَ خَوْفًا وَطَمَعًا وَيُنشِئُ ٱلسَّحَابَ ٱلثِّقَالَ ﴿١٢﴾ وَيُسَبِّحُ ٱلرَّعْدُ بِحَمْدِهِۦ وَٱلْمَلَٰٓئِكَةُ مِنْ خِيفَتِهِۦ وَيُرْسِلُ ٱلصَّوَٰعِقَ فَيُصِيبُ بِهَا مَن يَشَآءُ وَهُمْ يُجَٰدِلُونَ فِى ٱللَّهِ وَهُوَ شَدِيدُ ٱلْمِحَالِ ﴿١٣﴾

ᵃ The rise and fall of the communities of the world do not happen at random, but rather under the care of and by the decision of God. When God blesses a community with His bounties, He continues this blessing so long as that community keeps its competency intact. After losing this competency, that community necessarily loses God's grace also, for example, after losing internal unity, its impact on the world, is lessened.

Whatever a community achieves in this world, it achieves by the law of God and whatever a community loses, it loses it by the law of God. There is nobody here who is capable of giving or capable of taking away except God.

ᵇ When there is lightning, sometimes it carries the message of pleasant weather. But sometimes it falls on the earth like a thunderbolt and burns things down.

Similarly, when the clouds gather, they sometimes shower beneficial rains upon the earth. But sometimes they are the forerunners of storms and floods.

This means that in this world, one and the same thing can have the aspects of both fear and hope. The One who manages the affairs of the world sends His blessings to the people of the earth by means of various phenomena. He can turn an ostensibly beneficent thing into the most destructive punishment. This state of affairs warns man that he should never consider himself to be safe from God's scourge. ▶

¹⁴ The only true appeal is to God alone; those they appeal to instead of Him will never respond to them in any way. They are like a man who stretches forth his hands toward the water, so that it may reach his mouth, but it never does. The calls of those who deny the truth are all in vain.

¹⁵ All who dwell in heavens and on the earth submit to God alone, willingly or unwillingly, as do their shadows in the mornings and in the evenings.ᵃ

لَهُۥ دَعْوَةُ ٱلْحَقِّ ۖ وَٱلَّذِينَ يَدْعُونَ مِن دُونِهِۦ لَا يَسْتَجِيبُونَ لَهُم بِشَىْءٍ إِلَّا كَبَاسِطِ كَفَّيْهِ إِلَى ٱلْمَآءِ لِيَبْلُغَ فَاهُ وَمَا هُوَ بِبَالِغِهِۦ ۚ وَمَا دُعَآءُ ٱلْكَٰفِرِينَ إِلَّا فِى ضَلَٰلٍ ۝ وَلِلَّهِ يَسْجُدُ مَن فِى ٱلسَّمَٰوَٰتِ وَٱلْأَرْضِ طَوْعًا وَكَرْهًا وَظِلَٰلُهُم بِٱلْغُدُوِّ وَٱلْءَاصَالِ ۩ ۝

Heedless human beings always wait for some unique and magical sign. But those whose consciousness is alive are successful in finding every kind of sign—of an inestimable value—in the daily affairs happening around them. They feel their hearts beat faster with the roll of thunder and the flash of lightning and when they look at the raindrops, a flood of tears flows from their eyes. The condition which the angels face on seeing the power of God directly, are one and the same as those faced by true human beings, even when they have not seen the power of God directly.

ᵃ If you spread your hands and call upon the ocean, it will never happen that it responds to your call and its waters come out of the depths to quench the thirst of your fields and gardens. But, by the laws of nature, the waters of that same ocean rise into air in the form of water vapour, leaving behind the salt. Then under the influence of heat, gravitational pull and the force of the winds, it spreads over town and country and pours down in the shape of fresh, sweet water and irrigates the land. This shows that the ocean, in spite of being gigantic, is really helpless. It has no innate power either to act on its own, or to respond to another's call.

This is the condition of all the things of this world. As such, the wise person is one who worships the Creator and not the creations—one who concentrates on the Lord of the things and not on the things themselves.

¹⁶ Say, 'Who is Lord of the heavens and the earth?' Say, 'God.' Say, 'Why do you take protectors other than Him, who can neither benefit nor harm even themselves?' Say, 'Are the blind and the seeing equal? Is darkness equal to the light? Or have they assigned partners to God who create as He creates, so that both creations appear to them alike?' Say, 'God is the Creator of all things. He is the One, the Almighty.' ᵃ

قُلْ مَن رَّبُّ ٱلسَّمَـٰوَٰتِ وَٱلْأَرْضِ قُلِ ٱللَّهُ قُلْ أَفَٱتَّخَذْتُم مِّن دُونِهِۦٓ أَوْلِيَآءَ لَا يَمْلِكُونَ لِأَنفُسِهِمْ نَفْعًا وَلَا ضَرًّا قُلْ هَلْ يَسْتَوِى ٱلْأَعْمَىٰ وَٱلْبَصِيرُ أَمْ هَلْ تَسْتَوِى ٱلظُّلُمَـٰتُ وَٱلنُّورُ أَمْ جَعَلُوا۟ لِلَّهِ شُرَكَآءَ خَلَقُوا۟ كَخَلْقِهِۦ فَتَشَـٰبَهَ ٱلْخَلْقُ عَلَيْهِمْ قُلِ ٱللَّهُ خَـٰلِقُ كُلِّ شَىْءٍ وَهُوَ ٱلْوَٰحِدُ ٱلْقَهَّـٰرُ ۝

ᵃ God expects man to bow down before Him. This 'bowing down', is the religion of the whole universe. Everything in this world is totally subject to God's command. A physical sign of this subjection is the casting of shadows towards the west in the morning and towards the east in the evening. This daily happening is the material symbolising of that self-prostration which man is expected consciously to perform.

A study of the universe in all its vastness reveals that all of it is bound by one universal law. This proves the fact that its Creator and Lord is one and only one. Rational and intellectual studies do not in any way prove that more than one power is active in this universe. In view of this, the notion of an additional god other than the one and only God is an absolutely baseless presumption.

Observation with the help of the 'eye' indicates the existence of one and only one God. So, those who believe in the existence of more than one God, only prove their 'blindness', that they have assumed the existence of many gods due to their blindness and not on the basis of knowledge and observation in the real sense.

17 He sends down water from the sky that fills riverbeds to overflowing, each according to its measure. The torrent carries along swelling foam, akin to what rises from smelted ore from which man makes ornaments and tools. God thus depicts truth and falsehood. The scum is cast away, but whatever is of use to man remains behind. God thus speaks in parables.[a]

أَنزَلَ مِنَ ٱلسَّمَآءِ مَآءً فَسَالَتْ أَوْدِيَةٌۢ بِقَدَرِهَا فَٱحْتَمَلَ ٱلسَّيْلُ زَبَدًا رَّابِيًا ۚ وَمِمَّا يُوقِدُونَ عَلَيْهِ فِى ٱلنَّارِ ٱبْتِغَآءَ حِلْيَةٍ أَوْ مَتَٰعٍ زَبَدٌ مِّثْلُهُۥ ۚ كَذَٰلِكَ يَضْرِبُ ٱللَّهُ ٱلْحَقَّ وَٱلْبَٰطِلَ ۚ فَأَمَّا ٱلزَّبَدُ فَيَذْهَبُ جُفَآءً ۖ وَأَمَّا مَا يَنفَعُ ٱلنَّاسَ فَيَمْكُثُ فِى ٱلْأَرْضِ ۚ كَذَٰلِكَ يَضْرِبُ ٱللَّهُ ٱلْأَمْثَالَ ﴿١٧﴾

---

[a] God has created this world in such a way that here material events have become the symbols of moral realities. Whatever Almighty God expects from man at the level of consciousness is being demonstrated in the rest of the world at the material level. In the Quran two events of nature have been mentioned here. One is that when there is rainfall, its water flows and reaches rivers and streams. At that time a great deal of foam surfaces on it. In the same way when silver and other minerals are heated in order to clean them their impurities appear in the shape of foam, but immediately thereafter the foam, which is useless for man, evaporates in space and the water and minerals which are useful for man remain intact.

These are the events of nature through which God shows symbolically what principles He has laid down for the success or failure of life. One principle is that, in this world, only that person has a place who proves useful to others. The individual who has lost his capacity to benefit others has no place in this world created by God. The same is true of communities and groups.

¹⁸ There will be the best of rewards for those who respond to their Lord: while those who do not respond to Him—if they possessed all that is on earth and twice as much, they would surely offer it as ransom [on the Day of Judgement];—will have the worst reckoning and their goal is Hell: and how evil a resting-place! [a]

لِلَّذِينَ ٱسْتَجَابُواْ لِرَبِّهِمُ ٱلْحُسْنَىٰ وَٱلَّذِينَ لَمْ يَسْتَجِيبُواْ لَهُۥ لَوْ أَنَّ لَهُم مَّا فِى ٱلْأَرْضِ جَمِيعًا وَمِثْلَهُۥ مَعَهُۥ لَٱفْتَدَوْاْ بِهِۦٓ أُوْلَٰٓئِكَ هُمْ سُوٓءُ ٱلْحِسَابِ وَمَأْوَىٰهُمْ جَهَنَّمُ وَبِئْسَ ٱلْمِهَادُ

---

[a] It is the law of God in this world that dirt and foam may emerge and surface for some time, but finally what receives a place here is that which gives benefit. In the Hereafter also, the same is true of human beings. In the world some people may be prominent due to some skill but, in the Hereafter, only those who possess real qualities will receive a higher status.

People do not respond to the call for the Truth in this world because they always feel that, by advancing towards unadulterated Truth, they will lose worldly benefits. The rewards for ignoring the Truth which such people receive are invariably honour, popularity and prosperity in this world. They appear to be occupying seats of high status by rejecting the Truth.

In the Hereafter, all these people will have been thrown out as like fast disappearing foam. And only those people will figure as prominent who surrendered themselves to the Truth, ignoring timely benefits.

People give so much importance to worldly status and worldly benefits that they ignore the truth. In the Hereafter these things will appear unimportant to them, so much so that they would want to give this whole world and one more world equal to it, to ransom themselves from divine punishment.

¹⁹ Can one who knows that whatever has been sent down to you from your Lord is the Truth, be equal to one who is blind? It is only those who are endowed with insight who pay heed;^a ²⁰ they who are true to their bond with God and never break their covenant; ²¹ and those who join together what God has commanded to be joined, and fear their Lord and dread the harshness of the reckoning; ²² those who are steadfast in seeking the favour of their Lord, and pray regularly and spend secretly and openly out of what We have provided them with, and ward off evil with good. Theirs shall be the final abode.

۞ أَفَمَن يَعْلَمُ أَنَّمَا أُنزِلَ إِلَيْكَ مِن رَّبِّكَ ٱلْحَقُّ كَمَنْ هُوَ أَعْمَىٰٓ إِنَّمَا يَتَذَكَّرُ أُوْلُواْ ٱلْأَلْبَٰبِ ۝ ٱلَّذِينَ يُوفُونَ بِعَهْدِ ٱللَّهِ وَلَا يَنقُضُونَ ٱلْمِيثَٰقَ ۝ وَٱلَّذِينَ يَصِلُونَ مَآ أَمَرَ ٱللَّهُ بِهِۦٓ أَن يُوصَلَ وَيَخْشَوْنَ رَبَّهُمْ وَيَخَافُونَ سُوٓءَ ٱلْحِسَابِ ۝ وَٱلَّذِينَ صَبَرُواْ ٱبْتِغَآءَ وَجْهِ رَبِّهِمْ وَأَقَامُواْ ٱلصَّلَوٰةَ وَأَنفَقُواْ مِمَّا رَزَقْنَٰهُمْ سِرًّا وَعَلَانِيَةً وَيَدْرَءُونَ بِٱلْحَسَنَةِ ٱلسَّيِّئَةَ أُوْلَٰٓئِكَ لَهُمْ عُقْبَى ٱلدَّارِ ۝

---

^a There are always two kinds of human beings—one who use their reason granted by God and give serious thought, with an unbiased approach, to the matter of truth. Finally when their minds are addressed they adopt the truth by their conscious decision.

The other kind of human beings think within the sphere of their social traditions. They view things in the light of customs and not in the light of reasoning. And then they adopt as truth whatever appears to them to be popular with the masses.

According to the Quran, the first type of person is one who has become a believer in the light of knowledge; as opposed to this the other type of man is blind. The first knows truth and falsehood by his own realization, while the other is swayed only by hearsay. He considers that thing false which others consider false and he believes that thing to be true which others generally think of as true.

The call for the Truth seeks out those who are able to take decisions using their wisdom. Such a call does not benefit those who are blind, in spite of having eyes.

²³ They shall enter the eternal Gardens of Eden, along with the righteous from among their fathers, wives and descendants. From every gate the angels will come to them, saying, ²⁴ 'Peace be upon you for all that you have steadfastly endured. How excellent is the final abode!' *ᵃ*

²⁵ As for those who break the covenant of God, after having confirmed it, who cut asunder what God has commanded to be joined and spread corruption in the land, a curse shall be laid on them; they shall have an evil abode.

جَنَّتُ عَدْنٍ يَدْخُلُونَهَا وَمَن صَلَحَ مِنْ ءَابَآئِهِمْ وَأَزْوَٰجِهِمْ وَذُرِّيَّٰتِهِمْ ۖ وَٱلْمَلَٰٓئِكَةُ يَدْخُلُونَ عَلَيْهِم مِّن كُلِّ بَابٍ ۝ سَلَٰمٌ عَلَيْكُم بِمَا صَبَرْتُمْ ۚ فَنِعْمَ عُقْبَى ٱلدَّارِ ۝ وَٱلَّذِينَ يَنقُضُونَ عَهْدَ ٱللَّهِ مِنۢ بَعْدِ مِيثَٰقِهِۦ وَيَقْطَعُونَ مَآ أَمَرَ ٱللَّهُ بِهِۦٓ أَن يُوصَلَ وَيُفْسِدُونَ فِى ٱلْأَرْضِ ۙ أُوْلَٰٓئِكَ لَهُمُ ٱللَّعْنَةُ وَلَهُمْ سُوٓءُ ٱلدَّارِ ۝

ᵃ God created man; He provided the best world for him to live in; at all times He looks after him. All these things bind a man with his Creator and Lord by a natural bond. This bond demands that man should not become arrogant but should accept the realities and bow down before God.

Man's life in this world is marked by different types of relationships and connections. It is a requirement of man's subordination to God that he should develop relations with those liked by God and he should cut off relations as commanded by God. His realization of God's Majesty should be so intense that he bows down before Him: a regular form of this obedience is prayer (*salat*). And he should give to others from his assets as God has given to him from His assets. If he is badly treated by somebody, he should for his part respond with good treatment in order that in the Hereafter God should overlook his evil side and treat him with Grace and Mercy.

All this requires constant patience. It calls for the believer to hold out against the inducement of the self, to be steadfast in the face of loss of benefit, and to stand up to the pressure of his surroundings.

For the sake of paradise the believer has to exercise patience in all such cases. Patience is the price of paradise. Nobody can attain eternal paradise without paying the price of patience.

²⁶ God gives abundantly to whom He will and sparingly to whom He pleases—[those who deny the truth] rejoice in the life of this world; yet the life of this world is but a fleeting pleasure compared with the life to come.

²⁷ Those who deny the truth ask, 'Why has no Sign been sent down to him by his Lord?' Say, 'God lets go astray those whom He wills and guides to Himself those who turn to Him,' ²⁸ those who believe and whose hearts find comfort in the remembrance of God—surely in the remembrance of God hearts can find comfort.ᵃ

اللَّهُ يَبْسُطُ الرِّزْقَ لِمَن يَشَاءُ وَيَقْدِرُ وَفَرِحُواْ بِالْحَيَوٰةِ الدُّنْيَا وَمَا الْحَيَوٰةُ الدُّنْيَا فِي الْآخِرَةِ إِلَّا مَتَٰعٌ ۝ وَيَقُولُ الَّذِينَ كَفَرُواْ لَوْلَا أُنزِلَ عَلَيْهِ ءَايَةٌ مِّن رَّبِّهِ ۗ قُلْ إِنَّ اللَّهَ يُضِلُّ مَن يَشَاءُ وَيَهْدِى إِلَيْهِ مَنْ أَنَابَ ۝ الَّذِينَ ءَامَنُواْ وَتَطْمَئِنُّ قُلُوبُهُم بِذِكْرِ اللَّهِ ۗ أَلَا بِذِكْرِ اللَّهِ تَطْمَئِنُّ الْقُلُوبُ ۝

ᵃ Man is bound to God by the bond of nature and to his fellow beings by the bond of humanity. Breaking both bonds leads to creating mischief on God's earth. Living a peaceful life on God's earth means making his life subject to the above-mentioned bonds. In liberating himself from these bonds – caring nothing for the rights of God or men—he only creates mischief.

Those who act thus incur the curse of God. Such as these will not share in the Grace of God. They have fouled God's earth, so they deserve to be pushed into the foulest of places—Hell.

In this world one receives less and another receives more. The one who receives more develops a superiority complex, while the one who receives less suffers from an inferiority complex. But, in the eyes of God, neither attitude is correct. The correct reaction is that if one receives more, he should become grateful to God; one who receives less, should strive to remain patient and be contented with what he has.

Worldly-oriented people invariably ignore the preacher of Truth. The reason for this is that a worldly person recognizes only worldly glories. As the preacher is in possession of only sublime truths, he is not recognized and is ignored as an unimportant person. But, when the veil over reality is torn asunder, man will come to know at that time that the apparent glory which he considered everything, was absolutely valueless. The truly valuable thing was reality which, because it was unseen, could not claim his attention.

²⁹'As for those who believe and do righteous deeds—blissful is their end.'^a

³⁰Thus We have sent you to a people, before whom other peoples have passed away, so that you may recite to them what We have revealed to you. Yet they deny the Gracious God. Say, 'He is my Lord; there is no god but He. In Him I put my trust and to Him I shall return.'^b

ٱلَّذِينَ ءَامَنُوا۟ وَعَمِلُوا۟ ٱلصَّٰلِحَٰتِ طُوبَىٰ لَهُمْ وَحُسْنُ مَـَٔابٍ ۝ كَذَٰلِكَ أَرْسَلْنَٰكَ فِىٓ أُمَّةٍ قَدْ خَلَتْ مِن قَبْلِهَآ أُمَمٌ لِّتَتْلُوَا۟ عَلَيْهِمُ ٱلَّذِىٓ أَوْحَيْنَآ إِلَيْكَ وَهُمْ يَكْفُرُونَ بِٱلرَّحْمَٰنِ قُلْ هُوَ رَبِّى لَآ إِلَٰهَ إِلَّا هُوَ عَلَيْهِ تَوَكَّلْتُ وَإِلَيْهِ مَتَابِ ۝

---

^a The reason for the rejection of the preacher of truth is generally that the people do not find any tangible glories around this person. But this amounts to being unsuccessful at the very point where a man has to prove successful. God wants man to recognize the truth in its absolute shape and to surrender himself to that truth. Now, one who insists that he will not accept the Truth without tangible feats will be fated in this world never to find the truth according to the law of God and he will always be deprived of God's guidance.

This world is a testing ground. Here man can find God at the level of remembrance; he cannot find God at the level of 'observation'. Those who agree with this godly plan will find God and those who do not will be unsuccessful in finding Him, just as one who insists on seeing the sun with his naked eyes will be unsuccessful in doing so.

In this world only that person succeeds who accepts God's plan and who moulds his life according to it, because it is God who is the Creator of this world and not man.

^b Signs having been shown to those who asked for them, a final verdict should be pronounced upon them. Now, if at the instance of human beings, God did show any tangible signs and if, even after that, they did not accept Him, they would deserve immediate destruction. But God, ignoring human demands for tangible signs, goes on, in His special Grace and Mercy, conveying the Truth through His messengers in the language of advice and reasoning. In this way people have a longer period in which to reform themselves and become entitled to God's Grace.

In view of this, it is necessary for the missionary not to be disturbed by the foolish demands of his addressees. He himself should be agreeable to God's plan and should continue to call upon them to accept it likewise.

³¹ Even if there were a Quran by which mountains could be set in motion, by which the earth could be rent asunder, or by which the dead could be made to speak [they would not believe in it]. Surely all things are subject to God's will. Are the faithful unaware that, had He pleased, God could have guided all mankind? Calamity shall not cease to strike those who deny the truth because of their misdeeds or to strike near their homes, until God's promise be fulfilled. God will not fail to keep His promise. ³² Other messengers were also mocked before you; but though I granted respite to those who denied the truth, at last I seized them, and how awful was My punishment.ᵃ

وَلَوْ أَنَّ قُرْءَانًا سُيِّرَتْ بِهِ ٱلْجِبَالُ أَوْ قُطِّعَتْ بِهِ ٱلْأَرْضُ أَوْ كُلِّمَ بِهِ ٱلْمَوْتَىٰ بَل لِّلَّهِ ٱلْأَمْرُ جَمِيعًا أَفَلَمْ يَا۟يْـَٔسِ ٱلَّذِينَ ءَامَنُوٓا۟ أَن لَّوْ يَشَآءُ ٱللَّهُ لَهَدَى ٱلنَّاسَ جَمِيعًا وَلَا يَزَالُ ٱلَّذِينَ كَفَرُوا۟ تُصِيبُهُم بِمَا صَنَعُوا۟ قَارِعَةٌ أَوْ تَحُلُّ قَرِيبًا مِّن دَارِهِمْ حَتَّىٰ يَأْتِىَ وَعْدُ ٱللَّهِ إِنَّ ٱللَّهَ لَا يُخْلِفُ ٱلْمِيعَادَ ۝ وَلَقَدِ ٱسْتُهْزِئَ بِرُسُلٍ مِّن قَبْلِكَ فَأَمْلَيْتُ لِلَّذِينَ كَفَرُوا۟ ثُمَّ أَخَذْتُهُمْ فَكَيْفَ كَانَ عِقَابِ ۝

ᵃ The real reason for denial of the truth is not any shortcoming in reasoning. It is due rather to man having been given the freedom to accept it or not. As long as a man has the freedom to reject, he can seek an excuse to reject anything.

If an argument is presented to him using a particular mode of expression, he will find some other mode of expression to reject it. If reference is made to some signs of the universe, he will produce some explanation of his own devising to contradict it, so much so that if mountains were made to move on the surface of the earth, or dead bodies were brought to life, even then nothing could prevent him from saying that this was all magic.

Sometimes it happens that a rejecter apparently demands an explanation, but in actual fact he is indulging in ridicule; he wants to show that whatever the missionary is presenting is not the truth. Had his message really been true, the missionary would have had an argument with him which everyone would have been compelled to accept.

God has given mankind a period of respite, due to which people have become fearless, but when this period ends and God catches hold of people, then man will see that he had all along been powerless, though he had supposed himself to be powerful.

33 Is then He who watches over every soul and its actions [like any other]? Yet they ascribe partners to God. Say, 'Name them! Or do you presume to inform Him of something on the earth of which He does not know? Or, is all this only your verbal assertion?' Indeed, their devices seem fair to those who deny the truth, and they are kept back from the right path. There can be no guide for those whom God lets go astray. 34 Punishment awaits them in the present life: but harsher is the punishment of the Hereafter—no one will defend them against God.[a]

أَفَمَنْ هُوَ قَآئِمٌ عَلَىٰ كُلِّ نَفْسٍ بِمَا كَسَبَتْ وَجَعَلُواْ لِلَّهِ شُرَكَآءَ قُلْ سَمُّوهُمْ أَمْ تُنَبِّئُونَهُ بِمَا لَا يَعْلَمُ فِى ٱلْأَرْضِ أَم بِظَٰهِرٍ مِّنَ ٱلْقَوْلِ بَلْ زُيِّنَ لِلَّذِينَ كَفَرُواْ مَكْرُهُمْ وَصُدُّواْ عَنِ ٱلسَّبِيلِ وَمَن يُضْلِلِ ٱللَّهُ فَمَا لَهُۥ مِنْ هَادٍ ۞ لَّهُمْ عَذَابٌ فِى ٱلْحَيَوٰةِ ٱلدُّنْيَا وَلَعَذَابُ ٱلْءَاخِرَةِ أَشَقُّ وَمَا لَهُم مِّنَ ٱللَّهِ مِن وَاقٍ ۞

---

[a] Research shows that there is a system of recording in this universe. Whatever a man says or whatever a man does is immediately recorded by a universal arrangement. In view of this, only such a Being can be treated as God of this universe who possesses the powers of Hearing and Observing. But the so-called partners of God, presumed to be such by human beings, are all such as possess no power of hearing or power of observing. In view of this, how can they be the Creator and Lord of a world like the present universe? How can one who is not capable of hearing create the capacity to hear in his creations, and how can he make other things capable of observing, when he himself is not capable of observing?

There is so much uniformity in this universe that it leaves no scope for the idea of partnership. The universe rejects any kind of partnership in godhead.

'Indeed, their devices, seem fair to the unbelievers' — here 'devices' means their utterances. Whenever a man rejects the truth, his mind invents something to justify his rejection, though what he says may be a combination of pointless words, but, those who are not serious in the matter of truth, are prone to utter empty words and think that they have justified their rejection, irrespective of the fact that the words uttered by them may not have any value outside their own minds.

Such false words can give solace or satisfaction to a man only in the present world. In the Hereafter, when the reality of everything will be made plain, these beautiful words will carry so little weight that a man will be ashamed of repeating them.

³⁵ Such is the Paradise which the righteous have been promised: it is watered by running streams: eternal is its fruit, and eternal is its shade. That is the recompense of those who are righteous, but the recompense of those who deny the truth is the Fire.^a

³⁶ Those to whom We sent the Scriptures rejoice in what has been revealed to you, while some factions deny parts of it. Say to them, 'I have been commanded only to worship God and not to associate partners with Him: to Him I pray and to Him I shall return.'

مَّثَلُ ٱلْجَنَّةِ ٱلَّتِى وُعِدَ ٱلْمُتَّقُونَ ۖ تَجْرِى مِن تَحْتِهَا ٱلْأَنْهَٰرُ ۖ أُكُلُهَا دَآئِمٌ وَظِلُّهَا ۚ تِلْكَ عُقْبَى ٱلَّذِينَ ٱتَّقَواْ ۖ وَّعُقْبَى ٱلْكَٰفِرِينَ ٱلنَّارُ ۝ وَٱلَّذِينَ ءَاتَيْنَٰهُمُ ٱلْكِتَٰبَ يَفْرَحُونَ بِمَآ أُنزِلَ إِلَيْكَ ۖ وَمِنَ ٱلْأَحْزَابِ مَن يُنكِرُ بَعْضَهُ ۚ قُلْ إِنَّمَآ أُمِرْتُ أَنْ أَعْبُدَ ٱللَّهَ وَلَآ أُشْرِكَ بِهِ ۚ إِلَيْهِ أَدْعُواْ وَإِلَيْهِ مَـَٔابِ ۝

---

^a The price of paradise is the fear of God, that is, such an intense realization of God's Majesty that it turns into awe and permeates the human heart. Those who are God-fearing in this world will be the ones who will be lodged in the abodes of the Hereafter where man will have nothing to fear and around which there will be gardens that will enhance their beauty.

The condition of the people who were without fear of God in this world will be just the opposite. In the Hereafter, they will find themselves surrounded by the fire of hell.

³⁷ Thus We have revealed it as a [clear] commandment in Arabic. If you followed their desires after all the knowledge which has come to you, you would have no protector or shield against God.ᵃ ³⁸ We sent down messengers before you and gave them wives and children. Yet it was not possible for a messenger to bring a sign, save by the command of God. Every age has had its revelation.

وَكَذَٰلِكَ أَنزَلْنَٰهُ حُكْمًا عَرَبِيًّا ۚ وَلَئِنِ ٱتَّبَعْتَ أَهْوَآءَهُم بَعْدَمَا جَآءَكَ مِنَ ٱلْعِلْمِ مَا لَكَ مِنَ ٱللَّهِ مِن وَلِيٍّ وَلَا وَاقٍ ۝ وَلَقَدْ أَرْسَلْنَا رُسُلًا مِّن قَبْلِكَ وَجَعَلْنَا لَهُمْ أَزْوَٰجًا وَذُرِّيَّةً ۚ وَمَا كَانَ لِرَسُولٍ أَن يَأْتِيَ بِـَٔايَةٍ إِلَّا بِإِذْنِ ٱللَّهِ ۗ لِكُلِّ أَجَلٍ كِتَابٌ ۝

ᵃ When the Quran was revealed, the Jews and the Christians were divided into two groups. Among these people, those who were God-fearing and who followed the true teachings of Moses and Jesus, treated the Quran as their inner voice and accepted it happily.

But those who thought communal prejudice and groupism to be the real religion, could not recognize the truth appearing outside their familiar sphere and became its opponent. Their being without fear of God made them fearless of opposing the call of truth.

One who becomes the opponent of truth solely on grounds of communal prejudice and groupism is, in fact, a follower of the desires of the self instead of God. As such he has turned away from the path of God. Making changes in the call of truth in consideration of such people is not permissible for one who preaches the word of God. It is necessary for him to be firm on pure truth in thought, word and deed. In the case of deniers, he has to be firm and persevering and not adopt the way of compromise.

If a man continues to follow the dictates of his self in spite of the knowledge of truth being brought to him in his own understandable language, he incurs the risk of being completely deprived of God's help.

³⁹ God abrogates or confirms what He pleases; with Him is the source of all commandments.ᵃ

⁴⁰ Whether We show you part of what We have promised them or cause you to pass away [before that], your mission is only to give warning; it is for Us to do the reckoning.

يَمْحُوا۟ ٱللَّهُ مَا يَشَآءُ وَيُثْبِتُ ۖ وَعِندَهُۥٓ أُمُّ ٱلْكِتَٰبِ ۝ وَإِن مَّا نُرِيَنَّكَ بَعْضَ ٱلَّذِى نَعِدُهُمْ أَوْ نَتَوَفَّيَنَّكَ فَإِنَّمَا عَلَيْكَ ٱلْبَلَٰغُ وَعَلَيْنَا ٱلْحِسَابُ ۝

ᵃ Whatever prophets came on behalf of God were all human beings just like other ordinary human beings and had worldly connections. Then why, in spite of this did communities accept their previous prophets and reject their contemporary prophet? The reason for this was that the prophets of yore had a factor in their favour which the contemporary prophets did not have, namely, historical glory. Communities accepted the previous prophets due to the historical glory attached to them and rejected the contemporary prophet for want of this.

It is a weakness in man that he cannot discern reality in its abstract form. The contemporary prophet was possessed of reality in the abstract form. So man could not recognize him. The past prophets had additional characteristics like material glory, so man recognized them and became their follower.

Umm al-Kitab (the mother of the Book) means God's original scripture, which is in His possession, and which contains the instructions and principles which God expects man to follow. The scriptures revealed to different prophets were based on this original book. God revealed this book sometimes in one language and sometimes in another language; sometimes a symbolic method was adopted and sometimes a direct method. Sometimes the responsibility for its safety after revelation was given to a human being and sometimes this responsibility was taken on by God Himself.

⁴¹ Do they not see how We come to [their] land and shrink its borders? God decides—no one can reverse His decision—and He is swift in reckoning. ⁴² Those before them did also devise plots; but in all things the master planning is God's. He knows what each soul does. Those who deny the truth shall soon know for whom is the final abode.ᵃ

أَوَلَمْ يَرَوْاْ أَنَّا نَأْتِى ٱلْأَرْضَ نَنقُصُهَا مِنْ أَطْرَافِهَا ۚ وَٱللَّهُ يَحْكُمُ لَا مُعَقِّبَ لِحُكْمِهِۦ ۚ وَهُوَ سَرِيعُ ٱلْحِسَابِ ﴿٤١﴾ وَقَدْ مَكَرَ ٱلَّذِينَ مِن قَبْلِهِمْ فَلِلَّهِ ٱلْمَكْرُ جَمِيعًا ۖ يَعْلَمُ مَا تَكْسِبُ كُلُّ نَفْسٍ ۗ وَسَيَعْلَمُ ٱلْكُفَّارُ لِمَنْ عُقْبَى ٱلدَّارِ ﴿٤٢﴾

ᵃ The result of the rejection of God's religion becomes apparent in the Hereafter, but if the addressees of a prophet reject his call, the consequences start manifesting themselves in the present world itself. However, there is not one fixed principle for this worldly outcome. This has appeared in different forms during the periods of different prophets.

In the case of the Prophet Muhammad, by the special dispensation of the Almighty, the followers of the Prophet were made dominant over his opponents.

In the last stage of the Makkah period, when the tribal chiefs of Makkah had rejected him, the call of Islam was gradually spreading within Madina and among the tribes outside Makkah. In other words, Islam's missionary power was conquering the surroundings of Makkah and was advancing towards Makkah itself. In the case of the Prophet Muhammad the will of God appeared in the shape of missionary conquests.

Here Dawah strategy is called divine strategy. This shows its importance. When the Quraysh expelled the Prophet Muhammad from Makkah, they thought that they had finished him. At that time he was a person whose means of livelihood had been destroyed; a person who was deprived of the support of his own tribe.

After doing all this, the Quraysh were very happy. They thought that they had buried the problem of the Prophet once and for all. But they could not understand that the mission of Dawah is the greatest weapon of a missionary, and this is something which nobody can snatch from him. All other deprivations of the missionary only result in increasing the force of his missionary call; these do not reduce this force in any way. Accordingly, at the very moment when the Quraysh thought that they had deprived the Prophet of everything, his missionary call was spreading all round among the Arab tribes. People's hearts were won over by him. This process was quietly but constantly going on. And the conquest of Makkah was, in fact, its culminating point. Those who had been considered only "tens of hundreds" by the people of Makkah and had been uprooted from their homes, in only a few years' time became "ten thousand and returned to Makkah in such strength that the people of Makkah did not have the courage to prevent them from entering their city. ▶

⁴³ Those who deny the truth say, 'You are not God's messenger.' Say, 'Sufficient is God as my witness between me and you, and those who have knowledge of the Book.'^a

وَيَقُولُ ٱلَّذِينَ كَفَرُوٓا۟ لَسْتَ مُرْسَلًا ۚ قُلْ كَفَىٰ بِٱللَّهِ شَهِيدًۢا بَيْنِى وَبَيْنَكُمْ وَمَنْ عِندَهُۥ عِلْمُ ٱلْكِتَٰبِ ۩

Those whose interests are adversely affected by the call for acknowledgement of truth try to suppress it by adopting various devices against it. But in the end, devices are in the hand of God. He has power over everybody. The initial manifestation of God's superiority is taking place in the present world. The perfect manifestation of this will take place in the Hereafter, when even the blind will see it and even the deaf will hear it.

^a When those who are carried away by appearances, do not find signs in terms of miracles in the preacher of truth they are in doubt about the veracity of his message. But Truth is its own proof, however, its realization is possible for that person only who has developed in himself an eye which observes the reality by passing beyond outward appearances. Otherwise, one whose eyes are arrested by appearances will reject the truth, considering it baseless, though at that very time reason in its favour will be in existence right before him.

14. ABRAHAM

In the name of God,
the Most Gracious, the Most Merciful

[1] *Alif Lam Ra*

We have revealed to you this Book
so that, by their Lord's command,
you may lead men from darkness to
the light: to the path of the Mighty,
the Praiseworthy One, [2] to God, who
possesses whatever is in the heavens
and whatever is on earth. Woe to
those who deny the truth, for they
shall be sternly punished! [a]

الٓرۚ كِتَٰبٌ أَنزَلۡنَٰهُ إِلَيۡكَ لِتُخۡرِجَ
ٱلنَّاسَ مِنَ ٱلظُّلُمَٰتِ إِلَى ٱلنُّورِ بِإِذۡنِ
رَبِّهِمۡ إِلَىٰ صِرَٰطِ ٱلۡعَزِيزِ ٱلۡحَمِيدِ ۝
ٱللَّهِ ٱلَّذِى لَهُۥ مَا فِى ٱلسَّمَٰوَٰتِ وَمَا فِى
ٱلۡأَرۡضِ ۗ وَوَيۡلٞ لِّلۡكَٰفِرِينَ مِنۡ
عَذَابٖ شَدِيدٍ ۝

---

[a] Faith enables man to discover God as a Being who is all powerful and possessed
of all the good attributes. Such a mental state is not merely a formal belief. It, in
fact, signals the emergence of a man from the darkness of ignorance and his
entering into the light of knowledge. It amounts to the observation and realization
of the Hereafter, while actually remaining in this world. Faith in reality is a
conscious attainment and not the spiritless repetition of certain combinations of
words. The Book of God aims to lead man to this higher stage of consciousness.

Receiving guidance at the command of God would appear to attribute the matter
of guidance to God. But these words are, in fact, aimed at man himself. There is
an immutable law of God, which He has established for the guidance or
misguidance of man. According to this law, a man's serious desire for guidance is
the only condition which will take him towards it. When a man receives guidance
in this world, it is not simply because of the efforts of the missionary, but because
it is available to him by the law of God which lays down that only that person will
receive the bounty of guidance who himself is desirous of receiving it. Nobody can
receive guidance without his own personal desire to have it.

728

³ Woe to those who love this life more than the Hereafter; who turn others away from the path of God and seek to make it crooked. They have gone far astray.ᵃ

⁴ Each messenger We have sent has spoken in the language of his own people, so that he might make the message clear to them. But God lets go astray whom He will and guides whom He pleases. He is the Almighty, the All Wise.ᵇ

ٱلَّذِينَ يَسْتَحِبُّونَ ٱلْحَيَوٰةَ ٱلدُّنْيَا عَلَى ٱلْأَخِرَةِ وَيَصُدُّونَ عَن سَبِيلِ ٱللَّهِ وَيَبْغُونَهَا عِوَجًا ۚ أُوْلَٰئِكَ فِى ضَلَٰلٍ بَعِيدٍ ۝ وَمَآ أَرْسَلْنَا مِن رَّسُولٍ إِلَّا بِلِسَانِ قَوْمِهِۦ لِيُبَيِّنَ لَهُمْ ۖ فَيُضِلُّ ٱللَّهُ مَن يَشَآءُ وَيَهْدِى مَن يَشَآءُ ۚ وَهُوَ ٱلْعَزِيزُ ٱلْحَكِيمُ ۝

ᵃ God has made the path of guidance extremely clear and well illumined; signs are spread all around on the earth and in the sky; the Book of God provides undeniable arguments in its favour; human nature bears testimony to its veracity; in other words, all the evidence in nature are in its favour. This being so, those who do not seek out guidance certainly refrain from doing so in consideration of their worldly interests and not for any real reason, though such people advance a number of 'arguments' in order to justify their behaviour. But the actual purpose of these 'arguments' is to find something wrong with a straightforward statement. They are intended purely to justify their rejection of divine guidance in the eyes of the people.

In view of this, only that person will be deprived of guidance whose love of self-interest and worldly inducements have made him completely blind and deaf.

ᵇ It was the way of God to raise prophets from among the addressees' own community, fully taking into account their mentality, so that they might be able to call upon the people in their own understandable language to accept the truth. But it was very strange that the way adopted for the betterment of the people led to the very opposite effect. When they saw that the prophet was a man like themselves and talked in their own familiar language, they rejected him, considering him to be an ordinary man. The way adopted to make the process of guidance easier was turned by them into a source of misguidance.

It is not the way of God to display magical feats in order to attract people towards Himself, for example, by sending to a community a prophet who speaks a strange language or making the people wonderstruck by discoursing in a magical style. God does not cater to the wonder-loving nature of human beings. God's way is that of simplicity and realism. He has established His world on the basis of realities; therefore, He also carries into effect His scheme for the guidance of man on the basis of realities, not of magic.

⁵ We sent Moses with Our signs, saying, 'Lead your people out of the darkness into the light, and remind them of God's Days. In that there are signs for every patient, grateful person.'ᵃ

وَلَقَدۡ أَرۡسَلۡنَا مُوسَىٰ بِـَٔايَٰتِنَآ أَنۡ أَخۡرِجۡ قَوۡمَكَ مِنَ ٱلظُّلُمَٰتِ إِلَى ٱلنُّورِ وَذَكِّرۡهُم بِأَيَّىٰمِ ٱللَّهِ إِنَّ فِى ذَٰلِكَ لَأَيَٰتٍ لِّكُلِّ صَبَّارٍ شَكُورٍ ۝

ᵃ Here, 'Our Signs' means those signs of the universe which prove the statements of God to be true. 'God's Days' (ayyamullah) means those events of history when the decision of God was made manifest and, with the special help of God, truth was victorious over falsehood.

But it is very strange that these things remain almost untraceable in our world. The signs of God have been masked by wrong interpretation and wrong explanation, and the Days of God were not considered worth mentioning, the utmost attention was given to writing instead about 'the Days of the Human Being' (ayyamul insan).

In view of this, the only way for a subject of God to emerge from the darkness of falsehood is to exercise patience and remain grateful.

Modesty is necessary to find the truth. In order to find the truth, one has to lose oneself and this cannot be attained by anybody without the exercise of patience. Then the realization of truth shows a man that the division of resources in this universe is a matter between the giver and the receiver. God is the Giver and man is the receiver. The proper feeling which develops in man after the discovery of this reality is known as gratefulness. That is to say that, in order to reach reality, man has to exercise patience and, in order to assimilate this reality within himself, he has to be grateful.

⁶ Moses said to his people, 'Remember God's goodness to you when He delivered you from Pharaoh's people who were treating you cruelly, putting your sons to death and sparing only your daughters. Surely that was a great trial from your Lord. ⁷ Remember also the time when your Lord declared, "If you are grateful, I will surely bestow more favours on you; but if you are ungrateful, then know that My punishment is severe indeed."' ⁸ Moses said, 'Even if you should deny the truth, and all who dwell on earth together, God is self-sufficient, praiseworthy.' ᵃ

وَإِذْ قَالَ مُوسَىٰ لِقَوْمِهِ ٱذْكُرُوا۟ نِعْمَةَ ٱللَّهِ عَلَيْكُمْ إِذْ أَنجَىٰكُم مِّنْ ءَالِ فِرْعَوْنَ يَسُومُونَكُمْ سُوٓءَ ٱلْعَذَابِ وَيُذَبِّحُونَ أَبْنَآءَكُمْ وَيَسْتَحْيُونَ نِسَآءَكُمْ وَفِى ذَٰلِكُم بَلَآءٌ مِّن رَّبِّكُمْ عَظِيمٌ ﴿٦﴾ وَإِذْ تَأَذَّنَ رَبُّكُمْ لَئِن شَكَرْتُمْ لَأَزِيدَنَّكُمْ وَلَئِن كَفَرْتُمْ إِنَّ عَذَابِى لَشَدِيدٌ ﴿٧﴾ وَقَالَ مُوسَىٰٓ إِن تَكْفُرُوٓا۟ أَنتُمْ وَمَن فِى ٱلْأَرْضِ جَمِيعًا فَإِنَّ ٱللَّهَ لَغَنِىٌّ حَمِيدٌ ﴿٨﴾

ᵃ The speech of Moses referred to in these verses is perhaps the one which he had made in the Sinai desert to the Children of Israel, a few days before his death. This speech is recorded in detail in the present Bible.

The sum and substance of this speech of Moses is that if they remained in this world as the people of God and made the affairs of God the subject of their discussion, then all the things of the world would support them; all communities would bear the stamp of their domination; God would subdue their enemies; so much so that if a river obstructed their way, God would give the command and the waters of the river would separate and give way to them, while their enemies would be drowned in that very river.

He added that if they did not do as he said, they would be laid low in the eyes of God, that is, they would be deprived of God's grace; the product of their labour would go to benefit others; they would fail in all their tasks and they would become intellectually and physically subordinate to other communities.

This law of God is not only for Jews but for every community who is given the Book of God. This has been the way of God with every community bearing the Book irrespective of whether they were people of ancient times or whether they are people of the present day.

⁹ Has not news come to you concerning those who preceded you, such as Noah's people, and the ʿAd and Thamud, as well as those who came after them? Only God knows who they were. The messengers came to them with clear signs, but they put their hands to their mouths saying, 'We deny the message you have been sent with. We have grave doubts about what you are inviting us to do.'ᵃ

أَلَمْ يَأْتِكُمْ نَبَؤُاْ ٱلَّذِينَ مِن قَبْلِكُمْ قَوْمِ نُوحٍ وَعَادٍ وَثَمُودَ وَٱلَّذِينَ مِنۢ بَعْدِهِمْ لَا يَعْلَمُهُمْ إِلَّا ٱللَّهُ جَآءَتْهُمْ رُسُلُهُم بِٱلْبَيِّنَٰتِ فَرَدُّوٓاْ أَيْدِيَهُمْ فِىٓ أَفْوَٰهِهِمْ وَقَالُوٓاْ إِنَّا كَفَرْنَا بِمَآ أُرْسِلْتُم بِهِۦ وَإِنَّا لَفِى شَكٍّ مِّمَّا تَدْعُونَنَآ إِلَيْهِ مُرِيبٍ ۝

ᵃ All of the prophets who came to various communities, had the same experience: everywhere efforts were made to silence them, for every community opposed its prophet.

What was the reason for this? The reason for this was the people's 'doubt'. This doubt existed because the religion of their forefathers held sway and was widely believed in. By contrast, here was the divine religion being introduced by an apparently ordinary man. The arguments appeared to favour the religion of the Prophet. But historical glory and public popularity seemed to be on the side of their forefathers' religion. The addressees of the Prophet were themselves in a dilemma: they did not have the power to reject the arguments and at the same time they could not understand how they could consider their leaders and great men to be on the wrong path. This double-edged puzzle pushed them further into a dilemma. Attached as they were to their ancestral religion, they could not accept the truth inspite of being convinced of the strong arguments.

10 Their messengers said, 'Is there any doubt about God, the Originator of the heavens and earth? He calls you to Him in order to forgive you some of your offences and to reprieve you for a specific period.' They said, 'You are only human beings like ourselves! You want to divert us from what our forefathers have been worshipping, so bring us some clear authority.'[a]

قَالَتْ رُسُلُهُمْ أَفِى ٱللَّهِ شَكٌّ فَاطِرِ ٱلسَّمَـٰوَٰتِ وَٱلْأَرْضِ يَدْعُوكُمْ لِيَغْفِرَ لَكُم مِّن ذُنُوبِكُمْ وَيُؤَخِّرَكُمْ إِلَىٰٓ أَجَلٍ مُّسَمًّى قَالُوٓا۟ إِنْ أَنتُمْ إِلَّا بَشَرٌ مِّثْلُنَا تُرِيدُونَ أَن تَصُدُّونَا عَمَّا كَانَ يَعْبُدُ ءَابَآؤُنَا فَأْتُونَا بِسُلْطَٰنٍ مُّبِينٍ ۝

[a] This verse is related to ancient communities. However, a special characteristic of the Quran is that it presents God's eternal teachings in such a way as to relate them to both the immediate addressees and to the later generations.

The word 'Originator' as used here to translate the Arabic word, *fatir*, does not reflect the original, literal sense of 'one who tears'. Literally translated, the question would read, 'Is there any doubt about God who is the tearer of heaven and earth?' It is important to understand this aspect of the Creator, for this provides a proof of the existence of God in terms of today's laws of physics. Modern research shows that the matter constituting heaven and earth was initially in the shape of the solid ball known as the super atom. According to the known laws of nature, all its parts were attracted towards its centre with extreme intensity. The present extensive universe came into existence due to the explosion of this super atom. In this verse the word *fatir* (the Tearer) refers to this universal event—an absolute proof of the existence of a Creator, because the parts of the super atom which were completely attracted inside could not move in an outward direction by themselves. An intervention was required for this. If one accepts that the explosion did take place (that is, the Big Bang) then one must also accept the theory of external intervention. The other name for this intervening power is God.

¹¹ Their messengers replied, 'We are indeed mortals like yourselves. But God bestows His grace on such of His servants as He chooses. We cannot give you miracles, except by God's leave. In God let true believers put their trust—¹² and why should we not put our trust in God when He has already guided us to our paths? We will, surely, bear with patience all the harm you do us. So in God let those who trust put their trust.'ᵃ

قَالَتْ لَهُمْ رُسُلُهُمْ إِن نَّحْنُ إِلَّا بَشَرٌ مِّثْلُكُمْ وَلَٰكِنَّ ٱللَّهَ يَمُنُّ عَلَىٰ مَن يَشَاءُ مِنْ عِبَادِهِۦ وَمَا كَانَ لَنَا أَن نَّأْتِيَكُم بِسُلْطَٰنٍ إِلَّا بِإِذْنِ ٱللَّهِ وَعَلَى ٱللَّهِ فَلْيَتَوَكَّلِ ٱلْمُؤْمِنُونَ ۝ وَمَا لَنَا أَلَّا نَتَوَكَّلَ عَلَى ٱللَّهِ وَقَدْ هَدَىٰنَا سُبُلَنَا وَلَنَصْبِرَنَّ عَلَىٰ مَآ ءَاذَيْتُمُونَا وَعَلَى ٱللَّهِ فَلْيَتَوَكَّلِ ٱلْمُتَوَكِّلُونَ ۝

ᵃ When the people rejected each contemporary prophet in turn, saying 'You are a human being like us,' the real reason was not that they considered it necessary for the prophet to be superhuman. The real reason was the difference they observed between previous prophets and the contemporary prophet.

The fact is that the past prophets were also, in their time, just like the contemporary prophet. But subsequently their followers weaved a halo of magical stories around them, so that their personalities were given a dramatic colour which they did not initially possess. Now the communities had before them on the one hand prophets, supposedly capable of performing certain tricks and feats and, on the other, a prophet of realistic calibre. In this comparison the previous prophets became perfect examples. When communities viewed the matter by these standards, they found the contemporary prophet a lesser man than the charismatic prophets of the past. So they rejected him with contempt.

The prophets told their addressees that they could only exercise patience in answer to their objections, i.e. they wanted guidance at a superhuman level, while God had given them (the prophets) the capacity to give guidance only at a human level. The prophets said, 'Under these circumstances, what can we do except tolerate your persecution and entrust the whole matter to God?'

¹³ Those who deny the truth said to their messengers, 'We shall banish you from our land unless you return to our ways.' But their Lord inspired the messengers, saying, 'We shall destroy the evil-doers, ¹⁴ and settle you on the land to succeed them. That is [in store] for anyone who is in awe of meeting Me, and who heeds My warnings.' ^a

وَقَالَ ٱلَّذِينَ كَفَرُواْ لِرُسُلِهِمْ لَنُخْرِجَنَّكُم مِّنْ أَرْضِنَآ أَوْ لَتَعُودُنَّ فِى مِلَّتِنَا فَأَوْحَىٰٓ إِلَيْهِمْ رَبُّهُمْ لَنُهْلِكَنَّ ٱلظَّٰلِمِينَ ۞ وَلَنُسْكِنَنَّكُمُ ٱلْأَرْضَ مِنۢ بَعْدِهِمْ ذَٰلِكَ لِمَنْ خَافَ مَقَامِى وَخَافَ وَعِيدِ ۞

^a The religion adopted by the various communities was severely shaken by the call of the prophets. Those treated as great men by their people were reduced in status by the analysis of the prophets, and this angered them. They could not rebut the prophets' arguments. However, thanks to the system prevailing at that time, they had great powers in their hands. In their superior position they decided that the prophets should be made homeless and landless. What could not be countered by arguments was opposed by power.

When man is in possession of land, this possession is by way of a test and not as a right. If a man realizes that all these things are from God, which has been given to him as a test, he will develop a modest mentality. He will be afraid that what has been given by God may be taken away from him. But those neglectful of religion consider it as a personal right and this feeling makes them tyrannical and proud.

When the call of the prophet reaches its conclusive stage, it means that the period of respite given to the addressee community as a test has come to an end. Thereafter, the world is completely changed for them. The things in which they had reposed their hopes and on which basis they had made boastful plans suddenly leave them. So much so, that a time comes when the land is wrested from them and given to others who are more deserving.

¹⁵ When they sought Our Judgement, every stubborn oppressor was frustrated. ¹⁶ Beyond him is Hell, and he shall drink putrid water; ¹⁷ he will sip and will not find it easy to swallow it. Death will approach him from every quarter, yet he will not die. More intense suffering will lie ahead of him.ᵃ

وَٱسۡتَفۡتَحُواْ وَخَابَ كُلُّ جَبَّارٍ عَنِيدٍ ۝ مِّن وَرَآئِهِۦ جَهَنَّمُ وَيُسۡقَىٰ مِن مَّآءٍ صَدِيدٍ ۝ يَتَجَرَّعُهُۥ وَلَا يَكَادُ يُسِيغُهُۥ وَيَأۡتِيهِ ٱلۡمَوۡتُ مِن كُلِّ مَكَانٍ وَمَا هُوَ بِمَيِّتٍ وَمِن وَرَآئِهِۦ عَذَابٌ غَلِيظٌ ۝

ᵃ In the eyes of God, man's greatest crime is his adoption of an attitude of arrogance and obstinacy when he is called upon to submit to God. For such people there shall be disgrace in this world and in the Hereafter. Their punishment will be so severe that they will find themselves constantly on the verge of death and destruction.

When a man becomes tyrannical and arrogant towards others, he does it with some backing. The opponents of Islam felt their position to be impregnable because they followed the religion of their 'great men'. In comparison the Prophet and his Companions appeared to them to be lesser mortals. It was this mentality which prompted them to consider legitimate all types of persecution of the Prophet and his Companions. It was due to their linking themselves with their 'great men' that they became bold enough to take all sorts of punitive action against the so-called 'small men'.

¹⁸ The works of those who deny their Lord are like ashes which the wind scatters on a stormy day: they shall gain nothing from what they do. To act thus is to stray far into error. ¹⁹ Do you not see that God has created the heavens and the earth for a purpose? He can eliminate you if He wills and bring into being a new creation: ²⁰ that is no difficult thing for God.^a

مَّثَلُ ٱلَّذِينَ كَفَرُواْ بِرَبِّهِمْ أَعْمَٰلُهُمْ كَرَمَادٍ ٱشْتَدَّتْ بِهِ ٱلرِّيحُ فِى يَوْمٍ عَاصِفٍ لَّا يَقْدِرُونَ مِمَّا كَسَبُواْ عَلَىٰ شَىْءٍ ذَٰلِكَ هُوَ ٱلضَّلَٰلُ ٱلْبَعِيدُ ﴿١٨﴾ أَلَمْ تَرَ أَنَّ ٱللَّهَ خَلَقَ ٱلسَّمَٰوَٰتِ وَٱلْأَرْضَ بِٱلْحَقِّ إِن يَشَأْ يُذْهِبْكُمْ وَيَأْتِ بِخَلْقٍ جَدِيدٍ ﴿١٩﴾ وَمَا ذَٰلِكَ عَلَى ٱللَّهِ بِعَزِيزٍ ﴿٢٠﴾

---

^a The people of Arabia who rejected the Prophet Muhammad were those very people who had already accepted God and religion. Then why did they reject him? The reason for this was that in his case Truth was revealed in its abstract form, while they used to consider as true only that which had reached them through their 'ancestors'. They recognized the religion of their 'National Heroes', but failed to recognize the religion of 'Muhammad ibn 'Abdullah'.

Those who find religion under the influence of national traditions make a display of religiosity, but are, in fact, engaged in superficial activities in the name of religion. This has nothing to do with the spirit of the religion. What God requires is real religiousness and not just performance of certain rituals.

God approves of a man who has discovered the truth by means of his own mental striving; who has made observations of God in the realm of the unseen; who has recognized truth in its absolute form and supported it; whose soul has bathed in God's sea; who is restless in God's love and whose eyes have shed tears with the fear of God.

The religiousness of the first type of people is entirely superficial and outward, and of no value in the eyes of God. On the contrary, the religion of the second type of people is the real one. This is imbedded in the innermost recesses of human existence.

A study of the universe reveals that its creation is based on realities; in such a universe only good deeds have value and not suppositions and wishful thinking.

²¹ They shall all appear before God and the weak will say to those who behaved proudly, 'We were your followers. Can you protect us from God's punishment?' They will reply, 'Had God given us guidance, we would have guided you. It is all the same whether we are patient or impatient; there is no escape for us.' ᵃ

وَبَرَزُواْ لِلَّهِ جَمِيعًا فَقَالَ ٱلضُّعَفَٰٓؤُاْ لِلَّذِينَ ٱسْتَكْبَرُوٓاْ إِنَّا كُنَّا لَكُمْ تَبَعًا فَهَلْ أَنتُم مُّغْنُونَ عَنَّا مِنْ عَذَابِ ٱللَّهِ مِن شَىْءٍ قَالُواْ لَوْ هَدَىٰنَا ٱللَّهُ لَهَدَيْنَٰكُمْ سَوَآءٌ عَلَيْنَآ أَجَزِعْنَآ أَمْ صَبَرْنَا مَا لَنَا مِن مَّحِيصٍ ۝

ᵃ In reality, man is always under the eye of God. But, in the present world, man does not realize that God is watching him. In the Hereafter this veil will fall. At that time man will realize that he was completely visible to God, and to such an extent that nothing about him was hidden from Him.

Those who ignore the truth do so relying on their "great men." Whatever the common man does is done at the instance of leaders. In the Hereafter, when these people find themselves completely helpless, they will turn for assistance to their 'great men' on whom they had relied for guidance in this life. But the 'great men' will confess that their misguided leadership ended with the previous world. This being the case, how can they be expected to extend any help to them? They will tell their erstwhile followers that they are all destined to face the consequences of going astray, just as they themselves shall have to do. They will add that, whether they like it or not, they shall have to face this fate.

22 When the Judgement has been passed, Satan will say to them, 'God made you a true promise; I too made you promises, but I failed you. I had no authority over you, except that I called you and you responded to me. Do not now blame me, but blame yourselves! I cannot help you, nor can you help me. I reject your former act in associating me with God.' The wrongdoers will have a painful punishment.[a]

وَقَالَ ٱلشَّيْطَٰنُ لَمَّا قُضِىَ ٱلْأَمْرُ إِنَّ ٱللَّهَ وَعَدَكُمْ وَعْدَ ٱلْحَقِّ وَوَعَدتُّكُمْ فَأَخْلَفْتُكُمْ ۖ وَمَا كَانَ لِىَ عَلَيْكُم مِّن سُلْطَٰنٍ إِلَّآ أَن دَعَوْتُكُمْ فَٱسْتَجَبْتُمْ لِى ۖ فَلَا تَلُومُونِى وَلُومُوٓا۟ أَنفُسَكُم ۖ مَّآ أَنَا۠ بِمُصْرِخِكُمْ وَمَآ أَنتُم بِمُصْرِخِىَّ ۖ إِنِّى كَفَرْتُ بِمَآ أَشْرَكْتُمُونِ مِن قَبْلُ ۗ إِنَّ ٱلظَّٰلِمِينَ لَهُمْ عَذَابٌ أَلِيمٌ ۝

---

[a] The world of God is the world of reality and is not based on imagination. Here, relying on the promises of Satan amounts to building on an unrealistic basis.

Suppose an individual ignores the caller of Truth and himself takes the credit for doing dawah work, but he indulges in other activities besides dawah. He takes no account of the Hereafter but, relying upon self-made suppositions, still builds up the hope of salvation. He does not live his life in accordance with the commandments of God, yet hopes that his name will be included in the list of God's most favoured subjects. All these actions stem from relying on the false promises of Satan and, in the Hereafter, man will come to know that only God's promise was the true one and all other promises were only false hopes, which were never likely to be fulfilled.

In this world of God, placing hopes on anyone or anything other than God amounts to polytheism (shirk). It is those who ignore divine realities and want to construct their lives on other things will find that nothing except God can give them any support. But this realization will be of no avail to them on that day.

²³ But those who believed and did good deeds will be brought into Gardens with rivers flowing through them. They shall abide there forever by their Lord's permission, and will be welcomed with the greeting, 'Peace'! ᵃ

وَأُدْخِلَ ٱلَّذِينَ ءَامَنُوا۟ وَعَمِلُوا۟
ٱلصَّٰلِحَٰتِ جَنَّٰتٍ تَجْرِى مِن تَحْتِهَا
ٱلْأَنْهَٰرُ خَٰلِدِينَ فِيهَا بِإِذْنِ رَبِّهِمْ
تَحِيَّتُهُمْ فِيهَا سَلَٰمٌ ﴿٢٣﴾

ᵃ To say *assalamu alaykum* or 'peace be with you' at the time of meeting is not simply a formal social custom. This is in fact an outward symbol of a heartfelt connection.

Those who have lived their lives in this world with feelings of benevolence towards others, who have known how to forget their grievances and love others wholeheartedly, who have always spoken of others with respect, who have chosen for others what they desired for themselves, who have always longed in their heart of hearts for the well-being of others and who have rejoiced in seeing others in a state of well-being—such will be the people who will be entitled to take up their abode in the splendid world of paradise. The greeting *assalamu alaykum* has always given expression to their feelings of love and well-wishing whenever they met their brothers; in the Hereafter, when they greet their heavenly neighbours, this salutation will assume a powerful and more aesthetic form.

²⁴ Do you not see how God compares a good word to a good tree? Its root is firm and its branches are in the sky, ²⁵ it yields its fruit each season with its Lord's permission—God makes such comparisons for people, in order that they may take heed— ²⁶ but an evil word is like an evil tree torn out of the earth; it has no foothold.[a]

أَلَمْ تَرَ كَيْفَ ضَرَبَ ٱللَّهُ مَثَلًا كَلِمَةً طَيِّبَةً كَشَجَرَةٍ طَيِّبَةٍ أَصْلُهَا ثَابِتٌ وَفَرْعُهَا فِى ٱلسَّمَآءِ ۞ تُؤْتِىٓ أُكُلَهَا كُلَّ حِينٍ بِإِذْنِ رَبِّهَا ۗ وَيَضْرِبُ ٱللَّهُ ٱلْأَمْثَالَ لِلنَّاسِ لَعَلَّهُمْ يَتَذَكَّرُونَ ۞ وَمَثَلُ كَلِمَةٍ خَبِيثَةٍ كَشَجَرَةٍ خَبِيثَةٍ ٱجْتُثَّتْ مِن فَوْقِ ٱلْأَرْضِ مَا لَهَا مِن قَرَارٍ ۞

[a] In the present world Almighty God has appointed outward symbols for different realities. For example, a good tree is a symbolic representation of the believer.

It is the special characteristic of a tree that it makes the whole world its 'dining table', and in this way develops from the stage of a seed to establish itself on the earth as a majestic tree. The tree absorbs from the earth water, minerals and salts in order to grow: at the same time it obtains nourishment from the air and light from the sun. It takes nourishment from below as well as from above.

Using all these through the process of photosynthesis, the tree is able to make food throughout. This is what is meant by yields its fruit all the time.

This is also true of the believer. While the common tree is materially a tree, the believer is a conscious tree. The believer observes in the world God's creation and, looking to the system governing it, derives from it a proper lesson and guidance. Moreover, he continuously receives God's blessing from 'above'.

Fruit ripens on the tree in the proper season. Similarly, a believer adopts such behaviour as is proper for every occasion. Whether it is under economic constraints or in economic prosperity; whether it is in a moment of happiness or sorrow; whether it is a matter for complaint or commendation, whether it is in a condition of strength or weakness, on every occasion his language and behaviour express the reverence which he is expected to show as a true subject of God.

The opposite example is that of the evil tree, i.e. the wild bush. Its appearance suggests that it is provided with extremely unwholesome food, as a result of which it is covered with thorns, and bitter fruits with an unpleasant taste grow on its branches. It receives anyone who goes near it with a bad smell. Nobody likes such a tree. Wherever it grows, it is uprooted and thrown away. ▶

²⁷ God will strengthen the believers with His steadfast word, both in the present life and in the Hereafter. God lets the wrongdoers go astray. He does what He wills.ᵃ

يُثَبِّتُ ٱللَّهُ ٱلَّذِينَ ءَامَنُواْ بِٱلْقَوْلِ ٱلثَّابِتِ فِى ٱلْحَيَوٰةِ ٱلدُّنْيَا وَفِى ٱلْءَاخِرَةِ وَيُضِلُّ ٱللَّهُ ٱلظَّٰلِمِينَ ۚ وَيَفْعَلُ ٱللَّهُ مَا يَشَآءُ ۩

This is the case with the unbeliever, who from the beginning has always been *persona non-grata* on this earth. To him, the universe, despite its superlative features, has no argument in its favour and teaches no lesson. Though there is no end to the liberality of God's blessings, he has no share in them; God's magnanimity is not reflected in his character or his dealings.

ᵃ Being steadfast in the world means persevering in righteousness and doing good deeds at every turn in one's life. Being steadfast in the Hereafter means having been successful at the time of questions and answers in the grave.

Man is at every moment in the position of being put to the test. He faces different types of favourable and unfavourable events. On these occasions, only those who have grown 'the tree of faith' inside themselves behave in a correct and godly way. In the prevailing circumstances, they manifest the most appropriate reaction expected of them according to the will of God. In contrast to this, the man whose personality has grown like a wild bush evinces bitterness at every event; on every occasion he proves to be a thorn and emits a bad smell.

When these two types of person are tested finally at the stage of the grave, the one who proves himself to be the 'good tree' will be ushered into the Garden of Paradise. And the one who proves to be the 'evil tree' will receive the appropriate punishment of being uprooted from this world in order to be thrown as fuel into the fire of Hell.

²⁸ Do you not see those who, in exchange for God's favour, offer only ingratitude and cause their people to descend into the Abode of Ruin? ²⁹ In Hell shall they burn; an evil place to stay. ³⁰ They have set up rivals to God to lead people away from His path. Say, 'Enjoy yourselves awhile: you will then proceed to the Fire.'^a

۞ أَلَمْ تَرَ إِلَى ٱلَّذِينَ بَدَّلُواْ نِعْمَتَ ٱللَّهِ كُفْرًا وَأَحَلُّواْ قَوْمَهُمْ دَارَ ٱلْبَوَارِ ۝ جَهَنَّمَ يَصْلَوْنَهَا ۖ وَبِئْسَ ٱلْقَرَارُ ۝ وَجَعَلُواْ لِلَّهِ أَندَادًا لِّيُضِلُّواْ عَن سَبِيلِهِۦ ۗ قُلْ تَمَتَّعُواْ فَإِنَّ مَصِيرَكُمْ إِلَى ٱلنَّارِ ۝

^a These verses are primarily addressed to the chiefs of the Quraysh. But they apply generally to all those leaders who wage campaigns for the rejection of truth.

Only those who enjoy special benefits and opportunities become the great men of a community. The best use of these benefits and opportunities is that when the call of truth makes its impact upon them, they should stand up for it and, drawing upon all their resources, they should support it in every way. God has greater rights over the things which are given by Him than anybody else has.

But in most cases, the position is the opposite. Such people not only reject the truth, but even lead movements against it. The reason for this is that accepting the truth arising from outside themselves amounts to belittling themselves in comparison. And people who have, for whatever the reason, attained high status, very rarely agree to do so.

Human beings want a God—a Being who can be given the greatest position in their lives. But whenever their attention is diverted from the one and only God, they become inclined towards some non-God. Leaving God is always at the cost of setting up some non-God as God. Furthermore, those who divert people from God invest some non-God with those high qualities which are found in God, otherwise people would not be inclined towards it. That is why, when a man gives up worshipping the one God, he necessarily becomes superstitious. In this world the only alternative to believing in God is superstition.

³¹ Tell My servants, those who are true believers, to keep up prayer and to give alms secretly and openly out of what We have given them, before the Day comes when there will be neither trading nor befriending.^a

قُل لِّعِبَادِيَ ٱلَّذِينَ ءَامَنُوا۟ يُقِيمُوا۟ ٱلصَّلَوٰةَ وَيُنفِقُوا۟ مِمَّا رَزَقْنَٰهُمْ سِرًّا وَعَلَانِيَةً مِّن قَبْلِ أَن يَأْتِىَ يَوْمٌ لَّا بَيْعٌ فِيهِ وَلَا خِلَٰلٌ ۝

---

^a When a man confronts troubles, he tries his utmost to save himself from them; if he has friends, he uses their strength; if he has wealth, he spends it in that connection. A man's anxiety to save himself compels him to rush towards both these solutions.

Prayer (*salat*) and spending (*infaq*) are, in fact, the worldly manifestations of man's feelings about the problem of the Hereafter. Prayer (*salat*) is running towards God's protection so that one may thereby save himself from God's wrath in the Hereafter. In the same way, openly and secretly spending in this world is like donating one's earnings for the cause of God, so that it may become the means of obtaining relief from the rigours of the Hereafter. In the Hereafter, one may wish to spend, but one will have nothing with which one could ransom oneself from the suffering there.

³²It was God who created the heavens and the earth. He sends down water from the sky with which He brings forth fruits for your sustenance; He has made ships subservient to you, so that they may sail across the sea by His command; and has subjected the rivers to you. ³³He has also subjected to you the sun and the moon, both steadfastly pursuing their courses. He has subjected to you the night as well as the day; ³⁴He has given you all that you asked of Him; and if you try to reckon up God's favours, you will not be able to count them. Truly man is very unjust, very ungrateful.ᵃ

اللَّهُ الَّذِى خَلَقَ السَّمَٰوَٰتِ وَالْأَرْضَ وَأَنزَلَ مِنَ السَّمَآءِ مَآءً فَأَخْرَجَ بِهِۦ مِنَ الثَّمَرَٰتِ رِزْقًا لَّكُمْ وَسَخَّرَ لَكُمُ الْفُلْكَ لِتَجْرِىَ فِى الْبَحْرِ بِأَمْرِهِۦ وَسَخَّرَ لَكُمُ الْأَنْهَٰرَ ۝ وَسَخَّرَ لَكُمُ الشَّمْسَ وَالْقَمَرَ دَآئِبَيْنِ وَسَخَّرَ لَكُمُ الَّيْلَ وَالنَّهَارَ ۝ وَءَاتَىٰكُم مِّن كُلِّ مَا سَأَلْتُمُوهُ وَإِن تَعُدُّوا نِعْمَتَ اللَّهِ لَا تُحْصُوهَآ إِنَّ الْإِنسَٰنَ لَظَلُومٌ كَفَّارٌ ۝

ᵃ To the most wonderful extent, the present world bears testimony to God's existence. The rotation of stars and planets in the vastness of space; the provision and sustenance for life on the earth, the abundance of water; man's ability to run his vehicles on land, sail on water and fly in space; the earth's being favourable to man with the help of rivers and mountains; the regularity of the seasons and the occurrence of day and night with the help of the sun and the moon—all these are phenomena too great to be adequately expressed in words. There is such perfect co-ordination between man and the universe that every imaginable, or unimaginable necessity of man has already been provided for here in abundance.

All these things are so wonderful that they should shake a man and should overwhelm him with feelings of submission to God. In spite of this, why, on seeing the universe, is he not filled with wonder and why does he not tremble at the concept of the Creator of the universe? The reason for this is that man sees the universe as soon as he is born. By seeing it again and again he takes it to be an ordinary thing; he does not find any uniqueness in it, and takes it for granted.

Moreover, when a man receives anything in this world, it appears to be available to him through the 'cause-and-effect' process. On this basis, he thinks that whatever he attains is due to his own diligence and talents. That is why the feeling of gratitude to God, the Giver, does not develop in him.

35 [Remember] when Abraham said, 'My Lord, make this a city of peace and help me and my children to keep away from worshipping idols. 36 My Lord, they have led so many men astray! Anyone who follows me is with me, but if anyone turns against me, You are surely forgiving and merciful.*a*

وَإِذْ قَالَ إِبْرَٰهِيمُ رَبِّ ٱجْعَلْ هَٰذَا ٱلْبَلَدَ ءَامِنًا وَٱجْنُبْنِى وَبَنِىَّ أَن نَّعْبُدَ ٱلْأَصْنَامَ ۝ رَبِّ إِنَّهُنَّ أَضْلَلْنَ كَثِيرًا مِّنَ ٱلنَّاسِ فَمَن تَبِعَنِى فَإِنَّهُ مِنِّى وَمَنْ عَصَانِى فَإِنَّكَ غَفُورٌ رَّحِيمٌ ۝

---

a Prior to the advent of the period of Abraham, the condition of countries and communities had become such that polytheism (ascribing partners to God—*shirk*) had become the order of the day. The sun, the moon and other natural phenomena had become objects of worship. In ancient times, polytheism became so dominant over all activities of life that it thrived from one generation to the next. It seemed impossible that people could be taken away from the atmosphere of polytheism and brought into the sphere of belief in the unity of God—monotheism (*tawhid*). At that time, at the especial behest of God, Abraham left Iraq and entered the Arabian desert, which was a desolate place, far away from civilization. In this isolated atmosphere, he settled his wife, Hagar (Hajrah), and his son, Ishmael (Isma'il), so that a new generation would grow up, which would be cut off from the polytheistic trend prevalent at the time, and which, having been brought up in a free atmosphere, would follow its true nature in its formation. Abraham's statement reveals this particular fact in prayer-like style.

This was God's plan in settling the children of Ishmael in a dry and deserted place. Now, the people who made the unity of God (*tawhid*) the voice of their hearts, were, so to say, the true fruits of the Garden of Abraham. By contrast, the people of this place who reverted to the way of polytheism (*shirk*) would be treated as the poisonous weeds of this Garden.

37 O Lord! I have settled some of my offspring in an uncultivable valley near Your Sacred House, Lord, so that they might establish their prayers. So, make people's hearts incline towards them and provide them with fruits so that they may be grateful.[a]

رَبَّنَآ إِنِّىٓ أَسْكَنتُ مِن ذُرِّيَّتِى بِوَادٍ غَيْرِ ذِى زَرْعٍ عِندَ بَيْتِكَ ٱلْمُحَرَّمِ رَبَّنَا لِيُقِيمُواْ ٱلصَّلَوٰةَ فَٱجْعَلْ أَفْـِٔدَةً مِّنَ ٱلنَّاسِ تَهْوِىٓ إِلَيْهِمْ وَٱرْزُقْهُم مِّنَ ٱلثَّمَرَٰتِ لَعَلَّهُمْ يَشْكُرُونَ ۝

[a] The hilly and desert world of ancient Makkah was a natural training ground for the realization of God; the entire panorama of nature was an encouragement to man to remember Him. The only sign of human construction here, which claimed man's attention, was the stone mosque, the Ka'bah, built by Abraham and Ishmael. Here man could enter and engage in the remembrance of God.

In this atmosphere, the children of Ishmael were miraculously provided with water from the Zamzam spring. Moreover, it was so arranged that they received sustenance (*rizq*) from produce which was not grown there. This was, in fact, a special arrangement to make them grateful. With the provision of extraordinary bounties, extraordinary feelings of gratefulness arise in man. This was the wisdom which was hidden in Abraham's prayer that in the desert they should be provided with sustenance in the shape of fruits.

³⁸ Lord, You have knowledge of all that we hide and all that we reveal: nothing in heaven or on earth is hidden from God. ³⁹ Praise be to God who has bestowed upon me, despite my old age, Ishmael and Isaac. Surely my Lord is the hearer of prayer. ⁴⁰ Lord, grant that I may keep up the prayer, and so may my offspring. My Lord, accept my prayer. ⁴¹ Forgive me, Lord, and forgive my parents and all the believers on the Day of Reckoning.'^a

رَبَّنَآ إِنَّكَ تَعْلَمُ مَا نُخْفِي وَمَا نُعْلِنُ وَمَا يَخْفَىٰ عَلَى ٱللَّهِ مِن شَيْءٍ فِى ٱلْأَرْضِ وَلَا فِى ٱلسَّمَآءِ ۞ ٱلْحَمْدُ لِلَّهِ ٱلَّذِى وَهَبَ لِى عَلَى ٱلْكِبَرِ إِسْمَٰعِيلَ وَإِسْحَٰقَ إِنَّ رَبِّى لَسَمِيعُ ٱلدُّعَآءِ ۞ رَبِّ ٱجْعَلْنِى مُقِيمَ ٱلصَّلَوٰةِ وَمِن ذُرِّيَّتِى رَبَّنَا وَتَقَبَّلْ دُعَآءِ ۞ رَبَّنَا ٱغْفِرْ لِى وَلِوَٰلِدَىَّ وَلِلْمُؤْمِنِينَ يَوْمَ يَقُومُ ٱلْحِسَابُ ۞

^a In this prayer of Abraham, one sees glimpses of all those emotions which emerge in the heart of a true subject of God while addressing a prayer to Him. His submissive attitude compels him to admit his humility before God; whatever he requests is on the basis of his being needy and not on the basis of any entitlement; on the one hand, he admits to the bounties already available to him and, on the other, presents his request with all due respect. He admits that God is the Giver and man the beneficiary.

He prays to God to make him live in the world as His worshipper. He makes this request for himself, for his family members and for all believers also. At the time of prayer, the greatest problem before him should not be that of the world but that of the Hereafter, where a man has to live forever.

The prayer then made is prophetic in nature, and if such a prayer comes from a true heart, it will necessarily be accepted by God.

⁴²Do not think God is unaware of the wrongdoers' actions. He only gives them respite till the Day on which all eyes will stare fixedly in horror. ⁴³They will hurry on in fright, their heads lifted up, their gaze directed forward, their minds utterly void.ᵃ

وَلَا تَحْسَبَنَّ ٱللَّهَ غَٰفِلًا عَمَّا يَعْمَلُ ٱلظَّٰلِمُونَ إِنَّمَا يُؤَخِّرُهُمْ لِيَوْمٍ تَشْخَصُ فِيهِ ٱلْأَبْصَٰرُ ۝ مُهْطِعِينَ مُقْنِعِى رُءُوسِهِمْ لَا يَرْتَدُّ إِلَيْهِمْ طَرْفُهُمْ وَأَفْـِٔدَتُهُمْ هَوَآءٌ ۝

ᵃ When the Truth presents itself to a man, he sets himself against it. He shows such fearlessness in the face of it, as if there were nobody else in the world more courageous than he.

But this very Truth which is made manifest by a preacher of God's word in the present world, will become evident in the Hereafter at the level of God; the opponents of Truth will then lose all their bravado. After seeing the horrible scenes of the Hereafter, their condition will be such that their eyes will leap from their heads; they will not even be able to wink. Tilting their heads back, they will rush towards the ground where all will be gathered and their hearts will be terror-struck.

44 Warn men of the Day when the punishment will come upon them, and when the wrongdoers will say, 'Our Lord, grant us respite for a short while. We will respond to Your call and will follow the messengers.' [But God will answer], are you not those who swore that you would never suffer any decline? 45 You lived in the dwellings of those who wronged themselves, and it was made clear to you how We had dealt with them and We gave you many examples. 46 They hatched their plots; but these plots were all within God's knowledge. Though their plots were such as to shake the mountains, God will bring their plots to nothing.*

وَأَنذِرِ ٱلنَّاسَ يَوْمَ يَأْتِيهِمُ ٱلْعَذَابُ فَيَقُولُ ٱلَّذِينَ ظَلَمُوا۟ رَبَّنَآ أَخِّرْنَآ إِلَىٰٓ أَجَلٍ قَرِيبٍ نُّجِبْ دَعْوَتَكَ وَنَتَّبِعِ ٱلرُّسُلَ ۗ أَوَلَمْ تَكُونُوٓا۟ أَقْسَمْتُم مِّن قَبْلُ مَا لَكُم مِّن زَوَالٍ ۝ وَسَكَنتُمْ فِى مَسَٰكِنِ ٱلَّذِينَ ظَلَمُوٓا۟ أَنفُسَهُمْ وَتَبَيَّنَ لَكُمْ كَيْفَ فَعَلْنَا بِهِمْ وَضَرَبْنَا لَكُمُ ٱلْأَمْثَالَ ۝ وَقَدْ مَكَرُوا۟ مَكْرَهُمْ وَعِندَ ٱللَّهِ مَكْرُهُمْ وَإِن كَانَ مَكْرُهُمْ لِتَزُولَ مِنْهُ ٱلْجِبَالُ ۝

---

a Man's behaviour is such that he does not realize his fate right to the very end. If he attains some power or status, he becomes boastful and conceited as if these things were never going to be snatched away from him. He rejects the call of God and forgets that the things on the strength of which he rejects the call were all given to him by God Himself. Arguments are presented to him, but he pays no attention to them. The ultimate fate of the arrogant people of the past is well known to him, but he thinks that whatever happened was meant for others and that this will never happen in his case.

Those who have been given opportunities for betterment in the present world feel proud of ignoring the Truth. But after death, when they see the result of their arrogance, they will be so ashamed of their past that they will want to return to the past, so that they can contradict themselves and accept that very truth which they had earlier proudly rejected. Opposition of Truth amounts to opposition of God. Opponents of the Truth which is supported by God, are always unsuccessful, even if they come with preparation of Himalayan proportions.

47 Never think that God will fail in His promise to His messengers. God is mighty and capable of retribution. 48 On the Day when the earth shall be changed into another earth, as shall be the heavens, they will all appear before God, the One, the Most Supreme. 49 On that Day you shall see the guilty bound in chains, 50 their garments shall be of pitch and the fire shall envelop their faces. 51 God will requite each soul according to its deeds. Swift is God's reckoning. 52 This is a message for mankind. Let them take warning from it and know that He is but one God. Let those possessed of understanding may take heed.ᵃ

فَلَا تَحْسَبَنَّ ٱللَّهَ مُخْلِفَ وَعْدِهِۦ رُسُلَهُۥٓ إِنَّ ٱللَّهَ عَزِيزٌ ذُو ٱنتِقَامٍ ۝ يَوْمَ تُبَدَّلُ ٱلْأَرْضُ غَيْرَ ٱلْأَرْضِ وَٱلسَّمَٰوَٰتُ وَبَرَزُوا۟ لِلَّهِ ٱلْوَٰحِدِ ٱلْقَهَّارِ ۝ وَتَرَى ٱلْمُجْرِمِينَ يَوْمَئِذٍ مُّقَرَّنِينَ فِى ٱلْأَصْفَادِ ۝ سَرَابِيلُهُم مِّن قَطِرَانٍ وَتَغْشَىٰ وُجُوهَهُمُ ٱلنَّارُ ۝ لِيَجْزِىَ ٱللَّهُ كُلَّ نَفْسٍ مَّا كَسَبَتْ إِنَّ ٱللَّهَ سَرِيعُ ٱلْحِسَابِ ۝ هَٰذَا بَلَٰغٌ لِّلنَّاسِ وَلِيُنذَرُوا۟ بِهِۦ وَلِيَعْلَمُوٓا۟ أَنَّمَا هُوَ إِلَٰهٌ وَٰحِدٌ وَلِيَذَّكَّرَ أُو۟لُوا۟ ٱلْأَلْبَٰبِ ۝

ᵃ A prophet bears testimony to the religion of God to the fullest possible extent. So, God gives him His perfect support. Subsequent followers of the prophet will also go on becoming entitled to the help of God to the extent that they live up to the example set by the prophet.

Today, on the earth, man feels that he is the lord of land and sea; he is able to control spaces and vacuums; he has the power to use or not to use the resources available here. But, all this is possible only because God has subjected heaven and earth to man for as long as the period of testing lasts. The moment the period of testing is over, these conditions will completely change. Thereafter, the earth will be a different earth and heaven also will be a different heaven. Man will suddenly find himself in a whole different world.

Where man saw himself as a ruler, now God will hold sway. Where everything was subservient to his orders, all men and all things will now disobey him. Those who had become great men in the present world, will all appear to be helpless criminals on that day. Bodily adornments will now be like tar smeared all over the body. Glorious faces will be ravaged. All this will happen to those who were not ready to live as subjects of God in the world and who ignored the declarations made on His behalf.

The fact being a fact is not enough for man to accept it. For the acceptance of a fact, it is necessary for man to be willing to accept it. Only one who is serious about fact finding, who hears things with an open mind, will be successful in coming to grips with reality.

15. THE ROCKY TRACT

In the name of God,
the Most Gracious, the Most Merciful

¹ *Alif Lam Ra*

These are the verses of a clear Book, the Quran. ² A time will surely come when those who are bent on denying the truth will wish that they had surrendered themselves to God, ³ so leave them to eat and enjoy themselves and let them be beguiled by vain hopes; for soon they will realise [the truth]. ⁴ We have never destroyed a township without a definite decree having been issued; ⁵ no people can forestall their doom, nor can they delay it.ᵃ

الٓرۚ تِلْكَ ءَايَٰتُ ٱلْكِتَٰبِ وَقُرْءَانٍ مُّبِينٍ ۝ رُّبَمَا يَوَدُّ ٱلَّذِينَ كَفَرُوا۟ لَوْ كَانُوا۟ مُسْلِمِينَ ۝ ذَرْهُمْ يَأْكُلُوا۟ وَيَتَمَتَّعُوا۟ وَيُلْهِهِمُ ٱلْأَمَلُ فَسَوْفَ يَعْلَمُونَ ۝ وَمَآ أَهْلَكْنَا مِن قَرْيَةٍ إِلَّا وَلَهَا كِتَابٌ مَّعْلُومٌ ۝ مَّا تَسْبِقُ مِنْ أُمَّةٍ أَجَلَهَا وَمَا يَسْتَـْٔخِرُونَ ۝

ᵃ The freedom enjoyed by man will last only for the duration of the period of testing. This is a very critical issue. If a man seriously thinks this problem over, he will feel that the period which is going to end tomorrow has, as it were, ended today itself. This thought will shake him terribly. But man lives his life in 'today'. He does not pay attention to 'tomorrow'. Reality lies exposed before him, but he remains engrossed in wishful thinking. He seeks out some imaginary supports of his own devising and thinks that they will help him on the Day of Judgement.

But such wishful thinking will not come to his rescue when the period of testing is over and God's angels come to take him away from the world of trial to the world of retribution.

At a time like this, he starts remembering the occasions when he had tried to reject a genuine argument by mouthing false words; when he had ignored the voice of his conscience and followed the desires of the self; when purely out of self-interest he had ignored the divine preacher of truth, in spite of seeing glimpses of God in him. When he sees that no device of his has been of any avail, he will say, 'Alas! I should not have done what I have done! I should have adopted the way of one who surrenders to the Truth instead of the way of one who rejects the Truth.'

⁶ They say, 'You to whom the Reminder^a [the Quran] has been sent down, you are surely possessed. ⁷ Why do you not bring down the angels upon us, if you are truthful?' ⁸ But We send down the angels only to bring justice and then they will not be reprieved.^b

وَقَالُواْ يَـٰٓأَيُّهَا ٱلَّذِى نُزِّلَ عَلَيْهِ ٱلذِّكْرُ إِنَّكَ لَمَجْنُونٌ ۝ لَّوْ مَا تَأْتِينَا بِٱلْمَلَـٰٓئِكَةِ إِن كُنتَ مِنَ ٱلصَّـٰدِقِينَ ۝ مَا نُنَزِّلُ ٱلْمَلَـٰٓئِكَةَ إِلَّا بِٱلْحَقِّ وَمَا كَانُوٓاْ إِذًا مُّنظَرِينَ ۝

---

^a The Quran.

^b The addressees of the Prophet Muhammad suspected him of being mad. What was the reason for this? The reason for this was his declaration that he was a representative of God; that one who accepted his word would be successful, while one who did not would remain a failure.

But the addressees themselves actually perceived things to be just the opposite. They were of the view that the prevalent system had bestowed the position of leadership on them. On the contrary, the Prophet, due to his being a preacher of an unconventional religion, was a stranger and a man without a status in the prevalent system. Because of these apparent shortcomings, the addressees were emboldened to say that he (the Prophet) appeared to them to be a madman. They said, 'God has given us all kinds of worldly glories, yet still you say that success lies with you and your supporters.'

But such thinking was caused by a difference in perception. The addressees regarded whatever was material in their possession as 'rewards', though all of these things were simply a means of trial, given to all and sundry on a temporary basis.

They also used to say, 'You claim that the angels of God come to you. Then why are these angels not visible to us?' This comment too was due to a difference of point of view. An angel who comes to a prophet is the angel of revelation. He brings God's words to the prophet. Besides this angel there are other angels of God who come to the people in order to uncover the reality to them. But they come after the process of conveying the truth to the people is over. And when they come, it is the time for judgement and not the time for calling people to the faith.

⁹ It is We who have sent down the Reminder *ᵃ* and We will, most surely, safeguard it.*ᵇ*

إِنَّا نَحْنُ نَزَّلْنَا ٱلذِّكْرَ وَإِنَّا لَهُ لَحَٰفِظُونَ

ᵃ The Quran.

ᵇ The Quran, revealed by God in an age steeped in tradition—many centuries before the modern, scientific age—was a controversial book which presented a challenge to the whole of humanity. It set a definite standard for mankind to observe until Doomsday. If it was to survive, it needed a strong group to protect and preserve it. But there was no such group. The early Muslims were extremely weak as compared to their many enemies. Morever, in the seventh century A.D., paper and the printing press had not yet come into existence. Yet the Quran has remained intact, in the original Arabic, till the present day. There are several reasons for its survival. One is that the absolute veracity of its statements have stood the test of time. Another is that strenuous efforts were immediately made to write down the divine revelations and commit them to memory. But the most compelling reason was that God Himself had ensured its safekeeping, 'We will, most surely, safeguard it.'

10 We sent messengers before you to the previous peoples, 11 but there was never a messenger who came to them but they mocked him: 12 thus We cause this [habit of mocking] to enter into the hearts of the sinful. 13 They will not believe in it, though they have before them the example of former peoples, 14 and even if We opened to them a door from heaven, and they began ascending through it, 15 they would still say, 'Our eyes have been dazzled. We are bewitched.'ᵃ

وَلَقَدْ أَرْسَلْنَا مِن قَبْلِكَ فِى شِيَعِ ٱلْأَوَّلِينَ ۝ وَمَا يَأْتِيهِم مِّن رَّسُولٍ إِلَّا كَانُوا۟ بِهِۦ يَسْتَهْزِءُونَ ۝ كَذَٰلِكَ نَسْلُكُهُۥ فِى قُلُوبِ ٱلْمُجْرِمِينَ ۝ لَا يُؤْمِنُونَ بِهِۦ ۖ وَقَدْ خَلَتْ سُنَّةُ ٱلْأَوَّلِينَ ۝ وَلَوْ فَتَحْنَا عَلَيْهِم بَابًا مِّنَ ٱلسَّمَآءِ فَظَلُّوا۟ فِيهِ يَعْرُجُونَ ۝ لَقَالُوٓا۟ إِنَّمَا سُكِّرَتْ أَبْصَٰرُنَا بَلْ نَحْنُ قَوْمٌ مَّسْحُورُونَ ۝

ᵃ God's prophets were scoffed at in every age. The reason for this was that people judged their worth as representatives of God by self-devised, imaginary standards. The contemporary prophets did not appear to match up to the said standards, and so were dismissed as objects of ridicule.

In order to discover a new reality, it is necessary for a man to think with an open mind and be prepared to form an opinion purely on the basis of facts. Those who reject the truth do so mostly because the truth appears to them strange in relation to their own familiar standards. Over a long period of time those familiar standards permeate their hearts to such an extent that it becomes impossible for them to think of accepting alternatives. Till the last moment they are unable to emerge from the sphere familiar to them and recognize the truth.

The result of this attitude in communities was that the people belonging to them, in spite of being shown miracles, did not embrace the faith. Once they judged a prophet to be an ordinary man, basing their opinion on purely material factors, the person so judged could never be anything more than ordinary in their eyes. Even if he performed supernatural feats in front of them, their ideas were so rooted in the earlier traditions that he went on seeming unimportant, and so they would hold that his feats were just magic or some optical illusion and not a proof of his being a representative of God.

16 We have placed constellations in heaven and have beautified it for beholders, *a* 17 and We have guarded it from every accursed devil: 18 but if anyone eavesdrops, he is pursued by a bright flaming fire.*b*

وَلَقَدْ جَعَلْنَا فِى ٱلسَّمَآءِ بُرُوجًا وَزَيَّنَّـٰهَا لِلنَّـٰظِرِينَ ۝ وَحَفِظْنَـٰهَا مِن كُلِّ شَيْطَـٰنٍ رَّجِيمٍ ۝ إِلَّا مَنِ ٱسْتَرَقَ ٱلسَّمْعَ فَأَتْبَعَهُ شِهَابٌ مُّبِينٌ ۝

a This does not refer simply to the wonderful appearance of the sky at night. There are innumerable stars spread out in the universe, grouped in clusters, called constellations. Our own constellation is called the 'Milky Way.' During the night, when the atmosphere is free of clouds, dust, etc., when one stands on open ground and casts a glance at the sky, the array of twinkling stars in the vastness of the heavens is so wonderfully glorious that, on seeing it, man becomes overwhelmed by the feeling of God's greatness and majesty.

Those who used to tell the Prophet he should show an angel descending from heaven were asked, 'Is the scene of the stars in the sky shown to you every day not enough to awaken your consciousness and is it not enough to melt your hearts? Must you then demand further miracles?'

b Satan too has been allowed to settle along with human beings on the earth. Here, he enjoys full freedom to go wherever he likes. But in God's world beyond this earth, insurmountable hindrances have been placed in the path of Satan, so that he is unable to go beyond a certain limit.

¹⁹ We have spread out the earth, and set upon it firm mountains and caused everything to grow in due proportion. ²⁰ We have provided therein a means of livelihood for you and for all those creatures for whom you do not provide.[a]

وَٱلۡأَرۡضَ مَدَدۡنَـٰهَا وَأَلۡقَيۡنَا فِيهَا رَوَٰسِىَ وَأَنۢبَتۡنَا فِيهَا مِن كُلِّ شَىۡءٍ مَّوۡزُونٍ ۞

وَجَعَلۡنَا لَكُمۡ فِيهَا مَعَـٰيِشَ وَمَن لَّسۡتُمۡ لَهُۥ بِرَٰزِقِينَ ۞

---

[a] When initially deep seas and oceans were created on the earth, high hills emerged at various places on the earth in order to balance them.

After this, vegetation and animals came into existence and flourished in profusion, each one of them having a great capacity to grow. But it is clear that there is a fixed measure for everything. Everything goes on growing but, at a certain limit, it stops; it is not able to go on any further.

For instance, plants and trees have such an immense capacity for reproducing themselves that if one plant were allowed to grow in accordance with its internal capacity and without any restriction, within a few years that same plant would be seen covering the whole surface of the earth and there would be no room for anything else. But it is clear that there is a powerful Organizer, Who has control over everything. The same is true of animals. They too, have an unlimited capacity for procreation, but the number of offspring produced by each stops after reaching a certain limit. Similarly, the animals have the capacity to grow in size, but only to a certain degree. If a tiny fly were allowed to grow without restriction, it would be equal in size to an elephant. But natural control restricts its size to a certain limit. If the growth of these things was not restricted to certain limits, the life of man on this earth would be impossible.

Human beings require innumerable things for their sustenance and for civilization to develop. All these things have been made available on earth in exact accord with human needs. The provision for all these things and the assurance of their continued existence is of God's devising. If we were required to provide sustenance for ourselves, we would find it well-nigh impossible to do so.

²¹ There is not a thing but its storehouses are with Us. But We only send down each thing in an appropriate measure: ²² We let loose fertilizing winds, and bring water from the sky for you to drink; and you could not have stored it up for yourselves.ᵃ

وَإِن مِّن شَيْءٍ إِلَّا عِندَنَا خَزَائِنُهُۥ وَمَا نُنَزِّلُهُۥٓ إِلَّا بِقَدَرٍ مَّعْلُومٍ ۞ وَأَرْسَلْنَا ٱلرِّيَٰحَ لَوَٰقِحَ فَأَنزَلْنَا مِنَ ٱلسَّمَآءِ مَآءً فَأَسْقَيْنَٰكُمُوهُ وَمَآ أَنتُمْ لَهُۥ بِخَٰزِنِينَ ۞

ᵃ The principle of keeping within limits is inherent in all the things of the universe. The wind, although sometimes developing into a gale or a tornado, never exceeds certain limits. Except for minor variations due to its elliptical orbit, the distance of the earth from the sun remains constant. If the earth were to move further away, it would become frozen like ice. If it were to come nearer the sun, it would become like a burning oven. The pull of gravity remains at the most suitable level. Had the size of the earth been double, its gravitational pull would have increased so much that man would have found it difficult to walk on the earth, as his weight would have pulled him down. And had the size of the earth been half of what it is now, its gravitational pull would have decreased to such an extent that man and his dwellings would have become too light to have any stability. This is the condition of all those things amongst which man lives. There are fixed parameters for everything: natural phenomena go neither above nor below fixed limits.

The life of man and all living things on earth depend on water. From the underground reservoirs of water to the clouds spread throughout the atmosphere, the system of providing water is so complex and functions on such a large scale that its establishment could never be within the powers of man. This wonderful and gigantic arrangement is continuously maintained by God in exact accordance with human needs.

The human being is an extremely delicate creature. Any difference in atmospheric pressure and composition would be enough to upset his existence. The atmosphere, in spite of having innumerable possibilities, is stable as regards its particular composition and pressure which are suitable for a creature like a human being. This balance and this proportion could not have been accidental. Certainly, this is so thanks to the earth's most Majestic Creator and Sustainer. In view of this, one who does not accept God, or believes God to have partners, merely proves his own lack of reason and not the unreasonableness of the concept of the one God.

²³ Truly, it is We who bring to life and We who cause death and We are the inheritor of all things. ²⁴ We know those who lived before you and those who will come after you. ²⁵ It is your Lord who will gather them. He is all wise and all knowing.^a

²⁶ We created man out of dry clay, from moulded mud, ²⁷ and the jinn We had created before from flaming fire.^b

وَإِنَّا لَنَحْنُ نُحْىِۦ وَنُمِيتُ وَنَحْنُ ٱلْوَٰرِثُونَ ۝ وَلَقَدْ عَلِمْنَا ٱلْمُسْتَقْدِمِينَ مِنكُمْ وَلَقَدْ عَلِمْنَا ٱلْمُسْتَـْٔخِرِينَ ۝ وَإِنَّ رَبَّكَ هُوَ يَحْشُرُهُمْ إِنَّهُۥ حَكِيمٌ عَلِيمٌ ۝ وَلَقَدْ خَلَقْنَا ٱلْإِنسَٰنَ مِن صَلْصَٰلٍ مِّنْ حَمَإٍ مَّسْنُونٍ ۝ وَٱلْجَآنَّ خَلَقْنَٰهُ مِن قَبْلُ مِن نَّارِ ٱلسَّمُومِ ۝

---

^a The settling of human beings in the world and then their being taken away from here are events which occur at the behest of God. Had this been dependent on the will of man, he could never have come here and after coming here, he would never have gone on to the world of the Hereafter. This also proves that before the creation of human beings, heaven and earth belonged to God and thereafter they will also belong to God.

There are innumerable things on earth, but everything has its own individuality. Everything performs the special role assigned to it. This proves that the Creator of the earth has knowledge of each and every thing. He has allocated a particular function to everything, so much so that the thumb impression of one man is different from that of any other man.

For such a Powerful and Knowledgeable Being (that is, God) it is not difficult to keep every man's reckoning separately and deal with him in exactly the way he deserves to be treated.

^b The existence of man is a combination of two things—one is body and the other is soul. The body is totally made up of materials of the earth. The analysis of the body shows that it consists of the same elements that are commonly known as water and earth. In other words, as far as the body is concerned, man is the name of a completely lifeless and unaware existence. But when God infuses a soul into it through His Will, this very body suddenly becomes the possessor of such capacities as are not found in any other creation in the known universe.

The other creatures here on earth are known as 'jinn'. The jinn, rivals of human beings, are made out of fire. They are fiery creatures, and just as the earth keeps itself away from the fiery sun, so that it should not burn out, similarly, man should keep himself away from the jinn, otherwise they will scorch him in the spheres of morality and religion.

²⁸ Your Lord said to the angels, 'I am about to bring into being a man wrought from mud. ²⁹ When I have formed him and breathed My spirit into him, fall down in prostration before him,' ³⁰ then the angels all prostrated themselves together. ³¹ But Satan did not; he refused to join those who prostrated themselves. ³² God asked him, 'What is the matter with you, that you are not among those who have prostrated themselves?' ³³ He replied, 'I am not one to prostrate myself to a man whom You have created out of a clay of moulded mud.'

³⁴ God said, 'Then get out of here; for you are accursed,ᵃ ³⁵ and the curse shall be on you till the Day of Judgement!' ³⁶ Satan said, 'O my Lord! Grant me respite till the Day of Resurrection.' ³⁷ He said, 'You are granted respite ³⁸ till that Appointed Day.'ᵇ

وَإِذْ قَالَ رَبُّكَ لِلْمَلَٰئِكَةِ إِنِّي خَٰلِقٌ بَشَرًا مِّن صَلْصَٰلٍ مِّنْ حَمَإٍ مَّسْنُونٍ ۝ فَإِذَا سَوَّيْتُهُۥ وَنَفَخْتُ فِيهِ مِن رُّوحِي فَقَعُوا۟ لَهُۥ سَٰجِدِينَ ۝ فَسَجَدَ ٱلْمَلَٰئِكَةُ كُلُّهُمْ أَجْمَعُونَ ۝ إِلَّآ إِبْلِيسَ أَبَىٰٓ أَن يَكُونَ مَعَ ٱلسَّٰجِدِينَ ۝ قَالَ يَٰٓإِبْلِيسُ مَا لَكَ أَلَّا تَكُونَ مَعَ ٱلسَّٰجِدِينَ ۝ قَالَ لَمْ أَكُن لِّأَسْجُدَ لِبَشَرٍ خَلَقْتَهُۥ مِن صَلْصَٰلٍ مِّنْ حَمَإٍ مَّسْنُونٍ ۝ قَالَ فَٱخْرُجْ مِنْهَا فَإِنَّكَ رَجِيمٌ ۝ وَإِنَّ عَلَيْكَ ٱللَّعْنَةَ إِلَىٰ يَوْمِ ٱلدِّينِ ۝ قَالَ رَبِّ فَأَنظِرْنِيٓ إِلَىٰ يَوْمِ يُبْعَثُونَ ۝ قَالَ فَإِنَّكَ مِنَ ٱلْمُنظَرِينَ ۝ إِلَىٰ يَوْمِ ٱلْوَقْتِ ٱلْمَعْلُومِ ۝

ᵃ Satan's ostensible reason for not prostrating himself was that a human being was lower in status than he. But, in fact, the real reason was Satan's own inferiority complex. He resented it that all creatures were not made to honour him by prostrating themselves before him, as they did before Adam, considering that he had been created before Adam, a human being, whom he considered inferior to himself. He could not agree to pay homage to an undeserving being.

It is this type of pride and envy which are collectively at the root of all evils. In the present world such circumstances confront man again and again. One who does not become envious on such occasions has, in effect, followed the example of the angels and one who becomes a victim of envy has, in effect, followed Satan.

ᵇ The turn of events after the creation of the first human made Satan the permanent enemy of humanity. Now, till Doomsday, man is within the range of Satan's evil. It is imperative that man should be vigilant against the fraudulence of Satan. It is in this present world that the decision is taken about both a man's success and his failure.

³⁹ He said, 'My Lord, since You have let me go astray. I shall make the path of error seem alluring to them on the earth and shall mislead them all, ⁴⁰ except for Your chosen servants.'^a

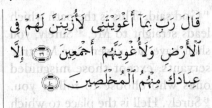

قَالَ رَبِّ بِمَآ أَغْوَيْتَنِى لَأُزَيِّنَنَّ لَهُمْ فِى ٱلْأَرْضِ وَلَأُغْوِيَنَّهُمْ أَجْمَعِينَ ۞ إِلَّا عِبَادَكَ مِنْهُمُ ٱلْمُخْلَصِينَ ۞

^a An opportunity was presented to Satan to take a test and he failed in it. Now the best course would have been to admit his failure. Instead of that he levelled allegations against God, that whatever He had done was meant to misguide him. He wanted to blame God for that which had proved his own weakness. To blame others for one's defeat amounts to following this characteristic of Satan.

The reason given by Satan for refusing to prostrate himself before a human being was that the human being was made from earth, while he (Satan) had been made from fire. There is no particular reason to believe that fire is superior to earth. But according to Satan's way of thinking, earth became contemptible and fire became a thing of a higher grade. This is known as glorification (taz'in). This is a psychological error and not a rational stand. Instead of admitting his mistake, Satan decided that he would make others commit the same mistake; that he would make all human beings suffer from that psychological weakness of which he himself was a victim.

Satan said that he would misguide all except the selected servants of God. And who are these selected servants of God? They are those who have adopted the straight path commanded by God, that is, the path of submission. In other words, Satan would not be successful in leading astray those men and women who have realised their real position, that is, a position of total helplessness in comparison to that of the All-Powerful God.

⁴¹ God said, 'This is the path which leads straight to Me. ⁴² Surely, you shall have no power over My true servants, except those misguided ones who choose to follow you. ⁴³ Surely, Hell is the place to which they are destined, ⁴⁴ it has seven gates: and each gate has a portion of them allotted to it.ᵃ

قَالَ هَٰذَا صِرَٰطٌ عَلَيَّ مُسْتَقِيمٌ ۝ إِنَّ عِبَادِى لَيْسَ لَكَ عَلَيْهِمْ سُلْطَٰنٌ إِلَّا مَنِ ٱتَّبَعَكَ مِنَ ٱلْغَاوِينَ ۝ وَإِنَّ جَهَنَّمَ لَمَوْعِدُهُمْ أَجْمَعِينَ ۝ لَهَا سَبْعَةُ أَبْوَٰبٍ لِّكُلِّ بَابٍ مِّنْهُمْ جُزْءٌ مَّقْسُومٌ ۝

ᵃ According to Mujahid, Hassan and Qatada, the meaning of 'straight path' is reported to be the 'way of Truth', which leads towards God and ends there. (*Tafsir ibn Kathir*). If a man adopts the path of polytheism, that path will not let him reach God but will lead towards the supposed partners of God. If he adopts the way of arrogance, his goal will be his own self. If he leads an unrestricted life, he will wander aimlessly hither and thither; his journey never leading to God.

But if a man makes God his entire centre of attention and, considering Him everything, lives his life focused on God, it is quite natural that his journey should carry him towards God and that finally he should reach God. God is All-Powerful and man is totally powerless. So there can be only one true relationship between God and His subject and that is one of man's subordination. Adopting the way of subordination to God is the means of establishing a perfect relationship with God, and Satan has no power over one who has done so. One who does not do so develops a relationship with Satan. Then he follows the suggestions of Satan, to such an extent that he reaches that very place where Satan is finally destined to arrive.

Hell, which is the final destination of Satan and his companions, consists of seven stages. Ikrama says seven gates means seven stages. (*Tafsir ibn Kathir*). People consigned to Hell will be divided into seven big groups according to their different deeds and, on that basis, they will find a place in one of the seven sections of hell.

⁴⁵ Truly, the God-fearing shall dwell amid gardens and fountains— ⁴⁶"Enter therein in peace and security!"—⁴⁷ We shall cleanse their hearts of all traces of ill-will; they will be like brethren seated on couches facing one another. ⁴⁸ They will not be affected by any weariness there, and they will never be made to leave.' ⁴⁹ Tell My servants that I alone am the Forgiving, the Merciful One, ⁵⁰ and that My punishment is a painful punishment.^a

إِنَّ ٱلْمُتَّقِينَ فِى جَنَّـٰتٍ وَعُيُونٍ ۝ ٱدْخُلُوهَا بِسَلَـٰمٍ ءَامِنِينَ ۝ وَنَزَعْنَا مَا فِى صُدُورِهِم مِّنْ غِلٍّ إِخْوَٰنًا عَلَىٰ سُرُرٍ مُّتَقَـٰبِلِينَ ۝ لَا يَمَسُّهُمْ فِيهَا نَصَبٌ وَمَا هُم مِّنْهَا بِمُخْرَجِينَ ۝ نَبِّئْ عِبَادِىٓ أَنِّى أَنَا ٱلْغَفُورُ ٱلرَّحِيمُ ۝ وَأَنَّ عَذَابِى هُوَ ٱلْعَذَابُ ٱلْأَلِيمُ ۝

---

^a The life of Paradise will be a life without fear. Only those who were mindful of God in this world will be considered eligible for this life. The fear of God in the present world is the price of a life without fear in the Hereafter.

Mutual ill-will is of two types: one is due to arrogance and the other is due to misunderstanding. Engendering ill-will or enmity out of sheer arrogance is the greatest social evil. The people of the Faith should put an end to it in this very world itself. Those who do not do so incur the risk of Hell in the Hereafter.

The type of ill-will which occurs due to misunderstanding, sometimes comes to an end, but sometimes, in spite of sincerity on both sides, continues till the very end. This second type of ill-will will completely end in the Hereafter, because the Hereafter is the world where realities are laid completely bare. When all the realities are unveiled before a sincere man, he will have no further reason to entertain feelings of ill-will against his brother.

The life of Paradise is so aesthetic and refined that one cannot imagine it in the present world. However, the pleasures and luxuries of the present world are a preliminary introduction to the ensuing world of pleasures and luxuries. When this introduction to Paradise is so pleasing, one can imagine how pleasing Paradise itself is going to be.

A man may accumulate all kinds of pleasure-giving things and luxuries in the world; but even then, various kinds of unpleasantness make all his accumulation meaningless. Paradise, however, is a place where pleasures and luxuries will be free of all unpleasantness. It is recorded in a tradition of the Prophet Muhammad that the people of Paradise will be told, 'Now, you will always be healthy and will never be ill; now, you will be alive for ever and will never die; now you will always be young and you will never grow old; now you will always be here and you will never have to leave this place.'

⁵¹ Tell them about Abraham's guests:
⁵² when they came to him they
greeted him with: 'Peace.' He
said, 'We feel afraid of you.' ⁵³ They
said, 'Do not be afraid. We come to
you with good news. You shall have
a son who shall be endowed with
great knowledge.' ⁵⁴ He said, 'Do you
bring me such news despite my old
age? What kind of good news are you
bringing me?' ⁵⁵ They said, 'We have,
indeed, given you glad tidings in
truth; do not therefore despair.'
⁵⁶ He said, 'Who but the misguided
despair of the mercy of their Lord?' ᵃ

وَنَبِّئْهُمْ عَن ضَيْفِ إِبْرَٰهِيمَ ۝ إِذْ
دَخَلُوا۟ عَلَيْهِ فَقَالُوا۟ سَلَـٰمًا قَالَ إِنَّا
مِنكُمْ وَجِلُونَ ۝ قَالُوا۟ لَا تَوْجَلْ إِنَّا
نُبَشِّرُكَ بِغُلَـٰمٍ عَلِيمٍ ۝ قَالَ
أَبَشَّرْتُمُونِى عَلَىٰ أَن مَّسَّنِىَ ٱلْكِبَرُ فَبِمَ
تُبَشِّرُونَ ۝ قَالُوا۟ بَشَّرْنَـٰكَ بِٱلْحَقِّ
فَلَا تَكُن مِّنَ ٱلْقَـٰنِطِينَ ۝ قَالَ
وَمَن يَقْنَطُ مِن رَّحْمَةِ رَبِّهِۦٓ إِلَّا
ٱلضَّآلُّونَ ۝

ᵃ Angels visited Abraham in the shape of human beings. In an exchange of questions
and answers, they said that they had come with the command of God. What was
this command for which the angels had come to Abraham? This was the good news
of an extra-ordinary reward which could not be expected under ordinary
circumstances. When God wants to confer an extraordinary benefit on man, He
sends His special angel to him in order to accomplish the task.

Angels of this kind come to prophets as well as to ordinary mortals. The difference
is that when a prophet is visited by angels, he sees them and consciously grasps that
those are angels, but ordinary men do not have this kind of certain knowledge or
consciousness. However, the close proximity of angels may evoke unusual feelings
in him. Such feelings can convey hints of the fact that at that time he is possibly
in the company of the special angels sent by God.

⁵⁷ Then he asked, 'What then is your business, O messengers?' ⁵⁸ They said, 'We have been sent forth to a guilty people.' ⁵⁹ Except for Lot's household, all of whom we shall rescue, ⁶⁰ except his wife. We have decreed that she will be among those who remain behind [and will be lost].ᵃ

قَالَ فَمَا خَطْبُكُمْ أَيُّهَا ٱلْمُرْسَلُونَ ۝ قَالُوٓاْ إِنَّآ أُرْسِلْنَآ إِلَىٰ قَوْمٍ مُّجْرِمِينَ ۝ إِلَّآ ءَالَ لُوطٍ إِنَّا لَمُنَجُّوهُمْ أَجْمَعِينَ ۝ إِلَّا ٱمْرَأَتَهُۥ قَدَّرْنَآ إِنَّهَا لَمِنَ ٱلْغَٰبِرِينَ ۝

ᵃ Abraham was living in Palestine along the coast of the Dead Sea. His nephew, Lot, lived nearby. He preached the word of God to the people settled in this area, but they were not willing to reform themselves. Their arrogance went on increasing, so much so that God decided that they should be destroyed. These angels had come to carry out God's will.

Probably nobody, except for a few family members of Lot, had embraced the Faith at his instance. It is very difficult for those who are not members of the missionary's household to accept him, because, for them, so many psychological impediments come in the way. However, for his own blood relations, such impediments do not exist. So, they rally the more easily to his cause.

This is what happened in the case of Lot. Probably, only his daughters embraced the Faith in response to his call. The special relationship which children have with their father inclines them to listen to his call. These girls were therefore saved along with Lot. But, his wife could not become a believer from the bottom of her heart. So she was killed along with other guilty persons. In the Law of God, no concession is given to anybody.

61 When the messengers came to Lot and his family, 62 he said, 'You are strangers [to me].' 63 They said, 'No, but we bring you news about what they disputed, 64 and we have come to you with the truth, and surely we are truthful, 65 so leave with your family some time in the latter part of the night, and walk behind them. Let none of you look back. Go where you are commanded.' 66 We communicated to him Our decree that the guilty ones would be destroyed by the morning.[a]

فَلَمَّا جَآءَ ءَالَ لُوطٍ ٱلْمُرْسَلُونَ ۝ قَالَ إِنَّكُمْ قَوْمٌ مُّنكَرُونَ ۝ قَالُوا۟ بَلْ جِئْنَٰكَ بِمَا كَانُوا۟ فِيهِ يَمْتَرُونَ ۝ وَأَتَيْنَٰكَ بِٱلْحَقِّ وَإِنَّا لَصَٰدِقُونَ ۝ فَأَسْرِ بِأَهْلِكَ بِقِطْعٍ مِّنَ ٱلَّيْلِ وَٱتَّبِعْ أَدْبَٰرَهُمْ وَلَا يَلْتَفِتْ مِنكُمْ أَحَدٌ وَٱمْضُوا۟ حَيْثُ تُؤْمَرُونَ ۝ وَقَضَيْنَآ إِلَيْهِ ذَٰلِكَ ٱلْأَمْرَ أَنَّ دَابِرَ هَٰؤُلَآءِ مَقْطُوعٌ مُّصْبِحِينَ ۝

---

[a] It was one command with which the angels had gone to Abraham. It was another command with which they reached Lot. The first command was in the shape of a special gift from God and the second one was in the shape of God's special punishment.

Those angels had come to Lot in the shape of human beings. Their task was to carry into effect God's verdict upon the prophet's rejectors. According to the angels' advice, Lot along with other people of the Faith, left the town in the darkness of the night. Thereafter, in the early morning the whole area was devastated by the explosions of a severe earthquake. All the deniers were summarily killed.

Where did this devastation take place? It took place in this very world which they had considered their own world; in which all appeared to them their comrades and supporters. That very plan which a man considered his key to success becomes an instrument of destruction for him, if God so commands. That very palace of which a man is so proud is turned into a ruin, like a heap of debris descending upon him.

⁶⁷ The people of the town came along, revelling, ⁶⁸ and he told them, 'These are my guests, so do not disgrace me. ⁶⁹ Fear God and do not shame me.'^{a 70} They said, 'Did we not forbid you to extend hospitality to strangers?' ⁷¹ He said, 'Here are my daughters,^b if you must act in this way.'

وَجَآءَ أَهْلُ ٱلْمَدِينَةِ يَسْتَبْشِرُونَ ۝ قَالَ إِنَّ هَٰٓؤُلَآءِ ضَيْفِى فَلَا تَفْضَحُونِ ۝ وَٱتَّقُوا۟ ٱللَّهَ وَلَا تُخْزُونِ ۝ قَالُوٓا۟ أَوَلَمْ نَنْهَكَ عَنِ ٱلْعَٰلَمِينَ ۝ قَالَ هَٰٓؤُلَآءِ بَنَاتِىٓ إِن كُنتُمْ فَٰعِلِينَ ۝

---

^a The angels who went to the town of Lot's community took the shape of extremely handsome youths. This was like the last examination paper to test this community which was steeped in debauchery. In their overweening arrogance, they made a rush towards these youths with the intention of molesting them, as usual. But they did not know that those they looked upon as charming youths were, in fact, the angels of punishment who had come only to leave them disgraced and dishonoured.

^b This means that 'here are the young girls of the city for you to marry'. When Lot saw that, in spite of his opposition, the rogues were rushing upon his guests, he said, 'For God's sake! Please don't dishonour me in the eyes of my guests. If at all you want to do something, here are the daughters of the community. You can marry any of them you like.'

⁷²By your life, they wandered on in their wild intoxication ⁷³and thereupon the blast [of Our punishment] overtook them at sunrise. ⁷⁴We turned the town upside down and rained upon them stones of clay. ⁷⁵There are certainly signs in that for those who can learn a lesson—⁷⁶it is still there on the highway—⁷⁷surely in this there is a sign for those who believe.ᵃ

لَعَمْرُكَ إِنَّهُمْ لَفِى سَكْرَتِهِمْ يَعْمَهُونَ ۝ فَأَخَذَتْهُمُ ٱلصَّيْحَةُ مُشْرِقِينَ ۝ فَجَعَلْنَا عَلِيَهَا سَافِلَهَا وَأَمْطَرْنَا عَلَيْهِمْ حِجَارَةً مِّن سِجِّيلٍ ۝ إِنَّ فِى ذَٰلِكَ لَآيَٰتٍ لِّلْمُتَوَسِّمِينَ ۝ وَإِنَّهَا لَبِسَبِيلٍ مُّقِيمٍ ۝ إِنَّ فِى ذَٰلِكَ لَآيَةً لِّلْمُؤْمِنِينَ ۝

ᵃ Why did the community of Lot go beyond all limits of arrogance? The reason for this was that they saw this matter in relation to Lot. Since they were more powerful than Lot, they thought that they could do anything they liked and there was nobody to prevent them.

Had they seen this matter in relation to God, the situation would have been just the opposite. Then they would have come to know that their arrogance was absolutely ridiculous, because nobody has any standing before the power of God. As a consequence, early in the morning, they were struck by a severe storm of thunder and lightning. At the command of God, the winds started showering pebbles on the towns of Lot's community (Sodom and Gomorrah). In a very short time, the whole community was destroyed.

There is a lesson in this event for those who give it serious consideration, i.e. in this world one's dealings in reality are with God and not with human beings. If a man realises this fact, all his arrogance will come to an end.

⁷⁸ The people of the Wood were also surely wrongdoers. ⁷⁹ So We took vengeance on them. Both are still there on the highway, plain for all to see. ⁸⁰ The people of al-Hijr also rejected Our messengers: ⁸¹ We gave them Our signs, but they turned away from them. ⁸² They carved out dwellings in the mountains, and lived in security—⁸³ the blast overtook them early one morning. ⁸⁴ All that they had acquired was of no avail to them.ᵃ

وَإِن كَانَ أَصْحَٰبُ ٱلْأَيْكَةِ لَظَٰلِمِينَ ۝ فَٱنتَقَمْنَا مِنْهُمْ وَإِنَّهُمَا لَبِإِمَامٍ مُّبِينٍ ۝ وَلَقَدْ كَذَّبَ أَصْحَٰبُ ٱلْحِجْرِ ٱلْمُرْسَلِينَ ۝ وَءَاتَيْنَٰهُمْ ءَايَٰتِنَا فَكَانُوا۟ عَنْهَا مُعْرِضِينَ ۝ وَكَانُوا۟ يَنْحِتُونَ مِنَ ٱلْجِبَالِ بُيُوتًا ءَامِنِينَ ۝ فَأَخَذَتْهُمُ ٱلصَّيْحَةُ مُصْبِحِينَ ۝ فَمَآ أَغْنَىٰ عَنْهُم مَّا كَانُوا۟ يَكْسِبُونَ ۝

ᵃ The people of the Wood, or al-Aykah, refers to the community of Shuʿayb. The real name of this community was 'Banu Madyan' (the children of Madyan). These people were settled in the area presently known as Tabuk. The people of Hijr refers to the community of Thamud to whom Salih was sent as a prophet. This area was located to the north of Madinah.

The arrogance of the people of al-Aykah not only made them polytheists but also pushed them into committing the worst moral crimes. When, in spite of Shuʿayb's admonition, they did not mend their ways, God commanded the earth. Thereafter, the earth which had been a cradle of comfort and luxury for them became a cradle of punishment.

The community of Thamud were experts in the art of stone-carving. They had cut into the hills and had turned them into lovely dwellings. They thought that they had made complete provision for their safety. When they ignored the call of God, He gave a command and their magnificent dwellings turned into magnificent graves.

85 We have created the heavens and the earth and all that is between the two in accordance with the requirements of truth and wisdom. The Hour is surely coming. So overlook [their faults] with gracious forgiveness. 86 Surely your Lord is the All Knowing Creator! [a]

وَمَا خَلَقْنَا ٱلسَّمَٰوَٰتِ وَٱلْأَرْضَ وَمَا بَيْنَهُمَآ إِلَّا بِٱلْحَقِّ ۗ وَإِنَّ ٱلسَّاعَةَ لَآتِيَةٌ ۖ فَٱصْفَحِ ٱلصَّفْحَ ٱلْجَمِيلَ ﴿٨٥﴾ إِنَّ رَبَّكَ هُوَ ٱلْخَلَّٰقُ ٱلْعَلِيمُ ﴿٨٦﴾

[a] The study of heaven and earth reveals that the entire system is marked throughout by wisdom. Here everything is as it should be. In this entire system, only human beings set themselves up against reality. This contradiction between human beings and the universe implies that it must come to an end. From this point of view, belief in the Day of Judgement is absolutely rational and logical, because nothing other than the Day of Judgement can eliminate this contradiction.

Graciously overlooking or turning away from others' improper behaviour is an essential part of the preacher's task in spreading the word of God. That is, when the addressee of his call starts some irrelevant discussion or picks a quarrel, politely ignoring him instead of answering him is the best policy. Without adopting this principle, the propagation of the word of God cannot be effectively performed.

87 We have given you the seven oft-recited verses and the great Quran. 88 Do not strain your eyes towards the worldly benefits We have bestowed on some of them, nor grieve on their account. Lower your wing of mercy for the believers 89 and say, 'I am, indeed, a plain warner,' 90 such as We send down for those who are divisive, 91 and who have broken the Scripture into fragments—92 by your Lord, We shall question them all 93 about whatever they had been doing! *a*

وَلَقَدْ ءَاتَيْنَٰكَ سَبْعًا مِّنَ ٱلْمَثَانِى وَٱلْقُرْءَانَ ٱلْعَظِيمَ ۝ لَا تَمُدَّنَّ عَيْنَيْكَ إِلَىٰ مَا مَتَّعْنَا بِهِۦٓ أَزْوَٰجًا مِّنْهُمْ وَلَا تَحْزَنْ عَلَيْهِمْ وَٱخْفِضْ جَنَاحَكَ لِلْمُؤْمِنِينَ ۝ وَقُلْ إِنِّى أَنَا ٱلنَّذِيرُ ٱلْمُبِينُ ۝ كَمَآ أَنزَلْنَا عَلَى ٱلْمُقْتَسِمِينَ ۝ ٱلَّذِينَ جَعَلُوا۟ ٱلْقُرْءَانَ عِضِينَ ۝ فَوَرَبِّكَ لَنَسْـَٔلَنَّهُمْ أَجْمَعِينَ ۝ عَمَّا كَانُوا۟ يَعْمَلُونَ ۝

---

a The 'seven oft-repeated verses' refers to the first chapter of the Quran. It is the essence of the whole Quran, and the rest of the Quran is an elaboration upon it. Undoubtedly, the Quran is the greatest gift of God. Its being a book of guidance offers the guarantee of success in the Hereafter to its believers and its being the last book makes it essential that it should necessarily overcome its opponents, because if it does not prevail, it cannot exist as the last book.

The preacher of God's word should not be despondent over those who have not embraced the Faith, but should be satisfied looking at those who have embraced the Faith and devote his full attention to making them contented and giving them training.

Fragmenting the Quran (the scriptures) means fragmenting the Torah. The ancient Jews had divided their holy scriptures into two parts. They used to leave out those teachings that went against the desires of the self, while those that were consistent with the wishes of the self were welcomed by them. The first type of verses were kept only as holy relics but were disregarded. Because these verses did not find favour with them, they did not propagate them, whereas they gave wide publicity to the other type of verses which were in consonance with their desires. In other words, they had made the Book of God subservient to their self-interest, instead of it being a means to encourage human beings to obey the commands of God.

There are two ways of finding a thing. One is to find its parts and the other is to find it in its totality. When a man recognises a tree in its totality, he says: 'This is a tree.' But if he does not recognise it in its totality, he will mention its trunk, branches, leaves, flowers and fruit. He will not be able to utter that one word, on uttering which different parts become rooted in one root and take the shape of one unit.

The same is true of God's Book. There are many different commandments in God's Book. At the same time it has its totality and its central point. Those who are engrossed in God's Book will find God's Book in its totality. ▶

⁹⁴ Proclaim openly what you are commanded, and avoid the polytheists. ⁹⁵ We will, surely, suffice you against those who mock, ⁹⁶ who set up another god with God, but they shall soon learn. ⁹⁷ We do indeed know how your heart is distressed at what they say. ⁹⁸ But glorify your Lord with His praise, and prostrate yourself: ⁹⁹ and worship your Lord until what is certain [death] comes to you.^a

فَٱصْدَعْ بِمَا تُؤْمَرُ وَأَعْرِضْ عَنِ ٱلْمُشْرِكِينَ ۝ إِنَّا كَفَيْنَاكَ ٱلْمُسْتَهْزِئِينَ ۝ ٱلَّذِينَ يَجْعَلُونَ مَعَ ٱللَّهِ إِلَـٰهًا ءَاخَرَ فَسَوْفَ يَعْلَمُونَ ۝ وَلَقَدْ نَعْلَمُ أَنَّكَ يَضِيقُ صَدْرُكَ بِمَا يَقُولُونَ ۝ فَسَبِّحْ بِحَمْدِ رَبِّكَ وَكُن مِّنَ ٱلسَّـٰجِدِينَ ۝ وَٱعْبُدْ رَبَّكَ حَتَّىٰ يَأْتِيَكَ ٱلْيَقِينُ ۝

On the contrary, when those who are engrossed in themselves see God's Book, it appears to them only as a collection of miscellaneous commandments. From these they pick and choose a part which suits their taste and condition and start laying stress upon it, as if only that was what mattered most.

When the roots of a tree are watered, the water reaches all of their parts. Similarly, if the central aspect of God's Book is revivified, the moment this happens, all the remaining parts come necessarily to life. As opposed to this, if some parts are selected to the exclusion of all others and much emphasis is laid on them, there can be a great deal of outward fanfare about this, but the real revival of religion does not take place, because its core features have been ignored. And the revival can take place only by reviving its central point.

^a In the present world, every man has been given the liberty to say or do as he likes. So, when the preacher starts urging his hearers to bow to God, many meaningless points are raised. People bring up different types of irrelevant issues to confuse the preacher (*da'i*). On such occasions, it is necessary, for the preacher to turn away without taking any notice. If, on such occasions, he starts picking quarrels with people, he will not be able in any positive way to perform the tasks relating to his divine call of Truth.

There is only one positive way for the preacher of Truth to follow and that is not to become involved with the mischief makers, but to announce in full detail the Truth as revealed to him. He should entrust to God every matter for which he himself has not enough strength to tackle. When the unfavourable conditions of the world trouble him, he should divert his attention towards the Hereafter. When the heedlessness of human beings annoys him, he should occupy himself with the remembrance of God.

The way of a true preacher of God's word, when he is overcome by woeful conditions, is to devote himself body and soul to God. Whatever he cannot get from human beings, he tries to obtain from God. He derives satisfaction or consolation from standing before God in prayer (*salat*). The burden on his heart is lightened by the shedding of tears. By engaging himself in whispers with God, he feels that he has gained whatever he wanted to gain.

16. BEES

In the name of God,
the Most Gracious, the Most Merciful

¹ The decree of God is at hand, so do not seek to hasten it. Holy is He, and exalted far above what they associate with Him. ² He sends down the angels with revelations by His command to whoever of His servants He pleases, saying, 'Warn mankind that there is no god save Me, so fear Me.' ³ He created the heavens and the earth for a true purpose. He is exalted above anything they associate with Him.*

---

a The reality of religion is that man should apprehend the Being of God and His workmanship in the universe so intensely and realistically that the Being of the one God should become everything for him; man should fear only Him and on Him alone, should he build up his hopes. The one God should be the entire focus of his heart and mind.

This is what constitutes the act of making God the object of worship (*ilah*) and amounts to praying to Him. All the prophets came into the world in order to bring about this condition. Those who prove to have this sense of submission to God will be treated as successful on Judgement Day, but those who go against this will be left without hope. For the general people, this decision will be taken on Doomsday (Judgement Day), but for the addressees of the prophet, it starts in this world itself.

There is perfect unity in the universe and at the same time, there also is perfect meaningfulness. Unity in the universe makes it unwarranted for anyone to make somebody other than the one God the centre of his attention. And it is the natural consequence of its meaningfulness that it should meet a meaningful end. In this way, the system governing the universe provides arguments in favour of both the unity of God (*tawhid*) and the existence of the Hereafter.

⁴ He created man out of a [mere] drop of sperm: yet he shows himself to be openly contentious! ⁵ He has created cattle for you: from them you derive food and clothing and numerous other benefits; ⁶ how pleasant they look when you bring them home in the evenings and when you take them out to pasture in the mornings. ⁷ They carry your loads to places which you could otherwise not reach without great hardship—surely, your Lord is compassionate and merciful—⁸ He has created horses, mules and donkeys, so that you may ride them, and also so that they may be put on show, and He creates other things beyond your knowledge.ᵃ

خَلَقَ ٱلْإِنسَـٰنَ مِن نُّطْفَةٍ فَإِذَا هُوَ خَصِيمٌ مُّبِينٌ ۝ وَٱلْأَنْعَـٰمَ خَلَقَهَا لَكُمْ فِيهَا دِفْءٌ وَمَنَـٰفِعُ وَمِنْهَا تَأْكُلُونَ ۝ وَلَكُمْ فِيهَا جَمَالٌ حِينَ تُرِيحُونَ وَحِينَ تَسْرَحُونَ ۝ وَتَحْمِلُ أَثْقَالَكُمْ إِلَىٰ بَلَدٍ لَّمْ تَكُونُوا۟ بَـٰلِغِيهِ إِلَّا بِشِقِّ ٱلْأَنفُسِ إِنَّ رَبَّكُمْ لَرَءُوفٌ رَّحِيمٌ ۝ وَٱلْخَيْلَ وَٱلْبِغَالَ وَٱلْحَمِيرَ لِتَرْكَبُوهَا وَزِينَةً وَيَخْلُقُ مَا لَا تَعْلَمُونَ ۝

ᵃ Man's life begins from a humble fluid. But when man grows up, he tries to take a stand in opposition to God. If he were to keep in view the reality of his origin, he would never allow himself to become arrogant in this world.

Animals, in particular, cattle, are among the various bounties with which man has been blessed in the present world. These are just like living machines of nature that are engaged in catering to the various requirements of man. Cows consume grass and fodder and convert them into meat and milk for his consumption. Sheep produce wool on their bodies which is used for his clothing. The owner of these animals includes them in his assets and this enhances his prestige.

'He creates other things beyond your knowledge' refers to those benefits that are available through sources other than animals. A part of these other sources was available to man even in ancient times. Man has discovered the major part of it in modern times and, for instance, is utilizing machines in place of animals.

Man's innumerable worldly endowments have not been created by him but have been provided for him by God. This shows that the Creator of this world is a kind Creator. Thus it necessarily follows that man should be grateful to his Creator and discharge the obligations due to Him as his Benefactor.

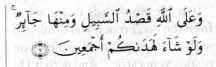

⁹ The straight way leads to God and there are ways which deviate from the right course. If He so wished, He would guide you all.ᵃ

ᵃ Generally, of the various highways the traveller has to choose from, there is a recognized route by which he can go straight to his destination. But, running parallel with, or connecting to each highway, there are always many lanes and by-ways. If the traveller chooses to drive along one of the latter, thinking he is on the right road, he will never reach his destination, but will stray many miles to the right or left of it.

The same is true of reaching God. God has already shown man which way will lead to Him. This is the way of the Unity of God (*tawhid*) and the fear of God (*taqwa*). One who follows this path will reach God and one who goes another way will be lost by the wayside; he will never be able to reach his Lord.

Everything in the world treads the path fixed by God. Had God so wished, man also would have been compelled to follow the path fixed by God. But the scheme of the creation of man is different from that of the creation of other things. Other things are required only to follow a regulatory discipline. But in the case of man, what is required is voluntary obedience to this discipline. The result of there being this opportunity to voluntarily submit to regulation is that while one person will take the right path, another will leave it and become lost on paths of his own devising.

¹⁰ It is He who sends down water from the sky. From it you drink and with it trees grow on which you pasture your cattle. ¹¹ And with it He grows for you corn, and the olive and the date-palm and the grape, and all kinds of fruits. Surely, in that is a sign for a people who reflect.^a

هُوَ ٱلَّذِىٓ أَنزَلَ مِنَ ٱلسَّمَآءِ مَآءً لَّكُم مِّنْهُ شَرَابٌ وَمِنْهُ شَجَرٌ فِيهِ تُسِيمُونَ ۞ يُنۢبِتُ لَكُم بِهِ ٱلزَّرْعَ وَٱلزَّيْتُونَ وَٱلنَّخِيلَ وَٱلْأَعْنَٰبَ وَمِن كُلِّ ٱلثَّمَرَٰتِ إِنَّ فِى ذَٰلِكَ لَءَايَةً لِّقَوْمٍ يَتَفَكَّرُونَ ۞

---

^a The clouds send down rain from the sky and, thanks to this, extremely fruitful results appear on the earth down below. This coordinated and harmonious action of 'heaven and earth' clearly proves that the God of earth is the same as that of heaven.

There is perfect harmony among the different parts of the universe. This harmony is definite proof of the fact that the Creator and Lord of the whole universe is only one. In the present structure of the universe, there is no scope for more than one God, and when the real Creator and Lord is one God, making any thing other than Him an object of worship will be absolutely indefensible.

¹² He has made the night and the day and the sun and the moon subservient to you; and all the stars are subservient to His command. Surely in this there are signs for men of understanding. ¹³ On the earth He has fashioned for you objects of various hues: there is certainly a sign in that for people who pay heed.^a

وَسَخَّرَ لَكُمُ ٱلَّيْلَ وَٱلنَّهَارَ وَٱلشَّمْسَ وَٱلْقَمَرَ وَٱلنُّجُومُ مُسَخَّرَٰتٌ بِأَمْرِهِۦٓ إِنَّ فِى ذَٰلِكَ لَءَايَٰتٍ لِّقَوْمٍ يَعْقِلُونَ ۝ وَمَا ذَرَأَ لَكُمْ فِى ٱلْأَرْضِ مُخْتَلِفًا أَلْوَٰنُهُۥٓ إِنَّ فِى ذَٰلِكَ لَءَايَةً لِّقَوْمٍ يَذَّكَّرُونَ ۝

---

^a The sun, the moon and the stars all revolve continuously in the vastness of space with total precision. On the earth, there are innumerable examples of God's creation (animals, vegetation, rocks and minerals, etc.). The former phenomenon highlights the totally submissive aspect of creation, (*musakhkharatun bi amrihi*), while the latter phenomenon highlights the endless variety of creation (*mukhtalifan alwanuhu*). The first scene reminds man of the limitlessness of God's power, while the second scene reminds him of the multiplicity of God's attributes.

These scenes are so wonderful that the keen-eyed observer cannot remain unaffected by them. In these things, he will see God's majesty and His role as Sustainer; he will discover unseen realities hidden in external occurrences; by looking at God's creations, he will be immersed in the realization of the Creator.

¹⁴ It is He who subjected to you the sea, so that you may eat its fresh seafood and bring forth from it ornaments to wear. You see the ships cleaving through it. All this, so that you may seek His bounty and feel grateful.ᵃ

وَهُوَ ٱلَّذِى سَخَّرَ ٱلْبَحْرَ لِتَأْكُلُوا۟ مِنْهُ لَحْمًا طَرِيًّا وَتَسْتَخْرِجُوا۟ مِنْهُ حِلْيَةً تَلْبَسُونَهَا وَتَرَى ٱلْفُلْكَ مَوَاخِرَ فِيهِ وَلِتَبْتَغُوا۟ مِن فَضْلِهِ وَلَعَلَّكُمْ تَشْكُرُونَ ۞

ᵃ If an iron bar is put into the sea, it will immediately sink to the bottom. But if the iron is moulded in the shape of a ship, it will start floating on the surface and will be capable of carrying heavy loads and going from one country to another.

This is a special law of God by means of which He has made as huge a creation as the sea subservient to man's interests. Similarly, by a wonderful under-sea arrangement, fresh food is provided in the shape of fish and, for the ornamentation of man, valuable pearls are formed in the oysters which live in the ocean.

As for the disposition of the world's natural features, God could have made various other arrangements. For example, there might have been no oceans or seas on the earth; or man could have been made capable of walking on the sea as he walks on land. But this was not God's way. His purpose was to create in man a feeling of gratefulness. Not being able to walk on the sea, when a man boards a boat or a ship, he experiences a sense of gratefulness; he thinks that since he is unable to traverse the sea with the help of his legs, God has been kind enough to make it traversable by means of a boat or a ship; he again thinks that since he is not able to fly in space, God has created such conditions as now permit him to fly at great speed in an aeroplane.

Such divine preferences have been built into the system of nature in order to awaken man's consciousness and to create in him feelings of gratefulness and obligation towards his Lord, the Sustainer.

¹⁵ He has set up on the earth firm mountains, lest it shake under you, and rivers and tracks, so that you may find your way, ¹⁶ and He has set up other landmarks. By these and by the stars people set their course.^a

وَأَلْقَىٰ فِى ٱلْأَرْضِ رَوَٰسِىَ أَن تَمِيدَ بِكُمْ وَأَنْهَٰرًا وَسُبُلًا لَّعَلَّكُمْ تَهْتَدُونَ ۞ وَعَلَٰمَٰتٍ وَبِٱلنَّجْمِ هُمْ يَهْتَدُونَ ۞

---

^a Here, two things are mentioned: maintenance of balance on the earth by raising mountains and the provision of signs to guide people on their way.

Geographical studies show that when the oceans were formed, the earth started shaking. Thereafter, high mountains emerged on the surface of the land, and in this way as a result of the two-phased action, balance was restored on the earth. Had there been no such balance on the surface of the earth, human life here would have been impossible, or at least extremely difficult.

Similarly, on his travels, the human being needs signs with the help of which he can make out the correct direction and reach his destination without going astray; here too the perfect arrangement is in existence. The human being of ancient times used to find his way with the help of such things as rivers and the stars. Nowadays, he finds his way with the help of magnetic instruments. Speedy flights on land and water as well as in space are possible with their help. Had signs of such a type not been in existence, human activities would have remained confined to a very limited sphere.

¹⁷ Is He, then, who creates like him who does not create? Will you not, then, take heed? ¹⁸ If you tried to count God's blessings, you would never be able to number them. God is ever forgiving and most merciful. ¹⁹ God knows all that you conceal and all that you reveal.^a

أَفَمَن يَخْلُقُ كَمَن لَّا يَخْلُقُ ۗ أَفَلَا تَذَكَّرُونَ ۝ وَإِن تَعُدُّوا نِعْمَةَ ٱللَّهِ لَا تُحْصُوهَآ ۗ إِنَّ ٱللَّهَ لَغَفُورٌ رَّحِيمٌ ۝ وَٱللَّهُ يَعْلَمُ مَا تُسِرُّونَ وَمَا تُعْلِنُونَ ۝

^a Whatever things there are in the world, none of them has the power of creating (i.e. bringing non-existent things into existence). It stands proved therefore that this world is not its own creator. Only that being can be its creator who has the inherent power in Him to bring a thing into existence which does not already exist. Therefore the belief in one God is absolutely natural. There can be no rational explanation of the universe without accepting the existence of God who possesses the perfect capability to create.

Whatever partner-gods the polytheists have concocted or whatever things the atheists have tried to establish as substitutes for God—none of them has its own inherent capability to create anything. This, in itself, is enough to prove that all gods concocted by people are absolutely imaginary, because it is absolutely baseless to claim that one who has no power of creativity in him/it, is the god of a universe which has been created. How can one who has no substantial existence, give existence to other things?

The best that God can expect from His subjects is their gratefulness for His bounties. Though God's bounties far outweigh human gratitude, being above all that, He accepts a very little gratitude for His very great blessings. However, this gratitude should be genuine and not simply a kind of formal recitation of praises.

²⁰ Those you call on besides God cannot create anything. They are themselves created. ²¹ They are dead, not living; nor do they know when they will be raised to life. ²² Your God is the One God. As for those who do not believe in the Hereafter, their hearts refuse to admit the truth and they are arrogant. ²³ God surely knows what they conceal and what they reveal. He does not love the arrogant.ᵃ

وَٱلَّذِينَ يَدْعُونَ مِن دُونِ ٱللَّهِ لَا يَخْلُقُونَ شَيْئًا وَهُمْ يُخْلَقُونَ ۝ أَمْوَٰتٌ غَيْرُ أَحْيَآءٍ وَمَا يَشْعُرُونَ أَيَّانَ يُبْعَثُونَ ۝ إِلَٰهُكُمْ إِلَٰهٌ وَٰحِدٌ فَٱلَّذِينَ لَا يُؤْمِنُونَ بِٱلْءَاخِرَةِ قُلُوبُهُم مُّنكِرَةٌ وَهُم مُّسْتَكْبِرُونَ ۝ لَا جَرَمَ أَنَّ ٱللَّهَ يَعْلَمُ مَا يُسِرُّونَ وَمَا يُعْلِنُونَ إِنَّهُ لَا يُحِبُّ ٱلْمُسْتَكْبِرِينَ ۝

ᵃ As a matter of course, polytheists start worshipping their self-devised saints of previous generations, treating them as holy and close to God, though such worship is absolutely foolish. These great men lying dead in their graves, to whom people pray for the fulfilment of their needs, are themselves in the interim stage after death before Judgement Day. In fact, they do not even know when they will be raised from the dead, not to speak of their being able to help others.

'They are arrogant' does not mean that they are arrogant towards God. Who would have the courage to set himself up against the Creator of heaven and earth? In fact, this means that they are haughty towards God's messenger and not towards God Himself. The subject of God who sets out to be a preacher of the unity of God (*tawhid*) is lesser in status from the worldly point of view in comparison with his addressees. The addressee being a proponent of the traditional religion, would enjoy a high position in the scheme of things at the time, while the bringer of Truth, being the representative of the 'new religion', would be devoid of such status and position. From the material point of view he, therefore, appears to the addressees to be inferior to themselves. So they develop a superiority complex and ignore what he has to say, thinking that his word carries no weight.

This is a case of pride on the part of such people, but they present their case as if it were one of principles and ideology. But God very well knows the inner workings of people's minds and will treat them in accordance not with their mouthings but with what they really are as human beings.

²⁴ When they are asked, 'What is it that your Lord has sent down?' they say, 'Stories of the ancients.' ²⁵ Let them bear all their own burdens on Resurrection Day as well as some of the burdens of those whom they lead astray without any knowledge. How evil the load with which they shall be burdened! [a]

وَإِذَا قِيلَ لَهُم مَّاذَآ أَنزَلَ رَبُّكُمْ قَالُوٓاْ أَسَٰطِيرُ ٱلْأَوَّلِينَ ۝ لِيَحْمِلُوٓاْ أَوْزَارَهُمْ كَامِلَةً يَوْمَ ٱلْقِيَٰمَةِ وَمِنْ أَوْزَارِ ٱلَّذِينَ يُضِلُّونَهُم بِغَيْرِ عِلْمٍ أَلَا سَآءَ مَا يَزِرُونَ ۝

---

[a] It has been recorded in traditions that when the Prophet Muhammad declared his prophethood in Makkah, the news gradually spread and reached the other Arab tribes. Whenever they met the chiefs of Makkah, they used to ask their opinion about the man who had claimed to be a prophet. In reply to this, the chiefs of Makkah used to cast doubt upon his personality and his discourse. (*Tafsir al-Mazhari*).

One of the ways of doing this was to distort or twist whatever was said. For instance, there is some mention of prophets in the Quran. This they could have referred to as 'the history of previous prophets', but they called it 'the stories and tales of the ancient people'. Turning people away from the call of Truth or making them doubtful made them guilty of the worst crime in the eyes of God, because not only had they themselves gone astray, but they had become the means of misguiding others.

²⁶ Those who went before them also plotted. But God struck at the foundations of their building, and the roof fell down upon them from above. The punishment came upon them from where they did not expect. ²⁷ Then on the Day of Resurrection He will disgrace them, and say, 'Where are My partners for whose sake you opposed [My guidance]?' Those given knowledge will say, 'This Day humiliation and affliction will surely befall those who have been denying the truth.'^a

قَدْ مَكَرَ ٱلَّذِينَ مِن قَبْلِهِمْ فَأَتَى ٱللَّهُ بُنْيَٰنَهُم مِّنَ ٱلْقَوَاعِدِ فَخَرَّ عَلَيْهِمُ ٱلسَّقْفُ مِن فَوْقِهِمْ وَأَتَىٰهُمُ ٱلْعَذَابُ مِنْ حَيْثُ لَا يَشْعُرُونَ ۝ ثُمَّ يَوْمَ ٱلْقِيَٰمَةِ يُخْزِيهِمْ وَيَقُولُ أَيْنَ شُرَكَآءِىَ ٱلَّذِينَ كُنتُمْ تُشَٰقُّونَ فِيهِمْ قَالَ ٱلَّذِينَ أُوتُوا ٱلْعِلْمَ إِنَّ ٱلْخِزْىَ ٱلْيَوْمَ وَٱلسُّوٓءَ عَلَى ٱلْكَٰفِرِينَ ۝

^a When those who have attained a high status on a false basis, see the call for Truth gaining ground, they feel that their position is at risk. For the protection of their position, they adopt the strategy of spreading mischievous statements against the divine call in order to make people doubtful about it and desist from rallying to it.

But the devices of such people against the call for Truth are never successful. The basic structures on which the opponents of Truth rely prove to be so weak that their roof literally caves in on them. Sometimes it happens that an earthquake shakes their foundations and causes their buildings to fall down on them. Sometimes their companions leave them and join the ranks of the truth-followers, so that in losing their supporters, they are compelled to surrender to the call of Truth. This end, in its final and perfect form, will appear on Doomsday when those who denied the truth will see their eternal degradation and will be helpless in the face of it.

²⁸ Those whose lives the angels take while they are wronging their own souls will offer submission saying, 'We were not doing anything evil!' 'Indeed!' the angels will reply, 'God is aware of what you have been doing, ²⁹ so enter the gates of Hell. There you shall abide forever.' Evil indeed is the abode of the arrogant.ᵃ

ٱلَّذِينَ تَتَوَفَّىٰهُمُ ٱلْمَلَٰٓئِكَةُ ظَالِمِىٓ أَنفُسِهِمْ فَأَلْقَوُا۟ ٱلسَّلَمَ مَا كُنَّا نَعْمَلُ مِن سُوٓءٍ بَلَىٰٓ إِنَّ ٱللَّهَ عَلِيمٌۢ بِمَا كُنتُمْ تَعْمَلُونَ ۝ فَٱدْخُلُوٓا۟ أَبْوَٰبَ جَهَنَّمَ خَٰلِدِينَ فِيهَا فَلَبِئْسَ مَثْوَى ٱلْمُتَكَبِّرِينَ ۝

ᵃ Arrogance is the worst crime. God will pardon every wrongdoing of man, but He will not pardon arrogance.

Haughtiness expresses itself in two ways. One is that which commonly prevails among God's subjects. An individual, for example, finds himself better endowed with power, wealth, property and other goods as compared to others and so he starts behaving haughtily towards them.

The other more serious type of haughtiness is that which is directed against God's envoy, who works towards the general call of truth. The true servant of God responds to the call of God's religion. But those who have attained a high status on the basis of false religion feel that they are adversely affected by this call and that by the standards of true religion, their worth is severely diminished. So they flare up over this and ignore the preacher of Truth in their arrogance.

A man behaves haughtily with someone, because he thinks that the other person cannot harm him. But when the angels of death approach and reduce him to helplessness, he will then realise that he had not been dealing with a man but with God. One man can be stronger than another, but who can be stronger than God? When God's angels take things under their control, then every man will surrender. But a true subject of God is one who surrenders to God before this.

³⁰ When those who fear God are asked, 'What has your Lord sent down?' Their reply is, 'Goodness!' The reward of those who do good works in this world is good, but the abode of the Hereafter is even better. The home of the righteous is indeed excellent. ³¹ They will enter Gardens of Eternity, where rivers will flow at their feet. There they will have all that they wish for. Thus God rewards the righteous, ³² those whose lives the angels take in a state of purity, saying [to them], 'Peace be on you; enter the Garden, because of [the good] which you did [in the world].' ᵃ

۞ وَقِيلَ لِلَّذِينَ ٱتَّقَوْا۟ مَاذَآ أَنزَلَ رَبُّكُمْ ۚ قَالُوا۟ خَيْرًا ۗ لِّلَّذِينَ أَحْسَنُوا۟ فِى هَٰذِهِ ٱلدُّنْيَا حَسَنَةٌ ۚ وَلَدَارُ ٱلْءَاخِرَةِ خَيْرٌ ۚ وَلَنِعْمَ دَارُ ٱلْمُتَّقِينَ ۝ جَنَّٰتُ عَدْنٍ يَدْخُلُونَهَا تَجْرِى مِن تَحْتِهَا ٱلْأَنْهَٰرُ ۖ لَهُمْ فِيهَا مَا يَشَآءُونَ ۚ كَذَٰلِكَ يَجْزِى ٱللَّهُ ٱلْمُتَّقِينَ ۝ ٱلَّذِينَ تَتَوَفَّىٰهُمُ ٱلْمَلَٰٓئِكَةُ طَيِّبِينَ ۙ يَقُولُونَ سَلَٰمٌ عَلَيْكُمُ ٱدْخُلُوا۟ ٱلْجَنَّةَ بِمَا كُنتُمْ تَعْمَلُونَ ۝

ᵃ When those who are of a haughty mentality hear any discourse about God, their minds start working in perverse ways and they are, therefore, unable to learn a lesson from it.

But one who fears God in his heart, will hear the discourse about God with full receptivity. For such a person, it becomes a source of spiritual realization; in it he sees glimpses of a higher reality.

One of the main features of paradise is that everything is available there that a man desires. There are things there which are not available in this world to anybody — not even to the greatest kings. In the present world, due to man's limitation and due to the unfavourable nature of external conditions, it never happens that man obtains whatever he wants. The concept that in paradise, man will find whatever he desires is of such allure that whatever sacrifice has to be made to enter paradise is negligible by comparison.

³³ Are they waiting for the angels to come to them, or the fulfillment of your Lord's will? Those who went before them did the same. God did not wrong them; rather they wronged themselves. ³⁴ The evil results of their deeds overtook them, and that which they used to mock at encompassed them.^a

³⁵ Those who associate [others with God] say, 'If God had so willed we would not have worshipped anything besides Him, neither we nor our fathers, nor would we have forbidden anything without His sanction.' So did those who went before them. The duty of the messengers is only to convey the message clearly.^b

هَلْ يَنظُرُونَ إِلَّا أَن تَأْتِيَهُمُ ٱلْمَلَـٰٓئِكَةُ أَوْ يَأْتِىَ أَمْرُ رَبِّكَ كَذَٰلِكَ فَعَلَ ٱلَّذِينَ مِن قَبْلِهِمْ وَمَا ظَلَمَهُمُ ٱللَّهُ وَلَـٰكِن كَانُوٓا۟ أَنفُسَهُمْ يَظْلِمُونَ ۝ فَأَصَابَهُمْ سَيِّـَٔاتُ مَا عَمِلُوا۟ وَحَاقَ بِهِم مَّا كَانُوا۟ بِهِۦ يَسْتَهْزِءُونَ ۝ وَقَالَ ٱلَّذِينَ أَشْرَكُوا۟ لَوْ شَآءَ ٱللَّهُ مَا عَبَدْنَا مِن دُونِهِۦ مِن شَىْءٍ نَّحْنُ وَلَآ ءَابَآؤُنَا وَلَا حَرَّمْنَا مِن دُونِهِۦ مِن شَىْءٍ كَذَٰلِكَ فَعَلَ ٱلَّذِينَ مِن قَبْلِهِمْ فَهَلْ عَلَى ٱلرُّسُلِ إِلَّا ٱلْبَلَـٰغُ ٱلْمُبِينُ ۝

^a Initially, arguments are used to explain the discourse about God. If man does not accept the Truth despite these arguments, a time will come when it is brought home to him—individually at the time of death and collectively on Doomsday.

If the facts about God are explained to a man rationally and he still ignores them, it is as if he is waiting for God and his angels to manifest themselves at some later stage. Then, of course, he would be compelled to accept the Truth. But accepting it at that time will gain him no credit, whereas if he had accepted it when he had the opportunity, prior to God's appearance, that would have been to his own great credit.

^b An unheeding person justifies his departure from the truth in various ways and one such way is to maintain that everything in this world happens according to the will and pleasure of God. In view of this, his present behaviour can be treated as a result of the will of God. He maintains that he would not have been able to do wrong if his misdeeds had not been backed by the will of God. He says that if his actions were not to God's liking, He would not have allowed him to continue those actions. In other words, it should have been the rule that whenever he did something against the will of God, He should have prevented him from doing it.

Man talks in this way because he is not serious about truth and untruth. Had he been serious, he would have immediately understood that the liberty of action pertains to the creation plan of God according to which man is being tested in this world. It has nothing to do with God's approval.

³⁶ We raised among every people a messenger who enjoined, 'Worship God alone and shun the evil one.' Then among them were some whom God guided and among them were others who became deserving of ruin. So travel across the earth and observe what was the end of those who rejected the messengers. ³⁷ Though you [Prophet] may be eager to guide them, God does not guide those whom He lets go astray, [because of their refusal to give a positive response to the truth]. They will have no supporters.ᵃ

وَلَقَدْ بَعَثْنَا فِى كُلِّ أُمَّةٍ رَّسُولاً أَنِ ٱعْبُدُواْ ٱللَّهَ وَٱجْتَنِبُواْ ٱلطَّٰغُوتَ ۖ فَمِنْهُم مَّنْ هَدَى ٱللَّهُ وَمِنْهُم مَّنْ حَقَّتْ عَلَيْهِ ٱلضَّلَٰلَةُ ۚ فَسِيرُواْ فِى ٱلْأَرْضِ فَٱنظُرُواْ كَيْفَ كَانَ عَٰقِبَةُ ٱلْمُكَذِّبِينَ ۞ إِن تَحْرِصْ عَلَىٰ هُدَىٰهُمْ فَإِنَّ ٱللَّهَ لَا يَهْدِى مَن يُضِلُّ ۖ وَمَا لَهُم مِّن نَّٰصِرِينَ ۞

ᵃ At some points God sent his prophets directly to mankind and at other points He arranged to convey His message indirectly through the deputies of prophets and their representatives. All of them advised man that God alone is entitled to be worshipped and prayed to. Satan tries to dissuade or divert man from such worship and prayer. Therefore, man should save himself from satanic inducements; otherwise he will be pushed into worshipping false gods. Though divine guidance is clear, its acceptance or rejection depends upon the extent of man's seriousness about it.

One who gives serious consideration to guidance will not take long to find the truth. But one who is not serious about it will remain enmeshed in trivial issues. Such a person can never find the Truth.

³⁸ They swear their strongest oaths by God that God will never raise the dead to life—nonetheless, it is a promise truly binding on Him, even though most people do not realize it—³⁹ this is so that He may make clear to them what they have differed about and so that those who are bent on denying the truth may realize that they were lying. ⁴⁰ When We will something to happen, all that We say is, 'Be!' and it is.ᵃ

وَأَقْسَمُواْ بِٱللَّهِ جَهْدَ أَيْمَٰنِهِمْ لَا يَبْعَثُ ٱللَّهُ مَن يَمُوتُ بَلَىٰ وَعْدًا عَلَيْهِ حَقًّا وَلَٰكِنَّ أَكْثَرَ ٱلنَّاسِ لَا يَعْلَمُونَ ۝ لِيُبَيِّنَ لَهُمُ ٱلَّذِى يَخْتَلِفُونَ فِيهِ وَلِيَعْلَمَ ٱلَّذِينَ كَفَرُوٓاْ أَنَّهُمْ كَانُواْ كَٰذِبِينَ ۝ إِنَّمَا قَوْلُنَا لِشَىْءٍ إِذَآ أَرَدْنَٰهُ أَن نَّقُولَ لَهُۥ كُن فَيَكُونُ ۝

ᵃ The present world is so constituted that Truth and untruth are not always clearly distinguishable from each other due to the trial of man. As such there is always scope for denial of the truth. Ways of contradicting valid arguments can always be found and some device or the other can be resorted to to cast doubt on established facts.

This is entirely against the scheme of the universe. In physical sciences it is possible to reach some definite results. Similarly, in respect of human beings, the truth should be brought out into the open. This proves the need for the Judgement Day to take place. Shah Abdul Qadir Dehlavi writes, 'In this world many things remained doubtful; some accepted God and some denied Him, so there must be another world where disputes are resolved; truth and falsehood are distinguished; and the accepter and the rejecter are rewarded according to their deeds.'

⁴¹ As for those who, after persecution, migrated from their homes for the cause of God, We will provide them with a goodly abode in this life: but truly the reward of the Hereafter will be greater, if they only knew it. ⁴² They are the ones who are steadfast and put their trust in their Lord.ᵃ

وَٱلَّذِينَ هَاجَرُواْ فِى ٱللَّهِ مِنۢ بَعْدِ مَا ظُلِمُواْ لَنُبَوِّئَنَّهُمْ فِى ٱلدُّنْيَا حَسَنَةً ۖ وَلَأَجْرُ ٱلْأَخِرَةِ أَكْبَرُ ۚ لَوْ كَانُواْ يَعْلَمُونَ ۝ ٱلَّذِينَ صَبَرُواْ وَعَلَىٰ رَبِّهِمْ يَتَوَكَّلُونَ ۝

ᵃ Most of the commentators of the Quran have held that this verse relates to the eighty companions of the Prophet who had become victims of persecution by opponents of Islam and finally migrated to Abyssinia (now called Ethiopia) leaving their native place. This event occurred in the Makkan period before the Hijrah (migration) to Madinah.

With regard to the Truth, there are always two groups—one group consists of those who undervalue Truth to such an extent that they are unwilling to sacrifice anything for its sake or re-plan their lives. The other group consists of those who adhere to the Truth in such a way that it becomes the most important thing for them, and they are willing to suffer all sorts of trouble for its sake; they make Truth their most important issue; they can sacrifice all else, but they cannot sacrifice the Truth.

Naturally, these two kinds of group cannot share the same fate. Those who gave Truth the most important place in their lives, will be treated as entitled to God's eternal bounties, but those who ignored the Truth will be ignored by God likewise; they will not be able to secure any place of honour in the eyes of God; neither can they have any share in God's bounties.

43 Before you also the messengers We sent were but [mortal] men to whom We vouchsafed revelation. Ask the People of the Book, if you do not know. 44 [We sent them] with clear signs and scriptures. We have sent down the Reminder to you, to enable you to make clear to mankind what has been sent down to them, so that they may reflect upon it.*a*

وَمَآ أَرْسَلْنَا مِن قَبْلِكَ إِلَّا رِجَالًا نُّوحِىٓ إِلَيْهِمْ ۚ فَسْـَٔلُوٓا۟ أَهْلَ ٱلذِّكْرِ إِن كُنتُمْ لَا تَعْلَمُونَ ﴿٤٣﴾ بِٱلْبَيِّنَٰتِ وَٱلزُّبُرِ ۗ وَأَنزَلْنَآ إِلَيْكَ ٱلذِّكْرَ لِتُبَيِّنَ لِلنَّاسِ مَا نُزِّلَ إِلَيْهِمْ وَلَعَلَّهُمْ يَتَفَكَّرُونَ ﴿٤٤﴾

a 'The People of the Book' (*ahl az-zikr*), i.e. those who have a knowledge of historical facts relating to past peoples and past prophets. What had to be ascertained from them was not about truth or untruth: they were to be asked about whether the prophets appearing in past ages were human beings or not. The fact that the Prophet Muhammad was a human being was treated by the people of Makkah as evidence of his not being the prophet of God. They were told to ascertain from the communities among whom prophets had been appearing (just as in the case of the Jews) whether the prophets who appeared among them were human beings or angels.

A prophet appears for the purpose of 'reminding'. This reminding is, in fact, done with the help of arguments. However, it is also necessary for the preacher to prove himself to be absolutely serious in this regard. If a man makes people aware of heaven and hell, but at the same time engages in such activities as prove him to be flippant about heaven and hell, his dawah efforts will become ridiculous in the eyes of the people.

However, even if the call of the preacher is of a high standard and is presented in a perfect manner, it will benefit only those who pay attention to it. Those who do not pay attention can never be benefited by the call of truth.

⁴⁵ Do those who devise evil plans feel secure that God will not make them sink into the land, or that a punishment will not come upon them from where they least expect? ⁴⁶ Or that He will not seize them suddenly in their daily activities and they will not be able to frustrate Him? ⁴⁷ Or that He will not punish them by giving them a fright? Indeed, your Lord is kind and merciful.ᵃ

أَفَأَمِنَ ٱلَّذِينَ مَكَرُواْ ٱلسَّيِّئَاتِ أَن يَخْسِفَ ٱللَّهُ بِهِمُ ٱلْأَرْضَ أَوْ يَأْتِيَهُمُ ٱلْعَذَابُ مِنْ حَيْثُ لَا يَشْعُرُونَ ۝ أَوْ يَأْخُذَهُمْ فِي تَقَلُّبِهِمْ فَمَا هُم بِمُعْجِزِينَ ۝ أَوْ يَأْخُذَهُمْ عَلَىٰ تَخَوُّفٍ فَإِنَّ رَبَّكُمْ لَرَءُوفٌ رَّحِيمٌ ۝

ᵃ This verse pertains to the last stage of the Makkan period when the opponents of the Prophet Muhammad were conspiring to kill him. The Prophet is God's representative on God's earth. Therefore, hatching such a conspiracy against a prophet must necessarily be the handiwork of such persons as are absolutely fearless of God's retribution.

The fact is that God is the Possessor of such control over man that He can cause him to be buried deep in the earth if He so desires, or He may wreak vengeance on him at the very place which he considers safe; or God may seize him in the course of his activities and he will not be able to save himself. God may even seize upon him when he is conscious of the risk and fully aware of the situation.

In short, God may seize upon man at any time and in any situation. If He sees people doing mischief, yet lets them go unpunished, they should not become fearless, because His restraint is due to His consideration of 'test' conditions and not to His being powerless.

⁴⁸ Have they not observed the things God has created, casting their shadows right and left, prostrating themselves before God in all humility? ⁴⁹ Everything in the heavens and all the creatures on the earth prostrate themselves before God, as do the angels, and they do not behave proudly: ⁵⁰ they fear their Lord above them, and do what they are commanded.^a

أَوَلَمْ يَرَوْاْ إِلَىٰ مَا خَلَقَ ٱللَّهُ مِن شَىْءٍ يَتَفَيَّؤُاْ ظِلَٰلُهُۥ عَنِ ٱلْيَمِينِ وَٱلشَّمَآئِلِ سُجَّدًا لِّلَّهِ وَهُمْ دَٰخِرُونَ ۝ وَلِلَّهِ يَسْجُدُ مَا فِى ٱلسَّمَٰوَٰتِ وَمَا فِى ٱلْأَرْضِ مِن دَآبَّةٍ وَٱلْمَلَٰٓئِكَةُ وَهُمْ لَا يَسْتَكْبِرُونَ ۝ يَخَافُونَ رَبَّهُم مِّن فَوْقِهِمْ وَيَفْعَلُونَ مَا يُؤْمَرُونَ ۝

---

^a Man indulges in arrogance in a world where all the things surrounding him are teaching him lessons in obedience. For example, the shadows of material things. The shadow of a thing standing erect falls on the ground. In this way, it symbolizes kneeling down (*sajdah*). It shows symbolically how a man should bow down before his Creator.

Though angels are not visible to man, the running of this immense universe in the most regulated manner proves that the agents appointed by God to run it are extremely powerful. These angels, in spite of being extraordinarily powerful, are totally obedient to God. If they were not so, the system of the universe would not function continuously with so much precision and uniformity.

In view of this, to be entirely correct in his behaviour, man can do no other than surrender himself to God, do obeisance to Him and become His most obedient subject.

⁵¹ God says, 'Do not take two gods. He is only One God. So fear Me alone.' ⁵² To Him belongs whatsoever is in the heavens and on the earth, and obedience is due to Him alone. Will you then fear anyone other than God?ᵃ

۞ وَقَالَ ٱللَّهُ لَا تَتَّخِذُوٓاْ إِلَٰهَيْنِ ٱثْنَيْنِ إِنَّمَا هُوَ إِلَٰهٌ وَٰحِدٌ فَإِيَّٰىَ فَٱرْهَبُونِ ۝ وَلَهُۥ مَا فِى ٱلسَّمَٰوَٰتِ وَٱلْأَرْضِ وَلَهُ ٱلدِّينُ وَاصِبًا أَفَغَيْرَ ٱللَّهِ تَتَّقُونَ ۝

ᵃ God has warned man through His prophets that he should not hold to any god except the one and only God. The God of this universe is only one. Man should fear only Him; he should be obedient to Him alone.

If a man fully realizes that it is God who is the sole Creator and Lord of all, and that his life completely depends upon Him, the feeling that develops in him as a result of this realization is fear of God (*taqwa*).

Eternal obedience is the due of God alone in this heaven and earth. Everything here is completely bound by divine law. In such a world, to pray to or to worship or to repose hope in anybody else is absolutely irrational. The present universe is such that it completely rejects polytheism or ascribing partners to God (*shirk*).

⁵³ Whatever blessing you have is from God, and to Him you turn for help when distress befalls you, ⁵⁴ yet no sooner does He relieve your distress than some among you set up other partners besides their Lord, ⁵⁵ showing no gratitude for what We have given them. Enjoy yourselves awhile; but soon you will know! ⁵⁶ They even appoint a share of what We have provided for them [to false gods] they know nothing of. You shall surely be questioned about the lies you have been fabricating.ᵃ

وَمَا بِكُم مِّن نِّعْمَةٍ فَمِنَ ٱللَّهِ ۖ ثُمَّ إِذَا مَسَّكُمُ ٱلضُّرُّ فَإِلَيْهِ تَجْـَٔرُونَ ۝ ثُمَّ إِذَا كَشَفَ ٱلضُّرَّ عَنكُمْ إِذَا فَرِيقٌ مِّنكُم بِرَبِّهِمْ يُشْرِكُونَ ۝ لِيَكْفُرُوا۟ بِمَآ ءَاتَيْنَٰهُمْ ۚ فَتَمَتَّعُوا۟ ۖ فَسَوْفَ تَعْلَمُونَ ۝ وَيَجْعَلُونَ لِمَا لَا يَعْلَمُونَ نَصِيبًا مِّمَّا رَزَقْنَٰهُمْ ۗ تَٱللَّهِ لَتُسْـَٔلُنَّ عَمَّا كُنتُمْ تَفْتَرُونَ ۝

ᵃ From time immemorial, whenever a man finds himself in such trouble that he is absolutely helpless, he starts remembering God. Even polytheists and others who deny the truth behave in this way. This shows that the concept of God is embedded in human nature. When man has no further recourse, he turns at last to God.

But strangely, man is so neglectful that when he is relieved of his trouble, he once again becomes preoccupied with the remembrance of his imaginary gods and attributes the benefit received by him to somebody other than God.

Satan has introduced different types of false rites among the general people in order to perpetuate and strengthen their belief that imaginary gods are worthy of worship. One of them is to set apart a share of their income for them. Such ceremonies are a sort of falsity in the world of God, because this amounts to giving thanks to entities other than God for the benefits received from Him.

⁵⁷ They assign daughters to God—glory be to Him!—but for themselves [sons] that they desire to have. ⁵⁸ When the birth of a girl is announced to any of them, his face darkens and he is filled with gloom. ⁵⁹ In his shame he hides himself away from his people, because of the bad news he has been given. Should he keep her and feel disgraced or bury her in the dust? How ill they judge! ⁶⁰ The attribute of evil applies to those who do not believe in the Hereafter, while to God applies the highest attribute, for He is Mighty, the Wise.ᵃ

وَيَجْعَلُونَ لِلَّهِ ٱلْبَنَـٰتِ سُبْحَـٰنَهُۥ وَلَهُم مَّا يَشْتَهُونَ ۝ وَإِذَا بُشِّرَ أَحَدُهُم بِٱلْأُنثَىٰ ظَلَّ وَجْهُهُۥ مُسْوَدًّا وَهُوَ كَظِيمٌ ۝ يَتَوَٰرَىٰ مِنَ ٱلْقَوْمِ مِن سُوءِ مَا بُشِّرَ بِهِۦٓ أَيُمْسِكُهُۥ عَلَىٰ هُونٍ أَمْ يَدُسُّهُۥ فِى ٱلتُّرَابِ أَلَا سَآءَ مَا يَحْكُمُونَ ۝ لِلَّذِينَ لَا يُؤْمِنُونَ بِٱلْأَخِرَةِ مَثَلُ ٱلسَّوْءِ وَلِلَّهِ ٱلْمَثَلُ ٱلْأَعْلَىٰ وَهُوَ ٱلْعَزِيزُ ٱلْحَكِيمُ ۝

ᵃ Why does a man want children? It is for the purpose of compensating for his shortcomings. But God is above such things. The Majesty and Power of God, which is evident in the existence of the universe, shows that God is far above any shortcomings to compensate which He would feel the necessity of creating a son or a daughter. The fact is that if God were deficient in any way, He would not have been God at all. God is God because He is entirely flawless.

⁶¹ If God were to take people to task for their wrongdoing, He would not leave even one living creature on earth, but He gives them respite till an appointed time: when their time comes they cannot delay it for an hour, nor can they bring it forward.^a

وَلَوْ يُؤَاخِذُ ٱللَّهُ ٱلنَّاسَ بِظُلْمِهِم مَّا تَرَكَ عَلَيْهَا مِن دَآبَّةٍ وَلَٰكِن يُؤَخِّرُهُمْ إِلَىٰٓ أَجَلٍ مُّسَمًّى فَإِذَا جَآءَ أَجَلُهُمْ لَا يَسْتَـْٔخِرُونَ سَاعَةً وَلَا يَسْتَقْدِمُونَ ۝

^a One way of dealing with transgression is immediately to seize upon the transgressor and punish him severely. But this is not the way of God. If God acted in this way, nobody would be left on the face of the earth. God has given a definite period of respite (*ila ajalim musamma*) to every person and every community. During this period God gives man the opportunity to listen to the voice of his conscience or to an external warning and to reform himself. This applies likewise to communities. As soon as people reform themselves, all their past crimes are pardoned: it is as if they had started a new life. Just as God has taken it upon Himself not to seize upon anybody during the period of respite, He has similarly taken it upon Himself after the expiry of this period to necessarily seize upon people. After that no individual or community will be given any further opportunity for reform or repentance.

⁶²They attribute to God what they themselves dislike and their tongues utter the lie that all good things are for themselves. Without doubt, the Fire awaits them, and they shall be hastened on into it.ᵃ

وَيَجْعَلُونَ لِلَّهِ مَا يَكْرَهُونَ وَتَصِفُ أَلْسِنَتُهُمُ ٱلْكَذِبَ أَنَّ لَهُمُ ٱلْحُسْنَىٰ لَا جَرَمَ أَنَّ لَهُمُ ٱلنَّارَ وَأَنَّهُم مُّفْرَطُونَ

ᵃ The main reason for man's going astray is his underestimation of God, Lord of the Universe. Many wrong beliefs have come into existence because God was judged to be a lesser entity than He really is.

It is the result of such underestimation of God that people, though believing in God, remain fearless of Him. They form the belief about very ordinary things that these will be a source of proximity to God and that all the bounties of the Hereafter will be allotted to them as their share. The belief is entertained that a thing which does not make even an ordinary man happy, will please God. This amounts to adding arrogance to wrongdoing, which can never be pardoned by God.

63 By God! We have sent messengers before you to other nations. But Satan made their [foul] deeds seem fair to them and today he is their patron. They shall have a painful punishment. 64 We have only sent down the Book to you so that you can make clear to them that concerning which they differ, and as a guidance and a mercy to people who believe.*

تَٱللَّهِ لَقَدْ أَرْسَلْنَآ إِلَىٰٓ أُمَمٍ مِّن قَبْلِكَ فَزَيَّنَ لَهُمُ ٱلشَّيْطَـٰنُ أَعْمَـٰلَهُمْ فَهُوَ وَلِيُّهُمُ ٱلْيَوْمَ وَلَهُمْ عَذَابٌ أَلِيمٌ ﴿٦٣﴾ وَمَآ أَنزَلْنَا عَلَيْكَ ٱلْكِتَـٰبَ إِلَّا لِتُبَيِّنَ لَهُمُ ٱلَّذِى ٱخْتَلَفُوا۟ فِيهِ ۙ وَهُدًى وَرَحْمَةً لِّقَوْمٍ يُؤْمِنُونَ ﴿٦٤﴾

---

a When God's messenger calls for the truth, his addressees feel that his call is clashing with their traditional religion. Now, since they are familiar with this traditional religion and since many of their interests are attached to this religion, they want to continue to adhere to it. At the same time Satan furnishes them with beautiful words by which they can prove that rejecting the Prophet's religion and adhering to their traditional religion is justified.

If a man accepts the word of the prophet in a straightforward manner, this amounts to making God his companion. On the contrary, if he takes the help of beautiful interpretations, to reject it, this amounts to making a friend of Satan.

By sending the last of the prophets, God has arranged for people to find the true divine path amidst the jungle of religious differences. This situation prevails even today. If a person is in search of the way of God and for this purpose he studies the different religions, he will definitely become confused, as the teachings of other religions, in the form they exist today, have serious differences among themselves. The seeker of Truth is therefore unable to understand what he should treat as correct or incorrect.

This being so, the religion brought by the last of the prophets is a blessing for the subjects of God, because unlike other religions, his religion is the 'preserved' one. From the point of view of history, it is completely authentic. It can, therefore, be taken for granted that the religion brought by the Prophet is, in reality, the religion which God desires his subjects to adopt.

⁶⁵ God sends down water from the sky and with it revives the earth when it is dead. There is truly a sign in this for people who listen.ᵃ

وَٱللَّهُ أَنزَلَ مِنَ ٱلسَّمَآءِ مَآءً فَأَحْيَا بِهِ ٱلْأَرْضَ بَعْدَ مَوْتِهَآ إِنَّ فِي ذَٰلِكَ لَأٓيَةً لِّقَوْمٍ يَسْمَعُونَ ۝

ᵃ The system of rains and vegetation has a great lesson in it. Due to the concerted action of various factors, water vapours rise in the air and form clouds and again fall on the earth in the form of rain. Then this rain causes the growth of lush green cover on the earth.

In this happening, there is firstly a lesson that, in this universe everywhere, the activism or workmanship of the one God is manifest. Had many gods been active here, there could not have been such wonderful coordination in the various forces of the universe that could result in such a unified harmonious process. The unity in the system of the universe is a clear proof of the fact that its Creator and its Lord is only one and not more than one.

Secondly, there is the lesson that the power and majesty of God are so great that they can revivify a dead body; cause the growth of a lush green garden, and produce colour, fragrance and taste in dry and barren things.

There is proof of unity in the first occurrence and the second one shows symbolically that for human souls also, there is similar godly 'rain', and that is 'revelation'. One who wants to give a new life to his dead and dry soul, should have himself drenched in the rain of godly revelation.

[66] There is also a lesson for you in cattle. From the contents of their bellies, from between the dung and blood, We give you pure milk to drink, pleasant for those who drink it.[a] [67] From the fruit of the date palm and the grapes you derive intoxicants as well as wholesome food. Surely in this there is a sign for men of understanding.[b]

وَإِنَّ لَكُمْ فِى ٱلْأَنْعَٰمِ لَعِبْرَةً ۖ نُّسْقِيكُم مِّمَّا فِى بُطُونِهِۦ مِنۢ بَيْنِ فَرْثٍ وَدَمٍ لَّبَنًا خَالِصًا سَآئِغًا لِّلشَّٰرِبِينَ ۝ وَمِن ثَمَرَٰتِ ٱلنَّخِيلِ وَٱلْأَعْنَٰبِ تَتَّخِذُونَ مِنْهُ سَكَرًا وَرِزْقًا حَسَنًا ۗ إِنَّ فِى ذَٰلِكَ لَءَايَةً لِّقَوْمٍ يَعْقِلُونَ ۝

---

[a] A characteristic peculiar to milch animals is that whatever they eat is converted into dung and blood yet there emerges along with these a liquid, milk, which is the most valuable food for man. This is also true of the trees. Mud, water and other such things enter them and under the influence of their internal system, they take the shape of juicy fruits which hang from the branches.

These occurrences are meant to remind people of God. Through them man should start seeing glimpses of His Majesty. This realization should be so intense that he should spontaneously exclaim, 'Oh God! You cause milk to come out from non-milk. God, let favourable results emerge from the unfavourable situations I am faced with. God, you transform mud and water into fruits, please turn my valueless life into a valuable one.'

[b] This gives a hint that the things created by God in this world can be used rightly as well as wrongly. Dates and grapes, if eaten in their natural forms, provide healthy and wholesome food, which give energy to the body and mind. But if through some human process, they are converted into intoxicants, they become harmful to the body and mind.

⁶⁸ Your Lord inspired the bee, saying, 'Make your homes in the mountains, in the trees, and also in the structures which men erect. ⁶⁹ Then feed on every kind of fruit, and follow the trodden paths of your Lord.' From its belly comes a drink with different colours which provides healing for mankind. Indeed, in this there is a sign for people who give thought.^a

وَأَوْحَىٰ رَبُّكَ إِلَى ٱلنَّحْلِ أَنِ ٱتَّخِذِى مِنَ ٱلْجِبَالِ بُيُوتًا وَمِنَ ٱلشَّجَرِ وَمِمَّا يَعْرِشُونَ ۝ ثُمَّ كُلِى مِن كُلِّ ٱلثَّمَرَٰتِ فَٱسْلُكِى سُبُلَ رَبِّكِ ذُلُلًا ۚ يَخْرُجُ مِنْ بُطُونِهَا شَرَابٌ مُّخْتَلِفٌ أَلْوَٰنُهُ فِيهِ شِفَآءٌ لِّلنَّاسِ ۗ إِنَّ فِى ذَٰلِكَ لَآيَةً لِّقَوْمٍ يَتَفَكَّرُونَ ۝

---

^a The honey-bee is the most wonderful masterpiece of God's creation. It constructs its beehive to a standard pattern, strictly following the relevant mathematical principles. Then, in the best planned manner, sucks the nectar from the flowers, brings it back and, in a perfectly systematic manner, stores it in the hive. Then, in accordance with hygienic principles prepares honey, which serves as a valuable food as well as a remedy for human ailments. All this takes place in such an amazingly regulated manner that voluminous books have been written on it and still the description is not complete.

The miraculous honey factory is more complicated than all the human factories and at the same time is more successful. It is run by bees who have not received any training in this technology. They are not even conscious of their own actions. This proves that there is a Being who is having this work done through the bees by giving them instructions. Anyone who observes the bees, will have a live example of God's workmanship and will see a glimpse of God in their wonderfully meaningful activities.

There is another aspect of the example of the bees given here. The bee works very hard to suck the nectar from flowers and to prepare honey which is a health-giving food for human beings. In the same manner, the servant of God should acquire wisdom from the universe by giving it deep consideration after intense observation of it, and such pieces of wisdom as he picks up should be spiritual food for him as well as a panacea for all his moral ailments. The things which are 'nectar' for the bees becomes intense realization (*ma'rifah*) at the level of human beings.

70 God created you; then He shall cause you to die: and some shall have their lives prolonged to abject old age, ceasing to know anything after once having had knowledge. God is all knowing and powerful.^a

71 God has given some of you more provision than others. Those who have been given more are unwilling to pass their provision to the servants they possess so that they become their equals. Will they then deny the favour of God?^b

وَٱللَّهُ خَلَقَكُمْ ثُمَّ يَتَوَفَّىٰكُمْ وَمِنكُم مَّن يُرَدُّ إِلَىٰٓ أَرْذَلِ ٱلْعُمُرِ لِكَىْ لَا يَعْلَمَ بَعْدَ عِلْمٍ شَيْـًٔا إِنَّ ٱللَّهَ عَلِيمٌ قَدِيرٌ ۝ وَٱللَّهُ فَضَّلَ بَعْضَكُمْ عَلَىٰ بَعْضٍ فِى ٱلرِّزْقِ فَمَا ٱلَّذِينَ فُضِّلُوا۟ بِرَآدِّى رِزْقِهِمْ عَلَىٰ مَا مَلَكَتْ أَيْمَٰنُهُمْ فَهُمْ فِيهِ سَوَآءٌ أَفَبِنِعْمَةِ ٱللَّهِ يَجْحَدُونَ ۝

^a Life as it manifests itself on the earth presents many aspects—one who was non-existent comes into being in the world; then everybody dies, but not at one time. Somebody dies in childhood and another in youth and yet another in old age. Then it is a very strange occurrence that at the last stage of his life, a man loses his mental powers, his knowledge and his physical strength completely. Man is apparently free in the present world. But he has no control over any aspect of his life.

All this happens to show man that perfect knowledge and power belong only to God. Man has no say in the above-mentioned type of events that occur in a man's life: he is not capable of bringing about any change in them. This proves that whatever is happening is happening at the instance of some other being; man's life as a whole, right from childhood up to his death, bears testimony to the fact that here all knowledge belongs to God and all power rests with God—man's helplessness is the proof of the all-powerful existence of God.

^b With the help of a simple analogy here, the belief that God has some partners and that these so-called partners have been given some powers has been shown to be wrong. In this world the division of material assets is not uniform. It is generally seen that one person has a great deal while another has so little that he is compelled to be the servant or slave of one who has plenty. Now an affluent person does not distribute his wealth among his servants in order to remove the difference between him and them. So, by analogy, it is not correct to believe that God has distributed His powers among others.

Nobody denies his own greatness. Then how can God want to do something which even a man would not like to do? The fact is that a man has no possessions of his own, while the possessions of God are His own and not gifted by others. The fact is that all such beliefs are inconsistent with the image of God!

72 God has given you wives from among yourselves, and given you children and grandchildren from your wives, and provided wholesome things for you. Will they then believe in falsehood and deny God's favours? 73 They worship, instead of God, things that have no control over their provision from the heavens or the earth in any way, nor do they have any power [to do so]. 74 Do not compare God with anyone. God has knowledge, but you have not.ᵃ

وَٱللَّهُ جَعَلَ لَكُم مِّنْ أَنفُسِكُمْ أَزْوَٰجًا وَجَعَلَ لَكُم مِّنْ أَزْوَٰجِكُم بَنِينَ وَحَفَدَةً وَرَزَقَكُم مِّنَ ٱلطَّيِّبَٰتِ أَفَبِٱلْبَٰطِلِ يُؤْمِنُونَ وَبِنِعْمَتِ ٱللَّهِ هُمْ يَكْفُرُونَ ۝ وَيَعْبُدُونَ مِن دُونِ ٱللَّهِ مَا لَا يَمْلِكُ لَهُمْ رِزْقًا مِّنَ ٱلسَّمَٰوَٰتِ وَٱلْأَرْضِ شَيْئًا وَلَا يَسْتَطِيعُونَ ۝ فَلَا تَضْرِبُوا۟ لِلَّهِ ٱلْأَمْثَالَ إِنَّ ٱللَّهَ يَعْلَمُ وَأَنتُمْ لَا تَعْلَمُونَ ۝

ᵃ The human being is a creature who has countless needs and the perfect arrangement to fulfill all these needs exists in this world.

All this is provided by God, but in every age human beings have made the mistake of attributing all these blessings of God to some entities other than God. Polytheists attribute these blessings to gods or goddesses or to some living or dead beings other than God. Those who are atheists attribute them to the result of the blind activity of natural laws. This system of Divine blessing was brought into existence by God in order to ensure that a feeling of gratitude emerged in human beings. But due to man's self-devised imaginings, this system nourished in him the feeling of disbelief in God.

Generally, misguidance in belief has occurred due to false parallels being drawn. Since man has sons and daughters, it has been assumed on the same basis that God also has sons and daughters. In this world, people of high position have some individuals who are close to them and who enjoy the position of intermediaries. On the basis of this example it has been assumed that, even in the court of God, there are beings who are close to Him and that their recommendations are effective in His eyes.

Many types of polytheism (shirk) and misguidance have come into existence through reference to such analogies. But this amounts to placing the Creator on a par with that of His creatures, which shows absolute ignorance. The Creator is different from His creatures in every way. Explaining something with the help of an example is not wrong in itself. But the example will be useful only when there is an awareness of the original as well as its analogy. When man does not know the reality of God, how can he formulate an analogy with any true relevance to it?

⁷⁵ God makes a comparison between an owned slave possessing no power over anything, and someone to whom We have given plentiful provision, who gives out from it privately and openly. Are they equal? Praise be to God! But most people do not know it.ᵃ

۞ ضَرَبَ ٱللَّهُ مَثَلًا عَبْدًا مَّمْلُوكًا لَّا يَقْدِرُ عَلَىٰ شَىْءٍ وَمَن رَّزَقْنَٰهُ مِنَّا رِزْقًا حَسَنًا فَهُوَ يُنفِقُ مِنْهُ سِرًّا وَجَهْرًا هَلْ يَسْتَوُۥنَ ٱلْحَمْدُ لِلَّهِ بَلْ أَكْثَرُهُمْ لَا يَعْلَمُونَ ۝

ᵃ Here, a simple and common example has been given to clarify the incorrectness of polytheistic analogies. Take the individual who has considerable property and compare him with another who has no possessions whatsoever. These two individuals are perforce very different in their outlook and style of living. So any analogy drawn about the one would not apply to the other. In the case of God and His subject, this difference is of infinite magnitude. This being so, how can it be possible for an analogy to be drawn for God on the basis of the human condition? In this universe, the relation between God and all other things is that of a Creator and His creatures, and not that of God and His partners. The Being of God is that Entity who is endowed with all kinds of miraculous attributes; He is the sole provider of all kinds of bounties. In this universe there is no joint performer with God. To make such an assumption is unrealistic and runs counter to the facts.

76 God makes another comparison between two men, one of whom is dumb and cannot do a thing, and is a burden on his master. Wherever he sends him on an errand, he brings [him] no good. Is he equal to someone who commands justice and is on a straight path? *a*

وَضَرَبَ ٱللَّهُ مَثَلًا رَّجُلَيْنِ أَحَدُهُمَآ أَبْكَمُ لَا يَقْدِرُ عَلَىٰ شَىْءٍ وَهُوَ كَلٌّ عَلَىٰ مَوْلَٰهُ أَيْنَمَا يُوَجِّههُّ لَا يَأْتِ بِخَيْرٍ هَلْ يَسْتَوِى هُوَ وَمَن يَأْمُرُ بِٱلْعَدْلِ وَهُوَ عَلَىٰ صِرَٰطٍ مُّسْتَقِيمٍ ۩

---

a In the foregoing verse, No. 75, it was shown that the concept of partners in relation to God was baseless. Now in this verse No. 76, it is clarified that also in relation to the Prophet, those beings on the strength of whom a man ignores the guidance of the Prophet, are also without any basis in reality.

God, by giving His special attention to a prophet, guides him towards a path which is the highway of Truth and which directly leads towards Himself. The Prophet and his companions not only tread this highway themselves but also guide others towards it. Unlike them, there are others who beckon people towards ways other than the ways of the Prophet. They are like blind and deaf people. They do not have ears to hear the voice of God. They do not have eyes to catch glimpses of God's glories. They do not have the heart and mind to discover the signs of God spread throughout the universe.

Man was granted the ability to hear, observe and realize by means of the heart and mind, so that he should see the Glory of God, the Creator, through the medium of created things. But man has utilized these capacities in such a way that he has become obsessed with the creatures themselves.

805

⁷⁷ God alone has knowledge of the hidden reality of the heavens and the earth; and the coming of the Hour [of Judgement] is like the twinkling of an eye, or even quicker. Surely God has full power over everything.ᵃ

⁷⁸ God brought you forth from the wombs of your mothers while you knew nothing, and gave you hearing and sight and hearts, so that you might be grateful.ᵇ

وَلِلَّهِ غَيْبُ ٱلسَّمَوَٰتِ وَٱلْأَرْضِ وَمَآ أَمْرُ ٱلسَّاعَةِ إِلَّا كَلَمْحِ ٱلْبَصَرِ أَوْ هُوَ أَقْرَبُ إِنَّ ٱللَّهَ عَلَىٰ كُلِّ شَيْءٍ قَدِيرٌ ۝ وَٱللَّهُ أَخْرَجَكُم مِّنۢ بُطُونِ أُمَّهَٰتِكُمْ لَا تَعْلَمُونَ شَيْـًٔا وَجَعَلَ لَكُمُ ٱلسَّمْعَ وَٱلْأَبْصَٰرَ وَٱلْأَفْـِٔدَةَ لَعَلَّكُمْ تَشْكُرُونَ ۝

ᵃ Immanent in the outward visible world, there is an unseen system. This unseen system was established by God. Due to our limitations, we do not see this unseen system; but everything about us is open and obvious to this unseen system. Remaining unseen, God is keeping a watchful eye on every big and small thing of His world. He has the most accurate assessment of everything. When God decides that the period of man's trial is over, at that very moment He will just make a sign, and then, in the twinkling of an eye, the whole existing system will break down, and a new, differently based system will come into existence, so that everyone may be placed in the position in which he belongs in actual fact and not in the position he had occupied by underhand means.

ᵇ When a human being is born, he is already the possessor of eyes, ears, and a brain, yet he is quite helpless and totally dependent on others. He might possibly—under a different scheme of things—have been born with the ability to use his wonderful faculties of seeing, hearing and thinking in the way that an adult would. But if things did not happen in this way, it was by design. Man was meant to experience his own helplessness as a baby and then to appreciate his mental and physical growth through adolescence to maturity as a gift from God. This process was meant to engender in him feelings of gratitude and a deep sense of obligation to his Maker.

But such feelings emerge only when a man utilizes his God-given capacities in the right manner. His eyes, ears and heart should not be so attracted to worldly, ephemeral glamour that these may stop one from penetrating the realms of the unseen.

⁷⁹ Do they not see the birds held poised in the vault of heaven? Nothing holds them up except God. Truly, there are signs in this for those who believe. ⁸⁰ God has made your houses places of rest for you and made tents for you out of cattle hides, which are light for you to carry, both when you are travelling and when you are staying in one place. He provides for you from the wool and fur and hair of cattle, household goods and articles for use for a time.ᵃ

أَلَمْ يَرَوْا إِلَى ٱلطَّيْرِ مُسَخَّرَٰتٍ فِى جَوِّ ٱلسَّمَاءِ مَا يُمْسِكُهُنَّ إِلَّا ٱللَّهُ إِنَّ فِى ذَٰلِكَ لَآيَٰتٍ لِّقَوْمٍ يُؤْمِنُونَ ۝ وَٱللَّهُ جَعَلَ لَكُم مِّنۢ بُيُوتِكُمْ سَكَنًا وَجَعَلَ لَكُم مِّن جُلُودِ ٱلْأَنْعَٰمِ بُيُوتًا تَسْتَخِفُّونَهَا يَوْمَ ظَعْنِكُمْ وَيَوْمَ إِقَامَتِكُمْ وَمِنْ أَصْوَافِهَا وَأَوْبَارِهَا وَأَشْعَارِهَا أَثَٰثًا وَمَتَٰعًا إِلَىٰ حِينٍ ۝

ᵃ The flight of birds in the atmosphere is possible thanks to the magnificent planning of nature. (The shape of birds, most suitable for the purpose of flight, is imitated in the shape of aeroplanes). Just as ships could not have sailed without the existence of water on the surface of the earth, birds would not have been able to fly if there had not been the superior arrangment of continuously maintaining air on the earth's surface by means of the earth's gravity.

If man reflects deeply upon these phenomena, he will feel as if he is seeing God in action in His universe; he will discover the Creator in the creative system; he will see the glory of the Manufacturer in the artefacts.

At the human level, take the house. The house is a shelter and a resting place for man. But how is a house built? There are many arrangements of God—thanks to which the construction of a house on earth is possible. All the elements by means of which a house is built have been placed in advance in our world. The earth has exactly the right gravitational force, thanks to which houses stay stable on the surface of the earth—otherwise they would have flown away from the earth, which is moving at a speed of one thousand miles per hour. Then there are things like the hides of animals from which man makes tents and basic crops such as cotton and flax from which fabrics can be made to decorate and protect the human body in the changing seasons.

All such things are provided so that man should develop a deep feeling gratitude for his Lord and Sustainer; and for the bounties granted by Him, he should fall down on his knees before God in the full realization of His Majesty and Powers.

81 God has granted you shade out of what He has created, places of shelter in the mountains, garments with which to protect yourselves from the heat and coats of mail to shield you in battle. Thus He completes His favour to you, so that you may submit wholly to Him.[a] 82 But if they turn away, you are responsible only for conveying the message clearly. 83 They recognize the favour of God, yet they deny it; and most of them are ungrateful.[b]

وَٱللَّهُ جَعَلَ لَكُم مِّمَّا خَلَقَ ظِلَـٰلًا وَجَعَلَ لَكُم مِّنَ ٱلْجِبَالِ أَكْنَـٰنًا وَجَعَلَ لَكُمْ سَرَٰبِيلَ تَقِيكُمُ ٱلْحَرَّ وَسَرَٰبِيلَ تَقِيكُم بَأْسَكُمْ ۚ كَذَٰلِكَ يُتِمُّ نِعْمَتَهُۥ عَلَيْكُمْ لَعَلَّكُمْ تُسْلِمُونَ ۝ فَإِن تَوَلَّوْا۟ فَإِنَّمَا عَلَيْكَ ٱلْبَلَـٰغُ ٱلْمُبِينُ ۝ يَعْرِفُونَ نِعْمَتَ ٱللَّهِ ثُمَّ يُنكِرُونَهَا وَأَكْثَرُهُمُ ٱلْكَـٰفِرُونَ ۝

---

[a] The importance of the shade of a roof or trees can be imagined when a man finds himself in a desert where there is no shade of any kind. The result of the sun's heat being so well regulated is that an ordinary barrier gives us comfortable shade. Had the sun's heat been more than at present, which is quite possible, our shaded dwellings would have become burning hot ovens. There being caves in hard rocks where man can make his dwellings and there being such materials in the world which, made into thin fibres provide clothes for the protection of man's body, are very important factors for a creature like a human being, so much so that if they had not been available, there would have been no human beings and no human civilization on the earth.

This realization develops two kinds of feelings in man—firstly, the feeling of obligation towards God, because He is the one who has given to man such valuable bounties and, secondly, a feeling of fear, because if God were to take away these bounties, man would have no other recourse. If such feelings awaken man's inner self to such an extent that he spontaneously kneels down before his Lord, then this is indeed true worship (la'allakum tuslimun).

[b] One who studies the universe, whether he be a common man or a scientist, always experiences a few moments when, while pondering over God's creations, his mind is diverted towards the Creator. He starts feeling that these wonderful things have neither come into existence of their own accord, nor have they been made by so-called gods; their Creator is none other than Almighty God.

But acceptance of God necessarily demands a change in man's own life. It takes away a man's freedom. So, when he undergoes this experience, after being temporarily affected, he directs his mind elsewhere. After finding God, he leaves Him.

⁸⁴ On the Day when We raise up a witness from every people, those who were bent on denying the truth will not be permitted to put forward excuses, or to make amends. ⁸⁵ When the wrongdoers face their punishment, it shall not be lightened for them, nor shall they be granted any reprieve.^a

وَيَوْمَ نَبْعَثُ مِن كُلِّ أُمَّةٍ شَهِيدًا ثُمَّ لَا يُؤْذَنُ لِلَّذِينَ كَفَرُوا۟ وَلَا هُمْ يُسْتَعْتَبُونَ ۞ وَإِذَا رَءَا ٱلَّذِينَ ظَلَمُوا۟ ٱلْعَذَابَ فَلَا يُخَفَّفُ عَنْهُمْ وَلَا هُمْ يُنظَرُونَ ۞

---

^a The coming of prophets and prophets' followers as preachers of the Truth to communities and nations would seem to be an ordinary event. The world has treated these events as being so insignificant that, excepting the last of the prophets (the Prophet Muhammad), there is no prophet whose work has been treated as worthy of mention in contemporary histories.

But their task assumes great importance and seriousness when it is seen linked with the Hereafter. In the majestic court of the Hereafter, these very prophets and bearers of the Truth will be testifiers on behalf of God and, on the strength of their testimony, the eternal future of people will be decided. Those who, according to the testifiers, accepted the Truth and surrendered themselves in submission to it will be treated as people of paradise in the eternal world there; and those who, according to these Godly testifiers, rejected the Truth and were not willing to submit to it, will be consigned to eternal hell.

If in a community or nation, true envoys of God make their appearance and that community does not accept their word, then it is a definite proof of that community's being blameworthy. Thereafter that community loses the right to plead that they were not aware of Judgement Day, Paradise and Hell and that, as such, they should be saved from the punishment of Judgement Day.

⁸⁶ When those who associate partners with God see their associate gods, they will say, 'Our Lord, these are our associate gods whom we used to call upon instead of You.' But they will throw back their words at them, [saying], 'Indeed you are liars,' ⁸⁷ and on that Day they will offer total submission to God: and all that they used to devise will fail them. ⁸⁸ Upon all who were bent on denying the truth and who turned others away from the path of God, We will heap punishment upon punishment, in return for all the corruption that they brought about.^a

وَإِذَا رَءَا ٱلَّذِينَ أَشْرَكُوا۟ شُرَكَآءَهُمْ قَالُوا۟ رَبَّنَا هَٰٓؤُلَآءِ شُرَكَآؤُنَا ٱلَّذِينَ كُنَّا نَدْعُوا۟ مِن دُونِكَ فَأَلْقَوْا۟ إِلَيْهِمُ ٱلْقَوْلَ إِنَّكُمْ لَكَٰذِبُونَ ۝ وَأَلْقَوْا۟ إِلَى ٱللَّهِ يَوْمَئِذٍ ٱلسَّلَمَ وَضَلَّ عَنْهُم مَّا كَانُوا۟ يَفْتَرُونَ ۝ ٱلَّذِينَ كَفَرُوا۟ وَصَدُّوا۟ عَن سَبِيلِ ٱللَّهِ زِدْنَٰهُمْ عَذَابًا فَوْقَ ٱلْعَذَابِ بِمَا كَانُوا۟ يُفْسِدُونَ ۝

---

^a On Judgement Day this fact will finally be clear that nobody in this universe has any power except the One and Only God. At that time, when the worshippers of false gods see the gods whom they worshipped, they will make excuses to try to prove their innocence. In other words, they will represent these false gods as having deceived them and made them worship non-gods. But the false gods will immediately contradict this and will say, 'This was your own arrogance. In order to avoid obedience to God, you yourself devised false gods and in their names you "proved" your self-loving religion to be legitimate.'

There are some who do not accept the call of Truth, and there are others who, further to this, try by various methods to prevent others from doing so. The first type of behaviour results from being misguided, while the second type is that of deliberate misguidance. The punishment given to misguided people will be doubled in the case of those who knowingly misguided others.

89 The Day will come when We raise up in every people a witness against them from amongst themselves, and We will bring you as a witness against these people. We have sent down the Book to you to make everything clear, a guidance, and a mercy, and glad tidings for those who submit to God.[a]

وَيَوْمَ نَبْعَثُ فِى كُلِّ أُمَّةٍ شَهِيدًا عَلَيْهِم مِّنْ أَنفُسِهِمْ ۖ وَجِئْنَا بِكَ شَهِيدًا عَلَىٰ هَٰؤُلَآءِ ۚ وَنَزَّلْنَا عَلَيْكَ ٱلْكِتَٰبَ تِبْيَٰنًا لِّكُلِّ شَىْءٍ وَهُدًى وَرَحْمَةً وَبُشْرَىٰ لِلْمُسْلِمِينَ ۝

---

[a] It is the way of Almighty God that He entrusts the task of delivering warnings and of giving good news to a community through an individual selected from that very community. This is why the prophets who came to various communities were members of those communities. Now the Muslim community is required to fulfil the responsibilities of calling for the Truth and of testifying in every community till the Day of Judgement.

The preachers of the various communities of this world will in the Hereafter be God's witnesses or testifiers of those communities. It will be on the basis of their testimony that decisions will be made regarding the reward or punishment to be given to all individuals of the community.

There are descriptions in the Quran of all matters of major moral and practical importance. Indeed, every revealed book which has come to mankind on behalf of God has contained such descriptions. However, the main focus is not on worldly knowledge, but on success or failure in the Hereafter. This is true of the Quran, which lays down broad principles covering the entire range of conduct which will lead to success in the Hereafter. (Neglect of these principles will lead to failure.) Those who are guided by them will merit divine blessings, while those who neglect them will only give grounds for their own destruction.

⁹⁰ God commands justice, kindness and giving their [due to] near relatives, and He forbids all shameful deeds, and injustice and transgression. He admonishes you so that you may take heed! [a]

۞ إِنَّ ٱللَّهَ يَأْمُرُ بِٱلْعَدْلِ وَٱلْإِحْسَٰنِ وَإِيتَآيِٕ ذِى ٱلْقُرْبَىٰ وَيَنْهَىٰ عَنِ ٱلْفَحْشَآءِ وَٱلْمُنكَرِ وَٱلْبَغْىِ ۚ يَعِظُكُمْ لَعَلَّكُمْ تَذَكَّرُونَ ۝

---

[a] How a subject of God should live in the world has been clearly described in this verse. In view of its importance, Caliph 'Umar ibn 'Abdul 'Aziz included this verse in the weekly sermon.

The first thing an individual must ensure is that justice ('adal) is done. This means that whatever right one person has over another should be fully discharged, be the claimant weak or strong. In the fulfillment of rights, only the nature of the right will be considered and not any other factors.

The next thing is showing consideration (ihsan). This means that while honouring rights, one should be broadminded. Human consideration should be added to the demands of justice. One should exhibit generosity and sympathy beyond the legal requirement. Man should have the courage as far as possible to reconcile with whatever is rightfully due to him and try to give to others more than is rightfully their due.

The third thing is 'giving their due to near relatives' (wa i'ta zil qurba). This means that just as a man becomes anxious when he sees his wife and children in need and fulfills that need, he should be similarly sensitive about the needs of others who are close to him. No well-to-do person should behave as if only he himself and the members of his household are entitled to his property: he should also include in his responsibilities the fulfillment of the rights of his relatives.

After this three things have been prohibited in this verse.

The first thing is moral evil (fahsha') which is clearly judged to be such by the human conscience and universally considered shameful.

The second is the perpetration of such deeds as are judged improper by common moral standards. This includes all those things which are considered as evil by man and which man's nature refuses to accept. Munkar is the opposite of ma'ruf. Ma'ruf consists of such things as are considered good in every society.

The third thing is transgressing all limits (baghi). This includes arrogance when a man exceeds his recognized limit and attacks another person; his engaging in sinful behaviour in order to harm another's life, property and honour; his making use of his strength and influence to gain an illegitimate advantage.

⁹¹ Fulfill the covenant of God when you have made one; and do not break your pledges after their confirmation. Indeed you have made God your surety; for God knows all that you do. ⁹² Do not, like the woman who unravels her yarn after its strands have been firmly spun, use your oaths as a means of deceiving one another, just because one community could become bigger than another. God is only testing you by means of this. On the Day of Resurrection He will make it clear to you what you differed about.^a

وَأَوْفُوا بِعَهْدِ اللَّهِ إِذَا عَهَدتُّمْ وَلَا تَنقُضُوا الْأَيْمَنَ بَعْدَ تَوْكِيدِهَا وَقَدْ جَعَلْتُمُ اللَّهَ عَلَيْكُمْ كَفِيلًا إِنَّ اللَّهَ يَعْلَمُ مَا تَفْعَلُونَ ۞ وَلَا تَكُونُوا كَالَّتِي نَقَضَتْ غَزْلَهَا مِنْ بَعْدِ قُوَّةٍ أَنكَٰثًا تَتَّخِذُونَ أَيْمَنَكُمْ دَخَلًا بَيْنَكُمْ أَن تَكُونَ أُمَّةٌ هِيَ أَرْبَىٰ مِنْ أُمَّةٍ إِنَّمَا يَبْلُوكُمُ اللَّهُ بِهِۦ وَلَيُبَيِّنَنَّ لَكُمْ يَوْمَ الْقِيَٰمَةِ مَا كُنتُمْ فِيهِ تَخْتَلِفُونَ ۞

---

^a The spinning of cotton involves the hard work of combining separate fibres so that articles useful to man may be woven from it. If someone spins cotton, working hard the whole day, but in the evening tears the spun thread to pieces, then the entire hard work will go waste. The same is true of those who enter into a mutual agreement and one or the other party breaks it without any valid reason. Shredding the cotton thread after spinning it amounts to wasting one's labour. Similarly, the breaking of an executed agreement nullifies the whole process by which a matter of mutual unity had come into existence.

In the present world a man spends his life along with other human beings. Every man has to do his work among many other men. For this reason, great importance is given to mutual confidence and trust. In order to maintain this collective social life, agreements and decisions between one man and another man are frequently entered into, sometimes by oath and sometimes without an oath. Now, if people start breaking such agreements without any real justification, social life will be greatly disturbed and constructive development of any kind will no longer be possible.

There are two ways of making an agreement in the name of God. In one case a pledge is made formally, uttering the words of the oath. In the second case the words of the oath are not uttered, but reference to God in some form is included in the agreement executed. In all such cases the undertakers of oaths are as if making God the witness or surety in the matter. The breaking of an agreement in which the name of God is also included is much more serious, because this shows that it is only when a man needs to win the confidence of others that he makes use of God's name, but when he is overcome by the requirements of his own interests, he ignores God. ▶

⁹³ Had God pleased, He would have united you in one community; but He lets go astray whoever He will, and guides whoever He will, and you will surely be called upon to account for all your actions.ᵃ

وَلَوْ شَاءَ ٱللَّهُ لَجَعَلَكُمْ أُمَّةً وَٰحِدَةً وَلَٰكِن يُضِلُّ مَن يَشَآءُ وَيَهْدِى مَن يَشَآءُ وَلَتُسْـَٔلُنَّ عَمَّا كُنتُمْ تَعْمَلُونَ ۞

There are two types of agreements between individuals or communities—one is based on principles, and the other is based on interest. In ancient times, the position was that whenever there appeared to be any advantage in making such an agreement, it was executed, but whenever it seemed beneficial to break it, it was broken. Things are no different today. As opposed to this, Islam requires that agreements should be subject to the principles of Islamic law and morality.

ᵃ There are unfathomable aspects of this world. Truth and untruth are not separate and distinct. The reason for this is to be found in the plan of God by which He created this world, a plan designed to ascertain the true moral fibre of each and every individual on this earth. Indeed, man has been brought into this present world for the purpose of being tested. This purpose would not have been served had man not been given the freedom to accept or reject God's word. He had to have the freedom to show truth to be untruth and to present untruth in the shape of truth. If God had not had this in view, he would have subjected all human beings to His orders, just as He did with the rest of the universe.

This state of affairs will be perpetuated till the Day of Judgement. On the Day of Judgement it will be clear as to who used his judgement correctly, and who ignored the Truth for the sake of self-interest. At that time God will mete out to each individual such treatment as will be commensurate with his or her performance during the period of trial in the present world.

94 Do not use your oaths to deceive each other lest any foot should slip after being firmly placed and lest you should taste the penalty for having hindered others from the path of God, for then you will have a terrible punishment. 95 Do not sell God's covenant for a paltry price. What is with God is better for you if you only knew.[a]

وَلَا تَتَّخِذُوٓاْ أَيْمَٰنَكُمْ دَخَلَۢا بَيْنَكُمْ فَتَزِلَّ قَدَمٌۢ بَعْدَ ثُبُوتِهَا وَتَذُوقُواْ ٱلسُّوٓءَ بِمَا صَدَدتُّمْ عَن سَبِيلِ ٱللَّهِ ۖ وَلَكُمْ عَذَابٌ عَظِيمٌ ۝ وَلَا تَشْتَرُواْ بِعَهْدِ ٱللَّهِ ثَمَنًا قَلِيلًا ۚ إِنَّمَا عِندَ ٱللَّهِ هُوَ خَيْرٌ لَّكُمْ إِن كُنتُمْ تَعْلَمُونَ ۝

[a] Executing an agreement on oath is the final shape of a firm agreement. From this point of view, all agreements are covered by this verse.

If Muslims enter into transactions involving agreements with others and thereafter, without any real reason and only for the sake of self-interest, break them, this will result in destroying the moral credibility of Muslims in general. This will create an atmosphere such as will discourage others from adopting the way of God. Ibn Kathir writes that when a rejecter of Islam sees that a Muslim has entered into an agreement, but goes against it, he will have no faith in the religion of Islam and will abstain from embracing the religion of God.

The act of breaking an agreement against the principles of Islamic law inevitably occurs when one partner to it sees that he will receive certain worldly benefits by doing so. But a believer's view is Hereafter-oriented. Whenever it is the self which makes a move to break the agreement, the person concerned curbs his self by saying that there may be some worldly benefit in breaking it, but he will gain no advantage thereby in the Hereafter. And the advantage of the Hereafter is definitely greater than any worldly benefit.

96 What you have shall pass away, but what is with God is lasting. We will certainly give those who are patient their reward according to the best of their actions. 97 To whoever does good deeds, man or woman, and is a believer, We shall assuredly give a good life; and We will bestow upon them their reward according to the best of their works.[a]

مَا عِندَكُمۡ يَنفَدُ وَمَا عِندَ ٱللَّهِ بَاقٍ وَلَنَجۡزِيَنَّ ٱلَّذِينَ صَبَرُوٓاْ أَجۡرَهُم بِأَحۡسَنِ مَا كَانُواْ يَعۡمَلُونَ ﴿٩٦﴾ مَنۡ عَمِلَ صَٰلِحًا مِّن ذَكَرٍ أَوۡ أُنثَىٰ وَهُوَ مُؤۡمِنٌ فَلَنُحۡيِيَنَّهُۥ حَيَوٰةً طَيِّبَةً وَلَنَجۡزِيَنَّهُمۡ أَجۡرَهُم بِأَحۡسَنِ مَا كَانُواْ يَعۡمَلُونَ ﴿٩٧﴾

---

[a] Supporting a messenger of God amounts to renouncing the customary religious system and becoming attached to a non-customary religion. This type of action is always most difficult for man. This involves ignoring the benefit to be received from human beings and proceeding towards the benefit which will be given by God.

The only virtue which is required if this type of decision is to be taken is 'patience'; that is, a man should be able to bear today's loss for the sake of tomorrow's benefit; he should have the ability to give more importance to a thing which is unseen in comparison to that which is seen; he should have the urge to adopt something at the cost of sacrifice, even if it means forfeiting some immediate benefit. The subjects of God who prove to have such high ideals deserve to be blessed by God with the highest type of bounties.

Those who support unadulterated pure Truth suffer a loss in the current system, so people think that such individuals are ruined. But there is a promise from God that He will fully compensate them for their sacrifices. In the eternal world after death, He will bless them with an extremely good life. Whatever they have lost temporarily will be restored by God in a better form and forever.

This promise of God applies equally to women. Before God in the matter of rewards, there is no distinction between men and women.

⁹⁸ When you read the Quran, seek God's protection from Satan, the rejected one. ⁹⁹ Surely, he has no power over those who believe and put their trust in their Lord; ¹⁰⁰ he has power only over those who are willing to follow him and associate others with God.ᵃ

فَإِذَا قَرَأْتَ ٱلْقُرْءَانَ فَٱسْتَعِذْ بِٱللَّهِ مِنَ ٱلشَّيْطَٰنِ ٱلرَّجِيمِ ۝ إِنَّهُ لَيْسَ لَهُ سُلْطَٰنٌ عَلَى ٱلَّذِينَ ءَامَنُوا۟ وَعَلَىٰ رَبِّهِمْ يَتَوَكَّلُونَ ۝ إِنَّمَا سُلْطَٰنُهُ عَلَى ٱلَّذِينَ يَتَوَلَّوْنَهُ وَٱلَّذِينَ هُم بِهِۦ مُشْرِكُونَ ۝

ᵃ There are two objectives in reading the Quran—one is for the guidance of the self and the other is to present it to others to encourage them to understand the Truth. Whether the actual words of the Quran are repeated or its meanings are explained, man should in any case seek the protection of God against Satan. It does not mean simply repeating some fixed words; it means consciously arming oneself so that Satan's attack becomes ineffective.

Satan is always lying in wait for man. He changes the meaning of the words of the Quran in the mind of the reader, and what cannot be included in the text he inserts in the commentary. In this way Satan raises controversial issues between the preacher and the addressee, as a result of which understanding the true meaning of the Quran becomes difficult.

However, God has given liberty to Satan only to misguide and instigate. He has not given power to him to lead anyone astray by force (laysa lahu sultan). His actions have no effect on those who have maintained their mental connection with God. But those who are neglectful of God and pay attention to the word of Satan become subject to Satan, who leads them towards his evil path.

101 When We substitute one revelation for another—and God knows best what He reveals—they say, 'You are but a fabricator.' Indeed, most of them have no knowledge. 102 Say, 'The Holy Spirit has brought it down as truth from your Lord, so that He may strengthen those who believe, and also as guidance and as good tidings for those who submit.' *a*

وَإِذَا بَدَّلْنَآ ءَايَةً مَّكَانَ ءَايَةٍ وَٱللَّهُ أَعْلَمُ بِمَا يُنَزِّلُ قَالُوٓاْ إِنَّمَآ أَنتَ مُفْتَرٍ بَلْ أَكْثَرُهُمْ لَا يَعْلَمُونَ ۝ قُلْ نَزَّلَهُۥ رُوحُ ٱلْقُدُسِ مِن رَّبِّكَ بِٱلْحَقِّ لِيُثَبِّتَ ٱلَّذِينَ ءَامَنُواْ وَهُدًى وَبُشْرَىٰ لِلْمُسْلِمِينَ ۝

a The Quran is the Book of dawah. Its various parts were revealed bit by bit over a period of twenty three years. In consideration of the training of the believers, a gradual approach was adopted in respect of certain commandments.

Taking advantage of such 'changes', the opponents of Islam used to say that the Quran was not the Book of God, but the Prophet Muhammad's own writings which he attributed to God. They used to say that, if it had come directly from God, there would not have been such changes in it.

Had these opponents been sincere and serious in the study of the Quran and had they looked upon the factor of change in the right perspective, they would have seen the wisdom of a gradual approach in giving orders. But when they saw the matter in the wrong perspective, changes appeared to them to be the result of a lack of human knowledge. A reasoned confirmation of these changes not being immediately forthcoming gave rise to the levelling of false allegations.

The Quran has been revealed to present the Truth—here Truth means the pure and unadulterated religion of God. Those who are seekers after Truth and who are not satisfied with adulterated religions, will find not only the answer to their search in the Quranic religion but also peace of mind therein.

¹⁰³ Indeed, We know what they say, 'It is only a human being who imparts [all] this to him!' But the tongue of him to whom they point is foreign, whereas this is plain Arabic speech. ¹⁰⁴ God will not guide those who will not believe in the signs of God; and theirs will be a painful punishment. ¹⁰⁵ Only those fabricate lies concerning God who do not believe in the signs of God, and these are the liars.^a

وَلَقَدْ نَعْلَمُ أَنَّهُمْ يَقُولُونَ إِنَّمَا يُعَلِّمُهُ بَشَرٌ لِسَانُ ٱلَّذِى يُلْحِدُونَ إِلَيْهِ أَعْجَمِىٌّ وَهَـٰذَا لِسَانٌ عَرَبِىٌّ مُّبِينٌ ۝ إِنَّ ٱلَّذِينَ لَا يُؤْمِنُونَ بِـَٔايَـٰتِ ٱللَّهِ لَا يَهْدِيهِمُ ٱللَّهُ وَلَهُمْ عَذَابٌ أَلِيمٌ ۝ إِنَّمَا يَفْتَرِى ٱلْكَذِبَ ٱلَّذِينَ لَا يُؤْمِنُونَ بِـَٔايَـٰتِ ٱللَّهِ وَأُوْلَـٰئِكَ هُمُ ٱلْكَـٰذِبُونَ ۝

---

^a In Makkah there were some non-Arab slaves. In various books of *tafsir* (commentary) their names have been given as Jabr, Yasar, 'A'ish, Ya'ish, etc. (there is some mention also of Salman al-Farsi who later became a Muslim). These slaves being either Jews or Christians were very knowledgeable about the ancient holy religions of Judaism and Christianity. From time to time they chanced to meet the Prophet Muhammad. On the basis of such meetings, the Chiefs of the Quraysh started saying, 'The non-Arabs tell Muhammad something and he presents it to the people, declaring it to be "divine discourse."'

Why was this ridiculous statement made by them? It was due to the same common wrong approach which is found in every period all over the world; i.e. the refusal to recognize the value of one who is one's own contemporary. The Prophet Muhammad was a contemporary personality for the Quraysh, and therefore, they failed to appreciate him.

This verse shows that those who feel nothing but contempt for their contemporaries can never be truly inspired to accept the Truth.

Instead of accepting the Truth, they fabricate false allegations against the messengers of the Truth; ignoring the greater facts, they seize upon irrelevant things amounting to hair-splitting in order to defame the preacher. They spend their entire lives in this way until the day of their death when they will be punished by God.

¹⁰⁶ As for one who denies God after he has believed, with the exception of one who is forced to do it, while his heart rests securely in faith, but one who opens his heart to a denial of truth shall incur the wrath of God; such as these will have a terrible punishment. ¹⁰⁷ This is because they prefer the life of this world to the Hereafter and because God does not guide those who deny the truth. ¹⁰⁸ These are the ones upon whose hearts and hearing and sight God has set a seal. It is they who are heedless, ¹⁰⁹ and in the life to come, they will surely be the losers.^a

مَن كَفَرَ بِٱللَّهِ مِنۢ بَعْدِ إِيمَٰنِهِۦٓ إِلَّا مَنْ أُكْرِهَ وَقَلْبُهُۥ مُطْمَئِنٌّۢ بِٱلْإِيمَٰنِ وَلَٰكِن مَّن شَرَحَ بِٱلْكُفْرِ صَدْرًا فَعَلَيْهِمْ غَضَبٌ مِّنَ ٱللَّهِ وَلَهُمْ عَذَابٌ عَظِيمٌ ۝ ذَٰلِكَ بِأَنَّهُمُ ٱسْتَحَبُّوا۟ ٱلْحَيَوٰةَ ٱلدُّنْيَا عَلَى ٱلْءَاخِرَةِ وَأَنَّ ٱللَّهَ لَا يَهْدِى ٱلْقَوْمَ ٱلْكَٰفِرِينَ ۝ أُو۟لَٰٓئِكَ ٱلَّذِينَ طَبَعَ ٱللَّهُ عَلَىٰ قُلُوبِهِمْ وَسَمْعِهِمْ وَأَبْصَٰرِهِمْ وَأُو۟لَٰٓئِكَ هُمُ ٱلْغَٰفِلُونَ ۝ لَا جَرَمَ أَنَّهُمْ فِى ٱلْءَاخِرَةِ هُمُ ٱلْخَٰسِرُونَ ۝

---

^a Before God, reality is what counts and not simply outward appearances. This is why liberal concessions have been made to man in Islam. If a person is truly loyal to God in his heart, but under serious compulsion and to save his own life he utters something against his faith, he will not be castigated for this by God. But those who have changed from the inside and who, under the influence of Satanic doubt or the pressure of circumstances, have willingly adopted some way other than God's way are not pardonable.

When an individual behaves faithlessly rather than as a man of faith, the reason for it is always worldliness. Looking to the salvaging of his worldly interests, he adopts the way of the unbeliever. Had he understood the value of the Hereafter, worldly interest would have appeared of so little worth to him that renouncing the Hereafter for the sake of the world would have seemed absurd.

If, in the eyes of any individual, worldly benefits appear to outweigh the gains of the Hereafter, the result is necessarily that he is not able to judge matters from the point of view of the Hereafter. He sees and hears, but due to his inclination toward the world, he loses sight of the various aspects of the Hereafter. He is only able to see those aspects which are connected with worldly considerations. Those who reach this stage of neglectfulness are fated to suffer eternal loss.

110 Surely, your Lord will be forgiving and merciful towards those who migrated after persecution and strove hard for the cause of God and remained steadfast. 111 On the Day each soul will come pleading for itself, and every soul will be repaid according to whatever it has done, and they will not be wronged.[a]

ثُمَّ إِنَّ رَبَّكَ لِلَّذِينَ هَاجَرُواْ مِنۢ بَعْدِ مَا فُتِنُواْ ثُمَّ جَٰهَدُواْ وَصَبَرُواْ إِنَّ رَبَّكَ مِنۢ بَعْدِهَا لَغَفُورٌ رَّحِيمٌ ۞ يَوْمَ تَأْتِى كُلُّ نَفْسٍ تُجَٰدِلُ عَن نَّفْسِهَا وَتُوَفَّىٰ كُلُّ نَفْسٍ مَّا عَمِلَتْ وَهُمْ لَا يُظْلَمُونَ ۞

---

[a] Whenever untruth dominates the current atmosphere, one who accepts the Truth faces severely trying circumstances: his surroundings force him to revert to the customary religion. Under these circumstances, if he remains steady in his adherence to the Truth and leaves everything (even his property and his native place), then he is a migrator (*muhajir*). One who strives and struggles (*mujahid*) for the cause of God, makes himself deserving of a huge reward.

What keeps a man steady on the path of Truth under the trying circumstances of the world is his remembrance of the Hereafter. Every man is soon going to face a Day so terrible that he will forget even his friends and relatives. At that time no one will be able to say anything on behalf of anybody, and no one will come forward in commendation of anybody. If a man fully realizes the meaning of that coming Day, he will be in a condition to bear any type of loss, but he will not abandon the Truth.

112 God makes an example of a town that was secure and at ease, with provisions coming to it abundantly from every quarter. Then it showed ingratitude for God's blessings and God afflicted it with hunger and fear because of what they did. 113 There came to them a messenger from among themselves, but they rejected him as false, so punishment overtook them, as they were wrongdoers.[a]

وَضَرَبَ ٱللَّهُ مَثَلًا قَرْيَةً كَانَتْ ءَامِنَةً مُّطْمَئِنَّةً يَأْتِيهَا رِزْقُهَا رَغَدًا مِّن كُلِّ مَكَانٍ فَكَفَرَتْ بِأَنْعُمِ ٱللَّهِ فَأَذَاقَهَا ٱللَّهُ لِبَاسَ ٱلْجُوعِ وَٱلْخَوْفِ بِمَا كَانُوا۟ يَصْنَعُونَ ۝ وَلَقَدْ جَآءَهُمْ رَسُولٌ مِّنْهُمْ فَكَذَّبُوهُ فَأَخَذَهُمُ ٱلْعَذَابُ وَهُمْ ظَٰلِمُونَ

[a] If a settlement of human beings is in a good condition and is well provided for, God raises one of His subjects from among them, who calls them to the Truth. Under these circumstances, either these people accept the truth and become deserving of more blessings from God, or they do not do so and then they are subjected to different types of affliction. These afflictions are not a punishment from God, but God's warnings. Their purpose is to awaken the people so that their sensitivity becomes keener and they become willing to give a positive response to the call of the preacher of truth.

If such warnings are not effective, then after the conclusion of the dayee's work the second stage comes: the destruction of that community. This is so that after reaching the world of the Hereafter, they face eternal punishment for their rejection of God's messenger.

¹¹⁴ So eat the lawful and good things which God has provided for you, and be thankful for the blessing of God, if it is Him you worship. ¹¹⁵ He has forbidden you only carrion, blood and the flesh of swine; also any [flesh] consecrated in the name of any but God. But if anyone is forced by dire necessity, not desiring it or exceeding his immediate need, God is forgiving and merciful towards him.ᵃ

فَكُلُوا۟ مِمَّا رَزَقَكُمُ ٱللَّهُ حَلَٰلًا طَيِّبًا وَٱشْكُرُوا۟ نِعْمَتَ ٱللَّهِ إِن كُنتُمْ إِيَّاهُ تَعْبُدُونَ ۝ إِنَّمَا حَرَّمَ عَلَيْكُمُ ٱلْمَيْتَةَ وَٱلدَّمَ وَلَحْمَ ٱلْخِنزِيرِ وَمَآ أُهِلَّ لِغَيْرِ ٱللَّهِ بِهِۦ فَمَنِ ٱضْطُرَّ غَيْرَ بَاغٍ وَلَا عَادٍ فَإِنَّ ٱللَّهَ غَفُورٌ رَّحِيمٌ ۝

ᵃ This verse relates to things which are eaten from day to day out of the eatable things created by God. All things are permissible (halal) with just a few exceptions. However, the ancient polytheists prohibited for themselves many things which were permissible. On the contrary, atheists have treated many things prohibited by God as being permissible for themselves. Both these approaches negate the spirit, which is intended to be developed in man through the bounties of food.

Food is the most important of all man's needs. It is a need which is experienced morning and evening. God desires that, whenever a man uses food, he should eat it considering it as a gift from God and he should be grateful to Him for it. But man has reversed the whole matter.

In the ancient polytheistic period, they attributed these foods to false gods and in this way made it the means of remembering false gods instead of the one and only God. In the atheistic modern period, man having made the whole matter subject to his personal tastes, those things prohibited by God have been treated as permissible by him. This has resulted in the things created by God becoming mere foodstuffs to cater to his tastes at the dining table.

If, under compulsion, anyone goes against the law of God regarding food, he should do it with a sense of shame and not with arrogance. In that way his mentality will be uncorrupted.

¹¹⁶ Do not falsely declare, 'This is lawful, and this is forbidden,' so as to invent a lie against God. Surely, those who invent a lie against God do not prosper—¹¹⁷ their enjoyment of this life is brief, and they shall have a painful punishment.^a

وَلَا تَقُولُوا لِمَا تَصِفُ أَلْسِنَتُكُمُ ٱلْكَذِبَ هَٰذَا حَلَٰلٌ وَهَٰذَا حَرَامٌ لِّتَفْتَرُوا عَلَى ٱللَّهِ ٱلْكَذِبَ إِنَّ ٱلَّذِينَ يَفْتَرُونَ عَلَى ٱللَّهِ ٱلْكَذِبَ لَا يُفْلِحُونَ ۝ مَتَٰعٌ قَلِيلٌ وَهُمْ عَذَابٌ أَلِيمٌ ۝

---

^a This verse is not connected with general law-making; it relates rather to the treatment of certain food items as prohibited or permitted. Man has always arbitrarily treated one set of food items as permitted and another set as prohibited. This has resulted either from the influence of superstition or from the desire to pander to the self. But the people responsible for this attribute it to religion.

The harm done by the above-mentioned prohibition and permission is that it develops a superstitious and self-loving mentality in people, whereas the correct approach for man is to live in this world as a God-worshipper.

In the present life, man has been given freedom in order to create the right conditions for putting him to the test. The opportunity available to him to make superstition or self gratification his religion is due to his having this freedom. When this period of testing ends, man will suddenly find that there was only one choice for him and that was making God-worship his religion. When he chose to do otherwise, this was only a misuse of the freedom of the test period and not the legitimate use of a right. When the testing period is over, he will face the same punishment as all the others who fail the test are destined to suffer.

Having turned things permitted by God into prohibited things, they put themselves to unnecessary trouble and then they made legitimate the list of prohibited items by enshrining it in their beliefs. In this way they became doubly guilty.

If, in adherence to any self-made concept, a man makes a legitimate thing illegitimate for himself and for that reason starts making sacrifices, then this will amount to self-oppression and not to a sacrifice made to God.

¹¹⁸ We forbade the Jews those things We told you about before. We did not wrong them; rather they wronged themselves. ¹¹⁹ Surely, your Lord is most forgiving and ever merciful towards those who do evil in ignorance and truly repent thereafter and make amends.^a

وَعَلَى ٱلَّذِينَ هَادُواْ حَرَّمْنَا مَا قَصَصْنَا عَلَيْكَ مِن قَبْلُ ۖ وَمَا ظَلَمْنَٰهُمْ وَلَٰكِن كَانُوٓاْ أَنفُسَهُمْ يَظْلِمُونَ ۝ ثُمَّ إِنَّ رَبَّكَ لِلَّذِينَ عَمِلُواْ ٱلسُّوٓءَ بِجَهَٰلَةٍ ثُمَّ تَابُواْ مِنۢ بَعْدِ ذَٰلِكَ وَأَصْلَحُوٓاْ إِنَّ رَبَّكَ مِنۢ بَعْدِهَا لَغَفُورٌ رَّحِيمٌ ۝

---

^a When feelings of arrogance and prejudice add up to evil, the individual in question will not be ready to steer clear of it, though many arguments may be advanced to prove his actions wrong. But there is another kind of evil which arises due to stupidity. A man sometimes errs due to his lack of knowledge or to his being dominated by his own desires. Such a man generally exhibits no bravado. When his mistake is made clear by argument, he immediately turns back and sets himself on the right path once again.

There is no question of pardon for the first category of people. But as for the second category, there is the good news that God will extend His grace to them because He is truly merciful on this subject.

¹²⁰ Abraham was a community ᵃ in himself devoted to God and true in faith, He was not one of the polytheists; ¹²¹ he was thankful for His blessings. God chose him and guided him to a straight path. ¹²² We gave him blessings in this world, and in the Hereafter he shall be among the righteous. ¹²³ Then We revealed Our will to you [O Muhammad], saying, 'Follow the religion of Abraham, the upright in faith; he was not one of the polytheists.' ᵇ

إِنَّ إِبْرَٰهِيمَ كَانَ أُمَّةً قَانِتًا لِّلَّهِ حَنِيفًا وَلَمْ يَكُ مِنَ ٱلْمُشْرِكِينَ ۝ شَاكِرًا لِّأَنْعُمِهِ ٱجْتَبَٰهُ وَهَدَٰهُ إِلَىٰ صِرَٰطٍ مُّسْتَقِيمٍ ۝ وَءَاتَيْنَٰهُ فِى ٱلدُّنْيَا حَسَنَةً ۖ وَإِنَّهُۥ فِى ٱلْءَاخِرَةِ لَمِنَ ٱلصَّٰلِحِينَ ۝ ثُمَّ أَوْحَيْنَآ إِلَيْكَ أَنِ ٱتَّبِعْ مِلَّةَ إِبْرَٰهِيمَ حَنِيفًا ۖ وَمَا كَانَ مِنَ ٱلْمُشْرِكِينَ ۝

ᵃ Literally 'Abraham was a community'. This means that Abraham combined within himself all virtues.

ᵇ In the Quran Abraham (Ibrahim) has been presented as a paragon of virtue. Why did he become such an exemplary person? Because in the face of the generally vitiated atmosphere, he was the only man who was steadfast in his Faith. All alone he stood for God, with nobody there to support him.

Abraham had completely surrendered to the will of God. In the world-wide polytheistic atmosphere, he had devoted himself to the Faith of monotheism. He considered all things to have been received from God, and for that his heart was full of gratitude to God. Due to his perfect Faith, God opened all the paths of guidance for him and selected him for prophethood, so that he might acquaint the people of the world with the religion of God.

Abraham was given the good things of this world (*wa ataynahu fi'd dunya hasanah*) as well as the good things of the Hereafter. It is known that in this world Abraham had neither crowds surrounding him nor the throne of power nor any of the other trappings of worldly glory. Nevertheless, the Quran testifies that he was given good things of the world at God's behest. This shows that in the eyes of God the betterment of the world hinges neither on public popularity nor on wealth or power, but on what are described here as the characteristics of Abraham.

¹²⁴ The Sabbath was only enjoined on those who differed about it. Your Lord will judge between them on the Day of Resurrection regarding the things about which they differed.^a

إِنَّمَا جُعِلَ ٱلسَّبْتُ عَلَى ٱلَّذِينَ ٱخْتَلَفُواْ فِيهِ ۚ وَإِنَّ رَبَّكَ لَيَحْكُمُ بَيْنَهُمْ يَوْمَ ٱلْقِيَٰمَةِ فِيمَا كَانُواْ فِيهِ يَخْتَلِفُونَ ﴿١٢٤﴾

^a For all the followers of the prophets, one day of the week has been specified for congregational prayer. The Jews celebrate it on Saturday (the Sabbath), the Christians on Sunday and Muslims have been given orders to arrange for it on Friday.

The leading lights among the ancient Jews did some hair-splitting and devised new regulations for the Sabbath. In this way, they bound themselves by artificial restrictions. Thereafter, when they found it impossible to follow those restrictions, they could not reject them in consideration of the holiness of their great men. But, in practice, they started going against these restrictions.

The differences created in God's religion by later scholars and other luminaries by means of their commentaries are not going to be resolved in the world, but when the Day of Judgement comes, God will then show what the real religion of God was and what the things were that the people themselves added to and included in their religion.

125 Call to the way of your Lord with wisdom and fair exhortation and reason with them in a way that is best. Your Lord knows best those who have strayed away from His path, and He knows best those who are rightly guided.

126 If you want to retaliate, retaliate to the same degree as the injury done to you. But if you are patient, it is better to be so. 127 Endure with patience; truly, your patience is possible only with the help of God. Do not grieve for them, or feel distressed because of their plottings,*

ادْعُ إِلَىٰ سَبِيلِ رَبِّكَ بِالْحِكْمَةِ وَالْمَوْعِظَةِ الْحَسَنَةِ وَجَٰدِلْهُم بِالَّتِى هِىَ أَحْسَنُ إِنَّ رَبَّكَ هُوَ أَعْلَمُ بِمَن ضَلَّ عَن سَبِيلِهِۦ وَهُوَ أَعْلَمُ بِالْمُهْتَدِينَ ۝ وَإِنْ عَاقَبْتُمْ فَعَاقِبُوا۟ بِمِثْلِ مَا عُوقِبْتُم بِهِۦ وَلَئِن صَبَرْتُمْ لَهُوَ خَيْرٌ لِّلصَّٰبِرِينَ ۝ وَاصْبِرْ وَمَا صَبْرُكَ إِلَّا بِاللَّهِ وَلَا تَحْزَنْ عَلَيْهِمْ وَلَا تَكُ فِى ضَيْقٍ مِّمَّا يَمْكُرُونَ ۝

---

* The preacher's call to the Truth is a process which emerges out of intense feelings of sincerity, seriousness and well-wishing. The realization of a man that he is answerable to God forces him to issue such a call to the subjects of God. He does so because he thinks that if he does not, he himself will be caught on the Day of Judgement. The natural result of such thinking is that the preacher speaks words of wisdom, gives good advice and engages in serious discussion.

Exhortations to accept the Truth can be effective only when they are supported by argument and reasoning, and when they take into account the mentality of the addressees. A reasoned discourse should readily convince them of the reality of things but if it ignores their intellectual capacity, it will miss the mark and will do nothing to bolster the status of the preacher.

Sympathy is a characteristic which develops in a discourse due to a well-wishing mentality (al-mu'izah al-hasanah). When the preacher whose personality has been radically transformed by his realization of God's majesty and glory speaks about God, the majesty of God will definitely shine through his discourse. The messenger of God who, after seeing heaven and hell, comes forward to show them to others will certainly in his discourse give glimpses of the joys of heaven and the terror of hell. The combination of these features will make his discourse so effective that it will melt hearts and bring tears to the eyes. ▶

¹²⁸ for God is with those who are righteous and those who do good.^a

---

Wisdom and good counselling are the staff of dawah work. However there are always those addressees who indulge in pointless discussions with the intention, who have no desire to understand the message but they only want to complicate matters. In such a case, the preacher must respond with gentleness; in the face of harsh words he must resort to reasoning and analysis and, in response to provocation, he must exercise patience.

The eye of one who calls on others to the Truth is not on his audience but on God, who transcends all. Therefore, he utters such statements as prove to be true in God's eyes rather than in man's assessment.

^a This verse indicates the character traits to be displayed by the dayee while facing up to his opponents. However, God says that if he is too sorely afflicted—allowing for human weakness in him as in other mortals, he is permitted to repay his tormentors in kind. But strictly speaking, the dayee is supposed to exercise patience whenever his addressees create trouble for him. Instead of adopting a retaliatory approach, he should leave all such issues to God.

If the addressee does not accept the Truth, being bent rather on destroying the dayee and his mission, then the best course to be adopted by him is that of patience, i.e. avoiding reaction or retaliatory actions, he should continue conveying the message of Truth in a positive manner. The missionary has really to prove that, in fact, he is always conscious of God. If he proves this, then thereafter in all other matters, God becomes sufficient for him. After that no device of his opponents can harm him. However, strong his opponents may be.

There are two kinds of human beings in this world. One is entirely focused on man and his activities, while the other is entirely focused on God. The latter see the powers of God with their own eyes. The former is never able to have control over impatience and anger. It is only the second type of person who can bear complaints and suffer bitterness and, for the sake of whatever he is going to receive from God, ignore whatever is meted out to him by his fellow men.

The dayee must not have a vengeful mentality, and must abstain from retaliatory action. The conspiracies and devices of his opponents are likely to make him afraid that they may completely derail the call of Truth and destroy the preacher himself. But whatever the circumstances, he has to rely on God; he is required to have the firm belief that God sees everything and that He will support the Truth and defeat the falsehood.

17. THE NIGHT JOURNEY

In the name of God, the Most Gracious, the Most Merciful

¹ Holy is He who took His servant by night from the sacred place of worship [at Makkah] to the remote house of worship [at Jerusalem]— the precincts of which We have blessed, so that We might show him some of Our signs. Surely, it is He who is All Hearing, and All Seeing.*

سُبْحَٰنَ ٱلَّذِىٓ أَسْرَىٰ بِعَبْدِهِۦ لَيْلًا مِّنَ ٱلْمَسْجِدِ ٱلْحَرَامِ إِلَى ٱلْمَسْجِدِ ٱلْأَقْصَا ٱلَّذِى بَٰرَكْنَا حَوْلَهُۥ لِنُرِيَهُۥ مِنْ ءَايَٰتِنَآ إِنَّهُۥ هُوَ ٱلسَّمِيعُ ٱلْبَصِيرُ ۝

---

a One year before the migration (*hijrah*) of the Prophet Muhammad to Madinah, the conditions at Makkah were extremely adverse. It looked as if the history of Islam might come to an end even before it could take any definite shape. At that very juncture, God arranged to show the Prophet a very great sign—a demonstration, in fact, that Islamic history would not only run its due course, but that certain conditions would also be created to ensure that what it brought to the world would be preserved and thus remain eternally alive. This was because it had to become the authentic source of God's religion for all nations till the Day of Judgement.

God so willed that the Prophet Muhammad be taken from Makkah to al-Masjid al-Aqsa in Palestine (Jerusalem). This was the first stage of a journey (*mi'raj*), which was spiritual rather than physical, in nature. Here, at al-Masjid al-Aqsa, God had also gathered all the previous prophets. Together, they engaged in congregational prayer, with the Prophet Muhammad leading them. This instance of the Prophet Muhammad leading the prayer symbolized God's decision that the shariah of the previous prophets were no longer an authentic source of divine guidance. Now, all the nations should have to draw upon the religion presented by the Prophet Muhammad in order to have the authentic knowledge of God' religion.

For this important happening, which came to be known as The Night Journey, or *isra'*, Palestine was the most suitable place, its having been the centre from which the majority of the previous prophets had issued their call of Truth. Hence God's selection of this particular area to announce His decision.

830

² We gave Moses the Book and made it a guide for the Children of Israel saying, 'Do not take anyone besides Me as a guardian, ³ you who are the descendants of those whom We carried in the Ark with Noah. He was a truly thankful servant.' *a*

وَءَاتَيْنَا مُوسَى ٱلْكِتَٰبَ وَجَعَلْنَٰهُ هُدًى لِّبَنِىٓ إِسْرَٰٓءِيلَ أَلَّا تَتَّخِذُوا۟ مِن دُونِى وَكِيلًا ۞ ذُرِّيَّةَ مَنْ حَمَلْنَا مَعَ نُوحٍ إِنَّهُۥ كَانَ عَبْدًا شَكُورًا ۞

---

a The implication of the above-mentioned event was that the Children of Israel, the Jews, were deposed from the position of the 'bearers of the Scriptures' in favour of the Children of Ishmael (Banu Isma'il). This event took place in accordance with the way of God, who has always chosen a particular group for the declaration of the truth. This is the greatest honour one can have in this world.

However, this selection is not based on race or community. A group is entitled to this honour only if it is able to demonstrate the necessary competence. The moment its competence becomes questionable, it must forgo its entitlement to this honour. This happened in the case of the respective communities of Adam, Noah, Moses, and Jesus—without exception. This is the law of God, moreover, for any future community and there can be no exception to it for anyone.

To qualify for this position, the chosen group must treat God as the sole guardian, (*wakil*), and, placing their full trust in the one and only God, should leave all their affairs to Him.

When man discovers God in all His majesty and power, it is but natural that he should make God his guardian. One who attains the true realization of God will make God his everything, and will lead the life of a true believer in the present world. In order to lead such a life, man has to find God as the greatest reality, that is, the Creator and Lord of all creation.

Moreover, only those who attain this status in the realization of God can properly discharge the responsibility of calling upon others to the truth. To preach the word of God, it is absolutely necessary to be completely selfless, for total concentration cannot be developed in a man unless all his hopes and fears are attached to God; God should be his everything.

⁴ We forewarned the Children of Israel in the Scripture, 'Twice you shall commit evil in the land. You shall become great transgressors.' ⁵ When the time of the first of these warnings came, We sent against you servants of Ours, of great might, who ravaged your homes. So the warning was fulfilled, ⁶ and after a time We allowed you to prevail over them once again and aided you with wealth and offspring and made you greater in number.ᵃ

وَقَضَيْنَآ إِلَىٰ بَنِىٓ إِسْرَٰٓءِيلَ فِى ٱلْكِتَٰبِ لَتُفْسِدُنَّ فِى ٱلْأَرْضِ مَرَّتَيْنِ وَلَتَعْلُنَّ عُلُوًّا كَبِيرًا ۝ فَإِذَا جَآءَ وَعْدُ أُولَىٰهُمَا بَعَثْنَا عَلَيْكُمْ عِبَادًا لَّنَآ أُو۟لِى بَأْسٍ شَدِيدٍ فَجَاسُوا۟ خِلَٰلَ ٱلدِّيَارِ وَكَانَ وَعْدًا مَّفْعُولًا ۝ ثُمَّ رَدَدْنَا لَكُمُ ٱلْكَرَّةَ عَلَيْهِمْ وَأَمْدَدْنَٰكُم بِأَمْوَٰلٍ وَبَنِينَ وَجَعَلْنَٰكُمْ أَكْثَرَ نَفِيرًا ۝

ᵃ The 'corruption', or *fasad,* referred to here occurred among the Children of Israel after the advent of Moses. This happened in two stages. The details of the first instance of corruption are found in the Old Testament books of Psalms, Isaiah, Jeremiah and Ezekiel.

The details of the second instance of corruption are found in the words of Jesus in the New Testament in the Gospels of Matthew and Luke.

The Prophet Muhammad was taken from Makkah to al-Masjid al-Aqsa in Jerusalem, in order to be shown 'the sign of God.' One of these signs is also the history associated with al-Masjid al-Aqsa.

The above verse just means a place of worship situated at a distance. It is called the farthest place of worship, because it was situated at a distance of 765 miles from Makkah. Al-Masjid al-Aqsa, in this context, refers to the Jewish place of worship, that is, the Haykal Synagogue.

This Jewish synagogue, built by Solomon in 957 BC, was razed to the ground in 586 BC by the king of Babylonia, Nebuchadnezzar II. After a long period of time, the Jews rebuilt their place of worship. This was gain reduced to ruins in AD 70 by the Romans.

This history is a manifestation of God's Law which lays down that if a community entrusted with the Holy Scriptures discharges the obligations attached to them, then it is given a high status in this world, as well as success in the Hereafter. If it fails to do so, it is made subject to oppressive communities, which make it a victim of their tyranny and exploitation.

The manifestation of this law has occurred again and again in the case of former bearers of the scriptures. Two important events of direct relevance have been referred to here, so that a lesson may be taken from them. ▶

7 [We said], 'If you persevere in doing good, you will be doing good to yourselves; but if you do evil, it will go against you.' When the time of the second warning came, [We roused against you others] to disgrace you utterly and to enter the place of worship as they had entered it before, utterly destroying all that they laid their hands on. 8 We said, 'Your Lord may yet have mercy on you, but if you do the same again, so shall We: We have made Hell a prison for those who deny the truth.' *a*

إِنْ أَحْسَنتُمْ أَحْسَنتُمْ لِأَنفُسِكُمْ وَإِنْ أَسَأْتُمْ فَلَهَا فَإِذَا جَاءَ وَعْدُ ٱلْآخِرَةِ لِيَسُۥٓـُٔواْ وُجُوهَكُمْ وَلِيَدْخُلُواْ ٱلْمَسْجِدَ كَمَا دَخَلُوهُ أَوَّلَ مَرَّةٍ وَلِيُتَبِّرُواْ مَا عَلَوْاْ تَتْبِيرًا ۝ عَسَىٰ رَبُّكُمْ أَن يَرْحَمَكُمْ وَإِنْ عُدتُّمْ عُدْنَا وَجَعَلْنَا جَهَنَّمَ لِلْكَٰفِرِينَ حَصِيرًا ۝

In the beginning God blessed the Children of Israel and delivered them from the Pharaoh's tyranny and permitted them to occupy Palestine and establish their rule there. But then, corruption set in among the Jews. They started engaging in polytheistic practices, became the victims of differences and schisms, and separated into different groups.

As a result of this repeated disobedience to God, the Children of Israel had to submit to Nebuchadnezzar, the King of Babylon, who established his dominion over Palestine. Thereafter, he chose a member of the royal family of the Jews and appointed him as his representative to rule over them. But, the Jews, considering this subordinate state damaging to their national pride, rebelled against it.

This was despite being advised against rebellion by one of their prophets, Jeremiah. The King of Babylon became so incensed that once again, in 486 B.C., he attacked Palestine with all his military might. The Jews were not only totally defeated, but their temple in Jerusalem, which was the last sign of their glory, was also completely demolished.

a Various calamities inclined the Children of Israel to turn back to God once again. They were then given divine assistance through the agency of Cyrus, the King of Iran, who attacked and captured Babylon in 539 B.C., having defeated its ruler. Cyrus showed his favour to the Jews by allowing them to leave Babylon and return to their native place, Palestine. There, after a long time, they constructed their temple once again.

However, the corruption, which had prevailed in the previous generation of the Jews, began to set in in the new generation also. In the meantime, they faced many vicissitudes. Their own prophets, John the Baptist and Jesus, who rose from among them, criticized their behaviour, revealing the irreligiousness they indulged in in the name of religion. This enraged the Jews. They went so far as to kill John the Baptist and were prepared to crucify Jesus. ▶

⁹ Surely, this Quran guides to the most upright way and gives good news to the believers who do good deeds, so that they will have a great reward ¹⁰ and warns those who deny the life to come with grievous punishment.ᵃ

إِنَّ هَـٰذَا ٱلۡقُرۡءَانَ يَهۡدِى لِلَّتِى هِىَ أَقۡوَمُ وَيُبَشِّرُ ٱلۡمُؤۡمِنِينَ ٱلَّذِينَ يَعۡمَلُونَ ٱلصَّـٰلِحَـٰتِ أَنَّ لَهُمۡ أَجۡرًا كَبِيرًا ۝ وَأَنَّ ٱلَّذِينَ لَا يُؤۡمِنُونَ بِٱلۡأَخِرَةِ أَعۡتَدۡنَا لَهُمۡ عَذَابًا أَلِيمًا ۝

Then the wrath of God descended upon them once again. In the year 70 A.C., the Roman King, Titus, attacked Jerusalem and destroyed it completely.

The Jews recognize these events as a part of their history, but when they mention these historical facts, they attribute them to the oppression of tyrants. The Quran, however, very clearly attributes them to the behaviour of the People of the Book themselves. This shows that political conditions are always subject to moral conditions. No tyrant oppresses any community unless the corruption of the religious and moral conditions of that community gives him the opportunity to do so, i.e. it allows him to make them his victims.

ᵃ The Quran calls upon all human beings to accept the Oneness of God, or *tawhid*, that is, belief in the one God and surrender to His will. It can truly be said that no other matter can be more correct, more reasonable and more natural. Undoubtedly, the Oneness of God is the greatest reality and also the greatest truth.

This position of the Oneness of God necessarily makes it the standard by which all human beings should be tested and the basis on which some should be treated as right and others as wrong, some as successful and others as failures.

But, in the present world this standard is seemingly not upheld and the testing of human beings is not, apparently, done on this basis. But this is due only to God's hidden way of applying His law of testing. For individuals, death, and for the general mass of the people, the Day of Judgement are the final limits of the test period. As soon as this limit is reached, human beings will be separated into two different groups: those who believed in one God in the full sense, and met all the demands of that belief, will find themselves in paradise, while those who did not, will find themselves in hell.

"Yet man asks for evil as eagerly as he should ask for good. Truly, man is indeed hasty. ¹²We have made the night and the day as two signs. We blotted out the sign of night and made the sign of the day illuminating, so that you may seek the bounty of your Lord and learn to compute the seasons and the years. We have set everything forth in detail.ᵃ

وَيَدْعُ ٱلْإِنسَٰنُ بِٱلشَّرِّ دُعَآءَهُۥ بِٱلْخَيْرِ وَكَانَ ٱلْإِنسَٰنُ عَجُولًا ۞ وَجَعَلْنَا ٱلَّيْلَ وَٱلنَّهَارَ ءَايَتَيْنِ فَمَحَوْنَآ ءَايَةَ ٱلَّيْلِ وَجَعَلْنَآ ءَايَةَ ٱلنَّهَارِ مُبْصِرَةً لِّتَبْتَغُوا۟ فَضْلًا مِّن رَّبِّكُمْ وَلِتَعْلَمُوا۟ عَدَدَ ٱلسِّنِينَ وَٱلْحِسَابَ وَكُلَّ شَىْءٍ فَصَّلْنَٰهُ تَفْصِيلًا ۞

ᵃ The system of night and day shows that it is the way of God that there should be darkness first and, thereafter, light should take its place. In God's eyes, both of them are equally important. Just as there are benefits in light, similarly, there are benefits in darkness. If there were no distinction between night and day, how would man allocate his time and how would he alternate work with rest?

Man should neither be afraid of darkness, nor should he constantly hanker after light, because eternal light is not possible in this world of God. One whose desires are such had better leave this world and go in search of another world.

It is strange that this is the greatest weakness of man: he never wants to have to face any period of darkness, but immediately wants to have light. His undue haste is a sign of this weakness. Haste is, in fact, the equivalent of not reconciling with the plan of God. And not reconciling with the plan of God is the real cause of all human destruction.

God wants man to be patient about acquiring the immediate luxuries of the world, so that he should keep to the right path on his journey towards the Hereafter. But man, due to his hasty nature, rushes to acquire ephemeral worldly luxuries, which prove to be impediments to his continuing his onward journey. Man's desire for instant gratification is the greatest reason for his being deprived of the bounties of the Hereafter.

This is likewise true of the world, where real success is achieved by means of patience and not by a hasty approach. ▶

¹³ We have tied the fate of every man about his neck; and We shall produce a book for him on Resurrection Day that he will find spread open. ¹⁴ It will say, 'Read your record, today there will be none but yourself to call you to account!' ¹⁵ Whoever chooses to follow the right path, follows it for his own good; and whoever goes astray, goes astray at his own peril; no bearer of burdens shall bear the burdens of another. Nor do We punish until We have sent forth a messenger to forewarn them.ᵃ

وَكُلَّ إِنسَٰنٍ أَلۡزَمۡنَٰهُ طَٰٓئِرَهُۥ فِى عُنُقِهِۦ وَنُخۡرِجُ لَهُۥ يَوۡمَ ٱلۡقِيَٰمَةِ كِتَٰبًا يَلۡقَىٰهُ مَنشُورًا ﴿۱۳﴾ ٱقۡرَأۡ كِتَٰبَكَ كَفَىٰ بِنَفۡسِكَ ٱلۡيَوۡمَ عَلَيۡكَ حَسِيبًا ﴿۱٤﴾ مَّنِ ٱهۡتَدَىٰ فَإِنَّمَا يَهۡتَدِى لِنَفۡسِهِۦ وَمَن ضَلَّ فَإِنَّمَا يَضِلُّ عَلَيۡهَا وَلَا تَزِرُ وَازِرَةٌ وِزۡرَ أُخۡرَىٰ وَمَا كُنَّا مُعَذِّبِينَ حَتَّىٰ نَبۡعَثَ رَسُولًا ﴿۱٥﴾

The Prophet Jeremiah advised the Jews that they should recognize the political domination of the King of Babylon for the present, and in the initial stage devote their efforts to constructive work and the preaching of God's word. He said that thereafter a time would come when Almighty God would give them the means of achieving domination and power. But, in their impatience, the Jews were not willing to accept his advice. Eager to enter the stage of 'light' before passing through the stage of 'darkness', they immediately started a political struggle against the King of Babylon. Since, in accordance with the system of God, it was not possible for them to succeed, only dishonour and degradation awaited them.

ᵃ In ancient times superstitious people tried to predict their fate by observing the flight of birds or the revolution of stars, or through different charms. In the present day, even those who do not believe in such superstitions, attribute their fate to some mysterious cause or the other. They think that it is some external factor which truly influences their destiny.

God, however, says that the human fate is not linked with the birds or the stars: neither is it connected with any external thing; indeed, the fate of every man hangs upon his own deeds. Whatever a man thinks or does is being recorded throughout his existence. On the Day of Judgement, therefore, man will find his life history written in the shape of a diary, which contains all matters, both great and small.

God raised prophets among the various communities and revealed the scriptures to them. He did this so that people should be aware in advance of the unforeseeable Day of Reckoning. Now it is for every man to decide what fate he wants to face in the future: eternal paradise as a result of his following the path of guidance, or an eternity in hell as a result of his straying from that path.

¹⁶ When We decide to destroy a town, We command the affluent section of its people, but they transgress therein; thus the word [sentence of punishment] is justified, then We destroy the town utterly. ¹⁷ How many generations have We destroyed since Noah's time. Your Lord is well aware of the sins of His servants and observes them all.^a

وَإِذَآ أَرَدْنَآ أَن نُّهْلِكَ قَرْيَةً أَمَرْنَا مُتْرَفِيهَا فَفَسَقُواْ فِيهَا فَحَقَّ عَلَيْهَا ٱلْقَوْلُ فَدَمَّرْنَٰهَا تَدْمِيرًا ۞ وَكَمْ أَهْلَكْنَا مِنَ ٱلْقُرُونِ مِنۢ بَعْدِ نُوحٍ ۗ وَكَفَىٰ بِرَبِّكَ بِذُنُوبِ عِبَادِهِۦ خَبِيرًۢا بَصِيرًا

---

^a The conduct of the leading group of a community is the chief indicator of the level of honesty or corruption of the community's members. Only this group has the understanding and resources to influence their inferiors. Only they can bear the cost of leadership.

This is why the reformation of the prominent group amounts to the reformation of the whole community and the corruption of this prominent group amounts to the corruption of the whole community. If a study is made of communities right from the time of Noah to the present day, the history of each community will confirm the correctness of this general principle.

Those leading lights, or elders of the community, who exploit the people to establish their leadership, teach the community emotionalism instead of realism; they teach the community to live in wishful thinking, instead of admitting the truth. In short, instead of making the community attentive to God, they turn it away from God by making it attend to worldly concerns. By thus misleading the community, they bring about its destruction.

When leaders of this kind dominate a community, it is to be expected that God has taken a decision to destroy it. Every event of this type happens by God's will, for no deed or misdeed of any person or community is hidden from Him.

¹⁸ We give whatever We will to whoever desires immediate gains; but then We have prepared Hell for him which he will enter, disgraced and rejected. ¹⁹ Anyone who desires the Hereafter and makes a proper effort to achieve it, being a true believer, shall find favour with God for his endeavours.ᵃ

مَّن كَانَ يُرِيدُ ٱلْعَاجِلَةَ عَجَّلْنَا لَهُۥ فِيهَا مَا نَشَآءُ لِمَن نُّرِيدُ ثُمَّ جَعَلْنَا لَهُۥ جَهَنَّمَ يَصْلَىٰهَا مَذْمُومًا مَّدْحُورًا ۝ وَمَنْ أَرَادَ ٱلْءَاخِرَةَ وَسَعَىٰ لَهَا سَعْيَهَا وَهُوَ مُؤْمِنٌ فَأُوْلَٰئِكَ كَانَ سَعْيُهُم مَّشْكُورًا ۝

ᵃ In the present world as man travels towards his ultimate destination, he finds himself standing before a fork in the road. One side leads to the path of immediate gains, while the other is a path on which everything is to be given on merit. One who follows the first path chooses instant benefit (*'ajilah*), whereas one who follows the other path chooses the Hereafter (*akhirah*).

On the one hand, man has before him the way of opportunism, which leads him straight to immediate honour and wealth. On the other hand, there is the way of infinite love of truth, the credit for which man will receive only when he begins his life after death. If a man has a grievance, one way of dealing with it is to become vindictive and vengeful. The other option is to forgive and, offering prayers to God, leave the whole matter in His hands. Similarly, man may spend his wealth in fulfilling his desires and furthering his ambitions, or he may spend it for the cause of God.

Likewise, there are two different ways of dealing with life's contingencies: one is to fulfil one's own desires, while the other is to dedicate oneself to the worship of God. One is to give importance to appearances, the other is to give credence to the reality of the unseen; one is the way of expediency, while the other is the way of principle. The former bears the mark of impatience while the latter makes manifest the virtue of patience.

The first way is associated with temporary gain followed by eternal deprivation. The second way is that of temporary loss followed by everlasting honour and success.

²⁰ Upon all, both these [who desire the world] and those [who desire the Hereafter] We bestow the bounty of your Lord: none shall be denied the bounty of your Lord—²¹ see how We have exalted some above others [in the present life]. Yet the Hereafter shall be greater in degrees of rank and greater in excellence.ᵃ

كُلًّا نُّمِدُّ هَٰؤُلَآءِ وَهَٰؤُلَآءِ مِنْ عَطَآءِ رَبِّكَ ۚ وَمَا كَانَ عَطَآءُ رَبِّكَ مَحْظُورًا ۝ ٱنظُرْ كَيْفَ فَضَّلْنَا بَعْضَهُمْ عَلَىٰ بَعْضٍ ۚ وَلَلْآخِرَةُ أَكْبَرُ دَرَجَٰتٍ وَأَكْبَرُ تَفْضِيلًا ۝

ᵃ Be it in this world or in the Hereafter, success results from availing of the opportunities provided by God. For those who have made success in the life Hereafter the goal of their lives, God has made such dispositions as will facilitate the spiritual journey leading to that success in the next world.

One can see that in this world some people are ahead of others, while some are lagging behind. Some have more and some have less. These are ways of telling us in the language of symbols, that there is no limit to opportunities in this world of God. The harder one works the more one achieves. Similarly, the more one is involved in Hereafter-oriented activities, the greater the reward one will receive in the Hereafter. Furthermore, whatever one receives in the next world will be eternal, while whatever one receives in this world will be ephemeral in nature.

²² Do not set up any other deity beside God, lest you incur disgrace, and be forsaken. ²³ Your Lord has commanded that you should worship none but Him, and show kindness to your parents. If either or both of them attain old age with you, say no word of contempt to them and do not rebuke them, but always speak gently to them ²⁴ and treat them with humility and tenderness and say, 'Lord, be merciful to them both, as they raised me up when I was little.' ²⁵ Your Lord knows best what is in your hearts; if you are righteous, He is most forgiving to those who constantly turn to Him.ᵃ

لَا تَجْعَلْ مَعَ ٱللَّهِ إِلَٰهًا ءَاخَرَ فَتَقْعُدَ مَذْمُومًا مَّخْذُولًا ۝ وَقَضَىٰ رَبُّكَ أَلَّا تَعْبُدُوٓاْ إِلَّآ إِيَّاهُ وَبِٱلْوَٰلِدَيْنِ إِحْسَٰنًا إِمَّا يَبْلُغَنَّ عِندَكَ ٱلْكِبَرَ أَحَدُهُمَآ أَوْ كِلَاهُمَا فَلَا تَقُل لَّهُمَآ أُفٍّ وَلَا تَنْهَرْهُمَا وَقُل لَّهُمَا قَوْلًا كَرِيمًا ۝ وَٱخْفِضْ لَهُمَا جَنَاحَ ٱلذُّلِّ مِنَ ٱلرَّحْمَةِ وَقُل رَّبِّ ٱرْحَمْهُمَا كَمَا رَبَّيَانِي صَغِيرًا ۝ رَّبُّكُمْ أَعْلَمُ بِمَا فِى نُفُوسِكُمْ إِن تَكُونُواْ صَٰلِحِينَ فَإِنَّهُ كَانَ لِلْأَوَّٰبِينَ غَفُورًا ۝

ᵃ For the human being God is everything. He is his Creator, Lord and Sustainer. But God remains in the unseen, He does not come before man to gain recognition. This means that when one acknowledges one's helplessness vis-à-vis the greatness of God, one does so out of choice rather than as a result of some visible compulsion.

In this respect, the case of elderly parents is somewhat similar in nature to that of God. The parents have no material power over their children. When the children treat their parents well, they do it of their own free will and not because of any material pressures.

This is the real test of man in the present world. Here he has to adopt the way of truth and justice, without being forced to do so. He has to perform of his own free will and at his pleasure such deeds as he would perform if God appeared before him in all His Omnipotence.

Such voluntary action poses a serious test for man. However, God has made it easy for man by his special Grace. He does not test man with the severity of a master who becomes overly exercised about petty things. If a man is basically loyal to God, He excuses his petty lapses. If a man turns over a new leaf after doing something wrong, He pardons him, regardless of how great a sin he may have committed.

²⁶ Give to your relatives their due, and also to the needy and the wayfarer. Yet do not spend extravagantly; ²⁷ spendthrifts are the brothers of Satan, and Satan is ever ungrateful to his Lord—²⁸ but if, while waiting for your Lord's bounty which you are expecting, you turn them down, then at least speak to them kindly.^a

وَءَاتِ ذَا ٱلْقُرْبَىٰ حَقَّهُۥ وَٱلْمِسْكِينَ وَٱبْنَ ٱلسَّبِيلِ وَلَا تُبَذِّرْ تَبْذِيرًا ۝ إِنَّ ٱلْمُبَذِّرِينَ كَانُوٓاْ إِخْوَٰنَ ٱلشَّيَٰطِينِ وَكَانَ ٱلشَّيْطَٰنُ لِرَبِّهِۦ كَفُورًا ۝ وَإِمَّا تُعْرِضَنَّ عَنْهُمُ ٱبْتِغَآءَ رَحْمَةٍ مِّن رَّبِّكَ تَرْجُوهَا فَقُل لَّهُمْ قَوْلًا مَّيْسُورًا ۝

---

^a A man has a right to spend on himself whatever he earns by his own hard work. However, the Islamic law lays down that he should avoid the habits of a spendthrift; he should spend his wealth on actual necessities and not on vanity or display.

Secondly, everyone must realize that others have a right to his earnings—be they relatives, neighbours, travellers or needy persons.

If one is to spend one's wealth according to the will and pleasure of God, one must first of all economize by refraining from pointless spending. Indeed, extravagance is a weapon used by Satan to induce one to neglect one's duties towards the poor and needy.

²⁹ Be neither miserly, nor so open-handed that you suffer reproach and become destitute. ³⁰ Your Lord gives abundantly to whom He will and sparingly to whom He pleases. He is informed and observant about His servants.ᵃ

³¹ You shall not kill your offspring for fear of want. It is We who provide for them, and for you.ᵇ Indeed, killing them is a great sin. ³² Do not commit adultery, for it is an indecent thing and an evil course.ᶜ

وَلَا تَجْعَلْ يَدَكَ مَغْلُولَةً إِلَىٰ عُنُقِكَ وَلَا تَبْسُطْهَا كُلَّ ٱلْبَسْطِ فَتَقْعُدَ مَلُومًا مَّحْسُورًا ۝ إِنَّ رَبَّكَ يَبْسُطُ ٱلرِّزْقَ لِمَن يَشَآءُ وَيَقْدِرُ إِنَّهُۥ كَانَ بِعِبَادِهِۦ خَبِيرًۢا بَصِيرًا ۝ وَلَا تَقْتُلُوٓاْ أَوْلَٰدَكُمْ خَشْيَةَ إِمْلَٰقٍ نَّحْنُ نَرْزُقُهُمْ وَإِيَّاكُمْ إِنَّ قَتْلَهُمْ كَانَ خِطْـًٔا كَبِيرًا ۝ وَلَا تَقْرَبُواْ ٱلزِّنَىٰٓ إِنَّهُۥ كَانَ فَٰحِشَةً وَسَآءَ سَبِيلًا ۝

ᵃ Islam favours moderation in all matters. According to Islam, the middle way, i.e. avoidance of extremes, is the best way. 'The best of matters is their moderation.' The same advice has been given in respect of expenditure. Man should not be so niggardly as to degrade himself in the eyes of others, but neither should he spend so much as to leave himself with nothing. It has been recorded in the traditions of the Prophet Muhammad, that one who adopts the way of moderation will not be a pauper.

Lack of moderation with regard to wealth generally develops in a man because he loses sight of the fact that the Giver is God. It is He Who in His wisdom gives less to one and more to another. God's dictum on this subject has been recorded in a divinely inspired tradition (*hadith qudsi*) of the Prophet Muhammad, 'There are some among My servants for whom poverty is better, that is, too much of wealth will lead them astray. If I were to make them wealthy, their faith would suffer. And there are some among My servants for whom being wealthy is better. If I were to make them paupers, their faith would suffer.'

ᵇ It was the Lord who created all living creatures and it was He who made provision for their sustenance. In view of this, man's action in killing anyone on the pretext of a lack of the means to survive amounts to committing a totally unjustifiable act. When God Himself undertakes the sustenance of all His creatures, nobody has the right to kill anybody for fear that another's continuing to exist will reduce his own chances of survival. 'It is We who provide (sustenance) for them, and for you.' Through these words the thinking of man is directed towards construction rather than destruction. It is worth considering that if human beings at present can earn their livelihood, it is by their utilizing the productive resources provided by God. This will hold good for future generations also.

ᶜ Literally 'do not go near adultery.' One of the evils, which God wants to root out completely, is adultery, or *zina*. That is what God says: 'Do not go near adultery.' ▶

³³ Do not take life which God has made inviolate—except by right. If anyone is killed wrongfully, We have given authority to his heirs to demand retribution, but let them not transgress the prescribed limits in exacting retribution; for then he will be assisted [by the law].^a

وَلَا تَقْتُلُوا ٱلنَّفْسَ ٱلَّتِي حَرَّمَ ٱللَّهُ إِلَّا بِٱلْحَقِّ ۗ وَمَن قُتِلَ مَظْلُومًا فَقَدْ جَعَلْنَا لِوَلِيِّهِۦ سُلْطَٰنًا فَلَا يُسْرِف فِّي ٱلْقَتْلِ ۖ إِنَّهُۥ كَانَ مَنصُورًا ٣٣

That is, adultery is such a great evil and is proof of such shamelessness, that man should abstain even from its initial stages. Here, only a basic command has been given on this subject. Detailed orders have been given in chapter 24.

^a The killing of anybody without the sanction of the Islamic law is totally prohibited (*haram*). One who is killed without the justification of the Islamic law must be regarded as having been wronged. In view of this, the surviving kin of the deceased have full rights over the killer; they may avenge the murder as per the law; or they may let the killer go, after taking compensation from him; or they may forgive him altogether. According to Islamic law, the real claimants are the surviving kin of the dead person and not the government. The duty of the government is only to help the surviving kin to enforce their will.

Murder is such a terrible crime that it is said in a tradition of the Prophet Muhammad that the killing of a human being is more undesirable that the annihilation of the whole world. In the eyes of God, this principle notwithstanding, the surviving relatives of the murdered person have no right to commit any excess on the killer in the avenging of the murder. They may not, for instance, disfigure the killer or kill one of his companions in his place, etc. If the surviving relatives of the killed person commit any excess in avenging the murder, in this case the government may step in to prevent this, in exactly the same manner as it would have assisted them in securing their right to retributive justice, or *qisas*.

This reveals the spirit of Islamic law: if a person, howsoever oppressed, wants to take revenge, he is allowed to do so only in proportion to the degree of oppression he has suffered. He is in no way allowed to take any action in excess of this.

³⁴ Do not go near the orphans' property,ᵃ except with the best of intentions, until they reach maturity. Keep your promises;ᵇ you will be called to account for every promise which you have made! ³⁵ Give full measure, when you measure, and weigh with accurate scales. That is fair, and better in the end.ᶜ

وَلَا تَقْرَبُواْ مَالَ ٱلْيَتِيمِ إِلَّا بِٱلَّتِى هِىَ أَحْسَنُ حَتَّىٰ يَبْلُغَ أَشُدَّهُۥ وَأَوْفُواْ بِٱلْعَهْدِ إِنَّ ٱلْعَهْدَ كَانَ مَسْـُٔولًا ۝ وَأَوْفُواْ ٱلْكَيْلَ إِذَا كِلْتُمْ وَزِنُواْ بِٱلْقِسْطَاسِ ٱلْمُسْتَقِيمِ ذَٰلِكَ خَيْرٌ وَأَحْسَنُ تَأْوِيلًا ۝

ᵃ Whenever an orphan's property is entrusted to the next of kin—the orphan being under age or not having reached maturity—it is incumbent upon the relatives to keep the orphan's wealth intact and, as soon as he is able to understand matters of profit and loss, to hand over to him his entire wealth.

ᵇ Keeping promises is a sign of nobility of character. One, who makes a pledge, but does not fulfill it, is a worthless person before God and men.

Literally 'a pledge must be accounted for to God'. These words make it quite clear that if one man makes a promise to another, it does not concern just the two of them: God actively participates in the capacity of the third party. One who breaks his pledge to someone weaker than himself should fear God—who is also present— for it is quite impossible to escape His wrath.

ᶜ Every kind of business in the world is based on weights and measures. Therefore, it has been ordained that weights and measures should be accurate.

There are two aspects to this. First, it is in accordance with human dignity, for the giving of short weight is a debasement of character. The second great merit is that it gives a stimulus to business, as total trust is the foundation of commercial progress. Proper weight and measurement are a sine qua non for the establishment of good business relations in any given society.

³⁶ Do not follow what you do not know; for the ear and the eye and the heart shall all be called to account. ³⁷ Do not walk proudly on the earth. You cannot cleave the earth, nor can you rival the mountains in height. ³⁸ All that is evil in the sight of your Lord, and is detestable.ᵃ

وَلَا تَقْفُ مَا لَيْسَ لَكَ بِهِۦ عِلْمٌ إِنَّ ٱلسَّمْعَ وَٱلْبَصَرَ وَٱلْفُؤَادَ كُلُّ أُوْلَٰٓئِكَ كَانَ عَنْهُ مَسْـُٔولًا ۝ وَلَا تَمْشِ فِى ٱلْأَرْضِ مَرَحًا إِنَّكَ لَن تَخْرِقَ ٱلْأَرْضَ وَلَن تَبْلُغَ ٱلْجِبَالَ طُولًا ۝ كُلُّ ذَٰلِكَ كَانَ سَيِّئُهُۥ عِندَ رَبِّكَ مَكْرُوهًا ۝

ᵃ Qatada, one of the early commentators of the Quran, said, 'Don't say, "I have seen" when you have not seen, don't say, "I have heard" when you have not heard, and don't say "I know" when you do not know.'

One who fears to be called to account before God, will never say anything without first verifying it. Man should use his eyes, ears and brain for the purpose they were designed and should talk of and act only upon such matters for which there is adequate evidence to warrant this. He should eschew all that is baseless, for example, bearing false witness, making false allegations, condemning someone on the basis of hearsay, justifying falsehoods merely on account of envy, placing credence on things that man does not know for sure because of his limitations. The ears, eyes and mind are apparently under man's control. But these are, as it were, entrusted to him by God, and so it is a must for a man to utilize them according to God's will, otherwise he will be taken strictly to task for their misuse.

Man, even with all the power given to him, cannot tear apart the ground on which he lives, while the sheer height of the mountains negates his every claim to greatness. This is a practical comparison illustrating the real status of man as opposed to the greatness of God. It emphasizes the fact that man should not be filled with pride in this world. He should tread the path of humility and submissiveness and not that of pride and rebellion.

³⁹ This is part of the wisdom that your Lord has revealed to you. Do not set up any other deity with God, lest you be cast into Hell, condemned and rejected.^a

ذَٰلِكَ مِمَّآ أَوْحَىٰٓ إِلَيْكَ رَبُّكَ مِنَ ٱلْحِكْمَةِ ۗ وَلَا تَجْعَلْ مَعَ ٱللَّهِ إِلَٰهًا ءَاخَرَ فَتُلْقَىٰ فِى جَهَنَّمَ مَلُومًا مَّدْحُورًا ۝

---

^a The injunctions given in the above verses come under the heading of 'wisdom' (*hikmah*). The meaning of 'wisdom' here stands for the firm reality, the sound truths of life. It is on the foundations of these realities that the healthy life is built. A human society devoid of them can expect little else but annihilation both in the present and in the next life.

The narration of the above-mentioned advice begins with the Oneness of God, or *tawhid* (verse 22) and finishes with the oneness of God (verse 39). This indicates that, for the foundation of all good deeds, man should believe in the one God. He should fear and love Him alone. The secret of a good life is concealed in the right relationship with God. If the relationship with God is not proper, no other thing can set right the affairs of human life. God is the beginning and the end of human life.

⁴⁰ What! Has your Lord then favoured you with sons and Himself adopted females from among the angels? What you say is monstrous. ⁴¹ We have explained [the truth] in this Quran in various ways, so that they may take heed, but it has only increased their aversion. ⁴² Say, 'If there were [other] deities along with Him, as they claim, then they would surely have tried to find a way to the Lord of the Throne. ⁴³ Glory be to Him! Exalted above all that they say! ⁴⁴ The seven heavens and the earth and all who dwell therein glorify Him. There is not a single thing but glorifies Him with His praise; but you do not understand their glorification. Truly, He is forbearing and most forgiving.'ᵃ

أَفَأَصْفَىٰكُمْ رَبُّكُم بِٱلْبَنِينَ وَٱتَّخَذَ مِنَ ٱلْمَلَـٰٓئِكَةِ إِنَـٰثًا ۚ إِنَّكُمْ لَتَقُولُونَ قَوْلًا عَظِيمًا ۝ وَلَقَدْ صَرَّفْنَا فِى هَـٰذَا ٱلْقُرْءَانِ لِيَذَّكَّرُوا۟ وَمَا يَزِيدُهُمْ إِلَّا نُفُورًا ۝ قُل لَّوْ كَانَ مَعَهُۥٓ ءَالِهَةٌ كَمَا يَقُولُونَ إِذًا لَّٱبْتَغَوْا۟ إِلَىٰ ذِى ٱلْعَرْشِ سَبِيلًا ۝ سُبْحَـٰنَهُۥ وَتَعَـٰلَىٰ عَمَّا يَقُولُونَ عُلُوًّا كَبِيرًا ۝ تُسَبِّحُ لَهُ ٱلسَّمَـٰوَٰتُ ٱلسَّبْعُ وَٱلْأَرْضُ وَمَن فِيهِنَّ ۚ وَإِن مِّن شَىْءٍ إِلَّا يُسَبِّحُ بِحَمْدِهِۦ وَلَـٰكِن لَّا تَفْقَهُونَ تَسْبِيحَهُمْ ۗ إِنَّهُۥ كَانَ حَلِيمًا غَفُورًا ۝

ᵃ The truth is so complete and perfect in itself that, if any untruth is placed next to it, the truth immediately stands out as such. One example of an untruth is ascribing partners to God.

Worshippers of deities call their supposed partners God's children, but this in itself is a refutation of their claim. Firstly, if these so-called partners are given feminine gender and called God's daughters, then immediately an objection may be raised, for the disbelievers hold that daughters belong to the weaker sex. Why then would God approve of a member of this weaker class as His partner? How surprising it would be if He gave man sons as his loving children and chose daughters for Himself!

Secondly, if the partner is taken to be God's son, —who, in the experience of man is a symbol of power and strength—this again would defy understanding, for, power is indivisible. If in any system there is more than one person invested with power, a struggle between them is bound to take place, for each one of them would want to have absolute power. Now, if there had been more than one powerful being in this universe, there would certainly have been a struggle for power and this would have created disorder and dissension. But, as there is no disorder or dissension in the universe, this proves that no such being or beings exist as have a share in God's power. ▶

45 When you recite the Quran, We place an invisible barrier between you and those who do not believe in the Hereafter. 46 We put veils over their hearts to prevent them from comprehending it, and We afflict their ears with deafness. When you mention your one and only Lord in your recitation of the Quran, they turn their backs in aversion.[a]

وَإِذَا قَرَأْتَ ٱلْقُرْءَانَ جَعَلْنَا بَيْنَكَ وَبَيْنَ ٱلَّذِينَ لَا يُؤْمِنُونَ بِٱلْأَخِرَةِ حِجَابًا مَّسْتُورًا ۝ وَجَعَلْنَا عَلَىٰ قُلُوبِهِمْ أَكِنَّةً أَن يَفْقَهُوهُ وَفِي ءَاذَانِهِمْ وَقْرًا ۚ وَإِذَا ذَكَرْتَ رَبَّكَ فِي ٱلْقُرْءَانِ وَحْدَهُ وَلَّوْا۟ عَلَىٰ أَدْبَٰرِهِمْ نُفُورًا ۝

Whether God's supposed partners are called sons or daughters, the notion of partnership clashes with reality. The truth is that the entire universe rejects all ideas that ascribe partners to God's divinity.

[a] When the Quran is recited to people, they fail to understand the message due to their deep conditioning. In fact, they are so frivolous about the world hereafter, that they ignore the message altogether.

People are so involved in their worldly matters that truth is no longer their concern. Their reluctance is due to the fact that they do not want to revise themselves.

The call of pristine truth always negates their worldly concerns. That is why they are greatly provoked on hearing this call. In their hearts they do not believe in the accountability of the Day of Judgement and this makes them non-serious in their approach to it. The mind which lacks seriousness is incapable of understanding anything of value.

⁴⁷ We are fully aware of what they wish to hear when they listen to you; and what they say when they converse in private; and when the wrongdoers say, 'You are only following a man who is bewitched!' ⁴⁸ See to what they liken you! But they are lost and cannot find the right path.ᵃ

⁴⁹ 'What!' they say, 'When we are turned to bones and dust, shall we be restored to life?' ⁵⁰ Say, '[yes] even if you turned to stones or iron, ⁵¹ or any other substance which you think unlikely to be given life.' Then they will ask, 'Who is it that shall restore us to life?' Answer them, 'He who created you the first time.' They will then shake their heads at you and say, 'When will that be?' Say, 'It may well be very soon.'

نَحْنُ أَعْلَمُ بِمَا يَسْتَمِعُونَ بِهِۦٓ إِذْ يَسْتَمِعُونَ إِلَيْكَ وَإِذْ هُمْ نَجْوَىٰٓ إِذْ يَقُولُ ٱلظَّٰلِمُونَ إِن تَتَّبِعُونَ إِلَّا رَجُلًا مَّسْحُورًا ۝ ٱنظُرْ كَيْفَ ضَرَبُوا۟ لَكَ ٱلْأَمْثَٰلَ فَضَلُّوا۟ فَلَا يَسْتَطِيعُونَ سَبِيلًا ۝ وَقَالُوٓا۟ أَءِذَا كُنَّا عِظَٰمًا وَرُفَٰتًا أَءِنَّا لَمَبْعُوثُونَ خَلْقًا جَدِيدًا ۝ قُلْ كُونُوا۟ حِجَارَةً أَوْ حَدِيدًا ۝ أَوْ خَلْقًا مِّمَّا يَكْبُرُ فِى صُدُورِكُمْ فَسَيَقُولُونَ مَن يُعِيدُنَا قُلِ ٱلَّذِى فَطَرَكُمْ أَوَّلَ مَرَّةٍ فَسَيُنْغِضُونَ إِلَيْكَ رُءُوسَهُمْ وَيَقُولُونَ مَتَىٰ هُوَ قُلْ عَسَىٰٓ أَن يَكُونَ قَرِيبًا ۝

ᵃ The call of the Prophet Muhammad was supported by such strong arguments that the common people of Arabia were awed by it. Seeing this, the Arab leaders felt afraid that, if the majority of the people converted to the new religion, their leadership would come to an end. They, therefore, employed a strategy to keep people away from it. They said that the great impact the Prophet's words had was due to his being possessed. They said, moreover, that the power of his words did not stem from his having discovered some truth, but from his possessing magical powers. That is, it was a mere matter of oratorical prowess rather than the communication of truth. In this way the majestic words of the Quran reflecting Truth came to mean to them a magic spell wrought by an individual.

Those who fail to judge such a call on the basis of its merit but look at it rather from the point of view of whether the words of the call support or reject their own stand, shall never succeed in finding the truth.

⁵²On that Day He will call you, and you will answer by praising Him, thinking that you have stayed for only a little while.'ᵃ

⁵³Tell My servants that they should always say what is best. Satan stirs up discord among them. Surely, Satan is an outright enemy to man.ᵇ

يَوْمَ يَدْعُوكُمْ فَتَسْتَجِيبُونَ بِحَمْدِهِ وَتَظُنُّونَ إِن لَّبِثْتُمْ إِلَّا قَلِيلًا ۞ وَقُل لِّعِبَادِي يَقُولُواْ ٱلَّتِي هِيَ أَحْسَنُ إِنَّ ٱلشَّيْطَٰنَ يَنزَغُ بَيْنَهُمْ إِنَّ ٱلشَّيْطَٰنَ كَانَ لِلْإِنسَٰنِ عَدُوًّا مُّبِينًا ۞

ᵃ Man's first existence clearly proves the possibility of his second existence, or re-creation, on the Day of Judgement. One who believes in the first creation of man has no real argument to back up his denial of man's second creation in the Hereafter. Furthermore, the concept of man's second creation is not at all difficult to understand for those who regard human beings as an amalgam of material elements, for the cells in the human body keep on breaking down and being replaced by new ones. In this world known to us, man's material existence is repeatedly terminated only to be rebuilt again and again through this continuous replacement of cells. In this way, man's body continually renews itself. It is said that every ten years the cells in our body replace themselves and a new body comes into being. The truth is what we already believe in and comprehend before death through our knowledge of the functioning of cells, i.e. what we have time and again experienced before death.

Doomsday is, in actual fact, the name of that day when the veil of the unseen is torn asunder and God in all His Power and Majesty appears before us. When this happens, the deniers will also be compelled to do what a true believer does today, namely, believe in God and life in the Hereafter. At that time all humanity will rush towards God in acknowledgement of His power and greatness.

ᵇ This verse alludes to the delicate relationship between the preacher and his addressees. However provocative the addressees may be, the preacher has been commanded to exercise patience and refrain from repaying in the same coin. For, if he is provoked by the addressees' ill behaviour, an atmosphere of hatred and obstinacy will develop. This tension between the preacher and the addressees might make it impossible for the latter to take his message cool-mindedly, with an open and unbiased mind. Any atmosphere of hatred and obstinacy between the preacher and the addressees favours Satan, who is thus able to make the call of truth unpalatable to the addressees. Therefore, if the preacher through any of his actions becomes responsible for producing a feeling of defiance and hatred, it is as if he were playing into the hands of Satan. It is like doing the enemy's job oneself.

54 Your Lord is fully aware of you. He may show you mercy if He will, or punish you if He will. We have not sent you as their guardian. 55 Your Lord knows best about everyone in the heavens and on the earth. We gave some prophets more than others: We gave David the Psalms.ᵃ

رَّبُّكُمْ أَعْلَمُ بِكُمْ إِن يَشَأْ يَرْحَمْكُمْ أَوْ إِن يَشَأْ يُعَذِّبْكُمْ وَمَا أَرْسَلْنَاكَ عَلَيْهِمْ وَكِيلًا ۝ وَرَبُّكَ أَعْلَمُ بِمَن فِي السَّمَاوَاتِ وَالْأَرْضِ وَلَقَدْ فَضَّلْنَا بَعْضَ النَّبِيِّنَ عَلَىٰ بَعْضٍ وَءَاتَيْنَا دَاوُۥدَ زَبُورًا ۝

ᵃ When a preacher calls for the truth and his hearers pay no attention to him, then certainly the preacher becomes exasperated, especially when the truth is as clear as daylight. Sometimes, he is so irritated that he cannot but vent his anger on the addressees by saying that they are not going to receive God's mercy. Such words as these do not befit a preacher. He does not have permission from God to utter such words.

Conveying the message of truth is one thing and meting out the divine reward according to the response given to the call of truth, another. The first is the task of a preacher and the second, that of God. A preacher should never make the mistake of crossing the limits set for him by entering the sphere reserved for God. Similarly, it happens sometimes that the preacher and the addressees engage in arguments regarding which of their respective prophets is the superior one. The energies of each side are then spent on proving that their own prophet enjoys a higher status with God, with the result that the discussion, which should have been focused on the principles of the prophet's message, is instead focused on personalities. This awakens in them feelings of prejudice and, as a result, places further obstacles in the path of the acceptance of the truth. Hence the explanation given in these verses that it is a matter pertaining to God as to what status He grants to His servants. What preachers have to do is avoid such heated discussions on irrelevant topics and convey the real message of truth to the people.

⁵⁶ Call upon those you claim to be deities besides God and you will know that they have no power to remove affliction from you or to bring about any change [that you may desire]. ⁵⁷ Those whom they invoke are themselves seeking a way of approach to their Lord, vying with each other to be near Him. They hope for His mercy and fear His punishment. Surely, the punishment of your Lord is to be feared: ⁵⁸ there is not a town [community] but We shall destroy or sternly punish it before the Day of Judgement. That is recorded in the Book.ᵃ

قُلِ ٱدْعُوا۟ ٱلَّذِينَ زَعَمْتُم مِّن دُونِهِۦ فَلَا يَمْلِكُونَ كَشْفَ ٱلضُّرِّ عَنكُمْ وَلَا تَحْوِيلًا ۝ أُو۟لَٰٓئِكَ ٱلَّذِينَ يَدْعُونَ يَبْتَغُونَ إِلَىٰ رَبِّهِمُ ٱلْوَسِيلَةَ أَيُّهُمْ أَقْرَبُ وَيَرْجُونَ رَحْمَتَهُۥ وَيَخَافُونَ عَذَابَهُۥٓ إِنَّ عَذَابَ رَبِّكَ كَانَ مَحْذُورًا ۝ وَإِن مِّن قَرْيَةٍ إِلَّا نَحْنُ مُهْلِكُوهَا قَبْلَ يَوْمِ ٱلْقِيَٰمَةِ أَوْ مُعَذِّبُوهَا عَذَابًا شَدِيدًا ۚ كَانَ ذَٰلِكَ فِى ٱلْكِتَٰبِ مَسْطُورًا ۝

ᵃ The entities given the status of objects of worship by man are themselves creations of God, for instance, pious people or the angels. They have not claimed divine status for themselves. It is their followers who worship and glorify them.

If one had the insight to perceive the unseen, one would see a strange sight. One would see that man gives the status of an object of worship to certain personalities at that very time when those very personalities shudder at the thought of God's Majesty: they themselves are forced to seek His mercy to attain salvation.

ᵇ Just as the law of annihilation (fana) applies to all individuals, similarly it applies to nations and civilizations. No matter how stable, splendid and vibrant with life a city might be, it is going to come to an end one day. It might either be destroyed due to the sins and insolence of its inhabitants or it might survive till the time of Doomsday, when it shall be destroyed along with the rest of the world.

⁵⁹ Nothing has prevented Us from sending signs, except the fact that previous peoples denied them. We gave the people of Thamud the she-camel as a clear sign, yet they mistreated her. We give signs only by way of warning.ᵃ

وَمَا مَنَعَنَا أَن نُّرْسِلَ بِٱلْأَيَٰتِ إِلَّا أَن كَذَّبَ بِهَا ٱلْأَوَّلُونَ ۚ وَءَاتَيْنَا ثَمُودَ ٱلنَّاقَةَ مُبْصِرَةً فَظَلَمُوا۟ بِهَا ۚ وَمَا نُرْسِلُ بِٱلْأَيَٰتِ إِلَّا تَخْوِيفًا ﴿٥٩﴾

ᵃ The extraordinary incidents which took place in the lifetime of the prophets were of two kinds. The first kind was in the nature of general help offered to a prophet and his companions. This help was like a support from God. The second kind was that taking place at the demand of polytheists, namely, miracles. The Prophet Muhammad—the last Prophet—and his Companions were given divine succour on a number of occasions. But the miracles, given to the previous prophets, were not given to Prophet Muhammad inspite of the demands of his contemporaries. The reason was that everything has certain demands: those who demand extraordinary signs will have extraordinary responsibility given to them too. Furthermore, according to the law of God, those who do not accept faith, even after being shown such extraordinary signs as miracles, are subsequently destroyed, having invited God's wrath and proved themselves deserving of God's scourge.

Now, since the Prophet Muhammad was the last Prophet and prophethood was going to be terminated with him, his addressees could not be dealt with in like manner, for in that case the entire community would have been wiped out by the divine scourge. Who would have remained then in the world to represent the Prophet? It was God's special mercy to the addressees of the last Prophet that in spite of their demands, they were not given tangible miracles. Had their demands been acceded to, they too—after their denial—would have faced the same fate as that of the Thamud community.

⁶⁰ We told you that your Lord encompasses mankind. We granted the vision which We showed you, as well as the tree that is cursed in the Quran, only as a test for mankind. We warn them, but this only increases their insolence.ᵃ

وَإِذْ قُلْنَا لَكَ إِنَّ رَبَّكَ أَحَاطَ بِٱلنَّاسِ وَمَا جَعَلْنَا ٱلرُّءْيَا ٱلَّتِى أَرَيْنَكَ إِلَّا فِتْنَةً لِّلنَّاسِ وَٱلشَّجَرَةَ ٱلْمَلْعُونَةَ فِى ٱلْقُرْءَانِ وَنُخَوِّفُهُمْ فَمَا يَزِيدُهُمْ إِلَّا طُغْيَـٰنًا كَبِيرًا ۝

ᵃ People often demanded some miracle of their own choice— a miracle, which they wanted in order to judge the veracity of the preacher, whereas if they had kept an open mind, they would have realized that they had already been given that miracle in the form of the special divine succour to the preacher. In answer to their demand for tangible miracles the Quran had this to say: 'Is this miracle not enough to open their eyes?' i.e. in the initial stages of conveying the word of God when the Prophet apparently had no power, it was declared that mankind had been encircled by God. This statement was corroborated with the spreading of Islam among the Arab tribes. It saw its completion with the victory of Badr, and the conquest of Makkah after the Hudaybiyyah Peace Treaty. Similarly, when the Prophet Muhammad announced on the morning following the Night Journey that the previous night he had been taken from the Ka'bah to al-Bayt al-Maqdis, people did not believe him. His opponents summoned those individuals who had actually seen al-Bayt al-Maqdis and the Prophet was then asked to describe the details of the building. This he did with great accuracy.

Still these happenings were not taken seriously. They scoffed at them, demanding proof of his veracity in the shape of miracles. The truth is that the actual problem is not one of showing tangible miracles but rather of serious thinking about the mission. When people are not serious about the divine call, they make a mockery of everything, even if it is of great importance.

When the Quran warned that in hell people would have to eat the fruit of the Zaqqum tree (37:62), Abu Jahal called for dates and butter to be brought, and asked others to eat them, saying that that was what Zaqqum was. (*Tafsir ibn Kathir*).

The fruits of this tree will serve as food for the inhabitants of hell. When this verse was revealed in the Quran, one of the leaders of the Quraysh remarked, 'Look at Abu Kabsha's son, he warns us of a hell which will burn up everything in it, even the stones. Then how does he think that a tree can grow in that fire? We all know that fire burns everything.' (*At-Tafsir al-Mazhari*).

⁶¹ When We said to the angels, 'Prostrate yourselves before Adam,' they all prostrated themselves except Iblis. He said, 'Am I to prostrate myself to someone You have created out of clay?' ⁶² and [further] said, 'Do you see this being whom You have exalted above me? If You reprieve me until the Day of Resurrection, I will bring all but a few of his descendents under my sway.' ᵃ

وَإِذْ قُلْنَا لِلْمَلَٰئِكَةِ ٱسْجُدُواْ لِأَدَمَ
فَسَجَدُوٓاْ إِلَّآ إِبْلِيسَ قَالَ ءَأَسْجُدُ
لِمَنْ خَلَقْتَ طِينًا ۝ قَالَ أَرَءَيْتَكَ
هَٰذَا ٱلَّذِى كَرَّمْتَ عَلَىَّ لَئِنْ أَخَّرْتَنِ
إِلَىٰ يَوْمِ ٱلْقِيَٰمَةِ لَأَحْتَنِكَنَّ ذُرِّيَّتَهُۥٓ
إِلَّا قَلِيلًا ۝

ᵃ The story of the angels and Satan shows the difference between the believers and the unbelievers. The believers see the truth as truth, therefore they do not find any difficulty in understanding it. They take no time in accepting it, just as the angels did at the time of the birth of Adam.

On the other hand, there is another category consisting of those who see the truth in relation only to their own selves. This is how Satan saw the truth—in relation to his own self. Since the command to prostrate himself before Adam appeared to make him a lesser being than Adam, Satan refused to comply. Seen in the context of the challenge given by Satan to God, everyone who ignores the truth because acceptance of the truth would amount to belittling his own position, has fallen a prey to Satan.

⁶³ God said, 'Go away! Hell will be your reward and the reward of any of them who follow you—an ample recompense. ⁶⁴ Go ahead and entice whomsoever of them you can, with your voice, and mount assaults against them with your cavalry and infantry and be their partner in wealth and offspring, and make promises to them—Satan promises nothing but delusion—⁶⁵ but over My true servants you shall have no power. Your Lord will be their all-sufficient guardian.'ᵃ

قَالَ ٱذْهَبْ فَمَن تَبِعَكَ مِنْهُمْ فَإِنَّ جَهَنَّمَ جَزَآؤُكُمْ جَزَآءً مَّوْفُورًا ۝ وَٱسْتَفْزِزْ مَنِ ٱسْتَطَعْتَ مِنْهُم بِصَوْتِكَ وَأَجْلِبْ عَلَيْهِم بِخَيْلِكَ وَرَجِلِكَ وَشَارِكْهُمْ فِى ٱلْأَمْوَٰلِ وَٱلْأَوْلَٰدِ وَعِدْهُمْ وَمَا يَعِدُهُمُ ٱلشَّيْطَٰنُ إِلَّا غُرُورًا ۝ إِنَّ عِبَادِى لَيْسَ لَكَ عَلَيْهِمْ سُلْطَٰنٌ وَكَفَىٰ بِرَبِّكَ وَكِيلًا ۝

ᵃ In the face of his threat to thoroughly mislead 'all but a few' of Adam's descendants, Satan has not been given any real power over man by God. The only thing he has the power to do is tempt people by his words and by putting evil thoughts into their minds. He glorifies things which will have no value in the Hereafter.

The words, 'but over My true servants you shall have no power' imply that, potentially, Satan does have considerable power over those who are not true servants of God. Now the question is how to save oneself in a world where Satan tries with all the strength at his command to mislead man. The only way is for man to make God his sole supporter in the real sense. One who does so will come under the protection of God, and then Satan will find himself helpless, despite the strength which God has allowed him to retain.

⁶⁶ Your Lord is He who causes the ships to move onward for you across the sea, so that you may go in quest of His bounty: He is most merciful towards you. ⁶⁷ When danger threatens you at sea, you call upon Him, and forget all others you are wont to invoke. But when He brings you safe to land, you turn away from Him. Man is ever ungrateful.ᵃ

رَّبُّكُمُ ٱلَّذِى يُزْجِى لَكُمُ ٱلْفُلْكَ فِى ٱلْبَحْرِ لِتَبْتَغُوا۟ مِن فَضْلِهِۦٓ إِنَّهُۥ كَانَ بِكُمْ رَحِيمًا ۝ وَإِذَا مَسَّكُمُ ٱلضُّرُّ فِى ٱلْبَحْرِ ضَلَّ مَن تَدْعُونَ إِلَّآ إِيَّاهُ فَلَمَّا نَجَّىٰكُمْ إِلَى ٱلْبَرِّ أَعْرَضْتُمْ وَكَانَ ٱلْإِنسَٰنُ كَفُورًا ۝

ᵃ God has imposed certain laws upon our world. This is what enables man to navigate the seas and fly in the air. All these dispositions were made so that he might realize God's mercies and become a thankful servant of God. But man thinks totally differently. He takes everything for granted, thinking that everything is happening as a matter of cause and effect. That is why he fails to receive any divine inspiration from life's events.

The concept of God is ingrained in human nature to the utmost extent. One demonstration of this is that when man is faced with a calamity, such as being on the point of being ship-wrecked, all artificial barriers are removed at that moment, and finding himself helpless, he starts calling out to the one and only God.

He is made to experience such adversity so that he may mould his conduct accordingly. This temporary recognition of God's godhead should become a permanent feature in his life. But, unfortunately, that same man who remembers God in the tempest forgets God as soon as he safely reaches the shore.

Accepting the godhead of God is monotheism (tawhid), while acceptance of beings and things other than God as the godhead is polytheism (shirk). What God desires from man is nothing other than acknowledgement. But man is so insolent that he is not willing to bow to God's will, even to this minimum extent.

⁶⁸ Do you then feel secure against His causing you to be swallowed up by the earth when you are back on land, or His sending a deadly sand storm upon you? Then you will find none to protect you. ⁶⁹ Or do you feel secure against His sending you back to sea once again, and raising a fierce gale against you and causing you to drown in requital for your ingratitude? You will find no helper against Us there.ᵃ

أَفَأَمِنتُمْ أَن يَخْسِفَ بِكُمْ جَانِبَ ٱلْبَرِّ أَوْ يُرْسِلَ عَلَيْكُمْ حَاصِبًا ثُمَّ لَا تَجِدُواْ لَكُمْ وَكِيلًا ﴿٦٨﴾ أَمْ أَمِنتُمْ أَن يُعِيدَكُمْ فِيهِ تَارَةً أُخْرَىٰ فَيُرْسِلَ عَلَيْكُمْ قَاصِفًا مِّنَ ٱلرِّيحِ فَيُغْرِقَكُم بِمَا كَفَرْتُمْ ثُمَّ لَا تَجِدُواْ لَكُمْ عَلَيْنَا بِهِۦ تَبِيعًا ﴿٦٩﴾

ᵃ Despite man's insolence, God does not seize upon him immediately. Rather He afflicts him with some natural calamity by way of warning. Man is awakened by this but is so heedless that, as soon as he is relieved of his distress, this feeling of wakening soon vanishes into thin air. He remains blissfully unaware of the fact that he is as much in God's grip as he was earlier. His coming home safely after the sea voyage does not rule out the possibility of suffering the same calamity again. Furthermore, the dangers and insecurity on land are no less than at sea. Tempests at sea are like earthquakes on land. There is no place where he can take refuge from God's chastisement.

⁷⁰ We have honoured the children of Adam, and have borne them on the land and the sea, given them for sustenance things which are good and pure; and exalted them above many of Our creatures.ᵃ

* وَلَقَدْ كَرَّمْنَا بَنِىٓ ءَادَمَ وَحَمَلْنَٰهُمْ فِى ٱلْبَرِّ وَٱلْبَحْرِ وَرَزَقْنَٰهُم مِّنَ ٱلطَّيِّبَٰتِ وَفَضَّلْنَٰهُمْ عَلَىٰ كَثِيرٍ مِّمَّنْ خَلَقْنَا تَفْضِيلًا ۞

ᵃ Of all the creatures in the world, man has been given special superiority. When the moon and the stars have not been endowed with consciousness, why has man been given consciousness and will power? Man exploits everything on this earth— trees, mineral ores, animals—but has the power to prevent any other creature from exploiting him. The animals have to rely upon their teeth, horns and hooves to do things with, but man makes tools and machines to achieve his ends. The only possible thing for a river to do is flow downwards, following the slope of the land over which it passes, while man can climb to any height, having the power to travel up or down, in any direction he wishes.

Man has been provided for on a large scale in this world. The tree leaves convert solar energy into chemical energy in order to prepare food for man. Cows eat grass in order that they may return it in the form of milk. The honeybee is engaged in hectic activities day in and day out, sucking the nectar of the flowers from all around it to transform it into precious honey for man, etc.

All these gifts of God to man demand that he should become His grateful servant. But he shows little if any gratitude to his Maker.

71 The Day will surely come when We shall summon every people with their leader. Then those who are given their records in their right hands will read their records [eagerly] and shall not in the least be wronged: 72 but whoever has been blind in this life will be blind in the life to come, and still farther astray from the path [of truth].*

يَوْمَ نَدْعُواْ كُلَّ أُنَاسٍ بِإِمَامِهِمْ فَمَنْ أُوتِىَ كِتَبَهُۥ بِيَمِينِهِۦ فَأُوْلَٰئِكَ يَقْرَءُونَ كِتَبَهُمْ وَلَا يُظْلَمُونَ فَتِيلًا ۝ وَمَن كَانَ فِى هَٰذِهِۦ أَعْمَىٰ فَهُوَ فِى ٱلْأَخِرَةِ أَعْمَىٰ وَأَضَلُّ سَبِيلًا ۝

a In this world all human groups have their leaders. Similarly, in the Hereafter all groups will be rated along with their respective leaders—good people with their good leaders and evil people with their evil leaders.

Subsequently, everyone will be given a full record of his deeds in the world he left behind. The record of good people will be placed in their right hands while the record of bad people will be placed in their left hands. This will serve as a tangible sign that the first group is God's favoured group and the second is the disfavoured group.

The division between bad and good in the Hereafter will be on the basis of who lead his life in this world like a deaf and blind man and who lead his life in this world like one possessed of sight. Since God does not converse with man directly in this world, His messages have to be learned through the silent signs of this universe and through the words of God's messengers. Those who apprehend this indirect communication of the divine message will be regarded as possessing sight in this world. And those who do not understand this 'indirect language' and wait for the day when God Himself will appear and speak, are the ones who are blind in the eyes of God. Ultimately, the direct words of God will be of no avail to them. They will remain as far from the reality of truth at that time as they are today.

73 They indeed sought to entice you away from what We revealed to you, hoping that you might invent something else in Our name; and then they would have accepted you as a close friend. 74 If We had not made you stand firm, you would almost have inclined towards them a little. 75 In that case, We should have inflicted a double punishment in this life, and a double punishment after death. Then you would have found no one to help you against Us.ᵃ

وَإِن كَادُواْ لَيَفْتِنُونَكَ عَنِ ٱلَّذِىٓ أَوْحَيْنَآ إِلَيْكَ لِتَفْتَرِىَ عَلَيْنَا غَيْرَهُۥ وَإِذًا لَّٱتَّخَذُوكَ خَلِيلاً ۝ وَلَوْلَآ أَن ثَبَّتْنَٰكَ لَقَدْ كِدتَّ تَرْكَنُ إِلَيْهِمْ شَيْـًٔا قَلِيلاً ۝ إِذًا لَّأَذَقْنَٰكَ ضِعْفَ ٱلْحَيَوٰةِ وَضِعْفَ ٱلْمَمَاتِ ثُمَّ لَا تَجِدُ لَكَ عَلَيْنَا نَصِيرًا ۝

ᵃ The actual point of the divine task undertaken by the Prophet Muhammad in Makkah was that God is only one and anything else worshipped by people in the form of idols is false; although the Makkans acknowledged a greater God, they believed in other gods as well.

Who were these other gods? They were their leaders and past and present saints whom they regarded as sacred. They made stone images of them and started bowing before them. The call of monotheism given by the Prophet Muhammad struck at this belief in these revered personalities and so they asked the Prophet to make some compromises. They said that they would accept his deity only if the Prophet stopped criticizing their deities.

In this world one who speaks out against the sacred men of others becomes an object of their anger. On the contrary, the easiest way to endear oneself to them is to endorse their saintly men. But the way of the Prophet was to announce the truth without caring whether or not it was going to have an adverse effect upon the sacredness of their supposed deities.

The actual aim of spreading the word of God is to communicate the truth in its entirety. That is why no concession can be made in this matter. Whether it is a prophet or an ordinary person who comes forward to proclaim the truth, he has to represent it exactly as it is, without resorting to any compromises, even if it is at the cost of losing all friends and supporters.

⁷⁶ Indeed they came near to unsettling you, so that they might expel you from the land, but in that case they themselves would not have stayed on for very long after you. ⁷⁷ Such was Our way with the messengers We sent before you, and you will find no change in Our ways.ᵃ

⁷⁸ Say your prayers from the decline of the sun, until nightfall;ᵇ and at dawn—the recitation at dawn is indeed witnessed.

وَإِن كَادُواْ لَيَسْتَفِزُّونَكَ مِنَ ٱلْأَرْضِ لِيُخْرِجُوكَ مِنْهَا وَإِذًا لَّا يَلْبَثُونَ خِلَـٰفَكَ إِلَّا قَلِيلًا ۝ سُنَّةَ مَن قَدْ أَرْسَلْنَا قَبْلَكَ مِن رُّسُلِنَا وَلَا تَجِدُ لِسُنَّتِنَا تَحْوِيلًا ۝ أَقِمِ ٱلصَّلَوٰةَ لِدُلُوكِ ٱلشَّمْسِ إِلَىٰ غَسَقِ ٱلَّيْلِ وَقُرْءَانَ ٱلْفَجْرِ إِنَّ قُرْءَانَ ٱلْفَجْرِ كَانَ مَشْهُودًا ۝

ᵃ Whenever a preacher of truth, who represents a religion free of human interpolation, calls upon the people to the true religion, he has to face the obstructive attitude of those already in possession of hallowed religious seats. Such a preacher is all alone, without any powerful supports, unlike those occupying high religious positions. This difference results in misunderstanding, so that those in power come to regard the preacher as a totally worthless person. They even go to the extent of wanting to expel him from their town or city.

Such people tend to forget that this earth has been created by God. Therefore, trying to harm the preacher of truth amounts to proving themselves sinners in God's eyes. Moreover, expelling God's preacher from any human settlement is the equivalent of expelling a representative of the government of the time. Such an expulsion serves only to condemn the expeller. Whenever a man wants to belittle another, it is he himself who is belittled in the eyes of the Lord of the world. For it is the Lord who has the actual power to elevate His creatures in status or lay them low.

ᵇ The literal translation of this verse is, 'keep up prayer from the declining of the sun till the darkness of the night.' These words appear to mean that right from the declining of the sun till the darkness of night prayer is to be said continuously. There is no doubt about it that the majesty of God and man's obligations to his Creator demand that His servants continue to say their prayers at all times. This verse has been explained by the Prophet in a *hadith* which makes this difficult command easy for the believers. According to this *hadith* except for four prayers appointed at specific times, *zuhr, 'asr, maghrib,* and *'isha* i.e. from afternoon till evening, people may keep their contact with God only by remembering Him (*dhikr*). ▶

⁷⁹ And during the night wake up and pray, as an additional prayer:ᵃ it may well be that your Lord will raise you to a station of praise and glory.'ᵇ

وَمِنَ ٱلَّيْلِ فَتَهَجَّدْ بِهِۦ نَافِلَةً لَّكَ عَسَىٰٓ أَن يَبْعَثَكَ رَبُّكَ مَقَامًا مَّحْمُودًا ۝

The literal translation of part of the next verse is, 'and the dawn (fajr) recitation of the Quran.' If this part too is taken in its literal sense, it will mean that the Quran must be recited during the whole morning. But according to a hadith, the specific meaning of this command is that one prayer should be said in the morning, the special feature of which should be a longer recitation from the Quran. This makes the observance of this command easier.

ᵃ Tahajjud, literally means keeping a vigil at night. The spirit of the tahajjud prayer is remembrance of God in the hours of solitude, i.e. during the night. When a man has slept for a short time, and gets up feeling refreshed, that is the best hour. When he directs his attention to God with full devotion and recites God's words in the form of prayer during this hour, it is as if he were the epitome of devoutness. When his mind is fully concentrated on the prayer, his entire personality is so engaged that this strong attachment to God makes its way through his eyes.

ᵇ The high status of the Prophet (maqam mahmud) has two aspects, one pertaining to this world and the other pertaining to the hereafter. In the latter case it is linked by the commentators with the Great Intercession. As we learn from traditions, all the prophets will intercede, by the will of God, on the Day of Judgement on behalf of the believers. This intercession will be a testament to their being true believers, and only after this intercession by the prophets will the believers who have been awarded Paradise by God be admitted to Paradise. The Prophet Muhammad will be the Intercessor for the largest group, for his followers will be greater in number than any other.

The worldly aspect of this exalted status of the Prophet Muhammad is his being acknowledged and acclaimed by the nations of the world on account of his having become a historical prophet. Indeed, the divine plan saw its completion with his prophethood; today the people of the world are compelled to acknowledge him as a prophet of God. His prophethood has become an established fact, instead of being the subject of controversy as it was during the early period of his prophetic career. That is to say, it is a prophethood in favour of which so much historical proof has accumulated that no room is left for doubt regarding the personality and teachings of the Prophet. Man, by his own established academic standard, is compelled to accept his prophetic position. The ultimate form of that acknowledgement and acceptance is praise. That is why such a status is described as exalted.

⁸⁰ Say, 'Lord, grant me an honourable entrance and an honourable exit, and sustain me with Your power.' ⁸¹ Say, 'Truth has come and falsehood has disappeared. Falsehood is always bound to wither away.'ᵃ

⁸² We send down in the Quran that which is healing and a mercy to those who believe; as for the evil-doers, it only increases their loss.ᵇ

وَقُل رَّبِّ أَدْخِلْنِي مُدْخَلَ صِدْقٍ وَأَخْرِجْنِي مُخْرَجَ صِدْقٍ وَٱجْعَل لِّي مِن لَّدُنكَ سُلْطَٰنًا نَّصِيرًا ۞ وَقُلْ جَآءَ ٱلْحَقُّ وَزَهَقَ ٱلْبَٰطِلُ إِنَّ ٱلْبَٰطِلَ كَانَ زَهُوقًا ۞ وَنُنَزِّلُ مِنَ ٱلْقُرْءَانِ مَا هُوَ شِفَآءٌ وَرَحْمَةٌ لِّلْمُؤْمِنِينَ وَلَا يَزِيدُ ٱلظَّٰلِمِينَ إِلَّا خَسَارًا ۞

ᵃ The Quraysh leaders wanted to denigrate the Prophet Muhammad by heaping all kinds of blame and abuses upon him, but God's plan was to grant him an exalted status. This divine plan materialised, by God's will, in the form of favourable circumstances being produced in Madinah to coincide with the Prophet's emigration to this city. According to the divine plan, the majority of the Madinans took no time in converting to Islam as a result of the efforts made by the Prophet and his Companions to spread the word of God. Finally, Makkah was conquered and then the whole of Arabia surrendered to Islam. This was the divine plan that has been expressed in the Quran in the form of a prayer enjoined upon the Prophet.

ᵇ The Quran is a declaration of pure truth. The communication of the pure truth amounts to adversely affecting the interests of all those who follow such 'truth' as has been vitiated by human interpolation. But when the pure truth is laid before those whose thinking is realistic, it is accepted by them as their absolute standard or criterion, as opposed to following their own instincts. They mould themselves to the truth instead of moulding the truth to themselves. Owing to their sincerity and realistic thinking, the Quran becomes a blessing for them. Unlike them are the arrogant ones who think that they are great, because of their particular mindset. When the truth comes to them in its pure form, their minds function in the wrong direction. They fail to understand that, if they adopted the truth, they would become right-minded persons. On the contrary, they believe that if they accepted the truth presented by someone else, they would become diminished in stature. So, in order to satisfy their egos, they are ready to belittle the truth by refusing to accept it, and attempting to show that it is not worth accepting.

⁸³ When We bestow a favour upon a person, he turns his back and draws aside; and when evil afflicts him he gives himself up to despair. ⁸⁴ Say to them, 'Everyone acts in his own way, and your Lord knows best who is rightly guided.'^a

وَإِذَآ أَنْعَمْنَا عَلَى ٱلْإِنْسَٰنِ أَعْرَضَ وَنَـَٔا بِجَانِبِهِۦ وَإِذَا مَسَّهُ ٱلشَّرُّ كَانَ يَـُٔوسًا ۝ قُلْ كُلٌّ يَعْمَلُ عَلَىٰ شَاكِلَتِهِۦ فَرَبُّكُمْ أَعْلَمُ بِمَنْ هُوَ أَهْدَىٰ سَبِيلًا ۝

^a When man is granted ease and affluence, he demonstrates great self-confidence, becoming stubborn and unwilling to accept any new proposition, as if he were made of iron that cannot be bent. It is when he is deprived of all material props that he experiences a state of helplessness. Then he loses all courage and falls a prey to frustration.

In the present world everyone undergoes this experience, but there is no one who discovers himself in the process. In this world, where man is granted full freedom, he shows total disregard for the truth and does not try to imagine what his plight will be when Doomsday comes to take away all his power. How weak man is, yet how powerful he considers himself to be!

^b People's circumstances and bent of mind gradually lead them into forming a particular mental framework (*shakilah*) within which their thoughts are conditioned. But the right way of thinking is that which accords with divine knowledge. And the wrong way is that which runs counter to divine knowledge. This is the point on which man is being tested. What man has to do is break this framework formed by his mental conditioning, so that he may see things as they are. That is to say that he should start seeing things from the divine viewpoint. Those who break free of this mental conditioning and discover the divine way of thinking are the ones who are rightly guided.

⁸⁵ They question you about the Spirit. Say, 'The Spirit is at my Lord's command, and you have been granted but little knowledge.' *ᵃ*

وَيَسْـَٔلُونَكَ عَنِ ٱلرُّوحِ ۖ قُلِ ٱلرُّوحُ مِنْ أَمْرِ رَبِّى وَمَآ أُوتِيتُم مِّنَ ٱلْعِلْمِ إِلَّا قَلِيلًا ۝

ᵃ 'The Spirit' here means divine revelation. The Arabs who used to question the Prophet were not deniers of revelation. Their questions arose not out of their ignorance of the fact that God reveals His message to His prophets, but out of their ignorance of the Prophet, that is, not considering him worthy of receiving divine revelation. It was at a time when history had not yet created an aura of greatness around the Prophet.

He appeared to people like a common man, so they could not believe that the angel would come to him with God's words, and if they questioned him, it was only to scoff at him. However, in answer to this question the Quran gives us a very important principle, that is, that man has been granted only a little knowledge, and not complete knowledge. That is why realism demands that he refrain from embroiling himself in such questions as he cannot answer because of his natural limitations.

In ancient times man could see only with his naked eye. So observation by the eye could work only over a specific distance, which is not enough to study the truth. For instance, something which appears from a distance to be a single object turns out to be two when we come closer to it.

Since so many gadgets have become available in latter times, man has come to look upon them as remedies for his limitations. He thinks that by means of these gadgets, things can be observed to the fullest possible extent. But when man reached the twentieth century this misunderstanding came to an end. Then he learnt that things were far more complex and mysterious than were imagined, even with the aid of these gadgets. This being so, remaining content with limited knowledge is now the demand of realism, not just the demand of some creed.

During the age of Newton, the world of scientific research was limited to the macro world. In those times, it was held that all things of the world, in their ultimate analysis, were a combination of atoms and the atom was something which could be weighed and measured. In the light of this theory, it was believed that anything that could be weighed and measured or was tangible had any real existence. Consequently an unseen God could not be believed in at a scientific level.

However in the 20th century in the era of Einstein, with the splitting of the atom, human knowledge reached the micro world from the macro world. Now it was demonstrated that the atom was composed of electrons and protons, which were nothing but intangible waves or energy which could not be seen. It could be apprehended only by means of indirect effect or by inference. ▶

86 If We pleased, We would certainly take away that which We have revealed to you—then you would find no guardian for you against Us—87 except through the special mercy of your Lord. His favours towards you has been great indeed. 88 Say, 'If all men and jinn gathered together to produce the like of this Quran, they could not produce one like it, however much they helped one another.'ᵃ

وَلَئِن شِئْنَا لَنَذْهَبَنَّ بِٱلَّذِىٓ أَوْحَيْنَآ إِلَيْكَ ثُمَّ لَا تَجِدُ لَكَ بِهِۦ عَلَيْنَا وَكِيلًا ۝ إِلَّا رَحْمَةً مِّن رَّبِّكَ إِنَّ فَضْلَهُۥ كَانَ عَلَيْكَ كَبِيرًا ۝ قُل لَّئِنِ ٱجْتَمَعَتِ ٱلْإِنسُ وَٱلْجِنُّ عَلَىٰٓ أَن يَأْتُوا۟ بِمِثْلِ هَٰذَا ٱلْقُرْءَانِ لَا يَأْتُونَ بِمِثْلِهِۦ وَلَوْ كَانَ بَعْضُهُمْ لِبَعْضٍ ظَهِيرًا ۝

Therefore, unobservable things that could be proved by inference also came to be considered as having a real existence. This led to the belief in the argument from design. "Where there is a design (Universe) there is a Designer". It was thus accepted that if we could see the effect of God, His design, or the Universe, we had to ultimately believe in the existence of the Designer or the Maker of the universe.

Our capacities are limited, but the world beyond us is unlimited. It is impossible for the limited to grasp the unlimited. Human limitation demands that man should remain content with indirect knowledge, and stop insisting on direct knowledge. In other words, knowledge acquired by indirect methods should be regarded as being as valid as that acquired by observation.

ᵃ The Quran used to be revealed to the Prophet Muhammad at particular times. Apart from this, the Prophet had no power to compose words such as those of the Quran; his own personal way of expressing himself was always quite different in style.

The Prophet was quite disturbed when for a long time no revelations were made to him. But it was not possible for him to compose verses like those of the Quran on his own or with the help of his Companions. It is a fact that there is a great difference between the language and style of the Hadith and the Quran. This difference can be seen even today by any Arabic scholar.

This is a clear proof of the fact that the Quran is not a composition of the Prophet Muhammad: it has come from a mind far superior to the human mind. Those who believed that the Quran was composed of human words, were asked to compose such words as those of the Quran. If what they believed was true, and it was a human composition, they too should have had the power to compose such scriptures. They might even seek the help of others, and strive to produce verses like those of the Quran. But no one was able to answer this challenge at that time. Even in later times, no stylist or scholar has been able to produce any composition paralleling the verses of the Quran. Events show that a number of people did in fact strive very hard, but they could not produce a single verse like that of the Quran.

89 In this Quran, We have set out all kinds of examples for people, yet most of them persist in denying the truth. 90 They declare, 'We will never believe in you until you cause a spring to flow for us from the earth; 91 or you have a garden of date palms and vines, and cause streams to flow plentifully in the midst of them; 92 or you cause the heavens to fall down on us in pieces, as you have claimed; or you bring God and the angels before us face to face; 93 or you have a house made of gold; or you ascend to heaven; and we will not believe in your ascension until you send down to us a Book that we can read.' Tell them, 'Holy is my Lord. I am but a human being sent as a messenger.' a

وَلَقَدْ صَرَّفْنَا لِلنَّاسِ فِى هَٰذَا ٱلْقُرْءَانِ مِن كُلِّ مَثَلٍ فَأَبَىٰ أَكْثَرُ ٱلنَّاسِ إِلَّا كُفُورًا ۝ وَقَالُوا۟ لَن نُّؤْمِنَ لَكَ حَتَّىٰ تَفْجُرَ لَنَا مِنَ ٱلْأَرْضِ يَنۢبُوعًا ۝ أَوْ تَكُونَ لَكَ جَنَّةٌ مِّن نَّخِيلٍ وَعِنَبٍ فَتُفَجِّرَ ٱلْأَنْهَٰرَ خِلَٰلَهَا تَفْجِيرًا ۝ أَوْ تُسْقِطَ ٱلسَّمَآءَ كَمَا زَعَمْتَ عَلَيْنَا كِسَفًا أَوْ تَأْتِىَ بِٱللَّهِ وَٱلْمَلَٰٓئِكَةِ قَبِيلًا ۝ أَوْ يَكُونَ لَكَ بَيْتٌ مِّن زُخْرُفٍ أَوْ تَرْقَىٰ فِى ٱلسَّمَآءِ وَلَن نُّؤْمِنَ لِرُقِيِّكَ حَتَّىٰ تُنَزِّلَ عَلَيْنَا كِتَٰبًا نَّقْرَؤُهُ ۗ قُلْ سُبْحَانَ رَبِّى هَلْ كُنتُ إِلَّا بَشَرًا رَّسُولًا ۝

---

a When the Prophet Muhammad called to the Truth, his contemporaries said that they would believe in him only if he could perform miracles for them. But all such demands go against the divine plan of creation. God has created man as a conscious being and throughout the entire universe, this consciousness is a unique phenomenon—a gift by which man may recognise the truth by his own powers of reasoning, rather than wait to be convinced by miracles.

The truth is that in the present world man is being tested at the level of argument. Here, everyone has to recognise truth in the language of reasoning and argument and adopt it as such. Those who cannot recognize truth in this way are the ones who will be failures.

94 Nothing has prevented men from believing whenever guidance came to them, save their query, 'Has God sent a human being as a messenger?' 95 Say, 'If there had been angels walking around on earth, We would have sent an angel down from Heaven as a messenger for them.' 96 Say, 'God suffices as a witness between me and you [all]. He is informed about and observant of His servants.' *a*

وَمَا مَنَعَ ٱلنَّاسَ أَن يُؤْمِنُوٓاْ إِذْ جَآءَهُمُ ٱلْهُدَىٰٓ إِلَّآ أَن قَالُوٓاْ أَبَعَثَ ٱللَّهُ بَشَرًا رَّسُولًا ۝ قُل لَّوْ كَانَ فِى ٱلْأَرْضِ مَلَٰٓئِكَةٌ يَمْشُونَ مُطْمَئِنِّينَ لَنَزَّلْنَا عَلَيْهِم مِّنَ ٱلسَّمَآءِ مَلَكًا رَّسُولًا ۝ قُلْ كَفَىٰ بِٱللَّهِ شَهِيدًۢا بَيْنِى وَبَيْنَكُمْ إِنَّهُۥ كَانَ بِعِبَادِهِۦ خَبِيرًۢا بَصِيرًا ۝

---

a Anyone studying such verses, will find the stubbornness of those who denied such a 'great' Prophet as Muhammad very strange. The cause of this astonishment is traceable to the fact that before him is the 'great' Prophet as he is known today, while the deniers of the first phase had before them a contemporary prophet who was at that time just Muhammad ibn 'Abdullah, as yet with no glorious history to commend him. A prophet to his contemporaries appears to be only a human being like any other, but later on, with the accumulation of historical proofs regarding his prophethood, people have no doubt about his being a real prophet. That is why all the prophets have been rejected by their contemporaries, save a tiny minority, while the next generation had no reason not to acknowledge their greatness.

Since man is in a state of trial in the present world, he will never be informed of the truth through the angels. Such a communication of the truth would mean unveiling reality to the ultimate extent. If reality were to be unveiled in this way, how would man be put to the test?

⁹⁷Those whom God guides are the truly guided, and for those whom He lets go astray, you will find no helper besides Him, on the Day of Judgement. We shall gather them together, lying upon their faces, blind, dumb and deaf. Their abode shall be Hell. Every time the fire dies down, We will make it blaze up again for them. ⁹⁸That is their recompense, because they rejected Our signs and asked, 'When we are reduced to bones and dust, shall we indeed be raised up as a new creation?'ᵃ

وَمَن يَهْدِ ٱللَّهُ فَهُوَ ٱلْمُهْتَدِ وَمَن يُضْلِلْ فَلَن تَجِدَ لَهُمْ أَوْلِيَآءَ مِن دُونِهِ وَنَحْشُرُهُمْ يَوْمَ ٱلْقِيَمَةِ عَلَىٰ وُجُوهِهِمْ عُمْيًا وَبُكْمًا وَصُمًّا مَّأْوَىٰهُمْ جَهَنَّمُ كُلَّمَا خَبَتْ زِدْنَهُمْ سَعِيرًا ۝ ذَٰلِكَ جَزَآؤُهُم بِأَنَّهُمْ كَفَرُواْ بِـَٔايَٰتِنَا وَقَالُوٓاْ أَءِذَا كُنَّا عِظَٰمًا وَرُفَٰتًا أَءِنَّا لَمَبْعُوثُونَ خَلْقًا جَدِيدًا ۝

ᵃ In this world man leads his life according to his material status. In the Hereafter he will rise or fall according to his spiritual status. That is why those who went astray in this world will be raised on Doomsday as blind, deaf and dumb. Their straying resulted from their not using their eyes, ears and tongues towards the end for which they were intended. They did not see the signs of God. They did not pay heed to the evidence of God. They did not speak out in support of the truth, in spite of being able to see, hear and speak. So far as the truth was concerned, they were as if without eyes, ears, and tongue.

After death when they reach the next world, they will find themselves in their real face. In this world they are given everything without deserving it; it is like having an unreal face which they have received in this world purely on a temporary basis, because the present life is a period of trial.

There are two types of misguided people, one uttering words of insolence, like 'How can we be resurrected when we have crumbled to dust?', the other acting in such a way as to convey the same sentiments. The latter are those who do not properly use their eyes, ears, or tongues: they use these things against the very purpose of creation, then they blissfully imagine that their actions will have no consequences in the Hereafter.

⁹⁹ Do they not see that God, who has created heavens and earth, is able to create the like of them? He has appointed a definite term for them; there is no doubt about it, but the wrongdoers persist in denying the truth.ᵃ ¹⁰⁰ Say, 'Even if you possessed the treasures of the mercy of my Lord, you would surely hold them back for fear of spending. Man is indeed niggardly!'ᵇ

﴿ ٭ أَوَلَمْ يَرَوْاْ أَنَّ ٱللَّهَ ٱلَّذِى خَلَقَ ٱلسَّمَـٰوَٰتِ وَٱلْأَرْضَ قَادِرٌ عَلَىٰ أَن يَخْلُقَ مِثْلَهُمْ وَجَعَلَ لَهُمْ أَجَلًا لَّا رَيْبَ فِيهِ فَأَبَى ٱلظَّـٰلِمُونَ إِلَّا كُفُورًا ٩٩ قُل لَّوْ أَنتُمْ تَمْلِكُونَ خَزَآئِنَ رَحْمَةِ رَبِّىٓ إِذًا لَّأَمْسَكْتُمْ خَشْيَةَ ٱلْإِنفَاقِ وَكَانَ ٱلْإِنسَـٰنُ قَتُورًا ١٠٠ ﴾

ᵃ The earth and the sky exist before us as an undeniable reality. Their existence proves that there is a living being who has the power to create something out of nothing. When this initial creation is possible, why should there not be a second creation? The truth is that after accepting the first creation, no scientific, rational argument comes in the way of believing in the second creation.

In the face of such clear evidence, anyone who does not accept the second creation is a transgressor. He treads on the ground of stubbornness instead of on the ground of reason and rationality.

ᵇ Man is narrow-minded. He wants to build up all kinds of status for himself or for his group. If the distribution of all kinds of blessings had been in the hands of man, surely the rich and the powerful would in addition have reserved prophethood for themselves.

But God sees everything in terms of merit rather than community biases. He looks at all human beings and selects the best person out of the entire human race for prophethood. Had prophethood been conferred by human beings, their choice would certainly have been characterised by communal biases and prejudices rather than by merit.

¹⁰¹ We did indeed give Moses nine manifest signs; you can enquire from the Children of Israel. When he came to them, Pharaoh said to him, 'Moses, I can see that you are bewitched.' ¹⁰² He said, 'You know full well that none has sent down these signs but the Lord of the heavens and the earth as eye-opening evidence. Indeed, Pharaoh, I can see that you are doomed.' ¹⁰³ So he resolved to scare them out of the land: but We drowned him along with all those who were with him. ¹⁰⁴ Thereafter, We said to the Israelites, 'Dwell in the land. When the promise of the Hereafter comes to be fulfilled, We shall assemble you all together.' ᵃ

وَلَقَدْ ءَاتَيْنَا مُوسَىٰ تِسْعَ ءَايَتٍ بَيِّنَتٍ فَسْـَٔلْ بَنِىٓ إِسْرَٰٓءِيلَ إِذْ جَآءَهُمْ فَقَالَ لَهُۥ فِرْعَوْنُ إِنِّى لَأَظُنُّكَ يَٰمُوسَىٰ مَسْحُورًا ۝ قَالَ لَقَدْ عَلِمْتَ مَآ أَنزَلَ هَٰٓؤُلَآءِ إِلَّا رَبُّ ٱلسَّمَٰوَٰتِ وَٱلْأَرْضِ بَصَآئِرَ وَإِنِّى لَأَظُنُّكَ يَٰفِرْعَوْنُ مَثْبُورًا ۝ فَأَرَادَ أَن يَسْتَفِزَّهُم مِّنَ ٱلْأَرْضِ فَأَغْرَقْنَٰهُ وَمَن مَّعَهُۥ جَمِيعًا ۝ وَقُلْنَا مِنۢ بَعْدِهِۦ لِبَنِىٓ إِسْرَٰٓءِيلَ ٱسْكُنُوا۟ ٱلْأَرْضَ فَإِذَا جَآءَ وَعْدُ ٱلْءَاخِرَةِ جِئْنَا بِكُمْ لَفِيفًا ۝

ᵃ When clear signs were shown to the Pharaoh, he said that this was magic. This shows how powerful an argument and how great the signs of God that are presented by the preacher to the addressee, it is still open to man to reject the message by uttering some words which he thinks to be logical. He may call divine signs a form of magic produced by man, or ignore its rational proofs as carrying no academic weight and as such unacceptable.

When the opponents fail in suppressing the call of truth by verbal opposition, they stoop to aggressive activities against the messenger of truth, forgetting that this was not a human, but a divine matter. Who can succeed in the matter of God by resorting to aggression?

¹⁰⁵ We have revealed the Quran with the truth, and with the truth it has come down. We have sent you forth only to give good news and to give warning—¹⁰⁶ We have revealed the Quran bit by bit so that you may recite it to the people slowly and with deliberation. We have imparted it by gradual revelation.ᵃ

وَبِٱلْحَقِّ أَنزَلْنَـٰهُ وَبِٱلْحَقِّ نَزَلَ ۗ وَمَآ أَرْسَلْنَـٰكَ إِلَّا مُبَشِّرًا وَنَذِيرًا ۝ وَقُرْءَانًا فَرَقْنَـٰهُ لِتَقْرَأَهُۥ عَلَى ٱلنَّاسِ عَلَىٰ مُكْثٍ وَنَزَّلْنَـٰهُ تَنزِيلًا ۝

ᵃ The Quran is a declaration of pristine truth. But this pristine truth is what is least acceptable to man. For this reason God did not burden the preacher of truth with the responsibility of forcing people to believe in him. All that is desired of him is that he should communicate the truth to the addressee to the fullest possible extent.

The Quran makes full allowances for the weaknesses of the addressees. Hence the Quran has been revealed at intervals, so that those who are serious about it, may have time to fully understand it; slowly and steadily it may become a part and parcel of their thoughts and actions.

107 Say to them, 'You may believe in it or not. Those to whom knowledge had been revealed, fall on their faces in prostration when it is recited, 108 and say, "Glory to our Lord! Our Lord's promise is bound to be fulfilled." 109 They fall down upon their faces weeping, and [the Quran] increases their humility.'ᵃ

قُل ءَامِنُوا بِهِ أَوْ لَا تُؤْمِنُوا إِنَّ ٱلَّذِينَ أُوتُوا ٱلْعِلْمَ مِن قَبْلِهِ إِذَا يُتْلَىٰ عَلَيْهِمْ يَخِرُّونَ لِلْأَذْقَانِ سُجَّدًا ۩ وَيَقُولُونَ سُبْحَـٰنَ رَبِّنَا إِن كَانَ وَعْدُ رَبِّنَا لَمَفْعُولًا ۝ وَيَخِرُّونَ لِلْأَذْقَانِ يَبْكُونَ وَيَزِيدُهُمْ خُشُوعًا ۩

ᵃ Divine words require humility from man, for God does not come Himself to the present world to convey His message to man. He selects a human being for this purpose. Now those who are filled with ego and arrogance think that surrendering to the truth is tantamount to surrendering to a human being. That is why they refuse to accept it.

On the contrary, those who are free of arrogance can see God in the words falling from the lips of His messenger. So through these words they come in contact with God. They discover their humility vis-à-vis God's greatness. This experience moves their hearts. They fall prostrate before Him with tears in their eyes.

The leaders of the Quraysh are examples of the former, while the People of the Book who believed in the Prophet in the first phase, are examples of the latter.

The virtuous people mentioned in this verse are the People of the Book. They had learnt from their ancient divine scriptures that a final prophet was going to come, and that those who believed in him and supported him, would be held deserving of special divine succour. Therefore, they had been eagerly waiting for the advent of the final prophet. That is why they took no time in recognizing the Prophet Muhammad. They were so greatly moved by the words of the Quran that, while reciting it, they would fall down in prostration before God with tears in their eyes.

However, this is not a matter of just one group. The same applies to all human beings. God has already vested in the soul of every human being born on this earth the ability to recognize the truth. It is as if every individual is already waiting for the call of truth. Now those who live in a state of awareness can undergo the same experience as that of the People of the Book mentioned here. Consciousness at the level of nature will enable them to recognize the truth and rush towards it wholeheartedly.

110 Say, 'Whether you call on God or on the Merciful One: His are the finest names.' Pray neither in too loud a voice nor in silence, but between these two extremes. Seek a middle way 111 and say, 'All praise is due to God who has never begotten a son and who has no partner in His kingdom; nor does anyone aid Him because of any weakness of His. Proclaim His greatness.'*a*

قُلِ ٱدْعُوا۟ ٱللَّهَ أَوِ ٱدْعُوا۟ ٱلرَّحْمَٰنَ ۖ أَيًّا مَّا تَدْعُوا۟ فَلَهُ ٱلْأَسْمَآءُ ٱلْحُسْنَىٰ ۚ وَلَا تَجْهَرْ بِصَلَاتِكَ وَلَا تُخَافِتْ بِهَا وَٱبْتَغِ بَيْنَ ذَٰلِكَ سَبِيلًا ۝ وَقُلِ ٱلْحَمْدُ لِلَّهِ ٱلَّذِى لَمْ يَتَّخِذْ وَلَدًا وَلَمْ يَكُن لَّهُۥ شَرِيكٌ فِى ٱلْمُلْكِ وَلَمْ يَكُن لَّهُۥ وَلِيٌّ مِّنَ ٱلذُّلِّ ۖ وَكَبِّرْهُ تَكْبِيرًا ۝

---

a Those who have not found the truth at a deeper level always find themselves embroiled in petty, superficial things. Some hold that God should be called by one name, others by another name. Some hold that the words of devotions should be uttered loudly, others that they be uttered quietly.

The Arabs were engaged in such debates and discussions in different ways. God said that all His names were good. He might be called by any of His names. Similarly, acts of devotion are not to be judged by quiet or loud utterances, but rather by the spirit they evince.

The spirit of prayer is one of a deep consciousness of God's greatness. Belief in God should become akin to discovering a perfect and great Being, who is independent of any help from anyone; who has no equal and no partner. When this discovery finds words and comes to the lips of the believer, it is called celebration of God's greatness (*takbir*).

18. THE CAVE

In the name of God,
the Most Gracious, the Most Merciful

¹ Praise be to God who has sent down to His servant—the Book, which is free from any ambiguity ² and which rightly directs, to give warning of stern punishment from Him, and to proclaim to the believers who do righteous deeds that they shall have an excellent recompense, ³ wherein they will remain [in a state of bliss] forever. ⁴ And to warn those who say, 'God has taken to Himself a son.' ⁵ They have no knowledge of this, nor did their forefathers have any either. What they say is monstrous: they are merely uttering falsehoods! [a]

---

[a] The Quran is the corrected edition of previous divine scriptures. In the case of previous scriptures, successive generations made the divine teachings complicated by indulging in hair-splitting. Furthermore, the original teachings were subjected to distortion by means of interpolation, and in this way the very direction of these teachings was deflected. The Quran is free of both these types of human interference. On the one hand, it contains religion in its natural, pure and simple form, and on the other, its direction is unwaveringly towards God, as in fact it should be.

Why is it that God has arranged for the revelation of scriptures to the people of the world? The purpose of this is to acquaint them with His divine scheme. God has created man in this world for the purpose of trial. Thereafter, He will take a reckoning of everybody, and according to his deeds, will send him to hell or settle him in the eternal gardens of heaven. God wants everybody to be aware of this before death, so that nobody should have any excuse for wrongdoing.

One cause of man's going astray in this world is his taking someone other than God as his supporter. This deviance is at its worst when someone is believed to be the son of God. All such beliefs are false, because there is nobody on earth or in heaven who wields any power or authority except God.

⁶ Perhaps you may destroy yourself with grief if they do not believe in this message. ⁷ We have adorned the earth with attractive things, so that We may test mankind as to which one is best in conduct, ⁸ but We shall reduce all this to barren waste.ᵃ

فَلَعَلَّكَ بَـٰخِعٌ نَّفْسَكَ عَلَىٰٓ ءَاثَـٰرِهِمْ إِن لَّمْ يُؤْمِنُوا۟ بِهَـٰذَا ٱلْحَدِيثِ أَسَفًا ۝ إِنَّا جَعَلْنَا مَا عَلَى ٱلْأَرْضِ زِينَةً لَّهَا لِنَبْلُوَهُمْ أَيُّهُمْ أَحْسَنُ عَمَلًا ۝ وَإِنَّا لَجَـٰعِلُونَ مَا عَلَيْهَا صَعِيدًا جُرُزًا ۝

ᵃ 'Perhaps you may destroy yourself'—this statement shows what condition a preacher of truth is driven into by the intensity of his feelings, if he is serious and sincere in his mission.

The call of truth which is very clear in reasoning, and which is made by one whose sincerity has reached such a pitch as to spark off serious discussion among the people. If, in spite of this, people do not accept it, then what is the reason for their rejection?

The reason is the enticements of this world. The present world is so attractive that a man finds it difficult to rise above it. Therefore, he cannot grasp the importance of the call for truth, which seeks to wrest his attention from the glamour of this world and divert it towards a world whose glamour is not immediately visible.

But, the attractions of this world are purely temporary. They exist till the period fixed for man's trial is over. Thereafter, the glamour of the earth will be taken away, so much so that it will be reduced to the condition of a barren desert.

⁹ Do you think that the Men of the Cave*a* and the Inscription*b* were one of Our wondrous signs? ¹⁰ When the young men sought refuge in the cave, they said, 'Our Lord, grant us Your special mercy and give us right guidance in our affair.' ¹¹ Then We caused them to fall into a deep sleep for many years inside the cave. ¹² Then We woke them up again so that We might see which of the two groups would better calculate the time they had stayed there.

أَمْ حَسِبْتَ أَنَّ أَصْحَٰبَ ٱلْكَهْفِ وَٱلرَّقِيمِ كَانُوا۟ مِنْ ءَايَٰتِنَا عَجَبًا ۝ إِذْ أَوَى ٱلْفِتْيَةُ إِلَى ٱلْكَهْفِ فَقَالُوا۟ رَبَّنَآ ءَاتِنَا مِن لَّدُنكَ رَحْمَةً وَهَيِّئْ لَنَا مِنْ أَمْرِنَا رَشَدًا ۝ فَضَرَبْنَا عَلَىٰٓ ءَاذَانِهِمْ فِى ٱلْكَهْفِ سِنِينَ عَدَدًا ۝ ثُمَّ بَعَثْنَٰهُمْ لِنَعْلَمَ أَىُّ ٱلْحِزْبَيْنِ أَحْصَىٰ لِمَا لَبِثُوٓا۟ أَمَدًا ۝

---

a The incident of the Men of the Cave shows symbolically the stages through which true believers have to pass in their lives and the hurdles which they have to surmount. We learn from this incident that true believers sometimes, by force of circumstances, are compelled to take refuge in a 'cave'. But, from this cave which, to all appearances, was a grave for them, emerged a flood of life and vitality. Where their opponents had planned to end the lives of these young men, a new history began for them from that very same place.

If the Men of the Cave are the same individuals known as the Seven Sleepers in Christian history, the story relates to the city of Ephesus. This once famous city, dating back to ancient times, was situated on the west coast of Turkey, where its majestic ruins can still be seen today. During the period 249 to 251 A.D., this area was under the rule of a Roman ruler, Desius. Polytheism was prevalent here and the moon was treated as a god and worshipped. During this period, the message of the Unity of God (monotheism) reached this area through the early followers of Jesus Christ and started spreading. The Roman ruler of this place, who was a pagan, could not tolerate the spread of this monotheistic religion and started persecuting the followers of Jesus Christ. The aforesaid 'Men of the Cave' were seven young men from noble families of Ephesus, who embraced the monotheistic religion probably in the year 250 A.D. and who became preachers of that religion. When they were harassed by the authorities, they fled the city and took refuge in a big cave on the side of a nearby mountain.

b 'Men of the Slab', a literal transaltion of *ashab ar-raqim*, is probably the other name for the 'Men of Cave'. *Raqim* means the written one. It is said that when the aforesaid seven young men of noble families were not traceable, their names and particulars were, written, by order of the king, on a lead slab which was kept in the Royal Treasury. For this reason they came to be known as 'the Men of the Slab'. (*Tafsir ibn Kathir*, vol. 3, p. 73).

¹³ We shall tell you their story as it really was. They were young men who believed in their Lord, and on whom We bestowed further guidance. ¹⁴ We strengthened their hearts, when they rose up and declared, 'Our Lord is the Lord of the heavens and the earth. Never shall we call upon any deity other than Him: for that would be an outrageous thing to do. ¹⁵ These people of ours have taken deities other than Him. Why do they not produce clear evidence about them? Who is more wicked than the man who invents a falsehood against God?^a

نَّحْنُ نَقُصُّ عَلَيْكَ نَبَأَهُم بِٱلْحَقِّ إِنَّهُمْ فِتْيَةٌ ءَامَنُوا۟ بِرَبِّهِمْ وَزِدْنَـٰهُمْ هُدًى ۝ وَرَبَطْنَا عَلَىٰ قُلُوبِهِمْ إِذْ قَامُوا۟ فَقَالُوا۟ رَبُّنَا رَبُّ ٱلسَّمَـٰوَٰتِ وَٱلْأَرْضِ لَن نَّدْعُوَا۟ مِن دُونِهِۦٓ إِلَـٰهًا لَّقَدْ قُلْنَآ إِذًا شَطَطًا ۝ هَـٰٓؤُلَآءِ قَوْمُنَا ٱتَّخَذُوا۟ مِن دُونِهِۦٓ ءَالِهَةً لَّوْلَا يَأْتُونَ عَلَيْهِم بِسُلْطَـٰنٍۭ بَيِّنٍ فَمَنْ أَظْلَمُ مِمَّنِ ٱفْتَرَىٰ عَلَى ٱللَّهِ كَذِبًا ۝

---

^a 'Why do they not produce clear evidence?' This question indicates that after embracing the new faith, there were prolonged discussions between these young men and the leaders of their community. But the statements made by these leaders in the course of discussions did not contain any convincing arguments in favour of polytheism (*shirk*). Therefore, they (the Men of the Cave) found it impossible to give up a faith whose merits stood proved for the sake of a belief which had no such advantage.

On being opposed as above, had they given importance to the 'greatness' of the leaders of their community, they would have fallen a prey to hesitancy and doubt. But, when they gave more weight to sound reasoning and convincing arguments, it enhanced their faith. For, in respect of reasoning and arguments, these 'great men' appeared small to them. In spite of their outward greatness, they were found to be standing on false grounds and not on the grounds of truth.

¹⁶ 'Now that you have withdrawn from them and from all that they worship instead of God, take refuge in that cave; your Lord will extend His mercy to you and will make fitting provision for you in your situation.'[a]

وَإِذِ ٱعۡتَزَلۡتُمُوهُمۡ وَمَا يَعۡبُدُونَ إِلَّا ٱللَّهَ فَأۡوُۥٓاْ إِلَى ٱلۡكَهۡفِ يَنشُرۡ لَكُمۡ رَبُّكُم مِّن رَّحۡمَتِهِۦ وَيُهَيِّئۡ لَكُم مِّنۡ أَمۡرِكُم مِّرۡفَقًا ۝

---

[a] When a man, on account of his devotion to truth, becomes isolated from his fellow-beings, he comes closer to God. He comes so close to his Lord that he can converse with God. He talks with his Lord and receives a response from Him. The new faith of the 'Men of the Cave,' their fearless preaching, their willingness to forego everything rather than to forego the right path, had all bestowed upon them the high status of nearness to God.

Whatever they had apparently lost was nothing compared to what they had gained. It was this sense of achievement which enabled them to tolerate the loss of all else but the truth. They reconciled themselves to the position that they were living in a cave, renouncing the comforts of their homes and their town, while still entertaining the hope that God would help them and ameliorate their condition.

Ibn Jarir has quoted 'Ata as saying that they were seven in number. While in the cave, they used to pray to God, used to cry and seek His help. (*Tafsir ibn Kathir*). Finally God made them fall into a long deep slumber.

¹⁷ The sun could be observed to incline away from their cave on the right, as it rose, and to turn away from them on the left, when it set, while they lay in the wide space inside the cave. This is one of the signs of God. He whom God guides is rightly guided; but for him whom He lets go astray, you will find no helper or guide.^a

وَتَرَى ٱلشَّمْسَ إِذَا طَلَعَت تَّزَٰوَرُ عَن كَهْفِهِمْ ذَاتَ ٱلْيَمِينِ وَإِذَا غَرَبَت تَّقْرِضُهُمْ ذَاتَ ٱلشِّمَالِ وَهُمْ فِى فَجْوَةٍ مِّنْهُ ذَٰلِكَ مِنْ ءَايَٰتِ ٱللَّهِ مَن يَهْدِ ٱللَّهُ فَهُوَ ٱلْمُهْتَدِ وَمَن يُضْلِلْ فَلَن تَجِدَ لَهُۥ وَلِيًّا مُّرْشِدًا ۝

---

^a In the days when the Men of the Cave were propagating their faith, the struggle between them and their countrymen increased. During this period, probably in anticipation of the possible danger, they had selected a particular cave, which was spacious enough to accommodate seven men. Moreover, it seemed to have been north-south oriented so that the sun's rays never entered it either in the morning or in the afternoon, with the result that no passer-by could detect that some human beings were living in it. If a man remains uncompromising in matters of truth and righteousness, even in the most difficult circumstances, and he turns to God with patience and gratitude, then God guides him and leads him along a path where his faith will remain secure and where, at the same time, his missionary efforts will not be adversely affected. This kind of divine help was fully available to the Men of the Cave in view of their special circumstances.

Furthermore, God had chosen them for His special plan. The spiritual heights that they had attained had entitled them, in the eyes of God, to be seen as tangible evidence of life after death. The Men of the Cave sleeping for such a long period of time, and their awakening at the end of this period serves as a proof of life after death.

18 You would have thought they were awake, though they lay asleep. We turned them over, to the right and the left, while their dog lay at the cave's entrance with legs outstretched. Had you looked down and seen them, you would have surely turned your back and fled in terror.[a]

وَتَحْسَبُهُمْ أَيْقَاظًا وَهُمْ رُقُودٌ ۚ وَنُقَلِّبُهُمْ ذَاتَ ٱلْيَمِينِ وَذَاتَ ٱلشِّمَالِ ۖ وَكَلْبُهُم بَاسِطٌ ذِرَاعَيْهِ بِٱلْوَصِيدِ ۚ لَوِ ٱطَّلَعْتَ عَلَيْهِمْ لَوَلَّيْتَ مِنْهُمْ فِرَارًا وَلَمُلِئْتَ مِنْهُمْ رُعْبًا ۞

---

[a] God had arranged a long period of unbroken sleep for the Men of the Cave and had taken different measures for their safety. For example, they used to turn on their sides regularly, as otherwise, in the words of Ibn 'Abbas, the earth would have eaten up their bodies, as happens with dead bodies. At the mouth of the cave, a dog was constantly keeping watch. This was perhaps to prevent the entry of any man or animal. In addition to this, the atmosphere inside was made so terrifying by God that, if an intruder had tried to peep in, he would have become terrified at the very first glimpse and would have run away.

¹⁹ In the course of time, We raised them up again so that they might question one another. One of them asked, 'How long have you stayed [here]?' They said, 'We have stayed a day, or part of a day.' But others said, 'Your Lord knows best how long you have stayed here. Let one of you go then with these silver coins to the town, and let him find out what food is purest there, and bring you back a supply of it. Let him conduct himself with caution and not disclose your whereabouts to anyone: ²⁰ for if they find you out, they will stone you to death, or force you back into their faith. In that case you would never prosper.'ᵃ

وَكَذَٰلِكَ بَعَثْنَٰهُمْ لِيَتَسَآءَلُوا۟ بَيْنَهُمْ قَالَ قَآئِلٌۭ مِّنْهُمْ كَمْ لَبِثْتُمْ قَالُوا۟ لَبِثْنَا يَوْمًا أَوْ بَعْضَ يَوْمٍۢ قَالُوا۟ رَبُّكُمْ أَعْلَمُ بِمَا لَبِثْتُمْ فَٱبْعَثُوٓا۟ أَحَدَكُم بِوَرِقِكُمْ هَٰذِهِۦٓ إِلَى ٱلْمَدِينَةِ فَلْيَنظُرْ أَيُّهَآ أَزْكَىٰ طَعَامًۭا فَلْيَأْتِكُم بِرِزْقٍۢ مِّنْهُ وَلْيَتَلَطَّفْ وَلَا يُشْعِرَنَّ بِكُمْ أَحَدًا ۝ إِنَّهُمْ إِن يَظْهَرُوا۟ عَلَيْكُمْ يَرْجُمُوكُمْ أَوْ يُعِيدُوكُمْ فِى مِلَّتِهِمْ وَلَن تُفْلِحُوٓا۟ إِذًا أَبَدًا ۝

ᵃ When the Men of the Cave woke up from their sleep, they naturally started discussing the duration of their sleep. But, time had stopped for them by God's order and as such the period which was spread over centuries for others appeared to be just one day for the Men of the Cave.

After getting up they felt hungry. Still having some silver coins in their possession, they sent one of their number out with a coin. They insisted on his searching for clean food thinking that perhaps 'halal' food would be available in the Christian localities of the city. Moreover, they advised the concerned person to handle the matter cautiously and wisely, because, on the basis of past experience, they were afraid that if their opponents came to know of their existence, they would try to persuade them to return to polytheism and, on their refusal, they would kill them.

²¹ Thus We disclosed things to them so that they might know that God's promise was true and there was no doubt about the Hour [Judgement Day]. The people argued about them among themselves. They said, 'Build a monument over them. Their Lord knows best concerning them.' Those who prevailed in their affair said, 'Let us surely build a place of worship over them.' [a]

وَكَذَٰلِكَ أَعْثَرْنَا عَلَيْهِمْ لِيَعْلَمُوٓاْ أَنَّ وَعْدَ ٱللَّهِ حَقٌّ وَأَنَّ ٱلسَّاعَةَ لَا رَيْبَ فِيهَآ إِذْ يَتَنَٰزَعُونَ بَيْنَهُمْ أَمْرَهُمْ فَقَالُواْ ٱبْنُواْ عَلَيْهِم بُنْيَٰنًا رَّبُّهُمْ أَعْلَمُ بِهِمْ قَالَ ٱلَّذِينَ غَلَبُواْ عَلَىٰٓ أَمْرِهِمْ لَنَتَّخِذَنَّ عَلَيْهِم مَّسْجِدًا ۝

---

[a] The span of a man's life in this world is hardly a hundred years or even much less than that. After he dies, to all appearances it seems that he is finished once and for all, but the fact is that he exists even after death and rises again in a new world where he receives perpetual comfort or perpetual punishment.

This is a very serious human problem and has always been the subject of discussion. In view of its importance, God arranged for tangible evidence in addition to logical arguments so that there should be no scope for doubt about 'life after death'. Such tangible evidence has been presented in different forms in different periods. In the fifth century A.D., the emergence of 'the Men of the Cave' from the cave after 'death' is an extraordinary incident of this kind. In the present age, the researches of meta-science have uncovered instances of a similar nature which establish the veracity of the theory of life after death.

When the Men of the Cave emerged from their cave, the condition of their city had completely changed. It has been estimated that it was in the year 250 A.D. that they left their city of Ephesus and went into hiding in the cave. At that time a pagan ruler Desius was ruling in that area. In the meantime, due to the efforts of the Christian missionaries, the Roman King, Constantine, embraced Christianity, and thereafter, Christianity spread over the entire Roman domain.

The Men of the Cave returned to their city in the year 447 A.D., at which time Christianity had become the dominant religion in their city.

When the seven young men came out of the cave and it was confirmed by means of slabs kept in the Royal Treasury and by other means, that these were the very individuals who had had to leave their city on account of their Christian beliefs, paganism being prevalent there, they immediately became the centre of the people's devotion. The new Roman Ruler, Theodosus, himself went on foot to see them and seek their blessings. When they died, a place of worship was built at their cave as a memorial.

²²Some will say, 'They were three, the fourth was their dog,' and others will say, 'They were five, the sixth was their dog,' guessing at random. And yet others say, 'They were seven, the eighth was their dog.' Say, 'My Lord knows best their number.' Only a few know anything about them. Therefore, do not enter into controversies over them, nor seek information about them from any of them; *ᵃ*

سَيَقُولُونَ ثَلَـٰثَةٌ رَّابِعُهُمْ كَلْبُهُمْ وَيَقُولُونَ خَمْسَةٌ سَادِسُهُمْ كَلْبُهُمْ رَجْمًا بِالْغَيْبِ وَيَقُولُونَ سَبْعَةٌ وَثَامِنُهُمْ كَلْبُهُمْ قُل رَّبِّى أَعْلَمُ بِعِدَّتِهِم مَّا يَعْلَمُهُمْ إِلَّا قَلِيلٌ فَلَا تُمَارِ فِيهِمْ إِلَّا مِرَآءً ظَـٰهِرًا وَلَا تَسْتَفْتِ فِيهِم مِّنْهُمْ أَحَدًا ۝

ᵃ Some of the citizens indulged in unnecessary arguments about the Men of the Cave. Some people said that they were three in number and the fourth was their dog. Some said that they were five and their dog was the sixth, while some maintained that they were seven and the dog was the eighth.

But such discussions indicate an unsound approach. When the spirit of religion is alive, the entire emphasis is laid on the essence of the matter. When a nation or community is on the decline, the real spirit is neglected while outward formalities become the subject of heated discussions. A true God-worshipper should not indulge in such discussions and, even if another raises such questions, he should evade the issue by giving a brief reply.

²³ never say of anything, 'I shall certainly do this tomorrow,' ²⁴ without [adding], "if God so wills." Remember your Lord whenever you might forget and say, 'I trust my Lord will guide me to that which is even nearer to the right path than this.' *a*

وَلَا تَقُولَنَّ لِشَأْىْءٍ إِنِّى فَاعِلٌ ذَٰلِكَ غَدًا ۝ إِلَّآ أَن يَشَآءَ ٱللَّهُ ۚ وَٱذْكُر رَّبَّكَ إِذَا نَسِيتَ وَقُلْ عَسَىٰٓ أَن يَهْدِيَنِ رَبِّى لِأَقْرَبَ مِنْ هَٰذَا رَشَدًا ۝

---

a The Quraysh of Makkah sent Nadar ibn Harith and 'Uqbah ibn Mu'it to Madinah to meet the Jewish scholars and ask for information about the Prophet Muhammad, because the Jews had knowledge about prophets. The Jews advised these emissaries to ask the Prophet Muhammad about three things, adding that if he could give information about these things, then he was the Prophet; otherwise he was merely a glib talker. Of these questions, one was about the young 'Men of the Cave', the second related to 'Dhul Qarnayn' and the third was about the spirit.

Before the age of the press the common people did not know about the 'Men of the Cave.' This story was recorded in certain Syrian manuscripts, a fact known only to particular scholars. When this question was put to the Prophet Muhammad, he said that he would give the required information the next day, in the hope that Gabriel would appear the next day and give him the necessary information, which he would then pass on to the questioners. But, Gabriel's arrival was delayed. He took fifteen days to bring the chapter entitled 'The Cave' (*al-Kahf*).

Due to this delay in revelation, The Prophet Muhammad's Makkan antagonists had a good opportunity to malign his name on this issue. God said, 'On the pretext of a small, ordinary incident, you are trying to make people doubtful about the truthfulness of a person whose truthfulness is going to be vouchsafed by far better and much more convincing arguments.' (*Tafsir al-Mazhari*, vol. 6, p. 27).

Now that so many arguments have accumulated to substantiate the truthfulness of the prophethood of the Prophet Muhammad, no sensible person could deny it. Today, his prophethood is a well established fact and not merely a claim.

²⁵ [Some say], 'They stayed in their cave three hundred years,' and to that some have added another nine years. ²⁶ Say, 'God knows best how long they stayed in it.' Only God has knowledge of the unseen in the heavens and on the earth. How well He sees and how well He hears! Man has no other guardian besides Him. He allows none to share His sovereignty.ᵃ

وَلَبِثُوا۟ فِى كَهْفِهِمْ ثَلَـٰثَ مِا۟ئَةٍ سِنِينَ وَٱزْدَادُوا۟ تِسْعًا ۝ قُلِ ٱللَّهُ أَعْلَمُ بِمَا لَبِثُوا۟ لَهُۥ غَيْبُ ٱلسَّمَـٰوَٰتِ وَٱلْأَرْضِ أَبْصِرْ بِهِۦ وَأَسْمِعْ مَا لَهُم مِّن دُونِهِۦ مِن وَلِىٍّ وَلَا يُشْرِكُ فِى حُكْمِهِۦ أَحَدًا ۝

ᵃ According to the respective Quranic commentaries of Qatada and Mutrif ibn 'Abdullah, the mention here of 300 years, or 309 years, is only a report of what people said and not information from God. On the basis of unauthentic stories, the people of the Book of those days used to believe that the period of stay of the 'Men of the Cave' in the cave was 300 years, according to the solar calendar, or 309 years according to the lunar calendar. (*Tafsir ibn Kathir*, vol. 3, p. 79). The Quran has merely reported this popular view, but at the same time has rejected it as baseless, saying, 'God knows best how long they stayed in it.'

The researchers of the present age have discovered that, according to the solar calendar, this period was of 196 years. This discovery proves that the Quran is the book revealed by God, who is aware of all past and future happenings, and that because of this knowledge He did not accept the aforesaid belief. Had the Quran been the product of human effort, it would have adopted the most popular belief prevalent at that time, which would have ultimately clashed with the findings of subsequent research.

²⁷ Proclaim what has been revealed to you from your Lord's Book. None can change His words. You shall find no refuge besides Him. ²⁸ Keep yourself attached to those who call on their Lord, morning and evening, seeking His pleasure; and do not let your eyes turn away from them, desiring the attraction of worldly life; and do not obey one whose heart We have made heedless of Our remembrance, one who pursues his own whims and becomes dissolute.ᵃ

وَٱتْلُ مَآ أُوحِيَ إِلَيْكَ مِن كِتَابِ رَبِّكَ لَا مُبَدِّلَ لِكَلِمَٰتِهِۦ وَلَن تَجِدَ مِن دُونِهِۦ مُلْتَحَدًا ۝ وَٱصْبِرْ نَفْسَكَ مَعَ ٱلَّذِينَ يَدْعُونَ رَبَّهُم بِٱلْغَدَوٰةِ وَٱلْعَشِيِّ يُرِيدُونَ وَجْهَهُۥ وَلَا تَعْدُ عَيْنَاكَ عَنْهُمْ تُرِيدُ زِينَةَ ٱلْحَيَوٰةِ ٱلدُّنْيَا وَلَا تُطِعْ مَنْ أَغْفَلْنَا قَلْبَهُۥ عَن ذِكْرِنَا وَٱتَّبَعَ هَوَىٰهُ وَكَانَ أَمْرُهُۥ فُرُطًا ۝

ᵃ In ancient Makkah, for those who supported the Prophet Muhammad and who had embraced a religion free from any human interpolation, it was not an easy task. This amounted to renouncing a system which served their interests and accept a belief which appeared to be quite the reverse. The believers had almost become strangers in the society, while those who denied the truth drew strength from the firm ground of the established order of the day. The believers' thinking is God-oriented, the importance of which would be known only in the Hereafter. As opposed to this those who deny the truth have a worldly approach. Their concern is this world, not the Hereafter. As such they are more successful than the believers in this present life. They are surrounded with worldly glory.

But a preacher of truth should not be impressed by the worldly glamour of these people. A dayee is not allowed to compromise on the matter of truth at any cost.

If he does so, he will be deprived of God's succour. In God's world he will be so isolated that no tree will give him shade, and no water will quench his thirst. Ibn Jarir, commenting on this verse, writes, 'God says, O Muhammad, if you do not recite (or convey) the Quran to the people, then you will have no refuge against God.'

²⁹ Say, 'This is the truth from your Lord. Let him who will, believe in it, and him who will, deny it.' For the wrongdoers We have prepared a Fire which will cover them like a canopy, and if they beg for water, they will be given water as hot as molten lead, which will scald their faces: how dreadful a drink, and how evil a resting place! ^a

وَقُلِ ٱلْحَقُّ مِن رَّبِّكُمْ فَمَن شَآءَ فَلْيُؤْمِن وَمَن شَآءَ فَلْيَكْفُرْ إِنَّآ أَعْتَدْنَا لِلظَّٰلِمِينَ نَارًا أَحَاطَ بِهِمْ سُرَادِقُهَا وَإِن يَسْتَغِيثُوا۟ يُغَاثُوا۟ بِمَآءٍ كَٱلْمُهْلِ يَشْوِى ٱلْوُجُوهَ بِئْسَ ٱلشَّرَابُ وَسَآءَتْ مُرْتَفَقًا ۝

---

^a The truth which comes from God is the absolute truth. It cannot, therefore, be altered to suit personal vagaries. The amendment of God's truth amounts to changing those standards on the basis of which tests will be undertaken and every person's position will be determined.

Those who want God's truth to be altered with a view to legitimizing their behaviour, are actually adding insolence to misbehaviour. Such people should expect nothing but the severest punishment.

30 As for those who believe and do good deeds—We do not let the reward of anyone who does a good deed go to waste— 31 they shall dwell in the Gardens of eternity where rivers flow at their feet. Reclining upon raised couches, they will be adorned with bracelets of gold, and will wear green robes of fine silk and heavy brocade. An excellent reward and an excellent resting place! [a]

إِنَّ ٱلَّذِينَ ءَامَنُوا۟ وَعَمِلُوا۟ ٱلصَّـٰلِحَـٰتِ إِنَّا لَا نُضِيعُ أَجْرَ مَنْ أَحْسَنَ عَمَلًا ۝ أُو۟لَـٰٓئِكَ لَهُمْ جَنَّـٰتُ عَدْنٍ تَجْرِى مِن تَحْتِهِمُ ٱلْأَنْهَـٰرُ يُحَلَّوْنَ فِيهَا مِنْ أَسَاوِرَ مِن ذَهَبٍ وَيَلْبَسُونَ ثِيَابًا خُضْرًا مِّن سُنْدُسٍ وَإِسْتَبْرَقٍ مُّتَّكِئِينَ فِيهَا عَلَى ٱلْأَرَآئِكِ ۚ نِعْمَ ٱلثَّوَابُ وَحَسُنَتْ مُرْتَفَقًا ۝

---

[a] The condition of those who are free from pride, consideration of self-interest and love of outward show is such that when God's Truth appears before them, they immediately recognise it, even though such Truth might have come through the medium of a human being like themselves.

They prostrate themselves before the Truth, and begin to mould their lives in submission to the Truth instead of attempting to mould the Truth to fit their lives. Those who prove to be worshippers of Truth in this manner are God's near and dear ones. They will be showered with splendid rewards in the life hereafter.

³² Recite to them the parable of two men! One of them We provided with two vineyards which We surrounded with date-palms, and placed a field of grain in between; ³³ each garden produced its fruit and did not fail to yield its best; We even caused a river to gush forth in the midst of them, ³⁴ and so he had fruit in abundance. While conversing with his companion, he said, 'I am wealthier than you are, and have a bigger following!' ³⁵ Having thus harmed his own soul, he entered his garden saying, 'I do not think this will ever perish, ³⁶ and I do not believe that the Hour will ever come. Even if I am returned to my Lord, I shall surely find a better place than this.'ᵃ

۞ وَٱضۡرِبۡ لَهُم مَّثَلًا رَّجُلَيۡنِ جَعَلۡنَا لِأَحَدِهِمَا جَنَّتَيۡنِ مِنۡ أَعۡنَـٰبٍ وَحَفَفۡنَـٰهُمَا بِنَخۡلٍ وَجَعَلۡنَا بَيۡنَهُمَا زَرۡعًا ۝ كِلۡتَا ٱلۡجَنَّتَيۡنِ ءَاتَتۡ أُكُلَهَا وَلَمۡ تَظۡلِم مِّنۡهُ شَيۡـًٔا ۚ وَفَجَّرۡنَا خِلَـٰلَهُمَا نَهَرًا ۝ وَكَانَ لَهُۥ ثَمَرٌ فَقَالَ لِصَـٰحِبِهِۦ وَهُوَ يُحَاوِرُهُۥٓ أَنَا۠ أَكۡثَرُ مِنكَ مَالًا وَأَعَزُّ نَفَرًا ۝ وَدَخَلَ جَنَّتَهُۥ وَهُوَ ظَالِمٌ لِّنَفۡسِهِۦ قَالَ مَآ أَظُنُّ أَن تَبِيدَ هَـٰذِهِۦٓ أَبَدًا ۝ وَمَآ أَظُنُّ ٱلسَّاعَةَ قَآئِمَةً وَلَئِن رُّدِدتُّ إِلَىٰ رَبِّي لَأَجِدَنَّ خَيۡرًا مِّنۡهَا مُنقَلَبًا ۝

ᵃ Take the example of a lush green garden which, due to a sudden natural calamity, is completely destroyed. This, figuratively speaking, will be the fate of one who achieves wealth and position in this world and becomes proud as a result.

Whatever share of wealth and position a man receives in this world is, in fact, a test from God. But an unjust and transgressing man takes it to be the result of his own efforts. Consequently he develops an attitude of arrogance. He looks down upon a person whose share of wealth and position in this world is comparatively inferior. He develops a certain type of mindset by which he thinks that his world will never come to an end, and that even if this world ends and another world comes into existence, there is no reason why he should not enjoy the same comfortable conditions as he is enjoying here.

He fails to differentiate between the world of trial and the world of reward.

37 His companion replied, in the course of their discussion, 'Do you deny Him who created you from dust, from a small drop of fluid, then formed you into a man? 38 But as far as I am concerned, God alone is my Lord and I set up no partners with Him. 39 When you entered your garden, why did you not say, "That which God wills [will surely come to pass], there is no power save with God?" Although you see I have less wealth and offspring than you, 40 my Lord may well give me a garden better than yours and send down thunderbolts from heaven upon your vineyard, turning it into a barren waste; 41 or its water may sink into the earth, so that you will never be able to find it again!' *a*

قَالَ لَهُۥ صَاحِبُهُۥ وَهُوَ يُحَاوِرُهُۥٓ أَكَفَرْتَ بِٱلَّذِى خَلَقَكَ مِن تُرَابٍ ثُمَّ مِن نُّطْفَةٍ ثُمَّ سَوَّىٰكَ رَجُلًا ۝ لَّٰكِنَّا۠ هُوَ ٱللَّهُ رَبِّى وَلَآ أُشْرِكُ بِرَبِّىٓ أَحَدًا ۝ وَلَوْلَآ إِذْ دَخَلْتَ جَنَّتَكَ قُلْتَ مَا شَآءَ ٱللَّهُ لَا قُوَّةَ إِلَّا بِٱللَّهِ إِن تَرَنِ أَنَا۠ أَقَلَّ مِنكَ مَالًا وَوَلَدًا ۝ فَعَسَىٰ رَبِّىٓ أَن يُؤْتِيَنِ خَيْرًا مِّن جَنَّتِكَ وَيُرْسِلَ عَلَيْهَا حُسْبَانًا مِّنَ ٱلسَّمَآءِ فَتُصْبِحَ صَعِيدًا زَلَقًا ۝ أَوْ يُصْبِحَ مَآؤُهَا غَوْرًا فَلَن تَسْتَطِيعَ لَهُۥ طَلَبًا ۝

---

a If God showers His blessings on a man, he should always remain grateful to Him. But, if he does not possess the right mentality, prosperity becomes the cause of arrogance and vanity developing in him. On the contrary, one who possesses the right mentality does not forget God, even in poverty. He is content with whatever he has, while entertaining the hope that God will give him more.

A man who lives in this world with open eyes will never indulge in impudence or arrogance. Man is brought up as a humble creature. He is subject to accidents, disease and old age. Neither the water nor the other things with the help of which he cultivates his 'Garden' in this world personally belong to him.

All this is in order to ensure that man should live in this world with humility and modesty. But the transgressor does not learn any lesson from any of these things. He does not come to his senses until he loses everything and only after being deprived of everything does he come to realise—after seeing it with his own eyes—that he possessed nothing but total helplessness.

⁴²So it was, and all his fruit was destroyed. The vines had all fallen down on their trellises, and their owner wrung his hands, bewailing all that he had spent on his garden. He said, 'Would that I had not associated anyone with my Lord!' ⁴³He had no party to help him against God, nor was he able to defend himself. ⁴⁴The only support is from God, the True God. He is the best in rewarding and the best in respect of the final outcome.ᵃ

وَأُحِيطَ بِثَمَرِهِ فَأَصْبَحَ يُقَلِّبُ كَفَّيْهِ عَلَىٰ مَآ أَنفَقَ فِيهَا وَهِيَ خَاوِيَةٌ عَلَىٰ عُرُوشِهَا وَيَقُولُ يَٰلَيْتَنِى لَمْ أُشْرِكْ بِرَبِّى أَحَدًا ۝ وَلَمْ تَكُن لَّهُ فِئَةٌ يَنصُرُونَهُۥ مِن دُونِ ٱللَّهِ وَمَا كَانَ مُنتَصِرًا ۝ هُنَالِكَ ٱلْوَلَٰيَةُ لِلَّهِ ٱلْحَقِّ هُوَ خَيْرٌ ثَوَابًا وَخَيْرٌ عُقْبًا ۝

ᵃ An individual may invest his money in a venture and also apply his talents to it, hoping that his investment and his talents will lead to a successful result and will bring him good returns. But, different types of untoward incidents occur and his hopes are dashed to pieces. No human device or human talent is able to save him.

In this world, time and time again God creates such situations, so that people should learn a lesson from them and should not commit the mistake of giving importance to anything except God.

45 Give them an example about worldly life. It is like the vegetation of the earth that thrives when watered by the rain, which We send down from the sky, and then it all becomes stubble which the wind blows away. God has power over all things. 46 Wealth and children are an ornament of the life of this world. But deeds of lasting merit are better rewarded by your Lord and a far better source of hope.[a]

وَٱضْرِبْ لَهُم مَّثَلَ ٱلْحَيَوٰةِ ٱلدُّنْيَا كَمَآءٍ أَنزَلْنَٰهُ مِنَ ٱلسَّمَآءِ فَٱخْتَلَطَ بِهِۦ نَبَاتُ ٱلْأَرْضِ فَأَصْبَحَ هَشِيمًا تَذْرُوهُ ٱلرِّيَٰحُ ۗ وَكَانَ ٱللَّهُ عَلَىٰ كُلِّ شَىْءٍ مُّقْتَدِرًا ۝ ٱلْمَالُ وَٱلْبَنُونَ زِينَةُ ٱلْحَيَوٰةِ ٱلدُّنْيَا ۖ وَٱلْبَٰقِيَٰتُ ٱلصَّٰلِحَٰتُ خَيْرٌ عِندَ رَبِّكَ ثَوَابًا وَخَيْرٌ أَمَلًا ۝

---

[a] Things in this present world make the world hereafter understandable to us. When the earth, after getting water, becomes fresh and green, it appears as if it will remain like this for ever. But thereafter the weather changes and all the greenery dries up and withers away.

The glamour of this world is no different. The charms of the world attract a man, but they are all quite ephemeral. Doomsday (the Day of Judgement) will soon destroy them in such a manner that it will appear as if they never existed.

The attraction of the world will not last, but here there is one thing that is going to endure forever and that is the good and pious deeds of a man. Just as plants in the garden grow by seeds being sown in the earth, so also there is a garden which flourishes by God being remembered and obeyed. This garden never has a winter season. Unlike the garden of the world, this garden grows in the life hereafter but it will be available there only to the sower of seeds.

⁴⁷ The Day We shall make the mountains move and you will see the earth laid bare, and We shall gather all mankind together and shall not leave any one of them behind. ⁴⁸ They will be ranged before your Lord, standing in rows and He will say to them, 'Now you have come to Us as We created you at first. But you supposed that We would not appoint the time for the fulfillment of Our promise to you.'ᵃ

وَيَوْمَ نُسَيِّرُ ٱلْجِبَالَ وَتَرَى ٱلْأَرْضَ بَارِزَةً وَحَشَرْنَٰهُمْ فَلَمْ نُغَادِرْ مِنْهُمْ أَحَدًا ۝ وَعُرِضُوا۟ عَلَىٰ رَبِّكَ صَفًّا لَّقَدْ جِئْتُمُونَا كَمَا خَلَقْنَٰكُمْ أَوَّلَ مَرَّةٍ ۚ بَلْ زَعَمْتُمْ أَلَّن نَّجْعَلَ لَكُم مَّوْعِدًا ۝

ᵃ The conditions made available by God in the present world exist merely for the purpose of trying and testing mankind. The moment the period fixed for this trial is over, these conditions will not remain as they are. After this, all the life-giving properties of the earth will be taken away. It will become so barren and lifeless that it will have nothing for anyone to boast about or be proud of.

The freedom man enjoys in this world is given to him due to the conditions of trial. But, Doomsday will suddenly bring all this favourable environment to an end. On that Day, in a state of helplessness, people will be gathered before their Lord. All of them will stand before Him to hear His Judgement. God will have with Him a complete record of the life of every person, according to which He will reward some, and punish others.

In the present world, there are two aspects of man's life. In one he is free, while in another he is helpless. If a man were to look at the helpless and humble side of his life, he would turn towards God and develop in himself feelings of devotion towards Him. But, in reality, he looks only at his freedom, and the result is that he becomes negligent towards God and develops an arrogant attitude.

⁴⁹ The Book [of deeds] will be placed before them and you will see the guilty apprehensive about its contents. They will say, 'Woe to us! What a record this is! It does not leave any deed, small or large, unaccounted for!' They will find everything they ever did laid in front of them: your Lord will not be unjust to anyone.ᵃ

وَوُضِعَ ٱلْكِتَٰبُ فَتَرَى ٱلْمُجْرِمِينَ مُشْفِقِينَ مِمَّا فِيهِ وَيَقُولُونَ يَٰوَيْلَتَنَا مَالِ هَٰذَا ٱلْكِتَٰبِ لَا يُغَادِرُ صَغِيرَةً وَلَا كَبِيرَةً إِلَّآ أَحْصَىٰهَا وَوَجَدُوا۟ مَا عَمِلُوا۟ حَاضِرًا وَلَا يَظْلِمُ رَبُّكَ أَحَدًا

ᵃ Whatever a man does is put on record by God's arrangement. Man's intentions, his sayings and his deeds are all imprinted on the screen of the universe. Today this arrangement or system is not visible, but on the Day of Judgement a curtain will be raised. At that time man will be terrified to see that whatever he had been doing in the world under the impression that nobody knew about it, is so clearly recorded here that neither the smallest nor the greatest thing has been left out.

On the Day of Judgement, the treatment meted out to a man by God will be based on thoroughly established facts, so much so that on that Day when he receives his reward or punishment for his deeds, he will know, beyond a shadow of doubt, that he is getting what he really deserves—nothing more and nothing less.

⁵⁰ When We said to the angels, 'Prostrate yourselves before Adam,' all prostrated themselves except Satan. He was one of the jinn and he disobeyed his Lord's command. Do you then take him and his offspring as protectors instead of Me, despite their enmity towards you? This is an evil exchange for the wrongdoers! ᵃ

وَإِذْ قُلْنَا لِلْمَلَٰئِكَةِ ٱسْجُدُواْ لِءَادَمَ فَسَجَدُوٓاْ إِلَّآ إِبْلِيسَ كَانَ مِنَ ٱلْجِنِّ فَفَسَقَ عَنْ أَمْرِ رَبِّهِۦٓ ۗ أَفَتَتَّخِذُونَهُۥ وَذُرِّيَّتَهُۥٓ أَوْلِيَآءَ مِن دُونِى وَهُمْ لَكُمْ عَدُوُّۢ ۚ بِئْسَ لِلظَّٰلِمِينَ بَدَلًا ۝

ᵃ By tradition, Satan (Iblis) was a God-worshipping jinn. Apparently he posed as being pious. But when God commanded him to kneel before Adam, he was not prepared to do so because of his vanity or pride. Now, those who under the influence of false pride refuse to kneel before 'Reality' or 'Truth', are all kith and kin of Satan, though they apparently seem to be God-worshipping people.

To kneel before God is, in fact, admitting one's own humbleness. If somebody is a kneeler before God in the real sense, then whenever he comes face to face with the Truth, he will immediately kneel down. Unlike him is the person who is only outwardly pious, because at the same time he nurses a sense of pride or egoism within himself. Such a person will readily kneel down on the occasions when his ego is not hurt. But, where his kneeling down is at the cost of surrendering his ego, he will suddenly become arrogant and refuse to kneel.

When the call of Truth is given and certain people, under the influence of Satan and his kin, do not respond to that call, they are in fact substituting Satan and his kin for God. When they are required to bow before the Truth for fear of God, they refuse to bow for fear of false gods. Such people are the worst transgressors. Soon they will come to know that those other than God on whom they relied will not be of any avail to them.

⁵¹ I did not call them to witness at the creation of the heavens and the earth, nor at their own creation; I do not take as My helpers those who lead others astray.[a]

⁵² On that Day He will say to them, 'Call on those whom you thought to be My partners.' And they will call on them, but their prayer will not be heard; and We shall place a barrier [of enmity] between them. ⁵³ The guilty shall see the Fire and realize that they are going to fall into it: they shall find no way of escape from it.[b]

* مَّآ أَشْهَدتُّهُمْ خَلْقَ ٱلسَّمَٰوَٰتِ وَٱلْأَرْضِ وَلَا خَلْقَ أَنفُسِهِمْ وَمَا كُنتُ مُتَّخِذَ ٱلْمُضِلِّينَ عَضُدًا ۞ وَيَوْمَ يَقُولُ نَادُوا۟ شُرَكَآءِىَ ٱلَّذِينَ زَعَمْتُمْ فَدَعَوْهُمْ فَلَمْ يَسْتَجِيبُوا۟ لَهُمْ وَجَعَلْنَا بَيْنَهُم مَّوْبِقًا ۞ وَرَءَا ٱلْمُجْرِمُونَ ٱلنَّارَ فَظَنُّوٓا۟ أَنَّهُم مُّوَاقِعُوهَا وَلَمْ يَجِدُوا۟ عَنْهَا مَصْرِفًا ۞

[a] Those who are regarded as powerful and as objects of worship by men, are in fact so powerless that they have no say either in the creation of the universe or in their own creation. Further, by playing the role of the one who misleads people ('mudil'), they prove themselves absolutely unworthy of trust. In a world where Truth reigns supreme, how can such personalities hold sway when their only goal is to dissuade the people from Truth?

[b] The leaders on whose backing man denies the Truth in this world will not be helpful to him on Doomsday. Today, they are each other's companions, but when realities are revealed, they will start hating each other. It will appear as if a deadly barrier has come between them. In the present world they consider themselves safe and secure, but on Doomsday they are fated to find themselves standing on the threshold of Hell, unable to find an escape from it.

⁵⁴ We have explained in various ways in this Quran, for the benefit of mankind, all kinds of examples, but man is most contentious. ⁵⁵ Nothing prevents people from believing when they are given guidance or from asking forgiveness of their Lord, but the fact that the fate of the previous peoples should befall them or to have the punishment come upon them face to face.ᵃ

وَلَقَدْ صَرَّفْنَا فِي هَٰذَا ٱلْقُرْءَانِ لِلنَّاسِ مِن كُلِّ مَثَلٍ وَكَانَ ٱلْإِنسَٰنُ أَكْثَرَ شَىْءٍ جَدَلًا ۝ وَمَا مَنَعَ ٱلنَّاسَ أَن يُؤْمِنُوٓا۟ إِذْ جَآءَهُمُ ٱلْهُدَىٰ وَيَسْتَغْفِرُوا۟ رَبَّهُمْ إِلَّآ أَن تَأْتِيَهُمْ سُنَّةُ ٱلْأَوَّلِينَ أَوْ يَأْتِيَهُمُ ٱلْعَذَابُ قُبُلًا ۝

ᵃ In the present world, the freedom given for the purposes of human trial allows man to find some excuse or the other for not admitting the Truth. He will find some word or the other to reject any proposition put to him. Sometimes it happens that an individual will try to counter convincing arguments by meaningless pleadings. At other times he simply ignores the argument given and demands something entirely different which, for some reason, has not so far been presented.

An extreme example of this is the Prophet presenting his message supported by clear arguments to his audience, their not paying any attention to it and, completely ignoring it, saying, 'Where is the punishment—in case of our refusal—about which you informed us? Bring it on us and let us see it.'

⁵⁶ We only send the messengers to bring good news and to give warning. Those who deny use fallacious arguments to nullify the truth, treating My revelations and My warnings as a jest. ⁵⁷ Who is more wicked than he who has been reminded of the revelations of his Lord, then turns away from them and forgets what his own hands have done? We have cast veils over their hearts lest they understand Our words, and made them hard of hearing. Call them as you may to the right path, they shall never be guided.ᵃ

وَمَا نُرْسِلُ ٱلْمُرْسَلِينَ إِلَّا مُبَشِّرِينَ وَمُنذِرِينَ ۚ وَيُجَٰدِلُ ٱلَّذِينَ كَفَرُواْ بِٱلْبَٰطِلِ لِيُدْحِضُواْ بِهِ ٱلْحَقَّ ۖ وَٱتَّخَذُوٓاْ ءَايَٰتِى وَمَآ أُنذِرُواْ هُزُوًا ۝ وَمَنْ أَظْلَمُ مِمَّن ذُكِّرَ بِـَٔايَٰتِ رَبِّهِۦ فَأَعْرَضَ عَنْهَا وَنَسِىَ مَا قَدَّمَتْ يَدَاهُ ۚ إِنَّا جَعَلْنَا عَلَىٰ قُلُوبِهِمْ أَكِنَّةً أَن يَفْقَهُوهُ وَفِىٓ ءَاذَانِهِمْ وَقْرًا ۖ وَإِن تَدْعُهُمْ إِلَى ٱلْهُدَىٰ فَلَن يَهْتَدُوٓاْ إِذًا أَبَدًا ۝

ᵃ God's words are supported by sound arguments, that is why those who do not want to accept this truth cannot find any real counter arguments. They entertain baseless notions by which they make unsuccessful attempts to suppress the Truth. They counter solid arguments with false objections, so that serious matters may be lost in ridicule.

The propaganda is aimed at discrediting the preacher in the eyes of the people. But they are oblivious of the fact that it is they themselves who are discredited in the eyes of God by such a campaign.

Man has been endowed with the capacity to think, so that he should be able to distinguish between Truth and falsehood. But, when he uses his thinking capacity in the wrong direction, it becomes impossible for him to see a thing in its right perspective and to grasp its true significance. He becomes 'eyeless', though having eyes and 'earless', though having ears.

58 Your Lord is the Forgiving One, the possessor of mercy. If He had to take them to task for the wrongs they have done, He would have hastened their punishment. They have an appointed time beyond which there will be no escape for them. 59 We destroyed these communities when they went on doing wrong, and We appointed a time for their destruction.[a]

وَرَبُّكَ ٱلْغَفُورُ ذُو ٱلرَّحْمَةِ لَوْ يُؤَاخِذُهُم بِمَا كَسَبُوا۟ لَعَجَّلَ لَهُمُ ٱلْعَذَابَ بَل لَّهُم مَّوْعِدٌ لَّن يَجِدُوا۟ مِن دُونِهِۦ مَوْئِلًا ۞ وَتِلْكَ ٱلْقُرَىٰٓ أَهْلَكْنَٰهُمْ لَمَّا ظَلَمُوا۟ وَجَعَلْنَا لِمَهْلِكِهِم مَّوْعِدًا ۞

---

[a] When a man flouts the Truth, but does not immediately receive the punishment for this, it makes him arrogant. The fact of his going scot free is only due to the latitude given to him during the period of trial, and not because of any real freedom.

If the individual is keen to learn a lesson, he must consider the fate of his predecessors, from which he may learn how to conduct his present life. On the face of this earth, different nations and different cultures have risen from time to time and have subsequently been destroyed. When earlier generations were punished for their disobedience, why should later generations not meet the same fate?

⁶⁰ Recall how Moses said to his servant, 'I shall not give up until I reach the place where both seas meet, even if it takes me years!' ⁶¹ But when at last they came to the land where the two seas met, they forgot their fish and it swiftly made its way into the sea. ⁶² After they had passed the place, Moses said to his young companion, 'Bring us our morning meal; we have indeed been fatigued by this journey.' ᵃ

وَإِذْ قَالَ مُوسَىٰ لِفَتَىٰهُ لَآ أَبْرَحُ حَتَّىٰٓ أَبْلُغَ مَجْمَعَ ٱلْبَحْرَيْنِ أَوْ أَمْضِيَ حُقُبًا ۝ فَلَمَّا بَلَغَا مَجْمَعَ بَيْنِهِمَا نَسِيَا حُوتَهُمَا فَٱتَّخَذَ سَبِيلَهُۥ فِى ٱلْبَحْرِ سَرَبًا ۝ فَلَمَّا جَاوَزَا قَالَ لِفَتَىٰهُ ءَاتِنَا غَدَآءَنَا لَقَدْ لَقِينَا مِن سَفَرِنَا هَٰذَا نَصَبًا ۝

ᵃ God continuously manages the affairs of this world through His angels. Since this system is not visible to man, he does not fully grasp its secrets. He harbours different types of doubts due to his deficient knowledge.

To remedy this, God has given the opportunity for indirect observation to certain of His selected subjects. He has arranged for them to observe His invisible world, so that they should see with their own eyes its wisdom and make others aware of it. Here, the incident relating to Moses is a similar type of exceptional event, by means of which he was given a glimpse of God's invisible system.

Moses is said to have undertaken this journey between Egypt and Sudan along with one young disciple Yusha' bin Nun (Joshua). By way of a sign, God had asked him to proceed on his journey until he reached a place where two seas came together. He was told that there he would find somebody (perhaps an angel in the shape of a human being), whom he was asked to accompany.

⁶³ He replied, 'Did you see when we were resting by the rock, that I forgot the fish? Satan made me forget it, so I did not mention it. It made its way to the sea in a miraculous way!' ⁶⁴ Moses said, 'That is just what we were looking for.' So they went back the way they had come, ⁶⁵ and they found one of Our servants to whom We had granted Our mercy and had given a knowledge from Ourself.

⁶⁶ Moses said to him, 'May I follow you, so that you may guide me by what you have been taught?' ⁶⁷ He replied, 'You will not be able to bear with me patiently. ⁶⁸ How could you be patient in matters beyond your knowledge?' ⁶⁹ Moses said, 'God willing, you will find me patient, and I will not disobey you in any thing.' ⁷⁰ He said, 'Well then, if you would follow me, do not ask me about anything till I speak of it to you.'ᵃ

قَالَ أَرَءَيْتَ إِذْ أَوَيْنَآ إِلَى ٱلصَّخْرَةِ فَإِنِّي نَسِيتُ ٱلْحُوتَ وَمَآ أَنسَىٰنِيهُ إِلَّا ٱلشَّيْطَٰنُ أَنْ أَذْكُرَهُۥ وَٱتَّخَذَ سَبِيلَهُۥ فِي ٱلْبَحْرِ عَجَبًا ۝ قَالَ ذَٰلِكَ مَا كُنَّا نَبْغِ فَٱرْتَدَّا عَلَىٰٓ ءَاثَارِهِمَا قَصَصًا ۝ فَوَجَدَا عَبْدًا مِّنْ عِبَادِنَآ ءَاتَيْنَٰهُ رَحْمَةً مِّنْ عِندِنَا وَعَلَّمْنَٰهُ مِن لَّدُنَّا عِلْمًا ۝ قَالَ لَهُۥ مُوسَىٰ هَلْ أَتَّبِعُكَ عَلَىٰٓ أَن تُعَلِّمَنِ مِمَّا عُلِّمْتَ رُشْدًا ۝ قَالَ إِنَّكَ لَن تَسْتَطِيعَ مَعِىَ صَبْرًا ۝ وَكَيْفَ تَصْبِرُ عَلَىٰ مَا لَمْ تُحِطْ بِهِۦ خُبْرًا ۝ قَالَ سَتَجِدُنِىٓ إِن شَآءَ ٱللَّهُ صَابِرًا وَلَآ أَعْصِى لَكَ أَمْرًا ۝ قَالَ فَإِنِ ٱتَّبَعْتَنِى فَلَا تَسْـَٔلْنِى عَن شَىْءٍ حَتَّىٰٓ أُحْدِثَ لَكَ مِنْهُ ذِكْرًا ۝

ᵃ Moses was told about a further sign, i.e. that when he reached the required destination, the fish kept for eating would go down into the water in a peculiar manner. And at a certain place this was exactly what happened. But the fish was with the disciple and he could not for some reason inform Moses about this incident. After proceeding a little further, Moses came to know of this incident. He immediately returned to that place and found Khidr there, the person for whom he had undertaken such a long journey.

ᵇ God had bestowed on this servant, Khidr, special knowledge and powers, so that he could bring certain extraordinary influence to bear upon the affairs of this world. In view of this knowledge, he used to act against the customary norms. That is why, on Moses' request to be allowed to accompany him, he said that he (Moses) would not be able to bear it.

⁷¹ So they set out, but, when they got into a boat, the man made a hole in it. Moses exclaimed, 'Have you made a hole in the boat to drown the people in it? You have indeed done a dreadful thing!' ⁷² He replied, 'Did I not tell you that you would never be able to bear with me patiently?' ⁷³ He said, 'Do not take me to task for what I have forgotten, and do not be hard on me on account of what I have done.' ⁷⁴ So they travelled on. Then they met a young boy and the man killed him. Moses said, 'Have you slain an innocent person without his having slain anyone? Indeed, you have done a terrible thing!' ^a

فَٱنطَلَقَا حَتَّىٰ إِذَا رَكِبَا فِى ٱلسَّفِينَةِ خَرَقَهَا قَالَ أَخَرَقْتَهَا لِتُغْرِقَ أَهْلَهَا لَقَدْ جِئْتَ شَيْئًا إِمْرًا ۝ قَالَ أَلَمْ أَقُلْ إِنَّكَ لَن تَسْتَطِيعَ مَعِىَ صَبْرًا ۝ قَالَ لَا تُؤَاخِذْنِى بِمَا نَسِيتُ وَلَا تُرْهِقْنِى مِنْ أَمْرِى عُسْرًا ۝ فَٱنطَلَقَا حَتَّىٰ إِذَا لَقِيَا غُلَٰمًا فَقَتَلَهُۥ قَالَ أَقَتَلْتَ نَفْسًا زَكِيَّةً بِغَيْرِ نَفْسٍ لَّقَدْ جِئْتَ شَيْئًا نُّكْرًا ۝

---

^a Damaging a good boat and killing a child do not appear to be good deeds. But, as the ensuing verses show, a profound sagacity was hidden in them. These apparently wrong deeds were in reality correct and useful acts.

This also provides an answer to what is known as the 'problem of evil'. In this world of human beings, there are many things which at first sight appear to be evils in the system. Yet, they are based on deep wisdom. It is true that in the present world this wisdom is hidden behind a veil. But, in the life hereafter, this veil will not be there. At that time, man will come to know that whatever happened was done according to the highest standards of justice.

75 The man said, 'Did I not tell you that you would not be able to have any patience with me?' 76 Moses replied, 'If I ever ask you about anything after this, do not let me accompany you. I will have given you sufficient excuse.' 77 So they went on until they came to a town. They asked its people for food, but were refused hospitality. They found a wall in the town which was about to fall down. His companion buttressed it and Moses said, 'Had you wished, you could have demanded payment for your labours.' 78 He answered, 'This is where you and I must part company. But first I will tell you the meaning of the things you could not bear with patiently.'ᵃ

۞ قَالَ أَلَمْ أَقُل لَّكَ إِنَّكَ لَن تَسْتَطِيعَ مَعِيَ صَبْرًا ﴿٧٥﴾ قَالَ إِن سَأَلْتُكَ عَن شَيْءٍ بَعْدَهَا فَلَا تُصَاحِبْنِي قَدْ بَلَغْتَ مِن لَّدُنِّي عُذْرًا ﴿٧٦﴾ فَانطَلَقَا حَتَّىٰ إِذَآ أَتَيَا أَهْلَ قَرْيَةٍ اسْتَطْعَمَا أَهْلَهَا فَأَبَوْا أَن يُضَيِّفُوهُمَا فَوَجَدَا فِيهَا جِدَارًا يُرِيدُ أَن يَنقَضَّ فَأَقَامَهُ قَالَ لَوْ شِئْتَ لَتَّخَذْتَ عَلَيْهِ أَجْرًا ﴿٧٧﴾ قَالَ هَٰذَا فِرَاقُ بَيْنِي وَبَيْنِكَ سَأُنَبِّئُكَ بِتَأْوِيلِ مَا لَمْ تَسْتَطِع عَّلَيْهِ صَبْرًا ﴿٧٨﴾

ᵃ The Prophet Moses and Khidr, God's favoured servants, who were very near to Him, wanted the local people of a place they had reached to treat them as guests and feed them. But they refused to do so. This shows that it is not enough for one simply to be in oneself righteous and truthful and to be in God's favour, in order to have a place in others' esteem. Had the people of that place recognized them, they would have certainly made them their guests and obtained their blessings. But due to their ordinary outward appearance, they ignored them. They could not see them in the light of their inner reality.

In spite of this inhospitable treatment, Khidr repaired a crumbling wall belonging to the local people. The behaviour of God's true and pious subjects with others is not retaliatory, but is always in accordance with the norms of justice and righteousness.

79 'The boat belonged to some poor people who made their living from the sea. I wanted to damage it because there was a king coming behind them who was seizing every boat by force.[a]

80 As for the youth, his parents were believers and we feared that he would trouble them by rebellion and denial of truth. 81 We wanted their Lord to replace him with someone purer than him and more compassionate.[b]

أَمَّا ٱلسَّفِينَةُ فَكَانَتْ لِمَسَٰكِينَ يَعْمَلُونَ فِي ٱلْبَحْرِ فَأَرَدتُّ أَنْ أَعِيبَهَا وَكَانَ وَرَآءَهُم مَّلِكٌ يَأْخُذُ كُلَّ سَفِينَةٍ غَصْبًا ۝ وَأَمَّا ٱلْغُلَٰمُ فَكَانَ أَبَوَاهُ مُؤْمِنَيْنِ فَخَشِينَآ أَن يُرْهِقَهُمَا طُغْيَٰنًا وَكُفْرًا ۝ فَأَرَدْنَآ أَن يُبْدِلَهُمَا رَبُّهُمَا خَيْرًا مِّنْهُ زَكَوٰةً وَأَقْرَبَ رُحْمًا ۝

---

[a] Khidr had not rendered the boat completely useless; he had only made it defective for the time being. The wisdom behind it was that, farther up the river where the boat was going, there was a king who, perhaps in connection with a war campaign, was forcibly confiscating good boats. So, the boat was made defective so that when the king's agents saw it, they should treat is as undeserving of attention and leave it.

This teaches us that a man should not lose heart if he has to face some untoward incident. He should reconcile with it, hoping that there should be some advantage hidden in whatever God has done, though man is not at that time fully aware of it.

[b] This incident of the child indicates the different ways in which God helps his subjects. He even helps them in matters of which they are not even aware and, not being aware of them, cannot pray to their Lord seeking a solution. Man should always demonstrate patience and gratitude to God. He should always hope for good from God in all circumstances. God is all-knowing and that is why He knows best. God knows better what is good for his subject while the subject himself cannot be aware of this due to his limited knowledge.

82 'The wall belonged to two young orphans in the town whose father had been a righteous man, and a treasure of theirs lay underneath it. So your Lord wanted them to come of age and then to dig up their treasure as a mercy from Him. I did not do [it] of my own accord. That is the explanation of the things about which you were not able to restrain yourself.'^a

83 They will ask you about Dhu'l-Qarnayn. Say, 'I will give you an account of him.' 84 We established him in the land, and gave him the means to achieve all things.^b

وَأَمَّا ٱلْجِدَارُ فَكَانَ لِغُلَـٰمَيْنِ يَتِيمَيْنِ فِى ٱلْمَدِينَةِ وَكَانَ تَحْتَهُۥ كَنزٌ لَّهُمَا وَكَانَ أَبُوهُمَا صَـٰلِحًا فَأَرَادَ رَبُّكَ أَن يَبْلُغَآ أَشُدَّهُمَا وَيَسْتَخْرِجَا كَنزَهُمَا رَحْمَةً مِّن رَّبِّكَ وَمَا فَعَلْتُهُۥ عَنْ أَمْرِى ذَٰلِكَ تَأْوِيلُ مَا لَمْ تَسْطِع عَّلَيْهِ صَبْرًا ۝ وَيَسْـَٔلُونَكَ عَن ذِى ٱلْقَرْنَيْنِ قُلْ سَأَتْلُوا۟ عَلَيْكُم مِّنْهُ ذِكْرًا ۝ إِنَّا مَكَّنَّا لَهُۥ فِى ٱلْأَرْضِ وَءَاتَيْنَـٰهُ مِن كُلِّ شَىْءٍ سَبَبًا ۝

^a It may be gathered from these examples that God is always actively taking care of this world. On the grounds of this world being for the purpose of trial or test, He has kept the system of this world functioning on the basis of 'cause and effect', yet He intervenes in this system again and again. God sometimes adopts a constructive method and sometimes a seemingly destructive method. But, on every occasion, from the point of view of broad inner wisdom, it is all attributable to His graciousness, and it is meant to ensure that in the course of the free play of cause and effect, the real purposes behind creation are not defeated.

^b The literal meaning of 'Dhu'l Qarnayn' is 'possessor of two horns' i.e. the king whose conquests encompass the further reaches of the world to the east and west. Here, Dhu'l Qarnayn is perhaps a reference to the ancient Iranian King Cyrus, or Khusro, who reigned during the 5th century B.C. He had conquered a major part of the known world of ancient times and was at last killed in a war. He was a just king.

85 He travelled on a certain road;
86 until, when he reached the setting
of the sun, he found it setting in a
spring of murky water and near it he
found some people. We said, 'Dhu'l-
Qarnayn! You can either punish
them or else you can treat them with
gentleness.' 87 He said, 'We shall
certainly punish him who does
wrong; then he shall be brought back
to his Lord who will punish him with
a grievous punishment, 88 but
whoever believes and does good
works shall have a good reward and
We shall facilitate his matter by Our
command.'[a]

فَأَتْبَعَ سَبَبًا ۞ حَتَّىٰ إِذَا بَلَغَ مَغْرِبَ
ٱلشَّمْسِ وَجَدَهَا تَغْرُبُ فِي عَيْنٍ
حَمِئَةٍ وَوَجَدَ عِندَهَا قَوْمًا ۚ قُلْنَا يَٰذَا
ٱلْقَرْنَيْنِ إِمَّآ أَن تُعَذِّبَ وَإِمَّآ أَن تَتَّخِذَ
فِيهِمْ حُسْنًا ۞ قَالَ أَمَّا مَن ظَلَمَ
فَسَوْفَ نُعَذِّبُهُۥ ثُمَّ يُرَدُّ إِلَىٰ رَبِّهِۦ
فَيُعَذِّبُهُۥ عَذَابًا نُّكْرًا ۞ وَأَمَّا مَنْ
ءَامَنَ وَعَمِلَ صَٰلِحًا فَلَهُۥ جَزَآءً
ٱلْحُسْنَىٰ ۖ وَسَنَقُولُ لَهُۥ مِنْ أَمْرِنَا يُسْرًا
۞

---

[a] Dhu'l-Qarnayn, in making his conquests, possibly proceeded in a westward
direction from Iran, and thus reached Asia Minor, halting only when he came to
the 'black water' of the Aegean Sea. If one stands on the sea-shore here and looks
out over the sea in the evening, it will appear as if the sphere of the sun is sinking
into the water and setting there. This is a figurative description of the furthermost
point which Dhu'l-Qarnayn reached.

Dhu'l-Qarnayn had reached this seashore not as a wayfarer but as a conqueror. Thus
he gained full control over the people inhabiting that area and established his rule
there. As a ruler he had full powers to deal with the inhabitants as he liked. But
Dhu'l-Qarnayn was a just king. He was not cruel to anybody. He made the general
announcement that he would deal severely only with anyone found indulging in evil
deeds and that no excess would be perpetrated upon those who maintained peace
and order.

⁸⁹ Then he followed yet another path, ⁹⁰ until he came to the rising-place of the sun, where he found it rising on a people for whom We had provided no shelter from it. ⁹¹ Thus indeed it was. We had full knowledge of him.^a

⁹² Then he followed still another path, ⁹³ until he came between two mountains. He found beside them a people who could scarcely understand a word [of his language]. ⁹⁴ They said, 'O Dhu'l-Qarnayn! Gog and Magog are causing corruption in the land, so may we pay you tribute on condition that you set a barrier between us and them?'^b

ثُمَّ أَتْبَعَ سَبَبًا ۝ حَتَّىٰ إِذَا بَلَغَ مَطْلِعَ ٱلشَّمْسِ وَجَدَهَا تَطْلُعُ عَلَىٰ قَوْمٍ لَّمْ نَجْعَل لَّهُم مِّن دُونِهَا سِتْرًا ۝ كَذَٰلِكَ وَقَدْ أَحَطْنَا بِمَا لَدَيْهِ خُبْرًا ۝ ثُمَّ أَتْبَعَ سَبَبًا ۝ حَتَّىٰ إِذَا بَلَغَ بَيْنَ ٱلسَّدَّيْنِ وَجَدَ مِن دُونِهِمَا قَوْمًا لَّا يَكَادُونَ يَفْقَهُونَ قَوْلًا ۝ قَالُوا۟ يَٰذَا ٱلْقَرْنَيْنِ إِنَّ يَأْجُوجَ وَمَأْجُوجَ مُفْسِدُونَ فِى ٱلْأَرْضِ فَهَلْ نَجْعَلُ لَكَ خَرْجًا عَلَىٰٓ أَن تَجْعَلَ بَيْنَنَا وَبَيْنَهُمْ سَدًّا ۝

^a Dhu'l-Qarnayn's next expedition was towards the east of Iran. He reached a place where a most uncivilised people were living. The description that there was no barrier (shelter) between them and the sun means perhaps that they were nomads and were living on open ground instead of in properly constructed houses.

^b Probably Dhu'l-Qarnayn's third campaign was in the north east, in the direction of Iran. He reached a place where savages were living. Because they could not have any interaction with any other community, they were hardly able to understand any other language but their own.

The 'two mountains' probably lay between the Caspian Sea and the Black Sea. Here savage tribes used to invade from other places and would then flee through mountain passes after indulging in plunder. Dhu'l-Qarnayn constructed an iron wall between the two mountains.

95 He said, 'What My Lord has given me is better [than any tribute]. Help me with a force of labourers and I will erect a barrier between you and them: 96 bring me blocks of iron.' Then, when he had filled the gap between the mountain sides [he said], 'Now blow on the fire with your bellows.' When the iron blocks were red with heat, he said, 'Bring me molten brass to pour on them.' 97 So they [Gog and Magog] were not able to scale it, nor were they able to bore through it, 98 and he said, 'This is a mercy from my Lord. But when the promise of my Lord comes to pass, He will level it to dust. My Lord's promise is ever true!' *a*

قَالَ مَا مَكَّنِّي فِيهِ رَبِّي خَيْرٌ فَأَعِينُونِي بِقُوَّةٍ أَجْعَلْ بَيْنَكُمْ وَبَيْنَهُمْ رَدْمًا ۝ ءَاتُونِي زُبَرَ ٱلْحَدِيدِ حَتَّىٰ إِذَا سَاوَىٰ بَيْنَ ٱلصَّدَفَيْنِ قَالَ ٱنفُخُوا۟ حَتَّىٰ إِذَا جَعَلَهُۥ نَارًا قَالَ ءَاتُونِي أُفْرِغْ عَلَيْهِ قِطْرًا ۝ فَمَا ٱسْطَٰعُوٓا۟ أَن يَظْهَرُوهُ وَمَا ٱسْتَطَٰعُوا۟ لَهُۥ نَقْبًا ۝ قَالَ هَٰذَا رَحْمَةٌ مِّن رَّبِّي فَإِذَا جَآءَ وَعْدُ رَبِّي جَعَلَهُۥ دَكَّآءَ وَكَانَ وَعْدُ رَبِّي حَقًّا ۝

---

a The high ranges of the Caucasus in what is now Russian territory running between the Caspian Sea and the Black Sea, serve as a natural dividing wall between Europe and Asia. In this mountainous region there were certain passes through which the savage Gog and Magog (Yajuj and Majuj) tribes from the south used to enter the northern part of Iran and plunder it. Here, till today, there are signs of an ancient wall. There is every probability that this was the very wall which was constructed by Dhu'l-Qarnayn for security purposes.

To erect an 'Iron Wall' to ward off enemies is a feat which generally generates a sense of pride in people. But even after constructing such an invincible wall, Dhu'l-Qarnayn did not lose his modesty and humility. He had set his eyes not on his own creations but on God's mighty powers, and a human being's power is nothing as compared to God's might.

⁹⁹ On that Day, We shall let them surge against each other like waves and then the Trumpet will be blown and We shall gather them all together. ¹⁰⁰ On that Day We shall lay Hell bare before those who deny the truth, ¹⁰¹ who have turned a blind eye to My reminder and a deaf ear to My warning.ᵃ

¹⁰² Do those who deny the truth, think that they can make My servants patrons instead of Me? We have reserved Hell as a lodging for those who deny the truth.ᵇ

وَتَرَكْنَا بَعْضَهُمْ يَوْمَئِذٍ يَمُوجُ فِى بَعْضٍ وَنُفِخَ فِى ٱلصُّورِ فَجَمَعْنَهُمْ جَمْعًا ۝ وَعَرَضْنَا جَهَنَّمَ يَوْمَئِذٍ لِّلْكَفِرِينَ عَرْضًا ۝ ٱلَّذِينَ كَانَتْ أَعْيُنُهُمْ فِى غِطَاءٍ عَن ذِكْرِى وَكَانُوا۟ لَا يَسْتَطِيعُونَ سَمْعًا ۝ أَفَحَسِبَ ٱلَّذِينَ كَفَرُوٓا۟ أَن يَتَّخِذُوا۟ عِبَادِى مِن دُونِىٓ أَوْلِيَآءَ إِنَّآ أَعْتَدْنَا جَهَنَّمَ لِلْكَفِرِينَ نُزُلًا ۝

ᵃ At the onset of Doomsday, the present world will no longer be the same. It appears that the present boundaries between mountains and rivers will disappear and huge crowds of human beings will lap against one other like the waves of the ocean.

Today, Hell is being shown to people through their 'mental eyes', but they fail to perceive it. On Doomsday, Hell will be shown to people through their physical eyes. At that time, everybody will see it. But this seeing will be of no avail except to one who had removed the veil from his eyes, having learned a lesson from divine advice in his pre-death life. The removal of veil on the Day of judgement, will be solely for the purpose of sending the arrogant and insolent disbelievers to their destined end in hell.

ᵇ Acceptance of the Truth (Reality) is in fact acceptance of God, while denial of the truth is in fact denial of God. Whenever a person refuses to accept the Truth, he does so banking on the apparent strength of some thing or some personality. Such reliance is false, because in this world nobody has any power except God. On the Day of Judgement there will be nobody to save him, because God is the only saviour and such a person would already have lost His support due to his disobedience.

¹⁰³ Say, 'Shall I tell you of those who will lose the most through their actions? ¹⁰⁴ They are those whose efforts have been wasted in the life of the world while they thought they were doing good. ¹⁰⁵ They are those who deny their Lord's signs and the meeting with Him.' So their works are in vain, and We shall give them no weight on the Day of Resurrection. ¹⁰⁶ Hell will be their reward, because they denied the truth, and made a jest of My signs and My messengers.^a

قُلْ هَلْ نُنَبِّئُكُم بِٱلْأَخْسَرِينَ أَعْمَلاً ۝ ٱلَّذِينَ ضَلَّ سَعْيُهُمْ فِى ٱلْحَيَوٰةِ ٱلدُّنْيَا وَهُمْ يَحْسَبُونَ أَنَّهُمْ يُحْسِنُونَ صُنْعًا ۝ أُوْلَٰٓئِكَ ٱلَّذِينَ كَفَرُوا۟ بِـَٔايَٰتِ رَبِّهِمْ وَلِقَآئِهِۦ فَحَبِطَتْ أَعْمَٰلُهُمْ فَلَا نُقِيمُ لَهُمْ يَوْمَ ٱلْقِيَٰمَةِ وَزْنًا ۝ ذَٰلِكَ جَزَآؤُهُمْ جَهَنَّمُ بِمَا كَفَرُوا۟ وَٱتَّخَذُوٓا۟ ءَايَٰتِى وَرُسُلِى هُزُوًا ۝

---

^a Man strives in this world and observes that, as a result, he gains wealth and honour. He does not see his work marred in any manner, therefore, he considers himself a successful man.

But, this is highly irrational. In the plan of God, the criterion of a successful life is in terms of the life of the Hereafter. Therefore, to consider success in this worldly life as real success amounts to taking a view of life which omits the life hereafter altogether. This is tantamount to substituting our own plan in place of God's plan and obviously those who do so can never be successful in the life hereafter.

God reveals His signs. But these signs of the life hereafter have no effect on those whose minds are preoccupied with the thoughts of this world. God discloses His arguments, but the arguments of the life hereafter do not appeal to those who are lost in the affairs of this world. Such people fail to accept guidance, even though they may be standing next to a guide. If they do not give any weight to God's word, how can they expect God to take their candidature into account for any divine consideration?

¹⁰⁷ Those who believe and do good works shall have the gardens of Paradise for their abode. ¹⁰⁸ They shall forever dwell in the Gardens of Paradise, desiring no change.^a

¹⁰⁹ Tell them, 'If the ocean became ink for writing the words of my Lord, surely the ocean would be exhausted before the words of my Lord came to an end—even if We were to add another ocean to it.'^b

¹¹⁰ Say, 'I am only a human being like yourselves. It is revealed to me that your God is One God. So let him who hopes to meet his Lord do good deeds and let him associate no one else in the worship of his Lord.'^c

إِنَّ ٱلَّذِينَ ءَامَنُوا۟ وَعَمِلُوا۟ ٱلصَّٰلِحَٰتِ كَانَتْ لَهُمْ جَنَّٰتُ ٱلْفِرْدَوْسِ نُزُلًا ۝ خَٰلِدِينَ فِيهَا لَا يَبْغُونَ عَنْهَا حِوَلًا ۝ قُل لَّوْ كَانَ ٱلْبَحْرُ مِدَادًا لِّكَلِمَٰتِ رَبِّى لَنَفِدَ ٱلْبَحْرُ قَبْلَ أَن تَنفَدَ كَلِمَٰتُ رَبِّى وَلَوْ جِئْنَا بِمِثْلِهِۦ مَدَدًا ۝ قُلْ إِنَّمَآ أَنَا۠ بَشَرٌ مِّثْلُكُمْ يُوحَىٰٓ إِلَىَّ أَنَّمَآ إِلَٰهُكُمْ إِلَٰهٌ وَٰحِدٌ فَمَن كَانَ يَرْجُوا۟ لِقَآءَ رَبِّهِۦ فَلْيَعْمَلْ عَمَلًا صَٰلِحًا وَلَا يُشْرِكْ بِعِبَادَةِ رَبِّهِۦٓ أَحَدًۢا ۝

---

^a To lead a life of faith and piety in this world is to give proof of tremendous sacrifice. It amounts to renouncing an apparent and visible heaven for the sake of a hidden, invisible heaven. This also means succeeding in the most difficult of tests, i.e. when man recognises the Truth on the strength of abstract arguments and then he turns his life in that direction, though there is no pressure on him to do so.

Those who exhibit such awareness (of truth) and perform such actions truly deserve to be admitted to gardens of eternal comfort and pleasure.

^b Those who do not accept God's message are in fact denying the most established of all established facts. It is so established that pens made from all the trees would not be sufficient to write God's words and the ocean turned into ink would become exhausted. But, what a pity that, in spite of all this, man fails to recognise the truth and does not mould his life in accordance with it.

^c The prophet is neither god nor angel. He is a human being just like any other human being. His only distinguishing feature is that he receives God's revelation through invisible means. In other words, a prophet is an individual who, outwardly, is a human being but who inwardly is a representative of God.

Because of this only those can recognize a prophet who can recognize his merit. Arriving at the Truth is possible only for one who can recognise reality in its essence, i.e. who is capable of recognising a 'prophet' at the level of a 'human being.'

19. MARY

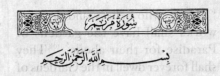

In the name of God,
the Most Gracious, the Most Merciful

¹*Kaf Ha Ya 'Ayn Sad*

²This is an account of your Lord's mercy bestowed upon His servant Zachariah, ³when he called upon his Lord in low tones, saying,ᵃ

كهيعص ۝ ذِكْرُ رَحْمَتِ رَبِّكَ عَبْدَهُ زَكَرِيَّآ ۝ إِذْ نَادَىٰ رَبَّهُ نِدَآءً خَفِيًّا ۝

ᵃ Zachariah, or Zakariyyah, who was the chief administrator of the Haykal (Solomon's temple) was married to Mary's mother's sister. Maryam was only five years old when her father, Imran, died. After his death, Zachariah was appointed in his place as the leader of the priests. At that time, Mary, in fulfillment of the pledge made by her mother, was placed in the service of the Haykal. As Zachariah was a close relative of hers and also the chief of the Haykal, he was given the responsibility of bringing her up.

Zachariah silently prayed to God and the prayer was granted in an astonishing and wonderful manner. This shows what real prayer is. True prayer is a spontaneous expression of the firm belief that all powers vest in God. Man receives every single thing only on His giving it to him, and no one can own a thing if He does not confer it on him. True prayer needs to be directed solely towards the one and only God. That is why true prayer gushes forth when one is alone—when there is nobody present except God and oneself.

4 'Lord, my bones have weakened and my head has turned hoary with age, but never, Lord, have I been disappointed in my prayer to you: 5 now I fear my kinsmen when I am gone. [I have no hope of their continuing my mission] for my wife is barren, so grant me a successor from Yourself, 6 to be my heir and to be the heir [of the blessings] of the House of Jacob; and make him, O my Lord, acceptable to you.' [a]

7 'Zachariah, We bring you good news of a son whose name shall be John. We have not given such a name to anyone before.' 8 'My Lord!' [said Zachariah], 'How shall I have a son when my wife is barren and I have reached such extreme old age?' [b]

قَالَ رَبِّ إِنِّى وَهَنَ ٱلْعَظْمُ مِنِّى وَٱشْتَعَلَ
ٱلرَّأْسُ شَيْبًا وَلَمْ أَكُن بِدُعَآئِكَ رَبِّ
شَقِيًّا ۝ وَإِنِّى خِفْتُ ٱلْمَوَٰلِىَ مِن
وَرَآءِى وَكَانَتِ ٱمْرَأَتِى عَاقِرًا فَهَبْ
لِى مِن لَّدُنكَ وَلِيًّا ۝ يَرِثُنِى وَيَرِثُ مِنْ
ءَالِ يَعْقُوبَ وَٱجْعَلْهُ رَبِّ رَضِيًّا ۝
يَٰزَكَرِيَّآ إِنَّا نُبَشِّرُكَ بِغُلَٰمٍ ٱسْمُهُۥ
يَحْيَىٰ لَمْ نَجْعَل لَّهُۥ مِن قَبْلُ سَمِيًّا ۝
قَالَ رَبِّ أَنَّىٰ يَكُونُ لِى غُلَٰمٌ
وَكَانَتِ ٱمْرَأَتِى عَاقِرًا وَقَدْ بَلَغْتُ مِنَ
ٱلْكِبَرِ عِتِيًّا ۝

---

[a] This is the prayer of one who had grown very old while pursuing a religious mission and failed to find among his family members anybody to carry on his task after him. The feeling of his own helplessness on the one hand, and the realization of the tremendous importance of his mission on the other, combine in the prayer expressed in these verses. In other words, this was not a mere prayer for a son in the usual sense: it was a prayer for a worthy successor capable of carrying on his prophetic mission after him.

[b] This prayer was answered by the granting of a son—an extraordinary happening, as a son is not ordinarily born to people in such circumstances. The birth of a child to a couple, where the husband was extremely old and his wife had been barren throughout her life, was really a most unusual event. On account of this, Zachariah's pleasure on receipt of this extraordinary and unexpected news spontaneously expressed itself as disbelief: how could he have a child when he and his wife were incapable of having children?

⁹ He said, 'It will be so! Your Lord says, "It is easy for Me for I created you when you were nothing before."' ¹⁰ He said, 'My Lord, grant me a sign!' He said, 'Your sign will be that you will not speak to anyone for three successive days and nights, although sound in body.' ¹¹ Then Zachariah came forth from the shrine to his people and told them by signs to glorify the Lord morning and evening.ᵃ

قَالَ كَذَٰلِكَ قَالَ رَبُّكَ هُوَ عَلَيَّ هَيِّنٌ وَقَدْ خَلَقْتُكَ مِن قَبْلُ وَلَمْ تَكُ شَيْئًا ۝ قَالَ رَبِّ ٱجْعَل لِّيٓ ءَايَةً قَالَ ءَايَتُكَ أَلَّا تُكَلِّمَ ٱلنَّاسَ ثَلَٰثَ لَيَالٍ سَوِيًّا ۝ فَخَرَجَ عَلَىٰ قَوْمِهِۦ مِنَ ٱلْمِحْرَابِ فَأَوْحَىٰٓ إِلَيْهِمْ أَن سَبِّحُواْ بُكْرَةً وَعَشِيًّا ۝

ᵃ Just as the creation of the first human being, without a father or a mother, was a miracle of God, the birth of a child through a father and a mother is also God's miracle, irrespective of whether the father and mother are old or young. The fact is that it is God who creates man. He created him in the first instance and He creates man even today. The seeming cause is not the real reason, though appearances would suggest otherwise.

Zachariah asked for a sign as a token of the mercy God should shower upon him. He was told that, in spite of being healthy, if he could not talk for three continuous days and nights, he should take it to be a confirmation of his wife's pregnancy. So, when the time came, his tongue would not utter a sound and he become mute. He came out of his place of worship and started exhorting the people by signs to remember God day and night, to worship Him and always obey Him.

Probably Zachariah was in the habit of delivering sermons and good advice to people every day. So when he was rendered speechless, he went to the usual meeting place and, as always, gave good advice to the people. But, since he could not speak, he counseled people by signs.

¹² To John We said, 'Hold fast the Book,' and while he was still a child, We bestowed upon him wisdom, ¹³ and tenderness [of heart] and purity. He was pious, ¹⁴ and dutiful towards his parents and was not haughty or disobedient. ¹⁵ Peace be on him on the day of his birth, and on the day of his death, and peace will be on him on the day he is raised up to life again.*

يَـٰيَحْيَىٰ خُذِ ٱلْكِتَـٰبَ بِقُوَّةٍ ۖ وَءَاتَيْنَـٰهُ ٱلْحُكْمَ صَبِيًّا ۝ وَحَنَانًا مِّن لَّدُنَّا وَزَكَوٰةً ۖ وَكَانَ تَقِيًّا ۝ وَبَرًّۢا بِوَٰلِدَيْهِ وَلَمْ يَكُن جَبَّارًا عَصِيًّا ۝ وَسَلَـٰمٌ عَلَيْهِ يَوْمَ وُلِدَ وَيَوْمَ يَمُوتُ وَيَوْمَ يُبْعَثُ حَيًّا ۝

---

*It is said that once during John's childhood, some children asked him to come and play with them. He refused and said, 'We have not been created for this.' This shows that from his very childhood he was conscious that life should be purposeful. Sensitive by nature and possessed of a feeling heart, he was free of psychological complexes. He scrupulously fulfilled his duties to his parents and was completely devoid of arrogance or willfulness.

These are the qualities that give man the ability never to diverge from the path of God's Book. It is the possessor of such qualities who is showered with God's mercy in this world and in the life hereafter.

¹⁶ Recount in the Book how Mary withdrew from her people to an eastern place ¹⁷ and kept herself in seclusion from them. We sent her Our angel, who presented himself to her as a full-grown human being. ¹⁸ When she saw him, she said, 'I seek refuge in the compassionate God from you; [do not come near] if you fear the Lord.' ¹⁹ 'I am only the messenger of your Lord,' he replied. 'I shall bestow upon you the gift of a son endowed with purity.' ²⁰ She said, 'How can I have a son when no man has touched me; and neither have I been unchaste?' ²¹ [The angel] replied, 'So shall it be; your Lord says, "This is easy for Me; and We shall make him a sign to people and a blessing, from Us. This has been decreed."' ^a

وَٱذْكُرْ فِى ٱلْكِتَبِ مَرْيَمَ إِذِ ٱنتَبَذَتْ مِنْ أَهْلِهَا مَكَانًا شَرْقِيًّا ۝ فَٱتَّخَذَتْ مِن دُونِهِمْ حِجَابًا فَأَرْسَلْنَآ إِلَيْهَا رُوحَنَا فَتَمَثَّلَ لَهَا بَشَرًا سَوِيًّا ۝ قَالَتْ إِنِّى أَعُوذُ بِٱلرَّحْمَٰنِ مِنكَ إِن كُنتَ تَقِيًّا ۝ قَالَ إِنَّمَآ أَنَا۠ رَسُولُ رَبِّكِ لِأَهَبَ لَكِ غُلَٰمًا زَكِيًّا ۝ قَالَتْ أَنَّىٰ يَكُونُ لِى غُلَٰمٌ وَلَمْ يَمْسَسْنِى بَشَرٌ وَلَمْ أَكُ بَغِيًّا ۝ قَالَ كَذَٰلِكِ قَالَ رَبُّكِ هُوَ عَلَىَّ هَيِّنٌ وَلِنَجْعَلَهُۥٓ ءَايَةً لِّلنَّاسِ وَرَحْمَةً مِّنَّا وَكَانَ أَمْرًا مَّقْضِيًّا ۝

---

^a Mary, in accordance with her mother's pledge, was placed in the service of the Haykal (Solomon's Temple). The eastern part of the Haykal of ancient times was set apart for women. Mary hung a curtain in a corner in this part to segregate herself from others and devote herself entirely to worship. Soon thereafter, she found a strong healthy man standing before her. It was only natural that this made her suddenly afraid. But the stranger said that he was an angel and that he had come from God to perform the miracle of giving Mary a son.

This miraculous birth of Jesus was a great sign from God. The purpose of this was to leave the people in no doubt as to his having been sent by God, so that they should accept whatever he said on His behalf. But, in spite of such clear signs, they refused to accept him.

22 So she conceived him and withdrew with him to a distant place. 23 The pains of labour drove her to the trunk of a date-palm. She said, 'Oh, if only I had died before this and passed into oblivion!' *a*

24 But a voice called out to her from below, 'Do not despair. Your Lord has provided a brook that runs at your feet, 25 and if you shake the trunk of this palm-tree, it will drop fresh ripe dates on you. 26 Eat and drink and rejoice. And if you see any human being say, "I have vowed a fast [of silence] to the Gracious God, and will not speak with any human being today."' *b*

فَحَمَلَتْهُ فَٱنتَبَذَتْ بِهِۦ مَكَانًا قَصِيًّا ۞ فَأَجَآءَهَا ٱلْمَخَاضُ إِلَىٰ جِذْعِ ٱلنَّخْلَةِ قَالَتْ يَٰلَيْتَنِى مِتُّ قَبْلَ هَٰذَا وَكُنتُ نَسْيًا مَّنسِيًّا ۞ فَنَادَىٰهَا مِن تَحْتِهَآ أَلَّا تَحْزَنِى قَدْ جَعَلَ رَبُّكِ تَحْتَكِ سَرِيًّا ۞ وَهُزِّىٓ إِلَيْكِ بِجِذْعِ ٱلنَّخْلَةِ تُسَٰقِطْ عَلَيْكِ رُطَبًا جَنِيًّا ۞ فَكُلِى وَٱشْرَبِى وَقَرِّى عَيْنًا فَإِمَّا تَرَيِنَّ مِنَ ٱلْبَشَرِ أَحَدًا فَقُولِىٓ إِنِّى نَذَرْتُ لِلرَّحْمَٰنِ صَوْمًا فَلَنْ أُكَلِّمَ ٱلْيَوْمَ إِنسِيًّا ۞

a Mary was an unmarried lady of a respectable and religious family. Being pregnant meant a calamitous trial for a lady like her; a trial of unparalleled severity. Ridden with anxiety, she quietly left the Haykal and went to far-off Bethlehem. When the time came and the labour pains began, she went out of town and sat under a date-palm tree. What a chaste, unmarried lady like her was going through at the time can be imagined from these words she uttered: 'Alas! Why didn't I die before this, so that my very existence would have been obliterated from people's memories?'

b In such difficult and trying circumstances, Mary could have had only one source of consolation, and that was that God's angel should appear and reassure her; and that is exactly what happened. At that very movement, an angel came and told her to have no fear and said that whatever was taking place was in accordance with God's plan. She was told that a spring of fresh water had been made to flow nearby, from which she might drink and that the palm tree would supply her with fresh fruits, which she might eat.

As far as the child was concerned, the angel comforted her by saying that the miraculously born child was himself sufficient to defend her. She was advised to take a vow of strict silence as was customary among the Children of Israel. If anyone approached her and made enquiries, she was advised to point to the child, who would himself give a reply and absolve her of any responsibility.

²⁷ Carrying her child, she brought him to her people. They said, 'O Mary, you have indeed done something terrible! ²⁸ Sister of Aaron, your father was not an evil man, nor was your mother an unchaste woman!'^a

²⁹ She pointed to the child. They said, 'How shall we talk to someone who is a child in the cradle?' ³⁰ [But] he said, 'I am God's servant. He has given me the Book and made me a prophet; ³¹ He has made me blessed wherever I may be, and has enjoined upon me prayer and almsgiving throughout my life. ³² He has made me dutiful toward my mother, and He has not made me arrogant or wicked. ³³ Blessed was I on the day I was born, and blessed I shall be on the day I die and on the day I am raised to life again.'^b

فَأَتَتْ بِهِۦ قَوْمَهَا تَحْمِلُهُۥ ۖ قَالُوا۟ يَـٰمَرْيَمُ لَقَدْ جِئْتِ شَيْـًٔا فَرِيًّا ۝

يَـٰٓأُخْتَ هَـٰرُونَ مَا كَانَ أَبُوكِ ٱمْرَأَ سَوْءٍ وَمَا كَانَتْ أُمُّكِ بَغِيًّا ۝ فَأَشَارَتْ إِلَيْهِ ۖ قَالُوا۟ كَيْفَ نُكَلِّمُ مَن كَانَ فِى ٱلْمَهْدِ صَبِيًّا ۝ قَالَ إِنِّى عَبْدُ ٱللَّهِ ءَاتَـٰنِىَ ٱلْكِتَـٰبَ وَجَعَلَنِى نَبِيًّا ۝ وَجَعَلَنِى مُبَارَكًا أَيْنَ مَا كُنتُ وَأَوْصَـٰنِى بِٱلصَّلَوٰةِ وَٱلزَّكَوٰةِ مَا دُمْتُ حَيًّا ۝ وَبَرًّۢا بِوَٰلِدَتِى وَلَمْ يَجْعَلْنِى جَبَّارًا شَقِيًّا ۝ وَٱلسَّلَـٰمُ عَلَىَّ يَوْمَ وُلِدتُّ وَيَوْمَ أَمُوتُ وَيَوْمَ أُبْعَثُ حَيًّا ۝

---

^a Mary gained confidence on hearing the words of the angel. She took the child and returned to her family. Seeing her in this condition, the Jewish people started condemning and scolding her. Maryam did as the angel had told her. She remained silent and pointed towards the child, meaning that this was not an ordinary type of child and in order to have proof thereof, they should talk to him and he, in spite of being an infant, would understand what they said and give a clear reply.

^b In spite of Mary's pointing toward the child, the people could not understand how they were supposed to talk to a small child. At that time, the child himself started speaking. In his miraculous utterances, there was, on the one hand, complete absolution of Mary and, on the other, advance evidence of his prophethood, so that when he grew up and declared his prophethood, there should be no scope for any doubt about it.

³⁴ Such was Jesus, the son of Mary. That is the whole truth, about which they still dispute: ³⁵ it does not befit the majesty of God that He should beget a son. Glory be to Him! He is far above that: when He decrees something, He says only, 'Be!' and it is.ᵃ

ذَٰلِكَ عِيسَى ٱبْنُ مَرْيَمَ قَوْلَ ٱلْحَقِّ ٱلَّذِى فِيهِ يَمْتَرُونَ ۝ مَا كَانَ لِلَّهِ أَن يَتَّخِذَ مِن وَلَدٍ سُبْحَٰنَهُۥٓ إِذَا قَضَىٰٓ أَمْرًا فَإِنَّمَا يَقُولُ لَهُۥ كُن فَيَكُونُ ۝

ᵃ The miraculous birth of Jesus was an extraordinary event; trying to explain it, Christian scholars have formulated peculiar dogmas. But there is always a limit one cannot cross in offering explanations; to account for the Messiah's extraordinary birth by suggesting that he is the son of God definitely amounts to going beyond all limits, because attributing children to God negates the very concept of the unity of God.

Quite apart from this, there are innumerable extraordinary and wonderful events in the universe that we see every day. In fact, every single thing in this world is in itself a kind of marvel. Now, if anyone comes across anything of this nature, he must realize that God has created it, just as He has created other countless wonders.

³⁶ God is my Lord and your Lord, so worship Him alone. That is the right path. ³⁷ Yet different groups differed among themselves. How awful it will be for those who have rejected the truth when a dreadful Day arrives! ³⁸ How sharp of hearing, how sharp of sight they will be when they come to Us. But today, these evil-doers are obviously lost in error.ᵃ

وَإِنَّ ٱللَّهَ رَبِّى وَرَبُّكُمْ فَٱعْبُدُوهُ ۚ هَٰذَا صِرَٰطٌ مُّسْتَقِيمٌ ۝ فَٱخْتَلَفَ ٱلْأَحْزَابُ مِنۢ بَيْنِهِمْ ۖ فَوَيْلٌ لِّلَّذِينَ كَفَرُوا۟ مِن مَّشْهَدِ يَوْمٍ عَظِيمٍ ۝ أَسْمِعْ بِهِمْ وَأَبْصِرْ يَوْمَ يَأْتُونَنَا ۖ لَٰكِنِ ٱلظَّٰلِمُونَ ٱلْيَوْمَ فِى ضَلَٰلٍ مُّبِينٍ ۝

ᵃ The Messiah and all the other prophets called upon the people to tread the same straight path, namely, that of taking God as their Lord and worshipping Him alone. But, it has always happened that, by willful misinterpretations and false explanations, there have been deviations from the straight path. Different people have emphasized different points of the doctrine. These divergent views have led to such major differences that a single religion has been divided into several religions.

The Truth is manifested in its entirety in this world too. But because here man has been given freedom of choice so that he may be put to the test, as the very purpose of his existence is trial, he may accept the Truth or he may not. Due to this temporary freedom, he falls a prey to misunderstanding and starts behaving arrogantly. He is shown the right path of God but, in spite of arguments in its favour, he does not accept it. Today his eyes and ears appear to be altogether devoid of the powers of seeing and hearing, but, in the Hereafter, when his freedom is snatched away from him, these very same eyes and very same ears of his will become so powerful that he will have no choice but to see and hear the Truth.

³⁹ Warn them of [the coming of] the Day of Remorse, when everything will have been decided, while they are heedless and do not believe. ⁴⁰ It is We who will inherit the earth and all who dwell upon it: they shall all return to Us.ᵃ

وَأَنذِرْهُمْ يَوْمَ ٱلْحَسْرَةِ إِذْ قُضِيَ ٱلْأَمْرُ وَهُمْ فِى غَفْلَةٍ وَهُمْ لَا يُؤْمِنُونَ ۞ إِنَّا نَحْنُ نَرِثُ ٱلْأَرْضَ وَمَنْ عَلَيْهَا وَإِلَيْنَا يُرْجَعُونَ ۞

ᵃ When a man meets with failure in this world, he has the opportunity to start his life afresh, and he feels himself fortunate to have friends and supporters who will offer him assistance. But, failure in the life hereafter allows of no chance of reversal. What keen regret a man feels when he learns that he had the opportunity to do what was right and proper, but did nothing until it was too late!

The root cause of all evil is that man takes himself to be his own master, while the fact is that this life is only a transient period in his existence. God was the Lord of everything in the beginning and He will be the Lord of everything till the end. In truth, there is nobody but God who may hold the position of a master.

41 Also recount the story of Abraham in the Book. He was a man of truth, and a prophet. 42 He said to his father, 'Why do you worship something that can neither hear nor see nor benefit you in any way? 43 Father, I have been given some knowledge which has not come to you, so follow me: I shall guide you along a straight path. 44 Father! Do not worship Satan—for, truly, Satan is a rebel against the Most Gracious One! 45 Father, indeed I fear lest a punishment from the Gracious One afflict you, and you become a friend of Satan.' a

وَٱذۡكُرۡ فِى ٱلۡكِتَٰبِ إِبۡرَٰهِيمَ إِنَّهُۥ كَانَ صِدِّيقًا نَّبِيًّا ۞ إِذۡ قَالَ لِأَبِيهِ يَـٰٓأَبَتِ لِمَ تَعۡبُدُ مَا لَا يَسۡمَعُ وَلَا يُبۡصِرُ وَلَا يُغۡنِى عَنكَ شَيۡـًٔا ۞ يَـٰٓأَبَتِ إِنِّى قَدۡ جَآءَنِى مِنَ ٱلۡعِلۡمِ مَا لَمۡ يَأۡتِكَ فَٱتَّبِعۡنِىٓ أَهۡدِكَ صِرَٰطًا سَوِيًّا ۞ يَـٰٓأَبَتِ لَا تَعۡبُدِ ٱلشَّيۡطَٰنَ إِنَّ ٱلشَّيۡطَٰنَ كَانَ لِلرَّحۡمَٰنِ عَصِيًّا ۞ يَـٰٓأَبَتِ إِنِّىٓ أَخَافُ أَن يَمَسَّكَ عَذَابٌ مِّنَ ٱلرَّحۡمَٰنِ فَتَكُونَ لِلشَّيۡطَٰنِ وَلِيًّا ۞

---

a Abraham was born in Iraq. His father, Azar, was a polytheist. When Abraham received prophethood, he advised his father to give up polytheism and start worshipping God, or face God's retribution.

Worship of Satan does not mean actually worshipping Satan himself, but worshipping something indicated by Satan. Although it is an inherent part of human nature to feel the need to glorify some being, place it in an elevated position and then bow down and pay homage to it, the real focus of such feelings should be and is God. But, Satan, by various methods, influences people and diverts their minds from this in order to make them worship things other than God, i.e. place them on a par with those who associate others with God and offer only to others what they should offer to God.

⁴⁶ [His father] said, 'Do you reject my deities, Abraham? If you do not desist, I shall surely stone you to death. Keep out of my way!' ⁴⁷ Abraham replied, 'Peace be on you: I will pray to my Lord for your forgiveness—He has indeed been gracious to me—⁴⁸ I will separate myself from you and from whatever you call upon besides God, and I will pray only to my Lord. It may well be that, in calling on my Lord, I will not be disappointed.' ^a

قَالَ أَرَاغِبٌ أَنتَ عَنۡ ءَالِهَتِي يَـٰٓإِبۡرَٰهِيمُ ۖ لَئِن لَّمۡ تَنتَهِ لَأَرۡجُمَنَّكَ ۖ وَٱهۡجُرۡنِي مَلِيًّا ۝ قَالَ سَلَـٰمٌ عَلَيۡكَ ۖ سَأَسۡتَغۡفِرُ لَكَ رَبِّيٓ ۖ إِنَّهُۥ كَانَ بِي حَفِيًّا ۝ وَأَعۡتَزِلُكُمۡ وَمَا تَدۡعُونَ مِن دُونِ ٱللَّهِ وَأَدۡعُواْ رَبِّي عَسَىٰٓ أَلَّآ أَكُونَ بِدُعَآءِ رَبِّي شَقِيًّا ۝

---

^a The statues criticized by the Prophet Abraham were not simply ordinary pieces of stone. Rather, they represented those entities, whose supposed magical greatness, enshrined in the legends of the past, had charmed the people and left a lasting impression on their minds. Compared to them, 'young Abraham' appeared to be an ordinary person, while the statues of Iraq seemed to be mountains of greatness. That is why Abraham's father contemptuously ignored his advice.

If the call to the Truth, initiated at a particular place, reaches a stage when the addresee though fully understanding it, stoop to violence, the believers have to move away from that place. Such a move is called Hijrah or immigration.

The call of Truth is a divine call. That is why, from the very outset, it is marked by God-oriented thinking. Even if those to whom the call is addressed deal contemptuously with the call-giver and oppress him, he still keeps a soft corner in his heart for them. Similarly, if he finds himself unsupported by his surroundings, he is not dejected, because his real support comes from God. He firmly believes that, as always, He is with him and will remain with him forever.

⁴⁹ So when he had separated himself from them and from what they worshipped besides God, We bestowed on him Isaac and Jacob, and We made each of them a prophet. ⁵⁰ We granted them Our mercy and bestowed on them true and high renown.^a

⁵¹ Tell also of Moses in the Book. He was indeed a chosen one, and was a messenger and a prophet. ⁵² We called out to him from the right side of the mount and made him draw near to be in close communion with Us; ⁵³ and We gave him as his helper, out of Our mercy, his brother Aaron, having made him a prophet.^b

فَلَمَّا ٱعْتَزَلَهُمْ وَمَا يَعْبُدُونَ مِن دُونِ ٱللَّهِ وَهَبْنَا لَهُۥ إِسْحَٰقَ وَيَعْقُوبَ وَكُلًّا جَعَلْنَا نَبِيًّا ۝ وَوَهَبْنَا لَهُم مِّن رَّحْمَتِنَا وَجَعَلْنَا لَهُمْ لِسَانَ صِدْقٍ عَلِيًّا ۝ وَٱذْكُرْ فِى ٱلْكِتَٰبِ مُوسَىٰٓ إِنَّهُۥ كَانَ مُخْلَصًا وَكَانَ رَسُولًا نَّبِيًّا ۝ وَنَٰدَيْنَٰهُ مِن جَانِبِ ٱلطُّورِ ٱلْأَيْمَنِ وَقَرَّبْنَٰهُ نَجِيًّا ۝ وَوَهَبْنَا لَهُۥ مِن رَّحْمَتِنَآ أَخَاهُ هَٰرُونَ نَبِيًّا ۝

---

^a Man is accustomed to living with his family and within his community. Under these circumstances, separating a man from his family and friends amounts to pushing him into an abyss of despair. But, through Abraham's lot, God has made it clear for all time that a man who is rendered homeless purely for the cause of God shall have a far better abode bestowed upon him by His Creator. In the long run God, by His Grace, honours with fame and good fortune one who has been thrust into oblivion for His sake.

^b Moses, while on his way from Midian to Egypt, passed by the Mount of Tur where God honoured him with prophethood. In every period in the past God selected his messengers (prophets) and entrusted them with His messages. These messages were always sent through the Angel Gabriel. But, in the case of Moses, he was given exceptional treatment, as God talked directly to him.

Moreover, Moses was granted a special provision in that God appointed another prophet, Aaron, to assist him. The reason for this special consideration might have been the exceptional circumstances under which he was required to perform his prophetic mission: on the one hand, he had to confront a tyrant, Pharaoh, and on the other, the community of Jews, which had reached the last stage of degradation.

God's Mercy and Help in such abundant measure are bestowed only on His prophets, though God favours his other faithful subjects in the same manner, albeit in varying degrees. God inspires them with divine guidance so that they may perform the task assigned to them. He instills His ideas in their minds. He arranges for them special support the like of which is not available to anybody under ordinary circumstances.

54 Tell also of Ishmael in the Book. He was true to his promise and was a messenger and a prophet. 55 He exhorted his people to prayer and almsgiving, and his Lord was pleased with him. 56 Tell also of Idris in the Book. He was a man of truth and a prophet. 57 We raised him to a high position.*a*

58 These are the ones whom God has favoured: the prophets from among the descendants of Adam and of those whom We carried in the Ark with Noah; the descendants of Abraham, of Israel, and of those whom We have guided and chosen. For when the revelations of the Merciful were recited to them, they fell down, prostrating themselves and weeping.*b*

وَٱذْكُرْ فِي ٱلْكِتَٰبِ إِسْمَٰعِيلَ ۚ إِنَّهُ كَانَ صَادِقَ ٱلْوَعْدِ وَكَانَ رَسُولًا نَّبِيًّا ﴿٥٤﴾ وَكَانَ يَأْمُرُ أَهْلَهُۥ بِٱلصَّلَوٰةِ وَٱلزَّكَوٰةِ وَكَانَ عِندَ رَبِّهِۦ مَرْضِيًّا ﴿٥٥﴾ وَٱذْكُرْ فِي ٱلْكِتَٰبِ إِدْرِيسَ ۚ إِنَّهُ كَانَ صِدِّيقًا نَّبِيًّا ﴿٥٦﴾ وَرَفَعْنَٰهُ مَكَانًا عَلِيًّا ﴿٥٧﴾ أُو۟لَٰٓئِكَ ٱلَّذِينَ أَنْعَمَ ٱللَّهُ عَلَيْهِم مِّنَ ٱلنَّبِيِّۦنَ مِن ذُرِّيَّةِ ءَادَمَ وَمِمَّنْ حَمَلْنَا مَعَ نُوحٍ وَمِن ذُرِّيَّةِ إِبْرَٰهِيمَ وَإِسْرَٰٓءِيلَ وَمِمَّنْ هَدَيْنَا وَٱجْتَبَيْنَآ ۚ إِذَا تُتْلَىٰ عَلَيْهِمْ ءَايَٰتُ ٱلرَّحْمَٰنِ خَرُّوا۟ سُجَّدًا وَبُكِيًّا ۩ ﴿٥٨﴾

---

a Ishmael was Abraham's son. Idris was a prophet who was probably born before Noah. Here, two special virtues of these prophets are described: first, their truthfulness and second, their diligence in exhorting people to pray to God and offer alms, or *zakat*, in order to give God's other subjects their rightful dues. God says here that these qualities have put the above prophets among His favoured servants, whom He shall raise on high.

The persons God selected for prophethood possessed these qualities to the fullest extent. However, the faithful in general are also expected to evince these qualities, and they too, in varying degrees, will forever partake of the divinely ordained fruits born of these qualities.

b Here, special mention is made of those prophets who were raised in the generations descending respectively from Adam, Noah and Abraham. God found them deserving of being blessed with His special guidance and of being selected to represent Him to the people.

Why did God shower His great blessings on these august personalities? God says that this was due to a virtue common to all of them, namely, their realization of God's greatness and majesty being so absolute that they would tremble on hearing His message and cry and fall down before Him on the ground. ▶

⁵⁹ But then they were succeeded by generations who neglected their prayers and were driven by their own desires. They will assuredly meet with destruction, ⁶⁰ except for those who repent and believe and do good deeds. These will enter Heaven, and they will not be wronged in the least.ᵃ

فَخَلَفَ مِنۢ بَعْدِهِمْ خَلْفٌ أَضَاعُواْ ٱلصَّلَوٰةَ وَٱتَّبَعُواْ ٱلشَّهَوَٰتِ ۖ فَسَوْفَ يَلْقَوْنَ غَيًّا ۝ إِلَّا مَن تَابَ وَءَامَنَ وَعَمِلَ صَٰلِحًا فَأُوْلَٰٓئِكَ يَدْخُلُونَ ٱلْجَنَّةَ وَلَا يُظْلَمُونَ شَيْـًٔا ۝

To cry and fall down in prostration, or *sajdah,* is the ultimate stage of the realization and admission of God's greatness and majesty. One who attains this stage has had a foretaste of that faith which is characteristic of God's messengers and prophets.

ᵃ A distinctive trait of those whose characters are moulded by the preaching of the prophets, is that they are no longer slaves of their base desires but rise above them. They turn into individuals who always remember God; indeed, the essence of religion is remembrance of God, the organized expression of which is prayer (*salat*).

If the generations that come after the prophets become negligent of God and start following their base desires, they will figure, in the eyes of God, as people who have gone astray. Being affiliated to a prophet shall be of no use to them. They shall receive what they deserve. Of them, only those shall be spared who return to the original religion, and adopt a life of faith and virtuous deeds.

Those who strive for the life Hereafter, do not immediately receive the fruits of their labours and sacrifices. For this reason, they may have misgivings that this is a path of pointless endeavour. But this is a mere misunderstanding. The fact is that, just as those who devote their efforts to worldly affairs achieve corresponding results, so also will those who strive for the life of the Hereafter be requited in full measure. Nobody need harbour any doubts about this.

⁶¹ Theirs shall be the Gardens of Eden, which the All Merciful has promised to His servants without their having seen them, and most surely His promise shall be fulfilled. ⁶² They will not hear therein anything vain, only greetings of peace. They will receive their provision there morning and evening. ⁶³ That is the Garden which We will grant to those of Our servants who have been God-fearing.ᵃ

جَنَّـٰتِ عَدۡنٍ ٱلَّتِى وَعَدَ ٱلرَّحۡمَـٰنُ عِبَادَهُۥ بِٱلۡغَيۡبِ إِنَّهُۥ كَانَ وَعۡدُهُۥ مَأۡتِيًّا ۝ لَّا يَسۡمَعُونَ فِيهَا لَغۡوًا إِلَّا سَلَـٰمًا وَلَهُمۡ رِزۡقُهُمۡ فِيهَا بُكۡرَةً وَعَشِيًّا ۝ تِلۡكَ ٱلۡجَنَّةُ ٱلَّتِى نُورِثُ مِنۡ عِبَادِنَا مَن كَانَ تَقِيًّا ۝

ᵃ This world being a place of trial, everyone has been given freedom. Here, those who perform good deeds are free and those who indulge in bad deeds are free too. Consequently, a true and righteous person never knows tranquillity in the present world. However righteous he may personally be, the fact that the unrighteous people take undue advantage of their freedom, and taint the surrounding atmosphere with ungodliness, constantly disturbs his peace of mind.

Paradise is a place from which all such wrongdoers will be excluded. There, only those noble persons will be lodged who have proved in this world that they do not live like thorns, but know how to live like flowers. A life shaped in the proximity of such people will undoubtedly be a haven of eternal peace—a paradise.

In this world, the hardest task is to abstain from vain pursuits and to lead one's life as an embodiment of peace. To this end, one has, of one's own free will, to change a life of freedom into a life of limitations. This is the most difficult sacrifice, which can be offered only by one who is truly God-fearing. Only those who fear God in this world can feel themselves to be accountable to God. They are the only ones who will be admitted to the eternal paradise of the Hereafter.

⁶⁴ We never descend except at your Lord's command. What is before us and behind us and all that lies between belong to Him. Your Lord is not forgetful. ⁶⁵ He is the Lord of the heavens and of the earth and of all that is between the two. So worship Him alone and be steadfast in His worship. Do you know of anyone equal to Him in His attributes? [a]

وَمَا نَتَنَزَّلُ إِلَّا بِأَمْرِ رَبِّكَ لَهُۥ مَا بَيْنَ أَيْدِينَا وَمَا خَلْفَنَا وَمَا بَيْنَ ذَٰلِكَ وَمَا كَانَ رَبُّكَ نَسِيًّا ﴿٦٤﴾ رَّبُّ ٱلسَّمَٰوَٰتِ وَٱلْأَرْضِ وَمَا بَيْنَهُمَا فَٱعْبُدْهُ وَٱصْطَبِرْ لِعِبَٰدَتِهِۦ هَلْ تَعْلَمُ لَهُۥ سَمِيًّا ﴿٦٥﴾

---

[a] When Dawah work is passing through a phase of being thwarted by opposition, it is a very difficult stage for the preacher (da'i). Not a day passes without the preacher wanting to take some new step to alleviate the difficulties of the situation, whereas God's will is that he should wait patiently.

Once the Prophet Muhammad experienced just such situation. In view of the gravity of the case, he awaited further guidance from God. According to a tradition, forty days passed and still Gabriel did not come. When Gabriel appeared, the Prophet asked him, 'Why did you take so long?' He replied that he was bound by God's will. When he received God's command, he came down to earth, otherwise he did not.

It was against this backdrop that the Prophet is given the advice about exercising patience. God is fully aware of the prevailing conditions and if, this being so, fresh guidance is not forthcoming from Him, it means that what is required is that the current conditions should be tolerated. Had the demands of wisdom been otherwise, then certainly fresh commandments would have been given. There is nobody who knows better than God, and there can be no guidance better than His.

It is not correct to seek a commandment on the issue of taking a practical step when the situation warrants maintaining the status quo. Doing so would amount to an attempt to have a commandment revealed prematurely.

⁶⁶ Man asks, 'When I am once dead, shall I be raised to life?' ⁶⁷ But does man not remember that We created him when he was nothing before? ⁶⁸ By your Lord, We shall most surely gather them and the devils too; and bring them close to hell on their knees.ᵃ

وَيَقُولُ ٱلْإِنسَـٰنُ أَءِذَا مَا مِتُّ لَسَوْفَ أُخْرَجُ حَيًّا ۝ أَوَلَا يَذكُرُ ٱلْإِنسَـٰنُ أَنَّا خَلَقْنَـٰهُ مِن قَبْلُ وَلَمْ يَكُ شَيْـًٔا ۝ فَوَرَبِّكَ لَنَحْشُرَنَّهُمْ وَٱلشَّيَـٰطِينَ ثُمَّ لَنُحْضِرَنَّهُمْ حَوْلَ جَهَنَّمَ جِثِيًّا ۝

ᵃ The Arabs, who were the primary addressees of the Quran, accepted the theory of life after death. All the words in the Quran relating to the life hereafter were already present in their vocabulary. But their acceptance was purely formal, as such it had no impact on their lives. In practice, they led their lives in a way that implied, 'The life of this world is the only life. Who is going to resurrect us after our death and who is going to call us to account?'

This indifference or denial, persists because man does not give serious consideration to this matter. If he did so, he would find that his initial, first birth is in itself an argument in support of his re-birth.

Here, the word 'Satan' stands for leaders who, with the help of deceitful words, mislead the common man. In this sense, they do the same work as Satan does. In the present world, these leaders are highly visible in their positions of greatness, and the people are therefore unable to ignore them. But, in the life hereafter, they will lose this 'greatness' and will be pushed into the pit of ignominy along with their followers.

⁶⁹ Then We shall carry off from every group those who were most stubborn in their opposition to the Gracious One—⁷⁰ We surely know best those most deserving of the fires of hell—⁷¹ and there is not one of you but shall pass through it: a decree from your Lord which must be fulfilled. ⁷² Then We shall save those who feared God, but the wrongdoers shall be left there on their knees.ᵃ

ثُمَّ لَنَنزِعَنَّ مِن كُلِّ شِيعَةٍ أَيُّهُمْ أَشَدُّ عَلَى الرَّحْمَٰنِ عِتِيًّا ۝ ثُمَّ لَنَحْنُ أَعْلَمُ بِالَّذِينَ هُمْ أَوْلَىٰ بِهَا صِلِيًّا ۝ وَإِن مِّنكُمْ إِلَّا وَارِدُهَا ۚ كَانَ عَلَىٰ رَبِّكَ حَتْمًا مَّقْضِيًّا ۝ ثُمَّ نُنَجِّى الَّذِينَ اتَّقَوا وَّنَذَرُ الظَّٰلِمِينَ فِيهَا جِثِيًّا ۝

ᵃ Not to accept the Truth is a crime, but to instigate a movement for the rejection of Truth is an even bigger crime. Those who become leaders of any movement to oppose the Truth deserve the worst punishment that God can mete out to them. In the life hereafter, they will be given double the punishment given to ordinary people.

From Quranic statements and certain traditions, it is learned that on the Day of Judgement Almighty God will let all people pass over hell. This will not be a passage through the interior of hell but merely across it from above. It will be just like a man passing across an open bridge over a deep river. He will see the dangerous waves of the river, but will not drown in them. The people's passing over hell on the Day of Judgement will be similar to this. The pious and righteous will go ahead and enter Paradise, while the evil ones will not be able to move on any further. Hell will recognize them and draw them in.

The purpose of putting men through this experience will be to make those who are sent to Paradise fully realize the magnitude of this great blessing of God, who has saved them from such a terrible place and sent them instead to an infinitely superior place.

73 When Our clear revelations are recited to them, those who deny the truth say to the faithful, 'Which of the two sides is better in respect of position and makes a more impressive assembly?' 74 We have destroyed so many generations before them, who surpassed them in material power and splendour.[a]

وَإِذَا تُتْلَىٰ عَلَيْهِمْ ءَايَٰتُنَا بَيِّنَٰتٍ قَالَ الَّذِينَ كَفَرُوا۟ لِلَّذِينَ ءَامَنُوٓا۟ أَىُّ الْفَرِيقَيْنِ خَيْرٌ مَّقَامًا وَأَحْسَنُ نَدِيًّا ۝ وَكَمْ أَهْلَكْنَا قَبْلَهُم مِّن قَرْنٍ هُمْ أَحْسَنُ أَثَٰثًا وَرِءْيًا ۝

[a] Those who do not care about what is right or what is wrong, who prefer the considerations of this world to those of the life hereafter and who choose to please other people rather than God, are always successful from the worldly point of view. They are surrounded by glamour and glitter. As opposed to this, those who in all their dealings are worried about right and wrong, who ignore the considerations of this world and prefer those of the life hereafter, and who care for God rather than the attitude of the public, are often bereft of external pomp and glory.

This difference gives rise to misunderstandings. It is thought that those who are better off from the worldly point of view are God's favoured ones and those who do not enjoy this position in this world are low in God's esteem. But this is a completely wrong assessment, and past history contradicts and disproves it. How many haughty heads of the past have rolled and are buried in the ground? And how many grand palaces are there still extant today that have not fallen into ruin?

75 Say, 'The Gracious One grants respite for a time to those who are in error until, when they are confronted with what they are promised, either in punishment [in the world] or in [the approach of] the Hour, they will realize who is worse in respect of position and who is weaker in resources.'*a*

76 God increases His guidance to those who follow guidance; and lasting good works are better in the sight of your Lord and are most rewarding.*b*

قُلْ مَن كَانَ فِى ٱلضَّلَـٰلَةِ فَلْيَمْدُدْ لَهُ ٱلرَّحْمَـٰنُ مَدًّا ۚ حَتَّىٰٓ إِذَا رَأَوْاْ مَا يُوعَدُونَ إِمَّا ٱلْعَذَابَ وَإِمَّا ٱلسَّاعَةَ فَسَيَعْلَمُونَ مَنْ هُوَ شَرٌّ مَّكَانًا وَأَضْعَفُ جُندًا ۝ وَيَزِيدُ ٱللَّهُ ٱلَّذِينَ ٱهْتَدَوْاْ هُدًى ۗ وَٱلْبَـٰقِيَـٰتُ ٱلصَّـٰلِحَـٰتُ خَيْرٌ عِندَ رَبِّكَ ثَوَابًا وَخَيْرٌ مَّرَدًّا ۝

---

a A rebel is given scope for his rebellious activities on account of his being on trial here, and not because it is his birthright. But it often happens that the person concerned is unable to understand this difference. He takes this temporary leeway to be a permanent feature. His eyes do not open until the respite given to him is declared to be at an end and until the opportunity for him to indulge in wrongdoing is taken away.

God in His wisdom sometimes has one man undergo this experience in this very world, whereas in the case of another, He allows him to remain in his ignorant condition until death overtakes him, and then He shows him what he was not prepared to see in this life.

b To be rightly guided means the arousal of one's consciousness and the turning of it in the right direction. Whatever the circumstances, and whatever events befall a rightly guided man, he interprets them correctly and his soul derives nourishment from them. In this way there is a constant increase in the guidance he receives in terms of faith and quality of life. The guidance received by him is not like a stagnant pool or a lifeless rock: it is like a living and ever-growing tree.

Just as one who keeps worldly interests in view progresses in this world, similarly, one who acts with the Hereafter in view keeps on accumulating his good deeds. But as they are being amassed and stored in the Hereafter, their build-up is not visible in this world. However, when Doomsday tears apart the veil, everybody will see how the guidance of the guided one was being enhanced and how, along with this, his righteous deeds were also accruing.

77 Have you seen him who denies the truth in Our revelations and says, 'I shall certainly be given wealth and children.' 78 Has he looked to the unseen, or has he made a pledge to the Merciful One? 79 Indeed not. We shall record what he says and shall prolong the punishment for him. 80 We shall inherit all that he boasts of, and he will come to Us all alone.ᵃ

أَفَرَءَيْتَ ٱلَّذِى كَفَرَ بِـَٔايَـٰتِنَا وَقَالَ لَأُوتَيَنَّ مَالًا وَوَلَدًا ۝ أَطَّلَعَ ٱلْغَيْبَ أَمِ ٱتَّخَذَ عِندَ ٱلرَّحْمَـٰنِ عَهْدًا ۝ كَلَّا سَنَكْتُبُ مَا يَقُولُ وَنَمُدُّ لَهُۥ مِنَ ٱلْعَذَابِ مَدًّا ۝ وَنَرِثُهُۥ مَا يَقُولُ وَيَأْتِينَا فَرْدًا ۝

ᵃ When a man acquires a certain amount of wealth and power, he develops a misplaced self-confidence, says things he should not and behaves in a manner that ill befits his true position.

An incident, which occurred in Makkah, illustrates behaviour of this kind. 'As ibn Wa'il, a pagan chief of Makkah, owed some money to one Khabbab ibn al-Arat. When the latter demanded his money back, 'As ibn Wa'il promised to repay the amount if Khabbab disowned allegiance to Muhammad. The latter answered: 'I will never disown Muhammad, even if you were to die and be born again.' Hearing this, 'As ibn Wa'il, answered that when he was born again, and possessed wealth and progeny, then he would repay the amount.

All this is false self-confidence and an empty boast, which are of no avail to anybody.

⁸¹ They have taken other deities besides God, so that they may be a source of strength for them. ⁸² But they shall reject their worship and turn against them.ᵃ

⁸³ Do you not see that We have appointed devils to incite those who deny the truth to disobedience? ⁸⁴ So take no hasty action against them; their days are numbered. ⁸⁵ The Day will surely come when We shall gather the God-fearing like [honoured] guests before the Compassionate God ⁸⁶ and We shall drive the sinful like a thirsty herd into Hell. ⁸⁷ No one will have power to intercede, except for those who have permission from the Lord of Mercy.ᵇ

وَٱتَّخَذُواْ مِن دُونِ ٱللَّهِ ءَالِهَةً لِّيَكُونُواْ لَهُمْ عِزًّا ۞ كَلَّا سَيَكْفُرُونَ بِعِبَادَتِهِمْ وَيَكُونُونَ عَلَيْهِمْ ضِدًّا ۞ أَلَمْ تَرَ أَنَّا أَرْسَلْنَا ٱلشَّيَٰطِينَ عَلَى ٱلْكَٰفِرِينَ تَؤُزُّهُمْ أَزًّا ۞ فَلَا تَعْجَلْ عَلَيْهِمْ إِنَّمَا نَعُدُّ لَهُمْ عَدًّا ۞ يَوْمَ نَحْشُرُ ٱلْمُتَّقِينَ إِلَى ٱلرَّحْمَٰنِ وَفْدًا ۞ وَنَسُوقُ ٱلْمُجْرِمِينَ إِلَىٰ جَهَنَّمَ وِرْدًا ۞ لَّا يَمْلِكُونَ ٱلشَّفَٰعَةَ إِلَّا مَنِ ٱتَّخَذَ عِندَ ٱلرَّحْمَٰنِ عَهْدًا ۞

ᵃ Man wants to be able to do whatever he likes in this world, but at the same time he does not want to be made to suffer the consequences of his wrongdoings. Naturally, such leniency is not to be expected from God. Therefore, man courts such beings as are supposedly near and dear to God and who could plead his case to Him.

But such a course of action, based as it is on false conjectures, will be of no avail to him or to anybody else. So much so that even those beings whom he had supposed to be partners of God and whom he ritually worshipped, will themselves disown him on Judgement Day. They will show him nothing but hatred.

ᵇ When Truth in its authentic form appears before a man and still he ignores it, this disregard of his paves the way for Satan's entry into his very soul. As a result, his mind is given over to obduracy. Now he is not able to accept any argument in a right and positive manner. God's signs may appear in front of him, but he offers self-devised explanations for them and even uses them to bolster his rebellious attitude and his arrogance.

One who assumes false supports to be his real supports, which he can safely lean on, falls a prey to the same foolishness time and again. But those who fear God consider God alone to be their real support. The fear of God makes the believers give no importance to such people as mislead others into the belief that they are their true support. Thus it is the believers alone who will be God's guests of honour in the life hereafter.

88 They say, 'The Gracious One has begotten a son.' 89 Assuredly, you have uttered a monstrous falsehood: 90 the heavens might well-nigh burst thereat, and the earth break asunder, and the mountains fall down in pieces, 91 because they ascribe a son to the Gracious One. 92 It does not become the majesty of the Compassionate God to take to Himself a son: *a* 93 there is none in the heavens or on the earth but shall return to the Merciful in utter submission— 94 He has counted them and numbered them precisely— 95 each one of them shall come to Him one by one on the Day of Judgement. 96 The Lord of Mercy will bestow affection upon those who believe and perform righteous deeds.*b*

وَقَالُوا۟ ٱتَّخَذَ ٱلرَّحۡمَٰنُ وَلَدًا ۝ لَّقَدۡ جِئۡتُمۡ شَيۡـًٔا إِدًّا ۝ تَكَادُ ٱلسَّمَٰوَٰتُ يَتَفَطَّرۡنَ مِنۡهُ وَتَنشَقُّ ٱلۡأَرۡضُ وَتَخِرُّ ٱلۡجِبَالُ هَدًّا ۝ أَن دَعَوۡا۟ لِلرَّحۡمَٰنِ وَلَدًا ۝ وَمَا يَنۢبَغِى لِلرَّحۡمَٰنِ أَن يَتَّخِذَ وَلَدًا ۝ إِن كُلُّ مَن فِى ٱلسَّمَٰوَٰتِ وَٱلۡأَرۡضِ إِلَّآ ءَاتِى ٱلرَّحۡمَٰنِ عَبۡدًا ۝ لَّقَدۡ أَحۡصَىٰهُمۡ وَعَدَّهُمۡ عَدًّا ۝ وَكُلُّهُمۡ ءَاتِيهِ يَوۡمَ ٱلۡقِيَٰمَةِ فَرۡدًا ۝ إِنَّ ٱلَّذِينَ ءَامَنُوا۟ وَعَمِلُوا۟ ٱلصَّٰلِحَٰتِ سَيَجۡعَلُ لَهُمُ ٱلرَّحۡمَٰنُ وُدًّا ۝

---

a Belief in the existence of God's children can be explained in either of two ways: that He is in need of assistants, or like ordinary people, He is desirous of having children. Both of these propositions are baseless.

The construction of the earth and the heavens is so perfect that it is unimaginable that their Maker and Mover could be prone to such weaknesses as man evinces. The grand, majestic image of the Creator, projected by His creations themselves, is not at all compatible with the concept of God being in need of children.

b It often happens that those who espouse the cause of unadulterated truth invite the wrath of the upholders of falsehood. Indeed, they become objects of hatred even in their own communities. But, in the life hereafter, the position will be reversed: the entire atmosphere will favour those devoted upholders of the pure and unadulterated truth; here in this world, having eschewed worldly honour and popularity in their staunch support of the truth, they will find in the afterlife, that they are rewarded with the highest possible esteem.

⁹⁷ We have made it [the Quran] easy, in your own language [Prophet], so that you may convey glad news to the righteous and give warning to a stubborn people. ⁹⁸ How many generations We have destroyed before them! Can you find a single one of them alive now, or hear so much as a whisper from them? ᵃ

فَإِنَّمَا يَسَّرْنَٰهُ بِلِسَانِكَ لِتُبَشِّرَ بِهِ ٱلْمُتَّقِينَ وَتُنذِرَ بِهِۦ قَوْمًا لُّدًّا ۝ وَكَمْ أَهْلَكْنَا قَبْلَهُم مِّن قَرْنٍ هَلْ تُحِسُّ مِنْهُم مِّنْ أَحَدٍ أَوْ تَسْمَعُ لَهُمْ رِكْزًا ۝

ᵃ God's book is in a language intelligible to human beings. Moreover, dealing with different topics, it takes into consideration all those aspects which make a book into a book of guidance. The Quran is nevertheless a source of guidance only to those who are serious minded, who are eager to know what is right and what is wrong, and who are ready to abstain from wrong deeds and build their lives in accordance with what is right. Those devoid of seriousness and the desire to learn will merely indulge in meaningless discussions on hearing the teachings of the Quran and will not be able to benefit from them.

Those who oppose the call for Truth err in thinking that, in doing so, they will not come to any harm. All around them there is ample evidence of the opponents of the Truth having been wiped out, but they do not learn a lesson from this. Till the last moment they harbour the impression that God's wrath may have descended on others, but that nothing is going to afflict them similarly.

But the law of God admits of no exceptions. Here, what happens to one person will happen to everybody else too; the fate of good people will be good, and vice versa.

20. *TA HA*

In the name of God,
the Most Gracious, the Most Merciful

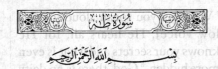

¹ *Ta Ha*

² We have not sent the Quran down to you to distress you, ³ but only as an exhortation for him who fears God; ⁴ it is a revelation from Him who has created the earth and the high heavens, ⁵ the All Merciful settled on the throne. ⁶ To Him belongs whatever is in the heavens and whatever is on the earth, and whatever lies in between them, and all that lies under the ground.ᵃ

طه ۝ مَآ أَنزَلْنَا عَلَيْكَ ٱلْقُرْءَانَ لِتَشْقَىٰ ۝ إِلَّا تَذْكِرَةً لِّمَن يَخْشَىٰ ۝ تَنزِيلًا مِّمَّنْ خَلَقَ ٱلْأَرْضَ وَٱلسَّمَٰوَٰتِ ٱلْعُلَى ۝ ٱلرَّحْمَٰنُ عَلَى ٱلْعَرْشِ ٱسْتَوَىٰ ۝ لَهُۥ مَا فِي ٱلسَّمَٰوَٰتِ وَمَا فِي ٱلْأَرْضِ وَمَا بَيْنَهُمَا وَمَا تَحْتَ ٱلثَّرَىٰ ۝

ᵃ The Quran is a reminder of the call to the Truth, but its full impact is felt only when the caller himself is fully dedicated to the cause of God, having sacrificed his own interests thereto. If he is to bring people to the right path, he must be seen to put others' welfare before his own, even if this brings him toil and trouble.

But no matter how perfect the presentation of the call to the Truth may be, only those will receive guidance from it who are capable of recognizing and appreciating the truth, and for whom the reasoned argument alone is enough to open their eyes. The August Being, who created the universe, has Himself revealed the Quran. Therefore, there is no contradiction between the Quran and nature. The Quran is a reminder of the truth. But its impact can only be commensurate with the ability —already innate in human nature—to recognise the truth.

⁷ Whether you speak aloud [or in a low voice], He hears all, for He knows your secrets and what is even more hidden. ⁸ God, there is no deity but Him. His are the most excellent names.*ᵃ*

وَإِن تَجْهَرْ بِٱلْقَوْلِ فَإِنَّهُۥ يَعْلَمُ ٱلسِّرَّ وَأَخْفَى ۝ ٱللَّهُ لَآ إِلَـٰهَ إِلَّا هُوَ لَهُ ٱلْأَسْمَآءُ ٱلْحُسْنَىٰ ۝ وَهَلْ أَتَىٰكَ

⁹ Have you heard the story of Moses? ¹⁰ When he saw a fire, he said to his family, 'Wait here. I can see a fire. Perhaps I can bring you a brand from it, or find some guidance at the fire.'*ᵇ*

حَدِيثُ مُوسَىٰ ۝ إِذْ رَءَا نَارًا فَقَالَ لِأَهْلِهِ ٱمْكُثُوٓا۟ إِنِّىٓ ءَانَسْتُ نَارًا لَّعَلِّىٓ ءَاتِيكُم مِّنْهَا بِقَبَسٍ أَوْ أَجِدُ عَلَى ٱلنَّارِ هُدًى ۝

ᵃ In this world, on the one hand, there are those whose creed is to compromise on their principles for the sake of their worldly interests and, on the other hand, there are the few who call people to the Truth and whose creed is based on remaining in consonance with God. The first group readily finds in its surroundings friends and supporters, and does not feel isolated. In contrast to this, those who give the call to the Truth stand apart, but on the firm foundation of God who is beyond the vision of mortal eyes.

Time and again the preacher becomes uneasy due to the disturbing nature of the prevailing conditions. Often he turns towards his God with prayers in his heart, and sometimes the words of prayer escape from his lips loud and clear in articulate form. To all appearances it seems that in this populous world, he is all alone and that there is nobody who is his friend or supporter.

But this is a matter of outward appearance. In reality, the preacher who gives a call to the Truth, stands on the firmest ground, because he calls for the support of God, who is aware not only of the prayers uttered in solitude but also of the whispering of the heart; such a preacher seeks to make that Being (God) his supporter who possesses all the imaginable and unimaginable powers that are required for giving anyone assistance.

ᵇ Moses was born in Egypt. There, by some mischance, a Copt got killed by him. Thereafter, he left Egypt and went to Madyan. After he had spent many years there and was married, he decided to return to Egypt, taking along with him his wife and his flock of sheep.

In the course of this journey, Moses passed through the Tur valley situated in the south of the Sinai peninsula. When night fell, he was unable to make out the way in the darkness. Moreover, it was winter time and the weather was bitterly cold. But soon he saw some far-off fire burning. Moses immediately set off in that direction to obtain some burning brands to keep them warm and also in the hopes of finding someone of whom he could ask the way.

¹¹ When he came close to it, a voice called out, 'Moses, ¹² I am your Lord! Take off your sandals, for you are in the sacred valley of Tuwa. ¹³ I have chosen you. So listen to what is being revealed. ¹⁴ I am God. There is no deity save Me; so worship Me alone, and say your prayers in My remembrance. ¹⁵ The Hour is coming. But I choose to keep it hidden, so that every human being may be recompensed in accordance with his labours. ¹⁶ Do not let anyone who does not believe in it and follows his own desires turn you away from it and so bring you to ruin.'ᵃ

فَلَمَّآ أَتَىٰهَا نُودِيَ يَـٰمُوسَىٰٓ ۞ إِنِّىٓ أَنَا۠ رَبُّكَ فَٱخْلَعْ نَعْلَيْكَ إِنَّكَ بِٱلْوَادِ ٱلْمُقَدَّسِ طُوًى ۞ وَأَنَا ٱخْتَرْتُكَ فَٱسْتَمِعْ لِمَا يُوحَىٰٓ ۞ إِنَّنِىٓ أَنَا ٱللَّهُ لَآ إِلَـٰهَ إِلَّآ أَنَا۠ فَٱعْبُدْنِى وَأَقِمِ ٱلصَّلَوٰةَ لِذِكْرِىٓ ۞ إِنَّ ٱلسَّاعَةَ ءَاتِيَةٌ أَكَادُ أُخْفِيهَا لِتُجْزَىٰ كُلُّ نَفْسٍ بِمَا تَسْعَىٰ ۞ فَلَا يَصُدَّنَّكَ عَنْهَا مَن لَّا يُؤْمِنُ بِهَا وَٱتَّبَعَ هَوَىٰهُ فَتَرْدَىٰ ۞

ᵃ The fire seen by Moses was not an ordinary fire, but the glowing manifestation of God's glory. Therefore, when he reached there, he was made to realise the importance of the audience he was having. He was asked to remove his shoes in order that, in all humility, he should be fully attentive. Then came the voice informing him that he was in the presence of God and that He (God) had chosen him as His messenger.

At that time, the instructions given to Moses were the same as were always given to all God's prophets, namely, to hold worthy of worship the one and only God, to pray to Him alone and to remember Him on all occasions. Then, Moses was informed of the fact that the present world was a world of trial, and that for a certain period God had kept the realities hidden in the realms of the unseen. On the Day of Judgement, this curtain would be torn asunder. Thereafter, the second phase of man's life would start, when everybody would be judged according to his deeds in the present world.

When emotions and desires get the better of a man, he becomes unmindful of the Hereafter and starts pursuing the ways of this world. To justify his misdeeds, he masks the true nature of the course of his action in beautiful and charming words. Others are impressed. On hearing this, they too become forgetful of the Hereafter. Under these circumstances, a man of faith needs to be extremely watchful about his own attitude and actions. He needs to save himself from being influenced by those who are unmindful of God and forgetful of the Hereafter.

¹⁷ 'What do you have in your right hand, Moses?' ¹⁸ He replied, 'It is my staff. I lean on it, and with it, I beat down the leaves for my flock; I also have other uses for it.' ¹⁹ God said, 'Moses, cast it down.' ²⁰ So he threw it down, and all of a sudden, it turned into a fast-moving serpent. ²¹ God said, 'Take hold of it, and have no fear: We shall return it to its former state. ²² Put your hand under your armpit: it will come out [shining] white, without any blemish. This shall be another sign.ᵃ

قَالَ ۞ وَمَا تِلْكَ بِيَمِينِكَ يَٰمُوسَىٰ

هِىَ عَصَاىَ أَتَوَكَّؤُاْ عَلَيْهَا وَأَهُشُّ

بِهَا عَلَىٰ غَنَمِى وَلِىَ فِيهَا مَـَٔارِبُ أُخْرَىٰ

۞ قَالَ أَلْقِهَا يَٰمُوسَىٰ ۞ فَأَلْقَىٰهَا

فَإِذَا هِىَ حَيَّةٌ تَسْعَىٰ ۞ قَالَ خُذْهَا

وَلَا تَخَفْ سَنُعِيدُهَا سِيرَتَهَا ٱلْأُولَىٰ

۞ وَٱضْمُمْ يَدَكَ إِلَىٰ جَنَاحِكَ تَخْرُجْ

بَيْضَآءَ مِنْ غَيْرِ سُوٓءٍ ءَايَةً أُخْرَىٰ ۞

ᵃ The question 'What do you have in your right hand?' was meant to awaken Moses's awareness. Its purpose was to impress afresh on his mind that his stick was but a stick, so that the next moment when, due to a miracle of God, it changed into a snake, he should be fully aware of its significance.

Moses' stick being changed into a snake was a miracle of transformation. But it must be borne in mind that all the things we see on earth are actually in a process of transformation. An acorn planted in soil and watered will one day grow into a mighty oak tree. Vapour condenses and turns into water, and water, when boiled, will turn into steam. Some of these processes are rapid and others are slow. Some are so slow—like the growth of a tree—that they are imperceptible to the human eye. The slower the process, the less strange it seems, because its slowness gives us time to familiarise ourselves with the phenomenon. When Moses' stick took the shape of a snake, it happened in an instant, and so seemed very strange and startling.

The fact is that whatever there is in this world, or whatever the events, all are 'miracles' of God, be it the emerging of a sapling from the earth or a stick becoming a snake. 'Extraordinary' miracles are shown through prophets to make man take notice of the everyday miracles wrought by God.

²³ We shall show you some of Our greatest signs. ²⁴ Go to Pharaoh; he has transgressed all bounds.'ᵃ

ᵃ Incidents in the lives of prophets of the past are mentioned in the Bible as well as in the Quran. But, at many places, there are meaningful differences in the versions respectively of the Quran and the Bible. For instance, in this case, the Bible says: Moses kept his hand on his chest and covered it, and when he brought it out and saw it, it was white like ice, due to leprosy (Exodus 4:7).

The Bible attributes the whiteness of Moses's hand to 'leprosy'. In this context, the Quran's describing of the miracle of the white hand and the adding of the words 'without any blemish' clearly indicate that the Qur'an is not derived from the Bible, but is directly from God, who is All-knowing. As such, it corrects the biblical version.

Moses was given two special miracles. The miracle of the snake was the sign of power, and the miracle of the bright white hand was a symbol of his standing for a luminous Truth.

Pharaoh transgressed all limits when, having attained power, he considered himself to be god. The literal meaning of 'Pharaoh' is the child of the sun. The ancient Egyptians used to regard the sun as the greatest god–the Mighty Lord. So Pharaoh had declared himself the representative of the sun god on earth. He had statues of himself made and installed in all the cities of Egypt and these statues were worshipped.

Power is a blessing conferred by God; when a man receives this blessing, he should be overwhelmed with gratitude. But if he is vain and arrogant, he not only feels no gratitude, but he also sets himself up as God's equal.

²⁵ Moses said, 'My Lord! open up my heart, ²⁶ and make my task easy for me. ²⁷ Loosen the knot in my tongue, ²⁸ so that they may understand my speech, ²⁹ and appoint for me a helper from among my family, ³⁰ Aaron, my brother. ³¹ Strengthen me through him, ³² and let him share my task, ³³ so that we may glorify You much ³⁴ and remember You much: ³⁵ You are surely watching over us. ³⁶ God said, 'You have been granted your request, Moses.'^a

قَالَ رَبِّ ٱشْرَحْ لِى صَدْرِى ۝ وَيَسِّرْ لِىۤ أَمْرِى ۝ وَٱحْلُلْ عُقْدَةً مِّن لِّسَانِى ۝ يَفْقَهُواْ قَوْلِى ۝ وَٱجْعَل لِّى وَزِيرًا مِّنْ أَهْلِى ۝ هَٰرُونَ أَخِى ۝ ٱشْدُدْ بِهِۦۤ أَزْرِى ۝ وَأَشْرِكْهُ فِىۤ أَمْرِى ۝ كَىْ نُسَبِّحَكَ كَثِيرًا ۝ وَنَذْكُرَكَ كَثِيرًا ۝ إِنَّكَ كُنتَ بِنَا بَصِيرًا ۝ قَالَ قَدْ أُوتِيتَ سُؤْلَكَ يَٰمُوسَىٰ ۝

---

^a After attaining prophethood, Moses might well have developed a sense of pride. But, at that time, the nature of his request to God reveals that he did not take prophethood as a matter of pride but as a matter of responsibility. At that time, the words he uttered were those of one who is fully conscious of the delicate and exacting responsibility attached to the work of a mission.

The opening of the heart for a man of the mission means that, according to the different occasions that may arise, appropriate guidance may enter it unhindered. The easing of the situation means that opponents should never succeed in impeding the work of the divine mission. Loosening the knot of the tongue means acquiring the capability to address large gatherings without hesitation in order to give the divine call. Almighty God granted all this to Moses to enable him to effectively discharge the responsibility of prophethood. Along with this, at his request, He made his (Moses') brother, Aaron, a powerful assistant to him.

This special assistance given to a prophet may also be given to a dayee, who is not a prophet, provided that he devotes himself fully to the work of the mission as the prophet had done.

Remembrance of God is the real purpose of religion. But, remembrance does not mean the mere oral repetition of certain words. It indicates rather that state which is quite naturally engendered by the discovery of Truth. At that time, a man experiences the perfection of God's attributes to the point of being quite swept away by them. He becomes so overwhelmed with godly feeling that he dedicates himself unstintingly to the divine cause.

³⁷ Indeed, We showed Our favour to you before also, ³⁸ when We revealed Our will to your mother, saying, ³⁹ "Put him into a chest, then cast it into the river. The river will cast it on to the bank, and there he shall be taken up by an enemy of Mine and his." I showered My love on you so that you might be reared under My watchful eye. ⁴⁰ Recall when your sister walked along and said, "Shall I guide you to one who will take care of him?" Thus We returned you to your mother, so that her eyes might be cooled and that she might not grieve. And you killed a man and We delivered you from sorrow. We tested you with various trials. You stayed for a number of years among the people of Midian, then you came upto the standard, Moses.ᵃ

وَلَقَدْ مَنَنَّا عَلَيْكَ مَرَّةً أُخْرَىٰ ۝ إِذْ أَوْحَيْنَآ إِلَىٰ أُمِّكَ مَا يُوحَىٰ ۝ أَنِ اقْذِفِيهِ فِي التَّابُوتِ فَاقْذِفِيهِ فِي الْيَمِّ فَلْيُلْقِهِ الْيَمُّ بِالسَّاحِلِ يَأْخُذْهُ عَدُوٌّ لِّي وَعَدُوٌّ لَّهُ ۚ وَأَلْقَيْتُ عَلَيْكَ مَحَبَّةً مِّنِّي وَلِتُصْنَعَ عَلَىٰ عَيْنِي ۝ إِذْ تَمْشِي أُخْتُكَ فَتَقُولُ هَلْ أَدُلُّكُمْ عَلَىٰ مَن يَكْفُلُهُ ۖ فَرَجَعْنَاكَ إِلَىٰ أُمِّكَ كَيْ تَقَرَّ عَيْنُهَا وَلَا تَحْزَنَ ۚ وَقَتَلْتَ نَفْسًا فَنَجَّيْنَاكَ مِنَ الْغَمِّ وَفَتَنَّاكَ فُتُونًا ۚ فَلَبِثْتَ سِنِينَ فِي أَهْلِ مَدْيَنَ ثُمَّ جِئْتَ عَلَىٰ قَدَرٍ يَٰمُوسَىٰ ۝

ᵃ The original inhabitants of Egypt were the Copts (Qibti) whose political and religious representative was Pharaoh. The other community there was that of the the Children of Israel (Israelites) who had migrated and settled there during the period of Joseph (Yusuf). At the time of Moses' birth, Pharaoh, intending the complete extermination of the Israelite race, had given orders for all male children born in Israelite homes to be killed. Moses's mother, inspired by God, placed her baby in a basket and set it adrift on the waters of the river Nile, in order to save him from being killed.

The basket floated down the river and reached a spot near the royal palace where Pharaoh and his wife saw him. Moved by pity for the small child, they took him and kept him in the palace. Thereafter, at the suggestion of Moses's sister, his mother was appointed to breast-feed him. It was a miracle of God that Moses was brought up and educated by that very Pharaoh who would have had him killed, had he known his identity, and who was later to become his greatest enemy.

When Moses grew up, he intervened in a quarrel between an Egyptian and an Israelite. When he took the Egyptian to task, the latter died quite unexpectedly. Then, orders were issued by the government for Moses to be arrested. But, Moses secretly left Egypt and reached Midian. ▶

⁴¹ I have chosen you for Myself. ⁴² Go, you and your brother, with My signs, and do not be remiss in remembering Me. ⁴³ Go, both of you to Pharaoh, for he has transgressed all bounds. ⁴⁴ But speak gently to him; perhaps he may yet take heed or even feel afraid.' *ᵃ*

وَٱصْطَنَعْتُكَ لِنَفْسِى ۝ ٱذْهَبْ أَنتَ وَأَخُوكَ بِـَٔايَـٰتِى وَلَا تَنِيَا فِى ذِكْرِى ۝ ٱذْهَبَآ إِلَىٰ فِرْعَوْنَ إِنَّهُۥ طَغَىٰ ۝ فَقُولَا لَهُۥ قَوْلًا لَّيِّنًا لَّعَلَّهُۥ يَتَذَكَّرُ أَوْ يَخْشَىٰ ۝

There in the desert, he had many new experiences. After the Egyptian's being killed, Moses prayed with great fervour to Almighty God, as a result of which He led Moses to understand that this incident could afford him valuable lessons.

ᵃ When, after a series of testing experiences, Moses reached the final stage of maturity, God assigned to him prophethood, so that he might communicate the divine message to man. Moses was given two pieces of advice—that he should never be remiss in the remembrance of God and that he should never be coercive in the performance of the mission of communicating the message of God to man.

Remembrance of God means belief in God being so all-pervasive that the thought of God comes to mind, time and time again. Every observation a man makes and every incident in his life should, coupled with his God-consciousness, be the cause of awakening for him. While ordinary people live on material food, the preacher of Truth lives on the remembrance of God. Remembrance of God is an asset to the faithful (*mu'min*) and to the missionary alike.

The second essential element is the adoption of a lenient approach in the communication of divine message to man. The very fact that Moses was so instructed when he had to approach such an arrogant person as Pharaoh shows that a tactful and considerate attitude in mission work is an absolute requirement in all cases. Even arrogance or harsh behaviour on the part of those who are the addressees, does not give the missionary any right to deviate from being kind and understanding in his approach.

45 They both said, 'Our Lord, We fear that he may commit some excess against us, or exceed all bounds in transgression.' 46 God said, 'Do not fear; I am with you both. I hear and I see. 47 Go to him and say, "We are both messengers from your Lord. Let the Children of Israel go with us, and do not oppress them. We have brought you a Sign from your Lord, and may peace be upon whoever follows the right guidance; 48 it has been revealed to us that punishment shall overtake him who rejects it and turns away!"' *a*

قَالَا رَبَّنَا إِنَّنَا نَخَافُ أَن يَفْرُطَ عَلَيْنَا أَوْ أَن يَطْغَىٰ ۩ قَالَ لَا تَخَافَا ۖ إِنَّنِي مَعَكُمَا أَسْمَعُ وَأَرَىٰ ۩ فَأْتِيَاهُ فَقُولَا إِنَّا رَسُولَا رَبِّكَ فَأَرْسِلْ مَعَنَا بَنِي إِسْرَٰٓءِيلَ وَلَا تُعَذِّبْهُمْ ۖ قَدْ جِئْنَٰكَ بِـَٔايَةٍ مِّن رَّبِّكَ ۖ وَٱلسَّلَٰمُ عَلَىٰ مَنِ ٱتَّبَعَ ٱلْهُدَىٰٓ ۩ إِنَّا قَدْ أُوحِيَ إِلَيْنَآ أَنَّ ٱلْعَذَابَ عَلَىٰ مَن كَذَّبَ وَتَوَلَّىٰ ۩

---

a Pharaoh was an extremely haughty and arrogant person. Having acquired power, he had started considering himself to be a god. So Moses feared that when the message of the real God was presented to him, he would flare up in anger. But God's messengers are under His protection. So Moses was commanded to proceed and to be rest assured that Pharaoh, despite his great might and power, would not be able to do him any harm.

The Israelites were monotheists like the Muslims. But, being in the midst of the polytheistic community of Egypt, they were badly affected by its polytheistic culture. Moreover, the rulers had subjected them to such privation and hard labour as to render them incapable of thinking about such higher realities as the oneness of God and the life hereafter. Therefore, Moses was instructed to remove the Israelites from this sphere and settle them elsewhere, so that they could be brought up and educated far away from this vitiating atmosphere of polytheism and ignorance.

⁴⁹ Pharaoh said, 'Who then is the Lord of you both, Moses?' ⁵⁰ Moses replied, 'Our Lord is He who has given everything its form, then guided it.' ⁵¹ Pharaoh asked, 'What about the previous generations?' ⁵² Moses said, 'My Lord alone has knowledge of that, recorded in a Book. My Lord neither errs nor forgets.' ᵃ

قَالَ فَمَن رَّبُّكُمَا يَٰمُوسَىٰ ۞ قَالَ رَبُّنَا ٱلَّذِىٓ أَعْطَىٰ كُلَّ شَىْءٍ خَلْقَهُۥ ثُمَّ هَدَىٰ ۞ قَالَ فَمَا بَالُ ٱلْقُرُونِ ٱلْأُولَىٰ ۞ قَالَ عِلْمُهَا عِندَ رَبِّى فِى كِتَٰبٍ لَّا يَضِلُّ رَبِّى وَلَا يَنسَى ۞

ᵃ Pharaoh's question, 'Who is your Lord?' did not mean that he was not aware of any god besides himself, or that he quite finally denied the existence of a superior god. All it showed, in fact, was contempt for Moses' utterance, rather than being a straight denial.

In Egypt, Joseph had preached the oneness of God. Moreover, hundreds of thousands of Israelites were still living there and they professed faith in the one God. In this way, belief in one superior God existed in Egypt, but the power, pomp and glory were Pharaoh's. According to the belief of the Egyptians, Pharaoh was the worldly manifestation of their greatest god, the sun. He was Egypt's god-king and idols and statues of him had become objects of worship throughout Egypt. Moses, in stark contrast to this, belonged to the Israelite community—a community held in low esteem because of its slave-labour status. Against this background, his faith could have no public significance in Egypt.

In this world there are innumerable things, each one of which has its peculiar structure and its own method of working. Everything functions according to immutable laws. Even an arrogant king like Pharaoh was not exempt from this system—which clearly proves the existence of a Superior Creator.

When Moses made this statement, Pharaoh felt that he had no direct reply to it; so he gave the matter a new turn. Finding himself weak in the field of reasoning and arguments, he wanted to incite prejudicial feelings and thus maintain his own superiority among his people. Therefore, he asked Moses—if whatever he said was true—what had happened to the great ones of the past, who, according to Moses, had died while in a misguided condition. Moses did not answer this question directly. Instead he said, 'You had better leave this matter to God and think about yourself.'

⁵³ It is He who has laid out the earth for you and traced routes in it and sent down water from the sky. We have brought forth every sort of plant with it, ⁵⁴ so eat and graze your cattle. In this there are signs for men of understanding. ⁵⁵ From the earth We have created you and We will return you to it, and from it We shall bring you forth a second time.ᵃ

الَّذِى جَعَلَ لَكُمُ ٱلْأَرْضَ مَهْدًا وَسَلَكَ لَكُمْ فِيهَا سُبُلًا وَأَنزَلَ مِنَ ٱلسَّمَاءِ مَاءً فَأَخْرَجْنَا بِهِۦ أَزْوَٰجًا مِّن نَّبَاتٍ شَتَّىٰ ۝ كُلُوا۟ وَٱرْعَوْا۟ أَنْعَٰمَكُمْ ۗ إِنَّ فِى ذَٰلِكَ لَءَايَٰتٍ لِّأُو۟لِى ٱلنُّهَىٰ ۝ ۞ مِنْهَا خَلَقْنَٰكُمْ وَفِيهَا نُعِيدُكُمْ وَمِنْهَا نُخْرِجُكُمْ تَارَةً أُخْرَىٰ ۝

ᵃ The creation of the earth, the institution of the system of rainfall, the growth of plants and greenery and other natural phenomena that have made the present world habitable for living things, are astonishingly great and wonderful manifestations.

They are 'signs' which prove that the Creator and Lord of this world can be none other than Almighty God. In order to bring into existence such a world as the present one, extraordinary power is required, which is available neither to any 'Sun' nor to any 'King'. This being so, there is no alternative but to admit that the One who has created our world and the One who controls it is a Superior Being, namely God.

This proves, moreover, that this world has not been created in vain; ours is not a world which has come into existence without purpose and which is likely to end in the same way. A meaningful world implies a meaningful end. Keen observation of this world provides proof of the oneness of God and also of the life hereafter.

⁵⁶ We showed Pharaoh all Our signs but he rejected them and refused to believe in them. ⁵⁷ He said, 'Have you come to us to turn us out of our land by means of your magic, Moses? ⁵⁸ We will certainly bring you magic to match it. So appoint a time between us and you, in an open space, which neither we nor you will fail to keep.'ᵃ

وَلَقَدْ أَرَيْنَهُ ءَايَتِنَا كُلَّهَا فَكَذَّبَ وَأَبَى ۞ قَالَ أَجِئْتَنَا لِتُخْرِجَنَا مِنْ أَرْضِنَا بِسِحْرِكَ يَـٰمُوسَى ۞ فَلَنَأْتِيَنَّكَ بِسِحْرٍ مِّثْلِهِۦ فَاجْعَلْ بَيْنَنَا وَبَيْنَكَ مَوْعِدًا لَّا نُخْلِفُهُۥ نَحْنُ وَلَآ أَنتَ مَكَانًا سُوًى ۞

ᵃ Moses continued to preach to Pharaoh over a long period of time, using rational arguments and also showing him miracles of a physical nature. But Pharaoh did not believe in Moses. In reality, admitting the truth of Moses's preaching would have amounted to a negation of himself—something which his proud and egoistic mentality would never permit.

Pharaoh tried to nullify Moses's rational arguments by means of irrelevant pleas. On the subject of his miracles, Pharaoh alleged that they were simply magic, i.e., something which had no relevance to God, and insisted that anybody could acquire the necessary expertise to perform such feats. In order to keep up his boastful assertions, he said that he, through his magicians, could perform the same feats or miracles as Moses had demonstrated. After some discussion, it was finally decided that, at the forthcoming national fair, magicians of the country should gather, and there should be a competition between them and Moses before all the people.

⁵⁹ Moses said, 'The day of the encounter will be the day of the festival, and let the people assemble when the sun has risen high.' ⁶⁰ So Pharaoh withdrew, devised his stratagem and returned. ⁶¹ Moses said to them, 'Woe to you! Do not invent lies against God, lest He destroy you by some calamity: whoever invents lies is bound to fail.' *ᵃ*

قَالَ مَوْعِدُكُمْ يَوْمُ ٱلزِّينَةِ وَأَن يُحْشَرَ ٱلنَّاسُ ضُحًى ﴿٥٩﴾ فَتَوَلَّىٰ فِرْعَوْنُ فَجَمَعَ كَيْدَهُۥ ثُمَّ أَتَىٰ ﴿٦٠﴾ قَالَ لَهُم مُّوسَىٰ وَيْلَكُمْ لَا تَفْتَرُواْ عَلَى ٱللَّهِ كَذِبًا فَيُسْحِتَكُم بِعَذَابٍ وَقَدْ خَابَ مَنِ ٱفْتَرَىٰ ﴿٦١﴾

ᵃ Pharaoh sent his messengers throughout the country with an invitation to all the expert magicians. When they had gathered at the fair grounds, before the start of the contest, Moses made a speech. This speech was nothing new to the people; it was in the nature of a reminder. The magicians and other people were already aware of what Moses' message was going to be. They knew that Moses upheld the unity of God as opposed to the belief in a multiplicity of gods, or in the existence of partners to God.

Against this background, Moses took this last opportunity to give the final admonition. He impressed upon Pharaoh and the magicians how vital it was not to treat this as mere conjuring. He said that it was an extremely serious matter to treat any sign from God as if it were magic and then to try to surpass it by human sleight of hand. This amounted to an attempt to counter actual reality by means of an absolutely unreal thing; this would certainly result in destruction. He clarified that while they were apparently bent on proving him false, what they were doing in reality, was trying to prove the falsity of God Himself. Those who give free rein to this type of arrogance can never succeed in the world of God.

⁶²Then they [the magicians] conferred among themselves, whispering to one another. ⁶³They said, 'Certainly they are both magicians who want to drive you out of your land by their magic, and destroy your best traditions. ⁶⁴Therefore, decide upon your plan and then come forward in ranks. Whoever gains the upper hand today shall surely triumph.'*ᵃ*

فَتَنَـٰزَعُوٓاْ أَمْرَهُم بَيْنَهُمْ وَأَسَرُّواْ
ٱلنَّجْوَىٰ ۝ قَالُوٓاْ إِنْ هَـٰذَانِ
لَسَـٰحِرَانِ يُرِيدَانِ أَن يُخْرِجَاكُم مِّنْ
أَرْضِكُم بِسِحْرِهِمَا وَيَذْهَبَا
بِطَرِيقَتِكُمُ ٱلْمُثْلَىٰ ۝ فَأَجْمِعُواْ
كَيْدَكُمْ ثُمَّ ٱئْتُواْ صَفًّا ۚ وَقَدْ أَفْلَحَ
ٱلْيَوْمَ مَنِ ٱسْتَعْلَىٰ ۝

ᵃ Moses' initial speech caused a difference of opinion among the magicians. One group said that this was the statement not of a magician but of a prophet. Others were opposed to it and held that Moses was a magician no different from themselves. (*Tafsir ibn Kathir*).

These magicians were certainly capable of recognising their co-professionals. The more experienced among them realised that what they were about to encounter were miracles, not magic. So now they felt afraid to enter the competition. However, at the instance of Pharaoh and his enthusiastic companions, they agreed to compete.

At that time, the entire structure of Egyptian life was based on polytheistic beliefs. The worship of Pharaoh as the personification of their super god (the sun) was the foundation of their political and social systems. Pharaoh provoked and exploited public sentiment by saying that the extant system based on the best traditions was their national system, and that if the upholders of God's unity succeeded in their mission, their entire national system would be overthrown.

⁶⁵ They said, 'Moses, will you throw down first, or shall we be the first to throw down?' ⁶⁶ Moses said, 'You throw down first.' Suddenly their ropes and staffs appeared to him, by their magic, to be moving about rapidly, ⁶⁷ and in his heart Moses became apprehensive, ⁶⁸ but We said, 'Do not be afraid. It is you who shall prevail.' ⁶⁹ Throw down that [staff] which is in your right hand—it shall swallow up what they have wrought, for what they have wrought is only a magician's trick. A magician shall never thrive, come whence he may. ⁷⁰ The magicians then prostrated themselves. They said, 'We believe in the Lord of Aaron and Moses.' ^a

قَالُواْ يَٰمُوسَىٰٓ إِمَّآ أَن تُلۡقِىَ وَإِمَّآ أَن نَّكُونَ أَوَّلَ مَنۡ أَلۡقَىٰ ۝ قَالَ بَلۡ أَلۡقُواْ ۖ فَإِذَا حِبَالُهُمۡ وَعِصِيُّهُمۡ يُخَيَّلُ إِلَيۡهِ مِن سِحۡرِهِمۡ أَنَّهَا تَسۡعَىٰ ۝ فَأَوۡجَسَ فِى نَفۡسِهِۦ خِيفَةً مُّوسَىٰ ۝ قُلۡنَا لَا تَخَفۡ إِنَّكَ أَنتَ ٱلۡأَعۡلَىٰ ۝ وَأَلۡقِ مَا فِى يَمِينِكَ تَلۡقَفۡ مَا صَنَعُوٓاْ ۖ إِنَّمَا صَنَعُواْ كَيۡدُ سَٰحِرٖ ۗ وَلَا يُفۡلِحُ ٱلسَّاحِرُ حَيۡثُ أَتَىٰ ۝ فَأُلۡقِىَ ٱلسَّحَرَةُ سُجَّدًا قَالُوٓاْ ءَامَنَّا بِرَبِّ هَٰرُونَ وَمُوسَىٰ ۝

---

^a The competition started with the magicians throwing their ropes and sticks on the ground where they seemed to move about in the shape of snakes. But this was an illusory effect. In other words, the ropes and sticks had not really changed into snakes. The magicians had simply created an optical illusion to play upon the imagination of the audience, so that it would temporarily appear to them as if the ropes and sticks were wriggling on the ground like snakes.

Then, in accordance with God's orders, Moses threw his stick on the ground where it immediately assumed the shape of a big snake, and started moving along the ground. At its touch, the magicians' spell broke, then all the things which had appeared to be moving about like snakes turned back into mere ropes and sticks.

The magicians had already been impressed by Moses' speech, and now that they had had a practical demonstration of his powers, they saw with their own eyes the truth of Moses' stand. They were now absolutely certain that the power Moses possessed was not that of human magic, but the actual ability to perform a miracle of God.

This conviction was so deep that they thereupon declared their conversion to Moses' faith.

⁷¹ Pharaoh said, 'Have you believed in him before I permit you? He must be your master who has taught you magic. I will cut your hands and feet off on opposite sides, and have you crucified on the trunks of palm-trees. You shall know whose punishment is more severe and more lasting.'ᵃ

قَالَ ءَامَنتُمۡ لَهُۥ قَبۡلَ أَنۡ ءَاذَنَ لَكُمۡۖ إِنَّهُۥ لَكَبِيرُكُمُ ٱلَّذِى عَلَّمَكُمُ ٱلسِّحۡرَۖ فَلَأُقَطِّعَنَّ أَيۡدِيَكُمۡ وَأَرۡجُلَكُم مِّنۡ خِلَٰفٍ وَلَأُصَلِّبَنَّكُمۡ فِى جُذُوعِ ٱلنَّخۡلِ وَلَتَعۡلَمُنَّ أَيُّنَآ أَشَدُّ عَذَابًا وَأَبۡقَىٰ ۝

ᵃ This was not merely a competition between two types of persons to see who could perform the greatest feats; it was actually a confrontation between monotheism and polytheism. In other words, this competition was to decide whether truth was on the side of the one true God or the many gods of the idolaters.

As Pharaoh's 'greatness' was completely based on polytheism, he could not tolerate its defeat and pronounced the severest punishment for the magicians, according to the law of ancient Egypt.

When Pharaoh was defeated in the field of arguments and reasoning, he tried to suppress the truth by force. This has been the general mentality of those in power in all ages, whether their power be dynastic or democratic in origin.

⁷²They said, 'Never shall we prefer you to all the evidence of the truth that has come to us. Nor to Him who has brought us into being. So decide whatever you will. Your jurisdiction only covers the life of this world—⁷³we have believed in our Lord so that He may forgive us our sins and forgive us the sorcery that you have forced us to practice. God is the best and the most abiding.'ᵃ

قَالُوا۟ لَن نُّؤْثِرَكَ عَلَىٰ مَا جَآءَنَا مِنَ ٱلْبَيِّنَٰتِ وَٱلَّذِى فَطَرَنَا فَٱقْضِ مَآ أَنتَ قَاضٍ إِنَّمَا تَقْضِى هَٰذِهِ ٱلْحَيَوٰةَ ٱلدُّنْيَآ ﴿٧٢﴾ إِنَّآ ءَامَنَّا بِرَبِّنَا لِيَغْفِرَ لَنَا خَطَٰيَٰنَا وَمَآ أَكْرَهْتَنَا عَلَيْهِ مِنَ ٱلسِّحْرِ وَٱللَّهُ خَيْرٌ وَأَبْقَىٰ ﴿٧٣﴾

ᵃ The magicians, on the one hand, were confronted by the cogent reasoning of Moses, and on the other, the towering personality of Pharaoh. The magicians preferred convincing arguments to authoritarianism, although they knew very well how dearly they would pay for their choice.

The magicians' faith was not of the hereditary or formal, ritual kind: it amounted to a 'discovery' for them. And faith received as a discovery is so powerful that under its influence everything else appears worthless—be it a great personality or some other worldly consideration.

74 Indeed, he who comes to his Lord a sinner shall be consigned to Hell; he shall neither die therein nor live. 75 But he who comes to Him as a believer, having done good deeds, shall be exalted to the highest ranks, 76 he will abide forever in the Gardens of eternity, through which rivers flow. That is the recompense for those who purify themselves.*a*

إِنَّهُۥ مَن يَأْتِ رَبَّهُۥ مُجْرِمًا فَإِنَّ لَهُۥ جَهَنَّمَ لَا يَمُوتُ فِيهَا وَلَا يَحْيَىٰ ۞ وَمَن يَأْتِهِۦ مُؤْمِنًا قَدْ عَمِلَ ٱلصَّٰلِحَٰتِ فَأُوْلَٰٓئِكَ هُمُ ٱلدَّرَجَٰتُ ٱلْعُلَىٰ ۞ جَنَّٰتُ عَدْنٍ تَجْرِى مِن تَحْتِهَا ٱلْأَنْهَٰرُ خَٰلِدِينَ فِيهَا ۚ وَذَٰلِكَ جَزَآءُ مَن تَزَكَّىٰ ۞

---

a What is meant by 'becoming a criminal or a delinquent'? Delinquency is that state to which a man descends when he has a sign from God shining brightly before his eyes, but fails to learn a lesson from it. Truth is revealed to him in the language of reason, but he ignores it. He is not capable of pulling himself out of the grip of worldly forces and material considerations to the point of admitting the Truth.

In the life hereafter there is the sternest punishment for such people. The troubles of this world, howsoever great, are necessarily limited in their severity by the very fact of being bound to come to an end—sooner or later—with death. But the hereafter is a place from which man, beset by unspeakable afflictions, will find it impossible to run away, for there, he will not even have death ahead of him to put an end to his torment.

Paradise is for one who purifies himself and purification consists of giving up a life of carelessness and neglect, and adopting a prudent way of living. The aspirant to Paradise abstains from all things that come in the way of Truth. He rids himself of the hindrance of any worldly considerations obstructing his path. He crushes the base desires of his self when they arise. If feelings of false pride and the urge to transgress raise their heads within him, he stifles them and buries them in his innermost self.

Such are men of true faith. In this world their faith takes the shape of a garden of pious deeds. In the life hereafter, it will be returned to them in the shape of heaven's eternally flourishing garden.

⁷⁷ We sent a revelation to Moses saying, 'Take away My servants by night and strike for them a dry path through the sea. Have no fear of being overtaken and do not be afraid.' ⁷⁸ Pharaoh pursued them with his hosts, but they were submerged by the sea, which was destined to overwhelm them. ⁷⁹ For Pharaoh had led his people astray and did not guide them. *ᵃ*

وَلَقَدْ أَوْحَيْنَا إِلَىٰ مُوسَىٰ أَنْ أَسْرِ بِعِبَادِى فَٱضْرِبْ لَهُمْ طَرِيقًا فِى ٱلْبَحْرِ يَبَسًا لَّا تَخَٰفُ دَرَكًا وَلَا تَخْشَىٰ ۝ فَأَتْبَعَهُمْ فِرْعَوْنُ بِجُنُودِهِۦ فَغَشِيَهُم مِّنَ ٱلْيَمِّ مَا غَشِيَهُمْ ۝ وَأَضَلَّ فِرْعَوْنُ قَوْمَهُۥ وَمَا هَدَىٰ ۝

ᵃ After the confrontation with the magicians, Moses remained in Egypt for many years. On the one hand, he persisted with his preachings to Pharaoh and his community, while on the other hand, he demanded that he be allowed to take his people along with him out of Egypt to the Sinai desert, so that they could freely pray to the one and only God. But Pharaoh neither accepted his advice, nor did he allow him to leave Egypt.

At last, at God's behest, Moses decided to migrate in secrecy. In accordance with a predetermined plan, all the Israelite as well as non-Israelite believers who were there in Egypt at that time gathered at a particular place and from there collectively marched onwards.

No sooner had this caravan reached the northern Gulf of the Red Sea than Pharaoh arrived there in pursuit of them with his army. Before them was the wide gulf like a vast sea and behind them was Pharaoh's army. Then, Moses struck the water of the gulf with his stick, and the water divided into two parts. Moses and his companions, walking on the dry land in the middle, reached the other side safely. On seeing this, Pharaoh also embarked on the same course. But as soon as Pharaoh and his army reached the middle, the two separate walls of the water gushed back in and joined together, so that they were all drowned. The same sea, which had provided a path of deliverance to God's faithful subjects, became a pit of death for His enemies.

Generally, people who rely on their leaders ignore the Truth. Pharaoh's example certainly shows that a leader's support can be very weak. In this world, those who chalk out their path by following God's signs rather than the dictates of some great national figure are the ones to enjoy real support.

⁸⁰ Children of Israel! We delivered you from your enemies and We made a covenant with you on the right side of the Mount. We sent down manna and quails for you, ⁸¹ 'Eat from the wholesome things with which We have provided you but do not transgress, lest you should incur My wrath.' [We said], 'He that incurs My wrath shall surely be ruined. ⁸² But I am most forgiving towards him who turns in repentance and believes and acts righteously and follows the right path.'^a

يَـٰبَنِىٓ إِسْرَٰٓءِيلَ قَدْ أَنجَيْنَـٰكُم مِّنْ عَدُوِّكُمْ وَوَٰعَدْنَـٰكُمْ جَانِبَ ٱلطُّورِ ٱلْأَيْمَنَ وَنَزَّلْنَا عَلَيْكُمُ ٱلْمَنَّ وَٱلسَّلْوَىٰ ﴿٨٠﴾ كُلُوا۟ مِن طَيِّبَـٰتِ مَا رَزَقْنَـٰكُمْ وَلَا تَطْغَوْا۟ فِيهِ فَيَحِلَّ عَلَيْكُمْ غَضَبِى وَمَن يَحْلِلْ عَلَيْهِ غَضَبِى فَقَدْ هَوَىٰ ﴿٨١﴾ وَإِنِّى لَغَفَّارٌ لِّمَن تَابَ وَءَامَنَ وَعَمِلَ صَـٰلِحًا ثُمَّ ٱهْتَدَىٰ ﴿٨٢﴾

---

^a After crossing the gulf, Moses and his companions pushed onwards until they reached the Sinai desert. They then went to the foot of Mount Tur, where they were given the code of ethics (*shari'ah*) in the form of ten commandments with due solemnity. These people remained in the Sinai Desert for almost forty years. Here, as a special gift of God, they were provided with water and food, manna (*mann*) and quails (*salwa*). This arrangement continued till a subsequent generation reached the fertile area of Palestine.

Almighty God's subjects can expect their Creator, as a matter of their right, to provide them with sustenance, whatever the circumstances. That is what they are entitled to. And God has the right to expect that his subjects will never under any circumstances be arrogant or disobedient towards Him. For those who remain grateful to God for His blessings, there shall be further blessings from Him, but for those who become arrogant, there shall be severe and unending punishment.

83 [When Moses was upon the Mount, God said,] 'O Moses, why have you come with such haste from your people?' 84 He said, 'They are following in my footsteps, while I have hastened to You, my Lord, to please You.' 85 But God said, 'We have tested your people in your absence. The Samiri has led them astray.' *a*

۞ وَمَآ أَعْجَلَكَ عَن قَوْمِكَ يَٰمُوسَىٰ ﴿٨٣﴾ قَالَ هُمْ أُوْلَآءِ عَلَىٰٓ أَثَرِى وَعَجِلْتُ إِلَيْكَ رَبِّ لِتَرْضَىٰ ﴿٨٤﴾ قَالَ فَإِنَّا قَدْ فَتَنَّا قَوْمَكَ مِنۢ بَعْدِكَ وَأَضَلَّهُمُ ٱلسَّامِرِىُّ ﴿٨٥﴾

---

a After Moses' departure from Egypt, Almighty God appointed a date for him to go to the same place at the foot of Mount Tur, where he had initially been awarded prophethood. Moses was required to reach this place along with his community in order to receive the Torah. But, in his enthusiasm, he proceeded quickly and reached the appointed place a few days earlier, leaving his community behind. Moses' absence proved to be a trial for his community. Some polytheistic-minded persons in the community, led by the Samiri, took advantage of Moses' absence to mislead the people into becoming calf worshippers, as was the common practice in Egypt in those days.

⁸⁶ Moses returned to his people in anger and great sorrow. He said, 'My people, did your Lord not make you a handsome promise? Was my absence too long for you? Did you desire that your Lord's wrath should descend upon you, when you broke your promise to me?' *a*

فَرَجَعَ مُوسَىٰ إِلَىٰ قَوْمِهِۦ غَضْبَـٰنَ أَسِفًا قَالَ يَـٰقَوْمِ أَلَمْ يَعِدْكُمْ رَبُّكُمْ وَعْدًا حَسَنًا أَفَطَالَ عَلَيْكُمُ ٱلْعَهْدُ أَمْ أَرَدتُّمْ أَن يَحِلَّ عَلَيْكُمْ غَضَبٌ مِّن رَّبِّكُمْ فَأَخْلَفْتُم مَّوْعِدِى ۝

---

a When Almighty God informed Moses that his community had gone astray, he returned to his community very emotionally upset. He reminded his people that God had only recently showered His blessings on them and had revealed His many signs to them. So, how was it that they had forgotten everything so quickly and gone astray?

Moses had gone to receive revelations from God for the Israelites and in the meantime the Israelites had started indulging in the worship of false deities at the instigation of certain misguided persons. This shows how deeply the polytheistic atmosphere of Egypt had influenced the Israelites and why it had become necessary to take them away from Egypt in order to restore them to the worship of the one God.

Whatever Moses did with regard to Pharaoh was in connection with his *dawah* mission, and whatever he did with regard to the Israelites was in the context of safeguarding true religion. He performed both these tasks simultaneously. This shows the importance of both these tasks. If the Muslims had gone astray, dawah activity could not be stopped on that account and, similarly, if dawah work had to be done, it was not to be at the cost of internal reform.

87 They answered, 'We did not break our promise to you of our own accord, but we had to carry loads of the people's ornaments and so we threw them [into the fire] for that was what the Samiri suggested,' 88 then he forged a calf for them—an image producing a lowing sound. They said, 'This is your deity, the deity of Moses; he has forgotten it.' 89 Why did they not see that it could not give them any response and had no power to harm or benefit them? *a*

قَالُواْ مَآ أَخْلَفْنَا مَوْعِدَكَ بِمَلْكِنَا وَلَٰكِنَّا حُمِّلْنَآ أَوْزَارًا مِّن زِينَةِ ٱلْقَوْمِ فَقَذَفْنَٰهَا فَكَذَٰلِكَ أَلْقَى ٱلسَّامِرِىُّ ۝ فَأَخْرَجَ لَهُمْ عِجْلًا جَسَدًا لَّهُ خُوَارٌ فَقَالُواْ هَٰذَآ إِلَٰهُكُمْ وَإِلَٰهُ مُوسَىٰ فَنَسِىَ ۝ أَفَلَا يَرَوْنَ أَلَّا يَرْجِعُ إِلَيْهِمْ قَوْلًا وَلَا يَمْلِكُ لَهُمْ ضَرًّا وَلَا نَفْعًا ۝

---

a According to ancient custom, the Israelite women were probably laden with heavy jewelry. During the journey when the community halted to set up camp, the women removed their jewels and put them all together in one place. Among the Israelites, there was one al-Samiri (the Samaritan) who was experienced in the old Egyptian art of making likenesses of deities. He melted these jewels down and made from them a calf-shaped statue. This calf was hollow from inside and shaped so skillfully that when the breeze passed through it, it gave out a sound like the lowing of a bull. Then al-Samiri said to the ignorant Israelite community, 'See, here is your real God, and Moses has gone in search of God, to which nobody knows.'

The 'Samiris' of every age fool the people in exactly the same way. They make a fetish of some tangible thing, then try to prove that it is the greatest reality. Being duped by their glib talk, large crowds of gullible people gather around them. Worship of material objects has been the greatest weakness of man from time immemorial till the present day.

⁹⁰ Aaron had already told them, 'O my people! You are only being tested by this. Your Lord is the All Merciful, so follow me and obey my command.' ⁹¹ They replied, 'We shall not cease to worship it until Moses returns to us.' *ᵃ*

وَلَقَدْ قَالَ لَهُمْ هَـٰرُونُ مِن قَبْلُ يَـٰقَوْمِ إِنَّمَا فُتِنتُم بِهِۦ وَإِنَّ رَبَّكُمُ ٱلرَّحْمَـٰنُ فَٱتَّبِعُونِى وَأَطِيعُوٓا۟ أَمْرِى ۝ قَالُوا۟ لَن نَّبْرَحَ عَلَيْهِ عَـٰكِفِينَ حَتَّىٰ يَرْجِعَ إِلَيْنَا مُوسَىٰ ۝

ᵃ After the departure of Moses, Aaron, entrusted with the responsibility of looking after the community, tried to guide his people, but he did not have as much influence over them as Moses did. So they did not desist from their wrongful practice of calf-worship, in spite of Aaron advising them against it. When Aaron's insistence increased, they expressed their determination to continue. They pointed out that it would be for Moses to take a decision in this matter on his return.

Had Aaron acted with sternness, it would have had no effect, because his supporters were few in number. He, therefore, preferred for the time being, to adopt a policy of patience, rather than launch himself on a futile course of action; in the meantime he prayed to God for the reformation of his people.

⁹²Moses said to Aaron, 'What prevented you, when you saw that they had gone astray, ⁹³from following me? Why did you disobey my command?' ⁹⁴Aaron said, 'Son of my mother! Do not seize me by my beard nor by my head. I was afraid that you would say, "You have caused dissension among the Children of Israel and did not pay heed to my words."'ᵃ

قَالَ يَهَٰرُونُ مَا مَنَعَكَ إِذْ رَأَيْتَهُمْ ضَلُّواْ ۝ أَلَّا تَتَّبِعَنِ أَفَعَصَيْتَ أَمْرِى ۝ قَالَ يَبْنَؤُمَّ لَا تَأْخُذْ بِلِحْيَتِى وَلَا بِرَأْسِى إِنِّى خَشِيتُ أَن تَقُولَ فَرَّقْتَ بَيْنَ بَنِى إِسْرَٰءِيلَ وَلَمْ تَرْقُبْ قَوْلِى ۝

ᵃ Moses took his brother severely to task. Aaron explained that it was not that he had not tried to reform the people, or that he had reconciled himself to their ignorance. On the contrary, he had tried with all the force at his command to dissuade them from adopting such idolatrous practices. However, the problem was that the majority of the people had been influenced by Samiri's guile and had become his supporters. When Aaron persisted, they were ready to fight and shed blood. Therefore, he was afraid that if he continued his efforts, there would be strife and bloodshed within the community.

Aaron said that when matters had reached this stage, he had to choose between two alternatives: either internal strife or postponement of the issue till Moses' return. Aaron adopted the second alternative as being the more advisable. In many instances, to avoid bloodshed, remaining non-commital is a better option, for the other option may prove to be greater evil.

95 Moses said, 'What was the matter with you, Samiri?' 96 He said, 'I perceived what they did not see. So I took a handful [of dust] from the footprint of the Messenger and threw it in [the calf]. That is what my inner self prompted me to do.' 97 Moses said, 'Begone! It shall be your lot to say throughout your life, "Do not touch me," and you will be faced with a fate from which there will be no escape. Now look at your deity to which you have become so devoted: we shall burn it up, and then scatter it into the sea. 98 Your only deity is God, there is no deity but Him. His knowledge encompasses all things.'*a*

قَالَ فَمَا خَطْبُكَ يَـٰسَـٰمِرِىُّ ﴿٩٥﴾ قَالَ بَصُرْتُ بِمَا لَمْ يَبْصُرُواْ بِهِۦ فَقَبَضْتُ قَبْضَةً مِّنْ أَثَرِ ٱلرَّسُولِ فَنَبَذْتُهَا وَكَذَٰلِكَ سَوَّلَتْ لِى نَفْسِى ﴿٩٦﴾ قَالَ فَٱذْهَبْ فَإِنَّ لَكَ فِى ٱلْحَيَوٰةِ أَن تَقُولَ لَا مِسَاسَ وَإِنَّ لَكَ مَوْعِدًا لَّن تُخْلَفَهُۥ وَٱنظُرْ إِلَىٰ إِلَـٰهِكَ ٱلَّذِى ظَلْتَ عَلَيْهِ عَاكِفًا لَّنُحَرِّقَنَّهُۥ ثُمَّ لَنَنسِفَنَّهُۥ فِى ٱلْيَمِّ نَسْفًا ﴿٩٧﴾ إِنَّمَآ إِلَـٰهُكُمُ ٱللَّهُ ٱلَّذِى لَا إِلَـٰهَ إِلَّا هُوَ وَسِعَ كُلَّ شَىْءٍ عِلْمًا ﴿٩٨﴾

---

a When Moses came to know that Samiri was the leader behind this episode, he made enquiries of him. Samiri cunningly made excuses and said that whatever he had done was done under the influence of divine inspiration (*kashf*) and that some earth taken from the footprint of the Prophet Moses himself had been included in the idol as being auspicious.

Samiri's attempt to deceive Moses and at the same time win cheap popularity in his community cast a more serious light upon his crime. For his sins, God punished him (according to the Bible) with the disease of leucoderma, with additional punishment to be meted out to him in the life hereafter. His body became so obnoxious that people used to shun him. He became the most hated person in his community.

In order to cleanse the Israelites' minds of the false impression they had formed of the greatness of the calf deity, Moses burnt it before their eyes and floated the ashes in the sea.

⁹⁹ Thus We relate to you the history of past events, and We have given you a reminder [the Quran] from Us. ¹⁰⁰ Whoever turns away from it will bear a heavy burden on the Day of Judgement, ¹⁰¹ which they shall bear forever. It will be a grievous burden for them on the Day of Judgement, ¹⁰² the Day when the trumpet shall be blown: We shall gather all the sinners on that Day. Their eyes will turn blue with terror ¹⁰³ and they shall murmur to one another, 'You stayed only ten days on the earth'— ¹⁰⁴ We know best what they will say. The most perceptive of them will say, 'You stayed only one day.' ᵃ

كَذَٰلِكَ نَقُصُّ عَلَيْكَ مِنْ أَنۢبَآءِ مَا قَدْ سَبَقَ ۚ وَقَدْ ءَاتَيْنَٰكَ مِن لَّدُنَّا ذِكْرًا ۝ مَّنْ أَعْرَضَ عَنْهُ فَإِنَّهُۥ يَحْمِلُ يَوْمَ ٱلْقِيَٰمَةِ وِزْرًا ۝ خَٰلِدِينَ فِيهِ ۖ وَسَآءَ لَهُمْ يَوْمَ ٱلْقِيَٰمَةِ حِمْلًا ۝ يَوْمَ يُنفَخُ فِى ٱلصُّورِ ۚ وَنَحْشُرُ ٱلْمُجْرِمِينَ يَوْمَئِذٍ زُرْقًا ۝ يَتَخَٰفَتُونَ بَيْنَهُمْ إِن لَّبِثْتُمْ إِلَّا عَشْرًا ۝ نَّحْنُ أَعْلَمُ بِمَا يَقُولُونَ إِذْ يَقُولُ أَمْثَلُهُمْ طَرِيقَةً إِن لَّبِثْتُمْ إِلَّا يَوْمًا ۝

ᵃ The fate which befell those who denied the truth brought into this world by the prophets was but a partial demonstration of God's judgement, which will only fully unfold itself on the Day of Judgement and be applicable to all humanity. The Quran is a reminder of this very reality.

When a person ignores the truth in this world, it seems to be a mere triviality, but in the Hereafter, this action of his will become a heavy burden upon him. When the divine trumpet (*sur*) announces that the period of trial is over, people will suddenly find themselves in another world. When it becomes clear to man that the world which he took to be his own was in fact God's world, he will be so terror-stricken that his entire being will undergo a transformation, and his face will be a reflection of it.

In the present world, man ignores the life hereafter, as if it were something very distant. But, after the advent of Doomsday, he will feel that the life of this world was nothing but a few numbered days, and the entire long life thereafter, stretching out before him into eternity, is the actual and ultimate reality.

¹⁰⁵ They ask you about the mountains. Say, 'My Lord will scatter them as dust ¹⁰⁶ and leave the earth level and bare, ¹⁰⁷ with neither hollows nor upthrust mounds to be seen. ¹⁰⁸ On that Day all will follow the summoning voice from which there is no escape; and all voices will be hushed before the Lord of Mercy, and nothing will be heard except a subdued murmur.^a

وَيَسْـَٔلُونَكَ عَنِ ٱلْجِبَالِ فَقُلْ يَنسِفُهَا رَبِّي نَسْفًا ۝ فَيَذَرُهَا قَاعًا صَفْصَفًا ۝ لَّا تَرَىٰ فِيهَا عِوَجًا وَلَآ أَمْتًا ۝ يَوْمَئِذٍ يَتَّبِعُونَ ٱلدَّاعِيَ لَا عِوَجَ لَهُۥ ۖ وَخَشَعَتِ ٱلْأَصْوَاتُ لِلرَّحْمَٰنِ فَلَا تَسْمَعُ إِلَّا هَمْسًا ۝

---

^a On Doomsday, the earth will be turned into a flattened plain. At that time there will be neither the heights of the mountains nor the depths of the seas. All human beings will be reborn and assembled on this ground. In this world when God's voice is directed to mankind through His spokesmen, it is ignored by many individuals. But, on Doomsday, when God will directly call the people, they will follow the direction of His voice without the slightest deviation. People will be so terrified that they will not be able to utter a single word. Except for the sound of dragging feet, no other sound will be heard.

¹⁰⁹ On that Day no intercession will avail, except from one who has received the sanction of the Merciful and of whose words He approves— ¹¹⁰ He knows what is before them and what is behind them, but they cannot encompass Him with their knowledge— ¹¹¹ on that Day all faces shall be humbled before the Living, Self-Subsisting One. Those burdened with evil deeds will come to grief, ¹¹² but he who does good works, being a believer, shall fear no harm nor any injustice.'ᵃ

يَوْمَئِذٍ لَّا تَنفَعُ ٱلشَّفَٰعَةُ إِلَّا مَنْ أَذِنَ لَهُ ٱلرَّحْمَٰنُ وَرَضِىَ لَهُۥ قَوْلًا ۝ يَعْلَمُ مَا بَيْنَ أَيْدِيهِمْ وَمَا خَلْفَهُمْ وَلَا يُحِيطُونَ بِهِۦ عِلْمًا ۝ ۞ وَعَنَتِ ٱلْوُجُوهُ لِلْحَىِّ ٱلْقَيُّومِ وَقَدْ خَابَ مَنْ حَمَلَ ظُلْمًا ۝ وَمَن يَعْمَلْ مِنَ ٱلصَّٰلِحَٰتِ وَهُوَ مُؤْمِنٌ فَلَا يَخَافُ ظُلْمًا وَلَا هَضْمًا ۝

ᵃ It is baseless to believe that recommendation in itself is effective. God, being fully aware of the condition of His subjects, needs no reports from others. Nor is He weak: He is not, therefore, amenable to pressures. However, under certain special circumstances, God Himself may be pleased to honour a request.

On the Day of Judgement, real importance will be attached to what the individual has brought with him in terms of his piety, his good deeds and his personal virtues. One who has founded his life on untruth is bound to meet with failure in the Hereafter. There, only those will be successful who recognised their Lord—who remained invisible in this world—and who shaped their lives in accordance with His will and pleasure.

113 We have thus sent down the Quran in Arabic and given all kinds of warnings in it, so that they may fear God, or may take heed— 114 exalted is God, the True King. Do not be impatient with the Quran before its revelation is completed, and say, 'My Lord, increase my knowledge.' *a*

وَكَذَٰلِكَ أَنزَلْنَـٰهُ قُرْءَانًا عَرَبِيًّا وَصَرَّفْنَا فِيهِ مِنَ ٱلْوَعِيدِ لَعَلَّهُمْ يَتَّقُونَ أَوْ يُحْدِثُ لَهُمْ ذِكْرًا ۞ فَتَعَـٰلَى ٱللَّهُ ٱلْمَلِكُ ٱلْحَقُّ ۗ وَلَا تَعْجَلْ بِٱلْقُرْءَانِ مِن قَبْلِ أَن يُقْضَىٰ إِلَيْكَ وَحْيُهُۥ ۖ وَقُل رَّبِّ زِدْنِى عِلْمًا ۞

---

a A dayee should have two major aims: to bring about a psychological revolution in his addressees so that they may become God-fearing or at least he should be able to raise questions in his hearers about his call.

During the Dawah campaign in Makkah, the addressees were raising all sorts of questions, creating problems for the Prophet. The Prophet naturally wanted that the intervals between the revelations could be reduced, so that he could receive God's guidance more frequently. This would have enabled him to deal more promptly and effectively with the questions and problems which arose daily during his dawah work in Makkah. He was told that the process of revelation was in accordance with a divine, pre-ordained plan. It would continue as the occasion warranted, and would reach its completion in due course. He was asked not to desire the revelation of future parts of the Quran before their divinely appointed time. However, he was advised to pray to God to increase his understanding of the vast wisdom enshrined in the verses of the Quran. Instead of wishing for an early revelation of Quranic verses, he was expected to have the desire to understand the reason for their being revealed gradually, on a pre-planned scale of priority.

¹¹⁵ We made a covenant with Adam before you, but he forgot, and We found him lacking in constancy. ¹¹⁶ When We said to the angels, 'Prostrate yourselves before Adam,' they all prostrated themselves, except for Satan, who refused, ¹¹⁷ We said, 'Adam, [Satan] is an enemy to you and to your wife. Let him not turn you both out of Paradise and thus make you come to grief.ᵃ

وَلَقَدْ عَهِدْنَا إِلَىٰٓ ءَادَمَ مِن قَبْلُ فَنَسِىَ وَلَمْ نَجِدْ لَهُۥ عَزْمًا ۝ وَإِذْ قُلْنَا لِلْمَلَـٰٓئِكَةِ ٱسْجُدُوا۟ لِءَادَمَ فَسَجَدُوٓا۟ إِلَّآ إِبْلِيسَ أَبَىٰ ۝ فَقُلْنَا يَـٰٓـَٔادَمُ إِنَّ هَـٰذَا عَدُوٌّ لَّكَ وَلِزَوْجِكَ فَلَا يُخْرِجَنَّكُمَا مِنَ ٱلْجَنَّةِ فَتَشْقَىٰٓ ۝

ᵃ To adhere steadfastly to God's commandments, unwavering determination is essential. If a man is influenced by irrelevant factors, he will undoubtedly deviate from the path of God. In order to remain steadfastly on the path of God, it is not enough to know what His commandment is; it is also absolutely necessary to have the will to resist all that goes against His commandment, and not to let himself be influenced by it.

When God ordered that all should kneel down before Adam, the angels immediately dropped to their knees. But Satan did not do so. The reason for this difference in behaviour was that the angels treated this matter as pertaining to God, whereas Satan, on the contrary, saw it as the affair of a mere mortal. When an issue concerns God, man has no option but to bow to His wishes. But when it is treated as relating to a human being, the person in question will appraise the human being before him. If the latter is comparatively stronger, he will kneel down; otherwise he will refuse to kneel down, even if such an action be the demand of truth and justice.

118 'Here you shall not go hungry or be naked, 119 you shall not thirst, nor feel the sun's heat.' 120 But Satan whispered evil to him, saying, 'Adam, shall I lead you to the tree of immortality and to a kingdom that never declines?' 121 They both ate the fruit of this tree, and so they became conscious of their nakedness and began to cover themselves with the leaves of the Garden. Thus Adam disobeyed his Lord and fell into error. 122 Then his Lord had mercy on him, accepted his repentance and guided him.ᵃ

إِنَّ لَكَ أَلَّا تَجُوعَ فِيهَا وَلَا تَعْرَىٰ ۝

وَأَنَّكَ لَا تَظْمَؤُاْ فِيهَا وَلَا تَضْحَىٰ ۝

فَوَسْوَسَ إِلَيْهِ ٱلشَّيْطَٰنُ قَالَ يَٰٓـَٔادَمُ

هَلْ أَدُلُّكَ عَلَىٰ شَجَرَةِ ٱلْخُلْدِ وَمُلْكٍ لَّا

يَبْلَىٰ ۝ فَأَكَلَا مِنْهَا فَبَدَتْ لَهُمَا

سَوْءَٰتُهُمَا وَطَفِقَا يَخْصِفَانِ عَلَيْهِمَا

مِن وَرَقِ ٱلْجَنَّةِ وَعَصَىٰٓ ءَادَمُ رَبَّهُۥ

فَغَوَىٰ ۝ ثُمَّ ٱجْتَبَٰهُ رَبُّهُۥ فَتَابَ

عَلَيْهِ وَهَدَىٰ ۝

ᵃ God kept Adam, with his spouse, in paradise, where he was freely and amply provided with all the necessities of life – food, clothing, water and shelter. Adam was not required to do anything in return for these blessings, unlike in the present world where man has to earn all these things by his own hard labour.

In paradise, the fruit of a certain tree was prohibited for Adam. But Satan came and described to him the eternal advantages of this fruit. Adam, influenced by what he said, ate it, then immediately felt that he was naked. This was symbolic of the fact that God had instantly withdrawn the guarantee of providing him with sustenance without his having to earn it by his own labour. Thereafter, on his supplication and repentance, he was pardoned. However, he was removed from a world where God's bounty had been freely given and sent to a world where he had to earn his living by the sweat of his brow. Such was the beginning of human existence on this earth.

123 God said, 'Go down, both of you, from here, as enemies to one another.' If there comes to you guidance from Me, then whoever follows My guidance will not lose his way, nor will he come to grief, 124 but whoever turns away from My reminder, will lead a straitened existence and on the Day of Judgement We shall raise him up blind 125 and he will ask, 'Lord, why have You raised me up blind, while I possessed sight before?' 126 God will say, 'Just as Our signs came to you and you ignored them, so will you on this Day be ignored.' 127 Thus We shall reward the transgressor who denies the signs of his Lord. But the suffering of the life to come is more terrible and more lasting.ᵃ

قَالَ ٱهْبِطَا مِنْهَا جَمِيعًا ۖ بَعْضُكُمْ لِبَعْضٍ عَدُوٌّ ۖ فَإِمَّا يَأْتِيَنَّكُم مِّنِّي هُدًى فَمَنِ ٱتَّبَعَ هُدَايَ فَلَا يَضِلُّ وَلَا يَشْقَىٰ ۝ وَمَنْ أَعْرَضَ عَن ذِكْرِى فَإِنَّ لَهُۥ مَعِيشَةً ضَنكًا وَنَحْشُرُهُۥ يَوْمَ ٱلْقِيَٰمَةِ أَعْمَىٰ ۝ قَالَ رَبِّ لِمَ حَشَرْتَنِىٓ أَعْمَىٰ وَقَدْ كُنتُ بَصِيرًا ۝ قَالَ كَذَٰلِكَ أَتَتْكَ ءَايَٰتُنَا فَنَسِيتَهَا ۖ وَكَذَٰلِكَ ٱلْيَوْمَ تُنسَىٰ ۝ وَكَذَٰلِكَ نَجْزِى مَنْ أَسْرَفَ وَلَمْ يُؤْمِنۢ بِـَٔايَٰتِ رَبِّهِۦ ۚ وَلَعَذَابُ ٱلْءَاخِرَةِ أَشَدُّ وَأَبْقَىٰ ۝

ᵃ God settled Satan as well as Adam on the earth and gave due warning in the very beginning that clashes of interest between the two would go on till Doomsday. Satan would make every possible effort to mislead mankind, therefore, people should make it a point to treat him as their greatest enemy and try to stay far away from his inducements.

To give further guidance to man, God periodically sent him His messengers, or prophets, who instructed him in the reality of life in a language which was clearly intelligible to him. Now, the success or failure of man depends on his own acceptance or rejection of the Prophet's guidance. One who accepts this guidance will once again be ushered into the comfortable life of paradise, whereas the life of one who fails to accept it will be a very severe one, from which he will never be able to escape.

Those who turn away from God's guidance will be reduced in the Hereafter to blindness, being deprived of both the eyes. The reason for this is that such people are given eyes in the world in order to be able to see and recognise God's signs. But they live in such a manner that, when they encounter God's signs, they fail to recognise them. Thus, they prove that, in spite of having eyes, they are really blind. So God will ask on that Day, what use it had been to give eyes to those who were determined to be blind.

128 Do they not learn a lesson from Our destruction of many generations before them in whose dwelling-places they walk about? Surely in this are signs for men of understanding. 129 But for a pre-ordained Word from your Lord, and a term [of respite] already fixed, immediate punishment would inevitably have taken place. 130 So be patient with anything they may say and glorify your Lord with His praise before the rising of the sun and before its setting; and glorify Him in the hours of the night and at the beginning and end of the day, so that you may find comfort.*ᵃ*

أَفَلَمْ يَهْدِ لَهُمْ كَمْ أَهْلَكْنَا قَبْلَهُم مِّنَ الْقُرُونِ يَمْشُونَ فِى مَسَاكِنِهِمْ إِنَّ فِى ذَٰلِكَ لَآيَاتٍ لِّأُوْلِى النُّهَىٰ ﴿١٢٨﴾ وَلَوْلَا كَلِمَةٌ سَبَقَتْ مِن رَّبِّكَ لَكَانَ لِزَامًا وَأَجَلٌ مُّسَمًّى ﴿١٢٩﴾ فَاصْبِرْ عَلَىٰ مَا يَقُولُونَ وَسَبِّحْ بِحَمْدِ رَبِّكَ قَبْلَ طُلُوعِ الشَّمْسِ وَقَبْلَ غُرُوبِهَا وَمِنْ ءَانَآئِ الَّيْلِ فَسَبِّحْ وَأَطْرَافَ النَّهَارِ لَعَلَّكَ تَرْضَىٰ ﴿١٣٠﴾

ᵃ If a community reaches the zenith of its progress in the world and then is made to face destruction or subjection, it is always because it has transgressed its limits. Every community so destroyed leaves a lesson for its successors. But there are very few people who care to learn a lesson from such events.

It is worth noting that the advice given here about the repeated glorification and remembrance of God and prayer was first given in Makkah; these practices were meant to be observed in the most trying and serious conditions of the Makkan period. This indicates that in the most difficult days of denial and tough opposition, prayers (*salat*) and remembrance of God are the best shields for the faithful. The principal benefit to man of these actions is that they lead to a smoothing of the paths to success in this world and the next.

¹³¹ Do not regard with envy the worldly benefits We have given some of them, for with these We seek only to test them. The provision of your Lord is better and more lasting. ¹³² Bid your people say their prayers, and be constant in their observance. We demand nothing from you. It is We who provide for you, and the best end is that of righteousness.ᵃ

وَلَا تَمُدَّنَّ عَيْنَيْكَ إِلَىٰ مَا مَتَّعْنَا بِهِ أَزْوَاجًا مِّنْهُمْ زَهْرَةَ ٱلْحَيَوٰةِ ٱلدُّنْيَا لِنَفْتِنَهُمْ فِيهِ ۚ وَرِزْقُ رَبِّكَ خَيْرٌ وَأَبْقَىٰ ۝ وَأْمُرْ أَهْلَكَ بِٱلصَّلَوٰةِ وَٱصْطَبِرْ عَلَيْهَا ۖ لَا نَسْـَٔلُكَ رِزْقًا ۖ نَّحْنُ نَرْزُقُكَ ۗ وَٱلْعَٰقِبَةُ لِلتَّقْوَىٰ ۝

ᵃ These verses are addressed not only to the Prophet, but to all of the faithful. In this world when a man dedicates himself to faith and dawah work, his life as a result becomes one of toil and struggle. In sharp contrast are those who, free from such responsibilities, spend their days in ease and comfort. Satan stresses this state of affairs and creates doubts and evil ideas in a man's heart. He tries to shake the faith of both the believer and the missionary by making them feel that if the path chosen by them had been the true path of God, they would not have had to suffer so much.

But, if the matter is examined in depth, it would appear that, beyond this temporary outward difference, there is another type of difference which is much more worthwhile. It is that whatever the world-loving people had received from God was only for the purposes of trial and purely of a temporary nature, leaving nothing in store for the eternal life of the Hereafter. On the other hand, what the believer and the missionary has received as a result of his devotion to God is much more valuable, i.e. God's remembrance, concern for the Hereafter, a life of piety and prayer, anxiety to save God's subjects from the reckoning of the Hereafter. This is also a form of sustenance (*rizq*). In fact, it is a higher type of sustenance, because this will be returned to the believer in the shape of boundless and inexhaustible blessings.

133 They say, 'Why does he not bring us a sign from his Lord?' Have they not been given sufficient proof in previous scriptures? 134 If We had destroyed them with a punishment before this, they would have surely said, 'Our Lord, why did you not send to us a messenger so that we might have followed Your commandment before we were humiliated and disgraced?' 135 Say, 'Everyone is waiting; so wait if you will. You shall know who has followed the right path, and who has found guidance.'[a]

وَقَالُوا لَوْلَا يَأْتِينَا بِآيَةٍ مِّن رَّبِّهِ أَوَلَمْ تَأْتِهِم بَيِّنَةُ مَا فِي ٱلصُّحُفِ ٱلْأُولَىٰ ۞ وَلَوْ أَنَّا أَهْلَكْنَٰهُم بِعَذَابٍ مِّن قَبْلِهِ لَقَالُوا رَبَّنَا لَوْلَا أَرْسَلْتَ إِلَيْنَا رَسُولًا فَنَتَّبِعَ ءَايَٰتِكَ مِن قَبْلِ أَن نَّذِلَّ وَنَخْزَىٰ ۞ قُلْ كُلٌّ مُّتَرَبِّصٌ فَتَرَبَّصُوا فَسَتَعْلَمُونَ مَنْ أَصْحَٰبُ ٱلصِّرَٰطِ ٱلسَّوِيِّ وَمَنِ ٱهْتَدَىٰ ۞

---

[a] Before the coming of Muhammad, the last of the Prophets, Almighty God had given intimation of his advent through the previous prophets.

These prophecies were found in the revealed books of the past, and may still be read, even today, in spite of all the alterations made to these books throughout the ages. This remains the most powerful argument in support of the veracity of the final Prophet. But, in order to understand the power of reasoning, seriousness is required—a rare phenomenon in this world.

21. THE PROPHETS

In the name of God,
the Most Gracious, the Most Merciful

¹ The time of reckoning has drawn near for mankind, yet they are heedless and turn away. ² Whenever any fresh admonition comes to them from their Lord, they listen to it, but do not take it seriously; ³ their hearts are distracted and forgetful. The wrongdoers confer together secretly, saying, 'Is not this man a mortal like you? Will you succumb to magic with your eyes open?' ⁴ Say, 'My Lord knows every word spoken in the heavens and on the earth. He is All Hearing, All Knowing.'ᵃ

 بِسْمِ ٱللَّهِ ٱلرَّحْمَٰنِ ٱلرَّحِيمِ

ٱقْتَرَبَ لِلنَّاسِ حِسَابُهُمْ وَهُمْ فِى غَفْلَةٍ مُّعْرِضُونَ ۝ مَا يَأْتِيهِم مِّن ذِكْرٍ مِّن رَّبِّهِم مُّحْدَثٍ إِلَّا ٱسْتَمَعُوهُ وَهُمْ يَلْعَبُونَ ۝ لَاهِيَةً قُلُوبُهُمْ وَأَسَرُّوا ٱلنَّجْوَى ٱلَّذِينَ ظَلَمُوا هَلْ هَٰذَآ إِلَّا بَشَرٌ مِّثْلُكُمْ أَفَتَأْتُونَ ٱلسِّحْرَ وَأَنتُمْ تُبْصِرُونَ ۝ قَالَ رَبِّى يَعْلَمُ ٱلْقَوْلَ فِى ٱلسَّمَآءِ وَٱلْأَرْضِ وَهُوَ ٱلسَّمِيعُ ٱلْعَلِيمُ ۝

ᵃ Every man who is living in this world is nearer to death than life. In this respect he is virtually on the verge of coming face to face with his Day of Reckoning. But man is so reckless that he does not pay heed to any sort of reminder from God, whether given through a prophet or anyone else. He ignores the advice of the preacher of truth and dismisses it as something uttered by 'a mere man'.

When in Makkah the Prophet Muhammad started calling upon people to God by means of the Quran. The divine discourse enshrined therein moved people's hearts. This became a serious matter for the Makkan leaders, because this jeopardized their leadership. The Quran urged people to accept the unity of God, whereas the great leaders of Makkah had maintained their supremacy on the basis of polytheism. In order to divert the attention of the people, they started spreading the notion that the effectiveness of the Prophet Muhammad's message did not derive from its being the word of God; the force behind it was not that of Truth but of magic. It was all mere human rhetoric and was in no way to be considred a divine discourse.

Albeit taking the name of God, those who indulged in such talk did not firmly believe that God was seeing and hearing them. Had they had real faith in God's being all-knowing, that is, His being One who knows the unseen—they would never have uttered such insincere words.

5 Some say, 'These are his confused dreams.' Others say, 'He has invented it himself,' and yet others say, 'He is a poet. Let him bring us a sign as previous messengers did.' 6 Before them, not one of the communities which We destroyed believed either. Will these believe?[a]

بَلْ قَالُوٓاْ أَضْغَٰثُ أَحْلَٰمِ بَلِ ٱفْتَرَىٰهُ بَلْ هُوَ شَاعِرٌ فَلْيَأْتِنَا بِـَٔايَةٍ كَمَآ أُرْسِلَ ٱلْأَوَّلُونَ ۝ مَآ ءَامَنَتْ قَبْلَهُم مِّن قَرْيَةٍ أَهْلَكْنَٰهَآ أَفَهُمْ يُؤْمِنُونَ ۝

---

[a] The messenger of truth always presents the truth on the strength of sound arguments. When the Prophet's opponents felt that they could not counter his arguments with their own arguments, they tried to dissuade the people from treading the path of truth by levelling different types of false allegations, such as saying that this (the divine discourse in the Quran) was mere poetry, that it was literary magic, that these were the senseless ramblings of a madman, that it was all self-devised, etc. Since the Prophet Muhammad did not perform any miracles before the people of Makkah, they cast aspersions on his prophethood by raising the issue of why he had not brought any miracle from God, like the other prophets in the past.

Throughout the history of religion, experience has shown that those who do not accept the truth on the presentation of sound arguments, refuse to accept it even after seeing a miracle. Therefore, it is essential for the well wishing of the people that admonition on the strength of arguments be continued, instead of concluding the process of preaching by performing a miracle, because the rejection of a miracle invites the wrath of God. Consequently, the next stage can only be the destruction of the deniers.

⁷ The messengers We sent before you were but men whom We had sent revelations. Ask the People of the Book if you do not know this— ⁸ We did not give them bodies that needed no food, nor were they to live forever. ⁹ Then We fulfilled Our promise to them and We saved them and those with them whom We pleased, and We destroyed those who exceeded all bounds.[a]

وَمَآ أَرْسَلْنَا قَبْلَكَ إِلَّا رِجَالًا نُّوحِىٓ إِلَيْهِمْ فَسْـَٔلُوٓا۟ أَهْلَ ٱلذِّكْرِ إِن كُنتُمْ لَا تَعْلَمُونَ ۝ وَمَا جَعَلْنَٰهُمْ جَسَدًا لَّا يَأْكُلُونَ ٱلطَّعَامَ وَمَا كَانُوا۟ خَٰلِدِينَ ۝ ثُمَّ صَدَقْنَٰهُمُ ٱلْوَعْدَ فَأَنجَيْنَٰهُمْ وَمَن نَّشَآءُ وَأَهْلَكْنَا ٱلْمُسْرِفِينَ ۝

---

[a] Those who refused to accept the prophethood of the Prophet Muhammad on the grounds that he was a human being like them, were told that if they were sincere and serious in their objection, they should not find it difficult to come to a correct understanding of the truth. The People of the Book, believers in past prophets, could be asked whether these prophets had been human beings or not. If they (the prophets of the past) were human beings, they had no reason to reject the present Prophet solely on the grounds that he was born of human parents, just like any ordinary human being.

The history of former prophets reveals that the people's acceptance or rejection of them was not an ordinary type of acceptance or rejection, in that it led to distinctly different results for the two groups. The acceptors enjoyed salvation, while the rejectors were destroyed. Therefore, this is a matter in which one has to be extremely sincere and serious.

¹⁰ We have revealed a Book to you which is admonition for you. Will you not then understand? ¹¹ How many communities of evil-doers We have destroyed, raising up other people after them. ¹² When they felt Our punishment coming upon them, they began to flee from it. ¹³ They were told, 'Do not try to flee, but return to the comfort and luxuries in which you exulted and to the places where you lived, so that you may be questioned.' ¹⁴ They said, 'Woe to us! We were indeed wrongdoers,' ¹⁵ and this they kept repeating until We caused them to become like a field mowed down, and reduced to ashes.ᵃ

لَقَدْ أَنزَلْنَآ إِلَيْكُمْ كِتَـٰبًا فِيهِ ذِكْرُكُمْ ۖ أَفَلَا تَعْقِلُونَ ۝ وَكَمْ قَصَمْنَا مِن قَرْيَةٍ كَانَتْ ظَالِمَةً وَأَنشَأْنَا بَعْدَهَا قَوْمًا ءَاخَرِينَ ۝ فَلَمَّآ أَحَسُّواْ بَأْسَنَآ إِذَا هُم مِّنْهَا يَرْكُضُونَ ۝ لَا تَرْكُضُواْ وَٱرْجِعُوٓاْ إِلَىٰ مَآ أُتْرِفْتُمْ فِيهِ وَمَسَاكِنِكُمْ لَعَلَّكُمْ تُسْـَٔلُونَ ۝ قَالُواْ يَـٰوَيْلَنَآ إِنَّا كُنَّا ظَـٰلِمِينَ ۝ فَمَا زَالَت تِّلْكَ دَعْوَىٰهُمْ حَتَّىٰ جَعَلْنَـٰهُمْ حَصِيدًا خَـٰمِدِينَ ۝

ᵃ The Book of God is not a mere book in the ordinary sense of the word. It is in fact a reminder. It is to remind man that the creation of mankind in the present world was not an accident. It took place in accordance with a divine plan, by which man was to be given temporary freedom for the purpose of putting him to the test, and thereafter rewarding him according to his deeds in this world. A partial manifestation of this fact has been given time and again in the shape of the destruction of transgressing communities. Its full manifestation will take place on the Day of Reckoning, when all past and present human beings will be re-created and gathered together in God's court.

As long as man possesses material means of support, he is not prepared to come out of his slumber of carelessness. But when the process of God's reckoning starts, all the material props on the strength of which the individual dared to ignore the call for Truth, will appear to be so burdensome that he would like to get rid of them. And it is only when he has to part company with his props that his eyes are opened. However, the opening of his eyes at that juncture will be of no avail, because at that time all things will have lost their power. Thereafter, only God and not the false deities—will have the power to help.

¹⁶ It was not in play that We created the heavens and the earth and all that lies between them. ¹⁷ Had We wished to find a pastime, We would surely have found it in that which is with Us, if such had been Our will. ¹⁸ We will hurl the truth at falsehood, the falsehood shall be crushed and will disappear. Woe to you for what you utter.^a

وَمَا خَلَقْنَا ٱلسَّمَآءَ وَٱلْأَرْضَ وَمَا بَيْنَهُمَا لَعِبِينَ ۞ لَوْ أَرَدْنَآ أَن نَّتَّخِذَ لَهْوًا لَّٱتَّخَذْنَٰهُ مِن لَّدُنَّآ إِن كُنَّا فَٰعِلِينَ ۞ بَلْ نَقْذِفُ بِٱلْحَقِّ عَلَى ٱلْبَٰطِلِ فَيَدْمَغُهُۥ فَإِذَا هُوَ زَاهِقٌ وَلَكُمُ ٱلْوَيْلُ مِمَّا تَصِفُونَ ۞

---

^a Those who are not serious about the divine call, consider the present world as a plaything of God which has no purpose except temporal entertainment. But judging by the immense wisdom and meaningfulness underlying the working of the present world, it would appear to be impossible that the Creator of this world could be a being who has created it merely for the sake of diversion.

In the present world, there is the special creation of God, namely, human beings, who by their very nature, have the ability to distinguish truth from falsehood. The existence in the world of such creatures, who can use their discretion and decide upon one path as that of truth and another as that of untruth, coupled with the frequent struggle between Truth and untruth, are all indications of the fact that a time is going to come when it will finally be clear as to what is really Truth and what is Untruth. And whoever sides with the Truth will attain success and whoever does not will be doomed to failure.

¹⁹ To Him belongs whosoever is in the heavens and on the earth and those that are with Him are never too proud to worship Him, nor do they grow weary; ²⁰ they glorify Him night and day without tiring.ᵃ

وَلَهُۥ مَن فِى ٱلسَّمَـٰوَٰتِ وَٱلۡأَرۡضِ وَمَنۡ عِندَهُۥ لَا يَسۡتَكۡبِرُونَ عَنۡ عِبَادَتِهِۦ وَلَا يَسۡتَحۡسِرُونَ ۞ يُسَبِّحُونَ ٱلَّيۡلَ وَٱلنَّهَارَ لَا يَفۡتُرُونَ ۞

ᵃ Every object on the earth and in the skies is God's creation. Everything behaves as has been divinely ordained. In the entire universe, it is only man who is arrogant and disobedient. Those who do not believe in God indulge in arrogance and disobedience on the plea that there is nobody to rule over them, and they are free to do as they like.

Those who believe in God also indulge in arrogance and disobedience, but they offer a different explanation for this behaviour. They take some particular individuals other than God as intermediaries and recommenders. They assume them to be closer to God and presume that if from time to time they are paid homage and obeisance, they will intercede with God for their salvation. Some assume angels to be the intermediaries, while others attribute such qualities to other human beings.

But all such theories are totally baseless. If one has such a deep insight as to have a clear vision of Reality at the universal level, he will see that those beings (who are supposed to have divine attributes) are themselves awe-struck by God's majesty and kneel down before Him. Ironically, it is in their name that man has adopted an attitude of arrogance and disobedience in the world.

²¹ Have they taken deities from the earth who can bring the dead to life? ²² If there had been in the heavens and on the earth, other deities besides God, both the heavens and earth would be ruined. God, Lord of the throne, is far above that which they ascribe to Him. ²³ None shall question Him about His works, but they shall be questioned.ᵃ

²⁴ Have they taken other deities besides Him? Say to them, 'Bring your proofs. This is the reminder of those who are with me and the reminder of those who were before me.' But most of them do not know the truth, and so they turn away from it. ²⁵ We sent all messengers before you with this revelation: 'There is no deity save Me, so worship Me alone.'ᵇ

أَمِ ٱتَّخَذُوٓاْ ءَالِهَةً مِّنَ ٱلْأَرْضِ هُمْ يُنشِرُونَ ۞ لَوْ كَانَ فِيهِمَآ ءَالِهَةٌ إِلَّا ٱللَّهُ لَفَسَدَتَا ۚ فَسُبْحَٰنَ ٱللَّهِ رَبِّ ٱلْعَرْشِ عَمَّا يَصِفُونَ ۞ لَا يُسْـَٔلُ عَمَّا يَفْعَلُ وَهُمْ يُسْـَٔلُونَ ۞ أَمِ ٱتَّخَذُواْ مِن دُونِهِۦٓ ءَالِهَةً ۖ قُلْ هَاتُواْ بُرْهَٰنَكُمْ ۖ هَٰذَا ذِكْرُ مَن مَّعِيَ وَذِكْرُ مَن قَبْلِي ۗ بَلْ أَكْثَرُهُمْ لَا يَعْلَمُونَ ٱلْحَقَّ ۖ فَهُم مُّعْرِضُونَ ۞ وَمَآ أَرْسَلْنَا مِن قَبْلِكَ مِن رَّسُولٍ إِلَّا نُوحِىٓ إِلَيْهِ أَنَّهُۥ لَآ إِلَٰهَ إِلَّآ أَنَا۠ فَٱعْبُدُونِ ۞

ᵃ The earth is not isolated from the rest of creation; it is inseparably bound with the cosmos. The existence of life on the earth and its flourishing and growth are possible only when it maintains total harmony with the rest of the universe. This balanced and harmonious interaction between the earth and the sky proves that the control of the earth and the sky rests in the hands of one single Being. Had it been with two beings, there would certainly have been frequent clashes between them and consequently the preservation of the existing life on earth would not have been possible.

The universe with all its immense majesty and meaningfulness projects the image of its Creator as a God who is absolutely above all shortcomings. To assume the Creator of all things to be a Being subject to shortcomings and weaknesses would be to grossly undervalue the existing universe.

ᵇ The assumption of there being anyone worthy of worship other than God is not based on any real reasoning, but on total ignorance. Those who assign partners to God have no argument in support of their belief—neither is it based on human knowledge nor on divine revelation. On hearing arguments in favour of the oneness of God, they become evasive and turn their backs, not because of the firmness of their belief based on sound reasoning, but purely because of their prejudice. ▶

²⁶ They say, 'The All Merciful has taken a son!' Glory be to Him! They are only His honoured servants: ²⁷ they do not try to speak ahead of Him, and they act at His command. ²⁸ He knows what is before them and what is behind them, and they cannot intercede without His permission. Indeed they themselves stand in awe of Him. ²⁹ Whoever of them should say, 'I am a deity besides Him,' shall be requited with Hell. Thus do We reward the wrongdoers.^a

وَقَالُوا۟ ٱتَّخَذَ ٱلرَّحْمَٰنُ وَلَدًا ۗ سُبْحَٰنَهُۥ ۚ بَلْ عِبَادٌ مُّكْرَمُونَ ۝ لَا يَسْبِقُونَهُۥ بِٱلْقَوْلِ وَهُم بِأَمْرِهِۦ يَعْمَلُونَ ۝ يَعْلَمُ مَا بَيْنَ أَيْدِيهِمْ وَمَا خَلْفَهُمْ وَلَا يَشْفَعُونَ إِلَّا لِمَنِ ٱرْتَضَىٰ وَهُم مِّنْ خَشْيَتِهِۦ مُشْفِقُونَ ۝ وَمَن يَقُلْ مِنْهُمْ إِنِّى إِلَٰهٌ مِّن دُونِهِۦ فَذَٰلِكَ نَجْزِيهِ جَهَنَّمَ ۚ كَذَٰلِكَ نَجْزِى ٱلظَّٰلِمِينَ ۝

On account of their biased attitude, they have become so rigid in their belief that they are not prepared to give it up, in spite of its being untenable on the basis of reasoning.

^a To consider one thing as right and some other thing as wrong curtails the freedom of human beings. Therefore, they have always attempted to find a theory according to which the difference between truth and untruth should vanish, so that they might live in the world in whatever manner they liked and have the satisfaction of not being answerable for what they did or for what they did not do. Irreligious people have tried to achieve this by denying the life hereafter while religious people have had recourse to polytheistic practices.

Angels are invisible creatures. Human beings were informed of the existence of angels through the prophets, so that they might realise God's power. But they (the human beings) formed the erroneous idea that the angels were the daughters of God and adopted the strange belief that they should perform certain rites of worship in the name of the angels, who would in turn recommend them to their 'Father', have them (the worshippers) pardoned and procure their salvation.

All such beliefs amount to a negation of the godhood of the Almighty. God is God only because He is free of all shortcomings. Had He been subject to shortcomings, He would not have been God.

³⁰ Do not those who deny the truth see that the heavens and the earth were joined together and that We then split them asunder? And that We have made every living thing out of water? Will they still not believe? ᵃ

أَوَلَمْ يَرَ ٱلَّذِينَ كَفَرُوٓاْ أَنَّ ٱلسَّمَٰوَٰتِ وَٱلْأَرْضَ كَانَتَا رَتْقًا فَفَتَقْنَٰهُمَا ۖ وَجَعَلْنَا مِنَ ٱلْمَآءِ كُلَّ شَيْءٍ حَيٍّ ۖ أَفَلَا يُؤْمِنُونَ ۝

ᵃ The solid mass which God 'tore asunder' probably refers to the earliest state of the earth and skies which, in this modern age is explained in terms of the 'Big Bang' theory. According to modern scientific calculations, the entire matter of the Universe was originally in the shape of a very big ball (a super atom). In obedience to known physical laws, all its parts were attracted towards its centre and were bound together very strongly. At some point, there was a huge explosion in this ball and its parts suddenly started hurtling outwards. In this way, finally the vast universe, which now extends before us, came into being.

The question that remains is what caused the highly compact particles of the super-atom to explode. The Big Bang proves the existence of an intervenor. When the intervenor is proved, the existence of God is proven in itself. In this way, the history of the origin of the universe clearly establishes the existence of a Being Who has a separate permanent existence outside the universe and, Who by His own independent power, exerts His influence over the universe.

In this world of ours the major component of every living thing is water. If there were no water there would be no life. Water is found in great abundance on the earth. In this extensive universe, the existence of so much water at one place clearly gives an indication of a 'special creation'. How surprising it is that in spite of such clear signs, man does not find God and continues to remain spiritually deprived.

³¹ We set firm mountains upon the earth lest it should sway under them, and We placed therein passages for paths so that they might find their way. ³² We have made the heaven a well-secured canopy; yet still they turn away from Our signs. ³³ It is He who created the night and the day, and the sun and the moon, each gliding in its orbit.ᵃ

وَجَعَلْنَا فِي ٱلْأَرْضِ رَوَٰسِيَ أَن تَمِيدَ بِهِمْ وَجَعَلْنَا فِيهَا فِجَاجًا سُبُلًا لَّعَلَّهُمْ يَهْتَدُونَ ۝ وَجَعَلْنَا ٱلسَّمَآءَ سَقْفًا مَّحْفُوظًا ۖ وَهُمْ عَنْ ءَايَٰتِهَا مُعْرِضُونَ ۝ وَهُوَ ٱلَّذِى خَلَقَ ٱلَّيْلَ وَٱلنَّهَارَ وَٱلشَّمْسَ وَٱلْقَمَرَ ۖ كُلٌّ فِى فَلَكٍ يَسْبَحُونَ ۝

ᵃ Here some prominent features of the earth have been mentioned which remind man of God in order to make him a grateful servant of God. One of these is the mountain ranges that have risen up on the surface of the earth in order to keep the dense matter beneath the seas well-balanced. Probably this refers to what is known as 'isostasy' in modern science. Similarly, it is also a sign of God that the earth is so made that man is able to make roadways sometimes on level plains, and sometimes as passages between mountains and rivers.

The roof of the sky, which is our upper atmosphere, is composed in such a way as to prevent certain harmful rays of the sun from affecting us in the form of the ozone layer. The atmosphere also prevents the majority of the continuous shower of meteorites from reaching us. In the same way, there are signs in the moving of the sun and the moon in their orbits without clashing with each other, resulting in the regular occurrence of day and night on the earth.

Innumerable such signs are found on the earth. If man examines them in depth, he will be overwhelmed by the realisation of God's blessings and His powers. But he ignores them. Even after seeing clear events and signs, he continues to turn a deaf ear and a blind eye to them.

³⁴ We have not granted everlasting life to any human being before you; then if you [Muhammad] should die, will they live forever? ³⁵ Every soul shall taste death; We test you with both good and evil [circumstances] as a trial. To Us you shall return.ᵃ

وَمَا جَعَلْنَا لِبَشَرٍ مِّن قَبْلِكَ ٱلْخُلْدَ أَفَإِيْن مِّتَّ فَهُمُ ٱلْخَٰلِدُونَ ۞ كُلُّ نَفْسٍ ذَآئِقَةُ ٱلْمَوْتِ وَنَبْلُوكُم بِٱلشَّرِّ وَٱلْخَيْرِ فِتْنَةً وَإِلَيْنَا تُرْجَعُونَ ۞

ᵃ Those who were opponents of the Prophet Muhammad in Makkah were more affluent and powerful in terms of material resources. They enjoyed respect and positions of superiority in the society of those days. According to them, this difference meant that they were on the right path and the Prophet Muhammad on the wrong path. But an excess or paucity of worldly effects bears no relation to superiority or inferiority, being purely for the purpose of trial. It is a trial imposed at the behest of God. If, after acquiring worldly resources, a man thinks highly of himself, he is as if proving himself unworthy of this blessing. The result will be that after death, in the life hereafter, he will be totally deprived of his riches.

The people of Makkah were engaged in strenuous efforts to defeat the Prophet Muhammad, to the extent that they wanted to eliminate him somehow in order to nip his mission in the bud. God says that those who conspired against the Prophet had forgotten the fact that those who dug a grave for others, have ultimately to enter the grave themselves. Then, after death, when they faced their Real Lord, what would they do?

³⁶ When those who deny the truth
see you, they laugh at you, saying,
'Is this the one who talks of your
deities?' Yet it is they who deny all
mention of the Gracious One.^a

وَإِذَا رَءَاكَ ٱلَّذِينَ كَفَرُوٓاْ إِن
يَتَّخِذُونَكَ إِلَّا هُزُوًا أَهَٰذَا ٱلَّذِى
يَذْكُرُ ءَالِهَتَكُمْ وَهُم بِذِكْرِ
ٱلرَّحْمَٰنِ هُمْ كَٰفِرُونَ ۝

---

^a The gods of the Quraysh were, in reality, the great ones of the community. On
the one hand, there was their imaginary greatness which was imbedded in their
minds. On the other hand, there was the Prophet, whose image at that time was
not more elevated than that of an ordinary man. In this comparison, the Prophet
appeared, indeed, to be an ordinary man with no special merit. They used to ask
contemptuously, 'Is this the man who criticises our great men, who rejects the
religion of these great men which we follow, and seeks to introduce a new religion?'

The Prophet Muhammad used to invite people to accept the oneness of God. But
these people were not interested in God. All their interests were centred round
their great men, whom they had elevated to the status of gods. As it was these false
gods who were affected by the call of the Prophet, their devotees became his deadly
opponents. They forgot that, by rejecting the false gods, he was presenting the
cause of the real God and not promoting his own self.

³⁷ Man is a creature of haste. Soon I will show you My signs, but do not ask Me to hasten them. ³⁸ They ask, 'When will this promise be fulfilled, if what you say be true?' ³⁹ If only those who deny the truth knew the time when they would not be able to ward off the fire neither from their faces nor from their backs. They will not be helped! ⁴⁰ Indeed, it will come upon them suddenly and confound them; and they will not be able to ward it off, nor shall they be reprieved. ⁴¹ Other messengers have been mocked before you, but those who scoffed were overwhelmed by the very thing they had mocked.[a]

خُلِقَ ٱلْإِنسَـٰنُ مِنْ عَجَلٍ سَأُوْرِيكُمْ ءَايَـٰتِى فَلَا تَسْتَعْجِلُونِ ۝ وَيَقُولُونَ مَتَىٰ هَـٰذَا ٱلْوَعْدُ إِن كُنتُمْ صَـٰدِقِينَ ۝ لَوْ يَعْلَمُ ٱلَّذِينَ كَفَرُواْ حِينَ لَا يَكُفُّونَ عَن وُجُوهِهِمُ ٱلنَّارَ وَلَا عَن ظُهُورِهِمْ وَلَا هُمْ يُنصَرُونَ ۝ بَلْ تَأْتِيهِم بَغْتَةً فَتَبْهَتُهُمْ فَلَا يَسْتَطِيعُونَ رَدَّهَا وَلَا هُمْ يُنظَرُونَ ۝ وَلَقَدِ ٱسْتُهْزِئَ بِرُسُلٍ مِّن قَبْلِكَ فَحَاقَ بِٱلَّذِينَ سَخِرُواْ مِنْهُم مَّا كَانُواْ بِهِۦ يَسْتَهْزِءُونَ ۝

---

[a] The people of Arabia, although believers in the life hereafter, denied that concept of the Hereafter, as described by the Prophet Muhammad. They were proud to be followers of a religion which guaranteed their success. When the Prophet contradicted this firm belief of theirs, they became incensed. Making a show of fearlessness, they said, 'Show us the retribution of God with which you are threatening us.'

God says that their haste was entirely due to the fact that they were still in the process of being tested, and as such, were distanced from God's retribution. But when this period of respite ended and they were overwhelmed by God's punishment, it would dawn on them that they had committed a huge blunder in not taking the Prophet's words seriously.

⁴² Say, 'Who will save you from the wrath of the Most Gracious, by night and by day?' Yet they turn away from the remembrance of their Lord. ⁴³ Do they have other deities who can defend them against Us? They cannot even help themselves, neither can they be aided against Us.ᵃ

قُلْ مَن يَكْلَؤُكُم بِٱلَّيْلِ وَٱلنَّهَارِ مِنَ ٱلرَّحْمَٰنِ بَلْ هُمْ عَن ذِكْرِ رَبِّهِم مُّعْرِضُونَ ۝ أَمْ لَهُمْ ءَالِهَةٌ تَمْنَعُهُم مِّن دُونِنَا لَا يَسْتَطِيعُونَ نَصْرَ أَنفُسِهِمْ وَلَا هُم مِّنَّا يُصْحَبُونَ ۝

ᵃ God's reckoning is not something which belongs to a distant future. It is latent in this very diurnal routine in which man feels so secure and protected. For instance, if the distance between the sun and the earth were to be reduced by half, our days would become so hot that we would be roasted as if by the flames of a fire. On the contrary, if the distance between the sun and the earth were doubled, our nights would become so cold that we would be frozen like ice.

The Being who has established such a highly favourable system of the earth and the heavens deserves to have homage paid to Him, to be worshipped and offered total loyalty, instead of false gods who are not capable of giving people anything.

⁴⁴ Yet We bestowed the good things [of life] upon their fathers for a great length of time. But do they not see how We are shrinking their borders? Is it they who will prevail? ᵃ

⁴⁵ Say, 'I warn you only through the Revelation.' But the deaf can hear nothing when they are warned, ⁴⁶ yet if even a breath of your Lord's punishment touched them, they would say, 'Woe to us! We were indeed wrongdoers.' ᵇ

بَلْ مَتَّعْنَا هَـٰؤُلَآءِ وَءَابَآءَهُمْ حَتَّىٰ طَالَ عَلَيْهِمُ ٱلْعُمُرُ ۗ أَفَلَا يَرَوْنَ أَنَّا نَأْتِى ٱلْأَرْضَ نَنقُصُهَا مِنْ أَطْرَافِهَآ ۚ أَفَهُمُ ٱلْغَـٰلِبُونَ ۝ قُلْ إِنَّمَآ أُنذِرُكُم بِٱلْوَحْىِ ۚ وَلَا يَسْمَعُ ٱلصُّمُّ ٱلدُّعَآءَ إِذَا مَا يُنذَرُونَ ۝ وَلَئِن مَّسَّتْهُمْ نَفْحَةٌ مِّنْ عَذَابِ رَبِّكَ لَيَقُولُنَّ يَـٰوَيْلَنَآ إِنَّا كُنَّا ظَـٰلِمِينَ ۝

ᵃ In ancient times, the people of Makkah were considered leaders of the Arab world. This leadership was God's gift to them, but it only gave rise to false pride and egoism. So, when the Truth was declared through the Prophet Muhammad, they refused to accept it on account of their egoistic mentality.

Such was the position of Islam in Makkah. But, among the people of other places who did not suffer from similar psychological complications, the truth of Islam was spreading. In Makkah, Islam was rejected, but in other places, Islam was being adopted by the tribesmen. The large-scale adoption of Islam by the people of Madinah had finally made it clear that the sphere of leadership of the people in Makkah was continually contracting. But those who suffer from a superiority complex do not learn a lesson from any warning, however open that might be.

ᵇ 'I warn you only through the Revelation' means warning people with the help of arguments. The giver of the call for the Truth always supports his statements with convincing arguments and people are required to recognise the truth solely on the basis of his reasoning. Those who are blind and deaf to arguments, are jerked into awareness only when God's power reveals itself openly after their death. Every arrogant and vain person will thereupon admit the Truth. But the acceptance of Truth at that stage will be of no avail.

47 We shall set up scales of justice on the Day of Resurrection, so that no soul can be in the least wronged. Actions as small as a grain of mustard seed shall be weighed. We are sufficient as a reckoner.ᵃ

وَنَضَعُ ٱلْمَوَٰزِينَ ٱلْقِسْطَ لِيَوْمِ ٱلْقِيَٰمَةِ فَلَا تُظْلَمُ نَفْسٌ شَيْـًٔا ۖ وَإِن كَانَ مِثْقَالَ حَبَّةٍ مِّنْ خَرْدَلٍ أَتَيْنَا بِهَا ۗ وَكَفَىٰ بِنَا حَٰسِبِينَ ٤٧

ᵃ In the present world, a 'balance (or scale)' is a device for finding out the weight of an object. Therefore, God has used this known term to explain the events on Judgement Day. Where the scales of the world weigh material things, on the Day of Judgement, the scales of God will weigh intangible facts and show their 'weights.' That is, the scales of the world can measure the material aspect of things but the divine scales will be able to measure the inner value of our deeds.

In this world, a man obtains things by paying for them. One who pays less receives less and one who pays more receives more. The same will be the position on the Day of Judgement. Things of high value will be available only on payment of their price which will be in terms of good deeds. Just as things are not available gratis in this world, similarly things will be available on the Day of Judgement only on making a suitable payment: the Quran is a book which indicates what the cost will be. According to the Quranic criterion, a believer will have to develop a spiritual personality in this world itself. This is the price which he has to pay if he wants to find an entry into the ideal world of Paradise.

⁴⁸ We gave Moses and Aaron the criterion of right and wrong and a light and reminder for the righteous, ⁴⁹ those who fear their Lord in the unseen, also dread the Hour of Judgement. ⁵⁰ This is a blessed reminder that We have revealed to you. Will you then reject it?ᵃ

وَلَقَدْ ءَاتَيْنَا مُوسَىٰ وَهَٰرُونَ ٱلْفُرْقَانَ وَضِيَآءً وَذِكْرًا لِّلْمُتَّقِينَ ۝ ٱلَّذِينَ يَخْشَوْنَ رَبَّهُم بِٱلْغَيْبِ وَهُم مِّنَ ٱلسَّاعَةِ مُشْفِقُونَ ۝ وَهَٰذَا ذِكْرٌ مُّبَارَكٌ أَنزَلْنَٰهُ أَفَأَنتُمْ لَهُۥ مُنكِرُونَ ۝

ᵃ The criterion or discernment (al-furqan), light and reminder or remembrance (dhikr), which were given to Moses, were the same things which all the prophets received from God. Al-furqan means that ideological standard which enables a man to distinguish between Truth and falsehood. Light means divine guidance which pulls a man out of the darkness of the wrong path and puts him on to the straight path. Dhikr means remembrance, i.e. the highlighting of the latent educative aspect of things, so that they do not figure simply as things, but as treasure chests of knowledge for the recognition and realisation of God and His Divine guidance.

In this way God has arranged for the guidance of man. But, it is possible for God's Guide Book to provide guidance in the real sense only when a man is anxious about his fate in the Hereafter, and this anxiety makes him so serious that he attaches more importance to Truth and righteousness than to all other things.

⁵¹ Before this We gave Abraham his guidance. We knew him well. ⁵² When he asked his father and his people, 'What are these images to which you are so devoted?' ⁵³ They replied, 'We found our fathers worshipping them.' ⁵⁴ Abraham said, 'Indeed, you and your fathers have been clearly misguided.' ᵃ

۞ وَلَقَدْ ءَاتَيْنَآ إِبْرَٰهِيمَ رُشْدَهُۥ مِن قَبْلُ وَكُنَّا بِهِۦ عَٰلِمِينَ ۝ إِذْ قَالَ لِأَبِيهِ وَقَوْمِهِۦ مَا هَٰذِهِ ٱلتَّمَاثِيلُ ٱلَّتِىٓ أَنتُمْ لَهَا عَٰكِفُونَ ۝ قَالُوا۟ وَجَدْنَآ ءَابَآءَنَا لَهَا عَٰبِدِينَ ۝ قَالَ لَقَدْ كُنتُمْ أَنتُمْ وَءَابَآؤُكُمْ فِى ضَلَٰلٍ مُّبِينٍ ۝

ᵃ It is God's principle to give according to the capability of the receiver. Abraham passed through different trials and tests and proved his mettle: God accordingly gave him guidance and divine knowledge. This is how God deals with His subjects.

Abraham was born in Iraq in the ancient city of Ur. At that time polytheism was all-pervasive. In spite of being brought up in this polytheistic atmosphere, Abraham was not influenced by it. He examined things rationally, rising completely above his immediate environment, he was able to discover the truth. He was living in a world where every worldly honour and progress were linked with polytheism. But he did not care for all this. Unmindful of all worldly considerations, he criticised the behaviour of his community and became ready to declare the Truth before it—these are the attributes which make an individual capable of receiving God's guidance.

⁵⁵ They said, 'Have you brought us the truth or are you jesting?' ⁵⁶ Abraham replied, 'Your Lord is the Lord of the heavens and the earth, who created them, and I bear witness to that. ⁵⁷ By the Lord, I will devise a plan against your deities after you have gone away and turned your backs!' ⁵⁸ He broke them all into pieces, except for the biggest one of them, so that they might return to it [for enquiry].[a]

قَالُوٓاْ أَجِئْتَنَا بِٱلْحَقِّ أَمْ أَنتَ مِنَ ٱللَّٰعِبِينَ ۝ قَالَ بَل رَّبُّكُمْ رَبُّ ٱلسَّمَٰوَٰتِ وَٱلْأَرْضِ ٱلَّذِى فَطَرَهُنَّ وَأَنَا۠ عَلَىٰ ذَٰلِكُم مِّنَ ٱلشَّٰهِدِينَ ۝ وَتَٱللَّهِ لَأَكِيدَنَّ أَصْنَٰمَكُم بَعْدَ أَن تُوَلُّواْ مُدْبِرِينَ ۝ فَجَعَلَهُمْ جُذَٰذًا إِلَّا كَبِيرًا لَّهُمْ لَعَلَّهُمْ إِلَيْهِ يَرْجِعُونَ ۝

---

[a] During Abraham's period, people's minds were in the grip of polytheistic ideas, so much so that in the beginning they took Abraham's criticism to be frivolous. Therefore, they asked him whether his utterances had been well thought out, or whether he was mouthing words out of sheer frivolity.

Abraham said that the fact that they considered matters of the greatest importance as frivolous was further proof of their ignorance. The truth is that the entire earth and the heavens bear testimony to the word of God. The next day, in an act of extraordinary courage, he broke down their deities. In this way, Abraham proved in practice what he had been saying in theory, namely, that the deities were absolutely worthless.

⁵⁹ 'Who has done this to our deities? He must be a wrongdoer.' ⁶⁰ Some said, 'We heard a young man, called Abraham, talking about them.' ⁶¹ They said, 'Then bring him here in the sight of all the people, so that they may act as witnesses.' ⁶² They said, 'Abraham, was it you who did this to our deities?' ⁶³ He answered, 'Rather this biggest one of them did it. Ask them, if they can speak.' ^a

قَالُوا مَن فَعَلَ هَذَا بِآلِهَتِنَا إِنَّهُۥ لَمِنَ ٱلظَّٰلِمِينَ ۝ قَالُوا سَمِعْنَا فَتًى يَذْكُرُهُمْ يُقَالُ لَهُۥٓ إِبْرَٰهِيمُ ۝ قَالُوا فَأْتُوا بِهِۦ عَلَىٰٓ أَعْيُنِ ٱلنَّاسِ لَعَلَّهُمْ يَشْهَدُونَ ۝ قَالُوٓا ءَأَنتَ فَعَلْتَ هَذَا بِآلِهَتِنَا يَٰٓإِبْرَٰهِيمُ ۝ قَالَ بَلْ فَعَلَهُۥ كَبِيرُهُمْ هَذَا فَسْـَٔلُوهُمْ إِن كَانُوا يَنطِقُونَ ۝

---

^a The next day when the people entered the temple and saw their deities broken to pieces, they were shocked. They eventually discovered that it was the handiwork of a young man who had deviated from their ancestral religion and spoken against it.

While demolishing the deities, Abraham had purposely spared the tallest one. When he was called by the people and enquiries were made of him, he pointed out that the big deity was still there, untouched and intact, and that people might put their questions to it. He said that if the big deity was god, then let it explain how the other deities had come to this pass.

Although Abraham did not answer their questions directly, it was his indirect statement that sufficed to convey his message effectively. This shows that sometimes indirect speech is more effective than direct speech.

⁶⁴ Then they turned to one another and said, 'It is you yourselves who are in the wrong,' ⁶⁵ then they hung their heads, and said, 'O Abraham! You know they cannot speak.' ⁶⁶ Abraham said, 'So, do you worship something instead of God that can neither benefit you nor harm you? ⁶⁷Shame on you and on whatever you worship instead of God. Can you not understand?' ᵃ

⁶⁸ They said, 'Burn him and help your deities, if you are resolved to do something.' ⁶⁹ But We said, 'Fire! Be cool and a means of safety for Abraham.' ⁷⁰ They had sought to do him harm, but We frustrated them.ᵇ

فَرَجَعُوٓاْ إِلَىٰٓ أَنفُسِهِمْ فَقَالُوٓاْ إِنَّكُمْ أَنتُمُ ٱلظَّٰلِمُونَ ۝ ثُمَّ نُكِسُواْ عَلَىٰ رُءُوسِهِمْ لَقَدْ عَلِمْتَ مَا هَٰٓؤُلَآءِ يَنطِقُونَ ۝ قَالَ أَفَتَعْبُدُونَ مِن دُونِ ٱللَّهِ مَا لَا يَنفَعُكُمْ شَيْـًٔا وَلَا يَضُرُّكُمْ ۝ أُفٍّ لَّكُمْ وَلِمَا تَعْبُدُونَ مِن دُونِ ٱللَّهِ أَفَلَا تَعْقِلُونَ ۝ قَالُواْ حَرِّقُوهُ وَٱنصُرُوٓاْ ءَالِهَتَكُمْ إِن كُنتُمْ فَٰعِلِينَ ۝ قُلْنَا يَٰنَارُ كُونِى بَرْدًا وَسَلَٰمًا عَلَىٰٓ إِبْرَٰهِيمَ ۝ وَأَرَادُواْ بِهِۦ كَيْدًا فَجَعَلْنَٰهُمُ ٱلْأَخْسَرِينَ ۝

ᵃ On hearing such replies from Abraham, the people could have accused him of insolence and taken him to task, as usually happens in such cases. But, in spite of their being polytheists, there seemed to be some sense of reason left in them. So, realizing the force of the rationality in his replies, they felt ashamed and admitted that they were wrong. Had they not subsequently fallen a prey to prejudices, this experience would have been sufficient to lead them towards the true faith.

ᵇ Those who enjoy power always resort to oppressive methods when they fail in the field of reasoned argument. This happened likewise in the case of the Prophet Abraham. After the incident of the demolition of the deities, when the leaders of the community felt that they could not counter Abraham's arguments, they started persecuting him. Finally, one day, intoxicated with power, they threw him in a pit of fire.

But, a prophet is God's representative on earth. Therefore, on this exceptional basis, God grants extraordinary help to prophets. So, in this case also, at God' behest, the fire cooled down for him. Help of this kind can be available to a non-prophet also, provided he completely identifies himself with God's plan to the same extent as a prophet does.

⁷¹ And We saved him and Lot [and brought them] to a land which We had blessed for all people, ⁷² We bestowed Isaac and then Jacob on him as an additional boon and We made all of them righteous. ⁷³ We made them leaders who guided people by Our command. We revealed to them the doing of good, observance of prayer and the giving of alms and Us alone did they worship.ᵃ

⁷⁴ To Lot We gave wisdom and knowledge and delivered him from the city which practiced abomination. They were indeed a wicked people. ⁷⁵ We admitted him to Our mercy; he was a righteous man.ᵇ

وَنَجَّيْنَـٰهُ وَلُوطًا إِلَى ٱلْأَرْضِ ٱلَّتِى بَـٰرَكْنَا فِيهَا لِلْعَـٰلَمِينَ ۝ وَوَهَبْنَا لَهُۥٓ إِسْحَـٰقَ وَيَعْقُوبَ نَافِلَةً ۖ وَكُلًّا جَعَلْنَا صَـٰلِحِينَ ۝ وَجَعَلْنَـٰهُمْ أَئِمَّةً يَهْدُونَ بِأَمْرِنَا وَأَوْحَيْنَآ إِلَيْهِمْ فِعْلَ ٱلْخَيْرَٰتِ وَإِقَامَ ٱلصَّلَوٰةِ وَإِيتَآءَ ٱلزَّكَوٰةِ ۖ وَكَانُوا۟ لَنَا عَـٰبِدِينَ ۝ وَلُوطًا ءَاتَيْنَـٰهُ حُكْمًا وَعِلْمًا وَنَجَّيْنَـٰهُ مِنَ ٱلْقَرْيَةِ ٱلَّتِى كَانَت تَّعْمَلُ ٱلْخَبَـٰٓئِثَ ۗ إِنَّهُمْ كَانُوا۟ قَوْمَ سَوْءٍ فَـٰسِقِينَ ۝ وَأَدْخَلْنَـٰهُ فِى رَحْمَتِنَآ ۖ إِنَّهُۥ مِنَ ٱلصَّـٰلِحِينَ ۝

ᵃ The Prophet Abraham was born in Iraq. When the people of his community and Iraq's ruler, Nimrod, became his enemies, he left his native place after fully conveying the divine message to them. At God's command he migrated to the lands of Syria and Palestine. Though his countrymen did not support him, God gave him sons and grandsons who followed in his footsteps. God accepted and appreciated his piety to the extent that He started a chain of prophets from amongst his descendants.

ᵇ Wisdom means realization of God (ma'rifah) and knowledge ('ilm) means divine revelation. All other prophets besides Lot also received these blessings. Now after the cessation of prophethood, the Quran is the sole purveyor of divine Revelation. As regards divine knowledge (hikmah or ma'rifah), non-prophets also receive a share of it according to their merits.

Those on whom God looks with kindness has God as their friend. He pulls them out of the environment of evil-doers and puts them in the environment of good people. He becomes their supporter at every turn of their lives. He bestows divine knowledge (hikmah) upon them, after which their whole life is bathed in God's mercy.

⁷⁶ Before him Noah cried out to Us, and We heard his prayer. We saved him and all his household from a great distress. ⁷⁷ We helped him against his people who rejected Our revelations. They were surely a wicked people, so We drowned them all.ᵃ

وَنُوحًا إِذْ نَادَىٰ مِن قَبْلُ فَٱسْتَجَبْنَا لَهُۥ فَنَجَّيْنَٰهُ وَأَهْلَهُۥ مِنَ ٱلْكَرْبِ ٱلْعَظِيمِ ۝ وَنَصَرْنَٰهُ مِنَ ٱلْقَوْمِ ٱلَّذِينَ كَذَّبُوا۟ بِـَٔايَٰتِنَآ إِنَّهُمْ كَانُوا۟ قَوْمَ سَوْءٍ فَأَغْرَقْنَٰهُمْ أَجْمَعِينَ ۝

ᵃ The Prophet Noah performed his divine task of giving the call for the Truth among his community over an extremely long period, but except for a few individuals, nobody was reformed. At last, Noah prayed for the destruction of his community. Thereupon, such a disastrous flood set in that even the mountain tops could not provide the people with safe havens.

Though this incident took place in relation to a prophet, there is solace in this for the common man also. It shows that those who make mischief in this world do not enjoy absolute freedom to do whatever they like, while one who espouses the cause of Truth is not all alone in this world. One who identifies himself with Truth, to the extent that he becomes the representative of Truth in the world, does not remain alone in this life, for God becomes his supporter; and who can overpower one who is supported by God?

⁷⁸ Tell of David and Solomon who both passed judgement on the field into which some people's sheep had strayed [and grazed] at night. We bore witness to their judgement. ⁷⁹ We gave Solomon the right understanding of the matter, and We bestowed wisdom and knowledge on both of them. We caused the mountains and the birds to celebrate Our praises along with David. We had the power to do this— ⁸⁰ We taught him the art of making coats of mail for you, to protect you in battle. Will you then give thanks? ᵃ

وَدَاوُدَ وَسُلَيْمَـٰنَ إِذْ يَحْكُمَانِ فِى
ٱلْحَرْثِ إِذْ نَفَشَتْ فِيهِ غَنَمُ ٱلْقَوْمِ
وَكُنَّا لِحُكْمِهِمْ شَـٰهِدِينَ ۝ فَفَهَّمْنَـٰهَا سُلَيْمَـٰنَ وَكُلّاً ءَاتَيْنَا
حُكْمًا وَعِلْمًا وَسَخَّرْنَا مَعَ دَاوُدَ
ٱلْجِبَالَ يُسَبِّحْنَ وَٱلطَّيْرَ وَكُنَّا
فَـٰعِلِينَ ۝ وَعَلَّمْنَـٰهُ صَنْعَةَ لَبُوسٍ
لَّكُمْ لِتُحْصِنَكُم مِّن بَأْسِكُمْ فَهَلْ
أَنتُمْ شَـٰكِرُونَ ۝

ᵃ In these verses two Israelite prophets have been mentioned—One David (Dawud) and the other, his son, Soloman (Sulayman). God had bestowed upon them the capability to settle human problems and take right decisions about them. The Prophet David used to offer prayers to God so eloquently that even the mountains and the birds would join in with him. Moreover, God also told him how to make use of iron.

It was the prophets of God who taught man how to pray to his Lord and praise Him. But it appears from these verses that other important things also came to be properly known to man through the prophets: for instance, the principles of social justice and the use of minerals and metals. Indeed, primary knowledge of every important thing in relation to life was probably granted to man through their good graces alone.

⁸¹ We subjected to Solomon the stormy wind, which blew at his behest towards the land which We had blessed. For it is We who have knowledge of all things— ⁸² We also subjected to him some of the jinn who dived for him in the sea and performed other tasks; We kept a watch over them.ᵃ

وَلِسُلَيْمَٰنَ ٱلرِّيحَ عَاصِفَةً تَجْرِى بِأَمْرِهِۦ إِلَى ٱلْأَرْضِ ٱلَّتِى بَٰرَكْنَا فِيهَا ۚ وَكُنَّا بِكُلِّ شَىْءٍ عَٰلِمِينَ ۝ وَمِنَ ٱلشَّيَٰطِينِ مَن يَغُوصُونَ لَهُۥ وَيَعْمَلُونَ عَمَلًا دُونَ ذَٰلِكَ ۖ وَكُنَّا لَهُمْ حَٰفِظِينَ ۝

ᵃ Here the taming of the winds means making navigation on the seas a possibility, for in ancient times ocean travel was revolutionised when man invented ships with sails. The sails were in fact a means of harnessing the winds and performed the function of engines for the ships of those days. The invention of ships with sales made the oceans not only navigable, but also suitable for transporting heavy cargo. This gives an indication that man was taught the science of navigation on the seas through the prophets.

Besides this, a group of jinn was made subservient to the Prophet Solomon (Sulayman). They used to execute for him large welfare projects which could not be done by ordinary men. In the modern machine age, such enormous tasks of human welfare are performed by machines. Before the machine age, in order to facilitate the performance of major projects, God had made the jinn subordinate to His prophets.

⁸³ Remember Job when he called on his Lord saying, 'I have been afflicted with great distress: but You are the most merciful of the merciful.' ⁸⁴ We heard his prayer and relieved his suffering, We restored to him his family, doubling their number as an act of Our grace, and as a reminder for the worshippers.^a

۞ وَأَيُّوبَ إِذْ نَادَىٰ رَبَّهُ أَنِّي مَسَّنِيَ ٱلضُّرُّ وَأَنتَ أَرْحَمُ ٱلرَّاحِمِينَ ۝

فَٱسْتَجَبْنَا لَهُ فَكَشَفْنَا مَا بِهِۦ مِن ضُرٍّ وَءَاتَيْنَاهُ أَهْلَهُ وَمِثْلَهُم مَّعَهُمْ رَحْمَةً مِّنْ عِندِنَا وَذِكْرَىٰ لِلْعَابِدِينَ ۝

---

^a God provides examples differing in kind and of the highest order through His prophets, the purpose being to give people a set of ideals. One of these examples is that of the Prophet Job (Ayyub). Job was an Israelite prophet probably some time in the ninth century B.C. According to the Bible, he was initially very rich. He was blessed with farms, cattle, houses, children, etc., to such an extent that it was said that nobody was his peer in the entire east. In spite of this, however, Job was a very grateful and faithful person. His life set an example of how a person may remain humble and modest, in spite of being blessed with great wealth and honour.

But, Satan reversed the lesson to be learned from this situation. He managed to convince people that Job's extraordinary reverence for God was on account of the extraordinary blessings that had been showered on him. If he were to be deprived of these blessings,—so Satan maintained—his entire gratefulness would vanish.

God thereupon set another example through him. Job's cattle died, his farms were destroyed, his children died and even his body was afflicted with a disease. All his friends and relatives left him, except his wife who remained with him. But Job reconciled himself with God's decision. He exercised the utmost patience. In the words of the Bible: 'Then Job, tore his robe and shaved his head; and he fell to the ground and worshipped. And he said:Naked I came from my mother's womb, and naked shall I return there. The Lord gave and the Lord has taken away; blessed be the name of the Lord. In all this Job did not sin, nor did he charge God with wrongdoing.' (Job, 1:20-22).

When Job showed so much patience and gratefulness, not only was a befitting reward set apart for him in the Hereafter, but his circumstances in the world were also changed. 'Then God gave him double of what he had before.' (Job:42:12). This very incident is thus figuratively described in the Prophet Muhammad's saying: 'When God changed the days of Job again, He sent a shower of golden grasshoppers on him.'

⁸⁵ Remember Ishmael and Idris and Dhul Kifl: they were all patient and steadfast. ⁸⁶ We admitted them to Our mercy. They were all righteous men.ᵃ

وَإِسْمَٰعِيلَ وَإِدْرِيسَ وَذَا ٱلْكِفْلِ كُلٌّ مِّنَ ٱلصَّٰبِرِينَ ۝ وَأَدْخَلْنَٰهُمْ فِى رَحْمَتِنَآ إِنَّهُم مِّنَ ٱلصَّٰلِحِينَ ۝

ᵃ Ishmael (Isma'il) was the Prophet Abraham's son. Some commentators (of the Quran) have held that Idris is the prophet who has been mentioned in the Bible by the name of Enoch. Similarly, Dhul Kifl is perhaps that prophet who has been mentioned in the Bible by the name of Hizti-El.

The prophets are refered to as patience personified. The reason for this is that the root of all God-worshipping actions is patience. Patience means abstaining from reaction. A person who is unable to refrain from reaction can never maintain himself on the path of the God-favoured life in this world of trial. The fact is that patience is the door leading to all God's mercies, in this world as well as in the life after death.

⁸⁷ Remember the man in the whale [Jonah] when he went away in anger, thinking We had no power over him. But he cried out in the darkness, 'There is no deity but You. Glory be to You! I was indeed wrong.' ⁸⁸ So We heard his prayer and delivered him from sorrow. Thus shall We deliver the true believers.ᵃ

وَذَا ٱلنُّونِ إِذ ذَّهَبَ مُغَٰضِبًا فَظَنَّ أَن لَّن نَّقْدِرَ عَلَيْهِ فَنَادَىٰ فِى ٱلظُّلُمَٰتِ أَن لَّآ إِلَٰهَ إِلَّآ أَنتَ سُبْحَٰنَكَ إِنِّى كُنتُ مِنَ ٱلظَّٰلِمِينَ ۝ فَٱسْتَجَبْنَا لَهُۥ وَنَجَّيْنَٰهُ مِنَ ٱلْغَمِّ ۚ وَكَذَٰلِكَ نُۨجِى ٱلْمُؤْمِنِينَ ۝

ᵃ Jonah (Yunus) was sent as a prophet to Nineveh, an ancient city of Iraq. At that time, Nineveh's population was just over one hundred thousand. For a long time, he invited the community to accept the unity of God and the Hereafter, but they were not ready to do so. Now, if any community remains adamant about their denial of a prophet, even after having had the divine message conveyed to them to the fullest possible extent, then God's way is to ask the prophet to leave the town and thereafter the community is subjected to punishment (in the shape of some disaster). But Jonah himself felt that the time had come for him to go, and he went away, leaving his community without waiting for God's command to do so.

He left the city and, reaching the sea coast, he boarded a boat. After setting sail, the boat started sinking. People thought that some slave who had fled from his master was on the boat. According to an old tradition, the solution to this problem was to discover the slave and cast him out. When lots were drawn, the name of Jonah came up and he was thrown overboard. At that moment a big fish (probably a sperm whale) appeared and swallowed him. The fish kept him in its stomach, then at God's command, ejected him and cast him up on the coast. There he recovered his health and returned to his community.

A prophet had to face this fate simply because he left his dawah mission before its completion. Then one can imagine the fate of those successors of the prophet who have been neglectful and completely unmindful of the task of spreading God's word.

⁸⁹ Remember Zachariah, when he
called out to his Lord, 'Do not leave
me heirless Lord, You are the best
of heirs.' ⁹⁰ So We heard his prayer
and bestowed John upon him and
made his wife fit to bear him a child.
They used to hasten to do good and
they called on Us in hope and fear,
and they were always humble
towards Us.ᵃ

⁹¹ Remember the one who guarded
her chastity; so We breathed Our
Spirit into her, and made her and her
son a sign for all people.ᵇ

وَزَكَرِيَّآ إِذْ نَادَىٰ رَبَّهُۥ رَبِّ لَا
تَذَرْنِى فَرْدًا وَأَنتَ خَيْرُ ٱلْوَٰرِثِينَ
﴿٨٩﴾ فَٱسْتَجَبْنَا لَهُۥ وَوَهَبْنَا لَهُۥ يَحْيَىٰ
وَأَصْلَحْنَا لَهُۥ زَوْجَهُۥٓ إِنَّهُمْ كَانُوا۟
يُسَٰرِعُونَ فِى ٱلْخَيْرَٰتِ وَيَدْعُونَنَا
رَغَبًا وَرَهَبًا وَكَانُوا۟ لَنَا خَٰشِعِينَ
﴿٩٠﴾ وَٱلَّتِىٓ أَحْصَنَتْ فَرْجَهَا فَنَفَخْنَا
فِيهَا مِن رُّوحِنَا وَجَعَلْنَٰهَا وَٱبْنَهَآ ءَايَةً
لِّلْعَٰلَمِينَ ﴿٩١﴾

ᵃ Prophets are those on whom God has bestowed His special Grace. A most
prominent personal characteristic of theirs is that their endeavours are directed
not towards the attainment of worldly goals but towards the attainment of things
that are valuable from the viewpoint of the Hereafter. They have discovered the
Majesty of God to the extent that in their eyes He is everything and nothing else
matters. In every circumstance they opt for the path of modesty and humility.

These qualities were found in full measure in Zachariah (Zakariyya) and other
prophets. On this account, God blessed them with His special grace. Common
believers too will be entitled to God's succour and His blessings, provided that they
possess the aforesaid qualities.

ᵇ The special quality of Mary (Maryam) is said to be that she guarded her chastity.
By way of a reward for this, she was made the mother of a prophet who was born
by a direct miracle of God.

This is true of common men and women also. Everybody is being tried in this world
by being required to keep his urges and desires under control. The more an
individual shows self-discipline on this score, the more he will share in God's special
blessings.

⁹² This community of yours is one community and I am your Lord, so worship Me. ⁹³ But they divided themselves into factions, but to Us they shall all return. ⁹⁴ He who does good works while he is a believer, shall not see his efforts disregarded: We record them all.ᵃ

إِنَّ هَـٰذِهِۦٓ أُمَّتُكُمْ أُمَّةً وَٰحِدَةً وَأَنَا۠ رَبُّكُمْ فَٱعْبُدُونِ ۝ وَتَقَطَّعُوٓاْ أَمْرَهُم بَيْنَهُمْ كُلٌّ إِلَيْنَا رَٰجِعُونَ ۝ فَمَن يَعْمَلْ مِنَ ٱلصَّـٰلِحَـٰتِ وَهُوَ مُؤْمِنٌ فَلَا كُفْرَانَ لِسَعْيِهِۦ وَإِنَّا لَهُۥ كَـٰتِبُونَ ۝

ᵃ God has sent all prophets with the same religion, namely, one according to which the one and only God should be one's God and that He alone should be worshipped. Had people been steadfast in this original religion, all of them would have continued as one Community (*ummah*). But, people on their own started entering into disputes and thus concocted different versions of the same religion. Individuals exercised their 'right' to choose whatever religion best suited their interests. Thus one religion came to be divided into many religions.

To God, faith and deeds have importance only when they signify true realization of Him and true obedience to Him. Anything other than these will not be appreciated by God, however much the individuals themselves may attach value to them.

⁹⁵ It is ordained that no nation We have destroyed shall ever rise again, ⁹⁶ but when Gog and Magog are let loose and swarm down from every hillside and they spread out, [leaping across every barrier of land and sea], ⁹⁷ when the true promise of God draws near, those who denied the truth will stare in amazement, crying, 'Woe to us! We have been so heedless of this. Indeed, we were wrongdoers.' ^a

وَحَرَٰمٌ عَلَىٰ قَرْيَةٍ أَهْلَكْنَٰهَآ أَنَّهُمْ لَا يَرْجِعُونَ ۝ حَتَّىٰ إِذَا فُتِحَتْ يَأْجُوجُ وَمَأْجُوجُ وَهُم مِّن كُلِّ حَدَبٍ يَنسِلُونَ ۝ وَٱقْتَرَبَ ٱلْوَعْدُ ٱلْحَقُّ فَإِذَا هِىَ شَٰخِصَةٌ أَبْصَٰرُ ٱلَّذِينَ كَفَرُواْ يَٰوَيْلَنَا قَدْ كُنَّا فِى غَفْلَةٍ مِّنْ هَٰذَا بَلْ كُنَّا ظَٰلِمِينَ ۝

---

^a When the Truth appears with clear arguments, a man is compelled to recognise it by the compulsion of his very nature. Now, those who accept the Truth after recognising it, remain in consonance with their nature. On the other hand, those who give importance to material things and, therefore, do not accept the Truth, are as if ignoring their nature—virtually casting a veil over it. Denial of Truth is always at the cost of shutting one's senses. The fate of those who run this risk is that their entry into Islam becomes absolutely impossible: they are no longer receptive to the truth.

Those who fail to recognise the Truth, though presented in rational arguments, will recognise it only when the Day of Judgement tears the veil away from their eyes. But, recognition at that stage will be of no avail, because it will be time not for acceptance itself, but for reaping the benefit of an earlier acceptance of the Truth.

⁹⁸ You and what you worship instead of God will be fuel for hell: to it you shall all come—⁹⁹ if those had really been deities, they would not have been led there; but there they will remain forever. ¹⁰⁰ They shall groan. They will not hear therein anything else. ¹⁰¹ But those who have been promised a good reward by Us will be kept far away from Hell—¹⁰² they will not hear the slightest sound of it, and they shall forever abide in a state of bliss, among everything their souls longed for. ¹⁰³ The great Horror [of the Day of Judgement] shall not grieve them, and the angels will welcome them, saying, 'This is your Day which you have been promised.' ᵃ

إِنَّكُمْ وَمَا تَعْبُدُونَ مِن دُونِ اللَّهِ حَصَبُ جَهَنَّمَ أَنتُمْ لَهَا وَارِدُونَ ۝ لَوْ كَانَ هَٰؤُلَاءِ ءَالِهَةً مَّا وَرَدُوهَا وَكُلٌّ فِيهَا خَالِدُونَ ۝ لَهُمْ فِيهَا زَفِيرٌ وَهُمْ فِيهَا لَا يَسْمَعُونَ ۝ إِنَّ ٱلَّذِينَ سَبَقَتْ لَهُم مِّنَّا ٱلْحُسْنَىٰ أُوْلَٰئِكَ عَنْهَا مُبْعَدُونَ ۝ لَا يَسْمَعُونَ حَسِيسَهَا وَهُمْ فِي مَا ٱشْتَهَتْ أَنفُسُهُمْ خَالِدُونَ ۝ لَا تَحْزُنُهُمُ ٱلْفَزَعُ ٱلْأَكْبَرُ وَتَتَلَقَّاهُمُ ٱلْمَلَٰئِكَةُ هَٰذَا يَوْمُكُمُ ٱلَّذِى كُنتُمْ تُوعَدُونَ ۝

ᵃ 'Abdullah ibn az-Zab'ari was a famous poet of ancient times. When this verse was revealed, he urged the people to ask the Prophet Muhammad if all those being worshipped other than God along with their worshippers would go to hell. He then pointed out that, in fact, they were worshipping angels, the Jews were worshipping the Prophet 'Uzayr and the Christians were worshipping the Messiah. The polytheists were very anxious to understand this point and asked the Prophet Muhammad about it. He replied that the one who was being worshipped, and liked to be worshipped instead of God, would accompany the worshipper. On hearing this reply, 'Abdullah ibn az-Zab'ari did not enter into any further arguments but embraced Islam. (*Tafsir ibn Kathir*, vol. III, p.199).

This shows that this verse refers to a deity made of stone, etc., or one who himself liked to be worshipped. One who worshipped anybody other than God and one who was so worshipped and liked to be so worshipped, would both be cast into hell in order to teach the people a lesson.

Doomsday will be a terrible day. But those who fear Doomsday before its arrival, will be safe from the terror of that day. They will be sent to a world full of heavenly pleasures.

¹⁰⁴ On that Day We shall roll up the heavens like a scroll of parchment. As We originated the first creation, so shall We repeat it. This is a promise binding on Us. Truly, We shall fulfill it. ¹⁰⁵ We have already written in the Psalms following the Reminder, 'My righteous servants shall inherit the earth.' ¹⁰⁶ Herein, surely is a message for true worshippers.*

يَوْمَ نَطْوِى ٱلسَّمَآءَ كَطَيِّ ٱلسِّجِلِّ لِلْكُتُبِ كَمَا بَدَأْنَآ أَوَّلَ خَلْقٍ نُّعِيدُهُۥ وَعْدًا عَلَيْنَآ إِنَّا كُنَّا فَٰعِلِينَ ۝ وَلَقَدْ كَتَبْنَا فِى ٱلزَّبُورِ مِنۢ بَعْدِ ٱلذِّكْرِ أَنَّ ٱلْأَرْضَ يَرِثُهَا عِبَادِىَ ٱلصَّٰلِحُونَ ۝ إِنَّ فِى هَٰذَا لَبَلَٰغًا لِّقَوْمٍ عَٰبِدِينَ ۝

---

* The expanse of the present universe was brought into existence for the purpose of creating a testing ground. Subsequently, when the time comes for creating the world of reaping results (the Hereafter), God will wind up this world, and perhaps with the same material will create another world which will fulfil result-and-reward-oriented purposes. The coming into existence of one world (the present world) itself provides sufficient proof of the fact that another world can be brought into existence.

In the present world, bad persons attain positions of greatness, but this is only for as long as the period of trial lasts. When the period of trial is over and God's eternal and perfect world is created, every kind of comfort and honour will be in evidence, but only for those who had proved to be God's true subjects in this world of trial. This has been set down in detail in the Bible, 'And do not envy the evil people....Trust in the Lord, and do good; dwell in the land, and feed on His faithfulness. He shall bring forth your righteousness as the light and your justice as the noonday – for evil-doers shall be cut off; but those who wait on the Lord, they shall inherit the earth. The righteous shall inherit the earth and dwell in it forever.' (Psalms, chapter 37, verses 1, 3, 6, 9 and 27).

¹⁰⁷ We have sent you forth as a mercy to all mankind. ¹⁰⁸ Say, 'It has been revealed to me that your God is but One God. Will you then submit to Him?' ¹⁰⁹ If they turn away, say, 'I have warned you all alike, though I do not know whether [the scourge] which you are promised is near at hand or far off. ¹¹⁰ God surely knows what you say openly and also knows what you conceal. ¹¹¹ Nor do I know whether it may mean a trial for you and a short reprieve.' ¹¹² Say, 'My Lord, judge with truth. Our Lord is the Gracious One whose help we seek against what you utter.' ᵃ

وَمَآ أَرْسَلْنَٰكَ إِلَّا رَحْمَةً لِّلْعَٰلَمِينَ ۝ قُلْ إِنَّمَا يُوحَىٰٓ إِلَيَّ أَنَّمَآ إِلَٰهُكُمْ إِلَٰهٌ وَٰحِدٌ ۖ فَهَلْ أَنتُم مُّسْلِمُونَ ۝ فَإِن تَوَلَّوْا۟ فَقُلْ ءَاذَنتُكُمْ عَلَىٰ سَوَآءٍ ۖ وَإِنْ أَدْرِىٓ أَقَرِيبٌ أَم بَعِيدٌ مَّا تُوعَدُونَ ۝ إِنَّهُۥ يَعْلَمُ ٱلْجَهْرَ مِنَ ٱلْقَوْلِ وَيَعْلَمُ مَا تَكْتُمُونَ ۝ وَإِنْ أَدْرِى لَعَلَّهُۥ فِتْنَةٌ لَّكُمْ وَمَتَٰعٌ إِلَىٰ حِينٍ ۝ قَٰلَ رَبِّ ٱحْكُم بِٱلْحَقِّ ۗ وَرَبُّنَا ٱلرَّحْمَٰنُ ٱلْمُسْتَعَانُ عَلَىٰ مَا تَصِفُونَ ۝

ᵃ All the prophets who were sent by God were sent here for one and the same purpose. Through them, God wanted to impart to man that knowledge of reality which would enable him to become an inhabitant of eternal paradise. But every time a prophet came, he was rejected.

All prophets were dispensers of God's grace on earth. But, what distinguished the Prophet Muhammad from the others was that God chose him as a means of sending a special kind of His blessings to His subjects. God decided that a door of guidance, which had hitherto been closed to them, should be opened forever. Accordingly, it was God's plan that his addressees' community should somehow be brought on to the right path, so that a strong band of his Companions could be formed, made up of stalwarts who could then bring about a revolution in the world and thus change the course of history. This gracious plan of God was indeed fulfilled, completely and perfectly, through the Prophet Muhammad and his Companions.

22. THE PILGRIMAGE

In the name of God,
the Most Gracious, the Most Merciful

¹ O People! Fear your Lord. The catastrophe of the Last Hour shall be terrible indeed: ² when that Day comes, every suckling mother shall forsake her infant and every pregnant woman shall cast her burden and everyone will appear intoxicated, although they are not: the punishment of God will be severe indeed.ᵃ ³ Yet there are some who dispute about God without having any knowledge and they follow every rebellious devil, ⁴ it has been decreed concerning anyone whom he befriends, that he shall mislead him and guide him to the punishment of the Fire.ᵇ

ᵃ This is a literal description of some of the horrors of Doomsday, a day which will throw people into such a state of sheer horror that the mother will forget the baby at her breast and the pregnant woman will miscarry.

The earthquakes occurring in our present world give only a slight foretaste of the events of Doomsday. The onset of the great earthquake of Doomsday will make man forget everything he had considered important and due to which he had forgotten Doomsday—so much so that on that Day he will forget even his most cherished possessions and his near and dear ones.

ᵇ Whatever the prophet says is based on knowledge and he establishes its veracity by sound arguments. But those who do not want to admit or recognise any Truth outside themselves, unnecessarily and falsely dispute the prophet's statements in order to establish that they are on the right path. Such behaviour amounts to arrogance directed against God. Those who use the shield of such false arguments in order to reject the message of Truth have, in effect, made Satan their guide. They prove that they are devoid of the fear of God. ▶

⁵O people! If you are in doubt about the Resurrection, remember that We first created you from dust, then from a sperm drop, then from clotted blood, then a lump of flesh, both shaped and unshaped, so that We might manifest to you [Our power]. We cause what We will to stay in the womb for an appointed time, then We bring you forth as infants and then We cause you to grow and reach full growth. Then, some of you will pass away early in life, while some of you will reach extreme old age in which they will know nothing of what they once knew. You see the earth, dead and barren, but no sooner do We send down rain upon it than it begins to stir and swell, and produce every kind of luxuriant vegetation: ⁶ that is because God is the truth. It is He who gives life to the dead and He has the power to will anything. ⁷ The Last Hour is bound to come. There is no doubt about it. God will raise up those who are in their graves.ᵃ

يَـٰٓأَيُّهَا ٱلنَّاسُ إِن كُنتُمْ فِى رَيْبٍ مِّنَ ٱلْبَعْثِ فَإِنَّا خَلَقْنَـٰكُم مِّن تُرَابٍ ثُمَّ مِن نُّطْفَةٍ ثُمَّ مِنْ عَلَقَةٍ ثُمَّ مِن مُّضْغَةٍ مُّخَلَّقَةٍ وَغَيْرِ مُخَلَّقَةٍ لِّنُبَيِّنَ لَكُمْ وَنُقِرُّ فِى ٱلْأَرْحَامِ مَا نَشَآءُ إِلَىٰٓ أَجَلٍ مُّسَمًّى ثُمَّ نُخْرِجُكُمْ طِفْلًا ثُمَّ لِتَبْلُغُوٓا۟ أَشُدَّكُمْ وَمِنكُم مَّن يُتَوَفَّىٰ وَمِنكُم مَّن يُرَدُّ إِلَىٰٓ أَرْذَلِ ٱلْعُمُرِ لِكَيْلَا يَعْلَمَ مِنۢ بَعْدِ عِلْمٍ شَيْـًٔا وَتَرَى ٱلْأَرْضَ هَامِدَةً فَإِذَآ أَنزَلْنَا عَلَيْهَا ٱلْمَآءَ ٱهْتَزَّتْ وَرَبَتْ وَأَنۢبَتَتْ مِن كُلِّ زَوْجٍۭ بَهِيجٍ ۝ ذَٰلِكَ بِأَنَّ ٱللَّهَ هُوَ ٱلْحَقُّ وَأَنَّهُۥ يُحْىِ ٱلْمَوْتَىٰ وَأَنَّهُۥ عَلَىٰ كُلِّ شَىْءٍ قَدِيرٌ ۝ وَأَنَّ ٱلسَّاعَةَ ءَاتِيَةٌ لَّا رَيْبَ فِيهَا وَأَنَّ ٱللَّهَ يَبْعَثُ مَن فِى ٱلْقُبُورِ ۝

Such a mentality deprives a man of the capacity to recognise Truth and accept it, and he easily becomes Satan's tool. Such a person will wake up only on hearing the terrifying roar of Doomsday. But, the earthquake of Doomsday will come to such individuals to open the door of Hell for them and not to give them guidance at that stage.

ᵃ Man is doubtful about the life hereafter for the simple reason that he is unable to understand how a human being who is dead and gone can come back to life. He wonders how a dead universe can become a live universe.

The reply to this question can be found in the structure of our present world itself. What is the present world? It is nothing but a change from one condition to another. What we call a 'live' existence is in fact the result of a change, a metamorphosis of a non-living existence. An analysis of the human body shows that it is composed of iron, carbon, calcium, salts, water, gases, etc. ▶

⁸ There are some who dispute about God without having any knowledge or guidance, or any enlightening Book. ⁹ They turn away arrogantly, leading people astray from God's path. Such men shall incur disgrace in this life and taste the punishment of the Fire on the Day of Judgement. ¹⁰ [God will say], 'This is the reward of your misdeeds. God is not unjust to His servants.' ᵃ

وَمِنَ ٱلنَّاسِ مَن يُجَـٰدِلُ فِي ٱللَّهِ بِغَيْرِ عِلْمٍ وَلَا هُدًى وَلَا كِتَـٰبٍ مُّنِيرٍ ۝ ثَانِيَ عِطْفِهِۦ لِيُضِلَّ عَن سَبِيلِ ٱللَّهِ لَهُۥ فِي ٱلدُّنْيَا خِزْيٌ وَنُذِيقُهُۥ يَوْمَ ٱلْقِيَـٰمَةِ عَذَابَ ٱلْحَرِيقِ ۝ ذَٰلِكَ بِمَا قَدَّمَتْ يَدَاكَ وَأَنَّ ٱللَّهَ لَيْسَ بِظَلَّـٰمٍ لِّلْعَبِيدِ ۝

These compounds which comprise the human body are all lifeless. But these inanimate soul-less things convert into animate objects having souls and start moving about in the shape of human beings. In the case of human beings, therefore, when non-living things have initially taken the shape of living things, the assertion that, once again, non-living things will change into living things, is not at all surprising.

Similarly, if one looks at the green vegetation growing on the earth, it will be seen that it is formed from a number of constituents found in the soil. All these constituents are initially devoid of the qualities found in vegetation. Yet this type of transformation takes place every day before our eyes. Then why should we have doubts about the recurrence of such a feasible event?

The fact is that the coming into existence of the first world in itself proves the feasibility of the coming into existence of the second world. After experiencing one world, the understanding of a second world, rationally and logically, is not at all difficult.

ᵃ The Arabs had adopted polytheism in the erroneous belief that it was the Truth. When the Prophet's call for belief in there being only the one God started shaking the faith of the idolators, those chiefs who had built their supremacy on the foundation of idolatory were perturbed, as they smelt danger. For the common man, the discarding of idolatory means only giving up the religion of his forefathers, while for a chief the destruction of idolatory amounts to the destruction of his supremacy. Therefore, in every age, the call for an uncorrupted faith is vehemently opposed by those who had built up and maintained their leadership on the strength of adulterated religion.

Such people indulge in unnecessary arguments against the call to Truth and the giver of that call. They make all-out efforts to see that the people under their influence become suspicious of such a call, so that they will remain within the fold of their traditional religions as a matter of course. ▶

¹¹ There are some who worship God half-heartedly, then, if some good befalls them, they are content with it, but if an ordeal befalls them, they revert to their former ways. They lose in this world as well in the Hereafter. That is a clear loss.ᵃ

وَمِنَ ٱلنَّاسِ مَن يَعۡبُدُ ٱللَّهَ عَلَىٰ حَرۡفٍ ۖ فَإِنۡ أَصَابَهُۥ خَيۡرٌ ٱطۡمَأَنَّ بِهِۦ ۖ وَإِنۡ أَصَابَتۡهُ فِتۡنَةٌ ٱنقَلَبَ عَلَىٰ وَجۡهِهِۦ خَسِرَ ٱلدُّنۡيَا وَٱلۡءَاخِرَةَ ۚ ذَٰلِكَ هُوَ ٱلۡخُسۡرَانُ ٱلۡمُبِينُ ۝

They thus oppose the Truth in order to maintain the false prestige and the supremacy which they had established on the basis of their self-made religion. They are more interested in themselves than in the Truth. Such people are the worst culprits in the eyes of God. On the Day of Judgement, nothing short of disgrace, humiliation and punishment will be their unmitigated fate.

ᵃ One who discovers Faith as the whole Truth, finds his heart and mind fully enveloped by his faith. He then surrenders himself to faith without any mental reservation. In his eyes, all other things assume a secondary place. Such an individual is a true believer in the eyes of God.

There are others whose acceptance of faith is purely on the surface. Such people are interested only in their own personal gain. Under some superficial influence, they may attach themselves to faith, but this attachment lasts only so long as they do not suffer any loss due to this attachment, and their interests are not affected. The moment they feel that their interests and the True Faith cannot go together, they revert to their personal interest and discard faith.

People of this second type are known as hypocrites. A hypocrite fails to succeed in the Hereafter as well as in this world, the reason being that he lacks the whole-hearted devotion which is a prerequisite for success either in this world or the life Hereafter. While a hypocrite is always deprived of this quality of the heart because of his dual orientation, he neither concentrates fully on the Hereafter nor on this world. Thus he is unable to pay the necessary price for either of the two. Such people become symbols of deprivation, both in this world and the Hereafter.

¹²He calls on, instead of God, something that can neither harm him, nor benefit him. That is indeed straying far away—¹³he calls on that which would sooner harm than help. Such a patron is indeed evil and such a companion is indeed evil. ¹⁴God will admit those who believe and act righteously into Gardens watered by flowing rivers. God does whatever He wills.ᵃ

يَدْعُواْ مِن دُونِ ٱللَّهِ مَا لَا يَضُرُّهُۥ وَمَا لَا يَنفَعُهُۥ ذَٰلِكَ هُوَ ٱلضَّلَـٰلُ ٱلْبَعِيدُ ۝ يَدْعُواْ لَمَن ضَرُّهُۥٓ أَقْرَبُ مِن نَّفْعِهِۦ لَبِئْسَ ٱلْمَوْلَىٰ وَلَبِئْسَ ٱلْعَشِيرُ ۝ إِنَّ ٱللَّهَ يُدْخِلُ ٱلَّذِينَ ءَامَنُواْ وَعَمِلُواْ ٱلصَّـٰلِحَـٰتِ جَنَّـٰتٍ تَجْرِى مِن تَحْتِهَا ٱلْأَنْهَـٰرُ إِنَّ ٱللَّهَ يَفْعَلُ مَا يُرِيدُ ۝

ᵃ Whenever a man, unmindful of God, strays from His right path or ignores it, the reason is that he has placed his entire reliance on something other than God. This could be either an idol or some other such object or being.

But, in this world, there is nobody who has any powers except the one and only God. Therefore, if a man relies on something other than God, he in fact parts from a powerful Being to seek the support of some imaginary thing which has no reality as a power. What action can be more wrong than this?

Moreover, one's association with God is not a simple matter. It is in fact an acceptance of reality. It is a right of God over man. Therefore, when a man leaves God and diverts his attention towards imaginary things, he is to be harmed by his own action. As far as any benefit is concerned, it can never be received from any object other than the one true God.

Those who seek the support of things other than God apparently consider those things to be on a higher plane than themselves, as they would not otherwise have had recourse to them. But the fact is that those whose support is sought and those who seek such support are equally helpless and powerless.

In such a world, the pure in thought, treading the God-favoured path with eyes fixed on the Hereafter, can distinguish God from a host of false gods. They are the most precious souls on this earth. God will show His appreciation for them by settling them in the perfect world of paradise, where they will experience eternal bliss.

¹⁵ Anyone who thinks that God will not help him [His messenger] in this world and the Hereafter, let him stretch a rope up to the sky; then let him cut it off and see if his plan can help to remove the cause of his anger. ¹⁶ We have sent down the Quran as clear evidence, and surely God guides whom He will.ᵃ

مَن كَانَ يَظُنُّ أَن لَّن يَنصُرَهُ ٱللَّهُ فِي ٱلدُّنْيَا وَٱلْأَخِرَةِ فَلْيَمْدُدْ بِسَبَبٍ إِلَى ٱلسَّمَآءِ ثُمَّ لْيَقْطَعْ فَلْيَنظُرْ هَلْ يُذْهِبَنَّ كَيْدُهُ مَا يَغِيظُ ۞ وَكَذَٰلِكَ أَنزَلْنَٰهُ ءَايَٰتٍ بَيِّنَٰتٍ وَأَنَّ ٱللَّهَ يَهْدِى مَن يُرِيدُ ۞

───────────────────────────────

ᵃ When the Prophet Muhammad called upon the people to the Truth, those who had built their castles on untruth became his enemies. Opposition went on growing until a stage was reached when it appeared that the flag-bearers of Untruth would overcome the flag-bearers of Truth. Under these critical circumstances, certain Muslims questioned why, if the truth were on their side, God was not helping them and why He remained neutral in the struggle between the Truth and Untruth.

God says that He always supports the Truth. But it is not the way of God to intervene immediately. He waits until matters reach the stage when one side's being on the right path and the other side's being on the wrong path are clearly established. When this stage has been reached, God intervenes without further delay and settles the issue.

This is the way of God. It is necessary for human beings to become reconciled to this, because no other course is possible in this universe. Any way other than this is the way of death and not of life.

¹⁷ God will judge between the believers, the Jews, the Sabaeans, the Christians, the Magians and the polytheists on the Day of Judgement. Surely God is witness to everything.ᵃ

إِنَّ ٱلَّذِينَ ءَامَنُوا۟ وَٱلَّذِينَ هَادُوا۟ وَٱلصَّٰبِـِٔينَ وَٱلنَّصَٰرَىٰ وَٱلْمَجُوسَ وَٱلَّذِينَ أَشْرَكُوٓا۟ إِنَّ ٱللَّهَ يَفْصِلُ بَيْنَهُمْ يَوْمَ ٱلْقِيَٰمَةِ ۚ إِنَّ ٱللَّهَ عَلَىٰ كُلِّ شَىْءٍ شَهِيدٌ ۝

ᵃ In this verse six religious groups or communities have been mentioned— Muslims, Jews, Sabaeans, Christians, Zoroastrians and polytheists (pagans of Makkah). The Jews owed allegiance to Moses. Similarly, the Sabaeans owed allegiance to John (Yahya), the Christians to Jesus, the Zoroastrians to Zoroaster and the polytheists of Makkah to Abraham.

All these communities were initially believers in and worshippers of the one God. But, later on, they distorted their religion. Now they continue to practice this distorted form. The Muslims are not immune to this. They could also in effect err in the same way. The Book of Muslims is unaltered and preserved in every detail, yet in this world of trial, Muslims' hands are not tied: they are not precluded from putting their own self-made interpretations on the Quran and the traditions of the Prophet Muhammad. They can form a self-styled religion, then by adopting that religion, they presumed to be following God's true religion.

God's original and true religion is only one, but on account of personal interpretations, it comes to have different versions. If people were to adhere to the original religion, unity and solidarity would flourish among them. But, with people following their self-made religion, religious differences crop up among them and these differences go on endlessly multiplying. But God is fully aware of everybody's circumstances, and He will make it clear on Judgement Day as to who was on the right path and who was on the wrong one.

¹⁸ Do you not see that whoever is in the heavens and whoever is on the earth, as well as the sun and the moon, and the stars and the mountains, and the trees and the beasts and many human beings—all submit to God? But there are many who have become deserving of punishment. Whoever God disgraces, will have no one to honour him. Surely, God does what He wills.ᵃ

أَلَمۡ تَرَ أَنَّ ٱللَّهَ يَسۡجُدُ لَهُۥ مَن فِى ٱلسَّمَـٰوَٰتِ وَمَن فِى ٱلۡأَرۡضِ وَٱلشَّمۡسُ وَٱلۡقَمَرُ وَٱلنُّجُومُ وَٱلۡجِبَالُ وَٱلشَّجَرُ وَٱلدَّوَآبُّ وَكَثِيرٌ مِّنَ ٱلنَّاسِ ۖ وَكَثِيرٌ حَقَّ عَلَيۡهِ ٱلۡعَذَابُ ۗ وَمَن يُهِنِ ٱللَّهُ فَمَا لَهُۥ مِن مُّكۡرِمٍ ۚ إِنَّ ٱللَّهَ يَفۡعَلُ مَا يَشَآءُ

ᵃ Just as there is a Law of God for human beings, so also is there a law for the rest of the universe. As far as the rest of the universe is concerned, it follows God's law strictly and without any deviations. It follows divine laws unitedly and with perfect harmony. It is only man who creates differences; by adopting self-made interpretations of these laws, he deviates from the straight path.

In the eyes of God, the worst culprits are those who create discord on the basis of religion; who want to live with conflicts in a universe which is free of conflicts. In a world where the lesson of harmony is being demonstrated everywhere on an extremely large scale, such people concern themselves with fomenting discord and disharmony.

God's universe is a demonstration of God's will. Those who go against this practical example set by the universe created by God, prove themselves to be deserving of God's punishment in this world itself. On the Day of Judgement the aforesaid verdict, which is being pronounced in practice at every moment against the culprits in this world of today, will require only verbal ratification.

¹⁹ These two groups, [the believers and those who deny the truth], dispute concerning their Lord. Those who deny the truth will have garments of fire cut out for them; and boiling water will be poured down over their heads, ²⁰ anything in their stomachs as well as their skins will be melted by it. ²¹ There will be maces of iron for them; ²² whenever, in their anguish they seek to escape from Hell, they will be driven back into it, and they will be told, 'Taste the punishment of Hell.'^a

۞ هَـٰذَانِ خَصۡمَانِ ٱخۡتَصَمُواْ فِى رَبِّهِمۡ‌ۖ فَٱلَّذِينَ كَفَرُواْ قُطِّعَتۡ لَهُمۡ ثِيَابٌ مِّن نَّارٍ يُصَبُّ مِن فَوۡقِ رُءُوسِهِمُ ٱلۡحَمِيمُ ﴿١٩﴾ يُصۡهَرُ بِهِۦ مَا فِى بُطُونِهِمۡ وَٱلۡجُلُودُ ﴿٢٠﴾ وَلَهُم مَّقَـٰمِعُ مِنۡ حَدِيدٍ ﴿٢١﴾ كُلَّمَآ أَرَادُوٓاْ أَن يَخۡرُجُواْ مِنۡهَا مِنۡ غَمٍّ أُعِيدُواْ فِيهَا وَذُوقُواْ عَذَابَ ٱلۡحَرِيقِ ﴿٢٢﴾

---

^a Broadly speaking, all groups fall into only two categories, namely, the upholders of Truth and their opponents. In the present world, those who quarrel with the proponents of the Truth erroneously imagine that they have innumerable arguments in their favour. It is their lack of seriousness which makes them enter into meaningless discussions, as if they had convincing arguments. Since they do not want to admit the Truth, they pick false and senseless quarrels with it. In the Hereafter, such people will be punished severely for their rejection of the Truth; and from this punishment they will never have any respite.

²³ God will admit those who believe and do good deeds to Gardens watered by flowing rivers; there they will be given bracelets of gold and pearls to wear and their clothing will be of silk. ²⁴ For they were guided to purity of speech. And they were guided to the path of the Glorious Lord.ᵃ

إِنَّ ٱللَّهَ يُدْخِلُ ٱلَّذِينَ ءَامَنُواْ وَعَمِلُواْ ٱلصَّٰلِحَٰتِ جَنَّٰتٍ تَجْرِى مِن تَحْتِهَا ٱلْأَنْهَٰرُ يُحَلَّوْنَ فِيهَا مِنْ أَسَاوِرَ مِن ذَهَبٍ وَلُؤْلُؤًا وَلِبَاسُهُمْ فِيهَا حَرِيرٌ ۝ وَهُدُوٓاْ إِلَى ٱلطَّيِّبِ مِنَ ٱلْقَوْلِ وَهُدُوٓاْ إِلَىٰ صِرَٰطِ ٱلْحَمِيدِ ۝

ᵃ In this world where the net of deceptive words is spread out everywhere and where people far away from Truth enjoy the position of dominance, it is undoubtedly the most difficult task to discover and recognise the truth of Faith; and it is even more difficult in practice to put oneself on the path of this faith.

Those who have been endowed with the ability to recognise and sift the noblest of words from the medley of senseless sounds, are the ones who will seek out the right path from a labyrinth of different paths. Those who show such great ability in this world are the cream of humanity. They deserve to be given an abode in the eternal gardens of paradise.

²⁵ As for those who deny the truth and debar others from God's path and from the Sacred Mosque which We set up for all people, natives and strangers alike, and all who seek to profane it by evil-doing—We shall make them taste a painful punishment.ᵃ

إِنَّ ٱلَّذِينَ كَفَرُواْ وَيَصُدُّونَ عَن سَبِيلِ ٱللَّهِ وَٱلْمَسْجِدِ ٱلْحَرَامِ ٱلَّذِى جَعَلْنَهُ لِلنَّاسِ سَوَآءً ٱلْعَٰكِفُ فِيهِ وَٱلْبَادِ وَمَن يُرِدْ فِيهِ بِإِلْحَادٍ بِظُلْمٍ نُّذِقْهُ مِنْ عَذَابٍ أَلِيمٍ ۝

ᵃ One instance of the denial of Truth is illustrated by an incident which occurred in ancient Makkah. The people of Makkah, intolerant of even the most peaceful activities of the Prophet Muhammad, imposed many restrictions on him. He and his companions became the target for atrocities, and were even prevented from entering the Ka'bah.

Such behaviour on the part of the Makkans, on top of their denial of the Truth, amounted to adding insult to injury. Those who indulge in this kind of sinful behaviour deserve the severest punishment from God.

²⁶ We assigned to Abraham the site of the House, saying, 'Do not associate with Me anything and purify My House for those who circumambulate [the Kabah] and those who stand upright, and those who bow and prostrate themselves.'ᵃ

وَإِذْ بَوَّأْنَا لِإِبْرَٰهِيمَ مَكَانَ ٱلْبَيْتِ أَن لَّا تُشْرِكْ بِى شَيْـًٔا وَطَهِّرْ بَيْتِىَ لِلطَّآئِفِينَ وَٱلْقَآئِمِينَ وَٱلرُّكَّعِ ٱلسُّجُودِ ۝

ᵃ The history of Abraham dates back four thousand years. During the period in which he lived polytheism was prevalent throughout the known and inhabited world, and had thus come to be a permanent feature of life, continuing from one generation to the next, without any break. Ultimately, the stage was reached when no new born child could learn anything other than polytheism from its surroundings.

Abraham was born in Iraq. God commanded him to leave the populated areas of Iraq, Syria and Egypt and go to the uninhabited area of Hijaz and settle his progeny in Arabia. The idea behind settling in a desert area was that here, in an isolated place, a new generation could be brought up, cut off from the influence of polytheism prevalent in the inhabited world of the time. In accordance with this plan of God, Abraham settled his progeny in a place known at present as Makkah, but which was totally unpopulated in those days. At that time, Abraham built a mosque (the Kabah) which was to be the centre of worship for the one God by the new generation, and finally by the whole world.

²⁷ Call mankind to the Pilgrimage. They will come to you, on foot, and on every kind of lean camel, by every distant track ²⁸ so that they may witness its benefit for them and, on the appointed days may utter the name of God over the cattle He has provided for them. Then eat their flesh, and feed the distressed and the needy—²⁹ then let the pilgrims purify themselves and fulfil their vows and perform the circumambulation of the Ancient House.ᵃ

وَأَذِّن فِى ٱلنَّاسِ بِٱلْحَجِّ يَأْتُوكَ رِجَالاً وَعَلَىٰ كُلِّ ضَامِرٍ يَأْتِينَ مِن كُلِّ فَجٍّ عَمِيقٍ ۝ لِّيَشْهَدُواْ مَنَٰفِعَ لَهُمْ وَيَذْكُرُواْ ٱسْمَ ٱللَّهِ فِىٓ أَيَّامٍ مَّعْلُومَٰتٍ عَلَىٰ مَا رَزَقَهُم مِّنۢ بَهِيمَةِ ٱلْأَنْعَٰمِ فَكُلُواْ مِنْهَا وَأَطْعِمُواْ ٱلْبَآئِسَ ٱلْفَقِيرَ ۝ ثُمَّ لْيَقْضُواْ تَفَثَهُمْ وَلْيُوفُواْ نُذُورَهُمْ وَلْيَطَّوَّفُواْ بِٱلْبَيْتِ ٱلْعَتِيقِ ۝

ᵃ The initial purpose in the constructing of the Kabah was to provide a centre of worship for those who were at 'walking' distance from that place. But, ultimately, it was to become a centre of worship of the one God for the whole world. And this purpose was fully achieved. The rites and customs which a pilgrim is required to perform after reaching here have been briefly described in the Quran, while full details are given in the traditions (Hadith) of the Prophet Muhammad.

'They may witness its benefits for them' means that they may actually see here the benefits of belief in a practical sense which they had so far been aware of solely as matters of faith.

Great historical importance is attached to the places a pilgrim visits during Hajj. Quite naturally, visiting these places and seeing them melts one's heart. Muslims of the whole world gather there, making the great international stature of Islam a visible reality. The annual gathering of Hajj promotes collectivism on a universal scale in Islam, and even the journey entailed affords the pilgrim many worldly and religious experiences which are helpful in the formation of his future life.

30 Such is God's commandment. Whoever honours that which is declared sacred by God may be sure that it counts for good in the sight of his Lord. Livestock is lawful for you, except that which has already been explicitly forbidden. Then shun the abomination of the deities and shun all falsehood.[a]

ذَٰلِكَ وَمَن يُعَظِّمْ حُرُمَٰتِ ٱللَّهِ فَهُوَ خَيْرٌ لَّهُۥ عِندَ رَبِّهِۦ ۗ وَأُحِلَّتْ لَكُمُ ٱلْأَنْعَٰمُ إِلَّا مَا يُتْلَىٰ عَلَيْكُمْ فَٱجْتَنِبُوا۟ ٱلرِّجْسَ مِنَ ٱلْأَوْثَٰنِ وَٱجْتَنِبُوا۟ قَوْلَ ٱلزُّورِ ۝

---

[a] What is permitted (halal) and what is prohibited (haram); what is sacred and what is not; which way of worship are proper and which improper—all these matters have been made absolutely clear by God through His prophets. Any changes in these matters are not permissible. Any change made in these things is highly wrong, in the eyes of God. Therefore, it is necessary for man to follow the Prophet's instructions. He should in no case increase or decrease what is prescribed by the Prophet.

These are matters the reality of which is known only to God. When a man on his own says something on this subject, he virtually claims, in effect, to have knowledge about things of which he has no knowledge. Obviously, what wrong can be greater than this.

³¹ Devote yourselves to God, not associating any partners with Him. Whoever associates anything with God is like one who falls from heaven and is snatched by the birds or carried away by the wind to a distant place.ᵃ

حُنَفَآءَ لِلَّهِ غَيْرَ مُشْرِكِينَ بِهِۦ وَمَن يُشْرِكْ بِٱللَّهِ فَكَأَنَّمَا خَرَّ مِنَ ٱلسَّمَآءِ فَتَخْطَفُهُ ٱلطَّيْرُ أَوْ تَهْوِى بِهِ ٱلرِّيحُ فِى مَكَانٍ سَحِيقٍ ۝

ᵃ The central force in this universe is only one, and it is the Being of the one God. One who attaches himself to God has, as it were, found his real abode. He stands on firm ground. Unlike him is one who does not attach himself to God or who only outwardly accepts God, but in his heart of hearts is attached to someone else. Such a person is in effect cut off from that centre, apart from which there is no other centre in the universe. The condition of this individual will be like that described in this verse.

³² Thus it is. He who honours the symbols set up by God shows the piety of his heart. ³³ You may benefit from the animals for an appointed time. Then they must be sacrificed at the Ancient House.ᵃ

ذَٰلِكَ وَمَن يُعَظِّمْ شَعَـٰٓئِرَ ٱللَّهِ فَإِنَّهَا مِن تَقْوَى ٱلْقُلُوبِ ۝ لَكُمْ فِيهَا مَنَـٰفِعُ إِلَىٰٓ أَجَلٍ مُّسَمًّى ثُمَّ مَحِلُّهَآ إِلَى ٱلْبَيْتِ ٱلْعَتِيقِ ۝

ᵃ The rites of worship or prayer in Islam have two aspects—the outward and the inward. The inward aspect is the real essence of worship. The outward aspect serves as a symbol (*sha'irah*, pl. *sha'a'ir*) of this inward aspect. The rites specified by God cannot be treated as being carried out properly if they are simply observed outwardly. In order to be properly observed, these deserve to be performed with a pure and God-fearing heart.

Animals specified for sacrifice are among God's symbols. They are the symbols of realities and not the realities themselves. In order to please God, it is not enough to colour these animals, or to abstain from riding them or utilizing them in any manner. God's pleasure lies in whatever is done being done purely for His sake. What God appreciates is the innermost feelings of the heart and not merely external trappings.

³⁴ For every people We have appointed rites of sacrifice, so that they may pronounce the name of God over the cattle which He has provided for them. Your God is One God; surrender yourselves to Him; and give good news to the humble ³⁵ whose hearts are filled with awe at the mention of God; who endure adversity with fortitude, say their prayers regularly and spend out of what We have given them.ᵃ

وَلِكُلِّ أُمَّةٍ جَعَلْنَا مَنسَكًا لِّيَذْكُرُواْ ٱسْمَ ٱللَّهِ عَلَىٰ مَا رَزَقَهُم مِّنۢ بَهِيمَةِ ٱلْأَنْعَٰمِ ۗ فَإِلَٰهُكُمْ إِلَٰهٌ وَٰحِدٌ فَلَهُۥٓ أَسْلِمُواْ ۗ وَبَشِّرِ ٱلْمُخْبِتِينَ ﴿٣٤﴾ ٱلَّذِينَ إِذَا ذُكِرَ ٱللَّهُ وَجِلَتْ قُلُوبُهُمْ وَٱلصَّٰبِرِينَ عَلَىٰ مَآ أَصَابَهُمْ وَٱلْمُقِيمِى ٱلصَّلَوٰةِ وَمِمَّا رَزَقْنَٰهُمْ يُنفِقُونَ ﴿٣٥﴾

ᵃ Whatever products a man avails of in this world—be they agricultural products, animal products or industrial products—they develop in him one of two different types of mentality. With one he either thinks that all the material things he possesses are the result of his talents and hard work, or he attributes their availability to the blessings of certain pagan gods. This mentality is entirely polytheistic.

With the other way of thinking, whatever a man receives is considered the gift of God. Charity and sacrifice are the prescribed methods of the external expression of these feelings. The individual offers a part of his earnings for the sake of God, and in this way, he admits that whatever he possesses is the gift of God and not the result of his talents.

If a man acquires knowledge of God (ma'rifah) in the true sense, the condition of his heart will be the same as is described as 'the humble' (al-mukhbitin) verse 34. Such a man will, with his body and soul, turn towards God. He will be overwhelmed with feelings of humility and modesty. He will tremble at the thought of God. He will start considering everything he has as belonging to God and not to himself.

³⁶ We have appointed for you the sacrificial camels as one of the symbols set up by God, in which there is much good for you. So invoke God's name over them as you line them up for slaughter, and when they have fallen down dead, feed yourselves and feed the needy—those who do not ask as well as those who do. We have thus subjected them to you so that you may be grateful. ³⁷ Their flesh and blood do not reach God: it is your piety that reaches Him. Thus God has subjected them to you, so that you may glorify Him for the guidance He has given you. Give glad tidings to those who do good.^a

وَٱلْبُدْنَ جَعَلْنَٰهَا لَكُم مِّن شَعَٰٓئِرِ ٱللَّهِ لَكُمْ فِيهَا خَيْرٌ فَٱذْكُرُواْ ٱسْمَ ٱللَّهِ عَلَيْهَا صَوَآفَّ فَإِذَا وَجَبَتْ جُنُوبُهَا فَكُلُواْ مِنْهَا وَأَطْعِمُواْ ٱلْقَانِعَ وَٱلْمُعْتَرَّ كَذَٰلِكَ سَخَّرْنَٰهَا لَكُمْ لَعَلَّكُمْ تَشْكُرُونَ ﴿٣٦﴾ لَن يَنَالَ ٱللَّهَ لُحُومُهَا وَلَا دِمَآؤُهَا وَلَٰكِن يَنَالُهُ ٱلتَّقْوَىٰ مِنكُمْ كَذَٰلِكَ سَخَّرَهَا لَكُمْ لِتُكَبِّرُواْ ٱللَّهَ عَلَىٰ مَا هَدَىٰكُمْ وَبَشِّرِ ٱلْمُحْسِنِينَ ﴿٣٧﴾

---

^a Had there been no animals like camels or cattle in this world and had there been only wild beasts like tigers, bears and wolves, man would have found it very difficult to put them to use, and it would have been absolutely impossible to offer them up for ritual sacrifice on a general scale. It is a great blessing of Almighty God that He created not only wild beasts but also some animals who, by their very nature, have the tendency to surrender themselves to human beings, this surrender takes its ultimate form when man can slaughter them for food and sacrifice.

The rites of sacrifice have been prescribed, not because God needs meat and blood, but purely as symbolic actions. The sacrifice of an animal is symbolic of the man who has sacrificed himself for the sake of God. This is, in fact, the sacrifice of one's own self which takes the shape of the sacrifice of an animal. Such people are fortunate for whom the sacrifice of animals becomes synonymous with the sacrifice of their own selves.

³⁸ God will surely defend the believers. God does not love the perfidious and the ungrateful. ³⁹ Permission to fight is granted to those who are attacked, because they have been wronged—God indeed has the power to help them— ⁴⁰ they are those who have been driven out of their homes unjustly, only because they said, 'Our Lord is God.' If God did not repel the aggression of some people by means of others, cloisters and churches and synagogues and mosques, wherein the name of God is much invoked, would surely be destroyed. God will surely help him who helps His cause—God is indeed powerful and mighty.^a

﴿ إِنَّ ٱللَّهَ يُدَٰفِعُ عَنِ ٱلَّذِينَ ءَامَنُوٓاْ

إِنَّ ٱللَّهَ لَا يُحِبُّ كُلَّ خَوَّانٍ كَفُورٍ ۝

أُذِنَ لِلَّذِينَ يُقَٰتَلُونَ بِأَنَّهُمْ ظُلِمُواْ

وَإِنَّ ٱللَّهَ عَلَىٰ نَصْرِهِمْ لَقَدِيرٌ ۝

ٱلَّذِينَ أُخْرِجُواْ مِن دِيَٰرِهِم بِغَيْرِ حَقٍّ

إِلَّآ أَن يَقُولُواْ رَبُّنَا ٱللَّهُ وَلَوْلَا دَفْعُ

ٱللَّهِ ٱلنَّاسَ بَعْضَهُم بِبَعْضٍ هُّدِّمَتْ

صَوَٰمِعُ وَبِيَعٌ وَصَلَوَٰتٌ وَمَسَٰجِدُ

يُذْكَرُ فِيهَا ٱسْمُ ٱللَّهِ كَثِيرًا

وَلَيَنصُرَنَّ ٱللَّهُ مَن يَنصُرُهُۥٓ إِنَّ

ٱللَّهَ لَقَوِيٌّ عَزِيزٌ ۝

---

^a When servants of God opt for the path of God, they are not alone in this world. When heedless, arrogant people make them the target of their persecution, God takes the side of the devotees against the persecutors. Initially God tests the sincerity of his proponents. But then He comes to the help of those who, having undergone this test have proved their sincerity. He creates such circumstances for them as may help them to overcome all kinds of hurdles and continue to adhere to the Truth.

The real task of the believers is solely to keep calling people to the truth. Once launched on this course, they remain steadfastly upon it. They sometimes wage war, if necessary, but their war is always defensive, never aggressive.

If a group remains in power for a long time, it becomes arrogant and boastful. Therefore, God has devised the law of 'repelling' for this world. He manages again and again, to dislodge one group from power through another group. Thus the political balance of power has remained steady throughout history. If God did not resort to this method, then human high-handedness would grow to such an extent that even sacred institutions like places of worship would not remain safe from the depredations of the wicked.

41 [They are] those who, if We established them in the land, would say their prayers regularly and pay the *zakat* and enjoin good and forbid evil. The final outcome of all affairs rests with God.[a]

ٱلَّذِينَ إِن مَّكَّنَّٰهُمْ فِى ٱلْأَرْضِ أَقَامُواْ ٱلصَّلَوٰةَ وَءَاتَوُاْ ٱلزَّكَوٰةَ وَأَمَرُواْ بِٱلْمَعْرُوفِ وَنَهَوْاْ عَنِ ٱلْمُنكَرِ ۗ وَلِلَّهِ عَٰقِبَةُ ٱلْأُمُورِ ۝

---

[a] The special condition for a man to be entitled to God's help is that he should not become corrupt, even if he comes to possess power. The elevation of his status should result in an increase in his modesty and humility. Those who are righteous in this manner before acquiring power are the ones who can prove to be righteous in the conditions prevailing after their acquiring power.

Such are those who, when given power, show humility before God, and fulfil and discharge the rights of their fellow human beings. In the affairs of life, they do whatever pleases God and refrain from doing whatever displeases Him.

 ⁴² If your opponents deny you, remember that, before them, the people of Noah and the tribes of ʿAd and Thamud denied their messengers likewise. ⁴³ So did the people of Abraham and the people of Lot, ⁴⁴ and the inhabitants of Midian also charged their prophets with falsehood. Moses was also rejected. I gave respite to those who denied the truth, but then I seized them. Consider then, how terrible My repudiation of them was.^a

وَإِن يُكَذِّبُوكَ فَقَدْ كَذَّبَتْ قَبْلَهُمْ قَوْمُ نُوحٍ وَعَادٌ وَثَمُودُ ۞ وَقَوْمُ إِبْرَٰهِيمَ وَقَوْمُ لُوطٍ ۞ وَأَصْحَٰبُ مَدْيَنَ ۖ وَكُذِّبَ مُوسَىٰ فَأَمْلَيْتُ لِلْكَٰفِرِينَ ثُمَّ أَخَذْتُهُمْ ۖ فَكَيْفَ كَانَ نَكِيرِ ۞

^a The people who denied Abraham and Moses were their contemporaries and not those living when this verse was revealed: by the time the Quran was revealed, all the people professed to be followers of these prophets.

The same thing happened in the case of all the other prophets. The people of their age disbelieved them, and it was the successors of these very people who elevated them to the status of greatness and holiness. The reason for this is that, in his own times, a prophet is simply a call-giver without the trappings of greatness, but in later ages, a history of greatness gathers round his name. The people of every age have proved that they are not capable of recognising a prophet,—a lonely herald of Truth. They can recognise a prophet only when greatness already attaches to his name. The Prophet Muhammad brought the same message as was brought by Prophet Abraham and Moses. But the people of his age, who were proud of being associated with Abraham and Moses, refused to accept him.

This shows which people are in reality believers in a prophet. The real believers in a prophet are those who recognise the 'call-giving' prophet while he is still at the stage of having no signs of greatness attached to him. Those who recognise him only when he has achieved greatness are simply believers in history and not real believers in the Prophet of God.

45 How many a town We destroyed which was given to wrongdoing, so that its roofs fell down, and how many a well is deserted and how many a lofty castle is in ruins. 46 Have these people not travelled through the land to make their hearts understand and let their ears hear; the truth is that it is not the eyes that are blind but the hearts that are in the bosoms that are blinded.*

فَكَأَيِّن مِّن قَرْيَةٍ أَهْلَكْنَٰهَا وَهِىَ ظَالِمَةٌ فَهِىَ خَاوِيَةٌ عَلَىٰ عُرُوشِهَا وَبِئْرٍ مُّعَطَّلَةٍ وَقَصْرٍ مَّشِيدٍ ۝ أَفَلَمْ يَسِيرُوا۟ فِى ٱلْأَرْضِ فَتَكُونَ لَهُمْ قُلُوبٌ يَعْقِلُونَ بِهَآ أَوْ ءَاذَانٌ يَسْمَعُونَ بِهَا ۖ فَإِنَّهَا لَا تَعْمَى ٱلْأَبْصَٰرُ وَلَٰكِن تَعْمَى ٱلْقُلُوبُ ٱلَّتِى فِى ٱلصُّدُورِ ۝

---

a Before God, people with eyes are those who look at things in order to learn a lesson or draw wisdom from them. Those who see things without learning a lesson from them, are blind in the eyes of God. Their seeing is like that of animals, not human beings.

God has spread on the earth innumerable lesson-giving things. Among them are the ancient memorials left behind by past nations. These nations once enjoyed pomp and power, but the signs of their existence today are nothing but a few dilapidated ruins.

This reminds everybody of the fate he is finally going to meet. But when people lose the mind's eye, the eyes on the face will fail to show them anything meaningful.

⁴⁷ They ask you to hasten the punishment; God will never go back on His promise. A Day with your Lord is like a thousand years in your reckoning. ⁴⁸ To how many a town We gave respite while it was given to wrongdoing. Then I seized it. To Me all things shall return.ᵃ

وَيَسْتَعْجِلُونَكَ بِٱلْعَذَابِ وَلَن يُخْلِفَ ٱللَّهُ وَعْدَهُۥ ۚ وَإِنَّ يَوْمًا عِندَ رَبِّكَ كَأَلْفِ سَنَةٍ مِّمَّا تَعُدُّونَ ۝ وَكَأَيِّن مِّن قَرْيَةٍ أَمْلَيْتُ لَهَا وَهِىَ ظَالِمَةٌ ثُمَّ أَخَذْتُهَا وَإِلَىَّ ٱلْمَصِيرُ ۝

ᵃ In this world, if an individual or a community rebels against God, God catches hold of that individual or community. But God does not make haste to do so. Man may lose patience in a day, but God does not become impatient even for a thousand years. God may observe disobedience among people, yet gives them ample opportunity to reform themselves, if they are so inclined. God catches hold of wrongdoers only when they have finally proved that they are guilty and incorrigible.

God treated people in this manner in the past and people of the future will also be treated according to His immutable method.

⁴⁹ Say, 'O people, I am sent only to give you clear warning.' ⁵⁰ Those who believe and do good deeds shall be forgiven and shall receive an honourable provision. ⁵¹ Whereas those who strive against Our signs, seeking to defeat their purpose, shall be the inmates of the Fire.ᵃ

قُل يَٰٓأَيُّهَا ٱلنَّاسُ إِنَّمَآ أَنَا۠ لَكُمۡ نَذِيرٞ مُّبِينٞ ۝ فَٱلَّذِينَ ءَامَنُواْ وَعَمِلُواْ ٱلصَّٰلِحَٰتِ لَهُم مَّغۡفِرَةٞ وَرِزۡقٞ كَرِيمٞ ۝ وَٱلَّذِينَ سَعَوۡاْ فِىٓ ءَايَٰتِنَا مُعَٰجِزِينَ أُوْلَٰٓئِكَ أَصۡحَٰبُ ٱلۡجَحِيمِ ۝

___

ᵃ The real matter is that man is going to enter a world where it is only believers and pious people who will have eternal comfort and not those who arrogantly ignore the Truth.

The real purpose of the Islamic call is to warn people of this coming Day. The sole duty of the giver of the call is to warn people. All other matters relate to God alone, for it is He alone who is at the helm of affairs.

⁵² Whenever We sent any messenger or prophet before you, and he recited anything [of Our revelation], Satan tampered with it. But God abrogates Satan's interjections and then He firmly reaffirms His revelations. God is all knowing and all wise. ⁵³ He makes Satan's suggestions a trial for those whose hearts are diseased or hardened—and, surely, the wrongdoers are far gone in error—⁵⁴ so that those who are given knowledge may realize that this is the truth from your Lord and thus believe in it, and so that in their hearts they may humbly submit to Him. God will surely guide the faithful to a straight path.ᵃ

وَمَآ أَرْسَلْنَا مِن قَبْلِكَ مِن رَّسُولٍ وَلَا نَبِيٍّ إِلَّآ إِذَا تَمَنَّىٰٓ أَلْقَى ٱلشَّيْطَٰنُ فِىٓ أُمْنِيَّتِهِۦ فَيَنسَخُ ٱللَّهُ مَا يُلْقِى ٱلشَّيْطَٰنُ ثُمَّ يُحْكِمُ ٱللَّهُ ءَايَٰتِهِۦ وَٱللَّهُ عَلِيمٌ حَكِيمٌ ۝ لِّيَجْعَلَ مَا يُلْقِى ٱلشَّيْطَٰنُ فِتْنَةً لِّلَّذِينَ فِى قُلُوبِهِم مَّرَضٌ وَٱلْقَاسِيَةِ قُلُوبُهُمْ وَإِنَّ ٱلظَّٰلِمِينَ لَفِى شِقَاقٍ بَعِيدٍ ۝ وَلِيَعْلَمَ ٱلَّذِينَ أُوتُوا۟ ٱلْعِلْمَ أَنَّهُ ٱلْحَقُّ مِن رَّبِّكَ فَيُؤْمِنُوا۟ بِهِۦ فَتُخْبِتَ لَهُۥ قُلُوبُهُمْ وَإِنَّ ٱللَّهَ لَهَادِ ٱلَّذِينَ ءَامَنُوٓا۟ إِلَىٰ صِرَٰطٍ مُّسْتَقِيمٍ ۝

ᵃ It invariably happens that when one proclaims the divine Truth, whether he is a prophet or not, his opponents bring up various types of irrelevant points with a view to casting doubt on the truth of the message.

Such points are always baseless. However, when they are raised, the preacher finds the opportunity to clarify his message and make it more cogent and well-established. This enhances the faith of sincere believers. Thereafter, their bonds with God become still stronger. But for those who are devoid of sincere understanding, these baseless objections become a source of trial for them. They are misled by them and move away from the Truth.

'God will surely guide the faithful to a straight path' means that those who are really sincere in their faith are not affected by false propaganda. They are never misled by the magic of false words. Their faith gives them deep insight into things, so that they are not carried away by outward appearances.

⁵⁵ Those who deny the truth will continue in doubt until the [Last] Hour suddenly comes upon them or the scourge of the woeful Day descends upon them. ⁵⁶ On that Day all control will belong to God. He will judge between them. Those who believe and do good deeds shall enter the Gardens of Bliss, ⁵⁷ but those who deny the truth and deny Our signs will receive a humiliating punishment.ᵃ

وَلَا يَزَالُ ٱلَّذِينَ كَفَرُواْ فِى مِرْيَةٍ مِّنْهُ حَتَّىٰ تَأْتِيَهُمُ ٱلسَّاعَةُ بَغْتَةً أَوْ يَأْتِيَهُمْ عَذَابُ يَوْمٍ عَقِيمٍ ۝ ٱلْمُلْكُ يَوْمَئِذٍ لِّلَّهِ يَحْكُمُ بَيْنَهُمْ فَٱلَّذِينَ ءَامَنُواْ وَعَمِلُواْ ٱلصَّٰلِحَٰتِ فِى جَنَّٰتِ ٱلنَّعِيمِ ۝ وَٱلَّذِينَ كَفَرُواْ وَكَذَّبُواْ بِـَٔايَٰتِنَا فَأُوْلَٰٓئِكَ لَهُمْ عَذَابٌ مُّهِينٌ ۝

ᵃ A prophet's call is marked by the greatness of convincing arguments. But those who are accustomed to seeing only outward greatness, are unable to detect the inner greatness of the prophet and consequently deny it. Such people are always in doubt because they want to see the Truth in external glory. And it is the way of God that He brings Truth in the abstract to people, so that those who recognise Truth may acknowledge it and attach themselves to it and those who are enamoured of outward show may ignore it and prove themselves finally guilty.

Denying the signs means that man ignores the Truth, even when it is supported by sound argument. He is not willing to accept the Truth, even if it is staring him in the face.

⁵⁸ As for those who left their homes for the cause of God and then were slain or died, God will give them a generous provision. Surely God is the Best of Providers. ⁵⁹ He will admit them to a place with which they shall be well-pleased. For God is all knowing and most forbearing.ᵃ

وَٱلَّذِينَ هَاجَرُواْ فِى سَبِيلِ ٱللَّهِ ثُمَّ قُتِلُوٓاْ أَوْ مَاتُواْ لَيَرْزُقَنَّهُمُ ٱللَّهُ رِزْقًا حَسَنًا ۚ وَإِنَّ ٱللَّهَ لَهُوَ خَيْرُ ٱلرَّٰزِقِينَ ۝ لَيُدْخِلَنَّهُم مُّدْخَلًا يَرْضَوْنَهُۥ ۗ وَإِنَّ ٱللَّهَ لَعَلِيمٌ حَلِيمٌ ۝

ᵃ A man who is sincere in his faith, tolerates the sacrifice of anything belonging to him. The one thing he is not prepared to sacrifice is his faith. In pursuing this course, if he is required to leave his home, he leaves it, and if he has to give something, he gives it. He is tied to faith forever until he dies.

Those who prove in the life of this world that they consider their faith to be the most valuable thing, will be highly appreciated by God and they will be given the most valuable thing in the life hereafter. There they will spend an eternal life of comfort and happiness.

⁶⁰ Thus it shall be. As for one who retaliates to the same extent as he has suffered and then is again wronged, God will surely come to his aid. God is merciful and forgiving.ᵃ

* ذَٰلِكَ وَمَنۡ عَاقَبَ بِمِثۡلِ مَا عُوقِبَ بِهِۦ ثُمَّ بُغِيَ عَلَيۡهِ لَيَنصُرَنَّهُ ٱللَّهُ إِنَّ ٱللَّهَ لَعَفُوٌّ غَفُورٌ ۝

ᵃ The people of faith were enjoined to adopt the ways of God who is forgiving and merciful, in that He repeatedly overlooks the excesses of the people and forgives them. Therefore, the respected companions (of the Prophet) were adherents of this divine code of ethics. They were subjected to atrocities, but they tolerated them. Provocative language was used against them, but they overlooked it.

Yet, it happened that when some excess was committed against some Muslims, they gave way to a sudden emotional outburst, and retaliated. Harm was inflicted on them, so they inflicted harm in return. Their opponents, taking advantage of this, started vigorous propaganda against the Muslims. Forgetting their own persecution and, treating trivial actions on the part of the Muslims as an atrocity, they started defaming them.

Such action shows the worst type of meanness. Those who indulge in such meanness are in reality challenging the honour of God. Apparently they are trying to prove a Muslim to be an oppressor: in reality they are themselves the worst oppressors and can bring no harm to the people of faith by their false propaganda. In consequence, they will meet with the severest punishment for their transgression.

⁶¹ That is because God makes the night pass into the day and makes the day pass into the night. God is all hearing and all seeing. ⁶² That is because God is the Truth while anything they invoke besides God is sheer falsehood. God is the Sublime, the Great One.ᵃ

ذَٰلِكَ بِأَنَّ ٱللَّهَ يُولِجُ ٱلَّيْلَ فِى ٱلنَّهَارِ وَيُولِجُ ٱلنَّهَارَ فِى ٱلَّيْلِ وَأَنَّ ٱللَّهَ سَمِيعٌۢ بَصِيرٌ ۝ ذَٰلِكَ بِأَنَّ ٱللَّهَ هُوَ ٱلْحَقُّ وَأَنَّ مَا يَدْعُونَ مِن دُونِهِۦ هُوَ ٱلْبَٰطِلُ وَأَنَّ ٱللَّهَ هُوَ ٱلْعَلِىُّ ٱلْكَبِيرُ ۝

ᵃ The system of this world, in its silent language, goes on teaching us a great lesson. Here, again and again, we see the phenomenon of the darkness of the night coming and enveloping the light of the day. Here, every day, the day dawns and dispels the darkness of the night. By analogy, if a group or community is enjoying pomp and glory, it should not harbour the misunderstanding that its pomp and glory will never come to an end. Similarly, if a group or community is oppressed, it should not think that it will remain oppressed forever.

God who, in the realm of the heavens, causes the light to be plunged into darkness, and who then restores it, can certainly cause similar events to occur in the world of human beings also. There is no power that can prevent Him from doing so.

⁶³ Have you not seen how God sends down water from sky, whereupon the earth becomes green? God is unfathomable, and all aware; ⁶⁴ all that is in the heavens and on the earth belongs to Him. Surely, God is self-sufficient and praiseworthy.ᵃ

أَلَمْ تَرَ أَنَّ ٱللَّهَ أَنزَلَ مِنَ ٱلسَّمَآءِ مَآءً فَتُصْبِحُ ٱلْأَرْضُ مُخْضَرَّةً ۗ إِنَّ ٱللَّهَ لَطِيفٌ خَبِيرٌ ۝ لَّهُۥ مَا فِى ٱلسَّمَـٰوَٰتِ وَمَا فِى ٱلْأَرْضِ ۚ وَإِنَّ ٱللَّهَ لَهُوَ ٱلْغَنِىُّ ٱلْحَمِيدُ ۝

ᵃ When a man builds up his life on the basis of Truth, he comes across different types of difficulties, such as being harassed by others at Satan's instigation. This reduces the worshipper of Truth to a state of abject despair.

But, the universe, in its silent language, declares that there is no question of despair for any of God's subjects. They have only to compare their condition to that of the earth when, due to extreme heat, it loses all its greenery and becomes dry and barren. To all appearances there is no hope of life. Then, as He does every year, God performs His wonderful miracle—He brings the rain—and all is green again.

This is an example of God's power which is made manifest every year at the material level. Can anyone then doubt His efficacy at the human level?

⁶⁵ Do you not see, how God has subjected everything on the earth to you, and the ships that sail on the sea by His command. He holds back the sky from falling down on the earth, except with His permission. God is most compassionate and most merciful to mankind—⁶⁶ it is He who gave you life. Then He will cause you to die. Then He will give you life again. Surely, man is most ungrateful.ᵃ

أَلَمْ تَرَ أَنَّ ٱللَّهَ سَخَّرَ لَكُم مَّا فِى ٱلْأَرْضِ وَٱلْفُلْكَ تَجْرِى فِى ٱلْبَحْرِ بِأَمْرِهِۦ وَيُمْسِكُ ٱلسَّمَآءَ أَن تَقَعَ عَلَى ٱلْأَرْضِ إِلَّا بِإِذْنِهِۦٓ إِنَّ ٱللَّهَ بِٱلنَّاسِ لَرَءُوفٌ رَّحِيمٌ ۝ وَهُوَ ٱلَّذِىٓ أَحْيَاكُمْ ثُمَّ يُمِيتُكُمْ ثُمَّ يُحْيِيكُمْ إِنَّ ٱلْإِنسَٰنَ لَكَفُورٌ ۝

ᵃ All the things of this earth maintain a harmonious balance. If this balance is upset, it will be harmful to us instead of being useful. If a piece of metal is put in water, it will sink immediately. But God has made water subject to certain rules on account of which if iron is given the shape of a boat, it will not sink in water. The numerous spheres floating in space should apparently have fallen down, but according to a set law of nature, they accurately maintain their orbits.

Man has not created himself. God has created him. Then He has maintained him in a world which is full of blessings. But after being given freedom, man has become so rebellious that he does not admit the graciousness of his greatest Benefactor.

⁶⁷ We have appointed for every community ways of worship to observe. Let them not dispute with you on this matter. Call them to the path of your Lord—for surely, you are rightly guided— ⁶⁸ if they should dispute with you, then say, 'God is well aware of what you do.' ⁶⁹ On the Day of Resurrection, God will judge between you regarding your differences. ⁷⁰ Do you not know that God has knowledge of what the heavens and the earth contain? All is recorded in a Book; all this is easy for God.ᵃ

لِكُلِّ أُمَّةٍ جَعَلْنَا مَنسَكًا هُمْ نَاسِكُوهُ فَلَا يُنَزِعُنَّكَ فِى ٱلْأَمْرِ وَٱدْعُ إِلَىٰ رَبِّكَ إِنَّكَ لَعَلَىٰ هُدًى مُّسْتَقِيمٍ ۝ وَإِن جَٰدَلُوكَ فَقُلِ ٱللَّهُ أَعْلَمُ بِمَا تَعْمَلُونَ ۝ ٱللَّهُ يَحْكُمُ بَيْنَكُمْ يَوْمَ ٱلْقِيَٰمَةِ فِيمَا كُنتُمْ فِيهِ تَخْتَلِفُونَ ۝ أَلَمْ تَعْلَمْ أَنَّ ٱللَّهَ يَعْلَمُ مَا فِى ٱلسَّمَآءِ وَٱلْأَرْضِ إِنَّ ذَٰلِكَ فِى كِتَٰبٍ إِنَّ ذَٰلِكَ عَلَى ٱللَّهِ يَسِيرٌ ۝

ᵃ There are two aspects of prayer—one is its spirit, i.e. its true inner aspect, and the other its outward ritual aspect. Inner reality is the true essence of prayer, and the outward form is extraneous. But when a group follows the outward form for a long period, it forgets the aforesaid difference. It gradually comes to consider carrying out only the outward formalities, as if they were the real prayer.

This means that the group has reached the stage of mental stagnation. Hence, it has been the way of God Almighty that when He sends a new prophet, He makes some changes in his *shariah* (i.e. outward ritual forms). His purpose is to shake the people out of their inertia, to break their addiction to outward formalities and to make them active and live worshippers in spirit. Now, those who think that outward formality and ritual in prayer are everything, refuse to obey the prophet. On the contrary, those who know the true spirit underlying prayer start to follow the prophet's instructions. This change infuses a new spirit into their prayers. It removes them from inert and frozen faith and takes them towards active and live faith.

This is the wisdom which accounts for the rites of prayer or worship having differed from one prophet to the next. When a prophet introduced new rites, those who were sunk in inertia would raise serious objections to them. But the prophets were instructed not to allow these matters to become the subject of serious discussions and to devote their full attention to the real and basic teachings.

71 Yet instead of God, they worship something for which God has sent no authority and about which they have no knowledge. The wrongdoers will have no helper. 72 Whenever Our clear revelations are recited to them, you will recognize the disgust on the faces of those who deny the truth. It is almost as if they are going to attack those who recite Our message to them. Say, 'Shall I tell you of something worse than this? It is the Fire that God has promised to those who are bent on denying the truth. What an evil destination!' [a]

وَيَعْبُدُونَ مِن دُونِ ٱللَّهِ مَا لَمْ يُنَزِّلْ بِهِۦ سُلْطَـٰنًا وَمَا لَيْسَ لَهُم بِهِۦ عِلْمٌ وَمَا لِلظَّـٰلِمِينَ مِن نَّصِيرٍ ۞ وَإِذَا تُتْلَىٰ عَلَيْهِمْ ءَايَـٰتُنَا بَيِّنَـٰتٍ تَعْرِفُ فِى وُجُوهِ ٱلَّذِينَ كَفَرُوا۟ ٱلْمُنكَرَ يَكَادُونَ يَسْطُونَ بِٱلَّذِينَ يَتْلُونَ عَلَيْهِمْ ءَايَـٰتِنَا ۗ قُلْ أَفَأُنَبِّئُكُم بِشَرٍّ مِّن ذَٰلِكُمُ ٱلنَّارُ وَعَدَهَا ٱللَّهُ ٱلَّذِينَ كَفَرُوا۟ ۖ وَبِئْسَ ٱلْمَصِيرُ ۞

---

[a] Inevitably, the call for pure monotheism is intolerable to those who have reposed their faith in many gods rather than in the one and only God. They become deeply agitated when their gods and beloved personalities are criticised. Being unable to refute by rational arguments the call of Truth, they resort to violence against the upholder of the call of monotheism, and want him to be eliminated altogether.

When told by God that their behaviour is unwise in the extreme, they are not prepared to bear even verbal criticism. But what will be their condition subsequently when they will be required to undergo the punishment of Hellfire on account of their opposition to the Truth?

73 People, here is an illustration. So listen carefully. Surely, those whom you invoke other than God cannot create even a fly, even if they were all to combine together to do it, and if a fly should snatch anything away from them, they cannot recover it from it. Both are indeed weak, the seeker and the sought. 74 No just estimate have they made of God. Surely God is powerful and mighty.*a*

75 God selects messengers from both angels and from mankind; God is all hearing and all seeing: 76 He knows what lies ahead of them and what is behind them. All things shall return to God.*b*

يَٰٓأَيُّهَا ٱلنَّاسُ ضُرِبَ مَثَلٌ فَٱسْتَمِعُوا۟ لَهُۥٓ إِنَّ ٱلَّذِينَ تَدْعُونَ مِن دُونِ ٱللَّهِ لَن يَخْلُقُوا۟ ذُبَابًا وَلَوِ ٱجْتَمَعُوا۟ لَهُۥ وَإِن يَسْلُبْهُمُ ٱلذُّبَابُ شَيْـًٔا لَّا يَسْتَنقِذُوهُ مِنْهُ ضَعُفَ ٱلطَّالِبُ وَٱلْمَطْلُوبُ ٧٣ مَا قَدَرُوا۟ ٱللَّهَ حَقَّ قَدْرِهِۦٓ إِنَّ ٱللَّهَ لَقَوِىٌّ عَزِيزٌ ٧٤ ٱللَّهُ يَصْطَفِى مِنَ ٱلْمَلَٰٓئِكَةِ رُسُلًا وَمِنَ ٱلنَّاسِ إِنَّ ٱللَّهَ سَمِيعٌۢ بَصِيرٌ ٧٥ يَعْلَمُ مَا بَيْنَ أَيْدِيهِمْ وَمَا خَلْفَهُمْ وَإِلَى ٱللَّهِ تُرْجَعُ ٱلْأُمُورُ ٧٦

a To clothe anybody except God with holiness is absolute stupidity, because holiness is given to a being who has inherent power, and as far as this world is concerned, there is no human being or non-human being who enjoys real power. A fly is an ordinary creature, but all the things of the earth and heavens together cannot bring into existence even this ordinary fly. Then where is the justification for holding anything other than God to be holy?

All these beliefs are, in fact, based on an underestimation of God's godhead. People do believe in God, but they are not fully aware of His majesty and power. If they believe in God as He should be believed in, then all deviant beliefs will strike them as meaningless to the point of being ridiculous. Then they themselves will give up all such beliefs.

b The scheme by which God created man and settled him on earth, necessitated His providing guidance to man and showing him which way leads to paradise and which way to hell. He, therefore, ordained the selection of certain human beings for prophethood and then sent them His messages by the angels.

By this arrangement, on the one hand, man is being made aware of the reality. On the other, Almighty God is keeping a watch on people's actions. Thereafter, when the period of testing is over, all the people will be brought back before God in order that they may be requited according to their performance.

77 You who are true believers, kneel and prostrate yourselves, worship your Lord and do good works, so that you may succeed. 78 Strive for the cause of God as it behoves you to strive for it. He has chosen you and laid on you no burden in the matter of your religion, the faith of Abraham your forefather. In this, as in former scriptures He has given you the name of Muslims, so that the Messenger may be a witness over you, and so that you may be witnesses over mankind. Therefore, say your prayers regularly and pay the *zakat* and hold fast to God. He is your master. An excellent master and an excellent helper![a]

يَـٰٓأَيُّهَا ٱلَّذِينَ ءَامَنُواْ ٱرۡكَعُواْ وَٱسۡجُدُواْ وَٱعۡبُدُواْ رَبَّكُمۡ وَٱفۡعَلُواْ ٱلۡخَيۡرَ لَعَلَّكُمۡ تُفۡلِحُونَ ۩ ۝

وَجَـٰهِدُواْ فِى ٱللَّهِ حَقَّ جِهَادِهِۦ هُوَ ٱجۡتَبَىٰكُمۡ وَمَا جَعَلَ عَلَيۡكُمۡ فِى ٱلدِّينِ مِنۡ حَرَجٖ مِّلَّةَ أَبِيكُمۡ إِبۡرَٰهِيمَ هُوَ سَمَّىٰكُمُ ٱلۡمُسۡلِمِينَ مِن قَبۡلُ وَفِى هَـٰذَا لِيَكُونَ ٱلرَّسُولُ شَهِيدًا عَلَيۡكُمۡ وَتَكُونُواْ شُهَدَآءَ عَلَى ٱلنَّاسِ فَأَقِيمُواْ ٱلصَّلَوٰةَ وَءَاتُواْ ٱلزَّكَوٰةَ وَٱعۡتَصِمُواْ بِٱللَّهِ هُوَ مَوۡلَىٰكُمۡ فَنِعۡمَ ٱلۡمَوۡلَىٰ وَنِعۡمَ ٱلنَّصِيرُ ۝

---

[a] The addressees of this verse were directly the companions of the Prophet Muhammad, and indirectly all the believers in the Quran. God chose this group for the special task of making all communities and nations aware of the true and eternal religion of God. The task of bearing witness was performed by the Prophet Muhammad for the people of his own times, and his followers were required to perform this same task for their contemporaries uptill Doomsday.

This obligation is a very delicate one. For this purpose, a vigorous and persevering struggle is required. It can be properly performed only by those who bow down before God in the real sense; who are well-wishers of others to the extent that they derive pleasure from spending their time and money on them; who rely on the one and only God; who rise above everything else; who fulfil in the real sense the requirement of the term 'Muslim', which term has been specially devised for them by God.

However, God has made a special dispensation in relation to the work of bearing witness, i.e. He has removed forever all the external hurdles in the way of this work. A revolution has been brought about through the Prophet Muhammad, which has resulted in the permanent abolition of such hurdles as once constricted the ways of the prophets of the past and their followers. Now there is absolutely no real obstacle to performing this work, unless the bearers of the Quran themselves create self-made difficulties out of ignorance, and thus make an easy task unnecessarily difficult.

23. THE BELIEVERS

In the name of God,
the Most Gracious, the Most Merciful

¹Successful indeed are the believers;
²those who are humble in their
prayer; ³those who turn away from
all that is frivolous; ⁴those who pay
the *zakat*; ⁵those who safeguard their
chastity ⁶except with their wives,
and what their right hands possess—
for then they are free from blame,
⁷but those who seek to go beyond
that are transgressors—⁸those who
are faithful to their trusts and
promises; ⁹and those who attend to
their prayers; ¹⁰these are the heirs
of Paradise ¹¹they shall abide in it
forever.ᵃ

ᵃ In this world of God, success is for one who is a true believer, one who devotes himself
fully to God and not to anybody other than God, and who leads a God-oriented life.

Realisation of God is not a simple matter. It brings about a revolution in the life
of a man. He becomes a worshipper of God and bows down before Him in
submission. His sincerity and seriousness increase to the extent that wasting time
in useless pursuits appears fatal to him. He sets aside a portion of his earnings in
the name of God and with that he helps the needy. He exercises control over his
sexual desires and gives free rein to them only within the limit prescribed by God
for the purpose. He lives his life in this world as a responsible person and never
misappropriates whatever is entrusted to him. Such a man never dishonours any
pledge undertaken by him.

Those who possess these qualities are the favoured subjects of God. These are the
people for whom God has kept ready the ideal world, namely, the gardens of
Paradise. After death they will be sent into this sublime atmosphere so that they
may savour its joys forever.

¹²We created man from an essence of clay, ¹³then We placed him as a drop of fluid in a safe place, ¹⁴then We developed that drop into a clinging form, and We developed that form into a lump of flesh, and We developed that lump into bones, and clothed the bones with flesh. Then We brought him into being as a new creation—glory be to God, the best of creators—¹⁵after this you shall surely die. ¹⁶Then you will be raised up again on the Resurrection Day.[a]

وَلَقَدْ خَلَقْنَا ٱلْإِنسَـٰنَ مِن سُلَـٰلَةٍ مِّن طِينٍ ۝ ثُمَّ جَعَلْنَـٰهُ نُطْفَةً فِى قَرَارٍ مَّكِينٍ ۝ ثُمَّ خَلَقْنَا ٱلنُّطْفَةَ عَلَقَةً فَخَلَقْنَا ٱلْعَلَقَةَ مُضْغَةً فَخَلَقْنَا ٱلْمُضْغَةَ عِظَـٰمًا فَكَسَوْنَا ٱلْعِظَـٰمَ لَحْمًا ثُمَّ أَنشَأْنَـٰهُ خَلْقًا ءَاخَرَ فَتَبَارَكَ ٱللَّهُ أَحْسَنُ ٱلْخَـٰلِقِينَ ۝ ثُمَّ إِنَّكُم بَعْدَ ذَٰلِكَ لَمَيِّتُونَ ۝ ثُمَّ إِنَّكُمْ يَوْمَ ٱلْقِيَـٰمَةِ تُبْعَثُونَ ۝

[a] The young one of a human being grows in the womb of his mother. In ancient times, the period from conception till child-birth was shrouded in mystery. It was only in the twentieth century that modern scientific developments made it possible to observe the development of a baby in the mother's womb and obtain direct information about it.

The vivid Quranic description of the various developmental stages of the formation and birth of human beings, is surprisingly identical with modern scientific findings. This provides a clear proof of the fact that the Quran is the Book of God. Had it not been so, such similarity between the findings of modern research and the statements of the Quran, revealed fourteen hundred years ago, would not have been possible.

The development of the embryo in the mother's womb shows that the Creator of this world is the most perfect Being. Our knowledge of the creation of man from the very beginning, is sufficient to make us believe that a second creation will take place and will occur in exactly the manner described by the prophets.

¹⁷ We have created seven paths above you; We have never been unmindful of Our creation. ¹⁸ We sent down water from the sky in due measure and lodged it in the earth—but if We please, We have the power to take it away—¹⁹ We have produced palm-groves and vineyards for you, in which there are abundant fruits for you; and you eat these, ²⁰ also a tree growing on Mount Sinai which produces oil and a condiment for those who eat it. ²¹ You have a lesson in livestock. We provide you with drink from what is in their bellies, and you have many other benefits from them; some of them you eat, ²² and you ride on them as you do in ships.^a

وَلَقَدْ خَلَقْنَا فَوْقَكُمْ سَبْعَ طَرَآئِقَ وَمَا كُنَّا عَنِ ٱلْخَلْقِ غَٰفِلِينَ ۝ وَأَنزَلْنَا مِنَ ٱلسَّمَآءِ مَآءً بِقَدَرٍ فَأَسْكَنَّٰهُ فِى ٱلْأَرْضِ وَإِنَّا عَلَىٰ ذَهَابٍۭ بِهِۦ لَقَٰدِرُونَ ۝ فَأَنشَأْنَا لَكُم بِهِۦ جَنَّٰتٍ مِّن نَّخِيلٍ وَأَعْنَٰبٍ لَّكُمْ فِيهَا فَوَٰكِهُ كَثِيرَةٌ وَمِنْهَا تَأْكُلُونَ ۝ وَشَجَرَةً تَخْرُجُ مِن طُورِ سَيْنَآءَ تَنۢبُتُ بِٱلدُّهْنِ وَصِبْغٍ لِّلْءَاكِلِينَ ۝ وَإِنَّ لَكُمْ فِى ٱلْأَنْعَٰمِ لَعِبْرَةً نُّسْقِيكُم مِّمَّا فِى بُطُونِهَا وَلَكُمْ فِيهَا مَنَٰفِعُ كَثِيرَةٌ وَمِنْهَا تَأْكُلُونَ ۝ وَعَلَيْهَا وَعَلَى ٱلْفُلْكِ تُحْمَلُونَ ۝

---

^a Man is a small creature. Compared to him, the universe is so large that it strikes terror into man. In the vastness of space, innumerable stars and planets revolve at high speed. Yet, the most wonderful aspect of the universe is that it is highly favourable to the existence of human beings. Moreover, exceptional the planet appear to have been made keeping all man's needs in mind. For example, man is able to domesticate a variety of animals and put them to various uses. The cow's stomach, for instance, is a wonderful factory which converts into a valuable commodity—milk.

All these factors warrant man's recognition of his Kind and Merciful God and his remaining ever grateful to Him.

²³ We sent Noah to his people, and he said, 'My people, worship God; you have no other deity except Him. Will you not fear Him?' ²⁴ The leaders of his people who denied the truth, said, 'He is only a human being like yourselves who wants to make himself superior to you. If God had wished, He would have sent down angels. We never heard about this from our forefathers. ²⁵ He is only a madman, so, as far as he is concerned wait for a while.' ᵃ

وَلَقَدْ أَرْسَلْنَا نُوحًا إِلَىٰ قَوْمِهِ فَقَالَ يَٰقَوْمِ ٱعْبُدُوا۟ ٱللَّهَ مَا لَكُم مِّنْ إِلَٰهٍ غَيْرُهُۥ أَفَلَا تَتَّقُونَ ۝ فَقَالَ ٱلْمَلَؤُا۟ ٱلَّذِينَ كَفَرُوا۟ مِن قَوْمِهِ مَا هَٰذَآ إِلَّا بَشَرٌ مِّثْلُكُمْ يُرِيدُ أَن يَتَفَضَّلَ عَلَيْكُمْ وَلَوْ شَآءَ ٱللَّهُ لَأَنزَلَ مَلَٰٓئِكَةً مَّا سَمِعْنَا بِهَٰذَا فِىٓ ءَابَآئِنَا ٱلْأَوَّلِينَ ۝ إِنْ هُوَ إِلَّا رَجُلٌۢ بِهِۦ جِنَّةٌ فَتَرَبَّصُوا۟ بِهِۦ حَتَّىٰ حِينٍ ۝

ᵃ The community into which Noah was born was not one made up of unbelievers in the common sense of the term. It consisted of the followers of Adam who were believers in God and prophethood. In spite of this, why did its members refuse to accept Noah as the prophet of God? It was because the Prophet Noah appeared to them as an ordinary man like themselves.

A prophet is a man born of human parents. Therefore, to the people of his age, he always seemed to be a man like themselves. It is in later history that a prophet appears to them as glorious, invested as he then is with legendary greatness. That is why a prophet's contemporaries fail to recognize him. To them the prophet appears to be a man who makes false claims to prophethood in order to be taken as a great man. They presume him to be a madman and ignore him.

It has been the story of every community that, as time has gone on, it has started following the traditions of its forefathers instead of following the real teachings of God. Whenever a prophet appeared and again preached genuine religion, they felt that the prophet's religion was different from the traditions of its forefathers. Given the mindset of these people, their forefathers appeared to be greater and the prophet appeared to be a comparatively lesser person. This is the main reason why the call of the prophets of every period seemed a strange cry to their contemporaries.

²⁶ Noah said, 'My Lord, help me! for they have rejected me,' ²⁷ then We revealed Our will to him: 'Build the Ark under Our watchful eye according to Our instructions. When Our command comes, and waters gush up out of the earth, take on board pairs of every species and members of your household, except for any of them on whom sentence has already been passed—do not plead with Me for those who have done wrong: they shall be drowned.ᵃ

قَالَ رَبِّ ٱنصُرْنِي بِمَا كَذَّبُونِ ۝

فَأَوْحَيْنَآ إِلَيْهِ أَنِ ٱصْنَعِ ٱلْفُلْكَ بِأَعْيُنِنَا وَوَحْيِنَا فَإِذَا جَآءَ أَمْرُنَا وَفَارَ ٱلتَّنُّورُ فَٱسْلُكْ فِيهَا مِن كُلٍّ زَوْجَيْنِ ٱثْنَيْنِ وَأَهْلَكَ إِلَّا مَن سَبَقَ عَلَيْهِ ٱلْقَوْلُ مِنْهُمْ وَلَا تُخَٰطِبْنِي فِي ٱلَّذِينَ ظَلَمُوٓاْ إِنَّهُم مُّغْرَقُونَ ۝

ᵃ The Prophet Noah admonished his community for a long time. But his community was not ready to accept his call. At last he prayed, 'Oh God! I have not been able to make my people accept the truth. Now, You reveal the truth to them!' But when the outermost limit of human effort has been reached, Divine action begins. It is then the time for reckoning and not for advice or admonition. So, God's retribution appeared in the shape of a devastating storm, which drowned Noah's entire community, with the exception of a few believers in Noah.

The refusal to acknowledge the Truth is the worst type of transgression. Those who indulge in this transgression are liable to be seized upon by God and then nothing can save them from their fate.

²⁸ When you and all your followers have settled in the Ark, say, "Praise be to God who has delivered us from a wicked people," ²⁹ and say, "My Lord, let me land with Your blessing in a blessed landing place. You alone can provide the best landings".' ³⁰ Surely there are clear signs in that. In this way We put people to the test.ᵃ

فَإِذَا ٱسْتَوَيْتَ أَنتَ وَمَن مَّعَكَ عَلَى ٱلْفُلْكِ فَقُلِ ٱلْحَمْدُ لِلَّهِ ٱلَّذِى نَجَّىٰنَا مِنَ ٱلْقَوْمِ ٱلظَّٰلِمِينَ ۝ وَقُل رَّبِّ أَنزِلْنِى مُنزَلًا مُّبَارَكًا وَأَنتَ خَيْرُ ٱلْمُنزِلِينَ ۝ إِنَّ فِى ذَٰلِكَ لَءَايَٰتٍ وَإِن كُنَّا لَمُبْتَلِينَ ۝

ᵃ In an environment fraught with idolatory, the few who had faith in Noah had that very day, in both the literal and the figurative sense, entered the Divine ark. When they boarded the wooden ship at the time of the storm, it marked the completion of the first stage of their decision. While they had intellectually saved themselves from evil, God saved them from the grim consequences of the Flood which would have been their fate, had they rejected the truth.

A man of faith attributes his every success to the blessing of God. Therefore, with each success he thanks God. And the relief afforded from Noah's flood was clearly an instance of God's help. At this juncture, the words that spontaneously came out of a believer's mouth have been recorded in this verse. He admits the grace of God bestowed upon him and solicits His further blessings in future, because he is sure that the present and future are both in the hands of God.

³¹ Then We raised another generation after them, ³² and sent a messenger to them from among themselves: 'Worship God alone. You have no deity other than Him. Will you not then fear God?' ³³ But the leaders of his people who denied the truth and denied the Meeting in the Hereafter, because We had granted them ease and plenty in their worldly life, said, 'This is only a human being like yourselves—he eats what you eat, and drinks what you drink—³⁴ if you obey a human being just like yourselves, then you will surely be lost.*ᵃ*

ثُمَّ أَنشَأْنَا مِنۢ بَعْدِهِمْ قَرْنًا ءَاخَرِينَ ۝ فَأَرْسَلْنَا فِيهِمْ رَسُولًا مِّنْهُمْ أَنِ اعْبُدُوا اللَّهَ مَا لَكُم مِّنْ إِلَٰهٍ غَيْرُهُۥٓ أَفَلَا تَتَّقُونَ ۝ وَقَالَ الْمَلَأُ مِن قَوْمِهِ الَّذِينَ كَفَرُوا وَكَذَّبُوا بِلِقَآءِ الْءَاخِرَةِ وَأَتْرَفْنَٰهُمْ فِي الْحَيَوٰةِ الدُّنْيَا مَا هَٰذَآ إِلَّا بَشَرٌ مِّثْلُكُمْ يَأْكُلُ مِمَّا تَأْكُلُونَ مِنْهُ وَيَشْرَبُ مِمَّا تَشْرَبُونَ ۝ وَلَئِنْ أَطَعْتُم بَشَرًا مِّثْلَكُمْ إِنَّكُمْ إِذًا لَّخَٰسِرُونَ ۝

ᵃ After being delivered in the Ark from the Great Flood, the generation of believers in Noah flourished, but again, with the passage of the centuries, they plunged into the same evils in which their predecessors had indulged. Here perhaps the community referred to is that which is known as the 'Ad. These people had neglected and forgotton God and were preoccupied with serving entities other than God. Once again a prophet of God, in this case Hud, appeared among them and made them aware of the Truth.

But, like their predecessors, the chiefs of the community ranged themselves against the prophet. These chiefs had assumed leadership of the people and were surrounded by plenty and prosperity. It is a common weakness of those who are fortunate enough to acquire wealth and power to presume that this is ample proof of their being on the path of Truth. This was also true of these chiefs. Their prosperity and power prevented them from thinking that they could be wrong.

They observed that the Prophet was not surrounded by heaps of wealth, nor was he seated upon a throne of power. So they considered him to be a lowly person. Due to the importance they attached to worldly glamour, they failed to understand the spiritual mission of the Prophet.

³⁵ Does he promise you that when you die and have become dust and bones, that you will be brought forth again? ³⁶ What you are promised is indeed far-fetched. ³⁷ There exists only our present life: we die and we live [but once], and shall never be raised up again. ³⁸ He is only a man who has invented a lie about God, and we are not going to believe him!'ᵃ

أَيَعِدُكُمْ أَنَّكُمْ إِذَا مِتُّمْ وَكُنتُمْ تُرَابًا وَعِظَٰمًا أَنَّكُم مُّخْرَجُونَ ۞ هَيْهَاتَ هَيْهَاتَ لِمَا تُوعَدُونَ ۞ إِنْ هِىَ إِلَّا حَيَاتُنَا ٱلدُّنْيَا نَمُوتُ وَنَحْيَا وَمَا نَحْنُ بِمَبْعُوثِينَ ۞ إِنْ هُوَ إِلَّا رَجُلٌ ٱفْتَرَىٰ عَلَى ٱللَّهِ كَذِبًا وَمَا نَحْنُ لَهُۥ بِمُؤْمِنِينَ ۞

ᵃ This verse refers to people's utterances regarding the Hereafter—some implicit and others explicit. Sometimes a man is so completely engrossed in worldly pursuits, that he seems to become forgetful of the Hereafter, as if he considered it to be only a remote possibility. And, sometimes it happens that his neglect of the Hereafter takes him to the extreme limit of arrogance, to the extent that he is outspoken, openly expressing the view that one should seize upon whatever one can today, and not lose today's certain benefits for the sake of tomorrow's imaginary gains.

Such people deride the Prophet by saying that he is an imposter who misrepresents God. Utterances such as these give people a reason for neglecting and ignoring the preacher of Truth.

³⁹ The messenger said, 'My Lord, help me, for they have rejected me.' ⁴⁰ God said, 'Before long they will be filled with regret.' ⁴¹ The blast justly struck them and We reduced them to rubble. Away with such wicked people!^a

قَالَ رَبِّ ٱنصُرْنِي بِمَا كَذَّبُونِ ۝ قَالَ عَمَّا قَلِيلٍ لَّيُصْبِحُنَّ نَـٰدِمِينَ ۝ فَأَخَذَتْهُمُ ٱلصَّيْحَةُ بِٱلْحَقِّ فَجَعَلْنَـٰهُمْ غُثَآءً فَبُعْدًا لِّلْقَوْمِ ٱلظَّـٰلِمِينَ ۝

---

^a The declaration of truth for which a prophet of God makes his appearance is the most serious reality of this world. But the prophet announces this reality only in the form of reasoning. The real believers are those who recognise the truth at a rational level and surrender themselves to it.

When a group conclusively proves that it is not capable of recognising the Truth in the form of reasoning, God reveals the Truth in the form of a blast (saihah). The Truth becomes such a loud roar that nobody has the strength to face it. But, when this stage is reached, i.e. when Truth appears in the shape of the roar, it is the hour of retribution and not an opportunity for the acceptance of the Truth. All that is left for man to do then, is to repent and pay for his foolishness for all eternity. For, despite seeing, he was blind, and despite hearing, he was dumb to the voice of Truth.

⁴²Then We raised up other generations after them—⁴³no community can advance or postpone its appointed time—⁴⁴then We sent Our messengers in succession. Every time their messenger came to a people, they rejected him. So We destroyed them one after the other, and let them become mere tales. So away with the people who will not believe!ᵃ

ثُمَّ أَنشَأْنَا مِن بَعْدِهِمْ قُرُونًا ءَاخَرِينَ ۝ مَا تَسْبِقُ مِنْ أُمَّةٍ أَجَلَهَا وَمَا يَسْتَئْخِرُونَ ۝ ثُمَّ أَرْسَلْنَا رُسُلَنَا تَتْرَا ۖ كُلَّ مَا جَآءَ أُمَّةً رَّسُولُهَا كَذَّبُوهُ ۚ فَأَتْبَعْنَا بَعْضَهُم بَعْضًا وَجَعَلْنَهُمْ أَحَادِيثَ ۚ فَبُعْدًا لِّقَوْمٍ لَّا يُؤْمِنُونَ ۝

ᵃ After the advent of each prophet, the succeeding generations of his community were always led astray. In order to reform them, prophets were sent to them again and again. In Adam's generation Noah appeared. In Noah's generation (the 'Ad), Hud appeared as a prophet. In Hud's generation (the Thamud), Salih appeared. But on each occasion those who had accepted the prophet of the past without question, were the very same people who were not at all prepared to accept the prophet of their own times.

The reason for this is that the prophet of the past, as a result of a wealth of traditions surrounding him, ultimately becomes a symbol of national pride, or national identity. He assumes the status of a national hero. By accepting him, one's superiority complex is satisfied. Obviously, who will refuse to accept such a prophet?

But, the case of the prophet during his lifetime is just the opposite. He has neither any halo of history around him nor any traditions of greatness to enhance his persona. Accepting him amounts to accepting an invisible reality. This is why those who accepted the prophet of the past have always refused to accept the prophet of their own times.

'So away with the people who will not believe!' Those referred to in this injunction are people who could recognize God's emissary only when, as a result of historical process, he had become their national hero.

⁴⁵ Then We sent Moses and his brother Aaron with Our signs and clear authority ⁴⁶ to Pharaoh and his courtiers, but they behaved insolently, for they were an arrogant people. ⁴⁷ They said, 'Are we to believe in two human beings like ourselves, while their people are subject to us?' ⁴⁸ So they rejected them both, and became those who were destroyed. ⁴⁹ We gave Moses the Book so that they might be guided.^a

ثُمَّ أَرْسَلْنَا مُوسَىٰ وَأَخَاهُ هَـٰرُونَ بِـَٔايَـٰتِنَا وَسُلْطَـٰنٍ مُّبِينٍ ۝ إِلَىٰ فِرْعَوْنَ وَمَلَإِيْهِۦ فَٱسْتَكْبَرُواْ وَكَانُواْ قَوْمًا عَالِينَ ۝ فَقَالُوٓاْ أَنُؤْمِنُ لِبَشَرَيْنِ مِثْلِنَا وَقَوْمُهُمَا لَنَا عَـٰبِدُونَ ۝ فَكَذَّبُوهُمَا فَكَانُواْ مِنَ ٱلْمُهْلَكِينَ ۝ وَلَقَدْ ءَاتَيْنَا مُوسَى ٱلْكِتَـٰبَ لَعَلَّهُمْ يَهْتَدُونَ ۝

^a Moses and Aaron belonged to the Children of Israel. At that time, in Egypt, the Children of Israel served as labourers to the ruling community. The inferior position of the Children of Israel and the superior position of Pharaoh and his companions became a stumbling block in the latter's acceptance of an Israeli prophet as God's representative. Though Moses gave them strong proofs, they did not carry enough weight to persuade them to rein in their sense of superiority and simply accept the truth coming from an 'inferior' person.

The result of this was that God Almighty finally gave His Prophet assistance and Pharaoh, despite all his power and its trappings, was engulfed in the Red Sea. Moreover, God favoured those who supported the Prophet by sending them a Book of Guidance, by following which a man might assure for himself success in this world and the Hereafter.

⁵⁰ We made the son of Mary and his mother a sign and gave them shelter on a peaceful hillside watered by a fresh spring.ᵃ

⁵¹ Messengers, eat what is wholesome and do good deeds: I am well aware of what you do. ⁵² Your religion is but one religion—and I am your only Lord, therefore, fear Me.ᵇ

وَجَعَلْنَا ٱبْنَ مَرْيَمَ وَأُمَّهُۥٓ ءَايَةً وَءَاوَيْنَٰهُمَآ إِلَىٰ رَبْوَةٍ ذَاتِ قَرَارٍ وَمَعِينٍ ۞ يَٰٓأَيُّهَا ٱلرُّسُلُ كُلُوا۟ مِنَ ٱلطَّيِّبَٰتِ وَٱعْمَلُوا۟ صَٰلِحًا إِنِّى بِمَا تَعْمَلُونَ عَلِيمٌ ۞ وَإِنَّ هَٰذِهِۦٓ أُمَّتُكُمْ أُمَّةً وَٰحِدَةً وَأَنَا۠ رَبُّكُمْ فَٱتَّقُونِ ۞

ᵃ The Messiah's birth without a father was an extremely strange occurrence. Why did it take place? It came as a symbol or sign from God. In ancient times, the Jews enjoyed the position of being a prophet-raising community. But, having continuously indulged in arrogant behaviour, they forfeited this entitlement. The time had come for this trust to be taken away from them and handed over to another community, in this case, the Children of Ishmael. Therefore, as a way of bringing to a conclusion the religious predominance of the Jews, God caused their last prophet to be born in a miraculous manner and gave him some additional miracles to perform. The Jews, however, persisted in rejecting him, and this finally proved that they did not deserve to be a community into which prophets should be born.

This was a very critical moment for the Messiah's mother, Mary. In these circumstances, she was in dire need of a corner where she could live away from the eyes of the people, and where the necessities of life should be available in a calm and peaceful atmosphere. When Almighty God placed her in this critical position, He also provided for her a peaceful place near her home.

ᵇ Religion is originally one, and the same religion was taught to all the prophets. Religion enhances man spiritually so that he may discover God as an Almighty Being. His mind and soul should be imbued with the idea of the one God, Who is watching his every move, and after his death will take a reckoning of all his deeds. This realization (ma'rifah) is the real religion. As a man enters the fold of realization, he begins to adopt righteous and pious methods in all his affairs. The realization of God essentially results in fear of God, and fear of God necessarily results in a pious life.

⁵³ Yet they divided themselves into factions, each rejoicing in what they had. ⁵⁴ So leave them in their bewilderment for a while. ⁵⁵ Do they imagine that the wealth and children We have provided ⁵⁶ have no other purpose except to help them in acquiring material benefits? No indeed. But they do not understand.ᵃ

فَتَقَطَّعُوٓا۟ أَمْرَهُم بَيْنَهُمْ زُبُرًا كُلُّ حِزْبٍۭ بِمَا لَدَيْهِمْ فَرِحُونَ ۝ فَذَرْهُمْ فِى غَمْرَتِهِمْ حَتَّىٰ حِينٍ ۝ أَيَحْسَبُونَ أَنَّمَا نُمِدُّهُم بِهِۦ مِن مَّالٍ وَبَنِينَ ۝ نُسَارِعُ لَهُمْ فِى ٱلْخَيْرَٰتِ بَل لَّا يَشْعُرُونَ ۝

ᵃ When the religion of God is revived in its true spirit, it instills the fear of God in people's minds but when religion loses its true spirit, it becomes a mere source of boasting and pride for its adherents. This is the time when men of religion split into a number of groups. Each group chooses for itself that aspect which feeds its pride. Groups which feed on pride are always many in number, while the religion of the God-fearing is always one. An absence of fear breeds a diversity of opinions, while a God-fearing mentality leads to uniformity of opinion.

In the present world, man is being put to test. During the period of respite allowed to an individual or a group at God's behest, all the amenities of life are provided. On account of this, negligent people think that whatever they are doing is right and that, if they had been wrong, their possessions and all comfort and convenience would have been snatched away from them. But, by God's method, a man's possession are taken away from him, not on his flouting God's will during the trial period, but in the world hereafter.

⁵⁷ Those who tremble with fear of their Lord; ⁵⁸ and believe in His messages ⁵⁹ and do not ascribe partners to Him; ⁶⁰ and those who give to others what has been bestowed upon them with their hearts trembling at the thought that they must return to their Lord; ⁶¹ it is they who vie with one another in doing good works and shall be the foremost in doing so. ⁶² We charge no soul with more than it can bear. We have a record which clearly shows the truth and they will not be wronged.ᵃ

إِنَّ ٱلَّذِينَ هُم مِّنْ خَشْيَةِ رَبِّهِم مُّشْفِقُونَ ۝ وَٱلَّذِينَ هُم بِـَٔايَـٰتِ رَبِّهِمْ يُؤْمِنُونَ ۝ وَٱلَّذِينَ هُم بِرَبِّهِمْ لَا يُشْرِكُونَ ۝ وَٱلَّذِينَ يُؤْتُونَ مَآ ءَاتَوا۟ وَّقُلُوبُهُمْ وَجِلَةٌ أَنَّهُمْ إِلَىٰ رَبِّهِمْ رَٰجِعُونَ ۝ أُو۟لَـٰٓئِكَ يُسَٰرِعُونَ فِى ٱلْخَيْرَٰتِ وَهُمْ لَهَا سَٰبِقُونَ ۝ وَلَا نُكَلِّفُ نَفْسًا إِلَّا وُسْعَهَا ۖ وَلَدَيْنَا كِتَـٰبٌ يَنطِقُ بِٱلْحَقِّ ۚ وَهُمْ لَا يُظْلَمُونَ ۝

ᵃ One whose discovery of God is such that he is awe-struck by Him becomes different from other men, in that his God-fearing mentality makes him extremely serious. His seriousness guarantees that he fully realises the weight of divine proofs and he submits to God completely.

In the present world, there are two ways in which a man may exert himself — one is the way of the world and the other is the way of the Hereafter. Those who possess the above-mentioned qualities, are exactly those who strive towards the Hereafter. However, in the present world, to strive towards the Hereafter is an extremely difficult task. It is one in which a man is prone to different types of shortcomings. But, Almighty God's requirement of every man is exactly commensurate with his capacity to fulfill it. Everybody's capacity and performance are both completely within the knowledge of God and this very fact ensures that, on the Day of Judgement, everyone will receive whatever concession he is justifiably entitled to and everyone will receive the reward which he actually deserves.

63 But their hearts are heedless of this. Moreover, there are other deeds besides this which they do. 64 But then when We seize the affluent among them, they will cry out for help. 65 Do not cry out for help this day, for surely you shall not be helped by Us. 66 My revelations were recited to you, but you turned your backs 67 in arrogance, as if you were abandoning a story-teller.a

بَلْ قُلُوبُهُمْ فِى غَمْرَةٍ مِّنْ هَـٰذَا وَهُمْ
أَعْمَلٌ مِّن دُونِ ذَٰلِكَ هُمْ لَهَا عَـٰمِلُونَ
٦٣ حَتَّىٰٓ إِذَآ أَخَذْنَا مُتْرَفِيهِم
بِٱلْعَذَابِ إِذَا هُمْ يَجْـَٔرُونَ ٦٤ لَا
تَجْـَٔرُوا۟ ٱلْيَوْمَ ۖ إِنَّكُم مِّنَّا لَا تُنصَرُونَ
٦٥ قَدْ كَانَتْ ءَايَـٰتِى تُتْلَىٰ عَلَيْكُمْ
فَكُنتُمْ عَلَىٰٓ أَعْقَـٰبِكُمْ تَنكِصُونَ ٦٦
مُسْتَكْبِرِينَ بِهِۦ سَـٰمِرًا تَهْجُرُونَ ٦٧

---

a Those completely devoted to the life of this world are not interested in any discourses about God or the Hereafter. Their interests are quite different from those of true men of faith. Talk of God and the Hereafter, however effectively presented, does not, therefore, appeal to them. They ignore all such talk, and are lost in their worldly pursuits.

But, with the onset of God's retribution, such people forget their recklessness and arrogance and start pleading humbly. At that time they bow down before God. But, doing so at that juncture is useless, because only that submission before God carries weight which is done on seeing God's sign. Bowing down when God Himself appears in all His Might, has no value.

⁶⁸ Have they not pondered over the word of God? Has something come to them that did not come to their forefathers? ⁶⁹ Or do they not recognize their Messenger, and so deny him? ⁷⁰ Do they say he is possessed? Rather he has brought them the truth, but most of them are averse to the truth. ⁷¹ If truth had followed their whims and desires, heavens and earth and all that lives in them would have been brought to ruin. Rather We have brought them their Reminder. Yet they keep avoiding their Reminder.ᵃ

أَفَلَمْ يَدَّبَّرُوا ٱلْقَوْلَ أَمْ جَآءَهُم مَّا لَمْ يَأْتِ ءَابَآءَهُمُ ٱلْأَوَّلِينَ ۝ أَمْ لَمْ يَعْرِفُوا۟ رَسُولَهُمْ فَهُمْ لَهُۥ مُنكِرُونَ ۝ أَمْ يَقُولُونَ بِهِۦ جِنَّةٌۢ بَلْ جَآءَهُم بِٱلْحَقِّ وَأَكْثَرُهُمْ لِلْحَقِّ كَٰرِهُونَ ۝ وَلَوِ ٱتَّبَعَ ٱلْحَقُّ أَهْوَآءَهُمْ لَفَسَدَتِ ٱلسَّمَٰوَٰتُ وَٱلْأَرْضُ وَمَن فِيهِنَّ بَلْ أَتَيْنَٰهُم بِذِكْرِهِمْ فَهُمْ عَن ذِكْرِهِم مُّعْرِضُونَ ۝

ᵃ Truth is that which is in consonance with reality. But, those given to self-indulgence want the Truth to be made subservient to their desires. Therefore, when a preacher speaks of the Truth, they are unhappy with him. They do not want to be subservient to the Truth. They want the Truth to be subservient to them. On account of this mentality they do not pay any attention to the call of Truth. The Truth appears strange to them, and they are, therefore, unable to recognise the real position of the preacher. Indeed, in order to show that they are on the right path, they try to prove him wrong.

In the universe, there appears to be perfect harmony. On the contrary, in the world of human beings one sees disturbance and turbulence everywhere. The reason for this situation is that the system of the universe is running on the basis of Truth (law of nature), i.e. whatever should happen actually happens, and whatever should not happen does not happen. If the system of the universe also started running on the basis of the desires of human beings, it would also become fraught with the same disturbance and turbulence as is found in the world of mankind.

Advice and criticism are to most people unpalatable. There are very few individuals who listen to advice and criticism with an open mind. Many people just go through life ignoring it, hence shutting the door of development upon themselves.

⁷² Or are you asking them for any reward? But the reward of your Lord is the best, for He is the Best of Providers, ⁷³ and, most surely, you are calling them to a straight path. ⁷⁴ But those who do not believe in the Hereafter have indeed deviated from that path.ᵃ

أَمْ تَسْـَٔلُهُمْ خَرْجًا فَخَرَاجُ رَبِّكَ خَيْرٌ وَهُوَ خَيْرُ ٱلرَّٰزِقِينَ ۝ وَإِنَّكَ لَتَدْعُوهُمْ إِلَىٰ صِرَٰطٍ مُّسْتَقِيمٍ ۝ وَإِنَّ ٱلَّذِينَ لَا يُؤْمِنُونَ بِٱلْأَخِرَةِ عَنِ ٱلصِّرَٰطِ لَنَٰكِبُونَ ۝

ᵃ A prophet does not anticipate any monetary gains from his addressee-community. The relationship between a prophet and his addressee-community is an extremely delicate one. If, on the one hand, the preacher gives the message of Truth and Hereafter, but at the same time seeks worldly benefits, his call for Truth will become ridiculous. This is why a prophet never makes any material demands upon his addressee-community, even though, due to this policy, he may himself have to suffer material loss.

The real remuneration of such a preacher of Truth is Truth itself. His discovery of God is his greatest asset. The divine experiences which he gains while leading his life as a preacher provide the best nourishment to his soul. His striving to uphold and to inculcate the highest ideals is the biggest source of satisfaction to him.

One who is ever anxious about the life Hereafter, will be the one who will give a positive response to the call for Truth. Realisation of the Hereafter makes a man serious, and seriousness is the sole factor which, with the support of convincing arguments, compels a man to accept the Truth.

⁷⁵ Even if We showed them mercy and relieved them of their afflictions, they would still persist in their transgression, wandering blindly. ⁷⁶ We seized them with the punishment, but they did not surrender to their Lord, nor will they humble themselves ⁷⁷ until We open before them a gate of harsh punishment and then they will be dumbfounded.^a

﷽ وَلَوْ رَحِمْنَـٰهُمْ وَكَشَفْنَا مَا بِهِم مِّن ضُرٍّ لَّلَجُّوا۟ فِى طُغْيَـٰنِهِمْ يَعْمَهُونَ ۝ وَلَقَدْ أَخَذْنَـٰهُم بِٱلْعَذَابِ فَمَا ٱسْتَكَانُوا۟ لِرَبِّهِمْ وَمَا يَتَضَرَّعُونَ ۝ حَتَّىٰ إِذَا فَتَحْنَا عَلَيْهِم بَابًا ذَا عَذَابٍ شَدِيدٍ إِذَا هُمْ فِيهِ مُبْلِسُونَ ۝

---

^a In the Makkan period of Islam when the Quraysh rejected the Prophet Muhammad, God imposed famine conditions on the people of Makkah for several years. In accordance with God's scheme of things, when a community adopts an arrogant attitude and does not accept good advice, He administers a warning punishment to that community in order to soften their hearts and make them pay attention to the Truth.

But, events show that man does not learn lessons either from good or adverse conditions. The purpose of both ease and adversity is that man should turn towards God. But, man thinks that the coming of good times is the result of his own talents, while he attributes hard times to the turn of events. In this way he fails to learn a lesson from either set of conditions.

Man remains heedless in this way until it is time for God's final verdict. At that time, he is wonderstruck that what he had considered unimportant and ignored, was the greatest and most important reality of this world.

⁷⁸ It is He who gave you ears, eyes and hearts, yet how seldom you are grateful!^a ⁷⁹ He it is who has multiplied you on the earth and to Him you shall all be gathered: ⁸⁰ He is the One who gives life and causes death and He controls the alternation of night and day. Will you not then understand?^a

وَهُوَ ٱلَّذِىٓ أَنشَأَ لَكُمُ ٱلسَّمْعَ وَٱلْأَبْصَٰرَ وَٱلْأَفْـِٔدَةَ قَلِيلًا مَّا تَشْكُرُونَ ۝ وَهُوَ ٱلَّذِى ذَرَأَكُمْ فِى ٱلْأَرْضِ وَإِلَيْهِ تُحْشَرُونَ ۝ وَهُوَ ٱلَّذِى يُحْىِۦ وَيُمِيتُ وَلَهُ ٱخْتِلَٰفُ ٱلَّيْلِ وَٱلنَّهَارِ أَفَلَا تَعْقِلُونَ ۝

---

^a In this universe the human being is a special creation who has been endowed with the exceptional powers of sight, hearing and thought. These capacities have been given to man for the special purpose of understanding the reality of life. He should use his ears to hear the voice of Truth. With his eyes he should recognise the signs of God that are spread around him and he should use his thinking powers to discover the Creator in His creations. Doing so amounts to being thankful to God and those who do not give evidence of such thankfulness in this world risk losing their entitlement to these gifts forever.

Among the attributes of God that are prominently visible in this world are His powers to create a life, to take it and revive it again (as in the case of a barren land). In the hereafter, God will assemble the entire mankind before Him. That Day, He will remove the veil of ignorance and the reality will stand fully revealed.

⁸¹ But they say the same as the ancients said, ⁸² 'When we have died and become dust and bones, will we be raised up again? ⁸³ We and our forefathers were promised this before. This is nothing but fables of the ancients.' ᵃ

بَلْ قَالُوا مِثْلَ مَا قَالَ ٱلْأَوَّلُونَ ۝ قَالُوٓا أَءِذَا مِتْنَا وَكُنَّا تُرَابًا وَعِظَـٰمًا أَءِنَّا لَمَبْعُوثُونَ ۝ لَقَدْ وُعِدْنَا نَحْنُ وَءَابَآؤُنَا هَـٰذَا مِن قَبْلُ إِنْ هَـٰذَآ إِلَّآ أَسَـٰطِيرُ ٱلْأَوَّلِينَ ۝

ᵃ Man has been endowed with wisdom, which gives him the capacity to go deep into matters and discover the underlying reality. But, it seldom happens that man uses his wisdom in the real sense. He forms opinions on the basis of outward appearances.

There are very few who consciously and openly deny the existence of the life hereafter. However, many can in fact be said to reject this belief. These are such as only formally accept the existence of the life hereafter, but in practice lead their lives as if they have no belief that they will be resurrected after death and presented before God to account for their deeds.

⁸⁴ Say, 'To whom do the earth and all therein belong? Tell me, if you have any knowledge?' ⁸⁵ They will say, 'To God.' Say, 'So will you not pay heed?' ⁸⁶ Say, 'Who is the Lord of the seven heavens, and of the Glorious Throne?' ⁸⁷ They will say, 'They belong to God.' Say, 'So do you not fear Him?' ⁸⁸ Say, 'In whose hands lies sovereignty over all things, protecting all, while none can seek protection against Him? Tell me, if you have any knowledge.' ⁸⁹ They will say, 'All this belongs to God.' Say to them, 'How are you then deluded?' ^a

قُل لِّمَنِ ٱلْأَرْضُ وَمَن فِيهَآ إِن كُنتُمْ تَعْلَمُونَ ۝ سَيَقُولُونَ لِلَّهِ قُلْ أَفَلَا تَذَكَّرُونَ ۝ قُلْ مَن رَّبُّ ٱلسَّمَٰوَٰتِ ٱلسَّبْعِ وَرَبُّ ٱلْعَرْشِ ٱلْعَظِيمِ ۝ سَيَقُولُونَ لِلَّهِ قُلْ أَفَلَا تَتَّقُونَ ۝ قُلْ مَنۢ بِيَدِهِ مَلَكُوتُ كُلِّ شَيْءٍ وَهُوَ يُجِيرُ وَلَا يُجَارُ عَلَيْهِ إِن كُنتُمْ تَعْلَمُونَ ۝ سَيَقُولُونَ لِلَّهِ قُلْ فَأَنَّىٰ تُسْحَرُونَ ۝

^a In these verses, a certain contradiction in thinking has been referred to by which the majority of people in every age have been afflicted.

Most people admit that the Creator of the earth and the heavens is the one and only God; that He is their Lord and He controls them; that He enjoys all the superior powers. Yet their lives do not in any way reflect this acknowledgement.

Such sublime truth demands that it permeates their thinking. The realisation of God should make them truly God-conscious. It should so become a part of their nature that, when they come face to face with the Truth, they admit it immediately. Their whole life should be moulded upon it. But, in actual fact, none of this happens. They accept God as a formal belief, but their real lives are not affected by it.

The conception of God does not cast any spell over such individuals. On the contrary, they remain enamoured of trivial things. How strange is man's behaviour!

⁹⁰ We have revealed to them the truth. But they are certainly liars. ⁹¹ God has not taken to Himself a son, nor is there any other deity besides Him; otherwise, each god would have walked away with what he had created. They would surely have tried to overcome one another. Glory be to God, above all that they ascribe to Him. ⁹² Knower of the unseen and the visible; He is exalted above all that which they associate with Him.ᵃ

بَلْ أَتَيْنَـٰهُم بِٱلْحَقِّ وَإِنَّهُمْ لَكَـٰذِبُونَ ۝ مَا ٱتَّخَذَ ٱللَّهُ مِن وَلَدٍ وَمَا كَانَ مَعَهُۥ مِنْ إِلَـٰهٍ ۚ إِذًا لَّذَهَبَ كُلُّ إِلَـٰهٍ بِمَا خَلَقَ وَلَعَلَا بَعْضُهُمْ عَلَىٰ بَعْضٍ ۚ سُبْحَـٰنَ ٱللَّهِ عَمَّا يَصِفُونَ ۝ عَـٰلِمِ ٱلْغَيْبِ وَٱلشَّهَـٰدَةِ فَتَعَـٰلَىٰ عَمَّا يُشْرِكُونَ ۝

ᵃ The nature of power is such that it does not tolerate division. If there are multiple power centres, each strives unceasingly to overpower the others.

Now take a look at the universe. The steller bodies follow their regime strictly and harmoniously. Had there been a separate god for every entity, each one would have distanced himself from the others along with his own part and no harmony would have existed among the different parts. Due to conflict among the various gods, the entire system of the universe would have been disturbed.

Given the above, it is clear that the theory of the unity of Godhead is the Truth while the theory of polytheism stands discarded.

⁹³ Pray, 'Lord, if you would show me that [the punishment] of which they have been warned, ⁹⁴ then do not place me, Lord, with the wrongdoers.' ⁹⁵ We certainly have the power to show you what they have been warned about.

قُل رَّبِّ إِمَّا تُرِيَنِّى مَا يُوعَدُونَ ۝

رَبِّ فَلَا تَجْعَلْنِى فِى ٱلْقَوْمِ ٱلظَّٰلِمِينَ

۝ وَإِنَّا عَلَىٰ أَن نُّرِيَكَ مَا نَعِدُهُمْ

لَقَٰدِرُونَ ۝

---

a This prayer illustrates that a believer is always a God-fearing man. Even when God's punishment is directed towards others, he starts trembling with fear. He starts addressing God in all humility, because he knows that, if he is to be saved, it will not be by any deed of his or by his own strength but by God's mercy.

⁹⁶ Repel evil with what is best—We are well aware of the things they say—⁹⁷ and say, 'My Lord, I seek refuge with You from the prompting of the devils. ⁹⁸ I seek refuge with You, Lord, lest they should come near me.'

اَدۡفَعۡ بِٱلَّتِى هِىَ أَحۡسَنُ ٱلسَّيِّئَةَ نَحۡنُ أَعۡلَمُ بِمَا يَصِفُونَ ۝ وَقُل رَّبِّ أَعُوذُ بِكَ مِنۡ هَمَزَٰتِ ٱلشَّيَٰطِينِ ۝ وَأَعُوذُ بِكَ رَبِّ أَن يَحۡضُرُونِ ۝

ᵃ When God's preacher calls for the Truth, it often happens that those whom he addresses, instead of acknowledging it, become his enemies. They make him the target of mischief and spread false propaganda against him. At that time, he has the urge to react. He feels that if he has been maltreated by others, he should also retaliate. He feels that if he keeps quiet, will be encouraged and they will be emboldened to engage in further opposition.

But all such thoughts are instigations of Satan. At this critical juncture, Satan confuses the issue with a view to leading man astray. On such occasions, one who is a believer should seek God's protection, will cast him into manifest error.

99 When death comes to any of them, he says, 'My Lord, send me back 100 so that I may do good works in the world I have left behind.' Never! It is indeed but a meaningless word that he utters. A barrier shall stand behind such people till the Day they are raised up again. 101 When the trumpet is blown, on that Day there will be no ties of relationship between them; neither will they ask about one another: 102 then those whose scales weigh heavy with good works will be successful. 103 But those whose scales weigh light will have ruined their souls; in Hell will they abide. 104 The Fire will scorch their faces and they will abide therein with their faces distorted. *a*

حَتَّىٰ إِذَا جَآءَ أَحَدَهُمُ ٱلْمَوْتُ قَالَ رَبِّ ٱرْجِعُونِ ۞ لَعَلِّىٓ أَعْمَلُ صَـٰلِحًا فِيمَا تَرَكْتُ كَلَّآ إِنَّهَا كَلِمَةٌ هُوَ قَآئِلُهَا وَمِن وَرَآئِهِم بَرْزَخٌ إِلَىٰ يَوْمِ يُبْعَثُونَ ۞ فَإِذَا نُفِخَ فِى ٱلصُّورِ فَلَآ أَنسَابَ بَيْنَهُمْ يَوْمَئِذٍ وَلَا يَتَسَآءَلُونَ ۞ فَمَن ثَقُلَتْ مَوَٰزِينُهُۥ فَأُوْلَـٰٓئِكَ هُمُ ٱلْمُفْلِحُونَ ۞ وَمَنْ خَفَّتْ مَوَٰزِينُهُۥ فَأُوْلَـٰٓئِكَ ٱلَّذِينَ خَسِرُوٓاْ أَنفُسَهُمْ فِى جَهَنَّمَ خَـٰلِدُونَ ۞ تَلْفَحُ وُجُوهَهُمُ ٱلنَّارُ وَهُمْ فِيهَا كَـٰلِحُونَ ۞

---

a As soon as man dies, he is separated from the present world and reaches a point of no-return.

Now, he realises that the life Hereafter, which he had hitherto ignored, was in fact the real target in life. The possessions of the pre-death period were for the purpose of earning credit towards the life Hereafter and not as ends in themselves. So, after death, he will immediately want to be sent back to this world. But this will not be possible, because in accordance with the creation plan of God, every man is given only one chance.

In the present world man relies on his friends and relatives, but on Judgement Day he will be all alone. There, only his good deeds will be of avail. Nothing else will save him.

¹⁰⁵ Were not My messages recited to you and did you not reject them? ¹⁰⁶ They will answer, 'Lord, misfortune overcame us and we became an erring people. ¹⁰⁷ Lord, deliver us from Hell. Then, if we revert again, we shall definitely be wrongdoers.' ¹⁰⁸ God will say, 'Stay there and do not speak to Me.ᵃ

أَلَمْ تَكُنْ ءَايَتِى تُتْلَى عَلَيْكُمْ فَكُنتُم بِهَا تُكَذِّبُونَ ۝ قَالُوا رَبَّنَا غَلَبَتْ عَلَيْنَا شِقْوَتُنَا وَكُنَّا قَوْمًا ضَالِّينَ ۝ رَبَّنَا أَخْرِجْنَا مِنْهَا فَإِنْ عُدْنَا فَإِنَّا ظَلِمُونَ ۝ قَالَ ٱخْسَئُوا فِيهَا وَلَا تُكَلِّمُونِ ۝

ᵃ After death, no one will be given the chance to come back and live rightfully in the present world.

The true test of a man is not in his acceptance of the realities after seeing them, but in his acceptance of them while they are unseen. A student is tested during the examination and not after it is over.

¹⁰⁹ Among My servants, there were those who said, "Lord, We believe, so forgive us and have mercy on us. You are the best one to show mercy." ¹¹⁰ But you made a laughing stock of them to the point where it made you forget My remembrance; and you went on laughing at them. ¹¹¹ I have rewarded them this Day for their steadfastness, and it is they who have triumphed.' ᵃ

إِنَّهُۥ كَانَ فَرِيقٌ مِّنْ عِبَادِى يَقُولُونَ رَبَّنَآ ءَامَنَّا فَٱغْفِرْ لَنَا وَٱرْحَمْنَا وَأَنتَ خَيْرُ ٱلرَّٰحِمِينَ ۝ فَٱتَّخَذْتُمُوهُمْ سِخْرِيًّا حَتَّىٰٓ أَنسَوْكُمْ ذِكْرِى وَكُنتُم مِّنْهُمْ تَضْحَكُونَ ۝ إِنِّى جَزَيْتُهُمُ ٱلْيَوْمَ بِمَا صَبَرُوٓاْ أَنَّهُمْ هُمُ ٱلْفَآئِزُونَ ۝

ᵃ During the life of this world, when the realities of the Hereafter were still hidden, there were still some servants of God who had recognised God in all His Majesty and perfection. In spite of hearing the call for Truth in a purely abstract form, supported only by rational arguments, they believed in it. But they had to pay the price for believing in an alien Truth in that they became the subject of ridicule in their immediate surroundings. Despite this, they did not break off this attachment.

Such steadfastness in thinking is the greatest form of patience and the reward for this is paradise in the life hereafter.

¹¹² He will ask, 'How many years did you stay on earth?' ¹¹³ They will say, 'We stayed a day or part of a day. Ask those who have kept count.' ¹¹⁴ He will say, 'You only stayed for a little while, if only you knew.ᵃ

قَلَ كَمْ لَبِثْتُمْ فِى ٱلْأَرْضِ عَدَدَ سِنِينَ ۝ قَالُوا لَبِثْنَا يَوْمًا أَوْ بَعْضَ يَوْمٍ فَسْـَٔلِ ٱلْعَآدِّينَ ۝ قَلَ إِن لَّبِثْتُمْ إِلَّا قَلِيلًا ۖ لَّوْ أَنَّكُمْ كُنتُمْ تَعْلَمُونَ ۝

ᵃ That joy which is everlasting is the real joy. Fleeting moments of joy have no meaning. In the life of this world, man is forgetful of this fact. But in the Hereafter, it will become abundantly clear to him.

Truth manifests itself to a man in this world, but he does not want to disturb his status quo, so he does not accept it. He is not prepared to forego the already available present gain for the sake of any promised future gain. The comforts and the considerations of this world appear valuable to him and he is unable to understand why he should ignore them all and attach himself to a 'non-thing,' or abstract promise.

115 'Do you imagine that We created you without any purpose and that you would not be brought back to Us?' 116 Then, exalted be God, the true King, there is no deity except Him, the Lord of the Glorious Throne. 117 He, who invokes another deity along with God—a deity of whose divinity he has no proof—will be brought to account by his Lord. Certainly, those who deny the truth shall never prosper. 118 Say, 'Lord, forgive us and have mercy. You are the best of those who show mercy.'ᵃ

أَفَحَسِبْتُمْ أَنَّمَا خَلَقْنَكُمْ عَبَثًا وَأَنَّكُمْ إِلَيْنَا لَا تُرْجَعُونَ ۝ فَتَعَلَى ٱللَّهُ ٱلْمَلِكُ ٱلْحَقُّ لَا إِلَهَ إِلَّا هُوَ رَبُّ ٱلْعَرْشِ ٱلْكَرِيمِ ۝ وَمَن يَدْعُ مَعَ ٱللَّهِ إِلَهًا ءَاخَرَ لَا بُرْهَنَ لَهُ بِهِۦ فَإِنَّمَا حِسَابُهُۥ عِندَ رَبِّهِ إِنَّهُۥ لَا يُفْلِحُ ٱلْكَفِرُونَ ۝ وَقُل رَّبِّ ٱغْفِرْ وَٱرْحَمْ وَأَنتَ خَيْرُ ٱلرَّحِمِينَ ۝

ᵃ There are two types of human beings: one leads a principled life, while another leads an unprincipled one. While one sacrifices himself for the sake of an unseen Truth, the other remains preoccupied with visible things. While one accepts the call for Truth—in spite of all its unfamiliarity—the other ignores it or even ridicules it. While one abstains from indulging in cruelty—solely because God has prohibited it, another becomes a tyrant at the very first opportunity, because his self-interest bids him do so.

The meaningfulness of the universe contradicts the theory that there is no purpose behind the creation of this world. The perfect system of the universe shows its Creator to be a highly intelligent Being.

The vast and perfect system of the universe introduces us to a Creator Who is perfect to the ultimate degree. It is inconceivable that such a Creator would countenance or tolerate the aforesaid two types of individuals meeting the same end. This is totally impossible. The Lord of this universe will certainly scorn those who scoffed at the Truth and will show His appreciation for those who valued it.

24. LIGHT

In the name of God,
the Most Gracious, the Most Merciful

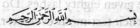

¹ This is a chapter which We have revealed and which We have made obligatory; We have sent down clear revelations in it, so that you may take heed. ² Flog the adulteress and the adulterer, each one of them, with a hundred lashes. Let no pity for them cause you to disobey God, if you truly believe in God and the Last Day; and let their punishment be witnessed by a number of believers. ³ The adulterer shall marry only an adulteress or a polytheist woman, and an adulteress shall marry only an adulterer or a polytheist man; such marriages are forbidden for believers.ᵃ

ᵃ This chapter was revealed in the year 6 A.H., after the campaign of Banu al-Mustaliq. A minor incident took place during this campaign, which the hypocrites of Madinah chose to misrepresent in order to defame 'A'ishah, the Prophet's wife, and create trouble for the Prophet Muhammad. In this chapter, on the one hand, 'A'ishah has been completely exonerated, and on the other hand, legal provisions to be enforced under similar social circumstances, have been laid down.

In Islamic law, *zina* i.e. an illicit sexual relationship (which includes in its definition fornication, adultery and rape) is an extremely serious offence. Giving a hundred lashes to a man or woman indulging in adultery is the punishment prescribed for illicit relations between unmarried persons.

The purpose of meting out punishment in public is to add a deterrent aspect to the penal provision. The idea is that, after seeing the fate of the guilty persons in question, anyone who has any intention of committing such a crime will desist from doing so.

If men or women guilty of illicit sexual relations repent and reform after punishment, they may again resume the lives of believers. But, if they fail to do so, they can no longer be accepted in Islamic society as being fit for marital relations.

⁴ Those who defame chaste women, but cannot produce four witnesses, shall be given eighty lashes. Do not accept their testimony ever after, for they are transgressors, ⁵ save those who afterwards repent and make amends, for truly God is forgiving and merciful.ᵃ

⁶ One who accuses his wife and has no witnesses except himself shall swear four times by God that his charge is true, ⁷ and the fifth time, that God's curse may be upon him if he is telling a lie.

وَٱلَّذِينَ يَرْمُونَ ٱلْمُحْصَنَـٰتِ ثُمَّ لَمْ يَأْتُوا۟ بِأَرْبَعَةِ شُهَدَآءَ فَٱجْلِدُوهُمْ ثَمَـٰنِينَ جَلْدَةً وَلَا تَقْبَلُوا۟ لَهُمْ شَهَـٰدَةً أَبَدًا ۚ وَأُو۟لَـٰٓئِكَ هُمُ ٱلْفَـٰسِقُونَ ۝ إِلَّا ٱلَّذِينَ تَابُوا۟ مِنۢ بَعْدِ ذَٰلِكَ وَأَصْلَحُوا۟ فَإِنَّ ٱللَّهَ غَفُورٌ رَّحِيمٌ ۝ وَٱلَّذِينَ يَرْمُونَ أَزْوَٰجَهُمْ وَلَمْ يَكُن لَّهُمْ شُهَدَآءُ إِلَّآ أَنفُسُهُمْ فَشَهَـٰدَةُ أَحَدِهِمْ أَرْبَعُ شَهَـٰدَٰتٍۭ بِٱللَّهِ ۙ إِنَّهُۥ لَمِنَ ٱلصَّـٰدِقِينَ ۝ وَٱلْخَـٰمِسَةُ أَنَّ لَعْنَتَ ٱللَّهِ عَلَيْهِ إِن كَانَ مِنَ ٱلْكَـٰذِبِينَ ۝

ᵃ If adultery is declared a serious crime, it follows, logically, that falsely accusing a person of adultery must be considered a serious crime too. Therefore, it is laid down that one who accuses another of adultery without being able to prove it, (as prescribed by the rules of the Islamic law), should be whipped eighty times. Moreover, his evidence should be treated thereafter as entirely unacceptable, and, according to the Hanafi School of jurisprudence, the evidence of such a transgressor may never again be legally accepted, even if he repents.

Levelling false allegations against anyone is, in fact, an attempt at moral assassination. Severe punishments are prescribed in Islam for such an offence. Even if a wrongdoer escapes punishment in this world, he cannot in any case escape punishment in the life Hereafter, unless he repents and seeks God's pardon.

8 The wife shall receive no
punishment, if she bears witness four
times in the name of God that her
husband has lied 9 and, a fifth time
that God's wrath will be upon her if
he is telling the truth.[a] 10 Were it not
for God's grace and His mercy upon
you, [you would have come to grief]
and God is wise, acceptor of
repentance.[b]

11 Those who brought up that slander
were a band from among you. Do
not regard it as a misfortune, for it
is good for you.[c] Every one of them
shall be held to account for the sin
he has committed; and he who took
the greater part in it shall have a
terrible punishment.[d]

وَيَدْرَؤُا۟ عَنْهَا ٱلْعَذَابَ أَن تَشْهَدَ أَرْبَعَ
شَهَـٰدَٰتٍۭ بِٱللَّهِ ۙ إِنَّهُۥ لَمِنَ ٱلْكَـٰذِبِينَ
٨ وَٱلْخَـٰمِسَةَ أَنَّ غَضَبَ ٱللَّهِ عَلَيْهَآ إِن
كَانَ مِنَ ٱلصَّـٰدِقِينَ ٩ وَلَوْلَا فَضْلُ
ٱللَّهِ عَلَيْكُمْ وَرَحْمَتُهُۥ وَأَنَّ ٱللَّهَ تَوَّابٌ
حَكِيمٌ ١٠ إِنَّ ٱلَّذِينَ جَآءُو بِٱلْإِفْكِ
عُصْبَةٌ مِّنكُمْ ۚ لَا تَحْسَبُوهُ شَرًّا لَّكُم
بَلْ هُوَ خَيْرٌ لَّكُمْ ۚ لِكُلِّ ٱمْرِئٍ مِّنْهُم مَّا
ٱكْتَسَبَ مِنَ ٱلْإِثْمِ ۚ وَٱلَّذِى تَوَلَّىٰ كِبْرَهُۥ
مِنْهُمْ لَهُۥ عَذَابٌ عَظِيمٌ ١١

---

[a] One of the issues, which is given special emphasis, is that of a man who, without having any witness to prove his case, accuses his wife of going astray; there is only his word for it. In such a case, the matter shall be decided by the taking of oaths, a legal procedure termed *la'an* under the Islamic law.

If a man takes an oath in the prescribed manner, and the woman does not protest—thus accepting the man's contention, the aforesaid punishment shall be imposed on the woman. But, if the woman too states under oath that she is innocent, then no punishment shall be imposed on her. However, separation of the husband and wife shall be enforced.

[b] Matters pertaining to social relations are extremely complex. If the legislation in these matters were left entirely to man, he would emphasize one aspect to the detriment of the other aspects. Divine law, however, simultaneously takes care of all aspects of these matters. Seen from this point of view, divine law is a provision of great mercy bestowed by God upon man.

[c] If a preacher is really treading the path of Truth, then any false propaganda issued against him in fact proves useful to him, because the Truth is ultimately bound to prevail. And when the reality becomes clear, it becomes even more evident that the preacher is on the right path, so that those wavering on this score enter the realm of certainty. They come to realize that indeed the opponents of God's envoy have nothing to offer except false allegations and baseless accusations.

[d] The main active participant in the campaign to vilify 'A'ishah was the notorious hypocrite, 'Abdullah ibn Ubayy. But he was not given any punishment whatsoever. ▶

¹² When you heard of it, why did not the believing men and believing women think well of their own people, and say, 'This is a manifest slander?' ¹³ Why did they not produce four witnesses? If they could not produce any witnesses, they were indeed liars in the sight of God!ᵃ

لَوْلَا إِذْ سَمِعْتُمُوهُ ظَنَّ ٱلْمُؤْمِنُونَ وَٱلْمُؤْمِنَـٰتُ بِأَنفُسِهِمْ خَيْرًا وَقَالُوا هَـٰذَآ إِفْكٌ مُّبِينٌ ۝ لَّوْلَا جَآءُو عَلَيْهِ بِأَرْبَعَةِ شُهَدَآءَ فَإِذْ لَمْ يَأْتُوا بِٱلشُّهَدَآءِ فَأُو۟لَـٰٓئِكَ عِندَ ٱللَّهِ هُمُ ٱلْكَـٰذِبُونَ ۝

He died a natural death, but severe punishment in the Hereafter was announced for him in the Quran. After the incident mentioned above, 'Umar suggested to the Prophet Muhammad that he, ('Abdullah ibn Ubayy), be put to death. The Prophet replied, 'Oh, 'Umar! What would happen if people started saying that Muhammad killed his own Companions?' We gather from this that policy considerations sometimes warrant even major criminals being spared the punishment they deserve in this world, leaving their ultimate fate to be decided in the Hereafter.

ᵃ Every right-minded believer must think well of his fellow believer. Entertaining bad opinions about others is actually exposing one's own evil nature and, conversely, holding a good opinion about others is a proof of one's own righteous nature.

The correct procedure is that whenever anyone speaks ill of any other person, proof should immediately be demanded of him. One who hears such an allegation should not simply start repeating it to others. On the contrary, he should ask the informer to furnish evidence according to the Islamic law to prove that he is right. What he has to say may be worth considering only if he produces witnesses, otherwise he himself becomes the guilty person. Nobody has the right to hold anyone guilty without proof.

¹⁴ Had it not been for the grace of God and His mercy on you in this world and the Hereafter, a terrible punishment would have afflicted you for your plunging headlong into slander. ¹⁵ When you were spreading it with your tongues and saying with your mouths things of which you had no knowledge, you considered it to be a trivial matter, but, in God's sight, it was very serious. ¹⁶ When you heard it, why did you not say, 'It is not right for us to speak of this. God forbid! This is a monstrous slander.'ᵃ ¹⁷ God warns you never to repeat the like of it again, if you are true believers. ¹⁸ God explains the commandments to you. God is all knowing and wise.

¹⁹ Those who desire that indecencies should spread among the believers, will have a painful chastisement in this world and the Hereafter.ᵇ God knows, and you do not know.

وَلَوْلَا فَضْلُ ٱللَّهِ عَلَيْكُمْ وَرَحْمَتُهُ فِى ٱلدُّنْيَا وَٱلْآخِرَةِ لَمَسَّكُمْ فِى مَآ أَفَضْتُمْ فِيهِ عَذَابٌ عَظِيمٌ ۝ إِذْ تَلَقَّوْنَهُ بِأَلْسِنَتِكُمْ وَتَقُولُونَ بِأَفْوَاهِكُم مَّا لَيْسَ لَكُم بِهِ عِلْمٌ وَتَحْسَبُونَهُ هَيِّنًا وَهُوَ عِندَ ٱللَّهِ عَظِيمٌ ۝ وَلَوْلَآ إِذْ سَمِعْتُمُوهُ قُلْتُم مَّا يَكُونُ لَنَآ أَن نَّتَكَلَّمَ بِهَٰذَا سُبْحَٰنَكَ هَٰذَا بُهْتَٰنٌ عَظِيمٌ ۝ يَعِظُكُمُ ٱللَّهُ أَن تَعُودُوا۟ لِمِثْلِهِ أَبَدًا إِن كُنتُم مُّؤْمِنِينَ ۝ وَيُبَيِّنُ ٱللَّهُ لَكُمُ ٱلْآيَٰتِ وَٱللَّهُ عَلِيمٌ حَكِيمٌ ۝ إِنَّ ٱلَّذِينَ يُحِبُّونَ أَن تَشِيعَ ٱلْفَٰحِشَةُ فِى ٱلَّذِينَ ءَامَنُوا۟ لَهُمْ عَذَابٌ أَلِيمٌ فِى ٱلدُّنْيَا وَٱلْآخِرَةِ وَٱللَّهُ يَعْلَمُ وَأَنتُمْ لَا تَعْلَمُونَ ۝

ᵃ The role of the Prophet Muhammad was that of a preacher of Truth. The position of a preacher, or da'i, is always extremely delicate. Even a slight mistake on his part can damage his entire mission. Those who lent an ear to baseless slander concerning a Muslim lady, namely 'A'ishah, and started spreading it all around, were thus acting in a highly irresponsible manner. Had it not been for the timely refutation of the allegations—by direct intervention of God—this would have caused irreparable loss to Islam. Muslims would then have been divided into two groups and would have started fighting against each other. The community, which, according to God's plan, was to serve as a means of eliminating the prevalence of polytheism from the world, would have destroyed itself in an internecine war.

ᵇ Criticism may therefore be legitimate or illegitimate. While the former is supported by strong arguments, the latter lacks any factual basis and must be refrained from. ▶

²⁰ But for the grace of God and His mercy upon you, and were not God compassionate and merciful, [you would have come to grief].

²¹ O you who believe, do not follow in the footsteps of Satan,ᵃ and whoever follows in the footsteps of Satan should know that he enjoins only indecency and evil. But for the grace of God and His mercy upon you, not one of you would ever be purified; but God purifies whom He pleases. God is all hearing and all knowing.

وَلَوْلَا فَضْلُ ٱللَّهِ عَلَيْكُمْ وَرَحْمَتُهُ وَأَنَّ ٱللَّهَ رَءُوفٌ رَّحِيمٌ ۞ يَٰأَيُّهَا ٱلَّذِينَ ءَامَنُوا۟ لَا تَتَّبِعُوا۟ خُطُوَٰتِ ٱلشَّيْطَٰنِ وَمَن يَتَّبِعْ خُطُوَٰتِ ٱلشَّيْطَٰنِ فَإِنَّهُۥ يَأْمُرُ بِٱلْفَحْشَآءِ وَٱلْمُنكَرِ وَلَوْلَا فَضْلُ ٱللَّهِ عَلَيْكُمْ وَرَحْمَتُهُۥ مَا زَكَىٰ مِنكُم مِّنْ أَحَدٍ أَبَدًا وَلَٰكِنَّ ٱللَّهَ يُزَكِّى مَن يَشَآءُ وَٱللَّهُ سَمِيعٌ عَلِيمٌ ۞

In practice, when it is an opponent against whom allegations are made, no great need is felt for any further investigation. The allegations are unquestioningly accepted and the story is spread far and wide. This is not only irresponsible, but is also a serious offence, which is punishable both in this world and the world Hereafter.

ᵃ To follow in the footsteps of Satan means acting upon his secret evil promptings. When for no reason at all the mind of an individual is suddenly flooded by feelings of suspicion, when a man begins harbouring negative thoughts about his opponents, it is the insidious work of Satan. Therefore, when such thoughts and feelings take shape, man should, instead of cultivating them, immediately root them out from his heart. To cultivate such feelings amounts to following Satan.

To raise a hue and cry against others is inconsistent with humility. There are certain individuals who have very high opinions of themselves, while holding unduly bad opinions about others. Neither trait is in consonance with faith. If a man cultivates faith-oriented humbleness, he becomes so engrossed in introspection that he has absolutely no time to engage himself in unfair criticism of others or in calling others to account.

²² Let not those who are possessed of means and plenty among you resolve to withhold their bounty from their kindred and the needy and those who have migrated from their homes in the cause of God.^a Let them forgive and overlook. Do you not wish God to forgive you? God is forgiving and merciful.

²³ Truly, those who accuse chaste, unwary, believing women are cursed in this world and the Hereafter. For them awaits a terrible chastisement.

وَلَا يَأْتَلِ أُوْلُواْ ٱلْفَضْلِ مِنكُمْ وَٱلسَّعَةِ أَن يُؤْتُواْ أُوْلِى ٱلْقُرْبَىٰ وَٱلْمَسَٰكِينَ وَٱلْمُهَٰجِرِينَ فِى سَبِيلِ ٱللَّهِ وَلْيَعْفُواْ وَلْيَصْفَحُواْ أَلَا تُحِبُّونَ أَن يَغْفِرَ ٱللَّهُ لَكُمْ وَٱللَّهُ غَفُورٌ رَّحِيمٌ ۝

إِنَّ ٱلَّذِينَ يَرْمُونَ ٱلْمُحْصَنَٰتِ ٱلْغَٰفِلَٰتِ ٱلْمُؤْمِنَٰتِ لُعِنُواْ فِى ٱلدُّنْيَا وَٱلْأَخِرَةِ وَلَهُمْ عَذَابٌ عَظِيمٌ ۝

---

^a 'A'ishah's father, Abu Bakr, had been giving financial help to Mistah ibn Uthatha, a poor migrant from Makkah, who was a distant relative of his. But when the latter actively spread slander against 'A'ishah, Abu Bakr was naturally hurt by this and vowed that he would never again help Mistah in any way.

In Islam, help is to be given to needy persons on account of their being needy and not on any other grounds. Therefore, the aforementioned Quranic verses were revealed ordering that those who could should not stop giving monetary help to those in need on account of personal grudges. They were asked whether they did not want to be pardoned by God and told that if they expected God's forgiveness, they too should adopt a forgiving attitude towards others. On hearing this verse, Abu Bakr said: 'Yes ! By God! We want You to forgive us; O! Lord of ours!' and he started helping Mistah once again.

In the eyes of a believer, God's commands are of the utmost importance. As soon as a believer becomes aware of God's injunction, he submits to it, even though it may be entirely against his wishes.

²⁴ On the Day when their own tongues, hands and feet shall bear witness against them about what they did—²⁵ on that Day God will justly requite them—and they will realize that God is the truth, that makes all things manifest.^a

²⁶ Corrupt women are for corrupt men, and corrupt men are for corrupt women; good women are for good men and good men are for good women. The latter are absolved from anything they may say; forgiveness and an honourable provision await them.^b

يَوْمَ تَشْهَدُ عَلَيْهِمْ أَلْسِنَتُهُمْ وَأَيْدِيهِمْ وَأَرْجُلُهُم بِمَا كَانُوا۟ يَعْمَلُونَ ۝ يَوْمَئِذٍ يُوَفِّيهِمُ ٱللَّهُ دِينَهُمُ ٱلْحَقَّ وَيَعْلَمُونَ أَنَّ ٱللَّهَ هُوَ ٱلْحَقُّ ٱلْمُبِينُ ۝ ٱلْخَبِيثَٰتُ لِلْخَبِيثِينَ وَٱلْخَبِيثُونَ لِلْخَبِيثَٰتِ وَٱلطَّيِّبَٰتُ لِلطَّيِّبِينَ وَٱلطَّيِّبُونَ لِلطَّيِّبَٰتِ أُو۟لَٰٓئِكَ مُبَرَّءُونَ مِمَّا يَقُولُونَ لَهُم مَّغْفِرَةٌ وَرِزْقٌ كَرِيمٌ ۝

^a Man often denigrates others. But he does not know that the words uttered by him reach God before reaching others. Man uses his hands and legs to harm and oppress others. But, he remains unaware of the fact that when the Day of Judgement arrives, his own hands and legs, being his no longer, will turn against him and act as God's witnesses.

This unawareness is the real root of all evils. If a man were to come to grips with the reality that he lives in a world where the eyes of God do not lose sight of him even for a single moment, and where every single action of his is being recorded by a divinely established system, his whole life would change. He would weigh every word before uttering it, and he would use the powers of his hands and legs with extreme caution.

^b A man is not bad simply because evil is spoken of him. Conversely, no one becomes good simply by popular acclaim. Critical comments genuinely apply to an individual only if they are in accordance with his nature. If evil people pass evil comments about good people, then such comments turn back upon the speakers themselves and good people are completely absolved of any blame.

Nevertheless, those who are personally good may become objects of calumny. It is certain, however, that in the Hereafter they will be considered innocent and no blame will attach to them. Rather, they will be showered with rewards, because they had to face false allegations on account of their breaking off with untruth and their complete attachment to the Truth.

²⁷ Believers, do not enter other people's houses until you have asked their owners' permission and greeted them. That will be the better for you, so that you may be heedful. ²⁸ If you find no one at home, do not go in until permission has been granted you. If you are told to go away, then go away. That is more proper for you. God knows well what you do. ²⁹ There is nothing wrong in your entering uninhabited houses if that serves a useful purpose: God knows all that you do openly, and all that you would conceal.^a

يَـٰٓأَيُّهَا ٱلَّذِينَ ءَامَنُوا۟ لَا تَدْخُلُوا۟ بُيُوتًا غَيْرَ بُيُوتِكُمْ حَتَّىٰ تَسْتَأْنِسُوا۟ وَتُسَلِّمُوا۟ عَلَىٰٓ أَهْلِهَا ذَٰلِكُمْ خَيْرٌ لَّكُمْ لَعَلَّكُمْ تَذَكَّرُونَ ۩ فَإِن لَّمْ تَجِدُوا۟ فِيهَآ أَحَدًا فَلَا تَدْخُلُوهَا حَتَّىٰ يُؤْذَنَ لَكُمْ وَإِن قِيلَ لَكُمُ ٱرْجِعُوا۟ فَٱرْجِعُوا۟ هُوَ أَزْكَىٰ لَكُمْ وَٱللَّهُ بِمَا تَعْمَلُونَ عَلِيمٌ ۩ لَّيْسَ عَلَيْكُمْ جُنَاحٌ أَن تَدْخُلُوا۟ بُيُوتًا غَيْرَ مَسْكُونَةٍ فِيهَا مَتَـٰعٌ لَّكُمْ وَٱللَّهُ يَعْلَمُ مَا تُبْدُونَ وَمَا تَكْتُمُونَ ۩

---

^a The demands of social life require people to meet each other frequently. One way for such a meeting to take place is for a visitor to go to the home of an acquaintance and, without giving any prior notice, walk straight into his house. This is troublesome for both the intruding guest and the householder. Therefore, taking advance permission has been included in the rules of social conduct.

If possible, the better course would be for the visitor to take a prior appointment with the person he intends to visit and then when he arrives, seek the host's permission before entering. Depending upon the cultural environment, there could be different ways of seeking permission, but in every case, observance of Islamic decency is most essential.

Islam wants all the dealings of the social life of a community to be based on consideration for others. The same sensibility should be observed with regard to meetings. If you go to meet someone, and that person, for some reason, wants to be excused from meeting you at that time, then you should return without any ill-feeling. However, this rule does not apply to those public places where, in principle, there is general permission for entry.

³⁰ Tell believing men to lower their gaze and remain chaste. That is purer for them. God is aware of what they do.ᵃ

قُل لِّلْمُؤْمِنِينَ يَغُضُّوا مِنْ أَبْصَٰرِهِمْ وَيَحْفَظُوا فُرُوجَهُمْ ذَٰلِكَ أَزْكَىٰ لَهُمْ إِنَّ ٱللَّهَ خَبِيرٌۢ بِمَا يَصْنَعُونَ ۝

ᵃ By way of guidance as to how men and women should behave at home and in society, two basic injunctions have been given here—one defines that portion of the body which must be covered (*satr*), while the other advises that the eyes should be cast down.

That portion of a male's body, which is required to be kept covered at all times, is from the navel down to the knees, including the knees. This is *satr*, which is obligatory before all except one's wife, or where some need arises by which prohibitions are relaxed, for instance, in the case of medical examinations.

The second important thing is that when a man and a woman happen to confront each other, the man should keep his eyes cast down. A casual meeting between a man and a woman who are not married or who are not very close relatives, should never be as informal as that between any two men. During any casual meeting between a man and a woman, the man should keep his eyes down and if a man happens to accidentally cast a glance at an unknown woman, he should immediately direct his gaze elsewhere and should not deliberately look at her again.

The instructions about looking down and concealing the private parts of the body are also applicable to women, as is made clear in the next verse (Verse 31).

³¹ Say to believing women that they should lower their gaze and remain chaste and not to reveal their adornments—save what is normally apparent thereof, and they should fold their shawls over their bosoms. They can only reveal their adornments to their husbands or their fathers or their husbands' fathers, or their sons or their husbands' sons or their brothers or their brothers' sons or their sisters' sons or maidservants or those whom their right hands possess or their male attendants who have no sexual desire or children who still have no carnal knowledge of women. Nor should they swing their legs to draw attention to their hidden ornaments. Believers, turn to God, every one of you, so that you may prosper.ᵃ

وَقُل لِّلْمُؤْمِنَٰتِ يَغْضُضْنَ مِنْ أَبْصَٰرِهِنَّ وَيَحْفَظْنَ فُرُوجَهُنَّ وَلَا يُبْدِينَ زِينَتَهُنَّ إِلَّا مَا ظَهَرَ مِنْهَا وَلْيَضْرِبْنَ بِخُمُرِهِنَّ عَلَىٰ جُيُوبِهِنَّ وَلَا يُبْدِينَ زِينَتَهُنَّ إِلَّا لِبُعُولَتِهِنَّ أَوْ ءَابَآئِهِنَّ أَوْ ءَابَآءِ بُعُولَتِهِنَّ أَوْ أَبْنَآئِهِنَّ أَوْ أَبْنَآءِ بُعُولَتِهِنَّ أَوْ إِخْوَٰنِهِنَّ أَوْ بَنِىٓ إِخْوَٰنِهِنَّ أَوْ بَنِىٓ أَخَوَٰتِهِنَّ أَوْ نِسَآئِهِنَّ أَوْ مَا مَلَكَتْ أَيْمَٰنُهُنَّ أَوِ ٱلتَّٰبِعِينَ غَيْرِ أُو۟لِى ٱلْإِرْبَةِ مِنَ ٱلرِّجَالِ أَوِ ٱلطِّفْلِ ٱلَّذِينَ لَمْ يَظْهَرُوا۟ عَلَىٰ عَوْرَٰتِ ٱلنِّسَآءِ وَلَا يَضْرِبْنَ بِأَرْجُلِهِنَّ لِيُعْلَمَ مَا يُخْفِينَ مِن زِينَتِهِنَّ وَتُوبُوٓا۟ إِلَى ٱللَّهِ جَمِيعًا أَيُّهَ ٱلْمُؤْمِنُونَ لَعَلَّكُمْ تُفْلِحُونَ ۝

ᵃ With regard to ladies, *satr* defines which parts of her body a woman must cover and which parts she may keep uncovered, either in or outside her house, and before whom, when and under what conditions.

The literal meaning of 'O! You Believers! Turn all together towards God,' is that in carrying out the instructions of the Islamic law, the most important virtues are the receptivity and sincerity of people's hearts. The male and female Companions of the Prophet Muhammad maintained the highest standard in this respect. 'A'ishah says, 'By God! I have never found anybody better than the women of the Ansar when it comes to honouring the Book of God and having faith in its instructions.' When the following verse of the chapter entitled *al-Nur*, 'They should put shawls over their bosoms', was revealed, the Ansar men returned to their houses and conveyed to their wives, daughters and sisters the instructions revealed for them by God.

Some untied their waist-belts while others used their covering sheets and made shawls out of them. The next morning when they offered prayers (*salat*) led by the Prophet Muhammad, it seemed as if crows sat on their heads (because of the scarves they wore). (*Tafsir ibn Kathir*, vol. III, p. 284).

³² Marry those among you who are single, and those of your male and female slaves who are fit [for marriage]. If they are poor, God will provide for them from His bounty, for God's bounty is infinite and He is all knowing. ³³ Those who do not have the means to marry should keep themselves chaste until God grants them enough out of His bounty. If any of your slaves desire a deed of freedom, write it out for them, if you find any promise in them, and give them some of the wealth God has given you. Do not force your [slave] maids into prostitution, in order to enrich yourself, when they wish to preserve their chastity. Yet if anyone forces them, once they have been forced, God will be forgiving and merciful to them. ³⁴ We have sent down clear revelations to you and the example of those who passed away before you and an admonition for the God-fearing.ᵃ

وَأَنكِحُوا۟ ٱلْأَيَـٰمَىٰ مِنكُمْ وَٱلصَّـٰلِحِينَ مِنْ عِبَادِكُمْ وَإِمَآئِكُمْ ۚ إِن يَكُونُوا۟ فُقَرَآءَ يُغْنِهِمُ ٱللَّهُ مِن فَضْلِهِ ۗ وَٱللَّهُ وَٰسِعٌ عَلِيمٌ ۝ وَلْيَسْتَعْفِفِ ٱلَّذِينَ لَا يَجِدُونَ نِكَاحًا حَتَّىٰ يُغْنِيَهُمُ ٱللَّهُ مِن فَضْلِهِ ۗ وَٱلَّذِينَ يَبْتَغُونَ ٱلْكِتَـٰبَ مِمَّا مَلَكَتْ أَيْمَـٰنُكُمْ فَكَاتِبُوهُمْ إِنْ عَلِمْتُمْ فِيهِمْ خَيْرًا ۖ وَءَاتُوهُم مِّن مَّالِ ٱللَّهِ ٱلَّذِىٓ ءَاتَىٰكُمْ ۚ وَلَا تُكْرِهُوا۟ فَتَيَـٰتِكُمْ عَلَى ٱلْبِغَآءِ إِنْ أَرَدْنَ تَحَصُّنًا لِّتَبْتَغُوا۟ عَرَضَ ٱلْحَيَوٰةِ ٱلدُّنْيَا ۚ وَمَن يُكْرِههُّنَّ فَإِنَّ ٱللَّهَ مِنۢ بَعْدِ إِكْرَٰهِهِنَّ غَفُورٌ رَّحِيمٌ ۝ وَلَقَدْ أَنزَلْنَآ إِلَيْكُمْ ءَايَـٰتٍ مُّبَيِّنَـٰتٍ وَمَثَلًا مِّنَ ٱلَّذِينَ خَلَوْا۟ مِن قَبْلِكُمْ وَمَوْعِظَةً لِّلْمُتَّقِينَ ۝

ᵃ Islam clearly approves of married life for both men and women. In case certain persons remain unmarried, due to lack of resources, it is necessary that all the members of society unanimously view it as a common problem and do not rest content until it is solved.

In the period when Islam came into existence, the system of owning slaves was prevalent in Arabia and, indeed, throughout the whole world. Islam, following its basic principles, started abolishing slavery in a very systematic though gradual manner. One of the methods followed was known as *makatibah*. The literal meaning of *kitab* or *makatibah* is 'writing'. Here this term denotes a bond by which a male or female slave promises his or her owner to earn for him a specified amount within stipulated time, after which he or she will be free.

Both male and female slaves were thus being set free either by *makatibah* or by other methods, so much so, that by the end of the period of early Islamic history (the period of the 'four rightly guided caliphs') the institution of slavery had been almost completely abolished. ▶

35 God is the light of the heavens and the earth. His light may be compared to a niche containing a lamp, the lamp inside a crystal of star-like brilliance lit from a blessed olive tree, neither of the east nor of the west.ᵃ The [luminous] oil is as if ready to burn without even touching it. Light upon light; God guides to His light whom He will. God draws such comparisons for mankind; God has full knowledge of everything.ᵃ

﷽ ٱللَّهُ نُورُ ٱلسَّمَٰوَٰتِ وَٱلْأَرْضِ مَثَلُ نُورِهِۦ كَمِشْكَوٰةٍ فِيهَا مِصْبَاحٌ ٱلْمِصْبَاحُ فِى زُجَاجَةٍ ٱلزُّجَاجَةُ كَأَنَّهَا كَوْكَبٌ دُرِّىٌّ يُوقَدُ مِن شَجَرَةٍ مُّبَٰرَكَةٍ زَيْتُونَةٍ لَّا شَرْقِيَّةٍ وَلَا غَرْبِيَّةٍ يَكَادُ زَيْتُهَا يُضِىٓءُ وَلَوْ لَمْ تَمْسَسْهُ نَارٌ نُّورٌ عَلَىٰ نُورٍ يَهْدِى ٱللَّهُ لِنُورِهِۦ مَن يَشَآءُ وَيَضْرِبُ ٱللَّهُ ٱلْأَمْثَٰلَ لِلنَّاسِ وَٱللَّهُ بِكُلِّ شَىْءٍ عَلِيمٌ ۝

In pre-Islamic times and even in the very early period of Islam, there were people who used to make their slave girls work as prostitutes. Abdullah ibn Ubayy had many slave girls whom he forced into prostitution and thus earned a profit out of them. When one of these slave girls embraced Islam and wanted to give up prostitution, Abdullah ibn Ubayy started harassing her. Ultimately, at the behest of the Prophet Muhammad, she was freed from his clutches by paying for her freedom.

ᵃ This is a metaphor with many layers of meaning. 'Light' symbolizes the guidance of God Almighty. 'Niche' is man's heart and 'lamp' is faith (*iman*), sheltered in that niche. The image is elaborated by two more points of reference: 'crystal of star-like brilliance' and 'luminous oil'. Faith, already compared to a 'lamp' standing in the 'niche' of the human heart, is safe and well protected from any external influence by the 'crystal' or the walls of the niche (human heart). The 'luminous oil' filling the lamp and ready to be lit at any moment, speaks of the eagerness with which faith waits for the Truth to appear before it, so that it may accept it without the slightest delay and sets itself ablaze.

The fact is that the only source of light in this universe is God. All receive light and guidance from this source alone. Furthermore, God instilled an intense longing for the Truth in the very nature of man. This desire is very strong and, if not diluted, constantly demands gratification.

By nature, man's receptivity to Truth is so immense and inflames so easily that it may be compared to petrol, which flares up as soon as a spark comes in contact with it. ▶

³⁶ [They worship] in the houses which God has allowed to be raised for the remembrance of His name, morning and evening, ³⁷ people who are not distracted by trade or commerce from the remembrance of God and the observance of prayer and the payment of the zakat—fearing a Day when hearts and eyes will be convulsed,ᵃ ³⁸ so that God may reward them according to the best of their deeds and give them more out of His bounty. God provides for whoever He wills without measure.

فِى بُيُوتٍ أَذِنَ ٱللَّهُ أَن تُرۡفَعَ وَيُذۡكَرَ فِيهَا ٱسۡمُهُۥ يُسَبِّحُ لَهُۥ فِيهَا بِٱلۡغُدُوِّ وَٱلۡـَٔاصَالِ ۝ رِجَالٌ لَّا تُلۡهِيهِمۡ تِجَٰرَةٌ وَلَا بَيۡعٌ عَن ذِكۡرِ ٱللَّهِ وَإِقَامِ ٱلصَّلَوٰةِ وَإِيتَآءِ ٱلزَّكَوٰةِ يَخَافُونَ يَوۡمًا تَتَقَلَّبُ فِيهِ ٱلۡقُلُوبُ وَٱلۡأَبۡصَٰرُ ۝ لِيَجۡزِيَهُمُ ٱللَّهُ أَحۡسَنَ مَا عَمِلُواْ وَيَزِيدَهُم مِّن فَضۡلِهِۦ ۗ وَٱللَّهُ يَرۡزُقُ مَن يَشَآءُ بِغَيۡرِ حِسَابٍ ۝

A seeker is one who has not let his natural instincts become impaired, so that, the moment he hears the genuine call for the acceptance of Truth, his instincts are aroused. The light of guidance coupled with the light of nature then illuminates his entire existence.

ᵃ A mosque in an inhabited locality has the same importance as the heart in the human body. The heart of a human being is illuminated by faith, while mosques are illuminated by prayers. Mosques are constructed so that within their sacred precincts, devotees may concentrate their thoughts on God and spend some time in offering prayers to Him. In the spiritual atmosphere prevailing therein, they turn quite naturally towards their Maker.

A human being, on whom God bestows the gift of divine guidance, learns to recognize the call of truth. His heart is filled with feelings of awe towards God and he decides to lead a God-oriented life. It is people such as these who become self-effacing and self-sacrificing God-worshippers. They are the ones who will receive the unlimited blessings of God.

39 As for those who deny the truth, their works are like a mirage in a desert. The thirsty traveller thinks it to be water, but when he comes near, he finds it to be nothing. He finds God there, who pays him his account in full. God is swift in His reckoning. 40 Or like darkness on a deep ocean covered by waves billowing over waves and overcast with clouds: darkness upon darkness. If he stretches out his hand, he can scarcely see it. Indeed, the man from whom God withholds His light shall find no light at all.^a

وَٱلَّذِينَ كَفَرُوٓاْ أَعْمَٰلُهُمْ كَسَرَابٍ بِقِيعَةٍ يَحْسَبُهُ ٱلظَّمْـَٔانُ مَآءً حَتَّىٰٓ إِذَا جَآءَهُ لَمْ يَجِدْهُ شَيْـًٔا وَوَجَدَ ٱللَّهَ عِندَهُۥ فَوَفَّىٰهُ حِسَابَهُۥ ۗ وَٱللَّهُ سَرِيعُ ٱلْحِسَابِ ﴿٣٩﴾ أَوْ كَظُلُمَٰتٍ فِى بَحْرٍ لُّجِّىٍّ يَغْشَىٰهُ مَوْجٌ مِّن فَوْقِهِۦ مَوْجٌ مِّن فَوْقِهِۦ سَحَابٌ ۚ ظُلُمَٰتٌۢ بَعْضُهَا فَوْقَ بَعْضٍ إِذَآ أَخْرَجَ يَدَهُۥ لَمْ يَكَدْ يَرَىٰهَا ۗ وَمَن لَّمْ يَجْعَلِ ٱللَّهُ لَهُۥ نُورًا فَمَا لَهُۥ مِن نُّورٍ ﴿٤٠﴾

^a In stark contrast to the person who revives his inner natural urge and consequently is blessed with the wealth of faith, there exists the other type whose 'oil' does not become ignited by the fire of Truth.

Of the second type, are those who follow a concocted religion. They build a palace of false hopes and are happy in it. Thus they live with their misconceptions till they are overtaken by death, which suddenly dispels the magical spell of their misconceptions. They then realise that what they thought of as their goal until now, was nothing but a pit of destruction.

Another category consists of open rebels and rejecters of Truth. Disregarding God's guidance, they become utter failures and grope in the dark forever.

41 [Prophet], do you not see that all those who are in the heavens and on earth praise God, as do the birds with wings outstretched? Each knows his own mode of prayer and glorification: God has full knowledge of all that they do. 42 To God belongs the kingdom of the heavens and the earth, and to God shall all things return.ᵃ

43 Do you not see how God drives the clouds, then joins them together, then piles them into layers and then you see the rain pour from their midst? He sends down from the skies mountainous masses [of clouds] charged with hail, and He makes it fall on whom He will, and turns it away from whom He pleases. The flash of His lightning may wellnigh take away the sight.

أَلَمۡ تَرَ أَنَّ ٱللَّهَ يُسَبِّحُ لَهُۥ مَن فِى ٱلسَّمَٰوَٰتِ وَٱلۡأَرۡضِ وَٱلطَّيۡرُ صَٰٓفَّٰتٍ كُلٌّ قَدۡ عَلِمَ صَلَاتَهُۥ وَتَسۡبِيحَهُۥ وَٱللَّهُ عَلِيمٌۢ بِمَا يَفۡعَلُونَ ۝ وَلِلَّهِ مُلۡكُ ٱلسَّمَٰوَٰتِ وَٱلۡأَرۡضِ وَإِلَى ٱللَّهِ ٱلۡمَصِيرُ ۝ أَلَمۡ تَرَ أَنَّ ٱللَّهَ يُزۡجِى سَحَابًا ثُمَّ يُؤَلِّفُ بَيۡنَهُۥ ثُمَّ يَجۡعَلُهُۥ رُكَامًا فَتَرَى ٱلۡوَدۡقَ يَخۡرُجُ مِنۡ خِلَٰلِهِۦ وَيُنَزِّلُ مِنَ ٱلسَّمَآءِ مِن جِبَالٍ فِيهَا مِنۢ بَرَدٍ فَيُصِيبُ بِهِۦ مَن يَشَآءُ وَيَصۡرِفُهُۥ عَن مَّن يَشَآءُ يَكَادُ سَنَا بَرۡقِهِۦ يَذۡهَبُ بِٱلۡأَبۡصَٰرِ ۝

ᵃ What God requires of man, is that he should always remain in the state of submission as demanded by acknowledgement of the Truth. This is the true religion. Viewed from this point, the whole Universe follows the religion of Truth, because everything in the Universe behaves in fact exactly as it should.

Take the example of a bird. When a bird spreads its wings and flies in the air, it presents the ultimate example of being in perfect harmony with the eternal world of reality.

There is a specific mode of prayer and a way of glorifying God prescribed for every single creature of God, which it is expected to adhere to. Similarly, there is a specific method of glorifying God as prescribed for a human being and he is expected to follow it. If a man indulges in heedless or rebellious behaviour on this score, he shall have to pay a heavy price for it.

⁴⁴ God alternates the night and the day—truly, in this there is a lesson for men of insight.ᵃ

⁴⁵ God created every creature from water. Some crawl upon their bellies, others walk on two legs, and others walk on four. God creates what He pleases. He has power over all things. ⁴⁶ We have sent down revelations clearly showing the truth. God guides whom He wills to the straight path.ᵇ

يُقَلِّبُ ٱللَّهُ ٱلَّيْلَ وَٱلنَّهَارَ إِنَّ فِي ذَٰلِكَ لَعِبْرَةً لِّأُوْلِى ٱلْأَبْصَٰرِ ۝ وَٱللَّهُ خَلَقَ كُلَّ دَآبَّةٍ مِّن مَّآءٍ فَمِنْهُم مَّن يَمْشِى عَلَىٰ بَطْنِهِۦ وَمِنْهُم مَّن يَمْشِى عَلَىٰ رِجْلَيْنِ وَمِنْهُم مَّن يَمْشِى عَلَىٰٓ أَرْبَعٍ يَخْلُقُ ٱللَّهُ مَا يَشَآءُ إِنَّ ٱللَّهَ عَلَىٰ كُلِّ شَىْءٍ قَدِيرٌ ۝ لَّقَدْ أَنزَلْنَآ ءَايَٰتٍ مُّبَيِّنَٰتٍ وَٱللَّهُ يَهْدِى مَن يَشَآءُ إِلَىٰ صِرَٰطٍ مُّسْتَقِيمٍ ۝

ᵃ Events of the physical world give direct introduction of the Creator, but only to those who possess insight. Rain for example, results after a series of events that comprise the rain cycle. The lightning and thunder, and the succession of day and night are likewise miraculous phenomena. On seeing such occurences an insightful man mentally journeys to reach beyond external appearances to grasp the higher, innate reality of things. This is called 'ibrah, meaning 'to traverse'.

ᵇ To all appearances, this is a world of multiplicity. Basing their belief on this view, the people of ancient times assumed the creators of all the numerous things of this world to be numerous themselves. But one who deeply observes nature finds that a certain uniformity is hidden in all its apparent multiplicity and diversity; this observation gives an entirely different hue to previous assumptions.

There are many different kinds of animals. But, an in-depth study shows that the underlying biological system of all animals is uniform. Given these facts, the multiplicity and diversity of life around us must be regarded as a miracle of nature's creation. Things which, seen from one angle, appear to manifest the multiplicity of creation, observed from another angle, demonstrate the proof of the unity of creation.

The present world is the one in which one has to discover reality amidst falsity. Here, one has to set oneself above things that are deceptive in order to perceive the Truth. Man has been given wisdom solely for this purpose. Only one who properly uses this divine torch of wisdom shall find the right path, while one who does not, shall descend into a state of moral chaos.

⁴⁷ They say, 'We believe in God and in the Messenger, and we obey.' But then, even after that a group of them will turn away. Those are surely not believers ⁴⁸ and when they are called to God and His Messenger so that he may judge between them, some of them turn away. ⁴⁹ But if the truth happens to be to their liking, they are quite willing to accept it! ⁵⁰ Is there a sickness in their hearts, or are they full of doubt? Or do they fear that God and His Messenger will be unjust to them? The truth is that they themselves are wrongdoers.ᵃ

وَيَقُولُونَ ءَامَنَّا بِٱللَّهِ وَبِٱلرَّسُولِ وَأَطَعْنَا ثُمَّ يَتَوَلَّىٰ فَرِيقٌ مِّنْهُم مِّنۢ بَعْدِ ذَٰلِكَ وَمَآ أُوْلَـٰٓئِكَ بِٱلْمُؤْمِنِينَ ۝ وَإِذَا دُعُوٓاْ إِلَى ٱللَّهِ وَرَسُولِهِۦ لِيَحْكُمَ بَيْنَهُمْ إِذَا فَرِيقٌ مِّنْهُم مُّعْرِضُونَ ۝ وَإِن يَكُن لَّهُمُ ٱلْحَقُّ يَأْتُوٓاْ إِلَيْهِ مُذْعِنِينَ ۝ أَفِى قُلُوبِهِم مَّرَضٌ أَمِ ٱرْتَابُوٓاْ أَمْ يَخَافُونَ أَن يَحِيفَ ٱللَّهُ عَلَيْهِمْ وَرَسُولُهُۥ بَلْ أُوْلَـٰٓئِكَ هُمُ ٱلظَّـٰلِمُونَ ۝

ᵃ While the Prophet was in Madinah, there was a group which had apparently accepted Islam, but which was not really sincere about religion. This group was called the hypocrites (*munafiqun*). These people mouthed their obedience to God and His Prophet, but in practice, at the time of need, their actions would belie their pretensions.

At that time, due to prevailing circumstances, a regular Islamic Court had not yet been established. The Jewish chiefs had been deciding cases as a matter of convention for centuries. But now the Prophet Muhammad had migrated to Madinah and established himself there. It was typical of the half-hearted hypocritical Muslims to agree to have their disputes (with other Muslims) settled by the Prophet Muhammad, provided they were sure that it would be decided in their favour. But when it seemed that the outcome might be unfavourable to them, these hypocrites (*munafiqun*) preferred going to a Jewish chief to have the matter decided.

To all appearances this was an act of great cleverness, but in actuality they were just wronging themselves. Such apparent winners shall have lost their case even before reaching the court of God.

⁵¹ The response of the believers, when they are called to God and His Messenger in order that he may judge between them, is only, 'We hear and we obey.' It is they who will prosper: ⁵² those who obey God and His Messenger, and fear God, and are mindful of their duty to Him, are the ones who will triumph.ᵃ

⁵³ They swear firm oaths by God that if you command them to march forth, they will obey you. Say, 'Do not swear: your obedience, not your oaths, will count. God is well aware of all your actions.'ᵇ

إِنَّمَا كَانَ قَوْلَ ٱلْمُؤْمِنِينَ إِذَا دُعُوٓا۟ إِلَى ٱللَّهِ وَرَسُولِهِۦ لِيَحْكُمَ بَيْنَهُمْ أَن يَقُولُوا۟ سَمِعْنَا وَأَطَعْنَا وَأُو۟لَٰٓئِكَ هُمُ ٱلْمُفْلِحُونَ ۝ وَمَن يُطِعِ ٱللَّهَ وَرَسُولَهُۥ وَيَخْشَ ٱللَّهَ وَيَتَّقْهِ فَأُو۟لَٰٓئِكَ هُمُ ٱلْفَآئِزُونَ ۝ ۞ وَأَقْسَمُوا۟ بِٱللَّهِ جَهْدَ أَيْمَٰنِهِمْ لَئِنْ أَمَرْتَهُمْ لَيَخْرُجُنَّ قُل لَّا تُقْسِمُوا۟ طَاعَةٌ مَّعْرُوفَةٌ إِنَّ ٱللَّهَ خَبِيرٌ بِمَا تَعْمَلُونَ ۝

ᵃ The believer is one who makes himself subservient to God and His Prophet. The moment the decision of God and His Prophet is made known to him, he unhesitatingly complies with it, irrespective of whether it is in accordance with his wishes or against them, whether it protects his personal interests or harms them.

In the life Hereafter, success will crown one who bows down before the commandments of God and His Prophet and whose realisation of God is such that he fears Him the most; to save himself from the displeasure of God becomes the greatest concern of his life.

ᵇ One whose heart has been deeply permeated by God-realisation always has his eyes downcast. His sense of responsibility prepares him for great sacrifices and makes him a man who is frugal with words as he is conscious of his accountability before God.

On the contrary, one who is remiss in his relations with God is assiduous in his relations with other people. He compensates for his shortcomings in deeds by an excess of words. Since he has no proof of good character, he remonstrates with big words in order to promote his image as a trustworthy and respectable person. Those who try to influence others by using the charm of words think that all matters are between human beings. Those who are certain that the real matter is rather between God and man experience a sea-change in their attitude.

⁵⁴ Obey God and obey the Messenger. If you turn away, then he is responsible for what he is charged with and you are responsible for what you are charged with. If you obey him, you will be rightly guided. The Messenger is responsible only for delivering the message clearly.

⁵⁵ God has promised to those among you who believe and do good works that He will surely grant them power in the land as He granted to those who were before them; and that He will surely establish for them their religion which He has chosen for them. He will cause their state of fear to be replaced by a sense of security. Let them worship Me and associate no other with Me. Whoever still chooses to deny the truth is truly rebellious.ᵃ

قُلْ أَطِيعُوا۟ ٱللَّهَ وَأَطِيعُوا۟ ٱلرَّسُولَ فَإِن تَوَلَّوْا۟ فَإِنَّمَا عَلَيْهِ مَا حُمِّلَ وَعَلَيْكُم مَّا حُمِّلْتُمْ وَإِن تُطِيعُوهُ تَهْتَدُوا۟ وَمَا عَلَى ٱلرَّسُولِ إِلَّا ٱلْبَلَٰغُ ٱلْمُبِينُ ۝ وَعَدَ ٱللَّهُ ٱلَّذِينَ ءَامَنُوا۟ مِنكُمْ وَعَمِلُوا۟ ٱلصَّٰلِحَٰتِ لَيَسْتَخْلِفَنَّهُمْ فِى ٱلْأَرْضِ كَمَا ٱسْتَخْلَفَ ٱلَّذِينَ مِن قَبْلِهِمْ وَلَيُمَكِّنَنَّ لَهُمْ دِينَهُمُ ٱلَّذِى ٱرْتَضَىٰ لَهُمْ وَلَيُبَدِّلَنَّهُم مِّنۢ بَعْدِ خَوْفِهِمْ أَمْنًا يَعْبُدُونَنِى لَا يُشْرِكُونَ بِى شَيْـًٔا وَمَن كَفَرَ بَعْدَ ذَٰلِكَ فَأُو۟لَٰٓئِكَ هُمُ ٱلْفَٰسِقُونَ ۝

ᵃ The promise of the grant of a dominant status applied initially to the Prophet Muhammad and his companions, but it also applies to the whole community of the believers. It is observed here that men of faith need not make the possession of power and dominance their target, for these are actually blessings of God, conferred upon deserving believers as a reward for their faith and good deeds.

The purpose of granting this dominant status is to provide the believers with stability in this world, so that they may be able to live peacefully and in safety, lead their lives as the subjects of the One God and pray to Him freely, without fearing their enemies. The dominant status of the people of faith shall continue so long as they remain grateful to God and do not lose their fear of God (taqwa).

Appointing a successor, khalifah, or 'one who comes afterwards', entails the conferring of dominant status and stability on one community in place of the community, which had earlier enjoyed this position. The dominant position is, in fact, a part of the divine trial. God gives this position to all communities, one after another, and thus puts them to the test. For people of faith, this position is a means of judging them.

⁵⁶ Attend to your prayers and pay the *zakat* and obey the Messenger, so that you may be shown mercy. ⁵⁷ Do not think that those who deny the truth can frustrate Our plan on earth; their abode shall be Hell; and it is indeed an evil resort.ᵃ

وَأَقِيمُوا ٱلصَّلَوٰةَ وَءَاتُوا ٱلزَّكَوٰةَ وَأَطِيعُوا ٱلرَّسُولَ لَعَلَّكُمْ تُرْحَمُونَ ۝ لَا تَحْسَبَنَّ ٱلَّذِينَ كَفَرُوا مُعْجِزِينَ فِى ٱلْأَرْضِ وَمَأْوَىٰهُمُ ٱلنَّارُ وَلَبِئْسَ ٱلْمَصِيرُ ۝

ᵃ The blessings of God refer to the position of dominance in the present world and Paradise in the Hereafter. Those who want to make themselves worthy of this blessing should foster three virtues in themselves: piety, charity and the willingness to follow the example of the Prophet.

The first quality is evinced in the regular saying of prayers. Observance of prayers regularly acts as a strong incentive to lead a life of sincerity, modesty and humility, rather than one of false pride and arrogance.

The second quality takes its practical form in *zakat,* the prescribed alms-giving, which means the setting aside of some amount at the prescribed rate from one's wealth and handing it over to *bayt al-mal* or the 'Public Fund'. *Zakat,* conveys the message that people should not be selfish but should be the well-wishers of others. Their well-wishing should go to the extent of fostering a feeling that others have a certain right over them.

The third quality is obedience to the Prophet Muhammad. During his lifetime, this meant obeying him personally, while beyond his lifetime, it means obeying his *sunnah* or tradition. In other words, in all matters of life, the ideal example for the people should be the life of the Prophet of God. People should accept only him as their guide and when confronted with his pronouncements, they should forego their personal opinions. The Prophet should be in the lead and all others should be behind him.

58 Believers, let [even] those whom you rightfully possess, and those who are under age ask your leave on three occasions when they come in to see you: before the morning prayer, when you have taken off your garments in the heat of noon, and after the evening prayer. These are the three occasions for your privacy. At other times, there is nothing blameworthy if you or they go around visiting one another. Thus God makes clear to you His revelations: God is all knowing and wise. 59 When your children have reached the age of puberty, let them still ask permission as their elders do. Thus God expounds to you His revelations: God is all knowing and wise. 60 There is no blame on elderly women who are past the age of marriage, if they take off their outer clothing, without revealing their adornments. But it would be better for them to guard themselves. God is all hearing, all knowing.ᵃ

يَـٰٓأَيُّهَا ٱلَّذِينَ ءَامَنُوا۟ لِيَسْتَـْٔذِنكُمُ ٱلَّذِينَ مَلَكَتْ أَيْمَـٰنُكُمْ وَٱلَّذِينَ لَمْ يَبْلُغُوا۟ ٱلْحُلُمَ مِنكُمْ ثَلَـٰثَ مَرَّٰتٍ مِّن قَبْلِ صَلَوٰةِ ٱلْفَجْرِ وَحِينَ تَضَعُونَ ثِيَابَكُم مِّنَ ٱلظَّهِيرَةِ وَمِنۢ بَعْدِ صَلَوٰةِ ٱلْعِشَآءِ ثَلَـٰثُ عَوْرَٰتٍ لَّكُمْ لَيْسَ عَلَيْكُمْ وَلَا عَلَيْهِمْ جُنَاحٌۢ بَعْدَهُنَّ طَوَّٰفُونَ عَلَيْكُم بَعْضُكُمْ عَلَىٰ بَعْضٍ كَذَٰلِكَ يُبَيِّنُ ٱللَّهُ لَكُمُ ٱلْـَٔايَـٰتِ وَٱللَّهُ عَلِيمٌ حَكِيمٌ ۝ وَإِذَا بَلَغَ ٱلْأَطْفَـٰلُ مِنكُمُ ٱلْحُلُمَ فَلْيَسْتَـْٔذِنُوا۟ كَمَا ٱسْتَـْٔذَنَ ٱلَّذِينَ مِن قَبْلِهِمْ كَذَٰلِكَ يُبَيِّنُ ٱللَّهُ لَكُمْ ءَايَـٰتِهِۦ وَٱللَّهُ عَلِيمٌ حَكِيمٌ ۝ وَٱلْقَوَٰعِدُ مِنَ ٱلنِّسَآءِ ٱلَّـٰتِى لَا يَرْجُونَ نِكَاحًا فَلَيْسَ عَلَيْهِنَّ جُنَاحٌ أَن يَضَعْنَ ثِيَابَهُنَّ غَيْرَ مُتَبَرِّجَـٰتٍۭ بِزِينَةٍ وَأَن يَسْتَعْفِفْنَ خَيْرٌ لَّهُنَّ وَٱللَّهُ سَمِيعٌ عَلِيمٌ ۝

ᵃ In some of the preceding verses certain instructions regarding social behaviour are given. Now these verses were revealed, perhaps as a supplement to and an elaboration of them. For instance, one of the instructions given initially to women regarding the covering of the body was that they should cover their bosoms with scarves or sheets (verse 31). In verse 60 those old women who are past the marriageable age have been exempted from the general rule, and it is laid down that there is no harm in their not following it. These two sets of instructions could have been revealed at one and the same time, but there are four intervening paragraphs (*ruku'*), in which different subjects have been dealt with. It is gathered from traditions that after the initial instructions had been revealed, some practical problems arose. Therefore, in clarification, these later verses were revealed. This shows that the Quran's method is one of gradualness and not that of taking sudden steps. It was possible for God to have revealed all the instructions together at one time, but He chose to reveal them bit by bit, according to the circumstances.

61 There is no harm if the blind, the lame, the sick or you yourselves eat in your own houses, or in the houses of your fathers, or mothers, or brothers, or sisters, or paternal uncles, or paternal aunts, or maternal uncles, or maternal aunts, or in those that you are in charge of or in the house of a friend. There is no objection to your eating together or separately. But when you enter houses, salute one another with a greeting of peace, a greeting from your Lord full of blessings and purity. Thus does God expound to you His commandments, so that you may understand.[a]

لَيْسَ عَلَى ٱلْأَعْمَىٰ حَرَجٌ وَلَا عَلَى ٱلْأَعْرَجِ حَرَجٌ وَلَا عَلَى ٱلْمَرِيضِ حَرَجٌ وَلَا عَلَىٰ أَنفُسِكُمْ أَن تَأْكُلُوا۟ مِنۢ بُيُوتِكُمْ أَوْ بُيُوتِ ءَابَآئِكُمْ أَوْ بُيُوتِ أُمَّهَٰتِكُمْ أَوْ بُيُوتِ إِخْوَٰنِكُمْ أَوْ بُيُوتِ أَخَوَٰتِكُمْ أَوْ بُيُوتِ أَعْمَٰمِكُمْ أَوْ بُيُوتِ عَمَّٰتِكُمْ أَوْ بُيُوتِ أَخْوَٰلِكُمْ أَوْ بُيُوتِ خَٰلَٰتِكُمْ أَوْ مَا مَلَكْتُم مَّفَاتِحَهُۥٓ أَوْ صَدِيقِكُمْ لَيْسَ عَلَيْكُمْ جُنَاحٌ أَن تَأْكُلُوا۟ جَمِيعًا أَوْ أَشْتَاتًا فَإِذَا دَخَلْتُم بُيُوتًا فَسَلِّمُوا۟ عَلَىٰٓ أَنفُسِكُمْ تَحِيَّةً مِّنْ عِندِ ٱللَّهِ مُبَٰرَكَةً طَيِّبَةً كَذَٰلِكَ يُبَيِّنُ ٱللَّهُ لَكُمُ ٱلْءَايَٰتِ لَعَلَّكُمْ تَعْقِلُونَ ۝

---

[a] Before the advent of Islam, Arab society enjoyed total freedom. Thereafter, however, Islam imposed some restrictions on entry into houses, as mentioned above. People thereupon felt that because of these restrictions, their social lives would become very constrained.

These verses were then revealed to clarify matters. It was made clear that the restrictions were meant to regulate and systematize social life and not to curtail legitimate freedom. For instance, if the blind, the lame and the sick were isolated from attendants, relatives, etc., it would amount to making them physically helpless. But this was never the intention of Islam. So, leeway has been made in the earlier provisions and their true spirit has been indicated.

It is stated that Islam's real purpose is that people should be each other's true well-wishers. When a man enters another's house, he should make a salutation, saying: 'Peace be on you and His (God's) blessings be showered on you.' If people are imbued with this spirit, most social evils will automatically cease.

⁶² They only are true believers who
believe in God and His Messenger.
When they are with him on some
matter of common concern, they
should not depart until they have
asked him for permission to do so.
Those who ask you for such
permission are the ones who truly
believe in God and His Messenger.
When they ask you for permission
to attend to some affair of their own,
then grant it to whoever you please
and seek forgiveness from God for
them. God is forgiving and merciful.^a

إِنَّمَا ٱلۡمُؤۡمِنُونَ ٱلَّذِينَ ءَامَنُوا۟ بِٱللَّهِ
وَرَسُولِهِۦ وَإِذَا كَانُوا۟ مَعَهُۥ عَلَىٰٓ أَمۡرٖ
جَامِعٖ لَّمۡ يَذۡهَبُوا۟ حَتَّىٰ يَسۡتَـٔۡذِنُوهُۚ إِنَّ
ٱلَّذِينَ يَسۡتَـٔۡذِنُونَكَ أُو۟لَـٰٓئِكَ ٱلَّذِينَ
يُؤۡمِنُونَ بِٱللَّهِ وَرَسُولِهِۦۚ فَإِذَا
ٱسۡتَـٔۡذَنُوكَ لِبَعۡضِ شَأۡنِهِمۡ فَأۡذَن لِّمَن
شِئۡتَ مِنۡهُمۡ وَٱسۡتَغۡفِرۡ لَهُمُ ٱللَّهَۚ إِنَّ
ٱللَّهَ غَفُورٞ رَّحِيمٌ ۞

---

^a Circumstances often merit holding consultations on common issues to seek co-operation collectively.

At such times, it may happen that certain people lose interest after a while and want to leave. This is not the correct Islamic attitude. However, even among those who are free of this attitude, there may be some who, because of some urgent need, want to leave the gathering before time. These persons must take proper permission from the responsible person (and during the period of the Prophet, it had to be taken from the Prophet himself). Furthermore, if the responsible person does not give them permission, they must ungrudgingly remain till the end of the proceedings.

One who is responsible for the collective affairs of Muslims should possess the temperament and attitude to willingly accede to any request to be excused made on the plea of having something more urgent to attend to. He should pray for the one making such a request to be helped by God Almighty.

⁶³ Do not treat being called by the Messenger like being called by one another. God knows those of you who slip away on some pretext. Let those who go against his order beware lest some affliction befall them or they receive a painful punishment. ⁶⁴ Surely, whatever is in the heavens and on the earth belongs to God. God knows well what condition you are in. On the Day when they return to Him, He will declare to them all that they have done. God has full knowledge of all things.ᵃ

لَّا تَجْعَلُوا دُعَآءَ ٱلرَّسُولِ بَيْنَكُمْ كَدُعَآءِ بَعْضِكُم بَعْضًا ۚ قَدْ يَعْلَمُ ٱللَّهُ ٱلَّذِينَ يَتَسَلَّلُونَ مِنكُمْ لِوَاذًا ۚ فَلْيَحْذَرِ ٱلَّذِينَ يُخَالِفُونَ عَنْ أَمْرِهِۦ أَن تُصِيبَهُمْ فِتْنَةٌ أَوْ يُصِيبَهُمْ عَذَابٌ أَلِيمٌ ۞ أَلَآ إِنَّ لِلَّهِ مَا فِى ٱلسَّمَٰوَٰتِ وَٱلْأَرْضِ ۖ قَدْ يَعْلَمُ مَآ أَنتُمْ عَلَيْهِ وَيَوْمَ يُرْجَعُونَ إِلَيْهِ فَيُنَبِّئُهُم بِمَا عَمِلُوا ۗ وَٱللَّهُ بِكُلِّ شَىْءٍ عَلِيمٌ ۞

ᵃ The commandment to obey the Prophet of God was directly applicable to his contemporaries and subsequently became applicable to all believing men and women.

Those who avoid devoting any efforts to collective affairs may think that they are strengthening their individual interests by not wasting their time on matters which are the concern of the entire community. But any group, which loses its collectivism, makes itself vulnerable to its enemies. The destruction that follows is of a general nature and the harm so caused affects everybody. It does not spare even those who were under the impression that they had made themselves safe by giving full attention to their own matters.

25. THE DISTINGUISHER

In the name of God,
the Most Gracious, the Most Merciful

¹ Blessed be He who has revealed the criterion^a [the Quran] to His servant that he may warn the nations. ² Sovereign of the heavens and the earth, who has begotten no children and who has no partner in His sovereignty, it is He who has created all things and measured them out precisely.

---

^a "The distinguisher" is the literal translation of 'al-furqan', which is the criterion for distinguishing between truth and falsehood. In this context "the distinguisher" means the Quran. God is all knowing and all aware and also the Absolute Sovereign. Revelation of the Book, on behalf of God, has two aspects to it. One is that it is certainly true and there is no doubt about its authenticity. The other is that, acceptance or denial of it cannot have the same outcome.

God alone is the Possessor of all Powers. Nobody can influence His decision and nobody can intervene between Him and His decisions. This very fact ensures that one who adopts the Quran as his mentor, will be successful, while one who ignores it will find it impossible to save himself from failure, which is the fate ordained by God for one who ignores the Truth.

³ Yet they have taken, besides Him, deities who create nothing and are themselves created, and who have no power to harm, or benefit themselves and who control neither death, nor life, nor resurrection.

⁴ Those who deny the truth say, 'This is only a forgery of his own invention in which others have helped him.' What they say is unjust and false. ⁵ They say, 'It is just fables of the ancients, which he has had written down. They are dictated to him morning and evening.' ⁶ Say to them, 'It has been revealed by Him who knows every secret that is in the heavens and on the earth. Truly, He is most forgiving and most merciful.' *ᵃ*

وَٱتَّخَذُوا۟ مِن دُونِهِۦٓ ءَالِهَةً لَّا يَخْلُقُونَ شَيْـًٔا وَهُمْ يُخْلَقُونَ وَلَا يَمْلِكُونَ لِأَنفُسِهِمْ ضَرًّا وَلَا نَفْعًا وَلَا يَمْلِكُونَ مَوْتًا وَلَا حَيَوٰةً وَلَا نُشُورًا ۝ وَقَالَ ٱلَّذِينَ كَفَرُوٓا۟ إِنْ هَـٰذَآ إِلَّآ إِفْكٌ ٱفْتَرَىٰهُ وَأَعَانَهُۥ عَلَيْهِ قَوْمٌ ءَاخَرُونَ ۖ فَقَدْ جَآءُو ظُلْمًا وَزُورًا ۝ وَقَالُوٓا۟ أَسَٰطِيرُ ٱلْأَوَّلِينَ ٱكْتَتَبَهَا فَهِىَ تُمْلَىٰ عَلَيْهِ بُكْرَةً وَأَصِيلًا ۝ قُلْ أَنزَلَهُ ٱلَّذِى يَعْلَمُ ٱلسِّرَّ فِى ٱلسَّمَٰوَٰتِ وَٱلْأَرْضِ ۚ إِنَّهُۥ كَانَ غَفُورًا رَّحِيمًا ۝

ᵃ Those who denied the truth used to denigrate the Quran as a false testament, but in fact the target of their allegation was the Prophet Muhammad. The Prophet appeared to them as an ordinary man. They were unable to understand how an ordinary man could be the possessor of an extraordinary Book.

The Quran touches upon various topics of a historical, psychological and social nature, etc., but no factual error has ever been pointed out in it. This proves that the Quran was authored by a Being who is aware of the secrets of the universe to the fullest extent. Had it not been so, the Quran also would have been full of mistakes—as are found in other man-made books. This fact in itself is the greatest argument in favour of the Quran being a Book of God.

Those who make baseless statements against the Quran, are indulging in undue bravado. Such people will definitely be seized upon by God. However, if they come back to the right path, it is not God's way to take revenge after their repentance. God looks at the individual's present and not his past.

⁷They say, 'What kind of a messenger is this who eats food and walks about in the market-places? Why has no angel been sent down with him to warn us?' ⁸Or a treasure should have been sent down to him, or he should have had a garden from which to eat.' The wrongdoers say, 'You are surely following a man who is bewitched.' ⁹Observe what kind of things they attribute to you. They have surely gone astray and cannot find the right way again.ᵃ

وَقَالُوا مَالِ هَـٰذَا ٱلرَّسُولِ يَأْكُلُ ٱلطَّعَامَ وَيَمْشِي فِي ٱلْأَسْوَاقِ لَوْلَآ أُنزِلَ إِلَيْهِ مَلَكٌ فَيَكُونَ مَعَهُ نَذِيرًا ۞ أَوْ يُلْقَىٰ إِلَيْهِ كَنزٌ أَوْ تَكُونُ لَهُ جَنَّةٌ يَأْكُلُ مِنْهَا وَقَالَ ٱلظَّٰلِمُونَ إِن تَتَّبِعُونَ إِلَّا رَجُلًا مَّسْحُورًا ۞ ٱنظُرْ كَيْفَ ضَرَبُوا لَكَ ٱلْأَمْثَٰلَ فَضَلُّوا فَلَا يَسْتَطِيعُونَ سَبِيلًا ۞

ᵃ Every preacher giving the call for Truth has had to face the same experience, as that of a Prophet. While his contemporaries looked down upon him with contempt, the people of succeeding ages venerated the preacher like a god. This is so because during his lifetime, a prophet lives the life of an ordinary human being and his contemporaries therefore fail to appreciate the wisdom he propagates. They see him cast in an overly idealized form, wearing the halo conferred by legend, and therefore, feel obliged to pay homage to him and glorify him in an exaggerated manner.

The minds of succeeeding generations develop such deep-seated notions about the extraordinary greatness of the prophet, that nobody is held superior to or even at par with him. A living prophet, however, is treated scornfully by the majority of his contemporaries. The few who develop a reasoned understanding of his message are also 'advised' to disassociate themselves from one who is "possessed". Having no rational arguments, the unrelenting contemporaries of a prophet, resort to unfair vilification of his image so as to curb the preaching of his message.

¹⁰ Blessed is He who, if He please, can give you better things than that; gardens watered by flowing streams, and palaces too. ¹¹ They deny the Hour. For those who deny that Hour, We have prepared a blazing fire. ¹² When it sees them from afar, they will hear its raging and roaring. ¹³ When they are thrown into a narrow space, chained together, they will plead for death. ¹⁴ But they will be told, 'Do not call today for one death, call for many deaths!' ¹⁵ Say, 'Which is better, this or the Paradise of immortality which the righteous have been promised? It is their recompense and their destination.' ¹⁶ Abiding there forever, they shall find in it all that they desire. This is a binding promise which your Lord has made.ᵃ

تَبَارَكَ ٱلَّذِىٓ إِن شَآءَ جَعَلَ لَكَ خَيْرًا مِّن ذَٰلِكَ جَنَّٰتٍ تَجْرِى مِن تَحْتِهَا ٱلْأَنْهَٰرُ وَيَجْعَل لَّكَ قُصُورًا ۝ بَل كَذَّبُوا۟ بِٱلسَّاعَةِ ۖ وَأَعْتَدْنَا لِمَن كَذَّبَ بِٱلسَّاعَةِ سَعِيرًا ۝ إِذَا رَأَتْهُم مِّن مَّكَانٍ بَعِيدٍ سَمِعُوا۟ لَهَا تَغَيُّظًا وَزَفِيرًا ۝ وَإِذَآ أُلْقُوا۟ مِنْهَا مَكَانًا ضَيِّقًا مُّقَرَّنِينَ دَعَوْا۟ هُنَالِكَ ثُبُورًا ۝ لَّا تَدْعُوا۟ ٱلْيَوْمَ ثُبُورًا وَٰحِدًا وَٱدْعُوا۟ ثُبُورًا كَثِيرًا ۝ قُلْ أَذَٰلِكَ خَيْرٌ أَمْ جَنَّةُ ٱلْخُلْدِ ٱلَّتِى وُعِدَ ٱلْمُتَّقُونَ ۚ كَانَتْ لَهُمْ جَزَآءً وَمَصِيرًا ۝ لَّهُمْ فِيهَا مَا يَشَآءُونَ خَٰلِدِينَ ۚ كَانَ عَلَىٰ رَبِّكَ وَعْدًا مَّسْـُٔولًا ۝

ᵃ The opponents of Truth frequently make the character of the preacher of Truth their target. In order to prove him untrustworthy, they indulge in all sorts of slander. Thus they give the impression that they would have accepted what the preacher had to say, had he been up to their standard. But this is not correct. Their real problem is not that they do not find the preacher of truth trustworthy. Their real problem is that they have no fear of the reckoning of Judgement Day. Therefore, they go on casting aspersions in an irresponsible manner.

The matter of Truth and untruth is important because they will be examined on this basis in the life hereafter. Those who are fearless about being censured in the Hereafter are consequently not serious about Truth or untruth. And when a man is not serious about something, he does not realise its importance, though numerous arguments may be advanced in its support. The meaningless utterances of such people will cease only when the terrible roar of Doomsday snatches away their words.

¹⁷ On the Day He gathers them all together with those they worship besides Him, He will say, 'Was it you who misled My servants, or did they stray away by themselves?' ¹⁸ They will answer, 'Hallowed be You! It was not proper for us to choose any guardian other than You. But You gave them and their fathers the comforts of this life, so that they forgot Your reminder and thus brought destruction upon themselves.' ¹⁹ [God will say], 'Now, they have given the lie to all your assertions, and you can neither ward off [your punishment] nor obtain any help.' For, whoever of you has committed evil, shall be caused by Us to taste great suffering!' ^a

وَيَوْمَ يَحْشُرُهُمْ وَمَا يَعْبُدُونَ مِن دُونِ اللَّهِ فَيَقُولُ ءَأَنتُمْ أَضْلَلْتُمْ عِبَادِى هَـٰٓؤُلَآءِ أَمْ هُمْ ضَلُّوا۟ السَّبِيلَ ۞ قَالُوا۟ سُبْحَـٰنَكَ مَا كَانَ يَنۢبَغِى لَنَآ أَن نَّتَّخِذَ مِن دُونِكَ مِنْ أَوْلِيَآءَ وَلَـٰكِن مَّتَّعْتَهُمْ وَءَابَآءَهُمْ حَتَّىٰ نَسُوا۟ الذِّكْرَ وَكَانُوا۟ قَوْمًۢا بُورًا ۞ فَقَدْ كَذَّبُوكُم بِمَا تَقُولُونَ فَمَا تَسْتَطِيعُونَ صَرْفًا وَلَا نَصْرًا وَمَن يَظْلِم مِّنكُمْ نُذِقْهُ عَذَابًا كَبِيرًا ۞

---

^a The Quranic commentator Ibn Kathir explains the reminder when he writes, 'They forgot the message You had sent to them through the messengers (prophets) about worshipping You alone and no other.'

The addressee communities of the various prophets were not deniers of the truth or polytheists per se. The prophets sent to them had brought to them the message of worshipping one God alone. But, with the passage of time, they became engrossed in worldly affairs, and developed the belief that their elders and prophets, etc. would become the intermediate means of obtaining God's pardon. But, on the Day of Judgement, all such beliefs will prove false. At that time, people will come to know that the only saviour from God's reckoning is God Himself and no other.

²⁰ We never sent any messengers before you who did not eat food and walk in the market-place. We make some of you a means of trial for others, to see whether you are steadfast. Your Lord is all seeing.^a

وَمَآ أَرْسَلْنَا قَبْلَكَ مِنَ ٱلْمُرْسَلِينَ إِلَّآ إِنَّهُمْ لَيَأْكُلُونَ ٱلطَّعَامَ وَيَمْشُونَ فِى ٱلْأَسْوَاقِ ۗ وَجَعَلْنَا بَعْضَكُمْ لِبَعْضٍ فِتْنَةً أَتَصْبِرُونَ ۗ وَكَانَ رَبُّكَ بَصِيرًا ۝

^a The initial addressees of the Quran were those who accepted as their prophets Noah, Abraham, Ishmael, Moses and others. Despite this, they refused to accept Muhammad. One of the reasons for this is that people of later ages always devise, of their own accord, legendary accounts of their past prophets with a view to glorifying them. In the light of these stories, the personality of their past prophet assumes an almost magical character. Subsequently, when the contemporary prophet comes before them, he strikes them as being an ordinary human being. In their minds, on the one hand, there is the image of the past prophet who appears to them as a superhuman personality, while on the other hand, there is the present, living prophet who appears to them simply in the form of a human being. In the light of this comparison, they find themselves unable to believe in the present prophet. While accepting the institution of prophethood, they reject the prophet.

For the disbelievers, the Prophet and the believers are a source of trial, and for the Prophet and the believers the disbelievers are a source of trial. The trial of those who deny the truth is that they should be able to recognise the latent greatness in the apparently ordinary appearance of the prophet, while for the believers it is that they should not lose patience with the meaningless and provocative utterances of the unbelievers.

²¹ Those who do not expect a meeting with Us say, 'Why are angels not sent down to us?' Or 'Why do we not see our Lord?' Surely, they are too proud of themselves and have greatly exceeded all bounds. ²² There will be no good tidings for the guilty on the day they see the angels; and they will cry out, 'Keep away, keep away!' ²³ and We shall take all that they did and turn it into scattered dust. ²⁴ The inhabitants of the Garden will have the best residence and the finest lodging on that Day.^a

وَقَالَ ٱلَّذِينَ لَا يَرْجُونَ لِقَآءَنَا لَوْلَآ أُنزِلَ عَلَيْنَا ٱلْمَلَٰٓئِكَةُ أَوْ نَرَىٰ رَبَّنَا ۗ لَقَدِ ٱسْتَكْبَرُوا۟ فِىٓ أَنفُسِهِمْ وَعَتَوْ عُتُوًّا كَبِيرًا ۝ يَوْمَ يَرَوْنَ ٱلْمَلَٰٓئِكَةَ لَا بُشْرَىٰ يَوْمَئِذٍ لِّلْمُجْرِمِينَ وَيَقُولُونَ حِجْرًا مَّحْجُورًا ۝ وَقَدِمْنَآ إِلَىٰ مَا عَمِلُوا۟ مِنْ عَمَلٍ فَجَعَلْنَٰهُ هَبَآءً مَّنثُورًا ۝ أَصْحَٰبُ ٱلْجَنَّةِ يَوْمَئِذٍ خَيْرٌ مُّسْتَقَرًّا وَأَحْسَنُ مَقِيلًا ۝

---

^a Those who demand, as a precondition, the physical appearance of God and His angels, before they accept a missionary's message, are not really sincere about it. Frivolous in their attitude, they do not know the implication or meaning of the appearance of God and His angels. The fact is that it is only when the Truth is revealed through a preacher of truth that they will have an opportunity to accept it. The moment Truth shows itself by the appearance of God and His angels, it will be the time for reckoning and judgement, and not the time for acceptance.

Many people labour under the misapprehension that on Judgement Day, when God asks them about their deeds, they will escape His verdict by showing off some good deed of theirs and by saying that they have the patronage of some saint or the other. But, on Judgement Day, all this wishful thinking will vanish into thin air, as if a drop of water had fallen on a red hot iron sheet and disappeared. On that Day, only righteous deeds will be of avail, and not false hopes.

²⁵ On a Day when the sky will split open with its clouds and the angels are sent down rank upon rank, ²⁶ true sovereignty on that Day will belong to the Gracious One, and it will be a hard Day for those who deny the truth. ²⁷ On that Day, the wrongdoer will bite his hands and say, 'Would that I had walked in the Messenger's path! ²⁸ Oh, would that I had never chosen such a one for my companion—²⁹ he made me forgetful of the warning after it had reached me. Satan is man's great betrayer.' ³⁰ The Messenger will say, 'Lord, my people did indeed discard the Quran,' ³¹ thus did We assign to every prophet an enemy from among the sinners; your Lord is sufficient as a guide and a helper.ᵃ

وَيَوْمَ تَشَقَّقُ ٱلسَّمَآءُ بِٱلْغَمَـٰمِ وَنُزِّلَ ٱلْمَلَـٰٓئِكَةُ تَنزِيلًا ۝ ٱلْمُلْكُ يَوْمَئِذٍ ٱلْحَقُّ لِلرَّحْمَـٰنِ ۚ وَكَانَ يَوْمًا عَلَى ٱلْكَـٰفِرِينَ عَسِيرًا ۝ وَيَوْمَ يَعَضُّ ٱلظَّالِمُ عَلَىٰ يَدَيْهِ يَقُولُ يَـٰلَيْتَنِى ٱتَّخَذْتُ مَعَ ٱلرَّسُولِ سَبِيلًا ۝ يَـٰوَيْلَتَىٰ لَيْتَنِى لَمْ أَتَّخِذْ فُلَانًا خَلِيلًا ۝ لَّقَدْ أَضَلَّنِى عَنِ ٱلذِّكْرِ بَعْدَ إِذْ جَآءَنِى ۗ وَكَانَ ٱلشَّيْطَـٰنُ لِلْإِنسَـٰنِ خَذُولًا ۝ وَقَالَ ٱلرَّسُولُ يَـٰرَبِّ إِنَّ قَوْمِى ٱتَّخَذُوا۟ هَـٰذَا ٱلْقُرْءَانَ مَهْجُورًا ۝ وَكَذَٰلِكَ جَعَلْنَا لِكُلِّ نَبِىٍّ عَدُوًّا مِّنَ ٱلْمُجْرِمِينَ ۗ وَكَفَىٰ بِرَبِّكَ هَادِيًا وَنَصِيرًا ۝

ᵃ Whenever a preacher of the Truth calls for its acceptance, those who represent untruth in the name of Truth, become his enemies. They raise a variety of objections and try to cast doubt upon his veracity. In so doing, they are successful in winning wide support.

On the Day of Judgement, those who, taken in by the assertions of false leaders, and not having co-operated with the preacher of Truth, will clearly see that the arguments of their leaders had no real basis in fact. They were simply false objections which they had accepted, as they suited their self-interests, and they had used them as excuses for distancing themselves from the Truth. On the Day of Reckoning they will regret having been taken in by the false arguments of their leaders and not supporting the preacher of God's word.

³² Those who deny the truth say, 'Why was the Quran not sent down to him in a single revelation?' We sent it in this manner, so that We might strengthen your heart. We gave it to you in gradual revelation. ³³ Every time they raise an objection, We will bring you the truth and the best of explanations. ³⁴ Those who will be dragged headlong into Hell shall have an evil place to dwell in, for they have strayed far from the right path.ᵃ

وَقَالَ ٱلَّذِينَ كَفَرُوا۟ لَوْلَا نُزِّلَ عَلَيْهِ ٱلْقُرْءَانُ جُمْلَةً وَٰحِدَةً كَذَٰلِكَ لِنُثَبِّتَ بِهِۦ فُؤَادَكَ وَرَتَّلْنَٰهُ تَرْتِيلًا ۝ وَلَا يَأْتُونَكَ بِمَثَلٍ إِلَّا جِئْنَٰكَ بِٱلْحَقِّ وَأَحْسَنَ تَفْسِيرًا ۝ ٱلَّذِينَ يُحْشَرُونَ عَلَىٰ وُجُوهِهِمْ إِلَىٰ جَهَنَّمَ أُو۟لَٰٓئِكَ شَرٌّ مَّكَانًا وَأَضَلُّ سَبِيلًا ۝

ᵃ When the Quran was revealed, it was not revealed all at once, but part by part over a period of 23 years. Those who denied the truth made this an excuse to say that this was a man-made book and not the book of God, because it would not have been difficult for God to prepare the whole book at one time.

It was clarified that the Quran was not simply the work of any author. It was a divine proclamation of the Truth. One of the strategies of preaching God's will is that it is presented to people gradually, so that it progressively takes root in society.

Every objection against such activity—which is based on perfect Truth—is a false one. Whenever such an objection is raised, but then is properly clarified, the authenticity of the preacher's call is reinforced; it is never in doubt at any stage.

³⁵ We gave Moses the Book, and appointed his brother Aaron as his supporter. ³⁶ Then We said, 'Go together to the people who have denied Our signs.' We utterly destroyed them! ³⁷ We drowned the people of Noah also when they rejected their messengers and We made them an example to all mankind. We have prepared a painful punishment for the wrongdoers, ³⁸ to 'Ad, and Thamud, and the people of al-Rass, and as We did for the many a generation between them. ³⁹ To each of them We gave warnings and each of them We destroyed completely. ⁴⁰ Indeed they must have come upon the town on which an evil rain had poured down. Did they not see it? Yet they have no faith in the Resurrection.ᵃ

وَلَقَدْ ءَاتَيْنَا مُوسَى ٱلْكِتَـٰبَ وَجَعَلْنَا مَعَهُۥٓ أَخَاهُ هَـٰرُونَ وَزِيرًا ۞ فَقُلْنَا ٱذْهَبَآ إِلَى ٱلْقَوْمِ ٱلَّذِينَ كَذَّبُوا۟ بِـَٔايَـٰتِنَا فَدَمَّرْنَـٰهُمْ تَدْمِيرًا ۞ وَقَوْمَ نُوحٍ لَّمَّا كَذَّبُوا۟ ٱلرُّسُلَ أَغْرَقْنَـٰهُمْ وَجَعَلْنَـٰهُمْ لِلنَّاسِ ءَايَةً ۖ وَأَعْتَدْنَا لِلظَّـٰلِمِينَ عَذَابًا أَلِيمًا ۞ وَعَادًا وَثَمُودَا۟ وَأَصْحَـٰبَ ٱلرَّسِّ وَقُرُونًۢا بَيْنَ ذَٰلِكَ كَثِيرًا ۞ وَكُلًّا ضَرَبْنَا لَهُ ٱلْأَمْثَـٰلَ ۖ وَكُلًّا تَبَّرْنَا تَتْبِيرًا ۞ وَلَقَدْ أَتَوْا۟ عَلَى ٱلْقَرْيَةِ ٱلَّتِىٓ أُمْطِرَتْ مَطَرَ ٱلسَّوْءِ ۚ أَفَلَمْ يَكُونُوا۟ يَرَوْنَهَا ۚ بَلْ كَانُوا۟ لَا يَرْجُونَ نُشُورًا ۞

ᵃ The names of many of the prophets to whom the Quran refers again and again do not find a place in the recorded history of humanity. This shows that the scholars who were their contemporaries did not attach any importance to them. They wrote zealously about kings and military heroes, because there was political colour in their lives, but they ignored the prophets, because there was nothing in their lives to feed their political tastes.

Surprisingly, this attitude is prevalent even today. Those who attain prominence on the political platform, immediately find a place in the media. Those who work in non-political fields are not considered either mentionable or memorable.

The most important thing required of a man is that he should learn lessons from events, but this is exactly what he fails to do. This is as true now as it was in the past.

⁴¹ Whenever they see you they only make a mockery of you—'Is this the one God has sent as His Messenger? ⁴² Indeed, he would well-nigh have led us astray from our deities, had we not been [so] steadfastly attached to them!' ᵃ When they behold the punishment, they shall realize who strayed furthest from the right path.

وَإِذَا رَأَوْكَ إِن يَتَّخِذُونَكَ إِلَّا هُزُوًا أَهَـٰذَا ٱلَّذِى بَعَثَ ٱللَّهُ رَسُولًا ۝ إِن كَادَ لَيُضِلُّنَا عَنْ ءَالِهَتِنَا لَوْلَآ أَن صَبَرْنَا عَلَيْهَا ۚ وَسَوْفَ يَعْلَمُونَ حِينَ يَرَوْنَ ٱلْعَذَابَ مَنْ أَضَلُّ سَبِيلًا ۝

ᵃ The response of those who fail to accept the truth shows that the reason for their being steadfast in their faith, was their prejudice and not the force of any argument. They had become defenceless in the matter of arguments, but they adhered to the religion of their forefathers on the strength of prejudice. This is the position of the majority of the people. The majority are simply swayed by prejudice, though they profess that their case rests on sound arguments.

There are two methods of opposing a mission. One is to reject it on the basis of arguments, while the other is to ridicule it. The first method is legitimate, while the second is quite improper. Those who heap scorn on a mission, actually demonstrate that they have lost the game when it comes to arguments, and that they simply want to cover up their defeat by falling back on ridicule.

43 Have you seen him who has taken his own desire to be his god?*a* Can you be a guardian over him? 44 Do you think most of them can hear or understand? They are like cattle.*b* Indeed, they are even more astray.

أَرَءَيْتَ مَنِ ٱتَّخَذَ إِلَٰهَهُۥ هَوَىٰهُ أَفَأَنتَ تَكُونُ عَلَيْهِ وَكِيلًا ۝ أَمْ تَحْسَبُ أَنَّ أَكْثَرَهُمْ يَسْمَعُونَ أَوْ يَعْقِلُونَ ۚ إِنْ هُمْ إِلَّا كَٱلْأَنْعَٰمِ ۖ بَلْ هُمْ أَضَلُّ سَبِيلًا ۝

---

a According to a tradition the Prophet is reported to have said, 'Among all the deities besides God being worshipped under the sky, the most serious before God is that desire which is followed.'

It is a fact that the greatest object of worship is the ignoble desire of man; Many deities have been devised simply to justify the religion of desire-worship.

b Responding to the lure of desire, a man descends to the level of an animal. Animals do not act as a result of thinking, but simply submit to the pressure of their natural instincts. Now, if a man does not utilise his thinking capacity and simply follows the dictates of his base desires, what is the difference between him and an animal?

⁴⁵ Have you not seen how your Lord lengthens the shadows? Had He pleased, He could have made them constant; then We placed the sun as an indicator for them, ⁴⁶ then We withdrew it to Us, a gradual withdrawal. ⁴⁷ It is He who made the night a mantle for you, and sleep for repose; and made the day a time for rising.ᵃ ⁴⁸ It is He who sends the winds as heralds of His mercy and We send down pure water from the sky, ⁴⁹ so that We may bring life to a dead land; and slake the thirst of Our creation; cattle and men, in great numbers.ᵃ

أَلَمۡ تَرَ إِلَىٰ رَبِّكَ كَيۡفَ مَدَّ ٱلظِّلَّ وَلَوۡ شَآءَ لَجَعَلَهُۥ سَاكِنًا ثُمَّ جَعَلۡنَا ٱلشَّمۡسَ عَلَيۡهِ دَلِيلًا ۝ ثُمَّ قَبَضۡنَٰهُ إِلَيۡنَا قَبۡضًا يَسِيرًا ۝ وَهُوَ ٱلَّذِى جَعَلَ لَكُمُ ٱلَّيۡلَ لِبَاسًا وَٱلنَّوۡمَ سُبَاتًا وَجَعَلَ ٱلنَّهَارَ نُشُورًا ۝ وَهُوَ ٱلَّذِى أَرۡسَلَ ٱلرِّيَٰحَ بُشۡرًا بَيۡنَ يَدَىۡ رَحۡمَتِهِۦ وَأَنزَلۡنَا مِنَ ٱلسَّمَآءِ مَآءً طَهُورًا ۝ لِنُحۡـِۧىَ بِهِۦ بَلۡدَةً مَّيۡتًا وَنُسۡقِيَهُۥ مِمَّا خَلَقۡنَآ أَنۡعَٰمًا وَأَنَاسِىَّ كَثِيرًا ۝

ᵃ The phenomenon which in the present age is known as the axial rotation of the earth has been set down here in layman's language. The earth rotates on its axis once in twenty-four hours, due to which day and night follow upon each other. This is a wonderful miracle of Almighty God's power. Had there been no axial rotation of the earth, half of it would have been continuously under the blazing sun, while the other half would have been continuously enveloped by night. Thus it would have been extremely difficult to live on the earth.

There are many lessons in this system of the earth. Just as the light of day necessarily follows the darkness of night; in the same way untruth will be followed by Truth. Similarly, waking up in the morning after sleeping at night is symbolic of resurrection in the life after death.

Likewise, there is a lesson hidden in the system of the rains. Just as the dead earth is revived thanks to the rains, so also does God's guidance instil faith and fear of God in a heart which otherwise would have become as lifeless as an arid land.

⁵⁰ We have explained it to them in diverse ways, so that they may take heed, but most persist in their ingratitude. ⁵¹ If We had so wished, We might have sent a warner into every town, ⁵² so do not yield to those who deny the truth, but strive with the utmost strenuousness by means of this [Quran, to convey its message to them].ᵃ

وَلَقَدْ صَرَّفْنَٰهُ بَيْنَهُمْ لِيَذَّكَّرُوا فَأَبَىٰ
أَكْثَرُ ٱلنَّاسِ إِلَّا كُفُورًا ۞ وَلَوْ
شِئْنَا لَبَعَثْنَا فِى كُلِّ قَرْيَةٍ نَّذِيرًا ۞
فَلَا تُطِعِ ٱلْكَٰفِرِينَ وَجَٰهِدْهُم
بِهِۦ جِهَادًا كَبِيرًا ۞

ᵃ In the Quran, the topics of the unity of God and the Hereafter have been described again and again in a number of different ways. If a man is serious, these discourses are enough to arouse his interest. But one who is unheeding is not influenced by any argument.

Undertaking the great *jihad* by means of the Quran means a peaceful struggle to spread the word of God. That is to say, peaceful struggle is the real *jihad*—nay, the greatest *jihad*. Even if opponents try to divert the attention of the believers from the realm of peaceful efforts, it should then be the endeavour of the believers to concentrate upon the field of preaching based on the teachings of the Quran. However, if, due to the distraction caused by opponents, the field of action appears to be changing at any time, then all possible efforts should be made to bring it back to the field of peaceful activity aimed at conveying the message of the Quran.

⁵³ It is He who released the two bodies of flowing water, one sweet and fresh and the other salty and bitter, and set up an insurmountable barrier between them.^a ⁵⁴ It is He who has created human beings from water and He has granted them the ties of blood as well as marriage.^b Your Lord is all powerful.

۞ وَهُوَ ٱلَّذِى مَرَجَ ٱلۡبَحۡرَيۡنِ هَٰذَا عَذۡبٌ فُرَاتٌ وَهَٰذَا مِلۡحٌ أُجَاجٌ وَجَعَلَ بَيۡنَهُمَا بَرۡزَخًا وَحِجۡرًا مَّحۡجُورًا ۝ وَهُوَ ٱلَّذِى خَلَقَ مِنَ ٱلۡمَآءِ بَشَرًا فَجَعَلَهُۥ نَسَبًا وَصِهۡرًا وَكَانَ رَبُّكَ قَدِيرًا ۝

^a When two rivers meet or a river flows down into the sea, at the point of confluence, in spite of coming together, the two waters remain separate and a line of demarcation can be seen for quite a distance. The writer of these words has witnessed this scene at the meeting place of the rivers Ganges and Yamuna at Allahabad. This happens under the natural law which in the present age is known as 'surface tension'. Similarly, at the sea coast when the tides are rising the salt sea water rides over the coastal river's fresh water. But the surface tension keeps the two waters separate, and when the tide goes out, the saltish water withdraws from above (without affecting the water below), and the fresh water below maintains its natural character. Due to this surface tension law, it has been possible to find reservoirs of fresh water in the very midst of salt sea waters to meet the needs of voyagers.

^b The main constituent of the human body is water. That wonderful creation, called the human being, came into existence with water. Then by the natural process of procreation, generation followed upon generation. If we identify and study similar events which take place on the earth, we will find symbols of God's power hidden in them.

⁵⁵ Yet they worship besides God that which can neither benefit them nor harm them. One who denies the truth is a helper [of evil] against his Lord. ⁵⁶ We have sent you only as a bearer of glad tidings and as a warner. ⁵⁷ Say, 'I do not ask you for any recompense for this except that anyone who so wishes should take the right path to his Lord.'ᵃ

وَيَعْبُدُونَ مِن دُونِ ٱللَّهِ مَا لَا يَنفَعُهُمْ وَلَا يَضُرُّهُمْ وَكَانَ ٱلْكَافِرُ عَلَىٰ رَبِّهِۦ ظَهِيرًا ۝ وَمَآ أَرْسَلْنَٰكَ إِلَّا مُبَشِّرًا وَنَذِيرًا ۝ قُلْ مَآ أَسْـَٔلُكُمْ عَلَيْهِ مِنْ أَجْرٍ إِلَّا مَن شَآءَ أَن يَتَّخِذَ إِلَىٰ رَبِّهِۦ سَبِيلًا ۝

ᵃ God has placed man in a world in which every thing and indeed the entire atmosphere bear testimony to the unity of God. But man does not avail of the light of guidance from it. He goes so far astray that he builds the system of his life on the basis of polytheism instead of the unity of God. If a servant of God takes up the task of proclaiming the unity of God, he meets with dire opposition.

However, the preacher of Truth is not allowed to go to the extent of indulging in violence. He has to pursue his mission keeping himself within the sphere of advice and admonition or persuasion. If his call is not being effective, it is not his duty to add violence to his preaching. The only additions he can make consist of praying to God, ending all material or worldly quarrels unilaterally and influencing people's hearts by selflessness and good behaviour.

⁵⁸ Put your trust in the One who is the Ever-Living [God], who never dies, and glorify Him with His praise. He is fully aware of the sins of His servants; ⁵⁹ it is He who created the heavens and the earth and all that is between them in six Days [periods],ᵃ then settled Himself on the throne—the Gracious One. Ask any informed person about Him.ᵇ ⁶⁰ When they are told, 'Prostrate yourselves before the Gracious One,' they ask, 'Who is this Gracious One? Shall we prostrate ourselves before whatever you will?' This increases their aversion.

وَتَوَكَّلْ عَلَى ٱلْحَيِّ ٱلَّذِى لَا يَمُوتُ وَسَبِّحْ بِحَمْدِهِۦ وَكَفَىٰ بِهِۦ بِذُنُوبِ عِبَادِهِۦ خَبِيرًا ۝ ٱلَّذِى خَلَقَ ٱلسَّمَـٰوَٰتِ وَٱلْأَرْضَ وَمَا بَيْنَهُمَا فِى سِتَّةِ أَيَّامٍ ثُمَّ ٱسْتَوَىٰ عَلَى ٱلْعَرْشِ ٱلرَّحْمَـٰنُ فَسْـَٔلْ بِهِۦ خَبِيرًا ۝ وَإِذَا قِيلَ لَهُمُ ٱسْجُدُوا۟ لِلرَّحْمَـٰنِ قَالُوا۟ وَمَا ٱلرَّحْمَـٰنُ أَنَسْجُدُ لِمَا تَأْمُرُنَا وَزَادَهُمْ نُفُورًا ۩ ۝

ᵃ Here 'six Days' means six Days of God. In the language of human beings, it may be called six stages or six periods. The Creation of the Universe in six stages indicates that it was done in a well planned manner. Whatever is brought into existence on the basis of a plan and a specific arrangement cannot be futile.

ᵇ In the question the stress is on the subject matter and not on the person to whom the question is put. The idea is that if a man is acquainted with God's wonderful marvels, he will be able to tell you how High and Mighty is the Merciful God. The research undertaken by scientists in modern times partially fits the meaning of this verse. If a man learns the secrets of the universe which have come to light as a result of scientific research, he will become extremely excited, his hair will stand on end and his heart will spontaneously bow down before the Might of the Creator.

⁶¹Exalted is He who put constellations^a in the heavens, a radiant lamp and an illuminating moon—⁶²it is He who has made night and day succeed each other, a sign for those who would take heed and would be grateful.^b

تَبَارَكَ ٱلَّذِى جَعَلَ فِى ٱلسَّمَآءِ بُرُوجًا وَجَعَلَ فِيهَا سِرَاجًا وَقَمَرًا مُّنِيرًا ۝ وَهُوَ ٱلَّذِى جَعَلَ ٱلَّيْلَ وَٱلنَّهَارَ خِلْفَةً لِّمَنْ أَرَادَ أَن يَذَّكَّرَ أَوْ أَرَادَ شُكُورًا ۝

---

^a This passage possibly refers to what is known as the solar system. The original Arabic word *buruj* literally means a castle or fort, but scholars differ as to its exact meaning in this context.

^b Among the numerous phenomena of our solar system is the constant revolution of the earth around the sun. Its revolution has a fixed orbit and is completed in one year. Due to the elliptical shape of its orbit and the sun not being at its exact centre, the different seasons occur. Besides its revolution, the earth rotates on its axis and this is completed in twenty-four hours. This rotation is the cause of day and night.

In the vastness of space, the revolution and rotation of the earth with extreme precision and their being greatly subservient to human beings' interests, are the most wonderful of happenings. One who ponders over these blessings will be overwhelmed with feelings of gratitude to God.

⁶³ The true servants of the Gracious One are those who walk upon the earth with humility and when they are addressed by the ignorant ones, their response is, 'Peace'; ⁶⁴ and those who spend the night prostrating themselves, and standing before their Lord, ⁶⁵ who say, 'Our Lord, ward off from us the punishment of Hell, for its punishment is a dreadful torment to suffer. ⁶⁶ Indeed, it is an evil abode and evil dwelling-place.' ⁶⁷ They are those who are neither extravagant nor niggardly, but keep a balance between the two;ᵃ

وَعِبَادُ ٱلرَّحْمَٰنِ ٱلَّذِينَ يَمْشُونَ عَلَى ٱلْأَرْضِ هَوْنًا وَإِذَا خَاطَبَهُمُ ٱلْجَٰهِلُونَ قَالُوا سَلَٰمًا ۝ وَٱلَّذِينَ يَبِيتُونَ لِرَبِّهِمْ سُجَّدًا وَقِيَٰمًا ۝ وَٱلَّذِينَ يَقُولُونَ رَبَّنَا ٱصْرِفْ عَنَّا عَذَابَ جَهَنَّمَ إِنَّ عَذَابَهَا كَانَ غَرَامًا ۝ إِنَّهَا سَآءَتْ مُسْتَقَرًّا وَمُقَامًا ۝ وَٱلَّذِينَ إِذَآ أَنفَقُوا لَمْ يُسْرِفُوا وَلَمْ يَقْتُرُوا وَكَانَ بَيْنَ ذَٰلِكَ قَوَامًا ۝

ᵃ A man's way of walking symbolises his whole personality. Those in whose hearts belief in God has taken firm root, become the embodiment of humility and modesty. The fear of God takes away any sense of superiority they may have. This sense of servitude to God permeates all aspects of their lives.

But this is not all. The realisation of God makes them (the believers) true advocates of His cause. In discharging this responsibility, they often face strong opposition from their addressees. The promulgation of the truth by the believers becomes unbearable to those who deny the truth and they take aggressive action against the preachers. But the fear of God prevents the believers from retaliating; they simply avoid conflict and pray for their opponents to be guided.

The realization of God results not only in their calling upon God during the daytime but also in their nights being filled with the remembrance of God.

Similarly, realisation of God makes them extremely prudent. They earn with a sense of responsibility and spend with a sense of responsibility. It is their sense of accountability to God which makes them moderate and cautious in the matter of income and expenditure. A tradition of the Prophet says, 'Wisdom lies in man adopting the path of moderation.'

⁶⁸ those who never invoke any other deity besides God, nor take a life which God has made sacred, except with the right to do so, nor commit adultery.ᵃ Anyone who does that shall face punishment: ⁶⁹ he shall have his suffering doubled on the Day of Resurrection and he will abide forever in disgrace, ⁷⁰ except for those who repent and believe and do good deeds. God will change the evil deeds of such people into good ones: He is most forgiving and most merciful. ⁷¹ He who repents and does good deeds has truly turned to God.ᵇ

وَٱلَّذِينَ لَا يَدْعُونَ مَعَ ٱللَّهِ إِلَٰهًا ءَاخَرَ وَلَا يَقْتُلُونَ ٱلنَّفْسَ ٱلَّتِي حَرَّمَ ٱللَّهُ إِلَّا بِٱلْحَقِّ وَلَا يَزْنُونَ ۚ وَمَن يَفْعَلْ ذَٰلِكَ يَلْقَ أَثَامًا ۝ يُضَٰعَفْ لَهُ ٱلْعَذَابُ يَوْمَ ٱلْقِيَٰمَةِ وَيَخْلُدْ فِيهِ مُهَانًا ۝ إِلَّا مَن تَابَ وَءَامَنَ وَعَمِلَ عَمَلًا صَٰلِحًا فَأُوْلَٰئِكَ يُبَدِّلُ ٱللَّهُ سَيِّئَاتِهِمْ حَسَنَٰتٍ ۗ وَكَانَ ٱللَّهُ غَفُورًا رَّحِيمًا ۝ وَمَن تَابَ وَعَمِلَ صَٰلِحًا فَإِنَّهُۥ يَتُوبُ إِلَى ٱللَّهِ مَتَابًا ۝

ᵃ Three sins have been mentioned in this verse—polytheism, the killing of a person without justification and adultery. These three forms of wrongdoing are great sins against God and His subjects. The sign of real faith in God is that a man abstains from them. Those who have indulged in these sins can save themselves from retribution by repentance, but for those who die without repenting and reforming, there will be severe punishment before God at God's behest, which they will in no way be able to avoid.

ᵇ Real virtue in the eyes of God is a man's becoming God-fearing. Any virtue which makes a man fearless of God is, in fact, a sin, while that sin which makes a man God-fearing is in fact, in terms of its result, a virtue.

If a man happens to commit a sin but later on, seeing the error of his ways rushes towards Him in repentance (*tawbah*) and seeks His pardon, then God will mercifully add this sin to the list of his virtues, because that had made him turn towards Him.

⁷² And those who do not bear false witness, and when they pass by frivolity, they pass by with dignity; ⁷³ who do not turn a blind eye and a deaf ear to the signs of their Lord when they are reminded of them; ⁷⁴ who say, 'Lord, grant us joy in our wives and children and make us a model for the righteous.'^b

وَٱلَّذِينَ لَا يَشْهَدُونَ ٱلزُّورَ وَإِذَا مَرُّواْ بِٱللَّغْوِ مَرُّواْ كِرَامًا ۝ وَٱلَّذِينَ إِذَا ذُكِّرُواْ بِـَٔايَٰتِ رَبِّهِمْ لَمْ يَخِرُّواْ عَلَيْهَا صُمًّا وَعُمْيَانًا ۝ وَٱلَّذِينَ يَقُولُونَ رَبَّنَا هَبْ لَنَا مِنْ أَزْوَٰجِنَا وَذُرِّيَّٰتِنَا قُرَّةَ أَعْيُنٍ وَٱجْعَلْنَا لِلْمُتَّقِينَ إِمَامًا ۝

---

^a In the present world, Satan has been at pains to glamourize wrongdoing and has taught the worshipper of untruth to present his case in the most appealing way. People, deceived by appearances, are therefore drawn towards evil. But if the outer covering of deceit could be removed, the wickedness thus uncovered would appear so ugly that people would be sure to keep their distance from it.

From this point of view, every bad thing in which a man indulges is a falsehood. In the present world, the test of a man is that he should recognise falsehood. He should be able to tear down the outer curtain and see things in the light of reality.

When a man is given advice which goes against his whims and fancies, he immediately becomes annoyed. In the eyes of God, such a person is blind and deaf, because he has not used his eyes to see reality and has not used his ears to hear the voice of Truth. If he has not welcomed the advice, it is because he is like a man deprived of the powers of hearing and seeing. In the eyes of God, a man capable of seeing and hearing is one who avoids pointless things when he sees them, but if true advice comes his way, immediately accepts it.

^b Every man with a family is the leader (*imam*) of his family. If his family members are God-fearing, he is the *imam* of God-fearing people. But if his family members are forgetful of God, he is at the head of those who are oblivious of God.

⁷⁵ These are the ones who will be rewarded with lofty mansions in Paradise, for their steadfastness. They will be received therein with greetings of welcome and salutations of peace. ⁷⁶ There they shall abide forever: a blessed dwelling and a blessed resting place. ⁷⁷ Say, 'What would my Lord care for you, if you do not call on Him. Because you have indeed rejected the truth and His punishment is bound to overtake you.^a

أُوْلَٰئِكَ يُجْزَوْنَ ٱلْغُرْفَةَ بِمَا صَبَرُواْ وَيُلَقَّوْنَ فِيهَا تَحِيَّةً وَسَلَٰمًا ۝ خَٰلِدِينَ فِيهَا ۚ حَسُنَتْ مُسْتَقَرًّا وَمُقَامًا ۝ قُلْ مَا يَعْبَؤُاْ بِكُمْ رَبِّى لَوْلَا دُعَآؤُكُمْ ۖ فَقَدْ كَذَّبْتُمْ فَسَوْفَ يَكُونُ لِزَامًۢا ۝

---

^a Those who had humbled themselves in this world for the sake of Truth, will be lodged in the loftiest dwellings of paradise. They lived with humility in this world, so in the Hereafter God will reward them with high status. This was expressed by Jesus Christ as follows: 'Blessed are those who are poor in this world. It is they who will enter the Kingdom of Heaven.'

Paradise is the place on high where all desires will be completely fulfilled; The qualities which take a human being to paradise may be developed by one who is prepared to exercise patience. For, in exercising patience, he will be able to fully curb his desires in this world. This is the price one has to pay for entering Paradise. One who is not prepared to pay the requisite price of patience in this world will be doomed to live forever in hell.

26. THE POETS

In the name of God,
the Most Gracious, the Most Merciful

¹ *Ta Sin Mim*

² These are the verses of the Book that makes things clear. ³ It may be that you will destroy yourself with grief because they will not believe. ⁴ But if We had so willed, We could have sent down to them a sign from the heavens so that their heads would be bowed down before it in utter humility. ⁵ Whenever there comes to them any fresh warning from the Merciful, they always turn their backs on it: ⁶ they have indeed rejected the message. But the truth of what they laughed to scorn will dawn upon them before long.ᵃ

طسمٓ ۝ تِلْكَ ءَايَتُ ٱلْكِتَبِ ٱلْمُبِينِ ۝ لَعَلَّكَ بَخِعٌ نَّفْسَكَ أَلَّا يَكُونُوا۟ مُؤْمِنِينَ ۝ إِن نَّشَأْ نُنَزِّلْ عَلَيْهِم مِّنَ ٱلسَّمَآءِ ءَايَةً فَظَلَّتْ أَعْنَقُهُمْ لَهَا خَضِعِينَ ۝ وَمَا يَأْتِيهِم مِّن ذِكْرٍ مِّنَ ٱلرَّحْمَنِ مُحْدَثٍ إِلَّا كَانُوا۟ عَنْهُ مُعْرِضِينَ ۝ فَقَدْ كَذَّبُوا۟ فَسَيَأْتِيهِمْ أَنۢبَٰٓؤُا۟ مَا كَانُوا۟ بِهِۦ يَسْتَهْزِءُونَ ۝

ᵃ The call for Truth reveals itself with total clarity. The sign of a call being Divine is that everything is clear and based on clear arguments. One may deny it, but nobody would be in a position to say that he has not grasped its message.

'It may be that you will destroy yourself.' These words show the very strong feelings of well-wishing that a preacher has towards his addressees. The desire to spread the word of God gushes forth from such pure feelings. So, when God's envoy observes that an addressee does not accept his message, he worries about him as a mother would worry about the welfare of her child. This sentence of the Quran is the confirmation of the benevolent feelings of the preacher and does not indicate criticism of his addressee.

The call for Truth is the call of God. God is that Being who is all-powerful but who nevertheless may be denied or rebelled against. But, this present position is in accordance with God's own plan. God wants such human beings to settle in paradise as are able to recognise the Truth in this world full of deception, and who bow down before Him without any compulsion. The selection of such individuals may be made only under conditions where everyone enjoys complete freedom of thought and action.

⁷ Do they not see the earth, and what beneficial kinds of things We have caused to grow in it? ⁸ Surely in this there is a sign, yet most of them would not believe: ⁹ truly, your Lord is the Mighty One, the Merciful.ᵃ

أَوَلَمْ يَرَوْاْ إِلَى ٱلْأَرْضِ كَمْ أَنۢبَتْنَا فِيهَا مِن كُلِّ زَوْجٍ كَرِيمٍ ۝ إِنَّ فِي ذَٰلِكَ لَءَايَةً ۖ وَمَا كَانَ أَكْثَرُهُم مُّؤْمِنِينَ ۝ وَإِنَّ رَبَّكَ لَهُوَ ٱلْعَزِيزُ ٱلرَّحِيمُ ۝

ᵃ The sprouting of a green and flourishing tree from the earth is as wonderful an event as the sudden emergence of a camel from the earth and its starting to walk on its surface. People are wonder-struck by the second type of incident, though more wonderful incidents are always happening on the earth without their learning any lesson from them.

Almighty God wants man to notice the extraordinary aspects of ordinary events which are not immediately apparent. In the events happening in the chain of cause and effect, he should be able to observe the direct role of God. Those who display this high degree of insight are the ones who will be treated as having faith in God and the ones who will be blessed with the eternal grace of God.

¹⁰ When your Lord called out to Moses, saying, 'Go to the wrongdoing people, ¹¹ the people of Pharaoh, will they not fear God? ¹² Moses replied, 'My Lord, I fear they will reject me, ¹³ and 'my breast is straitened and my tongue is not fluent; so send Aaron as well; ¹⁴ besides, they accuse me of a crime, and I fear that they may put me to death.' ^a

وَإِذْ نَادَىٰ رَبُّكَ مُوسَىٰ أَنِ ٱئْتِ ٱلْقَوْمَ ٱلظَّٰلِمِينَ ۞ قَوْمَ فِرْعَوْنَ أَلَا يَتَّقُونَ ۞ قَالَ رَبِّ إِنِّي أَخَافُ أَن يُكَذِّبُونِ ۞ وَيَضِيقُ صَدْرِي وَلَا يَنطَلِقُ لِسَانِي فَأَرْسِلْ إِلَىٰ هَٰرُونَ ۞ وَهُمْ عَلَيَّ ذَنۢبٌ فَأَخَافُ أَن يَقْتُلُونِ ۞

---

^a Moses was required to preach monotheism to Pharaoh of Egypt, the king of the greatest and most civilized empire of his times. Moses on the contrary, belonged to the Children of Israel, whose status in Egypt was like that of slaves and labourers. Another factor in his disfavour was that one of the Pharaoh's community had died accidentally at his hands. Moses had the feeling too that he was lacking in the necessary power of expression. Almighty God nevertheless chose Moses to carry out the mission of conveying His message.

The fact is that God looks at the inner self of a man rather than at his visible condition. If someone has inner strength, God chooses him on the basis of that to carry out the tasks of His religion. But man has first to reveal his inner capabilties himself. Thereafter, if there are any outward shortcomings, they are compensated for by God.

¹⁵ God said, 'Indeed not; go both of you with Our signs, We shall be with you, listening [to your call]. ¹⁶ Go to Pharaoh, both of you, and say, "We are messengers from the Lord of the Worlds: ¹⁷ let the Children of Israel go with us!"' ¹⁸ Pharaoh said to Moses, 'Did we not bring you up among us as a child? And you spent several years of your life with us. ¹⁹ Yet you committed the deed you did, surely you are one of the ingrates.'ᵃ

قَالَ كَلَّا ۖ فَاذْهَبَا بِآيَاتِنَا ۖ إِنَّا مَعَكُم مُّسْتَمِعُونَ ۞ فَأْتِيَا فِرْعَوْنَ فَقُولَا إِنَّا رَسُولُ رَبِّ الْعَالَمِينَ ۞ أَنْ أَرْسِلْ مَعَنَا بَنِي إِسْرَائِيلَ ۞ قَالَ أَلَمْ نُرَبِّكَ فِينَا وَلِيدًا وَلَبِثْتَ فِينَا مِنْ عُمُرِكَ سِنِينَ ۞ وَفَعَلْتَ فَعْلَتَكَ الَّتِي فَعَلْتَ وَأَنتَ مِنَ الْكَافِرِينَ ۞

ᵃ One chosen by God to represent Him is in every way under His protection. Moreover, he is given some special signs which indicate clearly that his mission is an affair of God. But, in spite of that, man has gone so far in transgression as not to admit this.

The Quran does not specify the details of the demand made by Moses on Pharaoh with regard to the Children of Israel. But the Torah elaborates upon the subject in the following sections: Exodus 4/18, 5/1, 8/25-27.

According to the description in the Bible, it appears that this journey of Moses was not for the purpose of migration but for instruction. In Egypt, the cow was considered holy. Due to this centuries-old tradition, even the the Children of Israel had been influenced by this belief. Now, Moses wanted to take the Children of Israel out of the polytheistic atmosphere of Egypt for a few days, keep them in a pure atmosphere and re-educate them.

²⁰ Moses replied, 'I did that when I was one of the misguided, ²¹ and I fled from you because I feared you. Then my Lord granted me wisdom and made me one of the messengers. ²² And this is the favour with which you taunt me—that you have enslaved the Children of Israel?'^a ²³ Pharaoh said, 'What is this: Lord of the Universe?'^b ²⁴ Moses said, 'Lord of the heavens and the earth and all that is between them, if only you would be convinced.' ²⁵ Pharaoh said to those around him, 'Did you hear?'

قَالَ فَعَلْتُهَآ إِذًا وَأَنَا۠ مِنَ ٱلضَّآلِّينَ ۝ فَفَرَرْتُ مِنكُمْ لَمَّا خِفْتُكُمْ فَوَهَبَ لِى رَبِّى حُكْمًا وَجَعَلَنِى مِنَ ٱلْمُرْسَلِينَ ۝ وَتِلْكَ نِعْمَةٌ تَمُنُّهَا عَلَىَّ أَنْ عَبَّدتَّ بَنِىٓ إِسْرَٰٓءِيلَ ۝ قَالَ فِرْعَوْنُ وَمَا رَبُّ ٱلْعَٰلَمِينَ ۝ قَالَ رَبُّ ٱلسَّمَٰوَٰتِ وَٱلْأَرْضِ وَمَا بَيْنَهُمَآ إِن كُنتُم مُّوقِنِينَ ۝ قَالَ لِمَنْ حَوْلَهُۥٓ أَلَا تَسْتَمِعُونَ ۝

---

^a Moses called for the acceptance of Monotheism in Pharaoh's presence and showed him the miracles of his rod and the shining bright hand. Then, in order to belittle Moses's importance, Pharaoh reminded him of two facts about his earlier life—one, that Moses had been brought up in Pharaoh's house in his childhood and the other that he was responsible for the killing of a Copt. In reply, Moses said that his (Moses's) being brought up in Pharaoh's palace had occurred due to his own (Pharaoh's) oppressive action. Since the latter had ordered the killing of the Children of Israel's offspring, Moses's mother put him in a basket and floated it down the river. It was Pharaoh's wife—the queen—who then retrieved Moses from the river and brought him up in her palace. As for the killing of the Copt, Moses said that he had not done it purposely. He had been defending his Israelite brother from the violent aggression of the Copt when the latter died accidentally.

After this incident, Moses left Egypt and went to Madyan where he lived for many years. Perhaps it was necessary for Moses's training to leave the artificial atmosphere of the city and to spend a few years in the free atmosphere of a village. When he was on his way back from Madyan to Egypt, Almighty God conferred prophethood upon him.

^b 'What is this: Lord of the Worlds?' This utterance of Pharaoh was meant to convey ridicule rather than ask a question. But Moses, without being irritated, replied to him in a normal manner. Again Pharaoh sought to show his disapproval of Moses by asking his courtiers, 'Did you hear?' Moses ignored this also and continued with what he had to say.

²⁶ Moses went on, 'He is your Lord and the Lord of your forefathers.' ²⁷ Pharaoh said, 'This messenger who has been sent to you is surely possessed!' ²⁸ Moses said, 'He is the Lord of the East and the West, and all that lies between them, if only you could understand.' ²⁹ Pharaoh said, 'If you take any deity other than myself, I will throw you into prison,' ³⁰ and Moses asked, 'Even if I show you a clear sign?' ³¹ Pharaoh said, 'Show it then, if you are telling the truth!' ³² So Moses threw down his staff and suddenly it appeared as a serpent, plainly visible. ³³ And he drew out his hand, and it appeared [shining] white to the beholders.ᵃ ³⁴ Pharaoh said to the chiefs around him, 'Surely this man is a skilful sorcerer. ³⁵ Who wants to drive you out of your land by his sorcery. Now what do you advise?'ᵇ

قَالَ رَبُّكُمْ وَرَبُّ ءَابَآئِكُمُ ٱلْأَوَّلِينَ ﴿٢٦﴾ قَالَ إِنَّ رَسُولَكُمُ ٱلَّذِىٓ أُرْسِلَ إِلَيْكُمْ لَمَجْنُونٌ ﴿٢٧﴾ قَالَ رَبُّ ٱلْمَشْرِقِ وَٱلْمَغْرِبِ وَمَا بَيْنَهُمَآ إِن كُنتُمْ تَعْقِلُونَ ﴿٢٨﴾ قَالَ لَئِنِ ٱتَّخَذْتَ إِلَٰهًا غَيْرِى لَأَجْعَلَنَّكَ مِنَ ٱلْمَسْجُونِينَ ﴿٢٩﴾ قَالَ أَوَلَوْ جِئْتُكَ بِشَىْءٍ مُّبِينٍ ﴿٣٠﴾ قَالَ فَأْتِ بِهِۦٓ إِن كُنتَ مِنَ ٱلصَّٰدِقِينَ ﴿٣١﴾ فَأَلْقَىٰ عَصَاهُ فَإِذَا هِىَ ثُعْبَانٌ مُّبِينٌ ﴿٣٢﴾ وَنَزَعَ يَدَهُۥ فَإِذَا هِىَ بَيْضَآءُ لِلنَّٰظِرِينَ ﴿٣٣﴾ قَالَ لِلْمَلَإِ حَوْلَهُۥٓ إِنَّ هَٰذَا لَسَٰحِرٌ عَلِيمٌ ﴿٣٤﴾ يُرِيدُ أَن يُخْرِجَكُم مِّنْ أَرْضِكُم بِسِحْرِهِۦ فَمَاذَا تَأْمُرُونَ ﴿٣٥﴾

ᵃ Moses continued the argument in favour of Monotheism with Pharaoh. Pharaoh then became irritated and called Moses a madman. But, even then, Moses did not lose his temper. Pharaoh then threatened him with imprisonment. Then, by way of argument, Moses demonstrated his final miracle. Now, Pharaoh had no scope to say anything further. Even then, he did not accept defeat. In order to belittle Moses's importance, he said that this was not any divine event, but simply a magical feat that any magician could perform.

ᵇ Moses's mission was totally peaceful and it had no direct relation with politics or government. But, just in order to incite his people against Moses, Pharaoh said that he (Moses) wanted to oust them from their country. Pharaoh's insincerity is clear from the very fact that Moses had already asked Pharaoh to allow him to take his community out of Egypt along with him. But Pharaoh twisted Moses' words and said that the latter wanted to oust him and his community from Egypt.

³⁶ They said, 'Let him and his brother wait a while, and send heralds into the cities, ³⁷ who shall bring to you every skilful sorcerer.' ³⁸ So the sorcerers were gathered on the appointed day ³⁹ and the people were told, 'Will you also gather together, ⁴⁰ so that we may follow the magicians, if they be the winners.' ⁴¹ When the magicians came, they asked Pharaoh, 'Shall we have a reward, if we are the winners?' ⁴² He replied, 'Certainly, in that case you will join my inner circle.'^a

قَالُوٓاْ أَرْجِهْ وَأَخَاهُ وَٱبْعَثْ فِى ٱلْمَدَآئِنِ حَٰشِرِينَ ۝ يَأْتُوكَ بِكُلِّ سَحَّارٍ عَلِيمٍ ۝ فَجُمِعَ ٱلسَّحَرَةُ لِمِيقَٰتِ يَوْمٍ مَّعْلُومٍ ۝ وَقِيلَ لِلنَّاسِ هَلْ أَنتُم مُّجْتَمِعُونَ ۝ لَعَلَّنَا نَتَّبِعُ ٱلسَّحَرَةَ إِن كَانُواْ هُمُ ٱلْغَٰلِبِينَ ۝ فَلَمَّا جَآءَ ٱلسَّحَرَةُ قَالُواْ لِفِرْعَوْنَ أَئِنَّ لَنَا لَأَجْرًا إِن كُنَّا نَحْنُ ٱلْغَٰلِبِينَ ۝ قَالَ نَعَمْ وَإِنَّكُمْ إِذًا لَّمِنَ ٱلْمُقَرَّبِينَ ۝

---

^a Pharaoh and his courtiers considered Moses's feats as magical in nature. So, they planned to counter them by magic. Their imagination took them no further than thinking that if Moses could change a rod into a snake, their magicians could also change sticks into snakes. They had no knowledge beyond that. They considered Moses's actions as those of a human being and that is why they wanted to counter them by human means. They did not know the secret that Moses's mission was a divine mission, and which human being can clash with God?

The annual national festival day of the Egyptians was appointed the day for the competition between Moses and the magicians. And for this purpose, a big open area was chosen so that a large number of people could gather and give as much encouragement to the magicians as possible.

43 Moses said to the magicians, 'Throw down whatever you are going to throw.' 44 So they cast down their ropes and staffs, and said, 'By Pharaoh's honour, we shall surely win.' 45 Then Moses threw down his staff, and it swallowed up all that they had conjured into being. 46 The magicians fell down prostrate, 47 saying, 'We believe in the Lord of the Worlds, 48 the Lord of Moses and Aaron.' ᵃ

قَالَ لَهُم مُّوسَىٰٓ أَلْقُوا۟ مَآ أَنتُم مُّلْقُونَ ۝ فَأَلْقَوْا۟ حِبَالَهُمْ وَعِصِيَّهُمْ وَقَالُوا۟ بِعِزَّةِ فِرْعَوْنَ إِنَّا لَنَحْنُ ٱلْغَٰلِبُونَ ۝ فَأَلْقَىٰ مُوسَىٰ عَصَاهُ فَإِذَا هِىَ تَلْقَفُ مَا يَأْفِكُونَ ۝ فَأُلْقِىَ ٱلسَّحَرَةُ سَٰجِدِينَ ۝ قَالُوٓا۟ ءَامَنَّا بِرَبِّ ٱلْعَٰلَمِينَ ۝ رَبِّ مُوسَىٰ وَهَٰرُونَ ۝

ᵃ The magicians threw down their ropes and sticks, and the spectators felt as if these ropes and sticks had changed into snakes and were running along the ground. But this was not a real change. It was simply an optical illusion, whereas, the changing of Moses's rod into a snake was a miracle of God. So when Moses's rod became a snake and started moving along the ground, it instantly nullified the spell cast by the magicians. Thereafter, the magician's ropes and sticks reverted to being the ropes and sticks that they actually were.

Earlier, the magicians had considered Moses to be a magician like themselves. But, the aforesaid experience opened their eyes. They were well versed in the art of magic. So, they immediately understood that this was not magic but prophethood. However, it was possible that they could have refused to accept the Truth and, like Pharaoh, could have uttered some falsities in order to reject Moses. But, it is impossible for a man who is intellectually alive not to accept the Truth when it fully reveals itself before him. The magicians were persons who were alive in this manner. So, they immediately accepted Moses's truthfulness.

⁴⁹ Pharaoh said, 'Have you come to believe in him, before I have given you permission? He is surely your master who has taught you magic. But you shall see. I will cut off your hands and feet on alternate sides and crucify you all.' ⁵⁰ They said, 'There is no harm. To our Lord we shall return. ⁵¹We hope our Lord will forgive us, as we are the first of the believers.' ᵃ

قَالَ ءَامَنتُمْ لَهُۥ قَبْلَ أَنْ ءَاذَنَ لَكُمْ إِنَّهُۥ لَكَبِيرُكُمُ ٱلَّذِى عَلَّمَكُمُ ٱلسِّحْرَ فَلَسَوْفَ تَعْلَمُونَ لَأُقَطِّعَنَّ أَيْدِيَكُمْ وَأَرْجُلَكُم مِّنْ خِلَٰفٍ وَلَأُصَلِّبَنَّكُمْ أَجْمَعِينَ ۝ قَالُوا۟ لَا ضَيْرَ إِنَّآ إِلَىٰ رَبِّنَا مُنقَلِبُونَ ۝ إِنَّا نَطْمَعُ أَن يَغْفِرَ لَنَا رَبُّنَا خَطَٰيَٰنَآ أَن كُنَّآ أَوَّلَ ٱلْمُؤْمِنِينَ ۝

ᵃ The embracing of the Faith by the magicians was a cause of great disgrace to Pharaoh. So, in order to salvage his position, he dubbed the whole incident a conspiracy. He alleged that they had colluded with Moses and that they had intentionally pretended to be defeated by him, so that Moses's greatness could be impressed on the people's hearts. Pharaoh announced his decision to the magicians that they would be punished for sedition; that their hands and legs would be cut off at random and they would be publicly crucified. In spite of these draconian orders, the magicians were not discouraged. Those very same magicians who had earlier pledged their allegiance to Pharaoh (verse 41) and asked to be rewarded, now fearlessly proclaimed that whatever Pharaoh did, they were not going to be dissuaded from accepting Moses's religion. The reason for this high morale of theirs was the discovery of Faith. A man bears a loss when, by this loss, he expects to find something greater. Before embracing the faith, the greatest things the magicians could hope to have now were Pharaoh's approval and his reward. But on embracing true religion, God and His Paradise now appeared to them to be greater than all else. That is why they were now ready to bear the losses of those very things which, prior to embracing the Faith, they had held too dear to part with.

⁵²Then We revealed Our will to Moses, saying, 'Set forth with My servants, in the night, for you will surely be pursued.' ⁵³And Pharaoh sent forth heralds to all the cities. ⁵⁴'These,' they said, 'are only a small band—⁵⁵and they have enraged us—⁵⁶we are a large and watchful force.' ⁵⁷So We made them leave their gardens and springs, ⁵⁸their treasures and their noble dwellings—⁵⁹and We made the Children of Israel inheritors of these bounties.ᵃ

﴿ وَأَوْحَيْنَآ إِلَىٰ مُوسَىٰٓ أَنْ أَسْرِ بِعِبَادِىٓ إِنَّكُم مُّتَّبَعُونَ ۞ فَأَرْسَلَ فِرْعَوْنُ فِى ٱلْمَدَآئِنِ حَٰشِرِينَ ۞ إِنَّ هَٰٓؤُلَآءِ لَشِرْذِمَةٌ قَلِيلُونَ ۞ وَإِنَّهُمْ لَنَا لَغَآئِظُونَ ۞ وَإِنَّا لَجَمِيعٌ حَٰذِرُونَ ۞ فَأَخْرَجْنَٰهُم مِّن جَنَّٰتٍ وَعُيُونٍ ۞ وَكُنُوزٍ وَمَقَامٍ كَرِيمٍ ۞ كَذَٰلِكَ وَأَوْرَثْنَٰهَا بَنِىٓ إِسْرَٰٓءِيلَ ۞

ᵃ In spite of the years spent by Moses in spreading the word of God, Pharaoh did not embrace the Faith. At last when Moses had striven his utmost to convey the divine message to Pharaoh, Almighty God instructed Moses to leave Egypt along with the Children of Israel. When Pharaoh came to know that all of the Children of Israel had left Egypt, he pursued them along with his army and courtiers. Obviously, this step taken by Pharaoh was meant to rout the Children of Israel, but as it turned out, it rebounded upon him. Unaware of their impending fate, Pharaoh and his companions left their palatial dwellings and reached the place where they were all destined to be drowned together in the sea.

Almighty God deprived Pharaoh and his companions of the royal amenities they had enjoyed in Egypt, because of their oppressive actions. But He blessed the pious people of the Children of Israel by eventually taking them to Palestine and, there, granting them all kinds of favours.

⁶⁰ Pharaoh and his people pursued them at sunrise, ⁶¹ and when the two groups saw each other, Moses' companions said, 'We are sure to be overtaken.' ⁶² Moses replied, 'No, My Lord is with me, and He will guide me.' ⁶³ Then We bade Moses strike the sea with his staff. And it parted, and each part was like a huge mountain. ⁶⁴ In the meantime We made the others approach that place. ⁶⁵ We delivered Moses and all those who were with him, ⁶⁶ then We drowned the others. ⁶⁷ Surely in that there is a sign; yet most of them do not believe: ⁶⁸ truly, your Lord is the Mighty One, the Merciful.ᵃ

فَأَتْبَعُوهُم مُّشْرِقِينَ ۞ فَلَمَّا تَرَٰٓءَا ٱلْجَمْعَانِ قَالَ أَصْحَٰبُ مُوسَىٰٓ إِنَّا لَمُدْرَكُونَ ۞ قَالَ كَلَّآ إِنَّ مَعِىَ رَبِّى سَيَهْدِينِ ۞ فَأَوْحَيْنَآ إِلَىٰ مُوسَىٰٓ أَنِ ٱضْرِب بِّعَصَاكَ ٱلْبَحْرَ فَٱنفَلَقَ فَكَانَ كُلُّ فِرْقٍ كَٱلطَّوْدِ ٱلْعَظِيمِ ۞ وَأَزْلَفْنَا ثَمَّ ٱلْءَاخَرِينَ ۞ وَأَنجَيْنَا مُوسَىٰ وَمَن مَّعَهُۥٓ أَجْمَعِينَ ۞ ثُمَّ أَغْرَقْنَا ٱلْءَاخَرِينَ ۞ إِنَّ فِى ذَٰلِكَ لَءَايَةً وَمَا كَانَ أَكْثَرُهُم مُّؤْمِنِينَ ۞ وَإِنَّ رَبَّكَ لَهُوَ ٱلْعَزِيزُ ٱلرَّحِيمُ ۞

ᵃ Pursued by Pharaoh, the Children of Israel reached a place where before them was the sea, and behind them were Pharaoh and his army. Seeing this critical situation, the Children of Israel were terrified. According to the Bible, they said to Moses, 'Were there no graves in Egypt that you have brought us from there to this deserted place to die?'

But Moses was sure that Almighty God would help them. So, in obedience to the commandment of the Almighty, Moses struck the sea-water with his rod. The water was thereupon split asunder. On both the sides, the water stood like high walls and in between there appeared a dry path. The Children of Israel traversed this path and reached the other side.

On seeing this, Pharaoh thought that he too could cross over by this path. He did not know that, only seconds before, the path had miraculously appeared by the order of God. Pharaoh set foot upon it along with his whole army. No sooner had they reached the middle than the standing sea water gushed from both sides and rose to a uniform level. Pharaoh and his entire army were immdediately drowned. At one and the same time, deliverance was planned for one group, and death and destruction for the other.

⁶⁹ Tell them the story of Abraham, ⁷⁰ when he asked his father and his people, 'What is that which you worship?'ᵃ ⁷¹ They said, 'We worship idols and will continue to cling to them.'ᵇ ⁷² He asked, 'Do they hear you when you call to them? ⁷³ Do they help or harm you?' ⁷⁴ They replied, 'But we found our fathers doing the same.'

وَٱتْلُ عَلَيْهِمْ نَبَأَ إِبْرَٰهِيمَ ۞ إِذْ قَالَ لِأَبِيهِ وَقَوْمِهِۦ مَا تَعْبُدُونَ ۞ قَالُوا۟ نَعْبُدُ أَصْنَامًا فَنَظَلُّ لَهَا عَٰكِفِينَ ۞ قَالَ هَلْ يَسْمَعُونَكُمْ إِذْ تَدْعُونَ ۞ أَوْ يَنفَعُونَكُمْ أَوْ يَضُرُّونَ ۞ قَالُوا۟ بَلْ وَجَدْنَآ ءَابَآءَنَا كَذَٰلِكَ يَفْعَلُونَ ۞

ᵃ Abraham's community went on doing whatever they saw their forefathers doing. But Abraham thought things over independently. He tried to discover the Truth by rising above his environment. This is the quality which particularly leads a man to realisation-based knowledge of God (maʿrifah), and one who reaches perfection in this quality is chosen by God as a messenger, or prophet, for His religion.

ᵇ Abraham's words indicate that during discussions with him, they found themselves unable to refute his views, in spite of which they did not yield. Despite being defeated at the level of arguments, they were steadfast in following the religion of their forefathers, simply on the basis of prejudice.

75 Abraham said, 'Have you really thought about what you have been worshipping, 76 you and your forefathers—77 they are all my enemies, not so the Lord of the Universe, 78 who created me. It is He who guides me; 79 He who gives me food and drink; 80 He who cures me when I am ill; 81 He who will cause me to die and bring me back to life; 82 and He who will, I hope, forgive me my faults on the Day of the Judgement.ᵃ

قَالَ أَفَرَءَيْتُم مَّا كُنتُمْ تَعْبُدُونَ ۝ أَنتُمْ وَءَابَآؤُكُمُ ٱلْأَقْدَمُونَ ۝ فَإِنَّهُمْ عَدُوٌّ لِّىٓ إِلَّا رَبَّ ٱلْعَٰلَمِينَ ۝ ٱلَّذِى خَلَقَنِى فَهُوَ يَهْدِينِ ۝ وَٱلَّذِى هُوَ يُطْعِمُنِى وَيَسْقِينِ ۝ وَإِذَا مَرِضْتُ فَهُوَ يَشْفِينِ ۝ وَٱلَّذِى يُمِيتُنِى ثُمَّ يُحْيِينِ ۝ وَٱلَّذِىٓ أَطْمَعُ أَن يَغْفِرَ لِى خَطِيٓئَتِى يَوْمَ ٱلدِّينِ ۝

ᵃ Man is an independent being. He has the wisdom to distinguish between good and bad, and make inferences from his continued sustenance on earth. When he falls ill, he finds that there is an abundance of resources from which to derive remedies. But then, man observes that in spite of all his apparent freedom, he is helpless in the face of death. He dies at the end of his allotted lifespan.

All these factors can be caused by none other than the one and only God. Then, how can it be legitimate and proper to worship anybody except Him alone? Moreover, a man should be extremely serious and sincere in this matter, because these factors also indicate that whatever God does is in preparation for the day when man will be called before Him to give an account of himself. Death marks the beginning of this process when man will be judged by God on the basis of the performance of his deeds on earth.

83 My Lord, bestow wisdom upon me; unite me with the righteous; 84 give me a good name among later generations; 85 and make me one of the inheritors of the Garden of Bliss; 86 and forgive my father; for he is one of the misguided; 87 and do not disgrace me on the Day when all people are resurrected, 88 the Day when wealth and sons will be of no avail, 89 and when he alone will be saved who comes to God with a sound heart.'ᵃ

رَبِّ هَبْ لِى حُكْمًا وَأَلْحِقْنِى بِٱلصَّٰلِحِينَ ۝ وَٱجْعَل لِّى لِسَانَ صِدْقٍ فِى ٱلْءَاخِرِينَ ۝ وَٱجْعَلْنِى مِن وَرَثَةِ جَنَّةِ ٱلنَّعِيمِ ۝ وَٱغْفِرْ لِأَبِى إِنَّهُۥ كَانَ مِنَ ٱلضَّآلِّينَ ۝ وَلَا تُخْزِنِى يَوْمَ يُبْعَثُونَ ۝ يَوْمَ لَا يَنفَعُ مَالٌ وَلَا بَنُونَ ۝ إِلَّا مَنْ أَتَى ٱللَّهَ بِقَلْبٍ سَلِيمٍ ۝

ᵃ These verses deal with right understanding, i.e. seeing things as they really are. For a subject of God, this is the greatest blessing next to prophethood. That is why it is mentioned in a tradition which says, 'If God wants to do something good to a man, He bestows on him the understanding of religion.'

Whatever Abraham asked for in his prayer was granted to him, but the prayer for the pardon of his father (Azar) was rejected. One can imagine from this that prayer (du'a) is mostly a matter between God and His subject. One man's prayer cannot obtain pardon for another man.

Before Almighty God, real value attaches to a pure heart (qalb salim). This means the right kind of pure heart, i.e. a heart which is free from the tendency to ascribe partners to God, feelings of hypocrisy, jealousy and ill-will. In other words, the believer should go before God with a heart as pure as it was at the time of his birth. He should not present himself before God with any other heart.

⁹⁰ When Paradise shall be brought near to the God-fearing ⁹¹ and Hell shall be revealed to the misguided, ⁹² they will be asked, 'Where are those whom you worshipped ⁹³ besides God? Can they help you or even help themselves?' ⁹⁴ Then they will be thrown headlong into Hell, both they and the misguided ones, ⁹⁵ and Satan's legions, all together. ⁹⁶ They will dispute between themselves therein, and will say, ⁹⁷ 'We were clearly misguided ⁹⁸ when we made you equal with the Lord of the Universe. ⁹⁹ It was the evildoers who led us astray, ¹⁰⁰ and we have no intercessors now, ¹⁰¹ and no sincere friend. ¹⁰² If we could only return to the world and be among the believers.' ¹⁰³ There is certainly a sign in that, but most of them would not believe: ¹⁰⁴ surely, your Lord is the Mighty One, the Merciful.ᵃ

وَأُزْلِفَتِ ٱلْجَنَّةُ لِلْمُتَّقِينَ ۝ وَبُرِّزَتِ ٱلْجَحِيمُ لِلْغَاوِينَ ۝ وَقِيلَ لَهُمْ أَيْنَ مَا كُنتُمْ تَعْبُدُونَ ۝ مِن دُونِ ٱللَّهِ هَلْ يَنصُرُونَكُمْ أَوْ يَنتَصِرُونَ ۝ فَكُبْكِبُوا۟ فِيهَا هُمْ وَٱلْغَاوُۥنَ ۝ وَجُنُودُ إِبْلِيسَ أَجْمَعُونَ ۝ قَالُوا۟ وَهُمْ فِيهَا يَخْتَصِمُونَ ۝ تَٱللَّهِ إِن كُنَّا لَفِى ضَلَٰلٍ مُّبِينٍ ۝ إِذْ نُسَوِّيكُم بِرَبِّ ٱلْعَٰلَمِينَ ۝ وَمَآ أَضَلَّنَآ إِلَّا ٱلْمُجْرِمُونَ ۝ فَمَا لَنَا مِن شَٰفِعِينَ ۝ وَلَا صَدِيقٍ حَمِيمٍ ۝ فَلَوْ أَنَّ لَنَا كَرَّةً فَنَكُونَ مِنَ ٱلْمُؤْمِنِينَ ۝ إِنَّ فِى ذَٰلِكَ لَءَايَةً وَمَا كَانَ أَكْثَرُهُم مُّؤْمِنِينَ ۝ وَإِنَّ رَبَّكَ لَهُوَ ٱلْعَزِيزُ ٱلرَّحِيمُ ۝

ᵃ A man's heaven and hell are not far away from him. Only a curtain intervenes between them. When Doomsday removes that curtain, every man will see that he was standing just on the edge of his heaven or hell, though the negligent man considered it something very distant.

There were false leaders (*mujrimun*), who enjoyed an elevated position in the society of their times. They did not accept the call for Truth simply because, thereafter, their greatness would be finished. Their false pride prevented them from accepting the Truth. As a result, their followers likewise did not consider the call for Truth worth responding to.

Equating the leaders with the Lord of the Universe means giving the same status to their utterances as to those of the Lord of the Universe. The Quranic commentator, Ibn Kathir, portrays them as carrying out the orders of their leaders 'as the orders of the Lord of the Universe are carried out.' Those who accepted the pronouncements of their leaders as if they were God's commandments in the world, will themselves, in the Hereafter, call those leaders blameworthy, but it will be of no avail. The place where one was required to recognise and differentiate between the falsifiers and the men of Truth was the world and not the Hereafter.

¹⁰⁵ The people of Noah also rejected the messengers. ¹⁰⁶ When their brother Noah said to them, 'Will you have no fear of God? ¹⁰⁷ I am a trustworthy messenger for you: ¹⁰⁸ fear God, and obey me. ¹⁰⁹ I ask of you no recompense for it, for my only reward is with the Lord of the Universe, ¹¹⁰ so fear God and obey me.' ¹¹¹ They replied, 'Are we to believe in you when your followers are but the lowest of the low?' ¹¹² He said, 'What knowledge do I have of their doings? ¹¹³ My Lord alone can bring them to account—if only you could understand—¹¹⁴ I am not going to drive away any believers. ¹¹⁵ I am only a plain warner.'ᵃ

كَذَّبَتْ قَوْمُ نُوحٍ ٱلْمُرْسَلِينَ ۝ إِذْ قَالَ لَهُمْ أَخُوهُمْ نُوحٌ أَلَا تَتَّقُونَ ۝ إِنِّي لَكُمْ رَسُولٌ أَمِينٌ ۝ فَٱتَّقُوا ٱللَّهَ وَأَطِيعُونِ ۝ وَمَآ أَسْـَٔلُكُمْ عَلَيْهِ مِنْ أَجْرٍ إِنْ أَجْرِيَ إِلَّا عَلَىٰ رَبِّ ٱلْعَٰلَمِينَ ۝ فَٱتَّقُوا ٱللَّهَ وَأَطِيعُونِ ۝ ۞ قَالُوٓا أَنُؤْمِنُ لَكَ وَٱتَّبَعَكَ ٱلْأَرْذَلُونَ ۝ قَالَ وَمَا عِلْمِي بِمَا كَانُوا يَعْمَلُونَ ۝ إِنْ حِسَابُهُمْ إِلَّا عَلَىٰ رَبِّي لَوْ تَشْعُرُونَ ۝ وَمَآ أَنَا۠ بِطَارِدِ ٱلْمُؤْمِنِينَ ۝ إِنْ أَنَا۠ إِلَّا نَذِيرٌ مُّبِينٌ ۝

ᵃ Noah's community rejected him, though his call was fully borne out by the strength of arguments. Besides, his character bore testimony to his truthfulness. The people of his community knew that Noah was a righteous and honest man. They knew that there was no vested self-interest attached to his call for the Truth. Indeed, his personal qualities were enough to prove his seriousness. And a person who is serious about God's creatures cannot be other than serious about their Creator.

Noah's community rejected his call for the Truth, though they could offer nothing but irrelevant matters to justify this rejection. To say that the companions of a preacher are ordinary people in order to justify rejection of his call, is not a contradiction of the call but amounts rather to self-contradiction. It means that nothing can be found by way of arguments to warrant saying anything against the call of Truth. Such a stance did no credit to Noah's community.

116 They said, 'Noah, if you do not desist, you will be stoned.' 117 Noah said, 'My Lord, my people have rejected me, 118 therefore, judge decisively between me and them; and save me and the believers who are with me.' 119 So We saved him, and those who were with him in the laden ark, 120 and drowned the rest. 121 There is certainly a sign in that; but most of them do not believe: 122 surely your Lord is the Mighty One, the Merciful.ᵃ

قَالُوا۟ لَئِن لَّمْ تَنتَهِ يَٰنُوحُ لَتَكُونَنَّ مِنَ ٱلْمَرْجُومِينَ ۝ قَالَ رَبِّ إِنَّ قَوْمِى كَذَّبُونِ ۝ فَٱفْتَحْ بَيْنِى وَبَيْنَهُمْ فَتْحًا وَنَجِّنِى وَمَن مَّعِىَ مِنَ ٱلْمُؤْمِنِينَ ۝ فَأَنجَيْنَٰهُ وَمَن مَّعَهُۥ فِى ٱلْفُلْكِ ٱلْمَشْحُونِ ۝ ثُمَّ أَغْرَقْنَا بَعْدُ ٱلْبَاقِينَ ۝ إِنَّ فِى ذَٰلِكَ لَءَايَةً وَمَا كَانَ أَكْثَرُهُم مُّؤْمِنِينَ ۝ وَإِنَّ رَبَّكَ لَهُوَ ٱلْعَزِيزُ ٱلرَّحِيمُ ۝

ᵃ Noah strove for centuries so that his community could realize the truth, but they refused to accept it.

The moral debasement of his people had reached its acme and the disbelievers now threatened Noah either to stop preaching or be stoned to death. Noah then prayed to God to judge decisively between him and the disbelievers. His prayer was answered.

At God's behest, Noah constructed a large boat, in which all his companions and the male and female counterparts of each animal species were accommodated. Thereafter, God sent a severe storm; water gushed out of the earth, and there was a heavy downpour of rain from the skies. All the living creatures, except those on the boat, were destroyed. This historical example is an embodiment of the fact that while true believers would remain protected, all others would face destruction.

123 The people of 'Ad, too, rejected the messengers. 124 Their brother Hud said to them, 'Will you not fear God? 125 I am a trustworthy messenger for you: 126 fear God, then, and obey me. 127 I ask no recompense of you; my reward is only with the Lord of the Universe. 128 Do you build monuments on every high place in vanity, 129 and erect castles hoping that you will live forever. 130 When you lay hands upon anyone, you do so as tyrants. 131 So fear God, and obey me; 132 fear Him who has aided you with all that you know— 133 He has bestowed on you cattle, and sons, 134 and gardens, and springs—135 indeed, I fear for you the torment of an awful day.' a

كَذَّبَتْ عَادٌ ٱلْمُرْسَلِينَ ۝ إِذْ قَالَ لَهُمْ أَخُوهُمْ هُودٌ أَلَا تَتَّقُونَ ۝ إِنِّي لَكُمْ رَسُولٌ أَمِينٌ ۝ فَٱتَّقُوا ٱللَّهَ وَأَطِيعُونِ ۝ وَمَآ أَسْـَٔلُكُمْ عَلَيْهِ مِنْ أَجْرٍ إِنْ أَجْرِيَ إِلَّا عَلَىٰ رَبِّ ٱلْعَٰلَمِينَ ۝ أَتَبْنُونَ بِكُلِّ رِيعٍ ءَايَةً تَعْبَثُونَ ۝ وَتَتَّخِذُونَ مَصَانِعَ لَعَلَّكُمْ تَخْلُدُونَ ۝ وَإِذَا بَطَشْتُم بَطَشْتُمْ جَبَّارِينَ ۝ فَٱتَّقُوا ٱللَّهَ وَأَطِيعُونِ ۝ وَٱتَّقُوا ٱلَّذِيٓ أَمَدَّكُم بِمَا تَعْلَمُونَ ۝ أَمَدَّكُم بِأَنْعَٰمٍ وَبَنِينَ ۝ وَجَنَّٰتٍ وَعُيُونٍ ۝ إِنِّيٓ أَخَافُ عَلَيْكُمْ عَذَابَ يَوْمٍ عَظِيمٍ ۝

---

a The 'Ad was a community which rose to prominence after Noah's people were destroyed (see 7:69). Almighty God blessed this community with everything—health, prosperity, power, etc. Had they been grateful for these blessings, they would have developed a feeling of humility. But, instead, they became proud, thinking that the best use of their resources was to upgrade their standard of living and to elevate their name. They considered the erecting of stone icons their greatest task.

If such people have any difference with or complaint against anyone, their pride makes them go beyond all limits. They consider any injustice perpetrated against one who is the object of their disapproval to be legitimate and proper. They simply want to crush him with all their might. Prosperity in the world makes them fearless of retribution in the Hereafter. Those who consider themselves safe from the ultimate reckoning can go to any extent to harm others.

People who enjoy prosperity and dominance develop a high degree of false self-confidence. This false confidence prevents them from understanding the Truth when presented to them by people who do not belong to their group. They do not give importance to the advice of the admonisher, who may be most trustworthy, and even though he be God's messenger. Such people accept the Truth only when they confront God's punishment, but such acceptance will be of no avail.

¹³⁶ They replied, 'It makes no difference to us whether you preach or do not preach, ¹³⁷ this is nothing but a habit of the ancients: ¹³⁸ and we shall not be punished.' ¹³⁹ So they rejected him; and We destroyed them. There is certainly a sign in that; but most of them would not believe. ¹⁴⁰ Surely your Lord is the Mighty One, the Merciful.[a]

قَالُوا۟ سَوَآءٌ عَلَيْنَآ أَوَعَظْتَ أَمْ لَمْ تَكُن مِّنَ ٱلْوَٰعِظِينَ ۝ إِنْ هَٰذَآ إِلَّا خُلُقُ ٱلْأَوَّلِينَ ۝ وَمَا نَحْنُ بِمُعَذَّبِينَ ۝ فَكَذَّبُوهُ فَأَهْلَكْنَٰهُمْ إِنَّ فِى ذَٰلِكَ لَءَايَةً وَمَا كَانَ أَكْثَرُهُم مُّؤْمِنِينَ ۝ وَإِنَّ رَبَّكَ لَهُوَ ٱلْعَزِيزُ ٱلرَّحِيمُ ۝

---

[a] The false self-confidence of the 'Ad community prevented them from accepting the preaching of their prophet and they went to the extent of ridiculing it. They took their prosperity in the world as God's reward. They failed to understand the secret that man is given worldly effects by way of trial and not because he deserves them.

When it was finally established that they were not going to accept the Truth, God had them lashed by stormy winds and heavy rains, which continued to wreak havoc for a week. The result was that the entire nation with its grand culture was destroyed. Now, the only sign of this nation, whose land had once been fertile and well populated is the desert which stretches far and wide between the present-day Oman and Yemen.

¹⁴¹ The tribe of Thamud also rejected the messengers. ¹⁴² When their brother Salih said to them, 'Will you not fear God? ¹⁴³ Truly, I am a trustworthy messenger for you, ¹⁴⁴ so fear God and obey me. ¹⁴⁵ For this I demand no recompense from you; my reward is only with the Lord of the Universe. ¹⁴⁶ Do you think that you will be left secure [forever]— ¹⁴⁷ in the midst of gardens and fountains, ¹⁴⁸ and cornfields, and palm-trees laden with fruit— ¹⁴⁹ hewing out houses in the mountains and taking pride in your skill? ¹⁵⁰ So fear God and obey me: ¹⁵¹ do not obey the bidding of those who are given to excesses, ¹⁵² those who spread corruption in the land instead of putting things right.'ᵃ

كَذَّبَتْ ثَمُودُ ٱلْمُرْسَلِينَ ۝ إِذْ قَالَ لَهُمْ أَخُوهُمْ صَٰلِحٌ أَلَا تَتَّقُونَ ۝ إِنِّى لَكُمْ رَسُولٌ أَمِينٌ ۝ فَٱتَّقُوا۟ ٱللَّهَ وَأَطِيعُونِ ۝ وَمَآ أَسْـَٔلُكُمْ عَلَيْهِ مِنْ أَجْرٍ إِنْ أَجْرِىَ إِلَّا عَلَىٰ رَبِّ ٱلْعَٰلَمِينَ ۝ أَتُتْرَكُونَ فِى مَا هَٰهُنَآ ءَامِنِينَ ۝ فِى جَنَّٰتٍ وَعُيُونٍ ۝ وَزُرُوعٍ وَنَخْلٍ طَلْعُهَا هَضِيمٌ ۝ وَتَنْحِتُونَ مِنَ ٱلْجِبَالِ بُيُوتًا فَٰرِهِينَ ۝ فَٱتَّقُوا۟ ٱللَّهَ وَأَطِيعُونِ ۝ وَلَا تُطِيعُوٓا۟ أَمْرَ ٱلْمُسْرِفِينَ ۝ ٱلَّذِينَ يُفْسِدُونَ فِى ٱلْأَرْضِ وَلَا يُصْلِحُونَ ۝

ᵃ After the 'Ad, the other community which gained ascendance was the Thamud (7:74). This community inhabited the area between Khaybar and Tabuk known as Al-Hijr. This community too was blessed with great prosperity and enjoyed dominance over others. But, the members of this community likewise devoted their full attention to the attainment of material prosperity. The art of constructing large houses by carving them out of the hills was perhaps started by this community and an improved form of this is found in the Ajanta and Ellora caves in India.

Unfortunately, all those who obtain worldly benefits harbour the misunderstanding that they are entitled to them and may use them as they like. But this is the greatest mistake. The fact is that these worldly things are there only for as long as the period of trial lasts. After that, everything will be snatched from them so that nothing remains.

One who exceeds the limit is one who, when he acquires wealth, develops the mentality of conceit instead of gratitude to God. When power falls to his lot, he indulges in vanity instead of being modest. If he is given high office, he uses it to glorify his name and not to serve others. Such misuse of available opportunities creates disturbance in society. The leaders of the Thamud community indulged in such type of excesses and the commoners followed them. Their prophet warned (the common people) that those they considered great were themselves misguided, and asked how they could then guide others.

¹⁵³ They replied, 'Surely you are bewitched. ¹⁵⁴ You are only a human being like ourselves. Show us a sign, if you are telling the truth.' ¹⁵⁵ He said, 'Here is a she-camel. She shall have her turn of drinking, as you have yours, each on an appointed day, ¹⁵⁶ so do her no harm, or the punishment of an awful day will befall you.' ¹⁵⁷ Yet they hamstrung her, and then they became regretful: ¹⁵⁸ so the punishment came down upon them. Surely in that there is a sign, but most of them would not believe. ¹⁵⁹ Your Lord is the Mighty One, the Merciful.^a

قَالُوٓاْ إِنَّمَآ أَنتَ مِنَ ٱلْمُسَحَّرِينَ ۝

مَآ أَنتَ إِلَّا بَشَرٌ مِّثْلُنَا فَأْتِ بِـَٔايَةٍ إِن كُنتَ مِنَ ٱلصَّٰدِقِينَ ۝ قَالَ هَٰذِهِۦ نَاقَةٌ لَّهَا شِرْبٌ وَلَكُمْ شِرْبُ يَوْمٍ مَّعْلُومٍ ۝ وَلَا تَمَسُّوهَا بِسُوٓءٍ فَيَأْخُذَكُمْ عَذَابُ يَوْمٍ عَظِيمٍ ۝

فَعَقَرُوهَا فَأَصْبَحُوا۟ نَٰدِمِينَ ۝ فَأَخَذَهُمُ ٱلْعَذَابُ إِنَّ فِى ذَٰلِكَ لَءَايَةً وَمَا كَانَ أَكْثَرُهُم مُّؤْمِنِينَ ۝

وَإِنَّ رَبَّكَ لَهُوَ ٱلْعَزِيزُ ٱلرَّحِيمُ ۝

---

^a When a prophet arises in a community, that community is not necessarily atheistic or irreligious. It is, in fact, a religious community in the fullest sense, but, the religion of its members is the religion of their forefathers, and what the prophet presents is God's religion. Those who consider the ways of their forefathers sacrosanct and stick to them, cannot understand the importance of other ways, even if those are presented by the prophet. To Salih's community (i.e. the Thamud), deviation from their forefathers' ways was so intolerable that they called Salih a madman. This struggle went on for a long time. Ultimately, they demanded that he show them a miracle. A miracle did appear, as commanded by God Almighty; it was both a miracle and the instrument of divine justice. It appeared in the form of a she-camel which had come into existence in other than the normal manner, i.e. in a miraculous way. Salih said that this was a she-camel of God. It would wander in their fields and gardens freely, and the water from the pond would be reserved for it exclusively on one day. The community tolerated the she-camel for a few days and then an arrogant man killed it. Soon thereafter the entire community was wiped out by a severe earthquake.

The crime of killing the she-camel was committed by a single person of the community, but the Quran uses the plural saying, 'They hamstrung her.' The reason for this is that at the time of killing, the people of the community did not prevent the person concerned from doing the deed, nor did they condemn him afterwards. Everyone spoke in his support and opposed Salih. While the killer had personally committed the crime, the rest of the people were his accomplices in that crime in their hearts and with their tongues. Therefore, in the eyes of God, all of them stood guilty.

¹⁶⁰ Then the people of Lot rejected the messengers. ¹⁶¹ When their brother Lot said to them, 'Will you not fear God? ¹⁶² I am a trustworthy messenger to you: ¹⁶³ so fear God and obey me. ¹⁶⁴ I ask of you no recompense for this; my reward is only with the Lord of the Universe. ¹⁶⁵ Do you, of all people, approach males, ¹⁶⁶ and leave your wives whom your Lord has created for you? You are a people who transgress all bounds.'^a

كَذَّبَتْ قَوْمُ لُوطٍ ٱلْمُرْسَلِينَ ۝ إِذْ قَالَ لَهُمْ أَخُوهُمْ لُوطٌ أَلَا تَتَّقُونَ ۝ إِنِّي لَكُمْ رَسُولٌ أَمِينٌ ۝ فَٱتَّقُوا ٱللَّهَ وَأَطِيعُونِ ۝ وَمَآ أَسْـَٔلُكُمْ عَلَيْهِ مِنْ أَجْرٍ إِنْ أَجْرِىَ إِلَّا عَلَىٰ رَبِّ ٱلْعَٰلَمِينَ ۝ أَتَأْتُونَ ٱلذُّكْرَانَ مِنَ ٱلْعَٰلَمِينَ ۝ وَتَذَرُونَ مَا خَلَقَ لَكُمْ رَبُّكُم مِّنْ أَزْوَٰجِكُم بَلْ أَنتُمْ قَوْمٌ عَادُونَ ۝

---

^a The community in which Lot appeared, had crossed all limits in debauchery. Not being content with their wives, they had started indulging in homosexuality. Lot taught them God-worship and piety and attempted to dissuade them from indulging in evil deeds.

Lot appeared in the community as a preacher whose personality was entirely free of falsehood and he never indulged in loose talk. Also, he completely abstained from raising matters of material interest. These events were enough to establish that Lot was fully serious about whatever he was saying. But as he spoke out against the behaviour of the community, they became his enemies. For Lot's words to carry any weight, it was necessary for the people to fear God. But the people of his community had become completely devoid of this very virtue. Then, how could they pay attention to the prophet's teachings?

167 They said, 'If you do not desist, Lot, you will surely be banished.' 168 He said, 'I am one of those who abhors your ways. 169 My Lord, save me and my family from their evil doings.' 170 We saved him and all of his family, 171 except for an old woman who stayed behind, 172 then We totally destroyed the rest, 173 and We poured a rain [of destruction] down upon them—and how evil was the rain which fell on those who were forewarned. 174 Surely in this there is a sign: but most of them would not believe: 175 your Lord is the Mighty One, the Merciful.ᵃ

قَالُواْ لَئِن لَّمْ تَنتَهِ يَـٰلُوطُ لَتَكُونَنَّ مِنَ ٱلْمُخْرَجِينَ ۝ قَالَ إِنِّى لِعَمَلِكُم مِّنَ ٱلْقَالِينَ ۝ رَبِّ نَجِّنِى وَأَهْلِى مِمَّا يَعْمَلُونَ ۝ فَنَجَّيْنَـٰهُ وَأَهْلَهُۥٓ أَجْمَعِينَ ۝ إِلَّا عَجُوزًا فِى ٱلْغَـٰبِرِينَ ۝ ثُمَّ دَمَّرْنَا ٱلْـَٔاخَرِينَ ۝ وَأَمْطَرْنَا عَلَيْهِم مَّطَرًا ۖ فَسَآءَ مَطَرُ ٱلْمُنذَرِينَ ۝ إِنَّ فِى ذَٰلِكَ لَـَٔايَةً ۖ وَمَا كَانَ أَكْثَرُهُم مُّؤْمِنِينَ ۝ وَإِنَّ رَبَّكَ هُوَ ٱلْعَزِيزُ ٱلرَّحِيمُ ۝

ᵃ The area to the south and east of the Dead Sea now appears to be deserted. But, from 2300 to 1900 B.C., it was a very flourishing area, inhabited by the people of Lot. In spite of his continuous preaching, they did not reform themselves. On the contrary, they were out to kill him. Then they were destroyed by a severe earthquake. One part of this area is buried in the Dead Sea, while the other part exists only in the shape of ruins. This event happened four thousand years ago.

Lot's wife could not rise above the traditions of her community. In spite of being the prophet's wife, she remained loyal to her community's religion. As a result, when God's punishment was administered, she was killed along with the common unbelievers.

¹⁷⁶ The dwellers of the forest also rejected the messengers. ¹⁷⁷ Shu'ayb said to them, 'Will you not fear God? ¹⁷⁸ I am a trustworthy messenger to you: ¹⁷⁹ so fear God, and obey me. ¹⁸⁰ I ask of you no recompense for this; my reward is only with the Lord of the Universe. ¹⁸¹ Give full measure, and cause no loss to others. ¹⁸² Weigh with correct scales: ¹⁸³ do not defraud people of what is rightfully theirs; and do not spread corruption in the land. ¹⁸⁴ Fear Him who created you and those who have gone before you.'ᵃ

كَذَّبَ أَصْحَٰبُ لْـَٔيْكَةِ ٱلْمُرْسَلِينَ ۝ إِذْ قَالَ لَهُمْ شُعَيْبٌ أَلَا تَتَّقُونَ ۝ إِنِّى لَكُمْ رَسُولٌ أَمِينٌ ۝ فَٱتَّقُوا ٱللَّهَ وَأَطِيعُونِ ۝ وَمَآ أَسْـَٔلُكُمْ عَلَيْهِ مِنْ أَجْرٍ إِنْ أَجْرِىَ إِلَّا عَلَىٰ رَبِّ ٱلْعَٰلَمِينَ ۝ أَوْفُوا ٱلْكَيْلَ وَلَا تَكُونُوا مِنَ ٱلْمُخْسِرِينَ ۝ وَزِنُوا بِٱلْقِسْطَاسِ ٱلْمُسْتَقِيمِ ۝ وَلَا تَبْخَسُوا ٱلنَّاسَ أَشْيَآءَهُمْ وَلَا تَعْثَوْا فِى ٱلْأَرْضِ مُفْسِدِينَ ۝ وَٱتَّقُوا ٱلَّذِى خَلَقَكُمْ وَٱلْجِبِلَّةَ ٱلْأَوَّلِينَ ۝

ᵃ Shu'ayb's community was the progeny of Abraham. The central city of the area which they inhabited was Tabuk. The old name of Tabuk was Ayka, which literally means 'the forest.' That is why, in the Quran, it is called Ashab al-Ayka (the dwellers of the forest).

The root cause of all moral and social evils is setting double standards. Just conduct for a man is to give others their rightful due, and take for himself what rightfully belongs to him. This is the Divine 'balance'. When this is upset, disturbance occurs in collective social life. The secret of maintaining this balance is the fear of God. If the fear of God goes out of the heart, nothing can make a man keep his moral equilibrium.

All the prophets who had appeared on behalf of God had told their addressee communities: 'I am a trustworthy Messenger to you.' This shows that a preacher should necessarily have the quality of trustworthiness. One aspect of this trustworthiness is that he should not raise any material or economic issue with his addressee community, so that there should never be any doubt about the selflessness of his purpose. This trustworthiness is so important that it should be fostered at any cost, even if the preacher of truth has, voluntarily, to forego his material rights for its sake.

¹⁸⁵ They replied, 'You are bewitched.
¹⁸⁶ You are only a human being like
ourselves. Indeed we think you are
a liar. ¹⁸⁷ So cause a fragment of the
sky to fall on us, if you are truthful.'
¹⁸⁸ He said, 'My Lord has full
knowledge of all your actions.'
¹⁸⁹ They rejected him, and then had
to suffer the punishment of a day of
overshadowing gloom. That was
indeed the punishment of an awful
day. ¹⁹⁰ Surely, in this is indeed a sign;
but most of them would not believe:
¹⁹¹ your Lord is the Mighty One, the
Merciful.ᵃ

قَالُوٓا۟ إِنَّمَآ أَنتَ مِنَ ٱلْمُسَحَّرِينَ ۝
وَمَآ أَنتَ إِلَّا بَشَرٌ مِّثْلُنَا وَإِن نَّظُنُّكَ
لَمِنَ ٱلْكَٰذِبِينَ ۝ فَأَسْقِطْ عَلَيْنَا
كِسَفًا مِّنَ ٱلسَّمَآءِ إِن كُنتَ مِنَ
ٱلصَّٰدِقِينَ ۝ قَالَ رَبِّىٓ أَعْلَمُ بِمَا
تَعْمَلُونَ ۝ فَكَذَّبُوهُ فَأَخَذَهُمْ
عَذَابُ يَوْمِ ٱلظُّلَّةِ إِنَّهُۥ كَانَ عَذَابَ
يَوْمٍ عَظِيمٍ ۝ إِنَّ فِى ذَٰلِكَ لَءَايَةً وَمَا
كَانَ أَكْثَرُهُم مُّؤْمِنِينَ ۝ وَإِنَّ رَبَّكَ
هُوَ ٱلْعَزِيزُ ٱلرَّحِيمُ ۝

ᵃ Shu'ayb's community had so much faith in the righteousness of their forefathers'
ways that the prophet's sayings seemed perverse and absurd. They said that
somebody might well have cast a magic spell on him to make him talk the way he
did.

They challenged Shu'ayb to bring down the punishment of the skies, if what he said
were true. They did this to deride Shu'ayb, feeling that the punishment would
certainly not descend because of him. The insolence of this community invited the
direct wrath of God, as a vast cloud plunged them in gloom and a raging fire
enveloped them, wiping out even the smallest trace of the community.

¹⁹² This surely is a revelation from the Lord of the Universe: ¹⁹³ the Faithful Spirit has brought it down ¹⁹⁴ into your heart, so that you may be a warner, ¹⁹⁵ in clear Arabic speech. ¹⁹⁶ Surely, it is foretold in the ancient scriptures. ¹⁹⁷ Is it not evidence enough for them that the learned among the Children of Israel have recognized this [as true]?ᵃ

وَإِنَّهُۥ لَتَنزِيلُ رَبِّ ٱلْعَـٰلَمِينَ ۝ نَزَلَ بِهِ ٱلرُّوحُ ٱلْأَمِينُ ۝ عَلَىٰ قَلْبِكَ لِتَكُونَ مِنَ ٱلْمُنذِرِينَ ۝ بِلِسَانٍ عَرَبِىٍّ مُّبِينٍ ۝ وَإِنَّهُۥ لَفِى زُبُرِ ٱلْأَوَّلِينَ ۝ أَوَلَمْ يَكُن لَّهُمْ ءَايَةً أَن يَعْلَمَهُۥ عُلَمَـٰٓؤُاْ بَنِىٓ إِسْرَٰٓءِيلَ ۝

ᵃ Though the Quran has been revealed in a language of human beings, its literary superiority is extraordinary, so much so that its language itself provides proof of the Quran being a superior Divine discourse of God. Another proof of the Truth of the Quran is that, the prophets, born long before the revelation of the Quran, had predicted it. This prediction is found even today in the Torah, Zabur (Book of Psalms) and Injeel (Bible). It was on the basis of these predictions that a number of the Christian and Jewish scholars of those days (for example 'Abdullah ibn Salam) embraced the faith. This trend continues even today.

The revelation of the Divine discourse of God with such special arrangements, could be only for a certain special purpose and this purpose is to warn the people of the coming Day of Judgement: Just as warning about the Hereafter was the special purpose of all the previous revealed Books, so is it the special purpose of the Quran.

¹⁹⁸ Had We revealed it to any one of the non-Arabs, ¹⁹⁹ and he had recited it to them, they would not have believed in it.^a ²⁰⁰ We have thus caused denial of truth to enter into the hearts of the sinners: ²⁰¹ they will not believe in it until they see the grievous punishment. ²⁰² It will come upon them suddenly when they are not expecting it. ²⁰³ Then they will exclaim, 'Could we have some respite?'

وَلَوۡ نَزَّلۡنَٰهُ عَلَىٰ بَعۡضِ ٱلۡأَعۡجَمِينَ ۝ فَقَرَأَهُۥ عَلَيۡهِم مَّا كَانُوا۟ بِهِۦ مُؤۡمِنِينَ ۝ كَذَٰلِكَ سَلَكۡنَٰهُ فِى قُلُوبِ ٱلۡمُجۡرِمِينَ ۝ لَا يُؤۡمِنُونَ بِهِۦ حَتَّىٰ يَرَوُا۟ ٱلۡعَذَابَ ٱلۡأَلِيمَ ۝ فَيَأۡتِيَهُم بَغۡتَةً وَهُمۡ لَا يَشۡعُرُونَ ۝ فَيَقُولُوا۟ هَلۡ نَحۡنُ مُنظَرُونَ ۝

---

^a The Quran was revealed in the Arabic language, which was also the mother tongue of the Prophet who presented it. This gave those who denied the truth the opportunity to allege that the Quran was this Prophet's own creation. They said that, being an Arab, he had authored the Quran in Arabic.

But the tenor of this objection itself clearly shows that it is lacking in seriousness. Indeed those who are not serious about matters of importance always find some flimsy excuse or the other to be critical of them. For example, if this Arabic Quran had been revealed to a non-Arab and if that person, in spite of not knowing Arabic, had recited the Arabic Quran to them, they would have immediately said that he was being tutored by some Arab.

For those who lead worldly lives, any admission of Truth amounts to negating themselves. When Truth appears before them and they do not accept it, having given more importance to personal considerations, they are so conditioned to their worldly ways, that they are unable to revise their thinking and acknowledge the truth, specially when it goes against their interests.

²⁰⁴ Do they want to hasten Our punishment? ²⁰⁵ Think! If We let them enjoy life for some years, ²⁰⁶ and then the promised punishment fell upon them, ²⁰⁷ of what avail would their past enjoyment be to them? ²⁰⁸ Never have We destroyed a town without sending down messengers to warn it, ²⁰⁹ as a reminder from Us: We are never unjust. ²¹⁰ It was not the devils who brought down the Quran: ²¹¹ neither are they worthy of it, nor are they capable of it, ²¹² indeed they are debarred from overhearing it.ᵃ

أَفَبِعَذَابِنَا يَسْتَعْجِلُونَ ۝ أَفَرَءَيْتَ إِن مَّتَّعْنَٰهُمْ سِنِينَ ۝ ثُمَّ جَآءَهُم مَّا كَانُوا۟ يُوعَدُونَ ۝ مَآ أَغْنَىٰ عَنْهُم مَّا كَانُوا۟ يُمَتَّعُونَ ۝ وَمَآ أَهْلَكْنَا مِن قَرْيَةٍ إِلَّا لَهَا مُنذِرُونَ ذِكْرَىٰ وَمَا كُنَّا ظَٰلِمِينَ ۝ وَمَا تَنَزَّلَتْ بِهِ ٱلشَّيَٰطِينُ ۝ وَمَا يَنۢبَغِى لَهُمْ وَمَا يَسْتَطِيعُونَ ۝ إِنَّهُمْ عَنِ ٱلسَّمْعِ لَمَعْزُولُونَ ۝

ᵃ When, on behalf of God, the call for Truth appears at the level of a prophet, it appears in its final and perfect shape. That is why it becomes necessary for God's punishment to visit any community which denies the prophet. However, until this punishment is actually administered, man considers himself safe from it. In order to prove the divine call baseless, he adopts various tactics. Sometimes he derides the prophet's personality and sometimes he calls the Divine revelation brought by him spurious. Sometimes he says that if God is against them, why does He not punish them?

The only responsibility of the prophet, or the preacher acting on behalf of the prophet, is that he should make the people aware of the Truth. All matters over and above that are the responsibility of God and He shows them this when He wills.

²¹³ So do not call on any deity besides God, lest you incur His punishment. ²¹⁴ Warn your nearest kinsmen, ²¹⁵ and extend kindness and affection to those of the believers who follow you. ²¹⁶ If they disobey you, say, 'I bear no responsibility for what you do.' ²¹⁷ Put your trust in the Mighty One, the Merciful, ²¹⁸ who sees you when you stand up [for prayer], ²¹⁹ and sees your movements among those who prostrate themselves: ²²⁰ He is the All Hearing, the All Knowing.ᵃ

فَلَا تَدْعُ مَعَ ٱللَّهِ إِلَٰهًا ءَاخَرَ فَتَكُونَ مِنَ ٱلْمُعَذَّبِينَ ۝ وَأَنذِرْ عَشِيرَتَكَ ٱلْأَقْرَبِينَ ۝ وَٱخْفِضْ جَنَاحَكَ لِمَنِ ٱتَّبَعَكَ مِنَ ٱلْمُؤْمِنِينَ ۝ فَإِنْ عَصَوْكَ فَقُلْ إِنِّى بَرِىٓءٌ مِّمَّا تَعْمَلُونَ ۝ وَتَوَكَّلْ عَلَى ٱلْعَزِيزِ ٱلرَّحِيمِ ۝ ٱلَّذِى يَرَىٰكَ حِينَ تَقُومُ ۝ وَتَقَلُّبَكَ فِى ٱلسَّٰجِدِينَ ۝ إِنَّهُۥ هُوَ ٱلسَّمِيعُ ٱلْعَلِيمُ ۝

ᵃ To take anybody other than God to be worthy of worship is the greatest crime in the eyes of God. No one guilty of this crime can escape punishment. It is the duty of the preacher to save himself from polytheism and to call the people to the Truth, primarily those who are near to him.

In order to support the Truth, one has to kill one's ego. That is why there are very few among the highly placed who are prepared to side with the Truth. It often happens that only those who occupy a lower position in society come forward to do so. This poses a serious trial for the preacher of God's word. He has to guard himself against holding these persons inferior as others do. They must be given equal status in an Islamic society.

The true emissary of the Almighty is one whose relation with his Maker is so strong that he passes his lonely nights in restlessness and is often forced to spring out of his bed. He holds his companions who are kneeling to pray to God in the stillness of the night in such high esteem that they become the centre of his attention.

²²¹ Shall I tell you upon whom the devils descend? ²²² They descend on every lying sinner, ²²³ who lends an ear to them, and most of them are liars. ²²⁴ And as for the poets—it is the misled who follow them. ²²⁵ Do you not see how they wander aimlessly in every valley, ²²⁶ preaching what they do not practice. ²²⁷ Not so the true believers who do good works and remember God with fervour and defend themselves only after they are wronged. The wrongdoers will soon know how evil a turn their affairs will take.ᵃ

هَلْ أُنَبِّئُكُمْ عَلَىٰ مَن تَنَزَّلُ ٱلشَّيَٰطِينُ ۝ تَنَزَّلُ عَلَىٰ كُلِّ أَفَّاكٍ أَثِيمٍ ۝ يُلْقُونَ ٱلسَّمْعَ وَأَكْثَرُهُمْ كَٰذِبُونَ ۝ وَٱلشُّعَرَآءُ يَتَّبِعُهُمُ ٱلْغَاوُۥنَ ۝ أَلَمْ تَرَ أَنَّهُمْ فِى كُلِّ وَادٍ يَهِيمُونَ ۝ وَأَنَّهُمْ يَقُولُونَ مَا لَا يَفْعَلُونَ ۝ إِلَّا ٱلَّذِينَ ءَامَنُوا۟ وَعَمِلُوا۟ ٱلصَّٰلِحَٰتِ وَذَكَرُوا۟ ٱللَّهَ كَثِيرًا وَٱنتَصَرُوا۟ مِنۢ بَعْدِ مَا ظُلِمُوا۟ وَسَيَعْلَمُ ٱلَّذِينَ ظَلَمُوٓا۟ أَىَّ مُنقَلَبٍ يَنقَلِبُونَ ۝

ᵃ The extraordinary nature of the Prophet's discourse was so telling that even those who denied the truth could not contradict what he had to say. So, they told their people, in order to satisfy them, that he was a magician or a sorcerer and that his superb preaching was due to his being a magician or a charmer, and not to his being a prophet. Similarly, they used to say that the Qur'an was the work of a poet. The answer to this was that it was enough to compare the prophet with the magicians and poets and then see the difference between them. A world of difference would be found between them and no serious-minded person would confuse the one with the other.

The basis of poetry is imagination and not facts and realities. That is why poets have flights of fancy, allowing their ideas to go hither and thither. Unlike the poets, the Prophet and his companions focussed their entire attention upon God—the greatest Reality. Their lives were ideal examples of harmony between preaching and practice. Deep knowledge of God (ma'rifah) made them remember their Creator on all occasions. They were extremely cautious and, if they took action against anyone, it was only in self-defence. One who is not serious about the life Hereafter cannot be serious about leading a God-oriented life in this world.

27. THE ANTS

In the name of God,
the Most Gracious, the Most Merciful

¹ *Ta Sin*

These are verses from the Quran, a book that makes things clear; ² it is guidance and good news for the believers ³ who pray regularly and pay obligatory alms and have firm faith in the Hereafter. ⁴ We have made those who do not believe in the Hereafter feel their actions appear good to them, so they wander blindly: ⁵ they are the ones who will have the worst of punishment, and in the Hereafter they will be the greatest losers. ⁶ You have received this Quran from One who is all-wise, all-knowing. *ᵃ*

طسٓ تِلۡكَ ءَايَٰتُ ٱلۡقُرۡءَانِ وَكِتَابٍ
مُّبِينٍ ۝ هُدًى وَبُشۡرَىٰ لِلۡمُؤۡمِنِينَ
۝ ٱلَّذِينَ يُقِيمُونَ ٱلصَّلَوٰةَ وَيُؤۡتُونَ
ٱلزَّكَوٰةَ وَهُم بِٱلۡأٓخِرَةِ هُمۡ يُوقِنُونَ
۝ إِنَّ ٱلَّذِينَ لَا يُؤۡمِنُونَ بِٱلۡأٓخِرَةِ زَيَّنَّا
لَهُمۡ أَعۡمَٰلَهُمۡ فَهُمۡ يَعۡمَهُونَ ۝
أُوْلَٰٓئِكَ ٱلَّذِينَ لَهُمۡ سُوٓءُ ٱلۡعَذَابِ وَهُمۡ
فِى ٱلۡأٓخِرَةِ هُمُ ٱلۡأَخۡسَرُونَ ۝ وَإِنَّكَ
لَتُلَقَّى ٱلۡقُرۡءَانَ مِن لَّدُنۡ حَكِيمٍ
عَلِيمٍ ۝

ᵃ When Truth appears before a man and he accepts it without any reservation, he immediately finds himself on the right path. His life becomes righteous in every respect. But, one who is not prepared to mould himself in accordance with the Truth, is forced to twist reality to suit himself. From this develops an attitude of perverseness which is expressed here as 'their actions appear beautiful to them' (*zayyanna lahum a'malahum*). One with such an attitude seeks self-made arguments to justify his behaviour. These so-called arguments gradually take hold of his mind in such a way that he believes them to be perfectly correct. In the light of his false reasoning, his misdeeds appear virtuous to him.

Those to whom God has made their misdeeds appear beautiful are those who are not serious about the call to accept the Truth. As a result of this thinking, they become completely unmindful of self-reformation. They have to pay a heavy price for this tendency of theirs to consider their wrong as right: the path they tread leads straight to hell.

⁷ Tell of Moses who said to his family, 'I have seen a fire. I will bring you news from there, or a burning brand for you to warm yourselves.' ⁸ When he came up to it, a voice called out, 'Blessed be whoever is near this fire, and whoever is around it! Glory be to God, Lord of the Universe!'ᵃ

إِذْ قَالَ مُوسَىٰ لِأَهْلِهِ إِنِّى ءَانَسْتُ نَارًا سَـَٔاتِيكُم مِّنْهَا بِخَبَرٍ أَوْ ءَاتِيكُم بِشِهَابٍ قَبَسٍ لَّعَلَّكُمْ تَصْطَلُونَ ۝ فَلَمَّا جَآءَهَا نُودِىَ أَنۢ بُورِكَ مَن فِى ٱلنَّارِ وَمَنْ حَوْلَهَا وَسُبْحَـٰنَ ٱللَّهِ رَبِّ ٱلْعَـٰلَمِينَ ۝

ᵃ Moses left Egypt and went to Midian (or Madyan), which was situated on the eastern coast of the Gulf of Aqaba. He spent eight years there. Then he left along with his wife for Egypt. During this journey, he reached the foot of a mountain which was situated on a peninsula projecting into the Red Sea. This mountain was called Tur in ancient days and is now known as Gebel Moses.

It was probably a winter night. Moses saw something, which to him looked like a fire far away on the mountain side. He went towards it. But on drawing near, he found that it was God's light and not a fire lit by human beings.

There is an ancient tree at the place on the mountain where Moses saw the light. It is said that this is the very same tree from which God's voice was heard by Moses. The Christians subsequently constructed a church and a monastery at this place which till today is a place of pilgrimage.

9 O Moses, I am God, the Powerful, the Wise. 10 Throw down your staff.' But when he saw it moving like a snake, he turned and fled. 'Moses, do not be afraid! The messengers need have no fear in My presence; 11 as for those who do wrong and then do good after evil, I am most forgiving, most merciful. 12 Now put your hand inside your cloak next to your bosom and it will come out [shining] white, without any blemish. This will be one of the nine signs for Pharaoh and his people: for truly they are a rebellious people.' 13 But when Our signs came to them in all their clarity they said, 'This is clearly sorcery!' 14 And they persisted in rejecting them wrongfully and arrogantly, while in their hearts they were convinced of their truth. Observe, then, how evil was the fate of the evil-doers.*a*

يَٰمُوسَىٰٓ إِنَّهُۥٓ أَنَا ٱللَّهُ ٱلْعَزِيزُ ٱلْحَكِيمُ ۞ وَأَلْقِ عَصَاكَ فَلَمَّا رَءَاهَا تَهْتَزُّ كَأَنَّهَا جَآنٌّ وَلَّىٰ مُدْبِرًا وَلَمْ يُعَقِّبْ يَٰمُوسَىٰ لَا تَخَفْ إِنِّي لَا يَخَافُ لَدَىَّ ٱلْمُرْسَلُونَ ۞ إِلَّا مَن ظَلَمَ ثُمَّ بَدَّلَ حُسْنًا بَعْدَ سُوٓءٍ فَإِنِّي غَفُورٌ رَّحِيمٌ ۞ وَأَدْخِلْ يَدَكَ فِي جَيْبِكَ تَخْرُجْ بَيْضَآءَ مِنْ غَيْرِ سُوٓءٍ فِي تِسْعِ ءَايَٰتٍ إِلَىٰ فِرْعَوْنَ وَقَوْمِهِۦٓ إِنَّهُمْ كَانُوا۟ قَوْمًا فَٰسِقِينَ ۞ فَلَمَّا جَآءَتْهُمْ ءَايَٰتُنَا مُبْصِرَةً قَالُوا۟ هَٰذَا سِحْرٌ مُّبِينٌ ۞ وَجَحَدُوا۟ بِهَا وَٱسْتَيْقَنَتْهَآ أَنفُسُهُمْ ظُلْمًا وَعُلُوًّا فَٱنظُرْ كَيْفَ كَانَ عَٰقِبَةُ ٱلْمُفْسِدِينَ ۞

---

a Moses had gone to the mountain to obtain a burning brand. But after reaching it, he came to know that he had been called there to have prophethood bestowed upon him. When Almighty God blesses any subject of His with a special gift, He gives it suddenly and unexpectedly, so that the recipient may attribute it directly to God and develop in himself the most profound feelings of gratitude towards Him.

On the one hand, the community of Moses (the Children of Israel), though a believing community, had degenerated. On the other, Moses had to proclaim the message of God to a tyrant king like Pharaoh. Therefore, Almighty God blessed him with the miracle of the stick at the very beginning of his mission. This stick was an enduring divine power for Moses, by means of which nine miracles were performed to awe the Pharaoh, apart from the miracles which were meant for the Children of Israel.

The miracles of Moses finally established his truthfulness. In spite of this, Pharaoh and his companions did not accept him. The reasons for this were their proneness to transgression, their false pride, and their unwillingness to curtail their freedom. Moreover, they knew that accepting Moses's preaching would amount to negating their own greatness. And who accepts Truth at the expense of his own greatness?

¹⁵ We bestowed knowledge on David and Solomon and they both said, 'Praise be to God who has exalted us above many of His believing servants.' ¹⁶ Solomon succeeded David. He said, 'Know, my people, that we have been taught the speech of birds and endowed with all good things. Surely this is God's manifest grace.'ᵃ

وَلَقَدْ ءَاتَيْنَا دَاوُۥدَ وَسُلَيْمَٰنَ عِلْمًا ۖ
وَقَالَا ٱلْحَمْدُ لِلَّهِ ٱلَّذِى فَضَّلَنَا عَلَىٰ
كَثِيرٍ مِّنْ عِبَادِهِ ٱلْمُؤْمِنِينَ ۝ وَوَرِثَ
سُلَيْمَٰنُ دَاوُۥدَ ۖ وَقَالَ يَٰٓأَيُّهَا ٱلنَّاسُ
عُلِّمْنَا مَنطِقَ ٱلطَّيْرِ وَأُوتِينَا مِن كُلِّ
شَىْءٍ ۖ إِنَّ هَٰذَا لَهُوَ ٱلْفَضْلُ ٱلْمُبِينُ ۝

ᵃ David was the prophet and king of the Children of Israel. His son, Solomon, succeeded him as prophet and king. Solomon's empire extended from Palestine to Transjordan. God had given him different kinds of useful knowledge. Also, he was blessed with many things by way of miracles, for example, his ability to understand the language of birds, train them and use them to transmit messages, etc. Solomon enjoyed extraordinary superiority over his contemporaries. But this superiority only created a feeling of humility in him. Whatever he had he considered a direct gift from God.

The period of Solomon's empire extended from 965 B.C. to 926 B.C.

¹⁷ Solomon's hosts of jinn and men and birds, were all gathered together in his presence and were ranged in battle order, ¹⁸ and when they came to the Valley of the Ants, one ant said, 'Ants! Go into your dwellings, in case Solomon and his hosts inadvertently crush you.' ¹⁹ Solomon smiled broadly at its words and said, 'Lord, inspire me to be thankful for the blessings You have granted me and my parents, and to do good deeds that please You; and include me, by Your grace, among Your righteous servants!' ^a

وَحُشِرَ لِسُلَيْمَنَ جُنُودُهُ مِنَ ٱلْجِنِّ
وَٱلْإِنسِ وَٱلطَّيْرِ فَهُمْ يُوزَعُونَ ﴿١٧﴾
حَتَّىٰ إِذَآ أَتَوْاْ عَلَىٰ وَادِ ٱلنَّمْلِ قَالَتْ
نَمْلَةٌ يَٰٓأَيُّهَا ٱلنَّمْلُ ٱدْخُلُواْ
مَسَٰكِنَكُمْ لَا يَحْطِمَنَّكُمْ سُلَيْمَٰنُ
وَجُنُودُهُۥ وَهُمْ لَا يَشْعُرُونَ ﴿١٨﴾
فَتَبَسَّمَ ضَاحِكًا مِّن قَوْلِهَا وَقَالَ رَبِّ
أَوْزِعْنِىٓ أَنْ أَشْكُرَ نِعْمَتَكَ ٱلَّتِىٓ أَنْعَمْتَ
عَلَىَّ وَعَلَىٰ وَٰلِدَىَّ وَأَنْ أَعْمَلَ صَٰلِحًا
تَرْضَىٰهُ وَأَدْخِلْنِى بِرَحْمَتِكَ فِى عِبَادِكَ
ٱلصَّٰلِحِينَ ﴿١٩﴾

---

^a In Solomon's army there were not only human beings but also jinns and birds. Once Solomon's army passed through a valley where there was a large number of ants. On this occasion, Solomon understood what the ants were saying to each other.

Such an incident would be enough to give rise to conceit and pride in an ordinary man. But, Solomon became the embodiment of gratitude on this account. He fully attributed to God whatever appeared to be his—and this is the way of a pious and righteous man.

20 Then Solomon inspected the birds, and said, 'How is it that I do not see the hoopoe? Is he absent then? 21 I shall surely punish him severely or order him to be executed, unless he gives me a good reason for his absence.' 22 But he was not long in coming, and said, 'I have learnt something you did not know. I have come to you from Sheba with reliable news. 23 I found a woman ruling over them, who has been given everything and she has a mighty throne. 24 I found her and her people worshipping the sun, instead of God. Satan has made their conduct appear good to them, and has thus diverted them from the right path, so that they might not be guided. 25 Should they not worship God who brings forth what is hidden in the heavens and earth and knows both what you conceal and what you make known? 26 He is God: there is no deity but He, the Lord of the mighty throne.' a

وَتَفَقَّدَ ٱلطَّيْرَ فَقَالَ مَا لِيَ لَآ أَرَى ٱلْهُدْهُدَ أَمْ كَانَ مِنَ ٱلْغَآئِبِينَ ۝ لَأُعَذِّبَنَّهُۥ عَذَابًا شَدِيدًا أَوْ لَأَاْذْبَحَنَّهُۥٓ أَوْ لَيَأْتِيَنِّى بِسُلْطَٰنٍ مُّبِينٍ ۝ فَمَكَثَ غَيْرَ بَعِيدٍ فَقَالَ أَحَطتُ بِمَا لَمْ تُحِطْ بِهِۦ وَجِئْتُكَ مِن سَبَإٍۭ بِنَبَإٍ يَقِينٍ ۝ إِنِّى وَجَدتُّ ٱمْرَأَةً تَمْلِكُهُمْ وَأُوتِيَتْ مِن كُلِّ شَىْءٍ وَلَهَا عَرْشٌ عَظِيمٌ ۝ وَجَدتُّهَا وَقَوْمَهَا يَسْجُدُونَ لِلشَّمْسِ مِن دُونِ ٱللَّهِ وَزَيَّنَ لَهُمُ ٱلشَّيْطَٰنُ أَعْمَٰلَهُمْ فَصَدَّهُمْ عَنِ ٱلسَّبِيلِ فَهُمْ لَا يَهْتَدُونَ ۝ أَلَّا يَسْجُدُوا۟ لِلَّهِ ٱلَّذِى يُخْرِجُ ٱلْخَبْءَ فِى ٱلسَّمَٰوَٰتِ وَٱلْأَرْضِ وَيَعْلَمُ مَا تُخْفُونَ وَمَا تُعْلِنُونَ ۝ ٱللَّهُ لَآ إِلَٰهَ إِلَّا هُوَ رَبُّ ٱلْعَرْشِ ٱلْعَظِيمِ ۩ ۝

a The Sabeans were a wealthy community of ancient times (1100 B.C. to 115B.C.). Their country was located in Ma'arib (Yemen), where its grand ruins are still in existence. During Solomon's period, this area was under the rule of a queen called Sheba (Bilqis). The people of this place used to worship the sun, Satan having taught them that the only thing worth worshipping was whatever was most prominent. As the sun was the most prominent of all visible things, only the sun, therefore, deserved to be considered a god and worshipped.

Solomon received detailed information about the Sabeans through the hoopoe bird. This hoopoe perhaps belonged to Solomon's army of birds and possibly received regular training.

²⁷ Solomon said, 'We shall soon see whether you have spoken the truth, or whether you are a liar. ²⁸ Go with this letter of mine and lay it before them, then withdraw from them and see how they respond.' ²⁹ The Queen of Sheba said, 'O Counsellors, an honourable letter has been delivered to me. ³⁰ It is from Solomon. It reads, "In the name of God, Most Gracious, Most Merciful, ³¹ do not exalt yourselves above me, but come to me in all submission." ³² Now advise me in this, Counsellors. I never decide any affair till I have conferred with you.' ³³ They said, 'We are strong and our prowess in battle is great, but the decision is in your hands, so consider what you will command.' ³⁴ She said, 'Surely, when mighty kings invade a country, they despoil it and humiliate its noblest inhabitants—these men will do the same—³⁵ but I shall send them a present and see with what reply my envoys will return.'ᵃ

قَالَ سَنَنظُرُ أَصَدَقۡتَ أَمۡ كُنتَ مِنَ ٱلۡكَٰذِبِينَ ۝ ٱذۡهَب بِّكِتَٰبِى هَٰذَا فَأَلۡقِهۡ إِلَيۡهِمۡ ثُمَّ تَوَلَّ عَنۡهُمۡ فَٱنظُرۡ مَاذَا يَرۡجِعُونَ ۝ قَالَتۡ يَٰٓأَيُّهَا ٱلۡمَلَؤُاْ إِنِّىٓ أُلۡقِىَ إِلَىَّ كِتَٰبٌ كَرِيمٌ ۝ إِنَّهُۥ مِن سُلَيۡمَٰنَ وَإِنَّهُۥ بِسۡمِ ٱللَّهِ ٱلرَّحۡمَٰنِ ٱلرَّحِيمِ ۝ أَلَّا تَعۡلُواْ عَلَىَّ وَأۡتُونِى مُسۡلِمِينَ ۝ قَالَتۡ يَٰٓأَيُّهَا ٱلۡمَلَؤُاْ أَفۡتُونِى فِىٓ أَمۡرِى مَا كُنتُ قَاطِعَةً أَمۡرًا حَتَّىٰ تَشۡهَدُونِ ۝ قَالُواْ نَحۡنُ أُوْلُواْ قُوَّةٍ وَأُوْلُواْ بَأۡسٍ شَدِيدٍ وَٱلۡأَمۡرُ إِلَيۡكِ فَٱنظُرِى مَاذَا تَأۡمُرِينَ ۝ قَالَتۡ إِنَّ ٱلۡمُلُوكَ إِذَا دَخَلُواْ قَرۡيَةً أَفۡسَدُوهَا وَجَعَلُوٓاْ أَعِزَّةَ أَهۡلِهَآ أَذِلَّةً وَكَذَٰلِكَ يَفۡعَلُونَ ۝ وَإِنِّى مُرۡسِلَةٌ إِلَيۡهِم بِهَدِيَّةٍ فَنَاظِرَةٌۢ بِمَ يَرۡجِعُ ٱلۡمُرۡسَلُونَ ۝

ᵃ The Queen of Sheba viewed the matter quite realistically. She realised that if she resisted the might of Solomon, there was a strong possibility of her being defeated and then her nation would be treated as every vanquished nation is treated by a victorious nation. On the contrary, she thought, she would be saved if she surrendered. However, the queen pursued the course of sending gifts to him by way of initial feelers, so that she might know whether Soloman desired wealth, or if not, whether he had any other demands based on some other principle.

³⁶ So when [the envoy] came to Solomon he said, 'What! Are you offering me wealth? But that which God has given me is better than that which He has given you. Yet you rejoice in your gift. ³⁷ Go back to them: we shall most certainly come upon them with forces which they will never be able to withstand, and shall most certainly cause them to be driven from their lands, disgraced and humbled!' ᵃ

فَلَمَّا جَآءَ سُلَيْمَٰنَ قَالَ أَتُمِدُّونَنِ بِمَالٍ فَمَآ ءَاتَىٰنِۦَ ٱللَّهُ خَيْرٌ مِّمَّآ ءَاتَىٰكُم بَلْ أَنتُم بِهَدِيَّتِكُمْ تَفْرَحُونَ ۝ ٱرْجِعْ إِلَيْهِمْ فَلَنَأْتِيَنَّهُم بِجُنُودٍ لَّا قِبَلَ لَهُم بِهَا وَلَنُخْرِجَنَّهُم مِّنْهَآ أَذِلَّةً وَهُمْ صَٰغِرُونَ ۝

ᵃ In comparison with the invaluable wealth, which Solomon had received in the shape of prophethood and the realisation of God, every other kind of wealth was worthless in his eyes. So, when gifts of gold and silver were presented to him on behalf of the Queen of Sheba, he did not even look at them.

In the way he conducted himself, Solomon gave the emissaries of the Queen of Sheba the impression that his real concern was that of principle and not of self-interest. The Quranic commentator Ibn Kathir, by way of explanation, paraphrases Solomon's words, 'Do you want to influence me with your wealth so that I should let you off along with your polytheism and allow you to keep your kingdom?'

The power and empire of Solomon were the gifts of God. Similarly, the manner in which he dealt with the kingdom of the Sabeans was also a godly matter. Shah Abdul Quadir (Dehlavi) writes in connection with verse 37, 'No other prophet spoke like this. Soloman had the force of God Almighty's empire behind him, so he spoke like this.'

³⁸ Solomon then said, 'O Counsellors, which of you can bring me her throne before they come to me in submission? ³⁹ A demon from among the jinn said, 'I will bring it to you before you get up from your seat. I am strong and trustworthy enough to do it.' ⁴⁰ But one of them who had some knowledge of the Book said, 'I will bring it to you in the twinkling of an eye.' When Solomon saw it placed before him, he exclaimed, 'This is by the grace of my Lord, to test whether I am grateful or ungrateful. Whosoever is grateful, it is for the good of his own self; and whosoever is ungrateful, then surely my Lord is self-sufficient and generous.' ^a

قَالَ يَٰٓأَيُّهَا ٱلْمَلَؤُاْ أَيُّكُمْ يَأْتِينِى بِعَرْشِهَا قَبْلَ أَن يَأْتُونِى مُسْلِمِينَ ۝ قَالَ عِفْرِيتٌ مِّنَ ٱلْجِنِّ أَنَا۠ ءَاتِيكَ بِهِۦ قَبْلَ أَن تَقُومَ مِن مَّقَامِكَ وَإِنِّى عَلَيْهِ لَقَوِىٌّ أَمِينٌ ۝ قَالَ ٱلَّذِى عِندَهُۥ عِلْمٌ مِّنَ ٱلْكِتَٰبِ أَنَا۠ ءَاتِيكَ بِهِۦ قَبْلَ أَن يَرْتَدَّ إِلَيْكَ طَرْفُكَ فَلَمَّا رَءَاهُ مُسْتَقِرًّا عِندَهُۥ قَالَ هَٰذَا مِن فَضْلِ رَبِّى لِيَبْلُوَنِىٓ ءَأَشْكُرُ أَمْ أَكْفُرُ وَمَن شَكَرَ فَإِنَّمَا يَشْكُرُ لِنَفْسِهِۦ وَمَن كَفَرَ فَإِنَّ رَبِّى غَنِىٌّ كَرِيمٌ ۝

---

^a Though Solomon was endowed with extraordinary power, he planned to subjugate the Sabean people by demonstrating his power rather than by using it. So, through a special agent of his, he arranged to have the Queen's throne shifted from her palace in Ma'arib to Jerusalem (Palestine). The idea of having the throne brought to him probably occurred to him when on the return of the presents, the Queen of Sheba started out from Yemen for Palestine, so that she could come to Solomon's court and have direct talks with him. This journey of the Queen, undertaken with much pomp and ceremony, must have started after her diplomatic deputation had returned and narrated to her the wise words of Solomon, testified to the nobility of his character and described the magnificence of his court.

The distance between Ma'arib and Jerusalem is about fifteen hundred miles. This long distance was covered in such a way that no sooner had the words of command fallen from Solomon's lips than the jewel-studded throne was there before him. In spite of this extraordinary power, feelings of pride did not arise in him. He remained the embodiment of modesty and kept bowing down before God.

⁴¹ He said, 'Disguise her throne. We shall see whether or not she will recognize it.' ⁴² When she came to Solomon, she was asked, 'Is your throne like this?' She replied, 'It looks as though it were the same, and we had been given knowledge [of your power] before this, and we have already submitted.' ⁴³ And that which she used to worship beside God had stopped her [from believing]; for she came of a disbelieving people. ⁴⁴ Then she was bidden to enter the palace; but when she saw it, she thought it was a deep pool of water, and bared her legs. But Solomon explained, 'It is just a palace paved with glass,' and she said, 'My Lord, I have wronged myself: now I submit myself along with Solomon, to God, the Lord of the Universe.'ᵃ

قَالَ نَكِّرُواْ لَهَا عَرْشَهَا نَنظُرْ أَتَهْتَدِىٓ أَمْ تَكُونُ مِنَ ٱلَّذِينَ لَا يَهْتَدُونَ ۝ فَلَمَّا جَآءَتْ قِيلَ أَهَٰكَذَا عَرْشُكِ قَالَتْ كَأَنَّهُۥ هُوَ وَأُوتِينَا ٱلْعِلْمَ مِن قَبْلِهَا وَكُنَّا مُسْلِمِينَ ۝ وَصَدَّهَا مَا كَانَت تَّعْبُدُ مِن دُونِ ٱللَّهِ إِنَّهَا كَانَتْ مِن قَوْمٍ كَٰفِرِينَ ۝ قِيلَ لَهَا ٱدْخُلِي ٱلصَّرْحَ فَلَمَّا رَأَتْهُ حَسِبَتْهُ لُجَّةً وَكَشَفَتْ عَن سَاقَيْهَا قَالَ إِنَّهُۥ صَرْحٌ مُّمَرَّدٌ مِّن قَوَارِيرَ قَالَتْ رَبِّ إِنِّي ظَلَمْتُ نَفْسِي وَأَسْلَمْتُ مَعَ سُلَيْمَٰنَ لِلَّهِ رَبِّ ٱلْعَٰلَمِينَ ۝

ᵃ The Queen of Sheba set forth from her country and reached Jerusalem. When she came to meet Solomon, the Queen, to her surprise, was asked whether her own throne resembeled the throne she saw at the palace. The Queen admitted that she was wonderstuck to see this throne which was exactly similar to her own. The throne which she had kept safe in her palace in Ma'arib, had mysteriously traversed a distance of fifteen hundred miles and reached Jerusalem.

After entering Solomon's palace, the Queen of Sheba reached a room where the floor was made of thick, transparent slabs of glass with water flowing beneath them. Mistaking the floor for a pool of water, the Queen quickly pulled up her garment to prevent it from getting wet. Seeing this, Solomon explained to her that it was just the floor and not water.

In this way, she was made to realise how outward appearances may deceive the understanding of men, the inner reality often being different from what meets the eye. Similarly, man starts worshipping the sun and moon because of their prominence, but the real God is beyond these visible phenomena.

The Queen of Sheba had so far been worshipping the sun under the influence of the conventions of her nation. ▶

⁴⁵ To Thamud We sent their brother Salih. He said, 'Serve none but God.' But they divided themselves into two factions contending with one another. ⁴⁶ He urged them, 'O my people, why do you wish to hasten on the evil rather than the good? Why do you not ask forgiveness of God, so that you may be shown mercy?' ⁴⁷ They said, 'We see you and your followers as an evil omen.' He replied, 'No, your evil omen is with God; the truth is that you are a people being put to the test.'ᵃ

وَلَقَدْ أَرْسَلْنَآ إِلَىٰ ثَمُودَ أَخَاهُمْ صَـٰلِحًا أَنِ ٱعْبُدُوا۟ ٱللَّهَ فَإِذَا هُمْ فَرِيقَانِ يَخْتَصِمُونَ ۝ قَالَ يَـٰقَوْمِ لِمَ تَسْتَعْجِلُونَ بِٱلسَّيِّئَةِ قَبْلَ ٱلْحَسَنَةِ لَوْلَا تَسْتَغْفِرُونَ ٱللَّهَ لَعَلَّكُمْ تُرْحَمُونَ ۝ قَالُوا۟ ٱطَّيَّرْنَا بِكَ وَبِمَن مَّعَكَ قَالَ طَـٰٓئِرُكُمْ عِندَ ٱللَّهِ بَلْ أَنتُمْ قَوْمٌ تُفْتَنُونَ ۝

But, in the company of Solomon, whatever she heard and whatever she saw, completely banished from her mind all impressions of the majesty of anything other than God. Consequently, she renounced the religion of polytheism and whole-heartedly embraced the religion of monotheism.

ᵃ When Salih started calling for belief in the pure unity of God, his community divided itself into two groups. The leaders of the community were too wrapped up in their own greatness to accept the pure and unadulterated religion preached by Salih. But, among the less important people, there were some who gave a positive response to his call.

The two groups began having controversial discussions. The leading luminaries of the community stated quite bluntly that they did not believe in God and that He might bring upon them whatever retribution He wanted as a punishment for their denial. If they faced any hardship, they were wont to say that it was the ill-luck brought upon them by the inauspicious presence in their midst of Salih and his companions. All these things were said in order to humiliate Salih and belittle his call, and not as a result of any serious thought. Their circumstances, whether good or bad, had come to them from God. But they took advantage of good circumstances to feed their false pride and cited bad circumstances to make false complaints.

The rising of a prophet from among them was in the nature of a trial devised for them by God. They were placed in this position in order to see whether they recognised the Truth and co-operated with it, or whether they remained blind and deaf towards it. They failed in this trial. They were so preoccupied with material things that they failed to comprehend the reality.

48 There were in the city nine men who spread corruption in the land, and would not reform. 49 They said, 'Let us bind ourselves by an oath sworn in the name of God that we shall attack Salih and his family by night, and to his protector [who demands retribution], we shall say, 'We were not present when they were slain. We are telling the truth.' 50 Thus they devised a plan, and We also devised a plan, but they were not aware of it. 51 See, then, what the consequences of their plan were. We destroyed them and their people utterly, all together. 52 Because of their wrongdoing, their houses are in ruins—in that surely there is a sign for people who have knowledge— 53 and We saved those who believed in and feared God.[a]

وَكَانَ فِي ٱلْمَدِينَةِ تِسْعَةُ رَهْطٍ يُفْسِدُونَ فِي ٱلْأَرْضِ وَلَا يُصْلِحُونَ ۝ قَالُوا تَقَاسَمُوا بِٱللَّهِ لَنُبَيِّتَنَّهُ وَأَهْلَهُ ثُمَّ لَنَقُولَنَّ لِوَلِيِّهِۦ مَا شَهِدْنَا مَهْلِكَ أَهْلِهِۦ وَإِنَّا لَصَٰدِقُونَ ۝ وَمَكَرُوا مَكْرًا وَمَكَرْنَا مَكْرًا وَهُمْ لَا يَشْعُرُونَ ۝ فَٱنظُرْ كَيْفَ كَانَ عَٰقِبَةُ مَكْرِهِمْ أَنَّا دَمَّرْنَٰهُمْ وَقَوْمَهُمْ أَجْمَعِينَ ۝ فَتِلْكَ بُيُوتُهُمْ خَاوِيَةً بِمَا ظَلَمُوا إِنَّ فِي ذَٰلِكَ لَءَايَةً لِّقَوْمٍ يَعْلَمُونَ ۝ وَأَنجَيْنَا ٱلَّذِينَ ءَامَنُوا وَكَانُوا يَتَّقُونَ ۝

---

[a] There were nine great chiefs in this community. In order to maintain their high position they made constant efforts to belittle the Truth, and efforts of this type undoubtedly constitute the greatest disturbance on God's earth.

Finally, these chiefs conspired to kill Salih. But, before they could take any steps against Salih according to their secret plan, God seized hold of them. In spite of all their might they were destroyed so utterly that, only dilapidated ruins of their ancient towns, still stand there as a memorial to them.

A great lesson is hidden in such historical events. But, this lesson may be learnt only by one who is capable of connecting such events with the eternal laws of God. Conversely, those who attribute such events to physical causes cannot learn any lesson from them.

⁵⁴ And tell of Lot. He said to his people, 'Will you commit evil knowingly? ⁵⁵ Must you go lustfully to men instead of women? Indeed, you are a people who are deeply ignorant.' ⁵⁶ The only answer of his people was, 'Drive out Lot and his family from the city. They are a people who make themselves out to be pure.' ⁵⁷ So We delivered him and his family—except his wife: We ordained her to be one of those who stayed behind— ⁵⁸ and We pelted them with torrential rain. How dreadful that rain was for those who had been warned! ⁵⁹ Say, 'All praise be to God, and peace be upon those servants of His whom He has chosen. Is God better, or what they associate with Him? ᵃ

وَلُوطًا إِذْ قَالَ لِقَوْمِهِ أَتَأْتُونَ الْفَاحِشَةَ وَأَنتُمْ تُبْصِرُونَ ۝ أَئِنَّكُمْ لَتَأْتُونَ الرِّجَالَ شَهْوَةً مِّن دُونِ النِّسَاءِ بَلْ أَنتُمْ قَوْمٌ تَجْهَلُونَ ۝ فَمَا كَانَ جَوَابَ قَوْمِهِ إِلَّا أَن قَالُوٓا أَخْرِجُوٓا ءَالَ لُوطٍ مِّن قَرْيَتِكُمْ إِنَّهُمْ أُنَاسٌ يَتَطَهَّرُونَ ۝ فَأَنجَيْنَهُ وَأَهْلَهُ إِلَّا امْرَأَتَهُ قَدَّرْنَهَا مِنَ الْغَابِرِينَ ۝ وَأَمْطَرْنَا عَلَيْهِم مَّطَرًا فَسَآءَ مَطَرُ الْمُنذَرِينَ ۝ قُلِ الْحَمْدُ لِلَّهِ وَسَلَامٌ عَلَىٰ عِبَادِهِ الَّذِينَ اصْطَفَىٰ ءَآللَّهُ خَيْرٌ أَمَّا يُشْرِكُونَ ۝

ᵃ The community of Lot, in its excessive sexual indulgence, had stooped to homosexuality. Lot, trying to stir their conscience, said, 'O, subjects of God! You have been given eyes to observe things and the moral sense to be able to differentiate between good and bad. Then, how can you indulge in conduct which amounts to open shamelessness?'

The community had no reply to this. They could not reject the prophet's words on the basis of logical arguments. So, they resorted to violence against him. But, when this stage is reached, the time comes for God's final decision to be made without further delay. So they were destroyed by a volcanic eruption. Lot's wife was also not exempt from this fate either, as she was one of the unbelievers. God deals with individuals according to their personal conduct and not on the basis of their being someone's relatives or on the basis of their worldly connections.

One who gives serious consideration to the aforesaid events of history, will cry out with feeling, 'I express my heartfelt gratitude to God, who has arranged for the guidance of humanity in every age!' And then his heart will be filled with respect for those who dedicated their lives to God and completed the mission of providing God's guidance to everyone.

⁶⁰ Who created the heavens and the earth and sends down water for you from the sky, by which We make luxuriant gardens grow—you could never make such trees grow in them—is it another deity besides God? No indeed, but they are a people who equate others with Him. ⁶¹ Who is it that made the earth a stable place to live in? Who made rivers flow through it? Who set mountains upon it and placed a barrier between the two seas? Is there another deity besides God? Indeed, most of them have no knowledge.ᵃ

أَمَّنْ خَلَقَ ٱلسَّمَٰوَٰتِ وَٱلْأَرْضَ وَأَنزَلَ لَكُم مِّنَ ٱلسَّمَآءِ مَآءً فَأَنۢبَتْنَا بِهِۦ حَدَآئِقَ ذَاتَ بَهْجَةٍ مَّا كَانَ لَكُمْ أَن تُنۢبِتُوا۟ شَجَرَهَآ ۗ أَءِلَٰهٌ مَّعَ ٱللَّهِ ۚ بَلْ هُمْ قَوْمٌ يَعْدِلُونَ ۝ أَمَّن جَعَلَ ٱلْأَرْضَ قَرَارًا وَجَعَلَ خِلَٰلَهَآ أَنْهَٰرًا وَجَعَلَ لَهَا رَوَٰسِىَ وَجَعَلَ بَيْنَ ٱلْبَحْرَيْنِ حَاجِزًا ۗ أَءِلَٰهٌ مَّعَ ٱللَّهِ ۚ بَلْ أَكْثَرُهُمْ لَا يَعْلَمُونَ ۝

ᵃ Expressed as a chain of cause and effect, the theories propounded by atheists or agnostics, remain woefully inadequate to explain the creation of the unimaginably vast universe.

Be it the creation of the innumerable heavenly bodies that float in boundless space, or the elaborate arrangements that make the earth habitable—all these and many other such phenomena are too great and too wonderful to have been wrought by any idol or occasioned by any blind physical law.

The fact is that any explanation of the universe on bases other than God amounts to giving a false explanation of reality. This is merely a fabrication and not a genuine explanation.

⁶² Who responds to the oppressed when he calls out to Him, and relieves his suffering and who will make you inheritors of the earth? Then, is there a god besides God? How little you pay heed! ⁶³ Who guides you in the darkness of the land and sea? Who sends the breezes as heralds of His mercy? Then, is there a deity besides God? Exalted is God above what they associate with Him. ⁶⁴ Who originates creation, then regenerates it, and who gives you sustenance from heaven and earth? Then, is there a deity besides God?' Say, 'Bring forward your proofs, if you are telling the truth.'ᵃ

أَمَّن يُجِيبُ ٱلْمُضْطَرَّ إِذَا دَعَاهُ
وَيَكْشِفُ ٱلسُّوٓءَ وَيَجْعَلُكُمْ خُلَفَآءَ
ٱلْأَرْضِ أَءِلَهٌ مَّعَ ٱللَّهِ قَلِيلًا مَّا
تَذَكَّرُونَ ۩ أَمَّن يَهْدِيكُمْ فِي
ظُلُمَٰتِ ٱلْبَرِّ وَٱلْبَحْرِ وَمَن يُرْسِلُ
ٱلرِّيَٰحَ بُشْرًۢا بَيْنَ يَدَيْ رَحْمَتِهِۦ
أَءِلَهٌ مَّعَ ٱللَّهِ تَعَٰلَى ٱللَّهُ عَمَّا
يُشْرِكُونَ ۩ أَمَّن يَبْدَؤُاْ ٱلْخَلْقَ
ثُمَّ يُعِيدُهُۥ وَمَن يَرْزُقُكُم مِّنَ ٱلسَّمَآءِ
وَٱلْأَرْضِ أَءِلَهٌ مَّعَ ٱللَّهِ قُلْ هَاتُواْ
بُرْهَٰنَكُمْ إِن كُنتُمْ صَٰدِقِينَ ۩

ᵃ The needs of man are fulfilled as a result of the perfect co-ordination between all the factors in the Universe. We must ask who, other than Almighty God, can assemble all the favourable factors on such a large scale?

Similarly, the displacement of a nation or race and another nation taking its place, the sailing of a ship, and in the modern age the flying of an aeroplane in darkness as well as in daylight by taking advantage of technological advances, the rising of water vapour from the sea and its subsequent descent in the shape of rain. The creation of things out of nothing and their resurrection, the provision of all kinds for man on a large scale—all these result solely from the instrumentality of Almighty God.

This is true of all of the world's events. Here, to cause a single event to take place, it is necessary to activate innumerable factors, and this can be done only by that Being who has control of the whole universe. In this context, how foolish it is to make anybody other than God the centre of adoration and worship!

⁶⁵ Say, 'No one in the heavens and the earth has knowledge of the unseen except God.' They do not know when they will be raised up again. ⁶⁶ Indeed, their knowledge of the life to come stops short of the truth: they are [often] in doubt as to its reality: in fact, they are blind to it. ⁶⁷ Those who deny the truth say, 'When we have turned to dust like our fathers, shall we be brought back to life again? ⁶⁸ We and our fathers were promised this before; these are but old stories.' ⁶⁹ Say, 'Roam across the earth and observe what was the end of the sinful ones.' ᵃ

قُل لَّا يَعْلَمُ مَن فِى ٱلسَّمَٰوَٰتِ وَٱلْأَرْضِ ٱلْغَيْبَ إِلَّا ٱللَّهُ وَمَا يَشْعُرُونَ ﴿٦٥﴾ بَلِ ٱدَّٰرَكَ عِلْمُهُمْ فِى ٱلْءَاخِرَةِ بَلْ هُمْ فِى شَكٍّ مِّنْهَا بَلْ هُم مِّنْهَا عَمُونَ ﴿٦٦﴾ وَقَالَ ٱلَّذِينَ كَفَرُوٓاْ أَءِذَا كُنَّا تُرَٰبًا وَءَابَآؤُنَآ أَءِنَّا لَمُخْرَجُونَ ﴿٦٧﴾ لَقَدْ وُعِدْنَا هَٰذَا نَحْنُ وَءَابَآؤُنَا مِن قَبْلُ إِنْ هَٰذَآ إِلَّآ أَسَٰطِيرُ ٱلْأَوَّلِينَ ﴿٦٨﴾ قُلْ سِيرُواْ فِى ٱلْأَرْضِ فَٱنظُرُواْ كَيْفَ كَانَ عَٰقِبَةُ ٱلْمُجْرِمِينَ ﴿٦٩﴾

ᵃ The addressees of the prophets were not absolute and total deniers of the life Hereafter, but they denied that particular concept of the Hereafter, which was presented by the prophets. People were under the impression that the issue of the Hereafter was meant not for them but for others to ponder over. The prophets told them that the Hereafter was as serious a problem for them as it was for others. Yet they clung to the belief that their attachment to some saints or holy persons would redeem them in the Hereafter. The prophets told them, however, that in the Hereafter only God's grace and not attachment to any saint or holy person would be of any avail.

That is why they were mentally confused about the Hereafter. Hot-headed individuals would, of course, articulate their denial of the Hereafter. However, the common people's position was that they did not deny the Hereafter altogether. But, since acceptance of the concept of the Hereafter resulted in the curtailment of their various liberties, their selfish side was not prepared to accept it. So, in reply, they used to talk as if they doubted it. Due to this mentality, they never gave serious consideration to the arguments in favour of the Hereafter. They remained blind and deaf to them.

The fact is that the powers required to decide the fate of nations or races are vested solely in the All-Knowing God. In the present world, He enforces His decisions partially, but in the Hereafter, He will enforce His decisions fully in respect of all nations.

⁷⁰ Do not grieve over them, nor feel distressed at their schemes. ⁷¹ They ask, 'When will this promise be fulfilled, if what you say be true?' ⁷² Say, 'It may be that a part of what you would hasten on is close behind you.' ⁷³ Truly, your Lord is bountiful to mankind, but most of them are not grateful. ⁷⁴ The Lord knows full well what they conceal in their hearts and what they disclose: ⁷⁵ there is nothing hidden in heaven and on earth, but is recorded in a clear Book.ᵃ

وَلَا تَحْزَنْ عَلَيْهِمْ وَلَا تَكُن فِى ضَيْقٍ مِّمَّا يَمْكُرُونَ ۝ وَيَقُولُونَ مَتَىٰ هَٰذَا ٱلْوَعْدُ إِن كُنتُمْ صَٰدِقِينَ ۝ قُلْ عَسَىٰ أَن يَكُونَ رَدِفَ لَكُم بَعْضُ ٱلَّذِى تَسْتَعْجِلُونَ ۝ وَإِنَّ رَبَّكَ لَذُو فَضْلٍ عَلَى ٱلنَّاسِ وَلَٰكِنَّ أَكْثَرَهُمْ لَا يَشْكُرُونَ ۝ وَإِنَّ رَبَّكَ لَيَعْلَمُ مَا تُكِنُّ صُدُورُهُمْ وَمَا يُعْلِنُونَ ۝ وَمَا مِنْ غَآئِبَةٍ فِى ٱلسَّمَآءِ وَٱلْأَرْضِ إِلَّا فِى كِتَٰبٍ مُّبِينٍ ۝

ᵃ The words 'do not grieve' are not meant to prevent the preacher from grieving. It is, in fact, meant to contradict the impression that Truth is helpless. It means that, in spite of unfavourable conditions, the Truth and supporters of the Truth will finally meet with success.

When the adversaries of the preacher of Truth contradict him, they think that they are dealing with a human being. They do not understand that this is tantamount to setting themselves up against God Himself and not merely opposing an ordinary mortal. This state of affairs (i.e. the temporary success of the opponents) continues only till the expiry of the period of human trial. As soon this period is over, God will appear and all these opponents will vanish into thin air. There is no foolishness greater than mistaking the temporary respite during the trial period for unconditional and unlimited liberty to indulge in arrogance.

76 This Quran explains to the children of Israel much of what they differ over, 77 certainly it is guidance and a blessing for the believers. 78 Certainly your Lord will decide between them in His wisdom—He is the Almighty, the All Knowing— 79 so put your trust in God. Surely you are on the path of manifest truth. 80 You cannot make the dead hear, nor can you make the deaf hear your call, when they turn their backs on it, 81 nor can you guide the blind out of their error. You can make only those hear you who believe in Our revelations and surrender themselves to Us.*

إِنَّ هَـٰذَا ٱلْقُرْءَانَ يَقُصُّ عَلَىٰ بَنِىٓ إِسْرَٰٓءِيلَ أَكْثَرَ ٱلَّذِى هُمْ فِيهِ يَخْتَلِفُونَ ۝ وَإِنَّهُۥ لَهُدًى وَرَحْمَةٌ لِّلْمُؤْمِنِينَ ۝ إِنَّ رَبَّكَ يَقْضِى بَيْنَهُم بِحُكْمِهِۦ وَهُوَ ٱلْعَزِيزُ ٱلْعَلِيمُ ۝ فَتَوَكَّلْ عَلَى ٱللَّهِ إِنَّكَ عَلَى ٱلْحَقِّ ٱلْمُبِينِ ۝ إِنَّكَ لَا تُسْمِعُ ٱلْمَوْتَىٰ وَلَا تُسْمِعُ ٱلصُّمَّ ٱلدُّعَآءَ إِذَا وَلَّوْا۟ مُدْبِرِينَ ۝ وَمَآ أَنتَ بِهَـٰدِى ٱلْعُمْىِ عَن ضَلَـٰلَتِهِمْ إِن تُسْمِعُ إِلَّا مَن يُؤْمِنُ بِـَٔايَـٰتِنَا فَهُم مُّسْلِمُونَ ۝

---

a The human being is a creature who has been blessed with the ability to see, hear and think. If these capacities are utilised in an open-minded way, realities may be seen and recognised with the utmost clarity. But, if a man is wrongly conditioned, truth may come before him unveiled, but he will remain unaware of it, as if he were blind and deaf. The fact is that, in this world, one can be guided to the right path, only if one wants to be guided. For one who has no burning desire to find the right path, no guidance of any kind will be of any avail.

In order to become a seeker of Truth, the qualities most needed in a man are those of acceptance. In this world, only that man receives guidance who possesses the quality of readily accepting that which is well established by arguments and following that whole heartedly.

Those who do not answer God's call have finally to bow down before God's verdict, but bowing down when the time for testing is over will be of no avail to anybody.

⁸² When God's word is justly carried out against them, We will produce a *dabbah*^a from the earth which will tell them that mankind had no real faith in Our signs. ⁸³ On that Day We shall assemble together a host from every community of those who cried lies to Our revelations and they will be grouped ⁸⁴ then, when they have arrived, He will say, 'Did you deny My revelations, even though you did not have proper knowledge of them? Or what was it that you were doing?' ⁸⁵ The verdict will be given against them, because they did wrong, and they will be speechless. ⁸⁶ Do they not see that We have made the night for them to rest in and the day to give them light? There are certainly signs in that for people who believe.

وَإِذَا وَقَعَ ٱلْقَوْلُ عَلَيْهِمْ أَخْرَجْنَا لَهُمْ دَآبَّةً مِّنَ ٱلْأَرْضِ تُكَلِّمُهُمْ أَنَّ ٱلنَّاسَ كَانُوا بِآيَٰتِنَا لَا يُوقِنُونَ ۝ وَيَوْمَ نَحْشُرُ مِن كُلِّ أُمَّةٍ فَوْجًا مِّمَّن يُكَذِّبُ بِآيَٰتِنَا فَهُمْ يُوزَعُونَ ۝ حَتَّىٰ إِذَا جَآءُو قَالَ أَكَذَّبْتُم بِآيَٰتِي وَلَمْ تُحِيطُوا بِهَا عِلْمًا أَمَّاذَا كُنتُمْ تَعْمَلُونَ ۝ وَوَقَعَ ٱلْقَوْلُ عَلَيْهِم بِمَا ظَلَمُوا فَهُمْ لَا يَنطِقُونَ ۝ أَلَمْ يَرَوْا أَنَّا جَعَلْنَا ٱلَّيْلَ لِيَسْكُنُوا فِيهِ وَٱلنَّهَارَ مُبْصِرًا إِنَّ فِى ذَٰلِكَ لَآيَٰتٍ لِّقَوْمٍ يُؤْمِنُونَ ۝

---

^a At the time when Almighty God takes the decision that the present history of the earth should be brought to an end, some extraordinary signs will appear to usher in the last phase. Among these signs will be the appearance of a communicator (*dabbah*). This will be the bell announcing the end of the examination period and not its beginning. Mass communications, particularly the internet and multimedia, are probably what is meant by *dabbah* here.

When all the people gather on the Day of Judgement, they will be divided into groups. The believers will be ranged on one side and those who denied the truth on the other. Then those who denied the truth will be asked what academic or rational arguments made them deny the Truth. At that time their silence will prove their denial was based on stubbornness and bias, though they advanced false arguments to show that they were right. At that time, it will be clear to them that over and above the verbal message of the preacher , even the alternation of day and night was non-verbally and tacitly conveying to them the words of Truth. Sleep during the night stood for death and waking up in the morning stood for resurrection. In spite of these extraordinary arrangements for the proclamation of the Truth, they were unable to discover it.

⁸⁷ On the Day when the trumpet is blown, whoever is in the heavens and whoever is on the earth will be struck with terror, except for those whom God wishes to spare. All shall come to Him in utter humility. ⁸⁸ You see the mountains and think them firmly fixed. But they shall pass away as the clouds pass away. Such is the work of God, who has ordered all things to perfection: He is fully aware of what you do. ⁸⁹ Whoever does a good deed, shall be rewarded with what is better, and will be secure from fear of that Day, ⁹⁰ and those who do evil will be flung down on their faces in the Fire. Are you not rewarded according to your deeds? ^a

وَيَوْمَ يُنفَخُ فِى ٱلصُّورِ فَفَزِعَ مَن فِى ٱلسَّمَـٰوَٰتِ وَمَن فِى ٱلْأَرْضِ إِلَّا مَن شَاءَ ٱللَّهُ وَكُلٌّ أَتَوْهُ دَٰخِرِينَ ۝ وَتَرَى ٱلْجِبَالَ تَحْسَبُهَا جَامِدَةً وَهِىَ تَمُرُّ مَرَّ ٱلسَّحَابِ صُنْعَ ٱللَّهِ ٱلَّذِى أَتْقَنَ كُلَّ شَىْءٍ إِنَّهُۥ خَبِيرٌ بِمَا تَفْعَلُونَ ۝ مَن جَاءَ بِٱلْحَسَنَةِ فَلَهُۥ خَيْرٌ مِّنْهَا وَهُم مِّن فَزَعٍ يَوْمَئِذٍ ءَامِنُونَ ۝ وَمَن جَاءَ بِٱلسَّيِّئَةِ فَكُبَّتْ وُجُوهُهُمْ فِى ٱلنَّارِ هَلْ تُجْزَوْنَ إِلَّا مَا كُنتُمْ تَعْمَلُونَ ۝

---

^a In the present world, the real reason for denial of the Truth is the lack of fear of God. It is due to this mentality of fearlessness that man ignores the Truth, and setting himself up against it, indulges in arrogant behaviour. But, when the period of examination is over and, as a sign, the Judgement Day trumpet is blown, people will suddenly come to know that their fearlessness was simply based on ignorance. On that Day, all greatness will be washed away like a wall of sand. This will be such a terrible moment that not only human beings, but even the mountains will crumble. At that time, all humility will be on one side, while all the power will be on the other.

At that time, all the things which were considered important in this world, will become unimportant. On that Day, only righteous deeds will carry weight. On that Day, the 'losers' will become the successful ones and the 'successful ones'—in the world—will face deprivation forever.

⁹¹ Say, 'I am commanded to serve the Lord of this town, which He has made inviolable and to whom everything belongs; I am commanded to be one of those devoted to Him; ⁹² to recite the Quran.' ᵃ Whoever follows its guidance, follows it only for the good of his own soul; and as for him who goes astray, just say, 'I am only a warner.' ⁹³ Then say, 'Praise be to God! He will show you His signs and you will recognize them. Your Lord is not unaware of what you do.' ᵇ

إِنَّمَآ أُمِرْتُ أَنْ أَعْبُدَ رَبَّ هَـٰذِهِ ٱلْبَلْدَةِ ٱلَّذِى حَرَّمَهَا وَلَهُۥ كُلُّ شَىْءٍ وَأُمِرْتُ أَنْ أَكُونَ مِنَ ٱلْمُسْلِمِينَ ۝ وَأَنْ أَتْلُوَاْ ٱلْقُرْءَانَ فَمَنِ ٱهْتَدَىٰ فَإِنَّمَا يَهْتَدِى لِنَفْسِهِۦ وَمَن ضَلَّ فَقُلْ إِنَّمَآ أَنَا۠ مِنَ ٱلْمُنذِرِينَ ۝ وَقُلِ ٱلْحَمْدُ لِلَّهِ سَيُرِيكُمْ ءَايَـٰتِهِۦ فَتَعْرِفُونَهَا وَمَا رَبُّكَ بِغَـٰفِلٍ عَمَّا تَعْمَلُونَ ۝

ᵃ The reference to 'this town' (Makkah) here is in relation to the first addressees of the Quran. However, indirectly, this verse reminds all mankind of the eternal reality that there is only one right way and that is to become worshippers of the one God.

It is the duty of a preacher to address others, i.e. to give the call of Truth. In this call of the preacher, which has apparently no power behind it, the hearer has to see the might of God. Those who prove their ability to do this, will be of those who will be treated as deserving of the eternal blessing of God.

ᵇ One aspect of this prediction relates to the first addressees of the Quran (the Quraysh of Makkah) who were shown God's signs in the earlier period of Islam through events such as the conquest of Makkah. The other aspect concerns the issue of the eternal guidance offered by the Quran. Thus the scientific evidence appearing in the modern period are also included in the wider scope of this prediction.

28. THE STORY

In the name of God,
the Most Gracious, the Most Merciful

¹ *Ta Sin Mim*

² These are verses from the Book that makes things clear. ³ We shall narrate to you some of the story of Moses and Pharaoh, with truth, for people who would believe. ⁴ Pharaoh behaved arrogantly in the land, and divided the people into groups, seeking to weaken one section, slaying their sons and sparing their daughters—he was one of those who spread corruption— ⁵ We wished to favour those who were oppressed in the land, and to make them leaders and make them inheritors [of Our bounties], ⁶ and to give them power in the land; and to show Pharaoh and Haman and their hosts that very thing which they feared.[a]

---

[a] Pharaoh is mentioned here as being guilty of creating great unrest in his land. He gave every conceivable advantage to his race (Egyptians) and deprived the Israelites of all facilities. Not only this, he also started having their newborn children killed so that their race should gradually be exterminated. Pharaoh's unfair discrimination between the two races of Egypt amounted to interference with the system of nature that is, '*fasad*,' in terms of God's laws.

Decisions regarding honour and dishonour are made by God. God's decision was contrary to Pharaoh's will. God decided to give honour and power to the Children of Israel and to destroy Pharaoh along with his armies. On conclusion of the missionary process through Moses, Pharaoh, though given a last chance to reform, proved himself to be deserving of punishment. Therefore, God ordained that he be drowned in the sea so that nothing should be left of his influence in Egypt. Subsequently, Children of Israel who had left Egypt were made rulers of Syria and Palestine.

7 We inspired Moses' mother saying, 'Suckle him, and then, when you fear for him, cast him into the river, and have no fear and do not grieve, for We shall return him to you, and shall make him one of the Messengers.' 8 Then Pharaoh's household picked him up—later to become for them an enemy and a source of grief for them: Pharaoh and Haman and their hosts were wrongdoers—9 and Pharaoh's wife said, 'He will be a joy to the eye for me and you! Do not slay him: he may well be of use to us, or we may adopt him as a son.' They did not realize what they were doing.ᵃ

وَأَوْحَيْنَآ إِلَىٰٓ أُمِّ مُوسَىٰٓ أَنْ أَرْضِعِيهِ ۖ فَإِذَا خِفْتِ عَلَيْهِ فَأَلْقِيهِ فِى ٱلْيَمِّ وَلَا تَخَافِى وَلَا تَحْزَنِىٓ ۖ إِنَّا رَآدُّوهُ إِلَيْكِ وَجَاعِلُوهُ مِنَ ٱلْمُرْسَلِينَ ۝ فَٱلْتَقَطَهُۥٓ ءَالُ فِرْعَوْنَ لِيَكُونَ لَهُمْ عَدُوًّا وَحَزَنًا ۗ إِنَّ فِرْعَوْنَ وَهَٰمَٰنَ وَجُنُودَهُمَا كَانُوا۟ خَٰطِـِٔينَ ۝ وَقَالَتِ ٱمْرَأَتُ فِرْعَوْنَ قُرَّتُ عَيْنٍ لِّى وَلَكَ ۖ لَا تَقْتُلُوهُ عَسَىٰٓ أَن يَنفَعَنَآ أَوْ نَتَّخِذَهُۥ وَلَدًا وَهُمْ لَا يَشْعُرُونَ ۝

ᵃ In the period when Moses was born, the children of the Israelites were being killed. Moses' mother was worried on this account. At that time, probably by means of a dream, she was shown how he could escape if she put him in a small box and floated it down the river Nile. Three months later, she floated Moses in a small boat. While floating, this boat arrived in front of Pharaoh's palace. Pharaoh's wife (Aasia) who was a virtuous lady, was filled with pity on seeing the innocent and charming face of Moses. So, on her advice, Moses was kept in Pharaoh's palace.

Tradition has it that at this juncture, Pharaoh's wife said that the baby may become a source of happiness for them. Pharaoh replied saying, 'For you, not for me.' Pharaoh might have said so because of being emotionally unattached but it later turned out to be true.

¹⁰ Moses' mother's heart was full of anxiety—she would have disclosed his identity had We not strengthened her heart so that she might be a firm believer [in Our promise]. ¹¹ She said to Moses' sister, 'Go, and follow him.' So she watched him from a distance, like a stranger, without anyone noticing her. ¹² We had already made him refuse all wet nurses. So his sister said to them, 'Shall I tell you of a family who will bring him up for you and take good care of him?' ¹³ Thus We restored him to his mother, so that she might be comforted and not grieve any more, and so that she would know that God's promise was true. But most of them do not realize this. ¹⁴ When Moses reached full manhood and maturity, We bestowed upon him wisdom and knowledge: this is how We reward those who do good.ᵃ

وَأَصْبَحَ فُؤَادُ أُمِّ مُوسَىٰ فَٰرِغًا إِن كَادَتْ لَتُبْدِى بِهِۦ لَوْلَآ أَن رَّبَطْنَا عَلَىٰ قَلْبِهَا لِتَكُونَ مِنَ ٱلْمُؤْمِنِينَ ۝ وَقَالَتْ لِأُخْتِهِۦ قُصِّيهِ فَبَصُرَتْ بِهِۦ عَن جُنُبٍ وَهُمْ لَا يَشْعُرُونَ ۝ ۞ وَحَرَّمْنَا عَلَيْهِ ٱلْمَرَاضِعَ مِن قَبْلُ فَقَالَتْ هَلْ أَدُلُّكُمْ عَلَىٰ أَهْلِ بَيْتٍ يَكْفُلُونَهُۥ لَكُمْ وَهُمْ لَهُۥ نَٰصِحُونَ ۝ فَرَدَدْنَٰهُ إِلَىٰ أُمِّهِۦ كَىْ تَقَرَّ عَيْنُهَا وَلَا تَحْزَنَ وَلِتَعْلَمَ أَنَّ وَعْدَ ٱللَّهِ حَقٌّ وَلَٰكِنَّ أَكْثَرَهُمْ لَا يَعْلَمُونَ ۝ وَلَمَّا بَلَغَ أَشُدَّهُۥ وَٱسْتَوَىٰ ءَاتَيْنَٰهُ حُكْمًا وَعِلْمًا وَكَذَٰلِكَ نَجْزِى ٱلْمُحْسِنِينَ ۝

ᵃ The process of the protection of Moses is attributed entirely to God, though the sequence of events seems to have taken place as per the 'cause and effect' principle. One can gather from this, that in the present world of trial, God's will manifests itself in terms of the 'cause and effect' chain and not in the form of supernatural wonders or magical feats.

Moses was set afloat in the river in a state of helplessness, but he reached the bank safe and sound. The king ruling at the time planned to kill him, but God ordained that he be brought up by that very king. He was born in an ordinary family, but God so arranged matters that he became connected with the royal palace and became acquainted with the learning and etiquette of the highest standard. This is an example which shows that Almighty God's powers are unlimited and there is nobody who can prevent His plans from coming into effect.

¹⁵ He entered the city unnoticed by its people, and there he encountered two men fighting with one another—one of his own people and the other one of his enemies. The one who belonged to his own people cried out to him for help against his foe—whereupon Moses struck him down with his fist, thereby causing his death. Moses said, 'This is Satan's doing; he is an open foe, leading man astray.' ¹⁶ He prayed, 'Forgive me Lord, for I have sinned against my soul.' God forgave him; for He is the Forgiving One, the Merciful. ¹⁷ He said, 'My Lord, because of the favour that You have shown me, I vow that I will never be a helper of the guilty.' ^a

وَدَخَلَ ٱلْمَدِينَةَ عَلَىٰ حِينِ غَفْلَةٍ مِّنْ أَهْلِهَا فَوَجَدَ فِيهَا رَجُلَيْنِ يَقْتَتِلَانِ هَٰذَا مِن شِيعَتِهِۦ وَهَٰذَا مِنْ عَدُوِّهِۦ فَٱسْتَغَٰثَهُ ٱلَّذِي مِن شِيعَتِهِۦ عَلَى ٱلَّذِي مِنْ عَدُوِّهِۦ فَوَكَزَهُۥ مُوسَىٰ فَقَضَىٰ عَلَيْهِ قَالَ هَٰذَا مِنْ عَمَلِ ٱلشَّيْطَٰنِ إِنَّهُۥ عَدُوٌّ مُّضِلٌّ مُّبِينٌ ۝ قَالَ رَبِّ إِنِّي ظَلَمْتُ نَفْسِي فَٱغْفِرْ لِي فَغَفَرَ لَهُۥٓ إِنَّهُۥ هُوَ ٱلْغَفُورُ ٱلرَّحِيمُ ۝ قَالَ رَبِّ بِمَآ أَنْعَمْتَ عَلَيَّ فَلَنْ أَكُونَ ظَهِيرًا لِّلْمُجْرِمِينَ ۝

---

^a This incident happened in the capital of Egypt before Moses received prophethood. One day, he saw an Egyptian and an Israelite fighting with each other. The Israelite called upon Moses (who was an Israelite himself) to help him. Moses wanted to separate them, but the Egyptian turned on Moses who in self-defence, gave him a blow. Accidentally, the blow led to the death of the Egyptian.

The Egyptians at that time were committing atrocities on the Israelites on a large scale. In this context, had Moses viewed the matter from the communal point of view, he would have treated it as a heroic feat and boasted about it. But, on the contrary, he was very sorry about the Egyptian's death. He immediately turned towards God and prayed for His forgiveness.

'I will never be a helper of the guilty' means, 'I will not support anybody without investigating the matter.' A person's apparently belonging to an oppressed community and his soliciting support by accusing another person of oppression are not enough to prove that the latter is really an oppressor and that the former (the complainant) is really the oppressed person. Therefore, the right approach on such occasions is for the matter to be properly investigated and support should be extended to a complainant only when, on impartial investigation, his being oppressed has been established.

18 The next morning, when he was walking in the city, apprehensive, and watchful, and the man who had sought his help the day before cried out to him again for help. Moses said to him, 'You are clearly a misguided man.' 19 When he wanted to catch the one who was an enemy to them both, the man said, 'Moses, do you want to kill me just as you killed a man yesterday? You only want to become a tyrant in the land; you do not want to set things right.' 20 A man came running from the far side of the city, and said, 'Moses, the authorities are conspiring to kill you, so leave the city. I am one of your well-wishers.' 21 So Moses departed from the city, fearful and vigilant, and prayed, 'My Lord, save me from these unjust people.'^a

فَأَصْبَحَ فِى ٱلْمَدِينَةِ خَآئِفًا يَتَرَقَّبُ فَإِذَا ٱلَّذِى ٱسْتَنصَرَهُۥ بِٱلْأَمْسِ يَسْتَصْرِخُهُۥ قَالَ لَهُۥ مُوسَىٰٓ إِنَّكَ لَغَوِىٌّ مُّبِينٌ ۞ فَلَمَّآ أَنْ أَرَادَ أَن يَبْطِشَ بِٱلَّذِى هُوَ عَدُوٌّ لَّهُمَا قَالَ يَٰمُوسَىٰٓ أَتُرِيدُ أَن تَقْتُلَنِى كَمَا قَتَلْتَ نَفْسًۢا بِٱلْأَمْسِ إِن تُرِيدُ إِلَّآ أَن تَكُونَ جَبَّارًا فِى ٱلْأَرْضِ وَمَا تُرِيدُ أَن تَكُونَ مِنَ ٱلْمُصْلِحِينَ ۞ وَجَآءَ رَجُلٌ مِّنْ أَقْصَا ٱلْمَدِينَةِ يَسْعَىٰ قَالَ يَٰمُوسَىٰٓ إِنَّ ٱلْمَلَأَ يَأْتَمِرُونَ بِكَ لِيَقْتُلُوكَ فَٱخْرُجْ إِنِّى لَكَ مِنَ ٱلنَّٰصِحِينَ ۞ فَخَرَجَ مِنْهَا خَآئِفًا يَتَرَقَّبُ قَالَ رَبِّ نَجِّنِى مِنَ ٱلْقَوْمِ ٱلظَّٰلِمِينَ ۞

^a The next day Moses found that the same Israelite was fighting with another Egyptian. This gave a clear indication that he was a quarrelsome person and was in the habit of picking quarrels with someone or the other every day. So, inspite of his being an Israelite, Moses held him guilty. The proof of the Israelite's being guilty was further strengthened by the fact that, when the Israelite found that Moses was not supporting him on that day and was on the contrary blaming him, he stooped to meanness. In an irresponsible manner, he revealed the secret of the previous day's killing, which till then had not come to anybody's knowledge. When the killer's name was made public by the Israelite, many people heard about it. In a few days the news spread everywhere. Ultimately, there was a discussion among the rulers about killing Moses. One virtuous man who came to know about it, met Moses secretly and advised him that it would be better if he went away. So, he left Egypt and set forth for Midian (Madyan). Midian was situated on the west coast of the Gulf of Aqaba and outside the limits of Pharaoh's empire.

²² When he made his way towards Midian, he said, 'I am sure, my Lord will guide me to the right way.' ²³ And when he arrived at the well of Midian, he found around it a group of men watering their flocks, and he saw two women standing apart from them, who were holding back their flocks, so he asked, 'What is the matter with you?' They replied, 'We cannot draw water until the shepherds take away their sheep. Our father is a very old man.' ²⁴ So Moses watered their flocks for them; and returned into the shade and prayed, 'Lord, I am truly in need of whatever blessing You may send down for me,' ᵃ

وَلَمَّا تَوَجَّهَ تِلْقَآءَ مَدْيَنَ قَالَ عَسَىٰ رَبِّىٓ أَن يَهْدِيَنِى سَوَآءَ ٱلسَّبِيلِ ﴿٢٢﴾ وَلَمَّا وَرَدَ مَآءَ مَدْيَنَ وَجَدَ عَلَيْهِ أُمَّةً مِّنَ ٱلنَّاسِ يَسْقُونَ وَوَجَدَ مِن دُونِهِمُ ٱمْرَأَتَيْنِ تَذُودَانِ قَالَ مَا خَطْبُكُمَا قَالَتَا لَا نَسْقِى حَتَّىٰ يُصْدِرَ ٱلرِّعَآءُ وَأَبُونَا شَيْخٌ كَبِيرٌ ﴿٢٣﴾ فَسَقَىٰ لَهُمَا ثُمَّ تَوَلَّىٰ إِلَى ٱلظِّلِّ فَقَالَ رَبِّ إِنِّى لِمَآ أَنزَلْتَ إِلَىَّ مِنْ خَيْرٍ فَقِيرٌ ﴿٢٤﴾

ᵃ Moses's departure took him on a journey towards an unknown destination. Moses had the same intense feelings as a believer's heart experiences under such circumstances. Proceeding on the strength of prayers, he reached Midian after a ten day journey.

Following his urge to help the weak, Moses helped the two girls of Madyan. The father of the girls was an elderly gentleman who belonged to the progeny of Abraham through his son Midyaan. Incidentally, Moses also belonged to the progeny of Abraham through his son Isaac (Ishaq), which made them blood relations.

At that time, this prayer spontaneously fell from Moses's lips, 'Lord, I am truly in need of whatever blessing You may send down for me.' This prayer shows the condition of a believer in such circumstances. He entrusts all his affairs to the care of God. He has the firm belief that whatever a man receives comes from God, and that whatever is received from God is 'good'.

²⁵ and then one of the two women came walking shyly up to him and said, 'My father is asking you to come so that he may reward you for watering our flocks for us.' When Moses came to their father and gave him an account of himself, he said: 'Don't be afraid! You have escaped from those wrongdoing people.' ²⁶ One of the girls said, 'Father, hire him! For the best man to hire is someone strong and trustworthy.' ²⁷ The father said, 'I would like to marry you to one of these two daughters of mine on the condition that you stay eight years in my service. But if you wish it, you may stay ten. I do not want to impose any hardship on you. God willing, you will find me a fair person.' ²⁸ Moses said, 'That is agreed between me and you; whichever of the two terms I fulfil, there will be no blame on me. God is witness to what we say.' [a]

فَجَاءَتْهُ إِحْدَىٰهُمَا تَمْشِى عَلَى ٱسْتِحْيَاءٍ قَالَتْ إِنَّ أَبِى يَدْعُوكَ لِيَجْزِيَكَ أَجْرَ مَا سَقَيْتَ لَنَا ۚ فَلَمَّا جَاءَهُ وَقَصَّ عَلَيْهِ ٱلْقَصَصَ قَالَ لَا تَخَفْ ۖ نَجَوْتَ مِنَ ٱلْقَوْمِ ٱلظَّٰلِمِينَ ۞ قَالَتْ إِحْدَىٰهُمَا يَٰأَبَتِ ٱسْتَـْٔجِرْهُ ۖ إِنَّ خَيْرَ مَنِ ٱسْتَـْٔجَرْتَ ٱلْقَوِىُّ ٱلْأَمِينُ ۞ قَالَ إِنِّى أُرِيدُ أَنْ أُنكِحَكَ إِحْدَى ٱبْنَتَىَّ هَٰتَيْنِ عَلَىٰ أَن تَأْجُرَنِى ثَمَٰنِىَ حِجَجٍ ۖ فَإِنْ أَتْمَمْتَ عَشْرًا فَمِنْ عِندِكَ ۖ وَمَا أُرِيدُ أَنْ أَشُقَّ عَلَيْكَ ۚ سَتَجِدُنِى إِن شَاءَ ٱللَّهُ مِنَ ٱلصَّٰلِحِينَ ۞ قَالَ ذَٰلِكَ بَيْنِى وَبَيْنَكَ ۖ أَيَّمَا ٱلْأَجَلَيْنِ قَضَيْتُ فَلَا عُدْوَٰنَ عَلَىَّ ۖ وَٱللَّهُ عَلَىٰ مَا نَقُولُ وَكِيلٌ ۞

---

[a] That day, the girls returned home earlier than usual. When their father asked the reason, they told him that a traveller had arranged for their cattle to be watered early. The girl's father asked them why they had not brought him home so that he could partake of their meal. So, one of the girls went back to the well and brought Moses along with her.

It took only a few days to show that Moses was hard working as well as honest. So, the old gentleman, agreeing with his daughter's opinion, kept Moses in his service permanently. The fact is that, honesty and hard work embrace all the necessary qualities. If any candidate has to be chosen, there is no better standard than these two qualities by which to judge him.

At a later stage, the old gentleman gave one of his daughters in marriage to Moses. However, as he was in dire need of a young man to look after his household and property, he made Moses agree to reside with him for eight years or ten years, thereafter he could go anywhere he liked.

²⁹ When Moses completed the term and set out with his family, he noticed a fire in the direction of Mount Tur. He said to his family: 'Stay here, I can see a fire. Perhaps I can bring you news, or a burning brand from the fire with which you may warm yourself.' ³⁰ And when he came to it, he was called by a voice from a bush in a blessed spot, on the right side of the valley: 'O Moses, I am God, Lord of the Universe. ³¹ Throw down your staff.' And when he saw it move as though it were a serpent, he turned his back and fled, and did not look back. 'O Moses,' said the voice, 'come forward and have no fear; you are quite safe. ³² Put your hand into your bosom; it will come out [shining] white, without blemish; now draw your arm close to your body to calm your fears. These are two credentials from your Lord for Pharaoh and his nobles. Surely, they are a rebellious people.'^a

فَلَمَّا قَضَىٰ مُوسَى ٱلْأَجَلَ وَسَارَ بِأَهْلِهِ ءَانَسَ مِن جَانِبِ ٱلطُّورِ نَارًا قَالَ لِأَهْلِهِ ٱمْكُثُوٓا۟ إِنِّىٓ ءَانَسْتُ نَارًا لَّعَلِّىٓ ءَاتِيكُم مِّنْهَا بِخَبَرٍ أَوْ جَذْوَةٍ مِّنَ ٱلنَّارِ لَعَلَّكُمْ تَصْطَلُونَ ۞ فَلَمَّآ أَتَىٰهَا نُودِىَ مِن شَـٰطِئِ ٱلْوَادِ ٱلْأَيْمَنِ فِى ٱلْبُقْعَةِ ٱلْمُبَـٰرَكَةِ مِنَ ٱلشَّجَرَةِ أَن يَـٰمُوسَىٰٓ إِنِّىٓ أَنَا ٱللَّهُ رَبُّ ٱلْعَـٰلَمِينَ ۞ وَأَنْ أَلْقِ عَصَاكَ فَلَمَّا رَءَاهَا تَهْتَزُّ كَأَنَّهَا جَآنٌّ وَلَّىٰ مُدْبِرًا وَلَمْ يُعَقِّبْ يَـٰمُوسَىٰٓ أَقْبِلْ وَلَا تَخَفْ إِنَّكَ مِنَ ٱلْـَٔامِنِينَ ۞ ٱسْلُكْ يَدَكَ فِى جَيْبِكَ تَخْرُجْ بَيْضَآءَ مِنْ غَيْرِ سُوٓءٍ وَٱضْمُمْ إِلَيْكَ جَنَاحَكَ مِنَ ٱلرَّهْبِ فَذَٰنِكَ بُرْهَـٰنَانِ مِن رَّبِّكَ إِلَىٰ فِرْعَوْنَ وَمَلَإِيْهِۦٓ إِنَّهُمْ كَانُوا۟ قَوْمًا فَـٰسِقِينَ ۞

---

^a Moses was in Midian probably for ten years. During this period the former Pharaoh died and another member of the Pharaoh dynasty ascended the throne of Egypt. Then, Moses along with his wife (and, according to the Torah, with two children) left again for Egypt. On the way, he underwent the divine test on Mount Tur (Mount Sinai).

God, who directly talked to a man on Mount Sinai, can also directly address all other human beings and apprise them of His will. But this is not the way of God. Direct address means removal of the curtain, while the considerations of human trial demand that the curtain should remain in place. So God reveals His message only to a selected person and causes this message to be delivered indirectly through him to others.

³³ Moses said, 'My Lord, I have killed one of their people and fear that they may kill me. ³⁴ My brother Aaron is more eloquent than I am. Send him with me to support me and back me up. For I fear that they will reject me.' ³⁵ God said: 'We shall strengthen your arm through your brother, We shall give you both power, so that they shall not be able to harm you. Set forth with Our signs. You, and those who follow you, will surely prevail.'ᵃ

قَالَ رَبِّ إِنِّى قَتَلْتُ مِنْهُمْ نَفْسًا فَأَخَافُ أَن يَقْتُلُونِ ۝ وَأَخِى هَرُونُ هُوَ أَفْصَحُ مِنِّى لِسَانًا فَأَرْسِلْهُ مَعِىَ رِدْءًا يُصَدِّقُنِى إِنِّى أَخَافُ أَن يُكَذِّبُونِ ۝ قَالَ سَنَشُدُّ عَضُدَكَ بِأَخِيكَ وَنَجْعَلُ لَكُمَا سُلْطَنًا فَلَا يَصِلُونَ إِلَيْكُمَا بِـَٔايَتِنَآ أَنتُمَا وَمَنِ ٱتَّبَعَكُمَا ٱلْغَلِبُونَ ۝

ᵃ When God appoints somebody as His missionary, He provides him with all that is essential for the performance of the task. Similarly, provision was made for Moses according to his special circumstances. By way of authority for his appointment, he was blessed with the ability to perform certain miracles and he was to be aided by his brother. Moses was endowed with an impressive personality so that Pharaoh's community may not dare to mishandle him. And it was ordained by God that Moses and his companions should finally be supreme.

³⁶ When Moses came to them with Our clear signs, they said, 'This is nothing but contrived magic. We never heard of this among our forefathers.'*^a ³⁷ And Moses replied, 'My Lord knows best who comes with guidance from Him and who will attain the heavenly abode in the hereafter. The wrongdoers shall never prosper.' ³⁸ Pharaoh said, 'O nobles, I know of no god for you other than myself.^b So, Haman, burn me bricks of clay, and build me a high tower, so that I may have a look at the God of Moses, though I consider him to be one of the liars.'

فَلَمَّا جَاءَهُم مُّوسَىٰ بِـَٔايَٰتِنَا بَيِّنَٰتٍ قَالُوا۟ مَا هَٰذَآ إِلَّا سِحْرٌ مُّفْتَرًى وَمَا سَمِعْنَا بِهَٰذَا فِىٓ ءَابَآئِنَا ٱلْأَوَّلِينَ ۝ وَقَالَ مُوسَىٰ رَبِّىٓ أَعْلَمُ بِمَن جَآءَ بِٱلْهُدَىٰ مِنْ عِندِهِۦ وَمَن تَكُونُ لَهُۥ عَٰقِبَةُ ٱلدَّارِ إِنَّهُۥ لَا يُفْلِحُ ٱلظَّٰلِمُونَ ۝ وَقَالَ فِرْعَوْنُ يَٰٓأَيُّهَا ٱلْمَلَأُ مَا عَلِمْتُ لَكُم مِّنْ إِلَٰهٍ غَيْرِى فَأَوْقِدْ لِى يَٰهَٰمَٰنُ عَلَى ٱلطِّينِ فَٱجْعَل لِّى صَرْحًا لَّعَلِّىٓ أَطَّلِعُ إِلَىٰٓ إِلَٰهِ مُوسَىٰ وَإِنِّى لَأَظُنُّهُۥ مِنَ ٱلْكَٰذِبِينَ ۝

---

^a If an individual thinks highly of himself, and if someone of apparently ordinary status comes before him and voices outright criticism of him, he immediately flares up. He ridicules his critic and makes different types of derogatory statements with a view to undermining him. This is what Pharaoh did in the case of Moses.

^b Literally, 'I do not know any being other than myself who is worth worshipping.' This was not a serious statement. In uttering these words Pharaoh did not intend to state any fact. He only wanted to denigrate Moses. Similarly, when Pharaoh ordered his minister Haman to prepare fired bricks and construct a high tower so that he could peep into the sky and see Moses's God, this was not a genuine order. Its sole purpose was to make a mockery of Moses.

³⁹ He and his hosts behaved arrogantly in the land without any justification—thinking that they would not be recalled to Us— ⁴⁰ so We seized him and his hosts and cast them into the sea. Consider the fate of the wrongdoers. ⁴¹ We had made them leaders, but they called people to the Fire; and on the Day of Judgement they will not be helped. ⁴² We have caused a curse to follow them in this world and, on the Day of Judgement, they will be among the wretched. ⁴³ After We had destroyed the earlier generations, We gave Moses the Book to give men insight, and as guidance and a blessing for people, so that they might take heed.^a

وَٱسْتَكْبَرَ هُوَ وَجُنُودُهُۥ فِى ٱلْأَرْضِ بِغَيْرِ ٱلْحَقِّ وَظَنُّوٓاْ أَنَّهُمْ إِلَيْنَا لَا يُرْجَعُونَ ۝ فَأَخَذْنَٰهُ وَجُنُودَهُۥ فَنَبَذْنَٰهُمْ فِى ٱلْيَمِّ فَٱنظُرْ كَيْفَ كَانَ عَٰقِبَةُ ٱلظَّٰلِمِينَ ۝ وَجَعَلْنَٰهُمْ أَئِمَّةً يَدْعُونَ إِلَى ٱلنَّارِ وَيَوْمَ ٱلْقِيَٰمَةِ لَا يُنصَرُونَ ۝ وَأَتْبَعْنَٰهُمْ فِى هَٰذِهِ ٱلدُّنْيَا لَعْنَةً وَيَوْمَ ٱلْقِيَٰمَةِ هُم مِّنَ ٱلْمَقْبُوحِينَ ۝ وَلَقَدْ ءَاتَيْنَا مُوسَى ٱلْكِتَٰبَ مِنۢ بَعْدِ مَآ أَهْلَكْنَا ٱلْقُرُونَ ٱلْأُولَىٰ بَصَآئِرَ لِلنَّاسِ وَهُدًى وَرَحْمَةً لَّعَلَّهُمْ يَتَذَكَّرُونَ ۝

---

^a Moses' mission was to bring about a godly revolution in the human individual. His aim was that man should develop fear of God. This was aimed at all individuals, including the individual who occupied the throne of the country.

It is common for one who attains to power and authority to develop a false sense of pride. This was equally true of Pharaoh. Moses warned Pharaoh that if he conducted himself arrogantly, he would be seized upon by God. But Pharaoh refused to accept his advice. The result was that he was drowned.

44 You were not present on the western side of the Mount when We gave Our Command to Moses: nor were you among the witnesses— 45 We brought into being many generations who lived long lives— nor did you live among the people of Midian and recite our revelations to them—it is We who send messengers— 46 you were not on the side of the Mount when We called out to Moses, but We have sent you as a mercy from your Lord, so that you may warn people to whom no warner has been sent before you, so that they may take heed,ᵃ

وَمَا كُنتَ بِجَانِبِ ٱلْغَرْبِيِّ إِذْ قَضَيْنَا إِلَىٰ مُوسَى ٱلْأَمْرَ وَمَا كُنتَ مِنَ ٱلشَّٰهِدِينَ ۞ وَلَٰكِنَّا أَنشَأْنَا قُرُونًا فَتَطَاوَلَ عَلَيْهِمُ ٱلْعُمُرُ وَمَا كُنتَ ثَاوِيًا فِي أَهْلِ مَدْيَنَ تَتْلُوا۟ عَلَيْهِمْ ءَايَٰتِنَا وَلَٰكِنَّا كُنَّا مُرْسِلِينَ ۞ وَمَا كُنتَ بِجَانِبِ ٱلطُّورِ إِذْ نَادَيْنَا وَلَٰكِن رَّحْمَةً مِّن رَّبِّكَ لِتُنذِرَ قَوْمًا مَّآ أَتَىٰهُم مِّن نَّذِيرٍ مِّن قَبْلِكَ لَعَلَّهُمْ يَتَذَكَّرُونَ ۞

ᵃ With the help of the Quran, the Prophet Muhammad described the events of Moses' life in full detail, as if he were standing there on the spot at that very time and seeing and hearing everything, though the fact is that he was born in Makkah two thousand years after Moses. This is clear proof that the contents of the Quran are the words of God, because no human being can have the ability to make such statements on his own.

In the times of the Prophet Muhammad there were no books such as we have today. At that time an account of Moses' achievements were to be found in some non-Arabic books of the Jews, a few copies of which were preserved in Jewish temples, these were definitely beyond the reach of the Prophet Muhammad. Moreover, there are significant differences in many statements contained in the Quran and the Jewish books and academic assessment shows that the Quranic version is the more accurate. For example, according to the Quran, the Egyptian's death at the hands of Moses had occurred accidentally, whereas the Bible says of Moses:

'And he looked this way and that way and when he saw that there was no man, he slew the Egyptian and hid him in the sand.' (Exodus: 2:12.)

It is very obvious that it is the Quranic statement, and not the statement of the Torah, which is in consonance with the holy and righteous personality of Moses. Then, how is it that the Prophet Muhammad was able to present in the Quran the incidents of Moses' life so correctly without any apparent help? There could be no reply to this question except that the All Knowing God (He, who knows the past and the unseen future) had revealed these facts to him through His divine revelation.

⁴⁷and may not say, if an affliction should befall them on account of their misdeeds: 'Lord, if only You had sent us a messenger, we might have followed Your message and become believers.' ⁴⁸But when the truth came to them from Us, they said, 'Why has he not been given the like of what Moses was given?' But did they not reject what Moses was given before? They said, 'Both [Moses and Muhammad] are kinds of sorcery, each assisting the other.' And they add, 'We reject both of them.'ᵃ

وَلَوْلَآ أَن تُصِيبَهُم مُّصِيبَةٌۢ بِمَا قَدَّمَتْ أَيْدِيهِمْ فَيَقُولُواْ رَبَّنَا لَوْلَآ أَرْسَلْتَ إِلَيْنَا رَسُولًا فَنَتَّبِعَ ءَايَـٰتِكَ وَنَكُونَ مِنَ ٱلْمُؤْمِنِينَ ﴿٤٧﴾ فَلَمَّا جَآءَهُمُ ٱلْحَقُّ مِنْ عِندِنَا قَالُواْ لَوْلَآ أُوتِىَ مِثْلَ مَآ أُوتِىَ مُوسَىٰٓ ۚ أَوَلَمْ يَكْفُرُواْ بِمَآ أُوتِىَ مُوسَىٰ مِن قَبْلُ ۖ قَالُواْ سِحْرَانِ تَظَـٰهَرَا وَقَالُوٓاْ إِنَّا بِكُلٍّ كَـٰفِرُونَ ﴿٤٨﴾

ᵃ At the time when Moses conveyed his message as a prophet to the ancient Egyptians, he also performed miracles. But, they did not accept the miracles as such and said that it was magic. When the Prophet Muhammad gave the call for the Truth in ancient Arabia on the basis of arguments, people said that if he was a prophet, why did he not perform miracles like Moses?

All these objections are the products of non-serious minds. In the present world the most important condition necessary for someone to accept the Truth is that he should be earnest and serious. One who is not serious in matters of Truth and Untruth, nothing can force him to admit the Truth. On each occasion, he will seek fresh excuses for not doing so and will find new words to refute all arguments.

⁴⁹ Say to them, 'Bring down from God a scripture that is a better guide than these two and I will follow it, if what you say be true.' ⁵⁰ If they do not respond to you, then know that they follow only their own desires. Who could be more astray than he who follows his own likes and dislikes with no guidance from God? God does not guide the evil-doers. ⁵¹ We have conveyed Our Word to them, in succession, so that they may give heed.ᵃ

⁵² Those to whom We gave the Book before this believe in it [the Quran], ⁵³ and, when it is recited to them, they say, 'We believe in it. Indeed it is the truth from our Lord. Even before it came, we had submitted ourselves.'

قُلْ فَأْتُواْ بِكِتَـٰبٍ مِّنْ عِندِ ٱللَّهِ هُوَ أَهْدَىٰ مِنْهُمَآ أَتَّبِعْهُ إِن كُنتُمْ صَـٰدِقِينَ ۞ فَإِن لَّمْ يَسْتَجِيبُواْ لَكَ فَٱعْلَمْ أَنَّمَا يَتَّبِعُونَ أَهْوَآءَهُمْ وَمَنْ أَضَلُّ مِمَّنِ ٱتَّبَعَ هَوَىٰهُ بِغَيْرِ هُدًى مِّنَ ٱللَّهِ إِنَّ ٱللَّهَ لَا يَهْدِى ٱلْقَوْمَ ٱلظَّـٰلِمِينَ ۞ ۞ وَلَقَدْ وَصَّلْنَا لَهُمُ ٱلْقَوْلَ لَعَلَّهُمْ يَتَذَكَّرُونَ ۞ ٱلَّذِينَ ءَاتَيْنَـٰهُمُ ٱلْكِتَـٰبَ مِن قَبْلِهِۦ هُم بِهِۦ يُؤْمِنُونَ ۞ وَإِذَا يُتْلَىٰ عَلَيْهِمْ قَالُوٓاْ ءَامَنَّا بِهِۦٓ إِنَّهُ ٱلْحَقُّ مِن رَّبِّنَآ إِنَّا كُنَّا مِن قَبْلِهِۦ مُسْلِمِينَ ۞

ᵃ The real criterion for the acceptance or rejection of the message of Truth is its assessment on the basis of its inherent worth. If the message itself establishes that it is inherently a greater Truth, then that is sufficient to warrant its acceptance.

Only Truth can answer Truth. If a man denies a truth and is unable to produce any other superior truth in its place, it indicates that he is denying the Truth as a result of following the dictates of his base desires. Those who behave in this way, have gone astray and are the worst of people. Such people will be treated as transgressors by God.

54 Such people as these will receive a double reward, because they are steadfast and repel evil with good, and give alms out of what We have given them, 55 and when they hear vain talk, they turn away from it and say, 'We have our actions and you have yours. We wish you peace. We will have nothing to do with the ignorant.' 56 You cannot guide whoever you please: it is God who guides whom He will. He best knows those who would accept guidance.*a*

أُوْلَٰٓئِكَ يُؤْتَوْنَ أَجْرَهُم مَّرَّتَيْنِ بِمَا صَبَرُواْ وَيَدْرَءُونَ بِٱلْحَسَنَةِ ٱلسَّيِّئَةَ وَمِمَّا رَزَقْنَٰهُمْ يُنفِقُونَ ۞ وَإِذَا سَمِعُواْ ٱللَّغْوَ أَعْرَضُواْ عَنْهُ وَقَالُواْ لَنَآ أَعْمَٰلُنَا وَلَكُمْ أَعْمَٰلُكُمْ سَلَٰمٌ عَلَيْكُمْ لَا نَبْتَغِى ٱلْجَٰهِلِينَ ۞ إِنَّكَ لَا تَهْدِى مَنْ أَحْبَبْتَ وَلَٰكِنَّ ٱللَّهَ يَهْدِى مَن يَشَآءُ وَهُوَ أَعْلَمُ بِٱلْمُهْتَدِينَ ۞

---

a There are two types of acceptance of any proposition. One is by virtue of it being the Truth. The other by reason of it being current in one's own circle. It is those who accept the Truth for the sake of Truth who are guided by God: it was people of this kind who placed their faith in the Quran and the Prophet in the earlier period of Islam.

A number of Christians and Jews embraced the faith as soon as they heard the Quran. These were such as had been steadfast in their acceptance of the true teachings of previous prophets. They had, therefore, quickly recognised the last of the Prophets, just as they had recognised the previous prophets. But, in order to maintain their ability to do so, they had to go through various stages of 'patience.'

They kept their minds free of those influences which render a man incapable of recognising the Truth, these being historical and social factors which create that frame of mind which causes a man to change the religion of God into the religion of a group. Man reaches the stage when he is able to recognise only the religion which he inherits from his group. He fails to recognise the religion which comes to him from outside. To keep oneself free of these influences, one has to make great psychological sacrifices. That is why this process has been called 'patience'. Those who exercise patience will be given a double reward: one because of their sacrifice in not allowing their erstwhile faith to become a group faith, and the other because of their capacity to recognise truth on merit, in the sense that when the new prophet came before them, they recognised him and rallied to his support.

It is in those who have the ability to recognise the Truth that high moral qualities develop. They are good even to those who harm them. They help others so that God may help them. They pursue a course of turning away from useless discussions, so that they may not become involved in futile debates.

⁵⁷ They say, 'If we were to follow your guidance, we should be uprooted from our land.' But have We not established for them a safe haven to which fruits of every kind are brought as a provision from Ourself? But most of them have no knowledge.ᵃ

⁵⁸ How many townships have We destroyed where the people had become arrogant on account of their affluence? Since then their dwelling-places have scarcely been inhabited—We became their inheritors.

وَقَالُوٓا۟ إِن نَّتَّبِعِ ٱلْهُدَىٰ مَعَكَ نُتَخَطَّفْ مِنْ أَرْضِنَآ أَوَلَمْ نُمَكِّن لَّهُمْ حَرَمًا ءَامِنًا يُجْبَىٰٓ إِلَيْهِ ثَمَرَٰتُ كُلِّ شَىْءٍ رِّزْقًا مِّن لَّدُنَّا وَلَٰكِنَّ أَكْثَرَهُمْ لَا يَعْلَمُونَ ۝ وَكَمْ أَهْلَكْنَا مِن قَرْيَةٍ بَطِرَتْ مَعِيشَتَهَا ۖ فَتِلْكَ مَسَٰكِنُهُمْ لَمْ تُسْكَن مِّنۢ بَعْدِهِمْ إِلَّا قَلِيلًا ۖ وَكُنَّا نَحْنُ ٱلْوَٰرِثِينَ ۝

ᵃ When a man's interests are linked with a system, he starts thinking that whatever benefits he receives are derived solely from that system. Man generally looks to his immediate gains of the present and is unmindful of potential gains in the future.

This was the time of the ancient polytheists of Makkah. They had installed in the Ka'bah deities worshipped by all the tribes of Arabia. In this way, they had captured the religious leadership of the whole country. Moreover, the offerings to these deities constituted their main source of income. But it was a system marked by narrow-mindedness. Now the Prophet Muhammad was inviting them to accept a religion which was to bestow upon them the leadership of the whole world, yet these polytheists ignored it in favour of a religion which had nothing to offer except mere tribal leadership of the country.

⁵⁹ Your Lord would never destroy a people until He had sent messengers to their capital cities, reciting to them Our revelations. Nor did We destroy a town unless their people became wrongdoers.ᵃ

⁶⁰ Whatever you are given in this life is nothing but a temporary provision of this life and its glitter; what God has is better and more lasting. Will you not then understand? ⁶¹ Can someone to whom We have made a gracious promise and who will see it fulfilled, be compared to someone We have allowed to enjoy a worldly life, awhile, and who will be brought up [before God] for his accounting on the Day of Resurrection?ᵇ

وَمَا كَانَ رَبُّكَ مُهْلِكَ ٱلْقُرَىٰ حَتَّىٰ
يَبْعَثَ فِىٓ أُمِّهَا رَسُولًا يَتْلُواْ عَلَيْهِمْ
ءَايَٰتِنَا ۚ وَمَا كُنَّا مُهْلِكِى ٱلْقُرَىٰٓ
إِلَّا وَأَهْلُهَا ظَٰلِمُونَ ۞ وَمَآ
أُوتِيتُم مِّن شَىْءٍ فَمَتَٰعُ ٱلْحَيَوٰةِ ٱلدُّنْيَا
وَزِينَتُهَا ۚ وَمَا عِندَ ٱللَّهِ خَيْرٌ وَأَبْقَىٰٓ ۚ أَفَلَا
تَعْقِلُونَ ۞ أَفَمَن وَعَدْنَٰهُ وَعْدًا
حَسَنًا فَهُوَ لَٰقِيهِ كَمَن مَّتَّعْنَٰهُ مَتَٰعَ
ٱلْحَيَوٰةِ ٱلدُّنْيَا ثُمَّ هُوَ يَوْمَ ٱلْقِيَٰمَةِ مِنَ
ٱلْمُحْضَرِينَ ۞

ᵃ In the world, if anyone achieves material stability, he develops a superiority complex, though history has repeatedly taught that the material stability of any person or any community (nation) is not permanent. Whenever a community (nation) ignored the Truth, it was destroyed, despite all its pomp and glory.

In the peninsula of Arabia, various communities or nations had come into prominence before Islam, for example, the 'Ad, Thamud, Saba', Madyan, and Lot's people, etc. Everyone of them indulged in ill-founded pride, but their pride was nullified by the times, and finally they became nothing but stories of the past. The ruins of these communities spreading far and wide diminished the glory of human beings. In spite of this, in the times of the Prophet Muhammad, the great ones among his contemporaries rejected him, as if the events of the past had no lesson of interest to them.

ᵇ At the time of death, a man, however great, finally parts with his possessions. After death, the things which go along with him are his righteous deeds and not his worldly honours or his material possessions.

In these circumstances, wise counsel demands that a man give preference to eternal success over temporary worldly success—he should take care to build up his Hereafter rather than build up his worldly position.

⁶² On that Day He will call to them, and say, 'Where are those whom you claimed to be My partners?' ⁶³ And those on whom sentence has been passed, will say, 'Our Lord, these are the ones who led us astray. We led them astray as we ourselves were led astray. We now dissociate ourselves from them before You; it was not us that they worshipped.'ᵃ

⁶⁴ Then they will be told, 'Call upon your partners.' And they will call upon them, but will receive no answer. They shall witness the punishment. If only they had allowed themselves to be guided. ⁶⁵ On that Day God will call out to them, saying, 'What answer did you give to Our messengers?'

وَيَوْمَ يُنَادِيهِمْ فَيَقُولُ أَيْنَ شُرَكَآءِىَ
ٱلَّذِينَ كُنتُمْ تَزْعُمُونَ ۝ قَالَ
ٱلَّذِينَ حَقَّ عَلَيْهِمُ ٱلْقَوْلُ رَبَّنَا هَـٰٓؤُلَآءِ
ٱلَّذِينَ أَغْوَيْنَآ أَغْوَيْنَـٰهُمْ كَمَا غَوَيْنَا
تَبَرَّأْنَآ إِلَيْكَ مَا كَانُوٓا۟ إِيَّانَا يَعْبُدُونَ
۝ وَقِيلَ ٱدْعُوا۟ شُرَكَآءَكُمْ فَدَعَوْهُمْ
فَلَمْ يَسْتَجِيبُوا۟ لَهُمْ وَرَأَوُا۟ ٱلْعَذَابَ لَوْ
أَنَّهُمْ كَانُوا۟ يَهْتَدُونَ ۝ وَيَوْمَ يُنَادِيهِمْ
فَيَقُولُ مَاذَآ أَجَبْتُمُ ٱلْمُرْسَلِينَ ۝

ᵃ On Judgement Day, the adherents of misguided leaders (*sharik*), whose word they accepted as if it were the word of God, will find themselves in a strange predicament. They will find that those great ones, whom they had been so proud to follow, have led them straight to Hell. They will then, in disgust, blame their leaders for their plight. But their leaders will retort that they have nobody to blame but themselves. They will allege that if their followers obtensibly bowed to their will, it was only because it was in accordance with their own desires. They will further accuse their followers of being slaves to their own desires. But they will then admit that they too had given in to temptation and that since leaders and followers had to face the same fate, there was no point in blaming each other.

66 They will be left speechless on that Day, and they will not be able to consult each other. 67 But as for him who repents and believes and does good deeds, he can hope to find himself among the successful.

68 Your Lord creates whatsoever He wills and chooses whomsoever He pleases. They have no choice. Praise be to God—exalted is He over anything they may associate with Him! 69 Your Lord knows what they conceal in their hearts and what they disclose. 70 He is God: there is no god but Him. All Praise is due to Him in this world and the hereafter. His is the Judgement and to Him you shall be returned.a

فَعَمِيَتْ عَلَيْهِمُ ٱلْأَنۢبَآءُ يَوْمَئِذٍ فَهُمْ لَا يَتَسَآءَلُونَ ۝ فَأَمَّا مَن تَابَ وَءَامَنَ وَعَمِلَ صَٰلِحًا فَعَسَىٰٓ أَن يَكُونَ مِنَ ٱلْمُفْلِحِينَ ۝ وَرَبُّكَ يَخْلُقُ مَا يَشَآءُ وَيَخْتَارُ مَا كَانَ لَهُمُ ٱلْخِيَرَةُ سُبْحَٰنَ ٱللَّهِ وَتَعَٰلَىٰ عَمَّا يُشْرِكُونَ ۝ وَرَبُّكَ يَعْلَمُ مَا تُكِنُّ صُدُورُهُمْ وَمَا يُعْلِنُونَ ۝ وَهُوَ ٱللَّهُ لَآ إِلَٰهَ إِلَّا هُوَ لَهُ ٱلْحَمْدُ فِي ٱلْأُولَىٰ وَٱلْءَاخِرَةِ وَلَهُ ٱلْحُكْمُ وَإِلَيْهِ تُرْجَعُونَ ۝

---

a When a man denies the Truth in this life, he does so after placing his reliance on something or someone. In the Hereafter he will be asked to invoke those on whom he relied, so that they may save him from the consequences of his denial. But this will be the Day of God's appearance and who can help anybody against God?

In the world, man does not just silently accept defeat. Here he finds words to counter any argument. But all these words will prove false on the Day of Judgement. Then he will regret that, for the sake of small gains, he gave up a very great blessing.

Almighty God creates human beings. Then He selects some individuals from among them for some particular work. This selection is not made on the basis of any mysterious reason, but depends on God's own decision. Therefore, to treat such persons as holy and to give them the status of God is absolutely baseless. There is no scope for this in this world of God.

Man denies the Truth on the basis of some personal (selfish) considerations, but talks as if his arguments were based on rationality. In the Hereafter this veil of pretence will be removed. At that time it will be known clearly that what he had in his heart, was very different from what he was saying—purely to maintain his prestige.

71 Ask them, 'Tell me, if God were to extend perpetual night over you till the Day of Judgement, is there any deity other than God that could bring you light? Will you not listen?' 72 Say, 'Tell me, if God were to extend perpetual day over you till the Day of Judgement—is there any deity other than God that could bring you night, in which to rest? Will you not then see?' 73 In His mercy He has made for you the night and the day, during which you may rest, and seek His bounty and be grateful.[a]

قُلْ أَرَءَيْتُمْ إِن جَعَلَ ٱللَّهُ عَلَيْكُمُ ٱلَّيْلَ سَرْمَدًا إِلَىٰ يَوْمِ ٱلْقِيَٰمَةِ مَنْ إِلَٰهٌ غَيْرُ ٱللَّهِ يَأْتِيكُم بِضِيَآءٍ أَفَلَا تَسْمَعُونَ ۝ قُلْ أَرَءَيْتُمْ إِن جَعَلَ ٱللَّهُ عَلَيْكُمُ ٱلنَّهَارَ سَرْمَدًا إِلَىٰ يَوْمِ ٱلْقِيَٰمَةِ مَنْ إِلَٰهٌ غَيْرُ ٱللَّهِ يَأْتِيكُم بِلَيْلٍ تَسْكُنُونَ فِيهِ أَفَلَا تُبْصِرُونَ ۝ وَمِن رَّحْمَتِهِ جَعَلَ لَكُمُ ٱلَّيْلَ وَٱلنَّهَارَ لِتَسْكُنُواْ فِيهِ وَلِتَبْتَغُواْ مِن فَضْلِهِ وَلَعَلَّكُمْ تَشْكُرُونَ ۝

---

[a] The earth, which is inhabited by human beings, has innumerable wonderful aspects. One of these is that it is constantly revolving around the Sun. Its axial rotation as it passes around the sun is such that it completes one full circle in twenty four hours. This is what produces the phenomenon of the repeated alternation of day and night. Had it not been for this axial rotation of the earth, there would have been perpetual night in half portion of the earth and perpetual day in the other half. The result of this would have been that the comfortable earth we know would have become a punishment chamber horrible beyond expression.

The constant rotation of the earth in space with perfect precision is so great a phenomenon that even the combined efforts of all men and all jinn could never have sufficed to bring it into existence. Nobody except the All Powerful God is capable of setting in motion such a great event. In view of this, it would be most misguided of man, to experience feelings of fear and love for anybody other than the One and Only God.

74 And on the Day He shall call out to them and say, 'Where are those whom you alleged were My partners.' 75 And We shall bring forth from every people a witness and We shall say to them: 'Bring your proof.' Then they will know that truth belongs to God alone, and that which they used to invent will fall away from them.[a]

وَيَوْمَ يُنَادِيهِمْ فَيَقُولُ أَيْنَ شُرَكَآءِىَ الَّذِينَ كُنتُمْ تَزْعُمُونَ ۝ وَنَزَعْنَا مِن كُلِّ أُمَّةٍ شَهِيدًا فَقُلْنَا هَاتُواْ بُرْهَٰنَكُمْ فَعَلِمُوٓاْ أَنَّ الْحَقَّ لِلَّهِ وَضَلَّ عَنْهُم مَّا كَانُواْ يَفْتَرُونَ ۝

---

[a] The Prophet and the Prophet's true missionaries will, on the Day of Judgement, be asked to act as witnesses of God. They will describe the reaction of the communities to whom it had been their duty to convey God's message. On that Day, all the false props of these communities will collapse. Those who denied the Truth, while relying on others except God, will try to put up a defence, but they will not find the words to defend themselves.

76 Korah was one of Moses' people, but he behaved arrogantly towards them. We had given him such treasures that their very keys would have weighed down a band of strong men. His people said to him, 'Do not exult in your riches, for God does not love the exultant. 77 But seek the Home of the Hereafter by means of that which God has bestowed on you; do not forget to take your portion [of the Hereafter] in this world. Be good to others as God has been good to you and do not strive for evil in the land, for God does not love the evil-doers.' a

﴿ إِنَّ قَارُونَ كَانَ مِن قَوْمِ مُوسَىٰ فَبَغَىٰ عَلَيْهِمْ ۖ وَءَاتَيْنَٰهُ مِنَ ٱلْكُنُوزِ مَآ إِنَّ مَفَاتِحَهُۥ لَتَنُوٓأُ بِٱلْعُصْبَةِ أُوْلِي ٱلْقُوَّةِ إِذْ قَالَ لَهُۥ قَوْمُهُۥ لَا تَفْرَحْ ۖ إِنَّ ٱللَّهَ لَا يُحِبُّ ٱلْفَرِحِينَ ۝ وَٱبْتَغِ فِيمَآ ءَاتَىٰكَ ٱللَّهُ ٱلدَّارَ ٱلْأَخِرَةَ ۖ وَلَا تَنسَ نَصِيبَكَ مِنَ ٱلدُّنْيَا ۖ وَأَحْسِن كَمَآ أَحْسَنَ ٱللَّهُ إِلَيْكَ ۖ وَلَا تَبْغِ ٱلْفَسَادَ فِي ٱلْأَرْضِ ۖ إِنَّ ٱللَّهَ لَا يُحِبُّ ٱلْمُفْسِدِينَ ۝ ﴾

---

a Korah or Qarun was one of the Children of Israel, but he cut off his relations with his community and shifted his loyalties towards Pharaoh, as a result of which he became Pharaoh's courtier. On account of his worldly wisdom, he accumulated great wealth, so much so that he became the richest man in Egypt. Having acquired wealth, he should have been duly grateful, but, instead he allowed his wealth to give him a sense of false pride. With the help of his resources, he should have earned the reward of goodness, but he did not do so.

What is meant by creating 'evil in the land?' According to verse 77, one of the ways of creating a disturbance on earth is for a man acquiring a lot of wealth, to spend it only on himself. Water from various parts of land gathers in a sea. The sea again scatters the water back over the whole land after turning it into vapour. This is an example of peaceful activity (islah) which is the opposite of creating discord (fasad) in this world of God. The very same approach is required of man. If, for any reason, wealth is accumulated by someone, he should by different methods, return it to those less favoured in the distribution of wealth. In other words, circulating accumulated wealth promotes islah, while hoarding accumulated wealth brings about fasad.

⁷⁸ But he said, 'I have been given it only because of the knowledge I possess.' Did he not know that God had destroyed before him people who were stronger than he and possessed even greater resources? The guilty are not required to offer explanations of their sins.^{*a*}

⁷⁹ Then he went forth before his people in all his pomp. Those who were eager for the life of this world said, 'If only we had the like of Korah's fortune! He really is a very fortunate man,' ⁸⁰ but those who had been given knowledge said, 'Woe to you, God's reward is better for those who believe and do good deeds: and it is awarded only to those who are steadfast.'^{*b*}

قَالَ إِنَّمَآ أُوتِيتُهُۥ عَلَىٰ عِلْمٍ عِندِىٓ أَوَلَمْ يَعْلَمْ أَنَّ ٱللَّهَ قَدْ أَهْلَكَ مِن قَبْلِهِۦ مِنَ ٱلْقُرُونِ مَنْ هُوَ أَشَدُّ مِنْهُ قُوَّةً وَأَكْثَرُ جَمْعًا ۚ وَلَا يُسْـَٔلُ عَن ذُنُوبِهِمُ ٱلْمُجْرِمُونَ ۝ فَخَرَجَ عَلَىٰ قَوْمِهِۦ فِى زِينَتِهِۦ ۖ قَالَ ٱلَّذِينَ يُرِيدُونَ ٱلْحَيَوٰةَ ٱلدُّنْيَا يَٰلَيْتَ لَنَا مِثْلَ مَآ أُوتِىَ قَٰرُونُ إِنَّهُۥ لَذُو حَظٍّ عَظِيمٍ ۝ وَقَالَ ٱلَّذِينَ أُوتُوا۟ ٱلْعِلْمَ وَيْلَكُمْ ثَوَابُ ٱللَّهِ خَيْرٌ لِّمَنْ ءَامَنَ وَعَمِلَ صَٰلِحًا وَلَا يُلَقَّىٰهَآ إِلَّا ٱلصَّٰبِرُونَ ۝

---

^{*a*} The character of Korah described here is the same as is invariably found in men of wealth. A wealthy man thinks that whatever he has acquired is thanks to his own talents. But with all his knowledge, the rich man never stops to wonder how his wealth is going to save him in this ephemeral world from the same fate as all his rich predecessors met with—namely death and destruction.

^{*b*} All the glamour of the world gathers around a person who possesses wealth. Seeing this, many foolish persons envy his lot. But those who possess real knowledge are quick to realize that this glamour is ephemeral, and that something so unenduring has no value.

Knowledge of reality is the most valuable thing in this world. But to acquire this knowledge, one must have the patience to mould one's mind without being influenced by external pressures, and while forming one's opinion to ignore things of temporary charm. This is of course the most difficult type of patience to exercise, but after passing this crucial test, man is rewarded with the precious attributes of knowledge and wisdom.

⁸¹ Then We caused the earth to swallow up him and his home: there was no one to help him against God, nor could he defend himself. ⁸² Those who had coveted his position the day before now began to say, 'Ah! It is indeed God alone who gives abundantly to whom He will and sparingly to whom He pleases. Had not God been gracious to us, He would have caused us to be swallowed up also.' Alas indeed! Those who deny the truth will never prosper.ᵃ

فَخَسَفْنَا بِهِۦ وَبِدَارِهِ ٱلْأَرْضَ فَمَا
كَانَ لَهُۥ مِن فِئَةٍ يَنصُرُونَهُۥ مِن دُونِ
ٱللَّهِ وَمَا كَانَ مِنَ ٱلْمُنتَصِرِينَ ۝
وَأَصْبَحَ ٱلَّذِينَ تَمَنَّوْاْ مَكَانَهُۥ
بِٱلْأَمْسِ يَقُولُونَ وَيْكَأَنَّ ٱللَّهَ يَبْسُطُ
ٱلرِّزْقَ لِمَن يَشَآءُ مِنْ عِبَادِهِۦ وَيَقْدِرُ
لَوْلَآ أَن مَّنَّ ٱللَّهُ عَلَيْنَا لَخَسَفَ بِنَا
وَيْكَأَنَّهُۥ لَا يُفْلِحُ ٱلْكَـٰفِرُونَ ۝

ᵃ According to the Bible, Moses cursed Korah for his evil deeds, and God caused him, his companions and his treasure to be swallowed up by the earth. This was visibly demonstrated by God as an example to clarify what the final result would be of leaving off the worship of God and adopting the worship of wealth.

The amenities of the world are in fact given as a trial of human beings. These are provided to man, by the will of God in greater or lesser quantities. It is the duty of man to be patient if he receives fewer amenities and to be grateful if he receives more. This is the only way to the salvation and success of man.

⁸³ As for the abode of the Hereafter, We shall assign it to those who seek neither self-aggrandisement on the earth nor corruption. The righteous shall have a blessed end. ⁸⁴ He who does good shall be rewarded with something better. But he who does evil shall be requited according to his deeds.ᵃ

تِلْكَ ٱلدَّارُ ٱلْأَخِرَةُ نَجْعَلُهَا لِلَّذِينَ لَا يُرِيدُونَ عُلُوًّا فِى ٱلْأَرْضِ وَلَا فَسَادًا ۚ وَٱلْعَٰقِبَةُ لِلْمُتَّقِينَ ﴿٨٣﴾ مَن جَآءَ بِٱلْحَسَنَةِ فَلَهُۥ خَيْرٌ مِّنْهَا ۖ وَمَن جَآءَ بِٱلسَّيِّئَةِ فَلَا يُجْزَى ٱلَّذِينَ عَمِلُوا۟ ٱلسَّيِّئَاتِ إِلَّا مَا كَانُوا۟ يَعْمَلُونَ ﴿٨٤﴾

ᵃ Those whose hearts are free of false pride are the ones eligible to be settled in paradise. They are so imbued with a sense of God's greatness that everything else seems insignificant.

If a man does not act in consonance with God's scheme, i.e. he acts against God's will in God's world, it creates discord (fasad). Those who are free of false pride are the truly virtuous. They will be settled in the eternal gardens of God.

85 He who has entrusted you with the responsibility of the Quran, will surely lead you to a successful end. Say, 'My Lord knows best who is rightly guided and who is in gross error.' 86 You never expected that this Book would be revealed to you. Yet, by the grace of your Lord, you have received it. So do not support those who reject the truth. 87 And let no one divert you from God's revelations, once they have been sent down to you. Call people to your Lord. Never be of those who ascribe partners to God. 88 Invoke no god other than God, for there is no god but Him. All things are bound to perish except Himself. His is the judgement, and to Him you shall be returned.ᵃ

إِنَّ ٱلَّذِي فَرَضَ عَلَيْكَ ٱلْقُرْءَانَ لَرَآدُّكَ إِلَىٰ مَعَادٍ ۚ قُل رَّبِّي أَعْلَمُ مَن جَآءَ بِٱلْهُدَىٰ وَمَنْ هُوَ فِي ضَلَٰلٍ مُّبِينٍ ۝ وَمَا كُنتَ تَرْجُوٓاْ أَن يُلْقَىٰٓ إِلَيْكَ ٱلْكِتَٰبُ إِلَّا رَحْمَةً مِّن رَّبِّكَ ۖ فَلَا تَكُونَنَّ ظَهِيرًا لِّلْكَٰفِرِينَ ۝ وَلَا يَصُدُّنَّكَ عَنْ ءَايَٰتِ ٱللَّهِ بَعْدَ إِذْ أُنزِلَتْ إِلَيْكَ ۖ وَٱدْعُ إِلَىٰ رَبِّكَ ۖ وَلَا تَكُونَنَّ مِنَ ٱلْمُشْرِكِينَ ۝ وَلَا تَدْعُ مَعَ ٱللَّهِ إِلَٰهًا ءَاخَرَ ۘ لَآ إِلَٰهَ إِلَّا هُوَ ۚ كُلُّ شَىْءٍ هَالِكٌ إِلَّا وَجْهَهُۥ ۚ لَهُ ٱلْحُكْمُ وَإِلَيْهِ تُرْجَعُونَ ۝

ᵃ The Prophet's cause is in every way God's cause. Prophethood is voluntarily given to him by God without any request on his part. Throughout his entire existence he remains steadfast in adhering to the Truth. He is appointed to announce the plain, unvarnished Truth, even if it is unpleasant to people. He is destined to reach his appointed goal and no impediment shall bar his path.

After the Prophet, the same will hold true for those who rise, in conformity with the Prophet, as missionaries of Truth. To the extent that they resemble the Prophet in conduct, they will go on being entitled to succour promised by God to His prophets in His Book.

29. THE SPIDER

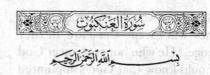

In the name of God,
the Most Gracious, the Most Merciful

¹ *Alif Lam Mim*

² Do people think that once they say,
'We believe,' they will be left alone
and not be put to the test? ³ We
certainly tried those who have gone
before them, so God will certainly
distinguish between those who are
truthful and those who are lying.*a*

---

a The question of whether a man is a true believer is decided on the basis of how
he conducts himself in extraordinary rather than in ordinary circumstances. It
becomes clear, on such occasions through a man's overt actions whether he is in
actual fact what he claims to be. Those who prove to be steadfast in their belief
and convictions under extraordinary circumstances, will be treated by God as
believers in the true sense.

To pass the divine test means to become a man of faith by adopting the way of
sacrifice, that is to say, to accept and confirm the Truth when people in general
reject it; to be staunch in one's beliefs when people harbour doubts; to be a believer
even at the cost of curbing one's ego; to accept the Truth even when rejection of
it does not entail any loss; to spend when restraint would appear to be more
prudent; to be steadfast and firm when circumstances warrant fleeing; to surrender
when the occasion demands that one save one's skin; to bow down in submission
when there is an occasion for arrogance; to support and co-operate when it
amounts to surrendering and sacrificing everything.

The inner man is revealed on such extraordinary occasions. Thereafter, no one is
left with the opportunity to make fictitious claims about what in actual fact one
is not.

⁴ Do those who do evil imagine that they will escape Us? How ill they judge! ⁵ He who hopes to meet God should know that God's appointed hour is sure to come. He is the All Hearing, the All Knowing. ⁶ And whoever strives, strives only for himself—God is independent of all His creation—⁷ as for those who have faith and do good works, We shall certainly cleanse them of their evil deeds and reward them according to the best of their actions.ᵃ

⁸ We have enjoined man to show kindness to his parents. But if they bid you associate with Me something about which you have no knowledge, do not obey them. To Me you shall all return, and I shall tell you about all that you have done. ⁹ We shall surely admit those who believe and do good deeds to the company of the righteous.ᵇ

أَمْ حَسِبَ ٱلَّذِينَ يَعْمَلُونَ ٱلسَّيِّئَاتِ أَن يَسْبِقُونَا سَآءَ مَا يَحْكُمُونَ ۝ مَن كَانَ يَرْجُواْ لِقَآءَ ٱللَّهِ فَإِنَّ أَجَلَ ٱللَّهِ لَآتٍ وَهُوَ ٱلسَّمِيعُ ٱلْعَلِيمُ ۝ وَمَن جَٰهَدَ فَإِنَّمَا يُجَٰهِدُ لِنَفْسِهِۦٓ إِنَّ ٱللَّهَ لَغَنِىٌّ عَنِ ٱلْعَٰلَمِينَ ۝ وَٱلَّذِينَ ءَامَنُواْ وَعَمِلُواْ ٱلصَّٰلِحَٰتِ لَنُكَفِّرَنَّ عَنْهُمْ سَيِّـَٔاتِهِمْ وَلَنَجْزِيَنَّهُمْ أَحْسَنَ ٱلَّذِى كَانُواْ يَعْمَلُونَ ۝ وَوَصَّيْنَا ٱلْإِنسَٰنَ بِوَٰلِدَيْهِ حُسْنًا وَإِن جَٰهَدَاكَ لِتُشْرِكَ بِى مَا لَيْسَ لَكَ بِهِۦ عِلْمٌ فَلَا تُطِعْهُمَآ إِلَىَّ مَرْجِعُكُمْ فَأُنَبِّئُكُم بِمَا كُنتُمْ تَعْمَلُونَ ۝ وَٱلَّذِينَ ءَامَنُواْ وَعَمِلُواْ ٱلصَّٰلِحَٰتِ لَنُدْخِلَنَّهُمْ فِى ٱلصَّٰلِحِينَ ۝

ᵃ To be a believer is often synonymous with going against the trend of the times. This amounts to being a God-worshipper in an atmosphere of hero-worship; to subscribe to principles in an atmosphere where importance is given to desires; to endeavour to live for the Hereafter in an atmosphere where people live for worldly interests.

This kind of life requires an earnest struggle, and only those who have absolute faith in God and who have made God's expected reward their sole focus, are capable of remaining steadfast on this thorny path.

ᵇ Of all the creatures, a man's parents have the greatest right over him. But, just as everything has a limit, so also do the parent's rights have a limit, in the sense that—according to the Prophet's tradition—'no obedience may be shown to any creature if it means disobedience to the Creator.'

The rights of parents must be observed, but only so long as they do not clash with the rights of God. ▶

¹⁰ Some profess to believe in God, but when they suffer for God's cause they mistake the persecution of man for the punishment of God. But when help comes to you from God, they will say, 'We have always been with you.' Is not God fully aware of what is in the hearts of all creatures? ¹¹ Most certainly God will mark out those who believe and mark out those who are hypocrites.ᵃ

¹² Those who deny the truth say to the faithful, 'Follow our way, and we will bear the burden of your sins.' But they will bear none of their sins. They are surely lying. ¹³ They shall bear their own burdens, and other burdens besides. On the Day of Resurrection they shall be questioned about their false assertions.ᵇ

وَمِنَ ٱلنَّاسِ مَن يَقُولُ ءَامَنَّا بِٱللَّهِ فَإِذَآ أُوذِيَ فِى ٱللَّهِ جَعَلَ فِتْنَةَ ٱلنَّاسِ كَعَذَابِ ٱللَّهِ وَلَئِن جَآءَ نَصْرٌ مِّن رَّبِّكَ لَيَقُولُنَّ إِنَّا كُنَّا مَعَكُمْ أَوَلَيْسَ ٱللَّهُ بِأَعْلَمَ بِمَا فِى صُدُورِ ٱلْعَٰلَمِينَ ۝ وَلَيَعْلَمَنَّ ٱللَّهُ ٱلَّذِينَ ءَامَنُوا۟ وَلَيَعْلَمَنَّ ٱلْمُنَٰفِقِينَ ۝ وَقَالَ ٱلَّذِينَ كَفَرُوا۟ لِلَّذِينَ ءَامَنُوا۟ ٱتَّبِعُوا۟ سَبِيلَنَا وَلْنَحْمِلْ خَطَٰيَٰكُمْ وَمَا هُم بِحَٰمِلِينَ مِنْ خَطَٰيَٰهُم مِّن شَىْءٍ إِنَّهُمْ لَكَٰذِبُونَ ۝ وَلَيَحْمِلُنَّ أَثْقَالَهُمْ وَأَثْقَالًا مَّعَ أَثْقَالِهِمْ وَلَيُسْـَٔلُنَّ يَوْمَ ٱلْقِيَٰمَةِ عَمَّا كَانُوا۟ يَفْتَرُونَ ۝

The moment a parent's order clashes with God's order, it becomes as necessary at that time not to follow his or her order as it is necessary to follow his or her order in ordinary circumstances. In Islam the rights of parents means service being due to them, but not worship.

ᵃ When one who calls himself a believer, or *mu'min*, shows himself to be such only when some advantage is to be gained, but otherwise recants, he reveals himself to be what the Quran calls a hypocrite, or *munafiq*. A believer in name only, he is not prepared to pay the price of his faith. He and other people like him fail at the very juncture where they are most required to prove their moral worth.

ᵇ Inventing a lie, or *iftira*, consists of saying something of one's own concoction and then attributing it to God. All manner of wrongful innovations in religion, or *bid'ah*, and wrong interpretations are included in this definition. One of the forms of *iftira* is prominent people among the deniers of God asking the less enlightened to follow their path and reassuring them that they will be responsible if the latter are questioned before God. But God has not given this kind of right to anybody. Therefore, to make such a statement amounts to uttering a falsehood in the name of God. ▶

¹⁴ We sent Noah to his people and he lived among them for fifty short of a thousand years; then the deluge overtook them, for they were wrongdoers. ¹⁵ But We saved him and those who were with him in the Ark and made the event a sign for mankind.ᵃ

وَلَقَدۡ أَرۡسَلۡنَا نُوحًا إِلَىٰ قَوۡمِهِۦ فَلَبِثَ فِيهِمۡ أَلۡفَ سَنَةٍ إِلَّا خَمۡسِينَ عَامًا فَأَخَذَهُمُ ٱلطُّوفَانُ وَهُمۡ ظَٰلِمُونَ ۝ فَأَنجَيۡنَٰهُ وَأَصۡحَٰبَ ٱلسَّفِينَةِ وَجَعَلۡنَٰهَآ ءَايَةً لِّلۡعَٰلَمِينَ ۝

Human beings say many things for the sake of saying them. But if they were to understand the consequences of their words, they would not utter them. When such people who have spoken idly see the horror of the Day of Judgement, their condition will be entirely different from what it seems to be in today's world.

ᵃ Noah lived for nine hundred and fifty years. Even before he was given prophethood, he was a righteous person and followed the Shariah or religious code of Adam. After receiving prophethood, he became a regular missionary of God and issued warnings to his people. But, even after he had put in efforts for hundreds of years, his people rejected him. In the end, the whole community, barring a few reformed individuals, was destroyed in a terrible flood.

There is a high mountain known as Ararat in the mountain ranges of Eastern Anatolia on the border between Russia and Turkey. Its height is more than five thousand metres. The pilots of planes flying over this mountain say that they have seen a boat-like object on the snow-clad peak. So, constant efforts are being made to reach this boat. Scholars hold the view that this is that very boat known in religious traditions as Noah's Ark.

If this information is correct, it means that Almighty God has preserved Noah's Ark till today, to serve as a sign to show that, in order to save themselves from a storm which will destroy them all, human beings required the special protection of a prophet's boat. Nothing else could save them from His wrath.

¹⁶ Tell of Abraham. He said to his people, 'Worship God and fear Him, that would be best for you, if only you knew. ¹⁷ You worship idols besides God and fabricate falsehoods. Those whom you worship besides God have no power to provide sustenance for you. So seek your sustenance from God and worship Him and be grateful to Him, for to Him you shall return. ¹⁸ If you reject the truth, other communities before you also rejected the truth. The messenger's responsibility is only to convey the message clearly.'ᵃ

وَإِبْرَٰهِيمَ إِذْ قَالَ لِقَوْمِهِ ٱعْبُدُوا۟ ٱللَّهَ وَٱتَّقُوهُ ۖ ذَٰلِكُمْ خَيْرٌ لَّكُمْ إِن كُنتُمْ تَعْلَمُونَ ۝ إِنَّمَا تَعْبُدُونَ مِن دُونِ ٱللَّهِ أَوْثَٰنًا وَتَخْلُقُونَ إِفْكًا ۚ إِنَّ ٱلَّذِينَ تَعْبُدُونَ مِن دُونِ ٱللَّهِ لَا يَمْلِكُونَ لَكُمْ رِزْقًا فَٱبْتَغُوا۟ عِندَ ٱللَّهِ ٱلرِّزْقَ وَٱعْبُدُوهُ وَٱشْكُرُوا۟ لَهُۥٓ إِلَيْهِ تُرْجَعُونَ ۝ وَإِن تُكَذِّبُوا۟ فَقَدْ كَذَّبَ أُمَمٌ مِّن قَبْلِكُمْ ۖ وَمَا عَلَى ٱلرَّسُولِ إِلَّا ٱلْبَلَٰغُ ٱلْمُبِينُ ۝

ᵃ Making anybody other than the One God the centre of one's noble feelings is a sin, because it amounts to presuming that divine attributes inhere in beings other than God. It is this attribution of the lofty qualities unique to God to some thing other than God, that makes it possible for a man to become the worshipper of some entity other than Him.

In the earlier days of polytheism, man used to presume that idols possessed such qualities. Today man is behaving no differently. It is just that the names of the idols of the present day vary from those of yore. The sole difference between ancient and modern times is that ancient man used to attribute the lucrative produce of his field to the kindness of some imaginary god, while the man of today says, 'Our green revolution is a miracle of our agricultural science'.

¹⁹ Do they not see how God originates creation, then reproduces it? That surely is easy for God. ²⁰ Tell them, 'Roam the earth and see how He originated creation. Then God will bring into being your second life. God has power over all things. ²¹ He punishes whom He will and shows mercy to whom He pleases. And to Him you shall be returned. ²² You cannot defeat His purpose on earth or in heaven; nor have you any friend or helper besides God.' ²³ Those who deny God's revelations and the meeting with Him—it is they who have despaired of My mercy. They will suffer a grievous punishment.^a

أَوَلَمْ يَرَوْا كَيْفَ يُبْدِئُ ٱللَّهُ ٱلْخَلْقَ ثُمَّ يُعِيدُهُ إِنَّ ذَٰلِكَ عَلَى ٱللَّهِ يَسِيرٌ ۝ قُلْ سِيرُوا فِي ٱلْأَرْضِ فَٱنظُرُوا كَيْفَ بَدَأَ ٱلْخَلْقَ ثُمَّ ٱللَّهُ يُنشِئُ ٱلنَّشْأَةَ ٱلْآخِرَةَ إِنَّ ٱللَّهَ عَلَى كُلِّ شَيْءٍ قَدِيرٌ ۝ يُعَذِّبُ مَن يَشَآءُ وَيَرْحَمُ مَن يَشَآءُ وَإِلَيْهِ تُقْلَبُونَ ۝ وَمَآ أَنتُم بِمُعْجِزِينَ فِي ٱلْأَرْضِ وَلَا فِي ٱلسَّمَآءِ وَمَا لَكُم مِّن دُونِ ٱللَّهِ مِن وَلِيٍّ وَلَا نَصِيرٍ ۝ وَٱلَّذِينَ كَفَرُوا بِآيَٰتِ ٱللَّهِ وَلِقَآئِهِ أُوْلَٰئِكَ يَئِسُوا مِن رَّحْمَتِي وَأُوْلَٰئِكَ هُمْ عَذَابٌ أَلِيمٌ ۝

^a Man was non-existent and came into being only at a certain point in time. In view of this, why should it not be possible for the creation which occurred once, to take place once again? Shah Abdul Qadir Dehlavi has written this meaningful observation, 'You have seen the beginning, you can now guess that it can be repeated in future.'

Each man himself is an example of the First Creation. If he needs further examples, he should observe and study this wide world of God. He will see that the whole world is replete with living examples of this event. God has provided these examples in this world so that man may understand what the Second Creation means and then perform such deeds as will be of avail to him in the next stage of existence.

²⁴ The only response of Abraham's people was, 'Kill him or burn him!' But God saved him from the fire. Surely in this there are signs for people who believe. ²⁵ Abraham said, 'You have taken up the worship of idols, instead of God, to promote friendship between yourselves in the present life. But on the Day of Judgement, you will disown and curse one another. Your abode will be the Fire and you will have no helpers.' ²⁶ Lot was the one who believed in him and said, 'I shall migrate to another land for the sake of my Lord. He is the Mighty One, the Wise One.'ᵃ

فَمَا كَانَ جَوَابَ قَوْمِهِ إِلَّا أَن قَالُوا اقْتُلُوهُ أَوْ حَرِّقُوهُ فَأَنجَاهُ اللَّهُ مِنَ النَّارِ إِنَّ فِي ذَٰلِكَ لَآيَاتٍ لِّقَوْمٍ يُؤْمِنُونَ ۝ وَقَالَ إِنَّمَا اتَّخَذْتُم مِّن دُونِ اللَّهِ أَوْثَانًا مَّوَدَّةَ بَيْنِكُمْ فِي الْحَيَوٰةِ الدُّنْيَا ثُمَّ يَوْمَ الْقِيَٰمَةِ يَكْفُرُ بَعْضُكُم بِبَعْضٍ وَيَلْعَنُ بَعْضُكُم بَعْضًا وَمَأْوَىٰكُمُ النَّارُ وَمَا لَكُم مِّن نَّٰصِرِينَ ۝ فَآمَنَ لَهُ لُوطٌ وَقَالَ إِنِّي مُهَاجِرٌ إِلَىٰ رَبِّي إِنَّهُ هُوَ الْعَزِيزُ الْحَكِيمُ ۝

ᵃ Any social custom, which assumes the position of a national tradition, soon becomes a standard requirement for every individual of the society in question. It is solely on this basis that mutually good relations are formed. All interests are linked with it and a man's worth is assessed in accordance with it. In ancient times polytheism had assumed the status of such a national tradition.

Abraham told the people of Iraq that the polytheism practiced by them was only a national custom and not based on actual Truth, and that its importance would vanish as soon as the present life came to an end. But his only support came from his nephew Lot. His own people became so hostile to him that they threw him into a fire. However, God saved him. He was blessed not only with the supreme reward of the Hereafter, but also with righteous descendants among whom the institution of prophethood continued for the next four thousand years. His son Isaac and his grandson, Jacob, were also prophets and thereafter the chain of prophethood continued in that family down to Jesus. Among the descendants of Madyaan (another son of Abraham), yet another prophet, Shu'yab was born. Similarly, Abraham's son, Ishmael, was himself a prophet and among his descendants was born the Prophet Muhammad, whose prophethood will continue undiminished in its influence till the Day of Judgement.

In this history of Abraham, there is a lesson for the worshippers of falsehood, as well as there being a source of light for those who stand on the firm base of Truth.

²⁷ We gave him Isaac and Jacob and granted prophethood and the Book to his descendants. We gave him his reward in this life and in the Hereafter he shall dwell among the righteous.

²⁸ We sent Lot to his people and he said to them, 'Indeed you commit obscenity such as no people before you have ever committed. ²⁹ You approach men and waylay them on the road and commit depravities within your gatherings.' But his people's only reply was, 'Bring down God's punishment upon us, if what you say be true.' ³⁰ Lot prayed, 'Lord, help me against this wicked people.'ᵃ

وَوَهَبْنَا لَهُ إِسْحَاقَ وَيَعْقُوبَ وَجَعَلْنَا فِى ذُرِّيَّتِهِ ٱلنُّبُوَّةَ وَٱلْكِتَابَ وَءَاتَيْنَاهُ أَجْرَهُ فِى ٱلدُّنْيَا وَإِنَّهُ فِى ٱلْأَخِرَةِ لَمِنَ ٱلصَّالِحِينَ ۝ وَلُوطًا إِذْ قَالَ لِقَوْمِهِ إِنَّكُمْ لَتَأْتُونَ ٱلْفَاحِشَةَ مَا سَبَقَكُم بِهَا مِنْ أَحَدٍ مِّنَ ٱلْعَالَمِينَ ۝ أَئِنَّكُمْ لَتَأْتُونَ ٱلرِّجَالَ وَتَقْطَعُونَ ٱلسَّبِيلَ وَتَأْتُونَ فِى نَادِيكُمُ ٱلْمُنكَرَ فَمَا كَانَ جَوَابَ قَوْمِهِ إِلَّا أَن قَالُوا۟ ٱئْتِنَا بِعَذَابِ ٱللَّهِ إِن كُنتَ مِنَ ٱلصَّادِقِينَ ۝ قَالَ رَبِّ ٱنصُرْنِى عَلَى ٱلْقَوْمِ ٱلْمُفْسِدِينَ ۝

ᵃ Lot left Babylon and settled in Jordan. God made him a prophet and assigned to him the task of reforming his community. This community inhabited the town of Sodom near the Dead Sea and was addicted to the unnatural habit of sodomy. Through this evil, other evils had become prevalent among them. But they would not reform themselves.

The words, 'Bring down God's punishment upon us' were directed at Lot and not at God. Lot's people so looked down upon Lot that, according to them, it was impossible that, on disobeying him, they would have to face God's scourge. So, they challenged him to bring God's punishment down on them if what he said was really true.

³¹ When Our messengers brought Abraham the good news [of the birth of Isaac] they [also] said, 'We are indeed going to destroy the people of this city, for the people of this city are truly wrongdoers.' ³² Abraham said, 'But, Lot lives here.' They answered, 'We well know who lives here. We shall surely save him and his whole family, except his wife, who will be among those who stay behind.' ³³ When Our messengers came to Lot, he was troubled and distressed on their account. They said, 'Have no fear or grief. We shall certainly save you and your household, except your wife—who will be among those who stay behind— ³⁴ We are surely going to bring down a punishment from heaven on the people of this town because of their depravities.' ³⁵ Surely the ruins We left of that city are a clear sign for a people who use their reason.ᵃ

وَلَمَّا جَآءَتْ رُسُلُنَآ إِبْرَٰهِيمَ بِٱلْبُشْرَىٰ قَالُوٓاْ إِنَّا مُهْلِكُوٓاْ أَهْلِ هَٰذِهِ ٱلْقَرْيَةِ إِنَّ أَهْلَهَا كَانُواْ ظَٰلِمِينَ ۝ قَالَ إِنَّ فِيهَا لُوطًا قَالُواْ نَحْنُ أَعْلَمُ بِمَن فِيهَا لَنُنَجِّيَنَّهُۥ وَأَهْلَهُۥٓ إِلَّا ٱمْرَأَتَهُۥ كَانَتْ مِنَ ٱلْغَٰبِرِينَ ۝ وَلَمَّآ أَن جَآءَتْ رُسُلُنَا لُوطًا سِيٓءَ بِهِمْ وَضَاقَ بِهِمْ ذَرْعًا وَقَالُواْ لَا تَخَفْ وَلَا تَحْزَنْ إِنَّا مُنَجُّوكَ وَأَهْلَكَ إِلَّا ٱمْرَأَتَكَ كَانَتْ مِنَ ٱلْغَٰبِرِينَ ۝ إِنَّا مُنزِلُونَ عَلَىٰٓ أَهْلِ هَٰذِهِ ٱلْقَرْيَةِ رِجْزًا مِّنَ ٱلسَّمَآءِ بِمَا كَانُواْ يَفْسُقُونَ ۝ وَلَقَد تَّرَكْنَا مِنْهَآ ءَايَةً بَيِّنَةً لِّقَوْمٍ يَعْقِلُونَ ۝

ᵃ A severe earthquake destroyed the region where Lot's community lived in the towns of Sodom and Gomorrah. The green and flourishing valley, inhabited by this community for four thousand years, was filled with the dense salt water of the Dead Sea.

According to the Quran, this incident of destruction had occurred through the agency of God's angels. But, geologists and archeologists say that as a result of a natural geological process when mountains appeared in this area, a chasm was formed, the southern part of which was later filled by sea water. In this way, a stretch of dry land came under water. It is now known as the Shallow Southern Coast of the Dead Sea. The event, which seems to be only a physical occurrence in non-Quranic observation, is, according to the Quran, a sign from God.

It is the view of the experts that the ruins of the area which was laid waste are still extant at the bottom of the sea. Undoubtedly, there is a lesson in this. But this lesson is only for those who try to study things in depth.

³⁶ To the people of Midian We sent their brother Shu'ayb. He said, 'My people, worship God, and look forward to the Last Day, and do not commit evil and spread corruption in the land.' ³⁷ But they rejected him, so the earthquake overwhelmed them and they were left lying prostrate on the ground in their homes.^a

³⁸ The same happened to the tribes of 'Ad and Thamud: this must be clear to you from their ruins. Satan made their actions seem good to them, and turned them away from the straight path, even though they were intelligent people.^b

وَإِلَىٰ مَدْيَنَ أَخَاهُمْ شُعَيْبًا فَقَالَ يَـٰقَوْمِ ٱعْبُدُواْ ٱللَّهَ وَٱرْجُواْ ٱلْيَوْمَ ٱلْأَخِرَ وَلَا تَعْثَوْاْ فِى ٱلْأَرْضِ مُفْسِدِينَ ۝ فَكَذَّبُوهُ فَأَخَذَتْهُمُ ٱلرَّجْفَةُ فَأَصْبَحُواْ فِى دَارِهِمْ جَـٰثِمِينَ ۝ وَعَادًا وَثَمُودَاْ وَقَد تَّبَيَّنَ لَكُم مِّن مَّسَـٰكِنِهِمْ وَزَيَّنَ لَهُمُ ٱلشَّيْطَـٰنُ أَعْمَـٰلَهُمْ فَصَدَّهُمْ عَنِ ٱلسَّبِيلِ وَكَانُواْ مُسْتَبْصِرِينَ ۝

---

^a The community, to which Shu'ayb was appointed as prophet, was a trading community. Its members, however, became so greedy that they resorted to earning through unfair and fraudulent means. This was how they spread corruption in the land. Legitimate trade is the rightful method of earning, while fraud and exploitation are sinful.

Shu'ayb exhorted his people not to be unmindful of the Hereafter while in pursuit of worldly gain. He beseeched them to adopt a way of life by which they could hope for a better fate in the Hereafter. But, despite the best efforts of the prophet, his community did not pay heed to his exhortations, with the result that, in accordance with the Laws of God, it was destroyed. Their homes, which had reverberated with life, became houses of death and destruction for them.

^b God's retribution was likewise meted out to the 'Ad and the Thamud. They were very shrewd in their worldly affairs, but they proved most foolish in the matter of the Hereafter. They learned the secret of carving houses out of rocky mountain sides, but not the secret of shaping their lives under the guidance of their prophet. The reason for this was what is known as false glorification of deeds, or taz'in. Satan misled them into thinking that building up their worldly position was the genuine aim of life, and that if worldly success were achieved, nothing would pose any problem after that. But this deception was of no avail to them and neither will such fraudulence be of any avail to anybody at any time.

In ancient times the 'Ad people inhabited the area of southern Arabia, which is now known as Yemen, Ahqaf and Hadramouth. Similarly, the Thamud people inhabited the areas located in the northern part of Hijaz stretching from Rabegh to Aquaba and from Madinah and Khyber to Tyma and Tabuk.

³⁹ Korah, Pharaoh, and Haman: Moses came to them with clear signs but they were arrogant in the land. They could not escape Us. ⁴⁰ So We seized each one for his sins; some We struck with a violent storm; some of them were overcome by a sudden blast, some were swallowed up by the earth and some We drowned. God did not wrong them: they wronged themselves.^a

وَقَـٰرُونَ وَفِرْعَوْنَ وَهَـٰمَـٰنَ
وَلَقَدْ جَآءَهُم مُّوسَىٰ بِٱلْبَيِّنَـٰتِ
فَٱسْتَكْبَرُوا۟ فِى ٱلْأَرْضِ وَمَا كَانُوا۟
سَـٰبِقِينَ ﴿٣٩﴾ فَكُلًّا أَخَذْنَا بِذَنۢبِهِۦ
فَمِنْهُم مَّنْ أَرْسَلْنَا عَلَيْهِ حَاصِبًا
وَمِنْهُم مَّنْ أَخَذَتْهُ ٱلصَّيْحَةُ وَمِنْهُم
مَّنْ خَسَفْنَا بِهِ ٱلْأَرْضَ وَمِنْهُم
مَّنْ أَغْرَقْنَا وَمَا كَانَ ٱللَّهُ
لِيَظْلِمَهُمْ وَلَـٰكِن كَانُوٓا۟ أَنفُسَهُمْ
يَظْلِمُونَ ﴿٤٠﴾

^a Whenever the addressee communities rejected the prophets sent to them, they were destroyed by calamities which burst upon them either from the heavens or from the earth. Lot's community was subjected to the curse of high-velocity winds that bore stones. The 'Ad, the Thamud and the people of Midian were punished by thunder and lightning sent down upon them. Korah, at God's behest, was swallowed by the earth. Pharaoh and Haman were drowned in the sea.

The common reason for all these punishments was the false pride of the concerned persons, i.e. their rejecting the call of Truth for the reason that it would put an end to their high status.

⁴¹ Those who take protectors other than God can be compared to the spider which builds itself a cobweb, but the frailest of all structures is the house of the spider, if they but knew it. ⁴² God surely knows what they invoke besides Him. He is the Mighty, the Wise One. ⁴³ Such are the comparisons We make for people, but only those understand them who have knowledge. ⁴⁴ God has created the heavens and the earth for a purpose; surely in this there is a sign for true believers.ᵃ

مَثَلُ ٱلَّذِينَ ٱتَّخَذُوا۟ مِن دُونِ ٱللَّهِ أَوْلِيَآءَ كَمَثَلِ ٱلْعَنكَبُوتِ ٱتَّخَذَتْ بَيْتًا ۖ وَإِنَّ أَوْهَنَ ٱلْبُيُوتِ لَبَيْتُ ٱلْعَنكَبُوتِ ۖ لَوْ كَانُوا۟ يَعْلَمُونَ ۝ إِنَّ ٱللَّهَ يَعْلَمُ مَا يَدْعُونَ مِن دُونِهِۦ مِن شَىْءٍ ۚ وَهُوَ ٱلْعَزِيزُ ٱلْحَكِيمُ ۝ وَتِلْكَ ٱلْأَمْثَٰلُ نَضْرِبُهَا لِلنَّاسِ ۖ وَمَا يَعْقِلُهَآ إِلَّا ٱلْعَٰلِمُونَ ۝ خَلَقَ ٱللَّهُ ٱلسَّمَٰوَٰتِ وَٱلْأَرْضَ بِٱلْحَقِّ ۚ إِنَّ فِى ذَٰلِكَ لَءَايَةً لِّلْمُؤْمِنِينَ ۝

ᵃ It is shown here that one who sees a spider's web and learns a lesson about reality from it, is a learned person in the true sense. This clealy demonstrates who are the truly learned in the eyes of God. They are not those who have become expert in bookish discourses, but individuals who are capable of imbibing the sound advice given by God's signs scattered throughout His world, and whose minds are capable of magnifying small events into great lessons. When this very learning reaches the final stage of *ma'rifah* or 'knowledge with intense realization of God,' then it is called by its other name: faith or *iman*.

⁴⁵ Recite what has been revealed to you of the book,ᵃ and pray regularly. Surely prayer restrains one from indecency and evil and remembrance of God is greater. God has knowledge of all your actions.ᵇ

أَتْلُ مَا أُوحِيَ إِلَيْكَ مِنَ ٱلْكِتَٰبِ وَأَقِمِ ٱلصَّلَوٰةَ إِنَّ ٱلصَّلَوٰةَ تَنْهَىٰ عَنِ ٱلْفَحْشَاءِ وَٱلْمُنكَرِ وَلَذِكْرُ ٱللَّهِ أَكْبَرُ وَٱللَّهُ يَعْلَمُ مَا تَصْنَعُونَ ۝

ᵃ 'Recite what has been revealed to you of the book' here means 'the propagation of the revelation' i.e. reciting the Quran before people and making them aware of the will of God. This work of propagation is a task calling for great patience. To perform this work well, one has to be the well-wisher of one's opponents, one has to ignore their excesses and one has to look at one's addressees as one's invitees, even if they are rivals and opponents.

Just as prayer restrains a man from evil in everyday life, similarly, it saves a missionary from unmissionary-like behaviour. Only that man can become preacher of God's message whose heart is full of God's remembrance and who bows down before God in all sincerity.

ᵇ Prayer, or *salaat*, restrains the human being from committing evil. If a man bows down or prostrates himself (performs *ruku'* and *sajdah*) before God in all earnestness, he develops a sense of responsibility and humility. The character which forms in a man as a result of this makes him do that which he should do and desist from that which he should not do.

When a man attains perfect knowledge through intense realization of God, or *ma'rifah*, the result is that the thought of God permeates his very existence. This is what is meant by remembrance of God (*dhikr*). This spring of God's remembrance, or *dhikr*, wells up and flows through his body and soul. Reaching this height of spirituality, man begins uttering noble words in praise of God, and this is undoubtedly the highest form of prayer or worship.

46 Believers, argue only in the best way with the People of the Book, [but contend not at all] with such of them as are unjust. Say, 'We believe in what has been revealed to us, and what has been revealed to you; our God and your God are one; and to Him we submit.'[a]

47 Likewise We have sent down the Book to you. Those to whom We gave the scripture believe in it, and so do some of your own people. Only those who deny the truth reject Our revelations. 48 You were not able to read any book before this, nor did you write one down with your hand. If you had done so, the followers of falsehood would have had cause to doubt it. 49 But the Quran is a revelation that is clear to the hearts of those endowed with knowledge. Only the evil-doers refuse to acknowledge Our revelations.[b]

۞ وَلَا تُجَٰدِلُوٓا۟ أَهْلَ ٱلْكِتَٰبِ إِلَّا بِٱلَّتِى هِىَ أَحْسَنُ إِلَّا ٱلَّذِينَ ظَلَمُوا۟ مِنْهُمْ وَقُولُوٓا۟ ءَامَنَّا بِٱلَّذِىٓ أُنزِلَ إِلَيْنَا وَأُنزِلَ إِلَيْكُمْ وَإِلَٰهُنَا وَإِلَٰهُكُمْ وَٰحِدٌ وَنَحْنُ لَهُۥ مُسْلِمُونَ ۝ وَكَذَٰلِكَ أَنزَلْنَآ إِلَيْكَ ٱلْكِتَٰبَ فَٱلَّذِينَ ءَاتَيْنَٰهُمُ ٱلْكِتَٰبَ يُؤْمِنُونَ بِهِۦ وَمِنْ هَٰٓؤُلَآءِ مَن يُؤْمِنُ بِهِۦ وَمَا يَجْحَدُ بِـَٔايَٰتِنَآ إِلَّا ٱلْكَٰفِرُونَ ۝ وَمَا كُنتَ تَتْلُوا۟ مِن قَبْلِهِۦ مِن كِتَٰبٍ وَلَا تَخُطُّهُۥ بِيَمِينِكَ إِذًا لَّٱرْتَابَ ٱلْمُبْطِلُونَ ۝ بَلْ هُوَ ءَايَٰتٌۢ بَيِّنَٰتٌ فِى صُدُورِ ٱلَّذِينَ أُوتُوا۟ ٱلْعِلْمَ وَمَا يَجْحَدُ بِـَٔايَٰتِنَآ إِلَّا ٱلظَّٰلِمُونَ ۝

---

[a] Rather than become entangled in unnecessary discussions and bickering, it is best if the preacher (da'i) greets his antagonists formally and then avoids them. But, to those who are sincere and serious, he should try to explain and clarify the Truth. Furthermore, the preacher's words should be full of wisdom—a wisdom made manifest in the way he takes into account the mental make-up of the addressee. He should present his message in a way which appeals to the addressee, so that his mind is addressed. The message should consist of sound advice and should not be argumentative.

[b] There are two types of individuals—one who already possesses a knowledge of the Truth and the other who apparently does not. However, the second type also are acquainted with the Truth at the level of their inherent nature. The former are the bearers of the book, while the latter draw on the resources of their own nature.

If people are really sincere and serious, they recognize the Truth immediately. One group might recognize it as a Divine Book from heaven, while the other might recognize it as a Book of Nature. To each one, the Truth will manifest itself as a matter after his own heart. ►

⁵⁰ They say, 'Why has no sign been given to him by his Lord?' Say, 'The signs are in the hands of God. I am but a plain warner.' ⁵¹ Is it not sufficient for them that We have sent you down the Book to be recited to them? In this surely there is a blessing and an admonition for a people who believe. ⁵² Say, 'God is sufficient as a witness between you and me. He knows all that is in the heavens and the earth. Those who believe in falsehood and reject God will surely be the losers.'ᵃ

وَقَالُوا لَوْلَا أُنزِلَ عَلَيْهِ ءَايَتٌ مِّن رَّبِّهِۦ قُلْ إِنَّمَا ٱلْأَيَتُ عِندَ ٱللَّهِ وَإِنَّمَا أَنَا۠ نَذِيرٌ مُّبِينٌ ۞ أَوَلَمْ يَكْفِهِمْ أَنَّا أَنزَلْنَا عَلَيْكَ ٱلْكِتَبَ يُتْلَىٰ عَلَيْهِمْ إِنَّ فِى ذَٰلِكَ لَرَحْمَةً وَذِكْرَىٰ لِقَوْمٍ يُؤْمِنُونَ ۞ قُلْ كَفَىٰ بِٱللَّهِ بَيْنِى وَبَيْنَكُمْ شَهِيدًا يَعْلَمُ مَا فِى ٱلسَّمَوَٰتِ وَٱلْأَرْضِ وَٱلَّذِينَ ءَامَنُوا بِٱلْبَطِلِ وَكَفَرُوا بِٱللَّهِ أُوْلَٰئِكَ هُمُ ٱلْخَسِرُونَ ۞

But, people often become enmeshed in a variety of psychological problems, due to which they adopt a rigid attitude of denial. They go on denying the Truth, even though there may be many factors in its support, and even if many arguments are advanced in its favour.

ᵃ People used to raise the objection that the Prophet Muhammad had not been given signs of God such as had been given to others, such as Moses, God's answer to them was that signs or miracles were matters pertaining to Him and not to the prophets. The real support of the Prophet's call of Truth are the sound arguments. Owing to certain considerations, God sometimes does give His signs or miracles to a prophet, but sometimes He does not.

Faith is a conscious experience. Faith finds its place in a man's heart once he is convinced by arguments in its favour. One who accepts something after testing it in the light of arguments is a protagonist of Truth, and one who indulges in irrelevant discussions is a worshipper of falsehood.

⁵³ They ask you to hasten the punishment. Had there not been an appointed time for it, the punishment would already have come to them. Indeed it will come down upon them suddenly and catch them unawares. ⁵⁴ They ask you to hasten the punishment, but surely, Hell is [already] encompassing those who deny the truth. ⁵⁵ On the Day the punishment envelops them from above them and from underneath their feet, they will be told, 'Taste [the punishment] for what you used to do!' ^a

وَيَسْتَعْجِلُونَكَ بِٱلْعَذَابِ وَلَوْلَآ أَجَلٌ مُّسَمًّى لَّجَآءَهُمُ ٱلْعَذَابُ وَلَيَأْتِيَنَّهُم بَغْتَةً وَهُمْ لَا يَشْعُرُونَ ۝ يَسْتَعْجِلُونَكَ بِٱلْعَذَابِ وَإِنَّ جَهَنَّمَ لَمُحِيطَةٌۢ بِٱلْكَفِرِينَ ۝ يَوْمَ يَغْشَىٰهُمُ ٱلْعَذَابُ مِن فَوْقِهِمْ وَمِن تَحْتِ أَرْجُلِهِمْ وَيَقُولُ ذُوقُواْ مَا كُنتُمْ تَعْمَلُونَ ۝

---

^a Man's deeds make his Paradise and his deeds make his Hell too. Were it possible to view the consequences of the deeds of one who had adopted the way of denial and insolence, it would be seen that his apparently great deeds actually signalled the punishment which he merited and which lay in wait for him. Death is but to come and dispatch him to the world he has built for himself.

Most of a man's arrogance is nothing more than the result of his ignorance of the reality pertaining to his own existence. If this ignorance were to be replaced by knowledge, he would become a completely different man.

⁵⁶ My servants who believe, My earth is vast, so worship Me alone. ⁵⁷ Every soul shall taste death and then to Us you shall return. ⁵⁸ We shall lodge forever those who believe and do good works in the mansions of Paradise beside which rivers flow. How excellent is the reward of those who labour, ⁵⁹ and who are steadfast and put their trust in their Lord. ⁶⁰ How many creatures cannot fend for themselves! God provides for them and for you. He is the All Hearing, the All Knowing.^a

يَـٰعِبَادِىَ ٱلَّذِينَ ءَامَنُوٓاْ إِنَّ أَرْضِى وَٰسِعَةٌ فَإِيَّـٰىَ فَٱعْبُدُونِ ۝ كُلُّ نَفْسٍ ذَآئِقَةُ ٱلْمَوْتِ ثُمَّ إِلَيْنَا تُرْجَعُونَ ۝ وَٱلَّذِينَ ءَامَنُواْ وَعَمِلُواْ ٱلصَّـٰلِحَـٰتِ لَنُبَوِّئَنَّهُم مِّنَ ٱلْجَنَّةِ غُرَفًا تَجْرِى مِن تَحْتِهَا ٱلْأَنْهَـٰرُ خَـٰلِدِينَ فِيهَا نِعْمَ أَجْرُ ٱلْعَـٰمِلِينَ ۝ ٱلَّذِينَ صَبَرُواْ وَعَلَىٰ رَبِّهِمْ يَتَوَكَّلُونَ ۝ وَكَأَيِّن مِّن دَآبَّةٍ لَّا تَحْمِلُ رِزْقَهَا ٱللَّهُ يَرْزُقُهَا وَإِيَّاكُمْ وَهُوَ ٱلسَّمِيعُ ٱلْعَلِيمُ ۝

---

^a Sometimes a change is necessary in the mode of performing a task. This may require a change in the sphere of influence, in the way that the Hudaybiyah Pact shifted the scene of action from the battlefield to the field of missionary work. But more often, it requires a major step, like migration, for example, the migration of the Prophet from Makkah to Madinah.

In these verses the faithful living in Makkah were told that if the people of Makkah were harassing them, they should leave Makkah, migrate to some other place, and carry on God's worship there. This shows that the exercise of patience and trust means being steadfast in prayer and not persisting in clashing with enemies. Had it been God's will that they should engage in hostilities under any circumstances, then the instructions would have been to continue fighting with their opponents and not in any event to move away.

⁶¹ If you ask them who it is that has created the heavens and the earth and subjugated the sun and the moon, they will say, 'God.' How then are they turned away? ⁶² God gives abundantly to whom He will and sparingly to whom He pleases. God has full knowledge of all things. ⁶³ And if you ask them who it is that sends down water from the sky and revives the earth with it after its death, they will surely answer, 'God.' Then praise be to God. But most of them do not understand.ᵃ

وَلَئِن سَأَلْتَهُم مَّنْ خَلَقَ ٱلسَّمَٰوَٰتِ وَٱلْأَرْضَ وَسَخَّرَ ٱلشَّمْسَ وَٱلْقَمَرَ لَيَقُولُنَّ ٱللَّهُ ۖ فَأَنَّىٰ يُؤْفَكُونَ ۝ ٱللَّهُ يَبْسُطُ ٱلرِّزْقَ لِمَن يَشَآءُ مِنْ عِبَادِهِۦ وَيَقْدِرُ لَهُۥٓ ۚ إِنَّ ٱللَّهَ بِكُلِّ شَىْءٍ عَلِيمٌ ۝ وَلَئِن سَأَلْتَهُم مَّن نَّزَّلَ مِنَ ٱلسَّمَآءِ مَآءً فَأَحْيَا بِهِ ٱلْأَرْضَ مِنۢ بَعْدِ مَوْتِهَا لَيَقُولُنَّ ٱللَّهُ ۚ قُلِ ٱلْحَمْدُ لِلَّهِ ۚ بَلْ أَكْثَرُهُمْ لَا يَعْقِلُونَ ۝

ᵃ Creating the earth and the sky was such a major event that only Almighty God could perform it. The movement of the sun and moon, the falling of rain and the sprouting of greenery from the soil of the earth are phenomena too great to have been brought into existence by anybody other than God.

Those who indulge in polytheism do not themselves believe that they have brought these great wonders into existence. In spite of this, many people worship beings others than God in the hope that they will increase their worldly blessings. However, when all powers are vested in God, who else but He can exert influence on the distribution of the daily sustenance?

⁶⁴ The life of this world is nothing but sport and a diversion. It is the life of the Hereafter which is the only true life, if they but knew it. ⁶⁵ When they board a vessel, they call on God, sincere in their faith for Him alone; but when He brings them safe to land, they begin to ascribe partners to Him. ⁶⁶ And thus they may show utter ingratitude for Our favours; let them enjoy themselves for a time. But they will soon come to know.ᵃ

وَمَا هَٰذِهِ ٱلْحَيَوٰةُ ٱلدُّنْيَآ إِلَّا لَهْوٌ وَلَعِبٌ وَإِنَّ ٱلدَّارَ ٱلْآخِرَةَ لَهِىَ ٱلْحَيَوَانُ لَوْ كَانُوا۟ يَعْلَمُونَ ۝ فَإِذَا رَكِبُوا۟ فِى ٱلْفُلْكِ دَعَوُا۟ ٱللَّهَ مُخْلِصِينَ لَهُ ٱلدِّينَ فَلَمَّا نَجَّىٰهُمْ إِلَى ٱلْبَرِّ إِذَا هُمْ يُشْرِكُونَ ۝ لِيَكْفُرُوا۟ بِمَآ ءَاتَيْنَٰهُمْ وَلِيَتَمَتَّعُوا۟ فَسَوْفَ يَعْلَمُونَ ۝

ᵃ The real reason for a man going astray is that he is so completely engrossed in the glamour and problems of the world that he cannot rise above them and think independently.

In order to arrive at the Truth, one has to raise oneself above external and superficial appearances. Most of the people cannot do so, and that is why they do not find the Truth.

In the world, time and again, man has experiences which remind him of his helplessness. At that time all his conditioning fall away from him and the real and natural man in him is awakened. But as soon as conditions return again to normal, he becomes as neglectful and arrogant as before. Among these crucial experiences is that of a voyage, which is mentioned in the verse.

Man should know that the chance to exercise freedom is given to him during this life for only a few days. After death, he will have to face a completely new world with a completely different set of problems.

⁶⁷ Have they not seen how We have granted them a safe sanctuary, though all around them people are snatched away? Would they still believe in falsehood, and deny the favour of God? ⁶⁸ Who does greater wrong than he who invents a lie about God or rejects the truth when it comes to him? Is Hell not the home for those who deny the truth. ⁶⁹ We will surely guide in Our ways those who strive hard for Our cause, God is surely with the righteous.^a

أَوَلَمْ يَرَوْا أَنَّا جَعَلْنَا حَرَمًا ءَامِنًا وَيُتَخَطَّفُ ٱلنَّاسُ مِنْ حَوْلِهِمْ أَفَبِٱلْبَطِلِ يُؤْمِنُونَ وَبِنِعْمَةِ ٱللَّهِ يَكْفُرُونَ ۝ وَمَنْ أَظْلَمُ مِمَّنِ ٱفْتَرَىٰ عَلَى ٱللَّهِ كَذِبًا أَوْ كَذَّبَ بِٱلْحَقِّ لَمَّا جَاءَهُۥ ۚ أَلَيْسَ فِي جَهَنَّمَ مَثْوًى لِّلْكَفِرِينَ ۝ وَٱلَّذِينَ جَهَدُوا فِينَا لَنَهْدِيَنَّهُمْ سُبُلَنَا وَإِنَّ ٱللَّهَ لَمَعَ ٱلْمُحْسِنِينَ ۝

---

^a The Sacred House of Makkah, i.e. the Kabah, is a wonderful gift of Almighty God. God fills the hearts of people with awe whenever they see it, so that even the overbearing and arrogant drop their evil ways on reaching there. This sanctity of the Kabah was one of the signs of God's power. It called for people to open their hearts to God. But what the worshippers of falsehood did was to ascribe God's attributes to entities other than God and wrongly divert people's instinct of devotion towards them. But even worse, when the Prophet Muhammad advised them to renounce the imaginary gods and bow down before the one real God, they became hostile to him.

In such an atmosphere the loss suffered by the believers in the world is more than made up for by the rewards bestowed on them by God. Distancing themselves from material comforts, they come closer to the state of spiritual experience. The outward glitter of things is no longer in view, but the inner realities of things are laid bare to them.

30. THE ROMANS

In the name of God,
the Most Gracious, the Most Merciful

[1] *Alif Lam Mim*

[2] The Romans have been defeated [3] in a nearby land. They will reverse their defeat with a victory [4] within a few years: [for] with God rests all power of decision, first and last. On that day the believers too will have cause to rejoice, [5] with the help of God. He helps whom He pleases: He is the Mighty, and the Merciful.[a]

---

[a] At the time of the advent of Islam, there were two very great empires in the world —the Christian Roman Empire and the Zoroastrian Persian Empire. There were constant clashes between these two. In the year 603 A.D., Iran (Persia) attacked the Roman Empire, taking advantage of certain weaknesses in the latter. The Romans suffered defeat after defeat, so much so that by the year 616 A.D., a large part of the Roman Empire, including Jerusalem, had been captured by the Iranians. The Prophet received the prophethood in the year 610 A.D. and he started upon the task of explaining the Oneness of God in Makkah. This was the period of the struggle between monotheism and polytheism in that city. The polytheists of Makkah, taking their cue from the events on the border, told the Muslims that their polytheist brothers, the fire-worshipping Zoroastrians, had defeated the possessors of the Book and brothers of the Muslims (namely, the Christians) and that in the same manner they (the polytheists of Makkah) would finally overwhelm the Muslims. At that time, completely against the prevailing trend, the Quran predicted that within ten years, the Romans would regain supremacy over the Iranians. Roman historians say that immediately thereafter the vanquished King of the Romans, Heraclius, started undergoing a mysterious change, so much so that in the year 623 A.D., he led a retaliatory attack on Iran. In the year 624 A.D., he achieved a decisive victory over Iran. By the year 627 A.D., he had recovered all his occupied territories from the Iranians. Thus it was proved that the Quran was a revelation from God, as nobody else except God could have made such statements about the future so accurately. Moreover, these events indicate that victory or defeat are directly in the hands of God. It is according to His decision who gains and who loses power. The downfall of a nation and the rise of another nation, to all appearances seem to be ordinary, normal, worldly events, but appearances have an inner aspect to it. ▶

⁶ [This is] God's promise. Never does God fail to fulfil His promise—but most people do not know this; ⁷ they only know the outward appearance of the life of this world, and they are neglectful of the Hereafter.

⁸ Do they not ponder about their own selves? God has created the heavens and the earth and all that is between them for a purpose and for an appointed time? Yet many deny they will ever meet with their Lord. ⁹ Have they not travelled through the land and seen what end their predecessors met? They were mightier than them: they cultivated the earth more and built more upon it than these have ever built. Their own messengers also came to them with clear signs: God did not wrong them; they wronged themselves. ¹⁰ Then the end of those who committed evil was evil, for they belied the signs of God, and they derided them.ᵃ

وَعْدَ ٱللَّهِ لَا يُخْلِفُ ٱللَّهُ وَعْدَهُ وَلَـٰكِنَّ أَكْثَرَ ٱلنَّاسِ لَا يَعْلَمُونَ ۝ يَعْلَمُونَ ظَـٰهِرًا مِّنَ ٱلْحَيَوٰةِ ٱلدُّنْيَا وَهُمْ عَنِ ٱلْآخِرَةِ هُمْ غَـٰفِلُونَ ۝ أَوَلَمْ يَتَفَكَّرُوا۟ فِىٓ أَنفُسِهِم مَّا خَلَقَ ٱللَّهُ ٱلسَّمَـٰوَٰتِ وَٱلْأَرْضَ وَمَا بَيْنَهُمَآ إِلَّا بِٱلْحَقِّ وَأَجَلٍ مُّسَمًّى وَإِنَّ كَثِيرًا مِّنَ ٱلنَّاسِ بِلِقَآئِ رَبِّهِمْ لَكَـٰفِرُونَ ۝ أَوَلَمْ يَسِيرُوا۟ فِى ٱلْأَرْضِ فَيَنظُرُوا۟ كَيْفَ كَانَ عَـٰقِبَةُ ٱلَّذِينَ مِن قَبْلِهِمْ كَانُوٓا۟ أَشَدَّ مِنْهُمْ قُوَّةً وَأَثَارُوا۟ ٱلْأَرْضَ وَعَمَرُوهَآ أَكْثَرَ مِمَّا عَمَرُوهَا وَجَآءَتْهُمْ رُسُلُهُم بِٱلْبَيِّنَـٰتِ فَمَا كَانَ ٱللَّهُ لِيَظْلِمَهُمْ وَلَـٰكِن كَانُوٓا۟ أَنفُسَهُمْ يَظْلِمُونَ ۝ ثُمَّ كَانَ عَـٰقِبَةَ ٱلَّذِينَ أَسَـٰٓـُٔوا۟ ٱلسُّوٓأَىٰٓ أَن كَذَّبُوا۟ بِـَٔايَـٰتِ ٱللَّهِ وَكَانُوا۟ بِهَا يَسْتَهْزِءُونَ ۝

Every event is caused by a number of angels of God, though they are not visible to ordinary human eyes. Similarly, there is an invisible aspect of the present, outward world and it is the world of the Hereafter.

ᵃ Constant remembrance (through prayer, etc.) and deep contemplation lead a man towards finding God. It is by profound thought that a man finds God. In the present world, God has scattered His signs everywhere—in the human environment, in the surrounding universe and also in the teachings of the Prophet. Those who give serious consideration to these signs of God will find God.

Argument in favour of God is God's representative on earth. If rightful argument is presented to a man and he ignores it, it is as if he has ignored God Himself. For such people there is nothing before God except eternal deprivation.

¹¹ God originates the creation, and shall repeat it, then to Him you shall be returned. ¹² On the Day the Hour arrives, the guilty will be struck dumb with despair, ¹³ and they will have no intercessors among those partners they ascribed to God. They will deny these partners. ¹⁴ When the Last Hour dawns—on that Day they will be sorted out: ¹⁵ those who believed and did good deeds will rejoice in a Garden, ¹⁶ and as for those who denied the truth and belied Our signs and the meeting in the Hereafter—they shall be brought to the torment. ¹⁷ So glorify God in the evening and in the morning—¹⁸ and praise be to Him in the heavens and on the earth—and glorify Him in the late afternoon, and at midday.ᵃ

اللَّهُ يَبْدَؤُاْ ٱلْخَلْقَ ثُمَّ يُعِيدُهُۥ ثُمَّ إِلَيْهِ تُرْجَعُونَ ۝ وَيَوْمَ تَقُومُ ٱلسَّاعَةُ يُبْلِسُ ٱلْمُجْرِمُونَ ۝ وَلَمْ يَكُن لَّهُم مِّن شُرَكَآئِهِمْ شُفَعَٰٓؤُاْ وَكَانُواْ بِشُرَكَآئِهِمْ كَٰفِرِينَ ۝ وَيَوْمَ تَقُومُ ٱلسَّاعَةُ يَوْمَئِذٍ يَتَفَرَّقُونَ ۝ فَأَمَّا ٱلَّذِينَ ءَامَنُواْ وَعَمِلُواْ ٱلصَّٰلِحَٰتِ فَهُمْ فِى رَوْضَةٍ يُحْبَرُونَ ۝ وَأَمَّا ٱلَّذِينَ كَفَرُواْ وَكَذَّبُواْ بِـَٔايَٰتِنَا وَلِقَآئِ ٱلْأَخِرَةِ فَأُوْلَٰٓئِكَ فِى ٱلْعَذَابِ مُحْضَرُونَ ۝ فَسُبْحَٰنَ ٱللَّهِ حِينَ تُمْسُونَ وَحِينَ تُصْبِحُونَ ۝ وَلَهُ ٱلْحَمْدُ فِى ٱلسَّمَٰوَٰتِ وَٱلْأَرْضِ وَعَشِيًّا وَحِينَ تُظْهِرُونَ ۝

ᵃ The existence of a perfect and complete world is a definite proof of the First Creation. If the first creation was possible, why should the second creation not be possible? If one accepts the present world, but does not accept the Hereafter, it amounts to denying a natural corollary of a fact which one has oneself accepted as such.

'The guilty' refers to the influential people who led the campaign against the Truth, and who provided arguments in support of the denial of Truth. When the Doomsday explosion dislocates the system of the world, the guilty ones will suddenly realize that the supports of which they had been proud were without foundation. The words which, according to them, supplied uncontradictable arguments in favour of their stand, will all prove false. When they see conditions which are quite contrary to their expectations and which shatter their illusions, they will be dumbfounded.

On the Day of Judgement, human beings will be divided into two groups—one consisting of those who glorify God and offer praises to Him, and the other consisting of those who do quite the reverse. The people of the first group are those who realize God to such a degree that He becomes the sole topic of their conversation. A definite manifestation of this glorification of God and offering praises is the prayers offered five times a day. In this verse, the offering of praises 'in the morning' means the *fajr*. ▶

¹⁹ He brings forth the living from the dead and the dead from the living. He gives life to the earth after its death, and you shall be raised to life in the same way. ²⁰ One of His signs is that He created you from dust and, behold, you became human beings and multiplied yourselves throughout the earth. ²¹ Another of His signs is that He created for you from among yourselves spouses, so that you might find repose in them, and He created between you affection and kindness. Truly there are signs in this for people who reflect.ᵃ

نُخۡرِجُ ٱلۡحَيَّ مِنَ ٱلۡمَيِّتِ وَنُخۡرِجُ ٱلۡمَيِّتَ مِنَ ٱلۡحَيِّ وَنُحۡىِ ٱلۡأَرۡضَ بَعۡدَ مَوۡتِهَاۚ وَكَذَٰلِكَ تُخۡرَجُونَ ۝ وَمِنۡ ءَايَٰتِهِۦٓ أَنۡ خَلَقَكُم مِّن تُرَابٍ ثُمَّ إِذَآ أَنتُم بَشَرٌ تَنتَشِرُونَ ۝ وَمِنۡ ءَايَٰتِهِۦٓ أَنۡ خَلَقَ لَكُم مِّنۡ أَنفُسِكُمۡ أَزۡوَٰجًا لِّتَسۡكُنُوٓاْ إِلَيۡهَا وَجَعَلَ بَيۡنَكُم مَّوَدَّةً وَرَحۡمَةًۚ إِنَّ فِى ذَٰلِكَ لَأٓيَٰتٍ لِّقَوۡمٍ يَتَفَكَّرُونَ ۝

The prayers of *maghrib*, and *'isha* are included in the words 'in the evening'. Prayer at midday is called *zuhr*, while that of in the late afternoon is called *'asr*.

ᵃ A wonderful miracle of the present world is growth and development. Here, one finds an inert, non-growing material turning into a material which is capable of growing and increasing. Here, lifeless earth, in other words, earth's elements, undergo a change and take the shape of moving and talking human beings. On account of this, human civilization has survived for thousands of years now. This change, and that too a well-organized, proportionate and harmonious change, would not be at all possible unless it were the work of an all-powerful God.

The fact is that if a man gives deep consideration to God's creations, he will feel that the presence of God is reflected in everything.

²² Another of His signs is that He created the heavens and earth, and the diversity of your languages and colours. There truly are signs in this for those who know. ²³ Among His signs are your sleep, at night or in daytime, and your seeking His bounty. There truly are signs in this for people who hear. ²⁴ Among His signs is this: He shows you the lightning, giving rise to [both] fear and hope, and sends down water from the sky, giving life thereby to the earth after it had been lifeless: in this, behold, there are signs indeed for people who use their reason! [a]

وَمِنْ ءَايَـٰتِهِۦ خَلْقُ ٱلسَّمَـٰوَٰتِ
وَٱلْأَرْضِ وَٱخْتِلَـٰفُ أَلْسِنَتِكُمْ
وَأَلْوَٰنِكُمْ إِنَّ فِى ذَٰلِكَ لَـَٔايَـٰتٍ لِّلْعَـٰلِمِينَ
﴿٢٢﴾ وَمِنْ ءَايَـٰتِهِۦ مَنَامُكُم بِٱلَّيْلِ
وَٱلنَّهَارِ وَٱبْتِغَاؤُكُم مِّن فَضْلِهِۦٓ إِنَّ
فِى ذَٰلِكَ لَـَٔايَـٰتٍ لِّقَوْمٍ يَسْمَعُونَ
﴿٢٣﴾ وَمِنْ ءَايَـٰتِهِۦ يُرِيكُمُ ٱلْبَرْقَ
خَوْفًا وَطَمَعًا وَيُنَزِّلُ مِنَ ٱلسَّمَآءِ مَآءً
فَيُحْىِۦ بِهِ ٱلْأَرْضَ بَعْدَ مَوْتِهَآ
إِنَّ فِى ذَٰلِكَ لَـَٔايَـٰتٍ لِّقَوْمٍ
يَعْقِلُونَ ﴿٢٤﴾

---

[a] The Universe in all the elements of its existence is the sign of God. Its coming into existence from nothingness and the enormous variety found in it indicates His vast powers. The utmost meaningfulness in all things reflects His quality of mercy. The existence of destructive things like lightning acquaints us with how God takes punitive actions. The revival of greenery on earth after its being dry and barren demonstrates re-creation and resurrection.

All these are the signs of God. But these signs are only for those who lend their ears to the silent call of the Universe—for those who put their wisdom and their knowledge to the correct use.

²⁵ Another of His signs is this: the heavens and the earth stand firm by His command and afterwards when He calls you, behold, from the earth you will come forth. ²⁶ All those in the heavens and on the earth belong to Him. All are obedient to Him. ²⁷ He is the One who originates creation, then repeats it, and it is very easy for Him. His is the most exalted state in the heavens and on the earth; He is the Mighty, the Wise One.^a

وَمِنْ ءَايَـٰتِهِۦٓ أَن تَقُومَ ٱلسَّمَآءُ وَٱلْأَرْضُ بِأَمْرِهِۦ ثُمَّ إِذَا دَعَاكُمْ دَعْوَةً مِّنَ ٱلْأَرْضِ إِذَآ أَنتُمْ تَخْرُجُونَ ۞ وَلَهُۥ مَن فِى ٱلسَّمَـٰوَٰتِ وَٱلْأَرْضِ كُلٌّ لَّهُۥ قَـٰنِتُونَ ۞ وَهُوَ ٱلَّذِى يَبْدَؤُا۟ ٱلْخَلْقَ ثُمَّ يُعِيدُهُۥ وَهُوَ أَهْوَنُ عَلَيْهِ وَلَهُ ٱلْمَثَلُ ٱلْأَعْلَىٰ فِى ٱلسَّمَـٰوَٰتِ وَٱلْأَرْضِ وَهُوَ ٱلْعَزِيزُ ٱلْحَكِيمُ ۞

---

^a In the vastness of space, the earth, the sun, the planets and stars—all wonderfully rare phenomena—proclaim by their very existence that there exists a Maintainer at whose behest, they continue to function. If this Being were taken away from the cosmos even for a moment, the whole system would be scattered helter-skelter. In this world, even an ordinary aeroplane will be destroyed if the pilot loses control. Then, how can the huge system of the Universe be run without the control of a Controller?

Given the Great Power exhibited in the Universe by its Creator, it appears an easy task for Him to re-create or resurrect man after his death. In the light of the feat of the first creation, which is being performed in the universe at every moment, to accept the possibility of the second creation is just like accepting a proven fact. In the universe, God's powers and His wisdom find expression at such a high level that attributing any remarkable feat to God on this basis is in no way a remote possibility.

²⁸ He sets forth for you an example taken from your own lives. Do you make your servants full partners with an equal share in the wealth We have bestowed upon you? Do you fear them as you fear each other? In this way We explain the signs to people who use their reason. ²⁹ And still those who are unjust follow their own desires without having any knowledge. Then who can guide those whom God has let go astray? There shall be none to help them.^a

ضَرَبَ لَكُم مَّثَلًا مِّنْ أَنفُسِكُمْ هَل لَّكُم مِّن مَّا مَلَكَتْ أَيْمَنُكُم مِّن شُرَكَاءَ فِى مَا رَزَقْنَكُمْ فَأَنتُمْ فِيهِ سَوَاءٌ تَخَافُونَهُمْ كَخِيفَتِكُمْ أَنفُسَكُمْ كَذَٰلِكَ نُفَصِّلُ ٱلْءَايَتِ لِقَوْمٍ يَعْقِلُونَ ۝ بَلِ ٱتَّبَعَ ٱلَّذِينَ ظَلَمُوٓا۟ أَهْوَآءَهُم بِغَيْرِ عِلْمٍ فَمَن يَهْدِى مَنْ أَضَلَّ ٱللَّهُ وَمَا لَهُم مِّن نَّصِرِينَ ۝

---

^a If there is common property, all those who share it have a right to it, and every partner has to think of the other partners. But, God's position is not of this kind. God alone is the Lord of the entire Universe. The relation between God and His creatures is the same as that between master and servant on a larger scale, and not that of sharers of a property. Nobody gives his servant a status equal to that of himself. Similarly there is no one in the entire universe who enjoys a status equal to that of God. Lordship is for God, while for all other creatures there is only subjection. Apart from this, any other equation propounded will be based only on supposition and not on any real ground.

³⁰ Devote yourself single-mindedly to the Religion. And follow the nature [constitution] as made by God, that nature in which He has created mankind. There is no altering the creation of God. That is the right religion. But most people do not realize it. ³¹ Turn to Him and fear Him, and be steadfast in prayer, and do not be one of those who associate partners with God, ³² those who split up their religion and became divided into sects; each one exulting in what they have.ᵃ

فَأَقِمْ وَجْهَكَ لِلدِّينِ حَنِيفًا ۚ فِطْرَتَ ٱللَّهِ ٱلَّتِى فَطَرَ ٱلنَّاسَ عَلَيْهَا ۚ لَا تَبْدِيلَ لِخَلْقِ ٱللَّهِ ۚ ذَٰلِكَ ٱلدِّينُ ٱلْقَيِّمُ وَلَٰكِنَّ أَكْثَرَ ٱلنَّاسِ لَا يَعْلَمُونَ ۝ مُنِيبِينَ إِلَيْهِ وَٱتَّقُوهُ وَأَقِيمُواْ ٱلصَّلَوٰةَ وَلَا تَكُونُواْ مِنَ ٱلْمُشْرِكِينَ ۝ مِنَ ٱلَّذِينَ فَرَّقُواْ دِينَهُمْ وَكَانُواْ شِيَعًا ۖ كُلُّ حِزْبٍ بِمَا لَدَيْهِمْ فَرِحُونَ ۝

ᵃ The true religion is one, and it has been revealed in its perfect form to every prophet. That religion is turning towards God, fear of God, worship of God and giving one's attention to God with all one's heart and soul. This is the religion of nature and it eternally pervades the inner soul of man. All prophets preached this one religion, but their followers in latter generations split it into many religions.

This results from the additions made by later generations to the original teachings of Prophets. Hair-splitting innovations in beliefs, new interpretations of religion with the changing times—all these things have created many religions out of one. When these additions are made people start laying more stress on them than on the original religion, due to which different groups set themselves up in opposition to each other. One group emphasizes one set of additions, while another group empasizes another set. At last a stage is reached when the followers of a single religion become divided up into many religious factions.

³³ When an affliction befalls men, they cry out to their Lord, turning to Him in repentance; but then, when He has made them taste His mercy, a section of them associate partners with their Lord, ³⁴ and are ungrateful for what We have given them. So enjoy yourselves for a while, but soon you will come to know. ³⁵ Have We sent down to them any authority which speaks in favour of what they associate with Him?ᵃ

وَإِذَا مَسَّ ٱلنَّاسَ ضُرٌّ دَعَوْا رَبَّهُم مُّنِيبِينَ إِلَيْهِ ثُمَّ إِذَا أَذَاقَهُم مِّنْهُ رَحْمَةً إِذَا فَرِيقٌ مِّنْهُم بِرَبِّهِمْ يُشْرِكُونَ ۝ لِيَكْفُرُوا بِمَا ءَاتَيْنَٰهُمْ فَتَمَتَّعُوا فَسَوْفَ تَعْلَمُونَ ۝ أَمْ أَنزَلْنَا عَلَيْهِمْ سُلْطَٰنًا فَهُوَ يَتَكَلَّمُ بِمَا كَانُوا بِهِۦ يُشْرِكُونَ ۝

ᵃ Under ordinary circumstances man finds himself possessed of certain powers. Therefore, he assumes an air of arrogance. But, when critical conditions make him feel his helplessness, the veils are removed from his mind. At that time he is cut down to size, and realizing his helplessness, he starts calling upon God for help.

This is the psychological proof of the Oneness of God. In this way, the reality is mirrored in the personal experience of the individual. But man is so foolish that, as soon as the circumstances become favourable, he reverts to his neglectfulness and arrogance.

³⁶ When We give mankind a taste of Our blessing, they rejoice therein: but if they encounter tribulation because of their own actions—they fall into despair. ³⁷ Do they not see that God gives abundantly to whoever He pleases, and sparingly to whoever He pleases? In that truly there are signs for those who believe. ³⁸ So give the near relative, the needy, and the wayfarer their due—that is best for those who seek God's pleasure: such men are the ones who will surely prosper. ³⁹ Whatever you lend out in usury to gain in value through other people's wealth will not increase in God's eyes, but whatever you give in alms in your desire for God's pleasure will be multiplied.^a

وَإِذَآ أَذَقْنَا ٱلنَّاسَ رَحْمَةً فَرِحُوا۟ بِهَا ۖ وَإِن تُصِبْهُمْ سَيِّئَةٌۢ بِمَا قَدَّمَتْ أَيْدِيهِمْ إِذَا هُمْ يَقْنَطُونَ ۝ أَوَلَمْ يَرَوْا۟ أَنَّ ٱللَّهَ يَبْسُطُ ٱلرِّزْقَ لِمَن يَشَآءُ وَيَقْدِرُ ۚ إِنَّ فِى ذَٰلِكَ لَءَايَٰتٍ لِّقَوْمٍ يُؤْمِنُونَ ۝ فَـَٔاتِ ذَا ٱلْقُرْبَىٰ حَقَّهُۥ وَٱلْمِسْكِينَ وَٱبْنَ ٱلسَّبِيلِ ۚ ذَٰلِكَ خَيْرٌ لِّلَّذِينَ يُرِيدُونَ وَجْهَ ٱللَّهِ ۖ وَأُو۟لَٰٓئِكَ هُمُ ٱلْمُفْلِحُونَ ۝ وَمَآ ءَاتَيْتُم مِّن رِّبًا لِّيَرْبُوَا۟ فِىٓ أَمْوَٰلِ ٱلنَّاسِ فَلَا يَرْبُوا۟ عِندَ ٱللَّهِ ۖ وَمَآ ءَاتَيْتُم مِّن زَكَوٰةٍ تُرِيدُونَ وَجْهَ ٱللَّهِ فَأُو۟لَٰٓئِكَ هُمُ ٱلْمُضْعِفُونَ ۝

---

^a A believer considers that both difficulties and ease come from God. Therefore, he turns towards God in good times and in bad. When in comfortable circumstances, he thanks God, and in adverse circumstances, he exercises patience. As opposed to this, one who denies the truth solely relies upon himself. So, when in easy circumstances, he is boastful. When his energies fail him, he is desperate, because he feels that he has reached the final limit. This is nature's indication that the former type of mentality is the truly virtuous one, while the latter is improper and unworthy.

One sign of a believer is that he spends his wealth for the pleasure of God. So, he shares his wealth with other needy persons who may or may not be his relatives. He spends his wealth to reap the benefits of the Hereafter and not to earn profits in this world like a usurer.

A man's creation, his being provided with the necessities of life day and night, his meeting death—all these events are so great that a universal power is required to bring them about. And no Being except the Creator of the Universe possesses such Universal powers. The fact is that the principle of the Oneness of God (monotheism) is its own proof and polytheism is its own contradiction.

⁴⁰ God is He who created you, then provides for you, then will cause you to die and then bring you back to life. Can any of your 'partners' do any one of these things? Glory be to Him and exalted be He above anything they associate with Him!ᵃ ⁴¹ Corruption has appeared on land and sea because of the evil which men's hands have done:ᵇ and so He will make them taste the fruit of some of their doings, so that they may turn back from evil. ⁴² Say, 'Journey through the land, and see how those before you met their end—most of them, ascribed partners with God.'

اللَّهُ ٱلَّذِى خَلَقَكُمْ ثُمَّ رَزَقَكُمْ ثُمَّ يُمِيتُكُمْ ثُمَّ يُحْيِيكُمْ هَلْ مِن شُرَكَآئِكُم مَّن يَفْعَلُ مِن ذَٰلِكُم مِّن شَىْءٍ سُبْحَٰنَهُۥ وَتَعَٰلَىٰ عَمَّا يُشْرِكُونَ ۝ ظَهَرَ ٱلْفَسَادُ فِى ٱلْبَرِّ وَٱلْبَحْرِ بِمَا كَسَبَتْ أَيْدِى ٱلنَّاسِ لِيُذِيقَهُم بَعْضَ ٱلَّذِى عَمِلُوا۟ لَعَلَّهُمْ يَرْجِعُونَ ۝ قُلْ سِيرُوا۟ فِى ٱلْأَرْضِ فَٱنظُرُوا۟ كَيْفَ كَانَ عَٰقِبَةُ ٱلَّذِينَ مِن قَبْلُ كَانَ أَكْثَرُهُم مُّشْرِكِينَ ۝

ᵃ If human beings adopt the one God as their object of worship, then everyone's centre of attention is one. This creates an atmosphere of unity among human beings. On the contrary, if numerous entities are made objects of worship, and people individually worship different things, their attention becomes divided. Because of this, differences amounting to enmity develop between individuals and nations. The land, the sea and the atmosphere become fraught with discord.

The end result of man's wrongdoing will appear after death. But the temporary result of man's wrongdoing is shown in this world for the time being, purely to serve as an admonishment and a warning.

ᵇ Man deviated from God's scheme and completely ignored His creation plan, in that he single-mindedly pursued worldly comforts. He very soon realized that modern civilization, which he had thought would fulfill his limitless hidden desires and ambitions, was only a source of utter destruction and chaos.

The present global warming is an apt illustration of this point: the modern culture of consumerism and greed for more and more has given an immense boost to industrialization, which has resulted in global climate change. Scientists now believe that the modern industrial age spells total catastrophe and that the world is careering head on to its doom. The damage is so severe and irreversible that, very soon, life on this earth will be impossible.

⁴³ [Prophet], set your face to the
right religion, before that Day comes
from God which cannot be averted.
On that Day, mankind will be parted
in two. ⁴⁴ Those who rejected the
truth will bear the burden of that
rejection, and those who did good
deeds will have made good provision
for themselves. ⁴⁵ For then He will
reward out of His bounty those who
believe and do good deeds; He does
not love those who reject the truth.ᵃ

فَأَقِمْ وَجْهَكَ لِلدِّينِ ٱلْقَيِّمِ مِن قَبْلِ أَن
يَأْتِيَ يَوْمٌ لَّا مَرَدَّ لَهُۥ مِنَ ٱللَّهِ يَوْمَئِذٍ
يَصَّدَّعُونَ ۝ مَن كَفَرَ فَعَلَيْهِ كُفْرُهُۥ
وَمَنْ عَمِلَ صَٰلِحًا فَلِأَنفُسِهِمْ
يَمْهَدُونَ ۝ لِيَجْزِىَ ٱلَّذِينَ ءَامَنُوا۟
وَعَمِلُوا۟ ٱلصَّٰلِحَٰتِ مِن فَضْلِهِۦٓ إِنَّهُۥ
لَا يُحِبُّ ٱلْكَٰفِرِينَ ۝

ᵃ In the present world there is a mixture of good and bad people. In the Hereafter
these two types of people will be separated. On that day, God's reward will be
bestowed upon those who lived in this world entirely as men of God, and those
whose interests were linked to any beings other than God will be eternally deprived
of God's blessings.

⁴⁶ Among His signs is this: He sends out the winds bearing good news so that He may make you taste His mercy, and ships sail at His command, so that you may seek His bounty, and be grateful. ⁴⁷ Surely, We sent messengers before you to their own people, and they brought them clear signs. Then We took vengeance on the guilty. It was certainly Our duty to help the believers.ᵃ

وَمِنْ ءَايَـٰتِهِۦٓ أَن يُرْسِلَ ٱلرِّيَاحَ مُبَشِّرَٰتٍ وَلِيُذِيقَكُم مِّن رَّحْمَتِهِۦ وَلِتَجْرِىَ ٱلْفُلْكُ بِأَمْرِهِۦ وَلِتَبْتَغُوا۟ مِن فَضْلِهِۦ وَلَعَلَّكُمْ تَشْكُرُونَ ۝ وَلَقَدْ أَرْسَلْنَا مِن قَبْلِكَ رُسُلًا إِلَىٰ قَوْمِهِمْ فَجَآءُوهُم بِٱلْبَيِّنَـٰتِ فَٱنتَقَمْنَا مِنَ ٱلَّذِينَ أَجْرَمُوا۟ وَكَانَ حَقًّا عَلَيْنَا نَصْرُ ٱلْمُؤْمِنِينَ ۝

ᵃ The blowing of a cool breeze before the start of the rains announces the fact that the God of this world is the most Kind and Merciful. Sailing across the seas is very important for the promotion of civilization. But, this is possible only when the winds blow within certain limits. Similarly, in the present age, the possibility of air-travel is dependent upon the fact that God has arranged to maintain a layer of air on the surface of the earth and given human beings the knowledge of aerodynamics needed to design air worthy plans.

All these arrangements have been made with a view to ensuring that man lives in the world as a grateful subject of God. The prophets of God appeared in the world in order to draw the attention of the people to these facts. But, while some accepted them others rejected them. Then, God helped those who accepted them and destroyed the deniers. The same fate on a larger scale awaits these two categories of human beings in the life Hereafter.

⁴⁸ It is God who sends out the winds so that they raise the clouds. Then He spreads them in the sky as He wills and places them layer upon layer and you see the rain issuing forth from their midst. When He causes it to fall on whichever of His servants He pleases, behold! they rejoice; ⁴⁹ though before that—before it was sent down upon them—they were in despair. ⁵⁰ Look, therefore, at the signs of God's mercy; how He resurrects the earth after its death. Truly, the same God will resurrect the dead; for He has power over all things. ⁵¹ Yet if We send a wind and they see their harvest turn yellow, they will then begin to deny [Our favours]. ⁵² You [Prophet] cannot make the dead hear and you cannot make the deaf hear your call when they turn their backs and leave; ⁵³ just as you cannot lead the blind [of heart] out of their error, you cannot make anyone hear your call save those who are willing to believe in Our revelations, and thus surrender themselves to Us and are submissive to Our will.ᵃ

اللَّهُ الَّذِى يُرْسِلُ الرِّيَـٰحَ فَتُثِيرُ سَحَابًا فَيَبْسُطُهُ فِى السَّمَآءِ كَيْفَ يَشَآءُ وَيَجْعَلُهُ كِسَفًا فَتَرَى الْوَدْقَ يَخْرُجُ مِنْ خِلَـٰلِهِۦ فَإِذَآ أَصَابَ بِهِۦ مَن يَشَآءُ مِنْ عِبَادِهِۦٓ إِذَا هُمْ يَسْتَبْشِرُونَ ۞ وَإِن كَانُوا مِن قَبْلِ أَن يُنَزَّلَ عَلَيْهِم مِّن قَبْلِهِۦ لَمُبْلِسِينَ ۞ فَانظُرْ إِلَىٰٓ ءَاثَـٰرِ رَحْمَتِ اللَّهِ كَيْفَ يُحْىِ الْأَرْضَ بَعْدَ مَوْتِهَآ إِنَّ ذَٰلِكَ لَمُحْىِ الْمَوْتَىٰ وَهُوَ عَلَىٰ كُلِّ شَىْءٍ قَدِيرٌ ۞ وَلَئِنْ أَرْسَلْنَا رِيحًا فَرَأَوْهُ مُصْفَرًّا لَّظَلُّوا مِنۢ بَعْدِهِۦ يَكْفُرُونَ ۞ فَإِنَّكَ لَا تُسْمِعُ الْمَوْتَىٰ وَلَا تُسْمِعُ الصُّمَّ الدُّعَآءَ إِذَا وَلَّوْا مُدْبِرِينَ ۞ وَمَآ أَنتَ بِهَـٰدِ الْعُمْىِ عَن ضَلَـٰلَتِهِمْ إِن تُسْمِعُ إِلَّا مَن يُؤْمِنُ بِـَٔايَـٰتِنَا فَهُم مُّسْلِمُونَ ۞

ᵃ When a man treads the path of Truth, he has frequently to face great difficulties, as happened with the Prophet and his companions in the early days. But, in that case, there was no question of anybody being disappointed. God is so merciful that, when a field under cultivation needs water, He moves the universal system and waters it. Naturally, He will certainly help those who tread His path. However, this help will be forthcoming only according to God's plan. So, if there is some delay in the process, man should not be disappointed or disheartened.

The word of God is very clear and reasonable. But only those who study things in depth, who listen carefully, whose nature it is to accept things that address their mind, who adopt the path which they find to be right, will repose their faith in the word of God.

⁵⁴ God is the One who has created you in a state of weakness; then He has granted you strength following [your] weakness; later on He has given you infirmity and grey hairs in place of strength. He creates whatever He wishes; He is the All Knowing and All Powerful. ⁵⁵ On the Day the Last Hour arrives, the evil-doers will swear they have not even tarried for an hour—they have always been deluded—⁵⁶ but those endowed with knowledge and faith will say, 'Indeed, you did tarry, as God ordained, till the Day of Resurrection, and this is the Day of Resurrection: but you were not aware of it.' ⁵⁷ So on that Day their pleas shall be of no avail, nor will they be allowed to make amends.^a

۞ ٱللَّهُ ٱلَّذِى خَلَقَكُم مِّن ضَعْفٍ ثُمَّ جَعَلَ مِنۢ بَعْدِ ضَعْفٍ قُوَّةً ثُمَّ جَعَلَ مِنۢ بَعْدِ قُوَّةٍ ضَعْفًا وَشَيْبَةً ۚ يَخْلُقُ مَا يَشَآءُ ۖ وَهُوَ ٱلْعَلِيمُ ٱلْقَدِيرُ ۞ وَيَوْمَ تَقُومُ ٱلسَّاعَةُ يُقْسِمُ ٱلْمُجْرِمُونَ مَا لَبِثُوٓاْ غَيْرَ سَاعَةٍ ۚ كَذَٰلِكَ كَانُواْ يُؤْفَكُونَ ۞ وَقَالَ ٱلَّذِينَ أُوتُواْ ٱلْعِلْمَ وَٱلْإِيمَٰنَ لَقَدْ لَبِثْتُمْ فِى كِتَٰبِ ٱللَّهِ إِلَىٰ يَوْمِ ٱلْبَعْثِ ۖ فَهَٰذَا يَوْمُ ٱلْبَعْثِ وَلَٰكِنَّكُمْ كُنتُمْ لَا تَعْلَمُونَ ۞ فَيَوْمَئِذٍ لَّا يَنفَعُ ٱلَّذِينَ ظَلَمُواْ مَعْذِرَتُهُمْ وَلَا هُمْ يُسْتَعْتَبُونَ ۞

^a When a man is born, he is but a weak child. Then after experiencing the strength of youth, followed by middle age, he again faces the weakness of old age. This means that a man's strength is not his own. He receives it when it is given to him. It is in the power of the Giver to give when He likes and take away when He likes.

In the life of this world, man cares nothing for the Hereafter, because the Day of Judgement appears to be very far away. But, this is only due to his ignorance. When the Day of Judgement arrives, —the stage for the next world—he will feel as if he had lived in the previous world for only a moment.

⁵⁸ Truly, We have set forth for men in this Quran every kind of parable and indeed, if you bring them a sign, those who are bent on denying the truth are sure to say, 'You are only making false claims!' ⁵⁹ In this way God seals the hearts of those who do not [want to] know [the truth], ⁶⁰ so have patience [O Muhammad]! God's promise is true; let not those who will not be convinced make you discouraged.ᵃ

وَلَقَدْ ضَرَبْنَا لِلنَّاسِ فِى هَـٰذَا ٱلْقُرْءَانِ مِن كُلِّ مَثَلٍ وَلَئِن جِئْتَهُم بِـَٔايَةٍ لَّيَقُولَنَّ ٱلَّذِينَ كَفَرُوٓا۟ إِنْ أَنتُمْ إِلَّا مُبْطِلُونَ ۝ كَذَٰلِكَ يَطْبَعُ ٱللَّهُ عَلَىٰ قُلُوبِ ٱلَّذِينَ لَا يَعْلَمُونَ ۝ فَٱصْبِرْ إِنَّ وَعْدَ ٱللَّهِ حَقٌّ وَلَا يَسْتَخِفَّنَّكَ ٱلَّذِينَ لَا يُوقِنُونَ ۝

ᵃ The people of Makkah used to tell the Prophet, if he was really a prophet, he should perform a superhuman, supernatural miracle. But, this demand was not acceded to, because an exhibition of the paranormal was not expected to serve the real purpose. The real purpose of Islam was to ensure that people's course of action changed, and such a change can be initiated only by bringing about a change in ways of thinking and not by stunning people with supernatural feats.

The Quran, therefore, lays the utmost emphasis on reasoning. It wants to change the minds of the people on the strength of arguments. It wants to make people capable of seeing things in the proper perspective and of forming correct opinions. In fact, the real problem of man is that he falls short of right thinking. If right thinking is not engendered in man, even after seeing wonderful feats and miracles, he will utter the same foolish words in the same mindless manner as he did earlier.

One's heart being sealed means one's not being capable of understanding things due to ignorance and wrong thinking. If an individual lacks the ability to form correct opinions, he can neither see things in their proper perspective nor learn fitting lessons from them.

A subject of God who comes forward with the pure call for Truth always has to face a discouraging reaction from the people. The dayee talks exclusively of the Hereafter, while people's minds are engaged in solving worldly problems. For this reason, people look down upon him. They always try to defeat him in every way, so much so that an atmosphere is created in which the preacher's words appear to be lacking in weight.

Such circumstances place the dayee in a situation of trial along with his addressees. At that time it becomes necessary for him not to lose his conviction. If, under the pressure of circumstances, he loses his conviction, he will start saying such things by way of compromise as may be important in the eyes of the general public, but which in the eyes of God will be of negligible importance.

31. LUQMAN

In the name of God,
the Most Gracious, the Most Merciful

¹ *Alif Lam Mim*

² These are the verses of the Book of wisdom, ³ a guide and a mercy for those who do good, ⁴ for those who attend to their prayers and pay the *zakat* and who have firm faith in the Hereafter: ⁵ these are rightly guided by their Lord: and these are the ones who will prosper.ᵃ

الٓمٓ ۝ تِلْكَ ءَايَتُ ٱلْكِتَبِ ٱلْحَكِيمِ ۝ هُدًى وَرَحْمَةً لِّلْمُحْسِنِينَ ۝ ٱلَّذِينَ يُقِيمُونَ ٱلصَّلَوٰةَ وَيُؤْتُونَ ٱلزَّكَوٰةَ وَهُم بِٱلْءَاخِرَةِ هُمْ يُوقِنُونَ ۝ أُوْلَٰٓئِكَ عَلَىٰ هُدًى مِّن رَّبِّهِمْ ۖ وَأُوْلَٰٓئِكَ هُمُ ٱلْمُفْلِحُونَ ۝

ᵃ In this world, the criterion of the proper performance of a task (*ihsan*) is that it should be in accordance with the facts. From this point of view, one who carries out a task in this way is one who admits the reality (*muhsin*); his actions become a manifestation of his spirit of submission.

Those who have it in their nature to mould themselves according to the factual position, are those who, when the Truth presents itself to them, accept it without suffering from any psychological complications. They immediately start fulfilling its practical requirements—they become regular offerers of prayers (*salat*), which is symbolic of fulfilling God's will. They give prescribed alms (*zakat*), which amounts to honouring the rights of God's subjects in the economic sphere. They shun the worship of worldly achievements and begin to think fondly of the Hereafter, because they know that the place where the question of success or failure shall finally be decided is nowhere other than the Hereafter.

⁶ But among men there are some who spend their time in idle diversions only to lead people astray from the path of God, and without knowledge, hold it up to ridicule: for such there is a humiliating punishment in store. ⁷ Whenever Our messages are conveyed to such a person, he turns away in his arrogance, as though he had not heard them—as though his ears were sealed: give him, then, the tidings of grievous suffering [in the life to come]. ⁸ Surely, those who believe and do good works shall enter gardens of bliss, ⁹ wherein they will abide forever. That is God's true promise; He is the Mighty, the Wise One.ᵃ

وَمِنَ ٱلنَّاسِ مَن يَشْتَرِى لَهْوَ ٱلْحَدِيثِ لِيُضِلَّ عَن سَبِيلِ ٱللَّهِ بِغَيْرِ عِلْمٍ وَيَتَّخِذَهَا هُزُوًا أُوْلَٰٓئِكَ لَهُمْ عَذَابٌ مُّهِينٌ ۝ وَإِذَا تُتْلَىٰ عَلَيْهِ ءَايَٰتُنَا وَلَّىٰ مُسْتَكْبِرًا كَأَن لَّمْ يَسْمَعْهَا كَأَنَّ فِىٓ أُذُنَيْهِ وَقْرًا فَبَشِّرْهُ بِعَذَابٍ أَلِيمٍ ۝ إِنَّ ٱلَّذِينَ ءَامَنُوا۟ وَعَمِلُوا۟ ٱلصَّٰلِحَٰتِ لَهُمْ جَنَّٰتُ ٱلنَّعِيمِ ۝ خَٰلِدِينَ فِيهَا وَعْدَ ٱللَّهِ حَقًّا وَهُوَ ٱلْعَزِيزُ ٱلْحَكِيمُ ۝

ᵃ Utterances are of two types—one offering good advice and the other entertainment. The former make one realize one's responsibilities and urge a man to do good rather than commit any impropriety. However, in every age those who have taken an interest in words of advice have indeed been very few. It has always been in the nature of man to prefer being entertained. Books which give good advice, are plentiful but he is always the more frequent purchaser of books which divert his mind and which do not demand any serious action on his part.

The guilt of one who goes to the length of inducing others to indulge in purely entertaining (i.e. wasteful) pursuits is greater, because he has made himself the leader of dissipation, keeping people preoccupied with pointless activities and rendering them incapable of giving their attention to more serious affairs.

Conceit is the worst trait in a man. If Truth presents itself before a conceited individual, he will not accept it, because he thinks too highly of himself. He will contemptuously overlook it and press on regardlessly. Just the opposite is true of the believers. Their advice-loving nature compels them to accept the truth and to surrender their life to it completely.

¹⁰ He has created the skies without any support that you could see, and has placed firm mountains upon the earth, lest it sway with you, and has caused all manner of living creatures to multiply thereon. And We sent down water from the skies, and thus We made every kind of excellent plant grow there: ¹¹ this is God's creation. Show me then what those besides Him have created! The wrongdoers are in manifest error.ᵃ

خَلَقَ ٱلسَّمَٰوَٰتِ بِغَيْرِ عَمَدٍ تَرَوْنَهَا وَأَلْقَىٰ فِي ٱلْأَرْضِ رَوَٰسِيَ أَن تَمِيدَ بِكُمْ وَبَثَّ فِيهَا مِن كُلِّ دَآبَّةٍ وَأَنزَلْنَا مِنَ ٱلسَّمَآءِ مَآءً فَأَنۢبَتْنَا فِيهَا مِن كُلِّ زَوْجٍ كَرِيمٍ ۞ هَٰذَا خَلْقُ ٱللَّهِ فَأَرُونِي مَاذَا خَلَقَ ٱلَّذِينَ مِن دُونِهِۦ بَلِ ٱلظَّٰلِمُونَ فِي ضَلَٰلٍ مُّبِينٍ ۞

ᵃ The universe exists in infinite space. The continuous revolving of innumerable large stellar bodies in this universe is a great and awe-inspiring phenomena. Amidst these, exists an extremely exceptional sphere—the earth, upon which numerous factors and arrangements have made the human life possible. Be it the maintenance of balance on the earth by the high mountains, or the opulence of valuable resources like water, greenery, etc., everything is indicative of a perfect system of management.

Who then, except Almighty God can manage this huge system? As such, is it legitimate for man to worship things, other than God?

[12] We bestowed wisdom on Luqman, saying, 'Be grateful to God: he who is grateful, is grateful only for the good of his own soul. But if anyone is ungrateful, then surely God is self-sufficient and praiseworthy.' [13] Luqman said to his son, counselling him, 'My son, do not associate anything with God. Associating others with Him is a terrible wrong.'[a]

وَلَقَدْ ءَاتَيْنَا لُقْمَـٰنَ ٱلْحِكْمَةَ أَنِ ٱشْكُرْ لِلَّهِ وَمَن يَشْكُرْ فَإِنَّمَا يَشْكُرُ لِنَفْسِهِۦ وَمَن كَفَرَ فَإِنَّ ٱللَّهَ غَنِىٌّ حَمِيدٌ ۝ وَإِذْ قَالَ لُقْمَـٰنُ لِٱبْنِهِۦ وَهُوَ يَعِظُهُۥ يَـٰبُنَىَّ لَا تُشْرِكْ بِٱللَّهِ إِنَّ ٱلشِّرْكَ لَظُلْمٌ عَظِيمٌ ۝

---

[a] Little has been recorded in history about Luqman, except that he was a wise and God-fearing man. The Quran says that Luqman was a grateful subject of God and who, as a father, advised his son to save himself from polytheism. Polytheism holds that beings other than God are man's benefactors and that, man should direct his feelings of gratitude towards them. The belief in the oneness of God stems from the intense realisation that God is the sole benefactor of man and as such all his gratitude should be shown only to that One.

14 We have enjoined man to show kindness to his parents—for his mother bears him, in hardship upon hardship, and his weaning takes two years. [We said] Give thanks to Me and to your parents; all will return to Me. 15 But if they press you to associate something with Me about which you have no knowledge, do not obey them. Yet be kind to them in this world and follow the path of those who turn to Me. You will all return to Me in the end, and I will tell you everything that you have done.[a]

وَوَصَّيْنَا ٱلْإِنسَٰنَ بِوَٰلِدَيْهِ حَمَلَتْهُ أُمُّهُ وَهْنًا عَلَىٰ وَهْنٍ وَفِصَٰلُهُ فِى عَامَيْنِ أَنِ ٱشْكُرْ لِى وَلِوَٰلِدَيْكَ إِلَىَّ ٱلْمَصِيرُ ۝ وَإِن جَٰهَدَاكَ عَلَىٰ أَن تُشْرِكَ بِى مَا لَيْسَ لَكَ بِهِۦ عِلْمٌ فَلَا تُطِعْهُمَا وَصَاحِبْهُمَا فِى ٱلدُّنْيَا مَعْرُوفًا وَٱتَّبِعْ سَبِيلَ مَنْ أَنَابَ إِلَىَّ ثُمَّ إِلَىَّ مَرْجِعُكُمْ فَأُنَبِّئُكُم بِمَا كُنتُمْ تَعْمَلُونَ ۝

---

[a] After God, a man's parents have the first claim upon his loyalty. But, if the parents' desire clashes with God's will, then preference has to be given to God's will and the parents' wishes have to be accorded the second place. However, it is necessary even then to continue to serve the parents as usual.

Striking this balance between two different requirements is the highest example of wisdom of Islam, and the secret of all successes is hidden in this wisdom.

16 [Luqman further said,] 'O my son! Though it be but the weight of a grain of mustard seed and though it be hidden in a rock, or in the heavens or on the earth, God will bring it forth. Truly, God is the knower of all subtleties and He is aware. 17 O my dear son! Say your prayers regularly, and enjoin good, and forbid evil, and endure patiently whatever may befall you. Surely, this is something which requires firm resolve. 18 Do not avert your face from people out of haughtiness and do not walk with pride on the earth: for, behold, God does not love arrogant and boastful people. 19 Walk modestly and lower your voice, for the ugliest of all voices is the braying of the ass.'[a]

يَبُنَىَّ إِنَّهَا إِن تَكُ مِثْقَالَ حَبَّةٍ مِّنْ خَرْدَلٍ فَتَكُن فِى صَخْرَةٍ أَوْ فِى ٱلسَّمَٰوَٰتِ أَوْ فِى ٱلْأَرْضِ يَأْتِ بِهَا ٱللَّهُ إِنَّ ٱللَّهَ لَطِيفٌ خَبِيرٌ ۝ يَٰبُنَىَّ أَقِمِ ٱلصَّلَوٰةَ وَأْمُرْ بِٱلْمَعْرُوفِ وَٱنْهَ عَنِ ٱلْمُنكَرِ وَٱصْبِرْ عَلَىٰ مَآ أَصَابَكَ إِنَّ ذَٰلِكَ مِنْ عَزْمِ ٱلْأُمُورِ ۝ وَلَا تُصَعِّرْ خَدَّكَ لِلنَّاسِ وَلَا تَمْشِ فِى ٱلْأَرْضِ مَرَحًا إِنَّ ٱللَّهَ لَا يُحِبُّ كُلَّ مُخْتَالٍ فَخُورٍ ۝ وَٱقْصِدْ فِى مَشْيِكَ وَٱغْضُضْ مِن صَوْتِكَ إِنَّ أَنكَرَ ٱلْأَصْوَٰتِ لَصَوْتُ ٱلْحَمِيرِ ۝

---

[a] In the present age, the progress of science has proved that distances and barriers are relative terms. 'X' rays are able to look into the interior of the body. The telescope and the microscope make such objects visible as cannot be seen by the naked eye. These possibilities which we experience in a limited fashion in the present world, exist with God on an unlimited scale.

To follow religion or to call others to follow religion are both patience-trying tasks. While performing them, one has to think deeply before (following a course of) action, and one has to go against one's own desires instead of pursuing them. One has unilaterally to surrender one's ego instead of protecting it. One has to bear the troubles inflicted by others.

All these tasks require the utmost courage, and the other name for courageous character is Islamic character.

²⁰ Have you not seen that God has subjected to you whatever is in the heavens and whatever is on the earth, and has completed His favours to you, both seen and unseen? Yet there are some who dispute concerning God, without knowledge or guidance or an enlightening Book. ²¹ When they are told to follow the [Revelations] that God has sent down, they say, 'No, we shall follow the ways that we found our fathers [following].' Yes! Even though Satan is inviting them to the punishment of the burning Fire? *ᵃ*

أَلَمۡ تَرَوۡاْ أَنَّ ٱللَّهَ سَخَّرَ لَكُم مَّا فِى ٱلسَّمَـٰوَٰتِ وَمَا فِى ٱلۡأَرۡضِ وَأَسۡبَغَ عَلَيۡكُمۡ نِعَمَهُۥ ظَـٰهِرَةً وَبَاطِنَةً ۗ وَمِنَ ٱلنَّاسِ مَن يُجَـٰدِلُ فِى ٱللَّهِ بِغَيۡرِ عِلۡمٍ وَلَا هُدًى وَلَا كِتَـٰبٍ مُّنِيرٍ ۝ وَإِذَا قِيلَ لَهُمُ ٱتَّبِعُواْ مَآ أَنزَلَ ٱللَّهُ قَالُواْ بَلۡ نَتَّبِعُ مَا وَجَدۡنَا عَلَيۡهِ ءَابَآءَنَآ ۚ أَوَلَوۡ كَانَ ٱلشَّيۡطَـٰنُ يَدۡعُوهُمۡ إِلَىٰ عَذَابِ ٱلسَّعِيرِ ۝

ᵃ The present world has been made in such a way that it is entirely favourable to human existence. That is, the present world contains in abundance everything which a human being needs. In spite of this, man is not thankful to the Creator of the universe. Indulging in useless discussions, he wants to turn people's attention away from God.

Generally, the reason for a man's going astray is that he does not use his mind. He does not think of getting out of the rut of common customs. If a man rises above those rigid customs, the mind given to him by God, will be enough to lead him in the right direction.

²² He who submits himself completely to God, and is a doer of good, has surely grasped a strong handle, for the final outcome of all events rests with God. ²³ But if any reject the Faith, let not his rejection grieve you: for to Us they shall return, and We shall tell them the truth about their deeds: for God knows well all that is in the human hearts—²⁴ We shall let them enjoy themselves for a little while, but then We shall drive them to a harsh punishment.ᵃ

۞ وَمَن يُسۡلِمۡ وَجۡهَهُۥ إِلَى ٱللَّهِ وَهُوَ مُحۡسِنٌ فَقَدِ ٱسۡتَمۡسَكَ بِٱلۡعُرۡوَةِ ٱلۡوُثۡقَىٰ وَإِلَى ٱللَّهِ عَـٰقِبَةُ ٱلۡأُمُورِ ۝ وَمَن كَفَرَ فَلَا يَحۡزُنكَ كُفۡرُهُۥ إِلَيۡنَا مَرۡجِعُهُمۡ فَنُنَبِّئُهُم بِمَا عَمِلُوٓاْ إِنَّ ٱللَّهَ عَلِيمٌۢ بِذَاتِ ٱلصُّدُورِ ۝ نُمَتِّعُهُمۡ قَلِيلٗا ثُمَّ نَضۡطَرُّهُمۡ إِلَىٰ عَذَابٍ غَلِيظٖ ۝

ᵃ Every man's nature has a direction in which he, along with his whole thought, action and his very existence, is inclined. The believer is one whose direction is entirely towards God. The life of a believer is a completely God-oriented life, and an unbeliever's life is a non-God-oriented life.

One who turns towards God is going in fact in the direction of the right goal, where he will find success. On the contrary, one who becomes neglectful of God and diverts his attention towards someone other than God becomes direction-less and goal-less. He may receive some temporary benefits for the time being but, in the permanent life of the Hereafter, there will be nothing for him except punishment.

²⁵ If you should ask them, 'Who created the heavens and the earth?' They will surely answer, 'God.' Say, 'Praise be to God!' But most of them do not understand. ²⁶ Whatever is in the heavens and the earth belongs to God. Assuredly, God is self-sufficient and praiseworthy. ²⁷ If all the trees on earth were pens, and the sea [were] ink, with seven [more] seas added to it, the words of God would not be exhausted: for, truly, God is Almighty and Wise.ᵃ

وَلَئِن سَأَلْتَهُم مَّنْ خَلَقَ ٱلسَّمَٰوَٰتِ وَٱلْأَرْضَ لَيَقُولُنَّ ٱللَّهُ قُلِ ٱلْحَمْدُ لِلَّهِ بَلْ أَكْثَرُهُمْ لَا يَعْلَمُونَ ۝ لِلَّهِ مَا فِى ٱلسَّمَٰوَٰتِ وَٱلْأَرْضِ إِنَّ ٱللَّهَ هُوَ ٱلْغَنِىُّ ٱلْحَمِيدُ ۝ وَلَوْ أَنَّمَا فِى ٱلْأَرْضِ مِن شَجَرَةٍ أَقْلَٰمٌ وَٱلْبَحْرُ يَمُدُّهُۥ مِنۢ بَعْدِهِۦ سَبْعَةُ أَبْحُرٍ مَّا نَفِدَتْ كَلِمَٰتُ ٱللَّهِ إِنَّ ٱللَّهَ عَزِيزٌ حَكِيمٌ ۝

ᵃ The universe is so extensive and so great that no one can claim that anybody other than God has created it. But despite accepting this fact, man's tragedy is that he gives to things other than God, a place of prominence and greatness. This irrational behaviour is otherwise known as polytheism, or ascribing partners to God (*shirk*).

The Majesty of God is too great to be expressed in words. The history of physical sciences is spread over thousands of years. But, in spite of innumerable researches, there are still many things about which it has not been possible to obtain complete information. For example man does not know the exact number of stars that exist in space, nor the number of species of animals and vegetation found on the earth. He remains unaware about the true nature and composition of the leaf of a tree or a grain of sand or even the many wonders hidden in the sea. In short, there are few things, big or small, in this world, about which man has obtained full information. This in itself is enough to prove that if all the trees of the world are chiselled into pens and all the seas become the ink, it will still not suffice to record the innumerable feats of God.

²⁸ Creating and resurrecting all of you is just like creating and resurrecting a single soul. Truly, God hears all and observes all. ²⁹ Have you not seen that God makes the night pass into the day, and makes the day pass into the night, and that He has pressed the sun and the moon into His service, each pursuing its course for an appointed term, and that God is well aware of what you do? ³⁰ That is because God is the Truth, and what they call upon besides Him is falsehood. God is the Most High, the Supreme One.^a

مَّا خَلْقُكُمْ وَلَا بَعْثُكُمْ إِلَّا كَنَفْسٍ وَاحِدَةٍ إِنَّ ٱللَّهَ سَمِيعٌ بَصِيرٌ ۝ أَلَمْ تَرَ أَنَّ ٱللَّهَ يُولِجُ ٱلَّيْلَ فِى ٱلنَّهَارِ وَيُولِجُ ٱلنَّهَارَ فِى ٱلَّيْلِ وَسَخَّرَ ٱلشَّمْسَ وَٱلْقَمَرَ كُلٌّ يَجْرِى إِلَىٰ أَجَلٍ مُّسَمًّى وَأَنَّ ٱللَّهَ بِمَا تَعْمَلُونَ خَبِيرٌ ۝ ذَٰلِكَ بِأَنَّ ٱللَّهَ هُوَ ٱلْحَقُّ وَأَنَّ مَا يَدْعُونَ مِن دُونِهِ ٱلْبَٰطِلُ وَأَنَّ ٱللَّهَ هُوَ ٱلْعَلِىُّ ٱلْكَبِيرُ ۝

---

^a Man's existence in itself is the proof of creation. And when one's existence is possible, the coming into existence of other lives is equally possible. It is on a parallel with man's experience of hearing one voice and seeing one scene, which leads him to feel that it should be possible to hear many voices and see many scenes.

The merging of night into day and day into night is the visible manifestation of what is known in the present age as the axial rotation of the earth. The continuous rotation of the earth on its axis with perfect precision and several other events of similar type show that the Creator and Lord of this Universe is unimaginably great. In these circumstances, who else can be worshipped except He? And who can be given the place of supreme importance in one's life? The fact is that giving a position of greatness to anybody other than God is nothing but falsehood, because nobody except God possesses greatness.

³¹ Have you not seen how the ships sail on the sea by God's grace so that He may show you some of His signs? Surely therein are signs for every steadfast, thankful person. ³² When the waves engulf them like shadows [of death], they call to God, sincere [at that moment] in their faith in Him alone: but as soon as He has brought them safe ashore, only some of them take the right course. And none denies Our signs save the perfidious and ungrateful person.ᵃ

أَلَمۡ تَرَ أَنَّ ٱلۡفُلۡكَ تَجۡرِى فِى ٱلۡبَحۡرِ بِنِعۡمَتِ ٱللَّهِ لِيُرِيَكُم مِّنۡ ءَايَتِهِۦٓ إِنَّ فِى ذَٰلِكَ لَأٓيَتٍ لِّكُلِّ صَبَّارٍ شَكُورٍ ﴿٣١﴾ وَإِذَا غَشِيَهُم مَّوۡجٌ كَٱلظُّلَلِ دَعَوُاْ ٱللَّهَ مُخۡلِصِينَ لَهُ ٱلدِّينَ فَلَمَّا نَجَّىٰهُمۡ إِلَى ٱلۡبَرِّ فَمِنۡهُم مُّقۡتَصِدٌ وَمَا يَجۡحَدُ بِـَٔايَٰتِنَآ إِلَّا كُلُّ خَتَّارٍ كَفُورٍ ﴿٣٢﴾

ᵃ If sea-bound vessels safely transport passengers and goods without any fear of sinking, it is thanks to Almighty God who endowed man with the skills to build seaworthy ships and gave him the knowledge about winds and currents. Undoubtedly, this is a great sign. But only patient and grateful people can learn a lesson from it. A patient person is one who abstains from being influenced by improper feelings and a grateful person is one who is capable of admitting the truth that exists beyond his realm.

However, if the ship gets caught in stormy weather and the sea becomes rough, then the ships' crews and passengers realize their utter helplessness. At that time, they forget the awe of the so-called great and start calling out to God alone. People should derive a lesson from the above experience and remain steadfast on the path of Truth and justice, but there are very few people who actually do so. Many people habitually remember God when in trouble and as the matter improves, they revert to their ways of arrogance and ingratitude.

³³ O men, seek protection with your Lord and fear the Day when neither will the father be of any avail to his son, nor will the son be of any avail to his father. God's promise is surely true. So let not worldly life beguile you, nor let the Deceiver deceive you concerning God. ³⁴ Truly, God alone has knowledge of the Hour. He sends down the rain, and He knows what is in the wombs. No soul knows what it will earn tomorrow, and no soul knows in what land it will die. Surely, God is all knowing, all-aware.^a

يَـٰٓأَيُّهَا ٱلنَّاسُ ٱتَّقُوا۟ رَبَّكُمْ وَٱخْشَوْا۟ يَوْمًا لَّا تَجْزِى وَالِدٌ عَن وَلَدِهِۦ وَلَا مَوْلُودٌ هُوَ جَازٍ عَن وَالِدِهِۦ شَيْـًٔا إِنَّ وَعْدَ ٱللَّهِ حَقٌّ فَلَا تَغُرَّنَّكُمُ ٱلْحَيَوٰةُ ٱلدُّنْيَا وَلَا يَغُرَّنَّكُم بِٱللَّهِ ٱلْغَرُورُ ۝ إِنَّ ٱللَّهَ عِندَهُۥ عِلْمُ ٱلسَّاعَةِ وَيُنَزِّلُ ٱلْغَيْثَ وَيَعْلَمُ مَا فِى ٱلْأَرْحَامِ وَمَا تَدْرِى نَفْسٌ مَّاذَا تَكْسِبُ غَدًا وَمَا تَدْرِى نَفْسٌ بِأَىِّ أَرْضٍ تَمُوتُ إِنَّ ٱللَّهَ عَلِيمٌ خَبِيرٌ ۝

---

^a In the present world, people have been given a certain amount of liberty as a means of putting them to the test. Man takes this trial-oriented freedom as the real freedom. This is the greatest illusion. All human evils are born out of this illusion. Apparently, it seems that a man is free to do whatever he likes in this world and there is nobody to check him. But the fact remains that a very difficult period is awaiting him, when even father and son will not be able to support one another.

Isn't asking the question, 'If Judgement Day is coming, then when is it going to come?' transgressing human limits? Man is unaware of the immediate future of the known and familiar things surrounding him. For instance, he is unable to make an accurate prediction about the rains, the growth of a baby in the mother's womb, his future earnings, the time of his death, etc. Despite his limited knowledge, man accepts these facts as realities. Similarly, man should believe in the coming of the Day of Judgement on the basis of the brief indications he has of it.

32. PROSTRATION

In the name of God,
the Most Gracious, the Most Merciful

¹ *Alif Lam Mim*

² This Book has beyond all doubt been revealed by the Lord of the Universe. ³ Do they say, 'He has invented it himself.'? No indeed! It is the truth from your Lord to warn a people to whom, before you, no warner came, so that hopefully they may be rightly guided.ᵃ

ᵃ On the face of it, this is an ordinary statement consisting of just a few words. But this is a very serious and portentous claim, which in the entire history of religion, nobody has had the courage to profess, except those chosen few to whom the Book of God was in actuality revealed. Other than the appointed person, anyone who mustered the audacity to utter these words, was either a trifler or a madman.

The Quran is a proof in itself. Its miraculous style, its claims that have not been proved wrong even after centuries have elapsed,—all these and similar considerations prove that it is a book sent by God. And since it is a book of God, it is absolutely necessary that everybody should pay heed to its warnings and gives serious thought to them.

⁴ It was God who created the heavens and the earth and whatsoever is in between in six Days, and then He established Himself on the throne. You have no patron nor any intercessor besides Him. So will you not pay heed? ⁵ He directs all affairs from heaven to earth. Then all will again ascend to Him on a Day whose length is a thousand years by the way you measure. ⁶ Such is the Knower of the unseen and the visible, the Powerful, the Merciful, ⁷ who gave everything its perfect form. He originated the creation of man from clay, ⁸ then He made his progeny from an extract of a humble fluid. ⁹ Then He moulded him; He breathed His Spirit into him; He gave you hearing, sight, and hearts. How seldom you are grateful! ᵃ

اللَّهُ الَّذِى خَلَقَ السَّمَوَاتِ وَالْأَرْضَ وَمَا بَيْنَهُمَا فِى سِتَّةِ أَيَّامٍ ثُمَّ اسْتَوَىٰ عَلَى الْعَرْشِ مَا لَكُم مِّن دُونِهِ مِن وَلِيٍّ وَلَا شَفِيعٍ أَفَلَا تَتَذَكَّرُونَ ۝ يُدَبِّرُ الْأَمْرَ مِنَ السَّمَآءِ إِلَى الْأَرْضِ ثُمَّ يَعْرُجُ إِلَيْهِ فِى يَوْمٍ كَانَ مِقْدَارُهُ أَلْفَ سَنَةٍ مِّمَّا تَعُدُّونَ ۝ ذَٰلِكَ عَلِمُ الْغَيْبِ وَالشَّهَدَةِ الْعَزِيزُ الرَّحِيمُ ۝ الَّذِى أَحْسَنَ كُلَّ شَىْءٍ خَلَقَهُ وَبَدَأَ خَلْقَ الْإِنسَنِ مِن طِينٍ ۝ ثُمَّ جَعَلَ نَسْلَهُ مِن سُلَلَةٍ مِّن مَّآءٍ مَّهِينٍ ۝ ثُمَّ سَوَّىٰهُ وَنَفَخَ فِيهِ مِن رُّوحِهِ وَجَعَلَ لَكُمُ السَّمْعَ وَالْأَبْصَرَ وَالْأَفْئِدَةَ قَلِيلًا مَّا تَشْكُرُونَ ۝

ᵃ The gradual creation of the universe, in six days meaning six stages, along with the system full of wisdom governing it, is indicative of the fact that the Creator has some special purpose behind this creation. Moreover, numerous processes are incessantly going on in the universe. This further proves that its Creator is running it in a well-planned manner. The human being is a wonderful living organism, but if his body is analyzed, it will be found that it is composed of earth elements. Then this creation does not end there, but continues eternally through the process of procreation and regeneration.

If the individual gives deep and serious consideration to these facts, his mind will be free of feelings of awe for anything except the Majesty of God. He will become a grateful subject of God. But there are very few who give deep consideration to anything. That is why there are very few people who offer praises to God and are grateful to Him.

¹⁰ They say, 'When we are lost in the earth, how can we then be recreated?' Indeed, they deny they will ever meet their Lord. ¹¹ Say, 'The Angel of Death who has been given charge of you will gather in your souls. Then you will [all] be returned to your Lord.' ¹² If only you could see the evil-doers hanging their heads in shame before their Lord, 'Our Lord, we have seen and we have heard, so send us back again and we will act rightly. For we do indeed now believe.' ¹³ Yet had We so willed, We could indeed have imposed Our guidance upon every human being: but My word shall come true: 'I will fill Hell with jinns and men all together.' ¹⁴ We shall say to them, 'Taste this—for you forgot you would ever meet this Day. We too will forget you—taste the chastisement of Eternity for your [evil] deeds!'ᵃ

وَقَالُوٓاْ أَءِذَا ضَلَلْنَا فِى ٱلْأَرْضِ أَءِنَّا لَفِى خَلْقٍ جَدِيدٍ بَلْ هُم بِلِقَآءِ رَبِّهِمْ كَٰفِرُونَ ۝ قُلْ يَتَوَفَّىٰكُم مَّلَكُ ٱلْمَوْتِ ٱلَّذِى وُكِّلَ بِكُمْ ثُمَّ إِلَىٰ رَبِّكُمْ تُرْجَعُونَ ۝ وَلَوْ تَرَىٰٓ إِذِ ٱلْمُجْرِمُونَ نَاكِسُواْ رُءُوسِهِمْ عِندَ رَبِّهِمْ رَبَّنَآ أَبْصَرْنَا وَسَمِعْنَا فَٱرْجِعْنَا نَعْمَلْ صَٰلِحًا إِنَّا مُوقِنُونَ ۝ وَلَوْ شِئْنَا لَأَتَيْنَا كُلَّ نَفْسٍ هُدَىٰهَا وَلَٰكِنْ حَقَّ ٱلْقَوْلُ مِنِّى لَأَمْلَأَنَّ جَهَنَّمَ مِنَ ٱلْجِنَّةِ وَٱلنَّاسِ أَجْمَعِينَ ۝ فَذُوقُواْ بِمَا نَسِيتُمْ لِقَآءَ يَوْمِكُمْ هَٰذَآ إِنَّا نَسِينَٰكُمْ وَذُوقُواْ عَذَابَ ٱلْخُلْدِ بِمَا كُنتُمْ تَعْمَلُونَ ۝

ᵃ Man's creation for the first time is enough to convince mankind of the possibility of creation for the second time. But when a man does not believe in his accountability before God, he ridicules the possibility of a second creation, and he talks flippantly of it.

But, this amounts to taking liberties throughout the period of freedom given for the purpose of putting man to test. And when this period expires and a man dies and is made to stand before Almighty God for the purpose of giving an account of himself, he will find himself speechless. At that time, the arrogant will say that they now accept the reality and will request that they be sent back into the world, so that they may perform righteous deeds. But this admission at that stage will be useless. Had God desired that people should accept reality in this way, He could have compelled them to accept it in the present world itself.

Before God, that acceptance carries weight which is made without the reality being visible. Acceptance after seeing the reality has no value.

¹⁵ The people who truly believe in Our messages are those who fall to the ground in prostration when they are reminded of them, and glorify their Lord with praise and are not arrogant. ¹⁶ They forsake their beds, calling upon their Lord in fear and in hope, and spend out of what We have provided them with. ¹⁷ No soul knows what joy is kept hidden in store for them as a reward for their labours.ᵃ

إِنَّمَا يُؤْمِنُ بِآيَاتِنَا ٱلَّذِينَ إِذَا ذُكِّرُواْ بِهَا خَرُّواْ سُجَّدًا وَسَبَّحُواْ بِحَمْدِ رَبِّهِمْ وَهُمْ لَا يَسْتَكْبِرُونَ ۩ تَتَجَافَىٰ جُنُوبُهُمْ عَنِ ٱلْمَضَاجِعِ يَدْعُونَ رَبَّهُمْ خَوْفًا وَطَمَعًا وَمِمَّا رَزَقْنَٰهُمْ يُنفِقُونَ ۞ فَلَا تَعْلَمُ نَفْسٌ مَّآ أُخْفِيَ لَهُم مِّن قُرَّةِ أَعْيُنٍ جَزَآءَۢ بِمَا كَانُواْ يَعْمَلُونَ ۞

ᵃ For an individual to avail of guidance, his willingness to accept the Truth is the most important factor. Only those who, by temperament, are ready to accept the Truth whenever it presents itself before them—whether it be revealed through a person of lesser importance, whether such acceptance be a tacit admission of one's own error, or whether such acceptance leads to upsetting the existing system of one's life—are capable of availing of guidance. Only those who have such a capacity will find the Truth. Those who want to accept the Truth, but at the same time want their 'greatness' to remain intact, will never find it.

A man who sacrifices his greatness for the sake of Truth actually finds the greatest thing, namely, the greatness of God. God enters his life in such a way that he sleeps thinking about Him and wakes up with memories of God. His hopes and fears are all linked with God. He surrenders all his possessions to God to the point of not keeping back anything for himself. Such people will forever relish the bounties of the eternal Gardens of Paradise.

¹⁸ So, is someone who believes equal to someone who defies God? No, they are not equal. ¹⁹ Those who believe and do good deeds shall be lodged in the Gardens of Paradise as a reward for what they have done. ²⁰ As for those who defy God, their home shall be the Fire. Whenever they try to escape it, they shall be driven back into it, and they shall be told, 'Taste the torment of the Fire, which you have persistently denied.' ²¹ And most surely We will make them taste a lesser punishment before the greater punishment, so that perhaps they may return to Us in repentance. ²² Who does greater wrong than someone who, when revelations of his Lord are recited to him, turns away from them? We shall inflict retribution on the guilty.^a

أَفَمَن كَانَ مُؤْمِنًا كَمَن كَانَ فَاسِقًا لَّا يَسْتَوُۥنَ ۞ أَمَّا ٱلَّذِينَ ءَامَنُوا۟ وَعَمِلُوا۟ ٱلصَّٰلِحَٰتِ فَلَهُمْ جَنَّٰتُ ٱلْمَأْوَىٰ نُزُلًۢا بِمَا كَانُوا۟ يَعْمَلُونَ ۞ وَأَمَّا ٱلَّذِينَ فَسَقُوا۟ فَمَأْوَىٰهُمُ ٱلنَّارُ كُلَّمَآ أَرَادُوٓا۟ أَن يَخْرُجُوا۟ مِنْهَآ أُعِيدُوا۟ فِيهَا وَقِيلَ لَهُمْ ذُوقُوا۟ عَذَابَ ٱلنَّارِ ٱلَّذِى كُنتُم بِهِۦ تُكَذِّبُونَ ۞ وَلَنُذِيقَنَّهُم مِّنَ ٱلْعَذَابِ ٱلْأَدْنَىٰ دُونَ ٱلْعَذَابِ ٱلْأَكْبَرِ لَعَلَّهُمْ يَرْجِعُونَ ۞ وَمَنْ أَظْلَمُ مِمَّن ذُكِّرَ بِـَٔايَٰتِ رَبِّهِۦ ثُمَّ أَعْرَضَ عَنْهَآ إِنَّا مِنَ ٱلْمُجْرِمِينَ مُنتَقِمُونَ ۞

---

^a A believer (*mu'min*) is one who accepts the Divine Truth and a sinner (*faasiq*) is one who rejects it for the sake of self-protection. These are two separate characters—entirely different from each other—and the fate of individuals who are entirely different in character cannot be the same.

In the present world, one who accepts the Truth, proves that he gives prime importance to Truth. Such a person will have greatness conferred upon him in the Hereafter. As opposed to this, one who considers himself great, while ignoring the Truth, shall have a lesser position in the real life of the Hereafter.

²³ We gave Moses the Scripture—so [Muhammad] do not doubt that you are receiving it—just as We made it a guide for the Children of Israel. ²⁴ We appointed leaders from among them, guiding by Our command when they were steadfast and when they had firm faith in Our signs. ²⁵ Surely your Lord will judge between them on the Day of Resurrection concerning that wherein they used to differ. ²⁶ Does it not guide them [to see] how many generations We destroyed before them, among whose ruined dwellings they now walk about? There truly are signs in this—will they not listen? *ᵃ*

وَلَقَدْ ءَاتَيْنَا مُوسَى ٱلْكِتَٰبَ فَلَا تَكُن فِى مِرْيَةٍ مِّن لِّقَآئِهِۦ وَجَعَلْنَٰهُ هُدًى لِّبَنِىٓ إِسْرَٰٓءِيلَ ۝ وَجَعَلْنَا مِنْهُمْ أَئِمَّةً يَهْدُونَ بِأَمْرِنَا لَمَّا صَبَرُوا۟ وَكَانُوا۟ بِـَٔايَٰتِنَا يُوقِنُونَ ۝ إِنَّ رَبَّكَ هُوَ يَفْصِلُ بَيْنَهُمْ يَوْمَ ٱلْقِيَٰمَةِ فِيمَا كَانُوا۟ فِيهِ يَخْتَلِفُونَ ۝ أَوَلَمْ يَهْدِ لَهُمْ كَمْ أَهْلَكْنَا مِن قَبْلِهِم مِّنَ ٱلْقُرُونِ يَمْشُونَ فِى مَسَٰكِنِهِمْ إِنَّ فِى ذَٰلِكَ لَءَايَٰتٍ أَفَلَا يَسْمَعُونَ ۝

ᵃ The awarding of the Book of God to a group is tantamount to bestowing the keys of world leadership upon that group. But, such status is conferred on a group only when it exercises patience. 'When they were steadfast' has been explained as 'When they were patient with the world.' (*Tafsir ibn Kathir*). In other words, they attained the position of leadership when they exercised patience in the face of the adversity of this world.

People accept that person (or group) as a leader or *Imam* who appears to be at higher level than their own—who lives for principles when others live for self-interest, who supports justice when others take the side of their own community; who shows tolerance on being wronged when others seek revenge; who reconciles with deprivation when others rush to find gains; who offers to make sacrifices for the sake of Truth when others know only how to sacrifice for self-interest. Such virtues are rooted in patience, and those who exercise this patience become leaders of the world.

Man does not often learn lessons from events until the same disaster befalls him as has befallen others. Those who make innovative interpretations of religion and thus cause differences to arise, incur the risk of final rejection on the Day of judgement and thereafter experience nothing but unending denigration.

²⁷ Have they not seen that We drive the water to the barren land and produce thereby crops of which their cattle and they themselves eat? Will they not then see? ²⁸ And they say, 'When will this judgement come, if you are telling the truth?' ²⁹ Say, 'On the Day of Judgement it will be of no benefit to those who were bent on denying the truth, if they [then] believe! They will be granted no respite.' ³⁰ So turn away from them and wait. They too are waiting.^a

أَوَلَمْ يَرَوْاْ أَنَّا نَسُوقُ ٱلْمَآءَ إِلَى ٱلْأَرْضِ ٱلْجُرُزِ فَنُخْرِجُ بِهِۦ زَرْعًا تَأْكُلُ مِنْهُ أَنْعَٰمُهُمْ وَأَنفُسُهُمْ أَفَلَا يُبْصِرُونَ ۝ وَيَقُولُونَ مَتَىٰ هَٰذَا ٱلْفَتْحُ إِن كُنتُمْ صَٰدِقِينَ ۝ قُلْ يَوْمَ ٱلْفَتْحِ لَا يَنفَعُ ٱلَّذِينَ كَفَرُوٓاْ إِيمَٰنُهُمْ وَلَا هُمْ يُنظَرُونَ ۝ فَأَعْرِضْ عَنْهُمْ وَٱنتَظِرْ إِنَّهُم مُّنتَظِرُونَ ۝

---

^a In ancient Makkah the polytheists were dominant, while Islam was in a very weak position, so much so that the polytheists used to ridicule Islam and Muslims. In response to this, Almighty God has given an example: He asks people to consider a land which is dry and barren. To all appearances, it seems impossible that it will ever become covered with greenery. But, God causes the clouds to pour rain-water on it. In a few days time, the dry land is replaced with lush green fields. Similarly, God's powers can cause Islam to flourish and become the predominant ideology of the world.

33. THE CONFEDERATES

In the name of God,
the Most Gracious, the Most Merciful

¹ O Prophet, have fear of God and do not yield to those who deny the truth and the hypocrites. God is all-knowing and all-wise. ² Follow what is revealed to you from your Lord. God is aware of all that you do. ³ Put your trust in God; God is sufficient as a Guardian.ᵃ

ᵃ The Prophet Muhammad was the call-giver of the purest Truth. In this world, one who rises as such has to face the most discouraging circumstances. He remains a stranger in his surroundings. The prevalent creed, based as it is on worldly considerations, does not accord with the Hereafter-oriented religion of the missionary. Time-serving tendencies clash with his fearless policy of following the Truth. Religion has been made subservient to communal beliefs, while the missionary demands that religion should be based purely on worship of God.

Under these circumstances, if a preacher succumbs to the pressure of his surroundings and makes compromises, he may attract many supporters. If he is firm in the way of Truth, he will find no support except that of the one and only God. But, the call-giver must not adopt the first alternative under any circumstances. He has to trust in God, stick to the unadulterated Truth and hope that as God is All-knowing and Wise, He will definitely help His subject.

⁴ God has not placed two hearts in any man's body, nor has He made your wives—from whom you keep away by saying, 'Be as my mother's back'—your [real] mothers, neither He has made your adopted sons as your own sons. These are merely words which you utter with your mouths: but God speaks the truth and gives guidance to the right path. ⁵ Call them after their own fathers; that is closer to justice in the sight of God. If you do not know their fathers, regard them as your brothers in faith and your protégés. You will not be blamed if you make a mistake, you will be held accountable only for what in your hearts you have done intentionally. God is forgiving and merciful.ᵃ

مَّا جَعَلَ ٱللَّهُ لِرَجُلٍ مِّن قَلْبَيْنِ فِى جَوْفِهِۦ ۚ وَمَا جَعَلَ أَزْوَٰجَكُمُ ٱلَّـٰٓـِٔى تُظَـٰهِرُونَ مِنْهُنَّ أُمَّهَـٰتِكُمْ ۚ وَمَا جَعَلَ أَدْعِيَآءَكُمْ أَبْنَآءَكُمْ ۚ ذَٰلِكُمْ قَوْلُكُم بِأَفْوَٰهِكُمْ ۖ وَٱللَّهُ يَقُولُ ٱلْحَقَّ وَهُوَ يَهْدِى ٱلسَّبِيلَ ۝ ٱدْعُوهُمْ لِـَٔابَآئِهِمْ هُوَ أَقْسَطُ عِندَ ٱللَّهِ ۚ فَإِن لَّمْ تَعْلَمُوٓا۟ ءَابَآءَهُمْ فَإِخْوَٰنُكُمْ فِى ٱلدِّينِ وَمَوَٰلِيكُمْ ۚ وَلَيْسَ عَلَيْكُمْ جُنَاحٌ فِيمَآ أَخْطَأْتُم بِهِۦ وَلَـٰكِن مَّا تَعَمَّدَتْ قُلُوبُكُمْ ۚ وَكَانَ ٱللَّهُ غَفُورًا رَّحِيمًا

ᵃ A man does not have two hearts in his chest. This shows that contradictory thinking does not fit in with the scheme of creation. When a man has been given one heart, his thinking should also be one. It cannot be that in one and the same heart, sincerity coexists with hypocrisy, devotion to God with a time-serving mentality, justice with oppression and vanity with modesty. Of the two alternatives, man can have only the God-fearing one, and that is as it should be.

ᵇ This is a matter of principle, and under it are covered the pre-Islamic conventions of divorce (zihar) and adoption. It was the custom among pre-Islamic Arabs that if a man said to his wife, 'You are like my mother's back for me', then his wife was treated as forbidden for him forever, just as his mother was forbidden for him. Similarly, in the matter of an adopted son, they held the belief that he became just like a real son. He was given the same status as a real son in every respect. The Quran abolished this custom completely. It has been made clear in the Quran that it is against the system underlying creation for the status of a real mother to be the same as that of an adoptive mother or the status of an adopted son to be the same as that of a real son.

If a man commits an error unknowingly, he is pardonable before God. But, if a man is fully aware of the reality of an affair, and in spite of that he does not desist from wrongdoing, he ceases to be pardonable.

⁶ The Prophet has a higher claim on the believers than [they have on] their own selves, and his wives are their mothers. Blood relatives are closer to one another in God's Book than are believers and the Emigrants except that you want to show your friends a kindness. That is decreed in the Book.*

ٱلنَّبِىُّ أَوْلَىٰ بِٱلْمُؤْمِنِينَ مِنْ أَنفُسِهِمْ وَأَزْوَٰجُهُۥٓ أُمَّهَٰتُهُمْ وَأُو۟لُوا۟ ٱلْأَرْحَامِ بَعْضُهُمْ أَوْلَىٰ بِبَعْضٍ فِى كِتَٰبِ ٱللَّهِ مِنَ ٱلْمُؤْمِنِينَ وَٱلْمُهَٰجِرِينَ إِلَّآ أَن تَفْعَلُوٓا۟ إِلَىٰٓ أَوْلِيَآئِكُم مَّعْرُوفًا كَانَ ذَٰلِكَ فِى ٱلْكِتَٰبِ مَسْطُورًا ۝

ᵃ A Prophet during his life-time is, in person, of prime importance to the faithful and after his death he is so in principle. The reason for this is that Prophet is God's representative on earth. In order to maintain the dignity and importance of the Prophet's teachings, it is necessary that his existence should be sacred in the eyes of the people. Even his wives should be held in high esteem as mothers. After the prophet and his wives, relations with other members of society or community are determined on the basis of the principle of 'blood-relatives being the nearest' and, accordingly, people have rights over each other. Sometimes, in fulfillment of requirements in religious matters, the sharing of rights among non-relatives may be established temporarily, as was done after the migration (*hijrah*) to Madinah in the early days. But, as a permanent social arrangement, real relatives have preferential claims and it will be so always.

⁷ We took a solemn pledge from the prophets, from you and Noah, Abraham, Moses and Jesus, the son of Mary—We took a solemn pledge from all of them. ⁸ So that God might ask those men of truth as to [what response] their truthfulness [had received on earth]. But for those who deny the truth, He has prepared a woeful punishment.ᵃ

وَإِذْ أَخَذْنَا مِنَ ٱلنَّبِيِّـۧنَ مِيثَٰقَهُمْ وَمِنكَ وَمِن نُّوحٍ وَإِبْرَٰهِيمَ وَمُوسَىٰ وَعِيسَى ٱبْنِ مَرْيَمَ ۖ وَأَخَذْنَا مِنْهُم مِّيثَٰقًا غَلِيظًا ۝ لِّيَسْـَٔلَ ٱلصَّٰدِقِينَ عَن صِدْقِهِمْ ۚ وَأَعَدَّ لِلْكَٰفِرِينَ عَذَابًا أَلِيمًا ۝

ᵃ The plan according to which Almighty God has created human beings is designed to put man to the test. To this end he is provided with all the amenities of life and sustained in an atmosphere of freedom. Thereafter to confer upon him, according to his deeds, eternal rewards or eternal punishment.

The life of a man being for the purpose of trial requires that he be made fully aware of the real position, in advance. For this purpose, Almighty God established the institution of prophets. Prophethood is not fulfilled by making announcements on a loudspeaker. It is a task which is extremely trying to the patience. Therefore, all the prophets were made to vow that they would perform this crucial task of conveying the message of God, all the while observing its every requirement and doing full justice to it without the slightest shortcoming.

⁹ You who have attained to faith, remember God's blessings upon you when mighty armies massed against you. We sent a violent wind against them and hosts that you could not see. God sees all that you do. ¹⁰ When they came against you both from above you and from below you, your eyes rolled [with fear] and your hearts leapt up to your throats, and you entertained [ill] thoughts about God. ¹¹ There the faithful were put to the proof and they were shaken as if by an earthquake.*a*

يَـٰٓأَيُّهَا ٱلَّذِينَ ءَامَنُوا۟ ٱذْكُرُوا۟ نِعْمَةَ ٱللَّهِ عَلَيْكُمْ إِذْ جَآءَتْكُمْ جُنُودٌ فَأَرْسَلْنَا عَلَيْهِمْ رِيحًا وَجُنُودًا لَّمْ تَرَوْهَا ۚ وَكَانَ ٱللَّهُ بِمَا تَعْمَلُونَ بَصِيرًا ۝ إِذْ جَآءُوكُم مِّن فَوْقِكُمْ وَمِنْ أَسْفَلَ مِنكُمْ وَإِذْ زَاغَتِ ٱلْأَبْصَـٰرُ وَبَلَغَتِ ٱلْقُلُوبُ ٱلْحَنَاجِرَ وَتَظُنُّونَ بِٱللَّهِ ٱلظُّنُونَا۠ ۝ هُنَالِكَ ٱبْتُلِىَ ٱلْمُؤْمِنُونَ وَزُلْزِلُوا۟ زِلْزَالًا شَدِيدًا ۝

---

a At the battle of Ahzab (in the fifth year of Hijrah) there was a combined attack by Arab tribes and Jews on Madinah. The number of attackers in this battle was about thirteen thousand and the Muslims were not capable of fighting this huge army. But, Almighty God, by His special devices, caused Islam's enemies to become so terror-stricken that they themselves abandoned the siege of Madinah and retreated.

Such difficulties befall the Islamic mission firstly in order to separate the sincere from the insincere and secondly to show to the enemy forces that God Himself is a supporter of His religion. He will not allow it to be vanquished.

¹² The hypocrites and people with sickness in their hearts said, 'God and His Messenger have promised us nothing but delusions.' ¹³ Others said, 'People of Yathrib, you cannot withstand [the enemy] here: so go back!' Yet others asked leave of the Prophet, saying, 'Our houses are exposed and [defenceless].' They were in truth not exposed: they only wished to flee. ¹⁴ If their town had been stormed, and they had been incited to sedition, they would have rebelled with little hesitation. ¹⁵ They had already vowed before God that they would never turn their backs: and a vow made to God must be answered for. ¹⁶ Say, 'Flight shall not avail you: if you manage to escape from death or killing, you will enjoy life only for a short while.'^a ¹⁷ Say, 'Who is there to shield you from God if He wishes to harm you? If God wishes to show you mercy, who can prevent Him.' Besides God they shall find none to protect them, and none to bring them succour.^a

وَإِذْ يَقُولُ ٱلْمُنَٰفِقُونَ وَٱلَّذِينَ فِى قُلُوبِهِم مَّرَضٌ مَّا وَعَدَنَا ٱللَّهُ وَرَسُولُهُۥ إِلَّا غُرُورًا ۝ وَإِذْ قَالَت طَّآئِفَةٌ مِّنْهُمْ يَٰٓأَهْلَ يَثْرِبَ لَا مُقَامَ لَكُمْ فَٱرْجِعُوا۟ وَيَسْتَـْٔذِنُ فَرِيقٌ مِّنْهُمُ ٱلنَّبِىَّ يَقُولُونَ إِنَّ بُيُوتَنَا عَوْرَةٌ وَمَا هِىَ بِعَوْرَةٍ إِن يُرِيدُونَ إِلَّا فِرَارًا ۝ وَلَوْ دُخِلَتْ عَلَيْهِم مِّنْ أَقْطَارِهَا ثُمَّ سُئِلُوا۟ ٱلْفِتْنَةَ لَأَتَوْهَا وَمَا تَلَبَّثُوا۟ بِهَآ إِلَّا يَسِيرًا ۝ وَلَقَدْ كَانُوا۟ عَٰهَدُوا۟ ٱللَّهَ مِن قَبْلُ لَا يُوَلُّونَ ٱلْأَدْبَٰرَ وَكَانَ عَهْدُ ٱللَّهِ مَسْـُٔولًا ۝ قُل لَّن يَنفَعَكُمُ ٱلْفِرَارُ إِن فَرَرْتُم مِّنَ ٱلْمَوْتِ أَوِ ٱلْقَتْلِ وَإِذًا لَّا تُمَتَّعُونَ إِلَّا قَلِيلًا ۝ قُلْ مَن ذَا ٱلَّذِى يَعْصِمُكُم مِّنَ ٱللَّهِ إِنْ أَرَادَ بِكُمْ سُوٓءًا أَوْ أَرَادَ بِكُمْ رَحْمَةً وَلَا يَجِدُونَ لَهُم مِّن دُونِ ٱللَّهِ وَلِيًّا وَلَا نَصِيرًا ۝

---

^a Realizing that the situation at the battle of Ahzab, was fraught with danger, the hypocrites were terrified and started exploring ways and means of fleeing. But the true and faithful ones firmly placed their reliance on God. They knew very well that God was before them and He was behind them. To run away from the danger of the enemies of Islam amounted to placing oneself in danger of God's chastisement, which was by far the greater hazard. They firmly believed that if they were steadfast in the face of their enemies, God's help would be forthcoming. On the other hand, they knew that if they fled the Islamic front, they would not be able to save themselves from either destruction in this world or God's terrible scourge in the Hereafter.

¹⁸ God knows exactly who among you hold the others back, who say to their brethren, 'Come over to our side,' and they seldom take part in the fighting. ¹⁹ Begrudging you all help, but when danger comes, you can see them looking at you with rolling eyes as if in their death throes; but once their fear has passed, they come to you and do glib-talking in their greed for wealth. Such men have no faith, so God has foiled their actions. This is indeed easy for God. ²⁰ They thought the confederate tribes would never withdraw. Indeed, if the confederates should come again, they would prefer to be in the desert, among the Bedouins. There they would ask news of you [from a distance]. But if they were with you, they would take very little part in the fighting.^a

﴿ قَدْ يَعْلَمُ ٱللَّهُ ٱلْمُعَوِّقِينَ مِنكُمْ وَٱلْقَآئِلِينَ لِإِخْوَٰنِهِمْ هَلُمَّ إِلَيْنَا ۖ وَلَا يَأْتُونَ ٱلْبَأْسَ إِلَّا قَلِيلًا ۝ أَشِحَّةً عَلَيْكُمْ ۖ فَإِذَا جَآءَ ٱلْخَوْفُ رَأَيْتَهُمْ يَنظُرُونَ إِلَيْكَ تَدُورُ أَعْيُنُهُمْ كَٱلَّذِى يُغْشَىٰ عَلَيْهِ مِنَ ٱلْمَوْتِ ۖ فَإِذَا ذَهَبَ ٱلْخَوْفُ سَلَقُوكُم بِأَلْسِنَةٍ حِدَادٍ أَشِحَّةً عَلَى ٱلْخَيْرِ ۚ أُوْلَٰئِكَ لَمْ يُؤْمِنُوا۟ فَأَحْبَطَ ٱللَّهُ أَعْمَٰلَهُمْ ۚ وَكَانَ ذَٰلِكَ عَلَى ٱللَّهِ يَسِيرًا ۝ يَحْسَبُونَ ٱلْأَحْزَابَ لَمْ يَذْهَبُوا۟ ۖ وَإِن يَأْتِ ٱلْأَحْزَابُ يَوَدُّوا۟ لَوْ أَنَّهُم بَادُونَ فِى ٱلْأَعْرَابِ يَسْـَٔلُونَ عَنْ أَنۢبَآئِكُمْ ۖ وَلَوْ كَانُوا۟ فِيكُم مَّا قَٰتَلُوٓا۟ إِلَّا قَلِيلًا ۝ ﴾

---

^a There are those who lag behind at the time when sacrifice is required, but who feel ashamed of this shortcoming. Then there are others who do not make sacrifices when they are called for, but who feel no shame on this account. This amounts to adding arrogance to neglect of duty. A shortcoming may be pardonable, but arrogance is not.

Even if some apparently good deeds are performed by those who are flawed by arrogance, they are worthless, because the essence of a good deed is sincerity, and that is the very thing which is lacking.

Shirking the duty of making sacrifices for a religious cause is invariably the result of a love for worldly affairs. Man loses his faith for the sake of saving his worldly assets. When materially-minded people see that worldly advantage is coupled with religion, they display their oratorical skill in speaking in favour of religion, in order to show off their connection with religion and then they extract the maximum advantage from this. But when following religion means sacrifice, they lose interest in becoming men of religion.

^b Wandering Arabs.

²¹ You have indeed in the Prophet of God a good example for those of you who look to God and the Last Day, and remember God always. ²² When the believers saw the confederates, they said, 'This is what God and His Messenger have promised us. Surely the promise of God and His Messenger has come true.' It served to increase them in faith and submission. ²³ Among the believers there are men who have been true to the pledge they made with God. Among them are such as have fulfilled their vow, and some who [still] wait, without having changed [their resolve] in the least. ²⁴ God will surely reward the truthful for their truthfulness and punish the hypocrites, if He so wishes, or He may accept their repentance, for God is forgiving and merciful.ᵃ

لَّقَدْ كَانَ لَكُمْ فِى رَسُولِ ٱللَّهِ أُسْوَةٌ حَسَنَةٌ لِّمَن كَانَ يَرْجُوا۟ ٱللَّهَ وَٱلْيَوْمَ ٱلْأَخِرَ وَذَكَرَ ٱللَّهَ كَثِيرًا ۝ وَلَمَّا رَءَا ٱلْمُؤْمِنُونَ ٱلْأَحْزَابَ قَالُوا۟ هَـٰذَا مَا وَعَدَنَا ٱللَّهُ وَرَسُولُهُۥ وَصَدَقَ ٱللَّهُ وَرَسُولُهُۥ وَمَا زَادَهُمْ إِلَّآ إِيمَـٰنًا وَتَسْلِيمًا ۝ مِّنَ ٱلْمُؤْمِنِينَ رِجَالٌ صَدَقُوا۟ مَا عَـٰهَدُوا۟ ٱللَّهَ عَلَيْهِ فَمِنْهُم مَّن قَضَىٰ نَحْبَهُۥ وَمِنْهُم مَّن يَنتَظِرُ وَمَا بَدَّلُوا۟ تَبْدِيلًا ۝ لِّيَجْزِىَ ٱللَّهُ ٱلصَّـٰدِقِينَ بِصِدْقِهِمْ وَيُعَذِّبَ ٱلْمُنَـٰفِقِينَ إِن شَآءَ أَوْ يَتُوبَ عَلَيْهِمْ إِنَّ ٱللَّهَ كَانَ غَفُورًا رَّحِيمًا ۝

ᵃ The lives of the Prophet and his companions were of an exemplary, godly character and were meant to be followed by all the faithful till the Day of Judgement. They set an example to show what it means to seek God's pleasure and merit success in the Hereafter; what is meant by remembering God; how to be steady and persevering in difficult times; how reliance is placed on the promises of God; what ever-increasing faith is and how it is achieved; and how to fulfill the vows taken before God.

The Prophet and his companions set the final example in all these matters. Under the most difficult circumstances, they did not falter. They were the embodiment of Islamic thought and Islamic character in all matters. Before the arrival of the moment of trial, they were firm in their acceptance of Truth and even after the arrival of that moment they remained unwavering.

Then, it was the life of the Prophet and his companions which set an example and showed that no decision was taken by God, unless one was put to the test. It is the way of God that He creates severe conditions so as to separate the truly faithful from the false claimants. In this Divine precept and practice, there was no exception earlier and neither will there be any exception in future.

²⁵ God turned back those who denied the truth in their rage, without their having gained any advantage. God was enough to [protect] the believers in battle. God is strong and all-powerful. ²⁶ He brought down from their strongholds those People of the Book who supported the aggressors and filled their hearts with terror. Some of them you killed and others you took captive. ²⁷ He made you heirs to their lands, and their houses, and their possessions and lands on which you had not set foot before. God has power over all things.ᵃ

وَرَدَّ ٱللَّهُ ٱلَّذِينَ كَفَرُواْ بِغَيْظِهِمْ لَمْ يَنَالُواْ خَيْرًا وَكَفَى ٱللَّهُ ٱلْمُؤْمِنِينَ ٱلْقِتَالَ وَكَانَ ٱللَّهُ قَوِيًّا عَزِيزًا ۝ وَأَنزَلَ ٱلَّذِينَ ظَاهَرُوهُم مِّنْ أَهْلِ ٱلْكِتَٰبِ مِن صَيَاصِيهِمْ وَقَذَفَ فِى قُلُوبِهِمُ ٱلرُّعْبَ فَرِيقًا تَقْتُلُونَ وَتَأْسِرُونَ فَرِيقًا ۝ وَأَوْرَثَكُمْ أَرْضَهُمْ وَدِيَٰرَهُمْ وَأَمْوَٰلَهُمْ وَأَرْضًا لَّمْ تَطَئُوهَا وَكَانَ ٱللَّهُ عَلَىٰ كُلِّ شَىْءٍ قَدِيرًا ۝

ᵃ At the Battle of Ahzab, or the Trenches, conditions were very severe. But, in this battle the stage of regular fighting was never reached. Almighty God sent stormy winds and an army of angels against the enemies and terrified them to such an extent that they themselves fled the battlefield.

The Jews of Madinah (the Banu Qurayzah) had entered into a pact of peace with the Muslims, but on the occasion of the Battle of Ahzab, they betrayed the Muslims. In breach of the pact, they supported the idolaters. Therefore, when the army of the attackers left Madinah, the Prophet Muhammad, as ordained by God, invaded the areas occupied by the Banu Qurayzah and the Islamic forces besieged their forts. The siege lasted for twenty five days. When they surrendered, everything that they possessed was forfeited.

²⁸O Prophet, say to your wives, 'If you seek the life of this world and all its finery then come, I will make provision for you, and release you honourably. ²⁹But if you seek God and His Messenger and the abode of the Hereafter, then know that God has prepared a great reward for those of you who do good deeds.' ³⁰Wives of the Prophet! Any one of you who commits a flagrant act of misconduct shall be doubly punished. That is easy enough for God.ᵃ

يَـٰٓأَيُّهَا ٱلنَّبِىُّ قُل لِّأَزْوَٰجِكَ إِن كُنتُنَّ تُرِدْنَ ٱلْحَيَوٰةَ ٱلدُّنْيَا وَزِينَتَهَا فَتَعَالَيْنَ أُمَتِّعْكُنَّ وَأُسَرِّحْكُنَّ سَرَاحًا جَمِيلًا ۝ وَإِن كُنتُنَّ تُرِدْنَ ٱللَّهَ وَرَسُولَهُۥ وَٱلدَّارَ ٱلْأَخِرَةَ فَإِنَّ ٱللَّهَ أَعَدَّ لِلْمُحْسِنَٰتِ مِنكُنَّ أَجْرًا عَظِيمًا ۝ يَـٰنِسَآءَ ٱلنَّبِىِّ مَن يَأْتِ مِنكُنَّ بِفَٰحِشَةٍ مُّبَيِّنَةٍ يُضَٰعَفْ لَهَا ٱلْعَذَابُ ضِعْفَيْنِ ۚ وَكَانَ ذَٰلِكَ عَلَى ٱللَّهِ يَسِيرًا ۝

ᵃ The Hijrah (migration to Madinah) had greatly disrupted the economy of the Muslims. Moreover, after the Hijrah, the enemies of Islam kept the Muslims continuously engaged in wars. As a result, the economic condition of the Muslims had seriously deteriorated.

The greatest impact of this condition was on the Prophet Muhammad. It was difficult to provide even the bare necessities of life to the members of his household. Things reached the stage when his consorts were forced to demand maintenance.

What his consorts asked for was basic necessities, but this was mentioned by God as a demand for worldly glitter—possibly too forceful an expression, just like the expression 'shameful acts' (fahishah). The Prophet had been assigned the most important mission in history, i.e. bringing to an end the age of polytheism and ushering in an era of monotheism. Under these circumstances, it was not possible for him to give importance to anything else. So, the consorts of the Prophet were told that either they should live contentedly with the Prophet and display greater endurance or, if that was not acceptable, to seek separation gracefully, but that raising domestic problems and thus diverting the attention of the Prophet could not be countenanced.

³¹ But those of you who obey God and His Messenger and do good deeds, shall be doubly rewarded. For them We have made an excellent provision. ³² Wives of the Prophet, you are not like any other women. If you fear God, do not be too soft-spoken in case the ill-intentioned should feel tempted. Speak in an appropriate manner.ᵃ

۞ وَمَن يَقْنُتْ مِنكُنَّ لِلَّهِ وَرَسُولِهِ وَتَعْمَلْ صَلِحًا نُؤْتِهَآ أَجْرَهَا مَرَّتَيْنِ وَأَعْتَدْنَا لَهَا رِزْقًا كَرِيمًا ۝ يَنِسَآءَ ٱلنَّبِىِّ لَسْتُنَّ كَأَحَدٍ مِّنَ ٱلنِّسَآءِ إِنِ ٱتَّقَيْتُنَّ فَلَا تَخْضَعْنَ بِٱلْقَوْلِ فَيَطْمَعَ ٱلَّذِى فِى قَلْبِهِ مَرَضٌ وَقُلْنَ قَوْلًا مَّعْرُوفًا ۝

ᵃ The consorts of the Prophet had the position of leaders in the society. Such people have to make greater sacrifices than those made by ordinary people. That is why God has promised a double reward for such people. They use more will power than others in the performance of a (good) deed and that is why they receive greater credit for it.

The Prophet's consorts in view of their qualities used to come in contact with others very often. People used to come to them to seek guidance on religious matters. That is why they were instructed to adopt a slightly dry tone while talking to others and not talk to them informally and familiarly as one is likely to do in the case of near relatives (in respect of whom marriage is not permissible).

³³ Stay in your homes and do not flaunt your charms as in the former times of ignorance. Attend to your prayers, pay the *zakat* and obey God and His Messenger. Women of the [Prophet's] Household, God seeks only to remove all impurity from you, and to make you completely pure. ³⁴ Bear in mind all that is recited in your homes of the revelations of God and of wisdom. God is all pervading and all aware.^a

وَقَرْنَ فِى بُيُوتِكُنَّ وَلَا تَبَرَّجْنَ تَبَرُّجَ ٱلْجَٰهِلِيَّةِ ٱلْأُولَىٰ وَأَقِمْنَ ٱلصَّلَوٰةَ وَءَاتِينَ ٱلزَّكَوٰةَ وَأَطِعْنَ ٱللَّهَ وَرَسُولَهُۥٓ إِنَّمَا يُرِيدُ ٱللَّهُ لِيُذْهِبَ عَنكُمُ ٱلرِّجْسَ أَهْلَ ٱلْبَيْتِ وَيُطَهِّرَكُمْ تَطْهِيرًا ۞ وَٱذْكُرْنَ مَا يُتْلَىٰ فِى بُيُوتِكُنَّ مِنْ ءَايَٰتِ ٱللَّهِ وَٱلْحِكْمَةِ إِنَّ ٱللَّهَ كَانَ لَطِيفًا خَبِيرًا ۞

---

^a Here, addressing the Prophet's consorts about correct behaviour, instruction is indirectly given to Muslim women as to how they should conduct themselves. Unlike worldly women, it should not be their aim to show off their charms and finery. Their attention should be entirely directed towards the worship of God. They should spend their wealth for the cause of God and their time in understanding the teachings of Islam.

This style of life makes one pure and righteous and it is only the pure and righteous who are approved of by Almighty God.

³⁵ Surely, for men and women who have surrendered [to God]— believing men and believing women, obedient men and obedient women, truthful men and truthful women, patient men and patient women, humble men and humble women, charitable men and charitable women, fasting men and fasting women, men and women who guard their chastity, men and women who are ever mindful of God—God is ready with forgiveness and an immense reward.^a

إِنَّ ٱلْمُسْلِمِينَ وَٱلْمُسْلِمَٰتِ وَٱلْمُؤْمِنِينَ وَٱلْمُؤْمِنَٰتِ وَٱلْقَٰنِتِينَ وَٱلْقَٰنِتَٰتِ وَٱلصَّٰدِقِينَ وَٱلصَّٰدِقَٰتِ وَٱلصَّٰبِرِينَ وَٱلصَّٰبِرَٰتِ وَٱلْخَٰشِعِينَ وَٱلْخَٰشِعَٰتِ وَٱلْمُتَصَدِّقِينَ وَٱلْمُتَصَدِّقَٰتِ وَٱلصَّٰٓئِمِينَ وَٱلصَّٰٓئِمَٰتِ وَٱلْحَٰفِظِينَ فُرُوجَهُمْ وَٱلْحَٰفِظَٰتِ وَٱلذَّٰكِرِينَ ٱللَّهَ كَثِيرًا وَٱلذَّٰكِرَٰتِ أَعَدَّ ٱللَّهُ لَهُم مَّغْفِرَةً وَأَجْرًا عَظِيمًا ۝

---

^a This verse shows what Almighty God wishes a man or woman to be like. The ten virtues He would like them to possess are as follows: Islam (submission to God), Faith in God, obedience, truthfulness, patience, sincerity, charity, fasting, chastity and remembrance of God.

These ten virtues encompass all the aspects of the Islamic faith and Islamic character. Briefly speaking, one who hopes to receive God's pardon and His rewards should bow to His injunctions, thus showing his total belief in God. There should be no contradiction between his words and his deeds. He should stand firm, regardless of the circumstances. The realization of God's greatness should have made him modest and he should consider the meeting of others' needs as his own responsibility. He must fast regularly and, in the context of sexual desires, he is chaste and pure. His days and nights are spent in the remembrance of God.

Just as these qualities are required of men, so also are they required of women. Although their manifestation may in some respects be different, as far as the qualities themselves are concerned, they are the same for both. A human being, whether a woman or a man, will be considered acceptable to God only when he or she approaches God endowed with these ten qualities.

36 It is not fitting for a believing man or woman to exercise any choice in his or her own affairs once God and His Messenger have reached a decision upon them. Anyone who disobeys God and His Messenger is in manifest error.[a]

وَمَا كَانَ لِمُؤْمِنٍ وَلَا مُؤْمِنَةٍ إِذَا قَضَى اللَّهُ وَرَسُولُهُ أَمْرًا أَن يَكُونَ لَهُمُ الْخِيَرَةُ مِنْ أَمْرِهِمْ وَمَن يَعْصِ اللَّهَ وَرَسُولَهُ فَقَدْ ضَلَّ ضَلَالًا مُّبِينًا ۝

---

[a] Man has been created independent, but he has to surrender his independence to God. This is the real test of man in this world. One who passes this crucial test is the one who is on the right path.

An example of this is the marriage in the early period of Zayd and Zaynab. Zayd was a freed slave, unlike Zaynab, who belonged to a highly placed family of the Quraysh, being the daughter of Aminah, daughter of Abdul Muttalib. The Prophet Muhammad wanted Zayd to marry Zaynab but Zaynab's people were not ready for this. Zaynab herself said, 'I am of higher birth than he.' But, when the Quran's aforesaid verse was recited to them, they showed their willingness immediately. In the year 4 AH the marriage took place.

This is the Islamic temperament and this should be the temperament of every Muslim male and every Muslim female.

³⁷ You said to the man who had been favoured by God and by you, 'Keep your wife to yourself and have fear of God.' You sought to hide in your heart what God wished to reveal. You were afraid of people, whereas it would have been more proper to fear God. When Zayd divorced his wife, We gave her to you in marriage, so that there should be no restriction on believers marrying the spouses of their adopted sons when they have divorced them. The commandment of God must be fulfilled.[a]

وَإِذْ تَقُولُ لِلَّذِىٓ أَنْعَمَ ٱللَّهُ عَلَيْهِ وَأَنْعَمْتَ عَلَيْهِ أَمْسِكْ عَلَيْكَ زَوْجَكَ وَٱتَّقِ ٱللَّهَ وَتُخْفِى فِى نَفْسِكَ مَا ٱللَّهُ مُبْدِيهِ وَتَخْشَى ٱلنَّاسَ وَٱللَّهُ أَحَقُّ أَن تَخْشَىٰهُ ۖ فَلَمَّا قَضَىٰ زَيْدٌ مِّنْهَا وَطَرًا زَوَّجْنَٰكَهَا لِكَىْ لَا يَكُونَ عَلَى ٱلْمُؤْمِنِينَ حَرَجٌ فِىٓ أَزْوَٰجِ أَدْعِيَآئِهِمْ إِذَا قَضَوْا۟ مِنْهُنَّ وَطَرًا ۚ وَكَانَ أَمْرُ ٱللَّهِ مَفْعُولًا ۝

---

[a] Zayd's marriage with Zaynab took place in the year 4 AH, but the marriage was a failure and the next year they separated. When Zayd expressed to the Prophet, his intention of giving a divorce in this case, the Prophet of God asked the reason for it. Zayd said that she had a superiority complex over him due to her being from a noble family. However, the Prophet Muhammad urged him not to divorce her. However, on Zayd's insistence, he permitted them to separate.

When Zayd and Zaynab got married, they broke an old convention and it was ordained that a difference in social status should not come in the way of marriage. But when they separated, it was the will of Almighty God that Zaynab should be made the means of breaking yet another erroneous custom.

By tradition, in the old pre-Islamic period, an adopted son was treated just like a real son, enjoying the same rights and titles. The best way of breaking this custom was that after her divorce, Zaynab should marry the Prophet Muhammad. Zayd was the adopted son of the Prophet Muhammad, and was known as Zayd bin (son of) Muhammad. Under these circumstances, the Prophet's marrying the divorced wife of his adopted son amounted to a disastrous contravention of the old custom, which held that a man's marrying a woman formerly married to his adopted son, and then divorced by him, was prohibited because she was no different from a woman married to and then divorced by his real son.

The Prophet Muhammad was told in advance that if there should be a separation between the aforesaid couple, then as a device to break the old pre-Islamic custom, Zaynab would be given in marriage to him. Since such a marriage in the prevailing atmosphere would have given him a bad name, the Prophet urged Zayd not to divorce Zaynab, so that he might be spared this very trying ordeal. But, whatever was ordained by God, did happen.

Zayd divorced Zaynab and, so as to break the old custom, Zaynab was married to the Prophet in the year 5 A.H.

³⁸ No blame shall be attached to the Prophet for doing what is sanctioned for him by God. This was God's way with those who went before him—and the command of God is a decree determined. ³⁹ Those who conveyed God's messages and fear Him only: God suffices as a reckoner. ⁴⁰ Muhammad is not the father of any of your men, but is God's Messenger and the seal of the Prophets. God has knowledge of all things.ᵃ

مَّا كَانَ عَلَى ٱلنَّبِيِّ مِنْ حَرَجٍ فِيمَا فَرَضَ ٱللَّهُ لَهُۥ سُنَّةَ ٱللَّهِ فِي ٱلَّذِينَ خَلَوْاْ مِن قَبْلُ وَكَانَ أَمْرُ ٱللَّهِ قَدَرًا مَّقْدُورًا ۝ ٱلَّذِينَ يُبَلِّغُونَ رِسَٰلَٰتِ ٱللَّهِ وَيَخْشَوْنَهُۥ وَلَا يَخْشَوْنَ أَحَدًا إِلَّا ٱللَّهَ وَكَفَىٰ بِٱللَّهِ حَسِيبًا ۝ مَّا كَانَ مُحَمَّدٌ أَبَآ أَحَدٍ مِّن رِّجَالِكُمْ وَلَٰكِن رَّسُولَ ٱللَّهِ وَخَاتَمَ ٱلنَّبِيِّـۧنَ وَكَانَ ٱللَّهُ بِكُلِّ شَىْءٍ عَلِيمًا ۝

ᵃ After the above-mentioned incident, there was as expected, a great deal of propaganda against the Prophet Muhammad. It was alleged that the Prophet had married his own daughter-in-law and such a marriage was illegal. To counter this, it was clarified that, in Muhammad's case, the fact was that he had only daughters— no sons. Zayd, son of Harithah, was only his adopted son and not his real son. So how could a woman, married to and divorced by him, be illegal for one who was not his real father?

Why is it that the Prophet had to face so many ups and downs, in spite of being the Prophet? The reason is that though the Prophet received divine revelation, he had to lead his life as a common man. In the world of trial, he faced the same circumstances as others had to face. Had it not been so, the Prophet's life would not have been an example for the common people. That is why prophetic guidance is given within the framework of realistic events, rather than under unrealistic or artificial conditions.

The Prophet Muhammad was the seal of the prophets. The word 'khatam' is used for 'seal', i.e. the final act. To seal an envelop means closing it finally, after which nothing can either be extracted or inserted into it. That is why in Arabic, the 'khatam' of a community means the last person of that community.

The announcement that the Prophet Muhammad was the 'khatemun-Nabiyyin' means that no prophet was going to come after him and, as such, it was necessary that all godly matters be revealed through him.

41 Believers, remember God often.
42 Glorify Him morning and evening.
43 It is He who sends blessings to you,
as do His angels, so that He may
bring you out of the darkness into
the light. He is most merciful to the
believers. 44 On the Day they meet
Him, they will be welcomed with the
greeting, 'Peace!' He has prepared an
honourable reward for them.ᵃ

يَـٰٓأَيُّهَا ٱلَّذِينَ ءَامَنُوا۟ ٱذْكُرُوا۟ ٱللَّهَ ذِكْرًا
كَثِيرًا ۝ وَسَبِّحُوهُ بُكْرَةً وَأَصِيلًا ۝
هُوَ ٱلَّذِى يُصَلِّى عَلَيْكُمْ وَمَلَـٰٓئِكَتُهُۥ
لِيُخْرِجَكُم مِّنَ ٱلظُّلُمَـٰتِ إِلَى ٱلنُّورِ
وَكَانَ بِٱلْمُؤْمِنِينَ رَحِيمًا ۝
تَحِيَّتُهُمْ يَوْمَ يَلْقَوْنَهُۥ سَلَـٰمٌ وَأَعَدَّ لَهُمْ
أَجْرًا كَرِيمًا ۝

ᵃ When an adulterated religion is dominant, the adoption of true religion is always
the most difficult task. Under such circumstances, the hearts of the faithful
sometimes harbour feelings of dejection and disappointment. There is one certain
method of saving oneself from this and that is to keep looking for the silver lining
in the dark clouds.

Common people live on the strength of materialism, while the Faithful live on the
strength of ideas. To live on the level of ideas means that a man lives for the
remembrance of God. The angels' inaudible discourse should be audible to him.
He should give the utmost importance to his intellectual and spiritual development.

⁴⁵ O Prophet, We have sent forth you as a witness, as a bearer of good news and a warner. ⁴⁶ As one who calls people to God by His leave, and guides them like a shining light. ⁴⁷ Convey to the believers the good news that God has bounteous blessings in store for them. ⁴⁸ Do not yield to those who deny the truth and the hypocrites: ignore their hurtful talk. Put your trust in God; God is your all sufficient guardian.ᵃ

يَـٰٓأَيُّهَا ٱلنَّبِىُّ إِنَّآ أَرْسَلْنَـٰكَ شَـٰهِدًا وَمُبَشِّرًا وَنَذِيرًا ۝ وَدَاعِيًا إِلَى ٱللَّهِ بِإِذْنِهِۦ وَسِرَاجًا مُّنِيرًا ۝ وَبَشِّرِ ٱلْمُؤْمِنِينَ بِأَنَّ لَهُم مِّنَ ٱللَّهِ فَضْلًا كَبِيرًا ۝ وَلَا تُطِعِ ٱلْكَـٰفِرِينَ وَٱلْمُنَـٰفِقِينَ وَدَعْ أَذَىٰهُمْ وَتَوَكَّلْ عَلَى ٱللَّهِ وَكَفَىٰ بِٱللَّهِ وَكِيلًا ۝

ᵃ The witness (*shahid*), the bearer of good news (*mubashshir*), the warner, (*nadhir*) and the giver of the call for the Truth (*da'i*) all represent different aspects of the same reality. It is the Prophet's mission to make people aware of the realities of life and inform them about heaven and hell. This is an action related to the call of the Prophet and on this basis only, will the Prophet give evidence in the Court of the Hereafter as to which of his addressees accepted the message of Truth, and which did not.

The Prophet's mission is also the mission of the followers of Islam. While treading this path, one has to face trouble from the people in getting support; while some give timely support, they later desert, uttering falsehoods. Under these circumstances, it was Trust in God alone which kept the Prophet (or his follower-missionaries) firmly on the true path of their missionary work. To be tolerant of whatever is negative in the people, to ignore it and under all circumstances to keep one's eyes fixed on God: these are the real assets of one who performs work.

⁴⁹ Believers, if you marry believing women, and divorce them before the marriage is consummated, you are not required to observe a waiting period: make provision for them and release them in an honourable way.ᵃ

يَٰٓأَيُّهَا ٱلَّذِينَ ءَامَنُوٓاْ إِذَا نَكَحْتُمُ ٱلْمُؤْمِنَٰتِ ثُمَّ طَلَّقْتُمُوهُنَّ مِن قَبْلِ أَن تَمَسُّوهُنَّ فَمَا لَكُمْ عَلَيْهِنَّ مِنْ عِدَّةٍ تَعْتَدُّونَهَا ۖ فَمَتِّعُوهُنَّ وَسَرِّحُوهُنَّ سَرَاحًا جَمِيلًا ۝

ᵃ If a man marries a woman, but divorces her before the marriage is consummated, the waiting period ('iddah) does not have to be observed, as happens in ordinary cases. But Islamic ethical considerations demand that the separation of husband and wife should be as dignified as their coming together was. If some alimony (mahr) was fixed for the concerned lady, then the man shall have to repay half of that. Otherwise, she should be graciously sent off after being given some amount commensurate with her status and the man's capacity to pay. The woman is permitted to enter into a second marriage immediately, if she wants to do so. There is no need for her to oberve the waiting period.

50 Prophet, We have made lawful for you the wives to whom you have given their dowers, as well as those whom your right hand possesses from among the captives of war whom God has bestowed upon you. and [We have made lawful to you] the daughters of your paternal uncles and aunts, and the daughters of your maternal uncles and aunts, who have migrated with you; and any believing woman who gives herself to the Prophet, provided the Prophet wants to marry her. This applies only to you and not to the rest of the believers. We know what We have prescribed for them concerning their wives and those whom their right hands may possess, in order that there may be no blame on you. God is most forgiving, most merciful.[a]

يَـٰٓأَيُّهَا ٱلنَّبِىُّ إِنَّآ أَحْلَلْنَا لَكَ أَزْوَٰجَكَ ٱلَّـٰتِىٓ ءَاتَيْتَ أُجُورَهُنَّ وَمَا مَلَكَتْ يَمِينُكَ مِمَّآ أَفَآءَ ٱللَّهُ عَلَيْكَ وَبَنَاتِ عَمِّكَ وَبَنَاتِ عَمَّـٰتِكَ وَبَنَاتِ خَالِكَ وَبَنَاتِ خَـٰلَـٰتِكَ ٱلَّـٰتِى هَاجَرْنَ مَعَكَ وَٱمْرَأَةً مُّؤْمِنَةً إِن وَهَبَتْ نَفْسَهَا لِلنَّبِىِّ إِنْ أَرَادَ ٱلنَّبِىُّ أَن يَسْتَنكِحَهَا خَالِصَةً لَّكَ مِن دُونِ ٱلْمُؤْمِنِينَ قَدْ عَلِمْنَا مَا فَرَضْنَا عَلَيْهِمْ فِىٓ أَزْوَٰجِهِمْ وَمَا مَلَكَتْ أَيْمَـٰنُهُمْ لِكَيْلَا يَكُونَ عَلَيْكَ حَرَجٌ وَكَانَ ٱللَّهُ غَفُورًا رَّحِيمًا ۝

---

[a] For Muslims in general the permitted maximum number of wives has been restricted to four. But, in the case of the Prophet Muhammad, this restriction was not applicable. By the special permission of Almighty God, he took more than four wives. The wisdom behind it was that the Prophet should experience no problem in the performance of his mission.

'Restriction' here refers to the problems encountered in the execution of the prophetic mission. In view of various missionary and reformative imperatives, the Prophet felt the need to marry more than four women. In view of these religious considerations, Almighty God did not apply the restriction of four wives in his case. For example, the advantage of the Prophet's marriage to Umm Salmah and Umm-Habibah was that Khalid ibn Walid, the famed general, and Abu Sufyan ibn Harb, the influential leader no longer opposed him. And the wisdom in the Prophet's marriage with 'A'ishah was that a young and intelligent lady should be in his company permanently, so that after him she could teach religion to people for a long period. Accordingly, 'A'ishah acted as a recorder of the Prophet's thoughts, words and deeds, and for half a century after his demise, went on nobly serving the cause of Islam by promulgating his ideas.

⁵¹ You may defer [the turn of] any of them that you please, and you may receive any you please: and there is no blame on you if you invite one whose [turn] you have set aside. That is more proper, so that their eyes may be cooled, and so that they may not grieve, and so that they will be satisfied with what you have given them. God knows what is in your hearts; and God is all knowing, and forbearing. ⁵² It is not lawful for you to marry more women after this, nor to change them for other wives, even though their beauty may please you, except any that your right hand possesses. God is watchful over all things.ᵃ

۞ تُرْجِى مَن تَشَآءُ مِنْهُنَّ وَتُـْٔوِىٓ إِلَيْكَ مَن تَشَآءُ ۖ وَمَنِ ٱبْتَغَيْتَ مِمَّنْ عَزَلْتَ فَلَا جُنَاحَ عَلَيْكَ ۚ ذَٰلِكَ أَدْنَىٰٓ أَن تَقَرَّ أَعْيُنُهُنَّ وَلَا يَحْزَنَّ وَيَرْضَيْنَ بِمَآ ءَاتَيْتَهُنَّ كُلُّهُنَّ ۚ وَٱللَّهُ يَعْلَمُ مَا فِى قُلُوبِكُمْ ۚ وَكَانَ ٱللَّهُ عَلِيمًا حَلِيمًا ۝ لَّا يَحِلُّ لَكَ ٱلنِّسَآءُ مِنۢ بَعْدُ وَلَآ أَن تَبَدَّلَ بِهِنَّ مِنْ أَزْوَٰجٍ وَلَوْ أَعْجَبَكَ حُسْنُهُنَّ إِلَّا مَا مَلَكَتْ يَمِينُكَ ۗ وَكَانَ ٱللَّهُ عَلَىٰ كُلِّ شَىْءٍ رَّقِيبًا ۝

ᵃ Where a number of ladies are involved, the scope for complaint increases. The Prophet Muhammad had many wives. In view of this, there was a possibility that these ladies might have grievances about inequalities in conjugal rights, as a result of which giving his full concentration to the performance of his missionary work might have been hampered. So, it was laid down that his case was a special one and that he was not subject to the provisions regarding the observance of equality in conjugal rights which were applicable to Muslims in general. If there had been any clash between the provisions regarding conjugal rights and those regarding Islamic rights, then it would have been legitimate for the Prophet to give preference to Islamic rights. The purpose of granting exemption to the Prophet from the general provisions, was to prevent the growth of resentment among his wives; as a matter of fact, the Prophet hardly ever took advantage of these powers in practice.

⁵³ Believers, do not enter the houses of the Prophet, unless you are invited for a meal. Do not linger until a meal is ready. When you are invited enter and when you have taken your meal, depart. Do not stay on, indulging in conversation. Doing that causes annoyance to the Prophet, though he is too reticent to tell you so, but God is not reticent with the truth. When you ask [the wives of the Prophet] for anything, ask them from behind a curtain. That will be purer for your hearts as well as their hearts. It is not right for you to cause annoyance to the Messenger of God or for you ever to marry his wives after him. Indeed that would be an enormity in the sight of God. ⁵⁴ Whether you reveal anything or hide it, God is aware of everything.ᵃ

يَـٰٓأَيُّهَا ٱلَّذِينَ ءَامَنُوا۟ لَا تَدْخُلُوا۟ بُيُوتَ ٱلنَّبِىِّ إِلَّآ أَن يُؤْذَنَ لَكُمْ إِلَىٰ طَعَامٍ غَيْرَ نَـٰظِرِينَ إِنَـٰهُ وَلَـٰكِنْ إِذَا دُعِيتُمْ فَٱدْخُلُوا۟ فَإِذَا طَعِمْتُمْ فَٱنتَشِرُوا۟ وَلَا مُسْتَـْٔنِسِينَ لِحَدِيثٍ ۚ إِنَّ ذَٰلِكُمْ كَانَ يُؤْذِى ٱلنَّبِىَّ فَيَسْتَحْىِۦ مِنكُمْ ۖ وَٱللَّهُ لَا يَسْتَحْىِۦ مِنَ ٱلْحَقِّ ۚ وَإِذَا سَأَلْتُمُوهُنَّ مَتَـٰعًا فَسْـَٔلُوهُنَّ مِن وَرَآءِ حِجَابٍ ۚ ذَٰلِكُمْ أَطْهَرُ لِقُلُوبِكُمْ وَقُلُوبِهِنَّ ۚ وَمَا كَانَ لَكُمْ أَن تُؤْذُوا۟ رَسُولَ ٱللَّهِ وَلَآ أَن تَنكِحُوٓا۟ أَزْوَٰجَهُۥ مِنۢ بَعْدِهِۦٓ أَبَدًا ۚ إِنَّ ذَٰلِكُمْ كَانَ عِندَ ٱللَّهِ عَظِيمًا ۝ إِن تُبْدُوا۟ شَيْـًٔا أَوْ تُخْفُوهُ فَإِنَّ ٱللَّهَ كَانَ بِكُلِّ شَىْءٍ عَلِيمًا ۝

ᵃ Here, the Prophet Muhammad's instructions have been given to Muslims as to what their domestic and social behaviour should be; that whenever they enter anybody else's house, they should do so with permission; when they are invited by somebody to partake of food, etc., they should remain in the house only as long as necessary, and leave soon afterwords. If they visit somebody, they should desist from unnecessary talks; in case they have any work in connection with women, they should do it with a curtain in between, etc.

In social life, a man should not simply concern himself with his own interests, needs and desires, but should very seriously ensure that his actions do not give trouble to others. Pointless chatter should not result in wastage of others' time.

⁵⁵ There shall be no blame on them for appearing before their fathers, their sons, their brothers, their brothers' sons, their sisters' sons, their women or those whom their right hands may possess. Women, fear God. God observes all things.ᵃ

لَّا جُنَاحَ عَلَيْهِنَّ فِىٓ ءَابَآئِهِنَّ وَلَآ أَبْنَآئِهِنَّ وَلَآ إِخْوَٰنِهِنَّ وَلَآ أَبْنَآءِ إِخْوَٰنِهِنَّ وَلَآ أَبْنَآءِ أَخَوَٰتِهِنَّ وَلَا نِسَآئِهِنَّ وَلَا مَا مَلَكَتْ أَيْمَٰنُهُنَّ ۗ وَٱتَّقِينَ ٱللَّهَ ۚ إِنَّ ٱللَّهَ كَانَ عَلَىٰ كُلِّ شَىْءٍ شَهِيدًا ۝

ᵃ In the foregoing verse, men were prohibited from coming before the Prophet's consorts. In this verse, it has been clarified that near relatives (with whom marriage is not permissible) and frequent lady visitors are exempt from these restrictions. In the range of relations mentioned here, other relations will be included which come within the ambit of this instruction, further details of which are contained in chapter 24, verse 31.

The sum and substance of all these instructions is that men and women should have the fear of God in their hearts. They should lead their lives bearing in mind that God is keeping a watch on them at all times.

⁵⁶ God and His angels bestow blessings on the Prophet. O believers, you also should invoke blessings on him and give him greetings of peace. ⁵⁷ Those who annoy God and His Messenger shall be cursed by God in this world and in the Hereafter. God has prepared for them a humiliating punishment. ⁵⁸ Those who affront believing men and believing women without their having deserved it [done any wrong] shall bear the weight of slander and flagrant sin.ᵃ

إِنَّ ٱللَّهَ وَمَلَـٰٓئِكَتَهُۥ يُصَلُّونَ عَلَى ٱلنَّبِىِّ ۚ يَـٰٓأَيُّهَا ٱلَّذِينَ ءَامَنُوا۟ صَلُّوا۟ عَلَيْهِ وَسَلِّمُوا۟ تَسْلِيمًا ۝ إِنَّ ٱلَّذِينَ يُؤْذُونَ ٱللَّهَ وَرَسُولَهُۥ لَعَنَهُمُ ٱللَّهُ فِى ٱلدُّنْيَا وَٱلْءَاخِرَةِ وَأَعَدَّ لَهُمْ عَذَابًا مُّهِينًا ۝ وَٱلَّذِينَ يُؤْذُونَ ٱلْمُؤْمِنِينَ وَٱلْمُؤْمِنَـٰتِ بِغَيْرِ مَا ٱكْتَسَبُوا۟ فَقَدِ ٱحْتَمَلُوا۟ بُهْتَـٰنًا وَإِثْمًا مُّبِينًا ۝

ᵃ The Prophet Muhammad was sent into this world to convey the divine religion to man. The subject of God who undertakes such a divine mission receives the full support of God and his angels. To favour him is as good as favouring God and His angels, and to evade him amounts to evading God and His angels.

Those who harassed the Prophet Muhammad were, to their way of thinking, making life difficult for a mere man, but they forgot that they were actually dealing with a representative of God. And those who harass God's representatives have always rendered themselves accursed in the eyes of the Lord of the Universe.

⁵⁹ O Prophet! Tell your wives and your daughters and wives of the believers that they should draw over themselves some of their outer garments [when in public], so as to be recognized and not harmed.^a God is most forgiving and most merciful. ⁶⁰ If the hypocrites^b and those who have tainted hearts and the scandal mongers of Madinah do not desist, We shall surely give you authority over them and their days in that city will be numbered. ⁶¹ Accursed, wherever they are found, they will be seized and killed.^a ⁶² Such has been God's way with those who have gone before them. You shall find no change in the ways of God.

يَـٰٓأَيُّهَا ٱلنَّبِىُّ قُل لِّأَزْوَٰجِكَ وَبَنَاتِكَ وَنِسَآءِ ٱلْمُؤْمِنِينَ يُدْنِينَ عَلَيْهِنَّ مِن جَلَـٰبِيبِهِنَّ ذَٰلِكَ أَدْنَىٰٓ أَن يُعْرَفْنَ فَلَا يُؤْذَيْنَ وَكَانَ ٱللَّهُ غَفُورًا رَّحِيمًا ۝ لَّئِن لَّمْ يَنتَهِ ٱلْمُنَـٰفِقُونَ وَٱلَّذِينَ فِى قُلُوبِهِم مَّرَضٌ وَٱلْمُرْجِفُونَ فِى ٱلْمَدِينَةِ لَنُغْرِيَنَّكَ بِهِمْ ثُمَّ لَا يُجَاوِرُونَكَ فِيهَآ إِلَّا قَلِيلًا ۝ مَّلْعُونِينَ أَيْنَمَا ثُقِفُوٓا۟ أُخِذُوا۟ وَقُتِّلُوا۟ تَقْتِيلًا ۝ سُنَّةَ ٱللَّهِ فِى ٱلَّذِينَ خَلَوْا۟ مِن قَبْلُ وَلَن تَجِدَ لِسُنَّةِ ٱللَّهِ تَبْدِيلًا ۝

---

^a When a Muslim woman leaves her house on an errand, she should be so clad as to give the impression that she is a well-bred, respectable, modest woman, and that she has left her home for some serious need and not to make merry or to go in search of entertainment.

Simple apparel, a modest gait, the body properly covered, etc.—these are the symbols of that approach.

^b Hypocrites here refers to those who indulged in acts of treason by siding secretly with the enemies of the Prophet.

⁶³ People will ask you about the Hour. Say, 'God alone has knowledge of it. Who knows? The Hour may well be near at hand.' ⁶⁴ God has rejected those who deny the truth and prepared for them a blazing Fire. ⁶⁵ There they will live forever, and they will find therein neither friend nor helper. ⁶⁶ On the Day when their faces are turned over in the Fire, they shall say: 'Oh, would that we had obeyed God, and obeyed the Messenger!' ⁶⁷ They shall say, 'Our Lord, we paid heed to our leaders and our elders, but they led us away from the right path. ⁶⁸ Our Lord, give them double punishment and curse them with a mighty curse.' ^a

يَسْـَٔلُكَ ٱلنَّاسُ عَنِ ٱلسَّاعَةِ قُلْ إِنَّمَا عِلْمُهَا عِندَ ٱللَّهِ وَمَا يُدْرِيكَ لَعَلَّ ٱلسَّاعَةَ تَكُونُ قَرِيبًا ۞ إِنَّ ٱللَّهَ لَعَنَ ٱلْكَٰفِرِينَ وَأَعَدَّ لَهُمْ سَعِيرًا ۞ خَٰلِدِينَ فِيهَآ أَبَدًا لَّا يَجِدُونَ وَلِيًّا وَلَا نَصِيرًا ۞ يَوْمَ تُقَلَّبُ وُجُوهُهُمْ فِى ٱلنَّارِ يَقُولُونَ يَٰلَيْتَنَآ أَطَعْنَا ٱللَّهَ وَأَطَعْنَا ٱلرَّسُولَا۠ ۞ وَقَالُوا۟ رَبَّنَآ إِنَّآ أَطَعْنَا سَادَتَنَا وَكُبَرَآءَنَا فَأَضَلُّونَا ٱلسَّبِيلَا۠ ۞ رَبَّنَآ ءَاتِهِمْ ضِعْفَيْنِ مِنَ ٱلْعَذَابِ وَٱلْعَنْهُمْ لَعْنًا كَبِيرًا ۞

---

^a Enquiring about the exact day when the Day of Judgement would arrive did not mean that the enquiries had no belief whatsoever in Judgement Day. This was not meant to mock the Day of Judgement, but to ridicule the person who gave news of that Day. They did not deny that Judgement Day would actually come, but they did not believe in the nature of that Day, of which the Prophet and his companions gave specific details.

Their real fault was that they gave undue importance to the leaders of their community, rather than showing due respect to the Prophet. That is why the words of the prominent persons of their community appeared to them more worthy of consideration than the words of the Prophet. But, on the Day of Judgement when the reality is revealed, they will regret that they could not differentiate between real greatness and false greatness, and that; having been deceived by false greatness, they went astray.

⁶⁹ Believers, do not behave like those who slandered Moses. God cleared him of their allegations. He was honourable in the sight of God. ⁷⁰ Believers, fear God, and say the right word. ⁷¹ He will bless your works for you and forgive you your sins. Whoever obeys God and His Messenger has indeed achieved a great success.ᵃ

يَـٰٓأَيُّهَا ٱلَّذِينَ ءَامَنُوا۟ لَا تَكُونُوا۟ كَٱلَّذِينَ ءَاذَوْا۟ مُوسَىٰ فَبَرَّأَهُ ٱللَّهُ مِمَّا قَالُوا۟ ۚ وَكَانَ عِندَ ٱللَّهِ وَجِيهًا ۞ يَـٰٓأَيُّهَا ٱلَّذِينَ ءَامَنُوا۟ ٱتَّقُوا۟ ٱللَّهَ وَقُولُوا۟ قَوْلًا سَدِيدًا ۞ يُصْلِحْ لَكُمْ أَعْمَـٰلَكُمْ وَيَغْفِرْ لَكُمْ ذُنُوبَكُمْ ۗ وَمَن يُطِعِ ٱللَّهَ وَرَسُولَهُ فَقَدْ فَازَ فَوْزًا عَظِيمًا ۞

ᵃ The injunction refrains believers from harassing the Prophet Muhammad, as did the Jews to the Prophet Moses. The verse was revealed in the backdrop of the following incident. Once when the Prophet was in Madinah, he received some goods, which he distributed among the people. Subsequently, one of the Ansars (followers of the Prophet who hailed from Madina) criticized him, saying: 'By God, Muhammad has sought neither the pleasure of God nor a home in the Hereafter, by this distribution.' When this incident was brought to the notice of the Prophet, he said, 'May the Mercy of God be on Moses. He was given much more trouble, but he remained patient.' (*Tafsir ibn Kathir*).

There are two types of utterances—the straightforward and the devious. The straightforward utterance is that which exactly conforms to the facts; which is based on factual analysis and which is presented with the support of solid arguments. As opposed to this, the devious utterance is that which is not reality-oriented, which is based on guesses and conjectures and simply amounts to expressing an opinion: it is not factual reporting. The first mentioned is the utterance of the believer (*mu'min*), while the second is that of the hypocrite.

72 We offered the Trust to the heavens and the earth and the mountains, but they refused to bear it, because they were afraid of it. But man bore it: he surely proved unjust and ignorant. 73 God will punish the hypocrites, both men and women, and polytheists, both men and women, but God will turn in His mercy to believing men and believing women; God is most forgiving and most merciful.ᵃ

إِنَّا عَرَضْنَا ٱلْأَمَانَةَ عَلَى ٱلسَّمَٰوَٰتِ وَٱلْأَرْضِ وَٱلْجِبَالِ فَأَبَيْنَ أَن يَحْمِلْنَهَا وَأَشْفَقْنَ مِنْهَا وَحَمَلَهَا ٱلْإِنسَٰنُ إِنَّهُۥ كَانَ ظَلُومًا جَهُولًا ۝ لِّيُعَذِّبَ ٱللَّهُ ٱلْمُنَٰفِقِينَ وَٱلْمُنَٰفِقَٰتِ وَٱلْمُشْرِكِينَ وَٱلْمُشْرِكَٰتِ وَيَتُوبَ ٱللَّهُ عَلَى ٱلْمُؤْمِنِينَ وَٱلْمُؤْمِنَٰتِ وَكَانَ ٱللَّهُ غَفُورًا رَّحِيمًا ۝

ᵃ The offering of 'trust' here means a transference of power, to be used at man's discretion. This power is something with which God has entrusted man temporarily, by way of trial, so that man of his own volition, should become obedient to God. Acceptance of this trust amounts to becoming God's representative. One has to impose upon oneself what the stars and planets do under compulsion. In other words, surrender voluntarily to God's will.

In this universe, only God is the Lord and all things are His subjects. But, Almighty God willed that He should create independent creatures who, without any compulsion, would voluntarily do whatever God wanted them to do. This voluntary obedience constituted a great trial for mankind. The heavens, the earth and the mountains could not undertake it. However, man accepted it, in spite of the serious risks involved. Now man is God's trustee in this world. He has to apply the rule of God to himself just as God applies it to others according to His will. Man is being put to the test and the present world is a vast examination hall.

God's trust is an extremely crucial responsibility, because it gives rise to the problem of reward and punishment. Other creatures, being helpless, are bound to conform to the will of God. So there is no question of reward or punishment for them. But, man enjoys freedom and this being so, he is deserving of reward or punishment. There is a tradition handed down from 'Abdullah ibn 'Abbas, which says that when Almighty God mentioned the subject of trust to Adam, he asked what was meant by trust. Almighty God replied: 'If you perform good deeds, you will receive a reward, but if you perform bad deeds, you will be punished.' (*Tafsir ibn Kathir*).

The will of God has been enforced on the whole world. This same will of God has to be imposed on man of his own accord.

In the name of God,
the Most Gracious, the Most Merciful

¹ Praise be to God, to whom belongs all that the heavens and the earth contain and praise be to Him in the Hereafter. He is the All Wise, the All Aware. ² He knows whatever goes into the earth and whatever comes forth from it, and whatever descends from heaven and whatever ascends into it. He is the Merciful, the Forgiving.ᵃ

ᵃ This Universe is an introduction to its Creator. Its terrifying vastness reveals the majesty of its Creator. The utter perfection of its harmony indicates that its Creator is a perfect and complete being. The fact of the Universe being extremely congenial and conducive to the nourishment of human life clearly shows that its Creator is extremely kind and merciful towards His creations.

One who ponders over the mysteries of the Universe will be totally absorbed in the realization of God's majesty and perfection. He will be convinced that from the beginning of time till the end of eternity, all majesty pertains to the one and only God and to none other than Him.

³ Those who deny the truth declare, 'The Hour will never come upon us.' Say, 'Yes, by my Lord, it will surely come upon you! Who knows the unseen. Not the smallest particle in the heavens or the earth, or anything less or greater than that escapes Him; all is recorded in an open Book. ⁴ He will surely reward those who believe and do good deeds: they shall have forgiveness and an honourable provision.' ⁵ But those who strive against Our signs, trying to defeat them, will suffer a painful torment. ⁶ Those who have been given knowledge know that what has been revealed to you from your Lord is the truth, and that it guides to the path of the Almighty, the Praiseworthy.ᵃ

وَقَالَ ٱلَّذِينَ كَفَرُوا۟ لَا تَأْتِينَا ٱلسَّاعَةُ قُلْ بَلَىٰ وَرَبِّى لَتَأْتِيَنَّكُمْ عَـٰلِمِ ٱلْغَيْبِ لَا يَعْزُبُ عَنْهُ مِثْقَالُ ذَرَّةٍ فِى ٱلسَّمَـٰوَٰتِ وَلَا فِى ٱلْأَرْضِ وَلَآ أَصْغَرُ مِن ذَٰلِكَ وَلَآ أَكْبَرُ إِلَّا فِى كِتَـٰبٍ مُّبِينٍ ۝ لِّيَجْزِىَ ٱلَّذِينَ ءَامَنُوا۟ وَعَمِلُوا۟ ٱلصَّـٰلِحَـٰتِ أُو۟لَـٰٓئِكَ هُم مَّغْفِرَةٌ وَرِزْقٌ كَرِيمٌ ۝ وَٱلَّذِينَ سَعَوْ فِىٓ ءَايَـٰتِنَا مُعَـٰجِزِينَ أُو۟لَـٰٓئِكَ لَهُمْ عَذَابٌ مِّن رِّجْزٍ أَلِيمٌ ۝ وَيَرَى ٱلَّذِينَ أُوتُوا۟ ٱلْعِلْمَ ٱلَّذِىٓ أُنزِلَ إِلَيْكَ مِن رَّبِّكَ هُوَ ٱلْحَقَّ وَيَهْدِىٓ إِلَىٰ صِرَٰطِ ٱلْعَزِيزِ ٱلْحَمِيدِ ۝

ᵃ The addressees of the Quran were not disbelievers in the Day of Judgement. It was just that they did not believe that Judgement Day would bring them humiliation and punishment. The world they lived in appeared safe to them and they could not, therefore, understand how they would be in jeopardy on reaching the world Hereafter.

This truth about life and the Universe is found in all divine scriptures. It is the Quran's mission to reveal this reality in its pure and unadulterated form. Now, those who take a stand in opposition to this mission are indulging in the most improper bravado. Before God, they will be treated as deserving of the severest punishment.

7 Those who deny the truth say, 'Shall we point out to you a man who will tell you that when you are broken up into particles, you will be put together again in a new creation? 8 Has he invented a lie about God, or is he afflicted with madness?' Indeed no. It is those who do not believe in the Hereafter who will suffer torment, for they have strayed far into error. 9 Do they not observe how they are encompassed by what is before them and what is behind them in heaven and on earth? We could, if We pleased, cause the earth to swallow them up, or cause a piece of the sky to fall upon them. In that certainly there is a sign for every servant of Ours who turns to us.[a]

وَقَالَ ٱلَّذِينَ كَفَرُوٓاْ هَلْ نَدُلُّكُمْ عَلَىٰ رَجُلٍ يُنَبِّئُكُمْ إِذَا مُزِّقْتُمْ كُلَّ مُمَزَّقٍ إِنَّكُمْ لَفِى خَلْقٍ جَدِيدٍ ۞ أَفْتَرَىٰ عَلَى ٱللَّهِ كَذِبًا أَمْ بِهِۦ جِنَّةٌ بَلِ ٱلَّذِينَ لَا يُؤْمِنُونَ بِٱلْءَاخِرَةِ فِى ٱلْعَذَابِ وَٱلضَّلَٰلِ ٱلْبَعِيدِ ۞ أَفَلَمْ يَرَوْاْ إِلَىٰ مَا بَيْنَ أَيْدِيهِمْ وَمَا خَلْفَهُم مِّنَ ٱلسَّمَآءِ وَٱلْأَرْضِ إِن نَّشَأْ نَخْسِفْ بِهِمُ ٱلْأَرْضَ أَوْ نُسْقِطْ عَلَيْهِمْ كِسَفًا مِّنَ ٱلسَّمَآءِ إِنَّ فِى ذَٰلِكَ لَءَايَةً لِّكُلِّ عَبْدٍ مُّنِيبٍ ۞

---

[a] The people of Makkah held the Prophet and his companions in contempt, and used to mock them. They did so due to their disbelief in the Hereafter and because in their hearts they were not fearful of God's scourge; this made them quite flippant about the affairs of the Hereafter.

The worst punishment for a man in this world is to be incapable of right thinking. One so punished is not capable of seeing things in their proper perspective. He is unable to learn lessons even from obvious realities. For example, innumerable stones of varying sizes, fall towards the Earth's surface but get destroyed as soon as they come in contact with our atmosphere. If these stones were to start falling on human habitation, the entire humanity would be wiped out. A major part of the centre of the earth consists of hot molten lava. If that lava were to erupt and flow unchecked over the surface of the earth, everything in its path would be burnt to a cinder. But God, having made special arrangements, does not allow such catastrophic events to occur. There are clear signs in heaven and on earth which show man's helplessness. But when a man is incapable of right thinking, no sign of God can give him guidance.

¹⁰ We bestowed upon David great favour. We said, 'O mountains and birds! Join with him in celebrating Our praise.' We softened iron for him, saying, ¹¹ 'Make full-length coats of mail, measuring the links well. And do righteous deeds. Surely, I see all that you do.'ᵃ

۞ وَلَقَدْ ءَاتَيْنَا دَاوُدَ مِنَّا فَضْلًا يَٰجِبَالُ أَوِّبِى مَعَهُۥ وَٱلطَّيْرَ وَأَلَنَّا لَهُ ٱلْحَدِيدَ ۝ أَنِ ٱعْمَلْ سَٰبِغَٰتٍ وَقَدِّرْ فِى ٱلسَّرْدِ وَٱعْمَلُوا۟ صَٰلِحًا إِنِّى بِمَا تَعْمَلُونَ بَصِيرٌ ۝

ᵃ When a believer who is fully absorbed in the remembrance of God recites the praises of God, he is in fact in consonance with the entire Universe; all things in heaven and on the earth join him in chorus, albeit in silent language. But, God had so specially blessed David that the hills, mountains and birds used to audibly join him when he recited the praises of God.

Similarly, God taught David (through angels) the skills to make use of iron. He developed the technique of melting and moulding iron to such an extent that he could make the very fine links of which chain mail is composed. The suits of armour made from this could be worn like ordinary clothes. At that time, this technique was unknown to the world.

A believer can make great advances in the fields of industry and science. But, it is essential that he should direct this human progress towards peace and goodness. Whatever he accomplishes should be done with the realization that, finally, he has to appear before God and be answerable to Him.

¹² We subjected the wind to Solomon; its morning course was a month and its evening course a month; and We caused a fount of molten copper to flow for him. And of the jinn there were some who worked under him, by the command of his Lord. If any one of them turned away from Our command, We would make him taste the punishment of the burning fire. ¹³ They made for him whatever he desired: palaces and statues, basins like reservoirs, and large cooking vessels fixed in their places. We said, 'Give thanks, house of David, for few of My servants are truly grateful.' ^a

وَلِسُلَيْمَـٰنَ ٱلرِّيحَ غُدُوُّهَا شَهْرٌ وَرَوَاحُهَا شَهْرٌ وَأَسَلْنَا لَهُۥ عَيْنَ ٱلْقِطْرِ وَمِنَ ٱلْجِنِّ مَن يَعْمَلُ بَيْنَ يَدَيْهِ بِإِذْنِ رَبِّهِۦ وَمَن يَزِغْ مِنْهُمْ عَنْ أَمْرِنَا نُذِقْهُ مِنْ عَذَابِ ٱلسَّعِيرِ ۝ يَعْمَلُونَ لَهُۥ مَا يَشَاءُ مِن مَّحَـٰرِيبَ وَتَمَـٰثِيلَ وَجِفَانٍ كَٱلْجَوَابِ وَقُدُورٍ رَّاسِيَـٰتٍ ٱعْمَلُوٓا۟ ءَالَ دَاوُۥدَ شُكْرًا وَقَلِيلٌ مِّنْ عِبَادِىَ ٱلشَّكُورُ ۝

---

^a Solomon had brought about great developments in seafaring and sea trade and it was at his behest that high quality sail-fitted ships were built. With God's further blessing, his ships always had favourable winds. Similarly, the technique of melting copper and the production of different artefacts from it were well-developed in his period. Solomon utilized these extraordinary powers for constructive and peaceful purposes. Among them was the preparation of the things mentioned in this verse.

The entire existence of man is the gift of God. From head to foot, he is the manifestation of His Grace. Therefore, he should have in him feelings of the utmost gratefulness and indebtedness towards God. But, this is the very feeling with which a human being is least imbued. The reason for this is that whatever a man may receive in this world is in the guise of the result of the cause and effect chain. Therefore, he considers it as such—the result of some cause. But this is the real test of man. It is expected that he should see the hand of God in whatever he ostensibly receives through cause and effect. Whatever he obtains, apparently on account of his talents and diligence, should be treated by him as direct gifts from God.

¹⁴ When We decreed Solomon's death, nothing indicated his death to them except a worm from the earth, which was eating away at his cane. When he fell down, the jinn plainly realized that if they had known what was unseen, they would not have had to continue with such humiliating labour.ᵃ

فَلَمَّا قَضَيْنَا عَلَيْهِ ٱلْمَوْتَ مَا دَلَّهُمْ عَلَىٰ مَوْتِهِ إِلَّا دَابَّةُ ٱلْأَرْضِ تَأْكُلُ مِنسَأَتَهُ فَلَمَّا خَرَّ تَبَيَّنَتِ ٱلْجِنُّ أَن لَّوْ كَانُوا۟ يَعْلَمُونَ ٱلْغَيْبَ مَا لَبِثُوا۟ فِى ٱلْعَذَابِ ٱلْمُهِينِ ۝

ᵃ When it was time for Solomon to die, he was leaning on a stick and having some constructive work done by the 'jinn'. The angel of death took away his life-spirit, but his lifeless body, with the support of the stick remained upright. The jinn continued with their work under the impression that he was nearby supervising the work. It so happened that some white ants infested the stick and after some time, when the white ants had made the stick hollow, his body fell on to the ground. It was then that the jinn came to know that Solomon had died.

This incident suffices to remove the erroneous popular belief that the jinn have knowledge of the future.

15 For the people of Sheba there was a sign in their homeland: two gardens, one on the right hand and the other on the left. We said to them: 'Eat what your Lord has provided for you, and be grateful. You have a good land and a Lord most forgiving.' 16 Yet they turned away [from the truth]. So We let loose on them a flood from the dam and replaced their two gardens by two others bearing bitter fruits, tamarisks, and a few lote trees. 17 We requited them in that way because of their ingratitude. We requite no one in that way but the ungrateful.ᵃ

لَقَدْ كَانَ لِسَبَإٍ فِي مَسْكَنِهِمْ ءَايَةٌ جَنَّتَانِ عَن يَمِينٍ وَشِمَالٍ كُلُوا۟ مِن رِّزْقِ رَبِّكُمْ وَٱشْكُرُوا۟ لَهُۥ بَلْدَةٌ طَيِّبَةٌ وَرَبٌّ غَفُورٌ ۝ فَأَعْرَضُوا۟ فَأَرْسَلْنَا عَلَيْهِمْ سَيْلَ ٱلْعَرِمِ وَبَدَّلْنَٰهُم بِجَنَّتَيْهِمْ جَنَّتَيْنِ ذَوَاتَىْ أُكُلٍ خَمْطٍ وَأَثْلٍ وَشَىْءٍ مِّن سِدْرٍ قَلِيلٍ ۝ ذَٰلِكَ جَزَيْنَٰهُم بِمَا كَفَرُوا۟ وَهَلْ نُجَٰزِىٓ إِلَّا ٱلْكَفُورَ ۝

ᵃ Sheba (Saba') was a very developed community of ancient times. It was spread over the area at present known as Yemen. Its centre was the city of Maa'rib. In the period before Christ, it had made great progress and remained at its zenith for about one thousand years. The inhabitants of Sheba had spread their trade far and wide across land and sea and had constructed dams for irrigation purposes. Near Ma'rib, there was a large dam which was 14 meters high and about six hundred meters long. By this means, water from mountain streams was stored and distributed to the adjoining lands. In this way this whole area had become lush green and luxuriant gardens could be seen everywhere.

All these developments had been possible thanks to the provision made by God. Therefore, the people of Sheba should have been grateful to their Lord. But, instead, they became neglectful and arrogant, as generally happens in the case of prosperous communities. Thereafter, the Ma'arib Dam started developing cracks. This was an initial warning, but they did not come to their senses. An earthquake shattered the dam irreparably in the seventh century A.D., as a result of which there were devastating floods and the whole area was destroyed. Moreover, due to the destruction of fertile soil, only wild bushes survived in this area. (*The Encyclopaedia Britannica*).

¹⁸ We had placed between them and the towns that We had blessed, other towns situated close to each other, and We fixed the stages [of journey] between them, saying, 'Travel between them in safety by night and day,' ¹⁹ but they said, 'Our Lord! Make the stages of our journeys longer.' Thus they wronged themselves and We made them bygone tales and scattered them throughout the land. There are certainly signs in that for everyone who is steadfast and thankful.ᵃ

وَجَعَلْنَا بَيْنَهُمْ وَبَيْنَ ٱلْقُرَى ٱلَّتِى بَرَكْنَا فِيهَا قُرًى ظَهِرَةً وَقَدَّرْنَا فِيهَا ٱلسَّيْرَ سِيرُوا۟ فِيهَا لَيَالِىَ وَأَيَّامًا ءَامِنِينَ ۞ فَقَالُوا۟ رَبَّنَا بَعِّدْ بَيْنَ أَسْفَارِنَا وَظَلَمُوٓا۟ أَنفُسَهُمْ فَجَعَلْنَٰهُمْ أَحَادِيثَ وَمَزَّقْنَٰهُمْ كُلَّ مُمَزَّقٍ إِنَّ فِى ذَٰلِكَ لَءَايَٰتٍ لِّكُلِّ صَبَّارٍ شَكُورٍ ۞

ᵃ 'The town that We had blessed' refers to the green and fertile area of Syria. In this lush green area from Yemen to Syria, there were rows of beautiful townships. Travelling in this area was a pleasant experience, enough to kindle the spirit of thankfulness and devotion in man. It was as if God had put up a signpost there to say: 'Go ahead without any fear and thank your Lord!'

But the unheeding people of Sheba were unable to read this inscription of God. On account of their improper behaviour, they lost their right to avail of these divine blessings. They were so totally destroyed that it was as if they had never existed. After the destruction of their homeland, the various tribes of Sheba scattered and migrated to far-off places.

These incidents are known facts of history. But the real assessor of these events is one who learns the lesson that if he achieves prosperity, he should not be vainglorious. On the contrary, he should treat everything that he receives as a gift from God and be grateful to Him.

²⁰ Satan was correct in his assessment of them and they all followed him— except for a band of true believers— ²¹ but he had no authority over them; We only desired to distinguish those who believed in the Hereafter from those who were in doubt concerning it. Your Lord is watchful over all things.^a

وَلَقَدْ صَدَّقَ عَلَيْهِمْ إِبْلِيسُ ظَنَّهُۥ فَٱتَّبَعُوهُ إِلَّا فَرِيقًا مِّنَ ٱلْمُؤْمِنِينَ ۝ وَمَا كَانَ لَهُۥ عَلَيْهِم مِّن سُلْطَـٰنٍ إِلَّا لِنَعْلَمَ مَن يُؤْمِنُ بِٱلْءَاخِرَةِ مِمَّنْ هُوَ مِنْهَا فِى شَكٍّ ۗ وَرَبُّكَ عَلَىٰ كُلِّ شَىْءٍ حَفِيظٌ ۝

---

^a Satan (Iblis) and his representatives, are forever hatching plots against human beings. On such occasions, it is man's duty not to fall a victim to them and thus render their plotting unsuccessful. But, the people of Sheba did not prove to be wise. They were influenced by and succumbed to the satanic inducements and trod the path to destruction. There were but a few (true believers) who were successful in this test.

God has not given Satan or his representatives any actual powers over anybody. Satan has the power only to seduce. This has been so arranged for the purpose of putting man to the test. One who passes this test will rise above satanic inducements and remain firm on the path of reality and Truth.

²² Call upon those whom you set up beside God! They possess not an atom's weight either in the heavens or on the earth, nor have they any share in either, nor has He any helpers among them. ²³ No intercession avails with Him, except on the part of one to whom He grants permission. When their hearts are relieved of fear, they will enquire from those to whom permission is granted, 'What has your Lord said?' They will answer, 'The truth. He is the Most High, the Supreme One.' *a*

قُلِ ٱدْعُوا۟ ٱلَّذِينَ زَعَمْتُم مِّن دُونِ ٱللَّهِ لَا يَمْلِكُونَ مِثْقَالَ ذَرَّةٍ فِى ٱلسَّمَـٰوَٰتِ وَلَا فِى ٱلْأَرْضِ وَمَا لَهُمْ فِيهِمَا مِن شِرْكٍ وَمَا لَهُۥ مِنْهُم مِّن ظَهِيرٍ ۝ وَلَا تَنفَعُ ٱلشَّفَـٰعَةُ عِندَهُۥٓ إِلَّا لِمَنْ أَذِنَ لَهُۥ ۚ حَتَّىٰٓ إِذَا فُزِّعَ عَن قُلُوبِهِمْ قَالُوا۟ مَاذَا قَالَ رَبُّكُمْ قَالُوا۟ ٱلْحَقَّ ۖ وَهُوَ ٱلْعَلِىُّ ٱلْكَبِيرُ ۝

---

a Every age has had many believers in the Hereafter, yet Satan has propagated such erroneous beliefs as have made the unbelievers fearless of the Hereafter. One of these is the false belief that certain beings enjoy such an elevated status before God that they can secure God's pardon for others.

Any such belief amounts to underestimating the powers of God. It is ridiculous that while these beings are themselves awe-struck by the majesty of God, they are expected by their adorers to use their influence for their salvation. Ironically, it is believed that this would suffice before God.

²⁴ Ask them, 'Who provides sustenance for you from the heavens and the earth?' Say, 'It is God'; either you or we are rightly guided or in manifest error.' ²⁵ Say to them, 'You will not be called to account for our sins and we shall not be called to account for what you do.' ²⁶ Tell them, 'Our Lord will gather us together; then He will judge between us with truth and justice. He is the Just Decider, the All Knowing.' ²⁷ Say to them, 'Show me those whom you have joined with Him as partners. No indeed! For He alone is God, the Mighty One, the Wise One.'ᵃ

* قُلْ مَن يَرْزُقُكُم مِّنَ ٱلسَّمَٰوَٰتِ وَٱلْأَرْضِ قُلِ ٱللَّهُ وَإِنَّآ أَوْ إِيَّاكُمْ لَعَلَىٰ هُدًى أَوْ فِى ضَلَٰلٍ مُّبِينٍ ۝ قُل لَّا تُسْـَٔلُونَ عَمَّآ أَجْرَمْنَا وَلَا نُسْـَٔلُ عَمَّا تَعْمَلُونَ ۝ قُلْ يَجْمَعُ بَيْنَنَا رَبُّنَا ثُمَّ يَفْتَحُ بَيْنَنَا بِٱلْحَقِّ وَهُوَ ٱلْفَتَّاحُ ٱلْعَلِيمُ ۝ قُلْ أَرُونِىَ ٱلَّذِينَ أَلْحَقْتُم بِهِۦ شُرَكَآءَ كَلَّا بَلْ هُوَ ٱللَّهُ ٱلْعَزِيزُ ٱلْحَكِيمُ ۝

ᵃ The Universe is unimaginably great. Moreover, perfect wisdom and meaningfulness is inherent in it. Such a universe can be the accomplishment of the All-powerful, All-wise God alone. No one can seriously believe that those beings, whom ancient or modern man has invented can be the creators or lords of this universe. This being so, who other than God can be the one who enjoys the position of supremacy in this Universe?

The fact is that the study of the universe invalidates all polytheistic theories. As such, only that theory can be correct which is based on the oneness of God. Any theory which projects the instrumentality of any being other than God is self-contradictory.

²⁸ We have sent you as a bearer of glad tidings and a warner for the whole of mankind, but most people have no knowledge. ²⁹ They ask, 'When will this promise be fulfilled, if you are truthful?' ³⁰ Say, 'A Day has already been appointed for you which you can neither delay nor advance by a single moment.'ᵃ

وَمَآ أَرْسَلْنَٰكَ إِلَّا كَآفَّةً لِّلنَّاسِ بَشِيرًا وَنَذِيرًا وَلَٰكِنَّ أَكْثَرَ ٱلنَّاسِ لَا يَعْلَمُونَ ۞ وَيَقُولُونَ مَتَىٰ هَٰذَا ٱلْوَعْدُ إِن كُنتُمْ صَٰدِقِينَ ۞ قُل لَّكُم مِّيعَادُ يَوْمٍ لَّا تَسْتَـْٔخِرُونَ عَنْهُ سَاعَةً وَلَا تَسْتَقْدِمُونَ ۞

ᵃ Every prophet did missionary work directly with his people (community). That alone was practicable. Similarly, the Prophet Muhammad also became the direct dispenser of good news (*mubashshir*) and a direct warner (*munzir*) for his own people (6:92). But, since the institution of prophethood ended with him, he is now, by order, *mubashshir* and *munzir* for all the nations in the world. Just as he discharged both these functions in relation to his first addressees (in his own times), so in the same way, his followers as deputies had to discharge these functions in relation to all other addressees in later periods. This will be treated as continuity of his prophetic mission. The missionary work done by him during his life-time is directly within the ambit of his prophetic functions, while the work done after his life in this world, will be indirectly so.

The mission of a prophet is always to convey the message of God. Thereafter, the reward or punishment, according to the response of the people, is for God to decide—in this world as well as in the Hereafter.

³¹ Those who deny the truth say, 'We shall believe neither in this scripture nor in [any] that [came] before it.' Could you but see when the wrongdoers will be made to stand before their Lord, casting blame on one another! Those who had been weak will say to the arrogant ones, 'Had it not been for you, we should certainly have been believers!' ³² The haughty ones will then reply to the weak ones, 'Did we keep you away from the guidance when it came to you? Indeed not. You yourselves were the guilty ones.' ³³ Those deemed weak will say to those deemed great, 'No, it was your scheming night and day when you commanded us to reject God and assign equals to Him.' But they will show their remorse when they see the punishment. We will put iron collars round the necks of those who had been bent on denying the truth. They will be requited only in proportion to their misdeeds.ᵃ

وَقَالَ ٱلَّذِينَ كَفَرُوا۟ لَن نُّؤْمِنَ بِهَٰذَا ٱلْقُرْءَانِ وَلَا بِٱلَّذِى بَيْنَ يَدَيْهِ ۗ وَلَوْ تَرَىٰٓ إِذِ ٱلظَّٰلِمُونَ مَوْقُوفُونَ عِندَ رَبِّهِمْ يَرْجِعُ بَعْضُهُمْ إِلَىٰ بَعْضٍ ٱلْقَوْلَ يَقُولُ ٱلَّذِينَ ٱسْتُضْعِفُوا۟ لِلَّذِينَ ٱسْتَكْبَرُوا۟ لَوْلَآ أَنتُمْ لَكُنَّا مُؤْمِنِينَ ﴿٣١﴾ قَالَ ٱلَّذِينَ ٱسْتَكْبَرُوا۟ لِلَّذِينَ ٱسْتُضْعِفُوٓا۟ أَنَحْنُ صَدَدْنَٰكُمْ عَنِ ٱلْهُدَىٰ بَعْدَ إِذْ جَآءَكُم ۖ بَلْ كُنتُم مُّجْرِمِينَ ﴿٣٢﴾ وَقَالَ ٱلَّذِينَ ٱسْتُضْعِفُوا۟ لِلَّذِينَ ٱسْتَكْبَرُوا۟ بَلْ مَكْرُ ٱلَّيْلِ وَٱلنَّهَارِ إِذْ تَأْمُرُونَنَآ أَن نَّكْفُرَ بِٱللَّهِ وَنَجْعَلَ لَهُۥٓ أَندَادًا ۚ وَأَسَرُّوا۟ ٱلنَّدَامَةَ لَمَّا رَأَوُا۟ ٱلْعَذَابَ وَجَعَلْنَا ٱلْأَغْلَٰلَ فِىٓ أَعْنَاقِ ٱلَّذِينَ كَفَرُوا۟ ۚ هَلْ يُجْزَوْنَ إِلَّا مَا كَانُوا۟ يَعْمَلُونَ ﴿٣٣﴾

ᵃ Denial of Truth is the greatest crime. The result of this crime does not become apparent to an individual in this world. Therefore, he goes on fearlessly denying the Truth. But, in the Hereafter, when the adverse effect of denying the Truth impinges on the deniers, they will be caught in a state of turmoil.

The common people, in this world, were proud of their leaders, but once in the Hereafter, they will curse them. In reply, their leaders will say, 'Don't blame us to cover up your ignominy. It was not we who misguided you but your own desires. You were with us simply because our words were in consonance with your own desires. You wanted a religion in which you could get credit for being righeous without taking much trouble and without changing yourself, and we provided you with it. You put our noose around your neck of your own accord; otherwise, we had no power to do so.'

³⁴ For it has been thus whenever We sent a warner to any community. Its affluent ones said, 'We reject what you have been sent with.' ³⁵ They say, 'We have more wealth and children; and we are surely not going to be punished.' ³⁶ Say to them, 'My Lord increases the provision for whoever He pleases and decreases it for whoever He pleases; but most people do not know it.' ³⁷ It is not your wealth or your children that will confer on you nearness to Us. It is those who believe and act righteously who will be doubly rewarded for their good deeds, and will dwell in peace in the high pavilions [of paradise], ³⁸ while those who strive to thwart Our messages, seeking to defeat their purpose, shall be summoned to punishment. ³⁹ Say to them, 'It is my Lord who increases the provision for such of His servants as He pleases, and decreases it for such of them as He pleases. Whatever you spend, He will recompense you for it. He is the best of providers.' ^a

وَمَا أَرْسَلْنَا فِى قَرْيَةٍ مِّن نَّذِيرٍ إِلَّا قَالَ مُتْرَفُوهَا إِنَّا بِمَا أُرْسِلْتُم بِهِۦ كَٰفِرُونَ ۝ وَقَالُوا۟ نَحْنُ أَكْثَرُ أَمْوَٰلًا وَأَوْلَٰدًا وَمَا نَحْنُ بِمُعَذَّبِينَ ۝ قُلْ إِنَّ رَبِّى يَبْسُطُ ٱلرِّزْقَ لِمَن يَشَآءُ وَيَقْدِرُ وَلَٰكِنَّ أَكْثَرَ ٱلنَّاسِ لَا يَعْلَمُونَ ۝ وَمَآ أَمْوَٰلُكُمْ وَلَآ أَوْلَٰدُكُم بِٱلَّتِى تُقَرِّبُكُمْ عِندَنَا زُلْفَىٰٓ إِلَّا مَنْ ءَامَنَ وَعَمِلَ صَٰلِحًا فَأُو۟لَٰٓئِكَ لَهُمْ جَزَآءُ ٱلضِّعْفِ بِمَا عَمِلُوا۟ وَهُمْ فِى ٱلْغُرُفَٰتِ ءَامِنُونَ ۝ وَٱلَّذِينَ يَسْعَوْنَ فِىٓ ءَايَٰتِنَا مُعَٰجِزِينَ أُو۟لَٰٓئِكَ فِى ٱلْعَذَابِ مُحْضَرُونَ ۝ قُلْ إِنَّ رَبِّى يَبْسُطُ ٱلرِّزْقَ لِمَن يَشَآءُ مِنْ عِبَادِهِۦ وَيَقْدِرُ لَهُۥ وَمَآ أَنفَقْتُم مِّن شَىْءٍ فَهُوَ يُخْلِفُهُۥ وَهُوَ خَيْرُ ٱلرَّٰزِقِينَ ۝

---

^a Those who acquire wealth and power, rise to places of prominence in this world. This creates a sort of false confidence in them. Such people do not give due importance to the Hereafter, even when they are warned of it. They cannot believe that God, Who has given them honour in this world, will dishonour them in the Hereafter.

This false confidence in every age has been the greatest cause of the rejection of the call for Truth by the influential members of a society; and when they look down upon something, men of lesser stature also hold it in contempt. In this way the common people as well as the elite are prevented from accepting the Truth.

The wealth and other material things of this world are for the purpose of putting human beings to the test and are not meant as rewards. A surfeit of worldly effects is not a sign of nearness to God; nor does their shortage indicate being at a distance from Him. ▶

⁴⁰ On the Day when He gathers them all together, He will ask the angels, 'Was it you that these people worshipped?' ⁴¹ They will say, 'Glory be to You! You are our protector, not them. Indeed no! They worshipped the jinn; it was in them that most of them believed.' ⁴² Today you possess no power to benefit or harm one another. We shall say to the wrongdoers, 'Suffer the punishment of the Fire that you persistently denied.'ᵃ

وَيَوْمَ يَحْشُرُهُمْ جَمِيعًا ثُمَّ يَقُولُ لِلْمَلَٰئِكَةِ أَهَٰٓؤُلَآءِ إِيَّاكُمْ كَانُوا۟ يَعْبُدُونَ ۝ قَالُوا۟ سُبْحَٰنَكَ أَنتَ وَلِيُّنَا مِن دُونِهِم ۖ بَلْ كَانُوا۟ يَعْبُدُونَ ٱلْجِنَّ ۖ أَكْثَرُهُم بِهِم مُّؤْمِنُونَ ۝ فَٱلْيَوْمَ لَا يَمْلِكُ بَعْضُكُمْ لِبَعْضٍ نَّفْعًا وَلَا ضَرًّا وَنَقُولُ لِلَّذِينَ ظَلَمُوا۟ ذُوقُوا۟ عَذَابَ ٱلنَّارِ ٱلَّتِى كُنتُم بِهَا تُكَذِّبُونَ ۝

Only those who always remembered God and kept themselves within the limits laid down by Him, while availing of His divine bounty, are really close to God. These are the people who will be treated as deserving of God's eternal blessings and rewards in the Hereafter.

ᵃ Angels are not visible to human beings. It was the prophets who told human beings of the angels. This they did as they wanted the people to realize the majesty of God and devote themselves to prayers. But, Satan, in his devious manner, misled them by saying that it was difficult to achieve nearness to God directly and, as such, they should first worship the angels and through them come near to God. So, throughout the world, idols of angels were set up and worshipped. The concept of gods and goddesses stems in fact from this perverse belief in angels. For example the angel who was appointed for rains was considered the rain-god; and the angel for winds was taken as the god of winds, etc.

In the Hereafter, the angels will dissociate themselves from such worshippers and neither God nor the angels will give them any support. Such people will become eternally helpless.

⁴³ Whenever Our messages are conveyed to them in all their clarity, they say, 'This [Muhammad] is nothing but a man who wants to turn you away from what your forefathers worshipped.' And they say, 'This [Quran] is nothing but an invented falsehood.' And they who are bent on denying the truth speak thus of the truth when it comes to them, 'This is clearly nothing but plain sorcery!' ⁴⁴ We had not given them books to study, nor have We sent them a warner before you. ⁴⁵ Their predecessors also rejected the truth. These have not attained to one tenth of the power that We had bestowed upon the earlier people. But they rejected My messengers. Then how terrible, was My chastisement! ^a

وَإِذَا تُتْلَىٰ عَلَيْهِمْ ءَايَٰتُنَا بَيِّنَٰتٍ قَالُواْ مَا هَٰذَآ إِلَّا رَجُلٌ يُرِيدُ أَن يَصُدَّكُمْ عَمَّا كَانَ يَعْبُدُ ءَابَآؤُكُمْ وَقَالُواْ مَا هَٰذَآ إِلَّآ إِفْكٌ مُّفْتَرًى ۚ وَقَالَ ٱلَّذِينَ كَفَرُواْ لِلْحَقِّ لَمَّا جَآءَهُمْ إِنْ هَٰذَآ إِلَّا سِحْرٌ مُّبِينٌ ۝ وَمَآ ءَاتَيْنَٰهُم مِّن كُتُبٍ يَدْرُسُونَهَا ۖ وَمَآ أَرْسَلْنَآ إِلَيْهِمْ قَبْلَكَ مِن نَّذِيرٍ ۝ وَكَذَّبَ ٱلَّذِينَ مِن قَبْلِهِمْ وَمَا بَلَغُواْ مِعْشَارَ مَآ ءَاتَيْنَٰهُمْ فَكَذَّبُواْ رُسُلِي ۖ فَكَيْفَ كَانَ نَكِيرِ ۝

---

^a The Quran presented clear arguments to its opponents which they were unable to counter. In spite of this, they were successful in dissuading the common people from accepting the truth. The sole reason for this success was that the disbelievers played on the sentiments of the common people and stirred them up by saying that it (the Quran's message) was against the traditions of their forefathers. The miraculous literary value of the Quran was undeniable, and therefore, attempts were made to convince people that its supposed greatness depended solely on magical feats of expression which had nothing to do with divine revelation; it was only a miracle of penmanship and not the result of the knowledge of reality. It is most interesting that as a matter of historical record, for people of every period, prejudice has proved stronger than rational arguments.

The Quran's addressees could have put forward rational arguments to reject it or they could have referred to any other divine scriptures from which a contradiction to the Quran could have been produced. But none took recourse to either of these possibilities. If people so blatantly deny the call for Truth, it is due to nothing but stubbornness.

⁴⁶ Say to them, 'I exhort you to do one thing: and that is to stand up before God in pairs, or singly, and then reflect. You will thus realize that your companion is not afflicted with madness. He is only a warner, warning you of an impending severe chastisement.' ⁴⁷ Say, 'If I have asked you for any recompense, you can keep it. It is God alone who will reward me: He is the witness of all things.' ᵃ

۞ قُلْ إِنَّمَآ أَعِظُكُم بِوَٰحِدَةٍ أَن تَقُومُواْ لِلَّهِ مَثْنَىٰ وَفُرَٰدَىٰ ثُمَّ تَتَفَكَّرُواْ مَا بِصَاحِبِكُم مِّن جِنَّةٍ إِنْ هُوَ إِلَّا نَذِيرٌ لَّكُم بَيْنَ يَدَىْ عَذَابٍ شَدِيدٍ ۝ قُلْ مَا سَأَلْتُكُم مِّنْ أَجْرٍ فَهُوَ لَكُمْ إِنْ أَجْرِىَ إِلَّا عَلَى ٱللَّهِ وَهُوَ عَلَىٰ كُلِّ شَىْءٍ شَهِيدٌ ۝

ᵃ The contemporaries of the Prophet rejected his call of Truth, but this rejection was purely due to stubbornness and prejudice. Had they thought over the matter, either individually or collectively, with open minds, they would have discovered that their Prophet was not a madman. His earlier life would have testified to his seriousness. His sympathetic way would have shown that whenever he spoke, his words showed the deepest concern. His style of discourse, replete as it was with wisdom would have been sufficient evidence of its veracity. His working without demanding remuneration shows that he had undertaken this task only for God's pleasure and not as a personal concern. Viewing him dispassionately, people would have come to know that his restlessness was not out of madness but because of the danger which he was required to warn against. But they were never serious about the call to accept the truth, and that being so, the above-mentioned facts, albeit so obviously true, did not impress them.

⁴⁸ Say to them, 'My Lord hurls forth the Truth [at falsehood] and He is the knower of hidden things.' ⁴⁹ Say to them, 'The Truth has come and will endure. Falsehood has no power to originate any good, nor to reproduce it.' ⁵⁰ Affirm, 'If I am in error, I shall carry the burden thereof; and if I am rightly guided, it is because of what my Lord has revealed to me. Truly, He is all-hearing and near at hand.'ᵃ

قُلْ إِنَّ رَبِّى يَقْذِفُ بِٱلْحَقِّ عَلَّٰمُ ٱلْغُيُوبِ ۝ قُلْ جَآءَ ٱلْحَقُّ وَمَا يُبْدِئُ ٱلْبَٰطِلُ وَمَا يُعِيدُ ۝ قُلْ إِن ضَلَلْتُ فَإِنَّمَآ أَضِلُّ عَلَىٰ نَفْسِى وَإِنِ ٱهْتَدَيْتُ فَبِمَا يُوحِىٓ إِلَىَّ رَبِّىٓ إِنَّهُۥ سَمِيعٌ قَرِيبٌ ۝

ᵃ The world has been created on the basis of Truth. Here, all emphasis is on Truth and all arguments support the Truth. Under these circumstances, Truth should prevail and untruth should carry no weight. But, it is not always so. In this world, sometimes Truth is unable to triumph over untruth.

The reason for this is that this world is a testing ground, and the rules pertaining to the human trial are prevalent here. So, even untruth has the opportunity to flourish here. But this situation will last only till the end of the trial period. On the Day of Judgement, this unrealistic situation will end once and for all. At that time, all evidence will substantiate the Truth, and untruth will be completely valueless.

This event will become a reality on the Day of Judgement. But if and when God wishes, He shows a glimpse of it in this world itself, so that people may learn a lesson from it. A demonstration of this was when Makkah fell and monotheism overcame polytheism, the Prophet of God recited this verse, 'Truth has arrived and falsehood has perished, for falsehood is bound to perish.'

⁵¹ If you could only see when those who denied the truth are terrified, and there is no way out, and they are seized from a place nearby; ⁵² then they will say, 'We now believe in Him.' But how will they attain to faith, having gone so far away from it? ⁵³ They had rejected it before, while they indulged in conjectures from far away. ⁵⁴ And between them and their desires a barrier shall be placed as was done in the past with people of their ilk; for they were indeed in disquieting doubt.ᵃ

وَلَوْ تَرَىٰٓ إِذْ فَزِعُواْ فَلَا فَوْتَ وَأُخِذُواْ مِن مَّكَانٍ قَرِيبٍ ۝ وَقَالُوٓاْ ءَامَنَّا بِهِۦ وَأَنَّىٰ لَهُمُ ٱلتَّنَاوُشُ مِن مَّكَانٍۭ بَعِيدٍ ۝ وَقَدْ كَفَرُواْ بِهِۦ مِن قَبْلُ وَيَقْذِفُونَ بِٱلْغَيْبِ مِن مَّكَانٍۭ بَعِيدٍ ۝ وَحِيلَ بَيْنَهُمْ وَبَيْنَ مَا يَشْتَهُونَ كَمَا فُعِلَ بِأَشْيَاعِهِم مِّن قَبْلُ إِنَّهُمْ كَانُواْ فِى شَكٍّ مُّرِيبٍ ۝

ᵃ When an individual rejects the Truth in the present world, the result of doing so is not immediately apparent. This position emboldens him to reject the Truth; he does not consider the call for Truth worth giving serious attention to. He describes it with contempt and rejects it carelessly.

But the day when the system of the present world collapses, the whole picture will change. He will come to know that this reality which he had ignored was the most important of all. The bubble of vanity will be pricked and he will start spontaneously appreciating and admitting the Truth, which he had considered unworthy of attention in the pre-death period. But, by then, the moment for this would have passed, and he will be told that acceptance at a time when realities were as yet invisible would have had value, whereas acceptance at a time when the truth is plainly visible has no value.

This is the picture of the psychological condition of those who deny the truth. The Truth which was presented to them in this world was so powerful that they found themselves unable to reject it on the basis of reasoning. But, as this Truth fitted ill with their mental mould, they were not ready to accept it either. This ambivalent condition had pushed them into and kept them in a peculiar state of inner conflict, till the angel of death arrived and lifted the veil from their eyes, which they themselves should have removed but did not.

35. THE CREATOR

In the name of God,
the Most Gracious, the Most Merciful

¹ All praise be to God, Creator of the heavens and the earth, who made the angels His messengers, with wings—two, or three, or four pairs. He adds to His creation whatever He wills; for God has the power to will anything. ² No one can withhold the blessings God bestows upon people, nor can anyone apart from Him bestow whatever He withholds: He is the Almighty, the Wise One.ᵃ

ᵃ God created angels to carry messages and execute orders. But, Satan misled people to believe that the angels had a distinct identity of their own and that they could be the source of bringing blessings in this world and salvation in the Hereafter. So, some communities drew imaginary pictures of them, giving them names 'Lat' and 'Manat' and started worshipping them. Some communities treated them with the reverence due to gods and goddesses. In the present age, reverence for the 'law of nature' is the modern version of a similar misconception. But the fact is that both the angels and the law of nature are subject to the will of One God alone.

³ People, remember God's favour to you. Is there any creator other than God who provides for you from the heavens and the earth? There is no God save Him. How then are you turned away from the truth. ⁴ If they reject you, other messengers have been rejected before you. To God all affairs will be returned.ᵃ

يَـٰٓأَيُّهَا ٱلنَّاسُ ٱذْكُرُوا۟ نِعْمَتَ ٱللَّهِ عَلَيْكُمْ هَلْ مِنْ خَـٰلِقٍ غَيْرُ ٱللَّهِ يَرْزُقُكُم مِّنَ ٱلسَّمَآءِ وَٱلْأَرْضِ لَآ إِلَـٰهَ إِلَّا هُوَ فَأَنَّىٰ تُؤْفَكُونَ ۞ وَإِن يُكَذِّبُوكَ فَقَدْ كُذِّبَتْ رُسُلٌ مِّن قَبْلِكَ وَإِلَى ٱللَّهِ تُرْجَعُ ٱلْأُمُورُ ۞

ᵃ Man is in need of innumerable things to sustain his life, for example, light, water, air, food, minerals, etc. Each of these elements require the combined and concerted actions of universal forces to come into existence. Who else except the one God is capable of bringing about such a big event? When the Creator and Organiser of all these things is the One God, then how could it be reasonable for people to worship any entity other than Him?

It is a peculiar historical experience that those who accord a position of greatness to things other than God are intractable when it comes to re-assigning that greatness to God, even though the call for this may be made by a prophet in person. The reason for this is that people find it easy to continue with previously accepted notions; whereas accepting a new prophet would mean putting one's faith in something different. For the individual to acquire this type of 'iman' (faith), he must activate his own thinking powers; he should discover the Truth through his own insight. Undoubtedly, this has always been the most difficult task for a man to perform.

⁵ O Men. The promise of God is true.ᵃ Let not the life of this world deceive you, nor let the Deceiver deceive you about God. ⁶ Surely Satan is your enemy: so treat him as an enemy: he calls on his followers only so that they should become inmates of the burning Fire. ⁷ Those who are bent on denying the truth will have a severe punishment, while those who believe and do good deeds will have forgiveness and a great reward.ᵃ

يَـٰٓأَيُّهَا ٱلنَّاسُ إِنَّ وَعْدَ ٱللَّهِ حَقٌّ ۖ فَلَا تَغُرَّنَّكُمُ ٱلْحَيَوٰةُ ٱلدُّنْيَا ۖ وَلَا يَغُرَّنَّكُم بِٱللَّهِ ٱلْغَرُورُ ۝ إِنَّ ٱلشَّيْطَـٰنَ لَكُمْ عَدُوٌّ فَٱتَّخِذُوهُ عَدُوًّا ۚ إِنَّمَا يَدْعُوا۟ حِزْبَهُۥ لِيَكُونُوا۟ مِنْ أَصْحَـٰبِ ٱلسَّعِيرِ ۝ ٱلَّذِينَ كَفَرُوا۟ لَهُمْ عَذَابٌ شَدِيدٌ وَٱلَّذِينَ ءَامَنُوا۟ وَعَمِلُوا۟ ٱلصَّـٰلِحَـٰتِ لَهُم مَّغْفِرَةٌ وَأَجْرٌ كَبِيرٌ ۝

ᵃ On the face of it, the facts of life (and hereafter), though conveyed to us by God through His prophets, appear to be figments of human imagination, because they are not immediately encountered. Conversely, the things of the present world appear to be real, because man encounters them today itself.

Sudden death, the upheaval of earthquakes and other such incidents shake a man's composure. These, in fact, remind one of Doomsday, before its actual occurrence. But, Satan immediately diverts the attention of the people by saying that these events have natural causes and are not a result of divine intervention. That day is bound to come when a distinction will be drawn between the true and the false; righteous people will be rewarded for their virtue and wrongdoers will be punished for their evil deeds.

⁸ Is he whose evil deeds are made alluring to him so that he looks upon them as good, [equal to the man who is rightly guided]? God leaves to stray whom He wills, and guides whom He wills. Do not destroy yourself with grief for them. God has full knowledge of all their actions.^a

أَفَمَن زُيِّنَ لَهُۥ سُوٓءُ عَمَلِهِۦ فَرَءَاهُ حَسَنًا فَإِنَّ ٱللَّهَ يُضِلُّ مَن يَشَآءُ وَيَهْدِى مَن يَشَآءُ فَلَا تَذْهَبْ نَفْسُكَ عَلَيْهِمْ حَسَرَٰتٍ إِنَّ ٱللَّهَ عَلِيمٌ بِمَا يَصْنَعُونَ ۝

---

^a Almighty God has blessed every man with the capability to think and distinguish between truth and untruth. One who utilizes this innate talent, receives proper guidance and one who does not is left to go astray.

When Truth appears before a man, he has two options before him. If he accepts the Truth, his mind starts off in the right direction and he becomes a wayfarer journeying towards the Truth. But if some extraneous consideration or some psychological complication comes in his way and, under its influence, he refuses to accept the Truth, he then starts devising ways and means of justifying his rejection of it and tries to prove that his bad deeds are actually good deeds. Those who suffer from such psychological barriers never admit the Truth. It is only when, after death, they come face to face with God that they reap what they have sown.

⁹ It is God who sends forth the winds so that they raise up the clouds. We drive them to a dead land, and by them bring the earth to life after its death. Such is the Resurrection. ¹⁰ If anyone seeks glory, let him know that glory belongs to God alone. Good words ascend to Him and righteous deeds are exalted by Him. Those who plot evil deeds shall be sternly punished and their plotting will come to nothing.ᵃ

وَٱللَّهُ ٱلَّذِىٓ أَرْسَلَ ٱلرِّيَٰحَ فَتُثِيرُ سَحَابًا فَسُقْنَٰهُ إِلَىٰ بَلَدٍ مَّيِّتٍ فَأَحْيَيْنَا بِهِ ٱلْأَرْضَ بَعْدَ مَوْتِهَا ۚ كَذَٰلِكَ ٱلنُّشُورُ ۝ مَن كَانَ يُرِيدُ ٱلْعِزَّةَ فَلِلَّهِ ٱلْعِزَّةُ جَمِيعًا ۚ إِلَيْهِ يَصْعَدُ ٱلْكَلِمُ ٱلطَّيِّبُ وَٱلْعَمَلُ ٱلصَّٰلِحُ يَرْفَعُهُۥ ۚ وَٱلَّذِينَ يَمْكُرُونَ ٱلسَّيِّئَاتِ لَهُمْ عَذَابٌ شَدِيدٌ ۖ وَمَكْرُ أُوْلَٰٓئِكَ هُوَ يَبُورُ ۝

ᵃ The present world gives us an introduction to the Hereafter. Rain, a common phenomenon, indicates that a force is at work which is beyond our ken. Rain results from the action of universal forces. The sun, the air, the sea, gravitational force and many other factors combine with each other in perfect co-ordination to produce the rain which makes dry land come alive.

This process of rain-making proves that the Organizer of the universe has full powers over it. He brings about an event according to His plan.

Re-vitalizing a barren piece of land and resurrecting a dead man are both feats of the same calibre. If the possibility of the first event is proved, then by analogy, the possibility of the second event automatically stands proved.

The present world is a testing ground. Therefore, here even an undeserving person may temporarily receive honour, but in the Hereafter all the honours will fall to the lot of those who are really deserving of them. The criteria for judging worthiness will be righteous words (al-kalim at-tayyib) and pious deeds (al-'amal as-salih), that is, man's expression—in thought, word and deed—of his discovery of God and the devotion of all his strength to the service of the Almighty. Those who build their lives in piety are bound to secure God's help.

" God has created you from dust, then from a drop of semen and then divided you into pairs; no female conceives or gives birth without His knowledge; and no one's life is prolonged or shortened, but it is recorded in a Book. That surely is easy for God.ᵃ

وَٱللَّهُ خَلَقَكُم مِّن تُرَابٍ ثُمَّ مِن نُّطْفَةٍ ثُمَّ جَعَلَكُمْ أَزْوَٰجًا ۚ وَمَا تَحْمِلُ مِنْ أُنثَىٰ وَلَا تَضَعُ إِلَّا بِعِلْمِهِ ۚ وَمَا يُعَمَّرُ مِن مُّعَمَّرٍ وَلَا يُنقَصُ مِنْ عُمُرِهِ إِلَّا فِى كِتَٰبٍ ۚ إِنَّ ذَٰلِكَ عَلَى ٱللَّهِ يَسِيرٌ ۝

ᵃ God first created man from the elements of the earth. By dividing human beings into men and women, God caused the human race to multiply. This exemplifies the power of the Creator.

At the time when a child starts developing in his mother's womb, he finds that all the factors essential to his growth are provided without asking. This shows that the Creator of the child knew his requirements beforehand, otherwise how could He have made such perfect arrangements in advance?

The same is true of a man's age. Nobody has the power to determine his own life-span. It appears that this lies wholly in the hands of an external Being. He takes away one person at a young age, while He gives another a longer life. In all these events, nobody has any say, except God. Then, how can it be proper for a man to have fears or entertain hopes of any being other than God?

¹² The two seas are not alike. The one is sweet, thirst-quenching, and pleasant to drink from, while the other is salty and bitter. Yet from each you eat fresh fish and extract ornaments to wear, and in each you see the ships ploughing through the waves so that you may seek His bounty and so that you may feel thankful. ¹³ He makes the night pass into the day and He makes the day pass into the night. He has subjected the sun and the moon, each running for an appointed term. Such is God, your Lord: His is the kingdom. Those whom you invoke besides Him do not own so much as the skin of a date stone; ¹⁴ if you invoke them, they do not hear your call; and even if they could hear, they would not respond to you. And on the Day of Resurrection they will disown your having associated them with God. No one can tell you [the Truth] like the One who is all knowing.ᵃ

وَمَا يَسْتَوِي ٱلْبَحْرَانِ هَٰذَا عَذْبٌ فُرَاتٌ سَائِغٌ شَرَابُهُ وَهَٰذَا مِلْحٌ أُجَاجٌ وَمِن كُلٍّ تَأْكُلُونَ لَحْمًا طَرِيًّا وَتَسْتَخْرِجُونَ حِلْيَةً تَلْبَسُونَهَا وَتَرَى ٱلْفُلْكَ فِيهِ مَوَاخِرَ لِتَبْتَغُوا۟ مِن فَضْلِهِ وَلَعَلَّكُمْ تَشْكُرُونَ ۝ يُولِجُ ٱلَّيْلَ فِي ٱلنَّهَارِ وَيُولِجُ ٱلنَّهَارَ فِي ٱلَّيْلِ وَسَخَّرَ ٱلشَّمْسَ وَٱلْقَمَرَ كُلٌّ يَجْرِي لِأَجَلٍ مُّسَمًّى ذَٰلِكُمُ ٱللَّهُ رَبُّكُمْ لَهُ ٱلْمُلْكُ وَٱلَّذِينَ تَدْعُونَ مِن دُونِهِ مَا يَمْلِكُونَ مِن قِطْمِيرٍ ۝ إِن تَدْعُوهُمْ لَا يَسْمَعُوا۟ دُعَآءَكُمْ وَلَوْ سَمِعُوا۟ مَا ٱسْتَجَابُوا۟ لَكُمْ وَيَوْمَ ٱلْقِيَٰمَةِ يَكْفُرُونَ بِشِرْكِكُمْ وَلَا يُنَبِّئُكَ مِثْلُ خَبِيرٍ ۝

ᵃ There is a large store of water on the earth—salt water in the oceans and seas, and fresh water in rivers, lakes and springs. This water is the source of innumerable advantages for man. It is used for drinking and irrigation. The creatures which live in water provide valuable food for man. The oceans and seas, spread over three-fourths of the Earth enable transportation and form a vast storehouse of valuable objects like pearls, mineral ores, etc.

God causes the earth to revolve around the sun and rotate on its axis in a regulated manner, thereby causing the seasons, and the alternation of day and night. There are similar innumerable arrangements which have been brought into being by the all-powerful God. As such, who else is there other than God who deserves man's utmost gratitude? It is God with His unfathomable powers who can fulfill the needs of man, and not those imaginary gods who possess absolutely no powers.

¹⁵ O men! It is you who stand in need of God—God is self-sufficient, and praiseworthy— ¹⁶ if He so wished, He could take you away and replace you with a new creation; ¹⁷ that is not difficult for God. ¹⁸ No burden-bearer shall bear another's burden, and if some over-laden soul should call out for someone else to carry his load, not the least portion of it will be borne for him, even though he were a near relative. You can only warn those who fear their Lord in the unseen, and pray regularly. Anyone who purifies himself will benefit greatly from doing so. To God all shall return.ᵃ

۞ يَٰٓأَيُّهَا ٱلنَّاسُ أَنتُمُ ٱلۡفُقَرَآءُ إِلَى ٱللَّهِ وَٱللَّهُ هُوَ ٱلۡغَنِيُّ ٱلۡحَمِيدُ ۝ إِن يَشَأۡ يُذۡهِبۡكُمۡ وَيَأۡتِ بِخَلۡقٍ جَدِيدٍ ۝ وَمَا ذَٰلِكَ عَلَى ٱللَّهِ بِعَزِيزٍ ۝ وَلَا تَزِرُ وَازِرَةٌ وِزۡرَ أُخۡرَىٰ وَإِن تَدۡعُ مُثۡقَلَةٌ إِلَىٰ حِمۡلِهَا لَا يُحۡمَلۡ مِنۡهُ شَيۡءٌ وَلَوۡ كَانَ ذَا قُرۡبَىٰٓ إِنَّمَا تُنذِرُ ٱلَّذِينَ يَخۡشَوۡنَ رَبَّهُم بِٱلۡغَيۡبِ وَأَقَامُواْ ٱلصَّلَوٰةَ وَمَن تَزَكَّىٰ فَإِنَّمَا يَتَزَكَّىٰ لِنَفۡسِهِۦ وَإِلَى ٱللَّهِ ٱلۡمَصِيرُ ۝

ᵃ Man is an extremely vulnerable creation. His whole existence depends on a particular balance of natural factors. If this balance were to be disturbed, the very existence of man would be threatened.

If, for instance, the sun reduced its distance from the earth and came near it, then all human beings would be burnt and reduced to ashes. Also, a large part of the inside of the earth consists of an extremely hot, semi-liquid material. If this hot matter moved upwards, the surface of the earth would experience terrible earthquakes which would reduce all human settlements to ruins. Moreover, meteors constantly fall upon Earth from outer space, but the atmosphere shields us against their effects. If the present balanced arrangement of this phenomenon were to be disrupted, the shower of meteors might turn into such a terrible barrage of stones that it would be impossible to save humanity from it. Man is surrounded by innumerable deadly possibilities of this kind; being totally dependent explains why man needs God and not vice versa.

The burden of Doomsday will be that of one's sins. Were it only a question of a physical burden, any individual could share another's burden. But, the denigration and pain one suffers due to one's bad deeds are of an extremely personal nature and there is no question of anybody else sharing them.

The Truth is very clear, but it is understood only by one who wants to understand. One who is not serious about knowing what is Truth and what is Untruth, cannot be made to understand anything.

¹⁹ The blind and the sighted are not equal, ²⁰ nor are the darkness and the light; ²¹ shade and heat are not alike, ²² nor are the living and the dead. God causes whom He will to hear Him, but you cannot make those who are in their graves hear you. ²³ You are but a warner—²⁴ We have sent you with the truth as a bearer of good news and a warner—there is no community to which a warner has not come. ²⁵ If they reject you, so did their predecessors. Messengers came to them with clear signs, with scriptures, and with the enlightening Book, ²⁶ but in the end I seized those who were bent on denying the truth and how terrible was My punishment.^a

وَمَا يَسْتَوِى ٱلْأَعْمَىٰ وَٱلْبَصِيرُ ۝ وَلَا ٱلظُّلُمَـٰتُ وَلَا ٱلنُّورُ ۝ وَلَا ٱلظِّلُّ وَلَا ٱلْحَرُورُ ۝ وَمَا يَسْتَوِى ٱلْأَحْيَآءُ وَلَا ٱلْأَمْوَٰتُ ۚ إِنَّ ٱللَّهَ يُسْمِعُ مَن يَشَآءُ ۖ وَمَآ أَنتَ بِمُسْمِعٍ مَّن فِى ٱلْقُبُورِ ۝ إِنْ أَنتَ إِلَّا نَذِيرٌ ۝ إِنَّآ أَرْسَلْنَـٰكَ بِٱلْحَقِّ بَشِيرًا وَنَذِيرًا ۚ وَإِن مِّنْ أُمَّةٍ إِلَّا خَلَا فِيهَا نَذِيرٌ ۝ وَإِن يُكَذِّبُوكَ فَقَدْ كَذَّبَ ٱلَّذِينَ مِن قَبْلِهِمْ جَآءَتْهُمْ رُسُلُهُم بِٱلْبَيِّنَـٰتِ وَبِٱلزُّبُرِ وَبِٱلْكِتَـٰبِ ٱلْمُنِيرِ ۝ ثُمَّ أَخَذْتُ ٱلَّذِينَ كَفَرُوا۟ ۖ فَكَيْفَ كَانَ نَكِيرِ ۝

^a It is a fact that the expectations one has of light are not applicable to darkness. What one gets from the shade cannot be derived from sunlight. The same is the case with man. Among human beings, some have vision and some are blind. A man with eyes immediately sees his way and recognizes it. But one who is blind will simply go on groping in the dark.

Similarly, with regard to insight there are two types of people, —one consisting of the living and the other consisting of the dead. The living man is one who sees things in depth—who tears apart the deceptive veil of words and grasps hidden meanings—who goes beyond superficial matters and tries to understand the inner reality—who assesses intrinsic values and not outward appearances—whose eyes are concentrated on real facts and not on irrelevant hair-splitting theories—who, after knowing the Truth, submits to it—he is the one who is alive. He is one who has been fortunate enough in this world to accept the Truth. Those whose behaviour is the very reverse of this are dead. They never come anywhere near accepting the Truth in this world of trial. They remain deaf to the call for Truth, until after death, when they go to God to face the result of their blindness.

²⁷ Did you not see how God sent down water from the sky with which We bring forth fruit of diverse colours. In the mountains there are streaks of various shades of white and red, and jet-black rocks; ²⁸ in like manner, men, beasts, and cattle have their diverse hues too. Only those of His servants, who possess knowledge, fear God. God is almighty and most forgiving.^a

أَلَمْ تَرَ أَنَّ ٱللَّهَ أَنزَلَ مِنَ ٱلسَّمَآءِ مَآءً فَأَخْرَجْنَا بِهِۦ ثَمَرَٰتٍ مُّخْتَلِفًا أَلْوَٰنُهَا ۚ وَمِنَ ٱلْجِبَالِ جُدَدٌۢ بِيضٌ وَحُمْرٌ مُّخْتَلِفٌ أَلْوَٰنُهَا وَغَرَابِيبُ سُودٌ ۝ وَمِنَ ٱلنَّاسِ وَٱلدَّوَآبِّ وَٱلْأَنْعَٰمِ مُخْتَلِفٌ أَلْوَٰنُهُۥ كَذَٰلِكَ ۗ إِنَّمَا يَخْشَى ٱللَّهَ مِنْ عِبَادِهِ ٱلْعُلَمَٰٓؤُاْ ۗ إِنَّ ٱللَّهَ عَزِيزٌ غَفُورٌ ۝

---

^a The same rain cycle causes rain everywhere in the world but it causes different types of things to grow—useful plants as well as wild bushes. Similarly, there exist varied fauna; while man domesticates some and put them to use, others remain wild.

God showers His blessings to all His creations without any discrimination, but in the case of man, the advantage taken depends upon individual capacity. The grace of God which presents itself in the form of the call for Truth is available to all, but its impact on different people varies, depending upon individual temperaments. Some find in it nourishment for the spirit and therefore, immediately accept the Truth and associate themselves with it. However, the mindset of others may present an impediment to their acceptance of the Truth, they may refuse to submit to it. Some even go to the extent of taking a stand against it.

One who finds the call for Truth to be in consonance with the inner voice of his heart, is truly a man of knowledge; the natural Divine light of God was aflame in his heart, and that is why he recognized the Truth the moment it appeared. Unlike him, there are those who, out of ignorance, have hidden their natural divine light behind a screen and so fail to recognize the Truth when it reveals itself to them.

³² We have bestowed the Book on those of Our servants whom We have chosen. Some wrong their own souls, some keep half-way [between right and wrong]; some, by God's leave, excel others in good deeds. This is a great bounty of God: ³³ they shall enter the Gardens of Eternity, where they shall be adorned with bracelets of gold and pearls, and wear silk garments. ³⁴ They will say, 'Praise be to God who has taken away all sorrow from us. Our Lord is forgiving and appreciative. ³⁵ Through His grace He has admitted us to the everlasting Abode, where neither toil nor weariness affects us.' *ᵃ*

ثُمَّ أَوْرَثْنَا ٱلْكِتَـٰبَ ٱلَّذِينَ ٱصْطَفَيْنَا مِنْ عِبَادِنَا ۖ فَمِنْهُمْ ظَالِمٌ لِّنَفْسِهِۦ وَمِنْهُم مُّقْتَصِدٌ وَمِنْهُمْ سَابِقٌۢ بِٱلْخَيْرَٰتِ بِإِذْنِ ٱللَّهِ ۚ ذَٰلِكَ هُوَ ٱلْفَضْلُ ٱلْكَبِيرُ ۝ جَنَّـٰتُ عَدْنٍ يَدْخُلُونَهَا يُحَلَّوْنَ فِيهَا مِنْ أَسَاوِرَ مِن ذَهَبٍ وَلُؤْلُؤًا ۖ وَلِبَاسُهُمْ فِيهَا حَرِيرٌ ۝ وَقَالُوا۟ ٱلْحَمْدُ لِلَّهِ ٱلَّذِىٓ أَذْهَبَ عَنَّا ٱلْحَزَنَ ۖ إِنَّ رَبَّنَا لَغَفُورٌ شَكُورٌ ۝ ٱلَّذِىٓ أَحَلَّنَا دَارَ ٱلْمُقَامَةِ مِن فَضْلِهِۦ لَا يَمَسُّنَا فِيهَا نَصَبٌ وَلَا يَمَسُّنَا فِيهَا لُغُوبٌ ۝

ᵃ Jacob was Abraham's grandson. From Jacob up to the time of Jesus, all the prophets were from among the tribes of the Children of Israel. In this way, the chain of Jewish prophets remained unbroken for about two thousand years. But, latter day Jews did not remain capable of bearing aloft the Book of God. Therefore, another community, the Children of Isma'il, was selected to be the guardian of the divine scriptures. The Prophet Muhammad was born into this tribe.

When the Prophet Muhammad presented the Quran before the tribe (Children of Isma'il), three groups emerged—one which consisted of those who stood in opposition, a second which adopted a middle way, and a third which believed in the message he presented. It was the last group, who stood by the Prophet at all times. They had to forego every comfort and lived lives of gruelling hard work during which time they exhibited great patience. As a reward for their sacrifice God admitted them in the everlasting gardens of paradise where no sorrow or trouble could ever affect them.

³⁶ Those who deny the truth shall remain in the fire of Hell. Death will not be decreed for them, so that they could escape by way of death, nor will its torment ever be eased for them. Thus do We requite every ungrateful person.ᵃ ³⁷ There they will cry out, 'Lord, take us out! We shall do good deeds, and behave differently from the way we used to.' But He will answer, 'Did We not make your life long enough to take warning if you were going to? The warner did come to you. So now have a taste of the punishment.' Wrongdoers will have no supporter.

وَٱلَّذِينَ كَفَرُواْ لَهُمْ نَارُ جَهَنَّمَ لَا يُقْضَىٰ عَلَيْهِمْ فَيَمُوتُواْ وَلَا يُخَفَّفُ عَنْهُم مِّنْ عَذَابِهَا كَذَٰلِكَ نَجْزِى كُلَّ كَفُورٍ ۝ وَهُمْ يَصْطَرِخُونَ فِيهَا رَبَّنَآ أَخْرِجْنَا نَعْمَلْ صَٰلِحًا غَيْرَ ٱلَّذِى كُنَّا نَعْمَلُ أَوَلَمْ نُعَمِّرْكُم مَّا يَتَذَكَّرُ فِيهِ مَن تَذَكَّرَ وَجَآءَكُمُ ٱلنَّذِيرُ فَذُوقُواْ فَمَا لِلظَّٰلِمِينَ مِن نَّصِيرٍ ۝

ᵃ Those who deny the Truth in this world will admit the Truth in the Hereafter. But this will be of no avail, because in the Hereafter, such an admission will be made under compulsion, whereas God seeks voluntary submission from man. It is the denial and obstinacy of such wrongdoers which will make them incur the eternal wrath of God.

³⁸ God knows the hidden reality of the heavens and the earth. He has full knowledge of what is in the hearts of men; ³⁹ it is He who has made you inherit the earth. He who denies Him shall bear the burden of his denial. God's displeasure with the deniers will only be increased by their denial of the truth, it will only increase their loss.^a

إِنَّ ٱللَّهَ عَلِمُ غَيْبِ ٱلسَّمَـٰوَٰتِ وَٱلْأَرْضِ إِنَّهُۥ عَلِيمٌۢ بِذَاتِ ٱلصُّدُورِ ۝ هُوَ ٱلَّذِى جَعَلَكُمْ خَلَـٰٓئِفَ فِى ٱلْأَرْضِ فَمَن كَفَرَ فَعَلَيْهِ كُفْرُهُۥ وَلَا يَزِيدُ ٱلْكَـٰفِرِينَ كُفْرُهُمْ عِندَ رَبِّهِمْ إِلَّا مَقْتًا وَلَا يَزِيدُ ٱلْكَـٰفِرِينَ كُفْرُهُمْ إِلَّا خَسَارًا ۝

---

^a In this verse, being given 'the earth to inherit' (*khalifah*) means that 'after the decline of the previous nations, a new nation was settled on the earth in their place.' It is the way by which God gives a nation the opportunity to settle and make progress on the earth. If the nation proves itself incapable, He replaces it by another nation. This process of the transfer of power shall continue right until Doomsday.

The advancements in the present age have made it possible even to take photographs in the dark and make an apparently inaudible sound audible to the human ear. Such possibilities indicate that the Creator of this universe is a Being who knows the unknown and is aware of the secrets hidden in one's heart. Man therefore, is accountable before the all-knowing and all-powerful God from whom no offence remains concealed.

⁴⁰ Say, 'Have you ever considered your associate gods whom you call on besides God? Show me what it is that they have created on earth. Or have they a share in the creation of the heavens?' Or have We given them a book so that they may act on evidence from it? Indeed, the wrongdoers' promises to one another are nothing but deception. ⁴¹ Surely, God holds the heavens and the earth, lest they should deviate [from their places]. Were they to deviate, none could hold them after Him. Surely, He is forbearing and most forgiving.ᵃ

قُلْ أَرَءَيْتُمْ شُرَكَآءَكُمُ ٱلَّذِينَ تَدْعُونَ مِن دُونِ ٱللَّهِ أَرُونِى مَاذَا خَلَقُوا۟ مِنَ ٱلْأَرْضِ أَمْ لَهُمْ شِرْكٌ فِى ٱلسَّمَـٰوَٰتِ أَمْ ءَاتَيْنَـٰهُمْ كِتَـٰبًا فَهُمْ عَلَىٰ بَيِّنَتٍ مِّنْهُ بَلْ إِن يَعِدُ ٱلظَّـٰلِمُونَ بَعْضُهُم بَعْضًا إِلَّا غُرُورًا ۝ إِنَّ ٱللَّهَ يُمْسِكُ ٱلسَّمَـٰوَٰتِ وَٱلْأَرْضَ أَن تَزُولَا وَلَئِن زَالَتَآ إِنْ أَمْسَكَهُمَا مِنْ أَحَدٍ مِّنۢ بَعْدِهِۦٓ إِنَّهُۥ كَانَ حَلِيمًا غَفُورًا ۝

ᵃ The creation of the universe, with its unlimited space and the innumerable astronomical bodies suspended in it, is an awe-inspiring phenomenon. Such colossal creation—an unimaginally gigantic feat—cannot be wholly or even partially attributed to any of the beings whom people worship as deities.

The fact is that worship of entities other than God is entirely based on fraudulence. Such practices will continue only till Doomsday, for on that Day, they will vanish as if they had never existed.

42 They swore their most solemn oaths that if a warner should ever come to them, they would be better guided than any other community. But when a warner did come to them, it only increased their aversion, 43 and they behaved arrogantly in the land and plotted evil. But the plotting of evil only rebounds on those who plot. Are they but looking for the way the previous peoples [sinners] were dealt with? You will never find any change in the ways of God; nor will you ever find God's decree averted.[a]

وَأَقْسَمُوا بِٱللَّهِ جَهْدَ أَيْمَٰنِهِمْ لَئِن جَآءَهُمْ نَذِيرٌ لَّيَكُونُنَّ أَهْدَىٰ مِنْ إِحْدَى ٱلْأُمَمِ فَلَمَّا جَآءَهُمْ نَذِيرٌ مَّا زَادَهُمْ إِلَّا نُفُورًا ۝ ٱسْتِكْبَارًا فِى ٱلْأَرْضِ وَمَكْرَ ٱلسَّيِّئِ وَلَا يَحِيقُ ٱلْمَكْرُ ٱلسَّيِّئُ إِلَّا بِأَهْلِهِ فَهَلْ يَنظُرُونَ إِلَّا سُنَّتَ ٱلْأَوَّلِينَ فَلَن تَجِدَ لِسُنَّتِ ٱللَّهِ تَبْدِيلًا وَلَن تَجِدَ لِسُنَّتِ ٱللَّهِ تَحْوِيلًا ۝

---

[a] When the Arab people used to hear that the Jews and other people had flouted and disobeyed their prophets, they used to say enthusiastically that if any prophet appeared among them, they would accept him wholeheartedly and obey him. But, when their prophet did appear among them, they became his dire opponents.

This mentality in some form or the other exists in all people. In this world, every man presents himself as a protagonist of Truth. He professes that whenever Truth appears before him, he will readily accept it. But, when the Truth emerges before him with clear supporting arguments, he ignores it and even opposes it.

The denial of Truth therefore, is not the peculiarity of any particular community, but is an outcome of man's psychology. The acceptance of Truth very often amounts to damaging one's own importance, and naturally man does not want his stature to be diminished. That is why he refuses to accept the Truth. He forgets that although he has the option to reject the Truth, he has no power to save himself from the result of doing so.

⁴⁴ Have they not travelled around the earth and seen the fate of those who preceded them? And they were far superior to them in strength. Nothing in the heavens or the earth can ever frustrate God's [plans]. He is all-knowing and all powerful.

⁴⁵ If God were to take men to task for their misdeeds, He would not leave a single living creature on the surface of the earth; but He grants them respite until an appointed time; and when their appointed time comes, then they will know that God is indeed observant of all His servants.ᵃ

أَوَلَمْ يَسِيرُوا۟ فِى ٱلْأَرْضِ فَيَنظُرُوا۟ كَيْفَ كَانَ عَـٰقِبَةُ ٱلَّذِينَ مِن قَبْلِهِمْ وَكَانُوٓا۟ أَشَدَّ مِنْهُمْ قُوَّةً ۚ وَمَا كَانَ ٱللَّهُ لِيُعْجِزَهُۥ مِن شَىْءٍ فِى ٱلسَّمَـٰوَٰتِ وَلَا فِى ٱلْأَرْضِ ۚ إِنَّهُۥ كَانَ عَلِيمًا قَدِيرًا ۝ وَلَوْ يُؤَاخِذُ ٱللَّهُ ٱلنَّاسَ بِمَا كَسَبُوا۟ مَا تَرَكَ عَلَىٰ ظَهْرِهَا مِن دَآبَّةٍ وَلَـٰكِن يُؤَخِّرُهُمْ إِلَىٰٓ أَجَلٍ مُّسَمًّى ۖ فَإِذَا جَآءَ أَجَلُهُمْ فَإِنَّ ٱللَّهَ كَانَ بِعِبَادِهِۦ بَصِيرًۢا ۝

ᵃ Man has been given freedom of action in the world, but he misuses it. His wrongs are so many that if he were caught hold of immediately for his wrongdoings, the entire human race would be wiped out from the world. But, human freedom is purely for the purpose of putting man to the test, and there is a period fixed for this. The period for an individual lasts till his death and the period fixed for humanity as a whole is till Doomsday. For this reason, the human race is still extant in the world. However, just as it is a fact that God does not seize hold of anybody before the expiry of the trial period, it must also be seriously considered that after the expiry of the trial period, He will definitely do so and nobody will escape the trial.

36. YA SIN

In the name of God,
the Most Gracious, the Most Merciful

¹ *Ya Sin*

² By the Quran, full of wisdom, ³ you are indeed one of the messengers ⁴ on a straight path, ⁵ with a revelation sent down by the Mighty One, the Merciful, ⁶ so that you may warn a people whose fathers were not warned and so they are unaware.^a

---

^a The Quran itself is the proof of Muhammad being the Prophet of God. The Quran calls mankind towards the right path, i.e. the path of righteousness. None of its contents clash with reason and nature. Even fifteen hundred years after the Quran was first revealed, nothing has been detected in it which can be called as irrational or unnatural. This distinct characteristic of the Quran is the greatest proof of its being the book of God.

'So that you may warn a people.' Here, 'people' refers to the Children of Isma'il. Every prophet is raised primarily to address his contemporaries. Accordingly, the first addressees of the Prophet Muhammad were his own tribesmen. But although the institution of prophethood ended with him, the Prophethood of Muhammad shall continue until Doomsday—the difference being that, with the Children of Isma'il, he personally and directly fulfilled his mission, while in respect of all other nations after him, the task of giving the call and fulfilling the mission shall have to be performed by his followers.

7 The word has been proved true against the greater part of them: they will not believe. 8 We have put yokes round their necks right up to their chins, so that they cannot bow their heads 9 and We have set a barrier before them and a barrier behind them, and We have covered them up so that they cannot see. 10 It makes no difference to them whether you warn them or do not warn them: they will not believe. 11 You can warn only those who would follow the Reminder and fear the Gracious God, unseen. Give them the good news of forgiveness and a noble reward.*a*

12 We shall surely bring the dead back to life and We record what they send ahead and what they leave behind. We have recorded everything in a clear book.*b*

لَقَدْ حَقَّ ٱلْقَوْلُ عَلَىٰ أَكْثَرِهِمْ فَهُمْ لَا يُؤْمِنُونَ ۝ إِنَّا جَعَلْنَا فِىٓ أَعْنَاقِهِمْ أَغْلَٰلًا فَهِىَ إِلَى ٱلْأَذْقَانِ فَهُم مُّقْمَحُونَ ۝ وَجَعَلْنَا مِنۢ بَيْنِ أَيْدِيهِمْ سَدًّا وَمِنْ خَلْفِهِمْ سَدًّا فَأَغْشَيْنَٰهُمْ فَهُمْ لَا يُبْصِرُونَ ۝ وَسَوَآءٌ عَلَيْهِمْ ءَأَنذَرْتَهُمْ أَمْ لَمْ تُنذِرْهُمْ لَا يُؤْمِنُونَ ۝ إِنَّمَا تُنذِرُ مَنِ ٱتَّبَعَ ٱلذِّكْرَ وَخَشِىَ ٱلرَّحْمَٰنَ بِٱلْغَيْبِ فَبَشِّرْهُ بِمَغْفِرَةٍ وَأَجْرٍ كَرِيمٍ ۝ إِنَّا نَحْنُ نُحْىِ ٱلْمَوْتَىٰ وَنَكْتُبُ مَا قَدَّمُوا۟ وَءَاثَٰرَهُمْ وَكُلَّ شَىْءٍ أَحْصَيْنَٰهُ فِىٓ إِمَامٍ مُّبِينٍ ۝

---

a If a man's neck is encircled by chains, his head will stay raised and he will not be able to see anything below. This is the picture of those proud individuals who are so engrossed in self-aggrandisement that they are unable to see any reality beyond themselves. Such people never admit the Truth.

It is very important for a man to be inclined to admit the Truth in order to avail of guidance; he should always be conscious and fearful of having to appear before God; he should never settle for anything less than the whole and absolute Truth. People who are so inclined towards the Truth as soon as it appears, consequently receive the greatest reward from God.

b Modern research has established that whatever a man utters remains preserved in the atmosphere in the form of vibrations or waves. Similarly, the image of the actions which a man performs remains preserved in the form of light waves. In other words, every individual in this world is being constantly video-recorded. It should be borne in mind that in this world, without a man's knowledge and quite independent of his will, his utterances and actions, being completely recorded and preserved, could be replayed any time later.

¹³ Recount to them the example of the people to whose town Our messengers came. ¹⁴ When We sent them two messengers, they rejected them both, so We strengthened them with a third. They said, 'Truly, we have been sent to you [by God] as messengers.' ¹⁵ They replied, 'You are nothing but mortal men like us and the Merciful God has not revealed anything. You are surely lying.' ¹⁶ They said, 'Our Lord knows that we have been sent to you. ¹⁷ And our duty is only to convey the message to you clearly,' ¹⁸ but they answered, 'We see an evil omen in you. If you do not stop, we shall certainly stone you, and you will suffer a painful punishment at our hands.' ¹⁹ They said, 'Your evil augury be with you! Is it because you are admonished about the truth? Surely, you are a people transgressing all bounds!' *ᵃ*

وَٱضْرِبْ لَهُم مَّثَلًا أَصْحَٰبَ ٱلْقَرْيَةِ إِذْ جَآءَهَا ٱلْمُرْسَلُونَ ۝ إِذْ أَرْسَلْنَآ إِلَيْهِمُ ٱثْنَيْنِ فَكَذَّبُوهُمَا فَعَزَّزْنَا بِثَالِثٍ فَقَالُوٓا۟ إِنَّآ إِلَيْكُم مُّرْسَلُونَ ۝ قَالُوا۟ مَآ أَنتُمْ إِلَّا بَشَرٌ مِّثْلُنَا وَمَآ أَنزَلَ ٱلرَّحْمَٰنُ مِن شَىْءٍ إِنْ أَنتُمْ إِلَّا تَكْذِبُونَ ۝ قَالُوا۟ رَبُّنَا يَعْلَمُ إِنَّآ إِلَيْكُمْ لَمُرْسَلُونَ ۝ وَمَا عَلَيْنَآ إِلَّا ٱلْبَلَٰغُ ٱلْمُبِينُ ۝ قَالُوٓا۟ إِنَّا تَطَيَّرْنَا بِكُمْ لَئِن لَّمْ تَنتَهُوا۟ لَنَرْجُمَنَّكُمْ وَلَيَمَسَّنَّكُم مِّنَّا عَذَابٌ أَلِيمٌ ۝ قَالُوا۟ طَٰٓئِرُكُم مَّعَكُمْ أَئِن ذُكِّرْتُم بَلْ أَنتُمْ قَوْمٌ مُّسْرِفُونَ ۝

ᵃ The township referred to in these verses was perhaps a settlement in Egypt where two prophets, Moses and Aaron were sent to admonish the people. But they rejected both of them. Then, a third person from amongst their own community came forth to support the Prophets, but this angered His fellow-men so much that they threatened to stone him, if he did not stop.

At all times, the bitterest pill for a man to swallow is the piece of advice which is not to his liking. He flares up as soon as he hears it. Consequently, he cannot consider it with a balanced mind and does not assess it in the light of reason. Swayed by obstinacy and hatred, he goes on saying irrelevant things against it. Making assessments in the light of reason is to remain within reasonable limits but irrational opposition amounts to transgressing those limits.

²⁰ Then, from the furthest part of the city, a man came running. He said, 'My people, follow the messengers. ²¹ Follow those who ask no recompense of you and are rightly guided.'ᵃ

²² 'Why should I not worship Him who has brought me into being, and to whom you shall all be recalled? ²³ Shall I take others besides Him as gods? If the Gracious God should intend me any harm, their intercession will be of no avail, nor can they deliver me. ²⁴ In that case I should indeed be in manifest error. ²⁵ Indeed, I have believed in your Lord, so listen to me.' ²⁶ We said to him, 'Enter paradise,' and he exclaimed: 'Would that my people knew ²⁷ how my Lord has forgiven me and placed me among the honoured ones!'ᵇ

وَجَآءَ مِنْ أَقْصَا ٱلْمَدِينَةِ رَجُلٌ يَسْعَىٰ
قَالَ يَٰقَوْمِ ٱتَّبِعُوا۟ ٱلْمُرْسَلِينَ ۝
ٱتَّبِعُوا۟ مَن لَّا يَسْـَٔلُكُمْ أَجْرًا وَهُم
مُّهْتَدُونَ ۝ وَمَا لِىَ لَآ أَعْبُدُ ٱلَّذِى
فَطَرَنِى وَإِلَيْهِ تُرْجَعُونَ ۝ ءَأَتَّخِذُ مِن
دُونِهِۦٓ ءَالِهَةً إِن يُرِدْنِ ٱلرَّحْمَٰنُ بِضُرٍّ لَّا
تُغْنِ عَنِّى شَفَٰعَتُهُمْ شَيْـًٔا وَلَا يُنقِذُونِ
۝ إِنِّىٓ إِذًا لَّفِى ضَلَٰلٍ مُّبِينٍ ۝ إِنِّىٓ
ءَامَنتُ بِرَبِّكُمْ فَٱسْمَعُونِ ۝ قِيلَ
ٱدْخُلِ ٱلْجَنَّةَ قَالَ يَٰلَيْتَ قَوْمِى
يَعْلَمُونَ ۝ بِمَا غَفَرَ لِى رَبِّى وَجَعَلَنِى
مِنَ ٱلْمُكْرَمِينَ ۝

ᵃ Both the prophets at that time were powerless. Nevertheless, this third man associated himself with them. In the struggle between truth and untruth, man has to take the side of the truth, even if it amounts to supporting the weak against the strong.

The third man urged the people of his community to pay heed to the words of the earlier Prophets who were on the straight path and who did not seek any return for guiding rightly. This shows that in spite of a man being selfless and well-intentioned, his words will be examined in the light of reason, and will be deemed to be of value only if they measure up to the standard of reason.

ᵇ The believer had risked his own life to support the call of the prophets before him. This action of his was of such great worth that he was sent to Paradise. After entering Paradise he did not speak ill of his people, although they were transgressors. On the contrary, he felt that, had they seen his reward, they would not have opposed the truth. This is the picture of a true believer. He is the well-wisher of others under all circumstances, even if he is oppressed by them.

²⁸ After him We did not send down against his people a host from heaven, nor do We send down such hosts: ²⁹ it was but one great blast and they fell down lifeless. ³⁰ Alas for human beings! They ridicule every messenger that comes to them. ³¹ Do they not see how many generations We have destroyed before them? Never shall they return to them. ³² All of them, gathered together, will certainly be brought before Us.ᵃ

﷽ وَمَآ أَنزَلْنَا عَلَىٰ قَوْمِهِۦ مِنۢ بَعْدِهِۦ مِن جُندٍ مِّنَ ٱلسَّمَآءِ وَمَا كُنَّا مُنزِلِينَ ۝ إِن كَانَتْ إِلَّا صَيْحَةً وَٰحِدَةً فَإِذَا هُمْ خَٰمِدُونَ ۝ يَٰحَسْرَةً عَلَى ٱلْعِبَادِ مَا يَأْتِيهِم مِّن رَّسُولٍ إِلَّا كَانُوا۟ بِهِۦ يَسْتَهْزِءُونَ ۝ أَلَمْ يَرَوْا۟ كَمْ أَهْلَكْنَا قَبْلَهُم مِّنَ ٱلْقُرُونِ أَنَّهُمْ إِلَيْهِمْ لَا يَرْجِعُونَ ۝ وَإِن كُلٌّ لَّمَّا جَمِيعٌ لَّدَيْنَا مُحْضَرُونَ ۝

ᵃ When a decision is taken by Almighty God to destroy a community, it is enough for Him to direct the forces of nature against it: He does not need to utilise heavenly forces for the purpose.

People always mock or ridicule the one who appears to them to be of a low status. This was the case with the prophets. The prophets' personalities were underestimated by the people and they were considered of too low a standing to represent the Divine Truths.

³³ There is a sign for them in the lifeless earth. We revive it and We produce grain from it of which they eat. ³⁴ We have placed in it gardens of date palms and vines, and caused springs to gush [forth] from it, ³⁵ so that they may eat its fruit, though it was not their hands that made this. Will they not then be grateful? ³⁶ Holy is He who created all things in pairs; of what the earth grows, and of themselves, and other things which they do not know.^a

وَءَايَةٌ لَّهُمُ ٱلْأَرْضُ ٱلْمَيْتَةُ أَحْيَيْنَٰهَا وَأَخْرَجْنَا مِنْهَا حَبًّا فَمِنْهُ يَأْكُلُونَ ۝ وَجَعَلْنَا فِيهَا جَنَّٰتٍ مِّن نَّخِيلٍ وَأَعْنَٰبٍ وَفَجَّرْنَا فِيهَا مِنَ ٱلْعُيُونِ ۝ لِيَأْكُلُوا۟ مِن ثَمَرِهِۦ وَمَا عَمِلَتْهُ أَيْدِيهِمْ أَفَلَا يَشْكُرُونَ ۝ سُبْحَٰنَ ٱلَّذِى خَلَقَ ٱلْأَزْوَٰجَ كُلَّهَا مِمَّا تُنۢبِتُ ٱلْأَرْضُ وَمِنْ أَنفُسِهِمْ وَمِمَّا لَا يَعْلَمُونَ ۝

---

^a The accumulation of fertile soil on the surface of the earth; the provision of water, sun and air and the potential in the seed to germinate and grow—these and other such innumerable known and unknown factors combine to produce the food-grains, fruits and vegetables which nourish human beings. This entire system of nature is not the handiwork of man. Its existence and sustenance clearly illustrate the grace of the Creator. Thoughtfully pondering over these facts would overwhelm man with gratitude towards God.

Studies show that the 'principle of pairing' is in operation in all the things of this world. When the system of this universe is based on the principle that all objects achieve completion by way of pairing, the present world by this logic should also have its counterpart. This crucial insight establishes the possibility of a Hereafter.

37 They have a sign in the night: We withdraw from it the [light of] day— and they are left in darkness. 38 The sun, too, follows its determined course laid down for it by the Almighty, the All Knowing. 39 We have ordained phases for the moon until finally it becomes like an old date-stalk. 40 The sun cannot overtake the moon, nor can the night outpace the day: each floats in [its own] orbit.*a*

41 Another sign for them is that We carried their offspring in the laden Ark. 42 We have created for them the like of it in which they ride. 43 If it were Our will, We could drown them: then there would be no helper [to hear their cry], nor could they be saved. 44 It is only by Our mercy that they are granted provision for a time.*b*

وَءَايَةٌ لَّهُمُ ٱلَّيۡلُ نَسۡلَخُ مِنۡهُ ٱلنَّهَارَ فَإِذَا هُم مُّظۡلِمُونَ ۞ وَٱلشَّمۡسُ تَجۡرِى لِمُسۡتَقَرٍّ لَّهَا ذَٰلِكَ تَقۡدِيرُ ٱلۡعَزِيزِ ٱلۡعَلِيمِ ۞ وَٱلۡقَمَرَ قَدَّرۡنَٰهُ مَنَازِلَ حَتَّىٰ عَادَ كَٱلۡعُرۡجُونِ ٱلۡقَدِيمِ ۞ لَا ٱلشَّمۡسُ يَنۢبَغِى لَهَآ أَن تُدۡرِكَ ٱلۡقَمَرَ وَلَا ٱلَّيۡلُ سَابِقُ ٱلنَّهَارِ وَكُلٌّ فِى فَلَكٍ يَسۡبَحُونَ ۞ وَءَايَةٌ لَّهُمۡ أَنَّا حَمَلۡنَا ذُرِّيَّتَهُمۡ فِى ٱلۡفُلۡكِ ٱلۡمَشۡحُونِ ۞ وَخَلَقۡنَا لَهُم مِّن مِّثۡلِهِۦ مَا يَرۡكَبُونَ ۞ وَإِن نَّشَأۡ نُغۡرِقۡهُمۡ فَلَا صَرِيخَ لَهُمۡ وَلَا هُمۡ يُنقَذُونَ ۞ إِلَّا رَحۡمَةً مِّنَّا وَمَتَٰعًا إِلَىٰ حِينٍ ۞

---

a The earth, the moon and the sun have their fixed orbits, in which they move with the utmost precision, and due to which different celestial phenomena take place: for instance, the occurrence of day and night on the earth and the waxing and waning of the moon, serve as a heavenly calendar. This system has been in existence for millions of years now, and there is still no deviation of any kind in it.

This observation is purely an introduction to the fathomless and unlimited powers of God. If man learns lessons from these phenomena, the majesty of the One God will prevail over his mind to such an extent that all other impressions of greatness will be automatically erased from it.

b God has created vast possibilities in this world, so that man may travel by land, sea and air.

All these forms of travel are possible due to the grace of God and if man consciously reflected, he would prostrate himself before God and never develop an attitude of arrogance.

45 When they are told, 'guard yourselves against what is before you and what is behind you, in order that you may be shown mercy,' [they turn away]. 46 Indeed, not one of your Lord's signs comes to them without their turning away from it, 47 and when they are told, 'Give to others out of what God has provided for you,' those who are bent on denying the truth say to the believers, 'Why should we feed those whom God could feed if He wanted? You are clearly in error!' *a*

وَإِذَا قِيلَ لَهُمُ ٱتَّقُواْ مَا بَيْنَ أَيْدِيكُمْ وَمَا خَلْفَكُمْ لَعَلَّكُمْ تُرْحَمُونَ ۝ وَمَا تَأْتِيهِم مِّنْ ءَايَةٍ مِّنْ ءَايَتِ رَبِّهِمْ إِلَّا كَانُواْ عَنْهَا مُعْرِضِينَ ۝ وَإِذَا قِيلَ لَهُمْ أَنفِقُواْ مِمَّا رَزَقَكُمُ ٱللَّهُ قَالَ ٱلَّذِينَ كَفَرُواْ لِلَّذِينَ ءَامَنُواْ أَنُطْعِمُ مَن لَّوْ يَشَآءُ ٱللَّهُ أَطْعَمَهُۥ إِنْ أَنتُمْ إِلَّا فِي ضَلَلٍ مُّبِينٍ ۝

---

a Behind a man are his actions and before him lies the Day of Reckoning. Life, in other words, is a journey from the world of actions towards the world of results. This is a very crucial state of affairs. If a man actually realises his position, he will start trembling. But he does not consider this; nor does any sign open his eyes. He tries to justify his actions by false interpretations until the day he dies.

⁴⁸ They say, 'When will this promise be fulfilled, if you are truthful?' ⁴⁹ They must be waiting for but one single blast, which will overtake them while they are still disputing. ⁵⁰ They will have no time to make a will, nor shall they return to their own people. ⁵¹ The trumpet will be blown and, at once, they will rise up from their graves, and hasten to their Lord. ⁵² 'Woe betide us!' they will say, 'Who has roused us from our sleep?' This is what the Lord of Mercy promised: the messengers spoke the truth! ⁵³ It will be but one blast, and they will all be brought before Us together.ᵃ

وَيَقُولُونَ مَتَىٰ هَٰذَا ٱلْوَعْدُ إِن كُنتُمْ صَٰدِقِينَ ۝ مَا يَنظُرُونَ إِلَّا صَيْحَةً وَٰحِدَةً تَأْخُذُهُمْ وَهُمْ يَخِصِّمُونَ ۝ فَلَا يَسْتَطِيعُونَ تَوْصِيَةً وَلَآ إِلَىٰ أَهْلِهِمْ يَرْجِعُونَ ۝ وَنُفِخَ فِى ٱلصُّورِ فَإِذَا هُم مِّنَ ٱلْأَجْدَاثِ إِلَىٰ رَبِّهِمْ يَنسِلُونَ ۝ قَالُواْ يَٰوَيْلَنَا مَنۢ بَعَثَنَا مِن مَّرْقَدِنَا هَٰذَا مَا وَعَدَ ٱلرَّحْمَٰنُ وَصَدَقَ ٱلْمُرْسَلُونَ ۝ إِن كَانَتْ إِلَّا صَيْحَةً وَٰحِدَةً فَإِذَا هُمْ جَمِيعٌ لَّدَيْنَا مُحْضَرُونَ ۝

ᵃ Those who do not believe in the Hereafter pay scant attention to it and remain heedless of it as if it were a faraway thing. Among them, those who are of a frivolous nature will even go to the extent of mocking the concept of the Hereafter. People such as these will remain reckless until the arrival of Doomsday. Then Doomsday will seize them suddenly and in such a way that they will be unable to save themselves.

It has been recorded in the Hadith that the Angel Israfil is looking towards the throne ('arsh) of God with the trumpet (sur) to his mouth awaiting His orders, ready to carry out the command instantly. The blowing of the trumpet will be like the ringing of a bell which signals the end of the examination. Immediately thereafter, the system of the world will change: the stage of the appearance of results will commence, leaving behind the stage of actions (the present world).

⁵⁴ On that Day no soul shall suffer the least injustice. You shall be rewarded only according to your deeds. ⁵⁵ The people of Paradise shall be happily occupied on that Day— ⁵⁶ they and their wives—shall recline on couches in the shade. ⁵⁷ They shall have fruits therein, and all that they ask for. ⁵⁸ 'Peace!' shall be the greeting from the Merciful Lord.ᵃ

فَٱلْيَوْمَ لَا تُظْلَمُ نَفْسٌ شَيْئًا وَلَا تُجْزَوْنَ إِلَّا مَا كُنتُمْ تَعْمَلُونَ ۞ إِنَّ أَصْحَٰبَ ٱلْجَنَّةِ ٱلْيَوْمَ فِى شُغُلٍ فَٰكِهُونَ ۞ هُمْ وَأَزْوَٰجُهُمْ فِى ظِلَٰلٍ عَلَى ٱلْأَرَآئِكِ مُتَّكِئُونَ ۞ لَهُمْ فِيهَا فَٰكِهَةٌ وَلَهُم مَّا يَدَّعُونَ ۞ سَلَٰمٌ قَوْلًا مِّن رَّبٍّ رَّحِيمٍ ۞

ᵃ The final result of man's deeds (in the present world) will be declared in the Hereafter. One who remained immersed in the pursuance of his petty interests here, will enter the eternal world of the Hereafter empty-handed, unlike those who lived a life of high purpose and who will be very pleased with the good results they achieve.

⁵⁹ [And God will say], 'Separate yourselves from the righteous this Day, you criminals. ⁶⁰ Did I not enjoin you, sons of Adam, not to worship Satan*ᵃ*—for he is your sworn enemy, ⁶¹ but to worship Me? Surely, that is a straight path. ⁶² Yet he led astray a great multitude of you. Why did you not then understand? ⁶³ This is the Hell you were promised. ⁶⁴ Enter it this Day on account of your denial of the truth.' ⁶⁵ Today We shall seal up their mouths and their hands will speak to Us, and their feet will bear witness to their misdeeds.*ᵇ*

وَٱمْتَٰزُوا۟ ٱلْيَوْمَ أَيُّهَا ٱلْمُجْرِمُونَ ۝ أَلَمْ أَعْهَدْ إِلَيْكُمْ يَٰبَنِىٓ ءَادَمَ أَن لَّا تَعْبُدُوا۟ ٱلشَّيْطَٰنَ إِنَّهُۥ لَكُمْ عَدُوٌّ مُّبِينٌ ۝ وَأَنِ ٱعْبُدُونِى هَٰذَا صِرَٰطٌ مُّسْتَقِيمٌ ۝ وَلَقَدْ أَضَلَّ مِنكُمْ جِبِلًّا كَثِيرًا أَفَلَمْ تَكُونُوا۟ تَعْقِلُونَ ۝ هَٰذِهِۦ جَهَنَّمُ ٱلَّتِى كُنتُمْ تُوعَدُونَ ۝ ٱصْلَوْهَا ٱلْيَوْمَ بِمَا كُنتُمْ تَكْفُرُونَ ۝ ٱلْيَوْمَ نَخْتِمُ عَلَىٰ أَفْوَٰهِهِمْ وَتُكَلِّمُنَآ أَيْدِيهِمْ وَتَشْهَدُ أَرْجُلُهُم بِمَا كَانُوا۟ يَكْسِبُونَ ۝

ᵃ In the present life, good people and bad people live in the same world. But in the life of the Hereafter, these two groups will be separated; the followers of Satan will be with Satan and the subjects of the Most Beneficent God will be with God. Nobody worships Satan per se, but the worshipper of anybody other than God is in fact indirectly the worshipper of Satan.

ᵇ Modern research has proved that a man's skin is a form of record on which his utterances are recorded and from where they can also be reproduced. This is a sign which makes it understandable that in the Hereafter man's entire being would bear witness to his deeds.

⁶⁶ If it had been Our will, We could have put out their eyes. They would have struggled to find the way, but how could they have seen it? ⁶⁷ If it had been Our will, We could have paralysed them where they stood, so that they would not be able to go forward or turn back. ⁶⁸ If We extend anyone's life, We reverse his development. Can they not use their reason?[a] ⁶⁹ We have not taught him any poetry nor would it be fitting for him. This is merely a Reminder and a clear Quran ⁷⁰ to warn all who are truly alive, and to justify the word [God's verdict] against the deniers.[b]

وَلَوْ نَشَآءُ لَطَمَسْنَا عَلَىٰٓ أَعْيُنِهِمْ فَٱسْتَبَقُواْ ٱلصِّرَٰطَ فَأَنَّىٰ يُبْصِرُونَ ۝ وَلَوْ نَشَآءُ لَمَسَخْنَٰهُمْ عَلَىٰ مَكَانَتِهِمْ فَمَا ٱسْتَطَٰعُواْ مُضِيًّا وَلَا يَرْجِعُونَ ۝ وَمَن نُّعَمِّرْهُ نُنَكِّسْهُ فِى ٱلْخَلْقِ أَفَلَا يَعْقِلُونَ ۝ وَمَا عَلَّمْنَٰهُ ٱلشِّعْرَ وَمَا يَنۢبَغِى لَهُۥٓ إِنْ هُوَ إِلَّا ذِكْرٌ وَقُرْءَانٌ مُّبِينٌ ۝ لِّيُنذِرَ مَن كَانَ حَيًّا وَيَحِقَّ ٱلْقَوْلُ عَلَى ٱلْكَٰفِرِينَ ۝

---

[a] Man has been endowed with eyes, hands and legs and numerous such blessings, but instead of being thankful, he takes these blessings for granted. It is a fact that these features were not created by man himself, instead his Creator blessed him with them. He must therefore realize their importance, for what would man do, if the Creator decided to withdraw His blessings.

Man gets a glimpse of this possibility at the onset of old age. When a man grows very old, all his powers are taken away from him, so much so that he becomes as weak and helpless as he was as a small child. But, man is so foolish that he does not learn a lesson from this.

[b] The miraculous literary style of the Quran also attracted listeners. The opponents of the Prophet used this to deride the importance of the Quran by referring to it as a poetic work and not a Divine Discourse.

This was a baseless assertion. The extremely serious tone of the Quran; the unveiling of hidden facts; its teachings concerning the realisation of God; its rare unity of thought from the beginning till the end and the indescribable glimpses of God that it provides—all these firmly indicate that it is much more than a work of man-made poetry.

The Quran's veracity will be evident only to those whose souls are truly alive, and only such people will admit the Truth.

71 Do they not see that, among the things which Our hands have fashioned, We have created for them cattle of which they are the masters, 72 We have subjected these to them, so that some may be used for riding and some for food, 73 some for milk to drink and some from which other benefits may be received? Will they not be grateful? 74 They have set up other gods besides God, hoping to be helped by them, 75 but they are not able to help them: rather they will be brought before God as their allied host. 76 Let not their words grieve you. We have knowledge of all that they conceal and all that they reveal.*a*

أَوَلَمْ يَرَوْاْ أَنَّا خَلَقْنَا لَهُم مِّمَّا عَمِلَتْ أَيْدِينَآ أَنْعَـٰمًا فَهُمْ لَهَا مَـٰلِكُونَ ۝ وَذَلَّلْنَـٰهَا لَهُمْ فَمِنْهَا رَكُوبُهُمْ وَمِنْهَا يَأْكُلُونَ ۝ وَلَهُمْ فِيهَا مَنَـٰفِعُ وَمَشَارِبُ ۖ أَفَلَا يَشْكُرُونَ ۝ وَٱتَّخَذُواْ مِن دُونِ ٱللَّهِ ءَالِهَةً لَّعَلَّهُمْ يُنصَرُونَ ۝ لَا يَسْتَطِيعُونَ نَصْرَهُمْ وَهُمْ لَهُمْ جُندٌ مُّحْضَرُونَ ۝ فَلَا يَحْزُنكَ قَوْلُهُمْ ۘ إِنَّا نَعْلَمُ مَا يُسِرُّونَ وَمَا يُعْلِنُونَ ۝

---

a Cattle and other domestic animals are living examples which show that this material world has been created by its Creator in such a way that man should be able to harness it according to his needs. On this amenability of the material world stands the entire structure of human civilization. If horses and bulls were to be as wild as bears and wolves, or if iron and petroleum were to be as uncontrollable as volcanic lava, the evolution of human civilization would become impossible.

Therefore, man should be extremely grateful to his Gracious Creator. But, he worships beings other than God and when he is advised to desist, he pays no heed. Undoubtedly, this is the worst type of disobedience to the divine rule, the aftermath of which nobody can escape.

⁷⁷ Does not man see that We created him from a drop. Yet there he is, flagrantly contentious, ⁷⁸ producing arguments against Us, and forgetting his own creation. He asks, 'Who can give life back to bones after they have rotted away?' ⁷⁹ Say, 'He who brought them into being in the first instance will give them life again: He has knowledge of every type of creation: ⁸⁰ He who produces fire for you from green trees and from this you kindle fire.' ⁸¹ Is He who created the heavens and earth not able to create others like these people? Of course He is! He is indeed the Supreme Creator, the All Knowing: ⁸² when He decrees a thing, He need only say, 'Be!' and it is. ⁸³ So glory be to Him who has control over all things. It is to Him that you will all be brought back.^{*a*}

أَوَلَمْ يَرَ ٱلْإِنسَـٰنُ أَنَّا خَلَقْنَـٰهُ مِن نُّطْفَةٍ فَإِذَا هُوَ خَصِيمٌ مُّبِينٌ ۝ وَضَرَبَ لَنَا مَثَلًا وَنَسِيَ خَلْقَهُۥ قَالَ مَن يُحْىِ ٱلْعِظَـٰمَ وَهِىَ رَمِيمٌ ۝ قُلْ يُحْيِيهَا ٱلَّذِىٓ أَنشَأَهَآ أَوَّلَ مَرَّةٍ وَهُوَ بِكُلِّ خَلْقٍ عَلِيمٌ ۝ ٱلَّذِى جَعَلَ لَكُم مِّنَ ٱلشَّجَرِ ٱلْأَخْضَرِ نَارًا فَإِذَآ أَنتُم مِّنْهُ تُوقِدُونَ ۝ أَوَلَيْسَ ٱلَّذِى خَلَقَ ٱلسَّمَـٰوَٰتِ وَٱلْأَرْضَ بِقَـٰدِرٍ عَلَىٰٓ أَن يَخْلُقَ مِثْلَهُم بَلَىٰ وَهُوَ ٱلْخَلَّـٰقُ ٱلْعَلِيمُ ۝ إِنَّمَآ أَمْرُهُۥٓ إِذَآ أَرَادَ شَيْـًٔا أَن يَقُولَ لَهُۥ كُن فَيَكُونُ ۝ فَسُبْحَـٰنَ ٱلَّذِى بِيَدِهِۦ مَلَكُوتُ كُلِّ شَىْءٍ وَإِلَيْهِ تُرْجَعُونَ ۝

---

^{*a*} Man has not created himself. This calls for man to possess the quality of humility or modesty. But, instead of being realistic, he indulges in discussions which are not in accordance with his humble position.

The creation of man and the universe for the first time itself furnishes ample proof of the fact that such creation for the second time is also possible. But ignoring this, man argues about how a dead man can come back to life. The changing of the dead into the living, will no doubt occur on the Day of Judgement, but this possibility is seen in other things even today. One may take the example of a tree. The tree is apparently green and fresh, but when it is cut up and burnt as sticks, it takes on a completely different shape, that of fire.

The metamorphosis of one thing into another is an established fact. God makes this possible today with regard to different things. As for man, however, He will make it possible on the Day of Judgement, but this will not be for the purpose of making the people admit this fact. It will be in order to punish them for their insubordination.

37. THE RANKS

In the name of God,
the Most Gracious, the Most Merciful

¹ By those [angels] who range themselves in close ranks ² and those who drive away [the wicked] with reproof ³ and by the reciters of the Reminder: ⁴ your God is One, ⁵ Lord of the heavens and the earth and everything between them; Lord of the Easts.ᵃ

ᵃ One of the secrets revealed through the Prophet is the existence of angels. Here, three special aspects of the angels have been mentioned. First, they are completely obedient to God. Without the slightest hesitation or objection, they carry out His orders. Then there is a group of angels which implements the punishments imposed by God on human beings, either in the shape of calamities or untoward incidents or in any other manner dictated by Him. The angels also bring God's advice to man in the form of inspiration or intuition (*ilham*) and as revelation (*wahi*) to the prophets.

⁶We have adorned the lowest heaven with the beauty of the planets; ⁷and guarded it against all rebellious devils: ⁸they cannot overhear the Higher Assembly for they are pelted from every side, ⁹driven away, and will suffer eternal punishment. ¹⁰But if anyone does succeed in snatching a glimpse [of such knowledge], he shall be pursued by a piercing flame.ᵃ

إِنَّا زَيَّنَّا ٱلسَّمَآءَ ٱلدُّنْيَا بِزِينَةٍ ٱلْكَوَاكِبِ ۞ وَحِفْظًا مِّن كُلِّ شَيْطَٰنٍ مَّارِدٍ ۞ لَّا يَسَّمَّعُونَ إِلَى ٱلْمَلَإِ ٱلْأَعْلَىٰ وَيُقْذَفُونَ مِن كُلِّ جَانِبٍ ۞ دُحُورًا وَلَهُمْ عَذَابٌ وَاصِبٌ ۞ إِلَّا مَنْ خَطِفَ ٱلْخَطْفَةَ فَأَتْبَعَهُ شِهَابٌ ثَاقِبٌ ۞

ᵃ 'The lowest heaven' (as-sama' ad-dunya) perhaps refers to that part of space which is nearer to man and which can be seen with the naked eye. The creatures such as the jinn attempt to fathom information about the unknown. But in the lowest heaven itself the arrangement is such that any such brazen endeavour is disrupted by occurrences like the shower of meteors.

¹¹ So, ask those who deny the truth if it was harder to create them than all the other things We have created? We created them from sticky clay. ¹² No wonder you are surprised as they laugh with scorn. ¹³ When they are reminded, they do not pay heed, ¹⁴ and whenever they see some sign, they ridicule it, ¹⁵ saying, 'This is plain sorcery!' ¹⁶ 'What! When we have died and become dust and bones, will we be brought back to life again, ¹⁷ along with our forefathers?' ¹⁸ Say, 'Yes indeed, and you will be brought low.'ᵃ

فَٱسۡتَفۡتِهِمۡ أَهُمۡ أَشَدُّ خَلۡقًا أَم مَّنۡ خَلَقۡنَآ إِنَّا خَلَقۡنَٰهُم مِّن طِينٍ لَّازِبِۭ ۝ بَلۡ عَجِبۡتَ وَيَسۡخَرُونَ ۝ وَإِذَا ذُكِّرُواْ لَا يَذۡكُرُونَ ۝ وَإِذَا رَأَوۡاْ ءَايَةً يَسۡتَسۡخِرُونَ ۝ وَقَالُوٓاْ إِنۡ هَٰذَآ إِلَّا سِحۡرٌ مُّبِينٌ ۝ أَءِذَا مِتۡنَا وَكُنَّا تُرَابًا وَعِظَٰمًا أَءِنَّا لَمَبۡعُوثُونَ ۝ أَوَءَابَآؤُنَا ٱلۡأَوَّلُونَ ۝ قُلۡ نَعَمۡ وَأَنتُمۡ دَٰخِرُونَ ۝

ᵃ The universe as we observe from the earth is so complicated and so extensive that the re-creation of human beings in the next world appears to be a work of comparatively smaller magnitude. A greater specimen of the creative power of the Creator is before us, then why should it be impossible for that Creator to engage in creation on a lesser scale?

On analysing the human body, it appears that it is a combination of earthly components. Man is made up of substances found on earth, such as water, calcium, iron, sodium, etc. All these are found in our world in abundance, then by utilising the same elements from which He once created human beings, can He not re-create man?

¹⁹ There will be but a single blast and then their eyes will open. ²⁰ They will say, 'Woe to us! This is the Day of Reckoning.' ²¹ [It will be said], 'This is the Day of Judgement which you have been denying.' ²² But We shall say, 'Assemble those who did wrong together with their associates and what they worshipped ²³ besides God, and lead them to the path of the Fire; ²⁴ and stop them there for questioning: ²⁵ "But what is the matter with you that you cannot help one another?"'—²⁶ indeed, on that Day they will surrender themselves.ᵃ

فَإِنَّمَا هِيَ زَجْرَةٌ وَحِدَةٌ فَإِذَا هُم يَنظُرُونَ ۞ وَقَالُواْ يَـٰوَيْلَنَا هَـٰذَا يَوْمُ ٱلدِّينِ ۞ هَـٰذَا يَوْمُ ٱلْفَصْلِ ٱلَّذِى كُنتُم بِهِۦ تُكَذِّبُونَ ۞ ۞ ٱحْشُرُواْ ٱلَّذِينَ ظَلَمُواْ وَأَزْوَٰجَهُمْ وَمَا كَانُواْ يَعْبُدُونَ ۞ مِن دُونِ ٱللَّهِ فَٱهْدُوهُمْ إِلَىٰ صِرَٰطِ ٱلْجَحِيمِ ۞ وَقِفُوهُمْ إِنَّهُم مَّسْـُٔولُونَ ۞ مَا لَكُمْ لَا تَنَاصَرُونَ ۞ بَلْ هُمُ ٱلْيَوْمَ مُسْتَسْلِمُونَ ۞

ᵃ In the present world, tidings of the future life or life in the Hereafter, are regularly communicated. But man attaches no importance to this. In the Hereafter, the reality of future life will seize man. At that time, man will forget his arrogance and will prostrate himself before God. This will be an indescribably terrible scene. The position in which people will be, when they have gathered to be judged, on the Day of Resurrection (*hashr*) has been described in the above verses.

27 They will turn upon one another, and question one another. 28 They will say, 'You used to come at us from the right.' 29 They will say, 'No! It was you who would not believe— 30 we had no power over you; but you yourselves were a rebellious people. 31 But now our Lord's word has come true against us: truly, we are bound to taste [the punishment]. 32 We led you astray as we were ourselves astray.' 33 On that Day they will all share the punishment:a

وَأَقۡبَلَ بَعۡضُهُمۡ عَلَىٰ بَعۡضٍ يَتَسَآءَلُونَ ۝ قَالُوٓاْ إِنَّكُمۡ كُنتُمۡ تَأۡتُونَنَا عَنِ ٱلۡيَمِينِ ۝ قَالُواْ بَل لَّمۡ تَكُونُواْ مُؤۡمِنِينَ ۝ وَمَا كَانَ لَنَا عَلَيۡكُم مِّن سُلۡطَٰنٍ بَلۡ كُنتُمۡ قَوۡمًا طَٰغِينَ ۝ فَحَقَّ عَلَيۡنَا قَوۡلُ رَبِّنَآ إِنَّا لَذَآئِقُونَ ۝ فَأَغۡوَيۡنَٰكُمۡ إِنَّا كُنَّا غَٰوِينَ ۝ فَإِنَّهُمۡ يَوۡمَئِذٍ فِى ٱلۡعَذَابِ مُشۡتَرِكُونَ ۝

---

a This is a dialogue between leader and his community. On the Day of Judgement, the latter will attribute their miserable condition to their misguided leaders and say that they were misled by their leaders in different ways. The leaders will deny this allegation and say, 'Nobody misleads anybody. You yourselves were full of arrogance. So you found whatever we said in consonance with your nature and you accepted it. In fact, you have followed your own desires and not our dictates. Both of us are equally guilty.'

The fact is that, on the Day of Judgement, leaders and followers will be given the same treatment. Neither will the so-called greatness of the leaders save them, nor will the followers' excuse that they were ignorant and that they were misguided by their leaders be of any avail.

³⁴ that is how We deal with evil-doers. ³⁵ When they were told, 'There is no deity but God,' they turned away with disdain, ³⁶ and replied, 'Shall we then give up our deities at the bidding of a mad poet?' ³⁷ 'Surely, he has brought the truth, confirming those who were sent before; ³⁸ you shall surely taste the painful punishment, ³⁹ and be rewarded only according to your deeds.' ^a

إِنَّا كَذَٰلِكَ نَفْعَلُ بِٱلْمُجْرِمِينَ ٣٤ إِنَّهُمْ كَانُوٓاْ إِذَا قِيلَ لَهُمْ لَآ إِلَٰهَ إِلَّا ٱللَّهُ يَسْتَكْبِرُونَ ٣٥ وَيَقُولُونَ أَئِنَّا لَتَارِكُوٓاْ ءَالِهَتِنَا لِشَاعِرٍ مَّجْنُونٍ ٣٦ بَلْ جَآءَ بِٱلْحَقِّ وَصَدَّقَ ٱلْمُرْسَلِينَ ٣٧ إِنَّكُمْ لَذَآئِقُواْ ٱلْعَذَابِ ٱلْأَلِيمِ ٣٨ وَمَا تُجْزَوْنَ إِلَّا مَا كُنتُمْ تَعْمَلُونَ ٣٩

---

^a When they were told that there was nobody worth worshipping except God, they behaved haughtily. This does not mean that their haughty behaviour was directed against God. The majesty of God is too lofty to allow any individual to be so presumptuous. Their haughty behaviour, in fact, was aimed at His messenger.

The leaders in whose name others indulged in polytheistic acts, were adversely affected by the Prophet's call for belief in the oneness of God. On the one hand was the Prophet and on the other, the polytheistic leaders. Since the Prophet appeared to be of a lesser stature than the leaders, most people ignored him, considering him a person of little or no account. The force of argument was undoubtedly on the side of the Prophet, but apparent greatness seemed to reside in their leaders and history is replete with examples where the force of reason has proved ineffective in the face of apparent greatness.

⁴⁰ But the chosen servants of God;
⁴¹ shall have a known provision—
⁴² fruits of various kinds; and they
shall be honoured, ⁴³ in the Gardens
of Bliss, ⁴⁴ seated on couches, facing
one another. ⁴⁵ A drink will be passed
round among them from a flowing
spring: ⁴⁶ white and delicious to
those who drink it, ⁴⁷ causing no
headiness or intoxication. ⁴⁸ With
them will be spouses—modest of
gaze and beautiful of eye—⁴⁹ like
closely guarded pearls.ᵃ

إِلَّا عِبَادَ ٱللَّهِ ٱلْمُخْلَصِينَ ۝ أُوْلَٰٓئِكَ

هُمْ رِزْقٌ مَّعْلُومٌ ۝ فَوَٰكِهُ وَهُم

مُّكْرَمُونَ ۝ فِى جَنَّٰتِ ٱلنَّعِيمِ ۝

عَلَىٰ سُرُرٍ مُّتَقَٰبِلِينَ ۝ يُطَافُ عَلَيْهِم

بِكَأْسٍ مِّن مَّعِينٍ ۝ بَيْضَآءَ لَذَّةٍ

لِّلشَّٰرِبِينَ ۝ لَا فِيهَا غَوْلٌ وَلَا هُمْ

عَنْهَا يُنزَفُونَ ۝ وَعِندَهُمْ

قَٰصِرَٰتُ ٱلطَّرْفِ عِينٌ ۝ كَأَنَّهُنَّ

بَيْضٌ مَّكْنُونٌ ۝

ᵃ The present world is a world of trial. Here people are given the opportunity to
act freely so that God may separate the good from the bad. Those who prove by
their words and deeds that they deserve to savour the joys of Paradise, will be
selected by their Lord for this purpose. Special favours will be bestowed on them
and they will be asked to remain forever in these gardens which afford every
comfort and enjoyment.

⁵⁰ They will turn to one another with questions: ⁵¹ one of them will say, 'I had a friend, ⁵² who used to ask, "Do you really believe that ⁵³ after we die and become dust and bones, we shall be brought to judgement?"' ⁵⁴ Then he will say, 'Shall we look for him?' ⁵⁵ Then he will look and see him in the midst of the Fire. ⁵⁶ He will say, 'By God! You almost brought me to ruin! ⁵⁷ If it had not been for the blessing of my Lord, I would also have been taken to Hell.' ⁵⁸ Then he will say [to his blessed companions], 'Are we not going to die, ⁵⁹ except for our first death? Are we not going to be punished? ⁶⁰ Truly, this is a great victory!' ⁶¹ It is for the like of this that all should strive.ᵃ

فَأَقْبَلَ بَعْضُهُمْ عَلَىٰ بَعْضٍ يَتَسَآءَلُونَ ۝ قَالَ قَآئِلٌ مِّنْهُمْ إِنِّى كَانَ لِى قَرِينٌ ۝ يَقُولُ أَءِنَّكَ لَمِنَ ٱلْمُصَدِّقِينَ ۝ أَءِذَا مِتْنَا وَكُنَّا تُرَابًا وَعِظَـٰمًا أَءِنَّا لَمَدِينُونَ ۝ قَالَ هَلْ أَنتُم مُّطَّلِعُونَ ۝ فَٱطَّلَعَ فَرَءَاهُ فِى سَوَآءِ ٱلْجَحِيمِ ۝ قَالَ تَٱللَّهِ إِن كِدتَّ لَتُرْدِينِ ۝ وَلَوْلَا نِعْمَةُ رَبِّى لَكُنتُ مِنَ ٱلْمُحْضَرِينَ ۝ أَفَمَا نَحْنُ بِمَيِّتِينَ ۝ إِلَّا مَوْتَتَنَا ٱلْأُولَىٰ وَمَا نَحْنُ بِمُعَذَّبِينَ ۝ إِنَّ هَـٰذَا لَهُوَ ٱلْفَوْزُ ٱلْعَظِيمُ ۝ لِمِثْلِ هَـٰذَا فَلْيَعْمَلِ ٱلْعَـٰمِلُونَ ۝

ᵃ Paradise will be a world of aesthetic and noble activity. There will be interesting meetings; there will be enjoyable experiences; intellectually stimulating conversations and all kinds of limitations and unpleasantness will have come to an end.

Believing in the Hereafter does not mean a simple acceptance of it but rather considering the existence of the Hereafter as so very real and so very important that its concept should prevail over one's entire life and one should be prepared to risk one's all for its sake. Those who had thought of believers who were ever conscious of the Hereafter as being mad will be wonderstruck on seeing their success in the Hereafter. On the other hand, the believers in the Hereafter themselves will be surprised to see their own glory, finding it difficult to believe that God could have rewarded them so generously for their small acts of goodness. How strange is one who does not pine for such a heaven and who does not perform such deeds as will help him achieve it.

⁶² Is that better by way of hospitality or the Zaqqum tree, ⁶³ which We have made as a test for the wrongdoers. ⁶⁴ For it is a tree that springs out of the bottom of Hellfire: ⁶⁵ and its fruits are like devils' heads. ⁶⁶ They will eat from it and fill their bellies with it; ⁶⁷ then in addition to it they shall have a draught of boiling water to drink; ⁶⁸ then surely they shall return to Hell. ⁶⁹ They found their fathers had gone astray; ⁷⁰ so they are rushing to follow in their footsteps. ⁷¹ And assuredly many of the ancients went astray before them, ⁷² though We had sent warners among them. ⁷³ See how those who were warned met their end! ⁷⁴ Not so the chosen servants of God.ᵃ

أَذَٰلِكَ خَيْرٌ نُّزُلًا أَمْ شَجَرَةُ ٱلزَّقُّومِ ۝ إِنَّا جَعَلْنَـٰهَا فِتْنَةً لِّلظَّـٰلِمِينَ ۝ إِنَّهَا شَجَرَةٌ تَخْرُجُ فِىٓ أَصْلِ ٱلْجَحِيمِ ۝ طَلْعُهَا كَأَنَّهُۥ رُءُوسُ ٱلشَّيَـٰطِينِ ۝ فَإِنَّهُمْ لَـَٔاكِلُونَ مِنْهَا فَمَالِـُٔونَ مِنْهَا ٱلْبُطُونَ ۝ ثُمَّ إِنَّ لَهُمْ عَلَيْهَا لَشَوْبًا مِّنْ حَمِيمٍ ۝ ثُمَّ إِنَّ مَرْجِعَهُمْ لَإِلَى ٱلْجَحِيمِ ۝ إِنَّهُمْ أَلْفَوْا۟ ءَابَآءَهُمْ ضَآلِّينَ ۝ فَهُمْ عَلَىٰٓ ءَاثَـٰرِهِمْ يُهْرَعُونَ ۝ وَلَقَدْ ضَلَّ قَبْلَهُمْ أَكْثَرُ ٱلْأَوَّلِينَ ۝ وَلَقَدْ أَرْسَلْنَا فِيهِم مُّنذِرِينَ ۝ فَٱنظُرْ كَيْفَ كَانَ عَـٰقِبَةُ ٱلْمُنذَرِينَ ۝ إِلَّا عِبَادَ ٱللَّهِ ٱلْمُخْلَصِينَ ۝

ᵃ It is stated in the Quran that there will be a Zaqqum tree in hell and that its fruits will be eaten by the inmates of hell when they are overwhelmed by hunger. (See 56: 52).

When this revelation was made in the Quran, the people of ancient Arabia started mocking it. One of the chiefs said, 'How can a tree grow amidst the fire of hell?' Another chief said, 'Muhammad is terrifying us by talking of Zaqqum, when the fact is that dates and butter are called Zaqqum, in the Berber language.' Abu Jahl took some people home and asked his maidservant to bring some dates and butter and when they were brought, he said to his companions, 'Eat this. This is the Zaqqum with which you are being threatened by Muhammad.' (*Tafsir al-Mazhari*).

Such Quranic statements were misused by unbelievers to demonstrate the untrustworthiness of the Quran. God might well have refrained from using such a word as would give unbelievers the opportunity to raise unnecessary issues, but He did not do so. The reason is that this creates the very situation in which a man is meant to be tried. In order to achieve salvation, he has to prove that by avoiding unnecessary issues he has given his full attention to the truth; that, by carefully avoiding misunderstandings, he has managed to discover the real purpose of the argument; that he has concentrated entirely on facts, although there were many opportunities for his mind to be diverted from them. ▶

75 Noah cried to Us, and how excellent was Our response! 76 We saved him and his people from great distress, 77 and We made his offspring the only survivors. 78 We left mention of him among later generations. 79 Peace be upon Noah among all the peoples! 80 That is how We recompense the righteous: 81 he was truly one of Our faithful servants. 82 We drowned the rest.*

وَلَقَدْ نَادَىٰنَا نُوحٌ فَلَنِعْمَ ٱلْمُجِيبُونَ ۝ وَنَجَّيْنَـٰهُ وَأَهْلَهُۥ مِنَ ٱلْكَرْبِ ٱلْعَظِيمِ ۝ وَجَعَلْنَا ذُرِّيَّتَهُۥ هُمُ ٱلْبَاقِينَ ۝ وَتَرَكْنَا عَلَيْهِ فِي ٱلْأَخِرِينَ ۝ سَلَـٰمٌ عَلَىٰ نُوحٍ فِي ٱلْعَـٰلَمِينَ ۝ إِنَّا كَذَٰلِكَ نَجْزِي ٱلْمُحْسِنِينَ ۝ إِنَّهُۥ مِنْ عِبَادِنَا ٱلْمُؤْمِنِينَ ۝ ثُمَّ أَغْرَقْنَا ٱلْأَخَرِينَ ۝

God's selected few are those who rise above traditional religion and discover the real Truth; who rise above outward appearances and realise the real meaning of occurrences; who recognise God's representative and become his supporters.

a When Noah's own people turned against him, he called upon God to help him in his struggle with them. God helped him to steer clear of his difficulties. This indicates that when a subject of God calls out to Him, he receives a superlative response. But such response succeeds a tireless strife of the implorer. Noah had been trying to spread the message of God for about nine hundred and fifty years, exercising patience, wisdom and all along wishing well for his people. After a long period of time elapsed in this way, Noah finally called out to God for His succour.

Noah's opponents were utterly destroyed in a terrible flood: indeed, the whole race was wiped out. The succeeding generation came into existence through those few individuals who were saved along with him in his ark.

83 Abraham was of the same faith:
84 he came to his Lord with a sound
heart. 85 'Behold!' he said to his father
and to his people, 'What are these
that you worship? 86 Would you
serve false deities instead of God?
87 What do you think of the Lord of
the Worlds?'[a]

۞ وَإِنَّ مِن شِيعَتِهِ لَإِبْرَٰهِيمَ ۞

إِذْ جَآءَ رَبَّهُۥ بِقَلْبٍ سَلِيمٍ ۞ إِذْ قَالَ

لِأَبِيهِ وَقَوْمِهِ مَاذَا تَعْبُدُونَ ۞

أَئِفْكًا ءَالِهَةً دُونَ ٱللَّهِ تُرِيدُونَ ۞

فَمَا ظَنُّكُم بِرَبِّ ٱلْعَٰلَمِينَ ۞

---

[a] Abraham (Ibrahim) was of the same religion as Noah. All the Prophets were sent
so that man can be made aware about the creation plan of God and be given the
aim of purifying himself during his pre-death period. God created man and sent
him into the world with a righteous nature. He must pass the test of resisting the
inducements of this world and go before God having kept himself free of all the
base desires of self and satanic defilement. Such souls will be welcomed into
Paradise.

To ascribe partners to God (*shirk*) amounts to belittling God. In this case, man
does not discover God as the greatest Being and that is why he is lost in other so-
called forms of greatness and stoops to worshipping them.

88 He looked up at the stars. 89 And said, 'I am sick,' 90 so they turned their backs on him and went off. 91 He turned to their gods and said, 'Do you not eat? 92 What is the matter with you that you do not speak?' 93 then he turned on them, striking them down with his right hand. 94 His people came rushing towards him, 95 but he said, 'How can you worship things you carve with your own hands, 96 when it is God who has created you and all your handiwork?' 97 They said, 'Build a pyre for him and throw him into the blaze!' 98 They wanted to harm him, but We humiliated them all. 99 He said, 'I will go to my Lord: He is sure to guide me. 100 Lord, grant me a righteous son.' 101 We gave him the good news that he would have a patient, forbearing son.[a]

فَنَظَرَ نَظْرَةً فِى ٱلنُّجُومِ ۝ فَقَالَ إِنِّى سَقِيمٌ ۝ فَتَوَلَّوْاْ عَنْهُ مُدْبِرِينَ ۝ فَرَاغَ إِلَىٰٓ ءَالِهَتِهِمْ فَقَالَ أَلَا تَأْكُلُونَ ۝ مَا لَكُمْ لَا تَنطِقُونَ ۝ فَرَاغَ عَلَيْهِمْ ضَرْبًۢا بِٱلْيَمِينِ ۝ فَأَقْبَلُوٓاْ إِلَيْهِ يَزِفُّونَ ۝ قَالَ أَتَعْبُدُونَ مَا تَنْحِتُونَ ۝ وَٱللَّهُ خَلَقَكُمْ وَمَا تَعْمَلُونَ ۝ قَالُواْ ٱبْنُواْ لَهُۥ بُنْيَٰنًا فَأَلْقُوهُ فِى ٱلْجَحِيمِ ۝ فَأَرَادُواْ بِهِۦ كَيْدًا فَجَعَلْنَٰهُمُ ٱلْأَسْفَلِينَ ۝ وَقَالَ إِنِّى ذَاهِبٌ إِلَىٰ رَبِّى سَيَهْدِينِ ۝ رَبِّ هَبْ لِى مِنَ ٱلصَّٰلِحِينَ ۝ فَبَشَّرْنَٰهُ بِغُلَٰمٍ حَلِيمٍ ۝

---

[a] The people of Abraham's community were perhaps going out of town to participate in some festival. Members of his household invited him to accompany them, but he managed somehow to excuse himself. When all the people had left, he entered the temple during the night and broke the deities kept there. It is important to note here that Abraham did so after continuous logical persuasion had failed to yield any result. When his people did not realise or accept the falsity of the deities by means of rational pleadings, by breaking the deities Abraham demonstrated that they were just a sham. Had they been genuine deities, they would have saved themselves from being smashed.

This infuriated the people of Abraham's community so much that they decided to kill him and throw him into a fire. But God saved him from it. Thereafter, he left his native place, Mesopotamia (now called Iraq). At that time, he prayed, 'O, God ! Bless me with a pious and righteous offspring so that, by teaching and training, I may make him a believer and a Muslim who, after me, will continue to perform the mission of preaching the oneness of God.'

¹⁰² And when he reached the age when he could work with him, he said, 'O my son, I have seen in a dream that I am sacrificing you. So tell me what you think of it!' He replied, 'O my father, do as you are commanded; and God willing, you will find me steadfast.' ¹⁰³ When they had both submitted to God, and he had laid his son down on his face, ¹⁰⁴ We called out to him, 'Abraham, ¹⁰⁵ you have fulfilled the dream.' It is thus indeed that We reward those who do good—¹⁰⁶ that surely was a manifest trial—¹⁰⁷ We ransomed him with a great sacrifice, ¹⁰⁸ and left him thus to be succeeded by a group [of followers] among later generations: ¹⁰⁹ 'Peace and salutation to Abraham!' ¹¹⁰ That is how We recompense the righteous: ¹¹¹ truly, he was one of Our faithful servants. ¹¹² We gave Abraham the good news of Isaac—a prophet and a righteous man—¹¹³ and blessed him and Isaac too: some of their offspring were good, but some clearly sinned against their souls.ᵃ

فَلَمَّا بَلَغَ مَعَهُ ٱلسَّعْىَ قَالَ يَـٰبُنَىَّ إِنِّىٓ أَرَىٰ فِى ٱلْمَنَامِ أَنِّىٓ أَذْبَحُكَ فَٱنظُرْ مَاذَا تَرَىٰ ۚ قَالَ يَـٰٓأَبَتِ ٱفْعَلْ مَا تُؤْمَرُ ۖ سَتَجِدُنِىٓ إِن شَآءَ ٱللَّهُ مِنَ ٱلصَّـٰبِرِينَ ۝ فَلَمَّآ أَسْلَمَا وَتَلَّهُۥ لِلْجَبِينِ ۝ وَنَـٰدَيْنَـٰهُ أَن يَـٰٓإِبْرَٰهِيمُ ۝ قَدْ صَدَّقْتَ ٱلرُّءْيَآ ۚ إِنَّا كَذَٰلِكَ نَجْزِى ٱلْمُحْسِنِينَ ۝ إِنَّ هَـٰذَا لَهُوَ ٱلْبَلَـٰٓؤُا۟ ٱلْمُبِينُ ۝ وَفَدَيْنَـٰهُ بِذِبْحٍ عَظِيمٍ ۝ وَتَرَكْنَا عَلَيْهِ فِى ٱلْءَاخِرِينَ ۝ سَلَـٰمٌ عَلَىٰٓ إِبْرَٰهِيمَ ۝ كَذَٰلِكَ نَجْزِى ٱلْمُحْسِنِينَ ۝ إِنَّهُۥ مِنْ عِبَادِنَا ٱلْمُؤْمِنِينَ ۝ وَبَشَّرْنَـٰهُ بِإِسْحَـٰقَ نَبِيًّا مِّنَ ٱلصَّـٰلِحِينَ ۝ وَبَـٰرَكْنَا عَلَيْهِ وَعَلَىٰٓ إِسْحَـٰقَ ۚ وَمِن ذُرِّيَّتِهِمَا مُحْسِنٌ وَظَالِمٌ لِّنَفْسِهِۦ مُبِينٌ ۝

ᵃ In the days of Abraham, polytheism was so dominant that its continuity in history had been long established. Now, any child born into this situation was influenced by the surrounding atmosphere and was so immersed in polytheism that no effort even at the level of the Prophet was successful in weaning him away from it. When Abraham left Iraq, after a long missionary struggle, there were only two believers with him—one his wife Sarah and the other his nephew, Lot.

People did not adhere to the concept of the oneness of God, despite the utmost struggle on the part of Prophet Abaraham. So, Almighty God planned that a new race be brought into existence which should be nurtured far away from the atmosphere of polytheism. For this purpose, the area of Hijaz was selected. This area, being dry and without any vegetation, was desolate and uninhabited. The plan was that a devotee should be settled in this area where he would become the progenitor of a pure race. ▶

114 We also bestowed Our favour on Moses and Aaron: 115 We saved them and their people from great distress; 116 and We helped them, so that they were victorious; 117 and We gave them the Book which helps to make things clear; 118 and guided them to the straight path; 119 and We left them thus to be succeeded by a group [of followers] among later generations: 120 'Peace be upon Moses and Aaron!' 121 This is how We reward those who do good: 122 truly they were among Our faithful servants.*

وَلَقَدْ مَنَنَّا عَلَىٰ مُوسَىٰ وَهَـٰرُونَ ۝ وَنَجَّيْنَـٰهُمَا وَقَوْمَهُمَا مِنَ ٱلْكَرْبِ ٱلْعَظِيمِ ۝ وَنَصَرْنَـٰهُمْ فَكَانُوا۟ هُمُ ٱلْغَـٰلِبِينَ ۝ وَءَاتَيْنَـٰهُمَا ٱلْكِتَـٰبَ ٱلْمُسْتَبِينَ ۝ وَهَدَيْنَـٰهُمَا ٱلصِّرَٰطَ ٱلْمُسْتَقِيمَ ۝ وَتَرَكْنَا عَلَيْهِمَا فِى ٱلْءَاخِرِينَ ۝ سَلَـٰمٌ عَلَىٰ مُوسَىٰ وَهَـٰرُونَ ۝ إِنَّا كَذَٰلِكَ نَجْزِى ٱلْمُحْسِنِينَ ۝ إِنَّهُمَا مِنْ عِبَادِنَا ٱلْمُؤْمِنِينَ ۝

Hijaz (Mecca and Medina) was a waterless desert and to settle anyone in such arid surroundings amounted to sacrificing him alive. God ordered Abraham to offer his son Ishmael as a sacrifice, and in all obedience, Abraham submitted to God's will.

Abraham's second son was Isaac. Prophethood continued in his line of descent until the advent of the last prophet who belonged to the Children of Ishmael (the younger brother of Isaac). The Prophet Muhammad brought about a revolution, which destroyed polytheism as a dominant school of thought.

a God helped the Prophet Moses and his community and relieved them from the oppression of Pharaoh. This was made possible through the dawah work performed by Moses. He preached the truth before Pharaoh. After the completion of the tenure of his dawah mission came the time for Pharaoh to be pronounced guilty and to be destroyed; and for Moses and his community to be victorious and dominant.

In this context, one of the meanings of 'showing the straight path' is that the right solution to the problem of Pharaoh was revealed to them. Though this was a problem faced at the community level, its solution nevertheless lay in communicating the divine message. So, the victory and supremacy which they achieved was the result of *dawah* efforts and was not due to any national struggle or rebellion against Pharaoh in the usual sense.

¹²³ Elijah too was one of the messengers. ¹²⁴ He said to his people, 'Have you no fear [of God?] ¹²⁵ Do you call on Baal and abandon the Best of Creators, ¹²⁶ God your Lord and Lord of your forefathers?' ¹²⁷ but they rejected him, and thus will certainly be called to account; ¹²⁸ except the chosen servants of God. ¹²⁹ We left him thus to be succeeded by a group [of followers] among the following generations— ¹³⁰ 'Peace be on Elijah and his people!' ¹³¹ It is thus indeed that We reward those who do good: ¹³² surely he was one of Our believing servants.ᵃ

وَإِنَّ إِلْيَاسَ لَمِنَ ٱلْمُرْسَلِينَ ۝ إِذْ قَالَ لِقَوْمِهِ أَلَا تَتَّقُونَ ۝ أَتَدْعُونَ بَعْلًا وَتَذَرُونَ أَحْسَنَ ٱلْخَٰلِقِينَ ۝ ٱللَّهَ رَبَّكُمْ وَرَبَّ ءَابَآئِكُمُ ٱلْأَوَّلِينَ ۝ فَكَذَّبُوهُ فَإِنَّهُمْ لَمُحْضَرُونَ ۝ إِلَّا عِبَادَ ٱللَّهِ ٱلْمُخْلَصِينَ ۝ وَتَرَكْنَا عَلَيْهِ فِى ٱلْءَاخِرِينَ ۝ سَلَٰمٌ عَلَىٰٓ إِلْ يَاسِينَ ۝ إِنَّا كَذَٰلِكَ نَجْزِى ٱلْمُحْسِنِينَ ۝ إِنَّهُۥ مِنْ عِبَادِنَا ٱلْمُؤْمِنِينَ ۝

ᵃ Elijah (Elias or Ilyas) was probably a descendant of Aaron (Harun). He lived in the ninth century B.C. at a time when Israel (Palestine) was governed by the Jewish King, Ahab, while Lebanon, was ruled by Phoenicians, polytheists who worshipped Baal (ba'l). Ahab married the daughter of the King of Lebanon. Under the influence of their Queen, the Jews began worshipping Baal. Then, Elijah calling upon the Jews to worship One God, which was their original (ancestral) religion. A detailed account of Elijah is given in the Bible.

Only a few Jews supported Elijah in his mission. Many of them opposed him to the extent of hatching plots to murder him. But Elijah subsequently attained a high status among the Jews. Now, in Jewish history, he is treated as a great prophet.

¹³³ Lot was also one of the messengers. ¹³⁴ We saved him and all his people—¹³⁵ except for an old woman who stayed behind—¹³⁶ and We destroyed the rest. ¹³⁷ You pass by their ruins morning ¹³⁸ and night: will you not take heed? ª

وَإِنَّ لُوطًا لَّمِنَ ٱلْمُرْسَلِينَ ۝ إِذْ نَجَّيْنَٰهُ وَأَهْلَهُۥٓ أَجْمَعِينَ ۝ إِلَّا عَجُوزًا فِى ٱلْغَٰبِرِينَ ۝ ثُمَّ دَمَّرْنَا ٱلْءَاخَرِينَ ۝ وَإِنَّكُمْ لَتَمُرُّونَ عَلَيْهِم مُّصْبِحِينَ ۝ وَبِٱلَّيْلِ ۗ أَفَلَا تَعْقِلُونَ ۝

ª Lot was Abraham's nephew. He was sent to give guidance to the people of Sodom and Gomorrah (in the Dead Sea area). The inhabitants of this place indulged in the worship of beings other than God. But they did not accept Lot's guidance. At last, they had to face the wrath of God and all were killed except Lot and his companions.

The ruins of the towns inhabited by the people of Lot lay along the Dead Sea coast, and the Quraysh tribesmen used to pass by these ruins while on their way to Syria and Palestine to engage in trade. But unfortunately, man takes note of incidents that befall him but seldom learns lessons from the fate of others.

¹³⁹ Jonah too was one of the messengers. ¹⁴⁰ He fled to the overloaded ship. ¹⁴¹ And then they cast lots and he was the one who lost, ¹⁴² and the fish swallowed him while he was blaming himself. ¹⁴³ Had he not been one of those who acknowledge the glory of God, ¹⁴⁴ he would certainly have remained inside the fish till the Day of Resurrection. ¹⁴⁵ But We caused him to be cast forth on to the beach, sick as he was, ¹⁴⁶ and We caused a gourd tree to grow over him. ¹⁴⁷ We sent him as a messenger to a hundred thousand people or more, ¹⁴⁸ and they believed in him: so We let them live in ease for a while.^a

وَإِنَّ يُونُسَ لَمِنَ ٱلْمُرْسَلِينَ ۝ إِذْ أَبَقَ إِلَى ٱلْفُلْكِ ٱلْمَشْحُونِ ۝ فَسَاهَمَ فَكَانَ مِنَ ٱلْمُدْحَضِينَ ۝ فَٱلْتَقَمَهُ ٱلْحُوتُ وَهُوَ مُلِيمٌ ۝ فَلَوْلَآ أَنَّهُۥ كَانَ مِنَ ٱلْمُسَبِّحِينَ ۝ لَلَبِثَ فِى بَطْنِهِۦٓ إِلَىٰ يَوْمِ يُبْعَثُونَ ۝ ۞ فَنَبَذْنَٰهُ بِٱلْعَرَآءِ وَهُوَ سَقِيمٌ ۝ وَأَنۢبَتْنَا عَلَيْهِ شَجَرَةً مِّن يَقْطِينٍ ۝ وَأَرْسَلْنَٰهُ إِلَىٰ مِا۟ئَةِ أَلْفٍ أَوْ يَزِيدُونَ ۝ فَـَٔامَنُوا۟ فَمَتَّعْنَٰهُمْ إِلَىٰ حِينٍ ۝

---

^a Jonah (Yunus) lived in the eighth century B.C. and was sent as a prophet to the ancient city of Nineveh in Iraq. After performing his dawah mission for a certain period of time, he came to the conclusion that his people were not going to embrace the true faith, and left the city. To proceed with his journey, he boarded a boat, perhaps on the bank of the River Tigris. The boat was overloaded; and halfway to its destination it was feared that it would sink. In order to lighten the burden of the boat, lots were drawn to decide who should be thrown out of the boat. The name of Jonah was drawn and so the sea-men threw him over-board. Then, at God's behest, a huge fish swallowed him, took him to the river bank and cast him ashore. Jonah had left his people before time, in this way God ordained him to return to his people. He went back and started preaching once again, with the result that all the one hundred and twenty five thousand inhabitants of the area became believers.

This incident shows that it is absolutely essential for a preacher to have patience, even at a time when his community becomes hostile towards him.

149 Now ask them whether your Lord has daughters, whereas they have sons. 150 Did We create the angels females, to which they were witnesses? 151 No indeed! It is one of their fabrications when they say: 152 'God has begotten children.' They are truly liars. 153 Has He chosen daughters over sons? 154 What is the matter with you? How do you form your judgement? 155 Will you not then reflect? 156 Or have you clear evidence? 157 Then produce your scriptures, if you are telling the truth.*a*

فَٱسْتَفْتِهِمْ أَلِرَبِّكَ ٱلْبَنَاتُ وَلَهُمُ ٱلْبَنُونَ ۝ أَمْ خَلَقْنَا ٱلْمَلَـٰٓئِكَةَ إِنَـٰثًا وَهُمْ شَـٰهِدُونَ ۝ أَلَآ إِنَّهُم مِّنْ إِفْكِهِمْ لَيَقُولُونَ ۝ وَلَدَ ٱللَّهُ وَإِنَّهُمْ لَكَـٰذِبُونَ ۝ أَصْطَفَى ٱلْبَنَاتِ عَلَى ٱلْبَنِينَ ۝ مَا لَكُمْ كَيْفَ تَحْكُمُونَ ۝ أَفَلَا تَذَكَّرُونَ ۝ أَمْ لَكُمْ سُلْطَـٰنٌ مُّبِينٌ ۝ فَأْتُواْ بِكِتَـٰبِكُمْ إِن كُنتُمْ صَـٰدِقِينَ ۝

---

a Satanic inducements, together with erroneous interpretations and interpolations made by human beings distorted the facts. One such belief is that the angels are the daughters of God. This was a baseless assertion and contradicted the polytheists themselves who considered women to be weaker. If the logic of the polytheists were to be upheld, God should have created sons for Himself. Producing such preposterous assertions is a crime and those who do so shall be held accountable for their utterances on the Day of Judgement.

¹⁵⁸ They claim that He has kinship with the jinn, yet the jinn themselves know that they will be produced before Him [for judgement]. ¹⁵⁹ God is far above what they attribute to Him—¹⁶⁰ but not so the true servants of God—¹⁶¹ neither you nor what you worship ¹⁶² can lure away from God any ¹⁶³ except those who will burn in Hell. ¹⁶⁴ [The angels say], 'Every single one of us has his place assigned: ¹⁶⁵ we are those who stand ranged in ranks. ¹⁶⁶ We glorify God.'^a

وَجَعَلُوا۟ بَيْنَهُۥ وَبَيْنَ ٱلْجِنَّةِ نَسَبًا ۚ وَلَقَدْ عَلِمَتِ ٱلْجِنَّةُ إِنَّهُمْ لَمُحْضَرُونَ ۝ سُبْحَـٰنَ ٱللَّهِ عَمَّا يَصِفُونَ ۝ إِلَّا عِبَادَ ٱللَّهِ ٱلْمُخْلَصِينَ ۝ فَإِنَّكُمْ وَمَا تَعْبُدُونَ ۝ مَآ أَنتُمْ عَلَيْهِ بِفَـٰتِنِينَ ۝ إِلَّا مَنْ هُوَ صَالِ ٱلْجَحِيمِ ۝ وَمَا مِنَّآ إِلَّا لَهُۥ مَقَامٌ مَّعْلُومٌ ۝ وَإِنَّا لَنَحْنُ ٱلصَّآفُّونَ ۝ وَإِنَّا لَنَحْنُ ٱلْمُسَبِّحُونَ ۝

---

^a A belief has it, that the 'jinn' are both the opponents and equals of God. But those who hold this belief are greatly misguided. They also think that the forces of evil are in the hands of the jinn and forces of righteousness are in the hands of the angels; both having the power to create trouble or bring success to anybody they like. Similarly, the Zoroastrians believe in the duality of the godhead. According to them, Yazdan is the god of righteousness and Aherman is the god of evil.

Man, on the basis of his false assumptions, worships angels when angels themselves proclaim the greatness of the one and only God, at all times.

¹⁶⁷ They say, ¹⁶⁸ 'If we had had with us a Book like that of the people of old, ¹⁶⁹ we would surely have been God's chosen servants,' ¹⁷⁰ but they have rejected it, [the Quran] and they shall soon learn! ¹⁷¹ And surely Our word has gone forth respecting Our servants, the messengers: ¹⁷² that it is certainly they who will be helped; ¹⁷³ and that it is Our host that would certainly triumph. ¹⁷⁴ So turn away from them for a while. ¹⁷⁵ Watch them: they will soon see.ᵃ

وَإِن كَانُوا۟ لَيَقُولُونَ ۝ لَوْ أَنَّ عِندَنَا ذِكْرًا مِّنَ ٱلْأَوَّلِينَ ۝ لَكُنَّا عِبَادَ ٱللَّهِ ٱلْمُخْلَصِينَ ۝ فَكَفَرُوا۟ بِهِۦ فَسَوْفَ يَعْلَمُونَ ۝ وَلَقَدْ سَبَقَتْ كَلِمَتُنَا لِعِبَادِنَا ٱلْمُرْسَلِينَ ۝ إِنَّهُمْ لَهُمُ ٱلْمَنصُورُونَ ۝ وَإِنَّ جُندَنَا لَهُمُ ٱلْغَٰلِبُونَ ۝ فَتَوَلَّ عَنْهُمْ حَتَّىٰ حِينٍ ۝ وَأَبْصِرْهُمْ فَسَوْفَ يُبْصِرُونَ ۝

ᵃ In ancient times, when the Arabs heard that the Jews and other peoples had rejected their prophets, they used to proudly say, 'These people are unfortunate. If a prophet had come to us, we would have appreciated him and supported him.' But, when God did send a prophet among them, they rejected him just as others had rejected their prophets. The Truth which affects others is readily seen by a man, but the Truth which affects him personally, seldom catches his eye.

Throughout history, people have ignored the call of the preachers of Truth. They forget that the preachers of Truth endeavour to spread God's word which will in any case reign supreme, however much the unbelievers may oppose them.

¹⁷⁶ Do they really wish to hasten Our punishment? ¹⁷⁷ When it descends on their courtyards, how terrible that morning will be for those who were warned! ¹⁷⁸ So turn away from them for a while. ¹⁷⁹ And watch, for they will soon see. ¹⁸⁰ Glory be to your Lord: the Lord of Glory is far above what they attribute to Him. ¹⁸¹ Peace be upon the Messengers ¹⁸² and praise be to God, the Lord of all the Worlds.^a

أَفَبِعَذَابِنَا يَسْتَعْجِلُونَ ۝ فَإِذَا نَزَلَ بِسَاحَتِهِمْ فَسَآءَ صَبَاحُ ٱلْمُنذَرِينَ ۝ وَتَوَلَّ عَنْهُمْ حَتَّىٰ حِينٍ ۝ وَأَبْصِرْ فَسَوْفَ يُبْصِرُونَ ۝ سُبْحَٰنَ رَبِّكَ رَبِّ ٱلْعِزَّةِ عَمَّا يَصِفُونَ ۝ وَسَلَٰمٌ عَلَى ٱلْمُرْسَلِينَ ۝ وَٱلْحَمْدُ لِلَّهِ رَبِّ ٱلْعَٰلَمِينَ ۝

---

^a The prophets used to warn their community about the consequences of denying God's Message. But people did not attach any importance to their words and instead ridiculed them because their prophet did not seem important enough to invoke God's punishment on their rejection of his call.

However, in spite of their ridicule, God's punishment was not meted out to them immediately, because before that can happen, the dawah work should have been brought to completion. That is why the prophets have been exhorted by God to exercise patience and avoid confrontation until the period of respite given to the people has been brought to an end at God's instance.

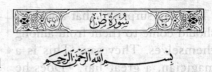

38. SAD

In the name of God,
the Most Gracious, the Most Merciful

¹ *Sad*

By the Quran, full of admonition!ᵃ
² Those who deny the truth are
steeped in arrogance and hostility.
³ How many generations We have
destroyed before them! And they
cried out when it was too late to
escape.

ᵃ The Quran calls upon people to accept the realities that already exist in human
nature. No statement of the Quran has so far been found to be against facts, which
is sufficient to prove the veracity of the Quran. If people still do not accept the
Quran, their rejection is certainly not based on arguments, but stems from the fear
that they may lose their sense of self-importance if they accept a greater Truth.

ᵇ The Quran is the continuation of that call to the oneness of God which was
propogated by various prophets throughout history. In every age, those who
rejected this call were destroyed. The non-believers of the present age should learn
a lesson from the fate suffered by non-believers of the past.

⁴ They are surprised that a warner should come to them from among themselves. They say, 'This is a magician, a great liar.'ᵃ ⁵ Does he make all the deities out to be one God? This is indeed a strange thing.' ⁶ Their leaders departed, saying, 'Walk away! Hold fast to your deities. This is clearly a conspiracy. ⁷ We have not heard of any such thing in the old religion. This is nothing but a fabrication. ⁸ Was the message sent only to him out of all of us?' In fact, they doubt My warning; in fact, they have not yet tasted My punishment.

وَعَجِبُوٓاْ أَن جَآءَهُم مُّنذِرٌ مِّنْهُمْ وَقَالَ ٱلْكَٰفِرُونَ هَٰذَا سَٰحِرٌ كَذَّابٌ ۝ أَجَعَلَ ٱلْءَالِهَةَ إِلَٰهًا وَٰحِدًا إِنَّ هَٰذَا لَشَىْءٌ عُجَابٌ ۝ وَٱنطَلَقَ ٱلْمَلَأُ مِنْهُمْ أَنِ ٱمْشُوا۟ وَٱصْبِرُوا۟ عَلَىٰٓ ءَالِهَتِكُمْ إِنَّ هَٰذَا لَشَىْءٌ يُرَادُ ۝ مَا سَمِعْنَا بِهَٰذَا فِى ٱلْمِلَّةِ ٱلْءَاخِرَةِ إِنْ هَٰذَآ إِلَّا ٱخْتِلَٰقٌ ۝ أَءُنزِلَ عَلَيْهِ ٱلذِّكْرُ مِنۢ بَيْنِنَا بَلْ هُمْ فِى شَكٍّ مِّن ذِكْرِى بَل لَّمَّا يَذُوقُوا۟ عَذَابِ ۝

ᵃ The Prophet Muhammad is a great name today, because subsequent history has glorified him. But when, in the seventh century A.D. he announced his prophethood, it was difficult for people to believe that this ordinary-looking person was chosen to receive God's revelations. It is crucial to understand that once history has taken shape, even a blind man can recognise a prophet, but before history takes shape immense sincerity is required to acknowledge a prophet.

The exceptionally different style of the Quran used to stun its opponents, but the ordinary image of the bearer of the Quran would cast them into doubt. Bent on rejecting him, these people used to denigrate the Prophet in various ways, called him a magician or a liar. They could not reconcile themselves to the possibility of their great men being in the wrong as against an ordinary man.

ᵇ 'Hold fast to your deities'. These words refer to the paucity of argument of those who oppose the Quran. Finding themselves helpless they try to keep their people away from the powerful effect of the Quran with the help of age-old traditions.

⁹ Do they possess the treasures of the mercy of your Lord, the Mighty, the Great Bestower? ¹⁰ Have they control over heavens and earth and whatever [lies] between them? Then let them climb up to heaven by ropes: *ᵃ* ¹¹ this host too, among other hosts, is bound to suffer defeat. ¹² Before them the people of Noah denied the truth, as did the 'Ad and Pharaoh of the Stakes, ¹³ and the tribe of Thamud, and the people of Lot, and the dwellers of the Wood— these were the confederates. ¹⁴ There was not one of them but treated their messengers as liars, so My punishment rightly overtook them: ¹⁵ they have only to wait for one single blast [of punishment]: it shall not be delayed by one whit. ¹⁶ They say: 'Our Lord! Hasten on for us our fate before the Day of Reckoning.'*ᵇ*

أَمْ عِندَهُمْ خَزَآئِنُ رَحْمَةِ رَبِّكَ ٱلْعَزِيزِ ٱلْوَهَّابِ ۞ أَمْ لَهُم مُّلْكُ ٱلسَّمَٰوَٰتِ وَٱلْأَرْضِ وَمَا بَيْنَهُمَا ۖ فَلْيَرْتَقُوا۟ فِى ٱلْأَسْبَٰبِ ۞ جُندٌ مَّا هُنَالِكَ مَهْزُومٌ مِّنَ ٱلْأَحْزَابِ ۞ كَذَّبَتْ قَبْلَهُمْ قَوْمُ نُوحٍ وَعَادٌ وَفِرْعَوْنُ ذُو ٱلْأَوْتَادِ ۞ وَثَمُودُ وَقَوْمُ لُوطٍ وَأَصْحَٰبُ لْـَٔيْكَةِ ۚ أُو۟لَٰٓئِكَ ٱلْأَحْزَابُ ۞ إِن كُلٌّ إِلَّا كَذَّبَ ٱلرُّسُلَ فَحَقَّ عِقَابِ ۞ وَمَا يَنظُرُ هَٰٓؤُلَآءِ إِلَّا صَيْحَةً وَٰحِدَةً مَّا لَهَا مِن فَوَاقٍ ۞ وَقَالُوا۟ رَبَّنَا عَجِّل لَّنَا قِطَّنَا قَبْلَ يَوْمِ ٱلْحِسَابِ ۞

ᵃ God's blessing of guidance is not meted out in such a way that one who is favoured with worldly greatness is also granted God's guidance. If worldly greatness were enough to make people great in the eyes of God, it would have become possible for them to confer God's grace on anybody they liked, while withholding blessings from all others. But the fact is that God bestows His grace by His own standards and not by those laid down by human beings on the basis of appearances.

ᵇ Those who rejected the Prophet used to say, 'Bring upon us God's punishment with which you are threatening us.' The non-believers were so audacious because they believed that they were not going to face God's punishment. The previous communities had also considered themselves safe and behaved insolently with their prophets, but all of them were destroyed.

¹⁷ Bear with their words patiently.^{*a*} Remember Our servant David, a man of strength who always turned to Us: ¹⁸ We made the mountains join him in glorifying Us at sunset and sunrise; ¹⁹ and the birds, too, in flocks, all turned to Him.^{*b*} ²⁰ We made his kingdom strong, and bestowed upon him wisdom and sagacity in judgement.^{*c*}

ٱصْبِرْ عَلَىٰ مَا يَقُولُونَ وَٱذْكُرْ عَبْدَنَا دَاوُدَ ذَا ٱلْأَيْدِ إِنَّهُۥٓ أَوَّابٌ ۝ إِنَّا سَخَّرْنَا ٱلْجِبَالَ مَعَهُۥ يُسَبِّحْنَ بِٱلْعَشِيِّ وَٱلْإِشْرَاقِ ۝ وَٱلطَّيْرَ مَحْشُورَةً كُلٌّ لَّهُۥٓ أَوَّابٌ ۝ وَشَدَدْنَا مُلْكَهُۥ وَءَاتَيْنَٰهُ ٱلْحِكْمَةَ وَفَصْلَ ٱلْخِطَابِ ۝

^{*a*} Islam attaches immense importance to patience, however an unpleasant situation can only be borne patiently by one who leads a God-oriented life.

^{*b*} David presents a good example of being a devout subject. God bestowed him with extraordinary strength, yet he remained ever grateful to Him. David used to sit in the foothills of the mountains and sing praises of God. He praised with such devotion that would turn the entire environment spiritual.

^{*c*} God also blessed David with a very strong empire. The secret of this strength was his wisdom (*hikmah*) and his decisiveness (*fasl al-khitab*) which made him capable of taking right decisions at the right time. These two attributes make a ruler efficient. His innate wisdom ensures that he does not take any action which will bring more harm than good. And his ability to distinguish between right and wrong ensures that his decisions will always be based on justice.

21 Have you heard the story of the disputants who entered his chamber by climbing over the wall? 22 When they reached David, he took fright, but they said, 'Do not be afraid. We are two disputants, one of whom has wronged the other: judge between us fairly—do not be unjust—and guide us to the right path.*a*

23 'This brother of mine has ninety-nine ewes and I have only one. He said, "Let me have charge of it," and got the better of me with his words.' 24 David said, 'He has certainly wronged you by demanding that your ewe be added to his ewes! Thus many partners wrong one another—[all] save those who believe [in God] and do righteous deeds: but how few are they!' And [suddenly] David understood that We were only putting him to the test, and so he asked his Lord to forgive him his sins; he fell to his knees, and turned to Him in repentance.

۞ وَهَلْ أَتَىٰكَ نَبَؤُاْ ٱلْخَصْمِ إِذْ تَسَوَّرُواْ ٱلْمِحْرَابَ ۝ إِذْ دَخَلُواْ عَلَىٰ دَاوُۥدَ فَفَزِعَ مِنْهُمْ قَالُواْ لَا تَخَفْ خَصْمَانِ بَغَىٰ بَعْضُنَا عَلَىٰ بَعْضٍ فَٱحْكُم بَيْنَنَا بِٱلْحَقِّ وَلَا تُشْطِطْ وَٱهْدِنَآ إِلَىٰ سَوَآءِ ٱلصِّرَاطِ ۝ إِنَّ هَٰذَآ أَخِى لَهُۥ تِسْعٌ وَتِسْعُونَ نَعْجَةً وَلِىَ نَعْجَةٌ وَٰحِدَةٌ فَقَالَ أَكْفِلْنِيهَا وَعَزَّنِى فِى ٱلْخِطَابِ ۝ قَالَ لَقَدْ ظَلَمَكَ بِسُؤَالِ نَعْجَتِكَ إِلَىٰ نِعَاجِهِۦ وَإِنَّ كَثِيرًا مِّنَ ٱلْخُلَطَآءِ لَيَبْغِى بَعْضُهُمْ عَلَىٰ بَعْضٍ إِلَّا ٱلَّذِينَ ءَامَنُواْ وَعَمِلُواْ ٱلصَّٰلِحَٰتِ وَقَلِيلٌ مَّا هُمْ وَظَنَّ دَاوُۥدُ أَنَّمَا فَتَنَّٰهُ فَٱسْتَغْفَرَ رَبَّهُۥ وَخَرَّ رَاكِعًا وَأَنَابَ ۩ ۝

---

a It is said that David had fixed each of the three days for different purposes—one day for holding court and deciding cases, a second day for spending with his family and a third day for remaining in solitude and praying to God. It happened once that on a day fixed for prayers, as he sat engrossed in his devotion, two men who had jumped over the wall of the palace, entered the room and stood beside him. This was an extraordinary occurrence and, therefore, he was somewhat afraid. But the two men allayed his fears and said that they were parties to a dispute and begged him to settle it for them.

²⁵ We forgave him his sins. His reward will be nearness to Us, a good place to return to.^{*a*}

²⁶ We said, 'David, We have given you mastery over the land. Judge fairly between people. Do not follow your desires, lest they divert you from God's path: those who wander from His path will have a severe punishment, because they ignore the Day of Reckoning.'^{*b*}

فَغَفَرْنَا لَهُ ذَٰلِكَ ۖ وَإِنَّ لَهُ عِندَنَا لَزُلْفَىٰ وَحُسْنَ مَـَٔابٍ ۝ يَٰدَاوُۥدُ إِنَّا جَعَلْنَٰكَ خَلِيفَةً فِى ٱلْأَرْضِ فَٱحْكُم بَيْنَ ٱلنَّاسِ بِٱلْحَقِّ وَلَا تَتَّبِعِ ٱلْهَوَىٰ فَيُضِلَّكَ عَن سَبِيلِ ٱللَّهِ ۚ إِنَّ ٱلَّذِينَ يَضِلُّونَ عَن سَبِيلِ ٱللَّهِ لَهُمْ عَذَابٌ شَدِيدٌۢ بِمَا نَسُوا۟ يَوْمَ ٱلْحِسَابِ ۝

---

^{*a*} The two intruders presented their case before David. The case was in allegorical language and bore a reference to some incident in the life of David himself and was meant as an admonition to him. While David gave his decision, he recounted the incident from his life, having quickly understood the analogy. Realising his mistake, he immediately asked for forgiveness and prostrated himself before God.

David enjoyed tremendous power at that time, but he did not punish or even scold the intruders. This is a sign of a true subject of God. He is never unduly stubborn and when his attention is drawn towards his shortcoming he readily accepts it and rectifies it, even if the person who pointed out the error does so in a rude manner.

^{*b*} A ruler always has two options before him—to decide cases according to his own whims or in consonance with principles of justice. The ruler who decides matters according to his own whims and desires, has in fact gone astray, and will ultimately have to suffer the scourge of God. But the ruler who decides cases by abiding by the principles of truth and justice, is the one who is on the right path. God will reward him immensely.

The divine injunction which is applicable to a ruler is equally applicable to his subjects and must be followed by the common man in his respective spheres of authority.

²⁷ We did not create heaven and earth and all that is between them in vain.ᵃ That is the opinion of those who deny the truth. Woe betide those who deny the truth, when they are cast into the Fire— ²⁸ shall We treat those who believe and do good works the same as those who spread corruption in the land; shall We treat the pious the same as the wicked? ²⁹ This is a blessed Book which We sent down to you [Muhammad], for people to ponder over its messages, and for those with understanding to take heed.

وَمَا خَلَقْنَا ٱلسَّمَآءَ وَٱلْأَرْضَ وَمَا بَيْنَهُمَا بَـٰطِلًا ۚ ذَٰلِكَ ظَنُّ ٱلَّذِينَ كَفَرُوا۟ ۚ فَوَيْلٌ لِّلَّذِينَ كَفَرُوا۟ مِنَ ٱلنَّارِ ۝ أَمْ نَجْعَلُ ٱلَّذِينَ ءَامَنُوا۟ وَعَمِلُوا۟ ٱلصَّـٰلِحَـٰتِ كَٱلْمُفْسِدِينَ فِى ٱلْأَرْضِ أَمْ نَجْعَلُ ٱلْمُتَّقِينَ كَٱلْفُجَّارِ ۝ كِتَـٰبٌ أَنزَلْنَـٰهُ إِلَيْكَ مُبَـٰرَكٌ لِّيَدَّبَّرُوٓا۟ ءَايَـٰتِهِۦ وَلِيَتَذَكَّرَ أُو۟لُوا۟ ٱلْأَلْبَـٰبِ ۝

ᵃ The system governing the functioning of our world is bound by wise and firm principles, when a random and unreliable system could very well have existed in its place. Between these two possibilities, the choice of the better one—the one which is governed by firm laws—is indicative of the fact that the Creator of such a world created it for a purpose. It follows that a world whose beginning was purposeful cannot have an end which is purposeless.

Similarly, every man in this world enjoys a certain amount of freedom. From amongst them, are those who submit to the truth and strive to lead their life on the principles of truth and justice whereas those who do not submit to the truth, indulge in unbridled talk and unrestrained actions. Such distinctly different persons cannot have the same fate.

³⁰ We gave David Solomon. He was an excellent servant who always turned to God. ³¹ When well-bred horses, which were fleet of foot were paraded before him near the close of day, ³² he said, 'I have put the love of good things above the remembrance of my Lord'—until [the sun] disappeared behind its veil and the horses disappeared from sight—³³ 'Bring them back to me!'—[he said] and began to stroke their legs and their necks.ᵃ

وَوَهَبْنَا لِدَاوُۥدَ سُلَيْمَٰنَ نِعْمَ ٱلْعَبْدُ إِنَّهُۥ أَوَّابٌ ۝ إِذْ عُرِضَ عَلَيْهِ بِٱلْعَشِيِّ ٱلصَّٰفِنَٰتُ ٱلْجِيَادُ ۝ فَقَالَ إِنِّيٓ أَحْبَبْتُ حُبَّ ٱلْخَيْرِ عَن ذِكْرِ رَبِّي حَتَّىٰ تَوَارَتْ بِٱلْحِجَابِ ۝ رُدُّوهَا عَلَيَّ فَطَفِقَ مَسْحًۢا بِٱلسُّوقِ وَٱلْأَعْنَاقِ ۝

ᵃ Solomon, the son of David was the ruler of a great empire. Once the thoroughbred horses of his army were brought before him and a race was held. The galloping horses moved further and further away until they were out of sight.

This was a magnificent moment upon witnessing which, an ordinary man would have become full of pride and vanity. But Solomon started remembering God. He said that he had not chosen these horses to flaunt his grandeur, but only for the sake of God. In the shape of the horses, he could discern the great workmanship of God, and by way of appreciating the greatness of God, he started to stroke the necks and legs of the horses. A believer, therefore, has the ability to observe the glory of God in everything, while a non-believer remains entrapped in the false notions of self-glory.

34 We tried Solomon by placing upon his throne a [lifeless] body; and thereupon he turned towards Us].
35 He prayed, 'Lord forgive me! Grant me such power as no one after me will have—You are the Most Generous Provider.'*a* 36 Then We subjected the wind to his power, so that it blew gently, at his behest, wherever he willed—37 and also the jinn—every kind of builder and diver 38 and others chained in fetters. 39 We said: 'This is Our gift, so give or withhold as you wish without reckoning.' 40 His reward will be nearness to Us, a good place to return to.

وَلَقَدْ فَتَنَّا سُلَيْمَـٰنَ وَأَلْقَيْنَا عَلَىٰ كُرْسِيِّهِۦ جَسَدًا ثُمَّ أَنَابَ ۝ قَالَ رَبِّ ٱغْفِرْ لِى وَهَبْ لِى مُلْكًا لَّا يَنۢبَغِى لِأَحَدٍ مِّنۢ بَعْدِىٓ إِنَّكَ أَنتَ ٱلْوَهَّابُ ۝ فَسَخَّرْنَا لَهُ ٱلرِّيحَ تَجْرِى بِأَمْرِهِۦ رُخَآءً حَيْثُ أَصَابَ ۝ وَٱلشَّيَـٰطِينَ كُلَّ بَنَّآءٍ وَغَوَّاصٍ ۝ وَءَاخَرِينَ مُقَرَّنِينَ فِى ٱلْأَصْفَادِ ۝ هَـٰذَا عَطَآؤُنَا فَٱمْنُنْ أَوْ أَمْسِكْ بِغَيْرِ حِسَابٍ ۝ وَإِنَّ لَهُۥ عِندَنَا لَزُلْفَىٰ وَحُسْنَ مَـَٔابٍ ۝

---

a Every human being is liable to err. But, for the pious and righteous subjects of God, a wrongful act leads them to great virtue, because after the misdeed, they turn towards their Lord with true repentance and devotion.

On one occasion, Solomon made an error in judging a matter. When the truth dawned on him, he turned towards God with the utmost devotion and repentance. God forgave him and rewarded him with a great empire; He was given such extraordinary powers as no other man had ever enjoyed.

⁴¹ Bring to mind Our servant Job who cried to his Lord, 'Satan has afflicted me with distress and suffering.' ⁴² We said, 'Stamp your foot! Here is cool water for you to wash in and drink,' ⁴³ We restored his family to him, doubling their number as an act of grace from Us, and as a reminder to all who are endowed with insight.*ᵃ* ⁴⁴ We said to Him, 'Take a handful of twigs in your hand and strike with that but do not break your oath.' We found him steadfast. What an excellent servant! He turned constantly to his Lord.*ᵇ*

وَٱذۡكُرۡ عَبۡدَنَآ أَيُّوبَ إِذۡ نَادَىٰ رَبَّهُۥٓ أَنِّى مَسَّنِىَ ٱلشَّيۡطَٰنُ بِنُصۡبٍ وَعَذَابٍ ۝ ٱرۡكُضۡ بِرِجۡلِكَ هَٰذَا مُغۡتَسَلٌۢ بَارِدٌ وَشَرَابٌ ۝ وَوَهَبۡنَا لَهُۥٓ أَهۡلَهُۥ وَمِثۡلَهُم مَّعَهُمۡ رَحۡمَةٗ مِّنَّا وَذِكۡرَىٰ لِأُوْلِى ٱلۡأَلۡبَٰبِ ۝ وَخُذۡ بِيَدِكَ ضِغۡثٗا فَٱضۡرِب بِّهِۦ وَلَا تَحۡنَثۡۗ إِنَّا وَجَدۡنَٰهُ صَابِرٗاۚ نِّعۡمَ ٱلۡعَبۡدُ إِنَّهُۥٓ أَوَّابٌ ۝

ᵃ Job was one of the Israeli prophets who lived probably in the ninth century B.C. He was very rich, but, far from being lost in his riches, he used to pray to God and call people towards God.

Some evil-minded people started saying that Job remembered God because he was blessed by God with so much wealth. In order to settle all argument God took away all His blessings from Job but he continued to be a sincere worshipper of God. He said, 'It was God who gave and God has taken away. Glory be to the name of God.'

Even then, mischievous people were not silenced. They said that the real test would be if he suffered physical affliction and remained patient and grateful. To prove his sincerity, God made Job contract a serious skin disease; yet he remained the embodiment of patience and gratitude. When the process of convincing the people was complete, God caused a spring to come into existence for Job's nourishment. By bathing in this spring, his body became healthy and, restoring him to his family, God gave him much more wealth.

ᵇ When God makes someone an example for the sake of religion and he surrenders himself to God without any reservation, God restores to him more than what was taken away from him during his period of trial.

⁴⁵ Remember Our servants Abraham, Isaac, and Jacob—possessors of strength and vision. ⁴⁶ We chose them for a special [purpose]—proclaiming the message of the Hereafter: ⁴⁷ and, in Our sight they were indeed among the select, the truly good! ⁴⁸ Remember [Our servants] Ishmael, Elisha, and Dhu'l-Kifl. Each of them was among the just.ᵃ

وَٱذۡكُرۡ عِبَٰدَنَآ إِبۡرَٰهِيمَ وَإِسۡحَٰقَ وَيَعۡقُوبَ أُوْلِي ٱلۡأَيۡدِي وَٱلۡأَبۡصَٰرِ ۝ إِنَّآ أَخۡلَصۡنَٰهُم بِخَالِصَةٍ ذِكۡرَى ٱلدَّارِ ۝ وَإِنَّهُمۡ عِندَنَا لَمِنَ ٱلۡمُصۡطَفَيۡنَ ٱلۡأَخۡيَارِ ۝ وَٱذۡكُرۡ إِسۡمَٰعِيلَ وَٱلۡيَسَعَ وَذَا ٱلۡكِفۡلِ وَكُلٌّ مِّنَ ٱلۡأَخۡيَارِ ۝

ᵃ For which special assignment does God choose messengers from amongst human beings? The special mission of prophets entails that they make men aware of the fact that their real destination is the Hereafter, and that they should prepare themselves for it. This is the most crucial problem for man, one which warrants utter seriousness.

⁴⁹ This is a Reminder. The righteous shall have a good place to return to: ⁵⁰ the Gardens of eternity with gates thrown wide open to them. ⁵¹ They will be comfortably seated; reclining, they will call for abundant fruit and drink; ⁵² with them, they will have pure, modest women of an equal age. ⁵³ This is what you were promised on the Day of Reckoning: ⁵⁴ Our provision for you will never be exhausted.[a]

⁵⁵ But the arrogant will have the worst return: ⁵⁶ they will burn, in Hell, an evil resting place—⁵⁷ all this will be theirs; let them taste it—a scalding, dark, foul fluid, ⁵⁸ and other such torments.[b]

هَٰذَا ذِكْرٌ ۚ وَإِنَّ لِلْمُتَّقِينَ لَحُسْنَ مَـَٔابٍ ﴿٤٩﴾ جَنَّـٰتِ عَدْنٍ مُّفَتَّحَةً لَّهُمُ ٱلْأَبْوَٰبُ ﴿٥٠﴾ مُتَّكِئِينَ فِيهَا يَدْعُونَ فِيهَا بِفَـٰكِهَةٍ كَثِيرَةٍ وَشَرَابٍ ﴿٥١﴾ وَعِندَهُمْ قَـٰصِرَٰتُ ٱلطَّرْفِ أَتْرَابٌ ﴿٥٢﴾ هَٰذَا مَا تُوعَدُونَ لِيَوْمِ ٱلْحِسَابِ ﴿٥٣﴾ إِنَّ هَٰذَا لَرِزْقُنَا مَا لَهُ مِن نَّفَادٍ ﴿٥٤﴾ هَٰذَا ۚ وَإِنَّ لِلطَّـٰغِينَ لَشَرَّ مَـَٔابٍ ﴿٥٥﴾ جَهَنَّمَ يَصْلَوْنَهَا فَبِئْسَ ٱلْمِهَادُ ﴿٥٦﴾ هَٰذَا فَلْيَذُوقُوهُ حَمِيمٌ وَغَسَّاقٌ ﴿٥٧﴾ وَءَاخَرُ مِن شَكْلِهِۦٓ أَزْوَٰجٌ ﴿٥٨﴾

---

[a] Paradise will be for those servants of God who submit to Him while He is invisible. They will be the fortunate ones who will relish the everlasting joy of the Hereafter.

The blessings bestowed upon men in the Hereafter will be of the same nature as those confered in this world. Yet there will be a tremendous difference between these two forms of divine grace. In this world, favours are given for the time being and in a rudimentary form whereas, in the Hereafter, these favours will be given forever and in their ultimate form. God will banish all kinds of fear in the Hereafter, which is not possible in the present world.

[b] Hell would also be everlasting and will be an amalgam of all troubles and tortures which can be imagined in the present world. When those who were arrogant in this world and rejected the truth gather in Hell, leaders and followers will quarrel with each other and curse one another. But, none of it would be of avail.

⁵⁹ [And they will say to one another: 'Do you see] this crowd of people rushing headlong to join you?' 'No welcome to them! Indeed, they are headed for the fire!' ⁶⁰ They will say to them, 'You are not welcome! It was you who brought this on us, an evil place to stay,' ⁶¹ adding, 'Our Lord, give double punishment to those who brought this upon us.' ⁶² And they will say, 'How is it that we do not see [here any of the] men whom we used to count among the wicked, ⁶³ [and] whom we made the target of our derision? Or are they here, and our eyes have missed them?' ⁶⁴ All this is certainly true— the inhabitants of the Fire will blame one another in this way.ᵃ

هَٰذَا فَوْجٌ مُّقْتَحِمٌ مَّعَكُمْ لَا مَرْحَبًا بِهِمْ إِنَّهُمْ صَالُوا۟ ٱلنَّارِ ۝ قَالُوا۟ بَلْ أَنتُمْ لَا مَرْحَبًا بِكُمْ أَنتُمْ قَدَّمْتُمُوهُ لَنَا فَبِئْسَ ٱلْقَرَارُ ۝ قَالُوا۟ رَبَّنَا مَن قَدَّمَ لَنَا هَٰذَا فَزِدْهُ عَذَابًا ضِعْفًا فِى ٱلنَّارِ ۝ وَقَالُوا۟ مَا لَنَا لَا نَرَىٰ رِجَالًا كُنَّا نَعُدُّهُم مِّنَ ٱلْأَشْرَارِ ۝ أَتَّخَذْنَٰهُمْ سِخْرِيًّا أَمْ زَاغَتْ عَنْهُمُ ٱلْأَبْصَٰرُ ۝ إِنَّ ذَٰلِكَ لَحَقٌّ تَخَاصُمُ أَهْلِ ٱلنَّارِ ۝

ᵃ When the people who rejected the truth see their miserable lot in the Hereafter, they will remember those who had taken the side of the Truth and as such had come to be regarded as inferior in their society. The rejectors of the truth used to say of the supporters of truth that the latter disrespected the great ones; that they had deviated from their ancestral religion and had made their own path separate from that of the community.

These rejectors of the truth had considered themselves to be on the right path. But in the Hereafter, the tables will be turned. At that time it will be clear to them that those whom they looked at with contempt and ridiculed, are the very people who are now enjoying the foremost position of success.

⁶⁵ Say, [Prophet], 'I am only a warner.
There is no god but God, the One,
the All-Powerful, ⁶⁶ Lord of the
heavens and earth and everything
between them, the Almighty, the
Most Forgiving.' ⁶⁷ Say, 'This is
momentous news, ⁶⁸ yet you ignore
it. ⁶⁹ I had no knowledge of the
Exalted Assembly when they argued
[against the creation of man]: ⁷⁰ it has
only been revealed to me that I am
a plain warner.' ᵃ

⁷¹ Your Lord said to the angels, 'I am
about to create a human being out
of clay; ⁷² and when I have formed
him fully and breathed My spirit into
him, prostrate yourselves before
him.' ⁷³ Thereupon the angels
prostrated themselves, all of them
together, ⁷⁴ but not Satan, who was
too proud. He became one of those
who deny the truth.

قُلْ إِنَّمَآ أَنَا۠ مُنذِرٌ وَمَا مِنْ إِلَٰهٍ إِلَّا
ٱللَّهُ ٱلْوَٰحِدُ ٱلْقَهَّارُ ۝ رَبُّ
ٱلسَّمَٰوَٰتِ وَٱلْأَرْضِ وَمَا بَيْنَهُمَا ٱلْعَزِيزُ
ٱلْغَفَّٰرُ ۝ قُلْ هُوَ نَبَؤٌا۟ عَظِيمٌ ۝ أَنتُمْ
عَنْهُ مُعْرِضُونَ ۝ مَا كَانَ لِيَ مِنْ عِلْمٍ
بِٱلْمَلَإِ ٱلْأَعْلَىٰٓ إِذْ يَخْتَصِمُونَ ۝ إِن
يُوحَىٰٓ إِلَيَّ إِلَّآ أَنَّمَآ أَنَا۠ نَذِيرٌ مُّبِينٌ
۝ إِذْ قَالَ رَبُّكَ لِلْمَلَٰٓئِكَةِ إِنِّي خَٰلِقٌۢ بَشَرًا
مِّن طِينٍ ۝ فَإِذَا سَوَّيْتُهُۥ وَنَفَخْتُ
فِيهِ مِن رُّوحِي فَقَعُوا۟ لَهُۥ سَٰجِدِينَ
۝ فَسَجَدَ ٱلْمَلَٰٓئِكَةُ كُلُّهُمْ
أَجْمَعُونَ ۝ إِلَّآ إِبْلِيسَ ٱسْتَكْبَرَ وَكَانَ
مِنَ ٱلْكَٰفِرِينَ ۝

ᵃ It is stated in the Quran that Satan had become man's enemy from the very first
day. He dissuaded Adam's progeny from adopting the right path by his glib and
deceitful talk. Man should therefore be wary of Satan and try to save himself from
his evil designs.

Satan pursues man at all times and, surreptitiously entering his thoughts, manages
to misguide him. Man must save himself from Satan and his promptings.

75 God said, 'Satan, what prevented you from prostrating yourself to what I created with My own Hands? Were you overcome by arrogance, or are you of those who think [only] of themselves as exalted?' 76 Satan replied, 'I am better than him. You created me from fire, but You created him from clay.' 77 'Begone! You are accursed: 78 My curse will remain upon you till the Day of Judgement!' *a*

79 But Satan said, 'My Lord, grant me respite until the Day of Resurrection,' 80 so He said, 'You are granted respite 81 till the Appointed Day.' 82 He said, 'By Your Honour, I will lead all of them astray, *b*

قَالَ يَٰإِبْلِيسُ مَا مَنَعَكَ أَن تَسْجُدَ لِمَا خَلَقْتُ بِيَدَىَّ أَسْتَكْبَرْتَ أَمْ كُنتَ مِنَ ٱلْعَالِينَ ۝ قَالَ أَنَا۠ خَيْرٌ مِّنْهُ خَلَقْتَنِى مِن نَّارٍ وَخَلَقْتَهُۥ مِن طِينٍ ۝ قَالَ فَٱخْرُجْ مِنْهَا فَإِنَّكَ رَجِيمٌ ۝ وَإِنَّ عَلَيْكَ لَعْنَتِىٓ إِلَىٰ يَوْمِ ٱلدِّينِ ۝ قَالَ رَبِّ فَأَنظِرْنِىٓ إِلَىٰ يَوْمِ يُبْعَثُونَ ۝ قَالَ فَإِنَّكَ مِنَ ٱلْمُنظَرِينَ ۝ إِلَىٰ يَوْمِ ٱلْوَقْتِ ٱلْمَعْلُومِ ۝ قَالَ فَبِعِزَّتِكَ لَأُغْوِيَنَّهُمْ أَجْمَعِينَ ۝

---

a God made man a creature of exalted stature and, as a token thereof, He ordered the angels and the jinn to prostrate themselves before him. When Satan (Iblis) did not bow before Adam, he became the eternally cursed one. But this incident was not only serious from the viewpoint of Satan; it was of the utmost importance for Adam himself.

By refusing to bow down before Adam, Satan forever became the enemy of the entire human race. This event foreboded that man's journey through life would not be an easy one, and would be full of serious impediments. Man would have to strive to keep himself on the right path and resist the inducements and promptings of Satan in order to reach his destination safely.

Satan's evil scheming stands between man and Paradise. Only one who keeps himself safe from Satan's machinations will enter the everlasting gardens of Paradise; those who fail to tear down the barrier of Satan's treachery, will be deprived of Paradise.

b In the present world of trial, Satan has been given every opportunity to misguide man. But Satan can do so only till Doomsday arrives. When the Day of Judgement tears apart the veil of falsehood, everything will become plain and clear. Thereafter, there will neither be anybody who can deceive nor anybody who can be deceived.

⁸³ except for those among them who are Your chosen servants.'ᵃ ⁸⁴ God said, 'This is the truth—I speak only the truth—⁸⁵ I will fill up Hell with you and every one of them who follows you.'

⁸⁶ Say, 'I do not ask you for any recompense for this, nor am I a man of false pretentions: ⁸⁷ this is simply an admonition to mankind, ⁸⁸ you shall before long know its truth.'ᵇ

إِلَّا عِبَادَكَ مِنْهُمُ ٱلْمُخْلَصِينَ ۝ قَالَ فَٱلْحَقُّ وَٱلْحَقَّ أَقُولُ ۝ لَأَمْلَأَنَّ جَهَنَّمَ مِنكَ وَمِمَّن تَبِعَكَ مِنْهُمْ أَجْمَعِينَ ۝ قُلْ مَآ أَسْـَٔلُكُمْ عَلَيْهِ مِنْ أَجْرٍ وَمَآ أَنَا۠ مِنَ ٱلْمُتَكَلِّفِينَ ۝ إِنْ هُوَ إِلَّا ذِكْرٌ لِّلْعَالَمِينَ ۝ وَلَتَعْلَمُنَّ نَبَأَهُۥ بَعْدَ حِينٍۭ ۝

ᵃ The chosen (*mukhlas*) subject of God is one who is free of mental perversion. While Satan has no practical power over man, he misguides human beings by supplying plausible justification for their wrong deeds; presenting untruth as Truth; enshrouding baseless facts in beautiful words; raising unnecessary issues in straightforward matters and raising doubts. However, only those who harbour complexes will be deceived by this beautification of Satan (*taz'in*). Those who retain their sincerity and are wise enough to objectively analyse a situation will immediately detect Satan's machinations. Such people are never misled by Satan's ruses.

ᵇ One basic virtue of a preacher is that he does not demand any remuneration from his hearers. Another is that he does not raise any material issues between them and himself. The call of the Quran is the call of the Hereafter. Therefore, if a man, on the one hand, gives the call of the Hereafter and of the Quran and, on the other, runs a campaign for material gain, then he figures as an insincere person. And who will pay attention to the pleadings of a person who has proved himself to be insincere?

Similarly, a preacher does not make statements concocted by himself. He simply passes on whatever he has received from God. Masruq Tabi'i (a contemporary of the Prophet's Companions) recounts a tradition of 'Abdullah ibn Mas'ud who said, 'O, people! One who knows should talk, and one who does not know should simply say that God knows better. He will seem wise if he states that God knows better (with regard to things which he does not know), because God said to his Prophet, 'Say, no reward do I ask of you for this, nor am I a pretender.' (*Tafsir ibn Kathir*, vol. IV, p. 44).

Similarly, it is also required of the preacher of truth to present his call in the shape of well-meaning advice. His discourse should be that of a well-wisher and should not be in the nature of debate or polemics.

39. THE CROWDS

In the name of God,
the Most Gracious, the Most Merciful

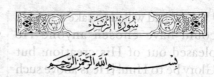

¹ This Book is sent down by God the Mighty, the Wise. ² It is We who sent down the Book to you [Prophet] with the Truth, so worship God with your total devotion: ³ it is to God alone that sincere obedience is due. And those who take other guardians besides Him say, 'We serve them only that they may bring us nearer to God.' Surely, God will judge between them concerning that wherein they differ. God does not guide anyone who is bent on lying and is a disbelieving liar.ᵃ

ᵃ The Quran is a divine statement of facts. Its sagacious style of expression and the exceptional nature of its discourses allude to it being the Book of God. No man is capable of presenting such a sublime work.

'So worship God with your total devotion,' means to worship only God, praying to Him, revering Him and devoting oneself entirely to Him. (*Safwat at-Tafsir,* vol. III, p. 69).

The instinct for worship and devotion is inherent in human nature, so he must consider a being as great and have feelings of awe for that being. Anyone for whom a man develops such feelings is considered most holy by him and man's entire existence submits before him. He expresses superlative respect and veneration for him and, his soul derives pleasure from remembering him. That being becomes the greatest support in man's life.

This is true devotion and such worship is the exclusive, rightful due of the one and only God. But what man does is that while accepting the one God, he accords divinity to beings other than God and starts worshipping them. This is the real error into which man falls because just as the godhead or divinity is indivisible, worship cannot be divided either.

⁴ If God had willed to take a son He could have chosen anyone He pleased out of His creation: but Glory be to Him! [He is above such things.] He is God, the One, the Omnipotent. ⁵ He created the heavens and the earth for a true purpose; He causes the night to succeed the day and the day to succeed the night; He has subjected the sun and moon, so that they run their courses for an appointed time; He is truly the Mighty, the Forgiving.*

لَوۡ أَرَادَ ٱللَّهُ أَن يَتَّخِذَ وَلَدًا لَّٱصۡطَفَىٰ مِمَّا يَخۡلُقُ مَا يَشَآءُ سُبۡحَٰنَهُۥ هُوَ ٱللَّهُ ٱلۡوَٰحِدُ ٱلۡقَهَّارُ ۝ خَلَقَ ٱلسَّمَٰوَٰتِ وَٱلۡأَرۡضَ بِٱلۡحَقِّ يُكَوِّرُ ٱلَّيۡلَ عَلَى ٱلنَّهَارِ وَيُكَوِّرُ ٱلنَّهَارَ عَلَى ٱلَّيۡلِ وَسَخَّرَ ٱلشَّمۡسَ وَٱلۡقَمَرَ كُلٌّ يَجۡرِى لِأَجَلٍ مُّسَمًّى أَلَا هُوَ ٱلۡعَزِيزُ ٱلۡغَفَّٰرُ ۝

---

* It is a natural instinct in man to rush towards God and worship Him. But it is always the endeavour of Satan to distract man from worshipping God. He implants the idea in people's minds that God's Court (throne) is very high and inaccessible and, therefore, one cannot reach God directly. So one should try to reach God through the mediation of saints. Similarly, he instils the belief that just as human beings have children, so does God, and an easy way to please God is to please His supposed children. Modern materialism is also a distorted form of this belief, in that it has diverted man's worshipping instinct from the Creator to the creation.

All this deviation amounts to a belittling of God. He Who is the Creator and Sustainer of the unfathomably vast universe is far above such ridiculous allegations.

⁶ He created you from a single soul, then produced its spouse from it, and He has provided for you eight heads of cattle in pairs.*ᵃ* He creates you stage by stage in your mothers' wombs in a threefold darkness. Such is God, your Lord. Sovereignty is His. There is no god but Him. So what has made you turn away?

خَلَقَكُم مِّن نَّفْسٍ وَحِدَةٍ ثُمَّ جَعَلَ مِنْهَا زَوْجَهَا وَأَنزَلَ لَكُم مِّنَ ٱلْأَنْعَمِ ثَمَنِيَةَ أَزْوَجٍ يَخْلُقُكُمْ فِى بُطُونِ أُمَّهَتِكُم خَلْقًا مِّنۢ بَعْدِ خَلْقٍ فِى ظُلُمَتٍ ثَلَثٍ ذَلِكُمُ ٱللَّهُ رَبُّكُمْ لَهُ ٱلْمُلْكُ لَا إِلَهَ إِلَّا هُوَ فَأَنَّىٰ تُصْرَفُونَ ۝

ᵃ God made man and created woman as his mate. In this way, through the first man and woman a generation of human beings came into existence. In addition, God made extensive provision to fulfil the needs of human beings. In the early days of civilization, sheep, goat, camel and cow (a couple from each totalling to eight) catered to economic and social requirements of man. As civilization entered the next stage, man harnessed nature's potential and used it for his progress.

ᵇ The 'three fold darkness' refers to the three membranes, that enclose the foetus inside mother's womb. It was impossible for a man to give such precise description lest it were revealed to him by the Creator Himself.

7 If you are ungrateful, remember that God has no need of you. He is not pleased by ingratitude in His servants; if you are grateful, He is pleased [to see] it in you.[a] No soul shall bear another's burden. You will return to your Lord in the end and He will declare to you what you have done: He knows well what is in the hearts of men.[b]

إِن تَكۡفُرُوا۟ فَإِنَّ ٱللَّهَ غَنِىٌّ عَنكُمۡ وَلَا يَرۡضَىٰ لِعِبَادِهِ ٱلۡكُفۡرَ وَإِن تَشۡكُرُوا۟ يَرۡضَهُ لَكُمۡ وَلَا تَزِرُ وَازِرَةٌ وِزۡرَ أُخۡرَىٰ ثُمَّ إِلَىٰ رَبِّكُم مَّرۡجِعُكُمۡ فَيُنَبِّئُكُم بِمَا كُنتُمۡ تَعۡمَلُونَ إِنَّهُۥ عَلِيمٌۢ بِذَاتِ ٱلصُّدُورِ ۝

[a] To accept God and be grateful to Him is sought by the soul of man. Such an acknowledgement amounts to the admission of the Truth, which undoubtedly is the greatest demand of rationality.

[b] In the Hereafter, a state of perfect justice shall prevail. Every man will receive the outcome commensurate to his deeds (in the pre-death period). The Hereafter will remove the shortcoming of the present world.

⁸ When man suffers some affliction, he prays to his Lord and turns to Him in penitence, but once he has been granted a favour from God, he forgets the One he had been praying to and sets up rivals to God, to make others stray from His path.ᵃ Say, 'Enjoy your unbelief for a little while: you will be one of the inmates of the Fire.' ⁹ Is he who prays devoutly to God in the hours of the night, prostrating himself and standing in prayer, who is ever mindful of the life to come and hopes for the mercy of his Lord [like one who does not]? Say, 'Are those who know equal to those who do not know?' Truly, only those endowed with understanding will take heed.ᵇ

۞ وَإِذَا مَسَّ ٱلْإِنسَـٰنَ ضُرٌّ دَعَا رَبَّهُۥ مُنِيبًا إِلَيْهِ ثُمَّ إِذَا خَوَّلَهُۥ نِعْمَةً مِّنْهُ نَسِيَ مَا كَانَ يَدْعُوٓاْ إِلَيْهِ مِن قَبْلُ وَجَعَلَ لِلَّهِ أَندَادًا لِّيُضِلَّ عَن سَبِيلِهِۦ قُلْ تَمَتَّعْ بِكُفْرِكَ قَلِيلًا إِنَّكَ مِنْ أَصْحَـٰبِ ٱلنَّارِ ۝ أَمَّنْ هُوَ قَـٰنِتٌ ءَانَآءَ ٱلَّيْلِ سَاجِدًا وَقَآئِمًا يَحْذَرُ ٱلْأَخِرَةَ وَيَرْجُواْ رَحْمَةَ رَبِّهِۦ قُلْ هَلْ يَسْتَوِى ٱلَّذِينَ يَعْلَمُونَ وَٱلَّذِينَ لَا يَعْلَمُونَ إِنَّمَا يَتَذَكَّرُ أُوْلُواْ ٱلْأَلْبَـٰبِ ۝

ᵃ Every man passes through times when he finds himself utterly helpless. At this juncture, he forgets everything and starts appealing to God. In this way, in times of helplessness, every man comes to know that there is nobody worth worshipping except the one and only God.

But, as soon as he is out of trouble, he resorts to his earlier ways. Man only becomes more arrogant and starts attributing his relief from affliction to beings other than God. For Some it becomes the miracle of cause and effect, while for others it is a feat of supposed gods. If a man keeps quiet after making a mistake, it involves the misguidance of only one man. But, if he starts giving false explanations in order to justify his mistakes, he becomes one who misleads others.

ᵇ There are two types of people: Those who make material interest their supreme concern; the other make God their supreme concern. It is this second type of individual who is a man of God. His realisation of God is his conscious discovery. He discovers God as the most Majestic and Supreme Being, so much so that all his hopes and all his fears are linked to that one and only Being. His restlessness keeps him out of bed at night. His loneliness is not the loneliness born out of unawareness, but the loneliness of the remembrance of God.

A man of knowledge is one whose mind is ignited by the remembrance of God, and that man is devoid of knowledge whose mind is ignited only by material factors. He is awakened only by material shocks and thereafter is lost, deep in slumber.

¹⁰ Say, '[God says] O My servants who have believed, fear your Lord. For those who do good in this world will have a good reward—and God's earth is spacious. Truly, those who persevere patiently will be requited without measure.'ᵃ

قُلْ يَـٰعِبَادِ ٱلَّذِينَ ءَامَنُوا۟ ٱتَّقُوا۟ رَبَّكُمْ لِلَّذِينَ أَحْسَنُوا۟ فِى هَـٰذِهِ ٱلدُّنْيَا حَسَنَةٌ وَأَرْضُ ٱللَّهِ وَٰسِعَةٌ إِنَّمَا يُوَفَّى ٱلصَّـٰبِرُونَ أَجْرَهُم بِغَيْرِ حِسَابٍ ۝

ᵃ When a man attains deep realisation of God, the essential result of this is that he becomes God-fearing. The realisation of the majesty of God makes him humble and he spends his life following the commandments of God. This makes him so serious that he renounces everything and leads a god-oriented life.

To build up one's life on the basis of faith involves a tremendous trial. Only those succeed in this trial for whom faith is the greatest wealth, for the sake of which they are prepared to forego everything else. A life of faith is a life of patience. Those who are prepared to become believers at the price of patience will be the ones who will be blessed with the superior grace of God.

¹¹ Say, 'I have been commanded to serve God, dedicating my worship entirely to Him. ¹² I have been commanded to be the first to submit.' ¹³ Say, 'I fear, if I disobey my Lord, the punishment of a Terrible Day.' ¹⁴ Say, 'It is God I serve, sincere in my faith in Him alone—¹⁵ as for yourselves, worship anything you please besides Him!' Say, 'The real losers will be those who lose themselves and all their kith and kin on the Day of Resurrection. That is the [most] obvious loss. ¹⁶ They will have sheets of fire above them and sheets of fire beneath them.' That is how God puts fear into the hearts of His servants. Fear me, then, My servants.ᵃ

قُلْ إِنِّي أُمِرْتُ أَنْ أَعْبُدَ اللَّهَ مُخْلِصًا لَّهُ الدِّينَ ۝ وَأُمِرْتُ لِأَنْ أَكُونَ أَوَّلَ الْمُسْلِمِينَ ۝ قُلْ إِنِّي أَخَافُ إِنْ عَصَيْتُ رَبِّي عَذَابَ يَوْمٍ عَظِيمٍ ۝ قُلِ اللَّهَ أَعْبُدُ مُخْلِصًا لَّهُ دِينِي ۝ فَاعْبُدُوا مَا شِئْتُم مِّن دُونِهِ ۗ قُلْ إِنَّ الْخَاسِرِينَ الَّذِينَ خَسِرُوا أَنفُسَهُمْ وَأَهْلِيهِمْ يَوْمَ الْقِيَامَةِ ۗ أَلَا ذَٰلِكَ هُوَ الْخُسْرَانُ الْمُبِينُ ۝ لَهُم مِّن فَوْقِهِمْ ظُلَلٌ مِّنَ النَّارِ وَمِن تَحْتِهِمْ ظُلَلٌ ۚ ذَٰلِكَ يُخَوِّفُ اللَّهُ بِهِ عِبَادَهُ ۚ يَا عِبَادِ فَاتَّقُونِ ۝

ᵃ The real call of the prophet yearns to make man discover and worship the one and only God, leaving aside the worship of everything else. A prophet pursues the dawah mission as a matter of personal concern. Not only does he guide his fellow-men but establishes an example by adopting the right path himself.

This nature of a prophet's work, indicates the nature of a dayee's work. The messenger of truth is one for whom the Truth becomes his personal problem. His call of Truth is the spontaneous expression of his inner experience and not merely a superficial call.

¹⁷ There is good news for those who shun the worship of false deities and turn to God, so give good news to My servants, ¹⁸ who listen to what is said and follow what is best in it. These are the ones God has guided; these are the people endowed with understanding.^a

وَٱلَّذِينَ ٱجْتَنَبُواْ ٱلطَّٰغُوتَ أَن يَعْبُدُوهَا وَأَنَابُوٓاْ إِلَى ٱللَّهِ لَهُمُ ٱلْبُشْرَىٰ فَبَشِّرْ عِبَادِ ۝ ٱلَّذِينَ يَسْتَمِعُونَ ٱلْقَوْلَ فَيَتَّبِعُونَ أَحْسَنَهُۥٓ أُوْلَٰٓئِكَ ٱلَّذِينَ هَدَىٰهُمُ ٱللَّهُ وَأُوْلَٰٓئِكَ هُمْ أُوْلُواْ ٱلْأَلْبَٰبِ ۝

^a The present world is one of trial. Here, realities do not reveal themselves in their true and final shape, which makes room for anything to be wrongly interpreted. Satan exploits this possibility and misguides people from the right path.

Whenever a Truth reveals itself, Satan tries to divert people's minds from it by misinterpreting it. He turns away the good aspect of a thing and brings to the fore whatever is unfavourable about it. This is a situation in which a man is really put to the test. Man has to prove his wisdom by distinguishing between right and wrong. He should be able to tear down the satanic veil of deception and see the reality. Those who have proved themselves to be in possession of such insight are the fortunate ones because they will find the Divine Truth; those who fail to prove this are fated to be enmeshed in the negative aspect of things, and are liable to be brought before God as worshippers of Satan.

¹⁹ But what of him against whom the sentence of punishment is justified? Can you rescue one who is already in the Fire? ²⁰ But for those who truly feared their Lord, there will be tall mansions, built up storey upon storey, beneath which there will be rivers flowing. This is God's promise: God never fails in His promise.^a

أَفَمَنْ حَقَّ عَلَيْهِ كَلِمَةُ ٱلْعَذَابِ أَفَأَنتَ تُنقِذُ مَن فِى ٱلنَّارِ ۞ لَكِنِ ٱلَّذِينَ ٱتَّقَوْا۟ رَبَّهُمْ لَهُمْ غُرَفٌ مِّن فَوْقِهَا غُرَفٌ مَّبْنِيَّةٌ تَجْرِى مِن تَحْتِهَا ٱلْأَنْهَٰرُ وَعْدَ ٱللَّهِ لَا يُخْلِفُ ٱللَّهُ ٱلْمِيعَادَ ۞

---

^a Every man has to live with the consequences of his deeds, for better or for worse. This means that the man worthy of Paradise lives in a paradisical atmosphere, while the man fit only for Hell lives in a hellish atmosphere. Only those possessing the insight to appreciate intangible things, will be able to perceive this difference.

Paradise would be the final and perfect manifestation of man's ambitions, which he wants to fulfill in this world, but cannot. The price of this Paradise is a God-fearing attitude. Those who fear God in this world will be made inhabitants of the perfect world of Paradise which would be free of any shortcomings.

²¹ Have you not seen that God sends down water from the sky, guides it to form springs in the earth, and then, with it, brings forth vegetation of various colours, which later withers, turns yellow before your eyes, and then He makes it crumble away? There is truly a reminder in this for those who possess understanding.ᵃ ²² Anyone whose heart God has opened up to Islam possesses a light from his Lord. But woe betide those whose hearts have been hardened against the remembrance of God! Such people are in obvious error.ᵃ

أَلَمۡ تَرَ أَنَّ ٱللَّهَ أَنزَلَ مِنَ ٱلسَّمَآءِ مَآءً فَسَلَكَهُۥ يَنَٰبِيعَ فِى ٱلۡأَرۡضِ ثُمَّ يُخۡرِجُ بِهِۦ زَرۡعًا مُّخۡتَلِفًا أَلۡوَٰنُهُۥ ثُمَّ يَهِيجُ فَتَرَىٰهُ مُصۡفَرًّا ثُمَّ يَجۡعَلُهُۥ حُطَٰمًا إِنَّ فِى ذَٰلِكَ لَذِكۡرَىٰ لِأُوْلِى ٱلۡأَلۡبَٰبِ ﴿٢١﴾ أَفَمَن شَرَحَ ٱللَّهُ صَدۡرَهُۥ لِلۡإِسۡلَٰمِ فَهُوَ عَلَىٰ نُورٍ مِّن رَّبِّهِۦ فَوَيۡلٌ لِّلۡقَٰسِيَةِ قُلُوبُهُم مِّن ذِكۡرِ ٱللَّهِ أُوْلَٰٓئِكَ فِى ضَلَٰلٍ مُّبِينٍ ﴿٢٢﴾

ᵃ The wonderful system of rains on the earth, the resulting growth of greenery and the subsequent preparations for harvesting, have countless meaningful lessons in them. But, these lessons are available only to those who devote themselves to deep thought.

On the one hand, God has created the external world in a way that everything in it has become a sign of great realities, and, on the other, He has endowed man with the ability to read these signs and understand them. Those who keep their natural capabilities alive and, by utilising them, give deep consideration to the things of the world, will have their minds filled with the deep realisation (ma'rifah) of God. Whereas those who do not keep these capabilities alive, will be unable to learn anything, even though surrounded by countless lessons. They will not be able to see, even after seeing, and will not be able to hear, even after hearing.

²³ God has sent down the best Message: a Scripture that is consimilar and oft-repeated: that causes the skins of those in awe of their Lord to creep. Then their skins and their hearts soften at the mention of God: such is God's guidance. He bestows it upon whoever He will; but no one can guide those whom God leaves to stray.ᵃ

ٱللَّهُ نَزَّلَ أَحْسَنَ ٱلْحَدِيثِ كِتَٰبًا مُّتَشَٰبِهًا مَّثَانِيَ تَقْشَعِرُّ مِنْهُ جُلُودُ ٱلَّذِينَ يَخْشَوْنَ رَبَّهُمْ ثُمَّ تَلِينُ جُلُودُهُمْ وَقُلُوبُهُمْ إِلَىٰ ذِكْرِ ٱللَّهِ ذَٰلِكَ هُدَى ٱللَّهِ يَهْدِى بِهِۦ مَن يَشَآءُ وَمَن يُضْلِلِ ٱللَّهُ فَمَا لَهُۥ مِنْ هَادٍ ۝

ᵃ God has blessed man with a guidebook in the form of the Quran. It has two special qualities. One of its qualities is that it is marked by utmost consistency. In other words, it is a book which has no contradictions. One part does not clash with another. If the Quran's statements had not corresponded exactly with reality, there would have been differences between and inconsistencies in its various parts.

The second quality of the Quran is its use of repetition, that is, its topics are often repeated in different styles. This quality in the Quran shows that it is a book of advice and guidance. An adviser always wishes that his words should establish themselves firmly in the mind of the hearer. For this purpose, he expresses the same statements in different ways. This wisdom is found in the Quran in its best form.

It is the nature of man that when he hears some terrible news, or he undergoes some hair-raising experience, his inner being is humbled and his heart is softened by the news. When a serious man reads the Quran he undergoes such spiritual experiences.

24 What about the one who will have only his bare face to protect him from his terrible punishment on the Day of Resurrection? The evil-doers will be told, 'Taste what you have earned.' 25 Those before them also denied the truth, and the punishment fell on them from where they did not expect. 26 God gave them a taste of humiliation in the life of this world, but the punishment of the Hereafter is greater, if they only knew it.[a]

أَفَمَن يَتَّقِى بِوَجْهِهِۦ سُوٓءَ ٱلْعَذَابِ يَوْمَ ٱلْقِيَـٰمَةِ ۚ وَقِيلَ لِلظَّـٰلِمِينَ ذُوقُوا۟ مَا كُنتُمْ تَكْسِبُونَ ۝ كَذَّبَ ٱلَّذِينَ مِن قَبْلِهِمْ فَأَتَىٰهُمُ ٱلْعَذَابُ مِنْ حَيْثُ لَا يَشْعُرُونَ ۝ فَأَذَاقَهُمُ ٱللَّهُ ٱلْخِزْىَ فِى ٱلْحَيَوٰةِ ٱلدُّنْيَا ۖ وَلَعَذَابُ ٱلْءَاخِرَةِ أَكْبَرُ ۚ لَوْ كَانُوا۟ يَعْلَمُونَ ۝

---

[a] Man always tries to save his face from injuries, but the punishment of Doomsday will so encompass man that it will not be possible for him to save any part of his body. In fact he will stand before the ineluctable punishment, as if using his face as a shield against it.

In the eyes of God, the greatest crime a man can commit is not to admit to the Truth when it reveals itself to him. Such people can never escape the scourge of God.

²⁷ We have set forth to men all kinds of parables in this Quran so that they may take heed: ²⁸ a Quran in Arabic, free from any ambiguity—so that people may be mindful. ²⁹ God sets forth a parable: there are two men— one belonging to many masters, all disagreeing with one another, and the other belonging entirely to one master: are those two equal in comparison? Praise be to God! But most of them have no knowledge. ³⁰ You will die and they too will die, ³¹ and, then on the Day of Resurrection you shall place your dispute before your Sustainer.^a

وَلَقَدْ ضَرَبْنَا لِلنَّاسِ فِى هَٰذَا ٱلْقُرْءَانِ مِن كُلِّ مَثَلٍ لَّعَلَّهُمْ يَتَذَكَّرُونَ ۝ قُرْءَانًا عَرَبِيًّا غَيْرَ ذِى عِوَجٍ لَّعَلَّهُمْ يَتَّقُونَ ۝ ضَرَبَ ٱللَّهُ مَثَلًا رَّجُلًا فِيهِ شُرَكَآءُ مُتَشَٰكِسُونَ وَرَجُلًا سَلَمًا لِّرَجُلٍ هَلْ يَسْتَوِيَانِ مَثَلًا ٱلْحَمْدُ لِلَّهِ بَلْ أَكْثَرُهُمْ لَا يَعْلَمُونَ ۝ إِنَّكَ مَيِّتٌ وَإِنَّهُم مَّيِّتُونَ ۝ ثُمَّ إِنَّكُمْ يَوْمَ ٱلْقِيَٰمَةِ عِندَ رَبِّكُمْ تَخْتَصِمُونَ ۝

---

^a The Quran's statements are in a language intelligible to man and within the sphere of his knowledge, so that nobody should have any difficulty in understanding them.

Here, in symbolic language, it has been explained that the principle of the Unity of God as compared to polytheism is more rational and consistent with nature. Indeed, the functioning of the external universe is indicative of the fact that a single Will is operative in it. Had there been many intentions operative therein, the system of the universe could not have run so harmoniously. Moreover, man's nature is also such that it prefers unity in loyalty. It is entirely against man's nature to subscribe to different kinds of loyalties, as a result of which he is unable to do justice to any of them.

All arguments and possibilities indicate that there is only one God, who is the Creator of man and who is worthy of being worshipped by him. In the present world, this fact is proclaimed through men like us. On the Day of Judgement, this will be declared by the Creator of the Universe Himself. At that time, denial of this fact will be impossible.

³² Who, then, is more unjust than he who lies about God and rejects the truth when it comes to him? Is not Hell an abode for those who deny the truth? ³³ He who brings the truth, and he who testifies to it as such—those are surely the people who are God-fearing: ³⁴ they will have everything they wish for from their Lord. Such is the reward of those who do good: ³⁵ God will efface their worst deeds from their record and give them their reward in accordance with the best of their actions.ᵃ

﴾ فَمَنْ أَظْلَمُ مِمَّن كَذَبَ عَلَى ٱللَّهِ وَكَذَّبَ بِٱلصِّدْقِ إِذْ جَآءَهُۥٓ أَلَيْسَ فِى جَهَنَّمَ مَثْوًى لِّلْكَٰفِرِينَ ۝ وَٱلَّذِى جَآءَ بِٱلصِّدْقِ وَصَدَّقَ بِهِۦٓ أُوْلَٰٓئِكَ هُمُ ٱلْمُتَّقُونَ ۝ لَهُم مَّا يَشَآءُونَ عِندَ رَبِّهِمْ ذَٰلِكَ جَزَآءُ ٱلْمُحْسِنِينَ ۝ لِيُكَفِّرَ ٱللَّهُ عَنْهُمْ أَسْوَأَ ٱلَّذِى عَمِلُواْ وَيَجْزِيَهُمْ أَجْرَهُم بِأَحْسَنِ ٱلَّذِى كَانُواْ يَعْمَلُونَ ۝

ᵃ Every ideology which is against the reality amounts to levelling a false allegation against God. In every age, people have been living on such falsehoods. The mission of the dayee is to prove the falsehood of such theories. Even then, there are people who are adamant in their adherence to such false ideologies. It is they who will be cast into the fire of Hell, whereas those who mend themselves, become supporters of the Truth and prove themselves to be God-fearing, will have the appreciation of Almighty God, who will overlook their failings and value them for their good deeds.

36 Is God not enough for His servant? Yet they try to frighten you with other [deities] besides Him! For such as God lets go astray, there will be no guide; 37 but he whom God guides cannot be led astray by anyone. Is God not mighty and capable of retribution? *a*

أَلَيْسَ ٱللَّهُ بِكَافٍ عَبْدَهُۥ وَيُخَوِّفُونَكَ بِٱلَّذِينَ مِن دُونِهِۦ وَمَن يُضْلِلِ ٱللَّهُ فَمَا لَهُۥ مِنْ هَادٍ ۝ وَمَن يَهْدِ ٱللَّهُ فَمَا لَهُۥ مِن مُّضِلٍّ أَلَيْسَ ٱللَّهُ بِعَزِيزٍ ذِى ٱنتِقَامٍ ۝

---

a The Prophet Muhammad preached the Unity of God. But he did not stop at only the positive declaration of 'God is one'. At the same time he used to negate those non-godly beings whom the people themselves had given the status of deities. This second part of his mission had become unbearable to the people.

Those non-godly beings were, in fact, their national heroes. For centuries exaggerated tales of their miraculous deeds had held the people in thrall. The greatness of these beings had captured people's minds to such an extent that when the Prophet Muhammad contradicted the idea of their holiness, they could not understand how they could be other than holy. They asked the Prophet Muhammad to desist from speaking against their gods, otherwise they warned that he would be destroyed.

The preacher of Truth was ordered not to pay heed to remarks of this kind, and to continue to perform the dual task of advocating the Unity of God and rejection of polytheism—all this while relying up on God and praying for the Truth to become clear and manifest.

³⁸ If you ask them who created the heavens and the earth, they will surely reply, 'God.' Say, 'Consider those you invoke besides Him: if God wished to harm me, could they undo that harm? Or if God wished to show me mercy, could they withhold that mercy?' Say, 'God is sufficient for me. In Him let the faithful put their trust.' ³⁹ Say, 'My people, do whatever is in your power—and so will I. Soon you shall come to know ⁴⁰ who will suffer a humiliating torment and on whom will descend an everlasting punishment.' ⁴¹ [O Prophet!] We have sent down to you the Book for mankind with the truth. Then whoever adopts the right way, will do so for his own soul, and whoever goes astray, injures his own soul. You are not their custodian.^a

وَإِن سَأَلْتَهُم مَّنْ خَلَقَ ٱلسَّمَـٰوَٰتِ وَٱلْأَرْضَ لَيَقُولُنَّ ٱللَّهُ قُلْ أَفَرَءَيْتُم مَّا تَدْعُونَ مِن دُونِ ٱللَّهِ إِنْ أَرَادَنِيَ ٱللَّهُ بِضُرٍّ هَلْ هُنَّ كَـٰشِفَـٰتُ ضُرِّهِ أَوْ أَرَادَنِي بِرَحْمَةٍ هَلْ هُنَّ مُمْسِكَـٰتُ رَحْمَتِهِ قُلْ حَسْبِيَ ٱللَّهُ عَلَيْهِ يَتَوَكَّلُ ٱلْمُتَوَكِّلُونَ ۝ قُلْ يَـٰقَوْمِ ٱعْمَلُوا۟ عَلَىٰ مَكَانَتِكُمْ إِنِّي عَـٰمِلٌ فَسَوْفَ تَعْلَمُونَ ۝ مَن يَأْتِيهِ عَذَابٌ يُخْزِيهِ وَيَحِلُّ عَلَيْهِ عَذَابٌ مُّقِيمٌ ۝ إِنَّا أَنزَلْنَا عَلَيْكَ ٱلْكِتَـٰبَ لِلنَّاسِ بِٱلْحَقِّ فَمَنِ ٱهْتَدَىٰ فَلِنَفْسِهِ وَمَن ضَلَّ فَإِنَّمَا يَضِلُّ عَلَيْهَا وَمَآ أَنتَ عَلَيْهِم بِوَكِيلٍ ۝

---

^a In every age, man has worshipped beings other than God, but nobody has had the courage to say that their deities created the heavens and the earth, or that the real causes of comfort or distress were in their power. It is very strange that, in spite of this uncertainty, people are not ready to leave their false gods.

When all the arguments and pleadings of a preacher prove ineffective in influencing his people, the only alternative left for him is to tell them to do whatever they like and to warn them that when the Day of Final Judgement arrives, it will be made clear who is on the right path and who is on the wrong one. This is an expression of certainty on the basis of arguments, and is always the final word of a missionary.

⁴² It is God who takes away men's souls upon their death and the souls of the living during their sleep. Then He withholds those for whom He has ordained death and restores the souls of others for an appointed term. There are certainly signs in this for those who reflect.^a

ٱللَّهُ يَتَوَفَّى ٱلْأَنفُسَ حِينَ مَوْتِهَا وَٱلَّتِى لَمْ تَمُتْ فِى مَنَامِهَا ۖ فَيُمْسِكُ ٱلَّتِى قَضَىٰ عَلَيْهَا ٱلْمَوْتَ وَيُرْسِلُ ٱلْأُخْرَىٰٓ إِلَىٰٓ أَجَلٍ مُّسَمًّى ۚ إِنَّ فِى ذَٰلِكَ لَآيَٰتٍ لِّقَوْمٍ يَتَفَكَّرُونَ ﴿٤٢﴾

---

^a While sleeping a man loses consciousness. In this sense, sleep is similar to death. When he wakes up from sleep, he regains consciousness. This is a foretaste of resurrection after death.

Through this system of nature, a man is shown today itself in an elementary manner how he will die and how he will rise up again. If he gives serious consideration to this matter, he will find in this very mundane event a great lesson of the Hereafter.

⁴³ Have they taken others for intercessors besides God? Say, 'Even though they have no power nor understanding?' ⁴⁴ Say, 'Intercession is entirely in the hands of God. He controls the heavens and the earth; you will all return to Him.' ⁴⁵ When God alone is named, the hearts of those who do not believe in the Hereafter shrink with aversion, but when others are named instead of Him, they are filled with joy. ⁴⁶ Say, 'O God! Originator of the heavens and earth! Knower of all that is hidden and all that is manifest, You will judge between Your servants regarding their differences.' ⁴⁷ If the wrongdoers possessed all that is on earth, and twice as much, they would offer it to redeem themselves from the awful suffering on the Day of Resurrection. For God will show them what they had never anticipated, ⁴⁸ the evil of their deeds will become apparent to them, and they will be overwhelmed by that which they used to mock.ᵃ

أَمِ ٱتَّخَذُوا۟ مِن دُونِ ٱللَّهِ شُفَعَآءَ ۚ قُلْ أَوَلَوْ كَانُوا۟ لَا يَمْلِكُونَ شَيْـًٔا وَلَا يَعْقِلُونَ ۝ قُل لِّلَّهِ ٱلشَّفَٰعَةُ جَمِيعًا ۖ لَّهُۥ مُلْكُ ٱلسَّمَٰوَٰتِ وَٱلْأَرْضِ ۖ ثُمَّ إِلَيْهِ تُرْجَعُونَ ۝ وَإِذَا ذُكِرَ ٱللَّهُ وَحْدَهُ ٱشْمَأَزَّتْ قُلُوبُ ٱلَّذِينَ لَا يُؤْمِنُونَ بِٱلْءَاخِرَةِ ۖ وَإِذَا ذُكِرَ ٱلَّذِينَ مِن دُونِهِۦٓ إِذَا هُمْ يَسْتَبْشِرُونَ ۝ قُلِ ٱللَّهُمَّ فَاطِرَ ٱلسَّمَٰوَٰتِ وَٱلْأَرْضِ عَٰلِمَ ٱلْغَيْبِ وَٱلشَّهَٰدَةِ أَنتَ تَحْكُمُ بَيْنَ عِبَادِكَ فِى مَا كَانُوا۟ فِيهِ يَخْتَلِفُونَ ۝ وَلَوْ أَنَّ لِلَّذِينَ ظَلَمُوا۟ مَا فِى ٱلْأَرْضِ جَمِيعًا وَمِثْلَهُۥ مَعَهُۥ لَٱفْتَدَوْا۟ بِهِۦ مِن سُوٓءِ ٱلْعَذَابِ يَوْمَ ٱلْقِيَٰمَةِ ۚ وَبَدَا لَهُم مِّنَ ٱللَّهِ مَا لَمْ يَكُونُوا۟ يَحْتَسِبُونَ ۝ وَبَدَا لَهُمْ سَيِّـَٔاتُ مَا كَسَبُوا۟ وَحَاقَ بِهِم مَّا كَانُوا۟ بِهِۦ يَسْتَهْزِءُونَ ۝

ᵃ Those believed by polytheists to be potential intermediaries between them and God were not simply stone statues. They were actually the statues of great men who lived among them. These supposed intermediaries were in reality their national heroes to whom they owed allegiance and who, they believed, would be adequate mediators before God.

Those who entertain such beliefs about beings other than God, gradually reach the point where their loyalty is dedicated solely to these beings. They are pleased to hear the praises of these beings; the proclamation of the Majesty of the One and only God does not nourish their souls.

With such people, howsoever one advocates the cause of the pure Unity of God, they do not accept it. Their eyes will open only when, on the Day of Judgement, the Majesty of God reveals itself. ▶

⁴⁹ When affliction befalls man, he appeals to Us; but when We bestow a favour upon him he says, 'All this has been given to me because of my own knowledge.' By no means! It is a trial: yet most of them do not realize it. ⁵⁰ Those who preceded them said the same thing but they gained nothing from what they did; ⁵¹ the very evil of their deeds recoiled upon them; today's wrongdoers shall also have the evil of their deeds recoil upon them: they will never be able to frustrate [Our plan]. ⁵² Do they not know that God grants abundant sustenance to anyone He wishes and gives sparingly to anyone He pleases? Surely there are signs in this for those who believe.ᵃ

فَإِذَا مَسَّ ٱلْإِنسَٰنَ ضُرٌّ دَعَانَا ثُمَّ إِذَا خَوَّلْنَٰهُ نِعْمَةً مِّنَّا قَالَ إِنَّمَآ أُوتِيتُهُۥ عَلَىٰ عِلْمٍ بَلْ هِيَ فِتْنَةٌ وَلَٰكِنَّ أَكْثَرَهُمْ لَا يَعْلَمُونَ ۝ قَدْ قَالَهَا ٱلَّذِينَ مِن قَبْلِهِمْ فَمَآ أَغْنَىٰ عَنْهُم مَّا كَانُوا۟ يَكْسِبُونَ ۝ فَأَصَابَهُمْ سَيِّئَاتُ مَا كَسَبُوا۟ وَٱلَّذِينَ ظَلَمُوا۟ مِنْ هَٰٓؤُلَآءِ سَيُصِيبُهُمْ سَيِّئَاتُ مَا كَسَبُوا۟ وَمَا هُم بِمُعْجِزِينَ ۝ أَوَلَمْ يَعْلَمُوٓا۟ أَنَّ ٱللَّهَ يَبْسُطُ ٱلرِّزْقَ لِمَن يَشَآءُ وَيَقْدِرُ إِنَّ فِى ذَٰلِكَ لَءَايَٰتٍ لِّقَوْمٍ يُؤْمِنُونَ ۝

Today, man is not even ready to offer words of acceptance, but at that time (on the Day of Judgment), he will wish to offer whatever he has as compensation in order to save himself. But, on that Day, nothing will be of avail to him except the merit of his own deeds.

ᵃ In the world, when man achieves anything, he is very happy to think that it is the result of his own talents. The fact is that the things of the world are meant as a trial for him and not as a reward for his talents. To know this fact is to have real knowledge. If a man considers that the things of this world are within his grasp because of his talents, he develops the mentality of pride and vanity. On the contrary, if a man considers them as items of trial, feelings of gratitude and humility will be engendered in him.

The increase or decrease in the provision of man in this world is a matter which is beyond human powers. It appears that there is a power beyond the human sphere which decides who should receive more and who should receive less. This shows that decisions regarding provision is not made on the basis of personal talents. It is decided on some other basis, and that basis is that this world is a testing ground and not a place for the handing out of rewards. So, whatever a man receives in this world is for his trial. The Examiner, at his discretion, gives one type of examination paper to one person and another type of paper to another. He tries one person under one set of conditions, while He tries others under a different set of conditions.

⁵³ Say, [God says] 'O My servants, who have committed excesses against their own souls, do not despair of God's mercy, for God surely forgives all sins. He is truly the Most Forgiving, the Most Merciful. ⁵⁴ Turn to your Lord and submit to Him before His scourge overtakes you, for then you shall not be helped.ᵃ

﴿ قُلْ يَـٰعِبَادِيَ ٱلَّذِينَ أَسْرَفُوا۟ عَلَىٰٓ أَنفُسِهِمْ لَا تَقْنَطُوا۟ مِن رَّحْمَةِ ٱللَّهِ إِنَّ ٱللَّهَ يَغْفِرُ ٱلذُّنُوبَ جَمِيعًا إِنَّهُۥ هُوَ ٱلْغَفُورُ ٱلرَّحِيمُ ۝ وَأَنِيبُوٓا۟ إِلَىٰ رَبِّكُمْ وَأَسْلِمُوا۟ لَهُۥ مِن قَبْلِ أَن يَأْتِيَكُمُ ٱلْعَذَابُ ثُمَّ لَا تُنصَرُونَ ۝

ᵃ When those who possess sensitive hearts are blessed with a deep realisation of God (ma'rifah), they start becoming worried as to what would happen about their past sins. Similarly, even after adopting a God-fearing way of life, a man is likely to display shortcomings from time to time, and his sensitive nature makes him worry again on this account. These feelings in some people can become so intense as to cause a deep sense of frustration.

For such people, God has declared in His Book that they should firmly believe that their God is Forgiving and Merciful. He does not look at a man's past but at his present. He does not look to his outward form but at his inner soul. He treats a man with broad-mindedness and not with petty-mindedness. That is why, when a man turns towards Him, He once again takes him into the fold of His Mercy, howsoever big a blunder the man might have committed.

⁵⁵ Follow the best aspect of what is sent down to you from your Lord, before the scourge comes upon you unawares, ⁵⁶ lest anyone should say, "Alas for me, for having neglected what is due to God, and having been one of those who scoffed!" ⁵⁷ Or, "If only God had guided me, I would surely have joined the God-fearing." ⁵⁸ Or, he may say as he sees the punishment, "Would that I had a second chance, so that I could be among the doers of good." ⁵⁹ No indeed! My revelations did come to you, but you rejected them: you showed arrogance, and were among those who deny the truth.' ⁶⁰ On the Day of Resurrection you will see those who uttered falsehoods about God with their faces blackened. Is there not enough room in Hell for the arrogant? ⁶¹ But God will deliver them who feared Him to their place of salvation. No evil shall touch them, nor shall they grieve.^a

وَٱتَّبِعُوٓاْ أَحۡسَنَ مَآ أُنزِلَ إِلَيۡكُم مِّن رَّبِّكُم مِّن قَبۡلِ أَن يَأۡتِيَكُمُ ٱلۡعَذَابُ بَغۡتَةً وَأَنتُمۡ لَا تَشۡعُرُونَ ۝ أَن تَقُولَ نَفۡسٌ يَٰحَسۡرَتَىٰ عَلَىٰ مَا فَرَّطتُ فِى جَنۢبِ ٱللَّهِ وَإِن كُنتُ لَمِنَ ٱلسَّٰخِرِينَ ۝ أَوۡ تَقُولَ لَوۡ أَنَّ ٱللَّهَ هَدَىٰنِى لَكُنتُ مِنَ ٱلۡمُتَّقِينَ ۝ أَوۡ تَقُولَ حِينَ تَرَى ٱلۡعَذَابَ لَوۡ أَنَّ لِى كَرَّةً فَأَكُونَ مِنَ ٱلۡمُحۡسِنِينَ ۝ بَلَىٰ قَدۡ جَآءَتۡكَ ءَايَٰتِى فَكَذَّبۡتَ بِهَا وَٱسۡتَكۡبَرۡتَ وَكُنتَ مِنَ ٱلۡكَٰفِرِينَ ۝ وَيَوۡمَ ٱلۡقِيَٰمَةِ تَرَى ٱلَّذِينَ كَذَبُواْ عَلَى ٱللَّهِ وُجُوهُهُم مُّسۡوَدَّةٌ أَلَيۡسَ فِى جَهَنَّمَ مَثۡوًى لِّلۡمُتَكَبِّرِينَ ۝ وَيُنَجِّى ٱللَّهُ ٱلَّذِينَ ٱتَّقَوۡاْ بِمَفَازَتِهِمۡ لَا يَمَسُّهُمُ ٱلسُّوٓءُ وَلَا هُمۡ يَحۡزَنُونَ ۝

---

^a The discourse of God maintains in all its parts a consistent level of perfection, so that in the Quran, one cannot say that some verses are better than others. Nor can it be said about the Quran in comparison with other divine books that one book is better to the exclusion of all others.

The fact is that in the present world of trial, man has freedom of action. He has the option of accepting divine words in their proper sense or of taking them wrongly. He may pay full attention to the real purpose of a talk, or he may try to ferret out insignificant points from it and interpret them wrongly. Ridiculing the Divine words is the result of such misconstruction. Man takes a verse and derives a wrong meaning from it, and then on the basis of that self-devised meaning, starts to make a mockery of it. ▶

⁶² God is the Creator of all things, He has charge of everything; ⁶³ the keys of the heavens and the earth belong to Him. Those who deny God's revelations will surely be the losers. ⁶⁴ Say, 'Ignorant men! Would you bid me worship someone other than God?' ⁶⁵ It has already been revealed to you and to those who have gone before you that if you ascribe any partner to God, all your works will come to nothing, and you will surely be among the losers. ⁶⁶ Therefore, you should worship God alone and be among the thankful.ᵃ

ٱللَّهُ خَلِقُ كُلِّ شَىْءٍ ۖ وَهُوَ عَلَىٰ كُلِّ شَىْءٍ وَكِيلٌ ۝ لَّهُ مَقَالِيدُ ٱلسَّمَـٰوَٰتِ وَٱلْأَرْضِ ۗ وَٱلَّذِينَ كَفَرُوا۟ بِـَٔايَـٰتِ ٱللَّهِ أُو۟لَـٰٓئِكَ هُمُ ٱلْخَـٰسِرُونَ ۝ قُلْ أَفَغَيْرَ ٱللَّهِ تَأْمُرُوٓنِّىٓ أَعْبُدُ أَيُّهَا ٱلْجَـٰهِلُونَ ۝ وَلَقَدْ أُوحِىَ إِلَيْكَ وَإِلَى ٱلَّذِينَ مِن قَبْلِكَ لَئِنْ أَشْرَكْتَ لَيَحْبَطَنَّ عَمَلُكَ وَلَتَكُونَنَّ مِنَ ٱلْخَـٰسِرِينَ ۝ بَلِ ٱللَّهَ فَٱعْبُدْ وَكُن مِّنَ ٱلشَّـٰكِرِينَ ۝

Man has kept himself hidden from reality, from what he really is. On account of false pride, he simply does not accept the Truth, but then talks glibly to give the impression that he is rejecting the Truth on the basis of principles. But, on the Day of Judgement, his face will reflect his inner condition. At that time his face will reveal that his rejection of the Truth was, in fact, the result of his false interpretation of divine words. Otherwise, the Truth was, in itself, very obvious and clear. At that time he will be full of regret, but regretting then will be of no avail.

ᵃ The existence of the Universe is proof of the existence of its Creator. Similarly, the conduct of the affairs of the universe in a meaningful and systematic manner proves that, at all times, a Supreme Caretaker is watching over it. If one gives serious consideration to these things, one will find in the universe the sign of its Creator and also the sign of its Organizer and Designer.

Under these circumstances, those who worship beings other than God are indulging in an action which has absolutely no value in the present universe, because as the Creator and Organizer is one and the same, worshipping Him alone will be of avail to man. Worshipping anybody other than that Being amounts to calling upon a totally non-existent entity.

⁶⁷ No just estimate have they made of God, such as is due to Him. But on the Day of Resurrection, the whole earth will lie within His grasp, while heaven will be folded up in His right hand—Glory be to Him! Exalted is He above all that they associate with Him—⁶⁸ the Trumpet shall be blown and whoever is in heaven and whoever is on earth will fall down in a swoon, except those who shall be spared by God. Then the Trumpet will be blown again and they shall rise and gaze around them. ⁶⁹ The earth will shine with the light of its Lord, and the Book will be laid open; the prophets and witnesses will be brought in; and judgement will be passed on them with fairness. And none shall be wronged. ⁷⁰ Every soul will be repaid in full for what it has done. He is fully aware of all that they did.ᵃ

وَمَا قَدَرُوا۟ ٱللَّهَ حَقَّ قَدْرِهِۦ وَٱلْأَرْضُ جَمِيعًا قَبْضَتُهُۥ يَوْمَ ٱلْقِيَٰمَةِ وَٱلسَّمَٰوَٰتُ مَطْوِيَّٰتٌۢ بِيَمِينِهِۦ سُبْحَٰنَهُۥ وَتَعَٰلَىٰ عَمَّا يُشْرِكُونَ ﴿٦٧﴾ وَنُفِخَ فِى ٱلصُّورِ فَصَعِقَ مَن فِى ٱلسَّمَٰوَٰتِ وَمَن فِى ٱلْأَرْضِ إِلَّا مَن شَآءَ ٱللَّهُ ثُمَّ نُفِخَ فِيهِ أُخْرَىٰ فَإِذَا هُمْ قِيَامٌ يَنظُرُونَ ﴿٦٨﴾ وَأَشْرَقَتِ ٱلْأَرْضُ بِنُورِ رَبِّهَا وَوُضِعَ ٱلْكِتَٰبُ وَجِا۟ىٓءَ بِٱلنَّبِيِّۦنَ وَٱلشُّهَدَآءِ وَقُضِىَ بَيْنَهُم بِٱلْحَقِّ وَهُمْ لَا يُظْلَمُونَ ﴿٦٩﴾ وَوُفِّيَتْ كُلُّ نَفْسٍ مَّا عَمِلَتْ وَهُوَ أَعْلَمُ بِمَا يَفْعَلُونَ ﴿٧٠﴾

ᵃ The root of many deviations is, in fact, the underestimation of God. Man is lost in admiration of other kinds of greatness, because he is unaware of God's unlimited Greatness. He considers attachment to great men the means of his salvation. When Doomsday removes the veils over people's eyes, they will come to know that God was and still is so great that the world could be enclosed in His fist like a small coin and the sky could be wrapped around His hand like an ordinary piece of paper.

Just as a bell rings as soon as an examination is over, similarly as soon as the time of the world is over, a trumpet will be blown. After that, the whole system will change. Thereafter, a new world will come into existence. This present world of ours is illuminated by the light of the sun, which is able to show us only tangible things. The world of the Hereafter will be directly illuminated by God's light (*nur*). So even the intangible realities of the world will become visible to man's eyes. At that time, people will be brought in to the Court of God. In the present world, people ignored the prophets and the preachers operating under their guidance. But, in the Hereafter, people will be wonderstruck to find that their future is decided on the basis of the support or rejection of these prophets and preachers.

⁷¹ Those who rejected the truth will be led to Hell in throngs. When they reach it, its gates will be opened and its keepers will say to them, 'Have messengers not come to you from among yourselves, who conveyed to you the revelations of your Lord and warned you about meeting [Him] on this Day?' They will answer, 'Yes, they did come.' But the decree of punishment has proved true against the deniers of the truth. ⁷² They will be told, 'Enter the gates of Hell, to stay therein forever.' What an evil dwelling place for the haughty.ᵃ

وَسِيقَ ٱلَّذِينَ كَفَرُوٓاْ إِلَىٰ جَهَنَّمَ زُمَرًا ۖ حَتَّىٰٓ إِذَا جَآءُوهَا فُتِحَتْ أَبْوَٰبُهَا وَقَالَ لَهُمْ خَزَنَتُهَآ أَلَمْ يَأْتِكُمْ رُسُلٌ مِّنكُمْ يَتْلُونَ عَلَيْكُمْ ءَايَٰتِ رَبِّكُمْ وَيُنذِرُونَكُمْ لِقَآءَ يَوْمِكُمْ هَٰذَا ۚ قَالُواْ بَلَىٰ وَلَٰكِنْ حَقَّتْ كَلِمَةُ ٱلْعَذَابِ عَلَى ٱلْكَٰفِرِينَ ۝ قِيلَ ٱدْخُلُوٓاْ أَبْوَٰبَ جَهَنَّمَ خَٰلِدِينَ فِيهَا ۖ فَبِئْسَ مَثْوَى ٱلْمُتَكَبِّرِينَ ۝

ᵃ There are varying degrees in rejecting and ignoring the Truth. In accordance with that would be the degrees or grades of Hell. In the Hereafter, people will be divided into different groups according to their degree and then every group will be put in that part of hell which it deserves. At the time of people's entry into hell, the conversation that will ensue among the angels watching over Hell has been described in the above verses.

The real reason for non-acceptance of the truth by the deniers of truth is always their false pride. However, the pride of the deniers is not really directed against the Truth but against the presenter of the Truth. To a man, the presenter of Truth appears to be a smaller person than himself. Therefore, that man also considers the Truth a smaller thing and contemptuously ignores it.

73 But those who fear their Lord will be led in groups towards Paradise. When they reach it, its gate will be opened, and its keepers will say to them, 'Peace be upon you. You have done well, enter Paradise and dwell in it forever,' 74 and they will say, 'Praise be to God who has fulfilled His promise to us and made us the inheritors of this land, letting us settle in the Garden wherever we want.' How excellent is the reward of those who labour! 75 You shall see the angels circling about the throne, glorifying their Lord with praise. And judgement will have been passed in justice on all and it will be said, 'Praise be to God, Lord of the Universe!' *a*

وَسِيقَ ٱلَّذِينَ ٱتَّقَوْا۟ رَبَّهُمْ إِلَى ٱلْجَنَّةِ زُمَرًا ۖ حَتَّىٰ إِذَا جَآءُوهَا وَفُتِحَتْ أَبْوَٰبُهَا وَقَالَ لَهُمْ خَزَنَتُهَا سَلَٰمٌ عَلَيْكُمْ طِبْتُمْ فَٱدْخُلُوهَا خَٰلِدِينَ ۝ وَقَالُوا۟ ٱلْحَمْدُ لِلَّهِ ٱلَّذِى صَدَقَنَا وَعْدَهُۥ وَأَوْرَثَنَا ٱلْأَرْضَ نَتَبَوَّأُ مِنَ ٱلْجَنَّةِ حَيْثُ نَشَآءُ ۖ فَنِعْمَ أَجْرُ ٱلْعَٰمِلِينَ ۝ وَتَرَى ٱلْمَلَٰٓئِكَةَ حَآفِّينَ مِنْ حَوْلِ ٱلْعَرْشِ يُسَبِّحُونَ بِحَمْدِ رَبِّهِمْ ۖ وَقُضِىَ بَيْنَهُم بِٱلْحَقِّ وَقِيلَ ٱلْحَمْدُ لِلَّهِ رَبِّ ٱلْعَٰلَمِينَ ۝

---

a Those who enter Paradise will be such as are God-fearing. If a man discovers the Majesty of God in such a way that he loses the sense of his own greatness, then the natural result of this will be that he will start fearing God. The realisation of his own humbleness vis à vis God's Powers makes him cautious and fearful. He will become extremely wary in matters concerning God. He will always worry as to how God will treat him in the Hereafter. Those who in this way were ever cautious and fearful in this world will be the ones who will be entitled to the fear-free life of the Hereafter.

The people of Paradise will be given the same treatment in the Hereafter as royal guests receive in this world. They will be escorted to their dwellings with utmost honour. When they see Paradise with their own eyes, they will spontaneously utter words of praise and gratitude for God. In Paradise they will not only have grand dwellings but there will also be no restriction on how they divert themselves or socialize. They will be able to move about and make contact with others as they please.

The Being who deserves all praises is the Being of God. But in the present world of trial the 'hymns' of God are not expressed in the real sense. The Hereafter will be the occasion for a full revelation of the praises of God. At this time the praises of God will be upon every tongue and the atmosphere will resound with hymns praising the Creator. All false greatness will come to an end. There will be only that Being there whose name will be worth taking. There will be only One Greatness in which one may become immersed and whose praises will be recited.

40. THE FORGIVER

In the name of God,
the Most Gracious, the Most Merciful

¹ *Ha Mim*

² This Book is revealed by God, the Almighty, the All Knowing. ³ The Forgiver of sin and the Accepter of repentance, who is severe in punishment and Infinite in His Bounty.ᵃ There is no God but Him. All shall return to Him.

ᵃ The appellations, the Almighty and All Knowing (*al-'Aziz* and *al-'Alim*), have been used here by way of argument in support of the Quran. At the time the Quran was revealed, this was in the nature of a forecast. Today it is an established fact.

The Quran was revealed before the age of science and in the most unfavourable of circumstances. But, exactly according to its claim, it won over its opponents. The polytheists of Arabia, the Jews and the great Roman and Iranian empires–all were its enemies. But, in a very short period, it overcame all of them. This is an event which amply proves that the Quran had been sent by the All-Powerful and Supreme God.

The other quality of the Quran is that it is a book based on facts. Even after the passage of fifteen hundred years, no statement of the Quran has been found to be at variance with the discoveries of science. This is proof of the fact that the Being who revealed it is All Knowing and All Aware. No matter relating either to heaven or earth is hidden from Him. He is uniformly aware of the past, present and future.

This is the very Almighty God who is truly worthy of worship by man. It befits His Power and Knowledge that He should gather all human beings and take stock of their deeds, and then decide everyone's fate with perfect justice, pardon those who turned towards Him and punish for their misdeeds those who rebelled against Him.

⁴ Only those who deny the truth dispute God's signs.ᵃ Do not let their activity in the land deceive you. ⁵ The people of Noah and later factions also rejected the truth and every community plotted against the messenger sent to them, aiming to lay hands on him, and they contended [against his message] with fallacious arguments, so that they might defeat the truth, therefore I seized them. How terrible was My punishment. ⁶ Thus has the word of your Lord come true against the deniers; they shall be the inmates of the Fire.

مَا يُجَٰدِلُ فِىٓ ءَايَٰتِ ٱللَّهِ إِلَّا ٱلَّذِينَ كَفَرُواْ فَلَا يَغْرُرْكَ تَقَلُّبُهُمْ فِى ٱلْبِلَٰدِ ۝ كَذَّبَتْ قَبْلَهُمْ قَوْمُ نُوحٍ وَٱلْأَحْزَابُ مِنۢ بَعْدِهِمْ وَهَمَّتْ كُلُّ أُمَّةٍ بِرَسُولِهِمْ لِيَأْخُذُوهُ وَجَٰدَلُواْ بِٱلْبَٰطِلِ لِيُدْحِضُواْ بِهِ ٱلْحَقَّ فَأَخَذْتُهُمْ فَكَيْفَ كَانَ عِقَابِ ۝ وَكَذَٰلِكَ حَقَّتْ كَلِمَتُ رَبِّكَ عَلَى ٱلَّذِينَ كَفَرُوٓاْ أَنَّهُمْ أَصْحَٰبُ ٱلنَّارِ ۝

ᵃ Here the 'signs of God' (*ayatullah*) means the arguments advanced to establish the veracity of the divine mission. Those who are not serious with regard to God, raise irrelevant points in these arguments and thus create doubt in the minds of the people that this call is not a true call but only a flight of imagination on the part of the preacher.

Bickering of this kind constitutes a very great sin. However, in the present world of trial, those who indulge in bickering are given respite only temporarily and for a fixed period. Thereafter, they are destined to face the same miserable fate as was faced by the communities of Noah, 'Ad, Thamud, etc. Those who considered themselves great were belittled, while those who were considered of no account by others were treated as great before God.

7 Those who bear the Throne, and those who are around it, glorify their Lord with His praise, and believe in Him. They ask forgiveness for those who believe, saying, 'Our Lord, You embrace all things in mercy and knowledge. Forgive those who turn to You and follow Your path. Save them from the punishment of Hell 8 and admit them, Lord, to the Eternal Garden You have promised to them, together with their righteous ancestors, spouses, and offspring: You alone are the Almighty; the All Wise. 9 Protect them from all evil deeds: those You protect from [the punishment for] evil deeds will receive Your mercy—that is the supreme success.' *a*

اَلَّذِينَ يَحْمِلُونَ الْعَرْشَ وَمَنْ حَوْلَهُۥ يُسَبِّحُونَ بِحَمْدِ رَبِّهِمْ وَيُؤْمِنُونَ بِهِۦ وَيَسْتَغْفِرُونَ لِلَّذِينَ ءَامَنُوا۟ رَبَّنَا وَسِعْتَ كُلَّ شَىْءٍ رَّحْمَةً وَعِلْمًا فَٱغْفِرْ لِلَّذِينَ تَابُوا۟ وَٱتَّبَعُوا۟ سَبِيلَكَ وَقِهِمْ عَذَابَ الْجَحِيمِ ۝ رَبَّنَا وَأَدْخِلْهُمْ جَنَّٰتِ عَدْنٍ ٱلَّتِى وَعَدتَّهُمْ وَمَن صَلَحَ مِنْ ءَابَآئِهِمْ وَأَزْوَٰجِهِمْ وَذُرِّيَّٰتِهِمْ إِنَّكَ أَنتَ ٱلْعَزِيزُ ٱلْحَكِيمُ ۝ وَقِهِمُ ٱلسَّيِّئَاتِ وَمَن تَقِ ٱلسَّيِّئَاتِ يَوْمَئِذٍ فَقَدْ رَحِمْتَهُۥ وَذَٰلِكَ هُوَ ٱلْفَوْزُ ٱلْعَظِيمُ ۝

---

a The subjects of God who set themselves the task of preaching the pure and unadulterated Truth are always harassed. They are made to feel lowly and small and treated as such wherever they may be. But, at the very time when this treatment is being meted out to them, the heavens and the earth are bearing testimony to their righteousness. The angels who have been charged with managing the affairs of the universe, will look forward to their ultimate glorious reward. Those who were looked down upon by the ignorant in this ephemeral world will be raised to such an exalted position that the angels nearest to God will pray for them.

¹⁰ Those who deny the truth will be told, 'God's abhorrence of you is greater than your hatred of yourselves. You were called to the faith but you denied it.' ¹¹ They will say, 'Our Lord! Twice You have made us die, and twice You have given us life! Now we have confessed our sins: is there any way out [of this]?' ¹² [They will be told], 'This is because when God alone was invoked you denied the truth, yet when others were associated with Him you believed in them.' Judgement rests with God, the Most High, the Most Great.ᵃ

إِنَّ ٱلَّذِينَ كَفَرُواْ يُنَادَوْنَ لَمَقْتُ ٱللَّهِ أَكْبَرُ مِن مَّقْتِكُمْ أَنفُسَكُمْ إِذْ تُدْعَوْنَ إِلَى ٱلْإِيمَـٰنِ فَتَكْفُرُونَ ﴿١٠﴾ قَالُواْ رَبَّنَآ أَمَتَّنَا ٱثْنَتَيْنِ وَأَحْيَيْتَنَا ٱثْنَتَيْنِ فَٱعْتَرَفْنَا بِذُنُوبِنَا فَهَلْ إِلَىٰ خُرُوجٍ مِّن سَبِيلٍ ﴿١١﴾ ذَٰلِكُم بِأَنَّهُۥٓ إِذَا دُعِىَ ٱللَّهُ وَحْدَهُۥ كَفَرْتُمْ وَإِن يُشْرَكْ بِهِۦ تُؤْمِنُواْ فَٱلْحُكْمُ لِلَّهِ ٱلْعَلِىِّ ٱلْكَبِيرِ ﴿١٢﴾

ᵃ God has showered His mercy in the form of guidance. But, people in general have not accepted it. As a result in the Hereafter, the rejecters of guidance will be completely deprived of God's grace. In the world, they ignored God's grace. In the Hereafter, God's grace will pass them by.

At that time, those who deny the truth will say, 'O God! You created us from the earth, that is, we were lifeless and you infused life into us. Afterwards, when our lifespan was over, we became lifeless for the second time. Now we have been raised again in the world of the Hereafter. In this way, you have twice given us life and twice given us death. Now, if you give us a third opportunity and send us back into the world, we will admit the Truth and live a life full of righteous deeds.'

But, this request of theirs will not be heard, because they proved that they could not recognise the Truth when it was hidden from their eyes. They were capable of recognising only so-called gods. They did not have the ability to recognise the real invisible God, and such people who are enamoured by outward appearances have no value in the eyes of God.

¹³ It is He who shows you His signs, and sends down provision for you from heaven; but none pays heed except the repentant. ¹⁴ Therefore call upon God, making faith pure for Him, averse as the deniers of the truth may be to it: ¹⁵ Exalted and throned on high, He lets the Spirit descend at His behest upon whichever of His servants He will, so that he may warn of the Day of Meeting, ¹⁶ the Day when they shall rise up [from their graves] and nothing about them will be hidden from God. 'To whom shall the kingdom belong that Day?' It shall belong to God, the One, the All Powerful. ¹⁷ That Day every soul shall be requited for what it has earned. On that Day none shall be wronged. And God is swift in reckoning.[a]

هُوَ ٱلَّذِى يُرِيكُمْ ءَايَٰتِهِۦ وَيُنَزِّلُ لَكُم مِّنَ ٱلسَّمَآءِ رِزْقًا ۚ وَمَا يَتَذَكَّرُ إِلَّا مَن يُنِيبُ ۝ فَٱدْعُوا۟ ٱللَّهَ مُخْلِصِينَ لَهُ ٱلدِّينَ وَلَوْ كَرِهَ ٱلْكَٰفِرُونَ ۝ رَفِيعُ ٱلدَّرَجَٰتِ ذُو ٱلْعَرْشِ يُلْقِى ٱلرُّوحَ مِنْ أَمْرِهِۦ عَلَىٰ مَن يَشَآءُ مِنْ عِبَادِهِۦ لِيُنذِرَ يَوْمَ ٱلتَّلَاقِ ۝ يَوْمَ هُم بَٰرِزُونَ ۖ لَا يَخْفَىٰ عَلَى ٱللَّهِ مِنْهُمْ شَىْءٌ ۚ لِّمَنِ ٱلْمُلْكُ ٱلْيَوْمَ ۖ لِلَّهِ ٱلْوَٰحِدِ ٱلْقَهَّارِ ۝ ٱلْيَوْمَ تُجْزَىٰ كُلُّ نَفْسٍۭ بِمَا كَسَبَتْ ۚ لَا ظُلْمَ ٱلْيَوْمَ ۚ إِنَّ ٱللَّهَ سَرِيعُ ٱلْحِسَابِ ۝

---

[a] There are countless signs in the universe which teach us lessons in symbolic language. One of these is the system of rains. This natural phenomenon is symbolic of God's inspiration. Just as rains are useful for fertile land and useless for barren land, similarly the inspiration from God brings forth fruit in some but not in others. This 'rain' enters the souls of those who have kept their hearts open and makes their existence lush green. On the contrary, those whose hearts are full of the greatness of beings other than God are like barren lands.

God is fully aware of His subjects. Whoever He finds capable, He chooses for the purpose of conveying His message. The main aim of this message is to warn the people of the fast approaching day when they will be presented before the Lord of the Universe, from whom nothing will be hidden and whose judgement will not be influenced by anybody.

¹⁸ [O Prophet] forewarn them of the approaching Day, when hearts will leap up to the throats and choke them; when the wrongdoers will have no friend, nor any intercessor who will be listened to, ¹⁹ [for] He is aware of the [most] stealthy glance, and of all that the hearts conceal. ²⁰ God will judge with [justice and] truth: but those whom they invoke besides Him, have no power to judge at all. Surely, God is all hearing, all seeing.^a

وَأَنذِرْهُمْ يَوْمَ ٱلْأَزِفَةِ إِذِ ٱلْقُلُوبُ لَدَى ٱلْحَنَاجِرِ كَٰظِمِينَ مَا لِلظَّٰلِمِينَ مِنْ حَمِيمٍ وَلَا شَفِيعٍ يُطَاعُ ۝ يَعْلَمُ خَآئِنَةَ ٱلْأَعْيُنِ وَمَا تُخْفِى ٱلصُّدُورُ ۝ وَٱللَّهُ يَقْضِى بِٱلْحَقِّ وَٱلَّذِينَ يَدْعُونَ مِن دُونِهِۦ لَا يَقْضُونَ بِشَىْءٍ إِنَّ ٱللَّهَ هُوَ ٱلسَّمِيعُ ٱلْبَصِيرُ ۝

---

^a The present world is full of opportunities, which make it possible for man to do whatever he likes. This leads him into a grave misunderstanding. He considers his temporary freedom to be a permanent condition. The fact is that whatever opportunities man has been given here are by way of trial and not on the basis of his deserving them. As soon as the period of testing is over, all the present opportunities will be snatched away from him. At that time, man will come to know that, except for his helplessness, he possesses nothing which will be a support to him.

Man wants to live an unrestricted life. On account of this, he associates beings other than God with the godhead, so that in their names he may be able to justify his misguided actions. But on the Day of Judgement, when reality reveals itself in an unveiled form, he will realize that there was nobody but God who had any powers.

²¹ Have they not travelled through the land and seen what was the end of those who have gone before them? They were stronger than them and made a more impressive mark upon the land, yet God destroyed them for their sins—they had no one to defend them against Him—²² that was because their messengers came to them with clear signs but they rejected them. So God seized them: He is powerful, severe in punishment.^a

﴿ أَوَلَمْ يَسِيرُوا۟ فِى ٱلْأَرْضِ فَيَنظُرُوا۟ كَيْفَ كَانَ عَـٰقِبَةُ ٱلَّذِينَ كَانُوا۟ مِن قَبْلِهِمْ ۚ كَانُوا۟ هُمْ أَشَدَّ مِنْهُمْ قُوَّةً وَءَاثَارًا فِى ٱلْأَرْضِ فَأَخَذَهُمُ ٱللَّهُ بِذُنُوبِهِمْ وَمَا كَانَ لَهُم مِّنَ ٱللَّهِ مِن وَاقٍ ۝ ذَٰلِكَ بِأَنَّهُمْ كَانَت تَّأْتِيهِمْ رُسُلُهُم بِٱلْبَيِّنَـٰتِ فَكَفَرُوا۟ فَأَخَذَهُمُ ٱللَّهُ ۚ إِنَّهُۥ قَوِىٌّ شَدِيدُ ٱلْعِقَابِ ۝

---

^a In the history of the world it has happened frequently that one nation or community rises to great heights, but is then annihilated. One finds that a nation once gave birth to a grand civilization and today that civilization is traceable only through its half buried ruins. A nation which once enjoyed the position of a live entity is today considered worthy of mention only as a matter of historical record.

Such events are a common occurence. But people have attributed them to geological phenomena or to historical revolutions. But the fact is that the fall of nations has always resulted from Divine decisions, which were imposed on the concerned peoples on account of their denial of the Truth. Had we possessed the insight to see the reality behind the events we will find that every event took place through the angels of God, though to all appearances, its causes were of a worldly nature.

²³ We sent Moses with Our signs and clear authority ²⁴ to Pharaoh, Haman and Korah. But they said, 'A magician, a liar.' ²⁵ When he came to them with the truth from Us, they said, 'Slay the sons of those who believe with him and spare only their daughters'—the schemes of those who denied the truth were futile.ᵃ

وَلَقَدْ أَرْسَلْنَا مُوسَىٰ بِـَٔايَٰتِنَا وَسُلْطَٰنٍ مُّبِينٍ ۝ إِلَىٰ فِرْعَوْنَ وَهَٰمَٰنَ وَقَٰرُونَ فَقَالُوا۟ سَٰحِرٌ كَذَّابٌ ۝ فَلَمَّا جَآءَهُم بِٱلْحَقِّ مِنْ عِندِنَا قَالُوا۟ ٱقْتُلُوٓا۟ أَبْنَآءَ ٱلَّذِينَ ءَامَنُوا۟ مَعَهُۥ وَٱسْتَحْيُوا۟ نِسَآءَهُمْ وَمَا كَيْدُ ٱلْكَٰفِرِينَ إِلَّا فِى ضَلَٰلٍ ۝

ᵃ In addition to arguments, the prophets were given miraculous supports which provided ample proof of their having been sent and commissioned by God. But, acceptance of the Truth by a man comes at the cost of negating his own self, which is the most difficult sacrifice for him. It was for this reason alone that Pharaoh and his courtiers did not accept Moses' prophethood, in spite of very clear arguments in its favour.

While, on the one hand, they started creating the impression among the people that Moses' claim to prophethood was baseless and his miracles were feats of magic. On the other hand, they decided to more vigorously implement their earlier policy of reducing the population of the Children of Israel, so that Moses should not be able to establish a firm foundation among his own community. But they did not know that they were using these strategies not against Moses but against God, and against God no strategy devised by any human being could be successful.

²⁶ Pharaoh said, 'Let me kill Moses—let him call upon his Lord—I fear that he may cause you to change your religion, or that he may cause disorder in the land.' ²⁷ Moses replied, 'I seek refuge with my Lord and your Lord from every arrogant person who does not believe in the Day of Reckoning.' ᵃ

وَقَالَ فِرْعَوْنُ ذَرُونِي أَقْتُلْ مُوسَى وَلْيَدْعُ رَبَّهُ إِنِّي أَخَافُ أَن يُبَدِّلَ دِينَكُمْ أَوْ أَن يُظْهِرَ فِي ٱلْأَرْضِ ٱلْفَسَادَ ۞ وَقَالَ مُوسَىٰ إِنِّي عُذْتُ بِرَبِّي وَرَبِّكُم مِّن كُلِّ مُتَكَبِّرٍ لَّا يُؤْمِنُ بِيَوْمِ ٱلْحِسَابِ ۞

ᵃ 'He may cause you to change your religion' here means that he might change the form of religion which had come down to them from their ancestors, so that a new religion might prevail among the people.

Pharaoh expressed his intention of slaying Moses, otherwise he might find supporters among the people of his community and, with their help, try to create unrest (*fasad*)in the country; he wanted him to be killed at the very outset.

The greatest impediment to the acceptance of Truth is man's overweening pride. In order to elevate himself, he wants to lower the Truth. But the supreme supporter of Truth is God, the Lord of the Universe. In the beginning, the opponents of Truth may apparently suppress it, but God's support guarantees that finally it will be the Truth which will prevail.

²⁸ A believer, a man from among the people of Pharaoh, who had concealed his faith, said, 'Would you slay a man merely because he says, "My Lord is God." He has brought you clear signs from your Lord, and if he is lying, the sin of his will be on his own head; but if he is truthful, a part of that of which he warns you will surely befall you. Certainly, God does not guide one who is a transgressor and a liar. ²⁹ My people! Yours is the kingdom today, you have dominion in the land; but who will help us against the scourge of God if it befalls us?' But Pharaoh said, 'I point out to you only that which I consider right; and I guide you to the right path.'^a

وَقَالَ رَجُلٌ مُّؤْمِنٌ مِّنْ ءَالِ فِرْعَوْنَ يَكْتُمُ إِيمَٰنَهُۥٓ أَتَقْتُلُونَ رَجُلًا أَن يَقُولَ رَبِّيَ ٱللَّهُ وَقَدْ جَآءَكُم بِٱلْبَيِّنَٰتِ مِن رَّبِّكُمْ وَإِن يَكُ كَٰذِبًا فَعَلَيْهِ كَذِبُهُۥ وَإِن يَكُ صَادِقًا يُصِبْكُم بَعْضُ ٱلَّذِى يَعِدُكُمْ إِنَّ ٱللَّهَ لَا يَهْدِى مَنْ هُوَ مُسْرِفٌ كَذَّابٌ ۝ يَٰقَوْمِ لَكُمُ ٱلْمُلْكُ ٱلْيَوْمَ ظَٰهِرِينَ فِى ٱلْأَرْضِ فَمَن يَنصُرُنَا مِنۢ بَأْسِ ٱللَّهِ إِن جَآءَنَا قَالَ فِرْعَوْنُ مَآ أُرِيكُمْ إِلَّا مَآ أَرَىٰ وَمَآ أَهْدِيكُمْ إِلَّا سَبِيلَ ٱلرَّشَادِ ۝

---

^a The true believer mentioned here was a member of the royal family of Pharaoh and was probably one of the high-ranking officials of the court. This venerable gentleman had been influenced by Moses' call to the Unity of God. However, he had kept his faith a secret. But, when he saw that Pharaoh intended to kill Moses, he openly came to his support. He defended Moses in a very wise and effective manner.

This event teaches us that the *dawah* process is in itself a power which creates its sympathisers and supporters in the camp of dire opponents also, even if the enemy be as tyrannical as Pharaoh.

³⁰ The believer said, 'My people! I fear for you a fate like that of the people of old: ³¹ like the fate of the people of Noah, 'Ad, Thamud, and those who came after them—God never wills injustice on His creatures. ³² My people, I fear for you the Day you will cry out to one another, ³³ the Day when you will [wish to] turn your backs and flee, having none to defend you against God: for he whom God lets go astray can never find any guide.ᵃ

وَقَالَ ٱلَّذِىٓ ءَامَنَ يَـٰقَوْمِ إِنِّىٓ أَخَافُ عَلَيْكُم مِّثْلَ يَوْمِ ٱلْأَحْزَابِ ۝ مِثْلَ دَأْبِ قَوْمِ نُوحٍ وَعَادٍ وَثَمُودَ وَٱلَّذِينَ مِنۢ بَعْدِهِمْ ۚ وَمَا ٱللَّهُ يُرِيدُ ظُلْمًا لِّلْعِبَادِ ۝ وَيَـٰقَوْمِ إِنِّىٓ أَخَافُ عَلَيْكُمْ يَوْمَ ٱلتَّنَادِ ۝ يَوْمَ تُوَلُّونَ مُدْبِرِينَ مَا لَكُم مِّنَ ٱللَّهِ مِنْ عَاصِمٍ ۗ وَمَن يُضْلِلِ ٱللَّهُ فَمَا لَهُۥ مِنْ هَادٍ ۝

ᵃ Pharaoh had threatened Moses with worldly punishment. In reply to this, the True Believer warned Pharaoh of the punishment of the Hereafter. This is always the method of the preacher of Truth. People fret about worldly affairs, but the preacher is focused on the Hereafter. People talk in terms of the world, while the preacher's discourse is always about the Hereafter. People consider worldly problems to be the most pressing, while, for the preacher, the most pressing problem is that which is connected with the Hereafter.

³⁴ Joseph came to you before with clear signs, but you never ceased to doubt the message he brought you. When he died, you said, "God will not send another messenger." In this way God leaves the transgressors and doubters to go astray—³⁵ those who dispute God's revelations without any authority are doing something that is greatly abhorrent to God and to the believers. That is how God seals up the heart of every arrogant oppressor.ᵃ

وَلَقَدْ جَآءَكُمْ يُوسُفُ مِن قَبْلُ بِٱلْبَيِّنَٰتِ فَمَا زِلْتُمْ فِى شَكٍّ مِّمَّا جَآءَكُم بِهِۦ ۖ حَتَّىٰٓ إِذَا هَلَكَ قُلْتُمْ لَن يَبْعَثَ ٱللَّهُ مِنۢ بَعْدِهِۦ رَسُولًا ۚ كَذَٰلِكَ يُضِلُّ ٱللَّهُ مَنْ هُوَ مُسْرِفٌ مُّرْتَابٌ ۝ ٱلَّذِينَ يُجَٰدِلُونَ فِىٓ ءَايَٰتِ ٱللَّهِ بِغَيْرِ سُلْطَٰنٍ أَتَىٰهُمْ ۖ كَبُرَ مَقْتًا عِندَ ٱللَّهِ وَعِندَ ٱلَّذِينَ ءَامَنُوا۟ ۚ كَذَٰلِكَ يَطْبَعُ ٱللَّهُ عَلَىٰ كُلِّ قَلْبِ مُتَكَبِّرٍ جَبَّارٍ ۝

ᵃ During the life of Joseph, majority of the people of Egypt did not accept his prophethood. It was only after his death, when the administrative system of the country began to deteriorate, that the Egyptians came to realise his greatness. Then, they started saying that Joseph's existence had been a great boon to Egypt. And they said that such a prophet would never come again. Though Joseph was a prophet of God, he was also a human being. This gave people the scope to say, 'It is not necessary that the feats performed by Joseph were on the basis of his being a prophet. It is quite possible that as a brilliant man, he was able to put up this excellent performance.' Under the influence of such opinions, the people of Egypt began to have doubts about his prophethood.

However clear and obvious the Truth may be, in this world of trial, it is always possible for a man to find shadows of doubt in it and then deny it. Those who are by nature arrogant and haughty, and those who think that by admitting the Truth, they will lose their greatness, can never overcome their doubts. Rather they nurture and exaggerate these doubts to such an extent that they come to prevail over their minds and souls. Consequently, they are unable to think about the Truth in an unbiased and objective manner. They remain its rejecters till the day they die.

³⁶ Pharaoh said, 'O Haman, build for me a lofty building so that I may gain access ³⁷ to the heavens,ᵃ so that I may look upon the God of Moses: I am convinced that he is a liar!' That is how Pharaoh's evil actions were made to look fair in the eyes of Pharoah,ᵇ and he was turned away from the path [of truth]. Pharaoh's scheming led to nothing but ruin.

وَقَالَ فِرْعَوْنُ يَـٰهَـٰمَـٰنُ ٱبْنِ لِى صَرْحًا لَّعَلِّىٓ أَبْلُغُ ٱلْأَسْبَـٰبَ ۝ أَسْبَـٰبَ ٱلسَّمَـٰوَٰتِ فَأَطَّلِعَ إِلَىٰٓ إِلَـٰهِ مُوسَىٰ وَإِنِّى لَأَظُنُّهُۥ كَـٰذِبًا ۚ وَكَذَٰلِكَ زُيِّنَ لِفِرْعَوْنَ سُوٓءُ عَمَلِهِۦ وَصُدَّ عَنِ ٱلسَّبِيلِ ۚ وَمَا كَيْدُ فِرْعَوْنَ إِلَّا فِى تَبَابٍ ۝

ᵃ What Pharaoh said to his minister, Haman, was not said seriously, but by way of a timely stratagem. He saw that the cogent and reasonable words of the true believer were having an effect on the people. So, he wanted to raise a frivolous point in order that Moses' call should not become the topic of serious discussion but appear rather as a mere triviality.

ᵇ This verse means that bad deeds (or rejection of the Truth) is often glorified by uttering pleasantries and this is the chief reason that leads man astray. In other words, giving importance to frivolous points rather than to genuine rational arguments; trying to cover up misdeeds by misrepresentation, etc. Those who attempt to trivialize the Truth, which is based on firm rationality, forget that it cannot be negated by raising baseless, trifling points.

³⁸ The believer^a said, 'My people, follow me! I will guide you to the right path. ³⁹ O my people, the life of this world is only a temporary provision; and the Hereafter is the permanent abode. ⁴⁰ Whoever does evil will be requited with evil; but whoever does good, whether male or female, and is a believer, will enter the Garden; where they will be provided for without measure. ⁴¹ My people! How is it that I call you to salvation, while you call me to the Fire?^b ⁴² You call upon me to deny God and to serve other deities about which I have no knowledge, while I call you to the Almighty, the Forgiver. ⁴³ Surely that to which you call me has no say in this world or in the life to come, that our return is to God alone, and that the transgressors shall be the inmates of the Fire. ⁴⁴ Soon you will remember what I say to you! I shall entrust my affair to God, for God is observant of all [His] servants.'

وَقَالَ ٱلَّذِىٓ ءَامَنَ يَٰقَوْمِ ٱتَّبِعُونِ أَهْدِكُمْ سَبِيلَ ٱلرَّشَادِ ۝ يَٰقَوْمِ إِنَّمَا هَٰذِهِ ٱلْحَيَوٰةُ ٱلدُّنْيَا مَتَٰعٌ وَإِنَّ ٱلْءَاخِرَةَ هِىَ دَارُ ٱلْقَرَارِ ۝ مَنْ عَمِلَ سَيِّئَةً فَلَا يُجْزَىٰٓ إِلَّا مِثْلَهَا وَمَنْ عَمِلَ صَٰلِحًا مِّن ذَكَرٍ أَوْ أُنثَىٰ وَهُوَ مُؤْمِنٌ فَأُو۟لَٰٓئِكَ يَدْخُلُونَ ٱلْجَنَّةَ يُرْزَقُونَ فِيهَا بِغَيْرِ حِسَابٍ ۝ وَيَٰقَوْمِ مَا لِىٓ أَدْعُوكُمْ إِلَى ٱلنَّجَوٰةِ وَتَدْعُونَنِىٓ إِلَى ٱلنَّارِ تَدْعُونَنِى لِأَكْفُرَ بِٱللَّهِ وَأُشْرِكَ بِهِۦ مَا لَيْسَ لِى بِهِۦ عِلْمٌ وَأَنَا۠ أَدْعُوكُمْ إِلَى ٱلْعَزِيزِ ٱلْغَفَّٰرِ ۝ لَا جَرَمَ أَنَّمَا تَدْعُونَنِىٓ إِلَيْهِ لَيْسَ لَهُۥ دَعْوَةٌ فِى ٱلدُّنْيَا وَلَا فِى ٱلْءَاخِرَةِ وَأَنَّ مَرَدَّنَآ إِلَى ٱللَّهِ وَأَنَّ ٱلْمُسْرِفِينَ هُمْ أَصْحَٰبُ ٱلنَّارِ ۝ فَسَتَذْكُرُونَ مَآ أَقُولُ لَكُمْ وَأُفَوِّضُ أَمْرِىٓ إِلَى ٱللَّهِ إِنَّ ٱللَّهَ بَصِيرٌۢ بِٱلْعِبَادِ ۝

---

^a This speech made by the true believer of Pharaoh's court is very clear. A model sermon, which shows what the mode of address of a preacher should be.

^b In other words the sentence, 'I call you towards the Lord of the Universe, whereas you call me towards one who is quite ineffectual both in this world and in the Hereafter.' This presents the gist of the speech of a true believer. This gives an idea of what was being discussed in Pharaoh's court. The discussion was on whether God or other man-made deities should be invoked. The true believer said that God is a living and dominant entity. Calling upon Him amounts to calling upon the real God. As opposed to this, he said that their deities were only the creation of their imagination or objects of superstition, and were of no avail either in this world or in the world Hereafter. When they (the deities) have no real existence, how can they confer any real advantage? (*Tafsir ibn Kathir*, vol. IV, p. 80).

⁴⁵ Thus, God delivered him from the evils which they plotted, and the companions of Pharaoh themselves were encompassed by a dreadful scourge; ⁴⁶ they will be brought before the Fire morning and evening. On the Day the Hour comes, [a voice will cry], 'Mete out to Pharaoh's people the harshest punishment!' *a*

فَوَقَىٰهُ ٱللَّهُ سَيِّئَاتِ مَا مَكَرُواْ وَحَاقَ بِآلِ فِرْعَوْنَ سُوٓءُ ٱلْعَذَابِ ۝ ٱلنَّارُ يُعْرَضُونَ عَلَيْهَا غُدُوًّا وَعَشِيًّا وَيَوْمَ تَقُومُ ٱلسَّاعَةُ أَدْخِلُوٓاْ ءَالَ فِرْعَوْنَ أَشَدَّ ٱلْعَذَابِ ۝

---

a The true believer of Pharaoh's court was not a prophet. But, in spite of his being alone, God saved him from the tyrannical plans of Pharaoh. This shows that even non-prophets—when they support the mission of truth—receive the same divine succour as was always promised by God to the prophets.

Though the final decision about the fate of human beings will be taken on the Day of Judgement, when a man enters the other world after death, it is immediately clear to him as to what he had done in the previous world and what fate he is ordained to face. In this way, at a conscious level, he becomes involved in his final fate immediately after death and, while at a physical level, he will face it on the Day of Judgement, when God's court is established.

47 When they dispute with one another in the Fire, the weak will say to those who deemed themselves mighty, 'We were your followers; will you then relieve us of some of the Fire?' 48 But those who had been arrogant will say, 'We are all in this together. God has judged between His servants.' 49 Those in the Fire will say to its keepers, 'Implore your Lord to relieve our torment for one day,' 50 but they will say, 'Did not your messengers come to you with clear signs?' They will say, 'Yes.' The keepers will say, 'Then pray [for help] yourselves.' But the prayer of those who deny the truth is of no avail.[a]

وَإِذْ يَتَحَآجُّونَ فِى ٱلنَّارِ فَيَقُولُ ٱلضُّعَفَٰٓؤُاْ لِلَّذِينَ ٱسْتَكْبَرُوٓاْ إِنَّا كُنَّا لَكُمْ تَبَعًا فَهَلْ أَنتُم مُّغْنُونَ عَنَّا نَصِيبًا مِّنَ ٱلنَّارِ ۝ قَالَ ٱلَّذِينَ ٱسْتَكْبَرُوٓاْ إِنَّا كُلٌّ فِيهَآ إِنَّ ٱللَّهَ قَدْ حَكَمَ بَيْنَ ٱلْعِبَادِ ۝ وَقَالَ ٱلَّذِينَ فِى ٱلنَّارِ لِخَزَنَةِ جَهَنَّمَ ٱدْعُواْ رَبَّكُمْ يُخَفِّفْ عَنَّا يَوْمًا مِّنَ ٱلْعَذَابِ ۝ قَالُوٓاْ أَوَلَمْ تَكُ تَأْتِيكُمْ رُسُلُكُم بِٱلْبَيِّنَٰتِ قَالُواْ بَلَىٰ قَالُواْ فَٱدْعُواْ وَمَا دُعَٰٓؤُاْ ٱلْكَٰفِرِينَ إِلَّا فِى ضَلَٰلٍ ۝

a In these verses a scene from Hell is depicted. Those who had assumed great positions in this world will forget their so-called greatness in the hereafter. Now, the common people, who were so proud of their heroes, will express their displeasure with them. Those who were not prepared to accept the Truth in this world will now humbly bow down before it. But this submissiveness in the Hereafter will be of no avail to any one.

⁵¹ Most surely We help our messengers, and those who believe, in the life of this world and on the Day when all the witnesses will stand up. ⁵² The Day when their excuses will be of no avail to the wrongdoers, the curse shall be their lot and they will have the most evil abode. ⁵³ We gave Moses Our guidance, and made the Children of Israel the inheritors of the Book—⁵⁴ a guide and an admonition to men of understanding. ⁵⁵ So be patient, for what God has promised is sure to come. Ask forgiveness for your sins; praise your Lord morning and evening.[a]

إِنَّا لَنَنصُرُ رُسُلَنَا وَٱلَّذِينَ ءَامَنُواْ فِى ٱلْحَيَوٰةِ ٱلدُّنْيَا وَيَوْمَ يَقُومُ ٱلْأَشْهَٰدُ ۝ يَوْمَ لَا يَنفَعُ ٱلظَّٰلِمِينَ مَعْذِرَتُهُمْ ۖ وَلَهُمُ ٱللَّعْنَةُ وَلَهُمْ سُوءُ ٱلدَّارِ ۝ وَلَقَدْ ءَاتَيْنَا مُوسَى ٱلْهُدَىٰ وَأَوْرَثْنَا بَنِى إِسْرَٰءِيلَ ٱلْكِتَٰبَ ۝ هُدًى وَذِكْرَىٰ لِأُوْلِى ٱلْأَلْبَٰبِ ۝ فَٱصْبِرْ إِنَّ وَعْدَ ٱللَّهِ حَقٌّ وَٱسْتَغْفِرْ لِذَنۢبِكَ وَسَبِّحْ بِحَمْدِ رَبِّكَ بِٱلْعَشِىِّ وَٱلْإِبْكَٰرِ ۝

---

[a] There is firm assurance of God's help to prophets and their followers. But entitlement to this help is achieved only after the exercise of patience. Patience has been given so much importance, so that those who uphold the Truth may be fully established as champions of the Truth and tyrants may be proved to be such. In order to reach the stage where this distinction becomes clear, the upholders of Truth have to exercise patience unilaterally. The patience they exercise makes them entitled to God's help in this world and, by virtue of this very quality, they become entitled to be God's witnesses against transgressors on the Day of Judgement.

The Book which comes from God comes only for providing guidance to human beings. But this guidance is useful only to those who are wise, i.e. those who are not bound by certain untoward considerations; those who keep themselves free of complexes; those who test matters on the basis of rationality and not on any other basis. Those who, unlike the former, indulge in an irrational interpretation of God's guidance are transgressors, while those who treat the guidance of God as a matter of logic are the ones who have achieved success.

⁵⁶ As for those who, with no authority to do so, dispute God's messages, there is nothing in their hearts but a feeling of greatness which they will never attain. Seek refuge in God, for He is the All Hearing, the All Seeing.ᵃ

ᵃ The Truth is so obvious and so rational that it is not difficult for anybody to understand it. But, whenever Truth reveals itself, it does so through a 'human being'. So, the admission of Truth practically becomes synonymous with the acceptance of the conveyer of the Truth. This is why those who have a superiority complex are not prepared to accept the Truth.

Such people fear that the moment they accept the Truth, they will lose their superiority in favour of the bearer of Truth. On account of this mentality, they become its opponents. But, God has ordained that, in His world, such people will never succeed.

⁵⁷ Certainly, the creation of the heavens and the earth is greater than the creation of mankind; but most people do not know this. ⁵⁸ The blind and the sighted are not equal, just as those who believe and do good works and those who do evil are not equal: how seldom you reflect! ⁵⁹ The Final Hour is sure to come, without doubt, but most people do not believe.ᵃ

لَخَلْقُ ٱلسَّمَـٰوَٰتِ وَٱلْأَرْضِ أَكْبَرُ مِنْ خَلْقِ ٱلنَّاسِ وَلَـٰكِنَّ أَكْثَرَ ٱلنَّاسِ لَا يَعْلَمُونَ ۝ وَمَا يَسْتَوِى ٱلْأَعْمَىٰ وَٱلْبَصِيرُ وَٱلَّذِينَ ءَامَنُوا۟ وَعَمِلُوا۟ ٱلصَّـٰلِحَـٰتِ وَلَا ٱلْمُسِىٓءُ قَلِيلًا مَّا تَتَذَكَّرُونَ ۝ إِنَّ ٱلسَّاعَةَ لَءَاتِيَةٌ لَّا رَيْبَ فِيهَا وَلَـٰكِنَّ أَكْثَرَ ٱلنَّاسِ لَا يُؤْمِنُونَ ۝

ᵃ The grandeur of the Universe is an indicator of the greatness of its Creator. This greatness is so immense that the resurrection and re-creation of a man is comparatively a very easy task.

And then, when one casts a glance upon human society, the advent of the world of the Hereafter seems like a moral necessity. There are some in society who have the insight to see the reality, while there are others who are totally blind to it. Similarly, there are some who in every case observe the principles of justice, while there are others who move away from the path of justice and adopt oppressive methods. The moral sense of man says that the final fate of these two types of human beings should not be identical.

If all these things are taken into consideration, it would appear that the coming of the Hereafter is a rational possibility as well as a moral necessity.

⁶⁰ Your Lord has said, 'Call on Me, and I will answer your prayers.' But those who are too arrogant to worship Me will certainly enter Hell, in disgrace. ⁶¹ It is God who has given you the night in which to rest and the day in which to see. God is truly bountiful to people, but most people do not give thanks. ⁶² Such is God, your Lord, the Creator of all things. There is no god but He. How then are you being turned away [from Him]? ⁶³ Thus, indeed, those who deny the signs of God turn away from Him.ᵃ

وَقَالَ رَبُّكُمُ ٱدْعُونِى أَسْتَجِبْ لَكُمْ إِنَّ ٱلَّذِينَ يَسْتَكْبِرُونَ عَنْ عِبَادَتِى سَيَدْخُلُونَ جَهَنَّمَ دَاخِرِينَ ۝ ٱللَّهُ ٱلَّذِى جَعَلَ لَكُمُ ٱلَّيْلَ لِتَسْكُنُوا۟ فِيهِ وَٱلنَّهَارَ مُبْصِرًا إِنَّ ٱللَّهَ لَذُو فَضْلٍ عَلَى ٱلنَّاسِ وَلَٰكِنَّ أَكْثَرَ ٱلنَّاسِ لَا يَشْكُرُونَ ۝ ذَٰلِكُمُ ٱللَّهُ رَبُّكُمْ خَٰلِقُ كُلِّ شَىْءٍ لَّآ إِلَٰهَ إِلَّا هُوَ فَأَنَّىٰ تُؤْفَكُونَ ۝ كَذَٰلِكَ يُؤْفَكُ ٱلَّذِينَ كَانُوا۟ بِـَٔايَٰتِ ٱللَّهِ يَجْحَدُونَ ۝

ᵃ The alternation of night and day and the existence of other life-sustaining processes on earth is too perfect and too great to have been brought into existence by any human being, or even by all God's creatures put together. This is a clear argument which urges that the Creator is the only one who is worthy of being worshipped. Man should bow down only before Him and entertain hopes solely of Him.

But, all too frequently, human beings are unable to establish any real relationship of worship and prayer with the Creator of the Universe because of being involved with someone or something other than God. Some are engaged in the worship of living or dead personalities, while others are totally occupied with themselves. Time and again, God reveals arguments which contradict such wrongful practices, but man ignores them, hiding behind false justification.

All such behaviour amounts to a lack of appreciation for the Creator of the Universe, and those who degrade Him will find no place for themselves except in hell.

⁶⁴ It is God who has given you the earth for a resting place and the heavens for a canopy. He shaped you, formed you well, and provided you with good things. Such is God, your Lord, so glory be to Him, the Lord of the Universe.ᵃ ⁶⁵ He is the Living One. There is no deity save Him. So pray to Him, making religion pure for Him [only].ᵇ Praise be to God, the Lord of the Universe!

ٱللَّهُ ٱلَّذِى جَعَلَ لَكُمُ ٱلْأَرْضَ قَرَارًا وَٱلسَّمَآءَ بِنَآءً وَصَوَّرَكُمْ فَأَحْسَنَ صُوَرَكُمْ وَرَزَقَكُم مِّنَ ٱلطَّيِّبَٰتِ ذَٰلِكُمُ ٱللَّهُ رَبُّكُمْ فَتَبَارَكَ ٱللَّهُ رَبُّ ٱلْعَٰلَمِينَ ۝ هُوَ ٱلْحَىُّ لَآ إِلَٰهَ إِلَّا هُوَ فَٱدْعُوهُ مُخْلِصِينَ لَهُ ٱلدِّينَ ٱلْحَمْدُ لِلَّهِ رَبِّ ٱلْعَٰلَمِينَ ۝

ᵃ The earth has been endowed with countless physical resources. This has enabled human beings to build their civilization in the world. Similarly, the atmosphere which envelopes the earth has such favourable arrangements, in which slightest of disturbance would make the whole system of human life go topsy-turvy. Then, the sublime constitution of man makes him the most superior creature in the world. So, who can be worthy of man's devotion and worship except the Creator who has created it all?

ᵇ This verse invokes a true subject of God to 'call upon Him, giving Him sincere devotion'. It means that any form of obeisance and worship should be for the One and only God.

66 Say, 'I have been forbidden to invoke those whom you invoke besides God—seeing that clear signs have come to me from my Lord; and I have been commanded to submit to the Lord of the Universe.' 67 It is He who created you from dust, then from a drop of fluid, then from a tiny, clinging form, then He brought you forth as infants, then He allowed you to reach maturity, then He let you grow old—though some of you die sooner—and reach your appointed term so that you may reflect.a 68 It is He who gives life and death, and when He ordains a thing, He says only, 'Be!' and it is.

﴿ قُلْ إِنِّي نُهِيتُ أَنْ أَعْبُدَ ٱلَّذِينَ تَدْعُونَ مِن دُونِ ٱللَّهِ لَمَّا جَآءَنِيَ ٱلْبَيِّنَتُ مِن رَّبِّي وَأُمِرْتُ أَنْ أُسْلِمَ لِرَبِّ ٱلْعَٰلَمِينَ ۝ هُوَ ٱلَّذِى خَلَقَكُم مِّن تُرَابٍ ثُمَّ مِن نُّطْفَةٍ ثُمَّ مِنْ عَلَقَةٍ ثُمَّ يُخْرِجُكُمْ طِفْلًا ثُمَّ لِتَبْلُغُوٓا۟ أَشُدَّكُمْ ثُمَّ لِتَكُونُوا۟ شُيُوخًا وَمِنكُم مَّن يُتَوَفَّىٰ مِن قَبْلُ وَلِتَبْلُغُوٓا۟ أَجَلًا مُّسَمًّى وَلَعَلَّكُمْ تَعْقِلُونَ ۝ هُوَ ٱلَّذِى يُحْىِۦ وَيُمِيتُ فَإِذَا قَضَىٰٓ أَمْرًا فَإِنَّمَا يَقُولُ لَهُۥ كُن فَيَكُونُ ۝

---

a These verses point to the phenomena of nature which exist so that man may reflect. In other words, these phenomena exist so that man may give them deep consideration and may uncover their hidden meaning.

The conversion of lifeless matter into living objects; the development of the human being in a gradual manner; man's passing through the stages of youth to old age; death of man, sometimes in old age and sometimes at a young age are events that introduce us to the various attributes of the Creator. It is revealed by these events that the Being who brought this universe into existence is the All Powerful and Wise God. He is Supreme and Dominant.

If man learns a real lesson from these facts, he will spontaneously opine that it is the one and only God who deserves to be worshipped. This picture of the Universe implicitly contradicts all the false gods set up by man instead of the real God.

⁶⁹ Do you not see how those who dispute God's signs, are turned away from the right path—⁷⁰ those who reject the Book and that with which We sent Our messengers shall soon know—⁷¹ when, with iron collars and chains around their necks, they are dragged ⁷² into the boiling water and then are thrown into the Fire, ⁷³ and then they will be asked, 'Where are those whom you associated [with God]?' ⁷⁴ They will say, 'They have been lost to us; nay, we did not invoke anything before [that had real existence].' Thus God leaves the deniers of the truth to stray; ⁷⁵ that is because you exulted in the land without justification and because you behaved insolently. ⁷⁶ Enter the gates of Hell to stay therein forever. The abode of the arrogant is evil.ᵃ

أَلَمْ تَرَ إِلَى ٱلَّذِينَ يُجَٰدِلُونَ فِىٓ ءَايَٰتِ ٱللَّهِ أَنَّىٰ يُصْرَفُونَ ۝ ٱلَّذِينَ كَذَّبُوا۟ بِٱلْكِتَٰبِ وَبِمَآ أَرْسَلْنَا بِهِۦ رُسُلَنَا فَسَوْفَ يَعْلَمُونَ ۝ إِذِ ٱلْأَغْلَٰلُ فِىٓ أَعْنَٰقِهِمْ وَٱلسَّلَٰسِلُ يُسْحَبُونَ ۝ فِى ٱلْحَمِيمِ ثُمَّ فِى ٱلنَّارِ يُسْجَرُونَ ۝ ثُمَّ قِيلَ لَهُمْ أَيْنَ مَا كُنتُمْ تُشْرِكُونَ ۝ مِن دُونِ ٱللَّهِ قَالُوا۟ ضَلُّوا۟ عَنَّا بَل لَّمْ نَكُن نَّدْعُوا۟ مِن قَبْلُ شَيْـًٔا كَذَٰلِكَ يُضِلُّ ٱللَّهُ ٱلْكَٰفِرِينَ ۝ ذَٰلِكُم بِمَا كُنتُمْ تَفْرَحُونَ فِى ٱلْأَرْضِ بِغَيْرِ ٱلْحَقِّ وَبِمَا كُنتُمْ تَمْرَحُونَ ۝ ٱدْخُلُوٓا۟ أَبْوَٰبَ جَهَنَّمَ خَٰلِدِينَ فِيهَا فَبِئْسَ مَثْوَى ٱلْمُتَكَبِّرِينَ ۝

ᵃ Who were the ones who were happy with untruth and indulged in false pride? These were men who held great stature in their times. They attained some worldly elevation, which alongwith their material possessions made them arrogant and vain. Their success in worldly matters had developed in them a false impression that they were the ones who had attained success, though in actual fact they were the truly deprived people.

As the high ranking men of a society become the rejecters of the Truth, the common people also follow them and start denying the Truth. In these verses, a scene of the world Hereafter has been described, when these people will be cast into Hell to be punished for their arrogant behaviour. Their overweening pride would have ultimately dragged them to such low levels that they will find no way to uplift themselves from their position.

⁷⁷ So be patient [Prophet], for God's promise is true: whether We show you part of what We have promised them in this life, or cause you to die first, it is to Us that they will be recalled.ᵃ

فَٱصۡبِرۡ إِنَّ وَعۡدَ ٱللَّهِ حَقٌّ فَإِمَّا نُرِيَنَّكَ بَعۡضَ ٱلَّذِى نَعِدُهُمۡ أَوۡ نَتَوَفَّيَنَّكَ فَإِلَيۡنَا يُرۡجَعُونَ ۝

ᵃ God has made a promise that He will help the preachers of Truth and defeat its opponents. But the fulfilment of this promise takes place after the adoption of the way of patience. The preacher has to put up with the harassment and provocative behaviour of the other party unilaterally, until, in accordance with God's methods, the time for the fulfilment of His promise arrives.

The real punishment of the opponents of the Truth is that which is awarded to them in the Hereafter. However, in the present world also, they are given a foretaste of what is to come, although this is not necessarily done in every case.

78 Before your time We sent other messengers: of them there are some whose story We have related to you, and some whose story We have not related to you. It was not [possible] for any messenger to bring a sign except by the leave of God: but when the command of God was issued, the matter was decided in truth and justice. There and then, those who stood on falsehoods perished. *a*

وَلَقَدْ أَرْسَلْنَا رُسُلًا مِّن قَبْلِكَ مِنْهُم مَّن قَصَصْنَا عَلَيْكَ وَمِنْهُم مَّن لَّمْ نَقْصُصْ عَلَيْكَ وَمَا كَانَ لِرَسُولٍ أَن يَأْتِيَ بِآيَةٍ إِلَّا بِإِذْنِ ٱللَّهِ فَإِذَا جَآءَ أَمْرُ ٱللَّهِ قُضِيَ بِٱلْحَقِّ وَخَسِرَ هُنَالِكَ ٱلْمُبْطِلُونَ ۝

---

a Events in the lives of the previous prophets have been described in the Quran, not as historical records, but by way of admonition. So, these descriptions of prophets in the Quran are restricted to whatever is deemed necessary (by God) for the purpose of admonition.

The real mission of a prophet is only to convey the message of God to the people, with all due respect to the requirements of propriety. As far as miracles are concerned, it is entirely at God's discretion whether they are demonstrated or not.

Miracles were shown mostly to communities who were destined by God to be destroyed on account of their arrogance. So, as a last measure, by way of fulfilling the conditions of fully conveying the divine message fortified by reasoned arguments, they were also shown miracles . But the case of the community of the last Prophet of God was different. A major part of this community was finally destined to be believers. They were the people who were potentially capable of becoming the first group in history who admitted the Truth simply on the strength of arguments and, in exercise of their free will, surrendered themselves to it.

⁷⁹ It is God who provides livestock for you, some for riding and some for your food: ⁸⁰ you have other benefits in them too. You can reach any destination you wish on them: they carry you by land, as ships carry you on the sea. ⁸¹ He shows you His signs; which then of the signs of God will you deny?^{*a*}

⁸² Have they not travelled in the land to see the fate of those who went before them? They were more numerous and mightier and left greater traces of their power on the earth; yet all that they accomplished was of no avail to them.

اللَّهُ ٱلَّذِى جَعَلَ لَكُمُ ٱلْأَنْعَـٰمَ لِتَرْكَبُوا۟ مِنْهَا وَمِنْهَا تَأْكُلُونَ ۝

وَلَكُمْ فِيهَا مَنَـٰفِعُ وَلِتَبْلُغُوا۟ عَلَيْهَا حَاجَةً فِى صُدُورِكُمْ وَعَلَيْهَا وَعَلَى ٱلْفُلْكِ تُحْمَلُونَ ۝ وَيُرِيكُمْ

ءَايَـٰتِهِۦ فَأَىَّ ءَايَـٰتِ ٱللَّهِ تُنكِرُونَ ۝

أَفَلَمْ يَسِيرُوا۟ فِى ٱلْأَرْضِ فَيَنظُرُوا۟ كَيْفَ كَانَ عَـٰقِبَةُ ٱلَّذِينَ مِن قَبْلِهِمْ ۚ كَانُوٓا۟ أَكْثَرَ مِنْهُمْ وَأَشَدَّ قُوَّةً وَءَاثَارًا فِى ٱلْأَرْضِ فَمَآ أَغْنَىٰ عَنْهُم مَّا كَانُوا۟ يَكْسِبُونَ ۝

---

^{*a*} Man needs many things for the upkeep of his existence and the development of human civilization, such as food, mounts, different types of industries, means of transportation etc. All these things exist in plenty in the present world. God has created the physical world in such a way that it is subservient and capable of being used by man for meeting his requirements.

All these things are, so to say, signs from God. Though this declaration is in indirect language, it is in man's interest to understand it, because when God resorts to direct communication, it will mark the end of the period allowed for the performance of good or bad deeds and not the beginning.

83 When messengers came to them with clear signs, they revelled in whatever knowledge they had, and so they were engulfed by the very punishment they mocked: 84 but when they saw Our punishment, they said, 'We believe in God—the One God—and we reject the partners we used to associate with Him,' 85 but believing after seeing Our punishment did not benefit them at all: this is the law of God to deal with His creatures, and thus the disbelievers were the losers.ᵃ

فَلَمَّا جَآءَتْهُمْ رُسُلُهُم بِٱلْبَيِّنَٰتِ فَرِحُوا۟ بِمَا عِندَهُم مِّنَ ٱلْعِلْمِ وَحَاقَ بِهِم مَّا كَانُوا۟ بِهِۦ يَسْتَهْزِءُونَ ۝ فَلَمَّا رَأَوْا۟ بَأْسَنَا قَالُوٓا۟ ءَامَنَّا بِٱللَّهِ وَحْدَهُۥ وَكَفَرْنَا بِمَا كُنَّا بِهِۦ مُشْرِكِينَ ۝ فَلَمْ يَكُ يَنفَعُهُمْ إِيمَٰنُهُمْ لَمَّا رَأَوْا۟ بَأْسَنَا ۖ سُنَّتَ ٱللَّهِ ٱلَّتِى قَدْ خَلَتْ فِى عِبَادِهِۦ ۖ وَخَسِرَ هُنَالِكَ ٱلْكَٰفِرُونَ ۝

ᵃ Knowledge is of two kinds. One is that which enables human beings to make worldly progress. The other is that which shows the path leading to success in the Hereafter. Those who possess worldly knowledge immediately receive the substantial benefits of this knowledge in the shape of worldly progress. Whereas the result of the knowledge of the Hereafter is not immediately visible in a tangible form. That is why the possessor of this knowledge comes to be degraded by worldly people.

This difference creates a superiority complex in those who are in possession of worldly knowledge. So, when prophets appeared among such people, they considered themselves superior and the prophets inferior. So much so, that they started ridiculing the prophets. But God caused them to be destroyed in spite of all their powers and superior development. Now their remains are to be found either in the form of ruins lying above or interred deep in the earth. In this way, God Almighty has set a historical example for human beings—that the secret of permanent success lies in the knowledge of the Hereafter and not in worldly knowledge.

The prophets were initially rejected by their communities. The prophets had all the force of argument on their side, but these communities were not prepared to accept their credo. Finally, God made them aware of the reality in the language of punishment. Only then did they bow down before the truth. But this was of no avail, because only that admission of truth is desirable and useful which is arrived at on the basis of arguments. Any such admission which is made after seeing the divine punishment is worthless.

41. REVELATIONS WELL EXPOUNDED

In the name of God, the Most Gracious, the Most Merciful

¹ *Ha Mim*

² A revelation from [God], the Most Gracious, the Most Merciful—³ a Book whose revelations are well expounded, an Arabic Quran for people who possess knowledge, ⁴ proclaiming good news and a warning. Yet most of them turn away and so do not listen. ⁵ And they say, 'Our hearts are encased against that to which you call us, and there is a heaviness in our ears, and there is a barrier between us, so do as you will and so shall we.' *ᵃ*

حمٓ ۚ ﴿١﴾ تَنزِيلٌ مِّنَ ٱلرَّحْمَـٰنِ ٱلرَّحِيمِ ﴿٢﴾ كِتَـٰبٌ فُصِّلَتْ ءَايَـٰتُهُۥ قُرْءَانًا عَرَبِيًّا لِّقَوْمٍ يَعْلَمُونَ ﴿٣﴾ بَشِيرًا وَنَذِيرًا فَأَعْرَضَ أَكْثَرُهُمْ فَهُمْ لَا يَسْمَعُونَ ﴿٤﴾ وَقَالُوا۟ قُلُوبُنَا فِىٓ أَكِنَّةٍ مِّمَّا تَدْعُونَآ إِلَيْهِ وَفِىٓ ءَاذَانِنَا وَقْرٌ وَمِنۢ بَيْنِنَا وَبَيْنِكَ حِجَابٌ فَٱعْمَلْ إِنَّنَا عَـٰمِلُونَ ﴿٥﴾

ᵃ The call of a prophet is the pure call of religion. However, people mostly follow the religion of their forebears. Their thinking is dominated by their national traditions and contemporary mores. For this reason, the prophet's unadulterated religion does not fit the pattern or mould of their thought. He appears a stranger to them. This difference acts as a mental barrier between the prophet and the common people. Unable to see the prophet's call in its proper perspective, they are not prepared to accept it.

The prophet's call is in itself extremely rational. It is in itself a proof that it has come from God. But the aforesaid mental barrier proves so impregnable that a man is unable to penetrate it in order to grasp the meaning of the prophet's call. Thus God opens the doors of His Grace to man, but he does not pass through them.

⁶ Say, 'I am only a human being like yourselves. It has been revealed to me that your God is One God. So take the straight path to Him and ask His forgiveness.' Woe to those who associate others with Him, ⁷ who do not pay the *zakat*, and who deny the Hereafter. ⁸ 'The ones who believe and perform good deeds shall have a reward which will never be withheld from them.'ᵃ

قُلْ إِنَّمَا أَنَا۠ بَشَرٌ مِّثْلُكُمْ يُوحَىٰ إِلَىَّ أَنَّمَا إِلَٰهُكُمْ إِلَٰهٌ وَٰحِدٌ فَٱسْتَقِيمُوٓا۟ إِلَيْهِ وَٱسْتَغْفِرُوهُ ۗ وَوَيْلٌ لِّلْمُشْرِكِينَ ۝ ٱلَّذِينَ لَا يُؤْتُونَ ٱلزَّكَوٰةَ وَهُم بِٱلْءَاخِرَةِ هُمْ كَٰفِرُونَ ۝ إِنَّ ٱلَّذِينَ ءَامَنُوا۟ وَعَمِلُوا۟ ٱلصَّٰلِحَٰتِ لَهُمْ أَجْرٌ غَيْرُ مَمْنُونٍ ۝

ᵃ Whenever the call for Truth is issued, it takes place at the level of human beings. But people are unable to understand how it is possible for a man to speak in the language of God, and therefore they deny his message. But God communicates his message through a human being. One who cannot see beyond the humanness of the prophet and recognise the divineness of the message delivered by him, must remain deprived of God's guidance in the present world of trial.

Only that belief in the Hereafter is reliable which is accompanied by a firm belief in the oneness of God and the giving of alms for the sake of God's pleasure. One who truly finds God can never be held in thrall by the greatness of any other being. Similarly, one who truly finds God cannot prevent himself from spending his wealth for the cause of God.

'So take the straight path to Him' means 'keep your worship purely for God', i.e. your whole attention should be directed towards God; the sole object of your prayers and worship should be the one and only God; your entire thinking should become God-oriented. God's perpetual blessings will be showered on those who conduct themselves in this way.

⁹ Say, 'What! Do you indeed deny Him who created the earth in two Days [periods] and do you set up equals with Him? He is the Lord of the Universe.' ¹⁰ He placed firm mountains on the earth, and blessed it. He measured out its means of sustenance all in four Days; this is for those who ask for it. ¹¹ Then He turned to heaven when it was vapour and said to it and to the earth, 'Come willingly or unwillingly.' They both said, 'We come willingly,' ¹² and in two Days He formed seven heavens, and revealed to each heaven its functions; and We adorned the lower heaven with brilliant lamps [stars] and guarded it. That is the decree of the Almighty, the All Knowing.ᵃ

۞ قُلْ أَئِنَّكُمْ لَتَكْفُرُونَ بِٱلَّذِى خَلَقَ ٱلْأَرْضَ فِى يَوْمَيْنِ وَتَجْعَلُونَ لَهُۥٓ أَندَادًا ذَٰلِكَ رَبُّ ٱلْعَٰلَمِينَ ۝ وَجَعَلَ فِيهَا رَوَٰسِىَ مِن فَوْقِهَا وَبَٰرَكَ فِيهَا وَقَدَّرَ فِيهَآ أَقْوَٰتَهَا فِىٓ أَرْبَعَةِ أَيَّامٍ سَوَآءً لِّلسَّآئِلِينَ ۝ ثُمَّ ٱسْتَوَىٰٓ إِلَى ٱلسَّمَآءِ وَهِىَ دُخَانٌ فَقَالَ لَهَا وَلِلْأَرْضِ ٱئْتِيَا طَوْعًا أَوْ كَرْهًا قَالَتَآ أَتَيْنَا طَآئِعِينَ ۝ فَقَضَىٰهُنَّ سَبْعَ سَمَٰوَاتٍ فِى يَوْمَيْنِ وَأَوْحَىٰ فِى كُلِّ سَمَآءٍ أَمْرَهَا وَزَيَّنَّا ٱلسَّمَآءَ ٱلدُّنْيَا بِمَصَٰبِيحَ وَحِفْظًا ذَٰلِكَ تَقْدِيرُ ٱلْعَزِيزِ ٱلْعَلِيمِ ۝

ᵃ A study of the universe reveals that its creation has been effected gradually in a phased manner. Creation in this way—in other words by stages, means planned creation; and when the creation of the universe has been so carried out, it essentially follows that it has a Planner who has purposefully created it according to a set plan.

Similarly, there are mountains on this earth at various places that maintain the balance of the earth. There are millions of species of living organisms on this earth and every species requires different types of sustenance, which are found in its habitat. Similarly, a study of the universe also shows that initially all things were in the shape of divided atoms. Then they combined to form different entities. It is further evident from such a study that all the things in this immense universe are uniformly governed by the laws of nature.

These observations clearly establish that the Creator of the universe is all-knowing and all-aware. He is all-powerful and dominant. So, who else can be there whom a man can treat as being worthy of worship?

13 If they turn away, then say, 'I warn you of a lightning-bolt like the one which struck the 'Ad and the Thamud: 14 when the messengers came to them from before them and behind them, saying, "Worship none but God!" They said, "If our Lord had willed, He would have sent down angels [to us]. Therefore, we shall never believe in your message."' a

فَإِنْ أَعْرَضُوا فَقُلْ أَنذَرْتُكُمْ صَعِقَةً مِّثْلَ صَعِقَةِ عَادٍ وَثَمُودَ ۝ إِذْ جَآءَتْهُمُ ٱلرُّسُلُ مِنۢ بَيْنِ أَيْدِيهِمْ وَمِنْ خَلْفِهِمْ أَلَّا تَعْبُدُوٓا إِلَّا ٱللَّهَ قَالُوا لَوْ شَآءَ رَبُّنَا لَأَنزَلَ مَلَٰٓئِكَةً فَإِنَّا بِمَآ أُرْسِلْتُم بِهِۦ كَٰفِرُونَ ۝

---

a Rejection of the call for Truth is the greatest crime in the eyes of God. If this rejection is of a call given by a prophet, the punishment for this starts right here in this world, just as happened in the case of the communities of 'Ad and Thamud.

The main point of the call for Truth has always been that man should become a worshipper of God. He should associate with the one and only God his feelings of fear and love. But in every age it has happened that the contemporaries of the Prophet opined that his personality was too unimpressive to have been chosen by God as His messenger. Therefore, they refused to accept his words.

¹⁵ As for the tribe of 'Ad, they behaved arrogantly in the land without any justification and said, 'Who is mightier than we in power?' Did they not see that God, who created them, was mightier than they in power? Still they continued to deny Our signs, ¹⁶ so We let loose upon them a raging wind over several inauspicious days, so that We might make them taste the torment of humiliation in the life of this world, and surely the torment of the Hereafter will be more humiliating. They shall have none to help them. ¹⁷ As for the Thamud We offered them Our guidance, but they preferred blindness to guidance. So the lightning-bolt of the punishment of humiliation seized them on account of their misdeeds. ¹⁸ We saved those who had attained to faith and were God-fearing.ᵃ

فَأَمَّا عَادٌ فَٱسْتَكْبَرُوا۟ فِى ٱلْأَرْضِ بِغَيْرِ ٱلْحَقِّ وَقَالُوا۟ مَنْ أَشَدُّ مِنَّا قُوَّةً أَوَلَمْ يَرَوْا۟ أَنَّ ٱللَّهَ ٱلَّذِى خَلَقَهُمْ هُوَ أَشَدُّ مِنْهُمْ قُوَّةً وَكَانُوا۟ بِـَٔايَٰتِنَا يَجْحَدُونَ ۝ فَأَرْسَلْنَا عَلَيْهِمْ رِيحًا صَرْصَرًا فِىٓ أَيَّامٍ نَّحِسَاتٍ لِّنُذِيقَهُمْ عَذَابَ ٱلْخِزْىِ فِى ٱلْحَيَوٰةِ ٱلدُّنْيَا وَلَعَذَابُ ٱلْءَاخِرَةِ أَخْزَىٰ وَهُمْ لَا يُنصَرُونَ ۝ وَأَمَّا ثَمُودُ فَهَدَيْنَٰهُمْ فَٱسْتَحَبُّوا۟ ٱلْعَمَىٰ عَلَى ٱلْهُدَىٰ فَأَخَذَتْهُمْ صَٰعِقَةُ ٱلْعَذَابِ ٱلْهُونِ بِمَا كَانُوا۟ يَكْسِبُونَ ۝ وَنَجَّيْنَا ٱلَّذِينَ ءَامَنُوا۟ وَكَانُوا۟ يَتَّقُونَ ۝

ᵃ Man is living in a world where the vastness of heaven and earth negates the greatness of man; where the event of death proves that man is a non-entity and truly powerless. In spite of this, man poses as being great and harbours no doubts of his power.

God, time and again, causes the Truth to be revealed and declared, thus disproving man's claim to greatness. But man does not learn a lesson until he is destroyed. The ruins of the 'Ad, Thamud and other communities are concrete examples of the results of human folly. The very days that these peoples considered auspicious became the very reverse at the behest of the Almighty.

Here 'inauspicious days' means winter, for the Arabs called winter inauspicious.

¹⁹ On the Day that the enemies of God shall be gathered together and driven to the Fire, they shall be formed into groups, and ²⁰ when they come close to it, their ears, eyes and skins will testify against them for their misdeeds. ²¹ And they will ask their skins, 'Why did you bear witness against us?' and their skins will reply, 'God, who gives speech to all things, has given speech to us [as well]—it was He who created you in the first instance and to Him you are [now] brought back—²² you could not hide yourselves from your ears and your eyes and your skins to prevent them from testifying against you, and you thought that God would never know much of what you did, ²³ but these thoughts which you entertained concerning your Lord, have brought you to destruction, and [now] you are among the utterly lost!' ²⁴ Even if they are patient, the Fire will still be their homes. And if they pray to be allowed to make amends, they will not be allowed to do so.ᵃ

وَيَوْمَ يُحْشَرُ أَعْدَآءُ ٱللَّهِ إِلَى ٱلنَّارِ فَهُمْ يُوزَعُونَ ۝ حَتَّىٰ إِذَا مَا جَآءُوهَا شَهِدَ عَلَيْهِمْ سَمْعُهُمْ وَأَبْصَٰرُهُمْ وَجُلُودُهُم بِمَا كَانُوا۟ يَعْمَلُونَ ۝ وَقَالُوا۟ لِجُلُودِهِمْ لِمَ شَهِدتُّمْ عَلَيْنَا قَالُوٓا۟ أَنطَقَنَا ٱللَّهُ ٱلَّذِىٓ أَنطَقَ كُلَّ شَىْءٍ وَهُوَ خَلَقَكُمْ أَوَّلَ مَرَّةٍ وَإِلَيْهِ تُرْجَعُونَ ۝ وَمَا كُنتُمْ تَسْتَتِرُونَ أَن يَشْهَدَ عَلَيْكُمْ سَمْعُكُمْ وَلَآ أَبْصَٰرُكُمْ وَلَا جُلُودُكُمْ وَلَٰكِن ظَنَنتُمْ أَنَّ ٱللَّهَ لَا يَعْلَمُ كَثِيرًا مِّمَّا تَعْمَلُونَ ۝ وَذَٰلِكُمْ ظَنُّكُمُ ٱلَّذِى ظَنَنتُم بِرَبِّكُمْ أَرْدَىٰكُمْ فَأَصْبَحْتُم مِّنَ ٱلْخَٰسِرِينَ ۝ فَإِن يَصْبِرُوا۟ فَٱلنَّارُ مَثْوًى لَّهُمْ وَإِن يَسْتَعْتِبُوا۟ فَمَا هُم مِّنَ ٱلْمُعْتَبِينَ ۝

ᵃ It is stated in the Quran that on the Day of Judgement a man's skin, ears, eyes and limbs will testify to his deeds. The theory of 'skin speech' of modern times has established the feasibility of such a happening. It has now been discovered that every utterance a man makes is recorded on the skin of his body and that it can be heard once again, just like a voice recorded by mechanical devices. Since God is not visible, man carries the impression that God does not see him. This misunderstanding gives rise to arrogance in man. But if a man realises that he is being observed by God at all times, his whole behaviour will change.

In the Hereafter, when he finally stands before God, man will express sentiments of obedience, but this will be of no avail, because obedience or submission has value or credibility only if it is practised at the 'unseen stage' and not after reality has been unveiled for all to see.

25 We assigned to them companions who made their doings appear fair to them. But the same decree [of punishment] proved true against them, which had proved true against nations of jinn and mankind who passed away before them. Surely they were the losers.[a]

وَقَيَّضْنَا لَهُمْ قُرَنَاءَ فَزَيَّنُوا لَهُم مَّا بَيْنَ أَيْدِيهِمْ وَمَا خَلْفَهُمْ وَحَقَّ عَلَيْهِمُ الْقَوْلُ فِي أُمَمٍ قَدْ خَلَتْ مِن قَبْلِهِم مِّنَ الْجِنِّ وَالْإِنسِ إِنَّهُمْ كَانُوا خَاسِرِينَ ۝

---

[a] In the present world, on the one hand, there are preachers of God who advise or instruct a man about the Truth. On the other hand, there are leaders who exploit people by making such speeches as please them. Those who pay no heed to God's advice fall a prey to leaders' smooth talks and without stopping to think, rush headlong to perdition.

Those who are deceived by the false utterances of such leaders and rush after them cannot but end by being destroyed forever.

²⁶ Those who deny the truth say, 'Do not listen to this Quran. Drown it out with noise, so that you may gain the upper hand.' ²⁷ Therefore, We will most certainly make those who are bent on denying the truth taste a severe punishment and We will most certainly requite them according to the worst of their deeds—²⁸ that is the reward of the enemies of God—the Fire will be their everlasting home, a reward for their rejection of Our revelations.[a]

وَقَالَ ٱلَّذِينَ كَفَرُوا۟ لَا تَسْمَعُوا۟ لِهَٰذَا ٱلْقُرْءَانِ وَٱلْغَوْا۟ فِيهِ لَعَلَّكُمْ تَغْلِبُونَ ۝

فَلَنُذِيقَنَّ ٱلَّذِينَ كَفَرُوا۟ عَذَابًا شَدِيدًا وَلَنَجْزِيَنَّهُمْ أَسْوَأَ ٱلَّذِى كَانُوا۟ يَعْمَلُونَ ۝ ذَٰلِكَ جَزَآءُ أَعْدَآءِ ٱللَّهِ ٱلنَّارُ ۖ هُمْ فِيهَا دَارُ ٱلْخُلْدِ ۖ جَزَآءًۢ بِمَا كَانُوا۟ بِـَٔايَٰتِنَا يَجْحَدُونَ ۝

---

[a] 'Abdullah ibn 'Abbas has explained that these words mean 'to find fault', i.e. attribute defects to the Quran and the possessor of the Quran and thus alienate people from both the book and the man (*Tafsir ibn Kathir*).

There are two methods of expressing an opinion about a thing or a person—one is criticism and the other is denigration. Criticism means analysing the matter under consideration on the basis of facts. Contrary to this, denigration means desisting from presenting any arguments in connection with the matter under consideration and simply trying rather to find defects in it, cast a slur on it, thus making it the target of condemnation.

The method of criticism is the most legitimate, while the method of ferreting out or imputing defects is the way of unbelievers. Moreover, the latter method amounts to denying the signs of God; because every true argument is a sign of God. Those people who do not bow down before an argument and try to belittle it by imputing defects to it and making false allegations against it are, in fact, denying the signs of God. Such people will be treated, in the Hereafter, as deserving of the severest punishment.

²⁹ Those who deny the truth will say, 'Our Lord, show us those jinn and men who misled us and we shall trample them underfoot, so that they may be among the lowest of the low.' ³⁰ As for those who affirm, 'Our Lord is God,' and then remain steadfast, the angels will descend on them, saying, 'Have no fear and do not grieve. Rejoice in the [good news of the] Garden that you have been promised. ³¹ 'We are your companions in this life and in the Hereafter. Therein you shall have all that your souls desire, and therein you shall have all that you ask for ³² as a rich provision from One who is ever forgiving and most merciful.' ᵃ

وَقَالَ ٱلَّذِينَ كَفَرُوا۟ رَبَّنَآ أَرِنَا ٱلَّذَيْنِ أَضَلَّانَا مِنَ ٱلْجِنِّ وَٱلْإِنسِ نَجْعَلْهُمَا تَحْتَ أَقْدَامِنَا لِيَكُونَا مِنَ ٱلْأَسْفَلِينَ ۝ إِنَّ ٱلَّذِينَ قَالُوا۟ رَبُّنَا ٱللَّهُ ثُمَّ ٱسْتَقَمُوا۟ تَتَنَزَّلُ عَلَيْهِمُ ٱلْمَلَٰٓئِكَةُ أَلَّا تَخَافُوا۟ وَلَا تَحْزَنُوا۟ وَأَبْشِرُوا۟ بِٱلْجَنَّةِ ٱلَّتِي كُنتُمْ تُوعَدُونَ ۝ نَحْنُ أَوْلِيَآؤُكُمْ فِي ٱلْحَيَوٰةِ ٱلدُّنْيَا وَفِي ٱلْءَاخِرَةِ وَلَكُمْ فِيهَا مَا تَشْتَهِىٓ أَنفُسُكُمْ وَلَكُمْ فِيهَا مَا تَدَّعُونَ ۝ نُزُلًا مِّنْ غَفُورٍ رَّحِيمٍ ۝

ᵃ There are two types of human beings. One consists of those who take Satan and those who misguide others as their leaders. In the world, these people are each other's best friends. But, in the Hereafter, the position will be just the opposite. There , when the followers see that their selfish leaders have caused them to be cast into hell, they will develop an extreme hatred for these 'so-called' leaders, and will wish to have the satisfaction of degrading and dishonouring them.

The second type of human beings comprises those who will fraternize with God's angels. Such people take angels as their comrades (companions) for the period extending from this world up to the Hereafter. The angels shower godly emotions on their hearts, and in difficult times give them peace of mind. Through fine aesthetic experiences, they convey to them God's good news. Subsequently, these angels will receive them in the Hereafter and lead them to the gardens of paradise.

³³ Who speaks better than one who calls to God and does good works and says, 'I am surely of those who submit'? ³⁴ Good and evil deeds are not equal. Repel evil with what is better; then you will see that one who was once your enemy has become your dearest friend, ³⁵ but no one will be granted such goodness except those who exercise patience and self-restraint—no one is granted it save those who are truly fortunate. ³⁶ If a prompting from Satan should stir you, seek refuge with God: He is the All Hearing and the All Knowing.^a

وَمَنْ أَحْسَنُ قَوْلًا مِّمَّن دَعَآ إِلَى ٱللَّهِ وَعَمِلَ صَـٰلِحًا وَقَالَ إِنَّنِى مِنَ ٱلْمُسْلِمِينَ ۞ وَلَا تَسْتَوِى ٱلْحَسَنَةُ وَلَا ٱلسَّيِّئَةُ ٱدْفَعْ بِٱلَّتِى هِىَ أَحْسَنُ فَإِذَا ٱلَّذِى بَيْنَكَ وَبَيْنَهُۥ عَدَٰوَةٌ كَأَنَّهُۥ وَلِىٌّ حَمِيمٌ ۞ وَمَا يُلَقَّىٰهَآ إِلَّا ٱلَّذِينَ صَبَرُواْ وَمَا يُلَقَّىٰهَآ إِلَّا ذُو حَظٍّ عَظِيمٍ ۞ وَإِمَّا يَنزَغَنَّكَ مِنَ ٱلشَّيْطَـٰنِ نَزْغٌ فَٱسْتَعِذْ بِٱللَّهِ إِنَّهُۥ هُوَ ٱلسَّمِيعُ ٱلْعَلِيمُ ۞

---

^a The call of the Quran is to invite people to God. Bringing man closer to his Lord and Sustainer; making him spend his whole life in remembrance of God; developing a feeling in man that he should make the one and only God the centre of his attention—these are the real aims of the Quranic call and undoubtedly there is no call better than this.

But, only that person becomes the preacher of God who is so sincere in his call that he, first of all, accepts whatever he wants others to accept. Whatever he exhorts others to do, he should have himself started doing from the outset.

The greatest weapon of a preacher of Truth is his ability to treat people well. Even if people are not good to him, he should be good to them. He should adopt the policy of avoidance in the face of provocation or irritating behaviour and exercise patience under trying circumstances. Almighty God has made it possible for unilateral good behaviour to be immensely persuasive. The preacher of God is aware of this God-given asset, and uses it to the utmost extent, even although it may involve crushing his own feelings and killing the urge to retaliate.

Whenever a caller to Truth has the feeling within him that it is necessary for him to retaliate against a particular instance of oppression in order to prevent the enemy from becoming so bold as to commit even greater excesses, he should immediately understand that this is a satanic inducement. It is the duty of every believer and preacher of Truth to seek the protection of God from such feelings instead of acting upon them.

t Reveal

37 Among His signs are the night and the day, and the sun and the moon. Do not prostrate yourselves before the sun and the moon, but prostrate yourselves before God who created them all, if it is truly Him that you worship. 38 If they grow arrogant, [remember that] those who are with your Lord glorify Him night and day and never grow tired.[a]

وَمِنْ ءَايَـٰتِهِ ٱلَّيْلُ وَٱلنَّهَارُ وَٱلشَّمْسُ وَٱلْقَمَرُ ۚ لَا تَسْجُدُوا۟ لِلشَّمْسِ وَلَا لِلْقَمَرِ وَٱسْجُدُوا۟ لِلَّهِ ٱلَّذِى خَلَقَهُنَّ إِن كُنتُمْ إِيَّاهُ تَعْبُدُونَ ۝ فَإِنِ ٱسْتَكْبَرُوا۟ فَٱلَّذِينَ عِندَ رَبِّكَ يُسَبِّحُونَ لَهُۥ بِٱلَّيْلِ وَٱلنَّهَارِ وَهُمْ لَا يَسْـَٔمُونَ ۝

---

[a] The greatest human blunder is having regard for outward appearances. In ancient times, the sun, the moon and stars appeared quite dazzling to man, so he took them as deities and started worshipping them. In the present age, it is the glamour of the material side of civilization which appears dazzling. So, materialism has now been given the same status as was enjoyed in former times by the sun and the moon, though the sun, the moon and other phenomena are all creations of God. A man should worship the Creator and not His creations.

The arrogance of the proud is not related to the call of Truth but to the preacher giving that call. It appears to the leaders of an age that the preacher of Truth is smaller in stature than themselves and that therefore the message conveyed by him is also of lesser import.

³⁹ Among His signs is this: you see the earth dry and barren, but when We send down on it water, it stirs and swells: most surely He who gives it life is the giver of life to the dead; surely He has power over all things. ⁴⁰ Those who distort the meaning of Our message are not concealed from Us. Who is better—someone who will be thrown into the Fire or someone who will arrive in safety on the Day of Resurrection? Do as you will, He sees whatever you do.ᵃ

وَمِنْ ءَايَٰتِهِۦٓ أَنَّكَ تَرَى ٱلْأَرْضَ خَٰشِعَةً فَإِذَآ أَنزَلْنَا عَلَيْهَا ٱلْمَآءَ ٱهْتَزَّتْ وَرَبَتْ إِنَّ ٱلَّذِىٓ أَحْيَاهَا لَمُحْىِ ٱلْمَوْتَىٰٓ إِنَّهُۥ عَلَىٰ كُلِّ شَىْءٍ قَدِيرٌ ﴿٣٩﴾ إِنَّ ٱلَّذِينَ يُلْحِدُونَ فِىٓ ءَايَٰتِنَا لَا يَخْفَوْنَ عَلَيْنَآ أَفَمَن يُلْقَىٰ فِى ٱلنَّارِ خَيْرٌ أَم مَّن يَأْتِىٓ ءَامِنًا يَوْمَ ٱلْقِيَٰمَةِ ٱعْمَلُوا۟ مَا شِئْتُمْ إِنَّهُۥ بِمَا تَعْمَلُونَ بَصِيرٌ ﴿٤٠﴾

ᵃ The phenomena of rains soaking dry land and thereafter greenery sprouting from it are a regular occurence. This is an allegorical reference to an inner reality. In this way man is informed that God has made extensive and elaborate arrangements in this world to refresh and invigorate his dry existence. The soil absorbs the water and allows it to percolate downwards, making the rain water a source of revitalization for it. Similarly, if man allows God's guidance to permeate his existence, he too will become reanimated upon receiving it.

The main reason for a man's not benefitting from God's guidance is that he distorts God's message. When God's guidance comes to him, he does not take it as it is, instead he tries to ferret out some points in it which he may misrepresent. In this way, God's guidance does not become a part of his mind. It does not nourish his soul.

For those who accept God's guidance as it is, there is the reward of paradise, and for those who distort its real meaning, there is the punishment of hell.

⁴¹ Those who reject the Reminder [the Quran] when it comes to them [are the losers]—truly it is a mighty Book: ⁴² falsehood shall not reach from before or from behind. It is a revelation from the Wise, the One worthy of all praise. ⁴³ Nothing is said to you but what was said indeed to the messengers before you; surely your Lord is the Lord of forgiveness but also the Lord of painful retribution.ᵃ

إِنَّ ٱلَّذِينَ كَفَرُواْ بِٱلذِّكْرِ لَمَّا جَآءَهُمْ وَإِنَّهُۥ لَكِتَٰبٌ عَزِيزٌ ۝ لَّا يَأْتِيهِ ٱلْبَٰطِلُ مِنۢ بَيْنِ يَدَيْهِ وَلَا مِنْ خَلْفِهِۦ تَنزِيلٌ مِّنْ حَكِيمٍ حَمِيدٍ ۝ مَّا يُقَالُ لَكَ إِلَّا مَا قَدْ قِيلَ لِلرُّسُلِ مِن قَبْلِكَ إِنَّ رَبَّكَ لَذُو مَغْفِرَةٍ وَذُو عِقَابٍ أَلِيمٍ ۝

ᵃ The Quran is a book of unsurpassable greatness. The proof of its being so is that untruth cannot enter it either from the front or from behind, i.e., there is no possibility of interference with it from any side. It cannot be distorted either directly or indirectly. And this holds true now and for all time to come.

This is a very extraordinary forecast to make. In terms of the cause-and-effect system of this world, if this forecast has to come true, it is necessary that a strong community should permanently exist as the bearer of the Quran; it should not be at variance with the teachings of previous prophets; nobody should ever be able to find fault with the Quran; the evolution of knowledge should never result in contradiction of any of its statements; the vicissitudes of history should not exert any influence upon it; the language of the Quran, Arabic, should always remain a living language.

Islam's long history after the revelation of the Quran shows that, surprisingly, all these factors in its favour have strongly resisted erosion. The very convergence of these factors is quite extraordinary: there is no other book except the Quran in respect of which so many positive factors have continuously remained accumulated for so long a period as one thousand five hundred years. This is sufficient proof that the Quran is the Book of God.

The greatness of the Quran must be discovered through argument and reasoning and not by a display of power. Its greatness will be apparent on the basis of power on the Day of Judgement. But then those who did not accept God's Truth on the strength of arguments would be compelled to accept this Truth by being humbled.

44 Had We sent this as a Quran [in a language] other than Arabic, they would have said, 'Why are its verses not clearly explained? What! An Arab Prophet, and a scripture in a foreign tongue?' Say, 'It is a guide and a healing to those who believe; but for those who do not believe, there is a deafness in their ears, and a covering over their eyes: they are [as it were] being called from a very distant place.'[a]

وَلَوْ جَعَلْنَٰهُ قُرْءَانًا أَعْجَمِيًّا لَّقَالُوا۟ لَوْلَا فُصِّلَتْ ءَايَٰتُهُۥٓ ءَا۬عْجَمِىٌّ وَعَرَبِىٌّ قُلْ هُوَ لِلَّذِينَ ءَامَنُوا۟ هُدًى وَشِفَآءٌ وَٱلَّذِينَ لَا يُؤْمِنُونَ فِىٓ ءَاذَانِهِمْ وَقْرٌ وَهُوَ عَلَيْهِمْ عَمًى أُو۟لَٰٓئِكَ يُنَادَوْنَ مِن مَّكَانٍ بَعِيدٍ ۝

[a] When the Quran was revealed in the Arabic language, opponents of Islam said that this was the Prophet Muhammad's mother tongue, and therefore it was not difficult for him to write some sort of book in Arabic and present it as holy scripture. They further said that had he really been a prophet, he would have delivered discourses in a strange language with the help of God.

Non-serious and insincere people alone indulge in such talk, and such people can never be satisfied. For example, if it had happened that the prophet had approached the Arab people and started talking to them in Greek or Syriac or Persian language, the people would have had grounds for saying; 'How strange is this prophet! He says that he has come to guide the people, but he speaks in a language which is not understood by his audience.'

The fact is that only those people are able to accept the Truth who are serious about it. Those who are not serious about the Truth are unable to understand even the clearest of its points. The analogy befitting them is that of a person who is called from a very far-off place. Such a person will hear some voice, but he will be unable to make out its real sense.

⁴⁵ We gave Moses the Book, but differences were created concerning it: and had it not been for a word that had already gone forth from your Lord, the matter would have been decided between them; and certainly they are in grave doubt about it. ⁴⁶ Whoever does what is just and right, does so for his own good; and whoever does evil, does so to his own detriment: and God is never in the least unjust to His creatures.ᵃ

وَلَقَدْ ءَاتَيْنَا مُوسَى ٱلْكِتَٰبَ فَٱخْتُلِفَ فِيهِ ۚ وَلَوْلَا كَلِمَةٌ سَبَقَتْ مِن رَّبِّكَ لَقُضِيَ بَيْنَهُمْ ۚ وَإِنَّهُمْ لَفِى شَكٍّ مِّنْهُ مُرِيبٍ ۝ مَّنْ عَمِلَ صَٰلِحًا فَلِنَفْسِهِۦ ۖ وَمَنْ أَسَآءَ فَعَلَيْهَا ۗ وَمَا رَبُّكَ بِظَلَّٰمٍ لِّلْعَبِيدِ ۝

ᵃ When the Truth was revealed through previous prophets, some people accepted it while others did not. The same thing happened when the last of the prophets was raised.

Why does man give the Truth such indifferent treatment? The reason for this is the existence of the present conditions for man's trial. In the present world of trial, whenever Truth appears, a veil is attached to it which screens it from human vision. This veil, which was required to be torn asunder, is then turned into a source of doubt.

But this doubt cannot be an excuse for anybody on the Day of Judgement, because it proves that man was not serious about the issue of Truth. Man is perfectly serious in the matter of his worldly interests and therefore he tears down all the veils and discovers the reality. Similarly, if he were to become serious about his 'other-worldly' interests, he would pull down all the veils of doubt and see reality as it actually is.

47 He alone has knowledge of the Hour [of Judgment]. And no fruit emerges from its husk, nor does any female become pregnant or give birth, without His knowledge. On the Day He will call out to them, 'Where are My associates?' They will reply, 'We declare to You that none of us can bear witness to them:' 48 [the deities] they invoked before will have vanished; they will know that there is no escape.ᵃ

۞ إِلَيْهِ يُرَدُّ عِلْمُ ٱلسَّاعَةِ وَمَا تَخْرُجُ مِن ثَمَرَٰتٍ مِّنْ أَكْمَامِهَا وَمَا تَحْمِلُ مِنْ أُنثَىٰ وَلَا تَضَعُ إِلَّا بِعِلْمِهِۦ وَيَوْمَ يُنَادِيهِمْ أَيْنَ شُرَكَآءِى قَالُوٓاْ ءَاذَنَّٰكَ مَا مِنَّا مِن شَهِيدٍ ۝ وَضَلَّ عَنْهُم مَّا كَانُوا۟ يَدْعُونَ مِن قَبْلُ وَظَنُّوا۟ مَا لَهُم مِّن مَّحِيصٍ ۝

ᵃ The springing of a fruit from a tree or the emerging of a live being from the womb of a mother is in essence the same as the emergence of the world of the Hereafter from the present world.

What is fruit? It is the change of the fruitless into the fruitful. What is a human being? It is a non-human entity turning into a human being. The Hereafter, too, in fact, is the change of present existence into the Hereafter. The first type of change occurs before us every day. Then why should another, but greater change of a similar nature (i.e. the change of the present world into the world of the Hereafter) be incredible?

The Day of the Hereafter will be the day of the final appearance of realities. When that Day arrives, all false bases on which human beings had built their lives will be demolished.

⁴⁹ Man never tires of asking for the good things of life; but if evil fortune befalls him, he abandons all hope, giving himself up to despair. ⁵⁰ When We give him a taste of some of Our mercy, after some adversity has touched him, he is sure to say, 'This is my due. I do not think that the Hour is going to come. And even if I return to my Lord, He will surely reward me well.' But truly We shall tell those who deny the truth [all] that they did, and shall make them suffer a hard punishment.ᵃ

لَا يَسۡـَٔمُ ٱلۡإِنسَٰنُ مِن دُعَآءِ ٱلۡخَيۡرِ وَإِن مَّسَّهُ ٱلشَّرُّ فَيَـُٔوسٌ قَنُوطٌ ۞ وَلَئِنۡ أَذَقۡنَٰهُ رَحۡمَةً مِّنَّا مِنۢ بَعۡدِ ضَرَّآءَ مَسَّتۡهُ لَيَقُولَنَّ هَٰذَا لِي وَمَآ أَظُنُّ ٱلسَّاعَةَ قَآئِمَةً وَلَئِن رُّجِعۡتُ إِلَىٰ رَبِّيٓ إِنَّ لِي عِندَهُۥ لَلۡحُسۡنَىٰ فَلَنُنَبِّئَنَّ ٱلَّذِينَ كَفَرُواْ بِمَا عَمِلُواْ وَلَنُذِيقَنَّهُم مِّنۡ عَذَابٍ غَلِيظٍ ۞

ᵃ The moment of crisis for a man is the moment of self-discovery. So, when he is confronted with adversity, he forgets self-conceit and starts remembering God. At that time, he realises that he is the subject or servant of God and God is his Deity.

But, when God gives him relief from his trouble and blesses him with amenities, he immediately forgets his earlier position. He links the grace of God bestowed upon him with the cause-and-effect chain and considers it to be result of his own devices and abilities. He develops a perverse mentality according to which he thinks that the only life is that of this world, and that there will be no reckoning in the Court of God. Furthermore, his prosperity leads him into the misunderstanding that since he is well-off here, he will definitely be well-off in the hereafter also.

⁵¹ When We grant a blessing to a man, he turns away and draws aside, but when any evil touches him, he is full of endless prayers! ⁵² Say to them, 'Have you considered, if this Quran is really from God and you still reject it, then who could be more astray than someone who has drifted far away from the truth?' *

وَإِذَآ أَنْعَمْنَا عَلَى ٱلْإِنسَٰنِ أَعْرَضَ وَنَا بِجَانِبِهِۦ وَإِذَا مَسَّهُ ٱلشَّرُّ فَذُو دُعَآءٍ عَرِيضٍ ۝ قُلْ أَرَءَيْتُمْ إِن كَانَ مِنْ عِندِ ٱللَّهِ ثُمَّ كَفَرْتُم بِهِۦ مَنْ أَضَلُّ مِمَّنْ هُوَ فِى شِقَاقٍۭ بَعِيدٍ ۝

---

* If God's bounties are bestowed on anyone, he should take it as God's Grace and be grateful to Him. But it is man's wont to become arrogant on receiving favours. When he gets into trouble, however, he starts pleading with God to help him. But invocations made under compulsion have no value in the eyes of God. Man would be truly virtuous only if he bowed down before God in times of comfort as well as in times of trouble.

The Truth does not compel anybody: submission to it should be voluntary. So, those who do not have any compulsion to make this obeisance ignore the Truth, for in material terms, they see no harm likely to befall them for doing so.

53 We shall show them Our signs in the universe and within themselves, until it becomes clear to them that this is the Truth. Is it not enough that your Lord is the witness of all things? 54 Yet they still doubt that they will ever meet their Lord. Surely, He encompasses all things.[a]

سَنُرِيهِمْ ءَايَـٰتِنَا فِى ٱلْأَفَاقِ وَفِىٓ أَنفُسِهِمْ حَتَّىٰ يَتَبَيَّنَ لَهُمْ أَنَّهُ ٱلْحَقُّ ۗ أَوَلَمْ يَكْفِ بِرَبِّكَ أَنَّهُ عَلَىٰ كُلِّ شَىْءٍ شَهِيدٌ ۝ أَلَآ إِنَّهُمْ فِى مِرْيَةٍ مِّن لِّقَآءِ رَبِّهِمْ ۗ أَلَآ إِنَّهُۥ بِكُلِّ شَىْءٍ مُّحِيطٌۢ ۝

[a] The story of all the people inhabiting this world is the story of the present. No story is the story of the future, because nobody's future could ratify its present. In such a world it was forecast by the Quran about itself one thousand five hundred years ago that the events and facts occurring after its advent would go on testifying to the correctness of the Quran. In the ensuing ages, the Quran will not only maintain its veracity, but will become clearer and more rationally established. The Quran will always be 'the book of the hour'.

All these forecasts in respect of the Quran have proved, quite wonderfully, to be one hundred per cent correct. Academic research, historical events and revolutions throughout the ages, have all built up evidence in favour of the Quran, so much so that even non-Muslim research has borne testimony to the fact that, in view of its rare qualities, the Quran itself provides the proof of its being a Book of God. No human writing can possess such eternal qualities.

Those who do not bow down before the veracity of the Quran, in spite of this clear reality, simply prove that their audacity has made them lacking in seriousness; it is only frivolous people who can indulge in the unreasonable behaviour of not accepting reality, in spite of clear evidence in support of it.

42. MUTUAL CONSULTATION

In the name of God,
the Most Gracious, the Most Merciful

¹ *Ha Mim* ² *'Ayn Sin Qaf*
³ Thus God, the Powerful, the Wise, sends revelation to you as He did to those before you. ⁴ All that is in the heavens and earth belongs to Him: He is the Exalted, the Almighty. ⁵ The heavens are almost split asunder from above as the angels sing their Lord's praise and seek forgiveness for those on earth. God is indeed the Most Forgiving, the Most Merciful. ⁶ And [as for] those who take protectors besides Him, God is watching them and you are not a guardian over them.ᵃ

ᵃ If man were to be blessed with boundless vision, he would see with his own eyes that there is one God alone who is the Lord of the heavens and the earth in their entirety. His Power is so immense that the Universe, so to say, dreads it and bursts with fear. The angels, who are directly aware of God's omnipotence, are awe-struck and continue to recite His praises at all times. Then man will also see that God, in exercise of His special powers, selects certain individuals as His messengers and sends them directly to mankind so that they may inform all God's creatures of the truth.

Although man does not see these facts directly, he can sense them indirectly by a process of reasoning. This is man's real test. It is man's responsibility to intuitively grasp those things which are not visible to his eyes. He should be able to recognise the voice of God in the voice of the prophets and bow down before it. He should accept the Unseen reality as if he were seeing everything with his own eyes.

On the Day of Judgement, the excuse that one was not able to see the reality directly with one's own eyes, will not be acceptable because, in this world of trial, it is not at all the divine intention to show reality directly. If the divine message reaches a person fully, in the eyes of God this is sufficient to conclude the process of argumentation.

⁷ Thus We revealed to you, this Arabic Quran so that you may warn the mother of cities [Makkah] and those around it, and warn them of the Day of Gathering which is sure to come: when some group will be in the Garden, and some will be in the Fire.ᵃ

وَكَذَٰلِكَ أَوْحَيْنَآ إِلَيْكَ قُرْءَانًا عَرَبِيًّا لِّتُنذِرَ أُمَّ ٱلْقُرَىٰ وَمَنْ حَوْلَهَا وَتُنذِرَ يَوْمَ ٱلْجَمْعِ لَا رَيْبَ فِيهِ ۚ فَرِيقٌ فِى ٱلْجَنَّةِ وَفَرِيقٌ فِى ٱلسَّعِيرِ ۝

ᵃ The real aim of the prophets' call was to make the people conscious of the fact that they were going to be presented before God, after which, in accordance with their deeds, the decision in respect of some would be eternal Paradise, while in respect of others, it would be eternal Hell.

The Prophet Muhammad came into this world to make people aware of this reality. His mission fell into two parts—one direct and the other indirect. His direct mission affected Makkah and the areas surrounding it. He completed this part of the mission during his lifetime. His indirect mission through his followers is for the whole world. This mission of his, still continues and will continue till Doomsday.

The Prophet Muhammad presented his message to the Arab people in the Arabic language. After him, his followers too, as his deputies, have to fulfill their dawah responsibilities by adhering to the same principles. They are required to convey the message of Truth to every nation in its own language. Only when a nation is presented the message in its own language, will they be treated as having discharged the responsibility of conveying the message.

⁸ Had God so willed, He could have made all of them one community, but He admits into His mercy whom He wills; and the wrongdoers have neither protector, nor helper. ⁹ Have they taken for themselves protectors other than Him? But it is God who is the real Protector. He resurrects the dead, and He has power over all things. ¹⁰ In whatever you may differ, [O believers] the verdict thereon rests with God. [Say, therefore], 'Such is God, my Lord: in Him I have placed my trust, and to Him I always turn.'^a

وَلَوْ شَاءَ ٱللَّهُ لَجَعَلَهُمْ أُمَّةً وَٰحِدَةً وَلَٰكِن يُدْخِلُ مَن يَشَآءُ فِى رَحْمَتِهِۦ وَٱلظَّٰلِمُونَ مَا لَهُم مِّن وَلِىٍّ وَلَا نَصِيرٍ ۝ أَمِ ٱتَّخَذُوا۟ مِن دُونِهِۦٓ أَوْلِيَآءَ فَٱللَّهُ هُوَ ٱلْوَلِىُّ وَهُوَ يُحْىِ ٱلْمَوْتَىٰ وَهُوَ عَلَىٰ كُلِّ شَىْءٍ قَدِيرٌ ۝ وَمَا ٱخْتَلَفْتُمْ فِيهِ مِن شَىْءٍ فَحُكْمُهُۥٓ إِلَى ٱللَّهِ ذَٰلِكُمُ ٱللَّهُ رَبِّى عَلَيْهِ تَوَكَّلْتُ وَإِلَيْهِ أُنِيبُ ۝

---

^a God Almighty has provided man with extraordinary access to His Grace, such as has not been provided for any other living creature: that is the grant of discretionary power to man to adopt His guidance voluntarily, and as a consequence thereof to become entitled to exceptional rewards from Him. The choice to opt for good or bad ways is the price of this freedom. This difference is certainly undesirable, but there is no other method to pick out the person of real worth.

God has created man free, but He has made provision for the guidance of man in his inner self as well as externally through the guidance of prophets and the Book of God, so much so that if man is really serious he will never take the wrong path. This being so, those who take the wrong path, are the worst transgressors. They will in no way be held deserving of pardon by God.

In this world, there can be no final verdict in respect of the differences arising between the proponents of Truth and followers of falsehood. The position in this world is that here one can produce words in support of the latter. Here it is possible even for falsehood to be shown in the shape of Truth. But, all this is restricted solely to the arena of the present life, it is one man against another. In the life Hereafter, it will be man versus God. There, it will not be possible for anybody to hide behind beautiful words.

"Creator of the Heavens and the Earth, He has made spouses for you from among yourselves, as well as pairs of livestock by means of which He multiplies His creatures. Nothing can be compared with Him! He is the All Hearing, the All Seeing. ¹² He is in complete control of heaven and earth; He gives abundantly to whoever He wills and gives sparingly to whoever He wills. He has full knowledge of all things.ᵃ

فَاطِرُ ٱلسَّمَـٰوَٰتِ وَٱلْأَرْضِ جَعَلَ لَكُم مِّنْ أَنفُسِكُمْ أَزْوَٰجًا وَمِنَ ٱلْأَنْعَـٰمِ أَزْوَٰجًا يَذْرَؤُكُمْ فِيهِ لَيْسَ كَمِثْلِهِۦ شَىْءٌ وَهُوَ ٱلسَّمِيعُ ٱلْبَصِيرُ ۝ لَهُۥ مَقَالِيدُ ٱلسَّمَـٰوَٰتِ وَٱلْأَرْضِ يَبْسُطُ ٱلرِّزْقَ لِمَن يَشَآءُ وَيَقْدِرُ إِنَّهُۥ بِكُلِّ شَىْءٍ عَلِيمٌ ۝

ᵃ The phenomena of the heavens and the earth before us are so gigantic that it is absolutely unimaginable that they were brought into existence by any of those false gods whom the people revere and respect instead of God Almighty. Similarly, the procreative and survival mechanism installed in the inner system of human beings and animals is so intricate and complex that it cannot really be attributed to any human being or to any of the gods other than the one and All Powerful God. All these arrangements are so extraordinary that they can be legitimately and properly attributed only to that Unparalleled Being, God.

The attributes of the Creator which come to our knowledge through observation of His creations are sufficient to prove how great the Creator is. He is All Knowing and All Observing. Most High and Almighty, He possesses all powers. Whatever one receives, is due to His Grace and whatever is taken away, is taken away by Him. He is Unique. There is nobody like Him.

¹³ God has ordained for you the same religion which He enjoined on Noah, and which We have revealed to you, and which We enjoined upon Abraham and Moses and Jesus, so that you should remain steadfast in religion and not become divided in it. What you call upon the polytheists to do is hard for them; God chooses for Himself whoever He pleases and guides towards Himself those who turn to Him.ᵃ

۞ شَرَعَ لَكُم مِّنَ ٱلدِّينِ مَا وَصَّىٰ بِهِۦ نُوحًا وَٱلَّذِىٓ أَوْحَيْنَآ إِلَيْكَ وَمَا وَصَّيْنَا بِهِۦٓ إِبْرَٰهِيمَ وَمُوسَىٰ وَعِيسَىٰٓ أَنْ أَقِيمُواْ ٱلدِّينَ وَلَا تَتَفَرَّقُواْ فِيهِ كَبُرَ عَلَى ٱلْمُشْرِكِينَ مَا تَدْعُوهُمْ إِلَيْهِ ٱللَّهُ يَجْتَبِىٓ إِلَيْهِ مَن يَشَآءُ وَيَهْدِىٓ إِلَيْهِ مَن يُنِيبُ ۝

_____

ᵃ The prophets came into this world with the same religion and that is the religion of the oneness of God. But the followers of these prophets subsequently divided themselves into separate factions. The reason for this was the shift in the centre of their attention. Initially, attention was centred wholly on God: the teachings of all prophets took the form of exhorting people to worship the one and only God. That was their original religion but their followers later shifted the focus of their devotion and they became the worshippers of beings other than God.

The ancient people of Arabia were initially the followers of Abraham. But, later on, the greatness of their leaders so captured their minds that they made them the sole centre of their attention. They even made idols to represent them and started worshipping them. The Jews were the followers of Moses, but they started considering their race a special one. Their attention became so concentrated on their own race, that godly religion became for them a racial matter. They rejected the last of the prophets simply because he was not born of their race. Similarly, Christians were the followers of Jesus Christ ('Isa). But they took him to be the son of God instead of His Prophet. In this way, in the religion they later adopted, the notion of Jesus being the son of God attained the utmost importance.

What God desires for His subjects is that they should be firm in the belief of the oneness of God. The one and only God should be the centre of all their attention. This constitutes real steadfastness in religion 'din'. Any shift in this centre of attention amounts to polytheism (shirk). Whenever polytheism gains ground with the people, variations and differences immediately start making their appearance, because in the case of 'shirk', many centres of attention come into existence. In the case of 'tawhid' (unity of God), on the contrary, the centre of attention is only one— God: this creates a greater sense of unity among the faithful. ▶

¹⁴ They became divided only after knowledge had reached them, out of mutual jealousy. Had it not been for a decree already passed by your Lord, [to reprieve them] till a specified period, the matter would surely have been decided between them. Those who inherited the Book after them are indeed in grave doubt, amounting to suspicion about it.ᵃ

وَمَا تَفَرَّقُوٓا۟ إِلَّا مِنۢ بَعْدِ مَا جَآءَهُمُ ٱلْعِلْمُ بَغْيًۢا بَيْنَهُمْ ۚ وَلَوْلَا كَلِمَةٌ سَبَقَتْ مِن رَّبِّكَ إِلَىٰٓ أَجَلٍ مُّسَمًّى لَّقُضِىَ بَيْنَهُمْ ۚ وَإِنَّ ٱلَّذِينَ أُورِثُوا۟ ٱلْكِتَٰبَ مِنۢ بَعْدِهِمْ لَفِى شَكٍّ مِّنْهُ مُرِيبٍ ۝

Though the religion of the Prophet of Arabia is a preserved religion as far as its text is concerned, his followers are disparate in their beliefs and practices. People however, are free to make new things their centre of attention, to make changes in the original religion by having recourse to explanations and interpretations of the text, and in this way turn one religion, in practice, into several religions.

ᵃ To differ after being given knowledge means that, even after receiving the call for Truth, man ignores it or opposes it. Through the Prophet Muhammad, God Almighty revealed religion (din) in its pure form. This meant that all those who were desirous of God should have joined it. But, they were not prepared to join the Prophet. By remaining attached to the previous prophets, they enjoyed the position of the pious ones among the people. They thought that this was enough for them, while the fact is that when the call of the True Religion is raised it becomes compulsory on the part of all the people to demolish their biases and prejudices and join the True Religion. Those who do not do so are guilty in the eyes of God, irrespective of their being ostensibly religious.

When the call of True religion is given, some people reject it out of jealousy or a false sense of pride (bagh'i), while others stay away from it because of their doubts. This is the case of such people as have attained an elevated status in society. Acceptance of Truth by them would involve stepping down from their high positions. As they are not prepared to lower themselves, they set about belittling the call for Truth in order to justify their stand.

The common people are generally beset by doubt and hesitation. The call of the preacher of Truth appears to them weighty on the basis of argument, but at the same time they find it difficult to ignore the great ones whose imagined greatness is already impressed on their minds. This dual pressure becomes a hindrance to their reaching a final decision. The first group ignores the Truth under the influence of a false sense of pride, while the second group does not accept it under the influence of doubt. In effect, both groups thus deprive themselves of the Truth.

¹⁵ So call people to that faith and hold fast to it yourself as you are commanded, and do not be led by their desires, but say, 'I believe in the Book which God has sent down, and I am commanded to do justice between you: God is our Lord and your Lord; we are responsible for what we do and you are responsible for what you do. There is no contention between us and you. God will gather us together, for to Him we shall return.' ¹⁶ As for those who argue about God after He has been accepted, their arguments will carry no weight with their Lord, and His wrath will fall upon them. Severe punishment awaits them.ᵃ

فَلِذَٰلِكَ فَٱدْعُ وَٱسْتَقِمْ كَمَآ أُمِرْتَ وَلَا تَتَّبِعْ أَهْوَآءَهُمْ وَقُلْ ءَامَنتُ بِمَآ أَنزَلَ ٱللَّهُ مِن كِتَٰبٍ وَأُمِرْتُ لِأَعْدِلَ بَيْنَكُمُ ٱللَّهُ رَبُّنَا وَرَبُّكُمْ لَنَآ أَعْمَٰلُنَا وَلَكُمْ أَعْمَٰلُكُمْ لَا حُجَّةَ بَيْنَنَا وَبَيْنَكُمُ ٱللَّهُ يَجْمَعُ بَيْنَنَا وَإِلَيْهِ ٱلْمَصِيرُ ۝ وَٱلَّذِينَ يُحَآجُّونَ فِي ٱللَّهِ مِنۢ بَعْدِ مَا ٱسْتُجِيبَ لَهُۥ حُجَّتُهُمْ دَاحِضَةٌ عِندَ رَبِّهِمْ وَعَلَيْهِمْ غَضَبٌ وَلَهُمْ عَذَابٌ شَدِيدٌ ۝

ᵃ Here the 'Book' means the original religion which was revealed through the prophets and 'desire' (ahwa) refers to the fabrications which human beings on their own added to the original religion of Truth. The Prophet was instructed to be firm on the original religion. Even on the grounds of dawah considerations, he was forbidden to make any concessions to man-made religions. He was told that his duty was to uphold justice, i.e. to take decisions about religious differences and show what was right and what was wrong; which part was from God and which was later added to religion by way of human interpolation.

'There is no contention between us and you' means that, in spite of your quarrelling with us, we will not start quarrelling with you. In other words, even if you introduce negative tactics, we will unilaterally adhere to our positive approach. The responsibility of a dayee is simply to convey the message of Truth. All other matters are left to God.

Harassing those who have accepted the Truth and embroiling them in unnecessary wrangling is the most oppressive and unworthy practice. Those who do so run the risk of incurring the wrath of God and facing severe punishment in the Hereafter.

17 It is God who has sent down the Book with the truth and the scales of justice. What will make you realize that the Hour might well have drawn near? 18 Those who do not believe in it seek to hasten it, but those who believe in it dread it, and know it to be the truth. Those who dispute the Hour have gone far astray.^a

اللَّهُ ٱلَّذِىٓ أَنزَلَ ٱلْكِتَٰبَ بِٱلْحَقِّ وَٱلْمِيزَانَ ۗ وَمَا يُدْرِيكَ لَعَلَّ ٱلسَّاعَةَ قَرِيبٌ ۝ يَسْتَعْجِلُ بِهَا ٱلَّذِينَ لَا يُؤْمِنُونَ بِهَا ۖ وَٱلَّذِينَ ءَامَنُواْ مُشْفِقُونَ مِنْهَا وَيَعْلَمُونَ أَنَّهَا ٱلْحَقُّ ۗ أَلَآ إِنَّ ٱلَّذِينَ يُمَارُونَ فِى ٱلسَّاعَةِ لَفِى ضَلَٰلٍ بَعِيدٍ ۝

---

a Just as a balance is meant for weighing material things, so in order to weigh intangible, ethereal realities God has revealed His book. God's book is the touchstone for distinguishing the Truth and separating it from falsehood. Everything will be tested by the standards set by God's book, instead of God's book being tested by the standards of other things.

The wrong attitude adopted by the opponents of the Prophet Muhammad during his lifetime caused them to assess the book of God by the standards of their current religion, which had been based on the traditions of their community and the words and deeds of their leaders. In fact, the right approach for them would have been to judge their national traditions and the words and deeds of their leaders in the light of the book of God. They should have accepted whatever befitted the standards of the book of God and rejected all else.

This assessment has to be done in this world by human beings themselves. In the Hereafter, this task will be carried out by God Himself. He is wise who weighs himself before he is weighed on Judgement Day, because the weighing on that Day will be for the purpose of the final decision and not in order to give any further opportunity for performing compensatory deeds.

¹⁹ God is most Gracious to His creatures: He provides sustenance for whoever He wills—for He alone is the Powerful One, the Almighty. ²⁰ To him who desires a harvest in the life to come, We shall grant an increase in his harvest; whereas to him who desires [but] a harvest in this world, We [may] give something thereof—but he will have no share in [the blessings of] the life to come.^a

²¹ Do they have associate gods who have laid down for them a religion without the permission of God? Had it not been for God's decree on the final Judgement, the matter would have been decided between them. Surely the wrongdoers shall have a painful punishment.^b

اللَّهُ لَطِيفٌ بِعِبَادِهِۦ يَرْزُقُ مَن يَشَآءُ وَهُوَ الْقَوِىُّ الْعَزِيزُ ۝ مَن كَانَ يُرِيدُ حَرْثَ الْأَخِرَةِ نَزِدْ لَهُۥ فِى حَرْثِهِۦ وَمَن كَانَ يُرِيدُ حَرْثَ الدُّنْيَا نُؤْتِهِۦ مِنْهَا وَمَا لَهُۥ فِى الْأَخِرَةِ مِن نَّصِيبٍ ۝ أَمْ لَهُمْ شُرَكَٰٓؤُاْ شَرَعُواْ لَهُم مِّنَ الدِّينِ مَا لَمْ يَأْذَن بِهِ اللَّهُ وَلَوْلَا كَلِمَةُ الْفَصْلِ لَقُضِىَ بَيْنَهُمْ وَإِنَّ الظَّٰلِمِينَ لَهُمْ عَذَابٌ أَلِيمٌ ۝

^a The life of this world is for the purpose of putting man to the test. Here, he is provided for, according to the requirements of the test. Now, a man who is Hereafter-minded, will use the provision of this world to build up his life in the Hereafter and consequently, he will be blessed with abundant rewards when he enters Paradise.

Contrary to this, all the actions of the man who loves this worldly life will be performed with worldly interests in view. Such a person may receive the fruits of his efforts in the present world, but he will be completely deprived of everything in the Hereafter. When he had done nothing for the sake of Hereafter, how could he possibly be given anything in the afterlife?

^b If a man insists that something is true, in spite of the fact that it is not so proved by the book of God, it means that he is holding others equal to God. In other words, he is giving to those other than God the right to devise his religion for him.

This is a very serious matter. The fact is that the right to decide upon or formulate anything in the nature of religion (*din*) rests with the one and only God. To entrust this right to anybody other than God is obviously engaging in polytheism (ascribing partners to God), and this is absolutely unpardonable in the eyes of God.

²² You will see the wrongdoers fearful of the consequences of their deeds, which will be inescapable. Whereas, those who have believed and done righteous deeds, will be in the meadows of the Garden and shall have whatever they desire from their Lord. That will be the supreme favour. ²³ These are the glad tidings which God gives to His servants who believe and do righteous deeds. Say, 'I do not ask of you any reward for it, except [that I am inviting you to God because of] love of kinship.' Whoever earns a good deed, We shall increase its good for him; God is most forgiving, most appreciative.ᵃ

تَرَى ٱلظَّٰلِمِينَ مُشْفِقِينَ مِمَّا كَسَبُوا۟ وَهُوَ وَاقِعٌۢ بِهِمْ ۗ وَٱلَّذِينَ ءَامَنُوا۟ وَعَمِلُوا۟ ٱلصَّٰلِحَٰتِ فِى رَوْضَاتِ ٱلْجَنَّٰتِ ۖ لَهُم مَّا يَشَآءُونَ عِندَ رَبِّهِمْ ۚ ذَٰلِكَ هُوَ ٱلْفَضْلُ ٱلْكَبِيرُ ﴿٢٢﴾ ذَٰلِكَ ٱلَّذِى يُبَشِّرُ ٱللَّهُ عِبَادَهُ ٱلَّذِينَ ءَامَنُوا۟ وَعَمِلُوا۟ ٱلصَّٰلِحَٰتِ ۗ قُل لَّآ أَسْـَٔلُكُمْ عَلَيْهِ أَجْرًا إِلَّا ٱلْمَوَدَّةَ فِى ٱلْقُرْبَىٰ ۗ وَمَن يَقْتَرِفْ حَسَنَةً نَّزِدْ لَهُۥ فِيهَا حُسْنًا ۚ إِنَّ ٱللَّهَ غَفُورٌ شَكُورٌ ﴿٢٣﴾

ᵃ 'I do not ask any reward for that, except (that I am inviting you to God because) of love of kinship.' The Prophet uttered these words at a time when the people of his own tribe, the Quraysh, were putting impediments in the way of his dawah activity. Under these circumstances, the aforesaid statement was meant to convey that they might not accept the Prophet's religion, if they did not want to, but they should at least take into account their relationship with him and refrain from tormenting him. In other words, he meant to say that even if they had religious differences with him, they should maintain a proper level of politeness, decency and moral values. In this way it was indirectly established that the opponents of his call for Truth were not only his personal opponents but were also morally guilty. They proved themselves wrong according to moral standards, the importance of which was established among them too.

²⁴ Do they say, 'He has invented a lie about God'? If God so willed, He could seal your heart. God wipes out falsehood and vindicates the truth by His words. He has full knowledge of what is in men's hearts—²⁵ He accepts repentance from His servants and pardons their sins. He knows everything you do. ²⁶ He responds to those who believe and do good deeds, and gives them more of His bounty; agonizing torment awaits the deniers of the truth.ᵃ

أَمْ يَقُولُونَ ٱفْتَرَىٰ عَلَى ٱللَّهِ كَذِبًا فَإِن يَشَإِ ٱللَّهُ يَخْتِمْ عَلَىٰ قَلْبِكَ وَيَمْحُ ٱللَّهُ ٱلْبَٰطِلَ وَيُحِقُّ ٱلْحَقَّ بِكَلِمَٰتِهِۦ إِنَّهُۥ عَلِيمٌۢ بِذَاتِ ٱلصُّدُورِ ۝ وَهُوَ ٱلَّذِي يَقْبَلُ ٱلتَّوْبَةَ عَنْ عِبَادِهِۦ وَيَعْفُواْ عَنِ ٱلسَّيِّـَٔاتِ وَيَعْلَمُ مَا تَفْعَلُونَ ۝ وَيَسْتَجِيبُ ٱلَّذِينَ ءَامَنُواْ وَعَمِلُواْ ٱلصَّٰلِحَٰتِ وَيَزِيدُهُم مِّن فَضْلِهِۦ وَٱلْكَٰفِرُونَ لَهُمْ عَذَابٌ شَدِيدٌ ۝

ᵃ According to the law governing this world, Truth appears here in the form of Truth and falsehood in the form of falsehood. A false soul cannot beget Truth. For this reason it is not possible for a non-prophet to use prophetic language. If an individual is not a prophet, but by telling lies, claims to be so, then the style of the false prophet will necessarily creep into his utterances. No ordinary person can speak in the style of a true prophet.

'If God so willed, He can seal your heart' means, 'Had you made false allegations against God, your heart would have been sealed by the will of God.' Under these circumstances, by the divine laws of nature, you would have found it impossible to deliver the pure, divine discourse, the signs of which are clearly seen in your utterances. The fact is that the sublime words of the Prophet themselves prove him to be a prophet of God. Had he not really been the prophet of God, such utterances would not have fallen from his lips.

Those who oppose the Truth do so, not at the dictates of their heart or conscience, but simply out of obstinacy and hostility. Such people are, so to say, held guilty in the court of their own conscience. God's judgement of them is final, except when they repent and seek God's pardon.

²⁷ If God were to grant His abundant provision to [all] His creatures, they would act insolently on earth, but He sends down in due measure whatever He will, for He is well aware of His servants and watchful over them: ²⁸ it is He who sends rain after they have despaired and spreads His mercy far and wide. He is the Protector, Worthy of All Praise.ᵃ ²⁹ Among His signs is the creation of the heavens and earth and all the living creatures He has dispersed throughout them: He has the power to gather them all together whenever He will.ᵇ

۞ وَلَوْ بَسَطَ ٱللَّهُ ٱلرِّزْقَ لِعِبَادِهِۦ لَبَغَوْا۟ فِى ٱلْأَرْضِ وَلَٰكِن يُنَزِّلُ بِقَدَرٍ مَّا يَشَآءُ ۚ إِنَّهُۥ بِعِبَادِهِۦ خَبِيرٌۢ بَصِيرٌ ۝ وَهُوَ ٱلَّذِى يُنَزِّلُ ٱلْغَيْثَ مِنۢ بَعْدِ مَا قَنَطُوا۟ وَيَنشُرُ رَحْمَتَهُۥ ۚ وَهُوَ ٱلْوَلِىُّ ٱلْحَمِيدُ ۝ وَمِنْ ءَايَٰتِهِۦ خَلْقُ ٱلسَّمَٰوَٰتِ وَٱلْأَرْضِ وَمَا بَثَّ فِيهِمَا مِن دَآبَّةٍ ۚ وَهُوَ عَلَىٰ جَمْعِهِمْ إِذَا يَشَآءُ قَدِيرٌ ۝

ᵃ Human life on earth depends on water, but the supply of water is completely in God's hands. If God does not provide water, man cannot obtain it on his own. Similarly, the distribution of sustenance is at the will of God. While doing so, God takes into account the depth of the human soul and, according to this, allocates sustenance to everybody. If people are given greater abundance than they can deal with with equanimity, they will become obstreperous and arrogant and, as a result, oppression and disturbance will prevail everywhere on the earth.

ᵇ We observe that when a farmer scatters seeds, he also has the power to reap the harvest therefrom. This observation is indicative of the fact that God too can marshall all His dispersed creations and gather them in His Court where the future of humanity will be collectively decided. For the Creator for whom it was possible to create and spread His creations far and wide, why should it be impossible to collect and re-assemble them after death?

³⁰ Whatever misfortune befalls you is of your own doing—God forgives much—³¹ you cannot escape Him anywhere on earth. You have no protector or helper other than God.ᵃ

وَمَآ أَصَٰبَكُم مِّن مُّصِيبَةٍ فَبِمَا كَسَبَتْ أَيْدِيكُمْ وَيَعْفُواْ عَن كَثِيرٍ ۝ وَمَآ أَنتُم بِمُعْجِزِينَ فِى ٱلْأَرْضِ وَمَا لَكُم مِّن دُونِ ٱللَّهِ مِن وَلِىٍّ وَلَا نَصِيرٍ ۝

ᵃ The present world has been created and made subject to the law of cause and effect. So, if an individual is beset by adversity, it is clearly due to his own shortcomings. However, it sometimes happens that a man commits a sin, yet remains unaffected by its baneful outcome.

All these events happen in the world in order that man should learn a lesson from them. When he sees that whatever people receive is commensurate with their deeds, he should infer that, in the Hereafter also, everybody will be rewarded according to his deeds. Similarly, when he sees that somebody has been guilty of a lapse, yet goes unpunished, he should learn the lesson that God is Merciful and Gracious, and that if a man turns towards Him, He, in His Mercy, will save him from the consequences of his shortcomings. If a man's Faith is deep, he comes to the point of discerning a picture of the Hereafter in the events of this world.

³² Among His signs are the ships sailing like mountains on the sea: ³³ if He willed, He could bring the wind to a standstill and they would lie motionless on the surface of the sea—truly there are signs in this for anyone who is steadfast and grateful—³⁴ or He may cause them to founder because of people's misdeeds—He pardons many of them—³⁵ those who dispute Our signs shall learn that they have no escape.ᵃ

وَمِنْ ءَايَٰتِهِ ٱلْجَوَارِ فِى ٱلْبَحْرِ كَٱلْأَعْلَٰمِ ۞ إِن يَشَأْ يُسْكِنِ ٱلرِّيحَ فَيَظْلَلْنَ رَوَاكِدَ عَلَىٰ ظَهْرِهِۦٓ إِنَّ فِى ذَٰلِكَ لَءَايَٰتٍ لِّكُلِّ صَبَّارٍ شَكُورٍ ۞ أَوْ يُوبِقْهُنَّ بِمَا كَسَبُوا۟ وَيَعْفُ عَن كَثِيرٍ ۞ وَيَعْلَمَ ٱلَّذِينَ يُجَٰدِلُونَ فِىٓ ءَايَٰتِنَا مَا لَهُم مِّن مَّحِيصٍ ۞

ᵃ Man sails his ships on the seas and flies his aircraft in the sky. This has become possible because God has made the laws of nature favourable to us. Had this not been so, neither would our boats have been able to sail the seas nor our planes been able to fly in the air.

Every event in life has a lesson for man in it. But if man is to derive food for thought from events, it is necessary for him to have patience and adopt a grateful attitude. One has to face many vicissitudes in life. In times of trouble, man has to rise above his circumstances, so that he may see things from different angles. And this is not possible unless one possesses the quality of patience. Similarly, in times of plenty, it is necessary for man to consider whatever he receives, apparently as a result of his own efforts, to be really the bounty of God, and this can be done only by one who has developed in himself that high degree of consciousness which is known as gratitude.

When in an event divine guidance is made manifest, and even then man does not accept it and tries to impute a different meaning to it, this in fact amounts to 'raising disputes over God's signs.' Those who do so are arrogant in the eyes of God. Such arrogant, rebellious people cannot receive God's blessing in the Hereafter.

36 Whatever you have been given is only a temporary provision of this life, but that which is with God is better and more lasting for those who believe and put their trust in their Lord;*a* 37 who refrain from heinous sins and gross indecencies; who forgive when they are angry; 38 who respond to their Lord and attend to their prayers; who conduct their affairs by mutual consultation and spend out of what We have provided for them; 39 who, when they are attacked, defend themselves.

فَمَآ أُوتِيتُم مِّن شَىْءٍ فَمَتَـٰعُ ٱلْحَيَوٰةِ ٱلدُّنْيَا وَمَا عِندَ ٱللَّهِ خَيْرٌ وَأَبْقَىٰ لِلَّذِينَ ءَامَنُوا۟ وَعَلَىٰ رَبِّهِمْ يَتَوَكَّلُونَ ۝ وَٱلَّذِينَ يَجْتَنِبُونَ كَبَـٰٓئِرَ ٱلْإِثْمِ وَٱلْفَوَٰحِشَ وَإِذَا مَا غَضِبُوا۟ هُمْ يَغْفِرُونَ ۝ وَٱلَّذِينَ ٱسْتَجَابُوا۟ لِرَبِّهِمْ وَأَقَامُوا۟ ٱلصَّلَوٰةَ وَأَمْرُهُمْ شُورَىٰ بَيْنَهُمْ وَمِمَّا رَزَقْنَـٰهُمْ يُنفِقُونَ ۝ وَٱلَّذِينَ إِذَآ أَصَابَهُمُ ٱلْبَغْىُ هُمْ يَنتَصِرُونَ ۝

---

a Only that person who reposes faith in God can be desirous of the Hereafter. In reality, whenever a man moves in the direction of the Hereafter, it appears to him that he is in danger of losing worldly benefits. Worldly considerations seem to be slipping from his grasp. This being so, the only thing which keeps a man steady on the path of the Hereafter is his unwavering reliance on the assurances of God. He should firmly believe that whatever he is losing in this world for the sake of God, will be multiplied many times over by God in the Hereafter.

The bounty of this world is of a temporary nature, while the good things of the Hereafter are eternal and never ending. A short-lived benefit in comparison with eternal bounty carries no weight whatsoever.

⁴⁰ Let harm be requited by an equal harm. But whoever pardons and amends will find his reward with God. He does not love the wrongdoers. ⁴¹ Those who defend themselves after they have been wronged cannot be held blameworthy, ⁴² blame falls only on those who wrong men and transgress on this earth without justification—such will have a painful punishment— ⁴³ whoever is patient and forgiving, acts with great courage and resolution.ᵃ

وَجَزَٰٓؤُا۟ سَيِّئَةٍ سَيِّئَةٌ مِّثْلُهَا ۖ فَمَنْ عَفَا وَأَصْلَحَ فَأَجْرُهُۥ عَلَى ٱللَّهِ ۚ إِنَّهُۥ لَا يُحِبُّ ٱلظَّٰلِمِينَ ۝ وَلَمَنِ ٱنتَصَرَ بَعْدَ ظُلْمِهِۦ فَأُو۟لَٰٓئِكَ مَا عَلَيْهِم مِّن سَبِيلٍ ۝ إِنَّمَا ٱلسَّبِيلُ عَلَى ٱلَّذِينَ يَظْلِمُونَ ٱلنَّاسَ وَيَبْغُونَ فِى ٱلْأَرْضِ بِغَيْرِ ٱلْحَقِّ ۚ أُو۟لَٰٓئِكَ لَهُمْ عَذَابٌ أَلِيمٌ ۝ وَلَمَن صَبَرَ وَغَفَرَ إِنَّ ذَٰلِكَ لَمِنْ عَزْمِ ٱلْأُمُورِ ۝

ᵃ When a man attains Faith in the real sense, this brings about a revolution in him and a new personality emerges. The qualities of a servant of God described here are the same that develop in a man as a result of the emergence of the aforesaid Faith-oriented personality. Such a man's nature develops to the point where he is ready to give due recognition to the reality. He fully realises the godliness of God and his being the subject of God and, under the impact of this realisation, bows down before Him. When God calls him, it becomes impossible for him not to respond positively. The consciousness springing out of Faith makes him sensitive to right and wrong. He does whatever is required to be done and abstains from doing whatever should not be done.

The realisation of his real position develops in him modesty and humility, which take away the anger, the propensity to transgress and the arrogance from his temperament. This humility enables him to benefit from others' advice in collective matters and requires him to desist from taking steps simply on the basis of his personal opinion. His relationship with others is that of well-wishing and not that of obduracy and exploitation.

One so inclined is never aggressive towards others. Whenever he takes steps against others, he does so in self-defence and only to the extent necessary to stop the oppression. Even when faced with extreme provocation, he is ready to forgive people and forget the wrong they have done him.

A believer does all this under the influence of his strong Faith. And God acknowledges his virtue by confering upon him the titles of 'Courageous' and 'Firm in Determination' and admits him to the Garden of unending bounties.

⁴⁴ Anyone whom God lets go astray will thereafter have no protector whatsoever: you will see the wrongdoers, when they face the punishment, exclaiming, 'Is there no way back?' ⁴⁵ You will see them exposed to the Fire, abject in humiliation, glancing furtively at it, while those who believed will say, 'The losers are those ones who have forfeited their souls and their people on the Day of Resurrection.' Truly, the wrongdoers will remain in everlasting torment; ⁴⁶ they will have no allies to help them against God; there is no way [forward] for those whom God lets go astray.ᵃ

وَمَن يُضْلِلِ ٱللَّهُ فَمَا لَهُۥ مِن وَلِىٍّ مِّنۢ بَعْدِهِۦ ۗ وَتَرَى ٱلظَّٰلِمِينَ لَمَّا رَأَوُا۟ ٱلْعَذَابَ يَقُولُونَ هَلْ إِلَىٰ مَرَدٍّ مِّن سَبِيلٍ ۝ وَتَرَىٰهُمْ يُعْرَضُونَ عَلَيْهَا خَٰشِعِينَ مِنَ ٱلذُّلِّ يَنظُرُونَ مِن طَرْفٍ خَفِىٍّ ۗ وَقَالَ ٱلَّذِينَ ءَامَنُوٓا۟ إِنَّ ٱلْخَٰسِرِينَ ٱلَّذِينَ خَسِرُوٓا۟ أَنفُسَهُمْ وَأَهْلِيهِمْ يَوْمَ ٱلْقِيَٰمَةِ ۗ أَلَآ إِنَّ ٱلظَّٰلِمِينَ فِى عَذَابٍ مُّقِيمٍ ۝ وَمَا كَانَ لَهُم مِّنْ أَوْلِيَآءَ يَنصُرُونَهُم مِّن دُونِ ٱللَّهِ ۗ وَمَن يُضْلِلِ ٱللَّهُ فَمَا لَهُۥ مِن سَبِيلٍ ۝

ᵃ In this world, guidance is revealed through logic, this being the law of God for this world. This means that in this world only that person will benefit from guidance who proves himself capable of understanding matters by a process of reasoning. The establishing of a fact by this method is enough to make him bow down before it. Those who do not accept facts in this way, can never receive guidance in this world.

One who does not yield to reason in this world, runs the risk of being laid low by God's power in the Hereafter. But bowing down on the Day of Judgement is of no avail to anybody, because then it will serve only to humble a man and not make him entitled to a reward.

⁴⁷ Respond to your Lord before a Day arrives that will not be averted [against God's will]. You will not find any refuge from God on that Day, nor will you have [any opportunity] to deny your sins. ⁴⁸ Now if they turn away, We have not sent you [O Prophet] as their keeper: your responsibility is only to convey the message. Man is such that when We let him taste Our mercy, he exults in it, but if an evil befalls him which is his own doing, he becomes utterly ungrateful.ᵃ

ٱسْتَجِيبُواْ لِرَبِّكُم مِّن قَبْلِ أَن يَأْتِيَ يَوْمٌ لَّا مَرَدَّ لَهُۥ مِنَ ٱللَّهِ ۚ مَا لَكُم مِّن مَّلْجَإٍ يَوْمَئِذٍ وَمَا لَكُم مِّن نَّكِيرٍ ۝ فَإِنْ أَعْرَضُواْ فَمَآ أَرْسَلْنَٰكَ عَلَيْهِمْ حَفِيظًا ۖ إِنْ عَلَيْكَ إِلَّا ٱلْبَلَٰغُ ۗ وَإِنَّآ إِذَآ أَذَقْنَا ٱلْإِنسَٰنَ مِنَّا رَحْمَةً فَرِحَ بِهَا ۖ وَإِن تُصِبْهُمْ سَيِّئَةٌۢ بِمَا قَدَّمَتْ أَيْدِيهِمْ فَإِنَّ ٱلْإِنسَٰنَ كَفُورٌ ۝

ᵃ The real test of man in the present world is his ability, irrespective of the circumstances, to give a proper and correct reaction. But man does not do so. When he meets with success, he turns into a vain braggart and when he gets into trouble, he can do nothing but express negative feelings.

Such people, who are unable to respond properly to the call for Truth, are by temperament unrealistic. The correct response to the call for Truth is that man should immediately admit to its being such. But he makes it a prestige issue. He thinks that by accepting the call, he will be lowering himself before the person who gives the call. This feeling comes in the way of his acceptance of the Truth. In spite of being convinced of its veracity, he ignores the call on account of personal considerations.

⁴⁹ God has control of the heavens and the earth; He creates whatever He will—He grants female offspring to whoever He will, male to whoever He will, ⁵⁰ or both male and female, and He leaves whoever He will barren; He is all-knowing and all powerful.ᵃ

لِلَّهِ مُلْكُ ٱلسَّمَٰوَٰتِ وَٱلْأَرْضِ يَخْلُقُ مَا يَشَآءُ يَهَبُ لِمَن يَشَآءُ إِنَٰثًا وَيَهَبُ لِمَن يَشَآءُ ٱلذُّكُورَ ۞ أَوْ يُزَوِّجُهُمْ ذُكْرَانًا وَإِنَٰثًا وَيَجْعَلُ مَن يَشَآءُ عَقِيمًا إِنَّهُ عَلِيمٌ قَدِيرٌ ۞

ᵃ Religion is based on the concept that every kind of power in the universe resides in the one and only God. Apart from Him, nobody else has any powers—whether these powers relate to managing the systems of heaven and earth or granting children to a human being. Whatever a man receives is at His behest and He alone may take it away whenever He wishes.

It is only this belief about God which develops in man that right type of feeling which is known as submissiveness, and it is this attitude towards God which compels man to adopt in life that behaviour which is commanded by the divine code of conduct.

⁵¹ It is not granted to any human being that God should speak to him other than by revelation or from behind a veil, or by sending him a messenger, so that the messenger may reveal, by His command, whatsoever He will. Truly, He is exalted and wise. ⁵² We have thus revealed a Spirit to you [Prophet] by Our command: you knew neither the Scripture nor the faith, but We made it a light, guiding with it whoever We will of Our servants. You are indeed guiding to the straight path, ⁵³ the path of God, to whom belongs all that is in the heavens and on the earth. Indeed all matters return eventually to God.ᵃ

۞ وَمَا كَانَ لِبَشَرٍ أَن يُكَلِّمَهُ ٱللَّهُ إِلَّا وَحْيًا أَوْ مِن وَرَآيِٕ حِجَابٍ أَوْ يُرْسِلَ رَسُولًا فَيُوحِيَ بِإِذْنِهِۦ مَا يَشَآءُ إِنَّهُۥ عَلِيٌّ حَكِيمٌ ۞ وَكَذَٰلِكَ أَوْحَيْنَآ إِلَيْكَ رُوحًا مِّنْ أَمْرِنَا مَا كُنتَ تَدْرِى مَا ٱلْكِتَـٰبُ وَلَا ٱلْإِيمَـٰنُ وَلَـٰكِن جَعَلْنَـٰهُ نُورًا نَّهْدِى بِهِۦ مَن نَّشَآءُ مِنْ عِبَادِنَا وَإِنَّكَ لَتَهْدِىٓ إِلَىٰ صِرَٰطٍ مُّسْتَقِيمٍ ۞ صِرَٰطِ ٱللَّهِ ٱلَّذِى لَهُۥ مَا فِى ٱلسَّمَـٰوَٰتِ وَمَا فِى ٱلْأَرْضِ أَلَآ إِلَى ٱللَّهِ تَصِيرُ ٱلْأُمُورُ ۞

ᵃ In the present world, no human being can directly talk to God. Man's humble position is the hindrance to such dialogue. Therefore the revelation of God's words to the prophets was made in an indirect manner. There are many methods of indirect revelation. Examples of these are found in the lives of the various prophets.

When a scholar writes a book or a thinker delivers his discourse, he has a scholastic background which may account or offer an explanation for his later successful academic or intellectual achievement. But the case of the prophet is entirely different. A prophet's life after attaining prophethood is entirely different from what it was before that event. The present work of a common man appears to be a continuation of or stems from his past life. But, in the case of a prophet, his utterances after the attainment of prophethood are so distinct from those of the earlier period, prior to prophethood, that they cannot be accounted for or explained on the basis of his past. This is a clear indication that a prophet's words are, in reality, divine in origin and not an ordinary human discourse.

What is special about the Prophet Muhammad is that the Quran (the divine message) conveyed by him and his own personal utterances have both been preserved and still exist in their original form. If one who knows Arabic makes a comparative study of both, he will find an obvious difference between these two. The language of the Hadith (sayings of the Prophet) is clearly that of Muhammad ibn 'Abdullah, while the language of the Quran is clearly that of God.

43. ORNAMENTS OF GOLD

In the name of God,
the Most Gracious, the Most Merciful

¹ Ha Mim

² By the Book that makes things clear, ³ We have made it an Arabic Quran so that you may understand. ⁴ Truly, it is inscribed in the Original Book, in Our keeping; it is sublime and full of wisdom.[a]

---

[a] The Original Book, or the Mother of Book (*ummul kitab*), refers to the preserved tablet (*lawh mahfuz*), which is with God. On this tablet, God Almighty has an imprint of the true religion, which He requires human beings to follow. This true religion, revealed to numerous prophets in various languages, was revealed to the Last of the Prophets in Arabic. Today, it is only this Arabic Quran which represents the true religion of God. It is now the responsibility of the bearers of the Quran to have it translated into every language and make it available to all the nations of the world, so that this religion may be understood by all other people, as it was understood by the Arabs.

These sublime scriptures, being full of wisdom, are in themselves proof of their being the Book of God. The language of the Quran and its contents do justice to the Majesty of God with the utmost exactitude. Had the Quran been couched in the words of human beings, it would not have possessed the extraordinary glory which it possesses till today.

⁵ Should We withdraw the admonition from you because you are a people far gone in transgression? ⁶ We have sent many a prophet to earlier peoples ⁷ but whenever a prophet came to them, they mocked him, ⁸ so We destroyed those who were mightier than these; such was the example of the earlier peoples.ᵃ

أَفَنَضْرِبُ عَنكُمُ ٱلذِّكْرَ صَفْحًا أَن كُنتُمْ قَوْمًا مُّسْرِفِينَ ۝ وَكَمْ أَرْسَلْنَا مِن نَّبِيٍّ فِي ٱلْأَوَّلِينَ ۝ وَمَا يَأْتِيهِم مِّن نَّبِيٍّ إِلَّا كَانُوا۟ بِهِۦ يَسْتَهْزِءُونَ ۝ فَأَهْلَكْنَآ أَشَدَّ مِنْهُم بَطْشًا وَمَضَىٰ مَثَلُ ٱلْأَوَّلِينَ ۝

ᵃ Today there are countless people in the world who speak of previous prophets with reverence. In view of this, it appears very strange that these very prophets (including the Prophet Muhammad) were ridiculed and mocked by their contemporaries.

The reason for this is not that the people of those days were savage and the people of today are civilized. It is simply due to a difference in the times. Today, after the lapse of centuries, every prophet is surrounded by an aura of historical glory. So, every superficial admirer of appearances recognises the prophet. But, to his contemporaries, the prophet appeared to be an ordinary person. At that time, in order to discover and recognise the reality of the prophetic position of a prophet, a deep insight was required to discover the reality and, undoubtedly, such insight has always been very rare in this world.

However badly a preacher's addressees may treat him, he unilaterally exercises patience and carries on the work of his mission, until the day comes when God's will is made manifest on what future course he should take.

⁹ If you ask them, 'Who has created the heavens and the earth?', they will surely answer, 'The Almighty, the All Knowing One has created them.' ¹⁰ Who has made the earth a cradle for you and made thereon paths for you so that, hopefully, you may find your way ¹¹ It is He who sends water down from the sky in due measure— We revive dead land with it and likewise you will be resurrected from the grave—¹² it is He who created all living things in pairs and gave you ships to sail in and beasts to ride upon*a*

وَلَئِن سَأَلْتَهُم مَّنْ خَلَقَ ٱلسَّمَٰوَٰتِ وَٱلْأَرْضَ لَيَقُولُنَّ خَلَقَهُنَّ ٱلْعَزِيزُ ٱلْعَلِيمُ ۝ ٱلَّذِى جَعَلَ لَكُمُ ٱلْأَرْضَ مَهْدًا وَجَعَلَ لَكُمْ فِيهَا سُبُلًا لَّعَلَّكُمْ تَهْتَدُونَ ۝ وَٱلَّذِى نَزَّلَ مِنَ ٱلسَّمَآءِ مَآءً بِقَدَرٍ فَأَنشَرْنَا بِهِۦ بَلْدَةً مَّيْتًا ۚ كَذَٰلِكَ تُخْرَجُونَ ۝ وَٱلَّذِى خَلَقَ ٱلْأَزْوَٰجَ كُلَّهَا وَجَعَلَ لَكُم مِّنَ ٱلْفُلْكِ وَٱلْأَنْعَٰمِ مَا تَرْكَبُونَ ۝

---

a In every period, the majority of people have admitted, that the Creator and Lord of the Universe is God, and that it is He who has provided them with the wherewithal for the sustenance of life. To bring the Universe into existence and to make every provision for life on the earth are such gigantic tasks that it is impossible to attribute their undertaking to anyone except the one and only God.

This assertion calls for man to devote his attention to God above all; his life should be a God-oriented life. But man sets himself other goals; he places entities other than God at the centre of his attention.

Almighty God has revealed the realities through His prophets. In addition to that, He has created the world in such a way that it has become the practical illustration, or analogy of hidden realities. For instance, it is a fact that human beings will be resurrected after death—a fact shown at the level of vegetation again and again. It is seen by man every year that the land becomes dry and dead. Then there are rains and the land is again covered with lush greenery. This phenomenon points to the fact that man will be brought to life again after death.

Another special feature of the present world is that it is most wonderfully favourable to human existence. Everything here has been created in such a way that it can be used by man for his own purposes as he wishes. This blessing demands that a feeling of gratitude should develop in man. Whenever he happens to use anything in God's world, he should spontaneously bow his head before God and words of acknowledgement and prayer should fall from his lips.

¹³ so that you may sit firmly on their backs. Then once you have mounted them, remember your Lord's favour and say, 'Glory be to Him who has subjected these creatures to us; we would never on our own have subdued them. ¹⁴ And to our Lord we shall surely return.'

¹⁵ Yet they make some of His servants partners in His divinity. Man is clearly ungrateful! ¹⁶ Has He then taken daughters out of His own creation and chosen sons for you? ¹⁷ When any of them is given the news of the very thing [i.e. a female child] which he himself has ascribed to the All Merciful, his face darkens and he is filled with grief— ¹⁸ ['Do you ascribe to God] one who is brought up among ornaments and who cannot produce a cogent argument?' ¹⁹ They consider the angels—God's servants—to be female. Did they witness their creation? Their claim will be put on record and they will be questioned about it.^a

لِتَسْتَوُرا۟ عَلَىٰ ظُهُورِهِۦ ثُمَّ تَذْكُرُوا۟ نِعْمَةَ رَبِّكُمْ إِذَا ٱسْتَوَيْتُمْ عَلَيْهِ وَتَقُولُوا۟ سُبْحَٰنَ ٱلَّذِى سَخَّرَ لَنَا هَٰذَا وَمَا كُنَّا لَهُۥ مُقْرِنِينَ ۝ وَإِنَّا إِلَىٰ رَبِّنَا لَمُنقَلِبُونَ ۝ وَجَعَلُوا۟ لَهُۥ مِنْ عِبَادِهِۦ جُزْءًا إِنَّ ٱلْإِنسَٰنَ لَكَفُورٌ مُّبِينٌ ۝ أَمِ ٱتَّخَذَ مِمَّا يَخْلُقُ بَنَاتٍ وَأَصْفَىٰكُم بِٱلْبَنِينَ ۝ وَإِذَا بُشِّرَ أَحَدُهُم بِمَا ضَرَبَ لِلرَّحْمَٰنِ مَثَلًا ظَلَّ وَجْهُهُۥ مُسْوَدًّا وَهُوَ كَظِيمٌ ۝ أَوَمَن يُنَشَّؤُا۟ فِى ٱلْحِلْيَةِ وَهُوَ فِى ٱلْخِصَامِ غَيْرُ مُبِينٍ ۝ وَجَعَلُوا۟ ٱلْمَلَٰئِكَةَ ٱلَّذِينَ هُمْ عِبَٰدُ ٱلرَّحْمَٰنِ إِنَٰثًا أَشَهِدُوا۟ خَلْقَهُمْ سَتُكْتَبُ شَهَٰدَتُهُمْ وَيُسْـَٔلُونَ ۝

---

^a One way of ascribing partners to God is to assume that He can have offspring, for example, holding angels to be the daughters of God, or Christ to be the son of God, or subscribing to the theory of the unity of existence (*wahdat al-wujud*) or monism which interprets all things of the universe to be part and parcel of God. All such beliefs are baseless suppositions or flights of imagination, which are not borne out by reasoning.

Here, certain of the gender characteristics of women have been dealt with under two headings—one is that by nature she is given to self-adornment and the other is that at times of dispute she is unable to vindicate herself. These weaknesses in a woman are facts, and that is why in Islam the distribution of work is such that the responsibility for outside work lies with the men and that of inside work with the women.

²⁰ They say, 'If the All Merciful had so willed, we would not have worshipped them.' They have no knowledge of that. They are only conjecturing. ²¹ Have We given them a Book before this, to which they are holding fast? ²² No indeed! They say, 'We have found our fathers following a certain course, and we are guided by their footsteps.' ²³ Whenever We sent a messenger before you to warn a township, the affluent among them said, in the same way, 'We saw our fathers following this tradition; we are only following in their footsteps.' ²⁴ Each messenger said, 'What if I should bring you better guidance than what you found your forefathers had?' They replied, 'We reject any message you have been sent with!' ²⁵ So We wreaked Our vengeance on them: now see what was the end of those who rejected [the Truth]! ^a

وَقَالُوا لَوْ شَاءَ الرَّحْمَٰنُ مَا عَبَدْنَٰهُم ۗ مَّا لَهُم بِذَٰلِكَ مِنْ عِلْمٍ ۖ إِنْ هُمْ إِلَّا يَخْرُصُونَ ۝ أَمْ ءَاتَيْنَٰهُمْ كِتَٰبًا مِّن قَبْلِهِ فَهُم بِهِ مُسْتَمْسِكُونَ ۝ بَلْ قَالُوٓا إِنَّا وَجَدْنَآ ءَابَآءَنَا عَلَىٰٓ أُمَّةٍ وَإِنَّا عَلَىٰٓ ءَاثَٰرِهِم مُّهْتَدُونَ ۝ وَكَذَٰلِكَ مَآ أَرْسَلْنَا مِن قَبْلِكَ فِي قَرْيَةٍ مِّن نَّذِيرٍ إِلَّا قَالَ مُتْرَفُوهَآ إِنَّا وَجَدْنَآ ءَابَآءَنَا عَلَىٰٓ أُمَّةٍ وَإِنَّا عَلَىٰٓ ءَاثَٰرِهِم مُّقْتَدُونَ ۝ ۞ قَٰلَ أَوَلَوْ جِئْتُكُم بِأَهْدَىٰ مِمَّا وَجَدتُّمْ عَلَيْهِ ءَابَآءَكُمْ ۖ قَالُوٓا إِنَّا بِمَآ أُرْسِلْتُم بِهِ كَٰفِرُونَ ۝ فَٱنتَقَمْنَا مِنْهُمْ ۖ فَٱنظُرْ كَيْفَ كَانَ عَٰقِبَةُ ٱلْمُكَذِّبِينَ ۝

---

^a A man may do whatever he wants in this world, because he has ample opportunities to do so. For this reason, people harbour the misunderstanding that whatever they do must be right. They argue that, had they been wrong, they would not have achieved success by adopting the course that they did. Arguments of this kind are generally advanced by those who belong to the well-to-do class.

But this is a serious misunderstanding. In this world, indulgence in any kind of behaviour may make headway because of the freedom given to human beings during their period of trial. But in the world of the Hereafter, the testing period will be over and, therefore, this opportunity will no longer exist for anybody there.

In every age, the religion of the prophets was opposed and most of all by ancestral religion. Ancestors assume the status of the 'great' ones in the estimation of nations. As compared to them, the prophet of their own days appears lowly in stature. It therefore becomes impossible for them to renounce the religion of their great men in favour of that of a lesser mortal. But it is on account of their denial of these 'small' men that these nations have had to face horrendous punishments.

²⁶ Call to mind when Abraham said to his father and his people, 'I disown utterly that which you worship.' ²⁷ [I worship] only Him who created me, and He will certainly guide me,' ²⁸ and he left these words to endure among his descendants, so that they might return [to God]. ²⁹ Yes, I gave the good things of this life to these [men] and their fathers, until the truth came to them, and a messenger expounding things clearly, ³⁰ but when the truth came to them, they said, 'This is sorcery, and we reject it.'ᵃ

وَإِذْ قَالَ إِبْرَٰهِيمُ لِأَبِيهِ وَقَوْمِهِۦ إِنَّنِى بَرَآءٌ مِّمَّا تَعْبُدُونَ ۝ إِلَّا ٱلَّذِى فَطَرَنِى فَإِنَّهُۥ سَيَهْدِينِ ۝ وَجَعَلَهَا كَلِمَةَۢ بَاقِيَةً فِى عَقِبِهِۦ لَعَلَّهُمْ يَرْجِعُونَ ۝ بَلْ مَتَّعْتُ هَٰٓؤُلَآءِ وَءَابَآءَهُمْ حَتَّىٰ جَآءَهُمُ ٱلْحَقُّ وَرَسُولٌ مُّبِينٌ ۝ وَلَمَّا جَآءَهُمُ ٱلْحَقُّ قَالُوا۟ هَٰذَا سِحْرٌ وَإِنَّا بِهِۦ كَٰفِرُونَ ۝

ᵃ Abraham's proclamation of the Unity of God as mentioned here was made by him during the last days of his mission. This was not simply a string of words: it was the sum and substance of a great history. When he attained the age of awareness, he discovered that the only Being worth worshipping by man was God. Except for Him, all other gods were false and without foundation. He built up his life solely on the basis of this belief and preached it among his family members and the people of his community. In complete disregard of personal or other considerations, he was steadfast in this belief for a very long time, so much so that his being a believer in the one God came to define his identity. After a lifetime spent in this way, when he left his native place and repeated the above-mentioned words, they naturally left a permanent impression. His words were such that people used to remember them whenever his name was mentioned.

This strong tradition laid down by Abraham should have served as a milestone for the coming generations. But absorption in worldly interests made them neglectful of it and they became so careless and forgetful of it that in a later period, when one of God's messengers came to remind them of this past lesson, they rejected him.

³¹ They said, 'Why was this Quran not sent down to one of the great men of the two cities?' ³² Is it they who apportion the mercy of your Lord? It is We who distribute among them their livelihood in the life of this world, and raise some of them above others in rank, so that they may take one another into service; and the mercy of your Lord is better than [the wealth] which they amass. ³³ If it were not that all mankind might have become one community [of disbelievers], We could have given all those who deny the Lord of Mercy, houses with roofs of silver, silver staircases to ascend, ³⁴ and silver doors to their houses and silver couches on which to recline, ³⁵ and ornaments of gold. But all of these are but the provision of this present life; it is the life to come that the Lord reserves for those who fear Him.ᵃ

وَقَالُواْ لَوْلَا نُزِّلَ هَٰذَا ٱلْقُرْءَانُ عَلَىٰ رَجُلٍ مِّنَ ٱلْقَرْيَتَيْنِ عَظِيمٍ ۝ أَهُمْ يَقْسِمُونَ رَحْمَتَ رَبِّكَ نَحْنُ قَسَمْنَا بَيْنَهُم مَّعِيشَتَهُمْ فِى ٱلْحَيَوٰةِ ٱلدُّنْيَا وَرَفَعْنَا بَعْضَهُمْ فَوْقَ بَعْضٍ دَرَجَٰتٍ لِّيَتَّخِذَ بَعْضُهُم بَعْضًا سُخْرِيًّا وَرَحْمَتُ رَبِّكَ خَيْرٌ مِّمَّا يَجْمَعُونَ ۝ وَلَوْلَا أَن يَكُونَ ٱلنَّاسُ أُمَّةً وَٰحِدَةً لَّجَعَلْنَا لِمَن يَكْفُرُ بِٱلرَّحْمَٰنِ لِبُيُوتِهِمْ سُقُفًا مِّن فِضَّةٍ وَمَعَارِجَ عَلَيْهَا يَظْهَرُونَ ۝ وَلِبُيُوتِهِمْ أَبْوَٰبًا وَسُرُرًا عَلَيْهَا يَتَّكِئُونَ ۝ وَزُخْرُفًا وَإِن كُلُّ ذَٰلِكَ لَمَّا مَتَٰعُ ٱلْحَيَوٰةِ ٱلدُّنْيَا وَٱلْءَاخِرَةُ عِندَ رَبِّكَ لِلْمُتَّقِينَ ۝

ᵃ When the Prophet Muhammad appeared in Makkah, he seemed to the people to be an ordinary man. They opined that had God wanted to send His representative to them for their guidance, He would have selected some great renowned personality from the central townships of Arabia such as Makkah or Taif. But, this showed a narrowness in their outlook. Man is able to look simply at the present, while far-sightedness was required to understand the greatness of the Prophet Muhammad. Since the people did not possess such an outlook, they failed to understand the greatness of the Prophet Muhammad.

The reason for the Prophet Muhammad being thought of as a small man was that people did not see any material pomp and show surrounding him. But these material things have no importance in the eyes of God. The fact is, these things are so unimportant in the eyes of God that, if He wishes, He may bless people with heaps of gold and silver. But God did not do this, as people's attention would have been diverted to riches and they would not have been able to proceed to find the truth.

³⁶ As for one who turns away from the remembrance of the Gracious God, We appoint for him a devil, who will become his intimate companion. ³⁷ Devils divert men from the [right] way, while they think that they are rightly guided. ³⁸ When such a person comes to Us, he will say [to his comrade], 'If only you had been as far away from me as east is from west. What an evil comrade!' ³⁹ It will be said [to such a person], 'You have done wrong. Having partners in punishment will be of no avail to you today.'ᵃ

وَمَن يَعْشُ عَن ذِكْرِ ٱلرَّحْمَٰنِ نُقَيِّضْ لَهُۥ شَيْطَٰنًا فَهُوَ لَهُۥ قَرِينٌ ۝ وَإِنَّهُمْ لَيَصُدُّونَهُمْ عَنِ ٱلسَّبِيلِ وَيَحْسَبُونَ أَنَّهُم مُّهْتَدُونَ ۝ حَتَّىٰٓ إِذَا جَآءَنَا قَالَ يَٰلَيْتَ بَيْنِى وَبَيْنَكَ بُعْدَ ٱلْمَشْرِقَيْنِ فَبِئْسَ ٱلْقَرِينُ ۝ وَلَن يَنفَعَكُمُ ٱلْيَوْمَ إِذ ظَّلَمْتُمْ أَنَّكُمْ فِى ٱلْعَذَابِ مُشْتَرِكُونَ ۝

ᵃ Man's turning away from good advice means his rejection of reality. Divine reality comes before him with undeniable, reasoned arguments. However, in order to protect his interests, he ignores it.

One who does so makes false statements against it in order to justify his stand. This is when Satan has the opportunity to get the better of him and turn his mind in the wrong direction. Keeping the man busy with false justifications, Satan goes on assuring him that he is on the right path. The spell of deceit is broken only when the man meets his death and is produced before God for the final reckoning.

In this world, man is wont to readily make friends with anyone who supports his falsehood, but in the Hereafter, he will curse all such companions. He will then want them to stay so far away from him that he should be able neither to see their faces nor hear their voices.

⁴⁰ Can you [Prophet] make the deaf
hear? Or guide either the blind or
those who are in manifest error?
⁴¹ Even if We take you away from the
world, We shall surely take
vengeance on them ⁴² or We shall
show you what We have promised
them; for surely We have complete
power over them. ⁴³ So, hold fast to
the Book that has been revealed to
you—you are surely on the right
path—⁴⁴ it is certainly a reminder to
you and to your people and you will
soon be called to account. ⁴⁵ Ask
those of Our messengers whom We
sent before you, 'Did We ever
appoint gods to be worshipped
besides the Beneficent One?'ᵃ

أَفَأَنتَ تُسْمِعُ ٱلصُّمَّ أَوْ تَهْدِى ٱلْعُمْىَ
وَمَن كَانَ فِى ضَلَٰلٍ مُّبِينٍ ۝ فَإِمَّا نَذْهَبَنَّ بِكَ فَإِنَّا مِنْهُم
مُّنتَقِمُونَ ۝ أَوْ نُرِيَنَّكَ ٱلَّذِى
وَعَدْنَٰهُمْ فَإِنَّا عَلَيْهِم مُّقْتَدِرُونَ ۝
فَٱسْتَمْسِكْ بِٱلَّذِى أُوحِىَ إِلَيْكَ إِنَّكَ
عَلَىٰ صِرَٰطٍ مُّسْتَقِيمٍ ۝ وَإِنَّهُۥ لَذِكْرٌ
لَّكَ وَلِقَوْمِكَ وَسَوْفَ تُسْـَٔلُونَ ۝
وَسْـَٔلْ مَنْ أَرْسَلْنَا مِن قَبْلِكَ مِن رُّسُلِنَآ
أَجَعَلْنَا مِن دُونِ ٱلرَّحْمَٰنِ ءَالِهَةً
يُعْبَدُونَ ۝

ᵃ Let a man close his eyes and he will see nothing. Let him close his ears and he
will hear nothing. Let him close his mind and he will understand nothing. It is futile
to offer guidance or advice to such a person, especially if the reason he has
suspended his thinking processes is that he wants to tread the path of his desires,
for desire draws a veil over the mind which the truth cannot penetrate.
Nevertheless, the preacher of the Truth has to continue the work of his mission
at all events, irrespective of the attitude of his audience, until the last stage of the
completion of arguments is reached.

Though the preacher of Truth is a human being, Truth per se is the concern of
God. After denying the preacher of Truth, a man thinks that he has saved himself
from being affected by the Truth, but at that very moment he comes within God's
striking distance. If a man came to know of this secret, he would tremble before
ignoring the preacher of Truth, because he would realise that ignoring him
amounted to ignoring the Truth itself and ignoring the Truth amounted to ignoring
God Himself.

46 We sent Moses with Our signs to Pharaoh and his nobles. He said, 'I am the messenger of the Lord of the Universe,' 47 but when he came to them with Our signs, they ridiculed them, 48 even though each sign We showed them was greater than the previous one. We afflicted them with torment so that they might return [to the right path]. 49 They said, 'Sorcerer, call on your Lord for us, by virtue of His pledge to you: we shall certainly accept guidance,' 50 but when We relieved them of the torment, they broke their word.ᵃ

وَلَقَدْ أَرْسَلْنَا مُوسَىٰ بِـَٔايَـٰتِنَآ إِلَىٰ فِرْعَوْنَ وَمَلَإِي۟هِۦ فَقَالَ إِنِّى رَسُولُ رَبِّ ٱلْعَـٰلَمِينَ ﴿٤٦﴾ فَلَمَّا جَآءَهُم بِـَٔايَـٰتِنَآ إِذَا هُم مِّنْهَا يَضْحَكُونَ ﴿٤٧﴾ وَمَا نُرِيهِم مِّنْ ءَايَةٍ إِلَّا هِىَ أَكْبَرُ مِنْ أُخْتِهَا وَأَخَذْنَـٰهُم بِٱلْعَذَابِ لَعَلَّهُمْ يَرْجِعُونَ ﴿٤٨﴾ وَقَالُوا۟ يَـٰٓأَيُّهَ ٱلسَّاحِرُ ٱدْعُ لَنَا رَبَّكَ بِمَا عَهِدَ عِندَكَ إِنَّنَا لَمُهْتَدُونَ ﴿٤٩﴾ فَلَمَّا كَشَفْنَا عَنْهُمُ ٱلْعَذَابَ إِذَا هُمْ يَنكُثُونَ ﴿٥٠﴾

ᵃ Moses presented the message of the unity of God to Pharaoh and showed him the miracles of the rod and the shining palm of his hand. On seeing this, Pharaoh and his courtiers started making a mockery of him. The reason for this was that they did not see Moses in the context of his mission but in the shape of a personality. They saw that to all appearances he was, as compared to themselves, a person of no account. Similarly, they thought that the miracles were simply feats of magic and that such magical feats could be performed by any other magician.

This always happens in the case of preachers of the Truth. People reject the call of Truth by simply looking at the personality of the preacher of Truth. They ignore the signs of God, considering them likewise to be nothing out of the ordinary.

When Pharaoh and his companions rejected Moses, God Almighty inflicted many admonitory punishments on them, so that they might turn back to the right path. Mention is made of these in chapter seven (verses 133-135). All these punishments were sent down, and also came to an end, in answer to Moses' prayers. This was one more reason why they should have felt inclined to return to the right path, but they did not do so. The fact is that those who do not reform themselves on the strength of reasoning are not affected by warnings until the irrevocable punishment of the Hereafter finally engulfs them.

⁵¹ Pharaoh called to his people, 'My people, is the Kingdom of Egypt not mine? And these rivers that flow at my feet, are they not mine? Do you not see? ⁵² Am I not better than this contemptible man who can hardly make his meaning clear: ⁵³ and why have not armlets of gold been bestowed on him and why is there not a train of angels accompanying him?' ⁵⁴ In this way he fooled his people and they obeyed him: they were a rebellious people. ⁵⁵ Then when they provoked Our wrath, We took revenge on them and drowned every one of them. ⁵⁶ We made them a precedent, an example for later peoples.*a*

وَنَادَىٰ فِرْعَوْنُ فِي قَوْمِهِ قَالَ يَـٰقَوْمِ أَلَيْسَ لِي مُلْكُ مِصْرَ وَهَـٰذِهِ ٱلْأَنْهَـٰرُ تَجْرِى مِن تَحْتِى أَفَلَا تُبْصِرُونَ ۝ أَمْ أَنَا۠ خَيْرٌ مِّنْ هَـٰذَا ٱلَّذِى هُوَ مَهِينٌ وَلَا يَكَادُ يُبِينُ ۝ فَلَوْلَآ أُلْقِىَ عَلَيْهِ أَسْوِرَةٌ مِّن ذَهَبٍ أَوْ جَآءَ مَعَهُ ٱلْمَلَـٰٓئِكَةُ مُقْتَرِنِينَ ۝ فَٱسْتَخَفَّ قَوْمَهُۥ فَأَطَاعُوهُ إِنَّهُمْ كَانُوا۟ قَوْمًا فَـٰسِقِينَ ۝ فَلَمَّآ ءَاسَفُونَا ٱنتَقَمْنَا مِنْهُمْ فَأَغْرَقْنَـٰهُمْ أَجْمَعِينَ ۝ فَجَعَلْنَـٰهُمْ سَلَفًا وَمَثَلًا لِّلْأَخِرِينَ ۝

---

a The rejecters of Truth have always done so after looking at the ordinary position of the preacher of Truth. Pharaoh enjoyed a prominent position in Egypt. He was the ruler of the country. The canals flowing out of the River Nile did so at his behest. He was surrounded by all the paraphernalia of pomp and glory. As compared to this, Moses was to all appearances an ordinary person. Pharaoh so mislead his people by highlighting this difference, that they joined him in rejecting Moses.

Apparently, on the basis of this reasoning, Pharaoh's community supported him. But the real reason for this was the weakness of Pharaoh's community rather than the strength of his arguments. At that time, supporting Moses meant the destruction of a well-settled life; and there are very few people who have the courage to take the side of Truth when it means sacrificing their well laid plans. Ultimately, the punishment of God afflicted Pharaoh as a result of his denial of Truth and his community was not spared either.

⁵⁷ When [Jesus] the son of Mary is held up as an example, your people raise an outcry on this, ⁵⁸ saying, 'Are our gods better or him?'—they cite him only to challenge you: they are a contentious people—⁵⁹ but he was only a servant We favoured and made an example for the Children of Israel: ⁶⁰ if We had so wished, We could have appointed angels in exchange for you to succeed you on the earth. ⁶¹ He is a sign of the Hour. Have no doubt about it. But follow me. This is a straight path; ⁶² do not let Satan bar your way. He is truly your sworn enemy.ᵃ

۞ وَلَمَّا ضُرِبَ ٱبۡنُ مَرۡيَمَ مَثَلًا إِذَا قَوۡمُكَ مِنۡهُ يَصِدُّونَ ۝ وَقَالُوٓاْ ءَأَٰلِهَتُنَا خَيۡرٌ أَمۡ هُوَ مَا ضَرَبُوهُ لَكَ إِلَّا جَدَلًا بَلۡ هُمۡ قَوۡمٌ خَصِمُونَ ۝ إِنۡ هُوَ إِلَّا عَبۡدٌ أَنۡعَمۡنَا عَلَيۡهِ وَجَعَلۡنَٰهُ مَثَلًا لِّبَنِىٓ إِسۡرَٰٓءِيلَ ۝ وَلَوۡ نَشَآءُ لَجَعَلۡنَا مِنكُم مَّلَٰٓئِكَةً فِى ٱلۡأَرۡضِ يَخۡلُفُونَ ۝ وَإِنَّهُۥ لَعِلۡمٌ لِّلسَّاعَةِ فَلَا تَمۡتَرُنَّ بِهَا وَٱتَّبِعُونِ هَٰذَا صِرَٰطٌ مُّسۡتَقِيمٌ ۝ وَلَا يَصُدَّنَّكُمُ ٱلشَّيۡطَٰنُ إِنَّهُۥ لَكُمۡ عَدُوٌّ مُّبِينٌ ۝

ᵃ In this world it is possible for a man to derive a perverse meaning from every statement. For instance, the Messenger of God once said: 'Whoever is worshipped other than God has no good in him.' On hearing this, his opponents pointed out that the Christians worshipped Jesus Christ. Did it mean that Jesus Christ had no good in him? Obviously, this was only irrelevant hair-splitting, because the saying of the Prophet of God was in relation to the worshippers and not the objects of their worship. Even if it is presumed that it was in relation to the latter, it obviously meant those beings who, while unworthy of worship, acquiesced in their being deified. If a man does not take a saying in its right sense, it is possible for him to clothe it in a perverse meaning, howsoever right and proper it may be. The personality of Jesus Christ in a way resembled that of an angel. In view of this, many people made him an object of worship. But, the Messiah's angel-like persona was an example of God's creative powers and not an example of the Messiah's personal powers. The fact is that creation of this kind is not at all difficult for God. If He so wished, He might convert the entire population of the earth into angels. Even so, the angels would still just be angels; they would not become gods and worthy of worship.

Jesus Christ was blessed with the miraculous power to bring a dead man back to life. He used to bring earthen statues to life by blowing his breath into them. This was in fact a sign of God which was displayed in order to demonstrate the possibility of life after death. But the people did not learn a lesson from this; on the contrary, they treated Jesus as superhuman and started worshipping him. The signs of God appear before us in different ways. If they are treated as such, they are a tremendous source of guidance. But if they are considered something other than divine portents, they may become the cause of man's going astray. ▶

⁶³ When Jesus came with clear signs, he said, 'Now I have come to you with wisdom, in order to make clear to you some of the things about which you dispute: therefore fear God and obey me. ⁶⁴ For God, He is my Lord and your Lord: so worship Him: that is a straight path.' ⁶⁵ The various factions among them differed—woe then to those who did wrong: they will suffer the punishment of a painful Day.ᵃ

وَلَمَّا جَآءَ عِيسَىٰ بِٱلْبَيِّنَٰتِ قَالَ قَدْ جِئْتُكُم بِٱلْحِكْمَةِ وَلِأُبَيِّنَ لَكُم بَعْضَ ٱلَّذِى تَخْتَلِفُونَ فِيهِ ۖ فَٱتَّقُوا۟ ٱللَّهَ وَأَطِيعُونِ ۝ إِنَّ ٱللَّهَ هُوَ رَبِّى وَرَبُّكُمْ فَٱعْبُدُوهُ ۚ هَٰذَا صِرَٰطٌ مُّسْتَقِيمٌ ۝ فَٱخْتَلَفَ ٱلْأَحْزَابُ مِنۢ بَيْنِهِمْ ۖ فَوَيْلٌ لِّلَّذِينَ ظَلَمُوا۟ مِنْ عَذَابِ يَوْمٍ أَلِيمٍ ۝

Satan has eternally striven to prevent man from learning a lesson from the signs of God. It is at this point that man's fate will be decided on the basis of whether Satan has succeeded in overcoming man or vice-versa.

ᵃ Here 'wisdom' means the spirit of religion and 'straight path' means the upholding of the virtues that are mentioned in the verse, namely, fear and worship of God, prayer to Him and obedience to the Prophet. This is the real religion. What the Jews did at a later stage was to lose the spirit of religion and indulge in hair-splitting over the basic principles of religion.

Due to these totally contrived additions, differing sects developed among them. One sect laid stress on one controversial issue, another laid stress elsewhere. In this way, with them, one religion turned into several religions. Jesus Christ was sent to the Jews to tell them that the really important aspect of religion was its spirit and not form; and also to inform them that they would achieve salvation on following the true religion sent by God and not that religion which they had themselves devised.

Jesus told them that the real religion was based on the fear of God, and that they should become worshippers of the one and only God and follow the example of the Prophet in everyday affairs. Beyond this, whatever innumerable problems they had created by their futile discussions and hair-splitting arguments were their own self-made additions. They were advised to give up all these additions and be steadfast in their adherence to the real religion. All these exhortations made by Jesus exist in the Bible even today.

⁶⁶ Are they merely waiting for the Hour, which will come upon them suddenly and take them unawares? ⁶⁷ On that Day, friends will become each other's enemies, except the righteous—⁶⁸ 'O My servants, you need not fear this Day, nor shall you grieve'—⁶⁹ those who believed in Our revelations and surrendered themselves to Us. ⁷⁰ 'Enter the Garden rejoicing, both you and your spouses!' ⁷¹ Dishes and goblets of gold will be passed around them with all that their souls desire and their eyes delight in. 'There you will remain forever: ⁷² this is the Garden which you will inherit by virtue of your past deeds, ⁷³ and there is abundant fruit in it for you to eat.'ᵃ

هَلْ يَنظُرُونَ إِلَّا ٱلسَّاعَةَ أَن تَأْتِيَهُم بَغْتَةً وَهُمْ لَا يَشْعُرُونَ ۝ ٱلْأَخِلَّآءُ يَوْمَئِذٍ بَعْضُهُمْ لِبَعْضٍ عَدُوٌّ إِلَّا ٱلْمُتَّقِينَ ۝ يَٰعِبَادِ لَا خَوْفٌ عَلَيْكُمُ ٱلْيَوْمَ وَلَآ أَنتُمْ تَحْزَنُونَ ۝ ٱلَّذِينَ ءَامَنُوا بِـَٔايَٰتِنَا وَكَانُوا مُسْلِمِينَ ۝ ٱدْخُلُوا ٱلْجَنَّةَ أَنتُمْ وَأَزْوَٰجُكُمْ تُحْبَرُونَ ۝ يُطَافُ عَلَيْهِم بِصِحَافٍ مِّن ذَهَبٍ وَأَكْوَابٍ وَفِيهَا مَا تَشْتَهِيهِ ٱلْأَنفُسُ وَتَلَذُّ ٱلْأَعْيُنُ وَأَنتُمْ فِيهَا خَٰلِدُونَ ۝ وَتِلْكَ ٱلْجَنَّةُ ٱلَّتِى أُورِثْتُمُوهَا بِمَا كُنتُمْ تَعْمَلُونَ ۝ لَكُمْ فِيهَا فَٰكِهَةٌ كَثِيرَةٌ مِّنْهَا تَأْكُلُونَ ۝

ᵃ Man is not free. At all events, he has to humbly accept reality. If he does not defer to the reasoning of the preacher of Truth, he shall have to submit to godly power. But godly power comes into play only at the time of the Final Judgement. Therefore, doing obeisance only at that time and not before will be of no avail to anybody.

In this world, when a man adopts any course which is opposed to the Truth, he finds many friends to support him. Man becomes bolder and bolder on the strength of such friendship. But all these friends will abandon him on the Day of Judgement. On that Day, only that friendship will last which has been established on the basis of the fear of God.

A life which is dedicated to the Truth is fraught with dangers. But in the Hereafter, it will be permanently relieved of every type of fear or trouble. Only those who firmly believe in this godly assurance will remain steadfastly on the path of Truth in this world. In the life Hereafter, God will bestow on them much more than they lost in this world for His sake.

⁷⁴ As for the evil-doers, they shall endure forever the torment of Hell, ⁷⁵ from which there is no relief: they will remain there in utter despair. ⁷⁶ We have not wronged them; it was they who were the wrongdoers. ⁷⁷ They will cry, 'Master, if only your Lord would put an end to us!' But he [the angel] will answer, 'No! You are here to stay.' ⁷⁸ We have certainly brought the truth to you: but most of you have an aversion for the truth. ⁷⁹ Have they determined upon a course? Then We too are determined. ⁸⁰ Do they imagine We do not hear their secret talk and their private counsels? On the contrary, Our messengers [angels] are at their sides, recording everything.ᵃ

إِنَّ ٱلْمُجْرِمِينَ فِي عَذَابِ جَهَنَّمَ خَٰلِدُونَ ۝ لَا يُفَتَّرُ عَنْهُمْ وَهُمْ فِيهِ مُبْلِسُونَ ۝ وَمَا ظَلَمْنَٰهُمْ وَلَٰكِن كَانُوا۟ هُمُ ٱلظَّٰلِمِينَ ۝ وَنَادَوْا۟ يَٰمَٰلِكُ لِيَقْضِ عَلَيْنَا رَبُّكَ قَالَ إِنَّكُم مَّٰكِثُونَ ۝ لَقَدْ جِئْنَٰكُم بِٱلْحَقِّ وَلَٰكِنَّ أَكْثَرَكُمْ لِلْحَقِّ كَٰرِهُونَ ۝ أَمْ أَبْرَمُوٓا۟ أَمْرًا فَإِنَّا مُبْرِمُونَ ۝ أَمْ يَحْسَبُونَ أَنَّا لَا نَسْمَعُ سِرَّهُمْ وَنَجْوَىٰهُم بَلَىٰ وَرُسُلُنَا لَدَيْهِمْ يَكْتُبُونَ ۝

ᵃ Hope always alleviates feelings of distress. Man's afflictions are many, but if, as he undergoes them, he entertains the hope that his troubles will some day come to an end, that very thought infuses him with the courage to bear with things. But the scourge of Hell will be so grievous that there will be no hope of relief from it. The appeal made by the people in Hell to the angels will be an expression of their helplessness; otherwise anyone making such an appeal must know that God's decision was final and that it could not be evaded.

The descent of anybody into Hell will be entirely as a consequence of his own shortcomings. God gave man a high degree of understanding and opened up for him the paths of Truth. But man knowingly and deliberately ignored the Truth. His arrogance so increased that he became bent upon the elimination of the preacher of Truth. In view of this, how could he escape being subjected to eternal punishment?

⁸¹ Say, 'If the All Merciful had a son, I would be the first to worship him.' ⁸² But—exalted be the Lord of the heavens and earth, the Lord of the Throne—He is far above their [false] descriptions. ⁸³ So leave them alone to indulge in vain discourse and amuse themselves until they come face to face with that Day which they have been promised.ᵃ

⁸⁴ It is He who is God in heaven, and God on earth: He is the Wise One, the All Knowing; ⁸⁵ blessed be He who has sovereignty over the kingdom of the heavens and the earth and all that lies between them. He alone has knowledge of the Hour, and to Him you shall be returned.ᵇ

قُلْ إِن كَانَ لِلرَّحْمَـٰنِ وَلَدٌ فَأَنَا۠ أَوَّلُ ٱلْعَـٰبِدِينَ ۝ سُبْحَـٰنَ رَبِّ ٱلسَّمَـٰوَٰتِ وَٱلْأَرْضِ رَبِّ ٱلْعَرْشِ عَمَّا يَصِفُونَ ۝ فَذَرْهُمْ يَخُوضُوا۟ وَيَلْعَبُوا۟ حَتَّىٰ يُلَـٰقُوا۟ يَوْمَهُمُ ٱلَّذِى يُوعَدُونَ ۝ وَهُوَ ٱلَّذِى فِى ٱلسَّمَآءِ إِلَـٰهٌ وَفِى ٱلْأَرْضِ إِلَـٰهٌ وَهُوَ ٱلْحَكِيمُ ٱلْعَلِيمُ ۝ وَتَبَارَكَ ٱلَّذِى لَهُۥ مُلْكُ ٱلسَّمَـٰوَٰتِ وَٱلْأَرْضِ وَمَا بَيْنَهُمَا وَعِندَهُۥ عِلْمُ ٱلسَّاعَةِ وَإِلَيْهِ تُرْجَعُونَ ۝

ᵃ This statement indicates that the belief declared by the Prophet was considered by him to be the absolute Truth. His stand was not on the ground of national tradition or group prejudice but on that of sound reasoning. He was the preacher of that Faith: all facts corroborated its truth. It can be imagined from this that what is vital to the caller to the truth is consciousness of reality and not the blind following of national tradition.

The vast creative system of God, which is spread out in the shape of heaven and earth, indicates that its Lord is the one and only God. The extensiveness of the system of the universe rules out the possibility of there being more than one God.

ᵇ Heaven and earth are continuously at work in perfect harmony. Perfect unity of wisdom and unity of knowledge are found in them. This proves that there is only one God Who is alone running the systems of both heaven and earth.

The universe introduces us to God's unlimited power and at the same time His unlimited mercy. These facts call for man to fear God most of all, and at the same time, entertain the greatest hopes of Him. Those who prove to have this consciousness and this character in this world are the only individuals upon whom—when they reach God—He will shower His infinite Mercy.

⁸⁶ Those whom they invoke besides God have no power of intercession, only those who bear witness to the truth and they know. ⁸⁷ And if you ask them who created them, they will surely say, God. How then are they turned away? ⁸⁸ The Prophet has said, 'Lord! Truly they are a people who do not believe.' ⁸⁹ Then bear with them [O Muhammad] and say, 'Peace.' They will soon come to know.ᵃ

وَلَا يَمْلِكُ ٱلَّذِينَ يَدْعُونَ مِن دُونِهِ ٱلشَّفَٰعَةَ إِلَّا مَن شَهِدَ بِٱلْحَقِّ وَهُمْ يَعْلَمُونَ ۝ وَلَئِن سَأَلْتَهُم مَّنْ خَلَقَهُمْ لَيَقُولُنَّ ٱللَّهُ فَأَنَّىٰ يُؤْفَكُونَ ۝ وَقِيلِهِۦ يَٰرَبِّ إِنَّ هَٰٓؤُلَآءِ قَوْمٌ لَّا يُؤْمِنُونَ ۝ فَٱصْفَحْ عَنْهُمْ وَقُلْ سَلَٰمٌ فَسَوْفَ يَعْلَمُونَ ۝

ᵃ In the Hereafter, on the Day of Judgement, human beings will stand in the divine court to be judged. Some will have accepted and supported the divine message conveyed to them, while others, having rejected it, will have stood in opposition to it. Whatever their condition, and knowing full well that God is omniscient, they will ask their erstwhile contemporaries to bear witness in their favour. All to no avail. The prophets and the preachers, on the other hand will be there—just as if in a court of law—to bear witness to matters of which they have first-hand knowledge, having personally observed and experienced them. It will not be their role to intercede for or condemn their fellow men. They will simply be required to present the facts.

On the Day of Judgement, nobody will have any power to recommend or intervene on behalf of any guilty person in order to change the Divine Judgement which had to be made on the basis of the facts. God is too High and Great for anybody to venture to do this before Him.

The task relating to the call for the Truth consists purely of giving advice and guidance. Even at the last stage, when the preacher is convinced that his hearers are going to reject his words outright, he prays to God for the people. Tolerating their torture, he remains their well-wisher.

44. SMOKE

In the name of God,
the Most Gracious, the Most Merciful

¹ *Ha Mim*

² By the Book that makes things
clear, ³ surely We sent it down on a
blessed night—We have always sent
warnings—⁴ on that night every wise
decree is specified ⁵ by Our own
command—We have been sending
messages, ⁶ as a mercy from your
Lord, He hears all and knows all,
⁷ He is the Lord of heaven and earth
and all that is between them—if only
you would really believe—⁸ there is
no deity save Him: It is He who gives
both life and death—He is your
Lord, and the Lord of your
forefathers,ᵃ

ᵃ The total clarity of the Quran is in itself proof of its being the Book of God, and
this being so, its tidings and forecasts are also definitive. There is no scope for any
doubt about them.

The beginning of the revelation of the Quran took place on a particular night—
a night fixed for important godly decisions. The revelation of the Quran was not
a simple event. It resulted from a decision regarding the dawn of a new era of
history. That is why it was revealed on this specially blessed night. Primarily, the
Quran was and still is a declaration of Truth. It came into existence in order to show
the falsity of polytheism and the truth of the Unity of God. Most importantly, it
provides man with a standard by which to distinguish between truth and falsehood.
The Quran was the distinguisher among nations solely on this basis.

⁹ yet, they toy with their doubts.
¹⁰ Wait, then, for the Day when the sky brings forth plainly visible clouds of smoke. ¹¹ That will envelop the people. This will be a painful punishment. ¹² Then they will say, 'Lord, relieve us from this torment, for truly we are now believers in You.' ¹³ How can they benefit from admonition, seeing that a messenger had already come to them explaining things clearly? ¹⁴ Then they turned away from him and said, 'He is a madman, taught by others!' ¹⁵ Were We to ease the torment for a while, you would still revert to denial of the truth. ¹⁶ On the Day We inflict the direst scourge upon all sinners, We will certainly exact retribution.ᵃ

بَلْ هُمْ فِى شَكٍّ يَلْعَبُونَ ۝ فَارْتَقِبْ يَوْمَ تَأْتِى السَّمَآءُ بِدُخَانٍ مُّبِينٍ ۝ يَغْشَى النَّاسَ هَـٰذَا عَذَابٌ أَلِيمٌ ۝ رَّبَّنَا اكْشِفْ عَنَّا الْعَذَابَ إِنَّا مُؤْمِنُونَ ۝ أَنَّىٰ لَهُمُ الذِّكْرَىٰ وَقَدْ جَآءَهُمْ رَسُولٌ مُّبِينٌ ۝ ثُمَّ تَوَلَّوْا عَنْهُ وَقَالُوا مُعَلَّمٌ مَّجْنُونٌ ۝ إِنَّا كَاشِفُوا الْعَذَابِ قَلِيلاً إِنَّكُمْ عَآئِدُونَ ۝ يَوْمَ نَبْطِشُ الْبَطْشَةَ الْكُبْرَىٰ إِنَّا مُنتَقِمُونَ ۝

ᵃ The subject about which these addressees of the Quran were in doubt was not the existence of God but the oneness of God. While accepting the existence of God in a traditional manner, they continued to practise the religion of their forefathers and their leaders.

The Quran proved the beliefs of their forefathers to be baseless, but they were not ready to accept this position. On the one hand, they found themselves without supporting arguments while, on the other, they found it impossible to banish from their minds the image of the greatness of their forefathers and leaders. This dual dilemma had pushed them into the realm of doubt. The preacher of God appeared to them too small a person for them to accept, or to act on his advice to abandon their so-called great men.

Those who do not accept the Truth through persuasion expose themselves to the danger of having to accept it under threat of punishment. They may accept it in the latter instance, but at that time their acceptance will be of no avail.

¹⁷We tried the people of Pharaoh before them: a noble messenger was sent to them, ¹⁸saying, 'Hand over God's servants to me. I am a trustworthy messenger for you. ¹⁹Do not set yourselves above God: I bring you clear authority. ²⁰I have sought refuge with my Lord and your Lord lest you stone me [to death]. ²¹If you do not believe in me, at least keep away from me.' ^a

ۜ وَلَقَدْ فَتَنَّا قَبْلَهُمْ قَوْمَ فِرْعَوْنَ وَجَاءَهُمْ رَسُولٌ كَرِيمٌ ۝ أَنْ أَدُّوٓا۟ إِلَىَّ عِبَادَ ٱللَّهِ إِنِّى لَكُمْ رَسُولٌ أَمِينٌ ۝ وَأَن لَّا تَعْلُوا۟ عَلَى ٱللَّهِ إِنِّىٓ ءَاتِيكُم بِسُلْطَٰنٍ مُّبِينٍ ۝ وَإِنِّى عُذْتُ بِرَبِّى وَرَبِّكُمْ أَن تَرْجُمُونِ ۝ وَإِن لَّمْ تُؤْمِنُوا۟ لِى فَٱعْتَزِلُونِ ۝

---

^a The call for Truth is, in fact, a manifestation of God's power in the shape of reasoning. In this way, God announces Himself through human beings, while He Himself remains unseen. The divine call, therefore, becomes a trial for its addressees. The truth seekers acknowledge it and bow down before it, while those who are enamoured of appearances consider it unimportant and ignore it.

But after rejecting the call to accept the Truth, man cannot avoid facing the consequences. During the lifetime of the Prophet, these ruinous consequences became apparent in this world itself, just as had happened in the case of the Pharaoh of Egypt. Where there was no immediate evidence of such divine retribution, the deniers had to face the consequences of their actions after death.

²² Then he cried out to his Lord, 'These are sinful people.' ²³ God said, 'Set out with My servants by night, for you will certainly be pursued. ²⁴ Leave the sea behind you parted; they are a host destined to be drowned.' ²⁵ How many gardens and fountains they left behind them, ²⁶ and cornfields and splendid buildings, ²⁷ and pleasant things in which they delighted! ²⁸ Such was their end, and what had been theirs We gave to other people to inherit. ²⁹ Neither heaven nor earth wept for them, nor were they allowed any respite.^a

فَدَعَا رَبَّهُۥٓ أَنَّ هَٰٓؤُلَآءِ قَوْمٌ مُّجْرِمُونَ ۝ فَأَسْرِ بِعِبَادِى لَيْلًا إِنَّكُم مُّتَّبَعُونَ ۝ وَٱتْرُكِ ٱلْبَحْرَ رَهْوًا إِنَّهُمْ جُندٌ مُّغْرَقُونَ ۝ كَمْ تَرَكُوا۟ مِن جَنَّٰتٍ وَعُيُونٍ ۝ وَزُرُوعٍ وَمَقَامٍ كَرِيمٍ ۝ وَنَعْمَةٍ كَانُوا۟ فِيهَا فَٰكِهِينَ ۝ كَذَٰلِكَ وَأَوْرَثْنَٰهَا قَوْمًا ءَاخَرِينَ ۝ فَمَا بَكَتْ عَلَيْهِمُ ٱلسَّمَآءُ وَٱلْأَرْضُ وَمَا كَانُوا۟ مُنظَرِينَ ۝

---

^a After prolonged effort on the part of Moses to bring Pharaoh's people to the right path, by preaching the word of God, his assignment to issue the call for the Truth came to an end. At that time, Moses was instructed to leave Egypt and move out along with his people (the Children of Israel). Accordingly, Moses set out and journeyed until he reached the banks of the Red Sea. The waters parted for him and a path appeared for him to cross over.

Pharaoh and his army were in hot pursuit of Moses and the Children of Israel. When Pharaoh saw a path being formed across the Sea, he thought that he could also cross it, just as Moses had done. But the path across the Sea was not simply a path in the ordinary sense. The waters had parted by the commandment of God and God's commandment was for the deliverance of Moses and the destruction of Pharaoh. So, when Pharaoh and his army entered the Sea, the waters rushed upon them from either side of the path and rose to their former level. Pharaoh was drowned along with his army.

One who receives the good things of life in this world often considers them as his personal possessions, though in reality, they do not rightly belong to him. God may give them to anybody whenever He wishes, then, taking them away from him, may give them to somebody else, just as He pleases.

³⁰ We saved the Children of Israel from their humiliating torment ³¹ at the hands of Pharaoh: he was a tyrant who exceeded all bounds. ³² We knowingly chose them above all other people ³³ and showed them signs in which there was a clear test.ᵃ

وَلَقَدْ نَجَّيْنَا بَنِي إِسْرَٰٓءِيلَ مِنَ ٱلْعَذَابِ ٱلْمُهِينِ ۝ مِن فِرْعَوْنَ ۚ إِنَّهُۥ كَانَ عَالِيًا مِّنَ ٱلْمُسْرِفِينَ ۝ وَلَقَدِ ٱخْتَرْنَٰهُمْ عَلَىٰ عِلْمٍ عَلَى ٱلْعَٰلَمِينَ ۝ وَءَاتَيْنَٰهُم مِّنَ ٱلْءَايَٰتِ مَا فِيهِ بَلَٰٓؤٌا۟ مُّبِينٌ ۝

ᵃ In this world, the downfall of one nation and the rise of another do not happen accidentally. Neither does it mean that a cruel nation has, on account of its oppressive methods, subjugated another. All such events take place in accordance with God's decision, for the trial of man. It is God who, at His discretion, decides upon domination for one and subjection for another. Whatever He decides, it is based on His knowledge and is not arbitrary.

God makes His decisions in accordance with His knowledge, in other words, whatever happens is on the basis of what one deserves. In the light of His total knowledge, God looks at the various peoples and then decides to give dominance to those nations whom He finds deserving: those whom He finds undeserving, He dethrones and commits to subjection.

In the lives of nations, there appear signs to show that whatever fate befell them was by the decision of God. If a man's insight is keen, he will be able to catch a glimpse of the causes leading to the decisions taken by God in respect of the various nations.

³⁴ Yet those who deny the truth say, ³⁵ there is nothing beyond our first death; we shall not be raised again. ³⁶ So bring our fathers [back], if what you say is true. ³⁷ Are they better than the people of Tubbaʿ and those who came before them? We destroyed them, because they were guilty of sin.ᵃ

إِنَّ هَٰؤُلَآءِ لَيَقُولُونَ ۝ إِنْ هِىَ إِلَّا مَوۡتَتُنَا ٱلۡأُولَىٰ وَمَا نَحۡنُ بِمُنشَرِينَ ۝ فَأۡتُوا۟ بِـَٔابَآئِنَآ إِن كُنتُمۡ صَٰدِقِينَ ۝ أَهُمۡ خَيۡرٌ أَمۡ قَوۡمُ تُبَّعٍ وَٱلَّذِينَ مِن قَبۡلِهِمۡ أَهۡلَكۡنَٰهُمۡ إِنَّهُمۡ كَانُوا۟ مُجۡرِمِينَ ۝

ᵃ In every period the root cause of a man's going astray has been his loss of belief in the life after death. The disbelief of some finds expression in their utterances. Others may not openly express it, but their hearts are devoid of the belief that they have to rise after death and face the reckoning of their deeds before God.

The reason for this misunderstanding is generally that man, in view of his strong position in this world, presumes that he is never going to lose his elevated status, though the history of past nations ought to be enough to dispel this illusion.

Tubbaʿ was the title of the Kings of the ancient Himyar tribe of Yemen. These people enjoyed prominence from 300 B.C. to 115 B.C. and their greatness was much talked about in ancient Arabia. The rise and fall of the Tubbaʿ people, a piece of history well-known to the initial addressees of the Quran (the Quraysh), gave proof of the fact that the law of 'crime and punishment' was prevalent in this world. Similarly, for every community there is a 'Tubbaʿ' which, by its example, teaches them a lesson. But, man is wont to take such occurrences as being nothing out of the ordinary. The result is that he does not learn those lessons which, by God's will, are latent in events.

³⁸ We did not idly create the heavens and the earth and all that lies between them; ³⁹ We did not create them save with a purpose, yet most people have no knowledge of this. ⁴⁰ Truly, the Day of Decision is the appointed time for all of them, ⁴¹ the Day when no friend shall be of the least avail to another, nor shall any be helped, ⁴² save those to whom God shows mercy. Surely, He is the Mighty, the Merciful One.ᵃ

وَمَا خَلَقْنَا ٱلسَّمَٰوَٰتِ وَٱلْأَرْضَ وَمَا بَيْنَهُمَا لَٰعِبِينَ ۝ مَا خَلَقْنَٰهُمَآ إِلَّا بِٱلْحَقِّ وَلَٰكِنَّ أَكْثَرَهُمْ لَا يَعْلَمُونَ ۝ إِنَّ يَوْمَ ٱلْفَصْلِ مِيقَٰتُهُمْ أَجْمَعِينَ ۝ يَوْمَ لَا يُغْنِى مَوْلًى عَن مَّوْلًى شَيْئًا وَلَا هُمْ يُنصَرُونَ ۝ إِلَّا مَن رَّحِمَ ٱللَّهُ ۚ إِنَّهُۥ هُوَ ٱلْعَزِيزُ ٱلرَّحِيمُ ۝

ᵃ If one ponders over the system of heaven and earth—indeed, of the entire universe, it will become clear that its creation was effected with a definite purpose. Had this not been so, it would have been impossible in this world for man to build up glorious cultures.

Its entire functioning being meaningful is an indication that it will end also in a meaningful and purposeful way. It is unimaginable that its end could be otherwise. Its end, in reality, will herald the commencement of the life Hereafter. And belief in the Hereafter is but an extension of universal meaningfulness.

The present stage of the world is that of trial. So, everyone finds his share in the meaningfulness of this world. But, in the Hereafter, only those who are actually deserving in the eyes of God, will find a share in the meaningfulness of the afterlife.

⁴³ Surely the fruit of the Zaqqum tree ⁴⁴ shall be food for the sinners: ⁴⁵ like the dregs of oil, it shall boil in their bellies, ⁴⁶ like the boiling of hot water. ⁴⁷ [A voice will cry], 'Seize him and drag him into the midst of Hell. ⁴⁸ Then pour boiling water over his head as punishment. ⁴⁹ Taste this; you who considered yourself the mighty, the honourable! ⁵⁰ This is what you doubted?'^a

إِنَّ شَجَرَتَ ٱلزَّقُّومِ ۝ طَعَامُ ٱلْأَثِيمِ ۝ كَٱلْمُهْلِ يَغْلِى فِى ٱلْبُطُونِ ۝ كَغَلْىِ ٱلْحَمِيمِ ۝ خُذُوهُ فَٱعْتِلُوهُ إِلَىٰ سَوَآءِ ٱلْجَحِيمِ ۝ ثُمَّ صُبُّوا۟ فَوْقَ رَأْسِهِۦ مِنْ عَذَابِ ٱلْحَمِيمِ ۝ ذُقْ إِنَّكَ أَنتَ ٱلْعَزِيزُ ٱلْكَرِيمُ ۝ إِنَّ هَٰذَا مَا كُنتُم بِهِۦ تَمْتَرُونَ ۝

---

^a The picture of Hell painted by the Quran here and at other places is sufficient to shake every man who is serious about his future; it will make him rush towards the path of Paradise and away from the path of Hell.

But those who are not serious about the Truth, who pay heed only to their own desires and who do not feel the necessity to consider the world of realities which lies outside their ambitions, will hear this and simply ignore it. For such people, these words will be like water running over a rock without a single drop penetrating its surface.

51 But those mindful of God will be in a safe place, 52 among gardens and springs, 53 dressed in fine silk and in rich brocade, and they will face each other: 54 so it will be. We shall wed them to maidens with large, dark eyes. 55 They will call therein for every kind of fruit, in peace and security. 56 They will not taste death therein, save the first death. God will save them from the torment of Hell 57 as an act of grace. That will be the supreme triumph.ᵃ

58 We have made this Quran easy to understand—in your own language—so that they may take heed. 59 Wait then; they too are waiting.ᵇ

إِنَّ ٱلْمُتَّقِينَ فِى مَقَامٍ أَمِينٍ ۝ فِى جَنَّٰتٍ وَعُيُونٍ ۝ يَلْبَسُونَ مِن سُندُسٍ وَإِسْتَبْرَقٍ مُّتَقَٰبِلِينَ ۝ كَذَٰلِكَ وَزَوَّجْنَٰهُم بِحُورٍ عِينٍ ۝ يَدْعُونَ فِيهَا بِكُلِّ فَٰكِهَةٍ ءَامِنِينَ ۝ لَا يَذُوقُونَ فِيهَا ٱلْمَوْتَ إِلَّا ٱلْمَوْتَةَ ٱلْأُولَىٰ وَوَقَىٰهُمْ عَذَابَ ٱلْجَحِيمِ ۝ فَضْلًا مِّن رَّبِّكَ ذَٰلِكَ هُوَ ٱلْفَوْزُ ٱلْعَظِيمُ ۝ فَإِنَّمَا يَسَّرْنَٰهُ بِلِسَانِكَ لَعَلَّهُمْ يَتَذَكَّرُونَ ۝ فَٱرْتَقِبْ إِنَّهُم مُّرْتَقِبُونَ ۝

ᵃ These words paint an idyllic picture of a world which man sees only in his dreams. Therein lies the existence he most yearns for, but is unable to have it in this present world. Only in Paradise will he enter such a world, and it will be even better than his 'dream' world.

This world, free of all kinds of fear, will be open to those who feared God in this world. The life there, which is replete with eternal benefits, will be the reward of those who sacrificed the temporary benefits of this world for its sake. The crowning glories of the Hereafter will be savoured only by those who had the courage to risk their worldly success for higher things.

ᵇ The Quran is undoubtedly a great book. It is, moreover, a very straightforward book. But its being easy to understand is in direct relation to the desire for guidance. In other words, one who seeks to discover the Truth through it will find it very simple to follow. But for one who is not serious or sincere in his search for Truth, the Quran can be impenetrable.

In the present world one of the conditions for a man's being serious is that he should not keep putting off his acceptance of the Truth. In other words, the appearance of Truth at the level of reasoning and arguments should be enough to make him accept it. One who does not accept the Truth on its being established at this level, is in effect waiting for the Truth to be laid bare before him. But when the Truth so appears, it does not do so in order to claim acceptance, but to have the accepters appreciate it and the rejecters pushed into the pit of blindness forever.

45. KNEELING

In the name of God,
the Most Gracious, the Most Merciful

¹ *Ha Mim*

² This Scripture is sent down from God, the Mighty and Wise One. ³ There are signs in the heavens and the earth for those who believe: ⁴ in your own creation and all the creatures He has spread about, there are signs for people of sure faith; ⁵ and in the succession of night and day, and in the means of subsistence which God sends down from the skies, giving life thereby to the earth after it had been lifeless, and in the circulation of the winds: [in all this] there are signs for people who use their reason. ⁶ These are God's revelations, which We recite to you in all truth. But if they deny God and His revelations, in what message will they believe?ᵃ

ᵃ To say that the Quran is a revelation from the All-Powerful and Wise God amounts to giving on His behalf a definite standard on the basis of which its veracity can be demonstrated. Its divine origin means, moreover, that it will prove to be unassailable. The Quran will, in any case, prevail over its opponents.

This statement was made in the Makkan period. At that time, circumstances were entirely against the Quran. But later history has most wonderfully testified to the veracity of this statement. The call given by the Quran met with the greatest success in history. Similarly, the notion of revelation from God the Omniscient and Almighty implies that all its contents must be based on knowledge and wisdom. The Quran was revealed before the age of science. But now, even in this age of science nothing mentioned in the Quran has been proved irrational. ▶

⁷ Woe to every sinful liar! ⁸ He hears God's revelations being recited to him, yet persists in his arrogance as if he had never heard them. Forewarn him of a painful punishment. ⁹ When he learns something of Our revelations, he derides them: for such there will be humiliating torment. ¹⁰ In front of them is Hell; and of no profit to them is anything they may have earned, nor any protectors they may have taken to themselves besides God: for them there shall be a terrible punishment. ¹¹ Such is Our guidance; those who reject their Lord's revelations shall suffer a woeful punishment.ᵃ

وَيْلٌ لِّكُلِّ أَفَّاكٍ أَثِيمٍ ۞ يَسْمَعُ ءَايَٰتِ ٱللَّهِ تُتْلَىٰ عَلَيْهِ ثُمَّ يُصِرُّ مُسْتَكْبِرًا كَأَن لَّمْ يَسْمَعْهَا فَبَشِّرْهُ بِعَذَابٍ أَلِيمٍ ۞ وَإِذَا عَلِمَ مِنْ ءَايَٰتِنَا شَيْـًٔا ٱتَّخَذَهَا هُزُوًا أُوْلَٰٓئِكَ لَهُمْ عَذَابٌ مُّهِينٌ ۞ مِّن وَرَآئِهِمْ جَهَنَّمُ وَلَا يُغْنِى عَنْهُم مَّا كَسَبُوا۟ شَيْـًٔا وَلَا مَا ٱتَّخَذُوا۟ مِن دُونِ ٱللَّهِ أَوْلِيَآءَ وَلَهُمْ عَذَابٌ عَظِيمٌ ۞ هَٰذَا هُدًى وَٱلَّذِينَ كَفَرُوا۟ بِـَٔايَٰتِ رَبِّهِمْ لَهُمْ عَذَابٌ مِّن رِّجْزٍ أَلِيمٌ ۞

Furthermore, all the things in the Universe spread out far and near are testimonies to the truth of the Quran's message. However, this testimony will be valid only for one who possesses a receptive and believing mind; who is capable of grasping the real meaning of such matters as are expressed in the language of signs.

ᵃ Very often, an admission of the Truth is synonymous with the surrendering of a high position. Since man does not want to lose his elevated status, he does not accept the Truth. But, not bowing down before the Truth amounts to a refusal to bow down before God. God will mete out the most severe of punishments to the recalcitrant.

Though a man turns away from Truth out of conceit, he nevertheless presents theoretical arguments meant to justify his behaviour. But these arguments are nothing but false utterances. The denier of truth misrepresents some facet of reality and makes this an excuse; and on the basis of this excuse ridicules the Truth and the preacher of Truth. Such individuals deserve the most severe punishment, because they compound their misdeeds with arrogance. What prompts them to behave arrogantly is the prominence of their worldly position. But, worldly position will be of no avail to anyone in the Hereafter.

¹² It is God who has subjected the sea to you so that you may sail thereon by His command, and so that you may seek His bounty, and so that you may be grateful. ¹³ He has subjected whatever is in heaven and on the earth to you; it is all from Him. In that are signs for those who ponder.^a

۞ ٱللَّهُ ٱلَّذِى سَخَّرَ لَكُمُ ٱلْبَحْرَ لِتَجْرِىَ ٱلْفُلْكُ فِيهِ بِأَمْرِهِ وَلِتَبْتَغُوا۟ مِن فَضْلِهِۦ وَلَعَلَّكُمْ تَشْكُرُونَ ۝

وَسَخَّرَ لَكُم مَّا فِى ٱلسَّمَٰوَٰتِ وَمَا فِى ٱلْأَرْضِ جَمِيعًا مِّنْهُ إِنَّ فِى ذَٰلِكَ لَءَايَٰتٍ لِّقَوْمٍ يَتَفَكَّرُونَ ۝

---

^a God has made water subject to such natural laws that large ships may sail back and forth across deep oceans and safely reach their destinations. Such is the case with the entire universe. The universe has been created in such a way that it is completely subservient to man's interests. Man may harness its resources in whatever manner he likes. It is thanks to the serviceability of this world that it has been possible for man to develop glorious civilizations.

We assume that the existing structure of the universe is unique and that it has taken its final shape. Yet it could have been created in a variety of other ways. What is truly miraculous is that, out of all the possible alternatives, it has taken a form which is useful to mankind. This is a sign of God which, if given deep consideration, will demonstrate a glorious lesson.

¹⁴ Tell the believers to ignore those who do not believe in the coming of the days of God. He will requite people for what they have done. ¹⁵ Whoever does what is just and right, does so for his own good; and whoever does evil, does so to his own detriment, and you shall all return to your Lord.ᵃ

قُل لِّلَّذِينَ ءَامَنُواْ يَغْفِرُواْ لِلَّذِينَ لَا يَرْجُونَ أَيَّامَ ٱللَّهِ لِيَجْزِىَ قَوْمًۢا بِمَا كَانُواْ يَكْسِبُونَ ۝ مَنْ عَمِلَ صَٰلِحًا فَلِنَفْسِهِۦ وَمَنْ أَسَآءَ فَعَلَيْهَا ثُمَّ إِلَىٰ رَبِّكُمْ تُرْجَعُونَ ۝

_____

ᵃ Those who do not firmly believe that the Day of Judgement is going to dawn on them, venture to oppress others. They harass the preacher of Truth in every possible way. At that time feelings of revenge may develop in the heart of the preacher, but he should be forgiving towards his addressees. He should concentrate all his attention on the work of his mission and leave the matter of dealing with others' evil deeds in the hands of God.

The value of the preacher's efforts is not assessed on the basis of the number of persons he has influenced and brought on to the path of Truth. The value of his performance in the eyes of God depends upon the extent to which he remained steadfastly dedicated to the Truth; and to what degree he himself exemplified the behaviour expected of him.

¹⁶ We gave Scriptures, wisdom and prophethood to the Children of Israel, and provided them with good things and favoured them over all other people. ¹⁷ We gave them clear arguments in matters [of religion]. It was only after knowledge came to them that they differed among themselves out of mutual rivalry. On the Day of Resurrection your Lord will judge between them regarding their differences. ¹⁸ Then We set you on a clear path [of religion]: so follow it, and do not yield to the desires of those who have no knowledge. ¹⁹ They can be of no avail to you against God. The wrongdoers are friends of one another, while the friend of the righteous is God. ²⁰ This [Book] brings enlightenment and guidance to mankind, and is a blessing for those who have firm faith.ᵃ

وَلَقَدْ ءَاتَيْنَا بَنِىٓ إِسْرَٰٓءِيلَ ٱلْكِتَٰبَ وَٱلْحُكْمَ وَٱلنُّبُوَّةَ وَرَزَقْنَٰهُم مِّنَ ٱلطَّيِّبَٰتِ وَفَضَّلْنَٰهُمْ عَلَى ٱلْعَٰلَمِينَ ۝ وَءَاتَيْنَٰهُم بَيِّنَٰتٍ مِّنَ ٱلْأَمْرِ فَمَا ٱخْتَلَفُوٓا۟ إِلَّا مِنۢ بَعْدِ مَا جَآءَهُمُ ٱلْعِلْمُ بَغْيًۢا بَيْنَهُمْ إِنَّ رَبَّكَ يَقْضِى بَيْنَهُمْ يَوْمَ ٱلْقِيَٰمَةِ فِيمَا كَانُوا۟ فِيهِ يَخْتَلِفُونَ ۝ ثُمَّ جَعَلْنَٰكَ عَلَىٰ شَرِيعَةٍ مِّنَ ٱلْأَمْرِ فَٱتَّبِعْهَا وَلَا تَتَّبِعْ أَهْوَآءَ ٱلَّذِينَ لَا يَعْلَمُونَ ۝ إِنَّهُمْ لَن يُغْنُوا۟ عَنكَ مِنَ ٱللَّهِ شَيْـًٔا وَإِنَّ ٱلظَّٰلِمِينَ بَعْضُهُمْ أَوْلِيَآءُ بَعْضٍ وَٱللَّهُ وَلِىُّ ٱلْمُتَّقِينَ ۝ هَٰذَا بَصَٰٓئِرُ لِلنَّاسِ وَهُدًى وَرَحْمَةٌ لِّقَوْمٍ يُوقِنُونَ ۝

ᵃ According to verse 16, God exalted the Children of Israel over the peoples of the world. This parallels what was said of the people (ummah) of the Prophet Muhammad, i.e. 'You are the best ummah (nation)' (3:110). To make a group the bearer of the Book of God is in fact making it responsible for guidance to other nations' and it is in this sense that the community that bears the Book is superior to all nations.

In principle, the Children of Israel were commanded to convey the message to the whole world, as is now the case with the Muslims. But the Children of Israel, by introducing deviations into their Book, lost this status forever.

There is always uniformity in the authentic teachings of religion. But additions to them by scholars create differences and undue complexities. Then every scholar makes additions according to his taste. Thereafter every scholar and his followers set about proving their additions to be correct and others' additions to be incorrect. In this way, religious sects start forming and finally a stage is reached when one religion becomes divided into several religions. ▶

²¹ Do those who commit evil deeds imagine that We shall deal with them in the same way as We deal with those who have attained to faith and do righteous deeds, that they will be alike in their living and their dying? How badly they judge! ²² God has created the heavens and the earth for a true purpose, so that every soul may be rewarded for whatever it has earned, and no one will be wronged.ª

²³ [Prophet], consider the one who has taken his own desire as a deity, whom God allows to stray in the face of knowledge, sealing his ears and heart and covering his eyes—who can guide such a person after God [has abandoned him]? Will you not take heed?ᵇ

أَمْ حَسِبَ ٱلَّذِينَ ٱجْتَرَحُوا۟ ٱلسَّيِّئَاتِ أَن نَّجْعَلَهُمْ كَٱلَّذِينَ ءَامَنُوا۟ وَعَمِلُوا۟ ٱلصَّٰلِحَٰتِ سَوَآءً مَّحْيَاهُمْ وَمَمَاتُهُمْ ۚ سَآءَ مَا يَحْكُمُونَ ۝ وَخَلَقَ ٱللَّهُ ٱلسَّمَٰوَٰتِ وَٱلْأَرْضَ بِٱلْحَقِّ وَلِتُجْزَىٰ كُلُّ نَفْسٍ بِمَا كَسَبَتْ وَهُمْ لَا يُظْلَمُونَ ۝ أَفَرَءَيْتَ مَنِ ٱتَّخَذَ إِلَٰهَهُۥ هَوَىٰهُ وَأَضَلَّهُ ٱللَّهُ عَلَىٰ عِلْمٍ وَخَتَمَ عَلَىٰ سَمْعِهِۦ وَقَلْبِهِۦ وَجَعَلَ عَلَىٰ بَصَرِهِۦ غِشَٰوَةً فَمَن يَهْدِيهِ مِنۢ بَعْدِ ٱللَّهِ ۚ أَفَلَا تَذَكَّرُونَ ۝

When the Children of Israel distorted their revealed religion, God thereupon revealed the Quran through the Prophet Muhammad. Since no other prophet was to appear after him, God caused the Quran to be preserved and kept safe by special arrangements, so that it should never again happen that the religion of God be lost in the labyrinth of human additions.

ª One who thinks that it is all the same whether a man leads a virtuous life or a life of evil—since either way he ultimately has to die and perish—is nurturing an extremely erroneous idea. This way of thinking runs counter to the consciousness of justice which is found in the very nature of every man right from his birth. Moreover, this amounts to denying the meaningfulness of the universe, which is immanent in it to the ultimate degree. The fact is that man's inherent nature and the vast universe around him both completely nullify the concept by which life is treated as being so purposeless as not to lead to any significant outcome.

ᵇ To make desire one's deity means giving it the supreme position in one's life. One who thinks and acts under the influence of desire has, in effect, made himself a slave to it. Man's mind is perfectly capable of distinguishing between right and wrong. But, when he mindlessly follows his desires, he closes the door to reason. Then when he encounters arguments in support of the Truth, he fails to feel their weight. In reply to every statement, he presents false arguments and rejects it. Such behaviour ultimately impairs his mental powers. ▶

²⁴ They say, 'There is nothing but our life in this world: we die, we live, nothing but time destroys us.' They have no knowledge of this; they only follow conjecture. ²⁵ Whenever Our clear revelations are recited to them, their only argument is to say, 'Bring back to us our forefathers, if what you say be true.' ²⁶ Say, 'God gives you life, then causes you to die, and then will gather you together for the Day of Resurrection, about which there is no doubt. But most people do not know it.'ᵃ

وَقَالُوا۟ مَا هِىَ إِلَّا حَيَاتُنَا ٱلدُّنْيَا نَمُوتُ وَنَحْيَا وَمَا يُهْلِكُنَآ إِلَّا ٱلدَّهْرُ وَمَا لَهُم بِذَٰلِكَ مِنْ عِلْمٍ إِنْ هُمْ إِلَّا يَظُنُّونَ ۝ وَإِذَا تُتْلَىٰ عَلَيْهِمْ ءَايَٰتُنَا بَيِّنَٰتٍ مَّا كَانَ حُجَّتَهُمْ إِلَّا أَن قَالُوا۟ ٱئْتُوا۟ بِـَٔابَآئِنَآ إِن كُنتُمْ صَٰدِقِينَ ۝ قُلِ ٱللَّهُ يُحْيِيكُمْ ثُمَّ يُمِيتُكُمْ ثُمَّ يَجْمَعُكُمْ إِلَىٰ يَوْمِ ٱلْقِيَٰمَةِ لَا رَيْبَ فِيهِ وَلَٰكِنَّ أَكْثَرَ ٱلنَّاسِ لَا يَعْلَمُونَ ۝

His ears hear the words, but fail to grasp their meaning. His eyes look at the Truth, but fail to learn a lesson from it. The message of truth reaches his heart, but fails to warm it.

God has made man's power of reasoning the entrance gate for guidance. But if a man enslaved by his desires shuts off his mind, how can guidance enter?

ᵃ 'Nothing but time destroys us.' These are not the words of the common man. Such maxims are typically uttered by a special calibre of individual. Such an individual, because of his intelligence, attains the status of an intellectual representative of society. However, whatever he says is based on conjecture and not on any real knowledge. On the contrary, whatever a prophet says is based on a concrete foundation.

Every day we witness the birth of a human being out of a death-like state of non-existence. It is as if here every man receives life after "death", then after being alive, he dies again. This is an indication of the fact that, just as life appeared after death-like non-existence for the first time, similarly, for the second time also, there will be life after death.

With this, the possibility of life after death is proved beyond doubt. Therefore, it is not correct to demand that those who are due to be resurrected in future should be brought back to life today for the purpose of demonstrating this truth, because the whole purpose of the present world is to put man to the test. If, today, the state of the future world were to be shown, the purpose of testing would be nullified.

²⁷ To God belongs the kingdom of the heavens and the earth; on the Day when the Hour comes, those who follow falsehood will be the losers. ²⁸ You will see every people on their knees,^{*a*} every people shall be summoned to its Record [and a voice will say], 'Today you will be requited for your deeds. ²⁹ This record of ours will declare the truth about you: We have been recording whatever you have been doing.'^{*b*}

وَلِلَّهِ مُلْكُ ٱلسَّمَـٰوَٰتِ وَٱلْأَرْضِ وَيَوْمَ تَقُومُ ٱلسَّاعَةُ يَوْمَئِذٍ يَخْسَرُ ٱلْمُبْطِلُونَ ۝ وَتَرَىٰ كُلَّ أُمَّةٍ جَاثِيَةً كُلُّ أُمَّةٍ تُدْعَىٰ إِلَىٰ كِتَـٰبِهَا ٱلْيَوْمَ تُجْزَوْنَ مَا كُنتُمْ تَعْمَلُونَ ۝ هَـٰذَا كِتَـٰبُنَا يَنطِقُ عَلَيْكُم بِٱلْحَقِّ إِنَّا كُنَّا نَسْتَنسِخُ مَا كُنتُمْ تَعْمَلُونَ ۝

---

^{*a*} Those who, in this world, rise with the Message of God, do so, in fact, on the basis of Truth; and those who stand up on any other basis, do so, in fact, on the basis of falsehood. In the Hereafter, the latter will have no footing; because whatever they had considered to be a solid foundation was nothing of the sort. It was a mere deceit or illusion which vanished on the appearance of reality.

^{*b*} Having one's deeds 'written down' does not mean having them written with pen and ink in the usual sense; it means rather having one's deeds recorded. Man's motives, his utterances and his deeds are all being recorded with precision in accordance with God's arrangements. This record will be so supremely real that it will not be possible for anybody to deny its correctness.

³⁰ Those who believed and did good deeds will be admitted by their Lord into His mercy—that shall be the manifest triumph. ³¹ But those who rejected the truth [will be asked], 'When My revelations were recited to you, were you not arrogant and did you not persist in wicked deeds? ³² When it was said to you, "God's promise is true: there is no doubt about the Hour," did you not reply, "We do not know what the Hour is. We think it to be nothing but a conjecture, and we are not convinced"?' ^a

فَأَمَّا ٱلَّذِينَ ءَامَنُواْ وَعَمِلُواْ ٱلصَّٰلِحَٰتِ فَيُدْخِلُهُمْ رَبُّهُمْ فِى رَحْمَتِهِۦ ذَٰلِكَ هُوَ ٱلْفَوْزُ ٱلْمُبِينُ ﴿٣٠﴾ وَأَمَّا ٱلَّذِينَ كَفَرُوٓاْ أَفَلَمْ تَكُنْ ءَايَٰتِى تُتْلَىٰ عَلَيْكُمْ فَٱسْتَكْبَرْتُمْ وَكُنتُمْ قَوْمًا مُّجْرِمِينَ ﴿٣١﴾ وَإِذَا قِيلَ إِنَّ وَعْدَ ٱللَّهِ حَقٌّ وَٱلسَّاعَةُ لَا رَيْبَ فِيهَا قُلْتُم مَّا نَدْرِى مَا ٱلسَّاعَةُ إِن نَّظُنُّ إِلَّا ظَنًّا وَمَا نَحْنُ بِمُسْتَيْقِنِينَ ﴿٣٢﴾

---

^a Here arrogance does not imply contempt for God, it is directed rather against the messenger of God. In the present world, accepting God's word is, in effect, synonymous with acceptance of the word of the messenger of Truth. Now, those who suffer from overweening pride consider it beneath their dignity to accept the word of a man like themselves. So they ignore it. Unlike them, those who are free of pride immediately bow down before it. While the wrath of God will descend upon the former, the latter will be blessed by the grace of God.

One who denies the Truth makes different types of statements in order to justify his stand. Sometimes he tries to prove the preacher untrustworthy and sometimes he tries to cast doubts upon his message. But it will be clear on the Day of Judgement that these attempts stemmed from a sinful mentality and not from a Truth-loving mind.

³³ The evil of their actions will then become clear to them. The punishment they mocked will engulf them. ³⁴ It will be said to them, 'This Day We shall forget you, as you yourselves forgot that you would meet this Day. Your abode shall be the Fire, and you shall have no helpers. ³⁵ That is because you made a mockery of God's revelations and were deluded by the life of this world.' Therefore, today they will not be brought out of the Fire, nor will they be allowed to make amends.ᵃ

وَبَدَا لَهُمْ سَيِّئَاتُ مَا عَمِلُوا۟ وَحَاقَ بِهِم مَّا كَانُوا۟ بِهِۦ يَسْتَهْزِءُونَ ۝ وَقِيلَ ٱلْيَوْمَ نَنسَىٰكُمْ كَمَا نَسِيتُمْ لِقَآءَ يَوْمِكُمْ هَٰذَا وَمَأْوَىٰكُمُ ٱلنَّارُ وَمَا لَكُم مِّن نَّٰصِرِينَ ۝ ذَٰلِكُم بِأَنَّكُمُ ٱتَّخَذْتُمْ ءَايَٰتِ ٱللَّهِ هُزُوًا وَغَرَّتْكُمُ ٱلْحَيَوٰةُ ٱلدُّنْيَا ۚ فَٱلْيَوْمَ لَا يُخْرَجُونَ مِنْهَا وَلَا هُمْ يُسْتَعْتَبُونَ ۝

ᵃ In the present world when a man commits evil, its bad results do not at once appear before him. This serves to embolden him. When he is warned about his bad deeds, he is not prepared to give any serious attention to this. But, in the Hereafter, the consequences of his misdeeds will appear before his eyes and he will be completely engulfed in them. At that time he will accept the Truth, which he had formerly ridiculed as being worthless.

In the Hereafter, man will accept the Truth which he denied in this world. But this will carry no weight there, as it is only acceptance of Truth at the 'unseen' level which is of value, not acceptance after the revelation of Reality.

³⁶ Praise, then, be to God, Lord of the heavens, and Lord of the earth, the Lord of all the worlds. ³⁷ All greatness belongs to Him in the heavens and earth. He is the Almighty, the All Wise.^a

فَلِلَّهِ ٱلْحَمْدُ رَبِّ ٱلسَّمَـٰوَٰتِ وَرَبِّ ٱلْأَرْضِ رَبِّ ٱلْعَـٰلَمِينَ ﴿٣٦﴾ وَلَهُ ٱلْكِبْرِيَآءُ فِى ٱلسَّمَـٰوَٰتِ وَٱلْأَرْضِ وَهُوَ ٱلْعَزِيزُ ٱلْحَكِيمُ ﴿٣٧﴾

---

^a The universe is of infinite immensity. So, its Creator and Lord must also be one who is of unlimited greatness: this mighty being cannot be anyone except the one and only God. Nobody can seriously venture to assume anybody except God to be the Creator and Lord of the universe. So, if the Creator and Lord of the universe is one and only one being, then it follows essentially that all praises should also be due to Him; man should devote his full attention to Him; he should make Him his all.

46. THE SAND DUNES

In the name of God,
the Most Gracious, the Most Merciful

¹ *Ha Mim*

² This Book is sent down from God, the Almighty, the Wise One. ³ We created the heavens and the earth and all that lies between them purely for just ends, and for a specific term, but those who reject Faith turn away from what they have been warned of.*

---

*The study of the universe reveals that inherent in it are wisdom and meaningfulness. Then, how can a set of systems which is so meaningful at its beginning become meaningless at its end?

Truth, monolithic and immutable, is the greatest power of the universe. In spite of this, why is it that people reject it when it is presented before them? The reason is that in the present world people are simply informed of the Truth. In the Hereafter Truth will impose itself on them and at that time those very individuals who treated the Truth as unimportant and ignored it, will break down before it.

⁴ Say, 'Have you thought about those you call upon apart from God? Show me what they have created on the earth. Or do they have a share in the heavens? Bring me a Book revealed before this or some other vestige of knowledge, if you are telling the truth.' ⁵ And who is more misguided than one who invokes, besides God, such as will not answer him until the Day of Resurrection, and who [in fact] are not even aware of his call, ⁶ and when mankind are gathered together, they will become their enemies, and will deny their worship? ᵃ

قُلْ أَرَءَيْتُم مَّا تَدْعُونَ مِن دُونِ ٱللَّهِ أَرُونِي مَاذَا خَلَقُوا مِنَ ٱلْأَرْضِ أَمْ لَهُمْ شِرْكٌ فِي ٱلسَّمَٰوَٰتِ ٱئْتُونِي بِكِتَٰبٍ مِّن قَبْلِ هَٰذَآ أَوْ أَثَٰرَةٍ مِّنْ عِلْمٍ إِن كُنتُمْ صَٰدِقِينَ ۝ وَمَنْ أَضَلُّ مِمَّن يَدْعُوا مِن دُونِ ٱللَّهِ مَن لَّا يَسْتَجِيبُ لَهُۥ إِلَىٰ يَوْمِ ٱلْقِيَٰمَةِ وَهُمْ عَن دُعَآئِهِمْ غَٰفِلُونَ ۝ وَإِذَا حُشِرَ ٱلنَّاسُ كَانُوا لَهُمْ أَعْدَآءً وَكَانُوا بِعِبَادَتِهِمْ كَٰفِرِينَ ۝

ᵃ Knowledge is in fact of two types: revealed and established. The former reached man through the prophets, while the latter was established as such by means of research and experiments carried out by human beings. Neither of these two types of knowledge indicates that there is any being worthy of worship except the one and only God. When neither supports the concept of polytheism, how can a polytheistic credo be appropriate for man? One who seeks the support of any thing or any being other than God, will find himself abandoned by that thing or being in the Hereafter.

⁷ And whenever Our clear revelations are recited to them and the Truth is brought to them, those who deny the truth say, 'This is plain magic.' ⁸ Do they mean to say that the Messenger himself has fabricated it? Say [O Muhammad], 'If I have fabricated it myself, you will not be able to do anything to save me from God. He knows quite well what talk you indulge in. He is enough as a witness between me and you; and He is the Forgiving, the Merciful One.'^a

وَإِذَا تُتْلَىٰ عَلَيْهِمْ ءَايَٰتُنَا بَيِّنَٰتٍ قَالَ ٱلَّذِينَ كَفَرُوا۟ لِلْحَقِّ لَمَّا جَآءَهُمْ هَٰذَا سِحْرٌ مُّبِينٌ ۝ أَمْ يَقُولُونَ ٱفْتَرَىٰهُ قُلْ إِنِ ٱفْتَرَيْتُهُۥ فَلَا تَمْلِكُونَ لِى مِنَ ٱللَّهِ شَيْـًٔا هُوَ أَعْلَمُ بِمَا تُفِيضُونَ فِيهِ كَفَىٰ بِهِۦ شَهِيدًۢا بَيْنِى وَبَيْنَكُمْ وَهُوَ ٱلْغَفُورُ ٱلرَّحِيمُ ۝

^a In ancient Arabia, the addressees of the Quran were too preoccupied by the greatness of their forebears to give its message any proper consideration. They said that it distressed them even to hear it, because it ran counter to the religion of their august predecessors and, on this account, they rejected it. But the Quran had another aspect to it and that was its literary supremacy. Every Arabic linguistic expert has felt that it is an extraordinary work. It is true that the works of certain human beings possess extraordinary literary value, but there is a limit to the merit of a composition by an ordinary mortal. Indeed, the literary majesty of the Qur'an is inconceivably greater than any possible feat of the human mind. In order, therefore, to lessen the importance of the Quran from this angle, its detractors held that it was magic, i.e. it was a feat of magical presentation and not a sublime rendering of facts.

When opponents stoop to obduracy, any serious person would remain silent after saying, 'The issue between you and me is now before God for His decision.' This is not defeatism but a forward-looking strategy. If one remains silent before an obstinate person, one actually distances oneself from the dispute and that brings one's opponent face to face with his own conscience, so that if there is any feeling of rectitude left in him, it should be aroused.

⁹ Say, 'I am not the first of God's messengers, and I do not know what will be done with me or with you: I do not follow anything but what is revealed to me, and I am merely a plain warner.' ¹⁰ Say, 'Have you thought: what if this Quran really is from God and you reject it? What if one of the Children of Israel testifies to its similarity to earlier scripture and believes in it, and yet you are too arrogant to do the same? God certainly does not guide evil-doers.'ᵃ

قُلْ مَا كُنتُ بِدْعًا مِنَ ٱلرُّسُلِ وَمَآ أَدْرِى مَا يُفْعَلُ بِى وَلَا بِكُمْ إِنْ أَتَّبِعُ إِلَّا مَا يُوحَىٰ إِلَىَّ وَمَآ أَنَا۠ إِلَّا نَذِيرٌ مُّبِينٌ ۝ قُلْ أَرَءَيْتُمْ إِن كَانَ مِنْ عِندِ ٱللَّهِ وَكَفَرْتُم بِهِۦ وَشَهِدَ شَاهِدٌ مِّنۢ بَنِىٓ إِسْرَٰٓءِيلَ عَلَىٰ مِثْلِهِۦ فَـَٔامَنَ وَٱسْتَكْبَرْتُمْ إِنَّ ٱللَّهَ لَا يَهْدِى ٱلْقَوْمَ ٱلظَّٰلِمِينَ ۝

ᵃ The Makkan polytheists regarded the Jews, whom they often met on trading expeditions, as a community of prophets and therefore very learned in religious disciplines.

When the Prophet Muhammad had become a controversial personality in Makkah, a number of these polytheists made enquiries of certain Jews about him. In the meantime a Jewish scholar told them that, according to their books, a prophet was due to appear in those parts, and that he (Muhammad) might be that very prophet. Evidently, this Jew had indirectly accepted the prophethood of Muhammad.

The events of history had already proved that God's messengers do appear along with God's books. It was written in ancient divine scriptures that such a messenger was due to appear among the Ishmaelites. In the life and sayings of the Prophet of God, all those signs were clearly found that signalled prophethood. In the face of such signs and portents, those who denied the prophethood of the Prophet Muhammad were not doing so on any rational grounds, but simply because, by accepting one who had hitherto been an ordinary individual in their eyes as the prophet of God, they would be damaging their own high position.

Those who are more concerned with their own pride and prestige than with the Truth, will always be led in the wrong direction by their warped mindset.

" Those who deny the truth say of the believers, 'If there were any good in this Quran, they would not have believed in it before we did.' And since they refuse to be guided by it, they say, 'This is an ancient fabrication.' *a*

وَقَالَ ٱلَّذِينَ كَفَرُوا۟ لِلَّذِينَ ءَامَنُوا۟ لَوْ كَانَ خَيْرًا مَّا سَبَقُونَآ إِلَيْهِ وَإِذْ لَمْ يَهْتَدُوا۟ بِهِۦ فَسَيَقُولُونَ هَٰذَآ إِفْكٌ قَدِيمٌ ۝

---

a Initially, of the people who became the companions of the Prophet of God, many were old and belonged to the slave class, for example, Bilal, 'Ammar, Shu'ayb, Khubbab, etc. At the same time, among those who had faith in him, there were also people who belonged to respectable families, such as Abu Bakr ibn Abi Qahafa, 'Uthaman ibn 'Affan, 'Ali ibn Abi Talib, etc. But the Prophet's opponents used to mention only the former and not the latter. The reason is that when anyone becomes biased against a particular individual, his attitude becomes one-sided. He ignores the latter's virtues and mentions only those aspects of him which give him the opportunity to degrade him.

Similarly, the call of the Prophet Muhammad was undoubtedly the same as that of all the previous prophets: he had come with an eternal truth. But his opponents, instead of calling it 'a very old truth', called it 'a very old falsehood.' This kind of injustice prevailed in former times and, even today, it is quite common.

¹² Yet the scripture of Moses was revealed before it as a guide and a blessing; and this is a Book in the Arabic language, fulfilling [previous prophecies], to forewarn those who do evil and to bring good news to those who do good. ¹³ Surely those who say, 'Our Lord is God,' and remain firm [on that path] shall feel no fear, nor shall they grieve: ¹⁴ it is they who are the people of Paradise, they shall abide therein as a reward for all that they have done.ᵃ

وَمِن قَبْلِهِۦ كِتَٰبُ مُوسَىٰٓ إِمَامًا وَرَحْمَةً وَهَٰذَا كِتَٰبٌ مُّصَدِّقٌ لِّسَانًا عَرَبِيًّا لِّيُنذِرَ ٱلَّذِينَ ظَلَمُوا۟ وَبُشْرَىٰ لِلْمُحْسِنِينَ ۝ إِنَّ ٱلَّذِينَ قَالُوا۟ رَبُّنَا ٱللَّهُ ثُمَّ ٱسْتَقَٰمُوا۟ فَلَا خَوْفٌ عَلَيْهِمْ وَلَا هُمْ يَحْزَنُونَ ۝ أُو۟لَٰٓئِكَ أَصْحَٰبُ ٱلْجَنَّةِ خَٰلِدِينَ فِيهَا جَزَآءًۢ بِمَا كَانُوا۟ يَعْمَلُونَ ۝

ᵃ One argument in favour of the veracity of the Quran is that the previous revealed scriptures predicted it. These predictions are still found in the Bible (Injeel) and the Torah. The Quran thus came as a realisation of earlier divine predictions, giving concrete shape to what had been foreseen many centuries before. This is a clear indication that the Quran is really a divine Book; otherwise how could it have been possible to give advance information about it hundreds and thousands of years ago? It is reported on the authority of 'Abdullah ibn 'Abbas that verse 13, broadly interpreted, means being steadfast in the discharge of duties attached to Faith. (*Tafsir ibn Kathir*).

Faith (*iman*) is a sacred pledge or vow. Time and again, moments of trial occur in the life of a man when he either keeps his pledge of Faith, or he breaks it. On such occasions, one who acts in accordance with his pledge of Faith, shows his steadfastness, while one who fails to do so, shows his lack of devotion.

Those unable to prove their steadfastness are transgressors, while those who prove to be steadfast are the ones who will be lodged in the eternal gardens of Paradise.

15 We have enjoined on man kindness to his parents: his mother bore him, in pain and in pain she gave birth to him, and his bearing and weaning takes thirty months. At length, when he reaches the age of full maturity and attains forty years, he says, 'O my Lord! Help me to be grateful for Your favours which You have bestowed upon me, and upon both my parents, and to do good deeds that will please You. Grant me righteousness in my offspring. Truly, I have turned to You and, truly, I submit to You.' 16 We accept from such people the best of what they do and We overlook their bad deeds. They will be among the people of Paradise—this is a true promise that has been given to them.ᵃ

وَوَصَّيْنَا ٱلْإِنسَـٰنَ بِوَٰلِدَيْهِ إِحْسَـٰنًا ۖ حَمَلَتْهُ أُمُّهُۥ كُرْهًا وَوَضَعَتْهُ كُرْهًا ۖ وَحَمْلُهُۥ وَفِصَـٰلُهُۥ ثَلَـٰثُونَ شَهْرًا ۚ حَتَّىٰٓ إِذَا بَلَغَ أَشُدَّهُۥ وَبَلَغَ أَرْبَعِينَ سَنَةً قَالَ رَبِّ أَوْزِعْنِىٓ أَنْ أَشْكُرَ نِعْمَتَكَ ٱلَّتِىٓ أَنْعَمْتَ عَلَىَّ وَعَلَىٰ وَٰلِدَىَّ وَأَنْ أَعْمَلَ صَـٰلِحًا تَرْضَىٰهُ وَأَصْلِحْ لِى فِى ذُرِّيَّتِىٓ ۖ إِنِّى تُبْتُ إِلَيْكَ وَإِنِّى مِنَ ٱلْمُسْلِمِينَ ۝ أُوْلَـٰٓئِكَ ٱلَّذِينَ نَتَقَبَّلُ عَنْهُمْ أَحْسَنَ مَا عَمِلُوا۟ وَنَتَجَاوَزُ عَن سَيِّـَٔاتِهِمْ فِىٓ أَصْحَـٰبِ ٱلْجَنَّةِ ۖ وَعْدَ ٱلصِّدْقِ ٱلَّذِى كَانُوا۟ يُوعَدُونَ ۝

ᵃ Human procreation takes place through a father and a mother who nurture their offspring through infancy to adulthood. This is, so to say, the natural system of man's training, which ensures that he develops a keen consciousness of his duties towards human beings along with the feeling that he must acknowledge the grace of his Benefactor and discharge his duties towards Him. This feeling teaches a man two things: firstly, to honour his pledges towards other men and, secondly, to fulfill important obligations to God, the Creator and Lord.

Those who learn a lesson from Nature, the great teacher, who activate their sense of moral awareness to the extent that they properly identify and appropriately fulfill their duties towards all, ranging from their parents right up to God, are the ones who will be treated as deserving of the eternal Grace of God in the Hereafter.

¹⁷ But he who says to his parents, 'Shame upon you! Do you threaten me with being taken out of the grave after death while many a generation has passed away before me and none has risen from among them?' The parents both cry for God's help and say to him, 'Believe! Alas for you! God's promise is true.' But he says, 'These are nothing but ancient fables.' ¹⁸ It is against such as these that the word of God has proved true, along with all the communities that went before them, jinns and humans: surely they are losers.^a

وَٱلَّذِى قَالَ لِوَٰلِدَيْهِ أُفٍّ لَّكُمَآ أَتَعِدَانِنِىٓ أَنْ أُخْرَجَ وَقَدْ خَلَتِ ٱلْقُرُونُ مِن قَبْلِى وَهُمَا يَسْتَغِيثَانِ ٱللَّهَ وَيْلَكَ ءَامِنْ إِنَّ وَعْدَ ٱللَّهِ حَقٌّ فَيَقُولُ مَا هَٰذَآ إِلَّآ أَسَٰطِيرُ ٱلْأَوَّلِينَ ۝ أُوْلَٰٓئِكَ ٱلَّذِينَ حَقَّ عَلَيْهِمُ ٱلْقَوْلُ فِىٓ أُمَمٍ قَدْ خَلَتْ مِن قَبْلِهِم مِّنَ ٱلْجِنِّ وَٱلْإِنسِ إِنَّهُمْ كَانُواْ خَٰسِرِينَ ۝

---

^a Children who are obedient to their parents are also obedient to God. Contrary to this, the behaviour of disobedient children is such that, when they grow up, they forget that their parents had to endure innumerable troubles to bring them to adulthood.

The best well-wishers of the individual are his parents. Whatever advice parents offer their children is based on absolutely selfless well-wishing. Therefore, one should give more weight to the advice of righteous parents. One who rebukes his righteous parents for their advice proves by his behaviour that he is a very hard-hearted person. It is such as he who will suffer heavy losses.

¹⁹ All will be ranked according to their deeds. We will requite them in full for their actions and they will not be wronged. ²⁰ On the Day when those who deny the truth are brought before the Fire, it will be said to them, 'You have had the good things of the life of this world, and you enjoyed them. Now this Day you shall be requited with humiliating punishment, because you were arrogant in the land without justification, and because you acted rebelliously.'^a

وَلِكُلٍّ دَرَجَٰتٌ مِّمَّا عَمِلُواْ وَلِيُوَفِّيَهُمْ أَعْمَٰلَهُمْ وَهُمْ لَا يُظْلَمُونَ ۝ وَيَوْمَ يُعْرَضُ ٱلَّذِينَ كَفَرُواْ عَلَى ٱلنَّارِ أَذْهَبْتُمْ طَيِّبَٰتِكُمْ فِى حَيَاتِكُمُ ٱلدُّنْيَا وَٱسْتَمْتَعْتُم بِهَا فَٱلْيَوْمَ تُجْزَوْنَ عَذَابَ ٱلْهُونِ بِمَا كُنتُمْ تَسْتَكْبِرُونَ فِى ٱلْأَرْضِ بِغَيْرِ ٱلْحَقِّ وَبِمَا كُنتُمْ تَفْسُقُونَ ۝

^a The Truth appears before a man, but, unwilling to relinquish worldly goals and material gain, he rejects it. This means that he sets worldly interests above the exigencies of the Hereafter; he wants to pursue the attractions of this world rather than seek the good things of the afterlife. Then, when he is required to demolish the structure of self-aggrandisement in order to accept the Truth, he prefers to reject it, so as to save his empty prestige: after all, he relishes the feeling of being a great man. At that point, in effect, he shows his preference for the enticements of this world over the blessings of the Hereafter, treating them as unworthy of consideration.

²¹ Tell of the brother of ʿAd; when he warned his people in the sand dunes—and indeed warners came and went before him and after him—saying, 'Worship none but God; surely I fear for you the punishment of an awful Day,' ²² but they said, 'Have you come to us to turn us away from our deities? Then bring down upon us what you threaten us with, if you are truthful.' ²³ He said, 'God alone knows when it will come, and I deliver to you the message with which I am sent, but I see you are a people who are ignorant.'ᵃ

﴿ وَٱذۡكُرۡ أَخَا عَادٍ إِذۡ أَنذَرَ قَوۡمَهُۥ بِٱلۡأَحۡقَافِ وَقَدۡ خَلَتِ ٱلنُّذُرُ مِنۢ بَيۡنِ يَدَيۡهِ وَمِنۡ خَلۡفِهِۦٓ أَلَّا تَعۡبُدُوٓاْ إِلَّا ٱللَّهَ إِنِّىٓ أَخَافُ عَلَيۡكُمۡ عَذَابَ يَوۡمٍ عَظِيمٍ ۝ قَالُوٓاْ أَجِئۡتَنَا لِتَأۡفِكَنَا عَنۡ ءَالِهَتِنَا فَأۡتِنَا بِمَا تَعِدُنَآ إِن كُنتَ مِنَ ٱلصَّـٰدِقِينَ ۝ قَالَ إِنَّمَا ٱلۡعِلۡمُ عِندَ ٱللَّهِ وَأُبَلِّغُكُم مَّآ أُرۡسِلۡتُ بِهِۦ وَلَـٰكِنِّىٓ أَرَىٰكُمۡ قَوۡمًا تَجۡهَلُونَ ۝

ᵃ The people of ʿAd once inhabited that area of southern Arabia which is now known as ar-Rub al-Khali. They made considerable progress, but their development pushed them into arrogance and neglectfulness. Then Almighty God made Hud, a member of that community, a prophet, and sent him to them.

Hud warned his community of God's displeasure but, unwilling to be reformed, it received its prophet with rudeness. Ultimately, God's wrath descended upon it and it received such a severe punishment that its glorious and lush green surroundings turned into a totally arid desert.

24 So, when they saw it in the shape of a dense cloud approaching their valleys, they exclaimed, 'This is only a heavy cloud which will bring us [welcome] rain!' [But Hud said]: 'By no means! It is the very thing which you sought to hasten—a wind bearing grievous suffering 25 which will destroy everything at its Lord's behest!' And in the morning there was nothing left to be seen save their [empty] dwellings: thus We repay the evil-doers.[a]

فَلَمَّا رَأَوْهُ عَارِضًا مُّسْتَقْبِلَ أَوْدِيَتِهِمْ قَالُوا هَـٰذَا عَارِضٌ مُّمْطِرُنَا بَلْ هُوَ مَا ٱسْتَعْجَلْتُم بِهِ رِيحٌ فِيهَا عَذَابٌ أَلِيمٌ ۝ تُدَمِّرُ كُلَّ شَىْءٍ بِأَمْرِ رَبِّهَا فَأَصْبَحُوا لَا يُرَىٰ إِلَّا مَسَاكِنُهُمْ كَذَٰلِكَ نَجْزِى ٱلْقَوْمَ ٱلْمُجْرِمِينَ ۝

---

[a] The people of Ad mistook the clouds of destruction for rain clouds. They understood the reality only when the raging winds entered their townships and reduced them to ruins. Man is so reckless that he does not accept the Truth even when on the brink of disaster. He accepts it only after the opportunity to repent has been taken away from him.

26 We had empowered them to an extent which We have not empowered you, [O people of later times]; and We had endowed them with hearing, and sight, and hearts: but neither their hearing, nor their sight, nor their hearts were of the least avail to them, since they went on rejecting God's revelations; and they were overwhelmed by the very thing which they had been wont to deride. 27 We have also destroyed other towns that once [flourished] around you—We had given them various signs so that they might return [to the right path]—28 so why did their gods not help them, those they set up as gods besides God to bring them nearer to Him? No indeed! They failed them utterly: it was all a lie, a fabrication of their own making.[a]

وَلَقَدۡ مَكَّنَّـٰهُمۡ فِيمَآ إِن مَّكَّنَّـٰكُمۡ فِيهِ وَجَعَلۡنَا لَهُمۡ سَمۡعًا وَأَبۡصَـٰرًا وَأَفۡـِٔدَةً فَمَآ أَغۡنَىٰ عَنۡهُمۡ سَمۡعُهُمۡ وَلَآ أَبۡصَـٰرُهُمۡ وَلَآ أَفۡـِٔدَتُهُم مِّن شَىۡءٍ إِذۡ كَانُوا۟ يَجۡحَدُونَ بِـَٔايَـٰتِ ٱللَّهِ وَحَاقَ بِهِم مَّا كَانُوا۟ بِهِۦ يَسۡتَهۡزِءُونَ ۝ وَلَقَدۡ أَهۡلَكۡنَا مَا حَوۡلَكُم مِّنَ ٱلۡقُرَىٰ وَصَرَّفۡنَا ٱلۡـَٔايَـٰتِ لَعَلَّهُمۡ يَرۡجِعُونَ ۝ فَلَوۡلَا نَصَرَهُمُ ٱلَّذِينَ ٱتَّخَذُوا۟ مِن دُونِ ٱللَّهِ قُرۡبَانًا ءَالِهَةًۢ بَلۡ ضَلُّوا۟ عَنۡهُمۡ وَذَٰلِكَ إِفۡكُهُمۡ وَمَا كَانُوا۟ يَفۡتَرُونَ ۝

---

[a] The worldly status enjoyed by the Quraysh chiefs had made them arrogant. Here they have been reminded of their neighbours, the people of 'Ad. From the point of view of civilization, they had been on a much higher plane than the Quraysh. Nonetheless, when God's ordinance was imposed, their entire grandeur and glory were destroyed. Whatever they had considered their supports, failed to come to their rescue.

A human being is, after all, going to be greatly reduced in stature before the majesty of God. But that apart, the system of the world has been devised in such a way that in this life man has to make himself small before others. This is shown by events which are the signs of God. If, before being cut down to size in the Hereafter, a man learns a lesson from these signs, he will voluntarily make himself small in this very life. Before facing the Hereafter, he will become realistic in this world itself.

Different kinds of events demonstrate God's signs, but man turns a blind eye and a deaf ear to them, for he is not prepared to learn any lesson from them.

²⁹ Remember how We sent to you a band of jinn who wished to hear the Quran and as they listened to its recitation, they said to one another, 'Be silent and listen,' and, then when it was finished, they went back to their people, to give them warning. ³⁰ They said, 'O our people, we have heard a Book, which has been sent down after Moses, fulfilling the predictions existing in previous scriptures; it guides to the truth, and to the right path. ³¹ Our people, respond to the one who calls you to God. Believe in him! God will forgive you your sins and protect you from a painful punishment. ³² But he who does not respond to God's calls can never elude [Him] on earth, nor can he have any protector against Him. Such people have clearly gone far astray.'[a]

وَإِذْ صَرَفْنَا إِلَيْكَ نَفَرًا مِّنَ ٱلْجِنِّ يَسْتَمِعُونَ ٱلْقُرْءَانَ فَلَمَّا حَضَرُوهُ قَالُوٓا۟ أَنصِتُوا۟ فَلَمَّا قُضِىَ وَلَّوْا۟ إِلَىٰ قَوْمِهِم مُّنذِرِينَ ۝ قَالُوا۟ يَٰقَوْمَنَآ إِنَّا سَمِعْنَا كِتَٰبًا أُنزِلَ مِنۢ بَعْدِ مُوسَىٰ مُصَدِّقًا لِّمَا بَيْنَ يَدَيْهِ يَهْدِىٓ إِلَى ٱلْحَقِّ وَإِلَىٰ طَرِيقٍ مُّسْتَقِيمٍ ۝ يَٰقَوْمَنَآ أَجِيبُوا۟ دَاعِىَ ٱللَّهِ وَءَامِنُوا۟ بِهِۦ يَغْفِرْ لَكُم مِّن ذُنُوبِكُمْ وَيُجِرْكُم مِّنْ عَذَابٍ أَلِيمٍ ۝ وَمَن لَّا يُجِبْ دَاعِىَ ٱللَّهِ فَلَيْسَ بِمُعْجِزٍ فِى ٱلْأَرْضِ وَلَيْسَ لَهُۥ مِن دُونِهِۦٓ أَوْلِيَآءُ أُو۟لَٰٓئِكَ فِى ضَلَٰلٍ مُّبِينٍ ۝

---

[a] In the tenth year of Muhammad's prophethood in Makkah, the life and work of the Prophet were becoming seriously jeopardized. At that time he went from Makkah to Taif in the hope that he might find some supporters there. But the people there received him rudely. While returning, spent the night at a place called Nakhla. He was reciting the Quran while offering prayers there, when a group of Jinn heard the Quran and became believers in it. One group rejected the Quran. But, at that very moment, another group accepted it and did so with such eagerness that they became its emissaries.

³³ Have they not seen that God, who created the heavens and the earth and was not wearied by their creation, has the power to bring the dead back to life? Yes, indeed, He has power over all things. ³⁴ On the Day when those who deny the truth will be brought before the Fire, they shall be asked, 'Is this not the truth?' They will reply, 'Yes, by our Lord.' He will say, 'Then taste the punishment, because of your denial of the truth.'ᵃ

أَوَلَمْ يَرَوْا أَنَّ ٱللَّهَ ٱلَّذِى خَلَقَ ٱلسَّمَٰوَٰتِ وَٱلْأَرْضَ وَلَمْ يَعْىَ بِخَلْقِهِنَّ بِقَٰدِرٍ عَلَىٰٓ أَن يُحْىِۦَ ٱلْمَوْتَىٰ بَلَىٰٓ إِنَّهُۥ عَلَىٰ كُلِّ شَىْءٍ قَدِيرٌ ۝ وَيَوْمَ يُعْرَضُ ٱلَّذِينَ كَفَرُوا۟ عَلَى ٱلنَّارِ أَلَيْسَ هَٰذَا بِٱلْحَقِّ قَالُوا۟ بَلَىٰ وَرَبِّنَا قَالَ فَذُوقُوا۟ ٱلْعَذَابَ بِمَا كُنتُمْ تَكْفُرُونَ ۝

ᵃ The coming into existence of the gigantic universe consisting of the heavens and the earth and then its functioning for millions of years in perfect harmony and with total precision proves that the Creator of this universe is the possessor of immense powers. Moreover, bringing the universe into existence did not exhaust His resources. Had the work of creation been fatiguing for Him, the universe after creation would not have been found running with such great exactitude.

The immense power of God being demonstrated throughout the universe suffices for us to be certain that the resurrection of human beings and the taking stock of their deeds is not at all difficult for Him.

In the present world reality comes before a man, but he does not accept it. This is because the result of the denial of reality is not immediately obvious. In the Hereafter, the terrible consequences will be there before every man; he will then become extremely serious and will readily accept the reality which he was not prepared to accept in the present world. However, acceptance of truth at that time will be of no avail.

³⁵ Have patience, then, as had the steadfast Messengers before you; and be in no haste about them. On the Day when they see what they are threatened with, it will appear to them as though they had not tarried longer than an hour of a day. [Your responsibility is] to deliver the message: and none but the disobedient shall be destroyed.ᵃ

فَٱصْبِرْ كَمَا صَبَرَ أُوْلُوا۟ ٱلْعَزْمِ مِنَ ٱلرُّسُلِ وَلَا تَسْتَعْجِل لَّهُمْ كَأَنَّهُمْ يَوْمَ يَرَوْنَ مَا يُوعَدُونَ لَمْ يَلْبَثُوٓا۟ إِلَّا سَاعَةً مِّن نَّهَارٍ بَلَٰغٌ فَهَلْ يُهْلَكُ إِلَّا ٱلْقَوْمُ ٱلْفَٰسِقُونَ ۝

ᵃ A preacher who calls for the acceptance of Truth has always to stand on the firm ground of patience. Patience in fact consists of unilaterally ignoring the tortures inflicted by his addressees. He should continuously exhort his addressees to enter his fold, in spite of their obduracy and their adamant rejection of his plea. He should always and in all cases be their well-wisher, regardless of the unpleasant experiences he has had on their account. This unilateral patience is necessary because, without this, God's plan for the addressees would remain unfulfilled.

All God's messengers and prophets of every period have performed the task of giving the call of Truth in a similar manner, with patience and perseverance. In future also those who perform this task as deputies of the prophets shall have to do it on the same pattern. In the eyes of God only those will be adjudged true preachers (da'is), who can unilaterally show the capacity for tolerance.

47. MUHAMMAD

In the name of God,
the Most Gracious, the Most Merciful

¹ God will bring to naught all the good deeds of those who are bent on denying the truth and bar [others] from the path of God. ² As for those who believe and do good deeds and believe in what has been revealed to Muhammad—and it is the truth from their Lord—God will remove their sins from them and set their condition right. ³ That is because the ones who deny the truth follow falsehood, while those who believe follow the Truth from their Lord. Thus God sets forth comparisons for mankind.ᵃ

ᵃ In ancient Arabia, the deeds of those who denied the prophethood of the Prophet Muhammad and opposed him, counted for nothing. In other words, since they did not prove to be religious on the level of moral awareness, their achievements, performed as a matter of conventional and traditional religiosity, became valueless.

The people of ancient Arabia used to consider themselves the community of Abraham and Ishmael. They also had the honour of being the custodians of the Kabah. The customs of prayer, fasting and Hajj in some form or the other were also prevalent among them. The serving of Hajj pilgrims, good treatment of relatives, and hospitality towards guests were also social requirements. Though the ancient Arabs acquitted themselves well on all these scores, their actions were not the outcome of their conscious religiousness. They performed all these deeds simply because it had been the custom to do so for centuries. In order to recognise the prophet of the time, it was necessary for them to have heightened their own awareness. At that time, the force of ancient traditions had not yet built up around the Prophet Muhammad. Therefore, only one who was capable of recognising reality through deep personal perception could have acknowledged him. In this context, when they rejected their contemporary prophet, it was clearly established that their religiousness was based purely on tradition and not on personal realization. And God requires religiousness in spirit not in form devoid of spirit.

Those, however, who embraced the faith of the Prophet of their own times, proved that they were capable of being religious at a heightened level of consciousness.

4 When you meet those who deny the truth in battle, strike them in the neck, and once they are defeated, make [them] prisoners, and afterwards either set them free as an act of grace, or let them ransom [themselves] until the war is finally over. Thus you shall do; and if God had pleased, He would certainly have exacted retribution from them, but His purpose is to test some of you by means of others. As for those who are killed in God's cause, He will never let their deeds be in vain; 5 He will guide them and improve their condition; 6 He will admit them into the Garden He has already made known to them.*a*

فَإِذَا لَقِيتُمُ ٱلَّذِينَ كَفَرُوا۟ فَضَرْبَ ٱلرِّقَابِ حَتَّىٰٓ إِذَآ أَثْخَنتُمُوهُمْ فَشُدُّوا۟ ٱلْوَثَاقَ فَإِمَّا مَنًّۢا بَعْدُ وَإِمَّا فِدَآءً حَتَّىٰ تَضَعَ ٱلْحَرْبُ أَوْزَارَهَا ذَٰلِكَ وَلَوْ يَشَآءُ ٱللَّهُ لَٱنتَصَرَ مِنْهُمْ وَلَٰكِن لِّيَبْلُوَا۟ بَعْضَكُم بِبَعْضٍ وَٱلَّذِينَ قُتِلُوا۟ فِى سَبِيلِ ٱللَّهِ فَلَن يُضِلَّ أَعْمَٰلَهُمْ ۝ سَيَهْدِيهِمْ وَيُصْلِحُ بَالَهُمْ ۝ وَيُدْخِلُهُمُ ٱلْجَنَّةَ عَرَّفَهَا لَهُمْ ۝

---

a Here, disbelievers or rejectors refers to those who did not embrace the Faith despite compelling arguments having been put forward in its favour. Moreover, they unjustifiably waged war against the Prophet Muhammad and thus compelled the Prophet to take defensive steps. As regards such people, it has been ordained that in case of confrontation with them, they should be fought against and crushed, so that they should not be able to place impediments in the way of the mission of Truth.

It has ever been the rule of God that those who rejected their Prophet would be destroyed after the conclusion of arguments. But in case of the last prophet, it was the will of God that, through him and his companions, the age of polytheism should be brought to an end and a new era of history should be brought into existence on the strength of the oneness of God. For this, epoch-making men were needed and their selection could be done only under the most trying circumstances: this purpose was achieved by sending the companions of the Prophet of God into the war waged by his opponents.

Paradise is the most familiar and best known concept for a believer. He not only hears about it from the Prophet, but also, by means of his developed inner knowledge (*ma'rifah*), gains an intuitive understanding of it. It is still this deep understanding of the unseen, hidden Paradise that inspires and encourages man to seek it, regardless of the sacrifices to be made. Had it not been so, nobody would have sacrificed today's world in the hopes of entering tomorrow's Paradise.

⁷ Believers! If you succour God, He will succour you and make your footsteps firm. ⁸ But as for those who are bent on denying the truth, destruction will be their lot, and [God] will make their deeds come to nothing. ⁹ It is because they are averse to what God has revealed that He has rendered their deeds futile. ¹⁰ Have they not travelled the earth and seen how those before them met their end? God destroyed them utterly: a similar fate awaits those who deny the truth. ¹¹ That is because God is the protector of the believers, and those who deny the truth have no protector at all.ᵃ

يَـٰٓأَيُّهَا ٱلَّذِينَ ءَامَنُوٓاْ إِن تَنصُرُواْ ٱللَّهَ يَنصُرْكُمْ وَيُثَبِّتْ أَقْدَامَكُمْ ۝ وَٱلَّذِينَ كَفَرُواْ فَتَعْسًا لَّهُمْ وَأَضَلَّ أَعْمَـٰلَهُمْ ۝ ذَٰلِكَ بِأَنَّهُمْ كَرِهُواْ مَآ أَنزَلَ ٱللَّهُ فَأَحْبَطَ أَعْمَـٰلَهُمْ ۝ ۞ أَفَلَمْ يَسِيرُواْ فِى ٱلْأَرْضِ فَيَنظُرُواْ كَيْفَ كَانَ عَـٰقِبَةُ ٱلَّذِينَ مِن قَبْلِهِمْ ۚ دَمَّرَ ٱللَّهُ عَلَيْهِمْ ۖ وَلِلْكَـٰفِرِينَ أَمْثَـٰلُهَا ۝ ذَٰلِكَ بِأَنَّ ٱللَّهَ مَوْلَى ٱلَّذِينَ ءَامَنُواْ وَأَنَّ ٱلْكَـٰفِرِينَ لَا مَوْلَىٰ لَهُمْ ۝

ᵃ The One who causes events to occur is God. But He does so through the chain of cause and effect. Such is the case with religion also. It is God's desire that the force of falsehood should be destroyed and Truth should eternally prevail throughout the world. But in order that this should happen, Almighty God requires certain individuals to serve as the human medium for this Divine Action. This process is termed here as 'assisting God'.

When a group rises to assist God it simultaneously performs another task, i.e. it proves unbelievers to be such. The individuals assisting God with extreme seriousness and sincere well-wishing call the people towards God. Distancing themselves from such behaviour as is opposed to the Truth, they bear testimony to the truth of religion (din). They establish the Truth as such to the ultimate degree. In this way, the process of the conclusion of argument in missionary work is completed; this is required by Almighty God for His judgement in the Hereafter. The upholders of truth become dominant over the upholders of untruth, provided the former do dawah work which is a prerequisite for seeking divine support.

¹² God will admit those who believe and do good deeds to Gardens through which rivers flow. Those who deny the truth may take their fill of pleasure in this world, and eat as cattle do, but the Fire will be their ultimate abode. ¹³ How many towns We have destroyed, greater in strength than your city which has driven you out, and there was no one to help them.ᵃ

إِنَّ ٱللَّهَ يُدْخِلُ ٱلَّذِينَ ءَامَنُوا۟ وَعَمِلُوا۟ ٱلصَّٰلِحَٰتِ جَنَّٰتٍ تَجْرِى مِن تَحْتِهَا ٱلْأَنْهَٰرُ ۖ وَٱلَّذِينَ كَفَرُوا۟ يَتَمَتَّعُونَ وَيَأْكُلُونَ كَمَا تَأْكُلُ ٱلْأَنْعَٰمُ وَٱلنَّارُ مَثْوًى لَّهُمْ ۝ وَكَأَيِّن مِّن قَرْيَةٍ هِىَ أَشَدُّ قُوَّةً مِّن قَرْيَتِكَ ٱلَّتِىٓ أَخْرَجَتْكَ أَهْلَكْنَٰهُمْ فَلَا نَاصِرَ لَهُمْ ۝

ᵃ The people of Arabia, who had rejected the Prophet of God, were forewarned by him that they should not imagine that they would remain unscathed, simply because they were free to eat and drink at that time. They were completely within the grip of God and the proof of this was that if they persisted in rejecting the truth, they would be destroyed in accordance with the system of God.

Things happened exactly according to the prediction. The upholders of Truth became dominant, while the rejectors of Truth were destroyed.

14 Can then he who takes his stand on clear evidence from his God be likened to those for whom the evil that they do is made to look beautiful, and who follow their own desires? 15 Here is a description of the Garden promised to the righteous: therein are rivers of water which is forever pure; and rivers of milk of which the taste never changes; and rivers of wine, a delight to those who drink it, and rivers of pure honey. And in it they will have all kinds of fruit, and will receive forgiveness from their Lord. Can those who enjoy such bliss be like those who abide in the Fire and who are given boiling water to drink so that it tears their bowels? *a*

أَفَمَن كَانَ عَلَىٰ بَيِّنَةٍ مِّن رَّبِّهِۦ كَمَن زُيِّنَ لَهُۥ سُوٓءُ عَمَلِهِۦ وَٱتَّبَعُوٓاْ أَهْوَآءَهُم ۞ مَّثَلُ ٱلْجَنَّةِ ٱلَّتِى وُعِدَ ٱلْمُتَّقُونَ فِيهَآ أَنْهَٰرٌ مِّن مَّآءٍ غَيْرِ ءَاسِنٍ وَأَنْهَٰرٌ مِّن لَّبَنٍ لَّمْ يَتَغَيَّرْ طَعْمُهُۥ وَأَنْهَٰرٌ مِّنْ خَمْرٍ لَّذَّةٍ لِّلشَّٰرِبِينَ وَأَنْهَٰرٌ مِّنْ عَسَلٍ مُّصَفًّى وَلَهُمْ فِيهَا مِن كُلِّ ٱلثَّمَرَٰتِ وَمَغْفِرَةٌ مِّن رَّبِّهِمْ كَمَنْ هُوَ خَٰلِدٌ فِى ٱلنَّارِ وَسُقُواْ مَآءً حَمِيمًا فَقَطَّعَ أَمْعَآءَهُمْ ۞

---

a Abiding by rational argument (*baiyyinah*) means building one's life on realistic facts, while following one's own desires (*ahwa*) means deviating from the truth. This is wanting to build one's own world in God's world against God's will.

In this present world of trial, both the realists and the self-indulgent apparently have equal opportunities. But in the real world of the Hereafter, only the first group will have a share in the eternal bounties of God, while the second group will be an utter failure and will be forever in disgrace.

16 Among them are those who listen to you, but then, when they leave your presence, say to those who have been given knowledge [Scripture], "What was that he just said?" Such are those whose hearts God has sealed, and who follow their own base desires. 17 But as for those who follow guidance, He adds to their guidance, and shows them the way to righteousness.[a]

وَمِنْهُم مَّن يَسْتَمِعُ إِلَيْكَ حَتَّىٰ إِذَا خَرَجُوا۟ مِنْ عِندِكَ قَالُوا۟ لِلَّذِينَ أُوتُوا۟ ٱلْعِلْمَ مَاذَا قَالَ ءَانِفًا ۚ أُو۟لَٰٓئِكَ ٱلَّذِينَ طَبَعَ ٱللَّهُ عَلَىٰ قُلُوبِهِمْ وَٱتَّبَعُوٓا۟ أَهْوَآءَهُمْ ۝ وَٱلَّذِينَ ٱهْتَدَوْا۟ زَادَهُمْ هُدًى وَءَاتَىٰهُمْ تَقْوَىٰهُمْ ۝

[a] It is characteristic of a hypocrite when he is in a serious-minded gathering, to seem to be outwardly very serious while his mind is busy with other things. He does not pay any attention to the words spoken by the preacher. When he comes out of the gathering, he asks other knowledgeable persons, 'What did the venerable gentleman say?'

This is the price they have to pay on account of their desire-worship. They mire themselves in desire-worship and then are overwhelmed by it. Instead of allowing reason to prevail, they follow their own desires. The result is that their sensitivities become blunted and their minds do not remain capable of grasping the finer shades of reality.

Unlike them, those who give importance to reality, and who bow down before true arguments, activate their intellect in the process. The inner knowledge and intense realisation of such individuals increase day-by-day. Their faith is never vitiated by their falling into a state of inertia.

¹⁸ Are they awaiting the Hour of Doom to come upon them suddenly? Its signs have already come. But of what avail will their admonition be to them when it has actually come upon them? ¹⁹ Know then that there is no god except God. Ask forgiveness for your wrongdoing, and for the men and women who believe. God knows both your movements and your lodging.^a

فَهَلْ يَنظُرُونَ إِلَّا ٱلسَّاعَةَ أَن تَأْتِيَهُم بَغْتَةً فَقَدْ جَآءَ أَشْرَاطُهَا فَأَنَّىٰ لَهُمْ إِذَا جَآءَتْهُمْ ذِكْرَىٰهُمْ ۝ فَٱعْلَمْ أَنَّهُۥ لَآ إِلَٰهَ إِلَّا ٱللَّهُ وَٱسْتَغْفِرْ لِذَنۢبِكَ وَلِلْمُؤْمِنِينَ وَٱلْمُؤْمِنَٰتِ وَٱللَّهُ يَعْلَمُ مُتَقَلَّبَكُمْ وَمَثْوَىٰكُمْ ۝

---

^a One who refuses to be on the alert on receipt of advance information about an earthquake, is in fact courting disaster, because every ensuing moment is bringing the earthquake closer to him. Similarly, man does not take warning from the portents of Doomsday. But when Doomsday breaks upon him, he will resort to pious avowals. But such avowals at that stage will be of no use, because only that testament to the truth has value which is made before the curtain rises. After the rising of the curtain, it has no value.

Begging God's pardon is, in fact, an expression of the feeling of one's humbleness. Firm belief in the horror of Doomsday, in God's power and the realisation of His being aware of everything, creates a psychological upheaval in man. This is evinced at every moment in the shape of sublime utterances. These take the shape of remembrance of God, prayer and the seeking of God's pardon.

²⁰ Those who believe ask why no chapter [about fighting] has been sent down. Yet when a decisive chapter that mentions fighting is sent down, you can see the sick of heart looking at you [Prophet] as if they were under the shadow of death. Therefore, woe to them! ²¹ Obedience and saying what is just would become them more; when the decision is taken, it would be better for them if they acted sincerely towards God. ²² Then if you turn away, you are likely to spread corruption on the earth and sever your ties of kinship. ²³ Such are those whom God has rejected, making their ears deaf and their eyes blind.ᵃ

وَيَقُولُ ٱلَّذِينَ ءَامَنُواْ لَوْلَا نُزِّلَتْ سُورَةٌ فَإِذَآ أُنزِلَتْ سُورَةٌ مُّحْكَمَةٌ وَذُكِرَ فِيهَا ٱلْقِتَالُ رَأَيْتَ ٱلَّذِينَ فِي قُلُوبِهِم مَّرَضٌ يَنظُرُونَ إِلَيْكَ نَظَرَ ٱلْمَغْشِيِّ عَلَيْهِ مِنَ ٱلْمَوْتِ فَأَوْلَىٰ لَهُمْ ٢٠ طَاعَةٌ وَقَوْلٌ مَّعْرُوفٌ فَإِذَا عَزَمَ ٱلْأَمْرُ فَلَوْ صَدَقُواْ ٱللَّهَ لَكَانَ خَيْرًا لَّهُمْ ٢١ فَهَلْ عَسَيْتُمْ إِن تَوَلَّيْتُمْ أَن تُفْسِدُواْ فِي ٱلْأَرْضِ وَتُقَطِّعُوٓاْ أَرْحَامَكُمْ ٢٢ أُوْلَٰٓئِكَ ٱلَّذِينَ لَعَنَهُمُ ٱللَّهُ فَأَصَمَّهُمْ وَأَعْمَىٰٓ أَبْصَرَهُمْ ٢٣

ᵃ It is characteristic of a hypocrite to talk big. But his words do not follow his actions; he talks of *jihad* but in times of defensive battle runs away from it.

It is the way of true people of faith that they are always ready to hear and obey and, when stringent measures are decided upon, they prove by their actions that they have fulfilled the pledge that they had taken before God as their witness.

In order to avoid participation in defensive battle, hypocrites make a pretence of being lovers of peace. But, in reality, whenever they have the opportunity, they start spreading bad blood, so much so that, completely careless of Muslims who are their relatives, they become the supporters of their enemies. In the eyes of God, such people are accursed. Being such means their thinking power is taken away from them. In spite of having eyes, they will not see, and in spite of having ears, they will hear nothing.

²⁴ Will they not, then, ponder over this Quran? Or are there locks upon their hearts? ²⁵ Surely, those who turn their backs [on this message] after guidance has been shown to them, [do it because] Satan has embellished their fancies and God gives them respite; ²⁶ because they say to those who abhor what God has revealed, 'We will obey you in some matters.' God knows their secrets. ²⁷ Then how will it be when the angels take their souls, beating them on their faces and their backs, ²⁸ because they followed the way that made God wrathful, and hated to adopt the way of His pleasure? So He made their actions come to nothing.ᵃ

أَفَلَا يَتَدَبَّرُونَ ٱلْقُرْءَانَ أَمْ عَلَىٰ قُلُوبٍ أَقْفَالُهَآ ۝ إِنَّ ٱلَّذِينَ ٱرْتَدُّوا۟ عَلَىٰٓ أَدْبَٰرِهِم مِّنۢ بَعْدِ مَا تَبَيَّنَ لَهُمُ ٱلْهُدَى ٱلشَّيْطَٰنُ سَوَّلَ لَهُمْ وَأَمْلَىٰ لَهُمْ ۝ ذَٰلِكَ بِأَنَّهُمْ قَالُوا۟ لِلَّذِينَ كَرِهُوا۟ مَا نَزَّلَ ٱللَّهُ سَنُطِيعُكُمْ فِى بَعْضِ ٱلْأَمْرِ وَٱللَّهُ يَعْلَمُ إِسْرَارَهُمْ ۝ فَكَيْفَ إِذَا تَوَفَّتْهُمُ ٱلْمَلَٰٓئِكَةُ يَضْرِبُونَ وُجُوهَهُمْ وَأَدْبَٰرَهُمْ ۝ ذَٰلِكَ بِأَنَّهُمُ ٱتَّبَعُوا۟ مَآ أَسْخَطَ ٱللَّهَ وَكَرِهُوا۟ رِضْوَٰنَهُۥ فَأَحْبَطَ أَعْمَٰلَهُمْ ۝

ᵃ The Quran is a book of guidance. But in order to have the benefit of it, it is necessary for the reader to be serious about it. If some improper feeling makes him flippant about it, he can never avail of the counsel offered, even although it has been presented in the best possible manner.

If any commandment of religion is issued by which an individual is required to sacrifice his desires and interests, Satan immediately gives him some excuse not to do so, and since the present world is a trial ground for mankind, he has the opportunity to make use of this lame excuse. But this holds only for a very short time. When death strikes, the whole position will be entirely different.

²⁹ Do the sick at heart imagine that God will not bring to light their malice? ³⁰ Now had We so willed, We could have shown them clearly to you, and then you could have identified them by their marks, but surely you will know them by the tone of their speech! God knows all that you do.ᵃ

أَمْ حَسِبَ ٱلَّذِينَ فِى قُلُوبِهِم مَّرَضٌ أَن لَّن يُخْرِجَ ٱللَّهُ أَضْغَـٰنَهُمْ ۝ وَلَوْ نَشَآءُ لَأَرَيْنَـٰكَهُمْ فَلَعَرَفْتَهُم بِسِيمَـٰهُمْ وَلَتَعْرِفَنَّهُمْ فِى لَحْنِ ٱلْقَوْلِ ۚ وَٱللَّهُ يَعْلَمُ أَعْمَـٰلَكُمْ ۝

ᵃ The hypocrite Muslims were jealous of their pious brethren in religion? The reason was that they felt that all progress made by Islam benefitted sincere Muslims, and this was very distressing to them. They used to wonder why they should sacrifice their lives and property in a campaign which enhanced the position of others, while conferring no greatness on them.

The hypocrites hid these inner feelings in their outward behaviour. But this did not remain concealed from people of understanding. Their artificial tone revealed that their connection with Islam was that of outward show and was not in any sense heartfelt.

³¹ Most certainly We will try you until We have discovered those among you who strive their hardest, and those who are steadfast, and will test your record. ³² Surely, they who are bent on denying the truth and on barring [others] from the path of God, and oppose the Messenger when they have been shown guidance, cannot harm God in any way. He will cause all their deeds to come to nothing.ᵃ

وَلَنَبْلُوَنَّكُمْ حَتَّىٰ نَعْلَمَ ٱلْمُجَٰهِدِينَ مِنكُمْ وَٱلصَّٰبِرِينَ وَنَبْلُوَاْ أَخْبَارَكُمْ ۝ إِنَّ ٱلَّذِينَ كَفَرُواْ وَصَدُّواْ عَن سَبِيلِ ٱللَّهِ وَشَآقُّواْ ٱلرَّسُولَ مِنۢ بَعْدِ مَا تَبَيَّنَ لَهُمُ ٱلْهُدَىٰ لَن يَضُرُّواْ ٱللَّهَ شَيْـًٔا وَسَيُحْبِطُ أَعْمَٰلَهُمْ ۝

ᵃ When a man struggles for the cause of religion, he has to undergo different experiences, which are a test of his Faith: he must prove his steadfastness of belief by making sacrifices, crush his self, ignore his material interests, tolerate harassment; and remain steadfast in his devotion to God, even at the cost of his life and property.

In order to place the believer in such circumstances, it is necessary for non-believers to have full freedom, so that they may indulge in all sorts of activities against the people of Faith. These activities, on the one hand, establish the guilt of opponents beyond doubt and, on the other, give the opportunity to the people of Faith to show that, by being steadfast in their Faith under the most trying circumstances, they are real believers and are entitled to be selected for the eternal afterlife in God's ideal world.

³³ Believers, obey God and obey the Messenger: do not let your deeds go to waste—³⁴ surely those who reject the truth and bar others from the path of God, then die as deniers of the truth, will not be granted forgiveness by God. ³⁵ So do not lose heart or appeal for peace when you have gained the upper hand. God is with you and will never let your works go to waste.^a

يَـٰٓأَيُّهَا ٱلَّذِينَ ءَامَنُوٓاْ أَطِيعُواْ ٱللَّهَ وَأَطِيعُواْ ٱلرَّسُولَ وَلَا تُبْطِلُوٓاْ أَعْمَـٰلَكُمْ ۝ إِنَّ ٱلَّذِينَ كَفَرُواْ وَصَدُّواْ عَن سَبِيلِ ٱللَّهِ ثُمَّ مَاتُواْ وَهُمْ كُفَّارٌ فَلَن يَغْفِرَ ٱللَّهُ لَهُمْ ۝ فَلَا تَهِنُواْ وَتَدْعُوٓاْ إِلَى ٱلسَّلْمِ وَأَنتُمُ ٱلْأَعْلَوْنَ وَٱللَّهُ مَعَكُمْ وَلَن يَتِرَكُمْ أَعْمَـٰلَكُمْ ۝

---

^a It is mentioned in a tradition that, during the period of the Prophet Muhammad, certain Muslims opined that if they professed, 'la ilaha illallah' (there is nobody worth worshipping except God), they would come to no harm by any sin. In that connection, this verse 33 was revealed. In this light the verse means that a man should combine obedience with Faith. He should carry out not only the harmless commandments but also those commandments for which he has to crush his self and jeopardize his interests. If he does not do so, his earlier deeds will be of no avail.

The position of weak Muslims is that they will support the Truth on the condition that they should not have to incur the displeasure of the great men of their day. When they see that supporting the Truth is becoming a cause of displeasure to them, they tilt towards them even if these great men are rejecters of the Truth or stubbornly resistant to it.

Those who reject the Truth or set themselves up as its opponents can never receive the grace of God. Then how can those who side with such rejecters of Truth meet with any other fate?

In Islam there is war as well as peace. But that war is not Islamic which is fought under provocation. In Islam only defensive war is permitted. Such a war should not be the consequence of an emotional reaction, but one which results from a proper decision, and is defensive by nature.

36 The life of this world is only a game, a pastime, but if you believe and are mindful of God, He will recompense you and will not ask you for your wealth. 37 If He were to ask it [wealth] of you, and continued to press you, you would be niggardly, and this would show your ill-will. 38 Behold! You are those who are called upon to spend for God's cause, but among you are those who are niggardly, and whoever stints does so against his own self. Indeed, God is self-sufficient, but you stand in need [of Him], and if you turn back, He will bring in your place another people, who will not be like you.ᵃ

إِنَّمَا ٱلْحَيَوٰةُ ٱلدُّنْيَا لَعِبٌ وَلَهْوٌ ۚ وَإِن تُؤْمِنُوا۟ وَتَتَّقُوا۟ يُؤْتِكُمْ أُجُورَكُمْ وَلَا يَسْـَٔلْكُمْ أَمْوَٰلَكُمْ ۝ إِن يَسْـَٔلْكُمُوهَا فَيُحْفِكُمْ تَبْخَلُوا۟ وَيُخْرِجْ أَضْغَٰنَكُمْ ۝ هَٰٓأَنتُمْ هَٰٓؤُلَآءِ تُدْعَوْنَ لِتُنفِقُوا۟ فِى سَبِيلِ ٱللَّهِ فَمِنكُم مَّن يَبْخَلُ ۖ وَمَن يَبْخَلْ فَإِنَّمَا يَبْخَلُ عَن نَّفْسِهِۦ ۚ وَٱللَّهُ ٱلْغَنِىُّ وَأَنتُمُ ٱلْفُقَرَآءُ ۚ وَإِن تَتَوَلَّوْا۟ يَسْتَبْدِلْ قَوْمًا غَيْرَكُمْ ثُمَّ لَا يَكُونُوٓا۟ أَمْثَٰلَكُم ۝

ᵃ The benefits of the world and its attractiveness act as impediments to the adoption of a life of Faith and righteousness. Man knows what kind of behaviour will lead him to success in the Hereafter. But immediate considerations overcome him and he goes astray. The fact is that God is most Merciful and Kind towards his subjects. He never demands of His subjects anything which is unbearable to them.

Islam is God's religion. But the tasks of its propagation and protection have to be carried out in this world of cause and effect by a group of human beings. Muslims constitute this group. If Muslims discharge their duty, they will demonstrate their worthiness in the eyes of God. But if they fail to discharge this duty, God will guide other nations towards the Faith and maintain the continuity of His religion through them.

48. VICTORY

In the name of God,
the Most Gracious, the Most Merciful

¹ Truly, We have granted you a clear victory ² so that God may forgive you your past and future sins and complete His favour to you and guide you to a straight path, ³ and so that God might bestow on you His mighty help.ᵃ

بِسْمِ اللَّهِ الرَّحْمَٰنِ الرَّحِيمِ

إِنَّا فَتَحْنَا لَكَ فَتْحًا مُّبِينًا ۞ لِّيَغْفِرَ لَكَ اللَّهُ مَا تَقَدَّمَ مِن ذَنبِكَ وَمَا تَأَخَّرَ وَيُتِمَّ نِعْمَتَهُۥ عَلَيْكَ وَيَهْدِيَكَ صِرَاطًا مُّسْتَقِيمًا ۞ وَيَنصُرَكَ اللَّهُ نَصْرًا عَزِيزًا ۞

ᵃ In the sixth year of the Hijrah, the Prophet Muhammad left Madinah for Makkah along with his companions, so that he could perform the rite of pilgrimage there. He had reached Hudaybiyyah when the pagans of Makkah came forward and barred his way, saying that they would not allow him to enter Makkah. Mutual negotiations followed, as a result of which a peace treaty was drawn up and signed by both sides.

This treaty was executed apparently on the unilateral terms and conditions dictated by the polytheists. As a consequence, the companions of the Prophet Muhammad were very disheartened: they considered it a degrading treaty. But on the way back from Hudaybiyyah, this verse was revealed, 'We have granted you a clear victory.' The reason for this was that according to this Treaty it was agreed that for ten years there would be no war between the Muslims and polytheists. The end of fighting was in fact synonymous to the opening of the door of *dawah*. After the Hijrah (migration to Madinah), due to incessant fighting, *dawah* activity had stopped. Now the truce had created an open atmosphere in which there could be a free exchange of thought between the opponents.

In this way, this treaty changed the sphere of combat. Formerly, the competition between the two sides had been held on the battlefield where the Muslims' antagonists had the upper hand. Now rivalry shifted to the field of intellect and in this, the theory of the one God clearly triumphed over polytheism. Here now was the 'straight path', i.e. the way which made the victory of the flag-bearers of monotheism an absolute certainty.

⁴It was He who sent down tranquillity into the hearts of the believers, to add faith to their faith—the forces of the heavens and earth belong to Him; He is all knowing and all wise—⁵and so that He might admit the believers, men and women, into Gardens through which rivers flow, to dwell therein forever, and so that He may remove their evils from them—that is, indeed, a supreme triumph in God's eyes—⁶and so that He might punish hypocritical men and women as well as the polytheists men and women who think evil thoughts about God; an evil turn of fortune will fall upon them, for God has become angry with them, and has rejected them and prepared Hell for them. How evil is such a destination. ⁷The forces of heavens and earth belong to God; He is almighty and all wise.ᵃ

هُوَ ٱلَّذِىٓ أَنزَلَ ٱلسَّكِينَةَ فِى قُلُوبِ ٱلْمُؤْمِنِينَ لِيَزْدَادُوٓاْ إِيمَـٰنًا مَّعَ إِيمَـٰنِهِمْ ۗ وَلِلَّهِ جُنُودُ ٱلسَّمَـٰوَٰتِ وَٱلْأَرْضِ ۚ وَكَانَ ٱللَّهُ عَلِيمًا حَكِيمًا ۝ لِّيُدْخِلَ ٱلْمُؤْمِنِينَ وَٱلْمُؤْمِنَـٰتِ جَنَّـٰتٍ تَجْرِى مِن تَحْتِهَا ٱلْأَنْهَـٰرُ خَـٰلِدِينَ فِيهَا وَيُكَفِّرَ عَنْهُمْ سَيِّـَٔاتِهِمْ ۚ وَكَانَ ذَٰلِكَ عِندَ ٱللَّهِ فَوْزًا عَظِيمًا ۝ وَيُعَذِّبَ ٱلْمُنَـٰفِقِينَ وَٱلْمُنَـٰفِقَـٰتِ وَٱلْمُشْرِكِينَ وَٱلْمُشْرِكَـٰتِ ٱلظَّآنِّينَ بِٱللَّهِ ظَنَّ ٱلسَّوْءِ ۚ عَلَيْهِمْ دَآئِرَةُ ٱلسَّوْءِ ۖ وَغَضِبَ ٱللَّهُ عَلَيْهِمْ وَلَعَنَهُمْ وَأَعَدَّ لَهُمْ جَهَنَّمَ ۖ وَسَآءَتْ مَصِيرًا ۝ وَلِلَّهِ جُنُودُ ٱلسَّمَـٰوَٰتِ وَٱلْأَرْضِ ۚ وَكَانَ ٱللَّهُ عَزِيزًا حَكِيمًا ۝

ᵃ Here tranquillity (*sakinah*) means not becoming irritated despite provocation. At Hudaybiyyah the opponents of Islam tried to goad Muslims in different ways into taking such action as would provide them with sufficient justification for aggression. But the Muslims for their part tolerated every attempt at provocation. Right to the end, they were firm on the policy of overlooking and ignoring such attempts.

Had God desired it, He could have subdued the forces of falsehood by means of His direct power and granted dominance to the Truth. Then, why is it that God created Hudaybiyyah Treaty-like conditions and made the Faithful undertake this journey? The purpose was to enhance the Faith by testing the Faithful. If a man curbs his urge to take revenge and enters into a treaty with an arrogant people simply because that is required by the task of disseminating the Truth, he does so by a conscientious decision. In so doing he makes his mind rule his heart. In this way, he increases his Faith-consciousness. He makes himself the recipient of such divine emotions as cannot be achieved in any other way. The advantage of this is that the people of Paradise and the people of Hell are separated in the process.

⁸ We have sent you forth as a witness and a bearer of good tidings and a warner, ⁹ so that you may believe in God and His Messenger, and may help him, and honour him, and so that you may glorify God morning and evening. ¹⁰ Behold, all who pledge their allegiance to you indeed pledge their allegiance to God: the hand of God is over their hands. Hence, he who breaks his oath, breaks it only to his own loss. Whereas he who remains true to what he has pledged to God, shall have a great reward bestowed upon him by God.ᵃ

إِنَّا أَرْسَلْنَاكَ شَاهِدًا وَمُبَشِّرًا وَنَذِيرًا ۝ لِتُؤْمِنُوا بِاللَّهِ وَرَسُولِهِ وَتُعَزِّرُوهُ وَتُوَقِّرُوهُ وَتُسَبِّحُوهُ بُكْرَةً وَأَصِيلًا ۝ إِنَّ الَّذِينَ يُبَايِعُونَكَ إِنَّمَا يُبَايِعُونَ اللَّهَ يَدُ اللَّهِ فَوْقَ أَيْدِيهِمْ ۚ فَمَن نَّكَثَ فَإِنَّمَا يَنكُثُ عَلَىٰ نَفْسِهِ ۖ وَمَنْ أَوْفَىٰ بِمَا عَاهَدَ عَلَيْهُ اللَّهَ فَسَيُؤْتِيهِ أَجْرًا عَظِيمًا ۝

ᵃ The real work of the Prophet is to be an exponent of the truth ('shaahid', as translated by Shah Waliullah). He should clearly show who will be entitled to God's Grace and who will deserve punishment from God in the eternal life after death.

The rising of such a 'shaahid' or witness of Truth poses the greatest trial for his addressees. They have to hear God's voice in the voice of a human being. They have to see a representative of God in the shape of human being. While giving their hand into the hands of a man, they have to think that they are giving their hand into the hands of God. For those who prove to have this superior insight, God has great rewards in store, but to those who fail in this test, God will mete out the most severe punishment.

¹¹ Those desert Arabs who remained behind will say to you, 'Our belongings and our families kept us occupied, so ask forgiveness for us.' They will say with their tongues what is not in their hearts. Say, 'Who then has any power at all [to intervene] on your behalf with God, if His will is to do you harm, or if He intends to do you good? Indeed, God is well aware of all that you do.' ¹² No. You thought that the Messenger and the believers would never return to their families; this prospect seemed pleasing to your hearts, and you conceived evil thoughts, and thus were doomed to perish. ¹³ For those who deny the truth, who do not believe in God and His Messenger, We have prepared a blazing Fire.ᵃ

سَيَقُولُ لَكَ ٱلْمُخَلَّفُونَ مِنَ ٱلْأَعْرَابِ شَغَلَتْنَآ أَمْوَالُنَا وَأَهْلُونَا فَٱسْتَغْفِرْ لَنَا يَقُولُونَ بِأَلْسِنَتِهِم مَّا لَيْسَ فِى قُلُوبِهِمْ قُلْ فَمَن يَمْلِكُ لَكُم مِّنَ ٱللَّهِ شَيْئًا إِنْ أَرَادَ بِكُمْ ضَرًّا أَوْ أَرَادَ بِكُمْ نَفْعًا بَلْ كَانَ ٱللَّهُ بِمَا تَعْمَلُونَ خَبِيرًا ۝ بَلْ ظَنَنتُمْ أَن لَّن يَنقَلِبَ ٱلرَّسُولُ وَٱلْمُؤْمِنُونَ إِلَىٰٓ أَهْلِيهِمْ أَبَدًا وَزُيِّنَ ذَٰلِكَ فِى قُلُوبِكُمْ وَظَنَنتُمْ ظَنَّ ٱلسَّوْءِ وَكُنتُمْ قَوْمًا بُورًا ۝ وَمَن لَّمْ يُؤْمِنۢ بِٱللَّهِ وَرَسُولِهِۦ فَإِنَّآ أَعْتَدْنَا لِلْكَفِرِينَ سَعِيرًا ۝

ᵃ The Prophet Muhammad had a dream in Madinah that he was undertaking a journey to Makkah for the purpose of performing *'umrah*. In accordance with this, he left for Makkah along with his companions. But at that time, the conditions were very adverse. There was a great fear that there would be a clash with the Quraysh and that the Muslims would be killed in large numbers. As they approached Makkah, the Quraysh did indeed start pelting the Muslim group with stones and attempted to provoke them in different ways, so that they would become overwrought and start fighting, and the Quraysh would thus have an excuse to do battle with them. But the unilateral tolerance shown and the overlooking of these acts on the part of the Muslims deprived the Quraysh of the occasion to fight them.

Many weak Muslims belonging to the areas surrounding Madinah did not join the pilgrims on their journey due to the fears mentioned above. When the Prophet had safely returned, these people came to him to profess their loyalty and started asking his pardon. But they were not pardoned, because their excuse was lame and false. Before God, a proper reason is acceptable at all times, while a false pretext is inevitably rejected outright. ▶

¹⁴ To God belongs the kingdom of the heavens and the earth. He forgives whom He pleases, and punishes whom He pleases. And God is most forgiving and merciful.

¹⁵ When you [believers] set off to gather the spoils, those that stayed behind will say, 'Let us come with you.' They want to change God's word, but tell them, 'You shall not follow us. God has declared this beforehand.' Then they will say, 'You are jealous of us.' But how little they understand! ª

وَلِلَّهِ مُلْكُ ٱلسَّمَـٰوَٰتِ وَٱلْأَرْضِ يَغْفِرُ لِمَن يَشَآءُ وَيُعَذِّبُ مَن يَشَآءُ وَكَانَ ٱللَّهُ غَفُورًا رَّحِيمًا ۝ سَيَقُولُ ٱلْمُخَلَّفُونَ إِذَا ٱنطَلَقْتُمْ إِلَىٰ مَغَانِمَ لِتَأْخُذُوهَا ذَرُونَا نَتَّبِعْكُمْ يُرِيدُونَ أَن يُبَدِّلُوا۟ كَلَـٰمَ ٱللَّهِ قُل لَّن تَتَّبِعُونَا كَذَٰلِكُمْ قَالَ ٱللَّهُ مِن قَبْلُ فَسَيَقُولُونَ بَلْ تَحْسُدُونَنَا بَلْ كَانُوا۟ لَا يَفْقَهُونَ إِلَّا قَلِيلًا ۝

They had no real excuse for their non-participation in the journey along with God's Prophet, except for their own feelings of uncertainty. They thought that they were protecting their interests by refusing to go on such a dangerous journey. They did not know that God is the Lord of all benefits and all harm. If God does not protect an individual, no protective armour can save him. Destruction will be the lot of such people in this world as well as in the Hereafter.

ª Before the Hudaybiyyah Treaty the Jews were very open in their hostility for the Muslims, because earlier they had had the full cooperation of Quraysh in this regard. The 'no-war' pact with the Quraysh at Hudaybiyyah cut off the Jews from the Quraysh and thereafter they were left on their own. For this reason, the morale of the Jews of Khybar, Tema, Fidak, etc. was lowered. So, three months after the signing of the treaty, when the Prophet besieged Khybar, the Jews of that place surrendered their arms without fighting and the Muslims acquired large amounts of booty on that occasion.

People of weak faith who did not accompany the Prophet on his Hudaybiyyah journey, considering it risky, now wanted to take part in the campaign against the Jews and thus have a share in the spoils, but they were prohibited from doing so. It is the rule of God that it is the one who takes risks who should receive the benefit. If a man wants to achieve something without taking a risk, he wants, in fact, to change Divine Law. But it is not possible for anybody in this world to change God's Law.

¹⁶ Say to the desert Arabs who stayed behind, 'You shall be called against a mighty people; then shall you fight, unless they submit. Then if you prove obedient, God will grant you a good reward, but if You turn back as you did before, He will inflict on you a painful punishment—¹⁷ the blind, the lame, and the sick will not be blamed.' God will admit anyone who obeys Him and His Messenger to Gardens through which rivers flow. But whoever turns back shall be severely punished by Him.^a

قُل لِّلْمُخَلَّفِينَ مِنَ ٱلْأَعْرَابِ سَتُدْعَوْنَ إِلَىٰ قَوْمٍ أُوْلِي بَأْسٍ شَدِيدٍ تُقَٰتِلُونَهُمْ أَوْ يُسْلِمُونَ ۖ فَإِن تُطِيعُواْ يُؤْتِكُمُ ٱللَّهُ أَجْرًا حَسَنًا ۖ وَإِن تَتَوَلَّوْاْ كَمَا تَوَلَّيْتُم مِّن قَبْلُ يُعَذِّبْكُمْ عَذَابًا أَلِيمًا ۝

لَّيْسَ عَلَى ٱلْأَعْمَىٰ حَرَجٌ وَلَا عَلَى ٱلْأَعْرَجِ حَرَجٌ وَلَا عَلَى ٱلْمَرِيضِ حَرَجٌ ۗ وَمَن يُطِعِ ٱللَّهَ وَرَسُولَهُۥ يُدْخِلْهُ جَنَّٰتٍ تَجْرِي مِن تَحْتِهَا ٱلْأَنْهَٰرُ ۖ وَمَن يَتَوَلَّ يُعَذِّبْهُ عَذَابًا أَلِيمًا ۝

---

^a Those who had shown weakness on the occasion of Hudaybiyah were deprived of the reward resulting therefrom, but still the door was not closed to them, because the campaign to promote Monotheism was to face many difficult situations. They were told that if they proved that they were imbued with the spirit of sacrifice on future occasions, they would once again be entitled to the Grace of God.

A test of this kind decides whether a man is a believer or a hypocrite. Only those who have some real difficulty are exempt from it. God pardons an error forced on a person because of circumstances which are beyond his control. But any other kind of shortcoming is not pardonable in the eyes of God.

¹⁸ God was pleased with the believers when they swore allegiance to you [Prophet] under the tree:ᵃ He knew what was in their hearts and so He sent tranquillity down to them and rewarded them with a victory near at hand ¹⁹ and with many future gains—God is mighty and wise.ᵇ ²⁰ God has promised you many future gains, and He has given you these in advance; and He has restrained the hands of men from harming you, so that it may be a sign for the believers, and so that He may guide you to a straight path. ²¹ And there are yet other [gains] which are still beyond your grasp, [but] which God has already encompassed [for you]: for God has power over all things.

۞ لَّقَدْ رَضِيَ ٱللَّهُ عَنِ ٱلْمُؤْمِنِينَ إِذْ يُبَايِعُونَكَ تَحْتَ ٱلشَّجَرَةِ فَعَلِمَ مَا فِى قُلُوبِهِمْ فَأَنزَلَ ٱلسَّكِينَةَ عَلَيْهِمْ وَأَثَبَهُمْ فَتْحًا قَرِيبًا ۝ وَمَغَانِمَ كَثِيرَةً يَأْخُذُونَهَا وَكَانَ ٱللَّهُ عَزِيزًا حَكِيمًا ۝ وَعَدَكُمُ ٱللَّهُ مَغَانِمَ كَثِيرَةً تَأْخُذُونَهَا فَعَجَّلَ لَكُمْ هَٰذِهِۦ وَكَفَّ أَيْدِىَ ٱلنَّاسِ عَنكُمْ وَلِتَكُونَ ءَايَةً لِّلْمُؤْمِنِينَ وَيَهْدِيَكُمْ صِرَٰطًا مُّسْتَقِيمًا ۝ وَأُخْرَىٰ لَمْ تَقْدِرُوا۟ عَلَيْهَا قَدْ أَحَاطَ ٱللَّهُ بِهَا وَكَانَ ٱللَّهُ عَلَىٰ كُلِّ شَىْءٍ قَدِيرًا ۝

ᵃ During the Hudaybiyyah journey, on one occasion, a rumour started circulating that the Quraysh had killed 'Uthman, who had gone to them as an envoy of the Prophet. This was an aggressive step. So, the Prophet sat under an acacia tree and took a pledge from the fourteen hundred companions that they would lay down their lives, but would not show their backs to the enemy. In the history of Islam, this pledge is known as the Pledge of Ridhwan.

The place at which this pledge was taken was two hundred and fifty miles from Madinah and only twelve miles from Makkah, i.e. the Muslims were far away from the centre of their activities, while the Quraysh were very near home. The Muslims had set forth with the intention of performing the minor pilgrimage ('umrah) as such they had only the basic equipments with them, while the Quraysh were well equipped for warfare. In such critical circumstances, it was the people's emotions of sincerity which prompted them to support the Prophet, in the absence of any external pressure.

ᵇ This refers to the unhappiness and uneasiness which had been created in the hearts of the companions over the outwardly one-sided Hudaybiyyah Treaty. However, they accepted this commandment of God with patience and in peace of mind. Within a few months, the benefits of this treaty, started becoming apparent. This treaty separated the Quraysh from their nexus with the Jews and in this way it became easy to subdue the latter. ▶

²² If those who deny the truth were to fight you, they would certainly turn their backs; then they would find neither protector nor helper: ²³ such was the law of God in the past; and you shall find no change in the law of God. ²⁴ It is He who withheld their hands from you, and your hands from them in the valley of Makkah, after giving you victory over them. God sees what you do.ᵃ

وَلَوْ قَٰتَلَكُمُ ٱلَّذِينَ كَفَرُوا۟ لَوَلَّوُا۟ ٱلْأَدْبَٰرَ ثُمَّ لَا يَجِدُونَ وَلِيًّا وَلَا نَصِيرًا ۝ سُنَّةَ ٱللَّهِ ٱلَّتِى قَدْ خَلَتْ مِن قَبْلُ وَلَن تَجِدَ لِسُنَّةِ ٱللَّهِ تَبْدِيلًا ۝ وَهُوَ ٱلَّذِى كَفَّ أَيْدِيَهُمْ عَنكُمْ وَأَيْدِيَكُمْ عَنْهُم بِبَطْنِ مَكَّةَ مِنۢ بَعْدِ أَنْ أَظْفَرَكُمْ عَلَيْهِمْ وَكَانَ ٱللَّهُ بِمَا تَعْمَلُونَ بَصِيرًا ۝

With the end of war-like conditions, the propagation of Islam increased manifold, so much so that the Quraysh themselves were subdued through the peaceful *dawah* process, for no ground was to be gained by fighting against them.

ᵃ It was the law of God that when the Prophet's initial addressees refused to answer his call, He destroyed them. On the occasion of Hudaybiyyah the Quraysh's refusal had finally been made known. Under these circumstances, had things reached the stage of battle, the angels of God would have come down to strengthen the Muslims so that they might defeat their enemies.

But, with regard to the polytheists, it was God's intention that they should not be destroyed so that their extraordinary human talents could be utilized for the purposes of Islam. Therefore, Almighty God guided his Prophet towards the No-War Pact.

²⁵ It was they who were bent on denying the truth, and who debarred you from the Sacred Mosque and who prevented your offering from reaching its place of sacrifice. And had it not been for the believing men and believing women [in Makkah] whom you might unwittingly have trampled underfoot, and on whose account you might have, unknowingly, become guilty, [God would have commanded you to fight it out with them; but He ordained it thus] so that He may bring whoever He will into His mercy. If they [the believers] had been clearly separated, We would have punished those who were bent on denying the truth with a painful punishment.ᵃ

هُمُ ٱلَّذِينَ كَفَرُواْ وَصَدُّوكُمْ عَنِ ٱلْمَسْجِدِ ٱلْحَرَامِ وَٱلْهَدْىَ مَعْكُوفًا أَن يَبْلُغَ مَحِلَّهُۥ ۚ وَلَوْلَا رِجَالٌ مُّؤْمِنُونَ وَنِسَآءٌ مُّؤْمِنَـٰتٌ لَّمْ تَعْلَمُوهُمْ أَن تَطَـُٔوهُمْ فَتُصِيبَكُم مِّنْهُم مَّعَرَّةٌ بِغَيْرِ عِلْمٍ ۚ لِّيُدْخِلَ ٱللَّهُ فِى رَحْمَتِهِۦ مَن يَشَآءُ ۚ لَوْ تَزَيَّلُواْ لَعَذَّبْنَا ٱلَّذِينَ كَفَرُواْ مِنْهُمْ عَذَابًا أَلِيمًا ۝

ᵃ The chieftains of the Quraysh had made themselves liable to be punished and engaged in battle. But in view of a greater and more important consideration, they were not fought against and instead of that a truce was reached with them. At that time there were among the Quraysh people who had in their heart of hearts given up polytheism and had faith in the oneness of God, or there were people who, because of their piety and righteousness, were likely to embrace Islam as soon as conditions normalised. If Almighty God did not cause a battle to be fought between the two sides, it was so that the aforesaid people might become believers and play their Islamic role in the world and receive God's rewards in the Hereafter. In the eyes of God, the importance of *dawah* work is greater than any other consideration.

²⁶ While those who deny the truth made it a prestige issue [in their hearts]—the bigotry of the days of ignorance—God sent His tranquillity down on to His Messenger and believers and firmly established in them the principle of righteousness, for they were indeed better entitled to it and more worthy of it. God has full knowledge of all things.ᵃ

إِذْ جَعَلَ ٱلَّذِينَ كَفَرُواْ فِى قُلُوبِهِمُ ٱلْحَمِيَّةَ حَمِيَّةَ ٱلْجَهِلِيَّةِ فَأَنزَلَ ٱللَّهُ سَكِينَتَهُۥ عَلَىٰ رَسُولِهِۦ وَعَلَى ٱلْمُؤْمِنِينَ وَأَلْزَمَهُمْ كَلِمَةَ ٱلتَّقْوَىٰ وَكَانُوٓاْ أَحَقَّ بِهَا وَأَهْلَهَا ۚ وَكَانَ ٱللَّهُ بِكُلِّ شَىْءٍ عَلِيمًا ۝

ᵃ From the heart of a man in which the fear of God is firmly embedded, the importance of everything other than God is driven out. He sets God above everything else in life. The occasion of Hudaybiyyah severely tested the companions, but they acquitted themselves well. On this occasion the opposite party had demonstrated brazen obstinacy and communal bias, but the companions simply reposed their trust in God. Their righteousness prevented them from obdurate retaliation and prejudice during this crucial trial period. Till the very end, they did not allow themselves to be provoked.

²⁷ God has in all truth shown His Messenger a true vision in which He said, 'God willing, you will most certainly enter the Sacred Mosque in safety and without fear, shaven-headed or with hair cut short'—God knew what you did not; and has given you a victory beforehand.ᵃ

لَقَدْ صَدَقَ ٱللَّهُ رَسُولَهُ ٱلرُّءْيَا بِٱلْحَقِّ لَتَدْخُلُنَّ ٱلْمَسْجِدَ ٱلْحَرَامَ إِن شَآءَ ٱللَّهُ ءَامِنِينَ مُحَلِّقِينَ رُءُوسَكُمْ وَمُقَصِّرِينَ لَا تَخَافُونَ فَعَلِمَ مَا لَمْ تَعْلَمُوا۟ فَجَعَلَ مِن دُونِ ذَٰلِكَ فَتْحًا قَرِيبًا ۝

ᵃ The Hudaybiyyah journey was undertaken as a result of a dream the Prophet Muhammad had. In his dream in Madinah, he had reached Makkah and was performing 'umrah. People took this dream as a good tiding and left Madinah for Makkah. But the Quraysh obstructed their path at Hudaybiyyah and ultimately he had to return without performing 'umrah. For this reason certain people thought that the Prophet's dream had not been true. But this surmise proved incorrect, because the dream did not specify that 'umrah would take place the same year, and according to the terms of the treaty itself, 'umrah was performed peacefully and properly the very next year in Dhu'l-Qa'dah in the seventh year of hijrah.

That year the postponement of 'umrah was agreed upon in the interests of something of greater importance, i.e. it facilitated the drawing up of a ten-year no-war pact with the Quraysh. When this was executed, it resulted in a proper atmosphere being created for dawah work. This in itself was a victory, because as a consequence, the door was opened for a final and total victory over the flag-bearers of polytheism.

²⁸ He is the One who has sent His Messenger with guidance and the true religion, so that He may have it prevail over all [other] religions. God suffices as a witness! *

هُوَ ٱلَّذِىٓ أَرْسَلَ رَسُولَهُۥ بِٱلْهُدَىٰ وَدِينِ ٱلْحَقِّ لِيُظْهِرَهُۥ عَلَى ٱلدِّينِ كُلِّهِۦ وَكَفَىٰ بِٱللَّهِ شَهِيدًا ۝

ᵃ The Prophet Muhammad had to play dual roles: one was that of a prophet (who strives to spread the message of God) and the other was that of the final Prophet, i.e. no other prophet was to appear after him. In his former capacity he had to do the same work as other prophets, namely to declare the oneness of God, to warn and to give good news about the Hereafter.

The latter role was different in that it required him to create those historical conditions which would be conducive to and a guarantee of the protection of both the Book of God and the prophetic traditions. No situation should occur which would necessitate the appointment of another prophet. It was thus a requirement of this second role that his *dawah* work should not end with a simple 'declaration' but should reach the stage of 'revolution'—revolution in the sense that change should be brought about in the history of the world. Those conditions should come to an end under which, time and again, God's guidance had been obliterated or distorted, thereby necessitating the selection of a new prophet to restore the divine guidance to its original form.

²⁹ Muhammad is the Messenger of God.ᵃ Those who are with him are firm and unyielding towards those who deny the truth, but compassionate towards one another.ᵇ You see them bowing and prostrating themselves, seeking the grace of God and His good will. Their marks are on their faces, the traces of their prostrations; they are described in the Torah and in the Gospel as being like a seed which sends forth its shoot, then makes it strong; it then becomes thick, and it stands firm on its own stem, delighting the sowers.ᶜ He seeks to enrage the disbelievers through them. God has promised forgiveness and a great reward to those of them who believe and do good works.

مُحَمَّدٌ رَّسُولُ ٱللَّهِ وَٱلَّذِينَ مَعَهُۥٓ أَشِدَّآءُ عَلَى ٱلْكُفَّارِ رُحَمَآءُ بَيْنَهُمْ تَرَىٰهُمْ رُكَّعًا سُجَّدًا يَبْتَغُونَ فَضْلًا مِّنَ ٱللَّهِ وَرِضْوَٰنًا سِيمَاهُمْ فِى وُجُوهِهِم مِّنْ أَثَرِ ٱلسُّجُودِ ذَٰلِكَ مَثَلُهُمْ فِى ٱلتَّوْرَىٰةِ وَمَثَلُهُمْ فِى ٱلْإِنجِيلِ كَزَرْعٍ أَخْرَجَ شَطْـَٔهُۥ فَـَٔازَرَهُۥ فَٱسْتَغْلَظَ فَٱسْتَوَىٰ عَلَىٰ سُوقِهِۦ يُعْجِبُ ٱلزُّرَّاعَ لِيَغِيظَ بِهِمُ ٱلْكُفَّارَ وَعَدَ ٱللَّهُ ٱلَّذِينَ ءَامَنُوا۟ وَعَمِلُوا۟ ٱلصَّٰلِحَٰتِ مِنْهُم مَّغْفِرَةً وَأَجْرًا عَظِيمًۢا ﴿٢٩﴾

ᵃ The Prophet Muhammad had to perform a historic role which is referred to in the Quran as making religion predominant. For this he needed a group of men of high calibre. Such men were available to him thanks to Ishmael, their progenitor, having been settled in the Arabian desert two thousand five hundred years before. With such ancestry it was the most vibrant group of history. When their full potential was tapped, thanks to Quranic instruction, the Arabs turned into a nation of heroes. The importance of this group was so great in the eyes of God that He informed the prophets about them in advance. In the Torah their individual qualities were mentioned while, in the Bible, their collective qualities were emphasized.

ᵇ The quality of the individuals in this group was made manifest in their unyielding behaviour towards the aggressors. Their behaviour was governed by principles and not by their desires or emotions. Their temperament was such that they bowed down before God and were engrossed in prayers to and praise of God.

ᶜ The prophecy of the Bible is clearly stated in Mark (Ch.4:1-20) and Matthew (Ch.13:3-9). This is a declaration in allegorical language that the call of Islam will start from Makkah like a plant springing from a seed. Then it will go on growing to become a strong tree. Its strength will so increase that it will please the true believers, while the deniers of Truth will be angry and jealous because they cannot harm it, though that is their earnest desire.

49. THE APARTMENTS

In the name of God,
the Most Gracious, the Most Merciful

¹Believers, do not push yourselves forward in the presence of God and His Messenger. Fear God—God hears all and knows all.ᵃ

يَـٰٓأَيُّهَا ٱلَّذِينَ ءَامَنُوا۟ لَا تُقَدِّمُوا۟ بَيْنَ يَدَىِ ٱللَّهِ وَرَسُولِهِۦ ۖ وَٱتَّقُوا۟ ٱللَّهَ ۚ إِنَّ ٱللَّهَ سَمِيعٌ عَلِيمٌ ۝

ᵃ To hold one's opinion superior to that of the Prophet is forbidden. During the life of the Prophet Muhammad, this attitude on the part of an addressee took the shape of indulgence in verbosity at his meetings, the object being to excel the Prophet's discourse. Subsequently, this meant the forming of opinions in disregard of the guiding principles laid down by God and His Prophet.

This sort of lapse occurs because man forgets that God is keeping a watch over him. If he came to know that his utterances reached God before they reached other human beings, he would prefer to remain silent rather than talk.

² Believers, do not raise your voices above the voice of the Prophet, and do not speak as loudly when speaking to him as you do when speaking to one another, lest your actions come to nothing without your realizing it. ³ Those who lower their voices in the presence of God's Messenger are men whose hearts God has tested for piety—they shall have forgiveness and a great reward—⁴ those who call out to you from outside your apartments are lacking in understanding. ⁵ If they waited patiently until you came out to see them, it would be better for them. But God is forgiving and merciful.ᵃ

يَـٰٓأَيُّهَا ٱلَّذِينَ ءَامَنُوا۟ لَا تَرْفَعُوٓا۟ أَصْوَٰتَكُمْ فَوْقَ صَوْتِ ٱلنَّبِىِّ وَلَا تَجْهَرُوا۟ لَهُۥ بِٱلْقَوْلِ كَجَهْرِ بَعْضِكُمْ لِبَعْضٍ أَن تَحْبَطَ أَعْمَٰلُكُمْ وَأَنتُمْ لَا تَشْعُرُونَ ۝ إِنَّ ٱلَّذِينَ يَغُضُّونَ أَصْوَٰتَهُمْ عِندَ رَسُولِ ٱللَّهِ أُو۟لَـٰٓئِكَ ٱلَّذِينَ ٱمْتَحَنَ ٱللَّهُ قُلُوبَهُمْ لِلتَّقْوَىٰ لَهُم مَّغْفِرَةٌ وَأَجْرٌ عَظِيمٌ ۝ إِنَّ ٱلَّذِينَ يُنَادُونَكَ مِن وَرَآءِ ٱلْحُجُرَٰتِ أَكْثَرُهُمْ لَا يَعْقِلُونَ ۝ وَلَوْ أَنَّهُمْ صَبَرُوا۟ حَتَّىٰ تَخْرُجَ إِلَيْهِمْ لَكَانَ خَيْرًا لَّهُمْ وَٱللَّهُ غَفُورٌ رَّحِيمٌ ۝

ᵃ The Bedouin tribes from the areas surrounding Madinah were not mature in understanding. When they used to come to the meetings of the Prophet Muhammad, they did not address him as 'O Prophet of God', but rather as 'O Muhammad.' Their manner of speech was not modest or humble, but overbearing. Such behaviour was prohibited. A Prophet is God's representative in this world. Rudeness to him of this nature amounts to rude behaviour towards God, which renders a man absolutely worthless.

After the demise of the Prophet Muhammad, the guidance brought by him stands in his place. Now this divine guidance necessitates obedience just as obedience to the Prophet personally was required during his lifetime.

Fear of God makes a man serious. If fear of God really enters a man's heart, he will come to know automatically, as a matter of instinct, all those realities of which others remain unaware in spite of being informed of them.

⁶ Believers, if an evil-doer brings you news, ascertain the correctness of the report fully, lest you unwittingly harm others, and then regret what you have done,⁷ and know that the Messenger of God is among you. If he were to obey you in many things, you would suffer for it. However, God has endeared the faith to you, and beautified it in your hearts, and has made denial of the truth, wickedness, and disobedience hateful to you. People such as these are rightly guided ⁸ through God's bounty and favour; God is all knowing, and wise.ᵃ

يَـٰٓأَيُّهَا ٱلَّذِينَ ءَامَنُوٓا۟ إِن جَآءَكُمْ فَاسِقٌۢ بِنَبَإٍ فَتَبَيَّنُوٓا۟ أَن تُصِيبُوا۟ قَوْمًۢا بِجَهَـٰلَةٍ فَتُصْبِحُوا۟ عَلَىٰ مَا فَعَلْتُمْ نَـٰدِمِينَ ۝ وَٱعْلَمُوٓا۟ أَنَّ فِيكُمْ رَسُولَ ٱللَّهِ ۚ لَوْ يُطِيعُكُمْ فِى كَثِيرٍ مِّنَ ٱلْأَمْرِ لَعَنِتُّمْ وَلَـٰكِنَّ ٱللَّهَ حَبَّبَ إِلَيْكُمُ ٱلْإِيمَـٰنَ وَزَيَّنَهُۥ فِى قُلُوبِكُمْ وَكَرَّهَ إِلَيْكُمُ ٱلْكُفْرَ وَٱلْفُسُوقَ وَٱلْعِصْيَانَ ۚ أُو۟لَـٰٓئِكَ هُمُ ٱلرَّٰشِدُونَ ۝ فَضْلًا مِّنَ ٱللَّهِ وَنِعْمَةً ۚ وَٱللَّهُ عَلِيمٌ حَكِيمٌ ۝

ᵃ If anyone provides information about another which takes the form of allegations against the latter, ready acceptance of this news on simply hearing it is absolutely against the precautions imposed by the Faith. It is essential on the part of the hearer of the news to make the necessary investigation about it, and whatever opinion he forms should be after impartial inquiry and not before.

It frequently happens that when information of this kind is received, there are immediate suggestions of taking punitive action. This is a case of gross irresponsibility. Nobody should form any opinion about such news before investigation; nor should others suggest direct action without a thorough probe.

Those who tread the path of righteousness and guidance develop an entirely different temperament from those who do not. They are averse to levelling allegations against others. They prefer to remain silent rather than talk about a supposed misdemeanour which is as yet uninvestigated. Being of such a nature is an indication of their having been blessed with a share in God's Graces. The Faith that has really permeated their lives now is being acknowledged in verbal form.

⁹ If two parties of believers fight against each other, make peace between them; then if after that one of them transgresses against the other, fight the party that transgresses until it submits to the command of God. Then if it complies, make peace between them with equity, and act justly. Truly, God loves the just. ¹⁰ Surely all believers are brothers. So make peace between your brothers, and fear God, so that mercy may be shown to you.ᵃ

وَإِن طَآئِفَتَانِ مِنَ ٱلْمُؤْمِنِينَ ٱقْتَتَلُوا۟ فَأَصْلِحُوا۟ بَيْنَهُمَا ۖ فَإِنۢ بَغَتْ إِحْدَىٰهُمَا عَلَى ٱلْأُخْرَىٰ فَقَٰتِلُوا۟ ٱلَّتِى تَبْغِى حَتَّىٰ تَفِىٓءَ إِلَىٰٓ أَمْرِ ٱللَّهِ ۚ فَإِن فَآءَتْ فَأَصْلِحُوا۟ بَيْنَهُمَا بِٱلْعَدْلِ وَأَقْسِطُوٓا۟ ۖ إِنَّ ٱللَّهَ يُحِبُّ ٱلْمُقْسِطِينَ ۝ إِنَّمَا ٱلْمُؤْمِنُونَ إِخْوَةٌ فَأَصْلِحُوا۟ بَيْنَ أَخَوَيْكُمْ ۚ وَٱتَّقُوا۟ ٱللَّهَ لَعَلَّكُمْ تُرْحَمُونَ ۝

ᵃ How should Muslims live and behave with each other? The short answer to this question is that they should live with each other as brothers. A religious relationship is in no way less important than a blood relationship. If two Muslims quarrel with each other, other Muslims should never add fuel to the fire. On the contrary, under the influence of brotherly feelings, they should make every effort to bring about a compromise between the two.

If two Muslims quarrel with each other, one alternative is for other Muslims to adopt a neutral posture. If they do intervene, or their family or group cause them to take the side of their 'own' people and fight against the other 'alien' people, either course is contrary to Islamic principles. The right Islamic way is to investigate the real issue, and the one who is right should be supported and the one in the wrong should be compelled to accept a just solution to the problem.

One who fears God can never relish the sight of people fighting with each other. In fact, he will be extremely uneasy at such a sight, and his true nature will compel him to make efforts to improve relations between the two parties. These are the people whose faith in God causes the opening of the door to God's graces.

11 Believers, let not some men among you ridicule others: it may be that the latter are better than the former: nor should some women laugh at others: it may be that the latter are better than the former: do not defame or be sarcastic to each other, or call each other by [offensive] nicknames. How bad it is to earn an evil reputation after accepting the faith! Those who do not repent are evil-doers.*

يَـٰٓأَيُّهَا ٱلَّذِينَ ءَامَنُوا۟ لَا يَسْخَرْ قَوْمٌ مِّن قَوْمٍ عَسَىٰٓ أَن يَكُونُوا۟ خَيْرًا مِّنْهُمْ وَلَا نِسَآءٌ مِّن نِّسَآءٍ عَسَىٰٓ أَن يَكُنَّ خَيْرًا مِّنْهُنَّ ۖ وَلَا تَلْمِزُوٓا۟ أَنفُسَكُمْ وَلَا تَنَابَزُوا۟ بِٱلْأَلْقَـٰبِ ۖ بِئْسَ ٱلِٱسْمُ ٱلْفُسُوقُ بَعْدَ ٱلْإِيمَـٰنِ ۚ وَمَن لَّمْ يَتُبْ فَأُو۟لَـٰٓئِكَ هُمُ ٱلظَّـٰلِمُونَ ۝

---

* From birth, there is hidden in every man an instinct to be 'great'. That is why, if a man finds some weakness in another man, he makes a point of highlighting it, so that in this way he may prove himself to be great and the other small. He ridicules the other person, finds fault with him and calls him by insulting nicknames, in order to satisfy his instinct for self-aggrandisement.

But the criterion of goodness or badness is not that which an individual himself decides upon. One is really good who is good in the eyes of God and one is bad if he is adjudged bad in the eyes of God. If a man really develops these feelings in himself, he will lose the desire to be known as 'great'. Ridiculing others, finding fault with others, giving nicknames to others will all become meaningless to him, because he will come to know that a man's true status and position are actually going to be determined by God. He will then ponder over the fact that if he considers anyone as small in this world and if later, in the real world of the Hereafter, he (the latter) is treated as worthy of respect, his way of thinking will prove to be absolutely meaningless.

¹² Believers, avoid much suspicion. Indeed some suspicion is a sin. And do not spy on one another and do not backbite. Would any of you like to eat his dead brother's flesh? No, you would hate it. Fear God, God is ever forgiving and most merciful.ᵃ

يَـٰٓأَيُّهَا ٱلَّذِينَ ءَامَنُوا۟ ٱجْتَنِبُوا۟ كَثِيرًا مِّنَ ٱلظَّنِّ إِنَّ بَعْضَ ٱلظَّنِّ إِثْمٌ ۖ وَلَا تَجَسَّسُوا۟ وَلَا يَغْتَب بَّعْضُكُم بَعْضًا ۚ أَيُحِبُّ أَحَدُكُمْ أَن يَأْكُلَ لَحْمَ أَخِيهِ مَيْتًا فَكَرِهْتُمُوهُ ۚ وَٱتَّقُوا۟ ٱللَّهَ ۚ إِنَّ ٱللَّهَ تَوَّابٌ رَّحِيمٌ ۝

ᵃ If a man harbours suspicion against another, everything about the latter appears wrong to him, for his mind starts drifting in negative and wrong directions. He starts searching for his shortcomings rather than his good points. It becomes his favourite ploy to describe his weaknesses and then to denigrate him.

The root of many social evils is unfounded suspicion. It is therefore necessary for man to be alert to this. He should not allow such suspicion to enter his mind.

If you are suspicious of someone, you can always meet him and talk frankly to him. But, it would be highly unethical to speak ill of a person, if he was not there to defend himself. An individual may occasionally make such mistakes. But, if he is God-fearing, he will not persist in doing so. His fear of God will warn him about his mistake and consequently he will give up his wrong approach and seek God's pardon.

¹³ Mankind! We have created you from a male and female, and made you into peoples and tribes, so that you might come to know each other. The noblest of you in God's sight is the one who fears God most. God is all knowing and all-aware.^a

يَـٰٓأَيُّهَا ٱلنَّاسُ إِنَّا خَلَقْنَـٰكُم مِّن ذَكَرٍ وَأُنثَىٰ وَجَعَلْنَـٰكُمْ شُعُوبًا وَقَبَآئِلَ لِتَعَارَفُوٓا۟ إِنَّ أَكْرَمَكُمْ عِندَ ٱللَّهِ أَتْقَىٰكُمْ إِنَّ ٱللَّهَ عَلِيمٌ خَبِيرٌ ۝

---

^a Human beings differ from each other in many ways, notably in terms of race and place of origin—some are black, some are white, some are from the rain forests, some are from the tundra. But all these differences are for the purpose of identification—not for the making of distinctions. Indeed, many evils have stemmed from these differences being used to discriminate between one person and another, between one community and another, between one nation and another. Humanity has been eternally torn asunder by such prejudice.

Human beings, in view of their origin, are all one. Among them, if at all there is any basis for distinction, it is as to who is fearful of God and who is not. Even this is known only to God and not to any human being.

¹⁴ The Arabs of the desert say, 'We have believed.' Say to them, 'You have not believed yet; say rather, "We have submitted," for faith has not yet entered into your hearts. But if you will obey God and His Messenger, He will not detract anything from your good deeds. God is most forgiving and ever merciful.' ¹⁵ The believers are only those who have faith in God and His Messenger and then doubt not, but strive, hard with their wealth and their persons for the cause of God. Such are the truthful ones.^a

۞ قَالَتِ ٱلْأَعْرَابُ ءَامَنَّا ۖ قُل لَّمْ تُؤْمِنُواْ وَلَٰكِن قُولُوٓاْ أَسْلَمْنَا وَلَمَّا يَدْخُلِ ٱلْإِيمَٰنُ فِى قُلُوبِكُمْ ۖ وَإِن تُطِيعُواْ ٱللَّهَ وَرَسُولَهُۥ لَا يَلِتْكُم مِّنْ أَعْمَٰلِكُمْ شَيْـًٔا ۚ إِنَّ ٱللَّهَ غَفُورٌ رَّحِيمٌ ۝ إِنَّمَا ٱلْمُؤْمِنُونَ ٱلَّذِينَ ءَامَنُواْ بِٱللَّهِ وَرَسُولِهِۦ ثُمَّ لَمْ يَرْتَابُواْ وَجَٰهَدُواْ بِأَمْوَٰلِهِمْ وَأَنفُسِهِمْ فِى سَبِيلِ ٱللَّهِ ۚ أُوْلَٰٓئِكَ هُمُ ٱلصَّٰدِقُونَ ۝

---

^a There were many small tribes around the Madinah township. After the immigration of the Prophet to Madinah, these people embraced Islam. But their embracing of Islam was not the result of any deep mental revolution. In the eyes of God, the person who genuinely adopts the faith of Islam is one who discovers Islam as a reality and enshrines it in the depths of his heart. Those who accept the Faith of God in this manner acquire eternal conviction. Their steadfastness is such they are ready to make any sacrifice.

One may perform some righteous deed then think it necessary to announce the fact, but such announcement actually has a nullifying effect. A truly righteous deed is one which is done purely for the sake of God. As God Himself knows everything, where is the necessity to advertise it?

¹⁶ Say, 'Do you presume to teach God your religion when God knows everything in the heavens and earth? God has knowledge of all things.' ¹⁷ They think they have done you a favour by becoming Muslims! Say, 'Do not consider your Islam a favour to me. No indeed! It is God who bestowed a favour on you by guiding you to the true faith. [Admit this], if you are telling the truth.' ¹⁸ God knows the unseen things of the heavens and the earth. God sees all that you do.ᵃ

قُلْ أَتُعَلِّمُونَ ٱللَّهَ بِدِينِكُمْ وَٱللَّهُ يَعْلَمُ مَا فِى ٱلسَّمَـٰوَٰتِ وَمَا فِى ٱلْأَرْضِ وَٱللَّهُ بِكُلِّ شَىْءٍ عَلِيمٌ ۝ يَمُنُّونَ عَلَيْكَ أَنْ أَسْلَمُوا۟ قُل لَّا تَمُنُّوا۟ عَلَىَّ إِسْلَـٰمَكُم بَلِ ٱللَّهُ يَمُنُّ عَلَيْكُمْ أَنْ هَدَىٰكُمْ لِلْإِيمَـٰنِ إِن كُنتُمْ صَـٰدِقِينَ ۝ إِنَّ ٱللَّهَ يَعْلَمُ غَيْبَ ٱلسَّمَـٰوَٰتِ وَٱلْأَرْضِ وَٱللَّهُ بَصِيرٌۢ بِمَا تَعْمَلُونَ ۝

ᵃ If anyone embraces Islam or some Islamic task is accomplished through him, he should realize that this has come about with the help of God. Faith and good deeds all depend on God's directive guidance. So, whenever somebody is in a position to do something good, he should thank God for it.

If, instead of so doing, the individual attempts to make his co-religionists feel obliged to him for what he has done, this would amount to his having acted not out of concern for God, but in order to figure well in the eyes of his fellow-men. God is directly aware of everything. One who performs any task for the sake of God, should firmly believe that God sees his work, and that there is no need to show it to Him.

50. QAF

In the name of God,
the Most Gracious, the Most Merciful

¹ Qaf

By the glorious Quran! ² Indeed, they are astonished that a warner should have come to them from among themselves. So these deniers of the truth say, 'This is indeed a strange thing, ³ to come back to life after we have died and become dust? That is most improbable!' ⁴ We know very well what the earth takes away from them: We hold a book which records all things. ⁵ But they denied the truth when it came to them, so they are in a state of confusion.ᵃ

ق ۚ وَٱلْقُرْءَانِ ٱلْمَجِيدِ ۝ بَلْ عَجِبُوٓا۟
أَن جَآءَهُم مُّنذِرٌ مِّنْهُمْ فَقَالَ
ٱلْكَٰفِرُونَ هَٰذَا شَىْءٌ عَجِيبٌ ۝ أَءِذَا
مِتْنَا وَكُنَّا تُرَابًا ۖ ذَٰلِكَ رَجْعٌۢ بَعِيدٌ
۝ قَدْ عَلِمْنَا مَا تَنقُصُ ٱلْأَرْضُ مِنْهُمْ
وَعِندَنَا كِتَٰبٌ حَفِيظٌۢ ۝ بَلْ كَذَّبُوا۟
بِٱلْحَقِّ لَمَّا جَآءَهُمْ فَهُمْ فِىٓ أَمْرٍ مَّرِيجٍ
۝

ᵃ The history of the prophets shows that their contemporaries were not ready to accept them. It was only in later times that people readily accepted their status as prophets.

The reason for this is that the prophet appears to his contemporaries as 'a person just like themselves'. They find it surprising that one whom they have always treated as their equal should suddenly become great and start advising them. But, as time passes, a history of greatness becomes attached to the prophet's name. So, he starts appearing to succeeding generations as a 'person greater than themselves.' That is why, in later periods people did not find it difficult to accept the prophetic status of a prophet. In other words, to the people of the early days, the prophet was a controversial figure, while to the people of later times he acquired the aura of an established personage. The people of the earlier period had to undertake a journey in consciousness in order to fill the gap between them and the prophet, while in the later period, this gap would have been filled by history itself.

In the eyes of those who entertain doubts about the prophethood of God's messenger, everything about him becomes doubtful—even those beliefs that are already enshrined in tradition. However, nothing can act as a shield or an excuse for the doubters. If the rejecters of the prophet were simply to consider the inimitable literary majesty of his book, they would be compelled to accept as a prophet the one who brought that book.

⁶ Have they not observed the sky above them and marked how We have built it and adorned it, leaving no flaws in it; ⁷ We spread out the earth and set upon it solid mountains and We brought forth from it all kinds of delightful plants, ⁸ as a lesson and reminder for every human being who turns to God; ⁹ and We have sent down from the sky blessed water with which We have brought forth gardens and grain to be harvested, ¹⁰ and tall palm-trees with their thickly-clustered dates, ¹¹ as a provision for human beings; and by [all] this We bring dead land to life. Such shall be the Resurrection.*ᵃ*

أَفَلَمْ يَنظُرُوٓاْ إِلَى ٱلسَّمَآءِ فَوْقَهُمْ كَيْفَ بَنَيْنَٰهَا وَزَيَّنَّٰهَا وَمَا لَهَا مِن فُرُوجٍ ۝ وَٱلْأَرْضَ مَدَدْنَٰهَا وَأَلْقَيْنَا فِيهَا رَوَٰسِيَ وَأَنۢبَتْنَا فِيهَا مِن كُلِّ زَوْجٍ بَهِيجٍ ۝ تَبْصِرَةً وَذِكْرَىٰ لِكُلِّ عَبْدٍ مُّنِيبٍ ۝ وَنَزَّلْنَا مِنَ ٱلسَّمَآءِ مَآءً مُّبَٰرَكًا فَأَنۢبَتْنَا بِهِۦ جَنَّٰتٍ وَحَبَّ ٱلْحَصِيدِ ۝ وَٱلنَّخْلَ بَاسِقَٰتٍ لَّهَا طَلْعٌ نَّضِيدٌ ۝ رِّزْقًا لِّلْعِبَادِ ۖ وَأَحْيَيْنَا بِهِۦ بَلْدَةً مَّيْتًا ۚ كَذَٰلِكَ ٱلْخُرُوجُ ۝

ᵃ The meaningfulness of the universe, its creative wisdom, its being free of shortcomings, and its being consistent with human needs compel every thinking and rational man to accept the sublimity of creation, and one who gives serious consideration to the system of the universe, will find the Creator in His creations. He will see a glimpse of the other world (the Hereafter) in this world, because, in fact, the world of the Hereafter is essentially another, more superior form of the present world.

¹² Before them, the people of Noah and the people of Rass denied this truth; and so did the people of Thamud. ¹³ And the tribe of 'Ad, and Pharaoh, and the brethren of Lot, ¹⁴ and the dwellers of the Wood, and the people of Tubba': every one denied their messengers, and so My warning came true. ¹⁵ Were We then worn out by the first creation? Yet they are in doubt about a second creation.*ᵃ*

¹⁶ We created man—We know the promptings of his soul, and are closer to him than his jugular vein—¹⁷ and the two recording angels are recording, sitting on the right and the left: ¹⁸ each word he utters shall be noted down by a vigilant guardian.*ᵇ*

كَذَّبَتْ قَبْلَهُمْ قَوْمُ نُوحٍ وَأَصْحَٰبُ
ٱلرَّسِّ وَثَمُودُ ۝ وَعَادٌ وَفِرْعَوْنُ
وَإِخْوَٰنُ لُوطٍ ۝ وَأَصْحَٰبُ ٱلْأَيْكَةِ
وَقَوْمُ تُبَّعٍ ۚ كُلٌّ كَذَّبَ ٱلرُّسُلَ فَحَقَّ
وَعِيدِ ۝ أَفَعَيِينَا بِٱلْخَلْقِ ٱلْأَوَّلِ ۚ بَلْ
هُمْ فِى لَبْسٍ مِّنْ خَلْقٍ جَدِيدٍ ۝
وَلَقَدْ خَلَقْنَا ٱلْإِنسَٰنَ وَنَعْلَمُ مَا
تُوَسْوِسُ بِهِ نَفْسُهُ ۖ وَنَحْنُ أَقْرَبُ إِلَيْهِ
مِنْ حَبْلِ ٱلْوَرِيدِ ۝ إِذْ يَتَلَقَّى
ٱلْمُتَلَقِّيَانِ عَنِ ٱلْيَمِينِ وَعَنِ ٱلشِّمَالِ
قَعِيدٌ ۝ مَّا يَلْفِظُ مِن قَوْلٍ إِلَّا لَدَيْهِ
رَقِيبٌ عَتِيدٌ ۝

ᵃ In the course of history, as presented by the Quran, it has happened again and again that as a result of the prophets' addressees rejecting them, the communities were destroyed. A few of these devastated nations are mentioned here by way of example. The destruction of these peoples is, in fact, a sample of the conditions in the Hereafter. A part of the punishment the rejecters of Truth are destined to receive in the Hereafter is shown here in this world of today.

The first creation of this world proves the possibility of the second creation. If a man is serious, he does not require any further proof, to make him believe in the Hereafter.

ᵇ The study of this world shows that there is an unerring system of 'recording' in operation here. Man's thoughts are impressed on the membrane of his brain. Every utterance a man makes is permanently preserved in the shape of sound waves in the air. Man's actions are preserved in the external world by means of heat waves in such a way that they can be repeated at any time. All these are known facts of today, and these known facts are what make the Quran's claim credible that man's intentions, his utterances and his actions, are all in the knowledge of his Creator. All affairs of all human beings are entered in the registers of the angels.

¹⁹ The trance of death will come revealing the truth: that is what you were trying to escape.' ²⁰ The trumpet will be sounded. This is the Day [you were] warned of. ²¹ Each person will arrive attended by an [angel] to drive him on and another to bear witness. ²² You were heedless of this, but now We have removed your veil, so your sight today is sharp. ²³ His companion attendant will say, 'I have here his record ready.' ²⁴ 'Cast into Hell every ungrateful, rebellious one, ²⁵ hinderer of good, transgressor, causing others to doubt, ²⁶ who has set up another god besides God: cast him into severe punishment'—²⁷ and his associate [Satan] will say, 'Lord, I did not make him transgress, he had already gone far astray himself.' ²⁸ God will say, 'Do not quarrel in My presence. I gave you the warning beforehand ²⁹ and My word shall not be changed, nor am I unjust to My servants.'ᵃ

وَجَآءَتْ سَكْرَةُ ٱلْمَوْتِ بِٱلْحَقِّ ذَٰلِكَ مَا كُنتَ مِنْهُ تَحِيدُ ۝ وَنُفِخَ فِى ٱلصُّورِ ذَٰلِكَ يَوْمُ ٱلْوَعِيدِ ۝ وَجَآءَتْ كُلُّ نَفْسٍ مَّعَهَا سَآئِقٌ وَشَهِيدٌ ۝ لَّقَدْ كُنتَ فِى غَفْلَةٍ مِّنْ هَٰذَا فَكَشَفْنَا عَنكَ غِطَآءَكَ فَبَصَرُكَ ٱلْيَوْمَ حَدِيدٌ ۝ وَقَالَ قَرِينُهُۥ هَٰذَا مَا لَدَىَّ عَتِيدٌ ۝ أَلْقِيَا فِى جَهَنَّمَ كُلَّ كَفَّارٍ عَنِيدٍ ۝ مَّنَّاعٍ لِّلْخَيْرِ مُعْتَدٍ مُّرِيبٍ ۝ ٱلَّذِى جَعَلَ مَعَ ٱللَّهِ إِلَٰهًا ءَاخَرَ فَأَلْقِيَاهُ فِى ٱلْعَذَابِ ٱلشَّدِيدِ ۝ قَالَ قَرِينُهُۥ رَبَّنَا مَآ أَطْغَيْتُهُۥ وَلَٰكِن كَانَ فِى ضَلَٰلٍ بَعِيدٍ ۝ قَالَ لَا تَخْتَصِمُوا لَدَىَّ وَقَدْ قَدَّمْتُ إِلَيْكُم بِٱلْوَعِيدِ ۝ مَا يُبَدَّلُ ٱلْقَوْلُ لَدَىَّ وَمَآ أَنَا۠ بِظَلَّٰمٍ لِّلْعَبِيدِ ۝

ᵃ A picture of death and Doomsday thereafter has been drawn in these verses. It shows what will happen to those who, finding themselves free in this world, became arrogant. This pictorial description is so terrible as to cause extreme unease in the minds of all living beings.

³⁰ On that Day, We shall ask Hell, 'Are you now full?' Hell will answer, 'Are there any more?' ³¹ Paradise will be brought near to the righteous and will no longer be far away. ³² This is what you were promised—this is for everyone who often turned to God and kept Him in mind, ³³ who fears the Compassionate One, though He is unseen, and comes to Him with a penitent heart; ³⁴ so enter it in peace. This is the Day of everlasting life. ³⁵ There they shall have all that they desire, and there is even more with Us.ᵃ

³⁶ How many a generation, far greater in prowess, have We destroyed before them! They searched the entire land: but could they find a refuge? ³⁷ There is truly a reminder in this for whoever has a heart, whoever listens attentively.ᵇ

يَوْمَ نَقُولُ لِجَهَنَّمَ هَلِ ٱمْتَلَأْتِ وَتَقُولُ هَلْ مِن مَّزِيدٍ ۝ وَأُزْلِفَتِ ٱلْجَنَّةُ لِلْمُتَّقِينَ غَيْرَ بَعِيدٍ ۝ هَٰذَا مَا تُوعَدُونَ لِكُلِّ أَوَّابٍ حَفِيظٍ ۝ مَّنْ خَشِيَ ٱلرَّحْمَٰنَ بِٱلْغَيْبِ وَجَآءَ بِقَلْبٍ مُّنِيبٍ ۝ ٱدْخُلُوهَا بِسَلَٰمٍ ذَٰلِكَ يَوْمُ ٱلْخُلُودِ ۝ لَهُم مَّا يَشَآءُونَ فِيهَا وَلَدَيْنَا مَزِيدٌ ۝ وَكَمْ أَهْلَكْنَا قَبْلَهُم مِّن قَرْنٍ هُمْ أَشَدُّ مِنْهُم بَطْشًا فَنَقَّبُوا۟ فِى ٱلْبِلَٰدِ هَلْ مِن مَّحِيصٍ ۝ إِنَّ فِى ذَٰلِكَ لَذِكْرَىٰ لِمَن كَانَ لَهُۥ قَلْبٌ أَوْ أَلْقَى ٱلسَّمْعَ وَهُوَ شَهِيدٌ ۝

ᵃ Who are entitled to the eternal Paradise of God? They are the people who, in this world, went in constant fear of God's punishment. Those who were afraid before they actually came face to face with their Maker will be the ones who will be safe from fear and grief on that Day, whereas others who knew no fear will be terror-struck. Fear of God creates heavenly attributes in man, while a lack of fear creates the attributes of Hell.

ᵇ Nations of the world progress and rise until they reach their zenith. But, when they are afflicted by God's scourge, as a result of their misdeeds, they are reduced to such a condition that they cannot find any place in the world to which they can run away or in which they might take refuge. There are great lessons in these events of history. But lessons can be learnt only by one who is mentally alive so that he may derive their unspoken message from events, or by one in whom the capacity to hear is unimpaired, so that when divine messages are conveyed to him, they go straight to the core of his innermost being unimpeded.

³⁸ We created the heavens, the earth, and everything between them in six days [periods] nor were We ever wearied. ³⁹ So bear with patience what they say, and glorify your Lord with His praise, before the rising and before the setting of the sun; ⁴⁰ proclaim His praise in the night and at the end of every prayer.^a

وَلَقَدْ خَلَقْنَا ٱلسَّمَٰوَٰتِ وَٱلْأَرْضَ وَمَا بَيْنَهُمَا فِى سِتَّةِ أَيَّامٍ وَمَا مَسَّنَا مِن لُّغُوبٍ ۝ فَٱصْبِرْ عَلَىٰ مَا يَقُولُونَ وَسَبِّحْ بِحَمْدِ رَبِّكَ قَبْلَ طُلُوعِ ٱلشَّمْسِ وَقَبْلَ ٱلْغُرُوبِ ۝ وَمِنَ ٱلَّيْلِ فَسَبِّحْهُ وَأَدْبَٰرَ ٱلسُّجُودِ ۝

---

^a The creation of the heavens and the earth in six days, in other words in six stages, indicates that God's method of doing things is a gradual one. When God, in spite of being the possessor of all Powers, brings things into existence gradually on a long-term basis, man should also desist from making undue haste, but rather try to reach his goals through action marked by patience.

Preaching, from beginning to end, is an act of patience. In this process one has to put up with the bitterness evinced by others, and persevere in one's task in spite of there being no favourable results in sight. This patience-trying process can be pursued only by one whose days and nights are spent in remembrance of God, who reposes all hope not in human beings but in God and who does not fall a prey to a feeling of frustration, in spite of having lost everything.

In the Bible it is mentioned that God created heaven and earth in six days and rested on the seventh day. This part of the verse '...nor were We ever wearied' contradicts and corrects the biblical statement. Rest is taken by one who becomes tired. God does not become tired and, as such, He does not need rest.

⁴¹ Hearken! The Day when the caller will call from near. ⁴² The Day when men will hear the fateful cry, they will rise up [from their graves]. ⁴³ Truly, it is We who give life and cause death, and to Us shall all return ⁴⁴ on the Day the earth will be rent asunder over them, and from it they shall emerge in haste. To assemble them all is easy enough for Us.ᵃ

⁴⁵ We know best what those who deny the truth say. You are not there to force them: so remind, with this Quran, those who fear My warning.ᵇ

وَٱسْتَمِعْ يَوْمَ يُنَادِ ٱلْمُنَادِ مِن مَّكَانٍ قَرِيبٍ ۞ يَوْمَ يَسْمَعُونَ ٱلصَّيْحَةَ بِٱلْحَقِّ ذَٰلِكَ يَوْمُ ٱلْخُرُوجِ ۞ إِنَّا نَحْنُ نُحْيِۦ وَنُمِيتُ وَإِلَيْنَا ٱلْمَصِيرُ ۞ يَوْمَ تَشَقَّقُ ٱلْأَرْضُ عَنْهُمْ سِرَاعًا ذَٰلِكَ حَشْرٌ عَلَيْنَا يَسِيرٌ ۞ نَّحْنُ أَعْلَمُ بِمَا يَقُولُونَ وَمَآ أَنتَ عَلَيْهِم بِجَبَّارٍ فَذَكِّرْ بِٱلْقُرْءَانِ مَن يَخَافُ وَعِيدِ ۞

ᵃ No day is fixed for Doomsday. Quite without warning, at the command of Almighty God, the angel Isra'fil will herald its commencement by blowing a trumpet (*sur*).

Those who are unmindful of God mistakenly imagine Doomsday to be something remote. But a true believer lives in the expectation that at any time the trumpet may be blown and Doomsday will arrive. After the blowing of the trumpet, the shape of heaven and earth will undergo a drastic change and all human beings will be assembled in a new world in order to receive eternal awards, such as befit their respective deeds.

ᵇ It has been recorded in the Quran, again and again, that the Prophet's mission was only to convey the message of God to the people and it was not his responsibility to change them. On the other hand, it has been stated in the Quran on more than one occasion that, through him, the Prophet Muhammad, God would cause the religion of Truth to prevail over all other religions.

These two statements, in fact, relate to different aspects of the Prophet Muhammad. From one aspect, he was the messenger of God. From another aspect, he was the 'last of the prophets.' As a messenger of God, his mission was the same as that of all other prophets, namely, to convey the Truth to the people in a proper manner. But, as he was the last of the prophets, it was the intention of Almighty God to create such conditions through him that the word of God should remain preserved for all eternity, so that there should be no necessity to send any further prophets. This second aspect of the Prophet necessitated that, through him, a revolution be brought about which should end the dominance of polytheism, thereby establishing Islam as a dominant force which would guarantee the continuance of Divine guidance forever.

51. SCATTERING WINDS

سُورَةُ الذَّارِيَات

In the name of God,
the Most Gracious, the Most Merciful

بِسۡمِ اللَّهِ الرَّحۡمَٰنِ الرَّحِيمِ

¹ By the winds that scatter the dust,
² and those that bear the burden [of
the rain], ³ and those speeding along
with ease, ⁴ and distributing the
command of God at His behest! *a*
⁵ What you are promised is certainly
true: ⁶ the Judgement will surely
come to pass—⁷ by the heaven full
of tracks, ⁸ surely you are deeply at
variance [as to what to believe]—⁹ he
is turned away from [the truth] who
is destined to be so turned away.

وَٱلذَّٰرِيَٰتِ ذَرۡوٗا ۝ فَٱلۡحَٰمِلَٰتِ وِقۡرٗا
۝ فَٱلۡجَٰرِيَٰتِ يُسۡرٗا ۝ فَٱلۡمُقَسِّمَٰتِ
أَمۡرًا ۝ إِنَّمَا تُوعَدُونَ لَصَادِقٞ ۝
وَإِنَّ ٱلدِّينَ لَوَٰقِعٞ ۝ وَٱلسَّمَآءِ ذَاتِ
ٱلۡحُبُكِ ۝ إِنَّكُمۡ لَفِي قَوۡلٖ مُّخۡتَلِفٖ ۝
يُؤۡفَكُ عَنۡهُ مَنۡ أُفِكَ ۝

---

a A picture of the natural system of rainfall has been depicted in these verses. First strong winds blow. Then, they make the clouds drift. Thereafter, the clouds shower beneficial rain on one group, while they wreak destruction on another group in the shape of floods.

These events indicate that in this world of God, the Law of the 'distribution of blessings' is prevalent. Here some receive less and some more, some are granted boons, while others are deprived of them. This is a hint which shows how, in the world to come after death, human beings are going to fare. There, this principle of the 'distribution of blessings' will be applicable in a perfect manner, with perfect justice; everybody will receive only that to which he is entitled and will receive nothing that he did not deserve.

There are countless stars in the sky. All of them are revolving in their respective orbits. This wonderful system indicates a deep, inherent meaningfulness. Those who exercise their mental powers will find a lesson in it. But for those who do not, it will be a meaningless charade.

¹⁰ May the conjecturers perish, ¹¹ who flounder in the depths of ignorance. ¹² They ask, 'When will the Day of Judgement come?' ¹³ It will be the Day when they are tormented at the Fire. ¹⁴ 'Taste your trial. This is what you sought to hasten.' ¹⁵ Surely the God-fearing will find themselves in the midst of gardens and springs. ¹⁶ They shall receive what their Lord will bestow on them. They have done good works in the past, ¹⁷ sleeping little in the night-time, ¹⁸ praying at dawn for God's pardon, ¹⁹ and sharing their possessions with the beggars and the deprived.^a

قُتِلَ ٱلۡخَرَّٰصُونَ ۝ ٱلَّذِينَ هُمۡ فِى غَمۡرَةٖ سَاهُونَ ۝ يَسۡـَٔلُونَ أَيَّانَ يَوۡمُ ٱلدِّينِ ۝ يَوۡمَ هُمۡ عَلَى ٱلنَّارِ يُفۡتَنُونَ ۝ ذُوقُواْ فِتۡنَتَكُمۡ هَٰذَا ٱلَّذِى كُنتُم بِهِۦ تَسۡتَعۡجِلُونَ ۝ إِنَّ ٱلۡمُتَّقِينَ فِى جَنَّٰتٖ وَعُيُونٍ ۝ ءَاخِذِينَ مَآ ءَاتَىٰهُمۡ رَبُّهُمۡۚ إِنَّهُمۡ كَانُواْ قَبۡلَ ذَٰلِكَ مُحۡسِنِينَ ۝ كَانُواْ قَلِيلٗا مِّنَ ٱلَّيۡلِ مَا يَهۡجَعُونَ ۝ وَبِٱلۡأَسۡحَارِ هُمۡ يَسۡتَغۡفِرُونَ ۝ وَفِىٓ أَمۡوَٰلِهِمۡ حَقّٞ لِّلسَّآئِلِ وَٱلۡمَحۡرُومِ ۝

---

^a To have a clear understanding of things of importance, seriousness and sincerity are essential. Those who are not serious pay no attention to reasons and justifications. So they are unable to understand the matter at hand. They ridicule it and try to show that it is not worthy of serious consideration. It is not possible to convince such people in any way. They will accept the truth only when their wrong approach brings down upon them overwhelming punishment, from which there will be no escape.

Serious people behave quite differently from this, for their seriousness makes them cautious. And they have no trace of arrogance in them. The extreme intensity of their feelings makes them spend sleepless nights: their time is spent in remembering God. They do not consider their wealth the result of their hard work, but take it as a gift from God. That is why they think that others have as much right to a share in it as they themselves.

20 On the earth, and in yourselves,
21 there are signs for firm believers.
Do you not see then?ᵃ 22 In heaven
is your sustenance, and also that
which you are promised. 23 By the
Lord of the heaven and the earth, it
is certainly the truth. It is as true as
your ability to speak.ᵇ

وَفِى ٱلْأَرْضِ ءَايَتٌ لِّلْمُوقِنِينَ ۝ وَفِى
أَنفُسِكُمْ ۚ أَفَلَا تُبْصِرُونَ ۝ وَفِى
ٱلسَّمَآءِ رِزْقُكُمْ وَمَا تُوعَدُونَ ۝
فَوَرَبِّ ٱلسَّمَآءِ وَٱلْأَرْضِ إِنَّهُۥ لَحَقٌّ
مِّثْلَ مَآ أَنَّكُمْ تَنطِقُونَ ۝

ᵃ Almighty God has created this known world in such a manner that it has become
the indicator of the coming unknown world. The material incidents taking shape
in this world and the feelings latent in man give information, albeit indirectly about
the events that will directly confront man after his death. Among these signs is the
capacity to speak.

It has been mentioned in a tradition of the Prophet Muhammad, that whatever
one receives in the Hereafter will be his own deeds which will be returned to him
('Indeed, these are your deeds that are returned to you'). In other words, the world
of the Hereafter is the double or duplicate of the present world. The capacity of
a man to speak is the partial manifestation of this possibility. If a man's voice is
recorded on a tape and if this tape is then played, a voice like the original one may
be heard, i.e. the voice of the tape is the double or duplicate of the original. In this
way, the phenomenon of voice demonstrates to us on a partial level that event
which is going to occur in the Hereafter on a full-scale level.

ᵇ Literally 'It is certain like your talking'. It implies that when one's voice can be
reproduced, it should be possible to reproduce one's existence. Perfect reproduction
of a part of a man's existence may be experienced in this world. It can be imagined
from this that reproduction of the whole existence of man is possible.

24 Have you heard the story of Abraham's honoured guests? 25 When they came to him they said, 'Peace!' He answered, 'Peace!' [saying to himself]. 'They are strangers.' 26 Then he turned quickly to his household, and brought a fatted calf, 27 and placed it before them. 'Will you not eat?' he said, 28 beginning to be afraid of them. But they said, 'Don't be afraid'; and they gave him the good news of a son who would be endowed with knowledge. 29 Then his wife came forward, crying and beating her brow. She said, 'I am surely a barren, old woman.' 30 'Such is the will of your Lord,' they replied. 'He is the Wise, the All Knowing.' *a*

31 Abraham asked, 'What is your errand, O messengers?' 32 They replied, 'We have been sent to a sinful people, 33 so that we may bring down upon them a shower of stones of clay, 34 which are marked by your Lord for the punishment of those guilty of excesses.'

هَلْ أَتَىٰكَ حَدِيثُ ضَيْفِ إِبْرَٰهِيمَ ٱلْمُكْرَمِينَ ﴿٢٤﴾ إِذْ دَخَلُوا۟ عَلَيْهِ فَقَالُوا۟ سَلَـٰمًا قَالَ سَلَـٰمٌ قَوْمٌ مُّنكَرُونَ ﴿٢٥﴾ فَرَاغَ إِلَىٰٓ أَهْلِهِۦ فَجَآءَ بِعِجْلٍ سَمِينٍ ﴿٢٦﴾ فَقَرَّبَهُۥٓ إِلَيْهِمْ قَالَ أَلَا تَأْكُلُونَ ﴿٢٧﴾ فَأَوْجَسَ مِنْهُمْ خِيفَةً قَالُوا۟ لَا تَخَفْ وَبَشَّرُوهُ بِغُلَـٰمٍ عَلِيمٍ ﴿٢٨﴾ فَأَقْبَلَتِ ٱمْرَأَتُهُۥ فِى صَرَّةٍ فَصَكَّتْ وَجْهَهَا وَقَالَتْ عَجُوزٌ عَقِيمٌ ﴿٢٩﴾ قَالُوا۟ كَذَٰلِكِ قَالَ رَبُّكِ إِنَّهُۥ هُوَ ٱلْحَكِيمُ ٱلْعَلِيمُ ﴿٣٠﴾ ۞ قَالَ فَمَا خَطْبُكُمْ أَيُّهَا ٱلْمُرْسَلُونَ ﴿٣١﴾ قَالُوٓا۟ إِنَّآ أُرْسِلْنَآ إِلَىٰ قَوْمٍ مُّجْرِمِينَ ﴿٣٢﴾ لِنُرْسِلَ عَلَيْهِمْ حِجَارَةً مِّن طِينٍ ﴿٣٣﴾ مُّسَوَّمَةً عِندَ رَبِّكَ لِلْمُسْرِفِينَ ﴿٣٤﴾

---

a In these verses that scene has been described in which angels came to Abraham in order to give him the good news of his having children in his old age. Abraham was born in ancient Iraq. For a long time he preached to his people about the Unity of God and the Hereafter. But, except for his wife and nephew, Lot, nobody was ready to accept his word, until he reached old age.

Now, in order to ensure the continuance of his mission, the second alternative was that he should have children who should be properly brought up by him. There is a blood relationship between father and son, which is a powerful factor in keeping a son attached to his father and make him like-minded whatever the conditions.

Almighty God granted Abraham two sons in his old age. One was Isaac (Ishaq), through whom the preaching of the Unity of God continued among the Children of Israel. The second was Ishmael (Isma'il), through whom a race was brought into being which was to support the Last of the Prophets in fulfilling his historic mission.

35 We saved all the faithful in the town. 36 We found in it only one household of true believers—37 and We left therein a sign for those who fear a painful punishment.ᵃ

38 There is another sign in Moses: We sent him to Pharaoh with clear authority. 39 But he turned his back, he and his courtiers, and said, 'This is a sorcerer or a madman.'ᵇ 40 Then We seized him and his army and cast them all into the sea: he himself [Pharaoh] was to blame. 41 There is another sign in the [tribe of] 'Ad, when We sent against them a life-destroying wind 42 and it destroyed everything over which it passed and reduced it to dust. 43 In the Thamud [there was another sign], when they were told, 'Make the most of your lives for a while.'

فَأَخْرَجْنَا مَن كَانَ فِيهَا مِنَ ٱلْمُؤْمِنِينَ ۝ فَمَا وَجَدْنَا فِيهَا غَيْرَ بَيْتٍ مِّنَ ٱلْمُسْلِمِينَ ۝ وَتَرَكْنَا فِيهَآ ءَايَةً لِّلَّذِينَ يَخَافُونَ ٱلْعَذَابَ ٱلْأَلِيمَ ۝ وَفِى مُوسَىٰٓ إِذْ أَرْسَلْنَٰهُ إِلَىٰ فِرْعَوْنَ بِسُلْطَٰنٍ مُّبِينٍ ۝ فَتَوَلَّىٰ بِرُكْنِهِۦ وَقَالَ سَٰحِرٌ أَوْ مَجْنُونٌ ۝ فَأَخَذْنَٰهُ وَجُنُودَهُۥ فَنَبَذْنَٰهُمْ فِى ٱلْيَمِّ وَهُوَ مُلِيمٌ ۝ وَفِى عَادٍ إِذْ أَرْسَلْنَا عَلَيْهِمُ ٱلرِّيحَ ٱلْعَقِيمَ ۝ مَا تَذَرُ مِن شَىْءٍ أَتَتْ عَلَيْهِ إِلَّا جَعَلَتْهُ كَٱلرَّمِيمِ ۝ وَفِى ثَمُودَ إِذْ قِيلَ لَهُمْ تَمَتَّعُوا۟ حَتَّىٰ حِينٍ ۝

ᵃ At that time Abraham was in Palestine. Nearby, around the Dead Sea there were the townships of Sodom and Gomorrah in which the contemporaries of Lot were settled. In spite of Lot's preaching for a long time, they were not ready to give up a life vitiated by forgetfulness of God. So, at God's behest, Lot and his companions departed. Then, the aforesaid angels destroyed the entire community by an earthquake, stormy winds and showers of pebbles.

The community of Lot was destroyed two thousand years ago, but their devastated habitat (south of the Dead Sea) exists even today to teach a lesson to those who have the inclination to learn from events.

ᵇ The Pharaoh of Egypt called the miracles of Moses magical feats. He interpreted Moses's firm belief (which indicated the latter's being on the right path) as madness. This is known as covering up (talbis) and this covering up has always been the way of those people who are not ready to accept the Truth, in spite of its being supported by sound reasoning.

44 But they rebelled against the command of their Lord. So the thunderbolt overtook them while they looked on: 45 they could not stand up again, nor could they defend themselves. 46 [We destroyed] the people of Noah before them. They were certainly a sinful people.ᵃ

47 We built the universe with Our might, giving it its vast expanse.ᵇ 48 We have spread out the earth—how well We have spread it out— 49 and We created pairs of all things so that you might reflect.ᶜ

فَعَتَوْا عَنْ أَمْرِ رَبِّهِمْ فَأَخَذَتْهُمُ ٱلصَّٰعِقَةُ وَهُمْ يَنظُرُونَ ۝ فَمَا ٱسْتَطَٰعُوا مِن قِيَامٍ وَمَا كَانُوا مُنتَصِرِينَ ۝ وَقَوْمَ نُوحٍ مِّن قَبْلُ إِنَّهُمْ كَانُوا قَوْمًا فَٰسِقِينَ ۝ وَٱلسَّمَآءَ بَنَيْنَٰهَا بِأَيْيْدٍ وَإِنَّا لَمُوسِعُونَ ۝ وَٱلْأَرْضَ فَرَشْنَٰهَا فَنِعْمَ ٱلْمَٰهِدُونَ ۝ وَمِن كُلِّ شَىْءٍ خَلَقْنَا زَوْجَيْنِ لَعَلَّكُمْ تَذَكَّرُونَ ۝

ᵃ People displaying such arrogance in the face of the Truth never escape God's scourge. Pharaoh was killed for this reason, and the communities of 'Ad, Thamud, and Noah were also destroyed for this very reason. They were given some benefit in this world, it being the test period. Beyond this small benefit they were destined not to receive any other.

ᵇ Literally 'We are broadening the sky.' This statement refers perhaps to that characteristic of the universe which has been only recently discovered, i.e. continuous expansion of the universe on all sides after the Big Bang. This expansion is proof of the fact that a Creator has created it, because this expansion means that it was initially in a contracted condition. According to the known laws governing matter, all the parts of the initial cosmic ball were attracted inwards. Then there was an explosion—the Big Bang—after which all matter started moving outwards. In view of this law, their movement towards the outside (or the Big Bang) could not have taken place without some external intervention. And once external intervention has been accepted, acceptance of God necessarily follows.

ᶜ The system of our world is a highly meaningful one. This proves that the creation of the present world has been brought about with some high purpose. But we see that man has wrecked disorder on the earth. In the meaningful universe, this meaningless development is incongruous and calls for a world which is free of all evils to come into existence. ▶

⁵⁰ Therefore hasten to God; truly, I am sent by Him to give you clear warning. ⁵¹ Do not set up another god, along with God. I come from Him to warn you plainly.

⁵² Likewise, there came no messenger to those before them, but they said, 'He is a sorcerer or a madman.' ⁵³ Have they handed this down to one another? They are certainly a people who exceed all bounds, ⁵⁴ so ignore them—you are not to blame—⁵⁵ but keep on exhorting them, for exhortation benefits the believers.ᵃ

فَفِرُّوٓاْ إِلَى ٱللَّهِ إِنِّى لَكُم مِّنْهُ نَذِيرٌ مُّبِينٌ ۞ وَلَا تَجْعَلُواْ مَعَ ٱللَّهِ إِلَٰهًا ءَاخَرَ إِنِّى لَكُم مِّنْهُ نَذِيرٌ مُّبِينٌ ۞ كَذَٰلِكَ مَآ أَتَى ٱلَّذِينَ مِن قَبْلِهِم مِّن رَّسُولٍ إِلَّا قَالُواْ سَاحِرٌ أَوْ مَجْنُونٌ ۞ أَتَوَاصَوْاْ بِهِۦ بَلْ هُمْ قَوْمٌ طَاغُونَ ۞ فَتَوَلَّ عَنْهُمْ فَمَآ أَنتَ بِمَلُومٍ ۞ وَذَكِّرْ فَإِنَّ ٱلذِّكْرَىٰ تَنفَعُ ٱلْمُؤْمِنِينَ ۞

In the present world provision has already been made for this, i.e. all things in this world come in pairs—in matter, positive and negative particles, in plants male and female and among human beings, men and women. This is the quintessence of the universe: the prevalence of the law of compensating for the shortcomings of any given thing through its pair or complement. This duality is an indication of the possibility of the Hereafter. In other words, the world of Hereafter is the other part which makes up a pair with the present world and this combination makes our world complete.

ᵃ If a serious man demands reasoning in support of any point at issue, he will concede to it if the argument presented is convincing. But those who are arrogant by nature, are never so persuaded. They will find some fresh excuse to reject the argument. Even if some proposition which cannot be countered is put forward, they will ignore it, saying that it is 'magic'.

This is the attitude of those who have reached a high status in their community. Their consciousness of being great becomes an impediment to their acceptance of the Truth as asserted by others. If such people reject the call for Truth, the preacher should not be disheartened. He will find supporters among others who are free of any false sense of prestige.

⁵⁶ I created the jinn and mankind only so that they might worship Me:ᵃ ⁵⁷ I seek no sustenance from them, nor do I want them to feed Me— ⁵⁸ it is God who is the great Sustainer, the Mighty One, the Invincible. ⁵⁹ The wrongdoers will meet the same fate as their predecessors—let them not ask Me to hasten on [the punishment]— ⁶⁰ woe, then, to those who are bent on denying the truth, when the Day arrives which they have been promised.ᵇ

وَمَا خَلَقْتُ ٱلْجِنَّ وَٱلْإِنسَ إِلَّا لِيَعْبُدُونِ ۞ مَآ أُرِيدُ مِنْهُم مِّن رِّزْقٍ وَمَآ أُرِيدُ أَن يُطْعِمُونِ ۞ إِنَّ ٱللَّهَ هُوَ ٱلرَّزَّاقُ ذُو ٱلْقُوَّةِ ٱلْمَتِينُ ۞ فَإِنَّ لِلَّذِينَ ظَلَمُوا۟ ذَنُوبًا مِّثْلَ ذَنُوبِ أَصْحَـٰبِهِمْ فَلَا يَسْتَعْجِلُونِ ۞ فَوَيْلٌ لِّلَّذِينَ كَفَرُوا۟ مِن يَوْمِهِمُ ٱلَّذِى يُوعَدُونَ ۞

ᵃ God Himself possesses all kinds of powers. However, He has created the angels to effect the administration of His vast domain. But, the case of human beings is different. Human beings were not created to fulfill any administrative or other need of God. The sole purpose of their creation was their devotion and servitude (*ibadah*) to God. This implies bowing down without any reservation before God completely and dedicating oneself entirely to Him.

The substance of this devotion is deep inner realisation of God (*ma'rifah*) (*Tafsir ibn Kathir*). In other words, it is required of man that God should be a discovery for him. He should recognise God without seeing him. This is essential to *ma'rifah*. The shape which the life of a man takes as a result of this *ma'rifah* is one of devotion and subservience.

ᵇ A pail when being filled with water sinks in water the moment it is full. Similarly, when the time given to a man to perform his life's work is over, he dies immediately. One who reforms himself before the overflowing of the pail may save himself, but one who remains careless and negligent till the last moment faces destruction.

If transgressors are not immediately seized upon, they should not imagine that they have been left free to do as they choose. They go free because it is not God's way to catch hold of human beings in haste. It is certainly not because God has no plan ever to bring them to book.

52. THE MOUNTAIN

In the name of God,
the Most Gracious, the Most Merciful

¹ By the Mount Sinai,ᵃ ² and by the
Scripture penned ³ on unrolled
parchment, ⁴ by the much-visited
House, ⁵ and by the lofty vault of the
sky, ⁶ and by the swelling sea, ⁷ the
punishment of your Lord shall
certainly come to pass— ⁸ there is no
one who could avert it— ⁹ on the
Day when the skies are convulsed,
¹⁰ and the mountains shudder and
shake. ¹¹ Woe on that Day to those
who deny the truth, ¹² who divert
themselves with idle chatter: ¹³ on
that Day they shall be ruthlessly
thrust into the Fire of Hell. ¹⁴ This
is the fire which you used to deny.
¹⁵ Is this magic or do you not see?
¹⁶ Now enter it. Whether you behave
patiently or impatiently will make no
difference: you are only being repaid
for what you have done.ᵇ

ᵃ Mount Tur is that mountain in the desert of Sinai where Moses was awarded
prophethood. The Scripture penned on unrolled parchment or the written Book
(*kitabun mastur*) here means the Torah. The frequented house (*al-bayt al-ma'mur*)
means the Kabah. The lofty vaults of the sky or high roof (*as-saqf al-marfu'*) means
the sky. The swelling sea (*al-bahr al-masjur*) means a sea with waves. All these things
bear testimony that the Day of seizure by God is certain to come. Almighty God
has repeatedly given these very tidings through the prophets. This has also been
mentioned in ancient holy scriptures. Heaven and earth announce this in their
silent language. The waves of the sea relate this story to every listener.

ᵇ Man will have to face the result of his actions. He is being forewarned of the
consequences. The negligence and arrogance of those who do not come to their
senses now with the forewarning, will ultimately suffer grievous punishment. When
they try to run away from this, they will find no refuge anywhere.

¹⁷ Truly, the God-fearing will dwell [on that Day] in gardens and in bliss,ᵃ ¹⁸ rejoicing in whatever their Lord has given them. Their Lord has saved them from the torment of the Fire, ¹⁹ 'Eat and drink with good cheer as a reward for your good deeds,' ²⁰ reclining on couches arranged in rows. And We shall wed them to fair maidens with large beautiful eyes.

إِنَّ ٱلْمُتَّقِينَ فِى جَنَّٰتٍ وَنَعِيمٍ ۝ فَٰكِهِينَ بِمَآ ءَاتَىٰهُمْ رَبُّهُمْ وَوَقَىٰهُمْ رَبُّهُمْ عَذَابَ ٱلْجَحِيمِ ۝ كُلُواْ وَٱشْرَبُواْ هَنِيٓـًٔا بِمَا كُنتُمْ تَعْمَلُونَ ۝ مُتَّكِئِينَ عَلَىٰ سُرُرٍ مَّصْفُوفَةٍ وَزَوَّجْنَٰهُم بِحُورٍ عِينٍ ۝

ᵃ The worst crime on the part of man is denial of Truth. And this is a crime which gives birth to other crimes. Similarly, the greatest virtue of man is his acceptance of Truth. All other virtues come into existence as a result of this.

By accepting the truth, man's sense of his own greatness or prestige is impaired. So such acceptance is the most difficult task for a man. Only those who have become truly serious out of extreme fear of God can undertake it. Those who prove to have this very great virtue deserve to have the doors to the eternal blessings of Paradise thrown open to them.

²¹To those who have attained to faith We shall unite their offspring who have also followed them in faith, and We shall not let any of their good deeds go unrewarded; every human being is a pledge for whatever he has earned. ²²We shall provide them in abundance with such fruit and meat as they desire. ²³There, they shall pass from hand to hand a cup which does not lead to any idle talk or sin. ²⁴They will be waited upon by immortal youths, like pearls hidden in their shells. ²⁵They will converse with one another, putting questions to each other, ²⁶'Before this, when we were among our families, we were full of fear of God's displeasure— ²⁷God has been gracious to us and has saved us from the torment of Hell's intense heat— ²⁸before this, we used to pray to Him. Surely, He is the Beneficent, the Merciful.'ᵃ

وَٱلَّذِينَ ءَامَنُوا۟ وَٱتَّبَعَتْهُمْ ذُرِّيَّتُهُم بِإِيمَٰنٍ أَلْحَقْنَا بِهِمْ ذُرِّيَّتَهُمْ وَمَآ أَلَتْنَٰهُم مِّنْ عَمَلِهِم مِّن شَىْءٍ كُلُّ ٱمْرِئٍ بِمَا كَسَبَ رَهِينٌ ۝ وَأَمْدَدْنَٰهُم بِفَٰكِهَةٍ وَلَحْمٍ مِّمَّا يَشْتَهُونَ ۝ يَتَنَٰزَعُونَ فِيهَا كَأْسًا لَّا لَغْوٌ فِيهَا وَلَا تَأْثِيمٌ ۝ ۞ وَيَطُوفُ عَلَيْهِمْ غِلْمَانٌ لَّهُمْ كَأَنَّهُمْ لُؤْلُؤٌ مَّكْنُونٌ ۝ وَأَقْبَلَ بَعْضُهُمْ عَلَىٰ بَعْضٍ يَتَسَآءَلُونَ ۝ قَالُوٓا۟ إِنَّا كُنَّا قَبْلُ فِىٓ أَهْلِنَا مُشْفِقِينَ ۝ فَمَنَّ ٱللَّهُ عَلَيْنَا وَوَقَىٰنَا عَذَابَ ٱلسَّمُومِ ۝ إِنَّا كُنَّا مِن قَبْلُ نَدْعُوهُ إِنَّهُۥ هُوَ ٱلْبَرُّ ٱلرَّحِيمُ ۝

ᵃ In the Hereafter, it will not happen that one man's sins are attributed to another, and nobody will be able to enter Paradise except on the basis of his faith and his own righteous deeds. But, the occupants of Paradise will be given one special privilege: if parents are in a high stratum of Paradise and their children in some other stratum, the children will be united with their parents so that their happiness should increase.

Only one who, in spite of being among his wife and children, has always been moved by the fear of God and who linked his hopes and fears with the one and only God, will be entitled to enter the sublime world of Paradise.

²⁹ Therefore continue to give warning, for by the grace of your Lord, you are not a soothsayer or a madman. ³⁰ If they say, 'He is but a poet; we are waiting for some misfortune to befall him,' ³¹ say [to them], 'Wait then: I too am waiting along with you!'—³² is it their minds that prompt them [to say] this, or are they merely insolent people? ³³ Or do they say, 'He has invented it himself'? Indeed, they are not willing to believe. ³⁴ Let them produce a scripture like it, if what they say is true.ᵃ

فَذَكِّرْ فَمَآ أَنتَ بِنِعْمَتِ رَبِّكَ بِكَاهِنٍ وَلَا مَجْنُونٍ ۞ أَمْ يَقُولُونَ شَاعِرٌ نَّتَرَبَّصُ بِهِۦ رَيْبَ ٱلْمَنُونِ ۞ قُلْ تَرَبَّصُوا۟ فَإِنِّى مَعَكُم مِّنَ ٱلْمُتَرَبِّصِينَ ۞ أَمْ تَأْمُرُهُمْ أَحْلَٰمُهُم بِهَٰذَآ أَمْ هُمْ قَوْمٌ طَاغُونَ ۞ أَمْ يَقُولُونَ تَقَوَّلَهُۥ بَل لَّا يُؤْمِنُونَ ۞ فَلْيَأْتُوا۟ بِحَدِيثٍ مِّثْلِهِۦٓ إِن كَانُوا۟ صَٰدِقِينَ ۞

ᵃ When a man has no argument against the call of Truth, and yet he does not want to accept it, he starts denigrating the personality of the preacher of Truth. He makes the character of the preacher rather than his statements the target of his attacks. It was becuse of this recalcitrant attitude that the addressees of the Prophet started calling him a 'poet' and a 'mad person'. They could not counter his call for Truth by reasoning. So, they started casting aspersions upon him.

But the prophet conveys what he receives from God. And the discourse of one who repeats what he receives from God's message is so distinctly different from that of others that it is not possible for anybody to equal it. This is the greatest proof of the fact that his discourse is Divine in origin.

35 Were they created out of nothing, or are they their own creators? 36 Did they create the heavens and the earth? No! They have no faith.[a] 37 Do they own the treasures of your Lord, or have they been given charge of them? 38 Have they a ladder up to heaven by means of which they can overhear? Then let their listeners bring a clear proof. 39 Does God have daughters while you have sons?

40 Or do you ask them for a reward, so that they are over-burdened by debt? 41 Do they possess knowledge of the unseen, so that they can write it down? 42 Do they want to hatch some plot? Those who deny the truth will be the victims of the plot. 43 Or have they a god other than God? Exalted be God over what they ascribe as partners [to Him]![b]

أَمۡ خُلِقُوا۟ مِنۡ غَيۡرِ شَىۡءٍ أَمۡ هُمُ ٱلۡخَٰلِقُونَ ۝ أَمۡ خَلَقُوا۟ ٱلسَّمَٰوَٰتِ وَٱلۡأَرۡضَ ۚ بَل لَّا يُوقِنُونَ ۝ أَمۡ عِندَهُمۡ خَزَآئِنُ رَبِّكَ أَمۡ هُمُ ٱلۡمُصَۜيۡطِرُونَ ۝ أَمۡ لَهُمۡ سُلَّمٌ يَسۡتَمِعُونَ فِيهِ ۖ فَلۡيَأۡتِ مُسۡتَمِعُهُم بِسُلۡطَٰنٍ مُّبِينٍ ۝ أَمۡ لَهُ ٱلۡبَنَٰتُ وَلَكُمُ ٱلۡبَنُونَ ۝ أَمۡ تَسۡـَٔلُهُمۡ أَجۡرًا فَهُم مِّن مَّغۡرَمٍ مُّثۡقَلُونَ ۝ أَمۡ عِندَهُمُ ٱلۡغَيۡبُ فَهُمۡ يَكۡتُبُونَ ۝ أَمۡ يُرِيدُونَ كَيۡدًا ۖ فَٱلَّذِينَ كَفَرُوا۟ هُمُ ٱلۡمَكِيدُونَ ۝ أَمۡ لَهُمۡ إِلَٰهٌ غَيۡرُ ٱللَّهِ ۚ سُبۡحَٰنَ ٱللَّهِ عَمَّا يُشۡرِكُونَ ۝

---

[a] The realities declared on behalf of God, are all perfectly rational and reasonable. If a man pays attention to them, he can easily understand them. So why do people reject them? The reason for this is people's disbelief in the Hereafter. People do not earnestly and actively believe that they will have to face any reckoning in the Hereafter. So, they are not serious about these matters and as such they are unable to understand them. If a man has a firm belief in the reward for good deeds, he will immediately understand matters which he hitherto found extremely difficult to appreciate.

[b] The addressees of a preacher invariably exist on the level of materialism. In view of this, if they have the feeling that the preacher of Truth wants to take some material thing from them, they immediately shy away from him. That is why a preacher of Truth never allows any material demand to crop up between his addressees and himself. To the very end, he maintains an atmosphere of selflessness between his addressees and himself. In so doing he may have to bear some material loss.

When a preacher proves his seriousness to this extent with regard to his call for Truth, he then becomes entitled to God's help, so much so that the unbelievers find all their tricks and devices recoiling on them, rendering them unsuccessful in gaining the upper hand.

⁴⁴ If they should see a part of the heavens falling down, they would say, 'A mass of clouds,' ⁴⁵ so leave them alone till they face the Day on which they will be struck dumb, ⁴⁶ the Day when none of their scheming will be of the least avail to them, and they will receive no succour. ⁴⁷ Truly, for those who do wrong there is a punishment besides that, though most of them do not know it.ᵃ

⁴⁸ So wait patiently for the Judgement of your Lord—you are certainly under Our watchful eye. And glorify and celebrate the praises of your Lord when you rise up [from your sleep]. ⁴⁹ Extol His glory at night, and at the setting of the stars.

وَإِن يَرَوْا۟ كِسْفًا مِّنَ ٱلسَّمَآءِ سَاقِطًا يَقُولُوا۟ سَحَابٌ مَّرْكُومٌ ۝ فَذَرْهُمْ حَتَّىٰ يُلَٰقُوا۟ يَوْمَهُمُ ٱلَّذِى فِيهِ يُصْعَقُونَ ۝ يَوْمَ لَا يُغْنِى عَنْهُمْ كَيْدُهُمْ شَيْـًٔا وَلَا هُمْ يُنصَرُونَ ۝ وَإِنَّ لِلَّذِينَ ظَلَمُوا۟ عَذَابًا دُونَ ذَٰلِكَ وَلَٰكِنَّ أَكْثَرَهُمْ لَا يَعْلَمُونَ ۝ وَٱصْبِرْ لِحُكْمِ رَبِّكَ فَإِنَّكَ بِأَعْيُنِنَا وَسَبِّحْ بِحَمْدِ رَبِّكَ حِينَ تَقُومُ ۝ وَمِنَ ٱلَّيْلِ فَسَبِّحْهُ وَإِدْبَٰرَ ٱلنُّجُومِ ۝

ᵃ Why were the people of ancient Makkah so inclined that, wherever they saw God's punitive devices falling from the sky, they would say that it was only a cloud? The reason for this was not that they did not accept God or His powers. The real reason for this was that they were doubtful of the Prophet really being a prophet. They were not convinced that the rejection of the person who was before them and who was apparently just like them could be so great a crime as to bring down a mountain of destruction upon them.

The personality of the Prophet Muhammad was a matter of controversy among his contemporaries. He had at that time no established reputation, as it would seem to people today. But, it is the real test of man that he should see the reality by tearing asunder the veils of doubt. He should be able to discover the essence of the established personality in the apparently controversial personality.

ᵇ This means that in spite of all sorts of unpleasantness on the part of the addressees, dawah work should be continued until it has reached its completion in the eyes of God. When this limit is reached, God's decision is made manifest; this in practice clarifies the difference between Truth and untruth, which had earlier been merely a matter of theory.

During this entire period, the preacher is completely under the protection of God. The task of the preacher is that he should focus on God and should believe that at all times he will remain under God's protection.

53. THE SETTING STAR

In the name of God, the Most Gracious, the Most Merciful

¹ By the setting star,ᵃ ² your companion has neither strayed nor is he misguided, ³ nor does he speak out of his own desire. ⁴ It [the Quran] is nothing but revelation sent down to him. ⁵ He was taught by [an angel] who is mighty in power, ⁶ and endowed with wisdom; who in time manifested himself; ⁷ standing poised at the highest point on the horizon, ⁸ then came down close ⁹ until he was two bow-lengths away or even closer ¹⁰ and revealed to God's servant what he revealed. ¹¹ The heart [of the Prophet] did not misconstrue what he saw. ¹² Will you then dispute with him as to what he saw? ¹³ And certainly he saw him descend a second time:ᵇ

ᵃ The setting of the stars is a symbol which hints at the stable and flawless system governing the revolution of stars. This is an indication that the spiritual system established with the help of revelation and prophethood should also be flawless.

ᵇ The experience of the Prophet with the angels and his being taught the revelation have been explained in the above verses. For corroborating the reality of these events the statement of the Quran is enough. The Quran's miraculous discourse proves that it is the Book of God. And every statement of that book which is established as God's Book shall have to be accepted as authentic.

¹⁴ by the lote tree beyond which none may pass ¹⁵ by the Garden of [Eternal] Repose, ¹⁶ when the lote tree was covered in mystic splendour. ¹⁷ His sight did not waver nor was it unduly bold. ¹⁸ He saw some of the greatest signs of his Lord.

¹⁹ Have you really considered al-Lat and al-'Uzza, ²⁰ and the third one, Manat? *^a*—²¹ 'What! For you the males and for Him the females?' ²² That indeed is an unfair division— ²³ these are nothing but names which you yourselves have devised, you and your forefathers. God has sent down no authority for them. They follow nothing but conjecture and what their own selves desire, even though guidance has already come to them from their Lord! ²⁴ Shall man have whatever he craves? *^b* ²⁵ But it is to God that the Hereafter and this world belong.

عِندَ سِدْرَةِ ٱلْمُنتَهَىٰ ۝ عِندَهَا جَنَّةُ ٱلْمَأْوَىٰ ۝ إِذْ يَغْشَى ٱلسِّدْرَةَ مَا يَغْشَىٰ ۝ مَا زَاغَ ٱلْبَصَرُ وَمَا طَغَىٰ ۝ لَقَدْ رَأَىٰ مِنْ ءَايَٰتِ رَبِّهِ ٱلْكُبْرَىٰ ۝ أَفَرَءَيْتُمُ ٱللَّٰتَ وَٱلْعُزَّىٰ ۝ وَمَنَوٰةَ ٱلثَّالِثَةَ ٱلْأُخْرَىٰ ۝ أَلَكُمُ ٱلذَّكَرُ وَلَهُ ٱلْأُنثَىٰ ۝ تِلْكَ إِذًا قِسْمَةٌ ضِيزَىٰ ۝ إِنْ هِىَ إِلَّآ أَسْمَآءٌ سَمَّيْتُمُوهَآ أَنتُمْ وَءَابَآؤُكُم مَّآ أَنزَلَ ٱللَّهُ بِهَا مِن سُلْطَٰنٍ إِن يَتَّبِعُونَ إِلَّا ٱلظَّنَّ وَمَا تَهْوَى ٱلْأَنفُسُ وَلَقَدْ جَآءَهُم مِّن رَّبِّهِمُ ٱلْهُدَىٰ ۝ أَمْ لِلْإِنسَٰنِ مَا تَمَنَّىٰ ۝ فَلِلَّهِ ٱلْءَاخِرَةُ وَٱلْأُولَىٰ ۝

---

^a Al-Lat, al-'Uzza and Manat were the deities of ancient Arabia. Al-Lat was located in Taif, al-'Uzza in Nakhla near Makkah and Manat in Qudayd near Madinah. These three, according to the popular belief of those days, were the daughters of god, and so they were worshipped. A belief of this kind was undoubtedly a baseless supposition. It is a contradiction in itself. These polytheists used to consider it a degrading thing to have daughters. So, God wanted them to ask themselves if He, who was the Creator of sons and daughters, were to create children for Himself, would He have created daughters for Himself?

^b Explaining the query in verse 24, 'Does man get all that he wants?' Shah Abdul Qadir Dehlavi writes, 'What does one get by worshipping deities? One gets whatever is given by God.'

²⁶ There may be countless angels in heaven, but their intercession will be of no avail until God has given permission to those whom he chooses and accepts. ²⁷ Those who do not believe in the life to come call the angels by female names. ²⁸ They have no knowledge to base this on. They merely indulge in guess-work which can never replace the truth.ᵃ

²⁹ So ignore those who turn away from Our revelation and seek nothing but the life of this world.ᵇ ³⁰ That is the ultimate extent of their knowledge. Surely your Lord knows best those who stray from His path and He knows best those who follow His guidance.

۞ وَكَم مِّن مَّلَكٍ فِى ٱلسَّمَٰوَٰتِ لَا تُغْنِى شَفَٰعَتُهُمْ شَيْـًٔا إِلَّا مِنۢ بَعْدِ أَن يَأْذَنَ ٱللَّهُ لِمَن يَشَآءُ وَيَرْضَىٰٓ ۝ إِنَّ ٱلَّذِينَ لَا يُؤْمِنُونَ بِٱلْءَاخِرَةِ لَيُسَمُّونَ ٱلْمَلَٰٓئِكَةَ تَسْمِيَةَ ٱلْأُنثَىٰ ۝ وَمَا لَهُم بِهِۦ مِنْ عِلْمٍ إِن يَتَّبِعُونَ إِلَّا ٱلظَّنَّ وَإِنَّ ٱلظَّنَّ لَا يُغْنِى مِنَ ٱلْحَقِّ شَيْـًٔا ۝ فَأَعْرِضْ عَن مَّن تَوَلَّىٰ عَن ذِكْرِنَا وَلَمْ يُرِدْ إِلَّا ٱلْحَيَوٰةَ ٱلدُّنْيَا ۝ ذَٰلِكَ مَبْلَغُهُم مِّنَ ٱلْعِلْمِ إِنَّ رَبَّكَ هُوَ أَعْلَمُ بِمَن ضَلَّ عَن سَبِيلِهِۦ وَهُوَ أَعْلَمُ بِمَنِ ٱهْتَدَىٰ ۝

ᵃ Making deities of stone and worshipping them, calling the angels 'daughters of God,' hoping to enter Paradise on the basis of recommendations—all these are non-serious beliefs. Non-serious beliefs are the product of minds that have no fear of God's wrath. Fear of God puts a stop to pointless talk: the mind of one who has no such fear will become a babel of useless chatter.

ᵇ There is no use arguing with those who do not fear God. Such individuals never pay attention to reason and rationality. So, they are not ready to accept the word of Truth. There is only one possible way to deal with them and that is to shun them. However, Almighty God knows the inner condition of everybody and according to that He will deal with each one.

³¹ Everything in the heavens and on the earth belongs to God and so He will requite those who do evil in accordance with their deeds and will reward those left with that which is best, for those who do good.ᵃ ³² As for those who refrain from committing grave sins and indecent acts, though they may commit minor offences, your Lord is unstinting in His forgiveness.ᵇ He knows you when He brings you out of the earth, and when you were embryos in the wombs of your mothers; so do not make claims to be pure. He knows best who is truly righteous.

³³ Have you [Prophet] considered the man who turned away, ³⁴ who at first gave a little, then later held back? ³⁵ Has he knowledge of the unseen, so that he sees?ᶜ

وَلِلَّهِ مَا فِى ٱلسَّمَٰوَٰتِ وَمَا فِى ٱلْأَرْضِ لِيَجْزِىَ ٱلَّذِينَ أَسَٰٓـُٔوا۟ بِمَا عَمِلُوا۟ وَيَجْزِىَ ٱلَّذِينَ أَحْسَنُوا۟ بِٱلْحُسْنَى ﴿٣١﴾ ٱلَّذِينَ يَجْتَنِبُونَ كَبَٰٓئِرَ ٱلْإِثْمِ وَٱلْفَوَٰحِشَ إِلَّا ٱللَّمَمَ إِنَّ رَبَّكَ وَٰسِعُ ٱلْمَغْفِرَةِ هُوَ أَعْلَمُ بِكُمْ إِذْ أَنشَأَكُم مِّنَ ٱلْأَرْضِ وَإِذْ أَنتُمْ أَجِنَّةٌ فِى بُطُونِ أُمَّهَٰتِكُمْ فَلَا تُزَكُّوٓا۟ أَنفُسَكُمْ هُوَ أَعْلَمُ بِمَنِ ٱتَّقَىٰٓ ﴿٣٢﴾ أَفَرَءَيْتَ ٱلَّذِى تَوَلَّىٰ ﴿٣٣﴾ وَأَعْطَىٰ قَلِيلًا وَأَكْدَىٰٓ ﴿٣٤﴾ أَعِندَهُۥ عِلْمُ ٱلْغَيْبِ فَهُوَ يَرَىٰٓ ﴿٣٥﴾

ᵃ The universe with its extremely stable system makes manifest the fact that its Creator and Lord is extremely powerful. This suffices to make it clear that He will sooner or later seize hold of man and when He does so, there will be no escaping His grasp.

ᵇ Man has been created with human weaknesses. So, it is not required that he be as pure as the angels. Almighty God has given full guidance to man as to what he should do and what he should not. However, man may be pardoned in the case of lesser offences (*lamam*), i.e. indulging in some mischief because of fleeting emotion, on the condition that he should immediately realise his lapse and, being ashamed of it, seek pardon of his Lord.

ᶜ There are many who become inclined towards the Truth, but only to a certain extent. Then the compulsions of their interests become too strong for them and they revert to their original position. In order to justify and explain their wrong behaviour, such people devise different types of engaging 'beliefs'. But this only increases their guilt because this amounts to adding insult to injury.

³⁶ Has he not been made acquainted with what was written in the scriptures of Moses? ³⁷ And with Abraham who kept his word: ³⁸ that no soul shall bear the burden of another; ³⁹ and that man shall have only that for which he strives; ⁴⁰ and that [fruit of] his striving shall soon be seen; ⁴¹ and in the end he will be repaid for it in full; ⁴² that all things in the end shall return to God; ^a ⁴³ that it is He who brings laughter and tears; ⁴⁴ that it is He who causes death and gives life; ⁴⁵ and that He Himself created the two sexes: male and female, ⁴⁶ from an ejected drop of sperm; ⁴⁷ and that He will bring about the Second Creation; ⁴⁸ that it is He who gives wealth and possessions; ⁴⁹ that He is the Lord of Sirius.^b

أَمْ لَمْ يُنَبَّأْ بِمَا فِى صُحُفِ مُوسَىٰ ۞ وَإِبْرَٰهِيمَ ٱلَّذِى وَفَّىٰٓ ۞ أَلَّا تَزِرُ وَازِرَةٌ وِزْرَ أُخْرَىٰ ۞ وَأَن لَّيْسَ لِلْإِنسَٰنِ إِلَّا مَا سَعَىٰ ۞ وَأَنَّ سَعْيَهُۥ سَوْفَ يُرَىٰ ۞ ثُمَّ يُجْزَىٰهُ ٱلْجَزَآءَ ٱلْأَوْفَىٰ ۞ وَأَنَّ إِلَىٰ رَبِّكَ ٱلْمُنتَهَىٰ ۞ وَأَنَّهُۥ هُوَ أَضْحَكَ وَأَبْكَىٰ ۞ وَأَنَّهُۥ هُوَ أَمَاتَ وَأَحْيَا ۞ وَأَنَّهُۥ خَلَقَ ٱلزَّوْجَيْنِ ٱلذَّكَرَ وَٱلْأُنثَىٰ ۞ مِن نُّطْفَةٍ إِذَا تُمْنَىٰ ۞ وَأَنَّ عَلَيْهِ ٱلنَّشْأَةَ ٱلْأُخْرَىٰ ۞ وَأَنَّهُۥ هُوَ أَغْنَىٰ وَأَقْنَىٰ ۞ وَأَنَّهُۥ هُوَ رَبُّ ٱلشِّعْرَىٰ ۞

^a The sum and substance of the reality revealed by Almighty God through His prophets is that every man has to receive the reward befitting his deeds. Nobody can save himself from the fate attending his deeds and nobody else can be his saviour. There is nobody more foolish in this world of God than those who are not affected by this prophetic warning.

^b Every event in this world arises from supernatural causes and nobody but God is capable of causing them to occur. Happiness and sorrow, life and death, the procreative system, riches and poverty—all these are the feats of a superpower. Ancient man used to consider the stars as the determining factors in life, while in the present age natural law is considered to govern all happenings. But the fact is that there is a Cause over and above these causes and factors and that is God, the Lord of the universe. Then, how is it legitimate for a man to make anything other than Him the centre of his attention?

⁵⁰ It was He who totally destroyed the former 'Ad ⁵¹ and Thamud tribes, ⁵² and before them the people of Noah who were even more unjust and insolent; ⁵³ and He overthrew the subverted cities [of Sodom and Gomorrah] ⁵⁴ and then covered them from sight forever. ⁵⁵ On which then of your Lord's signs do you cast doubt? ᵃ

⁵⁶ This is a warning just like those of former times. ⁵⁷ The Hour that was to come draws ever nearer. ⁵⁸ None but God can avert it. ⁵⁹ Do you then find these tidings strange? ⁶⁰ Why do you laugh rather than weep? ⁶¹ Will you remain proudly heedless? ⁶² Prostrate yourselves before God, and worship Him alone! ᵇ

وَأَنَّهُۥ أَهْلَكَ عَادًا ٱلْأُولَىٰ ۝ وَثَمُودَاْ فَمَآ أَبْقَىٰ ۝ وَقَوْمَ نُوحٍ مِّن قَبْلُ إِنَّهُمْ كَانُوا۟ هُمْ أَظْلَمَ وَأَطْغَىٰ ۝ وَٱلْمُؤْتَفِكَةَ أَهْوَىٰ ۝ فَغَشَّىٰهَا مَا غَشَّىٰ ۝ فَبِأَىِّ ءَالَآءِ رَبِّكَ تَتَمَارَىٰ ۝ هَـٰذَا نَذِيرٌ مِّنَ ٱلنُّذُرِ ٱلْأُولَىٰ ۝ أَزِفَتِ ٱلْءَازِفَةُ ۝ لَيْسَ لَهَا مِن دُونِ ٱللَّهِ كَاشِفَةٌ ۝ أَفَمِنْ هَـٰذَا ٱلْحَدِيثِ تَعْجَبُونَ ۝ وَتَضْحَكُونَ وَلَا تَبْكُونَ ۝ وَأَنتُمْ سَـٰمِدُونَ ۝ فَٱسْجُدُوا۟ لِلَّهِ وَٱعْبُدُوا۟ ۩ ۝

ᵃ A nation makes superb progress and surpasses other nations. It is apparently impossible for it to be overpowered. Thereafter, certain factors come into play and that nation is destroyed or faces decline and fades into oblivion. This indicates that there is a Super Power over human beings that decides about the future of nations. If even such events of history do not impart a lesson to a human being, what will?

ᵇ The history of the prophets as related in the Quran shows that the denial of Truth and its fatal result are as close to each other as two fingers of the same hand. If a man has the ability to comprehend, as soon as he indulges in denial of the Truth and becomes arrogant, he will sense that God's wrath is about to descend on him; he will consequently give up the way of arrogance and adopt the way of obedience. But man is so intoxicated that he is unable to see things which are right in front of him.

54. THE MOON

In the name of God,
the Most Gracious, the Most Merciful

¹ The Last Hour draws near and the moon is split asunder. ² Yet, when they see a sign they [who deny the truth] turn their backs and say, 'The same old sorcery!' ³ They deny the truth and follow their own whims—every matter has its appointed time—⁴ there has come to them many a tiding wherein there are warnings, ⁵ profound in wisdom, but all warnings have been of no avail: ⁶ so ignore them. On the Day when the Crier will call out about a horrible event, ⁷ with downcast eyes they shall come out of their graves, as if they were locusts milling about ⁸ hastening towards the Crier. Those who deny the truth will cry, 'This is such a hard day!' [a]

---

[a] God causes such events to take place in the present world as make the occurrence of Doomsday understandable in advance. An event of this type occurred in the days of the Prophet Muhammad a few years before the Hijrah, when people saw that the moon was 'cleft in two.' At that time, the Prophet told the people that just as the moon had broken into pieces, the world would also break into pieces and then a new world would be built.

Undoubtedly, there is a lesson to be learned from such events. But this is possible only when a man applies his mind to it. Those who are slaves to their own desires, will look at such events and simply say, 'This is magic'. They will interpret such events as they please and treat them as inapplicable to themselves. For such people even the most cogent reasoning is meaningless. They will come to their senses only when the blast of Doomsday bursts on them and deprives them of the opportunity to reform.

⁹ The people of Noah denied [the truth] before them. They belied Our messenger saying, 'He is mad!' He was rebuffed, ¹⁰ so he cried out to his Lord, saying, 'I am overcome, so help me!' ¹¹ So We opened the gates of the sky with water pouring down in torrents, ¹² and We caused the earth to burst with gushing springs: so that the waters met for a purpose which had been decreed. ¹³ We bore him on an [ark] which, made of planks and nails, ¹⁴ floated on under Our eyes: a vindication of him who had been rejected. ¹⁵ We have left this as a sign: but will anyone take heed? ¹⁶ How terrible then was My punishment and My warning. ¹⁷ We have made it easy to learn lessons from the Quran. Is there anyone who would receive admonition? *a*

۞ كَذَّبَتْ قَبْلَهُمْ قَوْمُ نُوحٍ فَكَذَّبُوا۟ عَبْدَنَا وَقَالُوا۟ مَجْنُونٌ وَٱزْدُجِرَ ۝ فَدَعَا رَبَّهُۥٓ أَنِّى مَغْلُوبٌ فَٱنتَصِرْ ۝ فَفَتَحْنَآ أَبْوَٰبَ ٱلسَّمَآءِ بِمَآءٍ مُّنْهَمِرٍ ۝ وَفَجَّرْنَا ٱلْأَرْضَ عُيُونًا فَٱلْتَقَى ٱلْمَآءُ عَلَىٰٓ أَمْرٍ قَدْ قُدِرَ ۝ وَحَمَلْنَٰهُ عَلَىٰ ذَاتِ أَلْوَٰحٍ وَدُسُرٍ ۝ تَجْرِى بِأَعْيُنِنَا جَزَآءً لِّمَن كَانَ كُفِرَ ۝ وَلَقَد تَّرَكْنَٰهَآ ءَايَةً فَهَلْ مِن مُّدَّكِرٍ ۝ فَكَيْفَ كَانَ عَذَابِى وَنُذُرِ ۝ وَلَقَدْ يَسَّرْنَا ٱلْقُرْءَانَ لِلذِّكْرِ فَهَلْ مِن مُّدَّكِرٍ ۝

---

a The leaders of Noah's community, consumed as they were by false prestige, were not prepared to accept Noah. The result was that they were afflicted by the retribution of God. This punishment came upon them in the shape of a terrible flood. The entire people and their dwellings were submerged in it. But, Noah and his companions, as commanded by God, boarded an ark. This vessel sailed forth and stopped at Mount Judi in the Mount Ararat range.

Ararat is in Turkey. The highest mountain of the region, it rises to 16,853 ft. Certain aeroplane pilots claim that, while flying over the snow-covered Ararat peak, they have seen some boat-like thing caught up in the snow there. If this is correct, then just as the dead body of Pharaoh (of Moses's period) was extracted from its pyramid in the late nineteenth century and became a sign of God (10:92), similarly perhaps Noah's ark may be discovered and become a sign of God for mankind.

¹⁸ The people of 'Ad too rejected the truth. How terrible was My punishment and My warning. ¹⁹ We sent a raging wind against them on a day of continuous calamity. ²⁰ It swept people away as if they were trunks of uprooted palm trees. ²¹ How [dreadful] was My punishment and My warning! ²² We have made it easy to learn lessons from the Quran: is there anyone who would receive admonition?^a

كَذَّبَتْ عَادٌ فَكَيْفَ كَانَ عَذَابِى وَنُذُرِ ۝ إِنَّا أَرْسَلْنَا عَلَيْهِمْ رِيحًا صَرْصَرًا فِى يَوْمِ نَحْسٍ مُّسْتَمِرٍّ ۝ تَنزِعُ ٱلنَّاسَ كَأَنَّهُمْ أَعْجَازُ نَخْلٍ مُّنقَعِرٍ ۝ فَكَيْفَ كَانَ عَذَابِى وَنُذُرِ ۝ وَلَقَدْ يَسَّرْنَا ٱلْقُرْءَانَ لِلذِّكْرِ فَهَلْ مِن مُّدَّكِرٍ ۝

---

^a The people of 'Ad merited divine retribution, so God unleashed a hurricane which made it difficult for them to remain upright. The winds lifted them and tossed them about violently and waves dashed them against the trees. Others were crushed when their roofs fell down on their heads. All this was a demonstration of the fact that man was absolutely helpless, and that he had no power or authority of any sort before God.

²³ The tribe of Thamud also rejected Our warnings: ²⁴ they said, 'Are we to follow a man from amongst ourselves? We would surely then fall into error and madness. ²⁵ Has the [Divine] message been revealed to him alone of all of us? No, he is a boastful liar.' ²⁶ [We said to him] 'Tomorrow they shall know who is the boastful liar, ²⁷ for We are [going to] send the she-camel as a trial for them, so watch them and be patient. ²⁸ And tell them that the water [of the well] is to be divided between them, and that each one should drink in turn.' ²⁹ But they called their companion who took a sword and hamstrung her. ³⁰ How [terrible] were My punishment and My warnings! ³¹ Then We sent a single blast against them and they became like dry stubble which has been trampled upon. ³² Indeed, We have made the Quran easy to learn lessons from. Is there anyone who would receive admonition? ᵃ

كَذَّبَتْ ثَمُودُ بِالنُّذُرِ ۝ فَقَالُوٓا۟ أَبَشَرًا مِّنَّا وَٰحِدًا نَّتَّبِعُهُۥٓ إِنَّآ إِذًا لَّفِى ضَلَٰلٍ وَسُعُرٍ ۝ أَءُلْقِىَ ٱلذِّكْرُ عَلَيْهِ مِنۢ بَيْنِنَا بَلْ هُوَ كَذَّابٌ أَشِرٌ ۝ سَيَعْلَمُونَ غَدًا مَّنِ ٱلْكَذَّابُ ٱلْأَشِرُ ۝ إِنَّا مُرْسِلُوا۟ ٱلنَّاقَةِ فِتْنَةً لَّهُمْ فَٱرْتَقِبْهُمْ وَٱصْطَبِرْ ۝ وَنَبِّئْهُمْ أَنَّ ٱلْمَآءَ قِسْمَةٌۢ بَيْنَهُمْ كُلُّ شِرْبٍ مُّحْتَضَرٌ ۝ فَنَادَوْا۟ صَاحِبَهُمْ فَتَعَاطَىٰ فَعَقَرَ ۝ فَكَيْفَ كَانَ عَذَابِى وَنُذُرِ ۝ إِنَّآ أَرْسَلْنَا عَلَيْهِمْ صَيْحَةً وَٰحِدَةً فَكَانُوا۟ كَهَشِيمِ ٱلْمُحْتَظِرِ ۝ وَلَقَدْ يَسَّرْنَا ٱلْقُرْءَانَ لِلذِّكْرِ فَهَلْ مِن مُّدَّكِرٍ ۝

ᵃ A prophet always appears in the shape of an ordinary man. So, man is not able to recognise him. Similarly, the she-camel sent by God was also apparently like an ordinary camel. So, the people of Thamud were unable to recognise it and killed it. Our world presents just this kind of test. Here, people are required to see the representative of God in the apparently ordinary person and the she-camel of God in the apparently ordinary she-camel. Those who fail in this test never find the path of righteousness.

Though the Quran is a deeply meaningful book, there is the utmost clarity in its style of expression. For this reason it has become very easy to understand the Quran, whether its readers be of greater or lesser education.

³³ The people of Lot rejected Our warnings. ³⁴ We sent a sandstorm against them which destroyed them all, except the family of Lot, whom We saved at the break of dawn, ³⁵ as a blessing from Us: this is how We reward the thankful. ³⁶ Lot warned them of Our punishment, but they disputed the warnings—³⁷ they even wanted to seduce his guests—but We blinded them, and said, 'Taste My punishment now that you have scorned My warnings!'—³⁸ and early in the morning the punishment decreed overtook them—³⁹ 'Taste My punishment now that you have scorned My warnings!' ⁴⁰ We have made it easy indeed to learn lessons from the Quran. Is there anyone who would receive admonition?^a

كَذَّبَتْ قَوْمُ لُوطٍ بِالنُّذُرِ ۝ إِنَّآ أَرْسَلْنَا عَلَيْهِمْ حَاصِبًا إِلَّآ ءَالَ لُوطٍ نَّجَّيْنَٰهُم بِسَحَرٍ ۝ نِّعْمَةً مِّنْ عِندِنَا كَذَٰلِكَ نَجْزِى مَن شَكَرَ ۝ وَلَقَدْ أَنذَرَهُم بَطْشَتَنَا فَتَمَارَوْا۟ بِالنُّذُرِ ۝ وَلَقَدْ رَٰوَدُوهُ عَن ضَيْفِهِۦ فَطَمَسْنَآ أَعْيُنَهُمْ فَذُوقُوا۟ عَذَابِى وَنُذُرِ ۝ وَلَقَدْ صَبَّحَهُم بُكْرَةً عَذَابٌ مُّسْتَقِرٌّ ۝ فَذُوقُوا۟ عَذَابِى وَنُذُرِ ۝ وَلَقَدْ يَسَّرْنَا ٱلْقُرْءَانَ لِلذِّكْرِ فَهَلْ مِن مُّدَّكِرٍ ۝

---

^a When Lot called to the Truth, there were a few individuals who responded positively. They accepted the greatness of Truth and, as compared to it, they conceded that they were small. But many did not concur. Instead of accepting sound arguments in support of Lot's call, they indulged in false reasoning just in order to reject it. This sort of rejection of the Truth is a major crime. So, while the accepters were spared, the rejecters were seized upon by God. This is an example which shows that, in this world, the fate of the rejecters of the call for Truth is destruction, while those who accept it earn salvation.

⁴¹ Surely warners came to the people of Pharaoh. ⁴² They, too, rejected all Our signs. So We seized them with the seizure of One Mighty, Omnipotent.ᵃ

⁴³ Are your people who deny the truth better than those? Or have you been given immunity in the Scriptures? ⁴⁴ Or do they say, 'We are a united group, and we are bound to prevail'? ⁴⁵ The hosts shall soon be routed and they shall be put to flight. ⁴⁶ Indeed, the Hour of Doom is their appointed time, and the Last Hour will be the most severe, and the most bitter. ⁴⁷ The evil-doers are indeed sunk in error and folly—⁴⁸ on the Day when they are dragged into the fire on their faces, it will be said to them, 'Now feel the touch of Hell!'ᵇ

وَلَقَدْ جَاءَ ءَالَ فِرْعَوْنَ ٱلنُّذُرُ ۝ كَذَّبُواْ بِـَٔايَٰتِنَا كُلِّهَا فَأَخَذْنَٰهُمْ أَخْذَ عَزِيزٍ مُّقْتَدِرٍ ۝ أَكُفَّارُكُمْ خَيْرٌ مِّنْ أُوْلَٰئِكُمْ أَمْ لَكُم بَرَآءَةٌ فِى ٱلزُّبُرِ ۝ أَمْ يَقُولُونَ نَحْنُ جَمِيعٌ مُّنتَصِرٌ ۝ سَيُهْزَمُ ٱلْجَمْعُ وَيُوَلُّونَ ٱلدُّبُرَ ۝ بَلِ ٱلسَّاعَةُ مَوْعِدُهُمْ وَٱلسَّاعَةُ أَدْهَىٰ وَأَمَرُّ ۝ إِنَّ ٱلْمُجْرِمِينَ فِى ضَلَٰلٍ وَسُعُرٍ ۝ يَوْمَ يُسْحَبُونَ فِى ٱلنَّارِ عَلَىٰ وُجُوهِهِمْ ذُوقُواْ مَسَّ سَقَرَ ۝

ᵃ Pharaoh was a very powerful ruler of his time, but on rejecting the truth he became valueless in the eyes of God. Thereafter, he was killed like any other helpless man. In this world, a man standing out against the Truth renders himself weak.

ᵇ For those who refused to accept the Prophet Muhammad, there was a lesson in the fatal incidents which befell those who rejected the earlier prophets. But they did not learn from this. This has been true of all the peoples. In spite of clear signs, every community has considered itself safe from God's ire and therefore exempt from religious obligations. Every community has indulged in the same arrogant behaviour as the previous communities, as a result of which they have had to suffer God's retribution.

⁴⁹ We have created everything in due measure; ⁵⁰ We command but once: Our will is done in the twinkling of an eye; ⁵¹ We have indeed destroyed many a people like you. Is there anyone who would receive admonition? ⁵² All their deeds are recorded in their books: ⁵³ every action, small or great, is noted down. ⁵⁴ The God-conscious will find themselves in gardens and rivers, ⁵⁵ in the seat of truth with an all-powerful sovereign.^a

إِنَّا كُلَّ شَىْءٍ خَلَقْنَـٰهُ بِقَدَرٍ ۝ وَمَآ أَمْرُنَآ إِلَّا وَٰحِدَةٌ كَلَمْحٍ بِٱلْبَصَرِ ۝ وَلَقَدْ أَهْلَكْنَآ أَشْيَاعَكُمْ فَهَلْ مِن مُّدَّكِرٍ ۝ وَكُلُّ شَىْءٍ فَعَلُوهُ فِى ٱلزُّبُرِ ۝ وَكُلُّ صَغِيرٍ وَكَبِيرٍ مُّسْتَطَرٌ ۝ إِنَّ ٱلْمُتَّقِينَ فِى جَنَّـٰتٍ وَنَهَرٍ ۝ فِى مَقْعَدِ صِدْقٍ عِندَ مَلِيكٍ مُّقْتَدِرٍ ۝

---

^a Just as everything in the world is governed by definite rules, so also are human beings bound to follow fixed principles. They have been given the opportunity to perform deeds in the present world, but by the same fixed principles they are removed from the site of action and taken to the place where rewards and punishments are meted out. The power of the Creator, which is everywhere manifested, is enough to ensure that this happening will occur exactly at the appointed time without delay. Similarly, the system of recording existing in the present world is advance intimation of the fact that (in the Hereafter) everybody will be given such treatment as will be strictly in accordance with his deeds. However, all such matters will be comprehended only by one who by nature is inclined to give deep consideration to events and who, going beyond appearances, is able to see the inner latent realities.

The present world is a world of trial. Here everybody has full freedom. So, in this world it is possible for a man to gain prominence, even if he lives a life of falsehood in order to obtain respect and status. But nothing of this sort will be possible in the Hereafter. In the Hereafter, the manifestation of the perfect authority of God will guarantee that standing on any ground except that of Truth will be of no avail to anybody.

55. THE MERCIFUL

In the name of God,
the Most Gracious, the Most Merciful

¹ The Merciful ² who taught the Quran—³ He created man ⁴ and He taught him speech. ⁵ The sun and the moon move according to a fixed reckoning; ⁶ the stars and the trees bend in prostration. ⁷ He raised the heavens and set up the measure, ⁸ so that you should not transgress the measure. ⁹ Always measure with justice and do not give short measure.ᵃ

ᵃ God created human beings. He granted them the unique power of speech—a power not bestowed upon any other creature or anything else in the whole known universe. Then, there is the practical example of the role of justice and fair play which inheres in the universe at God's behest. The whole world surrounding the human being is based on these principles of balance and justice, which God wants human beings to follow; and this is clearly set forth in the Quran. The Quran is the verbal expression of this Divine justice and the universe is its practical expression. It is imperative that the subjects of God weigh their words and deeds in this balance. They should not be unjust in either giving or taking.

¹⁰ He has laid out the earth for His creatures. ¹¹ On it are fruits and palm-trees with sheathed clusters [of dates], ¹² and grains with their husk and fragrant plants. ¹³ Which of your Lord's wonders would you deny? ¹⁴ He has created man, from dry ringing clay, like the potter's, ¹⁵ and He created the jinns from a flame of fire. ¹⁶ Which of your Lord's wonders would you deny? ¹⁷ He is the Lord of the two easts and the Lord of the two wests. ¹⁸ Which of your Lord's wonders would you deny? ¹⁹ He has set the two oceans in motion, converging together. ²⁰ Between them is a barrier, which they do not overrun. ²¹ Which of your Lord's wonders would you deny? ²² Pearls and corals come forth from both of them. ²³ Which, of your Lord's wonders would you deny? ²⁴ His are the lofty ships, that rear aloft on the sea like mountains. ²⁵ Which of your Lord's wonders would you deny? ᵃ

وَٱلْأَرْضَ وَضَعَهَا لِلْأَنَامِ ۝ فِيهَا فَٰكِهَةٌ وَٱلنَّخْلُ ذَاتُ ٱلْأَكْمَامِ ۝ وَٱلْحَبُّ ذُو ٱلْعَصْفِ وَٱلرَّيْحَانُ ۝ فَبِأَىِّ ءَالَآءِ رَبِّكُمَا تُكَذِّبَانِ ۝ خَلَقَ ٱلْإِنسَٰنَ مِن صَلْصَٰلٍ كَٱلْفَخَّارِ ۝ وَخَلَقَ ٱلْجَآنَّ مِن مَّارِجٍ مِّن نَّارٍ ۝ فَبِأَىِّ ءَالَآءِ رَبِّكُمَا تُكَذِّبَانِ ۝ رَبُّ ٱلْمَشْرِقَيْنِ وَرَبُّ ٱلْمَغْرِبَيْنِ ۝ فَبِأَىِّ ءَالَآءِ رَبِّكُمَا تُكَذِّبَانِ ۝ مَرَجَ ٱلْبَحْرَيْنِ يَلْتَقِيَانِ ۝ بَيْنَهُمَا بَرْزَخٌ لَّا يَبْغِيَانِ ۝ فَبِأَىِّ ءَالَآءِ رَبِّكُمَا تُكَذِّبَانِ ۝ يَخْرُجُ مِنْهُمَا ٱللُّؤْلُؤُ وَٱلْمَرْجَانُ ۝ فَبِأَىِّ ءَالَآءِ رَبِّكُمَا تُكَذِّبَانِ ۝ وَلَهُ ٱلْجَوَارِ ٱلْمُنشَـَٔاتُ فِى ٱلْبَحْرِ كَٱلْأَعْلَٰمِ ۝ فَبِأَىِّ ءَالَآءِ رَبِّكُمَا تُكَذِّبَانِ ۝

ᵃ A large part of this universe is filled with stars which consist entirely of fire. Jinn are also made of this fire. But human beings have been given special treatment by God in that they have been made of earth, or clay, which is an extremely rare thing in this extensive universe.

In the whole universe the earth is a unique exception. Here, all the factors that are conducive to the existence, survival and cultural development of man have been provided in the most appropriate proportions and in the most balanced manner. One of these arrangements is the system of 'two easts' and 'two wests' on the earth. In winter, the places on the horizon where the sun rises and sets are different from those in summer. In this way, there is a range of 'easts' and 'wests.' This seasonal difference occurs due to the axial tilt of the earth in space. This tilt is a most unique feature, and man receives many natural advantages on account of this. ▶

²⁶ All that is on the earth is doomed to perish, ²⁷ while your Lord's own Self will remain full of majesty and glory. ²⁸ Which of your Lord's wonders would you deny? ²⁹ Everyone in the heavens and on the earth entreats Him. Every day He manifests Himself in a new state.ᵃ

كُلُّ مَنْ عَلَيْهَا فَانٍ ۝ وَيَبْقَىٰ وَجْهُ رَبِّكَ ذُو ٱلْجَلَٰلِ وَٱلْإِكْرَامِ ۝ فَبِأَىِّ ءَالَآءِ رَبِّكُمَا تُكَذِّبَانِ ۝ يَسْـَٔلُهُۥ مَن فِى ٱلسَّمَٰوَٰتِ وَٱلْأَرْضِ كُلَّ يَوْمٍ هُوَ فِى شَأْنٍ ۝

The exceptional treatment of man and the earth in this universe is such a great manifestation of God's grace and bounty that man is in no way capable of thanking his Creator sufficiently.

ᵃ Nothing in this world possesses creative power i.e. the objects on which things depend for their continued existence are not self-created. This shows the boundless power of the Creator.

The signs of God in this world are so many that it is not possible for any thinking individual to ignore them. But man is such a transgressor that, even when surrounded by a host of signs, he denies them.

³⁰ Which of your Lord's wonders would you deny? ³¹ Soon We shall attend to you—two big groups [of jinn and mankind]. ³² Which of your Lord's wonders would you deny? ³³ O company of jinn and men! If you have the power to go beyond the realms of the heavens and the earth, pass beyond them: you cannot pass out but with [Our] authority. ³⁴ Which of your Lord's wonders would you deny? ³⁵ Flames of fire and molten brass shall be sent against both of you, and you will not be able to defend yourselves. ³⁶ Which of your Lord's wonders would you deny? [a]

فَبِأَيِّ ءَالَآءِ رَبِّكُمَا تُكَذِّبَانِ ۩

سَنَفْرُغُ لَكُمْ أَيُّهَ ٱلثَّقَلَانِ ۩ فَبِأَيِّ

ءَالَآءِ رَبِّكُمَا تُكَذِّبَانِ ۩ يَٰمَعْشَرَ

ٱلْجِنِّ وَٱلْإِنسِ إِنِ ٱسْتَطَعْتُمْ أَن

تَنفُذُواْ مِنْ أَقْطَارِ ٱلسَّمَٰوَٰتِ

وَٱلْأَرْضِ فَٱنفُذُواْ لَا تَنفُذُونَ إِلَّا

بِسُلْطَٰنٍ ۩ فَبِأَيِّ ءَالَآءِ رَبِّكُمَا

تُكَذِّبَانِ ۩ يُرْسَلُ عَلَيْكُمَا شُوَاظٌ

مِّن نَّارٍ وَنُحَاسٌ فَلَا تَنتَصِرَانِ ۩

فَبِأَيِّ ءَالَآءِ رَبِّكُمَا تُكَذِّبَانِ ۩

---

[a] The present world is a place of trial. So long as the period of testing lasts, everybody has the opportunity to be as arrogant as he pleases. But, in spite of this complete freedom, no jinn or human being has the power to go beyond the limits of the universe. This fact itself is enough to prove that man is completely in the grip of God. On the expiry of the test period, when He starts seizing hold of people, it will not be possible for anybody to save himself.

³⁷ When the sky is rent asunder, and becomes red like red leather, ³⁸ which of your Lord's wonders would you deny? ³⁹ For, on that Day, neither man nor jinn will be questioned about his sins. ⁴⁰ Which of your Lord's wonders would you deny? ⁴¹ The guilty shall be recognized by their marks so they shall be seized by their forelocks and their feet. ⁴² Which of your Lord's wonders would you deny? ⁴³ This is the Hell which the guilty called a lie. ⁴⁴ They will go round between its flames and boiling water. ⁴⁵ Which of your Lord's wonders would you deny?^a

فَإِذَا ٱنشَقَّتِ ٱلسَّمَآءُ فَكَانَتْ وَرْدَةً كَٱلدِّهَانِ ۝ فَبِأَيِّ ءَالَآءِ رَبِّكُمَا تُكَذِّبَانِ ۝ فَيَوْمَئِذٍ لَّا يُسْـَٔلُ عَن ذَنۢبِهِۦٓ إِنسٌ وَلَا جَآنٌّ ۝ فَبِأَيِّ ءَالَآءِ رَبِّكُمَا تُكَذِّبَانِ ۝ يُعْرَفُ ٱلْمُجْرِمُونَ بِسِيمَٰهُمْ فَيُؤْخَذُ بِٱلنَّوَٰصِى وَٱلْأَقْدَامِ ۝ فَبِأَيِّ ءَالَآءِ رَبِّكُمَا تُكَذِّبَانِ ۝ هَٰذِهِۦ جَهَنَّمُ ٱلَّتِى يُكَذِّبُ بِهَا ٱلْمُجْرِمُونَ ۝ يَطُوفُونَ بَيْنَهَا وَبَيْنَ حَمِيمٍ ءَانٍ ۝ فَبِأَيِّ ءَالَآءِ رَبِّكُمَا تُكَذِّبَانِ ۝

---

^a Denial and arrogance are always caused by an absence of the fear of God. When the terrible moment of Doomsday arrives, the guilty will shed their arrogance. The Truth which they were not ready to accept, in spite of the strong arguments in its favour in the present world, will be accepted by them on Doomsday without dispute. But, acceptance at that time will be of no avail. Acceptance of God's powers is valid only at the unseen stage and not after their open manifestation.

46 There are two gardens for one who fears standing before his Lord. 47 Which of your Lord's wonders would you deny? 48 [There will be two gardens with] spreading branches. 49 Which of your Lord's wonders would you deny? 50 In both of them, there are two springs flowing. 51 Which of your Lord's wonders would you deny? 52 In both of them, there will be two kinds of every fruit. 53 Which of your Lord's wonders would you deny? 54 They will recline upon carpets lined with rich brocade; and the fruits of both these gardens will be within easy reach. 55 Which of your Lord's wonders would you deny? 56 Therein are maidens of modest gaze, whom neither a man nor a jinn had ever touched before them. 57 Which of your Lord's wonders would you deny? 58 [There will be] maidens as fair as corals and rubies. 59 Which of your Lord's wonders would you deny? 60 The reward of goodness shall be nothing but goodness. 61 Which of your Lord's wonders would you deny? [a]

وَلِمَنْ خَافَ مَقَامَ رَبِّهِ جَنَّتَانِ ۝ فَبِأَىِّ ءَالَآءِ رَبِّكُمَا تُكَذِّبَانِ ۝ ذَوَاتَآ أَفْنَانٍ ۝ فَبِأَىِّ ءَالَآءِ رَبِّكُمَا تُكَذِّبَانِ ۝ فِيهِمَا عَيْنَانِ تَجْرِيَانِ ۝ فَبِأَىِّ ءَالَآءِ رَبِّكُمَا تُكَذِّبَانِ ۝ فِيهِمَا مِن كُلِّ فَٰكِهَةٍ زَوْجَانِ ۝ فَبِأَىِّ ءَالَآءِ رَبِّكُمَا تُكَذِّبَانِ ۝ مُتَّكِئِينَ عَلَىٰ فُرُشٍ بَطَآئِنُهَا مِنْ إِسْتَبْرَقٍ وَجَنَى ٱلْجَنَّتَيْنِ دَانٍ ۝ فَبِأَىِّ ءَالَآءِ رَبِّكُمَا تُكَذِّبَانِ ۝ فِيهِنَّ قَٰصِرَٰتُ ٱلطَّرْفِ لَمْ يَطْمِثْهُنَّ إِنسٌ قَبْلَهُمْ وَلَا جَآنٌّ ۝ فَبِأَىِّ ءَالَآءِ رَبِّكُمَا تُكَذِّبَانِ ۝ كَأَنَّهُنَّ ٱلْيَاقُوتُ وَٱلْمَرْجَانُ ۝ فَبِأَىِّ ءَالَآءِ رَبِّكُمَا تُكَذِّبَانِ ۝ هَلْ جَزَآءُ ٱلْإِحْسَٰنِ إِلَّا ٱلْإِحْسَٰنُ ۝ فَبِأَىِّ ءَالَآءِ رَبِّكُمَا تُكَذِّبَانِ ۝

---

[a] There are two classes of paradise. The Paradise with two gardens mentioned in these verses is that of the first category. In this Paradise, royal fare will be provided. Such bounties will be available to those who were so overwhelmed by thoughts of God that in the present world itself they made themselves stand, as if in the august presence of God. They related to God on the level of *Ehsan*, that is, experiencing the presence of God in this world itself.

⁶²Besides those two there shall be two other gardens. ⁶³Which of your Lord's wonders would you deny? ⁶⁴Both [gardens] of the darkest green. ⁶⁵Which of your Lord's wonders would you deny? ⁶⁶In both of them live springs gush forth. ⁶⁷Which of your Lord's wonders would you deny? ⁶⁸In both of them there will be fruit trees and date-palms and pomegranates. ⁶⁹Which of your Lord's wonders would you deny? ⁷⁰Therein will be maidens chaste and beautiful. ⁷¹Which of your Lord's wonders would you deny? ⁷²[There the blessed will live with their] pure companions sheltered in pavilions. ⁷³Which of your Lord's wonders would you deny? ⁷⁴Whom neither a man or jinn had ever touched before them. ⁷⁵Which of your Lord's wonders would you deny? ⁷⁶[They will live in such a paradise] reclining upon green cushions and the finest carpets. ⁷⁷Which of your Lord's wonders would you deny? ⁷⁸Blessed be your Lord's name, full of glory and majesty!ᵃ

وَمِن دُونِهِمَا جَنَّتَانِ ۝ فَبِأَىِّ ءَالَآءِ رَبِّكُمَا تُكَذِّبَانِ ۝ مُدْهَآمَّتَانِ ۝ فَبِأَىِّ ءَالَآءِ رَبِّكُمَا تُكَذِّبَانِ ۝ فِيهِمَا عَيْنَانِ نَضَّاخَتَانِ ۝ فَبِأَىِّ ءَالَآءِ رَبِّكُمَا تُكَذِّبَانِ ۝ فِيهِمَا فَٰكِهَةٌ وَنَخْلٌ وَرُمَّانٌ ۝ فَبِأَىِّ ءَالَآءِ رَبِّكُمَا تُكَذِّبَانِ ۝ فِيهِنَّ خَيْرَٰتٌ حِسَانٌ ۝ فَبِأَىِّ ءَالَآءِ رَبِّكُمَا تُكَذِّبَانِ ۝ حُورٌ مَّقْصُورَٰتٌ فِى ٱلْخِيَامِ ۝ فَبِأَىِّ ءَالَآءِ رَبِّكُمَا تُكَذِّبَانِ ۝ لَمْ يَطْمِثْهُنَّ إِنسٌ قَبْلَهُمْ وَلَا جَآنٌّ ۝ فَبِأَىِّ ءَالَآءِ رَبِّكُمَا تُكَذِّبَانِ ۝ مُتَّكِئِينَ عَلَىٰ رَفْرَفٍ خُضْرٍ وَعَبْقَرِىٍّ حِسَانٍ ۝ فَبِأَىِّ ءَالَآءِ رَبِّكُمَا تُكَذِّبَانِ ۝ تَبَٰرَكَ ٱسْمُ رَبِّكَ ذِى ٱلْجَلَٰلِ وَٱلْإِكْرَامِ ۝

ᵃ In these verses the second Paradise has been mentioned. This will also have two gardens like the first Paradise. This Paradise will be for ordinary righteous people. In comparison with the bounties of the present world, the bounties of this Paradise will also be unimaginably greater. Still, compared to the first mentioned Paradise, this will be a Paradise of the second degree.

56. THE INEVITABLE EVENT

In the name of God, the Most Gracious, the Most Merciful

¹When the inevitable event takes place, ²and there can be no denying its happening, ³some shall be abased and others exalted. ⁴When the earth is shaken violently, ⁵and the mountains are totally shattered and crumble to pieces ⁶and become like scattered dust particles, ⁷[on that Day] you shall be divided into three groups.ᵃ

إِذَا وَقَعَتِ ٱلْوَاقِعَةُ ۝ لَيْسَ لِوَقْعَتِهَا كَاذِبَةٌ ۝ خَافِضَةٌ رَّافِعَةٌ ۝ إِذَا رُجَّتِ ٱلْأَرْضُ رَجًّا ۝ وَبُسَّتِ ٱلْجِبَالُ بَسًّا ۝ فَكَانَتْ هَبَآءً مُّنۢبَثًّا ۝ وَكُنتُمْ أَزْوَٰجًا ثَلَٰثَةً ۝

ᵃ In the present world, man observes that he is free to do whatever he likes. So the question of retribution in the Hereafter makes no impact on his mind. But the formation of the 'other world' is just as possible as the formation of the present world. When that time comes, the whole system will be reversed. Those who were higher in position will go down and those who were lower in position will be elevated. At that time human beings will be divided into three groups, the forward group (as-sabiqun), the people of the Right (ashab al-yamin) and the people of the Left (ashab ash-shimal).

⁸ Those on the Right—how blessed are those on the Right! ⁹ Those on the Left—how unlucky are those on the Left! ¹⁰ The third to the fore shall be the foremost. ¹¹ They shall be the nearest to God. ¹² They will dwell in the Gardens of Bliss: ¹³ a large group of the early believers, ¹⁴ and a lesser number from the later generations. ¹⁵ Seated on couches wrought in gold and encrusted with precious stones, ¹⁶ reclining on them facing each other; ¹⁷ they will be waited on by ageless youths ¹⁸ carrying goblets and ewers and cups filled with the purest wine, ¹⁹ neither causing headaches, nor intoxication; ²⁰ along with fruits of their choice; ²¹ and the meat of any bird that they may desire; ²² and fair maidens with large, lustrous eyes ²³ like the pearls in their shells: ²⁴ shall be their recompense for their deeds. ²⁵ They will not hear therein any vain or sinful talk, ²⁶ only the words of peace and tranquillity.ᵃ

فَأَصْحَابُ ٱلْمَيْمَنَةِ مَآ أَصْحَابُ ٱلْمَيْمَنَةِ ۝ وَأَصْحَابُ ٱلْمَشْـَٔمَةِ مَآ أَصْحَابُ ٱلْمَشْـَٔمَةِ ۝ وَٱلسَّابِقُونَ ٱلسَّابِقُونَ ۝ أُوْلَٰٓئِكَ ٱلْمُقَرَّبُونَ ۝ فِي جَنَّٰتِ ٱلنَّعِيمِ ۝ ثُلَّةٌ مِّنَ ٱلْأَوَّلِينَ ۝ وَقَلِيلٌ مِّنَ ٱلْأَخِرِينَ ۝ عَلَىٰ سُرُرٍ مَّوْضُونَةٍ ۝ مُّتَّكِئِينَ عَلَيْهَا مُتَقَٰبِلِينَ ۝ يَطُوفُ عَلَيْهِمْ وِلْدَٰنٌ مُّخَلَّدُونَ ۝ بِأَكْوَابٍ وَأَبَارِيقَ وَكَأْسٍ مِّن مَّعِينٍ ۝ لَّا يُصَدَّعُونَ عَنْهَا وَلَا يُنزِفُونَ ۝ وَفَٰكِهَةٍ مِّمَّا يَتَخَيَّرُونَ ۝ وَلَحْمِ طَيْرٍ مِّمَّا يَشْتَهُونَ ۝ وَحُورٌ عِينٌ ۝ كَأَمْثَٰلِ ٱللُّؤْلُؤِ ٱلْمَكْنُونِ ۝ جَزَآءًۢ بِمَا كَانُوا۟ يَعْمَلُونَ ۝ لَا يَسْمَعُونَ فِيهَا لَغْوًا وَلَا تَأْثِيمًا ۝ إِلَّا قِيلًا سَلَٰمًا سَلَٰمًا ۝

ᵃ The group at the forefront (as-sabiqun) will comprise of those who, immediately accept the Truth when it appears before them, and surrender themselves to it without hesitation. According to the Prophet's wife, 'A'ishah, the Prophet said, 'Do you know, on the Day of Judgement, who will be the first to find a place in the protective shade of God?' People said that God and His Prophet knew best. Then he said, 'It will be those to whom Truth was presented and they accepted it. When Truth was demanded of them, they gave it. They gave the same decision with regard to others as they did with regard to themselves.' (Tafsir ibn Kathir).

In the early period of the call for Truth, for those who came forward and embraced Islam, it was a discovery. The generation coming after them, regarded Islam as a legacy. It is this difference between discovery and legacy which raises the status of first group over that of the second group. Naturally, the second group is larger in number than the first group. In the Hereafter, there will be ordinary rewards for the second group while, for the first group, there will be royal rewards.

²⁷ Those on the Right, how fortunate are those on the Right! ²⁸ They shall recline on high amidst lote trees without thorns ²⁹ and clustered bananas, ³⁰ and spreading shade ³¹ and flowing water, ³² and fruits in abundance, ³³ never-ending and unrestricted, ³⁴ on raised couches. ³⁵ We have created maidens perfectly ³⁶ and made them virgins, ³⁷ loving companions, matching in age, ³⁸ for those on the Right, ³⁹ a large group of the earlier people ⁴⁰ and a large group of those of later times.^a

وَأَصْحَٰبُ ٱلْيَمِينِ مَآ أَصْحَٰبُ ٱلْيَمِينِ ۝ فِى سِدْرٍ مَّخْضُودٍ ۝ وَطَلْحٍ مَّنضُودٍ ۝ وَظِلٍّ مَّمْدُودٍ ۝ وَمَآءٍ مَّسْكُوبٍ ۝ وَفَٰكِهَةٍ كَثِيرَةٍ ۝ لَّا مَقْطُوعَةٍ وَلَا مَمْنُوعَةٍ ۝ وَفُرُشٍ مَّرْفُوعَةٍ ۝ إِنَّآ أَنشَأْنَٰهُنَّ إِنشَآءً ۝ فَجَعَلْنَٰهُنَّ أَبْكَارًا ۝ عُرُبًا أَتْرَابًا ۝ لِّأَصْحَٰبِ ٱلْيَمِينِ ۝ ثُلَّةٌ مِّنَ ٱلْأَوَّلِينَ ۝ وَثُلَّةٌ مِّنَ ٱلْءَاخِرِينَ ۝

---

^a 'Those on the Right' (*ashab al-yamin*) means the ordinary people of paradise. This category includes all those people who, according to their belief and character, were pious. As regards faith, they were not in possession of a high degree of consciousness. However, they were sincere about God and His Prophet, and they maintained themselves on the path of justice and went in fear of God throughout their lives. In this category there will be a fair number of persons from the earlier period and a considerable number from the later period.

⁴¹ Those on the Left: how unfortunate are those on the Left![a] ⁴² They will find themselves in scorching wind and scalding water, ⁴³ and under the shadow of black smoke, ⁴⁴ neither cool nor refreshing. ⁴⁵ They had been affluent before, ⁴⁶ and they persisted obstinately in awful sin, ⁴⁷ and they used to say, 'What! After we have died and become dust and bones, shall we indeed be raised up again? ⁴⁸ And also our forefathers?' ⁴⁹ Say, 'Indeed, the earlier ones and the later ones ⁵⁰ will indeed be gathered together at a fixed time on an appointed Day. ⁵¹ Then you, you misguided ones, who deny the truth, ⁵² shall eat the fruit of the tree of Zaqqum, ⁵³ and fill your bellies with it, ⁵⁴ and shall drink boiling water on top of that. ⁵⁵ You shall drink it as the thirsty camels drink.' ⁵⁶ This shall be their entertainment on the Day of Judgement.

⁵⁷ We have created you: why then do you not accept the truth? ⁵⁸ Have you thought about [the semen] that you discharge—⁵⁹ did you create it or did We?[b]

وَأَصْحَٰبُ ٱلشِّمَالِ مَآ أَصْحَٰبُ ٱلشِّمَالِ ۝ فِى سَمُومٍ وَحَمِيمٍ ۝ وَظِلٍّ مِّن يَحْمُومٍ ۝ لَّا بَارِدٍ وَلَا كَرِيمٍ ۝ إِنَّهُمْ كَانُوا۟ قَبْلَ ذَٰلِكَ مُتْرَفِينَ ۝ وَكَانُوا۟ يُصِرُّونَ عَلَى ٱلْحِنثِ ٱلْعَظِيمِ ۝ وَكَانُوا۟ يَقُولُونَ أَئِذَا مِتْنَا وَكُنَّا تُرَابًا وَعِظَٰمًا أَءِنَّا لَمَبْعُوثُونَ ۝ أَوَءَابَآؤُنَا ٱلْأَوَّلُونَ ۝ قُلْ إِنَّ ٱلْأَوَّلِينَ وَٱلْءَاخِرِينَ ۝ لَمَجْمُوعُونَ إِلَىٰ مِيقَٰتِ يَوْمٍ مَّعْلُومٍ ۝ ثُمَّ إِنَّكُمْ أَيُّهَا ٱلضَّآلُّونَ ٱلْمُكَذِّبُونَ ۝ لَءَاكِلُونَ مِن شَجَرٍ مِّن زَقُّومٍ ۝ فَمَالِئُونَ مِنْهَا ٱلْبُطُونَ ۝ فَشَٰرِبُونَ عَلَيْهِ مِنَ ٱلْحَمِيمِ ۝ فَشَٰرِبُونَ شُرْبَ ٱلْهِيمِ ۝ هَٰذَا نُزُلُهُمْ يَوْمَ ٱلدِّينِ ۝ نَحْنُ خَلَقْنَٰكُمْ فَلَوْلَا تُصَدِّقُونَ ۝ أَفَرَءَيْتُم مَّا تُمْنُونَ ۝ ءَأَنتُمْ تَخْلُقُونَهُۥٓ أَمْ نَحْنُ ٱلْخَٰلِقُونَ ۝

---

a 'Those on the Left' (ashab ash-shimal) means those to whom is condign punishment will be meted out. Deceived by the amenities they had in this world, they had made things other than God the centre of their attention, and this is the greatest human crime. They had made themselves so forgetful of the Hereafter, it was as if it was not to become a reality at all. Such people will receive severe punishment on the Day of Judgement.

b The birth of a human being from the womb of his mother, the growing of crops from the earth, the falling of rain, the availability of fire from fuel—all these things come directly from God. They should be treated as gifts of God and not as the results of human effort. Man should be grateful to God for all the blessings He has showered upon him.

⁶⁰ It is We who have ordained death for all of you; and We cannot be prevented ⁶¹ from replacing you by others like yourselves or changing your forms and re-creating you in forms that you know nothing of. ⁶² You have certainly known the first creation. Why, then, do you not take heed? ⁶³ Have you thought about what crops you plant? ⁶⁴ Is it you who cause them to grow or do We? ⁶⁵ If We so pleased, We could turn your harvest into chaff. Then you would start lamenting, ⁶⁶ 'We are ruined, ⁶⁷ nay, we are deprived [altogether].' ⁶⁸ Have you considered the water that you drink? ⁶⁹ Is it you who cause it to descend from the clouds, or do We? ⁷⁰ If We so pleased, We certainly could make it salty. Why, then, are you not grateful? ⁷¹ Have you thought about the fire that you kindle. ⁷² Did you produce the tree that serves as fuel or do We? ⁷³ We have made it to be a reminder and a benefit for the wayfarers. ⁷⁴ So glorify the name of your Lord, the Supreme.ᵃ

نَحْنُ قَدَّرْنَا بَيْنَكُمُ ٱلْمَوْتَ وَمَا نَحْنُ بِمَسْبُوقِينَ ۝ عَلَىٰ أَن نُّبَدِّلَ أَمْثَٰلَكُمْ وَنُنشِئَكُمْ فِى مَا لَا تَعْلَمُونَ ۝ وَلَقَدْ عَلِمْتُمُ ٱلنَّشْأَةَ ٱلْأُولَىٰ فَلَوْلَا تَذَكَّرُونَ ۝ أَفَرَءَيْتُم مَّا تَحْرُثُونَ ۝ ءَأَنتُمْ تَزْرَعُونَهُۥٓ أَمْ نَحْنُ ٱلزَّٰرِعُونَ ۝ لَوْ نَشَآءُ لَجَعَلْنَٰهُ حُطَٰمًا فَظَلْتُمْ تَفَكَّهُونَ ۝ إِنَّا لَمُغْرَمُونَ ۝ بَلْ نَحْنُ مَحْرُومُونَ ۝ أَفَرَءَيْتُمُ ٱلْمَآءَ ٱلَّذِى تَشْرَبُونَ ۝ ءَأَنتُمْ أَنزَلْتُمُوهُ مِنَ ٱلْمُزْنِ أَمْ نَحْنُ ٱلْمُنزِلُونَ ۝ لَوْ نَشَآءُ جَعَلْنَٰهُ أُجَاجًا فَلَوْلَا تَشْكُرُونَ ۝ أَفَرَءَيْتُمُ ٱلنَّارَ ٱلَّتِى تُورُونَ ۝ ءَأَنتُمْ أَنشَأْتُمْ شَجَرَتَهَآ أَمْ نَحْنُ ٱلْمُنشِئُونَ ۝ نَحْنُ جَعَلْنَٰهَا تَذْكِرَةً وَمَتَٰعًا لِّلْمُقْوِينَ ۝ فَسَبِّحْ بِٱسْمِ رَبِّكَ ٱلْعَظِيمِ ۝

ᵃ For one who ponders over these events, there are countless lessons. In them there is proof of a second life after the present life. Similarly, there is a sure indication in them that He who has given things can also take them away. Then, there is the example of water. Reservoirs of water are mostly found here in the shape of seas containing salt water. About 98 percent of the water is found in seas and one tenth of its volume is made up of salt. It is a miracle of God's law that when water vapour rises from the sea, pure water rises and the salt is left below. The fact is that the system of rain is a huge universal desalination process. Had this natural arrangement not been in place, all of the water in the world would have been brackish just like sea water. ▶

⁷⁵ Nay, I swear by the setting of the stars*—⁷⁶ and, indeed, that is a most mighty oath, if you only knew— ⁷⁷ that this is indeed a noble Quran, ⁷⁸ in a well-guarded preserved Book, ⁷⁹ which none can touch except the purified. ⁸⁰ It is a revelation sent down from the Lord of the worlds. ⁸¹ How can you regard this discourse with disdain? ⁸² Do you make its denial your means of livelihood?*ᵇ

۞ فَلَا أُقْسِمُ بِمَوَٰقِعِ ٱلنُّجُومِ ۝ وَإِنَّهُۥ لَقَسَمٌ لَّوْ تَعْلَمُونَ عَظِيمٌ ۝ إِنَّهُۥ لَقُرْءَانٌ كَرِيمٌ ۝ فِى كِتَٰبٍ مَّكْنُونٍ ۝ لَّا يَمَسُّهُۥٓ إِلَّا ٱلْمُطَهَّرُونَ ۝ تَنزِيلٌ مِّن رَّبِّ ٱلْعَٰلَمِينَ ۝ أَفَبِهَٰذَا ٱلْحَدِيثِ أَنتُم مُّدْهِنُونَ ۝ وَتَجْعَلُونَ رِزْقَكُمْ أَنَّكُمْ تُكَذِّبُونَ ۝

The snow on mountain peaks, the water flowing in rivers would all have been extremely salty. In spite of the vast stores of water on the earth, the non-availability of fresh water would have presented an insurmountable problem for humanity. If man gave this matter consideration, his heart would be full of praises for God.

ᵃ The word '*mawaqi*' is the plural of '*mauqa'a*'. Its meaning is the place of falling. Here, the *mawaqi* of stars probably means the orbits of stars. In this universe, there are countless big stars. They are revolving in their respective orbits with extreme precision.

ᵇ This is a happening so great as to be owesome. A person who gives serious consideration to this system functioning in space, will be compelled to admit that the Creator of this universe is unimaginably Mighty. Then the Book coming from such a Creator should also be certainly great, and the Qur'an is undoubtedly such a great Book.

The Quran reached the Prophet through the angels in exactly the same condition as it was in the preserved tablet (*lawh mahfudh*) and it is still intact in that same condition today. There is no other book of ancient times which has been so perfectly preserved. This in itself is proof of the Book's (the Quran's) greatness. The misfortune of one who does not obtain guidance from such a book is incalculable.

83 Why, then, when the soul of the dying man reaches the throat, 84 and you are [at that moment] looking on [helplessly]—85 and We are nearer to him than you, although you cannot see Us—86 why, then, if you are not subject to Our command, 87 do you not cause the soul to return to him if you are truthful in your claim? 88 But if he [the dying person] is one of those brought near to God, 89 then for him there shall be comfort and plenty and a Garden of Bliss; 90 and if he is of those who are on the Right, 91 he will be greeted with, 'Peace be to you,' by those on the Right. 92 But if he is one of those who rejected [the truth] and went astray, 93 he will be welcomed with boiling water. 94 He will burn in Hell. 95 This is indeed the indubitable truth. 96 So glorify the name of your Lord, the Supreme.ᵃ

فَلَوْلَا إِذَا بَلَغَتِ ٱلْحُلْقُومَ ۞ وَأَنتُمْ حِينَئِذٍ تَنظُرُونَ ۞ وَنَحْنُ أَقْرَبُ إِلَيْهِ مِنكُمْ وَلَـٰكِن لَّا تُبْصِرُونَ ۞ فَلَوْلَا إِن كُنتُمْ غَيْرَ مَدِينِينَ ۞ تَرْجِعُونَهَا إِن كُنتُمْ صَـٰدِقِينَ ۞ فَأَمَّا إِن كَانَ مِنَ ٱلْمُقَرَّبِينَ ۞ فَرَوْحٌ وَرَيْحَانٌ وَجَنَّتُ نَعِيمٍ ۞ وَأَمَّا إِن كَانَ مِنْ أَصْحَـٰبِ ٱلْيَمِينِ ۞ فَسَلَـٰمٌ لَّكَ مِنْ أَصْحَـٰبِ ٱلْيَمِينِ ۞ وَأَمَّا إِن كَانَ مِنَ ٱلْمُكَذِّبِينَ ٱلضَّالِّينَ ۞ فَنُزُلٌ مِّنْ حَمِيمٍ ۞ وَتَصْلِيَةُ جَحِيمٍ ۞ إِنَّ هَـٰذَا هُوَ حَقُّ ٱلْيَقِينِ ۞ فَسَبِّحْ بِٱسْمِ رَبِّكَ ٱلْعَظِيمِ ۞

ᵃ The event of death is the last proof of the fact that man is completely helpless before the Divine powers. Every man will essentially die at a fixed time and nobody can save him from the angel of death. In view of this, man should be more concerned about his condition after death. Those who performed deeds deserving of paradise in their life before death, will be ushered into paradise in the life after death. However, those who shunned God in this world will be denied God's grace in the Hereafter. They will be greeted with scalding water and the fire will be their abode.

57. IRON

In the name of God,
the Most Gracious, the Most Merciful

¹ Everything in the heavens and earth glorifies God—He is the Mighty, the Wise One. ² He has sovereign control over the heavens and the earth. He gives life and brings death. He has power over all things. ³ He is the First and the Last, the Outward and the Inward. He has knowledge of all things. ⁴ It was He who created the heavens and earth in six Days [periods] and then ascended the throne. He knows what enters the earth and what comes out of it; what descends from the sky and what ascends to it. He is with you wherever you are; He sees all that you do; ⁵ He has sovereignty over the heavens and the earth. All affairs will return to God. ⁶ He causes the night to pass into the day and the day to pass into the night. And He knows all that is in the hearts of men.

⁷ Have faith in God and His Messenger and spend in charity from that of which He has made you trustees: those of you who believe and give alms shall be richly rewarded.[a]

بِسۡمِ ٱللَّهِ ٱلرَّحۡمَٰنِ ٱلرَّحِيمِ

سَبَّحَ لِلَّهِ مَا فِي ٱلسَّمَٰوَٰتِ وَٱلۡأَرۡضِ وَهُوَ ٱلۡعَزِيزُ ٱلۡحَكِيمُ ۝ لَهُۥ مُلۡكُ ٱلسَّمَٰوَٰتِ وَٱلۡأَرۡضِ يُحۡيِۦ وَيُمِيتُ وَهُوَ عَلَىٰ كُلِّ شَيۡءٍ قَدِيرٌ ۝ هُوَ ٱلۡأَوَّلُ وَٱلۡأَخِرُ وَٱلظَّٰهِرُ وَٱلۡبَاطِنُ وَهُوَ بِكُلِّ شَيۡءٍ عَلِيمٌ ۝ هُوَ ٱلَّذِي خَلَقَ ٱلسَّمَٰوَٰتِ وَٱلۡأَرۡضَ فِي سِتَّةِ أَيَّامٍ ثُمَّ ٱسۡتَوَىٰ عَلَى ٱلۡعَرۡشِ يَعۡلَمُ مَا يَلِجُ فِي ٱلۡأَرۡضِ وَمَا يَخۡرُجُ مِنۡهَا وَمَا يَنزِلُ مِنَ ٱلسَّمَآءِ وَمَا يَعۡرُجُ فِيهَا وَهُوَ مَعَكُمۡ أَيۡنَ مَا كُنتُمۡ وَٱللَّهُ بِمَا تَعۡمَلُونَ بَصِيرٌ ۝ لَهُۥ مُلۡكُ ٱلسَّمَٰوَٰتِ وَٱلۡأَرۡضِ وَإِلَى ٱللَّهِ تُرۡجَعُ ٱلۡأُمُورُ ۝ يُولِجُ ٱلَّيۡلَ فِي ٱلنَّهَارِ وَيُولِجُ ٱلنَّهَارَ فِي ٱلَّيۡلِ وَهُوَ عَلِيمٌ بِذَاتِ ٱلصُّدُورِ ۝ ءَامِنُوا۟ بِٱللَّهِ وَرَسُولِهِۦ وَأَنفِقُوا۟ مِمَّا جَعَلَكُم مُّسۡتَخۡلَفِينَ فِيهِ فَٱلَّذِينَ ءَامَنُوا۟ مِنكُمۡ وَأَنفَقُوا۟ لَهُمۡ أَجۡرٌ كَبِيرٌ ۝

---

[a] The universe, in its silent language, sings the praises of and describes the attributes of its Creator. In the Quran, those same attributes have been put into words. When a thing comes into being here, it has manifestly been brought into existence by the Supreme Being. Its end itself announces its termination by the Supreme Being. The fact is the universe is the vehicle of God's praises, while the Quran is their verbal recitation.

8 What could be your reason for not believing in God, when the Messenger calls on you to have faith in your Lord and He has already made a covenant with you, if indeed you are true believers? 9 It is He who sends down to His Servant clear revelations, so that He may lead you out of darkness into light. God is indeed compassionate and merciful to you. 10 Why should you not spend for the cause of God, when God alone holds the heritage of the heavens and the earth? Those of you who spent and fought before the victory will be higher in rank than those who spent and fought afterwards. Yet God has promised you all a good reward. He is aware of all that you do.ᵃ

وَمَا لَكُمْ لَا تُؤْمِنُونَ بِاللَّهِ وَالرَّسُولُ يَدْعُوكُمْ لِتُؤْمِنُوا بِرَبِّكُمْ وَقَدْ أَخَذَ مِيثَاقَكُمْ إِن كُنتُم مُّؤْمِنِينَ ۞ هُوَ ٱلَّذِى يُنَزِّلُ عَلَىٰ عَبْدِهِۦ ءَايَٰتٍ بَيِّنَٰتٍ لِّيُخْرِجَكُم مِّنَ ٱلظُّلُمَٰتِ إِلَى ٱلنُّورِ وَإِنَّ ٱللَّهَ بِكُمْ لَرَءُوفٌ رَّحِيمٌ ۞ وَمَا لَكُمْ أَلَّا تُنفِقُوا فِى سَبِيلِ ٱللَّهِ وَلِلَّهِ مِيرَٰثُ ٱلسَّمَٰوَٰتِ وَٱلْأَرْضِ لَا يَسْتَوِى مِنكُم مَّنْ أَنفَقَ مِن قَبْلِ ٱلْفَتْحِ وَقَٰتَلَ أُو۟لَٰٓئِكَ أَعْظَمُ دَرَجَةً مِّنَ ٱلَّذِينَ أَنفَقُوا مِنۢ بَعْدُ وَقَٰتَلُوا وَكُلًّا وَعَدَ ٱللَّهُ ٱلْحُسْنَىٰ وَٱللَّهُ بِمَا تَعْمَلُونَ خَبِيرٌ ۞

ᵃ When the call of Islam is given, it is based on clear reasoning in its preliminary stages. The second stage is marked by victory in its immediate surroundings. In the first stage, only those who have the capacity to see the inherent greatness of a thing solely on the level of reasoning are courageous enough to make sacrifices for Islam. But when Islam has already been crowned by success, every individual is able to see its greatness and everybody feels proud of coming forward and offering his life and property for its sake.

One who spends for the cause of Islam in the early stages has to do it without thought of reward, while in the latter stage, whatever a man spends is redoubled in this world itself, as a reward in various forms. That explains why, in the eyes of God, each group has a different status.

¹¹ "Who will offer God a generous loan? He will double it for him and give him a rich reward. ¹² On the Day, you [Prophet] shall see the faithful, both men and women, with their light streaming out before them and on their right hands, [and you shall hear a voice saying to them:] 'Glad tidings for you today! You shall enter gardens with rivers flowing through them wherein you shall forever dwell. That is the supreme triumph.' ¹³ On that Day, the hypocrites, both men and women, will say to the faithful, 'Wait a while for us, so that we may have some of your light.' They will be told, 'Turn back and look for a light elsewhere.' A wall will then be raised between them. It will have a gate on the inside of which will be grace and mercy and on the outside of which will be punishment. ¹⁴ The hypocrites will call out to the faithful: 'Were we not on your side?' They will reply, 'Yes, but you gave in to temptation, you wavered and doubted and were deceived by your wishful thinking until God's will was done; then the Deceiver [Satan] misled you about God.' ¹⁵ So this Day no ransom can be taken from you nor from those who were bent on denying the truth. Your home is the fire; that is your companion, and a hapless journey's end.ᵃ

مَّن ذَا ٱلَّذِى يُقْرِضُ ٱللَّهَ قَرْضًا حَسَنًا فَيُضَـٰعِفَهُۥ لَهُۥ وَلَهُۥٓ أَجْرٌ كَرِيمٌ ۞ يَوْمَ تَرَى ٱلْمُؤْمِنِينَ وَٱلْمُؤْمِنَـٰتِ يَسْعَىٰ نُورُهُم بَيْنَ أَيْدِيهِمْ وَبِأَيْمَـٰنِهِم بُشْرَىٰكُمُ ٱلْيَوْمَ جَنَّـٰتٌ تَجْرِى مِن تَحْتِهَا ٱلْأَنْهَـٰرُ خَـٰلِدِينَ فِيهَا ذَٰلِكَ هُوَ ٱلْفَوْزُ ٱلْعَظِيمُ ۞ يَوْمَ يَقُولُ ٱلْمُنَـٰفِقُونَ وَٱلْمُنَـٰفِقَـٰتُ لِلَّذِينَ ءَامَنُوا ٱنظُرُونَا نَقْتَبِسْ مِن نُّورِكُمْ قِيلَ ٱرْجِعُوا وَرَآءَكُمْ فَٱلْتَمِسُوا نُورًا فَضُرِبَ بَيْنَهُم بِسُورٍ لَّهُۥ بَابٌ بَاطِنُهُۥ فِيهِ ٱلرَّحْمَةُ وَظَـٰهِرُهُۥ مِن قِبَلِهِ ٱلْعَذَابُ ۞ يُنَادُونَهُمْ أَلَمْ نَكُن مَّعَكُمْ قَالُوا بَلَىٰ وَلَـٰكِنَّكُمْ فَتَنتُمْ أَنفُسَكُمْ وَتَرَبَّصْتُمْ وَٱرْتَبْتُمْ وَغَرَّتْكُمُ ٱلْأَمَانِىُّ حَتَّىٰ جَآءَ أَمْرُ ٱللَّهِ وَغَرَّكُم بِٱللَّهِ ٱلْغَرُورُ ۞ فَٱلْيَوْمَ لَا يُؤْخَذُ مِنكُمْ فِدْيَةٌ وَلَا مِنَ ٱلَّذِينَ كَفَرُوا مَأْوَىٰكُمُ ٱلنَّارُ هِىَ مَوْلَىٰكُمْ وَبِئْسَ ٱلْمَصِيرُ ۞

ᵃ While Islam was still unfamiliar, accepting it meant putting oneself through a great trial. At that time, the truth of Islam was veiled in doubt. Spending for Islam at that time was like giving a loan to somebody with flimsy hopes of getting any return. The atmosphere was pervaded by doubt and hesitation. ▶

¹⁶ Has the time not come for the faithful when their hearts in all humility should engage in the remembrance of God and of the revelation of truth, so that they should not become like those who were given the Book before them, whose hearts with the passage of time became hardened and many of whom were disobedient? ¹⁷ Remember that God brings the earth back to life after its death. We have made Our signs clear to you, so that you may fully understand.ᵃ

۞ أَلَمْ يَأْنِ لِلَّذِينَ ءَامَنُوٓا أَن تَخْشَعَ قُلُوبُهُمْ لِذِكْرِ ٱللَّهِ وَمَا نَزَلَ مِنَ ٱلْحَقِّ وَلَا يَكُونُوا۟ كَٱلَّذِينَ أُوتُوا۟ ٱلْكِتَٰبَ مِن قَبْلُ فَطَالَ عَلَيْهِمُ ٱلْأَمَدُ فَقَسَتْ قُلُوبُهُمْ ۖ وَكَثِيرٌ مِّنْهُمْ فَٰسِقُونَ ۝ ٱعْلَمُوٓا۟ أَنَّ ٱللَّهَ يُحْيِ ٱلْأَرْضَ بَعْدَ مَوْتِهَا قَدْ بَيَّنَّا لَكُمُ ٱلْءَايَٰتِ لَعَلَّكُمْ تَعْقِلُونَ ۝

As compared to the promises of God, the benefits right before people appear more certain to them. Under these circumstances, surrendering one's life and property for the cause of Islam requires a very strong decision-making ability. At such a time, only one who has the capacity to recognise the reality of things through wisdom and insight, has the courage to progress in the right direction.

For those who prove to have this insight in the world, it will become easy on the Day of Judgement; by making use of their insight, they will be able to pass more easily through the difficult stages there. The insight which had become their guide in this world will, by the grace of God, serve as a guide also in the Hereafter.

ᵃ When these verses were revealed, though Islam had not yet become a substantial power, it nevertheless had the full force of arguments and warnings behind it. Under these circumstances, one who did not feel the force of arguments and was not moved by Divine warnings is shown, by this, that he was suffering from a lack of awareness. Just as the earth becomes fresh and green when it receives water, so also should the individual awaken from his moral torpor when he hears clear arguments. How strange it is if he does not.

¹⁸ Alms-givers, both men and women, who give a generous loan to God, shall have it multiplied and shall have an honourable reward. ¹⁹ Those who believe in God and His messengers are the truthful ones and the witnesses in the sight of their Lord. They shall have their reward and their light. But those who are bent on denying the truth and reject Our signs shall be destined for Hell.^a

إِنَّ ٱلْمُصَّدِّقِينَ وَٱلْمُصَّدِّقَٰتِ وَأَقْرَضُواْ ٱللَّهَ قَرْضًا حَسَنًا يُضَٰعَفُ لَهُمْ وَلَهُمْ أَجْرٌ كَرِيمٌ ۝ وَٱلَّذِينَ ءَامَنُواْ بِٱللَّهِ وَرُسُلِهِۦٓ أُوْلَٰٓئِكَ هُمُ ٱلصِّدِّيقُونَ وَٱلشُّهَدَآءُ عِندَ رَبِّهِمْ لَهُمْ أَجْرُهُمْ وَنُورُهُمْ وَٱلَّذِينَ كَفَرُواْ وَكَذَّبُواْ بِـَٔايَٰتِنَآ أُوْلَٰٓئِكَ أَصْحَٰبُ ٱلْجَحِيمِ ۝

---

^a To give one's possessions to others and to spend on the requirements of religion are very great deeds. Those who spend like this, whether men or women, have proved their steadfastness in faith. In an atmosphere of doubt about the Truth, they were able to see the Truth. Such action on their part will become a beacon for them in the Hereafter. They will be treated as accepters of God's signs. They will be given the status of God's witnesses, i.e. presenters of the report of the deeds of the people in the Court of the Hereafter.

²⁰ Never forget that the life of this world is only a game and a passing delight, a show, and mutual boasting and trying to outrival each other in riches and children. It is like the growth of vegetation after the rain, which delights the planter, but which then withers away, turns yellow and becomes worthless stubble. In the life to come there will be a terrible punishment, or God's forgiveness and approval: the life of this world is nothing but means of deception. ²¹ Vie with one another for your Lord's forgiveness and for a Paradise as vast as heaven and earth, which has been made ready for those who believe in God and His messengers. Such is God's grace. He bestows it upon whoever He pleases. There is no limit to God's bounty.ᵃ

ٱعۡلَمُوٓاْ أَنَّمَا ٱلۡحَيَوٰةُ ٱلدُّنۡيَا لَعِبٌ وَلَهۡوٌ وَزِينَةٌ وَتَفَاخُرٌ بَيۡنَكُمۡ وَتَكَاثُرٌ فِى ٱلۡأَمۡوَٰلِ وَٱلۡأَوۡلَٰدِ كَمَثَلِ غَيۡثٍ أَعۡجَبَ ٱلۡكُفَّارَ نَبَاتُهُ ثُمَّ يَهِيجُ فَتَرَىٰهُ مُصۡفَرًّا ثُمَّ يَكُونُ حُطَٰمًا وَفِى ٱلۡأَخِرَةِ عَذَابٌ شَدِيدٌ وَمَغۡفِرَةٌ مِّنَ ٱللَّهِ وَرِضۡوَٰنٌ وَمَا ٱلۡحَيَوٰةُ ٱلدُّنۡيَآ إِلَّا مَتَٰعُ ٱلۡغُرُورِ ۝ سَابِقُوٓاْ إِلَىٰ مَغۡفِرَةٍ مِّن رَّبِّكُمۡ وَجَنَّةٍ عَرۡضُهَا كَعَرۡضِ ٱلسَّمَآءِ وَٱلۡأَرۡضِ أُعِدَّتۡ لِلَّذِينَ ءَامَنُواْ بِٱللَّهِ وَرُسُلِهِ ذَٰلِكَ فَضۡلُ ٱللَّهِ يُؤۡتِيهِ مَن يَشَآءُ وَٱللَّهُ ذُو ٱلۡفَضۡلِ ٱلۡعَظِيمِ ۝

ᵃ God has created examples of the Hereafter in this world. One of these examples is that of a field. When, after receiving water, the crops ripen, their greenery looks very attractive for a few days. But soon hot winds blow and they begin to wither away. Then, the crops are reaped and threshed.

Similarly, the glamour of this world is also temporary. It lasts but a few days. After coming into possession of it, man becomes misled. He starts thinking that it is his everything. But, afterwards, when he is taken back to God, it will be evident to him that the glories of the world were valueless.

²² No misfortune can affect the earth or your own selves without its first having been recorded in a book, before We bring it into being. That is easy for God to do; ²³ so that you may not grieve for what has escaped you, nor be exultant over what you have gained. God loves neither the conceited nor the boastful, ²⁴ nor those who, being miserly themselves, urge others to be miserly. He who turns his back should remember that God alone is self-sufficient and worthy of all praise.[a]

²⁵ We sent Our messengers with evidence and, with them, We sent down the Book and the Scales of Justice, so that men might act in all fairness. We sent down iron with its great inherent strength and its many benefits for mankind, so that God might know who would stand up for God, though unseen, and His messengers. God is powerful, and almighty.[b]

مَآ أَصَابَ مِن مُّصِيبَةٍ فِى ٱلْأَرْضِ وَلَا فِىٓ أَنفُسِكُمْ إِلَّا فِى كِتَٰبٍ مِّن قَبْلِ أَن نَّبْرَأَهَآ إِنَّ ذَٰلِكَ عَلَى ٱللَّهِ يَسِيرٌ ۝ لِّكَيْلَا تَأْسَوْا۟ عَلَىٰ مَا فَاتَكُمْ وَلَا تَفْرَحُوا۟ بِمَآ ءَاتَىٰكُمْ وَٱللَّهُ لَا يُحِبُّ كُلَّ مُخْتَالٍ فَخُورٍ ۝ ٱلَّذِينَ يَبْخَلُونَ وَيَأْمُرُونَ ٱلنَّاسَ بِٱلْبُخْلِ وَمَن يَتَوَلَّ فَإِنَّ ٱللَّهَ هُوَ ٱلْغَنِىُّ ٱلْحَمِيدُ ۝ لَقَدْ أَرْسَلْنَا رُسُلَنَا بِٱلْبَيِّنَٰتِ وَأَنزَلْنَا مَعَهُمُ ٱلْكِتَٰبَ وَٱلْمِيزَانَ لِيَقُومَ ٱلنَّاسُ بِٱلْقِسْطِ وَأَنزَلْنَا ٱلْحَدِيدَ فِيهِ بَأْسٌ شَدِيدٌ وَمَنَٰفِعُ لِلنَّاسِ وَلِيَعْلَمَ ٱللَّهُ مَن يَنصُرُهُۥ وَرُسُلَهُۥ بِٱلْغَيْبِ إِنَّ ٱللَّهَ قَوِىٌّ عَزِيزٌ ۝

---

[a] The receiving of things in the world or the losing of them is purely for the purpose of putting man to the test. Almighty God has settled in advance what shape man's test-paper should take. A man should pay real attention not to what he has received or what has been taken away from him, but to how he reacted on each of these occasions. The correct and required reaction is that a man should not be disheartened if he suffers some loss, nor should he develop feelings of pride and vanity if he gains something.

[b] Two things are required in religion. One is the following of religion and the other is the support of religion. The balance—or the Scales of Justice—is a symbol of the following of religion by its adherents. Just as man measures excess or shortage by means of a balance, similarly, God's book is also a balance for Truth. People should test their actions against the standard of God's book and find out how far they are right and how far they are wrong. ►

26 We sent forth Noah and Abraham and bestowed upon their offspring prophethood and the Book. Some of them were rightly guided, but many others were transgressors. 27 Then, in their wake, We followed them up with [others of] Our messengers and after them Jesus, son of Mary. We gave him the Gospel and imbued the hearts of those who followed him with compassion and mercy. But We did not prescribe monasticism for them: that was their own innovation by which they sought to please God. But then, they did not observe it in the way that it should have been observed. So We rewarded only those who were truly faithful, for many of them were disobedient.*a*

وَلَقَدْ أَرْسَلْنَا نُوحًا وَإِبْرَٰهِيمَ وَجَعَلْنَا فِى ذُرِّيَّتِهِمَا ٱلنُّبُوَّةَ وَٱلْكِتَٰبَ ۖ فَمِنْهُم مُّهْتَدٍ ۖ وَكَثِيرٌ مِّنْهُمْ فَٰسِقُونَ ۝ ثُمَّ قَفَّيْنَا عَلَىٰٓ ءَاثَٰرِهِم بِرُسُلِنَا وَقَفَّيْنَا بِعِيسَى ٱبْنِ مَرْيَمَ وَءَاتَيْنَٰهُ ٱلْإِنجِيلَ وَجَعَلْنَا فِى قُلُوبِ ٱلَّذِينَ ٱتَّبَعُوهُ رَأْفَةً وَرَحْمَةً وَرَهْبَانِيَّةً ٱبْتَدَعُوهَا مَا كَتَبْنَٰهَا عَلَيْهِمْ إِلَّا ٱبْتِغَآءَ رِضْوَٰنِ ٱللَّهِ فَمَا رَعَوْهَا حَقَّ رِعَايَتِهَا ۖ فَـَٔاتَيْنَا ٱلَّذِينَ ءَامَنُوا۟ مِنْهُمْ أَجْرَهُمْ ۖ وَكَثِيرٌ مِّنْهُمْ فَٰسِقُونَ ۝

Similarly, iron is the symbolic representation of the support for religion. Whenever, any problem about religion arises, a man should prove as strong as iron. He should defend religion with the strength of iron.

a All the prophets who came here on behalf of God brought the same religion. But successive generations, introduced innovations in the name of the prophet. An example of this is found in the followers of Jesus. Jesus was entrusted only with the task of conveying the Truth. His prophetic responsibilities did not include fighting. So, he laid more emphasis on missionary ethics, such as are based entirely on affection and compassion. He advised his followers to be affectionate and compassionate towards others. But after Jesus his followers could not fully appreciate this point. By temperament they tended towards renunciation. For the purpose of missionary work, they were only advised not to be engrossed in purely worldly considerations, but they went to the extreme of renouncing the world.

²⁸ Believers,ᵃ fear God and believe in His messenger. He will show you mercy in double measure and will provide a light for you to walk in. God will grant you forgiveness. He is forgiving and merciful. ²⁹ The People of the Book should know that they have no power whatsoever over God's grace. His grace is entirely in His hand and He bestows it upon whoever He wills. God is truly infinite in His bounty.

يَـٰٓأَيُّهَا ٱلَّذِينَ ءَامَنُوا۟ ٱتَّقُوا۟ ٱللَّهَ وَءَامِنُوا۟ بِرَسُولِهِۦ يُؤْتِكُمْ كِفْلَيْنِ مِن رَّحْمَتِهِۦ وَيَجْعَل لَّكُمْ نُورًا تَمْشُونَ بِهِۦ وَيَغْفِرْ لَكُمْ ۚ وَٱللَّهُ غَفُورٌ رَّحِيمٌ ﴿٢٨﴾ لِّئَلَّا يَعْلَمَ أَهْلُ ٱلْكِتَـٰبِ أَلَّا يَقْدِرُونَ عَلَىٰ شَىْءٍ مِّن فَضْلِ ٱللَّهِ ۙ وَأَنَّ ٱلْفَضْلَ بِيَدِ ٱللَّهِ يُؤْتِيهِ مَن يَشَآءُ ۚ وَٱللَّهُ ذُو ٱلْفَضْلِ ٱلْعَظِيمِ ﴿٢٩﴾

ᵃ 'Believers,' here refer to those who embraced the faith of Jesus. Those who had faith in the previous prophet and now, having discovered the Truth in the call of the Last of the Prophets, adopt his faith, are entitled to a double reward. Similarly, if those who are Muslims by birth study Islam afresh, and with renewed Islamic consciousness, become believers or Muslims, they too will be entitled to a double reward in the eyes of God.

58. THE PLEADING

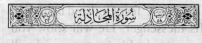

In the name of God,
the Most Gracious, the Most Merciful

¹ God has indeed heard the words of the woman who pleads with you about her husband and lays her complaint before God: God hears what the two of you have to say. God is all hearing, all seeing.ᵃ

قَدْ سَمِعَ ٱللَّهُ قَوْلَ ٱلَّتِي تُجَٰدِلُكَ فِي زَوْجِهَا وَتَشْتَكِىٓ إِلَى ٱللَّهِ وَٱللَّهُ يَسْمَعُ تَحَاوُرَكُمَآ إِنَّ ٱللَّهَ سَمِيعٌۢ بَصِيرٌ ۞

ᵃ Before Islam, it was the custom in Arabia that if a man said to his wife, 'To me you are like my mother's back' she was for ever forbidden for that man. This was called *zihar*. A Muslim of Madinah, Aws ibn as-Samit, once repeated these very words to his wife, Khawlah bint Tha'labah. She came to the Prophet and related the incident. The Prophet, taking into account the old custom, opined that she stood forbidden for Aws ibn as-Samit. Khawlah was worried that her house and her children would be destroyed, and she started crying and wailing. On this occasion these verses were revealed and the Islamic rules on *zihar* were laid down.

² Those who separate themselves from their wives by pronouncing, 'To me you are like my mother's back,'ᵃ must concede that they are not their mothers; none are their mothers except those who gave birth to them—surely they utter an evil word and a lie. God is pardoning, forgiving. ³ Those who put away their wives by equating them with their mothers, and then wish to go back on what they have said, must set free a slave before the couple may touch one another again. This is what you are exhorted to do. God is fully aware of what you do, ⁴ and anyone who does not have the means must fast for two consecutive months before they touch each other, and who is not able to do that must feed sixty needy people. That is to affirm your faith in God and His messenger. These are the limits set by God. Those who deny the truth shall have a painful punishment.ᵇ

اَلَّذِينَ يُظَٰهِرُونَ مِنكُم مِّن نِّسَآئِهِم مَّا هُنَّ أُمَّهَٰتِهِمْ إِنْ أُمَّهَٰتُهُمْ إِلَّا ٱلَّٰٓـِٔى وَلَدْنَهُمْ وَإِنَّهُمْ لَيَقُولُونَ مُنكَرًا مِّنَ ٱلْقَوْلِ وَزُورًا وَإِنَّ ٱللَّهَ لَعَفُوٌّ غَفُورٌ ۝ وَٱلَّذِينَ يُظَٰهِرُونَ مِن نِّسَآئِهِمْ ثُمَّ يَعُودُونَ لِمَا قَالُوا۟ فَتَحْرِيرُ رَقَبَةٍ مِّن قَبْلِ أَن يَتَمَآسَّا ذَٰلِكُمْ تُوعَظُونَ بِهِۦ وَٱللَّهُ بِمَا تَعْمَلُونَ خَبِيرٌ ۝ فَمَن لَّمْ يَجِدْ فَصِيَامُ شَهْرَيْنِ مُتَتَابِعَيْنِ مِن قَبْلِ أَن يَتَمَآسَّا فَمَن لَّمْ يَسْتَطِعْ فَإِطْعَامُ سِتِّينَ مِسْكِينًا ذَٰلِكَ لِتُؤْمِنُوا۟ بِٱللَّهِ وَرَسُولِهِۦ وَتِلْكَ حُدُودُ ٱللَّهِ وَلِلْكَٰفِرِينَ عَذَابٌ أَلِيمٌ ۝

ᵃ Saying to one's wife, 'To me you are like my mother's back'. This was an old pagan custom which was known as *zihar*, by which one's wife could be wrongfully divorced.

ᵇ Islam distinguishes between form and reality. That is why Islam has not recognised the old custom of a man's calling a woman 'mother', although she is not his real mother, and then treating her as such for the purpose of divorcing her. Any such action is absurd, because it cannot change the laws of nature.

It is clarified in the Quran that simply by acting in the above-mentioned manner, a man's wife does not stand divorced. However, it has been made compulsory for the concerned person to pay a penalty and then go back to his wife. After committing an error, if a man pays a penalty in this way, he revives his faith, which he had discarded due to negligence or stupidity.

⁵ Those who oppose God and His Messenger will be humiliated, as were their predecessors. We have sent down clear revelations. A humiliating punishment awaits those who deny the truth. ⁶ On the day God raises them all up from the dead, He will make them understand what they have done. God has taken everything into account, even though they have forgotten, for God is a witness to all things.ᵃ

إِنَّ ٱلَّذِينَ يُحَآدُّونَ ٱللَّهَ وَرَسُولَهُۥ كُبِتُوا۟ كَمَا كُبِتَ ٱلَّذِينَ مِن قَبْلِهِمْ وَقَدْ أَنزَلْنَآ ءَايَٰتٍۭ بَيِّنَٰتٍ وَلِلْكَٰفِرِينَ عَذَابٌ مُّهِينٌ ۝ يَوْمَ يَبْعَثُهُمُ ٱللَّهُ جَمِيعًا فَيُنَبِّئُهُم بِمَا عَمِلُوٓا۟ أَحْصَىٰهُ ٱللَّهُ وَنَسُوهُ وَٱللَّهُ عَلَىٰ كُلِّ شَىْءٍ شَهِيدٌ

ᵃ To oppose the Truth is to oppose God, and to oppose God means opposing that Being by opposing whom a man harms himself. Man can never hide anything from God, nor is it possible for anybody to elude His grasp.

7 Do you not see that God knows all that is in the heavens and on the earth? There is not a secret consultation between three, but He makes the fourth among them—nor between five but He makes the sixth—nor between fewer nor more, but He is in their midst, wherever they may be: in the end He will tell them the truth about their conduct, on the Day of Judgement. For God has full knowledge of all things. 8 Have you not seen how those who were forbidden to hold secret counsels yet revert to that which they were forbidden to do? And they conspire to indulge in wrongdoing, aggressive behaviour and disobedience to the Messenger. When they come to you, they greet you, but not in the words God would use, and inwardly they wonder, 'Why does God not punish us for what we say?' Hell will be a fitting punishment for them: they will burn in its flames—a wretched fate! [a]

أَلَمْ تَرَ أَنَّ ٱللَّهَ يَعْلَمُ مَا فِى ٱلسَّمَٰوَٰتِ وَمَا فِى ٱلْأَرْضِ مَا يَكُونُ مِن نَّجْوَىٰ ثَلَٰثَةٍ إِلَّا هُوَ رَابِعُهُمْ وَلَا خَمْسَةٍ إِلَّا هُوَ سَادِسُهُمْ وَلَا أَدْنَىٰ مِن ذَٰلِكَ وَلَا أَكْثَرَ إِلَّا هُوَ مَعَهُمْ أَيْنَ مَا كَانُوا۟ ثُمَّ يُنَبِّئُهُم بِمَا عَمِلُوا۟ يَوْمَ ٱلْقِيَٰمَةِ إِنَّ ٱللَّهَ بِكُلِّ شَىْءٍ عَلِيمٌ ۝ أَلَمْ تَرَ إِلَى ٱلَّذِينَ نُهُوا۟ عَنِ ٱلنَّجْوَىٰ ثُمَّ يَعُودُونَ لِمَا نُهُوا۟ عَنْهُ وَيَتَنَٰجَوْنَ بِٱلْإِثْمِ وَٱلْعُدْوَٰنِ وَمَعْصِيَتِ ٱلرَّسُولِ وَإِذَا جَآءُوكَ حَيَّوْكَ بِمَا لَمْ يُحَيِّكَ بِهِ ٱللَّهُ وَيَقُولُونَ فِى أَنفُسِهِمْ لَوْلَا يُعَذِّبُنَا ٱللَّهُ بِمَا نَقُولُ حَسْبُهُمْ جَهَنَّمُ يَصْلَوْنَهَا فَبِئْسَ ٱلْمَصِيرُ ۝

---

[a] The universe with its complex system bears testimony to the fact that it is under the careful watch of a Higher Power. The evidence of this vigilance over the universe proves that man is also constantly under the eyes of his Creator. In view of this, indulging in secret activities against Truth is the act of blind people who are unable to read the attributes of God either in the expressly worded Quran directly, or in the unworded message of the universe indirectly.

When certain hypocrites used to approach the Prophet Muhammad, instead of saying *assalamu alaykum* (peace be on you) they used to say *assamu alaykum* (death be upon you). This has always been the way of superficial persons. Such people derive pleasure from showing disrespect to true believers. They forget that at that very moment the whole of God's creation will acclaim the truthful person, while they, with their narrow mentality, will have exhausted every last word of contempt and rejection.

⁹ Believers, when you confer
together in private, do not confer in
support of sin and transgression and
disobedience to the Messenger, but
confer for the promotion of virtue
and righteousness. Fear God, before
whom you shall all be gathered.
¹⁰ Conspiracy for evil purposes is the
work of Satan, by which he means
to bring grief to believers. But he
cannot harm them in the least,
unless it be by God's leave. Let the
believers put their trust in God.ᵃ

يَـٰٓأَيُّهَا ٱلَّذِينَ ءَامَنُوٓاْ إِذَا تَنَـٰجَيۡتُمۡ فَلَا
تَتَنَـٰجَوۡاْ بِٱلۡإِثۡمِ وَٱلۡعُدۡوَٰنِ وَمَعۡصِيَتِ
ٱلرَّسُولِ وَتَنَـٰجَوۡاْ بِٱلۡبِرِّ وَٱلتَّقۡوَىٰ
وَٱتَّقُواْ ٱللَّهَ ٱلَّذِىٓ إِلَيۡهِ تُحۡشَرُونَ ﴿٩﴾
إِنَّمَا ٱلنَّجۡوَىٰ مِنَ ٱلشَّيۡطَٰنِ
لِيَحۡزُنَ ٱلَّذِينَ ءَامَنُواْ وَلَيۡسَ
بِضَآرِّهِمۡ شَيۡـًٔا إِلَّا بِإِذۡنِ ٱللَّهِ وَعَلَى
ٱللَّهِ فَلۡيَتَوَكَّلِ ٱلۡمُؤۡمِنُونَ ﴿١٠﴾

ᵃ As a rule, secret whispering is an undesirable action. However, sometimes for
some good reason, secret whispering has to be resorted to. In this case, the decisive
factor is intention. If it is done with good intentions, it is legitimate but if it is done
with evil intentions, it is sinful.

¹¹ Believers, if you are told to make room for one another in your assemblies, then do so, and God will make room for you, and if you are told to rise up, do so: God will raise in rank those of you who believe and those who have been given knowledge: He is fully aware of all that you do.^a

¹² Believers, when you come to consult the Messenger privately, give something in charity beforehand. That is best for you and most conducive to purity. But if you cannot find anything to give, know that God is Forgiving and Merciful. ¹³ Do you fear that you will not [be able to] give in charity before your consultation? Then if you are unable to do so, [know that] God has turned to you in His mercy; then observe your prayers and pay the prescribed alms and obey God and His Messenger. God is aware of all that you do.^b

يَـٰٓأَيُّهَا ٱلَّذِينَ ءَامَنُوٓاْ إِذَا قِيلَ لَكُمْ تَفَسَّحُواْ فِى ٱلْمَجَٰلِسِ فَٱفْسَحُواْ يَفْسَحِ ٱللَّهُ لَكُمْ وَإِذَا قِيلَ ٱنشُزُواْ فَٱنشُزُواْ يَرْفَعِ ٱللَّهُ ٱلَّذِينَ ءَامَنُواْ مِنكُمْ وَٱلَّذِينَ أُوتُواْ ٱلْعِلْمَ دَرَجَٰتٍ وَٱللَّهُ بِمَا تَعْمَلُونَ خَبِيرٌ ۝ يَـٰٓأَيُّهَا ٱلَّذِينَ ءَامَنُوٓاْ إِذَا نَٰجَيْتُمُ ٱلرَّسُولَ فَقَدِّمُواْ بَيْنَ يَدَىْ نَجْوَىٰكُمْ صَدَقَةً ذَٰلِكَ خَيْرٌ لَّكُمْ وَأَطْهَرُ فَإِن لَّمْ تَجِدُواْ فَإِنَّ ٱللَّهَ غَفُورٌ رَّحِيمٌ ۝ ءَأَشْفَقْتُمْ أَن تُقَدِّمُواْ بَيْنَ يَدَىْ نَجْوَىٰكُمْ صَدَقَٰتٍ فَإِذْ لَمْ تَفْعَلُواْ وَتَابَ ٱللَّهُ عَلَيْكُمْ فَأَقِيمُواْ ٱلصَّلَوٰةَ وَءَاتُواْ ٱلزَّكَوٰةَ وَأَطِيعُواْ ٱللَّهَ وَرَسُولَهُۥ وَٱللَّهُ خَبِيرٌۢ بِمَا تَعْمَلُونَ ۝

---

^a It happens sometimes that, according to the protocol of a meeting, one person has to take precedence over another. Similarly, it sometimes happens that, against all expectations, certain people are asked to leave. To make such things a prestige issue is a sign of petty-mindedness: one who avoids doing so proves that, with regard to religious awareness, he has reached an elevated plane.

^b It was the intention of Almighty God that only those who wished to meet the Prophet for some really serious purpose, should be allowed to come into his presence, while those who only wasted time in useless talk should be kept away. So, it became the rule that when one intended to meet the Prophet Muhammad, he should first give alms in the name of God, and if one could not afford to do so, he should perform some other righteous deed.

These injunctions were originally intended to apply to the Prophet, but even after the Prophet the same conduct will be required toward the leaders of the community, according to their status.

¹⁴ Do you not see those who have befriended a people who have brought down upon themselves the wrath of God? They are neither with you nor with them and they wittingly swear to falsehood. ¹⁵ God has prepared a severe punishment for them; surely what they have done is evil. ¹⁶ They have used their oaths to cover up their misdeeds and have thus turned others away from the path of God. A humiliating punishment awaits them.ᵃ

۞ أَلَمْ تَرَ إِلَى ٱلَّذِينَ تَوَلَّوْاْ قَوْمًا غَضِبَ ٱللَّهُ عَلَيْهِم مَّا هُم مِّنكُمْ وَلَا مِنْهُمْ وَيَحْلِفُونَ عَلَى ٱلْكَذِبِ وَهُمْ يَعْلَمُونَ ۝ أَعَدَّ ٱللَّهُ لَهُمْ عَذَابًا شَدِيدًا إِنَّهُمْ سَآءَ مَا كَانُواْ يَعْمَلُونَ ۝ ٱتَّخَذُوٓاْ أَيْمَٰنَهُمْ جُنَّةً فَصَدُّواْ عَن سَبِيلِ ٱللَّهِ فَلَهُمْ عَذَابٌ مُّهِينٌ ۝

ᵃ The hypocrites of Madinah, who were at that time living in the community of Islam, joined hands with other hostile tribes. This is always true of those who are unable to accept the Truth whole-heartedly. Such people are apparently in consonance with everyone else but, in reality, they are loyal only to their own interests, despite having given assurances on oath of their being devotees of the Truth.

¹⁷ Neither their wealth nor their children will be of the least avail [in protecting them] against God—they are the inheritors of Hell, and there they shall remain forever. ¹⁸ On the day God raises them all up from the dead, they will swear to Him just as they have sworn to you, thinking that they are on firm ground. But surely they are liars. ¹⁹ Satan has got the better of them and has caused them to forget the remembrance of God. They have gone over to the side of the devil, and it is as the devil's partisans that they shall be the losers: ²⁰ those who oppose God and His Messenger will [on Judgement Day] be among the most abased. ²¹ God has decreed, 'I and My messengers shall most certainly prevail.' Truly God is Powerful and Almighty.ᵃ

لَن تُغْنِىَ عَنْهُمْ أَمْوَٰلُهُمْ وَلَآ أَوْلَٰدُهُم مِّنَ ٱللَّهِ شَيْـًٔا أُوْلَٰٓئِكَ أَصْحَٰبُ ٱلنَّارِ هُمْ فِيهَا خَٰلِدُونَ ۝ يَوْمَ يَبْعَثُهُمُ ٱللَّهُ جَمِيعًا فَيَحْلِفُونَ لَهُۥ كَمَا يَحْلِفُونَ لَكُمْ وَيَحْسَبُونَ أَنَّهُمْ عَلَىٰ شَىْءٍ أَلَآ إِنَّهُمْ هُمُ ٱلْكَٰذِبُونَ ۝ ٱسْتَحْوَذَ عَلَيْهِمُ ٱلشَّيْطَٰنُ فَأَنسَىٰهُمْ ذِكْرَ ٱللَّهِ أُوْلَٰٓئِكَ حِزْبُ ٱلشَّيْطَٰنِ أَلَآ إِنَّ حِزْبَ ٱلشَّيْطَٰنِ هُمُ ٱلْخَٰسِرُونَ ۝ إِنَّ ٱلَّذِينَ يُحَآدُّونَ ٱللَّهَ وَرَسُولَهُۥٓ أُوْلَٰٓئِكَ فِى ٱلْأَذَلِّينَ ۝ كَتَبَ ٱللَّهُ لَأَغْلِبَنَّ أَنَا۠ وَرُسُلِىٓ إِنَّ ٱللَّهَ قَوِىٌّ عَزِيزٌ ۝

ᵃ When a self-seeking man opposes the call for Truth, he thinks that he is thus making himself safe. But in the Hereafter, when he sees that the things on which he relied are of no avail on the day of judgement, he will be struck with horror.

A hypocrite, in order to vindicate his position, indulges in tall talk to the extent of taking oaths as an assurance of his sincerity. After doing all this, he thinks that he has been very clever and that he has provided some support for himself. But when the blast of Doomsday opens the secrets of realities, he will come to know at that time that his attemptᶜ at vindication were simply a series of false words taught by Satan as 'certain proof' of his innocence.

²² You will find no believers in God
and the Last Day consorting with
those who oppose God and His
Messenger, even though they be
their fathers, their sons, their
brothers or their close relatives. He
has engraved faith on their very
hearts and has strengthened them
with a spirit of His own. He will
usher them into Gardens through
which rivers flow where they shall
dwell forever. God is well-pleased
with them and they are well pleased
with Him. They are God's party.
God's party shall surely enter into a
state of bliss.ᵃ

لَّا تَجِدُ قَوْمًا يُؤْمِنُونَ بِٱللَّهِ وَٱلْيَوْمِ
ٱلْأَخِرِ يُوَآدُّونَ مَنْ حَآدَّ ٱللَّهَ
وَرَسُولَهُۥ وَلَوْ كَانُوٓاْ ءَابَآءَهُمْ أَوْ
أَبْنَآءَهُمْ أَوْ إِخْوَٰنَهُمْ أَوْ عَشِيرَتَهُمْ
أُوْلَٰٓئِكَ كَتَبَ فِى قُلُوبِهِمُ ٱلْإِيمَٰنَ
وَأَيَّدَهُم بِرُوحٍ مِّنْهُ وَيُدْخِلُهُمْ جَنَّٰتٍ
تَجْرِى مِن تَحْتِهَا ٱلْأَنْهَٰرُ خَٰلِدِينَ فِيهَا
رَضِىَ ٱللَّهُ عَنْهُمْ وَرَضُواْ عَنْهُ أُوْلَٰٓئِكَ
حِزْبُ ٱللَّهِ أَلَآ إِنَّ حِزْبَ ٱللَّهِ هُمُ
ٱلْمُفْلِحُونَ ۝

ᵃ In this world success is for the believers (God's party). Who are the ones who
comprise this group of people devoted to God? They are those in whose hearts
Faith is firmly embedded as the greatest reality. They should have such a strong
relationship with God that they receive spiritual light from Him. Then, their
attachment to Divine Realities should be so deep that their friendships and
enmities should be based only on that. They should be nearest to those who have
adopted the Divine Truth, and they should remain far away from those who have
distanced themselves from the Divine Truth, even if they are their nearest and
dearest ones or closest relatives.

59. BANISHMENT

In the name of God,
the Most Gracious, the Most Merciful

¹Everything in the heavens and on the earth glorifies God. He is the Almighty, the All Wise. ²It was He who turned those People of the Book who denied the truth out of their homes in the first banishment. You never thought they would go, and they thought their strongholds would protect them against God. But God came upon them from where they least expected and cast such terror into their hearts that their houses were pulled down by their own hands as well as by the hands of the believers. Learn a lesson, then, you who are endowed with insight.ᵃ

ᵃ On the east side of Madinah, there was a settlement of the Banu al-Nadir, a Jewish tribe. There was a peace treaty between them and the Prophet Muhammad. But they committed breaches of this treaty time and again. At last in the fourth year of Hijrah, Almighty God created such conditions that they were compelled to leave Madinah. Thereafter, they settled in Khybar and Azra'at. But their conspiratorial activities continued. During the caliphate of 'Umar Faruq, they and some other Jewish tribes were made to leave the Arabian Peninsula. They subsequently went to Syria and settled there.

³ If God had not prescribed exile for them, He would surely have punished them in this world. But they shall have the torment of Fire in the Hereafter, ⁴ because they set themselves against God and His Messenger: God is stern in His punishment of anyone who sets himself against Him. ⁵ Whatever palm trees you cut down or left standing on their roots, it was by God's leave, so that He might disgrace the transgressors.ᵃ

وَلَوْلَآ أَن كَتَبَ ٱللَّهُ عَلَيْهِمُ ٱلْجَلَآءَ لَعَذَّبَهُمْ فِى ٱلدُّنْيَا ۖ وَلَهُمْ فِى ٱلْأَخِرَةِ عَذَابُ ٱلنَّارِ ۝ ذَٰلِكَ بِأَنَّهُمْ شَاقُّوا۟ ٱللَّهَ وَرَسُولَهُۥ ۖ وَمَن يُشَاقِّ ٱللَّهَ فَإِنَّ ٱللَّهَ شَدِيدُ ٱلْعِقَابِ ۝ مَا قَطَعْتُم مِّن لِّينَةٍ أَوْ تَرَكْتُمُوهَا قَآئِمَةً عَلَىٰٓ أُصُولِهَا فَبِإِذْنِ ٱللَّهِ وَلِيُخْزِىَ ٱلْفَٰسِقِينَ ۝

ᵃ Those who opposed the Prophet were destined to suffer such punishment. During the siege of the Banu al-Nadir, some trees in their gardens were cut down as a matter of military strategy. This was done on the direct orders of the government. However, this was not the general rule. This was an exceptional case concerning the immediate addressees of the Prophet.

⁶ Whatever God has given to His Messenger as spoils from them is by His grace; you spurred neither horse nor camel for them, but God gives power to His messengers over anyone He wills. God has power over all things—⁷ whatever gains God has assigned to His Messenger from the inhabitants of the town is for God and for the Messenger and for his kinsfolk and for orphans and the needy and the wayfarer, so that they may not become the property of those of you who are rich. Whatever the Messenger gives you, take it; and whatever he forbids you, abstain from it. Fear God; surely, God is severe in retribution. ⁸ It is for the poor refugees who were driven from their homes and possessions, desiring the favour and the pleasure of God and supporting God and His Messenger. Such people are the truthful.ᵃ

وَمَآ أَفَآءَ ٱللَّهُ عَلَىٰ رَسُولِهِۦ مِنْهُمْ فَمَآ أَوْجَفْتُمْ عَلَيْهِ مِنْ خَيْلٍ وَلَا رِكَابٍ وَلَٰكِنَّ ٱللَّهَ يُسَلِّطُ رُسُلَهُۥ عَلَىٰ مَن يَشَآءُ ۚ وَٱللَّهُ عَلَىٰ كُلِّ شَىْءٍ قَدِيرٌ ۝ مَّآ أَفَآءَ ٱللَّهُ عَلَىٰ رَسُولِهِۦ مِنْ أَهْلِ ٱلْقُرَىٰ فَلِلَّهِ وَلِلرَّسُولِ وَلِذِى ٱلْقُرْبَىٰ وَٱلْيَتَٰمَىٰ وَٱلْمَسَٰكِينِ وَٱبْنِ ٱلسَّبِيلِ كَىْ لَا يَكُونَ دُولَةًۢ بَيْنَ ٱلْأَغْنِيَآءِ مِنكُمْ ۚ وَمَآ ءَاتَىٰكُمُ ٱلرَّسُولُ فَخُذُوهُ وَمَا نَهَىٰكُمْ عَنْهُ فَٱنتَهُوا۟ ۚ وَٱتَّقُوا۟ ٱللَّهَ ۖ إِنَّ ٱللَّهَ شَدِيدُ ٱلْعِقَابِ ۝ لِلْفُقَرَآءِ ٱلْمُهَٰجِرِينَ ٱلَّذِينَ أُخْرِجُوا۟ مِن دِيَٰرِهِمْ وَأَمْوَٰلِهِمْ يَبْتَغُونَ فَضْلًا مِّنَ ٱللَّهِ وَرِضْوَٰنًا وَيَنصُرُونَ ٱللَّهَ وَرَسُولَهُۥٓ ۚ أُو۟لَٰٓئِكَ هُمُ ٱلصَّٰدِقُونَ ۝

ᵃ When the enemy have fled after defeat, their possessions are considered spoils of war (*ghanimah*). Sometimes the enemy retreats without fighting. On such occasions the booty acquired is described as abandoned property (*fay'*). As for the spoils of war, after a fifth part has been taken out, all of the remaining portion is the share of the army. While all the abandoned property in the case of *Fay* belongs to the Islamic government and is to be spent in the public interest.

It is the intention of Islam that wealth should not remain restricted to a particular class but should reach every class. In Islam, there is no concept of economy controlled by the State. However, its economic rules are so framed that wealth should not be concentrated, but should keep circulating in all groups.

⁹ Those who were already settled in the city [Madinah] and firmly rooted in faith, love those who migrated to them for refuge, and harbour no desire in their hearts for what has been given to the [latter]. They give them preference over themselves, even if they too are needy: those who are saved from their own souls' greed are truly successful. ¹⁰ Those who came [into the faith] after them say, 'Our Lord, forgive us and our brothers who preceded us in the faith and leave no malice in our hearts towards those who believe. Lord, You are indeed compassionate and merciful.' ᵃ

وَٱلَّذِينَ تَبَوَّءُو ٱلدَّارَ وَٱلْإِيمَٰنَ مِن قَبْلِهِمْ يُحِبُّونَ مَنْ هَاجَرَ إِلَيْهِمْ وَلَا يَجِدُونَ فِى صُدُورِهِمْ حَاجَةً مِّمَّآ أُوتُواْ وَيُؤْثِرُونَ عَلَىٰٓ أَنفُسِهِمْ وَلَوْ كَانَ بِهِمْ خَصَاصَةٌ وَمَن يُوقَ شُحَّ نَفْسِهِۦ فَأُوْلَٰٓئِكَ هُمُ ٱلْمُفْلِحُونَ ۝ وَٱلَّذِينَ جَآءُو مِنۢ بَعْدِهِمْ يَقُولُونَ رَبَّنَا ٱغْفِرْ لَنَا وَلِإِخْوَٰنِنَا ٱلَّذِينَ سَبَقُونَا بِٱلْإِيمَٰنِ وَلَا تَجْعَلْ فِى قُلُوبِنَا غِلًّا لِّلَّذِينَ ءَامَنُواْ رَبَّنَآ إِنَّكَ رَءُوفٌ رَّحِيمٌ ۝

ᵃ After the *hijrah*, the Muslims who left their native place and migrated to Madinah were in reality a burden on the inhabitants of Madinah, who were known as 'helpers' (*ansar*). But the helpers open-heartedly welcomed the migrants (*muhajirun*). Wherever the Prophet of God received any bounty, he shared it out among the migrants. In spite of that the Muslims of Madinah did not bear the migrants any ill-will. Ultimately, they fully acknowledged the migrants' services to Islam and used to pray for them from the bottom of their hearts. It is such broad-mindedness which will assure a group an honoured place in the annals of history.

¹¹ Have you not seen those who act hypocritically? They say to their disbelieving companions from among the People of the Book, 'If you are driven out we shall surely go out with you, and we shall never listen to anyone against you, and if war is waged against you, we shall help you.' God bears witness that they are indeed liars. ¹² If they are driven out, they will not go with them, nor, if they are attacked, will they help them. Indeed, if they go to their help, they will turn their backs in flight, and then they will not be helped.ᵃ

¹³ They are more in dread of you than of God, because they are people devoid of understanding. ¹⁴ They will never fight against you in a body except from within fortified strongholds or from behind walls. There is much hostility between them. You think they are united, but their hearts are divided, because they are a people devoid of reason.ᵇ

۞ أَلَمْ تَرَ إِلَى ٱلَّذِينَ نَافَقُوا۟ يَقُولُونَ لِإِخْوَٰنِهِمُ ٱلَّذِينَ كَفَرُوا۟ مِنْ أَهْلِ ٱلْكِتَٰبِ لَئِنْ أُخْرِجْتُمْ لَنَخْرُجَنَّ مَعَكُمْ وَلَا نُطِيعُ فِيكُمْ أَحَدًا أَبَدًا وَإِن قُوتِلْتُمْ لَنَنصُرَنَّكُمْ وَٱللَّهُ يَشْهَدُ إِنَّهُمْ لَكَٰذِبُونَ ۝ لَئِنْ أُخْرِجُوا۟ لَا يَخْرُجُونَ مَعَهُمْ وَلَئِن قُوتِلُوا۟ لَا يَنصُرُونَهُمْ وَلَئِن نَّصَرُوهُمْ لَيُوَلُّنَّ ٱلْأَدْبَٰرَ ثُمَّ لَا يُنصَرُونَ ۝ لَأَنتُمْ أَشَدُّ رَهْبَةً فِى صُدُورِهِم مِّنَ ٱللَّهِ ذَٰلِكَ بِأَنَّهُمْ قَوْمٌ لَّا يَفْقَهُونَ ۝ لَا يُقَٰتِلُونَكُمْ جَمِيعًا إِلَّا فِى قُرًى مُّحَصَّنَةٍ أَوْ مِن وَرَآءِ جُدُرٍ بَأْسُهُم بَيْنَهُمْ شَدِيدٌ تَحْسَبُهُمْ جَمِيعًا وَقُلُوبُهُمْ شَتَّىٰ ذَٰلِكَ بِأَنَّهُمْ قَوْمٌ لَّا يَعْقِلُونَ ۝

ᵃ When the Prophet Muhammad announced the banishment of the Banu al-Nadir, the hypocrites ostensibly rallied to their side. They asked the Banu al-Nadir to take a firm stand and assured them of their support. But the hypocrites uttered these words just to incite them to rise against Muslims; they were never sincere in their offer. So, when the Muslims besieged the Banu al-Nadir, nobody came to help them. This has been the character of self-interested people in every age.

ᵇ God's power is not outwardly visible. But the power of human beings is plainly visible. For this reason, those who are concerned only with appearances are fearless of God, but if they come across a human being who is stronger than the others, they feel afraid of him. Their lack of awareness with regard to God creates in them a lack of consciousness of the world also.

Those who become united for some negative purpose cannot remain united for long, because, for the purpose of long-lasting unity, a positive basis is required and that is precisely what they do not have.

¹⁵ Like those who went just before them, they have tasted the evil consequences of their doings. And they shall have a painful punishment. ¹⁶ They are like Satan, who says to man, 'Deny the truth!' but when man denied the truth, said, 'I disown you; I fear God, the Lord of the Universe.' ¹⁷ Thus, in the end, both will find themselves in the Fire, therein to abide: that is the reward of evil-doers.^a

¹⁸ Believers! Fear God, and let every soul look to what it lays up for the future. Fear God: God is aware of what you do. ¹⁹ Do not be like those who forgot God, so that He caused them to forget their own souls [their own true interests]. It is they who are the rebellious ones. ²⁰ The people of the Fire and the people of Paradise are not equal. The people of Paradise are the victorious ones.^b

كَمَثَلِ ٱلَّذِينَ مِن قَبْلِهِمْ قَرِيبًا ذَاقُوا۟ وَبَالَ أَمْرِهِمْ وَلَهُمْ عَذَابٌ أَلِيمٌ ۝ كَمَثَلِ ٱلشَّيْطَٰنِ إِذْ قَالَ لِلْإِنسَٰنِ ٱكْفُرْ فَلَمَّا كَفَرَ قَالَ إِنِّي بَرِيٓءٌ مِّنكَ إِنِّي أَخَافُ ٱللَّهَ رَبَّ ٱلْعَٰلَمِينَ ۝ فَكَانَ عَٰقِبَتَهُمَآ أَنَّهُمَا فِي ٱلنَّارِ خَٰلِدَيْنِ فِيهَا ۚ وَذَٰلِكَ جَزَٰٓؤُا۟ ٱلظَّٰلِمِينَ ۝ يَٰٓأَيُّهَا ٱلَّذِينَ ءَامَنُوا۟ ٱتَّقُوا۟ ٱللَّهَ وَلْتَنظُرْ نَفْسٌ مَّا قَدَّمَتْ لِغَدٍ ۖ وَٱتَّقُوا۟ ٱللَّهَ ۚ إِنَّ ٱللَّهَ خَبِيرٌۢ بِمَا تَعْمَلُونَ ۝ وَلَا تَكُونُوا۟ كَٱلَّذِينَ نَسُوا۟ ٱللَّهَ فَأَنسَىٰهُمْ أَنفُسَهُمْ ۚ أُو۟لَٰٓئِكَ هُمُ ٱلْفَٰسِقُونَ ۝ لَا يَسْتَوِىٓ أَصْحَٰبُ ٱلنَّارِ وَأَصْحَٰبُ ٱلْجَنَّةِ ۚ أَصْحَٰبُ ٱلْجَنَّةِ هُمُ ٱلْفَآئِزُونَ ۝

---

^a The hypocrites of Madinah who instigated the Banu al-Nadir against the Muslims had evidently learnt nothing from the total defeat of the Quraysh and Banu Qaynuqa' tribes who shortly before that had risen against the Muslims. This is always the case with those who take Satan's counsel. First of all they urge people to indulge in criminal actions. Thereafter, when the terrible results of this become evident, they attempt to absolve themselves of the responsibility by making all sorts of excuses. But these efforts cannot save such people from the grip of God.

^b Human life is divided into two parts: 'today' and 'tomorrow'. The present world is a man's 'today' and the world of the Hereafter is man's 'tomorrow'. Whatever a man does in the present world, he has to face the basic consequences in the ensuing longer life.

This is the truth and the other name for it is Islam. Man's success depends upon his always keeping this reality in mind. The whole life of one who is forgetful of this, will go wrong. In this matter, there is no difference between a believer or a non-believer. Believers will have the advantage only if they acknowledge realities. If they become forgetful of them, they will also meet the same fate as their precursors.

²¹ Had We sent down this Quran on a mountain, you would certainly have seen it falling down and splitting asunder, because of the fear of God. We set forth these parables to men so that they may reflect. ²² He is God: there is no deity save Him. He knows the unseen and the visible. He is the Compassionate, the Merciful. ²³ He is God, there is no deity save Him, the Sovereign, the Most Pure, the Source of Peace, the Granter of Security, the Protector, the Mighty, the Subduer, the Supreme, Glory be to God, who is far above what they associate with Him. ²⁴ He is God—the Creator, the Originator, the Giver of Form. His are the most excellent names. Everything in the heavens and earth declares His glory. He is the Mighty, the Wise One.ᵃ

لَوۡ أَنزَلۡنَا هَـٰذَا ٱلۡقُرۡءَانَ عَلَىٰ جَبَلٍ لَّرَأَيۡتَهُۥ خَـٰشِعًا مُّتَصَدِّعًا مِّنۡ خَشۡيَةِ ٱللَّهِ ۚ وَتِلۡكَ ٱلۡأَمۡثَـٰلُ نَضۡرِبُهَا لِلنَّاسِ لَعَلَّهُمۡ يَتَفَكَّرُونَ ۝ هُوَ ٱللَّهُ ٱلَّذِى لَآ إِلَـٰهَ إِلَّا هُوَ ۖ عَـٰلِمُ ٱلۡغَيۡبِ وَٱلشَّهَـٰدَةِ ۖ هُوَ ٱلرَّحۡمَـٰنُ ٱلرَّحِيمُ ۝ هُوَ ٱللَّهُ ٱلَّذِى لَآ إِلَـٰهَ إِلَّا هُوَ ٱلۡمَلِكُ ٱلۡقُدُّوسُ ٱلسَّلَـٰمُ ٱلۡمُؤۡمِنُ ٱلۡمُهَيۡمِنُ ٱلۡعَزِيزُ ٱلۡجَبَّارُ ٱلۡمُتَكَبِّرُ ۚ سُبۡحَـٰنَ ٱللَّهِ عَمَّا يُشۡرِكُونَ ۝ هُوَ ٱللَّهُ ٱلۡخَـٰلِقُ ٱلۡبَارِئُ ٱلۡمُصَوِّرُ ۖ لَهُ ٱلۡأَسۡمَآءُ ٱلۡحُسۡنَىٰ ۚ يُسَبِّحُ لَهُۥ مَا فِى ٱلسَّمَـٰوَٰتِ وَٱلۡأَرۡضِ ۖ وَهُوَ ٱلۡعَزِيزُ ٱلۡحَكِيمُ ۝

ᵃ The Quran is a declaration of the vital fact that man is not free, but is answerable for all his deeds to God who is all-powerful and who keeps a close watch on the actions of all mankind. This fact is of such grave import that it is enough to make even mountains tremble. But man is so negligent, forgetful and insensitive that, even after knowing this awesome fact, he is not perturbed.

The names of God mentioned here are, on the one hand, an introduction to God's Being. On the other hand, they show how Great is that Being who is the Creator of human beings and who keeps a constant watch over them. If an individual actually realises this, he will be completely engrossed in the remembrance and praises of God.

The universe, by virtue of its creative meaningfulness, mirrors the attributes of God. It is itself wholly taken up with singing the praises of God and urges human beings to follow suit.

60. SHE WHO IS TESTED

In the name of God,
the Most Gracious, the Most Merciful

¹ Believers! Do not offer friendship to those who are enemies of Mine and of yours. Would you show them affection when they have rejected the truth you have received; when they have driven you and the Messenger out [simply] because you believe in God, your Lord. If you have left your homes to strive for My cause and out of a desire to seek My goodwill, how can you secretly offer them friendship?ᵃ I know all that you conceal and all that you reveal. Whoever of you does this will surely stray from the right path.

ᵃ When the Prophet Muhammad decided to proceed against Makkah, he made his plans very quietly so that the Makkans should have no advance warning. At that time a Badri Companion, Hatib ibn 'Ali Balta'a, secretly wrote to the Makkans about the plan in a letter and sent it covertly in the name of some Makkans, so that the Makkans would be grateful to him and in return they would refrain from inflicting harm upon his family members who were staying in Makkah. But this betrayal became known through Revelation and the messenger was caught on the way. Every such action is against the demand of Faith.

² If they gain ascendancy over you, they will behave towards you as enemies and stretch out their hands as well as their tongues with evil intent; they long for you to renounce your faith.*³ Neither your relatives nor your children will be of any help to you on the Day of Resurrection. He will judge between you, and God sees all that you do.

⁴ Indeed you have an excellent example in Abraham and those who followed him, when they said to their people, 'We disown you and whatever you worship besides God. We renounce you. Enmity and hatred shall endure between us and you, until you believe in the one God.' [The exception was] when Abraham said to his father, 'I shall indeed pray for [God's] forgiveness for you; although I do not have it in my power to obtain anything from God on your behalf.' They prayed, 'O our Lord, in You we have placed our trust and to You we turn in repentance and to You is the final return.

إِن يَثْقَفُوكُمْ يَكُونُواْ لَكُمْ أَعْدَآءً وَيَبْسُطُوٓاْ إِلَيْكُمْ أَيْدِيَهُمْ وَأَلْسِنَتَهُم بِٱلسُّوٓءِ وَوَدُّواْ لَوْ تَكْفُرُونَ ۝ لَن تَنفَعَكُمْ أَرْحَامُكُمْ وَلَآ أَوْلَٰدُكُمْ ۚ يَوْمَ ٱلْقِيَٰمَةِ يَفْصِلُ بَيْنَكُمْ ۚ وَٱللَّهُ بِمَا تَعْمَلُونَ بَصِيرٌ ۝ قَدْ كَانَتْ لَكُمْ أُسْوَةٌ حَسَنَةٌ فِىٓ إِبْرَٰهِيمَ وَٱلَّذِينَ مَعَهُۥٓ إِذْ قَالُواْ لِقَوْمِهِمْ إِنَّا بُرَءَٰٓؤُاْ مِنكُمْ وَمِمَّا تَعْبُدُونَ مِن دُونِ ٱللَّهِ كَفَرْنَا بِكُمْ وَبَدَا بَيْنَنَا وَبَيْنَكُمُ ٱلْعَدَٰوَةُ وَٱلْبَغْضَآءُ أَبَدًا حَتَّىٰ تُؤْمِنُواْ بِٱللَّهِ وَحْدَهُۥٓ إِلَّا قَوْلَ إِبْرَٰهِيمَ لِأَبِيهِ لَأَسْتَغْفِرَنَّ لَكَ وَمَآ أَمْلِكُ لَكَ مِنَ ٱللَّهِ مِن شَىْءٍ ۖ رَّبَّنَا عَلَيْكَ تَوَكَّلْنَا وَإِلَيْكَ أَنَبْنَا وَإِلَيْكَ ٱلْمَصِيرُ ۝

---

*ᵃ During the state of war, when the position is that Islam and non-Islam have become polarised on separate fronts, it is the responsibility of the people of Islam to sever their relations with the non-Islamic front, even if their relatives and dear ones are part of it. Being a believer in Truth and at the same time having close relations with the enemies with whom one is at war is totally wrong.

⁵ Our Lord, do not make us a prey for those who deny the truth, and forgive us our Lord. For You alone are the Mighty, the Wise One.'ᵃ
⁶ Surely, there is a good example in them for you; for those who place their hopes in God and the Last Day. Whoever turns away will surely learn that God is self-sufficient and worthy of all praise. ⁷ It may well be that God will create goodwill between you and those of them with whom you are now at enmity—for God is all powerful, most forgiving and merciful.

رَبَّنَا لَا تَجْعَلْنَا فِتْنَةً لِّلَّذِينَ كَفَرُواْ وَاغْفِرْ لَنَا رَبَّنَا ۖ إِنَّكَ أَنتَ ٱلْعَزِيزُ ٱلْحَكِيمُ ۝ لَقَدْ كَانَ لَكُمْ فِيهِمْ أُسْوَةٌ حَسَنَةٌ لِّمَن كَانَ يَرْجُواْ ٱللَّهَ وَٱلْيَوْمَ ٱلْآخِرَ ۚ وَمَن يَتَوَلَّ فَإِنَّ ٱللَّهَ هُوَ ٱلْغَنِيُّ ٱلْحَمِيدُ ۝ ۞ عَسَى ٱللَّهُ أَن يَجْعَلَ بَيْنَكُمْ وَبَيْنَ ٱلَّذِينَ عَادَيْتُم مِّنْهُم مَّوَدَّةً ۚ وَٱللَّهُ قَدِيرٌ ۚ وَٱللَّهُ غَفُورٌ رَّحِيمٌ ۝

ᵃ In the beginning, Abraham conveyed the message of the oneness of God to his family in the manner of a well-wisher. After he had carried out his mission and had come to the end of his arguments, when his hearers persisted in their rejection of the Truth, he completely separated himself from them. But this was a very difficult stage, because his stated intention to distance himself from them amounted to an invitation to the rejecters of Truth to harass the Faithful in every possible way, ultimately degrading them by the use of force to make up for their own defeat in the field of arguments. That is why Abraham subsequently offered up this special prayer, 'O, Lord! Do not make us the target of the atrocities of the oppressors.'

To absolve oneself of the responsibility for the guidance of relatives does not entail enmity in the usual sense. It is simply the final expression of firm conviction. From this point of view this action becomes imbued with a missionary value. So, sometimes it happens that a person who is not affected by the language of a 'message', is successfully won over by the language of 'faith'.

⁸ He does not forbid you to deal kindly and justly with anyone who has not fought you on account of your faith or driven you out of your homes: God loves the just. ⁹ God only forbids you to make friends with those who have fought against you on account of your faith and driven you out of your homes or helped others to do so. Any of you who turn towards them in friendship will truly be transgressors.ᵃ ¹⁰ Believers! When believing women come to you as refugees, submit them to a test. Their faith is best known to God. Then if you find them to be true believers, do not send them back to those who deny the truth. These [women] are not lawful for them, nor are those who deny the truth lawful for these women. But hand back to those who deny the truth the dowers they gave them; nor is it an offence for you to marry such women, provided you give them their dowers. Do not maintain your marriages with those women who deny the truth: demand repayment of the dowers you have given them and let the disbelievers ask for the return of what they have spent. Such is God's judgement; He judges with justice between you. God is all knowing and all wise.ᵇ

لَّا يَنْهَىٰكُمُ ٱللَّهُ عَنِ ٱلَّذِينَ لَمْ يُقَٰتِلُوكُمْ فِى ٱلدِّينِ وَلَمْ يُخْرِجُوكُم مِّن دِيَٰرِكُمْ أَن تَبَرُّوهُمْ وَتُقْسِطُوٓاْ إِلَيْهِمْ إِنَّ ٱللَّهَ يُحِبُّ ٱلْمُقْسِطِينَ ۝ إِنَّمَا يَنْهَىٰكُمُ ٱللَّهُ عَنِ ٱلَّذِينَ قَٰتَلُوكُمْ فِى ٱلدِّينِ وَأَخْرَجُوكُم مِّن دِيَٰرِكُمْ وَظَٰهَرُواْ عَلَىٰٓ إِخْرَاجِكُمْ أَن تَوَلَّوْهُمْ وَمَن يَتَوَلَّهُمْ فَأُوْلَٰٓئِكَ هُمُ ٱلظَّٰلِمُونَ ۝ يَٰٓأَيُّهَا ٱلَّذِينَ ءَامَنُوٓاْ إِذَا جَآءَكُمُ ٱلْمُؤْمِنَٰتُ مُهَٰجِرَٰتٍ فَٱمْتَحِنُوهُنَّ ٱللَّهُ أَعْلَمُ بِإِيمَٰنِهِنَّ فَإِنْ عَلِمْتُمُوهُنَّ مُؤْمِنَٰتٍ فَلَا تَرْجِعُوهُنَّ إِلَى ٱلْكُفَّارِ لَا هُنَّ حِلٌّ لَّهُمْ وَلَا هُمْ يَحِلُّونَ لَهُنَّ وَءَاتُوهُم مَّآ أَنفَقُواْ وَلَا جُنَاحَ عَلَيْكُمْ أَن تَنكِحُوهُنَّ إِذَآ ءَاتَيْتُمُوهُنَّ أُجُورَهُنَّ وَلَا تُمْسِكُواْ بِعِصَمِ ٱلْكَوَافِرِ وَسْـَٔلُواْ مَآ أَنفَقْتُمْ وَلْيَسْـَٔلُواْ مَآ أَنفَقُواْ ذَٰلِكُمْ حُكْمُ ٱللَّهِ يَحْكُمُ بَيْنَكُمْ وَٱللَّهُ عَلِيمٌ حَكِيمٌ ۝

ᵃ As far as justice and fair play are concerned, they will be given to everybody— whether friend or foe. But having friendships with those who are at war with one is not proper.

ᵇ Here, allusion is made to certain Islamic rules relating to family affairs applicable in the light of the circumstances prevailing after the execution of the Hudaybiyyah Peace Treaty.

¹¹ If any of your wives desert you to go over to the disbelievers, and you subsequently have your turn, [by the coming over of a woman from the other side] give to those who have been deserted by their wives the equivalent of the dowers they gave them. Fear God in whom you believe.

¹² O Prophet! When believing women come to you and pledge themselves not to associate in worship any other thing with God, not to steal or commit adultery or kill their children or indulge in slander, intentionally inventing falsehoods, and not to disobey you in that which is right, then accept their pledge of allegiance and pray to God to forgive them their sins, for God is forgiving and merciful.ᵃ

¹³ Believers! Do not make friends with those who have incurred the wrath of God. Such men are indeed bereft of all hope of a life to come, just as those who deny the truth lying in their graves are bereft of all hopes.ᵇ

وَإِن فَاتَكُمْ شَىْءٌ مِّنْ أَزْوَٰجِكُمْ إِلَى ٱلْكُفَّارِ فَعَاقَبْتُمْ فَـَٔاتُوا۟ ٱلَّذِينَ ذَهَبَتْ أَزْوَٰجُهُم مِّثْلَ مَآ أَنفَقُوا۟ وَٱتَّقُوا۟ ٱللَّهَ ٱلَّذِىٓ أَنتُم بِهِۦ مُؤْمِنُونَ ۝ يَـٰٓأَيُّهَا ٱلنَّبِىُّ إِذَا جَآءَكَ ٱلْمُؤْمِنَـٰتُ يُبَايِعْنَكَ عَلَىٰٓ أَن لَّا يُشْرِكْنَ بِٱللَّهِ شَيْـًٔا وَلَا يَسْرِقْنَ وَلَا يَزْنِينَ وَلَا يَقْتُلْنَ أَوْلَـٰدَهُنَّ وَلَا يَأْتِينَ بِبُهْتَـٰنٍ يَفْتَرِينَهُۥ بَيْنَ أَيْدِيهِنَّ وَأَرْجُلِهِنَّ وَلَا يَعْصِينَكَ فِى مَعْرُوفٍ فَبَايِعْهُنَّ وَٱسْتَغْفِرْ لَهُنَّ ٱللَّهَ إِنَّ ٱللَّهَ غَفُورٌ رَّحِيمٌ ۝ يَـٰٓأَيُّهَا ٱلَّذِينَ ءَامَنُوا۟ لَا تَتَوَلَّوْا۟ قَوْمًا غَضِبَ ٱللَّهُ عَلَيْهِمْ قَدْ يَئِسُوا۟ مِنَ ٱلْـَٔاخِرَةِ كَمَا يَئِسَ ٱلْكُفَّارُ مِنْ أَصْحَـٰبِ ٱلْقُبُورِ ۝

ᵃ In this verse those terms have been mentioned on which a pledge is taken from a woman and after which she is taken into the fold of Islam. Among these conditions, two conditions are of basic importance, i.e. refraining from ascribing partners to God and obedience to the Prophet. The remaining stated and un-stated requirements are automatically included in these two conditions.

ᵇ The People of the Book who accept the revealed scriptures, but who are backsliders, and those who are not believers are on the same level as far as the Hereafter is concerned. Those who deny the truth do not expect any human being to be resurrected from his grave. The same is true of those People of the Book who, after embracing Faith have become forgetful of their religious duties and suffer from insensitivity. In spite of their verbal acceptance of the Hereafter, their practical life assumes the same pattern as that of those who deny the truth.

61. RANKS

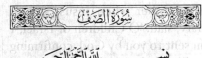

In the name of God, the Most Gracious, the Most Merciful

¹ Everything in the heavens and earth glorifies God—He is the Almighty, the Wise. ² Believers! Why do you say one thing and do another. ³ It is most hateful to God that you do not practise what you preach; ⁴ surely, God loves those who fight for His cause in ranks, as if they were a solid cemented structure.ᵃ

⁵ Remember when Moses said to his people, 'O my people, why do you cause me grief when you know that I am God's Messenger to you?' When they wavered, God let their hearts waver too. God does not guide transgressors.ᵇ

ᵃ In the universe, with the exception of the conduct of human beings, there is no inconsistency anywhere. In this world wood is always wood and anything which has the appearance of being iron or stone will be iron or stone in actual experience. Man should also be like this. There should be consistency in a man's sayings and doings, even if he is required to pay the price of facing all sorts of difficulties and has to become exceptionally patient.

ᵇ Moses came among the Children of Israel—at that time a people on the decline. They had no desire left to match their actions to their words. Their abasement was such that, on the one hand, they used to profess Faith before Moses while, on the other hand, they used to commit every sort of breach of trust and stooped to disobedience. They even used to make false allegations against Moses in order to justify the bad treatment they meted out to him. The relevant details have been set forth in the second chapter of the Bible, Exodus.

After making a pledge, man, by breaking it is taken even further away from the Truth than before.

⁶ Remember when Jesus, son of Mary, said, 'O Children of Israel, I am sent to you by God, confirming the Torah that came before me and bringing good news of a messenger to follow me, whose name will be Ahmad.' Yet when he came to them with clear signs, they said, 'This is merely sorcery.'ᵃ ⁷ Who could be more wicked than one who invents lies about God when called to submit to Him? God does not guide the wrongdoers: ⁸ they wish to put His light out with their mouths. But He will perfect His light, much as those who deny the truth may dislike it; ⁹ it is He who has sent His Messenger with guidance and the true religion, so that He may cause it to prevail over all religions, however much the polytheists may dislike it.ᵇ

وَإِذْ قَالَ عِيسَى ٱبْنُ مَرْيَمَ يَٰبَنِىٓ إِسْرَٰٓءِيلَ إِنِّى رَسُولُ ٱللَّهِ إِلَيْكُم مُّصَدِّقًا لِّمَا بَيْنَ يَدَىَّ مِنَ ٱلتَّوْرَىٰةِ وَمُبَشِّرًۢا بِرَسُولٍ يَأْتِى مِنۢ بَعْدِى ٱسْمُهُۥٓ أَحْمَدُ ۖ فَلَمَّا جَآءَهُم بِٱلْبَيِّنَٰتِ قَالُوا۟ هَٰذَا سِحْرٌ مُّبِينٌ ۝ وَمَنْ أَظْلَمُ مِمَّنِ ٱفْتَرَىٰ عَلَى ٱللَّهِ ٱلْكَذِبَ وَهُوَ يُدْعَىٰٓ إِلَى ٱلْإِسْلَٰمِ ۚ وَٱللَّهُ لَا يَهْدِى ٱلْقَوْمَ ٱلظَّٰلِمِينَ ۝ يُرِيدُونَ لِيُطْفِـُٔوا۟ نُورَ ٱللَّهِ بِأَفْوَٰهِهِمْ وَٱللَّهُ مُتِمُّ نُورِهِۦ وَلَوْ كَرِهَ ٱلْكَٰفِرُونَ ۝ هُوَ ٱلَّذِىٓ أَرْسَلَ رَسُولَهُۥ بِٱلْهُدَىٰ وَدِينِ ٱلْحَقِّ لِيُظْهِرَهُۥ عَلَى ٱلدِّينِ كُلِّهِۦ وَلَوْ كَرِهَ ٱلْمُشْرِكُونَ ۝

ᵃ The miracles of Moses, were the proof of the fact that he was the Prophet of God. But the Egyptians called them feats of magic and ignored them. Similarly, in the ancient divine scriptures there was a clear prediction made about the Prophet Muhammad. But when he actually appeared, both the Jews and Christians rejected him. Man is such a transgressor that he is not ready to accept even plain realities.

ᵇ In this verse 'He may cause it to prevail over all religions' means that in terms of intellectual supremacy, all non-monotheistic beliefs about God and religion in the world were to be demolished and monotheistic belief was to be promoted as the predominant belief. All other beliefs were to be intellectually overcome. This was a forecast made in the Quran under the most unfavourable conditions in the year 3 Hijrah. But it later turned out to be literally true.

¹⁰ Believers! Shall I guide you to a profitable course that will save you from a painful punishment? ¹¹ You should believe in God and His Messenger, and strive for God's cause with your possessions and your lives. That will be better for you, if you only knew^a—¹² and He will forgive you your sins and admit you into Gardens with rivers flowing under them. He will lodge you in fine dwellings in the Gardens of Eternity; that is indeed the supreme achievement. ¹³ He will give you another blessing which you desire: help from God and imminent victory. Give good tidings [O Muhammad] to believers!

يَـٰٓأَيُّهَا ٱلَّذِينَ ءَامَنُوا۟ هَلْ أَدُلُّكُمْ عَلَىٰ تِجَـٰرَةٍ تُنجِيكُم مِّنْ عَذَابٍ أَلِيمٍ ۝ تُؤْمِنُونَ بِٱللَّهِ وَرَسُولِهِۦ وَتُجَـٰهِدُونَ فِى سَبِيلِ ٱللَّهِ بِأَمْوَٰلِكُمْ وَأَنفُسِكُمْ ۚ ذَٰلِكُمْ خَيْرٌ لَّكُمْ إِن كُنتُمْ تَعْلَمُونَ ۝ يَغْفِرْ لَكُمْ ذُنُوبَكُمْ وَيُدْخِلْكُمْ جَنَّـٰتٍ تَجْرِى مِن تَحْتِهَا ٱلْأَنْهَـٰرُ وَمَسَـٰكِنَ طَيِّبَةً فِى جَنَّـٰتِ عَدْنٍ ۚ ذَٰلِكَ ٱلْفَوْزُ ٱلْعَظِيمُ ۝ وَأُخْرَىٰ تُحِبُّونَهَا ۖ نَصْرٌ مِّنَ ٱللَّهِ وَفَتْحٌ قَرِيبٌ ۗ وَبَشِّرِ ٱلْمُؤْمِنِينَ ۝

---

^a In trade, a man first invests and then receives a return on his investment. In the struggle for Faith also one has to invest his strength and his possessions. From this viewpoint, this is also a sort of trade. But, one receives the profit from worldly trade in this world, while in the religion-oriented trade, one receives the profit with further additions only in the Hereafter.

¹⁴ Believers, be God's helpers,^a as Jesus, son of Mary, said to the disciples, 'Who will be my helpers in the cause of God?' The disciples

يَـٰٓأَيُّهَا ٱلَّذِينَ ءَامَنُوا۟ كُونُوٓا۟ أَنصَارَ ٱللَّهِ كَمَا قَالَ عِيسَى ٱبْنُ مَرْيَمَ لِلْحَوَارِيِّـۧنَ مَنْ أَنصَارِىٓ إِلَى ٱللَّهِ قَالَ ٱلْحَوَارِيُّونَ

---

^a 'Be God's helpers' here means calling people to God (dawat ilal'lah). Since it is a task which is seen as desirable by God Himself and is performed by servants of God, it is, therefore, called 'helping God'. This is an exceptional honour which is granted only to a true believer.

The believer must of his own accord follow the commands of God relating to worship, morality and dealing justly with people. With this the believer proves his servitude and becomes eligible for God's rewards. But the case of the task of spreading God's word is different. According to the Quran, it is performed so that mankind may have no excuse or argument against God (4:165). Due to the exigency of putting man to the test, God wants this work to be given special priority. This is a divine mission which is carried out by individuals, on behalf of God, and they are, therefore, rewarded for it by God in the hereafter.

What is the meaning of helping God or being the helpers of God in this verse? It means giving oneself wholeheartedly to the divine task of preaching the truth. It means joining oneself with the divine plan whole-heartedly in both word and deed, so that mankind might have no argument against God on the Day of Judgement.

The noted commentator of the Quran, Ibn Kathir, explained that when Jesus asked his followers, 'Who will help me in the task of calling people to God?' The followers of Jesus replied, 'We are your helpers in the mission with which you have been sent forth, and we will be your helpers in this mission.' For this reason Jesus sent them to Syria to the Israelites and the Romans. In the same way the Prophet Muhammad used to go to people during the Hajj season and he would ask, 'Who among you will help me so that I may convey the message of God to people, because the Quraysh are stopping me from conveying to people the message of God?' (Tafsir ibn Kathir, vol. 4, p. 362).

The Prophet Muhammad was undoubtedly the messenger of God to the whole of humanity. Through him God conveyed His message in the form of the Quran for all eternity. But he lived in this world for a limited period of time and now the question arises as to how, after the Prophet's death, the prophetic responsibility had to be discharged. In his lifetime the Prophet performed this duty directly. After he had gone, this mission had to be carried forward indirectly by his followers, the Muslim ummah. It is incumbent upon the Prophet's followers to carry out this mission from one generation to the next and, in presenting the message of Islam to people of every age and time, bring people closer to God.

said, 'We shall be God's helpers.'
Some of the Children of Israel
believed in him and some denied the
truth; We supported the believers
against their enemies and they
triumphed over them.[a]

نَحْنُ أَنصَارُ ٱللَّهِ فَـَٔامَنَت طَّآئِفَةٌ مِّنۢ
بَنِىٓ إِسْرَٰٓءِيلَ وَكَفَرَت طَّآئِفَةٌ فَأَيَّدْنَا
ٱلَّذِينَ ءَامَنُوا۟ عَلَىٰ عَدُوِّهِمْ فَأَصْبَحُوا۟
ظَٰهِرِينَ ۝

---

[a] This issue can be further explained by a *hadith*, or saying of the Prophet, which
Ibn Hisham has quoted in his biography of the Prophet Muhammad. In this saying,
the Prophet mentions Jesus as well as himself. Ibn Hisham puts it thus on record,
'It has been narrated to me that the Prophet Muhammad came to his Companions
after the Peace Treaty of Hudaybiyyah and said, "O people, I have been sent as
a blessing for the whole of humanity. So do not differ with me in the way the
disciples of Jesus differed with him." The Companions asked, "O Prophet of God,
how did the disciples of Jesus differ with him?" The Prophet replied, "Jesus called
his disciples to the mission for which I am calling you." Those disciples whom Jesus
had asked to go to a nearby place made preparations for it. But those whom Jesus
asked to go to a distant place became unhappy and refused to go. Afterwards, Jesus
complained of this to God, so those who were not ready to go because of not
knowing the language of that area, miraculously started speaking the language of
the people to whom Jesus had asked them to go. Subsequently, the Prophet
Muhammad sent his Companions to different kings and rulers with his message.'
Ibn Ishaaq (the Prophet's earliest biographer) further writes that when the Prophet
Muhammad came to the Companions and reminded them of their duty to spread
the word of God, he said: 'God has sent me to the entire world as a blessing, so
you should carry out this responsibility on my behalf. God will show His mercy to
you.' (*Sirat ibn Hisham*, vol. 4, pp. 268-269).

There could be no greater honour under the sun than to be engaged in a mission
which is directly God's own mission. It is like working on behalf of God Almighty.
It is indeed so great an honour that no greater honour seems possible.

62. THE DAY OF CONGREGATION

In the name of God,
the Most Gracious, the Most Merciful

¹ Whatever is in the heavens and on the earth glorifies God, the Sovereign Lord, the Holy One, the Mighty, the Wise. ² It is He who has raised among the unlettered people a messenger from among themselves who recites His revelations to them, and purifies them, and teaches them the Book and wisdom, for they had formerly been clearly misguided— ³ and to others also, from among them, who have not yet joined them. He is the Mighty, the Wise One. ⁴ That is God's grace; He bestows it on whom He pleases; for God is limitless in His grace.ᵃ

يُسَبِّحُ لِلَّهِ مَا فِى ٱلسَّمَـٰوَٰتِ وَمَا فِى ٱلْأَرْضِ ٱلْمَلِكِ ٱلْقُدُّوسِ ٱلْعَزِيزِ ٱلْحَكِيمِ ۝ هُوَ ٱلَّذِى بَعَثَ فِى ٱلْأُمِّيِّـۧنَ رَسُولًا مِّنْهُمْ يَتْلُواْ عَلَيْهِمْ ءَايَـٰتِهِۦ وَيُزَكِّيهِمْ وَيُعَلِّمُهُمُ ٱلْكِتَـٰبَ وَٱلْحِكْمَةَ وَإِن كَانُواْ مِن قَبْلُ لَفِى ضَلَـٰلٍ مُّبِينٍ ۝ وَءَاخَرِينَ مِنْهُمْ لَمَّا يَلْحَقُواْ بِهِمْ وَهُوَ ٱلْعَزِيزُ ٱلْحَكِيمُ ۝ ذَٰلِكَ فَضْلُ ٱللَّهِ يُؤْتِيهِ مَن يَشَآءُ وَٱللَّهُ ذُو ٱلْفَضْلِ ٱلْعَظِيمِ ۝

ᵃ To send the prophets for the guidance of human beings is the expression of the same attributes of God at the level of humanity as those expressed in relation to material things at the level of the universe. The task of the Prophet Muhammad and other prophets was twofold—first, to convey the message of God to the people and, second, to awaken the consciousness of the people, so that they might understand godly matters and connect them with their real life. In future also, the work relating to *dawah* (the call for Truth) and reform will be twofold, i.e. the teaching of the Quran and intellectual and spiritual development.

5 Those who were charged with bearing the Torah, but did not do so are like an ass carrying a load of books. How unfortunate are those who belie the sign of God. God does not guide the wrongdoers. 6 Say, 'You who are Jews, if you claim that you are favoured by God out of all people, then long for death, if you are truthful.' 7 They will never wish for it, because of what their hands have sent forward. God has full knowledge of evil-doers. 8 So say, 'The death you run away from will certainly meet you, and thereafter you will be brought back to the Knower of the unseen and the seen, and He will declare to you what you have done.' *a*

مَثَلُ ٱلَّذِينَ حُمِّلُوا۟ ٱلتَّوْرَىٰةَ ثُمَّ لَمْ يَحْمِلُوهَا كَمَثَلِ ٱلْحِمَارِ يَحْمِلُ أَسْفَارًا ۚ بِئْسَ مَثَلُ ٱلْقَوْمِ ٱلَّذِينَ كَذَّبُوا۟ بِـَٔايَٰتِ ٱللَّهِ ۚ وَٱللَّهُ لَا يَهْدِى ٱلْقَوْمَ ٱلظَّٰلِمِينَ ۞ قُلْ يَٰٓأَيُّهَا ٱلَّذِينَ هَادُوٓا۟ إِن زَعَمْتُمْ أَنَّكُمْ أَوْلِيَآءُ لِلَّهِ مِن دُونِ ٱلنَّاسِ فَتَمَنَّوُا۟ ٱلْمَوْتَ إِن كُنتُمْ صَٰدِقِينَ ۞ وَلَا يَتَمَنَّوْنَهُۥٓ أَبَدًۢا بِمَا قَدَّمَتْ أَيْدِيهِمْ ۚ وَٱللَّهُ عَلِيمٌۢ بِٱلظَّٰلِمِينَ ۞ قُلْ إِنَّ ٱلْمَوْتَ ٱلَّذِى تَفِرُّونَ مِنْهُ فَإِنَّهُۥ مُلَٰقِيكُمْ ۖ ثُمَّ تُرَدُّونَ إِلَىٰ عَٰلِمِ ٱلْغَيْبِ وَٱلشَّهَٰدَةِ فَيُنَبِّئُكُم بِمَا كُنتُمْ تَعْمَلُونَ ۞

---

a When a book of God is given to a community, it is given for the purpose of its being followed. But a community which does not become the bearer of the book in that sense is like a donkey on which academic books are loaded without its being aware of what they are.

The Jews did not follow the teachings of their religion, but they had made it a sign of pride for themselves. But this sort of pride is not going to be of any use to anybody. Such pride is always false pride, and the proof of this is that no proud person is ready to make sacrifices for the religion which he had made a matter of pride. However, when death overtakes such people, they will come to know that the pride on which they were living in the world will bring them nothing but dishonour in the Hereafter.

⁹ Believers! When the call to prayer is made on the day of congregation, hasten to the remembrance of God, and leave all worldly commerce: this is for your own good, if you but knew it. ¹⁰ When the prayer is ended, disperse in the land and seek to obtain [something] of God's bounty; and remember God much, so that you may prosper. ¹¹ Yet when they see some merchandise or entertainment, they break away to go to it and leave you standing. Say, 'That which God has in store is far better than any merchandise or entertainment.' God is the most munificent Giver.ᵃ

يَـٰٓأَيُّهَا ٱلَّذِينَ ءَامَنُوٓاْ إِذَا نُودِيَ لِلصَّلَوٰةِ مِن يَوْمِ ٱلْجُمُعَةِ فَٱسْعَوْاْ إِلَىٰ ذِكْرِ ٱللَّهِ وَذَرُواْ ٱلْبَيْعَ ذَٰلِكُمْ خَيْرٌ لَّكُمْ إِن كُنتُمْ تَعْلَمُونَ ۝ فَإِذَا قُضِيَتِ ٱلصَّلَوٰةُ فَٱنتَشِرُواْ فِى ٱلْأَرْضِ وَٱبْتَغُواْ مِن فَضْلِ ٱللَّهِ وَٱذْكُرُواْ ٱللَّهَ كَثِيرًا لَّعَلَّكُمْ تُفْلِحُونَ ۝ وَإِذَا رَأَوْاْ تِجَٰرَةً أَوْ لَهْوًا ٱنفَضُّوٓاْ إِلَيْهَا وَتَرَكُوكَ قَآئِمًا قُلْ مَا عِندَ ٱللَّهِ خَيْرٌ مِّنَ ٱللَّهْوِ وَمِنَ ٱلتِّجَٰرَةِ وَٱللَّهُ خَيْرُ ٱلرَّٰزِقِينَ ۝

ᵃ In this world man is pulled in two different directions, firstly, by the force of economic considerations, and secondly, by the demands of religion. Each of these two considerations is ineluctable. But the divide between the two should be such that economic activities should be subordinate to the call of religion. A man is permitted to strive for economic betterment within legitimate limits. But it is essential that whatever economic success he achieves should be considered as a gift from God. Furthermore, in the course of earning his livelihood he should constantly go on remembering God. Similarly, whenever he is called upon to carry out some religious task, he should be ready to respond immediately, leaving aside all other work.

Once in Madinah, during the sermon of the Friday prayers, some people left the mosque and went to the market. These verses were revealed in that connection. These injunctions are directly in connection with the Friday prayers but, indirectly, they apply to every religious task. Whenever people have been called upon and are assembled for some special religious purpose, it will be highly inappropriate to leave the place without the permission of the Imam (leader of the gathering).

63. THE HYPOCRITES

In the name of God,
the Most Gracious, the Most Merciful

¹ When the hypocrites come to you, they say, 'We bear witness that you are indeed the Messenger of God.' God knows that you are indeed His Messenger, but God bears witness that the hypocrites are surely liars[a]— ² they use their oaths as a cover and thus they bar others from God's way: what they have been doing is truly evil—³ that is because they believed and then rejected their faith: their hearts are sealed up, so that they are devoid of understanding.[b]

إِذَا جَآءَكَ ٱلْمُنَـٰفِقُونَ قَالُوا۟ نَشْهَدُ إِنَّكَ لَرَسُولُ ٱللَّهِ ۗ وَٱللَّهُ يَعْلَمُ إِنَّكَ لَرَسُولُهُۥ وَٱللَّهُ يَشْهَدُ إِنَّ ٱلْمُنَـٰفِقِينَ لَكَـٰذِبُونَ ﴿١﴾ ٱتَّخَذُوٓا۟ أَيْمَـٰنَهُمْ جُنَّةً فَصَدُّوا۟ عَن سَبِيلِ ٱللَّهِ ۚ إِنَّهُمْ سَآءَ مَا كَانُوا۟ يَعْمَلُونَ ﴿٢﴾ ذَٰلِكَ بِأَنَّهُمْ ءَامَنُوا۟ ثُمَّ كَفَرُوا۟ فَطُبِعَ عَلَىٰ قُلُوبِهِمْ فَهُمْ لَا يَفْقَهُونَ ﴿٣﴾

---

[a] It is a sign of hypocrisy in an individual if he indulges in tall talk and resorts to swearing oaths to reassure others of the truth of his words. A sincere man is subdued out of fear of God. He speaks more from his heart than from his tongue. A hypocrite is eager for men to hear his voice, while a sincere man is eager for God to hear his voice.

[b] When a man embraces the faith, he makes a sincere vow. Thereafter, different practical occasions arise in life when he is required to act according to his vow. Now, one who, on such occasions, hears the voice of his heart and fulfils the requirements of his vow, has in effect revived and confirmed his vow of faith. On the contrary, one who hears his inner voice, ignores it and acts in breach of his vow, will gradually become less and less conscious of his vow and will eventually become completely insensitive about his vow of faith. This, in fact, is the meaning of 'their hearts are sealed up'.

⁴ When you see them, their outward appearance pleases you; when they speak, you listen to what they say. But they are like propped up blocks of timber. They think that every shout is directed against them. They are the [real] enemies, so beware of them. The curse of God be upon them! How they turn away! ⁵ When they are told, 'Come! The Messenger of God will ask forgiveness for you!' they turn their heads away and you see them walking away arrogantly. ⁶ It makes no difference whether you ask forgiveness for them or not. God will not forgive them: God does not guide such rebellious people.ᵃ

۞ وَإِذَا رَأَيْتَهُمْ تُعْجِبُكَ أَجْسَامُهُمْ وَإِن يَقُولُوا۟ تَسْمَعْ لِقَوْلِهِمْ ۖ كَأَنَّهُمْ خُشُبٌ مُّسَنَّدَةٌ ۖ يَحْسَبُونَ كُلَّ صَيْحَةٍ عَلَيْهِمْ ۚ هُمُ ٱلْعَدُوُّ فَٱحْذَرْهُمْ ۚ قَٰتَلَهُمُ ٱللَّهُ ۖ أَنَّىٰ يُؤْفَكُونَ ۝ وَإِذَا قِيلَ لَهُمْ تَعَالَوْا۟ يَسْتَغْفِرْ لَكُمْ رَسُولُ ٱللَّهِ لَوَّوْا۟ رُءُوسَهُمْ وَرَأَيْتَهُمْ يَصُدُّونَ وَهُم مُّسْتَكْبِرُونَ ۝ سَوَآءٌ عَلَيْهِمْ أَسْتَغْفَرْتَ لَهُمْ أَمْ لَمْ تَسْتَغْفِرْ لَهُمْ لَن يَغْفِرَ ٱللَّهُ لَهُمْ ۚ إِنَّ ٱللَّهَ لَا يَهْدِى ٱلْقَوْمَ ٱلْفَٰسِقِينَ ۝

ᵃ A hypocrite protects his interests by his compromising and self-interested approach. He does not involve himself in considerations of right or wrong. However, he maintains good relations with everybody, and when he speaks, he dwells upon the interests of his hearers. Therefore, everybody finds something agreeable in his conversation. But these apparently 'fresh green trees' consist in reality of 'dry sticks.' In the hypocrite's eyes, worldly interest is much more important than any religious interest. Such people, in spite of being vociferous claimants of Faith, are totally deprived of God's guidance.

7 They are the ones who say, 'Give nothing to those who follow God's Messenger, until they abandon him;' but the treasures of the heavens and the earth belong to God, though the hypocrites do not understand this 8 [and] they say, 'Indeed, when we return to Madinah, [we] the ones most worthy of honour, will surely drive out from there the contemptible ones!' [referring to poor Muslims]. However, all honour belongs to God, and to His Messenger and those who believe [in God]: but of this the hypocrites are not aware.[a]

هُمُ ٱلَّذِينَ يَقُولُونَ لَا تُنفِقُوا۟ عَلَىٰ مَنْ عِندَ رَسُولِ ٱللَّهِ حَتَّىٰ يَنفَضُّوا۟ ۗ وَلِلَّهِ خَزَآئِنُ ٱلسَّمَٰوَٰتِ وَٱلْأَرْضِ وَلَٰكِنَّ ٱلْمُنَٰفِقِينَ لَا يَفْقَهُونَ ۝ يَقُولُونَ لَئِن رَّجَعْنَآ إِلَى ٱلْمَدِينَةِ لَيُخْرِجَنَّ ٱلْأَعَزُّ مِنْهَا ٱلْأَذَلَّ ۚ وَلِلَّهِ ٱلْعِزَّةُ وَلِرَسُولِهِۦ وَلِلْمُؤْمِنِينَ وَلَٰكِنَّ ٱلْمُنَٰفِقِينَ لَا يَعْلَمُونَ ۝

---

[a] In old Madinah, there were two groups of Muslims—one, the Migrants (*al-Muhajrun*) and the other, the Helpers (*al-Ansar*)—the local hosts at Madinah. The Migrants had come to Madinah on being displaced from their native place, Makkah. Their best apparent supports were the local Muslims of Madinah, the Helpers. In the eyes of world-loving people, the Migrants seemed, therefore, to be people without honour in comparison with the Helpers who were respectable people. This was felt so keenly that on one occasion, 'Abdullah ibn Ubayy clearly stated, 'What is the status of these Migrants? If we expel them from our place, they will not find refuge anywhere in the world.'

Such words are uttered by those who are unaware of the reality that, whatever is there in this world, belongs to God. He gives to whomever He wishes and takes away from whomever He wishes.

⁹ O believers! Do not let your wealth or your children distract you from remembrance of God. Those who do so will be the losers. ¹⁰ And spend out of what We have provided you with before death comes to one of you and he says, 'My Lord! If only You would grant me respite for a little while, then I would give alms and be among the righteous.' ¹¹ But God will not grant a reprieve to a soul when its appointed time has come; God is well-aware of what you do.ᵃ

يَـٰٓأَيُّهَا ٱلَّذِينَ ءَامَنُوا۟ لَا تُلْهِكُمْ أَمْوَٰلُكُمْ وَلَآ أَوْلَـٰدُكُمْ عَن ذِكْرِ ٱللَّهِ ۚ وَمَن يَفْعَلْ ذَٰلِكَ فَأُو۟لَـٰٓئِكَ هُمُ ٱلْخَـٰسِرُونَ ۝ وَأَنفِقُوا۟ مِن مَّا رَزَقْنَـٰكُم مِّن قَبْلِ أَن يَأْتِىَ أَحَدَكُمُ ٱلْمَوْتُ فَيَقُولَ رَبِّ لَوْلَآ أَخَّرْتَنِىٓ إِلَىٰٓ أَجَلٍ قَرِيبٍ فَأَصَّدَّقَ وَأَكُن مِّنَ ٱلصَّـٰلِحِينَ ۝ وَلَن يُؤَخِّرَ ٱللَّهُ نَفْسًا إِذَا جَآءَ أَجَلُهَا ۚ وَٱللَّهُ خَبِيرٌۢ بِمَا تَعْمَلُونَ ۝

ᵃ The biggest problem for a man is the inevitability of the Hereafter. But the consideration of riches and children make a man unmindful of it. Man should know that riches and children are not the final goal but the blessings which are given to him so that he may utilise them for God's work. He should therefore use them to improve his life in the Hereafter. But man, in his stupidity, takes them to be his goal. When such people come face to face with their eventual final fate, they will experience only frustration and regret.

64. LOSS AND GAIN

In the name of God,
the Most Gracious, the Most Merciful

¹ All that is in the heavens and on the earth extols the glory of God.ᵃ To Him belongs the Kingdom and to Him all praise is due. He has power over all things. ² It was He who created you; and some of you are those who deny this truth, and some who believe [in it]. God sees everything you do. ³ He created the heavens and the earth for a purpose. He formed you and gave you the best of forms. To Him you shall all return. ⁴ He knows whatever is in the heavens and the earth. He knows all that you conceal and all that you reveal. God is aware of what is in your hearts.ᵇ

ᵃ This means that the universe is singing the praises of God; that the reality which is revealed in the Quran, is testified to by the entire universe. In its silent language, it confirms this to the extent of singing praises. Notwithstanding this two-fold declaration those who do not become believers, shall have to wait for the third announcement, when people will be gathered before God, so that they may hear the decision about themselves directly from the Lord of Universe.

5 Have you not heard about those who denied the truth before you and tasted the evil consequences of their conduct? They will have a painful punishment.[a] 6 That was because their messengers came to them with clear signs, but they replied, 'Shall mortals be our guides?' And so they rejected the truth and turned away. God has no need of such people; God is self-sufficient and worthy of all praise.

7 Those who deny the truth claim that they will never be raised up again. Say, 'By my Lord, most surely you will be raised up again and then you will be told of all that you have done; and that is easy enough for God.' 8 Believe then in God and His Messenger, and in the light[b] which We have sent down. God is fully aware of all that you do.

أَلَمْ يَأْتِكُمْ نَبَؤُاْ ٱلَّذِينَ كَفَرُواْ مِن قَبْلُ فَذَاقُواْ وَبَالَ أَمْرِهِمْ وَلَهُمْ عَذَابٌ أَلِيمٌ ۝ ذَٰلِكَ بِأَنَّهُۥ كَانَت تَّأْتِيهِمْ رُسُلُهُم بِٱلْبَيِّنَٰتِ فَقَالُوٓاْ أَبَشَرٌ يَهْدُونَنَا فَكَفَرُواْ وَتَوَلَّواْ وَّٱسْتَغْنَى ٱللَّهُ وَٱللَّهُ غَنِيٌّ حَمِيدٌ ۝ زَعَمَ ٱلَّذِينَ كَفَرُوٓاْ أَن لَّن يُبْعَثُواْ قُلْ بَلَىٰ وَرَبِّى لَتُبْعَثُنَّ ثُمَّ لَتُنَبَّؤُنَّ بِمَا عَمِلْتُمْ وَذَٰلِكَ عَلَى ٱللَّهِ يَسِيرٌ ۝ فَـَٔامِنُواْ بِٱللَّهِ وَرَسُولِهِۦ وَٱلنُّورِ ٱلَّذِىٓ أَنزَلْنَا وَٱللَّهُ بِمَا تَعْمَلُونَ خَبِيرٌ ۝

---

[a] The history made by the prophets in ancient times is an eternal source of admonition. For example, prophets appeared among the 'Ad, the Thamud, the people of Madyan, and the community of Lot. These prophets did not possess any supernatural powers to prove their veracity. They had only reasoning in their favour. Rejection of the Truth in spite of its being backed by reasoning made the doubters liable for punishment. This shows that in this world a man is tested by his ability to recognise the Truth on the basis of reasoning. One who fails to do so will always remain deprived of the Truth.

[b] The Quran.

⁹ When He shall gather you all for
the Day of Gathering, that will be
the Day of loss and gain;ᵃ and
whoever believes in God and does
good deeds shall be forgiven their
sins and admitted to Gardens
through which rivers flow, where
they shall dwell forever. That is the
supreme triumph. ¹⁰ But those who
denied the truth and rejected Our
signs shall be the inmates of the Fire,
there to remain—what an evil
destination!

¹¹ No affliction can befall man but by
God's permissionᵇ—He guides the
hearts of those who believe in Him:
God has knowledge of all things—
¹² obey God and obey the Messenger;
but if you turn away, remember that
Our Messenger is only responsible
for clearly conveying the message.
¹³ God! There is no god but He, so
let the faithful put their trust in
Him.

يَوْمَ تَجْمَعُكُمْ لِيَوْمِ ٱلْجَمْعِ ذَٰلِكَ يَوْمُ
ٱلتَّغَابُنِ وَمَن يُؤْمِنۢ بِٱللَّهِ وَيَعْمَلْ
صَٰلِحًا يُكَفِّرْ عَنْهُ سَيِّـَٔاتِهِ وَيُدْخِلْهُ
جَنَّٰتٍ تَجْرِى مِن تَحْتِهَا ٱلْأَنْهَٰرُ
خَٰلِدِينَ فِيهَآ أَبَدًا ذَٰلِكَ ٱلْفَوْزُ
ٱلْعَظِيمُ ۝ وَٱلَّذِينَ كَفَرُواْ
وَكَذَّبُواْ بِـَٔايَٰتِنَآ أُوْلَٰٓئِكَ أَصْحَٰبُ
ٱلنَّارِ خَٰلِدِينَ فِيهَا وَبِئْسَ ٱلْمَصِيرُ ۝
مَآ أَصَابَ مِن مُّصِيبَةٍ إِلَّا بِإِذْنِ ٱللَّهِ
وَمَن يُؤْمِنۢ بِٱللَّهِ يَهْدِ قَلْبَهُۥ وَٱللَّهُ بِكُلِّ
شَىْءٍ عَلِيمٌ ۝ وَأَطِيعُواْ ٱللَّهَ وَأَطِيعُواْ
ٱلرَّسُولَ فَإِن تَوَلَّيْتُمْ فَإِنَّمَا عَلَىٰ
رَسُولِنَا ٱلْبَلَٰغُ ٱلْمُبِينُ ۝ ٱللَّهُ لَآ إِلَٰهَ
إِلَّا هُوَ وَعَلَى ٱللَّهِ فَلْيَتَوَكَّلِ
ٱلْمُؤْمِنُونَ ۝

ᵃ People take the world to be a place of winning or losing (taghabun). One who is
successful here becomes very happy, but one who meets with failure is looked upon
with contempt. In this world, however, success is as valueless as failure is.

The place of true success or failure is the Hereafter. One is a failure if he fails in
the Hereafter and successful if he is successful in the Hereafter, and the criterion
of success or failure there is entirely different from that of this world, where it is
based on outward materialism: success or failure in the Hereafter will be on the
basis of Divine moral values. At that time, people will be surprised to see that the
whole complexion of things has completely changed. Gaining, which was considered
as such will actually turn out to be losing, while what was considered as losing will
turn out to be gaining in the real sense. Failure on that Day is real failure and success
on that Day will be real success.

ᵇ No trouble arrives of its own accord. Every tribulation comes from God, and it
afflicts man so that, through it, he should receive guidance. Trouble softens a man's
heart and jolts him out of his moral slumber. Trouble prods and sharpens a man's
mind. If he refrains from negative reaction, then trouble will become the best
Divine instruction for him.

14 Believers! [Even] among your wives and your children you have enemies: so beware of them.*a* But if you overlook their offences and forgive and pardon them, then surely, God is most forgiving and merciful. 15 Your wealth and your children are only a trial; God's reward is great: 16 so be mindful of God as best as you can; and listen, and obey; and spend in charity: it is for your own good. Those who guard themselves against their own greed will surely prosper: 17 if you give a good loan to God, He will multiply it for you and forgive you, for God is appreciative and forbearing; 18 God is the Knower of the unseen and the seen: He is the Almighty, the Wise One.

يَـٰٓأَيُّهَا ٱلَّذِينَ ءَامَنُوٓاْ إِنَّ مِنْ أَزْوَٰجِكُمْ وَأَوْلَـٰدِكُمْ عَدُوًّا لَّكُمْ فَٱحْذَرُوهُمْ ۚ وَإِن تَعْفُواْ وَتَصْفَحُواْ وَتَغْفِرُواْ فَإِنَّ ٱللَّهَ غَفُورٌ رَّحِيمٌ ﴿١٤﴾ إِنَّمَآ أَمْوَٰلُكُمْ وَأَوْلَـٰدُكُمْ فِتْنَةٌ ۚ وَٱللَّهُ عِندَهُۥٓ أَجْرٌ عَظِيمٌ ﴿١٥﴾ فَٱتَّقُواْ ٱللَّهَ مَا ٱسْتَطَعْتُمْ وَٱسْمَعُواْ وَأَطِيعُواْ وَأَنفِقُواْ خَيْرًا لِّأَنفُسِكُمْ ۗ وَمَن يُوقَ شُحَّ نَفْسِهِۦ فَأُوْلَـٰٓئِكَ هُمُ ٱلْمُفْلِحُونَ ﴿١٦﴾ إِن تُقْرِضُواْ ٱللَّهَ قَرْضًا حَسَنًا يُضَـٰعِفْهُ لَكُمْ وَيَغْفِرْ لَكُمْ ۚ وَٱللَّهُ شَكُورٌ حَلِيمٌ ﴿١٧﴾ عَـٰلِمُ ٱلْغَيْبِ وَٱلشَّهَـٰدَةِ ٱلْعَزِيزُ ٱلْحَكِيمُ ﴿١٨﴾

---

a Man has the utmost attachment for his children. He may talk of principles on every other subject, but where his children are concerned, he becomes unprincipled. That is why it is mentioned in a tradition of the Prophet Muhammad that children cause their parents to be timid and miserly. In another tradition it is mentioned that on the Day of Judgement a man will be brought before God, and it will be said of him that his wife and children ate away all his virtues.

Man, for the sake of his children, does not spend for the divine cause, though the truth is that if he spends for the sake of God, he will be recompensed by Him many times over.

65. DIVORCE

In the name of God,
the Most Gracious, the Most Merciful

¹O Prophet! When any of you divorce your wives, divorce them during their period of purity and calculate the period carefully: be mindful of God, your Lord. Do not drive them out of their homes—nor should they themselves leave—unless they become openly guilty of immoral conduct. These are the bounds set by God. He who transgresses God's bounds wrongs his own soul. You never know, after that, God may well bring about some new situation. ²And when their waiting term is ended, either keep them honourably or part with them in honour. Call to witness two reliable men from among you and bear true witness for God. This is an admonishment for those who believe in God and the Last Day. To one who fears God, He will grant a way out [of his difficulties], ³and God will provide for him from an unexpected source; God suffices for anyone who puts his trust in Him. God will surely bring about what He decrees. He has set a measure for all things.^a

---

^a Divorce is permitted in Islam in exceptional situations and a procedure has been prescribed for it which must be completed within a specific period. In this way the process of divorce has been subjected to certain conditions. The purpose of these limitations is that, till the last moment, the parties should have the opportunity for rapprochement, and the divorce should not create any disturbance in the family or society. Divorce is endorsed by Islam provided that, during the process, a God-fearing spirit is prevalent throughout.

⁴ In the case of those of your wives who have passed the age of menstruation, if you have any doubt, know that their waiting period is three months; and that will apply likewise to those who have not yet menstruated; the waiting period of those who are pregnant will be until they deliver their burden [give birth]. God makes things easy for those who are mindful of Him. ⁵ Such is the commandment which God has revealed to you. He who fears God shall be forgiven his sins and richly rewarded.ᵃ

وَٱلَّـٰٓئِى يَئِسۡنَ مِنَ ٱلۡمَحِيضِ مِن نِّسَآئِكُمۡ إِنِ ٱرۡتَبۡتُمۡ فَعِدَّتُهُنَّ ثَلَـٰثَةُ أَشۡهُرٍ وَٱلَّـٰٓئِى لَمۡ يَحِضۡنَ ۚ وَأُوْلَـٰتُ ٱلۡأَحۡمَالِ أَجَلُهُنَّ أَن يَضَعۡنَ حَمۡلَهُنَّ ۚ وَمَن يَتَّقِ ٱللَّهَ يَجۡعَل لَّهُۥ مِنۡ أَمۡرِهِۦ يُسۡرًا ۞ ذَٰلِكَ أَمۡرُ ٱللَّهِ أَنزَلَهُۥٓ إِلَيۡكُمۡ ۚ وَمَن يَتَّقِ ٱللَّهَ يُكَفِّرۡ عَنۡهُ سَيِّـَٔاتِهِۦ وَيُعۡظِمۡ لَهُۥٓ أَجۡرًا ۞

ᵃ The Shariah has subjected man to some regulations in respect of divorce and other matters. These regulations are apparently restrictive of man's free nature. But, in reality, these are blessings. The advantage of these regulations is that man is saved from many unnecessary and avoidable harms. Furthermore, the system of this world is so framed that every harm is compensated for in some way or the other. However, such compensation is available only to individuals who do not go beyond the sphere of nature.

⁶ Let the women [who are undergoing a waiting period] live in the same manner as you live yourselves, in accordance with your means; and do not harass them in order to make their lives difficult. If they are pregnant, maintain them until they give birth; if they suckle your infants, pay them for it; discuss things among yourselves in all decency—if you cannot bear with each other, let another woman suckle for you—⁷ let the man of means spend in accordance with his means; and let him whose resources are restricted, spend in accordance with what God has given him. God does not burden any person with more than He has given him. God will soon bring about ease after hardship.ª

أَسْكِنُوهُنَّ مِنْ حَيْثُ سَكَنتُم مِّن وُجْدِكُمْ وَلَا تُضَآرُّوهُنَّ لِتُضَيِّقُوا۟ عَلَيْهِنَّ ۚ وَإِن كُنَّ أُو۟لَٰتِ حَمْلٍ فَأَنفِقُوا۟ عَلَيْهِنَّ حَتَّىٰ يَضَعْنَ حَمْلَهُنَّ ۚ فَإِنْ أَرْضَعْنَ لَكُمْ فَـَٔاتُوهُنَّ أُجُورَهُنَّ ۖ وَأْتَمِرُوا۟ بَيْنَكُم بِمَعْرُوفٍ ۖ وَإِن تَعَاسَرْتُمْ فَسَتُرْضِعُ لَهُۥٓ أُخْرَىٰ ۝ لِيُنفِقْ ذُو سَعَةٍ مِّن سَعَتِهِۦ ۖ وَمَن قُدِرَ عَلَيْهِ رِزْقُهُۥ فَلْيُنفِقْ مِمَّآ ءَاتَىٰهُ ٱللَّهُ ۚ لَا يُكَلِّفُ ٱللَّهُ نَفْسًا إِلَّا مَآ ءَاتَىٰهَا ۚ سَيَجْعَلُ ٱللَّهُ بَعْدَ عُسْرٍ يُسْرًا ۝

ª Islam requires the individual to adopt the way of broad-mindedness and open-heartedness towards others, even at times of such difficult decisions as divorce. He should patiently tolerate such behaviour in others as goes against his nature and discharge his duties towards them in spite of unpleasantness on their part. When a man acts in this way, he does good not only to the other party but also to himself. In this way he creates a realistic nature within himself. And a realistic temperament is undoubtedly the most important factor in achieving success in this world.

8 How many a town rebelled against the commands of its Lord and His messengers and We called them sternly to account and punished them severely, 9 so they tasted the evil consequences of their conduct and the result of their conduct was ruin. 10 God has prepared a severe punishment for them. So, fear God, O men of understanding,[a] who have believed. God has sent down to you a Reminder 11 and a messenger who conveys to you God's clear messages, so that he might lead those, who believe and do good deeds, out of darkness into light. God will admit those who believe in Him and do good deeds into Gardens with rivers flowing through them, where they will remain forever. God has indeed made excellent provision for them.[b]

وَكَأَيِّن مِّن قَرْيَةٍ عَتَتْ عَنْ أَمْرِ رَبِّهَا وَرُسُلِهِۦ فَحَاسَبْنَٰهَا حِسَابًا شَدِيدًا وَعَذَّبْنَٰهَا عَذَابًا نُّكْرًا ۝ فَذَاقَتْ وَبَالَ أَمْرِهَا وَكَانَ عَٰقِبَةُ أَمْرِهَا خُسْرًا ۝ أَعَدَّ ٱللَّهُ لَهُمْ عَذَابًا شَدِيدًا فَٱتَّقُوا۟ ٱللَّهَ يَٰٓأُو۟لِى ٱلْأَلْبَٰبِ ٱلَّذِينَ ءَامَنُوا۟ قَدْ أَنزَلَ ٱللَّهُ إِلَيْكُمْ ذِكْرًا ۝ رَّسُولًا يَتْلُوا۟ عَلَيْكُمْ ءَايَٰتِ ٱللَّهِ مُبَيِّنَٰتٍ لِّيُخْرِجَ ٱلَّذِينَ ءَامَنُوا۟ وَعَمِلُوا۟ ٱلصَّٰلِحَٰتِ مِنَ ٱلظُّلُمَٰتِ إِلَى ٱلنُّورِ وَمَن يُؤْمِنۢ بِٱللَّهِ وَيَعْمَلْ صَٰلِحًا يُدْخِلْهُ جَنَّٰتٍ تَجْرِى مِن تَحْتِهَا ٱلْأَنْهَٰرُ خَٰلِدِينَ فِيهَآ أَبَدًا قَدْ أَحْسَنَ ٱللَّهُ لَهُۥ رِزْقًا ۝

---

a 'So, fear God, O men of understanding.' This statement indicates that the fountainhead of piety (taqwa) is the mind. Only by using his wisdom and consciousness does a man achieve that status which is called (taqwa) in the Islamic law.

b God sent His messenger 'so that he might lead those, who have attained to faith and do good deeds, out of darkness into light.' This statement at this juncture relates to family laws. In ancient times, superstition prevailed throughout the world. Different types of superstitious beliefs had caused the relations between man and woman to rest on an unnatural basis. The Quran banished these superstitions, and re-established the relations between men and women on a natural basis. Despite this, there are people who do not adopt the way of reform, and who can, therefore, expect nothing but loss on God's earth.

¹² It is God who created the seven heavens and the same number of earths.^a His commandment descends among them, so that you may know that God has power over all things; and that He encompasses all things with His knowledge.^b

اللَّهُ الَّذِى خَلَقَ سَبْعَ سَمَوَتٍ وَمِنَ الْأَرْضِ مِثْلَهُنَّ يَتَنَزَّلُ الْأَمْرُ بَيْنَهُنَّ لِتَعْلَمُوٓاْ أَنَّ اللَّهَ عَلَىٰ كُلِّ شَىْءٍ قَدِيرٌ وَأَنَّ اللَّهَ قَدْ أَحَاطَ بِكُلِّ شَىْءٍ عِلْمًا

---

^a 'It is God who created the seven heavens and the same number of earths'. This statement may refer to seven earths, but astronomy has not been able to discover this number. According to human knowledge (till the date of this writing) the present earth is an exception in this whole universe. Therefore, God knows the real meaning of this verse.

^b 'So that you may know that God has power over all things'. This indicates that what God truly requires of man is 'knowledge' i.e. the consciousness of God's Being. This vast system of the universe has been brought into being in order to make man recognise the Creator through it and have a deep and inner realisation of God's immense Power.

66. PROHIBITION

In the name of God,
the Most Gracious, the Most Merciful

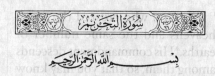

¹ Prophet, why in your desire to please your wives, do you impose a ban on what God has made lawful to you? God is forgiving and merciful. ² God has already ordained that you be absolved of such oaths. God is your patron. He is the All Knowing, the Wise One.ᵃ

ᵃ Due to some domestic problems created by his wives, the Prophet vowed that he would not take honey. But, a prophet's actions become examples for his followers. Therefore, God commanded the Prophet to pay expiation, the penalty prescribed by the Islamic law, and free himself from the his vow not to take honey, so that in future, his followers should not take it as a symbol of piety and stop taking honey.

³ The Prophet once told one of his wives something in confidence. She did not keep it secret and God informed him of this; he made known a part of it, and avoided [mentioning] part of it. When he spoke to his wife of this, she asked him who had told him about it. He replied, 'The All Knowing, the All Aware One.' ⁴ If only both of you would turn to God in repentance—and your hearts are already so inclined. But if you uphold each other against him, then surely God is his protector, and Gabriel and the righteous among the believers; and the angels too are his helpers. ⁵ Were he to divorce you, his Lord might well replace you with better wives—submissive [to God], believing, pious, penitent, devout in worship, given to fasting—previously married and virgins.ᵃ

وَإِذْ أَسَرَّ ٱلنَّبِيُّ إِلَىٰ بَعْضِ أَزْوَٰجِهِ حَدِيثًا فَلَمَّا نَبَّأَتْ بِهِۦ وَأَظْهَرَهُ ٱللَّهُ عَلَيْهِ عَرَّفَ بَعْضَهُۥ وَأَعْرَضَ عَن بَعْضٍ فَلَمَّا نَبَّأَهَا بِهِۦ قَالَتْ مَنْ أَنۢبَأَكَ هَـٰذَا قَالَ نَبَّأَنِيَ ٱلْعَلِيمُ ٱلْخَبِيرُ ۝ إِن تَتُوبَآ إِلَى ٱللَّهِ فَقَدْ صَغَتْ قُلُوبُكُمَا وَإِن تَظَـٰهَرَا عَلَيْهِ فَإِنَّ ٱللَّهَ هُوَ مَوْلَـٰهُ وَجِبْرِيلُ وَصَـٰلِحُ ٱلْمُؤْمِنِينَ وَٱلْمَلَـٰٓئِكَةُ بَعْدَ ذَٰلِكَ ظَهِيرٌ ۝ عَسَىٰ رَبُّهُۥٓ إِن طَلَّقَكُنَّ أَن يُبْدِلَهُۥٓ أَزْوَٰجًا خَيْرًا مِّنكُنَّ مُسْلِمَـٰتٍ مُّؤْمِنَـٰتٍ قَـٰنِتَـٰتٍ تَـٰٓئِبَـٰتٍ عَـٰبِدَٰتٍ سَـٰٓئِحَـٰتٍ ثَيِّبَـٰتٍ وَأَبْكَارًا ۝

ᵃ In the above-mentioned affair, some wives of the Prophet Muhammad had created complications in his house. By way of warning, his consorts have been addressed here in the manner of an ultimatum. This shows the importance of women in the affairs of life. The fact is that if a woman co-operates with her husband in the real sense, she becomes the husband's 'best half', and if she does not prove to be a true comrade, she may ruin the life's work of a purposeful man.

⁶ Believers, safeguard yourselves and your families from a Fire fuelled by people and stones, and watched over by angels, stern and strong: angels who never disobey God's commands to them, but promptly do as they are commanded. ⁷ You who are bent on denying the truth, make no excuses today: you are only being rewarded according to your deeds.ᵃ

يَـٰٓأَيُّهَا ٱلَّذِينَ ءَامَنُواْ قُوٓاْ أَنفُسَكُمْ وَأَهْلِيكُمْ نَارًا وَقُودُهَا ٱلنَّاسُ وَٱلْحِجَارَةُ عَلَيْهَا مَلَـٰٓئِكَةٌ غِلَاظٌ شِدَادٌ لَّا يَعْصُونَ ٱللَّهَ مَآ أَمَرَهُمْ وَيَفْعَلُونَ مَا يُؤْمَرُونَ ۝ يَـٰٓأَيُّهَا ٱلَّذِينَ كَفَرُواْ لَا تَعْتَذِرُواْ ٱلْيَوْمَ إِنَّمَا تُجْزَوْنَ مَا كُنتُمْ تَعْمَلُونَ ۝

ᵃ In the present world it often happens that a man knows that something is right, but excessive attachment to his wife and children compels him to shun the right path and do only that which his wife and children desire. But this is a terrible lapse on his part. Man should know that the children for whose sake he forgets to act with rectitude today, will be handed over tomorrow to fierce agents of Hell, who will be as heartless as robots and who will not make any concessions to them.

⁸ Believers, turn to God in sincere repentance. Your Lord may well forgive your bad deeds and admit you into gardens watered by running streams, on a Day when God will not abase the Prophet and those who have believed with him. Their light will shine out ahead of them and on their right, and they will say: 'Lord perfect our light for us, and forgive us; You have power over all things.' *a*

يَـٰٓأَيُّهَا ٱلَّذِينَ ءَامَنُوا۟ تُوبُوٓا۟ إِلَى ٱللَّهِ تَوْبَةً نَّصُوحًا عَسَىٰ رَبُّكُمْ أَن يُكَفِّرَ عَنكُمْ سَيِّـَٔاتِكُمْ وَيُدْخِلَكُمْ جَنَّـٰتٍ تَجْرِى مِن تَحْتِهَا ٱلْأَنْهَـٰرُ يَوْمَ لَا يُخْزِى ٱللَّهُ ٱلنَّبِىَّ وَٱلَّذِينَ ءَامَنُوا۟ مَعَهُۥ نُورُهُمْ يَسْعَىٰ بَيْنَ أَيْدِيهِمْ وَبِأَيْمَـٰنِهِمْ يَقُولُونَ رَبَّنَآ أَتْمِمْ لَنَا نُورَنَا وَٱغْفِرْ لَنَآ إِنَّكَ عَلَىٰ كُلِّ شَىْءٍ قَدِيرٌ ۝

---

a In the present world man has been kept in trial conditions and as such he is liable to commit errors. In compensation for this, he must turn towards God in repentance. In essence, true repentance comes from a sense of shame. If a man fully realises his mistake, he will feel ashamed, and this sense of shame will compel him not to indulge in such action in future. That is why a *hadith* says, 'Being ashamed is repentance.' A companion of the Prophet Muhammad said, 'True repentance is a man turning towards God and then not repeating that action.'

Repentance has to be borne out by actions. It is not just the repetition of some words. 'Ali ibn Abi Talib saw an individual who, after making a mistake, was simply repeating the words '*tawbah, tawbah*'. 'Ali said that this was repentance of liars. True *tawbah* is the light of the Hereafter and false *tawbah* is the darkness of the Hereafter.

⁹ Prophet, exert yourself to the utmost against those who deny the truth and the hypocrites. Deal severely with them. Hell will be their abode—a vile destination. ¹⁰ As an example to those who are bent on denying the truth, God cited the wife of Noah and the wife of Lot, who were married to two of Our righteous servants, but who betrayed them. So they could not help them against God, and they were told, 'Enter the Fire along with all the others.' ᵃ

يَـٰٓأَيُّهَا ٱلنَّبِىُّ جَـٰهِدِ ٱلْكُفَّارَ وَٱلْمُنَـٰفِقِينَ وَٱغْلُظْ عَلَيْهِمْ وَمَأْوَىٰهُمْ جَهَنَّمُ وَبِئْسَ ٱلْمَصِيرُ ۝ ضَرَبَ ٱللَّهُ مَثَلًا لِّلَّذِينَ كَفَرُوا۟ ٱمْرَأَتَ نُوحٍ وَٱمْرَأَتَ لُوطٍ كَانَتَا تَحْتَ عَبْدَيْنِ مِنْ عِبَادِنَا صَـٰلِحَيْنِ فَخَانَتَاهُمَا فَلَمْ يُغْنِيَا عَنْهُمَا مِنَ ٱللَّهِ شَيْـًٔا وَقِيلَ ٱدْخُلَا ٱلنَّارَ مَعَ ٱلدَّٰخِلِينَ ۝

ᵃ This means, 'Take hypocrites severely to task.' This is a regular permanent command. Elders and other responsible people should keep a watchful eye on all members of society, and if any Muslim adopts a wrong path, all possible efforts should be made to prevent him from doing so.

Only such deeds as are performed by a man himself will have meaning in the eyes of God. Even having connections with saints or being related to pious people will be of no avail. Noah and Lot were prophets of God, but their wives had nevertheless formed strong ties with the enemies of Truth. Consequently, in spite of being the wives of prophets, they were held liable to be sent to hell.

¹¹ To the believers God has given the example of Pharaoh's wife who said: 'My Lord, build me a house in nearness to You in Paradise and save me from Pharaoh and his misdeeds. Save me from all evil-doers.' ¹² [God gave another example in the story of] Mary, 'Imran's daughter, who preserved her chastity and We breathed Our spirit into her; she testified to the words of her Lord and His Scriptures, and was truly devout.^a

وَضَرَبَ ٱللَّهُ مَثَلًا لِّلَّذِينَ ءَامَنُوا۟ ٱمْرَأَتَ فِرْعَوْنَ إِذْ قَالَتْ رَبِّ ٱبْنِ لِى عِندَكَ بَيْتًا فِى ٱلْجَنَّةِ وَنَجِّنِى مِن فِرْعَوْنَ وَعَمَلِهِۦ وَنَجِّنِى مِنَ ٱلْقَوْمِ ٱلظَّٰلِمِينَ ۞ وَمَرْيَمَ ٱبْنَتَ عِمْرَٰنَ ٱلَّتِىٓ أَحْصَنَتْ فَرْجَهَا فَنَفَخْنَا فِيهِ مِن رُّوحِنَا وَصَدَّقَتْ بِكَلِمَٰتِ رَبِّهَا وَكُتُبِهِۦ وَكَانَتْ مِنَ ٱلْقَٰنِتِينَ ۞

---

^a Pharaoh was an unbeliever and a tyrant. But his wife Asiyah, daughter of Muzahim was a woman of Faith and a doer of pious deeds. So when she kept herself on the right path, her husband's wrong behaviour did not harm her. The husband was sent to hell and the wife found her place in the gardens of paradise.

From childhood till her youth, Mary kept herself pure and she preserved her chastity. Therefore, God chose her to give birth as a virgin to a miraculous prophet. According to some traditions, the angel Gabriel blew on the front of her shirt, which made her pregnant and the Messiah was born.

67. THE KINGDOM

In the name of God,
the Most Gracious, the Most Merciful

بِسْمِ اللَّهِ الرَّحْمَٰنِ الرَّحِيمِ

¹ Blessed is He in whose hand is the Kingdom: He has power over all things; ² He created death and life so that He might test you, and find out which of you is best in conduct. He is the Mighty, the Most Forgiving One. ³ He created seven heavens one above the other in layers. You will not find any flaw in the creation of the Gracious One. Then look once again: can you see any flaw? ⁴ Then look again and again. Your gaze will come back to you confused and exhausted.[a]

تَبَٰرَكَ ٱلَّذِى بِيَدِهِ ٱلْمُلْكُ وَهُوَ عَلَىٰ كُلِّ شَىْءٍ قَدِيرٌ ۝ ٱلَّذِى خَلَقَ ٱلْمَوْتَ وَٱلْحَيَوٰةَ لِيَبْلُوَكُمْ أَيُّكُمْ أَحْسَنُ عَمَلًا وَهُوَ ٱلْعَزِيزُ ٱلْغَفُورُ ۝ ٱلَّذِى خَلَقَ سَبْعَ سَمَٰوَٰتٍ طِبَاقًا مَّا تَرَىٰ فِى خَلْقِ ٱلرَّحْمَٰنِ مِن تَفَٰوُتٍ فَٱرْجِعِ ٱلْبَصَرَ هَلْ تَرَىٰ مِن فُطُورٍ ۝ ثُمَّ ٱرْجِعِ ٱلْبَصَرَ كَرَّتَيْنِ يَنقَلِبْ إِلَيْكَ ٱلْبَصَرُ خَاسِئًا وَهُوَ حَسِيرٌ ۝

---

[a] A study of the present world reveals a certain contradiction. The whole universe (except for human beings) is running quite perfectly and in the most well-organised manner. It has no defect in it anywhere. On the contrary, one finds many defects in human life. This is because the nature of man's creation is different. Man in this world is living under testing conditions. A test essentially demands freedom of action. This freedom of action has given the opportunity to human beings to create disturbance and imbalance in the world.

The transgression rampant in the human world is the price of human freedom. If such conditions did not exist, how could divine approval be given to those worthy persons who did not transgress, in spite of having opportunities to transgress and who abstained from arrogance in spite of having the power to be arrogant?

⁵ We have adorned the lowest heaven with lamps, and We have made them for driving away devils. For them We have prepared the punishment of the blazing Fire. ⁶ Those who are bent on blaspheming against their Lord will have the punishment of Hell: an evil destination. ⁷ When they are cast into it, they will hear its roaring as it boils up, ⁸ as though bursting with rage. Each time a group is cast into it, its keepers will ask them, 'Did no warner come to you?' ⁹ They will say, 'Of course, a warner did come to us, but we belied him and we said, "God has revealed nothing; you are in gross error".' ¹⁰ They will say, 'If we had only listened or understood, we should not now be among the inmates of Hell,' ¹¹ and thus they will confess their sin; far from God's mercy are the inmates of Hell.ᵃ

وَلَقَدْ زَيَّنَّا ٱلسَّمَآءَ ٱلدُّنْيَا بِمَصَٰبِيحَ وَجَعَلْنَٰهَا رُجُومًا لِّلشَّيَٰطِينِ وَأَعْتَدْنَا لَهُمْ عَذَابَ ٱلسَّعِيرِ ۝ وَلِلَّذِينَ كَفَرُوا۟ بِرَبِّهِمْ عَذَابُ جَهَنَّمَ وَبِئْسَ ٱلْمَصِيرُ ۝ إِذَآ أُلْقُوا۟ فِيهَا سَمِعُوا۟ لَهَا شَهِيقًا وَهِىَ تَفُورُ ۝ تَكَادُ تَمَيَّزُ مِنَ ٱلْغَيْظِ كُلَّمَآ أُلْقِىَ فِيهَا فَوْجٌ سَأَلَهُمْ خَزَنَتُهَآ أَلَمْ يَأْتِكُمْ نَذِيرٌ ۝ قَالُوا۟ بَلَىٰ قَدْ جَآءَنَا نَذِيرٌ فَكَذَّبْنَا وَقُلْنَا مَا نَزَّلَ ٱللَّهُ مِن شَىْءٍ إِنْ أَنتُمْ إِلَّا فِى ضَلَٰلٍ كَبِيرٍ ۝ وَقَالُوا۟ لَوْ كُنَّا نَسْمَعُ أَوْ نَعْقِلُ مَا كُنَّا فِىٓ أَصْحَٰبِ ٱلسَّعِيرِ ۝ فَٱعْتَرَفُوا۟ بِذَنۢبِهِمْ فَسُحْقًا لِّأَصْحَٰبِ ٱلسَّعِيرِ ۝

ᵃ At various places in the Quran, the picture of hell has been drawn. Though this hell is not observable today by man, it can be seen indirectly and imagined through the meaningfulness of the universe. The fact is that if there were to be no reckoning of the evil people brought to account in the Hereafter, the entire meaningfulness of the universe would become inexplicable.

The punishment of the Hereafter not being visible in the present world is precisely in accordance with God's plan. It is the intention of God to select such persons as are convinced of His greatness and who obey Him without actually having seen Him. And the assessment of such people cannot be properly made unless the fate awaiting everybody in the Hereafter is kept out of their sight, so that whatever a man does here, he does out of free will and not under any compulsion.

[12] As for those who fear their Lord in the unseen will have forgiveness and a rich reward. [13] Whether you speak in secret or aloud, He knows what is in every heart. [14] How could He who created not know His own creation, when He alone is the Most Subtle in His wisdom and the All Aware?[a]

[15] It is He who has made the earth subservient to you, so traverse its regions and eat its provisions. To Him you shall all be resurrected. [16] Do you feel secure that He who is in heaven will not cause the earth to sink beneath you and then begin to quake? [17] Do you feel secure that the One in heaven will not send against you a whirlwind to pelt you with stones, so that you will know how [true] My warning was? [18] Those who went before them belied [the truth]: then how great was My rejection of them.[b]

إِنَّ ٱلَّذِينَ يَخْشَوْنَ رَبَّهُم بِٱلْغَيْبِ لَهُم مَّغْفِرَةٌ وَأَجْرٌ كَبِيرٌ ۝ وَأَسِرُّوا۟ قَوْلَكُمْ أَوِ ٱجْهَرُوا۟ بِهِۦٓ إِنَّهُۥ عَلِيمٌۢ بِذَاتِ ٱلصُّدُورِ ۝ أَلَا يَعْلَمُ مَنْ خَلَقَ وَهُوَ ٱللَّطِيفُ ٱلْخَبِيرُ ۝ هُوَ ٱلَّذِى جَعَلَ لَكُمُ ٱلْأَرْضَ ذَلُولًا فَٱمْشُوا۟ فِى مَنَاكِبِهَا وَكُلُوا۟ مِن رِّزْقِهِۦ وَإِلَيْهِ ٱلنُّشُورُ ۝ ءَأَمِنتُم مَّن فِى ٱلسَّمَآءِ أَن يَخْسِفَ بِكُمُ ٱلْأَرْضَ فَإِذَا هِىَ تَمُورُ ۝ أَمْ أَمِنتُم مَّن فِى ٱلسَّمَآءِ أَن يُرْسِلَ عَلَيْكُمْ حَاصِبًا فَسَتَعْلَمُونَ كَيْفَ نَذِيرِ ۝ وَلَقَدْ كَذَّبَ ٱلَّذِينَ مِن قَبْلِهِمْ فَكَيْفَ كَانَ نَكِيرِ ۝

---

[a] Everything on earth is extremely well-balanced. It is this balance which has made the earth habitable for human beings. Should the slightest disturbance ever occur in this balance, man's life would be destroyed. We should be grateful to God for the balanced world provided to us and seek His gracious help against any destructive conditions that may develop as a result of the world's equilibrium being upset.

¹⁹ Do they not see the birds above them spreading and closing their wings? None save the Merciful sustains them. Surely, He observes all things. ²⁰ Who is there to defend you like an army, besides the Lord of Mercy? Those who deny the truth are in deception. ²¹ Who can provide for you, if He withholds His provision? Yet they obstinately persist in rebellion and avoidance of the truth.ᵃ

²² Is he who walks grovelling upon his face better guided, or he who walks upright upon a straight path? ²³ Say, 'It is He who brought you into being, and made ears and eyes and hearts for you, yet you are seldom grateful.' ²⁴ Say, 'It is He who has scattered you on the earth; and it is to Him that you shall all be gathered [on the Day of Resurrection].'ᵇ

أُوَلَمۡ يَرَوۡاْ إِلَى ٱلطَّيۡرِ فَوۡقَهُمۡ صَٰٓفَّٰتٍ
وَيَقۡبِضۡنَ مَا يُمۡسِكُهُنَّ إِلَّا ٱلرَّحۡمَٰنُ
إِنَّهُۥ بِكُلِّ شَيۡءٍ بَصِيرٌ ۝ أَمَّنۡ هَٰذَا
ٱلَّذِى هُوَ جُندٌ لَّكُمۡ يَنصُرُكُم مِّن دُونِ
ٱلرَّحۡمَٰنِ إِنِ ٱلۡكَٰفِرُونَ إِلَّا فِى غُرُورٍ
۝ أَمَّنۡ هَٰذَا ٱلَّذِى يَرۡزُقُكُمۡ إِنۡ
أَمۡسَكَ رِزۡقَهُۥ بَل لَّجُّواْ فِى عُتُوٍّ وَنُفُورٍ
۝ أَفَمَن يَمۡشِى مُكِبًّا عَلَىٰ وَجۡهِهِۦٓ
أَهۡدَىٰٓ أَمَّن يَمۡشِى سَوِيًّا عَلَىٰ صِرَٰطٍ
مُّسۡتَقِيمٍ ۝ قُلۡ هُوَ ٱلَّذِىٓ أَنشَأَكُمۡ
وَجَعَلَ لَكُمُ ٱلسَّمۡعَ وَٱلۡأَبۡصَٰرَ
وَٱلۡأَفۡـِٔدَةَ قَلِيلًا مَّا تَشۡكُرُونَ ۝ قُلۡ
هُوَ ٱلَّذِى ذَرَأَكُمۡ فِى ٱلۡأَرۡضِ وَإِلَيۡهِ
تُحۡشَرُونَ ۝

ᵃ Birds flying in the air, the emergence of man's sustenance from the soil and similar events are most wonderful. If one gives serious consideration to such things, one will become caught up in the realisation of God. But man is so forgetful that he indulges in arrogance in a world in which the natural phenomena visible all around him ought to teach him the lesson of obedience to God.

ᵇ Man has been granted the powers of hearing, seeing and thinking. Some individuals are so constituted that whatever they hear they follow, whatever they see they accept at face value, and whatever comes into their minds they uncritically retain. This type of person is like an animal which goes ahead with its head down, toeing a fixed line.

Quite another type of person is one who investigates whatever he hears, who tries to understand more accurately whatever he sees, and who discovers the Truth by coming out of his personal shell. This second type of person is one who straightens himself up and walks on a straight path—the qualities of hearing, observation and sensitivity have been given to man so that he may recognise the truth and not be as ignorant or unaware as a blind or deaf person.

²⁵ They ask, 'When will this promise be fulfilled, if you are truthful?' ²⁶ Say, 'God alone has knowledge of that; and I am only a plain warner.' ²⁷ But when they see it drawing near, the faces of those who deny the truth will turn gloomy and they will be told, 'This is what you were calling for.' ²⁸ Say, 'Have you thought: if God destroys me and those who are with me, or treats us mercifully, then who will protect those who deny the truth from a painful chastisement?' ²⁹ Say, 'He is the Most Gracious: we believe in Him and we put our trust in Him. You will soon come to know who is in evident error.' ³⁰ Say, 'Have you considered if your water were to sink into the ground, who could then bring you flowing water?' ᵃ

وَيَقُولُونَ مَتَىٰ هَـٰذَا ٱلْوَعْدُ إِن كُنتُمْ صَـٰدِقِينَ ۝ قُلْ إِنَّمَا ٱلْعِلْمُ عِندَ ٱللَّهِ وَإِنَّمَآ أَنَا۠ نَذِيرٌ مُّبِينٌ ۝ فَلَمَّا رَأَوْهُ زُلْفَةً سِيٓـَٔتْ وُجُوهُ ٱلَّذِينَ كَفَرُوا۟ وَقِيلَ هَـٰذَا ٱلَّذِى كُنتُم بِهِۦ تَدَّعُونَ ۝ قُلْ أَرَءَيْتُمْ إِنْ أَهْلَكَنِىَ ٱللَّهُ وَمَن مَّعِىَ أَوْ رَحِمَنَا فَمَن يُجِيرُ ٱلْكَـٰفِرِينَ مِنْ عَذَابٍ أَلِيمٍ ۝ قُلْ هُوَ ٱلرَّحْمَـٰنُ ءَامَنَّا بِهِۦ وَعَلَيْهِ تَوَكَّلْنَا ۖ فَسَتَعْلَمُونَ مَنْ هُوَ فِى ضَلَـٰلٍ مُّبِينٍ ۝ قُلْ أَرَءَيْتُمْ إِنْ أَصْبَحَ مَآؤُكُمْ غَوْرًا فَمَن يَأْتِيكُم بِمَآءٍ مَّعِينٍۭ ۝

ᵃ When the addressee is not convinced by reasoning, the preacher repeats his utterances of firm faith and thus stirs his inner self into awakening. Even if there is the slightest sensitivity in a man, these last utterances are enough to make him feel the urge to reform himself. But one whose conscience has been completely blunted, can never be awakened by any device.

68. THE PEN

In the name of God,
the Most Gracious, the Most Merciful

بِسْمِ اللَّهِ الرَّحْمَٰنِ الرَّحِيمِ

¹ *Nun*

By the pen, and all that they write!*^a*
² By the grace of your Lord, you are
not a mad man. ³ Most surely, you
will have a never ending reward. ⁴ For
you are truly of a sublime character.*^b*
⁵ Soon you will see, as will they,
⁶ which of you is a prey to madness.
⁷ Your Lord knows best who has
fallen by the wayside, and who has
remained on the true path.

ن ۚ وَالْقَلَمِ وَمَا يَسْطُرُونَ ۝ مَا
أَنتَ بِنِعْمَةِ رَبِّكَ بِمَجْنُونٍ ۝ وَإِنَّ
لَكَ لَأَجْرًا غَيْرَ مَمْنُونٍ ۝ وَإِنَّكَ
لَعَلَىٰ خُلُقٍ عَظِيمٍ ۝ فَسَتُبْصِرُ
وَيُبْصِرُونَ ۝ بِأَييِّكُمُ الْمَفْتُونُ ۝
إِنَّ رَبَّكَ هُوَ أَعْلَمُ بِمَن ضَلَّ عَن
سَبِيلِهِ وَهُوَ أَعْلَمُ بِالْمُهْتَدِينَ ۝

---

^a 'By the pen, and all that they write' refers to historical record. In historical records of human memoirs accumulated and preserved in the shape of history, the Quran is an exceptional book and the bearer of that book an exceptional personality. This quality of being exceptional cannot be explained unless the Quran is accepted as the book of God and Muhammad as His Prophet.

^b Having a sublime character means rising above the standard of others' behaviour. It should not be the believer's way to deal badly with those who are not good to him, while giving fair treatment to those who are good to him. On the contrary, he should do good to everybody, even though others may not do the same for him. The character of the Prophet was of the latter type, which proves that he was a man of principle. He was not a product of circumstances, but of his own high principles. His sublime character was consistent with his claim to be a prophet.

⁸ Do not give in to the deniers of truth. ⁹ They want you to make concessions to them and then they will reciprocate. ¹⁰ Do not yield to any contemptible swearer of oaths, ¹¹ or to any defamer or one who spreads slander, ¹² or to one who places obstacles in the way of good being done or to the wicked transgressor, ¹³ who is ignoble and besides all that, base-born; ¹⁴ just because he has wealth and sons, ¹⁵ when Our revelations are recited to him, he says, 'These are just ancient fables.' ¹⁶ Soon We will brand him on the nose.ᵃ

فَلَا تُطِعِ ٱلْمُكَذِّبِينَ ۝ وَدُّواْ لَوْ تُدْهِنُ فَيُدْهِنُونَ ۝ وَلَا تُطِعْ كُلَّ حَلَّافٍ مَّهِينٍ ۝ هَمَّازٍ مَّشَّآءِ بِنَمِيمٍ ۝ مَّنَّاعٍ لِّلْخَيْرِ مُعْتَدٍ أَثِيمٍ ۝ عُتُلٍّ بَعْدَ ذَٰلِكَ زَنِيمٍ ۝ أَن كَانَ ذَا مَالٍ وَبَنِينَ ۝ إِذَا تُتْلَىٰ عَلَيْهِ ءَايَٰتُنَا قَالَ أَسَٰطِيرُ ٱلْأَوَّلِينَ ۝ سَنَسِمُهُۥ عَلَى ٱلْخُرْطُومِ ۝

ᵃ 'Do not give in to the deniers of truth' means that the words of those who deny the truth are not worthy of acceptance. On the one hand, there is the upholder of Truth, who has taken his stand by virtue of reasoning. There is no contradiction between his words and his actions. On the other hand, there are his opponents who are of low character and have nothing to their credit except for false utterances. The missionary of Truth relies on Truth, whereas his opponents rely on their material status. The missionary of Truth is a follower of principles, unlike his opponents who are unprincipled, and whose views are highly inconsistent. For one who has a sound mind, this difference is enough to show who is on the right path and who is not.

¹⁷ We have tried them as we tried the owners of a certain orchard, who vowed to harvest all its fruits the next morning, ¹⁸ without saying, 'If it be God's will.' ¹⁹ A calamity from your Lord befell the orchard as they slept. ²⁰ And by morning it lay as if it had already been harvested, a barren land. ²¹ So they called out to each other at the break of dawn, ²² saying, 'Be quick to reach your orchard, if you want to gather all your fruits.' ²³ So they went off, whispering to one another, ²⁴ 'Be sure to stop any poor person from entering the orchard today.' ²⁵ They set out early in the morning, thinking they had the power to prevent. ²⁶ But when they saw it, they said, 'We must have lost our way. ²⁷ Indeed, we are utterly ruined!' ²⁸ The more upright of the two said, 'Did I not bid you to glorify God?' ²⁹ They said, 'Glory be to God, our Lord. We have surely done wrong.' ³⁰ Then they began to heap reproaches on each other. ³¹ They said, 'Alas for us, our behaviour was beyond the pale. ³² Maybe our Lord will give us a better orchard in its stead; we turn to Him.' ³³ Such was their punishment, [in this life]. But the punishment of the life to come is much more severe, if only they knew it!ᵃ

إِنَّا بَلَوْنَٰهُمْ كَمَا بَلَوْنَآ أَصْحَٰبَ ٱلْجَنَّةِ ﴿١٧﴾ إِذْ أَقْسَمُوا۟ لَيَصْرِمُنَّهَا مُصْبِحِينَ ﴿١٨﴾ وَلَا يَسْتَثْنُونَ ﴿١٩﴾ فَطَافَ عَلَيْهَا طَآئِفٌ مِّن رَّبِّكَ وَهُمْ نَآئِمُونَ ﴿٢٠﴾ فَأَصْبَحَتْ كَٱلصَّرِيمِ ﴿٢١﴾ فَتَنَادَوْا۟ مُصْبِحِينَ ﴿٢٢﴾ أَنِ ٱغْدُوا۟ عَلَىٰ حَرْثِكُمْ إِن كُنتُمْ صَٰرِمِينَ ﴿٢٣﴾ فَٱنطَلَقُوا۟ وَهُمْ يَتَخَٰفَتُونَ ﴿٢٤﴾ أَن لَّا يَدْخُلَنَّهَا ٱلْيَوْمَ عَلَيْكُم مِّسْكِينٌ ﴿٢٥﴾ وَغَدَوْا۟ عَلَىٰ حَرْدٍ قَٰدِرِينَ ﴿٢٦﴾ فَلَمَّا رَأَوْهَا قَالُوٓا۟ إِنَّا لَضَآلُّونَ ﴿٢٧﴾ بَلْ نَحْنُ مَحْرُومُونَ ﴿٢٨﴾ قَالَ أَوْسَطُهُمْ أَلَمْ أَقُل لَّكُمْ لَوْلَا تُسَبِّحُونَ ﴿٢٩﴾ قَالُوا۟ سُبْحَٰنَ رَبِّنَآ إِنَّا كُنَّا ظَٰلِمِينَ ﴿٣٠﴾ فَأَقْبَلَ بَعْضُهُمْ عَلَىٰ بَعْضٍ يَتَلَٰوَمُونَ ﴿٣١﴾ قَالُوا۟ يَٰوَيْلَنَآ إِنَّا كُنَّا طَٰغِينَ ﴿٣٢﴾ عَسَىٰ رَبُّنَآ أَن يُبْدِلَنَا خَيْرًا مِّنْهَآ إِنَّآ إِلَىٰ رَبِّنَا رَٰغِبُونَ ﴿٣٣﴾ كَذَٰلِكَ ٱلْعَذَابُ وَلَعَذَابُ ٱلْءَاخِرَةِ أَكْبَرُ لَوْ كَانُوا۟ يَعْلَمُونَ ﴿٣٤﴾

ᵃ Whatever a man earns in this world is apparently from farming or industry or other such pursuits. But, in fact, it is all given to him by the grace of God. If one considers it a gift from God and sets apart a portion of it for other subjects of God, Almighty God will bless his earnings. On the contrary, one who considers his earnings the result purely of his own talents and who is not, therefore, prepared to give others their dues, will find that his earnings will be of no avail. This is a strict law of God. In some cases, it manifests itself in this world, but in the Hereafter it will manifest itself for all, and none shall be exempt from it.

34 Those who are mindful of their Lord will be rewarded with gardens of bliss. 35 Should We treat the true believers and the wrongdoers alike? 36 What ails you? How ill you judge! 37 Have you a Scripture that tells you 38 that you will be granted whatever you choose? 39 Or do you have Our solemn oaths, binding upon Us till the Day of Resurrection, that you shall have whatever you yourselves decide? 40 Ask them, which of them will vouch for that! 41 Or have they other partners [besides God]? Let them bring forth their other partners, if what they say be true.*

إِنَّ لِلْمُتَّقِينَ عِندَ رَبِّهِمْ جَنَّتِ ٱلنَّعِيمِ ﴿٣٤﴾ أَفَنَجْعَلُ ٱلْمُسْلِمِينَ كَٱلْمُجْرِمِينَ ﴿٣٥﴾ مَا لَكُمْ كَيْفَ تَحْكُمُونَ ﴿٣٦﴾ أَمْ لَكُمْ كِتَٰبٌ فِيهِ تَدْرُسُونَ ﴿٣٧﴾ إِنَّ لَكُمْ فِيهِ لَمَا تَخَيَّرُونَ ﴿٣٨﴾ أَمْ لَكُمْ أَيْمَٰنٌ عَلَيْنَا بَٰلِغَةٌ إِلَىٰ يَوْمِ ٱلْقِيَٰمَةِ إِنَّ لَكُمْ لَمَا تَحْكُمُونَ ﴿٣٩﴾ سَلْهُمْ أَيُّهُم بِذَٰلِكَ زَعِيمٌ ﴿٤٠﴾ أَمْ لَهُمْ شُرَكَاءُ فَلْيَأْتُوا بِشُرَكَائِهِمْ إِن كَانُوا صَٰدِقِينَ ﴿٤١﴾

---

a A man who is not God-fearing gives importance only to visible material things, whereas the God-fearing person is one who is serious about the unseen reality. Such entirely different characters cannot have an identical fate.

⁴² On the Day when the truth shall be laid bare, they will be called upon to prostrate themselves, but they will not be able to do so. ⁴³ Their eyes will be cast down and they will be covered in shame; they were bidden to prostrate themselves, when they were safe and sound [but they did not obey]. ⁴⁴ So leave to Me those who reject this message. We shall lead them step by step to their ruin, in ways beyond their ken. ⁴⁵ I shall grant them some respite, for My plan is powerful.ᵃ

يَوۡمَ يُكۡشَفُ عَن سَاقٍ وَيُدۡعَوۡنَ إِلَى ٱلسُّجُودِ فَلَا يَسۡتَطِيعُونَ ۝ خَٰشِعَةً أَبۡصَٰرُهُمۡ تَرۡهَقُهُمۡ ذِلَّةٌ ۖ وَقَدۡ كَانُوٓاْ يُدۡعَوۡنَ إِلَى ٱلسُّجُودِ وَهُمۡ سَٰلِمُونَ ۝ فَذَرۡنِي وَمَن يُكَذِّبُ بِهَٰذَا ٱلۡحَدِيثِ ۖ سَنَسۡتَدۡرِجُهُم مِّنۡ حَيۡثُ لَا يَعۡلَمُونَ ۝ وَأُمۡلِي لَهُمۡ ۚ إِنَّ كَيۡدِى مَتِينٌ ۝

ᵃ On the Day of Judgement when God will reveal Himself, the true believers will fall prostrate before their Lord, just as they bowed down before Him in their previous life. On this occasion, the deniers will be inspired likewise to prostrate themselves (sajdah). But the backs of the people who offered 'false prostration' in this world, will grow stiff just as they virtually were in this world. Such people will want to prostrate themselves at that time of realisation, but they will not be able to do so. It will be the greatest sign of God's appreciation of sincere people of Faith that He Himself should appear and accept their offering of sajdah. On the contrary, it will be the moment of the greatest humiliation for those making false claims of Faith; in spite of their Creator and Lord being right there before them, they will not be able to do obeisance to Him.

⁴⁶ Do you demand some recompense from them that would weigh them down with debt? ⁴⁷ Is the unseen within their grasp so that they write it down? ⁴⁸ Wait patiently for your Lord's judgement; do not be like the man who, having been swallowed by a whale, called out in distress. ⁴⁹ Had his Lord's grace not been bestowed upon him, he would have been cast away in disgrace upon that desolate shore. ⁵⁰ But his Lord chose him for His own and made him one of the righteous. ⁵¹ When those who deny the truth hear the admonition, they would almost cause you to stumble with their evil eyes; and they say, 'He is certainly mad.' ⁵² Yet it is purely an admonition to mankind.*

أَمْ تَسْـَٔلُهُمْ أَجْرًا فَهُم مِّن مَّغْرَمٍ مُّثْقَلُونَ ۝ أَمْ عِندَهُمُ ٱلْغَيْبُ فَهُمْ يَكْتُبُونَ ۝ فَٱصْبِرْ لِحُكْمِ رَبِّكَ وَلَا تَكُن كَصَاحِبِ ٱلْحُوتِ إِذْ نَادَىٰ وَهُوَ مَكْظُومٌ ۝ لَّوْلَآ أَن تَدَارَكَهُ نِعْمَةٌ مِّن رَّبِّهِۦ لَنُبِذَ بِٱلْعَرَآءِ وَهُوَ مَذْمُومٌ ۝ فَٱجْتَبَٰهُ رَبُّهُۥ فَجَعَلَهُۥ مِنَ ٱلصَّٰلِحِينَ ۝ وَإِن يَكَادُ ٱلَّذِينَ كَفَرُوا۟ لَيُزْلِقُونَكَ بِأَبْصَٰرِهِمْ لَمَّا سَمِعُوا۟ ٱلذِّكْرَ وَيَقُولُونَ إِنَّهُۥ لَمَجْنُونٌ ۝ وَمَا هُوَ إِلَّا ذِكْرٌ لِّلْعَٰلَمِينَ ۝

ᵃ The relationship between the missionary and his addressees is a very delicate one. The missionary has to make himself pleasant-mannered unilaterally. The addressee may talk unreasonably, he may hold the missionary in contempt, and may make false allegations against him. In short, he may do anything of a discourageing nature, but the missionary must at all times abstain from negative reaction. His success is dependent upon two things—tolerance of excesses on the part of the addressee and having no expectation of material gain from him.

69. THE INEVITABLE HOUR

In the name of God,
the Most Gracious, the Most Merciful

¹ The Inevitable Hour! ² What is the Inevitable Hour? ³ And what will make you realize what the Inevitable Hour is? ⁴ The tribes of Thamud and 'Ad denied that disaster would strike them: ⁵ the Thamud were destroyed by a terrible storm of thunder and lightning; ⁶ and the 'Ad were destroyed by a furious wind ⁷ which God let loose against them for seven nights and eight days unremittingly, so that you could have seen its people lying prostrate as though they were the hollow trunks of palm-trees which had fallen down. ⁸ Do you see any vestige left of them now? ⁹ Pharoah and those before him and the inhabitants of the overthrown cities persistently committed grave sins. ¹⁰ They defied their Lord's messenger, so He seized them with an ever-tightening grip. ¹¹ But We bore you away in the Ark, when the waters rose high, ¹² so that We might make it a reminder for you and so that attentive ears might retain it.*

---

a Some deny the Hereafter openly, while there are others who may not explicitly deny the Hereafter, but who in their heart of hearts attach importance solely to worldly affairs. That is why there is no difference between the way of life of these people and that of those who make open denials. In essence, these two groups are the same. In the eyes of God, both of them are rejecters of the Hereafter—one group rejecting it by word of mouth and the other doing so in practice. ▶

¹³ When a single blast is blown on the trumpet, ¹⁴ and the earth and the mountains are lifted up and then crushed with a single blow, ¹⁵ on that Day the Great Event will come to pass. ¹⁶ And the sky will be rent asunder, for on that Day it will be so frail. ¹⁷ The angels will appear by its sides and, on that Day, eight [angels] will bear your Lord's throne above them. ¹⁸ On that Day you will be brought to judgement and none of your secrets will remain hidden.^a

فَإِذَا نُفِخَ فِى ٱلصُّورِ نَفْخَةٌ وَٰحِدَةٌ ۝ وَحُمِلَتِ ٱلْأَرْضُ وَٱلْجِبَالُ فَدُكَّتَا دَكَّةً وَٰحِدَةً ۝ فَيَوْمَئِذٍ وَقَعَتِ ٱلْوَاقِعَةُ ۝ وَٱنشَقَّتِ ٱلسَّمَآءُ فَهِىَ يَوْمَئِذٍ وَاهِيَةٌ ۝ وَٱلْمَلَكُ عَلَىٰٓ أَرْجَآئِهَا ۚ وَيَحْمِلُ عَرْشَ رَبِّكَ فَوْقَهُمْ يَوْمَئِذٍ ثَمَٰنِيَةٌ ۝ يَوْمَئِذٍ تُعْرَضُونَ لَا تَخْفَىٰ مِنكُمْ خَافِيَةٌ ۝

In accordance with the law of God, all such people are going to face destruction. In the days of the prophets, this destruction was made manifest in the present world, as for their successors it will become a reality in the Hereafter.

^a The present world has been made with a view to putting human beings to the test. When the period of testing is over, this world will be demolished and a new world fashioned to meet new requirements will be made. The majesty of God at present reveals itself indirectly, but at that time the Majesty of God will be directly manifested.

¹⁹ Then he who is given his record in his right hand will exclaim, 'Here is my record, read it. ²⁰ Surely, I knew that I should meet my reckoning,' ²¹ so he will live in a state of Bliss ²² in a lofty garden, ²³ with clusters of fruit within easy reach. ²⁴ We shall say to him, 'Eat and drink joyfully as a reward for the good deeds you did in days gone by.' ²⁵ But he who is given his record in his left hand will say, 'If only I had never been given my Record ²⁶ and knew nothing of my reckoning. ²⁷ How I wish my death had ended all. ²⁸ My wealth has been of no use to me. ²⁹ I am bereft of power.' ³⁰ Seize him and fetter him, ³¹ and then let him enter Hell. ³² Then fasten him with a chain seventy cubits long: ³³ for he did not believe in Almighty God, ³⁴ nor did he feel any urge to feed the needy, ³⁵ so today he has no friend here, ³⁶ and the only food he has is filth ³⁷ which no one will eat except the sinners.ᵃ

فَأَمَّا مَنْ أُوتِيَ كِتَٰبَهُۥ بِيَمِينِهِۦ فَيَقُولُ هَآؤُمُ ٱقْرَءُوا۟ كِتَٰبِيَهْ ﴿١٩﴾ إِنِّى ظَنَنتُ أَنِّى مُلَٰقٍ حِسَابِيَهْ ﴿٢٠﴾ فَهُوَ فِى عِيشَةٍ رَّاضِيَةٍ ﴿٢١﴾ فِى جَنَّةٍ عَالِيَةٍ ﴿٢٢﴾ قُطُوفُهَا دَانِيَةٌ ﴿٢٣﴾ كُلُوا۟ وَٱشْرَبُوا۟ هَنِيٓـًٔا بِمَآ أَسْلَفْتُمْ فِى ٱلْأَيَّامِ ٱلْخَالِيَةِ ﴿٢٤﴾ وَأَمَّا مَنْ أُوتِيَ كِتَٰبَهُۥ بِشِمَالِهِۦ فَيَقُولُ يَٰلَيْتَنِى لَمْ أُوتَ كِتَٰبِيَهْ ﴿٢٥﴾ وَلَمْ أَدْرِ مَا حِسَابِيَهْ ﴿٢٦﴾ يَٰلَيْتَهَا كَانَتِ ٱلْقَاضِيَةَ ﴿٢٧﴾ مَآ أَغْنَىٰ عَنِّى مَالِيَهْ ﴿٢٨﴾ هَلَكَ عَنِّى سُلْطَٰنِيَهْ ﴿٢٩﴾ خُذُوهُ فَغُلُّوهُ ﴿٣٠﴾ ثُمَّ ٱلْجَحِيمَ صَلُّوهُ ﴿٣١﴾ ثُمَّ فِى سِلْسِلَةٍ ذَرْعُهَا سَبْعُونَ ذِرَاعًا فَٱسْلُكُوهُ ﴿٣٢﴾ إِنَّهُۥ كَانَ لَا يُؤْمِنُ بِٱللَّهِ ٱلْعَظِيمِ ﴿٣٣﴾ وَلَا يَحُضُّ عَلَىٰ طَعَامِ ٱلْمِسْكِينِ ﴿٣٤﴾ فَلَيْسَ لَهُ ٱلْيَوْمَ هَٰهُنَا حَمِيمٌ ﴿٣٥﴾ وَلَا طَعَامٌ إِلَّا مِنْ غِسْلِينٍ ﴿٣٦﴾ لَّا يَأْكُلُهُۥٓ إِلَّا ٱلْخَٰطِـُٔونَ ﴿٣٧﴾

ᵃ In the world of the Hereafter, success is the fate of one who in the present world never ceases to fear God, whereas one who lives his life in this world without such fear and is arrogant towards the subjects of God will be affected with the severest punishment in the Hereafter.

³⁸ But nay, I swear by all that you can see ³⁹ as well as all that you cannot see: ⁴⁰ most surely, this is the word brought by a noble messenger, ⁴¹ it is not the word of a poet—how little you believe!—⁴² Nor is it the word of a soothsayer—how little you reflect! ⁴³ It is a revelation sent down by the Sustainer of the Universe: ⁴⁴ if he had invented any lies about Us, ⁴⁵ We would indeed have seized him by his right hand ⁴⁶ and would indeed have cut his life-vein, ⁴⁷ and none of you could have held Us off from him. ⁴⁸ And surely it is an admonition to the God-fearing. ⁴⁹ We know very well that there are some among you who reject Our signs—⁵⁰ it will be a source of bitter regret for those who deny the truth—⁵¹ it is the indubitable truth. ⁵² So glorify the name of your Lord, the Almighty.^a

فَلَا أُقْسِمُ بِمَا تُبْصِرُونَ ۝ وَمَا لَا تُبْصِرُونَ ۝ إِنَّهُ لَقَوْلُ رَسُولٍ كَرِيمٍ ۝ وَمَا هُوَ بِقَوْلِ شَاعِرٍ قَلِيلًا مَّا تُؤْمِنُونَ ۝ وَلَا بِقَوْلِ كَاهِنٍ قَلِيلًا مَّا تَذَكَّرُونَ ۝ تَنزِيلٌ مِّن رَّبِّ الْعَالَمِينَ ۝ وَلَوْ تَقَوَّلَ عَلَيْنَا بَعْضَ الْأَقَاوِيلِ ۝ لَأَخَذْنَا مِنْهُ بِالْيَمِينِ ۝ ثُمَّ لَقَطَعْنَا مِنْهُ الْوَتِينَ ۝ فَمَا مِنكُم مِّنْ أَحَدٍ عَنْهُ حَاجِزِينَ ۝ وَإِنَّهُ لَتَذْكِرَةٌ لِّلْمُتَّقِينَ ۝ وَإِنَّا لَنَعْلَمُ أَنَّ مِنكُم مُّكَذِّبِينَ ۝ وَإِنَّهُ لَحَسْرَةٌ عَلَى الْكَافِرِينَ ۝ وَإِنَّهُ لَحَقُّ الْيَقِينِ ۝ فَسَبِّحْ بِاسْمِ رَبِّكَ الْعَظِيمِ ۝

---

^a It literally means, 'whatever you see and whatever you do not see bear testimony to the veracity of this discourse' that is, whatever knowledge was at the command of humanity at the time the Quran was revealed and whatever was going to come within its reach thereafter, both go to prove the truth of the messenger's utterances. Neither the present available knowledge contradicts the Quran being the Truth, nor will future knowledge be able to do so. In spite of this, those who do not accept it simply prove that they are not serious about Truth and Untruth.

70. THE ASCENDING STAIRWAYS

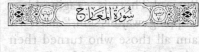

In the name of God,
the Most Gracious, the Most Merciful

¹ A doubter once demanded that punishment be immediately meted out, ² to those who deny the truth. No power can hinder God ³ from punishing them. He is the Lord of the Ascending Stairways, ⁴ by which the angels and the Spirit will ascend to Him in one Day which will last for fifty thousand years. ⁵ Therefore, [O believers] behave with seemly patience. ⁶ They see it [the Day of Judgement] to be far off, ⁷ but We see it near at hand. ⁸ On that Day the heavens shall become like molten brass, ⁹ and the mountains will become like tufts of wool, ¹⁰ and no friend will ask about his friend, ¹¹ though they shall be within sight of each other. The guilty one will gladly ransom himself from the torment of that Day by sacrificing his own children, ¹² his wife, his brother, ¹³ and his kinsfolk who gave him shelter, ¹⁴ and all the people of the earth, if that could deliver him.ᵃ

ᵃ The scenes of Doomsday cannot either be revealed in reality or truly described in the present world. However, in the Quran, these have been allegorically conveyed by allusions and examples, so that man should have a brief idea of their significance. When Doomsday arrives, it will be so terrible that man will forget this relations and the interests to which he gives the utmost importance today and for which he ignores the Truth.

¹⁵ But no! There is a raging blaze ¹⁶ stripping away his skin, ¹⁷ and it will claim all those who turned their backs [on the true faith] and turned away [from the truth], ¹⁸ and amassed wealth and hoarded it. ¹⁹ Indeed, man is born impatient: ²⁰ when misfortune touches him he starts lamenting, ²¹ and whenever good fortune comes to him, he grows niggardly.   ²² But not so the worshippers ²³ who are steadfast in prayer; ²⁴ those who give a due share of their wealth ²⁵ to those who ask [for help] and to the destitute; ²⁶ and those who believe in the Day of Judgement ²⁷ and are fearful of the punishment of their Lord; ²⁸ for none may ever feel secure from the punishment of their Lord; ²⁹ those who preserve their chastity ³⁰ except from their spouses and those whom they rightfully possess [through wedlock], for which they incur no blame—³¹ but those who go beyond that limit are transgressors; ³² and those who are faithful to their trusts and to their pledges; ³³ and those who stand by their testimony ³⁴ and are steadfast in their prayers. ³⁵ They will be honoured in the Gardens of Bliss.[a]

كَلَّا ۖ إِنَّهَا لَظَىٰ ۝ نَزَّاعَةً لِّلشَّوَىٰ ۝ تَدْعُوا۟ مَنْ أَدْبَرَ وَتَوَلَّىٰ ۝ وَجَمَعَ فَأَوْعَىٰٓ ۝ ۞ إِنَّ ٱلْإِنسَٰنَ خُلِقَ هَلُوعًا ۝ إِذَا مَسَّهُ ٱلشَّرُّ جَزُوعًا ۝ وَإِذَا مَسَّهُ ٱلْخَيْرُ مَنُوعًا ۝ إِلَّا ٱلْمُصَلِّينَ ۝ ٱلَّذِينَ هُمْ عَلَىٰ صَلَاتِهِمْ دَآئِمُونَ ۝ وَٱلَّذِينَ فِىٓ أَمْوَٰلِهِمْ حَقٌّ مَّعْلُومٌ ۝ لِّلسَّآئِلِ وَٱلْمَحْرُومِ ۝ وَٱلَّذِينَ يُصَدِّقُونَ بِيَوْمِ ٱلدِّينِ ۝ وَٱلَّذِينَ هُم مِّنْ عَذَابِ رَبِّهِم مُّشْفِقُونَ ۝ إِنَّ عَذَابَ رَبِّهِمْ غَيْرُ مَأْمُونٍ ۝ وَٱلَّذِينَ هُمْ لِفُرُوجِهِمْ حَٰفِظُونَ ۝ إِلَّا عَلَىٰٓ أَزْوَٰجِهِمْ أَوْ مَا مَلَكَتْ أَيْمَٰنُهُمْ فَإِنَّهُمْ غَيْرُ مَلُومِينَ ۝ فَمَنِ ٱبْتَغَىٰ وَرَآءَ ذَٰلِكَ فَأُو۟لَٰٓئِكَ هُمُ ٱلْعَادُونَ ۝ وَٱلَّذِينَ هُمْ لِأَمَٰنَٰتِهِمْ وَعَهْدِهِمْ رَٰعُونَ ۝ وَٱلَّذِينَ هُم بِشَهَٰدَٰتِهِمْ قَآئِمُونَ ۝ وَٱلَّذِينَ هُمْ عَلَىٰ صَلَاتِهِمْ يُحَافِظُونَ ۝ أُو۟لَٰٓئِكَ فِى جَنَّٰتٍ مُّكْرَمُونَ ۝

---

[a] These verses give a brief description of the qualities of two types of human beings: those who will be treated as entitled to enter Paradise and those whose deeds will cause them to be thrown into Hell on Doomsday.

³⁶ But what is the matter with those who deny the truth, that they come hastening towards you ³⁷ from the right and from the left, in crowds? ³⁸ Does every one of them aspire to be admitted into a Garden of Delight? ³⁹ Certainly not! They know quite well out of what We created them.ᵃ

⁴⁰ But nay! I call to witness the Lord of the Easts and the Wests,ᵇ that We have the power ⁴¹ to replace them with others better than them: nothing can prevent Us from doing this, ⁴² so leave them to indulge in vain idle talk and amuse themselves, until they face the Day which they have been promised, ⁴³ the Day when they shall come out of their graves in haste, as if they were racing to a goal, ⁴⁴ with downcast eyes and faces distorted in shame; such is the Day which they are promised.ᶜ

فَمَالِ ٱلَّذِينَ كَفَرُوا۟ قِبَلَكَ مُهْطِعِينَ ﴿٣٦﴾ عَنِ ٱلْيَمِينِ وَعَنِ ٱلشِّمَالِ عِزِينَ ﴿٣٧﴾ أَيَطْمَعُ كُلُّ ٱمْرِئٍ مِّنْهُمْ أَن يُدْخَلَ جَنَّةَ نَعِيمٍ ﴿٣٨﴾ كَلَّا إِنَّا خَلَقْنَٰهُم مِّمَّا يَعْلَمُونَ ﴿٣٩﴾ فَلَآ أُقْسِمُ بِرَبِّ ٱلْمَشَٰرِقِ وَٱلْمَغَٰرِبِ إِنَّا لَقَٰدِرُونَ ﴿٤٠﴾ عَلَىٰٓ أَن نُّبَدِّلَ خَيْرًا مِّنْهُمْ وَمَا نَحْنُ بِمَسْبُوقِينَ ﴿٤١﴾ فَذَرْهُمْ يَخُوضُوا۟ وَيَلْعَبُوا۟ حَتَّىٰ يُلَٰقُوا۟ يَوْمَهُمُ ٱلَّذِي يُوعَدُونَ ﴿٤٢﴾ يَوْمَ يَخْرُجُونَ مِنَ ٱلْأَجْدَاثِ سِرَاعًا كَأَنَّهُمْ إِلَىٰ نُصُبٍ يُوفِضُونَ ﴿٤٣﴾ خَٰشِعَةً أَبْصَٰرُهُمْ تَرْهَقُهُمْ ذِلَّةٌ ذَٰلِكَ ٱلْيَوْمُ ٱلَّذِي كَانُوا۟ يُوعَدُونَ ﴿٤٤﴾

ᵃ Those who stand by Untruth, feel that their high status is in jeopardy when the open and clear call to the Truth is delivered to them. In order to suppress this call, they try to smother it. Their unreasonable behaviour will take them straight to Hell, but with their false optimism, they go on thinking that they are fast approaching Paradise.

ᵇ The periodic change in the places where the sun rises and sets on the earth's horizon is due to that unique feature of the earth known as the axial tilt. This plus the fact that the sun is at one of the foci of the earth's elliptical orbit, and not at its centre, is responsible for the changing of the seasons. In the absence of such factors the earth would have been less useful to man.

ᶜ In this world when there is the example of an inferior thing being improved upon, the occurrence of similar other events is quite within the realm of the possible. Those who, in spite of such clear signs, do not learn any lessons are undoubtedly frivolous people. Such people learn lessons only when they are compelled to do so.

71. NOAH

In the name of God,
the Most Gracious, the Most Merciful

¹ We sent Noah forth to his people, saying, 'Warn your people before there comes upon them a grievous punishment.' ² [Noah] said, 'My people! I am but a plain warner to you, ³ that you should worship God [alone] and be conscious of Him. Pay heed to me. ⁴ He will forgive your sins and will grant you respite till an appointed time. When the time appointed by God arrives, it cannot be postponed, if you only knew.'ᵃ ⁵ He said, 'My Lord! I have called my people night and day ⁶ but my pleas have only increased their aversion.ᵇ

إِنَّا أَرْسَلْنَا نُوحًا إِلَىٰ قَوْمِهِۦٓ أَنْ أَنذِرْ قَوْمَكَ مِن قَبْلِ أَن يَأْتِيَهُمْ عَذَابٌ أَلِيمٌ ۝ قَالَ يَٰقَوْمِ إِنِّى لَكُمْ نَذِيرٌ مُّبِينٌ ۝ أَنِ ٱعْبُدُوا۟ ٱللَّهَ وَٱتَّقُوهُ وَأَطِيعُونِ ۝ يَغْفِرْ لَكُم مِّن ذُنُوبِكُمْ وَيُؤَخِّرْكُمْ إِلَىٰ أَجَلٍ مُّسَمًّى إِنَّ أَجَلَ ٱللَّهِ إِذَا جَآءَ لَا يُؤَخَّرُ لَوْ كُنتُمْ تَعْلَمُونَ ۝ قَالَ رَبِّ إِنِّى دَعَوْتُ قَوْمِى لَيْلًا وَنَهَارًا ۝ فَلَمْ يَزِدْهُمْ دُعَآءِىٓ إِلَّا فِرَارًا ۝

ᵃ Noah is perhaps the first prophet after Adam. The message that he gave to the corrupted people of those days has been put here in three words—worship ('ibadah), fear of God (taqwa) and obedience to the Prophet (ita'ah), i.e. the worshipping of God and renouncing the worship of anything other than God, leading one's life in the world with the fear of God in one's heart and considering the prophet of God an example to be followed in all matters. This has been the real message of all prophets in every age and this is the true message of the Quran itself.

ᵇ It is evident from the utterances of Noah that his way of delivering the divine message is identical with that adopted in the Quran for inviting people to the Truth. Noah based his reasoning on the events of the universe while urging others to reform. He addressed the people collectively and also had individual discussions. He spared no effort to bring people on to the right path. But his people were not ready to accept him.

⁷ Every time I have called to them, so that You might forgive them, they have only thrust their fingers into their ears, covered themselves up with their garments, grown obstinate, and given themselves up to arrogance. ⁸ Then I called them openly, ⁹ and spoke to them in public and in private.' ¹⁰ Then I said, 'Ask forgiveness of your Lord. Surely He is the most forgiving. ¹¹ He will send down abundant rain from the sky for you, ¹² increase your wealth and sons; and grant you gardens and waterways. ¹³ What is the matter with you that you deny the greatness of God,ᵃ ¹⁴ when He has created you through different stages of existence? ¹⁵ Do you not see how God has created the seven heavens one above another, ¹⁶ and made the moon therein a light, and made the sun a lamp, ¹⁷ how God has produced you from the earth and caused you to grow, ¹⁸ how He will then return you to it and bring you forth again, ¹⁹ how God has spread the earth out for you ²⁰ so that you may walk along its spacious paths?'

وَإِنِّى كُلَّمَا دَعَوْتُهُمْ لِتَغْفِرَ لَهُمْ جَعَلُوٓاْ أَصَٰبِعَهُمْ فِىٓ ءَاذَانِهِمْ وَٱسْتَغْشَوْاْ ثِيَابَهُمْ وَأَصَرُّواْ وَٱسْتَكْبَرُواْ ٱسْتِكْبَارًا ۝ ثُمَّ إِنِّى دَعَوْتُهُمْ جِهَارًا ۝ ثُمَّ إِنِّىٓ أَعْلَنتُ لَهُمْ وَأَسْرَرْتُ لَهُمْ إِسْرَارًا ۝ فَقُلْتُ ٱسْتَغْفِرُواْ رَبَّكُمْ إِنَّهُۥ كَانَ غَفَّارًا ۝ يُرْسِلِ ٱلسَّمَآءَ عَلَيْكُم مِّدْرَارًا ۝ وَيُمْدِدْكُم بِأَمْوَٰلٍ وَبَنِينَ وَيَجْعَل لَّكُمْ جَنَّٰتٍ وَيَجْعَل لَّكُمْ أَنْهَٰرًا ۝ مَّا لَكُمْ لَا تَرْجُونَ لِلَّهِ وَقَارًا ۝ وَقَدْ خَلَقَكُمْ أَطْوَارًا ۝ أَلَمْ تَرَوْاْ كَيْفَ خَلَقَ ٱللَّهُ سَبْعَ سَمَٰوَٰتٍ طِبَاقًا ۝ وَجَعَلَ ٱلْقَمَرَ فِيهِنَّ نُورًا وَجَعَلَ ٱلشَّمْسَ سِرَاجًا ۝ وَٱللَّهُ أَنۢبَتَكُم مِّنَ ٱلْأَرْضِ نَبَاتًا ۝ ثُمَّ يُعِيدُكُمْ فِيهَا وَيُخْرِجُكُمْ إِخْرَاجًا ۝ وَٱللَّهُ جَعَلَ لَكُمُ ٱلْأَرْضَ بِسَاطًا ۝ لِّتَسْلُكُواْ مِنْهَا سُبُلًا فِجَاجًا ۝

ᵃ Literally 'Why do you deny the greatness of God?' This has been explained by 'Abdullah ibn 'Abbas thus, 'You do not accept the Majesty of God as it should be accepted.' This shows that Noah's people did accept God, but the consciousness of the Majesty of God had not become ingrained as it should have done. The fact is that this acceptance of God's greatness is the real standard of God-worship. One who is living in the knowledge of the Majesty of God is a real God-worshipper, while one whose heart is not immersed in God's greatness is not a true believer.

²¹ Noah supplicated, 'Lord, they have disobeyed me, and followed those whose wealth and children have only added to their ruin;ᵃ ²² and they have hatched a mighty plot, ²³ and they said [to their followers], "Do not ever abandon your deities: abandon neither Wadd, nor Suwa', and neither Yaghuth, nor Yauq nor Nasr!"ᵇ ²⁴ They have led many astray; so lead the wrongdoers to further error.' ²⁵ They were drowned and sent to Hell for their misdeeds; they found no one to help them against God.

قَالَ نُوحٌ رَّبِّ إِنَّهُمْ عَصَوْنِى وَٱتَّبَعُوا۟ مَن لَّمْ يَزِدْهُ مَالُهُۥ وَوَلَدُهُۥٓ إِلَّا خَسَارًا ۝ وَمَكَرُوا۟ مَكْرًا كُبَّارًا ۝ وَقَالُوا۟ لَا تَذَرُنَّ ءَالِهَتَكُمْ وَلَا تَذَرُنَّ وَدًّا وَلَا سُوَاعًا وَلَا يَغُوثَ وَيَعُوقَ وَنَسْرًا ۝ وَقَدْ أَضَلُّوا۟ كَثِيرًا ۖ وَلَا تَزِدِ ٱلظَّـٰلِمِينَ إِلَّا ضَلَـٰلًا ۝ مِّمَّا خَطِيٓـَٔـٰتِهِمْ أُغْرِقُوا۟ فَأُدْخِلُوا۟ نَارًا فَلَمْ يَجِدُوا۟ لَهُم مِّن دُونِ ٱللَّهِ أَنصَارًا ۝

ᵃ Why did people deny Noah's pleas for reform? The reason for this was that they thought that, compared to the words of Noah, the utterances of those who had attained a higher status from the worldly point of view were more worth considering. The great ones of the time arrogantly rejected the call for Truth, while lesser mortals rejected it because the great ones had done so.

ᵇ The opponents of Noah devised many great schemes against him. One of these was to spread it about that Noah was against their great ones of old, viz., Wadd, Suwa', Yauq, Yaghuth and Nasr. All of them had been of great piety in ancient times. Gradually they became sanctified and ultimately people started worshipping them. It was easy to turn the people against Noah in the name of these men. So, they made Noah's mission look dubious to the people by saying that he was treading a new path, straying from the path of their revered forebears.

²⁶ Noah prayed, 'O my Lord! Do not leave on earth a single one of those who deny the truth*—²⁷ if You leave any, they will misguide Your servants, and they will beget none but sinners and deniers of truth—²⁸ Lord! Forgive me and my parents and every true believer who enters my house, forgive all the believing men and believing women; and bestow no increase upon the wrongdoers except in ruin.'

وَقَالَ نُوحٌ رَّبِّ لَا تَذَرْ عَلَى ٱلْأَرْضِ مِنَ ٱلْكَٰفِرِينَ دَيَّارًا ۞ إِنَّكَ إِن تَذَرْهُمْ يُضِلُّوا۟ عِبَادَكَ وَلَا يَلِدُوٓا۟ إِلَّا فَاجِرًا كَفَّارًا ۞ رَّبِّ ٱغْفِرْ لِى وَلِوَٰلِدَىَّ وَلِمَن دَخَلَ بَيْتِىَ مُؤْمِنًا وَلِلْمُؤْمِنِينَ وَٱلْمُؤْمِنَٰتِ وَلَا تَزِدِ ٱلظَّٰلِمِينَ إِلَّا تَبَارًا ۞

ª It appears from Noah's prayer that, in his own times, evil had reached its final limit. Misguided beliefs and thoughts had become so prevalent in society that any child born and brought up in this society would have gone astray. When this stage had been reached, Noah's people were destined to face nothing less than destruction by Noah's flood.

72. THE JINN

In the name of God,
the Most Gracious, the Most Merciful

¹ Say, 'It has been revealed to me that a band of the jinn listened [to the Quran] and they said, "We have heard a really wonderful recital, ² which guides to the right path; so we have believed in it and we will not associate anyone with our Lord— ³ and exalted is the majesty of our Lord—He has taken neither a wife nor a son. ⁴ And [now we know] that the foolish among us have been saying outrageous things about God. ⁵ We had supposed that men and jinn would never utter a lie against God. ⁶ Some men used to seek refuge with the jinn in the past, but that only increased their insolence. ⁷ They thought, as you did, that God would never raise up anyone from the dead.ᵃ

قُلْ أُوحِيَ إِلَيَّ أَنَّهُ ٱسْتَمَعَ نَفَرٌ مِّنَ ٱلْجِنِّ فَقَالُوٓاْ إِنَّا سَمِعْنَا قُرْءَانًا عَجَبًا ۝ يَهْدِىٓ إِلَى ٱلرُّشْدِ فَـَٔامَنَّا بِهِۦ وَلَن نُّشْرِكَ بِرَبِّنَآ أَحَدًا ۝ وَأَنَّهُۥ تَعَٰلَىٰ جَدُّ رَبِّنَا مَا ٱتَّخَذَ صَٰحِبَةً وَلَا وَلَدًا ۝ وَأَنَّهُۥ كَانَ يَقُولُ سَفِيهُنَا عَلَى ٱللَّهِ شَطَطًا ۝ وَأَنَّا ظَنَنَّآ أَن لَّن تَقُولَ ٱلْإِنسُ وَٱلْجِنُّ عَلَى ٱللَّهِ كَذِبًا ۝ وَأَنَّهُۥ كَانَ رِجَالٌ مِّنَ ٱلْإِنسِ يَعُوذُونَ بِرِجَالٍ مِّنَ ٱلْجِنِّ فَزَادُوهُمْ رَهَقًا ۝ وَأَنَّهُمْ ظَنُّواْ كَمَا ظَنَنتُمْ أَن لَّن يَبْعَثَ ٱللَّهُ أَحَدًا ۝

ᵃ In this world, in addition to human beings and angels, there is another set of creatures known as jinn. Human beings cannot see them but, in the Quran, they have been mentioned at several places. These verses show that among the jinn also there are guided and misguided types. Just as there are foolish leaders who misguide the common people, similarly there are foolish leaders among the jinn, who go on misguiding them with deceitful utterances. So far as the angels are concerned, they are not being put to the test, and thus do not have free will. They simply follow the commands given by God.

8 "We sought to reach heaven, but found it filled with strong guards and flames—9 we used to take up a position to listen, but whoever listens now finds a flaming fire lying in wait for him—10 we cannot tell if this bodes evil to those who dwell on earth or whether their Lord intends to guide them. 11 Some of us are righteous, while others are not; we follow divergent paths. 12 We have realized that we could never thwart God on earth and that we would never be able to thwart Him by flight. 13 When we heard the call to guidance, we believed in it. He who believes in his Lord has no fear of loss or of injustice. 14 Some of us are obedient while others are wrongdoers; it is the obedient who have found the right path, 15 but those who are wrongdoers will become the fuel of Hell." [a]

وَأَنَّا لَمَسْنَا ٱلسَّمَآءَ فَوَجَدْنَٰهَا مُلِئَتْ حَرَسًا شَدِيدًا وَشُهُبًا ۝ وَأَنَّا كُنَّا نَقْعُدُ مِنْهَا مَقَٰعِدَ لِلسَّمْعِ فَمَن يَسْتَمِعِ ٱلْءَانَ يَجِدْ لَهُۥ شِهَابًا رَّصَدًا ۝ وَأَنَّا لَا نَدْرِىٓ أَشَرٌّ أُرِيدَ بِمَن فِى ٱلْأَرْضِ أَمْ أَرَادَ بِهِمْ رَبُّهُمْ رَشَدًا ۝ وَأَنَّا مِنَّا ٱلصَّٰلِحُونَ وَمِنَّا دُونَ ذَٰلِكَ كُنَّا طَرَآئِقَ قِدَدًا ۝ وَأَنَّا ظَنَنَّآ أَن لَّن نُّعْجِزَ ٱللَّهَ فِى ٱلْأَرْضِ وَلَن نُّعْجِزَهُۥ هَرَبًا ۝ وَأَنَّا لَمَّا سَمِعْنَا ٱلْهُدَىٰٓ ءَامَنَّا بِهِۦ فَمَن يُؤْمِنۢ بِرَبِّهِۦ فَلَا يَخَافُ بَخْسًا وَلَا رَهَقًا ۝ وَأَنَّا مِنَّا ٱلْمُسْلِمُونَ وَمِنَّا ٱلْقَٰسِطُونَ فَمَنْ أَسْلَمَ فَأُو۟لَٰٓئِكَ تَحَرَّوْا۟ رَشَدًا ۝ وَأَمَّا ٱلْقَٰسِطُونَ فَكَانُوا۟ لِجَهَنَّمَ حَطَبًا ۝

[a] The jinn who heard the Quran not only accepted it immediately, but also became its propagators. This shows that whenever a true discourse reaches the ears of living people, it creates a two-fold effect—first, an open-hearted admission of its truth and second, a willingness to propagate its teachings.

¹⁶ If they had followed the right path, We would have provided them with abundant rain—¹⁷ so that We may test them by it—whoever turns away from the remembrance of his Lord shall be sternly punished. ¹⁸ The mosques are for God's worship—so do not invoke anyone else along with God—¹⁹ when God's servant stood up to pray to Him, they pressed close to him in great numbers, almost stifling him. ²⁰ Say, 'I call only upon my Lord and do not associate anyone else with Him.' ²¹ Say, 'It is not in my power to cause you either harm or good?' ²² Say, 'Surely no one can protect me against God, nor can I find besides Him any place of refuge. ²³ My duty is only to convey that which I receive from Him and His messages.' For those who disobey God and His Messenger there is the fire of hell, wherein they will abide forever.^a

وَأَلَّوِ ٱسْتَقَـٰمُواْ عَلَى ٱلطَّرِيقَةِ لَأَسْقَيْنَـٰهُم مَّآءً غَدَقًا ۝ لِّنَفْتِنَهُمْ فِيهِ وَمَن يُعْرِضْ عَن ذِكْرِ رَبِّهِۦ يَسْلُكْهُ عَذَابًا صَعَدًا ۝ وَأَنَّ ٱلْمَسَـٰجِدَ لِلَّهِ فَلَا تَدْعُواْ مَعَ ٱللَّهِ أَحَدًا ۝ وَأَنَّهُۥ لَمَّا قَامَ عَبْدُ ٱللَّهِ يَدْعُوهُ كَادُواْ يَكُونُونَ عَلَيْهِ لِبَدًا ۝ قُلْ إِنَّمَآ أَدْعُواْ رَبِّى وَلَآ أُشْرِكُ بِهِۦٓ أَحَدًا ۝ قُلْ إِنِّى لَآ أَمْلِكُ لَكُمْ ضَرًّا وَلَا رَشَدًا ۝ قُلْ إِنِّى لَن يُجِيرَنِى مِنَ ٱللَّهِ أَحَدٌ وَلَنْ أَجِدَ مِن دُونِهِۦ مُلْتَحَدًا ۝ إِلَّا بَلَـٰغًا مِّنَ ٱللَّهِ وَرِسَـٰلَـٰتِهِۦ وَمَن يَعْصِ ٱللَّهَ وَرَسُولَهُۥ فَإِنَّ لَهُۥ نَارَ جَهَنَّمَ خَـٰلِدِينَ فِيهَآ أَبَدًا ۝

^a The entire system of the present world has been formulated with the aim of putting human beings to the test. Therefore reality is revealed here solely to the extent of conveying the divine message. Had there been no human trial to be considered, and had the concealing veils been removed, the people would have seen that, from the angels to the righteous among the jinn, all acknowledge the god-head of God and the whole universe testifies to this.

²⁴ When they are confronted by what they have been promised, they will realize who is weaker in helpers and fewer in numbers. ²⁵ Say, 'I do not know whether what you are promised is imminent, or whether my Lord has set for it a far-off day.' ²⁶ He alone has knowledge of what is hidden. He reveals this to none, ²⁷ except the messenger whom He has chosen. He sends down guardians who walk before them and behind them, ²⁸ so that He may know that the messengers have delivered the messages of their Lord. He encompasses all that is with them and He keeps count of all things.ᵃ

حَتَّىٰ إِذَا رَأَوْاْ مَا يُوعَدُونَ فَسَيَعْلَمُونَ مَنْ أَضْعَفُ نَاصِرًا وَأَقَلُّ عَدَدًا ۝ قُلْ إِنْ أَدْرِىٓ أَقَرِيبٌ مَّا تُوعَدُونَ أَمْ يَجْعَلُ لَهُۥ رَبِّىٓ أَمَدًا ۝ عَٰلِمُ ٱلْغَيْبِ فَلَا يُظْهِرُ عَلَىٰ غَيْبِهِۦٓ أَحَدًا ۝ إِلَّا مَنِ ٱرْتَضَىٰ مِن رَّسُولٍ فَإِنَّهُۥ يَسْلُكُ مِنۢ بَيْنِ يَدَيْهِ وَمِنْ خَلْفِهِۦ رَصَدًا ۝ لِّيَعْلَمَ أَن قَدْ أَبْلَغُوا۟ رِسَٰلَٰتِ رَبِّهِمْ وَأَحَاطَ بِمَا لَدَيْهِمْ وَأَحْصَىٰ كُلَّ شَىْءٍ عَدَدًا ۝

ᵃ The messenger of Truth is apparently a common man. Therefore, the people who are affected by his call turn upon him. They forget that any action against him amounts to action against God Himself. And who can be successful by taking action against God?

73. THE WRAPPED ONE

In the name of God,
the Most Gracious, the Most Merciful

¹ O you who are wrapped up in your mantle, ² stand up to pray for much of the night. ³ It may be half the night or a little less than that ⁴ or a little more, but recite the Quran slowly and distinctly.ᵃ ⁵ For We are about to send down to you a message of considerable gravity.ᵇ

ᵃ Literally 'recite the Quran in slow, measured rhythmic tones'. This means 'recite, paying full attention to the import of the content'. When recited like this, a two-way process between Quran and its reciter comes into play. For him, the Quran is an address or speech by God and his heart starts answering this address at every verse. In the Quran where there is any mention of God's majesty, the reciter's entire existence is strongly affected by the realisation of His greatness. When God's blessings are enumerated in the Quran, the reciter's heart overflows with gratitude; when God's retribution is described in the Quran, the reciter trembles on reading it; when an order is laid down in the Quran, the feeling becomes intensified in the reciter that he should become the obedient subject of his Lord by carrying out that order.

ᵇ Literally 'weighty words' refers to that order for giving warning which is mentioned in the next chapter, 'Arise and give warning' (74:2). This means inform people about the hazards of the Hereafter. Undoubtedly this is the most difficult task in the world. For this, the missionary has to stand by the pure and unadulterated Truth, even if he becomes a stranger to all his people. He has to tolerate being tormented by the people, so that the relationship between him and his addressees remains unaffected till the last moment. He has to be unilaterally governed by the principles of patience and avoidance of confrontation, so that his status as *da'i* should not be damaged.

⁶ Surely, getting up at night [for worship] is the most potent means of subduing the self and most suitable for the word [of prayer]. ⁷ You have by day prolonged occupations [with Dawah work]. ⁸ Remember the name of your Lord, and devote yourself to Him wholeheartedly. ⁹ He is the Lord of the east and the west, there is no deity but Him, so take Him as your Guardian. ¹⁰ Bear patiently with what they say, and ignore them politely. ¹¹ Leave it to Me to deal with the deniers, who live a life of comfort, and bear with them a little longer. ¹² We have in store for them heavy fetters and a blazing Fire, ¹³ food that chokes and painful punishment ¹⁴ on the Day the earth and mountains shall shake and the mountains crumble into shifting sand dunes.ᵃ

إِنَّ نَاشِئَةَ ٱلَّيْلِ هِىَ أَشَدُّ وَطْـًٔا وَأَقْوَمُ قِيلًا ۝ إِنَّ لَكَ فِى ٱلنَّهَارِ سَبْحًا طَوِيلًا ۝ وَٱذْكُرِ ٱسْمَ رَبِّكَ وَتَبَتَّلْ إِلَيْهِ تَبْتِيلًا ۝ رَّبُّ ٱلْمَشْرِقِ وَٱلْمَغْرِبِ لَآ إِلَٰهَ إِلَّا هُوَ فَٱتَّخِذْهُ وَكِيلًا ۝ وَٱصْبِرْ عَلَىٰ مَا يَقُولُونَ وَٱهْجُرْهُمْ هَجْرًا جَمِيلًا ۝ وَذَرْنِى وَٱلْمُكَذِّبِينَ أُو۟لِى ٱلنَّعْمَةِ وَمَهِّلْهُمْ قَلِيلًا ۝ إِنَّ لَدَيْنَآ أَنكَالًا وَجَحِيمًا ۝ وَطَعَامًا ذَا غُصَّةٍ وَعَذَابًا أَلِيمًا ۝ يَوْمَ تَرْجُفُ ٱلْأَرْضُ وَٱلْجِبَالُ وَكَانَتِ ٱلْجِبَالُ كَثِيبًا مَّهِيلًا ۝

ᵃ Delivering the call for acceptance of the Truth means initiating the most difficult campaign. One who does so becomes persona non grata in his entire surroundings. In such conditions, the only Being whom the preacher of Truth finds as his sympathiser and supporter is his Lord. He not only goes on remembering his God in his heart, but he also stands before Him during the night. Night time is the time of leisure. In the dead silence of night man finds a better opportunity to turn towards God with full concentration. In the path of the mission of Truth, strewn as it is with difficulties, this is the only real weapon which the missionary has.

It is the way of a true preacher that, when he is troubled by an addressee, he does not inveigh against or argue with him, but rushes towards God. He abstains from negative reaction till the last moment. And to continue to work, rising above such a reaction, is the essential condition which makes a man a missionary of the Truth in the real sense.

¹⁵ We have sent a messenger who is a witness over you, just as We sent a messenger to Pharoah before you. ¹⁶ But Pharoah rebelled against the messenger, so We seized him with a strong, crushing grip. ¹⁷ If you persist in denying the truth how will you escape the Day that will turn the children's hair grey. ¹⁸ The Day when the heavens will be rent asunder and God's promise shall be fulfilled. ¹⁹ This, surely, is an admonition. So let him who will, take the right path to his Lord.^a

إِنَّآ أَرْسَلْنَآ إِلَيْكُمْ رَسُولاً شَٰهِدًا عَلَيْكُمْ كَمَآ أَرْسَلْنَآ إِلَىٰ فِرْعَوْنَ رَسُولاً ۝ فَعَصَىٰ فِرْعَوْنُ ٱلرَّسُولَ فَأَخَذْنَٰهُ أَخْذًا وَبِيلاً ۝ فَكَيْفَ تَتَّقُونَ إِن كَفَرْتُمْ يَوْمًا يَجْعَلُ ٱلْوِلْدَٰنَ شِيبًا ۝ ٱلسَّمَآءُ مُنفَطِرٌ بِهِۦ كَانَ وَعْدُهُۥ مَفْعُولاً ۝ إِنَّ هَٰذِهِۦ تَذْكِرَةٌ فَمَن شَآءَ ٱتَّخَذَ إِلَىٰ رَبِّهِۦ سَبِيلاً ۝

---

^a The arrival of a prophet was meant to ensure that the distinction between Truth and falsehood was clearly understood and that, finally, the Truth was opted for. Such a decision about these alternatives had taken place earlier between Moses and Pharaoh. Then the same type of decision had to be arrived at between the Prophet Muhammad and the Quraysh. Those who do not bow down before the missionary of God in this world, run the risk of having to bow down before God's punishment in the Hereafter.

20 Your Lord knows that you stand up praying for nearly two-thirds of the night, or one-half of it and sometimes one third of it, as do others among your followers. God determines the measure of night and day. He knows that you will not be able to do it, so He has turned to you in mercy. Recite, then, as much of the Quran as is easy for you. He knows that there will be some among you who may be sick and others who will be travelling throughout the land seeking God's bounty, and yet others who may be fighting for the cause of God. So, recite, then as much of it as you are able, and be constant in prayer, and spend in charity, and give to God a goodly loan. For whatever good deed you send on before you for your souls, you will find it with God. It will be improved and richly rewarded by Him. Seek God's forgiveness, He is most forgiving, most merciful.[a]

﷽ إِنَّ رَبَّكَ يَعْلَمُ أَنَّكَ تَقُومُ أَدْنَىٰ مِن ثُلُثَىِ ٱلَّيْلِ وَنِصْفَهُۥ وَثُلُثَهُۥ وَطَآئِفَةٌ مِّنَ ٱلَّذِينَ مَعَكَ وَٱللَّهُ يُقَدِّرُ ٱلَّيْلَ وَٱلنَّهَارَ عَلِمَ أَن لَّن تُحْصُوهُ فَتَابَ عَلَيْكُمْ فَٱقْرَءُوا۟ مَا تَيَسَّرَ مِنَ ٱلْقُرْءَانِ عَلِمَ أَن سَيَكُونُ مِنكُم مَّرْضَىٰ وَءَاخَرُونَ يَضْرِبُونَ فِى ٱلْأَرْضِ يَبْتَغُونَ مِن فَضْلِ ٱللَّهِ وَءَاخَرُونَ يُقَـٰتِلُونَ فِى سَبِيلِ ٱللَّهِ فَٱقْرَءُوا۟ مَا تَيَسَّرَ مِنْهُ وَأَقِيمُوا۟ ٱلصَّلَوٰةَ وَءَاتُوا۟ ٱلزَّكَوٰةَ وَأَقْرِضُوا۟ ٱللَّهَ قَرْضًا حَسَنًا وَمَا تُقَدِّمُوا۟ لِأَنفُسِكُم مِّنْ خَيْرٍ تَجِدُوهُ عِندَ ٱللَّهِ هُوَ خَيْرًا وَأَعْظَمَ أَجْرًا وَٱسْتَغْفِرُوا۟ ٱللَّهَ إِنَّ ٱللَّهَ غَفُورٌ رَّحِيمٌ ۝

---

[a] The compulsory duties in religion have been set forth in terms of the common man's capabilities. But these duties indicate only the minimum of compulsory limits. Beyond these limits there are certain requirements, but these are of a voluntary nature, for example, the offering of the post-midnight prayer (*tahajjud*) in addition to the five compulsory prayers (*fard salat*) said at different times throughout the day, or charity in addition to the prescribed alms-giving (*zakat*), etc. This is the test of a man's devoutness to see how many more good deeds he performs, thus making himself eligible for greater rewards.

74. WRAPPED IN HIS CLOAK

In the name of God,
the Most Gracious, the Most Merciful

¹ O, you, wrapped in your cloak, ² arise and give warning! ³ Proclaim the glory of your Lord; ⁴ purify your garments; ⁵ shun uncleanness; ⁶ do not bestow a favour in the expectation of receiving more in return; ⁷ and for the sake of your Lord, be patient.ᵃ

⁸ When the Trumpet is sounded, ⁹ that Day will be a hard and distressing Day. ¹⁰ It will not be easy for those who deny the truth. ¹¹ Leave Me alone [to deal] with him whom I have created alone, ¹² and to whom I have granted resources in abundance, ¹³ and sons to be by his side, ¹⁴ and whom I have provided with every resource, ¹⁵ and yet, he greedily desires that I give him even more! ¹⁶ By no means! He has been stubbornly hostile to Our revelation: ¹⁷ I shall force him to endure a painful uphill climb! ᵇ

ᵃ The real work of a prophet is warning the people, i.e. informing them of the serious nature of the events which will unfold in the Hereafter. This task can be performed only by one whose heart is overflowing with the realisation of God's Majesty, who possesses a noble character, who shuns all evil, who does good without aspiring to any recompense, who can be unilaterally tolerant and exercise patience in the face of trouble created by others.

ᵇ One who finds himself in an affluent position with a horde of companions, develops a false sense of confidence. He imagines that as he is well-to-do in this world, he will fare well in the Hereafter also. But with the advent of Doomsday, the whole situation will change. The individual who was in easy circumstances in this world, will then find himself surrounded by insurmountable difficulties.

¹⁸ For he thought and he plotted—
¹⁹ and woe to him; how he plotted!
²⁰ Let him be destroyed. How he
calculated! ²¹ Then he looked round;
²² then he frowned and scowled,
²³ and he turned his back and
behaved arrogantly ²⁴ and said, 'This
is nothing but sorcery from the
ancients. ²⁵ This is nothing but the
word of a mortal!'^a

إِنَّهُ فَكَّرَ وَقَدَّرَ ۝ فَقُتِلَ كَيْفَ قَدَّرَ
۝ ثُمَّ قُتِلَ كَيْفَ قَدَّرَ ۝ ثُمَّ نَظَرَ
۝ ثُمَّ عَبَسَ وَبَسَرَ ۝ ثُمَّ أَدْبَرَ
وَٱسْتَكْبَرَ ۝ فَقَالَ إِنْ هَـٰذَآ إِلَّا سِحْرٌ
يُؤْثَرُ ۝ إِنْ هَـٰذَآ إِلَّا قَوْلُ ٱلْبَشَرِ ۝

^a The greatest impediment to acceptance of the Truth is a man's egoism or pride.
Those who attain a high status in society do not accept the Truth for the simple
reason that, by such acceptance, their greatness will be diminished. In order to
cover up their rejection, they try to find defects in the discourse of the preacher
of Truth. They try to degrade him by making allegations against him.

²⁶ Soon I will cast him into hell.
²⁷ What could make you conceive
what hell-fire is? ²⁸ It does not allow
anyone to live, and neither does it
leave anyone to die; ²⁹ it scorches the
skin; ³⁰ there are nineteen [angels] in
charge of it—³¹ We have appointed
only angels to be wardens of the Fire.
We have specified their number
only as a trial for those who are bent
on denying the truth, so that those
who were given the Book might gain
in certainty, and those who believe
might increase in faith—and so that
neither those who have been given
the Scripture nor the believers might
have any doubts, and that those sick
at heart and those who deny the
truth might ask, 'What does God
mean by this parable?' In this way,
God lets go astray whom He wills,
and guides whom He wills. And
none knows the forces of your Lord
but He. This is but a Reminder for
man.ᵃ

سَأُصْلِيهِ سَقَرَ ۝ وَمَآ أَدْرَىٰكَ مَا سَقَرُ
۝ لَا تُبْقِى وَلَا تَذَرُ ۝ لَوَّاحَةٌ
لِّلْبَشَرِ ۝ عَلَيْهَا تِسْعَةَ عَشَرَ ۝ وَمَا
جَعَلْنَآ أَصْحَٰبَ ٱلنَّارِ إِلَّا مَلَٰٓئِكَةً ۛ وَمَا
جَعَلْنَا عِدَّتَهُمْ إِلَّا فِتْنَةً لِّلَّذِينَ كَفَرُوا۟
لِيَسْتَيْقِنَ ٱلَّذِينَ أُوتُوا۟ ٱلْكِتَٰبَ وَيَزْدَادَ
ٱلَّذِينَ ءَامَنُوٓا۟ إِيمَٰنًا ۙ وَلَا يَرْتَابَ ٱلَّذِينَ
أُوتُوا۟ ٱلْكِتَٰبَ وَٱلْمُؤْمِنُونَ ۙ وَلِيَقُولَ
ٱلَّذِينَ فِى قُلُوبِهِم مَّرَضٌ وَٱلْكَٰفِرُونَ
مَاذَآ أَرَادَ ٱللَّهُ بِهَٰذَا مَثَلًا ۚ كَذَٰلِكَ
يُضِلُّ ٱللَّهُ مَن يَشَآءُ وَيَهْدِى مَن يَشَآءُ ۚ
وَمَا يَعْلَمُ جُنُودَ رَبِّكَ إِلَّا هُوَ ۚ وَمَا هِىَ
إِلَّا ذِكْرَىٰ لِلْبَشَرِ ۝

ᵃ The conditions of hell described in the Quran relate to the unseen and hidden
world. There being nineteen angels in hell is also a fact of a similar nature. If one
resorts to hair-splitting, these matters will only increase one's doubts. But if the
way of complete faith is adopted, these matters will increase one's fear of the
Hereafter.

³² No, by the moon! ³³ By the night when it departs. ³⁴ By the dawn when it lightens! ³⁵ Surely, it is one of the gravest things, ³⁶ it is a warning to man, ³⁷ alike to every one of you, who want to go forward or hang back. ³⁸ Every soul is held in pledge against its own deeds, ³⁹ except those of the right hand ⁴⁰ who in their gardens will be enquiring ⁴¹ about the sinners. ⁴² 'What has brought you into the Fire of Hell?' ⁴³ and they shall reply, 'We were not among those who prayed; ⁴⁴ and we did not feed the poor; ⁴⁵ we indulged in vain arguments along with those who indulged in them; ⁴⁶ and we denied the Day of Judgement ⁴⁷ until the Inevitable End [death] overtook us.' ⁴⁸ So no intercession will avail them.ᵃ

كَلَّا وَٱلْقَمَرِ ۝ وَٱلَّيْلِ إِذْ أَدْبَرَ ۝ وَٱلصُّبْحِ إِذَآ أَسْفَرَ ۝ إِنَّهَا لَإِحْدَى ٱلْكُبَرِ ۝ نَذِيرًا لِّلْبَشَرِ ۝ لِمَن شَآءَ مِنكُمْ أَن يَتَقَدَّمَ أَوْ يَتَأَخَّرَ ۝ كُلُّ نَفْسٍ بِمَا كَسَبَتْ رَهِينَةٌ ۝ إِلَّآ أَصْحَٰبَ ٱلْيَمِينِ ۝ فِى جَنَّٰتٍ يَتَسَآءَلُونَ ۝ عَنِ ٱلْمُجْرِمِينَ ۝ مَا سَلَكَكُمْ فِى سَقَرَ ۝ قَالُوا۟ لَمْ نَكُ مِنَ ٱلْمُصَلِّينَ ۝ وَلَمْ نَكُ نُطْعِمُ ٱلْمِسْكِينَ ۝ وَكُنَّا نَخُوضُ مَعَ ٱلْخَآئِضِينَ ۝ وَكُنَّا نُكَذِّبُ بِيَوْمِ ٱلدِّينِ ۝ حَتَّىٰ أَتَىٰنَا ٱلْيَقِينُ ۝ فَمَا تَنفَعُهُمْ شَفَٰعَةُ ٱلشَّٰفِعِينَ ۝

ᵃ The earth rotates on its axis and the moon orbits the earth. For this reason, lunar dates change and night and day alternate on the earth. This system of rotation and changes is in fact an indication that the present order will change and that the period of the Hereafter will definitely arrive. Those who take this system into account will want to make full use of their 'day', before the arrival of 'night'. They will avoid all actions which could plunge them into Hell, preferring instead to act in a way which will lead them to Paradise.

⁴⁹ Then what is wrong with them that they turn away from admonition, ⁵⁰ like frightened donkeys ⁵¹ fleeing from a lion? ⁵² Indeed, everyone of them desires to have sheets of revelations unfolded before them—⁵³ No! They do not fear the Hereafter— ⁵⁴ but this is truly a reminder. ⁵⁵ Let him who will take heed: ⁵⁶ they will only take heed if God so wills: He is the Lord who is worthy to be feared: the Lord of forgiveness.ᵃ

فَمَا لَهُمْ عَنِ ٱلتَّذْكِرَةِ مُعْرِضِينَ ۞ كَأَنَّهُمْ حُمُرٌ مُّسْتَنفِرَةٌ ۞ فَرَّتْ مِن قَسْوَرَةٍ ۞ بَلْ يُرِيدُ كُلُّ ٱمْرِئٍ مِّنْهُمْ أَن يُؤْتَىٰ صُحُفًا مُّنَشَّرَةً ۞ كَلَّا بَل لَّا يَخَافُونَ ٱلْأَخِرَةَ ۞ كَلَّا إِنَّهُ تَذْكِرَةٌ ۞ فَمَن شَاءَ ذَكَرَهُ ۞ وَمَا يَذْكُرُونَ إِلَّا أَن يَشَاءَ ٱللَّهُ هُوَ أَهْلُ ٱلتَّقْوَىٰ وَأَهْلُ ٱلْمَغْفِرَةِ ۞

ᵃ Advice, howsoever reasonable and well-supported by arguments, can be effective only when the hearer is serious about it. If the hearer is not serious, the advice will not reach his heart. Such arguments as deeply move a serious-minded person, will only cause a frivolous person to engage in meaningless discussions.

75. THE DAY OF RESURRECTION

In the name of God,
the Most Gracious, the Most Merciful

¹ By the Day of Resurrection, ² and by the self-reproaching soul! ³ Does man think that We cannot [resurrect him and] bring his bones together again? ⁴ Indeed, We have the power to restore his very finger tips! ⁵ Yet man wants to deny what is ahead of him: ⁶ he asks, 'When is this Day of Resurrection to be?' ⁷ But [on that Day], when mortal sight is confounded, ⁸ and the moon is eclipsed, ⁹ when the sun and the moon are brought together, ¹⁰ on that Day man will ask, 'Where can I escape?' ¹¹ But there is nowhere to take refuge: ¹² on that Day, to your Lord alone is the recourse. ¹³ On that Day, man will be told of all that he has sent before and what he has left behind. ¹⁴ Indeed, man shall be a witness against himself, ¹⁵ in spite of all the excuses he may offer.ᵃ

ᵃ Man has the innate capacity to distinguish between good and evil. By his very nature he wants anyone indulging in evil to be punished and anyone doing righteous deeds to be rewarded. It is this consciousness which is called in the Quran the self-reproaching soul or *an-nafs al-lawwamah*. This faculty bears testimony at the psychological level to the reality of the world of the Hereafter. If, in spite of this inner testimony, an individual does not fulfil its demands, it means that he negates what he has already accepted.

¹⁶ [Prophet], do not move your tongue too fast in your attempt to learn this revelation: ¹⁷ We Ourself shall see to its collection and recital. ¹⁸ When We have recited it, follow its words attentively; ¹⁹ and then, it will be for Us to make its meaning clear.ᵃ

لَا تُحَرِّكْ بِهِۦ لِسَانَكَ لِتَعْجَلَ بِهِۦٓ ۝ إِنَّ عَلَيْنَا جَمْعَهُۥ وَقُرْءَانَهُۥ ۝ فَإِذَا قَرَأْنَـٰهُ فَٱتَّبِعْ قُرْءَانَهُۥ ۝ ثُمَّ إِنَّ عَلَيْنَا بَيَانَهُۥ ۝

ᵃ When revelations, *wahi*, were made to the Prophet Muhammad, he used to make haste to receive them. Here, he has been asked not to do this. It is further stated that he should pay full attention to that part of the Quran which had already been revealed and which had already been addressed to him and should not concern himself with that portion which had not till then been revealed and had not been addressed to him. This shows that the individual should pay the fullest attention only to that portion of the Quran for which he is accountable at that moment. To make a point of seeking out that portion of the Quran for which he has not yet been made accountable, is being over-hasty and is entirely against Quranic wisdom.

²⁰ Truly, you love immediate gain ²¹ and neglect the Hereafter. ²² Some faces will be radiant on that Day, ²³ looking towards their Lord; ²⁴ and some faces will on that Day be gloomy, ²⁵ dreading some great affliction. ²⁶ But when [man's soul] reaches the throat, ²⁷ and when it is asked: 'Could any magician save him now?'; ²⁸ and he knows that it is the time of parting; ²⁹ when his legs are brought together [when affliction is combined with affliction]; ³⁰ on that Day he will be driven towards your Lord![a]

كَلَّا بَلْ تُحِبُّونَ ٱلْعَاجِلَةَ ۝ وَتَذَرُونَ ٱلْأَخِرَةَ ۝ وُجُوهٌ يَوْمَئِذٍ نَّاضِرَةٌ ۝ إِلَىٰ رَبِّهَا نَاظِرَةٌ ۝ وَوُجُوهٌ يَوْمَئِذٍ بَاسِرَةٌ ۝ تَظُنُّ أَن يُفْعَلَ بِهَا فَاقِرَةٌ ۝ كَلَّا إِذَا بَلَغَتِ ٱلتَّرَاقِيَ ۝ وَقِيلَ مَنْ رَاقٍ ۝ وَظَنَّ أَنَّهُ ٱلْفِرَاقُ ۝ وَٱلْتَفَّتِ ٱلسَّاقُ بِٱلسَّاقِ ۝ إِلَىٰ رَبِّكَ يَوْمَئِذٍ ٱلْمَسَاقُ ۝

---

[a] There is only one reason for neglect of the Hereafter and that is the desire to obtain an immediate reward for all one's striving (kalla bal tuhibbuna'l 'ajilah). In relation to the Hereafter, the result of one's actions seems infinitely remote. Therefore, man disregards it. But in relation to this world, instant gratification appears to be a distinct possibility, so man rushes towards it. It is obvious that ultimately death overtakes every human being and nullifies all successes. Yet nobody learns a lesson from this, until he himself faces death—which takes away all opportunities for learning lessons.

³¹ He neither believed nor prayed, ³² but rejected the Truth and turned away! ³³ Then he went off to his people, swaggering. ³⁴ Woe to you, [O man!], yes, woe to you. ³⁵ Again, woe to you, [O man!], yes, woe to you! ³⁶ Does man, then, think that he is to be left to himself, to go about at will? ³⁷ Was he not once a drop of ejaculated semen, ³⁸ which then became a leech-like clot; then God shaped and fashioned him in due proportion, ³⁹ fashioning out of him the two sexes, the male and the female? ⁴⁰ Then is He not able to bring the dead back to life? ᵃ

فَلَا صَدَّقَ وَلَا صَلَّىٰ ۝ وَلَٰكِن كَذَّبَ وَتَوَلَّىٰ ۝ ثُمَّ ذَهَبَ إِلَىٰ أَهْلِهِۦ يَتَمَطَّىٰٓ ۝ أَوْلَىٰ لَكَ فَأَوْلَىٰ ۝ ثُمَّ أَوْلَىٰ لَكَ فَأَوْلَىٰٓ ۝ أَيَحْسَبُ ٱلْإِنسَٰنُ أَن يُتْرَكَ سُدًى ۝ أَلَمْ يَكُ نُطْفَةً مِّن مَّنِىٍّ يُمْنَىٰ ۝ ثُمَّ كَانَ عَلَقَةً فَخَلَقَ فَسَوَّىٰ ۝ فَجَعَلَ مِنْهُ ٱلزَّوْجَيْنِ ٱلذَّكَرَ وَٱلْأُنثَىٰٓ ۝ أَلَيْسَ ذَٰلِكَ بِقَٰدِرٍ عَلَىٰٓ أَن يُحْيِۦَ ٱلْمَوْتَىٰ ۝

ᵃ In the beginning a human being enters the womb of his mother in the form of a drop. Then he develops and takes the shape of a leech ('alaqa). He further develops and his limbs and features acquire their typical characteristics. Then, he emerges as a male or female. All these wonderful changes take place without any effort on the part of human beings. So, the system of nature which brings about such wonders every day, the creation of a new world after the present world should not be difficult. The fact is that the real impediment in the way of acceptance of Truth is egotism or conceit and not any dearth of arguments or reasoning.

76. MAN

In the name of God,
the Most Gracious, the Most Merciful

¹ Was there not a period of time when man was nothing worth mentioning? ² We created man from a drop of mingled fluid so that We might try him; We gave him hearing and sight; ³ We showed him the way, whether he be grateful or ungrateful.ᵃ

ساره الانسل

بِسۡمِ ٱللَّهِ ٱلرَّحۡمَٰنِ ٱلرَّحِيمِ

هَلۡ أَتَىٰ عَلَى ٱلۡإِنسَٰنِ حِينٌ مِّنَ ٱلدَّهۡرِ لَمۡ يَكُن شَيۡـًٔا مَّذۡكُورًا ۝ إِنَّا خَلَقۡنَا ٱلۡإِنسَٰنَ مِن نُّطۡفَةٍ أَمۡشَاجٍ نَّبۡتَلِيهِ فَجَعَلۡنَٰهُ سَمِيعًۢا بَصِيرًا ۝ إِنَّا هَدَيۡنَٰهُ ٱلسَّبِيلَ إِمَّا شَاكِرًا وَإِمَّا كَفُورًا ۝

ᵃ The Quran was revealed in the seventh century A.D. At that time nobody in the whole world knew that the formation of a human being in the mother's womb started with a drop or clot. It was only in the twentieth century that man came to know that a human being's (as well as an animal's) initial creative clot was formed by a combination of two parts—the ovum of a woman and the sperm of a man. When these two microscopic elements combined, that living thing started forming in the mother's womb which finally took the shape of a human being. The occurrence of the expression, 'a drop of mingled fluid' (*min nutfatin amshajin*) in the Quran one thousand five hundred years ago proves that the Quran is the Book of God.

There are many such examples in the Quran. These exceptional cases clearly establish that the Quran was divinely inspired. And when it has once been established that the Quran is the Book of God, its every statement has to be accepted as true, solely on the basis of its having been recorded in the Quran.

⁴ [Now,] behold, for those who deny the truth, We have prepared chains, iron collars and a blazing fire, but ⁵ the righteous shall drink from a cup mixed with the coolness of *kafur*,ᵃ ⁶ a spring from which God's servants will drink, making it gush forth in branches. ⁷ They keep their vows and fear a day the woe of which will spread far and wide; ⁸ they give food, despite their love for it, to the poor and orphans and captives, ⁹ saying, 'We feed you for the sake of God alone, we seek neither recompense nor thanks from you. ¹⁰ Truly, we fear from our Lord a woefully grim Day.' ¹¹ Therefore, God will ward off from them the woes of that Day, and make them find brightness and joy, ¹² and their reward for being patient will be a Garden and silk [clothing]. ¹³ Reclining upon couches, they will find therein neither the heat of the sun nor bitter, biting cold, ¹⁴ the shading branches of trees will come down low over them, and their clusters of fruit, will hang down where they are the easiest to reach. ¹⁵ Vessels of silver and goblets of pure crystal will be passed round among them ¹⁶ and gleaming silver goblets which have been filled to the exact measure,ᵇ

إِنَّا أَعْتَدْنَا لِلْكَافِرِينَ سَلَاسِلَا۟
وَأَغْلَالًا وَسَعِيرًا ۝ إِنَّ ٱلْأَبْرَارَ
يَشْرَبُونَ مِن كَأْسٍ كَانَ مِزَاجُهَا
كَافُورًا ۝ عَيْنًا يَشْرَبُ بِهَا عِبَادُ
ٱللَّهِ يُفَجِّرُونَهَا تَفْجِيرًا ۝ يُوفُونَ
بِٱلنَّذْرِ وَيَخَافُونَ يَوْمًا كَانَ شَرُّهُۥ
مُسْتَطِيرًا ۝ وَيُطْعِمُونَ ٱلطَّعَامَ عَلَىٰ
حُبِّهِۦ مِسْكِينًا وَيَتِيمًا وَأَسِيرًا ۝ إِنَّمَا
نُطْعِمُكُمْ لِوَجْهِ ٱللَّهِ لَا نُرِيدُ مِنكُمْ
جَزَآءً وَلَا شُكُورًا ۝ إِنَّا نَخَافُ مِن
رَّبِّنَا يَوْمًا عَبُوسًا قَمْطَرِيرًا ۝
فَوَقَىٰهُمُ ٱللَّهُ شَرَّ ذَٰلِكَ ٱلْيَوْمِ وَلَقَّىٰهُمْ
نَضْرَةً وَسُرُورًا ۝ وَجَزَىٰهُم بِمَا صَبَرُوا۟
جَنَّةً وَحَرِيرًا ۝ مُّتَّكِئِينَ فِيهَا عَلَى
ٱلْأَرَآئِكِ لَا يَرَوْنَ فِيهَا شَمْسًا وَلَا
زَمْهَرِيرًا ۝ وَدَانِيَةً عَلَيْهِمْ ظِلَٰلُهَا
وَذُلِّلَتْ قُطُوفُهَا تَذْلِيلًا ۝ وَيُطَافُ
عَلَيْهِم بِـَٔانِيَةٍ مِّن فِضَّةٍ وَأَكْوَابٍ كَانَتْ
قَوَارِيرَا۟ ۝ قَوَارِيرَا۟ مِن فِضَّةٍ قَدَّرُوهَا
تَقْدِيرًا ۝

ᵃ Camphor—a sweet smelling herb.

ᵇ Man has been created free in this world and then he has been shown two paths leading respectively towards a life of gratitude and a life of ingratitude. Now, it is for the concerned person to choose either of the two paths. For one who adopts the way of ingratitude, there will be the punishment of Hell in the Hereafter, and for one who adopts the way of gratitude, there will be the bounties of Paradise.

¹⁷ and they will be given a cup to drink flavoured with ginger, ¹⁸ from a flowing spring called Salsabil. ¹⁹ They will be attended by youths who will not age—when you see them you will think them to be like sprinkled pearls—²⁰ wherever you look, you will see bliss and a great kingdom: ²¹ they will wear green garments of fine silk and rich brocade. They will be adorned with silver bracelets. And their Lord will give them a pure drink. ²² This is your reward. Your endeavour is fully acknowledged.^a

وَيُسْقَوْنَ فِيهَا كَأْسًا كَانَ مِزَاجُهَا زَنجَبِيلًا ۝ عَيْنًا فِيهَا تُسَمَّىٰ سَلْسَبِيلًا ۝ ۞ وَيَطُوفُ عَلَيْهِمْ وِلْدَانٌ مُّخَلَّدُونَ إِذَا رَأَيْتَهُمْ حَسِبْتَهُمْ لُؤْلُؤًا مَّنثُورًا ۝ وَإِذَا رَأَيْتَ ثَمَّ رَأَيْتَ نَعِيمًا وَمُلْكًا كَبِيرًا ۝ عَلِيَهُمْ ثِيَابُ سُندُسٍ خُضْرٌ وَإِسْتَبْرَقٌ وَحُلُّوٓا أَسَاوِرَ مِن فِضَّةٍ وَسَقَاهُمْ رَبُّهُمْ شَرَابًا طَهُورًا ۝ إِنَّ هَٰذَا كَانَ لَكُمْ جَزَآءً وَكَانَ سَعْيُكُم مَّشْكُورًا ۝

---

^a This is the description of a higher plane of Paradise where people of a higher level of faith will be settled. Royal bounties will fall to the lot of the inhabitants of this Paradise.

23 Truly, it is We who have revealed to you the Quran, a gradual revelation. 24 So wait patiently for the command of your Lord, and do not yield to anyone among them who is sinful or ungrateful; 25 and glorify your Lord morning and evening; 26 and during the night prostrate ourself before Him, and extol His glory for a long part of the night. 27 Those people [who are unmindful of God] aspire for immediate gains, and put behind them a Heavy Day. 28 It was We who created them and made their constitution strong, but if We wish we can replace them with others like them. 29 This is a reminder. Let whoever wishes, take the right path to his Lord. 30 But you cannot will it unless God wills [to show you that way]—God is indeed all-knowing and wise—31 He admits whoever He will into His grace and has prepared a painful punishment for the evil doers.[a]

إِنَّا نَحْنُ نَزَّلْنَا عَلَيْكَ ٱلْقُرْءَانَ تَنزِيلًا ﴿٢٣﴾ فَٱصْبِرْ لِحُكْمِ رَبِّكَ وَلَا تُطِعْ مِنْهُمْ ءَاثِمًا أَوْ كَفُورًا ﴿٢٤﴾ وَٱذْكُرِ ٱسْمَ رَبِّكَ بُكْرَةً وَأَصِيلًا ﴿٢٥﴾ وَمِنَ ٱلَّيْلِ فَٱسْجُدْ لَهُ وَسَبِّحْهُ لَيْلًا طَوِيلًا ﴿٢٦﴾ إِنَّ هَٰؤُلَآءِ يُحِبُّونَ ٱلْعَاجِلَةَ وَيَذَرُونَ وَرَآءَهُمْ يَوْمًا ثَقِيلًا ﴿٢٧﴾ نَّحْنُ خَلَقْنَٰهُمْ وَشَدَدْنَآ أَسْرَهُمْ وَإِذَا شِئْنَا بَدَّلْنَآ أَمْثَٰلَهُمْ تَبْدِيلًا ﴿٢٨﴾ إِنَّ هَٰذِهِ تَذْكِرَةٌ فَمَن شَآءَ ٱتَّخَذَ إِلَىٰ رَبِّهِ سَبِيلًا ﴿٢٩﴾ وَمَا تَشَآءُونَ إِلَّآ أَن يَشَآءَ ٱللَّهُ إِنَّ ٱللَّهَ كَانَ عَلِيمًا حَكِيمًا ﴿٣٠﴾ يُدْخِلُ مَن يَشَآءُ فِى رَحْمَتِهِ وَٱلظَّٰلِمِينَ أَعَدَّ لَهُمْ عَذَابًا أَلِيمًا ﴿٣١﴾

***

[a] There are two particular reasons for the denial of Truth. Either man has his worldly interests in view, and the fear of being deprived of these prevents him from going ahead towards the Truth. Or man's false pride prevents him from recognising greatness in anyone other than his own self. Both types of people create obstacles in the way of the mission of Truth. But the preacher of Truth has been commanded to carry on his work with patience and without paying any heed to the hurdles he must surmount.

77. THOSE THAT ARE SENT FORTH

In the name of God,
the Most Gracious, the Most Merciful

¹ By the winds sent forth in swift succession, ² and then storming on with a tempest's force, ³ and the rain-spreading winds, ⁴ separating one from another, ⁵ by those who bring down the reminder, ⁶ to excuse some and warn others: ⁷ that which you have been promised shall be fulfilled.ᵃ

وَٱلۡمُرۡسَلَٰتِ عُرۡفًا ۝ فَٱلۡعَٰصِفَٰتِ عَصۡفًا ۝ وَٱلنَّٰشِرَٰتِ نَشۡرًا ۝ فَٱلۡفَٰرِقَٰتِ فَرۡقًا ۝ فَٱلۡمُلۡقِيَٰتِ ذِكۡرًا ۝ عُذۡرًا أَوۡ نُذۡرًا ۝ إِنَّمَا تُوعَدُونَ لَوَٰقِعٌ ۝

ᵃ Vapour rises from the surface of the sea. This rises in the atmosphere and forms clouds. The winds take these clouds from one place to another. Leaving some places dry, they shower rain at other places, causing freshness and the growth of greenery. This shows that the system of this world is based on the principle of differentiating between one thing or person. The manifestation of this principle is only partially evident in the present world, but in the Hereafter it will take a perfect shape.

This nature of the winds is a sort of reminder for man. Their being a mercy to some and bringing harm to others is to remind us of the fact that, as there are these two different types of persons in the present world, God's verdict in respect of these two types of persons will also appear in two different shapes in the next world.

⁸ When the stars lose their light, ⁹ and when the sky is rent asunder, ¹⁰ and when the mountains crumble into dust ¹¹ and when the messengers are brought together at the appointed time—¹² for what Day has this been appointed? ¹³ For the Day of Decision. ¹⁴ What will explain to you what the Day of Judgement is? ¹⁵ Woe on that Day to those who reject the truth. ¹⁶ Did We not destroy the earlier peoples? ¹⁷ We will now cause the later ones to follow them: ¹⁸ thus do We deal with the culprits. ¹⁹ Woe on that Day to those who reject the truth!ᵃ

²⁰ Did We not create you from a humble fluid, ²¹ then placed it in a secure repository [the womb], ²² for an appointed term? ²³ Thus We have determined the stages of development and Our power to determine is excellent indeed. ²⁴ Woe on that Day to those who reject the truth! ²⁵ Have We not made the earth a receptacle, ²⁶ for the living and the dead? ²⁷ Have We not placed high mountains upon it and given you fresh water to drink? ²⁸ Woe on that Day to those who reject the truth!ᵇ

فَإِذَا ٱلنُّجُومُ طُمِسَتْ ۝ وَإِذَا ٱلسَّمَاءُ فُرِجَتْ ۝ وَإِذَا ٱلْجِبَالُ نُسِفَتْ ۝ وَإِذَا ٱلرُّسُلُ أُقِّتَتْ ۝ لِأَيِّ يَوْمٍ أُجِّلَتْ ۝ لِيَوْمِ ٱلْفَصْلِ ۝ وَمَا أَدْرَىٰكَ مَا يَوْمُ ٱلْفَصْلِ ۝ وَيْلٌ يَوْمَئِذٍ لِّلْمُكَذِّبِينَ ۝ أَلَمْ نُهْلِكِ ٱلْأَوَّلِينَ ۝ ثُمَّ نُتْبِعُهُمُ ٱلْآخِرِينَ ۝ كَذَٰلِكَ نَفْعَلُ بِٱلْمُجْرِمِينَ ۝ وَيْلٌ يَوْمَئِذٍ لِّلْمُكَذِّبِينَ ۝ أَلَمْ نَخْلُقكُّم مِّن مَّاءٍ مَّهِينٍ ۝ فَجَعَلْنَـٰهُ فِى قَرَارٍ مَّكِينٍ ۝ إِلَىٰ قَدَرٍ مَّعْلُومٍ ۝ فَقَدَرْنَا فَنِعْمَ ٱلْقَـٰدِرُونَ ۝ وَيْلٌ يَوْمَئِذٍ لِّلْمُكَذِّبِينَ ۝ أَلَمْ نَجْعَلِ ٱلْأَرْضَ كِفَاتًا ۝ أَحْيَاءً وَأَمْوَاتًا ۝ وَجَعَلْنَا فِيهَا رَوَاسِىَ شَـٰمِخَـٰتٍ وَأَسْقَيْنَـٰكُم مَّاءً فُرَاتًا ۝ وَيْلٌ يَوْمَئِذٍ لِّلْمُكَذِّبِينَ ۝

ᵃ When Doomsday comes, the present system of the world will be thrown into disarray. Those who consider themselves strong in the present world—and on that basis ignore the call for Truth, will find that there is nobody weaker than they.

ᵇ The system of the present world has been so formulated that one who ponders over it sees the Hereafter in its mirror. So, there is no criminal worse than one who denies the Truth in spite of the above-mentioned scenario.

²⁹ Proceed to that which you denied.
³⁰ Proceed to a shadow rising in three columns: ³¹ affording neither shade, nor protection from the flames, ³² and throwing up sparks as huge as towers ³³ and as bright as a herd of yellow camels. ³⁴ Woe on that Day to those who reject the truth! ³⁵ On that Day they will be speechless, ³⁶ nor shall they be permitted to offer excuses. ³⁷ Woe on that Day to those who reject the truth! ³⁸ This is the Day of Judgement. We have assembled you all together with past generations. ³⁹ If now you have any strategy, use it against Me. ⁴⁰ Woe on that Day to those who reject the truth!^a

ٱنطَلِقُوٓاْ إِلَىٰ مَا كُنتُم بِهِۦ تُكَذِّبُونَ ۝ ٱنطَلِقُوٓاْ إِلَىٰ ظِلٍّ ذِى ثَلَٰثِ شُعَبٍ ۝ لَّا ظَلِيلٍ وَلَا يُغْنِى مِنَ ٱللَّهَبِ ۝ إِنَّهَا تَرْمِى بِشَرَرٍ كَٱلْقَصْرِ ۝ كَأَنَّهُۥ جِمَٰلَتٌ صُفْرٌ ۝ وَيْلٌ يَوْمَئِذٍ لِّلْمُكَذِّبِينَ ۝ هَٰذَا يَوْمُ لَا يَنطِقُونَ ۝ وَلَا يُؤْذَنُ لَهُمْ فَيَعْتَذِرُونَ ۝ وَيْلٌ يَوْمَئِذٍ لِّلْمُكَذِّبِينَ ۝ هَٰذَا يَوْمُ ٱلْفَصْلِ جَمَعْنَٰكُمْ وَٱلْأَوَّلِينَ ۝ فَإِن كَانَ لَكُمْ كَيْدٌ فَكِيدُونِ ۝ وَيْلٌ يَوْمَئِذٍ لِّلْمُكَذِّبِينَ ۝

^a When a man is confronted with the horrors of the Hereafter, he will find himself helpless. At that time, those who were wont to speak as if their vocabulary was inexhaustible, will be rendered speechless.

⁴¹ The righteous shall dwell amidst cool shades and fountains, ⁴² and shall have fruits such as they desire; ⁴³ [They will be told], 'Eat and drink with relish in return for what you did [in life]: ⁴⁴ this is how We reward those who do good.' ⁴⁵ [But] woe on that Day to those who reject the truth! ⁴⁶ Eat [your fill] and enjoy your life for a little while, O you who are lost in sin. ⁴⁷ Woe on that Day to those who reject the truth! ⁴⁸ When they are bidden to bow down, they do not bow down. ⁴⁹ Woe on that Day to those who reject the truth! ⁵⁰ In which word then, after this, will they believe?*

إِنَّ ٱلْمُتَّقِينَ فِى ظِلَالٍ وَعُيُونٍ ۞ وَفَوَاكِهَ مِمَّا يَشْتَهُونَ ۞ كُلُوا۟ وَٱشْرَبُوا۟ هَنِيٓـًٔا بِمَا كُنتُمْ تَعْمَلُونَ ۞ إِنَّا كَذَٰلِكَ نَجْزِى ٱلْمُحْسِنِينَ ۞ وَيْلٌ يَوْمَئِذٍ لِّلْمُكَذِّبِينَ ۞ كُلُوا۟ وَتَمَتَّعُوا۟ قَلِيلًا إِنَّكُم مُّجْرِمُونَ ۞ وَيْلٌ يَوْمَئِذٍ لِّلْمُكَذِّبِينَ ۞ وَإِذَا قِيلَ لَهُمُ ٱرْكَعُوا۟ لَا يَرْكَعُونَ ۞ وَيْلٌ يَوْمَئِذٍ لِّلْمُكَذِّبِينَ ۞ فَبِأَىِّ حَدِيثٍۭ بَعْدَهُۥ يُؤْمِنُونَ ۞

---

a God's bounties exist in the present world for the purpose of putting human beings to the test and only for a limited period of time. God's bounties will appear in the Hereafter in an ideal form and will be eternal. Today, everybody shares those bounties. But the bounties of the Hereafter will be shared only by those who were obedient when they had freedom, who bowed down when they were not compelled to do so. Those who accept the Truth purely on the strength of arguments, and as a matter of faith, deserve Paradise, while those who submit to the divine will only after experiencing the wrath of God will be cast into Hell.

78. THE TIDINGS

In the name of God,
the Most Gracious, the Most Merciful

¹ What are they asking each other about? ² About the awesome tidings [of resurrection]³ concerning which they are in disagreement!ᵃ ⁴ But they will soon come to know. ⁵ Surely, they will soon find out the truth! ⁶ Have We not spread the earth like a bed, ⁷ and raised the mountains like supporting poles? ⁸ We created you in pairs, ⁹ and gave you repose in sleep, ¹⁰ and the night as a cover, ¹¹ and made the day for earning a livelihood. ¹² We have built above you seven mighty heavens, ¹³ and We have set therein a glowing lamp. ¹⁴ From the rain clouds We send waters pouring down in abundance, ¹⁵ so that We may bring forth thereby grain and a variety of plants, ¹⁶ and gardens dense with foliage. ¹⁷ Surely, the Day of Judgement has an appointed time.ᵇ

ᵃ The Arab people were not disbelievers in the Hereafter. But they did not believe in a Hereafter of such a nature as is mentioned in the Quran. In other words, they doubted that by rejecting Muhammad, they would face degradation and humiliation in the world of the Hereafter.

ᵇ The physical events of the present world are indicative of the nature of the Hereafter. The 'present' of our world implies that it should have a 'future' consistent with it. Considered from this point of view, it must be accepted that there is going to be a great end to match a great beginning. This world is not going to finish without a befitting end.

¹⁸ On that Day when the trumpet shall be sounded, you shall come in droves, ¹⁹ and the heaven shall be opened, and become gates, ²⁰ and the mountains shall be made to vanish, as if they had been a mirage. ²¹ Surely, Hell lies in wait, ²² a home for the transgressors, ²³ where they shall remain for ages, ²⁴ and where they will taste neither coolness nor any drink ²⁵ save boiling water and a stinking fluid ^a—²⁶ a fitting requital, ²⁷ for they never expected to be called to account, ²⁸ and they rejected outright Our signs; ²⁹ but We have recorded everything in a Book. ³⁰ [So We shall say], 'Taste, then, [the fruit of your evil doings,] for now We shall bestow on you nothing but more and more suffering!'

يَوْمَ يُنفَخُ فِى ٱلصُّورِ فَتَأْتُونَ أَفْوَاجًا ﴿١٨﴾ وَفُتِحَتِ ٱلسَّمَآءُ فَكَانَتْ أَبْوَٰبًا ﴿١٩﴾ وَسُيِّرَتِ ٱلْجِبَالُ فَكَانَتْ سَرَابًا ﴿٢٠﴾ إِنَّ جَهَنَّمَ كَانَتْ مِرْصَادًا ﴿٢١﴾ لِّلطَّٰغِينَ مَـَٔابًا ﴿٢٢﴾ لَّٰبِثِينَ فِيهَآ أَحْقَابًا ﴿٢٣﴾ لَّا يَذُوقُونَ فِيهَا بَرْدًا وَلَا شَرَابًا ﴿٢٤﴾ إِلَّا حَمِيمًا وَغَسَّاقًا ﴿٢٥﴾ جَزَآءً وِفَاقًا ﴿٢٦﴾ إِنَّهُمْ كَانُوا۟ لَا يَرْجُونَ حِسَابًا ﴿٢٧﴾ وَكَذَّبُوا۟ بِـَٔايَٰتِنَا كِذَّابًا ﴿٢٨﴾ وَكُلَّ شَىْءٍ أَحْصَيْنَٰهُ كِتَٰبًا ﴿٢٩﴾ فَذُوقُوا۟ فَلَن نَّزِيدَكُمْ إِلَّا عَذَابًا ﴿٣٠﴾

---

^a In this world arrogance appears pleasurable to a man because it satisfies his ego. But, when man's ego appears in its real shape in the Hereafter, the position will be entirely different. Whatever seemed delightful in the world will become a horrible torture for him in the Hereafter.

إِنَّ لِلْمُتَّقِينَ مَفَازًا ۞ حَدَآئِقَ
وَأَعْنَابًا ۞ وَكَوَاعِبَ أَتْرَابًا ۞
وَكَأْسًا دِهَاقًا ۞ لَّا يَسْمَعُونَ فِيهَا
لَغْوًا وَلَا كِذَّابًا ۞ جَزَآءً مِّن رَّبِّكَ
عَطَآءً حِسَابًا ۞ رَّبِّ ٱلسَّمَاوَاتِ
وَٱلْأَرْضِ وَمَا بَيْنَهُمَا ٱلرَّحْمَٰنِ لَا
يَمْلِكُونَ مِنْهُ خِطَابًا ۞ يَوْمَ يَقُومُ
ٱلرُّوحُ وَٱلْمَلَٰئِكَةُ صَفًّا لَّا
يَتَكَلَّمُونَ إِلَّا مَنْ أَذِنَ لَهُ ٱلرَّحْمَٰنُ
وَقَالَ صَوَابًا ۞ ذَٰلِكَ ٱلْيَوْمُ ٱلْحَقُّ
فَمَن شَآءَ ٱتَّخَذَ إِلَىٰ رَبِّهِ مَئَابًا ۞ إِنَّا
أَنذَرْنَٰكُمْ عَذَابًا قَرِيبًا يَوْمَ يَنظُرُ
ٱلْمَرْءُ مَا قَدَّمَتْ يَدَاهُ وَيَقُولُ ٱلْكَافِرُ
يَٰلَيْتَنِي كُنتُ تُرَٰبًۢا ۞

³¹As for those who are mindful of God, they shall surely triumph: ³²theirs shall be gardens and vineyards, ³³and young maidens of equal age, ³⁴and overflowing cups. ³⁵There they shall not hear any idle talk, or any untruth:ᵃ ³⁶all this will be a recompense, a gift, that will suffice them, from your Lord, ³⁷the Sustainer of the heavens and the earth and all that lies between them, the most Gracious [and] none shall have it in their power to raise their voices to Him. ³⁸On the Day when the Spirit and the angels stand in ranks, no one will speak, except for those to whom the Lord of Mercy gives permission, and who will say only what is right. ³⁹That Day is sure to come, so whoever wishes to, let him take the path that leads towards his Lord. ⁴⁰We have warned you of a chastisement which is near at hand, on the Day when man shall [clearly] see what his hands have sent ahead, and when he who has denied the truth shall say, 'Oh, would that I were dust!'

ᵃThe atmosphere of Paradise will be free of all vain talk and falsehood. Therefore, only those who can prove that they have the inclination to live their lives in this world without indulging in trivialities and deceit, will be chosen to inhabit the pure and sublime atmosphere of Paradise.

79. THE PLUCKERS

In the name of God,
the Most Gracious, the Most Merciful

¹ By [the winds] that pluck out vehemently ² and those that blow gently, ³ and by [the clouds] that swim serenely and ⁴ by those that outstrip them suddenly, ⁵ and by those who regulate events. ⁶ On the Day when a violent convulsion will convulse [the world], ⁷ to be followed by further [convulsions], ⁸ hearts will be throbbing, ⁹ while eyes will be downcast. ¹⁰ They say, 'What? shall we be brought back to life, ¹¹ even after we have turned into decayed bones?' ¹² and they say, 'That indeed would be a losing return.' ¹³ But all it will take is a single blast, ¹⁴ and behold! They will all come out in the open.ᵃ

ᵃ Every year we experience periods of calm weather followed by gales bringing clouds and rainstorms. Soon it is clearly visible that where the land was desolate, a new world has sprung up. This event of nature indicates the possibility of the Hereafter. This shows in symbolic fashion that the emergence of the Hereafter from the present world is just as possible as the emergence of lush green foliage from dry barren land.

¹⁵ Have you heard the story of Moses? ¹⁶ His Lord called out to him by the sacred valley of Tuwa: ¹⁷ [saying], 'Go to Pharaoh, he has exceeded all bounds, ¹⁸ and say, "Will you reform yourself? ¹⁹ Do you want me to guide you to your Lord, so that you should fear Him?"' ²⁰ Moses showed him the great sign, ²¹ but he denied it and refused [the faith]. ²² Then he quickly turned his back. ²³ And he summoned all his people, ²⁴ and proclaimed, 'I am your supreme Lord,' ²⁵ but God seized him and meted out to him the chastisement of both the next world and the present: ²⁶ surely there is in this a lesson for the God-fearing.^a

هَلْ أَتَاكَ حَدِيثُ مُوسَى ۞ إِذْ نَادَاهُ رَبُّهُ بِالْوَادِ ٱلْمُقَدَّسِ طُوًى ۞ ٱذْهَبْ إِلَىٰ فِرْعَوْنَ إِنَّهُ طَغَىٰ ۞ فَقُلْ هَل لَّكَ إِلَىٰ أَن تَزَكَّىٰ ۞ وَأَهْدِيَكَ إِلَىٰ رَبِّكَ فَتَخْشَىٰ ۞ فَأَرَاهُ ٱلْآيَةَ ٱلْكُبْرَىٰ ۞ فَكَذَّبَ وَعَصَىٰ ۞ ثُمَّ أَدْبَرَ يَسْعَىٰ ۞ فَحَشَرَ فَنَادَىٰ ۞ فَقَالَ أَنَا۠ رَبُّكُمُ ٱلْأَعْلَىٰ ۞ فَأَخَذَهُ ٱللَّهُ نَكَالَ ٱلْآخِرَةِ وَٱلْأُولَىٰ ۞ إِنَّ فِي ذَٰلِكَ لَعِبْرَةً لِّمَن يَخْشَىٰ ۞

---

^a The life of Pharaoh and other deniers of the truth like him provides proof of the fact that one who denies realities is ultimately punished for it. These historical examples are enough to teach man a lesson. But an instructive event is such only to one who has a prudent mentality, and who examines an action from the viewpoint of its end-result and not just in relation to its beginning.

²⁷ [O Men!] Are you more difficult to create than the heaven which He has built, ²⁸ by raising its vault high and fashioning it flawlessly, ²⁹ and making its night dark and bringing forth its morning light, ³⁰ and the earth which He spread out, ³¹ after that bringing forth from it its water and its pasture land, ³² and making the mountains firm: ³³ [all this] as a means of sustenance for you and your animals?ᵃ

ءَأَنتُمْ أَشَدُّ خَلْقًا أَمِ ٱلسَّمَآءُ ۚ بَنَىٰهَا ۝ رَفَعَ سَمْكَهَا فَسَوَّىٰهَا ۝ وَأَغْطَشَ لَيْلَهَا وَأَخْرَجَ ضُحَىٰهَا ۝ وَٱلْأَرْضَ بَعْدَ ذَٰلِكَ دَحَىٰهَآ ۝ أَخْرَجَ مِنْهَا مَآءَهَا وَمَرْعَىٰهَا ۝ وَٱلْجِبَالَ أَرْسَىٰهَا ۝ مَتَٰعًا لَّكُمْ وَلِأَنْعَٰمِكُمْ ۝

ᵃ The magnificent phenomenon before us in the shape of the universe is so great that all other things are small in comparison to it. So, in the world when the occurrence of a big event is possible, why should the occurrence of a small event not be possible? There are already many factors in existence on a large scale which explain the Quran's declaration that man shall one Day have to face resurrection.

³⁴ When the great over-whelming event arrives, ³⁵ on the Day that man remembers what he strove for ³⁶ and Hell is there for all to see, ³⁷ anyone who has acted arrogantly ³⁸ and prefers the life of this world, ³⁹ will find himself in Hell; ⁴⁰ but one who fears to stand before his Lord and restrained himself from base desires, ⁴¹ shall dwell in Paradise. ⁴² They will ask you [Prophet] about the Hour, saying, 'When it will come to pass?', ⁴³ what have you to do with the mentioning of it? ⁴⁴ Your Lord alone knows when it will come; ⁴⁵ you are but a warner for those who fear it. ⁴⁶ On the Day when they see it, they will feel as if they had tarried in this world for only one evening or one morning.ᵃ

فَإِذَا جَآءَتِ ٱلطَّآمَّةُ ٱلْكُبْرَىٰ ﴿٣٤﴾ يَوْمَ يَتَذَكَّرُ ٱلْإِنسَٰنُ مَا سَعَىٰ ﴿٣٥﴾ وَبُرِّزَتِ ٱلْجَحِيمُ لِمَن يَرَىٰ ﴿٣٦﴾ فَأَمَّا مَن طَغَىٰ ﴿٣٧﴾ وَءَاثَرَ ٱلْحَيَوٰةَ ٱلدُّنْيَا ﴿٣٨﴾ فَإِنَّ ٱلْجَحِيمَ هِيَ ٱلْمَأْوَىٰ ﴿٣٩﴾ وَأَمَّا مَنْ خَافَ مَقَامَ رَبِّهِ وَنَهَى ٱلنَّفْسَ عَنِ ٱلْهَوَىٰ ﴿٤٠﴾ فَإِنَّ ٱلْجَنَّةَ هِيَ ٱلْمَأْوَىٰ ﴿٤١﴾ يَسْـَٔلُونَكَ عَنِ ٱلسَّاعَةِ أَيَّانَ مُرْسَىٰهَا ﴿٤٢﴾ فِيمَ أَنتَ مِن ذِكْرَىٰهَآ ﴿٤٣﴾ إِلَىٰ رَبِّكَ مُنتَهَىٰهَآ ﴿٤٤﴾ إِنَّمَآ أَنتَ مُنذِرُ مَن يَخْشَىٰهَا ﴿٤٥﴾ كَأَنَّهُمْ يَوْمَ يَرَوْنَهَا لَمْ يَلْبَثُوٓا۟ إِلَّا عَشِيَّةً أَوْ ضُحَىٰهَا ﴿٤٦﴾

ᵃ Man is between two domains. One is the present world, which is before him, and the second is the world of the Hereafter, which is hidden from view. The real test of man is that he should prefer the Hereafter to the present world. But this can be done only by one who has the courage to exercise control over the base desires of the self and not behave arrogantly.

80. HE FROWNED

In the name of God,
the Most Gracious, the Most Merciful

¹ He frowned and turned away ² when the blind man approached him, ³ for how can you know that he might seek to purify himself, ⁴ or take heed and derive benefit from [Our] warning? ⁵ As for him who was indifferent, ⁶ you eagerly attended to him—⁷ though you are not to be blamed if he would not purify himself—⁸ but as for one who comes to you, eagerly ⁹ and in awe of God ¹⁰ you pay him no heed. ¹¹ Indeed, this [Quran] is an admonition. ¹² Let him who will, pay heed to it. ¹³ It is set down on honoured pages, ¹⁴ exalted and purified, ¹⁵ by the hands of ¹⁶ noble and virtuous scribes. ¹⁷ Woe to man! How ungrateful he is! ¹⁸ Of what [stuff] has He created him? ¹⁹ Out of a drop of sperm! He creates and proportions him, ²⁰ He makes his path easy for him.ᵃ

ᵃ The Prophet Muhammad was once preaching to the chiefs of the Quraysh in Makkah, when a blind man, 'Abdullah ibn Umm al-Maktum, arrived at the gathering and said, 'O, Prophet of God! Please teach me something of what God has taught you.' The arrival of a blind person at this juncture displeased the Prophet. These verses were revealed on that occasion. In these verses the apparent addressee is the Prophet Muhammad, but actually it has been clarified with reference to this incident that, in the eyes of God, those prominent people who have turned away from religion have no value. Before God, the valued person is the one who is imbued with the God-fearing spirit, though apparently he may be a 'blind' person.

Then He causes him to die and be buried. ²²Then when He pleases, He will bring him back to life. ²³Yet man declines to do His bidding. ²⁴Let man reflect on the food he eats.ᵃ ²⁵We let the rain pour down in torrents ²⁶and then We cleaved the earth asunder. ²⁷We make the grain grow out of it, ²⁸and grape vines and vegetables, ²⁹and olive trees and date palms ³⁰and burgeoning enclosed gardens ³¹and fruits and fodder ³²as provision for you and for your cattle to enjoy.

³³But when the deafening blast is sounded, ³⁴on that Day a man shall flee from his own brother, ³⁵his mother, his father, ³⁶his wife and his sons: ³⁷on that Day every man among them will have enough concern of his own— ³⁸on that Day some faces will be beaming, ³⁹laughing, and rejoicing, ⁴⁰but some faces will be covered with dust ⁴¹and overcast with gloom: ⁴²those will be ones who denied the truth and were immersed in iniquity.ᵇ

ᵃ The driving force behind the true godliness required of a man is, in reality, his sense of gratitude. If he gives serious consideration to his creation and the various natural systems in operation around him, a sense of gratitude towards his Lord will eventually develop in him. The state of being resulting from these feelings of gratitude and obligation is known as godliness, or adoration of God in the real sense.

ᵇ Rejection of truth and being arrogant about it are the worst crimes. Arrogant people will have absolutely no personal worth in the Hereafter, while those who accept the Truth and bow down before it are the ones who will carry weight in the Hereafter. The honour and successes of the Hereafter will be theirs.

81. CEASING TO SHINE

In the name of God,
the Most Gracious, the Most Merciful

¹ When the sun is folded up, ² and when the stars lose their light, ³ and when the mountains are moved, ⁴ when ten-month pregnant camels are left untended, ⁵ and when all beasts are gathered together, ⁶ and when the seas are set on fire, ⁷ when the souls are divided into different classes, ⁸ and when the female infant buried alive is asked ⁹ for what sin she was killed, ¹⁰ when the records of men's deeds are laid open, ¹¹ when the sky is unveiled, ¹² and when Hell is set ablaze, ¹³ when Paradise is brought close: ¹⁴ [then] each soul shall know what it has put forward.ᵃ

إِذَا ٱلشَّمْسُ كُوِّرَتْ ۝ وَإِذَا ٱلنُّجُومُ ٱنكَدَرَتْ ۝ وَإِذَا ٱلْجِبَالُ سُيِّرَتْ ۝ وَإِذَا ٱلْعِشَارُ عُطِّلَتْ ۝ وَإِذَا ٱلْوُحُوشُ حُشِرَتْ ۝ وَإِذَا ٱلْبِحَارُ سُجِّرَتْ ۝ وَإِذَا ٱلنُّفُوسُ زُوِّجَتْ ۝ وَإِذَا ٱلْمَوْءُۥدَةُ سُئِلَتْ ۝ بِأَىِّ ذَنۢبٍ قُتِلَتْ ۝ وَإِذَا ٱلصُّحُفُ نُشِرَتْ ۝ وَإِذَا ٱلسَّمَآءُ كُشِطَتْ ۝ وَإِذَا ٱلْجَحِيمُ سُعِّرَتْ ۝ وَإِذَا ٱلْجَنَّةُ أُزْلِفَتْ ۝ عَلِمَتْ نَفْسٌ مَّآ أَحْضَرَتْ ۝

ᵃ The scenes of Doomsday, or the Day of Judgement, have been described at various points in the Quran. When Doomsday arrives, the present balance of the world will break down, and man will feel himself helpless. On that Day, all things except good deeds will lose their value. Then the oppressed person will have the right to take his revenge upon his oppressor.

15 I swear by the receding stars, 16 the planets that run their course and set, 17 and the night that falls, 18 and the first breath of morning.*a* 19 Truly, this is the word brought by a noble messenger,*b* 20 endowed with power and held in honour by the Lord of the Throne—21 who is obeyed there and is worthy of trust. 22 Your companion is not one possessed: 23 he truly beheld him [the angel] on the clear horizon. 24 He is not avid of the Unseen. 25 Nor is this the word of an outcast devil. 26 So where are you going? 27 This is merely a reminder to all mankind; 28 to every one of you who wishes to tread the straight path. 29 But you cannot will it unless God, the Lord of the Universe, so wills it [to show you that way].

فَلَا أُقْسِمُ بِالْخُنَّسِ ۝ الْجَوَارِ الْكُنَّسِ ۝ وَالَّيْلِ إِذَا عَسْعَسَ ۝ وَالصُّبْحِ إِذَا تَنَفَّسَ ۝ إِنَّهُ لَقَوْلُ رَسُولٍ كَرِيمٍ ۝ ذِي قُوَّةٍ عِندَ ذِي الْعَرْشِ مَكِينٍ ۝ مُّطَاعٍ ثَمَّ أَمِينٍ ۝ وَمَا صَاحِبُكُم بِمَجْنُونٍ ۝ وَلَقَدْ رَءَاهُ بِالْأُفُقِ الْمُبِينِ ۝ وَمَا هُوَ عَلَى الْغَيْبِ بِضَنِينٍ ۝ وَمَا هُوَ بِقَوْلِ شَيْطَنٍ رَّجِيمٍ ۝ فَأَيْنَ تَذْهَبُونَ ۝ إِنْ هُوَ إِلَّا ذِكْرٌ لِّلْعَلَمِينَ ۝ لِمَن شَاءَ مِنكُمْ أَن يَسْتَقِيمَ ۝ وَمَا تَشَاءُونَ إِلَّا أَن يَشَاءَ اللَّهُ رَبُّ الْعَلَمِينَ ۝

---

a The occurrence of day and night on the earth and the change of position of the stars as observed by man are due to the rotation of the earth on its axis. In this context, the meaning of these verses is that the system of axial rotation of the earth is a witness to the fact that Muhammad is the prophet of God and that the Quran is the word of God which has been revealed to him through an angel.

The axial rotation of the earth is one of the truly remarkable phenomena of this universe. It is, so to say, a model which makes the matter of revelation understandable to us. When you imagine that the earth, while rotating on its axis, also revolves round the sun in the vastness of outer space, you will feel as if there is a powerful remote control system which directs its movements with the utmost precision. The establishment of contact between man and God through an angel is also on a parallel with this. The controlled movement of the earth symbolically helps us in understanding the miraculous nature of man's contact with God through the angel.

b Angel-messenger, who brings divine revelation to man.

82. THE CLEAVING ASUNDER

In the name of God, the Most Gracious, the Most Merciful

¹ When the sky is cleft asunder; ² and when the stars are scattered; ³ when the seas overflow; ⁴ and when the graves are laid open: ⁵ then everyone will know what he has sent ahead, and what he has left behind. ⁶ O man! What is it that lures you away from your bountiful Sustainer, ⁷ who created you, fashioned you and proportioned you, ⁸ in whatever form He pleased? ⁹ Yet you deny the Last Judgement. ¹⁰ Surely, there are guardians watching over you, ¹¹ noble recorders, ¹² who know all that you do:ᵃ ¹³ the virtuous will dwell in bliss, ¹⁴ whereas the wicked will be in Hell; ¹⁵ which they shall enter on the Day of Judgement, ¹⁶ and from which they will find no escape. ¹⁷ What will make you realize what the Day of Judgement will be? ¹⁸ Again: what will make you realize what the Day of Judgement will be? ¹⁹ It will be a Day when no human being shall be of the least avail to any other human being, God [alone] will hold command on that Day.

ᵃ The Quran informs us that the Day of Judgement will finally come: all of humanity will be assembled on that Day and will be rewarded or punished according to their deeds. These tidings are absolutely consistent with the present condition of the world. Indeed, the meaningful creation of man has its justification in this announcement. Moreover, a system exists in the present world for the recording of the words and deeds of man. That becomes understandable in the light of what the Quran tells us. (For details regarding the recording of words and deeds, see the commentator's book titled: *God Arises*).

83. THOSE WHO GIVE SHORT MEASURE

In the name of God,
the Most Gracious, the Most Merciful

¹ Woe to those who give short measure, ² who demand of other people full measure for themselves, ³ but when they give by measurement or weight to others,ᵃ they give them less.ᵇ ⁴ Do such people not realize that they will be raised up, ⁵ on a fateful Day.

ᵃ Literally 'when they give by measure to others, or weigh out to them'.

ᵇ Every human being wants to have his dues paid in full. But it is only right and proper that, if he is a man of character, he should also take care to give to others their full and rightful dues. He should want for others whatever he wants for himself. Those who take full measure for themselves and give less to others, will reach the Hereafter in such an ill state of grace that they will be doomed to eternal perdition.

One who tries to ensure full measure for himself knows that everyone should receive his just deserts. In this context, if he gives less while giving to others, he lessens his realization of or sensitivity to the rights of others. If a man repeats this sort of misdeed again and again, a time will finally come when he will completely lose his sensitivity to others' rights. His heart will be completely corroded by his sinful actions.

In the present world many people are not at all keen to respect the rights of others or to give them their full dues. They are interested solely in recovering in full what is due to them from others. Such people will remain in a state of deprivation in the Hereafter. Wise are those who are eager to discharge others' rights and dues fully, because they are the ones who will be entitled to the great bounties of God in the Hereafter.

⁶ The Day when mankind will stand before the Lord of the Universe? ⁷ Indeed! The record of the wicked is in the Sijjin— ⁸ and what could make you understand what the Sijjin is?—⁹ it is a written record. ¹⁰ Woe, on that Day, to those who reject, ¹¹ those who deny the Day of Judgement. ¹² No one denies it except for the evil aggressor. ¹³ When Our revelations are conveyed to him, he says, 'Fables of the ancients!' ¹⁴ No! Their own deeds have cast a veil over their hearts. ¹⁵ Indeed! On that Day a barrier will be set between them and their Lord, ¹⁶ then they shall enter the Fire of Hell, ¹⁷ and they will be told, 'This is what you were wont to belie.'ᵃ

يَوْمَ يَقُومُ ٱلنَّاسُ لِرَبِّ ٱلْعَٰلَمِينَ ﴿٦﴾ كَلَّآ إِنَّ كِتَٰبَ ٱلْفُجَّارِ لَفِى سِجِّينٍ ﴿٧﴾ وَمَآ أَدْرَىٰكَ مَا سِجِّينٌ ﴿٨﴾ كِتَٰبٌ مَّرْقُومٌ ﴿٩﴾ وَيْلٌ يَوْمَئِذٍ لِّلْمُكَذِّبِينَ ﴿١٠﴾ ٱلَّذِينَ يُكَذِّبُونَ بِيَوْمِ ٱلدِّينِ ﴿١١﴾ وَمَا يُكَذِّبُ بِهِۦٓ إِلَّا كُلُّ مُعْتَدٍ أَثِيمٍ ﴿١٢﴾ إِذَا تُتْلَىٰ عَلَيْهِ ءَايَٰتُنَا قَالَ أَسَٰطِيرُ ٱلْأَوَّلِينَ ﴿١٣﴾ كَلَّا بَلْ رَانَ عَلَىٰ قُلُوبِهِم مَّا كَانُوا۟ يَكْسِبُونَ ﴿١٤﴾ كَلَّآ إِنَّهُمْ عَن رَّبِّهِمْ يَوْمَئِذٍ لَّمَحْجُوبُونَ ﴿١٥﴾ ثُمَّ إِنَّهُمْ لَصَالُوا۟ ٱلْجَحِيمِ ﴿١٦﴾ ثُمَّ يُقَالُ هَٰذَا ٱلَّذِى كُنتُم بِهِۦ تُكَذِّبُونَ ﴿١٧﴾

ᵃ Literally 'A prison'. It means a certain place in which the record of the deeds of the wicked is preserved.

18 But, the record of the righteous is [preserved] in the 'Illiyyin—19 and what will make you understand what the 'Illiyyin is? *—20 a written record, 21 which those angels closest to God will bear witness to. 22 The virtuous will surely be in bliss, 23 seated on couches and gazing around in wonder. 24 You will find in their faces the brightness of bliss. 25 They will be given a drink of pure wine, sealed, 26 its seal will be of musk—for this let the aspirants aspire—27 a wine tempered with the waters of Tasnim, 28 a spring at which those drawn close to God will drink. 29 The wicked used to laugh at the believers—30 when they passed by them, they would wink at one another; 31 and when they returned to their own people, they would speak of them jestingly; 32 and when they saw them, they said [scornfully], 'These men have surely gone astray,' 33 though they were not sent to be their keepers—34 so today those who believe shall [be able to] laugh at those who denied the truth 35 as they sit on couches, gazing around. 36 Have those who deny the truth [not] been paid back for their deeds? *

كَلَّآ إِنَّ كِتَبَ ٱلۡأَبۡرَارِ لَفِى عِلِّيِّينَ ۝ وَمَآ أَدۡرَىٰكَ مَا عِلِّيُّونَ ۝ كِتَبٌ مَّرۡقُومٌ ۝ يَشۡهَدُهُ ٱلۡمُقَرَّبُونَ ۝ إِنَّ ٱلۡأَبۡرَارَ لَفِى نَعِيمٍ ۝ عَلَى ٱلۡأَرَآئِكِ يَنظُرُونَ ۝ تَعۡرِفُ فِى وُجُوهِهِمۡ نَضۡرَةَ ٱلنَّعِيمِ ۝ يُسۡقَوۡنَ مِن رَّحِيقٍ مَّخۡتُومٍ ۝ خِتَمُهُۥ مِسۡكٌ وَفِى ذَٰلِكَ فَلۡيَتَنَافَسِ ٱلۡمُتَنَافِسُونَ ۝ وَمِزَاجُهُۥ مِن تَسۡنِيمٍ ۝ عَيۡنًا يَشۡرَبُ بِهَا ٱلۡمُقَرَّبُونَ ۝ إِنَّ ٱلَّذِينَ أَجۡرَمُواْ كَانُواْ مِنَ ٱلَّذِينَ ءَامَنُواْ يَضۡحَكُونَ ۝ وَإِذَا مَرُّواْ بِهِمۡ يَتَغَامَزُونَ ۝ وَإِذَا ٱنقَلَبُوٓاْ إِلَىٰٓ أَهۡلِهِمُ ٱنقَلَبُواْ فَكِهِينَ ۝ وَإِذَا رَأَوۡهُمۡ قَالُوٓاْ إِنَّ هَٰٓؤُلَآءِ لَضَآلُّونَ ۝ وَمَآ أُرۡسِلُواْ عَلَيۡهِمۡ حَٰفِظِينَ ۝ فَٱلۡيَوۡمَ ٱلَّذِينَ ءَامَنُواْ مِنَ ٱلۡكُفَّارِ يَضۡحَكُونَ ۝ عَلَى ٱلۡأَرَآئِكِ يَنظُرُونَ ۝ هَلۡ ثُوِّبَ ٱلۡكُفَّارُ مَا كَانُواْ يَفۡعَلُونَ ۝

---

a Duly registered and inscribed, with no possibility of error or effacement.

b One who disregards his worldly considerations for the sake of the Hereafter is regarded as a fool and becomes diminished in the eyes of the worldly wise. But when the Hereafter comes, it will appear that the really wise ones were those who were considered foolish in the present world.

84. THE BURSTING OPEN

سُورَة الانشقاق

In the name of God,
the Most Gracious, the Most Merciful

بِسْمِ اللهِ الرَّحْمٰنِ الرَّحِيمِ

¹ When the sky bursts open, ² and obeys its Lord as it must, ³ when the earth flattens out, ⁴ and casts out all that is within it and becomes empty; ⁵ and obeys its Lord as it must,ᵃ ⁶ O man, having striven hard towards your Lord, you shall meet Him: ⁷ he who is given his record in his right hand ⁸ shall have an easy reckoning ⁹ and he shall return to his people, joyfully, ¹⁰ but as for him whose record shall be given to him from behind his back, ¹¹ he will pray for utter destruction ¹² and he will enter the blazing flame. ¹³ He used to be happy with his own people; ¹⁴ for he never thought that he would have to return [to God]. ¹⁵ But he will indeed! His Lord was ever watching him.

إِذَا السَّمَاءُ انشَقَّتْ ۝ وَأَذِنَتْ لِرَبِّهَا
وَحُقَّتْ ۝ وَإِذَا الْأَرْضُ مُدَّتْ ۝
وَأَلْقَتْ مَا فِيهَا وَتَخَلَّتْ ۝ وَأَذِنَتْ
لِرَبِّهَا وَحُقَّتْ ۝ يَا أَيُّهَا الْإِنسَانُ إِنَّكَ
كَادِحٌ إِلَىٰ رَبِّكَ كَدْحًا فَمُلَاقِيهِ
۝ فَأَمَّا مَنْ أُوتِيَ كِتَابَهُ بِيَمِينِهِ
۝ فَسَوْفَ يُحَاسَبُ حِسَابًا يَسِيرًا
۝ وَيَنقَلِبُ إِلَىٰ أَهْلِهِ مَسْرُورًا ۝ وَأَمَّا
مَنْ أُوتِيَ كِتَابَهُ وَرَاءَ ظَهْرِهِ ۝
فَسَوْفَ يَدْعُو ثُبُورًا ۝ وَيَصْلَىٰ
سَعِيرًا ۝ إِنَّهُ كَانَ فِي أَهْلِهِ مَسْرُورًا
۝ إِنَّهُ ظَنَّ أَن لَّن يَحُورَ ۝ بَلَىٰ إِنَّ
رَبَّهُ كَانَ بِهِ بَصِيرًا ۝

ᵃ Whatever is related here about Doomsday refers apparently to an unknown world. However, such evidence exists as points to its veracity. An example of this is the present world itself. The very existence of the world proves that another similar or different world may come into existence. Furthermore, certain extraordinary aspects of the Quran prove that it is the Book of God. (For details see *The Quran: An Abiding Wonder* and *The Call of the Quran* by the commentator).

16 I swear by the glow of sunset, 17 by the night and what it covers, 18 and the moon when it grows full, 19 you will progress from stage to stage. 20 What is wrong with them that they do not believe? 21 When the Quran is read to them, why do they not fall to their knees? 22 Indeed, those who are bent on denying the truth reject it— 23 God is quite aware of what they are storing in their hearts. 24 Therefore, give them the news of a painful punishment.ᵃ 25 But for those who believe and do good works; for them there shall be a never-ending reward.

فَلَآ أُقۡسِمُ بِٱلشَّفَقِ ۝ وَٱلَّيۡلِ وَمَا وَسَقَ ۝ وَٱلۡقَمَرِ إِذَا ٱتَّسَقَ ۝ لَتَرۡكَبُنَّ طَبَقًا عَن طَبَقٖ ۝ فَمَا لَهُمۡ لَا يُؤۡمِنُونَ ۝ وَإِذَا قُرِئَ عَلَيۡهِمُ ٱلۡقُرۡءَانُ لَا يَسۡجُدُونَ ۩ ۝ بَلِ ٱلَّذِينَ كَفَرُواْ يُكَذِّبُونَ ۝ وَٱللَّهُ أَعۡلَمُ بِمَا يُوعُونَ ۝ فَبَشِّرۡهُم بِعَذَابٍ أَلِيمٍ ۝ إِلَّا ٱلَّذِينَ ءَامَنُواْ وَعَمِلُواْ ٱلصَّٰلِحَٰتِ لَهُمۡ أَجۡرٌ غَيۡرُ مَمۡنُونِۭ ۝

ᵃ In spite of such clear indications, there are those who do not believe in the Hereafter and live out their lives without ever taking it into account. Such individuals are certainly committing a crime which is deserving of the punishment mentioned above.

In the name of God,
the Most Gracious, the Most Merciful

¹ By the sky with its constellations, ² and by the promised Day, ³ by the Witness and the witnessed, ⁴ destroyed were the people of the trench, ⁵ the makers of the fuel-stoked fire! ⁶ They sat by it ⁷ to watch what they were doing to the believers, ⁸ whom they hated for no other reason than that they believed in God, the Almighty, the Praiseworthy, ⁹ to whom belongs the kingdom of the heavens and the earth. God is witness over all things. ¹⁰ Those who persecute the believing men and believing women, and then do not repent, will surely suffer the punishment of Hell, and the torment of burning. ¹¹ But those who believe and do good deeds shall be rewarded with gardens watered by flowing rivers. That is the supreme triumph.ᵃ

وَٱلسَّمَآءِ ذَاتِ ٱلۡبُرُوجِ ۞ وَٱلۡيَوۡمِ ٱلۡمَوۡعُودِ ۞ وَشَاهِدٍ وَمَشۡهُودٍ ۞ قُتِلَ أَصۡحَٰبُ ٱلۡأُخۡدُودِ ۞ ٱلنَّارِ ذَاتِ ٱلۡوَقُودِ ۞ إِذۡ هُمۡ عَلَيۡهَا قُعُودٌ ۞ وَهُمۡ عَلَىٰ مَا يَفۡعَلُونَ بِٱلۡمُؤۡمِنِينَ شُهُودٌ ۞ وَمَا نَقَمُوا۟ مِنۡهُمۡ إِلَّآ أَن يُؤۡمِنُوا۟ بِٱللَّهِ ٱلۡعَزِيزِ ٱلۡحَمِيدِ ۞ ٱلَّذِى لَهُۥ مُلۡكُ ٱلسَّمَٰوَٰتِ وَٱلۡأَرۡضِ وَٱللَّهُ عَلَىٰ كُلِّ شَىۡءٍ شَهِيدٌ ۞ إِنَّ ٱلَّذِينَ فَتَنُوا۟ ٱلۡمُؤۡمِنِينَ وَٱلۡمُؤۡمِنَٰتِ ثُمَّ لَمۡ يَتُوبُوا۟ فَلَهُمۡ عَذَابُ جَهَنَّمَ وَلَهُمۡ عَذَابُ ٱلۡحَرِيقِ ۞ إِنَّ ٱلَّذِينَ ءَامَنُوا۟ وَعَمِلُوا۟ ٱلصَّٰلِحَٰتِ لَهُمۡ جَنَّٰتٌ تَجۡرِى مِن تَحۡتِهَا ٱلۡأَنۡهَٰرُ ذَٰلِكَ ٱلۡفَوۡزُ ٱلۡكَبِيرُ ۞

ᵃ The perfect organisation of the system of the universe ensures that the Day of Final Judgement will come. Tidings of this very Day have been given by all the prophets and their true deputies. In spite of this, those who do not accept the Truth and even become the enemies of the preachers of the Truth, indulge in such aggressiveness and arrogance that they cannot save themselves from the dreadful consequences. However, those who give a positive response to the call for Truth, in spite of different kinds of difficulties, will receive the greatest possible reward from Merciful God.

¹² The grip of your Lord is indeed severe—¹³ it is He who begins and repeats [His creation]—¹⁴ and He is the Forgiving and Loving One. ¹⁵ The Lord of the Glorious Throne, ¹⁶ Executor of His own will. ¹⁷ Have you not heard the story of the hosts ¹⁸ of Pharaoh and Thamud? ¹⁹ Yet those who deny the truth persist in denial. ²⁰ God encompasses them from all sides. ²¹ It is indeed a glorious Quran, ²² written on a preserved Tablet.^a

إِنَّ بَطْشَ رَبِّكَ لَشَدِيدٌ ۞ إِنَّهُۥ هُوَ يُبْدِئُ وَيُعِيدُ ۞ وَهُوَ ٱلْغَفُورُ ٱلْوَدُودُ ۞ ذُو ٱلْعَرْشِ ٱلْمَجِيدُ ۞ فَعَّالٌ لِّمَا يُرِيدُ ۞ هَلْ أَتَىٰكَ حَدِيثُ ٱلْجُنُودِ ۞ فِرْعَوْنَ وَثَمُودَ ۞ بَلِ ٱلَّذِينَ كَفَرُواْ فِى تَكْذِيبٍ ۞ وَٱللَّهُ مِن وَرَآئِهِم مُّحِيطٌ ۞ بَلْ هُوَ قُرْءَانٌ مَّجِيدٌ ۞ فِى لَوْحٍ مَّحْفُوظٍ ۞

---

^a Of all the revealed scriptures, the Quran is an exceptionally protected book. This is a sign of the fact that the Quran is in the special care of God. Right till Doomsday there is no possibility of its being suppressed by anyone. For details, see the book 'Quran an Abiding Wonder', available on the website.

86. THAT WHICH COMES IN THE NIGHT

In the name of God,
the Most Gracious, the Most Merciful

¹ By the heavens and that which comes in the night—² and what could make you know what it is that comes in the night? ³ It is the shining star ᵃ—⁴ [for] no human being has been left unguarded. ⁵ Let man reflect on what he was created from. ⁶ He was created from spurting fluid, ⁷ issuing from between the backbone and the breastbone: ⁸ He certainly has the power to bring him back to life. ⁹ On the Day when secrets are disclosed, ¹⁰ [man] will have no power, and no helper. ¹¹ By the heavens, ever-revolving, ¹² by the earth cracking open with new growth. ¹³ It is surely a decisive utterance; ¹⁴ and is not to be taken lightly. ¹⁵ They are planning a scheme, ¹⁶ and so am I: ¹⁷ so bear with those who deny the truth, and let them be for a little while.

وَٱلسَّمَآءِ وَٱلطَّارِقِ ۝ وَمَآ أَدْرَىٰكَ مَا ٱلطَّارِقُ ۝ ٱلنَّجْمُ ٱلثَّاقِبُ ۝ إِن كُلُّ نَفْسٍ لَّمَّا عَلَيْهَا حَافِظٌ ۝ فَلْيَنظُرِ ٱلْإِنسَٰنُ مِمَّ خُلِقَ ۝ خُلِقَ مِن مَّآءٍ دَافِقٍ ۝ يَخْرُجُ مِنۢ بَيْنِ ٱلصُّلْبِ وَٱلتَّرَآئِبِ ۝ إِنَّهُۥ عَلَىٰ رَجْعِهِۦ لَقَادِرٌ ۝ يَوْمَ تُبْلَى ٱلسَّرَآئِرُ ۝ فَمَا لَهُۥ مِن قُوَّةٍ وَلَا نَاصِرٍ ۝ وَٱلسَّمَآءِ ذَاتِ ٱلرَّجْعِ ۝ وَٱلْأَرْضِ ذَاتِ ٱلصَّدْعِ ۝ إِنَّهُۥ لَقَوْلٌ فَصْلٌ ۝ وَمَا هُوَ بِٱلْهَزْلِ ۝ إِنَّهُمْ يَكِيدُونَ كَيْدًا ۝ وَأَكِيدُ كَيْدًا ۝ فَمَهِّلِ ٱلْكَٰفِرِينَ أَمْهِلْهُمْ رُوَيْدًا ۝

ᵃ A star shining upon a man is a symbolic reminder of the fact that an Observer is watching him. This Observer is recording man's deeds. He will resurrect man after his death and take the reckoning of all his deeds. It is the period of respite (during which man is put to the test) which acts as a 'wedge' between man and the aforesaid event. As soon as the period of trial is over, he will face the consequences—from which he seems to be far away today.

87. THE MOST HIGH

In the name of God,
the Most Gracious, the Most Merciful

¹ Glorify the name of your Lord, the Most High, ² who created all things and gave them due proportions, ³ who determines the nature [of all that exists], and guided it accordingly;ᵃ ⁴ who brings forth green pasture, ⁵ then turns it into black stubble. ⁶ [O Prophet!] We shall make you recite the Quran so that you will not forget any of it—⁷ except whatever God wills; He knows both what is manifest and what is hidden—⁸ We shall facilitate for you the Easy Way. ⁹ Remind, if the reminder can be of benefit. ¹⁰ He who fears [God] will heed the reminder, ¹¹ but it will be ignored by the most unfortunate, ¹² who will enter the Great Fire, ¹³ where he will neither die nor live. ¹⁴ He who purifies himself, ¹⁵ who remembers the name of his Lord and prays, shall indeed be successful. ¹⁶ But you prefer the life of this world, ¹⁷ although the Hereafter is better and more lasting. ¹⁸ This indeed is what is taught in the former scriptures— ¹⁹ the scriptures of Abraham and Moses.

ᵃ It is quite evident that there is planning in the creation of man and the world. This planning strongly implies that there must be some purpose behind this creation. And indeed, this purpose has been revealed to man through divine revelation. However, only that individual learns a lesson from revelation who is of a receptive nature. Such people will be introduced to the eternal bounties of God. But those whose arrogance prevents them from accepting guidance, will be doomed to being cast into the flames of the eternal fire.

88. THE OVERWHELMING EVENT

In the name of God,
the Most Gracious, the Most Merciful

بِسْمِ اللهِ الرَّحْمَنِ الرَّحِيمِ

¹ Have you heard about the Overwhelming Event? ² On that Day, there shall be downcast faces, ³ labouring, weary, ⁴ they shall enter a burning Fire ⁵ and will be made to drink from a boiling spring, ⁶ they shall have no food but thorns, ⁷ which will neither nourish nor satisfy hunger. ⁸ Some faces on that Day will be radiant, ⁹ well pleased with the result of their striving, ¹⁰ in a sublime garden, ¹¹ where they will hear no idle talk, ¹² with a flowing spring, ¹³ raised couches, ¹⁴ and goblets set at hand, ¹⁵ cushions ranged, ¹⁶ and carpets spread out. ¹⁷ Do they never reflect on the camels and how they were created,ᵃ ¹⁸ and on the sky, how it is raised aloft, ¹⁹ and on the mountains, how they are firmly set up, ²⁰ and on the earth, how it is spread out?

هَلْ أَتَاكَ حَدِيثُ الْغَاشِيَةِ ۝ وُجُوهٌ يَوْمَئِذٍ خَاشِعَةٌ ۝ عَامِلَةٌ نَّاصِبَةٌ ۝ تَصْلَى نَارًا حَامِيَةً ۝ تُسْقَى مِنْ عَيْنٍ آنِيَةٍ ۝ لَّيْسَ لَهُمْ طَعَامٌ إِلَّا مِن ضَرِيعٍ ۝ لَا يُسْمِنُ وَلَا يُغْنِي مِن جُوعٍ ۝ وُجُوهٌ يَوْمَئِذٍ نَّاعِمَةٌ ۝ لِّسَعْيِهَا رَاضِيَةٌ ۝ فِي جَنَّةٍ عَالِيَةٍ ۝ لَّا تَسْمَعُ فِيهَا لَاغِيَةً ۝ فِيهَا عَيْنٌ جَارِيَةٌ ۝ فِيهَا سُرُرٌ مَّرْفُوعَةٌ ۝ وَأَكْوَابٌ مَّوْضُوعَةٌ ۝ وَنَمَارِقُ مَصْفُوفَةٌ ۝ وَزَرَابِيُّ مَبْثُوثَةٌ ۝ أَفَلَا يَنظُرُونَ إِلَى الْإِبِلِ كَيْفَ خُلِقَتْ ۝ وَإِلَى السَّمَاءِ كَيْفَ رُفِعَتْ ۝ وَإِلَى الْجِبَالِ كَيْفَ نُصِبَتْ ۝ وَإِلَى الْأَرْضِ كَيْفَ سُطِحَتْ ۝

ᵃ Man observes that a serviceable animal like the camel is obedient to him. The sky in all its majesty is well disposed towards him. The earth, without any effort on our part, is subservient to our interests. All these phenomena remind a thoughtful man of God and the Hereafter. Those who derive the nourishment of remembrance from these arrangements of the world have established their entitlement to God's eternal bounties, while those who have remained lost in forgetfulness and neglect, have proved that they deserve to be deprived of every kind of bounty—forever.

²¹ So, [O Prophet] exhort them: your task is only to exhort,ᵃ ²² you are not their keeper. ²³ But whoever turns back and denies the truth, ²⁴ will be punished by God with the greatest punishment. ²⁵ Certainly, it is to Us that they will return. ²⁶ Then, surely, it is for Us to call them to account.

فَذَكِّرْ إِنَّمَا أَنتَ مُذَكِّرٌ ۝ لَّسْتَ عَلَيْهِم بِمُصَيْطِرٍ ۝ إِلَّا مَن تَوَلَّىٰ وَكَفَرَ ۝ فَيُعَذِّبُهُ ٱللَّهُ ٱلْعَذَابَ ٱلْأَكْبَرَ ۝ إِنَّ إِلَيْنَآ إِيَابَهُمْ ۝ ثُمَّ إِنَّ عَلَيْنَا حِسَابَهُم ۝

ᵃ Calling people to God aims at exhorting people through peaceful persuasion, to make them realize their Creator, the one and only God; to understand the purpose of their creation; the coming of the Hereafter, of their accountability to their Creator, etc.

The purpose of this exhortation is to awaken souls from their slumber. It is to put a lost person on to the right path leading towards God. It is to awaken man's insight so that he begins to see glimpses of God in the signs of the vast universe. It is to unveil the Creator in the mirror of His creation.

89. THE DAWN

In the name of God
the Most Gracious, the Most Merciful

[1] By the Dawn, [2] by the Ten Nights, [3] by the even and the odd, [4] and by the passing night, [5] is there not in this strong evidence for a man of sense? [6] Have you not heard of how your Lord dealt with the tribe of 'Ad, [7] the people of Iram, the city of many pillars, [8] the like of which has never been created in the land, [9] and with the Thamud, who cut out [huge] rocks in the valley, [10] and with Pharaoh of the stakes? [11] All of them committed excesses in their lands, [12] and caused much corruption in them: [13] so your Lord unleashed on them the scourge of punishment: [14] for, indeed, your Sustainer is ever on the watch! [15] As for man, when his Lord tests him, through honour and blessings, he says, 'My Lord has honoured me,' [16] but when He tests him by straitening his means of livelihood, he says, 'My Lord has disgraced me.'[a]

---

[a] Man passes through two sets of circumstances in the world—sometimes finding or receiving things and sometimes losing them. Both eventualities, meant to gauge human reactions to different conditions, are for the purpose of putting man to the test. If the individual starts to boast when he receives something and acts negatively when things are taken away from him, he has failed the test.

¹⁷ No indeed, but you show no kindness to the orphan, ¹⁸ nor do you urge one another to feed the poor, ¹⁹ and you greedily devour the inheritance of the weak, ²⁰ and you have a love of wealth which can never be satisfied. ²¹ No indeed! When the earth is crushed and ground to dust, ²² when your Lord comes down with the angels, rank upon rank, ²³ and Hell is made to appear on that Day, then man will be mindful, but what will being mindful then avail him? ²⁴ He will say, 'Oh, would that I had provided beforehand for my life!' ²⁵ On that Day no one will punish as He punishes, ²⁶ and none can bind with bonds like His! ²⁷ [But to the righteous, God will say], 'O soul at peace,^a ²⁸ return to your Lord, well-pleased, well-pleasing. ²⁹ Join My servants. ³⁰ Enter My Paradise.'

كَلَّا ۖ بَل لَّا تُكْرِمُونَ ٱلْيَتِيمَ ۝ وَلَا تَحَـٰٓضُّونَ عَلَىٰ طَعَامِ ٱلْمِسْكِينِ ۝ وَتَأْكُلُونَ ٱلتُّرَاثَ أَكْلًا لَّمًّا ۝ وَتُحِبُّونَ ٱلْمَالَ حُبًّا جَمًّا ۝ كَلَّآ إِذَا دُكَّتِ ٱلْأَرْضُ دَكًّا دَكًّا ۝ وَجَآءَ رَبُّكَ وَٱلْمَلَكُ صَفًّا صَفًّا ۝ وَجِا۟ىٓءَ يَوْمَئِذٍ بِجَهَنَّمَ ۚ يَوْمَئِذٍ يَتَذَكَّرُ ٱلْإِنسَـٰنُ وَأَنَّىٰ لَهُ ٱلذِّكْرَىٰ ۝ يَقُولُ يَـٰلَيْتَنِى قَدَّمْتُ لِحَيَاتِى ۝ فَيَوْمَئِذٍ لَّا يُعَذِّبُ عَذَابَهُۥٓ أَحَدٌ ۝ وَلَا يُوثِقُ وَثَاقَهُۥٓ أَحَدٌ ۝ يَـٰٓأَيَّتُهَا ٱلنَّفْسُ ٱلْمُطْمَئِنَّةُ ۝ ٱرْجِعِىٓ إِلَىٰ رَبِّكِ رَاضِيَةً مَّرْضِيَّةً ۝ فَٱدْخُلِى فِى عِبَـٰدِى ۝ وَٱدْخُلِى جَنَّتِى ۝

---

^a The other type of person is one who would bow down before God and thank Him when he received something, and when things were taken away from him, he would once again bow down before God and express his humility. It is the second type of person who has been called the contented soul or *an-nafs al-mutmainnah*.

The position of the contented soul is attained by one who ponders over God's signs in the universe; who derives spiritual nourishment, learns lessons and receives guidance from historical events; who proves that if there is a clash between the self and the Truth, he will ignore the self and accept the Truth; who, after once accepting the Truth, never renounces it, whatever the cost.

90. THE CITY

In the name of God,
the Most Gracious, the Most Merciful

¹ I swear by this city—² and you are dwelling in this city—³ and by parent and offspring, ⁴ that We have created man into a life of toil and trial.ᵃ ⁵ Does he think then that no one has power over him? ⁶ He says, 'I have spent enormous wealth.' ⁷ Does he then think that no one sees him? ⁸ Have We not given him two eyes, ⁹ and a tongue, and a pair of lips, ¹⁰ and shown him the two paths?ᵇ ¹¹ But he has not attempted the ascent. ¹² What will explain to you what the ascent is? ¹³ It is the freeing of a slave; ¹⁴ or the feeding in times of famine ¹⁵ of an orphaned relative ¹⁶ or some needy person in distress, ¹⁷ and to be one of those who believe and urge one another to steadfastness and compassion. ¹⁸ Those who do so are the people of the right hand, ¹⁹ and [as for] those who are bent on denying the truth of Our revelations, they are the people of the left hand, ²⁰ and the Fire will close in on them.

ᵃ Man has never been able to free himself from hardship. This shows that he is subordinate to some Superior Power. Similarly, man's eyes show that there is also a Superior Eye which is watching him. His power of speech indicates that there is One capable of speech over and above him, who has bestowed upon him the power of speech and showed him the right path. If a man realizes himself in the true sense, then he will certainly recognise God.

ᵇ God has commanded man to scale two heights—one is to treat others with justice, and help them in their hour of need. The other is to have firm faith in God. When such belief enters the inner depths of a human being, it does not remain confined to his own thinking but rather makes him become communicative. He then attempts to lead others along the path of Truth which he himself has adopted.

91. THE SUN

In the name of God,
the Most Gracious, the Most Merciful

¹ By the sun and its rising brightness
² and by the moon as it follows it,
³ and by the day as it reveals its glory
⁴ and by the night when it draws a
veil over it, ⁵ by the sky and how He
built it ⁶ and by the earth and how
He spread it, ⁷ by the soul and how
He formed it, ⁸ then inspired it to
understand what was right and
wrong for it. ⁹ He who purifies it will
indeed be successful, ¹⁰ and he who
corrupts it is sure to fail.ᵃ

وَٱلشَّمْسِ وَضُحَىٰهَا ۝ وَٱلْقَمَرِ إِذَا
تَلَىٰهَا ۝ وَٱلنَّهَارِ إِذَا جَلَّىٰهَا ۝ وَٱلَّيْلِ
إِذَا يَغْشَىٰهَا ۝ وَٱلسَّمَآءِ وَمَا بَنَىٰهَا
۝ وَٱلْأَرْضِ وَمَا طَحَىٰهَا ۝ وَنَفْسٍ
وَمَا سَوَّىٰهَا ۝ فَأَلْهَمَهَا فُجُورَهَا
وَتَقْوَىٰهَا ۝ قَدْ أَفْلَحَ مَن زَكَّىٰهَا ۝
وَقَدْ خَابَ مَن دَسَّىٰهَا ۝

ᵃ Almighty God has made threefold arrangements for the guidance of man. On the
one hand, the universe has been so constructed that it has become the practical
manifestation of God's will. On the other hand, the human psyche has been infused
with an intuitive consciousness of good and bad. Thereafter, it was arranged that
Truth and falsehood, justice and injustice be revealed clearly through the prophets
in a language understandable to the people. Even after this, if people do not adopt
the right path, they are undoubtedly transgressors.

¹¹ The Thamud tribe rejected the truth because of their arrogance, ¹² when the most wicked man among them rose up. ¹³ Then the messenger of God said to them, 'This is God's she-camel. Let her drink.' ¹⁴ But they gave him the lie, and hamstrung the she-camel. So their Lord destroyed them for their crime and razed their city to the ground. ¹⁵ He did not fear the consequences.^a

كَذَّبَتْ ثَمُودُ بِطَغْوَىٰهَآ ۝ إِذِ ٱنۢبَعَثَ أَشْقَىٰهَا ۝ فَقَالَ لَهُمْ رَسُولُ ٱللَّهِ نَاقَةَ ٱللَّهِ وَسُقْيَٰهَا ۝ فَكَذَّبُوهُ فَعَقَرُوهَا فَدَمْدَمَ عَلَيْهِمْ رَبُّهُم بِذَنۢبِهِمْ فَسَوَّىٰهَا ۝ وَلَا يَخَافُ عُقْبَٰهَا ۝

---

^a The she-camel of the Prophet Salih, in a way, symbolised the principle that one should respect the rights of others and discharge one's duties to them accordingly, even if they are helpless and weak. It is quite possible that a creature which, to all appearances, is only a 'she-camel', may be God's sign brought before people to test them.

92. NIGHT

In the name of God,
the Most Gracious, the Most Merciful

¹ By the night as it veils [the earth] in darkness, ² and by the day as it appears radiantly, ³ and by the creation of the male and the female.ᵃ ⁴ O men, you truly strive towards the most diverse ends! ⁵ As for one who gives [to others] and fears [God], ⁶ and believes in the truth of what is right, ⁷ We will pave his way to ease. ⁸ But as for one who is miserly and unheeding, ⁹ and rejects what is right, ¹⁰ We shall pave his way to hardship, ¹¹ nor will his wealth profit him when he falls [into the pit].

وَٱلَّيْلِ إِذَا يَغْشَىٰ ۝ وَٱلنَّهَارِ إِذَا تَجَلَّىٰ ۝ وَمَا خَلَقَ ٱلذَّكَرَ وَٱلْأُنثَىٰ ۝ إِنَّ سَعْيَكُمْ لَشَتَّىٰ ۝ فَأَمَّا مَنْ أَعْطَىٰ وَٱتَّقَىٰ ۝ وَصَدَّقَ بِٱلْحُسْنَىٰ ۝ فَسَنُيَسِّرُهُۥ لِلْيُسْرَىٰ ۝ وَأَمَّا مَن بَخِلَ وَٱسْتَغْنَىٰ ۝ وَكَذَّبَ بِٱلْحُسْنَىٰ ۝ فَسَنُيَسِّرُهُۥ لِلْعُسْرَىٰ ۝ وَمَا يُغْنِى عَنْهُ مَالُهُۥٓ إِذَا تَرَدَّىٰ ۝

ᵃ All things in this world are in pairs—male and female; night and day; positive and negative particles, matter and anti-matter. Everything in this world joins its pair and fulfils its purpose. This is a clear proof of the fact that this universe is purposeful. In such a purposeful universe it is impossible for both the good deeds and the bad deeds performed in it to have the same final consequences. This would not be consistent with the image of the Creator presented by the universe.

¹² Surely, it is for Us to provide guidance— ¹³ and to Us belongs the Hereafter as well as the present world— ¹⁴ I have warned you then about a raging Fire: ¹⁵ none shall enter it but the most wicked, ¹⁶ who denied [the truth], and turned away.^a ¹⁷ One who fears God shall be kept away from it— ¹⁸ one who gives his wealth to become purified, ¹⁹ and owes no favour to anyone, which is to be repaid, ²⁰ acting only for the sake of his Lord the Most High— ²¹ and before long he will be well satisfied.

إِنَّ عَلَيْنَا لَلْهُدَىٰ ۞ وَإِنَّ لَنَا لَلْأَخِرَةَ وَٱلْأُولَىٰ ۞ فَأَنذَرْتُكُمْ نَارًا تَلَظَّىٰ ۞ لَا يَصْلَىٰهَآ إِلَّا ٱلْأَشْقَى ۞ ٱلَّذِى كَذَّبَ وَتَوَلَّىٰ ۞ وَسَيُجَنَّبُهَا ٱلْأَتْقَى ۞ ٱلَّذِى يُؤْتِى مَالَهُ يَتَزَكَّىٰ ۞ وَمَا لِأَحَدٍ عِندَهُۥ مِن نِّعْمَةٍ تُجْزَىٰٓ ۞ إِلَّا ٱبْتِغَآءَ وَجْهِ رَبِّهِ ٱلْأَعْلَىٰ ۞ وَلَسَوْفَ يَرْضَىٰ ۞

---

^a The relationship of God with His subjects is not only that of a ruler but also that of a supporter. He smooths the path of those of His subjects who want to draw near to Him. Conversely, He lets those who adopt the way of arrogance to carry on in that way.

93. THE GLORIOUS MORNING LIGHT

In the name of God,
the Most Gracious, the Most Merciful

¹ By the glorious morning light; ² and by the night when it darkens, ³ your Lord has not forsaken you, nor is He displeased with you, ⁴ and the Hereafter will indeed be better for you than the present life;ᵃ ⁵ soon you will be gratified with what your Lord will give you. ⁶ Did He not find you orphaned and shelter you?ᵇ ⁷ Did He not find you wandering, and give you guidance? ⁸ Did He not find you in want, and make you free from want? ⁹ Therefore do not treat the orphan with harshness, ¹⁰ and do not chide the one who asks for help; ¹¹ but proclaim the blessings of your Lord.ᶜ

ᵃ The system of this world has been so formulated that here the day dawns and night also falls. Only with the occurrence of both is the system perfect. Similarly, for the proper development of a man, it is necessary that he should have hardship as well as easy circumstances. In this world, hardship befalls the servant of God in order to activate his latent capabilities. Impediments are put in his way so that he may strive to make his future brighter than his present.

ᵇ The Prophet Muhammad was born an orphan. Then God provided him with the best of guardians. He went eagerly in search of the Truth. Then God opened the door of Truth for him. He was apparently without wealth. Then God made him prosperous through his wife, Khadijah. These are historical examples which show how Almighty God helps His subjects.

ᶜ Man should help the weak so that he may be entitled to God's grace. His words should be full of the expression of God's grace, so that God may confer His blessings upon him.

94. COMFORT

In the name of God,
the Most Gracious, the Most Merciful

¹ Have We not lifted up your heart,
² and removed your burden ³ that
weighed so heavily on your back, and
⁴ have We not given you high
renown? ⁵ So, surely with every
hardship there is ease; ⁶ surely, with
every hardship there is ease. ⁷ So,
when you are free, strive hard, ⁸ and
to your Lord turn [all] your
attention.

ᵃ The Prophet Muhammad went tirelessly in the quest of knowledge about reality
and Truth. God blessed him with this knowledge, which opened his heart to the
deep realisation of Truth (ma'rifah). Then he started preaching the oneness of God
in Makkah, where he had to face stiff opposition, but it was thanks to this
opposition, that he became known throughout the country.

This is God's law in the present world. Hence, a man has to face difficult conditions
('usr) in the beginning, but if he perseveres with patience, this 'usr or hardship
becomes a stepping stone to new and easy circumstances (yusr). Therefore, a man
should always look towards God and continue to struggle according to his capacity.

95. THE FIG

In the name of God,
the Most Gracious, the Most Merciful

¹By the Fig and the Olive, ²and by Mount Sinai, ³and by this secure land,ᵃ ⁴We have indeed created man in the best of mould, ⁵then We cast him down as the lowest of the low, ⁶except for those who believe and do good deeds—theirs shall be an unending reward!ᵇ ⁷What then after this, can make you deny the Last Judgement? ⁸Is not God the greatest of the judges?

ᵃ Fig (*Tin*) and Olive (*Zaytun*) are the names of two hills in the vicinity of Jerusalem where Jesus's field of action was situated. Mount Sinai (*Tur Sinin*) refers to that hill where God made His revelation to Moses. The 'secure land' (*al-Baladu'l Amin*) refers to Makkah where the Prophet Muhammad was born.

ᵇ God has created man with superior capabilities. These capabilities have been given to man so that he should be able to recognise the Truth conveyed to him through the prophets, and to shape his life in accordance with it. Those who do so, will reach a high position of honour, which will be theirs for all eternity. On the contrary, those who do not make their God-given capabilities subservient to God's will, will have even the existing blessings taken away and they will have no place to take refuge. Their lot will be total deprivation. The raising of prophets and the end-results of their mission, bear testimony to the veracity of this fact.

96. THE CLOT

In the name of God,
the Most Gracious, the Most Merciful

¹ Read! In the name of your Lord,
who created: ² created man from a
clot [of blood]. ³ Read! Your Lord is
the Most Bountiful One ⁴ who
taught by the pen, ⁵ taught man what
he did not know.ᵃ

اقْرَأْ بِاسْمِ رَبِّكَ الَّذِي خَلَقَ ۝ خَلَقَ
الْإِنسَانَ مِنْ عَلَقٍ ۝ اقْرَأْ وَرَبُّكَ
الْأَكْرَمُ ۝ الَّذِي عَلَّمَ بِالْقَلَمِ ۝
عَلَّمَ الْإِنسَانَ مَا لَمْ يَعْلَمْ ۝

ᵃ The first five verses of this chapter were the very first verses which were revealed to the Prophet Muhammad. Almighty God created man out of ordinary material elements. Then He blessed him with the rare capacity to read and to understand the import of what he read. Then, man was given the additional capacity to use the pen and thus systematise and preserve his knowledge. While the capacity to read enables a man to acquire knowledge, the pen makes him capable of spreading this knowledge to others on a large scale.

The 'pen' is a symbol of knowledge. In other words, through written words the believers are enjoined to acquire and spread the knowledge of the truth, wisdom and beauty of Islam. Today, spreading the word of God will be done by means of printed material and through other means of communication which includes the internet and the multimedia. Translations of the Quran in various languages, Islamic books and other printed material on Islam should be distributed as a part of *dawah* work on a large scale, so that the word of God reaches each and every home—big or small as predicted in a hadith (Musnad Ahmed).

Thousands of men and women are dying every day without having had the message of God conveyed to them; without having had the opportunity to accept it, they have missed their chance of improving their lives in the Hereafter. In such a situation it is the solemn responsibility of the believers to desist from making excuses and seriously take up the mission of proclaiming the divine truth.

The conveying of the message of Truth to everyone, the responsibility for which has been placed on the Muslims, is not like an optional subject, which you may either take up or leave off on some pretext. This is a responsibility of such a nature that it has to be discharged at all costs. ▶

⁶ Yet man behaves arrogantly, ⁷ because he thinks himself self-sufficient: ⁸ truly, all will return to your Lord. ⁹ Have you seen one who prevents ¹⁰ a worshipper from praying? ¹¹ Do you think he is rightly guided, ¹² or enjoins true piety? ¹³ Do you see how he has denied the truth and turned away from it? ¹⁴ Does he not know that God observes all things? ¹⁵ Let him beware! If he does not desist, We will drag him by the forelock—¹⁶ his lying, sinful forelock. ¹⁷ Then let him call his associates; ¹⁸ We shall summon the guards of Hell. ¹⁹ No indeed! Do not obey him, but prostrate yourself and come closer to God.[a]

كَلَّا إِنَّ ٱلْإِنسَٰنَ لَيَطْغَىٰ ۞ أَن رَّءَاهُ ٱسْتَغْنَىٰ ۞ إِنَّ إِلَىٰ رَبِّكَ ٱلرُّجْعَىٰ ۞ أَرَءَيْتَ ٱلَّذِى يَنْهَىٰ ۞ عَبْدًا إِذَا صَلَّىٰ ۞ أَرَءَيْتَ إِن كَانَ عَلَى ٱلْهُدَىٰ ۞ أَوْ أَمَرَ بِٱلتَّقْوَىٰ ۞ أَرَءَيْتَ إِن كَذَّبَ وَتَوَلَّىٰ ۞ أَلَمْ يَعْلَم بِأَنَّ ٱللَّهَ يَرَىٰ ۞ كَلَّا لَئِن لَّمْ يَنتَهِ لَنَسْفَعًۢا بِٱلنَّاصِيَةِ ۞ نَاصِيَةٍ كَٰذِبَةٍ خَاطِئَةٍ ۞ فَلْيَدْعُ نَادِيَهُۥ ۞ سَنَدْعُ ٱلزَّبَانِيَةَ ۞ كَلَّا لَا تُطِعْهُ وَٱسْجُدْ وَٱقْتَرِب ۩ ۞

Dawah, which in the Quran is called 'warning and giving glad tidings', is directly the mission of God. So that men might have no argument with God on the plea that they were unaware, this task was passed on to the believers themselves after the preservation of the Quran. This exigency has opened up the opportunity for man to perform this great divine task. Those who come forward to carry out this divine mission of *dawah* will receive special succour in this life and will be held deserving of great honour in the life Hereafter.

[a] Those who wage aggressive campaigns against Truth or place impediments in the way of those who adopt the path of Truth, are destined to have a miserable fate. In such circumstances, the real prop for a preacher of Truth is his prayers to God. Having been disappointed by people, he should turn to God for fulfilment. He should distance himself from human beings and come close to the God of all humanity and submit to Him.

97. THE NIGHT OF DESTINY

In the name of God,
the Most Gracious, the Most Merciful

¹ We sent it [Quran] down on the Night of Destiny. ² And what will make you comprehend what the Night of Destiny is?ᵃ ³ The Night of Destiny is better than a thousand months; ⁴ on that night, the angels and the Spirit ᵇ come down by the permission of their Lord with His decrees for all matters; ⁵ it is all peace till the break of dawn.

إِنَّا أَنزَلْنَٰهُ فِي لَيْلَةِ ٱلْقَدْرِ ۝ وَمَآ أَدْرَىٰكَ مَا لَيْلَةُ ٱلْقَدْرِ ۝ لَيْلَةُ ٱلْقَدْرِ خَيْرٌ مِّنْ أَلْفِ شَهْرٍ ۝ تَنَزَّلُ ٱلْمَلَٰٓئِكَةُ وَٱلرُّوحُ فِيهَا بِإِذْنِ رَبِّهِم مِّن كُلِّ أَمْرٍ ۝ سَلَٰمٌ هِىَ حَتَّىٰ مَطْلَعِ ٱلْفَجْرِ ۝

ᵃ A particular night of the year (perhaps some night in the last days of the month of Ramadan) is the night of decisions by God. Certain tasks have to be performed in the course of the year in connection with the administration of the world, and the angels descend to the earth to arrange for them to be carried out. On a similar particular night, the revelation of the Quran began.

ᵇ This refers to the Angel Gabriel.

ᶜ It seems that on that night there is an abundance of angels on the earth. Those who are spiritually aroused are influenced by this atmosphere and, as a result, they become imbued with a spirituality which enhances the value of their religious deeds at that time as compared to such deeds as are performed in ordinary circumstances.

For this reason, as the month draws towards the last ten days, the worshippers give more time to prayers, give more in charity and read as much as possible from the Quran, beseeching their Lord for His mercy and forgiveness.

When the Prophet was asked by his wife, 'A'ishah, what one's prayer should be if one finds the Night of Destiny, *Lailatul Qadr*, he taught her this simple prayer: *Allahumma innaka afuwwun, tuhibbul afuwa, fa afuanni.* O Allah, You are forgiving, You love forgiveness, so forgive me.

98. THE CLEAR EVIDENCE

In the name of God,
the Most Gracious, the Most Merciful

¹ The deniers of truth from among the People of the Book and the polytheists would not desist from disbelief until they received clear evidence—² a messenger from God, reciting to them pure scriptures, ³ containing upright precepts.ᵃ

لَمْ يَكُنِ ٱلَّذِينَ كَفَرُوا۟ مِنْ أَهْلِ ٱلْكِتَٰبِ وَٱلْمُشْرِكِينَ مُنفَكِّينَ حَتَّىٰ تَأْتِيَهُمُ ٱلْبَيِّنَةُ ۝ رَسُولٌ مِّنَ ٱللَّهِ يَتْلُوا۟ صُحُفًا مُّطَهَّرَةً ۝ فِيهَا كُتُبٌ قَيِّمَةٌ ۝

ᵃ The Arab pagans and the followers of Divine scriptures (i.e. followers of previous prophets) used to ask the Prophet Muhammad to show them some miracles, as clear evidence, or demanded that an angel should descend from heaven and talk to them. Only then would they accept his prophethood. But those who make such demands are inevitably frivolous. Such demands had already been made by their forebears, but in spite of their demands being conceded to, they could not become believers.

⁴ Those who were given the Book did not become divided except after clear evidence was given to them. ⁵ They were commanded only to worship God, offering Him sincere devotion, to be sincere in their faith, to pray regularly; and to give alms, for that is the right religion. ⁶ Those of the deniers of truth among the People of the Book and the polytheists will dwell forever in Hell-fire. They are the worst of creatures. ⁷ Truly, those who believe and do good works are the best of creatures. ⁸ God has a reward in store for them: Gardens of eternity, through which rivers flow; they will dwell therein forever. God is well pleased with them and they are well pleased with Him. Thus shall the God-fearing be rewarded.

وَمَا تَفَرَّقَ ٱلَّذِينَ أُوتُوا۟ ٱلْكِتَـٰبَ إِلَّا مِنۢ بَعْدِ مَا جَآءَتْهُمُ ٱلْبَيِّنَةُ ۝ وَمَآ أُمِرُوٓا۟ إِلَّا لِيَعْبُدُوا۟ ٱللَّهَ مُخْلِصِينَ لَهُ ٱلدِّينَ حُنَفَآءَ وَيُقِيمُوا۟ ٱلصَّلَوٰةَ وَيُؤْتُوا۟ ٱلزَّكَوٰةَ وَذَٰلِكَ دِينُ ٱلْقَيِّمَةِ ۝ إِنَّ ٱلَّذِينَ كَفَرُوا۟ مِنْ أَهْلِ ٱلْكِتَـٰبِ وَٱلْمُشْرِكِينَ فِى نَارِ جَهَنَّمَ خَـٰلِدِينَ فِيهَآ أُو۟لَـٰٓئِكَ هُمْ شَرُّ ٱلْبَرِيَّةِ ۝ إِنَّ ٱلَّذِينَ ءَامَنُوا۟ وَعَمِلُوا۟ ٱلصَّـٰلِحَـٰتِ أُو۟لَـٰٓئِكَ هُمْ خَيْرُ ٱلْبَرِيَّةِ ۝ جَزَآؤُهُمْ عِندَ رَبِّهِمْ جَنَّـٰتُ عَدْنٍ تَجْرِى مِن تَحْتِهَا ٱلْأَنْهَـٰرُ خَـٰلِدِينَ فِيهَآ أَبَدًا رَّضِىَ ٱللَّهُ عَنْهُمْ وَرَضُوا۟ عَنْهُ ذَٰلِكَ لِمَنْ خَشِىَ رَبَّهُۥ ۝

ᵃ The true religion of God is that according to which man should pray to and worship the one and only God; he should love and admire God from the bottom of his heart; he should consistently say his prayers and pay *zakat* (prescribed alms-giving). This is the real religion which comes from God. The best of all are those who adopt this correct religion and the worst are those who do not do so, or who devise another religion instead of the proper one and call the new religion the true religion.

99. THE EARTHQUAKE

In the name of God,
the Most Gracious, the Most Merciful

بِسْمِ ٱللَّهِ ٱلرَّحْمَٰنِ ٱلرَّحِيمِ

¹ When the earth is shaken with its violent shaking, ² when the earth shakes off her burdens, ³ when man asks, 'What is happening to her?'; ⁴ on that Day it will narrate its account, ⁵ for your Lord has so directed it. ⁶ On that Day people will come forward in separate groups to be shown their deeds: ⁷ whoever has done the smallest particle of good will see it; ⁸ while whoever has done the smallest particle of evil will see it.ᵃ

إِذَا زُلْزِلَتِ ٱلْأَرْضُ زِلْزَالَهَا ۞ وَأَخْرَجَتِ ٱلْأَرْضُ أَثْقَالَهَا ۞ وَقَالَ ٱلْإِنسَٰنُ مَا لَهَا ۞ يَوْمَئِذٍ تُحَدِّثُ أَخْبَارَهَا ۞ بِأَنَّ رَبَّكَ أَوْحَىٰ لَهَا ۞ يَوْمَئِذٍ يَصْدُرُ ٱلنَّاسُ أَشْتَاتًا لِّيُرَوْاْ أَعْمَٰلَهُمْ ۞ فَمَن يَعْمَلْ مِثْقَالَ ذَرَّةٍ خَيْرًا يَرَهُۥ ۞ وَمَن يَعْمَلْ مِثْقَالَ ذَرَّةٍ شَرًّا يَرَهُۥ ۞

ᵃ The earthquake on Doomsday will be the announcement of the end of the testing period for man. This would mean that the freedom which was theirs on account of their being on trial, has now been snatched away from them. Now the time has come when human beings will be recompensed for their deeds. Today, God's world is silent, but when conditions change, everything found here will start talking. The inventions of the present day have proved that lifeless or inanimate things also have the capacity to 'talk.' A performance in a studio is fully reproduced by a video film and records. Similarly, the present world is, so to say, a big 'studio' of God. Whatever a man does or says or even thinks, everything is being recorded at every moment. And when the time comes, this world will repeat everybody's story in such a way that not a thing, great or small, will be left out.

100. THE SNORTING HORSES

In the name of God,
the Most Gracious, the Most Merciful

¹ By the snorting, panting horses, ² striking sparks of fire with their hooves, ³ as they gallop to make raids at dawn, ⁴ and raising clouds of dust, ⁵ forcing their way into the midst of the enemy, ⁶ surely, man is ungrateful to his Lord. ⁷ He himself bears witness to that. ⁸ Surely, he is ardent in his love of wealth. ⁹ Is he not aware of the time when the contents of the graves will be brought out? ¹⁰ And the hearts' contents shall be brought into the open? ¹¹ Surely, on that Day, they will know that their Lord had full knowledge of them all.ᵃ

ᵃ The horse is a very loyal animal. He sacrifices himself to the utmost for the sake of his master. Even in the battlefield, he does not leave his side. This is an example which shows how a man should conduct himself. Man should also be loyal to his Lord just as the horse is loyal to man. But, in practice, it is not like that.

In this world, the animal is grateful to his master, but man is not grateful to his Lord. Here an animal knows his obligations towards his master, but man does not know his obligations towards his Lord. Here an animal is totally obedient to his master, but man is not totally obedient to his Lord.

Man appreciates any animal which is loyal to him. Then, how is it possible that he does not comprehend that in the eyes of God only that individual is worthy of appreciation who is loyal to Him? It is the love of wealth which blinds him. He is unable to learn the truth even from his own experiences.

101. THE CLATTERER

In the name of God,
the Most Gracious, the Most Merciful

¹The Clatterer! ²What is the Clatterer? ³Would that you knew what the Clatterer is! ⁴[It is] a Day when mankind shall be like scattered moths ⁵and the mount-ains like tufts of carded wool. ⁶Then, the one whose good deeds weigh heavy on the scales, ⁷will have a most pleasing life. ⁸But as for him whose deeds are light on the scales, ⁹the Abyss shall be his home. ¹⁰What will convey to you what this is like? ¹¹It is a blazing fire.ᵃ

ᵃ The turmoil of Doomsday will smash everything. People will completely lose their bearings. Thereafter a new world will come into existence where only Truth will carry weight. All falsity will be set at naught. In the present world, the approval of the people prevails. Here things carry weight according to the likes and dislikes of men. The world of the Hereafter is the world of God, where everything will be subservient to His will.

In the present world the deeds performed are judged according to their appearance. In the Hereafter deeds will be judged according to their inner reality. The more sincere a man's deeds, the more importance they will be given. The deed which is devoid of sincerity will carry absolutely no weight in the Hereafter, however significant it might have seemed to the superficial people of the present world.

102. GREED FOR MORE AND MORE

سُورَةُ التَّكَاثُرِ

In the name of God,
the Most Gracious, the Most Merciful

بِسۡمِ ٱللَّهِ ٱلرَّحۡمَٰنِ ٱلرَّحِيمِ

¹ Greed for more and more distracted you [from God] ² till you reached the grave. ³ But you will soon come to know. ⁴ But you will soon come to know. ⁵ Indeed, were you to know the truth with certainty, ⁶ you would see the fire of Hell. ⁷ You would see it with the eye of certainty. ⁸ Then on that Day you shall be questioned about your worldly favours.ᵃ

أَلۡهَىٰكُمُ ٱلتَّكَاثُرُ ۝ حَتَّىٰ زُرۡتُمُ ٱلۡمَقَابِرَ ۝ كَلَّا سَوۡفَ تَعۡلَمُونَ ۝ ثُمَّ كَلَّا سَوۡفَ تَعۡلَمُونَ ۝ كَلَّا لَوۡ تَعۡلَمُونَ عِلۡمَ ٱلۡيَقِينِ ۝ لَتَرَوُنَّ ٱلۡجَحِيمَ ۝ ثُمَّ لَتَرَوُنَّهَا عَيۡنَ ٱلۡيَقِينِ ۝ ثُمَّ لَتُسۡـَٔلُنَّ يَوۡمَئِذٍ عَنِ ٱلنَّعِيمِ ۝

ᵃ Man wants to earn more and more so that he may accumulate more and more material assets. He remains immersed in that thought till the day he dies. After his death, man realises that what was worth accumulating was something else. But the realization after death will be of no avail.

Any increase in worldly goods increases a man's accountability. But man, in his foolishness, thinks that he is adding to his success.

103. THE PASSAGE OF TIME

In the name of God,
the Most Gracious, the Most Merciful

[1] I swear by the passage of time, [2] that man is surely in a state of loss, [3] except for those who believe and do good deeds and exhort one another to hold fast to the Truth, and who exhort one another to stead-fastness.[a]

---

[a] At every moment man is advancing towards his death. This means that if a man does not make the best of the time which is still available to him, he will finally face total destruction. In order to be successful, a man has to exert himself, while for failure he has to do nothing. It is itself rushing towards him.

A venerable gentleman tells us that he understood the meaning of this chapter of the Quran from an ice vendor who was shouting in market, 'O, people! Have mercy on one whose assets are melting away.' On hearing this shout, the gentleman said to himself that just as the ice melts and reduces, similarly the lifespan given to man is fast passing away. If the existing opportunity is lost in inaction or in evil action, this is man's loss. (Imam Razi, *Tafsir Kabir*).

One who utilises his time properly is one who adopts three courses in the present world. One is that of Faith (*al-ladina a'manu*), i.e. consciousness of Truth or reality and its acceptance. Secondly that of virtuous deeds (*wa a'milu as-salihat*), i.e. doing that which is required to be done as a matter of religious duty and abstaining from what is sinful. Thirdly that of advising people about Truth and forbearance. This follows upon such a deep realisation of Truth that the concerned person becomes its preacher.

104. THE BACKBITER

In the name of God,
the Most Gracious, the Most Merciful

¹ Woe to every fault-finding back-biter, ² who amasses wealth, counting it over, ³ thinking that his wealth will make him live forever. ⁴ By no means! He shall surely be cast into the crushing torment. ⁵ Would that you understood what that crushing torment is like. ⁶ It is a Fire kindled by God. ⁷ Reaching right into the hearts of men, ⁸ it closes in on them from every side ⁹ in towering columns.[a]

وَيْلٌ لِّكُلِّ هُمَزَةٍ لُّمَزَةٍ ۝ ٱلَّذِى جَمَعَ مَالاً وَعَدَّدَهُ ۝ يَحْسَبُ أَنَّ مَالَهُ أَخْلَدَهُ ۝ كَلَّا لَيُنبَذَنَّ فِى ٱلْحُطَمَةِ ۝ وَمَآ أَدْرَىٰكَ مَا ٱلْحُطَمَةُ ۝ نَارُ ٱللَّهِ ٱلْمُوقَدَةُ ۝ ٱلَّتِى تَطَّلِعُ عَلَى ٱلْأَفْئِدَةِ ۝ إِنَّهَا عَلَيْهِم مُّؤْصَدَةٌ ۝ فِى عَمَدٍ مُّمَدَّدَةٍ ۝

---

[a] If a man has a difference with another, he can settle it by argument. But it is not proper for him to denigrate the other person, defame him and make him the target of allegations. While the first course of action is legitimate, the second is not.

Those who resort to calumny, do so because they see that their worldly position is safe and strong. They think that they are not going to lose anything if they level baseless allegations against another. But this is mere foolishness. The fact is that their doing so amounts to jumping into a pit of fire—a pit of fire from which there will be no escape.

105. THE ELEPHANT

In the name of God,
the Most Gracious, the Most Merciful

¹ Have you not seen how your Lord dealt with the people of the elephant? ² Did He not foil their strategy ³ and send against them flocks of birds, ⁴ which pelted them with clay stones? ⁵ Thus He made them like stubble cropped by cattle? ᵃ

ᵃ Abraha was a Christian ruler of Yemen in southern Arabia in the sixth century A.D. Out of religious fanaticism, he attacked Makkah in the year 570 A.D. (the year of the Prophet's birth) with a view to destroying the Kabah by demolishing it. He had with him an army of sixty thousand soldiers and about a dozen elephants. That is why they were called 'the People of the elephant'. As these people approached Makkah, the elephants refused to move ahead. Besides that, flocks of birds flew over them carrying pebbles in their beaks and claws. They showered these pebbles on Abraha's army and the whole army was afflicted by a strange disease. The army was terrified and took flight. But many of its soldiers, including Abraha died on the way.

This was a sign that whoever set himself against the Prophet or his mission would be defeated like the army of the elephants.

This was Almighty God's way of showing that the Prophet was associated with domination. The divine book revealed to him would be preserved by God for all time to come for the guidance of all mankind.

106. QURAYSH

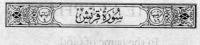

In the name of God,
the Most Gracious, the Most Merciful

¹For the security of the Quraysh:
²their security in their winter and
summer journeys. ³So let them
worship the Lord of this House,
⁴who provided them with food lest
they go hungry and saved them from
fear.*

---

a This chapter was revealed at Makkah, where the Quraysh tribe was the custodian
of the Kabah. Owing to this position they were held in high esteem throughout
Arabia. This gave them a number of privileges. The Quraysh was a trading
community. During the summer their traders' caravans used to go to Syria and
Palestine and in winter they would trade with Yemen. Their economy was
dependent upon these trading activities. In ancient times, when the robbing of
traders was common, the caravans of the Quraysh went unscathed. The reason for
this was their connection with the Ka'bah of which the Quraysh were the servants
and trustees. Since respect for the Ka'bah dominated the minds of the people, they
used to respect its servants and trustees also, and on account of this they did not
rob their caravans. Their tribe thus became prosperous.

Here, in connection with the call for the acceptance of Truth, the Quraysh have
been reminded of this blessing of God and called to Islam. They are told that it
would be highly ungrateful to enjoy the worldly benefits of the House of God—
the Ka'bah ('*Baytullah*') while shirking the religious responsibility incumbent upon
them.

They are enjoined to worship only God who confered all material benefits upon
them. This is to say, they are urged to give a positive response to the call of Truth
brought to them by the Prophet Muhammad and surrender to their Creator and
Sustainer. By extension, every believer is reminded here to be thankful to the Lord
and worship Him.

107. SMALL THINGS

In the name of God,
the Most Gracious, the Most Merciful

بِسْمِ اللَّهِ الرَّحْمَٰنِ الرَّحِيمِ

¹ Have you seen one who denies the Day of Judgement? ² Who turns away the orphan, ³ and who does not urge the feeding of the poor? ⁴ So woe to those who pray ⁵ but whose hearts are not in their prayer. ⁶ Those who do things only to be seen by others. ⁷ Who are uncharitable even over very small things.ᵃ

أَرَءَيْتَ ٱلَّذِى يُكَذِّبُ بِٱلدِّينِ ۝ فَذَٰلِكَ ٱلَّذِى يَدُعُّ ٱلْيَتِيمَ ۝ وَلَا يَحُضُّ عَلَىٰ طَعَامِ ٱلْمِسْكِينِ ۝ فَوَيْلٌ لِّلْمُصَلِّينَ ۝ ٱلَّذِينَ هُمْ عَن صَلَاتِهِمْ سَاهُونَ ۝ ٱلَّذِينَ هُمْ يُرَآءُونَ ۝ وَيَمْنَعُونَ ٱلْمَاعُونَ ۝

ᵃ This chapter, which has seven verses, draws our attention to the Day of Judgement, when we shall be held responsible for all our good or bad actions. It also deplores the ways of those who deny the Day of Judgement, treat the helpless with contempt and lead arrogant, selfish lives. They do not extend the slightest courtesy or kindness to their fellow human beings, their hearts being empty of Faith.

The hypocrites may put on a pretence of doing good deeds, but these hollow acts will not avail them. This chapter also warns those who are 'heedless in their prayer.'

Belief in the reckoning of the Hereafter makes a man pious. One who does not believe in this will be devoid of all goodness; he will be neglectful of prayer to God; he will not be ashamed of pushing over a weak person; he will not think it necessary to discharge the dues and rights of the poor; he will not even give to others such things as will cause him no substantial loss—even if it be only matchsticks or his good wishes.

108. ABUNDANCE

In the name of God,
the Most Gracious, the Most Merciful

¹ We have given you abundance.
² Pray to your Lord and sacrifice to
Him alone. ³ It is the one who hates
you who has been cut off.ᵃ

ᵃ This is the shortest chapter in the Quran, consisting of only three verses. It was
revealed at Makkah. The title is taken from the first verse. Al-Kauthar is the name
of a river which flows through paradise, its water being reserved exclusively for
God-fearing Muslims. The disbelievers used to taunt the Prophet that he had no
son, and therefore he had none to uphold his religion after him. But the Quran
says that it was in fact the Prophet's opponents who were cut off from all future
hope, in this world and the next, while the Prophet was granted abundance by God.

At the time when this chapter was revealed, the Prophet was facing stiff resistance
from the Makkan Quraysh. Only a handful of people had responded to his call. At
that difficult moment this chapter was a message of hope to the Prophet and to
the Muslims.

The Prophet Muhammad had arisen with the pure mission of calling all men to the
Truth. In the present world this is the most difficult task. So for the sake of this
mission, he had to forego his all. He was isolated from his community. His
economic position was ruined. The future of his children became dark. Nobody
except a few supported him. But under these very discouraging conditions, he was
told by Almighty God, 'We have given you abundance' i.e. the highest success of
every kind (*kawthar* here means *khayr kathir*). This prediction of the Quran was
fulfilled to the letter in later years.

This very promise was also applicable in various degrees to the followers of the
Prophet. For them also there was an 'abundance of good things' provided they rose
in the cause of the divine religion for which the Prophet and his companions had
risen. This 'abundance' extends from this world up to the Hereafter. It is never-
ending.

109. THOSE WHO DENY THE TRUTH

In the name of God,
the Most Gracious, the Most Merciful

¹ Say, 'You who deny the Truth,ᵃ ² I do not worship what you worship. ³ You do not worship what I worship. ⁴ I will never worship what you worship. ⁵ You will never worship what I worship. ⁶ You have your religion and I have mine.'ᵇ

ᵃ This chapter of the Quran, containing six verses, was revealed in the last days of the Makkan period. In the beginning the Prophet used to address people as 'O my people' or 'O my community'. But when in spite of completion of the arguments, the people did not accept him, he addressed them as 'You who deny the Truth'. At this stage, in fact, this is a statement given directly by God. No human being enjoys the right to declare anyone a denier.

God asks the Prophet not to force non-believers into the faith. The Prophet's duty was only to bear witness to the truth, spreading the message of God to everyone, without imposing it upon anyone. When, after 13 long years of unremitting efforts, people were not willing to believe, then the Prophet was told by God to say to the unbelievers, 'I do not worship what you worship, nor do you worship what I worship.' After the Prophet had fully conveyed God's message to the people, He was exempted from obligation towards those who rejected his call.

This chapter teaches us to practice tolerance towards non-Muslims and tells us to treat them with respect.

In his mission to invite the people of Makkah to God's path, the Prophet was filled with a sense of deep concern for the welfare of those he was addressing, and even though they heaped all sorts of oppression on him, he always beseeched God to guide them. The Prophet continued to do this steadfastly throughout the thirteen long years after receiving his prophethood in Makkah. Even after that, he did not refer to these people as *kafirs* on his own. It was only later that God revealed this commandment: 'Say, 'You who deny the truth'. From this it appears that it was only after these thirteen years of the Prophet's dedicated mission in Makkah that God declared, those whom the Prophet had addressed but who had rejected him, as 'deniers', and it was then that God revealed this commandment.

110. HELP

In the name of God,
the Most Gracious, the Most Merciful

¹ When God's help and victory come, ² and you see people entering God's religion in multitudes, ³ then glorify your Lord with His praise and seek His forgiveness. He is always ready to accept repentance.ᵃ

بِسْمِ اللَّهِ الرَّحْمَٰنِ الرَّحِيمِ

إِذَا جَاءَ نَصْرُ اللَّهِ وَالْفَتْحُ ۝ وَرَأَيْتَ النَّاسَ يَدْخُلُونَ فِي دِينِ اللَّهِ أَفْوَاجًا ۝ فَسَبِّحْ بِحَمْدِ رَبِّكَ وَاسْتَغْفِرْهُ إِنَّهُ كَانَ تَوَّابًا ۝

ᵃ This chapter is one of the last revelations of the Quran received by the Prophet. The place of its revelation was either the precincts of Makkah at his Farewell Pilgrimage in 10 AH, or Madina soon after his return from the Farewell Pilgrimage. God's special succour always accomapnies *dawah*, the spreading of the call of truth. The Prophet and his companions made untiring efforts in the path of *dawah*. Ultimately God's succour came and people began embracing Islam in their thousands. A number of neighbouring countries entered the fold of Islam. However, the victory of believers makes them all the more humble and conscious of their own failings. At such moments the faithful must be overwhelmed with the realization of God's Grace and Mercy. They must attribute all success to the goodness and mercy of God.

For a believer, victory increases his feeling of humility. Even for his apparently right action, he seeks God's pardon. Even the success he achieves, seemingly by his own efforts, is attributed by him to the will of God.

III. TWISTED FIBRE

In the name of God,
the Most Gracious, the Most Merciful

¹ May the hands of Abu Lahab perish, may he be ruined. ² Neither his wealth nor his gains will avail him. ³ He shall soon enter a Blazing Fire, ⁴ and also his wife who carries the fuel, ⁵ with a rope of twisted fibre round her neck.ᵃ

ᵃ This chapter, containing five verses, was revealed at Makkah. This is the only passage in the Quran where an opponent of the Prophet is denounced by name. Abu Lahab, whose real name was Abdul Uzza, was a first cousin of the Prophet's grandfather. He was the only member of the Prophet's clan who bitterly opposed him.

Abu Lahab made it his business to torment the Prophet, and his wife took pleasure in strewing thorn bushes in the path the Prophet was expected to take.

Consumed with grief on seeing many of the Quraysh leaders of the unbelievers killed at Badr, Abu Lahab died a week after Badr. Though this chapter refers, in the first instance, to a particular incident, it carries the general message that cruelty and haughtiness ultimately recoil upon oneself.

Abu Lahab, the name of an actual person, has come to denote a particular kind of character. 'Abu Lahab' who was an uncle of the Prophet Muhammad has come to be a symbol of such an opponent of the call for Truth as will stoop in his hostility to meanness. Just as the Prophet had to face this character, similarly others of his followers (ummah) may have to face just such a character. However, if the dayee has become active for the sake of God in the real sense, then God's help will be given to him. The inimical efforts of people like Abu Lahab will, by God's grace, become ineffective and, in spite of all their means and resources, the antagonists will perish. They will themselves burn in the fire of their own jealousy and enmity. Their aim may have been to ensure that the call of God came to a miserable end, but the opponents themselves will be the ones to suffer that everlasting fate.

112. ONENESS

In the name of God,
the Most Gracious, the Most Merciful

¹Say, 'He is God, the One, ²God, the Self-sufficient One. ³He does not give birth, nor was He born, ⁴and there is nothing like Him.'[a]

---

[a] The subject of the chapter is monotheism, or the oneness of God. The concept of God has been presented here in its purest form, ridding it of all polluting associations which people of every age have brought to it. There is no plurality of gods. There is only one God. All are dependent upon Him, but He is not dependent on anybody. He Himself has power over everything. He is far above being the progeny of anybody or having any offspring. He is such a unique Being that there is nobody like Him or equal to Him in any manner whatsoever.

This is an early Makkan chapter.

The doctrine of God's pure unity, or the Divine oneness, is clearly stated here: God is not many, He is only one. Everyone is in need of Him, but He is not in need of anyone. He reigns over all things of the heavens and the earth. Unlike human beings, He has no son or father. He is eternal, without beginning or end, and is thus a Unique Being who has no equal.

This chapter has been called the essence of the Quran. The Prophet Muhammad once described this chapter as 'equivalent to one-third of the whole of the Quran.' (Bukhari, Muslim)

113. DAYBREAK

In the name of God,
the Most Gracious, the Most Merciful

¹ Say, 'I seek refuge in the Lord of the daybreak ² from the evil of what He has created, ³ from the evil of darkness as it descends, ⁴ from the evil of those who blow on knots ⁵ and from the evil of the envier when he envies.'ᵃ

ᵃ This chapter, containing five verses, was revealed at Makkah. It is a prayer for protection. The title of the chapter is derived from verse no. 1, which asks people to seek refuge in 'the Lord of the Dawn or Daybreak' from every kind of ill arising from outer nature and from the envy and the dark and evil plottings of others.

God is the One who rends the darkness of night and brings out from it the light of dawn. It is this God who can remove the dark clouds of trouble overshadowing a man and bring him into the sunshine of well-being.

The present world has been made with a view to putting human beings to the test. So, here there is evil along with good. The only way for man to be safe from the ill effects of evil is to seek refuge in God against it. Evil is of different kinds. For example, the mischief indulged in by evil-hearted people in the dead of the night, and the practitioners of witchcraft. Similarly, there are individuals who, seeing others living prosperously, become jealous and make the latter the victims of their jealousy-inspired actions. A believer should seek refuge in God from the mischief of all such people, and undoubtedly it is God alone who has the power to protect man from all kinds of evil.

114. PEOPLE

In the name of God,
the Most Gracious, the Most Merciful

¹Say, 'I seek refuge in the Lord of people, ²the King of people, ³the God of people, ⁴from the mischief of every sneaking whisperer, ⁵who whispers into the hearts of people, ⁶from jinn and men.'ᵃ

ᵃ This chapter counsels the believers to 'seek refuge with the Lord of mankind.' It is a prayer to the Almighty to grant refuge from the mischief of evil-doers, both human and occult. In this case, protection is sought especially from the evil in man's own heart and in the hearts of other men.

This and the previous chapter are prayers for protection. The two chapters are known as *al-Muawwadhatayn*, two entreaties for refuge and protection. The previous chapter points to the necessity of seeking God's protection against such external factors as might affect an individual. Here the need of protection from internal factors, that is, the evil inclinations within man's own self is pointed out. So long as we put ourselves under God's protection, and trust in Him, evil cannot touch us in our inner life.

Man is a humble creature. He essentially needs protection. But this cannot be given to him by anybody except the one and only God. It is God who is the Lord and Sustainer of all human beings. It is He who is their King. It is He alone who is worth worshipping. Indeed, who except God can become the support of believers in their trials and tribulations?

The most dangerous mischief against which man should seek God's refuge is that of Satan. He is most dangerous because he always hides his real position. He misleads people by his deceitful ways. So, only one who is extremely alert; one to whom God has given the capacity to distinguish between Truth and Untruth; one who can understand what is reality and what is falsity can save himself from the machinations of Satan. Evil-inspirers are not only the known Satans, even among human beings there are certain Satan-like people who present themselves in artificial guises and, by means of deceitful words, brainwash others and put them on the path of misguidance.

Seeking refuge in God from mischief is a two-sided action. On the one hand, it entails obtaining God's grace. On the other hand, its purpose is to awaken one's awareness of mischief so that one may become capable of countering it more consciously.

Index

Index

Index

Index

Index

Index

by God, 67:23-24; 74:12-15; is impatient, 70:19-21; guilty of sins, 89:17-20; created into toil and struggle, 90:4; gifted with faculties, 90:8-10; strives for diverse ends, 92:4-11; created in best of moulds, 95:4

Mankind, one nation, 2:213; 10:19; created from single pair, 4:1; 39:6; 49:13

Manners, about entering houses, 24:27-29; in the home, 24:58-61; among the community, 49:11; in assemblies, 58:11

Marriage, with those who deny the truth, 2:221, to how many, lawful, 4:3; dower not to be taken back (in case of divorce), 4:20-21; prohibited degrees, 4:22-24; it' no means to wed free believing women, 4:25; if breach feared, two arbiters to be appointed, 4:35; if wife fears cruelty or desertion, amicable settlement, 4:128: turn not away from a woman, 4:129; with chaste ones among People of the Book, 5:6; of adulterers, 24:3; to those who are poor, 24:32; those who cannot afford marriage, to keep themselves chaste until God gives them means, 24:33; Prophet's Consorts, 33:28-29, 50-52; without cohabitation, no *'iddah* on divorce, 33:49; conditions for the Prophet, 33:50-52; Mary (mother of Jesus],

birth, 3:35-37; annunciation of Jesus, 3:42-51, 4:156; 19:16-21; in child birth, 19:23-26; brought the babe to her people, 19:27-33; guarded her chastity, 21:91; 66:12

Maryam, S.19

Masad, S.111

Ma'un, S.107

Measure and weight, give full, 17:35; 83:1

Miracles, see Signs of God

Mischief on land and sea, 30:41; 93:1-5

Monasticism disapproved, 57:27

Months, number of, 9:35-37

Moses, and his people, 2:51-61; advises Israelites, 5:23-29; guided by God, 6:84; and Pharaoh, 7:103-137; 10:75-92; 11:96-99; resists idol worship, 7:138-141; sees the Glory on the Mount, 7:142-145; reproves his people for calf-worship, and prays for them, 7:148-156; his people, 7:159-162; nine clear Signs, 7:133; 17:101; to the junction of the two Seas, 18:60-82; his call, 19:51-53; 20:9-56; 28:29-35; his childhood, mother, and sister, 20:38-40; 28:7-13; converts Egyptian magicians, 20:70-73; 26:46-52; indignant at calf-worship, 20:86-98; and the mystic Fire, 27:7-14; 28:29-35; his mishap in the City, 28:14-21; in Madyan, 28:22-28; guided to

straight way, 37:114-122; Books of, 53:36; 87:19; vexed by his people, 61:5

Mosques, 9:17-19, 28

Mountains, 20:105-107; 21:31; 31:10

Muddaththir, S.74

Muhammad, the Prophet, his mission, 7:158; 48:8-9, respect due to messenger, 2:104; 4:46; no more than a messenger, 3:144; gentle, 3:159; sent as favour to Believers, 3:164; 4:170; and to People of the Book, 5:21; a mercy to Believers, 9:61; mercy to all creatures, 21:107; his work, 3:164; 4:70-71; 6:107; not mad or possessed, 7:184; 68:2; 81:22; warner, 7:184, 188; 15:89; his teaching, 11:2-4; 12:108; 34:46-50; God is witness to his mission, 13:43; 29:52; 46:8; to invite and argue, in ways most gracious, 16:125-128; inspired, 18:110; 63:2-18; mocked, 25:41-42; 34:7-8; asks no reward, 25:57; 34:47; 38:86; 42:23; his duty, 27:91-93; 30:30; his household (consorts), 33:28-34, 50-53, 55, 59; 64:1, 3-6; close to Believers, 33:6; beautiful pattern of conduct, 33:21; seal of the Prophets, 33:40; universal Messenger to men, 34:28; fealty to him is fealty to God, 48:10, 18; Messenger of God, 48:29; resist him not, 58:20-22; foretold by

1758

Index

Index

Index

CONCORDANCE

Aaron
28:34 My brother Aaron is more eloquent than I am.

Abraham
16:120 Abraham was a community in himself devoted to God.

'Ad
89:6 ... how your Lord dealt with the tribe of 'Ad.

Adam
2:35 We said, 'O Adam! Live with your wife in Paradise...

Adornment
18:7 We have adorned the earth with attractive things.

Adultery
17:32 Do not commit adultery.

Ahmad
61:6 Whose name will be Ahmad.

Allah (see God)

Alms
9:60 Alms are for the poor and the needy...

Angels
42:5 ... the angels sing their Lord's praise...

Anger
3:134 Who restrain their anger

Animal
2:164 Scattering over it all kinds of animals.

Ants
27:18 and when they came to the valley of the Ants.

Ark
7:64 ...so We saved him and those with him in the ark.

Authority
12:40 ...names for which God has sent down no authority.

Azar
6:74 Remember when Abraham said to his father, Azar, 'Do you take idols as your gods?'

Backbite
49:12 And do not spy on one another and do not backbite.

Bakkah (Makkah)
3:96 The first house to be built for mankind was the one at Bakkah.

Balance
25:67 but keep a balance between the two.

Banu Israel (see the Children of Israel)

Bee
16:68 Your Lord inspired the bee.

Believer
23:1 Successful indeed are the believers.

Betray
8:27 O believers, do not betray God and His messenger.

Birds
34:10 We said, 'O mountains and birds! ...

Blessings
2:157 They are the ones who will have blessings and mercy from their Lord.

Blind
17:72 But whoever has been blind in this life will be blind in the life to come.

Blood
2:173 He has forbidden you only carrion, blood and the flesh of swine.

Body
10:92 So We shall save your body this day, ...

Bow down
2:34 When We said to the angels, 'Bow down before Adam';

Bridal Gift
4:4 And give the women their bridal gift.

Burden
6:164 and no bearer of a burden can bear the burden of another.

Call to prayer
62:9 When the call to prayer is made.

Camel
88:17 Do they never reflect on the camels and how they were created.

Cave
18:9 Do you think that the Men of the Cave and the Inscription were one of our wondrous signs?

Chapter
2:23 then produce a single chapter like it.

Charitable Deed
2:264 Believers, do not cancel out your charitable deeds with reminders and hurtful words.

Charity
57:18 For those who give in charity.

Children
64:15 Your wealth and your children are only a trial.

Children of Israel, the
3:49 He will make him a messenger to the Children of Israel.

Christian
5:82 The nearest in affection to them are those who say, 'We are Christians.'

Clay
3:49 I will make the shape of a bird out of clay for you.

Clothe, Clothing
22:23 and their clothing will be of silk.

Cloud
56:69 Is it you who cause it to descend from the clouds, or do We?

Consultation
42:38 Who conduct their affairs by mutual consultation.

Concordance

Corruption
2:205 God does not love corruption.

Covenant
2:83 We made a covenant with the Children of Israel.

Cradle
3:46 And he shall speak to men in his cradle.

Creator
39:62 God is the creator of all things.

Criterion
2:185 and the criterion by which to distinguish right from wrong.

Curse
3:61 and invoke the curse of God upon the liars.

David
4:163 And David to whom We gave the Psalms.

Death
3:185 Every human being is bound to taste death.

Deceive/Deceiver
31:33 nor let the Deceiver deceive you concerning God.

Deception
35:40 Indeed, the wrongdoers' promises to one another are nothing but deception.

Defraud
11:85 and do not defraud people by making short delivery

Delusion
4:120 Satan's promises are nothing but delusion.

Denial, Deny
3:77 Those who have bought a denial of truth at the price of faith

Desires
4:35 Do not, then, follow your own desires.

Destruction
2:195 do not cast yourselves into destruction by your own hands

Devotion
2:238 and stand up before God in submissive devotion.

Devout
39:9 Is he who pray devoutly to God.

Direction
2:148 Each community has its own direction in which it turns.

Disbelief
98:1 ...and the polytheists would not desist from disbelief until...

Disciples
3:52 The disciples said, 'We are God's helpers, we believe in God.'

Disease
2:10 In their hearts is a disease which God has increased.

Disobey
11:59 Such were the 'Ad who denied the signs of their Lord and disobeyed His messengers.

Dispute
4:65 They will not be true believers until they seek your arbitration in their disputes.

Dream
12:5 My son, do not relate your dream to your brothers.

Dust
80:40 Some faces will be covered with dust.

Earth
71:19 God has spread the earth out for you.

Eden
13:23 They shall enter the eternal Gardens of Eden.

Egypt
43:51 My people, is the kingdom of Egypt not mine?

End
30:10 The end of those who committed evil was evil.

Enemy
7:22 Satan was surely your open enemy

Enlightenment
7:203 This book is an enlightenment from your Lord.

Enmity
5:91 Satan seeks to sow enmity and hatred among you.

Error
7:60 We see that you are obviously lost in error.

Eternal
2:255 God: there is no deity save Him, the Living, the Eternal One.

Eternity
9:72 and fine dwelling places in Gardens of eternity

Evil
4:123 who commits evil will be rewarded accordingly.

Example
33:21 You have indeed in the Prophet of God a good example.

Expiation
5:45 But, if anyone forgoes it, this shall be for him an expiation

Faith
4:25 God best knows your faith

Faithful
26:193 the faithful spirit has brought it down.

False
25:72 Those who do not bear false witness

Falsehood
2:42 Do not mix truth with falsehood

Famine
90:14 or the feeding in times of famine

Fasting
2:183 Believers, fasting has been prescribed for you.

Fear
59:18 believers, fear God.

Feast
5:114 So that it may be a feast for us

Concordance

Fetters
13:5 Around their necks there shall be fetters.

Fire
2:24 Guard yourselves against the fire whose fuel is men and stone

Flame
37:10 He shall be pursued by a piercing flame.

Flood
34:16 So We let loose on them a flood.

Food
80:24 Let man reflect on the food he eats.

Forgiveness
3:133 And vie with one another for forgiveness.

Fornication
4:15 If any of your women commit fornication.

Fountain
15:45 the God-fearing shall dwell amid gardens and fountains.

Friend
4:125 Whom (Abraham) God chose for a friend

Gabriel
66:4 Then surely God is his protector, and Gabriel.

Gambling
2:219 They ask you about intoxicants and gambling.

Glory
10:65 Surely, all might and glory belongs to God alone.

Gnat
2:26 God does not disdain to give a parable about a gnat.

God
30:40 God is He who created you, then provides for you

Gog
18:94 Gog and Magog are causing corruption in the land.

Gold
18:31 They will be adorned with bracelets of gold.

Good
2:110 Any good you store up for yourselves, you will find it with God.

Good Deed
4:40 If there be good deed, He will repay two fold.

Gospel
57:27 We gave him the Gospel

Grace
2:105 But God singles out for His grace whom He wills

Grapes
16:11 with it He grows for you corn, and the olive and the date-palm and the grapes.

Grave
22:7 God will raise up those who are in their graves.

Greeting
10:10 their greeting in it will be: 'Peace!'.

Guardian
12:64 But God is the best of guardians

Guidance
2:120 Say, 'God's guidance is the only true guidance'.

Hajj (see Pilgrimage)

Haman
28:8 Pharaoh and Haman and their hosts were wrongdoers

Hardship
94:5 Surely with every hardship there is ease

Hatred
5:64 We have sown among them enmity and hatred

Heavens
6:73 It is He Who created the heavens and the earth ...

Hell
4:121 Hell shall be their home

Helper
61:14 Believers, be God's helpers.

Hereafter
2:86 Such are they who buy the life of this world at the price of the Hereafter.

Honey
47:15 ...and rivers of pure honey.

Honour
4:139 Surely all honour belongs to God.

House
66:11 My Lord, build me a house in nearness to You in Paradise.

Hud
11:50 To 'Ad We sent their brother Hud.

Hunger/Hungry
106:4 Who provided them with food lest they go hungry.

Hypocrite
4:145 The hypocrites shall surely be in the lowest depth of the Fire.

Immediate Gains
76:27 Those poeple aspire for immediate gains.

Indecency
7:33 Say, 'My Lord has forbidden indecency, both open and hidden.

Intercession
2:113 nor shall intercession be of any use to them.

Interpretation
12:37 I shall inform you of the interpretation of your dreams.

Intoxicants
2:219 They ask you about intoxicants and gambling.

Iron
57:25 We sent down iron with its great inherent strength.

Isaac
37:112 We gave Abraham the good news of Isaac

Ishmael
19:54 He (Ishmael) was true to his promise and was a messenger.

Jacob
21:72 We bestowed Isaac and then Jacob on him

Jesus
2:87 We gave Jesus, son of Mary, clear signs.

Concordance

Jinn
55:15 He created the jinns from a flame of fire

Job
21:83 Remember Job when he called on his Lord saying, ...

John
19:12 To John We said, 'Hold fast the Book'

Jonah
37:139 Jonah too was one of the messengers.

Joseph
12:7 Surely, in Joseph and his brothers there are signs for the inquirers.

Just, Justice
5:42 God Loves those that deal justly,

Ka'bah
5:97 God has made Ka'bah, the sacred House, a means of support.

Killing
2:191 Persecution is worse than killing

Kingdom
35:13 Such is God, your Lord: His is kingdom

Knowledge
17:85 You have been granted but little knowledge

Korah
28:76 Korah was one of Moses's people

Lawful
5:4 'All good things have been made lawful for you.

Lesson
79:26 Surely there is in this a lesson for the God-fearing

Lie, Lying
40:28 and if he is lying, the sin of his will be on his own head.

Life
3:185 The life of this world is nothing but an illusory enjoyment.

Light
24:35 God is the light of the heavens and the earth.

Loan
5:12 and give a generous Loan to God.

Luqman
31:12 We bestowed wisdom on Luqman

Magic
5:110 Who denied the truth said, "This is sheer magic..."

Magician
20:69 A magician shall never thrive, come whence he may.

Makkah
2:126 'My Lord, make this city a city of peace, ...

Mankind
51:56 I created the jinn and mankind only so that they might worship Me.

Manna
2:57 and sent down for you manna and quail

Marriage
2:236 When you have not yet consummated the marriage.

Mary
66:12 Mary, Imran's daughter, who preserved her...

Measure
11:84 Do not give short measure.

Men of Cave
18:9 Do you think that the Men of the Cave and the Inscription.

Mercy
12:87 Do not despair of God's mercy.

Migrate
2:218 But those who have believed, migrated, ...

Mischief-maker
2:220 God knows the mischief-maker from the reformer

Miserly
92:8 But as for one who is miserly and unheeding

Model
25:74 and make us a model for the righteous.

Modest
37:48 modest of gaze and beautiful of eye.

Monasticism
57:27 But We did not prescribe monasticism for them.

Moon
71:16 and made the moon therein a light.

Moses
43:46 We sent Moses with Our signs to Pharaoh and his nobles.

Mosque
72:18 The mosques are for God's worship.

Mother
39:6 He creates you stage by stage in your mothers' wombs

Mount Judi
11:44 The Ark came to rest on Mount Judi

Mount Sinai
95:2 and by Mount Sinai

Mount Tur
28:29 he noticed a fire in the direction of Mount Tur.

Muhammad
48:29 Muhammad is the Messenger of God.

Muslim
22:78 He has given you the name of Muslims.

Needy
22:18 Then eat their flesh, and feed the distressed and the needy

Neighbour
4:36 Be good to your parents, ...and the neighbour

Niggardly
3:180 What they are niggardly about shall be hung about their neck.

Noah
29:14 We sent Noah to his people

Oaths
16:94 Do not use your oaths to deceive each other.

Concordance

Obedience/Obey
24:54 Obey God and obey the Messenger.

Ocean
18:109 If the ocean became ink for writing the words of my Lord...

Olive
16:11 And with it He grows for you corn, and the olive...

Ornaments
24:31 Nor should they swing their legs to draw attention to their hidden ornaments.

Orphans
6:152 Stay well away from an orphan's property.

Paradise
10:26 They are destined for Paradise wherein they shall dwell forever.

Parable
30:58 We have set forth for men in this Quran every kind of parable.

Parents
2:83 Be good to your parents

Pastime
21:17 Had We wished to find a pastime, ...

Path
1:6 Guide us to the straight path

Patience
2:45 Seek help with patience and prayer

Patient
18:69 Moses said, 'God willing, you will find me patient.'

Peace
10:25 God calls man to the home of peace

Pen
96:4 Who taught by the pen.

People
9:11 We make Our messages clear for people who are willing to learn

Persecution
2:191 Persecution is worse than killing.

Pharaoh
73:6 But Pharoah rebelled against the messenger.

Piety
5:2 Help one another in goodness and in piety

Pilgrimage
22:27 Call mankind to the Pilgrimage

Pious
66:5 wives—submissive, believing, pious.

Pleasure
47:12 Those who deny the truth may take their fill of pleasure in this world.

Pomegranate
6:99 We produce vineyards and olive groves and pomegranates

Ponder
4:82 Do they not ponder on the Quran

Poor
24:32 If they are poor, God will provide for them.

Poverty
24:32 Do not kill your children for fear of poverty.

Power
2:165 all power belongs to God.

Praise
1:2 All praise is due to God.

Praiseworthy
35:15 God is self-sufficient, and praiseworthy.

Prayer
2:43 Attend to your prayers

Prison
12:33 Joseph said, 'O my Lord! I would prefer prison to what...

Prisoner
12:39 O my two fellow prisoners! Are many diverse lords better or God

Promise
2:80 God never breaks His promise

Property
2:188 Do not consume one another's property by unjust means

Prophet
3:81 when God made a covenant with the prophets

Prosper
10:17 Surely, the guilty shall never prosper

Prostration
48:29 Their marks are on their faces, the traces of their prostrations

Protector
7:155 You are our protector

Proud
2:34 He (Satan) refused and acted proudly

Provision
2:197 but surely, the best of all provision is God-consciousness

Punishment
2:104 For those who deny the truth, there is a painful punishment

Purity
58:12 That is best for you and most conducive to purity

Quarrel
50:28 Do not quarrel in My presence.

Quran
2:2 This is a book; there is no doubt in it.

Rain
2:22 It is He who sends down rain from above

Raiment of Righteousness
7:26 but the raiment of righteousness is the best.

Ramadan
2:185 The month of Ramadan is the month when the Quran was sent down

Ransom
2:48 when neither intercession nor ransom shall be accepted from it.

Concordance

Rebel
19:44 Truly, Satan is a rebel against the Most Gracious One

Recompense
20:76 That is the recompense for those who purify themselves

Reckoning
14:51 Swift is God's reckoning.

Religion
109:6 You have your religion and I have mine

Remembrance
13:28 Surely in the remembrance of God hearts can find comfort

Repentance
40:3 The Forgiver of sin and the Accepter of repentance

Resurrection
25:40 You shall receive your rewards in full on the Day of Resurrection

Reward
2:274 Those who spend their wealth... will receive their reward from their Lord.

Righteous
21:86 They were all righteous men

Rivers
4:122 We shall admit them to Gardens through which rivers flow

Roman
30:2 The Romans have been defeated

Sabbath
7:163 On their Sabbath the fish come to them near the surface.

Sacred Mosque
2:144 turn your face now towards the Sacred Mosque.

Sacred Valley
20:12 You are in the sacred valley of Tuwa.

Salih
7:73 To the Thamud We sent their brother Salih.

Satan
2:208 Do not follow in the footsteps of Satan

Scales
21:47 We shall set up scales of justice on the Day of Resurrection.

Scriptures
53:36 in the scriptures of Moses

Scroll
21:104 On that Day We shall roll up the heavens like a scroll of parchment

Sea
10:90 We brought the Children of Israel across the sea.

Serpent
26:32 Suddenly it appeared as a serpent

Ship
22:65 and the ships that sail on the sea by His command

Shu'ayb
29:36 To the people of Midian We sent their brother shu'ayb

Sign
41:53 We shall show them Our signs in the universe and within themselves

Sincere
98:5 offering Him sincere devotion, to be sincere in their faith

Sinful
4:107 God does not love one who is treacherous and sinful.

Sky
21:32 We have made the heaven a well-secured canopy

Slander
24:11 Those who brought up that slander were a band from among you

Sleep
2:255 Neither slumber nor sleep overtakes Him

Solomon
34:12 We subjected the wind to Solomon

Soul
2:48 on which no soul shall in the least avail another.

Spendthrift
17:27 Spendthrifts are the brothers of Satan

Spider
29:41 but the frailest of all structures is the house of the spider

Spoils of War
8:1 They (spoils of war) belong to God and His messenger.

Spring
2:60 And there gushed out from it twelve springs

Steadfast
70:23 Who are steadfast in prayer

Stone
2:24 Guard yourselves against the fire whose fuel is men and stones

Storm
69:5 The Thamud were destroyed by a terrible storm of thunder

Submission
3:20 If they submit themselves to Him, they are on the right path

Success
33:71 Whoever obeys God and His Messenger has indeed achieved a great success

Successful
23:1 Successful indeed are the believers

Sustenance
29:17 So seek your sustenance from God

Symbols
2:158 Safa and Marwah are among the symbols set up by God

Temptation
57:14 They will reply, 'Yes, but you gave in to temptation

Theft
12:81 Your son has committed a theft

Concordance

Threat
2:268 Satan threatens you with the respect of poverty.

Throne
2:255 His throne extends over the heavens and the earth

Thunder
2:19 Accompanied by darkness, thunder and lightning.

Torah
48:29 They are described in the Torah

Tranquillity
48:4 It was He who sent down tranquility into the hearts of the believers

Treasures
52:37 Do they own the treasures of your Lord

Trial
2:49 Surely in that there was a great trial for you from your Lord

Triumph
5:119 that is the supreme triumph

Trumpet
18:99 and then the Trumpet will be blown

Trust
3:160 In God, then, let the believers place their trust!

Trustworthy
28:26 the best man to hire is someone strong and trustworthy

Truth
2:149 this is the truth from your Lord

Truthful
12:46 'O truthful Joseph!' he said.

Unjust
2:140 And who could be more unjust than one...?

Unlawful
2:275 and made usury unlawful.

Unlettered
62:2 It is He who has raised among the unlettered people a messenger.

Usury
2:275 God has made trade lawful and made usury unlawful.

Verses
13:1 These are the verses of the Book.

Victory
48:1 Truly, We have granted you a clear vitory

Virtue
2:177 Virtue means believing in God...

Vows
2:270 and whatever vows you make are known to God.

Warner
29:50 I am but a plain warner.

Warning
50:14 and so My warning came true.

Waste
6:141 Do not waste anything

Wasteful
6:141 He does not love the wasteful!

Water
13:17 He sends down water from the sky

Whale
21:87 Remember the man in the whale [Jonah].

Wealth
8:28 Know that your wealth and children are a trial...

Weight
11:84 Do not give short measure and short weight.

Whirlwind
2:266 Stricken by a fiery whirlwind and utterly scorched

Wicked
38:28 shall We treat the pious the same as the wicked?

Wisdom
31:12 We bestowed wisdom on Luqman

Witness
33:45 We have sent forth you as a witness.

Women
4:7 Women shall have a share in what...

World
39:10 For those who do good in this world.

Worship
2:83 Worship none but God

Wrath
2:90 They have incurred wrath upon wrath

Wrong
7:177 They only wrong themselves

Wrongdoer
31:11 the wrongdoers are in manifest error

Youths
52:24 They will be waited upon by immortal youths

Zachariah
3:38 thereupon Zachariah prayed to his Lord

Zakat (see Alms)

www.goodwordbooks.com

www.goodword.net

The Quran

The Hadith

The Life of the Prophet Muhammad

Peace and Spirituality

Understanding Islam

Dawah Material

The History of Islam

Woman and Islam

Islam and Science

Quran Stories for Children

Children's Books

Islamic Games

DVDs and VCDs

A complete catalogue of Goodword publications can be downloaded from Goodword's website. It is also available from Goodword Books, 1, Nizamuddin West Market, New Delhi 110013, India.

Copies of the Quran and other publications can be ordered online at www.goodwordbooks.com or www.goodword.net

For more information on Islam, please visit:

www.goodwordbooks.com
www.cpsglobal.org
www.alrisala.org
www.online-quran.net
www.alquranmission.org
www.goodword.net